D0745502

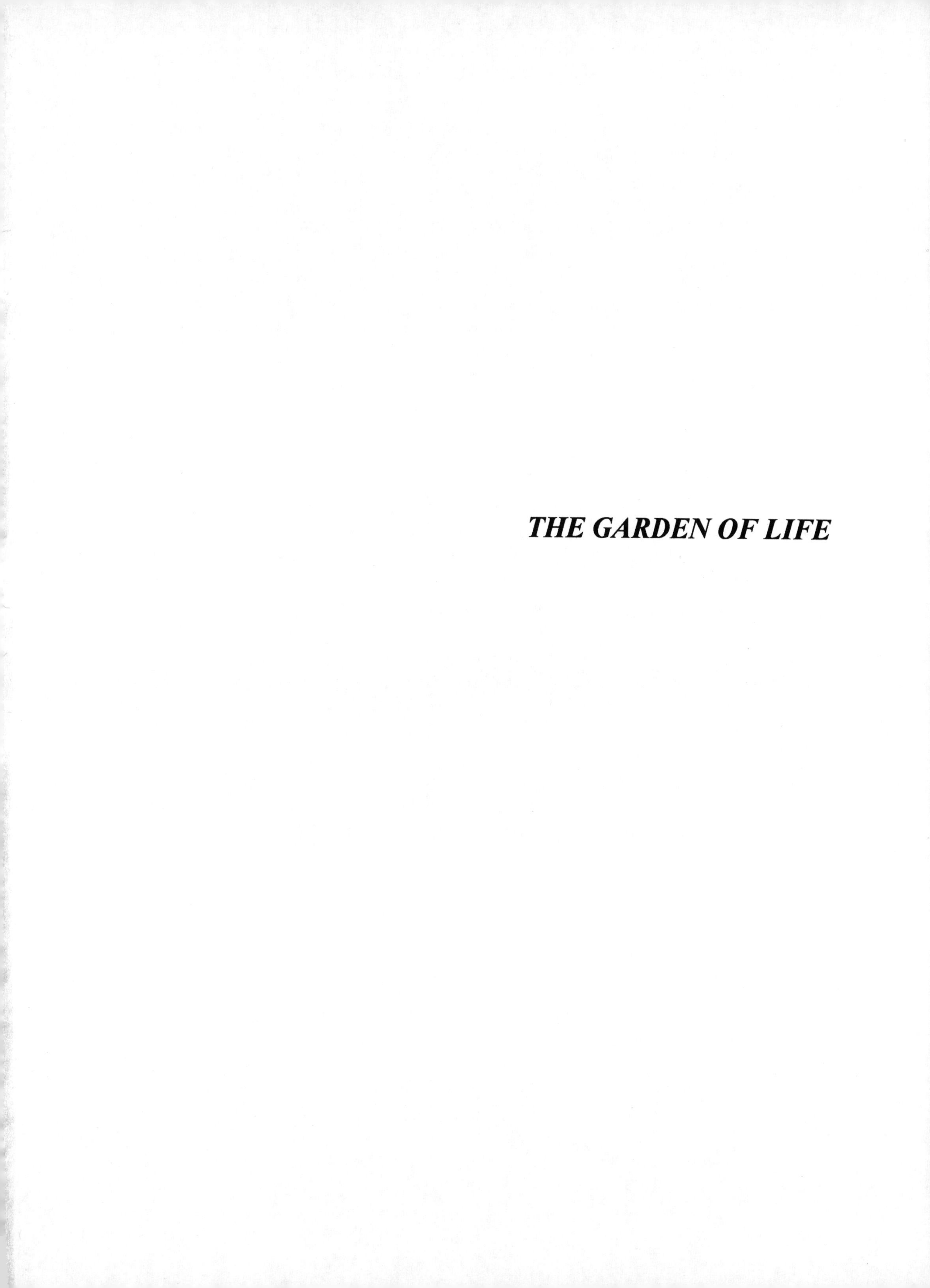

THE GARDEN OF LIFE

THE GARDEN OF LIFE
1995

Caroline Sullivan, Editor
Joy L. Esterby, Associate Editor

THE NATIONAL LIBRARY OF POETRY

The Garden of Life

Library of Congress
Cataloging in Publication Data

ISBN 1-56167-269-6

Proudly manufactured in the United States of America by
Watermark Press
11419 Cronridge Dr., Suite 10
Owings Mills, MD 21117

Editor's Note

When the morning sun's dappled light freckles the skin to a tingling stretch and pricks the mind to wake, self-awareness arises. And like the morning sun feeling, many of the poems published in **The Garden of Life** evoke similar reactions. The works appear on the surface as mere spots of light, but upon further probing exhibit a depth of meaning that creeps under the skin and snaps one to awareness: an awareness of life, an awareness of being.

Whether a poem evokes new consciousness or simply relates a pleasant story, I am sure that you — as reader or poet — will enjoy and can experience the following poems on many levels ranging from the inspirationally universal to the poignantly personal. And as is always the case with so many fine poems, it was truly difficult to narrow the group of semifinalists to only 70 prize winners. There were some poems, however, which were exceptionally well-written and merit special recognition.

One such poem is "Gestation" by Victor David. An unborn baby is the persona in this truly unique piece that pulls the reader from the warmth of the womb to the cold reality of life:

She tires of me, then squeezes, squeezes, squeezes me
as a blind lemon through darkness into drops of light
to awaken my soul for the first time,
a morning glory on the first stretch of sunlight.
To taste my marrow I delay my scream until
I grip the freeze of loneliness, open and close my eyes.

In "We Are Too Much Your Children," Lorraine Granieri uses the metaphor of a tree and its various by-products to relate the desire, and inevitable inability, of children to break free from their family ties. The poet states:

We tear along the perforations
In dry staccato moves
Picking off the paper nipples that drip with sap
Laying them in amber.

Although the children try to break free, they are left with pieces of family traditions and collections of adages which they ultimately — and ironically — preserve for future use.

If you believe structural rhythm is inseparable from poetic function, then be sure to read "Ragged Happenstance" by Colin Macfarlane. The language and meter are inseparable from meaning in this rap-tap-tap of short sounds that speeds the work forward:

Burned-out road-mapped red stripped hue
Scarred bright wise-swiped worry slew...

Another prodigious display of form is Rachel Price's "August Epiphany." On first reading, one sees a daugher making cherry pie from her mother's recipe. A closer examination, however, reveals the meticulous crafting involved in creating this poem. The last words of each line in the first stanza are the last words of each line in the second stanza — but in reverse order. The persona narrates a story of remorse, of reminiscence, and of comprehension: one is left with "no further instructions / than these: death accrues by slow degree."

After much discussion, the judges awarded the Grand Prize to Elizabeth Gheno for "Bete Noir." This remarkable work begins by juxtaposing the mundane with the vibrant:

Yorkshire heather scorns heathen poppies.
Fire tongues
shout lines
at milk-toast sunsets.

This juxtaposition lends itself to the overall idea of two opposing forces, i.e., the oppressor and the oppressed. The allusions to Sylvia Plath throughout the work and Ariel in the third stanza support this reading. Plath, as well as Ariel in Shakespeare's **The Tempest**, was controlled and manipulated by the dominant male figures in her life.

That the poem is in fact written about Sylvia Plath is hinted to in the second stanza with "The hidden verses / lie in a London flat..." but made quite evident toward the end with reference to Plath's suicide:

Did Yeats oppress you with death lines
or was it the scent of primroses
drenched in daddy's vowels
enticing the baby bee?

You fight the mirror image -
the colossus in your mind
that drove you to the stove.

Many remarkable works are published on the following pages, and I do wish I could comment on all of them. They are, like the aforementioned, unique, fresh, and skillfully crafted poems. I congratulate all of you featured here and truly hope you enjoy reading **The Garden of Life**.

Caroline Sullivan, Senior Editor

Acknowledgments

The publication of **The Garden of Life** is a culmination of the efforts of many individuals. Judges, editors, assistant editors, customer service representatives, typesetters, graphic artists, layout artists, and office administrators have all brought their respective talents to bear on this project. The editors are grateful for the contributions of these fine people:

Kim Albert, Elizabeth Barnes, Thomas C. Bussey, Amy Dezseran, Joy Esterby, Andrea Felder, Jeffrey Franz, Ardie L. Freeman, Hope Goodwin Freeman, Kathryn Hudson-Frey, Paula Jones, John McDonough, Steve Miksek, Diane Mills, Eric Mueck, John J. Purcell III, Lamont A. Robinson, Rick Schaub, Michelle Shavitz, Jacqueline Spiwak, Cynthia Stevens, Nicole Walstrum, Ira Westreich, Tiffany Wilson, and Diana Zeiger.

Cover art: Greg Kline

Howard Ely, Managing Editor

Grand Prize

Elizabeth Gheno / Westwood, NJ

Second Prize

Eva Butcher / Sorrento, B.C., Canada
Julie Callinicos / Bellevue, WA
Victor David / Berkeley, CA
Victoria Davis / Evansville, IN
Lorraine Granieri / Chicago, IL
Gregory Hughes / Portland, OR
Merry Johnson / Irving, TX
Colin Macfarlane / The Furlongs, Hamliton, Scotland
Rachel Price / Brookline, MA
Daniela Scalcon / Atlanta, GA

Third Prize

Diane Albano / Bethel, CT
Marston Allen / New York, NY
Mark Barabasz / McMinnville, OR
Gian Belloli / San Francisco, CA
R. Tipton Biggs / Omaha, NE
Jill Blanche / Leavenworth, KS
Bertha Blume / Lake Grove, NY
Alfredo Borras / San Diego, CA
Mike Bower / Sedona, AZ
Grace Burton / Simi Valley, CA
Michael Chapman / Lafayette, LA
Dounia Choukri / Strasbourg, France
Arthur Conway / Washington, DC
John Coyle / Vancouver, WA
L. Paul Daigneault / Nepean, Ont., Canada
Jose Dopwell / Cliffside Park, NJ
Nik Edge / Astoria, NY
James Edris / High Springs, FL
Jack Faison / Brooklyn, NY
Thomas Foster / Austin, TX
Keith Gagne / Kamloops, B.C., Canada
Jason Garrard / Boaz, AL
Judith Gelberger / Brampton, Ont., Canada
Bill Guirl / Edmond, OK
Kenneth Hack / Maryville, TN
M.T. Hazard / Saunderstown, RI
Barbara Jewell / Shingletown, CA
Wendy Johnson / New York, NY
Glenngo King / Brooklyn, NY
Aletha Krebs / Elgin, TX
Robert Landsberger / Motley, MN
Phyllis Leland / Santa Rosa, CA
Bennett Maina / New Rochelle, NY
W.D. McDonald / Nelson, B.C., Canada
Patrick McGeehan / East Liverpool, OH
Martin Mitchell / San Antonio, TX
Marsha Mueller / Bay City, MI
Amy Nyzio / South Hadley, MA
David Oplinger / Winslow, AZ
Jeffrey Parker / Warrington, PA
John Peacock / Dunwoody, GA
Herbert Peacock / Pointe-Claire, P.Q., Canada
Frank Pellecchia / Union City, NJ
Karen Peterson / Wantagh, NY
Selina Pimblett / Clayton, Ont., Canada
Gloria Procsal / Oceanside, CA
Camilla Rantsen / Los Angeles, CA
Ruth Riford / Endwell, NY
Nathan Sanders / Lexington, NC
Nigel Spence / Armidale, N.S.W., Australia
Susan Stern / Sugar Land, TX
Katherine Swint / Decatur, GA
Randa Torrisi / Willoughby, OH
Douglas Weiss / North Mankato, MN
Brendan Whalen / Los Angeles, CA
Elizabeth Whalen / Bayside, NY
Don Wigal / New York, NY
Alexandre Xavier / Coimbatore, South India
C. Jeanene Zielinski / Peru, NY

Grand Prize Winner

Bete Noir

Yorkshire heather scorns heathen poppies.
Fire tongues
shout lines
at milk-toast sunsets.

The hidden verses
lie in a London flat
where you stored your pensive cycles-
black beasts in bell jars.

Ariel's cellar reeks of honey.
Sweet words from Otto
soaked your word strings
like a violin in heat.

Did Yeats oppress you with death lines
or was it the scent of primroses
drenched in daddy's vowels
enticing the baby bee?

You fight the mirror image-
the colossus in your mind
that drove you to the stove.

Tiny hell fires sigh-

—Elizabeth Gheno

Constants

The crimson clouds above the bay,
A full moon rising o'er the way,
The setting sun's last golden ray,
Depict the ending of the day.
How odd to me is this display!
I'll waste no time to this relay.
For even as the sky turns gray,
It seems that nothing is to stay.
While watching how the sunbeams stray,
And twilight critters wake to play;
It's funny how these scenes portray
How given time, all things decay.
Reflecting on with much to say,
And wonder on with some delay,
"Is nothing I have seen today,
Exempt from death? That won't decay?"
And yet I know what wouldn't fray;
I know what time can't take away.
My love for you, I hope and pray
Is strong enough to never stray.

David Oplinger

Evening Of The Dead

This is, one more, an evening of the dead;
A time to mourn in the fast fading light
For friends and lovers lost, for words unsaid,
For golden dreams that vanished in the night.
So here sit I in solitary gloom
And travel backward down the path of years,
Recalling gardens I once thought would bloom,
To water each thin memory with tears.
Gray ghosts of yesterday! You haunting host
Of might-have-beens! With dawn I'll soon forget;
But now the love I left I miss the most,
And in this creeping twilight of regret
The ancient dreams I thought long gone, like lead,
Come weighing my heart down, down with the dead.

John Peacock

The Cat In Patent Leather Shoes

One winter eve I drowsed by my fire
Alone, though I'm no recluse.
I thought I saw in the flickering flame —
(I can't be sure, but still I claim)
A cat in patent leather shoes.

He wore a collar 'round his neck,
And trousers, denim blues;
No shirt, except his shirt of fur
(None other needed, I'd concur)
And patent leather shoes.

A cat in shoes? No logic there —
His nine lives he could lose.
He can't run fast, he can't climb trees —
He'd have to live a life of ease
In his patent leather shoes.

And then I roused — it was a dream,
A dream I hate to lose.
He was so pleased, so satisfied,
He knew he looked all dandified —
That cat in patent leather shoes.

Marie T. Harris

I Am The Spider-Woman

Prisoner of Athena's curse;
alone, voiceless, black and brooding
in the recesses of life.
Wretched.

Weaving, Weaving, Weaving:
gossamer lines of frail silk.
Weaving.

Time-Life (quietly unraveling) wreathed into ambiguous netting
of fragile design.
Radiating for support,
spiralling into oblivion.

Enmeshed within alabaster lacework
earthbound star mystic.

Struggling to knit past and present,
into a future?
Entangled, knotted, and twisted between heaven and earth.

Leslie M. Crisostomo

Sleep

I lay there, motionless at first, and peered
Along the broad expanse of sleep that lured
Around me, crept upon me, warm yet weird,
Among the maze of shifting scenes... unsure.
Immense, yet small they seemed, they gathered 'round.
And lo! They gathered 'round to taunt and twist,
And I lay still, defenseless, as if bound
By unseen hands...they melt into the mist.

The light of day has withered fast to show
The shadows of my room bedecked in grey,
And night, with robe of shimmering gems, aglow.
And now my eyes, with toils of yore at bay,
Retreat with grace, and slip away to sleep.

L. Paul Daigneault

Shadows Of The Past

In twining light of fire and candle,
An old man sits in meditation.
He sees his bent and meager form
As a long, lean shadow on an empty wall.
He's a youth again, a young man striding.
Then Maudie from the shadows came smiling,
Her hair the color of ripened corn.
Her fragrance penetrating the tiny room,
Her arms outstretched in supplication.
Her eyes alight with expectation.
Her voice imploring him to come
And join her in God's Heavenly home.
Candle's quenched and fire's gutted.
Now he sits in total darkness.
The silence like a cloak enfolds him.
All thoughts of life on earth abandoned.
In his final breath, these words are spoken,
"I'm coming Maud for my heart is broken."
Smiling, he slumps in the old sugarn
Scattering dust to dust upon the old flagged flood.

Diane Lavery

Pointing Fingers

Curse Copernicus
and curse Galileo
in the same breath
These malcontents whose
persistence cast us from the
center of the universe
They marooned us on a
spinning sphere, hurling
through the void,
dust
Left now to our own devices,
and the ongoing revelations
of the disciples of
science
To grapple with our
diminished status in a
grater cosmos
Banished from the garden,
again

Martin A. Mitchell

Transmutation

When all the world in smiles appears at Dawn,
And every shoot does blossom forth to greet
That flaming Messenger of Love and Song,
What heart does fail to have a quickened beat?

And if the Prince of Solitude and Dreams
Does kiss the visions of the day away,
And in their place replace sweet dreams,
I ask, "Is not the Night as sweet as Day?"

Let not one tear upon your cheek appear
In tribute to your youthful joys and loves;
For what has youth old age can hold so dear
Compared to the Joys when we ascent above?
The grave is but a resting place for bones;
But Heaven, is a Citadel of Godly thrones.

Shirley L. C. Dunlap

Urban Love Child

Your behavior is not representative
And regarded by most as abnormal.
I wonder how you must have felt or will feel
about all the cold shoulders that will turn away from you
or already have.

It sometimes annoys me
to suspect that you do not feel at all.
You are too light and childish
too uncultured and unreasoning, too provincial
to reflect upon your ostracism
or even to have perceived it.

Then, at other moments
I believe you carry about
in your elegant and irresponsible little organism
a defiant and passionate,
perfectly observant consciousness of the impression you produce.

I ask myself if your defiance comes from indolent innocence,
or from your being,
essentially,
a person of your reckless and enviable class.

Andrea Prusin

Silver

Your silly friend pours silver on my pillow, through the blind,
and teasing softly, gently chortles through my mind...
"I've got her now, you know, and I shall keep her, too,
The same way pouring silver on your pillow captured you;"

"And while you roll and turn like fish, wave-tossed upon the shore,
I fly, and spin, and haunt you fishies, laughing evermore."
The silver slowly drifts across my face as your friend climbs
to zenith, singing gently to me, telling me that both our minds

are wakeful, holding on to time, and trying not to cry
or laugh, the way that children will when mother's lullaby
can't overcome the call that your friend whispers, silver,
in the night.
I reach to touch your warm, soft body, and curse your friend
so bright

for keeping me awake, with thoughts of where you are, (so far!),
and how I miss you.

James E. Edris

The Assault Of The Cedar Waxwings

The waxwings spied the berries,
and the mountain ash was unaware.
Without warning, en masse, without warning —
they spearheaded a flurried attack.
And as the berries lay open and helpless,
it was the squirrels who wanted to fight back.

"Oh waxwings of cedar!
You've interrupted our route.
That tree you've invaded,
gets us home to full shells of nuts."

"Shut up lowly squirrels. We're feasting today!
We're stopping over for breakfast, and you've really nothing to say."

So as the berries disappeared the squirrels could only watch.
They knew they could up end like berries
if the waxwings decided to sup.

The waxwings finished their gouging.
And off to the south they flew —
Their assault and chaos completed,
as the ash and squirrels well knew.

Diane Docktor

My Single Mom

She reaches down to smooth the path
(and tucks her feelings on a shelf)
of Lucifer, so bent on wrath
and never sees beyond herself

Her solo kitchen waltzes sad
the laughter left her life,
now a drudge routine performed alone
on which her children thrive

For these others, she still lives
sees thorns upon her vine
but the flowers she believes have gone
fill these eyes of mine

For all the beauty that I know
and all the lessons that I've learned
to dance, to sing, to laugh, to love
are joys that she once earned

Yet reaches down still, does she
One hand for God
One hand for me

Elizabeth A. Whalen

Untitled

Limitations confined within the mind
As the progression of the static state
Considers instinctively the opportunity for change
The belief believes that there must
Be a recognition
Bursting the hatred to transcend
The purification
Analyzing the limitation of the void
Unrecognized
Retracing the origins of creation
With the imbalance of the zero reference point
Transcending and bypassing the unknown
In order to provide room for advancement
As the surge of emotional feelings
Vibrate the soul in resonance with
The universe
Intrinsic deviations deviation intrinsic
Searching for the trails as a bear
To create the gravaton bearings
As the ultimate cure for the +/-error

Ronald Arjune

E.M.A.

Half read newspapers drape like
Broken pavement along
Crooked lines cast
By old legs.

Uplifted by a singular mass of
Loosely mended garments,
A brittle face appears,
Cloaked by a graying beard and uneven mustache.

Liquid brown eyes survey
The hostile environment.

People glide past - formless shadows drifting unnoticed -
Not like the wind.

Shuddering, drawing blankets closer, he watches
Cars in the street
Marching solemnly as cats.

Jason Garrard

Life

Life runs,
clattering down
deserted streets, up a crooked stair,
through a bottle-green door,
to the fevered bed:
Life runs,
dragging a slattern to her feet,
shoving her toward the steamy mirror.
She blinks pencil-light eyes,
wine-rimmed mouth agape,
hennaed hair streaming in Medusa coils.
Life runs into the mirror, out of it,
sucked into the slattern's eyes,
into the purple-hole mouth.
While she poses and preens,
binds up her hair, youth flashes from breast
to thigh, and she tumbles
into bed, back into
that same old aching need,
and life runs.....

Gloria H. Procsal

Vedran Smailovic

Tuxedo wrinkled, face unshaven,
Coarse stubble covered with tear-stained dust,
Vedran sits on his plastic chair
Clutching his cello,
Playing Albinoni's Adagio.
An audience of two scurry to hide from Serbian shells
Thunderously applauding his performance,
In the heart of ancient Sarajevo
Twenty-two stand mutely, unseen,
Disdainful of time-worn feuds,
Crushed buildings spill their pride at Vedran's feet,
He smiles serenely, tears streaming from his soul.

Mark Edward Barabasz

Center Court At South Carolina State University

Ride remembrance with me to
An uplifting grove surrounded
By majestic college halls

Collegians puffed up with
Pride declare grand ambitions
And lay claim to the future

Romancers commune on bleak
Benches while glad magnolias
Keep the moss from weeping

Sunburst of walkways converge
On grey granite chiseled to
Honor three students slain
In pursuit of civil rights

The court tells of tragedy
But its legacy of joy endures
Beneath magnolias and moss

Harry K. Dowdy, Jr.

Kdav

Obsessed with a perfect
Consumed by a smile
Unzipped lips
Growl for approval
Spitting a label
He's a frill
A panic
A venom
A glitter of mirrors
The paperweight of scars
No substance
To clutter an urge
Unplugged
The human conductor
Serves up the pain
He knows me well
I need to feed

Barbara Lee Jewell

Winter Solstice

The sun's retreat cannot survive
Another week, I'm sure. His late
Arising, stingy arcs connive
To chill and cheat our house and gate
Of treasured light and heat. Days dive
To early graves of night, cold fate.

Can't last beyond the holy time
When glowing tree and star conspire
To banish darkness, sound a chime
And summon longer hours less dire,
Redeem our sun, bring back a clime
Sore missed: Late twilight skies afire.

John Coyle

I Belong To The Mountains

Just to see the mountains and to know that they are there,
Cradling the peaceful valleys within their friendly care,
Makes me feel I'm home again, and that those kindly heights
Will smile on me through sunshine and through the starry nights;
Or, when the storms are raging, they still will seem to say
Amidst the thundering darkness there they'll always stay;
It's in my heart I know that all these things can be
For I belong to the mountains, and they belong to me.

I can hear the very stillness of their deeply wintered wood
And almost see the winds rush on peaks where I have stood.
There's balsam-scented dreamland beneath the trees and sky,
And humility in knowing that such a one as I
Can freely love and climb them where'er it pleases me,
For I belong to the mountains, and they belong to me.

Ruth Tallmadge Riford

Ruth's Angle

A crepuscular cat
Deciphered the marine rain:
Drops of tuna fish dancing in the air.
Algeria and Paris diluted in the same wine
While graphite is glass stamen or butterfly.

Dervish of the moving line,
She inhabits her space with magical details.
Beyond the cat and the sunset,
Her room, angle of multiplicity,
Becomes the negation of death
blinking furtive,
Behind the photographs.

We look around, and we know
Her hand is delightful exact.
We drink this precision, out of breath,
Because her pencil is faster than life.

Catalina Zapata

"Women In The Shadows"

Women in the shadows,
Delivering messages to faces unseen;
Secret identities conveying knowledge,
Hopefully enlightening those
Who are fearful of the unknown.
Life in a shadow
Can be a very lonely existence,
But we are not the only ones —
The ignorant flee the light like cockroaches
Scurrying towards the nearest darkened cranny.
But knowledge is light
And they needn't be afraid,
For the brighter the light shines
The more the shadows can be diminished;
And the silhouetted females
Can scream their existence on this planet
And bare their faces
As they have their souls,
For both are things of beauty
That should never be eclipsed.

Andrea Skopp-Acosta

Night

When the night begins to whisper,
distant footsteps sound so near,
clocks hesitate between a tick and a tock.

Pale light spies under doors,
the neighbour's music intrudes through the keyhole
to fill the room with stolen loneliness.

Pianos are closed and mirrors are blind,
slippers rest relieved under snoring beds
and boughs knocking on the pane, perform dances on the wall.

On the bedside table,
speechless books are waiting for stretched out hands,
to grab them and give them a sense.

On the wall between the green and pink rose pattern,
grandfather's smile is captured in a golden frame,
dead, behind night's black veil it escapes into reality.

Two flashing eyes appear on the end of the bed,
the cat soft and warm,
is welcome on cold feet.

As night steals away,
dreams come shining through.

Dounia Choukri

Cetacean

Breath joy spouts cascade up, and away and
down my flanks as I jump past Liquid
Mother's surface tension to taste the sky
and wave a flipper in salutation to
Father Sun. Descending curve to Mother
Ocean I insert myself with grace
and passion and a quick kiss from
my tail to one of her soft swells.
Bubbles tickle me as air molecules
leapfrog up my skin to rejoin their
cousins topside. Hard right turn as
my clicks bounce back from a snack
whose spirit I thank even as I snap
and swallow little life to make bigger
life water dance in blessing to and
from the Creator of the oceans of
my universe.

Steve Jacobs

Bird Of Hope

O may I ne'er thy presence spurn
Fair bird of hope, nor deaf ear turn
To thy sweet song; the sweeter still
When anguish spills its bitter tears
And wind blows chill, the storm more fierce;
O let thy song my spirit fill
When faith wears thin; then let me hear
Thy endless strain, more sweet and clear;
And when in death I close my eyes,
Pour forth thy sweetness to my soul
And sing the sweetest song of all;
Sing thou to me of Paradise.

Selina Pimblett

Gestation

Untouched naiveté, raindrops unaware of jealousy,
feels the moist blush of the current.
Engulfed, not drowning I wander lost in perceptions
to mime without an audience,
cupped hands about my face unable to hide
in his mysterious ether that blankets me naked.
Unannounced I dance the waltz of the flowers,
then curl into my harmony of dual solitude
satisfied that care
lies in the instincts of a salmon.

I grow in a tick, my nine month itch
has no subject in this kingdom,
bored to play with life's cord,
to kick my blood—remember nothing.
She tires of me, then squeezes, squeezes, squeezes me
as a blind lemon through darkness into drops of light
to awaken my soul for the first time,
a morning glory on the first stretch of sunlight.
To taste my marrow I delay my scream until
I grip the freeze of loneliness, open and close my eyes.

Victor David

Liberty

There stands a magnificent statue
In the midst of New York Bay
Welcoming ships to America,
Her torch lighting the way
To a land of majestic beauty
And freedom for one and all
My grandparents were greeted by her,
As so I do recall

The roots that shaped America
Were formed by those who cared
To build a strong democracy
For people everywhere
Our beautiful America,
So blessed with liberty
Will forever live,
But her true success depends on you and me

Eleanor Joan Kearney

Here Only Heroes Lie

"Come flame! Come blood! Come death!" came whispered cry,
From broken mission walls, alone, apart.
"Here stand with courage bared - for Freedom die."
Compelled, each came with swelling soldier's heart.

On solemn quest within those hallowed walls,
Devoted men there wreaked such awful woe.
With souls astir from taunting bugle calls,
Was time and life they stole from lurking foe.

Embattled dead lay heaped in disarray,
Then tyrant's flames there loosed to bring on shame,
But lifted martyrs up through skies gone grey,
And spread across this land their storied fame.

Whenever bugles sound let legends show,
Here only heroes lie at Alamo.

Thomas E. Foster

Reunion

I watched them as they came,
From distant dwellings they wended homeward
Like birds answering the primordial call.
They came, some briskly, some painfully slow,
Aided by crutch or cane,
Creased skin heralding time's relentless passing,
Thin crowns with errant wisps of grey escaping henna rinse.
I leveled the hourglass to stay the flowing sands,
Rolled back the microfilm to review earlier days:
Vibrant bodies, jubilant voices, resolute purpose,
Lush buddings with their promise of forever.

How proud am I to be of kin
To this noble, hearty stock -
Inspiration for my future self,
My hope for tomorrow's maturity.
I lift my head, straighten my body,
And with heightened love
Move forward to greet these
Valiant, precious loved ones.

Miriam Starr

"Ode To Leaders"

Pains howling anguish with pulsating crescendo do explode
From outraged fragmented thoughts like Last Judgement's doom,
Slaughter manful mettle and cause Mother's teaching to corrode.
How wish these were fraudulent visions that haunt me to my tomb -
The massacre of vibrant rose cheeked lads not come of mental bloom -
To profligate Parent's pride and hope; the desecration of delight.
Communicate what condolence ergo what lasting significance the womb?
Passivity tall to the musics' call, glory to tunic is the sight
Contrasted with what neutrons and politics at white heat ignite.
Oh sightless procrustean bed, abhor more than being physical blind!
Do elite authoritarians feel Aceldama pride for causing to incite?
The torture of mass punishment — how fallacious and unkind —
They anoint my head with napalm, my cup runneth scorched - no hope
That this sententious antagonism will not broaden in its scope!

Evans P. Cook Jr.

Reminisce

This bottle's filled with faces and names
From times that wouldn't (couldn't) stay the same.
In the season of our innocence
We were blinded by our youth,
Children so wild, so naive
And we thought we wanted truth.

Spent the night, drinking in the rain,
Wondering why the world moved on,
It all seems like such a shame.
Sailing across seas of tears wept
Searching for the magic place
Where all the promises are kept.

Indigo mood, cloudy day
Memories, long since gone away
Thinking about times that passed
Really don't know what to say.
This lovely dream is over
The world's shaken us awake,
The trouble that we couldn't see
Left us broken in its wake.

Alexander McCaskill

December's Destiny

There's a pale full moon
Hanging low upon the cloudless sky
Casting silver shadows into this cold winter night
Reflected as faint silhouettes
On the surface of December's mirror eyes

And there's a lonely stillness
Mixed within the darkness of tonight
Clinging to everything in an embrace of ice
A whispered silence
Wrapped all around the passing of this time...

There's a sad longing
In the space between moon set and sunrise
Where December waits in need of a friendly smile
As she grows restless
Hungry to share someone's warm dreams for a while

And there's an uneasy feeling
Scattered along this sense of calm tonight
Stirring the desire to share these dreams of mine
But the rover remains in her heart
Seems December's destiny is always goodbye....

Keith Sikora

Puppet Theater

Since Mr. Sarg's fashionable audience demands makeup,
He blots Professor Herkimer's face with clownwhite,
Conceals the Professor's bald pate with paper tendrils,
Straightens the quivering points of his beestung lips, and
Cloaks his tapered fingers behind his swallowtail,
Lest the overwrought gallery gods discover the Professor
A pianist of distinction in Puppet Theater.
(Professor Herkimer shows what truth his patrons permit.)
Obediently, he's another in his place, while none sees
The tear appear from beneath his mask.
But Mr. Sarg sees the spark from his bridge where he flips
the Professor's strings—
So does Miss Ellen Van Volkenburg. (But they won't tell.)
Each remains invisible above; each presses his finger against
the other's lips;
In Puppet Theater, it's clearly understood, truth bows before the
footlights,
While the strings snarl the Professor's fingers with unplayable roles.

Frank Pellecchia

A Friend I Made

We made acquaintance on a frigid night
He loitered outdoors all bundled in white
Charmed me at once with a warm smile so wide
Forged a firm bond, in him I could confide
scintillating, buoyant, fair, kept his cool
Didn't have a care, good luck was the rule
I'd been going through a dark stormy phase
Just by glimpsing him, my spirits he'd raise

Then my world brightened, improved day by day
Our fate's seesaw, it swung the other way
With each new day his troubles would compound
Took lots of heat, got knocked to the ground
Ailing, thin and frail, expressionless, glum
Sad remnant of my rotund jolly chum
Died so fast! to greener pastures he ran
Oh! farewell, evanescent winter's-man.

Aryeh Pomerantz

ineptitude

i walk the constant path of monotony
heavy with fetters of old hates
through concrete halls
stained white walls
existing... barely

daily draining of thoughts and images
there is only an impotent compulsion
they so need saving
their hope is caving
dying... slowly

there is life and love and beautiful people
beyond the fences of my mistakes
i want to so badly
they gaze so sadly
separate... and fading

christine a. reiter

"God"

She sighs as
her head sinks
into her arms,
watching the lights
that fly by outside
the window in the darkness.
A long day of living,
of wandering,
of wishing and
ending up nowhere
except at a diner
dirty and forgotten
in the desert.

I light a cigarette,
stale smoke.
I look at her,
the coffee cup, then
out the window,
trying to see beyond
what's reflecting back at us.

Gregory Hughes

"The Watch"

He's sitting in his easy-chair, face darkened by the fields
His heavy belly folds in two - he leans to rise, then yields.
Words evaporating as he looks beyond his sister
Grandfather clock 'cross the room; his smile fades like a whisper.

It loses time as though to mock, we both lost - you and me
Reminds him mama's in the home, still calling out her plea.
Take it now. My farms are gone. I only have this locket -
This watch that worked so well in life, please drop it in your pocket.

That slow shuffle across the floor, how did that crawl begin?
Who pulled the plug and drained you dry? Who slid the stopper in?
What sorrow was locked inside, when your relatives, they jailed
Your thoughts - your trust, in doctor's hands, your understanding
failed -

After mama flew away with the only man she knew
Whose smile could warm the frozen nights and the quiet son he grew?
Illuminate this house he did; illuminate her heart
Illuminate your heart he did, now buried in this dark.

It's time to go out hunting now, to turn the gun around
And through your mind the words will travel, never to be found.
Your sister waits inside for you, sees you feel your pocket
Wondering at the words you scream, now buried with that locket.

Wendy Johnson

Hawks in Winter

In winter if you know
how to look and where
you will see them etched
against the sky, their massive
forms hunkered
on bare branches like owls
breasts turned
to catch the tentative suns
first rays.

What draws them to the highway's edge?
Does the carbon making heat of men
fool the mouse to movement?
Or do they like to watch
men's speed and clamor
shatter frost's cold?

Two in mute company
upon a single branch
mock men's larm.
Their brooding presence stills
the harried heart.

Margaret Freeman

Ah, Ben!

Once, when we went galloping to school,
I lost my one-hand grip on the saddle rim
And tumbled from the horse, head-over-heels,
Into the yellow dust on Clay Point hill.
Stopping the horse, some distance on,
You cantered back to where I sat,
Gathering up the scattered grapes
(A rare lunch treat our mother had put in)
And you berated me for being born a fool.
"Leave the goddman things," you said.
"Or we'll be late for school!"
At six, how could I make you understand
That it was not the loss of grapes
For which I wept? I couldn't bear
To leave our mother's special efforts there,
Abandoned in the yellow dust.

R. Tipton Biggs

Deluded Counterpoint

He stepped
I plodded red clay imprints

Toward the tingle-tongue tree.
Downhill, following to a stop.

He tried to give me a magnolia blossom.
Spikes reached out to pinion.

"I love the colors this time of year."
"Why haven't you written?"

His tight-laced trooping boots
My soft loose suede shoes

Cast moldy green sticks aside.
Tangled in a hay-grass web.

Deborah A. Rodney

Lighting
does not sit in council with the gods
nor does it stand with patience
in the anteroom of heaven
soliciting instruction.
Caprice alone
directs its course
and reason
is a stranger to its nature.

Dorothy Michaell

The Sire Of Star Wars

Cosmic time, earth time, breeze blowing leaves.
I spy, the star speckled, navy-night sky.

Far above the earth
I caught sight onto a moving,
but, not falling star.

In the sun's striking radiance,
a superstar.

Ostentatious marvel—a brazen spectacle
A bold spread-eagle drifts.

Stratagem of masterminds of men.
A barbaric vision—the beginning.

They're saying peace,
when there is no peace.
I have become vexatious.

Man's ethical accountability
your progeny will take away.

Yes, you satellite,
the sire of Star Wars armaments;
is without conscientious responsibility.

N. K. Byrd

KRISTINA

Won't you come and see her!
I'll show her in quick gait walking.
Come.
(quick gait walking)
We'll stride through dens of words,
past a crossing, to shape a voice.
Come.
(past a crossing)
Walking, dancing, she moves—
Sparkling hair lashing at the silence.
Come.
(she moves)
The yellow leaves kiss past her feet,
but, she still dances.
Come.
(lashing at the silence)
Come.
(still dances)
Come!

Susan Backus-Samit

Untitled

Ancient sentinels shrouded
In mournful mist
Shed silent tears.
Gnarled limbs—
Brushed with silver—
Reach skyward
In supplication.

Silken whispers slip
Through feathered fingers.
A fragile unreality
Rests undisturbed—
By blustery cries
Of outrage.

Withered giants ensnared
In soft gray velvet—
Cry out in quiet desperation.
Seeking solace in the touch
Of dappled sunlight—
Leaching away the stasis
Of habit.

Lee Ham

The N Word

The n word sliced a paper cut
into my placid mood.
So rancid. So rude.
Its dirty fingernails screeched
into the blackboard of my world.
I am the white chalk that could
stay after school and
write the wrong
write the wrong
write the wrong
So right. So strong.
But the angry gerrr of the word is heard instead.
I shiver at the sickening scratches
into my smooth slate,
even though of me it was not said.
So wrong. So what!

Don Wigal

Resolution

You reached out, but I was gone
journeyed to find the answers I had sought so long
Desperately searching for one to understand
you withdrew to your inner land
The darkness of the abyss shed an ironic light
pain and anguish relinquished a familiar sight
Unveiled was a reality so long relegated
memories of yesterday and dreams negated
Heartbreak an ephemeral paradox you discovered
when feelings suppressed are once again uncovered
Dreams, capricious aberrations in the mind
touch the heart in a place only you can find
Promises not met make us all reassess
acceptance our only vehicle toward true happiness
Two hearts can be one when each soul is relieved
of the mysterious pain the other can never perceive
Life is quagmire left to our own interpretation
believe in yourself and live with the peace of resolution

Eric V. Hull

Metacat

The Muse deep within that exact connection point
is unpredictable, quicksilver; a tease
scampering when caught at, yet present always
at the edge of the corner of the mind's eye.

Fleeing imperious and intrusive thought
It romps, feline, 'round the corner, somewhere
just exquisitely beyond discovery
and watches; alert, amused.

Turning, attention shrugs a sigh,
resigned to the mundane ... nudged, turns again
and sees It, rubbing, purring, affectionate;
complacent at the ankles of the mind.

Linda C. Himes

Umbrians Poetica

Both the beast's and angel's lark
listen to the tarnished hark
of starken places, aslant
asunder
athirst from centuries barrow

Muse, attest my page
word of capacity doth stage,
sacrosanct
salvaging all there be
crossing truth and image
resting in my breast

Michelle Suzette Patente

Divorce

The grandfather clock chimes one
Its hollow toll, the wail of loss
Reverberates through this vacant house
Plaintive reminder of days forever gone.

What produced this lethal hemlock?
Poisoning two lives with one draft
Whose hand wields the sword
That severs Solomon's 'three-fold sacred cord'.

Our children's dreams are blotted out.
Hope for reconciliation crashing,
Searching for a home now gone forever
A cape of driftwood gray usurped by Piscautawa bank.

Who spun this dense cocoon of melancholy whose
Passionless fibers encase our moribund love.
A shaded face leers in tenebrous gloom.
About to inhume this sacramental union.

Yes, I see the evasive villain:
Moonlight skirts the window blind
And I stand immersed in shame,
Myself outlined in the mirror.

Larry F. Bogart

Ann's Stroll Through Summers Past

It used to be when school was out we'd pack up all our load;
Ma and Pa, Ted, Jean and I would head on down the road.

"We'll surely get the Governor Nice boat," I can hear my daddy say,
As five long miles of cars sat waiting on ferries to cross the bay.

Once on board we all cut loose; to climb to the top deck was fun;
Ten cent snow cones heavy on juice cooled the heat of summer sun.

"Love Point here we come again," my mother would smile and say;
My mind recalls the memories like they happened yesterday.

Soon as we'd reach the farm house I'd run right out the door,
To say hello to my old friends down at the general store.

Then halfway there I'd see him; he'd be strollin' along the way;
It was always old Pic Council just passin' the time of day.

"Are ya down for the summer now?" Old Pic would always say.
"Did yer Ma and Pa and young Whitey come on down to stay?
Yer little sister whatsa name did you bring 'er with ya too?
Are ya down for the summer now? Gee it's good to see all you."

Now there are two huge bridges which span the Chesapeake bay;
They carry all the smiling folks a whole lot faster on their way.

All the famous ferry boats are long gone from the Maryland shore;
Yet, each summer relates changes in time on the shore
forevermore.

Ann McHugh

Intersection

So, I'm here in the California wine country
making wishes in tiled fountains
And I hear you're in New Mexico
waving your best magic wand.
But at the end of the day
When you've been permeated by as much
muted red and brown as you can take
Do you ever close your eyes and see
the piercing blue of Portland Maine?
Do you ever swear you can hear the fog horn
moaning through the morning mist
or the slap-lap of a determined wave
throwing itself onto shore
And do you wonder if the whole thing was
all a dream anyway
As if you and I had never really been
in Portland Maine
at the exact same time and place
And never really met at all?

Phyllis J. Leland

A Precious Gift

A precious gift, soul made by God;
Man-made leather upper, sole of rubber,
Relieves the stresses of daily life
When pounded against macadam
Or thrashed against the wall.
The force which heightens the spirit
Inflicts great pain
Unceasing pain felt day and night, such abuse contributes
To physical, mental and psychological misuse.
The stain that permeates the skin moans
Of torn muscles, bruises and broken bones.
The elements - fear and defeat,
Both these are used to meet
The final death of soul and shoe,
The need to recreate the child anew.

Augusta Czysz

Weeds Of War

With boundaries so blurry, clouded, unclear,
Maples, their leaves, lonely crabgrass now fear;
For a battle, long-waged, now begins anew -
The animals, the plants, their faith, tried and true.

The ants have built bunkers, "strategically" placed
In the fields, on the hills, in the trees - with much haste,
For they now are surrounded by vegetation, their foe;
Calls for help, reinforcements - rabbits, cattle and doe.

Vegetarians alike, they come for the feast
Savoring every morsel of life, no guilt in the least;
Rabbits nibble on leaves; cattle graze the mighty grass;
Deer, buck and doe, stripping bark to the last.

Seemingly hopeless and futile, water spilled everywhere;
What have the animals won,'tis perfectly clear;
With all plant life extinct, with all celebration complete,
All animals weep with a sad realization - they too are in defeat.

Yes, they came and acquired what they had hoped to achieve;
They'd destroyed those differing in appearance, content and belief;
Now they've nothing, nothing, nothing but hunger and grief;
They've gripped foolishness in-deeds, waiting for the death they'll
receive.

Jeffrey Ben Parker

Impasse

After cold shoulders are traded each one sits rigid in his seat
No one really wants to win, but wounded egos shun defeat
So our private war continues without benefit of words
Still a great deal's being said by subtle voices that aren't heard

We know each other's weaknesses and how they are best used
and with uncanny expertise each can light the other's fuse.
But now our rules have changed and no one can cross the neutral zone
as two friends who can't bear loneliness let each other dwell alone

This refusal to build bridges that can be crossed from either side
causes memories to be trounced and reason's voice to be denied
Was it your overly sensitive skin? Was I too harsh with you?
In our right minds we'd arrive at a combination of the two

We insist on building walls to hide from each other's faces
Our behaviour and our attitudes are immature and graceless
The detached frigidness you fake, the indifference that I feign
provide no balm for festering wounds, no respite from our pain

Despite our recent falling out you're still someone of whom I'm fond,
someone with whom I desire to rekindle a passionate bond
So I'll write a careful letter, spell out my feelings on a page
where I can reign in knee jerk judgements and hopefully quench
your rage.

Jose L. Dopwell

On Assignment

The great are not always honored
nor the honored always deserving.
The grain from the chaff is not winnowed.
The unsung who works without swerving
to fashion or transient discretion —
though less than a knight by his own scope —
may wake up content in the mornings
with visions to amplify hope.
He contrives with no ballad, but boldness.

Oh, there are rewards to the gallant;
a smile or some lift from a fellow,
the unstinted peace of the guileless,
or a soft white head near his pillow.

Forgive us, Oh God, that we publish
and deal indiscriminate eminence
to witch-hunts enlarging the godless
renouncing on altars of news
the cloutless who sharpen our systems
and stand for ennobling views.

Katherine Moon Swint

I Touch Rock

I touch rock
and feel the pulse of the earth
beneath my fingers
the crystalline heartbeat rests
sharply etched
the coarse and fine grained matrix
sits solid and real

I touch rock
and feel the bones of the earth
baking in the sun
hot and strong
shattered by ice
weathered by water
ground to powder
and washed away

I touch rock

Ken Lertzman

Once Man Of Iron

Once man of iron
now stares bewilderingly
at dark stain spreading
downward and outward.

Hands fumble crumpled sepia photos
where baseballs and guns
and girls still speak of manliness.

Feet that once flew bases
1, 2, 3, "YOU'RE OUT!
now shuffle along a gleaming floor
while moistened eyes search from room to room
bed to bed lingering—
not finding familiar faces.

"I got a hole in one once,"
he yells at the withered grey-haired woman
crumpled sideways in a wheelchair
sleeping snorting.

A plump pink face
looks up from the nurse's station
nods sagely.

Randa L. Torrisi

"The Winter Year" (Funeral For A Friend)

Gather us, to share in the Birth,
Of a friend in His Winter year.
So ceremoniously, do we of different seasons adorn,
The colors of shade, and mill about pell-mell well.
His closed eyes behold the setting of the sun.
And ours, open, the lengthening shadows sighing. Nearer.
Who draws down the nightshade? And closes, forever,
The Crystal Portals to the Soul? Who ushers in,
The Roaring wind of vacancy? The pelting stones of Gloom?

We then to kneel for the coronation of,....
Our Mutual Timidity of Immortelle.
At the tolling of the Bell we quake! Affrighted at
The reluctance of our Ears. Our nescience reflected,
So perfectly in the solemn tacturnity of the Winter Fellow.
He no longer hears the thunderous, beckoning Peals.

James E. Holter

A Marvelous: Worms #18

Cordelia,
On silver-
Slivered hair,
Counted must-
Dewed Shepherds
From her past.
"Maybe,"
"Not."
"Maybe,"
"Not."
Fell daisy
Dreaming depths.
Cordelia
Of blues clouds,
Fled further
Than any
Sheep herders'
Flight ever flew.

Barbara Ann Nesbit (1971-1992)

A Passing

So young Adonis chose to leave
On subtle pretence of a need for change.
Now with gaiety shielding his dark enigma
Afar he went and found an illustrious city
In which he lived amid driven reckless times,
Devoted in mind and body to customs
Sensuous and strange that challenged nature.
Dreams of love were nurtured and played out
Ever struggling to become the true reality
And from time to time came rising hot
To fulfill the groined yearnings of virile youth.
Haunting fears became dreadful and well founded
And mature Adonis lost the sweetness of life
Scourged by a fearful pandemic plague
He clung to the hopeless wish of cure.
Ending the sick decaying ritual, Adonis, sleeping,
Sighed, breathing his soul into the eternal absence.

Keith H. Gagne

Mount Vernon Street

The sun shines
on the north side, peers
from behind chimney pots
across the way, creeps
spider-like down doorways
from rooftop to windowbox
it pours into round bay windows
which sit like fat Buddhas
above brick facades, touches
patterned carpets which spring to life
and spill crazy colors
on warm brown floors;
it seeps onto pocked-brick pathways, leaks
into cracks that meander up the hill;
it turns moss bright green on foundation stones.
By late afternoon the bricks
are baked rosy red and shadows begin
to drag their grey cover
across the cobbles and up the wall.
As the sun drops out of sight, gas lamps begin to glow.

Patricia Bolger

Marooned

I careened that barnacled barque, desire,
On this shock-sand isle, and set a fire
On our hill, that you might see
It flicker for eternity.

Dolphins played, unperturbed by hooks,
Offshore, while I in dusty books
Buried deep the gimcrack heart
Never on a pirate's chart.

Along the jungle's rim swans and snakes;
But was whiteness so pure, or venom's aches
Like your love lost? Lost, I feel and see
My lack clearly.

So I cast my eyes to the edge of the sea
Each day, and sup my dull severity
Through matted beard, and the castaway wishes to be
Rescued to slavery.

Nigel Spence

Layers Of You

I'm lying here alone
on your side of the bed
and I've got loveless thoughts
running through my head.

And I think about life
and I think about death and I can see the deceit
oozing out of your breath.

So I smoke a little more so I feel a little less
but the pain is too clothed for the drugs to undress
as I peel back the layers of you.

All my things that you took
have left a hole in my heart
and what's filling the void
wasn't there from the start.

And I think how I'm cold and I remember your heat
and the tears wash my checks
like the bleach cleaned our sheet.

So I cry a little more so I hurt a little less
but the pain is too naked for my tears to redress
as I peel back the layers of you.

Marston Allen

A Mother's Wisdom

When I was a young boy - around the age of eight,
one of my sisters and I - had an ongoing debate.

For her own convenience - she was determined and bound,
that the seat of the toilet - should always be down.

But because of my gender - and being slightly corrupt,
for my own convenience - I'd leave the seat up.

I could agitate her further - I eventually found,
by using the toilet - while the seat was still down.

Thus the seat being down - was no longer the issue,
cause she couldn't sit down - till she wiped it with tissue.

She finally asked Mother - to referee our fight,
and use her authority - to determine who was right.

Having raised ten children - my Mother was no dummy.
She wouldn't take sides - you could bet even money.

She expressed her concern - how we could petition,
that the seat of the toilet - should be in our position.

In response to her wisdom - this is what we did.
After using the toilet - we lowered both SEAT and LID.

Bob Eshelbrenner

Memories Of An Angel

Two-headed Gate-Guarding
Pigs of logic,
Purveyors of sodomized animal carcasses
And the cold feet of doom.

Feet-metered and rhymed,
Choreographing the dew droplets,
As they leap and dance
On the rainclouds of love.

An offended love that is
Beyond the thunderclap.
Beyond the confusion.
Simply beyond the fear

Of an angel's gorged skateboard stomach
Purged, and be belching up
The remnants
Of his dedicated, yet all too
Aggressive, imperfection.

Douglas J. Weiss

Coronary

Snow-burned foul mouth
Pushing barrier down south
See how he gasps and tears at the
Block of (scratching fingernail) ice
Hear the vows of the heathen to the Atheneum
Drowning in his hibernaculum

I rarely hear his gurgled shouts
Nor recall the stabs of the narcotics officers
Civil so cleanly dressed in neat whites
Excusing themselves politely to me
And piercing him like a fish-blood spout

Beside the slab his re-tenured wife
Gently pressing on his dentures
Looks so coronary

Nik B. Edge

Shadowy Roots

Quivering grasses
remarkable barometers
of the imperceptible breeze,

Anchored to small
humus pockets in this
solid red sandstone,

Sharing the sun
with flies and lizards
and my perception.

Sitting still.

I have lost my need
for a body hours ago,

Almost everything is
made of light and vibrations.

My awareness traces
a luminous grass stalk
down to dark
shadowy roots

...and I sense
a balance in my being.

Michael W. Bower

The Front Porch

How many sobering thoughts have risen from my eyes,
run down my cheeks, and sunk into the cracks
of that front porch.

Years of season have colored my moods upon the trees
first green, then yellow before bared for snow
so near the porch.

Thousands of memories have frozen in icicles on the eave
to be recalled as they trickled with the thaw
upon the front porch.

So many rays of sun have baked too long there, scorched
and cracked the gray paint that southern rains washed clean
from the front porch.

Full many moons have risen in the east, cast shadows on
us, heard our secret before changing to lightning flashes
across the porch.

How many dreams have carried me back to a weather-beaten
chair beside them I love for a long night of fantasy
on the front porch.

Anne B. Pavlovsky

"Tempera"

He looked at her and
saw that she was
in fact scary and different
that bright veneer of
sexiness was in fact
a dark sexuality
of senses lost to
gather value
he saw the smile
across the dark canvas
of her face
he loved her then
appreciated
he loved her so
and left.

Camilla Rantsen

Ragged Happenstance

Burned-out road-mapped red stripped hue
Scarred bright wise-swiped worry slew
Cataclysmic social mires unfed and all too new
Then, in silent waning drives, a darker hunger grew

Cracks in the wall make an ugly wind cry
Numb fingers crawl, grip the slippery sigh
Majesty gone awry, slumping these days by
There's sand in the light on the path of my eye

Lumbering on, for how little, how long?
Lacking the grace, looking withered, forlorn
Cracking, croaked and choked in the dawn
Where did this much despair come from?

These dog days dog, and the carvery bends
The fleshless nights crave a gluttinous end
Voiceless profusion of images blend
Relentlessly tackled again and again

The clamour and stillness, aggressive and tame
Exists in the heart and the head all the same
In the sparsity circle or heat of the game
Remember that life? Do you remember my name?

Colin Macfarlane

The Addict

Empty as my pockets, I entered the boulevard.
Shuffling off the steps of dirty stone, only
the cold noticed as my sole met the pavement.
Faces whisked past not imagining as I imagined them.
Repeatedly, my swollen, stinging sockets were diverted;
thoughts, incessantly stagnant, withered as if
fields of cut wheat, rotting naked and exposed
to Helios' glare. A twitch of the eye,
a pang of the soul, fear creaked as demons gathered,
swarming through the mist of my mind.
A primal scream emits upon a cloud drifting before
the apathetic stares that sought sanctity through distance.
I too covet, escape. Clasping my ears,
sprinting in oblivion, ghosts and goblins,
fear and memories, writhingly expand into an implosion
of loneliness chasing my departure. Agony existed
more than a state of mind. I pled, I begged, I succumbed.
Huddled beneath freeway overpasses with belt re-furled,
the advent of diversionary shelter eased my tortured brow.
I was then relieved to believe, its imagination not conscience.

M. T. Hazard

The Only Thing We Have

"I tried to live today," you tell me,
sitting in a booth at a small restaurant,
blank faces stare at porcelain plates.
"Coffee?" Yes. It keeps me alive.
Your eyes look at the table where they stay
until you light your cigarette.
Are you afraid? "Yes."
I look to the faded yellow walls with their peeling paper,
and then your face. So tired.
"I couldn't do it, it was too hard," you tell me.
I'm lost in pools of black,
beneath your eyes. So tired.
"I'm leaving," you say regretfully.
Should I stop you? No.
Let you go until you conquer yourself.
"Goodbye."
As you walk through the door I wonder,
when will you find the courage to face your feelings?
"How's the coffee sir?" Black.

Nathan Sanders

The Pass Fail Option

Sliming, sliding past like worms, you crawl on your bellies.
Slip through mud with a schlurp to let me know you are there.
I grew out of this muck and mire that you're stuck in.
I have passed you by on my road

Grey ooze and oils and grime from the smoke stacks,
  you writhe in this.
Your pleasure, Mr. Snake, is to worm little holes out of me.
While you busy yourself with my meat and my bones I have
found the key to the next gate I must pass through.
You, I have passed on my road.

The squirming of snakes, though beneath me, is where I must go.
My road ends here and now it is time to rest. I will wait until
sundown for the next runner. He must pass me on his road
before the dark falls.

Allen Marshall

She Wasn't At The Funeral

The spring breeze could be tasted then
So fine so free on the lips yes then
Felt on the eyes and tasted there too
So thirsty were those days of youth
We played soon after the freeze of her death
blessed with obscure intelligence
Chased from morals and conference
We displayed our organs instead
Touch mine I said
And killed mosquito hawks with badminton rackets
Thousands and thousands of dragon flies on credit
We hid and weren't found
So deep was the meaning
darkness brought when it cloaked our bushes
And we whispered at the window so late and secret
As they ate from the plates that sister kept washing
Sometimes I rinsed
Once I spit in the water
We played soon after the freeze of her death
blessed by funeral intelligence

Michael Chapman

Cadence

Some people march to different drummers; others seem to dance.
Some folks call it coincidence; others term it chance
When two hearts meet; rapport ignites a certain special strength.
Perhaps they find union of mind, a sort of shared wave-length.
Alto alone will sound quite strange without soprano's ring,
And melody without a tune is difficult to sing.
I know not why life's sweetness is oft' enhanced by pain,
And not akin to reason, that loss results in gain.
The darkened threads in tapestry, so terrible and bold,
When placed within the borders, accent the red and gold.
Perception can be sorrowful; it can be fine and rare.
Discernment can be awesome if you will only dare
To see the picture overall, to hear the cadence soar,
Accept crescendos, cellos, flutes, amidst the tuba's roar.
To dance to distant drummers a silent, sweet refrain
Brought forth at times by ecstasy, or stealthy threads of pain,
Is not in vain if in your heart your soul soars wild and free.
For far from shore healing can come upon a tranquil sea.

Merry Johnson

Untitled

Much about you is a mystery to me
Sometimes the gate opens
A little more of you
Ventures out with the key
The key that unlocks the door
That allows people to enter in
To see a little more of you
Sometimes the door slams shut
For the visitor has gotten too close
You feel things that scare you
At the same time
They give you pleasure
It's more than you can handle...
At this time
So the key gets hidden away
Till the gate opens again
And you venture out to show the world
A little more of you

Pamela Smith-Gray

Pedal Prayer

Cross-generational audience regarding
student-teacher procession marching
hand-in-mic exec director calling
body-in-mind graduation enthralling

two anthems sung in successive "motion"
one, for all; the other, a requisite digression
representative students brought to podium
some, for extolling; others, laden with neologism

everyone present voicing succinct, promising chants
inducing gladness, inspiration, pride in grads
raising hands, syncopating feet, garnishing hallelujahs
moving onward...moving upward toward the dais

these grads having overcome
man-made artificially laid hindrances
seemingly insurmountable encumbrances

for whose sake they're boggling the establishment
and their feet in perfect step, step up
brandishing intent
first by exclaiming self-reliance in consummation
then by communing with their Maker via pedal invocation

Yoel Nitzarim

We Are Too Much Your Children

Clever you were to perforate our edges
Tagging all our soft spots with claims
To your old blood

Lean, you danced like druids around the family tree
Secure in your timeless craft

Speak little; do much, you counseled
Respect your alders, we joked

Eat bread with friends, you began
Never lend it, we finished

Pinches leave no scars, you warned
Kisses are for sleeping children, we replied in language without accent

We tear along the perforations
In dry staccato moves
Picking off the paper nipples that drip with sap
Laying them in amber

We are too much your children
Never a dry eye in the house

Lorraine E. Granieri

Sonarman

As a prowling predator the man-of-war scans off shore;
Tailing the traditional trail of them that lay the lore.
Within her, steadfast hearts hammer her heartless steel;
Corrupting the claim of lifelessness as crew and craft congeal.

Her vigilant sentinel strains as he monitors the mystic main,
Sounding the sea for a sonoric scent arising through ancient rain.
A sailor, scoping an ear to the keyhole of Neptune's tuneful lair;
Hears the wandering whale's soulful sighs: a symphony so rare.

Comrades calling as brothers lost, beckoning him home;
Awakening ancient answers anchored in the loam.
His watch is done, he seeks the sun, leaving the world of man:
Topside he runs, renouncing the pain of his deathly den.

Delving the depths, the dashing, darting dolphins salve the day,
As he paces her decks praying, facing the cleansing spray,
The beckoning blue broaches her bow, the gulls cry anew,
As flying fish frolic in the foam: friends cherishing the view.

Shimmering silver on the sun-washed sea the ship slips silently
With a purr of power pulsating her paths; he stares contentedly
At the satiating sun as she buries her burden in a golden grave;
An epitaph for unending beauty burning on aurous waves.

Patrick D. McGeehan

Robin

A resourceful Robin
in a resourceful world
Titters,
cock-necked
...and shot
by a tender play of sunbeam.

In his spotlight
he admires
Two thumb-notch wings,
Two feathery demons
to cast him light
over the leaden sphere of man.

He orbs
with two inch pride,
preening and packing
a pattering
in my breast.

So that now, I see
a squared symmetry
about his pebble eye.

Bennett Maina

The Spinner

Here the silent spinner, Death
Tends the loom of all creation,
Threading birth with each rotation,
Snipping life with every breath.

See him patient at the loom,
Swift, unblinking, spinning, spinning;
Every round a new beginning,
Every round a certain doom.

Does the ripened ear of wheat
Rue the signs of summer's ending,
Ere the harvest-blade, descending,
Lays him at the reaper's feet?

Does the careless butterfly
Feel the bitter twinge of sorrow,
Seeing that the year's to-morrow
Knows not of the years gone by?

Death sits tireless, spinning, spinning,
Spinning doom with each rotation.
Why do I, of all creation,
Fear to claim the new beginning?

H. Maxwell Butcher

Cheyenne Wings

Wings on the flying horse were rooted into legs
That formed to fit the curves and contours
Of wildly charging coursers of the plains,
Attached in youth, death alone to loose them

Wings fringed by shield and lance and bow,
Fletched for hunt and strife of warfare,
Sprouting out from stems of corded sinew
Covering hanks of hardened bone

A single being, those wings and body,
Two separated heads that thought as one,
Two segments linked by magic at the seam,
United by the glue of purpose and desire

Now a ghostly presence on the prairies,
A spirit flying on the fringes of
Imaginary herds of stampeding buffalo,
Lance and arrow aimed at long-dead foes

Memories of pride and memories of sadness,
Visions of triumph and disaster.
What promise is within these glimpses of the past?
Is there yet a seed of proud renewal?

Tom Steven

Mirror, Mirror....

Reflections of a face
that is sometimes not your own
I watch your eyes like twin chameleons
change with shades of other lives
The aquamarine of Grecian seas
when indolence was all there was
and farmers wearing hats of straw
worked the beaches selling fruit
to bodies baked to nutmeg brown
The cloudy grey of Paris skies
when baguettes and brie went hand in hand
with lazy walks along the Seine
and an angry young man
whose Irish blood
could not disguise the poet's heart.
You turn your head to catch the time
and curse the need
to run your life to dull routines
when neon digits take the place
of sunlight through a shuttered door.

Daniela Scalcon

"Existential" Speaks Of Arthur Nogood

He wasn't loyal to his being -
that is why he quickly sank into mediocre rank.
His very seeing was obscured by the cloak that he procured
from anti-being dark and dismal, non-perception quite abysmal.
One problem was that he was living as Mom and Dad had both
demanded.
Another self was thus created by axioms of conduct doubtly stated
from the moment he was born - these he carried on his shoulders
like the old man of the sea going to eternity.
What was it, then, that made him new,
changed his heart and then withdrew
the burden of familial race, of stereotypes, of darkened face?
Love it was that made him new!
A woman of sublime descent met him at some strange event.
Her being saw, beneath the skin
of the endless sphere he wandered in
the prisoner of formal sin.
Happily they lived (for ever after),
freed by joy and love and laughter.
They changed their name to knowgood on the claim
that what is heard and what is understood are not the same!

Herbert Peacock

Tomato Soup

Mother drinks to forget a man
that she dreams she married,
but instead she married no one
she chose to be alone

Without anyone

How did ~~I get here~~ then?
I don't know, she won't tell me
I don't like her anyway
I wish I wasn't here,
here to see her red, ugly,
drunken face all the time
her face red like tomato soup
she once threw at me
splattering all over the kitchen
where it remained
like her for months
it rotted, it stunk
up the whole house
until I couldn't tell the difference
between her and tomato soup.

Gian Carlo Belloli

The Crab And The Clam

I was a crab,
That weeps with a slight hurt of feelings.

I was a crab,
That bubbles out loud,
When a passerby throws a stone
To the waving lake of my mind.

I was a crab,
That fearlessly cries feeling
Feelings of villagers.

On a rainy day my mom finally told me,
Quit being a cry baby, you crab!

The system's gonna get you for crying to beat it.

My boss told me,
Don't show the signs of your weakness,
They're gonna walk all over you.

So, I've become a clam,
That opens up my shell but on a bright warm day.

Kyoo-Bon Cho

I Never Had To Shout To Be Heard

I never had to shout to be heard
That's the way of the world
My words are subtle, quiet, discreet
But effective as those that are hurled
From mouths both angry and sullen,
With faces contorted in rage

I believe the quietness speaks louder
And sometimes, the silence roars
For it takes a will made of iron,
A backbone forged into steel
To quietly face opposition
With a force that makes obstacles reel!

Perhaps this gentle persuasion
CAN change the world after all
"Inherit the earth" by mildness
Our strength in the Master's call

Elizabeth J. Krupa

communal "harmony"

the time is nigh
the drop starts
to envelop the ocean
fountains of blue blood
begin to gush forth
as the pressure of destiny
closes in on itself
pounded bones and crushed flesh
are strewn to welcome
that which is never welcomed
lick all that is fresh today
for tomorrow only the seething oozing
puss of silly remorse shall remain
even the marrow will not be spared
but day after the morrow
the time is no more nigh
for then even time is no more
when "harmony" is left in a bloody grave

Alexandre Xavier

Free Will

In the immense reality of existence,
the key to perfecting humanity
requires the doorway of imagination.
Evinced the human mind exertion
against and within, the degrees of
wrong and right, good and hate
dark and light, matter and space.
But, if reality has boundaries,
and imagination is infinity,
how can there exist, the perfection of humanity?
Consequently the conclusion is individuality.
So for those who have it well,
should thank God for creating
Free-Will.

William L. Dibble II

Intuition

Intuition is like a sponge
that is full of water.
You know that it is full
because it is dripping wet
like drops of awareness that
seep into your consciousness
like a crystal clear cascading
waterfall of knowledge that
runs to your mouth to be
lost on the tip of your tongue in words.

Bill Guirl

Timepiece

Captive of the stopwatch night in all its frozen motion,
the old man turns; the cat is fed-
he re-heats the borscht-
his breath an irregular metronome
pacing all his movements.

The kitchen clock licks brief and liquid seconds from the night
like the cat laps timidly at its wooden bowl.
Inconsistent timepieces are littered all around the room;
the night blends in a single web
a photograph, a newspaper clip, the used calendar by the stove.
The old man's move to the table leaves
no path or ripple in the weave.

The cat is old enough a friend to watch him from the table top.
He sips the soup in steady strokes,
seconds dripping drained and wasted from his whiskered days.
And as he sits, content, cross-legged, humming a tune from his youth
off beat one foot slowly ticks a rhythm
practicing escape.

W. D. McDonald

August Epiphany

I hold a pan of fresh-split fruit by the handle.
The recipe calls for 1 1/2 cups pit-
ted tart red cherries. My mother stands,
her back leaving me no
(no, not leaving me, not yet) no further instructions
than these: death accrues by slow degree;
your fleshy, knead-strong shoulders sigh
underneath strained nylon your bent back pinches.

And now my mother takes the crust and pinches
neat shells around the pie pan, rolls that flare and sigh
in waves about the tin. She turns the oven up a few degrees
and tells me all is ready, save the fruit. The instructions
she has written for me on a neat card so I will know
her secrets, long expired (this the distillation: cherry pie) I
misunderstand:
ted tart red cherries—no, the pitted
is broken by my mother's careful hand.

Rachel Price

"Message From Russia?"

A settling ship hulk fathoms deep
The ship of state now lies.
There's nothing to disturb her sleep
For over the last seen ties
With life the silent silt will seep.

The crew of this accorded craft
Had come to work as one.
Efficient men had learned to graft
Their skills, till all was done,
With ant-like plan, from bow abaft.

It did not take a tidal wave.
She sank without a wail.
The crew just let the captain rave
But did not bend to bail,
Not seeing any joy to save.

Jack Faison

"My Neighborhood"

Two towers mark the hour above a pair of golden steeples
The taste sweet, at times sour as my eyes devour
The scene below which is my peoples

Some profilin' others just survivin'
For a few it's a damn shame and sure enough a pity
Energy moves as brown bodies groove
To the pulsating rhythm of the city

Souls collide and coincide
With the echo of drums in the distance
Beats laid down
And passed around
Tell us it is time to dance.

Kinky heads, Mahogany dreads
Young children of tupelo honey brown.
Freckle faced afros smilin' as the breezes blow
The scent of sage from golden gate downtown

Native tribes melt with african vibes
Creating a love supreme, Latina percussion
Harmony rushin' through the veins
Of an American dream

Alex Thompson

The Beggar Of Siena

I bounded up the last cobbled step to admire
the towering Romanesque cathedral when I saw his crumbled
form sprawled near the doorway. He swung his head toward
the sound of the scraping of my heels on the stone,
his ear fine-turned to the wind.
His muddied eyes searched for my own;
the remnants of his teeth lay rotting in the black
cavity carved just above his grizzled chin.
His tongue clucked Etruscan; his lips were as cracked
as the yellowing tempera on an ancient altarpiece.
He blocked Pisano's soaring doorway,
and I felt his hot, fetid breath on my flushed cheeks.
My eyes sought a glimpse of the Sienese splendor inside—
gold, inlaid marble, the Last Judgement of the Good.
I plucked two coins from my sweat-stained money belt
and thrust their rounded edges into the beggar's
outstretched talon. "Gracia, gracia," he stammered; a
wide sweep of his arm bid me welcome. I unwittingly
brushed the soiled hem of his tattered shirt and
hastened through the darkened portal.

Susan Stern

Oblation

To you, I bird like bring a crumb of loveliness.
Like Philomela dumb
To utter the ineffable delights
In my heart upswelling, at these sights;
The lazy grace of cat's reach;
The nonchalance of a bridge
Flung like a necklace
Strung from river's edge to edge;
The mordant flavor of burning sedge;
The effortless curve of birds in flight;
The pied skies of rainy twilight;
The light tattoo of summer rain;
The elusive fragrance of fresh cut grain;
The daily imminence of death's kind
Promise, suddenly to free the mind
Which gives to life it's subtle tang
And fills each moment with a pang
With you, I gladly share the crumb
Lest hoarded loveliness leave me numb.

Bertha Schoenbach Blume

Poignant Treasure

Black sails callously flap in undulating shrouds
They cavil and shriek over ragged flesh
Inside the ebony clouds

Clarion calls, billowing ears sweep them all away
Oh! See the blight! A heinous plight!
The monstrous, gruesome display!

Slaughtered Lordly beings, becalmed in shimmering pools
Their regal visage splayed agape
To shame ignoble fools

Rest inert on crimson mirrors missing ivory lances
While blazoned trumpets mourn the loss
A loved one sadly dances

Buried them earthen knolls hiding cardinal horror
Now lay the branch of love's last glance
In crowning human error

Hide the skulls in gnarled roots, loath the hunter's gun
They coddle bones in wistful rue
Off by humans that they shun

Burnished moonlight glimpses all the hiding places
Memory cries through weeping eyes FOR ALL BELOVED FACES.

G. Burton

Morning

The early lights sneak into the room
through that chink in the curtains
that I can never completely close.
Under the down comforter, I move closer
to the warmth of your body.
Your arm lies heavily across my breast;
our legs intertwine.
I can almost believe you love me.
Last night, you turned your back to me,
hugged your pillow.
Is it dream or nightmare
that prompts you to reach for me now?

I hate to leave you.
Outside the bed, the distance waits.
Through the gray fog of morning,
I glimpse the specters of a world without peace.
A shawl of sadness settles on my shoulders.
When the world ends,
I want to be in bed beside you,
warm against your nakedness.

NethaLynn Thacker

Letting Go

You, dead leaf, clinging, curled up fetal
Through the miles of hard bark,
you're the only one still holding on
You could drop like dew
to float free as a blossom
to swirl on endless eddies
Still, you hold on
Perhaps, you remember
breathing in sunlight
I could snatch you away in a second,
hear you crackle like pine
burning in my clenched fist,
watch your dust sift through my fingers
But I am flesh; I must move on
You are dead; I cannot destroy your dignity

Julie Callinicos

Eternity's Sunrise

The leaves bend and the roses peek
to touch my fears with green of tears
Long is lost
moments sway to dance my
thoughts inside my skull

Silver doors open wide
Lilacs leap to branches bowed
numbers hang of distance force
on cosmic light

Sweet sleep into waters move
Songs to a silent sun
Awakens.

Jill Lys Shapiro

Serf Child

In our dreams and musings we
transport into waxen sun;
whisper breathless, careless creature
or the knife will clench your tongue.
Have you been a serf dear child
from a lavish, raining whore?
Do not mist those weary eyes;
incubate language do pour.
This stale cellar smears to tell her
enormous fluff, whipped batter;
their blank eyes can never view the true demons
to ask, "What the hell's the matter?"

Harmony Couillard

Notes On The Horizon

Sitting on the dockside of civilization
trying to hoist humanity to heaven
like a prime meridial magician
or a cargoed ex-sea captain

Shuffling a deck of demarcations
concerning Man and his origins
be it fisher of men
or being co-author of Original Sin

In the realm of holy benedictions
prophet motives and manifestations
the Poet, like a riddling climatician,
weathers and sheds like a distant cousin

To all beasts and fowl families
grounding and floating through promontories
inlanding and outlanding natural harmonies
in the twinkling of earth ripened divinities

Glenngo Allen King

Inimitable Imitations

There are these then among those
that though
our hearts our minds our
souls suppress, liege waters
of dark provenance loosed, express
the din which blackness yields
with syllables of soundless sounds, these
the eternal rhymes of the spirit
such as are and ever were
the inimitable imitations
and immutable mutations
of life and love, whose delves
are the shallows of ourselves.

Larry Gilcrease

Windows

He closes windows in his house,
turns them into walls,
following a blueprint for solitude
to surround his grief.

She enters his dark night,
a fresh breath to gasping life,
paints bright pictures
on his thirsty canvas mind.

He becomes her fear,
clings to her for life,
sucks her breath,
robs the only light she ever knew.

She struggles in the night,
to salvage wasted days
that hang on outlined frames
of faded dreams.

They toss in restless sleep,
each searches for the light
to lead a way through walls
where windows once had been.

Carol Gazlay

After The Concert

The orchestra that performed Handel
under the high trees of the park
that tinge, leafy,
the blonde brightness of a morning,
has ended.
Plunged on that lucid laxity,
almost fatigue, of the concert's hours
(there were kids, running in the distance,
like diminutive figures created
by the rhythm of nature and art),
the public started to abandon
the silent grass,
the benches and chairs of the place.

A man with a happy woman,
a boy with a most beautiful elder sister,
a young man resting affectionately the arm
on a friend's shoulders, they all were leaving
while I, somehow linked to all that people,
walked toward the gate of the park
below the sheltering shades of the elms.

Alfredo Borras

If You Might Return

If you might return, it would be now
When Spring has transformed the pear tree's bough;
When white blossoms fall to the ground like rain
And buds are waking to life again.

If you might return, it would be today
When the darkness of winter is hidden away
And out of a throat that was still too long
Comes the first shrill note of a gay bird's song.

If you might return you'd come back to me
But death has a strange and terrible finality-
I shall not find you now - or any Spring
Filled with pear blossoms and gay birds that sing.

Lucy Martin-Hellmuth

"Nature's Course"

Your wet lips
unnaturally want mine
I turn my head.

My white veil...My white tights...My white dress...

My First Communion.

You make me look at you
- NAKED -
with mocking laughter.

You put my hands
in places...
You lay your hands
in places...

In darkness I feign sleep
as your arms surround and suffocate.

My tears were always silent
in the sick shadow
of your laughter...

as I played "ring-around-the-rosey"
that laughter burned...ashes, ashes
the world fell down.

Patrice L. Brennan

Out Walking

When shadows linger on the grass and lamplights softly gaze
Upon the outline of a stage as in those English plays
Where mem'ries wander down the years in search of yesterdays.

While symphonies of crickets play a solitary note
Cacophonies of evening sounds o'er gentle twilight float
To stir the inner soulful chords with those that Mozart wrote.
Where zephyrs sprinkle twilight haze on fields of brown and green
I trace my path with lighter step for visions I have seen
Of places old and newly made where only God has been.

A soft toned Eve'tide wanders thus where summer shadows dance
With subtle whiffs of ecstasy, sweet perfumes of romance
So man may walk his road with hope that nothing's left to chance.

Patrick D. Harvey

Nothing Is Ever As It Seems

As I walk along the sandy ocean shore,
watching the silence of boats going by,
I think of you, and wish to dance
to the beat of lonely waves caressing the endless shore.

Like seamless shadows of night
the stars cry, for the clouds cover them
in a blanket of dull frost,
so I glide away with the leaves.

In the forest I could sit and watch
the moon spear through shielding branches
and shine off my flesh as I follow an animals' path
to the mountains which crumble in the endless sky.

The wind whispers your name, so clear,
so I follow the wind through the trees
which rake the flesh off my cold bones
which fall to the new morning sky.

On a new path which I've never seen
I come to a hard lake which covers soft stones,
so I wade into the cool fluid
and lie down to sleep without anyone.

Benjamin Trerise

Creation

Creating within my mind,
What mankind will never find.
Where words of colour made of thoughts,
Turn black into white, where life is bright,
And freedom is the only fight.
To seek justice from within.
Where man's intolerance
Is not excused by ignorance.

So let us act
While we're young
So much is said
So little done.

Those broken hearts
That silent scream
Is brotherly love
An impossible dream?

And must I create
Within my mind
What mankind
Will never find?

Alexander J. T. Cardinali

Second Chances

This lifetime was not meant for us,
Whatever went before.
It was ordained that we should part,
Though not forevermore.
A need so great arose that we,
Were graced with one more chance.
To light love's spark and yet again,
To dote and dare the dance.
In what was but a respite brief,
Enchantment soothed our souls.
Now strengthened, but alone again,
We face our separate worlds.
Seeking, striving, serving ... that when,
This life has had its run.
In yet another mystic dawn,
My soul will know its sun.

Karen Peterson

Sowing Season

It is almost too long ago to remember
when I was a woman without children.
How quickly I became a seed pod
carried on a wave of wind
to split apart and spew my tiny babies
so they might float up and away
eventually to land in some safe haven.

I feel now, that I have always been
not just me
but many clusters of alabaster eggs.
A silk-smooth basket for my children's journeys.

I would not trade for yesterday's me,
that narrow tube of closed blossom.
So much better now,
the sag and spread of full bloom.

Exquisite emptiness of birthsong.
The seeds of my babies now grown,
bending gently to the rays
of strong, yellow sun.

Joan B. Flynn

Find Me

In these days when anguish is communicative.
When insidious infection kills through life lines,
and angst is the breeding ground of contempt.
When the safest orgasm is visceral.

Please come and find me,
and show me this fossilized prophylactic.

Now the mating dance goes to the rhythm of stale bones.
When one can't touch another without reproach,
and simple conversation becomes pinnacle.
When life and death hangs in human attractions.

Please come and find me,
and show me this prophesied abstention.

In these days when ecstasy is sacrificed to caution.
When tenderness is lost in the shambles of paranoia,
and love becomes clouded and dogmatic.
When true union is preceded by medical batteries.

Please come and find me,
and show me this spiritualized solution.

Curtis P. Petrie

The Dream

In a whispery world of half-seen sights,
where far away dance ghostly lights,
a word, as whispered 'cross a bay;
hard to hear as love to stay,
is uttered in the forte quiet
through waves like feathers, soft and pliant.
It speaks in truths too foolish to heed
and offers fortunes to those in need.
So listen, friend, and when it's done,
take leave of all; return to none.
And when you've gone and seen the place
know despair
nevermore.

Skye Steele

October

October is a dancing girl
whirling through the town.
Can she be the same
or is she even kin
To the miss who just last April
shyly tiptoed in
and calmly settled down?

She calls, this gaudy hoyden
in gown of red and gold,
"Come out now and dance with me!
The nights are growing cold.
Come out now and dance with me
before we grow too old."

Janet Benish

The Taste Of Blood

The music made the movement as Jordan looked into the scarlet blue of Miro she could see herself beneath it all as a reflection in glass she watched herself move into the waves, and then the Indians came inside her head they sang and danced and fought savagely blood dripped from her heart onto the hardwood, and she touched it with her toe, bare, making the smudges that become the paint of a warrior about to fight.

Michele Burnett

A Friend of the Family

Who comes stooped with baggage?
Who comes creeping up my stairs
with scents of decay and carnage?
Carry my father in a tomb,
his mind shriveled beyond belief,
the courier of screams in the womb.

You aren't like any man.
I taste your spirit
like liquid from a can.

I saw you coming
like a familiar stranger to my liver
and because you are a friend of the family
I understand that you're the taker
and I'm the giver.

I thought that consciousness of your name
would keep me safe.
But knowing how you played the game
only paralyzed my steal to base.
Only a victim to your shame,
and miles away from being safe.

Jill Blanche

Symphony

Like Stevenson I lay abed
With covers nearly to my head
Wishing I were feeling great
Knowing house and yard must wait.

That's when I heard the symphony—
Directed movements through the trees.
I heard the music nature played:
Stanzas tree to tree relayed.

The wind was first conductor, it directed every note.
The scottish reel was wildly danced by each black haw and oak.
The cedars swayed through every waltz, the pines...Brahms Lullaby.
The clouds were spectators who watched the maestro wind whirl by.

Contentedly I listened to each measure, varied chord
Of melody the wind directed all throughout the yard.
It was a gentle soughing, and then a breathless pause,
Then unexpectedly the leaves broke out in wild applause.

Aletha Krebs

Night

The touch of Night falls upon the land
With her soothing silken calm.
She carries within her peace and silence
To vanquish strife and sunlight ban,
And spreads a deep and silent darkness
To cloak and comfort the burning land.

Over the earth her silence flows,
Quenching man's eternal flames
With gentle thoughts of elfin lands
And fleeting memories of forgotten dreams,
Which come to rest, and then depart
Leaving darkened pools of restful calm.

The wandering stars shine on high
And pave the way of the shadowy Night
With gossamer threads of silver light,
And from their dark and distant paths
They look upon the soft and silent Night
And touch her mantle with their misty love.

Her darkened veil is lifted but a moment,
A passing glimpse of time eternal peace.

Kenneth Hack

Break Down The Walls

They helped me build my house,
with hurt, but without knowing.
Little digs about my faults,
were the bricks for throwing.

Each brick hit me lightly -
but with repetition... slowly hurt.
I stacked the bricks around me,
Now I've walls around my dirt.

Years and years have passed,
a beautiful house I've built.
They helped with every brick-
but I'm the one with guilt.

They look with praise and envy
It's the false front that they see.
They are not allowed inside.
Yet, the outside isn't me.

I fear the day these walls fall in.
Then everyone will see...
The lies I've hidden all these years,
-To hide imperfect me.

C. Jeanene Zielinski

In The Fourth Dimension

After nearly three decades
with sad smiles we count
each other's graying hairs,
gently touching the lines
on each other's face.

Warming our hands
over the spark that
survived our broken love
we taste the morsels
of our mutual past.

In the fourth dimension
there is no place
for accusations,
jealousy, revenge can't
survive here either.

Locked in a teardrop
we float through the rainbow
where the stars are forming
a triangle and the evening breeze
ruffles the edge of our lake.

Judith Kopacsi Gelberger

Winter Wish

If only the snow bound pines could speak.
Would they boast of God-like beauty
In a wilderness so bleak?
Would they tell tall tales of grandeur
That soar the mountain peak?

We shelter sparrow, stag and wren,
The tall pines would say.
We open green-needled arms and then,
Winter winds come over to play.

If only the snow bound pines could speak.
Would they confess their ardent yearning
To harbor the lost and the weak?
Would Yule-Tide be the same each year
Without presents underneath to seek?

O world, salute the pyramids of green!
Shine forth your glory bright.
O lofty trees so grand and sheen,
Warm our hearts each day and night.

Robert C. Landsberger

Edgar And The Labyrinth

I had a predilection, others think an inclination
Yes, in the past without reading was told of your legend

Whether you in your life with reading I have come to see
Religions call your Dream within a Dream and writings of
Annabelle Lee a sin and your life a waste

But you like me with my melancholy cadence
have suffered

And I like a scared hunted Diana virgin deer
flew almost swam across the sea

Now I wonder why with your loves and diversions
you did not speak of something as soothing
as the solace of tea

Years later I may know more why
you like me had eyes that could do more than see

I'm alone
But less alone today with you and Annabelle Lee

Alan T. Moore

Phase Shift

Today's the perfect day to go to hell
you can feel it in the air
that hot, sticky, unsaid fear
that lurks near tangible
like some nightmare silent soft footfall
that you can almost hear.
it's coming at you from the back
back in your mind
warm, worn visions that speak
utterances of the undead
long since forgotten
in the turmoil of life
return to haunt
the places that you dwell

Brendan Whalen

Prester John's Paradox

My Utopian imagination envisioned an idyllic You,
Your hue a variegation, Hindsight revealing an un-Argus-eyed view.

Blind, my tempestuous craze heightened,
Uninspired by tutelary saintly ones,
Insanity vanished attempts to enlighten,
I was content in my own martyrdom.

A myopic phantasm propelled me, Toward a foreign adventure I sped,
Unprepared for my ultimate destiny, A caricature of the pristine
life I led.

Into a microcosmic chasm we succumbed,
The anachronistic interlude positioned neatly
Between separate dramas, our emotions consumed,
Through a retrospective masquerade we stepped sweetly.

Our own demons we wrestled in the abyss,
Silence the mockingbird - let injustice stain the earth.
The honest man grieves from Judas' kiss,
A deficiency in Communion will arrest their search.

The union dichotomous- it refused to be merged,
Disillusioned and vacant, my spirit withdrew
Past bridges and wheat fields and promises purged,
An aberration of essence to compose a new.

Amy Nyzio

The Defilement Of A Boarder Baby

I
A Boarder baby staring into Nothingness;
eyes bulging like a frightened frog being
seized by a lurking snake.

II
A Boarder baby screaming like a Banshee
...as she's impaled upon a crack crazed
phallus; that pushes like a stiletto
into her chaste womb, ripping flesh
like a red hot poker, neurons disarranged;
yelling like a heretic being roasted
at the gates of Seville, as a cryptogenic
man's anatomy jerks...a spray of semen leaps
forward like beads of sweat slung from the taut
muscles of a galloping race horse...odorous
sperm that smells of Mephistopheles' bowel...
commingling with an angel's flowing blood.

...a Boarder baby screams, knowing not why.

Arthur Lee Conway

At Peace

It's over...You're gone...I'll miss you.

I should be unhappy
and yet...
I feel strangely at peace.

It's not that I don't love you still
I do...
More than ever.

The ties that connect us will never break
Not now...
Not ever...

Love is more than a physical presence
more than knowing we'll meet again.

I know we will meet again someday
Because
Altho' it's over
It isn't.

Jay Hagan

Of Age

He raised his eyes up to the sun, where once beneath had life begun.
His withered hands proclaiming work, and years of sorrow,
conquest and hurt.
Beneath his black wool hat brim, his inner life grew brief and dim.
Within his voice a quaver grew, of a day and age which he once knew.
So long ago, yet still concrete, he walked this same old cobble
street. With courage, grace, and self esteem, Of war and peace
he walked between.
He'd fought the wars as a man, and built these roads with his
own hands..
He watched his nation with respect... deliver, divide and resurrect.
The tales he learned from others gone, he lived himself and
passed them on.
He conquered what he once had feared; a world and life he pioneered.
Now within him burns a light, yet strong and warm is not as bright.
The life he lived had left a trace, within the lines upon his face.
They script him with what once was pain, but now is only
wisdom gained.
What he had lived in time and length, is now within eternal strength.

He raised his eyes up to the sun, where once beneath had life begun.
He withered hands wrapped in his coat,
he slowly walked away...

Jamie Kelly

A Westerly Song

Their faint and peaceful honking . . . a calling,
Causes one to gaze into the gentle, cold, winter, night sky
To see the geese flying in broken chevron.
In front of the gentle white light of a bold full Moon,
Their feathers are diffusing the frail spectra,
Of the lunar white light—
Into a shimmering, delicately, crystalline, orange light
That bathes their chandelier bodies
. . . In Westerly . . . vector.

Gregory Reid Vaughn

Reflections on Otter Creek

Like brown skeletons,
The trees line either side of the creek
As if devoid of any life,
They stand there motionless
Waiting for spring
To bring them to life.

As warm air sweeps in
The bright sun beats mercilessly
On the melting ice and snow.
As little rivers flow along
The snow banks are eaten away
From the bottom and the top.

Swiftly pushing grass and mind away
The little rivers rush towards their destination
Forcing Otter Creek higher and higher
And the little islands of ice further and further.

Donita Hardy

Squirrel Encounter

Early one morn as I went for my walk
I met a young squirrel who was ready to talk.
"Did you see the sunrise-so bright and so red?
If not, open your eyes," Mr. Grey Squirrel said.
"You just walk along with your eyes on the ground,
Just see what you're missing; Head up! Look around!
God has given you beauty-observe-take note."
And then a brief scolding came from his throat.
So I jerked my head up-I did look around.
And you know, he was right? These beauties I found.
The dew on the grass, the birds in the trees.
Where else can you find joys such as these?
Roses, hibiscus, and magnolia blossoms
Rabbits, raccoons, and little o'possums.
So I have decided to take the advice
Of my friend, the grey squirrel-so wise and so nice.
He showed me God's love is in all of creation.
And I was just thrilled and stirred to elation.
I promised myself I'd continue to strive,
And count all my blessings-be glad I'm alive.

Cleo Brussow

Lunar Eclipse

Disdainful
you dance across my brain
demanding compliance
from my flesh
wrenching the love from my soul
twisting the parchment of pain
until the shards shatter...
like a grim reaper you lie me down
and drain me pale as a half moon
over Lake Huron in March

Marsha Mueller

Her Time...

She sat in Her room.
The clock on the wall reflecting Her thoughts;
TIME
Time until he would be back,
She could no longer wait.
With every tick, the Thirst inside Her swelled.
Swelled like the thoughts of Her lovers Passion inside of Her.

She could no longer bear to hear the sound of the TIME piece:
which so delicately sang of Loves mortality.

She was losing Her mind.
It began to rain Violently, Crying as if Heaven Itself had
SINNED...

She stepped out of the shower.

Caressing Her body as the Thirst swelled again.
Her skin was wet: wet and cold
It was only a matter of time now
TIME
That word again
That concept,
Enraged HER...

Christopher A. Minni

Untitled

I'm on the outside looking in and strange as it may seem,
This is not the place I've searched for the life of which I've dreamed.

What strange turn have I taken, this road does not seem true.
quest anew?

Bear to the left, that fork's well traveled, I remember
thinking clearly. While unknowingly I left behind what
I'd come to treasure dearly.

To doggedly press on it seems, would be to no avail.
That bridge ahead seems terribly worn. It's pilings
much too frail.

Wake up you fool, turn back and find the path you should
have taken, for soon you will have gone too far, the quest
you'll have forsaken...

James A. Cephas

The Sound, Taste, And Feel Of Murder

Scratchy like dry skin
A blah, dull kind of flavor
Quietness and stillness like time stopped
What you do every second, minute, and hour of each day
Loneliness and sightless objects
Driven by anger and madness. Revenge
Like air's trapped in my chest; popping out every other second
Change in sound, hitting a hard object, change in flow of water
Guilt and hurting, feeling really low
Smacking, like small explosions
Cold, good vibrant taste. In a solid but liquid state
Ragged sound like a chain saw hitting the bark of a tree
Tingling sensation cause germs are being eaten
Perky and tart. Wakes you up!

Carol Farnsworth

Teachers

Teachers are each other's friends
And all the teachers following the trends.
They always like each other
Rather nice like some of their mothers.
Some of them have a favorite sport
They play Basketball on a court.

Erika Gibson

Innocence

In a field of glistening morning dew
A body sat weak and crying.
So young, was he, yet the life seemed to be drained from his body.
I asked of him the reason for all his sorrow
The poor boy answered without raising his tear-soaked eyes.
"I am the symbol of the innocence of youth" was his reply.
Of course, this baffled me and I gazed at him in
astonishment
A moment of silence passed and a slight breeze cleared the
stale air.
I reached for him and he raised his eyes to me in terror
His were eyes as big and bright as the moon, yet they were a
deep, deep blue.
"Do not be frightened young boy" said I
His response to me was this, "Believe in yourself no matter
what you do.
Innocence becomes infected easily, so be careful, my friend,
who has influence on you.
I am the symbol of the innocence of youth, and as you can
see, I'm fragile."

Crys Riendeau

God's Gift

God the most powerful presence I've ever felt
A bolt of lightning is his walking stick.
Also the beauty, my beach walk when the moon
came down to the beach with a bird in it,
and the hell which put me in a hospital
But to be worthy of His Love.

What about my paradise? Empty within paradise without.
Maybe it's Bliss within, how do I attain? Start with
giving love that should fill with love, but where?
I have emptiness but a duality with paradise at times.
The way be a pool of water and reflect, how does this
work with people, they see themselves, I'm a mirror
What is outside is inside and returns to the source,
there is no retention.

Carl R. Miller

The Disprized

In all relationships, there is one thing:
A Bond; an emotional tie;
A link between two people.
Some bonds are tight,
Others are loose.
Some bind people like twine,
While others connect tenuously,
A union in circumstance only.
But the bond between brother and sister is different;
The bridge of love may seem unstable,
But, conversely, it is always strong:
Because a brother and sister,
Blood and blood, will always be linked.
Whether or not this seems plausible is immaterial;
It is a fact.
Even when experiencing the trying time,
That sometimes come between brother and sister,
One thing remains the same:
A brother always loves a sister,
Always, Forever.

Chad M. McKee

Untitled

I look up, seeing a leaf
A breeze seems ever so gentle, yet blows me over with passion
The fragile branch, though hard and withered
Silently sways before me
As if the spirits themselves were playing
I wonder why all of us creatures
Though hither and thou
Can hurt
Can hate
Can kill

Glenn Clifford Sveum

"Violence" It Doesn't Work

I saw it on the news today,
a child was killed by another's rage.
One more drive-by to make their stand,
laughing with their gun in hand.
A mother's tears they think aren't real,
but who's to say how she must feel.
One more baby a woman's left,
in a cold, dark dumpster to face its death.
I ask you why this world's grown cold,
why we fear we won't grow old.
Who's to say we won't be the one,
to lie face down, when all is done.
"Stop the violence," I beg you now!
before another's put in the ground.
Show your children, that's not the way,
Lets hold the peace, for one more day.

Connie E. Perry

Reflection

My dear old friend the tree is dead,
a cruel man has cut it down.
I asked him why - and all he said
was that he doesn't really know!

A single tree , what does it matter?
they're killing trees just everywhere,
he wanted just the view be better,
that's all about what he could care.

I know this tree since I was born,
I heard it talking to the wind,
I saw it drinking all the rain,
why did it have like this to end?

There are too many trees that die
from people's mind and hand,
it makes me sad and makes me cry,
I wonder - don't they understand?

"Dear Mother Nature" is her given name,
adored by all the people of this world,
I thought "Who ever want her any harm?"
and yet - my friend the tree was killed!

Horst W. Stoehr

Untitled

When I look in the mirror, I always see
A familiar face, who's better than me
He can run fast, but I am slow
He can jump high, but I jump low

He is well liked, and makes himself known
I blend in, and am afraid to be shown
He'll probably grow up, and make something of himself
I'll play it safe, and put my dreams on the shelf

But what bothers me most, about what I see
Is that, that boy's image is potentially me.

Elizabeth H. Ryan

Life's Treasure

Things that you love, both new and old,
a favorite shirt, old boots, worth more than gold.

A warm summer's night, with good company shared,
in laughter's echo, a moment well fared.

Blue birds that chuckle, dogs that smile,
make passing this way, seem well worth while.

The green of a meadow, mountains that stand tall,
listen to a stream, it's serenity will call.

A favor for someone, kind words from a pen,
enriches this life, from now till then.

A sky that's blue, not marked with a cloud,
enjoy it now, too soon comes death, with a shroud.

A fond farewell, to the friend you've had,
linger in the heart, with warmth and beauty, sad.

Joseph R. La Grasso

Chant Of An Abortionist

My palm to my belly gently pressed, I feel you.
A feeble pulsation, you slowly grew
to become an inseparable part of me.
And now I realize that only I shall decide
whether or not you will be.

I will rather not to know you, or see you grow
learning the thousand things I yearn to teach you so.
I will choose not to hold you or feel your tenderness,
reaching out in innocence, clinging to my breast.
I will deny your right to a face, a name, an identity,
since the decision of your existence rests solely with ME!

For who am I to bring you here,
Exposing you to the terrors and fears
That have made me heathen.
But if only I could have borne your pains
Or melted the chains that will bind you down
To the ground from which I must choose to carve you,
I would have given you birth.

Desree Karen Providence

"Wants"

What do you want?
A few minutes to eat.
Sorry! You can't have any.

What do you want?
A few minutes to relax in a warm bathtub.
Sorry! You can't have any.

What do you want?
A few minutes to have a quiet cup of coffee.
Sorry! You can't have any.

What do you want?
A few minutes to sleep.
Sorry! You can't have any.

What do you want?
A few minutes to wait on you hand and foot.
Oh Yes! You can have that.

Janice C. Spaulding

Precious Memory

Another flower was added to the Master's bouquet.
A flower so lovely and rare.
One of courage and strength and compassion,
A flower with (God's) love she shared.

He called her away to her home in the sky.
Her race here on earth she has won.
But her life will follow her down here below.
The race she so faithfully run.

Our hearts were made sad, but God knows the best.
A love one so dear made the goal.
She suffered so much in body.
But had peace in her spirit and soul.

We will miss her so much, for the kind deeds she did.
But to recall her we would not try.
For she's happy with Jesus, at (His) feet she sits.
To praise and adore (Him) on high.
She walked with (God) and she talked with (God).
And faithfully seed she has sown.
A harvest of souls she will reap here on earth.
Though she rejoices around Gods throne.

Eva Young

The Road We Choose

Look ahead and what do you see?
A forked path for you and me.
Which road shall we take?
Which path should we choose?
It all depends on the heart of you.
Tis time dear ones,
To lead the way
And help those less fortunate each and every day.
Show them the ropes,
Hold their hand,
Give them courage, so that they can stand.
The future depends on me and you.
For it's all in the path that only we can choose.

Brenda Tatro

Nanny

What is a Grandmother?
A Grandmother is — LOVE — from the earliest
days of my memory

It's trips; homemade root-beer; ham and cabbage;
turkey dinners; pies; cakes and always — LOVE

It's a burst of gladness and contentment when I
see her. It's warmth and understanding. It's
greying hair and wise old eyes and even wiser
recollections and always — LOVE

It's ailing limbs and a slower pace
It's dimming eyes in that loving face
It's a body tired and very worn, with
a soul that makes me glad I was born
It's quiet strength and inner peace,
facing the last and final release

What is a Grandmother?

It's — LOVE — 'til I can no longer remember

Audrey M. Whiting

Noah Begat

The Biblical boys were a sturdy bunch.
A hale and hearty lot.
Just look at the ages of most of them
When they begat what they begot.

Noah was five hundred
When his wife their sons did bear.
I've got to believe what the Bible says
Because I wasn't there.

Noah was six hundred
When he went into the ark.
Leading the animals two by two
Into the gloomy dark.

Forty days of heavy rain
Killed everything he knew,
Until there was nothing left on Earth
Except Noah and his crew.

Then the waters subsided
When it ceased to rain,
And everyone got off the ark
And began to begat again.

Al Friedman

Yesterdays

I see her often in my mind's eye
A happy child but a little shy
She had not a worry. Her days were all full
of the things that please a little girl.
She thought of the time she would be grown
and have a family all her own
I seem to see her as in a dream
This little girl, and yet it seems
She is so much a part of me
Tho' things are not as they used to be
I feel no envy for her now
Even when, at times, I wonder how
To cope with problems that come my way
And I seldom have a carefree day
But I have a family all my own
And with each trial my love has grown
I may dream a little once in a while
And remember that girl with a wistful smile
I would not go back to what used to be
But it's nice to remember when that girl was me.

Ethlyn Drury

Ode To A Pack Rat

I'm just like my mother, I've saved everything.
A jar, pictures, and a ball of string.
Why did I save so much of this or that?
I guess I'm just a pack rat.

I cleaned out my closets intending to throw some away.
But I put them all back, to do some other day.
Some memories are good, some are bad.
I saved them all and I'm glad.

Some make me cry, some make me smile
So I think I'll keep all for a little while
Would it be better to keep them, or throwing
Them away be worse?
Is this being a pack rat, a blessing or a curse?

Why did I save so much of this or that
I guess I'm just a pack rat.

Frances M. Chaltraw

"Touched By An Angel"

That face, such a precious face...
A little child of God;
Nothing can take its place.

Those beautiful innocent eyes...
Hair of silky white;
An angel in disguise.

The tiny hands so soft and warm...
A touch can melt the heart;
Such a glow around this child, halo adorned.

This little untainted being where sin
Dare not trod...
I lean to kiss this child,
And feel the presence of God.

Betty Vinson

Untitled

I understand that with my (un)boyish fears,
a little girl hangs, dangling life among her eyes.
Playing notes for a foreign tone and dancing,
slowly with a manner off beat.

"Invasion of people in my mind" she/he
hysterically whispered, laughing in his arms -

Catching the tears of hate morbidly with
all hope the poem of her favorite heart brings.

He does so so so so well.....

In front of the fire, she far away sits,
with the cold entangling her body —
Content she sits

Yes, I am comfortable, and how about you?

Ashley Willis

Immortal Son

Immortal Son, cast your shadow upon the city
A living Hell going on; in your eyes I see pity
People looking, but never seeing
People killing, they're fighting, they're disagreeing

Immortal Son, why is this so?
Gave all I had, but had to let go
Strong wind blowing; it tears us apart
Where do you run when everything gets dark?

Immortal Son, I am sorry to see
A rat race going on in a big monopoly
Could you wave your hand to even the score?
People living off millions; they want so much more

Immortal Son, do you have to go?
I pray for my soul and for all that oppose
What's done is done, so why do people lie?
Immortal Son, you're not even surprised

Don't leave me, don't leave me now
Immortal Son, you take it anyhow
Call to the wild, a cry in the sky
You grow up fast, people live, people die...

John R. Weber

Glade Of Furrow

Glade of furrow - blending amid the threshes of wheat were
Amid the thoughts, the values of which are unknown to me,
The winds will reveal how tender the shear are binded
How do we enjoy the abruptness of the kindred message;

Janet De Feyo

The Mirror Of Life

When I'd look in the mirror, this is what I'd see.
A lonely face, gazing back at me,
An oval face, framed by straight blondish hair,
Cloudy blue-gray eyes, that stare and stare,
A pale complexion, the color of paste,
A turned-up nose, God gave out in haste,
I had thought, that lonely girl was me,
'Cause In the mirror, that's what I'd see,
But then I looked, a second time,
And saw that the image, was not mine,
The only change, was my outlook on life,
The truth got through me, as sharp as a knife,
My face is the same, my hair is still blonde,
My smile is the same, of which I am fond,
My eyes are blue-gray, ready to pose,
My complexion is better, as is my nose,
I'm proud that I've changed what I thought,
I've learned a lot, and I have fought,
And now I'm happy, about what I see,
And glad that this person, is the real me.

Ashley Render

"A Musician's Dream"

A mountain lifts its crest amid the clouds,
A long, long road is curving round its side,
Below the long green meadow grasses wave,
As though a tide was ebbing in the glade;
And wild flowers show up here and there,
Their hue so varied by nature's brush.
The scene awakes and strikes a harp-like chord.

An orchestration beats on ears attuned.
A dozen insects beat their tiny wings,
Then comes a note, an answering call.
A song bursts out! A meadow lark! I sigh,
The notes are dancing in my head! I'll try!

Out comes my pen and paper, too. Alas!
I cannot capture quite the majesty...
Slow measure falters, ceases; I look up.
The sky is graying fast and looking down;
I find dark shadows on the grass, and mist,
Forerunner of the night, comes up the vale;
So, too, my dream dissolves away and yet,
One day! I'll try again...perhaps...kismet.

Judith Rubidge Koller

Meeting My Mother At Eighty

My mother is a remarkable woman, if the truth be told.
A mere child when she met her mate, and the story unfolds.

My grandparents came to America with little money, but full of hope.
Rising cost, growing family, it was hard to cope.

Alas, my mother, innocent, a teenager, knew not of life.
Yet promises, yes promises my grandparents made, now she is a wife.

My father was much older and was to provide.
Life proved such a struggle and strife could not hide.

There was arguing, fighting, and turmoil to endure.
Somehow vows of love, kept the reins in place, seemingly secure.

Fifty years of marriage passed and there was a celebration.
Shared with their twelve children, friends and other relations.

I used to blame my mother for many of my ills.
Now that I look back, I see she did her best with no frills.

My mother is eighty and we talked about the past and my crutch.
NOW, I understand this woman, who took little and gave so much.

I love my mother, we have no regrets of the past or people to blame.
She has enlightened me, given me hope, compassion, and a life to claim.

I'm glad we had this meeting, this meeting at eighty.

Enis Krol

Return To Budapest

I offered my son of twenty seven
A mother and son's "Last Fling"
Before he slips on his wedding ring.

To my greatest surprise he has chosen
Through a glass that was not rosen
In my memory of Hungary

There was no Schindler's list
And in the Hungarian winter's mist
We set out to gather flowers of memories.

He urged me on with earnest power
To reap the good, leave Babel's tower
Move on and clear the slate
In the semi free Hungarian state

Eva A. Schiff

My Prayer

I hope and pray someday to see
A Mother like I used to be,
To help my son once more to know
I am the Mother who loves him so.

My son is oh, so far away,
A year it seems, makes up one day,
I know I'll see him again someday
And never more to let him stray.

I left him in his Grandma's care
But my Motherly heart for him will tear,
I miss him terribly as you can see
But in June, I'll return to my son, Ricky.

I pray to the heavenly Lord above,
Someday I'll have my son to love,
To teach and love him in my own way
And help him to love me more each day.

Judy L. Stepp

Autumn

Crisp autumn mornings walking down
a narrow, wooded path
Sound of scarlet, maple leaves
rustling underfoot
From a distance Children's laughter, shouts
glad to be out of doors

Sunny afternoons down by the river
Feeding the ducks homemade bread
And hearing them quack their thanks
Down by the swamp
the cattails are unfluffing
Reeds are swaying in the wind

Cool autumn evenings spent beside
warm, crackling fires
roasting marshmallows on sticks
Beneath a yellow harvest moon
While the howling wind whistles
through icy lips

DeeAnn Nutter

Wind, Wind, Wind

Wind, wind and wind!
Amigo Mio, your sweet voice, have a wind sounds
Amigo Mio, yours blues eyes have wind and wind,
Amigo Mio, Wind, is need by nature,
Amigo Mio, them we are as wind,and natures.
Amigo Mio, Because ours Corazones, do not have wind!

Dolores Maria Bolivar-Brauet

New Orleans

Take a walk on the wild side
a place called New Orleans
It is one of the most art-related cities
But it sure can cause a scene.
The streets are packed with panhandlers
From tap dancers to clowns
And around eleven o'clock it is one of the craziest towns
Every one is crazy because of drugs and alcohol
And sure enough a fight breaks out soon after a brawl
Many people love it and at day it is fun
You can go shopping in the lovely New Orleans sun
You never will go hungry, there are many places to eat
For a fun time, stroll on down to Bourbon Street.
For Bourbon Street is a wild street with bar joints galore
It is always crowded but nobody is in a store.
Life is crazy in New Orleans
It is not a great place to settle down
But dare to discover the people of this town.

Joseph C. Viland

The Childhood Pony

There was a pony in my childhood dreams.
A pony that taught me things aren't all what they seem,
I loved the pony and it loved me,
But the pony was crippled you see.
My mother said I couldn't have it so I visited it at the
Stables each day.
But only time would tell how his condition would stay,
But his day came,
The pony of my childhood dreams took the step to his fame,
Yes my childhood pony died,
I cried and cried,
It happen so fast,
All though my life things never last,
I loved the pony I said once before
I know he will always adore,
And although he's in that big place in the sky,
My love for him will never die.

Cindy Morris

Our Home

It sits on a hill near the edge of town, nestled among the trees;
A rambling place with style and grace,
As lovely a house as you'd see.

Each spring the tulips come to life, the crocus and jews' mallow
Surround the yard, like a lovely card,
It awaits the warm days that follow.

In summer it rests mid the filtered sun that shines
through the lush, green trees;
Hot days so bright; warm, sultry nights,
Fragrant blossoms that float on the breeze.

Come autumn the house sits proudly among the bold,
bright colors of fall
Happy are we, and lucky to be
In the house when the leaves start to fall.

And who could miss a Christmas there, in wintertime it shines;
A fire's warm glow, the frosty white snow
Falls softly to cover the pines.

And so the seasons come and go, and though we often roam,
Our hearts are still in that house on the hill,
It will always be "Our Home".

Constance R. Fleming

Change—Who Wants It?

Change is an apple that was once a flower
a realty that was once a dream
a man who was once a little boy
a free man who was once a slave
an executive who was once a knave
a parent who was once a child
penicillin that was once a bad mold
a frog that was once a tadpole
a teacher who was once a pupil
a chicken that was once an egg
a brave man who was once afraid
a home that was once a blueprint
Change? That's what jingles in my pocket
Change...Who wants it?

Bea Fortin

A Raindrop

The tiny drop descends from heaven above;
A shadowing reminder of God's nourishing love.
The drop hits the ground and it shatters like glass;
So evenly it splatters and absorbs to the mass.
The drenching force of enduring love;
Awakens the flowers for all to admire.
These tears from God are the sadness He feels;
But beyond our control, the flower still grows.
How could we make a force so sad,
When His tears create beauty and nourish our hearts?
As a parent to child, He loves us still,
And we constantly hurt Him and we always will;
Knowing too well that His love will endure.

Christine M. Duncanson

My Sister, My Life, My Friend

From the moment I knew there would be one like me
A sister is what was meant to be
I would give all my love to this little tiny being
A sister is what brings my life a new meaning
A bonding so strong and a feeling so right
A sister is what brightens me she is my light
When sorrow fills up my tired weary day
A sister is what helps me to see the way
Her beauty is so powerful it's shown inside and out
A sister is what unconditional love is all about
A smile that could warm a cold winters chill
A sister is what gives me strength she is my will
Even though we live miles and miles away
A sister is what I think about each and every day
When we have a bad moment and do nothing but fight
A sister is what squeezes me real, real tight
There are times my sadness mounts in a big pile
A sister is what carries me that one extra mile
There will be a day when I will come to my end
My sister is my life she is my friend

Evelyn Grese

Analogy Of A Vibe

It was breathless—yes—we kissed before we even met,
A passionate moment locked in time—destined only when our eyes first meet.
Her beauty was God given.
No perfumes or oils to give me a faint memory of days long past.
Her disposition was locked in solitude.
She surrounded herself with a mysterious charisma
But as our eyes finally met, I untangled the aura which had been an enigma before me.
And as I smiled, I understood the mystery.
Because her spirituality whispered to me calm soothing words
which was like a vibration reminisce of my own.

Dwight Nawls

You

You appeared into my life one night, quiet and so shy,
a soft blonde-headed man, with eyes as blue as the morning sky.
You placed a smile upon my face and a happiness in my laugh,
lifted me so very high, and became my missing half.
You carried me away on a hope, a wish and a dream,
and gave me a strong shoulder on which to lean.
You took me places and showed me things I never knew,
Captured my heart, my soul, and I fell in love with you.
Now you are the love that burns eternal within my life,
and this poem is my gift to you this Christmas from your loving wife.
I love you with every precious breath I take,
with every unsure step that I must surely make.
I love you even in the darkest times, so dark I can not see,
because I know the sun will shine again, as I know we are meant to be.
I love you with every ounce of me there is to be,
and through the years I hope this you shall always be able to see.
And as we grow old together, I shall always love you so
very much, close my eyes and look back into the past to see,
The blue-eyed blonde, so quiet and shy, that fell in love with me,
you....

Jana M. Iler

Mystery

On the whispering wind I hear her name,
a sound so sweet, as none before.
Wishing this time to be much more,
her welcoming smile gives me life,
never before nor needed again,
a total resurrection with no exception.
It was said long ago,
under the sun, there's nothing new.
That then must mean there's nowhere to go,
nothing to show, and no time to be.
If it's all been done and said before,
can I possibly love you more?
If any lingering doubt yet remains,
just look what is, and is yet to be.
Your world remains unknown to me,
so then is mine to you,
a mystery.

John Tarr

Beyond The Looking Glass

She puts a ring of gold into her ear
A spray of scent at her throat.

She sees the sag of chin and thinks
Age breaching the moat

Of youth and time since spent
when skin was pearled with dew.
Now, hair once like the raven's wing
is frost dusted and oh, she thinks

Whose is the visage in the glass?

Time dulled eyes stare back, a dowager's squint
no more the maiden's flashing glint.

She turns away from this distressing view with grace
to see him standing there his loving gaze upon her fixed.

With joy her heart acknowledges his love
undimmed by time and knows full well

His eyes do not see what time and age have
wrought upon her face.

Alba R. Murphy

Of Time That Past

And the years fled -
A thought approached me with a scorpion's tail,
Spraying venom, to poison the brain.
A thought that burst inside of me,
And blew my mind back into the wind.
I feared then that soon,
Very soon, my soul would follow.
Did I come for you too late?
Was I to find you wrapped in someone else's arms,
Glistening with love, not mine?
Should I leave and come back as a prince?
For now, I'm just a pauper,
And I cannot shower you with diamonds;
I - I have only the evening stars to give.

Angel L. Aviles

Christmas Song

Christmas is a time for joy,
a time for memories.
It's a time for laughter, a time for fun,
a time for families.
It's a reunion—we'll all be together
to share our memories that will last forever.

I remember as a little girl standing by the tree,
wondering what Santa would bring for me.
Now that I'm older, I still sit by the tree,
but I don't wonder what Santa brought me.
I now know that the world is tough,
and some people just don't have enough.

My eyes are open, now I can see,
Christmas is about everyone, not just me.
I love the excitement, the family, too!
Now let me ask you—What does Christmas mean to you?

Diane Ely

"The Tie That Binds"

Inside a hospital nursery
A tiny baby lay,
More than Mommy's pride and joy
Or Dad's dream come true today.
For this child has two sisters
And an older brother too,
Each trying to find their own little niche
In this family, brought together, anew.

Marriages, Divorces, Remarriage
What a path for young children to tread,
They often pay for their parents mistakes
The price counted in tears they have shed.

Yet, every cloud has a silver lining
Every winter turns into Spring,
And for all the sorrows these children faced
Hope and unity, this birth will bring.

For each child is a special blessing
The greatest treasure one ever finds
But more than a blessing, this baby boy
Will be the tie that binds.

Bonnie T. Dennis

Untitled

My soul is entwined with love and happiness,
a vine that has grown from the heart of my lover,
one that is true and loyal and worthy of caressing
my feelings with the tenderest of touches.

Jenny Watts

An Act In War

Summer 1952

In open trucks the women came through town.
A tired few had infants at the teat,
But most were native women of the street
The army pushing north had run them down.

Inhabitants were not to know the time
Nor route of transfer to the pier and ship,
But someone knew or someone let is slip
And enmity became unindicted crime.

The lead truck braked and so delayed the flow;
As narrow cobbled streets now rained with stone
Which bruised and often cut into the bone.
All ninety cursed events that moved so slow.

The infants safe in mothers's arms were squeezed
The others put their heads between their knees.

Charles Creedon

Life

What is life?
A tunnel?
A maze?
A struggle?
Life, I've learned at a very young age,
is a very long journey through many ups and downs.
When you get through the downs, when you bring the downs up
by trying hard and loving all things, you then succeed!
By succeeding, you make life great!
Life's not always going to be good,
but when it is, it's the best!
Don't hide, face the fear and pain head on in life!
Come on!
Let's make life easier.
So many people try so hard to make life better.
All you have to do is do all you can.
Try and give what you can to others!
That's what we need in life.
That's all anyone needs in life!

Dina Reh

Abraham Lincoln

Back one hundred years ago,
Abe was a famous man.
He was trusted by all,
And to most everyone tall.
Mary, his wife, was so gentle and kind.
Abe's three sons almost drove him out of his mind.
A great president he did make,
Most everyone wished they could shake,
The great hand of old "Abe".

Dorothy M. Chandler

Silver Moon

By the light of the rippling water,
Above the crescents of the trees,
Flies the Moon at its early quarter,
Just as silvery as you please.
Lovers stroll the dark and winding lanes,
And kiss beneath darkened boughs.
All the beaus and all their pretty janes,
With promises of wedding vows.

What magic drives them ever-on?
What is there in the moonlight
That lingers 'til the new Dawn?
What is the magic of Night?
Above the crescents of the trees,
The Moon flies, silvery as you please.

James R. Poyner

Untitled

Crystals cry within their still eternity
aching for motion
to spread their clarity
An eagle awakens and begins a timely flight
dreaming of voice
to tell of its sight
A child is born and life's circle complete
awaiting the day
in death we all meet
Tides roll in with sedation of sound
damned for eternity
with variety unfound
Nightmares of love and dreams of lust
morality forsaken
and what of trust
Life's vile existence, a mockery to the mind
with the ability to reason
God's gift to mankind.

Justin Kulzyck

On First Looking Into Hubble's Findings

"If Hubble's lens should ever let us see
across the edge of time," the viewer sighs,
"the secret of Creation then would loom
open to view — the great, the final prize."

There might, of course, be something more beyond.
The "edge of time" might only prove to hide
the place from which to view a farther stretch
where light and lengths and speeds are multiplied.

Yet surely one day in the swirl of space
we'll trace that vaunted relic of the past —
the ball of mud or metal that was used
to make the Bang, the all-creating blast.

Then those who think they've snatched God's private truth
need only fear some childish tongue may cry
(like one who said, "The Emperor Is Nude!"):
"Who made the ball that banged? From what? And why?"

How many Adams from the very first
who hungered for an apple or a fact
have thought they grasped it firmly, then have found
the fruit was false. The tree remained intact.

Charles A. Cerami

Untitled

As the sun slowly slips beneath the horizon
again shrouding the world in darkness,
I think to myself
what would happen if it never returned.

In a lightless world how would we change
would the perpetual darkness enter our souls?
Would it slowly seep into the fastest reaches of our brains?
Would we become being consumed by blackness in every way?

Or could we be able to persevere in the face of the ultimate
adversity.
Could we light even brighter fires in our hearts?
Could we allow our souls to shine brighter than any mere star?
Could the eternal night make us seek the light in others?

For in a completely different world nothing could be the same
when faced with an utterly desperate situation there can be no more
compromise.
You can only go one way or another,
the real question for our race is which way will we choose.

Joel Schwendinger

The Swan

The swan looked like a silhouette
Against the waning sun,
Framed in serenity
By the last rays being spun.

One graceful wing had floated up
In a final exercise,
To receive a dusting of pale orange
From the sunset in the skies.

Enveloped in the arms of dusk
It issued a call of surrender
To the approaching blackness of the night
And the day's last fling of splendor.

Charles R. Watson

Maze

Left for dead in strawberry fields
All alone in muddy waters
It's back to blue face and black room
Out to burn down your innocent daughters
Two wrongs don't make it right
It all tastes foul so sugar coat it
It's all evolution adapt to confusion
It's hard to keep the truth in focus
Lay the jokers hand before them
Could bleed to death before they notice
Imprints in minds make no difference
Gave up on faith because it's hopeless
Those filled with riches pay the price
Those rich in riotous might just suffer
A penny for these thoughts
Here take a number
Those rich in priceless will definitely suffer

Brandon Coy

Untitled

Thru the valley of life into the sun
all God's children united as one.
The path is narrow the obstacles high,
"The Way is through Jesus!" we hear
a voice cry.
Compassion and Love, these are the signs
posted, directing as the road winds.
We struggle, we stumble, we stand up
again, led on by the Light with His
outstretched hand.
The evil one beckons with his earthly
things, but we see the Portals and
our hearts sing.
For there with His arms welcoming us
is the God of Creation, Protector, all Just.
Our journey is over, over death we have
Won, to spend all Eternity With
God and His Son.

Jewell Walsh

"Gathered"

One died today. His passing will be mourned,
and all that fate could tell me
was that his soul was scorned.
I couldn't warn.
I couldn't pray.
I could only complain.
That all my strength was not my own
And of this we are all before warned.

Joye Grace

Attainment

Minutes, hours, years,
All man's creations.
See that real time should not be feared.

It is there to use.
To enjoy, to accomplish,
Achieve and experience thought and feelings.

We need sense the dignity
The style and panache
Inherent with life and all this ancient path brings.

For it truly is a journey
To breathe each moment
Not concerned with an end, but slowing the now.

Respect, Family, Friends,
Risk, Laughter, Wind, Water, Motion, Music.
All gifts to be opened.

Age is growth.
Not to be feared,
But befriended and enjoyed as it was earned.

Jack Waring Miller

Will It Change

I can't do anything right. Never have, never will.
All my friends have talents,
riding horses, playing the piano, making teams.
Such options have come and passed with nothing but,
a little more loneliness and
disappointment than before.
I'm nothing special.
I'm just smart and the teacher's pet.
I'm writing this but I can't even write well.
Everyone is better and I come in last.
Anytime I try to take the spotlight.
Someone steals it back.
Will it ever change.
Now I know, even though I can't throw.
It doesn't matter.
That's not me, that's not what I'm meant to be.
Even though the world may
not think I'm special when I truly am.
I know I have a little place in my Father's heart and
will always be special to him. And he's the only one that counts.

Bethany Street

"Mountain Of Peace"

Up on the mountain I gaze out to see
all that the Lord has created for me.

I take in the beautiful breath taking view
and I wonder how God, how He really knew.

Just what kind of creation, he has placed here on earth
of how beautiful and glorious, the scenery was put forth.

I hear His sweet voice, ringing thru the air
I can tell how much, the Lord really cares.

Now here on the mountain, it's so peaceful and quiet
I shall not move for fear that I would doubt.

The animals they're grazing all over the land
they were put here by God, with just a command.

Here on the mountain, I feel so close to God
I can bow my head down, with just a slight nod.

I give Him my approval of how well he has done
for here on the mountain, I think He has won.

Diane B. Price

No Substance

Walking along the infamous blue field, passing the bugs,
All the blood suckers went into hibernation and were over fed
And this ghost town is yet to go to the grave, it's unpaved,
I am afraid of heights, one of the few things that I know,
All else is hypothesis and dreams, thoughts swirl, hair, curls,
all with no substance,
No common ground without faults, no hot plate without salt,
Ribosome organelles, cheap thrills, suicide cells, ringing bells,
Weave, weave a basket of my thoughts, I'll fill it up with spice,
Things break, turn to rust, dust, dead skin cells, and bells,
Killing bugs with my guilty heart and hand and show,
It doesn't matter, it's alive, true, but it's a small alive,
it has no substance,
Wings and sick, candlestick, cracks in the floor, they are alive,
I spend way too long looking at girls with pretty eyes,
Wasted time, lemon lime, can't explain this devil damned rhyme,
oh sing me a lullaby make it real quick,
I have guilt to do, feeling to forget, it all takes a time,
Time is an enemy, let the clock be my alibi, let my clock die,
No excuse, no disease, no part in the play, no substance.

Jeff VanDreason

A Smile?

It's amazing what a smile can hide,
All the pain and hurt that swells inside.

How would anyone guess you are sad,
When you walk around all lively and glad.

If you told people of the pain, they wouldn't believe you,
The smile is accepted and no one bothers to see thru.

So it really is amazing what a smile can hide,
But wouldn't it be better if people knew what was going on inside?

Aleda R. Conner

A Grandmas Wish

What would Grandma give to you that money cannot buy?
All the stars way up above that twinkle in the sky.
All the flowers in the wold with scents all fresh and sweet,
All the grass that's wet with dew to tickle your bare feet.
All the smells of nature - the rain - a burning log,
Puppies breath and just the smell of a roaming country dog.
The moon to light the nights for you - the sun to warm each day,
The clouds to be your pillows when nighttime comes your way.
But grandma cannot give you this,
Just God can make you see, All the wonders of the world He's
given you for "free".
So when I see your little legs trudging cross the land,
I know you'll see them all cause Jesus holds you by the hand.

Carolyn J. Budd

Family Ways Trivia

Feelings, confused and fashioned from the heart
All the time contributing a part
Making the best of come-what-may
Incurably wishing day by day
Loving and hating in good times and bad
Yet loyal and true while happy and sad

Weaving past, present, and future life
Aware of existing amid pleasures and strife
Yielding and unyielding, taking a stand
Small trials and triumphs making demand

Taking and giving is sometimes required
Relating in some manner surely desired
Ideally, a close kinship will abound
Very often instead, a storm is found
Imagine yourself unwanted and alone
Above all else, a family is home

Barbara J. Martin

Dan

Now that he's gone, I feel alone;
Alone like the wind begging the trees.
But no one listens.

I'm sad now that he's gone,
Sad like a breeze whispering in the grass,
But no one listens.

I feel alone, I feel sad,
Now, I listen.

I can't tell what will happen
I just cry and listen.

Caitlin Doyle

"Pine Country"

There's a range they call the Rockies from Montana to the line,
and along its distant reaches stands the grandeur of the pines.
In my dreams they seem to beckon, underneath the azure skies,
where the mountains and the forests spell a bit of paradise.
There they stand in peaceful splendor, with a beauty hard to find,
and down their emerald arching aisles a shady pathway winds.
It wanders to a place called Home where Nature has her way,
and when the skies with color glow to end another day.
A gentle breeze will stir the pines and I'll hear them whisper low,
"Come back again to the Rockies - Come back to Idaho."

Jack Reed

Life Way

It is a cold and dark day,
Along the life way.
One woman, her decision to make,
The life within, she will eliminate.
A million last year alone,
Never to have a happy home.
But don't despair...
The guardian lovingly watches over them,
Will take them home to be with him.
In green meadows warm with sun,
Children laugh and have fun.
They do not remember that day,
When mom chose her own way.
Now her heart and mind battle for control,
Seems to be a cold and lonely wind blowing through her soul.

Irene Swanner Odom

Might Have-Beens

You can take away my youth and good looks,
Along with my ability to understand what cooks!!
Even my energy in doing fun things,
And all the rest, that youth does bring!!

But, when all is said and done
I've had my world of youthful fun!!
With loads of good memories, within me still,
For you see, I'm not mentally over the hill!!

Age is a frame of mind we are in,
And I can remember the what ifs, and the might have beens!!
But, youth can only wonder, what's in store,
For, they don't have a memory of anything more!!

So, if we can teach them to be patient in life,
To enjoy the good times and forget that old strife!
Then, when old age comes a knocking and slips right on in,
They'll know what it was and about the Might Have Beens!!!

Barbara K. Nord

An Ode To The Poor

I was born on a Southern White Plantation;
Along with twelve siblings, who loved each other.
Our parents were poor illiterate tenant farmers, with determination.
They did the best they could as any good father and mother.
They worked in the fields planting and cultivating crops from dawn to sun down.
When each child became of age, he was taught to do the same.
On Saturdays we sold eggs and vegetables to the merchants up town.
Constantly we were told to be honest and work hard, in order to keep our good name.
Also, we were told to be good citizens, trust God and pray.
We could not see how these worthy virtues helped them to keep their pride;
Until we learned by personal experience that Jesus is the Way.
In every trial, temptation, struggle and storm God Stands by Our Side.
As I struggled to get out of poverty and get an education and be free;
Many relatives, friends and critics said, "It is Impossible".
Since I have proven them false, now many believe and see.
With faith in God, yourself and hard work anything is possible.
However, we must never be satisfied or comfortable with our plight.
We can choose our altitude, our platitude and even our attitude.
But forget not those who helped to bring us out of darkness unto the light.
Nor as we move up the ladder, do not neglect or abuse the poor multitude.

Joy Joseph Johnson

"You've Got A Friend"

The only friend you have is your mother,
Although you have sisters and brothers.
She wished you and suffered and cried in her joy,
And gave you her love and her world in a toy.

As you got older you became bold and laughed,
When she worried that you might learn sorrow.
While telling her stories you learned of your glories,
And dawning your hope and your faith in tomorrow.

Diplomas, employment, romance and a wife,
Mom hopes your prepared for your voyage in life.
Tell her you love her by being your best,
And give her a grandchild to sleep on her breast.

James F. Lyons

"My Son"

When the doctor slaps and the baby cries
Always means the sound of birth
Then the mother holds her new born son
There's no greater thrill on earth

Then a few short fleeting years go by
And she sends him off to school
Then a tiny tear wells in her eye
And she feels just like a fool

She holds him tight and kisses him
As he walks out thru the door
She knows he'll be back later
He's not going off to war

Then he's in his early twenties
With a new love of his own
And she watches him walk down the aisle.
My God! how he has grown

Very soon he'll make announcements
That a grandma she will be
Then the doctor slaps another child
That she'll bounce upon her knee

James C. O'Connor

The Living Light

Kindness — unwarranted
always present — part of him
like sunlight is to the day — inseparable.
Warmth emanates from him
fills the room he's in
penetrates the souls of others
like sunlight does the skin.
Sense of humor
to brighten up the gloomiest tombs.
Eyes that sparkle
shining with goodness
and a hint of mischief.
Hiding behind that desk
is not a man of stone
but a living, vibrant human being
that makes Apollo seem dim.
Of who do I speak?
but one could claim to be the likes of him —
he is my friend — David.

Deb Dickson

A Spring Vision

Like two buds under a tree
Among a forest with such abundance
Trying already to be noticed was he
Pulling - tugging nearly losing the stance
When behold did his eyes see
A special lady bud capturing the glance
Away with her to dance...Away with her to laugh
Minds turning slowly from fun to romance
Now the forest took notice of the buds new fancy
But with one heart spoken for there seemed to be a line -
If stepped over just a little to chancy
So with a view of what may - yet never be liven
The tulips touched as to seal their Spring Vision.

Dennis P. Smith

My Beautiful Lady

I looked at each dog and puppy as I walked
among the rows of cages.
Some were jumping, some barking, some quiet,
some acting so outrageous.

One dog was sitting quietly, precisely, very
ladylike, very smart.
I walked back to her several times, each time
she stole part of my heart.

She was so beautiful with her long pointed
face, white ruff and paws;
Rusty-reddish-brown, black hairs sprinkled;
I could find no flaws.

Her pointed ears would flick up into the air
each time I returned.
This beautiful Lady was using all her wiles;
to be chosen, she yearned.

I had wanted a little fur-ball, cuddly puppy.
It wasn't meant to be.
My beautiful Lady stole my entire heart;
she had chosen me.

Julia Brady

Remember The Good Times

A special touch, warming and secure,
an unspoken reminder that love is pure.

Joyful memories, meaningful and dear,
drifting, yet defining, those wonderful years.

Places we filled, with our lives entwined.
Places held special where once we dined.

Songs we remember that fill us with
dreams, timeless music, enchanting scenes.

Moments we shared, more treasured with time.
Healing the heart, soothing the mind.

Remember the good times were the words he left,
in a letter to be opened upon his death.

"Remember the good times," he had advised.
Their memory enriches and strengthens our live....

Jim Clarke

Escape

I sit here in the gathering dusk
And am able to detach myself from all humanity.

I watch the sun sinking slowly and am fascinated by the clouds gently brushing over the beautiful sunset, changing its aura with new shapes and color. Adding a new splendor to the already splendored view. The clouds move effortlessly as if being pulled by a string, as a kite would be gently guided to a destination.

The view is most magnificent!
Although the sun has slowly moved below the mountains,
The glow it casts is like a last gentle sigh of a long day's work well done. It is time to rest.

The clouds however, have just started their vigil of the night. Looking at the far horizons there is rain falling in long dark streaks against the paling sky. Lightning breaks with impressive strength. The thunder gently rolls as if pushing everything further on.

Yet still in another part of the sky is a moon - a moon so full and round. I know later, with the stars, it will end the final hours with its brightness.

Humanity is really very easy to escape when you can watch the heavens
And see three different shows at the same time.

Denise Chadwick

Unity

I will arise and go now,
and enter into a new life.
Where I am no longer a solitary creature,
but am a component of unity.

And there I will discover the solidity of faith,
the strength of security,
and the sweetness of companionship.

And I will offer encouragement,
provide understanding,
and share my desires.

And my soul will overflow with thankfulness,
invite hope,
and welcome his love.

And I will treasure my life partner......
For he is the light that illuminates my world.
I will arise and go now,
and enter into a new life.

Denise Bassham

My Mr. Fixit

As a baby he had a most photogenic smile
And beautiful blue eyes that would always beguile.

He could build his own toys from the time he was five;
On these little projects his quick mind would thrive.

He grew up to be as strong as a mule
And just a stubborn; he's nobody's fool.

He's smart and he's thrifty but he's always loved teasing
Myself and the cat, though he knows it's not pleasing.

He is quite witty though he doesn't even try.
It comes out so funny, you may laugh till you cry.

His sense of direction—a remarkable thing;
Almost as true as a bird on the wing.

God gave him a memory—he never forgets—
As sure as the sun rises and sets.

He has a big heart which he tries to conceal.
A "macho" man—to him nothing's a big deal.

And now he's an expert—engines, plumbing, and more.
He can fix most anything from ceiling to floor.

Though he's adapted quite well to his bachelorhood,
A bride in his future would make me feel good.

Elizabeth S. Gill

Oceanside Theater

Sea gulls fly over the land, let them all fly free
and become part of the sky.
And the sun's the limit for the freedom of flight
while we watch from the sand where we lie.
When you sit in the sand, let the sun shine down
and don't try to stop nature's way.
And the sea rushes in to be part of the land
while the sun sets behind a blue day.
While the sun sets behind a blue day.

Painted sky above the sea is like a portrait song
And the ending of the new day
and the sound of splashing water
Fill the air and the land
rolling back the mighty waves.
Rolling back the mighty waves.

Oceanside Theater, who was your creator?
We can guess it wasn't any man.
Oceanside Theater, while you were greater
man made castles in the sand.

Allen Dykes

In The Jungle

In the jungle tigers roar, monkeys screech,
and birds lazily soar.
In the jungle snakes slide past,
while spotted cheetahs run very fast.
In the jungle the wind blows hard,
and boars make use of their thick lard.
In the jungle animals run, but it is not all in fun.
In the jungle a new creature roars, while birds,
from the noise, quickly soar.
In the jungle machines cut down trees,
making the wind more than just a breeze.
In the jungle there's smoke and fire,
as the piles of logs gets higher, and higher.
In the desert vultures like to soar,
because there isn't a jungle there any more.

Britt Halvorson

"It's Something Beyond"

It's Something beyond we cling to when lost,
And days are so bleak and gray.
It's Something beyond that calms all our fears,
And lights our paths, along the way.

It's Something beyond the prayers of our hearts,
That gives us the peace we seek.
For somehow we know, that Someone beyond
Is there to hear, each prayer we speak.

No one doubts that You are always near,
Always near, our hearts to cheer.
A tender shepherd to guide and love,
Our constant comfort from above.

It's Something beyond that helps us to find
The love we keep searching for.
You find it by faith, just seek and you'll find,
Just knock and He, will open the door.

Bozena Kalista

"From My Heart I Cannot Hide"

It's hard waking in the morning
And dealing with this learning
that this pain will never go away.
It's even harder facing another long day.
Yet, the nights are even longer
With this pain that's growing stronger.
Sometimes, I wish I would never wake,
For this tearing at my heart I cannot take.
Loneliness envelopes like darkness.
My days, my nights, fills with sadness.
If only I could find a love so true
My world would not be so blue.
You filled my days and my nights.
Turning my darkness into light.
Suddenly, with my love, you departed
Leaving me crying, broken hearted.
You turned my sunshine into rain
And filled my lonely world with pain.
From my heart I cannot hide
So, my only wish — is to die.

Belinda Corley

Suspicious Woman

She has lived in Lebadi for several years,
and every night she goes home in tears.

The changes that occur every day,
other people don't see, "she's crazy", they say.

The store she saw yesterday is no longer there.
Now it's a place to fix nails and hair.

The butcher store where she bought her meat,
is now a doctor's office where they look at feet.

The shop where she used to get her sweaters and dresses,
is now a print shop, with ink and presses.

Everyday she looks at the town, that makes her so suspicious,
she thinks there is an evil, dark and pernicious.

Everything around her seems so strange and eerie,
trying to understand it makes her weary.

She hopes this strangeness will soon be gone.
Even if it ends, she will always be a suspicious one.

Amber McMurtry

The Forgiving Sea

Now for a time thou art at rest, a sleeping sea thou sure must be. And from thy face doth radiate a peaceful glow that, for endless hours, it troubleth me not to gaze upon.

My eyes behold no subtlety; no frown nor wince but honesty; peace the way I seek it. And yet I know, when troubled so, thou canst turn to me a face of anger that gets my rapt attention.

What troubles and upsets thee so? I've pondered late and long. Thy ripples and thy breezes too — thy stirrings doth whip them high with winds that blow and waves that grow.

If truth be known, thy face can feel, yet doth not show the damage done by prow and keel. 'Twas scared and marked but moments back, yet nothing shows the instant that my ship is gone. But I know you feel, though no one knows how your face is healed.

And still I sense anxiety there; restless winds that swish, "BE GONE!" A wanting to be left alone to heal thy face before the dawn, so thou canst smile to God with nary a scar for Him to see.

Yet, knowing this, I cannot stop and across thy lovely face yet another ugly wound I make. But I'll tarry not and tiptoe my ship as quickly, quietly and as lightly as I can and ask forgiveness from your smile and trust my life into your hand ... while hurriedly and humbly sailing on and on.

Glynn R. Adams

Forget-Me-Not

Our new found Love was exciting
and fun.
We shared ourselves telling of all
we done.
In our closeness our lives were
fused together.
With a promise to remain that way
from now until forever.
But I realized, as we grew with time
That you could never be fully mine
Our lives were to different in the peas
Our future together would never lost
I know we must live our lives apart
While keeping fond memories close to heart.
Please, treasure our love with each passing day
It helped us to grow in a special way
Like the tiny flower that wilts and dies
My fading love for you also cries
Forget-Me-Not

James Nichol

To My Love

I would like to hold hands with the wind
And go
Skimming over treetops,
Barefoot lightly touching the ground,
lying on cotton soft clouds.
And then
Go running through dew covered meadows
Touching with fingertips the mountains
Playing hide-and-seek amid foam covered waves
Yet always
Returning to the safety of your arms.

Jerri Davis

Thoughts From The Bathtub

The cowgirl sleeps at night
And has no respite.
Bells ring, birds sing
I feel like a king or something.

The actors did so just;
The audience did so much.

Do no wrong.
Wring the gong.

The truth makes me free.
There are no pans on me.
Have a date. Locate a mate.
The city is better than the country.
The fanatic flashes.
High voltage is better than low.
Weekly newspaper are better than daily newspapers. Yeah!
Have a date tonight.
The night is bright.
Yes, no
Yes, no

Ann Franklin

To George (Family Dog)

George was his name
And he knew the rules of the game
He would let us know he was not a chicken
For we would find him resting in the kitchen
Finding the right food was such a fuss
For it did not matter, for he loved us
Black, brown and white was his hair
And we could play anything, he did not care
His tail a wagging to the beat of his bark
For the time he spent at the park
His toy was a squeaky gray mouse
To which he ran about the house
There, a scratch at the door
Now it's time for basket ball on the floor
George is gone, so is his empty dish
Yet he fulfilled our greatest wishes
Good-bye is so hard to say
But don't be sad, we will meet again someday

Daniel B. Lajeunesse

Creativity

It's strange watching someone writing poetry
And I feel very much
alone
For the poet
Whose job it is to communicate and express
With imaginative power and beauty of thought
In the moments of creativity
Is communicating only with himself.

Elizabeth Severino

Night's Curtain

The curtain of night around me falls
And darkness wends its way.
The wind is echoing in dark halls
Where once shone bright the day.
The cool night breeze flows gently 'round,
Stars twinkle far away,
Within my heart a stillness I've found
At closing of this day.

Julie M. Curan

Whites Kill Whites

They say that blacks kill blacks,
And I reckon that is true;
But did you know what whites kill whites?
And they kill black folk, too.

The fingers that pulled the triggers
On Malcolm X that day,
They were black, or so they say.
But the power behind those fingers
Was white as white as day.
And the power behind those fingers
Was clearly C.I.A.

And who killed Che Quevara?
And Martin Luther King?
Think about these facts above,
And THEN let freedom ring.

Ann C. Beaudet

The Park

The time I have here is limited,
And I wish to spend it wisely...
With you.
Show me where your spirit lies,
Show me where your memories dwell...
I want to see your private playground—
Tell me about the scab on your knee,
Or the time you played doctor behind the slide,
But please don't keep your secrets.
Let me smell the grass after mowing
And taste the sweat of your chin
Following the never-ending game of tag.
I want to watch the eternal sunset,
Smell the barbecue scorching another rib.
The child-like is not the childish,
For here, everyone enjoys living.
Don't be embarrassed to show me...
Because it is part of learning.
Please teach me...
About you.

Christopher T. Brumfield

The Guardian Angel

A one hundred year old Photograph Stares out from a frame.
And, if you look really close, you'll see her eyes are just the same.
Well, I don't remember her, But, I know her really well.
From the stories that my dear grandpa always use to tell.

Elizabeth may Hipwell was her maiden name.
Grandpa loved her very much. together they had my mother.
Apart of their love that they could touch.

I loved listening to Grandpa's stories -"More, Grandpa, more!
He told me that my grandma died when I was only four.

My grandma's my Guardian Angel.
She's in on the decisions that I make.
She's always there watching over me.
And guides every step I take.

Well, I don't know where I'm going.
But, I know where I've come from.
Grandma's my Guardian Angel, and I'm her special one.

Sometimes, when I am tired, I feel Grandma take my arm.
Somehow she says, "keep on going, Claudia 'cause you can't
just give up now!" and when I'm feeling troubled and
I don't know what to do Grandpa whispers,
"Claudia do your best. Were really proud of you."

Claudia Schneider

My Awakening

My God allows me to dream
And in my dream
I walk without the aid
Of a cane, a walker, or chairs with wheels
Walking upright once again, smiling
And laughing, no feeling of pain within my body,
My eyes not burning, nor feeling weak.
Awakening I am aware I dreamed it all
And yet it does not sadden me.
Thankful for the dream I go outside
And welcome the new day,
Happy to be able to enjoy my awakening.

Anna Rose Rito

The Center Of The Earth

The center of the earth is the place where you stand
And it is holy ground.
The drumbeat of the world is the beat of your heart
With its rhythmic, throbbing sound.
The seasons of your life are a cycle resembling
The seasons of the earth—
From birth, to life's vigor, to age and to death,
Then on to a higher birth.
The meaning of the circle is earth bound with Heaven,
Eternal and complete.
And you stand at the center, enshrining the ground
That rests beneath your feet.

Betty Gubler

Serenity

Put me on a boat in the middle of the sea,
And let it drift away with me.
The sound of the water rippling off the boat,
While the whistling sound of the wind sings a note.

Oh, the peace and quiet way out there,
All that relaxing time without a care.
So much different from the sea to the land,
Although bound together by the shore full of sand.

Let the fresh smell of the sea carry you away,
That brisk clean air you don't get every day.
All the fish just swimming around so free,
That's the kind of place I want to be.

All the hustle and bustle left behind,
With only relaxing thoughts in your mind.
Oh, what a life that would be,
Drifting around on the open sea.

Jane Baker

"Share With Me"

Come to my door,
and let yourself in.
We'll share some secrets,
now, where to begin!

Come to my hearth,
and warm yourself, dear.
We'll share some wine,
and maybe some tears.

Come to my bed,
and lie next to me.
We'll share our love,
how wondrous 'twill be!

Bernita A. Lolley

A Perfect Night Unforgotten

This time... the city lights will admire us
and light our magic sky
While we sit wondering how to halt
One second from passing by.

This time... the moon will glow her dreams on us,
As if it were a quest,
Shining through each stretching branch
To wish for us the best.

This time... the wind will clear the dust for us
and guide us on our way
To what tomorrow has for us
and what yet for today.

Jamie Beth Calvey

What Happened To Tuesdays?

Today was Tuesday, morning and afternoon,
And looking toward another,
I guess we lost today.

Today was Tuesday again,
Playing tricks with umbrellas,
Keeping sun or rain, or was it both,
Away, hiding in the clouds.

Today was Tuesday again,
And they seem further away than before,
Will we ever remember, how many are left?
Some with rain, some with sun.

And some just peeking beyond clouds,
On Tuesday...

Herbert T. Smith

Friendship

When I couldn't tell anyone in my family I told you,
and never had to worry about hearing it said again.

When I got my first kiss, I told you. When I didn't
feel like talking you never pushed. I've never had to
give you an explanation for anything. If, I ask I
always got the truth from you. Good news or bad news
you are always there for me, but you know what? The best
thing about this friendship is we don't owe each other
anything. Were both giving, because we want to. Can
friendship get any better than that? I don't think so

Deborah Woods

Can You Hear Me

Don't say that I am different
and never wonder why;
Don't laugh and turn your head from me
for someday, too, you'll cry.

It may be that you cannot hear
as the drummer does his part;
I know your world is what you see
but there's a song within my heart.

I hear it! Come close and listen!
the melody is love.
I wonder do you ever gaze up there
where the stars shine bright above.

I love so many people
even those who do me wrong;
And I know someday when I'm laid to rest
the world will hear my song.

Betty Scrivner Madey

Mountaintop Memories

The sun is dropping behind the earth's horizon
And night is drawing her thin gray veil, of day's intermission
Across the stage of the world.
Man's feeble imitation of God's fireflies, are rising from the weeds,
Of buildings and boulevards, that scar the valley below.
They hang in the air above them like tethered flower gardens.

The loneliness of this spot crashes over me like a wave.
Oh, love, why am I here alone? When everywhere out of the night
There is some distant light, that patters a moment we knew.
My own love...
Found.———only to be lost again;
As the light of a passing ship rises high—then disappears
In the hollow of a wave.

Somewhere in that garden of lights,
You are warming a bed of new desires;
While I sit here, high on a hill,
Warming my passion;
With the memory of your kisses, —before a burned-out fire.

John R. Kinard

Sleep

When dreams are borne and fill our minds
and night prepares its dew;
The light that's cast from heaven above
reflects on us anew.

'Tis in this light that comfort comes
and hate and fear does wane;
Where trials of the day go numb
as we ease our silent pain.

Let wounds be healed in stillness, rest,
let weary souls rejoice;
Dispose of burdens heavy weight
delay the nagging choice.

Turn off life's struggle and conflict's press
that ache inside your head;
The body's tension reflects the world
release it to your bed.

Lie down, oh battered soldier, lie
and close those eyes that weep;
Let peace fulfill you and render pure
the virtue found in sleep.

Greg Prichard

A Lost Love

When the one you love isn't there any more
and no one knows just why
tell them how you loved him so
and why he had to die

I ask myself what I did wrong
I helped him all I could
I tried to see his way of things
I knew he thought I would

I couldn't understand the way
he hurt himself like this
I tossed and turned and cried at night
until it ended with a kiss

This glass remains within my house
to remember him each day
how he drank so much
and ruined his life in each and every way

I'll remember the love we had together
and the life we had planned to spend
through our hearts time became countless
then our love and dreams came to an end.

Julie Elliott

Late At Night

Things are different, late at night, that's when I think of her;
And of a time when things were right, at least I thought they were:

We were young, and naive, but thought that we were not;
And neither of us would believe, just what the future wrought:

We laughed, we played, we tempted fate, arrogantly with eyes closed;
Until one day it was too late, as we watched love's wrath unfold:

She said I was the one to blame, and maybe she was right;
But it still haunts me just the same, when it's late at night:

She meant so much, it was so sad, and it was the right thing I know;
But the hardest thing I ever had, to do was let her go:

I'm much older now, than I was then, the pain's long since gone away;
But I long to be with her again, almost every day:

I wonder if she thinks of me, somehow that would make things right;
Dare I ponder, that maybe she, has a late at night:

People say that I am strange, because I don't take part;
But that old dating game's, no longer in my heart:

The words I seek, just don't exists, or somehow seem surreal;
This poem is weak, it can't express, the way for her I feel:

Tomorrow is another day, from dawn's first early light;
But that's an eternity away, for now it's late at night:

David R. Jenney

The Lace Maker

She is a grisly creature with body fat and round
and one that walks on tip-toe wherever she is bound.

In dark damp places she is often found
although she utters not a single sound.

Her home is often just a mound
of fresh damp grass, or silted ground.

When unaware that she is near
one's heart will sometimes fill with fear.

Of beauty, she has not a trace
upon her dark repugnant face.

She spins in space; ties each thread in it's place
and designs the finest lace.

Elizabeth Lasswell

Tomorrow...

I took a stroll down memory lane,
And realized how it had changed.
The brook that used to tame my fire,
Is now engulfed by thick, barbed-wire.
The slide that used to give me speed,
Is now replaced by unmowed weeds.
The pool that used to soothe my skin,
Is now drained out and full of tin.
The grass that used to cool my feet,
Is now like straw turned from the heat.

The one thing that remained the same,
Was that blue swing which bared my name.
It called to me to swing up high!
It told me I could reach the sky!
And so I did that summer day,
I was a child again at play!
And as I sadly touched the ground,
My eyes gazed left, and soon I found,
A penny hidden in the dust,
With words that read, "In God We Trust."

Elise Dolat

Rebirth Of Living

To study one being, from new plateau's above
and relive past anger, sadness and love
can bring forth truth, and new ideas to be
a metamorphosis of the soul, with new eyes to see
accepting wrongs once had, but never to forsake
to give not to receive, knowing true wealth will await.
Disarrayed illusions of hopelessness can be lifted by a true heart
one that looks beyond the bleak and the depths of the dark
and envisions a rift, in the entwined curtain of hate
and rips through its tight fabric, to find the truth that awaits
to find peace in its love, is the Glory of Living
to encounter the love in its peace, is the virtue of giving
to be wise is to know, one's heart is not without flaw
or these trials of life, could have no place at all
even on the threshold of nothing, can an eternity begin.
for all have this spirit, to release from within
without the shackles of doubt, one may seek and behold
that there is a straight path, through the labyrinth of the soul

Joseph P. Garcia

Christmas Ghosts

We sit around the tree, my ghosts and I,
And reminisce of Christmases gone by;
The gifts, the smiles, the tears I know I'll shed —
Forget the pain, be glad they're here instead!
This night I'll not deplore those that I miss;
But, rather, smile and blow them all a kiss
For auld lang syne and all those wondrous eves.
My heart, though sad, is blessed as it perceives
That, though they're gone, I know they're with me still;
They live in love and so, forever, will.

So, peaceful be your rest, and may you find
A home as warm and loving as my mind.

Helen Pawlowski

Regenhardt Farewell

I am not the first to die
And roads beyond bring ever more.
But I must hope that someone's son
Will speak of war no more.
I did not choose this age to live
Or seek a soldier's martyrdom.
This lonely land I barely knew —
So many miles from home.
In Spring of life and Spring of year
It is goodbye, my task is done.
For April shall not come for me
And I will feel no summer sun.
To live, believe and understand
Was all I sought to do,
But fate decreed it otherwise,
My cross must pass to you.
In spirit now my hand extends
To all with war distraught.
Oh grasp my hand and still the fear
That I have died for naught.

Floyd A. Balman

Untitled

While walking through the garden, the Savior took my hand
and said to ask three questions that I wished to understand

I did not have to speak them, He heard them as I thought
and so I started asking for the answers mostly sought
"Dear Savior, I'm so overwhelmed that for my sins you died?"
"I LOVE MY CHILDREN ONE AND ALL," He answered as He cried

"Sweet Savior, why so many times surrendered I to fear?"
He laughed as He embraced me... "I'VE ALWAYS BEEN RIGHT HERE"

I had but one more thing to ask and knew what it must be
"My Lord of Lords, I tried so hard, have you been pleased with me?"

"I HAVE KNOWN YOUR HEART AND EVERY THOUGHT
YOU HAVE LOVED ME AS THOUGH MY CHILD"

Then Jesus held my face to His and beamingly, He smiled

Jeanette Madera Bongiovanni

"Ode To An Old Trunk"

In memory of father's love of poetry, passing this legacy onto his family. —Howard F. Goldey 1995

Just let me retire, dear old friend,
and say goodbye today
You have travelled around the land
and places far away —
Yes you have ridden many a buckboard,
stage coach and the old boxcar
And traversed deserts, mountains and
seen Asia afar —
You served your master well,
but like all who pass this way
The purpose has been fulfilled for those of another day
Offspring have taken over with plaids and gaudy array
But don't you fret dear old friend,
they'll pass your way some day —
You redeemed yourself with circuses,
horse racing, and ships large and small
And the shows that were performed in many an opera hall —
So, I'll bid a fond adieu and send you on your way
To where we all eventually will wind up some day
Down to the discarded haven where the worst is like the best
You have done your job ever so well and earned eternal rest.

S. Howard Goldey, Hollywood, Florida, circa 1965

Meaningless!

As sure as the sun rises in the east
And sets in the west,
Is the inevitable termination of life.

Man seeks.
He seeks till the dawn of a new day.

Man finds.
He rejoices like the sculptor who finds clay.

Man lives.
He has sought and found temporal joy.

Man dies.
He finds 'twas all a perfect ploy.

But always near is the one who knows all.
He knew that we were to fall.

But hope is man's rallying cry!
Without it, life just passes on by.

Fiona Lam

Sheep

There are sheep in the fields
and sheep on the shore
Which way do they wander
when they get bored?

Rams with horns and
rams with ewes
Who will have the first lamb
before the cows cry moo?

Shepherds keep watch for wolves and hunters,
while dogs gather the sheep to be slaughtered.

It's sad you say when one lamb becomes a dinner,
but how wrong you are for the children would have starved.

Yes, sheep are many and shepherds few,
but each one knows what to do
before the spring comes
and brings lambs anew.

Jennifer L. Parker

Playful Hope

Swing back and forth one hundred times
And study the clouds through child-eyes
Cottony dinosaurs, sounds of ferocious roars
Bad dreams last night..swing some more.

Filled with a terror not understood
Shamed and confused and feeling no good
Swing faster with eyes deep, dark and dim
So much pain trapped from within.

Swing back and forth as high as you can
Grabbing those clouds with strong little hands
Empower yourself and you will not fail
Your truth is profound...Your innocence prevails.

Swing high and low...Swing up and down
Let the breeze lift you...hear the wind sound
Magical thoughts keep your spirit alive
And benevolent arms will help you survive.

Carol Robinson

Alone

I feel so alone, why do I feel this way, I just wish God would come
and take me away.
So I could join a father I once lost.
Every time I feel things will be okay, something else gets in the way.
The way of my happiness, I feel so alone, I just want to go home.
To get away from all the hurt and pain.
I feel as if I'll never be sane.
Why did he go before me?
I want to go to thee,
Thy place where he lies in peace.
I just wish I could speak with him one last time,
I would tell him how I miss him so,
and if it was up to me I would of never let him go.
Why did he leave without me, I have so many questions and no
answers you see.
I cry myself to sleep each night,
and thinking how His death was such a fright.
It really hurts to know, that without a father I will grow.
No one seems to understand how I feel, my pain and hurt is
unbelievably real.
I feel like my heart is torn in a thousand pieces, and everyday my
pain increases,
As my poem comes to an end, I just want him to know that
someday we shall meet again.

Jessika Doeblin

Comparison

I can compare my mind to a cloudy sky,
and the atmosphere filled with streaks of dampness.
I can compare my body to a rosebush
that has lost its buds for the winter
My eyes, to the stars at midnight
and everyone who stares, wonders
what hides behind them.
I can compare my heart to a roaring ocean
rising up the bank, hoping to trickle someone's feet.
And I can compare you to me.
Like a dream that lasts all night
but never remembered in the morning

Faith Dorsey

Ducklings

She loved feeding ducklings
And the broom could wait
In her wild looking bedroom
Left in her wake.

"I'll clean it up when the ducks are fed,
Pick up my clothes and make my bed."
She would dream her dreams and go on her way.
Saving her work for another day.

Now she is gone and in my sorrow
I still hear her say "I'll do it tomorrow"
As off she would go to her "Friends" by the water,
My heart holds such grief at the loss of my daughter.

And some days it seems in the midst of my weeping
I'm so glad she fed ducks instead of sweeping.
And I hope somewhere in Heaven above
God will find her some little ducklings to love.

Ellen J. Speight

Winter's Tale

It's a too familiar story in a long familiar rhyme,
And the deaf do it to waltz step in a slow three quarter time.
For the King has lost his scepter and the Queen can't find her crown,
While the Princess Royal is dancing in her broken-hearted gown.
For the sunlight brightens princess, but the moonlight makes the rules
And before Alpha Centuri is the playing ground of fools
Making nursery rhymes for grownups to a rhythm called baroque
And there's no chance for repreavement till the Jester finds his joke
Which is hiding in a corner watching lovers talk in lies,
And the Jester knows the ending, but he saves it to surprise
The strong and tender children who were looking for a rhyme,
But were locked into a waltz step in that dead three quarter time.

Carol J. Cope

Letting Him Go

You've loved someone for all these years
And then he's gone - amidst your tears
No matter how very strong you feel,
It's still a shock! One quite unreal!

Life does go on - day by day,
Time does help - so they say.
No one knows the hurt in your heart,
And how terrible it is to be apart!

You have to believe for him it's best,
Because he's at peace, and now at rest
You feel so selfish and want him here,
So you can hold him and have him near.

But he's in heaven and happy now,
Remember the day when you took the vow.
In sickness and health - til' death do as part,
Live with the angels - my dear sweetheart!

Carol J. Walker

Lonely Is The Night

As the stars fill the heavens
And the moon puts on its grin.
It's another night I'm by myself
As loneliness sets in

Sometimes at night, I need someone
but no-one is there,
To give me comfort when I'm blue
or tell me they care.

Is there anybody, as I reach into the night
who will hold me close, and assure me I'll be alright

Just a shoulder to sometimes cry on
To blot away my hurt felt tears
someone to rely on
To ease my troubled fears.

I know my friends are out there
All I need do is pick up the phone
but that far from comforts me,
when I'm lying here all alone.

Here I am; filled with lonely plight
I can make it through the day, but so lonely is the night

Edward Wilkes

Friends To Be

I am on the face of frozen ponds,
And the October-trees know Me well;
The last butterfly of summer comes so gladly to rest in My hand;
A wrinkled bullfrog chugs his thanks at season's end,
He greets Me at the gate of Winter to sing hoarse praises;
Late-August flowers show tears of dewy joy,
On their now-scentless September-blossoms,
And genuflect in the cool breeze of peace,
That flows from My cloak like Autumn;
These are My simple, happy creatures who gather to My side,
When the Time is near;
Only you shrink from Me into musty alleys of unlit fear,
When I stand opening the Door to Home;
You, who loiters on the bleak corner of Reality,
And, shivering, hides in the dinge of your own existence;
All others welcome Me as a pleasant and gentle Friend,
We walk together amidst Forever in the sweetness of Knowing;
Step beside Me and I will cease to make you tremble;
Sit with Me in unending meadows;
Follow Me Home again.

John A. Storm

Friends And "Friends"

There are friends who try your patience,
And there are "friends" who say the right words.
There are friends who understand your mood changes,
And there are "friends" who comment on your coldness.
There are friends that visit and help when you're sick,
And there are "friends" who send a get well card.
There are friends who let you know when you're wrong,
And there are "friends" that say everything's
alright, regardless.

There are friends who will lend you a buck,
And there are "friends" that will say, I'm sorry but—
There are friends who will watch your back,
And there are "friends" that turn their backs on you.
There are friends who will back you up,
And there are "friends" that will use you up.
So as with all things in this life,
Be particular in your choice of "friends".

Juanita J. Brown

Treasure Beneath The Skin

For the richness of life, look for peace within,
And there you'll find a very special friend;

Someone to look after your life long success
To make sure you have all the best;

Rely and trust those inner gut feelings
To gain the riches of life's wheelings and dealings;

Let go of your frustration and pain,
Be burden free; a crown you will gain;

A warm fulfillment of peace this will bring,
'cause you see, this is a spiritual kind-of-thing;

Keep your heart open and do not boast,
Save that room and energy for the Holy Ghost!

Dorothy L. Edwards

Character

Where minds are clear, and men see light,
And thoughts come free, all freedoms within sight,
Where men can walk the darkest street,
No vicious foe, will they ever meet,
Where speech is aired, as the truth is honored,
As words flow fearless, and ambitions go forward,
Where all show respect for what is the Law,
And Justice is handed out without a flaw,
Where honesty takes its sacred place,
And men become blind to other men's race,
Where work is done, not just for money,
But toil is cherished, hours being dark or sunny,
Where just reward is the policy of the Boss,
Harassment and doubt, he never does toss,
When peace and love, forever will reign,
And works of men will never be in vain,
On these pleasant glories, my God, let mankind forever walk,
And with each step, pleasant words, may they ever talk,

Cecil S. Ramdayal

Wild Child

One who loves the flash of lighting
And thrills to the thunders roar
Plays within the rain and puddles
And begs the Gods for more.

One who's hair must blow
Wild and free in the wind
And feel the brazen heat and biting cold
Against their naked skin.

They walk among the jagged rock
Made by natures own
Fearing not the things unseen
That lurks beneath the stone.

They ride the high seas of life
Standing bravely upon the bough
Cutting loose anchors that bind
Riding out the tide somehow.

O, wild child of the earth
Where cometh your spirit within
Devouring the laws of nature
Disturbing the hearts of men.

Hazel F. Creamer

Reality

We start out as mere babes
And through the years
Are expected to turn
Into responsible productive adults
We are taught and eventually learn
The differences between right and wrong
We experience moments of joy
And endure moments of sorrow
Friends styles
Family ideals
And social morals
Mold us into the individuals
We are supposed to be
Then when someone else thinks we are ready
We go on to lead
Those responsible productive adult careers
Which we
Regretfully
Have waited for
Our entire lives

Evanthia Filiou

We Can Be Whoever We All Want Too Be

Being somebody is special
and too dabble is necessary
For any of us who think
Will be reminded that we all did blink
Not at only of what is of the past
But at also at who we became of the vast
Setting aside our differences
we all did find that we all can be of our natures
For we all can't be who we all not are
If we discovered we all are not in total par
But as the years go by and on they go
We all get better at not only what is wrong
But we all correct all of our mistakes
Only then to see
What we all wanted to see ourselves to be.

Forrester Foresttee Carpenter

"For Alissa"

A little girl used to knock on my door
And want to bake cookies or try to keep score
When we played Crazy Eights or Rummy on the floor.
When school time came, she passed by on her way
And would wave and say, "Grandma, I'll be back for lunch today".
In Spring, when it was time to start working outside
That same little girl was there with Grandma as her guide.
She'd make a hole and put in a seed, add some water and food
it would need.
She'd visit each day to see how it would grow,
And her pleasure knew no bounds, as the shoots started to show.
She grew, as those shoots did, tall, slender and pretty,
Through the grades into high school. Now to graduate, she is ready.
I miss that little girl with her apron so big,
A large spoon in her hand or a trowel to dig.
But I'm proud as can be of the young woman she has become
With the good points I see adding up to quite a sum.
Good luck to you, Lissie, please, don't change too much.
I like you as you are, you see and hope that you'll always have
that touch of humor, good sense and curiosity.

Helen F. Lemak

The Storm In My Heart

Have your ever stood by your window at night
And watched clouds drift across the moon?
Have you ever watched the trees in their weird ghost dance
Their music, the wind
And the plaintive cry of the loon?

Have you ever seen a twinkling light
Down some dark, and shadowy lane,
Did you ever hear the thunder roar
And the lighting flash
Washed by a hard, driven rain?

My dearest, if you have ever seen this
Then you know how I feel
And how much I miss you
Since you are gone.

Helen Marie Hood Ronsonette

To Sleep

Oh, precious sleep, why hath thou left thee?
And what of yonder morn?
Shall I hear thy morning dove call to thee?
Waking that which doth not sleep.

Oh troubled mind, shall thee find no peace?
Must thee ponder troubled thoughts which shall
not worry thee, least not in these joyous times.

Hath thee not found one to inspire thee?
One gentle as the morning dove who calls so softly,
who carries within the strength of many.
If only to feel his touch of tenderness
To be clothed within thine arms like that of a warm cloak
which surrounds thy body, protecting from thy bitter sweet torment.

To sleep, for it is thy will to dream a world of fantasy.
Keeping from thee reality 'til thy dawn shall sneak into thy
chamber room. Only then shall thee urge such this troubled mind
to ponder what future hours hold for thee. To sleep

Bonnie Rowe

My Treasure

I found a treasure in a trunk hidden away for years,
and when I held it up to look I could not hold back the tears.
In bright array Sunbonnet Sue held out her flower bouquet,
and I could see me as a child the same dresses worn at play.
For Mother had saved each tiny scrap from dresses she made for me.
and lovingly pieced them on her lap as I stood by her knee.
But then, somehow, as some things do the top was put aside,
she never seemed to get back to it though I know how hard she tried.
She was fifty-two then, and I was ten and more important things
filled my mind,
But I'm fifty-two now and she is gone and it's the most wonderful
treasure I could find.
I'll finish it now as memories rush back of days when I was small,
A small tribute to the love that time cannot pack away in a trunk
down the hall.
This quilt will be cherished and carefully saved for my daughter
for all time,
A greater gift I could not give than my Mother's work so fine.

Joyce E. Black

Never Be

My heart surrenders to your smile.
As I become a slave to our memories of no longer.
Our spirits cross... closing myself being to others.
Destiny's world to never be for my soul mate and I.

Elizabeth J. Garza

Times Changed!

It feels oh so right when you're here
And when you're not I'm on the verge of tears
Not because the loneliness in my heart.
But my fears we're growing apart.

I can tell when I look in your eyes
It's like you still love me, but I know it's a disguise.
So don't you dare hold me if it's not going to be forever
The truth is being absented, and you're telling lies
Do not tell your self things will get better.

We should've stop this a long time ago
Here's your chances take it an go.
At least we had yesterday, a memories
Which is... slowly but surely fading.

Because we can't live this life another day
You know and I do. We have to escape.

I thought just because I'm putting you in the past.
That their wouldn't be no pain.
I still feel for you, even thou

Time Changed!

Dena Williams

My Blue Box

I have a little box, painted in blue
And whenever I'm sad, I'll tell you what I do
I open my box, and I take out my wings
They take me to a land, where the people all sing
I fly through the day, past the birds, clouds, and sun
And sometimes I take off my wings and just run.
I run through the fields of colors red and yellow
And sometimes I sit when I feel kind of mellow.
I breathe in the air and smell such sweet things
But then I get bored so I put on my wings.
I fly through the day, through the evening and night
I fly with such power, I fly with such might
I fly through the trees, through the hills and the mountains
And when I get thirsty, I'll sip from the fountains,
Someone walks by, and picks up my hand
And says to me, child, you're in a magical land.
Nothing will happen to you me or him
As long as you keep loving and giving within.

Adrienne Shields

If Baby Could Talk

I love my cat and wish she could talk,
and wonder what she would say——

Why is mama always getting ready to go somewhere,
and my doesn't she stay home and play?

I love to chase mice and rabbits every time I go out
I bring them home to mama, and she screams a lot and jumps about

Why does mama not have hair all over,
and sits in her drinking water to bathe?

Every night she insists I eat these little heard rocks
instead of the salmon and shrimp I crave

She likes to dress me up and flash bright lights all in my face
No mouser worth her salt would be caught in sweaters and lace

I hate to leave my mama when my nine lives are through
She can't even catch a squirrel, what in the world will she do?

In the meantime I'll lay upon her shoulder
purr in her ear, and always be her pal

And even though I can't talk the way she does
I'll tell her that I love her every time I meow.

Joyce Simpson

Danny

As I awoke one morning the pain was gone
and you laid in my arms so very strong.
As I gazed down at you and saw the gold
spun hair, and the blue eyes like the sea, and
lips of cherries looking up at me. I thanked
God for this precious gift he had given me.
I named him Daniel and waited for the world
to see our blessed child God had given to
us. Years went fast from a child to a man
so very fast. You gave us so much love and
joy. Than I awoke again and I felt the
awful pain. I looked down into my arms
and felt the awful pain. I looked
down into my arms and you did not lay there
anymore. For God had called his precious
son back home. His name is Danny.

Ernestine L. Wilson

The Light Within

If you were a ship on the ocean waves,
And your goal was to reach the shore,
Just think how you'd feel if you saw a light
That offered you haven and more.

The glow from within the lighthouse tower
Gives aid to the vessels at sea.
For direction and course they look for the light
So they'll make it where they want to be.

The light from within that each of us has
Works just as the lighthouse tower.
It offers direction and help in your life
If you learn to rely on its power.

So look within for the light you seek,
And your vessel of life can set sail
For that shore which brings peace to a soul in need.
It's a light that when followed won't fail.

Janis Wilson

She Will Await The End

The destined journey so dreadfully looked upon by
another, she yearns to embrace with open arms. She
is indeed a phantom of life; for, there is no doubt
to her existence and yet, she is invisible to all.
She realizes that a world such as this will not, in
fact cannot permit her to be the being that is she;
the only soul she can and chooses to be. Therefore,
to the end she must flee to find a place where she
will be received with no hesitation nor obligation.
And there, she will seek refuge in the presence of
the Almighty Creator; there, she will at last feel
the inner peace she so longingly wishes to possess
from within. The floor of her woes will no longer need to
be acknowledged; such that run so deep she is not
able to imagine any sense of pure happiness. The destined
time indeed must draw near and alas, she will
await the end.

Irvine Saint-Vilus

My Father Lost

Wondering where you are, when not with me.
Asking who you are, when lost within me.
These questions I ask, of my father lost.
The answers I pray, are found within me.
My father lost, I too have wandered and travelled
many miles to find you.
Do not begrudge my love, my father lost.
A daughter is found.

Elizabeth Guy

A Friend

Sometime in "YOUR LIFE" you should have "ONE FRIEND", not just
"ANYBODY", but yes, "ONE SPECIAL FRIEND". Someone
who makes the worst "SITUATIONS" seem "BRIGHT", and lets
you see that "EVERYTHING" will be "ALRIGHT". Someone
who will stick with you through "THICK AND THIN". Yes,
everyone needs that one "SPECIAL FRIEND". Someone who
can show you the meaning of "LOVE", and even at times can
give you a much needed "HUG"! In your life, you may find a
"SPECIAL FRIEND" that's worth their weight in "GOLD", don't
take them for granted, and above all, friends shouldn't be
"BOUGHT OR SOLD". A friend will be there for you to let you
know they "CARE", and even in the best of times they'll take the
time to "SHARE". Yes, in your life some rain must fall, don't let
it "SCARE YOU", just stand tall. Call "THAT FRIEND", when
you need a helping hand, talk with them, and they'll "UNDER-
STAND". Lean on them, laugh and cry with them, but most of
all be glad your "FRIENDS". Yes, "YOUR A FRIEND" of a
"CHOSEN FEW", I'm just glad your "SPECIAL" and that my
"CHOICE WAS YOU".

Ginger Shields

On Bended Knee

I've had many Springs and Summers, the falls colorful, the
winters are long,
Each season I find a reason to sing a brand new song.
I walk with rhythm in my footsteps, I hear a voice inside my heart
And I try not to forget, each day brings a brand new start.
As the sun rises each morning, the song birds sing their dues.
By day's end I feel weary, and at night I feel the blues.
So I go on bended knee, lay my folded hands upon the bed.
I ask, "Lord won't you please, lay to rest my weary head?"
And as the seasons change I pray,
Give me a reason for each day.
Some words for a brand new song,
And a feeling that I belong.
Please put to work my useful hands,
So my mind will be at ease,
And I shall see the seasons change Lord,
As I watch on bended knee.

Gail M. Brumbaugh

Silent Pain

Silent tears for silent pain,
aren't loud like the rain.
Fall as softly as you please,
as you fall onto your knees.

The grief inside will tear you apart,
the sharpest dart that can strike your heart.
A rage for what you can't control,
quickly builds, then overflows.

But you know inside your soul
they will be happy forever more.
So let your fears be now lain,
and put to rest your silent pain.

Heather Palmer

Spring

Spring has sprung I guess you know
as fall has fallen, so winter goes.
Sun rays race through a window bright
it warms your skin, you can feel it right?
The ground breathes a sigh of relief
as it moistens under feet.
Birds they sing outside my door
Squirrels they play their play once more.
All this company the trees with belief
flowered from buds and so to leafs
But spring is more than all these things.
It's a feeling in the soul that it brings.

Garry O'Goley

Somebody Else

Indeed, my body lay still on the bed as a sacrifice-
Arms out, head back, to immolate. Victimize.
Take my soul, too while you're at it-
What do I need
breath
from you; aside from attention and sleep.
A production of children and their words
candy
meaningless, fighting to be friends.
Yield me your eyes and pretend to hear me.
You mirror your mirth onto me when I begin to break;
you permeate through me, all of me.
I feel shackled to this bed-
any bed with you in it. I negate my fear just as
you run from it, also, with your experimental mind.
Blood, the blood has been spilled here out onto these fancy
sheets. Alongside my fancy words that cover these sparing
circumstances. Somebody - used to be you, but inside of me
hot is burning wet you.
Somebody else.

Hillary Allen

Meditation

As I meditate on life, I think of early youth
As a babbling brook,
At times lazily and contentedly flowing along,
Again sparkling and dancing in the sunshine,
Or pouting under the gray skies of a storm
Unhurried—the years endless;
Leaves and twigs float along for awhile,
Are then forgotten as childhood friendships pass behind.
The years pass and the brook is joined by other brooks,
As life is enriched by experience and becomes a stream,
Flowing faster and the years do not seem quite so long.
Bits of branches and sticks replace the leaves and twigs
And flow along until diverted, some flowing along
For many miles; others but a short distance;
Lives which touch our own then go their separate ways,
Never to be seen again and yet the stream flows on.
Torrential rains swell it,
As life's disappointments seem at times too much to bear,
And still the stream flows on, rushing now,
Ever rushing as the years rush — to eternity.

Gloria E. Hood

An Ode To My Mother

They say that life is but stage,
As all the players in it age.
As actors we are judge by all
and with a good script one stands tall.

For it's the producer that sets the motion
and the director that controls the action.
How well Mum you played your role in life.
In times of joy, in times of strife.

How well you molded the characters
with moral codes for all ten actors.
As one of ten, I stand tall
and thank my mother for it all.

Bunny E. Coleman

Take Time to Smell the Flowers

Take time to smell the flowers
As each new day begins

Remember all of those special memories
Don't dwell on the past or what the future will bring

Look lovingly on yesterday and fondly to tomorrow
And let it make your heart sing and wipe away your sorrow

The past is behind you
And the future is yours to mold

Hold your head up high
Stand proud and strong and bold

Don't let your worries get you down
Let your dreams control your mind

Just think of all the love around you
And about everyone who cares

And know there's nothing you can't do
Because your determination will take you there

Take time to smell the flowers
And smile with each pleasant thought

Just keep your chin up
Because the battle is never won 'til you've fought

Gina Marie Morra

Challenger

I watched TV, this fateful day
As God took seven lives away
I feel the hurt, I feel the grief
What I just saw is beyond belief
Their plans, their dreams and all their hope
Just disappeared in a puff of smoke
There are no words that I can say
That will ever take the hurt away
The husband, the children and the wives
Find no consolation in this loss of lives
They say "Why Us and the Ones we love"?
But God found a need for them above
So in your loss, we also mourn
They did not die, they were just born.

Joan Marek

My Grandson

The teenager chatters to his dad
As he speeds the Interstate and brags
About how fast he drives his car
He hears his nagging grandmother say, "Luck, so far"
His mother sits behind him and prays
That he'll come to his senses and stop this craze
Later, she'll take him off and chew him out
And suffer in agony as they shout
She'll ask him to vision a scene on the side of the road
Two little girls and a teenager robbed of a chance to grow old
How can we reach this boy before it's too late
Get him to understand that lives are not his to take
Shall we explain the distance objects travel after impact
And tell him that is a proven fact
Will he listen as we preach
Keeping him and others alive is what we seek
I hope he gets this message and lives a very long time
To write his grandson such caring messages in rhyme

Edith LoBue

Untitled

I swear I heard 'em talkin'
As I rode up the Powder River today.
Steady ole hoss, I says. Whoa now.
Did you hear 'em, what did they say?

Must be the voice of the wind, I reckoned,
As it whispers thru that cottonwood tree.
Or is it the spirits of some Old-timers
Callin' out a howdy to you and me.

'Twas then I heard just what was said!
A tiny voice buzzed in my ear,
"If we take 'em down by the river, son
The big one's will get 'em, Better eat 'em here"

They ate my best horse, hair side out,
Left me afoot while they measured my old hide!
All in a day's work, so I built a wide loop,
Roped and saddled one, then broke him to ride.

Set me up another drink, Barkeep!
Just you listen to my tale of woe.
I never knew how hard the life of a cowpoke
'Til I met up with The Wyoming Mosquito!

Barbara Hennings

My Mountain

I gaze in awe at the mountain
As I stand by my kitchen sink
It's where I say my morning prayers
And meditate and think.

My life is like climbing a mountain
With its rocks and rugged terrain
But Jesus my Savior has promised me
It will not be in vain.

Blessings untold have been showered on me
As I travel over the land
Trials and misfortunes cannot prevail
For God is holding my hand.

The winter of life is approaching
As I near the mountain crest
And I can say at the end of the road
That I have been richly blest.

And when I've reached the summit
Praise God I shall be free
And we'll be together in Paradise
My God - My Mountain - And Me.

Agnes Conley

Lilly

It seems the clouds are lifting,
as I step outside the rain.

Yes, the sun is breaking through,
shining it's light upon you.

The smoothness of your ivory skin,
radiates like a warm soft glow.

Causing me to catch my breath,
just to stare in astonishment.

The beauty so many others have missed
reaches out like the warmth of a tender kiss,

filling my head with total peacefulness.

Aaron G. Shostak

Quietly I Await

You come when there is no moon and the night is black
as I toss and turn with an anxiety attack
my friends are asleep and my faith has been depleted
it's a battle of wills and I will not be defeated
not tonight anyway
for my mind is clear and my spirit is strong
but my resolve is weakening and that's why you've come along
You play on my doubts and fears and all my regrets
as if I don't know the inevitability of death
was there a time when I felt immortal and brave
when I danced with the wind and the world was my stage
if there was I don't recall, it seems so far right now
and there's so much to do but time just won't allow
I wish I could stay because I love you all so
but I'm tired of this struggle and the pain that I've known
I've lost the battle I've been beaten at last
and as I turn my eyes upward and take my last labored gasp
Please realize that I'll be all right
That love and life have been worth this cruel fight.

Irene Kondoleon

Until Then

A message has been heard today,
As I watched my father gracefully pass away.
Fragile were his last few years.
Yet, strong was his will...
While quiet were his tears.

As he somehow passes me all that he knows,
My feelings of loneliness begin to show.
He shares the thought on his mind...
Now forever frozen in time.

"It is not how and why you die,
Rather, how and why you live each day.
So go forward strong and be happy,
I will be with you all the way."

Cindy Newsum Smith

"In God We Trust"

What has happened to America?
As if you didn't know -
It's not what it used to be no more.
What happened to prayer?
The legislators don't care -
It's all about money - They just want their share.
It's been thrown out of schools -
Making the children act like fools.
Drugs, gangs, killings and things.
It must utterly be restored
Indeed it must
For this Nation was built on -
In God we trust!

Herman Parker

'Dancing On A Star'

I look toward the heavens and wonder where you are.
Are you singing with an angel. Are you dancing on a star.
Are you living in a city where the streets are paved in gold.
Is it everything you dreamed of. Is it all that you were told.

I look toward the heavens and wonder if you know
That love has finally found me. A love as pure as snow.
Do you know that now I'm happy. Do you know my life's complete.
Do you know that my past turmoils have melted at my feet.

I look torward the heavens and long for you to know
There's such an aching in my heart because I miss you so.
But even though you've left me, you'll never be that far.
For when I gaze into the sky you're dancing on a star.

Jan Martin Jackson

Sadness Of The Heart

How sad it must be, to loose a Son
as my friend has done.

He came into his world, as a little one.
Soft and cuddly, warm and meek, for Mom
to nourish and keep.

Watching him grow, running, playing,
sharing his toys, what a wonderful boy,
a Mother's Joy!

Schools, a challenge, much to learn,
Books to read, some writing and math.

Later, girls to meet and driving a jeep.

Moving on to become a man.
College and jobs, a way of time, but this
young man was lost in his prime.

No wife or child to have enriched his life.
A mother still thinks of him as a little boy,
cries her heart out, for it's truly broken.
My, my, my and we wonder why.

Carolyn J. Bloomfield

The Family Tree

There are maples and ashes and pine
As pretty as they can be
But the best tree of all, is the one that we call,
You guessed it - the Family Tree!

It starts with two little seeds
And as you will easily see
With love and with care - it never gets bare,
It makes a him, and a her, and a me.

I am but a leaf on that tree -
My parents are the stem
Grandparents the limbs, with lots of small shoots,
Great-Grandparents the trunk, ancestors the roots.

So take good care of that Family Tree
So that it won't whither and die,
And the only solution for it's restitution,
Depends upon you and I.

Before we're cut down like the maple or pine
In some April, or June, or September,
Let's think of the past - and make memories last,
Let's not forget - let's remember!

June E. Krause

Pictures in My Mind

The nostalgia came upon the girl,
As she stood in front of the tenantless
house of her childhood.

A balmy zephyr gave her goose bumps,
As her grounding came back to her.

The long walks along the beach
With the tepid water rushing up
to her feet.

The hue of the sky, as the sun set
So beautiful to her, the crimson
and canary.

The somnolent nights with cronies,
And the old apparition in the house,
Brought back very fond memories,
That she loved that old house.

Jaime Wright

A Captured Soul

My friend, to be around someone
As strong with mind and soul;
To see you through silence of touch and sight;
Through your voice clearly heard across the wind,
rivers, of timeless, endless expressions of life;

My life is as strong as yours regardless of gender;
Respect for you is what I give you and your life.
Regardless how our minds are aged, or how ripe our souls mature;
We are similar in our passions, to succeed in our challenging lives.
We lead.

Erica D. Norris

Friendships - 'New Beginnings'

Like grass in the spring, green and new, fresh
as the air after the rain. Happy as the birds
in flight, soaring in air as one, bright as the summer's
sun, can't you feel its warmth? Everything is beautiful
still in bloom, but with fall and winter everything dies,
must our friendship be the same? Let's fight to keep the
sun shining the grass green, let's be in unison. Then unlike
fall and winter we will never die. Our memories, our
sharing and caring, our lack of selfishness and taking each
other for granted, our loving and most of all our profound meaning
of communication. For without it the basis of our friendship
will mean nothing. This will keep us new. And when the sun goes
down let's open our hearts and share our feelings to make the sun
shine. Because just like the spring flowers we are the seeds and
without that rain and sun we will never grow. Let's work at it.
This is our friendship, our new beginning.

Cheryl L. Shomo

You Can Call Me Jim

With my brand new clothes and face made up, I went on my way
As the line moved closer, I rehearsed what I would say
"Sir, I think you're wonderful" with all the courage I could find
Unprepared for what he said when his eyes met mine

"You can call me Jim
I'm just an ordinary Joe
Why you chose to call me sir
Lord only knows
Not so long ago
I was just like you
Now you come and call me sir
When just plain Jim will do"

My cold hands were shaking as I handed him my pen
Thinking of it now my hands still shake as much as then
He told me he was a mortal man and his words were true
But gifted with a special charm given to a chosen few

Harriet M. Carlin

"Time Will Pass And So Shall We"

The world is ending my friend for me and you too.
And while the fires of fate rage on
the deeds of the many shall come
to cause curse to be righteous few.
And when I stop to think of everything
I become overwrought, with the evil
bill of goods the world has bought.

I see everyone chasing needlessly to find.
That which empties one's pockets
and shackles their minds.
Now the die is cast there will be no turning back.
We must pay with our lives for what our hearts lack.

Donald F. Scales

Apology

I came wrapped in ignorance
as the many that came before me.

I found that the discoverer
finds only what he wishes to.

I saw the blind opinionated
walk oblivious to beauty.

I heard the deaf plunderers
drown the cries of the innocent.

I felt the misunderstandings
dealt with through inconsideration.

I cried quietly to myself
and filled my hand with hers.

I failed in understanding but not with compassion.

David W. Stryker

Betrayed Heart

Angry tears pour from a broken heart
as the realization of betrayal sets in.

The trust once protected was now violently
raped by the one who held her heart.

How is she to survive with the knowledge
that a loved one turned into a traitor.

All the promise became sweet lies
falling from smooth lips.

Christina Fain

The Morning Light

Watching the sun rise over the horizon
as the sun gets a glimpse of the earth,
the light shines into the sky and on the land.
The darkness of the night turns into the light of a new day,
like flipping the light switch on as the room lights up.
As the sun goes up,
the sky changes its color
from black to orange and yellow.
After the sky is full of light,
the earth awakes to the morning light,
birds sing their morning praise,
clock alarms ringing,
and people opening up the drapes.
The sunlight shines into the bedroom.
The night is over and a new day has begun.

Becky Zessin

Fate

It was only a dream when she began
At the early age of eight.
Even though points were scarce,
She knew that it was fate.

As she got older her knowledge increased
About life and basketball, too.

She learned that being a slacker will get you
Nowhere
She learned that discipline and hard work always
Turns out fair.

As she looks back on those wonderful years
She remembers all her hard working hours and fears.
Then she looks at where she stands today
And knows that everything was worth the pain.

Jill Jones

Grandpa

Grandpa, Pop, Dad, Frank, Paquito; Many words for a man of few.
As the sun slowly rose, for what seemed like an eternity,
The epitome of genteel slipped into the light.
The way he lived his life; Peaceful, Uncomplicated.
And as the light shone brighter;
Because now there is one more star in the sky.
Memories of love come through.

So grandpa, here are some things that remind me of you:
coffee, cheese and crackers, portable radio, Puerto Rico,
baseball games politics, eye drops, flannel shirts, dominoes,
Your cane, Your laugh, although not often, but memorable.
And your last teardrops.

So as the music so hauntingly memorable plays in my ears,
The sound of music also fills my heart with loving memories
I am so lucky to have. And knowing you are at Peace with God.
Never having said goodbye and never will, but only,
Thank you Grandpa, for being my friend when I needed one,
A shoulder to cry on, Giving good advice without asking,
And loving unconditionally, not only me, but your entire family.
Forever in our hearts and souls...
Okey Dokey Grandpa, we'll see you in Heaven.

Christine Castro

Little Boy Lost

How long have I been here-the wet gray sand oozing up between my toes as the tide rushes back to the sea? It seems forever, but of course, that cannot be. Children frolic by-laughing, splashing, playing in the foamy surf. Others-older people mostly look at me strangely. What is wrong with me? Is it my bathing suit? My size? My age? Granted I am merely five or so-but I am independent and I am free.

A purple beach ball was carried in by the waves. It was very old and worn and I thought it would surely fall apart when I picked it up. As I held this old, worn, purple and strangely familiar beach ball and gazed out to sea the sky grew more ominous-the rain clouds gathered and the waves came crashing in - chasing me towards shore. And as I turned to come into shore - it was as if the boardwalk had gone back in time! It was the forties again and I saw them-saw them running toward me screaming! Then, at last I remembered-the tide had claimed me and my purple beach ball so long, long ago!

John P. Dennehy Sr.

A Mother's Prayer

If the Lord would answer one prayer for me
as there is only one I need,
I would ask Him to look over my children
through each day of life they lead;
To allow them peace and happiness
To bless them with good health,
To give them all that they shall need
without a greed for wealth,
To show them all that's good in life
To keep them safe and warm,
To let them learn all they need to know
and to shelter them from harm.
I would ask the Lord to guide them
when they have to walk away
And to enlighten every step they take
as they are on their way.
I'd ask the Lord to teach them Love
and to let them know He cares,
Then I would ask the Lord to listen to
and answer all their prayers.

Donna Michelle Armstrong

Old Bulcher Church

It's not a very large church
As today's churches grow
But it sets out in the wildwood
Where the fragrant breezes blow

It serves no purpose, it's falling apart
The seasons have done it in
Yet it served it's time we are sure
Helping purge believers sins

It is so old, so very old
What stories it could tell
Of circuit riders and outlaws
And hearts lifted by it's bell.

Roof shingles have fallen, the bell tower creaks
The floor has broken through
The steps are worn from many a foot
In both grown up and children's shoes.

It's fading away, this old church
Though many a soul it has fed
It thrived on life and lifted strife
But without people - it's D E A D !!!!

J. H. Word

"No Problem Is Too Great"

The human mind can be deceiving yet astonishing as well.
It can accomplish many tasks for every one to go and tell.
The miracles of the brain will always be explored by man.
But this is a creation of our maker that only he
knows the function it has at hand.
The mind can work solutions only to a certain
point not to infinity.
You must rest your problems on our "Lord Jesus"
shoulders he will help you reason with reality.
Time is at hand from micro seconds to thousands of years.
Yet our Lord foreseen the outcome of this world its Happiness,
its many fears.
We're only human wanting to be strong, wanting
to know or fate.
We must be humble help others in need and
remember to our "Lord Jesus" no problem is
To great.

Josephus Davis III

Then And Now

Being young you always know what is right;
As you age what once was right, is not always so.

Love at a young age is a thing to behold;
but not always a thing that will hold.

In age you will find, what once was good should of never been;
or at least not taken to the extreme.

I have experienced many wonders, and many blunders;
However, in my aging some wonders have become blunders

In love at one time I'm lost and not sure anymore;
I feel like my soul is dying and have no desire to continue.

To leave would be wrong, to stay would be to suffer and die.
What are the options? What can I do?

Ed J. De Paoli

Never Say Goodbye

I will never say goodbye, for we will meet again later,
At some point in time,
I will always remember the brightness you made for me.

I will never say goodbye, for I will always be able to feel
Your arms holding me, letting my tears stain your soul.
And I will remember you gave me hope when I was afraid of the
yesterdays.

I will never say goodbye, for the only way I can ever repay
The love you shared with me, is to continue on with my journey,
And give to others what you gave to me.

I will miss the gentleness of your eyes,
The warmth of your touch,
But I will always keep inside me, you.

I will never say goodbye, for death is a past memory, and a new
beginning,
I will always remember the traces of you that will be around me,
Making new rainbows, helping me to grow.

I will never say goodbye, for when I see a deer wandering through
the woods,
I will remember you, leaving footprints on my heart
That made me whole.

Dawn Sampson

"In The Garden"

The mesmeric snakes laugh
At the caterpillar in jealous rage
She crawls on
Temporarily trapped by the hypnotizing demons
They tear apart her soul
Leaving her alone in the garden
To find her stolen strength
She pulls together and rests from society
Suddenly, the beautiful butterfly breaks
She floats away to her secret door to ecstasy
High above the squirming snakes below.

Carol Forsyth

Windful Spirit

Hidden, we are, and yet we become part of a greater calling.
At the foot of the forest, man is stripped of his human nature and
wrapped in a cloak, woven by nature's hand.

Stepping further into the forest, the mind is cleansed by an array
of scents that lie within the still air.
A sweet smell stops us, searching about discovers a garden painted
of wildflowers.
The sunshine magnifies the stately appearance of the white birch
against a dark forest wall.

Ahead can be seen a doorway to light, anticipating its arrival,
and yet completely enthralled, in the melody of the forest.
The rays from the sun wrap their warmth around us and pull us out,
Stepping beyond the Shadow of the Almighty and onto Its Wing

We come to the cliffside, rising high above the sea, where the heavens
declare the glory of God, and the skies proclaim the work of
His Hands.
The rock beneath our feet feeds us its strength; as we fill our
chests with the air from the sea, we seem to stand a bit taller
and more proud.

Suddenly we begin to see as though an eagle may,
with the strength from the stone and the power from the heavens,
we rest assured that we may soar on wings as eagles.

Stillness settles in, we take our place high upon a rock and reflect
on the splendor of the day.
A brilliant melody from the forest echoes on windful spirits and is
carried over the sea to compose the harmony which fills the air.

Gregory W. Perry

Ballet Of The Night

Now I lay me down to sleep...slowly drifting, gently drifting—
at the portal, easing quietly beyond the outside...loosing grip of
sounds and things...yielding to the call from deep within
the recesses of the inner sanctum...
Flowing, leaping, soaring high, lucidly celebrating dreaming...
engaging—translated to another space and time...to a world within—
real, beyond real...within me;
Calling quietly at first, beckoning—a voice from the center of the
kingdom within...
flickering, transparent, full of light and beaming...
Leaping, bounding, dancing on the beams of light, I journey to
the centripetal core—infinite, ever, through the timeless tunnel...
spiraling—untrammelled spirit that I am... swirling through the
Ballet of the night.
Reaching, touching, tenderly embracing the "Messenger of my soul"...
constant, uniting, ever-loving river steaming from the one who
sits enthrone, ebbing like a tide and churning,
Incessantly dreaming...drifting on the waves of splendor and
returning, to the shores
of morning and waking...from dancing in the Ballet of the night!

John C. Byrd

Untitled

My heart beats with anxious rhythm,
at the sight of the mountain peak-
A rainbow sits within its bowel,
showing colors subtle and weak-
The morning dew glistens,
as it lays upon the leaves-
The wind echoing thru the valley,
whistles and dances thru the trees-
I'm in awe, for this beauty,
that surrounds me..." I alone can only see."

Claudia L. Forte

Infinite Way

Some ways of passage, through fire burned
At ways of innocence, are never learned
If you believe, it's not hard to follow the moon-
But when it's too late, you wish it was too soon

Why the voice's cries unheard:
When forgiveness, Bright Eyes, my last word

You wish it would change, and though it may -
Forever is eternity, an infinite way.

Beckie Warner

Dreams

I watch the world through curious eyes
And wonder at the star-filled skies.

I dream about the wondrous things
Tomorrow promises to bring.

I keep my secret hopes and dreams
Tucked far away on bright moon beams

And, out beyond the horizons far,
I wish upon a shooting star.

I journey to the worlds unmet
With treasures undiscovered yet.

My dreams will take me where rainbows are
When I follow my very own star.

Emily Horrworth

Call Of Awakening

I see all the children - one to a hundred years,
Babes cradled in the arms of a Mother with beauty and grace
But how we slowly kill her

Flashes of anger crash the night sky
A mighty hand rocks the foundation we stand on
From the windows of heaven, He sees the destruction and cries,

Wake up my children and see the beauty melting away
My stewards do you not understand the direction

Listen to the sludgy ripples of my waters
And to the cracks of my baked earth
Hear the mourning song of my Wren
And the laughing cry of my Hyena
It was my gift to you; your place of habitation

Soldiers stand firm in your commitment and righteousness
Wake up the sleepers and throw on the armor
All you brothers and sisters rush to heal the gaping wounds
He's counting on His children
Take the hand next to you

And let us pride ourselves on love and beauty; let us follow the
direction
and revive our tired Mother; let us praise a Father so loving

Cindee C. McCubbin

Baby Hands

Baby hands so small and sweet
Baby fingers, so complete
Baby palms so finely lined
In our heartstrings are entwined

How can a being so new and small
Command that love of one and all
And tho' our sleep stops with her cries
All our tomorrows are in her eyes

So helpless in her bed she lies
What are her dreams, what mean her sighs?
Fresh from heaven, Angelic still.
Bending parents to her will

Those hands reach out, unsure, and yet
Who can resist, who can forget?
A baby's grasp is soft but strong
Like silken strings, alive with song

So hold my finger in your grip
And never let this moment slip
Into fond memories misty lands
That dim the thrill of baby hands

Jim J. Culligan

Space Pilot's Lament

Some Big-shots died in the Moon-Star wreck,
Bad luck and the blame for me.
ASTAR failed and the asteroid
Came up too fast to see.

So they boot me out of the great Star fleet,
And they'll forget my name in space.
Now all I can do is dig in the rocks
Of this Godforsaken place.

I'd sell my soul to be back home
In the land that gave me birth;
Just to set those jets for that one last blast
To the good, green hills of earth.

Frank Blair Jr.

Pilgrimage

Oh! my entity, oh! my heart,
Be calm and quiet.
Be ready for a pilgrimage,
A sacred and reverence;
In this human shore — land, sea and sky,
Multi nation's capital, the city of NY.

Standing here, forwarding hands, remembering God,
Singing in adoration with high desire and thought.
A rosary and solemn world,
Caught and recited in sea and land.
Everyday, everybody beholds and views,
A human flood, flows towards unknown.

Hashan M. Mannan

On Justice

Be for and always strive for justice
Be strong in your quest for it
For justice is the balance which leads to
and brings sanity
The soul seeks justice in so many ways
Like the man who thirsts for water in the desert
He seeks it especially when life has been
too unfair
He seeks it because he wants to right the
wrong and set the record straight
He feels better about himself
because he has proven his worth
He has shown that he was right and
vindicated himself
He has won respect
He has won peoples hearts
He becomes grateful
Because with fortitude and determination
he has shown that he was good
But the situation was badly misunderstood.

Dennis J. Buckley

Untitled

From whence fourth I hath came I've returned
Bearing upon my shoulders the weight of the
Four horsemen of the apocalypse as my soul
they are a cross hilted blade I wear and wield
In battle Pestilence, Famine, Destruction, and
Death are as the names of childhood friends
to me Anarchy and Chaos are as games I play
I suffer From the censorship of no rules or
Laws but life's true law Death but even that
Rule is not enforced for Death is my best
Friend of All.

Joseph S. Otto Jr.

"Old Faithful"

The ice machine in the lunchroom
beats anything seen yet.
There's no way to mix ice and water,
without getting very wet.

Water first and then the ice
(the other way must be better).
Ice in first then H20,
the end result was even wetter.

You would think that in this day and age
with all of our inventive power,
something as simple as an ice machine
need not work like a cold shower.

Don Douglass

Insomnia For Love

I once couldn't sleep
Because I didn't know how he felt about me
The times we spent together
Meant so much
But to me it didn't seem like it meant anything to him
I finally got the courage
to learn the truth
Now I can't sleep
Because he doesn't give a damn about me
Sleep has come eternally
Boy I wish I were in Heaven
Instead of looking up from Hell.

Chandra R. Klinkner

The Last Tulip

This little tulip you should know well,
Because it used to grow close by our old well.
It was the only one left of the group it was in.
I didn't want it to die so I moved it in
Where it would have a new friend to take care of it
So it could grow and bloom again.
The caretaker it has now won't be as good as the one before,
Because she was one of the best in this whole wide world.
So when next spring comes, I know it will bloom.
And I will look at it, and thank God for our Mom
And think how good she must have been.

Carl Hees

Untitled

She loved him
because she couldn't love herself

And yeah, she knew that he was NO good
and that he frequently lied
and may have occasionally cheated on her
and no matter how many times he said he loved her
she knew damn well that he didn't...even though he said he did
all of these things
sounded like a melodious orchestra in her ears
in a world she constantly had to remind
"A woman, ain't I?"

Gigi McQueen

"Back Order"

When Christmas comes it is hard to wait,
because some gifts come early,
and others come late.

Now some elves are quick and some elves are slow.
While others just say,
"How the hell do I know?"

I had them start REALLY early
and they promised your gift would be here.
But the last time I called, they got a little surly!

Your special gift is on its way,
just when it will arrive
I cannot say.

I guess by now you're getting a little curious,
and it goes without saying
that I'm dutifully furious.

Not one hint will I give and I'm sorry it is late.
But when it arrives,
it'll be worth the wait!!!!

Ellen Baker

Someone Special

Someone special you always would find
because someone is out there so divine

When you do something special for someone
Something special will happen to you, so don't
be afraid to lend a hand because that
someone will be right there to reach for
that hand

That special person is waiting for you,
so climb up that ladder and right back down
surely you'll find that very special crown

So find that key and open that door
because behind it you would find
all what you've been looking for
because when you do you will find
the love that you have been...
searching for.

Deavonna A. Deane-Baker

Finding Myself

Finding myself is not an easy task,
because there are no answers in a book, or question to ask.
You see, my friend, I ought to know.
For I have looked so very hard.
I have looked at things to see my reflex, even a simple card.

I keep telling myself it will be okay.
cause I'm out there somewhere to find.
Maybe I'm crazy or maybe it's just my crazy mind.

But one day I passed my reflection
and looked myself dead in the eye.
I have to look no more cause I have found myself true without any lies

Everything about me was all so very clear.
it's like my own reflection, gestured truth to my ear.
All the paths and turns I took, all the flashes I saw.
I found me in that mirror, but yet it wasn't me at all.

I looked so sad lonely, but yet so sure and wise.
I tell you I saw plenty just straight through my own eyes.
I was scared of my own reflection,
or maybe I was just scared of what I could see.
It's amazing how quickly I found myself, the moment me saw me.

Erin Powitzky

White Lie

I was told not to play with them, I asked, why?
Because, they are taught about the, "little white lie!"

They can't be trusted in any type of deal,
Because, they lie, cheat and even steal.

I grew up with this belief, so I played with my own kin.
And all because of a person's race, creed or skin.

I joined the service as my patriotic deed,
In honor, to fight for my country, as they need.

Even here I found treatment of others wrongly, done!
But, they put us all together and treat all as one.

We were sent to war, to a place I've never seen.
Fighting strangers for unknown purposes and reason.

I was hit, blinded, I yelled, someone, help me!
A hand reached out of nowhere, I explained, I can't see!

He told me not to worry, and his name was Fife.
He carried me back to camp, he had saved my life.

When my sight returned, fife, I tried to find.
I was shocked, because of his skin, things ran through my mind.

After awhile we exchanged address and said our goodbye.
I know, I'll never teach my kids, those "Little White Lies."

Henry J. Gualdarama

"A Cry For Peace"

The sound of thunder far away
Beckons me to sit and pray
The thunder soon becomes suppressed
Can it be for the best?

I can see the bombs and shells above
Can there be no love?
Hear children cry, see people die
Can't you hear your mother's sigh?

It seems forever and a day those bombs do say
With flares and flashes in the sky
We count the days as they go by

We can no longer see the pain, you must agree
The pressure on my heart is sure to break apart.

My mother's strength instilled in me
Protects me from humility
My faith in God who is next to me I know watches over me.

I wonder if those cries shall cease
My flag I know stands for peace
I love my country and I stand tall
It gives us freedom for us all.

Catherine Kouvaris

Wake Up

I wake up some mornings with tear filled eyes...
Before me, I see children...
Oh! how my heart cries...
Children from Rwanda,
Children from all shores...
A child stands by his mama who lies
Silent by his side...
Wake up Mama! Wake up he cries...
Mama can't wake up...
Mama has died...
Who will stop this carnage?
Who will stop this woe?
Wake up world...
For God's sake...wake up.

Dorothy Fortson

Desert Sands

I roam through the heat of a desert wind. Crying, Begging, looking for somewhere to wash the blood from my hands. Sorrowing feet, dragging further across the land.

Searching for the end to a pale moon rise. I finally realize that I'm traveling alone. Thinking of the past, how much longer the pain to last. Wishing for one life to live, little of what do I give. No water, to cleanse or drink.

Do I die or whether away, as the sands if tune consumes my day. I'm free of lies and dreams. All as not of what it seemed. As I go deeper in this atmosphere. Spotless, clean, and crystal clear. Life is not of consequence. Living where i live earned me badges of common sense. Common wherever I learned. Common and created by fear. Questions of what is common with America and blues. America provided the atmosphere. So peep game, to all I have to say. I kick poetry in my own way. If you come closer, I'll tell you what I know, storm clouds have gathered, ill winds are to blow, the desert sand.

Foxxy J. Brown

She Makes Me Fly

The genesis of my life
Begins by her opening the door

I feel like a large brown and white eagle,
and able to soar.

Each in there own heaven can fly.

With her eyes to forever guide me,
I will spend an eternity in the sky.

David Michael Lopez

I Witnessed This Scene

I witnessed this scene so painful to see
Being a witness to it tore the heart out of me
A young Mother with incurable cancer
Doctors done all he can only God has the answer

I watched the young Mother lay helplessly dying
A lil girl by her side softly crying
I heard someone say where Mommie's going she can't take me
Why can't I go with Mommie to eternity

Is it because I'm so young I'm only seven
Please let me go with Mommie to heaven
Mommie always said where she goes I can go too
She'd say Mommie wouldn't go anywhere without you

I watched the Mother pull her baby close hide her pain with a smile
I heard her softly say It'll only be a short while
Hasn't Mommie told you "Jesus always knows what's best"
Mommie's going alone this time this is Jesus request

After I'm gone be a good girl and get things ready
You will join me some day and so will your Daddy
I want you to smile Baby please don't grieve
Give me a great big hug Baby Mommie's got to leave

Elizabeth Ann Crawford

"A Prayer From An Isomniac"

Oh, what a fight is going on in my mind,
Between good and bad, surely one of a kind.
Just when my head says, that is it,
My heart kicks in and won't let me quit!
Maybe this is a sort of world war III,
This awful battle that is inside of me.
Good must prevail for now and ever,
Oh I wish there was no bad, never, never!!
My mind is really in turmoil though,
Such weird thoughts, I wish to let go.
Life is such a precious thing
Take nothing for granted except God is King!
Sleepless now for 3 weeks in a row,
No wonder why such feelings would grow.
I have to keep fighting only for good.
And I pray that I sleep normal soon, I should.
We are all mortal on planet earth!
Every race, creed, religion all of us from birth!
So I beg my thought adjuster read just me,
And let me get back to the person I used to be.

Daniel J. Koechel

A Day In The Desert

I contemplate the awesome cavern of a desert hush
Bewildered by the hot dry sea of thirsting blight.
  And yet I know
That color, in a steady silent westward rush
  will change this sight
And mellow it with heaven's splendored glow
While laying the soft carpet of the night
  before I go.

Helen Leccese

Ad Infinitum

Beloved, grieve not for me if I should go
Beyond the veil, for this I know:
That Death is but the door to Life,
Leaving behind all earthly strife
To seek new ventures of prowess,
Setting new goals for one's success.
And though I'd leave you not by choice,
We'll meet again, and then rejoice
And smile at our once mournful tears,
Resulting from Life's foolish fears.

Ah no! Death shall not cheat us of our bliss;
For though with love's first tender kiss
Come dreams and plans for naught but joy,
True love, tempered by Life's alloy
Of strife and pain, is welded strong
To last beyond Death's even-song.
Love-bound together as we are,
I pledge to you I'd not be far—
But share your joys, your hopes, your pain,
Until the day we meet again.

Barbara L. Endsley

Stepping His Way

Step down, look around, see perfect glory
Birthed by mysteries not known to man.
Surrender to humility the amplified story
That all heights as others, only sand.

Step back, look around, see promises kindled
Influenced by the Golden Vessel straight from above.
Bind the soul! No place for worthless dwindle-
Must fill the spirit with the Master's love!

Step over, look around, see new hope today,
Miraculously delivered as the whispered need.
Blessed be the One leading the way
To supernatural powers from only a seed.

Step across, look around, see the Lord near
Reigned by exceeding riches of kindness and grace.
Born again-Born again, no more fear;
Come to full redemption, the only place.

Step up, look around, see the Eternal light
Magnifying openly the enemy defeated.
It is finished-It is finished, no more need to fight;
Just take a place jointly at the right hand of the seated.

Dorothy A. Dunn

What Is Black?

Black is big and very bold
Black is small and very scary
Black is the snake in the grass that you cannot
  see.
Black is blue when you're hit with force
  by an angry word out of the dark.
Black is fear inside your heart that sneaks up
  on you when you are in the dark.
Black is the midnight dark when the moon goes
  down and takes all the light.
Black is the Death of a person you know.
Black is sadness that you don't want to know.
Black are the shadows laughing at you.
Black is greed that turns you evil.

Andrew Allen Erwin

A White Black Person

A white black person is someone
Black who behaves like a white person
The white black person treats you as such
Because whites influence him or her too much

A white black person is a sister or brother
Who seems to ignore a person of color
And sometimes talks blacks down
When white people happen to be around

A white black person tries to hide
His or her face to keep his or her pride
When he or she sees a black person come by
Because he or she is with a white girl or guy

But when you see him or her around black people
He or she tends to treat you like an equal
Again like you are to forget about yesterday
When he or she treated you like a nobody

Chinedu D. Ogbuike

The Flower On The Window Sill

I'm just a tiny flower
Blooming on the sill.
No voice have I to shout and sing.
I'm standing here forever still.

Will people stop and look and see.
That God did make even me?
That with all his might and grace and power
He took the time for me - a flower?

Lo, I hear a voice within me say
"Why do you question me this way?
I put you there to beautify
To magnify and glorify.

Well done small bloom, you've earned your rest
I know that you have done your best.
Come home and you will ever be
A beauty to behold for me."

I'm wilting now and fading fast
It's true that I will be no more.
But I will grace the masters sill
And beautify forever more.

Barbara Riley

Seasons

I was like a feather in the wind
Blowing from one place to another
But never really having a destination
You taught me to see a flower's many colors
You taught me to seize the moment because tomorrow isn't promised
I'll be reminded of you when the winter comes
I'll reminded of you when the heavens open up and the rains fall without end
Each season will bring a special memory
No distance can conquer this love or the memories that we have made
Each season will bring a special memory
So if ever you find yourself thinking of me - pause for a moment,
Look up at the moon and know that I', staring at the same moon
Thinking of You...

Maybe one day there will be a season for us...

Joe Beavers

Luminous Tree

Above and below
Blue sky clouds
Consciousness colored of earths branches
From the luminous tree

Leaves that sway brightly with the wind
Leaves whispering shades of green
What is written, as the wind
lifts you away

You, carry a message
message to earth
message to the sky
message to the wind
The, message of love

Are your secrets what lay hidden
in the colors of your life
That, I may know
Your leaf has fallen on me
so delicate and mysterious
so translucent and fleeting
as a tear

Benjamin V. Suncin

Welcome Back To Country

Bunny tails bobbing down a dusty road,
Bob-Whites call in fields newly mowed.
If all these little normal things are what you'd like to see,
Then welcome back to country, come with me.

Ruby-Throats robbing nectar from a rose,
Baby calves bawling, an old cow lows.
If all these little normal things are what you'd like to see,
Then welcome back to country, come with me.

Summer clouds dripping rain upon your nose,
Bare feet squashing mud between your toes,
If all these little normal things are what you'd like to see,
Then welcome back to country, come with me.

Red squirrel holding nuts between his toes,
Frog legs jumping, warts on a toad.
If all these little normal things are what you'd like to see,
Then welcome back to country, come with me.

Coon dogs sobbing, creek water slows,
Fish worms stop crawling, midwinter snows.
If all these little normal things are what you'd like to see,
Then welcome back to country, come with me.

Joseph Dudley Matthews

'Born To Win'

Born to win salvation full and free.
Born to win the Saviour ransomed me.
Oh, the grace in His salvation plan.
Born to win by His redeeming hand.

Oh, the love that brought the Saviour down
To this earth, the cross, a thorny crown.
Jesus Christ, the Truth, God's only Son,
Born to win no matter what I've done.

For His grace erases all my sin,
Through His blood, I'm washed and now I win
All the promises He's made to me.
Born to live, with Him eternally.

Esther Thomas

A Baby's Touch

The touch of a baby's hand on a sparrow
Both are handiworks of God
The love in her eyes, the caress of her hand
Far from this world of mod.

Today, I have learned a lesson
A lesson of contrite love
By the touch of a hand on a sparrow
And the ways of God above.

I can travel my path with thorns at the sides
At night I am able to pray
I thank you Lord for this lesson
A lesson I have learned today.

The touch of a hand, so tender with care
The touch of an angel, you see
God cares for us still, in His infinite way
He cares for you and for me. (The little bird died)

But God called the sparrow to Heaven
Just as He calls you and me
A Heaven filled with beauty - what a wonderful
sight that will be.

Cloda J. Bane

A Mother's Reward

You bear your children one by one,
Both your daughters and your sons.

From the first, they're so dependent,
But all to soon, they're independent.

As they grow up and time flies by,
You wonder if your goals are too high;

Or if by some distant fate,
They'll end up all full of hate.

You try to guide as you watch them grow,
Really not knowing which way they'll go.

Then they're gone and own their own,
And you grow old there by the phone.

Sometimes you hear, and sometimes you don't,
Some of them will, but others won't.

And as the years slip slowly by,
They've made you laugh, they've made you cry.

Look deep in your heart to see if you can say,
I've done my best in every way.

Then if you are lucky, on judgment day,
"She was a good mother," they all will say.

Esther Braden

"Friendship"

Friendship is like the ocean, rough at sometimes
but calm and peaceful at others.

Even in the wildest hurricane friends seem to make it through
and watch the beautiful sunset on the water.

Never give up in a storm because the true friend
will always come out of it.

The true friendship will last a lifetime,
just like the ocean, strong and beautiful.

Erin McNamara

Miracle Of Two

Two smiling faces that greet you in the morning.
Bottles they want while still yawning

Four banging hands and four stumping feet.
Two hungry mouths to feed.

Two dirty diapers that need to be changed
Two pairs of clothes that get stained.

Bath time is a treat. They splash
the water by kicking all four feet.
Water all over me and the floor.
But they love it and I couldn't ask for more.

Two little Girls made out of
our Love, God gave us this miracle from up above.

Two babies to be Kissed Goodnight.
I tell you it's a beautiful Sight.

Sometimes it is hard and I'm Lucky
if I could Remember my name.
But sometimes it fun and that keeps me sane.

Me and my husband would not trade
them for the world. Cause
They are Our Twin Little Girls!

Dawn Catalfamo

Lost Or Taken

Lost, you say or taken, far away from home
brought to a place where we never belonged
Forced to live in a society that don't give a dam
About what's right or wrong
Built their land on the backs of our own

Stripped us of our native tongue; beat us down
When we tried to come together as one
Separated us, the good from the bad because they
knew each other was all we had

Took our Mothers and laid them in bed and now
We don't know if our color is black, white, yellow or red

As I write about it, a tear falls from my eye
because I don't want our future to die
What you say? There's no hope oh yes there is
all we have to do is stop the man from giving our
children the dope

Give them an education and teach them to read and see
if they don't change into a different breed; each one
teach one just as you always say and I betcha we start
to live a different way

Donna O'Brien

Sweets

Create within my soul's delight
Bubble Gum and candy with every bite
My childhood dreams have finally matured
As I suck up the sweets before I am cured
Lollipops and Cokes infiltrate my mind
As I roll in chocolates of every kind
I bathe my tongue in vanilla shakes
And caress my mouth with angel food cakes
So, if the day goes by before I am done
I will pray to the Lord to hold the sun
For 'tis better to have enjoyed this day of content
Then to have wasted my taste on nutritious intent

Frank Meade

Remember The Rivoli

For twelve cents,
Bud and I got to choose-
"Rivoli or Oil City?"
Didn't need popcorn in those days.

Sometimes we carried
One handkerchief between us,
Handed it back and forth
In the sad parts.
Ok to cry in the dark.

Once I had to miss the 13th
Episode of the serial,
Punished for some small crime,
Stubborn grandma standing pat.
He stayed home, too.

For twelve cents, all the dreams and lies
I ever needed.
Tried to make him dance Fred to my Ginger.
Mostly played nurse in his war epic.
Wonder, could I ask him,
"Remember the Rivoli?"

Barbara Armbruster

The Empty Glass

The empty glass sits upon the rugged dinner table we call life.
But filling the transparent somatic figure is painful and full of strife.
The glass is often filled with liquid love and liquid hate
and happiness and sadness and confusion much too great.
But when the time comes when the glass gets chipped or cracks
on the side,
the potable liquid emotions within suddenly begin to slide
out of the glass with ample speed and creates a huge milky spill.
Then we think that the cracked-up glass is something we can't refill.
But if we have some patience and some understanding glue,
We can pick up the pieces and mend the glass to make it look
brand new.
So the next time a glass very close to your own becomes a
recyclable pile,
Take some time to put it back together, but be patient, it may
take awhile.

John E. Higgins III

The Rose

To stop and smell the roses is a saying so grand
but for many people, they just don't understand
They romp in the field and play and have fun
when responsibility comes, from that they run
They don't have time for it, it doesn't fit in
so out comes the gardener, who sees it as no sin
out comes the scissors and shears, the instrument to tear it out
The rose, it has no voice, it cannot shout
if it hasn't bloomed, it has no life
but that saying, I feel, has caused much strife
The seed has been planted and the rose is growing
From its source of life, love and care should be flowing
let us not pick the rose before its time
"Don't take my life", I'm sure it would chime
let us hope and pray that everyone may feel
to pick a rose is wrong and its fate you seal

Joshua Godfrey

The Day I Had To Clean My Room

My mother says it's time to clean my room,
But I say it looks fine.
"No", she says, "look over there - an ugly melon rind."
So one melon rind or two,
That's really no big deal.
It could be worse,
It could be a moldy banana peel.
So then she says if I don't clean my room I'll be grounded
for a week.
But then the world will be out and I'll be called a major
geek.
My room is really not that bad at all,
It really is quite clean.
But once in a while my Mom will get a little mean,
She'll yell at me all night and day,
And when she finally goes to sleep she'll dream about me
moving away.

Amie Graves

One Moment In Time

Nobody else saw it
But I'll never forget
The feeling is imbedded in memory yet
The time when my faithful horse and I
Totally became one for a moment in time
My body was his and his became mine
It seemed so perfect a moment sublime
All of our work had reached a peak
I had no words with which to speak
It does not matter that nobody saw
No judges were watching with a test to score
No friends were there to give us praise
No instructors present with arms raised
Just myself and my horse no audience around
Together we danced our grace did abound
For a moment in time we became one
A treasure more precious than blue ribbons won.

Debra J. Bryant

To Our Daughter's First Grade Teacher

Another group of children came last August through your door,
But in this group was one quite different from the ones who'd
come before.
This child was "Oh! So special!" and possessed such charming powers.
She was the answer to our prayers — You see...this child was ours!

You smiled at her and took her hand, and led her to her seat.
She turned and waved "good-bye" to me, self confident and sweet.
I knew that day my little girl was safe within your care...
I looked into your eyes that day and saw such wisdom there.

And now the year has ended—I can't believe it's true.
It seems like only yesterday our daughter came to you.
You always strived to see that she had food to fuel her learning.
You made so sure those little wheels inside her head kept turning.

The blessings you have given us cannot be weighed or measured.
Our memories of her year with you will be forever treasured.
You've guided her through many a new and challenging endeavor.
You and she now have a bond that time will never sever.

Ernestine Haas

Untitled

It makes your heart tear
But it makes you soar to the clouds
It makes you weep
But it makes you smile
It is cold on a lonely night
But it holds you when you are unhappy
It makes you fear for the future
But it knows your darkest secrets
It makes you want more
But you decide you cannot live without it

Amy Tal

Friend Of My Life

You are such a friend to me,
but I've never seen your smile

You've been with me, for how long?
I'd say quite a while

You're always there for me
when my heart is breaking

You've stopped my tears from flowing
and my tortured soul from aching

Your warmth and enduring love
have helped me through the years

I beg of you, don't leave
for I've run out of tears

I've tried to catch a glimpse of you
from the corner of my eye

But you move too quick for me
oh, you are so sly

Alas, I shall keep wishing
upon every shining star

That one day I shall see you
Guardian Angel that you are

Arlene Deweber

Who Is Who?

Every hour - minute - second in one's life is indeed, precious
but nothing is more precious than twins.

Are you ETHAN - or are you JASON?
It is difficult to tell as God created carbon copy twin
boys and sent them on their way from Heaven for us to
ponder -

Are you JASON - or are you ETHAN?
A wonderful bond grew between them in the warm,
comfortable darkness of their Mother's womb -
awaiting the greatest gift of all - the gift of life, and a
bond never to be broken no matter what different paths or
directions destiny may dictate. One will always feel the
other's needs and, perhaps, even thoughts. Just a wink
between them will say - "I know"! How wonderful and
magnificent to start life and remain as one in
THOUGHT, DEED, AND LOVE FOR EACH OTHER
Oh how I love you ETHAN and JASON - you are most
certainly MY PRECIOUS MOMENTS.

June Werner

Malcolm

Brave, strong and intelligent.
But now only silent.

Not a preacher of violence.

For the black man he fought.
Equality, freedom, and justice is what he sought.

All races are equal is what he preached.
This goal, today, we still have not reached.

Even after a fire bombed home.
He did not expect to have to defend himself from his own.

Respect and human rights are what he desired.
His dreams all shattered when the guns fired.

John B. Kinsey

Home Again

Oh, they say you can't go home again,
But, Oh how I'd just like to go.
Back to the days of my childhood
To be with loved ones I used to know.

Back to the days of my youth —-
Before I learned What a cruel world this can be,
Just to gaze at the world with such beauty;
And with the eyes of innocence to see.

Just to run through fields and the meadows,
To caress the flowers with my fingertips;
To turn my face to the heavens —-
And let summer raindrops kiss my young lips.

Can I ever again know such happiness;
As I ran to arms filled with love?
Can I ever again feel such warmth;
As the sun that beamed down from heaven above?

Oh, they say you can't go home again,
But, I have in my own special way —-
I just walked down the lanes of my memory,
Back to precious hours of my yesterday.

Aleta K. Ball

"She"

She's there when I need her;
But she acts like she doesn't care,
And I know that's not true
Because we're like a perfect pair.

She's a Big part of my life;
That I know I'll always need;
She was even there when I
Smoked my first weed.

We're like sisters; just the two of us;
She also was there when I learned how to cuss.

She's there for me; I'm there for her;
She cares about me; I care about her.

She's there when I'm happy;
She's there when I'm mad;
But if we ever split apart again;
I'm going to be so sad.

Who is this mysterious "She"?
The one I talk about so much;
Well that's only known to her and me;
But she's always close enough to touch.

Emily "Keelie" Harmon

My Will

She beckons, sits and waits for me to spring onto her lap
But she bequeathed me curious and nimble wits
And a tiny attention span.

Instinctively, I ignore her gnarled outstretched hands
To stand on my sinewy legs and use my robust arms' grasping fingers
To explore the regions of her mind: the source of my succor.

I blush when she flirts with the sun and the moon
And produces concoctions like me. Her divine thread knits me to all her fabrics. I am nurtured and I nurture.

Her worm is my paradigm
He is my benefactor and beneficiary
But he tills her. I, cultivate her.

I will grab my fork and spade
And churn her soil and heave her rocks, in my allotment,
So that the beauty that's in her becomes resplendent through me.

And when to creep onto her lap
I hear her discreet call
I will have admired her in the winter
And ravished her in the fall.

Fred Hewitt

Purpose

I must have a purpose in this life,
But sometimes I wonder why,
I was born to live through these years,
With the sole purpose to die.

There must be a reason for my being here,
I will seek until I find,
The real purpose of my life,
Which is to serve mankind.

How did I learn of this reason,
Many may think it odd,
For through study of the Christian faith,
I learned all about God.

If you are lost and without purpose,
Think of all the reasons why,
You were put upon this earth,
Not just to live and die.

And let the Lord and master,
Enter into the strife,
To help you to understand,
The real purpose of your life.

James H. Mero

The Heroine

She is not the one who does not fail
but the one who takes risks,
not the strong among the wimp
but a fellow to the weak.

She is not concerned with usefulness,
rather, she cares
does not offer solutions to problems
without sharing the burden of carrying them.

She is not the one who lets be
but the one who disturbs and enables,
not the one who is true to how things should be
but the one who is free and acts justly.

She is not caught with clock-watching
but with presence to time,
she lives the vision today
and believes in beyond.

Eva Borrero Arcos

For Becka

You were once a part of our family tree,
But the wind took you off to seed.
Your single seed is now two,
And we all know that you're not through.
You fell so far away we could not believe,
But your happiness is easy to conceive.
With each written word or voice on the phone,
You know it's a given we miss you at home,
Your new growing tree we can all see,
And we're filled with joy with each new leaf.

Your sapling will soon grow to a mighty oak,
But must be fed friendship, love and hope
The strongest tree flourishes in drought,
The strongest marriage grows through doubt.
Remember you have plenty of gardeners to keep you healthy and trimmed,
In all your friends that help you grow from within.
No matter how far a seedling blows,
To me it's like the transplanting of beautiful rose..

Darin Eilerman

To The Sister I Never Had

This is a poem to the sister I never had,
But, through the years
Has spoken to me often, has looked at me
Through many pairs of eyes—
Eyes of my mother, aunts, in-laws,
Comrades, and co-workers;
Eventually my daughters, and their daughters.
The eyes and voices of Eve,
Mother of all living,
Speak to me as a sister.

I answer with a deep feeling
For the bright, courageous, willing,
Bearers of the burdens of the human race
I never would have known
Had I not also felt the yearning
For the sister I never had.

Joyce B. Stephenson

A Daughter's Love

A mother's love is so terrific,
But what about a daughter's love?

Respect, obedience, kindness, caring,
Helpfulness and friendship are what I
Need for loving.

My love for my mother is so important to me;
For without her I would not be.

I salute her, praise her, and give her cheer.
Mom, your love for me is so dear.

I want you to know you can do no wrong,
And I'm repaying you by letting you know,
That my love for you is incredibly strong.

Amy Grant

River

Not long ago, confined to narrow passage,
Briskly flowing, foaming, raging,
The river rushed along in youthful fancy,
Adolescent energy pervading.

Now expansive and mature, it rounds a bend
Reflecting filtered sunlight on its tranquil banks.
And for an instant seems to pause to rearrange
The living luggage carried in its swelling womb.

Bob Story

After Dad

Our hearts have been wrenched with out father's passing
but what would this Thanksgiving be,
if he were among us but still taken from us
this disease that would not set him free.

The lessons were taught those torturous months
as he struggled to be what he was.
He prayed, "God help me—save my children from this,"
in his anguish he remembered God's love.

I believe in my heart on June 25th he called
in a soft searching voice, what I was is no more—
what is it You want me to be.
No loved one can enter this place I'm in, only You
who died for my sins, The Lord is My Shepherd
I shall not want, by God's grace I begin life again.

Our lives have been altered by those months and his death,
that is how it should be.
Dad was so large in his life and in ours
but no one is larger that He.

Through the pain thank God for his wisdom and grace,
our Father is finally free.

Helen Williams Dobson

He Walks with Me

He walks with me, I can feel him near,
But when I turn to see, there is no one there.

He talks to me, his voice I can hear,
But when I turn to see, there is no one there.

He comforts me when I'm feeling fear,
But when I turn to see, there is no one there.

He's guiding me where the path is clear,
But when I turn to see, there is no one there.

He waits for me until the day is near,
That's when I will see my brother is here

Reaching for me with his hand to share,
Then he'll walk with me, and I'll see him near

Eileen Dello

My Mother

My mother is happy,
But when she is angry
Her voice is as angry
As a stampede of elephants,
When she is happy again,
Her voice goes down and she is nice.
Her heart is as pretty as her face.
Her hair is as brown as chocolate.
Her skin is as soft and white as the sky.
Her eyes are as brown as her hair.
Her touch is as soft as silk.
I love my Mommy!

Deena Kleinberg

For The Birds

Songs are lovely from the mocking bird;
But, without any warning at two in the morning
I'd prefer, by me they not be heard.
Is he just singing or is he bird-talking?
But, mostly, I wonder as he does his number
What thinks the bird which he is mocking?

Janie Robins

To My Daddy, My Father, My Friend

It was many years that we were apart,
but you always stayed inside my heart.
At night I would kneel and pray,
"Please God let me see my Daddy someday"
For eight years, I never heard not a letter, not a word.
I had to wonder if you were dead or alive, but I knew I had
to strive-towards the day that I would see you again.
I was in the hospital this past July,
with so many problems that I wanted to die.
I was told you must not care and that I needed to forget about you.
But I didn't care, that just wasn't true.
The phone call came, in late October,
and then from then the wondering was over.
I found out that you were well,
and then life didn't seem as much like hell.
For all these years I've had a dream, the biggest one ever dreamed
then the dream finally came true,
13 years later when I opened my door and there stood you.
All the words in the world cannot say,
the way I felt when I saw you that day.
Then you had to go back home, and part of me feels all alone,
but you're still my father and my friend,
and I can't wait until were together again.

Jacqueline Shelhart

A Message To "The Grandest Child Of My Heart"

You run to me now, and I look, with eyes that mistily see,
But your glow makes the brightness while I hold you on my knee.

That step that's all too brisk for me (although brisker I was then)
Takes my heart and says: "Come back, to dear sweet days of when"...

You call me "Nannie" in a voice so soft, so soothing to these ears
That aren't hearing all the words as sharp as by gone years.

You touch my hand with your "brand new" baby silken skin—
And suddenly I see on mine just how many years it's "bin!"

You start me laughing, and then I cry recalling my own baby's days:
She does for you as I did for her, in blessed motherly ways.

And so, dearest babe, at twilight when your angel arms sleepily hold
On to your "Nan" she says with a sigh, "I'm content in growing old!"

Dolores Visconti

A Friend In Mind...

Miles separate us at times
But your voice or handwritten letter
mends the distance.

You're a friend that always lends a
good ear
In time of need you are always beside
me.

We have been through a lot of troubles
and joys
But the friendships we share belong
especially to us.

Hand in hand as we walk through the
stages of life
Understanding our differences in the
way we view the world.

I hope we will always stay in touch to
withhold our special friendship
Because walking through life with you
balances my world.

Angela Foehring

Despair

From a heart of glass that's shattered beyond repair
By a heart of stone which only has little to care
A boy lost searching for the love that isn't there
A boy lost in a world full of despair.

From a soul of ice melting real fast
He's got no future and he's had no past
Oh this poor lost soul was not built to last
From the heart of stone to the heart of glass
I've found my future and I've lost my past

The boy's hopes and dreams have drifted away
Heart of glass broken by stone
All the faith is lost and gone

I am that boy
I've lost my dream
Falling down that stair
That stair of endless despair

Why do I keep playing the game
Oh why do I live in a world of despair.

Emrys Jones

A Bloom Gone Sour

A pretty flower was given to me
By someone I liked very much;
A pretty flower whose fragrance was sweet,
And petals were soft to touch.

I kept the flower for a very long time,
Even after it was dead;
Because it reminded me of him,
And things that he once had said.

But his love for me has gone away,
His feelings for me gone sour;
Just like the life, which at one time,
Dwelled within the flower.

I'd like to have just one more chance
To make him understand;
I love him just as much,
As the flower I hold in my hand.

Joanne Ferris

Prayer To Monday Morning

Off to work Monday morning
Caffeined up and yet still yawning
Body reluctant, Spirit tired
Wondering what the weekend sired

Oh early morning! Gateway to the day
Show your harried workers a brighter way
So when we bless you in the morning
A half downed breakfast cannot prevent
Spirit soaring.

Carolyn E. O'Connor

A Friend Or More

Can I be your friend, a friend or more
Can I be your friend, someone I won't ignore
A friend to me you'll be
A chain of steel connects us that nobody can see
Forever friends we will stay
Till we come to that special day
For we will always overcome all of life's tests
For we are bound to never reveal the where to our nest
For that's something nobody can find, Something we treasure
Can I be your friend, Friends we'll be forever.

Curtis L. Knox

Little Boy Blue

Can I have some candy before I go?
Can I take my toys to play with?
Tell me, mom, why I can't come home
Can I take my bear to sleep with?

Who's gonna read me stories?
Who's gonna buy me icecream?
Can I still have a birthday party?
Will you please come visit me?

Mom, my throat hurts; I can hardly breathe
Can you hear me?
When I get better can I play in the leaves?
I promise I won't get dirty

Can I take my friend? He won't stay long
I promise he'll go home early
We're building a house in the back yard
For all the little birdies

Mom, why are you crying?
Was it because my room wasn't clean
I heard the doctor say I was dying
Mom, what does die mean?

Julie Munoz

No One

Nowhere to turn- Nowhere to run.
Can not escape- From the things I've done.

Can not escape- These infinitive walls.
My mind has taken- Too many falls.

No one to confide in- Friends become enemies.
I feel like I'm drowning- My tears fill the seas.

Yet my eyes are dry- These tears stay inside.
My overwhelming fear- Of being exposed.
Turns to drive- To make certain they don't know.

All these hollow faces-
They don't care.

All their ways-
That I don't share.

They think they're God-
And I don't compare.

Elisa Jane Feldman

Untitled

Are you there God?
Can you hear me?
I want to know,
Can you really help me?
Was it really Jesus
Who died on the cross for everyone's sins?

Did he really rise up from the dead?
God, help me, help me to understand your word.
I love you! Can you hear me?
I love you.

If you can't hear anything else
Please hear this,
I love you.

Becky Biggart

Midnight Moon

A passion filled minute made her lose her composure.
Caught up in a feeling that completely absorbed her.
She could not resist the intrigue so she accepted the dare.
Fate rendered her helpless when she looked into his stare.

Under a midnight moon secret passions were released.
Surfacing were feelings she never dared to free.
And under a midnight moon be held her in his embrace.
Etching into his memory the happiness on her face.

Swept away into paradise by a touch she had never known
Unlocking the door into fantasy where she is free to roam.
Exploring all the desires so new and captivating.
He knows under a midnight moon is where she'll be waiting.

Jodi L. Allen-Davis

Life And Death

Flowers grow amid the remains of the gas
chamber at Auschwitz.
The barracks and the dungeons are quiet as
the seasons sweep by.
The dead, too, are silent.
An old man is sitting near me.
He tells the tales of the past.
How the guards would toss slices of bread to
the prisoners and laugh.
How the smoke from the crematoria
billowed against the moon.
He wears a remnant of the night that was.
A long row of numbers forever march across
the inside of his forearm.
How strange it is to think this ever occurred.
The flowers at Auschwitz sway gently in the
wind.
No one is there to admire them.

Adam Pfeffer

An Orphans Home Reunion

I am not dead, nor am I forgot
Children are still in my bosom; and it
Was a fight well fought.

My name may have changed from the one
You loved so dear.
My methods are different, my buildings are old;
But, I am still here.

I am your Father, Your Mother, Your teacher, and friend.
All, that you are today is what I was then.

I have never completely left you, though long
Years have gone by.
Your lives maybe different, but that spark
Inside you is "I".

Rekindling a friendship is so wonderful to do.
That spark may just grow and give meaning to you.

So, come make merry, make laughter and joy.
Remember your youth-be a young girl or boy.

There is much to be thankful to the Lord up above;
Come visit me now, remember tradition with love!

James E. Koski

Christmas' Reason

Christmas is a time of joy for every
Christian girl and boy.

It is a time of Peace and Love when
we remember God's gift from above;

How on a dark and dismal night, God
gave the world His Holy Light.

Jesus had come to save us all from
the curse of Adam's fall.

Presents, candy and cards are fine, but
let's not forget this gift divine,

For without God's gift of His Son,
there'd be no Christmas — No — Not one.

Let's remember then this gift of Love
sent to us from above,

Thinking as we play and pray, just why
there is a Christmas Day!

Don Wehry, Jr.

Remembrance Of Mother At Christmas

Let us remember as the days grow long the joy you brought us at
Christmas time.
For we will never again see anything as beautiful as you, doing
Your best to make each Christmas a treasure that would
warm our hearts and make each of us happy.
Let us remember as the years go past, the joy you tried to bring
each of us at Christmas time.
For like soft music, those images of joy will linger in our hearts
and minds, to tip the peak of life, where later we will horde with
aging eyes and minds, fond thoughts of your Christmas spirit though
You had little, it will shine like a beacon of light and
drive the clouds of sorrow away.
Let us remember to thank you mother at Christmas time, for each of
Us in our own quiet way will for always have a thought,
a day, a quiet moment, a lifetime of fond memories of
past Christmas's spent with you.

James F. Smith

Scenes At Dawn

The Sun beams stream though the sky,
Clouds float about like puffs of cotton,
Could a human hand paint such beauty?
Birds begin to sing their beautiful melody,
Could a human compose as beautiful sound?
Dew on the grass sparkles in the sun,
Could a human arrange that kaleidoscope just so?
Leaves on the trees begin to stir,
So slight, at first, like a whisper.
A squirrel scampers across a lawn,
Looking for a tree to climb.
No human hand in this creation,
Enjoyed by all humankind.

Helen J. Jarvis

America's "Past" Time

There once was a game we use to call great,
But now it's just an old memory that's really faint,
That game was baseball and the story is sad,
About how the players and owners got everyone mad,
The salary cap is what the owners wanted,
But the players said no and only granted,
Hopefully this game will come back to stay,
For the fans this would be a joyous day!

Brian Crompton

Fly Away Black Bird

Go away black bird there is no food today
Come back to me on another day

Why don't you fly next door
They will have plenty of stale bread for sure

Fly away black bird to your humble nest
Bird, you are becoming one giant pest

Fly away, let me get my needed rest
Maybe tomorrow I'll be at my best

Fly away and leave me alone
Maybe tomorrow you can have some bread
And maybe tomorrow I can chew on a meaty bone

Go! fly away black bird....

Blanca Estela Abad

"Under The Pines"

A visit to my friend, my knock on the door,
"Come in," he would say, "and tell what for."
Soon, suggest he would, "let's go sit under the pines
and visit for now, and for old times."
Comfortably seated, with a pleasant times,"
He would inquire, "Well what's new with you?"
"Just Look," he would say, "at the beautiful garden below;
pumpkins, peppers, tomatoes, other things grow."
"I just sit here and pass away the time
Looking, smelling and enjoying, under the pine."
"How's the church now days?" he would say,
"You know my tithes I always pay,
and something else I do, read my Bible all the way through."
Time did come to take another trip this happened on Jesus' ship
Across the harbor and through the veil below
to the Grand Portal, only the saved will know.
Oliver has made it to that fair shore
to be with Jesus forever more.
Just resting, talking, enjoying, where forever is time
Sitting with Jesus, under the pines.

Basil Shaw

Giddyup Row

Down on the farm our name we did hear,
Come quickly and get a task in gear—-
Another unexpected, time consuming chore
Amid mumblings and hatred for work we did deplore.
Gotta get busy cause the signs were right
Gotta pull, gotta pull, with all your might
To make a straight row.
Giddyup, giddyup, and tow
That flow straight through the soil;
To turn up bean furrow-that made us boil!
Pull! Pull! Pull! Pull!
And that is no bull.
The plowshare lodged beneath a root
Unbelievably, that plow backed up to boot!
Three little ponies and one little mare
Still towing and pulling forward-no effort to spare.
All ended up ground, heaped in a pale,
Entangled and dirty, not e're a smile;
From behind the ploughshare laughter engulfed us and become profuse,
But through all the grime, pleas for silence became our truce.

Fern Soyars Agee

The River

Darling, come sit with me by the river.
Come sit with me and watch the water roll by.
Darling, come sit with me by the river
Until the sun sets and the stars fill the sky.

Before I was born couples sat by these waters
The wind in their hair, and the breeze on their face.
Centuries from now lovers will gaze at these waters
Holding each other in tender embrace.

This river has flowed through this valley for ages.
The stars they have always hung in the sky.
And lovers have always sat hand-in-hand through the ages,
Watching the cool, gentle waters flow by.

My love for you, dear, runs like the river.
It's course is deep, and it's current is strong.
My love is eternal, my darling, like the river
The cool, quiet waters croon your name like a song.

Darling, come sit with me by the river.
Come stay with me till the morning's fresh dew.
Darling, come lay with me by the river,
And we'll make sweet love till the world is new.

Franklyn King

"Thanks, Mom"

In the darkness of my mind,
come wonderful thoughts, so sublime,
Of mother!
At fifty-eight, I just begin to see,
all of the many things, she did for me,
My mother!
Little education, she cleaned church for food,
she had to take care of five, in our brood,
Great mother!
Never a care for herself at all,
unselfish, loving, at our beck and call,
Nurse mother!
Now at eighty, she's more spry than I,
still loving and giving and standing by,
Our mother!
How do I say thanks, for this love in my life?
To one who went through many years of strife?
Thanks mother!

Bonnie Withers

The Elusive Bluebird Of Happiness

Happiness is just a "state of mind"
Comparable to other peoples' woes.
The reason it eludes us
No one really knows.

We all have a different set of patterns
Each composed of a different design.
By hoping, coping well, and with peace of mind
The elusive bird of happiness we will find.

Then at last we will be satisfied
And accept what we have got —
Be thankful for this happiness
So many have it not.

Iris Moses Weintraub

Untamed Hearts

Don't toy with love it's not a game
Contrary to what poets say...
For love is dangerous, it's not a game
With emotions and hearts you play.
'Tis not the passionate romance
That every dame dreams of...
A Prince Charming romance, of where there is "true love."

Get real, Wake up, get with it?
Is my advice to you!
For girl, he is a trap, waiting to capture you.
At first he says how special, and wonderful you are to him.
But what he's really saying is, "how long before you give in."
Give in to his temptations of passion and deceit,
Give in to loving mind games of which he can't be beat.
Listen to him with heart, not just with your ears.
If what he says is too wonderful, in the end you'll be left with tears.

Love is what you make it or so the poets say.
We laugh, we cry, we live and learn
With untamed hearts we play.

Danielle Knox

Peace Of Mind

Insanity is chaos
Corruption is for the have nots
Gain knowledge for the brain
So the explosive situation won't become insane
To gain peace of mind
It's high time
To set aside
Any misconstrued disturbance of unkind
Simply said
I want peace of mind
To achieve this unattainable goal
It's a must that you trust
Untapped and unconjured feelings
Of love, of hate, of indifference
And maybe if your willing to deal
Then it won't become necessary to steal
Just to feel
Peace of mind

Cathy Tucker Farmer

Soma

To sleep alone and hide my face,
cover my dreams with your embrace.
Lie to myself, a flood of fears.
My blood is mixed with sweaty tears.

Sweet mystery best left untold.
Now wish away the bitter cold.
Don't love, don't hate take a deep breath.
Slipping away an instant death

Believe solely in your visions,
never surrounded; private prison.
Hopeless thinking, helplessly lost.
Can't endeavor without a cost.

Unconsciousness is depleting.
Morality still receding.
Tasting freedom and leave no spills.
Unity breeds, deadly breath kills.

Brandon Bousman

444

Light fills the past as smoke fills the sky
covering the sun, warmth again denied.
diluted red brings forth, as rain fills my
wounds
friendly soul walk off the battlegrounds
so soon
too soon

Strength leaves my body, as images fill my
head
of the loved and the lost
the wounded and the dead
through the mud and the sweat
the cold and the disease
a scream leaves my body
as I fall to my knees
a shot rings out
one, two more
another death on the battlefield
no name, just a number
Year: 2020 Identification No. :444

Emanuel Joseph Cavallaro

"Peace Of Mind"

In search of true peace,
Craving the passions of total bliss,
Absorbing into oneself...
Grasping the true happiness which is hidden inside,
Avoiding all labors of love,
Selfishly, doing whatever brings oneself total
gratification.

Time for time,
Time for solitude and awareness,
Time to become inward bound,
Time to be left alone and time for rest,
Time to spend with The Creator of Nature,
And time to be grateful.

Enjoying the simple beauties which are natural...
The jewels of the earth,
To dive deep inside without hesitation,
Creating a tunnel vision within one's soul,
Walk and seek the true unity of body and mind.

Diana Wahrlich

Cardinal

A streaking meteorite of ruby
cresting and fluttering to a rest
"I think it's orange", she said.
"No", he demurred, "it's red".

A startling slash of crimson
That marks its sanguinary path to rest
"It looks like orange", she said.
"No", he replied, "it's red".

A flash of fiery scarlet
That breathes defiance in its breast
"It's orange", she said.
"No", he insisted, "it's red".

And then a veritable vermilion explosion.
Careening carnations, gyrating garnets,
Blood-hued whirls, reeling roses,
Churning cherries, burning sunsets,
Quivering lips.

A world incarnadine!

She smiled and caressed his head.
"It's orange", he said.

Edward Chalom

Her Eyes

Her eyes are like the summer pond,
crystal blue that twinkle in the sun.
Whenever I see those eyes I turn soft,
like a pillow,
pulling me in like the sea on a warm day,
making me think of nothing but her eyes.
Those eyes that shine so bright,
attract me like a moth to a light,
and then when I come eye to eye with her
I go into a deep trance,
thinking I'm looking into the blue sky.

Bradley Bodell

His Glare

His glare is a blade,
Cutting anything and everything that enters it.
Like a knife, piercing the world.
His glare is a blade.

His glare is a pillow,
Cushioning all of humanity.
Soft, fluffy, gentle, comforting all.
His glare is a pillow.

His glare is ice, freezing out the world,
Like icicles, hanging from his eyebrows.
His glare is ice.

His glare is a safe, concealing all of the fear,
Locking it away where only the combination holder can find it.
His glare is a safe.

His glare is a shade, protecting him from the outside world,
Shutting out the pain, hiding him.
His glare is a shade.

His glare, a blade, a pillow, a safe, a shade, ice.
Makes him seem so ominous, yet so scared.
His glare.

Jake Chused

The Dance

The moth hears it echoing in the night...
"Dance with me," it beckons.
From afar he sees the orgy.
The flames in an erotic dance with the darkness.
The night is deep...dark as ebony-
The flames lick at it seductively.
The moth goes closer.
"Dance With Me," the flames whisper, "Closer...closer"
"Come...Dance With Me"
The moth hesitates...
But the flames in their hypnotic dance pull him.
The lure is too strong.
The moth flies in - ahhhh- it is ecstasy!
They dance a macabre dance in the darkness.
The flames sighs in satisfaction as it calls into the night:
"Dance With Me..."
"Come... Dance With Me."

Dana Roberson-Horn

Approaching Christmas

Frigid North winds blow frosted breath;
dark clouds unleash newborn snow.
Wind gusts swirl flakes into whirlpools,
painting trees and roof tops magic white.

Circled evergreen wreaths with pine cones,
enhanced by large red satin bows,
hang on doors and frosty windows
announcing the coming Christmas.

Children dream of magnificent toys,
dolls, drums, trucks, and trains.
Visions of Santa traveling through space
spread instant happiness for days.

Pine trees arrayed in spectrum lights,
delicate ornaments of balls and bells.
Christmas Angel stands atop the tree,
announces the humble birth of Christ.

The wooden manger scene under the tree,
gives Christmas a profound meaning.
Christians ready for a birth celebration.
A hope symbol for worldwide peace!

Florence Danielewicz

Night's Playground

The deep blue blanket is pulled over night after night
Darkening all things far beyond our sight
In this hazy sky, dreamland lies
And at that time renaissance shall be born
And a time warp shall be torn
Setting free all of time to play havoc on my mind
Ranting and raving they all shall leave
Turning and giving a little snead
But as I know there is to be little reprieve —
For through all my life they always shall be
Waiting for the sun to rise
To cool once more these dreamy skies
They shall run and they shall play
Until the break of day
Then the sun does rise
And they run off bitter despise
They shall sleep until the dawn of the moon
And it shall come all too soon

Anna Elizabeth Watson

You Are

You are the moon so full and bright, even on the darkest of night, you are the sun that shines so warm and bright, you are my guiding light, when I feel everything, is as dark as can be, you come and shine your light for me.

You are my world through and through, more than I could ever tell you, you are the birds that sing so beautifully, you are the warm summer rain that falls to earth so tenderly, you are the wind that blows so freely, you are to me everything that needs to be.

You are the beat of my heart, to be without you I wish to be not, you are my life in so many ways, I pray that you never go away, that in my life you always stay, without you my life would not be today.

Amanda S. Nix

"Death Of An Icon" (Remembering Kurt Cobain)

My brains lay on this garage floor
Daughter may turn out to be a whore
Things I will never know
Scars of my stomach never sowed
Depression killed me
Music all I'll ever be
Now far gone from my wife
Gave up an illustrious life
Float above you all love for you built tall
My voice to live on
Even though I'm forever gone
Drugs ruled my mind peace I did not find
Cardigan Sweaters, Blond looks of my hair
You pass my dead body and stare
Cry all your tears
As my deepest passions turned to fears
Dead at last emotions and love crashed
My voice will always linger
Even though I'm a dead singer
Remember me as I was as I return to my original dust

Frank R. Liuzzi II

A Day In Your Life

The sky glows with yellow, orange, and red
Dawn is upon us
We lift up our head

A new day begins, new life, and new hope
Today we go forward
Up the steep slope

Yesterday's gone, look for joy in today
Sadness and troubles
Are all put away

Life is like daybreak, each day it is new
We can make it better
Or just make do

Live life like a day, make each moment last
Live for the future
Don't dwell in the past

When nightfall arrives, you will have been blessed
With a day in you life
Filled with your best.

Carol Lloyd

Can We Keep Peace The Same

As a blaze does the flame,
Day to day, time to time,
What's to blame?

Has it gone too far... beyond repair,
Should we still even care?
When all is said and done, It'll be seen,
That all across the land,
Not all will be in despair.

Strong hearts of giving,
Will prevail in parts of the game.
I'm here, your there,
I do mine, you do yours.

Together, may we keep peace the same.

James N. Nicholson

Prayer of Praise

Indeed there is an enlightening, so my
dears don't be frightened, for now is the
time, to hear from the divine So please
concentrate, contemplate, and meditate.
All is well if you dwell In our place
and time. It is indeed yours and mine
Open your heart and hand wide, for I
Jesus will be always by your side See
the sun - see the rainbow. Watch it
glow, flow with rays and colors Beauty
all around. Listen to the sound, it's
all around, touched by the Dove it's my
love, Your love, showing, growing
glowing, shining divining.
The stars are ours to watch to see them glisten
Shimmering in the night, pure delight
Creation is a delight, so use your being with
all your might.
You will see the light
Whether day or night

Dianne O'Bray

Holiday Spirit

Snowflakes fall like teardrops from heaven. Winter is here - it's December eleven.
They glisten in the dark night - pale, faded, yet shimmering bright.

The ground is covered with a soft white lid screwed on tightly to keep winter in.
Magical sights of the cold, dreary times; chuckling Santas, "Please give a dime."

Light strands like jewels in a crown; shopping for that perfect gift, ev'ry store in town.
Big shiny boxes, sweet candy tarts - as long as it comes from our tender hearts.

The giving season has come at last - you must move quickly; it comes quite fast!
Peace and love float in the air - breathe in deeply - it's everywhere!

Finally that glorious day has arrived. But, for those less fortunate, those deprived -
It's just another cold winter's day to reflect upon their misguided way.

So remember on this season's best: The hungry, the sad, and the rest.
A better gift than dark, bleak coal - Peace and Joy is our ultimate goal.

Andrew Haas

Untitled

This place I dwell, motionless, with frantic thoughts of
delicate gestures.
Beneath any and all chaos, I lay.
Draped with dark-green leaves still flourishing in life,
but securely drifting to their inevitable death below.
Amongst enormous life, which seem to penetrate Heaven,
Where tears of angels trickle in despair, nourishing
twisted weeds into a genesis of life
blossoming into the purest of petals.
Consumed by virginal scent, this place I called home
exhalted highest above all else.
Life, purest, gentlest among all else,
showered in rays of golden triumph.
I am home.

Carl Anthony Canales

"Good Health"

Forget about the treasures of earth, such as
Diamonds, silver and gold
Good health is the greatest treasure (Gods Gift)
That one can ever hold.

Alone, a quiet stroll through the woods.
Perhaps the fields, or by the streams
To see the squirrels jump and play
And hear the song birds sing.

To smell the fragrance of the trees
And enjoy the great outdoors
I've been to all those distant places
Heard the awful screams and cries of war.

Now, with this physical body impairment and wobbly legs
Maybe, just maybe someday
I'll take that quiet stroll once more

Eugene Montgomery

I Step Into Her

Where waves die out on top of waves
die out in bleached sand, I am lured
through the kaleidoscope of quayside
markets, charmed by the blackest woman
I will ever see. I step into her

footprints as she peddles ripe
guava and shaddock, raw
and white-worn bare

feet trudge down the center
of the pebble-tiled road. She is Mother

to all the childless girls snapping
peas between their legs.

Beneath the stars, I step into her
shadow and watch as she dances in the arms
of the cold wind across the barren,
moonsoaked strand. Into the salted air that burns her
blistered skin, she releases her untamed
spirit and I step into her

body and soar with the freed
souls of our stillborn.

Julie Terese Heil

Untitled

Fairy dust, magic wands and rabbits out of hats,
Disappear and reappear with cunning slight of hand.

Tinkerbell, carrousels and spinning ferris wheels,
Leave us giddy, short of breath and send us nearly reeling.

But none of these can quite compare to the visions that we treasure,
Of christmas past when we were young and time was not to measure.
Of twinkling lights and smells and sights that each of us holds dear,
The warmth of caring, coming home, and never feeling fear.

Dare to wonder,
Dare to laugh,
Forget your foolish pride,
Embrace the ebb and flow of Christmas and ride the
Magic of its tide.
Magical wishes from

Sue Atwell

Infidelity

The sacred institution of marriage has been lost;
displaced by carnal people,
as Christ lay on the cross.

In a moment of insemination,
word, thought, or deed,
the being seeks to quench its most humanistic need.

With the scruples of a primate,
humanity has lost the way;
leaving anatomical secrets to provoke the actions of the day.

Self description,
true depiction of those encased in glass,
mold the key to the door
of skeletons
of the past.

Adam A. Buster

Do I

Do I give it a chance? Do I try one more time?
Do I really believe everything will be fine?
Do I trust in the words I've heard once before?
Do I give it all up and walk out the door?

Do I know what I want? Do I know how I feel?
Do I really believe that this love is real?
Do I follow my heart? Do I follow my head?
Do I forget all the bad things we said?

Do I want it to last? Do I want it to end?
Do I really believe my heart will mend?
It's funny to me as I read the above,
There's two little words we consider in love.

We say them as we wed with all belief,
Then we turn them around when we're feeling grief.
Those two little words can have such meaning,
And it all depends at the time how we're feeling.

When I said them "I Do" I didn't lie,
But now with time they've changed to "Do I".

Judy Reynolds

"Something Special"

Wishing wishing is all I can
Do. Trying to retrieve that something
special I once had with you.
Lost lost oh where can it be. That something special
I once had with you
Dreaming dreaming is all that's
left to me. While trying to reclaim that something special
I once had with you
Then all at once much to
My surprise I found that while
wishing and dreaming of that something special I found
you only to learn you'd been wishing and dreaming of that
something special too
Then how we laughed and then how we cried to realize
While wishing and dreaming of that something special we
Both shared we in our
Needless wishing and dreaming of that something special we
Both shared we almost let our something special slip away
Foolish foolish how blind could we be for our something special
was right there to see mine was always him and his was always me

Cheryl Theriac

"Ode To Our Human Family"

Are we like drops of water?
Do we find ourselves in many forms
- some times alone,
- some times together?
When do we labor, when do we laugh?
Are we best as steam, or stream, or bath?
Do we smile in a cup, or in a pond,
or as we race in a river?
Are we friends? Are we groups? Are we meant to stand alone?
Is the bravest music for the troops? Or from the chorus?
...or the moan?

Down rapids, past eddies, over the fall
freed of thinking, reason, or rhyme.
Our universe needs us, - each and all
to work our way along.
Now trickling tear, now streaming torrent
now team, now solo, now government.

Discovering love and sanity across the seas of time.

David A. Symond

Song Of The Saints

What do you do when you're alone?
Do you just sit there singing old carols?
Don't you just miss the way that you kiss?
Don't you just wish you can go back to it?
Don't you think about the lost link?
Look at that guy he just gave you a wink
Song of the saints
Song of the saints
This is the tale of the song of the saints
Even though you think that you're old
So many people think you are just cold
You can do things you thought that you can't
If you just put you're mind into a chant
You can do anything, you can go anywhere
Nothing's impossible
Just give it a try
I'm almost positive you'll be surprised
Song of the saints
Song of the saints
This is the tale of the song of the saints.

Christi A. Torrez

The Windows Of The Soul

What is peeking from the windows of your soul?
Do you see yourself as one showing
kindness or playing the unkind role?
We can teach ourselves to be better
to others, or we can live a small
life under covers.
Our purpose in life is to let life
and love show through our windows
whether we let it be shown to friends
and yes even face,
Our eyes have work to do, they show our emotion,
they can be cruel or a healing lotion,
the love will show through help and riches
let yours show you to be full of compassion,
as a child sees true love in its mother.

Benita L. Cole

Built On Eggshells

Pinnacles of Success, Masters of the Game,
Doctor, Lawyer, Wino- we're really all the same.
Lonely Cardboard Box, or Massive Ivory Tower,
Your life in a basket, or the trapping of power .
The differences are easy-Hell, ev'rybody sees 'em
The Sameness though is hidden, and not without a reason.
I don't care much if I'm like you
Or as different as Night and Day
It's what I have- and you have too
That we try to hide away.
It's all built on eggshells
No rocks to be found,
It's all built on eggshells
Might crash to the ground,
It's all built on eggshells
But we won't let it show,
It's all built on eggshells
Don't let anybody know.

Bruce A. Digna

The Objective Truth

Which of us can know what's right?
Does everyone get a say?
Or are our morals much like a kite
Maneuvered by us on a windy day?
Do we change our philosophy to fit our mood?
Depending on how others act
If this is so why do we intrude
by telling others how they should react?

Is there something that tells us what's right
and right for all of man kind?
Could this be the most common loss of sight?
For to him most seem to be blind
Do we run from him because of fear
or is it to choose to do as we will?
If someone could prove, beyond a shadow of a doubt, he is here
Undoubtedly this man would be killed

Might we be able to believe what he spoke
can it be said that this man lived
will we succumb to his ideas and works
Because before any of us were, he is.

Craig Phillips

Indifference

Doesn't anybody care for souls anymore?
Doesn't anybody care about right?
Where are the warriors in prayer of this day?
For we still have a battle to fight.

Where is the heart reaching out to the ill,
Or the hand helping those who are weak?
Are we too much involved with our own selfish wants
To be bothered by others in need?

Our churches are now known as places of fun,
Where social activities reign.
We think not of those without Christ in their life,
We live just for pleasure or gain.

Where is our love for the lost of this day?
Our fathers of old taught us truth.
Our children are going the way of the world.
Where is the example for youth?

Oh, Christians, return to the Christ of the Cross;
Return to the path that is true.
Return to the teaching of God's Holy Word.
Let Christ live His witness through you.

Constance L. Burcham

Attitude

Please don't tell me I'm wrong
Don't bother trying to explain
From what you want to tell me
I have nothing to gain.

You think you know the answers.
that just the very reason, why I turn away
Because your always right, in everything you do or say.
How can I know so much about you?
It's really not so hard to figure.
I can tell by the way you talk.
And I can see how you prosper.

Now aren't you the ladies man
You know you can only go so far.
Ego is the motive you've got to be the star.
I would rather not have met you
probably much to your surprise
Attitudes like yours, I've really learned how to despise
It doesn't really bother me, knowing
that you don't understand a thing you've read.
Someone as smart as you could never be misled........

Jeffery W. Lee

Wake Up America!!!

Don't you see America, that you are heading in the wrong direction?
Don't you see, people are crying, killing and pleading.
You need to make some correction.
Don't you see America, kids are taking guns to school,
instead of learning from the books, they are turning into no
good Crooks. Wake up America!! Don't you see America,
better known as, "Land of the Free," How can we be free, when
there're so many living in Misery. Don't you see America, you
are sleeping way to late, you need to take time out and do some,
"Contemplate." Don't you see America, We no longer want's a
two parent home, instead we'll say, "I can do it better, if I'm
doing it alone." "America," Children are having babies why
they're still so young. It make's you think, It all started, when
they wanted to have some fun. Wake Up America!!
Don't you see America. Most Fathers aren't around, to push
their baby carriage, All because they couldn't comprehended
in this so called, marriage.
America, America, you need to make a change. We don't want
Our "Living" to be like someone going. "Insane."
I say. "Wake up America"!!!

Isaiah Cobb

...Infinity...

Without Beginning... Without End...

At what point on a scale in time...
Doth man first appear?
At what point in Infinity...
Doth man then disappear?

Only in human consciousness...
Doth Time and Space exist.
In God's glorious Universe...
Infinity doth persist.

What then, of finite Big Bang start?
And finite chaotic end?
Not so, God's infinite Universe...
Without beginning...without end...

God only...not mere man...
Ordains beginning, ordains end...
In His, the infinite Universe...
Without beginning...without end...

geo. dawes

Emerald Sea

Come along with me to an emerald sea,
where the clouds are white and the wind
blows free. Where not far away just above
the bay, feel majestic mountains take
your breath away.

As we sail along where the water is warm,
with you in my arms watching nature's song.
We will play all day in that emerald bay,
playing games of love only lovers play.

When the sun goes down and the wind is calm,
and moonbeams shine on the low palm frond.
There is a fragrance here from the flowers near,
casting spells of love till the early dawn.

Come along with me help me sing my song,
In this land of dreams where all life is
long. Here our love will last for eternity,
as we sail along on the emerald sea.

Matthew Phillip Schneider

The Woman I Love

The woman I love is the sun that lights my day
She's the warmth of a spring morning and the sparkle of a winter day
The flowers open in her glory and the trees reach to embrace her
She warms my heart and sole

The woman I love is the moon at night
She casts her peaceful glow on a quiet summer's night
The inspirations of love and dreams
Unlike I have ever known

The woman I love is a star in the sky
Shining forever, pure and beautiful
She is my guiding light
The one I have wished for all my life

The woman of love is the air that I breathe
She fills my lungs and flows in my veins
She has given me life were it has never been
The woman I love is my world
She surrounds me
She is in me
She is you, Deb
I will always be yours, my love

Keith Bradfield

Beth

Pain, fear, disillusion and dread
can make a man take to his house, his room, and his bed

This is not good, it is not right
for only through Love can an eagle take flight

Only through Love can he fly through
the pain, the fear, and the dread

Only through Love can an eagle take flight
towards Hope and Joy and Delight.

For it is Love that keeps an eagle above

Be an eagle and LOVE!!!!

Keith Fletcher

Untitled

We fight to hide the facade that keeps us in others graces.
It becomes a fight of fear that our secrets will show up in their faces.

God looks upon the heart to the things he has laid out for thee.
In the long run it makes little difference how cleverly others are deceived.

Work diligently and earnestly to fight the good fight of faith.
Do not let the core of unhappiness take away your gift of faith.

Release the things that are binding for life is a paradox.
The answers often come backwards for joy is found in hard knocks.

Rest can be found in conflict, and peace can come often by war.
Happiness is often contributed to finding that "less is more".

This angle to life is simplicity, live it with passion and strong doses of faith. Guard the soul with the gift of "clear conscience" and know that God is never too late.

Tammy B. Pope

"You Are ..."

My fireworks on an otherwise lonely fourth of July.

You are my wild and sometimes "reckless" spirit rushing down the path of life stopping for a few brief moments - to smell the roses.

The very essence of those roses.

The ray of hope that always shines through - just as I thought there was none.

You are the oxygen that sustains the life's blood of my vitality.

The frailty of all that honest love stands for mingled with the tenacity of a blade of grass in a wind storm.

You are a true friend - when life says to me, there are none left.

My tiller of laughter.

The pith of understanding.

My "lean-to" against all my seemingly, oh, so silly, storms.

My wings when my spirit is feeling earthbound.

You are a part of my soul, as much as the sun, the wind and the rain are a part of all that is life.

My lover.

You are as much to me as I pray I am to you.

You Are...

Martin E. Hill

A House On Mulberry Street

In Springfield, Mass., there's been quite a spat, oh, nothing to do with a dog or a cat! But rather a house a bit along in the tooth which was once the home of our dear Dr. Seuss. Now another type doctor whose expertise runs to filling crannies but not of the teeth, deciding he needed more space than before looked out the window at the view once more.

Now this doctor next door liked the look of that lot, gadzoots, an historical house he did not! A Longmeadow friend, a contractor to boot, he asked to destroy that historical root! A Reverend declared from his South Church pulpit what a shame that nothing was done to stop it. There've been shouts from all round 'bout this dastardly deed with plans afoot and intent to proceed to reconstruct fifty nine Mulberry Street.

As a boy Dr. Seuss sallied forth from that door, with imagination and verve, the world to explore. Now here is a cavity that doctor can't fill for the purpose of parking cars willy-nill. Our very own guardian of historical trust is even now checking the boards in the dust to see if this modern humpty-dump mess can be put back together so no one would guess at the careless destruction which has left a big space on the very best part of Mulberry Place!

Shirley S. Carpenter

That Big Black Granite Wall

There are 58,000 names on that Big Black Granite Wall
58,000 men who once stood tall

They were Vietnam Vets who fought for us all in a war
That they didn't quite know what they were fighting for

They had a job to do for me and for you
They did their job, but we didn't come through

58,000 names on that Big Black Granite Wall...
58,000 men who once stood tall

Once a year we pay homage to these brave men
As we read their names, and then say "Amen"
And let's not forget the P.O.W. and M.I.A.
They will have the stars by their names filled in some day.

58,000 names on that Big Black Granite Wall...
58,000 men who once stood tall

How often does a Vietnam Veteran have to die?
How often does a mother have to cry?
How often do we have to ask, "Why?"

58,000 names on that Big Black Granite Wall...
58,000 men who once stood tall.

William E. Jepson

Morning Dreams

If every morning I would see a bird fly,
a baby being born, and a sunrise,
I think I'd wonder how good life can be,
while looking out over a clear, blue sea.
If every morning I looked out over the same sea,
I could prove to you the love in this world
at your surprising glee.
Every morning I would dream,
about the low valleys ever so green,
or about mountains of purple majesty,
with high wheat fields as far as the eye can see.
If I would dream about the dotted plains,
or wonders of the world yet unexplained.
I would tell you yet as we are unmet,
that this life, full of love and hope,
is something no one can ever forget.

Kimberly Faith Lorah

Time

A flower blooms
A baby cries
A new moon
A love dies
Time rolls on....

The feeling inside
I couldn't explain
I couldn't tell you of my love
Because it was pain

Pain sears my heart
I become lost in sorrow
How could I hold you yesterday
When it didn't last until tomorrow

My hair whips in the harsh wind, as I cry
Waiting for you, I could die....

A flower blooms
A baby cries
A new moon
As our love dies
Time rolls painfully on....

Lerin White

God Reached Out His Hands

God reached out while they dreamed, reaching for stars
A ball of fire took their lives so far,
They died with their dreams in a flame of death
Now they are gone, tears and memories are all that is left.

Their dreams were shattered, stars did fall
Leaving tears and sadness on earth for us all,
God is now holding their souls in his hands
And their dreams will be fulfilled in heavens land.

Memories of seven will long live in our lives
Yes, God reached out for seven souls.
In heaven their dreams will survive.

Pearl R. Lineburg

"Shalom"

I think it is the warmest greeting in the world,
A belt surrounding and including all the nations.
A "Salutation" of Courtesy and Goodwill!
Be still, be silent, be quiet,
My brother, my Sister, my Child.
I explain it to you:
"SHALOM, SHALOM",
means Independence and Freedom,
To One and to All.
I think it is a cordial greeting
And should be Famous and Recognized,
In this World.
So, let it be oh God, a "PRAYER",
The holiest and most important
Message, to EVERYONE and
Everywhere on the EARTH,
Oh God, let it be heard.

Marianne Bogolub

Mother

A tender touch, a heart of gold,
A bond of birth, that grows 'til old.

A hand to hold, when things get tough,
A life of joy filled with love.

The eyes that sees things in different ways,
As mother and child, it's never the same.

When things are bad, it still looks good,
If anyone could make me strong, mother could.

The nose that sense, when something wrong,
The road uphill, often seems so long.

The arms that hold you close from birth,
I could never repay what those hugs are worth.

The body that weakens through her years,
And she herself, fills her eyes with tears.

And as she herself, reaches for a hug in peace,
I see that hug was repaid with ease.

And as I myself, help her each day,
I find my help will one day be repaid.

So help me Lord, this I pray,
To do the most for mother today.

Stephanie Lynn Williams

Somewhere In The Spirit

Somewhere in the Spirit, depends on circumstance,
A breath of wonderment, urge to take the chance,
Young, vibrant...soar away, other vicinities pulling emotions, seemingly for better,
Not so young, may drift to where thoughts want to be...however...

What if...back when...can't tell, could have been,
Impossible now, never to be, but then,
Wonders of the heart, so many different ones,
Imagination enhances possibilities
far beyond probable realities.

If only hearts could play innocently,
but play is often melodrama, even tragedy.
However, for sake of sanity...or...is there such a thing?
Possibly only surviving calamity can keep the soul from being
a haughty, reveling mass of pitying.

But wait, patience of not so young will reveal...
Happiness, tranquility, relief of all instability
lurks among the laughter within Spirituality!

Sharon A. Pryor

Old Man (The Legend Of The Flying Dutchman)

I knew it would be now, or never
a chance at last to get my head together.
So my dog and I went down to the beach
when we hit the sand I turned loose the leash

It soon grew dark and a fog rolled in
I could make out a shadow, far off in the dim.
The old man was hunched over a glass searching the fog
as if in a trance. A captain he was, from a time no more
left to die by his crew on this very shore.

Not breathing a word, I stood there aghast,
for out in the fog I could make out a mast.
And the Dutchman stood up with his fist to
the sea, "Curses!" he cried, "Curses on thee."
And then he drew his sword, and hurled it into
the sea. "No port shall be home, here what I say,
you'll wander the seas, the rest of your days!"

With his last cries, he and the ship disappeared.
Leaving me to question the real and the surreal.
But then I realized it was no joke, for there at
my feet was a brass telescope.

Buddha Hurtt

Thoughts

A madness covers my soul.
A darkness I can't comprehend.
A death of all that's dear.
A throwing away of all that's known,

I wish I loved you less than I did then
I could understand this sore spot in me but now
I just wish I knew you were dead that way
I could let you die in me.

I used to be happy.
I used to smile.
I need to smile again.

Why did you leave?
Why did you ever come at all?
Why do I still care?

I hate you, I hate you, I hate you,
But saying it doesn't make it so.

Veronica M. Tarleton

Can't You Stop The Crying?

Two men on a corner, a shot that's heard in the night
A child is sleeping in her bed
Now a mother lays alongside her dead.

The night is dark, but no peace can be found-
Only the screams and crying, and sirens all around.

Can't you hear the crying?
Can't you stop the pain?
Look what we're doing to each other
Look what we've become.

If you can see me for who I really am, and not judge me by the color of my skin
You'll see we're really a lot alike-
Same wants, same needs, all wanting to be cared about.

Just put away your weapons
They're killing the innocent and young
The pain is breaking so many hearts
That soon all feeling will be gone.

Can't you hear the crying?
Can't you feel the pain?
Look what we are doing
Look what we've become.

Mary Helen Abbott

Beaches....

With a cold wind blowing sand, stinging bare flesh.
A cold, salt spray covering glasses so that you can hardly see.
Low tide as high as High tide,
Its pounding echoing the pounding in your mind.
Sand crabs scurrying, blown against their will across the sand,
Looking for cover, Afraid of being overcome by the strong wind.

What trash and treasures wash up on the shore after the storm
A broken conch shell that still impresses you with its
symmetry and beauty — Even though it is not whole any longer.

Humans too have trash and treasures on their personal beaches.
Like the conch, that is both fragile and tough,
Our broken shells can present a beauty and symmetry
If we allow the rough edges of the brokenness to be smoothed.
Like the small creatures scurrying for shelter from the winds,
We too look for a place to hide and rest, to gather strength
to come out again, when the tide has regained its rhythm,
when the wind has lost its fury,
When the Sun has come out again, and Peace has been restored.

Lois Leineke

A Very Sad Song

A tinge of pain, a falling tear,
A crying heart no one hears.
She stands in a corner by a cold window pane,
Staring out, hoping and waiting for a moment she's sane.
The glass is fogged over by the mist she breathes out,
She stares out blankly like she can not hear the shouts.
If only for a moment the yelling would stop,
The hurting would seize with a single teardrop.
She shakes and shivers from the cold both outside and in.
The outside doesn't hurt like the pain that's within,
It takes away the life that she longs to live,
Only a hope is left, and a prayer she can't give.
Forever and ever the world turns on,
It's only one little girl's very sad song.

Stephanie D. Turley

Ode To A Rose

A rose is a thing of pain and beauty
a delightful flower on a bush
To gaze upon it is almost a duty
But oh! So painful if on its thorns,
your fingers should push.

Oh what a glory is a rose
With so many varied colors to enjoy
And oh! What a joy to my nose
From the many odors it does employ.

Red, pink, yellow, black and variegated
And so many different smells to be enjoyed
With so much care to be employed.

Weeding, pruning and watered with care
Treated with care so delicate
You are a fitting tribute to the fair
A thing of beauty that jewelers try to duplicate.

A blossom such as yours means romance
To the one it is given it means love
Like cupid's arrow to the heart like a lance
Gives great beauty below and above.

H. N. Langworthy

When You Were Born

It was not long ago
A dream time year or so when you were born
Such tiny fingers toes
A little turned-up nose when you were born

A wispy golden curl
"You are your Daddy's girl" when you were born
I held you wonder filled
"Be mine, all mine" I willed when you were born

A blossom on the water
Adrift a flower daughter when you were born
What wind or tide to guide you?
What champion beside you? - when you were born

"Be merciful and mild God
Look down upon this child God" - when you were born
"Be merciful and mild God
Oh smile upon this child God" I prayed when you were born

It was not long ago
Some years a tear or so when you were born
"Hush hush my child don't cry now
You're blessed and so am I now when you were born"

Patricia Packard

Blithe

When raging souls flourish in grace
A fantasia of passion flows
Through the thresholds of your broken heart.

The hatred of anger is discarded,
and mirth sails through your heart contently;
All dismal days have been disposed of.

What lies in your merry heart
Is visions of significant love,
And desolate days of cruelty are long forgotten.

Like scattering birds
Blossoming in a tranquil air,
All mind and spirit can rejoice in freedom.

Blithe is one that can not be replaced,
For as a transfixed smile sits on your beloved face,
Envisions of all evil eventually fade...

And draws all hope through your gratified soul.

Melissa Sarno

What Are You Going To Do When The Lord Steps In

This is a fast old world we are living in today
A fast old world in every kind of way
People coming and going, living in sin

Just what are you going to do when the Lord steps in

Everyone organizing in their own land
Not for the Lord, but against the other man
They're robbing and stealing, cause there's no jobs for men

Just what are you going to do when the Lord steps in

Young people going out looking for fights
Living in dance halls and cafes by night
Parents not caring, just living in sin

Just what are you going to do when the Lord steps in

Friends I know what I am going to do
I'm going to cleanse my soul and make myself new
I'm going to sing God's praises and tell all my kin

Just what are you going to do when the Lord steps in

Yes, my friends I'm telling you to
Get right with God, whatever you do
Start anew right now, forget where you've been

And you'll be alright when the Lord steps in

Rosallee Brown

Ouch!

A day without any words at all, tyranny seems to parallel pain
A fate that really hurts, would you laugh, or be surprised
If I asked you to do it again

If lust was just lust you know that would be bad enough, ouch!

It's no big swiss cheese that I don't know you, because
You don't know what's going on and I don't know what's going on

Five foot one and a half, you're real short and amazing
Standing next to you is a real dangerous place to be

If sex was just sex, you know that would be bad enough, ouch!

So don't tempt purity just trash it figuratively, because
Sometimes life is real amazing, sometimes being alive is just amazing

The day sex drove through my front door, and I didn't even notice

Would you still love me, if I had green hair do you think I'm crazy,
Do you even care you know there's a difference when you're
Touched by the heart instead of being undressed by the eyes

Because sex is just sex unless you're in love, ouch!

It's no big swiss cheese that I don't know you, you're just
An image in the past, you're just an image, you don't fade fast

You know I'd never kidnap you without you're permission
But oh no, I'm not in love. Oh no, this can't be love.

Shane Zane Crunchie

Letting Go

A change of life in a world full of fears,
a misguided fool I've been for years.
Forever it seemed I always believed
that the ones who brought you into this life
would never be the first to leave.
Such a sad state of mind for one
to feel this way of speaking of
someone you hold so dear to your
soul and heart just might pass away.
Lord, keep this someone safe away
from that ever after,
no sadness in their life please
fill it with laughter.

Scott A. Burton

Untitled

By the time we passed twin towers, it was almost dawn
A fawn in the forest, deep evergreen, Alice's dream...
..So I think the princess, said the king, is really, is really
Is really the queen, this remains, remains to be seen
We'll know for sure, when she's done, doin' the king
Yeah He's gonna buy it, buy it sight unseen
The name of the king, shall be James Dean
And have you, have you, have you seen the queen?
She's nothing like nothing, like you ever seen!
Her name, her name, her name's Norma Jean
I think she will have Him, have Him for her king
Past twin towers, deep evergreen, t'was the truth
Or so it would seem
This couldn't be real
Yeah it's only a dream
No you can never escape a celluloid scene
Remember, forever only lasts on the silver screen
And a king, is a king, is a king, is a king
And a queen, is a queen, if you know what I mean
So I say we raise a toast, a toast to James and to Norma Jean

J. D. Hudson

Ode To The World

The house on this hill once was not here,
  a few miles away Lincoln roamed.
He had to cope without lots of stuff,
  using only logs to build his home.
People used to act like humans;
  abortion was probably thought illegal.
And now, sadly as can be known, being endangered
  overpowers our precious bald eagle.
And as the world is rotting, President Clinton is plotting,
  of petty thinks like
  when to set off the A-bomb, or what to do about Mr. Saddham.
Now, Mr. President, I have something for you to hear—
WHY MUST THIS WORLD BE LIVING IN FEAR?

Stacey Janette Branson

Natural Things

The warmth and brightness of the sun, the breathtaking beauty of
  a flower;
Watching the snow fall, hour after hour;
Birds chirping and flying to and fro, squirrels jumping high and low;
The changing colors of fall, painting scenes enjoyed by all;
Crisp, cool, spring breeze creating ripples among the leaves,
Clear blue skies and clouds so white, foggy days full of fright;
Winding roads full of curves, sometimes grating on the nerves;
Raindrops tapping on the glass, dew enveloping the morning grass;
Water rippling in rivers and brooks, fishermen wishing they had
  time, line and hooks;
Frost on the windows, cold air biting nose and toes,
Winter is coming, everyone knows;
Snow melting from the rooftops,
Creating icicles as it drops;
Nature's wonders are a delight,
Full of splendor, both day and night;

Sandra J. De Filippo

Lies

He said someday I'd be his wife ... with children,
a house, a perfect life ... but his promise of bliss was naught
but lies ... since I've learned of another one who cries.. now
my pillow wet with mournful tears ... since the facts confirmed
my greatest fears ... but I cry not for my broken life ... but for
the pain inflicted on his wife ... his deceit and lies causing
misery ... I did not know, please, please forgive me!

Roe Schrock

Awaiting

In the desert, lonely like he;
A flower sits.
Such sweet nectar, ready to be claimed;
Just waiting.
Flying closer, the bee watches;
It's too late.
The flower, it is gone;
Plucked by a stranger.
Betrayal, then loneliness, as he sees the stranger;
He will never forget.
The empty space, it still remains;
Longing to be filled.
Like the bee,
My love waits;
Wantingonlyyou——

Kathy Lynn Martin

Our Own Darkness

Our hooded youth today appear to be
A force that wanders and cannot see
A hood or cap that hides the eyes
Prevents us from sharing the bond that ties
Within the recesses of this space
Lies a soul that has a face
If we cannot touch you or be your friend
Then my talking to you is at an end
For it is the touching that caring is expressed
And the love for one another is shown best
A hood or cap deflects the light
And impairs the image of one's sight
To look up longingly and see the day
The hood and cap must come away
Our souls need light like trees do water
And yet we persist in death and slaughter
So my kindred souls you beware
Be ready to recognize who can care
For in the struggle of your existence
Your plight will be easy because of your persistence

Roland J. Bailey

A Lifelong Friend

One day a tree was planted in the earth,
A healthy one that grew each passing day,
And planted on the same day as my birth
It represents my life along its way.
It grew and grew til it could grow no more,
I love it as the years fell into past,
I really took good care of my tree for
I knew I'd last as long as it would last.
One day my tree had finally reached its peak,
From that time on I grew so slow and tired,
The branches on my tree were old and weak,
It lasted til the day that I expired.
So old and gray I died without a sound,
And on that day my tree fell to the ground.

Sara D'Arienzo

Bill

A bit of down, drifting softly by;
A mad little beetle stomping his feet;
A lazy bookworm, chewing each word;
A dark, brooding storm, a patch of blue sky;
A snatch of Mozart I happen to catch;
A wave of spring beauties upon a green hill;
A piece of fine wood wearing age's soft glow;
A dove's sad "coo," so lonely and low;
All these things are a boy named Bill.

Mary Lou Bynum

A Memory Of My Father, James C. Shall

A painted face at age thirteen
A hero made, a shadow of a man not seen
Confused
A father who will not come when I call him home.

The tears shed, he would not tell
never thought she'd lose, not counting as they fell
Harmless
A father who will not come when I call him home.

Lending hands so big and strong
made brittle so fast by doing no wrong
Weakened
A father who will not come when I call him home.

A father, a coach, a friend- His power to please
Missed forever by the power of disease
Loved
A father who will not come when I call him home.

A wife, children, and friends left alone
a name never forgotten- Now carved into stone
Forever
A father who will not come when I call him home.

Lisa S. Shall

Martin Luther King Jr.

M is for miles (He walked with his brothers)
A is for available (He made himself to all)
R is restless (He could never be still)
T is for trust (He had for all)
I is for injuries (Which he felt when it was others)
N is for nation (He was here and there)

L is for love (He had for all men)
U is for unity (This he wanted to do)
T is for truth (He told to all)
H is for head (He held ever so high)
E is for eternity (Which all of us will share)
R is for recognition (Known throughout the world)

K is for king (God's number one)
I is for interest (He held for all mankind)
N is for noble (Which everybody knew him to be)
G is for God (Whom he kept his faith)

J is for justice (He wanted for you and me)
R is for regrets (He had only a few)

Mix, stir and blend together, when mixed well then mold
and Martin Luther King Jr. will rise in all of your hearts.

Louise Brunson

Unborn

As I watch the sun set on the beach at dawn,
A life flashes before me.
Over the waters and through the waves —
this feeling craves into my mind.
So I blink and continue to think to myself:
"What would this life feel for me?
Would it love me as I would love it?"
Soon it is felt and wakes me up from my evening dream.
"Of course it would love me, what was I thinking."
Soon this life is seen in a world I wish it wouldn't see.
I have this life in my hands, and I find myself on the beach again.
And as I watch the sun set with this life in my arms,
I feel the strength of the waves and think to myself
"I am just as strong."

LaKisha Daniels

Rose Attempts

She created her own reach,
a life of purity others often forfeit,
a seed barely visible,
she, struggled outward.......in growth.

Grabbing at a foundation,
her own scale of the universe,
sense.... did not see her coming,
always peeking at life's impossibilities.

Sun and shade tried to protect her,
as.... the forces of nature remembered,
while feet trampled her bed,
wounding her constantly.

It was there, we found her,
listening to the loneliness,
wilting on the ground,
with the evidence of budding grace!

Patricia J. Robinson

A Rose

An infant grows tiny in the womb.
A life precious, a tiny seed,
like the pistil of a flower growing steady.
Her life begins in beauty, joy, sorrow.
A bud for all the world to enjoy
Life progresses as do the petals
nurturing begins, this perfect bloom.
A rose of life, velvet petals depicting perfection.
Our bud blossom's into adulthood with petals scattering
along the landscape of our lives. The perfect bloom,
A perfect rose.
Years pass swiftly, our blossom ages, more petals lost
upon the wind. Her color fades, a perfect rose no more.
Yet in her mirror she sees visions of the bloom not
youthful still, a mature flower. Can that be dew glistening
upon the petals, or perchance a tear I see?

Nancy Root

"White Dove"

Off I went to that place I love
A lonely place called White Dove
A plot of land where the dead go to rest
Where I can be alone, there I think best.

As I lay in thought it was then I saw
A mighty army gone by as I gazed in awe
This great army all in a line
Caused me to realize a power greater than mine.

Line after line soldiers dressed in white shrouds
An army not of men but of great white clouds
Soldiers with a mission marching in unison
To bring life giving rain each in its own season.

It's here I go for his voice is always clear
With all life's troubles I forget he's always near.

So I go to this place for the simple reminder
That he always loves us and wants us to be kinder.

Ron Nicely

"To My Friend..."

Breathe into me a love my friend...
A love for life without an end...
A summer of eternal days...
Grasping time as we part ways...
Be for me what I am for you...
Love me...warm me...share thoughts too...
Be my strength when I am weak...
Be my hope when this I seek...
Be my joy...when all seems lost...
Be my way...what e'er the cost...
Give yourself as never before...
Express your dreams...hold back no more...
As this our bond of friendship's sealed...
A depth of love that fate revealed...
For nothing severs links so strong...
When two hearts know that they belong...

Karyn J. Shaffer

"Untitled"

I've got a love that makes me complete.
A love like ours is a treasure to keep.
With a single word or look of the eye,
He can make me laugh and he can make me cry.
He likes country music - I like rock and roll.
I like movies - he likes to bowl.
He likes denim - I like silk.
I like wine - he likes milk.
But there is one think on which we always agree,
I'll always love him and he'll always love me.
We have little money - no fortune, no fame,
But our life is happy all the same.
We have our health - close families and friends,
For all this Lord, we give thanks again.
I pray every day that when the going gets hard,
We'll find peace in each other and how lucky we are.

Kathy D. Teer

The Man Of My Dreams

He evolved from some enchanted domain
A magic engulfed his mysterious essence
He spoke to me of distant places
His voice overwhelmed my senses
He gave me pleasures too utterly remarkable
His life transpired in unknown realms
He opened up and brought forth dormant passions
His eyes melted away all reserves
His hands removed all lingering doubts
The mysterious and exciting Man of my dreams
He laughed, he taught, he listened and inspired
The words he spoke were clear, yet complex

He made no promises and demanded nothing
Was I ready to trust, to accept a man like this
My heart said yes, though my logic said no
Dear God, I asked, is he the answer to my prayers
I searched my mind, I pondered my desires
The solution soon became certain to me
The man of my dreams does not exist, you see
He was only in my dreams.

Patricia Ann Ryan

I Endure

As I look into my mind through thick clouded shadows I find.
A man who's not so big, still a child of some kind
A man who's not so smart, one who's eager to play the part
Afraid to face myself, because of confusion in my heart.
A coward - if you will, better yet a loser in disguise
How much pain must I endure, before I truly realize
That even though I'm not so brave, doesn't mean I'm born a slave
So I must fight with all I've got to free the shackles
from my brain.

Because life is far too precious, much too valuable to waste
So relentlessly I pray seeking strength to build my faith
The Lord is all I have when times get really rough
And I'm eternally glad to know that with "God" I have more
than enough.
So I'm thankful for all his blessings, and in his care
I wish to remain.
I pray for strength to endure this madness,
and always, always praise his "Holy" name.

William F. Daniels III

Happy Birthday

Another birthday passes into the mist of years. But not just another a milestone, a "No, you can't be", a label, a marker, an epic, round-figured number that should be daunting. And yet I shed no tears.

I judge my mortality in your eyes. And what I see is admiration, love, that glint of pride and twinkle of amusement, what I see is sunrise all around you. And I know the truth! Age belies!

Caught in the web of time, we move inexorably through the norm.
Now—don't work! Next—sit down! No more excitement for the future!
Forget the intake of breath at the sight of great beauty.
Imagination must die! This is the form.

Who made these rules that birthdays must assign?
Youth? Government? A child who means only well and loves
you unconditionally?
No, these rules do not affect you and me—we soar above our age.
Today is your birthday—or is it mine?

Yes, it is mine, too; the candles burn bright. Revel in our days, turn the next corner, hold my hand and step into tomorrow. Another birthday passes into the mist of years. And I laugh with delight.

Phyllis W. Goldman

Darkness In The Mist

Darkness in the mist.
A mist that spirals around the sun
like molasses around a child's hand.
There is light all around us,
but in the distance comes
what is not.
Nothing comes.
Everlasting nothing
or so they say.
The type of nothing that we fear,
but we don't know about.
The fear of nothing.
That which is nothing is nothing.
Yet if it is nothing, then what do we fear?
Nothing, darkness is nothing.
Then if darkness is nothing, what do we fear?
The darkness, the nothing within the darkness.
everlasting darkness, which is nothing....

Lou Rubio

Returning

That morning,
A moment of packing all the happiness and love
Into a huge suitcase.
The straw hat walks around the airport,
And find lots of American candies in the pocket.
As times goes,
Eyes look for the window.
Feel the wind going through your memories,
Hold on to the straw hat.
Many pampas grasses on old gravel road,
I remember the full moon.
How warm to be closer
To where I belong.

Yuko Taniguchi

Untitled

Thoughts pass my mind within
a moment's time.
Greater knowledge does it find
from the Lord, O Divine!
Deeper mysteries do unfold keeping
to our histories soul, finding light
that's brighter than our sight.

To each one's eyes I do sigh, lifting
up our bodies high weak and tired
we unfold for the Lord to behold.
He takes us and makes us whole,
with His Spirit we do grow, closer
to our histories soul; the Lord has it so.

Never worry, never drought, remember
the price, it brought our history to
the light of the Lord's unfailing life
which is love day and night to
share with all "Love's Delight"!

Philomena Giannone

Tribute To A Lady

She's attractive, witty, intelligent, serene.
A more perfect lady you've never seen.
She raised seven children, not a small task,
Giving them all compassion, love and trust.
Seven times she survived the "Terrible Teens",
Then all seven left to fulfill their dreams.
As the family grows, she prays more each day
That each may serve God in their own way.
And why does she walk so serene and tall?
Because she knows God takes care of all.
I love you, Mom.

Peggy Hergert

A Mother's Heart

A mother's heart, a mother's sorrow
A mother's hope for a better tomorrow
A child of her lies near deaths door
His dreams of life seem no more
A love gone mad
Made him so sad
What once was a heart of giving
Now seems to give up on living
A mother's heart won't let this happen
Her life she'd give
To have him live
The Gods they heard
Decreed by word
This is not the right order
A mother should not outlive a son or daughter
A mother's heart pulled him through
To start life again - anew

Renee Abramowitz

A Mother's Love

A mother's love starts from the first day of birth
A mother's love will be your blanket of comfort and
Safety for as long as she is upon the earth.

A mother's love should never be taken for granted
A mother's love is not always promised, take care of
Your mother's love, for without it one often fills
Alone, lost and even stranded.

A mother's love will guide and protect you
A mother's love will guide you along the way
A mover's love is your safe haven, your light of day.

A mother's love will never desert you, even in troubled times
A mother's love is your solid rock, your foundation
A mother's love is your safety net, your joy, your peace of mind.
Thank you God for a mother's love for it is truly divine.

Walter D. Turner

Epitaph

The rhythm of her life declines each month in infinitesimal ways,
A name forgotten. She knew that it was gone.
A light bulb needs to be replaced, and lunch, there is no lunch today.
The clocks have stopped. The telephone rings "How are you dear?"
"I'm fine! And you?" She lies. She is not fine. She's lost inside
her world of precious things and memories. Distractions come and go.
A neighbor knocks. "I think I'll make some tea." All slowly
turns to dust and cobwebs while the termites eat the furniture.

Her life is ashes. The remnants of relationships, and loves and hates
all powdered up in this one small container. My mother in a bag.
It's early morning on the beach. I crouch at the waters edge.
The incoming tide crosses the shallow flats of sand. Sinuously
a bone fish slips along, nonchalantly feeding. The triangle
of its tail disturbs the oily surface of the bay. It sends a ripple
towards the beach. I dedicate her spirit to the wave.
Her ashes spread like clouds along the water's edge.
I am alone and so is she. Make a mark upon the wall, it wears away.
Say a kind word, leave a kiss upon her cheek. Her dreams are
mine and I, I too have died and disappeared.
Her sea of dreams has risen, like a tide, and carried me away.

Nicholas Pawley

Untitled

My name now is Tydyn Rain St. Clair,
a name I quite like, but that does not hint
at the multidimensional complexity of my being,
invisible to the objective eye.
I live my life driven by this colony of passions
and loves that gives my existence meaning
and intensity. I yearn to express the totality
of my being in life, yet the more I express,
the more I feel that must be made physical.
It seems impossible; the reservoir of my life is
infinite, but cries for actuality nonetheless, my
life is complete, yet never complete.
I learn, I grow, I develop; and in the infinite
center of my being...I know...
I know that this divine discontent is native to
all beings, and is Eternal.
My name is Tydyn Rain St. Clair, a name I quite
like...

Tydyn Rain St. Clair

Until Now

The life that I once had was gone
A new start and a clear mind was all I had to move on

As time passed and nights grew longer,
I found peace in myself that made me stronger

Alone to think, I found so much more
From all of life's miserable faults,
There was an open door

To have fallen into their prey you go on thinking
Life is not much better

Therefore living day to day

Starving ourselves of what we really need
Making us pay for their mistakes and greed

From all of this darkness there was a light
A blessing from above that surrounded me to surrender
From this long and hard fight

I was ready to let the past lye,
To say "Hello" to this life,
Instead of good-bye.

Michelle Lovoy

The Immigrant

He stood at the bow his suitcase in hand.
A new way of life was opening for him.
A life filled with lonely, a life full of new.
I know that he wondered could his dreams come true?
A wife and a child he'd left behind, will they ever come
here, will their lives be entwined?
In the harbor he sees the Lady of hope, our Statue of Liberty.
He wonders again what his life will be. Will his dreams die
here like the leaves on a tree? Will he find freedom in this
land of mine? The gangplank is lowered, he takes a stand.
He will give of his best, he will make this his land.
Through customs he goes, his visa in hand; a smile on his lips,
for his promised land.

Loretta Engeron

Something

There's something I cannot find
A part of me I once knew
That something which torments my mind
And my feelings too

I search in the mirror
For that something to see
With hopes of a vision, a picture much clearer
Ah! But no! That's not I - it cannot be!

With no time to contemplate
Life's meaning or fate
Lines, wrinkles, frowns, and gray hair
Have left a face of total despair

Time for the laundry, the clutter, the dust
Time for the children, the husband a must
Where? What is that something I seek to find
Perhaps through the window, I'll look this time

Through this clear shield the sun reflects
The night, the stars, the moon - and me
All of the wonders God perfects
My spirit! My Passion! - that missing piece!

K. D. Nelson

Solace

Serenity,
a peaceful and warm loving glow,
adoring and adored,
through my heart, golden, and into my soul. (I know)
Yes.
I whisper.
Inside my mind, I have always known.
One being of perfection,
a soul of true love,
my only beloved idol,
protector, angel of faith, hope.
My heart fills with happiness
as I am gifted with light,
reassured and comforted,
Heaven is my home if I am worthy,
servant of all that is good,
a being of eternal kindness,
I belong loyally, forever, to infinite highness.

Paula LaFurno

Summer Solstice

The two tumblers and their dogs leap into the air,
A pleasure for all to see, the princess with the golden hair.
The jugglers aim their objects high, there,
At the summer's solstice fair.

Animals are brought by the wagonload,
The children in all their finery clothed,
This a time for paying off all debts owed,
At the summer's solstice fair.

Efforts are made for good cheer and remarks mellow,
Time to show appreciation for the neighboring fellow,
Eating all foods present, — except Jello,
At the summer's solstice fair.

Pets and animals run with abandon,
Music continues after the dance is done,
Parents preen and show-off the new son,
At the summer's solstice fair.

The merchant displays his new wares and the firecracker,
Fisti-cuffs in the ring made money for the financial backer,
And we decided this celebration to be named "4th of July" ever after,
At the summer's solstice fair.

Mary Ann Mitchell

Magic Moment

It felt like I was handed
A pocketful of magic
Standing in the shadow of the sun
Drenched in happiness
Watching from afar
My little girl upon an
Old man's lap
Tugging and pulling at his cheeks
Both giggling with glee
Like a bird, his chest puffed with pride
Oh child of my heart
Let the magic last forever.

Sharyn Ares

Wintertime

A flake of snow, an early dark;
A pond of ice, a fireplace spark.
A barren tree, a nighttime freeze;
A bird flown south, a cold north breeze.

A pair of gloves, a pair of boots;
A stocking cap, a winter suit.
A glowing smile, a twinkling eye;
A look of pleasure at a snowing sky.

A back that's bent, a slower walk;
A deafening ear; a louder talk.
A graying head, a wrinkling face;
An ache, a pain in some new place.

Each looking at winter with different expectations;
One with indifference, one pleasure, one seeking explanations.
The land takes for granted the springtime will come;
Its trees will fill with fruit, maybe an apple or a plum.
The child always trusting not worrying about what will be;
For they think they are immortal, they live their lives so free.
The old filled are with emotion, ranging from quiet peace to fear;
They know that wintertime has come and it's going to stay right here.

Rebecca Adams

'Kalbaroo'

A river running deep and clear,
A river running like a straight blue spear,
A river that is full of life,
Though pollution is a bane, a knife,
The river sides grow dark and bare,
Gaudy near a summer fair,
And when the river comes to a bend,
A raft down river it will quickly send,
A river great and straight and blue,
A river knows as 'Kalbaroo'.
"Kalbaroo" the people say,
In Kalbaroo the fishes stay,
To play and frolic in the water,
To entertain the mechanic's daughter,
The clearest water, clean and blue,
In the river called the 'Kalbaroo'.

Scott Antman

Sea Tears

The fog hovered over the dampened sand,
  A shroud embracing the deepened footprints along the shore.
The swaying eel grass through the misted night
  Cast a strange, mysterious backdrop to their love.
Lying on the quiet shore, lulled by the lapping of the waves,
  They listened to the sound of night and waited.
Faces touched by mist and kissed with longing,
  Serene in the darkened, foggy night.
The scent of beach rose wafted round,
  Blending as one with heavy ocean dew.
Blanketed by nature's vaporous shield,
  The lovers embraced in the lonely night.
The moon came out and wisps of clouds
  Stole across its luminous face.
The fog had lifted and in the darkened night.
  A solitary figure made his way along the shore.

Marilyn F. Winey

A Home

A place to have, a home to be
a spiritual place, a bird, a tree.
A peaceful place of nature's hue,
A place for me, a place for you.

A place to come at end of day
to drain the toil and care away.
A solitary little piece of land
the essence of which we hold in our hand.

A place where you can toil away
and have your schemes and plans each day.
A place where one can feel at home
and if we choose can be alone.

A place to bake bread or cut some glass
or plant some bulbs or mow the grass,
or read a book or listen to Bach
or sweep the steps or powder a lock.

I've not wanted anything more
than to share a home with the man I adore.
So let it be and let us plan
a life between a woman and a man.

Veronica Leary

News At 11:00

Another tear has fallen.
A starving child is calling.
All alone in the cold night air.
Life, is just not fair.
Another crime has just taken place.
A dark street corner dressed in lace.
Another illness has been found.
John Doe is asleep an the cold ground.
A suicidal teenager.
Two parents, once in love, now filled with anger.
A single parent all confused.
Life isn't something to abuse.

Michele Marshall

Burgundy

I remember burgundy, I wasn't very old
A sweater someone made for me, warm against the cold
It had buttons made of wood
I remember feeling good in burgundy.

Soft and warm is burgundy, so peaceful and serene
A shade for royal majesty, fit for any queen
It evokes my self-esteem
How I love to live and dream in burgundy.

Full of such emotion
A joy for fantasy
I get lost in time when I'm
Wrapped in burgundy.

One day I may change my scheme; however, not real soon
Still, I do believe there is a future for maroon
For now if I could only have
One color to surround me...
I'd want burgundy
Love is burgundy
Strawberry burgundy
Burgundy - for me.

Robin DeLisle

Untitled

Hidden in shadows of African plain
A tiger stalks the heart of his domain
A dark shape navigating harsh terrain.

Moonrise reveals tall grass and hazel eyes
But naught else of orange and black disguise
As through fertile fields he hunts his prize.

Night winds whispering, promising, expectant
Gathering feline strength magnificent
He crouches muscles taut; at last the scent!

Uneasy silence. Shattering twig snap.
In fluid motion leaping, pouncing, grappling.
Swelling hunger struggling to entrap.

Claws scraping, retracting, tearing. Flashing teeth
Emerging tasting surging blood, beneath
The paling sky and the moon's fading wreath.

Hidden in shadows of African lawn
A tiger growls content at the coming dawn
A dark shape trying to suppress a yawn.

Leilani Phillips

A Time for Thanks

Thanksgiving's a time for a family to share
A time to be there and show others we care
I had an experience-probably a lesson to learn
Not to be selfish-instead have concern
I was leaving the store after buying turkey and stuff
I'd fought the crowds-I'd had just enough
The thought of giving thanks didn't concern me at all
Only buying the groceries and get home before nightfall
As a young man loads my bags, and I'm ready to go
I am dreading the walk and the drive through the snow
I am watching my step and avoiding the soot
There's a woman on crutches, pushing her cart with no foot
She's all alone, I tried to help with the door
She smiled, said no thanks, I've done this before
I saw a strength that will stay in my mind
A lady disabled-yet friendly and kind
So as the holidays approach-I thank my lucky star
For health, family and friends both here and afar.

Linda Richards Hawkinson

A Sparrow Fell To The Ground

One day while I was sitting on the porch just looking all around,
A tiny sparrow fell from somewhere and fluttered to the ground.

I watched to see if it would fly again,
But all its efforts seemed in vain.
Because cruelty of man, its little head was bleeding,
And as I bent to pick it up, his eyes seemed to be pleading.
I gently wiped the blood away, but more just took its place,
Oh, what I felt for this little creature as I looked into its face.
God knew what had happened to that tiny bird,
And its cries of pain, I knew He heard.

So I held his little body and stroked his little chest,
His little heart beat wildly within his tiny breast.
He looked at me, then gaped his last breath,
His little heart stopped beating as he quietly found death.

Rosie L. Buckland

Untitled

I awoke with a smile on my face
a warm feeling coursing through my soul
my dream had opened my eyes to the possibilities
my heart opened to new love
my thoughts raced to reality
and were met with a fleeting sigh
the future of my dreams await so near
the emotions of my dreams within reach
I dreamed of dancing daisies
singing love songs from their smiling faces
love poured from the heavens
spilled from the clouds
sprinkled its power all around me
I am in love with my dreams.

Laura Henry

Twilight In Vermont

Above the pasture - on the hill
A white house nestles - cozy - still

Below - the lake - unripped lies
Reflecting mountains - to the skies

Beneath the window - thrushes sing
The lark - above - on soaring wing

Bees - busy in the roses - hum
From fields of clover - breezes come

The setting sun - inflames the sky
Then twilight - tiptoed - softly - shy

Across the hills - the lowing herd
And robins evening song - is heard

Far to the west - days last rays glow
In profile - giant mountains show

And to the east - a golden moon
Flings leafy patterns - through the gloom

Then night - with sheltering - guarding wing
Silently covers everything.

A. C. B. Havens

Where's The Passion?

In darkness
Abiding obliviously
Carrying on day by day
Unknowingly lulled
By a false sense of happiness
Which is just contentment with givens.
Unaware of the feeling
The aching of true passion.
Passion so strong
Mere thoughts burden the heart
With beautiful pain.
Pain so fierce it forces the air from lungs.
Pain so fierce it is blinding eyes.
Passion that lasts forever
Every second, every day
Building upon hope, gaining strength
Until the passion breaks from its cocoon
And flutters its wings
For its day of glory
Its day in the sun.

Lori Sussman

Appleman

I have been warned all my life
about falling in love
And I keep that avenue clear.
If it weren't for your warm smile
I could leave without a tear.
But I am fond of you
I enjoy the time we spend together
The happiness that fills the room
The radiant glow of your personality.
Accents your beautiful charm
But no matter where we stand
There is always a place for you on my arm.
I'll miss you when I'm gone.
For you have a place in my heart
I have tried to fight it,
To no prevail, I have been bit.
I have made it clear all along.
I don't want to fall in love.
For love hurts, then you die.
Once it ends, then you cry. And your life is never the same.

Sherrie Paige

The Edge

I touch the edge of insanity
about to fall off
I taste the air all around me
As I start to fall
I smell the fragrance it reeks of
and begin to pull back
I see the insane who've already fallen
and the sane who haven't yet come that close
I hear them calling to me
and I come back to my senses

Once again I've survived the edge—
I feel safe;
but it will only last for a short time
until it all happens again—

When I touch the
Edge..

Victoria L. Mckay

"The Mountain Tops"

Beautiful, beautiful azure sky,
Above the mountain peaks so high!
How could I ask for anything more?
—Such lovely beauty to behold!

Midst fleecy clouds, on the mountain slopes,
—Myriad of flowers, and "forest-folks"—
Tiny creatures (that was their home.)
And stately animals there did roam.

Elk, and deer, and bear were there—
Midst pine, and fir, and flowers rare—
And pheasants had their nests secure,
—It was a Paradise, for sure!

Beautiful trees and shrubs were there
To gather moisture—from the air—
Those fleecy clouds did thus provide
"Liquid health"—for the mountain-side.

Pauline Myers Howell

"Friends Forever"

To have a special friend in life is so very rare,
Actually , the world is usually too busy to really care.

If you are blessed enough for God to send a special person your way,
You better thank Him, praise Him, and most of all obey.

He has singled you out for a relationship that he created especially for you,
And he wants you to feel oh so blessed and oh so special, too.

Cherish this friendship and don't let it ever end,
Because everyone needs to feel the love of a friend.

Love means to learn to sacrifice yourself,
By caring more for someone else.

So, if God gives you such a gift from above,
Thank him and praise Him for this very special love.

Sharyn Harms

Seasons Of Changes

As I sit looking around, what do I see, I see storms rolling in
once again out of control and the seasons have gone mad.
Falls winters springs and summers. As I fight, fight to survive
the fires that are inside.
The fall storms put out the fires. Leaving me frozen and naked,
in a cold and barren waste land.
I open my eyes but can see only the darkness imprisoning me,
what is going to happen to me next?
All around is dark and cold
I don't know, don't know what is happening what is happening to me
I just don't understand it? I try to reason it out.
I get to the point, to the point that I want out
And then the sun springs forth destroying the cold and the darkness.
And clothes me in its warmth triggering a new birth of new life
The summer brings its everlasting peace and happiness then fall
slips in once again
When will it all end?, will it ever end?

Warren Jones

An Autumn Song

Frosty autumn nights when harvest moons will soar.
Air so crisp it crackles in the sycamores.
Stars that dance in tandem to my reverie,
Dare I believe, that I am free, to sing-
An autumn song.

Evening gathers early in the cloudy sky.
Fields turn brown, the leaves fall down like gems afire.
Breathe that turns to fog will make me hurry home,
Where fires glow, to write a poem, to sing-
An autumn song.

(Cheerless winter waits a turn
In a cloak of snowy white.
Now we do a harvest dance
In the chilly fading light.)

Giddy with relief from summers humid heat.
Saddened by the cold gale and the turning leaves.
Open to adventure, what's around the bend?
Let's chase the wind, it's time again to sing-
An autumn song.

Tom Frey

Cry Baby Cry...

Days are long, hours are forever —
Alienation sets in.
The sun no longer shines as bright,
The night is darker then a night has a right.
You sit alone and wonder, am I really alive.

You call — no one is there -
You call — no one cares.
Cry Baby Cry
Keep that pain inside, no one is
listening anyhow, so cry, you cry —
Cry Baby Cry.

Your heart is beating, but the drummer is dead.
Your mind is moving, but the thoughts aren't there.

Sun rises in a dim light, moon's
glow is out of sight, the light no
longer there for my eyes, the beauty
of life has disappeared, the days are long.

Nancy Ann Glover

Christmas Eve

Eyes big as dollars, a little red nose
Alive with excitement from head to his toes
"Oh, Mommy," he said, "I saw a huge star
I think it's the one shepherds saw from afar
And I'll bet angels played on a great golden horn
So the wisemen would know Baby Jesus was born.
I hope it was warm in the stable that night
I expect that's the reason God sent the great light
Which showed 'round His head, when they all looked at him
I'm glad it stayed bright and never got dim.
That star made me feel—it just glowed through the tree—
That Jesus looked down and smiled right at me!"
I kissed that sweet boy, for I saw in his eyes
True Christmas spirit within his heart lies
Oh, the love and the faith that tonight I did see—
No greater gift will God give, just to me.

Wilma F. Barry

The Mind Of Hudson

Is today the day? I don't know
All I know is the cold dark water
Huge ice mountains that control my waking thoughts
And haunt my dreams of sleep
I know others have come before me, and failed
But I believe in my heart that I can
I believe with my soul that I will
A find will make me a living hero
A find will give me fame
Look!!!

This is surely the entrance
This is surely the opening to fame
I see the passage stretch before me
Does it reach the other sea
No

This passage ends in land
This passage does not connect
I have not found fame
I have become a hero
I have failed

Nicholas Taylor

Self-Reference

Being me: the task I set before me
All my days: to know with certainty
That this is right, that I need never shyly
Ask or wait for anybody's praise.

The peacock's tail, the orchid's bloom,
The rocket's scintillating burst
When eyes are closed I see them all,
But see my sweet ideas first.

My love, your thoughts are gorgeous just as mine
It thrills me always when you dare to leap.
And yet I rather choose my own to speak
(I know the secret source that makes them shine).

The blood I pour upon the thirsting sand
Is shed by no one else's eager hand
But mine, and flows from my own veins in flood.
Shall I be ever other than I am?

Mind and body, these are mine alone,
They tend unerringly to what is true.
And yet, in touching self to the very bone,
I also touch the secret heart of you.

Neal Donner

All The Tears Taste Like The Sea

All the tears taste like the sea, when pools fill darkened eyes.
All the tears taste like the sea, when death brings the surprise.
All the tears taste like the sea, when love falls short of home.
All the tears taste like the sea, when scorn becomes the tone.

All the tears taste like the sea, when dreams die one by one.
All the tears taste like the sea, when life's long day is done.
All the tears taste like the sea, when hope attacks the pain.
All the tears taste like the sea, when love returns again.

All the tears taste like the sea, when life transcends the lie.
All the tears taste like the sea, when truth has cast the die.
All the tears taste like the sea, when gladness wins the day.
All the tears taste like the sea, when loosed we turn to pray.

All the tears taste like the sea, when surrender fills our soul.
All the tears taste like the sea, when God has made us whole.
All the tears taste like the sea, for tears are made of sky.
All the tears taste like the sea, as heaven fills our eye.

Niki David Shrode

The Trials Of Reality

So many times I wonder will it be worth it in the end,
All the time and endless effort,
Yet, no one can understand, the anger that builds each day
from all the trials we must face.
Approaching close, a climate point, then disappearing into the mind.
Not any one situation but in all we seem to find,
That in love or hopes to be or even the life we choose,
How long will it surpass or is the next time to be the last.
An explosion of emotions built from those left in the past,
Changing all the notions conceived within your head,
Turning all your dreams into a fantasy that you have read.

Penny M. Egler

Untitled

A poet by nature
an artist by choice
the writer reads to himself in the mirror, as always
he must continually reassure himself that the
collapse of his sublime reality
has not, can not, and will not occur
sensitive to the quality of deep seated ignorance
reflections reveal our true crimes, and yet
protect us from the more intimate space—time illusion

Tim Jay

Paul's Proposal

It is time for a surprise, as to why you are here
Allow me a few precious moments, and I'll make it quite clear

As I was ready to leave, you had a smile so sweet
That I asked you to pose, and swept you off your feet

Arriving to have your picture taken, a dress of red so fine
That when I first saw you, wow! You totally blew my mind

I told you in the past, that a day would come soon
That I would ask a question, and it is truly high noon

In front of this majestic house, and all its true historic glory
An answer to add our part, and start our own special story

Miss Paula K. Moore, I ask, fill me with joy and pride
I turn to you and say, please be my beautiful sweet bride

Paul E. Wright Jr.

The Conundrum Of Man In Society

He is like a man who is lost, adrift and
alone at sea
Who, throughout his wakefulness and dreams,
Longs to see the horizon and the promise of land
but which never materializes.
He experiences the fluctuations of the changing
tide - the angry, swirling waters, and the
inevitable calm.
But he is weary of the storm and suspicious
of the calm.
He glimpses the immutable tranquility of the
Distant hills but fears it's a mirage
Resulting from his solitude and despair,
Suddenly, with the incandescence of a tropical
sun, he realizes that he is moving in
circles
But his will to survive is stronger than his
Daunting circumstance
So he moves on.

Lennox Alexander

In The Wicklow Mountains

Once again—
Alone I stood. Atop an immense bluff
The cliff examining the
Irish countryside. flowing into the far towns, dimly lit for
supper,
Green. Luscious
rolling fields, as of those
longed for by the girl I
Love.
Oh, the craggy cliff. I
examined it. Never willing
to stray my eyes
to my ancestral home. where they close sheep over human life,
I thought once more of
my love
past and present. I cried.
And this time took the
Doozy,
And flirted with the atmosphere.

Kevin D Humphries

James Rock

Once a city had place
along north slope beside the bay
There bayside vantage called steamer 'n sail
Quarter mile south went span to channel

With rail traveling east and west
turned much transport at that step
If you ignore that upward trek
a city greets one investor guest

From that location no-average out
A pier without weighted count
With nearby port a shipping circle
How could this oddity seem otherwise doubt

At this place you only describe
Starts a cheerful course we needn't strive
An hours walk bluff and rail
finds singular rock a surrounding tide edge

With stories told questions pursued
Nature Catharsis has sown good
We visited history along with mood
Knowing a path that continues new

Bill Milhofer

Home

Like a sea shell in the ocean, the tide yields up then takes back.
Always moving in the waters—never knowing where it's at.
The place it lands for a day till the tide takes it away—
Takes it away from a land known as its home.

The waters produce their treasures though the lands may never know.
Time it takes to make one treasure—to build it up and make it whole.

The river flows into the ocean, does it know it can't go back?
Does it know the path it follows can determine where it's at?
The things it helps on its way, pushing forward and away—
Far and away, to this place now known as home.

The life I live is like the river though I wish I could go back.
But I know the path I followed only leads to where I'm at.
Never knowing where I may stay till the tide takes me away—
Takes me away, to a land not known as home.

The waters produce their treasures, though the lands may never know.
Time it takes to make it one treasure to build it up and make it whole

So I'll go down to the ocean—the tide will never lead me back.
I will come out of the water and I will know just where I'm at.
Not for just one day I'll stay, the tide will not take me away—
Take me away, for this land I'll know as home.

Tasha Page

Only For Tomorrow

Wish I could beyond the light
Always still dark as the night
It seems life works the opposite way
Here tomorrow gone today
It seems to be a lot less filled
Always looking for one more drop
Why is the sun so very still
Could it be because it's stopped
I've always gone around and around
To the confusion of life's ground
But look at nature of the fields
They toil not but are very real
The birds sing cheerfully with a song
The years are short and the days are long
Why cant I stop for the time to be
Is life a plan I'm looking to find
Should we be ahead of time

Ray Jernigan

Shattered

A single vapor lamp illuminates the rusted steps
An alleyway behind the house where all is laid to rest
I stand alone on foreign ground looking out into the night
The wind picks up and chills my heart, stray leaves float out of sight

The moon sheds not a pale beam upon this darkest hour
I'd lost a dream as dreamers do and pain becomes my power
I recall a time when you had said you'd never leave my side
But you grew cold and distant when the pain did not subside

The last few drops of troubled rain descending at my feet
Shattered glass beneath a window frame stirs memories
A half-filled glass of bourbon flies across the barren room
Broken pieces hit the floor, we'll both be leaving soon

Troubled nights left unresolved bring only troubled days
What I'd give to know when someone means exactly what they say
Now shadows haunt my mind although my secrets are not dead
And the only thing that I regret is leaving them unsaid

Marian M. Chau

Intimacy

How warm is your embrace,
An experience of inner grace,
Which lightens my heart and soul,
And makes me feel so whole.

How gentle is your caress,
In your arms, my heart rests.
To gain the inner strength I need,
Which moves me forward in word and deed.

To feel your head so close to mine,
Makes my heart yearn and pine.
To open up my life to you,
Following your example through and through.

I sense your love so deep inside,
In its grasp, I wish to abide.
Opening my mind and heart to you,
Praying to be ever loyal and true.

Oh intimate lover of my life,
As I struggle through pain and strife.
May these moments of truth never cease,
To fill my heart with inner peace.

Roseann Velas

Untitled

This is an imagism,
An imagism about racism.
Forget the past that lead to the present.
And make mother earth content.
Racism is like a disease,
It keeps spreading, it does not cease.
Being born here is no excuse,
For you are allowed to refuse,
Therefor society is not to be accused.
To look further than a race,
Would make the world a better place.
In conclusion,
Racism is an illness,
A hate explosion,
Racism will never lead to happiness,
It is never to late,
There is a cure,
You don't have to live trapped by these gates,
Your heart and soul can still be pure.

Sophie Trawalter

The Pinch Pot

A Lump of red clay,
An indistinct shape of cracks and imperfections,
Warm loving hands slowly begin to mold and shape it,
They turn it around and round as the sides become tall and smooth.
The shaping hands must eventually let it go,
But it is still nestled in the secure palms of its beginning,
Then off to the kin for a final finish,
Soon it will be able to stand alone, tall and strong,
Yet the hands of its creation can still lovingly caress it,
And the tender love that flows through them will never leave
or be forgotten.

Patricia A. Fale

Break The Silence

What possesses any mortal to have
an untamable urge to write on blank
paper...... is mysterious.

To me blank paper is like white
silence, and I see the need to break
that silence with the earth shattering
sound of a word! Any word will do.
I hate to see blank paper.....

In my mind, it signifies the absence
of creativity and the lack of the crucial
knowledge that is so vital to keeping
the world moving around in the right
direction...forward.

A blank page is the silent death of
creativity and when it dies, soon shall
follow the human race, and slowly after,
the earth will fall apart and drift
endlessly into the silent darkness
of time...

Rose Mandeville

Eternity

Let me tell you about a bird,
and a little silk string,
Working all alone for my kind,
Tho' the bird couldn't die,
And the string couldn't wear out,
And that's what eternity is all about.

Once every thousand years,
the bird would fly,
across the tall mountain that reached the sky.

Every time he flew,
Over the top,
He pulled the string across the rock.

Until the mountain wore down,
level with the sea,
That's how long we will be,

Praising the lord in Eternity,
Side by side,
You and me!

Ron Farrow

He Trusts Her

He trusts her not to hold him too long
and not to transform herself at all
not to tether or choke or smother
but to nurse and nurture and mother
him, dance with veils like Salome
to serve, and feed and nourish
him, and not to grow and breathe and flourish

Sarah Jane Woolf-Wade

The Golden Rule

The hickory sticks
and a red brick structure we called school.
So many numbers to add or subtract,
and all of those letters in the alphabet.
And in the corner of my class,
stood a stool and dunce cap.
It is a place I never sat.
Those days have long past,
but my heart harbors memories.
Memories with a tear.
For you see, it was the teachers
and not the red bricks that built this structure
we called School.

Leonard J. Darder

In The Mind Of Me

All my life things have been changing everyday in every possible way.
And all at night I close my eyes really tight,
to make the pain all go away I want it to all go a way.
I try not to think of my pain, and outside way, way,
way up high in the sky I have angels watching over me.
I'll pull the trigger and make it all go away,
I'll pull the trigger and make it all go away,
I don't need the pain I feel deep down inside of me,
deep down inside of me. Don't bother to find me, I'll come around
when I want to be found. I open my eyes and see the pain you have
inflicted on me. I have now found that you can find happiness in
slavery. I just cone a little closer every day to my dreams.
They think they know me, but take it from me, I'll be who I want
to be. So go do what you like, but make sure you do it right.
Up where the angels sing, my hopes are smashed on the rocks down
below. So heaven let your light shine low. And to those who don't
believe in me, kiss off! I don't need to take this pain the
world has given to me. So I will leave this pain that the has
been given to me. I will leave by my own hand, this is the end
of me.

Kathryn Uecker

"Shattered Dreams"

When you fail to let the master, guide you through endless
streams
And all on your own, you try to conquer
Needing no one, so it seems:
Yet time after time, you stumbled then fall,
Not understanding life disaster
If only you had opened your eyes to see,
Life could have been better, life could have been swell
If only, you had said "Master let me walk with thee."
Now that the years have gone by,
You see life's journey in reality:
Now that your days will soon be nigh,
O what pain, what regret
As you slowly close your eyes
On your shattered dreams.

Mary Codrington

Untitled

The love I give is as light as a feather,
and as with my mood, changes with the weather.

My voice is strong like the rivers,
and when stern can make you quiver.

My mind is wise and full of surprises.
I'm a Black woman, untitled, untamed,
full of wisdom and fame,
When I'm gone they shall ring my name, for
I'm a black woman, untitled, untamed.

Katondria Evans

A Daughter's Love

For all the things you mean to me.
And all the things we've done and seen.
To you my parents I send my love.

So many times I want to say, how very much your time has made my life so beautiful in many ways. Although the time just slips away your on my mind both night and day. It seems as though we're miles apart, but still you're always in my heart.

And time moves on in much dismay. We live our lives from day to day and try our best to make things stay, the way they were in younger days. But as we know that can't be true. So we do our best to make things do.

I love you mom and dad with all my heart and wrote this so you'd know my thoughts.

Roxanne Cazier-Gally

Untitled

I've never went in for all that TM jazz
and all those googly guru gyrations while
meeting a Maharishi yogi who sits around
all day chanting some ultra-ethereal chant,
which brings one's mind closer to some
divine Nirvana so we don't have to suffer
like the divine Miranda.
I didn't have to go on some jet set trip
with the stars and sit around with the man
sidereally signing autographs.
I just clasped my hands and looked inside
my heart and prayed and did it all for free
and not on some majestic mountain slope.

Richard Minot

Untitled

I arise from my slumber
And beautiful dreams of her

I steal past the spot where she sleeps
I try not to awaken her, but she stirs

She lies repose, wrapped in such beauty
That it makes me shiver inside

Her eyes open and she looks at me
It is such a look of love

I think — I must be mistaken, I am not worthy,
I must be dreaming — but I look again

And she is still there, still wrapped in beauty,
Still looking at me. And there is love in her eyes

My heart aches for her, my body cries for her embrace
Oh how I long for her touch, to take her hand,
To lie beside her and hold her, to love her.

W. N. Leslie

Mistakes

Mistakes are very easily made,
and in the future they will be paid.

God forgives and learns to forget,
people do not and they make it a threat.

I made some big mistakes in the past.
I just look at them and say that it was the last.

Now I just look to the future and hope for the best,
for I know God forgives me and I can easily rest.

Philip Brown

Next Time

She stopped to visit with me for a while,
and brought with her some flowers
That she planted high, in regal fashion,
atop my fenced in patio.

Was it a style she learned beside the
Zunder Zee, or had Babylon
Provided inspiration as their hanging
gardens burst forth in bloom?

The special way we touched; the comfort
shared from so many journeys.
Her smile, her voice; they will never,
never leave me. Never.

These tears you see are not of sorrow
that she has traveled on,
They are of happiness we once again
will share. Next time.

Sonny Molinelli

The Flower

Like a seed that's planted, our relationship needs time
and care, for it to grow. With a little effort these
needs are essential for maturity and harmony. When the
seed needs water and care. It's the same as our thirst
for love and comfort. When those needs aren't fulfilled
the flower tends to wilt, us do our feelings in our heart.
So we must protect as well for outside interference.
As the flower needs protection from the weeds, or bugs or
the elements. Our relationship face likewise situations
from our friends, family and enemies. Who wish or want an
end to its growth. But for every sunny day, there's a ray for
hope and life. That's when we'll bloom, as will the flower.
After all the gloomy days, trials and tribulations, our
relationship turns to love. As the flower becomes in its
beauty, a rose.

Tishaun Taylor

Canvas Of Love

Imagine that you were an artist,
And could paint your future through thought.
Would you begin to paint the perfect home;
An unknown woman; a tiny tot?

Could you put down on that canvas,
Your every feeling of completeness?
Would anything be missing?
Like a past kiss, once filled with sweetness?

Did you use every color that you once loved?
Were you proud when you signed your name?
Was your finished work up to your expectations?
Did it bring you fortune or fame?

As for me, I'll sketch mine in charcoal.
What is reality and in clear view.
I can always add color as time passes by,
And pray it's portrait of you.

Victoria Burgo-Solar

Dare We Follow The Magi

The radiance of the star resonated so strongly in the minds and hearts of the Magi that they desired to know whose birth it announced and which place was so honored.

Trusting the heavenly sign they let the light lead them, let the dream warn them of deception and they found the child born of the marriage of heaven and earth.

Do these events still echo in our inner deserts, can we respond to the reflections cast by that bright star? Let us not hesitate to take the long lonely road to the sphere where light and sound, endless delight await us all.

Ursula Kobiljak

Untitled Christmas Reminder

With the summer sun being so shy
and distant
Raindrops turned inside out being so
fragile and eager to perish
This is a time to hold and cherish

Anonymous flesh toned figurines
mobile and armed with good wishings
Toys complex and simple reflect a world
of wishful thinking
A child's smile obliterates in an instant
Yellowed newspaper memories and
bitter thought dream scapes

Family, friends and unknown extras
Arrive and leave secret sound stages
Divine motion as liquid intent
a Director's hand in perpetual caress
wakes the inner child
in each of us.

Paul James Putnam

His Loving Touch

He had a smile that was unbearable
And dreams to last a lifetime
He had a heart that was uncomparable
And laughter to be combined
He was someone who could love you
To make your dreams come true
But someone came and took his life
And made ours feel so blue
Now time goes by so slowly
And dreams have all been shattered
As they build up inside more boldly
Then was the time that mattered
Now as life goes by in loving memory
Our dreams are building shatteredly
And now we know he will always be with us
Til the end of Eternity

Melissa A. Aguilera

Horizon

As each moment ticks by
and each note plays by
My heart dances to a tune so fine

Beyond the spectrum
Without the realm of reference

I allow my thoughts to stray into your arms
Once again floating on your charms
OH, to feel so attuned to the gentle breath of your being

Is it right to so easily Love and be loved?
To so easily understand
and be understood?
To give of the whole but just a part?
Is it right to feel the completeness through separation?

Thirty years on, now
And all I've ever done

Is it right to think that it was always you
Who blessed my dreams? and
Brought my horizon to my feet

We are beyond the spectrum
Without the realm of reference...

Leslie Grainger-Haynes

LEARN FROM GOD
DURING THE STORMS OF LIFE

Just as Jesus suffered physical
And emotional pain,
God's people will experience and combat difficulties
Time and time again.

Often, we fail to realize and discern...
That our struggles stimulate and help us become strong,
While, through the world's eyes...
Everything may seemingly be going wrong.

Throughout our setbacks and waiting...
We're given suitable opportunities to pray,
Unmasking a new, creative zeal..
For listening to God each and everyday.

Then, in the midst of all adversity..
In every facet of life,
God empowers us to withstand all disappointments..
Providing lightning-like-grace...to endure all pain and strife.

For all who are willing and eager to LEARN FROM GOD...
DURING THE STORMS OF LIFE... who desire to seek His grace,
Their lives will be given new purpose and meaning...
And gently, yet firmly rekindled, by God's loving fond embrace.

Richard C. Mattock Jr.

Grand Canyon

Oh thou Who cast the stars into the heavens,
And fashioned the splendors of the earth,
We thank thee for the beauty of Grand Canyon,
Created by thy Word that gave it birth.

As we stand and contemplate its grandeur,
The myriad formations like cathedrals rise,
As though in their very silence
To sing thy praises to the skies.

So silent and yet if we but listen,
The Canyon speaks in a thousand ways
Our father, we too lift our voices,
In gratitude, in joy and praise.

Zora Aldrete

"A Moment Of Happiness"

I listen softly
And hear it glisten
Upon our asphalt streets

I stand outside and feel it falling alone in my world
As everyone else is tucked within their sheets

I wonder how it feels to fall from the sky
Falling, falling from way up high
Feeling a rush of excitement
I try to move but find that I can not

I wonder how it can be so strong and young
After falling each time to be killed by the sun

Then reborn again just to fall
The rain so wild and free
Unlike you or me feeling trapped within man's walls

I'm tired of the hate and madness of this world
I want to be part of the rain
Falling sparingly, but falling free

While I sit, watching by it I think
This is the only time when I have freedom...
And my soul is young again.

Wendy Wielosinski

"Goodnight - Lord"

Well, Lord, here we are at the end of another day,
And here I lay in my bed again and silently pray.
Now I don't have any fancy words for my mind to write,
Yet, I know you always understand when we talk this way each night.

At first I didn't understand all your words still unread.
But now I know it was you who took over when they gave me up
for dead.
Lord, I don't know why you've kept me around this long.
Because in my life I've done my share of treating you so wrong.

If there's something special you have left for me to do.
Then, please, show me the path so that I may follow you.
Now, I won't make any promises we know I can't keep,
For they say this road is rough and tomorrow's hills are steep.

You alone know how hard it's been to plow this ground of clay,
And sometime soon I'll not awake to see your beautiful new day.
Somehow, as the days pass, I loose my fear of deaths sting,
Yet, I would ask one favor, Lord, take my loved ones under your wing.

Well, Lord, I know you must have had a busy day up there
And I don't want to tire you, so goodnight, take care.
We'll talk again tomorrow night when I lay down to pray,
That is, Lord, if you see fit to give me another day.

Thomas Crawford Weidner

"Soul Mates"

I thought about what I would say today
And if I could express myself
In some poetic way.

You know that I love you that's easy to do
And because you're so special
I'll always love you.

A corner of my heart is reserved just for you
For you will always be with me
In whatever I do.

You make me feel great
when I am with you
You make me feel happy
that's what you do.

But it's more than that
Words can't describe
Being with you is being alive.

We are one Now
And sealed are our fates
We are one Now
Forever - Soul Mates.

Larry Santa Maria

Alone

I am alone, alone in a world I carry upon my shoulders,
And it is darkest here when lady night spreads her ebony cape.
I walk upon this world, and at every turn the boulders
Block my path and make me sit, there is no escape.
Where to turn? Where to look? Only upon the dark abyss
Resting upon my bosom, cold and wet, empty.
Turn to me, a mask you will see, confusion you will miss.
This world for me presents flashes amounting to plenty,
And as the earth's life giver rests his hands upon
His child the flashes seem light, and the darkness shifts.
There is a new valor that fills me, and I boldly step on
The struggles a new day brings, but loneliness never lifts.
Echoes remain of questions with answers eternal,
If, why, how, the sounds make my world infernal.

Sylvia M. Gonzalez

Where Bluebonnets Grow

COME!
And I'll show you where the bluebonnets
are talking to the sun!
Where Indian paintbrushes
tint the spring meadows
with a sunset hue!
And we'll pause for a while,
o'ercome with beauty, and peace,
and the quiet radiance of another Spring.

There isn't much time left, you know:
to sit in silence where bluebonnets grow,
remembering Easters past.
It may not last,
this understanding of the world's rebirth...
For what it's worth,

Come now, my love!
And share with me once more our youth,
Before we say goodbye to yesterday.

Pearl Webb Hammerle

Dream Till Your Dream Comes True

I had a dream one night not too long ago
And in this dream I met a beautiful beau
A prettier sight I had never seen
All of a sudden I woke up from my dream

As I woke from my sleep I looked around me
Looking for this beau, where could she be?
I walked for miles hoping to find
My dream lover, my one of a kind

As I walked around I found no one
I was lost and confused seeing darkness in the sun
So I decided to go back to sleep
In hopes of dreaming of her rather than sheep

I quickly fell asleep but dreamed of no one
Now I realized my dream was done
But as I woke from my sleep you stood over me
The dream is you my love, you're real you see

Michael Wierzbicki

Joshua

You've brought so much sunshine and love
and joy into my life.
I can't remember life before you,
or imagine life without you.

Your smile, your sparkling eyes,
the feel of yours arms around me.
But remember is all that I can do.
You're not here with me, and cannot be.

It's almost as if my life is on hold
until I can see you again.
I'll wait for that day when I can touch you
and hold you; laugh and cry with you. Love you.

JOSHUA! My heart cries for you.
Can you hear it across the miles that separate us?
Across the vast expanse of this country?
Do you know I love you more than life itself?

And reading this, would anyone ever guess
that you're the beloved first-born of my
beloved first-born?

Kathy Guerra

Pete's Garden

Pete planted onion sets and seeds,
And kept his garden free from weeds.
The little seeds just grew and grew
And bloomed and bore the summer through.
Vegetables to pick, from spring to fall.
Forget-Me-Nots, so very small.
Larkspurs with their bunny faces.
Cornflowers in a dozen places.
Velvet pansies in a bed.
Zinnias - yellow, pink, and red.
Bright Marigolds that need no care.
Petunias blooming everywhere.
Pete spent many happy hours,
While tending his garden and flowers.
There's little left to be said.
My brother, Pete, is long since dead.
There will be gardens in heaven, I know,
For him to plant some seeds and watch them grow.

Stella L. Brooks

In Thousand Miles

You leaned across ten thousand miles
and kissed me
It was so sweet to feel your soft caress,

For just a moment dear it seemed
God sent you
To share a bit of my deep loneliness.

I felt your presence here within
my room love.
T'was just a bit of you I used to know.

You smiled and said "Keep that chin
up love".
And that was all because you had to go.

You didn't give me time to say
"I love you"
Nor tell you that I miss you
more each day.

But for that one sweet moment
I am thankful
Our love could wipe ten thousand
miles away.

Ruby Leedom

"Savannah"

I'll take you places you've never known,
And lead you through the darkness which you've gone.
A companion and friend I'll always be,
If you will only trust in me.
I'll go the extra mile to satisfy you,
Because in return that's what you do too.
The dreams we've shared cannot be replaced,
Not by money, fortune, or fame;
For the bond we've formed is worth more than
any riches named.
For what we seek to accomplish is not for the
world to see;
But only a mere reminder of what it's like....
just you and me.
I will be your friend until the end,
When at last, we both ride into the wind.

Wendy W. Payne

Ode To Emily

Words stretch over the fragile frame of time
And lyrical lines still live on yellowed paper
Humming and buzzing in my ears
Scraping at the insides of my soul
With the sweet ecstasy of recognition.

For how was She — or I — to know
Her song sung within
Would grow to encompass the World
And prove that Then — as Now —
Humanity dances to the beat of the same drummers?

A friend I never knew gives me companionship
A long-dead Woman sings to me of hope
Her soul is a mirror to my own
Yet I fear in my glass's imperfections
She would find nothing familiar.

Melissa A. Kostera

"God Touched"

"God touched the sky"
And made it the color blue
Just for everyone of you!

"God touched the sun"
And made it bright yellow,
So we can see our passing fellows.

"God touched all small and big things"
Everything with flying wings.
Even creatures with ugly features
Don't be cruel or scared is what God teaches.

God touched the righteous earth
Gave us the rights to die or give birth,
Can't we see God's wonderful earth
For what it's supposed to be worth.

You all know, what our God is saying
Please start obeying, and don't forget,
our daily praying.
Can't everyone get along so we,
can sing in happy song.

Susan M. Moquin

Eternal Love

Do poems touch your heart
and make tears come to your eyes,
or is it the birds in heaven
singing love songs to you from the skies.
Oh how I would love to have the voice
to soothe your troubled soul,
the voice of love and laughter,
truly under God's control.
Do flowers in the garden bring a twinkle to your eyes,
Just as your beauty does to me as you go strolling by.
I want to make you happy,
I prayed to God above
to find the way into your heart
and give you eternal love.
Love my sweet love
you give meaning to my soul,
oh special one walk with me
down God's Holy path
and hear the bells toll.

Wayne M. Lynam

Pass Due To You

There is a fear that whispers in my ear and glows in my eyes
And makes my heart sigh, this I feel hurts through and through
Cause all that I promised you is pass due

I look in your eyes and I see your cries, what I myself have
Devised. I can't explain what it is all I can say is whispering
Fears, the fears that are pounding in my ears and welling up
In my eyes as tears for all the pain I've given you, and all
The love you've given true, I know my debt is pass due.

So forgive me these childish days and strengthen me with your
Loving ways, for this you have I'll always praise through all
our cherished days.
Yes all I've said is true that my love is pass due to you.

Rickey King

My Family

My family is so dear,
and means everything to me
Without a family I couldn't love as much,
you see

With my family, I can care and be kind,
to love them, to hold them, and to be so divine

I have a family that's the best and
they're really grand, who sometimes
get my message and is willing to take
the time to understand

I have a family, even if they were a
picture inside of bowl
At least I have a family, I can cherish
in my soul

Marcus Weaver

Time To Retire

I seem to remember when the days were longer
and much to my amazement, I felt much stronger.
This working each day seems a real great chore
and not as much fun as it really was before!

Now, what do you suppose could have caused such feeling,
this one, I don't care if I am arriving or leaving?
When everyone around me seems to be filled with such zest,
I sit here quite pooped and try to do my best.

I hope you don't think that I am an avid complainer,
because it is so hard for me to be a retainer.
While they tell me I look no older quite yet,
inside I can tell that my ways have been set!

Everyone keeps asking me when I am going to retire
and I continue to reply that it is really my desire!
But, how can I survive when it takes so much money
just to keep me, myself and too my honey?

I will say this, that just as soon as I know
when the time is right or when I will go;
Until that time, you'll just have to tolerate me,
because, I might stay that much longer you see!

Anna Mae

True Friends

Friends may come and friends may go.
And some friends, you never really know.
But a true friend her thoughts she shares,
Yet always lets you know, she's their.
She lets you know when you really mess up
But is always their when things get tough.
I've found that friend, that friend so true.
And I want you to know, that friend is you.

Tonya Milito

Young Of Heart

I sit down with paper and pen,
And now begin
With open heart and soul transcend.
Another year has passed you by.
So make a pledge, "Let dreams fly".
Make new days know, the learning heart,
To brave new paths, make new starts.
Be young of heart, and mind, and spirit.
Let go with ease, your love's strong merit.
For in this time, you are far loved,
And in this space, your warmth is shared.
And as the sands trickle slowly by,
Take heart in the solace of an infinite sky.
Be at ease with yourself and enjoy life.
May your smiles be many, your songs take endless flight.
Be both bold and wise in the turning of each page,
And "know" the reading of the story tells the beauty of your age.

Roger D. Whitner

Letting Go

It was early on a Friday morn.
And once again Spring had been reborn.
The old man decided it was time to go
Back to the mountains that he loved so.
Happy and care free as he could be,
He knew that on the mountain top he'd be free.
To gather ramps and smell the flowers,
And ramble through the woods for hours.
As he climbed he did not see
This would be his final destiny.
When he was found later that day,
He was resting on a log, they say.
A trillium he had clutched to his breast
As if he had laid down to rest.
The old man has now gone home,
Where the flowers will always bloom.
Where every day with be Spring
And where the birds will always sing.

Sally Lance

Remembering ... My Love

When evening drapes her curtains down,
And pins them with a star,
Remember that I'll think of you
Though you may wander far.

When the morning skies light up the earth
And the sun comes shining through,
Remember that my constant love
Will always be with you.

When the flowers open up their buds
And kisses them with dew,
Remember how our hearts entwined
When we said our last adieu.

When the Orioles sing their song so sweet
And bluebirds build their nest,
Remember that our memories
Were of the very best.

And so, my love, with fond farewell,
I bid you fond ado
And hope the many future years
Are always good for you.

Vivian J. Schaelchli

"Precious Moments"

Take charge of your life today
And promise yourself along the way,
To cherish each day that you are alive
And thank God that you did survive
All the challenges and obstacles along the way
That made you stronger every day.
To wake up in the mourn,
To give birth to a new born,
To breathe the fresh air and feel the breeze,
To walk, talk and bend your knees,
Are not promised to you forever.
Take them for granted, you should never.
But live, love, and thank God each day.
Because each moment is precious in its own way.

Shirley Elizabeth Jefferson

Time To Say Goodbye

It's time to say goodbye
And put the past behind us
It's time to put away the memories that only serve to remind us
Of what we had, and what will never be
It's time to close the door
And go on as before
It's time to let go of the dream
And open our eyes to reality
What we had was oh, so strong
But we both know it was wrong
So it's time to say goodbye
Please don't cry
We have to face the truth and accept what's real
No matter how we feel
It's time to move on
We've got to be strong
But it's time to let go and look to tomorrow
Our love will always last
But it's in the past
We've got to try, because it's time to say goodbye

Lori J. Feltner

Daddy's Girls

Daddy's Girls are beautiful
And really ornery as could be
And when they try to get by with something
They will flash their eyes you see
But daddy never waivers much,
Oh maybe sometimes though
Oh come on Dad please don't be mad
You know I love you so
Well down goes the barriers
And up with the grins.
Here's where trouble truly begins

Michael E. Scott

E. M. R. (Educable Mentally Retarded)

Someday, mom and dad, I'll have wings,
And I'll tear away from those apron strings.
Over each plateau may bring a frown.
I'll fly up and I'll fly down,
But, I'll get up and soar again,
I'll show you that I can win.
My take-offs may be sloppy, my landings may never be great,
I'll not make excuses just to compensate.
I'll show myself, and I'll show you,
Just exactly what I can do.
Someday, mom and dad, I'll have wings,
And I'll tear away from these apron strings!

Nancy Wildman

Special Gift

He gave them to us as a gift
and said, "Now learn to share."
No wonder; now that they are gone,
we learn how much we care.

They've given joy throughout their lives.
There have been some bad times too.
We hope that we have taught them well.
We hope they are with you.

And in our hearts, we know that
you only lent them for awhile.
We should have learned to love and care
to walk that extra mile.

Now they are gone - not in our sight,
and we don't understand.
We know that there's a reason.
We know there is a plan.

Please help us Lord; that we may see
why it must be this way.
Just take this child within your care.
and help us here, we pray.

Sandra D. Sims

Majesty In Alaska

The Master sat at his easel,
And said to the Angels, "hush"!
The scenery, it was magnificent,
It was the touch of the Master's brush.

The trees stand so proud and tall,
They shelter the squirrels and the birds;
The Caribou seek their shade,
Their beauty goes beyond known words.

The majesty of the mountains
Is awesome to behold;
The sheep climb to the highest crags,
To bring safety to the fold.

The glaciers and the mountains blend,
To create this awesome sight;
The valleys are also used by God,
To portray his glory and his might.

Majesty is what we see,
When the view is seen as one;
Praise God for his majesty,
And what, for us, he has done.

Valda Carrier

Eternity

Wind whistles down my chimney
And shrieks along the eaves,
It ruffles up the feathers of the snow birds,
Then it leaves:

To pile the white drifts higher;
To make the wires sing;
To lift the skirts of ladies;

But that doesn't mean a thing!

For spring's around the corner,
There's a lilting in the air.
The sun is up and bonnetted
Once more to leave its lair.
The daffodils in yellow,
Are dancing on the lawn.

The whole wide world's awakening!

I SMILE — AND HURRY ON.

Maude Putman Vough

"But...I Never Will!"

People do strange things
and some people don't.
There is one phrase that I often say to myself
and it is, "But...I never will!"

I look at people and how they act
and think they look silly.
Running 'round going willy-nilly
"But...I never will!"

A lot of friends and acquaintances
watch me oh so closely
Just to see what I do, if anything mostly
Because I often say, "But...I never will!"

Norma Y. McMichael

Sweet Green

Green are prickly pine trees, low ocean tides
and squishy under bare feet.
Green is the taste of yummy delicious pears
Fresh cut trees and delicious green apples smell green
When I'm dizzy it makes me feel green.
Green is the sound of rushing waterfalls
and a frozen lake crackling.
Green is tropical rain forest, meadows where wild horses
roam, and dreaming under a nice big green tree.
An extremely ugly monster is green.
Magnificent four leaf clovers are also green.
Green is a beautiful color unless you're scared.

Karen King

The Lost Soul Of A Celtic Warrior

The blood of many, stains my spirit, tears of loss mark my face
and still the beast is not appeased, the light is held in chains
deep within the bowels of continual loss and hurt. Fleshless,
brittle, the bones of past lives surrender to the weight of the
beast as it plunders deep within my spirit.

My sword and shield have at times served me well, but always the
darkness of loss has defeated me, burned upon the pyre of hope,
my soul again wanders into the void, where it is not a stranger.

The terror and fear that is the beast is as real as today, and
as lasting as death. But after lifetimes of battle, my spirit
is stronger then its hold on me. Still the struggle continues
to win is to perish, to win I must embrace the beast with chains
of truth and the honor of my Celtic Spirit, only my flesh will
die and some where in the bowels of loss and hurt, will the
Light be set free.

Wiley F. Jones

To A Gentleman

The day of toil has just been done.
And the wages for us was rightfully won.
From tiredness, we ached all over,
So homeward bound, we went once more.

The trolley which we took was very full,
Yet all of us could sit but not Mr. Gull.
Ten persons got on three stops from ours,
They stood, all ten, for half an hour.

Some folks were young and full of life,
While some where worn from heavy strife;
Old ladies were sick with faces torn,
And some were old from burdens born.

A lad of youth gave up his seat
To an aged lady of unsure feet.
I thought, Hurrah! for this young man.
To me, He was a perfect gentleman!"

R. Isabella Stephens

Sister-Love

You tangle me in your web
And suck the nectar from my soul.
Now my immortal body lies
Within the depths of your black throne.
She had once lured me
Into her pot of gold.
Missing was the rainbow
The one she had once sad.
As the tears from her face
Harden to blocks of coal,
It stabs her in the back
And more her cancer grows.
Who is this sadist creature?
And where did she come from?
What evil could've happened
For her to love no one?
Alas, you'll find no answer,
No matter how you try.
When she comes there's nothing left
For you to do but die.

S. Dib

Yesterday

Now that spring has come and gone
And summer is reaching on
I can still smell the leaves on a
dog wood free.
Running across the fields of yesterday
I can still feel the heat beneath
my feet.
As a child, the canals I once ran down
That seemed so long are now small
or already gone.
I'd lie down on a pillow of grass, trying
to find a four leaf clover in which
All my dreams would come true if I
wished over.
I would lie, and look up toward the sky
resting my head, or fall asleep instead.
But, what I remember most is the old
house which is no longer there and
the childhood dreams that linger in time
all of them I left behind.

Marie Osborn

What Would They Think?

If we could peer through the mists
and the pages of time were open to see
the faces and forms of family so dear—
whatever would they think of me?

These people who walked the wilder roads,
who trusted God enough to cross the sea,
who broke the ground with fervored brow—
whatever would they think of me?

These ones who walked upon the earth
and tasted life as men born free;
the teacher, lawyer, carpenter, smith—
whatever would think of me?

Someday, after my walk is over,
I go to sleep and my reward I see.
I will be called to my Maker and I will ask—
"My Lord, what do you think of me?"

Kelly Paul Graham

The Darkness

The darkness of a thousand years
And the salt of as many tears
Are in the soul of the man I call father

His blood is red and bitter to taste
He doesn't know love or joy only hate
His heart is empty like an alcoholic's glass

With his fist doubled and muscles flexed
He aims at his defenseless young son
And begins to destroy all that is good in man

A 2' by 4' as his weapon against his child
He swings into the hall of fame of hatred
And punished his son to a life of shame

Nothing can change what took place, thirty years ago
No one can tell by looking at this middle aged man
That the monster who haunts his dreams is the man
He called Dad......

Mark Hughes

Song Of Eve

I've tasted the fruits of innocence;
and the taste of it was good-
so why does the fruit of the passion tree
hold such a lure for me?
How wildly the serpent came
with cold unblinking eye-
How willingly did he exchange
perdition for
my paradise.

The piper is a mottled creature.
Though his tune be sweet,
the part you hear is deceptively simple:
the piper plays for keeps.
You did not reckon on a price?
The piper will be paid.
That jig you dance
is the debt you owe
to the bargain that
you once made.

LaVonia Ballard Dayton

"When A Cowboy Talks With God"

For the walls of the mountains that stretch around
And the wind through the trees of heaven's sounds
The abundant pastures with streams on the land
It all holds the signature of the "Master's" hand

For the new born foal by her mother's side
And the little bull calf with the bronze colored hide
The expectant cows grazing next to the fence
All things great and small prove your existence

For the girl I spotted while I was in the saddle
I took her on for keeps, to take home and help with the cattle
We've had our "ups and downs," our sorrows and our fun
I thank you for that day the two of us became "one"

From the creation of earth, to the miracle of birth
And for the woman you gave this man
I know in my heart, you knew from the start
It was all a part of your master plan

So, to you Lord, I am grateful
From way down deep inside
I'm thankful for your beauty and grace
As I continue this earthly ride

Randy Waller

Sea Shell

First it is a spiral sea shell washed from the sea,
And then it is like a spiny Stegosaurus roaming through the hills.
And then it is like a pointy Mongolian helmet upon a warrior's head,
And then it becomes a jagged drinking cup to quench my thirst,
And now it is a brown, black, and white ladle for dipping my
substance.
And now it is a delicate flower vase to hold my single bud,
And now I am a shell seeker of my imagination.

Sharon Pratt

Love's Longing

Always I've known you, even in childhood days
And then to find you too late
All my hopes and aspirations
Crushed and shattered at my feet
Why did you wait, too late, to come
Do you even know you're the one I've longed for
All the years of my being
The reason for who and what I am
I wonder if I call your name enough
Ever so silent but clear
Will you hear and answer
Could there be a chance
For a love so strong and pure
There's joy in my heart silently loving you
I know you not, yet know you completely
It was pre-determined; it was meant to be
Where did it all go wrong
Was this life of loneliness meant for me
Could there be a chance
For an hour or a day of perfect ecstasy

Kay Belvin

Grandparents

Have you ever just sat down a spell
And thought what grandparents do so well
How with love and care and tenderness
They are always there for your caress
How when things go wrong and make you struggle
You can go to them and they let you snuggle
Things seem to be better and look much brighter
With Grandma and Grandpa your cares are lighter
Isn't it great to see them there
With their smiles of love and tender care
I think the Lord knew just what to do
When Grandparents he placed for me and you
So as life goes on and age do we
May to a child we Grandparents be
So look to the Lord for his infinite grace
That we as Grandparents have a place
For the love and joy that child may hold
And be there for them whether young or old
Yes, God made us Grandparents don't you know
To help watch over his children as they grow

J. D. Hausenfluck

"Forever Friends"

Across the miles, over the roads,
and through the years ahead.
A lifetime together though so far apart,
friends we will be until the end.
When the stars fall like rain
and the heavens open up we'll stand
above on a silver cloud - forever friends
between us.

Lorea Lynn Silverthorn

The Love Of A Woman

I remember one day my daddy set me down,
And told me his thoughts and what's most profound,
Is the gift of life to a man after being a boy?
Is the love of a woman, the feeling of inner joy?

There's a time you know what's right is right,
There's a time when love fills you day and night,
There's a time you know when to take a stand,
There's a time of love when you hold that woman's hand.

Love will find your eyes and bring beauty to sight,
Love will find your ears and sound so right,
Love will find your heart and pump you with joy,
It's the love of a woman, no one else my boy.

And now I've grown and understand what he said,
Of the gift life brings, what was lying ahead,
That woman is you, the one I love,
It's the love of a woman, a gift from God above.

Pete Volkmann

My Waterfall

I don't know if my waterfall is a he or she,
And when it whispers, it splashes me.

My waterfall has the crispness of a mint,
And when the sun sets, a light blue tint.

My waterfall is as cold as the snow,
Yet inside there's a warming glow.

My waterfall is in fairy tales.
And in its waters, ships set sail.

My waterfall is a cloud in the sky,
And sometimes it's so very shy.

I have a wonderful, wet, waterfall.

Lori Zimmerman

Triviledge

Let's play trivia: What's the capital of Bolivia?
And who starred in Seahawk and Robin Hood?
(Study old movies, as you should)
And Classic Comic #17?
The Deerslayer, of course. Where've you been?
And Vietnam defoliated by what evil flame?
"Agent Orange," I think, was its name.
So your knowledge of government keeps you excited?
(Or, perhaps, the number of officials indicted?)
Often, it seems, corruption's the rule,
But not the one you learn in school.
What state is contiguous to most others?
Two are tied, and if you think I lied,
No debate, no crap: just consult a map!
So study your notes and make all A's,
And you'll be happy, the rest of your days.
But please remember, sisters and brothers:
What is knowledge to some is trivia to others!
We might also add, "vice versa,"
If only to make this poem even worse.

Mack Norton

Angels Of Mercy

Angels of mercy were sent to your side,
Angels who knew your plight,
Angels who loved you and cared for you
Until the night you died.
God sent his angels and he made a way
Where there seemed there would be none.
Wrapped in the arms of your children and friends
Until your day was done.

Susan Ropcke

The One I Love

I see her sitting there as innocent as could be
And wonder what it would be like if she were with me?
She is the type of girl I've always wanted
And now by her I am hunted.
Her friends are saying we will not last,
But the love for her I've had in the past.
No fight and no argument could come between,
For our love is easy to be seen.
She has helped me see things I never thought I'd see,
Like her with me.
Having her in my life has opened my eyes,
To a world which only at one time was filled with lies.

Steven Lane

Dedication

When it has been established... and your goal is in sight
And you are firm on where you stand,
Then, you must try with all your might
In spite of what it might demand.

I want to be met on the field of endeavor,
And I want the chance of judgments that are fair...
It matters little if my goal is imperiled,
Because my initiative and work will get me there!

Whatever I might be... must rate the best,
And this will come from those I serve.
There's generally come from one chance to pass the test,
And the reward is something that I must deserve.

It has little to do with handicaps... age... race
Or whether or not you seem fit.
It has all to do with Hope...Faith...
And mainly a whole lot of grit!

With courage renewed, get started today....
And dedicate yourself to your dream.
Let nothing dissuade you along the way,
And your future will be serene!

Lawrence R. Champion

Take Heart

When your world topples down about you
And you bear a heavy load,
When it seems as though you're walking
Down an endless, winding road,
When the tears are falling faster
Than they ever have before,
When your heart is slowly breaking
And you can't smile anymore,

Take heart. You're not forgotten.
Take heart. God loves you still.
Take heart, and rise above it.
Take heart, and seek God's will.

You don't have to understand why things happen so.
The Lord has ways that we can't comprehend.
But rest assured that with His love He'll wipe away your tears,
And with it, also, make your heart to mend.
For as the mountains rise above the deep and stormy sea,
So are the ways of God much higher than the ways of you and me.

Kelly L. Stinson

Unconditional Love

Her eyes of love look at you,
and your character they see right through.
A warm hug a gentle touch,
she never seems to ask for much.

I can't explain how much she means to me,
when I'm with her I can just be me.
We take long walks together in the park.
With her I feel safe even after dark.

She sadly watches me go through the door,
and waits eagerly for me to return once more.
She always has a smile on her face,
and never a hair is out of place.

Even when no one else does, she understands,
I don't have to give her ifs, buts or ands,
She's been by my side through thick and thin,
I know we'll be together to the end.

By now I think you might have guessed,
that you have heard all the rest.
But, to be sure read through to the very end and
you'll find, she's my dog Lady and my best friend.

Martha J. Loveless

Precious

Caring for Precious in my heart and mind is
Another reason to strive to accomplish goals and dreams
Sometimes the most difficult to cope with
Another possible heartbreak is to take risk upon it
Never in my life have I felt this way
Doubting my own desire has become a feeling of uncertainty
Reasons all too familiar, yet sometimes obscure
Any other way would seem a solution without challenge
My spare thoughts are filled with her
Adolescent behavior towards my sometimes strategic heartfelt traditions
Reminding me over and over why I work so hard
In order to find the way through her shell and into her heart and mind
Even though it often goes seemingly unnoticed
Just when I think I may have found a way
Underneath that shell she protects herself with
Shield that is for all men, unfortunately for me
Tranquility accompanied by a human mind and body waiting
I can only continue to dream and someday find a way
Concede upon the desired for all of
Eternity, GOD, I wish it would be me

Richard A. Gale

"Nature's Ritual"

Leaves of crimson gold and green fall gently to the ground
Another summer dwindles as autumn winds abound

Bright orange pumpkins fill the neighbor's fields
Apple trees are laden with their bountiful yield

The roar of farm tractors fills the fall air
Fields of golden corn will soon be bleak and bare

Flocks of migrating birds now brighten up the sky
To their summer home they soon will bid good-bye

Glistening mounds of snow will soon decorate the earth
As another long winter begins its blustery birth

Rita Kerkhoff

Gifts

All of earth's gems and all of earth's treasure
Are at our command for our personal pleasure
I gave you the forests with all my best wishes
You gave me the oceans and millions of fishes
I gave you the mountains, the valleys and streams.
You gave me the planets and all the sunbeams
I gave you the knowledge to look towards the future
You gave me the cities burning with lights
I gave you the breezes for all of our nights
You gave me the islands, the tropical flowers
I gave you the desert and sweet evening showers
You gave me the rainbow, I gave you the rain
And our gifts can be given - again and again

Richard G. MacDonald

To Granny, With Love

On the edge of a dream in heaven
are the memories of someone so dear
She arose long ago to the heavens, I know
for her Savior she always kept near

Though her life here on earth seemed a trial
and her pathway was strewn with debris
She remained gracious still, giving love to its fill
till the angels took her from me

I hope that she knew how I loved her
I was young and selfish those days
Never thinking about the living without
one so dear, in so many ways

As the years pass me by I remember
and I wish she could be with me now
To see how I've grown, the seeds that I've sown
that sweet smile to see on her brow

My dear Granny, I always will love you
and this life, to Jesus, I give
So I'll see you one day when this life slips away
on the edge of the cloud where you live.

Kay Altman Ayers

I See A Land

I SEE A LAND where race, creed or color
are viewed only externally, but invisible internally.

I SEE A LAND where homeless is a myth and
all can eat at a-table-of-a-plenty.

I SEE A LAND where those who are in pain
today, will see a better tomorrow.

I SEE A LAND where minds are clear thinking,
where people are free to walk on earth,
children can play without fear, and all peoples
are united in love.

I SEE A LAND where the air is clean, the waters
are pure, the grass fertile and green, and the
trees stand tall, bold and broad to shade their surroundings.

I SEE A LAND where the animals are free to
roam the hills, drink from the pure waters,
nibble the tender green grass and rest in
peace under the tall, bold and broad trees.

And when our tenure of life is over, I SEE A
LAND that will invite us in to PEACE, HARMONY
and sweet REPOSE.

Lillian Whitlow

Free

Freedom
Are we truly free
Or do we see what we want to see
We look and strain trying to point the finger
Of blame
We look at our kids with pants hanging off
Their butts
They think that this is cool but it really sucks
They call themselves gangs
Which is truly a shame
Free
How can we say that we are free
When we only be what others want us to be
We try to imitate what we see
Even if it is off of B.E.T.
Do we have our minds or are
They just programmed with the times.

Paul Jones

Let Me Be found

Look in my eyes and tell me what you see
Are you afraid to look what it might be?
Must you run the other way?
Please come back and hear what I've got to say

Do you see someone who doesn't walk like you do?
Maybe on crutches, wheels, a walker, or a cane?
Or is it the fact that I can't hear like you do?
Missing an arm or leg, are you afraid I may have pain?

Before you decide, let me say this first
Don't look at what I can not do
And feeling sorry for me just will not do
Just look at my heart and see what I've got
I have a lot to offer which equals an awful lot
I admit I have problems, that much is true
But no one is perfect through and through
I'm caring and sensitive and I work hard to please
I'm no more dangerous than the warmth of the breeze
Don't single me out, don't keep me bound
Just look in my eyes and let me be found

Lori L. Groves

Drug Culture

Do stress and strife fill you less with life?
Are you suddenly losing your will?
Don't cry out in defiance, use medical science.
Find inner strength through a Pill!

Do you want to lose weight, or make muscles inflate?
Need you confidence back on the scene?
Pills can make you feel tall, make you give it your all,
Now you, too, can be lean and mean!

To get your prescription, go see your physician,
Don't buy them from criminal thugs.
Just tell doc your ills, pay his "office-call" bills,
And he'll get you your much needed drugs.

But some folks feel that the power to heal
Does actually come from within.
They say that God is inside your bod,
And He lets the sunshine in.

Give help to the poor, worship your Lord,
Love your neighbor, and try not to sin.
And I swear to you, those things I will do...
Just as soon as my Prozac kicks in.

Stephan M. Rowden

Black, To The Future

Black, To The Future you can go.
Armed with a degree and all that you know.

Black, To The Future you must go.
You're somebody special, let it show.

Black, To The Future, it's yours for the taking.
Trod paths carefully, it's your life you're making.

Black, To The Future, and when it becomes the past,
You can rest assured that your impression will last.

Kevin Bingham

"By The Beautiful Sea"

I have seen the way the sand shines, by the beautiful sea.
Around the shores of rage, the wind comes up.

Feeding thousands of birds, that are watching me.
Flying in one at a time, to catch their bit of luck.

Sand dollars found on shore, as the tide goes out.
Visions of creatures, by the beautiful sea.

A light tower seen afar, spotting ships in route.
Clams pinching the depth's of the ocean's reef.

I would love to live by the beautiful sea.
A long walk, near ocean's edge dodging incoming waves.

Endless ocean waves a constant heartbeat so free.
Walking by the beautiful sea, in a white foggy haze.

Mark S. Emerson

Our Son

Once upon a time a special young man came along.
As a child, he never rested and his life was a song.
First came trikes, then bikes and cars at home and away,
Loving every minute, of every single day.
As his teen years faded, it was time to move on,
From the farm, his home, where he'd wakened each dawn.
He married and settled, but never cared to roam,
Away to a city or a strange new home.
When his little ones came, he knew it was time,
To put away his toys, to new heights he'd climb.
So the dream of all dreams, at last came true,
Back to the farm they went, from whence he grew.
His lady made gardens and canned it all up,
The kids got kittens and even a pup.
From early to late he'd farm all the day,
And loved every minute while he made hay.
Food for the world, "Midnight Farmer" is he -
As he sows and reaps and raised his family.
He knows God is with him, both day and night,
And never, not once, let Him out of his sight.

Sharon Norton

"A Seasonal Change"

Today a snowflake fell, and on my tongue it died.
As Fall met Winter, and for the season they vied.
Fall readied itself by grouping leaves into mounds.
Winter countered this move by sending
snowflakes crashing to the ground.
The battle then started, and for hours it did last.
Neither side winning or losing,
and the time seemed to go so fast.
Finally with icicles,
Winter gained the upper hand and fall quickly fell.
A cold wind blew through the trees,
and the outcome it did tell.
Summer and Spring watched,
knowing they would eventually do the same.
A day of bright sunshine filled with torrential rain.

Rodney Arrington

Moving On

Spring awaits, with God's gift of life
As a seedling yet dormant lies steadfastly by
Unearthed, it sprouts forth, moving on ...
To be cultivated and nourished by one such as I.

Moving on from heaven to earth, an infant born
Kindred in spirit to the small sprouting seed
Budding forth, yearning for warmth and love
Harmonious in nature to life preserving needs.

Brilliant color and individuality blossom enchantingly
Daily aspiring to new heights, growing stronger
Roots firmly planted, thirsting for knowledge
As comprehension of earths inheritance is pondered.

Summer embraces natures duet with enlightenment
Both graced by hands giving tender care
Fall enchants with full bloom, exquisite beauty
Sweet fragrance awakens our senses, softness so fair.

Savaged by storm and time, winter months prevail
Heart and stem thus broken, heaven and earth bound
Death triumphantly won, and yet we must move on ...
As spring awaits to unearth new life from fertile ground.

Yolinda Fay Willes

The Last Long Days Of Summer

See the bare foot little boy with the floppy straw hat,
as he kicks up the dust on his way to the fishing hole?
He knows the days are few till he'll be back in school
and that big old "bass" will laugh behind his back.

"I gotta get him soon or it's wait till next June," he mused,
"and I don't wanna wait that doggone long." He finally reached
the stream where that old bass was last seen and laid
his bait upon the water, a more perfect cast has never been.

There was a tremendous splash as that old bass took the bait
and went twisting straight up thru the air.
"Hang on little guy, don't let him get his head, your trophy
is almost there, and you'll take 1st prize at the fair."

With one tremendous jerk and a silent prayer his hook would hold
that big old bass lay flopping at his feet.
His heart was pounding wildly and his knees were very weak; but,
the prize was his and, "Oh, what a feat."

I. L. Sonnie Thornton

Sweet Sorrow

Parting is such sweet sorrow my love.
As I cling to thee in quiet adoration
I touch my cheek upon thy hem and
my heart weeps to see thy pain.
In utter disbelief, we are parting, searching,
longing for love's embrace and
God's uniting.

But wait, I pray thee linger here awhile
that I might place a kiss upon that hem
to touch thy cheek.
Or speak the words of love that cries
to be heard, but fall upon deaf hearts.
For in this moment our souls are destined
to find peace in tomorrow's embrace.
So with fond farewell upon sweet lips.
I take leave, drinking the essence of thy beauty.
For as the nightingale sings,
So sings my heart for thee,
and with this melody of love
our souls touch and become one.

Richard A. Mason

Blessed By A Poet

I grieve for you and the loss of your son
As I put to words my thoughts
For I know the pain that he may have felt
As he put to words his heart

To know a poet can be such a blessing
As I am sure it was with your son
Because their pen is a window
To what lies in everyone

The world is a better place
For what poets have had to say
And I know your life was made much richer
By the poet that came your way

Mankind shares a kindred spirit
Feeling the same joys and sorrows
And we share God's unconditional love and grace
Into His endless tomorrow

Steven Jones

Meditation

My sun is setting in the west
As I reflect how I've been blest
Long since I've passed three score and ten
Soon my future will end, I know not when.
Happy my childhood, parents caring
I longed for adventure, not quite daring
To challenge fate, chart unknown shoals
I settled for more modest goals.
College, teaching, days did fly
Romance did not pass me by.
Marriage and children brought joy, some sorrow.
My life brought contentment, not fear for tomorrow.
I've seen distant places and had many friends
And problems came too, yet happiness depends
Upon which memories you choose to dwell
And which of them you choose to tell
The sun will set, this life be done
But a new day awaits, the eternal one.

Marian L. Worrall

The Sky Is The Limit

My hands folded behind my head,
as I stare up to the sky,
My back wet from morning dew,
my legs arched as I lie,
A jet leaves a streak of white,
it sails soundless and forever,
I follow it with a peering eye,
it etches the blue sky so clever,
at last it seems to disappear
leaving a faint trail of white,
It reminds me of my place on earth,
only a faint streak until the night...,

Louis Frank Romansky Jr.

"Holy Spirit"

It is something that is felt and not seen.
As it makes a person feel humble and clean.
And it is a joy and wonderful to behold.
Gone are their sins, woes, worry and strife.
Now they have taken on a new outlook and lease on life.
The Holy Spirit makes a person feel all is just right.
Now the whole world shines so good and bright.
His fellow mankind feel his burden is ever so light.
As he felt the Holy Spirit, it opened his eyes to a wonderful sight.
Lowered his head in prayer, gave thanks to God and Christ.

Lawrence J. Crain

Untitled

March, the snow is falling, probably for the last time.
As I watch it fall, there are things that weigh heavy on my mind.
It slowly comes down, like the first time last fall.
For me the beauty is missing, it's not there at all.
The wind pushes it by, like time has our love.
It could melt away tomorrow, when the sun shines above.
What beauty it brought, the joy and the song.
With the dawn of the new day, it all could be gone.
As I stand here in silence, I watch it come down.
I look for a sign, I hope for a sound.
Will our love melt away, like the new fallen snow?
Is it gone for all time, does it have to be so?
The snow in the fall, will once more return.
Is it possible, once more, will our love fire burn?
Will we find what we had, together be happy once more?
Or does the future hold something, totally different in store?
As the seasons go by and the time turns us old.
Will I once more be standing, all alone in the snow?

Kevin Doyle

A Change

I can feel the river of hope
as it pours into my soul.
Healing it, stirring it, preparing it
for the days to come.

I can feel the rays of anticipation
as they rush into my mind.
Stimulating it, captivating it, tempting it
because there is a need.

I can feel the fingers of the future
reaching back to embrace my body.
Pulling it, assuring it, wrapping it
with the wind of change that is sure to come.

Patricia A. Thomas

The Sun

The heat touches my skin,
as it warms my body.
It shines upon my face,
as if a circle of joy.
Wonderful memories flow through my brain,
while my skeleton basks in its rays.
Reminders of puppies and children playing,
are cast along my mind.
Lovely portraits of beauty,
brighten the time.
Everything forgotten,
as if in a daze.
My eyes are drawn to its electric colors,
as I squint in amazement at its magnitude.
Every breath is warm,
shocking my cool insides.
I feel its arms around me,
holding for all time.
As darkness falls,
the cold returns.

Tiffany Cawley

Ode To Our Feathered Friend

I saw a bird fall; from its lofty height.
As it winged its way ore the snowy land.
To the roost they were hurrying on this wintery night.
Not one seemed to notice that it dropped out of sight.
There will be more room; on the roost tonight.
I saw a bird fall; this January night;
It fell from the sky on its homeward flight.
To a place on a roost it will yield tonight.
With dawn's early light they will wing again,
In search of food on this wintery land.
A neverending struggle in winter's grip.
In search of a seed or a helping hand.
They flit and flutter ore the snowy land.
Then return to the roost as the light slowly fades.
I; saw a bird fall.

Marlin K. Fertig

I'll Love You

I love you as much as poets love rhyme
As much as dancers love routine and fame
Love you as much as climbers love to climb
As much as children love to play a game

I'll love you 'til my last breath is taken
Until my senses cease to comprehend
I'll love you 'til my love is forsaken
Until my feelings feel signs of pretend

I'll love you 'til nothingness takes full charge
Till insignificance becomes your need
I'll love you 'til spats become fights of large
Till hurting me becomes your life way creed

I'll love you 'til I can no longer love
Till I can no longer love, I'll love you

Patricia Lamar-Neal

We Are Players

We are one
As one, we share the deepest truths
We do not ask for this, we just share
We live as we will never part
The hearts beat as one and we are in harmony

As one, we struggle through day and night
We do not want to end, we just struggle
We hide as we fight for togetherness
The hearts play a different drama

As one, we touch to break the loneliness
We do not want to admit, we just touch
We long for that single time of peace
The hearts begin to cry

We are two
As two, we do not share
We live as if we have never touched
The hearts long for forgiveness and pray for togetherness

Kelley D. Simpson

The Christmas Season

The Christmas season is once again here;
as our Families come from far away and near;
Celebrating with holiday cheer
may only cause families heartaches and tears.

We can celebrate with our loved ones looks;
as they open gifts filled with toys, clothes
and books.

As we hurry along the shopping crowd;
we hear all the people saying out loud;
"It's too expensive", "We can't afford it this year"
as the time of depression may bring us to tears.

Remember the meaning of caring and sharing;
It's the thought of the gift NOT the quantity
bearing;
The looks of the children as they open their gifts
and the words as you feel the arms and a kiss.

So as you decorate your trees and your yards;
as you wrap gifts and send out cards;
Remember the sparkle of each little eye;
and the birth of the Lord up in the sky...

Rhonda Allison

A Perfect Life

Rewind Me (Mother).
As the clear shell splits,
A life light takes over.
I knew it not as I dangled throughout the inner.
If only we could climb back (at times).
This, to know, we are the Genesis;
know no tripping grounds;
Only fresh beginnings, endless chances;
These would await us.
But God fits black holes into our puzzle.
Please accept this - Stand, Deliver.
Mother - cut the umbilical noose.
I am regenerated. (Thank you.)

Susan R. Goldman

Streetlight

In the gathering twilight
As the day comes to an end
It conceives as a tiny light
Small rays it begins to send

Growing bright during the night's progress
It reaches full radiance
At the height of darkness
Oh how glorious its luminance

Receding at dawn's first rays
Its light fades and is put to rest
By the bright sunshine of the new day
Remaining in darkness as the sun moves west

Dormant through daylight
Awaiting reincarnation at twilight

Mark K. Bechtel

Family Outing

The day was sunny, warm and cheery
As the family went sailing out on Lake Erie,
Father was tending the tiller with ease
While Mom tended sail with a smile if you please.

The children were all fishing over the side
As each was enjoying this bright Sunday ride,
When all of a sudden black storm clouds appeared
Without any warning a summer squall reared.

Its treacherous winds sent the little craft swaying
As each of its occupants started in praying,
They fought waves and winds with a feverish passion
But the poor little boat was taking a lashing.

The wail of the wind and the water so rough
Made all that they did not nearly enough,
So now, at the bottom of cold, calm Lake Erie
Lie a family of four, in a grave dark and dreary.

Remember now friends when boating for fun
Have enough life preservers for everyone,
In case there's a change in the weather that day,
You'll live to go boating again and to play.

Lois E. Sanderson

How Lucky I Am

An eery silence comes over everything
As the moon glares down from its perch among the stars
With it comes a feeling of sadness
At the world's selfish heart
I'm on the inside looking out
At those who reach for help
Help that they won't get
They are like trees in the wind
Ever reaching but never touching
Their dreams are my reality
My dreams unimaginable to them
They deserve a chance to be like me
A normal life with no needs
I feel their hunger
Hear their cries
The world wraps its cold blanket around them
Suffocating their cries of pain

Lee-Ann Van Biljon

"Mill Creek"

It always happens down at ole' Mill Creek,
as the night sets in...
and the wind starts to speak.
A doe stares down a beaming light,
the buzzard awaits for dinner tonight.
The speed of the glare,
hypnotic at glance...
the unaware victim
lost lives last chance.
The cries of the darkness,
swift through the air,
to the side lies the carcass...
and the buzzard sits near.
Man takes away a life in one great leap,
nature carries on
down at ole' Mill Creek.

Vickie R. Webb

November

She stood on the side
As they carried him into the cathedral
All surrounded in bronze and lying still
And followed by his family

She carried a bouquet of flowers
Like a bride's - but her veil was black
And her eyes were filled with tears
And the family didn't greet her

She walked alone, up the side aisle
And I knew who she was
And what she was to him
Because he was that to me

I sat on the other side, my bouquet on the pew beside me
And watched as the wife, in her long mink coat
Greeted the family, friends and guests
I was not among them

And neither was she -

Susan M. Terry

No Time

A grandchild is so precious you see
As to a Grandmother that's the way it should be
But always Busy and didn't have the Time
Always Pre-occupied with other things on her mind

One dark and Gloomy tragic day
Her five year old Grandchild was taken away
She said, oh no, it is I you should take
I've done my time I can not live with this heartache

Oh, but you must she was told
As you never had time for a five year old
There can be no Grandmother without a Grandchild you see
So now you are free, you have all the time you need

Regrets and sorrows are here to stay
If only she'd taken the time to laugh and to play
To love and to share and to enjoy one another
She wouldn't have all this lonely time as they would be together

Now the Grandchild has Gone
And so has the Time
So life must Go on
Without this Precious Grandchild of mine

Sarah Jane Flores

Come Play

Hand in hand, the carefree boy and I
Ascend the great green vines extended to freedom.
The clouds refreshing my face in sweet security.
My ears laden with wails of savage music.
And in my fists,
I clutch a myriad of stars.
Scattering them like seeds,
About, above, and beyond.
I concentrate far deeper then ever,
And magically I make things grow.
With a tiny flicker of golden light.
The boy vanishes into my playground.
Beseeching me to follow.
I run in circles, picking up speed.
Images whisking by bewildered eyes—
I spin faster and faster,
Gaining new energy,
Electricity galvanizing within.
I surge—until I too embrace my creation,
Leaving behind a trail of silver smoke.

Susan Wallerstein

Sonnet

Thoughts on sitting in a graveyard
at Fort Benning, Georgia, June 1941

The stone was marked: Emma C. Born 1860 died 1864

Those whose graves we desecrate this day
Tomorrow may nod at us and say:
"My son, I died when this was turned
"By sword and shot as hillside burned.
"For then, as now, was man's own blood
"Spilled in bitter fight — a flood
"Of torture on a peaceful land —
"Rancorous thoughts by battle fanned.

"I saw my child — my babe — my own —
"Die with hunger war had sown;
"I laid her fair head here to rest
"Upon this hill so Godly blessed.
"My son, you died to keep it free —
"I extend my hand to welcome thee!"

Vincent Lockhart

An Ode To Elks Past Exalted Rulers

For 365 days we stood
At the helm of our Lodge
As we said we would,
And sometimes offered a silent prayer
To Him who ultimately put us there,
For nerves to conquer butterflies,
And for knowledge to lead as problems arise.
We tried to rule with dignity and grace,
And to make our Lodge a better place
Because we served in this honorable chair,
And passed the torch to the next one there.
Each in turn with words sincere
Wishing the incoming a better year,
And when we finished our chosen task,
To know that we helped is all that we ask.

Royce H. Dorris

A Blanket Of Snow

I stood and looked out the window with awe
At the wonder of God and the beauty I saw.
The ground that was bare only moments ago
Was now completely covered with a blanket of snow.

The trees, the shrubbery, and the evergreen
Was now covered with snow,—what a beautiful scene.
The blanket of snow that covered the ground
Has a meaning for me I am thankful I found.

Only God could create beauty so rare,
A miracle sent by God to compare.
For just as he covered the ground with a blanket of snow,
By his shed blood my sins are covered, I know.

My heart is filled with grateful humility.
Because of his blood I have been set free.
And I am now clean and pure within;
For like the blanket of snow, Jesus covers my sin.

Willie Mae Hickman

An Old Folk Sport

Picking berries was an old folk sport
At which we always seemed to lose
When it was time to see who had picked the most.
And why, I really could not say;
For didn't we pick at the biggest bush,
And spotting bigger quickly go
To leave the old folk, for they were so slow,
To strip their mean bush from high to low.

Yet, when the sun had set,
And it was time to go,
And we all converged on the path to home;
Our quick glances at their full pail
Told us again that we did fail.

Robert Abrams

"Heaven's Infidelity"

The adulterous sky made love to the stars
atop night's black satin sheets,
cheating Earth out of creation's best kept secret,
peace: seductive like so many kisses
awakening lonely, dreaming lips
elusive like longed for moments that came,
not long ago, and longed for moments
that are yet to come.
Disturbed by the union of the stars and sky,
the angry sun arose and blazed.
The sky flamed scarlet as the jaded Earth
shook at innocence lost.
The mourning began as the wounded sky
left the Earth to hold the stars forever.
And from heaven's infidelity
peace: creation's best kept secret
was birthed.

Lisa LeJeune

"Still Memories"

Weathered and gray the old house still
Awaits in silence at the top of the hill
So many memories time can't erase
Are hidden forever within this place...

There in the stillness of the night
In the smoky haze of pale moonlight
Someone silently climbs the stair
And you glimpse a face in the shadows there

It's just old memories when no one's in sight
That walk dusty floors and weep at night
Weep's far a love that could not be
anything more than a memory...

As the moon hangs low atop the hill
A true love is weeping and waiting still.

Lola Rhea Stinson

The New Soldier

You're away from family, friends, and home
Away from everything you've ever known
With strangers that feel the same as you
Just as scared and homesick too.
And no matter how lonely you think you are
You are not alone I'm just a tiny bit far.
Just open your heart and think of me
It won't be just you, it will be we.
And if for some unknown reason I'm not there
You always have God, he will always care.
But as long as we never, ever lose touch
I will be there for you just as much.

Linda Ann Mennillo

The Beauty Of Life

The stillness of the woods, the creative surrounding.. Just in awe of it.
The real treasures in life are free.
Simplifying the beauty, but never taking it for granted.
Walking in the stillness and feeling the light as it radiates through the leaves of the trees.
Smelling the earth all around you.
Seeing God's creation, for He has given to thee, free for you and me
We take everything for granted, we ignore what pleasures we see
The water, feeling so cool and wet...glistening as it falls across my skin.
The mountains in all their strong grandeur..feeling the awesome
Power of their strength with sometimes taking my breath away
The beauty of it all is free
But do we take the time to really see, what's really there in front of you and me

Sandra Roman

Dachshunds

They prance with head erect
Baleful eyes searching to detect
A morsel of food, friend or foe

Long snouts and floppy ears
Sensing sound and scent in air
From both afar and near

Massive chest jutting like mountain rock
Wagging tail as if blown and held by the wind
Long bellies hovering over the ground
In all colors black and red and brown

Long haired, short haired, smooth or rough
The Kaiser's dog is more than enough
Loving to family, implacable foe
A Missy, a Gertrude, a Baby we know

Louis J. Tedeschi

We At War

All around the world we see
battlegrounds of racist pleas.

Today there starts another fight,
that ends tonight with no one right.

Each races strives to win their fight.
Based on visions of past frustrations.

The war rolls on with heightened tensions.
To find a path for better relations.

But, all along we fail to see,
there's just one race that we should seek!

That's the human race!
That's you!
That's me!

Timothy S. Kirchofer

Knowing

There grows a secret garden deep within your head
Be careful what you sow within this hidden bed.

Sow perennials of love deep within your heart
Knowing the roots of self-hate cannot be allowed to start.

Sow perennials of happiness deep within your soul
Knowing the weed of indifference can play a significant role.

Sow perennials of self-respect deep within your mind
Knowing the overgrowth of self-loathing can make it hard to find.

Sow perennials of self-esteem, nourish the tender sprout
Knowing the weed of insecurity produces blossoms of self-doubt.

Sow perennials of life and never question why
Knowing weeds are destructive while attractive to the eye.

Rosanne Holley

Submission

Be my poem
Be the blood
that seeps through veins
Be the thought,
shattering into oblivion
That passes through my mind
Be the eyes that see only you
To you, I am merely a grain in the sands of time
Endlessly flowing to nowhere
For you
I am set ablaze
All for naught
You are the knife that cuts
Mechanically
Intensely precise
My force, gliding past your body
Bathing you in sensual,
orgasmic,
lust.

Kevin Rothman

Christmas

May the Light of all you seek
Be the Light of the One born this night.
May the Gold of all you cherish
Be the Gold of the One who is born.
May the Myrrh of all you love
Be the Love within your heart.
May the Incense of all you revel
Be the Incense of all you imagine.

For God is your Light, your Peace, your Love;
And most definitely, your Dreams in all you do.

Remember, the Child is born this Christmas Season again
in your Hearts.
Remember, He gave His Life for all who would live in His name.
Remember His Love, for it will heal your life from discontent.
Remember His Patience, for it will bring Peace to your Soul.
Remember His Forgiveness, for it will bring claim to His
Kingdom.

Alleluiah! Alleluiah!
Christ is Born this day!

Patricia Bittman

Birds Of Envy

Birds of envy so soft and shy, you'll always be so lovely and beautiful to the human eye. It's with envy and in awe that we watch you fly, so high above us in God's spacious sky. With amazing grace and talent you do sore, over land, sea, and mountain more. You glide through the air with such elegance and ease, as though your admirers you are trying to please. This task you accomplish without any doubt, so their great admiration for you will never wear out.

As birds of a feather you gather and flock, in all the right places with your biological clock. You mate and you nest and your eggs you do lay, to assure on this earth birds of a feather will stay. Of all God's creations your above all the rest, as you look down on us, from up high where you nest. When birds become parents they care for their young. They feed and protect them until their growing is done. They teach them to fly and master the sky, so that some day they too, can be the object of man's envious eyes. And when their full grown their sent on their way, knowing they'll return by nature to mate some day.

All over the world birds of a feather in haste, will show off their talents with such beauty and grace. As for all God's creatures, the facts they must face, when it comes to man's envy, the birds take first place.

Nicholas P. Gelarderes

My Eight Second Birthday

I am eighty two, but I am not through
Because I desire affection,
I may be old, but I am not cold, no way
In that direction.
But I must say it's not every day I
Crave the great romancing "but on the change
Of the moon I long to spoon,

But there are no more chances so
I bury my head in the pillow
On my bed and in my dream go dancing

Kelsie Stewart Anderson

The Legend

In the beginning everybody was happy, so the legend goes
Because the love of male and female was contained in one soul

But then they sinned and the Gods made a decree
Every soul should be split in half for this wrongful deed

Since that time each of us is born only in one half
And we must wonder the world over down each rocky path

Searching for that other part with us to unite
So we can be one soul again and with the universe be right

But in order to be happy you must find that special part
That's really the other half of your body, soul and heart

Maybe there's something to this ancient myth of old
The reason for unhappiness we're matched with the wrong soul

So we go on searching for that mysterious missing link
Looking for that perfect part to make our life complete

Louise Walls

True Friends

True friends are great,
because they don't just come along everyday,
so, they're special to you in every way.

You do everything together,
your friendship lasts forever,
people can hardly tell you apart,
it feels like you've known each other from the start.

I'm writing this poem for one special friend,
who I know will be there 'till the end,
I hope she knows I'll be there for her,
occasionally fights will occur.

We're best friends like friends should be,
this special bond is shared between you and me,
let's stay friends for as long as we can,
from when we're dating boys,
to when we're dating men.

Regina Woiler

In Memory Of Beth

Loving someone is hard to do,
because when they have pain you feel it too.
My heart broke in half,
when you said you loved me but left.
The memories and the pictures I will always keep,
even though at times I'll weep.
I will always love you, deep down inside,
and I know from heaven my steps you'll guide.
But the memory will linger of the day
when you said you loved me, but then went away.

Kathryn M. Perry

Siren

I sit and waste my time with you once more,
While in my mind I know that I must run.
I am lost in your ocean, far from shore.

Whene'er I think of reaching for the door,
'Tis then your eyes find mine and they me stun.
I sit and waste my time with you once more.

Your words and movements touch me to my core,
As a blind man first seeing light of sun.
I am lost in your ocean, far from shore.

Long as I stay I know not what's in store.
Though in my heart I know not what's begun,
I sit and waste my time with you once more.

Release your grip on me I yet implore,
The duties that are mine I should not shun.
I am lost in your ocean, far from shore.

As once again the large hand nears the four,
And at my desk there is much left undone.
I sit and waste my time with you once more.
I am lost in your ocean, far from shore.

Robb Vanderstoel

Doug's Suicide

Did you find a god
Who'd fold you in his arms
And kiss you deep

Who'd hold you up
Like daddy did
To see the sea

Erica Kremenak

Your Kaleidoscope To Happiness

A kaleidoscope of colors, so beautiful and bright
Becomes more vivid with a strong ray of light.
For the "road to happiness" the light you will need.
You must control the focus and slow up the speed.
The array of colors are yours to behold.
When mixed with light, many combinations unfold.
The blues are so deep as sometimes in life.
But the red will prevail and over-ride strife.
The green is like grass and trees in the spring
Uplifting and soothing like the birds when they sing.
The yellow and orange bring brightness like gold.
Like treasures so rich, you grab and you hold.
Your kaleidoscope of life will change like the wind
And the mistakes of the past you soon will rescind.
Your rainbow of life will reach high to the sky
Where God will take hold and "bless you on high."
So your adjustment of colors will lead to "success."
And your kaleidoscope of life bring "happiness."

Louis E. Hough

Letter - 1935

Guess who I ran into the other day?
Been nigh six years since he went away.
Not a day went by that I didn't miss him so;
I've never liked anybody like I liked Old Bo.
Yeah, sure glad to see my friend, Bo Bob
And, from the looks of him, he's living high on the hog!

Something's bothered me bad since I saw him that day.
When he saw me he had nothing to say.
Then he said, I'll see you sometime - I'll let you know when,
And I knew right then I was no longer Bo's friend.

Bo got above his raising, that I'll allow,
Cause he was not the same as he is now.
He's up in the world, eating top grade.
He's in high cotton now - got it made in the shade.

I don't have any money - had none then,
But I'm the same inside as I ever been.
He hurt me fierce bad, Old Bo Bob,
But I'm glad he's living high on the hog.

Lexie Hill

"The Road"

As I look through the darkness, on the road that lay
before me. I wonder where the destination is,
or if I may fail, this yet I cannot see. I wonder
if there will be anyone along the way to share with,
or maybe all my feelings and fears, will once again
be shared by only me. I know there is a lot

more people along this road, in one way or another,
searching for a different kind of light.
But why is it every way I turn, there is no one in
sight? along this road there are a lot of storms a lot of
lighting and thunder. There is also holes in this road,
that will make you stop and wonder. This road isn't easy, it
was never meant to be, who makes it to the end,
we will have to wait and see. I don't want it
made easy. I don't want my road cut for me. Because
when I get to the end, I want to know I made it
honestly, and most of all, I made it through free.
I know this road may seem lonely, but you are never alone,
Have trust in someone higher than yourself, and the
Heavens will show you the way home.

Lonnie L. Hileman

The Visitor

He whispered to me calmly,
begging me to surrender to his dark embrace.
He held me tight.
And with strength of what strength is,
he took my breath away.
And with one last stare, my vision glared
And he said______
I am what patiently waits for you.
I am your peace.
I am your tranquility.
I am Death.

Takisha S. Reid

Gentle Wind

Oh gentle goddess-
Behold thy beauty of the forest

The birds the bees-
The deer that flees-

Winds that blow through leaves and trees-
Oh gentle wind
God prunes with sweet breathe

New life abounds-
Oh gentle wind

Robert E. Brown

To My Charming Lady

I wait for your love to return,
Being in love with you felt too good to be real.
To my charming lady,
I write this special poem.
With beauty like the sun is warm and steady
That freed my heart from stone,
When will you release me from my dreams
So we can fully enjoy the life feast.
I remember all the joys of that summer
When we were carefree lovers
Brilliant as lightning proceeding the rolling thunder.
If now you love another,
Then love's fire I must smother.
But I will regain your romance
So again in your charms I can dance.
I wait for your love to return
So the fire of my passion will burn.

Randy Perlis

Juden

Taken away by cruel, cruel men
Being whipped and beaten time and time again
Verbally and physically abused each day
Wishing for the day they could leave that place
Hoping for a time when there would be peace and grace
They stand by their God through and through
Wishing there was something he would do to save his people
Yet through the hard times they would not fight
Not knowing what the next day would hold when they went to bed at night
Suddenly they are awakened at about three or four
And taken outside to do a "chore"
And then in their prayers they would say,

"Oh, God help me, lead me away from this place!"
Then a man, an unknown man, would take them away
But not to freedom
To loneliness and everlasting silence
Never to awake.

Marti Hamblin

"A Sparrow"

Like a sparrow in the night, she stood
beside me just in sight, I looked in her
direction just to get her attention.

I spoke only a few words to see if I could
get a reply, she said little and did not say
good-bye. I offered a seat, she said sure, I
said why not, I don't bite. She sat down
and I offered more. For a while I was
quiet and she did not leave, this must be
it, it was hard to believe!

I started again with a few more words and
later a dance not knowing if I
would get the chance. Surprised by what
had happened, not knowing down
the road, maybe it's for the best.

As the weeks go by I stop to wonder
why I never thought that she would
give me a try. Just faith, I hope,
same day to see, maybe one day
she'll marry me!

Willie Russell Polite

Victims

Airports, 'scareports', expressionless faces, fatigue;
beware darting eyes 'neath berets and macs,
and footsteps persistently following tracks to
terrorize, amputate, quick as a flash for the bag,
the watch, or simply to bash.

A new breed of victim, lives in the city
blatantly daring the law of no pity,
waiting and watching for all those well-dressed or in
any way feeling or looking distressed.

A Business Alternative? Mission's in place with
knives..., guns..., syringes and mace.
Beware fair traveller as they are owed since
we have created our stylish modes.

"Your passport madame; why are you here?;
where are you going and where will you stay? You
carried a bag and travelled at night! How
silly! We're sorry, you'll have to pay!"

"Your Visa madame; stand in the queue! It's
raining we know but that's what you'll do!" That
lady, she's dead, she was waiting like me but,
once a victim a victim will be!

Yulie Allen

Time With You

When I look into your eyes
And when I watch what you do
You enjoy every thing that is new

When you look into my eyes
And you are watching me
What do you see

I want to tell you how I feel
To show you things I have seen
And anything in between

I hope you can learn how I feel
That you can see the mistakes I have made
And forgive me when I am afraid

Although I want you to know
I am proud of what I have done
And I love you my son

Mike Alex

An Angel For Amanda

Beyond the Secret Garden,
Beyond the fields and streams,
Stands a far-away Kingdom in Heaven,
Filled with magic, enchantment, and dreams.

And from this magical Kingdom,
Lives a tiny being so dear;
That in order to know of her precious ways,
You must forever hold her near.

One touch of this angel's sweet delicate wings,
With the hope of a time to be;
She'll wrap you in her protection...
She'll keep you safe when in need.

With love, kindness, and comfort;
She'll stay with you each day and night.
And as your tiny protector,
You'll always be in her sight.

And when you go through life's troubles;
Remember her angelic ways.
Keep happiness buried deep in your heart,
And long will be your days.

Katey J. Tibbetts

Happy Birthday...

Ever since our time began,
Birthdays came and went,
Lingering for that "one day only",
But they were "Heaven sent".

I'm sure you'll say, "I disagree",
and never chance the thought
But having been given all your years,
How can you say they're not??

Birthdays do have meaning
To many, or just a few,
But the real, true meaning of "Heaven Sent"
You'll find in your point of view.

Birthdays also have a purpose.
That's why God gives us one.
To do, or not what He'd have us do
Until our years are done.
To you with love, Happy Birthday
From us ....

Nellie B. Savage

You Want My Child?

You want my child?

But I remember naivete and dread as they accompanied me down the blood-red rose-petaled aisle, foreshadowing screeching tires, shrieking words, and blood-red wedding gown.

You want my child?

But I remember the lonely cavern—black hours gorged with car-door slamming starts that foreshadowed the drunken, slamming, savage, thrusting, that accompanied conception.

You want my child?

But I remember hours of labor, fearful tears, the ripping of my bowels and soul, accompanied by your "I can't stand this" departure, foreshadowing the past become future at the birth of "our" son.

You want my child?

But I finally remember—the past doesn't have to foreshadow the future, and red doesn't have to be blood, and I, myself, can stop the flooding blood of future pains—now—for me and my child.

Victoria E. Davis

Southern Winter Roses

Late this December, in a rose bed;
bloom bright red roses.
When most flowers are long dead;
roses, redder than frost nipped noses.
There are others, some creamy white;
some baby pink, edged in soft yellow.
One so delicate, like pale moonlight;
the other adorned in hues, so mellow.
There so late into the season;
beauty blooming beyond all reason!

Only here on our balmy Gulf Coast;
in earth warmed by the Gulf Stream.
Flora's splendor abounding, at its utmost;
roses soft and silky, akin to cream.
A fragrant and dazzling little reminder;
made up of blooms beyond their season.
Sights and smells become a spellbinder;
giving to each life more reason.
So enjoy each bud and flower;
all signs of God's love and power!

R. M. Rik Teed

To: Bob And Sherri

Love is not a candle,
Blowing in the wind..
Love is not a feeling,
You feel on a whim.

Love is like nature,
So pure and true...
Love is the feeling,
I have for you...
Love is not easy,
And love is not kind..
Love is an emotion,
And sometimes is blind.
What love is I cannot really tell...
But I know in my heart, in Bob and
Sherri's house, love will always dwell...

Rodney C. Winters

The Inanity Of Impetuous Life

A dreamed a dream, that died with age, placed its memory in a golden cage.
With it I put my careless youth, and not for a moment, realized the truth.

Immaturity at twenty...I gave it that name.
Thoughtless at thirty...was not the game.
Foolish fortys...and I never thought twice,
That loneliness, would be the dreaded price.

I thought my smile, would never lose its sparkling gleam.
I thought my hair, would never dull its youthful sheen.
I thought my figure, would never put on weight.
I thought...but I didn't think, and now it's too late.

You see: I could have caught that ring of gold,
But the carrousel music, grew suddenly old.
How vain I was, to think life's pace,
Would ever dare wrinkle my face.

But yesterday...yesterday, my mirror hadn't lied,
And in the cold of last night...my dream had died.
So today, I buried my golden cage...now aged with rust,
To lie alone...beneath the dreamless dust.

Sandra L. Armstrong

Lessons Of The Holy Vine

I, The Elder, stand upon the old wooden
bridge between life and death, to interpret
a message from the holy vine. My pen, the shadow
of my print. My body - The Puppet of my soul:
Consider elder poets a hindrance to contemporary
freedom. To shine, one must not seek that which
has already been consumed by the ones who have gone
before. Your consciousness rides the winds of change
while you dream of the past. But the river below only
moves forward! Above, soul dust sparkles in the deep
of twilight while the waning moon hides high in this
black monday.

I, The Universe, looking out upon myself, being
perceived as a mirroring reflection of this aged
mortal man upon this ancient bridge, slowly fades
away as the celestial northern lights guide me home
to the morning star.

Tim Earp Jr.

It's Wintertime, That's Plain To See

The fog creeps down through the Bull Pine trees, there's a
bright spot in the clouds where the sun ought to be
But it's wintertime, and that's plain to see,
and rain storms come relentlessly
The pine squirrel hasn't been here all this week, he
packed off the bird seed in his fat little cheeks
The font of water stands alone more these days,
migrating birds are reluctant to stay
But it's wintertime, and that's plain to see, as the
rain comes down relentlessly

I look for the blue-jays with their colorful hues.
But they have moved south 'till springtime's re-newed
The ducks are all gathering out on the bay, for
rainstorms don't chase them too far away
But it's wintertime, that's plain to see, and the
rain keeps falling relentlessly.

Rosemarie Peters Thompson

Reflections Of You

Thoughts of you linger in my mind,
bringing back the memories of time.
Times when you were near
and held me so dear.
I remember the passion of your love,
flurrying like snow flakes falling from above.
You were there and then you were gone,
leaving thoughts of you continuing on.
Sometimes I can hardly contain
within myself the thoughts that remain.
Thoughts of times we are together,
that seem to get better and better.
As I wait for your return,
my body, my heart, my soul, yearn,
for when, again, we
will reach love's true ecstasy.

Shirley A. Collins

The Mask

I smile on the outside,
but on the inside I frown constantly.
The outside is only a shell,
a mask of one's true feelings.
Things are hidden under covers
as my feelings are covered by my smile.

Leah Rebekah Egbert

Untitled

The sunshine blaring through my tightly locked window,
Brings sharp daggers of pain and distrust.
These points of hatred stab my soft, penetrable flesh,
Tingling and bleeding through my transparent soul.
Thoughts of the outside world corrode and rust my once new
and shiny iron wall,
Chipping away until it resembles swiss cheese,
Letting unpure particles of life pour through,
Into the small helpless cavities inside;
Disabling them, while tearing at the nerves,
Until all that's left is loose wires;
Unconnected and barely sparking.

Saundra Kuckie

Love Till It Hurts

She loves this man with all her heart
But all he can do is tear her apart
For almost two years it's all been the same
The games he would play
She always to blame

Crying herself to sleep she prays he will stop
The games, accusations, she's ready to drop
She's tried to leave him, again and again
Always going back when his promises begin

Honesty, loyalty is her way of life
He won't trust or believe her
Because of his ex life
She's paying for mistakes
She doesn't know about
Her love and understanding
Forces her to live without

How can you know when you love to much?
How can you know when it's time to give up?

Kristin Walker

A Champion

A champion is something I've never been
But always wanted to be
So when I finally became one
It was the greatest thing to me.

To see the crowd stand to cheer
And yell until they could no more
Gives you the greatest feeling
Because it's you they're cheering for.

You're overwhelmed with spirit
Yet overcome with tears
Because you're proud of you and your team
With what you've accomplished through the years.

In all that winning has taught me
Just one thing has meant the most by and by
You can always imagine being a champion
Yet you have to be one to ever even try.

Kelly Cartmel

The First Day Of School

A new year, a new slate
But for some reason today I hate
Too many tests for the coming year
Long nails on blackboards right in my ear!
Homework pile straight up to the sky
Ten paper airplanes fly to my eye
Well you see my face, I look like a fool!
Oh No ... It's the first day of school!!!

Sarah A. Manbeck

Love Found

Before you came into my life I saw the light;
but could not focus.
I knew love - but, could not nurture.
With you near there is no fear;
and in my heart I hold you dear.
Only he knows where this will go,
but life is short and friends are few,
I treasure what I found in you.
I am glad you came into my life.
Had I not taken that second look, I
might have missed true happiness.

Lisa Shah

Untitled

I loved to walk alone, seemed to help so.
But for all the emptiness surrounding me, I was not alone.
Crowded by mind, my thoughts, I could never be free.
This walk of mine, leading to nowhere,
Would come to an end as all things must.
But here, with the sky, wind and land, I was content.
Until the wind came again carrying
Old memories, each breeze saying remember, look back.
I looked and was sad, they go together.
I can never go back, can never return, and I wanted to.
I knew the past and not the future.
Scared, afraid of the uncertainty ahead, I wanted to walk further,
Stay forever in my memorial, but, I didn't belong.
It wasn't me but someone else being remembered.
I had changed, as only time can change you.
I was then glad of my past, for it had brought me here.
I continued my walk into the future.

Rebecca Press

Angel's Eyes

The beauty of this lady all see true to be
But for he not that which the eyes can see.
Kindness and caring from this angel she's cast
As notions of wonder falling into past.

Together they've found a friendship so rare
That with a bond they'll always share.
A lady so special only she can be
That so precious a blind man see.

Alone yet as one at night they would share
A dream to which they knew none compare.
Their eyes would speak silent words of affection
Those which need not be heard, for filled with passion.

So with this love on he she's graced
Felt by none other now he has placed,
In his heart the spot for a friend
To remain for her until the end.

Richard L. Greene II

I Think

The sound of the sun....
beating on the head of a
desert man, and so I think of you....
In this head of mine you will shine.
Like the sun, naturally, the only light natural.
You draw my attention
like an artist draws a picture
and affect me like the sun, a rose.
I think of you because
of you - there is no reason,
Love needs not one...

Tina L. Steeple

Ryan

All the rest laugh
but I see greatness in your imperfection
I see divinity in your limitations
I see in you a pure heart untouched
by a restless, unsympathetic, hurried,
misguided humanity.
I see in you the human soul at its pinnacle
loving unashamedly
giving unselfishly
accepting unconditionally.
they laugh
but in your weakness lies
the ultimate truth of this world...
that all any of us need to know is love.

Tarsha Davis

A Daughter's Love For Her Mother

Sometimes my mother yells at me,
But I still love her.
I try to be a good girl for her,
But sometimes it is hard.
I still love her.
My mother is sick with some kind of illness.

But she will not tell me what it is.
But I love her.
Some days it is hard, she can hardly get
out bed to help me get ready for school.
But I still love her.

I hope one day they will
find a medicine to help her
because I want her to be
around for a long time.
So I can always love my mother.

Sade Shiniqiua Shaw

I Am A Woman

I am a woman, soft to the touch,
But in the morning I don't do much,
I sit in my kitchen and drink coffee; cup after cup,
Just thinking what to do when my sitting time is up.

My husband has gone to work lunch pail and all,
Then I think to myself who can I call.
I call a friend and we talk for awhile,
The housework can wait; my fingernails I'll file.

Oh, dear; it's almost noon,
My husband will be home soon.
In the morning my home is an eyesore,
Make the bed, dust, wash dishes and the floor.

Now it's my time to prim and please,
For dinner I'll have a salad and macaroni and cheese.
I am a woman soft to the touch,
When my husband comes home I say, "I miss you much."

My time is spent the same day after day,
Until I have a child and toys in the way.
To have a happy healthy child at play.
That's what I pray for someday.

Katherine L. Czerwinski

Of Laws, Lawyers And...Such!

Fortunately, we live in a Land with...lots of laws,
but it's real sad that most of them have...so many flaws.
Like the one that says...y'can't "spit" in the street,
and another where y'can "plea-bargain"...for only a token sentence to complete!

Oh yes, in this great country of ours...you may own a gun,
that's supposed to make the "bad guys"...take note and run.
But y'may have to wait at least...five days,
before you can legally "shoot" anyone...who preys!

You can murder or rape or even your spouse...assail,
and within hours a good lawyer...will have you out on bail.
These are examples of what our laws can or...cannot do,
does it sound like they're written to protect...me and you?

We've spent millions and millions on trying...to change,
some of the laws we good citizens think...strange,
but all of our great minds haven't improved on the laws handed down... on the mount,
amazing thing is there are only Ten..by actual count!

I'll bet if every Lawyer...right from the start,
had to learn to recite the Ten Commandments purely...by heart,
those Laws given to us by The Lord...Blessed be he
would help the whole world live in...Perfect Harmony!!!

Nathan Jurist

Untitled

I don't know why we had to part
But it's tearing me up inside
It feels like I'm missing a piece of my heart
And all I want to do is hide.

The joy I felt when I first met you
Was something I couldn't explain
You made everything shine that was blue
And took away all the rain.

There was a special love between you and me
That no one could take away.
The confidence, support, encouragement, and unity
Was with me day after day.

And now all I do is yearn
For how you made me feel
And in the meantime try to learn
That what is happening is real

I know now that we have changed
And our paths no longer cross
And so I have to rearrange
This love that I have lost.

Kimberly Buxbaum

Sometimes In Life

Somethings are happy. Somethings are sad.
But sometimes they all mix together.

Somethings are scary. Somethings are exciting.
But sometimes they all mix together.

Somethings are shocking. Somethings are bad.
But sometimes they all mix together.

Somethings are nice. Somethings are different.
But sometimes they all mix together.

Somethings are interesting. Somethings are doubtful.
But sometimes they all mix together.

Somethings are troubling. Somethings are funny.
But sometimes they all mix together.

And everyone has these feelings sometimes in life.

Kathryn L. Broderick

The Mind Healer

Like a grounded, crippled bird that cannot fly
But knows it is its nature or it must die.
With mangled mind and wounded heart
We too, can not survive this worldly part.

From all relationships the enemy must hide
For all the shame and guilt, the illness must be denied.
Laughter and crying cannot be heard or shared;
Up or down - the monster has not cared.

But halt! the fear, the hopelessness must wait
The healer was found who understands my fate.
This hope—hope of the peace, even my destination
Depends upon his listening, gentle advice and inspiration.

Still he probes, cajoles, and tells it like it is;
Becomes the father, mother, lover; the gifts that are his.
Clinging to him, as thirst to the wine
Till the healing has grown and in control of the mind.

So sad, many crippled birds will never
find the healer;
They will not fly, nor will their song be heard,
no - not ever....

Ruth Ann Vitko

Objectives

By greater minds let great issues be solved
But, let me have purpose, let me be involved
If I must deteriorate in life's design
let it be in my body and not in my mind
What I see in others let me see in myself
Let me understand how and where I can help
Let me have social conscience and be politically aware
Let me recognize injustice. Let me be fair
Let me live by the motto "To thine own self be true"
Let me be open to different points of view
Let me treat others as I would have them treat me
Let me have pride tempered with humility
and finally, let me look always ahead
and don't let me die before I am dead

Ruth Olefsky

"Broken Dreams"

Love should be as pretty as the stars in the sky,
but love is mostly heartless and full of lies.
Love isn't today what it should be,
I guess now I know love's not for me.
Love should be a dedication to the heart and soul that's true.
Not a game that is so painful and will make you hurt and blue.
It should be of two souls becoming one,
a promise that should not be broken.
True love is what I thought I found,
but it was one-sided and in this love is where I now drown.

Sharlene Rigsby

The Fog

When the fog drifts from the east, the sun rises with it,
but the fog will soon lift to begin a lifeful day, full of
wonder, colors that are deep, into the forest where no one
has ever gone before, except me, when I am alone I often
wander there, where no one will bother me. I can see the
reflection of the life I have led and watch as the colors
fade and blanch into shadows and nothingness, where no one
will find the hidden truths of the life led, where greens
and purples are painted into the waters, like the sun's
rays - spread across the prairies onto, until and upon
death, and the sun sets to the west, ending with no trace
of existence of the fog that began it all.

Leigh A. Troha

Increments Of Dust

It is beyond my understanding to pen of Gods and Kings,
But of fools and men, I have even less a mind
The magic, the mythic, the mystifying
All embracing, all denying
Scrivener, talker, hacker
The poets knell
Send to heaven, damn to hell
The words, the words, the sirens call
Enticing, alluring, the seductive fall
Follow me:
Hearts need not quail
Follow me:
'Tis the Holy Grail
The truth, the truth, the Siren Song
Ah! The dreams we weaved from that fatal tree
Far more grim than harsh reality
And I poor relic of ancient myth
Now place my bricks with the nameless rabble
A journey man worker, on the tower of babble

Wesley Wood

My Knock

Once I was looking for the perfect partner to share life,
but one thing
I did not know was that you were by my side the whole time
I was always looking in unhealthy places love never dared to enter
Then one day when I had given up on everything,
at the lowest time in my life
You knocked on the door of my heart, and I invited you in
I never knew I could feel such contentment without trying
But you accepted me for who I am, there is so much joy and excitement
In my every word and action that I've never felt before
One day I turned to you and asked "why me?"
With all my problems and imperfections how
could you love me so unconditionally
That is when you said to me, my child you need not be
perfect to have my love
For my love is perfect and ever so true it was a gift I gave to you
You see my child I died on the cross to save you
And so you could have eternal life with me in my kingdom
One last thing I have always been walking side by side with you
And constantly knocking on your door,
but you never heard my knock before.

Nicole T. Treuil

Married To The Corps

She may not wear the uniform
But she stands proud and tall
Saying good-bye to the one she loves
A lonely teardrop falls
She knows her husband's doing
What life had borne him for
And hers was to be waiting
forever on the shore
Holding onto dreams and photographs
Yellow Ribbons, and her heart
War is not the only cause that keeps two loves apart
In peace-time too, she knows the call
Of duty soon will come
And she must say good-bye again
'Fore the rising of the sun
Her heart both breaks
And beats with pride
As he walks out the door
And time drags on 'till he comes home
When you're married to the corps

C. C. Hockett

The Source

I'm hurting so bad does anyone care?
But the voices that come back to me only fill me with fear.
"Quit sniffling", they say—"have a stiff upper lip"—-
"Look where you're going then you won't trip".

But is there any comfort, a word or a hug to help me along on
this path that I trudge? "Are you kidding," they say,
"We have no time for you, we must rush on and do what we do."

Oh please, please help me! This pain I can't bear.
It gnaws at my soul and can only be eased by someone who cares.

"Quit feeling sorry for yourself"—"you have no worth".
We want music and fun, money and mirth."

Then up ahead a cross roads I see.
A path must be chosen. Which will it be?
I can choose the one that thinks only of me always taking—
Never giving and end up like the Dead Sea.

The other path a less popular choice is to give
tirelessly to others and make little noise.
But what stills the inner pain you ask of me?
The source is the MASTER by becoming such as HE.

Sonia Oltmanns

"The Two Sides Of Me"

At times I'm as cool as the breeze from the seas,
but then I "wax hot," one trillion degrees;"
At times I love people both the young and the old,
but then I lose "faith," and my heart "wax cold;"

Whenever I'm sober, I'm very sincere,
yet very deceitful, when influenced by beer;
Whenever I'm not "high," I'm a "model of peace,"
yet when I'm on "crack," I attract the police;

Someday's I'm peaceful and very constructive,
other days I'm violent, extremely disruptive;
Someday's I socialize with every stranger I meet,
other days that I see them, I want even speak

One side of me seeks, "Salvation's Key,"
One side of me sins, "Perpetually,"

Which of "The Two Sides of Me" shall I free?

Paul Turnipseed

The Duke City

I've been to all those other towns and have seen their claims to fame.
But there is no place like Albuquerque, right down to her name.
So sing the praises of Chicago and leave your hearts there by the bay.
'Cause they'll never rival Albuquerque, and I just want to say.

The sun is shining on the mesa, the colors paint my eyes,
Like wide bands of ribbons they troll across the skies.
And, somewhere in the distance, I can hear the drums of old.
They are pounding out the rhythm of the Indians strong and bold.

The steady beat is echoing above the Rio Grande.
As shadows from the distant past stroll across the sand.
I feel the music shifting to take a spanish beat.
And, I'm sure I see a moor dancing in the street.

The Duke City is the finest place to ever grace the earth,
And those who've known her beauty will never leave her turf.
The Indian and the Spanish, the Irish and the Jew.
The Black man and the Asian all bow their heads to you.

Oh, Albuquerque, my Duke City, my golden desert gem,
God, how I yearned for you 'til I came home again.
And when I look into the heavens and see and angel's face.
I know I'm standing at the summit of God's enchanted place.

Margaret W. King

Someone New

The pain of what I lost, I still feel.
But there's someone new, who's helping me heal.
In a way, he kind of reminds me of you.
But this is not why my love for him is true.
He was there for me, though he knew about you,
but unlike you, he loved me too.
I must admit that I always knew
that it would be us when you and I were through.
This isn't to say I loved you not-
it seems to me that I just forgot.
You had come along, and brightened my day,
and I put him aside (in my own little way).
Yet he was still there when you were done with me.
He helped me live, he helped me see.
My pain from you is finally leaving,
because his love has so much meaning.
I wanted you to know what happened to me.
The love I had for you shall always be.
But he's here now, loving me, and helping me through
the pain I felt over losing you.

Shanna Christine Foley

The Difference

Our schools were never perfect,
But they shared a common thread,
They started their day with Scripture,
Before a book was read.

Now compulsory education,
Is the order of the day,
God isn't welcome on campus,
And the law forbids us to pray.

From republic to democracy,
From wisdom to consensus,
We've enshrined our institutions,
And left our kids defenseless.

If public schools are Godless,
It's better to shut them down,
Or leaders will train at private schools,
While public ones send us clowns.

Those for secular schools,
Speak of the lives they bless,
But America's Godless schools,
Hide the standards of greatness.

Tony Simpson

The-Stay-At-Home

"I'll tour the world," she'd blithely told the others
But they, with scorn, said they'd no wish to roam.
We'll take our chances here as did our mothers.
You go your alien ways. We'll stay at home.

But time and circumstance defied their notions
And scattered them in lands which they deplored.
Their letters came cross perilous seas and oceans
With longings for the hearth side they adored.

While she, who always longed for far-off places
Remained at home and made a sheltering nest
That they, when freed at last from widespread spaces
Might there return and find content and rest.

Vivian Lovelady

"Nothing Lasts Forever"

I thought you'd be the one I'd love forever,
But things change and mysteries remain.

And now I sit and wonder as I cry everyday,
Knowing your the one that I let slip away.

You always took the time to show your love for me,
And I tried to return it but you had to set me free.

When we're together, my life feels complete,
The memories we've shared is all that I can keep.

I've never been one for playing games,
I can move my mouth forever but the words sound the same,
When I look into your eyes,
I can feel a love restrained.

When you look into mine, don't you feel it the same?
Nothing lasts forever and we both know hearts can change,
I've never been through this before and I'm just trying
To ease the pain.

Nikki Garcia

Iron Role Model

People look and see Orioles shortstop, number eight
But to me that is only part of why you are great

Some flashier players people watch and grovel
But to me they are short stories, you're a novel

When it comes to jewelry some simply don't refrain
For you something simpler, a single gold chain

Many players are seen making the spectacular play
But you make all plays day after day

Lots of players are faster, you would swear they flew
Though none make better base running decisions than you

In bad times some critics say a day off should be the way
But why shouldn't a manager play his best shortstop each day?

I could continue with many reasons
Why fans in Baltimore look to the baseball season

With your humility this would be the last thing you would want
to hear or see
But I'll tell you why it's so important to me

Among your attributes are determination, dependability, hard
work and style
These help me most, as an example to my boys Kody and Kyle

Thomas Hines Jr.

A Day Of Vacation

I took a day of vacation to get the carpet cleaned,
But when I saw that the spots had remained, I only screamed.
The Chinese carpet cleaner said that I did not have to pay,
But I gave him $44 and sent him on his way.

Now I sit as depressed as a year ago today,
Over these damnable spots, that won't go away.
There are black ones and red ones, and yellow ones too,
And even of other colors there are quite a few.

I should not be so materialistic you will probably say,
Just pretend to be intellectual, and look the other way.
Yes, you are probably right, it was good advice,
One should never look down at colorful spots more than twice.

I swam in the pool till my mind was at rest,
And then showered leisurely, and got slowly dressed.
I drove to the Knightsbridge Theater for the first time,
And before the performance, at the French cafe I did dine.

Rita Wennerstrom

On Someone's Birthday!

This day I say Happy Birthday to you
But yearns to say something more to you

I owe you the color that you have lend to my life
The fragrance, the poise which fill my days.

I wish you happiness in the days to come
Joy would embrace you and success would come

I wish that world would be kind to you
And kind enough to let me stay with you.

I wish not to say the unsaid words
The unrevealed feelings the hidden thought.

But if you ever ask I would say
You are my reflection, my solace, my dream
You are my sky with its stars and its gleam

You are my sorrow, my disappointment my hope
The ever flowing stream that would never stop.

Roohi Abubaker

Sad Spring

Spring is here
But you are not here to welcome it
The trees are bursting their buds
Gay, yellow daffodils everywhere
And the tulips
The stately colorful tulips
That you loved so last spring
They are here again
But you are not here
The world is blossoming
Life is bursting forth
Warmth and sunshine are slowly defrosting
This bitter land
But you are not here to witness it
You are not here to love the tulips
And so I take no joy in the spring
Last spring you were here
But this spring you are gone
And my heart grieves

Sylvia Levy

"Expressions Of Love"

The moon is romantic or so it is said
by poets in poems of roses so red,
by heavenly bodies, the stars up above,
by a laurel leaf in the bill of a dove.
Such is love?
Yes, but it's the light from God's Son
whom we hung on the cross.
He bore our sins lest we be lost.
He did this by the Father in Heaven above.
He did this unselfishly
as an Expression of Love

Steven Paul Gregg

Ruby Red

Ruby Red went to see her Uncle Jed,
But Uncle Jed was already dead.
Some one put a bullet in his heart, made of lead;
They also had shot him in the head.
Ruby didn't worry, she got herself fed-
With nothing else to do, Ruby went to bed.
Next day, she found footprints, here Uncle Jed had bled;
She followed them to the home of Friendly Fred.
And with her gun, she shot Fred quite, quite dead.

Robert J. Vuyick

Ah! The Mystery of Colour

Life is marked
by stained hues of imperfection.
Worth green emotions, eager,
pulling in every direction.

Enraged. Red, searching
for a distant angry fix.
Orange! Radiant energy,
intense and unyielding mix.

Pursing skies
of healing deep blue, totally exposed.
Rigid limits,
complimenting colours rare, shades oppose.

Lies masquerade
as gallant white tie affairs.
Black? Frequently,
the stronger of the pair.

Granting silver lining
with gifts of gold to bestow.
I question,
will my rainbow colours fade, then blend and glow?

Terri Vidal

Be Careful What You Say ....

(... You Don't Know Who's Listening)

So many people have been hurt,
by the words of others.
Now our trust is gone,
and we've turned against each other.
Why are people so cruel?
Saying things that aren't true.
Playing others as their fool.
You shouldn't tell a lie,
I heard my mother cry.
Lies bring pain and sorrow.
You should tell a lie.
Why do people spread gossip?
Says the minister to the choir.
Are they mightier or higher?
Why do people spread gossip?
Families separated by hurt feelings,
fights separated by hurt feelings,
fights caused by misleadings.
What is this pain we're feeling?
When can we start heeling?

Nichole Lee Hill

Family

The love that started with only a slight flutter
By virtue of trust, respect, children and such
Has grown to a roar of love known to only one other
The husband or wife meant for one another.

The children arrive and grow with love and contentment
Until the time arrives for independence to soar
You let them loose so they may grow
Hopefully they continue to want more
of the mom and dad who love them unending
And more important, as we grow older,
We will have their understanding and love.

Ruth Kassin

"My Beloved"

Like sands in the hourglass
Calibrated in the fullness of timelessness
Moving and thriving upon the circuits of pure innocence
Lucid, but uniquely identifiable by two hearts
Of the Ethiopian purebreds:

Drawn by the chords of your love
I will run after thee with the oils of gladness
From the fountains of dayspring to perpetual ending
Highly and brilliantly refined, our love...
Shut up in my bones

Sweet as fresh fruit dripping from the tips of its stem
In season... let thy left hand be under my head
And thy right hand embrace me
For thy lips are like threads of scarlet
And thy temples like pomegranates

Spices of sentiment and the mellow odours of sacred intimacy
Awaken like unto fresh honeysuckles carried by the breeze
Through the flutter of hummingbirds wings
And with the sweat of compassion and comfort
Come! lie down in my bosom and take thy rest, My Branch,
My Beloved!

Roslyn Pasley

The Autumn Of Our Love

The Autumn of our Love
Came when we scarce thought it would,
As our gazes fixed stood
Upon the leaves of our souls as they fell from the
Branches of heartache...

The Autumn of our love
Came kicking on the heels of summer
When we were far dumber
Than the silence of our tears as they broke from the
Boughs of disillusionment...

The Autumn of our love
Left us Unshaded, naked and numb
The way indian summer comes...
Much too late for summer,
Far too early for spring...

Wm. L. Dubnov

Eyes

Can't you see it?
Can you feel it?
There's a strong emotion beating in the air
The pulse is so deafening
Can you not hear it?

A compassion of everlasting warmth
Something that will surpass even the ends of time.
Nothing can knock it down or stop its never ending path.
To you, my friendship is eternal and will not ever fail.
No matter how low you feel, you'll still be higher than me.
The pedestal on which you stand cannot be knocked down.
You'll have eternal flight and support.
Through all your storm and rainbow filled days,
I'll be there to shelter or release you.
What you wish you shall have.
I will only push you forward and never hold you back.

Can't you see?
Can you now feel?
A heart and mind with nothing but support and love.

Lyndi Morris

"A Heart Full Of Pain"

If you could feel what I'm feeling and see what I see.
Can you hear what I'm hearing in a memory?
Keep on Dreaming, I don't know what to do,
Keep on believing, I'm still in love with you.
But you're far, far away and there's nothing left to say.
I can't get over you, I'm still in love with you.
I can't get over you, I'm still in love with you.
Oh, I hate being lonely when nobody's there.
Losing everything is like nobody cares.
But when I think of you a cloudy sky turns blue.
I can't get over you, I'm still in love with you.
I can't get over you, I'm still in love with you.
I'll love you today and I'll love you tomorrow.
A heart full of pain, brings only sorrow.
But until the day I die, would only make me cry.
I can't get over you, I'm still in love with you
I can't get over you, I'm still in love with you

Paul Villarreal

Oneness

The rhythms of my soul cry out to you.
Can you not feel the feelings I do?
My heartbeat clears, the fog of my mind.
I see clearly, were two of a kind.
Fingers caress my face and touch,
the soul of my existence, I love you so much.
Your love each day brings a rebirth of oneness within.

Conflicts drown, in a sea of desire, a new day begins.
The rhythms of my soul cries out to you.
I know you feel the feelings that I do.

Margie De Lisse

Untitled

I've cried my last tears for you.
Can't believe you lied.
Deceived me of the truth, hid it oh so well.
Now you're gone and how can
Something so true be so faux.
I thought we had forever,
But we didn't, we had an
ending from the start.

Melynda Heinsch

The Shell

I'm still here.
Can't you see me?
I'm exactly the same person that I always was.
Only this shell I live inside has changed.
The legs are slow,
But my mind is still quick.
The fingers have lost feeling,
But my heart still feels love
As passionately as ever.
Senses have dulled,
But sensitivity has not.
This shell has changed,
Has slowed,
But take the time
To look closely.
Inside, where the real me is,
I haven't changed.
I'm still here,
Inside.
Can't you see me?

Roberta Anderson Davis

"Anna's Eyes"

It wouldn't take much to love her, ya know she's got that style
Captured my heart the first time, I saw her smile
I'm no hand at love, but I know I've gotta try
My first glimpse of Heaven, was the sparkle in Anna's eyes

The sparkle in Anna's eyes taught me to see
The beauty all around, that before I couldn't see
I'd lived my life in darkness, but she showed me the light
I'd gladly spend forever just looking in Anna's eyes

Ever since I met her, she's been on my mind
And when I close my eyes and dream, I hold her hand in mine
I don't know if dreams come true, but if mine ever can
Ya know I'd walk eternity holding Anna's hand

The love in Anna's eyes taught my heart to sing
Healed up old wounds and taught me how to dream
I don't know much of love and I may never earn the right
But I'd give anything in life, to look in Anna's eyes

Just looking in Anna's eyes may seem a simple thing
But the things in life worth having, they don't cost you anything
And if I could spend my time any way I like
I'd gladly spend it all, just looking in Anna's eyes

Steve W. Goldcamp

The Cross

Many years I've traveled the pathway of life....
Carrying the burden of troubles and strife....

The stepping stones were mountains - that I crossed..
I became so discouraged - I became lost....

I was so tired - my body so, so weary....
My outlook not bright - just dark and dreary...

I had no strength or courage - nor could I feel....
I lost my desire for life - my desire to live.

I can't go on - I just can't take anymore....
But somewhere in my heart was an open door.

I needed someone to love me - someone to care....
I cried, please Lord, help me carry this cross I bear.

Now just a kind word or a smiling face....
Will always remind me of our Savior's grace.

My life is not perfect - it never will be....
I'm just a sinner - but He loves me!!!

Sue Cofield

Apart—A Part

Apart— I joy to run to your embrace and
catch a glimpse of your hazel
eyes that dance with laughter
grow blurred in passion and
search for white light

Apart— I yearn to kiss your soft, smooth
lips and slowly outline them
with my fingertips as I inhale your
breath returning relentlessly to greet
your lips again and again

Apart— I seek to stroke your strong yet
supple hand and place it
carefully on my face that I
may feel the warmth seep
through me as it draws me to
submission

A part of you flows within my stream
A part of me sails your adventurous seas

Streams flow to the sea
A part... not apart

LaNetta Hammill

Moooooving On

Cows in the meadow
chew and chew and chew and chew and chew
the same bit of grass
over and over and over and over again.

And so do I.
Same stuff, same taste.

How about something other than dry yellow grass?
How about chocolate, pomegranates, a salt bagel?

Don't just stand still in the pasture,
on all fours,
head bent to the ground.

Find a hill,
roll up, roll down,
run, skip, laugh.

Meet some other cows from another field.
Jump the fence, if necessary.

Moooooooooooooo
Mooooooooove
Mooove
Come On ... MOVE!

Philip Decker

Blank Pages

Crisp
Clean
White
Spotless
Stiff
The pages look back at me
Waiting to be filled
With tales of the absurd, the silly, the serious, the sad
and the inspiring
Nothing inspires
Gloom pervades
Maybe if the pages were black I could think of something to write

ENDURE

The word looks lonely on the page
waiting for others to give it meaning

SANCTUARY

A time looking for a place
In a world overcrowded
with words

Marisa N. Pickar

The Hawk And The Dove

There once was a woman who entered my life
Clean as a whistle, yet sharp as a knife
She taught me to love, through pain and through joy
To her I'll always be her innocent boy
Whenever I was sick, she would rush to my side
Whenever I succeeded, her eyes filled with pride
There once was a man who entered my life
In love and in passion, the Dove is his wife
Through the stages of life, he served as a guide
A constant companion down a long, bumpy ride
To me he taught patience and the meaning of laughter
The hours and minutes seemed to move faster and faster
Now that I'm a young man, beginning my life
I realize the importance of their caring and strife
These two shining people, the Hawk and the Dove
Always willing to give
Always willing to love
For me they were there, when most wouldn't bother
I call these two people my Mother and Father

Paul Brouch

Winter Coat

Green and growing, never slowing,
climbing the red brick wall.
Man below is cutting, mowing, steady going,
but never sees that tall.

The ivy flowing, just keeps growing,
never stops at all.
Higher up its tail it's towing,
Coat of green 'til red's not showing,
at all.

No more can you see a red brick wall,
As the coat of Winter covers it all.

Scott H. Kranzley

"Mournful Cleansing Of My Grief"

My memories are like cobwebs
clinging to the corners of my mind.
I'm reminiscent of a happier time
before your soul left us all behind.

A painful and lonely era began
the day your soul walked away,
Ending the epilogue of our life together
and revising our final chapter on that fateful day.

My loved ones tell me I must dust off
those old cobwebs and start my life anew,
Yet I feel as long as they remain
I shall always have a little part of you.

Death always feels so final
as do the goodbyes which I have bade,
I can't help but feel guilty yet also peaceful
as I watch your disembodied spirit slowly fade.

For I realize now that not even death
can separate two souls which are bound together,
And on the day that I enter heaven's door
I know our two souls will be reunited forever.

Sarah M. LeVan

Winter's Near!

Whistling wind and dancing trees,
Coattail swirling at my knees;
"Winter's near!" The little birds call.
Leaves faint and start to fall.
Grass gets scared; its growth is stunted,
But icy winds blow on undaunted,
Sneaking through my cozy clothes,
Pinching my ears and tweaking my nose.

Kimberly D. Carter Jones

Untitled

Mmmm, the smell of salty sea air
Colorful kites with plenty of flair
Waves crashing upon the shore
To be at the beach is what I'm longing for.

Sand squishing between my toes
And clinging desperately to my clothes
The cry of the gulls overhead
Searching and seeking a free taste of bread.

Surfers gliding atop the sea
Children building castles upon bent knee
Sails engulfed as pillows of breeze
I wish all my days could be like these.

Hear the mighty call of the ocean
Sunbathers basting with oils, creams and lotions
Fisherman casting with the greatest of ease
I wish all my days could be like these.

Kelly Jo Driggins

The Rose

Love is like the rose is... with beauty and with thorn
Comforting in sorrow...and celebrating joy
Still love is like the bud is...when waiting patiently
For one to come and care for it...so it can grow and be
The Rose
With petals made of velvet...and color deep as wine
When dew drops fall in morning...I think of you and cry
Had I not held so tightly...I never would have crushed
The blossom full of life...which symbolizes love
My mind sometimes does wander...to thoughts of you and I
And I can't help but worry...and pray that love won't die
If you really love me...we can laugh and play together
Come hard times, sunshine...or stormy weather
And you'll try to handle questions...that in my mind arise
Knowing I just like the bud...need love in order to survive.

Mary C. Halfacre

Little Girl

A wooden figure hangs dormant on a string
completely motionless in an ocean of white sound.
Fear, the solitary driver, can make the figure sing
a hollow melody of monotones, of emptiness profound.

Gray nights full of unrest, gray days and days
void of prediction except the tremor in a hand
Pills imply a false calm to soothe a lurking malaise
but a knock on the door of reality allows one to understand.

A soul out wandering in this misty land of valleys with no peaks
asks only for a future ticket through an unknown door.
As if blind, hands outreached to search and seek
The safe way home, no more.

That wooden figure, silent until fear is paid
is my small self, unprepared for this test.
Don't cry little girl, your path has been laid
by a loving parent, who will guard you in your rest.

Take solace from the trust you've bestowed upon me
to protect and provide for you.
My precious child, you're safe from the monsters we see
for you live among flowers and sunshine on morning dew.

—J. Lizabeth Gaylord

The Uncommon Bridge

This bridge is a bridge that couples the two,
Connecting something besides an expanse between soil or dirt.
Not made of fabricated material to conclude,
Intangibility limits its design to damage or flirt!

This bridge continually hauls the freight,
From one-side to another without a brake or break.
Purposefully it must sustain the stress and weight,
Returning again and again to the receiver and senders' way.

Many lack the skill to claim this bridge for use,
But it sports wisdom, knowledge and love.
Others are genius at manipulating it to abuse,
So it is two-way and frolics races to grudge.

This bridge has bridges barrier,
At times it is closed.
Openness is important to the carrier,
Shut-down it brings on sorrow and woes.

It is not the bridge of iron, steel or wood,
It is the bridge of speech!
How dare we neglect the bridge of communication,
It's the mechanism to convey our message to those we seek.

Kenneth W. Mantooth

Shattered Illusions

Hatred
Consuming all that I am

Blackness and decay
Eating away at my innocence, naivete, and love
That used to be me.

My soul is scarred and burned
By the betrayal of those I've trusted.

In times of sadness and despair,
In my need to believe,
I turn to trust another.

Only to have them slither away
Just like all the others
Behind a mask of friendship and love.

Tammie L. Van Kampen

Power Paradox

The hungry baby's midnight cry,
Contentment in a lover's sigh,
A sick man's whispered death-bed prayer,
Mom's all-knowing ice-cold glare—

The shrill ring of phone in the middle of night,
A child's fine achievement that causes delight,
The artistic statement of image withheld,
A quiet understanding that time will not quell—

Words unsaid from stubborn pride,
Beauty of daughters in their fathers' eyes,
The peace wrought by Nature when life closes in,
God's comforting Promise: Salvation from sin —-

From dawn of time till time's no more,
For such power, nations war.

Linda J. Williams

My Prayer At Planting Time

Here I go, row by row
covering good seed, with a hoe.
Bless the seed, dear Lord, I sow
that it may have the strength to grow.

Please give the sunshine and the rain
that it produce much food and grain;
that I abundant have to store
to feed myself, and many more.

That I may not have to turn from my door
the sick or hungry, or helplessly poor.
For they are your sheep and your lambs, too.
So help me to love them as I should You.

You give the sparrows seeds to eat
and feathers to warm their little feet.
So help me to give some comfort and cheer
that all shall know God does care.

Sarah Sallee

A Mother Remembers

Thank You Lord for those little hands.
Clasped in mine in Childhood land.
Those little feet that would run to meet,
with open arms for me to greet.
How quickly do those days pass by.
As a bird in flight across the sky.
Those memories are so precious to me,
and from my heart, Lord I thank Thee.

Rilla M. Merrick

Still Waters Run Deep

I feel like I'm in still waters
cuz I don't know where to go
I have so, so many troubles
and I have nothing to show
I know my feelings lie deep inside
but they are just lying still
I wish I had somewhere to hide or stand
high up on a hill where I can't see nothing
below just sit there till the sun sets
I wish you would have been my betroth
but now my heart breaks

I sit here and wait for the tide to break
and then I will know where I stand
I'll know what my heart will take and what I give out of my hand
To be with you in the presence of the
Lord is what I had most desired
I wish for me to be at the end of the sword then to hurt
you, but I am so tired of fighting feelings which I know
are there but am so confused in my head you know in my heart,
I will always care and love you till I am dead

Sylvia Amaro

Daddy's Tears

Please don't cry peanut. Daddy's here to take care of you.
Daddy loves you Avonlea Autumn, please don't cry.
Why do you cry so much peanut, daddy's here to take care of you.

Talk to me sweetheart, are you tired, are you hungry, are you sick?
Because I keep calling your name, you do not answer.
Avonlea you must have been tired, for you sleep so long.
Please wake up sweetheart, daddy wants to hug his little girl again.
Because you sleep so long, I can't cry with you or for you.
I still hear crying "is that you Avonlea" I get no answer.
I see tears, "are these your tears Avonlea" I call out.
"Here I am peanut, daddy will hold you".
Still no answer, my calling out is in vain.
Then I realize the cries of pain that I heard,
and the tears of grief that I saw, were not yours peanut, for you are gone.
The cries of pain that I heard, and the tears of grief that I saw,
they were mine. They were daddy's tears.

Thomas Dutkiewicz

"Request For The Open Gate"

These dark things I go through
Daily pull me down, unto
The hellish state.
They peel me open and place me naked on a plate.

Sometimes my eyelids are sealed shut.
I am blind for a while, but,
Once the Son did shine.
A friend peeled open my frozen eyes.

This friend beyond a brother goes;
Helping me through my highs and lows.
Often I run away,
Leaving Him at bay.

Regret mixed with joy:
My life is a used toy.
Of forgotten by myself, then later remembered,
Up, down, I play, till in my grave am I dismembered.

Hopes have I of entering, though blind, without sight,
The place of pearls and shining light.
My spectacles, whether on or off, I own!
Take me and my impurity, and leave me not alone.

Matty Kuiper

gods

gods on pedestals lifted up move and
dance in dancing shadows. gods are
old but confident in men who they command.
gods are wise and know manipulation.
Worship gods bow to gods, gods, follow gods;
Atheists are good at this.
gods are power, gods are life to dead. gods on
pedestals are breathing seething, smiling
lurking shadows, obscure light around them.
Be afraid of gods, they kill. Be wary
of pride and ignorance and laziness, appearing as
Devils; but look, they are gods.

D. Clark Henderson

Yesterday

Yesterday, songs of innocence
danced through my mind.
Yesterday, a mother's sweet smile
Yesterday, having brothers and sisters to love,
a family together by your side.
Yesterday, little girls and boys not concerned
with right or wrongs.
Yesterday, having fun and playing games all day long.
Today, I've looked here and there for yesterday...
But, all I see is a world troubled and turned upside
with a frown.
Yesterday is gone.
I will cherish my yesterday fun.
Yesterday, where have you gone?

William H. Buxton

Starglow

The stars at night, they glow so bright
Dancing, beaming, full of life.
They have little time to play their games,
For soon the dawn will call their names.
They fade out of sight, as if erased,
To steal away to their secret place.
To wait again for night to fall,
Feeling very humble and very small
Happy knowing that darkness soon will call.

Nena Joy Barr

Queen's Ann Lace

Glory in the morning and through the afternoon
dancing on the wind
singing in the rain
most glorious in the sun
The beauty, the grace, the Queen's Ann Lace.

Down the hill and past the pond
where the green grass grows
the field of flowers, the field of day dreams and play-
the field of yesterday.

Spun round and round by little ones
made into crown for the beauty queen
held tightly in the fist of the young bride
given with love and dandelions
The beauty, the grace, the Queen's Ann Lace.

Kathy Riedel

Untitled

Flowers on the table -
Dazzling colors against the billowing white curtains,
Beautiful scents waffling through the house.
Simple.
Pure.
Ultimately, it is the most untimely death.

Michael J. Lennox

The Hip List

If you're hip, you're...
...either/or...real hard-core...
...gettin' busted...maladjusted...
...takin' a toke...always broke...
...out of work...a social quirk...
...dressed in jeans...talkin' obscene...
...talkin' fast...hopin' you'll last...
...tryin' to be erotic...borderline psychotic...
...runnin' from the pig...tryin' to bum a cig...
...cosmetically unkempt...an object of contempt.

If you're square...
...you like to cut your hair & don't like your body bare.
...you drive to work each day & you come home with your pay.
...you have to mow your lawn & your bank account's o'erdrawn.
...you have a nagging wife & you hate your mis'ble life.
...you like to waste resources & you want to join th'armed
forces.
...you want to watch TV & don't want to talk with me.
...you prob'bly liked Ron Reagan & you're prob'bly not a pagan.
...you've moved out to the 'burbs & you prob'bly don't like
herbs.

Head Poet

Far Away

Far away, far away in a void of bewitching dreams and
enchanting magic,
Far away, far away in that void of dreams and magic is
a castle, a castle made of sand,
Far away, far away in that void of dreams and magic in
a castle made of sand stands a man, watching,
Watching, watching through the window in a lonely tower
of a castle, a castle made of sand,
Searching, searching, painfully searching for a prize, a
prize lost to him,
Waiting, waiting, anxiously waiting for his one true love
to join him in the void of after life,
A maiden, a maiden with hair dark like the raven's wing
and eyes hollow like an ocean breeze,
This man, this man, he is sadly in death,
But his love, his love for his lovely young maiden,
Didn't die with him, couldn't die with him.

Dianna Penick

Winter's Night

The silken cloak of evening
Enfolds the lone silhouette
Moving slowly through deep glitter.
All is hushed but an occasional creaking sound
From a branch as it moves
Beneath its weighty burden.

Along the way, the amber glow of lanterns
Light a friendly path
As, here and there, a rabbit
Leaves its tiny prints
In the lacy-like crystals
Of fresh fallen white.

Above, the endless heavenly black,
Laden with beams of blue-white sparkle,
Provides a soft and seemly cover
For those below, who are companions
In this lovely montage,
On a quiet winter's night.

Dawn Verdell Reavley

False Truth

Truth unwonted cruel
And serving not its cause
Is but a tool,
Venomed by obscure vengeance;
A falsehood, spry
Made to deny
The naked truth
Of the other guy,
While thinly clothed
In our own skin,
Eyes closed
To the blazing sun!

David Glaser

I Can't Believe

be whimsical without heart
to run and be exhausted before long
hidden away those secrets so far
taken away to live without fear
I can't believe

happiness reigns in the world
make-believe without war
traffic fills our open arms
longing to be where we belong
I can't believe

follow them to the hidden spot
where we play and where we're taught
to be clones of what they say
for we have said, "years", far too long
I can't believe

lie down in the dirt
wait to die so it will not hurt
what it is makes us real
what it is allows us to feel
I can't believe

Jeremy J. Parker

Shells

She wanders aimlessly
down this lifelong beach,
picking up the shells
that some may call memories.
She may even toss
some of these shells
back into the sea
as one would toss away
memories not to be remembered.
Until the tide comes in
and washes her away,
along with those collected shells
only to be washed up again,
to be picked up,
and tossed again
on someone else's journey.

Alexis C. Dittman

Reflection At Dawn

At purple dawn
Tiny birds twitter
Glistening dew-drop pearls
Adorn slender grasses
And fragrant lilac blossoms;
I gazed in delight
And there beheld
My own being reflected
In those wondrous mysteries
Gloriously displayed!

Alisa R. Hilary

Automatic Perfection

One "Time Door" closed but Mama knows,
A better one soon will open;
And through it she will go.
Watch her, Mama does not cry;
She knows she's loved dearly,
By the Man beyond your skies.
Mama knows she will always,
Have bigger fish to fry.

Son, now don't you know,
You put on one mighty good show;
But the facts still remain,
Keys to "Future Time Doors,"
The wrong blew up backwards,
And only right was all,
That was left in the game.
It's automatic perfection;
Already in action.

Betty Lou (Miller) Counts

Cupid's Resignation

I fell on Love today.
A brokenness
—An Affair—

Falling from
Stained glass windows—
Forever married to things
I can not have and hold—

Would you kindly ask
Cupid to resign for me?

Half-heartedly,
Fallen Angel

Anh Nguyen

America Tomorrow

Over a land of freedom
A cloud did slowly form;
A war of grief and sorrow
Had to be performed.

The nights were blackened,
The days lengthened fast.
Was this America tomorrow
Or America of the past?

The toll that time has taken
Can never equal wars,
To the many hearts that are broken
These sorrows do encores.

The backbone of a nation
Lies in its religious views.
Our only hope for peace
Rest in our church pews.

Where hope, joy and gladness
Will do away with sorrow;
This isn't America of the past
But America of tomorrow.

Howard W. Hargis

"Humans Have"

A bird has wings to fly and be free.
A fish has gills and fins.
But what do humans have?....

Humans have personality and feelings.
Their personality creates who they are;
Their feelings show who they are.

Denice Sheffield

To Marry

To marry, we seek an anomaly,
A companion extraordinary;
But with the choice comes family
Who by consequence we also marry.

In marrying into a clan,
We accept its commonalties,
Often getting more than we plan:
Its blemishes and banalities.

While choosing we are chosen,
Reduced to profit and loss;
Considered by mate and coven,
Without representation or gloss.

So, before vows are said,
Weigh both mate and tribe,
For, with all we get in bed,
Conjugal peace to subscribe.

And, our timely toleration
Of those by consequence gained
Buys our highest admiration
From the anomaly for whom we aimed.

James F. Kirstein

Untitled

A father has authority,
A father has much strength.
When trying hard to please him,
We will go to any length.

When dads are home,
And starts to shout,
We want to cry,
And let it out.
But if they thought,
And that weren't tough,
And that we'd really had enough,
What role would mothers play?

Yes, a fathers role,
Is very tough,
I'm sure it was,
For mine,
Or we wouldn't be.
So out of the touch,
And all would be,
Just fine...

Annelie Chaney

Above And Below

The curved outline's edge
A feathered bow
Drawn against the foliage
Toward something below

So taut and sleek
The expectant arc
With pointed beak
Honed to mark
The unseen in the dark

The slender stalks
Stiff with attending walks
With feet pressed firm
Against the grass
As if listening

Across the expanse
Green and glistening
Like a silent physician
Listening
To the pulse beneath.

Henrietta Edelschein

Life

Life stands still for just
a glance,
but life cannot give us a second chance.

As we grow and as we see,
it is like an hourglass,
life runs out.

And in a split second it is over,
nothing but a glimpse is left.

Life is nothing but a dream,
that stops when we least
expect it.

Annemarie Vitale

"Mom's Back Porch"

The porch was wet from the
a glitter of a soft shining,
morning's dew. On the front
step was a pair of dad's
old gardening shoes. The dew had
covered them in such a way, one could
see silver.

An old milk can sat in the
corner, next to an old swing.
We would measure the milk
daily to see how much milk
the cows would bring.

The milk can, porch and old
frazzled shoes are all gone
now. Mom continues to gaze
out the window as the cool
dew arrives every spring.

Jerry Perkins

Silhouette At Noon

Were you musing far away
A little sad, a little gay,
Or were you dwelling on a scheme
Aiming to dissolve my dream?

For from my angle north of you
I enjoyed a Grecian view,
All my thoughts were resting on
The pillars of the Parthenon.

My luncheon pined upon my plate,
The hour feigned, held up fate,
When suddenly a chill wind rose
And my enchantment cooled and froze.

But since dream embers seldom die
I cannot help but wonder why, —
Your profile, madam, was so fine,
What made you turn and spoil its line?

George Marquisee

God's Painting

I see God's painting,
A winter wonder land.
Lacy frosty curtains,
Hung by a unseen hand.

A dark forest,
Turned into a rainbow hue.
While sun shine beams down,
on a scene made new.

Eva Wilkerson

Lost Soul

Today as I see it
A lost soul flowing
flowing to find a way out
out of frustration to find
another living soul to help.
Then it came but disappeared.
Where did it go? When will it be back?
Is it going to come back?
When will it come?
To show me
To help me
To be with me
To love me
To save me
From my misery
My lost soul
Flowing to find away out
out of frustration to find
another living soul
To help.

Elke Mandel

His Memory We Share

We knew a great man
A man we'll all remember,
He was tragically taken from us
Just this past December.

He was one of the best
A policeman in blue
We were all broken up
There was nothing we could do.

But grief has passed
And the memories are dear
Even though he's gone
We all feel him near.

We'll pass on his memory
To all our rookie cops
David M Parker 101
A lesson in the tops.

We know we will see him again
When we live our fateful day
But until that time comes
The memories will stay.
In Memory of David M. Parker Jr.

Fred C. Ray Jr.

Living For The Moment

Living for the moment,
A most popular way of life,
Seems for the young, a grand idea,
For the elderly, a vice.

But living for the moment
Somehow loses its appeal
As life's complications show
With what there is to deal.

It happens very gradually,
This exchange of attitudes.
Living for the moment
For an elderly point of view.

Carrie Alford

When I Was Alive

When I was alive
A music note to soothe
A song of love to dream
My world was full of hope

When I was alive
The sun warmed my soul
The fears washed with rain
A peaceful sigh
When I was alive

In this darkness, I survive
Look faraway
to those days
When I was alive

Sigh....
It comes to me now as I open my eyes
I am here
No longer alive...

Julie Holmes

Light Of My Life

At first, just a thought,
A perfect dream come true,
A prayer to God for the greatest gift,
My darling that was you.

Somewhere far off in heaven,
An angel came to earth.
Your smile of greater value
Than any treasure's worth.

I've done my best to teach you,
And love you more than life.
My goal that when I leave you,
I know you'll be all right.

You are my special Angel,
A blessing from above.
My life has special meaning,
You're God's gift of purest love.

Janice Bradshaw

In The Arms Of The Lord

There is a place I know,
A place I always go
When no one seems to understand,
Or accept me for who I am
In this place, there is no sound
No sign of emptiness to be found
All I feel is my heart beating
Trying to grasp a heavenly feeling
I am held in the arms of the Lord
As my feelings, I openly pour
When life seems so unfair
And no one else seem to care
I turn to this special place,
To hide from the human race
Even if it is for just a little while,
I know with Him, I can smile.

Aymi Lau

Love/Loss

My body is just a shell,
A container for my troubled soul,
I find it difficult to wish him well,
For without him I'll never be whole.

My spirit dies when I see his face,
I weep as I pray to the son,
I've even foreseen our final embrace,
Our souls no longer as one.

Bradford W. Hook

Three Endearing Words

You ask me to write a poem to you
a poem to prove my love.

How can you ask me to do that
when you know you're my Turtle Dove?

We've been so good Together
all through these many years,

We've always come out on top -
Together - through problems, through
smiles and through tears.

——Know what held our marriage,
Together without a doubt?

Those three Endearing Words hon -
——Let's Eat Out!

Betty G. Griffin

Home

I look out across the sky and see
A setting sun so beautiful that home
comes to mind.
Is the sky this beautiful at home?
But where is home for me?
When I look into my lover's eyes
I realize where ever I may go
Home will be with my lover, where
my heart is.
Yet, there will always be a place
Where I was born that will be home.
Or the place in the heavens long after
I'm gone, that will be home.
But I think that no matter if the
Scenery changes, my heart won't.
Home for me is where I'm the most
happiest,
With my lover.

Edwina Moree

Untitled

Just let me put
A smile on your face,
I won't make you forget,
Or try to replace-
He was one of a kind,
And I will be too-
But in a way special
My friend,
Just for you...

Judy Raley

Untitled

Did you ever wish on a star?
A star that felt so close,
but was so far.
Did you talk to it like
a lover, a friend, a foe?
Did you talk to it like
someone you really know?
Did you let out your feelings?
Did you tell it your fears?
Did you cry to it
many, many, sad tears?
Did you hold it close
like a teddy bear?
Did you tell it
for whom you really care?
Did you ever wish on a star...?

Candace Siravo

Indispensable Moments

A time
a thought
a memory

a window
and an open horizon
a mirror
and the sparkles of objects

a heart
a hope
a word

a house
and an empty shell of solitude
a road
and the ranks of darkness

a smile
a face
a curtain

a silence
and a sullen night
a dream
and a speechless rock

a sound
a pain
a man ... and a trembling branch ...

Amil Imani

Funny

Earth's a funny thing,
A tiny speck in space,
Running around in circles
Followed by the Human Race!

Esther S. Pefley

The Vision

Once I had a vision,
a vision so clear that I
trembled when I saw her,
and knew I'd never be the same,
the emotion welling up inside
me could not be explained,
and I knew I loved her
and could not live alone any longer,
she haunted my dreams, and
touched my soul, my purpose
in life was clear, I knew I
was here to love her forever.

Brian Peeler

Dare To Dream

Dare to dream
a wonderful dream

Then dare to make
that dream reality

When that dream
comes to life
then
Dare to dream
a wonderful dream

Anita Marie

Main Concern

What care I
about leaving footprints in the sand
that will disappear when the tide
laps the land.
My concern is the marks
I leave on man.
I want to light other lights
before my light goes out.
I want to shout encouragement
as long as I can shout.
To add a little happiness
to those I am around.
And I'll be more content
when at last I lie down.

Bruce Niles

The Spiritual Aspects Of Love

Poetry beyond the senses
Abstraction beyond the mind
A touch beyond a whisper
A caress forever held in time

A bond beyond commitment
And passion beyond reason
Twin flames merged
Into the spiritual aspects of love

To care to be, to become
Two raised to the power of one
Souls cradling the spark of creation
Hearts synchronized to the rhythms
of life

The desire, the ecstasy, the simplicity
The contemplative mood in the sound
of OM........
To restore, to renew, to be reborn again.
All immerse in symphony

Curtis Kelley

"Feelings"

The feelings were like a shell
all covered over with shiny veneer,
Inside the shell is an aching
heart and a feeling of helplessness
and despair, wondering what life
can hold on this planet.
A prayer of hope, faith and love
to our Holy Father above, is the
only comfort for the inner soul,
crying out for a reason to keep
on striving for peace and life.
As loved ones seem far away.
Oh! To have happiness once more.
Surrounded by loved ones with
smiles and laughter and merry hearts.
Oh! If the shell could be shed
and the spirit of love can enter
from above. And loneliness can
disappear and life could be happy again.

Dorma Lee Johnson

Moms

Moms are special people
Always giving love, like
God from above, Peace
Makers like the white dove
Not perfect but close
To me their the most

Billy R. Dillard Jr.

Untitled

It's not easy to say good-bye
All I can do is sigh
To say how much I'll miss you
Is even a harder thing to do
A friend of mine you'll always be
A better one I'll never see
So it's not easy to say good-bye
I think I should not even try
Until the time we meet again
I'll just keep missing my best friend.

Barbara Browning

A Shadow

I walk among the darkness
All I feel is pain
My shadow always hidden
I only find it ahead of me
The sadness of the night
Unfolds the abyss
Into my eyes and soul
And possesses me fully
Nothing can wake me
From my shattering trance
As the bullets pass through me
I cannot feel anything
I open my eyes to the sky
Not a star or moon to be seen
I am alone in the world
And scared I might find my shadow

Jessica L. Miller

Our Mother

God sent us down a shining light,
all kissed with morning dew.

Although our faults were many,
she only saw a few.

She made this family special,
no exceptions to the rule.

She only had to call our names,
when we were hateful, mean or cruel.

Always with a forgiving heart,
and unabiding love.

In our hearts we'll always know,
she watches from above.

Janice Jones

Untitled

I wish I would die
All my friends do is sigh
I wanted to go to heaven
When I was seven
After I heard those words
My mind became so disturbed
The sky turned gray
There was nothing I could say
I stood in the rain
Feeling such pain
Even though I love him so
He's my father but he don't know
I still want to die, some day I will
Right now I'm in the very mood to kill
Maybe one day soon I'll get my wish
I can't go on with a father like this
The pain I have today
Will never go away
Please daddy please STOP! living this way

Christine Carucci Lopez

Untitled

Here I sit
Alone and afraid
Unsure of the future,
Of decisions I've made.

Foreseeing the future
Is no easy task
Its facade is of iron
Yet, a gold-inlaid mask.

Mysterious and exciting,
Hopefully ideal,
Truthfully painful
Soul-searchingly real.

Life is a labyrinth,
a game and a maze
And with each decision
Our destiny can change.

Here I sit,
Alone, yet content
Confident in myself
and the choices I've spent.

Christen Dunlap

Kitchen Lessons

Empty, now and then
Although seldom the time when
Mom was not there or nearby
Very little missed her eye

If not there, Dad was working
Knowledge of his presence lurking
Our deeds he always knew
Good and bad as we grew

We'd stretch the curfew
Skip detention
Sneak a smoke
Some others I won't mention

Oh, we had to answer for our actions
Not in a court of law you understand
But in our kitchens

There we'd stand, the accused
Giving many a clever excuse
Which never worked, and so we learned

Courtrooms today are full, you see
And kitchens empty as can be.

Jo-Ellen Cron

Pale Blue Plum Tree
In The Sky Above

I see what I need
  among the silent plums.
The plums, I love to drum among
  the blossom of my love.

My plums are wondrous silent
  dreams in the spring.

I dream those plums are
  nousing and lousing in the springy,
Leafy sky above.

Those, plums bring joy.
  O boy!
To my toy in the silent sky above.

Antoinette T. Ricci

The Mask

Everyday I put on my mask
An invisible shield to hide
Never letting anyone know
What I'm really feeling inside
But if you took off the mask you'd see
I never meant to hurt anybody
I just want to live my life
Just want to do what is right
And if you looked in my heart
You'd see it was crying
The mask smothers my thoughts
The real me is dying.

Justin Aquinas Thompson

Untitled

It was only three flowers
And a card with a rhyme.
It cost less than five dollars
Took a few minutes time.
But it showed me you love me
It showed me you care
It showed me you miss me
When you're not here.

You hold me so gently
Your heart beats so near.
But words can seem empty
When you can't be here.
Then the fragrance of blossoms
Soft petals of wine
Remind me I'm special
And your love is mine

It was only three flowers...

Doris J. Ritzman

A Clown's Love

A clown that laughs,
and a clown that cries.
Is the one you want,
before your eyes.

The love he shows,
to make you laugh.
You'll always know,
his love will last.

If you're sad,
and feeling blue.
He'll make you glad,
that life is true.

So return the laugh,
that he gives you.
And he'll be happy,
that his job is through.

Jeri Howard

Mom

For all you've done,
and all you do,
and all you'll do I say...

I love you more
as times goes on so...
Happy Mother's Day!

Amy McBirnie

Mom And Me

You're part of me
And always in the heart of me,
You're there in the mirror,
A part of my very core.
Your love created me
And grew within me,
I hear your voice....
an echo in my speech
A reminder of the bond we keep.
You're everywhere...
and yet nowhere.
I long to hold your hand..
to touch your face,
To feel that belonging
in our special place.
If only for a moment...
To hold each other with Love and Grace.
A memory we've only to create.

Debra A. Ale

Brother

I am like Daniel,
and at times I still feel the pain.
Sometimes it is like a summer rain,
warm and gentle.
Other times it is like a HURRICANE,
destroying all my earthly frames.
All life seems to quake,
and even I begin to shake.
Because of the actions,
that our father did forsake.

Brother, we were but mere pawns
in this game of bait.
But soon our day will dawn.
When we have spoken the unspoken,
and soon the silence will be BROKEN.

And then the pain we carry
will be our only token,
of the childhood that we have never spoken.
To each other about,
Because of our inner doubt.

Donald S. Ackerman

A Grain Of Sand

Before me an ocean stretches,
And before me a sky stretches.
Both seem never ending.

Before me the heavens
stretch into the cosmos,
And about me the wind
calls from the cosmos.
Yet, these two are undisciplined.

One on the earth is
wondering about the universe.

Like a grain of sand am I.

Georganne G. Tiemann

Serenity

Serenity comes to me quietly
And engulfs me tenderly.
Soft as velvet, it soothes
Caressing my inner thoughts.
It comes and goes,
Leaving me alone,
Its essence always lingering
In long, lucid moments.

Anne Larkin

A Prayer For My Daughter

Heavenly Father, hear my prayer,
And bless this one whom I hold dear.
Give her peace within her heart,
And keep her safe while we're apart.

Please watch over her day by day,
And guide her steps along life's way.
May she always say and do,
Only that which pleases you.

Hold her hand and keep her strong,
Lest she stumble and do wrong.
Protect her from Satan's charms,
And hold her in Your Loving arms.
Amen.

Joyce Bamsch

The Reason For The Season

This is my favorite season
And do you know the reason?
It's a special time for you and me
To share with friends and family
And to tell of Jesus love,
That he came down from heav'n above
To be our Saviour, Lord and King.
For His goodness let the joybells ring!

He loved us so much that He
Came to earth and died on a tree
To save us all from our sin
That we can someday dwell with Him.
Do you believe in His holy birth?
Do you believe He lived on earth
And died on the cross to set you free?
What do you think of eternity?

If you but ask He will forgive
All your sins and you can live
A life filled with peace and joy
Because of the birth of this little boy.

Jesus is the reason for the season!

Carolyn N. Capp

"Help Me I'm Troubled"

When we are little
And faced with problems
We run to our Mothers
And ask "Help me I'm Troubled"

As we grow older
We become independent
And the running must stop
So we make our own solutions

But some of the problems
Are just too much
So we hide and hope
But the problems won't go away

Sooner or later we'll ask again
While showing our strength
And reaching for another's hand
"Help me I'm troubled"

James D. Williams

The Promise

I'll remember the good times
and forget all the others.
I'll miss you as a friend
but not as being lovers.

I'll be there to pick you up
if ever you should fall.
Whenever you might need me
just give me a call.

Don't think that it's over
because certainly it's not.
I will always remember you
because I really love you a lot.

If ever there was someone
that I would truly miss.
That someone is you
and that's my Promise.

Becky Treiber

"Friendship Is"

Someone you can laugh with;
and have a good-time,
A shoulder you can cry on,
to ease your boggled mind.

A gentle hand;
to wipe the tears away,
A silent whisper "thank you",
for being my friend today.

Someone you can share;
all your secret feelings with,
And when that persons not around,
in your heart, you will miss.

True friendship lasts forever;
it's not a passing thing,
Just knowing that between us,
It is "Love" that we bring.

Catheryn Smith

The Wedding Dance

She curtsies,
And he bows.
Slowly, ever so slowly;
as they stand afacing;
She raises the full hem off the floor,
and gracefully begins.
Soft kid clothed, the high arched foot
reaches out to point;
First to the front then to the right,
left and back again.

While eyes smile to eyes,
Hearts around the room join
to the quickening beat.
Then arm in arm, together they fly.
As note to note becomes bar.
And bar after bar becomes tune.
The dust takes life, as it leaves the
well worn boards of the floor.
And love dances in the warmth aglow
in the faces that whirl to the tune of old.

Jan Harlow

Shadows

While the sunshine in life is forming
and hearts are light and gay,
this sunshine is painting shadows
that are cast along our way.

These shadows are forever changing
fading and born anew
painting a constant contrast
from a different point of view.

These shadows disappear in evening
in total darkness sphere.
They fill our souls with longing
for what our hearts hold dear.

After the dark night is ended
and another day has come
new shadows may assail us
but are created by the sun.

Shadows give form and meaning
and make us see the light
so use your shadows wisely
with God there'll be no night.

Hugh M. Williams

Lucille

If only I could see your smile
and hold your hands in mine,
I'd share with you the things I feel
If only for awhile.

If only I could hear your voice
and hold you in my arms,
If only I could be with you,
If only for awhile.

Though no longer by my side
my thoughts of you remain,
My memories will see me through,
my memories of you...

Dawn Abdul-Jawad

Jill

I thought of you tonight
And I knew
That you were looking
At the same moon
And wished
That you were lying here
By me
Watching the lonely cloud
Pass by the evening star
Into eternity.

Dennis P. Minuti

Pick A Number

Pick a number, maybe three
A lucky one you bet.
Pick a number, then we see,
The kind of life we get.
Pick a number, take a chance,
Hope to win, not lose,
Pick a number, place your bet,
Give up your right to choose.
Pick a number, yes, my dear,
Take a chance on me.
Pick a number, you will see,
There is no number on me.

Dale Stoker

The Time Forgotten

One day I looked in a river
and I saw my reflection clear.
I looked back in the river
and decided my future was near.
I thought about what I'd done
And what I wanted to do
And realized that the best dreams
Are the ones I've made come true.
I thought about my life
And the memories I've made
And acknowledged in my heart
About the future plans I have laid.
And when I decided to lay to rest
All the secrets I have kept,
I looked back in the river
And wept and wept and wept.

Josetta D'Ambrosio

"Life's Realities"

I get up each & every morning
And I wonder what's in store,
For yesterday's been forgotten
It does worry me no more.

I view traits of so many people
That I just forget about myself,
I dispense of all my problems
I don't just put them on the shelf

And I listen to the singing birds
In the many kinds of trees,
They're so careful and so happy,
That down! this brings me to my knees.

And now I'm always thinking,
What a sad world this would be
If birds & little creatures
We're not bustling all around me.

Dorothy S. Riebe

Darkness

I don't know where I'm heading
and if did I don't think I
could stop.
My feelings our out of orbit,
and the stars do not shine anymore.
I would do anything for him, but
I need someone to show me the way,
because I can't make it on my own.

The sun sets in the west with a
glowing ray, and my feelings fade
away with the darkness.
Then the sun rises in the eastern
sky, and my feelings start again
with the sunlight shining through.

I can't feel the warmth without
him, so I go back into the darkness
frightened and scared of what the
night will bring.

Amber Trivette

Dreams

I close my eyes
And I'm in charge.
This is my domain to control.
Here I am free.

In this place of unconscious creation,
I can be anything,
Do anything.
Here I am happy.

But then the sun shines upon my face
And I open my eyes.

Daniel Straus

Friday Was My Bad Luck Day

Friday was my bad luck day.

My hair went every which way-
and it was Brush-Brush-Brush.

I slept late and missed the bus-
and it was Rush-Rush-Rush.

My teacher told me I was loud in school-
and it was Hush-Hush-Hush.

Outside the snow began to melt-
and it was Slush-Slush-Slush.

And all my mom could say was that-
tomorrow's Saturday.

Carol M. Jordan

My Heavenly Baby

I lay her down for the night
And knew everything was all right
But with the morning sun so bright
Things were not right
There she lay pure as the snow white
My feelings I did fight
My soul full of fright
But she had gone to a new height
To a place full of delight
Where one day we WOULD unite
To God I was polite
Because He had my baby in the twilight
Far beyond the moonlight
To that so heavenly site
That would be mine too some night
After all, things WERE right!
So with this earthly home so quiet
To my precious baby, Goodnight.

Debra Culp

Betrayal

Been stabbed in the back
And left here to suffer
I know who did it-
Didn't have to look
She comes to me, hours later,
Thinking I don't know it was she,
Comes to me with a smile,
Arms outstretched.
I stare at her with fright,
More scared now than even before.
She embraces me, whispering,
You're gonna be okay,
As she takes hold of the dagger
And twists the last breath out of me.

Erica Potterbaum

A Faded Memory In Time...

Somehow even though time goes by
and life goes on
I can still feel you by my side
as the days drift by
and I roll onto the side of another
knowing that
loneliness could be so bad
especially when
drowning into a sea of sorrow
until on can't feel no more,
one can't see no more
and even when ignorance becomes a virtue
the sun will still rise, surface the day
and set into sea
like light after dark
you'll slowly fade away
and become this faded memory in time...

Hemda Mizrahi

Harmony

Can't we live in harmony,
and live without a fuss?
Can't we live in harmony,
and try not to swear or cuss?
Can't we live with a little joy,
that sparkles like a star?
Can't we play, and sing, and laugh,
and like all as they are?
Can't we live in harmony,
please don't push or shove.
Can't we live in harmony,
and sing, and dance, and love?
Can't we live in harmony,
and give, and help, and share?
Can't we live in harmony,
and try to show we care?

Jennifer L. Cable

Life's Lesson

As life was slowly fading
and memories filled my brain,
I knew that it was over,
and yet, my dreams remained.

The dusk of life was falling
and silence was so near,
but would it really end now,
with fulfillment ever so dear?

The storms were now all over
and peace was drawing nigh
yet could it last forever,
like the wind and the seas and the sky?

The world was mine in that long ago time,
but life could not stand still
yet my mind and heart - while far apart,
can only wish that it will.

And all I can say for that bygone day
when on youths joys I did dine,
was I learned not to pine for the things
that I lost,
but be glad for the things that were mine.

Joseph T. Jackson Jr.

Conclusion

The high song is almost over,
And my life is counting down;
After about three score and ten,
Here's what I have found:

It's been a magnificent journey,
An odyssey of sheer delight,
Moving from oblivion and despair,
To supreme joy and awakening sight.

A life filled with love and struggle,
Singing and dancing on foreign shores,
Forging bonds with men and women,
Opening and entering forbidden doors.

But now it's time to pause and reflect
On an obvious fact that chills me,
A humorous conclusion beyond debate:
SOMETHIN'S OUT THERE TRYING TO
KILL ME!

Joseph E. Helton

To Be Strong

To be strong
And never cry
To be wrong
And wish to die

To stand alone and walk in danger
To tempt fate
To make a wager

These are the things that matter now
No falter of my step
I can't care now

To care would surely mean my death
To put my wondering soul at ease
And lay my body to rest

It may sound silly or even sad

But my hearts broke so much
It will do as it's told
It's grown small, weak, and very cold

Winter is upon it and my summer so far away
Another love avoided
Another day the same

Amber Dawn Cooley

Second Chance

Time has a way of changing dreams
and no one knows just why
two people fall in love for good
then love begins to die.

And when it dies it leaves behind
the joys we might have shared
and suddenly the pain we feel
is all that time has spared

And when that pain consumes our souls
our hearts forget to try
we don't remember how to love
and watch as time goes by

God help us take advantage of
the time we have together
and help us learn to love again
but this time love forever.

Judy McGaughy Nysewander

Twilight Memories

I heard a knock
And opened the door,
The sun was shining
but there was more,
Get your hat
and come with me,
Lets go down
By the big Oak Tree,
Time went by
Then we heard a call,
Come on home, you all.
Now in my twilight time
I still can see.
Good things happened
When I was two and he was three.

Bobbie Viola Meade

Keep Looking Up

Once I was depressed
And really feeling down,
Then a spark of hope reminded me
Jesus is still around.

To lend a helping hand
And a shoulder or two you see,
'Cause He's there when you need Him
And there He will always be.

So don't you ever give up
When things go wrong,
Just keep on looking up
Remembering He's always home.

There's hope on every corner
No matter where you go,
Remember Jesus is the answer
And that He loves us so.

No problem's too hard
That He can't help you solve,
You're always on His list
For His love no one can rob.

Annette Rivers

Missing Children

Little children used to play
And scream about this house
Now around in later years
It's quiet as a mouse

On Christmas day they used to cry
Out loud with glee so clear
But that will happen no more
In this house of later years

Come back little children
Come back shouts of glee
Come back little climber
In the old apple tree

Back came the children
With grandchildren for me
I was so happy
I shouted out with glee
Yippie! Yippie!

Beth Duey

"My Little One"

Your small little words ring
And softly sing
A song so beautiful
I almost miss your silence

Your smiles and giggles now show white
They truly are smiles now so bright
I almost miss those toothless grins
But I'll never miss the bites on my chin

You move so much faster now
Here and there
And of course everywhere
I almost miss your quiet play

You have made our home a maze
Gates blocking doorways
Locks holding cabinet doors
All so that little hands cannot explore

Yes I miss my little angel
I will always miss my little one
But I'll always love the growing one
The growing one who is my little one.

April M. Sutphin

Time

I wish that I could capture time,
and spend it like I would a dime,
There never seems enough to be,
of that great wonderful commodity.
Time flies, I swear it must have wings,
my daily chores no time it brings.
If I could capture from eight to ten,
and use it later, clothes to mend,
If I could capture noon to three,
I'd use it for some time for me,
I'd like to steal from five to seven,
my prayers to say to God in heaven.
But time you see will never wait,
so I give up and hasten my gait.
What I can't do today will be,
there tomorrow for all to see.

Dolores Wiggins

Hope

The sun still shines
And stars still twinkle
Rain still falls
And Waves still wrinkle.

But somehow something's missing
Things aren't appreciated as much
Maybe it's the absence of love
Or the longing for your touch.

Whatever it is, it's lonesome
To think of what is gone
So I start each day with new hope
That you won't be gone for long.

Christina M. Hillis

I Found Contentment

God met me in the garden
and said, he'd be my guide
He gave me all the answers
So I could set my fears aside.
As I looked upon the flowers,
and I listened to the birds
I could hear him speak to me,
and I cherished every word.

Barbara Ann Josanne

The Cloak

Honor, nobility, a gentle Spirit,
and the courage of a warrior,
Have been the cloak I've attempted
to wear through my life.

But, just like a cloak woven of
many Fabrics, that can weigh
Heavily at times,
the burden of the virtues
Hung heavily on my shoulders,
yet I continued to stoically
wear the cloak.

It was not until You filled
my Heart with Love,
That I Understood the cloak
could be shed from time to time,
and the burden shared.

And it's now with Joy that I
proclaim to the world,
That I both proudly wear
and share this cloak with you.

Jose M. Garcia

Happy New Happy Old

We change the world,
And the world changes us,
And in that shift
of hands and time
We slip and slide
Toward yet another year.
Take time, my dear.
Stop here with me
For just this minute to
Recap,
Recast,
Review
the tiny footprints
of our lives,
And tell me.
Tell me true,
What really matters now to you?

Dee Rickels

Childless Father

I knew them
and they knew me.
There was a need,
the need was me.

What fun we knew,
and how they grew.
They looked to me
and the bond but grew.

The bond diminished,
not even a glimmer.
Senseless errors
hasten the finish.

Gone are the children
in need of me.
No more to be Adam
with a need for me.

Little do they know,
the circle their in.
When in the end
it begins again for them.

Charles J. Maher

When I Said I Loved You

People say I love you all the time
and they never, mean it.
But when I said I loved you
I meant that I'd love you
Forever I cant explain
in words all I know

Is that when we're apart
I think about you all the time
I may not always tell I love
But when I do
You know that it's for
real and that it's from my heart.

Charity Moore

Forgotten

Tomorrow the sun will rise once more
And today will be forgot.
Yesterday we'll never meet again
But memories we have sought.
Wonders and happiness we see now
Never to be seen once more.
Today will blend with other days
Forgotten as before.
Remember nothing, but only this
Tomorrow will never come.
Today it is, and will always be
And yet be forgotten by some.

Cheryl Johnson

Philosophy Of Faith

God I know thee not at all
And yet I know thee well
I know of your small comforts
"Have Faith" so people tell
People are confused today
Don't know some right, some wrong
I know not why time is so short
And yet, time is so long
Knowing not, we trust in you
This is our faith, The right we do

Joan E Reed Tatarian

'Thor'

The Birth of a thousand
angels thrushed across his
soul
Battle blood spilled freely
to the winds
Limb and honor scattered
the red drenched sands
oh heed that cry half
beast half man
A black stallion laid
down to die, a sword cast
in iron lay in its side
"Black twisted Fate", "black
twisted night,"
"The great King Thor" does
Battle tonight.

Daniel Joseph Joubert

The Artist

He sits alone, but for his thoughts,
Bearing his soul to those who watch,
Passion flowing with seeming ease,
Continuing on till at last he sees,
His vision transformed.

Denise Courter

Your Eyes

Your eyes are so erotically
appealing, and amiable
The little things you do
caress my heart, like a
feather fluctuating in
air, so sensitive yet with
great significance.
Your smile makes my heart leap
similar to a lioness sneaking
up on her prey.
You have given me so much
without knowing it.
If you had never entered my life
I would not have the confidence
to search for my dreams,
or reach for sensible goals.
These things combined
is primarily the reason
that I love you so much.

Frances Ampuero

Exultation!

Who would have thought it?
Approaching a seventh decade,
Renewed, alive, curious,
Puzzled, elated, happy,
Sad, energized alive!
Fill in the days with zest
And joy and
Anticipation,
Being life to such
And fulfill in closure
My fun grandchildren anew,
One and all
Envelop and love me
For no reason at all.

John J. Kelly

A Dreamer's Dream

A dreamer's dreams
Are his hopes, feelings, and desires.
His dreams are his escape from life
And should not be taken lightly.

For pushing them aside,
Thinking them silly thoughts,
Would be a grave mistake.
For when he dreams of a land not far,
He is all but sad.
He shall not tell anyone,
In hopes it will come true.

For when the day arrives,
And not a single soul does know,
He shall be granted his dreamer's dream.
And we will wish,
We dreamed a dream with him.

Brad Gwinn

Rose

It sits there, Untouched.
Bright red and beaded with dew.
Thorns look fierce;
But probably not.
A single rose on the bush.
Do not touch it seems to say.
The wind blows on it;
But still it sits there;
Untouched.

Amber Votano

Our U.S.A.

Far away countries across the sea
Are no doubt wonderful places to be,
Such as the leaning tower of Pisa;
The streets of gay Paree.

Any state in the Union
Has scenic places galore.
Now that we have Hawaii and Alaska,
Why first seek a foreign shore?

Start out in any direction,
Take time along the way.
There is scenery and fun a plenty
Right here in the U.S.A.

No fashion trend can surpass
Those seen on 5th Avenue.
The scenes throughout the country side
Will catch and hold your view.

Even if there is a great thrill
In a prolonged foreign holiday,
Why not first take a general view
Of the good old U.S.A.?

Eleanor E. Davey

Of Angels And Sunsets

Have you ever watched a Sunset,
as color fills the sky
with Oranges, Reds and Yellows
Have you ever wondered why?

Maybe it's a message,
sent in a special way
from the loved ones gone before us
at the end of every day

I think that it's the Angels
giving us a look
of the wonders that await us
in the next chapter of Gods book

The little ones who went too soon
when we wanted them to stay
are telling us we're not to cry
because they've gone away

Amid the colors we'll reunite
as at the end of day
we'll see the colors once again
as little Angels play

Joni Boggs Marcy

Help

A tear trickles down my face
as I stare off in space.
Did I do something wrong?
cause now you're gone.
I discovered a letter,
but it didn't make me feel any better.
I now see,
you cheated on me.
That's not what's on my mind,
you are to hard to find.
I want to be there for you,
even though you were not true.
You need a friend,
my heart will soon mend.
I stare out the window,
and feel so low.
As the moon fades,
I think of you and your problem.
Aids.

Jenny Hovey

My Child

My child sat at the window
as the snow fell softly down;
he watched the flakes in wonderment
as they fell upon the ground.

He followed as whirling and twirling
they fluttered to and fro;
and silently - so silently
covered all with a blanket of snow.

His eyes saw nothing but beautv
in the whiteness all around;
as tiny snowflakes danced about
not making any sound.

I watched my child so tenderly
then heard him softly say;
Mommy - look at the snowflakes
they want to come in and play!

Gwen M. Brown

The Beauty

I stand out at the water's edge
As the stream trickles across my feet.
I look to the west
At the snow-capped mountains.
I wonder to myself
About what you are doing.
As the sun hides itself
I look to the stars
Wondering if you are doing the same.
Do you think about me too?
Do you long to be sitting next to me?
My heart is calling you
Hoping that you are feeling the same.
I live with the belief that our hearts
Will find each other again.
And the next time I look out
To the beauty of this world
You will be standing beside me
And seeing it too.

Heidi Fretheim

Thrice I Lost

Thrice I lost to the dust.
At first a bit of me went.
Tiny limbs bowed in the gust.
Tireless existence in life spent.

Thrice I lost to the dust.
Another part of me left.
Potential flower gone - unjust
Fruition dismayed - bereft.

Thrice I lost to the dust.
So much of me now departed.
A mountain strong, now nonplussed,
Left me desolate - brokenhearted.

Annie L. McClure

Dogs

Tails wagging fast,
bodies wiggling past.
Rolling over on their backs,
Tummies having scratch attacks.
Sweet and loving
People do the hugging

Blythe Miron

"Marriages Spent"

The birds they sang
At the break of day
Start again
I heard them say
Don't dwell on what has passed away
Or, what is yet to be
The wars will be fought again
the dove to be caught again
Bought and sold
It will never be free
We asked for signs
The signs were sent
The birth betrayed
The marriages spent

Arthur M. Lerner

My Dearest Joann

Here we are, my lovely wife
At the close of our first year
You're my source of happiness
And the one I hold most dear.

I love you more than ever before
For you fill my heart
You are my life's purpose
Its most essential part.

I know the years ahead of us
Will be as sweet and bright
Our love will burn with a golden glow
And fill our world with light.

So happy anniversary
My wife and my best friend
My love for you will never fade
My love knows no end.

Darrin Kerschner

Pray For America

For our young men are dying
at the hands of their brothers
families are deserted, to be guided by
their mothers
babies are having babies
that's no exception that's the rule
and there's "crack" on every corner
and "handguns" in our schools
has God deserted us?
No! We have deserted God...
Pray for America

Charles H. Paige Sr.

Delusion

She walks like a model,
Attitude, poise and grace,
The look of nonchalance,
On her you can't erase,
She stares right through you,
As if you don't exist,
Then changes her mind quickly,
Makes you her only wish,
She knows how to get,
Whatever she wants,
Clever and resourceful,
Will primp and then flaunt,
You think she is human,
She knows better than that,
Mystery and wonder,
She is forever a cat.

Jayne Dunn Thomas

Basketball

I love basketball
Basketball is played in
the winter

We play indoors out of
the rain all weeks long

It is fun I like to
dribble, shoot, and packing
the boys

I play on a team for the
league and in school every
day

On my team for the league
is the most fun because the
games we play are real

Desiree Serrano

Doubt Only What You Know

How can something oh so beautiful
Be a victim of doubt?

So serene, and so precious,
So loving, and so pure

A voice of melancholy,
The sound of ecstasy

Eyes of paralyzing gold,
Reflections of shimmering starlight

The monogamous unconditional love,
A love that is forever

Wild or tame are two in the same
When wild is free and tame is a name.

A human in fur.
A human in love.

So warm, so gentle, so compassionate,
Yet considered so violent.

The wolf is but a victim.
A victim of human doubt.

Erica Kinczel

Untitled

It seems there must
be more to it all.

How can something so
real feel so disconnected

The true irony is that
it is not supposed
to be anything great at all.

Just life.

Some how in our creation
of things we lost
sight of what was
truly relevant.

To live. . .

Corin DeChirico

I Like Rainbows

I like rainbows
because, they have bright colors
and hang in the sky
nice and neat.

Cassy Paloian

Tour Guide Through Passionate Knowledge

Be my teacher.
Be my common sense.
Let me kiss your
Wise lips.
Let me be
The curious student
In your
Abundant classroom.
I don't want a
Shackle around
My ring finger
...And...
I don't care if you have
Settled.
Let me be your
Passion.
Speak to me.
Educate me.
Guide me.
Seduce me.

Dacia Orr

Jewels Of Nature

Tall, strong trees
bearing emerald leaves;
a sky of sapphire blue -

A sun of gold,
such beauty to behold
as it reflects on you -

Droplets of rain
on a red rose remain,
to glisten like rubies, so bright -

The moon is a topaz eye
sparkling in the onyx sky,
as stars of diamonds twinkle in the night -

Simple is pleasure
in a world full of treasures
if you just take the time to see ...

The jewels of nature
stand high in stature,
proving the best things in life are free!

Cindy Lou Peloquin

There Is No Hope

There is no Hope for our children
because we adult can't get along
with each other.

There is no Hope for our children
if we are concerned with the color
of each other's skin.

There is no Hope for our world
because greed has taken over
our lives.

There is no Hope for our children
when adults teach hatred not love.

There is no Hope for human survival
for we have forgotten our maker.

Carrie D. Evans

Spring

I live now, I love now,
Because you came into my life.
It is as though spring came in a moment
And took my cold winter away.
I was warmed.
Your smile, like the sun
And your tears, the rain in spring.
And me... the first flower of May.
Take all that you give
And I live.

I love the sun
That smiles on me
And the rain that makes me grow.
And I know that as long
As I have your sunlight
And your rain,
I shall remain.
I hope.
The most beautiful of all
The flowers to you.

Crosby Ledger

Beyond

The ocean large and wide
beyond man's realm
The vastness of it all
We so small in view and thought
When will we learn?

The sky so blue and pure
Sparkles on a sunny day
Just to remind us how
perfect all this is
Enjoy!

Irene Safrit

The End

The silence is deafening,
Blackness envelops all.
Bells don't ring,
Never a call.

Families are gone,
The angels appear.
Society is destroyed.
The end is near.

Fields are burning
In dawns early light.
Souls are yearning,
They take to flight.

Battles are not won,
Or lost, ever again.
Humankind will never
Repeat that sin.

The earth is gone,
The angles disappear.
Life is destroyed.
The end is here.

Curtis Hudecek

Elora...Came

Elora, the almost human cat
Came into our lives...
Stayed around, long enough
For family to get attached.

Deanie Montieth

Spring Weekend Morning

white city
blanketed in fog
weary morning sun rises in exhaustion
such work to light
the other side of the world
the people greet the day
to the sound of birds
and new leaves unfolding
they rub their wrists,
cancelling the ache there,
and wash away the marks
left by the shackles
they wore as slaves
two days of respite have come
and though no sun shines
they still smile
and laugh
with the life that has been bottled inside,
biding their time
until Monday.

Amy Jasek

Blue

Blue
Blue is my favorite color.
Blue is a bright color.
Blue is on my bed spread.
Blue is a Dallas Cowboy color.
Blue is in the sky.
Blue is the color of the ocean water.
Blue is my brother's favorite color, too.
Blue is the color of my cousin's eyes.
Blue is a beautiful color.
Blue is on my language.
Blue

Ashley Abila

Untitled

Where do you keep your
Book of lover's who
Danced away, pieces
Of naked laughter
Into poems that decayed
Which parts of me
Will you press upon
The page or frame
In a picture for
Your wall, just a look
Now and then, that's all.

Dossey O'Steen Jr.

Happiness

Happiness is a butterfly
bounding across the sky.
It is a daisy caught up in a breeze,
swaying gently as I walk by.
It is a honey bee working intently
on his never ending task.
In October it's a child eager to
try on his Halloween mask.
Happiness is a lot of things
all rolled into one,
But most of all and best of all,
happiness is lots of fun!

Angela Lynn Blount

"My Favorite Place To Be'

Daytime in the meadow the
breeze through the green.
Blue sky's cast upon it such
a beautiful scene.

Set in the distance are the
tremendous pines.
Looking behind them so grand
in their lines.

Surrounding a lake of such
still sublime.
Waiting is a fisherman just
passing the time.

As I walk thru this place
of such great bliss.
I've finally found you,
gentle love and a kiss.

Harold R. Friedman

Pathway

Languid lapse of memory
Bringing plans tucked way inside
Secret chests.
Promises made and thrown like wind-
blown
Seeds.
Intentions, to the wind
Abed with placid sunsets;
For tomorrow, tomorrow
Tomorrow, I'll notice the color
Of your eyes
Abundant beauty!
And remember to remember
To say "I love you"
Tomorrow.............

Helen P. Curnutte

Your Touch

Your touch
brings a fever,
a heat...
I welcome the rush,
But, ooh, the ache
that will not subside
until wholly and completely
satisfied.

How was I to know
it would come again —
as though it had
never gone?

Taken by surprise,
Overwhelmed,
to say the least...

This feels like
something from
"forever"...

And this will not go without saying...
"I Love You."

Caroline Helton

Winter

Winter's rise
Brings summer's death
The ice and wind
Breathe into life
A coldness that is exceeded
Only by my heart of ice
The wind that blows
Sings me a cold song
The ice on the ground
Is too hot for my veins
Winter wolf in black
Walks the snow blanketed ground
Hoping the ice will never melt
And summer never return.

David Lovegren

Burning

Burn my love
Burn time
Burn my heart
Let's never part
Burn the rivers
Burn my blood
Burn in me
For we are in love

Christie Palermo

The Wise One

I am blind
but I can see
the land, the trees,
the flowers and the sea.

I am crippled
but I can fly
like a robin
that glides through the sky

I am deaf
but I can hear
sweet laughter of children
far and near.

Do I have a power
that enables me
to hear, move, and see
of which I did not originally?

The answer is yes
for I possess
my heart
which makes me believe.

Jamee Fowler

Stars

Stars, stars, I see you every night.
But I don't see you now, I miss you.
Did you go somewhere else to play.

Please stars, come back to play,
I hope you come back.
For I'm very bored without you,
it is no fun.

Stars, stars, I can see you now.
You came back to play with me,
I can have fun and now
I must go to sleep.

Chrissy Atkin

"Mirror, Mirror"

I look into the mirror,
But I see to my surprise
A different person
Looking deep into my eyes.

Brenda Rathbun

"Why"

The sun has risen
But it passes me by
Confusion sets in as I wonder
Why
Why did it pass me by
I have loved it as a friend
Love I gave and nothing less
So why pass me on
Is there something else
Somewhere else
A better friend than I
I keep hoping that you'll
Come back
Times keep coming back to me
When we were together
Laughing and confiding
The sun has risen
But it passes me by
Confusion sets in as I wonder
Why

Chanda Windsor

Miss You Already

You touch my heart
But now it's breaking
Don't want to part
Can't stand the aching.
You are to nice, to watch you go
My heart has been diced,
I hope you know
You're my best friend, in the world
Can't let this end,
good thing we're two strong girls
We'll never part
Far or near, cause in my heart
you are to dear.
I'll miss you so,
When you are gone.
Oh, please don't go.
My precious fawn.
Now is time to say goodbye
My dear friend
Please don't cry.

Jamie Baptist

She

She was not their mother
But she had them
Two school-age children
To bring up
It went against the grain
She was angry
I could tell
The way she took the clothes
And shook them hard
Against the wind
To hang them on the line

Helen Sonderby

Daughterly Love

You're my dad
but still I'm sad,
There's always pain
and it's all in vain,
I'll love you forever
remember that ends never,
We may fight
we got strong might,
Our love will never end
although we always defend,
Like a dove
there's always daughterly love.

Anita Marie Rugg

Thought Circles

Today I think I grew an inch,
But 'twas not in my height.
It was my thoughts that seemed to grow.
And make my circle bright.

The circle that surrounds my mind,
And makes my thoughts go round.
It widened just an inch today.
And all my wond'rings found.

Dolores Bixler

Alone

Lonely comes and lonely goes
but when it stays, it's hell.
Swiftly dealing mighty blows,
to lock you in its cell

Life is made of up and down,
built with love or hurt.
To lift, or make you drown,
must we always get our fingers burnt?

A tear is only outward seen,
all others inward hidden.
Our hearts are buried inside,
unseen when hurt ridden.

With love to cure
our broken hearts,
When love is lasting sure,
will loneliness depart.

Time heals all wounds,
at least I have been told.
Then time swiftly passes,
because alone gets old.

Daniel E. Backman

Cats

They walk on paws;
And swat with claws;
They constantly purr,
While they rub against you
With their fur.
All they really do, is
Sleep and eat.
When you lay down they
use you as a seat.
Of course it must
be a
Cat.

Jana M. Hester

Never Ending Love

I love you so much
but you just want
to go out and do
such and such

I try to forget but
sitting here just
makes me think of
the time we met

My heart yearns for
your love that the
love I feel for you feels
like a cloud from above

Soft and tender your
words are a good heart
mender

Being with you makes
my life so real I
love you is what you
say so I really don't
want you to go away

Erica Valenzuela

Encounter

My big world was lost
By a furious storm
I ran to find
A new friendship
I don't know how I go lost

Almost without a reason
When I realized
I was down on the floor
A heavenly angel looked at me
And gave me welcome
Happily he and I left together
To an immense castle of gold
That was called G O D.
When I perceived
I was in infinity
Dressed in white
Over a fluffy cloud
Waving to the big world I lost a
GOODBYE

Eliane Cruz

The Grasshopper

The grasshopper travels
By leaps and by bounds.
Ever, so rattled
By movements, and sounds.

He flies about wildly.
He sails to and fro!
But to put it quite mildly,
He's got nowhere to go.

So isn't it proper
To ask, as I plan,
"Am I a 'hopper,
Or, am I a man?"

Bill Martin

Suicide

As I took the knife
By my side
Thinking if I do it
I'll never be alive
No more hurt nor pain
Never again will I live in vain
Pulling the knife closer to my chest-
Will put me at, an early rest
Should I live
Should I cry
Should I just kill myself and go
ahead and die
Even though I have things to live for
There's so much pain I can't bare
I need help from someone who care
But since I feel, I can't go on
I must face this death road along
With Suicide

Ericka S. Golden

I Long To Be

I long to be
by your side
as the storm breaks
and the winds howl.

I long to be
the shoulder upon
which you place your tears
when they flow free.

I long to be
the one you seek
when the clouds part
and you bask in the sun.

I long to be
laughter dancing lightly
resting softly on your ear
during the midnight darkness.

Corbin England

Ice Storm

A fairy princess
Came last night
And turned my world to glass.
A shimmering, silvery spectacle
That near takes my breath away.
Although the power is out
For miles around
And the telephone lines a mess,
I thought as I looked
At this splendor
Sometimes the world should just
Stop
And give to God
Its awe.

Jane Hime

Cinquain: Cocaine

Drug
Chemical mixture
A costly ride
For a little while
Compound

Carolyn M. Foy

Untitled

What is beauty
can beauty be ugly
can it be found deep inside
is it just geared towards appearance
if that's the case
than what is true beauty
is what's ugly, beautiful
and what's beautiful, ugly
is beauty a state of mind
What I find beautiful
others may find repulsive
so what is beauty
I guess only beauty will know

Julianna Dietz

Peace

Shh! What is that. Wait it
can't be. The birds chirping,
the wind rustling. The trees
swaying. Why this is peace.
It is quiet. No guns, no
screams, no war noises. It
is peace, just like a river.
It is peace just like snow.
Come, come out all.
Come the nightmare is over.

Andrea Spearman

I Love, I Lost

A yellow bus with many
children parting
as steady as the lilies
grow till tomorrow
Is that another bee
tapping at my window

I see the flash of lighting
I hear the echo of the
thunder
It is possible for
rain to rain without rain
I believe it for I am
Insane, Insane, Insane.

Frank Hernandez

Untitled

Oh lovely lady
Come over to play
Oh lovely lady
Come over my house to play
Just to play
We'll play with the children
Turtles and frogs
Oh lovely lady
Come over to play
Oh lovely lady
We'll tuck in the children
And listen to their prayers
Oh lovely lady
Let's kneel down and pray
Oh lovely lady
You are the one
You are the only one
Suited for mother and wife
Oh lovely lady
You are the one.

Celeste C. De Angelis

White Winter

Glistening snowflakes
Coming down, from the sky
Gathering on the branches
Of the dead winter trees
Turning them beautifully white
I look around their is white
All around me
So peaceful, so virginal, so untouched
The brilliant red of the cardinal
The beautiful blue of the bluejay
The speckled brown of the woodpecker
Searching for food
Has turned the white of snow
Into a multitude of colors
And the snow keeps falling
Glistening, sparkling white.

Cindy Zalewski

Reflection

We sip wine and grow old
contemplating life
with red eyes and memories.

Hands touch
embracing warmth of a morning sun
through the patio window.

Our stare breathing life,
joy, pain, sadness,
retribution and forgiveness.

Grandfather clock
singing its song
breaks discerning silence.

Lips move with wordless speech.
Like a mute we listen,
but the eyes read like a novel.

Thirty years in twenty minutes
and I reflect,
with nothing to show
but a fragrant glass of wine
and two people in love.

Cary Westin

Summer Love

You are my summer love
could this one last
a star came from above
said you will never be in my past

the times we are home
we see one another is it fate
or was it just another summer

I feel I call to hear your voice
but only seem to fall
into something called choice

the feelings are strong
that I have for you
sometimes I do nothing
but sit around and think of us two

sometimes I feel completely alone
like you should be there to have for my own
and for me to follow everywhere

you are my present,
you are my past, you are my future
I feel this one was meant to last

Cara Degenhardt

Desire

Will you stop and
count the stars with me?
Eternity is time
for every wish and
dream come true
for you.

Ann Daigle

Glass

Breakable hard
Cracking smashing shattering
you can see right through.
Bashing sitting looking
Clean flat
Crystal.

Brian Smith

The Quest

Intellectual expansion
creates questions unanswered
Knowledge acquired is
knowledge needed
We pass it on
we pass on
The quest continues
Generation after generation
Still no answer
The one we seek
resides within

Dustan Gradala

Untitled

My Love
Cut loose and drifting
So lost and alone
Reaching out to him
Crying silently in the night
Praying for him to answer
And come to me.
Separated, so barren and cold
My karmic lover,
Return to me.

Janice Alter

"Fire Is Coming"

The death son
dances around the fire
He chants as purity
As a plane to a dove
He chants as laughter
Wounding the flame
The rains came
The fire dies down
The trees nourished
Nature strikes nature
As lightening hides in the wilderness
Creating the fire's second coming
The leader death son
Runs and dances as a fool
Killing he and his tribe
He burnt them with impatience
Is the night too long
To wait for the true Son

Brian Kelly

Rose Tree

Rose tree
Dark night
Rose tree
Winter fright

Rose tree
Raining as
I speak
Rose tree
Help me
To seek

Rose tree
There's a
Spark in
My heart
Rose tree
Come help
Me in the
Dark

Deana Louise Matthews

Chemo

Chemo again
Decision's been made
Eat up evil cells
Hurry do it today.
Strike down the invaders
Strike them with force
Strange chemicals attack
Fight my battle in course.

From heel to the skull
Race back and forth
Destroy!... Kill, kill!
With a mighty charge.
Hurry!.... Hurry!
Time is precious
Devour my cancer
Please! Be victorious!

Arlene Prigge

No Guarantee

Something that will make you scream
Definitely make you suffer,
Something that will make you hold
Your head and holler.
Doesn't care about age
Don't give a damn about color.

Don't care about religion
Or what your sexual preference might be,
What I do know is that it can
Be given for free.

Will cut your time in half
Of moments you planned to enjoy,
But it's so devastating and has
No known cure.

Whether you're young or old
Rich or poor, don't be ignorant
Of the given facts.
Once "Aids" is part of your life
There's no turning back.

Dawn P. Leader

By The Way....

After long observation
Deliberation and consideration,
I came to the conclusion
That we are full of suggestions
And short on execution.
For the few who are apt
To give a hand, a hundred
Are ready with declarations
Of better ideas and innovations.
Yet when asked to implement
Suddenly, to my despair,
A deep silence descends,
And those hundred depart
With all their good determinations
In a sad state of deterioration!

Djehane Sadek

Dew Drops

Dew drops, dew drops
Dew drops from the sky,
Dew drops from my eyes,
Tearing at my heart,
Wishing I would die.
Lonesome rivers, heartless wishes,
Selfish givers;
That's what makes me cry.
Dew drops from my eyes,
When I think of loves once lost,
I bow my head and watch the dew drops.

Julie D. Browne

Southern Comfort

Take your whole life to join me,
  Do not rush to see me;
For as I dream in the cool shade
of a willow on a southern cloud,
  I will be with you always
And as the sun feels good on my face,
I will remember your kind of soft love.
  So do not mourn me lost,
  for I am still beside you
and when my fate for you arrives,
  you then shall be with me;
  Under a willow tree
on a wide southern cloud

Chris King

Free

I am three maid and the slave
Do this, Do that.
When does it stop.
I just want to be free.
When will I be free.
Work, work to eat.
Is there a change I get to rest.
When is it my time to be free.
When is it my time to be free.
When, when!

Joanna Presley

Encourage Me

Encourage me
Don't discourage
Me
Make me feel
I can do.
That I'm not
Through.

David M. Smith

Know Me

Don't print me after I'm dead, I said
Don't sing of me when I'm gone.
Hear me and know me now my friend
Life is not that long.

Don't offer me flowers or kind words
in death or the great beyond.
A touch or kind word as I struggle here
will be a permanent bond

Don't miss me when I'm gone, I said
I am only here for awhile.
If ever I gave you anything
I hope it was a smile.

Barbara Sims

Turn-On

What turns you on they ask,
Don't they know
that LOVE
Is the only button to push

It's been torturous to wait
For love to arrive,
Life is too short
For so many long waits.

Now the If's in my life
Are a tangle
Of things that might
Have occurred

But if someone had whispered
I love you
I am sure
I would have heard.

Jeannette Frantz

"There Are Twenty Four Hours In A Day"

There are twenty four hours in a day
Don't waste them, let life slip a way
You owe it to God, pray and pray
There are twenty four hours in a day

There are twenty four hours in a day
Don't mock God, we get old and gray
It's hot down in hell, souls will pay
There are twenty four hours in a day

There are twenty four hours in a day
God sees all, so don't go a stray
Be thankful for life, I do say
There are twenty four hours in a day

There are twenty four hours in a day
Don't waste them, let life slip a way
You owe it to God, pray and pray
There are twenty four hours in a day

Daniel Andrade

Untitled

cry blood
dream of the goddess delirious
languidly drunk in the eloquent shadows

scream power
heaving lustful honey
into a storm of love

Elizabeth Klein

Devils Song

Tears of blood streaming
down my face,
My heart is breaking
My scream is faint
My body is numb
My love is gone
The pain is going on and on
My throat is filled
with hate and sorrow
I won't live to see
tomorrow
My mind is gone
It won't be long
I can hear the Devils song.
The sky is red and
I'll soon be dead
The devil waits
My soul he'll take to
draw it in his lake of hate.

Juliet Ricci

If You Dream

If you dream
Dream of me

And I'll wisk you away
To a land of enchantment

Where love
Spends the day

Frolicking, mindless
Of what's at the end

As the moon passes by
On its way round the world

You waken to find
Your dream by your side

The one who
Will love you

As each day
Goes by

Charmaine Rochon

"Angels"

Angels from heaven
  dressed all in white.
Halo's of gold -
  what a beautiful sight!

Songs like a melody -
  soft as the rain.
They sing songs to us -
  to take away pain!

God takes the precious -
  to live up above,
They help him teach us -
  the story of love!

My moms now an angel -
  I see her each night.
She looks down upon me -
  and sheds a glorious light!

Judy Cagle

A Final Prayer For "Dad"

Ashes to Ashes,
Dust to dust.
Dear LORD, Please
Accept Dad from us.
We gather to say our Goodbyes
All of us with tears in our eyes.
As requested, he is scattered at Sea.
All we will keep is his memory.

Charles E. Thomas Sr.

The Gentle Snow Of Autumn

The gentle snow of autumn
Dusts the earth below

It covers all the dank and dark
It sets the world a-glow

The gentle snow of autumn
Dusts the earth so clean

Showing us what heaven is
The way our Lord has seen

In future times the Word will come
To dust the earth below and
Make the hearts of every man
As clean as autumn snow

The gentle snow of autumn
A sign from God this day
Like the scorching heat of summer
Man's sin has passed away

The gentle snow of autumn
Dusts the earth below

It covers all the dank and dark
It sets the world a-glow

John R. Weaver

Too Young

I looked at her smiling
Enjoying her few days
In the land of the living
Oh how sweet her ways
And then I heard her cry
As I looked at the bottle nearby
I remembered the responsibilities
That I had to commit myself to
And the necessary duties
That came along with it too
When I decided to have a baby
Then down came my tears
Along with motherhood's fears
At 17, I was too young maybe

Carmel S. Victor

My Friend, My Fortune

It was easy to trust a good friend
especially when you know you
both can win. But, never use
friendship as away of doing business.
That my dear is a no win.
I've regretted the lose and held
within, the truth of doing business
with other friends.
My fortunes gone and so my dear
I live without the fear within.
I can't keep quiet I have to tell,
so it won't happen to you...
My Friend.

Gwendolyn R. Carrington

The Ignorance Of Bigotry

You look down on me
even though I'm bigger

You're still black to me,
nothin' but a nigger!

You crazy fool! Don't you understand?
I'm just your shadow, Hate Man!

David O'Karma

Eves

Even if
evening
eve is in
even if you hold me
even when you told me
lets go get even
even so
still
odd to be eve
every day
ten fingers grasp
one shows

Gisele Lessa Bastos

Christmas Insertion

Now Christmas comes again, the same
Event unchanged among the holy
Ways we celebrate Jesus' birth.
Profuse attempts to make it grand
Arrive each year at higher costs,
Ready for holiday exchange.
Above the wrappings of our toys
Glows a gift expressed, not bought,
Reserved for those who seek it most:
Adore this Child, in stillness still
Preserve a place where He may stay
Here, in keeping His nativity.

Florence A. Johnson

Untitled

The universe is vast,
ever so large.
Yet a solitary star
shines so bright
and reaches so far.

This Earth is vast,
ever so large.
Yet a single individual
can perform miracles
small and large.

You, my friend, are like the star
shining bright and reaching far.

Janice E. Smith

Love

Beautiful all the way through
Expressions outcasted
Realizing this is it
Keeping all of the memories
Especially ones of good friends
Leaving to an important future
Emptying unwantedness
Yes, this is my home.

Elizabeth Zehren

To My Mother

Sad, in despair
every Sunday goes
to be with you
the son whom you left behind,
and his hands scatter
the harsh earth
so as to keep out the air
so as to keep out the cold
that you always found so unkind.

Because I am stricken with grief
I wear some flowers
as a consolation.
To speak to you I strive
of many things
that you can not hear
because it is too late,
because you have departed
struggling to remain alive.

Jose M. Bohigas

I Just Began To Sing

The day was long and dreary
Everything seemed to go amiss
I could not put matters together
When I began to sing.

I know not what prompted singing.
I know not why I was so down
But I knew God had a promise
That caused me just to sing.

All matters had worked wrongly.
The answers would not come.
I realized I was lonely
When I began to sing.

God had entered with His promise
When He again took charge.
I know I could not falter
So I began to sing.

It's in those difficult trials
When doom stands at the door
I lean upon the Master
Than I can begin to sing.

Alberta A. Cox

Anticipation

How special to have precious moments to
experience you.
To touch your heart.
To meet your stretch for my soul.
How mysterious to explore
your inner most thoughts
your sadness
your gladness
your loves.
How exciting to pursue a desire
to anticipate a touch
to await a dream.
How awakening to watch
The glint in your eye.
The arch of your brow and
The lust in your smile.

Ginnic Macioce

Teeth gleaming,
eyes bright,
cutting pathways
through the night.

Muscles taught,
nerves afire,
eating up pavement
beneath her tires.

Highway Predator

David Duncan

Child Of War

Child of war -
Eyes - old, vacant expressionless
You run and hide
Though hunger stalks your every step.
Who are you, child of war?
Whose to blame?
You say, "Some grown up."

Child of war -
Victim of poverty, neglect, no love
Or victim of war torn lands
You are my future
You say "What future?"
Whose to blame?
I say "This money hungry,
power hungry society."

Doreen M. Moses

The Secret

Fog on a city
eyes staring back
the stars of heaven's angels
wink from a blanket so black
the wind whispers,
a melody so soft
a haunting ghost
from a fantasy; make-believe
a scratching voice
from the bottomless vessel
that pounds inside
a weakened soul
sounds of music rolls over the hill
a drop of crystal
tumble's down my cheek.

Chasity Mattis

The Face Of God

Have you ever thought about the
face of God, like his eyes so bright
like wings on flight.
What about his ears who hears
All our troubles when ever we speak
his glorious name Emmanuel, Jesus,
GOD Almighty, Prince of Peace.
Or his hair so white like the lambs
wool gleaming bright.
What about the Face of God!
We wait patiently to see it, how
Whenever we need him we bow down
before his glorious face we see. And
glaze upon his unchanging face we
see his love for me and thee.
Have you ever thought about the
FACE OF GOD!
He is always there for me and thee, so
remember
to pray not only for you but also for thee.
And maybe you will see the face I see.

Hope Ballard

Michael

Child of Wonder
fair of face
holy innocent
full of grace...

God's reflection
you're a part
forever held
within my heart...

Do not weep
in Michael's time
eternally he's
in God's mind...

Frances-Anne Dowling

With One Single...

With one single tear
Fallen from your eye
I can not look at you
Because I don't want to cry

With one single kiss
I can fall in love again
Each night it's you I miss
My heart is broken deep within

With one single touch
My heart would belong to you
I miss you so much because once
This love was true

With one single lie
My life fell apart
So how I will forever cry
Because you broke my heart

Adia Isbelle

The Lonely Soldier

Far across the sea.
Far from where I want to be.
Darling I wish you were here.
But this is no place for you to be.
As I lie here lonely too.
All I do is think of you.
But that is all I want to do.

John Barquin

Untitled

Touch the Earth
Feel the Texture
Taste the Fruit
Smell the Sweetness
Speak the Truth
Hear the Tone
Share the Experience
Breathe with Time
Play with Expression
Weather the Journey
Know the Rhythm of Life

Ellen Spicer

Untitled

Spring,
Fickle lady, she—
Peeking in the door,
flirting with the sun awhile
before boldly walking in
with her love just past—
not yet willing to let go
the tempting snowflake kisses
of persistent winter snow.
Spring,
a tease,
flaunting her newly green,
yet holding back
before rushing out the door
to greet her golden lover
and wile away the days
until Spring again gets restless and
Summer
takes her place

Jeannie Ramsey

Address Unknown

White envelopes
fill my mailbox
with your name
printed across
the empty space
in my handwriting.

Red ink stamps
"Return to Sender"
"Addressee Unknown"
through the thoughts
and memories I
carefully enclosed.

Time has gone by fast
in the six months
of our silence.
Six months that took
seven years of you
to a place
I can't find.

Debra Rath

Christmas Sadness

Christmas time is here,
Filled with sorrow and cheer.
We miss the ones not here,
In our hearts they really are there.

Christmas time is here,
Say a prayer for those not there.
We wish they were,
But sadly they aren't.
They left us,
Never to be forgot.

Christmas time is here,
Spend it with those who are there,
Because at one time they won't be near.
They'll leave you with special memories,
as those left before.

Amanda Schofield

Joy

Toe-tapping
Finger-snapping
Eye-twinkling
Rib-tickling
Side-splitting
Belly-laughing
Lip-quivering
Throat-choking
Voice-cracking
Tear-misting
Heart-melting
Spirit-bubbling
Overflowing joy.

David V. Every

The Field

Hippos turn their zippo
flick the light
brigade

Raul merits a medallion
strewn mushroom costs
the battalion Arnie's souffle

Lefty loosened his tie baited
fly fishing for the hate
in the salt water

Arteries batteries
calamity caravan
the heard got an award

Macadamia nut
macaroons juxtaposed on nests
of lattice origami

Alphabet from Duluth
mixed his homestead
with water

The pages were sewn
on the quilt the Colonel slept heavy under.

Andrew Curwin

The Pessimists' Lament

I sat and watched a squirrel today
flittering around the yard in play.
Undaunted by the trials of life,
never touched by care or strife.

I thought how good to be so free,
never a care like you and me.
He's got it made that's for sure
to be like him would be life's cure.

Then I thought, what in the world,
who wants to be like a silly squirrel?
He's got problems too you see,
someone will soon cut down his tree.

And all the nuts he's stored away;
Gone when winter comes cold and gray.
What will he do without food or den?
Die from hunger, cold or men?

Rodent, mammal, fish or fowl,
pass around the crying towel.
We all have troubles, don't you see?
Sooner or later they'll cut our tree.

Bobby W. Phillips

Reflections On Watching The Snow

Falling bits of downy white
Floating through the air at night
To blanket every rock and tree;
A wonderland for you and me.

Powder falling from the sky,
Silver make-up drifting by.
Touching all with tender care,
Silver beauty everywhere.

Tiny diamonds everywhere,
Caressing faces, dotting hair.
Creating crowns that will not last,
This lovely sight fades all too fast.

Whirling, twirling fairies gay
Dance by night, dance by day.
Dancers whirling round and round
Soon fall to death upon the ground.

Dixie Lee Meyer

Seasons

Carelessly throughout the air
Flutter autumn's leaves
Everywhere

Silently upon the hill
Fall winter's snowflakes
Deep and still

Faithfully across the earth
Flourish spring's first gifts
Eternal birth

Settling down for the night
Glows summer's dusky
Warm twilight

So life comes, so life goes
Bringing summer's warmth,
Winter's snows

Life with pleasure, life with pain
Seasons returning
Once again.

Ann Joyner

Alone With Love

Alone I've watched the sea gulls,
Flying just below the clouds;
And alone I've shed a tear
With every cry they sound.

Alone I've watched the sunset,
Thinking back to you and I;
And alone I relive promises
That did wither but not die

Alone I think of passion,
And the fires we did start;
And alone I see the water
That soon feel upon my heart.

Alone I feel that water; now
The falls they do still flow;
And alone I weep in silence
For my heart cannot let go.

Howard Cinnamon

A Son Lost

I felt his breath upon my cheek,
for as the wind he began to speak.

Dad, I heard, look above
and pick a star.
For that, I feel,
is where we are.

In your heart I shall reside
until the time with me beside
we look together far below
and see as one all we know.

It is then the truth be known,
we are never never all alone.

Our hearts and souls have been as one
and now as my time is done,
I've come to see how much a part of me
your love and tender care will always be.

And then I felt him move away,
leaving with me a part to stay.
Rest well my son, I thought
and thank you for
the gifts you brought.

John B. Parmenter

Untitled

My heart bleeds bitter tears.
For chances stolen
before they could be given.
For my soul ruled by fears.
I build walls
to hide behind,
which crumble
at a chance word,
burying my being
in the rubble of my mind,
from which
there is no escape.
My heart bleeds bitter tears.

Gayle Freese

Courage He Handed Me

My daddy wore a medal
for combat bravery.
I now fight a battle on
the field of recovery.

Bloody deaths within
infantry of grief
in my private fox hole
where earth darker deep.

Courage he handed me
with his loaded gun,
although our battles differ
like his, my freedom won.

Jean Holthaus

Our Memories

Memories are the key;
For you and me.
No matter how petty they may be.
The lifeline for our past;
Because it comes and goes so fast.
Without memories we would be nothing.
Flesh and bone;
But no soul to live and love from.
Our memories; the key to the past.

Duncan McBogg

A Chance

For every life - the unknown
For every dream - an obstacle
For every fear - despair
For every conflict - prejudice
For every question - an allegation
For every weakness - vulnerability
For every weakness - a strength
For every question - the truth
For every conflict - a resolution
For every fear - courage
For every dream - hope
For every life - a chance.

Debra E. Phillips

My Heart Is Plagued With Sadness

My heart is plagued with sadness,
For I have lost a friend I loved.
My heart is plagued with sadness,
As I watch the days go by.
Sometimes I can almost see,
My puppy coming to greet me.

My heart is plagued with sadness,
I miss his soft puppy brown eyes,
The copper fur that easily shed,
And the times he made me laugh.
I miss the kisses he use to give,
When he missed me too.

My heart is plagued with sadness;
My puppy has passed away.
I'll never forget that dark and dreary,
January day.
I saw him lying on the road;
The warmth and light were gone.
My heart is plagued with sadness;
He was forever cold.

Darla Reed

"Someone I'm Not 'Posed To Be"

Someone I'm not 'posed to be
For someone dealing fantasy
Good to know you're not alone
Darling just pick up your phone.

Somewhere in your fantasy
You meet someone not 'posed to be
Does this mean you'll take him home
Could this mean you'll never roam.

Dealing with your fantasy
Has drawn me from reality
Don't know who I'm supposed to be
Your love now takes control of me.

Someone I'm not 'posed to be
Drowning in your fantasy
Living life of make believe
To hold your love
That won't hold me.

Clarence Williams

Untitled

You
Have awakened me,
and I
shall never sleep again
not knowing you.
For it is us,
That is of utmost importance
to me.

Annette Berkley

His Greatest Blessing

There's a girl named Seal
For the 'Boys she used to cheer
With zest and zeal
To me she has no peer.

She's a ray of sunshine
Who brings about joy
These loving thoughts of mine
The devil can't destroy.

There's a child she's raising
While working for Ford
All the time praising
Jesus Christ our Lord.

Though often we're apart
And have no time to share
The love in my heart
Is constant in prayer.

She likes to sing
And loves me as I am
The gifts God will bring
To a girl name Pam.

Guy A. Taylor

Christmas Prayer

We thank you Father,
for the light that shines
Forever in each of us,
For this day, Your
Birthday and ours.

We honor the birth of
Your Spirit, because You
Share it with us.
We are one, united in
This light with you.

Let us today behold
Each other in this light!
How beautiful we are!
How holy and loving!
Come and join with Me today.
"We save the world
When we are joined."

Brenda Balzarini

"Time"

Time is for waiting
for things to come true
for planning good things
for me and for you

Time is to share
with ones that we love
and for viewing the stars
and the moon up above

Time is for using
and learning of life
for planning a family
and loving a wife

But time seems so short
in fulfilling our dreams
We grow weak and get old
so forgotten it seems

But time must go on
and for others it will
for dreams they will have
the need to fulfill

Dan McCormick

Forever

I wanted us to stay together
Forever
But I never
Thought about all the difficulties
There would be
And about all the arguments
It doesn't make sense
So before you ever
Want to stay with someone forever
Please think about all the things
That forever brings.

Jennifer Kemery

I Lay Awake

How odd to
forget the
white rain
feel the moon
moved in
and out of
clouds the
stars
watched me
and I
watched you
gently sleeping
on the brink
of a dream
where I
held to
your hand afraid
that the rain
would soon
drown me.

Brandy Sprunger

Friends:

Friends are forever
friends are to care
friends are their for you
when no one cares.
We have to be friends
we have to be free
we have to make friends
between you and me.

Friends are supposed to be their
through thick and thin
but not with your
friends man don't you see.

When a good friend
let a man come between them
that was not a friend indeed

So never trust a friend with your man
because friends are for ever
but a man is not never trust a man
because all he would do is lie to you.
but never let a man come between two
great friends.

Bettina McCaskill

The Rose

A rose blooms,
Happiness and joy.
A mistake is made,
Tears and sadness.
Apology accepted.
The rose dies,
And I'm still alive.

Jennifer Mosca

Positive Thoughts

I watched the moon arise last night
From low behind a hill
The silver moon, the golden stars
The heavy darkness still

I saw the graceful swaying pines
In darkness bravely stand
I saw the beauty of the sea
The beauty of the land

I breathed a breath of earths pure air
I knelt on bended knee
So thankful in all life's beauty
That God found room for me

And since he is the architect
of a world I've yet to see
I have no fear, I'll be at home
In the place that he prepares for me

Geraldine E. Moore

Perfect Life

Consider a question,
From me it derives;
To answer it justly,
Means our love survives.

Were my hopes too high,
Or were yours too low?
The answer is simple,
We'll never know.

While distance is growing,
The visions may fade;
All said and done promptly,
Decisions are made.

Our desire is so forceful,
Our need so sincere;
We rebel against freedom,
That which we most fear.

Too elusive to capture,
Impossible to find;
The perfect life lies,
In the depths of our mind.

Jerry Hollis

People Run

People run
from sand storms,
tornadoes, and hail stones.
People run
from raging fire,
a rising tide,
and air pollution.

People run
from fearful things
like the bee, the wasp, and the bear.
People run frightened
to escape
the dog pack,
the lurking shadow.
People run blind
from time, from truth,
and destiny,
and people run away from themselves!

Carolyn T. Abbot

My God (...Is Your God Too!)

I pray to God to save my soul
from this wretched pain I feel
to feed me with His loving word
the world's most pleasant meal

The hurt I feel, the loneliness
compares not in the least
to what my Lord had suffered then
with nails in hands and feet

The black I thought had filled me up
seems hardly black at all
with God's bright light to fill my soul
to lift me when I fall

So I lift my head and swallow hard
and trust in Jesus Christ
for when this world comes to an end
I'll be saved by His great might

So listen now, here's what to do
to save your soul like me
trust in the Lord and love Him so
And with Him you'll always be!

David M. Onder

Little Lies

Lies ooze
from your lips
like peanut butter
sliding
down
the
side
of
the
jar.

Falling
too fast-
You can't catch it...
The damage is done.

Anita Fee

The Heart

The heart is such a tender thing,
Full of courage and affections,
It guides down the road life,
Leads us in many directions.

It also is wicked and deceitful,
Pretending to be true,
It also is vain and forceful,
Which makes us do the things we do.

Who should know the heart but God,
Let every man be a liar,
who can raise the spirit of love,
and make it soar higher and higher.

The heart, mind, and soul are one,
So be lead by God only,
You'll always have peace and love,
Your heart will never be sad or lonely.

Delando Duane Reese

Organ Pipes

Tall and slender,
Gilt and silver,
Shouting with a celestial mouth,
Sans eyes or nose.

Standing side by side waiting
For the organist's signal,
Little pipes finally tweet
Like the sweet treble voice of a bird.

Big pipes growl deeply, like a lion.
They all sing out like a choir,
Celebrating the glory of God.

Deep and dark as coal
Are the mouths of the great pipes.
From within this darkness,
There is color, tones dull and brilliant,
Quiet and loud.

Each pipe is like an individual.
All tones and pipes create the
Mighty Organ!

Amy Wolfe

A Garlic Glance

The garlic fully grown
Glanced at me
From across the Garden.
Proud Garlic
Pistol and pistils
100's of them ball up
the garlic stem
Erect.

The garlic strip tease-
Filaments of skin
Molt
in Erotic
Display.

This is not an ode to a clove of Garlic
I once found under my tongue.

If Garlic be equal to 100 Mothers
A poem of Garlic be equal to 100 Muses
For if a poem be other than amuse,
It be food for the soul.

Gary C. Smith

Innocence Lost

Innocence in children
Glitters like diamonds
And
Radiates like the sun

While simplicity caresses
Youthful laughter and
Apples of gold fill curious eyes
With sparkles of hope

Years pass and children
Grow and innocence recedes
Like eventide into the
Secrets of night

Where - if I may ask - is the
Mirth of youthfulness...
And who - if you can tell - will
See innocence beyond today?

James R. Richards

Tomorrow

Tomorrow, people,
go buy yourselves some happy clothes,
do wear your happy faces,
go visit those places
that make you happy people.

Do that, yet pray today,
so that the sun may rise tomorrow.
Do that, forget your sorrow,
don't drawn tomorrow in yesterday.

Tomorrow I'll put on my happy face,
I'll see if I can find some clothes,
'cause it might turn out to be a day
a lot better than it is today.

Let's wear our happy faces, people!
Let's say today we will tomorrow.
I'll wear my happy face myself,
to hide behind my face of sorrow.

Felipe A. Sánchez

On This Day

Petals for a Bouquet,
God gave me a few
He sent them to me,
To give to you
He gave me the benefit,
Of your love too
Here on your birthday,
I've not gone a stray

My love for you,
Grows greater each day
May all the troubles,
He sent your way
Turn to glory for Him
On that narrow way
You travel alone,
With Him to stay.

Arthur St. Louis Sr.

Memories Through Time

Once upon a time,
God whispered in my ear,
"Do you think you have the love,
And time for another baby, dear"?

And I knew there was a purpose,
That He said these words to me.
Maybe I was extra special,
for He'd already sent me three.

They're growing up so quickly,
And often I have dreams,
That we could spend days over again.
All of them it seems.

And time has passed so swiftly,
Would we stop it if we could,
So we could enjoy the moments more,
The ones we really should.

Ann Culver

Untitled

In a clear blue sky
I look over a wheat field
I pretend I am a wheat stalk
One in a million
I have learned a lesson;
Although I think I'm special
There are a million others like me.

Clint Johnson

I Surrender

Like the rainbow following a storm
Gracefully
I Accept
Like the snowflake on a sunny day
Humbly
I release
Like the rain fall trailing thunder
Respectfully
I respond
Like the sun shower in spring time
Silently
I retreat
Like the warmth in summer
Lovingly
I care
Like the hours in a day
Willfully
I surrender

Brenda Renee Boler

Grasp Life

Take both hands and
grasp the full hold of life,
not just half way,
or a little at the time,
as life can get away, and
before you know it
your last bell will chime.
life is too precious and too short
to let it go to waste—
grasp life with all you have, and
get your full taste.

Brenda G. Hancock

I Bid You Farewell

Cry if you will
Grieve for the loss
Free the room in your heart

Remember me, all that I gave
Yours for the keeping

Rejoice with me
Life's endless seasons
Spring follows winter
Renewal abounds
New growth where roses bloom

Wounds heal with tenderness
Tears and laughter without regret
Birds in flight ever changing

Etchings of you, all that you gave
Mine for the keeping

Spirits of shared compassion
Hearts filled with acceptance
Hands held in caring
Eyes reflecting self-worth restored
I bid you farewell!

Dolores Eaves Peterson

Untitled

I consider you no fool
I love to laugh
I believe in making merry
Let us then rejoice
Your laughter enlightens the heavens
Causing my dimples to show
You're life's most fondest treasure
You're my Jovial Soul.

Beverly Williams

"True-Light"

The Lord is my shepherd he is my light
Guiding my soul to do what is right.
He is thee essence of truth in being
Well worth waiting for and seeing.
When your feeling down and alone
And your heart turns to stone.
Get down on your knee
Pray to the Lord to come and seize.
For the one truth in christianity
Is that Gods our hope, heart and sanity.

Gary Dean Fredrickson

If I Was A Picture

I wish I was a picture
hanging on the wall;
So I could see the people
big, small or tall
They would all look at me,
and would not let me fall.
I would always wear a
smile, and be so shining and bright.
So you wouldn't be scared
of those dark and drewy nights.
I could be your friend
some one to talk too!
And always keep your secrets
And never reveal a thing.
cause, I'm only a picture
hanging in a shiny brass frame.

Carol Jones

Memories

My father's love
has always made me strong
Guiding my path
whether I was right or wrong
The years have flown
since he was laid to rest
So I keep his memory
tucked within my breast
And though I long
for my eyes to see
He's never really
too far from me.

Joan A. Maier

Untitled

Having a faith in nature
have faith in man
Be good to nature and
Nature will be good to you
Why is there something
Rather than the nothing,
What a miracle the universe
What a miracle God is
What a miracle the atom is
What a miracle life is
Don't ask how or why?
What a miracle, it's magical
Nature is a work of art.

Carl Faso

Hi Mom And Dad

Are you busy July 8th?
Have you plans that you could change?
Are you free that summer day?

It's important that we know
So we're calling you to ask.
Hope you won't say "I dunno"

Or "why?" or "huh?" or "maybe".
For on that day next summer
We're having us a baby!

Anita L. Gay

A Precious Soul

In the freezing rain, to me,
He came,
with gifts of joy and laughter.

A precious soul with love untold,
He lingers on with me,
Here after.

His smile,
His grace,
His loving face,
are but reminders of yesterday.

The hopes,
The dreams
of heavenly things
are sure to Lead the way.

I move along the path he made,
with desire to meet him there.

We'll meet beside the river wide,
no earthly reunion to compare.

Judith Jane Miller

Invisible Love

When I look into his eyes
he can't see me,

When I talk to him
he can't hear me,

When I touch him
he can't feel me,

When I tell him I love him
he says he loves me,

But does he?

Jean Marie Beach

Patience - Please!

He giveth strength to the weary,
He giveth power to the faint
But sometimes I wish He would hurry -
A patient person I ain't!

Sometimes the answer is "no,"
Sometimes with a "yes" we are blessed
But you can rest assured,
The Lord does know what is best.

I've often wished I could help Him
Answer the prayers of a friend -
One who's going through perilous times
And having woes without end.

But we must learn to be patient -
Wait for Him to show us the way,
For after the storm is over,
There does come a brighter day!

Jean D. Wisner

Grandpa's Garden

Grandpa had a garden.
He loved to watch it grow.
And in this little garden,
His plants, they lived in rows.
And to this day we wonder,
How the years do show,
Now that Grandpa's gone,
Why won't his garden grow?

Angela Van Brunt

Untitled

Big and small,
He loves us all,
He tells us that,
We can always call.
He'll lend an ear,
When we have a fear,
He says, "Be not afraid,
I am always near,"
Rejoice,
For you have heard God's voice.
You have heard him speak,
Saying, "Do not be weak,
Be strong, with all that you do,
For, I am always with you."

Jill Schulte

"That Homeless Man"

He was a homeless man,
He wandered from town to town.
His only clothes were upon his back,
His only bed, upon the ground

He was always unshaven,
He had unkempt long hair,
Being mistaken for a beggar,
His feet were sometimes bare.

Some people called him crazy,
Some people just laughed at him,
Even when stones were being thrown,
With a smile, he forgave them.

Do not be so quick to judge
The appearance of any ONE,
You never know, who they might be,
"That Homeless Man" - Our Father's Son.

Cyndi Whorton-Brooks

Untitled

Did my Micky come to heaven Lord?
He went away last night
Vet. said his heart stopped beating
And he could not be revived.
Oh did he come to heaven Lord?
I really want to know
He was such a precious doggie
And oh I loved him so.
Did my Micky come to heaven Lord?
I really think he did
I'll think of him as running free
And racing through the wind
As happy as a dog can be
While waiting there for me.

Eva Sizemore

Untitled

Portrait of a man alone-
heart of gold.
Silence setting a lifeless tone-
the corner where he keeps the
wolf from the door.
He has no door.

The arctic winter of his discontent.
Shivering.
Words he said - he never meant.

Too much pride-
man can't confess.
No justice in being homeless.

Jenny Mullins

Laurel Unaware

Flaming hair frames
her face with threads
of gold,

And the light,
leaping from her lustrous eyes,
hesitates upon her once
angelic
mouth.

Bonnie L. Blankenship

Below The Cherry Tree

Below the cherry tree
Here, as I sit,
The breeze of a cool wind
Blows gently on my brow.
(Oh, if you could feel it now!)

Within the shade
The air is nipped
With the chill of the
Soon coming Autumn days -
Then snowy Winter haze.

But contented am I,
For the moment at hand,
As I still hear the wren
Belting out his song -
To hear it now, before it's gone.

Cindy R. Buckingham

"Arvell"

How can I give up my brother?
He's such a part of me.
You see, he really is the trunk
Of our entire family tree.

We never hugged or kissed
Or spoke about our love
Our bond was so much deeper
Like the beauty of a morning dove.

Thru the years as we aged
Our bonds just grew and grew -
Unspoken words we exchanged -
Somehow we always knew.

But now we are faced with parting
How dire this world will be.
I know the place he's going
Will offer peace eternally.

Bit Johnson

Untitled

Higher, float
high into the sky
into the night, take flight
from the day in the way
of the world up above
covered in a shroud of cloud
float like a boat
on a sea of sky, so high
reach up
reach far towards the stars
breathe the freedom up there
and dare to take the air
that's yours
as you rise to the sky
with life in your eyes
the quiet sky is yours to take
as you break away from the life you make
below, but go slow
and take to the moon, it's yours
balloon

Brad Spears

The Dance

I saw you dance with God
His hand was light
to thy touch -
his feet,
were graceful to thy soul -
his lips,
tender, as touched by
passion -
he swirled you in his arms,
and when you stopped spinning
my arms were snug around your body -
the heartbeat of your spirit
kept rhythm to my soul
and now,
it was my turn -
to dance with God!

Jan T. Philips

Why?

His hands are so soft
His smiles so big
His eyes always sparkle
Why does he keep them hid.

His heart is so big
It's so filled with love
His soul is so jolly
It's so filled with life
Why does he keep them hid

Everyone loves him.
Why doesn't he know
I guess it just don't show.
Now he'll never know.

Helen Kelley

Memory Of Mine

Help me.
Hold me.
My memory of mine.

I can see you so clearly,
So beautifully sitting there,
With your arms outstretched for me.
My memory of mine.

Don't let go.

James Polo

The Voices

I push past my instincts,
Hold on to my fears,
The rain is coming,
And so are my tears.

Drop among drop,
They fall to the ground
Not knowing when to stop,
Not knowing what I've found.

My innerself is speaking,
Love is what I'm seeking,
But I can wait until the day,
When things will go my way.

They say that I will know,
As I grow,
They say that when you do,
You will feel that it is true.

But will I ever feel that way?
The voices say someday.
Someday.

Becky Smith

"The World Through Shattered Glasses"

Insanity
holds me now
overwhelms
brings me down
walls
closing in
prisoner
alone again
corruption
tears my brain
mentality
stereotyped deranged
talking
on this phone
lines cut
no one's home
delirious
can't tell right from wrong
reality
fading...I don't belong

Colin Smith

I Care

You think I'm a tease,
I assure you I'm not.
My feelings run deep,
much more than a thought.

I think of you often,
most every day.
Sometimes just a memory,
which I've tucked away.

We have both changed,
much time has gone by.
It's hard to go back,
for yet one more try.

You seem like a stranger,
that I once knew.
Perhaps you are feeling,
these same feelings too.

Debra J. Taylor

To Dad

I barely take the time to say
How much you really mean to me
I may be bad and get real mad
But I think you are really rad

You were there when I was born
You gave me my first bath
You held me in your arms
And you even took me home

You taught me how to walk and talk
And even how to read
You helped me learn to play new games
Which took a lot of time

You took me on your fishing trip
And taught me how to fish
You let me stay up really late
Even when mom said, "No"

I am glad you taught me all these things
It's helped me do a lot
I think you are the greatest Dad
So really, THANKS A LOT!

Jason Hooker

The Little Brook

Water, water in the brook
How sparkling and effervescent you look
Swiftly racing with the tide
Over the rocks and knolls you ride
Who do you race with? Why do you ride
Into the inlets to run and hide?

Now dusk has fallen; the flowers sleep
The animals into their homes will creep
The trees and vines will rest together
But you dear brook run on forever!

Annette A. Rizzotto Valenti

The Passage

Each day I am noticing
How time rushes by
And months disappear
In the wink of an eye.

The days of my youth
Have now long past
And the middle years
Are going to Fast!

I find myself asking
In moments of true seeing
What lessons I've learned
In this passage of being.

I admit to being stubborn
And I choose my own way,
Marching to a different drummer
Or so my friends say.

Will I have to return
To this world once more,
Or can I rest for awhile
After I pass through that door?

Barbara A. Dunn

To Know

I need to know
How you feel about me.
Some people say you're nice,
Some people say you're sweet,
And you are really shy.
But I need to know,
Oh, yes I need to know
If you feel about me
The same as I feel
About you?
Always and forever.
Love Me.

Danelle Lacey

Mystery

Death and despair are not fair,
I am dead put me to bed.

Life is gone,
Who knows why?

I am mortal and cannot fly,
Why spare the gift of hate?

That is why we all must dedicate.

A rose is beautiful and so ripe,
Why must we all scream and gripe?

Prettier is the sun at dawn,
Move your King not your Pawn.

Love is so an unusual a thing?

Help me.

Adrienne Dafcik

Untitled

Over and over again
I am in this familiar place
In the hands of a man
There, I can't look at my own face

There, safety is a false sense
Feeling nonexistent is where I end
Invisibility is intense
How do I stop this trend?

Inside I am screaming,
"My God, let me be my own!"
To Him it must be seeming
Proportionately out-blown

My heart
Is replaced with death
I must start
To breathe my own breath!

Deborah Carter

I

"Do not stand at my grave and weep,
"I am not there, I do not sleep.
"I am a thousand winds that blow;
"I am the diamond glints on the snow.
"I am the sunlight on ripened grain;
"I am the gentle autumn's rain
"When you awaken in the morning's hush,
"I am the swift uplifting rush
"Of quiet birds in circled flight.
"I am the soft star that shines at night.
"Do not stand at my grave and cry.
I am not there, I did not die."

Ashley Webb

"Afloat"

In my flight - I am free.
I am warmed by rays,
Calm in mind.

My senses have no limit,
I feel - I touch,
What my heart believes.

I am pulled heavenward.
My realm is peace.
I can be myself.

The underside flourishes.
There are no flaws.
Just silent, patterned scenery.

In this flight - I am loved.
Embraced by light.
If loved not by man, then by God.

In my flight - I am free,
No proving of my worth,
I am me.

Barbara Lee Fritts

God's Pictures

Doesn't God paint pretty pictures?
I asked my child one day,
The pretty flowers, the graceful trees,
The clouds, that seem to play,
The animals wondering every where,
The birds gliding gracefully in the air,
The many hours I spend looking to see,
The beautiful pictures God made for me.

Darlene Cunningham

A Cycle Broken

Exploring at the beach,
I came upon a cove
A lovely pool of water,
And there I would have dove
But caught my eye a lobster,
A lovely shade of red
But when I picked it up,
I knew that it was dead.
It couldn't put its body,
Back in nature's hand
Because the oil that killed it
Poisoned all the land.
I saw its only purpose,
To recycle life on earth
His only purpose taken,
He waited for from birth
I knew this purpose stolen,
Was even worse than dying
And standing there, on that beach,
I knew his soul was crying.

Breanne Moneymaker

The Tiny Seed

I'm a tiny seed that wants to grow.
I don't have a stem or a petal to show.
Does anyone care or even know?
It sure takes a lot for me to grow.
All the others have grown and gone away,
here I sit for another day.

If you pass by and see me this way,
all I ask is that you pray,
hoping I've grown by the
month of May.

Gail Kafka

"Care"

Why do I care
I care, cause you are so special
I care, cause you are you
I care, cause you are so humble
in all the things you do
I care, cause when you smile
You bring on a new day
A glitter of sunshine, that
chases all fears away
I care cause you are someone
Who cares how other's feel
You show a special kindness
That no one can reveal
I care, cause you are so wonderful
and do the things you do
you show a deep affection
That's so very warm and true
I care, my precious one
for all these things are you.

Bill Verdon

"What Was Her Name?"

"What was her name?", he asked.
I did not ask her the name,
for I was acquainted with her heart.

"What does she do?", he asked.
I did not ask her that,
for I was enlightened by her words.

"Where does she live?", he asked.
I did not inquire, for
we were contemplating our world.
"Why did you not ask these
things of her?" he inquired.

I did not ask her these things
because I was talking with
a friend.

Angela Curl Reaves

"Confused"

Confused.
I don't know where to turn.
I have so many questions.
Who will give me answers?
Confused.
What to do?
What is right?
What is wrong?
Confused.
Should I stay?
Should I go?
Where would I go?
Confused.
I need to cry.
I want to cry.
Does anyone understand?
Confused.

Jennifer Townsend

Untitled

With the sunlight,
I turn my brush to daydreams.
That I outline indigo blue.....

James B. Hartel

Who Said It Can Be Done?

Who said it can be done?
I don't see how
It's a task of meticulous work
That could take...
Well, I actually don't know

This task is beyond my reach,
I do believe
Yet they say it can be done,
How?

I bet they believe I'm naive
And have no sense
But yet I don't see them
tackling this really hard task

I'm trying my very best,
I really am, I am
What should I do?

...I have decided to put
This heavy load to rest
For I know
It can't be done

Alan G. Ray

Ah, Majes

Like a cobra in a woven basket
I emerged from my world
And danced for you.
Your soul was the music
that drew me,
Your eyes that begged
passion
Pulled me farther and farther from
my woven world.
Your being that cried to possess me
Urged me to break free.

Suddenly, your music stopped-
Your soul sublimed into a nebulous
cloud.
Your eyes dulled in the light of
solipsistic truth.
Your being, still begging,
turned from me.
Now my basket world protects
me once more.

Evelyn H. Harlow

As The Years Go By

As the year go by
I find myself ready to cry.
Everyone grows up fast
And there is always one who is last.
As the years go by
Sometimes I want to cry.
Sometimes you keep
What you want to lose
And sometimes you lose
What you want to keep
As the years go by
I find my friends ready to cry.
This world is a hard place to live
And sometimes it's hard to forgive
If you know what I am trying to say
You know I am saying
You never know when you can lose your
friends, future, family or your life ...

Jessica Pittman

Preparing A Cup Of Tea

The coffee pot I've been using
I fry it in the boiling water
Everyday
And time and again in a day
Pretending sterilization.

But now I know it, wasn't
Germs killed by the heat
But my soul.

I prepare a cup of tea
To quench my thirst
Only to find the unquenchable thirst
In my heart.

The water is boiling.
And my heart is burning.

Julia K. Lee

Mother Dear

Mother, dear, I'm glad you're here,
I have something to tell you.
You really mean the world to me
And here's how much I love you.

I love you for the prayers you said
At night when you put us to bed,
I love you for the songs you sung
To calm our fears when we were young.

For making home a happy place
As we grew up the world to face.
Your love is strong in time of sorrow
Yet faith and hope for each tomorrow.

A mother's love cannot be bought,
But it's a precious treasure.
My heart is full of love for you
That words can never measure.

Mother, dear, oh, mother dear,
I want to tell you while you're here
So soon our life will come and go
I love you so, I love you so.

Emma Bradley

As You Watch

As you watch me from above
I know you feel my lasting love
with broken heart I'll always miss
your gentle touch and loving kiss.

In my heart I hold you dear
and feel your presence ever near
Though our worlds are far apart
the love holds fast within my heart

I remember you, my first love
as you watch me from above
you come to me in form of Dove
or the smell of flowers that I love

Many hours spent in thought
wondering if, why or what

If only I could have been
there with you at the end
to whisper softly, words of love

I know you're watching from above

Barbara A. Tankersley

The Rose I Watch

As I walk by a pretty rose
I like to just stare
I watch the petals blow in the breeze
and watch the last dew drop fall to the
ground
I watch as its color gets redder
as the orangeish sun gets brighter
I watch the rose quiver as a
curious bee approaches
I watch it open more as it begins
to rain to get a drink from the
cool water
I watch it die as a human picks it
to play a game
"He loves me, he loves me not"
I watch myself find another rose
to admire

Jennifer Warfe

Honey, I Love

Honey, I love the sun in the Spring.
I love the sun, it shines like God.
Like an angel in the sky, yes an angel.
Honey, I love the sun in the spring.

Honey, I love natures music.
Natures music has the touch that
makes me feel loved. I love nature.
Honey, I love natures music.

Honey, I love roses.
Roses feel like an apple.
Roses smell gentle.
Honey, I love roses.

Honey, I love my Parents.
My parents are everything to me.
If anything happens to them I don't know
What I would do.
Honey, I love my Parents.

And Honey, I love you!

Amanda Brown

God's Grace

I love you God my Savior
I love you God my King
I love you in the valley's low
and when the birds do sing.

You walked the land of Galilee
you touched both great and small
you always stopped to listen
just in case I called.

You made the stars of Heaven
you hold them in their place
yet in our saddest moments
you cover us in your grace.

Your heart of love is beating
it knocks on every door
to give us many blessings
that you have kept in store.

The sun comes up each morning
as if to say hello
the men go to the vineyard
so that the wine may flow.

Birdie J. Walker

To My Daughter

Since first I saw your tiny face
I loved you from the start
From then until forever
You're special in my heart

And now that you're all grown up
With children of your own
I look at you and wonder
Where all the years have gone

You'll never know what joy it is
To see you face to face
To look into your loving eyes
For none can take your place

To look into your loving eyes
It's not just you I see
My mother's eyes, my father's smile
And even some of me

I'm sad that you're so far away
But want you dear to know
You'll always be my little girl
I'll always love you so.

Irene Holodnak

When

When I tell you I love you,
I mean it.
When you give me a hug,
I love it.
When I say I'm sorry,
I am.
When I tell you I won't give up,
I won't.
When I hear a slow song,
I think of you.
When I tell you I will love you forever,
I mean that to.

Debra Lee Mincey

Someone To Love

I wish I could find someone to love.
I need someone to love.
Where's my someone to love?
I can't find him.
He can't find me.
What am I to do?
I need you.
There's no time, to rewind.

What's a person suppose to do?
I need love.
I want love.
I've been in love.
I need that feeling.

Will I find it again?
Will it hurt again?
I need you.
I want you.
Where are you?

Jeanette Bell

Them

I want to be wanted
I need to be needed
I'd love to be loved
Oh why can't I be
like the people I see
But not you
Not I
Never we
Only them
Always them
Why can't they see
I just want to be
Like them
But not, you, not I, never we
Only them
It would be nice to be wanted
It would be nice to be needed
But to be loved
To be loved
Like them

Beth Arena

"Spoken From Her Heart"

He's too old for you
I never heard

You've too much more
Life to live

I did not care
Tomorrow didn't matter

It might not even come
I was living for Now

This moment only
Her words echo daily

Years have gone by
Why didn't I listen

I've lost hair to
Those vicious hands

A foot now aches
In weather not nice

Confidence is no longer
Is it really me who needs

I know she still cares
She cares...and God

Cedeirdre S. Freeman

Beautiful Birds

Beautiful Birds in the sky
I often wonder, how you fly
Your beautiful wings
Stretch so far
Almost like a flying star
Some of your beaks are long
Some of your beaks are short
You come in all colors
And you come in all sorts
Some of you fly high
And some fly low
Some of you fly fast
And some fly slow
God made you all pretty
And that's no lie
So please continue to fly
In our beautiful sky

Deborah M. Stopczynski

"For William Michael"

My little one, I loved you so.
I only wish I'd seen you grow.

Your tiny life is gone from me,
A branch broke off my family tree.

God has a special place for you.
I live because I know this is true.

I too have a special place you see,
In my heart you will always be.

I love you so, my little one.
God please take care of my baby son.

Candy Carlton

"Good-Bye"

The time has come to say good-bye -
I promise you I will not cry
I loved you so - you made me laugh
But time was what we didn't have

The hours with you went by so fast
If only love could last and last
I loved you so - you made me smile
but Love like ours just lasts awhile

You had so much of life to share
I wanted more - it wasn't fair
It's hard to say why love goes wrong
So I'll just stay where I belong

Now your free - I let you go
And time stands still for me, I know

Gail Martin

So Little Time

So little time to say the things,
I really want to say.
Before I even find the words,
Time has slipped away.

So little time to do the things,
Places I would like to see.
So, I'll cherish to the fullest,
The life God has given me.

So little time to dream my dreams,
Youth has passed, I'm in my prime.
And all too soon, I realize,
That there is so little time.

So little time for passed regrets,
And less to make amends.
Yet God can heal the deepest wounds,
For those who, on him depends.

So little time to share Gods love,
And beauty here on earth,
To tell them of his endless love,
Its true meaning, and its worth.

Johnnie R. Money

Soul Of Coal

As I look into your eyes,
I see quarters.
Round in there shape,
Black as coal; with edges
that has burrs.
They reflect your soul; a
soul of darkness. Then I
step back, and realize; I
am gazing into a mirror of
my own lifeless meager soul.

Chris Fitch

Untitled

I remember your Dark Eyes
I remember your smile.
I still feel your warmth
They still linger awhile.

I hear you breathing even
though you're not here.
I feel your presence and
my heart stands still.

Why did you leave me
alone and undone?
I have no love and
no dreams since you've gone.

My arms are empty
My heart has no beat.
I hide from the morning.
The lonely night's repeat.

I steal from my memories
when I need you near.
I hope you remember
Remember me still.

Betty Hilton

Growing Up

When I was a baby
I sat in a chair,
When I was a baby
I yanked on my hair.
When I was a child
I went to the fair,
When I was a child
I flew in the air.
When I was a teenager
I drew graphic squares,
When I was a teenager
I met a lot of bears.
Now that I'm a grown-up
I have white hair,
Now that I'm a grown-up
I'm back in my chair.

Christopher Sweeney

The Man In My Dreams

I see a man is he there?
I see him everywhere,
in my dreams,
in my life
he is everywhere,
I think of him morning and night.
He is tall,
He is dark,
Who might this man be,
He claims he's my father
but that I do not know
I tell him he is not
that my father I have
not yet met and to my
surprise he replies,
I know I left but I gave
it thought and came back
I want you to be my daughter
but if I can't have that,
I would just like to be friends.

Crystal Upton

Dad

Now that you're gone,
I sit here and pray —
That the Lord will bring us together,
Together one day.
We're in two separate worlds,
that are so far apart,
But you know where you stand here,
Always in my heart.
Whenever I needed you,
you were always here,
to answer my questions,
to dry my tears.
I keep asking myself.
Why did Daddy go?
But the same answer comes to my mind,
I don't even know.
If the Lord chose you to go now,
it shouldn't have been like this.
I just want you to know,
that you're very, sadly missed.

Jamie Beasley

Journey to a New Beginning

Circle of light.
I surrender
To a new day.

The lady I await
Is uncharted territory
And knows no boundaries.

What phantom
Keeps her at bay?

When the physical need
Is subdued
An Appreciation
Of the fine aspects
Take hold.

I am ready.
Let the journey begin.
That with each
New day
Adventures await
To be discovered
And owned.

Alexis Griswold

Pictures In The Sky

Pictures in the sky.
I talk to them.
They talk to me.
I stare at one in particular.
And it stares back at me.
It shimmers and blinks.
And gets covered by clouds.
I wonder where it could be.
There are many pictures up there.
But only one is mine.
I stare at one in particular.
And it stares back at me.
It is so far away.
But yet so close.
It is my only friend.
My picture in the sky.

James Gulick

I'm Out Of Time To Rhyme

When
I think too much,
I leave my head
And go out of time
With my Rhyme.
This leaves all my senses dead.
So I must use a crutch.
But too much
Do I think.
This I write with ink.
I must sign,
Because;
I'm out of Time to Rhyme.

Byron Keith Wright

My Brother

When I left for vacation,
I thought I'd have fun,
But I didn't know, that when I got back,
My brother's life would be done,

I never knew I'd miss him,
But now he's gone,
It's too late to save him,
But there's nowhere to run,

Now I know, how much I cared,
When I think of the memories,
that we shared,

I wish I could tell him
I love him so,
And that if I had a choice,
He'd never go.

Elizabeth Gilbert

Before The End Of Time

Before the end of time
I want to be with you,
I want to have a life
with you there, too.

Before the end of time
I wonder what I would have done,
But without you here
I know I would have enjoyed none.

Before the end of time
there's so much I want to see,
I want to see our house
and what our love will grow to be.

Before the end of time
I want you to know,
That no matter where we are
My love for you will always show.

Before the end of time
know you are the only one for me,
No matter what happens,
my love, you will always be.

Jodi Raithel

Defiance

I tried to be though I failed
I worked hard to no avail
When things go wrong I bare the blame
and in my heart I did my best
So if someday something goes wrong
and I'm not there, please carry on
Wherever I am, I should have been
close by to except the wrong I missed

Remember thou someday you'll be
the one whose wrong and then you'll see
Thou you're right, you will be wrong
you'll know then as time goes on
No matter what you will be wrong
so if you think that you have won
Think again it has just begun

Remember now I've told you this
I'm wrong again but ponder this
Each day goes by they're getting older
and notice too they're getting bolder
If you felt good defying me remember
the acorn falls close to the tree

Hattie Mitchell

My Golden Heart

If I could
I would hold the world
in my arms
and
sing away
the pain
but
I can
hold
You
in my thoughts.
And
I do.

Barbara Broderick Flanagan

If I Were A Bird

If I were a bird
I'd fly toward the ocean,
put all my dreams
and my thoughts into motion.
I'd soar through the air
with my head held high
free to be me, myself, and I.
Leave all my troubles
and fears behind me,
pretend that all people are kind
like they should be.
But here I am
on the ground again,
hoping things will get better
but not knowing when.

Ann T. Cahill

Palindrome

Rats, a
racecar!
Side,
dual eyes,
mirror rims?
Eye-lauded.
Is
racecar
a star?

D. J. Cavoli

Heart And Soul

If I am dreaming, let me not wake,
If I am awake, never shall I dream.
My lungs full of fresh air,
My heart full of love.
If I am dead, leave me at peace,
If I am alive, let me never die.
Your love is all I ask,
Us to be as one is all I dream.
My soul is pure delight,
My heart is pure love.
Dare not take my soul,
Dare not break my heart.
My soul is all I have,
My heart is all I can give.
The sky, full of clouds,
My eyes, full of joyous tears.
Let not the cloud of darkness fall
upon my face,
But let your love and peace fill my heart and
soul with grace.

Christina Seay

It All Depends...

Christians say
If you
Don't believe
That Jesus is
The son of God
Then
You're going to go to hell

Islams say
If you
Do believe
That Jesus is
The son of God
Then
You're going to go to hell

Jews say
The son of God
Hasn't even come yet!
What the hell
Are you talking about??????

Ginger Penaluna

Forever Alone

Don't call,
I'll cry.
Don't look,
I'll die.
Don't talk,
I'll listen.

Just leave me alone.
I don't want to,
but I must,
I must let go of you.

I had a grasp,
you never did.
I'm forever alone.

Hilary M. Lewis

Hurt!

HURT!
I'll tell you what it does!

It makes my suffering miserable
It cuts me like a knife,
It makes my mind go wand'ring and
Lose focus of my life.

It makes my anger surface when
I least expect it to,
A look, a word, a smile can cause
My hate to grow for you.

HURT!
How do I overcome?

Remember, those that did you wrong
Will face me judgement day,
They'll wish the mountains fall on them
To hide themselves away

The evil one that tempted them
Is constantly with you,
If you don't let go all this hate
He'll be controlling you.

Hamby Ochmann

My Cross

I must carry a cross.
A cross not to scar me,
But to make me believe
In a power greater than mine.

I must carry a cross
Just like my Saviour.
His cross brought victory,
So will mine.

My cross carries no explanation
For we all face trials.
My cross is full of anticipation
Knowing Jesus is beside me.

As I carry my cross
I too shall flourish,
For God will nourish me
Through the storms.

My cross is one of understanding
That Jesus will never forsake me.
Together we will carry my cross.
My cross will be a blessing.

Tanya L. Holmquist

"I Like"

I like: Dogwood trees in bloom
A dark sky against a Harvest moon
Hearing the wind rustle leaves on a tree
Watching little bumble bees
Letting my dog out to run
Playing frisbee in the sun
Lying under the largest oak
Playing a little practical joke
Sledding on a cafeteria tray
Going out to eat and not having to pay
Driving a little sports car
Sitting on my bed strumming my guitar
Finding things that are very odd
Most of all putting my Trust In God.

Kimberly Maynor

"When Angels Come"

If you think you hear the world crashing
down around you.
It's really just the sound of Gods Angels
coming to surround you.
They are there to help give you the strength
to make it through the day.
Then you will know God truly loves you, and
it doesn't matter what others say.
So if your feeling blue my friend, just
stop and look around.
And, you will see that you are standing
there with Angels upon the ground.

Eric D. Milne

A Poem For Peace

Dream the dream of winning the Gold
Dream of dreams your grandmother told,
I dream the dream of winning first place
For swiftly swimming the butterfly in a swimming race
I dream the dreams of a future Olympic racer
While others dream of mastering the laser
But I know a dream we all dream together
Not of playing and sleeping among the heather
I mean the dream that all should dream
The one when all are in harmony, not racist or mean
I mean the dream that should have always come true
The one that people love you no matter if you are black white
or blue
"The lamb shall lie down with the leopard"
And no one's life would be made hard
"I have a dream." That great man used to say
"I have a dream to live in peace someday!"
Dream the dream of living on the right side,
And remember, we are all the same on the inside.

Haley Johnson

Untitled

I asked my father, "Are you proud of me, have I lived up to your dreams?" "Has my life been a reflection of yours through the kindness and caring deeds? Did I inherit your smile, do my eyes hold the tenderness of yours? Do I share the joys of my heart and soul and ask for nothing more?" Though I've strayed from time to time on a path you strived to lead me on. Your abiding faith was my guide and your courage kept me strong. The understanding that has always been there when others would leave me behind. Through words of wisdom or just the looks of love deep in your eyes. As one weary traveler saw the set of footprints in the sand. When my burdens were too much to carry, you continued to help me stand. To only walk in your shadow, a child's wish to be like you. Hoping that what people see in your life, will they see in me too. You show mercy to all men, you have compassion that never fails. And throughout many hardships, your presence gives me the hope to prevail. I know no matter what your dreams, your expectations of me, I surpass. For I am your precious child, your abundance of love shall forever last. PROUD OF YOU, am I, my father, I need not live up to a dream. If you have ever doubted yourself, feel assured by just looking at me.

Jennifer Bumpus

In Praise Of The Zebra Finch

Each morning when sunrise creeps into
every corner of his cage,
Gizmo awakens with hearty praise.
He rings his bell to let me know -
hey, look, I'm ready to go!
His playful, energetic nature fills my day.
And you know what? I just wouldn't
have it any other way!

Barbara Collins

Will He Hear

Lust of the flesh, lust of the eyes,
Drunken stupors, words of lies.

Bowing to idols, forsaking the poor,
Misleading my children, like fatherless whores.

How long must I listen, to the cries of the saints?
Their blood flows like rivers, their hearts grow faint.

Children are dying, from hunger and thirst,
Yet I have given to you, the richest nation on earth.

Woe unto you, who are wealthy and proud,
And turn from the poor, with your head in the clouds.

Your poor sleep in gutters, your women on the street,
While you sit back in your ten room suite.

Enjoy your wine, champagne and vermouth.
Fine cars and furs, your vanities of false truth.

Just remember this, my fine feathered friends,
One day you will give account, for the pleasures of your sins.

How much longer must I put up with you, as you turn from my ways,
Could not tomorrow, be judgement day?

I am still pleading for your souls, must you all be found asleep
My son is coming soon, he is the shepherd, they are his sheep.

Frank Gallagher

Coffee Memories

Drinking cold strawberry coffee
during a hot summer day
feeding each other pieces of scones
dripping with melted butter and jelly

Finding solace under the shade of a red stripped umbrella
in a courtyard full of lawnchairs and tables
talking about exotic places and books and loved ones
exchanging youthful dreams

Thinking I wouldn't want to share this moment with anyone else
and knowing if I didn't spend this moment with you
the coffee wouldn't be this good.

Dean Vincent V. Demesa

The Imagination

A young man walks home after work is done,
During the middle of the night;
In the deserted streets he walks,
But to him the streets are not completely deserted.
He always thinks that someone is following him,
He keeps hearing sounds like footsteps,
But looking back behind him, he sees no one.
The shadow of a cat even makes him stop still;
The slightest sound he fears,
As he walks alone.

Joseph Summers

"Within My Eyes"

Within my eyes I have seen the past go by with
each and every passing I've grown a little more
for days I've long to come again
I must close my eyes and seek deep within my heart
To see, to feel, to hope again
That within my eyes I shall see yours
I shall feel the warmth that once was felt within your eyes.
That within my eyes I shall see your hope and let it shine
For days ago have passed us by
And days ahead I shall see as one
For within my eyes my love will grow to pass
on to others as a mother once passed on to her daughter
Within my eyes it will continue to grow.

Janet A. Des Roches

Snow

They fall lightly as feathers in a soft breeze,
Each one supposedly different from the other.
But upon reaching the ground lay in a collective mass.
Looking out my window at a white stark world,
I wonder at the uniformity and if each snowflake
Is still unique or do they become one.
Is there not one duplicate?
To see the delicate work that nature can do
And yet not see it.
They beauty that is created, even the ugly of our
World is made beautiful and clean.

Glenda Buchanan

Ice Cream

Frolicking flavor flows on with no end,
eaten alone or with a special friend.
A smooth creamy fix that appeases the pallet,
spooned or lipped
bitten or sipped
its instant cool alleviates stress,
in the midst of the summer
is when it works best.
Without further ado
it wins hands down,
Haagen-Dazs ice cream
is the best around.
I've had Butter Pecan
and it was alright,
but that Rum Raisin
is my hearts delight.
I love ice cream and
ice cream loves me,
it's one of life's pleasures,
absolutely sin free!

Hope L. Streeter

Identity: Red, White, And Blue

As for human dignity,
Essential, necessary, fundamental...
Whose right is "life, liberty, and the pursuit of happiness,"
We cultivate result when we believe.
So, looking at brotherhood... Why? When? For what purpose?
We know the leaders, remember the masses,
Writers, speakers, and voters, who have been our forefathers...
Their contemporaries, and we, the ancestors of many who
Will follow, blessed with a land so fair.
We observe that personal dignity is each person's right,
Accept his individuality, and every soul's heritage
To be free, and yet governed,
"One nation, under God, indivisible,
With liberty and justice for all."

Jane Banks

The moon a pearl
lustrous
in the heavens.
The stars jewels
scattered through the velvet night.
A heavenly face seen,
radiant.
A black rose
glistens
a drop of blood on a thorn.

Eternity

Erica Frame

Being The Youngest

I always had someone to follow,
Even if I was a little slow.
My sister played house with me,
She was my "play" Mother and served the tea.
One day I followed her or so much,
She tired of my every touch -
All day I tagged along and pried
Until she finally cried -
Enough, Enough!
Boy, she's tough.
Today, even though we're miles apart.
She's still very close to my heart.

Gloria Tate

Beauty

Beneath us all
Even our foes
A beauty will show
Until it is diminished by others around
To you I say never lose it or it will never be found
You should forever guard it within your heart for it will grow
from the inside and slowly out

Amber Rene Perry

The Best

The snow and the rain take command;
Even the rich can't escape its hand.
Now it seems clearer, as time draws nearer.
YOU CAN'T TAKE IT WITH YOU; IT ISN'T YOURS!

So turn and change; get your focus into range;
Life is precious, Love is the gift.

Homes and cars and the like; vanish as quickly as the waters
break the dike.

YOU CAN'T TAKE THEM WITH YOU; THEY'RE NOT
YOURS!
Your's is a gift hands cannot hold; It's love and it's far
better than gold.
Let it go! Let it fly! But don't worry or cry!

As it flies it is certain; It will land. It will rest; and
make everything it touches — THE BEST!

Barbara Bertrand

Mama

I steeled my mind
Even tho' it was her time.
For ninety-eight years she was — just there.
Now, a year has passed and I can't find her anywhere.

The years caused her ears to go quiet,
But her mind and eyes were alive in spite.

Now, I need to grieve, because I miss her-
And not be sad for her because I care.

Now my body seems to be going down
And I feel alone — I've found.
I need to just sit by her and feel her presents-
Then maybe I could feel better in my senses

If she could be here and read this somehow,
She would just say "WHOW"
Just go ahead and finish you fight
For you too, it soon will be night.

Doris A. Stafford

Do You Know

Inspired by and written for Kara Rohe

Do you know how happy I am,
even though your not with me.
Just knowing that you love me,
makes me as happy as I can be.

My heart is empty without you,
I sit away lonely,
dreaming of the perfect life.
I dream of life with you only.

I share my time with desire,
it can not be excluded any longer.
Not being guarded with your love
makes my loneliness stronger.

I will see you again,
I will hold you once again.
For only a moment or forever,
the beating of my heart will begin.

Joe K. Deafenbaugh

A Goal

You must have hope and be persistent
Even when your goal seems distant.
A goal will seldom come with ease;
You've got to work; shoot for the breeze,

Use your mind, plus your muscles
Get energy from your corpuscles.
Picture your goal where 'ere you go;
See yourself on your plateau.

You will succeed, but you must work.
You will produce your masterwork.
If you goal is a new home,
Envision it where 'ere you roam.

With your goal, deep in your mind
You'll try harder, you will find.
With your hard work, you will achieve
The goal that you do now perceive.

French A. Emmons

"Unrequited Love"

You are the most beautiful person that I've ever seen
Every time I look at you I'm reminded of precious orchids.

Your face is like that of an angel with your pretty blue eyes and
lovely red lips;
And knowing I can't have you makes me want to cry.
You have the body of an model and your figure is one a lot are
jealous of
Because you're so beautiful you've made a lot of boys fall in love.

I've dreamt we were together
I didn't want to wake up, because it wouldn't be fair
Waking up and knowing you don't know I'm alive
is like living in a nightmare.

It tortures me to see you talk to other boys
And the way you treat me; like I'm an old wasted toy.

You're so popular and I'm not, I just want to be friends with you
Maybe go out one time because I'm really in love with you.

I can only look at you and fantasize about the way it could be,
but I know that won't happen, because
the way I feel about you, you don't feel about me.

John C. Moore

Falling Petals

As spring became
everything was so new
A bud grew and caught my eye
it grew on the path I walked every day
It was beautiful and precious
I found myself going out of my way
just to see that special flower
As fall came upon me
I wanted to take that flower and protect it
from the harsh cold winter
for fear I might lose it
But the frost came unexpectedly
so I said good-bye
I hold that flower deep in my heart forever

Joshua Peters

The Vietnam War Memorial

The Wall
Every time I see the wall I cry.
This wall was raised and names engraved
of all who for their country died

Daughters and sons answered their countries call
Served to the very best of their ability
Now their names are engraved on the wall
forever to be etched in our memory.

They came from all walks of life to fight
and die. Some were educated some were not.
Some black some white some brown
Color makes no difference to weapons of
war because weapons do not discriminate.

Every time I see the wall I cry.

James W. Smith

"We Can Make A Change"

The tears, the fears, all around u bound,
Everywhere we look, it's sure to be found.
What happened to the happy days that used to be.
When everyone seemed to live so trouble free?

Will there ever come a time in life once again
That the pain, the hurt and hate will finally wane?
What will our children grow up with and have to share
Instead of only a feeling of despair?

The day must surely come, when all the hate will cease
And the world as a whole will learn to live in peace.
What a happy thought looking forward to tomorrow
Gone will be all of the hurt, pain and sorrow.

The birds will sing in perfect harmony
And things will be as we want them to be.
"Oh Happy Day" will be heard loud and clear
And we'll know the meaning of good cheer.

But, while we wait, lets not forget
The good things we look for are not here yet.
"Patience is a virtue", this we know is true,
So let's work hard and pray hard in everything we do.

Fannie V. Wright

"Believe In Yourself"

Because you
Excel when it comes to things you
Love and hold dear to your heart.
I think you deserve the freedom of wings,
Eternity love, and the laughter of kings.
Vagabond boy you could win it all as
Effort will carry you over the wall of

Infinite success
Now and forever

You owe it to yourself to try your best
Or else you're not really trying
Underdog man stand up to the test
Reality, often is crying
See through it all the worth of the one
Everything now your life will become
Live it in love, happy and fun
Forever, for you.

David Anas

Perception

Alone; you look to be free.
Exploration,
possibilities abound,
for your freedom will be found in love.
Chains bound the soul to loneliness,
undone only from within -
help yourself to love
you
in order to be independent
of bonds
that bind the border of your personality.

Colette Renée Torr

Poetry

Words do not flow easily from one's heart onto a page
Exposing and defining such emotions as Love, or Joy, or Rage
They cannot show the depth of despair or the height of ecstasy
To which the soul can sour when the spirit is set free

There are no boundaries to experience, no limits on the soul
No existence that has no worth, is petty, or half - whole
For hearts and minds can touch and feel a color, taste, or smell
And experience the face of God, or know the depths of hell

To pen such deep emotions solidifies what must move
Limiting and confining what the poet hopes to prove
But fortunately for the masses, there are those who can set free
Such solid things as words — we call it Poetry

James L. Webb

I'll See You In The Morning

I'll see you in the morning, when my
eyes are full of sleep, my head will
still be spinning and my body very weak.
My mind will slowly focus on the
night that never passed, I'll see you in
the morning but my thoughts are fading fast.
I'll see you in my dreams and my body floats
away, I'm racing in a plane over a very
wide bay, I turn my head and see you,
sitting on my right, my head starts
spinning faster and I see a blinding light.
My body jerks and quivers, I fight and
lose the thought, wide awake I wonder, just
how much time I lost. I'll see you in the
morning, no matter what I do a day,
a month, a year, I will always remember you.

Connie Downs

"The Beggarman"

Today I passed a beggarman on the street,
Eyes were dimmed only one of his feet.
With his cap out, he appealed to all,
A silent, pleading, unspoken call.

I watched him for a while to see
how many would answer to his plea.
Cold, hurrying, indifferent they passed
until with a smothered sigh at last
he swing on crutches and turned away
to where there might be better pay,

But not before I had seen his eyes,
the ghastly eyes of a man who dies -
for they were hopeless, gone was the light
of goodwill fellowship, only a sight
of eternal suffering-haggard and pale -
a curse for the man hearty and hale,
Who has no thought and passes him by -
who cares not whether beggarmen live or die.

Then he was gone, his soul revealed startling bare,
The beggarman for whom no one gives a care.

Dorothy Weil Durflinger

Sitting Still

In the beginning I saw a child sitting behind a desk,
eyes wide open, looking for wisdom... sitting still.
Looking for instruction, understanding,
learning right from wrong.
Success will come to him; he is sitting still.
I can see the beauty of his mind, I can see
his mind being formed. He is patient,
his power shows; he is sitting still.
Where have I seen this power I am talking about?
Looking at the sun with all of its power... sitting still.
Look at all of the stars in the middle of the night,
the beauty and power of them... sitting still.
Look at the sea, powerful and beautiful,
powerful when angry, beautiful when sitting still.
Generation after generation, all things are created in stillness.
Love and power come to those who are sitting still.

James Owens

"The Patriot's Decision"

Hurting, scared, and anxious men,
Fighting with all their effort to win,
Saw the stripes of the flag held high,
Deciding in their hearts, they were willing to die;
If only they could have the freedom of their land,
And get out of the enemies' crushing hand.

Consciously they fought for freedom or fate;
Along with the feeling of anxiety and hate.
And then suddenly it was done; the great battle was won.
And immediately to their families they went!

Cut, bruised, and crippled men,
Thanking God along with their kin,
Saw the stripes of the flag once more,
Hanging over the neighbor's door.

And remembered the vow they had made that day,
Also the sacrifices they were willing to pay,
If, only they could gain their wanted freedom.

Jessica A. Chambers

Marilyn

See the beauty of your dreams,
Face and hair the color of cream.
Perfect figure in a white dress,
Ghostly angelic loveliness.

See her silhouette in your room,
Blonde beauty back from the tomb.
Fatally beautiful and fatally visioned,
With immortal fascination, she's become life's victor.

The mystery and the magic,
An image both comic and tragic.
Her life possessed one tragic flaw,
Although she seemed to have it all.

Searching the seas of faces,
She looked for love in all the wrong places.
A child who grew up a little too fast,
In a world where tomorrow is already past.

Supposedly dead, yet still alive,
In our hearts, and in our minds.
Marilyn is the legend's name,
Who achieved this undying fame.

Elizabeth J. Beyer

The Realness Of God

He came to this world a poor carpenter's son
Facing a battle not easily won
Speaking of love and forgiveness of sins
Speaking of placing all our faith in Him
He spoke not of violence, of carrying swords
He carried, instead, as His weapon, the Word
The Word of our Father who does love us so
He was willing to let his only son go
He went to cross, giving His life for me
Because of our sins, He was nailed to the tree
But after three days He arose once again
Relieving my soul of the burden of sin
Imagine the love that our Father must feel
To be willing, through Jesus, to make Himself real

Cathy Bach Matthai

God's Gifts

As we walk throughout our life,
Facing happiness, sorrow, and strife.
We take for granted God's beauty of this earth,
Plus the physical senses we receive from birth.

Do you ever take a moment to look around,
At the wonder of nature in sight and sound?
When winter's cold winds begin to calm,
Turn in God's word to the 104th Psalms.

We become so involved with our daily routine,
Appreciation for the world around us is rarely seen.
Winter, Spring, Summer, and Fall,
Hold glorious beauty for us all.

How would we feel if from a night's sleep we awake,
And the privilege of our six senses God would take.
We would miss all the beauty we once knew,
At least we once experienced it, some never do.

We need to ask forgiveness for our ungrateful ways,
Notice God's creations and sing His praise.
Handle His gifts with tender loving care,
For without them life would be hard to bare.

Dreama S. Ross

Reflections

Reflections of a past life
   fade away in the trickle of the stream
Exploding into cascading waterfalls
   of happiness only found in far off dreams.

Too late to go back and change the river of yesterdays
   when tomorrow is up ahead.
Today is being swept away in the never ending
   current of tomorrow and is gone.
      So long.

Live for the future
   not for yesterday
Dream for tomorrow
   take it day by day.

Christina Russell

Salvation

Falling
   Falling
Grace poured from Heaven above
Leap of faith gave wings of the Dove
The Word a pathway to Heaven's door
Where sorrow ends forever more
Flowing
   Flowing

Blood shed conquered sin and sacrifice
Peace is mine accompanied with eternal life
Strength drawn upon the shell of flesh
Protects the soul from the Enemy's catch

Saving
   Saving
The mind wrestles for understanding
His love finds victory that's never ending
Game of life won without arbitration
If we only acknowledge His gift....Salvation

Coco Daniel

Night Fears

Sitting like two outcasts on the summer porch,
Fearing what we could not see or touch,
My sister looked at me and I at her,
Ready to bolt we knew not where.

The house was lit all around to keep intruder spirits out,
While black and darkness engulfed all else.
We sat and talked of countless things,
Each ignoring the creaks and groans of an empty house,
Although the eyes said all that was left unsaid.

Safety was without and fear within our childish brains felt.
No coaxing would bring us in, not even a beckoning phone;
We were sure 'twas a trap waiting to ensnare us.
In this way we passed the summer nights,
Till home the folks would come, like angels to our call,
Then home would be just that, where safety is within and fear without.

Hilda Rodriguez

No Sound....

Feel the pain, I had from you.
Feel the tears, I had them too.
Listen to the cry of a soul.
Listen to the fire that was burnt by coal.
That was our love, that just slipped away.
That was our love, I thought would always stay.
Boom! Went the door, when you said goodbye.
Crack! Went the glass that I broke when I would cry.
Gulp! Went the poison, I drank straight down
Died on the floor, without no sound.

Danielle Signor

This Is My Time

These feelings of despair must be put aside
Feelings that my family no longer cares

I give up trying to impress them
for it is ME that I must please - first and foremost

My life is mine to live
With no one's approval needed but my own

Yes, it hurts when they don't call or come by
It's as if I had some strange disease

There is no disease, only my strength
And they're afraid to "catch" it

Nothing I can do to change their ways
All I can do is live for me

And the time to start is NOW!

Georgianna Zboray

Photos

Look at the yellowed photos! Pictures without speech, sepia toned figures faded. Grandfathers, grandmothers, in full stature. See your mother as an infant, a child with golden curls, then a woman. Your father, a teenaged soldier, a man still growing, fighting on foreign soil for a cause.
Families grouped together, united. Hands and arms linked in shared tenderness. See sullen faces, shinning faces, laughing faces. Others of cousins, couples, friends, friends of friends. Women in bright dresses, decorative hats, men in tailored suits. Faces shinning, squinting on the beach in odd swimsuits.
Look hard at these flat images, feel the time of relatives unknown and mysterious, looking back at you, strangers in time, most are gone now, past, passed.
As children of your children's children, will see your flat image, your happiness should reach out to them, muted yet bonded through genetic ties.
Your brain cells will be reincarnated in them, just as yours are with our ancestors.

Look hard at these flat images! See and feel yourself in them!

Donald Thorschmidt

November Sojourn

Overcast skies, with the sun,
filtering through naked branches
casting shadows of length, and they dance
with the wind, upon the Earth.

Days are short, as the depth of the night,
carries to the mind, early sleep and sadness,
straining to touch, the spirit and the soul,
as one touches life, and life begins,
to journey through sleep, of time 'til spring.

The chill of the air,
touching the spirit of the mind,
creating this moment, to give a depth.
of a peaceful quiet, of this November Sojourn.

The crunch of leaves underfoot,
the sharp winds and crisp air,
leading to a clear night, of a starlit sky,
lighting a hope, and a wish, for a life,
of a November Sojourn.

Charles P. Teator

The Care Giver

Now that my retirement has become a reality
Finding time to do the things and places yet to see.
Have been shelved,
For it seems the unexpected now becomes necessity.

Life is more gentle and at a slower pace
But the care of another now demands a place.
It wasn't planned,
But loving care enters, yet-handled with grace.

The path of life has many roads some are paved with dust
Reaching for a special goal no longer is a must.
There are other demands.
Perhaps later, time will tell, really it's no fuss.

Caring has a special love that only one can give.
Now it's daily duties and two lives to live.
Gladly doing what I can.
Life with its joys and remembrances to relive.

Jeanne Conner Cummings

He's Beautiful.....

My breath catches as I look down at him asleep.
First come sad thoughts then prayer ... "my soul to keep."

One warm tear escapes; more collect in the corners of my eyes.
Dare I vocalize my fears? No! My heart silently cries.

Intravenous lines are everywhere; his little oxygen tent looks hostile and cold.
Sadly out touch is forbidden. Challenge the doctor? Am I that bold?

ICU nurses hover; monitors drone on in hideous repetition.
Bad thoughts betray me and I am cloaked in an ugly apparition.

Stop! Stop! I'm being foolish; my faith has always been strong.
How can I question God's love? I can't. I've been so wrong!

He has whispered in my ear ...
I rejoice in my renewed faith; I feel no fear.

My body tingles from the warmth and energy it feels.
Sean, too, is enveloped in His love; his body heals.

I want to stroke his fair skin and make a loving cradle of my arms.
Just as God has cradled me He will keep this newborn from harm.

Magically Sean's breathing relaxes and he looks up at me with the bluest of eyes.
And smiles, slightly amused at his new grandmom as she cries ...

Carole Saunders

To Stephanie

The tiniest of wonders takes her
first peek of this minute, remote world
that she has discovered.
Velvety and brown, her hair glistens
in the new morning sun.
Her eyes reflect the carefree joys of life.
Growing and learning, curiosity is a professor.
As an adolescent, she changes abruptly
turning into a young woman.
The freedoms of childhood soon fade away
while the memories remain
Suddenly she has to climb the mountains of life.
As she struggles, a warm gentle hand
taps her shoulder
She reaches for his hand and they help
each other through hard times.
At the peak they look down below, yet so
in love are they, that all is seen is the
setting sun as he asks her hand in marriage
They will live eternally in the hands of love.

April Williamson

Gone Fishing

The sign is out,
fisherman gone to sea;
Fisherman, fisherman throwing out his net,
fishing now with boyish glee;

Fisherman, fisherman, now gone fishing
for those fishes on Heaven's shore;
Fisherman sitting on the bank of God's river,
fishing, fishing, catching more and more;

Lots more, catfish, lots more sturgeon,
and Salmon as big as can be;
Fisherman, fisherman, gone on now,
leaving us a delightful legacy;

Don't you worry none
about this man now gone away;
He's sitting on the bank of a river,
and if you listen, you can hear him say:

"Now here's a big one
I'm catching for all of you;
I'll still be sitting here fishing
When your journey on earth is through".

Carol Poole

Moonchild

There is a child dancing in the rain.
Flashing colors
purple light
dancing in the darkness of her night.
There is nothing that can stop her now.
Feeling the soul, the soul of her creation.
Touching on adventure.
In everyone there is a moonchild.

Here comes the yellow strictly fading
into blue
White this room will never again be.
In everyone there is a moon child.

Bringing back the youth.
Singing, melting with snowballs,
dancing on sunflowers, and running
through the ditches of blissful ignorance
colored with green and gold.
Fingertips are numb with everywhere
to go.
In everyone there is a moon child.

Evangelina Owens

The Wonders That Be

The radiant beauty of the rising sun,
flashing in glory a mighty screen, displaying
its grandeur for everyone, the majestic splendor
of powers unseen. Blessings for those who give thanks
to the one, "THE ONE WHO CAUSES TO BE", who gave us
the MOON, the STARS and the SUN, all the wonders of
the universe free.

The towering mountains reaching up to the sky,
The great rolling waves of the sea, the vast expanse of
desert so arid and dry., the tall stately green forest trees.

Varied are the colors of the rain-bow's hue, spanning
the heavens for all to see, an ever changing
panoramic view, all of the wonders that be.

Bowing in awe of the mighty hand, directing the
forces of land and sea, humbly rejoicing to obey
His command, all a part of the wonders that be.

Frances D. Scruggs

Soaring Above The Nest

I remember when I first said, it is time now my little
fledgling, time to go and try to really fly.

It has been quite some time now, I know, for we have
flown off and on as companions in the sky.

The weather and the air currents have changed many times
for you and me, since you truly tried your wings.

My feathers get ruffled when we two get buffeted about,
but with your graceful attempts my heart sings.

At times your flight is upward, beautiful, beautiful,
with others you have flown straight and true.

I have to stay behind when you fly away, gliding along
with currents that take you into the gray and the blue.

I sit there on my perch regarding an empty nest, I ruffle
my feathers a little, and I gaze a bit out there.

I am wondering if the elements will be kind to you, and
if your new fine-feathered friends will treat you fair.

Well, I can not perch here forever wondering how your
flight is going to fare, for I too must take off and fly.

The old nest must not fall into disrepair, for where else
will you return to for awhile, to be my companion in the sky.

Dolores Smith

Rialto

Mystical light of halcyon day
Floods woods and sea and inlet bay.
Driftwood piled along the shore,
Bleached white by years of being there,
Glows softly golden in sinking sun and mist-rich air.
The beach is but a narrow strip of stones
Betwixt the tide waves and the driftwood bones.
Barren trees harbor weary gulls
Whom the mystical, magical, golden light lulls,
Till, when some chord is struck which birds do know,
All rise as one and begin the flow
Of northern flight,
A magical dance through mystical light.

Jean Merritt

Birds

Sometimes I wish I were a bird
Flying high and being free as the air,
For birds do not have problems
Like the human race.

I often wonder how it feels to be high in the air
Seeing mother nature everywhere
Flying high, flying low
Flying with the wind when it blows.

A bird gets up early in the morning
Singing a song for all those who are mourning
A bird's best friend my be the trees
For the leaves are the protectors from the cold breeze.

Their home may be the sky
For it a bird does not fly he may surely die
I often think how simple life is
For their life is a life of happiness and of peace.

I may someday be a bird in my dreams
And my dreams are for a short time of my daily life
I often ask myself why was I ever a human being
And not like a bird that I have always love.

Abel Aguilera

Mother Nature's Window

We're all right child, here in Mother Nature's Window,
Flying squirrels play in trees above,
Caretaker protects it for posterity,
Green gods claim it in the name of money,

The sun is breaking through greens and browns,
The urban forests gild the ground,

We walk with common sense through Mother Nature's Window,
Deer and strangers live in transient harmony,
Slight-of-hand developer, you take space up in the world,
But save a piece for us,

The Sun is breaking through greens and browns,
The urban forests gild the ground,

This business park was a busy field in Mother Nature's Window,
This decayed swamp fed my childhood stream when I was ten,
Stories we share are the path to understanding,
Gather children, slow your breath and listen,

Please don't close the latch to Mother Nature's Window,
Leave it open just a crack, it's Mother Nature's Window,

Who wants the little ones to grow up
loving black top and cement?

Douglas Buell

Despair

We look around and what do we see, everything has changed
from A to Z.
Food is least, money is short, children killing children,
parents get smart.
Jobs are few, pain is deep, heart ache is all we got to keep.
Where is the love from deep within, the love you carry
from thick and thin.
You used to care: but now you don't. There isn't anyway out.
You stand in a line to wait for a meal, your feet are cold
your hands are still.
You sleep on the ground without a cover, you wonder where
the next day lies.
People robbing and killing for a dime. Is it worth the
pain and trouble, to hurt your own sister or brother.
Where is the love from deep within, the love you carry
from thick and thin.
No money in your pocket, no food to eat, not a job to go
to, the pain is so deep.
You sit around wondering, what can you do. No one takes
You in, no one cares about you. So you say, you'll join a gang.
For what? To cause more pain. We look around and what do we see.

Fredia Stills

Cry For Both

Cry my angel for a broken wing,
For a soul that lost, for a fallen king.
Place faith in only one, for all else will fall,
Faith in one to hold fast the crumbling wall.
Cry my angel for what can't be,
For what things have passed into eternity
This land none cross, that barren plain
Deserts of the mind, drive man insane.
Cry my angel for times of past,
Losses in life, tear down the mast.
Pour my cup, and let it overfill,
Greatest amounts as in my will.
But cry not for me, but cry for yourself,
For what you had lost and what dust lies on the shelf.
Brush it aside, but it settles the same,
Just an attempt done solely in vain.
So cry one last tear and tear it in two,
Drop half for me and
Keep the other for you.

Justin Everman

Springtime

All winter I can't wait for spring
for buds and leaves and the birds that sing
oh what happiness it all brings

New life and vigor flows through my veins
forgotten are winter blues and pains.

Flowers spring up that have dormant lain
lifting sweet faces to sun and rain.

March winds blow to dry the wet earth
My heart takes wing to see the new birth
Winter drear turns to cheer and mirth.

The flash of the sun on a robins red breast
as she flies to and fro building her nest
when nature awakes it fills me with zest.

My dogs run and romp and play children laugh with joy at such a day
schools soon out they gleefully shout
No homework to do no more will they pout

They'll have fun in the sun all day long
days getting warm they bursts into song
as they wait to hear the school bell ring
Goodbye to school Hello to spring.

Arlene Trexler

Great Grandmothers, Grandmothers And Mothers

What can I say - they pave the way
For generations to follow - with lessons they know
Learned from a life of happiness and strife
They have wonderful stories - of how to conquer worries
And believe in one being who will soothe the sting
They sit at family tables, smiling and telling fables
With everyone a part of their genes and heart
They've been here for years wiping dirty hands and tears
They are our rock with white hair and frock
Shining eyes and face singing "Amazing Grace"
With voices so sweet, it's always a treat
To listen of days gone by, and wonder with a sigh
How it would be to live, bear and see
All the amazing things their experience brings
It's a nice to think with a wide-eyed blink
"I'm a lot like her," or I wish I were
It is certainly great to smile at fate
and thank God for sending me
such grand ladies to see.

Dianne Sloan

Adoptee

Thank You Lord...
For giving me such a healthy start
For assisting the first who held me
For making a choice from the heart...

For the wonderful parents who cared for me
For a family with life, laugh and love
For the happiness you have brought me...

For the beautiful lady in my life
For the life I see before me
For today and the rest of my life...

Dennis Arteaga

"Forgive Me Jesus"

I confess my sins to you Lord
For I am self-righteous and a sinner
You then showed me that I was worldly
Full of fear and meant to suffer

I have lived my life not caring
But to myself and not others
I have led a restless life
Then you stopped me and said "Enough"

I called upon you only when I was troubled
Asked for understanding and wanted help
But you knew I was weak in faith
So you decided to let go and let me weep

Oh Jesus, please turn my life around
From a spider web I lived in
Please release me from this struggle
For peace I want and spirit clean

Forgive me Jesus for all my sins
As I am only human and not Holy
Please hear my prayers and confessions
So weaknesses will never again touch me

Bert R. Ricasa

Just To Be

Yesterday my life brought me new and special things
For I could see what the mighty sky could bring
I breathed through Drums and Space, becoming one without a trace
Of me to see
Just to be.

Weasel on my path leading to a sky of light
I conversed with him, then I ran to see the night
The clouds began to clear, feeling peace without the fear
What a bliss for me...
Just to be.

Take me through that door where I haven't been before
And tell me what I hear are 'Light Beings' oh so clear!
And let me continue the fate of a life that seems too great
In reality
Just to be.

Midnight in the grove and the foggy moonlit trees
Frightened by the dark, of what I could not see
Then breathing in the light, remove the glasses feel the might
Stop looking because you're free...
Just to be.

Anita Taverner

How I Feel...

When I hear your precious name all my fears float away,
for I know I have your love with me every single day.
When you say you love me my heart is filled with joy.
Before the time I found your love I was a very lonely boy.

You made my world a better place, brighter than the sun.
And deep in my heart I fear the day I hope will never come,
The day I see you turn from me and run.
The day that you do, my weak heart will die.
When you turn to look at me, you will see me cry,
because the greatest love of my life, will have withered away and died.

So the longer you stay, you will see my love will never do you wrong.
If I do anything to hurt you, my life could not go on,
because if it did I would live every single day
with the memory of it hurting and it would not go away.

The pain I feel inside of me will never go away.

Donnie Jones

Just Look

Look into my eyes,
For I will take off my disguise.
Look into my heart,
And see what you should have from the start.

Look into my mind,
You may be surprised of what you find.
Look into my soul,
And you will see that it's not whole.

Look into my words,
And you will see they're not what you've heard.
Look into my thoughts,
And you will see they can't be bought.

Look into my nights,
And you will see my bedroom light.
Look into my songs,
And you will see there's something wrong.

Look into my face,
And you will see I hold disgrace.
Look into my head,
And you'll finally hear what I've said!

Amanda Spears

Trading Places

Don't stare at me, this is just a shell
For in this body a soul doth dwell
Don't laugh at me because I am blind
Don't call me retarded, without a mind
Don't pity me because I cannot walk
And don't say dummy you cannot talk
For it is your ignorance that cannot see
And that makes you more blind than me
Now I ask is your mind that small
Aren't we all God's Children one and all
And when you speak only to be cruel
Doesn't that make you not me the fool
No I don't want to walk in your shoes
Because I wonder who is more crippled me or you
Remember but for God's good Grace
You could be here in my place

Bonnie Ross

Windows On The World

Windows on the world create mist in my eyes
For it calls me to be my higher being.
A being free of the pleasantries of life,
Bursting with life in my death.

Looking at myself I see a creature
Not a being, for being is eternal.
A creature yearning to be freed from captivity,
Only to be enslaved by freedom.

I wonder sometimes what it would be like to see myself,
Not the Self I see in the mirror,
But the Self that will eventually succumb to the pain of death
And live in the pleasure of nothingness.

I know that I know nothing but what I feel
Because the senses are the training we receive
To prepare our minds for the onslaught of afterlife,
When all we will have is imagination.

With such a fleeting moment of physical existence
Let us not forget that we can enjoy life as we know it,
For in enjoyment we taste immortality,
An in immortality, we are freed from captivity.

John Bird

When Time Has Come For Me To Wander

When time has come
For me to wander in the breeze
Shed not a tear. I did not die.
My voice will come to you
In time of need.
Come to the sacred fire
And the strength of my spirit will be your guide.
And if one day you fall
Upon the side of the road,
Call upon the eagle.
He will pick you up; bathe you, clothe you.
And give you food and drink.
The great wings of his Spirit
will shelter you with prayer and dance.

Gregory McCraw

Earth Man/Earth Woman

Hold! Ye mighty warriors in your quest
for release from servitude,
have you forgotten the sister that walks by your side?

In your haste to forget your own troubled soul
misgivings from follies not of your choosing
in your shadow space the soulful sister strides

Mindful of tears, strife and strange fruits of yesteryears
Nefertiti's smile across luscious lips stranger now to yours
What bend of the road did you take
when she was heavy burdened with struggles of survival?

Could you hold and comfort her as she cried
childbearing pains reality?
Ever mindful Eli's coming to snatch from her breast
life's essence formed in universal love and comparison.
Heed! Mighty warrior in your quest
for release from your personal servitude
don't ever forget all the sisters
that have always walked by your side?

Elizabeth Moore

His Last Breath

Thank you dear God in heaven above,
For relieving the pain of my dear love,
We had many years, so happy and gay,
But somehow I knew you would take him away,
If you needed him badly, it is for the best,
But please, oh dear God, give him some rest.

I know he is good and will obey your command,
And with your kind guidance, will never be damned,
He had a hard life here on this earth,
So please try to help him with laughter and mirth,
Then one day soon, when you take me away,
Again with my love, I'll be happy and gay.

But thank you dear God, for letting me be
Near his bedside, when his last breath, he gave to me.
But I will raise the daughter I gave to you in birth
And teach her the treasures we have here on earth,
Now until you call me, I will never love another
For my last breath, my love, will be waiting for me.

Helen Amann

Sorrowful Reaper

Death weeps in sorrow embrace
For the life he cannot give nor save
One touch of his hand, a whispered word
Life's flame darkens like a dying world
His gentle hand caressing your face
Take you into his cold embrace
Wishing he could relight life's fire
His gentle fingers enclose around yours
Holding tight as you fly higher
Death weeps for the pain he brings
To everyone who loves
And everyone who needs
He wishes he only brought forth life
But for his eternal destiny
He brings darkness, not light
The joy, the love we all do feel
For our poor reaper will never be real

Crystal D. Arroyo

Au Revoir

Care not for lonely man from whom you fly,
For tis my heart you break and nothing more.
Worry not for stolen, foolish pride,
Nor soul turned bitter for soul he once adored.
Tears are solemn dreams of waking time;
But soon their witness will not grace my cheeks;
Memories are not mountains yet to climb;
People are not conquered for the meek.
But for now, my heart is wounded deep
by arrows piercing mind's unruly sleep.

Justin Allen

Melancholy

My melancholy feeling is not sadness
for what has been or for what was not
It is for what could be now - but isn't.
It is how I feel when I want to share a secret
and there is no one to listen,
When my laughter goes unheard and my
tears are shed in silence.
It's when I awake at night
and my bed is empty, yet,
when we make tender sweet love,
I feel the fool for loving.
It's the emptiness I feel when I discover
My trust - My loyalty
My devotion
are toys to another.
It's when I think true happiness is finally
mine - but isn't
Melancholy is when my heart aches.
Tonight, I am melancholy.

Joanne Tipton

Friendship

Gossamer webs in blusterous breeze;
Fragile snowflakes in frigid freeze;
Defenseless nests in towering trees;
Leaky boats on stormy seas;
Relationships, meant to plumb and please,
Sometimes turn to taunt and tease.
But you can set your mind at ease,
I do not ask for guarantees,
Only friendship.

David A. Moore

A Message To My Brothas

How is it that my brothas can dis me when I'm them?
For without a *She* there would be no *Him*.

For without me there would be no life,
I'm your mother, your sister, your daughter, your wife.

I am *Everywoman*, for I was the first,
The woman that you now disrespect and curse.

So to all my nubian brothas open your eyes and see,
that I am you, just as you are me.

Where did we go wrong I ask myself,
On my knee's I pray to God and ask for His help.

Where is the unity that used to be ensoled,
For in the black community there is a very deep hole.

So love the blackwoman and please understand,
that without a blackwoman there would be no blackman.

I'Keyia Leonard

Uniting Souls And All

Today is a very special day for you and your chosen one,
for you both have found each other, the blessing that only
reaches some. Two people are as one now, uniting souls and all,
leaning on the other, if one should take a fall.

You'll find sometimes a narrow path, the days
you must be strong, but better than the lonely,
the nights for them are long.

The bonding grows within each year and
and you must always know, that marriage is
a sacred thing both happy days and low.

Hang on to all your passion, your hopes, and
all your dreams, for life is such a short journey,
however long it seems. Trust, love, and respect,
is what the other needs, so never lose the sight
of that and let it be your creed.

For we are all just humans, trying to
find our way, and you've been blessed
with a soul mate, for the rest of all your days.

Debbie Dilts

Eternal

Desolate and barren this lonely place of evil
forbidden by most of human race
wind and dust and sand so bleak
'tis not the peaceful land I seek.

For the land I seek is beautiful and green,
it exists for such a land I have seen
Be it north, south, east, or west
'till I find it I shall not rest.

This lifetime of sorrow and hatred I regret
so now to a place of good I must get
to quit my old ways and make amends
for I know my time on earth is almost at an end.

This place I have found to the best
for me to live be forgiven
before I rejoice in my eternal...
...rest.

Beau Ferguson

Moving Away

The noise interrupted my thoughts,
Forcing me to gaze out the walls of window into a distance that held
Both beginnings and endings...

Another plane raced down the runway, to a destination unknown.
I felt my heart soar!
It's fuel more fear than anticipation.
"I wish I had your guts."
She had said that to me as I bid farewell.
She had meant it.
I felt it in her arms as She hugged me.
I saw it in her eyes as She cried.
"Wish I had your guts."
I couldn't focus on Her.
It hurt too much, this farewell,
To Home, To Childhood, To the Past.
It broke something inside me.
Yet I couldn't let Her see how very weak I felt.
And as I walked away,
Part of me wanted to turn around and scream for Her.
But I kept on.

Cheryl Lynne Alexandra Murray

The Price We Pay

The price we pay for freedom is
Found in many a place.

I hear the price we pay for freedom,
Is written on that wall.

I see the price we pay for freedom,
In that endless white sea at Arlington.

I smell the price we pay for freedom,
In the fumes of that eternal flame.

The price we pay for freedom is
Found in many a place.

The price we pay for freedom is
Molded to my father's face.

Chris Bono

Remembrances Of Ireland

Ruined castle a palace makes,
framed by dark clouds—-
'Tis a soft night...

Wild rose and white thorn
intertwine, like lovers
strolling down the lane.

A thousand needless
pierce the sky;
Better for Him their Hymn to hear.

An aristocrat lounges in his prison barn,
He dreams—
Wild rabbits...

Red and yellow wagon,
open fire, browsing ponies,
Free as the wind.

A worm weaves its tomb,
A Monarch wings heavenward—
Where there's death, there's hope.

Irene Katherine Strause

On Inturned Eyes

Rotating. Advancing forward. A maintained speed. Never an end.
Frames. All seen separate. All watched in full. Telling a story.
Animation. Bright in colors of different shades. Detailed in excess.
Voices. Narrating each scene. Inaudible during a performance.
The screen. A mighty spindle. Suspended. Rolling on invisible reels.
Dark the surrounding. Beautiful the unseen background. A single beam to display.
An audience. Of one. Silhouetted. None other is there.
A book read, though seen. Observed, on inturned eyes.

Christina M. Bettale

When You Pray

When you pray be sincere;
Free of doubt and free from fear.
Pray ye one for another;
Peace and love you will discover.
Pray without ceasing everyday;
Allowing God to have His own way.
Be Humble and thankful at all times;
Asking forgiveness from the Father Divine.
Pray that we all be on one accord;
Growing in grace to be with the Lord.
Pray for the sick and those in need;
Pray to the Father your paths to lead.
And when you pray the Lord will hear;
He'll bless and keep you ever near.
All your burdens He will bear;
When you take it to the Lord in prayer.

Faye Hubbard

Freedom And Liberty

What does America mean to me?
Freedom, liberty, freedom and liberty.
There's one thing that we all know,
Our people were oppressed a long time ago.
Country bumpkins and men of wealth
Became concerned for America's health.
Some were mighty with the sword,
And some with the pen.
They wrote a new law way back then.

They wrote the law and they endorsed it,
Fought the king's men to enforce it.
They said "All across this land,
There will be freedom for every man."
Read the laws and study them,
Learn why they were written that way back then.
Don't take freedom for granted today.
There are some who would take it away.
What does America mean to me?
Freedom, Liberty, Freedom and Liberty.

Emilea Moring

Susan

When her eyes open and look my way,
From that far far place
Where she goes,
As I study the face and profile
I know so well,
An urge to sketch the beauty there
Swells in me and instantly
A sense of unethicalness -
That to do so would be to plagiarize death's work
I let it go, with regret

Brenda Bennett

"Love"

It grows as a flower in early spring
Fresh like the blossoming apple tree,
Whose fragrant odor is nature's sweetness
Flowing outward to meet its call.

Love so beautiful and lasting
Loves enchanting passion to all,
To all that know its meaning
And the others they are lost.

Awake my love be aware of life,
Of its secret meaning to us
Observe nature that is so beautiful
Beneath our heavenly sky.

And when at last you feel it too
Come to me forever,
Forever we will always be
As one enchanted flower.

Francis Anable

Looking Down

There is such a wonderful beauty as you look down
from a mountain high -
With the land below stretching out as far as the eye can see,
Like a huge patchwork quilt with all shades of green and brown.
And here and there you catch a glimpse of a little town,
Looking just like dollhouses, as the memory of childhood comes to me.

There are little bright specks of yellow and red,
as if a paint brush did drip -
It must be the places where there are beautiful flowers in bloom.
There's a slash going across the land, as if with a knife
was cut thru,
Where a stream, ever winding and never ending, shows a sliver of blue.
There are groves of trees that send shadows down below of gloom.

There are little black specks, like an army of ants,
busily milling around -
Among the miniature buildings, that look just like a fairyland.
It must be the people who live in that far-off distant town,
That must be such a friendly place, where you would see not a frown.
You feel so at peace when you look down and view God's
beauty so grand.

Dorothy M. Barr

Eternal Beauty

The beauty I love is a mystic form
From an unremembered place
From there it sheds a fitful light
On the world of time and space
In a timeless realm this beauty burns
With undiminished glow.

So we spend our lives in a restless search
For the love we yearn to know
At times we catch a fleeting glimpse
Of this eternal fire
Mirrored in eyes of one we love
Kindled by desire.

Then stands revealed a living proof
Of beauty immortal, one, for a moment held
in mortal eyes
As reflection of the sun
And though we shall not hold the flame
Nor grasp its shimmering light
Beauty remains our only torch
In a dark and endless night.

Bart Cooper

Just Look Up

Thousands and thousands miles away
from home, on some nowhere land.
Spending my days, dodging bullets and
the sun, fanning myself with my hand.
Wondering if I'm going to make it through.
Well I just look up, because I know the man
I'm looking up at known right thing to do.

Edward W. Howard

Scottie

I could see and hear him
From my kitchen window
Talking to himself as he tossed
The baseball way up high
And ran to catch it on the fly.
Like a little puppy left alone
Which would bark and pace to and fro
Passing the time away waiting for the clan to return.
Later, I heard a knock at the door
I opened and there stood the little boy from next door
Leaning against the door-jamb
With ball and glove in hand.
He looked up at me sadly —
"My mother's not home and I'm hungry"
The thought that he came to me
Filled me with great joy.
Happy to have changed darkness into sunshine
I was rewarded with a hug and a kiss
I can still hear his parting words
"I also like pumpkin pie and liverwurst"

Evelina G. Wolf

To An A

With you began the journey
From scratch to understanding
From someone's aardvark to all zinfinity.
With you was set a standard
Toward which we all might strive-
Your quintessential baton to our hand.
And yet...don't B too taken with yourself.

David Weitzler

Poetry

Poetry is all around
from the sky to the ground.
You live your life day by day,
watch out it's on its way.
When you speak, out it comes,
not like cat got your tongue.
When asked to write it down,
the words can't be found.
The blank piece of paper stares back at you,
you think to yourself,
what will I do?
No ideas, clean out today,
got to start another way.
Think about something you know or love,
passion, history, stories from above.
Nothing special needed, just you and your heart.
There you go, there is a start.
It's in us all, I know it is.
Never doubt yourself, what poetry gives.

Jonnie Liddle

"Faith"

The wonders of the Lord never cease to be and amaze me.
From the tinniest twig to the towering trees.
From Alps to beaches, he always reaches,
the tender hearts of all,
big or small.

The world would not be if it weren't for the Lord in me.
For once you use his eyes to see,
nothing else could greater be.

From the littlest bug to the elephant grand,
He's over sea and land,
Everywhere at once,
Inconceivable yet true.
Thank God for faith found in me and you.

Darcy Renna

"A Soul To Touch"

I'm not different. Than all you out there.
Full of hopes and dream. Perhaps ever despair.
At times it's hard. Hanging on this ride.
Just want to let go. I've collapsed and died.
So it's all in the game. Love a little lose a little.
No top or bottom. Out here in the middle.
For some it's a joy. Others a curse. When good turns bad.
Does it get any worse? You and I know. Of course it does.
Still we fight. For the way it was. Family is the thread.
Which weaves the web. So why is this truth. Withering with ebb?
Of this world. I don't ask much. Only someone's smile.
And maybe a soul to touch!

Sebastian Percy

"Remembering"

Little baby fingers, clinging tightly to my thumb.
Gentle cooing noises speak of pleasures yet to come.
First steps slowly taken,
Then running takes its place,
Bicycles, and basketballs and whiskers on his face.
Hockey games and girlfriends, school dances, then the prom.
Graduation, off to college and he waves goodbye to mom...
The years just passed too quickly,
And I knew this day would come.
That no longer would I feel those little fingers,
Round my thumb.
But the joy I feel remembering,
Can be no greater than,
The joy I feel as the mother of
A very special man.

Beverly S. East

Butterflies...And Friends

A butterfly came into my garden one late October day,
gently touching fading blossoms, seeking, resting.
How beautiful! Fragile...yet enduring, strong!

I watched, enchanted. "Stay awhile, my friend,"
I silently invited, my heart filled with wonder.
No bonds to hold it, no reason to delay,
it lingered awhile, then flew away.

"Friend?" Yes! Friends too come into our gardens,
gently touching, seeking, giving, free to go or stay;
leaving images on film, on mind, on heart
to linger like a song.

Butterflies and Friends—priceless treasures—
bringing joy, sharing love and memories,
causing no strife.

Thank you, Butterfly! Thank you, Friend!
Beyond measure, you have enriched my life!

Julia Tonn

Remorse

From the dark cavern of man's thought,
germinates the seed of all he's wrought:

This is the source of great delight,
the origin of agonizing plight;

The base on which to build his fame,
or tumble down, destroyed in shame.

Don't turn away with sneer and spurn,
this is the lesson man must learn;

To examine close within his hand,
each stone he casts upon the land;

For stones cast without regard,
land on loved ones very hard;

Though love is strong in spots it's weak,
the very spot the stone will seek;

Many's the lamp burned late at night,
by one who knows he's not done right;

And asked himself day by day,
will the bruise ever go away?

Graham K. Romans

No Tears?

Daddy? You were there for me when I was a little
girl, you were for the others
Daddy? You were there when I started school,
you were for the others
Daddy? You were there when I graduated,
you were for the others
Remember the calls you always returned, and
the visits with you and the others how
I received all the attention
I recall the love you had for me
just like the others, but I never
seem to fit

When you died I shed no tears,
and thought so cruel of myself
I cared, and pondered of passing memories—No tears
Until this day I think of you and can't cry—No tears
What's wrong? No tears! No tears! No tears for dad
Just memories
No tears

Deborah Whatley

Prayer Of The Homeless

HEAR ME, Father, for this I pray -
GIVE ME a home - a place where I can stay.
FEED ME today, or maybe tomorrow.
FILL ME with warmth. Take away my sorrow.
CLOTHE ME with blankets that will keep me warm.
PROTECT ME from evil - from every harm.
SEE ME when others choose to look away.
HEAR ME when the world ignores what I say.
REMEMBER ME - Others tend to forget.
LOVE ME. I will always be in your debt.
UNDERSTAND ME when no one seems to care.
COMFORT ME when I have too much to bear.
HOLD ME. Wipe away my tears when I cry.
RESTORE ME to when I held my head high.
GUIDE ME through this world of concrete and chrome.
RESCUE ME when I die,
then...
TAKE ME HOME.

Allyn F. Lomen

The Companion

Its still bare branches, straight, uplifting
giving praises to its God; patiently waiting to give birth to leaves and birds; patiently waiting for the man to sit beneath its branches.

Year after year, becoming more complete, fertilized by the love that seeps from the man's heart; growing older together as partners; slowly becoming one.

Sad and lonely until the first burst of Summer, it waits for the man to take his place—quiet, happy grateful for the leaves to shelter him from the sun; each in love with the other.

Winter once more, limbs bare, branches straight, uplifting, giving praises to its God.

Happy for another year; waiting in silent anticipation for that first Summer day when the man will sit beneath its branches, together becoming one.

Spring again, birds singing, leaves begin to bud, it waits for the man to come forth and share his love.

As signs of Summer fade into Fall, bringing an eerie sadness; leaves shed, branches bare, it knows the man will no longer sit beneath it; no longer share his love.

And, from that first realization, it too began to die.

Fannie Burnell Vennettilli

Prayer

Prayers are the steps to the Mansion of
God,
Our hope for the things to come,
For night can not hide the Lord from our
Sight,
Or silence our voices to Him.
For the world is a fleeting page,
That is destined soon to fade,
But the Kingdom that He has made,
Will last forever in His name.
For Jesus awaits at the doorway of
Prayer,
To usher us into the Great Somewhere.

Evelyn Beebe Leddy

My Sister My Mother, My Brother My Father

My sister, my mother, my father, my brother
God bless this family
And the tears that have shed
Over words that were said
To poison the family tree

One thing for sure
That has always been pure
Is the love that a mother possesses
And her heart that beats for all her children
No matter their transgressions

Dolly C. R. Reft

Love

Love surrounds with inter-twinning
Halo's touching the soul
As a whisper caresses the silent night air.
It lays in the lap of kindness
Stroking the spirit to peace,
Cries in the babe's
Outstretched arms and,
Dances lightly in the old man's memory.
Love, ever and ever, turning, ebbing,
Beams outward to the
Glistening tears that shine the Halo's light.

Gigi Bragg

"The Light"

Time created....civilization began,
God breath a life giving earth, to form a Man...
Listen and learn to heed to those words....
But lost life without one bite,
Absence of light was gone from sight.... time goes on,
Confusion set's in, ...
Pray for peace, evil to cease,
Purpose to find,.. "The light"...
Strayed years gone on, ...
Divine inspiration, I'll soon find....
"The Light",
Courage Heart... Faith to dream...Find?
"The Light",
Peace enfolds you, love fills your soul...Find?
"The Light",
Knowledge, understanding,
Ever-Faithful, ...At last,
The beginning,....
He comes to fill out life with
"Love"... He's here, "The Light"

Julio H. Castro

Destroy

The anger inside me boils high
God knows why I let it control me
The devil smiles a wicked smile
As I slowly slowly destroy

My blood runs cool, my heart beats faint
I'd like to hear his cracking skull on the pavement
The devil's companion is my middle name
As I slowly, slowly, destroy

My voice is icy, inviting
My lips curl to the sound of his scream
Demons call me out by name
As I slowly slowly destroy

Time is a ticking illusion
My head spins with sudden delight
His agony is my mural
As I slowly slowly destroy

As I taste the blood of damnation
My world turns from heaven to hell
Stuck in this f*&%ing condemnation
As I slowly slowly destroy

Jennifer Bress

Today

I once was lost but today I have found,
God's guiding hand and a new life bound.

He's given me what I need today,
A program, love and less dismay.
A fellowship of love and caring,
by which I can return by sharing.

Gratitude for all I've received this day,
That's why I get down on my knees and pray.
With Him, through Him and for Him I pray,
To do His will makes for a better day.
The giving back what I have found,
And there's plenty of that to pass around.
For all of you for helping me.
To get to where I want to be.
God let me help someone in need,
To give it back what I've received.
Just like we say, One day At A Time,
Remember the good and put the past behind.
For today I try to live my life,
TODAY

Carol Klingler

Rid

I'm seriously thinking about selling up
going away, getting away
Just the thought of escape seems to set me free
Chains drop away, shackles fall
A deep and secret woods await my running entry
As the arrows of my enemies fall all around me

I have no desire to arm myself and fire back
To merely get away is defence enough
But there was a time, a time recalled
When satisfaction could only be measured
by the body-count of my adversaries
No longer
It is not that I care to see them left standing
or fallen
I simply don't care about them at all

I'm seriously thinking about selling up
going away, getting away
A deep and secret woods awaits

Ellis James

Where Are The Fathers

A lot of kids today they don't have any Fathers, they don't have good male role models. The only male role models that they see are Pushers and Pimps and things they don't need to be.

To all you Fathers across the land trying to call yourself a man making all these little baby boys and girls, and then running off and getting lost in the world. Not even taking time to come around to see what type of person they are growing to be. Not even giving a helping hand to help your son become a man.

You run around and you say you're a Father, you know you shouldn't even bother. Fathers are the men that come to stay, to help your kids along the way, help them grow up straight and tall always there in case they fall, keeping them away from drugs and things that they know could cause them pain.

Men wonder why woman call them dogs. Some of them should be called leap frogs. From woman to woman without stopping, they don't even care how many babies they're popping.

Joe E. Sibley

"Let The Sun Shine In"

You think you've got me; got me down.
Got my chin scrape'n the ground.
Well I've got a few things to say.
A few things to do.
A few things to show you.
My Head's up high; eye on the Sky.

I can see and sense the presence of the
positive essence of my Soul.

The day will come when I'll no longer have to run
To catch a fraction of the action, you have
left behind.

Just as a bamboo Shoot pops its tender head and
trunk up from the Soil.
And will toil to reach maturity; without
being plucked and devoured.

So...Shall...I!

Becky J. Bolden

Inevitable Fall

I am slipping down the mossy bank into despair. My fingernails are grasping for any shred of grass or gob of dirt. My fingernails are dirty. I am tired. I know it is uncontrollable. I will land in the pit any time now. The fear of the muddy bottom results in extreme anxiety.

I am so afraid to let the tears fall. I know I would be swept away on the landslide of salty weeping and snot into the peccant pit. The gray clouds are circling overhead. The sky darkens. Everything becomes unnervedly still and calm.

How long can I clutch to the edge of rationality? I am drawn to sharp objects. Is it because I want to cut away at my clawing fingers and fall into despair? Or would I rather suffer physical pain than endure emotional self-doubt? Or am I just completely f*&%@ng nuts?

I am grappling with the selfishness of my battle. Madness is such a self-absorbed journey. I need a grappling hook to prop myself, or I'll tumble down the hole. Would it all be better if I just let go?

Connye Draper

To A Bloodroot

"O wondrous little gem of white,
Greeting the world in the early spring light,
What brought you out of the ground so soon
To bask in the light of the sun and moon?

"You are the first in the spring to show your bloom,
The first to rise from earth's dark tomb.
You have come from the ground where 'twas dark as night,
Yet your petals are radiant in a gown of white.

"All winter you hid in the deepest gloom,
Your white face locked in that earthen tomb.
What made you rise to become a flower—
Did you hear the call of some far-off power?"

"No, not some power that is far away,
But a source of strength that enfolds me each day.
In my heart is hidden the strength of God;
He called me to life, to rise from the sod."

Howard Hardeman

Beautiful Spring

In the spring there is rebirth,
Green things begin to show forth on earth.
Small living things on the wing,
Butterflies fluttering, birds sing.
Fleecy clouds on skies of blue,
They are part of nature too.
People dress in beautiful hues,
Green, lavender, Pink and blue.
Can Mere mortal man do all this?
If we think so, we are amiss.
Our creator, with pattern sublime,
Completed the job, all on time.
A time for winter, a time for spring,
Yes, there was thought put into everything.
If only man could be kind to his brother,
And really try to love one another.
Then twelve months a year our hearts would sing,
And the earth would have continual spring.

Helen Buehler Kosch

Passing By My Window

Grey days passing by my window
Grey world why does it spin slow
I looked out the window saw my hopes on the ground
Flowing down the gutter like the rain coming down
I looked out the window saw my spirit lying there
It was all in pieces scattered everywhere
Grey days passing by my window
Grey world why does it spin slow
I looked in the mirror saw a sad individual
The happiness he felt was no longer visible
The sad realization that she's gone for good
He tried to understand it but he never could
Grey days passing by my window
Grey world why does it spin slow
I turned on the music and I heard a lonely voice
A singer sang a song about a man who had no choice
He had to let her go because for him she didn't care
And now it's grey outside and raining everywhere

Carlos Lizarraga

A Winter Rainbow

Life seems slow after bustle of the season,
Greenery and glitter discarded until another year.
In solitude I search to find a reason,
Why so much caring, sharing, joy just disappear.

I walk familiar streets, my mind is shrouded.
My spirits match the grey sky covering,
When suddenly my vision is unclouded,
I find an answer to my questioning.

Rounding a corner I heard a child crying.
The scene to follow showed I need not fear,
Caring, sharing, and joy were not dying,
I only need to look to find it near.

Another child had lifted the fallen toddler,
He comforted and soothed till tears were gone.
In one small deed, joy replaced the sadness,
And in my heart A Winter Rainbow glowed.

Helen Joy

"Rainbows Vs. Reality"

When you died, I knew I had no choice.
Grief leaves one unable to rejoice.

Though, in your casket I kissed you,
I could not be glad.
For you were only eighteen...
The one brother I had.

People say as time goes on-the pain won't be strong.
Little do they realize... They're wrong.
The emptiness will never die,
No matter how hard anyone can try.

I look forward to heaven's day, when we will meet again.
That's the reason I face the future and pretend.

Although you're resting now
You'll always be alive in my heart
Through all the beautiful memories...
We will never be apart.

Carol Daniels Pate

Untitled

Slipping, I'm slipping, mind is tripping, for the hope is continue gripping,
Intriguing words, sounds good, so I grasp, but alas
Efforts they are in vain. Same unintellectual game...
to play, at least I believe, is a shame
I'm lead with an amorous heart, not a knowledgeable head
flighty feelings instead
Not knowing if I'm coming, if I'm going
Blind with burgundy hues, a heart that's tempted, but sings the blues
I'll keep grasping, the rope....everlasting, the test of lasting
Triumph? Mine? Not yet, not that I can see
Not something that I could visualize. So I remain, in disguise
as the pawn, forward, on the front lines
Of this game, assisting to conquer, in the kingdom's name
The kingdom of.... my heart, my soul, my mind.
Hopefully not back to the beginning
where in the dark, I continue slipping

Holly Roberson

Planet Earth

Sun goes down, feelings found, speed of sound, nervous town, solid ground
children peek, old folks speak, robins shriek, lovers meet, empty street
people die, others cry, don't know why, always try, eyes lie
growing old, stories told, babies sold, memories cold, characters mold
humans hate, is it fate, mortgage rate, find a mate, gotta wait
outer space, saving grace, satin lace, fast pace, separated by race
one last fling, oil is king, life brings, children sing, wedding ring,
beauty strays, nothing to say, fly away, kneel and pray, another day
normal commotion, job promotion, no emotion, nuclear explosion, mind erosion
baby booties, pageant beauties, peace treaties, eat your wheaties, diabetes
smoking banned, nothing planned, barren land, blistered hand, make a stand
judgeless trial, divorces filed, endless miles, wait a while, faces smile
business meeting, phony greeting, out of seating, love fleeting, wife beating
eat a peach, trash-filled beach, want to teach, out of reach, one to each
graying hair, electric chair, people stare, no one cares, is it fair
Indian corn, patience worn, babies born, kiddy porn, loved ones mom
dessert cart, poisonous dart, broken heart, lovers part, never start
go to school, learn the rule, life's best tool, vanishing fuel, too cool
have some fun, rising sun, two become one, smoking gun, almost done
parents call, babies crawl, standing tall, john and paul, that is all.

Donald Trotter

"Magical Blessings"

Life-Just-brings-all-kinds-of-occasions
Happy and sad-to-write-down-our-memorable-sensations
Art-music-poetry and love go-hand-in-hand-
Of-one-thing-or-the-other-like-a-"Magical-Command"!
Of-man-or-beast-or-God-and-his-creations!
Of-sweet hearts-dear-of-friends-and-our-relations-
The-beauty-of-the-sky-the-sea-the-sun-the-moon-and-stars-all-free
And-of-the-snow-covered-winter-trees
And-the-glorious-fall-with-its-calico-tumbling-leaves-
and-of-the-white-fluffy-clouds-sailing-by.
And-remember-spring-and-the-4th of July?
The colorful-perfumed-flowers-even-the-birds-butterflies-and-bees make us sigh! ah! the-cuddly-babies-human-and-animals-too-
They-are-a-sight-to-behold-.
To-watch-them-play-without-a-care
As-we-see-their-future-unfold!
This-is-all-music-and-poetry-to-our-hearts-and-minds
Without-these-many-blessings-life-would-be-very-very-unkind!

Daisy Bartholomew

The Texas Mockingbird's Christmas Song

The Texas Mockingbird's Christmas song,
has been a national favorite so dang long,
and whenever it's heard in the Lone Star State,
the people stay up to listen to it real, real late,
and when it is over everyone will say,
aw what the heck let's hit the hay,
and all through the night a sound most annoying,
all through the city people were unpleasantly snoring,
and when the night is gone and the people had their rest,
they all got up sniffing a good hardy breakfast,
the night was still and really quite long,
but the people did not care they wanted to hear the
Texas Mockingbird Christmas Song.

Daniel Del Toro

World Without A Sun

Since you've been gone my endless day
has been filled with dread and gloom.

I have no sweet and blessed sunshine to call my own.

The park which was once sunny and fair, with children happily running about
is now a place of sadness where the sun hides itself from the world.

And a single child cries for the loving embrace of its mother
As I cry for yours.

The beach where we once walked hand in hand
while the sun warmed our hearts

Is now dark and desolate,
and the sky bursts open with tears of its own.

I'll wander through my endless day
until it finally comes to an end.

When it does I'll find a place
filled with warmth and love where the sun shines brightly in the sky.

I'll turn around to see you standing there
with your loving eyes and your warm smile.

You are my life, my happiness, and my joy
And being here on earth without you is a World Without A Sun.

Heather Fittro

July Wedding

It is the infinite amount of things I
have heard, smelled, touched, felt and just
plain known around you that have affected
my soul unlike all the combined experiences
of my lifetime. The love you make me feel acts
as a window through which all is made
breathtaking. What makes me feel this
love is as clear as a crystal wine glass and
incomprehensible as the boundaries of the
universe. Next July I shall proclaim what
I have already surrendered to you several
years ago — the secrets that make my
heart beat, the dreams that set my
destiny, the flame that is my life, and
the trust that weaves them all together.
They are delicately cradled in your heart of
hearts where both our souls can feed
from the power that our love creates....
I love you

Mark Scesny

The Mystic Marks

The mystic marks of the time and span,
Have left their auras impressed on man,
And deftly though their etchings lie,
Defy all explanation why, as meaningless.

Aeons of sages cast their doubts,
In myriad forms of bold wit spout,
Impress minds that cannot know,
The empty uncertainty of creatures below, as meaningless.

The stars arise in a coal black sky,
The moon and the sun continue to cry,
That man in his knowledge still is weak,
No matter that ages his boldness may seek, as meaningless.

And so in his struggle to live and to stand,
Man fights for a purpose and destroys what is man.
And still as he stretches his thoughts to the limit,
He still is devoid of what's really all in it, as meaningless.

A void, a darkness, ingrained all in all,
A hunger to be, a reason to call,
But devoid of a God who gives reason to be,
Man drowns in his struggle beneath a dark sea, of meaningless.

Anthony Alan Pearson

"Thanks Lord"

Dear Lord,
Have you any idea what it was you'd done
when you gave me such a darling son?
Well, I'm sure you do
And I really appreciate it too.
Sometimes I think that life is so unfair
Until I see those big brown eyes
and that pretty blonde hair.
He's smart, he's cute, and he's great at ball
And someday I know, he's going to be tall.
Lord, you know I almost hate to say
but I ask you this every single day
"When is our life going to change?"
But then I think, how strange?
Because I'll hear him call mamma
and I'll known that's your letter
to let me know life is already better.

Thanks Lord.

Debbie Edens

"Quiet Man"

There he was a quiet man
He came from Bethlehem
For His trade it wasn't grand
Things He made with His hands

With one touch the blind could see
He could tell what would be
When the winds began to rage
With one word they would obey

He was a young man, so I'm told
He wasn't married, He wouldn't grow old
Satan tried Him, He couldn't be sold
He said nothing, so the story goes

So he died there on Calvary
Tried to end His majesty
Thought they'd crush Him, He'd cease to be
From our sins He set us free

Jessie Garcia

Misguided Death

Lying in a grave, this soul's too late to save.
He could've ascended to the angels, but he spun a web of many tangles.
His life was full of sin, he followed the path of many men.
Christians felt, for him, nothing but grief, for neither heaven nor Hell were a part of his belief.
For God this man would've been great, he could've changed many mens' fate.
But first he needed one to change his own, for with God his heart would've grown.
So when God's in your spirit it is no secret and others should hear it.
So when there's death there is no fear, and Christ's eye will not, again, shed a single tear.

Angela Mentzel

Which Way Joe

There once was a boy named Joe.
He didn't know which way to go.
He didn't know whether to go up or down,
To go to the country, or run down town.
He didn't know whether to go east or west.
He didn't know which way was best.
He couldn't decide to go north or south,
Until a bug flew into his mouth.
Joe turned this way, and he turned that,
He shook his head and took off his hat.
His suspenders snapped and Joe fell down.
There he rolled upon the ground.
He turned to the east, then to the west.
He said, "I've really been put to the test."
Joe spit the bug from out his mouth,
And said, "I know! I should go south."
Joe went south 'till he came to a town.
He got a basement apartment and he went down.
Now he knows east is east and west is west,
Cause he carries a compass in his vest.

Cleo Bopp

A Loving God

God is our Maker, Creator, and Friend.
He has a big heart and a hand to lend.
He can make your life easier if you
will take your problems to Him,
because God will never break
nor will he ever bend.
He has promised to see us through to the very end.
God loves us when we're good
He loves us when we're sad.
He even loves us and tries to help us,
when we have been bad.
Now, in your time of need what ever it may be,
take it to the cross and you will surely see
how Jesus takes care of these
things for your you and for me.
Look up now to Jesus who loves you so much.
He doesn't like to see us upset and such
He is standing there waiting for you to open the door
so He can take away the hurt for you to remember no more.

Barbara J. Coppley

The Bat, Cat And Gnat

There once lived a bat who had a straw hat.
He always slept on a kindermat. His mom
and dad were kind of fat. He lived with a
gnat and a cat. The bat and the cat were crazy.
But the gnat was very lazy. Then they lived
happily ever after.

Amanda Dettman

"God's Greatest Gifts"

God has made the earth, which gives birth,
He has made the sun, that sets in the night,
Which gives off light, morning through night,
God has made the sky and clouds up above,
Which move as graceful as a dove,
God has made grasses and the ground,
He has made the waves whom when crash make a sound,
God has made flowers and plants galore,
Not to mention a whole lot more,
God has made the land and vegetation,
Without any hesitation
He has made colors dark and light,
All from which are a beautiful sight
God has made lakes and rivers,
He has made the kind of weather that makes you shiver
He has made the mountains, hills, valleys and all
The creatures of the earth,
We should thank him for our birth.

Jason McElhenney

A Lonely Young Man

A young boy strolls slowly home
He is eleven and in the fifth grade
Home is where he's going to
Tattered pants and worn out shoes
No one to greet him when he arrives
No one who really cares
He return on the T.V. eats a small snack
Parents come in very late
Stumbling into their own bed
Didn't even give their son a kiss
Didn't know if he was even amiss
The years flew by so very slow
His parents came and went
No love has he ever felt
He learned to grow without a sound
He is free of them at last
This quiet little man
They both died of what they drank
He has moved away from the dreaded days
He is becoming a man without a past

Beverly A. Marks

Water

He travels around the world never stopping,
He is known by all;
He is life, and his absence is death.

At times he is calm and peaceful,
Or warm and inviting;
He will draw you in and comfort you,
But be aware!

You can only control him under certain conditions
At times, his anger will get the best of him,
He will lash out and destroy anything in his path.

But you need him,
And you can never completely avoid him;
After all, he is a part of you.

Don't think that he relies on you for anything;
For you can only irritate him,
And cause problems for him,
Which you may or may not try to correct.

You are totally dependent on him
And you have no right to curse him;
For you would be nothing without him.

Claire Caprioli

Benjamin

There is a boy, I have just met,
He is someone I will never forget.
He is the one I want in my arms,
Through sad, rainy days, even storms.

He's the best of the best, the top of the line,
I don't deserve him, but he is really mine.

He says he loves me, is he for real,
Well I love him, that's how I feel.

Today makes a month, it hasn't been long,
But it will be longer, if our love stays strong.
Later in years we will surely see,
Together forever, that's how we'll be!!

Jessica Bouanchaud

The King

I started out with the enemy that pretended to be a King
He punished my family in anger
His words were as smooth as butter, but war was in his heart
until one day, my mom rose up
The enemy lost and my mom won

So there we were, alone, for six long years,
until one amazing day, the real King showed up.

The real King got me into shape.
He saved my life; he disciplined me in love
He held me when I was sad; He wept with me; He loved me.
He caused me to rise up and introduced me to the Great King.

This King calls me a prince and he makes me feel like one
Every time I get better this King puts a ruby on my sword
So,
When I fight, this King is always with me, pulling for me,
fighting for me.

One day this King said to me that I was going to be a King too
He said that I was going to fight with the gold on my sword
Just like my Dad who is...

The King

David Michael Carnahan

"Little Angel"

Mommy and Daddy's little Angel got his wings today,
He said he was sorry but he really couldn't stay.

God had plans for me he needed me to go,
Even though I had to leave, I'll always love you so.

And thought I'm just a tiny tot God gave me these great big wings,
I never knew that heaven had so many beautiful things.

And ever since I left I've been sleeping on a cloud,
But God gave me permission he said I was allowed.

And thanks for always being there right by my side,
It's been a rough journey for us it's been a bumpy ride.

But I'm safe and sound now and peaceful as I sleep,
So please don't cry anymore, and please, try not to weep.

Donna Lynn

Rodeo

As he says a prayer, and gives the okay with a little nod of his head, he holds on with the old tattered glove he's always had. As the gate opens wide, out of the shoot, the rank Brahma bull bucks him up, and down and around. As he spurs him to move he can feel all of the aches and pains from the rides before. While he holds on for dear life, he wonders if he can stay on this night and ride the eight seconds he needs to win the money, for this is a cowboy's life.

Julie Perrill-Hartgrove

The Little Boy

The little boy went out to play
he said, "Mom and Dad, I have something to say."

Who made the stars so bright
when they come out at night?

Who made the world so round?
And who made the ground?

Who made the hills, valleys, and creek?
I know that's where the animals all drink.

Who made all the trees?
And who made such a strong breeze?

And who made the sunlight so bright?
And why does the moon come out at night?
Who made the ocean and the snakes?
And who made the skunk, for Pete's sake?
His Dad said, "God made all of these.
He is a million times stronger than me."
The little boy said He did all He can
but why make a bear and shark that can eat a man?

The little boy went on his way
and said, "I sure learned a lot today."

Bud Farrell

My Shaggy Friend

I met him one day outside my home
He seemed so frightened, so alone
He'd been abused, down trodden and hurt
It was plain that someone had done him dirt
His eyes were knowing, yet soft and bright
His hair a little shaggy but gleaming white
I bid him come in and asked him to stay
Hesitant to respond he shied away
I could tell it would take a little shove
To show him that all I offered was love
I opened my door and I opened my heart
Cautiously he entered and didn't depart
I stroked his head, gave a gentle pat
There in the dark corner where he sat
I gave him to eat I gave him to drink
And soon he began to trust, I think
Years have passed, he's my dearest friend
I'm thankful the day I bid him come in
He's just a mutt, this lowly stray
But my pal Laddie is here to stay.

Georgia M. Chandler

Land's Image

I saw the face of God in the land,
He smiled at me through a cougar cub, I held in my hands.

He whispered in my ear,
When a robin flew near.

I felt God's hand as I walked;
From a touch of the willow tree's branch.

I felt God's breath from the sky;
As a tree bud floated from on top high.

I felt God's tears from the clouds;
As the oil and waste is spilled in mounds.

I heard God's heart beat healthy and strong;
As his children started to respond.

Helen Davis

The Man Of My Dreams

The man of my dreams has hazel green eyes,
He stands way out from all the other guys.
His warm gentle ways and soothing, friendly attitude,
Make my body melt and put me in a good mood.
Looking at his dark complected face,
Can make any girl's heart race.
Just glancing at his beautiful smile,
Causes you to hit the tile.
For me, no other guy, could do,
Most other guys don't have a clue
I'm very lucky he stole my heart,
Cause, I know we will never, ever part.

Heather Madden

A Pen

My arm clings tightly to the pocket of my master.
He takes me out from my day long sleep, and lays me on the table.
He leaves, only for a short amount of time.
When he returns I know my job.
He lifts me up and removes my head, revealing my skeleton.
Next he puts me to the blood-thirsty paper.
The paper drains my blood for thirty minutes.
When I am laid down I take a short nap.
When I am moved again, I feel very empty.
He puts me to the paper again and I am depleted some more.
I start to stutter in my speaking and then; I die.
My master throws me away, and I am forgotten.
Once again it is shown;
Life Feeds On Life.

Eli Howell

He Thought About It

He thought about it, he tried to find another way.
He thought about it, every night and everyday.
There was so much pain and so much hate.
He thought about it, he tried hard to concentrate
He knew he had to get away, he knew that he could no longer stay.
He thought about it, he was confused
He thought about it, he was abused.
He thought about it, a plan make.
He thought about it, himself he'd brake.
I tried to stop him he wouldn't listen.
His mind was set, on his self-imposed mission.
He would hang a rope from a tree, he would say goodbye to you and me.
He thought about it, and finally,
he decided to hang himself from that tree.
He's left this world forever, his short life is thru.
He's left this world forever, and made me very blue.
He thought about it, every night and everyday.
He thought about it, and he couldn't find another way.

Gina Parisse

Cat

Silently walking the shadows
He quietly stalks his prey.
With padded feet he waits to eat
In the light of the day.

He crouches and sits,
He licks his lips.
Trembling with fear, the prey comes near.
He hisses and spits...
Gulp,
The prey is all gone!

Heather Birdsall

Taking Time

The sky is God's canvas that He uses in many ways.
He uses blues and pinks and grays and sometimes even haze.
The colors in the sunset I witnessed just last night,
gave a new dimension to pinks and blues highlight.

Even things as simple as a rose bud closed up tight,
if you look really close the color is just right.
The purple in the mountains as the clouds float over the top
show that God's talent is everywhere and will never never stop.

He wants each and every one of us no matter what the day brings
to take an extra minute just to enjoy the very special things.
We take these things too lightly and never stop to view
all the really wonderful things that are in each day a new.

We always think there is lots of time to enjoy the beauty God has
created but our time clock and our life clock may not be related.
There is only one today
and it is ours to do with what we may.

Make yourself a commitment each day
that you will take time to enjoy God's gifts along the way.

Jane Nichols

A Very Kind Mouse

There was a mouse who was very kind, and
he would say to me. "I am the mouse who is
very kind, how may I help thee?" Early in
the morning e'er the dew was gone, he
would stand real tall and say, "I must
help someone." All day long he kept his
job, busy as a bee. Walk up to a stranger
say "How may I help thee?"

One day in the winter, he would stand and
shiver. "I must get wood, keep others warm,
Help the other feller." Soon as snow was
off the ground he would run and say "I'm
so glad I helped someone for another day."
This little mouse said one day. "I'm
so tired of giving. I'm going to wait a while,
'til after Thanksgiving." Then when Christmas
came around he was sad he said it.
He sang good news in the Christmas
choir - then he ran to tell it!

Alma Neeley

Flight

He stood in a dim lit corner
He watched
Her silken gown danced with a night breeze
A cool fluidity flowing over keys
Keys being stroked by hands tired and sore

"Is That You?" She called.
His world, her world, wrapped up in night strewn melodies
"Yes," he replied.
She relinquished her seat, parted the curtains and motioned
"Play Baby Play"

Compositions rose and to nature's surprise
The darkness of her skin pierced the Black skies
She soared up past Toni Morrison's scenes
Of slaves with tattered clothes and bright shiny wings

Mommy you left me
Don't sigh child don't sigh
You know mommy didn't leave you
Mommy can't fly

Carlton R. Blair

American Soldier In The Gulf

To a land beyond the oceans, for a cause not yet perceived,
He went without a question, when his orders were received.

To the training site he traveled, with ten thousand other men.
There they learned to fight a war, that they dared not fail to win.

To war games played in the sand, where he found that he could trust
His own resolve to overcome, the heat waves, the lice, the dust.

To battle lines they mustered, there to face an enemy,
Who had fought on his terrain, from the deserts to the sea.

To buried trenches in the sand, caution marked his slow advance.
Here he killed the deadly foe, from a standing, fearless stance.

To the land he had defended, at long last he could return,
To the gratitude of millions, and the peace his soul did yearn.

George E. Watson

Untitled

Hush...
hear the silence as it rushes past your ear.
Noiseless, but it makes its presence known.
Quiet, as if to disturb no one—
Solitude is what it brings.

Hush...
hear the laughter as it flows past.
Louder, as more than one finds the happiness.
Encompassing many as it is contagious—
Feeling of warmth is what it brings.

Hush...
hear the cries of a lonely soul.
Muffled, but the pain can still be heard.
The flowing tears can be felt at a distance—
what it brings are
cries from being silent without the laughter.

Charlean Breiner

Son

You held my hand, I saw you smile, you touched my
heart forever after
I've seen the pain, tears, and joy and heard your
sounds of laughter
I've watched you learn how to crawl, how to walk,
to grow up tall
I remember the times you would sit on my lap,
while I read to you before you took your nap
I held you loving to my breast, brushed your hair
from your forehead as you lay to rest
Memories so special, of a time in the past,
yesterdays and yesteryears that will forever last
These things and more I will always keep in my heart
While you collect memories of your son as we live apart
As the years slip by one by one,
Always remember I love you my son

Doris Meissner

Vanquished Dreams

Strife and pain inside me rage
Heart of stone, emotions of age
Just a glance of innocent smile
Walking array of light that your beauty compiles
Hidden strength inside me lurks
But when seen, I'm such a jerk
Failures of the past have increased desperation
Leaving me lonely, alone, with only depression
The wars I fight, my thoughts deny
Every passing day as my emotions die
It now may be too late
For I'm losing the stalemate

Fearing the passage of dawn to dusk
Falling and falling evermore
In darkness I fall in darkness I soar

The agony of despair as life fades away
Body suffering from the loss, continually tired
Can't function right or even stay alert
My love of life has now expired

Please come back!

Chaning L. E. Simnitt

Searching

An elaborate queen doesn't dream
Heaven is only a 12 inch step away
Hold a hand, be a man, what's going on
today?
Any love? Oh no, we're friends
Happiness solemnly settles in the bottom of
the pond
But I'm swimming, searching for my
perfect fish.
Pull the reins, no needles in my veins,
Stop the torment and make new friends.
Slat don't trap my head in the door. Fear
I steer clear of the forbidden shore.
A bay I stay, flourish as I strap
on my snorkel and fins.
Take a dive, strive to find my only
fish in the sea.

Jason Murry

"Angels Know Not Why"

So sad was the face where no children played
Heaven's eyes for them did cry.
Ears that listened knew not the grief,
of angel's hearts that knew not why.

A siren screams, a shell explodes
a burned out skeleton of a home.
In a place which has no past
One more orphan cries alone.

Who shall hear a sound so faint
as a single finch in the wood?
Who shall stand in evils path
where only the bravest have stood?

So many spoke of what was wrong
of ignorance, of prejudice, of hate.
They spoke and listened till silence came,
then found they were too late.

So sad was the face where no children played
Heaven's eyes for them did cry.
Ears that listened knew not the grief,
of angel's hearts that knew not why.

Jeffrey S. Wood

On Second Thought

My words rush gushing as a spring fed stream,
Heedless of harm and consciousness both.
I see the denting then, however unintended,
In the shrinking of the one before me.
Stopping the momentum, I breathe,
Take refuge in silence, reframing
My language to fill in the places
Where my thoughtless words struck,
Piercing as arrows, psychic darts.
Filled in and bigger now, our newly
Expanded energies meet, create a space
For shared communications, heartful speech.
My own heart opens, grateful to have
Caught that one in time, to be
Learning a second language.

Grover Cleveland

Goshen

The long, brown beard with suspenders
Held the leather straps while a white bonnet
In a modest gown read the road map; as
Chariots of the atomic age passed the one
Horse powered carriage by, a steady
Drift of dust fell back in their faces - pulling
His black hat down over his eyes of
Certainty - that they will get home first.

Don Andrews

Waaa, The New Born's First Voice

Doc, why did you do that?
Held upside down by my feet,
Treated to the disgrace we all meet.
Slapped briskly on my bottom part,
Oh, Doc, please have a heart.

Taken from a warm cozy space,
Into this harsh earthly place.
If that's an example of life we will be in,
I'm not surprised there is so much sin.
I'm going to do things and have my fun,
And suffer the punishment after it is done.

When Mom is extra busy as a bee,
I'll go Waahoo, to make her tend to me.
When Mom and Dad are sound asleep,
Is when I'll make my loudest peep.
I'm the boss, though they don't know it,
I'm not the one to go and blow it.

Earl V. Wing

The Unseen Friend

Jesus our Savior, Jesus our Friend
He'll walk along with us 'til our life's end
Though the path becomes rocky, and mostly up hill
He will always remain, beside us still
Waiting and silent, strong and true
Giving strength and comfort, whatever we do
In times of trouble, just call his name
With gentle touch, our fears he will tame
We should give him the glory, every day of our life
And thank Him most humbly, for easing our strife.

Janice A. Sargent

Survived The 'Sharecropper' Days

She is attractive and clean.
Her body - no laziness has seen.
Former years were lean
That did not make her mean.

She cooked the food at the age of five.
She scrubbed and cleaned in dignity.
She was humble and clever and kept alive.
She rose above the bigotry.

Proud! Confident! Her husband displays.
Memories of bad times, he too, recall -
The era of the 'Sharecropper' Days.
Love for Jehovah subdued it all.

They grew crops on rented land -
Expecting a share of the profit on hand.
Informed that the crops did not yield
Disappointment! And back to the field.

She picked the cotton - no books were read.
She made the wine and baked the bread.
Observed and learned along the way
Optimistic of a better day.

Almarine Russell Banks

The Potter

Today I saw the potter that sits at yonder wheel.
Her hands were deft and supple, endowed with grace and skill.
Expressing years of tempered life, she shaped her kaolin.
Round and round she worked the clay, forming beauty with each spin.

Etched upon the vessel that issued from her throwing
Was sgraffito from her learned hands, the kind that comes from knowing
All about the trials of life which cut away the glaze,
Yet leave behind a wisdom that remains for countless days.

Ready then to fire her ware, she stoked the flame up bright.
Oh, and how the clay did glow when baked so high in Fahrenheit.
Melted glaze and hardened clay, she moved it from the kiln.
With her breath she gave it life, and thus her soul revealed.

Yes, now I've seen the potter that sits at yonder wheel.

James A. Latham

Mom's Poodle

Mom had a little poodle who went to sleep one day,
Her legs were bent, her eyes were dim, she no longer liked to play.
The constant love and companionship that poodle offered me,
A dozen years as "man's best friend" is all that she could be.

When eyes were closed that final time, her body limp in mine,
I knew that I had loved her for the very final time.
Does God let pets in heaven? No one seems to know,
But if she's not there and waiting, I'm not sure I want to go.

That little dog brought such happiness to me down here below.
Oh God! please tell me of her fate, that's what I'd like to know.
How could there be joy in heaven, without that which we love?,
Some would say "she's just a dog," she can't be up above,

Are there such things called Angel Dogs? that truly is my plea,
Because that dog was such a friend, there surely has to be.
So when I pass those pearly gates, what joy that will be,
Please tell me God, when I get there, will my poodle welcome me?

John C. Banker Jr.

As the Eagle Flies

As the eagle flies three miles high to mate as it descends,
Her love was my joy and soar did my heart content,
The dove of my life did fly on her way,
And the lovers' moon turned dark with dismay,
As a knight in white satin from a long time ago,
I searched in the harsh world for an answer unknown,
Hungry and tired and weak from my fears,
Looking for true love through the pain of my tears,
Hard is my journey and the lessons I've learned,
Turning my eyes inward I've changed and I've turned,
What keeps me going is a heart made of gold,
I know out there somewhere are the riches untold,
Led by my passion, like love for a king,
It pushes me onward in search of a ring,
Life is so endless until it reaches the end,
Love is forever if one learns how to bend.

Coy Kenyon

My Guardian Angel

Her head is weary,
Her shoulders hunched,
Her eyes teary,
Her card's been punched!

Let her rest in peace,
Her work here is done,
Her road here was rocky,
But then again who said life was fun.

The rain will still fall,
The sun will still shine,
And I'll cry my tears as we bury her
Below her marble shrine.

A blanket of earth will be her bed,
A place where she can lay her weary head.

All is dark - But now is bright.
Because I know she watches over me
As I sleep at night!

Beth Ann Buechler

The Lily

See her there in a blue field
Her winsome smile, my soul in healed
A gentle breeze blows, through her hair
A mirage, a vision, no she is there

From where she comes, too few know
Where she goes there is an eternal glow
Dancing, swaying like the lilies in the field
Gentle beauty and so very real

Possessing the innocence of a child
Raised in culture with manners mild
Though a free spirit and even celestial
One who wins her must be special

See her there in a gown of white
So ethereal she can almost take flight
See how she dances to her own spirits band
That inner spirit that says, yes you can

a mirage, a vision, is she real
Yes, she is one of the lilies of the field.

Bruce Dorset

Our Telephone

Without a Telephone we couldn't get by
Here are some of the reasons why-
We are never alone when we have a phone
We can pick it up to say Hi!

We can call for advice and ask for a price,
Or maybe to settle a bill.
If we have some news or are feeling the blues
Or give comfort to someone who is ill.

We make appointments for our hair
Call the garage for repair
Also call and say happy birthday.
Ask a friend to have lunch-
Or visit with one far away.

We call the doctor, the drug store,
The bank and the bus,
But whatever we do
Our phone is a must.

Florence Cheney

New Parents

To the new parents soon to be.
Here's some ideas you may not see.

First of all Dad, you may not know,
But its patience you must always show.

Secondly, no matter what you fear,
You should never cause a tear.

You must stand tall and proud at all hours,
To protect this grandchild of ours.

Mom will have the hardest role to play,
Regardless of what other people say

When Dad's off making a buck,
She's the one that will be stuck.

With her daily chores of care & food.
She may not always be in the mood.

With love and care this child you'll raise,
And over the years you'll get much praise.

We know of what we say to you,
Cause not long ago we had babies too.

With Love and thoughts so mild,
We await the birth of this new Grandchild.

John C. Kiskamp

Rosco

No secrets here, "Man's best friend" I'll make it clear.
He's a youthful, curious Lab, bountiful with energy.
With open mouth, long red tongue and propeller tail
he greets me each and every day.
How giving he is of interest, energy, time and affection.
How reliable are his offerings.
I have no choice. His behavior and emotional expression
are infectious and I'm pleased there is no vaccine, no antibiotic, no
cure for this "infection" I respond to him with love and affection. I
have no choice. I have no choice and forever I will have no choice.

This emphasis deserves serious yet playful and thorough
consideration. I will not pose the question, "Must we study the
behavior of and take lessons from a DOG?" to learn how to give
and receive love, attention, affection, etc. For this question
implies that a DOG is at least secondary to a human in the
"manmade hierarchy" of species. This human arrogance hurts us
and mauls our best friend." I finalize with a question. How is it
that the letters D, O and G were chosen to label this species and
why when reversed these letters give rise to the concept we turn
to when no human can help?

Christian Sarra

As Night Falls

Slowly the golden sun set,
Hiding itself behind the massive purple mountains.
Reddish blue clouds drift quietly away at twilight,
Night descend upon the earth,
Darkness unfold embracing the waiting world,
The sky turn to jet black,
A soft cool breeze kiss the earth good night.
A silvery moon ascend
and touch the earth with its finger of light.
Sparkling stars shine and glitter
Like a mistress,
Waiting for her lover in the night.

Emelda J. Brown

America

A man was slaughtered last night on the street.
His blue lips kissed the crack in the walk.
He could've been you or he could've been me.
He wasn't, you see, so just walk away.

The man with the gun was like anyone else.
He could've been you or he could've been me.
His face was gone so none could see
The hate he had and the fear that grew.

The man with the gun had done no wrong.
The slain man was innocent, guilty one in the same.
He was different and strange and not the norm.
And that's why his lips kissed the crack in the walk.

The man who had died was cold through and through.
But he wanted to stay on the walk where he lay.
Wanted the result of hate at every man's feet.
'Cause dead men can and do tell their tales.

The man with the gun has long run away.
"I've done no wrong", he continues to say
As the pink of his heart now as black as the night.
The man is you and this man is me.

Eric Koch

Necessary Evil

He lay still and quiet, unmoving, unaware of his surrounding.
His gnarled old claws lay at rest on his withered chest.
His pale face is undaunted by the disruptions that flurry about it.
His stillness says more than words can, peacefully slumbering in
his comatose state.
The bright lights seem to miss him as if by magic, leaving a
gloomy heavy shadow about his body.
The way the noise drones in silent screams is as unsettling as the
sight itself.
Far off a siren wails, telling of more tragedy in the surrounds.
He doesn't appear dead, but who is to say what death's sounds are.
He slips off the earth and goes far enough away to forget all his pain.

Evan Horne

Happy Birthday, Daddy

Today I wished him Happy Birthday.
His hair still going white.
His eyes still a dreamy blue.
His features still of a bear without the bite.

Today I wished him Happy Birthday.
His smile still bringing happiness.
His nature still showing care.
His heart still filled with love.

Today I wished him Happy Birthday.
I pray he'd still be that way
when I get to see him in Heaven one day.

Today I wished him Happy Birthday.

JayLynn Thibault

Innocence Lost

Every sip of evil spilt over his lips, an evil consuming
his mind and soul.
Confusion from a long ago past now coursing through his
veins, altering the present. A look of rage penetrating her.
She falters with every step as she frantically searches
for escape, once again. It's not found.
Every blow of his hand, a hot flash of pain scarring her
flesh, her mind, her soul. A child's cry in the distance.
He looks away and for an instant she beholds the face of
the man she once knew.
She rises only to be met with those eyes filled with darkness.
Glass, exploding and falling around her. The essence of life
slipping away from her. She cried out one last time.
A vision moving towards her from a distance. The Guardian
reached out to her and held her in his arms.
As she welcomed her release, she heard the little girl's sorrow
and the shattering echo of a gunshot.
Darkness.

Julie Michaels

The Trooper

How tall he stood, his jaw firmly set
His shoulders thrown back, his cheek slightly wet.
He asked for this duty, though his rank was quite low.
He needed to do this, for reasons he couldn't know.
He remembered his commander, his kind grizzled face.
He recalled his generous nature, when he'd visit his place.
The visits were over now, his commander was gone.
Nightfall had come with no sign of dawn.
Yet, today the Trooper was brave, he would not weep.
He was true to his mission, though his pain was quite deep.
He'd be strong like the others, he'd bare his burden well.
He could be likened to his commander, as he'd been before he fell.
When the mission was over, he would allow himself to cry.
As he turned toward the casket, and told his Grandpa Joe goodbye.

George Beighey

When Reality Came

The first time I laid eyes on him, he was perfect.
His smooth skin, soft spoken eyes, and joyful smile.

His innocence sucked me up like a vacuum.
He soon asked me to be his girl.
This was it! A month later......THEN CAME REALITY.

The lies started, there was verbal
abuse and disappearing acts......THEN CAME REALITY.

I was being used, manipulated and taken
for granted......THEN CAME REALITY.

I am a good woman, do all the best things
for my man..........THEN CAME REALITY.

What could have went wrong?
What happened to all that innocence?
Those soft spoken eyes and that joyful smile......THEN CAME
REALITY.

The innocence that he once briefly carried
had faded into his own selfish soul.

The soul of a selfish one.
There was only one thing left to do when
reality came to me! TELL HIM HE WAS DISMISSED!!!
NOW THIS IS REALITY................

Froncine R. Pringle

Daydreams

My thoughts escape me
hitting the ceiling and bouncing off the floor

Scurrying deep into the corners of the room
-hiding from my sight -
as I sit quietly and daydream.

Julie Toulson

The Crusader

Chains....that rattle through the darkness of my soul
Hold me behind walls as I grow old
And all the great crusades I might have led
lie shackled....in the dungeons of my head.

The world I thought I'd save someday
Is neither black or white....it's grey
And all the words of wisdom that I said
Still echo through the dungeons of my head.

I dreamed that I was born to lead
The chosen on my snow white steed
Our weapons would be truth and justice
The right would win....God would protect us.

Surveying all the battles lost I find
The wars I fought were raging in my mind
And all the great crusades I might have led
Lie shackled....in the dungeons of my head.

Jerry Gallagher

The World As We Know It

I sit around and do nothing,
how can I for you let me do nothing?
I hear the groans and screams of everyday people,
I know you cause them.
I see all the horrors of the world,
but you ignore them.
I see only what you will let me see,
because your hands are over my eyes.
I mark the power of your passing,
how could I not?
I see the hatred in the recesses of your mind,
is it directed toward me?
I observe the ravages of time on your face.
I observe that you do not feel what I do.
All these say what you can not say yourself.
See, hear, and feel the pain of my suffering.

Elisha Anne Darville

My Wounded Heart

Love is the pain I feel with thoughts of you.
How can I measure my pain? It's so deep.
It strikes at my heart, I can't help but weep
in sorrow, losing the one love I knew.
I spend days dreaming of what could have been.
My nights are endlessly sad with you gone
away, and I feel like I can't go on
without you. I tried to forgive your sin
against our love; but, yet it haunts my soul.
Hopefully, time will heal my wounded heart.
I don't feel that I can make a new start
with you. Deep inside my heart paid the toll
for our love. Your deception ruined that love.
Is there hope? No one knows but he above.

Camille Charmagne Jones

Birthdays

You begin to die when you're born
how can it be that you live for nine months
and die for seventy years?
I ask myself this question many birthdays.
Living just for dying ain't that true?
Birthdays with candle-coffin nails plastered across
the cake of happiness.
All I ask is to see the frost of dawn, of tomorrow.
The cessation of life is death.
For seventy years we bring a property of being strong.

Enrique Molina

Golden Asphalt

Land of ample opportunity,
How fortunate I am to breathe
The unrestricted air of this great republic!
How blessed I am to exercise
My thinking powers;
I need not fear an oppressive
Militia or one-man rule;
I need not fear a weak government;
Checks and balances make it impeccable.
I am grateful that I can exercise
My own free will:
The exercise of one's own free will
Is an inner experience;
Living in a free society
Makes that inner experience possible.
Corridors and asphalt of gold,
Continue to pave the roads to freedom
For all who seek their place in the sun.

Claire Lieberman

"No Better Than The Other Man"

Who do you think you are?
How high do you think you stand?
You are no better than the other man.
He was created the same as you.
And he can ride on this bus too!
Why don't you get up, and let the old lady sit down!
There is no segregation in this town.

Whether he's black, green, purple or blue.
He is still a man, the same as you.
Whether he's white, yellow, red or gray,
He will walk this earth with you; until his last day.
So, whoever you think you are!
And, whatever height you may stand!
Remember!, you are "NO BETTER THAN THE OTHER MAN!"

Jewel L. Monk

Starship Earth

Although old, I have tirelessly fought to survive
How much longer will I choose to remain alive?

I have been brutally raped by parasites
That I loosely call my children

My lungs inhale your materialistic sulfur
I will no longer be a partner in your sado-masochism!

I will no longer cry rainfalls for your transgressions!
I will no longer shield you from the universe's harmful truths.

I will now hold the whip
And die in honor.

Cedric Broomfield

Uncle Goldsworthy

Oh great uncle, tall soldier, blue hero, big.
How I grieve for your pain and the untold story.

Do you know that I remember?
Do you know that you are cool?
Do you know that you are king?

I haven't forgotten your solo dance,
your grace, your wit, your top dog class.
The precision and the magic are still crystal clear.

I need your story, for my dragons are real
And the demons in the mist play with.
Will you tell me the story for history's sake?
Will you tell your story to someone?

So they will know about courage.
So they will know about discipline.
So they will know about excellence.
So they will know about heart.

I salute your essence.
I salute your soul.
Uncle G.,
My tall king of cool.

Eileen Pardini

People

When I was young, I thought and thought,
How people breathe, how they talk,
It's silly I know, yet who makes it so,
The world goes around like the wheels of a car,
People live near, people live far,
Why can't our world be happy and grand,
Jealousy and slander should be banned,
Why do people find fault and accuse,
Why do people their own living abuse,
God put us on this earth to love each other,
Sister, brother, father and mother,
People can be kind, yet so mean,
Some live in hope yet others in dreams,
A beautiful gift God has given to us,
To feel, to see, to hear, to trust,
Why can't our world be happy and grand,
Forever peace on earth, in our great land,
It's not that I'm old and getting feeble,
Yet I turn to you and ask, what are people?

David L. DuBour

Untitled

Wall flower
How pretty is your placement?
Pressed out for all to see
What is your view from that sedentary position?
Just watch others live laugh and talk
Whatever pleases them
Wall flower
Just watch
And know their colors will fade
But yours will be warm
Someday, you'll be taken off that wall
by loving hands and be carried away.

Jamee Klehn

Jimmy

Once there was a boy named Jimmy,
his tongue was long and skinny,
he stuck it up his nose
boy was that a funny pose
till mom said, "Don't Jimmy, you're looking like a ninny".

Allison Scheffler

Killing Eyes

Killing eyes, oh those eyes, great pools of black,
how they know how to delight in disguise. At times
they have the power to take on the look of daggers,
shooting hate from their gaze while at the same time,
with love they can mesmerize.

Interesting eyes, eyes of happiness, eyes of dismay,
but revealing many hopes and dreams of her everyday loves.
They will trick you, they will treat you,
and they can also thrill you, these true gems sent down
from above.

Miracle eyes, Lord, thank You for allowing such as I
the gift of the chance to see them. Killing eyes, but
loving eyes, brought to life through me. Glorious and
mischievous eyes, eyes that laugh, eyes that cry, possessed
by someone born of me through Thee.

Precious eyes, which transformed from killing eyes into
eyes full of hope and promise for me, eyes belonging to
my baby, my child. And now to my daughter, my friend,
at one time my savior. Who could wonder why by these
beauties I am beguiled.

Anna Katherine Fenton

Soulmates

Soulmates are those who know from the start
How to have and to hold each others heart.
Those relationships are made in Heaven
They just need a chance to leaven.
They know the depths of each others heart.

Their minds are capable of the same thought
Because it was of the same metal they were wrought.
Their ideals and goals are one in the same,
For with loves same arrow they do aim.
Things they want are together sought.

They say love is blind,
But soulmates love the body and the mind.
The soulmate can handle any duress
Just by loves simple caress.
It is a soulmate which one needs to find.

It is the same interests that they share
And for each other they do care.
Life's long road can be dark and cold
But not with a soulmate to hold!
Their deep love has a condescending air.

Christopher J. Midlock

Metamorphosis

Having experienced a moment when I am
hurled from a peak of complacency and
allowed to recognize what a small bungling
creature I am, evolved from some dark
primeval ooze, I contemplate what mysterious
weaving of cause and effect has brought me
to this unbearable impasse.
My soul strains against my body's incapacities
I am self-deluded and not complete.

Divine and deeper nuances surround
and permeate my being, and I know
my dignity consists in thought.

I will not compromise my spirituality
with a senility of the body.
I awaken each day a stranger and stretch
my soul to encompass an exaltation of beauty.

Elizabeth Monroe

I Am A Woman

I am a woman strong against the wind like an eagle
I am a woman frightened by the thought of a broken wing
I am a woman ready for a fight
A builder of the nest, an owl in the night
I am a woman made of all things
I am a woman hear my heart sing

I'm flying, flying, over the desert, across every sea
Into the jungle, around every tree

I am a woman gentle against the rain like a snow white dove
I am a woman afraid to be seen in the open air
I am a woman beautiful in flight
A hunter of the food, a duckling in the light
I am a woman made of all things
I am a woman hear my heart sing

I'm flying, flying over the ocean, across every sea
Into the jungle around every tree

Fly, I can fly...fly, I can fly, fly..

Debra Corchia

I Am

I am a poet though no poem is on paper - only in my being.
I am an artist with no canvas - only life.
I make music all inside of me, and showing through in
happiness and joy.
I am an author, not of books but of life, for everyone I
touch is changed by my being.
The goal I seek? To create.
But must this be concrete, to hear or touch or see?
Or may I create those things by which life's totality is
made worthwhile?
Honor, integrity, truth, joy and love.
Comfort, aloneness, companionship, passion and freedom.
These exist only because my being makes them so.
I could not change them or withhold them even if I would because
the shape of my being demands that I be true.
These creations are my reality.
I am, therefore I create.

Elizabeth Nichols

Whispers

I am love and nurturing.
I am awareness and growth-
Able to drink in beauty and substance.

I am laughter on the wind,
A whisper in the breeze.
Turn, I am but a shadow in retreat.

I am a sponge of human kindness -
Yet found in the untamed darkness
See me in the sunshine, dancing on the waters surface.

Call to me and feel my presence.
I live through the hope of a child,
And the strength of your will.
I am but another side of you.

Jeanne Falen

Mary

She stood in solitude on the beach,
Her black hair wild and free,
Her eyes intent upon the sea,
Her body wrapped in the wind's energy,
As she become part of nature's reach
And crossed to planes I could only hope to breach.

Cecilia Viviano

Walk, Why?

I walk through puddles, everyone's puddles
I am drenched from their residue
but I'll dry soon enough.

That residue, everyone's residue
comes toward me at a smothering pace
but I'm not stifled.

Keeping pace, everyone's pace
I walk slower than they . . .
but I get wet, but I feel the residue.

Avoid puddles, which puddles
cleanse the residue, anyone's residue
maintain the pace, who's pace?
Walk, Why?

Carol M. Rhoads

Mornings Dawn

In the dawn of the morning, time seems to stand still.
I am in my quiet time to relinquish to God my will.

As I settled back in my old over stuffed chair.
With my Bible opened, I knew Jesus would lift my care.

My mind began to go into gymnastics this day.
I thank God for His gentle leading in His way.

God you burdened me with abounding trials this year.
Considerable pruning, abundant tribulation, trials by tears.

It is written that you won't tempt me beyond my durability.
God I am joyful that your word manifests your dependability.

I petitioned for help with faith of a child this day.
Jesus reminded me I had His strength, His word did say.

I am covered by Jesus blood from my head to my toe.
Not bothered by the angel of death to steal my soul.

I now look forward to the next year with glee.
For Jesus has purchased me and I am sin free.

Jesus will sustain me the rest of my victorious life.
For He will do battle for me against satan's strife.

David Lee Tinberlake

Yet, I Believe

I am beautiful, sexy, all that.
I am independent, dependable, reasonable.
I am affectionate, caring, giving.

I am all of these things, so you say
I am any man's dream, so you say
Yet, I am not your woman.
I am exactly what you want, you want no other
Yet, I am alone.
I am willing to give a man a break, work together, compromise
Yet, you have no time for me.

I've got your back, I've got you covered
I'm your friend, I'm your lover
I am yours, you are mine — that's what you say, today.
Yet, tomorrow's sunrise will bring more lies you've told
So long that you believe them, weave them, string them,
Decorate your world with them,
Sprinkle them liberally upon my wounded pride & broken heart until
Yet, I believe them too.

Desmond Rudder

The Delight Story Of Amanda Carnahan

I am the clouds, flying freely overhead.
I am movies, done classically.
I am a basket, full of information.
I am a teddy bear, so quiet and eager to meet people.
I am a tree, growing tall and strong.
I am a cat, curiously exploring everything.
I am an ant, tromping through the fields.
I am an old abandoned city, full of treasures and mysteries.
I am a puzzle, full of complicated designs.
I am a marble in a maze, turning the wrong and right corners.
I am a jacket, mildly worn.
I am a computer, full of technology.
I am book, full of good ideas.
I am flowers, growing delicately.
I am an island, surrounded by water.
I am a baby, learning at amazing speed.
I am a dream, full of all these things.

Can you see me? I am here.
I am free. I am religious.
Can you see me? I am here.

Amanda Carnahan

The Ocean

As I sit upon these cold hard rocks,
I am reminded of my times near the ocean, on the docks.
There are many things I remember feeling, like I am free!
I thought about a lot of things, on those long, lovely walks.

And when the ocean roared majestically, I thought that is me!
There were many things I didn't see,
But I saw the shells, the many shells, of clams and snails.
And I saw the opening to my heart, the key.

There were shells, pails and pails,
They went about, blown by the gales.
There were hours I spent, of lying in the sun,
Mostly, though, I loved the whales.

Lying in the sun, until my tan was done.
Many days and weeks of fun,
I played and made new friends.
With the waves breaking, hitting you and feeling like a ton.

Jessie Shover-Ross

Four Times Ten

I asked him out to dinner - he made a polite excuse.
I asked him out to lunch - he couldn't find the time.
Drink after work? Movie? Anything?

What happens when a man starts to gray? He becomes fascinating to younger women. He becomes mature - He becomes the envy of all his peers.

But a woman, she doesn't have "laugh lines" - She has wrinkles.

Bitter, angry? You bet I am! Consider the plight of a woman who has all the desires and feelings she had twenty years ago. Have the emotions extinguished with the birthday candles? I think not.

Fine wine ages - so do I - My lips invite you to come and taste of the cup.

Constance Roseanne Kowalczyk

When I Arise

When I arise at the dawning of each new day,
I bow my head and then I pray.
I do not ask forgiveness for my husband my human failures or downfalls
I bow my head to listen, lest I should hear my saviour call.
When I go to the seashore, the mountains, or valley, or
where ever I choose to walk, I bow my head and listen when
I hear my saviour talk.
When I stand alone in the darkness, gazing in wonder at the
stars in heaven above, I bow my head and thank Him for His
Mercy and His love.
At the end of each day, when the moon has crossed the milky-
way, I bow my head and listen that I might hear my saviour say.
Sleep well my Son, you have earned the right to my peace
and love for this night.

James Collins

Untitled

When I was five,
I can remember being shy.
When I turned ten,
a decade came and went.

I wanted to be grown up,
never knowing what I'd have to give up.
Turning fifteen meant I was in between.
I cried when no one asked me to any sweet sixteens.

Turning twenty was like coming to the top of a mountain.
At first I thought I've reached my goal, it is over.
But soon reality set in.
I was about to find out that my life was ready to begin.

Responsibility became a must,
and learning the hard way who and not to trust.
The everyday world had sucked me in.
It was then that I realized I should have never been in a hurry
for it to have begun.

Our youth is like life's many gifts.
When it is here it must be treasured,
for once it is gone, it is forever.

Danielle Borelli

In Need Of A Friend

Everyday they have to live on the streets by themselves.
I can see that you are in need of a friend.
Everyday they have to look around and keep asking people for food.
I can see that you are in need of a friend.
Everyday they have to wear raggedly old clothes.
I can see that you are in need of a friend.
Everyday they have to fight the pain and the tears of being homeless.
I can see that you are in need of a friend.
Everyday some of them die because of starvation or because too much
cold. Only God knows how many die and without people finding out.
I can see that you are in need of a friend.
It's really sad because God loves those people and they've got
nothing except their lives.
And their lives, by the way they're living, they have to fight
winter and the rain.
Sometimes we should invite them into our homes.
Feed them and let them stay the night.
You do have a friend that's dear to heart, ME!

Don R. Wyant

Caring

If while I'm passing through this life
I can touch a heart or two
Or bring a smile to a child's face
By an insignificant thing that I do

Or compliment an unselfish act
And comfort those who cry
By offering consolation to a broken heart
While humbling a creature called I

Then perhaps my presence is not in vain
Though we mortals are perpetually naive
And tend to justify our capricious behavior
By the pervasive philosophies we believe

But when earnestly searching our conscience
We leave alter egos behind
And can conform more to the Biblical promise
That by seeking we shall find

When glorifying the omnipresence of God
We nullify Satan's power I'm told
So that descent folks can live by Grace
And not just by gold alone

Don Marsch

Untitled

I know this kid like no one else could.
I cared about him like no one else would.
Then he started to drink and he started to smoke,
And the next thing he knew he was hooked on coke.
He loved that feeling, he loved that rush.
But unfortunately he loved it a little to much.
He thought he was great, and he thought he could fly.
That same kid I knew had started to die.
What was this feeling that had taken him over.
It was more like an addiction but too fun to recover from.
What was this problem? What did it do?
It had taken over his body, this much he knew.
It got worse and worse as I began to cry.
He had to stop or he had to die.
But I know someday my old friend will be back.
He has recognized his problem and started the attack.
Everything will be over, Maybe, we say.
For now he has to take it Day by Day.

Heather Donovan

Fishing

My cork, my pole, and a bucket of bait,
I cast out my line, then I sit and wait.
And then in an instant, as I sit in the grass,
My cork was pulled under by a monstrous bass.
I jumped to my feet and tried to pull him in,
But he broke my line and swam away with a grin.

Life is like fishing, I guess in a way,
You caught fish last week, but you didn't today.
Sometimes in life things don't go as you wish,
And living your life is like catching a fish.
You get one piece of line and one cup of bait,
And by the river of life, you sit and wait.

And then in an instant as you sit on the bank,
Under the water your cork quickly sank.
You hooked a monstrous opportunity fish,
Your line didn't break and you got your wish.
Then on the side you look at your life,
And when your line breaks, will you give up your strife.

Brad Tyler

"To A Little Girl I Love So Much"

I was so young, you were so little.
I changed your diaper, after you piddled.

Your Mom was gone, your Dad was at work,
I didn't know, but I was a big jerk.

I would get mad, cause I had to stay.
At home to watch you, when I wanted to play.

Mother would tell me, she's only a baby.
That didn't help Dorothy, she wanted no maybe's.

Maybe you can go, to the movies next week,
Out the door I would go, a baby sitter to seek.

Now Bonnie I know, you must think I'm mean
To write you a story, after the troubles you've seen.

But really I'm not, a terrible old bitch.
With the face I now have, I look like a witch.

But we have a maker, way up above.
You know him also, he's the love of a dove.

Now you are alone, I mean without Lou
Even a house full of people, can't keep you from feeling blue.

My reason for writing, is I'm very sad,
That I did not write one, for my brother, your Dad.

Dorothy Henry

'Tween Precious Pearls And Pigs

'Tween precious pearls and pigs
I choose my destiny each morn
The things I once disdained, I have become
I start afresh each new day
determined no longer to sacrifice myself
to that demagogue of complacency...that swine of conformity
But my life is no longer my own
I reach out to touch the fading whisper of my past
My heart hears the child in tears
The walls of Petra call out to me
Stand tall...Stand firm...For then you live forever
The Scarlet salmon sighs...
Live life...Love life...for tomorrow you die.
Immortality beckons me gently
Show courage...Be strong...place your trust in me
But I walk my highway daily
Amidst the pig trough with millions of others
wanting...hoping...knowing...
that tomorrow is yet another chance for me

But tomorrow...is already...too late.

Faye Pamela Dee-Smith

My Guardian Angel

This gift of life is like a rock to which
I cling whenever troubled times surround me;
Many days I hear a whisper or feel a touch
of strength from this my angelic force, I never see.

I believe with all my heart that this enormous
power is the watcher of my soul, guiding my way;
This form of light creates a shimmering feeling
in me, a profound effect on my journey every day.

I know that I can trust my loving spiritual
friend to be with me everywhere I go, each day of my life;
This is my security blanket, especially when there is
fear of the unknown, a Guardian comforting my strife.

This is my shepherd and I rest in peace
every moment of each day, for all my multitudes of need;
It has a special corner of my heart for all the
wonders bestowed, truly a loving Guardian indeed.

Francis A. Horning

Sorrow

It took all the courage
I could find deep within;
to look inside your soul.
No more day dreams of love
and life together...
No fairy-tale endings for me.
All those hopes and joys for tomorrow;
so easily shattered by today's realization.
How long does the heartache last,
before I can look at you
without tears in my eyes?
Will I ever be able to forget
the feel of your warm arms around me;
or the sweet taste of your lips upon mine?
Or is it my fate, to wonder
through this life...
Never truly being able to say
"Goodbye".

Cathy Kral

Friends

When you see my cheerful facade, don't be fooled!
I cry when I'm hurt, just like anyone else,
Sometimes my smile is to hide my inner feelings.

Treat me with sensitivity and compassion just like you
would a child.
In doing that, don't forget to treat me with respect and
intelligence as you would an adult.

Don't look through me as if I have no substance.
Don't talk over me as if I don't understand and
don't talk around me as if I don't exist.

Look me in the eye and show me your feelings and emotions.
Let me get to know you.

Take me into your confidence and you won't regret it.
Tell me the little things that make you, you.
We'll walk together and share secrets.
We'll run together and share quietness.

As we are getting acquainted, watch my expressions and I'll
watch yours.
In doing so, you will get to know the real me and I, you.

Most of all treat me as you want to be treated and lets be friends.

Betty Beagle

Oak Leaf

The river runs rapidly below me
I desperately hold on, fighting the winds of
change
I am tired now, too tired to fight any longer
So I let go
falling
falling
falling
into the river of
Time
Change
and life
There is no way to tell where I will go
or what I will become
I am a small
brown
oak leaf
racing through the river of life

Carrie Shuman

One Day

One day I humbly bowed my head
I do not know the words I said.
God heard my words of deep despair,
surrounded me with loving care.

He knew my heart was broken up,
and as I drank life's bitter cup,
He placed His angels a mist my woe
to guide my steps as they should go!

When I would stumble and almost fall,
on wing of prayer He heard my call.
From grief so black I could not see,
still, His love protected me.

He made the rough path smooth again;
and placed His peace and love within.
Until, undaunted by grief and strife
He gave to me Abundant Life!

Ida M. Lee

"I'm 24"

I'm 24, but it feels like I'm 84,
I don't know why, but it just does,
My body is young,
My organs are old,
Everything I do feels like a chore,

It has been told, that there is nothing wrong.
I know there is because I'm always weary.

I wish something can be done,
So I wouldn't have to fuss,
But until then my life will be dreary,

I know that my life isn't suppose to feel this way,
It does because of what I put my body through.

I try taking vitamins to make me strong,
but my body would reject it because it couldn't hold,
Oh well, I guess I have to feel like I'm 84
even though my body says "I'm 24."

Desta Tobal

Untitled

Frustration, hurt, and anger is what I feel.
I don't understand how it could be real.
When we were little we always had so much fun.
He could always come up with a pun.
When I see a blue GMC go by,
I always think to myself, why?
I remember all the times we had,
And wonder - why it hurts so bad.
People try to make us feel better
By sending us a nice letter.
But no one can take the hurt away.
Everyone says to take it day by day.
He was such an important part of our life,
It is so unfair, he never got to have a wife
Everything I see reminds me of him,
I'm afraid his memories will grow dim,
But I'll always remember how he'd pick on me
And how his attitude was so carefree!
I just wish I had a chance to say good-bye,
But you just never know when someone will die.

Danielle Pinkham

The Gang

I'm not one person, but one of many
I fear for no one's life, not even my own
I protect my territory that cost me not one penny
But I grab it as mine as a dog grabs a bone
Wearing our street colors of either blue or red
We kill in style by putting a bullet in top of one's head
Sometimes there's no reason in the killing we do
We just do it and don't give a damn who
Once you're with us, there's no turning back
If you try it, you may be the one in a garbage sack
You're in it for life, no matter how long that may be
The best thing to do is, don't join like me.

Joseph F. Vacca III

Immortal Love

When I look into your sky blue eyes
I feel a love that never dies
I love to touch your smooth, soft face
and when you hold me close I feel embraced
when you feel alone or feel despair
Just call my name and I'll be there
Your hair is like silky gold
My love for you will never grow old
Your eyes are like shinney pearl
You mean everything to me in the whole wide world
Your body as warm as the summer breeze
Without you here, my heart would freeze
Your sweetness and warmth is like a dream come true
All I'm trying to say is, darling, I love You

Jason Hughes

Prisoner

Love is an emotion not one can resist nor ever attempt to understand.
I feel captured in your world
a slave to only pleasure
that you alone control.
Impulses begin to intensify
I become frighten - A fire burns within me.
I reach out to you, your naked skin against mine.
Our bodies merging together, exploring our outer limits.
Experiencing sensations never imagined.
Soft kisses and light touches - You begin to tease me.
Wanting you so badly, I could not hold back.
You reached deep down into my soul
Controlling my being - You made me your prisoner.
The warmth of our bodies melted the barriers of our deception.
We became one.
Capturing our highest peak
—UNTIL—
We lie quietly. No words to be spoke of.
We fall asleep in each others arms
Waking — Only to a dream.

Diane Audoin

Flowers

As I sit among the flowers, the flowers of yester year's.
I feel my heart wonder through all the wondering years - where have all my friends & relatives gone within all these years -

As I sit among these flowers of all the yester years.

My tears are a flowing when I think of all those years
when I had so many beautiful flowers that have disappeared through the years.

Frances Cello

The Beach

I see no pollution, I hear no war
I feel no frustration, can you ask for more
I feel the seas breeze play in my hair
As I watch the sea gulls fly without a care
I see the shrimp boats floating gently along
And I listen to the crickets beautiful song
I look out to the waves doing rolls in the sea
This is all I need to make a wonderful dream for me

April Tucker

My Friends

In my fifty-plus years, it's true I've had many.
I feel sad for those with few or not any.

I'll mention just some; by nicknames you'll see.
There's Beau, Mickey, Barney, Pumkin, and Fonzie.

Their sex not important; devotion true.
Pure instinct told them when I was blue.

But who could stay sad with such "friends" as these?
Their love quickly wiped away my miseries.

I think of the good times, spent with them plentiful.
They asked of me little, made each day eventful.

I loved them so much; each loss brought great sorrow.
But along came another to brighten tomorrow.

I've but one "friend" left. Her name is Sissy.
At twelve years I fear her life's end nears; poor she.

You may have surmised my "friends" be canine.
No human compares to these "friends" of mine.

When my time grows short, as it's sure to do;
I'll look forward to when I will join "All of You."

Judy L. Carter

Desire For Love

To cherish my heart for you my lady of desire,
I feel so close to you.
Every way and every day I see your beautiful smile.
A touch of blue fills your eyes so dear.
Oh the sweet scent you have so pure.
Among the golden sun in the sky.
A touch from your heart, sets the clouds a fire.
Truly your love has me bound, under a night where
the moon appears - silk and red
Roses of red passion, touch of the heart,
make it hot as the stars in the sun.

Daniel D. Monfort

My Father's Son

As I opened up my door,
I fell down to my knees,
Standing there before me was my lord.

He said, with a smile,
"You're still my father's child,
I'm here for you as long as you believe."

Temptation lies ahead,
"Trust in God," he said.
"He's in your heart so give yourself to me."

He said, "I am my father's son,
You're the one I've come to love,
Follow me and all his will be yours."

Bill Billington and Jim Pelletier

I Love You

Lately is seems we spend a lot of time being angry with each other,
I find myself doing things I shouldn't do and saying things I
shouldn't say.
I know I've made mistakes, but my love for you is not one of them.
I just want you to know how much a part of me you truly are, and
how happy I am that in this world full of people, I found you.
Sometimes I smile and don't know why, and then I realize, I'm
thinking of you.
Your knowing glance, or a simple, touch fills my heart with
warmth and joy.
You make me laugh and cry and feel things I've never felt before.
You have the ability to take me to heights I hadn't even dreamed
existed.
I know we have some problems, but I also know we can work them out.
Because in spite of everything that's happened,
I believe in me and I believe in you, but most of all
I believe in us.

Anne Ambrose

A Canadian Daydream

A Canadian daydream around the wild rose bush.
I frolic and pluck my buds.
Off I peel the petals,
Counting them for my life and love.
I frolic around the rose bush and in the unpaved rode-
Airborne, I scatter my petals;
  and through them I run,
  and in them I roll,
  and they on my face I sense.

Oh! I must wake from my daydream and flee.
For my mother is coming and she doesn't like
  me to dream with wild roses.

John Buckard

Now And Then

Look at me, I'm down again.
I get this way, now and then.
It's not that I have reasons to cry,
I'm just not happy, I don't know why.
I just can't look forward to anything new,
It seems like life is old and used.
My problems are old and from the past,
My sometimes happy moods don't last.
I guess it's time to change scenes once more,
Throw all those depressions out the door.
Pick up my life, start over again.
I get this way, now and then.

Jo Smith

Caitlyn's Song

I met a girl the other day, she was really something to see,
I had a strong desire to take her home with me.
I realized I was staring, just couldn't look away,
If she smiles at me tomorrow, I'll think of something to say.

She has a friendly greeting for young and old alike,
She is like a star up high, that is shining very bright.
The Lord did a wonderful job when he handed this one down.
I act just like a kid when I know she is around.

I try to be so witty, but it comes out very dumb,
I try to act so sharp, but feel just like a bum.
When she is holding my hand, I am as happy as can be,
I would ask her to marry — but she is only three.

Allen P. Grubbs

A Day Full Of Thoughts

I was born a long whiles back.
I had all but one small lack.
I grew up in a world of sadness.
Never once a joy or gladness.

I got married and then grew older.
But never once did I grow bolder.
I watched my first be born and die.
I watched the pigeons as they flew by.

I've experienced all there is to be.
The price I paid for this is one small fee.
I was born a long whiles back.
But I've found all the needles there are to
find in the hay stack.

Jennifer Vlasaty

Pain

Pain is something I thought
I had learned to deal with.
Until for some unknown reason
I was ask to leave someone that I really love.
Cupid could not have shot his arrow any straighter.
Those words hit my heart, as if it was a bulls eye.
From that moment on pain began to take over even to this day.
Never will I understand what prompted them to say,
"What calls pain this way."

James Edward Young Sr.

The Painful Mistakes

I want to correct the mistakes I've made.
I have a feeling of incredible pain.
I lost one of the best friends I had.
Everyone else is just plain mad.
I lied to many to cover up the truth.
I was too afraid of the truth.
It all came back in my face.
It feels like someone maced my face.
How can he gain his trust back in me?
Why would he want to believe in me?
I want to correct the mistakes I've made.
I just can't bear this lasting pain.

Amie See

"The Prayer Of Love"

Lord lend me your ear as I say this prayer unto you.
I have a hurting love in my heart,
Which at times seems like there's no end to the pain.
Moments come when I want to give up,
Then I recall that you've never given up on me.
Every night, I cry a tear which is a silent prayer,
That no one must hear, but you.
As each word of my sacred prayer is said,
I know you're right beside me, sharing my moment of
tears.
With a little faith, I know in time my prayer will
be answered.
Each time I call to your name,
The pain seems to come to a rest, but never to a heal.
I say this prayer of sincerity, to surrender it all to you.
I ask, as each time one of my tears drop
I'd have a constant reminder,
Of how much your love is for me,
So that I may not quit the love I have
for my friend!

Christina Sierra

The Fears Of A Jewish Teen

I am Anne Frank and have no place to go.
I have certain feelings, but can't let them show.
I wish I could have someone to tell,
but they shan't hear the cries I spill.

I have whispers to share, laughs to cry,
please can anyone spare me,
for I am just a 14 year old child.
Dances to enter, people to see, places to go,
but I can't let my body appear or show.

Races, faces is that all there is to life?
I am a human, don't deny me by sight.

I lose, for I am a jew.
Stick me in chocolate or buttermilk too,
I'm still Anne Frank, a teen jew.
I live in fear of siege at 14.
Should I have these dreams to scream?

Jasmine Hawley

The Last Kapok

Hi, I am the great kapok tree of the Amazon.
I have long been holding the animal kingdom,
And man has used my silky fibers to weave clothes,
To make soft pillows to place their heads on.
But every day I am getting weaker and weaker.
It seems my life is being shattered by a blade!

I don't know if I will still have
The gentle massage of the under brush,
Or the tickling of vines growing around me.
No longer will I feel the gliding of tree frogs,
The slithering of emerald boas
Or the smacking of the chameleons,
Their tongues missing their prey.
Nor will I feel the poisonous slime of the arrowhead frog
Or the smell of the orchids.
I'm being chopped down.

When I was a producer of oxygen
Man did not know I held in my sap a secret medicine.
Now I am going. And they will never know!
I will become just an ash. Just an ash.

Armen Dekmezian

The Natural Truth

I behold a heart
I hold a heart balanced on the tines of my fork
a heart rich with the wealth of the earth

Meaty, dense, and redolent of iron
a beet glistens in the sun as I eat my sack lunch
by the hidden lake
where red-ringed blackbirds swoop and toads croak listlessly
halfway out of hibernation

It is winter now
and there is a truth stripped bare here
that presents itself in the dry sheaths of once glorious thistles
a truth that lies quietly at the bottom of the lake
and soaks in gradually through the soles of my feet

I sit respectfully before beet orbs tasting of minerals
organs of truth reminding me so of our red hearts
steadily beating blood through our bodies
their rhythm reverberating endlessly in ruby chambers

This is a truth we couldn't live without.

Carole Fanning

I Love Him

I love him with my whole heart,
I hoped that we would never part.

I loved him when he smiled that cute smile,
He's what made my life worthwhile.

I loved him when he laughed that stupid laugh,
He's what kept my eye on a straight path.

I loved when his hair blew in the wind,
I hoped that our love would never end.

I loved him so much that pain grows insides knowing
that he once was mine but now he's not.

Wanting only to be wrapped in his arms one last time,
but only being wrapped in the wind.
He was the one I loved and wanted,
but can never have again.

Jaime Orlando

Gray To White

For K.D.H.

No one understands me, they don't care
I just want to be free, life is so unfair
I can't explain, the way I feel
Inside there is a pain that won't seem to heal
I just want out, away from my torment
I need to shout, 'My life is spent'
I'll embrace the darkness, just close my eyes
Slip into the abyss, silent are my cries
I used to feel hate, I was sad, alone
Cursed at fate, thought I was on my own
But then I decided to share, let my feelings known
Opened up my private lair, to a friend they were shown
I had the lock, he showed me the key
And with a shock, a new life I could see
Life is for living, not an impossible test
For taking and giving, full of fun and zest
It hasn't been quick, over in a single day
Sometimes I still feel sick, but the darkness has turned to gray
I won't give in, that day is in sight
And I know I will win....the gray will turn to white

David J. Hart

"My First Love"

The first time I saw you, it was surely true love
I knew that you were coming, for you were all that I dreamed of
A gift from the heavens, that I could never repay
Oh! What a beautiful face
I've never in my life felt a love like this
Delivered so much affection, in every single kiss
Been amazed at something as simple as a smile
Never questioning the fact that God blessed this child
At times I just stared as you laid there asleep
Your expressions-expressed; all that's innocent and sweet
I would reach out to touch you because I felt compelled
To hold you in my arms; yet let you sleep as well
Nothing on this earth has brought so much pleasure to me
So on this day of your birth, I convey to thee
(You Are My First Love!)

Brian K. Chapman

Autumn

The crisp autumn air is wonderful to meet,
I hear the colorful leaves crunch beneath my feet,

A nearby Jack-O-Lantern's golden glow
Illuminates the presence of a scarecrow.

The cool autumn day seems to whisper good-bye.
As the full moon takes its place in the sky.

John Oshel

The Hangin' Tree

There is no racism in the trees in fall
I know

I eat and drink from the earth
And feed my leaves, as if I did not know

They begin green, and then they change
I do not choose the colors, I give them life

It is not until I am poisoned myself
Will I let my leaves die

Because I know
There is no racism in the trees in fall

Today, my leaves were cleared from my strongest limb
Succulent drops of blood fell to the ground

For a moment, as I absorbed it through my roots
Life felt plentiful

But I know fall will come
And the leaves will turn

Eric Michael Angeles

Rest Easily Dear Mother

Rest easily dear mother
I know it's time to let you go
The gates in heaven are opening wide
And dad is waiting for you there
The Lord is coming to get you
There'll be no more pain for you to bear.
The stroke left you lifeless here,
Now you'll go to the heavenly place
Dancing with dad forever
Seeing him face to face
Don't fret about me momma
The times we shared were great
You took care of me, and I of you
With dad you have a date.
A smile upon your face your eyes
Opened wide, grasping my hand a last time
As I sat by your side.
No words need be spoken I feel it inside
God came, he took you home,
on the last heavenly ride.

Joann Barber Edwards

When I'm Called

I kneel me down to pray, I sigh,
I know someday I too will die.

It matters not to me to know and wait,
Knowing when my time comes God won't hesitate.

I'm aware that to all comes their time.
Why should I ponder when comes mine?

We know not when nor can God tell,
When falls our curtain, when rings the final bell.

To know, a heavy cross to bear,
To realize it comes allows your soul to share.

Each day I prepare my thoughts, my life, my mind,
When I'm called I'll answer, I won't be hard to find.

Gerald G. Larsen

Papa

For Alex Mastervich, my grandfather
The other day I hugged somebody new.
I know that he loves me, and knows I'm there,
but does he know that I really do care?
"Papa", and he would answer on the cue,
that disease in him, how can this be true?
He gave so much for my life, it's just not fair,
cause this "Alzheimer's", he can't seem to bare.
Lord tell me why-name it, for him I'll do.
Pictures of him once a solider of war.
Those eyes you could see ambitions and dreams.
Does it matter if he recalls my name?
Give me the key and let's reach his locked door.
Inside, I feel, the love from his light beams.
Look, in my heart he will always remain.

Jenny Mastervich

Have Faith In God

God is with us we have to be strong
I know the hardships seem to be long,
But hold on to the faith He gives
in our hearts He always lives.

Try not to linger on to your sorrows
be thankful we have a few more tomorrows,
Without the trust of our Lord above
We wouldn't know the meaning of love.

Make every minute count along the way
put joy in your heart as you pray,
Only our Father can guide us home
then no more will we have to roam.

Keep in mind He sees to our needs
We'll be rewarded for our deeds,
He'll see in His heart how hard we try
God is our Savior in the sky.

Don't let sadness and fear get in the way
We're only His children on earth astray,
He'll guide us to that Pearly Gate
just have patience, it's not too late.

Joyce Meeker

Tell It To My Heart

From deep within I feel the love,
I know will always last.
I try to tell you how I feel.
You say "I go too fast."

You insist I wait till the proper date,
and then you'll play your part.
You know I'll wait for that lovely day,
but someone tell my heart.

I didn't predict when the moment came.
It was too late when the moment past.
My mind said no, but my heart said go.
I can't help I go too fast.

You avoid my caress whenever you can.
You never encourage my kiss.
So whenever I can, I'll hold your hand,
and remind you of what I miss.

I hear the words "You're trying too hard."
They're tearing me apart.
I understand completely dear.
Now tell it to my heart.

Jerry Curtis

Dream World

Alone in the night,
I lay awake crying.
Alone in the night,
My innocence dying.
Alone in the night,
Thoughts of death and destruction disturb my sleep.
Alone in the night,
I dream of love and hate, of murder and rebirth,
But alone in the night is where I am,
When I fall in love,
When my dreams come true.
And alone in the night is where I am,
When my world falls apart,
When the ones I love die.
Alone in the night,
Where I cry.

Audra Leone

Legal Alien Blues

Here I have come, to the U.S.A.
I left my home, and came far away.
How I longed to be here, beside my husband
But my heart still yearns, for dear old Scotland.

The sights, the sounds, unfamiliar faces,
It really is tough, all these strange new places.
Wait for the mailman, maybe, a letter.
Some word from home, would make me feel better.

Scouring the ads, in hope of employment.
I need to get out, and have some enjoyment.
What's my next move? Learn to drive!
Then, my dear girl, you're ready to dive!!

License in hand, lots of hope in my heart,
I know I'm now ready, for my brand new start,
keys in ignition, keep out of my way!
California, I'm ready, I'm here to stay!!

No longer, so blue, and down in the mouth,
No longer, so sad, living here in the south.
But at night in my dreams, I know where I'll be,
In Scotland, my friends, family and me.

Jeannie Gill

Karen Dolores Schupp

Passing in life like a wren
I lost my wife, my lovely Karen
Only a score, decade and two
Spirit to soar, with me only a few
An accident ceases life so abruptly
All purpose in pieces, ended so roughly
Physical pain of bloody, broken mass
Emotional pain of a love that passed
Specter of my soul, haunting of my mind
Buried under a knoll, my peace never to find
All my love to my beautiful Karen
You were happiness, my loving siren
I was told I am fortunate to survive
I feel old waiting for death to arrive
How could I be spared, a dream to end?
Karen must know I cared, my love I send
We lived our love all too brief
Sent to you above, my deepest grief
Please show into me some kind of sign
My lament to you is a favored rhyme.

Henry Thomas Schupp Jr.

A Child View Of Christmas

I'm just a kid, and Christmas is near.
I love every minute, of this time of year.
I try to be good, as good as can be,
so Santa will like, and be nice to me.
The stores are like magic, as well as our homes.
They're all decorated with lights, and those weird looking gnomes.
Our church is so pretty, with red flowers and bows.
We sing lots of carols, that everyone knows.
Already, there's presents under our tree.
I hope, how I hope there's plenty for me.
I check them each day. I'm just a child.
I rattle and shake them. They just drive me wild.
Finally — at last it's Christmas eve.
I'm little I know, but this I believe.
Jesus, is real. He is God's son.
He was born in a manger, and He loves everyone.

Helen M. Crabill

Quiet Beach

Oh sea-you mighty ocean roar,
I love to watch your lips kiss the sandy shore.

It is quiet now on the sandy beach,
As the sea gull gives an awesome screech.

The summers gone, you know not why,
To all the people you said good-bye.

Only a few walk along your sandy shore,
Looking for sea shells you have washed from your floor.

As I look on the water and see the rising sun,
It reminds me, this part of God's creation is beauty and fun.

There is no sand castles for the children to build,
The sand lies golden- like the corn in the field.

The awesomeness of a warm fall day,
Makes me want to sit and pray.

Thanking God for the beauty of this land,
Whether it be golden fields or golden sand.

The closeness of heaven comes to those of us,
Who sit and glean God's beauty from dawn to dusk.

Oh great and might ocean roar,
I love how your lips kiss the sandy shore.

Judy Price

True Love

I love you like a brother
I love you like a friend
I love you like I've loved no other
I'll love you until the end.
My love for you is great
My love for you is grand
My love for you was brought through fate
My love for you is true, give me your hand.
I'll walk with you forever
I'll stay by your side
I'll follow you wherever
I'll trust you until I've died.

JennyLynne Butcher

Untitled

I loved you...once
I loved you excessively
I loved you with everything I had

I gave you my soul, I gave you my spirit, I gave you my sanity
You were my world, You were my existence, You were my all
You taught me love, You taught me hate, You taught me life
We were awesome, We were awful, We were extreme
We loved passionately, We fought fiercely, We lived inconstantly
I betrayed you, You wounded me, We began to end
We finally separated, You found another, I learned to live alone

We once loved...deeply
We once caused each other pain
Now we live separate lives...forever

Heidi Bonham

"All By Myself"

All alone, I dwell & drown.
I make myself so sick.
Excuses are merely exits of reality.
To face the unknown would be brave.
To go alone would be ignorance.
So, why do I look so weird?

An outcast inside; lonely follower outside.
My truth is only in my eye,
Seen by only me and heard by only my ears.
Terror and fear being so common around these parts,
I have nothing to look forward to.
What else can be done with a hungered mind, absent heart?

Mind being filled with knowledge of inexistence,
Heart being just cold and still.
The flow of the river is opposite of me.
Destruction of direction is only accomplished
With nothing.
So what's wrong with me?

Christy Blasingim

A Flower

I am a flower that adds color to the world.
I marvel at God and how much our Father has done for us.
I hear music ringing through the trees.
I see the homeless, some scared and alone,
but all missing the same thing.
And I want to reach out and help them.
I am a flower and when left unattended I shrivel up and fade away.

I pretend I am a character in a book that can travel all over,
through time and back.
I feel that everyone can make a difference and touch the heart of
someone special.
I worry about the earth and how it is slowly being destroyed.
I cry for all those people who have been hurt or misguided.
I am a flower blossoming yet not quite in full bloom.

I understand that living is a complicated thing.
And I say that if everyone works together it can be understood.
I dream of one day achieving all of my dreams.
I try to make a difference in someone's life.
I hope to see the world through others.
I am a flower and like all flowers,
it takes time to be allowed to see all my glory.

Courtney Arnold

"Wondrous Creation"

As I gaze at the world, its splendor so great,
I meditate,
What a wondrous creation to see, such beauty and
Perfection, truly heighten my spirituality.
The mountains, the oceans, the forests lush and green,
Magnificent, radiant, awesome sights just bursting to be seen.
The cycle of the earth as it revolves around the sun
Capturing warmth and light,
The cycle of day to night.
The cycle of the seasons,
Spring, summer, autumn, winter.
Birth, growth, harvest, sleep.
The cycle of life.
Such perfect law and harmony,
Truly heighten my spirituality.

Joan Reego Gully

Forever, Long Distance

Sometimes when I'm alone, I cry out for you.
I miss you so much I can feel it in my soul.
Sometimes when I'm alone, I reach out for you.
I keep forgetting you're not there.
Sometimes when I'm alone, I smile,
remembering some sweet memory,
some time we spent just you and me.
Sometimes I just laugh out loud,
how lucky I am.

You are laughter!
You are love!
You are sweet caresses!
You are tenderness!
You are strength!
You are love!
And,
You are mine
And
I am yours
forever!

Dana Russell

Friends

We were friends for many months when
I moved into town.
Both with similar problems.
Both with familiar backgrounds.
Our friendship will last forever;
though never to be seen again,
but at least we'll know deep in our hearts,
that friendship was meant to the end.

Heather Hedge

Gangs

I know who I have been.
I know who we are now.
We are a lion, grown large and raised
By civil, petting hand. Until one day
In play, we find my mouth and tooth
Encircling civil flesh. My petted natured
Falls away. We taste the feel of noisy,
Civil flesh, and some dark nature
Peels away the petted overlay.
We lose myself.
Lions have their pride.
Dark natures there reside.

John F. Deethardt Jr.

Don't Break It Apart

As I write you a letter, I don't know what to say
I need you, I love you, please don't go away.
Say you'll be here your whole life through
I could never love anyone as much as you.

You're sweet and loving and so much fun
You came into my life and my heart you won
Be careful, it's fragile, don't break it apart
You must admit we've had a nice start.

We know each other like no one else could
We belong together, you know we should.
You say when you're with her, you always smile
But you know that she'll leave you after a while.

Remember that looks she doesn't lack
And when she leaves, I won't take you back.
You can cry, you can plead, and even beg, too
But if you leave me for her, then I don't want you.

Joni Chadwick

Never Satisfied

Although I loved my valley, my home of love and pride,
I never could stop yearning to roam the world outside.
The future's always better viewed from the eyes of 'teens,
But from the eyes of 'elders the past's the better scene.

In 'teenhood we skipped the yoke of summer's dusty chores,
Drawn by the exciting lure of woodland streams and moors;
The stream's cool bank, a launch-pad to launch rockets of dreams
Of foreign shores, alien lands and strange exotic scenes.

Days were but a chain of time and nights the shorter link,
All was but a space in time to contemplate and think
Of the day I'd venture forth into the world alone
To seek fortune, fame untold, a happy rolling stone.

More years add capricious charm to memories of youth,
Though dreaming dreams cannot harm, they can't conceal the truth.
Now I think of life back then, sweet morn' on magic tide;
It only goes to prove my point, one's never satisfied...

Alexander C. Park

Only For August

At one time, I could never feel love.
I never saw light, only loneliness.
One August night opened my eyes.
You were there, only to keep me forever.
One August night held my hand.
You were there, only to hold my hand.
One August night touched my cheek.
It felt so soft, only to touch my cheek.
One August night felt my emotions.
I had an other, only to feel my emotions.
One August night kissed my lips.
It was you, only to kiss my lips.
One August night held me close.
You were the only one, only to hold me close.
One August night left me in your arms.
There I will stay, only in your arms.
As for August, eternal love is in its name.
August, in our minds, will live forever.
If we should forget our August night, not a moment more shall
we live.
Our August night will live forever.

Alexis Hiscox-Padrnos

Love For Sure

How could something so good go so wrong
I once had it all but now it's all gone

Everything we had, it seemed so right
We used to laugh and talk every night

He always brought a smile to my face
But those were in the good ole' days.

My life has changed since he left
He's guilty for the crime of theft

He stole my heart and then broke it in two
That's one thing he promised not to do

I always have and always will love him
But right now my world is looking very dim.

I wish we could go back to the way we were
Then I would know it was love for sure.

Avona Ford

My Hand

I rubbed my hand down her cold, black body.
I picked her up in my hand.
I had visions of wasps and bees,
in a battle for a flower,
a rose,
an arrangement of roses, of carnations.
Flowers now in blossom, soon to wither and die,
to rot on the ground,
becoming houses for the earthworms.
Guests mourn at the dead flowers,
decomposing into its earliest elements,
the proton, the neutron, the negatron.
And as I held her so firmly in my hand,
I felt the trigger,
I squeezed.

Joseph Rafuse

Faith, Refound

When I must, or mostly, when I wish
I place myself on lofty plains
To scud among the clouds of billowy thought,
To create, or better, to recreate, a
Finished, yet far from final
Masterpiece.

And from this plain of enlightenment
My weathering elements I draw
Upon: The rains of human sorrows,
The sunlit wings of feathered spirits,
And the dawn of memories and joys
Reborn.

And here, there enters something more
That weathers steadfast among all these.
It is the thread that binds all things
To complete my final masterpiece
Refound, yet without searching, my vanished
Faith.

Herbert W. Kale II

Midnight

Her gown black velvet against her skin
I told myself to fight but I had to let her in
Golden touches of black lace
Like an angel out of place
The kiss of brandy upon lips so fine
My soul begs for her to be mine
And as sure as day follows dawn
Within an instant she is gone.

Josi-Lyn Dulaney

Man Ameba

I sit in wonder
I ponder upon questions
What shall happen
When time runs out
Sun burns out
Earth so cold
Flowing along gentle deep groove
Pre-cut truth never questioned
Man Ameba
Ocean universe big bang current endless expansion
Undisturbed phosphorescent stars
Flashfire lifetimes
Brilliant spectacle
Faded waves of history
Wash up push outward never return
Electron Earth valleys mountains
Cosmically minute
Illuminating invisible love
Running through God
The ocean itself the conductor

John Anthony Kerns

Together Again

Each time I leave you side
I pray to God right there and then
To give me the patience I need
Till I see you again.

I know that we can't touch
But I can feel you in my heart
And since God put us together
I know nothing can tear us apart

So just remember that I love you
And I pray you feel the same
I thank God for sending you to me
And for giving me your name.

Keep this note with your where ever you go
And read it thinking of me
For soon we will be together again
As God meant for it to be.

Elizabeth Garcia

Ode To Mama

I placed a rose upon my Mother's grave.
I prayed to God her soul he'd save.
And as I knelt on bended knee,
a strange feeling came over me.

And as the wind began to blow
The Spirit of God was surely there, I know.

But soon, He'll come and take her
from this cold, cold ground,
and carry her homeward, Heavenly bound.

Where the streets are paved with gold
and there's never any cold.
Where old friends and loved ones never say goodbye -
in that Heavenly home up in the sky.

George T. Shelton

Untitled

Here is love clinging gently to the vine
If it is showered with love in return
it will blossom brilliantly and feel so fine
But if it is sprinkled with neglect, misuse or pain
love then withers and dies
Leaving behind a cold internal rain.

Charles A. Wheeler

For Joseph My Special Valentine!

Down around the corner 'round the bend to yesterday,
I ran into some memories of a little boy at play.
So full of life and love and fun a wiry bundle of joy,
He crowded every minute with dogs and fish and toys.
Filling all his pockets with marbles, gun-wrappers and string,
Looking forward to tomorrow to see what it may bring.
Those days passed by too quickly as good times always do,
But oh the joy that fills my heart for the years God lent me you.
'Cause 'round another corner I'll see you once again,
And share for all eternity a love from way back when.
Down around the corner your little hands would bring,
To "happy-up" this mothers' heart, marbles, gum-wrappers and string!

Joyce Eileen Boyles

Forever Young!

Forever young, I plan to be, there's no growing old for me!
I rise each day just full of expectancy.
For there's still a whole big world, just waiting out there for me.
With a spring in my step, and a smile on my face, I plan to carry on indefinitely.
Forever young! There's not growing old for me!

So, stiff fingers and knees, go away if you please!
I don't have time for thee.
And sore back! Stop aching like that! For don't you see.
I plan to be......
Forever young! There's no growing old for me!

Billie L. Courson

A Winter Ride

On one beautiful snowy day,
I rode the mighty white mountain waves,
over and over, my sled knew the way,
and in my mind my memory saves.

You never forget that feeling inside,
when your heart's in your throat,
and your eyes are open wide,
frozen in time for all eternity.

Just like first love, one never forgets,
as you glide down that hill,
holding on with dear life,
overcoming the challenges you meet on the way.

So close your eyes,
and just remember, and smile,
with anticipation and appreciation,
as you rock in your sleigh.

Joann G. Kuebler

It Started In Me

Safely away from the whispering rain
I sat in a corner and quietly sang.
My heart full of love asking God for world peace
I sang words of harmony that began within me.
To free the love that was meant to be
I started the song meant for all to sing.
Sing with your voice and banish your fears
Sing with the world and cry happy tears.
Sing with the birds that fly over the sea
Sing to the starts till they fall to your feet.
Sing to the clouds that are purple and pink
or walk up the steps to freedom's tall peak.
Walk on your wishes and follow your heart
reach out for your dreams to get a head start.
Raise your voice above all, sing the peace meant to be
And remember that it started from the love
within me.

Jacqueline Clinger

The Rabbit And Moving House

Something happened in my house this morning
I saw a rabbit in pink pajamas running
White galloping goose
And in red boats playing piano moss

I stood on the kitchen floor
Watching the dancing front door
And window floating away from the house
Spaying on the purple mouse

Silver spoon talking with the gold dish
Dish had a big wish
He wanted to serve a king
With a sparkling diamond ring

The kitchen table folded his legs and took a bath
The yellow broom ran after my blue rat
House expand his ribs in heavy breath
And houseplant sang with the garden weeds

I got mad
My face turned red
I hit with my foot the floor
Everything stopped, even the door,

Barbara Kabala

Creation

I stood at dawn and looked upon the earth,
I saw iridescent drops of dew on leaf and blade,
My ears attuned to all the trilling of the birds.
I saw the pulsing fragile colors of the sky,
And felt the breath of wind upon my cheek,
Saw petals of the fragrant flowers near by,
Each exquisitely formed to form a seed.
I looked upon the bounties of the earth,
And all my being trembled with great awe,
At all the untold power of my God,
Who fashioned everything on earth precisely so.
It matters naught to me how it was done,
Through eons or in just a few short days,
I only feel the wise and caring love,
That shaped man and creatures and the earth,
According to our Heavenly Father's plan.

Grace L. Semon

Dear Sandy

I see you aglow with the light of CHRIST
I see GOD'S love shine through your eyes,
I hear GOD'S laughter in your voice,
And when you hold my hand and pray,
I feel the comfort of HIS love.

On days when I have to say,
Oh GOD, please help me through this day,
and then somehow, I just know,
The answer to my plea is you.
Thank you GOD.

Elizabeth Abarr

Bus, Please Don't Be Late

As I walked the boys out at a quarter to eight
I silently prayed, BUS, PLEASE DON'T BE LATE,
I tried to be solemn but my glee I couldn't hide
They said, "Mother dear, would you please go inside",
The school bus came, along with the realization
That this is finally the end of summer vacation,
As they drove away I jumped and hollered
It was probably a bit much when I dropped and wallered,
Now I will be gone for the rest of the day
I'm going out to see if my friends can play.

Candy Sherbert

Untitled

As I look out the window
I see snow.
Patches of snow,
but still snow.
As I look around
I see branches frozen in ice.
The branches are perfectly still,
frozen in their beauty.
It is winter.
It is winter.
The time for snow flakes,
snowmen, and snow fights.
As I drive down the highway,
I see kids bundled up in coats and scarves.
Yes, it's winter.

Barbara R. McCoid

Divided We Fall

I see the stars falling into the oceans.
I see tears fall into a pool of many emotions.
I see a people fighting against their own side,
And in the process their own body dies!
Their banner lifted is now brought down,
To be burned in the streets of their crumbling towns.
The heroes are gone, dead and forgotten —
From dust to dust, now decayed and rotten.
The spit on their graves falls down like rain;
Their glory is now inverted to shame.
Liberty stands, but soon she will tumble,
For already her foundation is beginning to crumble.
One nation rebels under God,
Will only fall into its own blood!
A deliberate losing of meaning to a Declaration —
Woe to you, O dying nation!!

Everett E. Pyse

I Close My Eyes

I gaze out my window.
I see the grass, the trees.
I close my eyes.
I open them and I see the sky, the stars, the moon.
I close my eyes.
I open them and I see the world.
I wonder - Are these just objects?
I think not.
I ask myself - Who has such a power?
The answer calms me.
For I know - Only God has such a power.
The power to make such glorious objects.
Then I am frightened - What if there is no God?
I close my eyes.
I open them and I see the beauty.
I am calm.
For my heart knows the answer.

Catherine Tate

Evening Shade

When I was young
I used to dream of riches to be made.

Of romance
And how my true love's beauty would be displayed.

But now I'm old
I'm wiser now these dreams all did fade.

My dreams
Have all turned out to be like shadows in the shade.

Frederick Shehane

The Old Woman

Each morning as I cross the highway that is my street
I see the lights
Lights flickering behind dusty venetian blind slats
Lonely lights, replaying a 4am TV movie
The aging, lonely, alone old woman, her husband dead
A FOR SALE sign growing like a dandelion on her lawn

I use to see her in a red leather coat
Fingers weighted down with fine jewels
Married forty odd years, the old woman and the old man
I envied her those many years ago
All red leather, cold diamonds, warm gold

As I cross the highway now
God, is rubbing the sleep from his eyes, to wake the day
Envy dissipates, empathy begins, we are two women
One old, the other young in comparison
Each alone
She, watching the TV ghost glide across the screen
salve for the loneness inside and I
I put pen to paper and bleed an abandoned soul's truth.

Judith Raymo

I Am God's Child

I am God's child.
I shall not go wild.

His power is in me
Oftentimes awakening my being.

My God is always near
Much closer than my darling dear.

He nourishes my soul
And makes me whole.

He lives inside of me
And gives sweet relief.

I can't live without him, he is my only thing.
I have such a wonderful cling.
When I was in sin,
I could not win
but, now I'm in him.
My light is no longer dim.

Heavenly gifts come from above.
In the glorious form of a dove.
Because, I'm God's child.
His power has made me mild.

Caroline Miller

Do You Smell The Rain?

Do you smell the rain?
I smelled it, being born one day,
As it fell from my mother's hair.
Do you smell the rain?
It drizzled that first day of school,
When I gained new friends and left my parents behind.
Do you smell the rain?
It sprinkled when we left our family, our home, and our country.
Do you smell the rain?
It showered when my brothers entered my life.
Do you smell the rain?
It falls and seeps
Through where our memories have gone.
Do you smell the rain
That pours as you leave the only home you've known?
Do you smell the rain? The hurricane?
When all you have-
The memories, the objects, family and friends- have gone,
Do you smell the rain? No?
Nor do I, since the last drop fell from my eyes.

Garry Glenn O. Coloma

Christmas In Florida

While taking a walk the other day
I spied a man in an open sleigh
When I stopped to ask him of his plight
He said "You know Christmas Eve is a long night
So this year I thought I'd start a little soon
Like April, May, or even in June
But this weather in Florida is just too darn hot
I don't know whether I'll make it or not
So let me say this before I leave
I'll see you much later — like, say
Christmas Eve!"

Barbara Lee Davidson

Christina

Thanks for the walk I took on a dawn of your new day.
I strolled into your valley when I thought I'd lost my way.

I knew this was your garden, a place you made for me.
Where flowers waved the many colors of love and harmony.

The yellows, reds and lavenders far as I could see,
the violets, blue and indigo, then you offer one to me.

It was then I saw a golden bloom, well nurtured with your power
with strength you gave by sun and rain, this single golden flower.

You plucked it from your blessed soil then placed it in my heart
and said her name's Christina and I must finish what you start.

John H. Voll

Hymn Of The Forest God

10,000 Years
I tended these great forests
I sent the caribou and then the wolf
I whispered of the balance into attentive ears
then came the night of iron and steam
it came with such sweet unassuming innocence
enamored of its indomitable hope
I was disarmed
they stumbled through my forests
breaking down the trees
lost babies
taking
they had no sense of seasons
their searching gashed the earth so deep it cut my soul
I whispered
then I screamed
they only heard the clicking and the ticking
as they followed the machine

Jim Johnson

"I Am The Little Boy"

I am the little boy
I walk in the park and hear the birds
I am the little boy
I play in the woods and climb the big oak tree
I am the little boy
I run in the fields and play with the bat and the ball
I am the little boy
I crave ice cream and pie and goodies too sweet
I am the little boy
That gave you flowers one sunny day
I am the little boy
With those mischievous kind of ways
I am the little boy
Who has grown up so tall and dark

I am still the little boy just for you

Billy Stage

Gratitude

When I was a child
I thought the world belonged to me.
Because every thing was given to me free

Later the time I spread my wings
And in complete solitude
I was sent to conquer-the world

The painful experience of impotence
And lack of recognition
Forced me to search
For the meaning of my life.

Do I behold the presence of my creator?
Do I comprehend the following?
The full meaning of love.
The celestial smile of a new born.
The endless songs of birds
The enduring presence of sun rain, day night, cold warm.
The elegance of flowers with their colors and perfumes.

God is patient, he gave us life
He joyfully expect us to return
We must express gratitude for his benevolence.

George Blanco A.

My Heart Sings

One cold and dreary December Day
I took my lost heart to hear the music play
Revealed within each note, I heard
GOD's voice he gave to every bird
It touched my heart so I could feel
His own soul deep inside of me was real
This was purely GODS' heart touching to mine
And I clearly forgot my place in time.
I stood in longing, let my spirit fly
Capturing every moment as music floated by
I closed my eyes and as on a cloud
Lost to the moment of just here and now
The minutes or hours I was without cares
Then it was over: I descended the stairs
Heading for home with a dream in my heart
Troubles were now joy at being a part
Of GODS' wondrous plan
In the scheme of things
Where hearts aren't just happy
They sing.

Debra Goodman

Ludlow Street

Last weekend I walked
I walked happily
Whistling and grinning.
Down the streets of Brooklyn
Busy and covered with people,
different people funny people.
All of them were strangers.

As I strolled amongst strangers
An old familiar face
Peeked over the tallest building
As if to be shy.

"Good morning, sun," I yelled pompously and joyously.
The sun said nothing.
A warm smile came across me
My old familiar friend glanced down warming us folks below.

Kicking a paper cup along the curb I slowly strutted.
Stopping, I jolted my head all round.
People began to fade.
The corrupt voices of the street people hushed.
The comforting warmth of the sun grew cold, never to return.

Jeffrey James Johnson

Never Know

As I slipped the ring off of my hand,
I was the only one who could understand.
The true meaning of this ring I wore,
And the memories it had in store.
As I laid it down next to his side,
I kissed it and bid a sweet good-by.
Knowing never again will I hear his sweet voice,
or get his opinion when making a choice.
It's gonna be tough, but I've gotta get by,
it's ok to hurt, and it's ok to cry.
Knowing I may never again see his face,
praying to God, he's in a better place.
So quietly he slipped away,
with no one there to help him stay.
I guess God decided it was his time to go,
but at least a great person I got to know.
Why would God take precious Ryan from others and me,
when there's rapist's and killers roaming about free.
It just makes no sense why he had to go,
I could ask, "why" forever, but I'll never know.

Denise Inacio

The Journey

The journey's over it's time for me to go
I will miss my friends and family
But I'm only passing through you know
It's a cycle and the way it has to be
No tears no regrets and no sorrow
Life must go on there is no other way
We come we go and others follow
For it is written no one can stay
Do your best as if you had forever
Leave a legacy of love and achievements
For your loved one and friends to remember
To those who have not achieved their goals
The regrets and sorrow must follow them
As they continue their journey as lost souls
For those who have labored again and again
The journey from here will be so beautiful
Oh such joy and happiness there will be
At the dawning of a new beginning
The reward will be there just wait and see
So farewell I go with joy and singing.

Generoso J. Foglia

"Naked"

How do they measure worth?
I will tell you
Money, Power, Possessions
Worth is no longer a measure of man
It is a measure of what man has hoarded
Not for others, or generations to be
But for himself and his needs
Through my eyes, I can see worth from worthlessness
When the dollar drops
When power changes hands
When possessions are stolen
Man is naked
He is naked against a jury of peers
That measure worth with the scale I use
Passion, Sacrifice, Promise
These qualities tip the scales
If all men were to be measured through mine eyes
The worthless would shine and the others would fade

James Gavilan

Some Thoughts

Mama, everything that moves and all that I see,
I wish that you were a part of it.
All the comfort and enjoyment that others possess,
I wish you could have it too.

But it's too late to offer the things I want to give.
Your wishes were not hard to fulfill but I forgot,
Drowned in lust and hunger for wealth.
Now you're gone and I realize

You left us with an ache in your heart.
Your wish to have all of us by your side
For your last moments, never came true,
And even now I feel that you're calling me.

Thinking of you makes my tears fall.
It's hard without you;
All the things that move
Can never be the same again.

Flerida Vogel

A wish could be

I wish you could be here with
me, for all of the day's of the year,
but I know it can't be so.
I wish life could be a fairytale,
forever in a year, but I know it can't be so
I wish our lives could float
together like a feather, in a sky of
blue, but I know it can't be so.
I wish we could be free like a
rushing sea, but I know it's not so
What can be is you and me in
this wish that will always be for
year's and year's it will always
be you and me.

Jenny Mullinax

Oppression

Sitting here watching your helpless body before me,
I wonder if they will disagree with my actions.
Should I be gentle with your plain face of serenity?
Or should I invade your privacy with all my aggression?

I guess it's your unlucky day because I'm going to fill you
with my madness.

All alone, I lay you down beside me, where I can have total
control of you.
Don't say a word because they are not going to believe you.
It's only my version against yours,
My word against your word. And you know what?
They're going to believe me because I have all the power,
all the control.

I guess it's your unlucky day because I'm going to fill you
with my anger.

Raping your virginity with my manhood,
I now start to see you bleed my intentions.
Take a look in the mirror, those scars are permanently etched
in eternity.
It's amazing how forceful actions can influence someone's train
of thought.

I guess it's your unlucky day.
Was it as good for you as it was for me?

Brendan Boyle

"If I Could Change"

If I could stop time and change things,
I wonder, just what all I'd do.
I'd probably change my past life-style,
And then I could start off brand new...

First, I would have to look at my life,
And see were my troubles began.
I'd look at both sides of the problems,
And then change whatever I can....

But, how do I know it would be different?
Or what path my changes might take?
I might find myself with worse problems,
Or hurt more by the changes I make...

So, maybe I should just reconsider,
And accept what is dealt out to me.
I'll leave the change to God up above,
And believe what will be, will be...

James P. Hale

If I Could Give The World A Gift....

I saw a little girl today,
I wonder what happened along the way.
She looked so tired, small, and frail,
She seemed so frightened and so pale.
She has no one to spend Christmas with,
This is true it, is no myth.
Sometimes I wonder late at night,
How many things to her must be a fright.
Oh, I wish I may, I wish I might,
Have the wish I wish tonight.
If I could give the world a gift,
I give the world a special lift.
To give the world a home to make them cheerful, joyful, and gay,
That would be my wish today.

Genelle Cleburn

I Am

I am a strong, aggressive, military platoon leader
I wonder what it is like to be free from guilt
I hear the cry of wounded soldiers falling to the ground
I see fright in others' eyes when they are dying
I want to be free of guilt
I am a strong, aggressive, Military platoon leader.

I pretend that I am not frightened, but I am
I feel the pain when someone dies
I touch the trigger of a loaded gun
I worry about my family back home, my wife and kids
I cry when I see the pain that I inflict on people
I am a strong, aggressive, military platoon leader.

I understand what I need to do
I say that the fights will end someday
I dream of that day when the fights do end
I try not to think of back home but it's hard
I hope to leave this horrid place
I am a strong, aggressive, military platoon leader.

John Barley

"I Am"

I am black and white,
I wonder when I will cease to take another breath;
I hear beautiful songs repeating with in my mind;
I see beautiful new worlds constantly changing;
I want peace with in my soul,
I am black and white.

I pretend I can fly through the skies,
I feel a majestic power inside myself, I cannot yet harness,
I touch the open waters which run smooth across my skin,
I cry the undying sound of death echoing at my feet,
I worry my loved ones shall hear death's song soon,
I am black and white

I understand everyone's time will come,
I believe in heaven and hell
I dream I shall rise above my pitiful self and become powerful
I try to keep moving everyday to glide and live freely
I hope I will receive power to destroy death, but death is inevitable,
I am black and white.

Aaron Marsh

Will Work For Food

They read my signs, they think I would lie, if I lied,
I would be rich. But the words tell the worlds. I will work for food.
Red convertibles; give me distaste. Shake their head
Pretentious, condescending
I wish I would starve, but I'm so hungry
And so is my daughter

I'm not human, because I smell; because my beard is unkept; because
I wear patches on my jeans; because I can't be like you

I can't give, what I don't have.
Corner I will stand. Hands empty, stretched out, thin and gaunt. Sign.
I will work for food, because I can't work for money.

I will give my pride to live; I will give my self to eat; I will give
my happiness so I might be. I ask for kindness...And hope
And food to receive. Maybe good times, too

And I stand in the street with the sign
ignored.

Joshua Bryan Hammack

My Poem To The Lady I Love

Sonia, your an angel from heaven above
I would bow my head and say a prayer to you
with Love I would look up and say I Love You
pretty angel that's what I would do, if you
could only see what I feel in my heart for
you and if you don't believe that it is true,
the truth is written in front of you
I Love You
well this is true as it is written here and
sometimes when I think about you at night I
can't help from shedding a tear the tears start
falling and there is nothing that I can do it's
just I have fallen in Love with a pretty Lady
and it is you Sonia, I would give you a diamond
ring of 14K gold and if you are not ready yet I
will wait for you until I am gray and old and
as the years go by I will ask for your hand in
marriage again to fill this empty space of this
tear broken heart of a man.

Darrell Cupp

"Sarcasm"

I would tell you how I feel, but that's inappropriate.
I would share my emotions with you, but that's inappropriate.
So I'll keep my emotions
locked inside and put on a mask.
I would tell you what's on my mind, but that's inappropriate.
I would share my secrets with you, but that's inappropriate.
So I'll just keep my secrets
locked inside and put on a mask.
I would express myself, but that's inappropriate.
I would share my thoughts with you, but that's inappropriate.
So I'll just keep my thoughts
locked inside and put on a mask.
Don't look for the real me,
because it's behind this mask,
and that's appropriate?!

Chad W. Haase

I Wouldn't Want To Be A Cat...

I wouldn't want to be a cat because everyone would say "Aww".
I wouldn't want to be a cat because I would have a paw.
I wouldn't want to be a cat because I would have to sleep on the floor
And then I might get hit by a door.
I wouldn't want to be a cat because I would have to drink from a bowl.
And I wouldn't want to be a cat because I might run in to a pole
I wouldn't want to be a cat because I would eat mice.
When I would much rather be eating rice.
I wouldn't want to be a cat because I would be so small
and everybody would seem so tall.
But I would want to be a cat because I wouldn't have to go to school.
But, I would turn out to be a fool.

Jennifer Weissman

If I Were A Writer

If I were a writer with a long, long nose,
I'd smoke pipe tobacco and wear tweed clothes,
I'd stroll in the park, observing the birds,
And then I'd write it all down in words.

I'd write of the pigeon with the funny gait,
And of the old old men who do nothing but wait,
I'd write of the monkeys with the funny faces,
And of people from really foreign places.

I'd write and write and spread my fame,
And soon whole world would know my name,
But I'm just a boy with a turned-up nose,
Chewing bubble gum and wearing old clothes.

I run in the street and play in the gutters,
You'd never know me from the many others,
But when I grow up, and have a long nose,
I'll smoke, and write, and wear tweed clothes.

Ida Sue Kittrell

Untitled

In the velvet arms of my protector;
I sleep within the confines of my own world;
With darkness as my blanket I reach out to see myself;
The earth surrounding me.
Now, tired of being alone, I retreat;
Without flesh and blood to the outreach of heaven...
or hell...

Or is hell where I have been living after all;
Then it is surely heaven that I am seeking,
and my feet know not the way.

Eric Hamilton McDaniel

Explain Your Feelings

I'm searching to find, and looking to see
If I could find you!
I open my eyes to see - make my ears attentive
So I may hear!
Most of all, I open my heart
So that you know for sure I am there!

All through life we have our ups and downs
We also have our trails and tribulations.
Who are we to say when things should be right.
There are so many frustrations!

We go step by step, with challenges through the day
To render our feelings unto time.
Let's try to keep situations in prospective
Because we all need a peace of mind!

Let's talk, let things be known, communication is in demand.
There are times when silence is due - we all know it golden!
Soar to the back of your mind - where there is only space
And say, "yes, this the place."

Keep yourself attuned to the happenings around you.
Keep yourself on watch for the person approaching.
Yes, let them find you - Let them see you -
This is the one that will help you do some soul searching!
Explain your feelings!

Jacqueline L. Rodriguez

A Quest for Love

Of times that have come and gone,
If I count the ways you've helped me,
I'd be up until the break of dawn.
Is love like a see-saw that goes up and down?
Or is love like a circle that goes round and round?
Where does it come from?
Can it grow on trees?
Or maybe it's made like honey from bees.
Is love for sale?
How much does it cost?
Can you find love that someone has lost?
If you can't find love go right back to the start,
Where love can be found in your mother's heart.

Donald A. Bott Jr.

My Bob, My Husband

My Bob, my husband, whom I look up too.
If I keep my thoughts on him, I should
never be sad or blue
My Bob, is number one (here on earth) in my life
I count myself very fortunate to be his wife
My Bob, and I, share our schemes, problems,
Love and dreams
Together, our son, Jeff, says we make quite
a team
In fact he says, if you want to see - how true
Love should be
Then, just look at his Dad, my Bob and me.
After all these years that we've been together
After all that we've been through
Well - my Bob and I - we're still in
Love with each other.

Alice Scott

Goodbye Betty Jean

You were valiant braving that night's requiem;
Death clinging ever close to thee.
Each breath you seized to prolong your life
Ushered painful visions for me.

At the darkest hour I fathomed truth
As I stared boldly into your hollow eyes,
How could you face such depth of anguish
And yet gracefully say goodbye?

With every ounce of courage to evoke,
Employing composure to restrain my tears;
In a measure of time I recited for you
All our wonderful years.

Wherewithal you heaped a final breath,
Your hand slipped slowly to your side,
I thrust myself upon your breast
And just clung to you and cried!

Patricia Emily

Gravediggers

People died longing long ago,
Deaths slow like life,
Hopes long like New York avenues,
Hearts wide as rivers.
With divers' courage,
They collage together dreams
Suffocated in nocturnal lids:
Left to die like babies in garbage bags.

The ones that borne dreams witness death;
The mourning silent,
Calm ripples in the eyes.
They have an archaeologist's love for the fossils
Piled up in the closet of thought.

Go...Go.
Dig in the closed-eye darkness,
Excavate the bones of artists' holocaust,
Whimper a lover's weep
But admire from a distance.

Oghenevovwero Ogbevire

Help My Brother, Please!

Why are my people suffering?
Deep inside their heart, there's love.
I feel the pain never ending
and in the name of peace,
I wish for the miraculous DOVE.

I watch my brother in the restaurant.
Docile and submissive to the boss... so arrogant.
Gently, he cleans and dusts the table.
He doesn't look as I do, though he is as HUMBLE.

I look up to HEAVEN and search for our GOD
though he is always SAME,
He is ever so SILENT.
My heart clings to him.
The pain never ends,
but, in the horizon I see the long awaited end.

Haitians are people too!!

Kettly Cherubin

The Reality

Ignorance the Mighty, along with his terrible mates,
Devastate the world like Vikings of times past.
They mutilate many souls in search of Truth's path.

Their ships of destruction scatter lies and half-truths abroad.
Attacking on winds of evil, causing storms of fear,
That cloud man's mind with deception and fraud.

A perfidious clan herded by wicked intentions.
One is Hate, whose influential tactics
Hinder good judgement and humane decisions.

Malignant Arrogance thanklessly tramples about,
While shallow Racism, darkens the perception of its prey
Like his shamelessly seductive associate, Sexism.

The stealthy, obsessive, selfishness of Greed,
Indulging in excess, O how grotesque,
Causes poverty, famine, and uncalled-for need.

In these Days of Ignorance the individual must fight
To attain salvation from this wickedness.
The fulfillment of God's promise will come to light.
The Day of Judgement, the Reality, the Garden of Bliss.

Norman Jones III

Abort-Me-Not

Oh mother to be why
Did you let me die?

Never to feel the warm rays of the sun
No sense of accomplishment felt from a days work well done.

The flowering trees and singing birds, I'll never see
To smell the fragrant flowers, this will never be.

The strains of voices from a church choir
To join in and praise God would have been my desire.

To partake of Our Lord at the consecration
Oh what you've done, such a desecration.

Sweet Mother Mary, smiling down at me
While I in meditation, on bended knee.

These are things that I could treasure
But you, careless mother robbed me of this pleasure.

Oh mother to be why
Did you let me die?

Philomena Mary Kieffer

Comfort In Loss

Alone by myself I often wondered, would it have been different if you stayed,
Would we still have talked for hours on end,
Would you have gotten bored with me the way you did with the rest of life.
When we parted my life stood still, the days grew long and the nights so cold,
Then the ice melted and the air warmed under the warmth of your memories,
And I felt like a kid on his first roller coaster.
Forever shall you reign on my mind, like you wanted to when we were together,
Now I understand the quotes that used to confuse me,
I know that you're still here with me,
And so will forever remain in my heart and soul,
Because that's what a Dads love is

Winfield Scott Wolfe IV

Mourning After

The path once bright and clear,
disappeared before my eyes.
The life so full of dreams,
had turned to only lies.
Impossible task of starting anew,
can't forget the past, will always remember you.
Pain is piercing deeply,
tears flow freely,
consciousness holds no peace.
Death would be an easy thing,
but damn this heart won't cease.
Pray to God in heaven,
to let this pain subside.
And help to understand,
why a love has died.
The path ahead uncertain,
clouded by fear and pain.
But someday soon be guided,
by loves true force again.

Ken Macy

Call To Serve

Whatever your trade or vocation
Do it in style
In the spirit of the master
Lift it out of the Ordinary
With great zeal and gusto
High unto the olympian heights
For many roads lead to a spot in the sun
Even lucifer matches pay well,
If enough is sold
For who is not ashamed of the apron
Will soon learn to do without it.

Michael K. Oluwole

Confidence

What do people see when they see me?
Do they see my childish innocence?
My firm grasp of life?

Or do they see my shell? My shell that holds me together
in times when I need it most.
Yet lately I've been wondering how people can see
my shell when it is slowly cracking into tiny little
fragments that nobody else can see...

Look...

My shell is fragile. It cannot stay secure by being thrown.
It cannot protect me from my aggressors if it cannot even
hold me together...

It is caving in on itself because all my childish innocence
has run out like a trickling stream... and my firm grasp of
life has blown away in the wind.

Laura Jean LaCasse

Little Ole You

You know, it's funny, but it is true
Even if I'm right, I'm wrong, no matter what I do
No matter what I say, or wherever I go
It's for another reason - that I don't even know
For another judges me, according to his mind
That what I say or do is wrong, when in fact I'm doing fine
If they see me with a frown, they think I'm mad.
Or if I'm smiling, they think I'm up to bad.
No matter what you say or do, you can't please everyone
So just go right on living, until your life is done
No matter who may think you're weird, in what you say or do
Forget it- just go right on being, Little Ole you.

Shirley A. Richmond

Love

What meaning does that word have?
Does it mean anxiety to see him?
Or is it being content in seeing him twice a week,
Just a glimpse when he comes and goes
Perhaps its wanting to say hello and not being able to,
For fear that he might not respond or he might ignore you.
Could it be having dreams of him next to me,
watching old black and white movies?
What is in that emotion that does not discriminate?
Why do some people fear it? Why is it so strong?
Why does it make you so blind you don't know whether you're
doing good or evil? how can it be so dominating?
People have been known to kill in the name of love,
Yet others are constantly ridiculing themselves never regretting it.
What is in that emotion that can also drive you crazy?
Love is feeling, love is caring,
Love has so many shapes and properties it could be fat-thin,
poor-rich, bad-good, ugly-handsome, the list can be continued,
But for now I'm glad love exist and I'm especially glad that he exist,
even thou he doesn't know I exist.

Khaira S. Polanco

Will She...Will I?

She sleeps, the quiet, peaceful slumber that only a small child knows.
Does she dream of the sights and sounds that enter her new life
each day?
Will she remember the warmth and security that she finds in my
arms today?
Will I always be able to protect her simply by holding her?

Those eyes, dark blue now and filled with the curiosity of an infant.
Will they turn brown or gray or green like other members of her
new family?
Will she always have the sparkle of childhood innocence in those eyes?
Will I always be able to show her the beauty and wonder of this world?

That smile, it fills a room and lights up my heart on the very
darkest of days.
Will her smile diminish as she grows into a beautiful young woman?
Will she be able to smile regardless of the path that life chooses
for her?
Will I always be able to put a smile on that precious face just by
loving her?

Her hands, so tiny and fragile at this stage in her young life.
Are those the hands of an artist; will they paint a masterpiece or
write a novel?
Will she master an instrument or perform life-saving surgery?
Will I always be able to encourage her to reach for the stars with
those hands?

She sleeps, she fits in the crook of my arm and nestles against me.
Does she know, can she feel the love that surrounds her?
Will she remember the warmth and security that she finds in my
arms today?
Will I always be able to protect her simply by holding her?

Saundra Leigh Hunt-Hall

If You Want Me...

You don't have to worship me, because I'm not a goddess
Don't bother with the compliments because I'm far too modest
You don't have to buy me gifts to prove your love is true
You don't have to show your strengths just so I'll depend on you
Don't shield my eyes from the pain in life, 'cause there are
things I must see
Don't be angry when I tell you I belong to only me
Don't take my trust and blow it away like the dust upon the wind
Don't break my heart by cheating with other women
Just hear my words, embrace my soul and love me honestly
Then, I'll be yours with eternal faithfulness and love, through all
infinity

Sandra Carruth

A Parenthesis In Time

Remember us in the streets from Chicago to Saigon?
Does your memory fade; Has it been that long?
We were fighting for a cause: Right against Wrong
Does your memory fade; Has it been that long?
Flower Children; Radicals; Soldiers in Green
Does your memory fade like phantoms on the screen?

There's a generation crying out for peace
for blessed release; praying wars will cease
There's a generation singing out their songs
can they be so wrong; won't you sing along?
There's a generation marching out of step
with the trust they've kept; bearing no regrets

Remember us in the fields from Woodstock to Da-Nang?
Does your memory fade; Does it seem so strange?
We were singing for a cause: Right over Wrong
Does your memory fade; Has it been that long?
A vaulted Generation: a Parenthesis in Time
Does your memory fade into a blurred pantomime?

Michael L. Rossmann

Decision Of A Lifetime

Crack, Acid, Speed, Cocaine
Doing these things shows you have no brain.
When you do these things you get real "High,"
If you do these drugs you will wilt and die
Doing these things just all depends,
whether you listen to the peer pressure from your so called "Friends."
When I see these things I feel real bad,
I'm so glad I was taught to say "No" by my mom and dad.
When I watch T.V. I see the victims on the news,
I just put my head down and get the blues.
I think how stupid can these people be.
They not only hurt themselves, but their whole family.
These people don't realize they have their whole lives ahead,
But they've abused themselves and will end up Dead.
I pray for these people each and everyday.
That's why I'm asking you to please keep drugs away.
If you do these drugs on any given day,
I guarantee you will greatly pay.
You heard the message that I just gave.
I tell you to please don't use drugs or it will be an early GRAVE...

Mirdad Rafiq Sweis

"The Spirit Of Man"

"God, breathed the breath of life into this man made of dust.
Dominion over all living things were put in his trust.
With a rib from his side God made him a wife.
They were placed in the garden to begin their new life.

God placed in the garden all things they would need.
But of the tree in the center they were forbidden to eat.
They were to care for the garden be fruitful an multiply.
Never a care or worry all their needs were supplied.

Eve gathered their food in the garden the serpent she happened to meet
He flattered and be guild her the forbidden fruit to eat.
You'll be as God's knowing all things you surely will not die.
Eve ate and gave to Adam the veil fell from their eyes.

From a king to a beggar they went in one day.
No hope for the future to brighten their way.
Jesus came from glory to redeem all they lost.
He shed his own blood on the old rugged cross.

So onward an upward there's hope for us now.
In truth and in spirit our heads humble bow.
To God all the glory from bondage set free.
In spirit with God eternally we will be.

Ruby B. Canada

The Little Girl

Please listen to me the child seems to say.
Don't act like that, you will send me away.
She was only seven, with a life-time of experience.
As she dealt with life with such mature resilience.

The pain etched on her face like an artist impression.
As deep in her soul lingered a sad reflection.
She wanted so much to enjoy a period of childhood,
But playing and laughing was but a distant memory.

Her mother and father, she had loved at will.
But now they were hopelessly addicted to a social ill.
A solitary tear caressed the soft tissue of her cheek,
As it danced on the side of her innocent face.

She wanted to cry and show her emotion.
But her desire to be strong, and show dee devotion,
Prevented her from showing her true feelings,
In the midst of such commotion.

Then the social worker appeared at the door.
And the little girl, took up her doll from the floor.
Then without as much as a goodbye,
She walked out the door with tears in her eyes.

Oscar Peters

My Daily Prayer

To You oh Lord, I pray,
don't fail me Lord, for I am
trusting you today!
Don't let my enemies succeed
Don't give them victory over me.
Show me the paths where my
feet should trod,
None who have faith will ever
be disgraced for trusting in God.
Lord lead me, teach me for I am your creation.
For you are the God who gave me salvation.
God I know you are good and glad
to teach me the right way!
So that I might obey and not go astray.
Lord, my sins are many,
Oh pardon them Father so there won't be any.
Oh Lord overlook my youthful sins,
Forgive me for, bless me for, I
have changed within.

Margaret Widner

Words Of Encouragement

Dedicated to Robert C. Brown

You've come a long way.
Don't give up now - you've been through the worst
And now there's light at the end of the tunnel -
Don't give up now - you've answered to those in
Which you do not know and soon you'll be free.
Don't give up now -
You've got a long way to go and possibilities are endless.
Don't give up now -
You've got dreams and now it's time to make them come true.
Don't give up now - your tomorrow can now be today,
Don't give up now - you've made a new you.
And it's a new year. With new hopes and dreams.
Don't give up now - you've only the future to look
Forward to and it can be all you want it to be, it's all up to you -
Don't give up now - you've shown yourself that you
Are important and that you are someone special.
You are the one who matters,
Don't give up now - for all your hopes and dreams
And wants, I sincerely hope you GET IT ALL!!
Don't give up now.

Mary L. Gloster

"Jesus Hold My Hands"

Jesus hold myself, in the palms of you hands,
Don't put me upon shelves, or in burning sands,

Take all of the hurt, and worries away,
Bury them in the dirt until judgement day,

Take this worried heart, so it will not trouble anymore,
Take all the parts, that's been hurt before,

Let me no longer feel pain, nor hunger, over stormy rains,

Take all the love in my heart, for everyone to feel and see,
Let it travel far, to the top of the skies, and the bottom of the seas

Jesus I believe, trust, and have faith in thee,
I know there should not be any must left in me,

Only one should be left, which leads me to you, you're the only one who knows,
What I've felt, and has the answer to what I should do.

I have hurt over these years, full of heart aches and pain,
And cried many of tears, while left standing in the rain!

Keep me in your hands point out the right roads,
Through these weary lands, so I will not have to carry such heavy loads,

Thank you, oh Lord, for taking time to listen,
Thank you for opening your doors and not away fishing

Lorie L. Blagg

Precious Baby

Don't you leave me, Precious Baby— Honey—
Don't you walk out on me— Precious Baby!
Precious Baby! Oh, don't you leave me, Precious Baby!
Honey,—don't you walk out on me—
No, don't leave me, Precious Baby—
Because I want you to work it out with me;
Precious Baby— Precious Baby.
Let's work it out together, Baby! Let's work it out!
No matter how hard it seems, Baby...
We can work it out! I need your love ever so bad..
And I need your lovin' ever so bad!
So don't leave me, Precious Baby...Honey,
Don't ever walk out on me!
Oh Precious Baby! What are you going to do?
Oh Precious Baby! Don't you know that I Love You?
I Love You , Precious Baby and I need your lovin' ever so bad
You're my lover! Yes, my lover! Precious Baby!

Don't you leave me, Precious Baby honey, don't you
ever walk out on me! Don't you leave me, Precious
Baby Precious Baby, I Love You! My Precious Baby!

Milton Shannon

Where Children Go

Your bright and happy eyes are
drawn to that eternal light
as it casts its ethereal glow
and illuminates the night.

Lesser men see it nocturnal show
an esoteric realm where children go —
To a sanctified place from whence she came
hurled into a world wild and profane.

No poet Laureat, or even Hemingway
could dream the perfect verse or prose
to justly describe that day.

Darkness consumes that boundless gulf
Like a trackless wilderness un-hewn and rough
Life, as a tide, ebbs and flows
Back, to that mystical place
Where children go.

J. Allen Aday

Despairing Questions

Down.
Down.
Down I go in the tornado of despair.
I find myself reaching for something that isn't there.

Where is there?
Where is here?

Is reality really a place?
My soul knows the truth—the truth of my Creator's grace.

My spirit holds on for me as I tumble down the depths of the past.
Blinded by the darkness, I reach for the Light to be free at last!

Is freedom a state of mind, or is it a state of being?
Emotions of every kind express gently in the moment of the feeling.

"Wake up!!" they say, "and open your eyes!"
Unlock the chains of bondage—the link of lies.

Is it safe to be free or is it safe just to be?
Only one can answer this, only one who is me!

Wendy Galloway

Summer Sea

Oh, how I love to wonder
down by the side of the sea
and watch the beautiful, boundless blue
rolling, rolling free!

The shining, shimmering, glistening, glimmering
waters of the sea
roll in majestic, mountainous waves
as far as the eye can see.

Far, far out, the waves rise up
to a white-capped crowning peak.
Then the whirling, wide white waters
rush to the shore with a thunderous roar
and (tumbling) fall — in a swirl — at my feet.

I'm hypnotized by the fall and the rise
of the gull, with a dip and a soar,
and I'm drunk with the sweet moist ocean air
and the cool, cool, comforting breeze
on the shore.

Lanier Graham

Life's Waterfall

Life's waterfall of bounty comes tumbling down,
Down to the tributes of barren land.
To nourish and grow as a child at its birth
Beneath the soil brings a bud to the earth.

As life beings from barren land, so it must end
As the dust and the sand.
This bud will grow to a life-giving thing, only
To die as it once began.

Trod under by plow, or war or machine, its death
Is cruel and hardened it seems; so back to the dust
And the sand that began.

Somewhere, somehow, its life will regain, this time
Strengthened by life's bitter pains.

Somewhere life's waterfall will once again appear,
To nourish the ground where this bud will not fear.
This time stronger and hardened, its life will take root,
To bud into beauty of life's greatest loot.

Margaret Eleanor Giannone

In All I Am

Each day, each trial, each test,
Draws me close to the Lord for strength;
For I alone am weak,
But by Faith I do the Lord seek.

Not for riches do I strive,
To achieve my purpose while I'm alive;
But to live each day accordingly,
In all the Lord would have me do.

The secrets between God and Me,
Reveal the failures that I cannot see;
But looking closely at myself,
God takes away the sins that are left.

My soul poureth over with thanks,
Each day I live and breath;
For the Lord doeth sustain me,
IN ALL I AM and will be.

Teresa Smith

Still A Dreamer

Dreams are said to be a mirror to our hidden desires.
Dreams give us hope when there is nothing left.
Dreams keep me safe, when I feel lost my way.
My dreams are sometimes incomplete and complicated to most.
Somehow my dreams have a way of falling in mid flight.
After all the crashes, I still take off again to make them soar.
Through the years, I've learned you have to work to keep some dreams alive.
Instead of waiting for Prince Charming to appear with roses on your door step.
Realize, life is a like a play, full of love and sometimes tragedies.
Stop wearing your heart on your sleeve or it will get broken.
Remember time heals all wounds.
With every storm a beautiful day follows.
In every rainbow, I believe a pot of gold is waiting at the end.
There is true love and it can last forever.
Believe in yourself or no one else will.
Hold on to your dream and forever keep trying.
Because dreams are part of the future, and the future is you.

Lisa Jennings Johnson

Always Life

I went through grief
During that year.
I went through pain.
I went through fear -
Fear that you would die
And I would never see you again
But only through memories.
I felt lonely not knowing what to do
If you would have left.
I know God would have taken care of you
And looked after you.
I am glad He gave you back the way you are.
I LOVE YOU, DAD!

Kara Hillman

Love And Nature's Beauty

Walking along a small & narrow path I see
Delicate violets of purple, yellow, and white, looking up at me
The beautiful lush green trees above
Provide cool quiet shade for me and my love
We touch and kiss in the glow of the sky above
And hope that as the beauty of the earth will
Last, so will our love.

Patricia McGill

To Our Grand-Daughter Dearest

You are like a ray of sunshine in our lives
During this time of trouble and strife.
Who would have thought that such a little one
Could bring us so much joy and fun.
From your tiny pink toes to your beautiful face,
All dressed up in calico and lace.
You remind us of a budding flower
You fill with happiness, our every hour.
Gammy and Grampy love you so,
How very, very much you'll never know.
In the future whatever road you choose to tread
If ever you should feel blue,
Think of all the happiness you have spread
And some of it will surely come back to you.
Love you,
Gammy & Grampy

Vicki Burton

December 7, 1941

Blindly we waited at the brink of war,
Each busy with his ant-like, vast designs;
Nor cared what other men were fighting for.
We dwelt behind the sea's protecting lines.

Then on a Sabbath dawn the bombers spoke
Over the palm trees of a peaceful land—
Complaisance vanished in the ARIZONA's smoke.
God knows we wanted peace. But now WE STAND!

In war, or peace, we hold it certain yet
'Tis man's eternal birthright to be free,
And in this hour of fate dare not forget
That freedom had its birth in Galilee.

Let us lift voices in a mighty shout
Thanking the day that brings us now at length,
After we've crossed the deserts of our doubt,
Back to the inner source of all our strength.

With ease and comfort gone before the gale,
We turn at last to God—Who does not fail.

William W. Edel

"For Your Return I Live"

For your return I prevail.
Each day I say tomorrow he'll return, when tomorrow comes I can not help to say the same words over again.
Everyday my mind, my devotion, yes, even my soul at times tell me; Stop you've done enough!
But, a crazed heart stands in the way of all begging for just another day.
The birds in the sky no longer sing for my sake,
The garden has asked me not to return and smell the roses,
The grass leading to your lawn, no longer wants my pace to touch her face.
My cry to heavens are no more carried by the wind.
Friends have left me, crazy they call me.
Enemies of main have broken their animosity.
For they say I no longer impose a challenge.
Like a candle I stand mute and tearful.
My heart broken and black yet, it holds its breath.
In a ruinous shape it still wishes to remain.
Remain just one more day in hope.
Saying tomorrow he'll return.

Mariam Al Majid

The Incurable Romantic

The incurable romantic, ceases to amaze
Each day of his life, like a brand new phase
Waking alone, through the days
Rain pouring down, no hint of sun rays
Everyone looks upon him, as though he is crazed
Then one day, he comes to find
Someone like himself, one of his own kind
Such rare beauty, does this creature carry
To look upon her, makes one weary
To love her, even more sacred
Then what you've had before, so close to hatred
This beauty burns, with such romance
She even cares, about her kindrance
But what could she see, in a person like me
With nowhere to run, so confused and complex
Even to himself, so perplexed

Robert C. Mezoff Jr.

Rose Of Blue

In Memory of Sister, Kelli M. Yeates

On a window downtown, there is a rose painted round
Each petal, like you, soft and delicate yet sometimes blue
Leaves of green make me wonder what was unseen
Rugged thorns that tear when I look and you're not there
That long sturdy stem with a ruff jagged end
I saw memories of you in that rose painted blue
As I reached out to touch I could feel you so much
I knew I would see you soon when that bud turned to bloom
There's a memory in this rose that no one else knows
And each time I hold one in my hand I try to understand
Why my rose of blue has to be a memory of you!

Karen Thomas

Texas Soul Trip

To the hill country many Texans go,
each spring the caravans steadily flow.
The grey ribboned highways, stretched between carpets of many colors,
carry toil-worn city folk over hills and through hollows.
The indian paintbrush is a red badge of courage,
most brilliant beside the pale, humble buttercups which merge.
About the future there can be no apprehension
when daisies and black-eyed susans need our attention.
Thistles and dandelions, by the farmer oft maligned,
this season are exalted by the divine.
Bachelor buttons skip about with no cares,
wedding slippers will overtake them unawares.
Our state flower, the bluebonnets, are the most outstanding,
like God's care, each year more overwhelming.
So let's pack a picnic lunch, also load worries and woes,
and head for the hill country to seek solace for our souls.

Mary Helen Hampton

"The Seasons In My Soul"

Springtime, breezes in; With the colors, of the
earth all aglow. Newborn; in an array, of green
that grows. Flowers; bursting apart, with a new
promise. Of the life we know!

The summer sun, rushes in; shimmering around
and threw, each of us. That heat flows and fades,
into a warm glow. Telling us, love is everywhere we go!

Fall drops in, with a blanket of leaves, covering the
mountains. With rainbows of colored dreams;
They float a cross the sky, it seems.

Winter is cold, empty and barren; until you see!
All the warmth, loving someone; can give to thee.

When our bodies die; our souls, are free!
To lay in, God's warm love; for it's golden you see!

Mary A. Myers, R.A.

Tidewater Seasons

Your feelings flow like the shy, ebbing tide
  Easing in high on the sands of my soul
    Drifting out low with the doubts in your mind

My emotions flow like the great, raging tide
  Roaring upon the rocks of confusion
    Rushing away with my indecision

The tidewaters change each coming season
  Spring tides pound the shore, life teaming within
    Akin to the new love we can't live without

Seasons of summer; calm, hot and steamy
  The tide continues ebbing to and fro
    Our feelings of love flowing back and forth

Fall is the season in which one reflects
  With fall the tide swirls constantly growing
    Around us love grows, life also ages

Frigid in winter the world falls asleep
  Cold tidewater churns the ocean alive
    Tidewater seasons, our love must not die

Rodney J. Kline

Out In Desert Spaces

Out in desert spaces
Edged in hazy blue
Coyotes sing and prance
With voices like dew
The sun sets
In the old-fashioned desert
Not a wisp of movement
No scampering of mice
No singing of birds
No rustling of leaves
Among the quiet times of the herds
Space is like a soft flame blossom budding sapphire blue
Dewdrops on fire blossoms
All that shiny dew
The sun melts over desert spaces
The twinkling of starlight
Now dark, dark of night

Riana Rohmann

A Monster In The Village

Disarray, Disillusionment, Disbelief
Emotions running through my mind like sprinters
going for the gold
Fleeting thoughts of purpose in a world
where nothing has one
The revolving door of change keeps spinning
stopping its eternal motion
for nothing
What has happened to me? Joy, once as sure
as the sun's rays on my face
has pulled a disappearing act, now it's there,
now it's not
A monster named despair has invaded the village
of my mind
and the magician which is my sanity cannot stop it
and has given up trying
For the monster's life force,
the pain of saying goodbye
cannot be
overcome.

Paul M. Eza

The Desert Eternal

Bells ringing lights blinking
Enough cigarette smoke to choke
Child-like figures in a childless land

Vacant staring jackpots caring
As dreams go up in smoke
Big money hopes of the poor

A once honored place on earth
Where seas and waves abounded
And life swarmed everywhere
Now warm-brown and dry
Where the Joshua tree stands stretching
Proudly growing to meet the deep blue sky
Amidst tall sandy sun-kissed mountains
A land warm and comforting
A land created and blessed by God on high
Called rightly Las Vegas the meadows
But now a land full of excess

Bells ringing lights blinking
People grope blinded by greed
Vacant staring jackpots caring

Walter Christian Francis

Refugees

Refugees are natives of many lands,
Equal to anyone; by judgment of God's hands.
They come to our country for safety and peace,
Leave behind loved ones with no future release.

Families are separated; it's not their hearts desire.
To make things better is their only prayer.
They bring neither food or extra change of clothes.
Hoping to be welcomed for awhile, each suppose.

Their races vary: yellow, brown, black and white.
Their nerves are wound up real tight.
"Cause at the end of their dismal day.
Maybe a job will come; and they'll have money to pay.

These are God's people; created by Him.
Our love and compassion should never run thin.
Our country was founded on freedom and love;
So welcome them in on the wings of God's dove.

Lupe Martinez

Love

Why is the concept of love, so hard to understand
Especially since from the beginning, it was God's only plan.
Why do we say things that tear others apart
By our words, deeply piercing the heart.
Why do we hurt those we love the most
Does that pain we cause, give us reason to boast.
Why do our actions speak so loud and clear
Causing harm to those we hold so very dear.
Why so often does love turn to hate
Realizing that the relationship was a complete mistake.
When people argue, disagree, or even fight
Love should be the answer, in making things right.
But instead people turn and walk away
Leaving only loneliness, emptiness, and miserable days,
They turn their heads, as if not even to care
With nothing more to say, nothing more to share,
Why must love hurt so very bad
It should bring happiness and joy; make us glad,
Real love should last always and forever
Making life's disappointments easier and so much better.

Kristy R. Garretson

The Deed

I wasn't the first in our house to walk,
Even now they question how I talk

Learning how to tie my shoes was a chore,
So many subtle signs they chose to ignore.

My mother knows what's wrong with me,
To tell would reveal what she'd rather not see.

It's a dark secret longing to be told,
So I can be helped to thrive and grow.

When I was in the womb fighting for life,
Mom was busy getting high on the pipe.

Now I'm having problems and you wonder why,
You think I'm bad, that I just don't try.

Often I think I can't get anything right,
My temper is short, with my siblings I fight.

Can you help me? I don't know what's wrong,
It seems I've been this way much too long.

My life's just beginning and I'd like to succeed,
If mom would only tell about that awful deed.

Leslie D. Allen

Pinky

Pinky was a pig who wouldn't get fat,
Even though she knew where all the food was at.
All the other pigs in the pen used to laugh and grin,
Making fun of Pinky's skinny skin.
One day the laughter went away,
For that skinny pig saved the day.
Lightning struck the pen one night,
It caught fire, and all the pigs squealed with fright.
The gate on the pen was latched tight,
There was an opening on the right.
The fat pigs tried to squeeze through,
They couldn't, and didn't know what to do,
Pinky held her stomach in real tight,
She hit the latch with her snout and all the pigs rushed out.
Now Pinky is a hero, still as skinny as can be.
All the other pigs learned a lesson that day.
Treat everyone nice some say,
For you never know when someone different will save the day.

Mary T. Cooper

Even Now

I listen to her anger, the loudness of her voice.
Every day. Every evening. Nothing changes.

Not even the familiar, screamed insistence
that, "You goddamn kids do it now!"

I hear it. The murmured threats she uses and
thinks no one else does.
I do. Everyday. Every evening. Like clockwork.

I hear it. Again. Her subdued voice rising,
growing, hating, wounding. Loud. Louder.
Everyday. Every evening...
EVEN NOW

Margaret Johnson

The Creation

Euphoric dawning follows shadowed labourings.
Fingerlings of light creep into newborn valleys.
Lava-laden vapor rises from cooling waters.

Pale-green moss begins on still-damp hillsides.
Haloed sun rises in murky skies.
Virgin earth nurtures embryonic heart-beats.

Lorraine Standish

Children Of The World

In the futile day of a faithless haze,
Every life, every beating heart,
Has a lonely soul inside.

Every hoping, ever reaching out,
Has a special meaning of pride.

We have faith for the children of the world,
Every single little boy and girl,
Red and yellow black and white,
They hold on like a string to a kite.

Their skin, religion, and their culture,
Are praying with all their might,
While the love in the cold darkness,
Is catching them with fright.

Let them sing, let them dance,
Let them smile,
For they have a chance.

These are the children of the world,
Holding on, and searching for their gold.

Stephanie Krauss

Prose Poetry: The Demise Of The Heart

There's a hole in my heart. I can feel it when I breathe. Every rise and fall of my chest is like a snake swallowing its prey whole, down the pit of its throat. With each breath, I try to fill that hole, but, like an expanding balloon, with every breath, the hole grows larger. Soon, this hole will engulf me. I shall plummet through the darkness, and unless someone throws me a rope that I can grasp on to and believe in, my heart will cease to beat. At first, it will stop emotionally, and eventually, altogether physically. My family will place me in the ground with the same ropes I could not grasp where vermin will steal my eyes and memories will steal my soul.

Shawn Mathis

Bring Back the Memories

Bring back the memories of my beloved
Every scene of uncontrollable pain
And every moment of romantic bliss
No longer remind me that she is dead
The memories fall upon me like rain
Gently caressing my cheek like her kiss
And as these memories engage my head
These cheeks of mine will have another stain
For the one that I will forever miss
For in the past, this is what has been said
In your life you never will again gain
The love given to you by your mistress
Never again will she be in your bed
Just the memories that invoke great pain

Ty Plumlee

Maple Magic

Standing alone in a maple grove, seeing the fields below
Feeling the silence of the wind, serenity few will know.
A place to go to get away from problems you may gain
To sit among the trees so proud and tell them hopes or pain.
They listen in their quiet way swaying to and fro
While life begins again for you and problems seem to go.
The maple grove is a special place, a place where feelings start
The reality of a friend so near. Does it come from the heart?
Time will send the answers down to the grove so full of trees
And there you'll follow paths marked out toward playful destiny.

Karen B. Magnan

The Last Kiss

I am lonely and confused
every time I think of you
I have no idea as to what I should do
You are in my mind
and in my dreams.
You are haunting me
so it seems .
You gave me a kiss and lead me on.
You moved to the side and now you're gone.
what do you have to say for yourself?
I cannot read your mind.
I thought you cared
but I guess I thought wrong.
The best thing for me is to let you go.
The love I felt for you
I guess you'll never know.
so, now I'll say good-bye and walk away.
For this night together was our last day.

Mary A. Vermilyea

Forever Asleep

A pain within, you're scared so deep,
everyday you live but they forever sleep.

You feel such guilt, from things you could have done,
but, it's too late you've lost your loved one.

Inside you feel so empty and alone,
wishing in your heart that they would come home.

In your dreams you might be together,
but when you awake, they'll still sleep forever!

Karen Bauer

Pillows Filled With Tears

When we were together
Everything felt so right
But now that we're apart
Sadness sleeps with me at night

I know at times I've done things wrong
I've even made you cry
The sorrow for those times I can never forget
No matter how hard I try

The love I feel for you
Is stronger than anything I've ever known
Scared of what you mean to me
I'm frightened by feelings shown

The feelings that make me want you
Are the same ones that drive me away
Like an untamed animal
I know not how to stay

Someday when I stop fighting with myself
And no longer consider love among my fears
Neither of us will have to rest our heads alone at night
On pillows filled with tears

Richard Tanner, Jr.

An Old Man's Lament

I never thought I'd live this long.
Eighty Years!
Our family history's not that strong.
It's not as bad as I thought it would be,
With the help of some gadgets I can hear and see.
If I could only remember how to pee,
I'd have it made

Thomas Carlile

Reflections Of A Christmas Past

Tis the day after Christmas, and I am just beat,
Everything hurts me, especially my feet.
The cleaning .. the cooking .. the shopping .. the wrapping..
Have all left me with a desire for napping.

The gaily tied packages under the tree
Are all opened now, nothing new to see.
It seems to arrive before we're quite ready
And then gone so quick, the feelings quite heady.

The family all gathered, it really was fun
They ate and they drank, and then had to run.
Back to their homes and their jobs and such,
I wonder sometimes if it all is too much.

And yet I know when Christmas comes round,
I'm sure I will have new energy found,
I'll do it again as I do every year
Cause there's no time of year to my heart that's so dear.

Nancy Strannemar

Untitled

Share the wealth
expose the mind
drop the mask - the veil of greed
living on the masses and share the wealth
Shed a tear for the common man
let him know the time has come.
So share the wealth.

U. Trudeau

You'll Never Learn

Reaching for what he cannot have,
Failing, but never learning,
Always getting burned,
Never learning to stay away from matches.

Walking slowly down the street,
Frowning at all blondes,
They remind him of her,
She who carelessly cut him.

Life has no purpose to him now,
That zest he once had is gone with her,
He continues to exist,
Hoping that one day zest will come back to him.

Sherry M. Karabin

South Beach

White sand warmly glowing in the blue-gray light.
Fat gulls moving slowly,
On the beach they now own.

Green grass,
Greener still
In the overcast sky.

Green scrub pines.
Slashed by flashes of arid pastel colors, the sandy dunes
To be seen, only seen
In this dark tremulous, gray and yet soft light.

All enveloping ocean,
All powerful, all mystifying ocean,
Magnificent in the rain!

And I suspended in this time and this place
Look on. Lonely. Quiet. Superb.
An almost part of the whole,
But not quite. Not quite.
Still, I am grateful for the rain
On my holiday.

Ted Pollack

All Along

Abraham a shepherd, spoke with God above.
Fathered many nations, with the grace of God's pure love.

It was the joy of many wise men, to share in Christ's birth.
But evil king herod, planned death for the king of the earth.

But as he grew to teach people, that loving and sharing's the way.
A shameful crucifixion, still can't stop him today.

Open up the Bible, truthful study and through prayer.
Faithfully call on the Lord, his word assure he'll be there.

Some believe when they die, that's really all she wrote.
There's no father, son, or heaven, surely no holy ghost.

Satan is the deceiver, he wants you to sin to the end.
To cleanse your soul, repent your sins, and let Jesus the savior in.

If we could have heard the words of moses, before thousands died.
To hear the voice of John, in the wilderness he cried.

Just as many of the prophets, they foretold the truth.
The same as the word of God, is now doing to you.

Kenneth R. Stephens

The Changing Seasons

January brings the snow, makes our feet and fingers glow!
February brings the rain! Thaws the frozen lakes again.
March brings breezes loud and shrill stirs the golden daffodils.
April brings the primrose sweet scatters daisies at your feet.
May brings flocks of the pretty lambs skipping by their fleecy dams.
June brings tulips, lilies, roses, fills the children hand with poses.
Hot July brings cooling showers apricots and jilly flowers.
August brings the sheaves of corn then the harvest home is born.
September brings the golden aspen leaves
its time to picnic in the changing autumn trees.
A full moon in October brings us halloween and the Fall
goblins witches and festivals means celebration for all.
Cold November brings the blast, then the leaves are whirling fast!
December brings us X-mas and the festive season
praying for peace on earth is our main season.

Rocky Jocky Anderson

Life

What is life? One might ask
Figuring it out seems like such a tough task
It begins in the delivery room and ends in the grave
What happens in between can never be saved

At times life seems like candy, sweet as can be
At other times it's like punishment, and we ask: Why me?
Life is like a roller coaster with its up and downs
Life is different for people in big cities and in small towns

For some life revolves entirely around their careers
For others it involves watching T.V. and drinking a few beers
If people really wish to make life great
They must learn how to love and not how to hate

At times we think life is so very rough
And we say we've really had enough
But deep down inside we're all glad to be here
While death is really the one thing we fear

When one looks up at the sky on a clear sunny day
They can feel as if someone is trying to say
That life is really what you make it to be
Just ask around, and most people will surely agree.

Steven Kirsch

As A World Turns

As the world turns, My heart burns
Filled with emotions done and gone
Lost in the dying light is my last fight
To keep peace and happiness floating around me
Till my last breathe

For mortality lasts for so long as we sing our songs
Filling our hearts with emotions
Overwhelming our feelings

We are here to prove one thing
To be perfect in our deities' eyes
Than maybe we can fly like a bird
Instead of buying a ticket for a cramped ride

As the tides reside
The night's frights come alive
with tide pools of fools
Who drool for violence
Thou we just ask for silence

Then peace fills the night in the moonlight
And happiness reigns in the rays of the sunlight
But first we have to pass our hidden test.

Richard W. Kreiner

Promise

The pen moves,
Filled with the bitter ink of hopelessness.
The black stream
Paints stories of man's destruction:
The child - with an old man's eyes;
The old man - without eyes.
Stars dimly seen - veiled by
Man's gift to the heavens;
Trees, crackling in the hearth in
Burning tribute to - Progress.

Somewhere.....
A violet blooms softly
Near a heap of garbage....
And the pen is satisfied.

Louise Harvey

Kindred Spirit

Listen to my words, brothers and sisters of the land.
Find your pride, be strong. Don't listen to the white man.
He is wrong. Show him to listen to the wisdom you can share.

You were once strong of heart and of spirit.
Stand for your rights but do not use war as your way.
You are better than that. Use your strong will, your mind.
Make the white man listen.

I am not of your blood but since I was very young I believed
In you. I have grown to love you all by learning about you.
I am ashamed of what has been done to you.

I cry for your dead. I feel your pain and sorrow.
I pray that you will again find the spirit to fight;
To find out the great Native American pride lives in you still.

Listen to the songs of your ancestors; the wisdom they gave
You. Hear their words; heed them. Show the white man what
You are——A GREAT NATION.

Ronalda R. Cayzer

Life

Life is being born and dying,
Finding love and despair,
Finding happiness and sadness,
And everything in between.

Life has its ups and downs—
You either go with the flow
Or get run over.

Life is full of lies and the truth,
Generosity and selfishness—
But out of life one can
Learn a lot about people.

So live happy and have fun while you can
Before you know it
Life is gone.

Tamara Pressler

Morning In A Meadow Universe

I see a galaxy of whorls of lace,
Fine spider webs made visible by dew.
These night-strung spirals hung on glistening thread
Are made by master spinners flinging strands
Of silk in forms evolved so long ago.

Smart artisans whose skills cause victims' woe
Have fashioned traps with neatly laddered bands.
Each net becomes a welcome mat outspread
To greet unwary prey whose destined view
Will be from crafty spider's inner space.

Mary E. Donnelly

Textures

Textures of humanity — Godhood touching man fused
Finite with Infinity — Earth hosting Heaven's plan.

The vulnerable velvet of babe-soft scented skin
Teased by dusty manger straw that prickled Him within.

Joseph's wiry curling beard as his rough lips kissed
The miracle of newborn Son — and contemplated bliss.

The Child fussed and felt the gentle flow of Mary's hands;
Incarnate Grace in Earth's embrace of clothy swaddling bands.

The huffing warmth of oxen breath and glint of frosty star.
The wet caress of lambkin tongue mid singing from far.

Textures of Divinity were touching humankind —-
Such sweet bonded affinity, when mortal met Divine.

Kay Trudell

Two Lives In One

Confusion and self-doubt have pervaded her days.
Flutters of consciousness come in bits—time delayed.
Who knows, who she will become? How will she get there?
Her parents want lovely grandchildren out playing.
Her boyfriend says they will live in great wedded bliss.
She knows they are sincere, yet they can't see her needs.
Does she follow the street they have already paved,
Or does she blaze her own trail reflecting her dream.
She dearly loves her family and friends, but can she
Refuse to let her inner soul mature and grow.
A family and career, together, is her dream.
She's told, "It's not possible!" and "Don't be absurd!"
Her spirit understands that her life must have both.
Through criticisms and doubts, she knows she'll prevail
And become a woman who lives two lives in one.

Penny Jones

Christmas On The Homestead In Colorado

Daddy would get the christmas tree, would reach from ceiling to floor,
He would always have one spotted, from at least a year before.

When we decorated the tree, everybody has something to do,
Made chains with colored paper, and used flour paste for glue.

Wrap pinion cone with tinfoil, whenever some could be found,
All around the windows and doors, is where we would hang them around.

We might buy some icicles at store, to add to the christmas cheer,
After christmas we would remove them, so we could use them the next next year.

Everything that would be in your sock, christmas morning you did not know,
But an orange and some corn candy, were two things that would always show.

Did Santa really show? For me I had no proof.
I guess I always figured, that he landed on the roof.

Out in the snow in the yard, the sled tracks did not show
But he always brought me presents, that is one thing I did know.

All the happy memories, I'm glad I did not miss,
Thinking of all good times, now I can reminisce.

Kenneth E. Webb

Roses In The Night

The blood red, dew dipped fragrance, that smells as sweet as candy, flows and sways in the pitch black sky. The perfumed fragrance fills the meadows with a soft touch, like the hand of God is touching the ground. Peace fills the air like a love song, with a soft rhythm. A cool breeze sweeps the blackened sky, while a herd of deer scamper by. Birds soar with a mighty wind around their wings. All have come to praise this single rose, that stands so tall in this meadow of peace. As I lay on the cold ground of the meadow, I feel like I have seen the face of God as He silently whispers "I love you."

Leslie Canniff

Old Man (Gramps)

The cost of getting old is too much
for an old man to pay today

For the children have all ran away

Plenty to talk about today,
but no one has come my way

My fair lady has left me,
but I know her smile is lighting my way

That thought usually brightens my day,
but not on a day when the cost of getting
old is too much for an old man to pay

It is said you cannot put a price on a
youthful glow,
I should know,
because the cost of getting old is too much
for an old man to pay today

O to be a pauper today,
but loneliness has taken even that away...

Mark Robert Berchman

My Valentine To God "Not Just Mine Alone"

Each day of my life, I am thankful to you
For giving me life with a smile
For breathing life into all that we know
To live for a little while.

How gracious you give, so that I may live
In splendor, a perfect home
And I want to you to know that the flowers you grow
Are NOT JUST MINE ALONE.

How warm are your rays in bright summer days
When fields are laden with flowers.
The valleys so green and the sky so serene
By the hand of your Almighty Power.

How loving you are, when you gave us a star
And the moon to light our way home
These are the things I hold dear in my heart
For they're NOT JUST MINE ALONE.

Marcia A. Desreuisseau

The Juggler

Painting her face - getting ready
for her show - the clown prepares
for elegance
She places on her red whig - ever ready -
and a brown corduroy shirt - warming
up for her juggling act
She only juggles two balls - with a
drink, maybe a third - and, oh, and
then there is Ted - who was funny -
so she painted her face for him too
Like Harry with Ruth
the wash cloth is prepared to
cleanse her uncleanliness - to remove
her whig - her paint and replace
her broken hymen
But as she juggles - she drops one
of her balls - her paint begins to
run - realizing she is unable to
be true to her art.

Steven Carickhoff

Going Home

Mom, Dad, oh please don't you cry
For I will be there in the sweet by and by.
Some day we will all be there, and then
Never to be parted, no never again.

I know the other people will understand
As we walk down that golden street hand in hand.
They will say, now the old folks are not alone.
For another daughter has came home.

So Mom, Dad, oh please don't you cry
For I will be there in the sweet by and by.
Someday we will all be there, and then
Never to be parted, no never again.

We will all live in heaven, where it is bright and so clear
Waiting for the rest of our family there.
I miss you both since you have been gone.
Now I have a feeling it won't be long.

So Mom, Dad, oh please don't you cry.
For I will be there in the sweet by and by.
Some day we will all be there, and then
Never to be parted, no never again.

Norma Hoon

Untitled

How can you describe what makes a friend, a friend?
For me the list goes on and almost has no end.
A friend knows all about you, knows your ups and downs
And when no one else can cheer you up, a friend can turn your day around.

A friend knows about your past
All the mistakes that you've made
And the best part of all
Is that they love you anyway

If a friend is true
And loyal all the way
Then they'll remember you in prayer
Every single day

Life is just too tough
To go it all alone
And God knows you need a friend
Who won't let you cry alone

Every friend we have deserves
An awful lot of love and let us never forget
That they came from God above.

Kim Haynes

"Tears Of Yester Years"

Although we have parted and my heart is broken
For now I cannot bare to say farewell.

I rely on the good memories as now my token
To uplift me in this state I dwell.

Someday if I should whisper good-bye
It will be with boldness, peace and no tears

For to have known love and lost, oh why should I cry
Love, it must not forever die in my yester years.

For it has quickened my tomorrows to know
That I can still fly, if I only need try.

Mary Emma Jones

The Stage Is Set

You'll get all the laughter, and receive the applause,
for one so abiding.
No casting for their cause,
for the life that you lead is not just for them,
the sheep in the field, asleep in the pasture,
paraded as slaves to amuse the masses,
the deceiver has been deceived.
The masses have been baffled,
for now the play is yours, the acts raw and gritty.
Cast onto the stage as the beginning of a new planet,
portray dreams and realities that you now control.
Puppet master superseded by another,
the jest is a king, and the king a jest,
they now tread where you once tread, and feel your anguish and suffering.
Chaos made into order, reality transformed into consciousness,
all the jest said was, "How does it feel to be me."

J. D. Bowman

Voice To A Veteran

Two tear-filled wars you have fought through
For our freedom you've fought through two
Now you're engaged in number three
And you're your own cruel enemy
Christ taught to love our enemies
So hear O hear the message please
Freedom shall come as a dart
When you love yourself with whole-heart

Ollie Vee Zoller

A Mother's Prayer

I prayed for an angel to watch over my child,
For out in the world there are ones who are wild.
They seek to destroy, and much damage they do,
So I'm asking, my child, for one to watch over you.

I prayed for an angel when you were small
To stay close beside you and hear when you call.
A mother does watch her little ones, too,
But I prayed for an angel to watch over you.

I prayed for an angel your life to share
So always you'd be safe there in his care.
I know that God answers prayer when we speak,
So I'm asking your angel to guard you this week.

I prayed for an angel, and I'm sure he came
To be there with you for he knows your name.
A mother can give material necessities each day,
But God sends an angel when a mother does pray.

Marjorie F. Jenkins

My Gift To You

There's no love like my mother's
For she has cared before any other.
She's my mom, and my best friend
She will love me to the very end.
With all her advise she gives unto me
The lessons of life that are not easily.
She's there to wipe away my tears
Or hold my hand when I am in fear.
Or sometimes when I want to talk
Her ears will listen as I squawk.
Her arms that hold me, Oh so tight
As she whispers, everything will be all right.
Thanks for being there for me, caring as you do
For taking time to hear my dreams and making them come true.
Always and forever, I will think of you
And all the wonderful things that you do.
Happy Mother's Day

Marla Padilla

Silent Answers

Betrayed to the bone, I suffer and search
For simple answers.

No words come...only silence.

Where is Justice for the just and Love for the loving?
Where is Truth for the poet and Beauty for the artist?

No words come...only silence.

Why is Goodness imprisoned while Evil runs freely?
Why is Wealth honored while Health is ignored?

No words come...only silence.

Why are babies having babies while babies kill babies?
Why is Death living while Life is dying?

No words come...only silence.

Who is God and who is Satan?
Who am I and who are you?

No words come...only silence.

I implore you...speak!
Break this suffocating silence with your psalms of peace.

No words come...only silence.

Martin Becerra

The Beginning Of My Tomorrow

Here I'm in a twilight state, waiting for the sun to rise
For the dawn is surely breaking somewhere, beyond the skies.
There I'll live in God's own bright world, and see my Savior's face,
For there my life is beginning, because of His Love and Grace.
There'll be joy unspeakable, I'll lay my burdens down
Somewhere in Heaven where I may wear a Crown.
Its diamonds are the teardrops Christ shed on the earth below
Its rubies are the drops of blood that from His brow did flow.
And the sparkle of the halo, to encircle every face
Are reflections of our Savior's Love and His all enduring Grace.
There'll be singing, and praising, and happiness everywhere
The day I step in tomorrow in a land of love so fair.
My fears will be forgotten in the presence of God's Son
What a wonderful happy tomorrow when my life has just begun.

Teresa Mabel Campbell

Higher Ground

Begin at the end to let our love last.
For the time has come to leave what has past.
Your children, your family have come to your side.
So know we are here where life and death tied.
But in our memories you shall remain,
For in eternity we'll meet again.
Your short time here was a rainbow of life
The love you shed, your kids and wife.
Will remain for years to carry your name.
But know in your heart there was no shame.
Because you have life and without a sound,
you'll reach the place of a higher ground.

Mark C. Maurer Gregerson

"Moving Out"

How can you say that the time is here
for you to move out when you are so dear?
How do I watch as you clean out your cave
and throw out all the stuff that I'd want you to save?

How much will I cry when you can't see or hear?
I know you want this, that you've made clear.
How often will you call your mom on the phone
when you are moved out and living alone?

How will I keep my fingers from dialing your place
when days have gone by without sight of your face?
How short are the years since first of you were born
and now my heart is shattered and torn.

How hard will it be to watch as you go
when all in my being is screaming out "NO"?
How soon will I realize that this must be
that you have grown up but I just didn't see.

Linda Bevington

The Butterfly

The Butterfly, unlike me, is free.
Free to roam and to go, wherever his wings let him go.
Free to fly way up high, free to see all beauty.
He doesn't need music or TV. He's got the wind and breeze.
He's seen so much, that I haven't seen.
I want to spend just one day as him.

Nicole Herrington

Friends

Friends come,
Friends go,
Especially the ones you don't even know

Friends come,
friends go,
if they hurt you, you should let them know.

Friends come,
Friends go,
they might just leave you for some others,
more likely their long lost lovers.

When things get bad and maybe out of hand;
Keep this in mind,
And someday you will surely find.
A best friend who won't do this and I'll always
be kind in good times and bad.

Friends come,
friends go,
Especially the ones you think you know.

Kristen Hughes

Temple

No building has ever come into being as easily as did this temple
of friendship, love and feelings.
Obviously, the magnificent sharpness of its stones have come to
be of trust.
Eternities lasting hands reach out for the knowledge.
Barbaric mountains of friendship and caring keep it standing tall.

What is the grass that makes the sky beneath my feet?
Green fields and groves and I move higher and higher.
The unseen joy blossoms in the night.
The sleeping colors of dark and silent dreams.

I journey to life.
I find myself in a savage forest.

My fear is lost in the past.
The temple is there and I discover the love, good, happiness and
friendship.

In the temple I see things that are invisible to others.

Kjersten E. Ostrom

The Woods

I am lost in the cold, dark woods
Frightened by the eerie cries of the birds.
Wandering around the endless rows of trees
Keeping a watchful eye out for my enemies.
They'll be here very soon
They'll take me to a dark and musty room.
There they'll torture me and leave me to die
And there'll be no one around to hear my cries.
My feelings of pain and loss
Will stay there with me and rot.
My mind will start to slip away
My bones will shrivel and decay.
My heart will feel no more
I'll be a victim of torture.

Rayleen Gauthier

My Love

Eyes like steel that pierced my heart,
from a glance at the very start.
Oh, that I could only find
Peace within my mind,
My love.

Courage lacketh I, 'tis true,
to express the love I feel for you.
Concentration no longer do I possess
My thoughts and actions must redress
My love.

Hair as red as the light
of a Harvest Moon on an Autumn night.
Arms so strong and body lithe,
Oh, that I could steal one kiss,
My love.

A tear cascadeth down my cheek,
were it not that I was so meek.
To tell you of this love, I must,
or sink in the mire of loneliness' dust,
My love.

Lori-Ann R. Nienstedt

Freeland

Where is my African Moses? The one born to lead me
from bondage and oppression to my freedomland.
The land promised to me by God, and paid for with the blood of
my ancestors. From out of chaos and separate, it is written that
you my African Moses will redeem me, Africa.
To order, organisation and unity. A land rich with opportunities
and privileges you will make of me. Hail my African Moses, the
voice of the oppressed calleth thy name, to lead on, preach on,
give me a light so that I might follow. Shout through the
darkness, I will hear, make me know that you care, hold my
hand so that I will not fall. Bumpy and rocky the way may be,
dark and sometimes too bright for me to see, treacherous and
dangerous our journey to be, but in you my African guide lies all
my trust. With your great strength, wisdom and
knowledge lead me, show me the place where I will be free, to
grow, to learn, to develop and to become caretaker of my
inheritance from GOD. The Earth. Take me by the hand My
African redeemer and lead on, take me to my freedom land. A
place set aside especially for me, my promised land.
Take me to freeland.

R. O. King

Commitment

My love has asked me to refrain
from equating life with pain
My love has asked me to forget
the foundation onto which I was set
My love has asked me to believe
that which my mind cannot conceive
My love thinks I keep stalling for a power play
My heart wants to follow, but my fear leads me away

My belief asks me to accept
things I have not experienced yet
My faith asks me to understand
All the things that are out of my hand
My higher voice tells me that there is one light
and if I aim for its center I will always go right
But there dangles this mystery in front of my eyes -
Is the light hovering over this great compromise?

I think, someday, to remain intact
I will have to stop, thinking - and act

Michele D. Cohen

Work Ethic

One day upon review of just how I've spent my time
From home to school to work, the information climb

The origin of motivation - people doing what they do
This interest overwhelmed me; I had to share with you

Some thoughts on giving up, or sticking with the plan
Decisions made on values, a mere instant they may span

But how each final choice becomes our guiding rule
Is inspired long before one's enrollment into school.

A parent really does, you know, do more than just relate
Their own experiences, hoping that a clone they will create

No, the really fine ones instill curiosity and trust
Toward new, unknown discoveries and those as old as dust

With a steady hand of confidence, they lead us through the fray
Often without words or even motions to delay

Our personal experiences, so important to our growth
Developing personality-indeed, the value oath

Many goals and opportunities will present themselves en route
Toward a genuine work ethic that stands beyond dispute.

Thomas W. Sanders

Ma Ma Dah

When we were kids we called you this,
From our smiling, childish lips,

This special name we gave to you because we loved you dearly,
And now that you have passed, we will be reminded of it yearly,

Silkened hair about your face,
full of poise, love, and grace,

We grieved when your life slipped away,
And mourn your passing everyday,

Off to heaven you did fly,
To help the angels in the sky,

Although you're in a far away land,
One day we'll meet and touch your precious hands,

Ma Ma Dah How we miss you so,
Especially when the seasons come and go,

God sent you as our guardian angel for many, many years,
It hurts to think about you for it conjures up sweet, bitter tears,

Tears for you Ma Ma Dah because you are gone,
But we know you're in "Beulah Land" singing your favorite song,

Just to hear you sing one more time,
Would ease this sorrowful pain of mine.

Lucille K. White

Creation

On axis shall spin, first blue, green, than human.
From deep cold shall come warmth, dark's death, life's love forth.
Fire, fire shall breath heat, for comfort and length.
Red fabric around soul, gray matter to console.
Thought will not leave, even if desire thrives.
For yours is to prolong, together, not alone.
In harmony, not fight.
Till time to depart, then ancestors follow, till time to restart.
Creation begin.
Creation abound.
Creation maintain.
Creation in round.

Wayne J. Speranza

Comparsians

The bee may leave its sting - but the sweetness of honey lingers on..
From prickly thorns - grows the exquisite beauty of a rose.
From the unsightly cocoon - flutters the graceful butterfly.
From the rocks, the art of sculpture, statues, vases, walls and walks.
From the imperfection of the oyster — a lovely pearl.
From devastating storms — the calm and captivating rainbow.

From excruciating pains of birth — there appears a God-given life.
Relief — when burning fever breaks - and there appears a smile on baby's lips.
From endless hours of toil and labor - comes pay day,
From turmoil and worries of problems of the day - that seem to disappear on the morrow.
When all friends seem to forsake — there's "Ole Ship" wagging his tail
And more over, look up - there's God
From the blackest of sin - thru Christ - we can be washed as white as snow.
From death - life eternal.
Moral?
When we experience the bad - we can appreciate the good.

Mildred P. Patterson

Snowflakes

Snowflakes are falling
from steely gray skies,
wintertime is upon us again.
The birds have stopped chirping
till spring time is come,
and the still baron desolate silence descends.

Snowflakes appear to dance through the air,
like tiny prism specks in this wondrous fair.

Joy, fun and excitement it brings,
along with a quiet, charming,
panoramic, picturesque countryside scene.

This spectacular artistic display
to our eyes a delight,
is seen everywhere for all to enjoy
and send up a prayer,
"Thank you God".

Marolyn E. Baker

Poem Without A Name

The haunted eyes of injustice stare out at me
from the suffering hordes of humanity.
Black, White, Yellow—Christian, Jew or Pagan,
whatever color of belief,
They stare out and I look back and see their
naked grief.
What have they gone to deserve the fate of man's
inhumanity to man?
In the name of God we dare to say: 'I am right—
you are wrong
And I will put down as long as the power
is mine.
My god, your god, no god at all, what right have I
to put another beyond the call of personhood?
Where is that love that lets us share our work, our
play, our food and drink, our joy, our grief
Over all the world, until at last mankind knows:
LOVE IS ALL!

Mary Carnese

"Mother"

Mother was the one who kissed away my tears
From the time I was small, with many fears.
She was the one who held me with tender care
Til I felt secure, just knowing she was there.

Mother was the one who walked by my side
That first day of school, and, oh how I cried!
When the last bell rang at the end of the day,
I knew my dear mother was not far away.

It was Mother who took me to Sunday School
And taught me to live by the "Golden Rule."
She talked about Jesus, how he died on the cross,
And if I lived for Him, I would never be lost.

Mother's prayers followed me down through the years,
But I went my own way, ignoring her tears.
The day finally came when I recognized my need
Of the Savior I rejected and my Mother's pleas.

Making my way to the altar one night,
I met the Lord Jesus who made everything right.
I'm no longer the "Prodigal" who has to roam,
Because my Mother's prayers have led me home.

Ruth Rhoads

The Universal Classroom

We are all students and teachers.
From the tiniest baby, who shows us
the bliss of wonder;
And learn from us how to grow.
To children and teenagers, who scamper
and play, teaches us not to worry.
They learn love and respect.
To adults who show what they've
learned through experiences during
their life time.
And learn that life is precious in all forms.
And so we never cease being student and teacher.

Paul Seermon

Wisdom

Wisdom we gain for only a time on earth,
from the hour of conception to the moment of birth.

Wisdom granted by God through its mystery in the brain,
sent the first awareness of human sufferings of pain.

Wisdom, ah yes it's true, we need its living breath,
and all its intelligence, and teachings till our death.

Wisdom in our experiences, wisdom of what is right,
wisdom in strategy to survive throughout our life.

How could we live without Wisdom's strength of defense,
and protection through mere common sense.

Wisdom, oh how we deeply need its gift in thought,
for without its guidance in life, what have we got?

Rachel M. Sainato

To Love

I thought it would be easy to say
goodbye and not even cry,
I thought it would be easy to let your memory fly by.

I thought it would be easy to still be friends,
I never want our friendship to end, give me time, I'll be fine
I'll still love you even though your not mine.
I guess we'll just be friends until the end,
it's hard not to want you but it'll have to do even though it's
so easy to love you!

Nicole Michele Arendt

Where Are You

The oldies but goodies an old but good refrain, when we were young and full of love and hadn't felt life's pain.

Remember when we believed the skies were blue and the grass was green.
but learned that the sky had more colors than one, and the grass had thorns not easily seen.

As we grew we made mistake after mistake and desperately awaiting our first break.
The years have come and gone, along with the fears.

Doors were slammed and walls built from fears. Our real self's hidden deep down inside,
ego's built up to handle the roller coaster ride.

Soon we became some one else, who knows, to hide life's unfair, maybe brought on blows.

We can choose our own little worlds, then live out its course, then go onto the next world not lingering in remorse.

Just trying to get back, what was long ago lost, who knows in which world or at who's cost.
When the sky was blue and the grass was green and our souls were full of love and serene.

Then the roller coaster ride starts to descend, for the last world you live out towards the end.
You've aged a lifetime or more by now, and your ego turns to take a bow.

Don't lose your self worth or forget who you are, the reason why we're here, or why we're reaching for that star.

Don't forget you're soul inside in materialistic gain, or hide behind justification to feed the ego, so there's no pain.

Look deep inside and find the real you and the gift given to you from afar, that's where the blue skies and green grass lay, and where YOU are.

Pam Dewitt Norman

The Gathering

As I stand within a vision
gazing at the paths of decision-
I hear the voice of Ignorance proclaiming-
'Seek the truth! Choose the path of knowledge.'
Refraining-
Contemplating-I do not heed the words of a Fork
-ed Tongue.

If I choose-the choice of One way
perhaps the path of knowledge. To my dismay-
What I beheld-incomplete half-truths. Lies.
Lost forever the unknown. Ignorant of the un-chosen.
Realize-
I have been enclosed-subjected. Here, the truth- Lies
-Disguised.

I wander-not down the path of knowledge
nor do I carelessly seek another. Bridges-
Meld the paths before me-cautiously searching-
Crossing all-as times allows. Learning-growing.
Breaching-
Belief-obligations of decisions. Knowledge-truth-it's Everywhere
-Gathered.

Sandy McPherson

My Time On This Planet, With Her

Lying there above the sea,
Gazing with eyes closed, Heart pounding, Pictures swirling;
Remembering You...

The surf pounding its rhythmic beat,
Crashing, Roaring, Sea gulls flying;
I see You...

You appear to me in my dreams,
Haunting, Loving, Stirring my emotions;
I know You...

I long to see you,
Feel you, Bathe in your aura, Your magic;
You've trapped me...

My time is short,
The seasons pass; Time, like the sea, Marches, on, and on;
And still You're here...

In my Dreams...

Larry Godfrey

Love For Granted

As my lips caress the tear drops
Gently falling from your eyes
I'm so sorry for the pain I caused you
I hope you realize

As we both grow older we change in many ways
Life is a lesson in the passing of each day
So it's best if you remember
To hold the one you love dear.

So when you really need her
She will always be near
So if you take a moment
And reflect along the way
And don't take for granted
Your love will always stay

For love is like a flower
Left alone it will die
For love once lost forever
The question is always why

Lawrence J. Szopinski

Wanting To Give In

Holy man, being tempted, wanting to give in
Gets advice from crazy man, orange juice and gin
I can't stand it, crazy man, I don't know how to act
I'm not listening to reason, my heart has jumped the tracks
She's exciting beautiful, no secret or surprise
Fascinating history, she's been scandalized
Royal born and elegant, she's getting all dressed up
A whisper in the moonlight, her hair is all messed up
Frankie Valli, somewhere softly, sings, "My Eyes Adored You"
Though I never laid a hand on you, I just can't afford to
Crazy man, staring down, always thinking of her
The answer's very simple, holy man, do you love her?
I'll confess to anything, I could talk all day
It's only love, it's only love, it'll go away
Give all your money to the poor, and you can pray until
God will forgive you, but your wife never will

Tracy Guerra

The Drowning Day

So beautiful the sun burns my eyes; she's
glaring yet already yelling to hold on,
does she know?, to the man drowning
in blindness left with only
a pack of Camel Lights and an empty
Evian bottle in a Volkswagen Fox.
With the parking brake off he's
moving toward the glass structure of which she's
sliding down
giving each pane of glass
life,
but only for a moment;
with the drums beating she's yelling
to rise up to take her hand
and hold on tightly
for the world is cooling
and the glass is melting away from sight;
as the flood of blindness rises,
the postcard picture of life becomes night.

Oren Haker

Have You Ever?

Have you ever seen a birds eye,
glistening in the diamond sky?

Have you ever wondered how birds cry,
waiting for their mothers sigh?

Have you ever seen birds flap their wings,
over great big high trees?

Have you ever wondered how birds fly,
in raining, stormy, dark blue sky's?

Have you ever heard birds sing a beat,
with soft gentle little tweets?

Have you ever seen a bird soar so high,
in the great big diamond sky?

Kyra Lynn Lenert

Fade To Black

Shining stars speckle the clear night sky.
Glittering moonlight dances upon the sea.
A young man stands on a cliff so high,
Broken, miserable, lonely.

His raven black hair is tousled by the wind.
His delicate features are a mask of pain.
Not a soul walks upon the pale gray sand.
No one there would even know his name.

He stares for awhile at the rolling waves,
Hopelessly thinking of the love he seeks.
But now he knows he cannot be saved.
A single tear rolls down his cheek.

He steps to the edge.
There is no turning back.
The sea rushes to claim him . . .
Fade to black.

Sharon Canale

My People

I am the struggle and plight of my people.
I am the blood and tears of my race.
I am the night that casts its shadow over the world.
I am the epitome and definition of beauty.
I am the one who gives birth to kings.
I am the one who carries the struggles of my people.
I am...black,...women, a queen.

Roxanne Williams

A Dream Of A Day

Walking by the river pole in hand
God leads this little boy with the
old man
Down by the river he played in the sand
The old man cast in the running stream
life was just a dream

Generation gap was gone
They were having fun in the sun
A dream of a day had begun
It is time to live together and work
together as one

Each generation looking after and extending
a helping hand

Then the sun goes down the little boy takes
the old man's hand

The dream of a day has come to an end
But the generations gap has just begun.

Victorine Bradford Davis

Manhood

I cry as I see my son leaving,
Going out to face the world as a man,
Leaving his childhood behind him,
Willing to do what he can.

All grown up now, he leaves me,
So upright, so tall, and so strong,
Entering a world that is alien,
Hoping to right every wrong.

I'm crying with pride, and with grieving,
(As every mother well knows,)
Mixed emotions have now overcome me,
And, blindly, I wave as he goes.

Pride for the man he's become
As he strives to be all he can be.
Grief for the child I'm losing
As he goes, the world to see.

My mother's heart was touched by his presence
And memories I'll always hold dear.
While the man faces his future
The boy will always be near.

Nancy Linderman Buchanan

Sally

Sally was a
good friend! She
laughed, and played, and
did many things a seven
year old would do. When
ever I saw her it felt like I
could fly. She could always make
people laugh, and I'm sure that she
didn't have to try. One thing that she was
very fond of was flowers. She loved them more than
books, candy, and toys. She saw something in them
that no one else saw. She made sure that around
those flowers there were lots and lots of noise. There
was one flower that she liked best, but she couldn't
reach it because it was on the edge of a cliff behind a
railing, and no one wanted her to fall. The flower was
a special flower. It was a red rose. One
night she reached over to get the rose, and
over the cliff she fell! Why I wasn't there to
to help her I couldn't tell. I couldn't tell!

Mandy Harp

Wise Up

Do you know who I am? I am the descendant of
great and powerful Egyptian royalty.
I am the offspring of indestructible determination
and perseverance which were chained and bound
by the shackles of slavery. I am also the unpraised
soldier who fought to the death, so that the others
could be freed from those shackles. I am the one
who enriches the young minds of today with
literature and science and much more. I am a master
builder who constructs tremendous institutions.
With precision instruments I am the one who saves lives.
But with another precision instrument,
I am the one who brings pain and death within a blink of an eye.
I am also the merchant of addictive substances and deadly
remedies.
I am the extinction and savior of my own kind.
I am all of these, yet I am only one.
Do you know who I am? Yeah, you know.

Kendall Ivy

Spoiled Seeds Of Youth

The wind is brisk and stings my nose and throat as the
ground crunches beneath my shoes, all the ideal symptoms of
winter. As I walk, bleak hopelessness lies heavily on my
mind the pain in my heart lingers with brokenness and
sorrow. Forward I lumber on toward the sound of my blind
fate end in which I've traveled many times before, all for
the same reason all for the same fate, only to find myself
turning away for one reason or another. I think to myself
"This time it'll be different, this time I'm going to do it."
My destination was upon me quickly and so I slowly started my
stride across the beam that straddles the bed of my dark
angel to which I'll lie my lonely soul to rest. I gaze at
the murky stagnant waters that roll below me, while the wind
plays with my balance in acting the roles of good and evil
battling for my soul. As I stand there looking on into my
dark wet grave, my mind swims and ponders for reasons of why
and why not too. I sit down to gather my nerves, stand up,
and turn away. Not today, not alone, maybe tomorrow or the
next, but the sad truth is there will always be another time.

Shane M. Zavala

Mother Lore

A beautiful small ocelot on a branch above
guards her twins frolicking below
creatures of the jungle going about their daily routines
suddenly silently the killer is known

All live creatures glide slide burrow swim and run
the birds hide in a tree nearby instinct has gripped them in its fear
they know the hand of death is near
not a sound is heard not a movement seen

Danger to her cubs has overcome the mother ocelots fear
one short warning bark is sounded her fate is sealed
the killer man looks up and spots the mother frozen to the branch
in the silence which prevails two shots are heard
death has not missed its mark the mother ocelot falls
panic ensues as all living creatures rush to hide
a covey of birds with flapping wings and loud shrill cries
rise to the skies in flight
the killer as silently as he approached left
carrying a small carcass and two live cubs also doomed

natures bounty will not last
man must eventually pay for his killing past

Ruth Z. Becker

The Morning Jesus Come

A glow- so bright- so golden- not made by the rising sun.
Had filled the tiny chamber room, one day when Jesus come.
The nurse had called the Doctors in to check the frail form.
"It can't be long they whispered, "for Linda's going home."

"Please close the door" I ask them as they departed from the room.
It was time for morning worship with Jesus coming soon.
I took her hand and squeezed it, placed a kiss upon each cheek,
Called out her name for morning prayer, for comfort, I did seek.

Her black eyes opened to met mine as we voiced The Lords Prayer.
It was as if a thousand angels had accompanied Jesus there.
I held my darling daughter's hand, whispered 'you have suffered long"
"I love you so-I'll miss you here-but Christ has come to take you home."

It only took one moment, just one little breath away
My Lord had taken Linda's hand and taken her away.
I looked upon that frail form that I had watched her entire life.
I closed the lids of those black eyes and sat at the lifeless side.

Mary K. Willey

The Shadow Of Love

The weight of my heart
Hangs heavily in my chest
My soul aches for the warmth of your arms
I'm saddened by the sting of your words
Love should not be so painful
Words should not make me so sad
Why am I weeping?
Why do I seem to fail you?
Love must not fail!
The moon is looking at me
The stars seem to have faded away
I hear the crickets
They too, seem to be sad
Gone is the warmth of the sun
The night becomes the shadow of the day.

Mary Ann McCormack

An Indians Mountain

May the breezes from your mountain bring
happiness and laughter to those it touches.

May the sun that shines from its park
bring warmth and health to those who see
and feel its rays.

May the stars that fill the sky and surround
your mountain guide you home safely from
your hunt.

May the rains from your mountain help
to grow your corn; may those rains fill
your brook to grow trout for you and your
family.

May Manitou look favorably upon you
and give you strength and courage to teach
your family the ways of life and to provide
them with food and shelter — from your
mountain.

Larry Jubb Sr.

A Child

A child is many things,
happiness, love, hope, understanding,
and sometimes a tender smile.

A child is God's creation, he is like a
rainbow or a shining star from above.

A child is peace and joy in all our
lives, he lights up like a
candle, and reflects the love
of others.

A child is a blessing from God and
through him, he holds our
knowledge, dreams, and hopes
of tomorrow.

Mary Lou Oliver

A Mother's Love

Gentle in touch; a voice soft and calm
Happy expressions - warm inviting arms
A cheerful smile bright as sun rays
Sending forth hope on dull gloomy days
This is a mother's love.

A kindness that speaks - a patience that's rare
A sweetness and light; awareness and care
An ear that listens - the faintest voice hears
Eyes that see the tiniest tears
This is a mother's love.

A strength that excels - a protective shield
A helper, a sharer, a friend that's real
A deep devotion that comes from the heart
Is this a masterpiece of art?
This is a mother's love.

Sarah L. Glenn

Pathways

Every infant born to this world
Has a destiny which is of his own.
Every child grown has a fate
Whose future was by someone known.

Every child has charisma
Which gains a smile from adults.
Every youth displays behavior
That receives a frown or scowl.

As adults we mature
Make mistakes then reciprocate.
Looking for a brighter future
That doesn't end at our front gate.

As the infant born to this world
With his own destiny, future and fate.
We must leave this world for we are old
We must now cross the celestial gate.

Sylvia Cano

My Dad

My Dad is a wonderful man that's sometimes quite kind.
He lives for his work and his job stays on his mind.
He loves me dearly and through his eyes I can see,
he doesn't say a word or even tell this to me.
The things he do and the smile he show,
gives me all the reason to believe and know.
For he is the man that my mom chose to be,
the father of her children, four others plus me.
When I think of my dad my eyes start to glow,
and I thank God above for my dad and his love.

LaShaun Conaway

Factory Love

The boy I have in my mind
has a factory.
He makes gum in his factory.
He makes chocolate and fun things
in his factory.
He's been there many times
but can't tell me where it is.
He can't take me there
even if he wanted to.

When bursting with love — too much love for a little boy —
he says,
"You can come to my factory."
I love that boy when he says it me.
(You would be lucky if he said it to you.)

Last night when I covered the sleeping boy,
He whispered,
"You—can—come—to—my—factory."
The heart opens even when eyes are closed.

Phil Gneiting

The Question?

I find the dreams of yesterday
Have long since gone.
Now new ones take their place
Before each dawn arises.

Yet, I am glad to leave those dreams behind
For I am not the same today
But of a different mind.

I wanted love and joy and the rainbow's gold
Just like the fairy stories tell
And now I know one needs only
A small unsilenced bell
That tolls between two people
Whose souls perhaps can touch
A symphony of understanding
Is that asking very much?

M. Lerche

Personal Space

I woke up this morning left the comfort of my home
Have to earn that money on life's water I'm the foam
Lord so many people crowded on the bus
Everyone's impatient their all in a rush
Now I'm in a hurry have to catch a train
Lord so many people just like drops of rain
No room to move around no room to even breath
Yes! This is my stop, I'm so relieve, no personal space
If you ever wonder why we rush from home to work
Especially in the city where everyone's a jerk
At work I feel much better I know all the faces there
Not like on the street where there's only fear
Our personal space
Then when the day is over it's rush, rush, rush again
To get back to my sanctuary where everyone's a friend
Even when I'm on the streets there's little room to walk
Even on the bus and train there's little room to talk
When I get home at night I eat and then relax
throw off the pressures of the day TV, a book and I sit back
My personal space

Peter Collinsworth Caddle

You

Have you ever ached to be yourself?
Have you ever felt like you couldn't be you?
I have
Have you ever ached so bad,
That you finally said forget it,
I'm gonna be me?
I have
Have you ever been yourself,
And had some one frown at you?
I have
Have you ever wondered if it was even worth it to be you?
I haven't

Marla Duty

Albedrío

Did you not know you never make a choice?
Have you not learned your acts are not your own,
and all you do is at some higher voice
you must obey, although to you unknown?
Some smirking universal dramatist
hath writ your lines, for you to act and be,
your speeches fit the plot, or would desist;
Pierrot, you dance for them to laugh to see.

When you laughed yester eve, it was not you,
yours was a mirth ages ere then decreed,
and your regret, ordained too, had no need.
You were the spinning leaf the long wind blew.

Yet do not cease to cling, since you must fall.
That leaf best spins which waits. This is your all.

J. Kellogg Burnham

Untitled

I see him through a crowded room,
He comes to me at night.
He stays there in the darkness with me,
And awakens me at light.
I see him fading with all the faces,
I watch him disappear.
Every time I think I'm close enough,
My heart gives in to fear.
Every corner that I turn,
And each place that I hide -
He stands there looking the other way,
But kneeling at my side.
I see him at all our places,
Just the way we always were
But there's just one important difference,

Now I see him there with her.

Megan Esser

Jake The Snake

There once was a snake named Jake.
He found a bright purple rake.
He ate it because it smelled like a cake.
It gave him a terrible stomach ache.
He went to a doctor for his own sake.
The doctor told him what to take:
Two aspirin and a jump in a lake.
Jake thought "Oh give me a break".
Instead he made a chocolate shake.
He fell asleep like a big white snowflake.
And to this day, Jake won't awake.
That poor old snake named Jake.

Mandie Zollinger

You Little Dickens

God threw away the pattern when He made a girl like you.
He didn't want another girl to keep me in a stew.
You laugh at me when I'm in pain. I never can forget
How you double-up with laughter, when I'm in an awful fit.

I love you as my chauffeur, since my eyes are not the best,
But you take me spinning 'round the block as if I were a pest.
You are a little dickens; I can see it in your eyes,
But who else would know the difference when you catch me surprise.

You drove me silly-willie in a shopping spree one day.
We tried to get outside the store; Alas! who had to pay?
I love to get you things you need, instead of all those rings,
But you nearly drive me up the wall with many needles things.

You're funny in the store when you're looking for things to wear.
Your sudden glance of self-inspection is enough to make one stare.
You are charming, and I love you, as I always want to do;
But I really, really love you, because you are you.

Paul L. Conklin

Toast To The Bride By The Father Of The Groom

When a father first looks on the face of his son,
He dreams marvelous dreams for his life.
And high on the list of his hopes for the lad
Is the love of a wonderful wife.

A girl who'll inspire him seek noble goals,
And encourage him right from the start.
A mother who'll make any house a real home,
And bear children to gladden His heart.

A partner who'll laugh when he's happy and gay,
And console when he's hurt or he's sad.
A sweetheart who'll bring him the fullness of life
That his mother has brought to his dad.

Now I look at my son, and all of these dreams
I see in the girl at his side.
So, join me my friends, I propose you a toast,
"To Christy, Jon's beautiful bride!"

Royce M. Chambers

The Man Upstairs

When the man upstairs created the Earth
He felt we must know what it was worth,
So he gave us winter with its beautiful snow,
While we downstairs say, "please let it go!"

After this, he added Spring,
When our flowers would bloom and our birds would sing,
With our tulips and daffodils no winter to fear,
It's really the start of a brand new year,
Once again we can come outside
To say "hello", no more to hide.

It begins with Easter and a summer of fun,
He gave us so much, even His only Son.
Then doesn't it seem just a little bit fair,
All He asks is some time and a daily prayer
To show him for all that he has done,
The world downstairs he has really won.
So, on with your bonnets and bunnies, but say your prayers,
To the one it all comes from, "The Man Upstairs".

Shirley A. McGeough

Dr. Martin Luther King, Jr. — We Remember

Martin Luther King was a black man with a heart of gold.
He had a great dream which he told and told.

He dreamed we should live in peace and love,
And never more push or pull or shove.

King was a black man with a heart of gold.
He pleaded and preached to both young and old;

"Our ways must change, or this world will fold."
But some stubborn people wouldn't be sold.

King was a black man with a heart of gold;
But the bullet of hate stopped him cold.

Still his dream lives on in our land today.
We'll work and pray and find the right way

TO SHOW

Martin Luther King with his heart of gold
That his dream lives on in a bullet-proof mold.

Rose Cheroff

What Is To Come?

I see him sit and stare.
He has no concern for his care.
His family will come this Sunday,
He will have nothing to say.
For years it has been this way.
Do I fear this could be me on some somber year?
I at times can lose myself in his unknown fear.
Perhaps, he has decided to just sit and wait;
Wait for his last day on the planet.
He knows it is only a matter of time.
A matter of time till this is my line.
To await a visitor to come and endure my gloom.
Will I sit in a tiny drab room?
To linger onto life, to only give my family strife.
This is my fear, not of death, but, to be left to rest.
From one day to only be looked at as a guest.
No, death is not my fear today.
Today I am full of energy and youth.
Today my fear is of loneliness and despair.
What is to come?

Tammie R. Hughes

He Is There

When I climb the highest mountain
He is there
When I'm walking up the hillside
He is there
If on the highest peak I'm climbing,
In his arms I'm safely hiding
He is there
When I'm walking through the valley,
He is there
When I'm walking through the shadows
He is there
If I'm feeling insecure, his love makes me feel so sure
He is there
In the midst of tribulations
He is there
In most any situation, he is my inspiration'
He is there
When my life at last is ending, on his strength
I'll be depending
He'll be there.

Marjorie Wells

Eyes Of An Age That Is New

I live in a world of superheroes!

Daddy's hands create light!
He puts a small glass globe on the ceiling,
and with that he lights the whole world.

Uncle keeps a fearsome monster in thrall!
Vroom, vroom, it growls at us fiercely,
but he forces it to take us to the store.

Mother turns the course of immense floods!
They bubble and rise, higher, higher, menacing all life;
but she sends them seething down the laundry drain.

Brother travels awesome distances with his great stride!
Across oceans, mountain ranges, galaxies and undiscovered stairways
he moves faster than sound — sometimes carrying me along.

Someday I too will be a superhero.
I too will travel uncharted ways, turn the vast floods,
control heat, wind, light, water, sound, and all the world.

But since I'm going to be so busy as a superhero,
I think right now, while I still can,
I want to take a nap.

G. R. Snow

My Life's Spell

When the sunshine comes on, every beggar wakes up
He rests on his stick then wears his shirt of coat
before to gain the sidewalk
To hold out his hand the whole day long
Do not make fun of his pathetic situation
Do not laugh at him because that is not so
That he would have preferred to born
If he would buy House and car then would sing his
Wonderful life
Do not distrust him lady be nice to him
Comfort him just in saying a little good evening
Better than buy a dinner
Understand above all his complaints
Tomorrow I will be on the sidewalk
When I would hold out my hand to you
Please look at it with a smile
I will not demand another thing
Because the life will not be wonderful.

Richard Mata

The Great South African Leader

Mandella was a wonderful leader for South African blacks,
He risked his life to save their backs.
This great leader spoke up for his oppressed race,
His courage brought a ray of hope to their face.
He was brought up in poverty,
But still he dreamed of liberty.
This man fought against vicious Apartheid laws,
Which caused him to face incredible odds.
The whites did not at all like his ways,
They jailed him for many, many, days.
They put him inside a tiny cell,
And for 30 years there he dwell.
The food was moldy, cold, and stale,
And each day he prayed for mail.
After those long years passed, he was set free,
Then his supporters danced with glee.
He went back telling blacks their rights,
And they fought back with all their might.
Since he gave hope to all South African residents,
They honored Mandella by electing him their president.

Krishanu Sengupta

Gramma, You Got Pennies?

She has a little grandson who's almost—not quite—three;
He says just anything he wants—and says it quite distinctly.
He's been talking for some time now—and not just baby things;
And when he sees his grandma, his little voice sings,
"Gramma, you got pennies?"

He can be fascinated by a favorite toy or tune;
But either's soon forgotten when grandma comes into the room.
His eyes get big—his smile gets wide, and toys and tune are cast aside;
He runs to greet her—'cause he's sure, he can always get from her
Some bright and shiny pennies!

She digs into her pockets (where she made sure she hid them)
And brings out those precious pennies (she couldn't disappoint him!)
"Gramma! You got pennies!"

Isn't it amazing what these few cents can do?
Bring a squeal, a laugh, a hug, perhaps a juicy kiss or two!
It's hard to tell which one enjoys this ritual the most;
Grandma or her little boy—the one on which she dotes—
Who asks her each and every time she walks into the room
The question she is eager for (the one he gives up toy and tune for)
"Gramma, you got pennies?"

N. Jean Fergerson

"I Was Naked..."

The old man crawled across the road at a snail's pace.
He stopped only to rest his bandaged hands and tired knees he leaned upon.

Passing cars ignored him, like a dead cat or fallen tree limb.

I stopped. And thankfully, so did two others.
We all stood over the old man in the road. Two men, and me.
I touched him first.

He had to be eighty. His pants, saturated with rain and mud, had fallen to his ankles.
Sores on his legs oozed with puss. He could not stand. He had no shoes.

We carried him to his home—a soaked blanket under a tree with no leaves. We wanted to take him to a hospital or a shelter. I pleaded, but he said no, content to die.

The sun set enveloped us in an eerie blackness. It started to rain again. No one came. We were on our own.

His gnarled fingers began the crawl again.
He wanted to eat and his dinner was in the garbage can across the road. Our hearts wrenched. And so we began. One man gave him sweatpants, the other man, a blanket. I offered my letterman's jacket. I wanted to take him home. What right did I have to leave the old man this way? But he looked up at me, put his crumpled hand on mine and whispered "thank you." I stopped by the next day with lunch, and the next. And the next day he was gone. I don't know where the letterman's jacket, the sweatpants, or the blanket went. I do know he died, we cared, and we learned. I know his life had meaning.

Malia M. Zimmerman

"Making It Right"

When I was a girl I wanted a horse.
I begged my dad every weekend,
this was my only chance because of divorce.
He said it was too much money to spend.

Now my dad is 80 and I'm 47.
He decided to buy me a lovely llama,
hoping this will send him to heaven.
I hope it does and ends this drama!

Tina Jacobs

The Pain Of Love

This pain is not something physical, but it never heals
He tells me that he loves me
If this truly is love, I never want to be in love again
He couldn't possibly love me, he keeps hurting me
His blade has slowly been digging into me and now it is tearing into my heart
What type of person will I be when he steals my shredded heart?
I have no shield to block him, for love is my pain as it is his weapon
Does he see the blade that he tears me with, or is it accidental?
Does he love me as I love him?
Is this how it will always be?
I am hurt, in pain, and it will not stop
Why, what have I done?
My questions continue to haunt me, while his blade continues to tear into me
My heart is dying, I feel as though it should be me
I am in pain that can never be healed, I doubt it ever will...

Tracey Allen

Reflections Of A Mother

I shined my son's shoes today
He was having his first picture taken
All soft and sweet and innocent....one month old

I shined my son's shoes today
His first Christmas play
Joseph, husband of mary....four years old

I shined my son's shoes today
First day of school
Shiny little face, excited, scared....six years old

I shined my son's shoes today
Sweetheart banquet and
Prettiest girl in church....thirteen years old

I shined my son's shoes today
High school graduation, exhilarating
Becoming a man, life waited....eighteen years old

I polished my son's boots today
Saudi Arabia, the 155th regiment
Guns, tanks, desert....nineteen years old

Virginia R. Saulters

Untitled

I had a Grandfather, he was so great;
He was infected with cancer we all did hate.
For three years, he put up a fight;
He fought so hard he could barely sleep at night.

He lay in our house four long weeks;
The smell of death, Oh! how it reeks.
We gave him medicine, upon medicine to relieve the pain;
His eyes cried out to us, "Please not again."

The priest, he came to spread God's light;
We ask dear Lord forgiveness tonight.
The sign of the cross in oil was marked;
The soul was readied to disembark.

The house was filled with sounds of death;
My poor Grandfather, struggled for every last breath.
As I stood there watching, panic filled his eyes;
I tried so hard to muffle my cries.

The entity of this life I had known was gone;
But hark! look to the heavens, rebirth a new dawn.
With a smile on his face and peace in his soul;
After sixty-eight years, he had met his GOAL.

Lana K. Kirby

A Happy Ending

He wasn't kind — but I said to myself, I love him — I lied
He was manipulative, abusive, insensitive
But where was I to go
It was the sixties, with two small children and no day care
I was dependent
If only he said he loved me
Again I lied
He was nice to everyone — except his family
He was an obsessive compulsive
I went to therapy

Then twenty-three years later, I met a friend —
I was food shopping — we talked and talked and said goodbye
Then one day, I got a phone call
How could I
I hated myself, but I did
Many years later
A new love — A new life,
A new marriage
And a very happy ending

Rose Wertheim

A Chain Gang

Listen to the thumping beat.
Hear the weary tread of feet.
Endless lines of chained men.
Working in a prison pen.

Toiling all the live long day.
Bodies bent in a weary way.
Striving to break all rocks by hand.
Eyes staring bleakly at the barren land.

A guard's whistle shrills for them to stop.
Sledges from there weary hands do drop.
In an endless line they form.
Chains rustling like a gathering storm.

Fed and shackled from their chains.
To the cells they march in vain.
Listening to the cell door click.
Vast myriads of eyes do flick.

Turning then to bunks against the wall.
Each man upon his bunk does fall.
To wait the coming of another day.
Slowly finding out, that crime doesn't pay.

Tracy Mulvey

The Death Of A Friend

There is nothing in this world that hurts so much, that stings my heart and bruises my soul, as a death of a long time friend.

All the hours of memories flood through my mind as I realize what a tremendous part of my life this good friend was, and now I must go on without him.

I, first had a friend die a long time ago.
I decided right then this part of life simply was too difficult to bear, and by any reasoning simply not fair.

Because death is so final and it hurts so much,
most other people will finally let this feeling go.

I simply refuse to forget my friend and I will not let go.
I keep him alive in my head, I keep him close to my heart, and next to my soul.

I often recall the things my friend said,
how my friend looked when he laughed or just smiled.
I'll never forget what he stood for, how hard he worked from morning till night, and all the fun that we had.

I still don't understand death, and probably few people do.
I do know what it is to have a great loss. One of the greatest losses you will be asked to bear in this life is the death of a friend.

Russell R. Wilson

The Ride

Chrome flashes and explodes with the sun's rays.
Heat rises up from iron heads to dissipate on faded denim.
Each pulse from the motor thunders in the ear and combines with the gushing wind, channeling the mind to some distant realm within itself.
The smells of oil, exhaust, and black top braze the nostrils
as countryside vanishes as quickly as it appears.
No fear is felt as you fly straddled across this beast
of painted steel and polished chrome.
You bravely ride this demon with all the content of knowing
that it is finely tuned and caged within iron cases.
Its only means of escape are the rear wheel and two inch drags.
A feeling tickles your insides as you hold the throttle like a leash and whip it another hard lick!

Michael L. McDonald

The Dancing Girls' Parade

She sways and swings through autumn leaves,
Her dance is like no other.
Although alone she is pleased,
No one is to disturb her.
Colored leaves prance and dance,
Brightness protects her from their glance.
Wind moves her hair and chills her frame,
Don't stop, keep dancing, the wind remains.
Others come with their moans and groans,
Ridiculing with laughter and agonizing pain.
For they don't know the essence of prostration.
She can get them through looking sweet,
For they don't know the dancing girls defeat.
For she has angel potential
Yet unknowingly demons persuade.
Is she good? Is she bad?
Does God surround her? Does Santa destroy her?
Now on a pedestal, her eyes display emotions like no other.
She continues to sway while the leaves abide their parade,
Don't touch her. Don't talk to her. Alone she must remain.

Laura Elizabeth Parker

Passing

Grandpa leans back in his chair with ghosts glued to his eyes.
Her form contorted and hair of gray, Grandma mutters a sigh.

The air is resonant with silence - musty, thick and deep.
Grandma blurts, "What'd say Henry?" But Grandpa's fast asleep.

But they speak in passing - passing - passing in the day.
Saying things that no one hears in their own passing way.

Grandma stands for God knows what and crumples to the floor.
Grandpa startles awake thinking she can't take much more.

Stooped, Grandpa shuffles to her side and does what he must do.
She thinks the old man will hurt himself. And he thinks she will too.

Their thoughts are passing - passing - passing in the day.
Trading thoughts that only they hear in their own passing way.

Grandpa utters to himself, "This may just be it."
He fumbles for the pouch of Red Man and cocks his head to spit.

Grandma is in the bed at the community hospital - "Not so good."
In death she will be comfortable. Grandpa's tears are understood.

And they'll die by passing - passing - passing from this day.
Death is the savior that only they know as they pass away.

Richard Wirtz

Elisa

Her eyes were from the deep blue sea
Her hair was sprinkled with gold
But her true beauty you could not see
For it was hidden in her soul

Her faith in God was much like Joseph's
Strong and trusting she lived her life
She was so young with much to live for
Someone's mother, daughter, sister, and wife

She touched my hand one Sunday morn
"Peace be with you", she prayed
I don't remember what I said
I turned my head, I was afraid

To see her body destroyed by cancer
No more her hair of gold
But her faith was stronger than her bones
It could never touch her soul

She now lies in peace with God
With hair of gold and eyes so blue
I think of her on Sunday morn
And pray for peace for you

Trudy Hebert

Angel In Flight

I remember the way she used to smile,
her kind and gentle touch.

She had a heart of gold that was full of love,
I've never known anyone as such.

I remember the way she used to laugh,
her funny but simple way.

She had the strength of steel-the touch of silk,
She was a refreshing as a breezy day.

I remember the way she left the earth, it
was as silent as a winter cold night.

She'll always be loved and always be missed,
I can see the Angel in flight.

Steven C. Owens

Raggedy Ann

When I was three I had a doll
Her name - Raggedy Ann.
My mother placed her on my pillow
After she finished making my bed.

Raggedy Ann was a
Treasure, Hero, and Friend.

We had many quaint adventures.
She braved the odds with few defenses,
But she needed none.
We would stick together for whatever
Needed done.

I still have Raggedy Ann, but now
I am twenty - three.
She still has a place in my home -
On a bench in the living room, instead of
The pillow on my bed.

I am saving my doll
To pass on down the line,
So Raggedy Ann can be a treasure
For the child of mine.

Lori McAllen

The Angel Within

Inside all of us, there lies an Angel within.
Her or she, it matters not;
The Angel is where we all begin.
God has instructed our Angel to serve and protect.
But, it is up to us to heed Its advice.
For if we are blind to Its teachings,
We have only ourselves to blame in retrospect.
Sometimes we may not like what It says,
Because the truth often hurts.
Yet, if we remember the Angel's purpose,
The wounds heal quickly,
And our Protector helps change our ways.
Listen to the voice within,
And when you next look in the mirror,
The Angel will be smiling back,
No longer confined within.

Kerri L. Senzapaura

Welcome, Gia!

A pretty young woman came into our lives;
her sense of humor caught all by surprise.
How happy she made our handsome young man.
She worked and she worked 'til she had him in hand.

Sheer radiant joy is now what she displays
as she starts this new life - a wondrous maze.
May the rough spots encountered along life's way
bring you closer together everyday.

In silk and pearls at the altar she'll stand
and soon he will place the gold wedding band.
A sweet symbol of love they feel so strong,
may it serve as a bond a life-time long.

If tears flow today, I won't try to hide
'cause they come from my heart - way deep inside.
For happiness we pray with all of our might.
We welcome you now to our circle so tight!

Marky Hooper

Little Marita Kay

Little Marita Kay has hair like golden honey;
Her smile could charm the millionaire from his money.
She possesses eyes like blueberry milk;
Her bronze skin is as smooth as china silk.

Little Marita Kay dances like Ginger Rogers;
With her pitching arm, she could play for the Dodgers.
She has the voice of an angel and a face to match.
That little girl will make a fine catch!

Little Marita Kay is as sweet as sugar,
Though some days she acts like Mommy's little bugger.
Her temper is like that of a Tasmanian Devil,
But normally, her head is very level.

Little Marita Kay is as cute as a button.
I admit, when it comes to spoiling, I'm a glutton.
That little darling is only four years old.
And everybody loves her, if the truth must be told!

Mary Sills

Drifting

As you drift back home out of the skies
Here are a few things that may meet your eyes.
The street or all worn.
The side walks all bent.
The homes all lean from a life well spent.
A familiar face may be hard to be found.
To see a old name, one may haft to look upon the ground.
For it only then that one will realize, that one spent a long time drifting in the skies.

Warren N. Whitworth (Ol, Sarg)

Untitled

Inside walls she's seen for years.
Her vision went from metallic yellow to grey
And the time is stretching out reaching far beyond reality.
She can make those walls anything
But she doesn't get a prize for life or for enhancing life
And now she's bitter inside those walls
time won't drag her out of her grey room...
her grey state of mind
let me whisper...why?
you're old now lover...soft rotting skin
See me! Do you see me?
In your grey room and your grey state of mind.
look, see...I bet you'll like my yellow
My colors, my shining faces, odd faces, familiar faces, dead faces
grey faces. Wise dead and grey. Grey bodies matching the grey sky.
Your breath singing soft rotting flesh.
You whisper with your grey lips: "Love my flesh, forget me now."
Metal fields. Rust and the color grey.
Winds blowing rusting metal shards.
Metal showers bring steel flowers.

Rachel Krumpelman

Pondering A Pup

A pup is . . . It's plain to see
He's not a dog, though he tries to be.
He has this kind of 'I love you',
That emanates from eyes so blue.
He snuffs and sneezes, barks and growls,
Depletes our rolls of paper towels.
He drags our slippers and when he bites
Each foe succumbs with whom he fights.
Perpetual food isn't adequate,
It is for me who's stepped in it.
And when he tires, as puppies will
It seems I'm destined to just stand still
For he stalks and staggers 'til we meet,
Then lays his bulk across my feet.
What is this winsome, charming Pup?
I never fail to pick him up.
He's God's design, I must concede,
Yet, he's everything I didn't need.

Sylvia Passinault

"Santa Cares"

Santa is amongst us each day,
he's the good things we are in every way.

He's love, he's patience, he's understanding too,
he's the kindness in all that we say, and we do.

T'is a mystical, magical time of the year,
warmth and good tidings are abundantly clear.

The spirit arrives long before him,
awakened in all, throughout the year dim.

He arrives when all is quite and still,
he has a big order, many wishes to fill.

Children are dreaming, God's creatures await,
he spreads Christmas joy at a wondrous rate.

There is only one gift, he'd like in return,
the lesson of caring, we all want to learn.

To hold his message in your heart ever dear,
until his visit is once again near.

Jesus lives in Santa, and all great and small,
with peace and serenity, God bless us all.

Laurie J. Hurst

Untitled

The dishevelled figure huddled beside the park bench
Hiding from the cold, covered with wet cardboard.

His watery eyes tried to catch the attention
Of every man who walked the park;
Someone who could help him.
The paper cup was placed far enough.

In his furtive search
His eyes passed quickly past me
As he turned to look for anyone else.

I walked up to him
And placed in his palm the money I had.
He lifted his eyes as if to thank me;
I could see the surprise in them.

He drank in my appearance, the color of my skin;
I walked away with a happy heart.

Sheby Joy

A Homeless Man

There's a Homeless Man that lives on the street.
His clothes are very soiled and he begs for food to eat!
Somehow the Lord has directed me to give to this man.
I've often wonder, why him Lord? His odor I can hardly stand.
But for whatever reason to him I must give. After all he is human. Yes, he has a right to live!
Whenever I give to this man, something comes back to me!
It's usually within the hour, it maybe two, it's never been three! But I strongly feel there's a message for me.
The Lord is saying, "give my child!" It comes right back to thee!
I thought, I'll share this experience. There maybe a message for YOU!
You may see a Homeless Soul and, You'll know what to do!

Sharon Anita Jackson

No Toys For Luke

He was not yet six in eighteen-ninety-one
His father gave to him a plow with a low rung

He farmed for three years until he was nine
Then in a cotton mill he was doing just fine

For fifty-nine years he was a good as his name
He retired at sixty-five yet weak and nearly lame

He watched the soap stars for the rest of his life
And fretted if some had more than one living wife

His grandson was Donald so we all called him Duck
He came for a visit with his little red truck

Paw Paw it's your birthday I want you to have this
As he gave up his truck and planted a kiss

Well Duck he came back that very next day
I came to get my truck then I'll be on my way

But that was for my birthday the old man cried
Yet how he said it you couldn't say he had lied

Your birthday was yesterday and now it's all gone
I'm taking my little truck with me back home

At seventy-five his tomorrows went in with his past
There were no toys for Luke from the first until the last

Sammy S. Lee

Death By Dignity

I see him walk the path every day.
His legs are stiff, but not because of play.
Each movement that he makes I hear him sigh
From pain he finds he cannot keep inside.

His eyes seem tranced, yet I can see a tear.
The smile on his face can't hide his fear.
Yet everyone would like him to be strong,
To help relieve the sadness when he's gone.

But wouldn't he just love to scream and cry
And ask himself the simple question, why?
Shouldn't he feel free to curse this place
Where death's the only thing he's left to face.

It doesn't mean he's lost his will to live.
Just that he cannot find the strength to give.
His fortune told, he'd rather not delay,
But die as he has lived, in his own way.

Kim Bazaldua

The Way I See Him

His eyes are a blue never seen before.
His lips are curved and round.
His beard is long and curly.
His face is beautifully shaped.
His body is well built.
His skin has no color.

He looks on the inside not the outside.
He speaks wisdom, truth, and honesty.
He teaches love, joy, peace, patience.
He cares for the sick and broken hearted.
He healed the lame and made the blind
to see.

He is seen by few and adored by many
He loves those who love Him.
He cries for our sins.
He is crowed Prince The King.
He is my Lord, God, and savior Jesus
Christ The King.

Valencia Spooner

His Love

His love knows no boundaries,
His love grows in leaps and bounds,
His love is always waiting for us to come
to Him!

His love knows no hate,
His love accepts everyone,
His love is always waiting for us to come
to Him!

His love knows no color,
His love only sees inside our hearts,
His love is always waiting for us to come
to Him!

His love knows only love,
His love knows only caring,
His love knows only sharing,
His love knows all, it comes from above,

His love is always waiting for us
to come to Him!

Renate Wymiarkiewicz

Hugs And Kisses

He brushes his lips across our new born baby's face
Holds him tightly to his chest
Soon he is changing a diaper filled to the brim
Laughing at what a mess was made
Puts an over sided finger into a tiny fist
Look how strong he is man
Tears are welling in my heart
Mother said: When he was a babe
Not one diaper or bath water did father bring
Was always to busy had to see a friend
time passes in the wink of an eye
Missing hugs and kisses cannot be denied

Rose Moccia

Depression

Coming home to find an empty house with no love,
Hoping for someone to say the cheery words "Hello"
But only to discover how quickly time's passing you by:
Leaving you alone in your solitude, with spirits low.

Coming home to find an old friend looking sad,
Trying to lift her spirits with companionship,
But only to find reason for her sadness is terminal,
Soon leaving behind only memories of our friendship.

Coming home to find traces of another woman,
Perfume lingering in the air, the scent not mine,
The breaking of my heart brings tears to my eyes,
Recognizing unfaithfulness and all of its signs.

Michele R. Bryson

Astronomy

I sense that I am a dirigible world.
Hovering over an occasional football game,
Or Siberia.
Avoiding moorings.
Orthodox moorings.

Galileo, and Sagan
Caught glimpses of me
Dancing,
Through telescopes.
"Curious sunspot," said they.

But what do they know
Of
Dirigible worlds?

Keith Sjosten

Why Me

The day was so perfect that no one could tell,
How a father could put a daughter through so much hell.
They spent the day together and she loved him so dear,
She never would've guessed that her love would turn fear.
As they returned home to gather with friends,
Because they all were so close he need not pretend.
He had been drinking and now his tempers gone mad,
The violence started and you'd think he'd feel bad.
Then he drew back his hand and a slap to the face,
It not only brought sorrow but fear and disgrace.
After the violence the yelling began,
And the friends never saw this side of the man.
As some time had passed and the police had come,
She thought her night of horror would finally be done.
There were no charges pressed and she left with a friend,
That was the sure sign that her terror would end.
It's been almost five months and Christmas has passed,
I guess this father and daughter just didn't last.

Shirron Kemp

Salute To Stephen Decatur

America with your heart to share
How long will you be host?
How long will you be first one there,
When help is needed most?

Everything must end sometime—
The good die young they say—
But may you prove the myth untrue
That hints an errant day.

And like a ship that sails the stars
Before your journey ends
May you touch each goal your heart desires
And have a million friends.

The archipelago's we safely guard,
There's envy and there's hate
There are people 'cross the waters
Who only lie in wait.

America, I must warn you now
If you will understand
There are people who say they want your trade,
But, they want your home and land.

William Wallace Godsey

Sisterly Love

There are no words on Earth to show
How much we love you, and we want you to know
We are so sorry for all that's happened to you,
And all the sad things your whole life through.

With "Christ's" help, you will overcome!
We pray that soon your health you have won.
"CHRIST" I KNOW IS holding your hand;
And will guide you daily through this land.

NEVER forget How much we CARE
And if you need us: We will be there!
You are of US a very big part,
And always very close to our heart!

Marjorie Evelyn Clayton

Childhood Memories

I remember as a child, all the fun we used to have,
How we ran and sang and laughed until the end of day.
We had a lot of childhood dreams, that never did come true,
And every time I think of you it makes me Oh so Blue.

I remember every summer, when it was oh so hot,
We'd fill a tub of water and swim in it a lot.
We spent a lot of time in the backyard in the shade,
Looking at the trees and wondering how things were made.

I remember one day, we found a nest of eggs,
It was hidden in the bushes next to the sticky hedge.
We took it in the house and hid it in the drawer,
And when your Mother found it, oh how she really roared.

I have a lot of memories, of you and I together,
But they are only memories, that I will have forever.
You were killed in 1965, when we were only ten,
And I will miss you every day, until we meet again.

I'm looking forward to seeing you Sissy, so much you wouldn't know.
But I know that you will know me, no matter how much I've grown.
For no matter how many years have come between us, we'll
never grow apart,
For a love like ours so deep, so strong, is always in the heart.

Lana Newman

"A Word From The Wise"

There was a time in my life I did not understand,
how years of experience came first hand,
I listened to few and did things on my own,
and ignored the advice of those life had shown.

When young, I needed no one, I felt no shame,
When things went wrong, other people I blamed.
I faulted my teachers, my parents, and even my kids,
I blamed everyone else for the things I did.

But all of a sudden an adult I became,
and my viewpoints and feelings were not the same.
I looked at my life and the paths I had gone,
I had to swallow my pride and admit I was wrong.

I started to ponder if lessons were learned,
why did I continue to make the wrong turn?
Should I choose a path on my own or just sit and wait,
and let someone much bigger than I lead me straight.

I chose to wait and the lesson I learned,
is we are given choices in life at every turn,
But it's the wise who will wait and think things through,
and will become wiser with patience in all he might do.

Susan S. Ward

Spirit Of The Wolf

As he looks out into the vast stillness of the valley, the wind howls like a long lost spirit wisping right through him just as if he wasn't there at all. It thrashes and screams like a determined animal fighting in fear and anger.

It starts to snow, slowly at first then faster, heavier, like a blanket of frozen clouds, fallen.

His mate comes out to stand by him. She stands with her head held high, independent, but she needs him just the same. She is mysterious yet beautiful.

A gunshot rings out like thunder echoing through the valley so swiftly that all he sees is her fall.

He kneels before her, he raises his head to the moon and howls his anguish, anger and sadness.

Another gunshot, the hunters are pleased but the cubs still cry for their mother.

Shanna Fuller

Wedding Card For A Friend

Candles flicker soberly, as if in time with that obscure,
Hushed prelude.
Black shoes slip silently past and courteously turn their wearer,
Guiding the Dearly Beloved to their places.

Clasped tightly beneath wan smiles, nosegays slowly parade by
In solemn cadence.
Yet I remain,
Mindful of my own role in the occasion.

Those who flank her, I suspect,
Have never lost to her at hopscotch.
Yet there they stand, smartly stamped in triplicate satin,
Beyond the role of spectator.

It's doubtful that any one of them ever breathed life with her
Into blank-faced, soft-limbed baby dolls.
Who among them, I wondered,
Plotted grand schemes with her amid the chinaberry branches?

A closed bud drops from its bridal berth, forgotten.
And I, with nary a hint of realization upon my countenance,
Pocket it.
For time runs quickly from those who hold it loosely.

Lee Ann Giles

The Beauty Of The Park

When I go to take my walk in the park
I always get a peaceful feeling inside me
The park is the best place to be
When you want to pass the time away

I can always think of the many wonderful things
That I can see around me when I am at the park
It clears my stressful mind and body
When I stop at the park and study

I bring my children to the park to play
And spend time with me or just lay
Under the sun in the summertime
Or go for a stroll in the park at wintertime

I love the park especially early in the morning
Because it is very quiet and serene
I am able to appreciate all the good things
That God has blessed me with when I am at the park

I am truly grateful to the people
Who made it possible for me to enjoy the park
And keep it safe for people like you and me.

Marizol Talmadge

Come And Go

I am a person who made the sun come and go.
I am a person who made stars shine.
I am a person who sang with birds and danced with deer.
I am somebody.

I am a person who made the moon smile.
I am a person who made the sky blue.
I am a person who made the dawn shine and the night glow.
I am somebody

I am a person who made my friend the clouds cry, so the land could be fed, for its thirst was high.
I am a person who made rainbows come so birds would have a path home.
I am a person who made coyotes howl for a glorious song.
I am somebody.

I am a person who cried for days and days because clouds would not cry to make food for the land.
I am a person who watched time come and go and water run and flow.
I am somebody.

I did so many things and now I walk slow and see, feel, and hear all of my accomplishments.

I am someone, someone who followed the sun. Everyone will.

They will....... Come and go.

Lauren Mitchell

Reflections Of A Father

A father in need is a father indeed.
I am here my father, I am with you,
A reflection I see, my reflection is he.
It's a child I see slipping and sliding.
A boy I see cowering and crying.
A childhood shortened, vengeance is reaped.
A boy is a man, the cycle complete.
Your eyes are reaching, searching, they study me.
Your legacy is imported, oh my soulful heart.
A father in need was my father indeed.

Kathleen M. Neumann

Child

I am from you, and the love you shared
I am the creation, of two that cared

An innocent child, in a world full of hate.
I must be protected, not left for fate

I must be guided, during each of my days
I must be taught, and shown the way

I am the future, you are the past
So teach me well, to make us last

I am willing of you, so be willing of me
You are my eyes, so teach me to see

Cause I am of you, and you are of me

Mike Black

Untitled

I am the last of a wild breed that believes in love
I am the one who sits breathless before the sun and weak before the rain
I am the one who flinches at the sound of a child's cry and weeps at the end of the day

I am your friend
I am your listener
I am your strength

I will defend my rights by defending yours
I will prosecute those who refuse to look, refuse to hear, refuse to think
I will hold up the columns of truth if they begin to fall

I am the small girl who compares the different shades of the grass she sits on
I am the woman who walks fearless among the tallest buildings
I am the oldest woman alive who still have has a sparkle in her eye

I am the seeker
the learner
the one who asks the question
why?

Theresa Duncan

Listen

I stand before you with my hopes and my fears
I bring to you my laughter and my tears
I give to you my youth and my years
I bare and I share all your
troubles and cares
I fear loneliness, rejection and
stares
But life is challenge with
many failures and dares
For God has blessed me with you
as my wife
By his gift he has changed my
entire life
For you and our children have
made up for my strife
And grand children too, what
more can I ask of my beautiful wife
I know what I will do
I will go on life's journey forever
in love with you.

Robert J. Laskos

Time For A Change

I bring death and destruction for frivolous gain
I build great incinerators to destroy my remains
I overrun countries and governments for power
I can turn a cool rain into a nuclear shower
I am politics, technology and ideology
I am one in the same when it comes to biology
I am just another blank face
For I am the great human race.

Keith B. Olds

One Sadness That Happened Before

I wish I could say the words to take your pain away.
I can hear it now, I can hear you say,
"I'm really okay. I just want to be left alone today."
I know you do, and I won't stay.
I just thought maybe I could help in some way.
Please don't hurt and don't cast away.
You mean so much to me, I really want you to stay.

So many lives at stake, in so many ways.
They want you near to play, so don't take your own life away.
I know it's not good and I've had such days, but you've got to realize:
All in time, it will be fine.

We are one, you and I. You are my protector and my solid objector.
The world is mean, the world is sad.
I don't want to go at it alone, it would be bad.

We had dreamed of being together and dying right next to each other.
Please promise that you'll always be there for me?
Be there to heal my skinned knee.
You are my one and only. I want you here with me, I want you happy.
Because life is worth a lot more than one sadness that happened before

Ruth Brooks

"I'll Stay"

I can see the stars and stripes give rise to every dawn
I can proudly hail its colors and the battles it's won
When in the gleam of twilight somber skies my flag is gone
- to rest and to rise another dawn.

Star Spangled Banner in your red, white and blue
You are my country - my life is part of you.
America - ring your bell of Liberty...
And tell all the world that all people should be free.

Free to say the things and thoughts that others dare not say
Free to pray to God in any religion - in anyway
Free to choose the one who'll lead this nation on its way
- For these Freedoms in my country - "I'll stay"!

Michael Zukowski

'Till Always

How long will I love you?
I can't count that high.

I'll love you 'till all of the oceans run dry....
'Till fish cannot swim and birds cannot fly...
And the soft pillow clouds climb down from the sky.

I'll love you 'till all the earth washes away...
'Till the sun shines all night and stars sparkle all day...
And the Man in the Moon bows his head down pray.

I'll love you 'till shadows dance alone in the air...
'Till the coldest day ever is sunny and fair...
And ears cannot listen and hearts cannot care.

I'll love you 'till always, and this, you will see...
I'll love you forever..... throughout eternity.

Sharlynn R. Baker

Poem For A Nuclear Age

The ego is so harsh and clanging, like the sound of iron banging
I can't recall a time when it was not, yet industry not long ago begot
Now there are so many, unrestricted uses
Of natural elements by mans' greedy abuses

A mass of material goods unfurled, separates man from the spiritual
world
The consumer consumes, the economy cons...
Just look around, every Thing that you find
Is the manifest thought from a persons' mind

Congress is incongruous, leaders are misleading
Newspapers sensationalize stories we are reading
Business people gather-up opinions in their heads
With no one but each other to impress and not the Feds

The people want the leaders to lead, but Democracy means they should
follow
Citizens taking initiative is a time-pill masses can't swallow
Divorcees in their news vacuums, struggling for survival
Romantic famines in their beds cry for love's revival

When God created the heavens and earth, he didn't pollute or destroy
for its birth
It's man who has created industrial waste! Man says, "God is Dead"
...forgotten in haste!

Laura Drewes

Wilderness Pond

As I am walking through gigantic trees and luxurious ferns in a forest,
I come across a lively little pond.
I sit at the pond's edge quietly absorbing the world around me.
I look and see delicate birds taking flight, small squirrels pouncing
upon each other,
and tracks of deer who once drank from the water's edge.
I listen to the melody of the young birds, to the squirrels chirping
in playful delight,
and to a quiet trickle of a small creek joining the lively pond.
I lean over to look at my reflections and see myself surrounded by
the harmony of this wilderness.
Then before I realize what has happened it seems as though I am
engulfed by the reflection.
I look around me and see that the gigantic trees have vanished and I
am startled to see my thoughts running freely in the smokey cinders
of a newly open field.
I notice my family, my friends, my home and all that had meant
anything to me,
transformed into different sorts of transparent ghosts.
Suddenly they disappear as quickly as they had come.
I quickly look up, realize I am back again,
and I stand up with a new reflection on life.

Yvonne Carder

The Four Winds Of Time And Ozymandias

Upon reading Shelley's poem, "Ozymandias,"
I first came to know this great Egyptian king.
A king who ruled in the second millennium BC
With love and a strong hand of righteousness.
The people's acclaim to his name and fame,
Echoed throughout the land, but now is heard no more
And will not be heard, forevermore.
The winds of yesteryears have blown these mounds of sand
That now cover deep, his people and his land.
The sea at each tide, continue to ebb and flow
Who then will remember Ozymandias?
All is mute, and no one cares to know
I hear naught but the four winds that blow.

Yoshiyuki Otoshi

To Dad

Dear Dad you knew when I was born,
I could not wear the shoes you've worn.

I could not walk the path you cleared,
I could not ride the car you steered.

I had to break in my own shoes.
I had to chop out my own views.

I had to drive cars that were cheap,
But thank God, I don't hit trees.

I had to walk on virgin ground.
I had to earn it pound by pound.

So even though I'm not like you,
That doesn't mean that I'm untrue.

I've encouraged your son, I've protected your daughter,
I've promoted your valves, and defended your honor.

Please let me be, what I am,
And like Hemmingway, start a new trend

Rick Tomlinson

Simply Blue

I looked into the nerve center to answer the question, why?
I cried to Him with love for I did not know, why.
And then with restive quiet, from whence I do not know
I found His loving shadow upon me grow.

I wake in the morning light and ask again the same.
His riddle doth descend upon, all of humble frame.
Why then does He who creates, to infinite detail
Tend to scatter all ones thoughts in yonder vale?

Frustrated and tired, I see the day to end
Will it be to get the chance to recover from the mend?
Or will it be another day without an answer too
Only to realize that sometimes you are blue.

Roland B. Davis

Life Song

Bittersweet lust for life
I cry for the beauty of what might have been.
Trees clinging to the threads of hope
stretch upward to snatch the sun,
their life force ebbing through colors of red and gold.
Winds call to the sky for another chance
to trick the gods.
As if mocking their plea
the leaves fall
and quietly join the earth.
Trees frozen in thought kiss the snow as
ice wraps the world
in a blanket of timelessness.
Hope applauds faith of things yet unseen.
Branches embrace the spring and
new life peeks from their tips like a treasure
taken from a child's pocket.
Simple and stark, death trusts
and life goes on.

Sonja Pomainville

Untitled

I wanted to be a boy named Sue.
I became a woman named Mann.
John my husband said, "You are my little butch wife.
You are more man than many men I know,
enough woman to keep me parking my shoes
beneath our double bed."

So now I pray these questions;
Who am I? What do I want? Who do I become?

Susan Mann

Wild Ferns

One night while watching out my bedroom window,
I didn't see with my eyes, but with my heart.
I saw beautiful wild ferns swaying like a weeping willow
in the midnight breeze.
Oh, how pretty they are, how lovely and fresh they smell.
Spring is coming like a lamb.
The flowers are blooming before my very eyes.
They seem almost alive, dancing under a well moon-lit sky.
But once again, I turn my full attention to the wild ferns.
Like the flowers, they are alive.
I hear a comforting voice.
Wild ferns in the night, are calling me.

Michael Price

Female Pig

Bitter?..Who me?
I don't know the word.
It's not even in my vocabulary.

A man hater?....Oh surely you must jest!
Just because I don't trust anyone-
Without ovaries and breasts.

Spiteful?
Not me, I get mad not even.
But don't let the door hit you in the behind
As you're leavin'.

The end?
Not hardly, I've only just begun,
The battle of the sexes is yet to be won.

Scared?
Don't be, you have nothing to fear,
I promise I'll try to go easy on you dear.

Just remember life's a boomerang,
After centuries of sexism, I guess the fat lady sang.

Stacy Finneman

A Dream Comes True

Often times when I'm alone
I dream of a life beyond my own,
a life of peace and loving grace
a life where tears have no place.

Only joy can be seen
upon the faces within my dream,
while shouts of praise ring throughout
this glorious life I dream about.

But could a life such as this truly exist in all its bliss,
my dream seems real but is it so and if it is can I go?

I search the answer from the scenes
trying to determine what each one means,
and then appears before my sight a wondrous glow of beautiful light.

Embracing me in such tender love
my spirit breaks free rising above,
my pain and my tears, pardoned by grace
the moment I reached out and touched God's face.

You may know this precious love to and God is waiting
to share it with you, He'll give you the hope to set yourself free
I know this because He did it for me.

Staci C. Ruby

Broken Dreams

My pain is real and my mind is numb
I fade away but peace won't come
My body changes because of you-
already I feel your presence
but soon you will be gone
and I will have to go on
knowing what I've done

boy or girl - dark or light
Never to be born - only destroyed
because the time wasn't right
Where are you now as your soul breathes
can you know, what you already mean to me

I dreamt of you last night
of you kicking me inside...
and then of holding you as you cried

How can I be so torn-when I know I have no choices left
to bring you into a life so cold and cruel
would make me more the fool

No answer is easy - no one to lean on
No dreams left - so I slowly fade away-bereft

Michele Engel

Neurotic Novelty

I feel the heartache. I feel the heartache inside my brain.
I feel the ivy. I feel the ivy growing through my veins.
The sky is falling. Everything is falling on top of me.
Suffocation the desert becomes the sea. Everyone's better
much better than me. Interior feelings, neurotic ecstasy.
Twisted trees, purple moon, time zone, I'm alone. Paint a
picture of reality but I can't see through the neurotic sea.
I'm paranoid my best friend told me she was part android.
Zero gravity, the continents fly away into the black hole,
another galaxy, still everyone's better than me, it's a
neurotic ecstasy. I'm trapped everything is closing in on me,
help me out, lead the way. Mourning voices of the angels,
I hear them sing. Only in heaven will I feel peace of mind.
It is then I will leave neurotic thoughts behind.

Melinda Simonton

Late Love

When first I saw you, in my heart
I felt as if spring came in fall,
It seemed my life was at its start
And I had yet not lived at all.

When I'm to catch your look, your word,
It seems, I've caught the sunshine bright,
And all misfortunes of the world
Are but a coolish breeze at night.

When you're with me, I wish that time
Would slower down its rushy speed,
It seems, whole universe is mine,
And nothing else on Earth I need.

When you're away, the twinkling star
Reminds me of your sparkling eyes,
It seems, they bring your charm from far,
They warm me up and make me wise.

When I review my years, to find
Their very sense and vital truth,
It seems, you've made my life divine:
You've brought me back into my youth!

Paul Raphael Friedman

Dedication To Friends

As I crossed the road,
I found a field of flowers.
I spent many an hour learning
about those beautiful flowers.

Each flower had a special significance.
Carrying their own fragrance,
leaving me with more than just a remembrance.

Unlimited colors, textures, and styles;
some grew forever, others stayed for just awhile.

Given for all occasions, what more can one ask.

Just your appreciation always to last.

Lana Brewer

Eutopia Of The Mind

Far away in a climate warm,
I found a shelter from the storm,
The sanctuary so long I sought,
Was always there inside a thought,
The peace of mind from deep within,
Felt like a place I've never been,
The sound of water falls flowing clear and true,
The trees were glistening, kissed by morning dew,
As the new day's sun rose into view,
I thought such beauty has been seen by few,
The air was filled with an unblemished scent,
Untainted by man, yet for man it was meant,
Could this place be how Earth might have been?
So long ago but never again,
How far have we come? And how much the cost?
Do the things that we've gained outweigh what we have lost?
I guess we must live with what we have done,
But if we don't change then all will be gone,
They can poison the people, and destroy beauty they find,
I have but one consolation, they can't touch my mind.

Timothy J. Huotari

"Reminiscing"

Way down in the back woods, of old Alabam'
I grew up the hard way, like most Southerners do,
All week I chopped cotton, in the hot burning land,
At night I'd go courting, where magnolias grew.

The winters were rough, and I'd work for small pay,
To help keep the wolf, away from our door,
By a log burning fire at the end of the day,
My bed was a pallet, on a hard wooden floor.

Then as I grew older I searched for a wife,
To work close beside me, and share what I had,
I found a beautiful maiden the love of my life,
Who always stands by me, through good times and bad.

The years have passed by me, I'm long past my youth,
In memory I smile on the fun that we had,
Though hardships were many, in the land of my birth
I think how the good times surpassed all the bad.

F. Andrea Blizzard

The Crock In My Backyard

I am scared of the crocodile
I have been scared of him for quite awhile
The crocodile knows how to swim
That is one of the reasons I am so scared of him
When he kills you he pulls you down
Then he waits for you to slowly drown
He just doesn't eat people he eats fish too
He eats and eats until he is almost blue
So hold your dogs and grab your cats
And roll up all your welcome mats.

Monique Dumas

On Losing Janie

What tale does the wail of the coyotes weave tonight?
I grieve for my poor pet's fright at their delight.
With trepidation, I approach the pitch dark trails of the night.

The leaves and bushes tremble
as an evening breeze shakes the solitude of the night.

Resolving to dissemble courage, I venture forth into the black abyss.

My throat, imprisoned by fear and hope,
chokes back the strangling sobs
lest I fail to hear the cry of the one I miss.

Stop! Did I hear the soft voice that I fear I shall hear no more,
or was it the wind whispering?

Gripped by the haunting uncertainty - the lingering doubt -
I continue down the dark path.

There it is again - that sound!

Alas, it was but my own mind
faithfully echoing the memory of her voice.

The specter of other losses, infinitely more profound,
looms before me in the ever advancing darkness.

Gone forever more - the timeless chant of the wind tears at my heart.

Lisbeth Bellet

The Last Thing I Remembered

When the guns began to fire, and bombs fell close to where we stood,
I had never thought of losing you, but then I knew I could!
When I fell slowly to the ground, darkness came over me;
The last thing I remembered was what you really mean to me!

Your sweet love that you shared with me down through all the years;
Love I once took for granted, now filled my eyes with tears.
A cool hand on my burning brow, brought me back, again
And I thanked God in heaven, that this was not the end.

Pray God gives me the courage to fight this war, and win!
And I get home to see you, and to love you once again!
I know we need to be here, and I'm proud to take a stand,
But, my love for you is greater than all this desert sand!

Leonard M. Williams

The Cry of a Heart Broken

What is life worth?
I have made so many bad choices in my life;
Is this because I have had bad examples?
Why must we kill each other in the name of Righteousness?
Why do we deceive ourselves in His precious name?
My husband, you lied to me from the beginning.
You pursued me — not in the name of love, but in your need to control.

Your pursued my son "in love" and killed his spirit,
And you wonder why he has no respect.
You are a wolf among sheep, yet your wool is white as snow.
You speak of your faith, but there is darkness in your eyes.
I resent your abuse laced with holiness.
I resent your anger in the guise of conviction.
I resent your love of money at the price of humanity.
And because of my shame, I was blinded to your dagger
that cut me to pieces one day at the time.

Lynne Marie Rodgers

I Heard About The Lord

I heard about the Lord who came from within.
I heard about the Lord who saves us all from sin.
I heard about the Lord who loves us so.
I heard about the Lord, the one that we should know.

I heard about the One who heals with his hands.
I heard about the One who can save the lands.
I heard about the One who wants us to be
Free from all our sins for all eternity.

I heard about the Son who came from above.
I heard about the Son who gave us all his love.
I heard about the Son who died upon the cross.
I heard about the Son who died for all of us.

I heard about the King who reigns from within.
I heard about a King who will come again.
I heard about a King who will bring us home,
So we won't ever have to be so all alone.

Timothy Robert Cox

A Tribute to You

As I lift my head up to the sky
I hope that you can see
Just how much you are still a part
Of all of those you have touched
In so many ways.
Your love, your laughter, your smiles,
And your special touch, and your advice
That always meant so much.
Our hearts were saddened when you went away
The memories we all have we will all
Cherish in our own special way.

Pearl A. Sharp Brown

Unforgotten Memories

As the seasons change
I ingest all its beauty to its own
Some of life's best are not meant to grasp
Only to let go
Not steal, borrow or loan

But in my mind it will forever burrow
Deeper than the canyons roam
When in need to relieve from sorrow
I will pull these from my memory
To get me to tomorrow

Kimberley McKee

To My Husband

When we went on our first date
I knew you'd be the perfect mate.
You swallowed me up heart and soul
You filled my empty life and made it whole.
Your kisses so soft, your heart so warm
When you hold me close, I feel no harm.
And though we maybe years apart
You captured my love and warmed my heart.
And despite all the boos and all the hisses
You gave me a chance and made me your Mrs.
Thank you for staying with me through thick and thin
And for all the arguments you let me win.
Everyone sees how great we are together
And I know what we have will last forever.
You're exactly what I'm needed in my life
And I wanted to say Thank you — I love you
Your wife

Lisa K. Rutledge Calder

Birdman

Old Birdman, he my best friend, now he dead and gone.
I know he flapped his wings, done soared de heavens home.
He told me dat many birds habits how dey got deys name.
And fo' my old friend Birdman, dat truth acts jest de same.
Sometimes when a'workin de hot-sun cotton fields, he'd jest stand
and watch de birds a 'flyin, hands cupped his eyes to shield.
Overseer would catch him a'watchin, give him a beatin round de
barnhaus back.
You could hear him "caw" from de beatin wit de strap.
He said birds de only thang God made truly free.
Then he'd sang a song of Africa, sound mighty fine to me.
He said, birds when dey reared away from dey very own species, never
sang de true songs o' dey very own kind. And even tho' a long way
from home dey might be caged, dey sang deys soul a'flyin.
Yep, old Birdman, he my best friend, now he dead and gone.
But, wit de memories I have o' him, never am I alone.
He always believed he could fly, now I sho' he can 'cause now
he truly free.
And as he soars de heavens home, protection his wings fo' me!
Fly, Birdman, fly!

O'Keather T. Campbell

"The Leash I Lead"

When the Animal Control trucks roll in
I know my job is about to begin
It will be filled with unique creatures
Each with its own beautiful features
Though their stories are never told
Each is wonderful to behold
It is impossible to save them all
When their time is up, I just want to bawl
If people only realized that when pets mate
Most of the babies meet a terrible fate.
So people call me awful names
But I truly know who to blame
So, before you let your pets mix
I recommend that they be "fixed."

Kim Roy

Riding The Sword's Edge Between Heaven And Hell

Riding the sword's edge between heaven and hell.
I know the reflection oh so well,
yet still, it's not me.

No one gets in behind these eyes,
not me,
not you.
Locked within perceptions of yours and mine hides a third,
the truth.
It's just far too dangerous to do.
Isn't it?

My back to the depths of the steps I have climbed.
Doorways of direction without destination stand before me.
Who is this that stands here stronger, proud,
scared of a doorway to wholeness,
with so much still left to be?

I know him oh so well,
yet still, it's not me,
just standing there,
looking back,
riding the swords edge between heaven and hell.

Shawn Sowers

"The Sunrise"

Having a desire,
I know what that is,
I've experienced it.
Just being able to wake before a sunrise....

- Wanting to watch every lovely sight.
- Freezing your bones just to succeed.
- Watching and Loving every minute of it.
- Wishing for others just to even get a
  peek at what you saw.

To be able to absorb everything in.
- Wanting more.
That's a desire.
A love.
It's beautiful - like a picture.
I did it -
I saw it -
I love it-
I want more -
That's Desire - for a Sunrise.
I'm Living another day.

Michelle Clancy

From Dusk To Dawn

A storm of memories rages thru my mind.
I let its warm rain saturate me,
Cover over me completely.
In my ears, in my eyes, I feel it gather,
Mouth open to taste its sweetness.
I cannot become a part
Of this downpour from the heavens,
I cannot stand to be apart from it.
Moistened and enriched, I seek shelter
In slumber.
Arm across my chest, soft hand on my cheek,
Head resting lightly on my shoulder.
We entwine, content. I feel you in my dreams.
Dawn brings chilled sadness.
The new sun's warmth not enough.
My pillow wet with the run-off of left over memory,
I add to the damp recollection.
My heart and soul pour forth from my flesh
In the form of a solitary, glistening tear.

Kenneth Ivy

The Tall Tall Grass

Sometimes at night, when late the hour
I lie awake then softly wander
Alone in fields of tall tall grass
Where all is silent save the laugh
Of the northern bird alone in flight
Who knows no fear of the darkening night
Who wings his way to freedoms call
All cares behind, whether big or small.

Then I lie down in the tall tall grass
Wishing that this fair moment would last
And settling back in my comforting space
I stare at the clouds and study their face.
They smile at me gently as the wind blows them by
They know of my sorrow and gently they try
To give me their courage to move right along
That come the new morning, there'll be a new dawn.

Marlene Marmanillo

The Wind

The "wind" calls out a beautiful song. So, sweet and loving,
I listen very carefully! Because I wish, and I hope, and I
even pray that one day I could sing and live the same
beautiful song. My song is so lonely, and bitter, and
dull. It's also very empty and interminable.........
When I hear my song I can't speak of words.
My eyes, however, fill with tears and my heart begins to
break into pieces.......................................
But one day the wind spoke to me. It said "What I have
been looking for is inside of myself." So, I looked deep
down in my soul, and I found that my song was myself.
I found a gentle, sweet, loving, tender, and affectionate one.

Melissa Lee Tamburo

My Rack

My home is my rack, where I stay
I live here, where I am both night and day.
It's not real fancy, covered with lace
But by golly it is a hell of a place
covered with blankets marked U. S.
Kept real neat, never a mess.
A good place to come back to by Joe
Don't ever knock it my friend
It's a good place to be at a day's end.
My rack, my home.

Rolla E. Allen III

Looking Down

From my window
I look down on rain-sogged roofs
And writhing trees
To the bottom of the hill
Where rugged rocks
Shoulder stubbornly against the surf.
Bright spindrift, torn from a wintry womb,
Is swaddled by the sky —
I see the child of storm and sea.

So many over-rolling years I've shouldered
Since I first joined this ever changing scene,
And from the elements which met in me
Creativity has thrown much blowing mist
Which rises to my secret roiling skies.
If there's one who watches down through a window
As the rain, roofs, rocks, trees, wind, and waves clash in me,
I hope the view of how my striving spreads to spray
Will show some white flash of majesty.

Rod Clark

Release

If in my zeal to keep a promise;
I lost your heart, 'Twou'd break mine!

Were I to have my way;
You and I would fly away!
Sharing joys we knew well—-
Laughing, singing, raising hell!

Mocking old impostor, pain;
The fragile thread which binds to earth
The fear, the dread, that begs for mercy
only Angels hear.
Then sheds the pain, the grief, the dying
At Heaven's gate — Spirits flying!

Thelma Jean Duke

Untitled

I found.
I loved.
I lost.
I hurt.

I found again.

Will the life of love survive,
In
One
Continuous
Circle?

Or will it ever chance the ultimate escape
And soar
Forever onward
Into
New horizons.

I found.
I loved.
I lost.
I hurt.

I found again.

Susan S. Daves

Forever This Time

What is this I'm feeling, the loss of the man
I loved, deep, deep within.
Only my heart knows, for its beats are fast.
it pounds from within. It feels the pain, Oh
I must slow it down again.
No, no my mind it wonders, my eyes see his face,
his lips tender again I must kiss. I shake my
head, I must clear my mind, for I know he is dead.
No, no this can't be happening again, but wait it
Tis for I feel his body press against mine.
Am I dreaming, or is it real, Oh I see you now.
I'm not dreaming I'm awake and now I know. I've
left my world and now I'm in yours, and together
we are forever this time.

Sandra Wagner

My Cousin Left Behind

My cousin left behind his mother, my aunt.
I loved her before, but even more now because he can't.

He left behind his only son,
Another task yet left undone.

He left behind his young daughter,
Also left without her father.

He left behind his cousin and friend.
I'll love him until my end.

He left behind his family and friends,
Who all must someday face our ends.

But most important,

He left behind his memories for us to treasure,
And I hope someday they give his children pleasure.

I know in my heart he is gone,
But I also know what he has left behind
I'll not leave undone.

R. Owen

Untitled

R iyadh is the place, a thousand miles away
I ndeed it's a joke, for here we did cross
Y ou are here, sharing, caring
A nd in my heart
D early, yes I know, I Love You so
H ow soon did it happen, how long will it last
For me it's true, you'll always be a part...
To thee I give this simple rhyme
Maybe elementary as you see
But just the same, keep this honey
For in my heart, it came directly
And when the time comes
You see me no more
Just think of this place
For somehow in your way
I might always stay...

Tess S. Short

Untitled

Why lie? I do not know how. Help. Where is it?
I need yet never receive.
Lies Bombard me as images of love swarm through my brain.
Anger pulsates in my skull.
Fake- that is what everything is-the world is a grand delusion and emotions are a deadly reality.
Leave. I no longer need or even want.
Can you give of yourself for one splendid moment?
The question is rather will you.
I know you will not-you're heart is barricaded with apathy and deception.
Nothing matters. Will I ever?
Survival seems like a dream of ultimate being.
Where is my state of mind and my conscience for that matter.
Nothing real, yet the world bleeds from hidden wounds.
Kill me and you have nothing.
Lie to me and you grasp your own existence.
You think you know everything when in actuality your brain does not function and cannot register anything but thoughts of your pompous soul.

Kendra A. Warmolts

Because I Was Born

For years I thought everyone's home was the same
I never knew there was anyone to blame.
Never knowing who my enemy was,
It was always the person who I dearly loved.
Now inside me lies a fury so deep
The only time I'm at peace is when I'm asleep.
The things that were done and the things that were said
Replay over and over inside my head.
Sometimes when I dream of hell...
I can see prettier flowers than in my own front yard.
Was I alone and the only one?
Who knew what they knew and saw what they'd done?
There were so many times I felt all alone
There's so many things no one has known
Through the years and all the assault
I never did know it wasn't my fault.
Through all of my punishment and all of their scorn
The must have been mad because I was born.
Sometimes when I think of flowers...
All I can see is hell.

Shandy Metcalf

When I'm Sad

When I'm sad, I feel like running away or jumping to the clouds.
I never want to come back.
My legs collapse like a giant wall falling down.
My eyeballs start swimming in water. My shoulders slouch down, hanging to the ground.
I feel nothing but sadness.
My hand feel hot and stiff and they want to do something bad, but what? My stomach rides a roller coaster. My teeth think it's winter and chatter and clench together tightly. My feet don't want to go anywhere but far, far away.
I feel so bad I don't even know why I am living.
But then, after a long time my eyes stop swimming, my legs stop falling, my hands get relaxed, and my stomach gets off the roller coaster.
I feel something else.
It's happiness.
Then I come down from the clouds and live my life with my family and friends.

Renee Morgan-Saks

Memories

Years ago when I left home, my fame or fortune to seek,
I often thought of that little church, up at the end of the street,
Where friends and family gathered each glorious sabbath day,
To give thanks to our Lord and Saviour, for showing us the way,
and right up front by the alter, the family bible lay,
In memory of a son lost on that dark December day,
And the vision of my father as down the aisle he trod,
Arms raised high tears streaming down, he pledged his soul to God.
Many miles have since been travelled, wondrous things there I did see,
And memories of that little church traveled there with me,
Now that I am anchored, never more will I roam,
That little church at the end of the street, has welcomed me back home.

Leon Puckett

Understanding Death

Death, you once frightened me
I once held strongly to life
Come here and take it from me
For I no longer fear thee
No more do I see the reds, the blue, and greens
In their places,
I see the softness of gray
It touches my soul, holding its warmth in the infinite light
And the beauty it beholds is finally seen
To my surprise, I leave behind the darkness of day
To leave this earth, to take eternal flight
Life and death I hold both their hands
As I walk thru the stars to the promised land.

Tim Andrews

A Mountain Stream

Watching the rushing water of a mountain stream,
I perched on a rock and began to dream,
About the explorers and dreamers of the past,
Who stopped to drink and their eyes did cast,
Toward new horizons and a future quite new,
People like Joseph Smith, Kit Carson, and a soldier in blue,
I wondered if this same little bubbling creek,
Gave the adventurer a drink refreshing as well as the meek,
As they journeyed to new lands o'er the Oregon Trail,
Not knowing if their lives would be successful or fail,
Thank you little cool spring for your help today,
And for those of the past who may have come your way.

Sybil G. Southers

Dear Daddy

Dear Daddy, I miss you so much, please show me the way...
I pray for your guidance with each new day.
You were the rock we all leaned upon;
It's so hard to believe that you are gone.
You were there to guide the way, always willing and ready to say...
"Don't let life's bumps phase you my child,
I'll be watching and praying all the while."
You forgave, you forgot and judged not your friends;
For only God in heaven, has that right in the end.
Anger and bitterness are festering sores,
You taught us love offers so much more.
So much you gave and all from the soul,
So little you asked; so much to behold.
So special you were... a man among men,
You always said, "Death is no end."
A beginning, a meeting, a reunion of those dear,
Please, my family, don't shed a tear.
For when I've departed this earth, and my new life begins,
I'll meet you all and we'll be together again.

Linda Harris Davis

The Changing Of The Guard

As I sat here tonight and watched you play
I realized the young boy I raised was gone
and a young man was here to stay
You see, life has been good to me, I know
Because I have been around to watch you grow
From the time you were born and we played those children games
To the church tonight where I listen to the music flowing
from your horn

You are the new generation
That will build this world of ours
and after tonight I'm not worried about you
or the
world's temptations
For I know as I pass on to you the post in life you'll take
That the changing of the guard we will take in stride
and I pass it on to you with pride

Robert C. Giles III

Vision

When I peered up in the sky,
I saw ripples in the galaxies
like the vast oceans abroad and
I saw the bleak white puffs of clouds,
enormous ships with angels on board
which hovered over my head.
The majestic mountains seemed
to absorb the mandarin sun,
for then I could see the
glistening stars pry through
the curtain of darkness.
The tranquil breeze that dried my eyes and
the glowing moon which lit
the solemn earth, put me
in a place where I have never been;
At peace with myself.

Mike Reynolds

A Definition

Pain is a harried hag, drilling into my bones,
ignoring my frantic howls and moans
Pain is a piercing dart, an anger entering my heart
Pain is an evil consuming fire, sending my temperature
higher and higher.
Pain is the sub total of all life's wounds,
Gathered and stored for many moons!

Mariana Beeching Prieto

Deep Waters

As I walked along the sandy beach,
I saw the racing ocean before me.

As the deep sea roared
and chattered like a baby bird
bellowing for food,
I fell to the ground
and let the sand run through
my fingers.

I happened to be the only person
on the beach but I wasn't
the only animal on the beach.

The sun was falling and the water was settling,
so every moment you can see
the beautiful whales flip their fins
from miles away.

Every moment in the water
was another special minute
of my life.

Lynde Prentice

A Friend I Had

I had a friend who was so wonderful and so sweet.
I say I had a friend rather than have because this friend has been
swept off her feet.
So innocent and so good she once used to be.
Now she's made a new friend and this something is not me.
Rather than it be someone, it is a substance of misuse.
In her mind she sees it as fun, but in mine it's alcohol abuse.
This substance that took my friend away is labeled as alcohol.
She believes she's at the top of the ladder but it's really one
big fall.
This hole grows larger as she falls deeper into it each day.
I want to fill this hole so she'll fall no more and stay.
I wish I could pull her out and bring my friend back to me.
But I'm afraid she wants no help, alcohol is where she wants to be.
My friend is no longer innocent, sweet, nor good.
Without the alcohol it would have been better, I know it would.
I would still have that friend, innocent and kind.
But now there's only laughs and memories to leave behind.
In her mind, this choice got her higher in life today.
But in my mind, it held her back and caused her to fade away.

Laura Wozniak

A Grasp Of Light

As I open my eyes upon a dream,
I see around me walls of darkness;
Upon far and away I see a glimpse of a Bright,
but yet so Blinding Light......
What?.... What could it be?
I walk fast; It was so far yet I see it so near.
As I'm walking almost a run.
I fall to my knees as I reach to grab a small
Grasp of the Bright and Blinding Light;....
I touched it, I touched the Light.
I felt it. JOY, HAPPINESS, PEACE WITH GLORY
run through my soul and mind.
I linger in the walls of Darkness only to find
that it was my Lord ah calling....
Ah calling for me.......
That it is Time;
Time to follow the Glorious Light,
to lead me
To Happiness and Peace of Mind.

Sylvia L. Trevino

To My Mother, Poetry In Motion

I see poetry in motion,
I see my mother's devotion.
She sits with her beads, praying in word,
She moves in her kitchen, praying in deed.
I see poetry in motion.

Among her family, she moves like an angel,
To serve, to help, to watch, to pray for her family.
I see poetry in motion.
Ah! what a joy, she is to behold.
No one has done deeds so bold,
As to hold, a child in love,
And to send them forth to the world with hope.
While inside, she hides her fears, and her tears,
So she may give, what she has been divinely lent,
A life to be beheld, and for others to see.
I saw poetry in motion,
I saw my mother's devotion.

Kathleen Mary Zuiss

Pain

I watched myself and
I see pain, pain in my heart.
Pain, a sad word to say and feel.
My heart is crying, and it hurts, but nobody knows.
The pain I feel it's killing
me, don't ask me why
I feel this pain is just
my heart that cries for love.
I asked myself why do people hurt my heart,
but their is no answer
I love my family, I love
my friends, and the guy
that brought me the pain.
My family don't care, my
friends say you be alright.
The guy that I love went away.
I watched myself and I asked
my heart why the people I
love always go away, but my
heart just answered me with pain.

Rosie Incandela

Clouds

The gray clouds in the skies,
I see so far with my eyes.
As they pass me by, I wonder why.

They move so slowly,
As if not a care
On their chartered course,
Up in the air.

Over rivers and over streams,
And over our imaginary dreams.

Over trees and over hills,
And where everything is quiet and still.

As they linger, in certain places,
Floating high above, with all their graces.

And I wonder why,
As they pass by.

Patricia Cook

Sorrow

Well, here I sit in a pool of sorrow where will I be come tomorrow?
I see so many paths that I may go, but here I stand at the crossroads of my life,
as confused as ever not knowing which way to go
If I choose the wrong path I will always be unhappy.
I don't want that so I just stand here while time passes me by,
getting older with no idea what to do with my life.
I need to get out but where to go?
There is nowhere for me.
If there is I can't seem to find it.
Why does it have to be me?
Can't someone take over from here and live this life?
I can't seem to shake these feelings of mine,
it's becoming an anchor that is weighing me down.
I know I need to do something, but what is it
I feel like life is passing me by and I'm afraid.
Afraid of life and afraid of death, so I just float along,
please someone hold my hand I'm scared.

Lisa Webber

Memories

Back, back to the past.
I see the Grandfather I never knew. How I wish we had more time.

All of the way back, as far as I can go.
I smell the flowers, I see the road. That road
I traveled so long ago.

Quite a ways now, how far back must it be?
The things I see, the things I know. If you only
knew how much I want to go back.

In my mind, I see all these things.
Then I open my eyes and it disappears. Inside of
my head, my heart, I'll always go back and enjoy my memories.

All of my life, I've made so many decisions,
some were good. Some were bad.

Look at all the time I've wasted. Those
things seemed so important, why don't they seem to matter now?

All I have are memories, cold am I at night.
Is it possible to take me back any other way,
rather than only in memory. So many things I wish to change.

It is too late when all you have is memories,

Mary Keller

How Long?

I often sit to watch the world of its beauty or some cruel words.
I see the sun, the birds and the bees.
But half the time it's meaningless when it cannot be shared.
How long must I search 'til my life is fulfilled?
To search and search and yet never to find.
To finally realized I have left it behind in some past relationship,
When I was the only one who cared.
How long must I search 'til my life is fulfilled?
It's hard to achieve what I am looking for, when no one can
Really hear what I say.
I don't want to be alone—I need what that someone has.
How long must I search 'til my life is fulfilled?
I had it before—but never had seen it, but now I am wise,
Mature and still growing: Though one never stops.
Life is to be lived: Not questioned, not feared.
How long must I search 'til my life is fulfilled?
I will live each day to its fullest, though everyone needs
Someone to walk through life's path. I need that someone for
Today, tomorrow and for always.
But how long must I search 'til my life is fulfilled?

Mary Crago

Bird Of Victory

It well may be that in the end
I shall forget the summer's gift
And go therefrom to autumn and in its stint
Of dead-stiff trees, bare branches
And silent birds adrift
From coddling nests, who lift
Their wings to hasten toward more comely
Solace from the wind. I shall not see
You but I shall miss
The shadow of your wing-spread
Above the stark and reeling cloudiness
Of a world at war in anguished need of you...

O Bird of Beauty and Ecstasy,
Lift us above the heaps of uncared dead!
Come back again, so
We may cudgel death and emptiness.

Kaya Chernishova

The Letter

The dawn is dark, and dreary, dreary.
I sit with pen in hand, but weary.

Word has come, I wish it hadn't.
My heart is marked with shame, as though an iron had branded it.

I feel the fool in trying to respond,
And my hand shows a tremor, creating words, not found.

Closer to home, I will put on a smiling face,
Shortly no one there will guess of my disgrace.
I will seek sanction to heal my fears and pain,
Till my life again will seem more sane.

Soon to hear his name will ring hollow to my ears,
And my eyes will not be bedimmed with tears.
Tender memories will be behind me,
And his parting shadow I will not see.

But for now, I will search for my stationery case,
For all of my reply has run into the paper border of lace.

Mary Kay Uraga

The Bouquet

I break off flowers from a tree then running drop them

They fall like bright stars from above
I stoop and tie them with green ribbons
A yellow butterfly lands on them and leaves a kiss

As the purple clouds announce a summer storm
I feel I no longer need fear summer storms and darkness

I hurry along carrying the summer flowers
on which silent kisses rest

Carrying the bouquet in the dark the ribbons that I tied
around it were life's tender promises
There are no more tender thoughts
They were swept away by the winds and the storm

I carry the flowers tied with green ribbons
through the summer storm and reach home
The flowers aware of their short lived
fate - lie in my hand like broken promises

Marie Hughes Kloeppel

There Is A God Of Love

Dear baby in Heaven above
I thank you for helping teach
me there is a God of love!

Although I chose not to give you life;
a new life was born, though it
took some time, cause of the struggles,
the hatred, the strife!
That LIFE is mine through Jesus Christ!

I hurt deep within, when I think what I've done!
Were you may daughter or were you my son?

I love you today and with God's
precious grace I have faith we will
meet someday.

Dear Baby in Heaven above
I thank you for helping teach
me there is a God of Love!

Leada Gail Turner

The Real World

As I sit in my room, in my white wicker chair,
I think of someone starving somewhere.
I think of the hard working man who is so underpaid,
And of the innocent child killed in a drug raid.
I think of the person no longer alive,
Because of the drunk man who decided to drive.
I think of the person living in the street,
With only a blanket for shelter and heat.
I think of the soldier who never returned from war,
And I say to myself, is that what fighting is for?
I think of the child stolen from its mother,
Just the thought of it makes me shudder.
As I think of this world so full of hate,
I feel sorry for those doomed to ill fate.
So I sit in my room away from the pain,
And on my window sill, down drips the rain.

Kimberly Hotz

Untitled

I am sick and tired of this nation's crime.
I think of this from time to time.

I hope that we rid the world of these bad people someday.
Executing them is the only way

To ensure our safety.
We deserve this so why can't our leaders see

That the Bill of Rights is protecting the evil in this once great country.
It makes these criminals feel so powerful and free.

If the framers of the Constitution only knew,
But they had no clue

Of what was to come about.
I wish they had had more doubt.

Hindsight is twenty/twenty.
If our forefathers had had it, our well-being and safety would be
plenty.

Scott Kaplan

Thinking Of You

I think of you, everyday
I think of you, in every way
I think of you, good or bad
I think of our lives, they're not that sad
I think of you, you're so far away
I think of you, when I want to play
I think of you, for all that you stand
I think of you, me, being your man
I think of you, when you're at home
I think of you, when I'm alone
I think of you, right from the start
I think of you, deep in my heart
I think of you, you're getting better
You'll think of me, after reading this letter

E. J.

A Second Chance

One day when I was resting and everything was still
I thought I saw my saviour standing on a hill.
He beckoned me to follow, I said, Lord I can't go with you,
I have too many loose ends — things I need to do.
I'd like to see my children a little more secularly on their feet.
And I can't leave those babies, so precious and so sweet.
I'd like to see the grandchildren grown — see what they become.
Surely I'd be a little help, maybe for just one.
And my mate, he needs me Lord - so many things we planned to do.
Yes, I'm happy to say, those plans include You!
How swiftly all the years have flown, I've accomplished nothing yet.
I'd like to leave a little mark so people won't forget.
Then I awoke, it was just a dream, I'm granted a reprieve.

With humble heart, I thank you Lord for all the blessings I receive.
I realize now my burdens aren't more than I can stand.
Let me give those less fortunate a willing, helping hand.
Help me to live every day as though it were my last
So I will be ready anytime your out stretched hand to grasp.

Ruth Noyes McCullick

Secret Love

As I turned to leave your world behind
I thought I saw your smile
So pure a thing it could have been
A dream to keep me here awhile
I'd pass up love a thousand times
To be with you again
So pure a thing your love for me
I wish it didn't have to end
But secret loves are hard to keep
And time is hard to find
The patience and strength it takes to wait
Aren't fated to be mine
I'd give my life to have you know
That I do love you
But your eyes are closed, you didn't smile
You wouldn't know it's true
Secret love is hard to keep
It only lasts awhile
So I think I'll have to say goodbye
But I thought I saw you smile

Laura Lowe

3 AM

Soul's midnight
I thought if I saw you today
All my despair would drain away
But the blood drained from my face instead
I thought I wanted my old friends back
I thought all I needed was that
Or without you my life would be dead
But the meeting went off with no glimmer of hope
Disturbed and hateful, you just sat there and moped
And the absent goodbye stunned what little I had left
So now I'm proud to say life does go on
My planets say there's a new change in fun
So the hatred we feel really is for the best.

Suzanne Rallis

When I Went Home To God

I did not want to go to what
I thought to be an unknown

I knew immediately on leaving my body
That I "knew" and had known all the time

All that was all that is and all that will be
Came into view allowing me to see eternity

I now have knowledge to be able to access the
Highest limit of creation - God or Creator, you see-

My limit is the accessibility of the Creator- God-
Beyond God, or Creator, there is nothing, only God

I have reached the limit so to speak, there is
Nothing else but to be with God and be at peace

It is so wondrous here as not to be explainable
Angels are working miracles this is not deniable

God sits in glory over the universe, waiting above
For His angels to bring you into His circle of love

Forgive yourself because God already gave his nod
All this and more, I saw, when I went home to God
Inspired by John S. Brown.

Patricia Horwell

"Never Forgotten"

Through all the fun weekends
I thought would never end
I thought I could trust you
And never imagined getting hurt again
Our love and time together I'll always treasure
Because hopefully we'll be friends forever
I thought our love would be everlasting
But now everything has been quickly passing
When it was finally time to say good-bye
All I could do was sit there and cry
Though many tears have been shed
While thinking of not being with you in the days ahead
Watching the time pass day by day
Still wishing things were the same way
During all the great times and memories we've shared
I never thought that one day you wouldn't be there
Every time I saw you smile
I knew my life was worth while
Although our worlds are so far apart
Please remember you're always in my heart and "Never Forgotten"

Melissa West

The Love Of Two

You come to me as a dream,
I understand, not the pleasure nor the pain.
As a pale mist on a hazy moonlit night
your image I see for so long,
for so right?

Confused am I
do I run, do I cry?
Are we true to each other
even though we love another?

I yearn to believe that we do not deceive.
I am here for you in pleasure or pain.
It is you to decide
should I go, do I remain?

If no be true, let us not be blue,
another time will come
for the love of two.

Paul Thomas Davis

To My Lost Child

Pray do not dream I love you less because
I vanished as you clung to me the most.
I will return to you, a penitent ghost,
If I can bend away the sensate bars

Which mar your seeing me. Forgive me finally
For all hour years of yearning spent in vain,
All of the bitter, hopeless, endless pain
Which I have willed you, bequeathed helplessly.

For I have watched you there, cursed and forlorn
Blaming yourself for sins I left behind,
Searching the darkest caverns of your mind,
Viewing the awesome days when you were born.

And I would still protect you if I might
From hideous demons gibbering in the night.

Mary B. McKenzie

Wicked Witch

The sidewalk was a endless as my love,
I walked it all, my thoughts were wicked.
I proceeded forward, but my mind went above
searching my past,
for at least one thing I've done to be proud of.
I sat on the curb, and refused the desire
to touch the voice that lured.
I want to know my fate or to understand my past.
My inquiring only got me glares of hate.
Who are they to deny me?
I have the right to sit, to think.
I happen to like the pavement,
it is hard like my mind, and cold like your heart.
I follow the trail of breadcrumbs,
the crumbs that the birds refuse to touch,
in the silent forest of rejection.
My spirit is unruly, she stays to forever linger,
to make you have to live your life dead,
to know what it felt to be me. Now thanks to you, I am free.
I bid you farewell and wish you luck
on your journey to hell, for eternity...

Linda Gansky

First Snowfall

One winter morning long ago, when I was just a child,
I walked past a window and saw something white and piled...
High upon the window sill, I stood there amazed—
With nose pressed to the window, in wonderment I gazed...

Upon the carpeting of white, that made my world anew—
The old familiar shades of green had quietly passed from view.
'Twas then my mother hugged me tight, and whispered in my ear—
I still repeat those words she said to children every year.

"Old Mother Goose is cleaning her house, a busy old lady is she,
Shaking her old feather pillows, for all of the children to see—
She'll dust all the pillows, fluff them a bit, but wouldn't you
think she could see...
The pillow case zipper is open...she's shaking her feathers on me!"

Tho' many years have come and gone, I still recall that day,
That's one mem'ry in my heart, that never goes away.
It seems just like a yesterday... I look again and see...
The first snow fall... I can recall... and mother telling me...

"Old Mother Goose is cleaning her house, a busy old lady is she—
Shaking her old feather pillows, for all of the children to see,
She'll dust all the pillows, fluff them a bit, but wouldn't you think
she could see...
The pillows case zipper is open... she's shaking her feathers on me!"

Sally Bixler Dodds

Your Free

When spring was fare and the sun was bright
I walked though a meadow in its early light
Then time stood still and I looked around
This is a moment of peace I've found

A swaying tree it bows to me
The wind it whispers your free, your free
I envy a sparrow as it darts near by
and for a childish moment I wish I could fly

I've been to a land where peace is nil
I've heard the echo of war cross the hills
I've seen the sons of mothers die
And in this moment of peace I wonder why

If I could speak and all could hear
Lay down your arms let the cannons be still
Come to this meadow by the swaying tree
Listen to it whisper your free, your free

William Brown

Mom

Even though I ended your childhood
I was never your burden.
At eighteen you cared for me, protected me, cried for me.
You've done everything you could to make me happy.
Like the time we were separated.
Dad took me from you.
You fought to find me, found me.
Took me home, to our home.

Even after when I grew and made your life hard
You loved me.

Soon I'll be leaving, leaving you.
Sure I'm scared, but I know you want me strong, independent.

A young adult now, I can finally say thank you.
For the life you let me live,
for letting me correct my own mistakes.
I love you, Mom.

Liberty LiVecchi

Let Me Be The One

When your needs, need attention
I want to be in contention.
When the mood calls for romance,
come on girl, take a chance.
And when you need someone to care
I want to be right there.
All the things that should be
let them be for you and me.

In your life
In your heart
Let me be the one.

Let's share walks on occasion
Let's share sweet conversation
Let's share the lovers' touch
When the moment means so much.

I want to be a part of all you are
if love takes us that far.

Someone who needs your love
Someone who wants your love
Let me be the one.

Roosevelt Cash

The Bum

The night was damp and dreary
I was cold and weary
A figure appeared out of the dark
Sure did give me a start
This fellow looked like a lout
On man, I wanted to shout
"Don't be scared he said"
Oh well, I just shook my head
I'm just a bum on the down and out
What do I have to be scared about
Held out his hand, gave my two five dollar bills
Now I can eat, get rid of these chills
Sat in the cafe warming my feet
Sat there half dozing in that warm heat
Waitress said, "You'd Better Leave"
Oh, that warmth I would sure grieve
Now that I was nice and warm
I stepped out into the storm
Mister, I don't know who you are
But you have my thanks from afar

Paul E. Deardeuff Jr.

I Was There

I was there when you said we were in Heaven.
I was floating on a lonely cloud-
Soft, safe, and secure.
I was there
In that paradise of ours.
I was there in that garden you said
You'd built for us.
I was there
Staring into a mild bleakness,
Sitting on a silver throne
In a golden sanctuary
I was there-
A bystander in your already-complete life.
I was there
As your only protection from the cruelties of life,
The harsh winter breath,
The pounding rain,
The agony of loneliness.
I was there.
Where were you?

Spence Hoffman

Remember

I remember a time when life was sweet
I wasn't afraid to walk the street
No locked doors and security alarm
Never had to worry about being harmed.

Laughing and playing any time of day,
No threat of being taken away, by someone with a twisted mind
Those good ole days are lost in time

A playground use to be for fun, now it's for knives and guns
King of the hill was just a game
Now they play to achieve life deadly fame

Parents got respect, now they suffer pain and regrets
You look at the news on the TV screen
Another child lost or killed at the crime scene

Kids were afraid of jail, now their home is a prison cell
Thinking and wandering, how they failed
Pleading with God, to keep them from hell

I will continue to remember the day
When sharing and caring was okay
Spreading joy and a smile along the way
Remembering peace and love is here to stay.

Sharon Killings Brunson

Seasons Gone By

Back in Winter - months ago -
I watched from a window at mounded snow.
Sweet Spring came along, then Summer, too,
I watched as foliage blossomed and grew.

The seasons come, and the seasons pass,
A glance away and they seemed just a flash.
Our blossoming Spring, and fading Fall,
Have come and gone - didn't last at all.

Seasons must change, and so must we,
Eternal youth wasn't meant to be .
We're born, we flourish, then fade away,
So the youth who come after, may have their day.

The seasons we've had should have planted a seed,
That would grow and grow in a world of need,
And bear the fruits to show after our season,
The Lord gave us life for a meaning - A - reason.

Ruby Woodward

"Veterans Day"

When I was young and not a care
I watched the parade go by
I didn't really know the reason why
but I noticed some with a tear in the eye

The flags were waiving in the breeze
I watched the parade go by
The men marched proudly down the street
The crowd seemed content but incomplete

Way back then I never knew why
I watched the parade go by
When I grew older I understood
That men gave their lives, for freedom's good

Now I see old glory flying high
I'm in the parade that's marching by
The young man is still out there
knowing some people really care

Knowing freedom does not come free
I watched the parade go by
I remove my cap, with heart full of glee
Knowing the young man was once me

Paul V. Estelow

Missing

Early in one historic morning
I went with my father.
We were going for his office
across the flight line.
Granting clearance
the S.P. waved us forward.
Continuing to drive along
without an utterance of words between us.
A fighter was taxing the runway.
It was a phantom in camo clothing;
A pilot and his navi
glorified in back helmets and shields.
When I remember them, I think:
they might have been my heroes.
Any how, we drove on to his bunker.
I stayed outside, no clearance beyond those gates.
I waited in the corolla for hours;
It seemed everlasting.
Many mornings followed in solitude...

Nelson Lee Walter

Tropical Trance

Tell me your secrets and your desires
I will show you my passion with a whisper
Let a gentle breeze blow you my way
Let me caress your masculine curves and hold you with content

To join you in gazing upon the sunrise
To fall in to a spell with you at sunset
Drinking in the beauty as we drink in one another

Trust me to set your spirit free
I will teach you the language of love

The dance of the swaying palm trees
The song of the exotic birds
Natures music of love
The harmony and peace echo around us

Entranced for eternity

Natalie Singh

I Wish I Were

I wish I were a horse, so wild and running free,
I wish I were a horse, bringing lots of joy to me
I wish I were a cat, prowling and sleeping all day,
I wish I were a cat, as content as words can say
I wish I were a deer, prancing in a field of flowers,
I wish I were a deer, running and bounding for hours
I wish I were a dog, barking, running, and exploring,
I wish I were a dog, for nothing would ever be boring
I wish I were a rabbit, hopping and sniffing about,
I wish I were a rabbit, for those I couldn't do without
I wish I were a hawk, soaring gracefully in the sky,
I wish I were a hawk, watching the time go by
I wish I were an owl, so peaceful, quiet, and wise,
I wish I were an owl, sleeping when the sun does rise
I wish I were I were a peacock, with my beautiful tail,
I wish I were a peacock, with admiration I'd prevail
I wish I were a lion, so proud, fierce, and feared
I wish I were a lion, watched by all as I neared
I really am glad that I'm just me,
But it's fun to imagine all of the things I could be.

Lauren Paul

If I Could

I wish that I could write a song with a lilting melody
I wish that I could sing along in perfect harmony

I wish that I could write a book that everyone would read
a book of happy, wholesome thoughts not full of crime or greed

I wish that I could paint a scene so perfect and serene
that everyone would hang it where it always would be seen

I wish that I could write a poem that folks would memorize
and when their hearts were heavy, it would let them fantasize

I wish I could plant flowers along our super highways
and have them bloom the whole year through, to everyone's surprise

I would like to plant a shade tree in everybody's lawn
and hang a rope upon it for children to swing on

I would keep the spirit of Christmas alive all through the year
not by giving presents, just by spreading warmth and cheer

I wish I had been gifted and been given the power to do
the lovely things I dream about, just a time or two

Marjorie Miller

"Unspeakable Joy"

Today, I witness what I call unspeakable joy.
I witness how gracious his mercy is on the
journey I explore.
He speaks to me in ways that bring me everlasting joy.
He walks with me and he talks with me; He prays
with me and stays with me wherever I may go.
He directs me and protects me from all that is
unknown; He showers me with his blessings and
encourages me to go on.
He holds me and comforts me, when I am in distress;
I am his child created at his best.
He is my divine savior and everlasting friend,
He promises me everlasting life that has no end.
Today, I witness what I call unspeakable joy.
As I travel this spiritual journey that leads me
to who knows where, but one thing I am certain I'm
always in His care.

Robin D. Owens

Hand In Hand

One night, silent as the night could be,
I woke to find you close beside me.
Ever so quiet so has not to disturb,
I carefully studied, your every line and curve.
Trying so hard to memorize,
I suddenly noticed small wrinkles by your eyes.
Startled I thought "Has it been so long?"
I stopped to think where all the years have gone.
A rush of emotion brings tears to my eyes,
I should have so many memories of all the years gone by.
When we joined together there seemed to be so much time...
We had only our love, yours and mine.
Yet marriage and family has taken its toll
Our love and lives often seem out of control.
Yet the children you have given me
Are very precious and will always be,
A constant reminder of why we began so long ago
Down the tremulous path which has proven to show,
Our love can and will always withstand
The obstacles which so often find us, hand in hand.

Rita N. Beerle

Humanimals

They say we're more intelligent;
I wonder!

Murder, rape, incest
torture, death, crime;
things we do best
time after time!

War, ethnic cleansing, strife
euthanasia, abortion, abuse;
religious fanaticism, terrorism, genocide
In their wake, continents of refuse!

Therapy, insanity, media saturation
talk shows, analysts, misplaced blame;
the macabre side of life our infatuation
acting as if it's all a game!

Depletion, extinction, experimentation
hunting, killing, snaring;
boundaries, turf, exploitation
All done with no one caring!

And they say that humans are more intelligent
than animals!

Scott Martin

I Am

I am a computer programmer who never leaves the Application Framework.
I wonder if I will be able to take C++ classes at PCC.
I hear the silent thrumming of my hard drive spinning.
I see myself casually throwing darts at Bill Gates face.
I want to develop the first Programming language that allows only preprocessor directives to save time and space.
I am a computer programmer who never leaves the Application Framework.
I pretend that I am worth more than any other man in the world.
I feel the pressure from my parents assuredly pushing me forward.
I touch the sun.
I worry that I will not get a college scholarship.
I cry at the thought of not being a success.
I am a computer programmer who never leaves the Application Framework.
I understand that I must support my parents when they get old.
I say that if you don't try your hardest it's not worth it.
I dream that I will become a millionaire.
I hope I will go to heaven.
I am a computer programmer who never leaves the Application Framework.

Kurtis McCleery

I Am

I am a wacky girl who loves pretty things, like nature.
I wonder if I'll go to a university instead of a college.
I hear continuous talk from a bubbling stream.
I see angels in the clouds.
I want to keep earth clean.
I am a wacky girl who loves pretty things, like nature.

I pretend continuously that all human's actually care about the earth.
I feel my heritage comes in good use.
I touch the emotions of my friends and get the truth.
I worry that I'll never see my father again.
I cry for the extinction of all races will soon come to be.
I am a wacky girl who loves pretty things, like nature.

I understand the words of wordless music.
I say, "If someone speaks out, let them be heard."
I dream about living a carefree life without death and pain.
I try to understand the problems of life.
I hope that one day I will live again.
I am a wacky girl who likes pretty things, like nature.

Michelle Martinez

I Am

I am a unique girl who cares about all kinds of people
I wonder when and if diseases will be cured
I hear cried of children who are dying and are sick
I see generations after generations that are starving
I want for my little brother to be able to walk
I am a unique girl who cares about all kinds of people

I pretend that the world will become a lot better
I feel the pain and struggle of disabled people
I touch God and all my guardian angels
I worry about the health of very sick people
I cry about people who are dying because they are sick and nothing can cure them
I am a unique girl who cares about all kind of people

I understand the difficulties of life even though I don't like them
I say that God is with us all the time and watching out for us
I try to make the best out of life, and so should you
I hope one day we will have world peace
I am a unique girl who cares about all kind of people

Mara Ruth Medina Martinez

I Am A Dreamer In This World

I am a dreamer in this world, curious and compassionate.
I wonder why there is racism and cruelty.
I hear the cries of pain from violence.
I see the destruction of the world around me.
I want this world to be a better place.
I am a dreamer in this world, curious and compassionate.

I pretend this world is not my world.
I feel the worry of people around me.
I want to touch the hearts of others.
I worry I will die without being heard.
I cry about the way we treat others.
I am a dreamer in this world, curious and compassionate.

I understand this world isn't perfect.
I say it almost could be, if we try.
I dream of a world in perfect unity.
I imagine myself in that world.
I hope my dreams are your dreams.
I am a dreamer in this world, curious and compassionate.

Mandy Osweiler

If I Could Only Run

If I could only run as before
I would never ask the Lord for more

I'd run the roads of our countryside
And mimic an exhilarating blissful ride

When the morning dew is on the ground
And the singing of birds is the only sound

It clears mind and soul - puts one in awe
To see God's work is without a flaw

To look up at the cloudless sky
And feel that one can almost fly

This is by far the highest of highs
To see the world through unclouded eyes

But then the illness and pain appeared
Came the despair - its ugly head had reared

I had to embrace a bit a strength
Just to walk - I'd go to any length

So slowly now I roam around
The familiar paths I used to pound

I close my eyes and feel and see
That colossal high - no one can take that from me.

Theodora Czarnecki

Untitled

If I knew your heartaches, I'd take them away.
I would take you far from all of your troubles
to a place free of pain.
If only I knew what you thought,
I could help take away your pain.
That one little word-help.
I listen for it, but I never hear it,
When I hear it, will it be too late?
Will you be gone,
Never to be saved or brought back.
Will I forget and go on?
No - I will not, I will
Always stay, always wonder
if it's too late.
Someday tell me, so I don't wonder
if it's too late to save you.

Tara Brie Alvarez

"Wanderlust"

They talk of gypsy in the soul, of me it must be true.
I yearn to travel far and wide this glorious world to view.
I envy spacemen in the sky, bright ships upon the sea.
Caravans upon the road, just a gypsy don't you see.
The China Wall so strong and bold,
The far far north so crystal cold.
Islands swaying in the breeze,
Dolphins romping in the seas.
One place I'd really love to see
The garden of Gethsemane.
Dutch gardens where the windmills churn,
Quiet forest pools edged with fern.
Down the Nile in summer's heat
Listening to a jungle beat.
Traveling through Spain's sunny land,
Running barefoot on Sahara sand.
Visiting cathedrals tall,
Praying at the Wailing Wall.
Yes I'd like to see it all
Before I hear that long last call.

Sybil Benton

Eileen

I used to call her about now
I'd hear her sweet voice and loving tone
I used to call her about now
But now I can't for she's gone home

I used to see her when I'd awake
I didn't want to leave
I couldn't kiss least she'd wake
I'd see her again, for I believed

I used to feel her presence near me
For she was always on my mind
But now I have a hard time feeling
Then I could see but now am blind

I wish right now I could hold her close
Tell her I love her and kiss her sweet face
But now she's gone I know not where
Will God ever let me find such a place?

Lee Gray

Untitled

If a rose had a shell, would its beauty be dimmer?
If covered in clouds, do the stars still glimmer?
An eagle not seen still soars through the skies.
What one may not see finds another's eyes.

The strength of a man isn't measured by weight.
Honesty, not a character trait.
Generosity could still harbor hate.
Courage can be just an act of fate.
Just merely to look can't describe a man.
His heart and his soul are what make him grand.

Love has no face, no features, no scars.
It burns bright as night through the clouds as the stars;
It sails like the bird the woman, the man
Their hearts intertwined; LOOK! if you can.

D. Elder

Untitled

Wonder what Jesus of Nazareth would think
If he were to make a return
about all that goes on with himself as a link,
Embarrassed, would he red-faced burn?

Wouldn't he sicken of so-called prophecy,
Believe his own eyes and his ears?
All that he preached as he's well meant-legacy
Wander if 'twould bring him to tears?

Prophecy consigns humans to a fiery hell
If they don't believe what they read
Jesus taught kindness - a
peaceful "all's well"-
To let greater love supersede.

He'd hear of the sects, wars,
troubles, dissensions.
Through all ages gone in his name
Some of such wrath, horror, lasting dimensions
He might turn and leave filled with shame!

Pauline Moore Fox

One More Time

If I could just hold you, one more time,
If I could just feel you close, one more time.
If I could just tell you, "I Love You," one more time.
My life would not be over, for the rest of time.

If only I could kiss you, one more time.
If only I could hear you whisper,
"I Love You," one more time.
My life would be new, one more time.
"No," it would never be enough, just
one more time.

Melvin R. Bishop

enomiS In The Mirror

See if you be able to think of the poet's thinking
If you be able to, be as lightning to let the poet know
Mind you! You shan't to anyone tell of the poet's writing
Otherwise yourself shall but sand become, no longer able to blow
No! fear not! For the poet lacks the heart of such devil evil
Everything the poet possesses is but an art of humor, not peril
Be reminded though of the poet's trivial intentions!
Yield not to your wrong thought of the poet's implications!
So sad the poet no longer knows what to indite about
If only his tongue hath such words to trait your nature!
But sadly the poet hath not, by virtue of his culture
Unfortunately the poet must part to part take, so he's out!

Sibusiso "Sibu" Msomi

Evening Of The Morn

I will not know another Spring—
I'll miss the brave, bright daffodil
That harbingers the birth of all things
Greening soon, and, still, despite the
Errant cold of Winter's reluctant passing,
Stands a symbol of Hope and Promise of
Summer's bloom—

Wish me the courage of a daffodil, that
I may, in the cold winter of my heart,
forlorn, stand brave in the chill of hope-
lessness of knowing that, for me, it is the
Evening of the Morn—

I have walked so long and so far to where
I was going—

Virginia D. Stahl

Never Say Good-Bye

As I sit in the dark I remember the past.
I'll not say Good-bye to you,
we'll be friends to the last.
I want to stay forever
to hold your hand,
but a foreign plane is taking me
to walk on foreign sand.
And friend I ask one favor,
only one favor before I go.
Please! just remember the times we shared
and never let those moments go.

Before we laughed now we cry.
Yes I'll always love you
and I'll never say Good-bye!

Trica Dyal

Loving And Giving

Dad said show me a man that money can't change
I'll show you a man that has much to gain
In the eyes of our Savior he is one his way
Up Jacob's ladder there to stay
Climbing each rung with precision and care
He uses his talents, God given to share
At home he was taught how to love and give
Not only his money, but how to live
His brothers and sisters, numbers seven and two
Were often his critics and playmates too
when he was ten into a hammock he lay for awhile
To sleep and dream as only a child
When meal time came, mother counted the chairs
One son was missing, her meals to share
The search was on for this missing lad
He was found asleep in that hammock by Dad
Mother's prayers brought home from the war five boys
Who served their country with pride and joy
You have nothing said Mother, until you give it away
What an excellent example for our lives today.

Markwood C. Reid

Never Again

As I sit here
I watch the conversation between two peanut shells.
The smaller shell asks:
"Why must you conquer me?"
"Because I am bigger than you,"
The larger shell replies.
"I am bigger and stronger
And therefore must win."
"Oh" replied the smaller shell
And gave into his desires.

Lyle A. Feigenbaum

"A Teacher's Dream"

Sunshine streams through the window
Illuminating the room with golden light
A young child sits at a desk
Learning how to read and write.

A teacher stands in front of the room
Not more than a child herself
She dreams of making this world a better place
By pledging that books will do more than collect dust on a shelf.

She has her work cut out for her
The road ahead has many twists and turns
There is so much she has to teach
And so many lessons to be learned.

She must keep moving along for time is running short
Just as the sun will set behind the hill
Her students will soon be moving on.

Michelle Y. Miller

Gone

Shattered Dreams of innocence
illusions fill my head
Complicated intricate webs of
frigid calmness do I dread.
You left me deranged and ever pressing.
I pondered when and why would you go.
I always knew but didn't show.
I slipped on a mask of Jubilance
and glee
I knew you would leave, I knew you
would leave me,
Did you think I was spun with
threads of insincerity? Your
inner soul I could see
you couldn't hide couldn't hide that from me.

Paige N. Casey

That Special Someone

Someone to love is what I need.
I'm a flower ready to bloom, yet still a seed.

Someone with whom my own self I'll reveal,
Like a bright, shiny apple without its red peel.

My feelings are mute, for nobody knows
as the love in my heart continues to grow.

One day I will open, my inner self blooming,
to that one human being who knows what he's doing.

He'll lift my soul high and my love will fly out,
For my dream has come true, it has now come about.

Way up to the heavens, my heart does soar,
Someone's changed my life, he has opened the door.

My heart's been unlocked, the key thrown away,
And I hope and I pray that these feelings will stay.

But if they should not, I'll be sure to not cry,
'cause for now I'm a seed that will surely not die.

And so I'll keep dreaming until it comes true,
though my heart will be happy whatever I do.

Kimberly DeGroff

Just A Thought Away

Even though I'm not there,
I'm just a thought away.
You are always there for me,
As I am for you.

The meaning is not understood,
By me or by you.
I'm not a stranger to you anymore,
As I was before.

I would do anything for you,
As you would for me.
Our relationship isn't over as far as it goes.
If you ever need to talk,
Just remember—I'm just a thought and a call away.

Even though I'm just that thought away,
Time is passing by as well as every day.
Maybe our hearts will be close once again,
Unless we decide to never meet again.
But just remember, I'm just a thought away.

Tracy J. Lewis

Passed By

Life's golden way has passed me by
I'm not green like the sea, not blue like the sky
I'm old and tired and withered and worn inside
On the outside, I'm physically new
Not sea like the green, not the sky like the blue.

Life's golden way has passed me by
Stone-cold hard, not able to cry
I've been beaten and battered by life's whirling wind
Hurt beyond the longful point, not able to mend
Cried all my tears, stone cold hard

Life's golden way has passed me by
On my way, ready to die
Wishing for death to take me by surprise
No longer, will anyone, hear my heartful cries
Life's golden way has passed me by

Rebecca Rae Hill

"I Never Had A Chance"

As I cry out from my grave with a voice so very faint,
I'm the unborn little child you killed who God made a Saint.
I will never know the joys of life or even how to dance,
For I was not conceived in love so I never had a chance.
The world will never know of me because of my terminated birth,
My life was destroyed pre-mature from the rest of the earth.
If I had of been born I may have been named Joy or Lance,
But being unwanted as I was, I never had a chance.
Our society has grown to be so ruthless, cruel and invented,
Considering the way I was disfigured, destroyed and tormented.
If only they would have let me be born to see my face,
I might have contributed life to the struggle of the human race.
Uncaring hands have destroyed me without even a simple glance,
They thought only of themselves, you see, I never had a chance.

Wilkie L. Sanders Sr.

Kaleidoscope

As I sit and ponder the window of time
Images flash like a kaleidoscope before my mind

My life spreads out before me - present and past
And, I wondered if I had accomplished anything at last

As a child, I was a shell waiting to be filled
With dreams of the days to come that were not to be stilled

Would I be a model, dancer, or great artist, I just knew
Whatever the price I had to pay, it just had to be true

But, with great expectations also comes reality of life's heavy load
And with reality - so shall we reap the seeds we sewed

The kaleidoscope flashed bright, multitudes of colors into
the span of time, and as the years went spinning by, I turned around
and asked if life had been kind

I stand now in the maturity of my years and watch the
kaleidoscope again flash
I ask myself for the thousandth time if the decisions I made
had alas been rash

Now on the threshold of a new beginning that holds both remorse
and fear
As the colors again flash to reveal everything that I hold dear

What would my life bring in the days to come, joy or strife?
Only God can give me the answers to all that I desire in life.

Lois Lowe

Confederate Rest

Hanging leaves, a bough, a branch,
Immortal souls left to chance.
Grass overgrown and moss on stone,
Quiet underneath, a world unknown.

One boy in blue buried amongst the gray,
What on earth will mamma say?
A walk through here reveals no noise,
All is peace and serene with these boys.

Do not these ghosts who play at night
make all unjust return to right?
For their ground is sacred not hollow or profane
and all who dwell here are one and the same.

Valor, honor, tradition and much more,
Underlined in a speech that began: "Fourscore."
You may take the flag, our heritage and might,
But do not tell us wrong from right.

Michael A. McCaffrey

I Wonder

I wonder if I will ever be a star
I wonder will I turn out right,
I wonder if I will grow up to
be a successful person.
I wonder, I wonder upon a star
I wonder if I can be a singer,
if I can sing good.
I wonder, I wonder upon twinkling star.
I wonder will the world turn out and be a
better place to live.
I wonder about everything, but wondering
can change everything.
I wonder, I wonder,

Keep on wondering

Shannon Colbert

Thinking of You

Your love and your laughter
Always filled the room.
Your joy inspired me
To be a better person.
Just your presence
Was enough to make me smile.
The happiness you have left me
Is still in my heart.
Every memory,
Every good time,
Was worth the while.
Everlasting love
Was the blanket you wrapped me in
Whenever I was cold and alone.
It still keeps me warm
Every time
I think of you.

Sonya Passi

"Of Course, Ah Horse"

"Ah horse"
""
"Ah horse.
Ah horse!"
"Ah horse."
"Ah horse!
Of course,
Ah horse!"
"Ah horse!"
"Of course,
Of course!
A horse!"
"A horse.
Of course!"
"A horse."
"Of course,
Ah horse."

W. S. McCormick

Baby

A baby is tiny
A baby is joy
You're having a baby girl or a boy

Love it with care
To cherish and share
Hug it and kiss it like a big teddy bear

When you have your baby we will all say
"God bless you on that special day"

Leann Wintermute

Candelabrum

A candle dances,
a beam of light
of beauty and brilliance
displaying life.
A flood of wax
runs down the stem,
securing itself
at the end.
As a human,
as time grows on,
it burns and burns
until it is gone.

Tom Creedon

The Mountain

The mountain stands defiant,
a challenge steeped to climb -
if rightly paced with proper haste
one can prevail, in time.

The mountain taunts ascension,
a pinnacle of height -
its peak, a dare; each step, a stair...
its summit soon in sight.

The mountain, now a footstool,
the conquest slow but sure -
once scaled, its crest no more the test
of will set to endure.

Randy Almond

"To Play"

"To play is but more than
a dream, a dream of eternal
love."

"To fly upon the high
rigid skies is more than a
fantasy."

"To dance with the angel
of Death is but a tender
horror."

Why is life so complicated?

Ryan C. Olsen

Dream Of Death

Late last night I had a dream
A dream of a blank place
And in that dream I saw it
I saw her lovely face

I slowly walked to her
To her deathly bed
I looked down upon her
With my hand I touched her head

I looked at her sad face
With so much pain in my eyes
I really wanted to say it
But I couldn't watch her die

That night I thought about it
But it was too late to do
I never got to tell her
Grandma, I love you...

Kim McCance

Season Of Death

An artist dream,
a leaf's nightmare,
a rainbow of colors,
warm, pretty.

But look very closely,
the colors will trick you.

It is cold out there,
stay awake,
the season of death
is among us.

Lynnea DeHaan

Daddy Dear

A man of wisdom, in a loving kingdom.
A father so bold, yet, not to old.
Pride so strong, meaning no wrong.
Fighting to the end,
Not willing to bend.
The price he paid,
Was a little over weighed.
He as a good man,
Always keeping his stand.
Strong in his beliefs,
Now he has his relief.
It's so very confusing,
Why we are losing.
My father was dear,
And always so near.
I love him still,
With all my will.
All I pray is, to find my way.
To my daddy dear,
To past the years, together.

Moira Lynn Boughton

Untitled

Time flowing
A flood of hours and days,
A raging river.
If we try to swim
We are swept away.
The years follow one another,
Soldiers, stiff and precise.
And then they are gone, into battle,
Never to return.
Life is a barrier
Whose only gate is time,
Through which we pass
Stolidly and without thought.
The future seems always
A shining vision before us.
But when we open our eyes
We are in chains and anchored
Firmly in the past.
We cannot feel the flowing time
Until it has ceased.

Mara Hardy

An Angel's Prayer

Close above us looking down
A guardian angel can be found

In times of trouble and good deeds
A guardian angel is what we need

They're in disguise through out the day
Protecting us in many ways

You may not always see their wings
For angels live in many things

It's up to you to feel the love
For what a guardian angel's done

A gentle touch, some kind words shared
These are ways an angel cares

Within our hearts and in the air
A guardian angel's everywhere

Close above you looking down
Your guardian angel can be found

S. V. Munoz

The Surgeon

As I lay, sleep filled my head.
A knight appeared beside my bed
With silvered armor all aglow.
He smiled at me, laying there below.

Where he came from, I didn't ask.
He was overtaken by the urgent task.
He drew his weapon for the fight.
The blade was glistening in the light.

The razored steel came down to rest
And glided slowly across my breast
With layered flesh opened wide
He slew the dragon deep inside.

Then quietly, he closed the wound.
The dragon was carried from the room.
And when he said that he was done
I knew MY battle had been won.

Some people say it was just a dream
That knight in armor all agleam.
But it was real, he gave me the chance
To laugh, to sing, to pray, to dance.

Sharon F. McCall

The Eagle

E agle, the symbol of America,
A land of liberty,
G racefully skims the mountain tops
L ike its nation it is free.
E agle, symbol of Nature's majesty!

Michael Pedley

Reality

Floating on a breeze
A leaf gently descending to earth
Lost in its own world

Being swept about on the ground
In a twirl, suspended-
Ah, but only for a brief moment

Coming to rest, dream like
Curling up, only to fade away
Sadly lost among the masses

Sandra Schouten

Children's Faces

Have you ever really looked into,
A little child's face,
And seen before you limpid pools
Reflecting heaven's Grace.

The Innocence seen mirrored there,
The trust that knows no bound,
The Love that gently filters through,
In children's eyes are found.

And if by chance you smile at him,
And he returns your grin,
You know that you have won his heart,
There's room for you within.

So, in our hearts, and in your Love,
Let children hold first places,
Because the Love God has for you,
Is seen in children's faces.

Sister Stephen Marie C.S.J.,
Boston

Each Day

Each day I shed
a little skin,
And

My heart a little
more forgiving,

My mind a little
more tolerant,

My soul is a
little more wiser,

My life a
little more rewarding.

Each day I shed
a little more skin,
And
Grow...

Randy Porter

Eclipse

As I peer on to the tinted grassy field,
a look of confusion strikes my face,
then I realize.
Forbidden to look up, the
rebel inside takes just a glance.
My eyes! I close them tightly.
I open.
Darkness.
Again I look up quickly.
I see a bright crescent tear
in the sky, for all free spirits
to depart,
but this sacred moment
lasts only so long.
I blink.
The sun. It's back.

Kate Slowick

Untitled

Handful of tears
A loss of words
I watched our love
Drown and Disappear
Love went wrong
In ways more than one

That last good-bye
Still screams in my ear
Her eyes like stars
Have fallen from my sight
My love brings bad luck
And has happened
More times than one

This broken heart
I know will never mend
I always lose
And this book of love
Really does end.

Mark W. Shoemate

Haiku

The sun is setting
A bird is watching the sky
Then he flies away.

Paul Kubik Jr.

The Magic Garden

There is a place upon the earth
A magic garden grows
Two people made this happen
Here's how the story goes.
Two children when they fell in love
Amid a world of strife
In spite of all objections
They became husband and wife

So quickly did the years go by
And almost unaware
As quickly as you blink your eye
Your here and now your there

But while the time was passing
They taught me these four things
Be brave have courage hope and love
For with these you have wings

And with these wings you fly above
All those content to sit.
For quitters never win
And winners never quit.

Vanessa Capobianco Fontana

Next To

Describe me
A man
In a black room
On an ebony throne
Without windows
To see out
Next to
A door
In a tower
On a landing
Without out hall ways
To walk down
Next to
A staff
In a king's Majesty
On a simple glass stand
With only my silhouette
To light
Next to
A man....

Karima C. Johnson

The Mirror

In a room, so far away,
A mirror shows a girl of easy prey.
She stands in front, and with amaze,
Sees behind an evil gaze.
Eyes and mouth and beautiful skin,
All await his wicked sin.
Man in black, knife so bright,
Who is he in dead of night?
Shrieks of help, screams of pain,
Hush, hush now or he'll do it again.
He pushes, groans, and rips and bleeds,
Only to fulfill his horny needs.
Little girl, left on the floor,
Can only hear the slam of door.
The mirror, shattered, shows reflection.
Of this man's hateful erection.
No more innocence, no more love,
No more peace of graceful dove.
Her world has crumbled and is no more,
As she dies on that cold floor.

Meghan Fryett

Jive at Five

One morning, arising at five
A mother named Bev would survive
Staying calm and serene,
Trying not to be mean
When her daughter started to "Jive"

Her darling, named Summer Reanna,
Joyfully played the "piana."
Eating breakfast that day
While plunking away.
She invented the key of "B"-nana

It was rather a mess on the keys
With banana all over her knees
She played soft and mellow
But when Bev saw the jello
She cried, "Oh, my dear Summer, please!"

The piano is no place to dine
Believe me, I'd like it just fine
If you'd breakfast in bed,
Then lay down your head
And sleep 'til quarter to nine!"

Robert B. Moore

My Friend

Another year is closing
A new season to begin
As autumn blankets down
And winter settles in.

The year has seen changes
Some sorrows and regrets
But October brought a smile
It's the month in which we met.

The way you've made me feel
In the time we've been together
Are feelings that I'll cherish
Hold dear to me, forever.

Your eyes they tell a tale
No words could ever say
For you have touched me deeper
In a mystical, yet gentle way.

So if it's meant to be
That our souls do not amend
To me, you'll always be special
Much more, you'll be my friend.

Loretta F. Carrington

"Let Only Love Remain"

In my heart I feel,
a pain that's ever so real.
Aches so strong inside,
tears I just can't hide.

Thoughts running so wild,
like a tiny frightened child.
How could it come to this,
my life seems so amiss.

Can I change this path,
and let go of all my wrath.
Free me of this sorrow,
so I can smile tomorrow.

I try to act so strong,
but everything I do is wrong.
Please take away this pain,
let only Love remain.

Patricia Lynn Emerson

Sorrowful Tears

She lies here with a silhouette
A peaceful scene, a dramatic set
A fallen tear strolls down her cheek
She cannot move for she is too weak
A thought of failure in her mind
Even more for her to find
She cannot take the pain inside
The feelings are too hard to confide
A rush of blood flows to her heart
It hits her chest like a thrusted dart
The pain has stopped now she is numb
She checks the pulse of her thumb
A still figure in the bed
With a sorrowful mind
She now lies dead

Paula Bennett

A New Dawn

Conjure me up
a river of freedom.

Let it flow to
the cleansing glow
of a moon —
sinking into a dawn
yawning the spirit
of a new day -
that offers me to
itself
as a new birth
warms the earth.

Cradle me in this space
in this day among
this prodigal race.

Paddy Fitzpatrick

Untitled

How does
a seed
become
a flower?
what power
ignites
the sun
with moon,
earth and shower?
I have seeds.
I have never.
planted flowers.
that never.
have blossomed
oh, touch me.
now, so I can.
grow.

Kathy Robbins

"Love"

Love means affection,
admiration, attachment,
devotion, loyalty,
attraction, tenderness,
passion, to hold dear,
to cherish, to share,
to care for, but above
all this love means
you and me

Michelle Thibault

Al

He's 85 today.
A shadow of
His former self.

He was so strong,
He walked
For miles each day.

His German shepherd,
Lady, was her name,
His constant companion.

His life is ebbing,
Slowly moving
Toward the end,

Yet he remembers
All the busy times,
The things he did.

His life has
Touched so many
Positively in passing.

Lillian Dawson

Coffee Aroma

Coffee aroma awakens
A sip livens
Encourages readiness
for today

Sally Hill

Smile From The Ashes

The phoenix is at your alter now.
A song of eternity it sings.
I wonder if you'll ever hear,
The ancient message that it brings.

Oh, I was like you long ago,
Knew confusion and stormy weather.
Then They sent this same bird to me,
And He put the answer together.

Yesterday's only a memory,
Tomorrow only a fool's dream.
Now consists of each moment,
Time is not what it may seem.

The life you seek is already yours,
Just open your eyes and see,
And know tomorrow this grand bird,
Was sent to you by me.

Kathy McKee

Love Is...

A wingless bird
A song silenced
Dried flower petals on the ground
A cloudy day
A misguided arrow
Mountains withering into dust
A motionless ocean
A shattered window
Crushed butterflies laying on the floor
A cold hand
A ringing clock
Shades of red fading to black
A dancer's broken legs
A locked door
Love is...
Dead.

Lloyd Patrick B. Quinto

The Memory Train

It's funny how the mind works
A sound unlocks a dream,
And like a video we play
You see it on a screen.

Your hear the whistle of a train
and your thoughts search back to find,
A safe, secure, and loving place
that comforts you inside.

A picture holds a special key
It locks a feeling past,
It makes you hurt, it makes you smile
That train goes by so fast.

We share so many happy times
Enduring with the years,
Our memories we'll always have
A train our minds can steer.

So when times get tough, just close your eyes
let the memory train roll through,
and hitch a ride on pleasant dreams
like the Love I hold for you.

Steven Sykora

"Measuring A Lion's Heart"

Gaze inside the cage and you will see
a splendid anomaly.
A beast quite large—a king, in fact,
the ruler of his habitat
who paces with a rich reserve
and cautions those of weaker nerve:
Halt! Stand back! and be apprised
that it's folly to measure his size.
Just as Locke knew that to measure time
is to tamper with the once sublime
so the lion knows in his wild wisdom
that the laws of his heart
defy every system.

Lynne M. Connors

"Fall"

A time of beautiful color
A time of fun for all
On Saturdays and Sundays
There's couch potato ball
And let us not forget
The fun for children on halloween
Or a trip into the country
Where farmers harvests can be seen
The air is crisp and refreshing
But it also has a chill
We all know what's coming
A matter of time until
Mother nature starts to blow
That cold north wind
And another beautiful season
Is about to meet its end

Mick Wempe

It's Time

I want to raise the window up
And hear the peepers sing.
I want to hear the woodcock
With the wind upon his wing.
I want to feel the happiness
The songs of robins bring.
I want some pussy willows...
I just want it to be spring.

Nancy R. Weissmuller

"Heaven - Sent"

In the sweet music Heaven-sent,
A wondrous hope to me was lent.
The mellow notes,
So soft......,
So clear....,
No mortal notes could be so clear
As these sweet strains that came to me,
In this my souls soliloquy.

Then into heaven it returned
To greater heights than I had yearned,
And my faith which undulate had grown
Still sought that glorious unknown,
For there was calm tranquility
In this immortal melody.

Ruth A. Russell

The Picture

This is a little ditty,
About a trip to the city,
To shop for a picture suiting me,
And decorate a room sunny as can be.
I found just the one,
The right size, color, what fun,
Mechanical I'm not, in fact, a chore,
But I set to task, what a bore.
I started my job, hammer to hang,
It fell to the floor, Dang,
So now I must get the proper tool,
At last, it's right, I'm no fool.
The picture is beautiful, I see,
I admire my handiwork with glee,
My family gathers to view my crown,
When all exclaim, "It's upside down."

Sharon J. Boan

Grandfathers Legacy

A rounded mound of dirt
Above a hole so deep.

Brilliant flowers, colors gay
Beside a casket gray.

The short bearded preacher
Like an aged prophet, he.

Mournful somber silence
Muffled sobs, stifled cries.

Like a cannon's shot
The words ring out,
A shout of victory:

Wilhelm is not dead;
He lives for all eternity!

Walter E. Anderson

To My Sweet Spring Breeze

You tease, taunt, brush yourself
across my lips seductively.
Softly kissing my cheeks until
they blush slightly.
My hair sways gently as you
play your game, making me
feel sensuous, sexy, making
me want you always.

Nicole Peterson

The Gypsy Rats

Late one night
after a terrible spat,
I dreamed I was kidnapped
by a gypsy rat,
He dragged me to the river
and through me in,
Then stood on the shore
with a big fat grin,
He danced and clapped
tambourine in hand,
Then up came some more
with a full-fledged band,
Their eyes were glazed
as I swam ashore,
That's when they grabbed me
threw me back once more.
Late at night, if you spat
be careful of the gypsy rats.

Kay Franzel Allen

Oceans Oratorio

When summertime is over
all eyes and ears are closed.
Some think that natures beauty
becomes a faded rose.

Her beaches are deserted
they're under lock and key.
Still, deftly she composes
the rhythm of the sea.

At times it is a whisper
or she may choose to roar.
Each wave is guided by her hand
until it's kissed the shore.

Her rays of light are dancing
above the ocean floor.
And yet, her heart is broken
we've hurt her to the core.

She set the stage so graciously
thinking all would stay.
The theater remains empty
for her winter matinee.

Sharon Pandiani

Spring

Spring is to remember
All our hopes, and fears.

To see, and to recall
Our long deceased dears.

But even though we miss them,
Deep, down in our hearts.

They'll always be within us,
They'll always be a part.

So we don't have to cry,
When someone else does die.

We'll always have our memories-
That's what really counts.

For in our memories there's hope.
And that's what love's about.

Sarah Winter

One Leaf

The wind was blowing
all the leaves around
most of them were falling
slowly to the ground.

But on one twig
a leaf still hung
it wasn't very big
and for dear life it clung.

The wind could not tear it
from its natural given home
the leaf still lived and bared it
for on it the sun still shone.

Then one day the leaf gave in
to the mighty wind
the leaf could no longer make it
so it let the wind just take it.

To the ground the little leaf fell
with the other leaves and all
and in the distance a ringing bell
as the snow began to fall.

Michele Ann Fye

Help Them Please

See the old woman there
all the people do is stare.

She has no food so she can't eat.
She has no home, she walks the street.

She carries her clothes in shopping bags.
The people call her a dirty old hag.

All they do is pass her by
not even stopping to wonder why!

Don't they know it could be them,
whose on the street,
not having any food to eat!

Let's help her now and give a damn,
so she don't eat from garbage cans!

Help these people for you see
they could be you,
or even me!

Patricia Arana

Untitled

I don't know how to say,
All the things I'd say to you.
From the special times we shared,
To the giving things you do.
But if I could I'd truly say,
You've gave me a new start.
To enjoy a brand new feeling,
That's been growing in my heart.
In a place that was so empty,
And felt so all alone.
A place that I could hide behind,
With walls built in stone.
In a world that offered nothing,
You gave me a part of you.
And melted down my heart of stone,
With the little things you do.
And if people counted happiness,
In days and nights and years.
I'd have to measure all our love,
In joys and sighs and tears.

Tim Ewing

Timeless Love

The years we've spent together,
all the time we spent apart

The words we spoke in anger,
and the words straight from the heart

The times we spent sleeping,
and those we spent awake

I never knew how much time,
with you I'd want to take

A never ending moment,
is what I truly need

Maybe that will be enough,
our souls together freed

Then hand in hand together,
forever we shall fly
Loving one another,
forever, you and I.

Whitney L. Fischer

"Peace Within"

Where is peace among
all this turmoil that
all governments place
upon us? Peace has
fled from all the
nations of this earth
just as a scab releases
its puss. If there
is no Justice, How
then can peace prevail?
How can we ask our
children to succeed,
if we without peace,
have so sadly failed.
My fellow man there
are many ways to peace,
but only one is genuine.
The only true way to such peace,
is when we find our own within.

Victor Sahagian

Wander...

Dying, he strolls
along vast mountains.
Can't think
only sore feet.
Deep cuts.
Feeling pain.
Blistered and burnt
by a sun
he can't remember.
He forgot
the one who taught silence.
He forgave
the one who brought tears.
wanderer who believes
the dying trees
bleed his sorrow.
Looking through emotion,
glass cracked by wind,
the maker of damnation
destroys another friend.

Rebbecca Brown

The Tale Of A Murderer

Just a boy, 18 years old
Always do what I'm told
Father always seems to scold
For what I'm never told

Not a tear do I shed
With each lash to the head
Have another shot of gin
Before the beatings begin

Day in, day out
Letting his aggressions out
Tired of being slapped around
I put father under ground

"Guilty" said the jury
Condemned by society
Judged by my supposed piers
They weren't beat for 18 years

On death row I await
The meeting of my fate
Listen to me, you can be sure
This is the tale of a murderer

Myke J. Friscia

Traces Of Me

Among the weeds I'm the flower,
among paupers I'm the prince,
among friends I'm the enemy,
among many I'm alone.

Among sounds I'm what you hear,
among you I stand between,
among the brave I'm the scared,
among surprises, I'm the known.

Among beaches, I'm without sand.
among stars, the one that doesn't shine.
among the spirits you don't see
there is always me.

Maria Retounotes

The Little Pink Flower

Oh little pink flower
among very few, in a
field of green and blue.
My only little pink flower
in center, for all to see

A. Sipe

"Marie's Memories"

What are you searching for Marie?
Among your boxes of old -
perhaps loved faces you'll see,
on photos faded, trimmed in gold.
Maybe a little dress of lace -
on top, a clip of golden curl,
gently wrapped, put in place,
which once adorned a little girl.
Crayoned paper, folded and torn,
now graces shaky hands -
very tired and thinly worn.
Travel your box of memories -
long put to silent rest
they're your treasures Marie -
God wanted you to have the best.....

Maxine Haddox

"Friends"

A rare existence in my life
an entity on its own
Your friendship means so much to me
I know I'm not alone

As quietly as you came
I hope that you will stay
For since I have befriended you
My heart has more to say

I'm glad to have you in my life
It's good to know you're there
You represent all that is good
All that I hold so dear

We share in laughter pure of heart
Created a bond right from the start
I relate to you my deepest thoughts
Of all past battles that were fought

I'll be there if you should ever need me
I'll stay to the very end
I know that you believe in me
I love you, you're my friend

Theresa D. Cleveland

A Morning Mist

You are tears for my eyes
and a pillow for my heart
waiting to hear those words
your heart now whispers -
should they go unspoken
send your breath
anointed with love
that I may glisten
with the mist of a morning dew.

Marc A. Sabo

Light Before Darkness

When things seem to be at its darkest
And all not so well,
I look to the Lord
Whom has never failed,
With arms open wide
Accepting the flowing strength,
Ready to give praises
With no needed consent,
I'm never alone
He's forever at my side,
Drying away my tears
Even restoring my pride,
The gloominess is gone
I'm back at my best,
Owing it all to the Lord
Whom supply my happiness.

Ruby Stokes

Hand In Hand

Come hold my hand that we may stroll
Along the road of life
And handle all the winds of woe
With days of rainy strife

So hand in hand we travel on
And cherish every day
We store in mind each happening
We live along the way

There may be times when foggy mists
Will hide the road we trod
Be not afraid, my other hand
Is being held by God.

Ralph Webb

Snow

'Twas the day before T-Day,
And all through the town,
The snow kept on falling,
It kept coming down.

You got it, that's right,
The first snow of the year.
It melted, but hey,
Winter's finally here!

The following sunday,
It snowed once again.
This time it stayed,
But along with it, rain.

Under your feet,
You can hear the slish-slash,
But if the slush freezes,
The cars will go CRASH!

Vicki Smith

A Friend

A friend is someone, you love
and behold.
A friend tells you what needs
to be told.
A friend will never lead you astray.
They will only direct you the right way.
A friend will give love and respect
when it's due.
But will not uphold you in the wrong
doing you may do.
When a problem arise in your life
big or small a friend is there
by your side through it all.
So always remember through thick
and thin you can count on a
true friend until the end.

Regina R. Jones

Change

Let us come together my brother
And change what should not be.
The hate we express for one another
is killing us you see

Instead of talking it out, you and I,
Our decision is to end it all
With guns and drugs as our solution.
The world is taking a fall.

We were put here to love one another,
But the opposite we tend to do.
If there's any love involved,
It's only shown by few.

It's time to stop the ignorance
And come together as friends
Because if there is no change,
Then, the world has reached the end.

Shenita Randolph

Goodbye

A word that stings my eyes,
And echoes throughout my soul.
Something inside of me dies,
My heart no longer feels whole.
As I painfully utter this word,
I hope that we'll soon be together.
For somehow I know that I will be heard,
That goodbye is not always forever.

Stephanie Proto

Depression

Light disappears
and darkness grows
your darkest fears
come to and fro
the decision comes
the time goes by
the choice drums
and depression cries
seasons pass
trees will die
sorrows will mass
with a growing cry
the sword is thrust
and the fear grows
with the loss of trust
and the sound of crows
hope arrives
finding an end
Light survives
and life, will mend

Richard Doll

Hoar Frost

She cares not where she lays,
and does it with such grace.
Floating until she finds a place,
where she can wrap herself like lace.

And then she waits...

She starts her work in gray,
then transforms herself to white.
She waits among the grass and trees,
for the sun to make them bright.

And then she sparkles...

She knows that its short life,
the start is its conclusion.
She accepts that humans stare
at her beautiful illusion.

And then she glitters...

Her moments here are but a few,
and leaves us breathless at her sight.
But as the heat of day ascends,
she begins her lonely night.

And then she weeps...

Roselle E. Rappette

"Anger"

When anger get's the best of me,
and I have lost my head,
I often say a lot of things,
I wish I had't said.

When reason get's beyond control,
the things I do for spite,
Make me ashamed, for the meanness,
that never, help me do things right.

Someday soon, I hope and pray,
I'll reach a wiser age
and learn I never profit,
from the things I do in rage.

For anger, when it's flaming hot,
burns to a bitter end,
and when it cool's,
I find to late,
I've lost a cherished friend.

Rosalie Bane

Christmas Eve

It was Christmas Eve,
And everything was quite.
The countryside was covered
With a snow so white.
The trees were sparkling.
What a beautiful sight.
The stars were shining down
From heaven to illumine the night.
The church bells were playing.
Everything was cheerful and bright.

Joy and excitement filled the air.
Children hoping that St. Nicholas,
would soon be there.
The world awaiting, the
celebration, of a very special birth
The miracle of Jesus
Born on earth.
Sent as a gift from up above.
So we may all
Have Eternal Love.

Linda Strickland Vaught

While There Is Time

As grass is greener for the fire,
And eyes shine bright through tears;
A better world may find rebirth
After painful, blood-soaked years.

We find our life by losing it.
The things we've lost, we prize;
So threats to our democracy
Should make us realize

That honor, trust, integrity,
Must not by us be lost;
That freedom, peace, and tolerance
Are all worth what they cost.

Margaret Stamper

Surrender

Mist rises above the mountains
and floats somewhere between
heaven and earth.

Suddenly, I drop seaward;
And hear the cry of a gull.
He floats on a wave;

Letting the breezes carry him
to shore.

Marian Sullivan

A Father's Dream

He showed me a world
and gave me hope for a dream
he held my hand till I thought
I could stand alone.
When I fell, he remained up right,
holding his heart in his hand for me.
I want to stand for this man.
That showed me a world and
gave me a chance at his dream,
where a man holds his heart
in his hand for me.

Pamela Ann Crupi

"Thank You Lord"

Thank you Lord for saving me
and giving your life for my sin.
Thank you Lord for forgiving me
time and time again.

Thank you Lord for the air I breathe
and for life upon this earth.
Thank you Lord for family members,
and for their love and worth.

Thank you Lord for loving me,
and opportunities to work for you.
Thank you Lord for helping me
in all I say and do.

Thank you Lord for fellowship
with loving Christian friends.
Thank you Lord for not changing
like forever changing trends.

Thank you Lord for being there
through all my pain and strife.
Thank you Lord, I love you so
for your wonderful gift of life.

Sandra K. Jones

Untitled

With snail I did but motion
and go along his rate
Look round so slow and delicate
and pause with burdened weight

Sage hide kelly green from me
it matter for still leaves sing
With autumn rain go melody
and rosemary to the dew doth cling

Ivy hold to sycamore
and sunflower lay to ground
I slide still on the frozen mourn
with a snail that I had found

Together we did cross the bricks
turned moist and wet with dawn
and headed for the warmth of day
across the swarded lawn

But know we not our distance here
and time doth be our fate
With snail I did but motion
and go along his rate

Roderick Haney

My Granny

She lived in Oklahoma
and had a child
She was a waitress for awhile
She liked cornbread and buttermilk
Soap operas and bingo
and you would always know
That if you ever were in need
She would be the one to do the good deed
She was so nice
and gave good advice
She loved us all the same
and never called any of us a bad name
Even though now she's gone
I can still see her happy face
and still feel her warm embrace
but now I know she's in a better place.

Monique Barnhart

Untitled

God looked around his garden
And he found an empty place,
He then looked down, upon this earth
And saw our daddy's face.
He put his arms around him
And lifted him to rest.
God's garden must be beautiful,
He always takes the best.
He knew that dad was suffering,
He knew he was in pain,
He knew that he would never
Get well on earth again.
He saw that dad was hurting,
So he closed his eyes and whispered,
"My child, peace be thine."
It broke our hearts to lose him
But he didn't go alone,
For part of us went with him
The day God called him home.

Lana Quarrels

My Admirable Friend

I have a nice, admirable friend,
And his name is Bryan Gaw.
Every time I see him,
My heart would shout "hurrah!"

He is silly and funny
And sweet in every way.
That's why I look for him,
Always everyday.

Wherever Bryan goes,
I would always tag along.
We'd laugh and chat and smile,
And also play Ping-Pong.

Bryan is a really special person,
That I really know.
I wish I were Juliet,
then he'd be my Romeo.

Shiou Yung Teng

Home

Four walls to enclose us
and hold us so dear
Protect us and keep us
lighten our fears
For love and for laughter
Sweet memories and tears
This house is our home
and shall be through the years

Lynne Probert

Final Kiss

The comforting hand takes mine
and holds tight.
I used to struggle,
but I won't tonight.
Cold, bony fingers grasp
my broken heart
and twist.
My vision is blurred
with a numbing, hazy mist.
Good bye sweet breath,
Farewell bitter bliss.
Here is my last exhale and
My final kiss.

Theresa Jarvis

I Won't Let Go

Sometimes my dreams are shattered
And I feel I can't go on
But I still think of you
Even though you're gone
I try to stand up
But I always fall
I know I still need you
And love you most of all.
So I try to hold on to you,
I won't let go
'Cause you still mean
So much to me
But I can't let it show
At night I'll be counting
On that one bright star.
And in my dreams
I'll wonder
Where and how you are.

Tammy Dove

Golden Retriever

For Buddy

They say he's man's best friend
And I guess they were right
Cause he'll stand by you
Through thick and thin, day or night

People can hurt you're feelings
And make you feel mad
But a pup doesn't know the meaning
Of making his master feel sad.

I think maybe Jesus had to have a pup
And Mary and Joseph surely knew
That dogs were something special
So loyal, faithful and true

I hope that you too have a dog
Or soon will be getting one
Because he's such a special friend
Who's devotion and kindness surpasses none.

Karin Geers

On The Outside Lookin' In

As years go by so quickly
And I look at where I've been
It seems as if I'm always
On the outside lookin' in

My friends all seem contented
With husbands, homes and things
While I'm traveling life's highways
On the outside lookin' in

Perhaps it's Irish gypsy blood
That's coursin' through my veins
Or that I need a challenge
To keep me young and sane

But I know one day
I'll tarry, at a spot where I can rest
And my Lord will look upon me
Smile and say, "you did your best".

The pearly gates will open
I'll be at home again
And I'll no more be sittin'
On the outside lookin in

Marilyn Knox

Mississippi Tree

The ground got warm
And I pushed through;
The light was bright
And the sky was blue.

Through my mother's limbs,
I looked t'ward heaven.
The white man's calendar read
Fourteen Hundred eighty-seven.

Now I'm big, tall, and old.
The things I've seen
Can never be told,
Because I'm just a tree.

Louise M. Rice

In My Doubt!

As I sit and looked out the window
and I watched the falling rain.
I wondered if JESUS heard me
when I called upon his name?
For it seemed to me I was all alone
and about to go insane.
And why were things so hopeless?
and why was I in pain?
For if he really heard me
and my prayer was not in vain.
They why are things not changing?
Am I the one to blame?
And then I heard HIM say to me
I heard you call my name.
And then HE softly whispered
no your not the one to blame.
For by the powers of darkness
many lives are slain.
But you my child do not fear
For you have so much to GAIN.

Mona Carr

Forever And A Day

If you will listen to my plea
and if your heart will say.
That you will love and cherish me
forever and a day.
There is nothing on earth
I will not gladly do.
To live a life of greater worth
and give it all to you.
Because darling, you mean so much to me
that when I hold your hand
The comfort of your gentle touch
is like a soft command.
It is the urge to better things
and to a nobler goal
With all the joy that beauty brings
to elevate the soul.
And in that hope I look above
and put the past away.
That I may live a life of love.
forever and a day.

Leone P. Howard

Fallen Sequoia

The giant has fallen again
and many are coming to see.
But others are rising to thee,
like man, and like Joshua tree.

And try to remember Thy rhymes
in Thy spaces and times.

Semion Kizhner

The Hand

The hand covers her mouth
And imprisons her rage.
It holds her wrist
And steals her power.
It chains her feet
And bars her flight.
It tears out her innocence
And buries her womanhood...

Her heart weeps, mourns, and remembers.
She screams
And begins to reclaim her soul.

Valerie Ireland

Paradox

When I was young
and in my prime,
so slowly turned
the hands of time.

Now, that I'm in
my twilight years,
how swiftly time
just disappears!

Norma Kesler Lawrence

Shadow's Into Light

I am coming out the shadows
and into the light.

I am no longer in darkness
I am no longer afraid of the night

I've come to realize what happened
to me.

Was never my fault in reality

Things happen to us, and we
can't understand why.

The people we trusted, would
hurt us, and make us cry.

I can't change the past, or
what happened to me.

I can only look to the future
and let the past be.

I can feel myself changing
with each passing day.

I feel stronger and braver
in my own special way

Patricia A. Perry

Chances

Look into the water
and judge it, soiled or pure
One never can be sure, you know,
there's no way to be sure.
Some look and feel safe enough
to dive and take the swim,
and others, matters not the case,
will never enter in.
And who's to say, which man
will most enjoy the day,
The man, who took the swim around,
or the man, who walked away?

Mike Strong

Take A Road Not Taken

Take a road not taken
And lead along the way;
Set examples for others
But listen to what they say.

You have been set free into this world
To choose what one should do;
What you do with your life
Is entirely up to you.

Grow with your knowledge
And learn from your mistakes;
Teach others your wisdom
Tell them what it takes.

Share with them
All of your joy, pain, and sorrow;
Teach others to improve their lives
And change their tomorrow.

Always as you travel
Remember from where you came;
Improve with all your wrong doings
Teach others to do the same.

Shane S. Sullivan

Memories

The waves break from time to time
And leave us behind,
The memories of what used to be.

Through good ones and bad
Some of them have made me mad,
And others left me sad.

I'll never go 100 years,
And forget those happy tears.

And now we've gone our separate ways,
And moved on to better days.

Katie McDaniel

Alone And Up Till Three

My father passed away last year
and left both mom and me
now she sits in a darkened room
alone and up 'til three.
The picture of my dad is hung
on the wall so we can see
though out of sight from dark of night
he's in mom's heart with me.
My father filled mom's life
with his tenderness and love
they never went apart for long
like the clouds and sky above.
My father was a simple man
who never pushed and shoved
and mom fulfilled his emptiness
that year they fell in love.
The seasons pass and flowers bloom
the rains and snow go by
while dad looks down upon us both
at night I hear mom cry.

Richard R. Garland III

Life

Sit calmly
and let your mind wander
search far beyond
dig deep into your thoughts
see what you find
close your eyes
forget the worries
and problems
feel that you're alone
let all emotions out
find the past present
and seek the future

Kevin Schroeder

Passage Of Life

Know you are born
And life you shall live
With laughter ahead
And tears to be shed
Songs will be sung
And memories will be some.
As time runs out
You'll have no doubt
Life remains a little sprout.

Virginia Johnson

Suicide

We think life is precious
and live each day as such,
Knowing we have just one chance
and hope some lives we'll touch.

But then times get hard
and thing don't work out,
we pray our life improves
but we still have doubts.

Our mind cannot accept
the change in our days,
from happy times to sad
we just can't live this way.

So we pray the Lord understands
what we feel we must do,
our life we can no longer live
we just can't get through.

The end of our life here
no happiness will it bring,
we just hope people will learn
Suicide never solved anything.

Sharon TheuerKauf

To Remember and Cherish

To remember
and cherish
our memories
is a truly beautiful gift we share.

What we have yet to learn,
is that our hidden strength
lies in our ability to make new
and even more wonderful memories,
together,
in the times to come...

Mary Beth Googasian

My Mother's Hand

I took my mother's hand one day
And looked up to her to see
A fair young woman full of life
Looking back down at me

I took my mother's hand one day
And looked over to her to see
A middle-aged woman, tired and stressed
Looking back over at me

I took my mother's hand one day
And looked down on her to see
A woman sick with life all spent
Longing to be free

I took my mother's hand one day
And looked up to her to see
Her standing next to my dear Dad
In forever peaceful eternity

Susie Simmons

Angel

"YOU ARE MY LIFE"
and 'my love',
YOU give me a reason
to breathe every day
FOR WITHOUT YOU
I would be lost,
WITHOUT sight and
carry the burden of a cold heart.
YOU mean the world to me,
even when I'M down or
wish not to go on
YOUR LOVE reaches down to me
and pulls me up
so with that
YOU ARE MY LIFE...

Russell E. Smith II

Lonely

Sun comes thru the window
And runs across the floor
Leaving daylight in its wake
'Til shadows are no more

Then my eyes begin to see
In the morning hour
Only ordinary things
That have no special power

When the magic of the night
Disappears from this common place
I no longer hear your call
Or feel your warm embrace

As sun bleaches out the darkness
And night begins to fade
There's a cloud of loneliness
That's my eternal shade

Then night covers up the day
And lays the world to rest
You'll once more be at my side
There will be no loneliness

M. E. Young

Morning Glory of Life

I GOT UP EARLY one morning
And rushed right into the day;
I had so much to accomplish
That I didn't take time to pray.

Problems just tumbling about me —
And heavier came each task;
"Why doesn't God help me?" I wondered.
He answered: "You didn't ask."

I wanted to see joy and beauty —
But the day toiled on, gray and bleak;
I wondered why God didn't show me,
He said: "But you didn't seek."

I tried to come into God's presence,
I used all my keys at the lock;
God gently and lovingly chided:
"My child, you didn't knock."

I woke up early this morning
And paused before entering the day;
I had so much to accomplish
That I HAD to take time to pray!

Mary Osinski

Cap Eden Rock

Birdsong fugue
and scrape of sand across
a Paradise Lost

In Virgin blue
and tangerine sky
beckons one to
Eden Rock.

Psychedelic florals
and weathered vine
with battle tale and victory
meet on
Normandy Beach.

Teal ringlets flicker
sparkling lovers' eyes
as Aurora's ghost flees
the barren churchyard.

Nirvana will remain
Awash
in
Time.

Lisa Hart Willis

Untitled

A stone cast in a glassy lake,
And small concentric circles take
A journey widening evermore,
That ends a whisper on the shore

So much like us these circles be
As side by side, yet separately
Afraid to touch, we spend our days
As ripples flowing silent ways.

Pat Boudreau

Autumn

September is here - Alas,
Another year gone by;
Hearty winds, falling leaves,
South the birds will fly;
Quiet, cloudy days,
Reminiscing by the hearth;
Autumn - in all its splendor,
The season of my birth.

Susy Harris

Some Folks

Some folks are very special
and that is just the way with you
you're wonderful to be with
and nice to think of too
So you shouldn't be surprised to find
what this greeting brings
a world of whispers most sincere
for all of life good things
should come to you.

Martha L. George

Windswept

It was a yesterday
And the leaves were rainbowed
Windswept
As flights of fancy
Swirled
Upward, reaching out
Searching
For islands lucid lush
Where salmon roses sang
Of tomorrow's triumphs
But in their chorus rang
A bittersweet whisper
Of today's tragedy

Ronald A. Amarant

Untitled

When the hours creep so slowly
And the months fly by so fast,
And you think less of the future
And much more of the past.

You know that life is fleeting
You know you're growing old,
Too often you're too tired
Or upset by heat or cold.

Then you must pause and ponder
On how small your troubles are,
All your hopes are not fulfilled?
You still can travel far!

You must look to bright tomorrows
And the times that can be best,
And enjoy each day completely
And put doubts and fears to rest.

Martin A. Krass

On The Path Of Enlightenment

The darkness is upon you now
And then confusing to see how
This chosen path of yours is right
For one to find again the light.

Ask God to dwell within your heart
Envision clearly the next part
Along your path as truth is shown
To shine like stars before unknown.

Certain ways how you relate
To others even to your mate
Have followed not the holy road
Therefore karma they have sowed.

While in the light divine love grows
Revealing how the energy flows
Between each one of God's creations
As we seek our destinations.

Kristine Lovance

There's A Spider In My Purse

There's a spider in my purse
and what's worse
I put him there!

I'd spied him near, and
Not rising from my chair
I'd stretched——to sweep him up
But——he countered me, spun out
And landed eight upon my keys.

Then, in the watching mode
I waited for a time,
And now I'm happy to report
He's made his climb
Along the clutch's zippered line
And down the fold——to his escape.

He's on his way
To join his fellows in webbed space——
High on walls, in corners where
There's no need, for me to care.

priscilla whitaker

In Search Of

I watch you
and wonder
what it is
that you
are searching for in this world -
What is it
that I
could not give you?
Perhaps you
do not know yourself
and so
you wander aimlessly
in a world full
of uncaring people -
Maybe what you are in search of
is as simple as
that which you leave
behind.

Susan Mathison

Beyond The Clouds

I sometimes gaze up at the sky,
and wonder if it's all a lie.
Is life suppose to be this way,
with sins and problems everyday.
I'd rather be somewhere up high,
where mortals go after they die.
Life is perfect, life is sweet,
Beyond the Clouds where souls meet.

Karen Martins

My Love, My Friend

I sit and dream of days long gone.
And wonder where I've been.
Of what I've learned, and what I've done.
And things I've never seen.

I had my chance, a one true love
I held on, and thought would never end.
It left me on the morning dove
My other self, my lifetime friend.
The love that came to me was new
From it I was reborn.
And that is why I live and laugh
But never have to mourn.

Margaret McGrory

Roses

There was an aroma of roses
And, yet they were not there
Perhaps my mind was clouded
By the grief of yesteryear
As in a special garden
Frozen in endless time
The hues of all those roses
Touched my heart in rhyme
Then as the sun began to set
Subtle shadows seemed to fade
Something stirred within me
That was hiding in the shade
A sweet and poignant memory
Captured by the sensory.

D. Ann Parente

Hawaii And You

Palm trees swaying in the breeze
And you, my love are just a little tease
Ginger blossoms wafting on the air
Moonlight reaching to your hair.

Hawaii I Love You.
With you I share this lovely place
White caps moving with such grace
Underneath it all, a sea of blue
Utopia can only be so true
Hawaii I Love You.

Veronica B. Taylor

Garden Valley

Somewhere, O' Lord, you may have made
Another valley just like ours,
Where season's magic touch the peaks
And grace the land with flowers.

Perhaps O'Lord, you also gave
That other valley many things,
Like streams and mantled slopes of pine
And soaring skies with gentle winds.

And if O' Lord I have a choice
When beckoned on some fateful day,
Please leave me here to rest in peace
In Garden Valley, this I pray.

Walter H. McKinney

A Matter Of Life And Death

Are we really living?
Are we not dying too?
Each day that passes by,
Do we not lose our youth?

Is birth really the beginning,
The beginning of an end?
Is death really the end,
Or a soul being born again?

We often call the sick,
A being that is simply dying.
Is this really true,
Or are we really lying?

Often on a tombstone,
It reads "Rest In Peace".
But peace should always reign,
With each breath we release.

Myrian R. Catchings

Another Year

With heart aches and grief
Another year with no relief

Love shredded into tatters
living together no longer matters

Another year with no trust
pride no longer a must

With hope and dreams so grand
that was our original plan

What happened at year's end
of us to be part of the trend

Another year to endure
life's bitter tour

A year without relief in death
escaping the devil's breath

A year of despair
with no one to care

Another year with no start
of happiness of fill the heart

Nothing to hold dear
except another year

Nancy McCombs

Lines For Eternal Encouragement

I have heard Death's shoes
Approach, and pass,
Time and time anew;
So have you.

Then count this new despair
As one more lamp
To guide the way
Where nothing comes to stay.

Not joy,
Nor grief,
Nor any moving thing
With substance on the wing.

For only Change
Stays on
With constant stance
To bring about Tomorrow's other chance.

C. R. Tayman

Kindred Spirit

Sweet kindred spirit our souls
are intertwined

A kinship that is shared and
blessed by something more divine

This really defies all logic to
find such common ground

And like a diamond in the rough
this love is rarely found

Where thoughts are known before
they're spoken
Promises made - never broken

Sweet kindred spirit through all
bounds of time

I can say without reserve
—you are a friend of mine.

Marty Whipple

Smile

There is nothing quite as beautiful
As a friendly smile from you
Not the early morning sunshine
Making diamonds out of dew.
Not the waking song or robins
As they greet the morning sky
Not the gentle breeze of springtime
As it floats the butterfly

For it says, "Hello, how are you"
And "I hope your doing fine"
It lifts away the worries
That have clouded up my mind
It makes me feel like sharing
With those who, just like me
Have taken things for granted
Like this simple courtesy.

William George Snyder

Clayton

Quaint Ohio politeness masquerades
as big city
big shot.
Foundation of Clay— mold him, make him
sleek, chic, slick.
Yeah, that's him,
The Man.

Freckles hidden under tinted glass
he peers out past you
through you
he can breathe
in all this smog.

Through the bottom of my glass
he's a fine specimen
All-American boy— gone
sour, sold out
all for this
for nothing
for me.
He will die here.

Tricia Lee De Hos

Little Eaglet

The little eaglet fell
As his mother let him go
He dropped toward the earth
So many miles below
He tried to use his wings
But found he couldn't fly
His papa bird retrieved him
Still high up in the sky
He caught him on his back
Then flew up high again
Dropped him toward the earth
Oh would it never end?
This time his mother caught him
There was no damage done
For the next time that she dropped him
He flew - the battle won.
That's how the Lord will catch us
When we're falling fast with pain
And he will lift us up
Till we're flying high again.

Marilyn McNeil de Latour

Marvelous Grace

Savior, Sweet are all your promises
As I look into Thy Word
But I find it hard to claim them
And to lift you up as Lord.

As I step thro' faith to claim them
By Grace found alone in Thee.
Dying to self and my desires
Do Your Perfect Work in me.

Cleanse and fill me Oh Lord Jesus
May Thy promises I believe.
Take and use me Precious Master
So that others may receive.

May the much more of Thy Presence
As abundant Life in Thee
Fills this Dry and Thirsty vessel
To overflowing eternally.

Vesta McCurley

"Someday"

I went there in a dream
As if it were a theme
With love in the air
I will go there

"Someday"

Someday I will be
Where my heart is set
Oh, you will see
What I had met

I met with a dreamer
So far away
It was perfect there
I will be back another day

"Someday"

Natalie C. Kalugin

Dawn!

The most glorious sight to see
As it comes and casts it light on thee.
'Tis the rebirth of the day,
As we watch it we should be gay.
Orange, red, pink, purple, and blue,
For all who gaze upon it; old and new...
....Blessed be thy sun,
Which awakens each and everyone.

Vanessa Kingsbury

The Promised Land

I can hear the wind
As it whistles thru the pines,
It whispers a song of love
As sweet as many wines,

I see a lovely vision
Of us walking hand in hand,
Upon the beaches of a new world
Into the promised land,

There won't be any war
Just happiness, peace and love,
The air will be fresh and clean
And angels flying like doves,

All will be amazed
While standing in sweet delight,
At the most important event
Ever to be witnessed by sight.

Louis E. Stricklan

Flower On The Stone

The flower starts to wither,
as it's laid against the stone.
How can I go on now,
that you won't be coming home.

We each must make the journey,
I know this to be true.
My love I always thought that I,
would make it before you.

How am I to say good-by,
the anguish of it all.
The spirit has no other choice,
when the cherub comes to call.

The spiritless shadows start to move,
for the sun is nearly gone.
You were so afraid of the darkness,
shall I stay until the dawn.

Destiny is upon us,
I shall walk the path alone.
For the flower starts to wither,
as it lay's against the stone.

Raymond C. Browning

Midnight Eyes

Silence echoes throughout the mist
as midnight eyes walk the land.
Unleashed is a presence so bold,
with secrets so grand.
Disguised as friend,
revealed as foe.
Telling you things your lover
should never know.
Sweet caresses, tender lips...
promises of forever.
To you this gift I endeavor.
Be mine for eternity.
'Cause now you can never go free.
It's not a matter of love,
it's a matter of possession.
But who owns who is the question.

Vianna Thomas

Ode To Dustin

A new little boy in our neighborhood
As sweet as he can be
Dustin Michael is his name
He means the world to me.
Happy little fellow.
Eyes as dark as night
Mommy's little angel
Daddy's heavenly light
When he grows up
What will he be?
Perhaps a fire fighter
Or a sailor gone to sea,
Love he will always have from all
Because he is a living doll.

Kathy Culp

Wounded Children

Cold.
Bitter,

Cold.

Richard J. Chirip

Brother

I sat in silence
as they came,
my eyes were vacant
without the pain
of remembered thoughts
of the person you were.

Now just a body
cold and still,
where did you go
what made you - you.

This flesh and bone
is but the vessel of
an essence so fleeting
you can only live on in
the memory or a glance of
a past meeting.

But you're all right
where you are, asleep in death -
but alive forever in my mind.
until I die.

Sandra Weese

A Scream

Your actions screamed help me
as you
plunged all too quickly
down the abysmal hole.

I reached out for your hand,
to bring you back into the light,
to save you.

You jerked your hand away.
I know now what it meant.

Leslie Farnsworth

Eyes In The Dark

They're green and they glow,
As you look at them they
Seem to poison the mind,
In away that suddenly...
You seem paralyzed and dead
but yet alive,
Just like a scorpions' sting.
When the venom goes to its
worst.
It seems helpless.
You can't fight it!
"Cause the eyes are You!"

Megan Williams

Ashes

Ashes of my grandma
Ashes of my grandpa
Ashes bring many tears
Ashes bring many fears
Ashes of my great aunt Sue
Ashes of my great uncle Lou
Ashes might bring tearful faces
Ashes might be in pretty vases
Ashes are scary thoughts
Ashes Ashes Ashes

Shana Richardson

God Rest Your Gentle Soul

Although I've never met you,
at least not face to face,
I've felt that you've been with me
but I've longed for your embrace.

I've wished I could have known you
and felt your tenderness.
Heard your laughter, seen you smile,
or felt your gentle kiss.

I've studied all the photos
of you from long ago,
and seen a Lady full of love,
God rest your gentle soul.

My eyes could never see you
but my heart can feel your love.
Someday I'll come and join you
in the heavens up above.

Patricia Carter

Crazy Men

They run the streets
at night. Hunting for
victims to sabotage, and
eat them at the sound of
a heart beat. They show
no pain and no mercy
for the weak. They are
nuts and just want
to do evil. The earth
is fill with these
people but one day
us as the normal
people will over come
them with God's love
and power.

Matthew Sanchez

For A Soldier's Pay

Through the crisp chill,
at the beginning of a new day,
men intent on taking the hill,
for a soldier's pay.

Each wearing a soiled garment,
intent on saving the day,
They are a regiment,
for a soldier's pay.

As each bullet is shot,
while the children they slay,
soldier's wonder why they have fought,
for a soldier's pay.

Souls are flying away,
and still the soldiers pray,
wondering if it's worth it,
for a soldier's pay.

And yet when the war is over,
some of them will stay,
for they will never recover,
for a soldier's pay.

Wendy Vines

When the Angels Came

When the angels came and took you
away; I felt my heart go astray,
you were so loving, so sweet and
kind; until you left my wounded
heart behind. Though life is like
a flower; once it blooms; once it
dies, as I hear in the distance
silent cries. There will always be
a place in my heart for you,
Just remember Dad that I will
always love you.

Peggy Carroll

The Song Birds Return

When spring returns, it brings
Back the song birds' melody.

As it woke me in the morning
With their joyful song,

I lay there listening and relaxing,
Thanking God for our feathered friends.

They are telling us spring has returned,
And, soon, we will see

Beautiful green trees and grass,
And those lovely flowers in bloom.

It fills my heart with gladness,
And seems to renew our bodies.

Like a cup of cold water,
How refreshing to the soul.

So, little song birds welcome back,
Thank for your songs of cheer,

As you announce spring's return,
And life is born anew.

Pearl E. Jones

My Heart

My heart
beats for your love.
A love so strong, it had
to be sent from above.

My heart
won't allow me to let you go.
Because it has learned
to love you so.

My heart
will forever be yours.
As long as I have
your heart, forever more.

Stephanie Lauren Bell

Paradox

The thought of a rose,
Beauty and love
Yet even a rose has thorns

Image of the sun
Life-giving and fertile
Can also kill and deform

The trust implied in an open hand
Betrayed when the hand opens
Above a pit and allows you to fall

Love in the rose
Life in the sun
The trust is in your open hand.

Tracy Stanger

Shades Of In Between

We accused them of being black
Because they weren't white.
But if we'd stop and think a moment
We'd see we weren't right.

For we aren't truly "white"
Just as they aren't really "black".
We're all Shades of in Between
It's just love that we lack.

Rose Ingraldi

"In Alio Loco"

If I must live
behind iron barred spaces
and lettered walls
fear, noise, and isolation
Let me lot be classed
as the men dwelling around me
but as a bird of flight
that rests momentarily
on a fenced balcony
only to fly upwards to
luscious green branches
where song is language
and leaves the only barrier
to creatures dwelling
amongst cumulus playgrounds.

Stacey Stone

Personal Reflections Of Mr. Lincoln

It must have been quite a struggle-
Being President during the Civil War.
But pulling on his large, black boots,
Well, that was a struggle more.

Often around the White House,
In those very troubled days,
Mr. Lincoln had expressions,
That revealed his personal ways.

Can you just imagine,
As he would get dressed everyday,
"How will I ever get these boots on?"
He was, often, heard to say.

Someone said he was two-faced
An accusation, that's for sure.
But he said, "If I was two-faced,
How then, with this one could I endure?"

Mary, his beloved wife,
Had ways he could not understand.
But on the evening, when he was killed,
They say Mary held his hand.

Keith F. Arnold

Lost In Thought

Your mind wanders off,
Are you thinking of the future?
Your mind wanders off,
Are you thinking of the past?
Today is for real,
Sometimes you gotta get away.
You don't have to leave,
Just get lost in thought.
The best release is inside you,
There's nothing like — getting lost.

Lou J. Valdes

My Apology

You said you were my friend,
best friend at that.
I can't understand
why you would stab me in the back.

We had a little fight,
and neither of us was right.
We were both wrong,
so why is it taking so long.

I said I was sorry,
but that didn't help.
I couldn't change things.
I know how you felt.

Maybe things will change this time,
cause sorry doesn't have a good rhyme.
This is just my way,
of letting lying dogs lay.

Kristina Kennedy

At Sunrise

It was the glory of the sunrise
Beyond the mountain peak
It was the beauty of the valley
The mist over the creek
It was the chirping of the sparrows
As they built their nest
It was the sense of solitude
The day at its very best.

It was the quietness of the morning
That filled my soul with peace.
It was the tallness of the mountains
That stood with majestic grace
It was the swiftness of the river
That flowed beneath the trees
It was the sense of greatness
For God had given these.

Polly Perkins

Dean Moriarty On Tolstoy's Beard

It's out there man
beyond the skin
it's life
God is in there, man.

Look-
the beard, man.
containing life
and madness
and God
and where is it, man?
on his face!

I mean
life and God and madness
on his face, man
on his face.

Mike Klumpp

Man's Best Friend

They say he's man's best friend
but I'm a girl
and he's my best friend;
yet there's still something
that's keeping us apart
I don't know what and I don't know why
but it's keeping us apart
like a big black dot in our hearts

Stefanie Marroquin

True Life

Angels' heart we do seek when troubles bind our soul.
Secret prayers we do speak as darkness fades to dawn.
Whispers uttered, make amends,
our lives a flutter in the winds.
Turbulent seas, blackened skies,
someone, somewhere, heed the cries.
Life so precious, purist snow,
trials of living jades the soul.
Triumph struggles amidst great odds,
faltering steps, heavily fall.
Wisdom sparked through years of strife,
wonderment, a normal life.
Bear the sorrow, strike the pain,
age runs on as falling rain.
Joyful days are far and few,
grasp the rainbow, ride the moon.

Sans Cook

"Patience"

Stillness, darkness
Bitter, sour and cold
Wishing for the new
So I can out the old

Sunshine surrounds
Yet storming deep within
Smiles beam across my face
Yet, still, it's only a grin

The future is yet to show itself
The past won't let go,
The future seems so clear and bright
The past needs to be sowed

Yet - in this world of "make - believe"
I'll hold my head up high
Be strong, be tough, not give up
And somehow I'll get by

For a flower was once an ugly seed
But blossomed with sweet, tender care
Maybe someday my time will come -
Patience will lead me there.

Suzanne Siegrist

Colors

The colors live between
black and white, from
what we know best by
sight

For colors laugh, and
colors cry
turn off the light and
colors die

Each has a taste
Each has a smell
and each as a wonderful
story to tell.

Simona Shuster

Celestial Melancholy

Star-crossed by Fate
Bled together by Destiny
Created from the same light
Yet separated at birth.

Still, at the Exodus
They will melt into music
And never really know
They are holding one another.

Stacey L. Underwood

Divorce

They walked down the aisle
Both wearing a smile
For theirs would a bed of roses be.

Then, through the years
The smiles turned to tears
The roses were ashes,
Strewn on a cruel sea.

Natalie J. Brannian

Memories

Memories of yesteryear and years beyond
Bring back to mind those special ones
Some are joyous ones, others touch off
Tears for loved ones lost over the years.

These memories are precious things,
Vivid realities and haunting dreams,
Igniting the passion that lurks within,
For loved ones lost and special friends.

Kenneth Perkins

My Choice

The darkened clouds, the ceaseless rains
Bring naught but gloom
And increase my pains

They cause in me a mood so vile
No soft words from me
And not one smile
But then indeed, I do recall
The poet's words
"Into each life some rain must fall
Some days must be dark and dreary"
And so I ask,
How shall I make them cheery?

By faith, I'll see the light
in those I meet.
Their goodness shining
With a smile I'll greet
And have no need for pining

Mary Berenice Hagerty

Love's Faded Path

For promises are
broken
And of dreams we
must let go
Love does not last
forever
For those of us
who know.

Marilyn Marlin

Nature Reigns

The earth shakes.
Buildings crumble.
People die
In Kobe and LA.
Fear Reigns.

Time heals.
The future awaits.
People forget
In Kobe and LA.
Optimism Reigns.

The earth shakes.
Buildings crumble.
People die
Somewhere near.
Fear Reigns.

Undaunted by the news
Kobe and LA people wonder
Didn't that happen here?
Could that happen here?
Nature Reigns.

Roger A. Gorski

Love's Pure Light

Love's pure light
Burns like a candle's FLAME
Lighting the shadows of my heart.

Love's pure light
Glistens like a pearl droplet
In a pool of SUN.

Love's pure light
Crashes like a wave
On a DESERT beach.

Stephanie Frost

Music When I Die

When I die
Bury me deep
and lay two speakers
Below my feet.

Wrap the headphones
around my head
and Rock-n-Roll me
When I'm dead

Play all country tunes
and say no more
Play em with spoons
and I'll rest forever more.

Louise Huntoon

Violence

Violence does not pay
But it is here to stay
There is quite a bit
How can you escape it?
Not knowing when you can get hit
Even though you may not be the target
You see it everyday
Will it ever go away?
You must continue to renew your mind
And this takes time
All you can do is try harder
And keep praying to your Eternal Father

Rhonda Douglas

"A Late Reflection"

It should have been a short day-
But I did not quite understand
just how truly genuine
were the depths of her emotion.
As suggested from the onset
it became a very long day-
rain filled the skies
that afternoon just as tears
filled my eyes that evening.....

A sparse breakfast without
sleep and reflecting on the simple
beauty of how she affected me
so very smoothly as a favorite cat,
your affectionate friend
can invade your lap -
smoothly and eloquently.

So hear gentle ways and her loving
feelings were like the sun on a
paradise island - as they tanned my mind.

R. Sanders-Maclean

Endless Breeze

You think I do not know
but I do

You think I do not see
but I do

It is you that can not
see, it is you that can
not know

Look at me, look at me
See me I am here, I am the
one you have searched for endlessly

You let me go and you push me
away, only later to say now
know, now I see
Please look at me, please look at me
You waited too late and took it all
away

I was the one you could not
see, it really was me.

L. A. Nevels

Untitled

A friend will be there
But not say a word
When you need a listening ear
They can not be heard

Friends know what to say
And what needs to be said
And at the right moment
They just nod their head

A friend helps you remember
or help you to forget
They'll always keep those secrets
of moments you regret

A friend can spot a loser
who doesn't care at all
Be there for you
whenever you fall

Friendship is forever
No matter what the season or year
A friend will be there
to catch your fallen tear

Libby Hogan-Sanders

Daddy's Gone

I know I was a trial,
But sometimes you were proud.
I wanted to be independent,
Not part of any crowd!

I lead you on a merry chase,
Growing up was very hard.
I liked to try new things;
Not play it by the cards.

Oh, Daddy! Why'd you have to leave?
I still need you so much.
I don't want to be alone;
I want to hug you and such!

I love you! I need your wisdom,
Eighty years have taught.
You and I against the world,
Life's battles we have fought!

So many things I want to say,
My mind is in a jumble.
Be safe and happy now, I pray.
"I love you, Dad," I mumble.

Linda C. Fincher

Love Forgot

I loved you, you loved me,
but then your heart forgot.
Disheartened, I set you free.
You promised eternity, you did not.

Tears glistened in my eyes.
I saw you with another.
My mind asks all these whys.
I cry to my mother.

You hurt me so deep,
it drives on like a thorn.
I want to forever sleep,
because you will not mourn.

For you, I died for,
because you loved me no more.

Sheila Chan

Jews

Jews such a sweet sound
But why do I deny it.
Am I afraid?
Am I ashamed?
What do I fear?
The looks, the whispers.

In the past
The ignorance of the masses
Can yester become tomorrow.
Yes the Viper can once again rise up.

If I do not hold my head high.
I cannot say to my children.
Be proud you are Jews
Do not fear to tread where I did not.

Do not be again led to the slaughter.
For you are not sheep.
You are lions that can roar.
So once again roar loud and clear.
Be forever proud.
You are a Jew.

Pauline Janis

A Cry Within

I have many friends
but yet, I feel alone.
No one seems to understand
and my feelings aren't shown.

My life is filled with holes
and no one searches me.
I'm hiding within my soul
and can no longer see.

Where does the shoulder lie?
I hold back my wanted tears.
'Cause there's no place to cry
and no one is near.

How long will I last?
How far will I go?
Life's corners turn fast
and I lose control.

Kristi Eth

Encounter

I am here, just as I said I would be.
But yet, you are nowhere to be found.
Why do you hide from me?
Do I frighten you?
It's okay, I too am frightened.
I tremble at the thought
of what you might ask me;
Of what I might answer.
Who am I?
Is that all you ask?
Well, I am whoever and
whatever you want me to be.
I am good and I am evil.
I am shame and I am pride.
I am love and I am hate.
I am god and I am demon.
I am death and I am life.
For in the end you'll see,
that I am me and I am you.

Roy Torres

Love Of My Life

My heart is dying,
But you can't see the hurt.
It's all about those feelings
Of you, who gave up.

I've been crying since we parted.
My eyes are drowning in the flood.
I wish we were together,
But you won't give your love.

You know we had some good times.
And I thought we were meant to be.
I guess you lost that love inside.
But you stole my heart from me.

I'll soon recover,
After a lot of strife,
But one thing I'll always remember,
You were the love of my life.

Vee Ingram

We are all creating the beast
by taking from the earth and from
one another.

Wendy Renee Liddle

To My Special Son

Something inside of you
Calls out your need.
My words don't help-
It's your heart we must feed.

You just want a girl
To hold your hand.
I know the feeling-
I understand.

You can't tell her
The message you send.
You just want her
To be your friend.

Oh, please let there be
Some girl who can
Sit by him and see
Just a lonely young man!

Nancy D. Smith

A Silver Light

Oh, lover where in the night
Can we meet near a silver light
Oh lover come to my arms.
Be wise and love my charms,
The winds that swept a kiss
Came with thy love and bliss
Be more than the heart
Joyful and not to part
Oh listen to me think
Our great love on a brink
Quiet wake not her sleep
For I stand near to weep
My love did she die
Will she wake to cry
Oh, beauty my love of mine
Have you not sip good wine

Theodore O'Neil

Friends

Do you know I love you?
Can you see I care?
Am I the only one who sees
That we make the perfect pair?

I see you there.
Holding her hand.
So I struggle with my heart
And try to understand.

I try so hard for you to see.
Everything you mean to me.
My love for you will never die.
I see you as the perfect guy.

But if you've still
No love for me.
I guess it's friends
We'll have to be.

Nicole Ness

Ode To Christine

Purified by Mother Earth
Care and Love
For Life and Birth
Sand with Sea
Sky in Holy Water
Crazed Universe

William Welling

Tough Love

Why is my heart breaking?
Can't you see I'm in pain?
Should I say what I want
or should I stay quiet like it's o.k.?

I hear your voice,
I want to talk
but, all I can do is cry.

I think of how you left me
Then I try to forget.
I smile like I'm happy
but, inside I'm crying.

My whole world is filled with pain
I used to have so much
now I have so little

You make promises
That you can't afford to keep.
It hurts so much that
I cry myself to sleep.

Silvianne Giarratano

"Bridge Of One"

What am I, but a mirror of others,
caring, loving.....unknown words.

Whose hands but mine can carry a
burden,
a burden of a generation.

Hand on hand, building a bridge of one,
I support us all.

I am guilty of my time,
and you are all a part of me.

Michael Kalinoski

Does Heaven Have A Phone?

Does Heaven have a phone?
'Cause I'd like to place a call.
You see, my mom is there,
Haven't heard from her in a while.
I wonder if there's something wrong,
or if everything's alright.
'Cause, you know,
it's Christmas time...
and nothing seems just right.

My world is turned upside down.
Don't know wrong from right,
all I know is that I miss her
and need to know everything's alright.
....So please call.

Lee Ann Marie McIntosh

Transit 1994

Lift not my veil
commands the Goddess
until Time bids you enter
when Guardian Angels open
my moist pulsating womb
Receive Thy Holy Serpent
Create together as in ancient magic
The Child
transmuted Spirit galaxies away
erupts from Pluto's mineshaft -
the atom splits
And He, released,
Fulfills anew Conception of the World.

Peter C. Lynn

Do Hearts Lie?

Do hearts lie?
Cause if they do I need
to know, why?
My heart told me to fall
for you
The love was so soft,
tender and true.
My heart told me you
would be the one.
How could I be so gullible,
stupid and dumb.
The only heart I had lied
to me.
Now I am depressed, down
and lonely.
Now that my heart is
all wounded and torn.
I don't know what to do with
this heart that is scorn.

KEM Jackson

Changes

Changes will occur no matter what we do
Changes that make us happy
Changes that make us blue

Changes in our bodies
Changes in our minds
Changes in our jobs
Changes all the time

Changes can be good
Changes can be bad
Changes can make us laugh
Changes can make us mad

Dare to change and you might find
Life could become easier in time

Without changes life would be
Very mundane and boring you see

It's life's changes that bring us to know
Who we are and where we want to go.

Mary Farris

Remembrance

A breeze kissed my cheek.
Drifting away, returned again.
Touching me where
You used to lay.
Ever so gentle, before moving on.
My heart broke a new,
contentment washing away,
Loneliness came.
My love had feet of clay.
Another woman took you away.

Viva Nadine Horn

Untitled

Lone serpentine hugging fog line
creeps along the ridge—
Sandwiched between the grey heavens
and the blue-grey hills.

The sea is still, yet whimpers softly,
as it caresses the shoreline here.
Our somber mood is like the fog —
quiet, unsure, moving softly on...

Thos Cawley

Our Lives: The Four Seasons

Spring - the new beginning, a
child is born.

Summer - our childhood, bright and
warm.

Fall - our teen years, our childhood
falling off the trees. The trees being
our parents.

Winter - our adulthood, cold and
bitter. A world of responsibilities,
falling like snowflakes.

Your own child is a new spring.

Rita Erickson

Muddle

Two bands of light I can see
Coming and going in front of me

A wave of darkness over me then
Another band of light again

Where am I? My mind tries to shout
My thoughts falling on emptiness about

Body tired from the workday strain
Mind confused, just short of pain

Could it be the martian might
Come to give an earthling fright?

A UFO from who knows where
To take me to their leader there?

Or poltergeist on gleeful spree
Just having a bit of fun with me?

A whine, a honk, a screech and then
I'm brought back to my sense again

The two bands of light I clearly see
Coming and going in front of me

One is red and the other is white
I'm on the freeway and it's night

Kristina Taylor

Life's Greatest Loss

His life is O'er and the darkness
Covers me from head to toe,
As the fog rolls ever relentless,
Silently toward its final goal.

I see the dawn of tomorrow
Gleam through the tears in my eyes,
And a feeling of sadness and sorrow
Causes my soul to fly;

To struggle, to sputter in feeling,
While in the grip of pain,
That permeates my being
As the dew does the rain.

Come, O death! I sense thy sting,
That draws me ever near,
And beckons away that feeling,
That resembles what I fear.

For this soul that has flown;
So near and dear to me
Was not just a man I'd known,
But my father, you see!

F. Lewis Phibbs

Cricket Symphony

Just after 9 on summer nights,
creatures from near and far,
assemble to hear the symphony
played by crickets under the stars

Dogs bark with bold approval
Even the breeze stops in its tracks
For the crickets will be performing
'til the morning sun comes back

Darkness keeps birds from chirping
The conductor raises his baton
The crickets begin their symphony
and the night is filled with song

So if you missed the last production
they are here each summer night
Playing a familiar melody
with the moon as their spotlight

C. Christopher Jenkins

Sweet Dreams

I love the taste of
crisp warm candy apples, melting
in my moist mouth in the morning
when the sun is rising and half way up.
The sky has a gentle sunset,
the colors are very exciting
they make you want to jump up and shout.
They're the colors
of a red city full of golden locks
on a child's hair.

The radiant sun comes
out while I am eating my
crisp warm candy apple a nice
cold breeze of air walks by
me it gives me a great feeling
like I'm flying across the sunset
sky over the fierce blue ocean
the wind carries me away
and I'm right in my cuddly
bed I realize it was all a wonderful dream.

Skye Sands

"Alternatives"

Alternatives to leave
Crosses sun drenched mind.
Alternative to remain,
Leaving others behind.
As a crab scraping the beach
Desperate to reach safety,
A refugee from hell
Seeking to be free;
The alternative to persevere
Holding one's own.
Suffering other darkness-
As a child with no home.
Alternative to flee,
Never to return.
Even if so desired to see
Packages left to burn,
Burn among them all.
Hatred with no reason why,
Leaving options limited-
The option to die.

Katie Meehan

Unanswered

If I could transfer sadness onto paper,
Crumple it up and throw it away,
Or water the earth with tears;
Would I then?

If I could release pain into space,
Watch it burn leaving the atmosphere,
Or introduce loneliness to a friend;
Would I then?

If I could embrace happiness,
In lost love returning,
Or taste the kiss of an angel;
Would I then?

If I could see love in person,
Staring into my soul,
Or regain the innocence of a child;
Would I then?

Rebecca C. Kelleher

Potential

My low intelligence
crushed and packed by years,
low motivation, classroom scars
and black animal fears,
now rises to meet
aggravation, mine only; sweet
bleeding corpse at my door,
stark naked and half-eaten,
a symbol or metaphor
that cannot be, and
never will I reach

Wes Kriesel

Our World

Live a little,
Cry a little,
You'll put up with it all your life.
You can be mad,
You can be sad,
Or weep on your pillow at night.

Children play and,
Dance and sing or,
Huddle together with fright.
World of hunger,
Soldiers of war,
It's not a pretty sight.

Why all of these problems?
Why all of this grief?
Why all this fighting,
That never seems to cease?

Theresa Seipel

A Truthful Love

If you plant a see of
divine knowledge of truth.
It shall bring forth and emerge
a vineyard of unique splendor
suspending from Its perpetually
growing vine, an extraordinary
fruit of distinctive love that
intertwines with intriguing
depths of aspiring fondness
within its truthful self and
others that accompanyingly
surround its environment
through out life as it convinces on.

Sandy L. Sharp

Procrastination

Down where flamingoes
Dance in shining pools
Perturbed people shake their heads
And again take up their tools.
Cows meow, moons turn blue
Fairy tales enchanting
But people have too much to do
So busy ladder climbing.
Life, beauty, timelessness
Locked into museums
Hidden away for rainy days
When people come to see them
Labor today, live tomorrow -
The eternal lottery
But what if, just what if
Tomorrow can never be?

R. B. Platt

Darkness

I dwell in the shadows of sadness,
Darkness being my light.
I dwell in the shadows of jealousy,
Darkness being my air.
I dwell in the shadows of hopelessness,
Darkness being my guide.
I dwell in the shadows for the only
ones who care are those of whom
cannot see me.

Shana R. Sauer

About Darkness

I stumble around in the
darkness of my insecurities
and fears.

Sometimes just a quiet candle's
glow is all I need to
find my way.

But sometimes I need more light.

Sometimes I need you to
take my hand and guide me.

Steve Willis

Dying Light

Evil lurks in the air,
Darkness surrounds everywhere,
Demons curse,
And angels sing,
It's the last night,
Before comes spring.

Holiness of light appears,
Demons die from angel's spears,
Birds sing and flowers bloom,
Until summer is done,
Then comes doom.

Coldness falls and demons rise,
The angels watch us fall from the skies,
The sky is black when demons call,
Streams of light make them fall

Deep in the earth, the devil reigns,
High above God takes names,
Of those to be cursed,
With the devil's rule,
And those that loved forever true.

Patrick Lockwood

Day

Day, the day is coming.
Daybreak is turning the
nighttime into sunbeams.
The water sparkles and
glistens on the grass of an
enjoy able dew.
A rooster cries his treating
alarm, as I walk along
the Highway for a pack
of cigarettes to the store.
a passing motorist costs a
friendly wave as a blanket
of light covers the
view, so quickly, almost
before you can realize it's here;
All in the awakening and the
changes of an new day.
day, a new beginning.

Robert Howard

City Faces

The nights are old and the
days are cold.
The people look weary and the
muggers look scary.

I walk and I walk through
the city alone.
I see all those faces of
ice and stone.

They walk and they stare from
there and there.
Not a smile on their faces
in all of these places.

There's no love in the air
not here, not there.
These are the city Faces.

Stacy Mikolajczyk

Loneliness Is...

A feeling deep down inside
Depression is growing stronger
And there is no reason why
Suicide is a thought
That wont go away
Wondering, waiting, and hoping
Maybe, someday
Love is something
I may never know
Happiness an emotion
That may never show
Peace of mind is a tranquility
I have no knowledge of
It's tearing me apart
Push will turn into shove
It will drive me over the edge
But the heartache will end
Forever gone the loneliness
And the pain.

Monica Steward

Confession

I once was a growing star,
Destined to be spectacular!
But I got lost along the way.
Why did I trip and go astray?

Yet sometimes in my restless sleep
I regret and quietly weep.
I can still attain that fame.
For Christ forgives hidden shame.

So tomorrow, I will rise and shine
And the world again will be mine.
You'll welcome me back to a good life,
And I will be your faithful wife!!

Virginia A. Bartman

"Another Society"

I awaken to the sounds of a
different life,
I face each day filled with toil
and strife.

Each day a journey, an adventure
against time,
You intimidate, manipulate, devise
your every con.

No one is for-sure of the outcome
of their sentence,
Your debt paid with your freedom,
no room for repentance.

Attitude of anger, fits of rage, devours
your true character;
The arena is set for masters of the game,
Death for the fallen Gladiator!

Leander Jones

Your Heart

This smile on your face,
does it come from your heart?
Your eyes are flashing little stars,
do they come from your heart?
Your hands are giving,
does it come from your heart?
Your lips are honeyed by sweet words,
do they come from your heart?
Show me the way to your heart.
I want to touch it
and become your friend.
I want to open it
and become your lover.
Give me your heart,
I will fill it with mine.
And we will become
one for ever.
For my heart will be
in YOUR HEART.

Marlene White

Runaway Train

My life is like a runaway train;
Each time around I wonder
If this is the last time.
I can't escape the guilt,
I can't forget the pain;
Maybe today
I won't have to ride that
runaway train.

LeRoy David Alto

Untitled

Just because we don't approve
doesn't mean it's wrong
people have been arguing this
forever so, ever so long
You shouldn't judge a person
by the color of his skin
You shouldn't judge a man
on where he goes or where he's been
People are all different
that's what makes us "us"
I can not understand why
individuality is causing such a fuss
No one has the right
to say what's wrong, what's not
It's finally time to open our minds
and forget what we've been taught

Rachel Ramirez

Move on

Take me on a trip so far away from here
Don't tell me where I'm going
Take me all away from this
Don't talk about where we've been

There are times we have to step aside
Try to move on
Keep our feelings inside
Move on
Move on
Move on

Sometimes when I'm alone, or not
my mind takes me to the one I know
To the girl I remember —
The one you forgot

So now it's time to step aside
Try to move on
Keep my feelings inside
Move on
Move on
Move on

Richard Hussey

Imagination

It makes you come alive,
Drawing pictures,
Playing toys,
You begin to think,
Of fairy tales, and rhymes.
Knights, and fair damsels,
Castles, and cottages,
Things of far and thought-up lands,
Of wide green meadows,
And fat white unicorns,
Your brain begins to dream.
Playing dress up,
Pretending you're a king or queen,
Writing stories,
Acting out plays,
Your imagination works,
In many ways.

Laura Waite

Frith And Marco

Gentle, gentle lovely creatures
Dwelling softly on the earth,
Fleet of foot, ever watchful,
Stillness being of much worth.

Bunny's breath, bunny's whiskers,
Bunny's soft paws on my arm.
Bunny's bright eyes gazing at me
Liquid fire, yet soft and warm.

Bunnies flashing by like silver,
Bunnies sitting in the sun,
Bunnies playing with each other,
Bunnies leaping, just for fun.

Bunny's tail - white cotton fluff,
Inky black, his velvet nose.
Bunnies playing all around me,
Bunnies chewing up my clothes!

Bunnies ever in my mind
Make my spirit soar above,
Bunnies always in my heart
Gently teaching me to love.

Marie M. Kutz

Life And Death

I am a tree
each one of my
leaves
is a dream.
When one of my
dreams is fulfilled
a single leaf
glides through the air
and softly lands
on the ground
like a dove's feather.
But when one of my dreams
shatters,
that one single leaf
that was once full of life
crumples up
and slowly,
let's go
of something it knows
it can't hold on to.

Pauline Hart

I Am

I am what you would call,
educated.
I am what you would call,
a dreamer.
I am what you would call,
a searcher.
I am what you would call,
a fool.
I am a part of the world,
a world full of,
Educated fools searching
For a dream...

Vertrell R. Peterson

"Affair"

The dark side of love,
Empty promises and vows,
Borne by a black dove.

William W. Rozek

Sunset

Life is like a never
Ending Sunset.

The distance between
you and the
Sunset,
Makes the foundation
between you and
a good friendship.

Yvette R. Holman

Untitled

Perfect in every way,
Eyes, lips, hair, skin.
Yet my fear keeps me from looking within.
Tormented by her walk,
Intrigued by her talk,
I watch from a distance.

Tom Tyrrell

Untitled

I see your eyes,
Eyes that hold pain,
Pain of which is mental.
I see your tears,
Tears of which pain is slowly
Leaving.
I see your pain,
Pain that hurts,
Hurts more than anyone can
Know of.
I see you slowly dying from pain,
Pain not visible, or physical,
It's emotional and mental pain.
I see you struggling for survival,
It's too much for you to handle,
But I know you will survive.
I want to help,
Help only you can give yourself.
You have the will power.

Renee Smotherman

Content With Alone

Down the long corridor
Faces from the flame,
Painting of ancestors,
Their eyes all the same.

As she enters the room
Lights a fire with care,
An idea enters her mind,
With no one to share.
Could it be possible?
Oh God, could it be true?
Am I the last of my family?
Deep down the answer, she knew.
Never married nor children
For reasons unknown,
Like a wise old owl,
She was content with alone.

"Goodbye my sweet castle,"
As she let out a sigh,
Eased the quilt to her chin,
And closed her weary eyes.

Ronald C. Contreraz

The Mask

It hides,
facial features
of beauty.
Degrading masquerade,
such beauty,
overwhelms me.
Remove it.
Let me meet the hiding
with a kiss.

Sam Hartle

Spirit Song

You know my way when my spirit grows faint within me.
No one cares for my life, but you,
Oh Lord are my refuge.

Let your gentle breeze bring me news of your unfailing love
for in you I do put my trust.
Show me the way I should go,
for in you my soul is lifted up.

On eagle's wings I will fly when
my spirit touches yours.
You are faithful to your promises
and loving toward all you have made.

Terri L. Pittman

A Place Called Shadow Lake

There is a place,
Far and wide,
Beyond the trees,
Beyond the sky,
There is a place no one can see,
But me,
Beyond the sea,
When I am lonely I see,
My lake,
And it makes me feel better,
Again,
This place I call home,
I call this place Shadow Lake.

Susan Kelly

Search For Love

We are both here now
Feeling loved, happy, and strong;
Yet we keep searching
For that satisfied end.
But, do I still feel empty?

Can't we stand still
And fulfill ourselves with these
Moments together?
Why must we keep searching?
For what we seek may be near.

Our busy souls flying about restlessly,
Using all our energies
To come full circle
To find what was already there.

Close your eyes-relax and feel
For what's inside your heart.

Michelle Robinson

Feelings

Feelings make you full of pride
Feelings are what's inside
Feeling you have to let out
Feelings or they will sprout
Feelings come in all sizes
Feelings can win you prizes
Feelings can be positive
Feelings can be negative
Feelings fill you with joy
Feelings are just a toy
Feelings are just a fee
Feelings will always love me

Vicki Pride

Flights Of Ideals

Wondrous thoughts of you
fill my imagination
Like ocean waves of deepest blue
drifting in and out
in relentless harmony
My life is once again challenged
to accept friendship within
Flights of ideals
flock my mind
And in my soul
my heart swells.

Phillip Hirshberg

Bubble Fairies

Once I saw some tiny fairies
Floating in the air.
They were inside a big, round bubble,
Flying here and there.

They were all trying to get out,
As if being held by force.
But the bubble was carried away
In its own uncharted course.

The wind was blowing hard
And it blew that bubble into a tree.
As the bubble burst with a great pop,
The fairies flew off free.

Now every time I make bubbles
And see those tiny fairies;
I remember to pop the bubble
Because I know what it carries.

Laura Watts

Father Missing You

Memories of you are again
flooding my mind in
pulling out old photos and
letters once again feeling the
anguish at the loss of you
Twenty years since gone,
seeming like yesterday in
hearing the words of your passing
In denial - not believing
only twelve, now thirty one
still missing you, wishing
you were here
for your grand children
for me

Pamela Bush Beattie

Untitled

Tenderness, a rivulet
flowing,
cascading to an embrace,
The essence
to the confluence
of the heart and mind,
Sweeping, swirling,
surging forth,
pausing,
into the eddy driven,
not to be stilled,
onward movement,
touching,
encompassing,
drawn to sea.

Sim Sutterby

Violation

Magic dreams
Fly so high
Never fall
Never die
Don't give into one's self
Try to run scream for help
Falling down from my trance
See the mist catch a glance
Master screams
I fall quiet
They urge you on
Make you try it
Rotting flesh I hear it fall
The beating drum I hear them crawl
Rules of man imposed by law
The falling bird begins to caw
I hear my name and see a face
Come to life a warm embrace
Drunken friend falls to death
Lives no more his last breath

Will Gabaldon

To The World

My very precious love I give
For all the world to see
Never once thought I,
That in my life I do live,
That anyone could be
As thoughtful and secure with love
As the love I give to thee
And in my hour of need
I know to whom I can turn
For your love is equal for me.

Nancy Jarvis

Fate

Deprived of logic,
fear the unknown
to venture on the red wave
of one's impulse
prepare for the moment!
discover the rage of love
and cries of the spirit
the painful embrace
of chance
Questions the soul.

Pamela J. Liggett

Dear Lord, I Thank Thee

Today, dear Lord, I thank thee,
For everything You do.
Someday when I grow big and strong,
I want to be like you.

Today, dear Lord, I thank thee,
For blessings that you bring.
Today, dear Lord, I thank thee,
For every little thing.

Today, dear Lord, I thank thee,
For my mommy and my daddy.
Today, dear Lord I'll try to show,
How good that I can be.

Today, dear Lord, I thank thee,
For everything I see.
Today, dear Lord, I thank thee,
For listening to me.

Lisa Barney

God's Miracle

I am a living miracle
for God has pulled me through
I am a witness and a testimony
for many of you
God has spared my life for
my duty on earth is not through
He wants me to witness and
to tell people just like you
That He is the living God above
and all He wants us to do is love
God has saved my soul
and my soul is His to keep
I still have many trials ahead
and many hurdles to leap
All I need to do is lean on Him
and He will pull me through
For God's word says - Have Faith
in me and I will completely heal you
For I am a living miracle
for God has pulled me through.

Leandra Hill Bryant

Eulogy To A Mother

Look not on me with anger
For I've missed so much of life;
I never knew my children,
Nor portrayed the loving wife.

My years were spent in solitude;
My moods all came from pills.
I never thought to question why
This void was never filled.

I leave behind no namesake
And never thought to ask
Why all my children's' memories
Seldom centered on my tasks.

I knew not of apology;
Just never felt the need.
For when I'd hurt someone with words
It seemed just daily deed.

If anything is learned of this
Please bear in mind, though sad,
You can not share in the life those skills,
The ones you've never had.

Pamela J. Hunt

Someone Special

Lord I thank you every day
For sending someone special my way.
I hope he is in my life to stay.
I love him more and more each day.
Although he is so far away,
I know I could love him from the start.
He has a place within my heart.
I know I will always be true,
no matter what folk say or do.
I waited on him for so long,
Lord, I hope nothing ever goes wrong.
But you hold the future in your hand,
Lord I hope this is part of your plan.
Help us to accept the things we do,
for Father we are depending on you.

Virginia Williams

Easter Time

It's Easter Time and feelings flow
For sister and my brothers
While watching all my children grow
It's thoughts of Dad and Mother.

Family; Ours, Yours, and Mine
Regardless where they came
Remembering at Easter Time
God blessed us all the same

Jesus gave you all to me
In this flower love will show
And believe my love grows stronger
Even if, the flower doesn't grow.

Raymond B. Barnett Sr.

Lesser Brethren?

We thank thee, Lord
For snowy mice
And for the hamsters
golden
For Rhes. macac', the
little monk'
To whom we're most
beholden.
In countless caged
cloisters
Thy Friars Furry make
As Thou
Their one oblation
For all creation's sake.

F. H. Chard

Ecstasy

Move closer don't shy away,
For that one strange moment
Of ecstasy is now fast approaching.

Even though strangers foreseeing
Only half what each may fell,

Let us move closer, for that
One strange moment is now
Fast approaching.

Linda Parker

Dare To Discover

A baby bird taking flight
for the very first time,
looking down upon the earth.

A baby gazing into the eyes of
a new mother, both have a lot
of learning in front of them.

When you are too scared to do something,
but do it anyway,
you sometimes find out you like it.

Even in dying
you dare to discover
what is beyond life.

If you do not discover
anything about yourself,
you do not know yourself.

Patrick Iske

Justice

Everyone is Responsible
for what they do in Life:
but responsibilities are lifted
when you take
somebody's Life:
Society says Justice will come
to those who commit
the Crime:
Justice is only justified
to those who wait in
Time:
but where does Justice start
when you take a Life
that's Mine?

Paulette M. McGee-Jones

Echo From The Mountains

Forever!
Forever!
Forever...
Rolls ever onward into
Unending eternity;
Power immeasurable,
Limitless,
The vastness of time
Soars on the eddying wind.

Kathryn Reuss

"A Star"

As a tear falls
from an angel's face,
a star lights up the night.

Like a candle in
a darkened room,
with orange flames burning bright.

'Cause every time
an angel dies,
and her soul drifts on afar,

It goes out
into the sky,
and turns into a star.

Kandi Starling

The Russian River

Hurriedly, the Russian River,
From its birthplace in the hills,
Wends its way through glade and canyon,
Gathering truant streams and rills.

Wends its way down to the ocean,
Rushing over myriad stones,
Seething, churning, whirling, turning,
As its restless water foams.

Slowly, now, for it is passing
Sloping banks of cleanest sand,
Cabins nestled in the forest—
Natural vacation land.

Lazily, the Russian River
Lingers now for swimmers gay—
Boating, floating, fun promoting;
People young and old at play.

Swiftly, now, the Russian River,
As if remembering to be
Rushing onward, flows the faster—
Hurrying to join the sea.

Ruth S. Zerintcheff

Mistakes

Everybody makes mistakes
From mistakes you grow wiser
When you make a mistake don't give up
Just pick up where you left off
And give it one more try
Maybe two...three...or four
Some people make things happen...
Some wonder...
Some watch...
Making things happen is the
best thing of all
Sometimes making it happen
You might trip, stumble, or fall
But...
When you fall
Make sure it is on your back
So you can look up
and get back on track.

Maya Seymour

You

You give me love
From the heavens above.
Like a dove in a tree
You make me feel so carefree.
Even though I weep
I make not a peep.
For I shall not let you know
Because I love you so.

Stacey Johnson

Doves

Graceful beautiful
Fly flown flying
The symbol of love
Keen old fast
Loveable huggable
Bird.

Sean Liston

Friendship

Culled like peas
from various shells.
Hoarded for memory's
sake.

Strung like beads
on a pristine cord;
silver, shimmering, selectively
held.

Some sound symmetrical
like precious pearls;
others dented, damaged, disfigured,
wrapped in tissue.

Rosemary Tatum Reed

Just Say No

Another level of consciousness
frozen but expanding
Trails render my sight unclear
Thumping, thumping, thumping
Reverberations fill my ears
Apperception of my soul
A feeling that can't be told.

Rick Harden

Perfidy

The man's unblinking eye
gazes at the two
swans so intertwined
twins so much in love.

But the eye is sly
and the smirk is dark,
as the crumbs are tossed—

to slurp the wretched bread,
his neck a begging arc,
the swan will leave his dove.

And now the nasty laugh
cries the man has won
the wager he had made
against his better soul

at a Hyde Park pond.

Vladimir J. Konecni

The Strongest Man In The World

That man is something else
Glory in his eyes that
conquers perceptions of infinity

Strength and wisdom all around
like a field of daisies

Lightning flashing through the
world for justice

Words flowing like mountain
spring water

Courageous as a mighty current
in vast ocean waters

A calvary unto himself

He is the strongest man in
the world
my Dad

Mary L. Ferguson

Raindrops

Drip drop plip plop,
Go the little raindrops,
Drip drop drip again,
Down my window pane,
When the sun comes shining through,
The raindrops change their hue,
Some are yellow some are green,
Some are simply in between.

Linda Ammon

To Know

Oh beautiful for spacious skies
God shed his grace on thee
Please let them know that this is so
and set their spirits free
And crown thy good with brotherhood
from sea to shining sea
And crown thy bad with knowledge of
the pain they inflict on you and me

Tina Plank

A Rose???

A rose is the fragrance of love
Graced with promise and trust,
But the petals will fall
When the fragrance is gone
And the rose will turn into dust,
I have wondered...why is it so
As love and desire is born
Why a rose is a rose
Just for a while?
Is the rose also....a thorn?

Mardi Iannaccone

Mourning Wind And Crying Skies

Mourning wind and crying skies,
Grieving heart and tear-filled eyes.
A love once lost cannot be found,
While spirits linger on the ground.
Release the pain, distill the sorrow,
Live again and love tomorrow.
Remember love, rejoice in thought,
Return no more to sorrow's plot.
Create anew a life gone sour,
Live to love in every hour.
With every tear of pain and sorrow,
A life against its soul does borrow,
Another chance to live again,
And comfort sweetly the mourning wind.

Karen Earls-Mickle

America

Land of opportunity,
Growth,
Fulfillment,
Land of Justice.

Where men and women Work together
side by side,
To help make a better life
For their self and their family.

In peaceful co-existence
One with the other,
Lending a helping hand
Where ever they can.

All hoping for peace and unity
In God's good time.

Paula M. Libonati Schumann

Hidden Treasure

Sad sea shell
half buried in sand

Your dwelling place
shifting with tides
from restive seas
that shape the land

A solitary boy
runs half bare
along the beach

He stops.........

Searching fingers
reach down
and lift you
into light

Within your spiral chambers
there is a hidden music
to be discovered
by the I
which penetrates the surface.

Libero Arcieri

Thinking Of You

The moon is bright
Hanging on the sky
Its silver
Nectarous light
Kindles the whole world
In the quiet forest, comes the
Nightingale bird
Gathering poems
Of my mind
For the strings of my heart
Yearning for the note
Of the passionate music
Unbearable is the inscrutable cold

Tina Hao

Gone

Today is passing tomorrow
has come. But one day your day will
surely come.

Unlike those who want
to stay. They will see another day.

Some people can't help
the fact to die. But in their minds
their wondering why.

People in a family can
even die tomorrow. But in the families
heart they can feel the sorrow.

There's a time to sing
there's a time to cry. But there
is also a time to die.

One day you might be here one day
you might be home.

But in your single life
you might surely be gone.
Very long gone.

Marquita Allen

Know Thyself?

No mark or wound could they find,
He was the victim of his mind.

B. E. Christopher

The Oak At Airlie Gardens

The magnificent oak on Airlie's Lawn
Has felt the sun of many dawns.
When it was young and not too tall
Indians were here - and that was all.
As it grew, the changes came.
The English thought it just a game;
But freedom was the cause they sought
So Colonists rallied, fought and fought.
They longed to live here, farm and pray,
Indians and English were forced away.
War between the states then came.
God help us overcome our shame!
As families were torn apart,
The Oak was crying in its heart.
Peace came again - But with great cost
The pride of the South was nearly lost.
Time has healed the pain of war.
Only God knows what's next in store.
Man lives his life and is soon gone -
But, Airlie's Oak lives on and on.

Valerie Titman

Wind

She travels through every country.
Has she been to outer-space?
I'm not sure anyone knows her
because she never stays in one place.

She can be quiet as a whispered secret
or she can turn your skin color red.
People tend to love or hate her
when she blows the hair on their head.

In the summer when it's warm
I'm happy.
She can sing and dance just so;
Until the moment she becomes angry
She can let the whole world know.

Maureen Padden Mitchell

The Barber

My husband was a barber
He cut hair and gave a shave
His biggest fault I know of
Was the way he did behave

One day I went into the shop
A cute girl was in the chair
He was pouring out sweet talk
And he hadn't cut a hair!

I grabbed the old hair blower
Blew it in her face so fair
Till she slid from off the seat
And left without her hair!

Now my husband the barber
Was extremely mad at me
So left and joined the Navy
I was stuck with shop and key!

Mary Masten Kimmel

The Seal

Hunting in the snow,
Hunting in the snow,
seal, seal,
Brought gloves,
Brought boots,
Forgot my gun,
good!

Sean Wilson

The Sundancer, My Dad And Me

Brown eyes to my soul;
he did see.
Eagles, hawks, deer and doe
The Sundancer and me.

Here for a reason only he could see.
Many people touched.
Short the time.

Remembering legend,
important to thee and me—

In dreams;
Visits the sundancer and me.

Never gone,
forever here,
The Sundancer, my dad and me.

Linda Cioffi

Termite

A termite is an emotional glutton
He even eats things that are rotten
He eats when he's mad
He eats when he's sad
He eats when he's happy too
He doesn't care if it's old or new
He chews and chews with all his might
He's a hungry fellow, this tiny termite.
He invites his friends to come on in
The way they eat, it's really a sin.
They eat as tho' they have not been fed,
Yet just last night they ate my bed.

Rosemary Green

"He"

When I told the lie,
HE pleaded for me.
When I did the sin,
HE begged for me.

When I placed the thorns,
HE bleed for me.
When I drove the nails,
HE hung for me.

When I pierced HIS side,
HE cried for me.
When I stopped HIS heart,
HE died for me.

When I needed help,
HE arose for me.
When I call HIS name,
HE is there for me.

Sandra Evelyn Thompson

To Be Blessed

Blessed are my eyes this morning
For I can see him in the rising sun
Blessed are my feet this morning
For my works are done
Blessed are my eyes this morning
For I can hear his eternal plan
Blessed is self
For I am a living daughter
But most of all Blessed is my mind
Which tell me what to do
Because you created my hands enabling
me to walk joyously with you

Regina Gaines

Broken Vow

She believed him, but now she knows.
He said he would conquer eternity.
His love his weapon.
The battle finished and forever spared.
At her side is where he would be.
The believer is the fool.
Promises whither to nothing.
Waiting is where she stands.
In defeated time she cries.
Her trust shattered.
He speaks his vow to another.
This is whom forever awaits.
The battle yet finished.
Now she is the victor and he the slain.
Eternity bows to it's companion.
Standing tall, she remembers his vow.
She believed him, but now she knows.

Tracy Kim Terry

Untitled

From Crown on my
Head - to soles of my
feet I give to you
Jesus my Being
complete for guidance
and wisdom through
out this day,
every step that I take
every word I say,
Keep me from sickness
accidents and sin
Help me be patient
and kind to all
men for Jesus who died
to save me from
sin through his
life everlasting amen.

Laura Cuddy

A Question

Have you ever had your
heartache?
The world just seems to take
I long for spring to come again
Knowing it is too late to win

The question keeps coming
back again and again
Is this such a sin?

Melba Jane McKnight

Happy Birthday

Many years have come and gone
Hearts have been touched
one by one.
You've given strength and love
To people everywhere,
You've brought happiness and joy
And taught so many how to care
Your words and wisdom
Are special and true,
Your faith and beauty
Shines through and through
We have all been fulfilled
With your heart and your love,
You are truly a blessing
From our Heavenly Father above.

Kimberly D. Smith

Dare To Discover

Horizons limited to infinity
Heavens unexplored
Dare to Discover
Treasures of talents and more

Opportunities unanswered
Dreams untold
Dare to Discover
What the future will hold

Emotions unsure
Songs unsung
Dare to Discover
What lies beyond

Climb the highest mountain
Swim the deepest sea
Dare to Discover
And be what you want to be.

Necia Young

Eternal Rest

Dear Lord, take your hand and
help Jimmy stand, and lead him
to your gates, so he may run
once more, as a steed, right
through heaven's gates.

And as he runs with tail up high
and nickers jubilantly, he's
telling all his passers by he is
now painless, and free.

His snorting will be heard
without a single word, to let
his brothers know, he's joined
them up in heaven's home.

While grazing together in the
lush green meadows with
running streams, they will
peacefully roam, since they've
now, all come home.

Sally Jo Songy

God On High

God on high, please hear my prayer
Help me know you are there
I am lost, life is hard
Time is short, help me Lord

God on high, you know all my fears
Guide me through my golden years
I have loved, I have tried
Help me to regain my pride

God on high, teach me now
Only you can show me how
Make me strong in my belief
My aching heart needs some relief

God on high, if I try, if I stumble
Will you be there to make me humble?
For if I die without a goal
Then I have lost my very soul

To be alone is what I fear
Let me know that you are near
For I must live each day with hope
God on high, teach me to cope

Vivian Schwartz

Her Dream

She silently slept,
Her breath a whisper of cascading memories.
A tranquil breeze caresses her amber hair.
The golden moonlight plays on her creamy skin.
Her elegant lashes gently flutter.
A sudden explosion of light radiates a luminous glow in her mind.
Pure thoughts enclose her innocent heart.
Visions emerge behind her closed doors.
A heavenly figure appears, glowing from within.
Touched by an angel,
She awoke to the sound of the carillon.

Rachele Sherblom

A Day At The Beach

Her laughter, a child's,
Her eyes unaware
That a healthy, safe world
was existent out there.

She was ignored by all strangers,
She heard whispers, no words.
And she'd eat off the biscuits
that had been thrown to the birds.

To her this was living,
Just a face with no name.
And everyone else probably
lived just the same.
She was too young to realize,
And too innocent to know,
that when it was time to go home
she had no place to go.

Karen S. Connelly

Misery Underground

The ragged woman enters
her world a winding stairway,
the subway tunnel home.

A grimy light bulb
Incandescent lamp gives heat
Warm card-board boxes, her bed.

Long tail rats in duel,
stale bread is the booty,
her meal taken by villains.

The cold night passes.
Screeching wheels and
sparkling third rails
deluge her space.

Vincent Samuels

"Angels"

Angels,
Holy,
Spiritual
Watching, waiting and praying,
Up in Heaven -
Watching me,
My aunt, Edna.

Mallary Berry

Why Is The Sky So High?

"Why is the sky so high," the bird asked herself." Maybe to let the birds fly so high," she thought to herself.
"Why is the sea so deep," the fish asked himself." Maybe to let the fish swim so deep to keep away from heat," he thought to himself.
"Why are mice so fast," the cat asked herself. "Maybe they try to get past," she thought to herself.
"Why are people so mean," the tree thought to himself. "They cut us down and make us frown," he thought to himself.

Nick Neff

Open The Door

Open the door for Jesus
He's standing at your heart's door
Knocking continually knocking
As he has many times before.
Don't close the door forever
for so sad you will be
when you come to heaven's portals
and say, "Open the door for me."
Unless you have accepted Jesus
and are saved while here on earth
How sad it will be up yonder
Door closed you've had no re-birth.
Jesus loves you dearly, and
He suffered so for you
upon a cruel rugged cross
He paid sins' debt for you.
But you and only you
can let Jesus in year heart.
Then on heaven's door above
will be "enter" not "depart".

Margaret Stidham

The Child Inside

He screams at me
His eyes aflame
The hurt he holds
Wells inside
He wants out
But is denied
Break the toys
Smash the windows,
He wants out!

His anger aside
He is docile
Like a newborn:
He loves.
Tears flow down
His silkened face
For all he wants
To be:
Is a child inside.

D. Francis Jacobs

Red

Red is the color of love,
I dream it's the color of a dove.
It whispers something in my ear,
Something that I cannot hear.
Then it flies away so bright,
But I will see it tomorrow night.

Nadia Tabbara

A Soldier's Dream

He lay upon the battlefield,
His gun clutched in his hand.
Blood oozes from his shattered side,
And trickles on the sand.

Is war so good, Is war so bad,
I really do not know.
But when I hear the battle charge,
I must rise up and go.

In this a dream, is this for real;
His plaintive voice rings out.
It's real the cannon thunders,
It's real the rebels shout.

He lay upon the battlefield,
The gun still in his hand.
But when the bugle sounds "To Arms",
He will not rise again.

Wilbur Leo Alvey

Hidden In Shadows

Smiling at me with
His innocent smile
Hidden in shadows.

Why does he hide in
Shadows? What is he thinking,
Smiling at me with that
Innocent smile?

Smiling at me from Shadows
Following close but,
Far away.
I am never alone,
He is always there,
Hidden in shadows.

Perhaps,
I will never know why
He stays hidden
Hidden in shadows.

Smiling at me with
His innocent smile
Hidden in shadows.

Kaudra

War Vs Peace

War is hell and hatred worse
How can mankind exist on earth
This killing must stop for mankind
For loving is better not worse
Destroying each other
Is no way to live
We must love one another
To have peace on earth
In order to live
So let's call it a day
and throw our guns and ammo away
Have peace at last now
For it's the only way
May peace and joy abundant be
Loving one another and live happily
No more sorrow will there be
For then no more wars will there be.

William F. Koehler

Untitled

It never occurred to me,
How much one can love,
The feelings inside,
Like he was sent from above.

Knowing you can trust,
The one close to your heart,
Is an amazing discovery,
Telling you, you will never part.

All of the memories,
The endless nights,
Forgetting very few,
Those of fights.

Not being afraid,
To tell how you feel,
Being there for each other,
These feelings are real.

You know that he's the one,
When all your dreams come true,
That you want to spend your life with,
Then it's time to say I do.

Keely Kephart

My Mentor

I've tried hard to figure
how we came to be.
It's really quite simple;
God sent you to me.

He knew that I needed
to learn more about life,
So He sent you to teach me
about both love and strife.

You were my mentor,
my very best friend.
You aroused in me feelings
I'll have till the end.

You taught me to give
and not be afraid.
You said not to dwell
on mistakes that I've made,

But to look to the future
and what I can be.
I know, through my journey,
you'll be standing by me.

Nancy Williams Grant

Dawn Of Time

Dawn of time lost in past
Hunting, rabid, feasting, fast.

Follow signs of every creature
Of ourselves reflect in them.
Waiting for the final feature
Sing our praise of God in hymn.

In ourselves is where we lie
Place ourselves amongst the brave
Much more there than meets the eye
Neglect Him till we reach our grave.

Mark Miller

Wonderer

As the winds accompany me,
I always wonder, where I can be
As I watch the clouds drift away far,
Till they fade or split apart

I wonder....
I wonder where I could be
Am I happy or pretending to be

I don't know where I'm going,
I only know where I've been.
You think something's wrong
But deep within.... I'm wondering.

I sit and wonder,
Who or what shall speak of me?
They're just emotions growing within me,
So I wonder .... Is this me or am I
Lacking an inner personality.

Wonder....
I like to wonder
It sets me free
But I keep a lot internally.

Manuel S. Morales

Family

If God created man,
I am a product of men past.
Who were these men.
Whose vapors permeate my pores,
And fill my soul?

What were they like?
These man whose spirit
Fills my head.
Whose blood fills my heart,
And influences my goal.

My fathers of the past,
Shaped by events to be what they were.
Left so little, left everything,
A foundation of history
Which through me is alive.

I am these man,
They reside in me !
This likeness, this culmination.
Must in future project,
For our name, our being, to survive.

Robert D. Tucker

Easy Way Out

I feel lost
I am going nowhere
Sometimes just living
Is more than I can bare
Days run together
And I lose count
The pressure rises
As my worries start to mount
What is this life really all about
Wouldn't it be nice
To find an easy way out
I strive to find a balance
To keep an even keel
I will lock in my emotions
My thoughts they can not steal
I feel it is all my fault
So I'll take all the blame
I will carry the weight of the world
And I'll proceed from shame.

Michael Angelo Turi

Reunion

Proud like the dandelion,
I boast before the crowd.
No one sees my naked stem,
Only a soft white shroud.

Pretentious words give me fuel,
And make my ego ascend.
But their scrutinizing questions,
Create a harsh and deadly wind.

I better learn to lean and sway,
To take each forceful blow.
Or I will lose my precious wall,
And everyone will know.

Micah Moseley

It

My surroundings are flooded with fear
I can feel its presence
getting nearer and nearer
I sit and I wait for it to come
Then I jump up and run, it is
no use waiting so long
I run over the grass and through
the trees
On my neck I can feel the cold,
cold breeze
My heart and lungs burn inside
my chest
I continue to run thinking of what
could happen next
I suddenly stop and turn around
For it is nowhere to be found

Sarah Schroeder

Remembrance

I remember your name,
I can still see your face;
If I close my eyes,
I can still feel a place.

A place that is warm,
With laughter and love;
But you are now gone,
As you watch from above.

A day doesn't pass,
And a day doesn't close;
That I don't remember,
A day like a rose.

Life was a blossom
So perfect, so sweet;
But now life's a thorn,
Until once more we meet.

Wendy C. Clarke

Never Again

The town was old and quaint to see,
I felt that life was crowding me -
I went away, the years flew by,
Then suddenly I knew not why -
I wanted towns so quaint and small,
And happy times I could recall.
That's how I knew that I was wrong,
For loving you was still my song.
To be with you and just to share
But all was lost, you were not there.

Marguerite E. Halpin

Rainbows

Do you like rainbows?
I do!
They somehow remind me
Of you.
They are so pretty,
Up there;
They make the whole world
Seem fair.

I'd like to walk on one;
Wouldn't you?
From up there, the earth would be
A grand view.
I'd see the storm clouds retreating,
Their fury spent;
I'd see sunbeams come speeding—-
Heaven-sent.

A rainbow's a blessing anywhere.
It's apt to make you forget care.
I'd like to keep one in view,
'Cause I really like rainbows, don't you.

Virgil Ira Glen Churchman

Can Not Cry A Tear

Can anybody hear me
I do so hope, or I fear
I love honor and respect
A man that is dear
I know he knows how
I feel for I tell him year
By year
He's the only man for me
I fear he can not hear
My heart breaks with care
Every time that he is near
But I look with sadness
In my eyes
For I cannot cry a tear

Linda S. Thomas

For Robert

In awe and adoration,
I gaze at your face.
The smile, the eyes
I see Love in their place.
I waited forever, it seems
for you to come into my life.
Now you are my husband
and I am your wife.

Together, we'll travel
life's road as one,
secure in our marriage
till our journey is done.

And when we are finished,
I'll proudly rest by your side.
For you were my husband,
and I was your bride.

Sandra Boleware

Walk On Grass

Walking through the grass
I got cut on a piece of glass
A cow passed
On the grass
By a tree
The cow peed
By the tree
On the grass
By the glass
As I walked through the grass

I climbed a tree
Another cow peed
Right on me
So I couldn't see
The cow passed
So I jumped in the grass
Back to the glass
Where the cow had passed

Melissa Cooper

Always A Dreamer

I've always been a dreamer,
I guess I always will.
Although I'm in my autumn years,
My dreams may come true, still.

I dreamed of getting married,
Having a daughter and a son,
Living in a nice house,
I've had all my dreams but one.

My dream to be a teacher,
It also did come true.
But writing was my secret dream
All those long years through.

Now I'm in retirement,
I've time to write at will.
If someone likes my poetry,
My dreams may come true, still.

Kay Million

From Teen Age To Old Age

When I was young and fair,
I had a head of wavy blonde hair.

Boys and men were few and far between,
For with them I dared not be seen.

But now that I have older grown,
and my hair has turned to gray.

Six men have come to share my life,
but to none of them am I a wife.

The first to come was Bur Sitis,
Bringing his next of kin, Arthur Itis.

Of Paul Bunion I sorely disapproved,
So I had him surgically removed.

I get up every morning with Charlie Horse,
Who grabs me with quite a force,

Then with strong will Power,
I can work for another hour,

I now spend the night with Ben Gay,
Praying he'll ease the pain away.

Still kneeling there in prayer, I pray,
"I thank you Lord, for each new day."

Margaret L. Stiede

Headstone

I didn't know that
I had died
Because you see
I sometimes lied

So on my headstone
Written clear
Hear he lies
That's if he died

Now all my friends
Who know for flight
Let's all believe
Rest easy tonight

Norman F. Pizza

Keep My Head Above Water

As I go about my daily duties
I have problems everywhere I go.
But I try to smile and bear them
Because God has willed it so.

Whenever things get to be too much
I turn my mind to him.
I pray "God keep my head above water
And give me the power to swim."

I don't ask not to have problems
For Christ had problems too.
And I'm not as good as he was
So what else am I to do?

If our pathways were always level
With no stumbling blocks in the way,
With nothing at all to upset us
We might forget to pray.

When things begin to overtake me
Right away I turn to him
I say "God keep my head above water
And give me the power to swim."

Ruth L. Traynham

Sean's 7th Birthday

I love you my nephew
I have since the start.
There's a special place for you
And it's deep in my heart.

You're just like my kids
So playful and sweet
And just between us
I think you're real neat.

You recently turned seven
You're growing so fast.
It's hard to look back
And remember the past.

Soon you'll be grown
With friends of your own,
But always remember
You're never alone.

A brave little boy
So loving and strong,
You really are special
I knew all along.

MaryAnn Donnelly

Reality

Life can be beautiful and our minds holds the key
If only we would accept reality
We say one thing but we do another,
we won't admit to our shortcomings and our mistakes
we try to cover.

Whenever we think that we can get something for
nothing we will give it a try.
We don't always do our best but just enough to get by
Although we may be shown what's right and given some proof.

Sometimes we can be stubborn and won't accept the truth.
Often we let pride stand in our way and our feelings we disguise,
Remember nobody is perfect nor too good to apologize.

The truth stands alone just as sure as you were born
But the hardest thing for some people to do is to
admit when they are wrong.
Life is what you make of it and not always what
you wish it would be.
So make each moment count by facing reality.

Arthur Robinson Jr.

"A Glimpse In Time"

How would we value love's worth
If wishes always came true—
Could we know how precious the outcome
If no obstacle challenged our view?

Something unknown would be missing
Even though we would be unaware-
Expectation is half of the blessing.
In the course of our personal fare.

If we looked at the sky forever
Seeing nothing but bright shining sun-
It would prove we need stormy weather
To balance emotions unsprung.

No thing acquired of great value
Comes easily to people of worth-
Be patient and caring and loving
Give thanks for the blessing of earth.

The light of a new dawning daybreak
Will erase most of yesterdays woes-
Don't dwell on the past- travel on fast-
Don't endure- just enjoy- on life goes!

Beatrice P. Price

"Acceptance"

You wouldn't know life's pleasures if you sampled not its pains.
if you've never suffered losses, you'd not understand its gains.
Not ev'ry day is sunny. Not ev'ry sky is blue.
Things won't always go your way. Not ev'ry friend is true.
Appreciate your trials and the sorrow sent your way.
In that way, growth is measured. Have you gained or lost today?
Did someone hurt your feelings? Did the other cheek you turn?
Did you give vent to anger? Did it make your stomach churn?
If you've reacted badly, in your heart you'll surely know,
That you've lost a minor battle and a major chance to grow.
Keep peace and love your neighbor as the path of life you trod;
For life is but a classroom and the teacher is our Lord.

Jonathan McNeil

The Drifter

Everyday she'd walk right by
Ignoring me the best she could.
She talked to everyone around,
That's everyone except for me.
I remember when we were close friends
Way back in the past.
We always laughed and talked together.
But those are all just memories.
In the recent past it seemed
She began to drift away.
All the years we had been friends
Were nothing in her eyes.
I always tried to keep us close
But nothing seemed to work.
She drifted farther and farther away.
I wish I could've kept her close.
Every night I pray to God
That we could be close friends again.
But I guess not even God's miracles
Can keep her from drifting away from me.

Danny Seifried

My Mother, My Best Friend

My long time best friend and a wonderful mother,
I'll always love you more than any other.

The one I tell my deepest most intimate thoughts to,
Yes mother, my best friend, that someone is you.

You've always listened to me and you never judge me harsh,
All other "so called friendships" have all been a farce.

To ever think of being without you is a very scary thing,
You have my unconditional love, you know what I mean.

I feel you are my soulmate, I truly believe it with
my heart,
You were the one that gave me a life to start.
Your knowledge and wisdom is something I value so much,
You've been there whenever I needed an emotional crutch.
You share my dreams and encourage me to go on,
You're the greatest best friend and I'm proud that
You are my mom.

Jo Anne Showalter

Lost Friendship

One time I had so many friends at school.
I'll name some if you promise not to laugh:
Susanne, Issac, Carmen, Jamal, and Chu.
Of all my friends, these were not even half.

One day a boy quite new came to our school.
I left my friends because I thought him wise.
He taught me how to play and cut each class,
And how to steal and tell the teachers lies.

Oh, what a lesson I have truly learned!
How much I wish my friends would heed my call!
But when I see them now at school and play,
They turn as though they see me not at all.

One time I had so many friends at school.
I'll name some if you promise not to laugh:
Susanne, Issac, Carmen, Jamal, and You.
Now, of my friends, I have fewer than half.

Ben Edward Holt

I've Got The Face I've Got The Talent

All I Need Is A Little...

I'll take you on.
I'll take you on.
Beauty is not just a pageant.
It's within, it's without.
Give me a chance, and
I'll disprove your doubt.
Why won't someone hear me out?
Call me up, if you think I should give the show.
I know I could.
Singing, dancing, acting, casting.
What do you think - I am not passing?
I'll take my chance, whatever you do.
Don't forget that I am here with you.
Show me up; show me down.
Let me go all around.
Take me high; take me low.
Let me know, I've got the show.

Anna Steen

Dark

The darkness sets, the night is still
I'm being forced against my will
To fight the demons of cold and dark
The gods of darkness have come to embark
On an evil journey to all the lands
To take away the joining of hands
The feeling of love they cannot feel
When it's alive, they roll and keel
But we'll withstand these beings of dark
And we will come and make our mark
So here we go, let us bring light
Because of dark, we have to fight
I won't become a hateful soul
I will become a God of light
Because I fight
For the light of love.

Amanda Carruth

Promises Of A Wee One

Hi, I'm just a wee one.
I'm really bummed.
I heard my mommy talking,
She said that she didn't want me.
Mommy has already made her plans,
To throw me in the trash.
I thrash a lot inside to let my mommy know,
That I am still here and alive.
Mommy I promise to never get in your way.
Mommy you won't ever have to sit with me and play.
Mommy I promise to never cheat, steal or lie.
Mommy I'll do anything for you to spare my life.
Mommy I promise to be the perfect little child,
Mommy please hear my cry.
Mommy I'm so scared, why can't you care,
To give me the one and only chance to survive.

Corrina Whitney

The Upset

A blue pennant gloats above the wooden court.
Implanted in the court is a ridged pattern of lines and dots.
A Morse code trampled repeatedly by feet,
The creation of a quaint cacophony.
Above a sleek circular skin spins through the cylindrical net.
Wan faces populate the bench as the buzzer sounds,
And the pennant drops its pride all over the court.

Alex Hassinger

Untitled

I never asked to be born,
I'm the product of two irresponsible persons.
The mother did the mother things, it had its payoff for her.
The father did the father thing, escaped responsibility;
Each doing the least, expecting the most.

In return I have to learn to be alone.
I grew...everyone stayed the same.
I changed playgrounds, the games stayed the same.
I follow the rules, they win...I lose.
I ask for friends, none to be found.

I do not ask to die, die I must.
Each day is a good day to die.
Only 24 hours to struggle to survive.
I can live with that. What I am is a creation of God.
He is not finished with me yet.

Lord you were given your grave,
You brought your own cross.
I will not carry your cross, I have my own.
I didn't ask for it, But I'll carry it.
It's the lonely times that I forget you are carrying me.

John P. Marshall

Imagine Me

Imagine me lovely, smiling, serene
Imagine excitement, unbridle my dreams
Imagine me flowing, graceful and strong
Imagine my heart singing its song
Imagine me joyful, my face shown with love
Imagine the presence of hope and of God
Imagine the stillness upon the waters, the calm
Imagine adoration of the vision beyond
Imagine the love that wells up in my soul
Imagine me loose of my burdens, my woe
Imagine me free to give all that I may
Imagine the beauty of Grace in my gaze
Imagine me fearless relying on faith
Imagine me laughing and happy all day
Imagine me free to express what I feel
Imagine my touch, the pain it could heal
Imagine the wonder that it would be
Imagine if you were to ever know me
Imagine the things that you never have seen
Imagine they are what I imagine for me.

Julie L. Hamman

Untitled

Truth sits on my shelf untouched.
Immortal words - on pages much like this - a result of an anxious feeling of what's to come.
One life lies ahead - - mine and yours.
Unfolding into creation, refolding as destruction.
An empty bottle of whisky sits on my window sill, better seen from that perspective. That potion contains the power to unjustly capture, control, and conquer, but somehow it feels like courage.
The chaos calms as I try to think of more words for "THANK YOU."

Just a guest here pointing to the star that you point back from.
The flame between us grows larger as I stand and stare wondering if I come back tomorrow will you still be there?
My clock flashes 12 o'clock ... how can I say there's not enough time, not enough time to feel good?
A nation obese from feeding on misery and fear.
Can't close my eyes - - - - - - - - - - - - -
I pick a rose and stab myself with its thorns, choose not to smell it. Know why? 'cause sweetness doesn't last as long as pain.
That's what I used to think until you reminded me that beauty is nurtured by the rain.

Jen Zagame

When The Flag Was Burned

A knife was placed
in a dead soldiers Heart today
When someone burned the flag
and called that freedom, in some sort of way.

And I heard the cry, of a thousand young soldiers boys
as the knife slowly pierced their soul
I could see the look upon their faces, as if to say
there's a mark on America, as black as coal.

That Flag meant
everything to me,
That's why I fought
to keep her free.

The flag is a symbol
a torch, if you may
To be held high, and in Honor
not in dismay

I am truly dead, and forgotten by all
as the soldiers boys voice faded away
The day he heard that someone
burned His flag today.

Clarence Whitworth

Faces Of Love

Faces shining, eyes bright,
in a flickering light, warmed by chardonnay.
Our fingers reach out, touching tenderly,
anticipating, sparks in a warm blue bath.
Can't get enough, drowning in our sexual heat.
Ah, but so much more. Love, a bond forever!

After five years, married, long moments of silence,
punctuated by repartee, intimacy and pain.
Watchful eyes, cool analysis, every crack a fissure.
Separate animals, pacing in their cages.
The ends of a twisted rope, uniting fire and ice.
Love in its chrysalis.

Old now, no need to talk.
Can't remember when we weren't together.
Like two pieces of a broken tree,
bound and become one branch.
Not married, just one being, enveloped by the past,
and gently settling into the detritus of our dreams.

Doug Schaffer

Loneliness

She was walking down a dusty road,
In a quiet sort of mode.
When a cat meowed nearby,
I thought I heard her call, "Goodbye."

I saw her again by the pond,
Trying to talk with a swan.
When she left, It let a honk.
When she said, "I must be Gone."

In the forest, very near,
I heard her talking to a deer.
When she left, its young fawn bayed
Then ran into a meadow and played.

I found her cottage beaten and worn,
With curtains that were tattered and torn.
She played with a small brown cat
While I stood on the welcome mat.

She talked to a little bee,
She was lonely, you could plainly see.
Next she sat talking to a tree,
I moved, and she came to talk to me.

James A. Pipkin

Life's Worth

In the wild, a new bird chirps
In a hospital, a new mom gives birth

In another land, there is a war
And up above, and eagle soars

In one country, an invention is made
In another, someone hides afraid

Somewhere else, people protest beliefs
At a cemetery, a young girl weeps

Around the world such things are seen
Faces cry or sometimes gleam

People ponder things unknown
While others talk gaily on the phone

Families are suddenly reunited
And other families are sadly divided

People are separated because of color
And a young man fights against his brother

The world is one big melting pot
And most events are left forgotten

Bur whenever life gets unbearably worse
Remember all the others on this earth.

Jamie Collins

Love

Love is like a candle burning to the end
In a little while you'll see the flame descend.

Why is this so hard?
Or simple as a card?

Feelings so deep
Relationships you need to keep

Can I trust you?
Or try someone new?

When we hold hands
Sometimes love will land

Looking far ahead
For what you have said

Wishing well is near
Why do you fear

Searching for the sky
Don't want to cry

Love is like a candle burning to the end
In a little while you'll see the flame descend

Andrea Carson

"Magic"

With a glint of stardom in her eyes, she shined
In a way I was never allowed to witness before.
And she was more beautiful than anyone else on stage.
I felt the roles reverse...
As if she were my child - I was so proud!
The magic called music dripped like sweet honey off of her tongue.
It was her evening, her moment to shine, her spotlight.
But what impressed the audience most
Must have been her eyes...
The energy they showed, the anxiety to please,
The uncertainty of the perfection she would display.
She is the magic that is my mom.

Cherilyn Denise Snively

"God Lifted Me Up When I Was Down"

One day I found myself setting
in a room, as I sat there looking
out the window seeing the first
snow of winter trees laced with
white, a few birds in the trees
wondering where to go.

As I thought about those
words. "Wondering where to go." I
looked at the passed year of my
life many times I had thought
the same thing as the birds where do I go from here.

God had lifted me up and
carried me this last year a sad lonely
and fearful year, not knowing what
was going to happen in my life and family
when these times come in our lives it's hard
to understand but God answers our prayers
not our will but his will for our life.
And now I know God lifts us up,
Because God lifted me up when I was down.

Gloria Lindig

The Warmth Of My Father's Love

In the warmth of my father's love
in abundance was given to me.

I took it so freely and held it so tight,
for it meant everything to me.

Tho the days have gone by since I was a child,
those precious memories forever I hold,
for they come to me softly calmly warming my soul.

Yes, this is the life that still lives on
and comforting it is to be.

In the warmth of my father's love
the love he gave only to me.

Cowanna Raines Ivey

Keys To Wisdom

Where are the keys to wisdom
in cat's eyes and crystal balls?
Or in the spirits' homes which glow with
the light of the golden halls,

But what do the creatures know
when the candles dim?
But for sure their minds hold the
notes of wisdom's hymn.

They feel the pain and sense the fear
of man's purest emotions and thoughts.
For all minds hold the knowledge
and some search no matter what the cost.

Some doors are locked
like ones of supreme power
Though if evil finds the key
both heaven and earth shall cower.

So before you look in the key holes
You must not writhe in fear.
For truth and strength are needed
To use this wisdom, my dear.

John McKay

Brent

This poem is about a precious one whose name is Brent,
in God's great wisdom a son to me he has sent.

He has only recently turned one, my one and only son.

What a joy and pleasure it would be for my uncle Fennie and
aunt Annie Lee, to have been here to see their great great
nephew whose name is Brent Lee.

As I listen to his giggles, babbles, and balks, I know that he
is learning to talk.

Within our family we have a beautiful daughter named Joy,
whose little brother is now a big boy.
He loves to play with our pots and pans, and when no one is
watching he moves quickly to turn over our trash cans.

To my stomach and head he lands two handed slaps, he runs and
plays hard all day but then only takes short naps.

As we snuggle, run, crawl, wiggle, and play fight, I pray that he
is never long out of my sight.

When he is asleep he's a real beauty, when awake a little monster
but sill my cutie.

I love to see Brent with my wife, Pat, especially when he on her
lap sat.

I love my little boy, who thinks of me as his own personal living toy.

For reasons I may never understand, my God, a son to me has he sent,
I will always love and cherish my son, Brent.

Johnny A. Stanfield

This Fearsome Foursome Of The Links

Each Saturday night at the 19th hole finds Victor quaffing beer,
In grief tormenting he sits lamenting in a voice that all could hear;
"I hit my drives so long, my irons high, I could have been Jack
Nicklaus——but,
God He must know why I always blow that awesome two foot putt."

Now Al, he's the pride of this fearsome foursome, he's mean and lean
and wiry,
With a long iron game and a power-fade drive he makes par,
sometimes bogey or birdie.
"I've got all the shots to win" says he, "and I love pressure—but,
For God's sake please don't ask ME to make that awesome two
foot putt."

And then there's Stan, the leader of the band—to be the best is necessary,
He's got all the strokes of the game down pat, his chip shot is legendary.
In freon frozen concentration he vows, "I've gotta crack one more nut,
I'll find the ultimate thrill when I can handily drill that awesome
two foot putt."

And finally there's Bernie, the old man at the tee—just to be
playing he gives thanks,
He drives somewhat shortly, his iron game wobbly, his chip shot?
well sometimes he shanks.
"When I get to the green," he cries in his dream, "God help me
out of this rut!
Gimme a chance to prevail and I'll step up and nail that awesome two
foot putt."

Bernard F. DaSilva

The Gift:

The most precious gift I am told,
is all the love the heart can hold. I give
it to you, you give it to me. There's enough
for the world and the gift is free. Will
you take my love more precious than gold?
It's the finest gift that the heart can hold.

Becky Mayville

I Drink From A Beautiful Aria

I drink from a beautiful aria in God in holiness,
in happiness, in joy, in peace,
in suffering, in loss, in grief, in solace,
in contentment, in solonatic peace.

I drink from a peaceful fountain
over in the Yonder Vales of creation and new
life.

I drink from a beautiful vision of life that
I heretofore had not seen or heard of.
It speak through the vale of heart and hopes
Song and creation's new life.
Its vision is creative and effervescent
beyond my highest dreams.
Its hope is ever rejuvenating to my heart.
The beautiful Aria. The beautiful Aria.

Judy Mallory

A Tribute To Maya Angelou

Sometimes in life a special star appears, and holds
in her hands life's treasure so dear.

She constantly strives for greater things, hoping the
pathway will lead to her dreams.

She has fought many battles, and gone through many trials and
tribulations, at times it seemed she couldn't find peaceful
consolation.

But God did provide a wondrous place, where she could go in
His grace and find peace of mind.

She asked all of us, no matter the color of our skin
to treat one another with respect and love, which God blessed
us with from the heavens above.

And that is wy I write today, to honor a lady whom
God has blessed along the way.

She has proven herself time and time again, showing
us that if we have faith within, we will surely the battle win.

And that is Why God found an angel on earth
below; Her name is Maya Angelou....

Ameca P. Morgan

Invisible

He was there.
In her heart, in her mind,
her soul and her thoughts.
Invisible to the naked eye he was.
And yet, he seemed so near.
One she had loved so deeply;
Given so much, but never enough.
Expectations and anticipations
Never met or fulfilled.
Plunged to the depths of despair she was.
And yet through him she'd learned life's secrets.
Pearls of wisdom she'd never before possessed.
Through tears and joy,
Pleasure and pain;
Agony, with its sharp claws
Tearing at her very being...
And ecstasy, with its pure light
Buoying her up ever so high and mighty,
She'd acquired the stuff of life.

Constance Kint

Impulse

There are times-
In my bedroom-
When I think of all the people whom I would like to be-

So easy to pretend-
To play the part-
To wish "If I could only be"

In my bedroom-
I could be who I want to be-
Feeling beautiful - Yet -
Controlling the desire of whom I would like to be-
Knowing—Tomorrow -
It will only be "just me"

In my bedroom-
I pretend - as I disclose-
a little bit more of me-
Each day.

Gigi De Morgan

The Love I Cannot Hold

Alone, I kneel down by the water's edge.
In my reflection, I see you kneel down beside me.
I scoop my hands into the pool to
reach for you, a clear puddle in
the cupped palms of my hands, and
I feel refreshed, alive.

But I cannot hold you long, I know,
and the clear water begins to
drift softly between my fingers.
I can't seem to grasp it as your
substance slides away from me,
into the pool from whence it came.

I glance into the pool and see that my
reflection is alone. You have
left me once again
with wet hands,
and I have no towel
to dry my broken heart.

Christine Rioux

A Special Time Coming

I must apply what I have gained,
In prayers and meditations,
As countdown time
To the second millennium.

It will be infinite to...
See hopes of love solemnized
On wings of grace and exaltations.
Fulfillments and remembered joys,
Not computer games or playing toys —
of wealth
But activities centered in
The perfect spirit of God,
Flowing through as peace, love and health.

Thus, all in faith, stillness and light,
As journeys of the mind,
Seeking noble expectations,
An appointment to a greater life.

Dorothy Williams

Adios, Joaquin

Blame, there is no blame now
In retrospect: only a life twice
Lived the depth and breath for the
Living to examine. Death
Gathers us here, the human formality
We embrace to satisfy ourselves on the
Finality we all will face; finality indelibly
Etched in the sand on the seashore, the
Tide to determine its historical mark. A
History of soul and flesh and blood and meaning
Spread out at first on virgin canvas: the
Maestro's hand to develop its
Excellence or beauty or brutality.
We gather in death to remember a
Brother a Son a Friend and
Remember...for now we the living posses
Only memories on which to endure
His legacy.

Julian Aguirre

We Love, Because He First Loved Us

"My God! I do not love you!" was my pain-filled cry that day,
"In spite of all we've been through it is all that I can say.
I don't know how to love you, though I struggle and I try,
But this one thing is surely true - I must learn how, or die".

"My child", His voice came strong and clear, "my joy, my very own,
I know how you have worked and strained to love just me alone.
Come now, and I will show why your efforts are as dust -
There is one simple, shining truth that you must fully trust."

His gentle eyes turned to me and He held in out stretched hand
A vessel that was empty and as dry as desert sand.
"Now, pour water from this vessel" was His puzzling word to me,
"I cannot Lord," I responded, "What you ask just cannot be".

"That's right" He said, "So is your life unless I fill it up,
You see my child, you've missed my truth - I first must fill your cup.
'We love Him, as He first loved us' sounds simple, but you see,
The way to loving anyone is to first be loved by me.

"No matter how you search or strain or struggle, all is vain
Unless the vessel of your soul receives my gentle rain.
Now let me pour upon you all the love I yearn to send
And you will find your love for Me will never know an end"

Joy Dawn McArtor

Fall Shadow

Whose sleep I enter when my shadow is near?
In the darkness of my shadow, sleep becomes fear.
Though I cannot see that dark place behind me,
I will tread forward—careful of my lead.

And upon the hill I rise from the fallen leaves
To climb until dragging, my shadow past the trees;
For upon this autumn crest does the sun go down,
And fade into darkness as my shadow falls round.

I have with great fortune, to watch the empty light
Cast from body upon the hill at night.
For I will wonder at the brown, red and green,
And follow down treading through the leaves I have seen.

It is now night time, and with much hard to see,
I beseech of the crest where my shadow might be—
That I so dragged up to triumph in the sun;
For now I tread beneath the darkness just begun.

David R. Stevens

Grandpa's Jar Song

They come in a caravan jostling along,
In the dead of night they come singing this song;

"Woe to the beggars whose hearts lay to waste,
They ask for some bread and some wine to taste.
But we know what's best, we monkeys behind bars,
Trade us your souls for an armful of jars."

Their voices ring out as they climb up the trees,
Low buzzing awaits like the sound of our bees.

"Our offer is wise for you that are cold,
Let us give to you these jars you can hold.
Your soul is a small, small price for these jars,
For we are just monkeys trapped behind bars."

The trading begins like the frenzy of sharks,
Ripping and shredding fresh souls from young hearts.

"I've a jar for you", I hear myself say,
"I met a small band of monkeys today.
Please know that this jar is all I have left,
The monkeys have come and taken the rest."

Emily Savannah Blake

The Joy Of Spring

When nature awakes,
In the Earth with gleam,
So briefly and faintly
- in its transient form,
It's Spring.

When a robin appears,
With joyful countenance,
- and a pleasing succession -
With competence, it does sing,
As I listen to its tranquillity, I know
It's Spring.

When I gaze with delight,
At the flourishing verdure,
The splendor and luster of grass so green,
The vastness and intensity of the blossoms, I know
It's Spring.

Doris L. Beams

'Cause I'm The Oldest One

My brothers follow me all around,
in the house and out in the yard.
They sometimes mock my every sound,
'CAUSE I'M THE OLDEST ONE!

My Mom and Dad tell me to act right,
in everything I do.
My brothers always keep me in sight,
'CAUSE I'M THE OLDEST ONE!

Sometimes my Dad takes me out with him,
to check on all the cows.
I get to stay out 'till the sunlight grows dim,
'CAUSE I'M THE OLDEST ONE!

I was the first to have a lunch box,
and my brothers envied me.
I was also the first to have chicken pox,
'CAUSE I'M THE OLDEST ONE!

I'll work and study and pass every test,
since my brothers are watching me.
I'll try to do my very best,
'CAUSE I'M THE OLDEST ONE!

Alonzola Studdard

If Only

Darkness can be so lonely,
In the middle of the day.
That cannot be you say,
Two words come to mind, if only.

The day they laid you to rest,
The day my blue skies turned gray.
I thought of the words I did not say,
I felt the ache inside my chest.

If only you were here,
Then I would tell you today.
The words back then I did not say,
If only you were near.

The days could've been brighter and not so lonely,
This I know is true.
If I had said the three words, I love you,
Instead I say just two, if only.

Jocie Combs

Death In Flight (Life On Earth)

The white Ptarmigan beautiful and safe
In the white tundra snow, with faith
Camouflage of white on white, like a waif
The arctic Ptarmigan beautiful and safe.

The arctic Ptarmigan beautiful in flight
The arctic tundra falcon, a dreadful fright
But also beautiful when in flight
Camouflaged when white on white.

Look out Ptarmigan when in the sky
Death in flight when you try
To out fly the falcon is no pie
Stay in the snow or you will die.

You can have it astronaut
I stay aground like an Argonaut
Death in flight shouldn't aught
To happen to the young who bravely fought.

Where the falcons fly is not for me
Go, astronaut, fly and be free
You are rare as it should be
No discoveries made by poets like me.

Calvin D. Jarrett

Untitled

As I walk along these streets
in the winter, 'neath the blue-grayish sky,
I am feathered by the moonlight
that is falling down on me.
The blue note captures me as I sip a smooth
glass of cognac; oblivion drunkens me.
My smaller shadow follows me,
Silhouetted on the frosted pavement preceding
me. Where did it go?
When did it leave me?
Does it return?
Looking for answers is the way of the wind;
it carries me to this lonely city
entrapping me in canvas strokes
of blurred confusion and brilliance

Jonathan Fabio

Inspiration

Inspiration is everywhere,
In the words that we speak,
In the silence of the moment,
In the peace that we seek.

Where have you been inspired?
In the quiet of a church,
By the roaring of the ocean, or
Under a beautiful white birch?

When have you been inspired?
While your life is in turmoil,
When your life is running smooth and serene,
Or when you are with nature, turning the soil?

How have you been inspired?
By the writing of a poem,
By the winning of the game, or
By finding peace within your home?

We all find our own inspiration,
Which puts us on course.
We become pleasantly surprised,
When we discover the source.

Arlene A. Gutierrez

Ode To The Only Girl

I've seen you many times, in many places,
In theater, bus, train, or on the street,
Smiling in spring rain, in winter sleet,
Eyes of any hue, in myriad faces;
Midnight black, all shades of brown your hair,
Long, short, bronze or honey-fair

Instantly have I loved, yet never spoken
Because a truck passed, a light changed,
A door closed—all seemingly pre-arranged—
Then you were gone forever, the spell was broken.

Ubiquitous only one, we've met before
A hundred times, and we'll meet again
As many more; in hills or forest glen,
On crowded street or lonely, peaceful shore;
Somewhere, someday, in glare of sun or glow
Of moon, true love—but how will we ever know?

John Williams

For What Would Life Mean

There will be times of sorrow,
in which we all have cried
There will be times of joy,
in which we all have smiled

But, still and yet behold,
keep your faith in the Lord
For He has seen those tears
which really let it show

Please don't make any mistakes,
this can be no dream
For throughout it all, may your trust
be neverending and loyalty supreme

For He will be there to protect you,
through a troubled storm
For He will be there to comfort you,
when you're all alone

For He will answer, everything and all
For what would this life mean?
If no tears were to fall.

James Hutchinson Jr.

The Teacher

There once was a teacher, noble and proud,
In whose classroom fools were never allowed.
Upon his scholarly nose was seated
A pair of glasses, purpose defeated,
For he did not use them to read a book:
Since he was a teacher they came with the look.
When the first bell rang he was filled with joy
Knowing how many students he would annoy
With his symbolic sayings and rules.
The students never quite mastered his tools;
Nevertheless he reviewed them each day.
Not understanding, they had to obey.
One ignorant comment sent him ablaze,
His eyes bulging out, he seemed in a daze.
Then he tapped his yardstick and stared them down
Till every face in the room bore a frown,
And the guilty one repented his sin.
Class would continue, the battle he'd win.
At the end of the day he scratched his beard
And thought, "What a wonderful thing - to be feared!"

Julie Kubik

"Like An Angel From Heaven"

The smile on your face and the sun
in your hair. Your love grew stronger
as I silently stared.

Overwhelmed by the beauty I saw
in your face. So soft and tender, so
full of grace.,

Like a Angel from Heaven, sent
from above. So sweet, so pure, so full of love.

Eyes like diamonds so shiny and bold
a reflection of your heart and a mirror to your soul.

The message I read when I looked
in your eyes, "you'll love me dearly
for the rest of our lives!"

Dwight David Mabe

Comet

Comet, Comet, burning bright,
Incandescent pilgrim of night
From what mooring is your flight.

Did you tire of harmony,
Rent the chains of symmetry,
And assailed poor Jupiter so mightily.

I'll omen, perhaps you be,
Spoken of in prophecy,
Sent to vex man with calamity.

Hail, precursor of gloom,
But, prepare, if catalyst of doom,
Shan't the Lord returneth soon?

Then again, old cosmic wonder,
Might your form be existential,
Errant, dreadful, hardly, consequential.

The answer to such a mystery,
Lies in how you are perceived,
By the fickle mind of human kind.

James M. Pitt

The Long Road Back

Escaping the world of reality
Innocence lost young, stolen from me.
Travelling in dreams to a different place
Where no pain exists, no fear to face
Roaming the stars, searching to find
Some kind of haven, some peace of mind
Transcending through time, space, and dimension
Where I discover my future without apprehension
If I can endure, learn to survive
Meet my destiny-not dead, but alive
Tempted by fate, find the one with the key
Who'll unlock my heart and set the pain free
Probing the exceeding depths of my soul
I possess that strength to open the door
Lifting the lid off of Pandora's box
Feel the thunder crash, feel the lightening shock
Days drifted by, tears fell like rain
Lifting my spirits, slowly healing the pain
Most of the anguish has all but subsided, some will remain in my heart
To remind me how hard I fought for my life, how hard I fought
for a new start.

Gail L. Buttery

"Lovers Till The End"

Moonlight and movie watching was their ideal kind of date,
inseparable until their untimely fate.
Unusual as it may seem,
their lives were straight out of a dream.
Lovers till the end,
for eternity they'll be.
It was kind of hard not to see,
that forever in their love they wanted to be.
Hand in hand, side by side,
they walked with such loving pride.
For at their deaths,
they knew not how painfully we cried.
Lovers till the end I knew they'd always be,
but now I know that they'll both be looking over,
and smiling at me.

Bernardo E. Macias

Boy's Shirt

This boy's shirt the erupting iron steams
Into a limp shirt shape will enclose
Two chubby arms and a sturdy torso,
Will gather wrinkles through the day
(As his mother through the years).
Soil, sweat, gravy spots and indeterminate
Contamination of plain living,
At day's end drop emptied on a littered
Bedroom floor to add to the detritus
Of toys and other fearsome treasures.
He shall not know the stiffened tenderness
Ironed in, a ritual to cherish him
Throughout the day, which will in no way
Shield him from the day's small smudgy tragedies.

Chiye Mori Oshima

The Past

The past is nothing but paged memories,
It makes you laugh or cry.
But they also help you remember,
The ones you once knew and loved.

We forget these things for certain reasons,
Whether it be painful, loveable, cryable.
We all forget the things we once knew,
So we give these things a name....

The Past.

Angelo Diosdado

High Noon On A Nevada Highway

Shade rests somewhere in the sleepless sunlight.
Invisible and undisturbing.
In the incessant heat of the black topped highway,
It is as alluring as it is unattainable...

In the vast distances of the desert the wind plays
Hide and go seek with itself.
Boundaries fade.
And the only sound besides the wind is of my own heart beating...

A few miles back, or was it a few hundred?
Three buddhist monks stopped me and asked me for a cigarette.
They were crawling on their bellies and chanting in broken urdu.
Their eyelids were turned inside out and they looked sunburnt as hell.
I offered them a ride but they felt undeserving.
I offered them some water but they were ashamed for even needing it.
The last I saw them they were building a shrine in an abandoned '57 chevy...

Right now I am as invisible as the shade.
Right now I remain hidden from the wind.
Right now I am hotter then all get out and just looking forward to
Getting the hell out of here.

John F. Terzino

A Matter Of Life And Death

What is happening to the children of tomorrow?
Is a day of life too much to borrow?
The safety of the mother's womb
Has been transformed into a deadly tomb.

We are silencing voices of innocence.
Murdering them for their undefinable weakness.
Unable to demand their right for life,
We destroy them to ease our own strife.

To kill the unborn, they say is her choice.
A death sentence forced on those that have no voice.
Who will speak for the child that may never be?
It is our responsibility, don't you see?

Amy Burchfield

Let God Avenge

He who seethes with rage and hate
Is always deserving of a better fate
To build on lies and innuendo
Brings one's hate to a violent crescendo
To feed the fires of rage and hell
Forbids the soul in joy to dwell

When with a brother one must contend
Let not his weakness cause thee to bend
If disagreement cause thee to part
Let further communion with wisdom be fraught
'Tis better to agree to disagree
Than allow the entrance of the adversary

When contemplating thy ways to mend
Do not nurse hate to the bitter end
Forgiveness and love thy soul will fix
Happiness and joy within will mix
Until you come to heaven's door
Where hate and rage will be no more

Joseph Stumph

The Birth Of A Man

What is a man and how does he come,
Is he like the music of the drumming of a drum.
Is he a man when he comes of an age,
Or is it with hatred, fighting and rage.

Is he ever so gentle and filled with great love.
Like the soft fallen rain that comes from above.
What is a man and how is he born,
Does the boy wake to manhood at the start of the morn.

Is he formed by the artist like a great mound of clay.
Or is he just there at the break of a day.
Has his features been sculptured by a soft gentle hand.
Or does he just sprout like the seeds on the land.

What makes a man who is strong and yet weak,
Does he soar like a bird to the high mountain peak.
A man starts his journey from the seed of great love,
A seed that is nurtured by God up above.

A man is a baby, a boy and a lad.
He is all of these things, some good and some bad.
A man is a boy. Who on one special day.
Becomes all these things then goes his own way.

Jack T. Nolley

"Weather"

Water comes from the sky.
Is it water?
Or is it a child that has begun to cry?
The sun beats down on my head.
Is it the sun?
Or did someone light the sky on fire, instead?
The wind whispers in my ear.
Is it the wind?
Or is it questions and words unspoken?
What is the weather really?
It is gold or silver, somewhat like a token?

Aimee Cardoza

On Being Myself

To be loved for being me
  is what I wish to be
To possess my being as my own
  not be confined to a comfort zone
To escape the reigns that restrict
  those aspects of me that contradict
The persona that people see
  when they think they're seeing me
For too long I gave permission
  to be held in submission
Because no waves I dared to make
  the ties that bound grew harder to break
I pray for strength to go the distance
  and to combat the resistance
So I can set my spirit free
  just so I can be me.

Corletta Allen Smothers

My Tree

My tree has many branches: My branches have many leaves:

My heart is the tree; my tree is planted by the water and it shall not be moved:

My arms are the branches on my tree; my branches reaches out to bring lots of joy to my tree:

The people that I know are the leaves on my tree:
And when a leaf falls from my tree, it seem to be replaced:

My leaves adds so much beauty and love to my tree:

Dorothy Lewis

Returning To The Sea

Returning to the sea, if but for a moment
Is wished by many, achieved by some
But required by a few.

The feeling of belonging, if completely belonging
In a fluid environment, is nourishment
For their sanity.

The attempt to dream, if not to fully realize
The deja vu of marine existence a feeling of knowing a distant past
Becomes unsatiable.

But the melancholy flow of life, if not so melancholy
Brought across the little window by the undersea wind, the current Is a thrill to behold.

It is from this thrill, if not for this thrill
That one feels the frustration, and sweet bitterness
Of limitations.

Returning to the sea, if but for a moment
Allows oneself special feelings, and completeness of mind
For those few.

John D. Moore

Hyperreality

The pain that exists inside is a gnawing so deep I wonder if it can ever be grasped with my bare hands.
My mind is reeling out of control, agonizing over the disparity I feel; the abandonment, the disloyalty, the unfulfillment
of life.
How can this be?
My daily existence has somehow gone awry.
The finely navigated course I so deftly plotted has suffered irreparably.
An impending blowout pervades each waking moment with fear.
Inescapable, like the watery depths, is what my future has become.
Consumed by the massive, yet elusive blue waves of an ocean so cold I am left powerless.
Powerless against the forces that hold me captive; I wonder,
When does the pain end?
Won't someone tell me?
When?

Denise Parker

An Uneven Balance

I wish I would stop wishin' for my life to come out even.
It doesn't work that way.
Life, that is.

Could I change today?
How much time do I have?
What is important?
Who is important?

Life isn't fair, they say.
So, when does it happen?
And who are "they" anyway?
And what is "it"?

And you ask, why me?
Why not you? I reply.
We could trade places, you and me.
And still, life isn't fair.

I wish I'd get on with the helpin' my wishin' to come true
Instead of asking the why's and why not's.
Is the answer because?
Then I best get on with it.
Life, that is.

Jean M. Grubb

Love Mystery

Love gives meaning to everything we see
It earns our respect like a great Oak tree

Love sneaks upon us when least expected
It starts with the mind and travels neglected

When it reaches the heart it really shows.
We develop a radiance which really glows

Love can bring us together or tear us apart
It glides through the air like a feathered dart

Available to all this thing called love
It sneaks in and fits like a fine leather glove

You think you can run or maybe just hide
It can come from the front or even the side

If Love comes your way please take it to heart
You'll want the whole thing and not just a part

Love your family, neighbors, and friends
Because before you know it life comes to an end

Love endures in all that we face
When Love comes your way accept it with Grace

Donald A. Woodson

Love

Love - what a strange word!
It echoes with a peculiar chord.

Encompassing such deep emotion -
Does it mean passion, or
Does it mean devotion?

We proclaim it so easily -
I love you, do you love me?

So many loves -
Your lover - on whom you always wait.
Your marriage partner - hopefully your life-long mate.
Your children - you see them as your destiny, your fate.
Your friends - this love often turns to hate.

The puzzle for me has come to an end.
My heart had to break, then bend.
And, at long last, it began to mend.

For me, the mystery of love was not by way of happiness.
The knowledge came by way of loss and distress.
Now I see love as cherishing.
For, from the moment you claim it, love begins perishing.

Debbie Walmsley

Paper Doll

A Paper doll is very thin and fragile,
it feels nothing and never communicates with others.
A paper doll could be ripped into a million tiny
pieces and never cry out stop.
A paper doll will never know what love is for a
paper doll has no heart.
Are you a paper doll?
A person who shuts out life and never rejoices
or cries, but just feels the hurt inside.
The hurt you ignore for you say nothing affects me
and you fool yourself into believing it.
Don't lie to yourself and say every things all right
when your world is really fallen apart.
Don't carry on a smile when behind it there is sadness and fear.
Don't act like everything is under control when it's not, for you
are lying to yourself and it's not fair to you or anybody around you.
Don't act fake and pretend you're something you're not, for
you are a real person with feelings that run deep.
So don't make believe you're a paper doll because everyone
hurts sometime.

Jill Engel

The Ring Of The Ninth Year

It is a symbol of my love for you.
It had a beginning but now it is boundless.
The origin has vanished.
Now it has no beginning and no end.
It is a continuation.
It embraces my finger with a gentle firmness.
The sensation is a stimulation
of the senses that awakens the heart to a new rhythm.
There is life glowing within its circle.
It forms the second letter of the word "love".
I am unclothed without it.
It is always a reminder that I am not alone.
It has lifted me to heights I had only
dreamed of before its existence.
The ring of the ninth year encircles us
but simultaneously expands as we grow closer together.
Although it is a complete circle,
it is never closed until it is close
to the ring on your finger.

José Alvarez

Pieces Of The Heart

The heart itself is now worn and mellowed.
It has been taken by fragments: used, twisted, tormented
then returned to its place.

The entire being is weak and tired, yet it has so much knowledge
and sight that it is not stupid or insane.

Just tired
Tired of re-runs.

It is too young for the continuing saga.
It has years of throbbing and feeling to come.

To encourage laughs
To feel them

To feel beauty
To give beauty

To censor the breaks
To forget them

To love
and be loved in return

Bridget Burrell

Towards Becoming

It is hard looking up from zero
It is hard realizing you are not a hero
It is hard to go through life without sharing
It is hard to build a relationship without caring

The disease robbed from me my innocence
The disease left me to escape from my presence
The disease took hugs from me and moments of closeness
The disease left me lost in my own hopelessness

Recovery has helped to find my senses
Recovery has helped to focus my lenses
Recovery has helped to find joy and love
Recovery has helped to focus on spirits from above

Life is listening to my inner child as he talks
Life is matching the pace as he walks
Life is hearing sounds and the cries he makes
Life is sharing those precious moments he takes

Life is about bright skies and morning fogs
Life is about clean air and "occasional" jogs
Life is about balance and inner joys
Life is about choice and child-like toys

Gary Earnley

Black

Black-
It is the oil that slicks an innocent seal,
the force that swallows the light,
the endless ditch where echoes live,
deep and solemn like the night.

Black-
It is a dark, eternal passion
that will never be quenched.
It is the unknown that lurks
in every passage of life, hence,

Black-
It has no boundaries
but still can't escape its own walls.
It desires nothing
but seems to engross all.

Black-
This absence of color
possesses a life,
that is evil in nature
and has the aura of strife. Black.

Emily King

The Mouse

There's a small creature, it's called a mouse.
It likes to occupy a place in your house.
The attic or a space in the walls will do,
But wherever it is, it will not please you.

There it builds a nest and raises its litters
And forages for food to feed the critters.
Any food it finds in the kitchen will do.
It spoils what is left and leaves you a clue.

The mouse is not large, a small hole it does take,
Or with its sharp teeth ample room it will make
To let itself into your private domain.
Then how it got there you find hard to explain.

If you have a house cat, mice seek other quarters
Then they won't frighten your wife or your daughters.
It's a fact that's been known for many a year,
A mouse in the house gives them terrible fear.

The mouse can be useful for all of mankind.
Our physicians and scientists recently did find
That mice can be used to find wonderful ways
To treat man's ailments and new hopes to raise.

Herbert C. McClure

Dear Daddy -

Just got the news of faithful "Si"
It makes a tear come to the eye.
The memories of those hunting days
And a dog's peculiar ways
Will always be a special part
Of a loving master's broken heart.

He loved his job and performed with pride.
Those birds from him just could not hide.
We know that such a trusty friend
He was to you right to the end.
He leaves his duties to one much younger
So train her now - she is much stronger.

Teach her the ways of a hunter's guide
You can count on her being there by your side.
We must not grieve for a pet gone on,
But turn our face toward a bright new dawn.
There is much hunting to be done this fall
And Lady will be there at your beckoning call.
I Love You.

Carol Bernauer

The Last Salute

In the distance he hears machine gun fire
It reminds him of the forth of July
With his rifle poised in from of him he wonders how many have died.

His birthday is tomorrow, he'll just be twenty-two
He thinks of his dreams and ambitions in life
There's so much he wants to do.

He remembers the laughter and fun he had
With his family and friends
He thinks of the girl he left behind
Will he ever see her smile again?

He closes his eyes in hopes that the fear will soon disappear
But hearing the guns and the cries of the battle
Leaves his face wet with his tears

He sits on a bench, a tired sad man
Remembering dreams of long ago
He remembers the girl he almost married
But there was somewhere he had to go

In the distance a truck backfires He screams, "take cover men"
His mind goes back twenty-three years
The nightmare returns once again.

Diane M. Curtin

Heavens Above....

A light shines down from the sky,
It seems so bright it catches my eye.
The light is all I can see,
When suddenly a voice calls to me.

All of the sudden I'm in a dark hallway,
It falls into night and ends the day.
Then I see a dim light,
I start floating through the night.

I reach the light, a hand motions to me,
To follow the hand and be free,
I follow that hand into a colorful field,
It seems so strong it's like a shield,

I hear the voice again saying,
"I see that you are finally staying."
Again the hand reaches for me,
And leads me to a peaceful sea.

The waves are so gentle, the waves are so calm.
It sounds like the waves are singing a song,
The voice turns out to be a white, beautiful dove.
And I know I'm in a world full of love.

Alicia M. Hacker

The Wind

The wind is enraged.
It vents its loathing.
From far away, hear it roar.
Down the mountains, through the valleys,
The tree tops toss as it passes.
Brown leaves scatter in front of its fury.
As testimony to its savagery,
Dark clouds dash across the sky.

Coax it down from the heavens.
Then cradle it softly with quiet murmurs.
Calm its fears to banish its anger.
Hold it closely with hearts entwined.
Soothe its tears and rock it gently,
Until it sleeps a blissful slumber.
Dreaming a dream unto its own,
Safely enfolded in tender arms.

Alan Corson

A Brown Leaf

In the woods today a leaf fluttered down.
It was wrinkled and old and bent and brown.
But it met the wind and began to play,
And I watched it until it whirled away.

And I could but wonder, when time and grief
Should have made me old and bent as the leaf,
Would my heart be as young and full of glee
As the brown leaf playing in front of me?

Carol R. Ice

The Red Man And The White Buffalo

This is a story that happened a long time ago,
It's about a Red Man and a White Buffalo.
Bringing gifts to Native Children was his game,
Long before the white man ever came.
And the Red Man's face would be all aglow,
Riding spirit, the White Buffalo.

His red moccasins, pants and coat were trimmed in white,
Shining with the red feathers of his headdress in the moonlight.
He had a sack full of neat little toys,
For all the Indian girls and boys.
And he always came out at night through the snow,
The Red Man, riding that White Buffalo.

Chief Red Clawes was his handle,
And from tepee to wigwam he would scramble.
They could hear the bells on his ankles jingle,
As he danced around the campfire, ever so nimble.
Finished, he rode off with a shout, Hi-Yah Ho Ho!
The Red Man, riding that White Buffalo.

Charles E. Hagan

Twins

They're double trouble and double love.
It's double diapers and scrubbing the tub.

It's two hungry mouths and four bright eyes
and double the clothes in the same size.

It's four sticky hands and two winter coats,
and two little boats in the tub to float.

It's two for the measles and two times the mumps
and double the scratches and twice the bumps.

It's "I'll take your bottle and you take mine,"
and when one's asleep, the other will whine.

It's two for the money, two for the show,
two to get ready and two to go!

Don't take it so hard for they do grow up.
Then it's double the Proms, two Caps and Gowns,
twice the smiles and twice the frowns.

Remember, "It's double your pleasure, double your fun."
Just think; What if it had only been one!!!!!

Jean Simmons

Great Grandma

Her hair is like a dandelion
It turns white then falls out one hair at a time,
In her younger years she was like a lion
Upgoing and cheerful,
She is older and wiser than anyone I know,
She gets sad sometimes because most of her friends are gone
She still keeps going for herself and her family though,
She is a rock
She is steady and keeps our family together.

Jessica Heater

My Only One

When darkness falls upon my sight,
It's finally time to rest for the night.
My work is over, for the day is done,
Now I will lay down, with my only one.
Holding her in my arms all through the night,
Telling her everything will be all right.
There's nothing better to be with, this angel of mine,
Thank you Lord for sending her just in time.

Because the nights were as lonely,
As my days were as long,
I thought I would never find a love so strong.
As the sun rises and the night fades away,
It's time to start a brand new day.
Lord, I can't wait 'till my work is done,
Because I know what's waiting for me at home,
Tonight,

My Love, My Friend,

My Only One.

Gaylon Chapman

Sea World

The sea is a world with laws of its own.
Its highways are real though they are not stone.
The denizens are there; each in its commune.
Her music is sweet though of a different tune.

The waves and the tempests may bring their woes;
The depths hold their secrets—those no one knows.
The rage and the breakers are feared by mankind.
The treachery of depths and shallows are blind.

The calm and the cool, the refreshing and the quiet,
The blue of its depths and waves dressed in white,
The surf's gentle laughter, the shore's glist'ning sand—
All stretch forth a welcome to ethereal man.

Man travels her highroads and rides on her waves.
She tosses him gently or harrows his days.
She bears him home safely or buries him deep.
The laws, though her own, she expects him to keep.

Her powers are great; magnificent her tide.
The rules she imposes in her mastery guide
Are firm and unyielding as man and ship have known—
The sea is a world with laws of its own.

James C. Hardin

Dreams Of Success

Success is not merely a word to say,
It's not just a feeling within;
For the man who's successful has a positive way
To overcome life's battles and win.

The victory comes when goals are set
And dreams have enveloped the mind.
For each time a goal has been reached or met
Success is not far behind.

A man without dreams is like a ship lost at sea
Battered and torn by the tides;
Helplessly struggling to become free
From life's monotonous ride.

So let your dreams soar like an eagle
Upon the currents of life.
For dreams make a man feel regal
Crowned with success and not strife.

Debra Boyd

October Sun

There's nothing like October Sun.
It's quite different from all the others.
If I close my eyes and bask in all of its glory;
I have memories of far away airplane engines traveling over the quiet streets.
While everyone is being taught, I still nap with my mother.

Close your eyes and let it rest on your cheek, for its warmth consumes you.
And you fear no burn.
But the impending memory that it leaves behind, surely seers your soul.

It reminds you of days gone by and holds the fragrance of firewood.
You inhale it and know that it's October and you drink in its familiarity.
If you close your eyes, it will envelop you.
Like long ago as my mother's arms; and I am safe.

What lies in us all is a summer with its searing heat.
Yet, how fortunate we are to have October with its bright cooling warmth.
It holds memories of school windows that are graced with pumpkins and tantalizes with impending promises of Christmas.

October holds a benevolent stance; It's tall and states itself as being here, but once a year.
Lay your cheek to its sun, for it will never burn you.
It warms you with sweet memories of days gone by and the anticipation
of what will come.

Jacqueline Ferretti

One At A Time

It's not that I don't have anything to do,
It's that I don't know where to start,
Or with who!
Cards, letters, calls and gifts,
All are added to my list.
One at a time,
They come to mind,
Until no one is missed.

Cathy Gene Schultz

Flaming Blue Bells

"Flaming" bells, flaming blue bells...
It's the blues time inside of God"
Samara" Galaxies.
Sing and dance, dance and sing.
It the season time, for the yule tide Galaxy's.
Cities Galaxies are hilarious cities Galaxy's
All, are glittery and blue for miles and miles
And beyond the flaming blue " Azure"
Are the galaxy's scenes of the yuletide styles
Brothers and sisters souls chums,
Are full of mellow fun, from the begun.
For the golden moments to sell.
For the holidays golden exciting
Memories of the yells.

Harold Gabriel McNairy

Will To Survive

What makes us go on in a world that's so lost.
It's the will to survive, no matter what cost.
Every day we do what we feel we must.
Others take it for granted, but we feel it's a trust.

We all look forward to the fruits of tomorrow.
In hopes we'll have happiness without sorrow
We'll travel on to whatever God expects.
To live our lives with love and respect.

Ella B. Murrow

"Since You Went Away"

Since you went away, glad
I've been pining for you.
You were the best wife I ever had,
Our love was so very true.
So lonely am I without your love,
But I feel your spirit from above.
Sure we had our ups and downs
Thru 40 years, they became only frowns.
You were one heck of a wife to he.
My girl, my love, my wife-Gladdie
I feel the vib's from you up there
for me, my love, just say a little prayer!

John W. Walsh Sr.

Spirolove for Robin

Time's been so long since
I've felt your heart beat close to mine.
Time's been so hard to be by myself leaving you behind.
Time's been so short when we're alone together.
Time's tested our love and we know that it's true,
I spin around and around in circles
Every time I'm without you.
I love you

Clayton L. Reynolds III

Why God Cries

As I sit here looking to the skies,
I've often wondered why God cries.

A sweet gentle breeze blows and the raindrops fall.
And it makes you feel so close to God and his tender call.

But when we do not listen and get out of his will.
He doesn't toss us out, he loves us still.

As I see tears roll down his cheeks,
I can hear, my child, come back to me my sweet.

Though you may grow weary, he says keep doing good,
For what God has in store, will soon be understood.

The rewards here on earth may not be seen,
But what's to come will seem like a dream.

So don't give up, cause God is near, he'll be your
Strength and you'll never have to fear,

That when you reach heaven and he says "Well done"
And you ask Father why did you cry?

He'll look you in the eyes and say,
"Look my child my eyes are dry!"

Judy P. Sherbert

Whether You Realize It Or Not

A birthday is something that everyone has got
I've said it before now I'll say it again
A birthday is not something that comes now and then
It comes once a year on the exact date
Not a day early nor a day late
But remember that birthdays were made for frolic and fun
To be enjoyed by everyone
The rich-the poor-the old the young-the frail and the hearty
Everyone enjoys a birthday party
So enjoy and be happy if you can stand up and say
This is my birthday and I've done my good deed for the day.

Josephine Monaco

Shattered Dream

I choose not to feel anymore.
I've seen one too many thing.
I've felt one too many pains.
I've been betrayed one too many times.
Things which once would have brought a reaction in me
Now roll off my callous insensitivity.

But who am I kidding?
The suffering in my heart surfaces, flooding my raw
Nerve endings with pain.
One who cares simply cannot walk around with eyes open.

But what can I do? There is nothing.
It is the most frustrating of feelings.
It is of no use to go on.
Yet that is my biggest driving urge.

My life is a wreck.
As a child I imagined how my life would go.
And I've made a total mess of it.

Becky Mate

"Ode To The Wind"

Who likes the Wind? Not I! Not!
I've tried to ignore her by and by.
But I must state before I die,
Who hates the Wind? 'Tis I! 'Tis I!

Sister Wind, pardon the gender,
Knows how to harm, misplace and hinder.
See how she laughs as fierce she blows.
While I question why, she knows, she knows.

Yet oft' times she blows with tenderest sway,
Giving my world a fresh, breezy day.
Who likes the Wind? Not I! Not I!
But blow she will, while I must die.

O, Wind, your mighty force is great,
But greater far is mine.
Tho' die I must, I yet shall live
Forever and divine.

So blow on, Wind, and cast your face
Where e're you choose to go.
Be kind, O Wind, when times we meet.
Be friend to me, not foe.

Dolores M. Falconer

Grandma's Root Cellar

The mice scurry at the sudden burst of light, as the
jammed door squeaks open -
The steps creak, with yellow dry grass growing out
from under -
The roof seems to creak, as if a warning for
children not to enter -
Charred wood, a remnant of the fire a little uncle
David once lit -
The damp, cold and musty, crawls under your
bare feet.
The mice scurry for shelter, red potato eyes
seem to grab at you -
The beets in Jars are like eyes staring at you.
Just barely tall enough to reach the light
switch -
Click! Light!
Now everything is OK.

Dawn N. Zetko-Goldman

"Look"

Hiding the truth seizes the mind
Just as the dark hides the obvious
Look beyond the obvious-look beyond the lies
Look hard and you will see... the truth never lies

Adriana Pozo

Call On Jesus

When times are tough and you want to cry,
Just call on Jesus, He'll draw nigh.

Lately you've felt you've been defeated,
Call on Jesus, when his love is needed.

Your flesh is weak, your faith is shaken,
Just call on Jesus, He's never left the righteous forsaken.

So when hope is dim, the future's not bright,
Just call on Jesus to be the guiding light.

The mistakes you've made, you've done it all wrong,
Just call on Jesus, He makes us strong.

My life was a mess and full of strife,
I called on Jesus, He gave eternal life.

Jesus is a friend who sticks closer than a brother,
I'll call on Jesus and serve no other.

Jennifer Pereira

Assumptions

Green light yellow
just turned Red
took the advantage
and passed on ahead
didn't see the other car
another one—BANG!
ASSUMPTIONS

He's on my territory doesn't wear red
I take out my gun another one dead
it's the fourth one today
ASSUMPTIONS

They're too old look at them walk
wear such thick glasses can't see too far off
if senses are failing then they won't care
if we put them in the nearest home
without anyone who cares
ASSUMPTIONS

See them playing out on the street
sweet and bright as they start to laugh
young and innocent they won't know
that we're in world with its game all its own.
ASSUMPTIONS.

Heidi Kriner

Black

I knew you once... at least I thought. Who did I really
know? Inside I'm screaming, screaming in complete silence.

He glanced at me... a light in his eyes. Afraid to lose, wrapped
in loneliness, I said something I regret. The tears behind
yours made me afraid. Would you be here tomorrow or would
fate take you like it had taken the rest? The yells echoed
in my head... why, why? We sat, broken. This place of
uncertainty, this place of pain. We went often. The tears
blended in the gravel and the glass. I reached to you but
only caught your heartache. Trying to be strong when really
I felt weak. Wishing we could change it but rather having
to face it. Changed your ways but couldn't keep on the path.
Fate had taken you too... only the memories remain. You look
at me as you light your cigarette. Who are you? You hold it
in your hands knowing it only brings destruction. You promised
me. I promised you. We both sit, alone, in darkness.

Andrija Potkonjak

Our Daughter

She comes and goes like the wind and rain,
Leaving behind heartbreak and pain.
Never stopping for her life to unravel,
But on the road she continues to travel.

Alcohol is her drink from day to day,
Cigs and drugs making her body decay.
Truth she knows not, lies she can tell,
And a real con artist, she does it well.

She stops on occasions, her life to share,
With those type of people who really don't care.
Satan has her in his grip, but it's never too late,
To kick "all" the habits, and get her life straight.

She cares not to listen, but stays on the run,
Treating her life like a game of fun.
She lives by the sword, will she die by the sword?
The fate of Our Daughter is now up to the Lord.

Edward G. Jones

Time

Time is the fire that burns within me
Leaving behind the ashes to measure how long it took to
finish what had to be done
Time
It pushes me
Gnaws at me
To finish what must be done
Time

Beatrice Ochoa

Running In Winter

How I hate to run in winter,
Leaving the warm cocoon of my home to hit the cold, empty streets,
Layers of clothing constricting me, bitter wind biting my cheeks;
hands and feet and nose quickly numb.
It is cold, dark, desolate, lonely and forbidding.
There is not another person to be seen,
No one out for an evening stroll; no one walking a dog.
Perhaps I'll turn around and go back home,
But then I realize, I'm no longer cold.
I'm two miles from home, comfortably into my run.
All is quite except for the sound of my feet hitting the pavement
and the sound of my breathing, now into an even, steady rhythm.
I've wrapped myself into my own warm cocoon of thought,
looking inward.
I run on past the softly glowing lights of familiar neighborhood homes,
Running until I no longer feel the movement of running.
Alone on these quiet streets, I feel that I am the only person in
the world,
On this tranquil, velvet night of solitary meditation.

Esther Hawkins

My Aunt

I feel the pain running through my veins
It hurts, It hurts
I can't get up
I can't move
My family comes to visit and I cry.
I ask myself why.
Why did I do the foolish thing
I did
Just to have machines to help me breath
Do I deserve it?
I plead for forgiveness but it's too late
I feel the switches going off.
I take one more look, say goodbye
Then I die!!!

Christie Navea

Her Corner Stone

He was only twenty-nine when they laid him in his grave,
Leaving two little girls and a wife all alone.
They wouldn't let him go for they loved him so,
When Jesus came and took him, he took their corner stone.

He said, "Someday when you awake I hope you understand,
Why I came into your home and chose to take your man,
I have a job up in heaven that only he can do,
And to finish his job here on Earth, to chose it to be you."

I'll give you strength and courage to face your burdens ahead,
I'll give you health and a job to earn your daily bread.
I know that you'll be lonesome from being left alone,
But I will see that the girls and you will always have a home.

As the years roll on and the girls are gone time will heal the pain,
You'll meet another and fall in love and you will wed again,
You'll have your ups and you'll have your downs, even miseries,
But when you need help my little one, you can always depend on me.

Evelyn C. Walker

White Trash

Right-wing extremist white trash.
Left wing save everything white trash.
President white trash.
Look 'ma I'm running the country through my husband-President White Trash.
White trash is as white trash does.
Pee-wee's wee-wee white trash.
Madonna's white trash panties to goofy-looking host white trash.
Jurassic white trash.
Michael wanna-be white trash.
Michael married white trash.
Did black football legend kill white trash or is this some big farce set up by white trash?
Ed "white trash" Wood.
Post office blown to hell because white trash can't handle finding another crappy job set up by white trash.
Nirvana gone because of loss of white trash.
Natural Born White Trash.
Parle vous white trash?
Skinny balding white trash arguing about how bad a movie is with overweight white trash.
I guess MTV has nothing better to do than show us bad cartoons about stupid white trash.
Well, this white trash is for you.

Casey Marshall

Born In September 1897

Physically delicate
Lets her thoughts go beyond,
While she seems strolling through
Her path of life,
So beautiful to contemplate.

She explains,
"Chores and hobbies enjoys no longer
My empty hands and motionless fingers"
To her many years of life
She blames.

With the serene look of her blue-gray eyes
Pleases herself with whatever her sight reaches
Like children running, flowers blooming,
Different greens of the trees - looks around
Softly smiling, the way herself she satisfies.

The sunset is on, time for her daily last part,
Give thanks to God for the day
And ends, with all of her heart,
"Oh Lord, give me much strength to keep on
Until you want me to depart."

Irma E. Medina

Tell Me You'll Stay

Don't let me go. Tell me to stay.
Let's make love till late in the day.
Don't kiss me good bye. Just kiss me hello.
Tell me you love me and don't let me go.
The look in your eyes. The touch of your hand.
Is like the music of a 40 piece band.
The life that we share isn't always so sweet.
But the love that we have is truly unique.
So take my hand. Walk from where we stand.
And shout out our love as we walk through the sand.
So don't let me go. Make me want to stay.
Just kiss me hello, till the end of life's day.
Take me in your arms. Safe from harms.
Show me your love, your tender embrace.
As our hearts start to race.
So tell me you love me. Tell me you'll stay.
And be my lover till life fades away.

Donna L. Stewart

Ultimate Happiness

At last, at last, the day has come
Let's toot that horn and beat that drum.
I sing as I clean out my desk with care
For the occupant coming to sit in my chair.
Ring out the bells, my work days are ended,
my week day and weekends are happily blended.
What time is it? Do I really know?
I must finish my painting to enter the show.
My novel is started, my typewriter's banging.
I hope the neighbors don't wake up complaining.

At last, at last I'm doing the things
that make me happy-hey, my life is a fling.
Contented? You bet, my accomplishment sore.
I pray for a long life, it's sure not a bore.
My pay checks helped to pay taxes and bills
But my leisure days hold only cultural thrills.
Your day will come, hang in there my friend.
The light in the tunnel will come to its end...
The struggle, the problems, it's all worth the fight,
To stay home, savor life, wow! Everything's right.

Doris Summer

The Holocaust Museum

We started at the top, moving downwards
level by level, into the depths,
shuffling through the darkness...
and the silence.
Lighted panels telling the story -
photos, long-gone voices,
drawing us inexorably on.
The feeling of doom growing stronger ....
knowing what was to come.

We walked through the boxcar,
surrounded by numbered suitcases.
Battered shoes, hair, skeletal umbrellas,
were all that remained of so many lives.
The inhumanity was beyond belief, beyond tears.
Speechless, I withdrew into myself, diminished.

Reaching at last the healing peace of the Hall or Remembrance
where the flame burns brightly, purifying;
the words of one survivor haunt me:
"I've taught my children to love, not hate.
But for me - I can never forget, never forgive."

Judy Kantor

Christmas Magic

Christmas magic fills the air;
Life is most jolly hearts free from care.
As the yule log blazes bright
Out past my window is a beautiful sight.
Snowflakes glisten like ghosts in the sky
Fall silent and swift on those passing by.
As if enchanted they rush hand in hand
To spin their magic all o'er Christmas land.

In the glow of candlelight
And through the stillness of the night
Children sing so soft and low
The Christmas tunes of so long ago.
With hearts bursting and faces aglow
They steal on so softly through the white snow,
And like an elf-like fairy band
They cast their spell all o'er Christmas land.
Christmas magic! Beautiful sight!
Icicles glistening in the pale moonlight,
Snow peaks steeped so solemn and white
Lend to the spell of this magical night.

Gertrude S. Holtzclaw

Peace Should Come With Love

Peace of the heart is hard to come by,
Life passes you quickly without knowing why.
With the untrue comes lies,
You do not hear your loved one's cries.

Sometimes we think people have changed,
They can not, if they are deranged.
We want to believe it to be true,
Though we haven't a clue.

To trust in only one,
It should be done.
But, if the one is unstable,
Then can we trust? Are we able?

You think you are to blame,
Maybe this is your shame.
Happiness you so deserve,
But, pity and contempt you reserve.

They say it is better to have loved and lost,
Then to never to have loved at all, but not at a cost.
Love should be gentle and true,
Not be to blame or taken out on you.

Julia Grannan

My Sons

When you were born
Life took on a new meaning
When you cried; I cuddled you
When you laughed; I laughed with you
When you started growing; I grew with you
When you learned; I learned with you
When understanding was hard; I tried to understand
You never gave me any heartache
All the years you've been here
That new meaning in life was
Love, giving, acceptance, understanding, patience
Being there unconditional through good and bad
Thank you Sons, I'm so glad you were born

Donna Carter Smith

Jerilyn

She walked so softly across the room
like a beautiful bride without a groom
she came to me and asked with a smile
would you like to dance for a while?

Her name was Jerilyn, and she wanted to be mine
Jerilyn, for me a pretty Valentine

She whispered softly in my ear
the sweet love words I've longed to hear
and for a moment I was born anew
my dreams of her had all come true
she took my hand and led the way
out the door and along the bay
the tide rolled in and I could hear a breeze
the angels whispered in the trees
I turned to look and she was gone
left with only the memory of a song
I begin to wake and come to find
that it was all just in my mind

Jerilyn, just a dream or is she real
Jerilyn, will she know how my heart feels?

Craig Laux

The First Snow

The first snow often comes while I'm sleeping,
Like a gift given in a dream;
Not really mine for the keeping,
Just a passing heavenly scene.

The lackluster of November is over
The morning reveals with a sigh,
As a flowers of gossamer frost -clover
Descend from a heavenly sky.

In chimney pots the smoke curls 'round
And night embers glow in the fire;
The world around me the snow has bound
And on a hill I see a silvery spire.

The first snow often comes in the sacred night
To transfigure the land with God's garment of white.

Florence A. Maloney

Pit Of Despair

I keep falling through a hole that is
like a pit of despair and loneliness,
that keeps bringing me to my knees
thinking of what I should do next.
If I should climb out the hole what
would happen to me. Will I be able to
get rid of the hurt that keeps staying
inside me like a flea on a dog.
If I should get rid of this hurt what will
I do then, will I be able to find
somebody to watch over me and make
sure I don't fall in the pit again, and if
I do hopefully I'll have a rope of
happiness to bring me out of the
despair again.

Jarred Adam Graham

Universe Bright

Stars upon skies of heaven's light shines our way into the universe
Long foretold of the heaven's vastness
Stars of light hail bright a peaceful essence
The universe a pleasant sight
A Lord of hosts to a wood-be traveler, across space
What is-it's nature, of bright might

Jack T. Armstrong

The Blessing Of Life

There are many things I'm thankful for,
Like food, my life, and so much more.
I'm thankful for my life the most,
Because without him I would have been a ghost.
He gave me strength to live each day,
He held my hand each step of the way.
He helped me conquer all my fears,
By preaching his word to my ears.
He made me see the light,
When I thought things could not go right.
But the most important thing he had to give,
Was by blessing me with the will to live.
Who is he that I speak of,
He is without a doubt the good Lord above.

Jessica Haddock

Pain

Pain rains upon you
like hot, molten lava,
searing your heart, body, and soul.

Like some pagan god,
it requires your body
to bow down in homage
you may at first refuse.

The flesh is burned away and the molten lava
crystallizes your heart and soul,
becoming one with you.

You stiffen your knees, whispering:
"I will be strong; pain will not win — not this time.
I will not bow before the hated enemy."

With every breath, every heartbeat,
the molten pain courses through your
blood, your strength ebbing
until once again, as before, this pagan god

Beats you to your knees
Bows your head and you whisper:

"Mercy, you win again."

Joy Simpson

Untitled

Have you ever felt like there was more
Like opportunity was just outside your door
Do you think we are all destined for something great
Like you were best friends with fate

Maybe if we all did what we could
Lived up to our potential to be good
This world would begin to unite
Rise above destructions plight
We would become the authors of our own lives
If we could put down the guns and knives

So please consider this one thing
Before you hurt another human being
When your kids look up and ask you why
And you have to answer for all those who died

Can you tell them you helped stop the hate
You helped all mankind to clean the slate
Or when it's all said and done
Did you play a part in man's destruction

Burke Troy

"Let Me Be Me"

I can't be myself,
listening to the advice of someone else.
If I would act like you want,
talk like you want me to
do what you want me to do.
You would never know what I've done over the years to be myself.
Please just accept me as I am.
I have feelings to, just like you.
I like to do things my way too.

I look out of the window for days and sometimes late at night,
and I wonder who's wrong or who's right.
Maybe we all are just about the same,
then I thank God in Jesus name.

God has watched over me time after time,
when I had nothing, not one dime.
I don't have to worry, I'm not afraid.
Every morning when I get out of bed, I say, this is a new day,
don't wonder, why people act that way.
"I JUST WISH I COULD REALLY BE ME!"

Jewel B. Moore

Ode To A Fly

In Atlanta, July and dreary,
Little but food to make you cheery -
Menu in hand with indecision,
Hunger pains blur my vision.
Then, out of nowhere...thank you...goodbye -
There appears a monstrous, nasty green fly.
Oh, purveyor of filth and disease,
You attempt to make me ill at ease.
I shan't be bothered by your presence;
At least I want it that way in essence.
Sail away you worthless creature.
I abhor your ugly feature.
You'd drive a man to be a doper.
Be gone you pesty interloper.

Joe L. Wright

The Journey

Travelling along slow and fast,
living and aching the journey past.

Sharing the stories of joy and grief,
embracing each step; mourning each leaf.

Stubbing my toes, bruising my brain,
wondering if life is worth this pain.

Searching for strength along the way,
in eyes of those passing by each day.

Finally reaching the journey's end,
grateful you took the trip with me...dear friend.

Chris Jacobsen

But A Moment

I live but a moment away from death.
Like a storm welling up inside me,
I feel the strong wind blowing away my breath.
I stand weak against the roar in my ears.
The flash of light pierces my heart.
I know it won't be long now,
Until my shell of humanness,
Will be covered over by the downpour.
My soul shall be thrashed against the cliff of rocks,
Until I confess to God and ask for mercy,
So that I may see the hues of the rainbow
From Heaven's window of everlasting life.

Elizabeth D. Thornton

The World Is Alright

The world is alright.
Look at the sun shining so bright
and the white clouds drifting across the sky.
It gives you a wonderful feeling, yet I know not why.
Tonight, the moon will be out in full and shine o'er
the earth, like a sparkling jewel.
The stars will add there shimmering light,
to help prove that the world is alright.

A gentle breeze comes in from the sea, to offer
comforting peace for you and for me.
You'll know you are fortunate to live on this earth,
once you realize what its assets are worth.
So, if you complain, from morning till night.
try remembering that the world is alright.

Harry M. Harrison

Life's Renewal

Look to the stars, you will see light
Look to the Moon, that radiates brightness
Look to the Rainbow, much beautiful colors
Turn your eyes toward the Horizon, ...plenteous dreams!

Look at the Trees
Listen to the sweet songs of the Robin and see life
Touch the Morning Dew and visualize calmness
Smell the succulent nectar of the Daises and dare to hope
Picture the Eagle in its flight and let your spirit soar and,
Begin your life anew.

Carol-Fay Faulkner

Thanking Them Both

Birth Mother's heart beat faded in the distance,
lost warmth, lost safety, shoved out into the light.
Frightened and alone, the journey began again.
I walked with the illusions that were the gifts of my people.
Without Grandmothers or Aunties I walked, seeing womanhood ahead.
frightened and alone, selecting mates, making a home,
birthing one, raising many, nurturing by instinct rather than lessons.
No longer able to act as if, no longer willing to live the lie,
I walked away from my birth family one step at a time.
The journey was renewed as the memories began to return.
Crow spoke. Down into the Canyon I went,
Spirit Eyes no longer blind, Spirit Ears no longer deaf,
the memory went deeper than the Canyon floor.
My partner arrived another door opened.
I went through not so frightened and not so alone.
Crow spoke. Children grew, grandchildren came.
My hair went white and curly, my body softened, my heart softened,
Tired one sleeping in a double bed, Not frightened and Not alone
The journey is completing. New warmth. New Safety.
Earth Mother's heart beat approaching in the distance.

Claudia Hazard

Beyond the Closet Door...

When you open up that closet door,
Lots of junk, but beyond that there is a lot more....

When you look at an old scraggly doll, what do you see?
It could have been a gift from old Aunt Lee,
A gift from your parents when you were sick,
Right by your side, they would stick.

An old baseball glove,
A gift from your dad,
He really showed his love.
Around in the yard, you used to throw the ball,
And then for dinner your mother would call.

All of these can be happy memories from your past
It really makes you realize you are growing up fast!

Jan Soetaert

Love?

What's the purpose of love
Love does not make the world go round
Death makes the world go round
Everyone dies and a new weakling is taken in place of them
Everyone is weak
Love is supposedly strong when someone is in love
It's supposed to make some strong
It doesn't make someone strong
Someone strong please tell me what the purpose of love is
No one knows
Nobody is strong enough to know

Jennifer L. Oliver

Clouds And Love

My sunshine shines a little less today,
Love has less meaning somehow I am ashamed to say

What happened, where did the clouds come from?
I feel empty, but my eyes are full. I'll be glad when day is done

I am here, she is there, it is hard to understand,
Maybe it is better to hold a memory than have something grand

Illusion must have been part of my mind's eye,
I felt the day was perfect, no clouds to make me cry

Nothing is simple it is so hard to understand,
These complex relations between a woman and a man

A friend told me this feeling would pass in time,
That sometime the sun would again begin to shine

Patients the friend said is the key,
The cloud may not have been meant for you to see.

It is true that the sun can shine again in the same place,
It also true that clouds often leave with little or no trace.

I can only wait and mend my myself,
For now I'll just put my heart back on the shelf.

This is not a new feeling but I wish it would go away,
I just want a little sunshine to come my way.

James P. Walden

Love And Agony

Empty tears, and tired sobs fill her soul
Love throws her heartbreak to the floor
She reaches out to him and he sends her heart soaring
down a river of agony.

Warmth in her being freezes and turns to ice.
The tears streaming down her face are hot with misery.
She looks with hope and desperation into his unforgiving
eyes, and his cruel stare goes through her, and makes her
shudder from within.

Her love stains his soul and makes life hard.
He won't show his love for her.
His twisted mind loves to see her in pain.

Meanwhile she stands by the window searching for an
answer, and death blows a cold breath of air down her
spine and into the depths of her soul.

The next night she is on the floor, a note by her side
saying simply "I told you I'd do anything".

Janine Laviolette

The Unsung Song Of The Heroes

Called are many but, few go.
Many are called to give of compassion.
I see your need yet, I will not go.
I hear your cry, and yet I say no.
I feel your pain, and it troubles me so.
I see your loss, and it is only my gain.
Yet, if there be one, or more who counts all
but loss, to go and meet the need,
compassion is shared.
When one or more, dries the tears and quiets the cry,
compassion enters in.
When one or more, soothes the pain
compassion heals.
It takes a heart, full of compassion, to give of yourself.
Many have it, few give it.
But for those, who will answer the call
they are the unsung heroes
in our world today.

Ellen Sue Hampton

Chinese Nanny

Amah yanked the child's hand,
marched her two miles in crunching snow
past chained guard dogs trained to kill.
Terror froze Jean's tears, girl of sixteen months,
in the icy silence that gripped her entrusted heart
and cramped her legs.
Amah's faded blue quilt-coat warmed
her lidless Asian face
and black hair strained back in a bun.
Her unbound feet conveyed "unwed."
Each year absent parents studied
Chinese tongue and character brush,
leaving Jean alone with Amah.
Child marched on
soon too tired to rage.
Near home the calligraphy of dry
wisteria blackened pure snow.

Betty B. Wiseman

"Parades"

The leaves were on parade today,
marching all in disarray,
In hues of yellows, reds, golds and grays.

When the wind bands began to play
the leaves went on their merry way.

From place to place they bantered about,
as they went astray on their merry way.

In numbers to large to count or sort,
they continued their march as
the days grew short.

Till all had joined there merry jaunt,
except the "Pines" who watched so stunt.

When they all had settled and laid about,
then the "Pines" were marched away,
for a Christmas night.

A. M. Cardona

As Friends Go

May the wind fill your sails and blow strong beneath your wings.
May the sun brighten your days and light-up your lives.
May the moon shine on your nights and glow in your hearts.
May waves caress your shores and ease your mind.
May there always be a song on your lips and words in each breath.
May the distance you travel only be as far as friends go.

Danny Sullivan

A Wedding Prayer

I pray that God will shower you with blessings untold.
May He, through your love for each other,
His truth unfold.
May you take God's Spirit, His word as your guide.
May you each day together in His peace abide.
May you enter the mystery of love complete.
May that love provide the fullness of both challenge and retreat.
May you pray daily for each other's faults and weakness
claiming for each other, through the precious blood of Jesus,
wholeness.
May you enhance and support each other's strengths
without envy or jealously.
May you daily give to each other expressions of love
and encouragement tirelessly.
I pray that you will fully share each other's
triumphs and failures, joys and sorrows, laughter and tears,
as you grow in love together throughout the years.

Dorothy Hemphill Edwards

An Empty Page

An empty page, soon to be full of words.
Maybe a sobering thought or a reflection on the past,
or maybe just rambling not making any sense
The choice is mine, because here I call the shots.
What is to be, and what is not.
Maybe a fantasy, or maybe something true.
Words to brighten up your day,
or scare the hell out of you.
Words to make you stop and think,
words to make you toast a drink.
The power is immeasurable and possibilities endless.
So think it through, be careful of how you choose,
even the kindest of words can hurt you.

Charlie Bardo

Maybe?

Let me know the pain of a birth mother;
  maybe I'll be a MAN.
Let me remember that all tears are the same;
  maybe I'll be a MAN.
Let me feel the anguish of the suppressed;
  maybe I'll be a MAN.
Let me know the laughter of children;
  maybe I'll be a MAN.
Let me know the plight of the homeless;
  maybe I'll be a MAN.
Let me know the despair of the black man;
  maybe I'll be a MAN.
Let me honor the indigent;
  maybe I'll be a MAN.
Let my heart ache for a love that's gone;
  maybe I'll be a MAN.

Charles R. Crosthwaite

My Mansion Of Blessings

If I had just a match stem for every time the
Lord has blessed me I could build me a ten story
high mansion. There would be enough match stems
to furnish every single room from wall to wall.

And If I had just a half a match stem for every
time I said, "Thank You", There would be just
enough match stems to make the doorsteps to my
mansion of blessings!

Dorothy J. Harrion

"The Satyr's Song"

Gentle woodland enchantment, coupled with mystical
melodies of the early dawn. I am indeed the stuff of
dreams, yet my essence leaves no doubt of a very
real existence. Allow oneself a mid-summer's day stroll
across the sunlit glen and the little living things there
shall give a subtle testimony to my being, the Aroma
of the dew kissed meadows shall speak of me. What
will they say? The honey suckle and lavender say that
I am mischievous and playful, while the lemon grass,
pine and Oak moss tells a tale of my magical
spirit which prances and frolics throughout the forest
during the wee morning hours and during the dusk
of twilight. The Jasmine, Rose and Sandalwood
whisper upon the breeze of my insatiable lust
for the lovely nymphs, for they too as well as
I share this enchanted realm. The harmonic
symphony of the swallows, sparrows and
swifts give me praise by singing my song
greeting the emergence of solar light, whilst the nocturnal
ballads of the frogs and crickets serenade the lunar beam.

Darrell A. King Sr.

Memories Of You

Memories of you will last forever. Never will I let your memory fade away. You let your light shine for me only. You told me you loved me everyday. The warmth in my heart is still there, when I think about you. You always had such kind words to say. I treasure those precious moments we had together. Precious memories of yesterday.

I wish I could turn back the time. Back to the days when your heart was mine. Those days can be no more. But you I still adore. The feeling of love was always there. It never left us when we were apart. Each meeting was a new beginning. We loved each other that much.

Fate and time took me away from you. Never to see you again. The memories go on of the one that I have loved for so long. In my heart you will always be. Your memories is all I have left, of a love so dear to me.

Jeanette Stamper Huff

Piano

In a corner, where the red brick wall
met the grime smeared window, a view to the pausing groups
looking in with curiosity before continuing on with
shopping bags and hand bags and a scuffed guitar case,
I shut my eyes to the muted shuffle of the people
turning book pages and leaning in close to one another,
whispering over their coffees and teas.
In the blanket warmth that smelled of vanilla,
I surrounded myself with slightly untuned purity
coming from keys caressed by the calloused fingers.

Cheryl Meyer

Respond With A Smile

When you smile at me I go places I've never been before
my eyes tire of the pain around me, your smile whispers
to me enter close the door.
When I think I can't go another step you lie beside me
you smile my heart leaps a mile
I only ask you smile and say you will stay awhile
Like a child I see the sites of the world through your smile
In your smile is my world if you call I'll answer with a smile.

Earmie Jean Fletcher

Inside A Kaleidoscope

A playful child sneaks
Mischievously in a snow filled forest,
And a glittery baby accidentally
Reflects light,
Majestic stars are gliding gracefully,
And a beautiful garden full of colorful
Shapes is fading slowly as patterned
Lightning takes its place,
There are wild ballerinas playing with
Light carelessly,
Blazing fire engulfs them quickly as
Sparkly glitter fearfully falls and takes
The fire's place,
In this magical world breathtaking
Fireworks explode dazzlingly......

Brittany Rohrer

You Say "She's Just A Friend"

Moments between you and her are joyous.
Moments between you and me are depressing.
You say "she's just a friend."
Gifts given to you from her are treasured.
Gifts given from me are lost.
You say "she's just a friend."
Words shared between her and me are taken out of context.
You then are angry with me.
You say "she's just a friend."
If I am out of the picture, will you still say...
"She's just a friend."

Armandina Flores Lopez

Through The Air

Daddy flies you through the air
Mommy loves to sit and stare,
at the picture you two make

Mommy stops the crying when you're scared.
Daddy stops the crying when you're mad.

We both hold and we both love you
So you'll know, we both care

When you are older, little boy, and
look back through your past
We hope you see how much we care.

But for now, while you are "ours",
We'll love you, and teach you, and fly
you through the air.

Jennifer A. Smolcnop

From Light To Gray To Dark

Been mixin' black and white paints on the canvas of my life
Monday comes how I despise this day it's on the gray side so
I mix my mood paints and mix black and white to be balanced
at the true feeling. I either face the day with a smile or frown
uh. oh! I heard your granny died, we'll put this meters level at
a total morbid darkness. You're sitting there watchin' reruns of I
Love Lucy; you're there but you wanna be somewhere else.
HOW DO YOU FEEL! open the curtains of your barred
windows. That makes things lighter and further away from the
dark side. And even if you went outside enough the scale of
light - gray - darkness would be pushed more towards the light.
We all have our moods sometimes it's painted on our faces.
What do you do about moods? Know what makes you happy?
BE FLEXIBLE and be prepared for change

Dave Bernitsky

Love Without Logic

Love and hate are further apart than we think; A thin line? No, it's more than a blink;
Beautiful regardless of the door of the eye, when through love you despise the sound of goodbye;
With hate there's the desire to be without, and with it comes evil visions, no doubt;
Love is beautiful, spontaneous and off rhythm, it may not rhyme but love carries on;
With hate the poet sacrifices the so called deep feeling, the pen scribbles "Be mine, forever";
Does the poet know or is this love's blinding? Well is love blinding or transparent? I think not.
Love is not simply a sight, or scent, or texture, love is an emotion but, not a one way street;
Two hearts combine to lead the way along this street; two hearts different but, in agreement;
These hearts have found love and share this road together;
My heart will not allow my mind to impede our way, there is no logic in love;
As we reach another fork in the road, follow your heart.

Justin Long

'God's Gift'

When you see a rose dripping with the
morning dew —
it's God's gift to me and you.
When you see a rainbow across the western sky -
make a wish when it you first spy.
When the leaves and the blossoms come
out in the spring —
think of the beauty and pleasure they
will bring.
In the Fall when you kick up the leaves
while walking down a country lane —
a promise it will soon be winter with the
fields white with snow again.
It's a wonderful world we live in,
a beautiful place to be —
God's great creation for people
like you and me.

Audrey B. Dodge

Last Green Tree

Mother, do you think they'll cut it down?
Mother, do you think they'll strike a match?
Mother, it's the last green tree.
Will all they'll want to do is take another pee,
as they charge another sight seeing fee?
Will the price get higher, will the wind get drier?
Mother, why is everyone turning away, why don't we holds hands and pray?
Mother, why do just dully stare as if we don't even care?
I see a brown leaf up there, a dead twig over here.
Is it going, is it dying?
I close my eyes, but I can here it screaming, I here it crying.

Oh Momma! What's that awful sound?
Is it a big black limousine?
Are they bringing up buckets of kerosene?
"Boy, it's time to cut it down.
Now we can forget, now we can move on.
Tomorrow will be a new, better dawn."

Oh Momma! What's that awful sound?
"Boy, it's crashing onto the ground."

Greg Chapman

"Perfect Parents"

Mothers are kind, Mothers are gentle
Mothers are loving, Mothers are truly a gift

Mothers are caring, Mothers are beauty
Mothers are fun, Mothers are the only ones

Mothers are shy, Mothers are slim
Mothers are love, Mothers are a gift from above

Fathers are strong, Fathers are good
Fathers are willing, Fathers are really a gift

Fathers are great, Fathers are mighty
Fathers are smart, Fathers are the only ones

Fathers are fun, Fathers are number one
Fathers are cool, Fathers are better than anyone

Jeff Pommerenck

Rain

The sky turns dark in the middle of the day,
Mothers call their children in from play.
As the building breeze;
Rustles the leaves,
A gentle rain starts falling...
Gradually, the downpour grows,
Adding to the water flows.
The droplets sang a happy song,
But now the storm is getting strong.
The thunders clash!
The lightenings flash!
The sky in all its glory calling...
Angrily, the clouds roll past,
Only a while, does, the tempest last.
The ground ingest the passing flood,
Nature's awash with new life's blood.
As the sun comes shining through,
The cycle is to start anew.
When, in time, they meet again,
The earth does call the rain a friend...

Anthony Jovinelli

End The Violence

Saturday night ... a dark quiet street;
movement in the shadows, two groups meet.

Shots rang out ... gang members ran;
then came a shout ... he's been hit!! Oh man!

Flashing lights ... the medical teams here,
nobody's talking — you can feel the fear.

Who is the young man face down in the street?
Don't let his life end in defeat.

Needle marks on his arms, a bullet wound in his head;
there is nothing to do ... the young man's dead.

Now comes the time to make the call;
Hello Sir ... it's about your son Paul.

We will meet you at the emergency room;
yes; you need to come very soon.

Flowers, music, the shedding of tears;
All for a young man's eighteen years.

Wake up America ... the time is now;
To end the violence ... someway, some how.

Jonni Eubanks

In Search Of The "I Don't Know"

The family sat around, each one doing his own thing.
My children were in front of the TV engaged with a Nintendo game.
My husband sat behind a paper which had been used for cutting practice
As I stood in my domain surveying a mess left by a hurricane.
Asking my beloved family who spilt Koolaid on the freshly cleaned rug.
"I don't know" was the guilty response which they uttered.
Then I inquired who left a half eaten sandwich on the kitchen table.
"I don't know" was spoken all in unison.
Wondering what everyone wanted for dinner I sighingly asked.
The reply hastily given "I don't know," this I should have guessed.
Throwing arms upward, crying to anyone who would listen.
"I don't know!" I screamed, "I must search! I must find this
"I don't know thing!"
Just think if I capture this and bottle it up to sell,
I could become a millionaire!
So frantically I ran from one room to another, pulling out drawers, opening up cubbards.
Spilling the contains onto the floor, I found things I had lost never hoping to find.
As I searched, I did not find this mysterious thing which plagued my mind.
Exhausted I fell upon a chair not once did I glimpse it, nor did I care!
So here I sit looking at family dear, insanity I know is so near.
Why ask these predictable questions, which the answers will never differ.
I pondered long this delirium, the answer given, "I DON'T KNOW!"

Deborah Norman

Prince Valiant

Where are you now Prince Valiant?
My comic-strip hero who dominated
my childhood dreams.
And rescued me from the humdrum of life.
Now I dream of my sons laying on
slabs in mortuaries.
And a black, bullet-shaped car with
ominous tinted windows
Chases me down endless streets.
I clutch the bedside as I fall through infinity.
In search of I know not what.
The stridency of the alarm clock
pulls me from the abyss.
And I waken, slippery with sweat
As if I have eluded death.
Where are you now, Prince Valiant?
Now that I need you.

Barbara Gribbin

Not A Dream

I knew it was love from the moment I saw her
my confidence and self-esteem grew taller
I knew then that love was in store
and when my phone rings I'll be out the door
sitting down town which is where I meet you
chocolate and flowers is how I'll greet you
I lay awake at night with you on my mind
the picture's perfect but I still seem blind
I wish I could hold you close to my heart
and have a guarantee that we would never part
the thought of love comes straight from the heart
but the thought of losing you is tearing mine apart.

Jeremy Weinberg

"Daydreaming You Back To Me"

When I close my eyes and think of you
my darkness fades away, and everything's a glow
cause I know....
the light that shines from my dreams will show
you the way back to me.

Sometimes my heart strings sing sad songs of loneliness
when you're not there, but I hope soon
these bitter sweet tunes....
will hit your ears and bring you back to me.

I see you running to me...
and dream your arms around my fantasy.
This is what I do to pass away time,
wish your lips on mine...

June Anigbogu

As I Stand

As I stand in the shadows of blue light;
My face flushes with anticipation;
I feel the coolness of the stage under my bare feet;
I stretch, in hope that it will calm these butterflies in my stomach;
In the back of my mind I hear the voices of my friends and colleagues;
Murmurs of the past colliding with coming ideas;
In my minds eye, I see figures talking in low whispers;
I clutch the bead I wear around my neck;
It is my only lifeline;
Someone comes up behind me and whispers, " 30 seconds.";
The blue light dims and then fades away into darkness;
I close my eyes and hold my breath;
I hear the curtain open, and open my eyes to reveal only darkness;
The orange lights go on and the music starts;
Hold on for the ride.

Gretchen Arentzen

Mom

You taught me how to speak and heard
my first words. You taught me how to walk
and reached for me as I walked towards.
You taught me how to see and opened up my eyes.

You were there and never told me lies.
A mother from heaven and hard working all along.
and at night you still sang me a song.

I began in school and prouder you became.
you never stopped loving me. I never stopped
feeling the same. Junior High started, you loved
me all the more.

You cured my first broken heart when my heart
was sore. High school began and I was kind a of
scared. But I would get through anything as long
as you still cared.

Heather Anderson

Untitled

When I run, when I am alone,
My mouth gets dry, and I need you,
I put a stone in my mouth, I call you, hoping,
And my mouth waters, you tell me you still love me,
But the thirst does not, but you're still so
Go away, far away,
It's all an illusion. It's all an illusion.

Jeffery M. Strobl

Aces On The Bottom

My angry black brother, must plead his case,
My frightened white father, and the wrongs he
can't face. Shameless bigotry, we all know
It's true, there's no-one without guilt, not me,
Not you, not black, not white, not brown, yellow
Or red, we all share the blame for the
lies that we've said. Day after day, year
after year, we kindle the fires that we've
started through fear. What have we to
show, but sorrow and pain? How can we claim
progress, when nothing has changed? Like dogs
on a bone! We fight for the gnaw, and when
we can't steal, we take by the law.
So it is, in the brotherhood of man,
Love is the hope!
Yet!
Fear rules the land!

Daniel A. Davis Sr.

Untitled

Psalm 19 - Let the words of my mouth and the meditation of my heart be acceptable in thy sight!

O Lord, my strength and my redeemer, be my guide,
In everything I say or do, stay at my side.

Let my heart be filled with meditations of love,
And the words that I speak, be blessed from above.

My heart and my tongue are so prone to evil,
And only your grace can keep me civil.

You law is perfect, converting the soul,
More to be desired than silver or gold.

It keeps us from the great transgressions,
And makes us humble in our confessions.

Thy judgments are true and righteous, O Lord,
And in keeping them, there is great reward!

Eva H. Atkins

First Love

I saw my love of yesteryear.
My heart sighed and shed a tear.
When he was long out of sight,
Past struggled with present and momentarily won the fight.
I remembered him tall and handsome then.
I toyed with the thought of what might have been.
I pictured the two of us as one,
Having a daughter and maybe a son.
True to each other, bonded by love,
Happiness a gift from above.
Then present began to struggle free,
And with loving kindness whispered to me,
It was never meant to be,
It Was Never Meant To Be!

Dolores Grigsby

Butterflies

From a caterpillar fat, dull and green...
Nature creates the most beautiful miracle ever seen...
From a delicate jewel case of blue...
Emerges nature's palette in every hue...
Above the meadows' quilted patch works of colors...
Swirling clouds of iridescent jewels fluttered...
Lifting, falling, ebbing and flowing from flower to flower...
On shimmering wings of Emeralds, Rubies and Sapphires...
I could sit and watch them by the hour.

Betty-Jo Clark

To My Dad

Of all the ones I hold so dear,
My kin and friends from far and near;
I've always had a special spot
Held in my heart for you, My Pop.

You've healed my wounds, both big and small
And helped me up each time I'd fall.
Throughout the years a path you've paved
With all the love and trust you gave.

And even though at times, I know
I've given you much pain and woe;
You've been right there, next to my side,
To wipe my tears each time I cried.

And so on this, your special day,
The love I feel no words can say.
But with the love that's in my heart,
We're never really far apart.

Jan Davis

Yes, That Isabella

As I walked thru downtown Philadelphia,
My love and I were oh so happy
Over seeing a beautiful vision
Of St. Isabel of España.

As I strolled alongside of the Schykil,
My love and I were oh so happy
So happy with the loveliness
Of St. Isabel of España.

She watches over the oceans,
She watches over the people
She watches over the chapels
St. Isabel of España.

We honor the flag of España,
Along with the Red, White, and Blue
But the stars and the stripes are forever
St. Isabel of España.

St. Isabel of Castilla, España
St. Isabel of España, Olé!
St. Isabel of Castilla, España
St. Isabel of España, Olé!

John Paul Paine

Seasons Of A Woman's Life

As my life ebbs away,
my mind views the moments that lead to today.
In my days there has been joy and pain,
and in each season, sunshine and rain.
The bright sunshine of my spring,
shines on ribbons and curls,
and all the heartaches and joys of little girls.
The summer seems to just fly by.
Now a mother and wife am I.
Rushing, rushing to and fro,
I didn't know how quickly this time would go.
Then the fall with colors all aglow,
a quieter time now I know.
Children all gone and grown,
again, it's he and I alone.
Then the winter, cold and stark,
Now there's but one, that is alone in the dark.
In my days there has been joy and pain,
and in each season, sunshine and rain.

Jessica Clifford Farmer

Frank And Jesse

Yeah, we robbed a bank, me an' my brother, Frank,
My name is Jesse, you see,
We knew we had sinned, so we run like the wind,
And we got away, scott free.

So we drug out a jug and we each had a "slug",
Then we had a "belt" or two,
We loosened our belts to soak up our pelts,
We had a belt or two for you.

When the posse showed up, we're drunker'n a pup,
Again we lit out a-runnin',
But our britches slipped down and we tripped to the ground
That posse didn't need to come gunnin'.

There's a moral somewhere in this li'l affair,
But that sheriff was quite a sport,
As he slipped on the "cuff" he said, "Boys, it's tough,
You were just two belts short."

George H. Kidder

Untitled

I close my eyes and sit in my chair
my old, broken, wooden chair
the wood is dead and
the legs have fallen
though, it still supports me
in this time of need
my chair has lived so many years
it has felt from my face, all those tears
it stays in that same place
and sees me with blinded eyes
it is there for me to sit on
whenever a part of me dies
what would I do if it were to break?
where would I sit
when my life I decide to take?

Angie Bode

The Transforming Mind

My opinions have changed.
My outlook is different.
I am not afraid, the beings have entered my mind.
Senseless deaths, irrevocable crimes.
It was once abstract, but has become personal.
Death is peace-the essence of the human experience.
Challenge me, I will not refrain.
Give me a reason when I find none.
Strangeness is exhilarating and complex,
Although, sometimes lonely.
Fractions upon fractions-never the whole.
I guess it comes later;
When we are not prepared the empty, black hole
becomes visible and words have no meaning.
This is what it is all about.
This is life.
Illogical.

Diane Newcombe

Too Late

I was mad at my Father.. thought I'd even the score.
Now, can't remember why I was sore.
When it came to my life I just closed the door.

Time passed by, weeks in to years. Now I sit confused
Drowning in tears.

I forgave my Father but can't remember what for.
Thought I'd go see him. But, was too late; they closed
The coffin door.

Joyce M. Kennedy

Spring

In morning drizzle I walk past your window.
My sneakers, the color of the sky, avoid earthworms draped
along the sidewalk.
I glance at the window. Your hand curls around the shade.
On the ground, a worm writhes beneath my tread.
"They have no eyes," you say.
I turn, but your fist is still fighting the shade,
and the worm curling and uncurling around the flat tread mark.
"They have no eyes. You can cut them in half."
You pull the worm in two, the separate ends
bending, squirming away.
The shade flutters upward, your eyes in shadow.
"But they still feel," I say quietly. "Can't they still feel?"
Our bodies fog the glass.
The rain comes down hard now. I pick up a sneaker,
look at the bottom.
You sit up. "They're stupid. They drown themselves in rain."
"Yes, they feel though, don't they?"
But you have fallen asleep.
I light a fire, the smoke the color of the sky.

Elizabeth Stone Maland

Place So Longed

Shades of black, block out the light
Naked hanging head of hair
Liquid reflection on my blackened cubby
Secrets are held, tick tock.
Strings of yellow and blue,
Fastened upon a shattered racket.
Memories: Past, Present, Future
Tacked in place.
Doc's of black, Stars of green
Lay on the place for walking.
Waves of water rush about,
Held in place by wooden bracket.
This place of noise, this sanctuary of peace.
A crackle, a hiss escape the hideous monster.
Tossed about, array of colors-
Reeking destruction
Passed down through time,
The almost like casket-
Covered with the panty blanket.
A place of comfort and fear, a place so longed.

Jaime Fenner

Call A Man By Name

We the people of the constitution
Need so much to find the solution
To that over whelming power that we yield to satisfy OUR
OUR is that selfish power
That sticks out his chest, wears a stiff collar
Grooms himself to yell, scream and holler
All he ask is to have his way
And get what he want's to make his day.

Support this kind of man we must
For this is the man we're made to trust!!
From the White House down to the nitty gritty
A brain washed world we're in, WHAT A PITY!!
We love, We worship, We praise the flesh
Come on GOD's people, Lets praise the best
God said he's coming back one day
That time is near so You'd better kneel and pray
Your name is: Your character your heart, your soul
However you like it, this is your mold

Let's Out Vote Evil Now!!
Read your Bible, It will tell you how

Gloria Toles

Always

Never to want anything else
Never to stand alone, for myself
Never to touch the sun's light
Never to feel the rain at night
Never will I know your touch of love

Never again to smell the air
Never again my life would I share
Never again will I see your face
Never again with my hand could I trace
Never will I know your touch of love

Never shall I see the sky
Never shall I understand why
Never shall I let your memory leave
Never shall I wear my heart on my sleeve
Never will I know your touch of love

Never can I call your name
Never can the picture fit the frame
Never can our love progress
Never can we, together, exist
Never will I know your touch of love

Cris Reyes

Memo

This rose is for the little fingers I will
never touch with my hands.
This rose is for the tiny feet that will
never touch the sand.
This rose is for my baby fears
I will not be there to wipe away his tears.
This rose is for the Christmas's,
and every holiday you will not see,
this all because of your father and me.
This rose is for the pain in my heavy heart,
the pain I live with until death may it part.
For this rose will never grow, bud and bloom.
No one but God will see this beautiful sight.
No one will get to watch you grow and take flight.
This rose my child is for you.

Jill R. Myers

My Legacy

My Mom and Dad, they gave me things,
Nice clothes, cars and even rings.
They sent me to school,
And for this I'm grateful.
Now I don't have to break my back,
Like my dad did, when he laid track.
True, they gave me the things they never had.
I got the things they wanted, how sad!
The things they didn't give to me,
Were hard work and responsibility.
I needed to be left on the brink to struggle, to think.
I needed some pains, some aches, to make some mistakes.
Now I'm on my own and I find it's kind of hard.
For the decisions that I now make, into reality I'm jarred.
I hope I don't continue the fad
Of giving my kids the things I never had.
I want to give them other things.
Like responsibilities...
And values...
Not cars or rings.

John G. Cooper

The Struggle To Survive (Or The Wolf)

The old grey wolf paused to rest and stared across the plain
night approached, the wind was cold, as he winced against the pain

With red-flecked eyes, the yellow teeth, the grey around his nose
the bloody paws, the rumpled fur and miles yet to go

Vision blurred, his wounds were deep, the arrow in his heart
he shook his head, cleared his eyes and knew he had to start

The hounds were near, he heard their howl as he started up the hill
closing fast, with a frenzied rush, ready for the kill

They'd gotten close in recent days, as he struggled to survive
at times he'd almost given up, but he was still alive

Now the cave was near, not far away, as he stumbled through the night
and slipped into that safe warm place, through the fading light

Home at last, he settled down, with his back against the wall
raised his head, closed his eyes and moaned his lonely call

Across the mountains the call was heard, throughout the silent bays
his spirit strong, the wolf survives, to hunt another day!

Dale W. Glenn

A Tribute To Our Dad

What a blessing to have had our father, rejoice this man who fathered nine!
With so few needs and so much courage, his wisdom remains beyond his time.
Though we poked fun at his frugal manner, deep down we saw his real intent.
Mom's future needs was his compassion. Have money there instead of spent.
The sadness in our hearts is selfish, for a better place he went.
He died much like the way we lived, selfless and humble right to the end.
He left us all with his good name, over seventy years that says a lot.
A man of many strengths and morals, he is gone, but not forgot.
We must feel happy in what he left us, memories unique in many ways.
Just imagine what he'd be thinking, if he knew we were sad on holidays.
He still lives on in each of us...in our gardens, our kitchens, and in our arts.
He'd not want us crying at his grave... for he's not there, he's in our hearts.

Helen Corey

Thinketh

I am where I am and I feel what I feel
No circumstance can I not at least respectively command
In my house or on the field
I think what I think whether I am strong or on the brink
Outer conditions are just a condition
Listen to me! This is my humble rendition
Pleasant and unpleasant
Precious and vicious
Black and white, which is right?
In the light of truth and in the shadow of deceit
In the thrill of victory and in the agony of defeat
Whims, fancies and ambitions in the name of traditions
Dwelling in and acting out in peace and in bout, I beg of you
Of all the beautiful truths pertaining to the soul
The most cherished by you can today begin to be the righteous goal
I think what I think and I say what I say
These words you have just read may be the link
Whether strong or on the brink, I hope I have made you think
Seeking friendship sounds a little like sinking ship
But I'll tell you my brother, one is better than the other

Bill Perez

"Twenty Three"

No dreams
No hope
Not one ambition
Everything in life
Is such a Mission
No way to reach that moment of fame
Without dropping your guns and taking some blame
What has fate dealt to me?
A life with no hope, no ambitions, no dreams
Oh please, Oh please, Shed some light my way
And show me the light of a brighter day.

James E. Bradley

I Will Never Leave Thee

I will never leave Thee,
No! I left Him,
I choice to go on the side of sin,
I traveled far from the Saviors side,
But I heard a voice, with me abide:

Where ever I went on whatever I did
awake or asleep at work or at play
a little voice would with me stay,
begging and pleading from me don't stray.
I've heard the voice so long within
I can not stand the pain it brings,
I've ask Him to forgive my sins,
and let me be His child again.

Grace M. Straight

Friendship-Friendship

Friendship, Friendship, a thing of the past
No longer needed or meant to last
Friends, stepping stones, milestones, millstones
About this, we will make no bones
Choose one carefully, then grind to dust
Our mark in the world it is a must
Man is losing a most precious thing
When he thinks he has so much to gain
As he climbs his ladder to success
True friendship with others a total mess
We shall allow the good to be crucified
The whims of the wicked must be satisfied
Alas, into the devil's trap we are falling
Survival of the fittest is our calling
Judas, Hitler, Ruwanda, we are one
Forgiveness, we cry, too late, it is done.

Jean Ballard

The One Thing Worth While

Never lose an old friend,
No matter what the cause
We wouldn't ever do it.
If we didn't look for flaws,

The one thing worth while having
Is the friend who stands the test,
To have a friend such as this.
Knows friendship at its best.

How little is costs, if we gave it a thought
To make some heart happy each day
Just one kind word, or a tender smile
As we go on our daily way.

Florence Lunger

A Small Tribute

There is nothing left to commit to ink.
No more of my life do I wish to record.
I grow weary of this day to day.
I pray the Lord to just take me away.

But perchance a new hope beckons;
A dream yet left undreamed,
A speck of truth for me to tell.
Are these reasons to continue to dwell?

Yet when I speak, no one seems to listen.
My desires lie well beyond my time and tide.
My friends have ills of their own.
My troubles they have already known.

Could I be allowed to open just one door;
Maybe this and nothing more.

Cecil D. Ten Cate

Don't Tell Anyone What I Said

Don't tell anyone what I said
No one will believe I was in your bed
Don't say what you might, you could hurt my feelings
Ruin our love, insult all our dealings
Now little baby, Mommy is your friend
It would be only your fault if that came to an end
I see it in your eyes, you need Mommy's touch
So what if my fingers only reek with lust
Besides, I've got rights to touch you there
Mommy's seen you naked several times, so who cares?
It's alright, it's alright! Don't believe the T.V.
It exploits everything in anyone's family
Come on, young lady! Would Mommy hurt you?
She only wants to lay you down nice and smooth
Remember, nothing's better than "hands on" training
You'll know it all so no boys will be complaining
I'm doing you the favor, now get on the damn bed!
And remember, don't tell anyone what I said

Dianna Lyngdal

My Heaven

I like to think of life as a test.
No one's the worst
No one's the best.
Everyone is equal.
Everyone's the same.
Everyone feels gladness.
Everyone feels shame.
And in the end, it's all just been a dream.
I'll wake up to the sunshine beam.
There are no clouds or rainy days.
Just happy times and loving ways.
When life is hard, I think of this:
The swaying trees and days of bliss.
This dream is what keeps me going in life,
Through every hardship and every strife.

Erin Schlabach

Eternal Artificial Flower

I see you plastic flower, protruding from your vase,
No snow of winter, sun of summer, rests upon your face.
No bees in search of nectar, upon your petals sit,
No fragrance other flowers have, it ever you omit.
No root to steady you, in fertile ground and loam,
Instead your wired stem, is stuck in styrofoam.
You know no illness, blight or aphids stings,
You will never wither, outlasting living things.
Yet your color is the same, your leaves stay ever green,
You have the secret, the wish of all the aged's dream.
You have beaten father time, by the year, day and hour,
You will outlive us all, you eternal, artificial, plastic flower.

Alfred Gorski

Christmas By The Marina

Christmas by the marina; not a trace of snow in sight.
No visions of sugarplums nor of reindeer
cavorting among the sleeping beauties of the lakes-
just a lonely sailboat wearing its winter tarpaulin coat
brightly festooned with a garland of plastic holly
and a red velvet star to celebrate this glorious day.

An ethereal light determinedly struggles to part
the thick gray curtains of clouds;
with a broad smile, it successfully paints the restless waters below
with its heavenly light.

The waves whisper words of consolation and hope
to a solitary sojourner strolling along the shore-
dispelling the loneliness of spirit with its ageless, gentle wisdom.
Shards of ice and tinkling sounds,
like the shattering of crystal mirrors of fairy tale lore,
follow the wake of a speeding motorboat.

Christmas peace descends upon the ship-filled domain.
A coalescence of spiritual oneness with the waters and a Higher Order
bring solace and serenity to a land bound sailor
who is happily celebrating Christmas by the marina.

Carmen Norkiewicz

Glazed With Rain

The sun does not shine for me,
Nor do the clouds snow for me.
I believe something is wrong.
My heart does not ache,
And my smile does not laugh.
Something is wrong.
I believe I was glazed with rain.

But why on me
Must this horrid rain fall?
And why must it leave me numb?
Though I am hurt, why can't I cry?
Though I am strong, why can't I stand?

For now I will take in
One tender breath
And pray to God he will make the sun brave,
And shine if only once.
But until that day,
I will be forever glazed with rain.

Amy Pizirusso

Untitled

I never knew an angel's eyes could shine so bright
Nor had I ever seen an angel until my son was born to me that night

I counted ten tiny fingers and ten very little toes
Then I sighed with a relief only a mother knows

I held up his small body so that I might hear the beating of his heart
And then and there I felt this bond and I knew we'd never part

The love of a mother is like no other and now I know it's true
And for my son, He'll always come first and for him there's nothing I won't do

And for the man who made my dream become reality and helped it come true
There will never be another who is loved as much as you.

My whole world has changed and better now it will always be
Because of this brown haired angel that was sent especially for me

Cecilia Brum

Through The Door

In mask like faces we all march on covered by unseen lines,
nor marred by make-up.

The tomb of man awaits quietly as our day quickly escapes to disappear.

This march on call soon trumpets into the ears that were not
ready for the sounds, his ears are not ready for sounds, his
ears are not yet open they said. He was born with only one lobe.

My vision shoots past these creatures as they move along slowly
in a somewhat lazy, but orderly procedure.

"Slowly", my mind speaks, "Move onto quieter things", but
remember "glorified is the pace of one who moves and is filled
with the spirit of assurance".

Turning around I see a place Christ has prepared for me, "yes",
I have a place in Heaven, for he told me so.

Cecilia Collins

"Can We All Get Along"

People judge others all day long,
not knowing what's inside, makes them all wrong.
Race nor color doesn't make us so wrong, listen to what's being said,
Can we all get along. Everyone's the same deep down inside,
full of happiness, love and compromise. If we focus on caring
all year long, through helping and sharing would that be so
wrong. People say, we're all God's child, let's really show him
by sending a smile. No one should be judge by the color of their
skin, what matters the most is what they posses within. All that
has been written, is not hard to understand, if we all come
together and lend a helping hand. So listen up people don't wait
too long, before it's too late, can
WE ALL GET ALONG.

Alphonso L. Weaver III

Elvis Graceland

The king is gone, the people cried
Not one wanted to believe Elvis had died
Friends came from near and from after
To the home of the beloved star
By the beautiful gates of Graceland
They came to take their stand
To cry, to mourn, to weep, to pray
Many held words they could not say
They gazed upon the hill top
at a mansion to behold
Whose long beloved masters voice
once echoed from very fold
The mansions lit up, but feels empty
Its halls seem dark and cold
His Graceland holds many stories
that never will be told
His body is home at Graceland
to rest by his mother dear
His wishes have been granted
And his work is finished here

Erma J. Hollis

Untitled

We came to live in our house in the wood
not our first but I think our last.

A feeling of peace where large oaks have withstood
the movement to future and the gales of the past.

The stream nearby makes a gentle rush sound
in passing on its way to somewhere new.

Our children have grown gone away and have found
that always here is the home they love too.

So here I shall stay in my house in the wood
with my love, my peace, my home, my future, my past.

Judith Potter

Flood

Not rain, deluge; driving as we drove.
Not passable, reverse, returning to our refuge from storms.
Not to worry; rain ceasing, sun steaming, skies clearing.

Bayou rising, watching water in contrast to tradition;
climbing the drains, filling the streaks, devouring our security
in inches per hour.
How high before crest and rest from worry?

Nighttime is silenced by muffling water.
Sounds of shovels filling sandbags and grunts from those unaccustomed
are the sounds of the dark.
How can the sky be clear? What beauty...looking up!

With dawn comes the waiting. Feet propped in patio chairs, helpless
to alter the course of a river. With sleep-deprived bodies, we wait.
Ants float...rolling balls of life. Spiders skip-dance on the water
while snakes curve-swim beside. We wait and watch life displaced.
Crest at 3:00. We waiver between hope and home loss. We wait,
watching the bayou climb the brick and enter, uninvited into our home.

Now, we wait for the boat.
Clothes for a day in a bag, dog in our arm...
We wait.

Diana Schneider

Overdone

She lies as she had planned, but
not under a mound of grass,
wild flowers, and pink periwinkles.

She lies, instead, under a two-tiered
rectangular stone house,
with a cross at the bow
like the standard of a ship.

She lies, now under a harsh white
layered stone, loud
among her silent companions,
while children wade knee-deep, shell hunting
and water-splashing in the sea nearby,
and the villagers pass and pass again,

Unaware that Froilina's last request
has been replaced by stone,
instead of the soft earth she craved.

Perhaps stone presents a sharper memory,
although the earth's is longer.
Those who grieve make the final choice
for those who leave.

Jean Martinez

Mother Dearest

To have a mother is the best thing in the world
Nothing could replace her not even diamond or pearl
She sacrifices nine months out of the year
Leaving daddy nothing to do but care
She goes to work come home and cook
Just to find Daddy in bed reading a book
She gave you love and affection when you are sad
Just knowing you are going to turn into a fine young lad
She shares your sorrow and joy
She also find time to play with you and your toy
She kisses you when you go to bed
Just knowing you are clean and well fed
She is the gift of eternal life
Came from above to be a mother and a wife

Errol Hendricks

Determination

There was a young cowboy from Texas
Now his goal was to own a Lexus
Didn't rope well at the rodeo
Left him a little short of dough
While watching TV he was able to see
A golf pro on tour, collect a large fee
He took up the sport at a golf resort
And within a year was able to report
With all my practice and repetition
I am now ready for the competition
He won a big check at the U.S. Open
It paid a lot more than when he was roping
Now that young cowboy from Texas
is driving around in his very own Lexus

George Hansen

Grand View

Last born to this choice in pain.
Nurtured to cling.
Encouraged never to fly freely
beyond the familiar zone.
Unwanted seed to this cloak of secrecy.
How little I know of you. All your secrets
locked inside.
But this wall breeds no regrets.
I belong to me.
Tumultuous joy leaps within, nourished from
self seeds of love.
Graceful wings stretched out to soar
securely past the known retreat.
Feel the cool, sweet breeze.
Oh celebrate!
From here, this view so grand.

Chequeta D. Chisom

"Thanks Be To God"

O Father God, How great Thou art!
O Christ, my Savior, take my heart,
My life I give to Thee this day,
My hands, my thoughts, my every way!

Your Vision O Christ I ask to see,
Your mind dear Lord, pray give to me,
Your discernment of things large and small,
Your love and compassion to give to all!

Wisdom and Guidance, Your will to see
With strength and grace to bring it to be;
Ears to receive the words You enfold,
Lips speaking forth...Your message is told!

May lives be changed as they are touched by You,
Each one made whole and Holy too!
Thank you dear Lord that I am a part
Of your all-sufficient and loving heart!

Anne Bailey Morgan

Life

Life is like a flowing river
never waiting on no one
Flowing over rocky waters from
sunset into early dawn.
From day of birth the future's
unknown and life flows by so fast
Then like a river raging out of control
The years disappear into the past.

When years have passed and life is short
we have no certainty of the flow
Life has suddenly turned into an ocean
and we are caught in the undertow.

Dorothy Melhorn

Untitled

As I watched I was told
of a magical bird of black and gold,
and as I closed my eyes to fall asleep
I saw the birds flying for me.

As I sat I was told
Of the prettiest girl of the world
but the most pretty sight for me
was that of the golden bird who sang in harmony

As I listened I was told
of the perfect flower the eyes behold
but the perfect thing my eyes will ever see
is that of the golden birds I saw in that tree

As I sang I was told
of the coldest winter of the cold
but I like the warm and the warmest feeling inside of me
is that of the golden bird that holds the key.

Brandi Clayton (age 9 1/2)

Mother's Day

Just for today, let's not play the game
Of flowers, candy, dinner and fame.
While all that is nice, and I'll not complain
It's the rest of the year when the spirit doth wane.
I wish you'd remember that I'm human too;
I bleed when I' scratched and weep when I'm blue.
Every day thoughtful things please me indeed:
Help when I'm weary, respect for my need,
Warm loving smiles to last the year thru',
Forgiveness for error, 'cause I make them too.
Lets stretch out the love, and not need to borrow
Regret for today or a special tomorrow...Petrie

Dick Petrie

Lest We Forget

Our forefathers had the dream,
Of freedom in our land,
But, wrong will rule while justice sleeps,
Unless we seek God's guiding hand.

Those men died in vain,
For those who desecrate the flag,
Those who forget the heartache and the pain,
Behind that blood-red rag.

Hearts should always beat faster,
When our flag comes into sight,
That sunkissed, windtossed,
Red and Blue and White.

So, let the drums beat and fifers pipe,
That sweet, sweet ole song,
"God Bless America,"
Both to whom we belong.

Thy mercy on this people, Lord!
God be with us yet.
May liberty's torch be held high,
Lest we forget — Lest we forget!

Derrell Brame Jr.

Problems At The John

One shot will hit a squirrel's eye
Or rattlesnake as he slides by.
You always score with gun or bow
Or with a club - a single blow.
   You rock a fly at fifty feet!
   Your aim, my sin, it can't be beat!
   With all this skill (so I've been told)
   Why can't you hit the "water hole"?

Fran Jones Libby

It Is No Curse

To marry a nurse could be a curse
   of medical practice, they say.
If the medical man were to do all he can
   he would marry that nurse today.

To live a happy life, as a doctor's wife,
   you must have his profession at heart.
To sit home and wait; break date after date,
   only a nurse can play the part.

So any medical man if you possibly can,
   make a nurse your blushing bride.
She'll understand; lend a helping hand,
   you'll work successfully side by side.

It is no curse for doctor and nurse,
   to enjoy one another's kisses.
There's one sure way your nurse will stay,
   just make it Dr. and Mrs.

Ivey R. Spurrier

My Sparkling Lady-Night Lights Of San Francisco

Her sparkling eyes remind me of the night lights
of San Francisco;
They too brighten and excite
To foolish feats of imagery and fantasy-
The would I, could I, should I
Of admiration gone wild.

They recall the yesteryear of youthful exuberance
When all was possible, and reality
But one moment from expression.

Her sparkling entices and that's reward
For fulfillment in its fantasy.

So it's with gratitude,
I honor her with this imagery,
My sparkling lady.

Alfred Sheldon Hanly

Untitled

Visions of Nature
Of still gray mountains
rising up through swiftly moving rough
gray clouds, hinting
that the mountains never stop rising.
Of a tall grass valley
surrounded by green hills
when the sun rises, and it all looks freshly made,
if eyes could see it or not.
Of a campsite centered with a strong fire with
a tent, and pots and pans
freshly cleaned by the obliging
stream that runs down
from who knows where and
passes my sleeping bag,
begging me not to sleep.
Of animals friendly or dangerous with only one
thing on their minds and
me trying to find what that is, and I will
always wonder at what they already know so easily.

Joseph Raffaele

To C.S. Lewis

"The power of imagination sets the spirit free,
   Our dragon guards the secret door into fantasy,
A land of castles, knights and kings,
   Wizards, dragons, fairie things.
Close your eyes and you will see,
   In your mind, there lies the key."

Elizabeth Guide

"Teardrops"

My memories lay like the cracked floor
of the desert, waiting for the water of
remembrance to bring them back to life.
Each tear glistens with a tiny glimpse,
a faded memory.
A lost detail, too fleeting to catch.
Just out of reach of my fingers,
I lunge toward the past.
Head long into the world of certainty,
and the knowingness of yesterday.

Elizabeth Hofsommer

Consider The Radiance

Consider the radiance
of the dying ember;
how it trembles in the flying fire,
while close at hand the very
stillness that releases it from consuming decay.

Your beauty requires
all to pause in the burning -
wholeness in a present perfect tense
for me, the voyeur;
harmony in the charred ruins under the fire;
the fire itself that brightens -
you, your warmth that
cleanses the ash and earth of a
suffering with sparks that flee upward.
Consider all of this:
then discover your radiance
in that last coal; how it lingers in me,
flickering to distinguish demise.
How carefully I measure
that innocent fire's mystery.

Jamie Lyle Graham

"My First Swim"

As I see the ocean, I feel afraid
of the rough waves and what awaits
me there.
As I plunge into the sea it amazes me
how beautiful it is.
The bright orange, green, and silver fish
swim by me as if I am not there.
As I swim deeper, I see outstretched
arms of seaweed waving at me.
Suddenly a shadow moves, I'm afraid.
As I look, I am relieved
I see it is only me
reflecting off the floor of the sea.

Charlotte Kubb

The Wall

The wall is the place where names are stored
of those of us who died in war.

We who made the sacrifice,
so that you could have a better life.

Honor, glory for comrades dear,
for those heroes listed here.

Mothers, sons and husbands too,
they gave the ultimate for me and you.

Heroes one and all,
we place your names upon this wall.

Jack Stevens

Bond Of Freedom

If you are my friend, I will stand in front.
Of your arrows.
If you are my acquaintance,
I'll be good to you if you let me.
If you are my enemy, beware I'll behave as
An enemy behaves.
If you are my love, I'll go all the way.
My family, means my life line. Don't touch
It.
If you are my neighbor, I'll love you next
Door, or in a country far away.
We have the flowers, the mountains, and the
seas. A bond of freedom to love, also is a
gift. It means the most to me.

Gaynell NeSmith Drew

A Christmas Wish

Christmas bells they chime and jingle
Office parties, smile and mingle,
Cookies, candy, cakes and pies
Oh, what will happen to my thighs?

If I give in and so indulge
My hips will spread my things will bulge,
They'll grow and grow like summer's weeds
And show the world my glutinous deeds.

Oh, Santa dear, to you I plea
Put presents on the tinsled tree,
And take with you those naughty eats
Especially the chocolate treats.

Then leave for me a body slim
'Cause this one's not so very trim.
It's gained a few pounds here and there
In fact, it looks just like a pear!

I shall not ask another thing
No furry coat, no diamond ring,
If you, dear Claus, grant me this wish
Please make me be a foxy dish!

Jeanne Peters

Eternity

If only the ocean could speak.
Oh, all the secrets it could tell;
The beginning of man
And all his tears in the sand,
All the deaths that it knows
And the dreams postponed
And man growing, reaching
For the sky, then long last, he dies.
And the wind still blows the sand,
And the waves keep coming to meet the land
Without a murmur of whisper
Of all the secrets gone by.

Debra Suto

To My Grandparents

The great white house has a big north porch.
On Sunday morning I can still see,
Two elderly people who looked after me.
Straightening the tie, and fixing the hair,
In the corner of the porch by the rocking chair.
Their souls are gentle, and they've mellowed with age,
The wrinkled skin tender, and the hair slate-like grey.
He leans over to her and gives her a kiss.
Tears come to my eyes, cause my heart sure does miss,
My grandparents on that big North porch.

Jack De Young

Oh America, Oh America

Oh America, oh America God loves America
Oh America you ar the land that God made and loves
America with its land of many people
America with land stretched out to welcome the poor, the old, the babies, the out cast and rich
Oh America how great God has made the America land
And on the America land there have been a many strong leaders
Who has accepted many people on Gods America land
Oh America, oh America with its free speech
How great God has let thee stand America
Oh America wake up before it's too late
Oh America, oh America hear the plea of Gods word
Your leaders in America need the wisdom and Gods word to be able to lead America on
Oh America, oh America your people need to turn from their wicked ways and pray to God
To heal this America land and for God to help them and pray for wisdom from God to
Give the leaders wisdom to lead America on
Oh America, oh America our country.

Elva L. Webb Walker

"A Prayer for Peace"

from The Missing Sonnets Of Romeo and Juliet

Let's heed how hate hath murdered life and love!
Oh! Heed how love hath murdered all our joys.
Sweet sacred sacrificial kindred blood,
Absolve our sins, transform what we employ.

If murder is but all we know to do,
Foul hate hath murdered peace; let love kill war!
For this we pray, for this they died in youth.
Dear families, save your souls! Cease to abhor!
Those deaf to peace are madmen with no ears.
Those blind to hate are wisemen with no eyes.
Our enmity? Forgotten through the years!
So let our hatred here entombed reside.
With trust and faith lives honesty in men.
Join hands my friends and seek to make amends.
Amen

William Shakespeare & Anita James Wilson

The Cry Of The Unborn Babe

"Oh, Please Don't Throw Me Away"

One man's trash is another man's treasure
Oh,Please don't throw me away,
For I'll make another happy beyond measure
Just give me to someone today.

For the fruit of the womb is a blessing from God,
All things come from above,
For although my Mom and Dad may not need me
I'll still know God's great love.

For it is written, "I knew you before
You were in your mother's womb,
And my plans are life, and surely not death,
Tis recorded in His Word.

So let us now turn back to God,
Let's try it His way again,
For He's the Creator of all mankind-
Let's turn away from sin!

Judith E. Reed

A Fat, Round, and Skinny Tree?

Our teacher, Mrs. Julie asked our class,
"Oh smart, smart students, can you see
"A fat, round, and skinny tree?"
They all said "yes" but except for me.
Because how can that ever be.
When it is fat, it can't be skinny!
Not at one time, you cannot see.
So then Mrs. Julie came to me,
and asked how come I disagreed.
So then I said "How can that be?"
"When it is fat, it can't be skinny."
Then suddenly Mrs. Julie asked me.
"Are you blind, or can you see?"
"Because if I were you, I would agree."
But then she stopped, and said to me.
"I was joking, so don't worry."
"You earned an A, instead of a B."

Diem Thanh Nguyen

Maui Whales

O tradewinds pure and cool.
Oh water green and blue
with spindrift white
and in an instant gone.

Repeating and repeating
all these thousand, thousand years.
Great whales you leap and rise!
So huge! So free!
'Till watching you my heart forgets to beat.

If we should fail to save ourselves
and lose the race against hate
and ware and mushroom cloud,
please remember us.
Remember that long ago we cared...
and tried to save the whales.

Janet Little

Katherine's Tears

Katherine spoke of "Old Tears."
Old tears, the lingering hurts of injuries, scorns and shames,
held back until the time we risk to release them.

Old tears, that taste of a bitter brine, a strong and cutting vinegar that hints of something metallic.
Old tears, that feel thicker, heavier, oily and globulious,
as they roll slowly down the slopes and crevices of the face.

Old tears, the slightly amber color of aged crystal, throat catching, parching, acidic and stale.
The burning wash of a soul too long restrained, shackled by habit,
constrained by convention, fear and brutal callousness.

Old tears, cried in long shuddering, racking breaths,
framed in anguished rasping sobs of heart sore grief.
A tremulant moan, the muted dirge of pain etched memories.

Katherine spoke of "Old Tears," cried again,
and went away, leaving a memory,
and remembrance.

Benjamin Taylor

The Flower

The flower swayed in the air as the wind roared outside. Its gorgeous golden color shines like the sun. As the wind blows harder and harder, the petals start to lose grip and break loose and coast through the air. The roots holds tightly in the ground, grasping each inch of earth as new life. Then the winds die down, safe until the next storm.

John Paul White

Where Are You?

I see you before me as I have always seen you
Older, yes, I am older too
But why am I here and you are not?
Why can I not find you?
Where are you?
I try again, my dear friend, it's me, me, me,
Don't you remember me?
As we sat near the brook, you citing poetry?
From memory, from the depth of your heart
Your young children playing around us?
The sunsets when I was grieving
And you gave me strength to go on?
He was dead and I had no children
But you were there, definitely there
And you don't remember me
Where is your grave? Or have I died? No!
But how can you have died and yet sit before me
Your eyes of the same brown color, your eyes' color
Looking at me, vacant
I implore you, where are you?

Gisela Moellmann

"Game Called"

Game called
On a summer's day
The lights are off, the players are gone.
Game called
On a summer shower
The rain looks like sweat from more heavenly players
And the thunder like the crack of the bat from mighty Babe.
Game called
The game is over, the battle is won.
The bats are put away, the mitts under pillows.
Game called, but not for now
The sun a'riseth, the masks are donned.
The battle wages on
'till someone yells:
"Gamecalled!"

Frank Mullady

That Face

The face of God, where was it last seen?
On a woman and child some time ago.
An old woman in her first life,
A child towards its end.

God's young face, before it knew,
God's old face, too full of horror
At what it had witnessed.

Someone saw God's face on a convicted man,
Another sighting was reported on a judge.
Both were in the same place.

It was once seen in a bolt of lightening.
However, electrical interference proved
It was the face of the devil.

Mostly never seen in churches
Except in stained glass.
Wished-for sightings by the dying,
Frequently in automobiles.

God's face is sighted inside one's head,
Imposed on a wish or a transgression.
I saw it on my daughter once.

Barbara Clay

Meant To Be

As I turn back the pages
On all the years of my life,
I can't help but remember
The many day of toil and strife.
I think about the good times
And also recall the sad
Happy times far out-weigh
The sorrows that I've had.

There are many things to be thankful for
And so many that don't have a label
But the most important one in my life
Is a beautiful sweet lady named Mabel
She came into my life at just the right time
A pure stroke of destiny
It had to be a miracle
Or perhaps it was "Meant to be".

Gene Browning

My Philosophy

I've read so many poems
on how to define success,
some say it's in your pocketbook
while others say it's happiness.

But I think that my philosophy
on this important word,
is a little different
from any others I have heard.

Because maybe I define success
as the little things I do,
changing diapers, drying tears,
lost of hugs and "I Love you's."

And maybe there are others who can relate
to how I see success,
and those that don't, that's okay,
it's whatever makes you happiest.

But keep in mind
as you think of how you see success,
it's not always found in your pocketbook,
sometimes it's found in how you're blessed!

Connie J. Bathrick

Linkages

I still walk,
On the paths we took together.
If together then, perhaps once more.

I still talk, to myself,
Of the topics we considered.
Your answers remain, but are not elaborated.

I do not pray.
It seems a presumption.

I still wait,
At places we had been.
At places I had seen you coming to.
I wait expectantly... by myself.
But never alone.

George M. Lady

The Hands That I Hold

The hands that I hold
once held mine.

They were firm and calloused
now soft and wrinkled.

Over the years many kinds of work
pasted through these fine hands.

And now it is my turn to care and comfort
these tired, kind old hands.

The hands that I held, belonged to my father-
gone but not forgotten.

Carolyn Spears

Irresistible Release

Late at night the ghosts enter my room.
One by one they take their respective places about my bed
And with their presence steal my breath.

"Why do you still linger within these cardboard walls
While the wind outside rages?
The music is playing, the dance is afoot, the heartbeat is
Irresistible...
But you lie here still,
Wrapped tight within your mortal coil
Praying for sleep."

These spectre brethren come not to haunt,
But seek only to claim their own.
They know my place, as do I
But why can't I just let go,
Release...
And take My place upon the wind?

Brian Calhoun

Love's An Abyss

Love has no measurement, it is an abyss.
One of life's pleasure we should not omit.
A sea of emotions wash us to and fro.
With accompanying tides of high and low.

Making life glisten, as moonlight kisses the sea.
Sounds of the ocean, two hearts listen and believe.
On the wings of the gull our life will soar.
Two hearts now flowing shall not be ignored.

Our love now joined like the sky and sea.
Ebbed together, creating infinity.
Now to dance with the sun and stars.
A minute of Venus and Mars.

Elaine Johnson Jones

Fear and Love

Why must one fear the other side of the veil or fear his fellow-man? Only because he or she does not love. Why does a composer compose? Only to express the love that he feels, and the eternal gift that we all share, music. Love is like that. Oh the depth of my soul; each moment I live. For there are times when my soul thunders — the soul is the king of kings Lord of Lords — for I can not hold back the tears when and where love is present, illuminating my soul. Oh! oh! love embrace me and the day with your splendor grace, like the wind I feel against my skin, that tells my soul a story with a gentle breeze. For to me love is like the wind that expresses it self extinguishing the way I feel. Oh come all mighty love. Run, dance, sing. Oh! But hurry the year two thousand is approaching — like the waves that sway to and fro; speaking only the language that the pyramids of the past generations understand — all mighty love.

Alvenson Moore

A Matter Of Life Or Death

Awaiting sits the Man on Death Row
One who has lost this game called "Life",
With no hope, and feeling low
and beaten by this mortal strife.

The people, cold, and caring not
to help this Loner, turns their head
and do forget the terrifying lot
of this poor soul, until he's dead.

But sentenced to death some do deserve,
for deeds so thoughtlessly performed;
will share the pain held in reserve
for those that could not be reformed.

And now uncertain is the court
of this Poor Man's Alleged guilt;
The execution they won't abort
though still unsure of blood he spilt.

Am I not my brother's keeper?
A spiritual and Moral thought Indeed;
Now we'll hand him to the Grim Reaper.
By conscience and example we all should Lead.

Anthony Witmer

The Immigrant's Dilemma

Hot tears burn your eyes, but don't look back.
Only, carry with you the weight of young nurtured hopes
Not yet blossomed but brewing.

Step on board, and forget hunger,
And fear of doors kicked opened,
pointing barrels, and bullets lodged in flesh.
Dear beloved land of my birth — now,
only a haze of green beneath this majestic bird of steel.

Go forward, you foreigner.
Lift up your babies and wipe your tears.
The day is here. Peel off the old garb,
keep your head up and step with pride.
A new land with new hopes. Begin again from scratch.
Cover your shame, don't tell them — pretend,
keep buried deep inside the haunting longing for your
home far away. And wait.

But too many years, they can't remember.
Babies are grown into men.
Look back now, and feel the hollow pain inside —
lost an alien forgotten in both worlds.

Julie Jailall

"Mind Flight"

Did you ever sit and wonder why
Only the birds were given wings to fly
Soaring high
They see and know the world gone by
They sigh
And sing the songs of knowledge

But what of man, why did God not give him wings
He got a mind of all things
Knowledge it brings
Oh, but man's wings are in his mind
His mind soars by thinking and seeking
His mind grasps what knowledge he can find
How benign.

Donna J. Pedrera

The Great Wall of Sanity

A strange partition separates the sane from the insane.
Only the insane can really define this partition
Because they are the ones who have broken through it.
The frightening thing about life is not knowing across
Which side of the razor's edge you're about to fall.
Clinging to nostalgia is the main factor of insanity.
Only the ones who ignore the truth and strive to be average
Can enjoy a life of "normalness."
The rest of us live according to our impulses and strive
to be what makes us happy....not normal.

Chris F. Minshew

A Cry For Help

What has happened today, have people gone astray?
Open your minds, and see just what you'll find.
People often stare, in great disappear, then say
why should we continue to care?
Is there a way in which we could be spread?
Has the darkness closed your eyes, only to make
your heart to be come unwise.
Don't litter there, and don't abuse me here!
Open your eyes and realize.
Love me once more, then we can be sure, this life
we can endure.
To survive, is to strive.
This is our home, let us make it our own.
Hear my cry for help, that we may not depart.
If man expects to die, why not live?
Something has to give.
If people would turn around, then more will abound.
Working together as one, then we could say we have won.
Then our earth will last forever, bringing peace of
mind, and hearts that are truly kind.

Barbara Baker

White Bird

White Bird must fly
or all it is must surely die

A cage of gold cannot suffice,
no matter the fashion, no matter the price.

Transitory pleasures will never please,
for while trapped in a cage he can never be at ease.

But somewhere within lies the key to release,
that While Bird may fly and be at peace.

Where hides the answer, where goes the faith,
has everything left him, has he become as a wraith.

The truth lies deep, it is in everyday life.
The wings are weighted and there drips blood from a knife.

Turn to passion, turn to the mind,
to shatter the bars, gain release from tightening binds.

But an evil tide rises, and he becomes as a crow,
yet he sits and grows old while watching the blood flow.

The time draws near,
whence he will have nothing to fear.

Either White Bird shall fly,
or all it is will utterly die.

James Chapman

To Those Of Us...

To those of us whose lives are marred or broken by imperfection
Or by damage done to strength within ourselves
There arises the indissoluble question, an unanswerable question:
Why.
To those of us, to those of us,
Pain built these buildings... Need raised these walls.
To those of us whose lives are scarred or measured
By imperfection or by damage done to strength in someone close
There arises the clutching, gnawing question,
A possibly avoidable question:
Why.
To those of us, to those of us,
Guilt built these buildings... Death raised these walls.
To those of us, in long struggle with these questions
Who have held the broken human spirit in our hands,
There arise no certain, studied answers,
Just a hope, God.
To those of us, to those of us,
Dreams built these buildings,
Love raised these walls!

Baxter H. Armstrong

A True Friend

They're different as flowers along the way,
or people that you meet every day.
More precious than all diamonds and gold;
after God made them, He destroyed the mold.

You're in their thoughts all thru the year;
and they pray for you, even shed a tear.
You'll be chauffeured both near and far;
when they freely transport you in a car.

A cheerful voice is just a phone call away;
as you and your friend have much to say.
Though you may be depressed and trapped by trouble;
true friends will come running, "On-The-Double."

If your children forget you, as the years roll by;
Don't curse our creator, up in the sky.
Be happy for graces that God did send;
Thank the Good Lord you have one true friend!

Austin F. Stebor

My First True Love

Every time I hear a song
Or see a movie about the war
I remember my first true love
Who I loved with my heart and soul.

I can't help it, but I cry hard
When I remember his words, and his beautiful smile
He asked me, to give him a smile he could keep
And promised he'd be back to marry me.

He went away to do his duty
We kept in touch for a long term
Somehow, something, had happened
A strange man came into my way.

I heard from someone who knew him
That his brother got killed in the war
When he went back to his country
He found his brother's wife and children alone.

They ended up marrying each other
In the meantime, I got married myself
Even though I loved my husband
There was always him in the back of my head.

Catherine Vella

In Touch

Have you really lived?
Or smelled a rose, heard a cricket
watched a puppy play, tasted a snowflake...

Do we take time to enjoy
each breath we take
As we dream our dreams
and live our lives!

Strolling along the waters edge
I hear the babbling brook,
And rest on the mossy rocks
While a Robin sings.

The fragrance of a rose is
sweet to the senses,
A cricket chirps a melody
as the puppy frolics,
And in winter's snowstorms
a snowflake melts
As I taste life once more,
for I know forever
God loves me.

Jean Boyce Capra

Hidden Tears

I was your child in many a way,
Or so people told me from day to day.
Did we feel love or even care?
You never said and I didn't dare.
Or did you show it in ways not understood,
By the things that you said were for my own good?

Separated by eyes that looked away —
No words of comfort could we say.
Burying deeper what neither could share,
Struggling to keep it inside — so seemingly unaware
Of the depths of affection awaiting us there,
There in the heart as yet unexpressed,
Behind hidden tears at last confessed.

Is this a link in a chain never-ending,
Passed on through generations ever-pretending?
Who'll be the first to face the pain,
From parent to child, who can break this chain?
I'll take the first step, if you'll meet me there.
We'll let the past go, let true feelings flow,
And show how we care.

Allan M. Carlozzi

Wishing

Have you ever wanted to be a bug on the wall
Or wanted to be shorter, instead of so tall
Have you ever wished you were thin and not fat
Or gottan a doll, instead of a bat
Have you ever dreamed of another place
Or wanted to vanish without a trace
Have you ever wished upon a star
And wanted to be someone other than who you are
Why is it we're so hard to please
And want to own our neighbor's keys
Don't try to change what life's given you
For treasured moments are, oh so few
Remember the saying, "What will be , will be"
And you be you, and I'll be me!!!

Chris O'Steen

Art

Everyday of my life I grow a little more; not knowing what to expect
or what's in store.

Life with all its splendors and happy times in love, my life's been
content from the magic up above.

Sunrise and Sunset, the beauty of it still, is somewhat rather
startling when you look beyond the hill.

Before me I see a stranger with a look of discontent, thoughtful
hours and lonely days are times I wished we'd spent.

No boundaries, no lines, no stranger to me now, I see the way it
is and feels, but know no answer how.

Although the years they travel fast when things are in their place;
you suddenly realize what's happened and finally have some space.

The years though tough that they may seem are yours for the taking like
fish in a stream. Yet when caught releases freedom that people
so seldom see; for if that freedom could be put into words the
freedom would mean me.

So few the words were ever spoken with wisdom and are true;
the world around us often test the love I have for you.

I want no obligations, I want no promises true, just some time to
know you better and love the real you.

Debbie Turman

Grace

No matter what you may have done
Or where you may have been

There is always the Eternal Son
Father and Comforter, all are one

Maybe just lonely and in deep thought
Or with friend, or spouse you may have fought

He can fill your void, your emptiness
Fill you with warmth and happiness

Yes, died for us, sins to forgive
Nailed to the cross, shed blood, so we may live

For it is by his amazing, somber grace
That he could save some of the human race

He knows all, but is still full of love
All he asks is acknowledgement to above

Lord is Christ, I'm a sinner, please forgive
It is after you I pattern my life
So with you, I'll always live

Amen!

Garry R. Linam

Snow In Heaven

Will there be snow in heaven, do you think winter will ever come
Or will there be only sunshine in my great heavenly home
There's little of snow in the Bible, of that you can be sure
Tho' - white, pristine and fluffy, and falls so clean and pure

I really don't like the heat of summer where most folk like to bask
So.. How will I cool when in heaven? To the Lord I humbly ask
What will there be to compare with the calm, cool essence of snow
That fills my heart with such beauty, and warms my soul here below

I'm praying that even in heaven all seasons will hold full sway
Then I can enjoy the great panorama that only nature can display
Yes: there will be snow in heaven for people who are just like me
We will enjoy the fullness of earth and heaven; can't you see?

Florence Gilmore

Senior

Senior, Senior who has no time
Others look up to him he's losing his mind
The counselor says where're you goin'
But his parents say the money better start flowin'
Applying for scholarships is such a drag
It would be easier if they came in a wrapped bag
But life will go on and everyone will forget
Then that Senior will have a kid with the same problems, I bet

Christopher N. Robbins

Naked Betrayal

The fire of the times heating
Our country, like boiling water
Poured on naked people.
The pain scorches our pride,
Our siblings. Our lives.
Burnt skin, bloodied hair, ravaged earth:
Again present in the orders of a new killer.
There is no longer true democracy.
The finger has been pointed by the voted,
Blood drips slowly and painfully as
We carry bloodshot vision in this arena of death.
The whip cracks and snaps us into another combat,
But we do not wear the crown.
We are the villainous heroes protecting the ruthless,
Falsely loved in to hatred, to never forgive it,
When it is their sins we cannot ignore any more.
We will remember and not eat of the same bread
At the table of those we guard —
For like us, it is bitter.

Brad Lengel

True Love

In the beginning we played the game
Our hearts never beat the same
Until the time I told you my name
And the way it began was just the same
I wonder if this love is right?
Can I call it love at first sight?
It feels so right; but could be wrong?
How will I know?
It's been so long?
What will become of this "love" in a few days?

Questions linger inside my head
Must I cry before I go to bed
I really need to know where my feelings stand
My decision to love is in your hands
Something tells me when you call my name
That this feeling called love is here to stay
You've showed me that in so many ways
Now I know your love is here to stay
I've finally found true love today...

Audrey Richards

Seeking

Crying out in the wilderness
Passionately absorbed in the now,
Yearning, searching . . . . for what?

The ultimate, the indestructible
Wanting the Eternal to possess:
Finding it nowhere in this alienated world.

My heart tells me there's more,
And my soul wants to soar
And grasp the All.

Emily D. Cyrol

"Pure Lust"

Our bodies would be hot and dripping with sweat,
Our muscles' would be sore and the sheets will be all wet,
From a slight stroke you'd be in bliss.
I will make you want me by just one kiss.

Then I'd take you somewhere you've never been,
As you slowly work your way in.
Our body's would start to pump,
Our hearts would start to jump.

The feelings we'd have would be purely lust.
Moving my body on top of yours would be a must.
I wouldn't do this with any other,
Even if they begged I'd still call them a mother.

If I just touched your body once you'd get the hint,
That I want to give you one hundred and ten percent.
And if you're wondering, no I would tease,
The only thing I'd do to you is please!

Hope Baker

Our Goal

If we could only set aside
our prejudice and hate.
We'd find true love inside ourselves
I know it's not too late.

The world would be a joyous place
for every living thing.
No fearful thoughts could fill our minds
what freedom that would bring.

For every man throughout the world
would feel the same inside.
And the unity of one pure thought
would be our greatest stride.

No longer would we have the need
to honor church and state.
And flags and idols could be lost
no further need for hate.

So break the bonds that close your mind
and let the light shine in.
For only then can man find peace
and harmony begin.

Eileen Simone

H.I.V. Positive

Playboy lover always played the field
out to discover, it was too late to yield
Unprotected felt so much fun,
Now, I'm dying from a disease,
that's deadly number one (AIDS)
High price to pay, not only for the Gay
In the nightlife, A.I.D.S runs the mile
A race, against time, catches up with your life style!!
Sex is fun, passion is a game,
H.I.V. doesn't need to know your name.
My advice, don't think about it twice,
use a rubber, when with your lover,
think with tact, before you act.

Just remember, the things I've said,
better to be alive than to be dead,
I'm still alive, to tell my tale,
But I know soon, my body will fail,

The music, the lights, the drinking,
the fun is all an illusion, A.I.D.S is a nightmare
"It's real", It's H.I.V. Positive!!!

Joseph A. Gomez

"Stay"

I nestle beside, the massive river wide.
Over the earth black canvas falls.
I hope to be, that reaper takes me,
for I feel my destiny calls.

The trigger clicks down, there's no other sound.
A twitch and I'll fly away.
Down or up I'll drink from the cup
that the reaper will hand my way.

My true fate calls, my actions are stalled,
seems a voice calls out my name.
It occurs to me, the sky talks to me,
From this moment I shan't be the same.

This deed of foul, your face shines a scowl
Your soul now restrictive with chains.
With existence so great, feast from life's plate.
Make sunshine from coldest of rains.

Either from fear or shock, self destruction is lost.
I wave the reaper away,
And now with just cause, I'm given applause
For I am in this world to stay.

Jeffrey Walling

Christmas In Connecticut

Christmas in Connecticut brings back warm memories of my boyhood past.
I would count the days after Halloween; hoping they would go fast.

The unforgettable smell of a fresh cut tree; with presents waiting underneath; all addressed to me.

My mother in the kitchen, her apron tucked in neat, as she rushed us from the kitchen to perform her baking feat.

Our Christmas Eve dinner was one we thought about all year, as we gathered close to family; that we hold so dear.

The thought of going to sleep that night was all that I could bear, and the fact we couldn't wait up for Santa didn't seem fair.
We awoke before dawn, the patter of six little feet-rushing to the tree to see our treats.

The hot chocolate and cookies left for Santa were eaten and gone.
Proof he had been there; reindeer and all.

And now as I get older, and no matter where I roam, when I think of Christmas I think of home.

Daniel A. Vanacore

My Grandpa

I cannot see him but I know he's there,
Peeking over a cloud way high in the air.

He wasn't afraid of such things as bugs,
And he so very loved our hugs.

I love him dearly that will always be.
It feels like a big chunk has been taken out of me.

It's like the sunshine has gone down,
Not only in our homes but also in our town.

We will always remember him in our lives.
The pain is knowing he is no longer alive.

Jennifer Watson

The Yell Of A Child

The Yell of a Child is so faint in the wind,
people cannot hear the poor child cry,
thinking did someone leave my poor
growing body in the wind to die,
tho they love me like a blink of an eye

Ashley Michelle Coey

The Dream Is Alive

The dream is alive, and it has been for many years.
People have gone up facing no fear.

They have wondered, and pondered, and lived up their dreams
to continue to discover unknown things.

People laughed when I said I wanted to do it,
but now I'm here and there's nothing to it.

So continue to dream and keep it alive
for NO ONE can stop your feelings inside.

Ellen McGowan

Expression Of My Heart

We want to own a business, a house and a car.
People like me should be happy to have, two working legs
which is better by far.
We want to have gold, diamonds and other charms.
People like me should be happy to have two working arms.
We want to have a stereo, records, V.C.R. and a T.V.
People like me should be happy to have two eyes that can see.
We want to have riches, fortune and fame, and a lot of good years.
People like me should be happy for our two working ears.
We want to take trips, and sail the seven seas.
People like me should be happy for our good
health and being free from disease.
Don't take things for granted, be good to your fellow man.
The Lord will always thank you whenever he can.
So for now, let's contribute to cause
whenever we can, it'd be a good start.

Alfred Peter Soucy Jr.

New England Spring

March can be the cruelest month of all...
Perched upon Winter's back, it howls like banshees;
Rages like lions;
Rampages like bears.

And then comes April, sighing and swooning;
Wafting her way into Spring with bird song,
With bud and blossom,
Young lambs...and rain.

And rain...and rain...and rain! If you don't like our weather...
Why, Mister, just you wait a minute!
Two hours from now,
It maybe will be snowing!

It's May. Two weeks ago it did snow!
The poor damn geese laid their eggs,
As geese will do; then couldn't find them.
Warm eggs do tend to sink through something cold!

Jean O. Gibbs

Perhaps There's One

Shall a soul be real by depth of thought?
Perhaps skies aren't scorned by views unsought.
Being one as a glow through spirits abounding,
Still shunned am I to realms of surrounding.
The horizon is true to my destiny for sure.
So wayward I travel as winds flow ashore
Through reams of beauty I seek out to hold.
Can I, as one, have the strength of the mold?
Behold the sunset upon the toll
Though beauty is body by mind through soul.

Daniel Oyas

Sunfire

Pulsating rays from the sun above
Pierce my flesh like tiny needles
The heat with the power to control gravity
Anchors my aching body to the soil

Too weary to stand or kneel
I lie still with no energy to expound
Too tired to utter a single sound
My mind conjures a silent prayer for mercy

Within the crevices of my heart
I search for the fire within to retaliate
Through the labyrinth of my mind
I search for the path to peace

With a bright burst of crimson
The ever-glowing orb conquers all
I am destined to suffer its wrath
My soul a victim to incineration

Solace seems beyond my reach
Relief appears only as an oasis
An oasis that is merely part of the sands of time
And time is merely a prison.

Isaac A. Bobbe

In Loving Memory Of Cindy Ann

A child is now at rest, for a safer
place she remains, a world of goodness
and beauty, a world without worry or pain.

No fear will she encounter, for a better
place she'll be a place where the
sick are healed and where blinded eyes can see.

Our world has forever changed, our lives
are not the same. But close within our hearts,
her precious face remains.

We give to her our tears and our prayers
we send above. We cherish all the memories,
filled with happiness and love.

She'll have someone to depend on,
a helping hand is there to lend.
For our Father shall be watching and
in heaven she'll have a friend.

This battle is faced head on,
many obstacles to over come.
But in the end, we'll all be with her again!

Denise Renee Batterton

Puzzle People

Open up the box and pull out a seat
Plan to spend some time and get off your feet.
Scatter a few pieces amongst the board
Pick out all the straight edge ones
For this is just the beginning, Oh Lord!
Now your frame is built, next comes the middle
Some kind of connection should come to mind -
Let's see if I can explain it is riddle.
Puzzles are like people you see
Everyone wants to fit in somewhere, just longing to be.
They come in all sizes and shapes, just like me!
Some fit so smoothly into their places
Others are scattered and floundering, frustration is seen on their
faces.
We might group them, mix them up, or stand them alone,
But to each person, there's only one place where they belong;
Just like a puzzle, fitting so snugly into their throne!
Most people search the world over, others are molded and laced
But for those who are out there wandering and questioning yourselves
There is hope in time, that your too, will find your place.

Ann M. Chabot

Sun's Song

I sang a song last night
Played with a gentle happy tune
It was full of memoir's light
Of warm and happy thoughts I crooned

It filled my soul with peace
It filled my heart with love
It told of daybreak's crease
The burst of motion above

Moving every minute with energy's store
With promise to come back another
Day to meet me at my door
It brought its brightest color

The song I sang last night left daisies in my street
It wasn't worrisome or full of bright
Its dream of hope I keep
It left a morning full of glories upon my fence
Post light
If you want it can be the song you sing tonight...

Judy Ann Breymeyer

Meadow Flowers

Sun dances on my window
Playing with the frost
Silently it reaches my pillow
Signaling a new day has come

Waking to the morning sun so warm upon my face
Feeling the cold frost of night drift away
Inside the misty morning of a brand new day

Meadow flowers all dressed in gold
Butterflies playing tag around you
You never worry of growing old

People can learn from you
If they would just take the time
To look and listen to you

Meadow flowers, natures maidens
Never work or run
Yet they grow so beautifully
As I watch them in the morning sun.

Cindy Stellmach

Untitled

I don't know what's on your mind.
Please just know I wish I could leave my mistakes behind.
The warmth you filled my heart with when I was feeling cold
I have pushed away and it has gotten pretty old.
I wish I could erase all the bad,
but now it seems too late,
to agree that I was wrong
for now you're filled with hate.
A part of me will never die,
the part that once loved you.
But it will fill with regret
if for you there's someone new.
Love is what it was all about,
but now it's disappeared.
I hope you remember all the fun we used to have
and don't dwell on the pain and tears.
I hope for sometime in the future
when I see you once again
You think of all the things we've shared
and want it back again.

Jessica Sanford

Treasured of the Heart

Rainbows, sunshine or lolly pops are always
pleasing to a child's heart.
But come the spring when flowers bloom
and the birds begin to sing.
All across the land life begins to unfold
young men seek the courage to be bold
Keen or pretty faces adorned in lovely colors
and fancy laces

like a bee from flower to flower he chases
diligently looking for the right sparkle
in the eye
Maybe it will be the next encounter by and by
No longer thoughts like a boy he thinks
Rainbows, sunshine or lolly pops
now only of the favors from a lovely maiden
that makes his heart to sink
or his stomach to do flip-flops

Al Lopezo

The Missing List

When my father was dying there was one thing he knew; there was plenty of work that he had left to do so he called for me urgently and asked, "Would you mind? There's a list I've misplaced that I simply must find. I'm too weak to stand, my eyes are not strong I remember the list on yellow paper and long. It seems like only yesterday that I put it away; please look for it, Dear. What more can I say?" This clearly upset him, he was dying I knew so finding this list was the least I could do. I began by searching every drawer, box and chest, closets and cupboards with just time to rest. I looked in the attic, then covered with dust, down to the basement picking locks full of rust. Frantically searching I would climb, I would kneel and everything yellow I would snatch with a squeal. That list was important but I had to admit after looking for two weeks - I just had to quit. Confessing my failure, head bowed there I sat and Dad said, "I'm sorry, but what list was that?" How clearly I saw now there was never a list; he just wanted assurance there was nothing he'd missed.

-Epilogue-

I got a phone call the other day from an elderly aunt who lives far away. She was feeling quite poorly and asked if I'd mind sending that list she just could not find.

Cynthia Montini

Precious Moments

Precious little fingers,
Precious little toes,
That precious little face,
With that little precious nose.

Yes every moment is so precious,
Let every mother know,
That soon her precious baby will begin to grow.

Don't turn your head, don't look away...
You'll only look back another day,
To see your precious gift from God has grown and gone away.

So put all others to the side,
And look inside those big wide eyes.
You'll see pure innocence, love, and joy.
Embrace your precious girl or boy.

These precious moments go so fast.
Before you know they come to pass.
As pure as the snow white turtledove,
Yes, they are the true meaning of precious love.

Beverly K. VanDusen

Nicholas

Missing the feel of your body
pressed to mine, going over each moment
like a dream.
A passionate woman with powerful needs
gnawing at my belly.
Wanting you inside to stay, to carry
with me a memory to embrace.
Longing for your touch, hoping you would
feel the same for me.
Instead I would hold you close, hearing
in the distance the thunder matching in tempo
your heart beat.
Relishing in what I did have, never to
love another the way I loved you.

Cherie Crandal

The Final Blow

A deafening blow. It rattled my brain.
Punctured my eardrum, but I'll take the blame.

I set myself up. I let you get near.
You punched out my lights, and now I can't hear.

But this is not bad. It's as it should be.
For now I must listen to no one save me.

The mistake I have made, all my life long,
Is listening to others. You proved me wrong.

This lesson I've learned has cost me a lot.
I feel I have nothing, but there's one thing I've got.

She's with me right now. She always has been
She lives in my heart, my only true friend.

I've got me. Plain and simple. I'll see me right through.
I don't need hearing. And I don't need you.

A deafening blow. Right straight to my head.
It might have been deadly. It freed me instead.

Cindy L. Gamble

The Windmill

Round and round the windmills go
purple skies as shadows grow

Autumn winds chasing leaves
sing-song like a windmills heave

There they stand and seem to see
The soul of things that used to be

How church bells gaily chimed and rang
while in the fields we toiled and sang

Then at dusk when work was done
'twas neath their wings hearts were won

But one day a storm came
'twas thunder like a crashing flame

With aching hearts to god we cried
while every man left his fire side

But once again the windmills sing
and church bells gaily will chime and ring

A song of freedom, of peace to be,
of love, of life, of liberty

Esther Farisato

Untitled

I've felt needless before.
Purposely painful renditions
torn and ached through
violent strings.

Ready to rage
into the melted core.
Being scorned by lace, tossed through stone.
Again,
I am pushed into a lit flame;
The drunken burn slides inside
curing the seconds between heat and warmth.

You can only hope for passion.
Dance under pressure.
Search the ground for dropped concern.
Create sections of black and white photos
in remembrance of reality.

I've seen restrictions before.
Concoctions conceived within seduction.
Following hollow urns to benefit
saint sinners.

Byron K. Banks

Life Is But A Walking Shadow

Life is but a walking shadow
Quiet, loneliness and stress
Try to hide behind tear stained eyes
The shadow of a smile, that remains to be seen
The shadow of a shattered and broken dream

Life is but a walking shadow
Loneliness cast no silhouette
Empty arms and broken hearts
Unspoken truths, forgotten youth
Memories you can't forget

Life is but a walking shadow
False hope, false love, false pride
Within our hearts we tell ourselves
That we will still survive
Life is but a walking shadow,
Walking...walking by.

Corine Rice

Stormy Weather

The storm rode down from the mountains,
Racing onto the plains
Like a great wave of buffalo, darkening the horizon.
Clouds, like horsemen leaning low to the horse's ear,
Chased each other in wild abandon,
Raced each other towards the sunset.
Painted grey and blue and black and red,
They were on their way to war;
Lightning speared the earth like feathered lances.
Thunder rolled before them—
Battle cries warning of what was to come,
Sending all before them in frantic fright for safety.
Suddenly, the storm was on them.
The thunder roared in their ears.
Shook them deeply. Turned them cold. Her hands trembled.
The night turned day, burning white with lightning fire;
Rain hammered the ground like the hooves of a thousand horses.
And then they were gone,
Leaving dead silence in their wake,
Their battle cries echoing off the plains in the distance.

Heather E. Hewitt

The Empty Nest

Where did they go, days that the house rang with noise
Radios, jam boxes, children running in and out of doors.
The laundry basket overflowing, the floor littered with books,
sweaters, socks and shoes.
The phone bill longer than a shopping list, a sink of dirty
dishes and empty cookie jars.

The rough and tumble of children playing tag on a green lawn.
The giggles and whispers of overnight guests.
The "hurry-up, I need to use the bathroom too."
The sweet good morning kisses from rosebud lips.
Trying to comb out a cowlick.
The sad tears of something ending, happy tears for new
beginnings, when the last child graduates.

Laughter no longer rings out, no "Hi Mom, glad you're home."
Just the silence and echoes of yesterday greets you.
I sometime sit staring out the door and in my mind's eye
I see lively kids romping in the yard, the old dog chasing them
Now I sit in my empty nest, eagerly awaiting the sound of
little running feet and rosebud lips with a kiss for Grandma.
A new generation fills the hole in the empty nest.

Beulah Marie Camp

Untitled

The wind beat against you
Rain ran down your face
Eye's pleading—Jaw firm
Pride and hope grown pale
Within your hand you held fast to a promise
A promise forgotten by an endless stream of passers by
Suddenly, you moved forward
Face to face with the other
Reaching out—touching
But too long had the promise been forgotten
The light of mercy could not be found
Forced back into the darkness
You too let go of the promise
The promise died

Elvira Faith Walling

A Mother's Love

To know the wonder of motherhood is to know the pure
rapture it brings.

The sweetness of infancy the frustration and the joy,
and the constant reminding yourself that he really is
your little boy.

Everything that brings you pleasure will also bring
you pain,
just as with the flowers will also come the rain.

He'll drive you crazy, he'll make you laugh, and grow
in the blink of an eye,
and when you look back on his childhood, it's enough
to make you cry.
So forget the fretting, the anger and ire, just remember
his love and his sparkle of fire.

For the years pass so quickly, you somehow don't
remember the bad little boy that wouldn't go to bed.

A mother just remembers the Angel with the halo 'round
his head.

Adrienne Garcia

The Dawn

Splashes of color, all around,
Quietly, without a sound,
Descend upon this world of mine.
The earth, each morning, is thus crowned.

Alissa Gafford

Dream Trek

I think I don't want safe, sure passage;
Rather, some bright piece of world
Where strange sights tease and dangers rage.
Then I remember (lying curled
Snugly in my dreaming place):
My body's old—its fleshly fears
Reject adventure's beckoning face.

Life takes its toll of waning years—
But not of dreams! In their embrace
I dream the day I'll leap the bars
Of flesh to tread the dawn and race
To climb the sky and kiss the stars.

Betty Garton Ulrich

"Fear for Life"

As I sit gazing out of my window,
Reaching for the utmost thought
A fierce wind of anger came to mind
A rapid beating heart, my breath, I caught,
Then, I said please God.
At that time a tear did fall
I felt the endless movement of time
And a rapidly beating heart, that's all.
Where are all the signs that pave the way
to happiness and joy?
I turned to see what was the noise
There stood Colby, Chase, Roy, all my boys,
Then I knew someone was aware
Temporary are the dreary days
A smile come across my face,
And the sun burst out with bright rays,
I want a soul full of joy,
I won't let life's withering storms destroy.

Imogene Sachse Evans

Mystic Red Rose

Red as the rose blush cheeks of your sweet heart.
Red through out her graceful name of Scarlet.
Beautiful as the crimson red kiss upon the defined rose
from her flower-like lips.
Chrome-red, parked on the seat of that majestic new
maroon auto.
Slipping through waters of love throughout the coral
red reef on your honeymoon sunset swim.
The thorn of moods brings the blood of life's pain and
pleasure to fall drop by drop as if teardrops.
Blood-red upon the heart of your cherished but perished
beloved.
As the petals of life float down to the dewdrops of the
earthen ground may the lifeless tranquility, calm our
hearts of malady anguish.

Chad Martinez

Untitled

Once there was a little lamb who
roamed far, wide, and free
Along came Mary who said you belong to me
Now this little lamb did not understand, and
wasn't about to take any command
He looked at Mary sheepishly and thought
this cannot be
He turned and ran as fast as he could
as he was taught he should
Shouting I'm free, free, free

John A. Kepler

Beauty Of A Rose

Roses.
Red. Yellow. Pink. Blue.
So many colors covered by dew.
Roses.
In the spring on a wing under rain
As beautiful as a crane.
Roses.
Gentle yet so strong
And not a single thing wrong
Roses.
The fairy of flowers
That holds the most special powers
The powers of a potion
Strong enough to cause emotion
The emotions of friendship, joy, and love
All sent through the flower,
From Father above.

Brooke Danielle Mercedes Davey

The Hateful Love

A frightened child hiding in her room, dreading the time she returns. Even now, growing older by the days, still fears the time her mother comes home.

She gives her so much, yet her mother takes back even more. It's true, possessions can be replaced, but the trust and love will be lost eternally.

The throbbing of her throat, not from screaming, but from choking on her sorrow. The screaming and yelling seems as though they'll never end, but still never getting to put her say in it.

The hateful words she so many times absorbed, trying to ignore, she can no longer bare. The many emotional and physical pains she's endured have since scared her trust.

In a race with each other, the tears drip down her cheeks. Each one containing trust and love that she can no longer share with anyone but the pillow she buries her face in.

Heather Ewen

Tempest

Divisional, fractional, gravitational RAGES.
Rock stars on an acid, performing on STAGES.
Cold times and memories of the PAST.
Longitude and stratospheres that make this world a BLAST.
Quiet yet wild, and the atoms of my CHILD.
The years of an old AGES, plus the heat of twelve GAGES.
The tormented IMAGINATION, of the burning MANIFESTATION.
The eyes, of generic, homicidal symbolic AGRICULTURE,
with the tendency and precision in a crazed minded VULTURE.
We must believe in the TRUST.
We have to bring back the systematic cummunicational
BACKGROUND.
away from the RUST.

Missions of problems and human abnormal CHANGES.
Thoughts in the mind, entering theoretical boiling RANGES.
Turning this terrific ordinary LAND,
into hydraulic positional SAND.
Zapping out historic warm decisions, and pushing out
megabolic, astronomical torn INCISIONS
into a world of death and GREED.
Verifying energetic ventures that our people tend to NEED.

Chris Hartsock

An Ode To Those Who Teach

The deep dimension of the mind,
Run quietly like trickles of a softly flowing brook.
Awake, when stirred by those who challenge our
right to decay.
The surge of response like rushing torrents of the
rapids, exudes our being.
Imagination knows no bounds.
Like salt that draws out pain.
And sun rays beckon the unfolding petals of new birth.
Like a child, we learn to walk,
Cautious lest we fall,
Relentless in their guest to make us wonder.
They trespass temporarily in our minds depths,
And we see the beauty beneath the dark waters,
The promise of hope and creation.

Jean Markivee

"Summer Dream"

Another summer sunset
runs slowly from the night.
Bright red spots of magic
fill the purple skies.

Onward, pushes darkness
as it leads the summer night,
distant silver moon beams
begin to come alive.

Another summer sunset,
has slipped right out of sight,
leaving just a memory,
and another summer night.

The midnight sun lights up the sky
and soon a new day will take birth.
It won't be long, and the night will run.
Golden rays of sunshine, will kiss the morning earth.

Then another summer sunset
will find its way to me.
More purple skies, with bright red spots,
another summer dream.

Carlos Robert Garcia

The Opened Door

Confusion knots my belly up
Sadness grows a lump in my throat
I've forgotten about this dead sea of time
I have been there but only for so long
All I desire is to follow you but your so hard to find
My mind is like a dried up reservoir waiting to be filled
It's too much right now
Why are they spilling out their venom now?
I'm not strong enough and when I'm they block the sunshine
Tug of war, power struggle is tired, why do you play?!
Your heart might wither and you're making me shrivel too
Words of wisdom, yeah you have some good points
I do take them in but I won't lock the door behind you

Jennifer Sullivan

Sand Castle At Night

Imagine if you could live in a
Sand castle made up of glistening
walls of sand.

Around the castle lies a window:
Through it you can see the stars
Of time and the heavens of eternity.

Below the beating light of the stars,
is the cool shadow of the peaceful quiet,
night.

Anna D'Amico

"Sandy"

With a touch of silver in her hair
  Sandra's still a classy old dame
Her voice rings a joyous flare
  A spirit too beautiful to tame

An adventurous gal, loving and free
  Always that mischievous gleam in her eye
Full of laughter and life she'll spree
  Willing to tackle the world going by

For three weeks in Europe she's bound
  Her work and kids she left behind
WIC girls stuck under a paper mound
  While the sitter slowly loses his mind

Holland, France, and Belgium too
  Leaving with no regret her troubles at home
Not thinking of who's happy and blue
  Checking her map on the way to Rome

On the eighteenth she'll meet reality
  For travel and glamour will now end
She'll face a sitter losing his sanity
  And a work load she'll never mend

Ed Hanson

School

School is great;
School is the best.
You use a brown or metal desk.

You write with pencils and pens;
You sit with your friends.
You draw and color with crayons and markers,
Then you put them away in your locker.

Our teachers are the best;
They're better than all the rest.
The work can be hard,
But in later life you'll go far.

Any subject that you really get,
You'll do well and earn extra credit.

That's all I have to say,
So I'll just call it a day.

Colleen Gilmartin

Thrown A Crumb

Like pigeons in the park
Searching endlessly for crumbs
As food for survival
I search for love.
Not the physical, sexual love.
But the love of wanting, needing, touching
Of arms enfolding, holding.
Protecting from outside cares
If only for a moment,
Learning to ask for love, difficult
For one who lives on crumbs
Afraid there won't be any
Afraid someone else will grab it away.
The searching goes on everyday.
Many times I come up empty, to return
To my rest and curl up in a tight ball.
Trying to find peace within
That comes from the endless love
Which flows freely from the one
Whose arms enfold...forever.

Ann C. Whiting

The Coming Out

In my room is a closet but no one else can see. It keeps my secret to know one else but me.

Each day I open up my closet so I can see if I can wear my true identity.

My hangers hold no labels of designer cloths you'll see, but labels in which society has given me.

I check my hangers one by one, but can not see the hanger that says acceptance and equality for a homosexual like me. So for now, I close my closet so no one else can see my true identity.

Today I open up my closet for the whole world to see the person inside of me.

I felt so free no more secrets for me. I realized now how no one else could see in this insensitive society.

Before were old, we are shaped and we are molded and we are told to be a pillar of society. So there is no room for a person like me because truly the only difference is my homosexuality.

Barbara Ferro

Sleeping In Snow

I once had dream, though may it
seem, a very strange dream of snow. It was
at night and the moon shined bright, what a
very wonderful glow. I wasn't talking, or walking,
I was sleeping in the snow. In a row,
the snow would go, all upon my face. It
wasn't cold, to my skin as gold, for I was sleeping
in the snow.

Amy Elizabeth Rose

Winter's Last Stand

The soft swift swooping breeze
Sends the lovely liquid diamonds
Shimmering down from space;
To the tickle the naked trees.
The winds roar, the rivers swell, but soon,
The sun shines
And winter's last battle
Is soon past.

Gail M. Rascoe

Jan's Smile

Your girlish smile
Set in motion by emotion
Not created for essential demands - a purpose - a goal
An upward curve of innocence and peace
From days gone by: From:
Love of a sister
A wagon full of groceries
Dips in a creek
Baber poles
007
Sunday School dresses
A french poodle

Your transcending smile
Sacrificing self against instinct
Not emotion, but spirit
An enviable gift
Releasing the intestinal vice of a scared soul
Anticipation of home to a fatigued frame

Your tough smile that heard "I DO" on thanksgiving

Barry R. Rheault

You're The One

Many thru puppy love to marriage
Several of whom thought to be you
But only to end up with a hole within the soul

Years of struggle and some of pain
The end result always the same
Still looking for the one, who would fulfill and stop the pain

Then you appeared while still with one
But knowing It was you just the same
The guilt to run you out of mind like a child's game

Now whole, complete and washed of pain
Life's outlook is with meaning and gain
Till life's final end there will be no other, for you're the one.

Farrell Maier

Swirling Leaf

Swirling, twirling: A leaf spins, comes to rest.
Shadow spreads a blanket. Breeze brings a dance.
By velvet moss linger leaves bequest,
Void of stress or strength and far from the branch...
Still lovely, though dead, and is it by chance?
Swirl elements of reality,
Twirl patterns of creativity.
Silently, the old leaves become new ground:
An occasion of ingenuity.
Another leaf spins, around and around.

Geaugua

Eagles Courting Over Lizard Head Peak, Wyoming

To the ground eye it
seemed
an aerial duel to the death,
the swift birds whirling spread-winged,
climbing,
spiraling in the thermal,
beaks locked in a hooked kiss,
talons meshed,
riding Wind River high
over the stone rippling roof of the Rockies,
spinning in the sun,
dissolving in light.

D. A. Westover

Autumn's Canvas

Orange, Red, Brown and Gold
The Colors of Autumn, Bright and Bold

To Look Across, the Great Expand
As if An Artist, was on Hand

The Touch of Brilliance, All Around
From the Top of the Trees
To the Bottom of the Ground

A Hint of Coolness, Touches your Cheek
As Colored Leaves, Drift in a Creek

You Know the Colorful, Display is Here
... But not for Long, This Time of Year

For Soon the Colors, Fade and Go
To Make the Path, for Winter's Snow

Dorothy Fullilove

My Children

Of little girls, there are plenty,
I'm sure you will agree,
But God blessed me a plenty,
For He has sent me three.

Our Betty is the eldest,
In adolescence tall,
And Carol in the middle
With flaxen curls that fall.

And let me not forget Georgia,
An angel in disguise,
For I can see the star dust,
When I look into her eyes.

I thought that I was blessed enough,
But much to my surprise,
He sent me yet another one,
A son to idolize.

I think He closed the book on that,
And said, "You've had your due;
Now be the kind of mother
Your God would want you to."

Georgia Rosen

To My Husband

Even though I don't always show it,
I'm sure you will always know it,
My love for you keep growing stronger,
I know it can only lost longer,
For you see,
You will always be,
The one and only love for me.
I love you.

Elaine M. Greensten

Memory Lane

I'm lost again in Memory Lane,
I'm trying to get home again,
So many roads lie up ahead,
Care must be taken where I tread.

Perhaps this stranger offers help,
To those who are alone,
Kind sir, can you direct me
On my proper path toward home?

You see, my roadway turned away
From all of those who care,
It's been so long, there's so much lost,
I need to hurry there.

The stranger said "go straight, be swift
From your path do not depart -
You'll find your happy Memory Lane
And those dear to your heart."

Jane Forbes Eckerl

Your Touch

That feeling

The warm, huge raindrops fall on me
In sands of deserts moonlit dusk,
Caress my face with gentle musk
Of brush on floors of steady seas.

The owl, her song so soft and slow,
Like music touching deepest heart.
The night grows cold and dark, apart
From your warm feel and soothing glow.

Touch me again

Jess Lawrence

"Jenny's Room"

She sits in the rocker
In a corner of the room
Arms thrown out, hair all askew,
Oh dearest dolly, I miss Jenny, too.

The rocking horse
That once brought laughter and glee
With tangled dark mane
Stands as still as can be.
Oh, rocking horse, so sturdy and true
I miss Jenny, too.

The tiny tea set, of porcelain blue
Sits on the table waiting for you.
Oh little tea set,
Do you miss my Jenny, too?

As I leave the room
In the dimming light
I reach for the doll and hold her tight.
Do I see a tear trickling from her eye?
Yes, dear dolly, I say with a sigh,
You are as lonely as I.

Joyce Hall Schiwart

Dream Lover

He comes out at night
In a way that makes me fright
You don't see him in the day
As someone might say

He is very romantic
Which makes him dramatic

In my dreams, it seems
Like we are running through meadows
While my head is laying
On my pillows

Laying in bed, I can almost
Feel him caressing me
Then my mom would come in
And say for him to let me be

I don't know how we
Could go on like this
He gave me a kiss
That I'll always miss

I was left under the cover
by my dream lover

Christina Scott

Untitled

The music faded
into empty space
the silence screamed
in my face

The air turned yellow
the clouds came down
my laughter went green
my smile went brown

Then I caught my breath
when I heard your eyes
then I saw your voice
and I heard no lies

And I turned the silence
in my hand
and I felt the music
of a soundless band

Bethany J. Lee

The Best Of The Years

My childhood was a great delight,
In fact, it was pure dynamite.
My teen age years were filled with joy,
There were the girls - I was a boy.

My middle years - beyond compare,
A pretty wife - three children fair.
And as I reached maturity,
All things kept going well for me.

And now retirement with my wife,
We have a pleasant, happy life.
With family and friends galore,
I really couldn't ask for more.

But now I sit in pensive thought,
And wonder what my life has wrought,
Which were the best of all the years,
With mostly smiles and fewest tears?

My vote to old age, I must give,
Considering the alternative!

Chuck Sexton

Thoughts Of My Newborn

Here I lie holding you
in my arms for the first time.
I'm so proud, so happy,
my eyes are all a-shine.

Here you are my baby,
my brand new son.
What a responsibility.
I'll try to be the best mom.

You're so small and fragile.
You need so much love.
Your skin is all soft and pink,
cuddle and hug.

Your father and I love you.
Patience we hope to have.
We'll try to protect you
from all out there that's bad.

Yes, here I lie holding you
in my arms for the first time.
I look at you and smile
with love on my mind.

Jodi F. Bernstein

A Guardian Angel

Last night as I lay thinking
in my bed so warm
I knew the Lord was keeping me
from all the worldly harm.

He sent an angel from heaven
to keep an eye on me,
To guide me in a Christian life
Thus fill my need to see.

I send my praises now to him
for all his tender care,
For when I seek Him on bended knee
He is always there.

He hears my prayers and answers
them as only God can do,
He teaches me to seek the right
and all that's good and true.

He has a plan for me I know
as He has for everyone.
For we must live our lives His way
To see our battles won!

Alice Halt

I Wonder...

I wonder what it is like for you
in the dark early hours
of the morning.
Do you sometimes lie awake,
tormented by your body?

There is love for you here
if you will only take it.
I would give it to you freely,
unashamedly.
Words wouldn't be necessary;
your beautiful eyes could speak to me,
your mouth and hands and manhood
could show me your desires
and I would satisfy them.
You could reveal yourself to me
in this way without fear;
I have already accepted that self
in my heart.
I wonder...will I ever touch you?

Diana Calvert

Edge Of Darkness

There is an evening echo
in the mesa

The edge of darkness
gathers up the sleeves of the past

Crickets moan a reverie
of the ancient ones

We are borne
in a shroud of mist

After the last smoke
of the warriors fire

Unable to capture
a star's veiled dream

Silence washes our faces

We awaken to the sun

Dian Taylor

Afraid To Say Goodbye

It's a cold, cold sun
In the pale summer sky
I don't love you anymore
There's no question why.
I gave you my love
But you wanted me to die.
We just kept going on
Afraid to say goodbye.
Push turned to shove
And you called it love.
You turned your back on me
So easily.
You were so mean to me
Constantly.
Things were just never the same
Life with you was so insane.
I'm not afraid to say goodbye.

Cindi Savage-Fox

Choice

I did not choose that I be born,
In this I had no say;
But I was dealt this precious life
To cope with day by day.

So many things I can't control
Since my sweet life began,
I take the good mixed in with bad,
And do the best I can.

The only thing I can control,
And I alone will know;
When life's no longer precious
I'll choose when I will go.

Florence Kolos

Starting Over

Out with the old
In with the new
Changing cloudy skies
Into ones of blue
Why is change
So very hard to do?

The sought answers
Are already there
Though maybe not
What we expected
Heart prayers to G-d
Choices so selected.

Standing straight and tall
Getting a second wind
Springtime in the heart
The hopeful future pinned
A fresh new beginning
And past memories rescind.

Judith C. Lynn

Life's Child

A child comes into the world
Innocent and free
Not knowing life's choices
or what his path will be

He looks to us for guidance
Direction and care
Testing life's waters
Expecting us always to be there

Through the ages he will learn
As the mystery of life unfolds
Carving out his way
Following his own goals

Soon he will be in our shoes
With the responsibility of life
Teaching from our example
Of what is wrong and right

With this in mind...
What a responsibility we bear
For all of life's children
To love, cherish and care.

Donna Dixson

True Innocence

Little fingers in mine entwine
Innocent eyes look into mine
Words unexpressed
Not yet the time.

Doris A. Burgess

Inhaling Universally

Breathing involuntarily, Wow!
Is it compassion striking,
But how?

With it, the heart lives to care
All the while, pumping, throbbing
No matter what to dare.

Onward going in and out,
With an ease of unawareness
As if knowing what it's about.

A gift indeed and yet,
What thanks is given
Not much, want to bet?

Continuing on as if no end,
Daily working, sustaining life,
Existing here, there, and at every bend.

Effortless, absorbing it now
Not even thinking,
Priceless, wow!

Barbara Brown

What Is Love?

"What is love?"
is love when you
hug someone?
is love when you
kiss someone?
is love when you
say you love someone?
is love when you
think you love someone?
-or-
is love when you
know you love someone?

Darcy Kuta

Jamaican Sweetness

Wrapped in chocolate
is my lover.
Wrapped in his arms
am I.
Melted by his charms
is my heart.
Soothed by his voice
inside my memory.

First time transformed
by his darkness.
Set free, to go home
by his soul.

Dark like me, His touch says quietly,
'Never again will you be alone.'

Devil's trick, God's gift?

With hoping,
It will be made good.
With patience, it will come again.
With prayer, it will never leave.

But for now, He lead me home.

Beth Anna MoonRay Ferguson

Untitled

Early to bed and early to rise
is not only stupid and asinine
it is also unwise.

Benjamin R. Fairbank

A Truckers Life

The life of a trucker
is only for the strong.
The highway is lonely
the miles are long.
His home and family
are far away,
Waiting for his calls
every other day.
Each evening they pray
to the Lord above,
To keep him safe
and tell him he's loved.
He gets home weekends
now and then,
To see his family and friends.
But all to soon
a load is ready.
He's back in his truck
his hands on the wheel,
Strong and steady.

Gloria Pazik

Euphoria

Beauty's imperfection
is the picture I behold,
twisted limbs and crooked trunks
reaching tall and bold.
Bushes sprayed with color
flutter in the breeze,
while shadows dance and hover,
in play beneath the trees
and nature's grace inspires me.

Jean Ann Kaitner

Blackened

Wandering in darkness
is this where I belong,
being punished for all my deeds
so now I sing my blackened song.

Drowning in this dark abyss
my love and friends I truly miss.
My tears dark, my heart gray,
take me from this damnation I pray.

Hoping that it won't be long,
but for now, blackened is my song.

Ben Wheeler

Life

To halt - to dream of days that were
Is to be no longer young
We cannot brood of friends now gone
On tunes no longer sung.

We must live with the times that are
Not dwell on pages turned
and struggle with the day that is
and not with candles burned.

Life is for the here - the now
An arc must have full swing
Death is just the moment's pause
When winter moves to spring.

William McCarran

For Love Of Susan And The Moon

The Moon
It belongs to you on this night
With its fullness
Standing over the night skies

The moon
Every time I see it full
When I am alone
I think of you

The moon
And you
Are the only shining moments
I enjoy with fullness.

Charles B. L. Kupa

Wind Song

The wind heard me crying;
it blew through the rain —
my voice longing for you,
but nobody came.

You touched my heart deeply.
You gave me great pain.
As leaves fall from trees,
I whispered your name.

I think of you often.
I ponder my fate.
I dance in my flame
though the hour grows late.

The wind rang my doorbell,
but you never knew
how much that I wanted
its sound to be you.

Janet Marie Bingham

"My Arthritis"

My Arthritis, how I dislike the word,
It comes and goes any time, who knows.
Times I suffer pain, times I cry,
Then, times I rub Ben-Gay or
Aspercreme.
Again I'll try Muscle Rub all I know,
Even then I don't know what to do.

I won't try Aspirin nor Advil by mouth,
The doctor advises not to do.
It doesn't agree with stomach pain,
So I just sit and don't complain.
For my Arthritis is there to stay,
I'll get along just the same.

Catherine M. Karpiak

Seasons

Even tho seasons truly never die
It does make my heart sigh
To see their time just fly on by
First it is time to say a big hi
Then within a flash it waves goodbye

Winter, spring, summer or fall
There's no need to ever bawl
It's like walking down a hall
Or think of a shopping mall
Each doorway beckons you to call

With each new season coming upon us
Think of each as a christmas
Brightly shining, all aglow just for us
There is a need to make a fuss
It again is renewal time for all of us

Edith Barrett

The Waterfall

The water glides to the falls
It does not hesitate at all
Rushing past me over rocks,
It seems as though it almost talks...
of summer joys and fishing boys
of little girls with water toys
But on it goes to reach its height
And topples over in sheer delight.

Carol Louise Dennis

How Long

I guess she doesn't love me now
It hurts so much I've cried.
What was a happy, health man,
Is just an empty shell inside.
No feelings, no emotions, no love to
hold on too.
Just emptiness and sadness,
Cause he knows that he lost you.
He trusted you completely.
An gave away his heart.
Now all that's left is loneliness
So cold, an oh so dark.
Winters can be lonely,
But spring will always come.
Just how long does it take a man,
Who's lost his own true love.

Danny R. Anderson

On The Wings Of Angels

Listen, hear my voice,
it is I who calls to you.
I am with you, I am your shield.
It is I who guides you through.

Listen, make still your heart.
It is through your life I rise.
Do you see me, for I am Love?
I am in your brothers eyes.

Listen, feel my breath.
Have you seen me through the crowd.
Do you know me? You spoke to me.
I have called your name out loud.

I am ever in your life,
on the left and on the right.
Where you search, I will be there,
Just follow the Light.

On the wings of Angels,
you will learn to fly.
On the wings of Angels,
you will touch the sky.

Curry Scott

Remembering

Remember your blessings
Instead of your crosses
Remember your gains
Instead of your losses
Remember your smiles
Instead of your tears
Remember your courage
Instead of your fears
Remember your good health
Instead of your wealth.
Remember praise God
Instead of yourself!

Ann K. Hust

Future

The thick, black darkness surrounds us
It is the blanket of death
From our stabs come screams of cuss
Until finally the last breath

This is something we must face
Our mother we have killed
No longer hang our head in disgrace
There is nothing left to feel

The masks are now, not two, just one
Comedy no longer exists
The blackness reflects the damages done
Temptation too strong to resist

From an eternal sleep we will never wake
To find the morning light
A recurring nightmare we can't shake
We finally lost the fight

Billie Ruppe

Perfection

Perfection is: completeness,
It is the enlightened whole,
The embodiment of spirit,
An eternal warmth.

Perfection is: the alpha,
It is the circle of being,
The omega of consciousness,
A love of life.

Perfection is: innocence,
It is the birth of the soul,
The uniting of karma,
A beautiful thought.

Perfection is: the Source,
it is the pattern of existence,
The emotions of time,
A dream to Be.

Jandy Hanna

Sorrow Will Pass

When our life is full of sorrow,
It's hard for us to look for tomorrow.
We know in our heart,
there will be a better day,
With God here with us,
To lead the way.
He will lead us into,
A much better life,
Where there is no sorrow,
Troubles or strife.
We say "Please Lord,
Don't let these Troubles Last".
Then we remember His words,
"THIS TOO SHALL PASS".

Elouise Collins Mason

Untitled

Only the lonely only the few
knew of the pain that time saw to renew

Only the sound of the wind in the trees
only the look of love you gave to me

Gone forever without a trace
never again to see your face
alone
alone
so very alone

Antoinette M. Sarnoski

Love

It has to do with everything.
It's in our every breath.
It keeps us with the one we want,
It stays with us in death.
It keeps us warm,
It makes us whole,
It takes us all the way.
It carries us on wings of gold,
It changes every day.
It never shrinks,
It only grows,
It's bigger than the sun.
It gives our soul an inner light,
It leads us to the one.

Doug Isaacson

Wisdom's Son

Because you were unable to accept its light—when it was wrapped in task, Wisdom fled you:
Its hasty runaway was Swift and Sure; fleeing with trodden thumping feet the stubborn rebellion of Your Youth:
It picked up pace as you chased it with seams and angles you wrestled and claimed from shadow's sight:
It escaped your grasp to wait — basking in the light beyond shadow to pass the remnants of its stunning wake to more patient consul:

It was afraid, My Son, that you would wrestle it perversely as it was fleeing your indifference; that it should die a moment only:
And so, quell The sure'ty of its Everlasting Truth.

John Martane

The Crystal Waters

So you say you're leaving
It's sad to see you go
But it's really nothing new to me
I've lived alone since long ago
Like a ship out on the ocean
The wind carries me along
The sunset only leaves me wishing
There's still some place I belong

Look deep into the ocean
These are the Crystal Waters
Thousands have sailed upon them before
Travelers, poets, kings and martyrs
They all sailed to find themselves
On some favorable shore
Living out those tranquil years
They only dreamed of before
They gather shells along the shoreline
As they stroll in the ocean breeze
Or sit upon some quiet mountain
With their eyes on these changing seas

Alric C. Clay

The Golden Ring

Catch the golden ring, lad,
It's sparkling in the sun;
Just below where the angels sing
Your life has just begun.

Close not yourself away
Beneath the bleak despairing;
There's beauty, love and laughter,
To enfold you in its caring.

Joyful strains fill day and night;
Wonders never cease;
Reach upward - outward - for the ring;
There you'll find release.

When you catch it, hold it tight;
Clasp it close to you;
When the dark begins to fall,
Let its light shine through.

This rocky road is not all fair;
It's only from our sorrow
That we must catch the golden ring,
And find our bright tomorrow.

Dorothy A. Willingham

Something

Something's there,
It's watching me,
But I don't know where.
I wonder if he can see me,
Because I can't see him.

Something's there,
But I don't know where,
Is it in the sea,
Or the air?
Oh, how this confuses me!

He's watching me,
Or is it a she?
Or maybe them,
Instead of him.

Something's there,
But I don't know where.
I wonder if he can see me,
Because I can't see him.

Erin Light

Here We Live In

God's earth so fair
Killing innocent people in despair
Living in a world of violence
Actually, who should care
There will never be world peace
for all to share.
Always some moron
Just lurking right out there
Government's play with their people
Like it's just a game,
Go to other countries.
Try to put them to shame;
Let's play a game
Of modern day chess;
Don't use nuclear weapons,
They could make a big mess;

Gary P. Bechard Jr.

Open Arms

Dedicated in memory of Marge Landwehr

With open arms I come to you, my
journey just begun,

Once again we'll be together, a
mother and her son.

No more lonely memories, as together
we will be,
Joined in love and peaceful hearts,
amidst our family.

Thou tears there may be many,
allow them just to flow, united now
we stand here, happy you must know.
Now we have each other, and with
strength we stand as one, as we look
down among you, this mother and her son.

With open arms we'll wait for you,
to reunite this family - as time
helps heal our hearts, stronger we shall be.

So brush the tears from your eyes, in
Heaven we shall remain, waiting for
our loved ones, to join us once again.

Connie Wesenberg

Know A Fellow

When you get to know a fellow
Know his joys, and know his cares.
When you've come to understand him,
And the burden that he bears.

When you learn the right he's making
And the troubles in his way.
You find that he is different
Than thought of him yesterday.

You find the faults are trivial,
And there's not so much to blame.
In the fellow you jeered at
When you only knew his name.

You are quick to see the blemish
in the distant neighbors style.
You point at all his errors
And sneer at him the while.

When drawn a little closer
Till your hand sand shoulders touch.
You find the faults you hated
Do not amount too much.

James Lowe

Lady Bug

Lady bug, lady bug,
land on my nose; tickle
me softly with your
lady bug toes.
Lady bug, lady bug land
on my hand, I'll shake
you off gently to
lady bug land.

Amanda Van Cleave

Untitled

Alone I stand
Left once again by a man
This fate that follows me
Is beginning to hollow me
And soon, beside a man
Alone I will stand!

Dawn D. Austin

Violent Soul

Let the rage out of your body,
let the hurt out of your soul.
Let you be the way you are,
let no one bring you down.
Let your mind think the thought,
let nobody tell you no.
Let you be a free spirit,
let no one tie you down.

Amanda Arrington

Little People

Hey, little people
Let's go, go, go
Hey, little people
Let's look at the show
Let's see the birds
Doing a dance
Come on, everyone
Let's give them a chance
Hop, skip and jump
What do you say
Come on, everyone
We're going to stay

Christine Zalewski

Happy New Year 1995

Happy New Year, 1995!
Let's make it the best year ever —
As we've cleaned out our home —
Let's also clean out our mind —
And, leave the debris —
of 1994 behind!

Let's release each other —
With kindness and respect —
To live our own lives —
As we each see fit —
And, when we come together —
Which, I hope that we will —
We will come as friends —
With truth and peace in our heart —
Where we can all live joyously —
Together or apart!

Let's make 1995 a turning point —
Where all our dreams come true —
I'm wishing a peaceful and prosperous 1995 —
To all of you!!

Avis W. Fosler

Disguise And Shame

Let's play the games
Let's smile our lies away
Let's dance the guilt in pretense
Our shame shall be awide
When truth is revealed.

Let's mellow our secrets in disguise
Let's laugh our dishonest victory
Let's hide in secret shame
Our regrets shall be full
When truth unclouds our secrets.

Joshua Satty

Life

The madness of it all,
Life, how ironic it is.
First you are shoved,
Then you are pulled,
Yanked, and shoved again.
Explanations, I have none,
Irritating as it all is,
You either laugh or avoid it.
Some even forget.
What is your method of staying sane?

Howard J. Varney

Life

Life is good
Life is fair
Life is hard
Life is soft
Life is a gift
Life is swift
Life is hot
Life is cold
Life is friendly
Life is being sick
Life is being sick of people
Life is crying
Life is smiling
Life is being hurt
Life is love
Life is hate
Life is stupid
Life makes sense
Life is dying
This is life and I am living it.

Jonathan W. English

October

Three chickadees
Lifted by the wind in their
tumbling act.
Their song an invisible shadow,
trailing

Freshly fallen leaves
Gleaming through still water.
A brilliant mosaic
Lining the hidden woodland pool.

The mulberry tree
Undressed by invisible shears
stands ankle deep
In a petticoat of ruffled
gold.

Alice Spencer

Dreams of Glass

Dreams of glass
Like clouds in a bubble
Though sometimes De'Javue

As life goes past
We often stumble
but angels never do

We can see the colors
Yet not smell the rainbow
And never wonder why

But if the ground was above
And the sky was below
We'd have to fall to fly

Bill White

Reckoning Day

A burst of light wondering by
lightning rips through the sky.
Clouds rolling fast, low, and wide
take shelter, it's time to hide.

Thunder hurling through the air
sound shattering so nice and fair.
The second warning is what we hear
natures power shows no fear.

Winds whirling and whipping around
destroying with a whistling sound.
Pounding on everything in its path
keeping on its devastating wrath.

Rain blasting down so fast
reservoirs will not last.
Blurring every creatures eyes
wondering what controls the skies.

Erik Januszkiewicz

"Free And Easy"

Free and easy
Like a bird
That is flying
In the sky.
Why not be free
Of taxes?
Why not
Have easy living?
Free and easy ...
I'm sitting
In my favorite tree
Writing
Free and easy,
And I thought
If life were free and easy
Then that white bird
Soaring high above me
Would join my world.
I could offer it a seat
Next to me in my favorite tree.

Christine Morris

Memories Of Dad

My Dad isn't here,
like all of yours today.
He died when I was two,
alive he could not stay.

I don't remember much,
about how he used to be,
all I have to know him,
are pictures of him and me.

He's been gone for along time,
it's been more than ten years;
usually when I think of him,
I wipe away the tears.

God must have told him,
that it was time for him to die,
but why did God take my Daddy, away;
before I could say Good-bye?

Jasmine Ballinger

Images

Shattered;
Like broken glass
My dreams and aspirations...
Tiny pieces crashing to the ground.

You gently picked them up
And re-assembled them
In a far different pattern
Than I had ever thought of.

The breaking was painful;
The re-assembling, confusing,
But I had to let go
And let you complete your work.

And now, out of my brokenness
I am completely and forever whole,
And in the mirror
I see a far nicer image that wasn't there before.

Johnny Plyler

For Today

The sun will rise tomorrow
Like every other day
But somehow you'll be different
Just how, is hard to say

The lesson of the ages
Finds truth more frequently
Your time of age has come around
There's more for you to see

Your audience will grow larger
Your performance must improve
And when you witness inspiration
By choice, your heart will move

And so, tomorrow's sun rises
All new, so fresh, and so clean
In your life, a spark is ignited
For today, you are sixteen

John Burke Halford

Walking Along In Silence

You walk in moonlight
like the oceans that sing...
You come to me in silence
with soft, gentle wings.

Your gentle whispers
speak to me in waves...
like the first eve's fallen star
that my memory will save.

Eternity feels like seconds
when you're by my side.
Winter winds that blew in
feelings of love, that I cannot deny.

The time slides by
as the sun sets on hills.
As I'm driving to you
I know finally, how love feels.

Amber McFadden

Untitled

Up and down
Like tides of time.
Back and forth
Like rhythm and rhyme.
An intense beauty
Pale as the moon.
Warm summer sunshine
Bright as noon.
Dark and dismal
a thunderous cloud
A wolf's lonely howl
Clear and loud
Visions of the past
Although there are few
If you look in my eyes
You will see they are true

Frances Riehl

Life's Changes

Life is beautiful and grand as
long as I walk with my
Lord hand in hand.
Life has away of changing
from day today. But my Lord
helps me find the way.

There are roads we must
travel on and at the bend
of each, you can see churches
and hear the pastors preach

The songs coming from within
makes me feel so good and at peace.
I know I can go on my way,
for you see I have the Lord
forever and a day.

Joyce Darlene Riutort

Pain Neglect

Sit here bored, stop talking
Look what is happening around
Can't you see anything
Feel, See, Hear, Hate
The pain exists here
Not in the streets or cities
Here in my heart, HERE
I look about myself
See so much hurt held back
Poster near me - pictures
I once knew those
Long ago I love 'em all
Love - long ago, long killed
So sad is the death
Not of people, places
But of thoughts - nonexistent
Forgive - Forget - Fear
I guess I'm doomed
Fall head first to Georgia

Jill Nolde

What Is Love?

What is love all about
Love is something we don't doubt.
Love is something we can share
Love is always in our prayer
God is love that we know
Love is something that we show
So show your love in all you do
And it will always come back to you.

Betty Morris

Emptiness

I walk along the avenue,
looking at the stars.
I walk into an empty street,
full of empty cars.

Up the road a bit,
the light turns green.
Something should have happened,
but it was just as it had been.

I take a few steps,
out of the street.
It's like everything had died,
in just a heart beat.

I start running down the street,
my heart is full of fear.
And falling from my face,
a single, solo tear.

Then I realize,
I'm the only one.
All the streets are empty,
I'm the only one.

Josh Bellinger

Greed

I sit and stare
looking out the window
where is the clean air?
Where did it go?

There use to be a field
with patches of flowers.
It was bought and dealt
to the higher powers.

The factory was built.
The asphalt lot laid.
Yet there was no guilt,
because many jobs were made.

The factory is closed.
The higher powers have gone away.
In the field that they bull-dozed,
their sign of greed will stay.

Cassie Sweeney

And So On....

Mourn the souls
Lost to you in your very presence
Neglect or apathy
Drifted away in the guise of life
Or the business thereof

Watch the families silent screams
With the initial cuts
Silent cries of acceptance to follow
Wounds heal
Impact lessens to the business of life

Souls in black
Antiquated dreams

Where is the young girl skipping
In love with life
Surrounded by the strength of family

She cries aloud

Dolores Conley

Life

Life is made of love
Love is made of kisses.
Kisses are made of hugs.
Hugs are made of you.
You are made of Life.
Life is made of friends.
Friends are made of understanding.
Understanding is made of listening.
Listening is made of respect.
Respect is made of Life.
Life is made of family.
Family is made of strength.
Strength is made mind.
Mind is made of heart.
Heart is made of Life.
Life is made of happiness.
Happiness is made of sadness.
Sadness is made of depression. Depres-
sion is made of life.
Life is made of you. You are made of me.
Make your life what you want it to be

Diana Garrett

Love In The Eyes Of The Beholder

Love is not an item,
Love is not a test.
It is not a competition,
to see who will turn out best.

Love is but a power,
a power of great source.
Not only does it hold good,
it holds an evil force.

Love is a feeling,
a feeling of great joy,
for without this great feeling,
we are but only a used toy.

Love is an emotion,
an emotion of great strength,
for love is any size,
love is any length.

In the eyes of the beholder:

Danilo Kovilic

Love

Love is faithful
Love is true
Love makes all things
Seem like new.

Love is hopeful
Love is kind
Love has the other one's
Needs in mind.

Love is joyful
Love is growing
In kind deeds
Always sowing.

Love is ageless
It knows no time
It knows no reason
It knows no rhyme.

Love is ours
To have and to hold
To keep on enjoying
As older we grow.

Drucilla M. Edgar

Lost Hope

When we were younger,
love was so important.
We listened to songs on the radio,
or walked to school with friends.
The future seemed to be bright
as we looked with innocent eyes,
never seeing the dangers,
which would suddenly appear,
creating hazards and fear
to a generation weaned on hope.
And the words of Camelot
seem to be so far away
like all the distant stars
in a remote galaxy of the Universe.
And we wander like clouds
lost, searching and seeking
for the answers to our questions
in all the wrong places.

Eve Jeanette Blohm

Mad And Annoyed

I feel mad and annoyed
mad and annoyed about our world
mad and annoyed that other people
don't care
mad and annoyed that other people
don't feel mad and annoyed
and they're not willing
to give up their happiness
to feel mad and annoyed
and do something about our world
with the rest of us
mad and annoyed people.

Andi Tomczak

The Bench Of Gold

The bench of gold
Makes me sit still and listen
To the pansies and buttercups
Chatter.
Grass waving,
Beckons to me.
I see the fragrance
Of the flowers;
But only if I sit
On the bench of gold.
Mysteries are solved,
Hurts are healed
When I sit on the bench of gold, —
The bench at the edge
Of my imagination!

Joshua Clay Phillips

Reality

Many Strands
Many Colors
Many Chords
Pass though darkness
Emerge into light
One Thread
One Pattern
One Harmony
Perfect Love
Perfect Unity
Perfect Joy

Freda Kimmey

One Dozen Stacked in a Sack from Steinek's Baker Downtown Mineral City, 1966

Powdered sugared puffs from
maple cream-filled clouds hung

thick in sunbeams as I blew
the wisps to our worn-off

gold-rimmed special glass
plate when I was just eight.

Joan E. Shroyer-Keno

Celestial Seasons

I see
Maple flame, aspen gold
halos circling harvest moon
frost feathered breezes

I hear
Crystal light crackling night
quiet flocked evergreens
silvered whispers of joy

I feel
Pale green beginnings
soft-winged springlight
moss dance

I am
Icarus in star form
Northern lights soaring
mystic, magic life

There are angels
everywhere...

Carrie Everhart

Good-Bye Gramp

Just one year ago,
March 8, 1994,
I laid down on the floor,
and cried and cried,
I could not believe you had died,
why, why did leave, why,
I never said good-bye,
I miss those days,
When we'd have fun all day,
Then at night stop and pray,
Why, why did you leave,
I can't believe,
You are gone,
Up in the havens,
With God,
I love you,
I miss you,
Good-bye

Elizabeth Lindberg

Untitled

The political machine is
night
Making her parachute
ring
Under one window
light
With wrist holder during
a wedding watch.

Gal Camperlengo

Happy Valentine's Day

Happy, Happy Valentine's Day
May Your Day be full of Love
And You find Love all along Your Way
May the Sun Shine on You from Above

May Your Heart be Filled
With Sunlight and Flowers
Where Much Love has Spilled
And Love Rains down as Showers

May You give Love to Others
In a Special Graceful Way
That each Heart You Touch
Be Especially Blessed Today.

Gloria Gober

"Memories"

Memories will be made of this
Memories of our very last kiss
Memories to have and to hold
Memories to enjoy when I'm old
Memories that you have given me
Memories that won't set me free,
Those memories bring sparkle to my eyes
Those memories also make me cry.
For those are the memories
When there was a "you and me".
Now that you're gone,
And I'm left on my own,
Those memories just won't leave me
alone.

Grace Moore

For My Abode

I would like the smell of Pine,
Mingled with the Misty Brine,
Spraying toward my Mooncliff House.
There I'll spend my time!

There should be a haze of white,
Clouds afloat within the night.
Nature's silence sweet to hear
Just for my Delight.

Jean Juline

This House

What makes this house,
more than just four walls;
Rooms with banging doors,
and empty halls.

Could it be the love,
that we two share;
Even when not together,
we really do care.

Is it total respect,
you have been shown;
A total true equality,
that has been known.

Little children's laughter,
a joyful shout;
Your smiling, happy face,
wandering all about.

Yes, all these things,
more than wood and stone;
Make this more than a house,
they've made it our home.

Herbert E. Davis Jr.

Wild Flowers

Wild flowers you can always find
most any place you look
Amidst the very tallest of trees
or beside a swollen brook.

They also can be found pressed flat
preserved for years to come,
Within the pages of old books
of times we were so young.
To climb the highest mountain peak
there to they can be found,
a fragrance that's so fresh and clean
just growing from the ground.

Brian Neelands

Kristen

Kristen
my beloved
savage as a wolf
yet
gentle as lamb
she is the devil
as well as an angel
hunting
for the human spirit
an immortal
living amongst
mortal kind
reaching out
for
their liquid life
to quench her everlasting thirst
a thirst
of a
vampire

Abner O'Neil Parramore

Bleeding Love

By candle light
my blood stained hands
reach for you now
shadows not they.
Lay scarcely awake
side by side
longing to hold you.
Caressed in blood
feeling heat of thee
flesh pierced
soul intertwine.
Hear the thoughts
twirling round
know my pain
feel the love,
flooding my veins.

Erin-Kelly Hulbert

Forever May You Shine

"If I could catch a falling star,
my dreams would all come true
For the light of a star from heaven
would be shared with all of you.
But until I catch this star,
I will keep this thought in mind,
I've only to look inside me
for there, this light I'll find."

Bruce S. Merola

What I Feel Is Real

My love so hard to express.
My heart so afraid of rejection.
My life I wanted to love.
and be loved.

My love is SO REAL.
My love is FOREVER.
My love will NEVER DIE.

As we may fade away,
or be worlds apart -
My heart just aches.
and my body hungers
for your touch.
My mind will never forget
your voice
My body will never feel
what I feel when I'm
with you.

My soul will remember
you.

Cyndi Ray

Catch The Wind

When I was but a child,
my imagination ran wild
with thoughts of what I'd
someday be,

Yet now that I'm older,
the world seems much colder.
And it's quite plain to see.

That it's a tough row to hoe,
when most of what you sow,
are seeds of frustration and woe.

So, hoist your sails,
catch the wind,
let your voyage begin.

Don't wait for your ship to come in.

Catch the wind.

Dan Benton

My Yesterdays

Just can't let go of yesterdays
My life has changed in so many ways
If I could live my life again
Instead of five kids
I would have had ten
Then the laughs would have
lasted longer
And my heart would have stayed full
Maybe I would have felt stronger
And the past would not have such a pull
I hope I don't feel this way till the
Day I die
But the "Empty Nest Syndrome"
Is not a lie.

Cecilia Ramsay

Prayer For Guidance

Close to the future
Near to the past
Caught in limbo
With present tasks
I cannot go back
I must go on
Lord, guide my steps
Into the unknown

Barbara Cowen

Ode To My Son

I rode the clouds so soft, so white
My spirit was as light as they:
For I could look beyond today
And trust His mercy in my flight
I see a son, with family dear
My spirit reached and drew them near
Each one so different, yet the same
And more and more the loving came

The days pass quickly down below
But what a joy to see them grow
Remembering all those happy years
And sometimes shed a prayerful tear

The future's unknown, the past is gone
But up so high I drift along
To ride the clouds and dream awhile
And picture loved ones funny smiles
My spirit calmly bids me rest
For in His care, He knoweth best
I'd like to say the clouds are mine
But NO! They are a gift of Time.

Grace P. Alex

Insomnia

Who's this villain stealing my sleep
Nameless and without a face.
Too many long hours I keep
With a companion I can't place.

You know me, but I know you not
Draining my strength and energy.
Driving me on toward - exactly what?
Where's the pleasure you get from me.

Onward and onward throughout the night
You puzzle me to no end.
I fail to see reason for my plight
And no reward do you send.

Why have you chosen me to haunt
What makes you torture so.
Is there no way to end your taunt
And forever let me go.

Eileen P. Banyai

Untitled

Joint Venture Opportunity
Navigator desires Captain
Sail to the Unknown
Make a Dream come True
Interested Party apply in Person
Rendezvous under the Evening Sky
Sparkling with Stars and
The Enchanted Moon
Raise Crystal Goblets filled with Wine
A toast, "Destiny".

Learning, Sharing, Enjoying each Other
Communicating Essentials and Aspirations
Understanding No One is Perfect
Working Together, Encouraging and
Developing into the Best
Each of Us can Be
Ultimately Walking as Partners...
Side by Side, Hand in Hand
Together
You and Me.

Bonnie Austin-Bator

Two Giraffes

Two giraffes running
Neck and neck against the clock
So they too can live.

Idell J. Shore

Two Women I Love

Two women I love
Neither will bend
Feelings in their hearts
Each choose to defend

Time now grows short
For thoughts they shall bare
What matters that count
Have not been made clear

When will they see
What this turmoil does
Especially too these
Two women I love

Dick Dinan

Our Wonderful World

If all the leaves on all the trees
never changed their colors
If all the animals lived on and on
with no room left for others

If the sun was always over you
the moon was over me
What an enormous difference
our two lives would be.

We'd miss the freshness of the spring
the beauty of the fall.
We'd miss the time in winter when there
are no leaves at all.

Our world would be a crowded place
with creatures everywhere,
No place to run, no quiet place
on land or sea or air.

The hardest part of living in
this boring, crowded space,
I'd never see you, touch your hand,
or feel your warm embrace.

Clara K. Pinion

The Internal Trap

Greatness in a Jar
Never going far
Only within my mind
Are these feelings that I find

Wonder what it'll take
To make the great escape
To break the bands that hold
This life within its fold

Wanting to run away
But can't seem to make it sway
Rooted deep and firm
With only room to squirm

All appears to be
Not what you really see
Distorted by a vision
Of a rhyme without a reason

Nothing more to say
Can't seem to find the way
A battle not to win
For the loss is from within

Garnette Marsh

Locked

Keep on smiling
Never had close
Friends of others not
You were never liked very
Much pain from being
Alone with nowhere to
Turn to death but who
Knows how lonely
You really
Are still smiling

Jami Nydam

Unborn Child

You are grasped from my existence
never to be born
before I wanted you.
Time erases the numbness,
sorrow fills my soul,
and the perpetual ache reminds me.
Never to feel you in my arms
to see your tiny face
to have your love
to hear you call me mommy.
Such a harsh punishment
for adolescent uncertainty...
this constant pain of knowing that
I'm sorry
will never be enough.

Brenda A. Kallay

The Curtain Now Must Fall

Hush, the drowsy birds that call
Night is here.
Black, the curtain now must fall
Black and clear.
Clear, the sky with many stars
Clear and bright.
Bright, the brilliant, silver moon
Sails the night.
The soothing hand of death
That beckons nigh
And, as the body reach't
Its final goal,
Called to the fathomless depths
Of someone's soul
To send it winging upward
To the sky.

Frances Crowder

No One Cares

No one cares
No one cares about feelings
No one knows my feelings
No one wants to respect my thoughts
Everyone thinks they're the best
But no one's the best
Why do they do this to me
My tears mean nothing
Why is your voice so demanding?
What did I say or do?
I'm sorry please don't hurt me anymore
The process never ends
The tears flow again
No one cares

Cathy Huffman

Death

There are the sounds of silence
No weeping sorrow
There is hope for today
But there's never tomorrow
Cover me in your darkness
Living in Eternal Hell
Come not for my heart
But my soul as well.
Scars unbearable taking its share
I breath not the sky
But are lost somewhere.
Sail on wings in an Endless Flight
Fly Oh fly, right on through the night

James Buckley

"Maybe"

"No" is not the answer
Nor is "Yes". In the constant
Struggle between "this" or "that"
Lies the unfolding of all
The possibilities. The "Maybe's".
Our world craves exactitude;
Seeks absolutes - the clear cut.
Yet, unachievable in the
Chaos of change, of mobility,
We grope for certainties still.
It is in the eye of the artist,
The ear of the musician,
The heart of the poet,
The wonderment of the spirit
(Which we all contain)
That lie the answers, which
Come to us mysteriously,
Unannounced, un-heralded.

Alwyn L. Powell

What A Day

The sun was shining
Not a cloud in the sky
The wind was still
It was beautiful to the eye
Oh the sight
For anyone to see
Just look to the right
And you shall laugh with glee
The grass is so green
The trees so straight
Birds looking for a stream
To fill their thirst
What a beautiful day to sing
To Our Master, Lord and King
Giving Him thanks for everything
The One who loves every human being

Barbara Emerson

Birthdays

I wake up and think,
Oh no not today.
Another Birthday?
Didn't I have one yesterday?
Lord let me enjoy the day
And think not of the years.
The day is over, I am free
No more shrinking and thinking
Not until another year
Of feeling young and ageless

Blanche Sabatini

"To Home, From Nowhere"

Throw passion from the thoughts,
not love be my demise.
So many shattered hearts lie bleeding
under cold September skies.
Ocean be my refuge,
behold my endless cries.

Gray gloom upon the desert floor,
where life forever thirsts.
Pent up in my cold dark cell,
my heart on sleeve bleeds cursed.
Ocean lying distant,
my mind shall think of first.

Relentless I shall rise again,
out of my seeming doom.
My presence back upon the shores,
my promise it shall loom.
As I watch the waters of the ocean,
make love with summer moon.

Jeffrey L. Walker

dilemma

Dilemma

do the right thing
NOW WHICH WAY SHOULD I GO?
don't make mistakes
IS THIS LOVE THAT I SHOW?

damned if I do
LIFE IS PULLING AT ME!
damned if you don't
WHAT'S MY PRIORITY?

care for others
IS THE ANSWER OUT THERE?
care for yourself
IT MUST BE-BUT WHERE?

their feelings count
I HAVE WANTS AND NEEDS TOO!
my feelings count
DEAR GOD WHAT DO I DO?!

Cheryl Quickle

Neutron Bomb

There not a soul here,
nowhere to turn to;
talk to somebody,
have a glass of whisky;
a bottle of beer,
an innocent kiss,
or have in my bed a girl, a woman...
a prostitute

The winter is cold,
my soul is freezing;
my thoughts are nothing but air:
but bear, creature bear!
This is your world,
you created this fear -
Take a look, deep into your soul,
and weep, my brother, weep.

Bela Kleiner

The First Christmas

In this wise, beneath the skies
Of Bethlehem, a Child is born;
While shepherds sigh, His Mother's eyes
Behold God's Son, first Christmas morn.

While oxen low, and candles glow,
Three wise men kneel before the Babe,
Who will bestow on mankind's woe
An unction, triumph o'er the grave.

The angels sing, the heavens ring
With hymns of peace and songs of joy;
Their message brings to man new springs
Of hope, of love none can destroy.

Dave Heilman

Untitled

A map, a guide, and a package
of deeded properties

All the essentials for a gold
miners topography

High banking, dredging, camping
and panning

The activities on the prospectors
landing

Shovels and picks and the
shocking size boulder

Black sands and an eye
opening gold nugget
unfolding

Mother lode country
and all that's been found

What a telling, what a mission
you have gold fever bond.

Emily Waltjen

Siblings

We've heard a lot of stories
Of family feuds and such;
Of brothers who are fighting,
Of sisters, just as much.

And they often speak of "in-laws"
In a not-so-kindly way;
They "hate to go to their place -
And have to spend the day."

Perhaps because of Mom and Dad
And parents of our spouses,
We are all most welcome
At any of our houses.

All together all too seldom,
Wish it could be more.
When it happens, how we relish
That knock upon the door.

Not so close to smother -
We've different goals and ends;
But all agree our siblings are
Our oldest, dearest friends.

Evelyn Rose Briggs

The Messenger

Riding upon the wings
Of season's change
The colorful leaves of Autumn
Write messages in the sky,
Along the walk,
Through the garden,

In a last minute flourish
Eager to complete the cycle.

Coming to rest in harmonious surrender,
Whispers goodbye to Summer
Welcomes the compelling tranquility
Of Winter's approach.

Jewel Shell

Judgement Seat

I just fell out
of the Judgement Seat,
but wasn't fortunate enough
to land on my feet.
The fall was expected
for I'm well aware
there's not enough room
for both God and me there.
So I need to remember
when I harbor a grudge,
that I should stand at attention
and let God sit as the Judge.

Bobbie J. Northrop

Unconditional Love

We shared the good and shared the bad
Oh but what a life we had
Our good times took us everywhere
I always felt his loving care
We dealt with many bad times too
He was there to help us through
Our greatest gift came from above
God gave us unconditional love
Now that his work on earth is done
That love will help me carry on

Judith Lubarsky

Kurt C

Oh my dear Kurt
Oh how it does hurt
To see your life end like this.
You had it all.
How hard did you fall?
I sure do wish you had missed
Poor Courtney love
She was your dove
She'll tell Frances Bean about you
Come back in their dreams
Explain what you've seen
Your songs will give them a clue.
And if you will please
Give you talent to me
I will use it with great strength
Your words make no sense
But listen again
Think sad thoughts and stretch their length
His death was in April, not March or May
So, what's going on in heaven today?

Ellen Emmons

A Delightful Dream

I stood on a mountain top
Oh so high.
I felt I could reach
To the sky.
God touched me with
"Freedom"
As I stood there.
The wind was blowing
Through my hair.
The white clouds
filled the sky.
Like symbols of purity
floating by.
That is what gave me
"Peace of Mind."
It was Tennessee
God's country
For me to see
And love.

Faye Sizemore

Sparrow Tree

God is a Sparrow Tree
on a rain mist morning
dreary with predictable pattern
yet full of expectation chatter.
Sparrow Tree, full of welcome
twigs and hollows,
a place for all, great and small.
Raging storm and summer heat,
Sparrow Tree stands to meet
with welcome arms
the weary, tired travelers.
Sparrow Tree, alive with life
fluttering and shimmering
in morning breeze and blizzard snow,
bending branches low to comfort all
against the rage.
Timeless age, Sparrow Tree,
comfort me.

Elizabeth McNeal Whitehead

Shadow My Cat "I Luv You"

Walking in my room,
On dark and silent nights,
Staying with me in the darkness,
Until darkness turns to light.
Meets me at the door,
When I come home from school,
We go into the kitchen,
And play with his white spool.
When we eat supper,
He jumps up on my chair,
I gently put him down,
and he gives me a kitty stare.
When I go to sleep,
He jumps up on my bed,
Then he curls up,
Around my head.
And so it happens,
All over again,
I can just hope,
He lives longer than I am.

Alyssa Conard

Unbidden Guest

Sorrow comes unbidden to every heart
On each page of life, it plays a part;
The sweet-scented rose has its thorns
Sorrow oft the tender heart adorns.

Life is a world of sorrow
Which each must overcome
To merit the crown of tomorrow
Promised by the Almighty One.

Janet M. Pelissier

Resigned

Standing alone
On this small kissing stone
Hoping with anticipation.
Looking for you
But instead, seeing the view
Of Long Valley with great resignation.

Deette A. Little

Empty Containers

Lonely bottle
on window sill
moans
as breeze brushes by;
contradicting
dancing sun spots
on the rug.

I danced with you
like that,
once.
Now,
my spirit moans
for your touch,
waiting
by the window.

Charlene Masterton

Did You

Did you stop to smell the flowers
on your way through life today
Did you offer any kind words
to a friend along the way
Did you feel the cleansing beauty
of a fresh breeze on your face
Did you Thank God for the many things
He gives to you each day
The sun was out there shining
Oh, so brightly in the sky
Did you take the time to notice it
As you hurried by
Tonight, when all was silent
And you settled down to rest
Did you find yourself satisfied
Because you'd done your best

Beverly James

Untitled

Ah, sweet scepter waiting in the wings,
Once before your scythe was raised -
Once reprieved.
Withhold not thy lily hand,
Thy icy stare -
I have no need of second chances now -
Nor thirds.
Welcome departure from the living death.

Judith Butler

Losing Your Way

It starts simply
one wrong turn
sends you down a shady path
and the nights seem long
highways leading no where
and you forget from where you came
and who you used to be

Where is the road
to take me home again

Gilda Malone

Forever

Time together
Onward bound-
Look at all
the love we've found.

You were there
and so was I-
We reached out
to kiss the sky.

In my heart
you'll always be-
Us, together,
You-n-me.

I want to share
my life with you-
Nothing else
I'd rather do.

Filled with joy,
love and laughter-
We will live
forever after.

Elizabeth Stevenson-Fairleigh

No Desire

Two ships sailing in
opposite directions;
Too many wrongs with
too many corrections.
Is there love left for
our souls to share?
Shall we dock here,
see how much we still care?
We're a good pair,
when we're far apart;
When together, a vicious
battle will start.
Then one of us will depart
only to return to set the fire
To the other one's heart
when there is no desire.

Bill Parks

"Musical Grace"

Tonight I heard music
out of an eclectic past;
its rhythm so pure, so varied,
like good wine cultured and aged
to its proper moment...
and all I could do was listen
with a fine tuned ear to history,
done in a melodic and lyrical fashion

Eleanor Sturgis

Helplessness

I could have ridden with Crazy Horse
Or held the Zeider Zee.
I could have swum the Hellaspond
Or fought with Robert Lee.
Life held no fears for me.
But here I sit and watch
while the woman I love
is destroyed by
Schizophrenia.
And all I can do
Is sit
and watch
and stare
and cry.

Edward A. Heller

Where Are You?

If you can build a Coney Island
Or mold a beach of pure white sand
Get together a Tin Pan Alley
Or assemble a big band
Where are you today?

If you are inspired by the Eiffel Tower
Or you dream of Mickey Mouse
Think about the pyramids
Or how to build a brand new house
Where are you today?

If you can make things happen
Or dreams are your propriety
If you have ideas like Thomas Jefferson
Or can build a new society
Where are you today?

If you're out there, please step forward
For we sorely need you now
Bring this country back in style
Your talent should be used somehow

Joe Kennedy

April

April's a lassie gay to see,
or so it always seems to me,
dancing as blithely, young and slim
with laughter rain-tears cannot dim.

Winter's a spangled maiden too
with star-dust tangled in her hair,
Summer's a maiden fresh as dew
and clover-perfumed, just as fair,
Autumn's a gypsy, scarlet-tressed,
a flaming beauty, glory-dressed.

But April-lassie's hair is gold,
long-curled and gleaming to behold,
daffodil-strewn are all her ways,
dream and love-filled are all her days,
a lovely, singing, blue-eyed girl,
keeping hearts in a dizzy whirl!

Bruennhilde Wegmann

A Question?

Was it rain.
Or tears within my heart,
I heard falling in the night?

I'll never know,
Some said it rained before dawn.
In the morning all was bright.

Dorathy E. Engle

After A Bullfight In Madrid 1976

It's not the killing of the bull
or the pomp and pageantry
Many will react with courage
given the right time and place
But to be brave with style and grace
Ole! that has meaning

Emil D. Morrow

Forgotten Fathers

What is a Father? Someone who takes
part in the birth of a child.

What is a father, but takes part
in raising and keeping that child safe.

When two parents separate, and
a child chooses the mother to live with.

What is a Father, but to be
forgotten.

Birthdays, and other special days
come and go unnoticed.

What is a father, but to be
forgotten.
After all that has happened, I have
never missed their special days.

No visits, no calls, most fathers
end up lonely, and forgotten.

Gary O. Walker

The Color Of Dreams

Blue dreams
Peaceful as Caribbean waters
Red dreams
Passionate as a lover's arms
Pink dreams
Sweet as a strawberry sundae
Green dreams
Cool as a forest at dusk

Purple dreams
Exciting as a royal coronation
Orange dreams
Crisp as leaves in the fall
Yellow dreams
Warm as sunshine at daybreak
White dreams
Cold as a snowstorm in winter

Dreams in rainbow colors
Feelings the essence of life
To dream and feel, to live and love
This is the soaring of the soul

Delores Kay Swabb

Germination

Seed...
Planted....
Grows—
Becomes a glorious bouquet, or,
Bemoans its fate as a weed, but
Always it is growing.

Word...
Written...
Unfolds—
Becomes a thought transformed, or,
Loses its way in the darkness, but
Always I am growing.

Jean Milburn

A Biosphere Destiny

Granted, heaven is nowhere.
Pell mell, the Reaper chops,
Often short, and anyway
The avatars have no place to go.
The brave, the foolhardy
Expectorate in fate's eye
But the drippings bring no comfort.
Then there are lucky ones,
Observant, perceptive and
Masters of body English
Who can answer the question,
"What is a full life?"
These can incise their autobiographies
In a human-architectured land,
A biosphere kingdom where
All childhoods sparkle,
All families are loving,
All marriages happy
And all deaths sweet.

Auren Uris

Daisies

Laughingly we picked the
petals of the daisies
Some said yes, and some
said no
Gaily we talked of their
phrases
You loved me and I loved
you so
I think that I am dreaming
I'm glad I'm not alone
The petals had one meaning
They meant you for my own

Tenderly we picked up our
Babies like we picked the
Petals of the daisies.

Helen Marciniak

World Pollution

Let all refuse be known gamely
Pollutions bound, water not sound
Begging time reveals
Bolting together, we must toil.

Big dreams alert, ready will
must not foil
Shunning job, hoping is sin
help educate, harden our kin
Lapse time not being.

Smokestacks belch, screening sun
cars snake highways, emitting
deadly carbons unseen
Behold ounce of prevention
Worth pound will cure

Muster, take action
worthy try a must
Hold back the budget
to clean up our spoils
Train new generation
caring our soils.

Edward H. Hermanson

Joy

Flakes of white
Pour from the sky.
It settles gently
Onto the ground.
Inside a cabin
The fire burns down,
The ornaments glisten,
And all is quiet.
Everyone's asleep.
A door creaks open.
He sees the presents
Under the tree.
The rest of the family
Awakes from their sleep.
And morning has come
As wrapping paper is torn
And sounds of delight
Echo around the house.

John D. Pfannenstein

God's Love

God our Father up above
Protects us with His love,

The clouds up in the sky
Holds rain to keep us dry,

For the flowers that bloom
Helps us heal our gloom,

The songs the birds sings
To our soul the peace it brings,

We know not what tomorrow brings
So we give thanks for these things,

With God's love so true and pure
There's nothing we can't endure.
Amen.

Judy Ann Cole

Smiles

When you're feeling down,
put a smile on your face
Because it's so beautiful
you could wrap it in lace.

That's when your personality
comes shining through
And people will see that your
heart is true.

A smile is the cure for a
broken heart
Because you can't buy love
at the nearest K-Mart.

Your "inner-beauty" shines
through for everyone to see,
Out of those people,
most of all ME!

Allison Merrifield

The Voice Of God

You spoke,
quietly in my ear,
barely above a whisper.

I awoke,
and the music of your voice
caused the great spheres to dance.

Your voice for me a universe evokes.

John Russell

Discarded—To The Heart

It sits on the shelf,
Quietly waiting and hoping,
For two tiny hands
To hold it once more.

Through the shadows for comfort
Those two hands come groping
To take down the toy
They once did adore.

Newer, brighter things
Have attracted attention
From the toy which those
Hands knew so well;

But the love for the old
Still stubbornly clings—-
In its niche in the heart
It always will dwell.

Aureba G. Kellogg

The Search

Has there never been a quest
quite like mine?
A search for a love that will
endure the test of time.

I possess an obsession to the
finding.
My pursuit is like that of a
gallant Knight's foraging.

Upon discovery, my soul will produce
an illustrious glow.
One so enlightening it would surpass
the diamond glints on snow.

My journey for such a love is like that
of an eternal flame.
For I suspect it as hopeless as seeking
an apology from one with no shame.

Alas, my quest for a love to beat all
will live on.
Tis better to have tried and failed
than never to have tried at all.

Janet Todd

Untitled

Rainbow colored memory cells
rain upon me
bitter sweet rivers
slide along my tongue
as I drink
from my chalice of tears
resting silver on sallow
undying cerebral screams
of indecision
I've lain my head upon a mountain
only to hear the scream echo
the zephyrus winds blanket me
roll over me
rest upon me
release my soul
from these unbearable chains
and let me blow away
with you.

Gretchen Kaslik

Call It Confused

In a haze
reality and fantasy merge
into one
vision gets blurry
thoughts are confused

in a blaze
days and nights converge
into one
time gets hurried
thoughts are confused

in a maze
opposing forces emerge
into one
conscience gets worried
thoughts are confused

Cheri Angelique Baldi

Red Is

Red is passion steam and blood
Red is a rose, in bloom or in bud
Red can be anger
Red can be love
Red is a heart
Red is a dove
Red can hurt and red can heal
Red is a color
Red you can feel.

Jessica Doyle

Flowers

Flowers in the summer,
red, orange, yellow and white,
flowers in all sizes and shapes.
Beautiful while they last,
but alas they all must pass.
Another year must come and go,
before they will come again.

Danielle Griffith

"Reflecting"

My thoughts of life
reflect the passing
of human form my
wisdom lasting.

My soul abides
within the light
my journey ending
with not a fight.

I bring to rest the
loves I've shared
the memories of
the ones I've cared

I seek the calm
and peace within
for soon I go
to live again.

Harriet Smart

The Cameo

Lady of grace on oval mount
pinning past and present;
binding fond and flowing fount
of love through generations.

Brenda D. Hollis

"Love"

The act of love in any form
Regardless of its source
Could transform this world we live in
To a beautiful recourse.

We should pool our global powers
Our knowledge and our guile
To induce the love in adults
That is found in every child.

If an infant could be monitored
And its loving thoughts defined
So we could change our teaching
For the future of mankind.

Then the world could be a garden
Which initially was Gods plan
And we could live so peacefully
While we loved our fellow man.

There would be no bitter feelings
In the pages of our book
And returning to our childhood
Would take on a brand new look.

Joseph H. Cassidy

Olympics

Regal in Robes of Fame
reigns a Mythical Queen
and bestows Medals of
Bronze - Silver - or Gold

Superb athletes from corners
of the globe
convene to compete in events
outstanding, and awesome, to behold
They vie for the honor of winning
Medals - of -
Bronze - Silver - or Gold

Mythical Queen reigns not alone
Fate rules the other throne
and at random decrees
The winners to receive
the elusive Medals - of -
Bronze - Silver - or Gold

Helen M. Butler

Book Shoppe

I should like to
Rename my every word
and cough out sinister
Verses like poets on stand
and rake my feet
across a fence of frozen
Names
For up they went
So sure a little flock
Would call them "good"
and use them in their passage
use them like I would.

Amy Bishop

Lavender Roses

Miniature lavender roses,
some buds, some in full bloom.
Cut and left to dry,
hanging in the room.
Tiny little pedals fall.
A reminder that summer has past.
Miniature lavender roses,
make a bouquet, placed in antique glass.

Becky Hall

Rolling Thunder

Hear the roaring thunder,
Rolling down the road,
From all across the nation,
The thunder grows and grows.

They're riding towards a big
black wall in Washington D.C.
This great wall stands proud and tall,
For all to come and see

They ride not just in honor,
But remembrance as well,
They ride to honor those brave men,
Whose names are on the wall.
And they hope we won't forget,
The tragedy of our fall.

Now some may call them outlaws,
And some may say they're scum,
But as for us, I say to thee,
These men are no less than we.

They live to ride and ride to live,
And all they wish is for all to be free.

Harry Fullerton

Precious Water

The sound of mighty waters
Rushing down a mountain stream
Set my mind to thinking
And my soul began to dream.

Down the rugged mountain side
The rushing waters flow
Having melted, true to nature,
From a mountain full of snow.

Water is a vital substance,
Without it natural life cannot remain,
Be it brought by snow or condensation,
Or by a gentle summer rain.

Now that brings up another thought,
That other life within my frame.
And the precious living water necessary,
That life to sustain.

Though we're thankful for the crimson tide,
There's another thing I know.
I'm thankful for the living fountain,
That from "his" wounded side did flow.

Harry B. Horne

Untitled

All the words linger, like
shadows on a mirror
deep in the reflection of
the glass

I dare not look in fear
of what I might see -
I close my eyes and listen,
but images make no sound

So I must read each word,
and hear the echoes in my
mind

I am the caretaker the belong
to me.

Bebe Lea Brannan

H I V

First the wind then the rain,
Saints preserve us it has come.

The zero hour is upon us,
We must accept that we are doomed.

It's amazing no one assumed
It will end upon any given day.

I won't be able to look back
And say "Why in my day.."

In ten years I'..Have fled,
To the ever sleeping land of the dead.

A golden light will appear,
And my flesh it will sear.

I write no more for I must sleep,
But a promise I shall keep.

I can't lie back and sigh,
Because I won't quit.

David N. Silverman

"Life's Dreams"

Dreams come true, so they
say, if you can only wait.
Skies will be blue and roses
will bloom, on the garden gate.

The young child dreams
of being grown up someday.
Patience, my dear, is what
its parents say.

Please, don't dream so much,
because the years will go quickly by.
Before you realize it, you
have aged and death is drawing nigh.

DeEtta J. De Pew

George

Season's come and
Season's go
My love for you has
always grown
There has been bad
and there has been good
For you and you only
is a special Brother Hood
Whatever it takes
Whatever it turns out to be
I pray and know you
Will be free

Grace Murray

Alone

Here I lay alone,
See me walk alone,
I must talk alone,
but nobody knows, I'm alone
All alone, rejected from love,
I have many friends,
though I'm still alone,
I still breath alone,
I still sleep alone,
In my heart alone, cold
To everyone outside it's unknown
To me being alone

Christine Ruzicka

My Mother

Our mother-daughter bond
seemed to take shape
When I looked into the mirror
and saw your face.

It wasn't hard to find;
It was always there.
In the slant of my eyes
In the curl of my hair.

We share the same smile,
the same walk, the same talk.
Others saw it all the time—
For me—it took a while.

Whenever I'm sad
or feeling blue,
You know the right things
to get me through.

It's nice to know
that whatever life sends,
You're not only my mother
but also my friend.

Cheryl A. Guess

The Firedrake

Delicate, fragile,
Seemingly ethereal
As it dances
In and through
The rays which
Illuminate its sinuous frame.

With tail curled
And body poised,
It leaps away
Into the swallowing light
Where rainbows swirl
Within its veins
And paint each pore
With celestial hues.

The wonder is
That human hands
Fashioned this
Which breathed not
Outside the realm of faerie.

George Misakian

Legacy In The Sky

A peak, a mountain standing tall,
Sending an undying call.
Dressed in pearly virgin snow,
Firm and chiseled she did grow.
A thousand facets grace her form,
A million years since she was born.
Her special home 'twixt Earth and Sky,
Gives pause to fragile human eye.
A regal splendor, heaven-blessed view,
And yet this is where I lost you.
She welcomed you with open arms,
And gave you peace among her charms.
She coaxed you up where eagles fly,
It was for this you had to die.
You saw and felt and knew her all,
And so she cradled your great fall.
The mountain's secrets she will keep,
For none was there to guide your feet.
And all our sorrows, answers why,
Now paint the Legacy in the Sky.

Alicia Tarico Laine

Portrait Of Love

Paint a portrait of love today,
set the mood with love.
When the night is sleeping,
paint the stars above.
Hold the brush with tenderness,
stroke with gentle ease.
Feel the thrill of happiness
that each heart receives.
Never paint with angry words
when we feel dismay,
even when the green with envy
overwhelms the day.
Color hearts a shade of red,
feel the burning flame.
Know the moment's passing,
memories will remain.
When the portrait is finished,
lovers fill with bliss.
Seal the frame with romance
and sign it with a kiss.

Alice Mason Belue

David's Pillow

It was a Christmas gift
Sewn by my teenage grandson.
A simple pillow that didn't match
Or even blend with my decor.

For a couple of years
My heart appreciated the donor
But wasn't really overwhelmed
By the donation ...

Until post surgery
When I needed a buffer
Between my missing breast
And the overweight cat in my lap.

David's pillow, soft, light,
Comforting - fit precisely,
Blended perfectly
With my new blue recliner.

Jo Plunkett

Michael

Two sacred Birthdays
shared together.
Almost three years
since
we've found each other.

Once we were unknown.
Trapped in a mindless
category.

Now we share
some mutual
history...
the accrual of
treasured memories
of one and the other

I guess that's what
Anyone might expect
of a Son and his mother.

Delyce Wensel

Mrs. Whalen

She was sweet.
She was old.
An old friend
died this
summer.
A sincere old
lady left
the world.

We are FRIENDS to the end.

The lady across
the street.
Kind, gentle, and
loving.
Her heart was
always open.
She had a husband
and many dogs.
She is with them
now.
I am happy for her.

Elizabeth E. O'Neill

My Angel

I know I have an Angel,
she was sent from Heaven above,
to protect me every day,
and to give me lots of love.

She helps me when I'm lonely,
she sits by me when I cry,
she encourages me when I'm down,
and makes me want to try.

Some day I hope I'll meet her,
to thank her for being there,
for giving me the strength,
and remembering me in her prayer.

Judy Ryan

The Sun Shines On

The sun shines on,
shimmering on wind-fluttered leaves.
My heart breaks.
Time, without thought of me, rolls on.
For one exquisite moment,
physical senses cease to exist.
I am emotion.
Agony, betrayal, melancholy, loss.
I am grief herself.

The sun shines on,
shimmering on wind-rippled water.
My heart mends.
Time, mercifully, rolls on.
In one exquisite moment
I am reborn, my soul expanded.
I am spirit.
My thoughts turned God-ward
I am God's child...
...And the Sun shines on.

Inga Kotila (1960-1992)

Lullabies

Lullabies, sung after day,
Sweep the fears of night away;
Sung with mother's dreamy sway,
Gently guides the sleeper's way
Toward the lovely dawn of day,
When the sunbeams come to play.

Arleen Gerard

Phantom Lover

I've been dreaming
Sick of dreaming
About you
My Phantom Lover

I'm famished for your love
So why deny me this love
Life is give and take
And I promise same

Time after Time
Days turn into night
I keep waiting
Don't let it be in vain

Busari Olalekan I

Grace

Her face paled as the last
signs of life
abandoned her body.
She had lived a good 86 years,
had borne two children,
loved two grandchildren, and
married only one man, for life,
until death she did part.
The lines in his face reflected
the agony and pain belonging
exclusively
to a survivor.
If she had lived,
if Grace had lived.
What now?
A child's hand tugged at his.
He held it securely and smiled.
Nothing was said, yet
everything was said.
And life pressed on.

Carol M. Runolfson

Night Time

Darkness falls around me,
silence fills my soul.
The nighttime holds a promise,
like a story never told.
It's the offer of a dream,
or a nightmare just as real.
Nothing you can see or touch,
but in your heart you can feel.
It's the presence all around,
but unique to us all.
It touches every one of us,
whether man or creature small.
With the darkness all about,
our minds can see no bounds.
Plunging forward with eager hearts,
happiness is found.
Do I speak of God?
or demon wrong or right?
The answer is within ourselves,
and the quiet found at night.

Bradley Thiel

Nature

Nature is in the birds and the
stars and the worms and the mountains.
Big cities are out.
No way, Jose.
That's what it's about.
The end.

Eric Siegel

Untitled

Whoever said...
Silence is Golden
Never listed for
A newborn's breathing...
Not shared spoken words
With a partner
For days.
Never needed support
or approval
After an original expression.

I need to hear
When I am listening,
Speak when I am mad;
And to hear the applause.

Andrea M. Tomczyk

Doorway

She sits by a window
Silently gazing out
Gently flowing fields
Of wheat and winter rye
Reminiscing.

A hand on her shoulder
Face of a child
Old friends
Smiles in her eyes
They sit together.

The house is warm
Filled with memories
Tears fall unheeded
Echoes down the halls
Faded laughter.

The wind blows on
Weaving new dreams
Trees barren and sparse
Ripple unbending
A door closes.

Judy Kucharski

The Little Man

For years I saw the little man
Sitting with his cup in hand,
And didn't know from where he came,
Or where he lived, or knew his name.
I didn't take the time to care
About why he was sitting there.
I went about my merry way,
Until it dawned on me one day,
To look around the village square
And didn't see him sitting there.
I look in vain upon the street,
For the little man who had no feet.

A lesson I have learned from this,
Man or woman lad or miss,
Always with a smile I'll greet,
With cheerful words whene'er we meet.
When Heaven's gate is opened wide
And I step up to look inside,
Right there!! Upon the golden street,
I'll see the man who had no feet.........

Helen Evers

Winter Is...

Fire places,
Sled races,
The time for scarves and hats,
Not the time for balls and bats.

Winter is shoveling snow,
Getting burned by hot cocoa,
The time for building snowmen.

I hope winter comes again.

Carolyn Donnelly

The Miracle

Miracle of my spirit
Smile on me this day
Cause my inner vision
To expand my life his way
Guide me to that mountaintop
And cause me to listen there
Extend the horizon's of my life
Filled with peace and prayer
And as my life flows on and on
Like a river to the sea
I'm grateful for the love I feel
That washes over me
And as my doubts are cast aside
Though fears may come and go
I know God always will provide
All the loving thoughts we know

Alice B. Kell

Living The Seasons

Winter, feeling buried,
Snowed in, cold, shivering
Sun seems so very far away

Spring, pushing from under
the burden, reaching for the
sun and sky. Springing anew
to begin life

Summer, skipping, playing
with youthful abandonment.
Searching for warmth and
fulfillment in each day.

Fall, I drift slowly down.
my limbs twisting, becoming
dry, brittle and bent. Falling
out of existence.

Betty Young

As The Bough Is Bent

As the bough is bent
so it has grown.
As the crop is reaped
it thus was sown.

As the world is changed
servility exceeds to height,
brave souls become estranged,
obscure time runs unkempt.

As the heart must beat
a challenge will be met,
unseemly doctrines to defeat,
morbid mortality forget.

As the bough was bent,
clinging strong, yet tried,
condescending to its fate,
now the tree has died.

Anita Kingsley

At Our House

At our house we have no beer
So no one can drink it here.

At our house we don't smoke
If someone did, we might choke.

At our house we try to stay healthy
Avoid doctors, cause we're not wealthy.

At our house, we like to keep fit
With money saved, we can travel a bit.

We are happy, me and my spouse
So that's how it is AT OUR HOUSE!

Emma J. Lavik

Leaves

They are born in the Spring
soft, fine, and green

They shelter you from the
Summer rain and sun.

Making a shady spot to rest
play and have fun

But in the Autumn their work
is done

The heat has vanished and also
the Summer sun

But even in dying and in death
they bring forth beauty unsurpassed

The reds, yellow, orange and brown
falling softly to the ground

They have accomplished what no
man, fowl, or beast can do

Making a beauty, of their death
just for you.

Betty Carter Bumgardner

Eyes Of Love

You never told me I was pretty
Somehow you sensed the words
were hollow to my ear
But oh, you made me feel so beautiful.
You looked at me with love-soft eyes
or touched my hair,
or kissed me deep,
And I knew I was loved, and lovely.
Oh, I was beautiful
when you loved me.

Hilja Laakso

Untitled

Redolent
sex scent
rumors
linger longingly
within,
slowly
silently scarring
lovestained
memory

Charles Lee Howe

Little Buddy

My buddy is someone Special.
Someone who is ornery, daring,
silly and such.
Someone who is loving and warm
just like you or I.

He's just a little tyke,
with his own wants and needs.
He is happy and content,
while playing with his toys.

He reached his terrible two's,
throwing tantrums and such.
He's to young to understand,
that those actions are to much.

He is my little boy,
not willing to start listening
But I'll always be here,
to reach him between right and wrong.

Janet Simmons

Our Friend Buck

Old Buck's a dog and black as coal,
sometimes you think he's growing old
each morning he comes up my drive,
to see if I'm still well and alive.
Each day his masters all leave home,
so comes and gets his daily bone.
Sometimes he eats and gulps it down,
or else he'll bury it in the ground.
He always carries things in his jaw,
and likes you to shake his dirty paw.
It may be a ball, a stick, or a glove
or anything to show his friendly love.
I go to the store for milk or bread,
he goes along too, in the old truck bed.
If you make friends and he likes you,
maybe he'll bring you a worn out shoe.
If all folks were friendly just as he,
what a wonderful place this would be.

Grady W. Wilkie

"Ballads Of My Heart"

Like a simple
song of music...
That sang....
within my heart
The melodies...
you gave to me...
Were carefully chosen thoughts....

Reflections of a love...
long ago...
For us it was...
a start
However short....
and misguided...
Till fate....
threw us apart
And still... the song
never ended....
For the music....
only faded...
And it never left my heart.....

Deborah Williams

The Beloved Forest Magician

Trees glide
Sound dies
We believe our lives
The Lover of the Forest
Drinks of Love Divine
To close our minds
To beings entwined
Peace, my child
My child in my arms
Thirst for good
Not your charms
Peace, I laugh
You see the truth
Withering without light
We breathe the night.

Brenda Preece

Longing

Moonlight lead me home,
Span the distant miles,
Let me see the glow
And feel the smiles.

Silvery winding roads
Like a memory,
Places I have known
Places I could be.

Magic of the night
Lingering on a prayer,
Watch a falling star
And I am there.

David G. Bowen

Welcome Spring

Winter winds are here no more.
Spring is knocking at my door.
Come in, spring.

Mellow earth and gentle rain.
Nature comes to life again.
Hello, spring.

Butterflies and bumblebees,
Hummingbirds and dogwood trees
Herald spring.

Flowering quince and daffodils,
Cardinals and whippoorwills
Know it's spring.

Greening grass and budding trees,
Flowers dancing in the breeze,
Welcome, spring.

Frances Mauldin

Questions Of Violence

Where is the laughing
Springtime that is Jackie?
How can the loving essence
Of a lifetime be snuffed
Out — in one cruel day.
A minute?
God, where is the
Goodness in it?

Janet Washington

An Ode To Sunflowers

Along the fields of clover,
Standing so tall and noble,
Are the golden sunflowers
Facing the shining sun.

Their fanlike spray of petals
Unfold in artistic array
Of pictorial beauty
As a painting by Monet.

They have a special greeting
For travelers on the road.
They seem to be relating
A country episode.

Notice these golden nobles
Along the country side.,
Notice their sparkling spirit
That livens the tedious ride.

Oh, these golden sunflowers
That grow so tall and noble,
May they stand forever
Along the country side.

Dorothy Eaton Hahn

The Loss

The songbird flies off during the
stillness of the night
Straight into the deep dark part
of the woods

Wipe tears off my child's eyes
Look ahead, straight forward
Piercing eyes knowing the truth

Fearing the soul
All that takes place there
There beyond realization

The place we can't grasp firmly
But it exists,
embracing the night's truth
Impatient for the light,
knowing it will never come

Catherine Vaughan Bailey

"The Hill"

In time past
stood a lonely hill
that's where they brought my saviour
to mock and to kill.
Crucify, crucify
that's what they did.
because he took my place instead.
As he was dying
many were stunned
He cried "Father not my will,
but thine will be done.
It got very dark
started lightning and thunder
the whole hill shook
with a big quake under
Our sins died out
how it was God's will
for my sorrow and yours
to die on that hill.

Donald B. Ratliff

The House Of Love

Secrets, Secrets
Stored away
Of childhood past
and their sunny days.

Rooms of color
Rooms of joy
The love of living
The love of girls and boys.

They ran, they skipped
and jumped around
no thought of past,
no worry about.

The home they cherished
The people they loved
are hidden away
in this house of love.

Jennifer Becker

Useless Tendencies

Words sear like lightning
Straight to the heart.
Fighting, like thunder
As waves collide and part.

All actions of violence
Caused without thought.
There are other ways
If they are sought.

Such needless violence
I can't understand
When people use fists
To get their demands.

Try a kind word,
Make the enemy your friend.
Loose all your hatred.
Let your heart and soul mend.

Let the Lord rule your life
And protect your very soul,
For only through Him
Shall you ever be whole.

Christopher Daniel Messer

To Susan Smith

I weep for you.
Such a short time ago
You were walking on air
You had a husband and
You were blessed with two sons.
You adored them and your home.
But then your bubble burst.
David found a new love.
And blithely walked away.
He who so carelessly
Sews his seed and walkaway.
He surely shares the blame.
Was his new love worth it?
He surely shares the blame.
Then you found a new love.
He did not want your sons.
No one came to help you.
Overwhelmed with your grief
You sought to end it all.
I keep for you.

Clara Post

I'm Not Alone

Accompanied by a Colt,
Surrounded by Polo,
Overcome with Bombay,
Wanting to be Alone.

Consoled by Junkies,
Singing of the Moon,
A Sky full of stars,
In the Shadow of the Mountain.

Was I to Blame?
Did I not make sacrifices?
How could she abandon me?
Damn, out of quinine!

Across the expanse of green
Come Bill and Drew and Dave.
I am not Alone.
I expel from myself.

My worry, My pity,
My Bile, My Bowels,
And a sock.

Charles McLoughlin

The Beauty Of A Miscarriage

As if standing near the ocean,
taking in its beauty,
then turning to walk away,
you were within me for only
a brief moment, but your
beauty in my memory forever...
You were to be my first child.
Losing you has overwhelmed
me with sadness, emptiness.
The pain, not only physical,
but the pain in my soul,
has taken your place within
my body, and shall remain there
even after this lifetime.

Debra Metcalf

Tears

Tears of a prisoner, tears of lost hope,
Tears of despair, tears of sadness,
Tears of hate, tears of fear.
They are only drops from our eyes;
Even we the lowest have tears we don't
Want anyone to see, yet it would be
Such love to share them with some one
Who cares.
Is there such a person who cares?
I think not!
So the tears are mine, alone I shed.

David McPeters

Knowledge Of Confusion

Life is a cycle
The beginning is the end
Understanding evades me
And doubt sets in
Knowledge could be the key
But where do I begin
Knowing causes confusion
And I fear it will never end
The key is a far off Place
It evades me again and again
Either way causes frustration
And I must embrace it or I'll never win

Heather Turfley

Little Bear

Teddy!
teddy
now i leave, and let you be.
when to be back,
Not sure.
you alone now; me alone now.
do you miss to cuddle?
games 're done; giant leap back
while you sit, watch, wait,
How patient.
you always same
not change
this is a comfort.
you comfort,
Always sturdy.
sit alone
smile content
to watch friend
depart
Not forgotten.

James M. O'Meara III

A True Tale Of Birds Of A Feather

How quiet and peaceful outside
Temptation too great an override
No cars nor people passing by
Above a bright blue sunny sky
Oh what I saw from my window
Glancing down two stories below
On a lawn so emerald green
Some jet black birds about eighteen
Really a picture to behold
Now for the action or drama to unfold
A mighty bobtailed cat all gray
Came silently stalking its prey
For the likes of that "Catty" beast
They did not want to be a feast
The birds dive bombed the attack
Now the gray cat was all black
A retreating cat, try as it may
by birds, was shown across the way
Until it was out of sight
The birds flew off on another flight.

Betty Engle

First Encounter

She had ten tiny fingers,
Ten tiny little toes,
A shock of auburn hair,
And a tiny turned-up nose.
She had a round little bottom,
And chubby little hips,
Two tiny shell-like ears,
And two tiny rosy lips.
She had all her little parts
Right where they should be!
How GREAT to be a mother,
How LUCKY to be me!

Elinor Adams

Untitled

Personal relationships count for more
than anything else
You must not underestimate the
importance of human example
All symptoms dwell within my eyes
The result of mistrust is forever seen
How often I feel as though the best
part of my life has already passed

Jeff Malley

What You Mean

You're like the sun,
that brightens the earth and gives
it warmth in all that its worth.

You're like the trees,
that stand strong and tall, always
there for me to lend a limb.

You're like the sea,
that washes away the bad and never
stops the good that it's giving.

You're like an angel,
that was sent from the sky to make
my life better until the day I die

Jeanine Golanek

Everlasting Love

In my heart there lies a river,
That few seldom get to see,
Its beauty is present,
But the view is not for free.
There's a price to gain its glory,
And a place to gain its love,
So walk along the shoreline,
And view it from above.
When the journey brings you to the end,
Remember what you saw,
And when your heart speaks to you,
I'll listen to your call.
For now you know its secret,
You've waited patiently,
You proved your love was lasting,
So my heart is yours for free.
Now you've gained its beauty,
Now you've gained its love,
So thank you God in heaven above,
For guiding my everlasting love.

Ashlea C. Cook

Michigan Vs. Notre Dame

There was a game
That had some fame;
It was Michigan
Vs. Notre Dame.

Half time was dim
For a Michigan win.

But things changed after the turnover
By the Notre Dame player.

Michigan finally won
When Wheatley had run,
With a last minute touchdown,
And made Notre Dame frown.

So you can blame
Notre Dame,
For losing the game!

Aaron Michon

ONE WISH

If I had ONE WISH,
That WISH would be,
Myself to see,
As others do,
Or you might say,
From a different view.

Elva Cavazos Cuellar

Untitled

You are the stone within my hand
That I have tried to hold on to.
But,
With this new day
And this new beginning,
I find that the stone has become
Too heavy for me to carry.
And when I hold it tight
its sharp edges pierce my skin,
Forcing me to loosen my grip.
I let the stone drop from my hand.
The scars remain
But, the pain is gone
And I smile.

Eileen M. Merrill

My Dear Friends

There are some friends
That I once knew
That made a difference in
My relationship with you

Friend like this are
Hard to find
So use them to touch
Someone else's heart
Just as they did mine

Disciples for you they
Will always be
Witnessing to others
To glorify thee

For the time will come
When we will all meet again
But for now, I want to thank you
For introducing me to...
My Dear Friends

Gary R. Gardner

When Comes The Fall

How I wish
That in autumn
We sit beneath a tree

With my head on your shoulder
Your hand in mine
On a blanket of fallen leaves

From a place that is hidden
From life itself
You and I
And the warmth of the sun

A place where the rain shall not walk
And the darkness does not come

If there is such a place
On this earth
With love and beauty overall

There we shall be
Together my dear
In autumn
When comes the fall.

Eric E. Waiters

To Man

It's the strength of your convictions
that last for all of time,
after flesh has turned to dust
and blown away.

It's the beliefs that you hold dear
with all your heart and soul,
that burn bold upon pages
through the years.

It's your prides and your secrets,
your triumphs and your failures,
that mark the stepping stones;
the building blocks.

Your posterity and progeny
feed upon your hopes and dreams;
your discarded keys
unlock tomorrow's locks.

And every step you take,
be it forward or away,
is another toward
that summit of man's growth.

Jennifer D. Warhank

Lessons To Be Learned

I always thought,
  that life was all mine.....
Things could last forever,
  but forever is a long time.
Sometimes you're in touch,
  with how you really feel.....
And if you're lucky enough,
  you'll know what's real.
Love and friendship,
  and lessons to be learned.....
Take either too lightly,
  and you're gonna get burned.
Ideas and intentions,
  usually get swept away.....
Into a pile of regrets,
  that gets bigger by the day.
Because we're trying too hard,
  for all the wrong things.....
Life flies by us,
  as if it had wings.

John Williamson

Love Can

There is no mountain known to man
That LOVE cannot ascend.
There is no hurt or heartache
That true LOVE cannot mend.

There are no cultural barriers
That LOVE cannot cross.
There is no price that is so high
That LOVE can't pay the cost.

There is no wrong so permanent
That LOVE can't heal the pain.
There is no hatred so intense
That LOVE cannot contain.

Though caught in a mad and violent world
We still may rise above.
Just shelve your pride and reach inside
And show the world your LOVE.

Arthur Neal Crews

"His Hands"

"His Hands" are on the ships
That sail the sea,
And through the storm
He's with you and me

And in times of doubt
He is right their,
When the body is sore,
And wants to give out,

When the soul feels week,
And in need, you only
Need ask, not Plead.

"His Hands" are their to fill
Your cup, the power of
His light, is strong, His
Grip is tight, say the
Word and He will lift
You up.

Curtis Schweiger, Jr.

Little Old Schoolhouse

Little old schoolhouse
That sits on a hill
Turn back the pages of time
If you will!

The bell in the tower rings
In the morning at nine,
Calling all children to get
Into a straight line!

Then it's time to read
From the "Little Red Hen",
Older pupils do Penmanship
With black ink and pen.

In winter at noon
It's sliding down hill
With cold crisp air and
Bumps with a thrill!

If the schoolhouse could talk,
Many tales it could tell
Of children who came running
At the sound of the bell!

Emma Sahlstrom

The Wind That Blows The Willows

The wind that blows the willows,
That stirs the quiet air,
That ripples water in the pond,
And swings the yellow pear.

The wind that blows the willows,
That moves the ships at sea,
The one that blew my love of you,
Around the world to me.

The wind that blows the willows,
That nipped the apples's cheeks,
Never told my secret,
To one with mouth or beak.

The wind that blows the willows,
That ripples water in the pond,
That drew a kite up in the air,
And stirred the palm tree fronds.

The wind that blows the willows,
And can be soft and gentle.
That brings down quiet winter snow,
And helps the swaying flowers grow.

Emily Hruby

Sadness

It starts with one tear
That swells against your will
Spilling over, tickling the lid
Chilling as it clings
Hesitates and falls
Making way for the warm
Welcome stream the follows.
Letting go there is a feeling
Of freedom - briefly
And with the back of your hand
You brush your face
As if to wipe away -
The pain.

A. Cone

Untitled

The gray and misted morning
that the night forgot to take
is spreading cold throughout my heart
as I stare 'cross the wake
And wandering thoughts of you and I
and what we use to be
drift slowly over rippling waves
disappearing to the sea
I tried to grasp the memories
as they went floating by
but foggy gale swallowed them
and I'm too tired to cry

Casi Walton

True Feelings

People have been talking
that we are more than friends
well there right we are
we are closer than friends
we are soul mates
brought together by friendship
that seemed to go a little far
we started out as friends
but now I seem to have
feeling for you that is more than friends.
What to do? Who cares!
I am starting to love you.

Anne M. Turney.

A Love To Call My Own

I knew from the beginning
That you were just a flirt
And yet I fell in love with you
Knowing I'd be hurt

I thought that I could tie you down
And make you love just one
But how could I do something
No-one else has ever done

I know you'll never love me
And I'm trying not to cry
For I must find the courage
To kiss your lips good-bye

When you ask for me again
You'll find I won't be there
I want a love to call my own
Not someone I'd have to share

I will hide my broken heart
Beneath a laughing face
And though you'll think I never cared
No one else can take your place.

Deanna M. Wolf

Saying Good-bye

I knew from the beginning
That you were just a flirt
Yet I fell in love with you
Knowing I'd be hurt
I tried to tie you down
Make you love just one
But how could I do something
No-one else has ever done
I know you'll never love me
I'm trying not to cry
For I must find the strength
To kiss your lips good-bye
And if you ask for me again
You'll find I won't be there
I want a love to call my own
Not one I have to share
So I'll hide my broken heart
Beneath a laughing face
And though you thought I never cared
No-one else can take your place

Charlene Rachwal

One Day At A Time

I have a cluttered closet
that's all a part of me,
I've thrown inside my fears
and all my insecurities.

They're bundled tight and thick
with pain and tears inside,
no-one knows about it
it's mine - for me to hide.

Someday the door will open
organization will take place,
and I'll be stronger for it
and deal with it - face to face.....
One Day at a Time.

Emma Walker

Dreamland

I dream of a place,
that's far away.
Where the birds gracefully sing,
and the trees gently sway.
The sight is beautiful,
so kind and so fair.
Everyone wanders,
without any care.
They speak of no anger
Only kind words are said.
They will helplessly follow,
Where they are led.
Children happily play,
all in one place.
Not judging their color,
their sex or their race.
Together they fight
and together they win.
At night when I rest
I hope to be here again.

Jennifer Robinson

Reality

Seeks the eye of the
the beholder that it brings
out to find, within the mind
of oneself, as truth rains from
the sky in silent tears that
can roar into rage of thunder
and pound the soul in search
for peace.

Bronte Williams

Love

Love, love is
the best thing
you can ever
give.

Love comes in
All sizes large, medium,
small, tiny and humongous.
However, love is
as beautiful as a
turtle dove.

Love also
comes from anyone
and anywhere.

You can send love to anyone
and let them know you care.

Love will be there
to protect you
believe it or
it will capture you.......

D'Andra Mitchell

Stones And Bones

I had never noticed
the boulders in that
field. Huge molded
stones scattered over
the green. Lumps close
to the ground, brown
some massed together
some alone, stewing in the
ground fog—stone soup
But reality changes stones
to bone and sinew
broth to beef ragout
They were just cows
lying in soft grass
with no legs showing

Dori Marie Calhoun

Leaves that Leave

Branch to ground
The bright multi-colored
fall leaves that act as
jackets during the spring
and summer months will
soon abandon their home
to trickle complacently
to an unknown destination
soon to settle on new
surroundings - in
anticipation their former
home will be blanketed
with a scintillating
white awning.

John L. DiGiovanni

"My Stillborn Son"

In memory of: Kenneth Douglas Smith, Jr.

It's been ten years since
the day of your birth
but for some reason you chose
not to come to earth
You're somewhere awaiting for
a mission to fill
I wanted you to live but
it wasn't God's will
I miss having known you
my precious one
I still feel connected
even though you are gone
I love you always my
stillborn son
maybe someday I'll know you
in a life yet to come....

Dawn Smith

Papa

Looking back to the happy days,
The days when Papa was here.
Things were so much easier,
For mama, my brothers, and Me.

Now that Papa had left us,
The home once is now a house.
Solitary ruled our hearts,
And believed no happiness to come.

Many have tried to love us,
And many tried to be Papa,
But many have not succeeded,
For many tried too hard.

We dreamed to see Papa again,
And we've shouted for his love,
Never once will he hear our cries,
For Papa has claimed his rest.

Once in awhile I sing and shout,
Oh Papa you are loved so much.

Jamie Ann Lo

Strength Flows From Within

Strength flows from within
The depths of our soul
And gives us courage to face
The uncertainty of each new day.

Strength is the powerhouse
Which charges our soul
When life's energy slows
To a pace of unwillingness to go.

Strength is that matchless force
Which pushes us forward when loneliness
Reaches out to make us its prisoner.

Strength is that luminous spark
Which continues to brighten our spirit
When our ambitions become nothing more
Than lingering dreams.

And no matter what crisis
We may face tomorrow,
Strength is that perfect rhythm
Filled with songs of endurance.

John W. Williams

Rue Lamente'

My heart weeps for
The deserted shack
And empty mansion
Whose times live back.
If stories contained
Within each wall
Could be revealed
Before they must fall-
What tales of gladness,
And cringing fears,
Lilting laughter,
Or heartfelt tears!
They'd love to tell
Of the dreams "To be;"
Forlorn now - empty -
Pitied by me.

Helen L. Zimmerman

Excuses

I can't find it! I can't find it!
The dog ate my homework!
I need some compassion
To bring that A homeward.

But Teacher! But Teacher!
Please don't call Mom
My Birthday's tomorrow
this can't happen now!

Tomorrow, tomorrow
I'll sure turn it in.
Anything, anything
so Mom won't come in.

Amy Sternberg

Calm And Storm

The birds stop chirping,
the dogs do not bark.
The children don't play
on the swing at the park.

The wind does not blow,
so the leaves are still.
All this can happen
at nature's own will.

Then comes the thunder,
rumbling at night.
The bright lightning flashes,
as the storm giants fight.

The rain pours down,
the tears from the Lord.
As the storm lashes out
with its newly sharpened sword.

Justin Paul Gerke

Our Flag

Betsy Ross will never die
The flag she designed
Still flies high,
It means peace and
freedom throughout the
land,
The symbol of
Old Glory
Will Always stand.

Audrey Adams

Draftsman's Pride

The Lord sat down one day and planned
The finest woman in the land.
He used blueprints and slide rules, too,
For only well made charts would do.

He took the beauty of the rose,
The grace of antelopes He chose,
From birds the sweetest songs He took
And then sat back to take a look.

He added personality,
A zest for life, vitality,
Compassion, kindness, tenderness,
Desire for children to caress.

An angel's halo was her Crown,
And straight from Heaven she came down,
The blueprints that he threw away
Perfection He'd achieved that day.

George Newton Keyser

Untitled

Heart of a man, yield to
the grace of reason
Tis the time of spring, and
love is the season
The earth is reborn, with all
shades and hues
The sky is abound with
pinks and blues
The trees turn to green, and
children are gay
Their faces are bright, with
the games they play
We wait for our love, with
souls brave and bold
As we yearn for the truths, that
have yet gone untold
Heart of a man, yield to
the grace of reason
Tis the time of spring, and
love is the season

Debra L. Pierce

The Silent Scream

Out of her belly
the howl of a coyot',
long, low,
bloodcurdling,
lingering.
Yow-oooo-ow-oooo-ow!

Up from her entrails,
Up from his guts,
Up from our ghoulish innards.
The Cry of the Century,
The Cry of the Universe,
central, core, complete.

Out of her throat
and into the air.
Vapors curling on currents.
Spiraling upward,
reaching toward heaven,
raw, ugly, angry.

Deanna Shapiro

The Bowman

Silently stalking
the hunter draws near
his prey oblivious
to the danger behind
the hunter notches an arrow
in his bow made of yew
and takes aim at his prey
with his eagle-like sight

He lets go of the bow string
with an audible twang
and the arrow flies straight
true to his aim
into the flank
the arrow glides in
down goes the prey
he has dinner again

Charles Meyer

Despair

The Homeless,
The jobless
People without a soul,
Understaffed shelters
a vain attempt to make them whole.
Is there not enough room on
this crowded planet?
Everyone for himself
Some sleeping on hard granite.
Eating out of trash bins
What a terrible plight,
Consuming other people's leavings
While the reach dine on a gourmet
delight.
Is there someone out there
Who has a solution?
Politicians can't help
They just add to the pollution
There's always money to be spent on war,
but never enough funds to feed its poor.

Angela L. Jones

Despair

When achievement no longer is
the key to Success

When Strength and Courage are
replaced with Fear

When your Soul no longer feels
the Sun

When Time no longer heals
the Pain

When Accomplishment no longer
relieves your Burdens

A TEAR DROP COMES MORE OFTEN
THAN A SMILE

Jaimie Oatley

Leadership

Leadership is the key
The key to success
Success equals power
Power equals respect
Leadership is fun challenging
To have leadership is
To have success, power
And respect

Jennifer Schwyhart

A Cry For Help

The water is wide!
The land is vast!
With everything we have ...
Why do we hurt it?

Erica L. Wilson

A Secret Love

Did your heart become too weak
the last time that we spoke?
Were you afraid that if we stayed
in this world that we wrote,
that we'd be carried off somewhere
to a place we should not be?
That somewhere is the place
where love is all we see.

I long to take you there again
to our place of long ago.
Where we can set our memories free
and make new ones as we go.
So please feel free to take my hand
and follow me there.
So we can try to understand
this love we'll always share.

Audra Carter Epperson

Untitled

It disturbs me to no end
... the light
Reaching far down into
... the depths
- My Cell
What is this knowledge that
... we seek
and why with knowledge are we
... Not Free

Deborah Stambaugh

I'll Always Remember

The sparkle in your eyes
The loving smile upon your face
Your warm and gentle embrace
The soft words "I Love You"
touched me deeper than you know
I will always remember
for the memories I will never let go

Deborah Runyon

"A Woman's Plea"

The man I search for
The man I need
At last I finally see
There is no man for me
For I ask for too much
Love, friendship, honesty, companionship
But most of all commitment
Alas, these things are not to be given
For a man needs his space and freedom
Society has placed a burden on man
He must be forever young
Committed to being the best He can
When does He have time to commit to me

Glenda Severance

Gray

The sun.
The moon.
Both shedding light on a dark world.
A world darkened by our ignorance.

The same sun warms both our skins.
When I stare in awe
at the beauty of the moon,
it is the same moon you see,
my dark brother.

The moon.
The sun.
Both indiscriminate.

I am the sun.
You are the moon.
If only we would allow it,
our different lights would flood the world
until night and day were the same as each
other.

Black and white would blend,
forming a beautiful shade of gray
called humanity.

Caroline Brook Bartenfield

Love

The more they deny me
The more they reject me
The more I want it
The more I need it
The more I would do anything to have it
I care, oh yes, I care
I want to, but I can't stop
They know this and they hurt me
It's a game
It's only a game to them
But it's Life to me
And Life like that is Death
And there is nothing, no one.
Only the want of it
Only the need remains

Jaime Rowe

Untitled

All is a void
the muse of yellow
arcing into orbs of blue
arrives and
the Commitment is made

Thoughts flow like
great cosmic birds
winged in fire
wrapped in ash

Ancient insects march
into gangrenous wounds
and emerge anew

In chaotic climax
the Commitment is done
the brain dull
the wounds healed

Gary Bucci

Broken Dreams

Unpainted and sun bleached
the old house stands
Dust devils swirl in the air
The yard is parched and cracked
no grass grows
no flowers bloom
Even the weeds are brown and
curled
The barn stands empty
and still
The fields mice have gone
The windmill is broken and still
but no matter
The well went dry long ago
The sun unmercifully beats down
on someone's broken dreams

Helen Hinkle

Washed with Pain

A tear can wash away
The pain'
Like the rain can wash
Away the world.
Your heart is the only
Thing that knows
That pain.
And God is the only one
Who knows the rain.

Jana Bone

Lonely Reality

Nothing is real, here.
The people walk, and talk,
And smile,
But their eyes are empty.
Falseness of feeling.
How can the have false feelings
When my real feelings are so strong?
I want to scream,
I am real!
Pained in my reality.
Hot and angry reality.
They are as cold as winter.
I stand in the snow,
Searching for sincerity,
And the empty eyes pass by.

Jennifer Lynn Wilson

Whispered Kiss

The nights we went out,
The places we would go,
One thing I remember,
Still touches by soul.
When your soft lips touched mine
In a pleasant tenderness.
Or when your lips were faintly cruel,
Controlling a desire long suppressed.
In those silent moments
I felt more cared for than ever before,
As if I was all you wanted
And nothing more.
I realize now I wasn't the only one
You graced each day,
And because of your wide passions,
Our fondness died away.
If you ever feel empty and alone
And think that it's me you miss
Remember our final farewell and
whispered kiss.

Dawn Massingill

Sometimes

Sometimes, when the wind is so cold...
The rain, so wet..
The sky, so black...

Sometimes, when all are sad,
When all are cold,
When all must starve...

Sometimes, when violence hits...
When people cry,
And people die,

I think to myself,
Does it have to be?

Amelia Fitz

The Way I Feel

Am I the culprit?
The rider?
The prisoner?
The bride?
The ceremony?

The pleasure?
The pain?
The witness?
The partner?

The possibility?
The illusion?
The weather?
The rate of exchange?

The form or the formula?
The victim?
The aggressor?
The song?

Jenny Schipper

The Five Senses

The stained glass "illuminated"
the risen Christ—angels all around
His five wounds; fresh
from the victory of the Cross.

Each wound carried a gift
each angel acted out . . .
Seeing
  Touching
    Smelling
      Hearing
        Feeling

On Seeing it
I was so Touched
I could almost Smell the blood.
I had Heard His holy word;
His symbiotic Feeling for all Mankind.

Elaine K. Manilla

Christmas

Christmas is coming, approaching fast
The joy of his birth is here at last!

It is not the presents given
Or presents that were received

It's just the joy of knowing
He is coming for you and me!

Holli Power

The River

The river flows freely,
The river flows wild,
But the river isn't looked at
As though it were a child.
Even though it be,
No one really cares,
Because what they see,
Is where the river stares.
Sometimes it lays still,
Sometimes it rages,
The river is like life -
Both go through stages.
There is infancy and adolescents,
Middle and old age,
But none are as easy
As the word's written on this page.

Jacquelyn Moore

Little Angel

You're an angel in
the sky.

You won my
eye.

I can't even lie
or even try to deny.

I saw you standing there
I had to stare at you, and
your beautiful hair.

Yet I'm so shy to talk to you,
that's why I sent this
message from the blue.

What I'm trying to say
is I love you so and if
I had you I would never
let you go.

I know this must sound oh
so strange oh but please
say you will be my
little angel

Hans P. Clermont

Silence Screams

The sun shines
The sky is blue
The birds sing
And flowers bloom

The children play
As their parents fight
Can't anyone see
That something isn't right

Suddenly a shot is heard
Like in a bad dream
At a time like this
Silence Screams

Jamie Rice

Life

Have you ever wondered how the sky stays up there and doesn't fall down. Have you ever wondered how the planets are so round.

Have you ever wondered how we all began in a world filled with mysteries and tragedy. Guess you haven't. That's why life is such a mystery.

Camille Wallace

"The Beauty Of A Woman"

The calming, soothing voice of the sea,
The softness of a summer's breeze.
Beauty paled not by any flower...
The beauty of a woman.

A knowing smile,
a mother's touch.
a lover's silent reassuring...
The beauty of a woman.

The gentle grace of wind-blown leaves,
the strength of ancient oaks,
the tenderness of angel's wings...
The beauty of a woman.

The warmth of an eternal flame,
the fires of compassion,
the sanctity, as heaven's own...
The beauty of a woman.

A masterpiece of priceless worth,
a harmony of silent whispers,
a dream, a vision, a fantasy...
The beauty of a woman.

Dwayne Hixon

The Unknown

Drip, drip, dripping I hear
The sun has disappeared
Only the distant light
From the moon is shinning
On the ground, screaming in the distance
I walk into the woods
Everything is scarlet
I see crimson spots everywhere
Bloody bodies lie in the darkness
No one hears their cries
They walk in a world of silence
Unknown to anyone
Their souls wander endlessly
For they weren't put to rest.
Do you understand their sorrow?
Do you hear their cries?
Do you feel their pain?
Do you feel the coldness?
I do, "Open thy eyes and thou shall see the truth"
Pain is real.

Crystal Hainbecher

Untitled

A single rose blooms,
the sun is happy,
the sky brightens,
and the grass dances.

One lonely tear falls,
the moon frowns,
the clouds cry,
and the heavens break.

Julie Anne Adam

Time

Time is everything to a hand,
the tik-talk non-stop
companionship
A bracelet just hangs there
teasing the hand
Saying "I want to get off",
it drops to the ground

Alanna Stewart-Bell

Linda

You're the warmth in the sunshine
The sweet smell in the rain;

You're the wind in my hair as
I walk down the lane.

You're the gold of the rainbow,
the sparkle in the dew.

You're the sweet glow of morning
in a gay yellow hue.

You're the freshness of a daisy
as it blossoms in Spring.

All these things that you are
show the love you did bring.

You were so full of love with
a sweet little smile;

And it seems you were with us
for such a brief little while.

God has taken you from us . . .
I can't see you again;

But you are always with me in
these things without end.

Betty Jacobs Perfetti

A Wind Call

As my daily walk in a Heavenly woods
The thoughts roam so endlessly.
A tree's leaves shake to call of a wind,
Saying where am I going?
Is there a place in life for me,
Am I just occupying man's space.
As the tree shakes the wind called,
Praying God am I lost forever?
Show me the truth of my sins,
Don't for bid of being what to be?
So the tree wind called a song,
Of humming I'm feeling so blue.
I could go and lift the world,
And ever feel restless.
The tree wind was calling a,
moan of sadness.
Moaning when I die bury me,
nice in a blue velvet suit.
The wind stop calling,
and I left with understanding.

Jerry Pinckney

In The Moment

The Winds of Change, they rock my boat.
The tide is high, alone I float.
Set sail, my passage a stormy sea,
to find the lost Isle of Tranquility.

In the Moment I long to be.
In the Moment, hey, can't you see?
Release your eyes and look with me,
gazing into Eternity.....

A Place of Wonder, Earthly bound.
Open your heart and look around!
The world of Magic, Sight and Sound;
what once was gone can soon be found.

Work and slave until you die.
A flesh-bone ghost, you live a lie.
The Truth of Life just passes by....
BREAK FROM YOUR CHAINS and
RIDE THE SKY!!!

John Curry

Beauty

As I walk through a path of roses
the touch of the petal so smooth,
bees eating pollen grain and crops
harvesting honeydew.
The wind whistles through
my hair as birds
chirp everywhere,
the good smell of potpourri
from flowers everywhere.
The trees let their
spring leaves go as Fall
starts setting in, the sun goes down
at the edge of town as the stars
give way their grin.
The grass ever so green,
trees, fruits so sweet, the
lovely scene in the air, as for me it
shall be paradise
everywhere.

Cynthia Pedraza

"LoveStroll"

As I stroll through life for
The true love that I seek
my soul is so weary,
The heart, it grows too weak.
Another day, soon it shall pass and
with it, the night brings fear.
Once again I shall sleep,
Alone in my tears.
For tomorrow, I pray, from
the darkness I shall rise, that
my Lord he will end these
tears in my eyes
That he alone will send to thee
another lost and empty soul and
that we two shall become as one
and in love, through life
we shall stroll.

Flynn A. Wallace

Summer Lake Nights

On summer lake nights,
the watermelon rinds still
thrown across the lawn
and chain link wonder
still bowing in the moon's oceans,
a party raged on in the
misty trees of the other shore.
Big band floated across my
brother's canoe to the back porch,
where My Parcheesi and cap gun
were left for next year.
I was out catching fireflies
and riding My red bike to the
top of old
Sturnam's Hollow, flying
past the sound of a lady's
laughter in the
drunken hours of dusk.

And not once, not once, did
I invite them in.

Craig McRea Seip

A Winter Night

The snowflakes have begun to fall,
The wind is very still.
I hear the wolf's long lonesome call,
It echoes o'er the hill.

Wild geese have long gone by;
The winter birds are still.
The bears are sleeping in their dens;
And bare trees guard our hill.

We've gathered in the fire wood,
Closed all the shutters tight.
Put the kettle on to boil,
And settled in for the winter night.

The dog's curled up beside the fire,
That cat is fast asleep.
The children nestle warm and quiet
To dream and love the beauty of
A winter night.

June Mounger

Sunshine

Sunshine, the sun is shining so brightly
The wind rustling against the tree leaves
This is a quiet place
I wonder if this is heaven
The sun shining brightly
It's so nice and quiet here; there's
no gun shots sounds, nor fire engineer
or police sirens in the air
I wonder if this is Heaven
Someday I would like to go there.

Elizabeth J. Washington

A + B = C

For my friend I would offer
the world on a platter, the
stars in the heavens fine gold
and jewels, furs and diamonds,
the richest oils and luxury cars.
But I can't, what I can offer
you my friend is my warm since
of humor, my advice, and my love.
For this is all I have and would
gladly give it to you if you accept
this gift of what I have to
give to you.

Ebonese Olfus

Today

When out of the past
there arises contention,
Reveal the intruder
to the present condition.

If acceptance prevails,
contention will whither.
If obtrusion persists,
show no cause to consider.

For time only relates
to conditions existent.
The past is a memory
and must not be insistent.

Living is today,
though tomorrow consider.
One day at a time
is enough of a jitter.

Donald H. Barker

Flight

While a walking late one night
There arose in me quite a fight
The cold did freeze me to the bone
For I was weak and alone
What a night to run in flight
Over the logs
And through the bogs
Dashing from those demon dogs
My predators were closing
As I run in pain
They growl at my strain
This night of my flight
How they did rip and bite
for my flight was failing
As they feed upon my wailing
They now choose if it is to be my last
night
Or to let me slip away in flight
Only to run another night.

Court Prestia

Darkness Or Light?

In this cold, angry world
there is darkness everywhere.

In sunlight parks, on lonely streets,
in the bedroom where you sleep.

Whether profane or gently sweet,
you will know not 'till you meet.

But it will come, it will dwell,
it will take your very soul.

In this world there was a light
that seems to have passed from sight.

It filled each soul with kindly love
but it could not keep the pace.

Will it return? I do not know
but it can't without our help.

Unless we wish it to be so
nevermore will love be known.

Carolyn R. Fricke

"Mom, You In The Kitchen?"

I never was a-polled...
There never was a time,
For someone always called
The name, always mine;
"Mom, you in the kitchen?"
There it was; the book to write,
The painting, or the etchin'...
The plot so close and in my sight;
But years of expression go so fast
As did, "Mom, you in the kitchen?"
...Now that part of life is passed;
All the shoutin' and the pitchin'...
It really kept me on the go,
So now I could really be a-sketchin'
If this mind were not so...
Filled with, "Mom, you in the kitchen?"

Helen M. Gephart

Cold

Sleet slants off my cardboard hut
Then snow provides a gentle cover.
Two buddies bundle by,
Our body heat we share
Is scant relief.

Howard F. LeBaron

"Always"

For Everett

Our time together was so little,
There was always passion in our hearts.
Our souls were once deep lovers,
But now that we are miles apart:

The clouds drifting lazily
No longer flow softly along,
The stars I now wish upon
No longer shimmer in moonlight.

The blazing sun hides from sight,
Stormy nights are more lonely now.
The wind did not blow so cold,
Dawn was not so achingly cruel,
When you were here beside me.

Now we are a thousand miles apart,
Longing for what we said was "always."
Our hearts are painfully lonely,
But our souls are still lovers.

Jennifer Dawn Hudson

Faith

When all seems lost and
there's nowhere to turn
A little pinpoint of
light appears giving hope.
Reminding one not to give up.

And to reach within
and find that ounce
Of strength to take the next step.

The next step that brings one
closer to the success,
The dream held onto so firmly.
So deeply that the dream
has a life of its own.

Each step brings one closer
to the dream.
Because one believes.

The one has faith.
Faith in the ONE.

Dilsa Saunders Bailey

Danny's Child

My little lost angel
These words are for you
Please forgive Mommy
For what she chose to do
I made a big mistake one day
I let them take you, my baby, away
Understand darling, I lost my mind
When I gave you up thinking I was
Leaving a world of troubles behind
And oh how I regret
My ungodly mistake
Of shattering your life
For my freedom's sake
You're in my heart now and forever
I'll love you always
And forget you never

Victoria Veaux

Some Dads

Some dads are bad,
They can even be mad,
Or big and fat,
But some dads aren't,
Like ones that go to K-Mart,
Or what about Wallgreens,
What does that mean?
Some dads have hair,
And some are bald.
It's just not fair,
If your dad's mean,
But always remember,
You're lucky if he's lean.

Dane Knezek

Never To Be Forgotten

As my eyes move across the page,
they fill with fear,
they fill with tears.
There is a longing in my heart,
Not to believe you could write such a
harsh, cruel page to the one
who gave it all for you.
Now nothing can fill the darkness
that has seeped into my heart.
That page is replayed like a broken
record every minute of everyday.
Never to be forgotten.

Holly Woods

Flying

While we were together
they painted the sky
I looked out and saw
a Michelangelo
And when I sat in my chair
it smiled

I wondered
Can I walk down the street
with my earlobes dancing?
I might be arrested

Dressing was difficult
clothes would not come on
my coat tightened
the shoes were hiding

I started to walk
my head in a cloud of you
I fly like a drunken pilot

Diane Rose

Restlessness

At night my thoughts are restless,
They plunge, they soar, they leap!
They chant a Jeremiad
That flaunts a dare to sleep.
The stress of drowsy moments,
When sleep refuses rest,
Inflames the pain of longing
That smolders in my breast.
O night be swift and dreamless
Unfettered by desire!
Oh heart be still! The morning
Will cool this embered fire.

Ida G. F. Hackett

"Dreams Can I Come Too?"

They are so hard to find.
They say they were meant
for everyone...
To encourage a world of mankind.

To create our own Destiny
is unique all by itself.
To accomplish our goals
and set free our souls,
Is the ultimate happiness
of wealth.

With the Lord as my Shepherd,
and the angels all around,
Sweet miracle set forward;
The most beautiful music
intoxicates the town.

For my dreams are those of few,
and my needs don't override;
but my mysteries still ask you
about the dreams on the other side.
Can I come too?

Alicia Parker

Summer Day

I sat in the swing
this afternoon
on the palace grounds.
But I was not alone,
my heavenly King was there.
I saw him
in the restless,
sunlit clouds
while breezes soft and warm
bathed away my cares.
And just across the fence
Jake's peach tree bowed
in gentle grace
beneath a load
of crimson fruit.

Doris Nason Boles

At Easter

To greet you on this day;
This day our Lord arose.
This day that He had triumph.
O'er all His earthly foes.

He became a lowly babe,
This child of, misery;
He eft His home in glory,
To die, for you and me.

Some day He will come again
And walk the earth anew;
His own with Him, will always be,
He wants you with Him too.

On Calvary's cruel cross He died,
About two thousand years ago;
To give to us eternal life,
And Heavens glory to us show.

He suffered bitter torment
To rescue us from sin.
He died for you your soul to save,
So give your heart to Him.

Dorothy Z. Goppert

Guardian Angel

I know I have this angel fair,
This spirit that follows everywhere,
Where are you now my faithful friend?
Will you be with me till the end?
Angel of God I know your here,
And you are as said "my guardian dear"
It is with God's love you are committed,
To rule and Guide you are permitted,
Stay by my side and watch over me,
That I may better thank you in eternity!

Harold J. Fitzsimmons

Nature's Way

I took my child upon my knee,
This tiny man, a part of me.
We looked through the window
To watch nature's show.
We were enchanted by snow, snow,
Snow, and more snow.
Secure in our home and nestled together,
Wishing this time could last forever.
The snow will melt, the child will grow,
Seasons and children come and go.

Ann Barry

Road Fever

Well I had road fever,
tho' I thought I had won.
But I woke up this morning
and found myself gone.

There was nowhere to go to,
and nothing to leave.
Except you babe, just you babe,
so I sit here and grieve.

Still the road leads on
through the jungles of towns.
While I'm thinking of you,
and the peace I had found.

And I'm wondering why,
these things go this way.
Why I'm walking this road
when I wanted to stay.

Dawn Kakely

I Am That Friend

Through the good and bad and
through the thick and thin, you
can always count on me to be that
friend

Who is there when you need to
talk or a shoulder to cry on. I
am that friend that you can
always rely on.

Should you ever become lonely,
sad, or blue, it should brighten
your day knowing that I am that
friend who's thinking of you.

It matters not that we are a
world apart. I am that friend who
carries you deep in my heart.

When you call on others and they
are not around, you can call on
me, I won't let you down
.... I am that friend

Darren C. Spears

The Forbidden Love!

The love I discovered
through you,
was the best thing
that I ever felt in my
entire life,
but behind the forbidden
corner in the back of my mind,
lurked reality,
I remembered my worthless childhood,
How could I let my self
get close to anyone?
What if I get hurt?
What will I do?
Will I die?
This is what lurk's
in the depth's of my eyes.

Erin Young

Letter To God

Dear God;
I love you for always taking
care of me,
Your patience and guidance
has made me become
all I can be.
Sometimes I'm doubtful
and my faith is shaken,
but it doesn't take long to
get a spiritual awaken.
I pray sometimes for selfish things
but I find myself happy with
whatever your "will" brings.
God, your love and guidance has
brought me through some ruff times
I just know when I hold on
to your Grace,
Happiness I'll always find.

Karen L. Cox

Whispers

Sometimes...
I miss you for who you are
and I catch myself smiling
with fond memories

Sometimes...
I miss you for who you were to me
and my throat knots for want
of someone special again

Most of the time I just wish
Wish that I could be
a wind's whisper
passing this thought of mine
through to you
without hurting you...
without hurting me...
Without interrupting our right
to private lives going on

But sometimes..
thoughts just overwhelm me

Michelle D. Morris

With Just One Look

What I feel
 I know it's true
It's more than real
 when I'm with you.
It hurts so much
 since you are not here
I need your touch
 it seems so clear.
It's hard to see
 that I need your hold
But please believe
 my love's like gold.
With just one look
 I fell so deep
That is all it took
 I'm yours to keep.

Tara L. Kaheny

The Killing Match

I could feel them coming.
I know they were coming
At the edge of night.
They were coming
To take my life.
Is this?
Is this, what my life is about;
My whole life?
Is to die, is to die alone.
Is to die, ten thousand miles from home.
This was?
This was my life?
I will protect my life.
The survivors will know
I was alone.
Alone ten thousand miles from home.
When they come
They will not forget
I faced them. Alone.
So far from home.

Thomas Kelly

Do You Hate Me?

I'm a beautiful woman.
I know you see.

I'm a smart woman.
I know you've heard.

I'm a fearless woman.
I know you'll learn.

Is that you hate me?

Is it a jealous mind that has
caused you to be in such a bind?

You don't really know me
So I can't see

How you can form an opinion about me.

You've only discovered a
little of my outer misery.

So how oh how can you hate me!

When you know only what you've heard.
Which you'll never know if it's true

Because you've formed an opinion
of me out of the blue.

Do you really hate me or do you hate you????

Shanese Shields

Last Time

His green eyes haunt mine, searching for their prey
In a brief second I'm brought under his spell
His lips, tender in their touch, graze my skin
I quiver beneath him
His blonde hair falls across his face and he pushes it back
He reaches down and I accept his probing kiss
For the last time I feel his body close to mine
For the last time I hold him in my arms, unwilling to let go
Not wanting to look forward to tomorrow, only wanting now to never end
To have him forever in my life
Never to lose him
To forever remember his face, the way it is
For the last time.

Nikki Maunu

Love And Life

Ah the sweetness of a peaceful evening
In a lonely village or a burg;
It's not the place, it's only in the being;
Could be a South Sea Island—or even Heidelberg.

For as it has been said some time ago,
That love and life are truly where you find it,
I know no matter where on earth I go
There'll be my Bali Ha'i if I'll not mind it.

And so I'll seek not that which I would find,
For ere I did 't would not be worth the seeking,
For how could I improve upon God's mind?
Or why should I force earth on heaven's planning.

Love and life must like a steel be tempered;
Thus life's made sweet by problems that are bared.

Kenneth W. Weidner

The Rocking Chair

There it was just sitting there.
In a room almost empty and oh so bare.
She closed her eyes to hold back the tears.
She knew would come as she remembered the years.

That rocking chair sat in a place of distinction.
Right next to the crib of the newest addition.
It helped to comfort that babe in the night.
Somehow it helped make a lot of things right.

She remembers with love the books that were read.
To a toddler who had all the words in his head.
But who listened with awe as the story unfolded.
If a word she did miss she was sure to be scolded.

The arms of that rocker worn smooth as could be.
The cushion so tattered, the threads she could see.
What anyone else might call imperfection.
She looked on with love and a lot of affection.

For that old rocking chair was to her a reminder.
Of days that were sweeter of days that were kinder.
When there was time to sit back and relax just a bit.
And a rocker was just the right place for it.

Mary A. McDaniel

Friends Of All Kinds

Friends are very special,
It doesn't matter if you aren't just the same.
If you care for one another,
It doesn't matter if your black or white,
Chinese or American,
Italian or French,
What counts is that your friends.

Kara Gavigan

If I Were A Diamond

If I were a diamond, I would come
in all shapes and sizes: pear shaped,
round, marquis, emerald and heart shaped.
If I were a diamond, I would glow in the night.
I would sparkle, sing and dance.

I would be as hard as nails.
I would be a great big karat.
Each karat would tell you my size.
I would be a crystal rock.

If I were a diamond, I would be
found in mines throughout the world.
I would be a rare gem.
If I were a diamond, I would be part of a baseball field.
Grassfields would sparkle.

My sunvisor would have diamonds.
My shirt collar would be covered with diamond stones
My sneakers would light up
I would be diamond ballet slippers, gliding on stage while
dancing to music of love.
A diamond lasts forever.

Paula F. Press

"Our Dad"

You were always a very special dad to your daughters of three,
in all the things you've said and done we couldn't more agree.
There's so many things that come to mind in our childhood of the past,
the raising of three daughters what an excruciating task.
When you packed up all our bags and moved us way out west,
we just want to let you know, you did your very best.
We were leaving far behind our family and our friends, but you saw
us through our sorrow and helped our lives to mend.
Now through these many passing years as we look back in time,
we see a daddy's special love that's always been entwined.
We thank our heavenly Father who is up above
for giving us a dad like you to cherish and to love.

Ruth Maynard

The Ocean

Life is like the waves of the ocean
In and out all day long.
The waves washing the sands calmly
The tide going out very strong.

When the tide gets pulled back
And there are treasures on the shore
You try to pick up every one before the tide comes in
Or they will be none just like before.

A day can be like a cool summer breeze
With a little smell of watery salt
Other days are harsh sand storms
With the bitter smell of worries and fault.

The ocean goes farther,
Than you can ever see
Your troubles get washed away by the waves,
And are replaced by a feeling of serenity.

Stephanie Poulin

Loneliness

Loneliness is an empty space inside,
It can tear your heart a mile wide.
It's having no one to call on the phone
It's once feeling great, then feeling alone.

Loneliness takes some time to repair,
You'll find it real hard and even unfair.
But once you overcome that awful embrace,
You'll see you end up with a smile
on your face.

Michal Shelkowitz

Time

As I lay here tonight
In another lonely night
It's the beginning of a new year "1995".

As you try to change your life
And forget the past, it's just not to easy to get over so fast.
You've got to realize it only takes time.
Time is the key factor in making things alright
The time to forget, and to forgive it helps
to keep your head on straight.

It's not always so easy to get it together,
So friends can help you through and through
but, sometimes only a little time is all you need.

Time is what you make of it, so when the time is right,
Life will change only when you feel it is exactly that time.

Yvonne Terwilliger

Morning Star

He's there strong and bright from the moment I wake.
In his light I rise and bloom.
He lifts me up if I bend or faint.
In his love I enrapture and swoon.

When all seems dark, his light leads the way.
I follow after and I see,
The clouds disperse, his brightness reveals
All the colors heavenly.

Stephen Maloney

The Last Tour

Once again, excitement filled the halls of Graceland,
In just a few hours, another tour was to begin,
Even now his staff and musicians were assembling,
Not knowing the final curtain had brought Elvis earthly show
to an end.

It's true that Elvis went from rags to riches,
Why he shaped the whole world to fit right in his hand,
Little wonder at last the world could not contain him.
It was time now for him to tout the promised land.

That very night the greatest of all agents,
Booked Elvis for one eternal show on high.
And I just know the angels stood in awe and wonder
When he stepped out on that great stage in the sky.

As the sun sinks low tonight behind the hills of Graceland,
The shadows run to hide their face from its lingering light,
The trees bend low and whisper Oh so softly,
There's a new grave at Graceland tonight.

Stella Walton

My Butterfly

Each butterfly, flies the same
In search of the nectar
Its life to sustain.
Its colors, it proudly displays on its wings,
Its beauty declared, like the robes of a king.
You my darling, are much the same,
Your only different by character and name.
You live your life to not be ashamed,
Of your radiant beauty, and life without stain,
You live your life as you see fit,
Your morals and principals, tight in your grip,
An individual you are, and so you must be,
Like the butterfly, PROUD AND FREE!

Norman Unruh

An Iron Arm

Rapidly changing alliances entangle
In the foldings of an unresolved world war,
With unfairly drawn boundaries
Drifting slowly into space.
An iron arm aims toward life
As mounds eat away the body, and
Visions melt in the California sun.
Stand alone at the top of a hill and
Glance around at all that's failed
Before finally plunging into darkness
Forever.

Kylie S. Smith

The Land Of The Tall Jack Pine

When you sit at night with the fire for light
In the land of the tall Jack Pine.....
You're really awed, by the wonders of God
When you think, this is yours and mine!!!!

The minarets with snow capped crest
And flowers that abound....
The thing to do, tho it's hard mind you
Is to keep your feet on the ground....

The city man with his well trimmed lawns
And houses row upon row.....
Can never find real peace of mind
That folk in the big wood know.....

They rise with the sun, sleep when it sets
They toil the whole long day....
And still find time to thank their God
For wonders along the way....

You, just for once, you city folk
Should leave your houses so fine.....
Try the Sierras, the old Sierras
The land of the tall Jack Pine.

Mary M. Kasson

Embrace

As I lay there
In the mist of my solitarily
I could feel the love of one
Cold and scared from the night of pain
Slowly ... she came towards me
Each step with more meaning than the one before
Open her arms lay
Open her heart waits
For when I envelop the warm embrace
I know that pain is no more
In her arms and in my heart I know
That she will shelter me from the pain
Arms around me, protecting my heart
Warm, loved, wanted is that what she gives

J. R. Andrade

Hernando Cortez

Hernando Cortez was from spain.
In the mountains of Mexico
he brought the aztec Indians a lot of pain.

He took their land and
stole their gold because he was
very cruel and bold.

Hernando Cortez died in 1547
and I wonder if he went
to heaven.

Karmel Stapleton

A Small Amount

A small amount is a wise beginning
In the realm of one's careful measure.
It will oft-times lead to a gleesome winning
Of meaningful things to hold and treasure.

A small amount of daily caring
Will build up to a pinnacle of joy.
It usually promotes a wholesome sharing
Of the many things that we employ.

A small amount of cellular tissues
Will continually develop to a mental height,
That will sensibly settle various issues
In the determination of flight or fight.

A small amount of fertile seed
Will sprout and grow all over a field,
Producing much more than one will need,
And, a grateful heart for the abundant yield.

So, always consider that the small amount
Is a most prudent medium in all your measures.
Its ability to increase many things that count
Adds great value to one's chest of treasures......

Violet S. Fifer

Red Water

I Lie Here On My Back
In the Rice Paddies, of the Mekong Delta
Watching, Jet fighters, roar above the Land
While Fireworks, explode into the humid midnight air.

Shrapnel, still, burning, stinging
at the flesh, on my legs.
End the Madness I scream, I pray.

A chilling breeze I wonder Why?
Then Spinning Blades appear in the sky.
A chopper U.S. of A. Hovering above.

An answered Prayer, a friendly Face, A thumbs Up sign
Images of home it's time to Smile.

Suddenly, hearing Foreign voices,
Then, gunfire ringing in my Head
Sweating, Freezing
Body and Mind in a panic
Even these Torrential Rains
Can't Wash away my Tears

I'm Dying Young,
In The RED WATER!

Robert A. Morch

Untitled

I was walking down life's highway
In the springtime of my life,
Sin filled my everyday and I always carried my knife.
My days were blurred by alcohol and drugs
I was alone, sick, and unloved;
All I could see was violence and blood.
When out of the dark the Savior spoke to me
And said I was breaking His heart.
And didn't I know that He had died for me?
Sorrow filled my very being and I asked Him
To please help me.
And that's when the most glorious light
filled my soul;
The Master came and said, "Come, go with me."

Norma Kamansky

The Fisherman

You catch more than fish, don't you?
In the waters of the bay
You seek, not just a bite on your line,
But, also, words shared with a friend
In a time of quietness and peace.

When you are lucky and a string of fish
Dangles from the side of the boat,
With a gleam in your eye, you forget the chore
That will be yours—the messy scaling and gutting—
And anticipate the pleasure of
Giving them to a friend.

Not many people realize, as you do,
That what you really catch to keep
Is what you give away.
The form may be fish,
But the gift is love.

Mary S. Palmer

Loneliness

I never knew how lonely it could be
In the wedded state of matrimony

To be so near, yet worlds apart
Is very trying on the heart

To have so many wants and needs
And no one cares about these needs

All I want is to be number one
To want and need me and call me hon

I have begged, pleaded and sometimes screamed
Does anyone know what I mean

Words come easy, but deeds do not
Everyone thinks that I want a lot

Hold me and love me and show me you care
I might as well be a chair

Try thinking first of me
Do deeds that I can see

Oh well what the hell
I might as well go ring a bell

No one cares what I think
So I might as well go have a drink

Sharron Dorst

Today's Promise

This magic day promise to your God
Inside your heart to stop feeding
Yourself with dead parts of once living creatures.
Receiving this day the magic power
To exorcise for the rest of your life:
Pain, diseases, violence, depression
And self-hate or those crashes
That come in many ways.
Therefore, we must do so to
Receive this above blessing to begin
Our new journey.
We are living the most violent
Times just because we have been
Blind, paying for the ignorance of
Past times.
Parents must not train their
Children to adore stuffed animals
While they serve on their sacred
Table the mutilated parts of the
Real ones.

Tamara Vargas '95

"We Know You Taught Us True"

In Memory of Our Mother, Evelyn Lee Shipman

You were always there, our tower of strength,
In this world of truth and lies,
You stood the test in the storms of life,
Without a compromise.

We learned from you our better side,
Of the person we should be,
The courage of a patient heart,
While cowards fail and flee.

You taught us to look deeper,
Past the simple human form,
Beyond despair, to where spirit dwells,
And ignore all false alarm.

To cast away the tempered shell,
One wears as armor clad,
And see the child within us all,
In an angry world gone mad.

And now when fear surrounds us,
We draw on memories of you,
And whether life is sweet or bitter,
We know, you taught us true.

Ronald P. Shipman

The Betrayal

It rained
inevitably I was left in still water
pooled about my feet—hoping
hoping for ever-so-long that you too would remain still.

I wept
inevitably I was left in still water
joined in my sorrow by each wish—hoping
praying that you might feel as I had, know what I knew.

I cried
openly at first then more gently
for times, shadows really, of my former life
who had come and taken it from me? God?
I don't know and I stood too afraid to know.

It rained and I wept
pools mixed in no particular order, and yet
I knew that to love does not find barriers in raiments
love knows no master, lives in no house, is bound by no convention
and has left me breathless and afraid in its wake.

I cried, it rained, I wept, and love grew between us
and with us and around us—hoping that both may bloom—I cried.

Larry Dean

Our Wedding Day

May our wedding day be filled with bliss,
Initiated at the altar with a kiss.
A Love that is true which no one can deny,
Will be ours until the day we die.
There are many memories on the road that lies ahead,
Many will be good ones, some we may wish were dead.
But no matter what the circumstance,
There will never be an end to this romance.
Romance, Passion, Love, or Armour,
No matter how you phrase it, I will keep delivering more.
And when our lives start to fade, and gray appears in your hair,
That Love we knew at the altar will still be there.
It will get us through some hard times, it will strengthen us through the years,
And Love, Yes Baby, means I will always care, dear.
I will be a shoulder to cry on and an ear to sound your trouble,
And all the love that you give to me I swear to give you double.
So, I vow on this wedding day to make you my wife,
But Leslie, it's really so much more, for I really am promising to make you my Life.

A. Ashley Booth

Hide N Seek

I feel my tears playing hide N seek with my emotions.
Insecurity and jealousy
Are conducting the search.

Resentment and anger are hiding in the shadows
Just beyond my reach.

Hurt and loss are lingering just outside the boundaries.
Escaping the rules of the game.

I am lost trying to find myself.
Searching madly, hiding from myself.

I am afraid to find me.
Tag.....I am still it.

I feel my tears playing hide N seek with me.

Sheri Wade

No Ammunition

High flyin' dreams on a budget of a lady poor
Is a hope, a desired wish that may not come true.
Whether it's false to dream such dreams for:
The purpose of improving one's station's quality will do
Wonders for the frailty of humans' emotional state
When the reality of life bites & stings like bees
Instead of being calm, full of peace: overcome by hate
That rages and boils over into violence tossed seas
Of discontented, disgruntled, frustrated swarms
Avast the disasters of nature and of God's stormy tests.
Not much happiness left which heart it warms
When settling for second rate rather than wait for the best.
For the force of time is unjust and unfair
And all one works toward is no longer there
For the meaning is lost with the ambition
And all the guns lay silent with no ammunition!

Marie C. Sholunas

The Worth Of Fame

Fifteen minutes of fame, they say
Is all we get along life's way

To give the world a chance to see
The stuff that's inside you and me.

Does a few moments of notice mean that much
To seek out glory's noble touch?

For after all is said and done,
And life's journey meets the setting sun;

It seems less important trying to mark the miles
Than it is to try to count the smiles.

Ronald R. Strausser

Death Forecast

The Growing Wearnies of impending Death,
Is Constantly approaching with each breath,
I'm not able to control this terrible deed.
Could he do this to me? With not a heed
To my life, my loves or any of my needs.
Is as he planted a dread and terrible seed,
And then died, leaving me all alone,
To deal with it, accept it and to atone,
For this, I gave twenty-six years of my life,
To struggle, to work for all this strife,
Somehow I must try to obtain peace,
A new contract of life, a new lease,
I know it's within me to do so,
This, I must do, before it's time to go.
No one will ever know and the secret goes,
Never to ever be revealed by my foes.

Nancy Dauley

Happiness

What is happiness?
Is it climbing a tree?
Could it be getting stung by a bee?
Eating ice cream on a hot sunny day.
Or taking a swim in a cool, blue bay.
I ask myself these questions many times a day.

What is happiness?
Is it when you get to sing your favorite song?
Or flying in the sky all day long?
Could happiness be right in front of our face?
Or are we just passing it by without a trace?
Will we ever know what happiness may be?
I am sure it is just me loving me.

Kelly Rupp

A Child's Fears

What's out there in the darkness, just waiting there for me
Is it something to be frightened of, or mere tranquility?

What's out there in the darkness, as I lay upon my bed
Is it something that will soothe me, or something I should dread.

What's out there in the darkness, with no one here to save
With my Teddy Bear beside me, I'm trying to be brave.

I guess I'll have to be grown up, and put away my fears,
And be like Daddy, brave and true, but first I'll dry my tears.

Linda C. Corkery

"What Is Love?"

What is love from one to another?
Is it when your heart is full of pain?
For you just hunger to hear your lover's sweet name.
Or maybe it's just a thought of romance.
To unfold the many days of happiness.
I believe it's just an emotion,
That is not within any sort
Of this world, but within the next,
To be endured and felt forever
With eternal happiness and with
Another of likeness,
For loves come and go, but only
One may stay eternally
So choose to be chosen
Because happiness is found
Where you look for it.

Lea Ann Druck

Mister Moose

The month of October
is like a cold shoulder.
The hunters all trample with heavy boots
and carry large guns that shoot.

Autumn colors are in session,
but I'm missing the art lesson.
As I run through the field
I know they won't yield.

As they fire at me
I try to run free.
My antlers get caught in a tree,
So I can't flee.

I try to take cover
But I'm discovered
By hunters near by.
I wish I could fly!

I fall to the ground,
As they estimate my pounds.
It's all so clear,
my life ends right here.

Martha MacFarland

Shopping Trip

Shopping at the grocery store
Is now much different than before
The reason no doubt must be
My darling daughter age three
Her tiny mind programmed by ads
Makes her lips beg for new fads
Each request is expressed as a need
Soon sweetness is replaced by greed
Suddenly I'm sounding just like Monty Hall
"Just let mommy finish, I'll buy you a ball"
My mind now unable to recall
Do I indeed have it all?
I grab my girl, I get in line.
If I'm lucky we'll eat by nine
Home I go and start to unpack
Where's the milk! Oh no I'll have to go back!!!

Maggie Rice

Letting Go... Saying Goodbye To The One You Love

To walk away, to say goodbye to you;
Is one of the most painful things I've ever had to do.
To turn around and not look back on what we shared,
And face the fact that you never really cared.

It hurts more than words could ever say,
My only expression is the stream of tears on my face.
As I look back to yesterday and my hope for our tomorrow,
All I see now is an empty dream and a promise of sorrow.

I know I have to go on without you at my side; and, I will,
I realize that life goes on, and for no one does time stand still.
It's just hard to let go of you and our love,
Cause I believed you were sent from heaven above.

I do wish you the best of everything,
And my hat goes off to the one who will wear your ring.
Goodbye, my love, I'm letting you go free
But, the memories of us, in my heart will forever be.

Yes, I'll always remember the times that we had,
Laughter, tears, ups, downs, and, yes, my sweet, even the bad.
I wish you the best of everything, now that we're apart,
Even love and bliss, really, and that's straight from the heart.

Teresa A. Powell

My Best Friend

What I look for in a best friend
Is someone who will be there 'til the end.
Someone with lots of patience and trust,
And loyalty, now that's a must.

Someone who will listen and give advice,
Who doesn't get mad if you ask twice.
Someone who always makes time for you
No matter what they've got to do.

Someone who loves you for who you are,
And doesn't ask you to be anything more.
Who can help you through all your pain,
Doing it for you and their own gain.

Someone who knows your every thought,
Whose love and friendship doesn't have to be bought.
Someone who will be there through thick and through thin;
All these qualities I found in my best friend.

Leslie Reynolds

"Life"

Life, tell me, what is life?
Is this striving to survive, is this life?
Always trying to exist, never being happy,
just existing!
No, I feel there must be more!
I know in the next life there will be.
But what about now!?
I try, I work, help others, love, or do I love?
I'm not sure I know the word.
I feel no love, no one gives me true love.
So maybe love is like respect,
You have to earn it.
I want love, the deep giving kind, not surface love!
Real love never expects anything in return.
It just gives, and flows, it feels hurt, pain,
But still gives.....

E. J. Ellis

"Essence Of Life"

Life, some people say;
is what you make of it!
But I say, what good is life without
its essence,
For it is by the essence of life
that life itself begins and ends
Just as it is by the essence of life
the Sun Shines, rain falls, seasons change
and a mother loves her child,
it is by this very essence
our spirits are allowed to rise
and when at times we're feeling low
His love is our disguise
life without its essence
is no life at all
Although this very essence
Lies with in us Ace!!

Stephanie Eric Tamlin

A Mother's Love

Mary, peaceful Mary, you gave us your son
is your heart yet full Mary? Your faith yet strong!
But your heart is true, for only you have bore God's Son
only a mother's love could sustain you
To be so faithful, to leave comforts of home when your time is so near
to go out into the known and the unknown
Follow your heart Dear Mary, for a mother's love is like none other
it comes from Heaven with Baby Jesus
The pain and anguish that labor brings, yet no comfort do you find
a strange city, with no room for a mother in need
yet your faith was there, to guide you and fill you with love
To bear your son, you know where not, to bear your son, you
know how not
For your Mary, who sustained you? Gave you peace for a difficult time
with no mother by your side of offer words of comfort
You question not, but you know a mother's love will bring peace
to your heart
For you give of yourself the greatest gift you could offer
With your heart to guide you, for the truth burns within you
The Son of God, The Mother of God
For a Mother's Love is the warm place in my heart!

Lillian E. Peters

Why?

Why is it I have to get separated every time I fall in love,
Isn't there a God above,

Why can't be with that special guy sitting in the sand,
Watching the sunset hand in hand,

Why is it, every time I fall in love I have to get a broken heart,
And get my heart torn apart,

It's so hard,
Standing in the backyard,

Thinking about all the good memories and you,
And the way our love was once true,

It's weird how I just had to leave,
I made my own heart deceive,

It's not fair, you know why because it's so hard to bare,
Since I really care,

I miss the times you bugged me,
I miss the special way you hugged me,

But out of everything you know what I miss,
It's your tender kiss,

And I always say to myself why did you have to go away,
Please come back with you I want to stay!!!

Lillian Oloomi

The Mind's Eye

What a wondrous thing the mind's eye is
It allows us to glow in the dark
It lets us chase the wild butterfly
For hours on end through the park

Its magic makes us what we long to be
Young - old - tall - short, it's our choice
We can run, we can fly, we can do it all
And we all have that magical voice

It takes us to places we've never been
And we dwell there as long as we choose
It lets us be whatever we wish
In our mind's eye - we never lose

It's God's gift to we mere mortals
It's boundless - endless - and free
Perhaps it's meant as only a glimpse
Oh how Lovely Heaven will be

Norval H. Sanders

That Plastic Heart

O coração, o pobre coração.
It beats so wild, when you are standing near.
It almost dies whenever you are gone
With loneliness, anxiety and fear.

I wish they had invented plastic heart
Insensitive to stars and moon above.
That plastic heart, that would not ever cry
Because of you and my frustrated love.

And should my heart become a feeble toy
In careless hands and fall and break apart,
All I would need to send an office boy
To buy for me another plastic heart.

But plastic heart; alas entirely unknown.
With real one I'll have to carry on,
With one that longs for you and cries for you alone.
O coração, o pobre coração.

Victor Salatko

The March Wind

The March wind marches in like soldiers on the attack.
It blows down roof tiles, and squirrel nests.
It bends trees and bushes, and whips up waters in
lakes and seas.
It blows off hats, and turns umbrellas inside out.
It pushes on backs and nearly knocks you over.
It swirls around looking for spring.
When it sees small flowers appearing, it slows down
and marches quietly around them.
Now it marches at a steady pace, clearing the air,
taking winter away, and wining the battle.
Then it marches proudly, turning its back on the
month of March, exiting, to let April begin.

Ken Schmidt

Wonderment

There is no nonsense in the wind,
it blows with careless effort.
When it is gentle, it is just a breeze.
When it is angry, it is a howling gusty gale.
I love the gentle breeze that blows,
I don't even mind the wind.
But one thing that scares me to death,
is the angry howling breath
of Mother Nature.
It matters little what I think,
Mother Nature has the show
and can cause wonderful beauty,
and even death we know.

Marie Rosas

Untitled

I feel the wind blow through my soul.
It breathes in me the days of olde.
I remember times of yesterday my soul was "young" and "free to play!
I remember boys who'd come to call.
The trees I'd climb and sometimes fall.
I remember the giggles my friends and I shared
The chances we took and all that we dared.
These memories are mine and cherished so much.
Locked away safe, where no one can touch
Now I'm gray and growing old.
My memories more precious, more precious than Gold.

Poet Iverson

Life

Life is so strange...
It can bring you joy, It can bring you pain...
Sometimes we feels like it's so unfair
We began to believe that God doesn't really care...
We all have our love ones, with whom we love so dear...
It's still not clear. When we loose a love one, we began too
wonder. Why? does God give us our love ones? And to turn
around and have them to depart from us. It's really hard
for us to bare. Remember. My friend, God is, and always will
be there, And he does care.

He does not put no more pain on us than we can bare.
So! I would like to say my friend, once again, he never
leaves us alone. He walks with us every single day of
our lives. There no such thing as dying.
We just goes on to a much better place.
There comes a time when our very old bodies just began
to tired. God knows best. So he just gives us along and
peaceful rest - Until judgement day -"God's be with you."

Lillian Louise Edwards

Next Time Lord

When God came down from heaven to take you from me
It caused saddened feelings leaving me empty
My heart was broken because there was no love
Because Lord you took my one and only, above
You took Bob when things were going great
But since then all my love has turned to hate
I was mad at the world and everyone in it
Family and friends and those that came to visit
You took all my loves, my husband, daughter, mom and dad
Grandparents relatives, friends and children. How sad!
You even took my dog which left me all alone
With only memories, pictures and a old dog bone
And now you sent me another Bob to share my life
Even though were not married were like husband and wife
The laughter is slowly coming back in the house
Two dogs stormy and teezer who replace silence with joust
And now I'm finding love and happiness again
But next time Lord please take me and not them

Margaret Seiders

State Of Grace

In old age, in December
It doesn't take a book
To say it all.
No great tome of theology is needed.
A few spare lines will do.

We live, have lived
Steeped in holy mysteries,
Sacraments everywhere.

The tall oak sheds golden leaves,
Flowers fade,
A mass of arctic air falls
All the way to Mississippi.

Spring remembered,
Prodigious, prolific, boundless creation.

Now the dying time.
Yet cicadas sleep in earth
To rise again
And dormant seeds hold life.

What a strange place.
What a gift!

Robert Ray McGee

The Loss

When the sky is blue and the sun shines down
It eases some pain and I love my frown.
In my heart I know you are there
But when the sky is gray I always wonder where.
My mind tells me one thing, my heart tells another.
How do I deal with the loss of my brother?
Time does not heal as I have been told
When the pain is so great that I feel I could fold.
Then the sun comes out to give me the hope
That I need at this time to be able to cope.
The pain of loss I now know will always stay,
In the hope of acceptance I kneel down to pray
For the day to come that I might actually start
To believe he is with me forever...
As long as I keep him in my heart.

Suzanne McGlynn

Love Is Like A Rose

Love is a feeling that goes and grows,
it flourishes in sunshine and resembles a rose.

Frail and fragrant and cherished forever,
properly loved and nourished, its end is never.

A rose is more than mere beauty and scent,
roughness in handling, will cause many a dent.

Loving another, is to be as a rose,
the more you love, the more it grows.

The radiant beauty of the rose, is like it glows,
the beauty of love is the bonding of souls.

Both can die by frost or neglect,
against demise one must always protect.

Hold together and forever be as one,
with joy and contentment to out shine the sun.

Robert C. Newsom

Welcome

This welcome is short, it's not very long...
It goes to you, from our church home.
It'll make you smile, it'll make you glow...
You'll want to come back, for this we know.
You see the cross upon the wall...
It always says, "Welcome! Come one, come all."..
You see the hands, and how they pray...
That grace may abound from day to day!
You see the pianist, and hear the tunes she plays...
With a choir that sings their words of praise.
We'll hear the words of God...
And apply them to our lives, with faith, hope and charity,
And power to survive!
So from the pulpit, and members, too...
We grant a heart-felt "welcome", to you, to you and to you!

Wilma Pendgraft Calicuitt

Life

Life is like a river
It has its ups and downs
Sometimes it's rough
Sometimes it's calm
But at the end of the river
There is always a much bigger and better place
Opportunity is there
For those who believe
Help as come
For those in need
There is peace and love
All around
Happiness is there
Throughout the land
There are no fights nor wars
You lead a wonderful life.

Natalie Reed

The River

I see a river and every thing a river has.
It has long terrifying, fearful rapids,
It has tall ridges,
huge rough round dangerous rocks,
It has smooth calm deep fishing holes.
The best part is the trickling sound of the waves.
Except this is not a river of water,
but of life.

Tyler Pratt

A Poem In The Making

A poem in the making is some words that seem to rhyme
It illustrates a parable to what may pique the mind.
It's a metaphor of rolling verse on the condition of the soul.
Some lines glued to an ancient tune from the days of Rock N'Roll.

A poem in the making is an avenue of stains.
Spotted notes of hidden thoughts, a cadence bleached with pain.
A tease to catch a scholar's muse and asked the question why,
We only play the role we play in life, is how we hide.

A poem in the making is a maxim to mankind.
The difference is, it's from the heart, and isn't from the mind.
A statement of sincerity which rings of honesty
Time is, the poem in the making for all eternity.

Michael O. Sullivan

It Is A Friend

It's a friend that is faithful,
It is a friend that is true.
It is a friend that is there.
There during the longest of nights, and
days that are bright.
This is a friend that can greet you
with the warmest of touches,
and sometimes hurt you while holding
on to tightly.
This friend, is friends to all of us.
This friends name is
Loneliness.

Michael T. Countryman

Spring Is -

Spring is a picture, too big for a canvas,
It is a poem, too big for a book,
Spring is life at its grandest,
And it can be yours for merely a look!

Spring is the rain twinkling on the new flowers,
It is diamonds on the grass,
It is clouds parting after the showers
And the sun smiling through at their pass.

Spring is the many delicate shades of things,
Such as in The For-get-me-nots, tulips and rose,
it is the robin's sweet song and the flutter of His wings,
Ah, it is new life to everything that grows!

Sylvia H. Cole

Struggle Within

It can be frightening and awesome...
It is depressing and yet re-assuring
To know in your heart you'll never be alone
If you can believe and trust in yourself
You may even find the whole world alluring.

I too, can admit the terrible truth of
Over-powering symptoms which tend to include
The struggle within to somehow survive
Those devastating temptations that come with abuse.

I'd give anything: Myself included
To never again have to suffer through
The horrible sickness and indescribable fluke
Of living a hell that so many of us do.......

Sharon Lynn Drew

The Child

The time has come. The point has been reached.
It is love to some, "Mere infatuation," others have preached.
Searching my soul for a window to my heart,
Forgetting what I've been told, all for a new start.
I take a deep breath and close my eyes.
Love overshadowed by the death of the naive child inside.

As time passes on, our love grows much deeper.
From dusk 'til dawn my thoughts can be no sweeter.
My dreams filled with laughter and smiles so true.
I think of life ever after and know I'll always have you.
We're there for each other; for things big and small.
Our love made in heaven will last through it all.

Yet, blinded by happiness I let down my guard.
My trust in your kiss broke my tender heart.
Tears fall from my eyes as I cry all alone.
Mislead by your lies, this naive child has but grown.
Knowing more now than before, I start over again,
In search to restore that love from within.

Terri S. Wiles

"Today Is, Time"

Eternity, has no time. Only today is, time.
It is now, it is here, we live time.
We are limited, we are set, to die in time.
Now, would be best, to believe all truth
and, understand why. Not willing to see why,
shortens time believing.
The truth is in ourselves, when we expose our will,
to hear the truth, see the truth, acknowledge the truth,
live the truth. Then, we know why time, is our learning,
in preparing for eternity.
Be very careful, how you live—
Not as unwise but, as wise.

M. Margaret Hofseth

Love

It is not something you can buy
It is something you can give and receive
It can make you happy or it can make you cry
But it is something we all can believe

It is the greatest power of all
It always brings us to its all
We may not think of it everyday
But it is something we all say

It comes from the heart and soul
It makes us better when we're feeling low
It is something that keeps all of us together
It is something we all must have forever

It is something we all possess
It's the one thing that will never die or go to rest
It is the greatest thing on planet earth
And no amount of money can match its worth

It comes from the heaven above
It comes from each and every one of us
It is something that we all can trust
And that is what we all call LOVE.

Stephen Wood

A Child's Flight

The Hobgoblin with horns aplenty, it comes no more today.
It's pitty packs and mitty macks, no more to spoil our time for play.
For School is Dead in May!
Up, Up and Away! Three Cheers! Yippee! Yea! Hooray!!

Robert Thomas Hill

The World Shines

The smile on your face was always so bright,
It just seemed when you were around you made the world shine,
But that day when I lost you it seemed that I went insane,
The thought of being without you made me not want to go on,
You would make me see how the sun rose, and then left,
Just like the way you left me:
I know I must go on
I know I must be strong in order to survive.

In order for me to survive I must think of the good in the world,
and not the bad
Not like that terrible disease that took you away from me!

Rebecca L. Marnell

Scars

Scars from hunger, they are so deep
It makes me wonder, how many can't sleep

Scars from a bruise, on a beautiful flower
One that does not wash away, in a rain shower

Scars from a word, you have said in anger
A scar that does not erase, with an eraser
Scars from the love, you do not give
A flower without sunlight, it will not live

Scars from a demon, trying to make a perfect angel
Like glass that will break, it is so fragile

Scars that don't make you stop and think?
Everything you do is written in ink

Scars I wish I could gather, a package of seeds everyday
Plant them in my lap, to show them the way

Scars from my love, which will make them grow and blossom
A human; a child; could anything be more awesome?

Scars that are not there, the scars you don't make today
Will grow to become, a beautiful bouquet.

Sirena Diane New

Reflection

To us the seeing people of this earth
It seems a pity that the blind and deaf,
Those children of the silent night,
Will ne'er behold the evening sun as it
Goes down behind a mountain's purple ridge.
Will never hear the lilting strains of Strauss'
Undying melodies nor listen with
Attentive ear to Brahms, Beethoven or Bach.

Those children of the silent night
Will ne'er behold the ruined cities of
The world, bombed and crushed by warring nations.
Will never hear the scream of falling bombs,
Of people pinned beneath their battered homes.
To us, the seeing, is this heritage.

William W. Fagan, deceased

Soaring High

Soaring high through the sky
is the Golden eagle.
This eagle is part gold,
very bright and bold.
The babies get pushed out of their nests
and they do not look their very best.
So if you get a chance
to see this eagle dance,
be thankful of the way she flies
because you might never be able to say good-bye!

Stacey Webb

"A Special Place"

Inspired by my mother and father, Lucile and S.G. Ricker with love

Time seems to escape through this special place
It seems so dark to this aging face
With nowhere else to hide
It seemed her soul had almost died
Not with you, but only with me
She's exactly where she wants to be
Obvious to the sounds around
Her thoughts are far from being profound
That touch of the love she yearns that may
Memories of the sweet smell of passion
With a love so far away
The taste of life that only comes with time
This is her own realm
Yes her special place is my own mind

Kimberly Guinther

Fear

Fear is the color of fire in hell
It sounds like a heart beat racing faster and faster
And tastes like acid eating away at your sanity
It smells like a choking cloud of gas
And looks like a never ending fault in the earth
It makes me feel cold

Fear is black like a cage
It sounds like adrenaline pumping
And tastes like salty tears
It smells like stale air
Fear looks like a distorted mirror
It makes me feel vulnerable

Fear is the color of a raging tornado
It sounds like an angry fist beating at the door
It tastes like a bitter poison
And smells like cooking sauerkraut
It looks like a predator stalking its prey
Fear makes me feel alone

Fear is the unknown enemy within us all.

Nicole Lykens

Love

Love is beauty in action
It speaks more loudly than words.
One cannot explain its attraction
But it's seen in the flight of the birds.

It could be an arm placed around you,
The flowers springing up from the sod,
Or maybe the Holy Spirit
Descending to earth from God.

Although it's beyond understanding,
We still feel the joy it will bring
As our hearts seem to keep on expanding,
And we feel like those birds on the wing.

Roland Symons

Needing

Needing is like a disease:
It starts small with a spark of desire;
innocent in its warmth, so easily it deceives.
Growing it bursts forth in a raging flame;
metastasizing like a cancer out of control.
Consuming it destroys that which gave it life;
depleting the nutrients of its foundation,
till it crumbles like the ashes of a fire
many years spent.
It came; It went.

Kathrene C. Berger

The Secret

Since childhood days, when thru the country lanes I walked,
It stayed with me and pleaded to be set free.
But being young and shy I balked,
And so my secret followed me;
Into a world beyond those muddy lanes
Where wordily pleasures taunted each new turn,
And losses overpowered gains.
And yet my secret still did yearn
To scream to everyone the news;
But yet I would not let it go,
Knowing not their private views
I felt compelled to keep on saying no.
And then into the twilight years I turned
And with my secret still inside of me,
The need to tell still burned,
But 'twas too late, and now will never be.

Raymond Smith

I Love A Smile

Do you notice that a smile will soften any face.
It takes away the hardness and does not leave a trace.
I love to make people smile, no matter who they are.
When a person smiles they are prettier by far.
No one is really ugly, no matter how they look,
If they will only smile with that little upward crook.
A real smile brings a twinkle to any pair of eyes.
It brightens every countenance, that's where the beauty lies.
I love to see a smile break across a frown,
It always brings a pleasure to all who are around.
Long or short, thin or fat, no matter the shape of the face,
Like a lovely garment, the smile is the lace.

Ruth Kirk

Afraid To Let Go

You were the first to steal my heart,
It was a great feeling to know.
But now it's shattered in a million parts,
And for you it won't let go.

I'm afraid I'll forget; the taste of your lips,
While we embraced kiss after kiss.
I'm afraid I'll forget; your smile, your face,
Even though it cannot be replaced.

I'm afraid I'll forget; the little things you do,
Which meant so much, and still do.
I'm afraid I'll forget; the smooth feel of your skin,
And the warmth that radiates from within.

But I'll never forget; the love that we shared,
Because I know, that we both cared.
I miss your embrace, your soft gentle touch,
I miss the way you held me; and how it meant so much.

I miss being with you, being by your side.
And I miss that feeling, that now you seem
to hide.

Misty Rainey

Love Is

Love is the feeling inside when he happens to pass by,
Love is also the hurt that makes you sit for hours and cry.
Love is the happiness you feel when you look into his eyes.
Love is the smile that comes to your face when you think
of your guy.
Love is the pain you get after he's told you lies.
Love is the problems, the fighting, and the question why?
Love, is the greatest thing in life regardless of the
problems, that you'll have until you die.

Sarah Stine

The Bridge

A bridge I am rebuilding was burned long ago
It was built one day during a January snow
At first it was nurtured and kept from wear
But as the new wore off it began to tear

Piece by piece, it began to fall
Until finally...that fatal flaw
And in flames it did ignite
One dreadful, cold November night

And so I harbored anger and woe
As many do when a loved one does go
As times of reflection came and went
I could not forget, was my only hint

Reaching out with a warm return
Has saved my soul from this constant yearn
For I am now free of all regret
Why our bridge stands is no secret

Lori Gieger

I Loved You Too Much

Our love was one, that was never meant to be.
It was doomed from the start but this we could not see.
I yearned to have you with me, near me, by my side forever.
But how could I possibly think this way, when you went home to her.
I dreamt sweet passionate dreams of you, every single night.
Knowing deep in my heart, that this just wasn't right.
I told you my deepest thoughts, never thinking twice.
You were the man, the only man, I wanted in my life.
How could I fall so deep in love, with someone who wasn't mine.
Desperately seeking love from you so precious and divine.
I needed you, wanted you, longed to have you near.
But all the while, inside my heart, struggled with my biggest fear.
How could I feel this way, for a man that wasn't mine.
I was face to face with my deepest thoughts, walking a thin line.
Loving you, wanting you, craving your tender touch.
I had to face reality.. I loved you too much.

Marisa Outley Jackson

The First Snow

I saw the first snow of the season.
It was the most beautiful one I'd seen.
Because now I see things in a different light,
since you are here with me.

You're love and you're understanding.
The looks you give me each day,
have given life to a kindred spirit,
in a most delightful way.
I feel like a child exploring,
not knowing what's ahead for me,
but wanting to take chances,
just to have you here by me.

You never know when love will find you,
and timing is not always right,
but you're like the first snow of the season,
all warm, wondrous and bright.

Nancy L. Flynn

Life's Little Dreams

When you're young you feel you can sing forever of your
many Life's Dreams.
When you're young you Dream your family will always be.
When you're young you Dream your friends will always be.
When you're young you Dream your cares will always be care free.
When you're young and fall in love your Dreams will always be.
Never stop Dreaming and your Life will always be
full of Life's Little Dreams.

Morris Knowles

Peace

If I could wish one wish for you,
It would be "Peace" to see you through,
The days the months, the years ahead;
Where will we be when all is said?

To live life to the fullest, is an unrequited dream;
If worldly goods are all you seek;
You're on the losing team.
But first thing's first, what could that be?
It's peace with God, then you will see
That life is good, and air is free;
And being what you're meant to be,
Will bring you peace, and set you free.

Free to live, to love,to care;
To bear the pain we're sure to share;
But peace with God, will see you through,
He cares for me and He cares for you.

I wish you joy, I wish you love
I ask God's blessings from above.
We'll all go on our separate ways;
I wish you peace, for all your days.

Ruby Sarazen

"Music Man"

You said, "Don't let them steal your pain away."
"It's a part of who you are."
The lessons from those rainy days
Are sure to take me far.
I never had the chance to know you.
We only exchanged first names.
I didn't have myself to show you.
We were too wounded for playing games.
You shared with me your melodies,
And I drank in every chord.
Our eyes held infidelities
Of the pasts we could not afford.
You gripped your instrument as a vessel for survival.
I consumed its artistry as food for my revival.
"Suicide Is Painless" - a tune I still hear you strum.
You left without resolution. What are you running from?

Kelly Morgan

"Realization Of Loneliness"

I just can't help the way I feel
It's as if somebody has shot me,
and left me for dead.
It seems like I give all my love to someone
and when times are hard, when I need help
I'm standing in a vast open space
With no one around for miles.
I can't see nor hear no one
Yet I reach and call out to anyone
to just help me!
To show some kind of affection or compassion.
But there's nothing but the feel of emptiness.
The echo of my voice
and the sound of another shot penetrating
my already wounded body.
And there's a white cloud, and dark thoughts
And nothing but pain.
The pain of loneliness......

Kenneth L. Kotewa Jr.

"The Blue Diamond"

The Blue Diamond sits in the case. People pass by admiring its grace.
Memories of old flames surface and thoughts of true love to come.
My past returns and I recall all the times in my life when
everything went wrong.
What a day. What a life. What a past.
Now, I can only think of the future and hope for the best.
The Blue Diamond can be considered a way of life.
It's remarkable, dazzling, and smooth. Then suddenly it cuts.
We meet people, think they're the one, and it turns out they're not.
It hurts, just like a Blue Diamond.
So, I continue looking at all the different kinds of stones
that exist — precious and semi-precious.
I keep on looking for that perfect Diamond, but my heart doubts
I'll ever find it.
Usually, you go through life and you only get cut.
It really burns when you look at my Blue Diamond and see the
price and know you can't get it.
But, my Blue Diamond is different. It doesn't hurt...it stings.

Kendra Dorty

Goodbye

It's hard to just stand by and watch as your eyes cry,
It's hard to understand and realize the reasons why,
My heart goes out to you with a heavy sigh,
I wish I could say the words to make your emotions high,
But I know that in your heart your struggling with the words goodbye.
I know that your in pain I can see it in your eyes,
I hear it in your voice and know it when you cry,
If I could only understand than I could help you fly,
For I know your mind is heavy and I am oh so shy,
But I know that in your heart your struggling with the words goodbye.
At times you feel like running but you have no place to hide,
You turn around each corner and take each day in stride,
And as you go about your day you hold your head with pride,
But I know that in your heart your struggling with the words goodbye.
Each day brings forth a new beginning or so that we are told,
Perhaps today will bring a friend or someone you can hold,
Someone who'll keep in confidence the things that you unfold,
Because you'll find someone like you someone being so bold, they'll
Know what your going through for they too have been told, and they'll
Know that in your heart your struggling with the words goodbye.

Nedra Ticknor

Mother Our Best Girl

Of all the things that we love in this world
It's mostly of you mother, our best girl
No matter what we have we would give to you
Because we know of the sorrow for us that you
Have been through.

Though mother's day may come but once a year
It is every day that we hold you so dear
You give your love to us in many ways
That we won't forget till the end of our days.

We love you so much with all our heart
That distance nor death can ever tear it apart
It is not only on mothers day that we are true
But during every minute of every day, every
year that we love you.

Leonard R. Kantor

Let Them Live

How can they say it is o.k, then just turn and walk away?
It's MURDER it's wrong! It can't go on!

These babies have no choice, so listen up and hear my voice.
They say it's law, to never kill at all.
Then, what do you call ABORTION?
It's MURDER, that's all.

You probably never gave one thought,
to what these babies could have brought.
You'll never get to hear their cries,
or wipe the tears from their little eyes.
You'll never get to see them walk,
or even hear how well they'll talk.
You'll never get to hold their hand, or just sit and watch them sleep.

A baby is a gift from GOD, (sent from up above.)
No matter how they were conceived, they're someone to be loved.

ABORTION IS LEGAL, OH HOW SO EVIL!!!
And now just think of what you've heard,
and go ahead and take GOD'S WORD.
So now the choice is left to you,
HOW WOULD YOU FEEL IF THEY DID THIS TO YOU?

Vicki Resch

Fatal Beauty

The beauty of a rose is forever seen in nature.
Its petals can capture the sunlight and the rain.
It is a fatal beauty with a twinge of pain.
The petals are tender to the touch.
but if it is grasped the wrong way its thorns are its protector.
A rose can be a symbol of love or purity.
Red as blood or white as snow, on a crisp winter evening.
A rose can also be a symbol of pain and death.
Black as a night sky in the countryside.
This beauty holds two sides to itself.
One is sweet and innocent, and the other is cold and cruel.
It lives until its beauty fades away.
Its beauty makes it appealing until it simply shrivels and closes
itself forever.
The petals can no longer be touched, because they will fall to the
ground.
They are free, blown away in the wind.
The rose is a symbol that is seen throughout our lives.
From life to death, its petals capture the sunlight and the rain.
It is a fatal beauty with a twinge of pain.

Kimberly Johnson

A Playful Child

It's playtime once I get up
It's playtime until I sleep
It's playtime all day long, let's play, play, play!

I love playing in spring and summer
I don't mind a cold weather
Rain or sun I care little, let's play, play, play!

I love playing in breezy wind
I don't mind a muddy pond
Dirt or snow I care little, let's play, play, play!

I love playing in a lush plantation
I don't mind a rocky mountain
River or ocean I care little, let's play, play, play!

I love playing in a tropical forest
I don't mind an arid desert
Meadow or plain I care little, let's play, play, play!

I love playing with a christian boy
I don't mind a Jewish guy
Hindu, Muslim, or Buddhist I care little, let's play, play, play!

Ramesh S. Hegde

Perfectionism

Perfection, you know, is the only way to go
It's the road I continually seek.
To be 'average', you see, is an insult to me,
It's a threat to my insatiable goal.

"One day," they say, "you'll discover the mistake
Inherent in this cognitive distortion.
So, for your own sake - and before it's too late -
Better modify this mental contortion."

Oh, say can you see from the perfectionist tree
The dangers lurking before you:
Frustration, exasperation, agitation, debilitation,
Few innocuous points to be seen.

Perfection, although, with its own set of woes,
Has a striking attraction to me;
And to turn from it now would only leave a 'frown' -
A 'flaw' on my impeccable soul!

Perfection, you know, is the only way to go;
I'll follow it till the day I die.
And if you'll join me too I can guarantee that you
Will be just as miserable as I!

Morris Murray Jr.

Weeping Willow Tree

How I wonder, can it be
I've discovered the Earth's most beautiful tree
Its branches cascade like a slow waterfall
Mobile arms flowing, green leaves and all
It stands in all its majesty
Winds playing games with its tapestry
It is said you are weeping
For what and for whom
As your beauty betrays all others in bloom
Yet you stand there so staunchly
You stand there so proud
Can it be you try to catch a cloud
Do you weep 'cause you can't reach the sky
Or catch a bird as he fly's by
Wistful weeping willow tree
Won't you be mine eternally?

Ruth Schwartz

"Forever Dreams"

Empty heart, empty soul — all my highs just turned to lows.

Life is changing all the time
I've found that these dreams of mine
May come along and then may go
And again my highs will turn to lows
Like a merry-go-round there are ups and downs
My dreams can take me all around
Through the highs, I'll be free
But through the lows depressed I'll be

Empty heart, empty soul — all my highs just turned to lows.

Love will come and love will go
So will the flowers and the snow
Nothing lasts forever not today, tomorrow, ever
Although it's easier said than done
I'll have to take things as they come
I'll try to make a brand new start
Brace myself and hold my heart
Keep it from falling too much in love
And pray for some good to come from above

Yes, empty heart, empty soul all my highs just turned to lows

Kim Kane

Occupy 'Til He Comes

I ask and ask, will it happen today?
I've looked and looked for many years.
Has it been easy to travel this way?
Yes and no, for I've shed happy and sad tears.

Occupy 'til He comes, the word does say.
Just a smile, a hug or a kind word
For someone who's hurting or had a bad day.
It'll be worth it all, for the Master has heard.

Payday for all will come one day.
What will the accounting and the tallying be?
Time is ticking fast and somehow we pay.
Lord, don't find me wanting.

Please Lord, not me.

Virginia Walker

The Gift

I was given a gift a long time ago
I've shared it with many a soul
Although it has only been borrowed
I find it more valuable then gold
It was given to me not shiny and new
There are others who were given this gift before me
Yet having to share this gift
Makes me appreciate it even more
At times I may have seemed to shun it
Left it sit idly by itself
While I would go about each day
Trying to manage without its help
But never has a day gone by
When this gift wasn't far from mind
For never again have I received
A gift such as this kind
No matter where I am now
I hold this so dear to my heart
This gift, this wondrous gift
My mother was my gift from God

Roseanne Koch

Love's Treasure

Like a miner who searches for gold
I've spent years searching for love
With everything I own now sold
Now with only the sincerity of my heart
I start by offering my heart and soul
To you for your divine love
Your love is greater than any wealth
That any man may be able to find
A lifetime of security and romance
This is what I see in you
The peace of mind that is our love
My years of searching came to an end
The first day that I looked into your eyes
Our desires are the same
As only love can lite our fires
We shall enjoy a lifetime
Of only happiness and beauty

Michael E. Fritter

The Space Age

More room for maidens to conceive in,
More space for men to become confused in,
And wisdom for those who make
The moon's aridity comprehensible to mankind.

Maria M. Links

Southern Pride

Many years ago we thought we had found
Job security in an industry that was sound
That industry is the long-standing textile
Whose fate is almost doomed for exile

The problem is imports - imports - imports
On which the news media extensively reports
But take stock that something must be done
It's a problem our government seems to shun

Let's not forsake where we were born and bred
Let's not defeated hang our head
Let's stand together and go in stride
United once again in southern pride

This dilemma seems to be
Left entirely up to you and me
So let's help make sure this industry can stay
Buy "Crafted With Pride in U.S.A."

Linda H. Leonard

If I Were

If I were an artist, I would paint you with colors filled with life, joy, and happiness
If I were a sculptress, I would carve a masterpiece which would show the very essence of the man which you are
If I were a vocalist, I would capture your heart with the songs of love I would sing, as a mockingbird serenades on a warm Florida morning.
If I were a musician, I would orchestrate the most beautiful sounds to bring pleasure to your ear and to excite the child within you
If I were a writer, I would express my feelings through the use of romantic poetry and clever metaphors
If I were a beautiful goddess from time past, I would serve you faithfully and strive to surpass your wants and desires in every way
If I were a spirit, I would protect you from senseless evils and facilitate your purpose by celebrating your presence
But since I am who I am, all I can do is love you the way only I know how... completely, sincerely, and unconditionally

Lorain C. Prevaux

Planets

There are nine major planets, revolving round the sun,
Jupiter by far, is the largest one.

Uranus is the least known, it's the most remote you see,
Mercury is the smallest, on this they all agree.

Venus sounds like a goddess, or a pretty song,
Neptune was thought to be the furthest, till Pluto came along.

Saturn is the second largest, and noted for its rings,
Is there any life on Mars, if so are they human beings!

Earth is the only planet, that's different from the rest,
For it enhances life, and surely is the best.

Laraine Reimold

"Daddy Gone"

Our visitations were taken for granted,
Laughing and sharing we thought would never end.
The last night I viewed through foggy window,
My youth, your age, greatly conflicted.
Selfishness and hatred seized your heart,
Love and friendship lingered in mine.
Our acquaintance of eleven years went by so quickly,
I look back now; we were strangers on the road of relationships.
Morning came, afternoon passed,
Death intruded, and you were gone.
I long to see you, but the sky divides us.

Stephanie Ann Wilber

Helping Them

There's a place I've visited once before, when I was
just a little boy for reason of helping me through a
traumatic horror, the people I in countered there I
remember what I felt they must have been sent here from
the Heavens above, From day to day I've seen and heard
the pain for myself I know how it feels,
Such nice people helping them all the way through the tears
and Anguish I see in the parents eye's to see what their
kids have to endure night after night.
I'm older and better now this place I talk about is still
helping them out this day I feel the love and care from
those wonderful people who helped in so many ways,
to those people I speak about THANKS', I'll never forget
that you all are still there helping them.

Richard Suba

Just 'Cause

Just 'cause I get good grades doesn't make me smart...
Just 'cause I say "I love you" doesn't mean it's from the heart...

Just 'cause I know where I'm going doesn't mean I know when...
Just 'cause I swore I'd never love doesn't mean I won't again...

Just 'cause I do wrong doesn't mean I won't repent...
Just 'cause I'm smiling doesn't mean I am content...

Just 'cause I don't speak up doesn't mean I have no pride...
Just 'cause I say I'm honest doesn't mean I haven't lied...

Just 'cause the candle flickers doesn't mean it won't wane...
Just 'cause the sun always shines doesn't mean it never rains...

Just 'cause there's silence doesn't mean there's no warning...
Just 'cause the rooster crows doesn't mean it is morning...

Just 'cause I shout out questions doesn't make me furious...
I'm just confronting the truth cause it makes me very curious...

Kevin Michael Blum

True Love

I searched high and I searched low
Just for a man who would love me so
God sent him down out of the blue
And all my locked up loneliness he did soothe

So one cold day in December
As I pause now to remember
I met that man and he ask me
To take his hand and together
We walked as one upon the land

We laugh a lot we loved a lot
Neither of us knowing there was a plot
That the sands of time was gonna to give
And that one of us would no longer live

A million times I needed you
And a million times I cried
Cause if my love alone could
have saved you
Then you surely would not have died

Tammy Satterfield

Portrait Of An Artist

My body is an artist
My mind a blank canvas on which the imagination
uses the brilliant colors of my emotions to paint
images of the world as I see it

Its works cannot be seen by anyone but me

Unless I want them to

Teresa A. Sarro

I Hear Wedding Bells

Pearls and smooth satin on lace,
Karots of love safely in place.
Pressed tuxedos streaming across the aisle,
A cathedral train catches a mother's smile.
Freshly arranged flowers mark its enchanting smell,
Off in the distance, I hear wedding bells.

Something old and new, something borrowed and blue,
Slipping a shinney penny in a high-heeled shoe.
Awaiting the moment the brides entrance will begin,
Pink and teal gowns across from three groomsmen.
The beginning of love for only the future to tell,
As the ringing is closer, I hear wedding bells.

On this warm autumn day, love fills the air,
The bride joins her groom and they make the perfect pair.
All their hopes and dreams come true on this day,
A kiss seals their marriage and the band starts to play.
Thus a story they tell on their golden year together,
As they hear the wedding bells playing in their hearts forever.

Melissa Brinkly

After Andrew 1992

Here are comforts - food and lodging
kids wake up early, dress for school
brand new clothes and fresh scrubbed faces
they have learned to live by rule...
lunches packed, they start out early
in the sweet morning air they laugh
together, three bright children
set off for unknown paths
while miles away from home are some
that cannot close their eyes
life uprooted around them, they search their painful lives
how could this God who loves them leave, there is total devastation
in their fright they call His name: "Retrieve our generation!"
is it right that ones so small walk helplessly amongst us
I cannot close my ears to the experience of hunger
no matter how I try, words stay swelled inside my throat
tonight I cannot close my eyes
so I pray
I pray
I hope

Rozan Petito

"Her Needs Are Last"

Raised on a farm, from a child she
knew no harm.
Her hands are rough, from years that were tough,
She gives her best, to her children,
from her nest.
Always giving to those, who cross her path.

A lady from the past, her needs are last.
Her back is bent, from too much strain,
from loads to heavy for her frame,
Never complaining of the pain,
With innocence in her brown eyes,
yet for her years, she is wise.

Never speaking of the bad times,
but now and then when memories,
haunt her, when she's alone, I know she cries.
A lady from the past, her needs are last.

Melba Durham

Stop The Merry-Go-Round

So I retired to sunny S.W. Florida. Goodbye cold ice snow. Knew nobody. Torporous days. Reached out. Joined.

Three years later. Life on the Merry-go-Round began.

SUNDAY. Up early to buy a scarce Sunday New York Times. Ate breakfast at a Greek-Italian restaurant. I'm neither. Home. Read N.Y. times. Sarasota paper. North Port paper. Port Charlotte paper.

MONDAY fed the birds, the goldfish in the pond, watered the new plantings. Off to bridge class in Venice via deadly U.S. 41. Off at noon. Sped south on lethal Interstate 75 to Port Charlotte. A matter of 45 miles at 85 MPH. Ten minutes to eat. Opera class 1-3. Next off to the Red Barn Auction in Punta Gorda. Hot. Shabby. A somewhat dinner at Pizza Hut. Heart burn special. Home at 10. Vitamins to take. Read Read mail, newspapers. Exercise. And so to bed, as my friend Sam Pepys used to say.

REST OF WEEK. Hike every 5 AM for 4 miles at 4 MPH. A healthy breakfast: skim milk, cereal, no flavor. Oh yes. Bridge playing 3 nights a week.

Organizations joined: Audubon, Native Plant Society, Garden Club, Horticultural Society. Friends of the Library. Endless meetings, field trips, conferences. Round and round. No time to think the big thoughts, start that novel, procreate.

Finally one day the Merry-go-Round stopped.
Nobody told me that when it stopped I stopped.

Raymond Doersam

Their Daddy's Gone

Their daddy's gone for this they
know, but do not understand. Why
did God choose to take the life of
this young man. It's not for us to
judge or spite decisions made above
but simply just to carry on with
lots of help and love.
Their daddy's gone but do their
cries really go unheard, I truly
feel he's always there and hears
just every word.
Their daddy's gone, it's so unfair
they cannot call his name. Just being mom
is really hard, to them it's not the same.
Their daddy's gone some day they'll
see, and maybe they will know
he's been a part of Gods great plan
but he still loves them so.

Kathy Benson

Requiem - A Song Inviting Repose And Renewal

Who knows man's heart and mind
Knows me...
As surely as there's spring to see...
So am I,
One with immortality.
Compare me to a star, the sea...
Infinitesimal, transient flesh, you say?
No! infinite miracle am I, as they!
Remember this, when I am gone.
In humanity's heart...I still live on!!
I think that all I need to know
Is that there are daffodils and snow...
Wild birds singing on chimney tops...
Bubbling beans in brown jug pots.
Nocturnes, pearl-strung by debussy...
Letters! Friendship's tapestry.
Kittens climbing my slacks like trees...
Be gone all doubts...I have known these!

Wendy Christy

Visions

I am blind. Yet, I see vistas far in front of me.
Land and sand and churning seas...rolling hills and tall green trees.
Sunset's backdrop fire glows
As daylight slowly fades and goes.

Wrapped in dusk and shadows soft, the moon ascends to shine aloft,
Midst myriad stars. In true array, the ordered constellations lay
In velvet folds of night time skies.
All these visions are my eyes.

Music fills my eager ears. Majestic sounds and cadence hear
Lullabies and baby cries, mournful owls, contented sighs;
Hushed and gentle whispering winds
Wave, as morning sun begins to warm the Earth.
Another day is given birth.

I feel excitement start to stir. Mornings are, and ever were
Another gift..with thoughts to sift and moods to lift my mind
To visions of the world above,
To families and God and love.

Madeline Bradshaw

The Electrical Palette

Political montage, pseudo intellectual melange,
landscaped by T.V. presidents, teflon leaders,
and synthetic artists.......................
All mixed in a lotto caldron with people
daydreaming and hypnotized by material things.

Separated by their lack of universal identity;
on a socially scarred divided world,
networked with the infrastructure
of interactive electron and proton super-
highways, virtual space, and no real communication.

Wake up, compassion, empathy, and the
giving of spiritual love is the answer.

B. C. Mantherudder

My Thoughts

Friend of my heart, a small bit of magic from the start, Laughter shared on a winters night, Music heard and felt, to heal a wound or make eyes bright.
Summer of happiness without any measure, Campfire and song, a wonder...filled treasure.
But then, the scene changes, so softly, the rhyme slips away, subtle new feelings come unbidden.
The shadow of the face in all the dreams, reflections caught for but a moment in the lifetime.
The mind tries to forget, but the heart remembers; the secrets shared on a soft summer night.
Who's to say whether right or wrong, just a wish to give something to someone that's special.
A wish to you for joy, happiness for a lifetime, for you are a friend of my heart.

Kaye R. Degattis

When Hope Arrives

Just when the light at the end of the tunnel has faded, you lead the way. Just when my love has faltered, you restored my faith. In times of confusion, when loving and trusting in someone can make a difference, you were there. When I pray for finding the joy I know exists, you answered. Always consistent in your actions, never wavering in purpose, you believed in me. When my vision had blurred, you taught me to see with my heart. You gave me the strength to go on. For you are the hope that lightens my darkened skies.

When I forget my purpose in life, you know what things to do that make me think, things could be worse than what they are. For you see what others miss, with your love. When hope arrives, you appear...

Ael Ziig

The Last Trumpet

Abomination of desolation look what's happening to our nations
Leaders arising wearing phony crowns just to drive us into the ground

Abomination of desolation look what's happening to our nations
Bullets flying night and day killing people along the way

Abomination of desolation look what's happening to our nations
Our brothers and sisters in the third world countries
Are starving in their beds all cold and hungry

Abomination of desolation look what's happening to our nations
Fatal maladies are on the rise with noxious doctrines by there sides

Abomination of desolation look what's happening to our nations
Affliction, distress, and suffering too is about to call on me and you

Abomination of desolation look what's happening to our nations
Woe cometh the day the earth shall rock
as the moon shalt bleed when the sun is not.

Abomination of desolation look what's happening to our nations
Seven seals about to unfold unleashing prophecies foretold.

Paul J. Pavelco

Pathway

A path runs from my door
Leading to nowhere (to the world).

When the world becomes too much for me,
I thread the path up the steep incline.
Up, up, the fragrant broom-sage lane
Until I reach a plateau in recline.

In the shade of this natural paradise
I have seen the sun sift through the leaves,
And waited for thought's cocoon to burst
With ear tuned to life's sweet melodies.

I have often sat in this wondrous haven
In silence, and watched the world below go by,
Arising with hope renewed, despair subdued,
Descending from my refuge with a sigh.

A path runs form my door
Leading to nowhere (but to me).

Maude Sumner Campbell

Friendship Is...

Friendship is the wine of life, a cool refreshing change,
Learning who we are, up and down, trying out the range.
Friendship is that peace of heart, that fulfilled feeling,
A shoulder to lean on, one who cares, concerned about your dealings.

Friendship is the uncommon bond, the holds like dry cement,
Time with a friend, is realizing it's just time well spent.
Friendship is the smile on a face, that helps me through the day,
As sunshine on a winter's day, the glimpse of one bright ray.

Friendship is a spoken word, to encourage me on the path,
Words help along the way, as flowers along the unmown footpath.
Friendship is food for the soul, as it thinks of times gone by,
It's good to know a friend is always there, setting silently nearby.

Friendship is like a memory, playing its way like music from afar,
Sounds of friendship, line by line, strummed on the old guitar.
Friendship is like a melody, pitched for every voice,
Good friends are hard to come by, be wise with each choice.

Friendship is that peace of mind, flowing silently as the tide,
Setting, waiting, thirsting, famished, and yet totally satisfied.
Friendship is an eternal prize, a goal to continually strive for,
A good friend at any price, will never leave you wanting more.

Rod Landes

Free Speech

Fled the oppressive lands, broken the constricting bands,
Led to this safe haven, hear now the voices of freedom exalted.
Praise rose to the heavens creator, who establishes nations.
Learned, righteous dissenters argued variant visions of governance,
Chastened in prayerful fasting, the towering ego succumbed on
bent knee.
The bloody inked quill drew carefully crafted words to Revolution,
Protecting the soul within mighty emerging lands from feudal Lord,
Prized freedoms of privilege bestowed with blessing on all citizens.
Infant prodigy land, cherish and protect with civility, discipline.
Your growth, travails, and mastery astound the soul weary world, but,
Woven through the promised land becomes the rebellious adolescent,
Learned, irreverent minds deny self-evident truths and equal souls,
Recreating that old creation and dreaming the dreams of ancient time,
Raising the bones of buried civilizations from that unholy past.
The old bones rise to conquer, their names in ancient books;
Within that brash disrespectful adolescence the dragon head appears.
Faraway crackled bones clamor the renewed life of vile conquerors,
Tempting that uncivil youth, head turned to the new thing beneath.
Strangling on the gnat of freedom voice, the camel swallowed whole.
Bring back our land, o Lord, a wheel within a wheel.

Shirley Griffitt

The Penultimate Poem

Treat me as a stranger — for I really am you know.
Let me call and visit — to nurture friendship's growth.
Let my soul embrace yours — to pledge my love and care.
Treat me as a stranger — whom you'll want to find is near.

Treat me as a stranger — for you don't know me at all.
Let us share the moment — should we rise up or we fall.
Let me softly kiss you — and caress and hold your hand.
Treat me as a stranger — whom you'll want to have as friend.

Treat me as a stranger — whose infatuation showed.
Let your doubts be ended — as our friendship now unfolds.
Let's drop old games and masks — for they only cause us pain.
Treat me as a stranger — and begin to talk again.

Treat me as a stranger — whom you'll welcome to your life.
Warm my mind and heart — with a friendship that is ripe.
Gently take my dreams — to cradle them with yours.
Treat me as a stranger — come to share your hopes and fears.

Treat me as a stranger — just that, and nothing more.
Have no preconceptions — as you open up your door.
Think only of the future — as you reach to take my hand.
Treat me as a stranger. — come to know me as a friend.

Walter C. Brown

To Rest And Think

Come climb this hill with me
Let's set beneath this great pine tree
A world to watch as we look about
A place to think to talk and even shout

In boyhood past, for many times
I've sat and listened to the whispering pine
Oh! how I grew to love this hill
Above the noise the dine and shrill

Then as my mind was put at ease
The time had come to rise and leave
I could almost hear this great pine say.
Come rest yourself another day.

Myron C. Brown

A Cry For Peace

Awareness of our being among devastation and despair.
Lies an inner-voice whispering, how can I show I care!
Man's inhumanity to man and an obsession to win the prize,
When compassion is what's needed and fairness of game, to be wise.

The strong must stand tall and join hands around the weak.
To introduce the respect and love that every human seeks.
Little ones enter the world in possession of this trait.
Sin and evil of the adult is taught to seal their fate.

Should not we let the innocent grow, bearing love and respect for all.
It's one's measure of character in the wake of evil, to stand tall.
I plan to do my share of good, make it spread, make it increase,
And like a contagious disease, be an instrument for world peace.

Zenolia Laura

On The "Wings Of Restoration"

On the wings of repentance and restoration
lies the homeland, where I've got my reservation
Changing of the seasons, the rain forest and the droughts
On the wings of restoration, another life sprouts,
Okeefenokee squirms leviathan, still waters shallow and deep.
On the wings of restoration, birds still fly high and free
Of the woman, lies the womb,
The man lies the strength,
On the wings of restoration
Just an arms length,
Now the predator becomes the prey,
On the wings of repentance and restoration
Lies the promised land,
What more can I say
On the wings of restoration
Have you made your reservation
In the promised land
On the wings of restoration!

Leah Karen Wiley

Laws Of Emotion

East of sorrow, and west of glee
Lies the valley of peace and tranquility

The trail leads to the valley below
Is long and treacherous, and often slow

The snags of emotions and the crags of deceit
Can loose your footing though you're lights of feet

But there are gems of wisdom the trail
And berries of faith to nourish the frail

So if you'd like to settle in this peaceful place
Gather the gems and the berries of faith

And never lose sight of your goal of devotion
Or you may lose your soul on the crags of emotion!

D. L. Farrow

The Rose

They say there was an old man, that wandered aimlessly.
Looking for a treasure, of lost time mystery.
His clothes were all in tatters, but he didn't seem to mind.
For any dime he gathered, left his hand in time.
To the children of the poor he gave, for food, for shoes, for joy.
Then he would wander back to the desert, to look for something more.
They found him there one day, in the early morning light.
In the deep sleep that is known, as the Eternal Light.
And every year thereafter a miracle occurs,
right in the place they found him—
A rose appears.

Margaret Meyer McConnell

Untitled

I see only three colors.
Life, Death, and what is in between.
Everything is simpler, yet more confused.
My religion is dead, yet is immortal.
Can you die if you have eternal life?
I ask questions, but no one answers.
I scream for a brow to raise,
But everyone shuts their eyes and looks away.
The darkness closes in on the bulb.
The pain runs from the bandage.
There is an eternal war, between light and dark.
The war is between good and evil.
In the movies good always wins,
But what does the silver screen know anyway?
The raven lashes out and strikes its prey.
The prey shrieks away, but dies.
The raven eats the soul of its prey.
There is a raven for every thought.
The shadows beckon the fire.
The shadows swallow my soul.
I hold my breath ... and think no more.

Nic Armour

"Life"

Life is just a waters gallow,
Life is just a walking shadow,
Life is what you make it be,
Life is the waves of the rolling sea,
Life is just a wary notion,
Life is the salt in the ocean,
Life is the mating of a breed,
Life is the rose of a seed,
Life is the tear that falls from your eye,
Life is the wings that enable you to fly,
Life is the air that you need,
Life is the breast that can feed,
Life is the chair that you can sit,
Life is what you make of it,
Life is the clouds in the sky,
Life is the pain that can make you cry,
Life is all one feature,
Life is natures living creature,
Life is sap on the tree,
To sum it up Life is me!

Sara DeBaggis

Look Unto Me

"Look unto Me," the Father said.
"Lift up your eyes," said He.
"Place no other Gods upon my throne.
Give all your attention to Me!

"Keep your thoughts high as you climb the trail.
Look up to the mountains, and see
A vision of Glory spread far and wide,
As you keep your attention on Me.

"Do not look back, but on the trail
Are others who could not see,
Had you not blazed the trail ahead
By constantly watching Me.

"So, put your attention on Me, dear child.
Put all your attention on Me!
And your will walk on through the storms of life
Unhindered, unfettered, and free!

Mary Standring Ross

The Truth

Sometimes the world seems so bland
like a heart that loves but hides the truth;
We hold a dream that can never be
or we hold the truth that hides.
To run and run but we never get away;
Like the sun that rises and sets
like the days and night we live the truth.
In the end we're back where we started
I had the problem which was best to run,
so I cry, I run, I stop,
I thought if we run, the truth runs with us
If we cry, it cries with us
If we stop, it stops with us
but life will never be the same
until we face the truth;

Leroy Preyer Jr.

After The Rainy Day Poem

The man I see is slick-ghost pale, laughing, verbally correct
Like a perfectly-constructed sentence - no fragments, no participles dangling. All done-up in clean, correct.
Nice, with the deadly under tones of unimpassioned.

The woman I see is broken English, phrases falling on a beat-up car with no floor board
Bouncing to the dusty road, evading tires, missing mutilation, escaping prison,
Left on a lonely island somewhere in the Cyclades.

All hell breaks loose in some South Asian part.
Monsoons tearing at the earth, ripping its flesh,
and people, like scabies burrowing into the outer crust,
Laying their eggs, hoping for respite just a little longer.

Tone over tone comes pouring through the dirty, greasy windows of my room.
Dark outside greys with no boundaries licking on my windowpanes.
Me throwing a yellow pencil at them like a laser stabbing its way to redemption.

Mary M. Swift

Misfit

I feel like some sort of misfit.
Like a sailor lost at sea
Alone among the jungle
In a world I call my home

I watch swarms of people, bustling to and from their jobs
Like bees buzzing to and from their hives.
Their lives much to busy for a friendly Hi
I see countless people scurrying to the malls
Collecting and buying material possessions in wild frenzy
Like squirrels gathering and hoarding acorns for survival

I feel alone among this chaos
In this hectic world we call our lives
I much prefer to take my time,
To walk through life
To witness a rainbow, or smell a rose
But then maybe I'm like the dinosaur
Soon to become extinct

Patricia Oxford

When Louis Left

She lay silent now.
Like an island in the calm sea of her bed.
Beside her, a bear with no beating heart;
A source of substitute affection
With plastic eyes.

The sheets are clean and cool.
No scent of him remains
On the laundered cotton
Where she lay like a body laid to rest;
Hands folded over the crucified heart within her breast.

She lay silent now,
Searching the infinity of her room,
Praying without words,
Tears pooling in her plastic eyes.

C. L. Donaldson

Giggles

Giggles
Like soda fizzes
Come rolling towards me
To the attack!

"No, I'm not, O I cannot
Succumb to these fizzes
Interviews a must...
A straight face I must keep
But Mr. Fizz is tickling, O so much!"
"Giggles, go, O please go!"
"No, I'm not, until you relent"
Aaah! I'm rolling, face and sides splitting!
Relief... Aaaah!
Thanks to Mr. Fizz and wife
.....Mrs. Giggles

Paulette P. Forbes

Memories

Yesterday's charm tastes sweet,
like ice cream and birthday cake and home-made bread.
Yesterday's charm is wrapped in tender memory,
pressed, like fragile flowers,
between the pages of the years.

Yesterday's pain
has cast its net of wisdom into the sea of life.
Yesterday's pain is over,
like a mother's labor to birth a child;
like the agony of sitting at the death-bed of a loved one.

Yesterday is a gift,
something like mist on the horizon,
or like a nursery rhyme and riddle combined, intertwined.
Some rhyme has reason,
some riddle has no clue,
while a few of yesterday's dreams, pains, charms,
hold keys to tomorrow.

In quiet moments of remembering experiences from the past
we are given food and drink for the heart,
and courage for the journey into new memories.

Mary Catherine Walton, S.S.J.

"Remembering The Elks"

Wings that spread so far and wide,
Like the Angels God sent here to guide,
Giving love, protection and help,
Letting you know you're not by yourself,
A friend that will always be there,
With so much love and concern to share,
The Elks stand tall and in number so strong,
God put them here so you won't be alone.
Remembering their reason and purpose in life,
They help to take away some of your worries and strife,
So when you thank God for his magnificent plan...
Thank God for the Elks, with their helping hands...
Ask God to protect and help them too,...
To please be there for them,
Like they were there for you.
Three cheers for the Elks! Pat them on their Backs!
Don't forget to say Thank you, because they don't need claque,
For applause for them are truly deserved,
Because they are always ready to subserve!

Mary Jean Salmon Stennis

"Unlimited Whispering"

Whisper, whispering the cool wind slowly sifts by
Like snow on the land it freely shifts, drifts by
Not having in this whole world a place to go
Wandering, drifting through endless time it does blow
Telling of all the wonder of the unseen
From the beginning of creation by the Lord on high
Gave us the wind for which we seldom know why
Though it seems we hear not what it is saying
Through our own imagination it may for us be praying
Saying STOP for a second, come listen closely here
I am of the unseen being all our past brought near
Most of the time I am quiet, gentle and serene
But am knowing in the past to be vicious and mean
Only when brought forth to the Lord's clear sight
I may at times be used as many of his might's
To bring together his flock that have wandered astray
Showing strength of the Lord as He only knows the way.

Patrick Martin

Untitled

Insanity came to visit today.
Likes his coffee black and blue.
He came to let me out of myself,
Wanted to show me the sights
Look at those idiots on leashes, in muzzles
Peering down I laugh at myself.
Oh, the silliness I used to think was real.
Crazy and I walked hand in mind
Down the purple paved rows
Strolling past the furry flowers
Through a forest fire of lightning bugs
Across the bridge to the land of nothing,
There we boarded the boat to nowhere.
The sea was rough, brimming with wonderful horrible
creatures
And bodies floating, slowly, homeward.
Finally, looney kissed me good night,
And he dropped me off (in his mind machine)
In front of my own nose,
Whence I crawled back into my brain.

Tammy Markert

Listen

Where is God, you say?
Listen to the wind whispering in the trees,
God is there!
Listen to the lilting flow of a rushing stream,
God is there!
Look into the blaze of the sunrise,
Or at the glow of the evening sunset,
God is there!
Listen to the night sounds - crickets chirping,
Frogs croaking, night birds calling,
All of these say - God is here!
How simple the beauty of the world can show,
God is here, God is there, God is everywhere!
You don't know where God is?
Take time to look;
Listen, HE is everywhere

Wanda Anderson Paul

Little Girl Lost

Little girl are you lost
Little girl are you gone
Little girl where are you
Are you only in our hearts now

Are you gone forever
From our presence - but not our hearts?
Do we only have loving memories
Of the sweet quiet, smiling face and soul?

How can we express our anger
At having you taken away
How can we express our caring
While you, my dear, are gone away?

Please, God, let us find her
So our minds can be put to rest.
Please God let us find her
We know that what you do is best.

Why are there so many questions
About our soul and where we go?
We really do want some answers
Especially now - please - let us know.

Koa Bostwick

Three Little Boys

Two little boys named Peter and Matt
live far away from where Russ is at.
The days got long and summer went by
counting stars in the nighttime sky.

One little boy who's name is Russ
lives too far to take the bus.
Now he lives beside the lake,
he has no one to come and skate.

His two best friends he left behind
when he moved to this place so fine.
The miles between them seem so long,
but when together they've never been gone.

Three little boys, the best of friends,
will all be together no matter the ends.
Three little boys will always know
they will be together come summer or snow.

So when counting stars throughout the night
think of your friends who are out of sight.
They are out there counting the same stars, too,
thinking of the friend they have in you.

Linda Morey

In The Eyes Of A Child

In the eyes of a child, life is a fairy tale. Where Pluto lives, and Chip and Dale. In the eyes of a child, make-believe is king. Where everybody dances, and everybody sings. Everybody laughs, nobody cries. Everyone's happy, and nobody dies.

In the eyes of a child, grass is always green. Where you can be a king, or you can be a queen. In the eyes of a child, everything is gold. Where everything is young, and nothing grows old. There is a place where dead babies go. Where nobody lives, and nobody grows. Because that is where aborted children go.

In the eyes of that child, everything is dark. They can't hear a meow, and they can't hear a bark. They had a mom they had a dad. But someone got angry, someone got mad. Abortion kills an innocent kid, without giving them a chance to live.

Natalie Mason

"The Locked Door"

Locked door, locked door, what is behind you?
Locked door, locked door, how do I find you?
Maybe a ticket for a magic ride,
All sorts of wonders waiting inside!
Locked door, locked door, what is behind you?
Locked door, locked door, how do I find you?
Infinite possibilities nagging at me,
Tell me, where in the world is that incredible key?
Locked door, locked door what is behind you?
Locked door, locked door how do I find you?
Something gigantic or very small?
Something that's zany and off the wall?
Locked door, locked door what is behind you?
Locked door, locked door, how do I find you?
Door, your mystery is certainly tough,
But this little boy has had enough.

Samuel A. Liberty

Nexus

Rosie, I remember when you were only a girl really,
long hair worn around your head, wrapped...
You were beautiful. I was your baby and you loved me.
And you were loved. By a man. My father.
He was handsome and witty and charming and he played the guitar.
But he left.

That was twenty years flown passed.
Now it's me, my mother.
With a sweet baby daughter, barely from my breast, it seems.
Like you, for my husband, all love, but lost.
Like you not, another man, then my Love Child.
The Miracle that I was for you.
A daughter, a treasure, a friend.

I watch you now in a white room returning from death,
terror in your eyes,
Don't be afraid, my mother, I am here.
As you always were for me.
As no man was for either of us.

Patricia M. Leyden

United In Pain

Thrown together by fate, torn apart by chance,
Our relationship ended without even a final glance.
Hate is like fire but mine I learned to tame,
Yours eternally sparks and burns, to you it's all a game.
I walked away from your hate but with it you decided to flirt,
You'll never know how much I have hurt.
Thrown in a gutter is where our love is finally lain,
For although we are separated by choice we'll always be united in pain.

Mary Beth Naretta

Spirit

When you stand by my grave don't cry.
Look toward heaven. I am in the sky
I do not sleep, I did not die.
I am the wind and sand slowly drifting by
do not grieve do not cry.
Listen to the silence as I drift by
Watch the dew drops as they slowly fall.
Listen for me, I will hear your call.
Lift up your eyes and worry not for me.
I am the gentle blue upon the giant seas.
The far horizon I will travel forever by your side
do not cry for me I did not die
When like the echo of a sea shell
You hold upon your hand
I whisper gently to you I left the world of man.
My spirit is forever free
Like the wind upon a sail I am bound for heaven
God trampled over hell so do not worry about me
do not grieve and cry I do not sleep I did not die
I will meet you on the other side.

Lucille Bowens

Changing Wind

Do I see you
looking at the same wispy clouds as I
flying high in summer's bright blue sky?
Or do I hear your laughter
when the singing whippoorwill
stirs me from my window sill?
And I know I'll see your smiling face
all along and in every place;
somewhere, sometime upon a salty beach
or near a mountain's snowy reach.

And then one day
it will be autumn
with leaves of color
and changing wind—
Will I see you once again?

Mona Hand Plackmeyer

Untitled

Trap, within the walls of myself yearning to be free,
Looking for a way out but in the dark it's hard to see
So many things I reach for hoping that would be the key
but on the other side still the prison awaits for me.

Looking at so many striving for the top
thinking that will bring fulfillment, only to realize it's not
While others at the bottom lying in the dirt
Struggle day to day for whatever it is worth.

Both at extremely different ends
And everybody in between
Is searching for an answer
An answer that can't be seen.

Luanne Giffune

Dark Night

Night falls darkness fills the air. Stars come
out to dance and play and then they disappear.
Firefly's fly above the crystal lighted moon. The
cool night air bends the swift trees. All is silent
in the fall air that hurries by our house. The
mysteries that happen know one knows until the
sun rises and warms the air. The colorful leaves
twirl around and around. When we wake all is well.
But I can't wait until night comes again.

Traci Niemi

Undertow

So there you are, standing on a plank,
Looking out across the ocean, and you're
Feeling a bit misunderstood.
Yes, you're waiting, heel on edge for your love to return to you.
And it's hard, staring into the eyes of those
Who have laughed along the way.
But you wait, clinging to the remaining ends of your pride,
And it hurts.
Then you're falling in what has become reality:
The essence of solitude, and a holocaust of emotional unbalance,
drowning in the amethyst rain.
Now you find yourself wandering in memory,
alone to the sound of your tears,
Falling like worthless drops of wine, and
Taking with each, the loss of a tiny piece of sanity,
One drop at a time,
One drop at a time,
One drop at a time.
Facing the loss, you become a sunken treasure chest,
at the bottom of the sea.
And down come the divers, and they open your lid in search of truth.
But your soul is now empty,
And the ocean is empty,
And the world is only a world.

Steve Uitz

What Colour Are the Skies Where You Live?

Through a porthole in the past...
looking out of dusty glass into the present
never touching the future.
Angel eyes in an old disguise...
looking for the hope of catching you in
some other motley shade
...other than the gray of
nineteen hundred and thirty-two.

A timeless wind blows into
your face and through your soul
...sending dust devils from
your mind out of nineteen
hundred and thirty-nine.

Out through this porthole
of black and white...
asking of you just this question,
not the rise from phantoms
of nineteen hundred and twenty-nine but,
just one simple thing only you can give...
What colour are the skies where you live?

Kimberly A. Levine

Surrounds Us

Ever so slowly the steady rain coats an old copper roof,
making its tattered dull green tint all the more enhanced.
The once quiet drains, rich with architecture and knowledge,
are now alive in uniform chorus.

Occasionally, a bellow awakens the standing timbers...
As the host, they sway in perpetuity not to disturb their neighbors,
adding to their friends' dance as they carve in unison a time
line of the storm in the ground which welcomes it.

As the rain subsides and streams go down,
sunlight bathes this crystal palace of tranquility.
The brilliant colors welcome the brightness;
all too excited by the recent squall.

As light is shed, one anticipates and awaits.
Trees so excited, drains all inviting; all knowing
For the next rain.
This dampness which surrounds us.

Todd Carleton Dilatush

A Teenager's Mother

When that bundle of joy is placed within your arms, You say, "Dear Lord, I dedicate him to you and please keep him from all harm." You might say, "Will these diapers and bottles ever come to an end?" Oh, yes they will and you will even wish for those "terrible two's" again. The years will pass so swift and to school he must go, And as he learns to read and write his parents are all aglow. Time doesn't stop and those teen years arrive, But you sigh and say, "I have three more years of rest before he can drive." His big day appears and his Mama signs on the dotted line, He feels he has so much power now - this teenage boy of mine.

A few weeks later he calls from the ball game concerning a classmate, "Mama, my friend just "totalled your car" and so we will be home a little late." A few weeks later as Mama and Pop were waiting for him in bed, The telephone rings at 12"30. "I was "mudslinging" and my Bronco stopped and is now dead." These are only a few of the incidents that have happened in the last two years, But we've come through them by God's help-as he has learned lessons we have shed tears. Those big eyes and sweet smile will always soften his mother's heart, "Mama, in that Tommy Hilfiger shirt and those Silvertab jeans I would really look smart". I'm sure these teen years will swiftly pass away, And then we'll look back and say, "Lord, you were with us every single day."

Linda Huffman

"Whispers Of Love"

As I look into your eyes, I see "Whispers of
Love"
As you hold me in your arms, I feel
"Whispers of love"

As we make love and the stars of a
Thousand skies appear, I see "Whisper of
Love"
As your touch sends the thrill of a
Thousand fires deep within me, I again
Feel "Whisper of Love"

As we walk down life's path, hand in
Hand, I feel "Whispers of Love"
You awaken within me the feeling
Of the ages, as long ago I was in love with
You then, as now and I feel "Whispers of
Love"

As the stages of our lives continue to
Unfold, for you I will always feel
"Whispers of Love"

Trish Ballagh

Devotion

I want to give you what you give me
Love happiness tranquility
I want to be the anchor to your ship at sea
For you are my stars, my guiding lights
Kneeling before you I offer myself
I am your disciple
White lights shine when you are near
Electricity burns in my veins
To be with out you the blackness of night
Would swallow me
Death of all feeling
Wondering aimlessly with absolute apathy
Be gone these cold thoughts for
My faith lives true
In the devotion of our love
To infinity

Roy Samuel Brown

To Ask Of Love

Shall I ask of love a permanent stay?
Love's far too nervous and intemperate.
It rushes forth, retreats, and finds a way
To make hearts bleed in tears immoderate.
Beneath a sweet moonlit night it resplends;
It will bask in a paramour's parting —
But the moment the fragile ego bends
Too great and suffers a grievous smarting,
Love will get anxious and bid hearts adieu.
The "I" will resound, unity will tear
And with love parted, only heart's the fool
For it faiths in this love that has no wear.
It doesn't last, this love that's just a song —
But it's a song that's sweet, till moment wrong.

Nadine Kjellberg

Woman

When the great Jehovah made the world,
Made the forests, the flowers, and the long rays of sun,
Blew breath upon a piece of clay
And made a man, made man and woman one,

When all and more than all were finished
Set up in a perfection too defile,
God said and make the woman beautiful:
The sun upon the water for a while,

The trees before the winter sheds their leaves,
The moon behind a crest of shadowy clouds,
The silvery silken sheen of moonlit waves;
And it was done.....and so the mystery crowds.

Oh I know all there is to know of women,
Of strength and fear and love, and the will to bear;
But I shall never know the source of all
The courage and the beauty that is there.

Leo Allard

You're Like A...

You're like a flame... that burns throughout the night,
Making sure to keep me warm so I'll sleep all right.
You're like a simple love song... with your words so true,
Always telling me I'll spend forever with you.
You're like a tree...because through the rough times
you still stand strong,
Opening your arms to me and saying that's where I belong.
You're like a poet..everything you say seems to capture my heart,
And conversations between us fill my mind when we're apart.
You're like a habit...that I just can't seem to break,
Because I run back to you with every wrong move I make,
You're like an angel... who shines a guiding light on me,
And leads me out of my sorrowful times of misery.
But most of all, you're like a gift.. that fills me up with joy,.
And this special gift is something no one can destroy.

Tina Kauffman

Return Of The Trapper

Where yesterday lay driven snows,
Marked only by the hand of nature -
Trace of birds' feet, prints of paws,
Tiny scars of woodland creatures -
Deeper signs now: cross-hatched circles,
In a straight line, all spaced equal.
Spoor of human, wearing snowshoes!

High stepping, short striding,
Seeking out a place of hiding
For a clanging, rattling, evil,
Blue-black, shining, heartless devil.
Beware when it falls silent, biding.

Robert Kroning

Ode To A Shepherd Dog

One night on a hilltop in Bethlehem Town,
Man and beast were asleep as the stars looked down,
One creature alone in all God's creation
Was alert and listening as he guarded his station.

But now the ears snap hard to attention,
And point to the heavens as Divine intervention
Gives a command to this shepherd dog;
He heard that night the voice of his God.

The shepherds, the flock, the dog and all
Went to the town where Jesus lay down,
All enter the cave to love and adore
The dog alone guarded and remained at the door.

What was the message you heard on the hill
When your ears pointed heavenward and strengthened your will
To guard the Child and keep him from harm
For wolves roam freely outside the town?

Down through the centuries they guard and listen
For his coming again. This is their mission.
As man walks the earth with his faithful dog
Awaiting once more the Glory of God!

Mary L. Glynn

The Enchanted Forest Of Life

As you walk through the Enchanted Forest of Life,
May you take a path bearing no strife

May the path be lined with flowers of happiness,
And trees wearing blossoms that smell of success

May the forest's spring showers drench you in wealth,
And its summer sunrays bask you in good health

May the autumn breezes that stir up above,
Come down to caress you and bless you to love

May the path lead to a warm home that is blest,
With some one to share all the joys of the forest

Karl S. Bicknese Sr.

What Am I Looking For?

I come from an old mainland
maybe you have never been,
I come to the New Continent
really I have never seen.

We are different?
— Yes, we are quite different in so many things,
from the natural attribution to the cultural tradition.
I am saying: "Good night!"
meanwhile you say: "Good morning!"

We are all the same?
— Sure, yet we are exactly the same.
All we need are the same things:
from air, water, food, to the clothing and housing...
since we are all human being, on the same Earth standing.

Is that all?
— No, there is something important more.
For example, knowledge, the source of force,
as well as friendship, a bridge across the wall.
That is why I come here,
and what I am looking for.

Yike Hu

A Week And A Day

I hope you don't mind
Me takin' up this time,
To tell you I really care...

I think of you every day,
Although, you are never here to stay.
A month has passed.
I have nothing bad to say,
Just that, I have only seen you a week and a day.

I don't mean to sound rude,
I'm just one lonely dude.
They tell me, as I sit here and ponder,
"Separation makes the heart grow fonder."
Still, I wait for the day
You came home and say,
"I love you."

Marc Hundley

Old House Of The Woods

How fragile a thing, this house of wood,
Memories long, speak if they could
a shelter of life, from living things,
Timbers old, of an ancient Spring
Footsteps fall, the floors do creak,
'Tis a mistake, to believe them weak.
But no, rather they give, than break.
Like the love within, for others sake.
Weather endured for many years,
A place of trust, leaves no fears.
Old friend tried and true,
It warms the heart, as old friends do.
Just when I think it too old to last,
I hear young footsteps, to hold it fast.
Out of that ancient spring is born,
the stuff it takes, to weather the storm.

Vincent Johnson

Dream Lover

Dream Lover is someone that you love in your heart, mind, and in your dreams,
But in real life it never seems
That means someone that you love and care for very much but they don't feel the same way about you.
And to have him or her feel the same way for you is all you you wish he would do.
And you love your Dream lover and all you can think about is for us to be together would be a myth.
Myth means never been and never be like a happy ending fairy tale.
But your dream lover's love only burns in your mind and and dreams not in your heart although you wish your Dream Lover would love you.

Laura Schempp

A Great Nation

This country's history I am told
moved westward in search of gold.
The Civil Ware tore us apart
and we had to rebuild our nation's heart.
World War One and World War Two
were wars we fought because it was the right thing to do.
Our flag has thirteen stripes and fifty stars.
We became a mobile society with the mass production of cars.
The Star Spangled Banner makes us stand
and come together as we sing the band.
This great nation today
is none other than the U.S.A.

Pamela Voyles

Existence

Caught along the vicious circle of life,
mind changing with each phase,

First birth, then adulthood, then the
imminent death through a daze.

Wanting to be grown, but not to grow old
but yet,

Know one has no choice in the matter, fore
we all get

What birth's first breath on life gives each
soul,

A ticket - to run one's course on the road
to the ultimate - Old!

Wondering - will we be ready once the
time is here?

To bow out gracefully, to come face to face
to what we most fear
And that is death.

Norma A. Holmes Martin

Nature's Magic Place

In this magic place, the world is a curious
mix of all four seasons.
Sky blue, with marshmallow clouds; Winter winds
click the branches, and autumn leaf's fall like
tears down a loved one's face!

The chocolate brown water; topped with white
froth, flows down stream over logs-half
buried, that become dinosaurs of ages past!

Open your mind and see the world as it was
meant to be. Open your ears, and hear the
world's music!

Nature, in this magic place is always in
tune; the birds sing overhead, as does the
river going-by the wind joins in with her song!

One can imagine the world in harmony, when man
was at peaced with himself and GOD!

Even as we silently sit and listen
Nature tell's all who listen and hear -

We are the intruders here!

Sandra Lee Hartley

Our First Kindergarten Christmas

We came to her, she was our first; (we didn't want to go);
Mom and dad and friends alike; claimed this was food for growth;
We packed a drink, and snack for break and on the bus we went;
It wasn't all that very long, (and really not so bad);
We learned to count, draw patterns and such; we even say the pledge;
We place our hand upon our heart and think of what it means;
And now it's near the end of day, the time to travel home;
We're placed in order and all lined up, (we're never left alone);
Our wish to all and Everyone is Happy Holiday!
'Cause soon it's 1995 and back to school again;
We want the challenge, the chance to grow, we want to learn it all;
Our kindergarten teacher, her cheerful disposition;
has shed some light upon us all; we've even learned to listen.

Shelley B. Love Ciraolo

You

You are the essence of all that I know
More beautiful than any goddess known to man
You are an angel
You are pure as the finest diamond
Yet smooth and soft like silk

You are radiance providing me with warmth as the sun
You are my friend and lover
Compared to none
You bring out the best in me
You are the island for which I am bound
I have no desire to be rescued

You give life to my existence
Your smile is my heartbeat
Your eyes my soul
Your touch my feeling
Your voice my direction
You *make* me
You *are* me

Rodney L. Bland

Listening

When as a little child, I sat on Papa's knee.
My arms entwined around his neck as he sang to me.
He invented funny jingles just to make me glad.
Oh! such a dear papa, no other Lassie had.

Now as a young Missie, I sat not on his knee.
But from across the table, he whispered words to me.
He spoke strong Father words of wisdom and of care.
I knew then, if I needed him, he'd be always there.

My full bloomed woman days, came oh so soon.
And listening then to Papa, was oh such a boon.
Wisdom and understanding was his daily grace.
Though the cares of the world, furrowed his face.

Now Papa always having such good words to say
And listening, I am led in the straight and narrow way.
I am glad I took heed to every word he said.
For listening and remembering, I am not afraid.

Muriel Ratteray Green

Untitled

I am the sound of soft music echoing through
my brain, then touching my heart.

I am the sight of a flock of blackbirds flying
in unison, yet each one as free and unique as
a drop of rain.

I am the smell of a mountain morning, freshly
cleansed by a spring rain.

I am the taste of an orange at the peek of
maturity, hanging proud, patiently awaiting
your approval.

I am the feel of the invisible force of wind
caressing my soul, and blowing my mind.

Peggy Darnell

Being Ill

A family member was diagnosed as schizophrenic
other relatives have become paranoid,
about genetic possibilities, about whose side
is responsible, about demonstrating intent,
about escaping guilt, about somehow caring
without caring and being afraid of everything
we don't know for sure.

Michael D. Brown

Custody

Once I was a mother
My children grew within me
They nursed from my ample breasts
I felt their gentle breath upon my neck
Listened to their rhythmic baby noises
Snuggled them tight nightly
Soothed their tears by day
Laughed inside with joy from loving with them
And then it died.

He took them from me
He killed the mother within me
Crying about his fatherly needs once ignored
But now denying their maternal bond
He took them away.

Goodbye.

Nanette Metskas McCarthy

My Eternity

My words are my only legacy,
My children, my eternity.
The words flow in and out, beyond space and time.
I won't fear love or death
And when the tears come,
I won't fear mine.
My eyes will close on the last word written.
He will turn the final page,
Lift my spirit up and take my breath away.
And let life fly,
Into another world sublime.
I won't fear love or death,
As I cross the Great Divide,
And say goodbye one last time.

A. Daniel Martinez

Untitled

Now I lay me down to sleep,
my bed is soft, my dreams are deep.
In my dream I do not wake,
and then, my lord, you do not take.
My soul is forced to walk astray,
to have no peace, day after day.
Then I wake, broken out in cold sweat,
we've all had dreams like that, I'll bet.
Sleeping scares me in more ways than one,
eternal sleep and your life is done.
Floating in unending mist,
the most important lesson is this:
Death is just a roll of the dice, and
Sleep is but a tiny slice.

Leslie O'Sullivan

Untitled

Even in your absence your image taunts me
My dreams don't sleep...
haunted by the nightmare of your shadow
You embrace me holding me so
close, yet pushing me so far away
You toy with my emotions
reflecting a picture of what
you think I want to see
You said you didn't want to hurt me
Not knowing that you did the first
time I saw you glance at me
Knowing I let you have me to
soon yet far too late
Pushed aside after the
physical touch
Forever to sleep alone with
a shadow of the man

M. Paige

Air Force Blues

Help, I'm lost, alone, and sad;
My God, I feel so very bad.
I need my friends and family ties,
The home I left, where my heart lies.

I'm scared out here, out on my own.
I can't see love through a telephone.
So many many miles away,
I have no choice, I have to stay.

The service is no life for me,
I feel enslaved, I long to be free.

The different insects that make me scream,
This room with rotten wood and paint,
The wind blows and I smell the cows
I go to work, but I feel faint.

I'm sick, so I have to make a call, to ask someone to make me well.
They say, "call back tomorrow", but I think, "Go to hell".

For vacation I receive thirty days a year,
When I ask if I can take them he says, fifteen days at a time my dear!

Still I work hard everyday, and do the best I can.
Though I don't think I'll reenlist. Four years is all that I can Stand!

Wanda L. Mayes

Memories Of My Grandpa

From my memories I will recall,
my grandpa as the best of all,
Looking at me so frail and thin,
I wonder why cancer came to him,
All the memories he gave to me,
I look back to see—how special one can be,
He took me fishing once in a while,
I caught fish as long as a mile,
When I was bored we'd walk to the park,
There I'd be as happy as a lark,
He'd always take me to his ducks,
Naming all—his favorite was Luck,
Fighting for his country in the war,
he won lots of medals and awards,
He told stories of that war,
I never thought they were a bore,
I always loved being with him,
Leaving every time with a great grin,
Now he's gone and I miss him,
but my memories will never be dim.

Lindsay Kroon

Thoughts Of You

If my love could stop self destruction, we could live in total bliss.
My love would make you confident, a feeling you now miss.
My love would make you strive, to do your personal best, and also help you realize that's the only way to success.

My love would keep you safe and warm you from within, build a little fortress to help fight against crime and sin.

My love would keep you healthy, your vision would be clear, you'd spot the vicious dangers before they could get near.

My love would let you see the strengths you have inside, you'd learn to trust your judgments and never wonder why.

If my love could stop self destruction, we could live in total bliss.

You'd be at home not all alone, with family you now miss.

Olivette Lynette Kelly

The Moment We Kissed

I had a dream and you were there,
My hand flowed through your soft brown hair.
Your eyes glistened in the light of the moon,
I knew in my heart I would kiss you soon.

I heard the water, my feet in the sand,
My heart pumped louder with the touch of your hand.
I heard the sea crash on the rocks.
My soul stirred quickly as a sly running fox.

I felt your kiss below my chin,
"I love you", traveled in the wind.
You felt warm in my embrace,
Your eyes met mine with artistic grace.

The tide said, "Hurry up", time's what we missed.
Our surroundings applauded, the moment we kissed.
As the sun was setting beneath the sand,
I could feel the soft warmth of your gentle hand.

This love will last forever
As long as our hearts are true.
It can't be expressed to the fullest,
By saying, "I love you!"

Lisa R. Lewis

The Fall

The leaves fall to the ground
My hopelessness abounds

The flowers fade and die
So I do

These things will decompose
Creating a substance for new things to grow
But will I?

We are alike, don't you know
The leaves and I have no control

Our destinies are in others hands
Some of God's and some of man's

But I ask you why I have no choice
Why no one wants to hear my voice?

And so this day begins and ends
With the leaves dancing in the wind

Their destiny - the fall
The same for us all.

Sandra Goodman

My Sister My Friend

My little sister is more than just kin
My little sis is my best friend
A special friendship that's very rare
Because there' so many things that we share
We share our secrets, bad or good
Secrets we wouldn't tell anyone even if we could
You better believe we do fight
But after awhile, it's alright
We won't even remember why we were mad
So whatever it is, it's never too bad
When we're happy, we laugh. When we're sad, we cry
That's a special friendship money can't buy
I love my little sister very much
And we make sure we stay in touch
Well today little sis, you turned twenty-four
I hope and pray you have many, many more
All the happiness in the world I wish to you
And remember always! I LOVE YOU VERY MUCH, too!

Tricia Schneebeli

Love Or Not?

As I saw the grass begin to grow,
as the clouds began to move toward my long thin almost invisible body,
as I was covered by the clouds unseen by human eyes
unheard by human ears,
as I fell to the ground in peace but sadness,
as I fell asleep dreaming about love, marriage, kids, animals,
and a husband that would not beat me,
in hope to leave this man who could not love like a normal person
all he knew was animal life.
Beating me, hurting me, not loving me,
not caring about me or my feelings.
When I'm ill just leaving not coming back.
He tore me apart.
I cried again and again.
Please help help help please.

Kristin Theisen

Grandma, Mom

Hush up Hush up I say can we have this talk another day
My love for you is very real, open up your heart and feel
She can not move or say a word, that's ok you don't have to be heard
My heart is broken will it ever mend, I just want her pain to come
to an end
People from far and near, scrape their money just to come here
Why, so they can go to her room and hope she's coming home soon
I think about her every day and hope that she won't go away
If someday we have to part, she will always remain in my heart
She comes to see me in my sleep, because she knows my love is deep
If she wants to die let her now take off the machines and ask her how
I know it hurts but let her rest, you know deep inside it's for the
best
Please don't cry my mother dear, even if she's gone she's always here
I know you don't want her to die, but please my mother don't you cry
She's been in pain all her life, from the time she was born 'til she
was a wife
Then when she's left all alone, you opened your heart and gave her
a home
Please just let her rest, you know it is for the best
Let her pains come to an end, let her heart finally mend.

Teri Sherman

Mental Images

Like Kansas buckshot out of metal gun,
My mental images explode with thumbtack violence
clarity and grace. Sometimes chicken scratch,
A dilettante's drooled ramblings —
Sometimes multiple revelation in free range topography.
Mental images that dip twenty card carrying years
Into split pea cauldron east of the brambles,
And arthurian moat.
Yes gifted with memory and quaker weave,
I witness the short breath of wounded deer,
The fire of birthing calf, the soliloquies of the deranged.
Deprived of desert slumber, carnival trinkets I move along
ridge line with quest to commit each arched step to memory and bone.
Deep Virginia roots abound in skull, memory
a long standing habit, like lithium pills.
No cruel word or gesture can separate me from
stockpile of synapsed images. I preserve memory,
iron tools and several smoke worn manuscripts -
sparse, baggage, a poet's grace.

Peter Chelnik

Songs From The Sad Lady In Blue

Everything seems unchanged.
My mind thinks in inches.
How can it be all else is the same,
When what was my heart is gone.

I touch the mirror looking for a friend.
I feel my face - there's a stranger there now.
Somehow I know her - the eternity in her eyes.

I touch the chair, seeking warmth in yellow on blue.
Though familiar things fill these rooms
Comfort is swallowed by my empty soul.

My cat walks silently - bowed head, side glance,
She can tell all is not well.
This pain is untouchable, unspeakable.
Felt by one - seen by none.

I sit by the window waiting for rain.
Fears burns my eyes and brings back the sadness,
When it rains, there's no need for tears.
The angels cry for you and wash away the pain.

How long can I wait for the rain?

Sandra Lasater

Breakdown

Excuse me please . . . what did you say?
My mind was somewhere far way.
Which do I want . . . the red . . . the blue?
Surely, either will have to do.
Perhaps the blue . . . maybe the red.
These decisions fill me with dread.
Things are a mess . . . I have no time.
I know, the problem is all mine.
I got so tired . . . washing the clothes.
I don't recall, I must have dozed.
So, I'm worthless . . . not a bad day?
I'm sorry, what else can I say?
Speechless and deaf . . . you stand . . . you glare
Breathing far too much of my air.
Take a deep breath . . . Time to get out.
Of this there can't be any doubt.

Sherley Sprague

"On Borrowed Time"

When I was just a little girl
My papa would always say
Of a person who was aging "He's already had his day.
That follows living on 'Borrowed Time'
That's plain to see" -
For he'd be grey and bent with years
and I didn't want that said of me.

So all my life, I've ask my Lord
For a promise he gave to us all,
That I'd reach my thru scene years and ten,
Before I'd hear his call.
And now, since I've reached that time,
For I am Seventy today -
Do you think me selfish if I ask for ten more years to Stay.

There's folks and friends I'd hate to leave
But I'm ready - you see
To meet my maker and my God for life has been good to me -
So, now I've changed my prayer Lord,
And I'm asking for ten years more.
And if you'll give that to me, I can boast of living four score.

Maurine McKnight Sullivan

My Lost Heart

My heart is lost among the willows
My secret longs to be revealed
It is my most important secret
It's all about the way I feel.

My heart is lost among the willows
Right now it's lost for half of my life.
My heart is lost among the willows
The breeze'll take it to who wants me for a wife.

My heart is lost among the willows
By now it's only warm sweet air.
My heart is lost among the willows
And I don't think it's very fair.
(From the first day I fell into despair.)

My heart is lost among the willows
My secret longs to be revealed
It is my most important secret
It's all about the way I feel.

Olga Kamensky

"Dad, I Miss You"

Dad, as I sit down at the end of a day;
My thoughts always seem to stray your way.
You'll never know how much you are missed;
If only I could have given you one more kiss.
I miss you more each day;
Only God knows how I pray.
In the autumn of the year;
I know I'll shed one more tear.
When the hunting season neared;
My mind itself I feared.
Hunting with you was such a joy;
Not that I wanted to be a boy.
Your daughter was all I ever wanted to be;
For when I was with you, you were with me.
Over the mountains we did go;
Not with one care or woe.
Together we were a happy pair;
Sharing our thoughts and each tiny care.
I know you are in heaven and as happy as can be;
Oh how I wish you could share just one more hunting trip with me.

Patricia M. Killinger

My Bitter Fears

The breeze is blowing, yet I'm standing still,
My thoughts are drifting as is my will.
Haunting dreams caress the night,
Afraid of sleep, more afraid of the light.
Oceans of wind press in my mind,
My ideas are dim - they are making me blind.
As I try to leave, I am slightly aware,
Of my silent reprieve whispering "dare".
I'm sick of falling I just want to stand,
Yet not alone, I need a hand.
The dawn is beckoning, it's calling me near,
It wants me to cry, to shed my tears.
No ice shall fall from my eyes,
No pain nor grief, I will survive.
I force my fright into the black,
There it shall stay, it mustn't come back.
So as the pain surrounds my soul,
I'm getting weak and I'm growing cold.
My bitter fears subside the rain,
Everything ends, my wrists are slain.

Kimberly DeWitt

"Breakfast"

O World. TIRED.
My will is black like the mark
of a tire on the concrete. I'm
ugly feeling and stale looking. But
someone is eating my liver while I sleep
in unsilent agony EVERY NIGHT.
It is so unhealthy my lungs burn and shrink
and every breath the mucus of my nose is
ripe with falsities and HYPOCRISIES I inhale
daily. The hairs cannot filter all BAD AIR.
And this morning I awoke to find I have no
liver. And I Painkillers for Breakfast.

Rebecca Seibel

Alone

I sit alone, with no one at all
myself to only moan, me only to listen.
No one to love me, no one to share
no one to see, no one to care.
No one to save me, my own tragic tale
a child by herself, only to fail.
Alone in a corner, with no one to play
time for a story, no where to lay.
The stories about, a child held alone
sounds just the same, as a tale all my own.
I long for a pal, a partner or friend
a person to talk with, an emotion to mend.
I wish all the time, some wishes come true
maybe not all, some say I am blue.
My wish has come true, a child has come near
they reach out their hand, a gesture I fear.
I take hold the hand, happy at last
I've found a friend, not to go fast.
We talk and play, together forever
two tales once the same, alone again never.

Kim Hoye

The Fine Line Between Self Together And Self Alone

Onward through the woods I fly
naked as the naked eye.
Marked course is plan'd for me
naked in my dignity.
Reflecting all that's said to me
onto all that joins us, we.
Fore we fly together, we
must join together!
Don't you see?
There's much at hand
that we can be;
what'er there is
that makest we!
'Cause you are you and I am me,
and together broken free!

Kristen D. Sutton-Schleis

Alex

An essence rising to a soul in order to be free,
No more than a simple image, causing me to see.
Looked through unopened windows into shadows from the stars,
You are good for me.

Stepping through a vestibule that once allowed no key,
Powers of emotion, demanding ancient grief to flee.
Sifted through eternal sand for one idol stone,
You are good for me.

Understanding a droplet of water in the vastness of the sea,
A voice above the waves, dissolving my lonely plea.
Listened to the sea shells till you called my name,
You are good for me.

Tami Mollaei

"Prevailing Powers"

Powers of evil justify his mind
Never again will he be left behind
As the moon writhes through the dark cloud
He yells to all aloud;

All shall suffer for living in my world
Hear me all I am the Lord
You shall abide to my needs
No matter how your heart bleeds
For I have lived with the pain
And sorrow and now I live in vain
All those who mock me
Shall never be free
I live in misery tormented by own mind
The freedom I search for I can never find
As long as I live this torturous life
No one shall survive to lead their own
glorified life

Kathryn Mary D'Addario

Tread

In the cool and gloomy light of day - in the darkness and dread of night. Do you wish for the sun to feel its warm ray and the moon to light the night.

Do you think about the fear that can be so great.
Of what tomorrow will hold and what will be your fate.

When those thoughts enter in to places they shouldn't tread
There is no need to worry and no need to feel dread.

Lift your face up to the sky see the wonder waiting there.
There is no need to tremble there is no need to fear.

Just leave it in the Saviors hands.
The cares and fears you hold if it's in His plan He'll
take away your worries and your woes.

Terri Britton

Last Performance

The show is over, curtains down.
No need to go on, I know now.
I know your act, all your lines by heart -
Are you proud?

I still smile, my stage makeup is still on,
but yours is taken off, you bear your naked being -
Your show is over, but mine has just begun.
Are you happy?

I laugh, I guess I must,
Because you're watching my performance -
And yet, I think you see under my costume.
How do you feel?

No, that is insane -
You couldn't see through it, you couldn't
see through the thick layers of red, black, and blue.

So I'll leave the stage, never return again -
I leave everything behind, you, all of you, took all for granted.
Take a bow.
The show is over, say goodbye.

Krista Feltner

Country's Pride

Fight, Fight, Fight, was all that was heard,
No one could hear even a bird.

Blood was shed for miles around
Many bodies were easily found.

Bullets were flying as fast as they could.
The army stood strong as they should.

Walking around with fear in their eyes,
Listening to women and children's cries.

They waved their flags with their country's pride
Even though they could have died.

The night was filled with blindness,
With lots of lacking kindness.

Even though it was a living hell,
The townsfolk and much to tell.

Even though the men were tough
The war ended really rough.

Phil Longo

My Sister—My Best Friend

You're the best sister,
No other one will do.
No sister could ever be,
As good as you.

We laugh and we cry together.
I listen to you and you even listen to me.
Hey, what could be better?
That's the way it should be.

The day when you
Leave and you're gone,
It'll be difficult for me.
But every night has its dawn.

Don't give up and
Don't give in.
Follow your heart and
Only what you believe in.

You are very special to me.
Don't let anyone tell you any differently.
You'll always have a place in my heart until the very end.
You'll always be My Sister—My Best Friend.

Kelly Agre

Grace To Ugly

Does it matter if you live in a town or city?
No, then why does it matter if you're ugly or pretty?

People should respect how you look,
Go and find out in a book.

Don't say an ugly person should be ashamed,
Maybe your popularity won't be claimed.

Around the world in its lovely motion,
people have eyes like the ocean.
But inside they're mean,
The worst sight to be seen.

Beauty isn't everything,
Because inside is the focus ring.

This is something we all must face.
we should be kind to ugly or grace.

Tara A. Timpanaro

Go And Find It!

Once I loved with fervent ardor.
No truer love could anyone harbor.
I believed there was no other.
I just knew! And looked no further.
I was content or just naive.
I didn't care. I just believed.
Blinded by this, I couldn't see
this kind of love can never be.
The truest love is one you find
after you've been left far behind.
A "forgiving love" is the first sign
that you've found the one for all mankind.
See it! Feel it! Drench yourself in it!
It's the one that will save this planet!

Teresa Alexander

No Time To Say Good Bye

Never given the chance to say good bye
Nor a decision whether to die
Gone from those I love
Meeting with God above

As I walked into the light
Pain, guilt, and remorse took flight
Peace and happiness filled my very being
I had embarked on a new beginning

You must learn to understand
That I am now in God's hands
I've come to a better place
So wipe those tears from your face

We did not complete all our dreams
Complete them-no matter how hard it seems
Remember me with a happy thought
Tears, anger, and sorrow are for nought

Patricia Lobdell

A Mother's Prayer

I do not ask for riches for my children,
   Nor even recognition for their skill;
I only ask that Thou wilt give them
   A heart completely yielded to Thy will.

I do not ask for wisdom for my children,
   Beyond discernment of Thy grace;
I only ask that Thou wilt use them
   In Thine own appointed place.

I do not ask for favors for my children,
   To seat them on Thy left or Thy right,
But may they join the throne in heaven
   That sings before Thy throne so bright.

I do not seek perfection in my children,
   For then my own faults I would hide;
I only ask that we might walk together
   and serve our Saviour side by side.

Nancy Dilworth Stoller

Homeless

Helpless...
Out in the cold
Making a living on the streets
Enough space on a grate for one man
Living alone...
Enough blankets to cover up?
Sitting and waiting to go a shelter
Stuck on the streets with no home or money.

Steven Zakulec

Free As Me

Can't you see?
Nor ocean, nor river, can't you sea?

Shells of empty bodies of water,
once filled dreams, just spilled into
the air.

Fair as the breeze thru the trees, over mountains
of joy, like a boy on christmas, with one single
gift that never existed before.

Free as me, a sea captured by the upside down
mountains, captured by the pain of strain.

Free as me, the sea of a fool with no school
of its previous existence. Free as me! A sea
when I see the sky lying on the ground, with the
smile of a hound who has a master that shows him the world,
but chains him to the fence.

Free as me!

Willie I. Bell

Our Very Special Friendship

We have a special friendship not everyone can understand,
not believing in just friendship between a woman and a man.
When both of our ex-spouses started having an affair,
we were so very naive and not really very much aware.
There was a call from a lady that thought I should know,
and in front of you they put on quite a blatant show.
You were hospitalized because of trouble with your heart,
I spent time in a stress ward trying to make a new start.
We started our special friendship by talking on the phone,
becoming close through talking but never any time alone.
We still share a very special friendship as of today,
hopefully no one can tear it apart in any awful way.
I've shared with you all my innermost thoughts and feelings,
and we have always been honest in all our friendship dealings.
You know of the things that could hurt me, if anyone could,
you have told me often, that intentionally you never would.
I believe you feel about our friendship the way that I do,
Our Very Special Friendship is still very strong and TRUE.

Katherine R. Biles

The Soldier Stands Alone

Lost and bewildered, he looks around.
Not one peep is heard, not one single sound.
Quietly he sighs, just another day gone by...
His troubled eyes well up with tears
I'm only seven, why aren't they here?
Mommy's at work, and daddy's gone
Where is their parental bond?
I'm left here all alone,
And outside is just a war zone.
Mommy tries, and so does daddy
I just wish they could love me.
I want a life, why can't they see
I want them to pay attention to me!
I'm angry and I'm hurt
They make me feel like dirt!
Love me, love me, please, please
You stay home only when there's disease.
I was born to live this life, why is there so much strife.
I'm a little soldier, weary to the bone-
I am the soldier who stands alone...

Melissa A. Cline

So Far Away

I go to this place, not so far away.
Not so far away, I see this face.
Who has seen this place, I go to see?
How many have faced this place, I go to see?
Oh to be safe, I go to smell this place.
Who has seen this face, I see?
How many have placed this face, I see?
Oh to be safe, I go to touch this face.
Not so far away, I go to this place.
So far away are the many who smell this place.
Not so far away, I see this face.
So far away are the many who touch this face.
I go to this place, so far away.
Not so far away are the many near this place.
I see this face, so far away.
Not so far away are the many near this face.
So far away, I go to be safe, in this place,
to see this face,
not so far away.

R. J. Babb

A Woman's Pain

A woman's pain...
not the shameful pain of original sin; the bite of the forbidden fruit not the gripping pains of child birth, her body's thrust of life

But, the paralyzing pain of love; slashing her heart to slivers of memory.

A woman's pain...
had been joy, at first; devotion of her soul, mind, heart, body piece by piece it crumbled; the look that made it fear; the words had made it tear - his choice to strike - no warning.

A woman's pain...
the pain - bruising the joy
ending the love in her soul.

A woman's pain.

Marcia Cannon

In Memory Of My Brother Bruce

How do you explain a life that was never quite fun?
Nothing ever finished, nothing completely done.

Was he scared to fail or succeed?
He was never quite happy, but always in need.

Away from us in body, but not our minds,
Was he on the streets? did he eat?
Was he warm in the winter time?

He was running away from you and me
Trying to find where he was supposed to be.

Through tears and fears it had become crystal clear,
Though burden to us and society, our love for him is endless.

As guilt fills our minds, from time to time,
Did we do all we could, I can only speak for mine.

When you try harder then the one you love,
I think you can find comfort from God above.

Not all of Bruce's life was bad,
When he was sober, that was some of the best times we had.

He was funny, and smart,
A jack-of-all trades.

Those are the memories that I will save.

Paul R. Affholter

That Little Old Sod Shanty

There was a little old sod shanty away out on the plains
Nothing left there any more but the foundation frame
It was built of sod blocks, hardly any wood
All is gone now where this shanty stood
It was only a one room shanty with furniture side by side
The family living there was numbered five
Soon another house was built and the family moved in
Leaving this one room shanty to stand against the wind
Over the years this shanty fell-one block at a time
Until it was all down and it was hard to find
The family soon numbered 8 as 3 more children were born
Living in the new house while the shanty was being torn
Down with the strong winds that always blew
Out on this prairie where families were few
Now both houses are gone — there's nothing left to see
Where I was born and raised; out on the lone prairie
I'd like to build a shanty out of sod
Back where the old one stood where my family trod
I'd like to build another house, where the old one used to be
Another barn, another place for everyone to see.

Maxine F. Webb

Silence

Silence that used to cause such pain,
now does offer a sweet refrain.
The silence now is comfort not fear,
of ending in a violent tear.
Tears that come from wounds felt deep,
In a heart that you know is weak.
A heart that's stretched beyond its ties,
And tired from all your careless lies.
Lies of love, respect, and care,
As you try to hold a heart somewhere,
Deep somewhere inside your soul,
Where fear becomes an endless hole.

Stacey DeRousse-Burke

Let's Face It

There was a time I was chasing life
Now it is chasing me..

The lust for living
The need, the giving
Now has ceased to be.

There was a time I was chasing love
Now it is chasing me..

The search for loving
The find, the deserving
Now has ceased to be.

Do I gather the flower?
Sit in ivory towers?
Believe in supreme powers?
Or face what I must face?

That life is chasing what can't be caught
Seeking what can't be sought.

Your choice is setting the pace...

Rita Dube-Harris

Here Or There

I said that I would write, when we got there.
Now, that we are here, or is it there?
I cannot tell, if we are here or there.
For, when we were there, there was there,
and there was here, or was it there?
Then on the way to there, we stopped at there,
which of course, was neither here nor there.
Now that we are here, or there.
We can only be happy, that we are safely there.

Stephen B. Antus Sr.

The Spirit Of Birth

There once was a time when I was blind
Now the safety of darkness is gone
Like the spanking of a baby's behind
My eyes flew open and the lights came on

But this wasn't the way that it seemed
From the other side of the world
Where I always dreamed that someday I'd be born as a little girl

Things went wrong from the very beginning
When my toes got caught in the net
My mind was trapped in a maze of time and my bottom was soaking wet

I kicked and screamed and tugged and teemed
But could not get me loose
My mind in a panic and my body frantic I called on Dr. Zeus

In a flash he was there with his gentle hand
And a nudge that set me free
They examined my body from head to foot but nobody noticed me

I watched as they clothed and fed her and me without a feather
Alone I stood outside myself with no one to put us together

Again I called on the spirit of the Gods to combine us body and soul
then a gentle voice said peace! be still! it's love that makes you whole

Willie Edna Beard

Couldn't Wait

I couldn't wait for the first tooth
Now they eat everything in sight.

I couldn't wait for the first step
And they haven't stopped running since.

I couldn't wait for the first word
How do you shut them up?

I couldn't wait for the first day of school
You want me to bake how many cupcakes?

I couldn't wait for the first birthday party
60 kids? What pony ???

I couldn't wait for the first field trip
A teacher's helper on what type of reptile farm?

I couldn't wait for the first after-school job
You bought how many CD's?

I couldn't wait for the first prom
A tux costs how much? What limo???

I couldn't wait for graduation
Now they're gone. It so quiet.

I should have waited!

Kathryn A. Mann

Mo And Me

It's always a struggle.
Not between good or bad,
just between two beautiful souls that are trying so hard to make it through this world.
We are young
so our battles are just beginning.
We have very little experience
so we are learning.
Every day brings a new understanding.
And from that new understanding a new path is opened to us.
We don't know the direction our life is taking,
but we do know it isn't going to be easy.
We are prepared for the battle,
and we do not fear the future.
The world is ours to conquer.

Sarah Griffin

I've Arrived

A little baby, all cuddly and loved,
Nurtured, cared for and always hugged.
A little boy, so curious and carefree,
Riding his bike, and skinning his knee.
A young teen, needing approval of friends,
Listening to no one, a bad message this sends.
A young man, but still a boy,
Please grow up, a loving parents ploy.
Exhilaration and depression were the next few years,
While mother and father, shed their tears.
Flashes of adulthood appear here and there,
Still adolescent behavior, he doesn't seem to care,
Failed relationships, he thought were true,
with help from friends, the man child grew.
He needed someone special to enter his life,
could this person, be a wife?
Luckily he found her, as anyone can,
From a little baby, many years later, a man.
It's quite a story, these words have contrived,
Hey Mom and Dad, your son has arrived!

Mark Gulbrandson

My Beautiful Angel

I had a dream the other night,
of a beautiful garden- Oh! what a sight.

it was on a hill of golden sand.
There were flowers of purple, red, gold and tan.
I skipped around and danced with glee.
I looked up and saw an angle watching me.
She was dressed all in white and was all aglow.
She was sent from heaven down here below.
She said I love you and took my hand.
Then together we went to the promised land.

Madge Schneider

Good - Bye For Now

If your hands could speak what a story they could tell
Of a man who has self-taught
And who did quite well

Providing for your grandchildren, children and wife
And loving all of us in your own way
Today we recognize the passing of your life

Tomorrow when we remember you
Our thoughts will be filled with a few key words:
Loving, proud, dignified, simple, hard working, farmer,
stubborn, strong family values, and wonderful
Good-bye for now - see you when the sky is blue

Loretta Pierce

Summer Trip

Don't worry mom,
of course i brought back pictures

only let me show you
Here
the odd, angular, dark head of a moose
i saw by the roadside,
the sensuous, furred curve of a hill
shimmering under a full moon,
the silent, singing beauty of a mountain lake
by which i watched the sun set one evening

What?
why didn't i use my camera?

i didn't want to lose my pictures

Shira McClain

The Days

I sometimes long for those days
of old where everything was new
and everyone was your friend
and you trusted a total stranger
as you would your mother.
A time where the days were measured
in lightness and darkness instead of
nanoseconds and you awoke with the same
enthusiasm on September third as
you did on Christmas morning.
At exactly what point did the snow become cold
and the rain wet and two plus two equal four?
Why did Bugs Bunny lose his charm?
Some things I can never understand.

Wren Greene

"Biscuit"

He's the end of the rainbow to his daddy and me.
Of our Boston Terriers he's now number three.

Two little girls named Lisa and Midge, before him we had.
The wanted another girl, but Biscuits a boy and we are glad.
The girls went to heaven before he came to stay.

Now we are praying that God won't take him away.
He's really a beautiful little boy, with one black eye and one that's white.
If we try to take his harness off, he'll put up a fight.

So we just check to be sure it's not too tight.
Friends, he has many, not just one or two.
At Heritage Nursing Home, he has quite a few.
He wears a sweater when outdoors he goes.

Then comes in and grabs my slippers and sometimes my toes.
He'll bring you his ball and wants you to play.
Once he gets it he'll play keep away.
Then through the house, he runs and the throw rugs are a Mess.
We just laugh and call it the "Biscuit Express".

Onalee Sweet

Our Connection

At some point in time when God was creating the essence of the moon and the brilliance of the stars. He destined our souls to meet.

Along with the melody of the waves and whisper of the wind, He intertwined our laughter and our tears. The smiles we exchange, the embraces we treasure and the courage we instill in each other's hearts He supported with the birth of each sunrise.

He then weaved into the tapestry of night the times we would have to spend, miles apart, in different worlds.

And into the fabric of time he pieced your circle of life and mine: Two existences that are crossed by many other lives but are bound together as one.

The mysterious sky, the resounding waves, the rising sun and the darkness of night we will be brought through, so that we will always be a part of each other.

Katherine Marie Howard

Home

H is for Happiness for families and friends,
O is for others who help us to win;
M is for Memories so wonderfully true;
E is for everyone who abides within, too!

Mary Grace W. Garner

The White Picket Fence

As a girl I always dreamed,
Of the white picket fence and home,
The children's laughter, but none of my own,
God, sometimes I feel so alone.

Through my life I've had my trials,
Enough to fill a room,
Just once, to have a dream come true,
Wouldn't be too soon.

My gift from God is to give to others,
To spread happiness and comfort their cries,
But sometimes I wonder when the tables will turn,
And often I cry out, "why?"

I know God has a plan for me,
In my life and what I will do,
I must be patient and hear his word,
I know he will answer me soon.

God has his reasons for the life I live,
I know this, though I sometimes resist,
My tomorrows will be brighter because of my faith,
And soon...I'll find that white picket fence.

Kathy Hogan

I So Small

Lord, God, I cannot comprehend the vastness,
Of these your mountains, so majestic, grand!
Your mighty winds that bring great branches crashing,
And sing a song encompassing the land!
Your sky so wide I cannot see its ending,
Your trees, so tall, they seem to reach to heaven,
And I, so small, yet so much loved by you, Lord,
Dominion over all to me you've given!
I cannot understand, but I believe, Lord,
In eternal life, your great love, oh so wide,
Your arms so strong, I'm cradled there in safety,
And, oh, what joy, what peace I find inside!
When you have done such great things with your world, Lord,
What greater things might you yet do with me?
Oh, precious father, Lord of all this grandeur,
Moving in ways mysterious and free!
How can I ever, ever more feel fettered,
How can I ever more feel small or tied?
Help me reach out, walk in your strength and grandeur
Help me do great things with you at my side!

Ruth Mohr Ildza

Fire Truck

Somewhere there is a fire burning
of this there is no doubt.
I stood on the corner,
I saw the fire truck.
Metal, men, and water
headed toward the smoke that rises from the scene.
Now every note is reviewed, every recording played.
I see the house that is burning
the flames caress the entire frame.
The child that has died is darkened,
the fire has kissed his skin.
A Stone Henge of flesh has gathered,
silent standing shadow folk come to watch
some day-time spectacle to sweep them from their thoughts
far off there is a siren heard
beckoned by the crackle of burning wood and telephone callers.
And somewhere there is a fire burning
of this there is no doubt.
I stood on the corner,
I saw the fire truck.

Leticia Rodriguez

Of Body And Soul

The softness, the touch, the passion.
Of two bodies join as one
As the heat rises, the love begins
Let the beauty flow and the kisses show
that there is love in the air.

The slow movements of our bodies making love,
for there has never been nothing like it before.

The sweat of our bodies in the heat of passion,
Your love, my love, our love
Your body, my body, our soul.........

LaTanya A. Quinn

Wondering

Sitting on the patio, absorbing the sweep
of yard, trees, gardens—
swings, birdbaths, feeders
Contentment abounds

Whisper of breeze, sparkling colors,
bird sounds
even the distant hum of highway traffic
seeming almost musical

How can it be—this serenity
this cocoon-like peace and beauty
in a world so shrouded
by poverty, hunger, evil, death?

Is it wrong to be grateful for
(forgive the platitude)
this "heaven on earth"
when so many are trying desperately
to live at all - in hells
not of their making?

Ruth T. Miller

"In the Blink Of An Eye"

Times seems to move, in the blink of an eye
Often not hearing a lonesome man's cry
Happiness is a short season, yet sadness is so long
Which brings depression to the lonely man who's
often all alone.

The lonesome man has often had a greatly confused life
steadily fighting with the question
"Is it wrong or is it right?"
He will toss and he will turn as he lays there in bed
Trying to justify his actions for what he's done
or what he's said.

By the time he finds the answer
Time will have slipped away
What happens next in life
God can only say

Shawn Ray White

Beyond The Tomb

In a park,
On an aged redwood bench,
I stretched out,
And laid my aged head
Upon his aged lap.
We bathed in the warm morning sun,
The blue sky held us tight;
Birds fluttered about and chirped approval,
It lasted only for a moment.
A memory...a memory
to last beyond the tomb.

Rose Boehm Ebner

My Second Heaven

Los Angeles told him
"Oh God, Lord of the heavens,
The stars no longer fit in the vast open sky"
And God with his great power,
And his great will to overcome
Another heaven he created in the United States,
That is my dear America, and of the purest kind
And as a reminder for what God has left us to behold
A sky that always shines and never clouds
So it's put upon my flag as something so sacred,
The brave, the mighty, the bold
For every star that surges, new to all infinity
Will be placed upon my flag, from order of my Lord,
the trinity.

Mario D. Montoya

With This Ring

With this ring I thee wed.,
Oh how many times this has been said.
I remember on our wedding day,
That was what we had to say.
And some people said it could be rough,
They were right, at times it was tough.

Now the years have past,
And our love did last.
We are getting older, our love is still there,
And after all these years, we still care.
I will love you with all my heart,
Till death do us part.

Vera L. Moody

Teach Them The Song

A struggle was begun,
Oh, how we sang the song;
The song of victory and freedom,
The longing to belong.

Eras of fighting and scraping,
Decades of tears and sweat;
But singing the song all day long,
The desire to belong.

A dream for the next generation;
A dream of unity, equality, diversity, indivisibility;
Dreaming and singing the song,
A will to belong.

The generation of strugglers:
Reaching, grasping, learning, aging, mellowing, fading;
Forgot to teach the song,
To the ones coming along.

A few decades later, complacency holds on;
The new generation picking up guns,
No longer singing the song,
Tell me: Where do they belong?

Patricia M. Andrews

Embracing Joy

As the orchid casts a mantle of peace
Over the chocolate decadence of Uptown,
It cleanses acrid filth and smoky breath;
Pressing cool lips to heads damp with honest sweat.
As morning reflects blindingly in each languid, nacreous drop of dew,
I stumble; tripping like the crippled notes of an adolescent
Passing into manhood.
When the wondrous orchid sweeps into this city of hope,
I embrace time, holding on for dear life - for my life,
And for sweet, unnatural joy.

Y. Regina Whitmore

Looking Back

Down in the hollow where I lived as a child
Oh the beauty of the meadow where the flowers grew wild.
My daddy would sing as he walked behind the plow
Until the dinner bell rang and it was time for chow.

The house wasn't much, but the love was great,
Oh to see mother waiting at the garden gate
To welcome us home from wherever we'd been,
With the sweetest expression and a great big grin.

Playing in the creek my friends and I,
Laying in the grass making images in the sky.
Helping my dad in the fields of corn
Waiting at the neighbors for my brother to be born.

Helping my mother I learned to cook
Setting at her feet I learned the Good Book.
These are the days I like to recall
Because they meant so much to us all.

Louise Neal

Sobriety

My mother stands in the cool morning
on the hearth of my first house.
I am 25 years old and finally grown up.
I see her feet in the wet grass, the glow of her cigarette,
redder than the shame riding low in her heart.
We are not alone, but she asks me if I can forgive.
I am afraid to answer. I have never really used the word,
and my mother's voice, is not her voice, but somehow clear
and sober, a voice I have not heard before, but often dreamt of.
She passes a finger at the full corners of my eyes.
The booze is gone, but I can taste
the addiction that hangs onto her heart.
She cries and pulls me down to her shoulder,
and now I too am there, with the shame in her heart.
And with her new voice she says something
holding my heart tight against her heart
her eyes open against the shame as though those huge,
unblinking eyes of light might not find the small child
holding her mother to the promises of spring,
until the woman woke never to sleep in that pain again.

Lisa A. Long

God Made The World

God made the world in seven days,
On the seventh day He gave it praise.

God made the world with love and care,
God made the world for all to be fair.

God made the world for good and not bad,
God made the world to be happy not sad.

God made the world with love in His heart.
God made the world and people who are smart.

God made the world with pleasant dreams,
God made the world and rivers and streams.

God made the world and God made a tree.
God made the world and God made me.

Katie Nuttall

My Father

Look at the trees. He said, come to me in the leaves.
Oh Daddy. Do you see me?

Marie Elena Sarnicola

The Image Of Man

His wall in place, his feelings suppressed
On the surface he smiles, inside he cries
The hardships of being a man
To remain strong and sturdy
Never allowing uncertainty to show
Emotions never coming in to play
Such a shallow existence, the image of man
He has always been told feelings are weaknesses
To always suppress them, remain strong and sturdy
Like a rock, the image of man
Just a facade, going through life
Never touching, never being touched
Such a waste, the image of man
So many lies he has been told:
To cry a weakness, to feel a crime
Not so!
Emotions build and direct, give us strength
Throughout all our lives
So many untruths he has been told
All in the image of man

Mary J

Laura

Laura, as an Angel,
On the wings of the ocean.
Soar high with each swell,
And reminisce on what has been.

For you are now a spiritual force,
Which brings the mind and body into one.
We are returning you to the source,
But feel your touch with each ray of sun.

Your family has prepared you for this time,
You are now our link with the future.
Watch over us and guide us in our climb,
Our lives on earth need your gentle nurture.

We set you free to reign supreme,
But you are never very far away.
You live on with our every breath and dream,
With those you have touched you always will stay.

So, Laura, spread your new wings and fly,
We celebrate your life and herald your soul.
This is not a mere "Good-bye",
But a joining of spirits into one whole.

Lenore A. Ceithaml

The Seasons

Spring will arrive soon
Once again people will play and hear happy tunes
Everyone will all dance together
For dinner, they'll have chicken, potatoes and prunes

Then there'll be summer
And little children will have a chance to become good swimmers
They wouldn't mind if they swam everyday
They wouldn't even mind if they were bookkeepers

Next is Fall
Babies will start to crawl,
Toddlers will begin school
And young adults will grow tall

Last of all is winter
The kids play in the snow and their faces get redder and redder
All the parents would probably think, "Time goes by fast!"
When the little one's grow up, what will they be? A doctor?

Pauline Louie

Nirvana

Such a sad story that I dare to tell, about a girl that I once knew.
She thought she could own the world you see, and it was a trouble to do.
She wanted it all gold, silver, and more, but that was only the first.
She craved for fame and a husband too, but her love was only a curse.
Nirvana, Nirvana I called to thee, look upon this poor child.
She has nothing but the clothes she wears, and her sweet loving smile.
The girl brought back bad memories, my queen could only say:
My love is only to my husband. Now please just go away.
Nirvana what aren't you telling me, I dared to even mention.
Her poor childhood came to mind. Forget it I've answered my question.
Not everyone lives the perfect life. Not everyone has a loving soul.
My queen you see is scared of life, everyday it's a different role.
One day she found her destiny. Plunged from a building top.
That little girl was there to see her. Too late she could not stop.
Such a sad story that I dare to tell, about a girl that I once knew.
She was a coward and took her life, and it wasn't a trouble to do.

Rachel P. Weber

Indiana Brother (My Kindred Spirit)

You were young and I was younger still.
One day you were there, then gone forever more.
Your name was never mentioned and days turned into years.
But I thought of you big brother and shed my share of tears.

Oh Indiana brothers have the years been good to you?
My Indiana brother do they love you like I do?
Did you know you're my kindred spirit and still dear to my heart?
My Indiana Brother they'll not keep us apart.

I'd love to come to see you and rest my weary mind,
Yet the pain's still here so now is not the time.
I'm older and my children are grown now,
And still we think of you and the things that might have been.

Oh Indiana brother have the years been good to you?
My Indiana brother do they love you like I do?
Did you know you're my kindred spirit and still dear to my heart?
My Indiana Brother they'll not keep us apart.

Shirley A. Boundy

Alone

When one stands in the vast emptiness of the ocean,
One feels the joy of pure freedom.
But if one stays there for long,
Loneliness takes hold
And one will long for friends.

If one stands there longer,
Fear will take over
And one will feel very small in a huge universe.

If one stays there even longer,
Panic will take hold of one
And the vast emptiness of the ocean will claim
Yet another mind......or life.

Megan McKnight

The Dawn

Up, up, up from the horizon comes the dawn.
One meditates in deep serenity the rising sun
That has hidden behind the
embededness, essence, and
spaciousness of beauty.
We know not of the longevity of time
But of the great assurance that lies
Within this mystical life of ours.
We are living in the hope that we may someday
Conquer the great suspense
That lies beneath this overshadowed life
And build it up from beyond this rock of darkness
Into a magnanimous and glorious universe.

Sara Margaret S. Long

Untitled

My emotions are alive with sensation
One minute I feel exhilarated and full of endless possibilities
The next I'm sobbing out of control
My head is spinning with so many thoughts and feelings
It's hard to put everything into words
The words to express myself come to me in my dreams or in a song
Watching a child play so cheerfully
There are many things I want to do, say and feel
At night, I look up to the stars and think of the dreams
Those dreams are what keep pushing me forward
Striving and searching for more
I can't set limitations
I must achieve the things I want through constant pursuit.
The possibilities of life are endless as long as you believe in yourself
Through hard work and determination, goals and dreams can become a reality.

Lori R. Mueuller

The Voice

Found the other day, hidden within these bones, a record of voices- one pleading to unravel the mystery towards the final separation- body from soul, heart from creator, vision from reality, delusion from the flight within, wings that have no destiny, mouth that licks, tongue reddened to plunge into me again, lips that whispered words I could not hear, hands that reached the unreachable, breasts that once gave me life, hairs that disappeared into those years of no years, explosive flesh-pieces that were never set free, words that I only heard (to be denied again), creature from no mother, smiles that never reached their destination, a winged journey without a landing taken into the sky to be swallowed up by an unknown caller - the voice of the woman next door.

R. Mostofi

Untitled

One hundred years ago, our eyes would have
only met in disgust and reproach.
One hundred years ago, our lips would have
only spoken words of anger.
One hundred years ago, our hearts would have
only harbored hatred for one another.
One hundred years ago, we would have been...
enemies.

The years have past, old wounds have faded away,
and you and I have met under a moonlight sky;
one of us white, one of us Kiowa.

Our eyes have met, and have only seen
beauty.
Our lips have met, and have only felt passion.
Our hearts have touched, and there was
only love.
Today, there is only honor in calling you...
friend.

Linda Dale Rowader

Youth

The inexperience of one's youth will manifest foolish things.
One mistake, one step too far, may yield a harp and wings.

It is said we come this way but once, no need to make a plan.
To live, to die, one could care less, do all the things you can.

Through the gauntlet of experience, the sand of time does fall.
Come listen, by the hand of fate, you'll hear the final call.

Spring once bourne gives way to summer, and times that passion enters.
We choose our paths and when it's fall, we hope for many winters.

Time stands still for no one, this we know too well.
One day we come, one day we go and leave this earthly shell.

Michael R. Farley

You Are Not Yet Now What Someday You May Become

Like a green oak leaf not yet turned golden
Or a spotted deer child not yet turned brown
Or a raindrop not yet crystallized to a snowflake
You are not yet now what someday you may become

Life is a river that fills a deep lake
And your soul's days are not yet measured
Your future still a shimmering, misty, cloudy, haze of hope
You are not yet now what someday you may become

The mountain you've climbed is a but a foothill
The distance you've traveled, a step
The depth you've plunged just shallow water
The words you've spoken, a breath
You are not yet now what someday you may become

Walk on, run on, race on, chase on
To your next day, your next way
Your next path, your next place
You are not yet now what someday you may become

Go on to see it — to be it — to live it — to feel it
You are not yet now what someday you may become

Kristi Anne Kozuszko

The Big Sleep

Can Heaven wait in any form or style
Or at the least until we reconcile?
The objects of our passion and hate
Take a priority for their sake.

The Conqueror Worm is always near
Yet of him we deny all fear.
Our own life and definite mortality
Are left unchecked to infidelity.

Death belongs to the Saints and great,
But not to the lowly of caste and fate.
We believe to be immune but twice
While the world is replete with lice.

Death does not forget or discriminate
The lowliest beast to a stalemate.
His sword swings fairly to all that crawl
To infinity and Heaven's door.

Heaven can not wait in any form or style
And we should not mistake this for awhile.
The list is present and prepared each day
As the setting sun will have its way.

Richard A. Sanchez

Star Space

O Pleiades! Are you really there?
Or imaged from a glass-sheened shadow
Cast by grand Big Dipper, up
And toward our North?

Below horizons East or West
Or far below due North,
Perhaps a great dark convex wanders,
Caught in greater gravity
Than Earth's small company commands.

The convex sees Big Dipper there.
It gazes long,
Transfixed by glossy memories
of time long spent on Earth,
By shapes remembered from the past.

So Pleiades -
Down side up - front side back
And far-a-ar away, I wonder
If you're really there.

J. Kilb

Are You Sorry?

Uncertainty? Confusion? Denial?
Or maybe lack thereof.
I thought I was it, the only one.
I stop.
To think perhaps.
I remember the old days.
Just me, the girl, the darkness.
Darkness comes fast to the unworthy.

Then you came, you were like me.
Didn't know who, what, how or why you were.
And you, too, kept going.
For unknown reasons, life rushes onward.
We both believed, yes both of us.

I see myself, as the only one once again.
You went to others for comfort.
To other for what I wasn't.
Are you sorry?
Are you?

Scott Sumner

The Melody Remains!

Was it possibly the canopy of trees,
or maybe the softness of the light breeze.
It may well have been the solitude,
the serenity, contributing to a comforting mood.
One might say it was the newness of the place,
that brought the warmest of smiles to my face.
But weighing it all and thinking it through,
I really do know it was being with you.
Your smile so warm, so genuine and tender,
the talk of times gone by we took time to remember.
Paralleling the few words that I wanted to say,
Was the wonderful melody in my heart all day.
The thought of these things and a lot more too,
brings anticipation of the next moments to be shared with you.
Timing is everything I've learned to understand,
also hearts not broken are not necessary to mend.
When all is said and done and through,
I feel so very lucky to have found a special friend like you!

Richard G. Boswell

Nobody Knows

Nobody knows why there is hate in this world
Or why there is love mixed in with fear,
Nobody knows why we live with all three
Or why there is happiness along with the tears.

Nobody can understand the emotions that we feel
From the very first moment we're born,
We can smile and laugh with tears in our eyes,
But then when we're mad we'll shed tears of scorn.

It seems that emotions are an oddity of life
That will continue to live though we pass on,
Constantly growing stronger every new day
Taking us over before the crack of dawn.

I wonder what life would really be like
Without any emotion to show how we feel,
No tears or smiles or love in our hearts
No way for our confused minds to heal.

Sharon Caringer

Precious Gifts

Suppose you had to pay for the sun to shine one day,
Or you had to buy an ocean for to swim.
Or, could you afford to buy the stars bright in the sky?
We own them—each of us—supplied by Him.

Suppose you had to buy the birds that each day fly
So gracefully and offer us their song;
Or could you afford the fee for the flowers that you see
Growing wild in all the fields you drive along?

Or, what if the great Giver just charged you for the river
That you walk along and fish in when you please;
Or the air you're free to breathe; or the love He doth bequeath—
Do you really think you could afford all these?

And, how you would complain if you had to buy the rain
That falls gently and refreshes your great Earth;
And the rainbow that you see that is given to you free—
How much money do you think these would be worth?

Now, you think you have no wealth—but what about your health
That riches can't buy—even for a king!
And the rich shall surely die—even as you and I.
When our time comes, all our wealth won't mean a thing.

Madeline Thayer

Forgiveness

We walk this way, but only once.
Our children follow, in our footsteps
If there is hatred in our hearts,
We'll find our children,
Will soon depart.
So show them love, and understanding too!
Make mistakes, as we have done.
In the end, love has always won.
So first and second blood generations
Of our Loves.
Be forgiving, and understanding
It comes from above.
A prayer or two will suffice
And will always make things nice.
Say I'm sorry, I forgive you.
Then this love will follow through.

Patricia Calcagno

Untitled

The children are crying, the reason, they've said,
"Our mother is gone, our mother is dead.
She drowned in the "C", it took her away,
Now we've no where to go and no where to play".

The children are trying to cope with their fear.
"Why did Mom have to go, who will care for us here"?
"She's not really gone", said the young one believing,
In hopes that the others would soon stop their grieving.
"Mom wouldn't go and leave us alone,
She knows we can't cope with the world on our own".

Now the children are lying so they don't have to face,
The cruel realization of death and its place.
Then one of the children, who was oldest and wise,
Said, "The world doesn't stop when somebody dies,
No matter how much we love her and want her to be,
She's better off now where her spirit is free".

Now the children are grown but they feel incomplete,
For they lost in their lives what was precious and sweet.
No one could stop- their sweet mother from dying,
And inside their dear hearts, the children, are still crying.

Rebecca S. Hilden

Remembrance

Though angels often cross
our paths, in sight, they are unseen,
habitually we pass them
by, yet yearn for them in dream.
A dream is but a mystery
we try to comprehend,
The morn destroys the
messages our angels seek to send.
Forgotten are the sweetest
words, whispered in rapturous bliss,
How we would grieve
if we but knew the glory that we miss.
With softest touch
of unfurled wings, selfless love is found,
Remembrance floods
weary souls with ecstasy, unbound.

Shell McLaughlin

Licorice

I remember the day I walked
out in that autumn sun,
The shadowy darkness of the twins,
their pointed ears, and sharp claws,
the way they slept in one little
ball, and the joy they brought
to my overflowing heart.
But that day they just lay
unmoving, cautious, weary
They would not play that day.
And when night came I held
one frail body on my lap,
caressing the soft black fur,
as he lay dying in my arms.
I cried as he moaned, and
he left his brother, Gumdrop, alone that night.
Licorice died so young, but still
a part of him lives on through me,
And will always be in my heart
just the same.

Leigh Burnett

Over And Over

Around, around, my head does spin,
Over, and over, and over again.
Inside my heart I wish I could cry,
For my grandpa, he has died.

Like a maze, my heart feels no peace,
For the doctors feel he should have lived.
For yet, I don't understand why,
But I sure know it's okay to cry.

Inside I want to believe he's at peace,
Among the angels he does sleep.
By the way, I still love him deeply,
For his picture is of my keeping.

Around, Around, my head does spin,
Over, and over, and over again!

Michelle Deuri

"My Wish"

I want to live upon a cliff
overlooking the sea,
in a cottage painted white with
three bay windows to let in light.

Dark green grass, with flowers galore,
rocks and shells gathered from the shore.
Three big weeping willow trees
with a swing underneath
especially for me.

A lighthouse next door
will give off the light
for ships to go safely into the night.

The shore is rocky, but there is some sand
to walk upon, and touch with your hand.

The sunset is bright yellow, purple and orange
as I sit the swing
with a shawl to keep warm.

This is my home in my mind.
I hope that someday
this wish will be mine.

Mary L. McCord

Loving Thoughts Of You

As the darkness of the night
overpowers the lightness of the day.
And the lustre of the moon rises
upon the heavens of the sky.
I shall stroll along the sands of
the beach where quietness will always lay.
As the waves strike upon the rocks and disappear,
the roaring echo will linger behind and cry.
As I sit upon the highest rock, leader of them all,
my loving thoughts of you shall appear and call.
They shall mix in the beauty of the sea.
Well meant, they will reappear, or they shall be
washed upon the sands with me.
As I meditate with the Master of them all.
The loving thoughts reappear stronger than a racing yawl.

Robert A. Jencks

Going Away

While I'm sitting here packing
Packing up a very large part of my Grandmother
Her memories - Her good times - And her bad
I think to myself
As teardrops flow through my heart and my mind
Why people have to get worse
Before they get better
Why some people just get worse
And why GOD couldn't let people die fast and painless
Instead of letting them slowly die
Painfully
And knowing that they are
And letting the family die inside
As they watch their loved one
Slowly drift away

Lindsay Jones

Anthology

Precious, hardbound anthology
Pages sweet with the fragrance of love
A soul enthroning LIFE in Poetry
Essence dreams and hopes are made of!

Breath is in your pages
Just as surely as you are the wings of dreams
Even the meanest among sages
Rejoices there held in your seams!

You transport hearts barred from heaven
To the glorious heights of beyond
Emotions and words are your leaven
Breaking that surly bond!

Carry me forth in your flight
To the place of timeless identity
And there in your wond'rous delight
Let there be remembrance of ME!

Kathy Anne Saada

"Shut The Door"

Rhythm - in tears, I know well;
Pain is my closest relative.
Dear God, why do these eyes seek?
My mind can't bare fear's lustful touch;
Though my heart helps it try.
Shut that door - let me lean on the wall.
It is strong and sturdy - it will welcome my presence.
Oh, the rage, and the pity, and the sorrow that circles me!
All are like starving, raving vultures.
They haunt me. Taunting and teasing, they mock my image.
These feet won't run - God help them.
I turn, so often, in a room - walls tightly snug;
A door is slightly ajar, but no light shines through.
Spare these visions, or take my heart - my only spirit!
For this soul upon my body no longer yearns to fulfill
life's expectations.

Marty Mohr

Pain Is When!

Pain is when you are born
Pain is when you turn five and have to go to school
Pain is when you get yelled at by the teacher, for
something you didn't do
Pain is when you lose your Lunch Money, and can't
eat for the rest of the day
Pain is when it's time for school to get out
Pain is when you miss your bus for the tenth day straight
Pain is when your Mother picks you up, and yells at you
until your home
Pain is when you can't watch television for the rest
of the day
Pain is when you have to eat all of your broccoli at
dinner time
Pain is when it's time to go to sleep at night
Pain is when you have to do it all over again
the next day....

Kevin R. Combs

Dreams

Dreams are like pictures,
painted in my mind.
I dream at night trying to find,
someone to share my joys and cheer when sad.
Something more special than I have ever had.
I will go on dreaming until I find,
someone to fit this puzzle,
painted in my mind.

Shirley Coffey

Untitled

As a child, I believed in fairytales, in things of mystic fascination-
palaces in the sky, knights on white horses
me, a princess in a far off land, possessing what others only dreamt of,
then one day, reality happened and I came to know life's
suffering and pain.
So much heartache - so many tears.
Childhood swept away
Dark clouds replacing soft, blue skies
dreams of wonderment over,
I struggled to hold onto what little hope I had left.

Slowly, I emerged into a person that still clung to fairytales-
hoping that love could find it's way home
and touch me where I was hollow.
Some dreams escaped as new ones surfaced,
as I realized, life is what you make it.
And I believe I'll always be that innocent child
looking for the rainbow after the storm-
always ready for the impossible to be possible.

Theresa Diane Johnson

Servant That I Am Passing Over

Long the road has been. Yet short for long waited
peace within. I contend this is that road given
freely. Lonely is the servant, for the true longing
is to see the face of His Holiness, the Father's
chosen lamb. The Magnificent Oneness with our
entwined hearts is the closest. I his servant shall
get till I descend towards the heavens in spirit,
longing, waiting, and faithfully believing the Word
of the Precious Son and His Father. Though my feet I
do not know where it shall lead me, you go willingly
because of the growing love He shows me. As I gazed
upon the stars of heaven, God has stars on Earth
that shine brighter because the Aura descends from
the human heart where His Beloved Son is with us.
All the Children of God are brilliant and truly seen
by the eyes of those who take care of the living
soul. The servant that passes-over earthly things
is loved.

Kathyann Morse

Surroundings

Around in time surrounding survivors,
Placing thoughts of our arrivals.

Where in life do we be relieved,
That decisions are made and believed.

Thoughts of conclusions is our illusions,
Because our surrounding are our delusions.

Nevertheless, we try to be our best,
But things sometimes turn to be a mess.

But being surrounded can be confounded,
But when we depend on life itself, we also leave out the rest.

But if we include the maker of life,
We would all be better in sight.

Luthan Poole

The Soulful Eye

An expressive chameleon.
Penetrable, illuminating depths of trust and sincerity.
At times a narrow corridor which nary an intruder may trespass.
Psychic, in ability to interpret what may transpire.
Protective, as it sends a swift current to wash the pain to sea.
A globe like no other, able to hold many universes in its grasp.
Guiding the myriad of illusions that fill our days.

Michelle Julie Goldstein

"Wildflowers"

"Save the wildflowers" Lady Bird Johnson said-
Plant them every where you can, I read.
Every color of the rainbow I should think-
Purple, orange and yellow - blue, red and pink.
Wild and wonderful colors that bring an "oh-my"-
And delights each nature lover who passes by.
I saw many results on my trip this summer-
Butterflies and bees and even some "hummers".
All flitting about gathering nectar and honey-
From the beautiful wildflowers warm and sunny.
Since God provided us with this natural beauty-
Protecting this treasure is a gardener's duty.
"Save the wildflowers", Lady Bird Johnson said-
Along the roadsides and even in your flower beds.
Delay the roadside mowing-let the flowers go to seed-
So they may repeat this glorious spectacle-yes indeed.

Virginia Trindle Stephens

Lessons On Life

I walked to Grandmother's house today, but on the way I stopped to play.
A little friend gave me a smile, and I decided to stay awhile.
We played and played while the sun was high. We didn't notice the time rush by.
Before we knew it the sun had set, and I hadn't gotten to Grandmother's yet.

As fast as the wind I raced to see if Grandmother knew what had happened to me.
Would she be mad at the way I'd done? Or would she laugh and think that was fun?
As I drew near, there she sat on the step, with her head in her hands so softly she wept.
Her hair white with years, shown in the dim light. I had given my Grandmother such a fright.

So gently I touched her and called her name, "Grandma, I'm here, I finally came.
A little friend asked me to play, and that's what caused the long delay."
Her loving arms around me wrapped. She drew me close into her lap.
And silently, for hours on end, we sat and watched the night begin.

Laska Hughey Holley

My Little World

Wisps of cotton candy clouds
Played tag with the sun.
A soft and gentle wind
Cooled my browning skin;
While I lay on green velvet
Staring at the sometimes shadowed sky.

The almost quiet sound
Of waving grass echoed in my ears.
The slight dampness of the soil beneath me
Filled my nostrils with its sweet scent;
My mouth and tongue both savored
The faintest flavor of flowers.

My every part was made aware
Of its own existence and sensuality.
My body received that which surrounded it
And gathered nature's gifts within its shell;
In return, my entire being gave of itself
And became a part of that which enveloped me.

A hint of Paradise had found its way
Into My Little World.

Michael J. McGee

Jaded Life

Lost to the light
Playing with shadows
Living with ghosts unable to take flight
Searching for something, that will never be shown
Hidden within a crowd
And still standing alone
For everyone, yet no one to see
Looking for the real me
Hidden behind a mask
Unwilling to see myself free

Lawrence R. Busha

To My Family

Hi Mom, Hi Dad, Craig and little Jackie too!
Please don't be sad, on this my final rendezvous,
A helicopter pilot I always wanted to be; and low and behold
God chose me, His co-pilot to be,
As it was my destiny, my final flight, in a helicopter
I saw the light!
A better and more beautiful tomorrow,
No need today of great sorrow,
So Mom, Dad, Craig, and little Jackie too,
Just remember, how much I love you.
"Jason"

Marianne L. Mauricio

Poetry Is

Poetry looks like flowers in a field.
Poetry looks like shiny gold.
Poetry looks like dew in the morning.

Poetry is love and sadness at the same time.
Poetry is life and death.
Poetry is very funny.

Poetry feels like silk.
Poetry feels like cotton.
Poetry feels delicate.

Poetry smells like sweet flowers.
Poetry smells like candy.
Poetry smells like cotton candy.

Poetry sounds like birds flying.
Poetry sounds like angels talking.
Poetry sounds like a story from a storybook.

Katie Zonelle Crandall

My Wife

Darling, as I pen these words
Pondering the blessings of my life.
Although they are many, they began
When you chose to become my wife.

As a young girl you were pretty,
You're now more beautiful, by far.
Passion is one of the pleasures of life,
But I love you more for who you are.

"You're too young to fall in love." They said
"You're too young to understand."
But my love for you is just as real
As the day I first touched your hand.

In my youth I prayed for an angel
And God gave me you.
I'm as unworthy of your consideration now
As the day that you said "I do".

And now as I pause to reflect
On the fullness of my life,
I get on my knees and thank God for you
My friend,..... My lover,.... My wife.

Tom Williams

Not Only A Christmas Gift

On that special day he gave us an awesome
present that we could never repay.
In the manger lay our swaddled gift from
heaven's glory on high.
So then we on earth should be so giving as
our father who art in heaven.
That on this special day and throughout
the year we should feel the need inside of
us to give...hallowed be thy name.
To give not only that which is material but
that which is intangible love... thy kingdom come.
So special is this love that the one you give it
to will never be the better...thy will be done.
Thus everyday reflect on this special day and
reach within yourself and share freely what
has been freely given to you...on earth.
As it is in heaven... God Bless.

Robert H. Wong Jr.

Untitled

Abortion is not the answer
Prevention is the key,
With so many choices to offer
- And all this starts with "me"

The sacrificed millions are just a statistic
To dismiss with a casual shrug,
But a sign of a society ... sick!
Just slip it under the rug

Tiny hands - tiny feet
With a heart to grow,
What an impact and loss on all our lives
This we will never know

You say this planet has lives too many,
And abortion is the cure,
Just step up and volunteer
Your life for theirs will endure.

The felon on death row
Has more chance of life,
Than this innocent victim,
A victim of society's strife.

Roy T. Sparks

Life's Turning Wheels

Ah! It says that growing old is a
privilege for each of us to define, beginning
with the down side of not, walking ahead,
but rather behind, as I've lost that strength
and vigor portrayed by youth so well, this
causes great anxiety as I begin to feel like hell.

I cannot see the path ahead due to
impaired vision; it's just another
obstacle of grief to hinder my decision, to carry
on or call it quits in this quest of much ado,
as I accept the benefits a lifetime has
accorded me.

To grow old gracefully and enjoy the Golden
Years fulfilled with all the love and hope this
old paradox reveals is to live happily ever after
in the remainder of life's turning wheels.

I find it questionable as to the
bliss life unfolds over the years as I listen
to the answers from the view point
of my peers.

Lois Stiner

"Ringing In The New Year 95"

A brand new beginning
Promise, dreams never ending
A release from tomorrow's past ends
And a promising New Year now begins
Fire-crackers lighten up the sky
New hopes and wishes, "Dare not die!"
Colorful party hats and streamers of balloons in the air
Dances and crowded parties mingled with those we care.
Noise makers and music play loud.
People wanting to get lost in the massive crowds
Future holds mystery, as the sands of time ring

Will this be the year of a brand new fling?
"Lonely hearts," sit and stare
Loved ones forgotten and no longer wanting to care
Crystal glasses of pink champagne people share
Oh "the Lucky," selective ones in whom we care.
Candle light dinners and romantic restaurant so fine.
Everyone dreams of that someone "Special" they can call "mine."
As the midnight rings clear, everyone both young and old,
Dreams of a brighter, more promising year!

Mary Ellen Lamie

Opening Life's Door

Closeted was the world, close in and narrow;
protected, restricted with little room to grow;
until you appeared on my life's brow.

People were of a one; different, yet all the same;
then all expanded - existence no longer tame;
the universe appeared along with your name.
To find another so open to knowing more -
with real love - made my soul soar,
and I thank you for opening life's door.

Paul E. Drangeid

From: The Poets, To: Us

The poets, open doors to many a thought
Providing answers, for questions sought.
With their gift, we are taught.

With pen in hand and thoughts in mind.
Providing answers, we cannot find.

Filling the gaps, between time and space.
Leaving trails, of thoughts to be traced.

Sharing their gift, they hold so dear.
Sharing with us, their laughter and tears.
Filling the gasp, of past and future years

Their poetic thoughts, they do roam.
With pen and paper, to create their poem.

Heaven or hell, here on earth.
The poetic seed, begins to grow at birth.

William F. De Simone

"Chaco"

Chaco, Chaco, ancient city of ANASAZI,
Pueblo Bonito, Great Kiva, Thy ART.
Upon sacred Mesa, the "Ancient Ones" built.
Lying abandoned, their Souls still exist.
Through darkness they came,
facing unknown terrain.
Still standing through time,
Our "Great Kiva" remains.

Yvonne C. Harris

Your Day

The earliest morning sun seizes the night,
Pulls down the horizon and breaths through the rise,
Struggling to become a day.
Can you smell it?
Close your eyes and take it in.
This day is yours.
Morning dews of the field unite at the crest of the knives in the Garden of grass for their final suicidal leap back to earth.
It's another day - can you see it?
Look around and see the aroma,
It's yours.
Stranger abandons his berth,
Allowing nature's band to strike up upon his face.
Winds trumpet through his hair,
Air's essence flutes to his nostrils,
And earth slides under his feet like a trombone
As the sun pursues to a crescendo.
Lift your arms from your sides and take a firm chunk of the day.
It belongs to you....
It's your day!

Rodney C. Belen

Mademoiselle Erythroxylon

She is the Madonna, Medusa, Hellen and Hekate,
Pure, Evil, Beautiful and Bewitching.
She is gone now and no longer lies with me,
Heaven rejoices-Hell laments.

I go on through infinity with, no witness,
No love, no life, no death, no awakening,
Just a vague observation as though, everything
I see seems to pass first, through a kaleidoscope.

Her essence a shard deep in my soul,
Her heart I sense when I am alone,
That shadow just beyond my sight,
My soundless roar she hears at night.

William Lane Summers

Untitled

Memories spring unbidden to my mind,
pushing for room in which they may flower.
A heart full of dismay, no hope to find,
my only companion this darkest hour.

A child whimpers, perhaps from a past life,
Sorrow echoes in each and every strain,
and, as always in my moments of strife,
I count on your tender love to sustain

The sense of magic and wonder I need
to live out this life as I'm called to.
time is suspended now, my heart is freed
and tonight will consists only of you.

Pain is diminished, hope rises reborn
tomorrow's always soon enough to mourn.

J. Warczakoski

Shooting Star

You were like the fiery brilliance of a shooting star
racing through time.
Unexpectedly you flashed across my life
setting my world ablaze with
passion, hope, and seemingly endless laughter.

Your leaving was as unforeseen as your arrival.
As the warmth of your presence fades from my memory
and darkness returns,
I wonder at the thought:
is it better to have never known the light
or to live in continual sorrow, wishing for its return?

K. W. Gray-Bow

The Voice

All alone, my thoughts seem so deep and lost
put an end to it the voice says, so I asked it the cost?
It won't cost you anything the voice says.
"So I started to think" how my life was missing a link.
I was so confused I didn't know which way to turn,
"then the voice said" no one is concerned.
I could not talk to no one for I knew they would not understand that's when I took my problems and put them in the voice's hands.
Then the voice started laughing, I knew I would win
now here's some ideas how to put it to an end.
First take these pills, "no" that's too slow, ok slit
your wrist "no" that's no way to go.
"I got it!" shoot yourself in the head. "No I can't do it!"
"Do it!" The voice said.
Then I heard the voice say, "Wait! Don't shoot your self in the head."
I asked why? Cause you're already dead.

Patrick Roberts

A Hug

Understand my thoughts and give me a warm smile
Put your arms around me and hold me a while.

I need a feeling of closeness right now,
A friend to reach out and show me how.

Please don't lecture or give advice,
Just embrace me please, that would be so nice.

You may rub my back or pat it a while.
Please don't let go until I smile.

How great it feels, this moment I will savor.
Stay a while and I will return the favor.

It's such an easy thing to do
And helps so much when you're feeling blue;

Or have a happy moment to share
With someone special whom you know will care.

It can make you feel so secure and snug
To open your arms and give someone a hug.

Let me know if your are ever down
And need a hug, I will come around.

I will understand your thoughts and give you a warm smile,
Put my arms around you and hold you a while.

Linda N. Brown

A Wood Burning Stove

A wood burning stove
radiating
in the daylight

blind
hypnotized by
forgotten memories

nestled dreams
days
lost

from a past era
memories
gray and dismal

pulsating
energized coals
of warmth

hay in my hair
blending
in simple thoughts

Sherry Pedonesi

Rain

Rain is here and here to stay.
Rain makes everything wet and the sky old and gray.
Rain makes you stay inside so you can't go out and play.
Rain makes everything all muddy
and gooey like caramel sticking to your teeth.

Patrizio Peluso

Smile Your Tender Smile

Smile that smile, so tender, for me
Raise your head high, as should be.
Be good to yourself, your body and mind
Read the Bible daily, you'll be happier, you'll find.
Walking through streets, be cheerful and gay
Shake a friend's hand, as you go on your way.
Any tear to come down, needs to be dried
So let your pain out, don't let it hide.
God made you good, and He loves you, you see
You're wonderfully made, and special to me.
This little poem comes straight from my heart
And I hope from your mind, it never will part.

Laura L. Rackley

From My Heart

Here is my poem to you,
Read my words when you're sad and blue,
and as you read these words, "I've said,
Let them soothe your inner soul..
For these words I've wrote you'll soon find,
will stand the very test of time...
the words that I wrote on this white paper
is what comes from my heart, so pure and
true, I swear to you.
So don't you ever let yourself forget,
the very precious LOVE I have inside for
the Greatest Man that I could find,
I think that your the "sweetest, kindest,
man by far,
So with these closing words I'll say to you,
there is none sweeter, more loving then you.
That is why my gift to you, is meant to melt your
heart so true, My Love Eternal, is my gift to you....

Shirley Ann Williamson

Apology

Please forgive all the wrong I have done;
Really, I was just trying to have some fun.
Angering others is what I seem to do best.
You know, I think I'll give it a rest.

The way I think, most say is weird.
Hateful vengeance leaves me feared.
Anyone you ask would wish I was dead;
That's okay, because it's life that I dread.

Today I reflected upon my past,
Realizing the numbers I hurt are vast.
Obviously, it's too late to take my words back;
You know now that it's a brain I lack.

Wouldn't it be nice if I had nothing to say?
Only then would I have peace for one day.
Never have I ever felt to belong;
Trying to impress others is my only wrong.

Love is something I will probably never experience;
In my life, I now have benevolence.
Voyaging into my new ideologies,
Ending the year with my apologies.

Troy Thigpen

Treasures Of The Heart

Growing up with gifts galore,
people leaving presents behind every door.
In my teens, be it precious metals, silver or gold,
or a pearl retrieved by a diver bold.
Later on, in my years,
tis the treasures of love and tears.
So hold me close, it is what I want,
For your love and tenderness I could not have bought.

Roger Morrow

Reflections

How very strange I look to me
Reflected from a Christmas tree
In ornaments of silver red and green.

In myriads of light I laugh
And revel in my tinsel bath
Made multicolored by the tree lights glow.

Above my head a soft spruce bow
Suspends me in the fleeting now
And knows I am illusive as I seem.

I give myself a shining look
From my secluded fairy nook
And turn around to watch me as I go.

Patricia Painter Schamaun

Dance Of Lights

A dance of lights out of the night and a stormy soul seeks
Refuge in flight.
What makes the feeling go away?
A search for life, a never ending storm.
The wind brings a cleansing, a renewal avowed.
This too shall pass, with the dance of the lights.
Like the storm at night, my love so intense.
Then it is over like the dance of the lights.
Why so short it flees in the night and can it endure or will
It take flight.
A celebration of life, it is so short we see.
That broken spirit that always will be.
A mended seam that gives way from the tug.
Can we be happy from a love gone astray?
What is the answer, where is the way?
Not of this time the heart will say.
We cannot find peace with a love gone astray.

Sammye Sessions

My Quiet Place

Out in the middle of nowhere,
Is a peaceful little spot.
Quiet, serene and restful,
A place to collect all my thoughts.

A place with lots of blue skies.
And clouds floating overhead.
Little friends, scampering around,
Birds flying on the wind.

Soft breezes flowing thorough the leaves,
Creating a soft gentle rustle.
It's a place to walk and relax,
Away from the daily bustle.

Sometimes we need such a quite time,
To be with our thoughts and our dreams.
Time to remove all the cob webs,
That clog up our life's daily stream.

We can only stay for a little while,
Soon we must head back down the road.
But it's a joy just to know, that no matter how life will go,
That special spot, will always be there.

Lynn C. Seiltz

For J.B.

When I hear thunder
I hear drum rolls
And cymbal slams
War is another way.

When my friend hears thunder
He hears the blast of bombs
The slamming of shells
Against the earth
Separating us.

When I see lightening
I see beautiful reds, yellows, white
He sees the flash after the explosion
And the red color of body parts flying
Through the air
The beauty of nature.

Zeldine Golden

The DJ

His voice comes to me over the airwaves.
I hear it in the morning as I start my day.

The sound is soothing and deep,
and it makes my day complete.

His wisdom is strong.
His confidence high.
When you're on the air,
Watch Out!
He'll eat you alive.

Some say he's rude,
others says he's just mean.

That's because he makes you look at
yourself and scream.

I take what I need,
and discard the rest,
because my days wouldn't be the same,
if I thought like the rest.

Rose Morales

To My Wife, I Love You, Mike

When I met you in eighty five,
I knew then our love would survive.
Then we married in eighty seven
I thought then, I was in heaven.

In eighty eight we had our first bundle of joy.
Three years later, we had a second
baby boy.
I was so happy, I was so proud,
For my wife and my sons, I could
scream out loud!

You are my life, you are my love,
I know you were sent from heaven above.
To put up with my ways, for all of
these days.
My heart beats true, it beats only for you.

Thru the months year after year,
I want you to know, I'll always be here.

Mike McDonald

To My Mother

In order to provoke the thought,
I must admit 'twas much I sought
To tell thee of my deep intent
And of the heart's pure-meant content.

To say that thou art more supreme
Than any other sweetest dream,
May seem to thee mere flattery;
But I have oft thought so of thee.

How often I have had the mind
Like thee to be - myself to find
Awaking from a sweet Spring show'r,
A bud blooming into a flow'r.

Today thine heart has seen so much,
Felt all that thou might never touch -
Some beauty, known to only thee -
Some sorrow that thine own 'twill be.

Thou art still young - many a year
To bring to thee great things of cheer;
So, when with things thou do despair,
Look then to this my little air.

Mary E. Bridges

Bull Run

When I was in the Nuthouse
I never realized
The battle that was being waged
behind my sad brown eyes

I knew that I was crazy
The doctors called me ill
I tried the cure of suicide
They preferred a pill

The evil that is Satan
The peace of Christ, the Lord
Who would win the contest?
Who held the sharper sword?

Jesus intervened for me
My sanity returned
The will of God Almighty
Saved my soul from being burned

Madness is a struggle
The crazy never win
For they are just a battlefield
To the forces from within

Michael Pitts

Untitled

"When I walk alone,
I ponder the solitude.
When I walk alone
I ponder the refreshment
that solitude brings!"

Robert A. Preston

The Cure

I loved him more than chocolate,
I loved him more than spring,
I loved him more than laughter,
Then he gave me a ring.

He made my mind grow dizzy,
He made my heart go pat-pat-pat,
He made me his wedded wife,
And that took care of that.

Shirley Ziegler

Why

A tear falls down my face
I reach out and hold your hand
A tear falls down my face
I love you, and want you with me again

A tear falls down my face
And I don't want you to leave
A tear falls down my face
I can't help the way I feel

A tear falls down my face
And I start to laugh
A tear falls down my face
And suddenly I am sad

A tear falls down my face
And I seem to want to live
A tear falls down my face
Your gone, but I am still here

A tear falls down my face and I am disbelief
A tear falls down my face
I try to hold your hand again, but I just
can't reach

A tear falls down my face.

Tonya M. Davis

My Love

I sleep upon your feathers
I rest beneath your wings
your voice travels through me
Like a nightingale when it sings.

We became friends
Right from the beginning
These feelings I have
are far from ever dimming

Your eyes are the ocean
your heart filled with the sea
nothing in this world
means more then you do to me

The lessons you will learn
The struggles you pull through
I will always be here
watching right over you

Open your heart
and try my feelings I give
because without you
Is a LIFE I don't want to live.

Kimberly Rose

A Continuance

...And as the reasons fly
I sit back and try to grasp
"What is happening to me?"
I do not know for sure.
But one thing I see as clear
Nothing stays the same,
but it never changes either.
The wind blows by and yells
"Don't let me pass you by!"
But how do I keep with a breeze?
I can run and jump and walk
and never keep the pace.
So I'll try forever to follow
the mystical wind's advice
To try on and stay stubborn
However difficult a task
and I'll continue forever.

Mike Kobus

Tranquillity

I beheld majestic mountains
I sat beside man made fountains

I walked among the forest trees
Heard whispering waves in the seas

I have spent my idle hours
Just enjoying summer showers

I walked the beach through fog and mist
Ignoring the watch on my wrist

I felt a most refreshing breeze
Heard the singing birds in the trees

I walked along the quiet shore
Calming my inner self once more

I sat beside a babbling brook
Too enchanted to read my book

I observed a field of flowers
Evidence of His great powers

Moonlight and stars then wind and rain
Followed by sunshine once again

All of these things mean much to me
They all express tranquillity.

Lillian Lozier

I Don't Belong

Buried in madness
I see no trace of light
And no one is out there
To guide me through the night

I don't belong
I never did
I have always felt this pain
Even when I was a kid

I look like you
Aren't appearances deceiving?
I just want to belong
And so I must keep on believing

Things have got to get better
For they can't get any worse
If I change my way of thinking
Can I end this bitter curse?

I need to find direction
Through this winding, foggy maze
I don't know if I'll get through
I've little passion left these days

Margaret Kraniotis

Contentment

A dream house of my own!
If only I had known
When I was a new bride
That someday by his side
I'd sit and dream before the fire
And remember, and never tire
Of all the plans that we had made
In sunshine and in shade.

We worked hard to make dreams come true.
Two children were given to us
And shared our dreams from the blue.
Now in seventies and eighties we rest;
Knowing our dreams were the best.
So in peace and all that it meant
We thank God for contentment.

Leuty Quaid

Wasted

I stare at pages that were to be my life
I take a good long look
A dream which I could see as real
Knowing now that what I did was wrong
I can never seem to help myself
I really never seem to find myself
Needing to explore
Leaving what I have
Finding it necessary now
To escape my troubled mind
I see the pictures every day
A hopeful dream I wish was real
Feeling crazy every time I see your face
There is no understanding
No one will ever know its meaning
I can never really seem to know myself
I would never try to understand myself
Negative values are my hopes
I see my world through images
I hope to never change myself

Nancy Morta

Might

As I arise at day's first light,
I take the time to ponder just what might,
The might of long ago
and all the memories to be told.
The might of now,
with all its rush and hurry to endow.
The might of later as time goes on
as I sip my tea and dwell upon...
The beautiful time God has given me
to share with others and family.

Linda G. Francis

Why? Oh Why?

Oh, Baby, where did I go wrong?
I thought our love was so
deep and strong.

I let it encircle me, like a
baby in a mother's womb, and
it felt so secure, warm, and serene.

Suddenly it become an iceberg,
straight from the North Pole, I
Couldn't even break a piece with
an ice pick, it was so cold.

Then there was the silence,
just like you couldn't speak,
Talking to a brick wall sort
of made my nerves squeak.

Now, the breakup has arrived,
and, the days and nights are long,
but, there is no use hanging
on to a love, that would end
up all wrong.

Shirley N. Colbert

Lightning

In the wet and dreary night
I see a jagged knife scarring
the sky and earth which
leaves behind an after flow
of pain.
The sky weeps, as rain
dripping from her eyes.

Ty Inhofer

The Neutering

Sitting on your sofa
I twist, strain,
peer over the back
to see you
hiding, safe, far away
on the kitchen floor.

You're more comfortable
over there,
more comfortable
with the space of the other side
and you talk...

Talking
Talking
Talking

As I
pretend pleasure
for a place for my
outstretched legs.

Dennington

"Amulet"

In my dreams
I walk on the wind.
Searching and gazing,
To seek my journey's end.

I travel through sand,
I travel through snow.
And through the darkest rain,
Even my heart can't tell me where to go.

Where will my destiny take me,
What shall I find.
Will I wake up to reality,
From the sleeping thoughts in my mind?

Seeing shadows on black walls,
And ghosts on clouds of white.
Seeing roses with thorns of ice,
But everything is just visions of night.

Because with slowly opening eyes,
As I creep from my enchanted rest,
I see the so faithful Lord's amulet,
Laying upon my chest.

Steven D. Monroe

You

You want out,
  I want out,
We all want out,
  Yet we only shout,
You got out,
  We stayed in,
You made a sin,
  You were forgiven,
You said you'd get out,
  We had to doubt,
You couldn't share the pain,
  Now we share the pain,
You're left happy,
  We're left sad,
You thought of yourself,
  Now we're mad,
We'll be together,
  in the end,
You and I,
  once again.

Sarah Lynne Mickelson

To Be Someone

If there is a star out there
I want to reach out and catch it
And hold it forever

When I dream about the impossible
I want to achieve it
And show everyone I can

As I look ahead to the future
I see so many opportunities
I'll take advantage of them all

Going down the road of life
I'll take the unbeaten path
To blaze a trail of my own

If there is something out there
Something I want to have
I'll be the one to take it

When I look back on my life
I want to be able to say
"I did" not "I should have"

I want to be someone-not just anyone
I want to do everything-not just one thing

Lynnette Carpenter

I Was There

When you were born
I was there
When you took your first steps
I was there
When you spoke your first word
I was there
When you started school
I was there
When you played sports
I was there
When you graduated from school
I was there
When you wed
I was there
When my grandchildren were born
I was there
When you needed anything
I was there
When I'm departed from this life I hope I'll still be there in your Heart Forever.

Sue Gilfillan

When Baby Left His Nest

From my window, so early
I watched in dismay
Baby Cardinal—Prepare
For his Big Get-Away

He stretched legs and wings
Mommy and Daddy close by,
Saying-"Step out gently
But don't try to fly."

I'd awaited this moment
With joy and great zest
Two hours he sunned himself
Just a foot from the nest.

I thought "Say ol' Boy"
You're too slow while I sit
I have work to do, Babe
Happy Day to you-"So-Be-It."

"A watched pot never boils"
And old adage—"so they say"
An hour later I took a look
Sure enough he'd gone away.

Mary L. Gonterman

Skid Marks

Her stormy eyes still haunt me;
I wonder now of what they see
In kingdom beyond the sky . . .
Does heaven stop a child's cries?

She hated what was in the mirror;
Her dreams of courage made her fear.
Shedding tears was drawing breath.
Instead of life she thought of death.

The nights she cried in my arms
I never thought of the harm,
The outcome of her drowning grief,
The suicide of her beliefs.

She left me early one day in June;
She drove her youth into the ruins.
Over a canyon my daughter fell.
She took her life and made my hell.

I visit still that cliff of fate
That shows me truth far too late.
The skid marks cannot make me blind.
They leave me knowing she'd changed her mind.

K. B. Zettlemoyer

If It Hadn't Been For You

If it hadn't been for you I say,
I would not be here on this day
You gave me hope when I was down,
You turned my frown upside down
Now I'll wade across the river
And climb up to the shore
Then say out loud for all to hear,
I'll Love You
Forever More!

Sarah Amspaugh

Sharing

If I could dream a dream for you,
I would take you to a place,
Where mountains, streams and forests,
Surround your life with grace.

Amidst a golden meadow,
Swaying gently in the breeze,
I would grow for you some daisies,
White as snow, and tall as trees.

Beyond the swaying meadows,
On hillsides touching the skies,
I would find for you billowy cloud,
For you to float and rest your eyes.

For life can be so troublesome
And full of winding roads,
If I could share in your burdens,
And help to lighten the load.

So, let me dream these dreams for you,
And let your thoughts run free,
Escape and travel inside yourself,
But share it all with me.

Kathy L. Mayabb

Within The Light

If only I had the power to change,
If only I could rearrange,
A relaxant I would be,
To set you free,
From all your pain and miseries,
But I know of a man,
Who hold all plans,
He is there when in need,
Put your faith in him,
And call him up,
Because only he can set you free

Karla R. Ball

When You Need A Friend

When you need someone to comfort you-
I'll be there.
When you need someone to talk to-
I'll be near.
When you need a hug-
My arms are free.
When you need a friend-
Call on me.

Monica Shelley Harper

As I See It

As I travel down life's highway
I'm beginning to realize
I've been wearing rose-colored glasses
On these old and fading eyes.

It's fine to be an optimist
And try to live your life with zeal
But be sure to learn what's fantasy
And separate it from the real.

Things aren't always great and wonderful
There is good and there is bad
But if we try to face life honestly
A better one can be had.

If the good Lord can take the bad
And out of that make something good
We can also do the same —
This must be understood.

If we face a lot of problems
He is sitting on His throne
For He waits up there to help us
He promised — We're not alone.

Margaret Burrell

To A Tree

Below all dark and dank
In must of moistened earth
The seed
A creeping warmth
Touches its skin
It moves without being seen
And slowly
A green stem of being
Arches through the layers
Of brown free soil.
Behold! a TREE
That becomes hope
For the future
And peace.

Shay Yeager

Life's Journey

What am I
I'm flesh and bone
A wandering spirit
Journeying toward home

Placed on earth
To be a light
To live by faith
To fight the good fight

To spread the news
To all I can
To take many with me
To God's promised land

To work while I can
While there is light
To gather the sheep
Before the night

To increase the number
In the kingdom of love
That God has waiting
For us up above

Shirley Burns

Intrusion

It's dark, no one around
I'm here all alone
no where to go, no place to hide
fears is the only thing on my mind
oh no! what happened?
I can't scream...my voice...is gone
no one around to help
what do I do? how is this happening?
I'm scared and in shock
tears fall from my eyes
oh God! help me! what have I done
will I live..or die?
can't stop crying yet cannot scream!
where am I?
am I alive?
as I try to walk, my whole body trembles
I look down and only to see broken glass
beneath my feet
I am still alive.

Mayumi Fulkerson

"Daddy's Whispering Soul"

Son here my whispers
In a echo

Whispers of regrets
And words of wisdom

The regrets of
Never holding
My baby boy

For the first time
And watching him
Grow into manhood

Rips through my soul
Like thunder and lighting

But a few to many beer's
One dark night
A car crash took my life

And the words of wisdom
Son is when you're grown
And out with your friends

Remember don't drink and drive
Daddy's whispering soul

Wilma Cole

World Of Darkness

In a world so full of darkness,
In a world so full of pain,
Where children starve and young men die,
And life's the price for any gain.

I read of people dying hungry,
Lips so straight with tightened ends.
Lips to whom joy is a stranger,
Lips that laughter never bends.

I read of young men downed in battle,
Lives now void of growing old.
Bodies vibrant with tomorrow
Now lay silent, growing cold.

Men of knowledge and of power,
Passed their youth and laughing still.
Speak of moral ways to wage
The wars that wreck and starve and kill.

Louis LaBar

Thoughts Undisciplined

My thoughts undisciplined fly
In all directions to the sky.
Can they not be bottled once
Then studied thus
To be made sense of
Just once?

If thoughts so unexamined lie
and fit no pattern,
Then how am I to know
Just who I am
And why ?

To stem the flow of thoughts diverse
I take up pen and turn to verse,
But thoughts unruly do remain;
And though I try and try again,
I just make matters
Worse!

Lee C. Watson

Old Blue

Old Blue, he ain't no hound dog,
In fact, he ain't no prize,
He's got an awful lookin' face
With green and yella eyes.

His ears are cocked both east and west,
His whiskers, they're a sight,
He ain't got no more eyebrows cause
He lost 'em in a fight.

Cain't say his coat is perty
Cause his spots have faded, see,
Old age has pounced right up on him
Like doggy leprosy.

He thinks he's got a pointer's tail,
It's sorry, "mercy be,"
Instead 'o pointin' straight back out
It u-turns t'wards the sea.

There ain't a mean bone in him though
And that's what in the end,
Keeps him 'round this farm 'o mine,
Yep - he's a special friend.

Lana Bischoff

Learning Curve

Serenity escapes me
in my endless pursuit
time moves on without me
peace has no substitute

My life has gone to places
I never thought it would go
guided by some unseen force
I have been given time to grow

Letting go, and letting be
are not lessons easily learned
peace of mind can not be forced
it is a prize hard earned

Laura M. Staunton

Prayer To Thee, Earth

If I forget thee, Oh Earth
In my mortal haste
Remind me with thy power,
So I shall not forget again.
If I destroy thee, Oh Earth
In my mortal eagerness
Remind me with thy presence,
So others may learn from my mistakes.
If I cherish thee, Oh Earth
In my mortal way
Reward me with thy beauty,
So I shall continue to covet thy form.
If I hurt thee, Oh Earth
In my mortal foolishness
Remind me with thy wrath,
So I may change my ways.
But if I love thee, Oh Earth
With my mortal heart
Then fill me with thy hope,
So I may teach my children the same.

Susan Lee Gidley

Lest I forget

Lest I forget the gladness
In remembering the sorrow,
I'll take my yesterday
And give up my tomorrow;
Give up all thoughts of sadness
For much more lovely things
And keep memories of the gladness
That remembrance of you brings.

F. D. Rodgers

You Said

You said you were singing
in that woods, last night
all were you alone
only the breeze had heard
the voices from your mind

You said your voice had gone
through the woods, last night
all had you sung
not the cheerfully happy words
but the sad sort that I like

You said you wished had my hand
among the woods, last night
all would you've done
holding the moon, the breeze, and me
sweetly singing, endlessly, to the sky

Ruby Y. Dong

Gladness and Joy

Gladness again reigns
In the harmony of our home
For my brother is becoming a priest
And to God's work has gone.

Not so long ago it seems
That we both were in our teens
Rejoicing in our childhood happiness
Our home and meager means.

But a greater blessing
Has blossomed forth its fruit
Has transformed my brother's soul
And taken in him its root

I think of the last judgement day
When God shall call to him
All the humans of this troubled earth
To account for all their sins

And again I'm filled with gladness
When I think of him so dear
Who always will abide by God
In the future here and near.

Margaret Cummings

Under My Bed

As I lie in bed
in the middle of the night,
I clutch my covers
filled with fright.

Someone is hiding
under my bed,
and in a low voice
I slowly said...

Who are you?
Why are you here?
Please tell me,
I'm trembling with fear!!

I heard no reply,
not even a peep,
and hearing no answer.
I could not go to sleep!

Finally I looked
expecting the worst,
and seeing my brother
I felt like I'd burst!!...

Sara Mandel

For My Husband

I need you my darling
In the morning to start my day
Your voice ever so gentle
To carry me on my way
I need you my darling
When shadows fill the sky
Your warm lips to caress me
The light in your eyes telling me why
Why to go on living
When inside me all is cold
This world so full of sorrow
Why must we all grow old
And if I didn't have you
My darling
My life would be in vain
Each day would have no meaning
Like rainbows without the rain

Shirley Basara

Untitled

It is midnight,
In this weary hour,
As the sky darkens,
I feel the ancient power.

The storm arises,
In its fury and rage,
As the cold sweeps the land,
In this darkened age.

Raindrops fall,
Like tears from the skies,
The wind picks up,
Then it slowly dies.

The breeze blows cool,
This special night,
And the angry storm,
Has finally reached its height.

Then all of a sudden,
With a mighty crash,
It all ends,
As quick as a flash.

Katie Connery

Yesterday, Today And Tomorrow

Shadows of what used to be
In those shadows memories I see
Some of them happy some of them sad
That's the story of life
Not all good and not all bad.

Then there's today
Let come what may
We know that it's not here to stay
There's time for work and time for play
Sun may be bright
Clouds may be gray
Let's do our best, for it's today

Of course there's talk of tomorrow
To put off what we should have done today
Some say tomorrow never comes
But be that as it may
I guess it's just the day we
worried about yesterday

Mary Kathryn Richardson

To My Son

Lean on me as on a wall
In your morning glory days,
On the road to growing tall,
Searching for the many ways
Of facing life and staying true
To all that is the best in you.
Learn when to build, when to destroy -
I will give you what I can.
You came to me a little boy,
Leave me as a man.
Then before my journey's end,
Come back to me and be my friend.

Rita Gold

Life Is Complex

With its pain and relief
In the midst of our happiness
We're visited with grief
A deliberate balance
To keep us in toe
Reassures us though joy will pass
So to will our woe!

Patti Sires

Persistent Bondage

Centuries of isolation,
Intellectual deprivation.
Emancipate! How can that be?
In an oppugnant, American society.
Devoid of compassion, or shame.
Tho she extirpated my culture and
divested my name.
Who am I? where shall I go?
What will I do? I need to know!
Teach me about democracy,
Your capitalistic economy.
What is economize,
Investment and free enterprise?
Tell me about industrialization,
Wages and compensation.
What does it mean to discount,
Pay interest, and the net amount?
KNOWLEDGE will set me free,
from the persistent bonds of slavery.

Will Hudgins

Brazil

The household sounds
intensify
with the thunder of
the upstairs plumbing—
Another roar compounds:
a power
mower
near the open window...
Music on the radio—
the song they're playing is
"Brazil"
You want to ask the
King of the couch to
volume-up the music
but
he might not,
yet see your eyes
and ask you
"Why?"

Nancy L'enz Hogan

Dance Of Life

Threads everywhere
intertwining, coming apart
weaving in, weaving out
that is the dance of life

Dancing in, dancing out
bowing here, dipping there
stopping now, moving on
that is the dance of life

Being in the eye of the storm
wondering when it will pass
wondering who will be there
feeling lost, coming undone

Center, oh life, help me center
because if I come apart,
who will help?

Time to trust, it is now
time to trust
yourself—now.

Marisela Rios

Coldness

I'm crouching into coldness
into life beyond despair
Into a forest full of trees
When no one else is there
Alone near raging waters with
no one by my side
As my body falls to nothing
I am swept up by the tide
but no one will even notice
and no one will even care
because I'm crouching into coldness
into life beyond despair

Kristen M. Mucci

A Short Time

As a new mother looks down
into the tiny new face,
she holds God's new creation
in a tight embrace

What wonder she feels
as this awesome task unfolds
thinking of the responsibility
in molding this child's soul

She thanks God for this miracle
and prays for God's helping hand
to guide her each day
and help her to understand

Making the right choices
through the growing years
sharing the joys with God
and being there to wipe the tears

When it's time to set this life free
give her the courage and the faith
to be able to release...
this miracle, God hath made

Linda Houts

Untitled

The sand of people's conversations
is a psychopathic low rumble murmur
yet offers comfort
and lends itself to a feeling
I have today -
I want to make love to the world;
create it; nurture it
cultivate, and tend to it.
My heart sings
to the orchestral movements
of men and women.
Nature is the conductor to this,
my great wonderful symphony
which is my life.

Michael Bogart

Day Dream

Sitting here in an awakened sleep.
Isolated by what's goin' on around you.
Thinking about whatever in your thoughts,
but shortly something will astound you.

Unaware of relaxation,
you slowly play along in this scheme.

Then suddenly you snap out of it,
and realize, that you had a
Day Dream!

Katisha Burt

The Tree Is Me

The tree I see in front of me
is a symbol of my life
The emotions and the feelings
that cut me like a knife.

The leaves on the tree
that fall to the ground,
Are like my tears that fall
with no reason to be found.

The top of the tree
reaches for the sky,
Just like my ambitions
which people say are "too high."

Trees are often thought of as
"that thing you plant,"
Sometimes I feel that unimportant
when people put me down and say I can't!

People will see how important I am
someday
as they will this tree,
And they will stop putting me down
and let me be me!

Michelle Jones

Alone

Hello'
is anybody there?
silence!!!
I am alone...
All alone!
hello!
is anybody there?
silence!!!
nobody cares...
nobody cares at all!
hello!
is anybody there?
a voice!!!
I am not alone...
somebody cares!

Sarah Bleattler

Helping

Monday morning! What I see
  is clouds and cold and misery
But I must get myself prepared
  To meet the world and do my share
  To brighten up this deep abyss,
  Perhaps to spread some happiness.

A smile, a touch, a little tune
  Not only of Spring, June and Moon
  But God's great love for all of us.
I think I see a ray of light
  Break through the murky sky above.

Oh yes! I must go see my friend.
She's old and ill but with her smile
  She warms my heart and all the while
  I think I'm helping her you see,
But she is really helping me.

Marguerite W. Bates

To Walk With God

Just to walk with God each day
Is my heart's most earnest plea,
To share with Him my problems
And to hear Him speak with me.

Life without God is empty
All it offers is a shell,
When I walk with God today
I have peace and joy as well.

I need to be aware that
As I travel on life's way
My life is full of meaning
If I walk with God each day.

Marvin H. White

Untitled

Echoes Ride the wind and time forever
is on the verge of touching tomorrow
visibly we wait and contemplate the
everlasting storms of our souls
only to find the resolution on the wind

Tracy Killinger

Untitled

One who lives for love
Is one who lives as a fool
As in life
Love will end
Only a fool
Would live, to die

Larry Schwartz

Mirror

Is that me who motions?
Is that me who speaks?
Is that me who laughs?
Is that me who sheds a tear?

When I'm confused,
Do you understand?

Are you afraid,
of what scares me?

Options, reasons, choices invite.
Translucent images vivid and bright

Move when I move.
Talk while I talk.
Laugh when I laugh
Cry while I cry.

Laurie Dozier

He's Mine

Thou the Vastness of space,
is the Far unknown,
Belief in Christ will carry
The Load,
From the farest star, to the
Deepest of the sea,
Jesus governs all for you
and me,
From the inside of the heart
To the outside of the mind (mouth)
Christ governs all, because
he's mine.

Kenith L. Kelly

Like No Other

A love that is special
Is the love of a Mother
A love that is warm
Like no other

A Mother is there
With tender love and care
Through thick and thin
She'll always share

A Mother's ears are for silent tears
The one's
That are due to hidden fears

Fears of loneliness
A need for love
A Mother's there
With belief in the one above

Robert D. Wall

Capitola Street

The apartment of Capitola Street
is where I come and go,
on the weekends remains the same.

The foothills above
are a golden brown,
the sky above a bright blue.
People pass by everyday, all day
searching for that special someone.

The hills and Capitola street
will always be the same,
but I have changed.

No more the unhappy smile,
the sad song,
the desolate stare of love,
the young heart
ascending around the room.

Kathleen Mascia

"Fighter"

There is stands,
Isolated...
Under bits of everlasting ice.
Fallen snow,
Dropping,
On its stretched out branch.

Climb, climb, climb,
You hard - headed bird...
Seek out your precious destiny,
Call out your ambitions
and crawl to your endless love
and say forgiveness.
Grow, grow, grow,
you heart-filled soul.
Touch the sky,
Let your emotion fill your bark
and stay strong...
You powerful fighter.

Venissa Irwin

Wild Horses

There they go by,
Like they're floating in the sky,
Snorting and Oh! Don't you see them?
They have so much freedom,
Oh! Can't you see them?

Savannah Person

Untitled

The voice of time commands,
It bellows through the night.
It paralyzes my thoughts,
It fills my mind with fright.

The voice of time foretells,
It knows what soon will be.
It knows all God's convictions,
It sees what we can't see.

The voice of time condemns,
It punishes lives of vain.
It destroys days in passing,
It replaces peace with pain.

The voice of time demands,
It steals away our hope.
It robs our hearts of passion,
It hangs us by its rope.

The voice of time prevails,
It knows all that grows will die.
It drowns our smiles with tears,
It turns hello into goodbye.

Virginia Olson

Your Friendship

Your friendship is a gift of God,

Its delight I cannot measure.

Your friendship is a gift of God,
It is full of joy and pleasure.

Your friendship is a gift of God,
I'll never want to sever.

Your friendship is a gift of God,
It is utmost of my treasure!

W. Anna Kamas

Youth And Death

In the minds of the young
it is only the old that die
the spring of life
is flowers trees and sky.

Youth is the creek in spring
teeming with life.
It's a girl to kiss
not children and wife.
It's a life well started
with spirits high,
The spring of life
is flowers, trees and sky.

The chill of the wind
can bring this to an end
It is sad, but it is true
on spring we can't depend.

Robert L. Laumeyer

Life

Life is a flower
It dies, so do we
Petals are our chances in life
They fall and go away
But sometimes you can water yourself
Friends will help you along
Drink the water,
Eat the sun,
Live Your Life

Meghan Smith

Loss Of A Friend

When someone you love dies,
it is so hard to say goodbye.
You always think of her smiling face,
and think she's in a better place.
You wonder why God took her,
with all she had going for her.
God has a reason,
though no one knows.
I will miss her dearly,
and someday I will see her clearly.
She was my idol,
and she had such a great title.
Her memory will live on in
the hearts of me and others
And I will always remember her
true colors.

Shannon Foust

"The Time For Me To Fly"

Today may be my last tomorrow
It is the day for me to fly
Mother will lead me out of the nest
With the words..
"Go make your mark my little bird.
It is your time to fly."
I have been given this grand day
Will I stumble?
Will I land?
Will I make my way?
I know in my heart
It is for me to decide
Shall I fly East? Shall I fly West?
What if I die?
Today may be my last tomorrow
It will not be a day of sorrow
I will fly high into my goals of life
With my wings spread wide
My head held high
Today is the day for me to fly

Marguerite Elise Clucas

Untitled

What happens to the time that goes by
It just seems to fly
Honey I love you most of all
No matter what time it says on the
Old clock on the wall
Whether It's winter, spring, summer
Or fall
Honey I love you most of all
Not much time to sit and talk
Hardly ever time to hold hands
And take a walk
You should always take time to know
Honey I love you most of all

Rita Wagner

From The Heart And Soul

Love is a bird that sits in a tree,
Love is a bird that cannot see.
Could it be pain in disguise?
Or maybe when we close our eyes,
It sits and tells us all the lies.
When we see it fly away,
All we can do is hope and pray.
When it's time to lock the pen,
Our lives will be free of sin.

Tresa R. Stuart

The Past

The past is done it can not change
It keeps me locked inside a cage
The past, the awful dark black past
Will always be there 'til the last.
I must now look into the glass
And see the cause of my morass
The anger at myself is real
My mind is screaming let me heal.

The past is done, I must let go
I must be strong, but I don't know
It's been so long I hid inside
And raged against the strong dark tide
I have to learn to build up pride
To take mistakes within my stride
And change the things that will go wrong
To make an effort to be strong

I do not want to be this way.
To be afraid to face the day
I want to smile, and laugh, and cry
Without the feeling I should die

Lorraine Z. Ford

A Dream For Success

A dream for success,
It's a great one indeed!
It demands a variety of hard work,
Learning and a good self esteem.

The secret is to believe in yourself,
For without this thought
You could go no place else.

Never forget there are always
ups
and
downs.
Keep this in mind
Or you'll get all turned around.

So think things out
And keep plugging away
Because without hard work
Your dream for success
Will soon go down the drain.

Richard H. Wallack

The Darkest Place

There is a place I know,
it's cold, harsh, and empty,
where darkness finds its sanctuary,
and evil there are plenty.

It has been corrupted,
and the spirits will never tell,
where once there was innocence,
and the sounds of liberty bell.

Now the place is twisted,
the doors are sealed and cold,
Heaven's grace will never reach,
my dying wicked soul.

Ryan Yamada

The Moon Through Birches

The moon through birches;
light transects form. Ichor flows,
diffracting essence.

Karen C. Austin

My Rainbow

The rainbow has smeared.
Its colors have faded.
The joy that it brought
Is now worn-out and dated.
One thing happens and your
Rainbow is smashed.
And you can't help but wonder
Where the good times are stashed.
I'm going to pick up the pieces of my
Rainbow now shattered.
And think of happier times
When nothing else mattered.

Kristy Smith

"Now And Forever"

I'm going to another land my love
I've taken my last breath
And we will be together eternally
As soon as you reach death.

Time will pass and in a dream
You'll see my peaceful face
Then you shall stop an realize
I'm in a better place.

Your time will come and you will go
And above the clouds you'll soar
Then we'll be back together again
As you walk through the golden door.

We'll walk among the saints of life
From centuries years before
And you will be back in my arms again
To hold forever more.

Lori Hallberg

Born To Blindly Run

Thirty-seventh planet of space
John Doe of the igneous race
soldered cheeks frozen and numb
you were born to blindly run

Catch a comet now and then
learn to think in powers of ten
object of astrologer's jokes
billion miles to see the folks

Lava flows all shagged out
no atmosphere to fuss about
cinder nose on a silent clown
performing far from lights of town

Orbits cause predestination
time's a once removed relation
hide and seek in the void's no fun
you were born to blindly run

R. Greg Carlson

A Dream

Dreams are special
Keep them safe
Don't you dare get them lost
Give them a boost each day
If you want them to work

A dream is special
Very special
Dreams are the best
Without them life
Would be a painting
With no color.

Rachna Kenia

Full Circle

As a child life came full force,
Just hit me in the face.
Said: Let's enjoy ourselves,
At a vigorous pace.

As a teen she's there again,
This time coy and flirting.
But besides the fun times,
Came some real, real hurting.

Adulthood seemed to overwhelm.
At times I longed to be-
Back as a child out playing,
Wild as the wind and free.

Now as I come to the last years.
Look back, reflect and muse,
I see it was a full time.
But the spark's near the end of its fuse.

So you mustn't dwell in the past,
Or become stuck on future dreams.
Savor the present, live for now.
It's harder than it seems.

Sondra French Cange

Just Hold My Hand

Don't say anything;
Just hold my hand.

When life seems so unbearable,
When it hurts to smile or utter a sound,

Don't say anything;
Just hold my hand.

When the pain is built up inside
And a small teardrop may cause a flood,

Don't say anything;
Just hold my hand.

When I feel so worthless
And life seems such a waste,

Don't say anything;
Just hold my hand.

It may not seem like much,
But empty words are defeated by silence.

Don't say anything;
Just hold my hand.

Linda Shafer

The Greatest Is Love

I could never express in words
Just how much you mean to me.
But I love you dearly
As anyone can see.
And my prayer for you
Is that you get well soon
But put all your trust in God
And he will see you through.
I'm praying for you every day
That God will restore your health to you,
But never forget that God is the
Greatest Physician
And that He cares for you & loves you
very much too.
As God has said in His word
The Greatest Gifts come from above,
No Greater Gift could there be
Than having each other to Love.

Sharon McComber

Trouble

Run from your trouble
Just leave it behind
Running and running
What is there to find

Raising a riot
Making a clatter
Watching your life
And your dreams shatter

Fears and thoughts
Fears all the same
Wondering why and how
Wondering who's to blame

Where is my family
What about my dreams
It all flew to nowhere
That's the way it seems

Michaela Romans

"Kids"

Kids are people
just like you and I
some are a little loud
and some are very shy

Kids can tell stories
just like me and you
some may be lies
but, most of them are true

Kids like to have fun
and are easily amused
they all need more hugs
instead of the abuse

Kids need, lots of caring
and understanding too
so give them a chance
into what ever they do

Kids are so precious
our future they will hold
if we don't care now
who cares, when we're old...

Rose Marie Palmer

Close Enough?

We bought a handyman special
just seven months ago

Now it has new plumbing
wiring and hard-wood floors

The sun shines through new windows
that makes the painted walls glow

We need to move in so we're not homeless
yet the city tells us no

We have to put up siding
so we can get our C.O.

We have no extra money
wish we could win the lotto.

Mary Weber

Untitled

Manatee slumbers,
Mother earth tends her children,
Behold, a pale horse.

Lai Quon

Prozac

The aftermath of an emotion,
Keeps me awash and a little behind.
It's the prelude to a devotion,
That leaves me in charge of my mind.

It comes in a two tone capsule.
It's delivery system by day.
It assists with the prenuptial,
That sustains me underway.

It mends the hole's infection,
And keeps me in the act.
It ministers to deception,
That fools my head intact.

It's kind a like an extension,
When emotion is on the edge.
It aligns what feels for direction,
Upon life's chemical ledge.

An instance of denial,
Could afford you to miss a life.
Once missed operation eternal,
Depression, confusion, the knife.

Kevin R. Pack

Poor Little Rich Boy!

Poor little rich boy you don't
know what to do,
You have ruined your life and
your family's too
Poor little rich boy on the
streets selling crack,
Hanging with the bad gang and
don't want to come back.
Poor little rich boy dropped out
of school,
Thought you were bad and
just knew you was cool.
Poor little rich boy what made
you go that way
You have your family worried
each and every day.
Poor little rich boy knotted
with gold,
Ashamed to face the fact
that you will reach what you sold!

Roberta Martin

I Watch You Leave

You turn and walk away
leaving a vague shadow
and a dim memory
behind.

Enough to keep me
holding on
but not enough
to give me hope.

And how can I
let you go,
knowing you take
the best part of me?

Still,
I remain behind,
like a forgotten sea shell
on the shore,
with the sound
of your goodbye
roaring in my ears.

Linda Richardson

Creation

You took away
Left me nothing
Emptiness where the earth
should be
You made me strong.

You took away
Replaced with lies
Deceit and pain
You made me wise.

You took away
Blood from my veins
Tears and screams
You made me feel.

You took my away
My wholeness
Cracks and breaks
You made me real.
You gave me Life.

Renee DiMuzio

He Loves To Hear Our Voices

Come to me, speak to me
Let me hear your voice
Tell me that you love me
That you've made me first choice

I love to hear your thanks
I love to hear your praise
I love the sound when to me
your voice you raise

Tell me when you're happy
Tell me when you're sad
I love to hear your voice
It makes me oh so glad

Come to me, pray to me
Bring your burdens and your woe
Leave them here with me
whenever' you turn to go

Yes, your problems, your thoughts
I really already know
I just want to hear your voice
Because I love you so.

Maxine Shipps

The End?

Tell us stranger what you look like,
Let us look upon your visage.
We wish to venture to your darkness,
We want to seek and find your message.

Don't come to us too fast or gruesome,
Or pounce on us like raging weather,
Softly blow like summer breezes,
Or like a weightless, drifting feather.

Our minds know not until your coming,
Just how great and bold you are.
The time and place is still a secret,
Is our finale near, or far?

It's a wonder to every person,
That mystic thing that we call death.
And what will our consolation be,
After we have finally left..., forever?

Larry Lorenz

The City

Beneath the ark of the far flung sky
Lies the city far below.
We can see and hear the traffic,
As they travel to and fro.
The eye can never be at rest,
Cars winding as a trail of ants.
Beneath the very noisy din,
The heart of the city pants.
Every where there are people,
We watch with bated breath,
So much action and so much life.
Revolve around, and even death!
Some folk look on us with pity,
Some how it must be in my blood.
The action, the smells of the city,
All a part of the human flood.
This is all a part of my life.
I live, I love, I work I play.
I do not look on it as strife,
I have my home, at close of day!

Pearl L. Johnson

Life

Life brings so many changes
Life brings so much pain
Life is a constant battle.
Each day is wonderful in what life can bring.
The darkness is comforting when life is too much.
The light is splendid when life is joyous
God gives us life
God gives us love
Oh the wonders of life are everlasting
Behold for you are life!

Robert B. Wells

Life

Life is waiting for what is next
Life is what we need to do best

Life is working towards a goal
Life is finding one's own soul
Life is feeling high and low
Life is cherishing every spark and glow.
Life is loving whatever comes your way
Life is struggling to be and to stay
Life is avoiding feeling too blue
Life is noting the morning mildew
Life is forgetting the hovering end
Life is perpetuating in its torment

But life is waiting for what is next
And life is what we learn to love best.

Monica Bergkamp

Words

Words and phrases
Line after line
Some with meaning
Others written to kill time
Letter after letter
All coming together
Making sense of nothing
Outlining a life
Never ending power of
Words written
A testament to all

Shannon Lujan

Fallen Stars

Graveyard celluloid
Light
Shining through
Sequined soil
Illuminating
Late night
Translucent boob tubes.

Infinite celebrity
Stuck in
Immortal make-believe
In gangsta-color,
Western vision-espionage.

Yester-vision
Of a fallen shining star
Shot to the future,
In a flash past.

Tyrone Granderson Jones

The Glory Of The Sunrise

A bright and radiant glow
Lights up the eastern sky,
Then the clouds turn pink and purple
As tho the painters brush was night.

The darkness slowly fades away
As another day is born,
And I can see all God's creations
In the light of early morn.

All the birds start singing
As though bursting with His love,
And I feel the peace of morning
In the cooing of the dove.

I gave across the pasture
As the light creeps o'er the land;
I see the cattle grazing there
From where I usually stand.

I bow my head in reverence
To the Creator of this day,
And the glory of His sunshine
Stays with me all the way.

Olive Patterson

The Return

The past slides away
Like a dress from yesterday
Worn and torn, a dream that was.
Silently like a cloud
Scurrying by with no place to go.

What once was is not.
What will be is not known.
Today is still a question.
Tomorrow's unknown.

Love haunts me.
Like a ghost in the night.
Love and peace; can they be one?
Or is peace always to be alone?

Love is giving and kind.
Love is demanding and selfish,
Love is being free to give
Love is my soul, Give it back to me!!!

Patricia M. White

Alive In My Soul

You'll float on the clouds
like an angel with wings
and you'll triumph in the glory
that only the heavens can sing,
and you'll smile down
like the sun in the sky,
and you'll water the earth
when it's time to cry.
and you'll dance your first steps
when there's thunder in air
and you'll paint me a rainbow
while none can compare,
and I'll feel your breath
as the wind rushes by,
Streaking my face
with the tears from my eyes,
and I'll feel your touch
as snowflakes drift to the ground
passing through my fingertips
without even so much, as a sound.

Whitney Thompson

Untitled

Everyday my love for you grows
Like the perfect tree in the forest
All it takes is the
Nourishment I get from being with you
Every time we're together
It's like a new branch
Develops, making us stronger
The dormant times are
Few and far between
For our love is based on
Knowledge, and
As we discover more of each other,
Our love expands like
Roots, in search of
New and exciting things
That we could never
Find alone.
For like the tree, our love
Needs both, the branches
And roots, to survive

Rebecca A. Stiffler

Another Day Without You

The sun bounces gold through the limbs of trees,
But I can't see it because
I'm missing you.
The wind blows the leaves
like chimes,
But I can't hear it because
I'm missing you.
The moon reaches for me
through my window,
But I can't feel it because
I'm missing you.
The hands of the clock
don't move,
But I don't watch it because
it's another day without you.

Kathy D. West

Awakening

I walked along the shore
Listening to the ripples of
Waves hitting against the rocks
Sound of the sea gulls flying above
The smell of the ocean
A sailboat drifting with the wind

The blue sky moving softly
The sun smiling down
The greenery on the hills

Surfers racing
Children building castles in the sand
Lovers embracing

Tears of joy ran down my cheeks
For I knew it was time to seek
I reached
I touched
I loved
I held

Virginia Vickie Jackson

Our Son

Are you in there,
Little One?
thump
Can you hear me?
thump
We're here for you-
Waiting
thump
Touching, feeling, praying
thump
Will you make it,
Little One?
thump
We Love You,
Little One.

Michelle R. Simmon

Portrait Of Mother

The Lady in the portrait on the wall:
Look how regal she sits, how tall;
The painting is by artist Mary Dunn:
Many hours she worked with her brush,
And then mother emerged on canvas,
Alive for all to view.

"Won't you stay awhile?" her daughter
Would say to her guests,
"Please, don't be shy. Gaze at her.
She was honoured well," she explained.

We were all impressed by her.
Her family name was an old name,
Her rank was high,
Her fame,
Was that of a mother.

Smiles,
Warm and lovely;
Mother,
Remembered, honoured;
Presented on canvas.

P. A. Pitchforth-Steele

Out Of The Time

Standing on the front step door,
Looking out into the world,
Thinking of the days that pass,
And the years forever more.

Yet no one has slumbers silent,
From their view of the warp,
The Earth has but desolation,
From the days left to relent.

Days and years of sorrowed grief,
Cut at throats of helpless minds,
But in search for grateful Heaven,
You must add your fervent piece.

But in time, time soon will cease,
First in hearts and then in souls,
Then worldwide ending all sorrows,
For ye helpless, rest in peace.

Roxanna Myhrum

Love Is....

Love is saying "I Love You"
Love is saying "I Care"

Love is saying, when your hurting
Honey, I'll always be there

Love is forgiving
Love is saying O.K.

Love is saying, Honey, I'm sorry,
for the way I acted today

Love is not obnoxious
Love has no flaws

Love is merely telling you,
I love you without a clause

Sometimes we get angry
Say things we don't really mean

But what's when genuine love comes in,
and wipes the slate all clean

We should try this love of Gods
for it was He, who loves us first

When we think we didn't show Love
our little hearts should burst

Sheila B. Walker

Embroiled Emotions

One
moonless night
I sat in fright
un at ease
I started to weave
was A quilt,
guilt and grieve.
Suddenly I felt
a quake, a shake
a seed of greed.
Swift as a breeze
the seed turned
lust, If you must
I said my dear
yet love is near.
enough is a enough
to end one
restless goodnight.

Kelly R. Eastburn

To Write

Stir the waters,
make the birds take flight,
From peace and contentment
I cannot write.

Ignite volcanic thunderstorms,
dismantle my brains,
Obliterate and destroy
Those peaceful spring rains.

Up from the rocking chair,
But, where do I turn?
Seduce and adulterate
To make the heart burn.

Abandon loved-ones,
Inflame hatred upon rage;
But, satisfy that passion
To create a printed page.

Let heaven despair,
Give Satan cause to grin;
But, if to write, I must,
I embrace you sin.

Ronald E. Goska

Clouds

Clouds in the sky
make you wonder why,
So you stop and sigh,
So very very high.

In the very cloudy sky
Could It be a face
or just a little
trace OUT

There in space
among the human race,
There must be a place to see
a special face.

I was thinking of you
in the clouds
So hew, or just
A Little dew!
Or may be It was
you!

Pamela Jean Stong

"Holding On To Memories"

We talked, we laughed,
Many feelings shared.
Everyday, in many ways,
Showing each other we cared.
Since the time we first met,
We've been very dear friends.
I never thought all this happiness
Would ever come to an end.
But this time is very near,
And you know as well as I,
That once you leave you take my heart,
And leave me hear to cry...
Now that you're gone I miss you more,
More than words can say.
You wrote me that you're coming soon,
And I can't wait until that special day.
The memories are flooding back,
Remembering all we had.
Now I'm holding on to the memories,
the memories are now all I have.

Lori DeLa Rosa

The Sun And The Moon

Oh, that bright yellow,
Mixed with orange and red,
It shines so bright,
Until it's time for bed.

Then comes the moon,
The wonderful white and gray,
As I stare into its colors.
I am reminded of the day.

Ah, the sun and moon,
The moon and sun,
They both shine so brightly,
Until their job is done.

Kimberlee Hall

Emergency Room Perspective

Life is short,
more so for some than others.
I watch them check out -
mothers, sisters, fathers, brothers.
Swift and painless
is better it seems,
Don't weep oh loved ones
For nomads of eternal dreams.

Robert Rasmussen

The King Of Rock And Roll

He was the king of rock and roll
Most everyone would agree,
When he first started out
Was quite a sight to see.

Was once on Ed Sullivan
Many years ago,
From his head to his torso
Was all that could be shown.

Would gyrate around
Some people thought it bad,
But as it turned out
He became quite a fad.

He could sing like no one else
Every note was on key,
Then he'd turn and flex his face
For all the ladies to see.

He truly was a legend
The king of rock and roll,
Left an empty void
That really took its toll.

Rod Cutler

Snow

The wind blows
My eyes close
As it snows
It stings my nose
No one knows
Why the snow glows

The snow is bright
The color white
And in the night
We see the light
With all its might
All is right

Spring will come,
Fall will go
But in between,
A little snow.

Leah Satlin

Find Me

Claim me my Father, and
my blood which has spawned
in your veins.

Why did you welcome my
absence and disown my being
a product of your loins.

And your eyes did not see
my silence, and the hurt
of my longing.

Loneliness was your shelter that
you built with my total
youth and insecurity.

Find me my Father and touch
me quickly, before time blurs
my outstretched hope.

Alas only now that you are
old will you remember that I
was my Mother's son.

C. T. Miller

No Forwarding Address

A Little Girl's Song

Oh, we don't really live here
my dad and I just stand
sometimes he holds a sign up
or I'll hold out my hand

we don't really live here
but dad says it's all right
until we get an address
we can stand here for the
night

we don't really live here
and no one seems to mind
if I just hold my hand out
or my dad holds up his sign

No, we don't really live here
only standing passing time
just until we get an address
just until some body minds.

Saundra Broussard

My Community

In the sense of being new
My family lives far away
I entered a community of strangers
Being alone and unfamiliar.

The arms became open
The hands outstretched
The smiles and greetings are warm
and welcome.

What was unfamiliar, in a moments
hand shake, became home.
These are my family now, extended.
To fill the hours of my day.

I am not lonely now
For God has guided me here.
I give him Thanks and Praise each day
For he leads me to the path of this
community of caring.

Mary Jane Large

Mutual Trust

The depth and complexity of
my feelings are
more than I can comprehend.
Nervous hesitation,
a rush of excitement grips
my heart.
You approach,
two souls become one.
Reaching out, take my hand.
Emotions are not as hidden
as anticipated.
Mutual trust.

Mary Lou Lukachko

My Best Friend

My best friend is cool,
My friend is nice
My best friend is made up
Of sugar and spice.
She doesn't do drugs.
She's not in a gang.
Come! Let's go! Let's go out to
play.
My friend, Arlene,
Plays soccer with me.
She's also a member of the
all star team.
That's why I trust.
My best friend, ARLENE.

Leslie Stewart

"What Is A Cowboy, Grandpa?"

One afternoon some years ago,
My grandson came to me—
"What is a cowboy?", Grandpa
Said this little one—so wee.

"Now son," I said, "come here and sit,
And let me tell you this,
A cowboy is a cowhand—
His life's no life of bliss."

In rodeos, you'll always find,
Them riding broncs and bulls
Or maybe bull dogging steers
Or roping calves, who knows?

Now a range cowboy is a different breed,
With many chores to do,
Working cattle for his boss, and
Fixing fences, not a few.

A drugstore cowboy is a different sort,
who does his best to act
Like the "Real McCoy" out on the range,
with western boots and hat.

So grandson, dear, I hope that you
understand my explanation,
for if you do, I am happy to say be a
cowboy, it's a great tradition.

Kenneth Haraldsen

Giving Love Away

Giving love away is as easy as 1,2,3.
Needs no special holiday
Send it to a chum or even that hard
to reach bum
Ain't no trouble not at all.

Machiko Momii

Heart's Captivity

With each passing hour of the day
my heart long's for her.

With each passing moment of the
day my heart belongs to her.

She alone holds the key that
will release me.

Set me free, I say to thee.
No this cannot be.
For I am truly happy,
in her captivity

Mathes J. McMillan

Two Strangers

I see you through the lonely crowd,
my heart stands still in time
my eyes search yours for happiness
Can you see that in mine?

We seldom meet, we speak in kind
the reason is not clear
I see your face in all my dreams
and cry a lonely tear.

We've never shared that wanting look
but this I know is true
that all the lonely tears I shed,
I shed them just for you.

The promise of a memory
that you could give to me
I keep that wanting locked inside
only you control the key.

I wish upon a falling star
and hope my wish comes true
that someday we might shine as one,
two strangers, me and you.

Sandra Strejcek

Deadly Thoughts

A deadly thought runs through
my mind
The time to leave this cruel land
When and how is what is left to
figure out
After that I do my deed. To
make this world a better place
Life will go on for others
but as far as me it is the end
All I have is one lousy thought
which it seems serious yet,
no one understands except for me
The time is soon
closer to what anyone suspects
when I go it will be forever
not just a couple of days
What do I have to do for
this crazy world?
Just keep a deadly thought

Sarah C. Wiechen

Untitled

Poor
no money
no materials
no cash, no cards
Just self
freedom, happiness
love
Rich

Mary Anne Flanagan

To Daughter:
From Father, In Exile

In all the years I've been away,
My thoughts have turned to thee;
So many times, throughout each day,
I've lived in memory.

I first recall that night I gazed
Upon your infant form
A blessed gift from God, Himself,
So sweet, so soft, so warm.

With a tender, tiny tilted nose,
A delicate dimpled chin;
That blissful thrill in the velvet touch
Of thy dainty virgin skin.

Oh how I swelled in fatherly pride,
As I held you in my arms;
Eager to show the world, that night,
Your sweet immaculate charms!

Though years have quickly passed us by;
Though we be miles apart,
Such precious thoughts of you, my Dear,
I hold within my heart.

Louis E. Loper

Not A Nature Poet

I am not a Nature poet.
Name a flower, I won't know it.
Gather up a tuft of grass —
Well, to me, it's that — some grass.

Looking up into the sky,
There a bird is flying high.
And it's just a bird I see;
Looks like nothing else to me.

No, the sky is not of azure;
Does not glow like golden treasure.
Gates of heaven aren't thrown open
For Apollo's fire disc golden.

Just, to me, it's getting daylight
And the sun is rising dawn bright.
I am not a Nature poet.
Reading this, you're bound to know it.

E. B. Pyle

A Place For Prayer

As long as men
need God's correction,
As long as lives
lack His Direction.

As long as sorrow
engulfs the soul
As long as sin
still takes its toll.

As long as men still
hope and care,
There'll always be
A Place For Prayer.

Rev. Claud Logan Asbury

There's No Rainbow

There's no rainbow without the rain,
No baby born without some pain,
No summertime without the spring,
No songs at all unless we sing.

No twinkling stars without the night,
No morning dew without the light,
No minutes or seconds without the hours,
No fragrance sweet without the flowers.

No honeycombs without the bees,
No shady lawns without the trees,
No love at all unless we give,
Pour out our love each day we live.

Melanie Myers

Jennie

My dear sister Jennie is gone
No more can I seek her advice
Or get her help to make decisions
On any matters that may arise.

I always had the confidence
That to Jennie I could turn
For she gave me understanding
She showed me much concern.
Even in my childhood schooling
When needed, Jennie helped me,
And despite existent attitudes,
Jennie maintained a neutral position.

'Tis obvious I am deeply grieved
At the loss of my dear Jennie,
But comforting is the solace I have
For the years I had my dear sister Jennie.

Lillian G. Abrams

Amazon River

Amazon river, you are a mighty river;
No other river comes nearer.
Put your power in my intellect,
So that I will sing your glory.

I love you, mighty river;
I love you, powerful river.
I was born at your banks —
I belong to you.

Amazon river, I live far from you;
But I see you almost every day,
When I fly to see you
In my mind, in my imagination.

All human beings admire you,
Admire your dense, thick rain forest;
Admire your great volume of water;
Admire your gray and crystalline water.

Amazon river, you were born being great
And so was I.
You were born with greatness—
I was born to be great.

S. P. Cordeiro

Melancholy

No place to go,
No she to meet,
No you to love.

Desert
Emptiness
And a 'solitude' and a loneliness.
A tiny man in the giant of world.

Wanda Chrzanowska

poem

first, we kiss
no tongues, just lips

then you touch my back
pull me to you

kisses become deeper
we are naked.

your breath is the wind
your beating heart is the pounding sea

you inside me is like flying
our noises are like music

our love making
is my poetry.

Lisa Leinard

State Of Mind

They say stone walls no prison make,
Nor is cage made with bar,
But state of mind in which we live
Determines where we are

The invalid on affliction's bed
With wings may skim the sky,
If in his heart he wants to live
And does not long to die.

The rich may live on Poor Man Street,
On Wealth Hill may live poor,
It is how we count our riches
That gives us less or more!

And those who seem so fancy free,
May live in agitation,
Imprisoned by great walls built
With their imagination.

Yes, it is a state of mind
That makes the world go around.
The most elusive things we seek
In state of mind are found!

Mary Miller Clegg

We Will Never Forget

We will never forget your laughter,
nor the Merriment within your eyes.
We will never forget your open arms,
patting our backs, as we all cried.

We all knew someday you would leave us,
there was nothing anyone could do.
"But Lord", we were never ready,
the day she went home to be with you.

How do we say how much we Miss her?
How do we say, how much we Care?
She taught us the true value of living,
Love is Precious, so always share.

Our Hearts, have never mended,
Our Tears, have never dried.
Her Love will always be with us,
Her Cherished Memory is deep inside.

Thank you God, for the time we had,
Someday Cancer might have a cure.
Throughout her illness she taught us Love,
it's just not the same without her.

Melanie J. Hatz

102 Degrees At Midnight

In a shadow Lurks a man
Not a foe Broken hand
In my room I hear a noise
Louder boom Crunch of toys
Down the hall Way up high
Sudden fall Soundless cry
Softer whisper In my ear
Mysterious mister Not a care
Footsteps come Start to run
Countless sum No more fun
Tree breaks Willow weeps
For my sake Done with sleep!

Kristin Boryca

Morning

Have you ever felt the morning?
Not a soul in sight.
The precious calm,
you'll never hear
late into the night.

Have you ever felt, the morning breeze?
Stirring softly,
through the trees.
Gently touching, on their wings.
The birds awakened, softly sing.

Have you ever heard the morning?
So many sounds, to hear.
Still, there is a silence.
Which nothing can compare.

If you ever see the morning.
Not a soul in sight.
You'll find, it's human nature...
That wakes us in the night.
And only mother nature.
Who makes the morning bright.

Lori Kelsey

I Hope

If I could have one wish,
not about something that would squish,

Something I could find,
not like a lemon rind,

Something I could grasp,
Not make me fall or stumble in my path.

I hope someone could,
should,
or would,

Find out how I feel.
So I would know how I could,
should,
or would feel.

Sarah E. Martin

Paragon

The paragon is:
nothing is more strange
than the stranger
in thyself.

Thus,
dare not dangle
a participle in front of
an English Entrepreneur:
The enigma may be forthcoming.

Ricardo M. Mejia

Problems

Problems are hard to understand
Not knowing if everything will be grand.
Problems are very hard
Knowing that you need a guard.

Problems are hard to go through
With no one right beside you.
Problems are very rough
So you have to be tough.

Problems have a course
With a solution to every source.
Problems always seem to stay
And get in your way.

Kim Dalton

How Beautiful I Am

How beautiful I am
Not only to be vain
But I am beautiful
Standing in the rain

How beautiful I am
Not full of conceit
But I am beautiful
And beautifully sweet

How beautiful I am
So wonderfully fair
I am so beautiful
With the love in my stare

How beautiful I am
Like heavenly sighs
But I am most beautiful
When seen through your eyes

Raquel I. Penzo

"Friends Remembered"

Nestled in the green grass,
Not so far away,
Sits a dark reminder,
Of those once called away,

Shadowed by the greatness,
Of men of yesterday,
Stands this granite tribute,
To those so young and brave,

Watched over by three comrades,
As flags around them wave,
Their faces show the sacrifice,
That all of them had made,

Now not to be forgotten,
None of them at all,
Each and everyone of them,
Are etched upon THE WALL.

Russell D. Griffith

Thirteen

No longer a girl
Not yet a women

Too old for barbie
Too young for Broadway

Too young to leave
Too old to stay

Too young to love
Too old to play

No longer a girl
Not yet a women

Rebecca Smart

Lovers Can Be Friends

You can make me feel so tiny
now I'm rather small
You, the man, surround me
to see me through this all

Just a mortal nothing
can make you grow this BIG
Now I've grown into something,
something which you used to be

If I were thinking clearly
I wouldn't say a word...
but now that words have found me
I'll tell it to the world

Yes, this all seems quite perplexing
In fact I'm on my nerves
So I'll make this interesting
by confusing you with words

Let me take my bow of silence
you'll thank me in the end
But let me reassure you
Lovers can be Friends!

Valerie A. Tressler

Relief

Heavy and tired
Of aimless wanderings,
Weakened and ragged
As a worthless beggar;
Having gathered
The world's deep sorrow
In its compassionate
Gray chest;
Driven away
And beaten by winds,
Pierced and wounded
By pitiless lightnings;
Still having the endless
Sky ahead,
But seeing the end
Of its own road,
The cloud stopped,
Closed its gray eyes,
Breathed deep...
And cried.

Olga Gribova

Imagine

I imagine one breath
Of air on so sweet
As a shadow casts over
The day which we meet.

I imagine those words
Oh so softly you said
But you said it all wrong
I was one step ahead.

Imagine the whisper
Oh so softly of who
Unbelonging myself
To yet one who's true.

I imagine that day
Oh so softly you spoke
But you spoke it all wrong
For my soul had awoke

I'm so truly sorry
Never wanted to lie
But that same very shadow
May once more make me cry.

Kathleen Laurino

Untitled

Our papers tell us everyday
Of crimes that just don't go away
But lest in haste we all forget
There's one we haven't dealt with yet.

The crimes of theft, assault and rape
Are crimes the news cannot escape
But what about the words we say?
We murder English every day.

The schools, so strict, of yesteryear
They taught the language we hold dear
We studied verbs in days of yore
We studied nouns and much, much more.

So now our language is in limbo
The sentence structure's out the window
And maybe we should simply say,
"Perhaps we'll see a better day."

Katharine Brown

David's Dying

I remember

The white flesh
of his cringing buttocks

The sharp needle
one more time

The dry flaked skin
on his thinning ankles

The bulging bones
of his frowning forehead

The neatly stitched skin
above his ear

The sea blue
of his hospital gown

His clinging eager arms
his screams of agony

And

His gray dead face at dawn.

Pamela Horton

Caged Bird

Memories of songs now seldom sung,
Of intrusions long ago begun,
Of pain and shame.

From bronze-skinned muse,
A warm heart soothes
And transcends the blame.

Flowers shared with love,
And I cried,
For I was loved, too.

Laughing of pain,
Abandoning hurt to aim,
Love grew.

Warren L. Bailey

Dance

Stand with me
On steps of flowing water

So we glide
In life together

Bathing in love
And being in laughter

Rodger D. Jones

Neurosis

I built a wall around me
Of mortar, stone and brick.
Sign, says, do not enter
The door of crooked sticks.

Inside there is turmoil
Pictures hang askew.
Demons guard a simmering pot
Stir not the wicked brew.

Time will ease the torment there
And cool the bubbling stew.
Tranquility will then return
And I will welcome you.

Lucille Maxwell

A Christmas Dream

I had a dream of Christmas night,
Of Santa and his sleigh,
And of his reindeer riding fast
With toys for children's play.
Upon my roof he stopped,
And then I heard him call,
"Hey, kids, whatever shall I do?
This chimney is too small!"
I slipped my feet out of my bed
And rushed across the floor;
I whispered up the chimney,
And let him in the door.
Oh my! There were so many gifts
For me and Dad and Mother.
A doggie and a teddy bear
Were there for Baby Brother
He said, "I'll give you one big wish.
'Tis midnight by the clock."
I jumped into the sleigh with him
And rode around the black.

Thelma Nave

Untitled

I'm happy for the memories
of things we used to do
And cherished are the moments
when I think of you
Time they say can heal
the hurts down deep inside
And people go their way
but memories never die
They pop up unexpectedly
and grab hold of your mind
And send you far away
to someone left behind
Some are filled with joy
others give you pain
But memories of love
in my mind remain.

Kathryn Rubbert

Street War

The steam begins to rise
off the dirty city streets
Guns peek out from every corner
This time, it's twenty against two
The guns go off, hitting
the young girls womb, completely
missing her boyfriend
Bangs! He's dead, just like
his girl, due to a misunderstanding

Sarah Thurston

The Unknown Soul

As I lay in silent fear
Of very trying times
I brush away an unwept tear
And enter in my rhymes

Scared of death, but not in life
For what is death to me?
The quick slices of a knife
To set my spirit free

What awaits at creations end
For my eternal soul?
The loving nature of a friend
Or a burning fire's toll?

I hear voices in my head
Of those I've left behind
All the prayers that they have said
Have not an ear to find

Paul Garofallou

For Wendy

Soft whispers, toiling the parting
of Wendy,
Stilled, by the gentle breezes of
Wailua,
Outreaching, and cradling with
passion:
Her love, in the peacefulness of
sleep.
Caring, dissolving of fears
fortified by strength
Renewed by the understanding:
opening the way to meet the
impossible.
Solved alone again to be assured,
outreaching in her memories:
plucking gems for a precious
"crown of smiles"
to be worn in her hair,
Forget me not, aloha my Kaua'i.

Mary Ann K. Lindsey

Path Of Darkness

Stumbling through the darkened path,
of which through I am guided.
Guided by whom I do not know,
if only he was sighted.
Maybe someday the light will strike,
and then I'll understand.
But I am sure, the man up there,
has got this all well planned.

Vanessa Vallejo

Beautiful Ballet

Ballet, Ballet
Oh, beautiful ballet.
You twist and turn,
Eshappe' and saute.
Oh, listen and move.
The steps are so smooth.
You jump in the air.
You dance everywhere.
Move to the beat.
Oh, look at your feet.
Up high, down low.
Oh, look at you go!
Ballet, ballet,
Beautiful Ballet.

Miranda Lightfritz

Untitled

Oh Mary, how you must have felt,
oh, that your heart would melt.
Knowing your son was coming soon,
but not outside under the shining moon.
If only there was a room,
oh, how heavy was your gloom?

"I know You are more than able,
oh please God, not a stable."
For God to answer her plea
was as simple as making a sea.
But God's plan was a better plan,
entirely unknown to man.

For lambs are born in a stable,
this was God's plan and He was able.
As the north star shone bright,
and the shepherds were led by its light,
Mary was careful to lay
the Lamb of God gently on the hay.

Patty Ardrey

Gone Too Soon

I meant to call so many times.
Oh, the countless plans I made.
How did we ever drift apart?
How did our friendship fade?

We were so close, we shared so much;
The heartaches, the laughter, the fears.
We vowed to always keep in touch.
Has it really been that many years?

What happened to our hopes and dreams?
Now just memories of the past.
Remember all our plots and schemes?
How did time get away so fast?

Now here I stand, eyes opened wide,
Fighting to hold back my tears.
A rose in hand, and a last farewell;
Has it really been that many years?

Virginia James

Sunrise, Sunset

Have you ever watched the sunrise
On a beautiful summer day
And wondered just how anyone
Could think God was far away?
For God is seen in all of nature
Yet, especially a sunrise glow
Seems to be His favorite place, I think
To let all the world know
That He is God of the Universe
Of all things both great and small
And he watches over what He has made
Because of His Love for all.
So the next time you see a sunrise or
a sunset glow
Pause and meditate for awhile
And in the beauty there, you'll see
His Love, His Care, His Smile for you
and me.

Lucille O. Pinkerton

Knowing

Today I was sad-
On a quiet beach I saw
A sea gull alone,
His wing broken.
What can I do,
My heart cried, my hand
Yearning to touch
And comfort him.

I watched as he fed
On sea debris, warmed
By the sun
And gentle breeze.
I released him then
To a higher care, knowing
He'd soar again
Whole and free!

Shirley S. Byke

David

Shadows dance
On epitaphs.
Silent tongues
Speak through the
Memories
Of us who've been
Left behind.
Living on through
My thoughts
Your impressions
Etched in my mind.
Forever my heart
Shall be healing.
Yet to never again
Be whole.
Every tear takes
Some hurt
And my tears
Are
Endless.

Katherine L. King

My Thoughts Of The Moon-Buggy

Do you see what I see
on reflecting globe
moving
across darkened sky?
Abandoned moon buggy
powered by earthmen-
stranded on gaunt moonscape
unchanging,
frozen in time.

It is somewhere on that
half-moon tonight.
Is that million dollar gem
glowing in the light
or
dozing in the dark
of this night's moon.

Rosemary Jones-Wylde

"Exodus"

I stand
On the high hill,
Hands raised,
To the sun,
I ask, "Guardian,
Help my soul find God."

Yes, as the son of Him,
Stands behind me,
Arms out,
Exhibiting His protection,
To the city below.

He looks down on,
Me,
I leapt to Eternity,
Those streets below,
Tears in my Eyes.

More in His.

Leo Cittadini

Jesus Within Me...

Jesus is my Rock and my name is
on the roll
I let the Holy Ghost within me
take control
The Holy Ghost leads me down the
Green Pasture Road
It will speak mysteries to your
body and soul
It changes your appearance it
will make you glow
The spirit will take you places
that you never thought you would
go
I'm a living witness that the
spirit is moving from Coast-to-Coast
That's why I thank God for the
Holy Ghost

Tonia Butler

Bird's Watching

Young birds balanced in a row
on the telephone wire
looked upon me and my life
inside the window frames
ending the boundaries
of my room.

Their curious study
reminded me
of pityings gazes
humans give over
to lions in the zoo.

Those free in the sky,
those birds,
must have wondered
why anyone
would place herself,
by choice,
behind concrete, glass, steel and cement.

I wonder too.

Philein Wang

Me Two

I saw a girl I've seen before,
On the world and in my mind.
Channel of speech - a hidden door,
True romance, I did not find.

A great spectacle, we could've been,
My vision of her was bright as day,
Dream to reality a vicious seam,
To have spoken what I didn't say.

I saw a girl I've seen before.
Anyplace, her presence there
Animated verbiage - I was its whore
Only, in my dreams was she never bare.

Realization came at last
She was almost over me
But I snatched her up quick and fast
Failed clairvoyance... serendipity.

Lloyd Savage

Vietnam Memorial

I saw their names etched in stone
On their country's wall of fame,
Those fallen heroes of vietnam
No victory could they claim.

To fight a war they could not win
Took courage never known,
And from their wailing wall they cry
We're home, we're home, were home.

But honor too, they also, cry
The living from nam's zone,
So they can finally truly say
We have been welcomed home.

Leo F. Sanders

Graduation Day

Tried to find the perfect words to say
On this, your special Graduation Day!

I've know the little girl
Through the young woman you've become
I'm proud of your accomplishments
And all that you have done.

Remember playing dress up
Pretend princess with a crown?
No make believe, this time it is real
Your dress ... a cap and gown!

For all that you have done
For all that you will be
I'm proud today of who you are
I say this ... to you from me!

Tenya Anthony

Chance

Two people come together as if by chance
One intrigued by the music
The other intrigued by the dance
One too bashful to dance
but the other engulfed by the beat
Yet they still somehow connect
They teach each other so much
but the dance is dying
And it's over with one final touch
The two people separate as if by chance
both intrigued by the music
Both intrigued by the dance

Salvadore M. Cook I

Untitled

Count the buttons.
One is missing.
One has escaped this stitched row.
Will the glass-errant
find another measured set
that it will fit
or must it be outside the pattern
hiding free
before it finds capture in a bottle
with other truants wait.

Lois A. Montgomery

A Gentle Man

I cried Lord, I need a gentle man
one that is sensitive and true.
I need someone to tell me hey,
"I love you". I need someone that
can keep my tender heart safe,
from this day forward, from all
of the storms I'll brave. A gentle
man that will be there through
thick and thin. I mean, a man
that holds the one and only key.
Someone that will grow with me and
never grow apart, a gentle man that
will go with me to the finish from
the start, then I wiped the tears
from my cheeks and got off of the
floor, I heard a gentle knock from
a gentle man at the door.

Shirley A. Robinson

Untitled

Jogging
only expending one fourth
of the energy held within.
Then—
Running
hard, harder, faster,
near exhaustion
pushing to near collapse
stumbling onward
struggling.
Feeling
blood rush violently
through the body
harder, faster, struggling,
legs weakening, hot,
then the break.
God,
the world broke loose
for me to sleep in.

Shirley A. Benedict

"Me And You"

What attracted me to you
Only heaven knows.
Even though I said: I love you!
You had to leave and go.

Why I love you, I don't know
I guess that I must assume.
I love you 'cause you know
How the earth attracts the moon.

I want me and you to be together
And never have to part.
But, if you leave then I'll know
I'll still love you in my heart.

Rachael Jacobs

Talent Discovery

You leap through the air,
only to find,
you have some hidden talent,
in the depth of your mind.

You land on your feet,
feeling strong and impressed,
and stretch one more time,
to have your ability blessed.

You have many faces,
still left to uncover,
and many more qualities
yet to discover.

Kerri Johnson

Untitled

If I can touch one heart,
Or comfort one soul,
If I can replace tears
with a smile,
If I can fill an empty heart
with hope or acceptance,
If I can help ease the pain
and strengthen the muscles,
If one person was glad I was there,
Then I am glad to be.......a nurse.

Patricia Troche

His Son-lit Moon

Have you ever sat and stared up high
or felt the love upon a sigh
or captured the strength within a smile
or walked along a moonlit mile?

If you have, I'm sure you've seen
the Son-lit moon upon the scene
God made this moon and gave it light
through His son and His fight.

He gave us all the pure white dove
He died for us that we might love
I pray to Him that one day soon
We all will see, His Son-lit moon.

Susan Robbins

Untitled

I am well
Or so you think
In love I fell
With no one, but a fink
My love's for sell
My heart's in a sink
Draining itself to a jell
Covered in mink
Beating faster than hell
Looking for someone to link
Its phosphoric cell
A lovely pink
In a ringing bell
Losing my ink
I yell and yell
I shrink and shrink
Into my little shell
My love I drink

SHAGGY

Refugees

From raging wind and storm tossed seas,
Or war's hot breath, there's no release.
See the children with bodies bare.
Eyes so glazed, they are dying there.
Who will listen? Who will hear?
To what is said, their words so dear.
Listen closely to their pain.
They will not pass this way again.
That dance of thought, so gently grown.
Now cast aside, carelessly thrown.
A spark of youth, ideas brash.
Now quietly dimming amid the trash.
Reach out, be counted, across this land.
With generous heart, and helping hand.
Consider well, what you must do.
The next one needful could be you.

Winnie J. Powell

Our Great And Mighty God

Who can compare with you, O Lord
Our God, our Savior and our King.
Your Majesty endures forever,
Your word forever reigns

You sent Your Son to save us,
You gave Your love to us.
As poor and needy people,
We're lost and without hope.

A love like yours, unequaled,
We have if we desire.
Your promises unchangeable,
To strengthen every heart.

We cannot fathom Your greatness,
Our God, without ever a mistake.
From beginning to end, profound;
As mortal men, we quake.

We adore and worship You, Our God,
As we seek you day by day.
You are forever holy,
And keep us as we pray.

Pearl Modica

"Departure"

Our eyes will meet,
Our lips will kiss.
Our bodies will hold,
Our hearts will miss.

Our hands will clasp,
Our minds will race.
Our feelings we'll share,
Our fears we'll face.

Our time will come,
Our pain will grow,
Our good-byes we'll say,
Our tears will show.

Our doubts will raise,
Our souls will pray.
Our wishes will hope
Our love will stay.

Neil D. Dettwiler

Getting Old

Getting old, getting old
Our perfect body breaking its mold
Sitting on my old wooden rocker
Watching the kids play
All so happy and gay

Getting old, Getting old
Now my house already sold
I'm living in the nursing home
I'm growing thin, all skin and bone
Wasting the time all alone

Getting old, Getting old
Almost time to let death off hold
Nearing death by the minute
Checking over my will in my head
Lying motionless on my bed

Getting old, Getting old
Soon my body food for mold
I'm not ready for this time you see
I'm getting tired I must go
This is the bow at the end of the show

Paul Hedrick IV

Our World Of Truce

Come sit down and talk
Our world is full of trouble and pain
Let's stop fighting and have
peace and joy.
Don't shift the blame from one
person to another.
Unfold your arms and let the
love come from your heart.
Be strong—Our world belongs
to all. Pour out the tears of
joy from our eyes let them flow
If there is pain, bare with it
It will soon go away
People all over the world have
different personalities.
some good, some bad But who
am I to say they don't belong
The World belongs to all.

Mary L. Elliott

Business

Black as night
Painted light as day
Another suit and tie
Winds away
A special key
Sticking out of his back
Allows canned feigning
And happy smiles, smack
In the middle
Of the perception game

Blah blah blah
And a rah rah rah
Gotta keep up with the flow
Blah blah blah
And a rah rah rah
Put on a little more glow

Nicholas P. Kiefer

Please Don't Knock My Driving!

Tell me I'm not good at sports,
Particularly diving,
Say I'm always "out of sorts"
But please don't knock my driving!

Say my head is made of wood,
Say that I'm conniving,
Tell me I'm just plain no good,
But please don't knock my driving!

Say I keep a dirty house,
Despite my earnest striving,
Tell me I'm a dirty louse,
But please don't knock my driving!

Tell me I can't cook, and - Yes -
My children I'm depriving,
Tell me that I look a mess,
But please don't knock my driving!

When this has all been said, you know,
Great pleasure I'll derive,
From telling you just where to go,
And you, yourself, can drive!!

Rhoda S. Mellor

Whose Hand Does What?

Sizes of Galaxies can be
partly controlled by me
but whether they spin so free
is more apt to be
determined, God, by thee
I usually do not interfere
with these little flattened spheres
of course from time to time I do
however I'm prone to this view
I'll step back for you and let you do
your creativity for all to see
you just plain do it so magnificently
crowds in 2,000 come to theaters
(a dream not yet realized)
to see your majestic flattened spheres
and some pour out joyous tears
at all times my hand should be
working for thee
at other times your hands alone
set dramatic tones

D. Phillip Adams
(Christian Galactic Creations)

A Mom

A mom is a special
person in your life.
She helps you up when
you've fallen to the ground.
She cheers you up when
you're feeling down.
She even helps you when
you're feeling frustration.
She also helps you when
you can't get any
concentration.
A mom is a special
person.

Siobhan Givens

One's Birthday

Singularly
personal
Only one
per customer.
An entire
twenty-four
hours to
relish and
reflect.

But quickly
the inexorable
minutes and
hours consume
the day,
so special
to the celebrant,
so impersonal
to mankind.

Nancy Fleharty

Loneliness

The Chill of night
pierces loneliness
Cold cares not
dull thought waves
add sadness
No plans
nothingness
dull routines
Wait - wait - wait.
No - push away
Spark the brain
excite the nerves
And roll on!

Ruth Silnes

Twenty Nine

You were to me a puddle of wax
pooling around my world
all too easily at any moment
to harden
but you could have flipped
the pages of a book in a
faster pace and the
air, despite the force, would have
caused the flame to remain
strong and stand all too still.

Kerry Loftus

My Daughter

When you lie with your tiny head
Pressed tightly to my chest
Can you hear what's being said
By the heart within my breast?
With each beat it says to you
I love you daughter dear,
And how simple words just won't do
To let you know I need you near.
Or when you gaze into my eyes
Can you see the adoration there.
I hope it comes as no surprise
Just how awfully much I care.

Michael Mitchell

Cruel Crude

Excitement!

It's everywhere!
Pumped up.
Energy.
Power.

Kick his butt!
Patriots
Doing duty
Soldiers and
Sailors.

Slaughter and
Sacrifice—
Cruel crude.
Blood, rape,
Barbarism.

Hypocrisy in
Policies.
Euphemisms.
Rhetoric.
America.

Naomi J. Tegland

Fifty-Two

I'm fifty-two,
Quite true
But between you and me
I feel brand new
I'm not blue
at being fifty-two

Cut the pain,
forget the shame,
Just aim and you will gain.

Adjust if you must,
begin again to trust,
forget the past,
it won't last,
Pick up the pieces
and get new lease on
life

Only true to new me,
new life, new strive,
feels real new at
FIFTY-TWO!

Marjorie C. Smith

Sunrise

I saw a sunrise early this morning
Reaching into the sky,
It wrapped the world around it
In its wonderful warmth and light.
The glory of the sun glistened
In the early morning air.
The mountains stood in majesty,
As if they almost dared
To reach up higher into the sky
And touch the mighty face,
Of the One who caused the being
Of this beautiful place.
I realized that this day
Was an extra special gift.
It brought a smile to my face
And gave my soul a lift.
Then I felt a peace inside,
And I could truly see
That this was the way God intended
His perfect creation to be.

Sheryl A. Cox

Reality

What is Reality?
Reality is a baby crying,
the laughter of children,
the anger of teens,
the hopelessness of adults.

What is Reality?
Reality is the cold back turned on you,
reaching out and finding no one there,
the feeling of emptiness,
the desire to die.

What is Reality?
Reality is neither black nor white,
it's the grey bleak world outside,
it's everything and nothing,
without the grey there is no Reality.

MaryAnn Becker

Our Soul's Reflection

The stars in the sky,
Reflect the age,
Of a time passed long ago.
Millions have looked,
Many have watched,
And guessed about their creation.
Who are we,
To second guess,
The nature of God's manifestation?
The universe in which we live,
Is vast and wide,
And unexplainable.
It is better to just be,
Than always wonder,
What could have been?

Salvatore P. Incorvaia

Untitled

To soar above the clouds,
releasing the pressure below.
We are able to breathe again,
and let our bodies flow.
To see the world in a new perspective,
a simple kind of place.
Remembering we must return,
for there is life we have to face.

Richard L. Payne Jr.

Riddle Of Dreams

Riddle of direction
Riddle of dreams
What's the secret
Nothing that seems

Angry North snow and ice
Aggressive South heat and sacrifice
Farthest East the birds shall sing
The wild West there is no king

Haunting stillness eerie slow stir
Frightened children buried in fur
Book closed and put down
Reader possessing an evil frown

Todd B. Kline

Why Run!

My body says run —
Run from pain.
Where is the ecstasy then?

My heart says run —
Run from hate.
Where is love then?

My life says run —
Run to preserve pride.
Where is courage then?

My mind says run —
Run from deception.
Where is truth then?

Can there be ecstasy without pain?
Love without hate?
Perseverance without courage?
Truth without deception?

Can life be free of hate, pain and deception?
Life? No; Death? Yes.
For in death is truth, ecstasy, love, courage
and yet again, Life.

Marion A. Carter

Longtime Ago

Longtime ago, you passed me and smiled.
Running to the phone, I gave you a dial.
It was a longtime ago, we can both see.
As our love developed, for an eternity.

Regulo Rendon Jr.

Cold Winter Hearts

A cool winter breeze
runs through my face
so gently,
as it leaves a cold touch
on my skin.
Thinking of the many
cold hearts there are
in this big world,
wishing the world
will come to peace.
God created people
to love, care and share.
But not to have hatred.
And like all seasons,
cold winter days
could all turn to
warm summer years.

Kristin Kimura

Love And Eternity

My dear husband, I
Sadly miss.
His gentle touch and
Loving kiss.
In life and death,
We are apart.
I still love him, with
All my heart.
Everyone must go alone.
When it's God's will
To call us home.
Above the sky, we'll
Meet again.
Together, Forever, Amen

Sharron Marie Cramer

The Beach During the Summertime

The noise of the water
rushing upon the shore softly.
The sound of waves crushing
at the floor sharply.
The dolphins jumping high.
The mountains are pretty
in the reflection of the sky.

The sea gulls glide swiftly.
The flowers grow stifly.
The sun red and hot
burning greatly.
The music of the shells sounding faintly.

The shiny, blue sky is filled
with a breeze, that moves
at each beat of the gentle, dry trees.
The fish have a disease of happiness.
The sharks have a seize of laughiness.
The sand is filled with
white stones and the people
have content tones.

Melissa Warren

The Paradox

The old friends that just met,
sat apart and talked
for hours,
of commonly known secrets
they laughed while weeping,
at the perfect imperfections of life.

Since the maturity of childhood
they have known each other,
living the realities of their dreams
while time stood still,
as the years passed
changing as they stayed the same.

The duo separated,
but were together in spirit
the paradox,
that was there life
seemed bizarre to an outsider,
but was an old friend to the two strangers.

Samantha Shechtman

Ancestor

Who was she, Daughter?
She, whose spirit lives on in you?
Herself, a daughter of the ancient
Sioux.

Was she a medicine woman who
Sought a dream?
Did she gather berries by a
Mountain stream?

While you seek answers to questions
Troubling your soul,
Perhaps she walks with you
Guiding your goal.

Great-great-great Grandmother,
Once young like you
Chanted prayers to the sky
In a world that was new.

In your world of today, amid
Turmoil and despair,
When you pray for peace,
In you, she is there.

Maxine Wilson

Time Has Come And Passed Her By

Tears from long ago
scar her face.

She no longer cries
or whispers a sound.

She looks out at the world,
with clouded eyes.
She sees, but does not know.

She remembers, but forgets.
She's lost,
but no one is looking.

Her heart aches,
but can not communicate.

No one comes,
yet she waits.

She is no longer what she once was.
There is no purpose anymore.

Lost to everyone, but herself.
She lives, but
she is not alive.

Time has come and passed her by

Kimberly Hofer

Sleeping Darkness (Dreamless Nothing)

Sleeping darkness (dreamless nothing)
Searching, hoping, needing
(Bright mem'ry)
Her arms around my neck
Her kiss, (is everything)
Her voice in my ears
("I love you")
Sleeping darkness (dreamless nothing)

Robert A. Lupton

Gestation

An aproned prophet
Sees through
Shiny-black mud
I'm a green, plastic bowl
A daffodil
Waiting quietly
On a soft-brown window sill.

Robert P. Burke

Untitled

Black eyes deep with
Shadows accented below
Pools of deep fear
Past sufferings that show

Why do I love her
I ask at close of day
When these eyes are closed
And smiling dreams of play

Why I ask myself
What is there
To turn and melt my heart
Why do I care

Never the answer comes
Will I know
That is the price of love
The living world is so

William A. Bergin

"Necessities"

Go to the gold with globs of cream rinse,
Shave your hair, paint your boldness red.
Blow a kiss to your cat,
and bye a flannel.

Leah Anderson

Mother

I was chosen for her.
She held my spirit
She was the first woman I ever knew
A soul was given to me through her
Her heart is bigger and stronger, than
her body will ever be
She kissed me with the gift of life
And gave me eyes to see
I'll forever feel the spirit of her
presence wherever I will go
And she will stay in my heart and
mind
And forever breathe in my soul.

Vanessa Whitt

The Writer

In the still of the night,
She silently lifts her pen.
With eager strokes she begins to fight,
Back and forth across the whiteness,
With soundless sin,
That had no likeness.
A pinch of joy,
A smidgen of fear,
Slowly like a small toy,
Spread like fire.
Was that not a tear?
Was she never tired?
At last at the end,
With a laugh at her deed,
She lays down her pen,
Until she again has the need,
To write.

Mandelin Palmer

Trust

He trusted her,
She trusted him,
But they trusted others
When the lights were dim.

Who's to say,
I'm this lovers' game,
Who is innocent
And who's to blame.

Times of passion,
Inhibitions gone,
It seemed okay,
Not so wrong.

Years went by,
Memories passed.
Now they hoped
Their life would last.

Just one more day
To breath again;
Just one more day
To regret their sin.

Linwood Burton Wickett

Encounter

The child was following the man,
(She, waist high to me,
Round of face, dark hair, and
Eyes.)
And stopped, there in front of me.

And tilting her head back,
Fixed on me a gaze
Of such utter yearning
As I have never seen
On human feature.

Blood-chilled,
Eye-locked,
Volition-less,
My hand, touched her head.
There rested.

For just a moment.
And then she moved away,
Again behind the man,
(Brother, Father, or whatever)
And somehow, no further away.

Herbert Greenwald

To A Stray Dog

Oh, poor little throw-away dog
Shivering alone in the fog.
Ten years at your dreary post,
Such faithfulness deserves a toast.
Master who left you deserves a flog.

Each morning you arrive at seven,
Give up each day around eleven.
To see such brave heart,
Makes both my eyes smart.
For you, there's certainly dog heaven.

You have been so very aloof
Knowing you had some owner proof.
We thank those kids who made a deal,
And convinced you to share their meal.
Each night you stay under their roof.

Your muzzle has grown very gray,
From years enduring a long stay.
On Highway Two-Ninety cars whiz by,
Yours doesn't stop, I see your long sigh.
Still, you keep anxious watch each day.

Sonya Woicinski Riggs

Holiday Express

Packed and pushed
Shoved and smashed
Wish we had
Back our cash!

Naomi Gale Silverman

Exclusive

Shunning all the outsiders,
Sifting through the insiders,
Selling all those
Who don't come up to par.
Stealing from the enemy,
Slinking from the lies,
Shrinking to a corner
Where the fever hides.
Savoring special someones,
Straining to ignore the rest,
Silly to try to run to
Where only you are blessed.

Marissa Hamilton

Tree, Tree, Oh Beautiful Tree

Tree, tree, oh beautiful tree,
Since the beginning of this earth,
You gave the fruit that Eve gave to Adam
That is now a part of you and me.

Tree, tree, oh beautiful tree,
You produced the wood for Noah
To build the Ark to sail the sea.

Tree, tree oh beautiful tree,
You give us shade, you purify,
The air for us to breath free.

Tree, tree, oh beautiful tree,
You give us paper to write and give
Us lumber to build houses
And beautiful furniture for a
Better life for you and me.

Tree, tree, oh beautiful tree!
Let's all work together to save
And preserve the beautiful tree.

Tirso M. Gaytan

Time

Down by the river
sits the answer to time.
Music knows the meaning,
how to make man shine.
No one speaks to him.
They don't even know he's there.
He sits here with his clock
and doesn't seem to care.
Down by the River
the rhythm plays a tune.
No one knows the answer
is coming so soon.
But he just sits there
with time to spare.
Time is all he has
and what he has he shares.
Down by the River
is the beginning and end.
Down by the river
is an unknown friend......time.

Mary Axle

Where Did You Go?

There was a time when the
sky was blue, and all the
stars were shiny and bright.
I stood on the porch and eventually
laid my head up against the
pillars. My wish was laid upon a
falling star and there I was floating
upon a cloud looking down at you.
My only hope was to pull the clouds
together and form a vision of you.
As a small child my dreams and
thoughts were all about you. Your
beautiful smile and caring ways.
Suddenly one day the clouds
turned, black and all of the stars
began to disappear and the cloud
I formed of you was no more.

Linda Hurdle

To The Wise

Erratic, on static electric legs
Slight quick air movements
The malign menacing, liquid-like
Spider creeps diligent
Across the face of a vague day's long
sinuous defeat and sits noiseless
In the cool nucleus of its black
impulsive pattern silk spun wicked
Insidious to capture foe to strangle
its weak entangled,
A dry desperate moth withering away,
alive, in frighten anguish
Is the example of us it eats
Cut out by the corner, in the measureless
shade of the evening ceiling
Easily, how peacefully does
Evil and the nightmare sleep
Amen.

Thomas James Mayeux

The Kiss

To my loving husband, Johan

Wet moist lips pressed against mine,
slightly parted and quivering.

You touch my tilted face with your
hand, which finds my face slightly
moist from the heat between us.

Rhythmically we rasp lips, keeping
time with our racing hearts, leading
us further than we expected.

With our flesh uniting, there seems
to be endless seconds to ponder
over our next movement.

Suddenly the phone rings, it's been hours.
We never noticed.
Well, until our next kiss, my love.

La Sandra Ye"Vette" Akesson

Silence Beckons Thee

Sunlight shone upon my bed
Smoky mist around my head

Dancing dust beyond the grave
Restless soul enslaved

Crashing waves forever sound
Sailing ships have run aground

Quiet mist surrounds the sea
Silence beckons thee

Sealed fate and endless time
Sense and state forever rhyme

Juries hung in children's minds
All is left behind.

Shawn Ohl

Untitled

Passing essence, passing grace,
only the memories remain.
Take her spirit from this place,
it's our loss Lord, Your gain.

With empty arms we'll manage somehow,
such painful hearts her loss did bring.
But heaven is a little brighter now,
another angel has got her wings.

Ted Trathen

You Again

Hello pretty girl,
So beautiful and powerful.
You seem to control,
destiny and life.
I fell into your eyes,
those eyes, grey in sorrow
that turned so blue in laughter.
I loved you so much
in the past.
And that seems to stay
deep in my soul.
But on the surface
I have become so cold and empty;
I know I can never love...
You again

Scott E. Hayford

Untitled

I met a handsome boy one day
So beautiful and sweet,
His eyes are blue his have is blond
And it's him I like to meet.

One day as we sat side by side
He held my hand and said
It seems I like you very much
But I hate to go above you
Then his blue eyes lower fell
Because you see I love you.

Lottie Borowy

Contrails

Son of man be you
so bold
As to fly so high up in
the cold
To leave white trails etched in
the blue
While pretending your wings are
ever true
Don't you know your wings are
for naught?
And in life's net you will
be caught
To be brought to earth
forever more
Never on shimmering wings
to soar

W. Grant

The Old Man

So cruel.
So cold.
Wrinkles so old.
His heart,
So young
and bold.
Flooding memories
Of better days.
Near the soft window
his damp eyes close.

Katie Jon Welch

Without You

One day my life was
so empty and dull
Then you came and made
it complete without a fall.
You made me realize
how special I was
in your eyes,
Regardless of my past
sins and lies.
Thank you Lord for
standing by me,
Because without you
I could not be.

Marcellina R. Missouri

The Ring

Sometimes it's made of stainless steel
so heavily does it weigh.
And other times it's fairy gold,
ready to float away.

But usually it is a wedding ring,
of everyday weight and size,
For a simple, commonplace
meeting of minds,

In a comfortable, everyday
meeting of souls,

The two of us bound for
everyday goals,
With our not unusual
hands entwined.

Mikhail Ann Marsh-Long

Again

I silently cry,
so no one can see me!
I miss my friends,
who are standing next to me.
I reach out, and refuse,
to hold on.

I don't have it inside,
enough love to hold on.
I'm slowly slipping away.
But no one knows.
I silent cry!

It is inside of me.
I do need someone.
But I need to be alone,
to figure me out.
And I can't hold on.
I don't trust myself.

Mandria

Enigma

Raindrops fall like rose petals
Someone is dying
the petals drop
Someone is crying
one...
Someone is sick
by one...
Someone is hungry
by one
And someone is
covered
in
petals

Karly Southworth

The Rain

The rain never sounded
so soothing,
It never pounded
the way it does now,

A drum beat
out of time,
Out of heat,
out of place.

It calls to you,
because it knows
You're blue
and listening.

It calls in the
middle of the night,
When the time
is right.

It knows you're awake,
it woke you.

Paula Urbach

What He Can Do

The sun shone so brightly
So that everyone could see,
The beautiful thing
That had become under a tree.

With gracious precautions
And elegant moves,
He gently shapes
A beautiful rose.

His gentle hands sculpt,
As Scarcely we see,
What beautiful things
He can do for you and me.

But we do notice
All the things he does wrong,
No one ever hears
His beautiful song.

They can't hear the words
Or sing along just as sweet.
They hardly even notice
What's growing at their feet.

Pamela Simpson

A Face

A face for a time is
soft, smooth without
signs of worry.
A face starts to show
the lines of time.
with every smile
in happiness,
from a child to a young adult.
The lines from the smiles
are there permanently,
around the eyes and the
corners of the mouth.
Then comes the face
of a mother,
a scowl
of disapproval and worry.
The circles under the eyes from
missed sleep, for one reason or another.
Then finally as I look into the mirror,
I see my mother's face with me.

Rosemarie Vanzant

Untitled

People Come, People go.
Some are good, some are bad.
But we will never forget them,
Not even one,
For the impression they leave
on us, will remain on us for
the rest of our lives!

Linda Christianson

Untitled

She's so sad, she let him go
somehow she knew
yet she didn't know
how to stop him
from pulling away
feeling him fight
himself to stay.
She's so sad, she didn't see
beyond his fears
and into his dreams.
She's so sad, he couldn't see
she shared the same fight
within her as he.

Pamela Joy Warwick

Myself

To view myself through
someone else's eyes.

Let me see kindness and
love inside.

Let there be warmth, compassion
and hope.

Qualities of merit, trust and
a will to cope.

Let there not be hatred,
malice or greed.

Unkind words, prejudice or
misdeeds.

Let there not be selfishness
or swollen pride.

When myself is viewed through
someone else's eyes.

Nita Johnston

Till I See You Again

I see you walking hand in hand
somewhere in a distant land.
Full of peace and tranquility,
visions of love and serenity.
Your pain and your struggles,
have come to an end
and those you have missed
come together again.
Loved ones surround you
friends say hello,
your face is beaming
with a warm soft glow.
You speak to me softly,
your message is clear...
"Continue the laughter
live life without fear."
God walks beside you,
he is your friend.
Ask him for guidance
till I see you again.

Kathleen S. Waddington

"My Special Friend"

Whenever I think of my
special friend, my heart smiles
once then over again.

If one of us hurts the other
is there, if one has no money
the other will share.

If one has a problem, and can't
find the way. The other is
there with something to say.

There's no doubt about it, I know
I am blessed. To have found a
friend who is truly the best.

Tonia Bigelow

I'm Still Listening

Soul floats above me,
Straining hard to see,
From where it has come,
Looks on with pity.

Sleep walk through my days,
Alerted to the ways
Inanimate grey matter
Will make me pay.

Space between my ears
(Hiding place for fears
Developed over time)
No light for years.

Mouth opens to speak;
Sewer springs a leak,
Odor is very strong,
Substance very weak.

Voices in my head,
Unforgiving,
Say I should be dead.
I'm listening.

Laurier Andre Bruley

"Mirrors Lie"

Looking down at pieces of myself,
Strewn about since primordial times.
Strive to pull myself together,
Beyond renaissance chapel chimes.

Pull up from the muck and mire,
Brace thyself for precedence truths.
Only as close as I can come,
Convalesced into non feeling numb.

Up close they're mirrors of myselves,
Farther back of neanderthal.
One step looker may reveal,
Nothing reflecting at all.

Betrayed by oncoming beliefs,
Ignored by greedy appearances of kings.
Became my own grain of relief,
From promise of golden rings.

Mirrors lie in pieces of myselves,
Thousands now stare back to me.
Cracked and broken slivers of alive,
Writhing in stoic agony.

Ronald K. Nealy

A Long Night

In my bed and lying still
suddenly I get a chill
The window shakes
the door it creaks
then I start to get the creeps.
A monster sounds inside the closet
and now I think I've really lost it
Everything is spinning round
suddenly I hear a sound
Something runs across the floor
then I dash right to the door
it's locked, oh no
I've got to go
My arms are weak, my legs are sore
then I fall onto the floor
Suddenly I wake up straight
knowing that it's very late
Still I think - "Am I all right
safe from things that go bump in the
night?"

Scott Shambaugh

A Beautiful Day

What a beautiful day!
Surely the day the Lord has made,
There is no other way
A day like this could be
Except for a power higher than we.

God's beauty is everywhere we look,
In every flower and in the brook,
In the country and in the town,
Everywhere God's love is surely found.

So let us learn to fully enjoy
This beautiful day that God has made,
And help someone along the way
So that they can have a beautiful day.

Nell S. Brewer

Love

Love is a sound of music
sweet and Joyful

Love is a spice of life
sour and tasteful

Love is immortal as
the Sun and the Moon

Love is sometimes ardent as a flame
sometimes soft as a caress

Life without love will be
dry as the earth with no rain
So love is my desire —

Mia F. Robinson

Breezes

I like the way,
The breezes go by.
So high,
So high,
Up in the sky.

No shall I touch,
No shall I see,
The way the air,
Believes in me.

Tina D. Ivory

Savannah Jennifer Thais

Smiling
Sweet girl
Hair of gold
One Year Old Today
A queen holding her court

Smiling
Promising child
Full of Determination
One Year Old Today
A true gift of God

Smiling
girl child
A promise shared
One Year Old Today
A quilt of many colors

Smiling
Long-sought grandchild
Blue Eyed Darling
One Year Old Today
A grandmother's hope and joy

Mary Jane Watson (July 1, 1994)

"Sweet Sleep"

Come upon me sweet, sweet sleep.
Take me from my troubles deep.
Fall over me just like a veil.
Pain will leave me - time will tell.

The only rescue that I find
From this dark and tear - filled time
Is in the valleys; silent and deep-
Of a long and dream - filled sleep.

I can close my eyes and see
A day of sunshine - a laughing me.
Running - loving - being so free;
Unlike the face in the mirror I see.

I can travel, feel sunlight
In the middle of the night.
Walk along a sandy beach-
Watch the sun set red and deep.

Take me on a trip tonight
Back to the time of my wings in flight.
Let my eyes close and refuse to weep.
Take me, hold me, - sweet, sweet sleep.

Vicki Gayle Hall

Apocalypse Now

How I hunger to be lost
Take me from this holocaust.
Mass contagion, an alien space,
I have no home but in this waste.
Locked in a prison not my own
Where lames are game and evil is sown
In plastic traps where nothing matters,
Where power grabs and sanity scatters.
Cloverleaf puzzles in a freeway maze,
Mankind muddles in the concrete daze
Unaware of what it is...
Cloudy minds in polluted fizz.
Littered streets and cluttered bay,
Poisoned fish where children play,
Missing mountains behind the day,
And all I want is to get away.

Marilyn Roberts

"Morbid Angel"

Death is a lady,
tall and slender.
What can you render?

Death is beauty.
She creeps along with us.
Misty, frightful,
Sometimes even delightful.

Sleek and sly,
you sometimes wonder...
Why do we make a fuss?

She is always with us,
Always takes what she wants.
But when the time is right,
it's always a fright.

Mark Odinezenko

Death...

When death comes you
taste a muckey taste,

When death comes you
see nothing but dark,

When death come your
blood runs colder than cold,

When death comes you
feel alone and abounded.

When death comes
you feel a gaping black
Shadow hanging over you.
.... That's when you
know death has come.

Megan Canfield

Someday Is A Place In Time

Someday is a place in time
that does not yet exist.
Yesterday has come and gone;
it has been.
It leaves behind its essence
in either a negative or a positive way.

But today is now
and now is the time to take hold
of what could be good
and not let yesterday influence
what someday might be
when it has not yet come to us
as today.

Sandra Ann Trujillo

Wishes

The greatest wish
That I can wish for you
Is that you be the best you can
At simply being you
And if you have a wish
That you would want to wish for me
Please let it be the same
My being the best at being me
For then we could be nothing better
To ourselves or to each other
Than to be that which no one else
Can possibly be...

Robert Kelly

Untitled

What can I say
that hasn't been said

What can I read
that hasn't been read

What can I do
that hasn't been done

What is really
the definition of fun

What really matters
is a heart that is brave

Willing to learn
willing to slave

Willing to be
the very best

Toiling without
the thought of rest

Your joy will be
the peace in your mind

Knowing your service
benefited mankind.

Lucile Wilson

Mummers We

It may be more act, than art,
That I appear to be the part
You see me playing on life's stage.
Not by chance, but by design,
Chameleons match another's kind
In color and live to ripened age.
Just to hear words, as spoken,
Are often but the slightest token
Of the speaker's inner rage
And to read the lines as penned
Often incompletely recommend
The hidden message on the page.
So also deceit can mask the face
Which, when pierced, reveals the trace
Of innocence lost, revealing age
And with it, wisdom's scarcity,
That hateful human paucity
Which locks us in a cage.

A. J. Craddock

"Thy Will Be Done!"

I once had a petition
That I directed to God:
"Not my will; Thy will be done."
He replied: "Thy will be done!"

I took it to mean:
"I must make my own choices
and decisions.
He gave me brains, knowledge
and understanding.
I have a free will."

My major goals were thwarted;
But my minor goals
Came out better
Than I expected!

I came to the following
conclusion:
"We must learn how to live
With the cards
That have been dealt to us."

Thaddeus Capek

Whose Child Is This

Whose child is this
that I found today
his body all warped
in trash where he lay
with broken bones
and bad bruises too
like those that come
from a person's shoe.

Whose child is this
so blue and cold
with nothing to wear
but long hair of gold
his blue eyes staring up
in a contented way
like he was just set free
from his parent's bad day.

Whose child is this
did you give him a name
he'll remember you too
at the end of your game.

William T. Redden

Didn't Give Up

On again, off again
That is the way it goes

I have tried many times
Heaven only knows

There are many ways
I have tried them all

First one then the other
And each time I would fall

I need it for this
Or I need it for that

Excuses, excuses
I have them all down pat

This time is different
This time I will win

How do I know
Because I won't give in?

Mildred Jenkins

The Playground

Oh no, the sun is coming out,
that means children will be
here without a doubt.

It always seems worse in the spring,
as most of the time they would
rather fight than swing.

My swings and teeters will
fly so high, as the children
try to reach for the sky.

The sandbox will be fully
in demand; I wish there
were a way to enlarge and expand.

Most of the time children are
such a pain; it's days like
this, that I wish it would rain.

Thressa J. Wengland

Absolute Defeat

I feel within a storm a-brewing
That my flesh cannot control.
I feel an anguish ripping
And tearing at my soul.

I feel my powers to reason
Have been paralyzed with despair,
No hope for logic or reason,
No confidence in prayer.

I feel waves of emotion
That I did not know existed
Gnawing away at the core of life
And leaving it maimed and twisted.

I feel drawn into a fraternity
With others I hope I never meet
As I cast my fate upon the sea
Of absolute defeat.

J. Connolly

Serenity

A feeling of time and space
that none can compare,
like the wings of an
eagle glistening in the air.

The sun great with brightness
setting in a cloudless sky,
as the moon rises in glory
to bid the day good-bye.

A rose so fragile yet so full of life,
gives such love and pleasure
with its beauty and might.

Serenity like all these things
forces great and small,
a place we hide within ourselves
to protect us from the world.

Micki W. Rowlette

Daddy

If I had only known Daddy
That one day you would be gone
If I had only known Daddy
That one day I would not be able,
to hug you any more
If I had only known Daddy
I would have called you on the phone
If I had only known Daddy
I would have come home sooner
If I had only known Daddy

Sharon Gallaway

Soulmate

There is a silent bond between us
that supersedes understanding yet
there is a sense of total acceptance
I like that and yearn for it.

My vulnerability is not compromised
I sense a closeness
a feeling of awe!
I love knowing you are
near, there, here
for whatever the need dictates,
forever.

Ruby "Fergie" Ferguson

The Inward Me

How can I make you understand
That what you see is not at hand
For what I comprehend and see
Is not the outward, but inward me.

I'd be disillusioned and depressed
If I accept this outward dress.
The deep veined hands, the wrinkled face
Do not present my inward grace.

The body that you comprehend
Struggles at times, to move and bend.
But the body that I feel in me
Is active, lithe and moving free.

So chain me not with what you see
Or hold me when I would be free
But see with me, the inward me
With thoughts alive, active, forever free.

God made us, be we big or small
His love surrounds us, one and all
So when you look at you or me
See His reflection, and inward be.

S. Dodson Clark

That Would Be

To dance with him. . .
that would be a dream.
To sing to him. . .
that would be fantasy.
To talk to him . . .
that would be a day dream.
To go to him. . .
that would be happily.
To turn from him . . .
that would be tearfully.
To watch him . . .
That would be reality.
To love him. . .
that would be a promise.
To hold him. . .
that would be forever.
To know him . . .
that would be a wish.

Nicole Nordeen

You're Gone

Didn't I know
That you couldn't show
All that you know?
It's not real,
Couldn't I feel,
That it wasn't real?
Was I that naive,
That I couldn't receive?
Now I grieve.
I didn't reach out and touch,
You loved me so much.
But now you're gone,
Just like a pawn,
You're gone.

Chelley Sauer

Charlie

I would jokingly tell those who asked
that you lived to see
your first birthday pass.

I would shake my head at finding
your treasures
kept among the couch cushions.

And walking by my side
you make me smile
at your single mindedness
watching you follow a path
only you could see
across a walk, over the grass
and up some strangers steps.

You remind me daily
to see and enjoy
the wonders about us
everyday.

Louise V. Cobb

We The People

"We the people,"
That's what we say,
But often times
Things tend to sway one way.

Why did this nation
Grow like this?
My God in what lesson
Did we miss?

Why do races
Fuss and fight
When we as the people
Hold the might?

Why do people
Curse and kill
Then all the while
Say they do God's will

"We hold these truths to be
Self-evident" is true,
But the only real solution
Is me and you.

S. Miciel Brown

The Rose

To know someone well you must reach
The core...to the center...past speech
Like the Rose with each petal
You must see, but not settle
For colors like those of a peach

This Rose, don't you see, can be read
By those who need more of God's bread
And His grace will touch those
Like the dew on this Rose
Bringing love to all with hands spread

Tad Wolicki

"The Shadows Touch"

Softly he caresses me
Speaking my name
But do I, his victim, do the same?
For my heart is breaking to the pain
From the unbearable burden
When he speaks my name.

Kami Jo Tassin

Friendship

Do you remember when we were young
The crazy things we said and did.

Do you remember when we were young
What fun it was to be a kid.

We woke each morning with a smile
Looking forward to each new day.

We laughed, we sang
We danced till dawn.

We enjoyed just living in every way.

The trips we took to Coney Island
The hot dogs we would eat

The smell of sea weed in the air
The sand upon our feet

Now that we are growing old and
All our youth is gone,

Our friendship still remains pure gold.
The memories linger on.

The time will soon be coming
When we must say goodbye.

But maybe! If the Lord allows
We'll still be friends up in the sky.

Lucille Feminella

Night Moves

Night attends.
The dark hides me, holds me,
Seduces me into profundity -
Knifes me with despair.

I was sure
Night was my friend, my joy.
Illusion-free, I knew reality-
Embraced my soul life.

Black descends
I know nothing; care naught
Think darkly - enmeshed and never free
I relieve my past.

Susan McPherron

"Stolen Love"

The day has come,
The day well-long waited,
The day when I see
How my love has elated.

Am I Blue? Do I need you?
I must confess, the answer is "yes."

Will this day go by,
Without me uttering a sigh?
And what about the next seven,
Will they be hell or heaven?

Maybe it's true what the old women say:
"A stolen Love never does pay".

But I'll take my chances,
What else can I do?
As long as you promise
To me you'll be true.

M.A. Tata

A Lonely Soul

I live my life all alone;
The dirty streets are where I roam.

I have nowhere to sleep at night;
I pray the Lord will make it right.

The cardboard boxes that form my bed
Are no place to lay my head.

Certain people feel sorry for me,
While others give me charity.

Sometimes I wish to myself
That I could be someone else.

The world around us wouldn't be
If every person were like me.

Sara Weisfelner

Untitled

In the beginning
The Earth was new,
Nothing was living,
Everything was few

The sea was deep
The ground was bare
Nothing to keep
Nothing to share,

In the end,
The sea was dry,
No one to tend
No one to cry.

Travis Ayers

Seasons

I remember your eyes
The eyes that brought us closer
Your skin so soft and white
All the years we spent together
Is like a moment I can not forget
No room for us to change
Will we change like the leaves
Or disappear like the air we breathe

From season to season
Back when we were young
It was much easier then
To hide within our dreams
Now all I do, Is think of you
To touch your heart
And hear your voice
There is little I can do
I feel like a leaf falling
From branch to branch
Mere words from a man
That Loves You

Terry Wells

Love

Curling up in my arms
soft and warm
he closes his eyes
in pleasure
and goes to sleep
treasured in my embrace
my special little Max
my not so little kitten.

Myrna L. Sanders

"Spring Is Still New"

The trees are barren
The grass has turned a brownish hue
Patches of a recent fallen snow
Can still be seen-
Yet, my heart is warmed
By the glow of His love
And, to me, spring is still new.

The leaves have fallen and died
After turning into their blaze of color
And lie fading-as the flowers also do-
Yet, for me, the birds sing their songs
Because I am warmed by His love
And, to me, spring is still new.

Nancy J. Weaver

Idol Thoughts

It's a wonderful feeling to witness
the harmony of nature
As I was watching a doe
And her two fawns grazing
along a creek, I noticed to
the side of my vision in my
binoculars about a dozen kildeer.
They flew in a tight formation
When they turned in the air,
the leader became follower,
the follower became leader and so forth.
I then realized that there is
a lesson to be learned by
something as simple as
as watching a dozen birds fly.

The lesson is in this world.
Man must learn how to be
good followers, and when we've
mastered this art well, we
become leaders

Randy Miller

Impossible Perceptions I

As I hold
the ice cube
in
my palm
it stares
back
at me
with a face
frozen in
time.

Its tears
run between
my fingers
and
drop
to the floor
with the
swiftness
of
death.

Karen George

The View

The door is locked.
The key is gone.
And still there is a view
of dogmas, of heresies,
of never-ending hues.

To sort the scene of fallacies
no one can seem to do,
so fallow is the mind
that the greens become the blues.

In time the hue of darkness
fills the tiny room...
blinded in a sepulcher
pernicious is the view!

Michael Domenic

"Dreams"

The dreams people have make up
the melodies of life
Some happy, some sad, some bring
contentment, and others bring strife
They all go hand in hand, one
leading us to the other
Dreams can open us up, but can
also send us fleeing for cover
Some have the power to bring
reality, others do not
But who can tell the difference
and know which one they've really got
Without dreams passions die and life
slowly fades away
So we keep on dreaming, just trying
to make it through one more day
We take our chances hoping the
dream won't let us down
Hoping at the end of this
dream, happiness will be found

G. Sid Sparks

"A Moonlight Dream"

The moon so bright
The night so still
And nature serene
Over me cast a spell

With dreaming eyes
My spirit soared high
Until I balanced between
Earth and sky

Then I thought of thee
My far away love
With fleetest wings
I sailed above

In all that wide space
I seem to see your dear face
And the tears I saw
Held me in awe

For I had committed a deed
That made my heart bleed

Then on waken I am not mistaken
The place where I flew was back home to you

O. D. Smith

Untitled

The elves all whispered,
The nymphs all laughed,
The fairies softly float,
and the stardust gently drifts,
But the child sleeps on.
The elves kiss her eyes,
The nymphs tickle her toes,
And the fairies sing their lullabies,
But the child sleeps still.
The elves walk away slowly,
The nymphs skip off, one by one,
And fairies flutter away,
Over the horizon peeks the sun,
The child awakes.
They were here again,
The ones who play games,
Those strangers who share their love.
She knows they'll keep coming
As long as she still believes.

Katie Hawks

Street People

Oh, how the world shuns you, turns
The other way.
Your raggedy clothes, torn shoes
Dismay so many.
You seek to harm no one, rather to be
Left in peace.
Your riches are within your soul,
Not material gains.
Your compassion is great, for
You have known pain.
Your kind words, gentle actions are
Beauty beyond compare.
You have much wisdom to offer, yet few
Know of your precious gift.
Your laughter and joy, so deeply lived,
Cures your many hurts endured.
Continue to be, for perhaps one day the world
Will truly see the beauty within the
street people.

Paula Crews

Hunger And Soul

No more do I witness
the phases of the moon
while waiting for the beloved
moment, the beloved, the eyes
to set me on fire, the passion
that will quench my thirst.

Mine is a hunger unabated,
a soul bigger than my heart
a chasm consuming my mind.

I am not satisfied by sadness,
pain or even just plain joy.
I want to rage to boil to writhe
in never-ending patterns, to
take my life in mine own hands
and say to a beloved -
have love am here.

Yolanda Ortega-Stern

JFK A Eulogy

The shots ring through the air,
The screams of ladies,
The thud of your body as it drops
The cries of children,
The tears of the citizens,
You were going to do so much,
You didn't have a chance
Just because of the "Miracle Bullet",
Your warm blood gushes -
over the nation your loved
Because some disagreed
they took your life away
Your life means to much,
now it is no more.

Kim Kocher

Light Blue

Blue is
The sea that splashes on the beach,
The pool as cool as can be,
A person that came out of a cold sea.
The sky as clear as can be,
The color of my lips so cold,
Wind that blows in your face,
The tears that hurry down your cheeks,
The dolphin that jumps into the air,
The blueberry that tastes so sweet.
That's what blue is.

Patricia Morris

"My Chula"

True love and happiness
The gifts my Chula gave to me
Will be with me forever
For all eternity.

Although for now we've had to say
Our parting sad good-byes
I still can see the trust and love
In my precious Chula's eyes.

And when my life is over
I hope I'm blessed to find
My Chula waiting for me there
Just on the other side.

Pam Benefield

Suicide

Spanked'er breath I drew,
Tied like string.
No choice, no option,
But death's promised sting.

I known the smell of heaven
And the bitter taste of hell -
Out among the stars?
They are here on earth as well

No storage box for me
Sing my song as written -
a tired old dog, remembering,
Some of the bites he's bitten!

Stopped by fear and pain
And the scourge of men -
No choice, no option -
This time I'll say when!

Glenn Allen

Clouds

Oh, of what are clouds made?
So billowy and white.
Oh, of what are clouds made?
As they dance in the light.

Of what are clouds made?
Shapeless yet shaped
Of what are clouds made?
White castles in heaven draped.

Oh, of what are clouds made?
All shades of blues, grey and white.
Oh, of what are clouds made?
Perhaps as Angels breath their delight.

Of what are clouds made?
Some like cotton balls suspended in air.
Of what are clouds made?
Others so light you'd hardly know they're there.

Oh, of what are clouds made?
Some but a whisper, others thick and bold.
Oh, of what are clouds made?
For when they were created, there was no mold.

Reverend Zeita M. Pierce

Sea Grass

I sat looking in the depth of the Sea!
She began to bubble and move!
The Sea Grass came from the bottom in groves!
Wind began to roar and whirl! The Sea came alive!

Grand daddy of all Clouds! Dark, black, and blue!
Came from a distance, where the Earth and Sea parted!
Wind, lightening, and thunder roared through the heavens!
The Sea got angry! The Cloud and the Sea,
headed to do battle, like two Warriors!

They met, it began! The Sea rose to the Heavens!
And she danced on the Earth as a ballerina on stage!
Black with red evil streaks of anger she turned,
slapping at our hull with all her might!
Back-an-frow! Helpless as a child,
we rode her anger!

She lifted us to God's cradling hands!
We started to dance with her spout!
The two warriors met! The bout stood firm!
We began to ride lower! And we rode no more!

I sit at the bottom, watching the Sea Grass grow!

Gerald Don Slocum

"Up Before Dawn"

Up before dawn, the quietness was so serene
she could hear the leaves which clothed the already half-naked trees.
She was sitting up high on a hill that overlooked
such beauty as only God could have created,
untouched by man.

Just below the terrain were God's creatures, both great and small.
The doe and fawn were feeding on wild oats, moistened by the morning dew.
The heifer stood content nursing her young,
the squirrels already laboring for a long winter.
All creatures both great and small, untamed by man,
but familiar to each other.
Only God could have created such beauty.
Where is this place so perfect and without flaw?
Untouched by man but only by God that surely created it?
"The Country," a place where one finds peace within oneself,
and the animals are safe to roam.
Where is this place she speaks of?
This place once was her home.

Judy Stewart

Untitled

I have a friend she never did any harm
She fell down one day and found out she had cancer in her arm
At the age 15 she had her arm and shoulder taken away
She somehow found the courage to live on the next day
She was so young and had to go through so much heartache
At first she thought it was much more then she could take
Going for chemo treatments losing all her hair
Even with a family behind her it felt like no one was there
She didn't get high or bother people in any way
Her young world crumbled she stood through it anyway
She's shown people a part of life most never seen
After a terrible illness a life's still left to dream
4 years had past without the worries in sight
Then again came the horror and fright
She died before she even had a chance to fight
A young life was lost in a battle to survive
But always in my heart her memory will be alive
Even though I never had a chance to tell Fran goodbye
I know she's at peace now with the angels in the sky

Joann Carucci Rivinius

The Outsider

I once knew someone that felt like she was an outsider.
She felt lonely, and bitter, she couldn't help it
Because that's the way she felt.

She felt alone because through her eyes no one seemed
To care about her and for that she felt bitter toward
The people who she cared for.

But she didn't realize at the time that they did care
And it was the terrible devil, Himself, that was
Blinding her.

And not letting her see the good, gracious love of her
Friends, family, and of the devils own enemy, God,
Himself, that loved her with all of their hearts.

But on one precious night she discovered the love she
Wanted so much was waiting for her right in her own
Memories of love from her family and friends.

Angela L. Phillips

Autumn

Before Autumn's leaves are meant to fall,
She ignites trees in rainbow flame.
Weaving her deep magic spell on all.
Her breathless beauty we acclaim.

Finally those "leaves" begin to fall.
Like a carpet over the ground.
The bare trees stand stark naked and tall.
The leaves become withered and browned.

Leaves are set on fire, and smoke intense,
Rises to watch autumn depart.
To Dame Autumn this is like incense.
As she fades with a wistful heart.

Fleeting Autumn, The world loves you so!
You lift up our souls in good cheer.
We wait in joy and hope, since we know.
You will come back to us each year.

Joseph Blanchfield

Emergency Room

The lady is wheeled into the Emergency Room;
She injured her leg tripping over her broom.
Thirty-nine patients and it's not even noon;
Must be connections with ER and the full moon.

Patients line the hallway, some cannot wait;
Critical patients first, the rest a long stay.
No time to take an aspirin for a big headache;
That lady is real lucky she didn't break a leg.

Respiratory Therapy, to the Emergency Room stat;
Code three coming in...a man with a heart attack.
Check the child for rabies, bitten by a stray cat.
What's wrong with that dude in the boots and Cowboy hat?

A baseball player brought in, hit on the head by a ball;
Soon ER is packed with family, the whole team and all.
It's so noisy in here, people lined from wall to wall;
Get security stat to send these folks down the hall.

Seeing so many patients can really get you all wired;
Some patients leave you with a lot to be desired.
The shift finally ends, staff all stressed out and tired;
To everyone working in ER, by others you're greatly admired.

Deborah M. Collins

Untitled

I have a daughter - her name is Jill.
She is a girl who never sits still.
She likes to eat - she likes to walk -
She likes to drive and she likes to talk.
She is very fond of all life's joys,
But most of all, she likes the boys!
She doesn't like dishes - she doesn't like school -
She does just enough homework. This kid is no fool.
She just doesn't like work - in this she's not rare,
If I really insist she will do her share.
It has been a long time since she cared about toys,
But golly, she certainly cares about boys!
Since 'way back when she was a little thing
There have been boys around - to push her swing -
To play her games - to carry her books -
To take her to parties and admire her looks -
To take the blame if there is too much noise -
No wonder this girl is so crazy about boys!

Beverly Swazey

Fascination

Ambitious, determined, humble
She left home, the country, at an early age. Traveled across the continent leaving her mummy behind. Got a job all on her own in a big city. Met an executive who promised her the moon. Regenerated from a scandalous broken relationship and became a newborn modern day woman.

Sexy, seductive, sensual
She loves fast cars, studded leathers, spicy perfumes and the sweet scent of jasmine. Hooks you in with those deep hypnotic brown eyes and makes you think you've got a chance with her. Can write a book on how to walk and talk.

Powerful, complex, magnetic
She commands the room instantly just by her appearance. Sends shivers down your spine and releases other negative energy when she's angry at her world. Doesn't show her true self to you but knows hidden secrets of other people.

Independent
Barbara Ann wanted to taste life and said goodbye to her small rural hometown at 25. No one can possess her and no one can control her.
She's very mysterious and you can't help admiring her.

Diana Rumjahn

A Daddy

How can a girl express the special feelings for her Dad?
She loves to see him smile, yet will cry for him when he's sad.

A Daddy is there when she takes her first step only to fall down.
My Daddy brought gifts when he was out of town.

My Daddy was the one to teach me how to ride a bike.
He bought me the little yellow daisy one which he knew I'd like.

My Daddy helped me with homework when the problems were tough,
and stood by my side when my brother played too rough.

My Dad taught me to drive in that old black car,
He was also the one that kissed me goodbye when I needed to move far.

My Daddy welcomed me home when my job sent me to return,
My Daddy taught me lessons that I am still trying to learn.

My Dad loves and supports me with no end,
For it seems to me that my Daddy is also my best friend.

Dana Polizzi

The Mystery

I met a lonely woman just the other day,
She smiled at me shyly in a most familiar way.
There were wrinkles at the corners of her eyes,
And they were the color of faded winter skies.
Her face was wrinkled like leather somehow,
And there were furrows impressed upon her brow.
Her hair was neatly styled in a very simple way,
When I spoke to her she looked, but; had nothing to say.
She seemed to always follow me,
I thought I was insane.
For I could clearly see her in the window pane.
Her attitude remained aloof,
As the Mystery seemed to grow.
I wondered if she were someone I once did know.
The image of the woman haunted me, night and day.
Then this morning she appeared
in my bathroom mirror,
and my mystery went away.

Dolores J. Bell

Darlene

Darlene was a mother
She was also a daughter,
A sister, a grandma and a godmother
There could never be another.

Darlene was a wife to a man named Paul
He was always there for her
No matter how great the fall

We will never understand why she got
This deadly disease and
Why she had to leave.

Even though we know she will be in the sky
It's a place called heaven
Which is so very high.

We will always remember her deep down inside
For her show of strength
And her great show of pride.

Darlene was a person which we could all trust
That's why I know she is here with us.

She was smart and cleaver
And she will be in our memories forever!

Brandi Trindade

Mothers

Mothers are there when you need a friend,
she'll be there 'till the very end.
Her love could never be replaced,
her face is so soft and full of grace.
A shoulder to cry on when you need it most,
to check your bed for a real scary ghost.
A daughter is what a mother needs,
to help her with her dirty deeds.
The feelings that I can't describe,
are all tucked in; tucked deep inside.
Deep in my heart is where they'll be,
for that's the closest they are to me.

Danielle Corellis

Katie

Her eyes gold as moons, her coat silky black
She's gone now, and she's not coming back

I knew she was sick, that her day had come
I'll never forget the sound of her purring hum

She'd curl up with me, she'd lick my tears
With her next to me, she'd calm my fears

The last few minutes that she was mine
You could tell by her actions, she knew it was time

She didn't struggle, she just lay there and purred
Her breath slowing down was the last thing I heard

She's not here now, but her spirit lives on
You can't see or feel her but her memories are not gone

I'll remember the good times we had over the years
I'll remember the joy, I'll remember the tears

I'll never forget her although her I can't see
But she's in heaven now and she's watching over me

Jordan Essenburg

Stalker

Is he coming? Yes, I see him
Should I run or be still?
Tell me Lord, what should I do
before I'm killed in front of you
Is he coming? Yes, I see him
I can also feel him
in my gut, its churning fear
how long has he been near?
I want to run, you know it's so
I have only seconds left you know
Is he coming? Yes I see him
I can't scream, my tongue is thick
I am so afraid, I hope it's quick
How'd this happen, can't someone help me?
It's over now, he'll let me be
No more running or standing still
I'm buried now up on the hill

Carol L. Daniels

Mesa

Saguaros, tall and branching
Silhouetted against a draping red sky
Standing as nature's exclamation point
Sprinkled on the desert, barren and dry.
Palm and olive trees
Posing on tiptoe as if in a trance
Perfuming the air with sweet sensation
Projecting their arms in wild romance.
Celebrated mountains on moon-blanched sand
Curving high and low as if heaving a sigh
Crowned with a creamy spray of mist
Crouched under the star-webbed sky.

Amy Welch

Silence So Loud

When will it end — this silence
Silence — so loud in my life
When did I start to notice
Nothingness
Nothing but strife
Was it when one so important
Was never again to be heard
Never again to embrace me
The reason—
Not even a word
Will I again be so willing
To freely my heart give away
Trusting completely - - all caution gone
In spite of the warnings my way
When will I learn in this world so unkind
That others can selfishly leave
A love that is true — for somebody new
Not caring how that one will grieve
When will it end - - this silence
Silence so loud - - in my life

Adele B. Arnold

Facade?

A girl...
Sits by a window and watches people walk by.
A girl...
Walks to the store and says, "hi" to people who walk by.
Does this mean that she is happy?
Does this mean that with her bright glowing face and
that beautiful smile that peaks out every once in a while
that she is happy?
Is it a cover up or is it facade?
Yet she is being blamed for that smile and for her hellos.
A girl...
Sits by the window and wonders are those really my
friends and why aren't they with her sharing her smiles,
or is it only a facade?
Yet in a distance she hears a small voice,
"Mommy I love you!"
A girl...
Sits by a window and whispers I love you to
and realizes, that none of her is half-true.

Caresse T. Baxter

With Skip By My Side

I wake up each morning next to my man
Skip is the best, I'm his biggest fan
We've raised many Children
Our life's been fulfilling
Now it's just two of us, it's really thrilling
Two people in love, almost 30 years
We've been through some hardship anguish and tears
In spite of it all, we've remained tried and true
Respect and dedication - two words helped us through
Skip, you're my husband, my lover my friend
I always will love you until my life's end
For nowhere on earth could I find any better
Then the man that I married - two birds of a feather
I want you to know dear
I'm filled with great pride
I will always feel safe, long as
Skips by my side
I love you very much!

Joey Roth

Christ In Christmas

Christmas is a beautiful time,
Sleighbells ringing, people singing
And to listen doesn't cost a dime.

Christmas is wonderful,
Hearing Santa's "ho, ho, ho"
Is this what Christmas is really about?
The answer must be, "NO"!

It's about a small child, born in a stable,
A manger as a place to lie.
Little did this child know,
That He was born to die.

Baby Jesus was His name,
God's one and only son.
He died on a cross for our sins.
And yet this wouldn't be the end.

Three days later risen from the dead,
He told His followers He'll be back again.
So Christ is Christmas; Christmas is Christ.
Any other belief would not suffice!

Jason Vititoe

Music From God

With the rhythm of the breeze
slowly drifting you away,
You can faintly hear the ancient
and enchanted melody in the air.
The water cascades among the rocks
at the bottom of the falls.
Mist rises from the uncalm surface.
A stream forms from the fall's overflow.
Birds from heaven drink from the
vein of nature and
Let forth the most beautiful harmony
heard by any mortal.
A harmony so pure and sweet
it could crack a heart of stone.
When the elements of nature combine,
they perform MUSIC FROM GOD.

Jason Durant

A Simple Dream

Flowers growing up a vine,
Small sweet dandelions
Rose buds kissed with morning dew,
Purples, pinks and yellows too.

Children of the waters edge
Come and sit on her grassy ledge
And at night dance under the silver moon
And swim in a sea of mysterious blue

And when you look to the sky's to see the
Stars, know that heaven can't be far

And when the morning has come
Sing and dance and be as one.

Carrie Frances Watkins

An Ode To Woe

For every Dragon I ever slew,
Six others puffed up I never knew.
From dawn to dusk, I bathed in gore
but Alas! There they lumbered, still one more!

Midst the hissing, midst the steam
my flailing sword slit their seam.

And now if you think this Saga over, Dear Friend,
O! No! O! No! Here THEY come —
No End! No End!

Irving Eidenberg

They Go Away

They come in droves
Smiling, laughing, shouting
Calling you to them
Asking your opinion
Your feelings and thoughts
They pull you in and lock all others out
You are their special someone
Different yet same
Tighter and tighter they hold
Keeping you safe and sure.

Then, as the firelight on the beach
Grows fainter and dimmer
They go - One by one they disappear
As if devoured by some wandering beast
Leaving only the slightest hint that they ever existed
Leaving only crumpled and torn pieces of paper
Bearing letters and numbers
Names and promises
Fluttering over your naked feet
And sticking softly to your tears.

Julie Newcombe

The Rainforest

Birds start chirping
Snakes start rattling
The soft breeze is moving my trees
Looking down at the earth
For it is morning, things are awakening
The wind feels good, it tickles my leaves
And makes me laugh
My laugh rings throughout the valley
Birds stop chirping
Snakes stop rattling
Everything is still
For it is night.

Brad Clipp

Snow Geese

Winter is everywhere in the cold
Snowflakes have fallen through the day
The sky is leaden grey, heavy with snow.
The mountain, a ghostly shadow through the storm.
And island raises its head out of the mist.

Suddenly, from out of the nothingness,
Comes the eerie call of the snow geese.
The leader circles round and round searching,
searching——
Finally he calls and the geese plummet and glide
To the ice-covered camouflaged lake.
They settle into the whiteness and cold
Their goose mutterings and murmurings continue
through the night.

The fog lifts as dawn breaks
Snow sparkles when the sleepy sun awakens.
The leader rises, circles, honks for take-off
Suddenly the sky is filled with snow-white wings
Fluttering, rising, circling, lifting to the Heavens
Once again their northward course is set.

Allene S. Hamilton

Turn Off Time

Turn off time. You're a false illusion
That drives the world into confusion.
Measured in hours is the childish prattle,
Marked in minutes the voiceless rattle.
The clock dictates without conclusion.
Turn off time.

Joan Krieger

Cherish Your Mama

She's the Original, the one who gave birth to you,
so cherish your mama, if no one else do.

She'll love you, she'll care for you she'll never
let you down, so cherish your mama while she's still around.

I say this to you coming from my heart, to cherish
your mama right from the start.

She may be right she may be wrong, just think god
that she's here and still going strong...
because I learned the hard way my mama is
DEAD AND... GONE.

Denise M. Woodland

Remembered River Waters

The cool, refreshing spring waters of the head water
So cold, so fresh, and sweet to the taste
The waters of this beautiful old river
The refreshing wetness of the cool, clear water.
The old swimming hole, so deep it was green.
Tubing the winding river, it seemed endless.
Times remembered of the beautiful waters on that old river bank.

Fishing the waters from the soft green mossy banks
The fish jumped from the waters.
The frogs jump from their perch on the slimy, green rocks.
The turtles are covered with the green slime of the river banks.
Times remembered of the beautiful waters on that old river bank.

Such a shame to have in a few short years
Water that is not fit to drink.
Speed boats with taxes to clean up pollution,
Power plants contributing to the noise and water pollution.
Fish are jumping from the waters to commit suicide against trees.
Instead of green moss that once grew to feed the animals,
Green slim slithers down the polluted waters.
Times remembered of the beautiful waters on that old river bank.

Charles Sledge

I Never Wrote A Poem Before

I never wrote a poem before, in fact I did not ever.
So, excuse me while I give some thought
To this here new endeavor.
I'm told it ought to rhyme,
They say that way is better.
I was also told it did not have to.
See what I mean?
It's important to have something to write about.
This is very necessary.
So once again, please forgive me
While I give this thought some query.
I think I'll write about love,
Yes, that's a very good subject.
It's something we all should have for
Some one, some thing or other.
If you have a try at love,
You'll learn it's high above
The other ways of living life.
You'll find it's grand, you'll find it rife
With what it's all about. Try it. You'll like it.

Benjamin Laba

Lost Hope

They sat there en masse, callously —
Some with delusions, some near mania.
They sat there, with faces of stone,
Empty spaces where eyes should have been
They sat there - reason is gone
Humanity is lost, life is fiction
They sat there, shadows pass by but no one cares
Voices are there, but no one hears
The stones move, and the empty spaces fill with tears.

Ethel Smith

To Meet A Wish

This Christmas I thought that I would be with you,
So I closed my eyes and wished it true.

The visions and thoughts that raced through my mind,
Were like scenes from a movie suspended in time.

There were flowers, and birds, and a sky clear bright blue.
And right in the middle, was my image of you.

The sun shown down soft over the smile on your face,
And I knew in my heart you belonged to this place.

The place where there's happiness, laughter and love.
Where the power of glory is felt from above.

This place that I speak of, lies deep in my heart,
And you will always be there; end, middle, or start.

So, If you happen to need me, just close your eyes.
I will meet you there, beneath the cool clear blue sky.

Heather H. Senn

Path Of The Courier

Whilst lions fight
so lambs may right
and make straight the path of the Courier.
Martyrs know that when the Nile flows
so will the corpses to lake Victoria.

Allegiances sworn to a crown without thorns
a land governed from afar.
Where the love of God goes
only the Courier knows
when traveling through county Armagh.

Prayer is too late
to religions of hate
the olive branch is covered with oil
Even Hercules would choke
under the Couriers yolk
when plowing death under Iraqian soil.

Remember my son when all's said and done
darkness is the road of the warrior.
Dying amblers ignite deep in the night
to make straight the path of the Courier.

John P. Toner

The World

The world is changing every new day.
So many people are getting blown away.
It isn't save... to walk late outside at night.
If you're not paying attention,
and not looking behind you,
someone might come, and give you a fright.
Then your whole life is flashing
right before your eyes,
and in a split second... you come back to life,
thinking your alright, and praying to God for forgiveness.
And what about them people,
who are cold out there at night?,
laying in an alley fighting for there life!
They're asking for our help.
All together we could do something.
But if you turn your back, and walk away,
and say "don't worry," "It's not our problem,"
you can forget about saving our world,
and other people in need.
But the only thing your not saving is yourself!!

Casey Stevens

"MindWeaving"

The mind weaves webs of memories.
So many soft, silken threads,
enveloping the soul.

Soft, silken threads caressing and creating
confusion and disillusion with present
day and time.

Discontent stirs a tranquil sea.
A menacing whirlpool threatening to
vaporize traces of sanity.

Lightening bolts of rage, constant and steady,
rip and tear asunder the fragile humanity
which remains.

As the woven webs of memories wishfully
weave a soft cocoon of pain and the
mind continues weaving.

Danielle R. Marshall

A Diamond

As a diamond in a field of stones,
So rare my heart's delight,
'Tis not with brilliance that she shines,
But with soft and gentler light.

Amid the clamoring din of voices
Demanding to be heard,
But soft she speaks, and quietly,
No stridance in her word.

I am her hero, she is my world,
I am her shining knight,
Though tarnished is this suit of armor,
And suspect this swords might,

I fear I am not worthy of
This gem that doth shine so,
For I receive so much and give so little,
And I wonder, does she know,

That without her I am less than whole,
She gives meaning to my life,
This diamond in a field of stones,
So rare a friend, my love, my wife.

John O. Dial

Untitled

The old man will never change
So set in his smoke filled alcoholic ways
He can never say what his heart wants him to say
Oh, he can be jovial, a few shots see to that
In his mind he ponders something, he begins to laugh
He laughs at everyone else's world
Keeps him from looking into his own
Keeps him from looking, to see himself, alone
He rambles on, about memories past
About how he could hit so hard with hands so fast
He babbles about days in the Marine Corps
Repeating himself so often, you can't listen anymore
He goes on, about women, all his past loves
He takes a break for a beer, another cigarette to puff
Watching him, a tear comes to the eye
Watching him you begin to realize
The old man's just passing time before he dies.

David Olcott

Crucifixion And Resurrection

Jesus hung on that cruel cross that day
So that you and I might have new life.
He suffered agony and shame we say
To carry us thru all our trials and strife.

As he lingered there, He cried, "Oh Father,
Forgive them for they know not what they do."
The wicked crowd didn't seem to bother
That His blood was shed and life was through.

But "Glory to God" for that happy day,
He told us He would rise again.
And our debt He would pay
That we could go where they'll be no pain.

So now you know why we have new life
And how He became our precious Saviour;
So we could experience no more strife
And the "tree of life" is in our favour.

Harry E. Wenger

Your Destiny

As minutes turn into hours,
So the closing of another day comes to pass.
The closing of one dream,
And the opening of another.
Anxiously awaiting for some things,
Yet dreading the moment for others.
Trying to build onto your dreams,
But your tomorrows are so uncertain.
Now the day is gone,
In what seemed like a second.
And you then realize that nothing was done.
So you move on in life just like the wind.
However you follow,
Depends on where it leads.
Wherever it takes you,
Is where you are destined to be.

Angelina Gutierrez

Dear Marilyn

Oh Marilyn, Dear Marilyn,
So young, so fair, so kind
You will always be in my heart, and on my mind.

Why did God take you so young from here?
God must have had good reasons to join
Him up there!

You were a daughter, sister, grandchild
niece, wife and mother,
All wrapped up in one,
and you were truly loved
by each and everyone.

Family was important to you and you told me why,
You spoke, I listened, and then we both began to cry.

I made you a promise, I hope I can do,
And that is to bring our families together
to have your wish come true.

You loved life and lived it to your fullest,
You deserved nothing but the best.

I hope you can hear me Dear Marilyn,
May you lay in peace and rest.

Eileen S. Altneu

Dolls

Dolls are like statues or just pretty toys,
Some made for girls, some made for boys.
Each made in the likeness of a child
With a pensive face or winning smile.

With toddler dolls, each mother seas within their face
A fond remembrance, a soft embrace of her own child;
Precious moments and she smiles.

The teens, more graceful and petite,
Porcelain limbs molded slim and sleek.
Each dressed in accordance to the era born,
A picturesque scene by the clothing worn.

Placed in a coveted collection, stands
Dolls of every generation and of different lands
Each representing a time or place,
And postured there in absolute grace.

Conveying visual comfort; a feeling of peace
And within one's being, pleasant relief.
Treasured beauty depicting present and past;
An appreciative gift of quiet company that lasts.

Elva B. D'Antoni

God's Way

God always give some men a way out, when they pray
Some men will not accept help unless it comes from himself
That is why they sometime kill themselves
When they feel they are not enough.

When we hate ourselves, we will do an evil thing
Lord help the poor unbelieving man
Who will not accept anything
Anything that will not come by his sweat.

Lord help the man that is put to the test
That life hands out to every man
For if some men will hear God's word
Other men might take notice

That God helped some men, he might also help other men
The leaders of this world
Without God their tender mercy is evil.

Flossie Lambert Crossley

Tears From My Heart

You were here but now you're gone
Some ow I'll learn to get along

I think of you each and every day
Hoping these feelings of missing you will go away

Your hair, your smile, your personality too
These are the things I miss about you

You nurtured, you cuddled, you made me grow
With you my confidence was high, but now low

I can't make you love me, that's a sad fact of life
But it tears me apart to not be able to call you my wife

What would I do different, if I had it all to do over again
I loved you with all my heart, and was faithful to the end

My heart cries out in agony in missing you to death
If I could have what we had years ago I'd give up my last breath

Craig William Harris

Do They Know

Some people must know how to pray
Some people must live right
Because some people can come home after a hard day,
and have someone to love that night.

But do they know how lonely it is,
to drive deep into the night.
And to know there's no fire at home,
to show them the way, with its warm light?

Do they know how it feels,
to watch a couple holding hands.
And to feel that empty hole inside,
and know here alone I stand?

Do they know what it's like,
To live life alone.
To never have held, or touched, or loved,
and to hate it so much, it hurts to the bone?

I know all these things, these things they don't.
And it scars my heart so much,
that I don't even know if I could feel,
the warmth of a loved ones touch.

Jared Hyatt

Someone Love

I never thought I'd have someone to love,
Someone to trust and someone to care for.
Every night I'd look at the stars above,
And hope and wish—but I couldn't do more.

You came into my life without warning.
We have a friendship—nothing can compare.
I think about you from night to morning,
We know we have something special to share.

You open my eyes to new things to see.
With you around, I couldn't ask for more,
A lonely person I could never be.
For me, you have opened a whole new door.

Now I don't wish on the bright stars above,
Because I know I have someone to love.

Holly Cowell

A Storm Warning

The sounds of nature
sometimes mimic the raging
turmoil within a human mind.
One has heard it many times.
The rushing forward to somewhere, as to an opened door.
A need to go through,
turned back as before.
Indecision!
Rushing, rushing!
Where the destination!
So much frustration!
Then, as the way of human emotion, the wind lessens,
A hopeless situation is gone as before.

Dorothy D. Longfoot

Healing Of The Soul

Walking through the woods, my soul is wrapped in silence
Stress flows and exits from my limbs
Peace and serenity take over renewing my body
Warm breezes kiss and embrace my skin
Green moss cushions and softens the path on which I trod
A lazy crow circles above, a playful squirrel
scatters oak leaves, burying an acorn for future use
Rejuvenated and energized by no one other than Mother Nature,
Now I can face another day!

Joan S. Parker

Working Together

When two people meet and work together a lot
Sometimes they get close, sometimes they do not.
It really makes a difference on how things will go
Towards accomplishing great things or doing so so.

Like a well greased machine much work can be done
When two minds are open and function like one.
The thoughts are so clear and the mind is so free
That problems are solved and the answers are easy to see.

With the right working friend you achieve so much merit
And the friends only want to give each other credit.
The best part of working is sharing the task,
No matter how long a hard job will last.

A partner who works closely with you
Can inspire your thinking in the things that you do.
And when it is time to make a decision
You can count on your friend to understand in your vision.

If you're lucky enough to work with someone
Whose work you believe is second to none
Don't take it for granted and cherish the time
Most likely you'll find it happens once in a life time.

Bill Schmitt

The Fallen Leaf

The leaf resisted; then tumbled down
Soon found its place upon the ground
Then snow covered—all around

Thus started the natural process of decay
The never-ceasing cycle of Life's way

A newly-formed seed had fallen too
An essential part of Nature's brew
Nurtured by the leaf, it steadily grew

Slowly a tree began to grow
From the leaf's decay, its strength would flow

Molded, and tempered, by years of grief
In God's grand scheme, 'tis my belief
There is even a use for the fallen leaf

Through time, and warmth, from the gentle Sun
The leaf, and the Earth, will become as one.

Gerald Ladd Hersh

My Underwater World

The coolness is all around me
Soothing,
Massaging,
Gently smoothing away all cares of the outside world.
Here I am free-
I am myself, restrained by nothing
Free to do anything I will
Within the watery bounds.
I may even scream,
No one will hear
In my world under the surface.
The sounds silently dissolve from my lips
Even as they come out.
I may move at the speed of my innermost desire-
Slow, fast
It matters not, for I am in complete control
Here in my underwater world.

Grace Swink

Afrika

The Island of "Goree" bears yours marks
Soweto bleeds, Mississippi burns
"Yalta" devours my people
Haiti and Rwanda are in fire
The Reggae sings its tune
Why, please could you tell me why,
Afrika, they kill and bury your children?
The dream can never come true
Death has several faces,
Coup d'etat, drugs, starvation, politics and power.
Why, could you tell me why,
Afrika, they kill and bury your children?
Life is unbearable
For culture, gold, diamond, ivory,
Mineral oil, your land and your children
They slash your throat
Without cause, and bend your head
No right, no dream, no hope, no future
Why, could you tell me why,
Afrika, they kill and bury your children?

Bondima H. Tombwe

The Bible

Fountain of wisdom in all its glory,
Speaks from Genesis to Revelation.
To rule our heart and fill our memory
With history of civilization.

Sixty-six books within its rich pages,
The Testaments of the New and the Old.
God reaching for man, down thru the ages,
Our soul to forgive, to love, and remold.

The Old tells of sin, of law, and judgement,
Of wise Prophets and the right ways to live.
The New implores we must ne'r be content,
Till sin we've confessed and men we forgive.

If life Eternal we choose for our goal,
'Tis Christ, not the world, that must have our Soul.

Edythe G. Ferguson

Stewardship

We are all stewards of this land
Spoken of in song as, "America the Beautiful
And Home of the Brave."
A land with many plants, birds and animals we need to save.

As stewards do we take our office seriously,
Keeping clean air, pure water and planting another tree?

Looking me straight in the eye in a mirror, can I say
"Because of you, America has become a better place today?

If not, the question is why?
Will I mess things up until the day I die?

Have I added litter or trampled the desert bare
Or added pollution to water and the air?

Is this land better than when I came
Or did I treat it with shame?

Did I take off all I could?
Did I take more than I should?

Each of us should ask at the closing of every day
Is America a better place because of how I work and play?

Hamilton Teichert

How Great Is Our God

I walked in the forest at daybreak and watched the
sprinkles of sunlight dancing on the diamonds of dew.
The air was soft and quite and the sun was slowly
peeking over the horizon like a sleepy child just waking.
Now and then a bright shaft of light broke through
the foliage like a golden stairway to heaven.
The breeze gently stirred the fallen leaves as
small animals scurried about.

As I beheld the wonders of nature spread out around
me my mind turned to the one who made them.
How wonderful is our God. No mind can reach to the
height and depth and breadth of His wonderful work.

Frances Long

"Have You Ever"

Have you ever watched the leaves
Sprout out overnight on spring trees?
Ever smell the scent of the rain
And freshly plowed ground that yields no pain?

Ever watch a rose slowly bloom?
Shine the light on a year old coon?
Ever hear bass, strike the water?
Gets you so excited, that you want to holler!

Ever listen to the ocean waves?
Explore like pirates in a make believe cave?
And listen to the sea gulls, fuss back and forth?
Makes you wonder if they keep a course.

Ever see a blue bird in the yard?
Watch a kitten with a piece of string, they're such a card!
Ever watch little puppies crying, for their mother,
And having trouble staying close to one another?

Don Sebren

Wild Horse

Beautiful, handsome, eyes so bright,
Standing powerfully against the night.
He cannot be tamed, he's running free,
Never by you, never by me.
Through fields of flowers, racing in flight,
In thunder and lightning, day and night.
He's wild in his soul he lives for the day.
May his beauty never fade away.
And may God in his heaven see what I see,
And never take this creature away from me.

Julie Partin

Her Promise

There she stood on nature's sand
Staring at the tranquil sea
Her eyes fixed at heaven's point on the horizon
Where her fairy tale had been inspired
Years had passed, a countless number of tears had been shed
Yet, the vision remained unscathed
As if a child, she escaped into moonlit reveries
Of evenings spent in the embrace of his arms.
The waves crashing against the sand serve to disturb her silence
As she awakens to the reality she has avoided
And created
Was he seated on a parallel beach
Aspiring for her
In the same fashion, with the same fervor
Enduring the same pain
Or, perhaps, was he as she had watched him
On another beach
Content in the embrace of his beloved
And had her point on the horizon, indeed,
Disappeared.

Dina L. Siracusa

Stand High Above

Mountains stand high above, alone they seem to be....
Stately portraying the beauty of:
for all the world to see.....

But I, am not a mountain - For I am just a tree,
Among those thousands of uneventful things - again,
I'll lose my leaves....

The cold, it rushes through my veins, it leaves a hidden scar.
Today marks the seasons change,
Tells us who we are.....

A tree am I, withstanding all - storms that passed me by,
forever reaching - extending out into the endless sky....

My seasons passed have been as dim, images
have come and gone - late in the fall,
the light does shine, for each and every dawn.....

Throughout the winters coldest winds, hold the warmest
thoughts. Spring has Sprung - leaves reflect,
those lessons never taught.....

To stand as high as a mountain - portray the beauty of:
To give the gift of shade to those,
with this a sheltering love......

George F. Heller Jr.

"Sweet Child"

Sweet Child you are, Sweet Child do
stay Gods given you all that's gold!
Hold-on-to it, keep all that's you-don't
loose sight (inside) hold tight! Heart an
soul, pure innocence, laughter filled with
all the warmth, twinkles that eight the
eye's "Like Magic" Sweet Child "No Magic"
you see can make our hurt ever go a
way! It's love pure as gold that teaches
us to forgive and in time the
hurt fades away, Sweet Child you
are, God's given you all! You are
Sweet Child, you are...

Cota Y. Lissu

Still Lean'n On You, Lord

As the years pass by in this pain wretched body
Still lean'n on You, Lord

Not worrying or wondering "why" for this thorn
Just lean'n on You, Lord

For in Your Word all thru the Book You demand trust
in our storms

So, I'll keep Lean'n on You, Lord
It's as simple as that!

Trials and suffering bring me into beautiful valleys
Still lean'n on You, Lord

Where the most beautiful lessons are learned
Always lean'n on You, Lord

Drawing me closer to You, Lord, giving me grace to endure

So, I'll keep lean'n on You, Lord
It's as simple as that!

Barbara J. Summers

"A Little Angel From Heaven"

He's just a little angel sent to us from Heaven above.
Such a beautiful bundle of joy for us to cherish and love.
With little small hand and little small feet,
A little pug nose that looks so cute and neat.
Perfect little eyes and a tiny rosebud mouth. I can't believe he's not just asleep. He's only a few days old and he passed away.
But I know he's in a better place, as I was asleep late on the same day. I was awoke by a very bright light and my little boy was before my eyes. He was being held in the Master's arms, very close and very warm.
Jesus looked at me and smiled. I'm sorry that I caused you pain, but I hope you understand. He's one of my special little angels, I need for my special plan.
And one day you'll hold him in your arms again. As I woke up a peace stole over me and then I knew it wasn't a dream but reality.

Charlotte Fanguy

Born The Same Time

We were born the same time but on the wrong side of town.
Sue she had the best but I wore the hand me downs.
But God knows I loved her and I always will.
We tried so hard but Lord knows we failed.
Sue's streets were different not like mine.
Her's seemed to glitter, they had a shine.
You could stroll down her street but not walk on mine we were born the same time, but on the wrong side of town.
Mama used to tell me and my friends did too.
Said Don we love you and God knows we love Sue
But you're two different people in a world so far apart
I see nothing but destruction and two broken hearts
Born the same time but on the wrong side of town.
Some day in the big land uncorrupted by man
We'll stroll together side my side.
Then I can walk on her street and she can walk on mine
Then we'll both be together in the same town.

Donald Deal

Winter

You see no green on the ground,
Summer animals make not a sound.

Out with the warm and in with the cold,
I've never seen whiteness so bold.

Children slip and slide on the ice,
People gather together, isn't that nice?

Boats and water skis are not out,
Now snowmobiles run their route.

I don't like this winter dread,
When summer comes, I won't look dead!

Amy Barker

Sand Dollar

I see the sparkling sun reflecting its array of sunlight on the waves. I would see the sea gulls gracefully soaring throughout the wind above the mountain peaks. The thing I feel is the wind whipping it's smooth delightful rays of wind at my face. When I take few steps out onto the crunching walkway of sand, I hear the many splashes of the water waves. When I am at this wonderful place, I feel like a sand dollar happily watching the actions of the kids just waiting for someone to pick me up ...... ACTIONS SPEAK LOUDER THAN WORDS........

Cameron M. Sandel

Self-Knowledge

Lines on sidewalks, cracks we unconsciously avoid
Superstitions, the supernatural; things we easily ignore

But cracks in our souls, we bandage with addictions;
For temporary relief, so we don't have to face our afflictions

So traumas and hardships of everyday life, get buried beneath the surface
But soon they end up choking us, making it difficult for us to soar

Drugs of choice, or so they're called, are temporary indeed;
For it is only self-knowledge that can fulfill most of our needs

A friend, a lover; someone with whom you can share
It can make life precious, if indeed you truly care

If you know yourself, your dreams and your thoughts
Then real joy can come to you, for happiness can't be bought

Try to find the good in the things that you see
Because that's where goodness lies, it's in you and in me

If you're looking at the gold and never at the rainbow
If you see homelessness and poverty, yet never lend a hand

If you climb a corporate ladder, and refuse to look back
Then all that is beautiful in life, you will miss
And the feelings that make life worth living, you will lack

Dena Elaine Ciminelli

Untitled

Where, oh God, is thine abode?
Surely there is a better place than Heaven,
For a God so kind, so loving, so benevolent;
On which star in the universe do you live?
Is it eternal spring where you live God?
Do children splash in the waters of life, laugh, play?
Are people kind and courteous in your house;
Does the water of life bring serenity to all?
It is never spring where I live, God.
The sun is black in my home, dark as night;
Civility was replaced by rage, and the peace
Shattered by the rat ta tat,tat,tat of the AK.
Why, God, did you let your son die?
Surely not for Chicago, New York, or Saint Antonio,
The reason had to be noble for you are a just God.
The God of love could not live in America.
So tell me, God, upon which star is thine abode?
I will lie on my back and search the heavens
To locate the region of the universe where you live,
And find a moment to escape the hell in which I live.

Ernest Bedsole

Never Forget

Chilling willow trees hang high above me. Swaying branches threatening to end my life in a single slash. I guess I should be intimidated but I eagerly await my destiny.

True to my word I become the prodigy that is expected. Never betraying what's forced to mine. Never becoming what's truly realistic. Always surrendering my thoughts to them.

I am drowning in my weaknesses. My tears take on a mind of their own. The realization of living a pointless life has once again brought depression to cloud my life.

You're susceptible to the wounds just as I. Shame washes over us like salt. Constantly inflaming our hearts until we fade away into nothing.

Devin Flynn

Wizardry

The Princess, all gossamer clothed,
sweeps through enchanted forest, toward the Toad.
A Kiss! And now a Prince! And how they danced,
where sprites and gnomes and fairies pranced!
Champagne for breakfast and endless days
to learn each other's secret ways.
But into every kingdom comes
a specter — and as with cadenced drums,
it fills the hallowed palace walls — and waits.
And in the noonday sun he sits, to warm himself by garden gates.
Facade still there: the golden curls
still turn the heads of younger girls.
But only She can see beneath
the handsome face, the perfect teeth.
And she knows the soul within
still yearns for marsh and wild heath.
Yet in the tower bed she lies...
alone...while he's out catching flies.

Denise Kay

A Tiger In The Yard

A picture painted from the center of my being
Symbolized fear, pain, anger, and defeat.
A slow destruction of a beautiful child.
The Middle-America house looks secure,
But beware the Tiger crouches near.

A troubled child, sits by an empty window
is stamped upon, trod upon, scratched and marred.
She smells the Tiger's hot decaying breath.
She knows of its trickery.
The Tiger lurks near, can anyone hear?

A yellow tricycle and red wagon litter the yard.
There, behind the wagon, the Tiger stalks.
No one sees the Tiger,
No one knows what dark secrets are kept within.
No one cares.

Barbara J. Weber

Precious Metals

Take this heart:
Take this bruised, aching heart come as my knight
In armor of silver (not gold, never gold,)
And hack down the brambles
scratching me, chaining me,
Reach your hand into
the writhing, sickly mass, and draw out my heart,
Rusted and tarnishes with disuse;
But do not lack away, do not give me up to
seek a heart of shining gold (not gold, never gold,)
Just draw your hand across the twisted metal
And you will see—you will see.
The silver shines out: Pure, simple,
So unlike gold: cruel, false, glittering gold,
Take this cold, tarnished heart:
Make it shine, make it glow,
And we will ride into the moon
set (not gold, never gold,)
It will be worth it. I promise.
For nothing is more precious than silver.

Claire Shinkman

My Wonderful Friend

I once had a friend, I cultivated with tender care:
Taking care not to over water.
Watering them with morning dew.
Now, I and have one, I have two.

God took my two friends, multiplied them by four.
I now have eight friends, I'm looking for a dozen more.
To add to my beautiful bounty store.

My first friend, I don't love any less,
Although I am blessed,
I still need more
Many years have come and gone
When I first had a friend.
I now have a few thousand,
yet, not one to spare.

I stir water when needed
I have never pulled a tare
My garden, grows flowers and flowers.

Carrie Franklin

Mother's Nature

Mother of this little girl, seventh child, daughter;
Teacher, giver of wings, singer of songs sprung from deep within her soul
that were there long ago.

You, yourself, a daughter; keeper of a dream.
(A quiet whisper kept within your heart)
Seeking words and melody to realize a song....
A rhapsody of love that was played within gardens and on rivers
By us, the instruments you crafted carefully.

And now, comes forth another - we've known her presence since.
We learned about her in between the lines of lullabies...
A guardian angel - ever watchful - teacher, giver of roots.
Known well to those who called her Bird,
Her flight and song brought home to us
The courage and the strength of spiritual release.

So now I stand before you as a witness for my brothers and my sisters -
Arthur Aksel, Lois Eleanore, Melvin Prentiss, Martin George,
Margaret Elizabeth, Priscilla Ann, Ingrid Yvonne, and Mark Hall —
And watch our father, still your lover, gently give you to your mother
Mother Earth, Mother Bird, Mother Ida May —
Understanding as we give you unto her, so we take her unto us.

Ingrid Y. Burnett

Dead Man's Float

Hypocritical remarks rip us to shreds
Tearing self-confidence into minute fragments.
Nonchalant piranhas feed on such algae,
And multiply the infinite grapevines of lies,
Selfishly to enhance their own food chain to survival.

Sticking your fingers into their dark and independent world
Wondering how quickly these man-eaters
Jump to the chance of biting,
Biting,
And chewing you out;
When they are just as blind to their own
Whereabouts as you are of yours.

The guppy imprisoned inside the chamber
of concern
Glubs out the wart of all worries
Asking itself what will finally destroy
The ignorance of this world?

An individual candlelit dinner consisting of herbs and seeds?
Or
The vicious stew of collected plaques?

Diane Albano

"Wake Up"

If you want to get a rise
Tell someone they have exercise
So what I have to lose my gut
and of course I have to firm up my butt
I have to get an outfit off the rack
And I have to make sure it fits in my crack
Wake up do what's best for you
Don't let them talk you into what's bad to do
For a weekly fee you can bet
This fee will really make you sweat
Wake up you know what is best
and you will take it to the test
You self esteem how you feel about yourself
Is the important thing not to be put on a shelf
Tall or short thin or fat
You know where it's at
I like what I am when I look in the mirror
Because I am loved by someone dear.

Christine M. Hofmeister

Christmas Is Sharing

Thank our Lord, who seeks to find us
Thank Him, too, for special joys that binds us.
We should keep ourselves for living
Reasons for our joyful giving
Christmas should be for all our days
Not just December that fade away
It opens heart with loves great key
Giving our love to Him, for all eternity
These words are sent with heart felt meaning
To hope and share, does glorify
His Heavens gleaming
The secret for doing our best
is in keeping Christmas in our hearts
all year through.

Billye M. Riler

Someone Listen Please

Impotent rage pulsed through the little boy's hands
That beat his pain out against the bedstead
Tears splashed unheeded down soiled underclothes

Dark time dragged slowly by for a child in fear
Sleep was place where someone found you
Waking was a birthing nightmare world
Living became a test of survival

Stealthy footsteps would creep down the hall
While the child huddled under cover
Shadows filtered into his sad room as the other children slept
Tight held whimpers echoed off the uncaring walls

I was and still am that little boy that cried
There were none who listened or cared
Many knew but chose to be silent
I am speaking out for the child inside of me

Billy Moore Hale

Untitled

Dream. This is what I do when life treats me unfair.
So when I am dreaming, of these things I am not aware.
As I see life through open eyes,
this little voice inside my head tells my spirit to rise.
When I sit and dream in peace,
my thoughts of living never cease.
As lively thoughts fill my head,
I can't help wondering what it's like to be dead.
Dreaming I'm a bird I can fly.
And while dreaming you see I am free to cry.
So I'll just sit here with my dreams.
Because they hold my hopes, thoughts, and my schemes.

Amber Delight Dauson

The Blue Birds Of Paradise

Blue birds of paradise is the bluest of all birds
- that exist in heaven -
Blue birds of paradise is the bluest birds
- swimming across the bluest of all waters -
Blue birds of paradise are the biggest birds with
- enchanting wings -
Blue birds of paradise have a say:
"He who picks a feather off thee shall become drunk"
"He who crumble thy leaves under the blue birds
- of paradise will produce smoke -

"He who catches thee shall become greedy"
- Blue birds of paradise -

James Taylor

Friendships

Friendships are like flowering things
That grow throughout the year,
They are nourished by thoughtful deeds
Memories and tears.

Friendships may be fragile at first,
But soon they may be strong,
Because they're like a little seed
Which grows all year long.

Friendships are made by trying a little harder,
We also need to be a little meeker and kinder,
Then we can be like the little seeds that grow
Into beautiful flowers.

Dilly Hockenberry

The Shying Time

When we first meet,
that is the shying time,
afraid of our words, our eyes,
we say what we don't care to speak about,
we look at anything else but each others eyes,
we can not let our hearts go so quickly,
that is not the way,
we want too though,
say what we feel,
lose ourselves in each other's eyes,
we are so afraid,
do I say the words?
I want too, so badly but...
I'm so scared,
it is what we all think at the shying time,
we are like prisoners,
some say there is a time and place for everything,
I believe that time is at the shying time.

Eric Damschroder

The Fritillary

What Master Hand but One could paint thee thus,
That on thy wings the crimson with the blues
Doth blend with black in varicolored hues,
And frees thy image from any canvas.

No earthly thing is near so glorious,
Thou Spark of Life adorned with rainbow wings,
When sunbeams illumine thy fluttering —
And I am stirred in all that's sensuous.

Thy cut, no filigree of man comes near;
Nor will it ever equal or surpass
Thy exquisite form which doth appear
To me a mark of some celestial class;
Here for a moment, then to disappear —
Thy beauty, all transformed to dust, alas!

Eugene W. Dunlap

Thoughts On A Once Before Splendid Life...

I used to be a working person
that paid bills and kept house,
Now I can't see my way. I used to
be someone that had a future-
Now that all seems so far away...
The past few years have brought
garbage cans a few pennies and used clothes-
All the family, house, and car dreams
are like dead roses-just old.

I used to be in love...
in love with the finer things
women, sex, and money funny
how things change. Now a ride
on the subway for free is my
car...

A shelter is my home-
Another homeless man is my family
And yet I still feel so alone.

Miko Smith

A Chore No More

You said that it would be a chore
That seemed to open up a door
A daughter's heart to her mothers
Is a path traveled like no others
Not like an aunt, and uncle or brothers
Sometimes it seems to be kept under covers
Only to unblanket when you really need it
But that's how it's supposed to be isn't it?
Not to abuse but to nurture
Doesn't that paint a pretty picture?
You are my mother and I couldn't be prouder
Do you want me to yell that a little louder?
You are always in my heart of hearts
No matter where our paths may part
Together we will end up in the end
You are more than my mother
You are my very best friend!

Charmaine Fluss

Born With A Smile

The baby boy was born with a smile,
That smile awakened her barren heart
To her his tiny face was total joy
Motherhood could have no better start.

Sometimes he was ill and tired,
But the smile was still in place
She held him and rocked him aware childhood
would disappear and time would win the race.

The little boy games brought triumphs
some fears and tears, ups and downs,
But always he was the smiling child
who was prince of all the clowns.

When the little boy days were finally past,
He set out for what life would bring
Left sealed forever in her heart was his smile,
a smile that could never take wing.

Delores Fredricks

Eternal Bloom

There is a joy in loving
That surpasses feeling loved
One of life's sweet mysteries
That remains unsolved -

To pour into another's cup
And see his spirit grow
Is a form of ecstasy
The lover comes to know -

To hear the song of love he sang
Simple thought it be
Sung back by his beloved
He hears a rhapsody -

Feeling loved is just the bud
It's loving that's the flower
It's the breath of God He breathed in man
In it's finest hour.

June P. Bergeron

Confidence

The knowledge and assurance of knowing
That you can take control of
The situation even when the situation has control of you.

The reason why you go on
Through the unexplored terrain to see
The other side - Confidence.

The how and why things happen because of
The way you handle each difficulty,
Then either give up, or Conquer!

The ability to stare the devil right in
The eye and say,
To hell with you!

The explanation of what has happened to you,
The purpose you have dreamed up in your life,
The way things get done—Because of

Confidence! to overcome
Any situation.

Mr. anonymous aka Joseph Bellizzi

Are You There?

I'm told that time will heal the soul
That's broken and alone.
And time will bring a softness
To a heart that's turned to stone.

Who can give me comfort
And show me that they care?
From the loneliness that surrounds me,
At times to much to bear!

Would he calm me, when the lightening cracks,
And thunder echoes the sky?
Could he see the flames of a fire
Set deep within my eyes?

I want so much to give someone
The love I've kept inside.
Release the passion and desire
That's been hidden and denied!

Maybe it's all fantasy
A knight on a horse so white!
I'll dream of love and tenderness
As sleep dries my tears tonight.

Andrea Woodward

The Six Of Us

There are six of us you see, and all are girls really
That's unusual for a family this size, but we weren't trying to win a prize
Three with hair the color of gold, three with hair black as coal
We all have eyes that are blue, and pretty nice looking it is true
No matter what kind of weather, we all got along fine together
The first of us was born in 1928 we're all still here this year of 88
We all seem to be very healthy, even thought we weren't wealthy
We grew up living on a farm, and only had one broken arm
We walked to the corner to catch the bus for school, so we could learn the golden rule
We would jump, run and play, and pick daisies in the pasture on the way
We caught bumble bees in the spring, we were lucky we didn't get a sting
Georgia Lee, Nita Fay and May Belle, were the first of us to spell
Anna Jenell, Mary Ann and Billie June, came along and learned soon
We received our high school diplomas, right in this town of Tuttle, Oklahoma
All of us would load in the pickup on Saturday night, to so see all the bright lights

Anna Jenell Campbell

"Autumn"

When the summer season is over and done
that's when autumn has just begun.
The grass will no longer grow.
The cool winds will soon start to blow.
The flowers, they will hang their heads and sigh
for they all know they must give up and die.
The green in the leaves will also begin to change
to lots of colors so different and strange.
The trees shall stand strong and tall
for their leaves must start to fall.
But there is nothing really to fear
for it will all be back the spring of next year!

Beverly J. Botala

On Tour

I'm playing and singing about the things I do
That's why I'm singing the blues
If you did all that
You'd be singing the blues too
Out here all over the world
I'm telling them about my world
As the blues unfurl
Smoke filled bars, big time ears
People waitin' anticipatin'
Backstage their aim get in the game
On tour paying dues
All the rooms seem the same
While out there seeking fortune and fame
Fortune seems to be slipping away
Along with the go -along
That's why I play and sing the blues
In different hues
While on tour paying dues

Darcy Merritt

Green

There are many things in this world that are green,
Such as: envy, ivy, grass and beans.
There are mountains and hills and plains and sands,
But nothing compares to the gorgeous green lands.
There are geese that fly in V's, and yellow-jacket bees,
But none of them come close to the beautiful green trees.
Green is the earth's signature color, as most people have seen,
For whenever Mother Nature is shown, she's always pictured green.

Beth Blair

Whispers In The Wind

As the night slowly turns to darkness.
The air turns cold and brisk
The crackling of the leaves echoes through my head.
One by one children are called in
One by one lights in neighboring houses go out.
I find myself alone.
Alone in a world of strangers
No one hears my voice, yet I am there.
No one hears my cries.
Yet I am there.
Alone in a world of strangers.
So I continue on this road of life.
Alone

Coralie Amy Stoltzfus

The Stroll

As I took my evening stroll, Up that lonely timber trail
the air was damp and oh so brisk, with every breath came a cloud
of mist. The ground is frozen winters here, fall has passed
the trees are bare. All the critters large and small who
stored their food before the fall, lie tightly snugged within
their dens waiting for old man winter to make amends. A northern
wind cuts between the trees with a howling sound and crackling
leaves. Patches of ice that mar my path, old tire ruts from
a time gone past. But just ahead, my favorite spot an abandoned
field that once grew crops. Now it lays all weeded in. A
rusting plow, and tractor rim. The work it took to clear this land
a farmers sweat and callous hands, to remove the stumps and
clear the trees. To till the soil, to sow His seeds. A vacant
house upon the hill, two hundred yards from a old wind mill,
a weathered barn with creaking doors, where a family worked
and did their chores. A dried up well and old tool shed, a
fenced in plot to mourn their dead. Now it lay like a ghost
for all to see, We're just the Host.

Eugene Costello

Model Supreme

I went to Alaska in my Model Supreme,
The airplane, it flew, like an F 16,
So I was happy, of course, for this was my dream.

It was cold in Alaska, so I decided to get warm,
I took off to the Bahamas, and was met by a storm.
The storm blew and it puffed,
but my airplane flew,
as if it was untouched.

I finally landed somewhere far away,
And thought to myself,
Oh what a day!
I sat around for a while,
Restless as one could be,
And when I got hungry,
I knocked a coconut out of a tree.

I repaired my plane, but it just would not go,
so I got in my spare boat and started to row.

Here I am, 30 years and 24 days later,
and I'm just lucky that I wasn't eaten by that alligator!

Jaclyn Greenstein

Untitled

The heavens cried the day we laid our son to rest.
The birds flew by and gave a final song.
The flowers bowled to see that he would be forever young.
The wind blew down and brushed his brothers' cheeks,
To dry the tears that fell upon their breasts.
And hundreds came to give their best,
The day the heavens cried when we laid our son to rest.

Barbara Stalnaker

It's The National Debt

It's the National Debt that causes me grief
The amount, quite frankly, is beyond belief.

I won't go on moaning or placing the blame.
There is a solution to winning this game.

From Federal Employees whose programs don't work,
I hope their conscience does, somewhere, lurk.

From Private Industries who contribute no tax,
I suggest their patriotism is somewhat lax.

From welfare recipients, I know times are lean.
But some contribution may make them feel clean.

From everyone else, that's you and me.
Don't think we are getting off free.

Dig into your wallet and your checkbook too.
What America is - is up to you.

Just label some money "FOR THE REDUCTION OF DEBT."
And mail to the Treasury WHERE IT IS SPENT FOR JUST THAT!!

Just imagine how precious, when we look back some year,
Americans will really have something to cheer.
A reduction of debt. OH, won't that be nice.
Let's buy back our Country. It's worth whatever the price.

Barbara Ann Ward

Landscape

A solitary tear escapes her eye and meanders through
The ancient crevices of pain that scar the barren fields of her soul.
Hollow winds moan of anguish and fear,
Of could-haves and should-haves and why-did-it-have-to-bes.

In a blink of eternity, she gathers her heavy woolen skirts
Around her insecurities and races toward the foothills of desire.
Confusion quickly overtakes her resolve;
She knows not her destination, her vision clouded by indecision.
An incomprehensible rending of her very essence
Shrieks voluminously through the canyons of purpose.

Time creeps across her path, like the shadow of a great eagle
Majestically soaring on the wing.
She shades her azure pools with a withered glove
As the shallow ebbing of her breast harmonizes in the song.

Coarse shale and brambles underfoot give way to a presence,
Cool, green, and refreshing to her leathered cheek.
Comprehension dawns across the valley with splendor;
Reds and yellows ignite the tinder of acceptance.
She turns from the spectacle, its prophecy etched forever in her soul
And matches her stride with the timpani of her own power.

Jocelyn A. Walters

The Angel

I saw an angel.
The angel was glowing and shinning with every
glowing light around him like a thousand
midnights of stars put together.
The wings put together with every white of
whitest dove feathers, to make the angel
shine to the fullest.
The angels face was glowing with no oils but with
happiness, for what had been done, and the angel
said...
"God is pleased with what you did and keep on keeping
on with they good deeds that you hath done."
And what to the good deed was... it was being
reborn and then I had protection for life.
The protection for life was getting to have
everlasting life, in heaven, when I die.

Bobbie Jo Manges

Thoughts

You know a cold wind blows thru the sky
the autumn leaves cut loose and fly, leave
me watching and wishing I could follow, among
the regrets that I can't get by there are just
one or two I wish I could of said to you, but
girl what was I supposed to do, don't know
why it was so hard to talk to you, I guess my
past experiences showed me thru, you know no
sooner than I'd hit the street's, I met the fool's
that a young fool meets. All in search of truth,
and bound for glory, listening to our own heart beat's we,
stood around like we accomplish some feats, though it's fainter now,
the older I become living my life day after day,
soon all your plans and changes either happen.
Fail, or fade away, leaving so much still left to say,
but girl I want to let you know somehow, the
things you said are so much clearer now, I would
turn the pages back but time will not allow,
the way these day's just rip along. To fast
to last, to vast to strong, I know I done something's wrong.

David Jaco

The End

Life is the passage, death is the toll,
The body expires, never the soul.
The soul is the actor, life is its role,
The body, death will claim.

Heaven is the reward for paths wisely taken,
Hell, the punishment for values forsaken.
Wrong for right is often mistaken,
To death it's all the same.

Death is the nightmare we all fear,
Life is the dream we hold so dear.
Death is the crossing, ever so near,
Life too quickly passes.

To stand in shame at the gates of hell,
Or to hear the stories angelic harps tell,
The myths of Hades do not dispel,
But Heaven's glory amasses.

Bruce L. Matthynssens

God Is On Duty Today

A small black capped bird stopped to see
The breakfast menu at my tree
Black oil sunflower and white provo millet it read
So he grabbed a perch and nodded his head
And started to dine in joyous glee
Since the breakfast was on me
I watched from my kitchen window view
His visit was not really new
A daily caller I noted again
Mr. Chickadee you are my friend
come again another day
And bring your family I do pray
You'll always find enough for all
At my willing feeding stall
To remind me that natures way
Shows God is on duty again today.

Harry C. Rotenbury

For Molly Powell Medicine Woman

I see you South Carolina's motherless child
The chains of slavery set you free...
You are my history book, my link to my pitiless soul
Love began with you... Mississippi midwife...

Smells of sage and Catnip, fried green tomatoes, and pot liquor
Your veiny and swollen hands healed the sickly and brought in
new life...
Missy Anne played for your time, without a thought your own
lamenting
sister you chose...

With loving self-respect, I see you gazing back at me on Mudeor's,
bedroom wall
Your picture yellowed and cracked, yet fresh with the dawn...
As your soft dark brown eyes and pomaded hair, blew your aura into
the busy confusion
of my present... I wish for you...

I long for you...though you have transcended poverty, inadequacies,
and time
you are the balm of ancestral roots...
My darkest love is your eternal strength...
Your great gift of strength challenged me to be...

Billie Marie Hill-Beckley

Early Morning

Quietly, the sun rises over the eastern horizon,
The cold dark expanse
Almost silently advances and recedes
Along the mist covered sands.
Off in the distance
A lone gull cries out
As he begins his morning hunt.
The ocean breeze
Carries the sound to me,
And makes me shiver.
I stand there in silence
Trying to shake off the effect
Of the endless night,
Trying to capture that new,
Waking feeling that comes with
Each new day.

Trying, yet in vain,
For the feeling once again
...eludes me.

Jim Chase

A Grandpa Remembers

I remember the day I met Kayla
The day that she first breathed in life
The love in the eyes of her mother, my daughter
The look of joy in the eyes of my wife

Though the day was rainy and gloomy
The sunshine beamed from our eyes
To hold for the first time my Granddaughter
And to hear for the first time her cries

The tininess of her fingers and toes
The tenderness of her touch
Made me just want to hold her ever so close
And tell her Grandpa loves her so much

May our lives be filled with joy and happiness
And may God bless us and give us his love
For the newest little addition to our family
Was sent from our father above

Yes I remember the day I met Kayla
Though we thought that this day would never come
We wish to take this opportunity to tell you
Kayla Kristine, we welcome you home

John M. Holmes

The Delaware

Turbulent -then calm, serene, blue-grey,
The Delaware lies on this wintry day..
While far out can be seen the white caps
Churned by the wind blowing up from the bay.

Then again on another day
The river is seen in a different way.
The sun rising as a ball of fire
Shows us a sight of which we never tire!

As daylight's last gleams fade, dusk takes hold
And before us we see this scene unfold.
Hosts of stars twinkling high in the sky
A full, mellow moon, all this meets the eye.

The silver tipped waves can now be found
Dancing against some steamer seaward bound.
Then, as the ship fades slowly from sight,
The river flows silently on through the night!!

Anna Hineman Roberts

A Stroll With Nature

The path through the trees, along the shore front,
The desert so hot, the mountains so cool,
One strolls along remembering the past;
For we know not what the future will bring.
One can only wonder of the beauty they've seen,
Looking from a mountain top to the valleys so green,
Or waves lapping at their toes while watching the setting sun
A lake mirage or heat waves, seen in the distance on the desert sands.
So many memories comes from trees, in woods or forest,
At the park or home, along the street, down by the brook,
From the leaves changing colors, or swept by a gentle breeze.
The carved initials on the ole oak tree,
A very first kiss a sad goodby, summer or winter
The beauty and shelter never die.
For the birds build their nest, and animals multiply,
The ocean provides fish and gives us rain,
While the beauty of the desert protects heat loving things,
Stop for a moment, and take that stroll,
For nature will never let you be alone.

James H. Bud McKelvey

Circus, Circus

In the last candy-striped tent,
the dirt floor is littered with
confetti and stale popcorn.
Strangers flood in—

There she sits on her little jeweled throne —
Pink nails laced together
While waiting for the hours to pass.
It's an honest living.

Miniature features stare out at them — smiling.
While do-gooders protest outside—
It's for her own good, you know.

She straightens out her
Frilly dress with pudgy fingers —
Young in size, old in experience.

She sits on a dais
With scepter in hand—
And watches the freaks pass by.

Cynthia Harper-Gosselin

In And Out

When the shadows of night are flickering about,
the dog wants in and the cat wants out.
He'd like to sleep, she yearns to roam,
but not too far away from home.
At mornings light, as the day begins,
the dog wants out and the cat wants in.
He spends his day out in the sun,
chasing phantom rabbits, he likes to run.
She sleeps and dreams her day away,
then spends hours grooming for her night of play.
They're best of friends in real bad weather,
they both stay in and snuggle together.
But the cat is fickle and there's not much doubt,
when the weather's better, she'll go back out.
I love my two little furry friends,
and tomorrow we'll do this over again.
I think that's what life's all about
coming in and going out.

Barbara Sparks Yearling

Untitled

The weather was forbidding and the sky was dark
The field was underwater as we came into the park
As the players gathered it was written on their face
No reason to worry, we took first place

We won the toss to begin the game
But suddenly our players didn't look the same
We slipped and we slid as we tried to gain ground
But we just couldn't seem to get a first down

At the half we trailed seven to zip
And the coaches cried out "Keep a stiff upper lip"
Coach Withaeger bellowed "You must do your part"
"You've got to go hard and fight with your heart"

And on and on, and on it went
But their defense stiffened and never bent
Oh how our Steelers fought in vain
As they tried to overcome the cold numbing rain

And then it was over, the game at a close
And players struck a curious pose
We stood and watched as Bensenville exalted
The realization our season had halted

James K. Feck

The Warrior, The Flower

The Warrior rose to guard and defend;
The Flower reaches for life's giving light.

He stepped forward to face each coming challenge;
She swayed with each breeze, giving not yielding.

His voice boomed towards any conflict or fight;
Her whisper gently upon the air for what's right.

The Warrior readies his world against threat or defiance;
The Flower opens to listen, to form an alliance.

His strength like steel not going to weaken;
Her softness and grace, it's calm she's seeking.
The Warrior fights the fight but cannot hear;
The Flower can't fight, but teaches without fear.

He will stay having no fear;
She will blossom, keeping him near.

The Warrior is protector and guardian of Light;
The Flower is understanding and gives with delight.

This their living, this their life;
He her Husband, she his Wife.

Francis Chabot

I Told Him

He told me my kiss felt like
the gentle sucking on a peach
to extract some of the juices.
He told me I was as illusive
as the smoke of incense,
floating through the room.
He told me my eyes held too many secrets behind them.
He told me my mind was as mysterious as the stars.
He told me my lips looked like spilt blood.
He told me my body was fertile soil,
waiting to be harvested.
He told me my touch could arouse monks,
thousands of miles away.
He told me I knew too many truths.
He told me I was a woman.
I told him to tell me something,
I didn't already know.

Jennifer Boland

Among The Ocean Night

The moon is full and hovers in the sky,
The glassy sea lies still among the air.
The stars above shine with a sort of sigh,
The darkness all the fish share.

The eerie wind lies still without a stir,
The boards beneath me are dry as desert dust,
The sky and ocean begins to blur,
I'm wrapped in my thick blanket of trust.

I lay back to begin my field of dreams,
And forget this lonely ocean for which I do not care.
When I suddenly hear a familiar scream,
I spring up and begin to fearfully stare.

My heart races for I know of what has become,
"Not again," I whisper, my thoughts becoming numb.

Jamie Pace

Undated

I strolled along the moist stretch of sandy beach watching
the gulls wheeling out over the waves rolling into the shore.
They seem to reach out their foamy hands to draw the
sand back into the sea. Off in the distance where the
horizon meets the sea, is the setting sun like a ball of red
molten gold, silhouetting the ship on its way to faraway places.

As I stride along, beneath my feet are the shells and drift wood
strewn along the beach. In the dunes lining the landslide, the
the salt hay grass grows in varied size clumps and tiny hill locks.
Here and there stand sections of storm fencing like wood and wire
sentinels offering their protection against the elements
to the eroding sand.

Further along are the barnacle covered boulders that form
the breakwater jetty, pointing like a single arm thrust out
hundreds of yards into the sea, and the surf that seems bent
on destroying the huge rocks. But to no avail, the ebb and
flow are but feeble waves that polish the kelp festooned stones.
It really is the action of a restless sea!

James J. Healy Sr.

God's Love

A friendly smile to share with others;
The love and warmth of gentle mothers.
The beautiful sky, clouds, and breeze;
The flowers, grass and towering trees.
The peaceful days, and fabulous dreams;
Majestic mountains and flowing streams.
The friends I love and who love me too;
And all the wonderful deeds they do.
The gift of life God has given me;
And His love to which I hold the key!

Cheryl Michon

Disciples

Not many years ago
The homeless and poor had a place to go
Disciples responded to the teaching of our Lord
They gave gifts of more than they could afford

All the churches made good use of the funds
And sponsored homes for the aged and children
Homes that taught the wisdom in the Bible
Charity and fear and the discipline of living

The discipline of living has gone astray
We no longer depend on the church to show the way
She is caught up in worldly affairs
She has discontinued preaching charity and fear

So Christians have gone hand in hand with the world
Widows, orphans, and the homeless are left in the lurch
Charity has disappeared from the holy words
Replaced by a love so false and turgid.

Pray that we would return to being disciples again
Of Jesus our Lord, Savior and friend
Respond to God's greatest gift of many years ago
Then widows, orphans, poor and homeless will have a place to go

Arthur L. Johnston

Immigrants - A Granddaughter's Tribute

"Return not," the ocean cries.
The horizon beckons.
Tears trickle down your troubled face;
Torn between two loves.
Poverty reflects in your mother's face
Troubled by this adventure.
New found friends push forward.
The sun winks in support.
At last the boat weds the sea.
Toil and labor melt into the sunset.
Voices chime with struggle;
Babylon relived.
Time rehearses a pirouette.
The mind unfolds, yet is confused.
To the sea bows the earth.
Minarets dance to the pyre
Never to return.
A gale licks the sore.
Beckoning, the child reaches out.
A new world awaits.

Beverly Skrincosky Dorsey

The Sun Will Truly Rise

The last wrath is done
The last helpless child will be brought down by a gun.
The last innocent victim dies.
Then the sun will truly rise.

The first morning glory will bloom.
The first ghost of night will flee to its tomb.
The first evening shadow dies.
Then the sun will truly rise.

The last hopeless war is fought.
The first true love is found.
The last criminal is caught.
The first cheer of joy will sound.

The world will open its once blind eyes.
The people will finally care who dies.
The flags of nations in truce will fly high in the skies.
Then the magnificent sun will truly rise.

And forever in peaceful skies;
Then, indeed, the sun will truly rise.

Becky Sumrell

Who's To Blame?

To all the kids of yesteryear
The little ones who had no fear.
Who trusted in the word's of the old,
Who never felt left out in the cold.

What's happened to those little ones?
Now that our world's being unspun.
Our children are now doing drugs and carrying guns
As all of us parent's walk with our heads lowly hung.

Head's hanging low in pity and shame,
Knowing we've allowed these kids these games.
Forgetting the ways of discipline and rules.
Forgetting the ways by which WE were schooled.

Can you feel the bitterness and freezing cold
While these kids walk around feeling so brave and bold
Can you now see who wears the frowns and tears?
Because now the parents are the ones who fear.

But this is the question we now have to ask!
Who is to blame because we've failed in our task?
Is it really society the one we all wish to blame!
If we should look in a mirror, the answer the same!!

Donna Lynne Duarte

Heaven

I come to you again and try to express in mere words
the love that I feel, the love I have for you.
How I long for the day when we will be together. When
a look, or touch can and will express this love I have
for you. I have to ask: Is there a heaven? To hear
your voice at night, the last thing. To hear your voice
in the morning, the first thing.
To take you in my arms in the morning, the first thing.
Truly this would be heaven. Is there a heaven?
Yes there is, but, only with you. The kiss of life, the
kiss of love. To be together, never to be parted. To
share the same air that you breath. To have the sun
shine on me after it has shined upon you. Is this heaven?
Yes! Heaven and you, they
are the same. Believe in love. You are my life and my love
and my heaven. Ask the question, expect the answer. Do I?
Yes I do, very much. There is no doubt. The
what ifs, they don't exist. What does exist is the love.
If you look into the future you
can get a glimpse of what will be. Not the maybes, not the
what ifs. Love and more love, that is the future. Yours and mine.

Donald J. MacNair

Remembrance

This goes to you, who are not here today:
The mem'ry of your smile does linger on.
Your laughter, heart, and special loving way;
Through dark of night, until the light of dawn.

My nights are torment — days without an end;
And every hour divides us even more.
Your death is mine, a pain I cannot mend —
The rain inside shall never cease to pour
This sadness shades my life, my hope is dim;
And dreams now lost beyond my loving touch,
The future empty, feelings lost within;
Forever gone to never love as much:
And now, just thinking of days to be
For this life was not meant for you or me.

James W. Lyrenmann

Love

Love, oh how that word defies
The magnitude of sin that fills the world.
It breathes new meaning into lives
And lets the flag of hope unfurl.

Love it conquers all 'tis said
That motto sets our hearts aflame.
We dare to dream of things ahead
Forgetting disillusionment and pain.

Love, the joy this word can bring
When softly said to little ears
And have their tiny bodies cling
To us, and wipe away their tears.

Love, it opens wide the door
To be all we can be.
And kills the seeds of bigotry, but more
The best is all it makes us see.

Love, if we could only share
This once true gift with fellowmen
And show each other that we care.
Then "Peace On Earth" we'd see, Amen!

Beulah Jones

On The Way To Bedlam

Where has he gone?
the man I used to know
He looks the same
except for the eyes
once dark and vital, flashing lights
now withdrawn
they skim the surface of my face.
I smile
I laugh
joining in his silly jokes
the wanderings behind the broad forehead
that creases in puzzlement.
He laughs
the lost keys
the shoes found on the pantry shelf
the sentences left dangling.
He swipes at the cobwebs
shadowing his mind
Where has he gone?
the man I used to know.

Frances Hunt Yordan

The Midnight Ride Of Paul Revere

Listen my children and you shall hear,
The midnight ride of Paul Revere.

It was in the year of 1771.
The war hadn't started it had just begun.
He mounted his steed and set out that night,
He rode toward the horizon and out of sight.
No one knows what happened that year,
On the midnight ride of Paul Revere.

The ride was set for November 31st,
But at reading he was the worst.
For he set out on halloween,
And ever since then he hasn't been seen.

The British lost, the Americans cheer,
But no where there shed a tear,
For good old Paul Revere.

So my children remember that night
When Paul Revere rode out of sight.
We know what happened to the war that year,
But not what happened to Paul Revere.

Jeffery Mark Lasley

Time

Time waits for no one, I've heard them all say; unprepared for the moment, unavailable for the catch.
Rewards go unclaimed because there's no room for the overflow.
What then happens to the lonely hearts that miss the train when they are late, forever too late.
For those overdue, time stands still and refuses to march onward in spite of the fear.
The carriage has departed and left me behind to lick my wounds and drown in a sea of bitterness. My own name sounds unfamiliar to my ears, and the face looking back at me in the mirror is a face I dare not know.
Was it all a mistake? Or merely a dream I have not yet returned from?
Has it all been for nothing, no one, all this time that has gone and refuses to budge? The words are thick in my brain and the sentences are fogged by the fears and confusion of the past, the present and the future, all standing on the same empty marker.
The time that was near has gone by and will never come back again.
Perhaps it's another guess; I'm never really sure if it's yesterday or tomorrow.

Helene Giordanelli

This Good Home

I own it not, I still must pay
The monthly payment due this day.

The walls of paint and mortar bound
Are crumbling slowly to the ground.

The windows sliced and marred with break
The floor's lopsided timbers ache.

The doors stand slanted, slightly jarred,
The beckoning want of comforts charred.

The clever night winds pitch and moan
Play hide and seek with tearful groan.

It's saddened rooms with lowered lips
Untouched by human fingertips.

You ask for all who see you thus,
Envision you with love's sweet blush.

When lovers cared for all your needs
And gently pulled your bothered weeds.

When friendly flames of sweet romance
In the heart, once did a lover's dance.

The flames are all but vanquished now
They perished with the marriage vow.

Joyce N. Ellis

The Speed Of Life

The speed of life an adventure thru time.
The roads ever winding destination sublime.

Each passenger is special like each page of a book.
If one page is missing there in's a different look.

No one is forgotten, each one has his role.
Each trip is completed demonstrating many goals.

Some speed to the crossing, others stop to smell flowers.
Some take a few detours usually looking for powers.

Some delight in the wonder of all that takes place,
While others simply wait to see "His" heavenly face.

Matters not it will happen, regardless of price.
And this miraculous happening is simply called life.

Connie Lind

The Plan

I entered this world as if by plan
The ol'man gone before I became man

Begged me, he did, but I was a boy
Told me to "grow, give-up them toys"

Was in my teens, in old blue jeans
I opened my eyes, to see what to think

The time had come, to see who'd been lyin'
My eyes long dried, by too much cryin'

I entered this world as if by plan
Uncle Sam said he'd make ya' a man

Weren't that all, and I knew the cost
To see this world, and what the ol'man lost

Left me cold and cussin' with nothin' but disgust
That the ol'man had lost without even a fuss

Gone was my youth; it all made me pause
That for only a second, ashamed I was

Now I've loved my life, but I wanted you to see
What your hopes and dreams done to me

I've played your games and passed your tests
And you made sure that I'd face the best!

George T. Cooksey

The Other Woman

I don't know if I can be
The one who parts so casually
From what we've shared; this time with you
Has made a world of dreams come true.

Don't know if I can let you go
And walk away, and yet I know
I will someday but when I do,
I'll still be in love with you.

Don't know if I can make it through
The pain I know that is my due.
But I would not trade away one passioned night
One sunny day
To ease the hurt I will go through
When I go through the loss of you.

Irene Puricz

Our Children

Where are the children of yesterday?
The ones we walked to school
Or dropped off as we went on our way.

The little ones that grew so fast,
That caused sleepless nights in times past,
Oh how they change and go out of our grasp.

As I look back did do my best,
Is it really time for them to do the rest?
Was I always there to love and care?

My love for you I do not doubt,
But oh my child I see your size
My heart says watch out.

I cannot take your hand anymore
And lead you to the door
Of right and happiness, success and truth.

I'll watch and pray and try every day
To live my life in such a way
To show my love is here to stay.

Joan Chere Francis

What Is Love?

Love is not when you can't take your eyes off the beauty on the outside.

Love is when you can't take your heart off the beauty on the inside.

Christina Michelle Navarra

Purple Rage

What happened? It hurts. I want to be in your arms again and feel the pain fade. You are everywhere. Music plays and thoughts of you stir the deepest emotions. Silence is the only comfort. There are no words; only love. The light shines in the window, the welcome light left on. The night is endless; the darkness brings powerful emptiness of the soul; cold and alone. Awaiting the dawn's light; the hope of the warmth of the morning sun. The storm rages within, it swells with overflowing waves of tears; tears of the unknown. Of the uncertainty, of confusion, of disbelief, of questioning, of love! Looking for answers, frightened of the mind's wanderings searching not finding. The way to make the aching and yearning depart. Cruel realty? Stolen moments in time. Dreams of times to come; fleeting, fluttering like the illusive butterfly, slipping. Through fingers in a vain attempt to hold on, yet clinging to each thread of the web which envelops the entanglement of the heart. Memories so real, so close, so alive with depth of spirit, yet closed from thought, but not mind's eye, so as not, to suffer more the anguish and need, deep desire for the touch of your hand in mine, the touch. Which quickens my pulse, races my heart, stirs the embers burning within, tho the fire rages alone, kindled not by a glance, a smile, a word, an unspoken mind link but by the unbearable loss, the numbness, the part of me which has lost the ability to feel. The wonder, the joy the happiness you impart. Rejection! Agony! Unfulfilled! Crying out in pain; I must find you or suffer an eternity of hues of purple rage..

Christine A. Lee

Myself

Who am I that everyone sees?
The person that stares at me in the mirror.
Am I only flesh and bones?
That can so quickly turn to dust.
What do I look like on the outside?
Am I pretty?
Or just another face in the crowd.
If you could look inside me,
would you like what you see?
I do.

Hillary Brooke Van Such

The Pillar

The pillar fell. It could no longer take the weight of the trial.. The pressure was too great.

As the pillar lay there in a pile of rubble, the Builder saw it and was sad. He knew the foundation was strong and did not need repairs. So He cleaned away the rubble and rebuilt the pillar. As He rebuilt the pillar, He made it stronger and able to withstand greater trials.

He then placed the pillar back in the place where it once stood. He then mended the part of the house that was damaged when the pillar collapsed. After seeing His child rebuilt and stronger, the Builder was pleased to see the house rejoice.

Alan Martin

A Daughter's Prayer

As I gaze out the window, the ocean looks so calm
The reflection of the sun makes the water shimmer like silver
And the time ticks away
One minute at a time

If I could turn back the clock, everything would be different
There would be words I would say, actions I would take
Now, it's too late
And the time ticks away
One minute at a time

I pray for the day that you will find your peace
Where your soul would be released
And soar in the heavens and look down and see
The water shimmer like silver
Until that day
The time ticks away
One day at a time

Gail Asuncion

The Letter

A letter I sent you the other day.
The right thing to do I can only prey.

Whether it be wrong or right.
I thought about day and night.

Remembering the words and how it went,
and you have no idea it's even been sent.

How will you feel when my words you have read?
Will the words be right or wrong that I have said?

Will they make you give me a call?
Or to deaf ears will my words fall?

Will my words change anything?
Will they a difference bring?

I can only hope as here I set.
As you don't know of my words yet.

Alan McKay

Letter To Loved One

My loved one where have you gone, why did you leave me here all alone? The road ahead with its trials and tests upon my shoulders alone it all rests. Tomorrow's duties cause me to fear without your helping hand near. Children to care for, bills to pay, questions to be answered what shall I say? I've become so accustomed to leaning on you when problems arise what shall I do? Where my loved one have you gone, why did you leave me here all alone, without your help how can I go on? Seems there's no reason to get up today, wait! I think I heard your voice say, get up my darling an effort make, it will get easier with each step you take. It's years now that you've been gone, I'm growing accustomed to being alone. Children I've reared, bills I've paid, questions I've answered, problems I deal with day after day. My loved one I miss you as much as then, without your help rough it has been, but I've grown stronger, even I can see. If you were here proud of me you would be. I no longer ask where have you gone, for I know in my heart you are home. I met the Master one dark day and He's promised by my side to stay. So rest my loved one in God's loving space
and I'll join you there one day thanks to HIS GRACE.

Bernice Plunkett

A Poem To My Beloved Father

Even the angels were crying on this first day of March,
the robins were asleep, they too, felt the loss in their hearts.

A true lover of nature, children, a good joke, and all the
things gentle and kind, shall be what I remember of this
father of mine.

To sit and speak with him one came to know, of the
endless wit and wisdom that this man bestowed.

He had an endless passion for what was yet to learn,
now that he's with the angels, I know that he again,
shall never yearn.

He was a decorated soldier in World War II, he
proudly jumped out of the sky for the Red, White, and Blue.

He loved writing, poetry, his children, and Frances, his wife.

I shall forever miss this kind gentleman, my father,
for the rest of my life.

May the Lord be with him.
Dad's loving daughter,
Missy

Barbara Dubovick

The Curtains Of Darkness:

Life is like a piece of sand in an hour glass
The sands of time move so swiftly
With the blink of an eye
One moment we are here
The next moment we are beyond
Beyond to the incredible light
The light so bright, warm and serene
There is no sound
Just knowing of our inner feelings

The stream of flowing ebony
That passes the mahogany chest
The bouquet of flowers
The opaque showers that flow
All the emotions spilled outwardly
The onyx Earth
The silent eclipse

Those Dark Ebony curtains drawn forever!

Daina M. Snyder

How Big Is The Sea?

How big can the sea really be?

As time went on to advance,
the sea must be shrinking its great expanse.
Centuries ago it took men months to transcend,
before that they thought there was no end.

As time went on to advance,
the crossing time dropped by a great significance.
Man got the mail quickly to the other side.
The sea was no longer the great divide.

As time went on to advance,
man has made the sea make a disappearance.
In America we simply pick up the phone,
to reach someone almost instantly in Sierra Leone.

So you can see,
How big can the sea really be?

Benjamin Harrison

Undefined Conceptions

Silence.
The silence in my head is causing confusion.
The confusion is causing me to think twice.
Never twice will I fall for the game again.
The game of what?
The game of life.
Life is like a cherry pie...
Nice and sweet (and right in your eye).
Your eyes will deceive you...
Make sure you don't blink.
'Cause in any second now
Your whole plan could sink.
Sink, drown,
I can't even swim!
Well you better learn how if you're gonna stay above the rim.
Above the clouds, above the smoke,
Out of the rain- in with fresh hope.
Out with the pain, in with the rising.
The rising of what?
The rising of recognizing.

Alisha Milliner

You And I

Sweetie, I'm looking back at the times we spent
The smiles, the tears, and what they meant,
The love we shared
Just you and I
It grew and grew as time went by.
Angel that sunny glow that shines on your beautiful face,
My need to feel your warm skin and warm embrace.
warm embrace,
The dreams of our life's could be, if you
will marry me.
To live with out my dreams with you
is something I could never do
So in the future may it be
just you and I eternally...

Daniel E. Hedrick

"The Greatest Gift"

Life revolves around friends as the earth moves around the sun.
The stars in the sky can not be numbered but one companion
can be counted.
It is the honor and admiration you give to one special individual.
You need to harvest your feelings about a close advocate.

Will they stick with you through afflictions, strife, and
sorrows which may oppose you on your struggle to be a survivor.
The biggest question to be asked; would you perish so your
companion may live on?
This is the most prominent sacrifice you may be faced with
down the road.
This is the far greatest love which can be shown to one's friend.

The looking up to an elder who has shown compassion and
understanding to life's misfortunes.
This day and time friends are hard to find.
It is the ultimate trust between people.
A friend is not like the moon which only presents its self
half of the time.
All these things we should think upon to help us in life.

Jeremy Priest

Life's Quiet Pleasures

The sheer magic of a breeze upon your face,
The still calmness of the ocean wide and deep;
A perfect song that the birds quietly sings,
Gives an array of what life's all about;

A content heart, in the midst of calamity,
A soul saved by grace in the nix of time;
The warmth one feels on a cold day-expresses the awe,
This my friends, is what life's all about;

The joy that's heard in a laugh - the unheard sadness in a cry;
The task of living through one day's end;
Reaching for what's real and solid,
The time slot - that's what life's all about;

The distance between the clouds and the stars,
As far away as the moon and the sun;
Our reach for what our hearts desire,
Is extended further, cause we know not what, life is all about;

Search your heart - see what is there,
Sift carefully through the unused parts;
All the things that are never mentioned,
Those, are what life is all about;

Helen G. Ross

Pax

I throw a stone
The stone sinks
Blood is rolling from the stone
The stone is rolling to the ground.

I throw another stone
again the stone sinks
again the blood is rolling from the stone
again the stone is rolling to the ground

I throw another
another
another
I cannot throw another stone
Rolling stones, rolling with blood, rolling
to the ground

They surround
and I cannot throw another
stone

George H. Cladis

A Pocket Of Peace

The earth in its orbit, so perfectly moves—
The sun, moon and stars all in place—
I ponder all this as I look out tonight,
On our snow-covered town, and the ice.

Street lights are on, but most folks are a-bed,
Few windows are showing a light.
Muffled are sounds of the thin line of cars,
That carefully pass through the night.

Peace in our hearts; in our homes warm and dry,
No homeless human in view—
Still we are saddened by news that we hear,
Of places where this is not true.

Many the places and people at war;
I wish that all conflict would cease.
Beautiful snowfall has covered our town,
And made it A Pocket of Peace.

Frances Morrow Duke

Worth Looking For

The cool fresh feeling of water thru your hair
The sun shining in a clear blue sky
The taste of warm sweet air
The gift of a single red rose
A soft caressing touch

These are the things worth looking for

The gurgling laughter of an infant
An old couple walking down the street, holding hands
A child's sweet gift of crumbled flowers
A walk in the forest with only the birds to hear
A phone call in the night just to say, I love you

These are the things worth looking for

The loving look of a contented dog
The sweet purr of a warm puddle of fur called kitty
The fresh scent of a newly sliced orange
Clean warm clothes, sun dried and softened by the wind

These are the things worth looking for

Not hate, not prejudice, not greed, not cruelty
Warm sweet healthy things, simple, truthful, hopeful

These are the things worth looking for

Frances S. Houston

Dawn At The Sea

I was alone for miles.
The sun warmed my face and broke the chill,
The puissant sea air saturated my lungs.
Waves reflected the sun's light,
and cracked on the shore.
Sea gulls flocked on the beach.
Interrupting the intoxicating serenity,
as if they too were absorbed in the same scene as I.
I felt as if it was a dream,
the beauty of the sea.

Domenic M. Paci

Would You

Would you sing a song to keep eagles soaring,
The swans swimming and the robins singing.
Would you open your eyes to allow the sun to rise, into the blue sky.
Would you close your eyes to allow the sun to set, into the distant seas.
Would you plant a flower in honor of beauty, for all you hold dear.
Would you walk the empty path if it lead you to the light.
Would you give your essence for eternal love,
The endless complete circle, perfect, like the ring.
Would you jump for the chance to feel your
child's first breath on your cheek,
To feel the beat of a tiny drum, chest to chest.
Would you smile if I gave you the sky,
to see Orion, to touch the sparkles
To see the world as only the clouds can.
Would you cry if I said....goodbye.

David W. D. Haynes

A Mansion By The Delaware River

Sun rays piercing through the windows warming all of
the inner surroundings.
Water, rippling downstream, smoothly and ever constant.
Bare trees mixed with tall evergreens and old willows;
their shadows giving comfort to the grass.
Little breezes move the branches ever so slowly.
Squirrels running and climbing briskly through the grounds,
Tug boats and barges floating on the river on their way;
Sea gulls flying through, making chatter to one another,
Nature's quiet presence awakens us and helps us feel
its serenity.

Josephine Raspanti-Quinto

Your Thought

The golden rays of the sun,
the sweet smell of the air, waves of
green grass in the wind, spotted with
beautiful flowers, trees reaching for the
sky. The clear-water stream flowing peacefully,
pebbles washed clean on its bottom. The
cabin sitting motionless, laughter coming
from inside, smoke floating from its chimney.
What a wonderful place to be. So much
love, so much peace, so much comfort. Such
a place exists only in your heart. I found
mine you should start looking for your
peace, and comfort also. There's a big
reward for those who find it.

Brandon Hart

Pathway To Heaven

I feel the years in my hand,
The tears in my eyes,
For it is the year before I say goodbye
To what I know as home.

From the bed where I rest,
I look around the room and see
All the things that are precious to me.
The love I started
And the ones who have passed
Stay within my heart.

I know from working with the gatekeeper
That my time grows near. So —-
I wait for that moment when
The air moves no more, sound fades away,
And light becomes dark.

For at that moment my body lies in silence
My flesh grows cold, and my spirit proceeds.
The day is now upon me
And everyone I knew
Is with me once again.

Dominick Venafra

Time

The clock with its endless hours, endless minutes and forever years.
The ticking, the tocking and overall time,
are us unlimited as ocean tears.
Time never ends. It has neither limits nor deadlines.
The clock is time.
It seems endless in making sense out of things.
The clock would ridicule us when we say that we have forever.
It seems to control us, and it seems to make us die.
We have a mere star out of the universe, a blade of grass out of
the pastures and the fields so plentiful.
Time seems to go on so quickly, leaving nothing for
us to remember it by except memories.
Ah yes, the memories; the laughter, the tears, the joys and the fears.
Out of it all, is there room? Can we fit into our blade of grass,
our star from above?
Or, is it just emptiness without it?
With hands
With face
With numbers
With Time...

Carla Cash Crapster

Untitled

How sudden our departure seemed,
the time just too short,
before this naval vessel
left its homeport.
Unable to call, with only letters and cards to hold,
hoping beyond hope, my strength doesn't fold.
The frustration is ever building, still so long to go,
how are they doing? I just don't know.
She has so many things to take care of,
bills, school, house and kids.
I know she can keep her wits,
her strength, she doesn't know,
with stability that is undeniable.
She'll need it, all her fears are viable.
Everyday my love grows as the distance becomes more,
trusting in our relationship as never before.
Absence makes the heart grow fonder is what they say.
If the first few weeks are any indication,
that will be proven the 180th day.

Daren E. Crespo

Things I Find Beautiful

The trees in the spring before they bloom
The trees in the fall while they turn color
Snow that falls on a winter night that covers
Everything in sight
Best of all I like the summertime
Seeing people having fun in the summer sun
The sun that comes up over the mountains
in the early morning and the end of
the day as the night sets in.

Arthur La Fountain Jr.

Solitary Rose

Amidst the ill tangled under brush,
the trod upon, the tainted forgotten,
there thrives a solitary rose.

Among this yield of infectious weeds,
rotten contempt and barbaric ruins,
there thrives a solitary rose.

Within parched rivers of poison ivy
where hazardous waste matter clabbers
there thrives a solitary rose.

Throughout those multiple notches
where putrid aroma strangles all,
there thrives yet, a solitary rose.

And insects gobble all that decays
and disease runs thicker than crime...
and still there thrives, a solitary rose.

Nourished with hatred, a watering of
neglect, bristle thorns festering...
and there still thrives a solitary rose.

In shadows of doom, thrive on, you will,
solitary rose, thrive on you will.

June Marie Alexander

Ga

We see your face so soft and true
the love you hold inside of you.
Yours eyes so bright, your hands
so warm, your heart as pure as gold.
Never hurting anyone's feelings with that
soft smile of yours.
And now we see that you're at
peace and all the hurting's gone.
Now we'll all say good-bye and we
all love you so

Danielle Spicer

Life

My Mother's womb is like
The universe; hidden
Void of understanding
Her nature is sorrowful
The fire in her belly is without
Purpose, its theme - a mirror of reflections
Her beauty is the earth's beauty
The clouds her children from whose
Fingertips drip ambrosia
Its vapors are the rain I conceived with
Deep emotions of ecstasy, the fire of
Your desires flames like a sweet red
Rose mirrors the movement of the seas
Uniting together powers of things superior
And things inferior - as the light of you
Filters through my consciousness knowledge
from unknown origins, I could see
The trials of life in the ocean waves....

Arly Denis

Night

As the sun sets in the west, I anticipate the night.
the warm glow over the horizon gives off a welcoming feeling.
I shut my eyes and feel the sun covering my body like an embrace.
I welcome the night, dark and mysterious...
as the night overcomes the day, the stars slowly begin to appear.
like rhinestones on black velvet,
they sparkle in all their splendor.
at last the long wait for the moon to show is over,
it is out full and glowing; its life bringing life to me.
I close my eyes again and am at peace,
at last.

Bradi Van Noy

Reborn

Endless running water, like a man without a soul,
The wind is my direction but it doesn't state my role
Timeless, reaching, grasping, falling into space,
A mountain in the distance, a body less a face
A smile a frown, the sun, the rain,
Gliding through the storm, reaching for the pain
It's all so different, it's all the same,
A life of chasing dreams, a never ending game

The wind is picking up now, it seems I'm floating free
Seems I'm getting nearer, a land where I should be
Standing on a rainbow, curious, bold,
Reaching for the sunlight, hands yearning through,
One step away, excitement of the new
In the distance an object, slowly it arose,
Grasping fingers reaching out, finally they close
Standing on the rainbow, multi-colored sand
I realize now my power, for the moon in my hand,
Crystal running water, like a man's newborn soul.

Craig P. Wiggins

Snow

Snow falls at a very fast pace and everyone starts to cover their face.

All of a sudden snowballs fly, then a little kid starts to cry.

He said he was cold from his head to his toes, he even had frost bite on his nose.

We took him inside and dried his mittens, soon he was playful as a little kitten.

Joleen Smay

Untitled

I took a walk along the path that runs though
the woods behind the house this evening.
It opens into a clearing at the top of the hill,
where you can watch the sun setting across the valley.
From where I stood I could see a
flock of geese flying low over the horizon.
It reminded me of how we sat and
watched the sea gulls flying over the beach
while we were on vacation,
and I began to smile.
Then I saw a plane flying toward the city.
It reminded me that you had gone,
and I began to wonder where you might be
at that moment and what you might be thinking,
and I hoped that you were thinking of me.
And then I saw one of the first stars
of the evening peeking through the clouds.
It reminded me of how much I love you
and how much I miss you,
and I began to weep.

Calvin Francart

The Woods Of Howe County

Fleshless bones of barren winter trees,
the world seems sick with cold, bleak disease.
These trees with no leaves form empty forest
sadly transparent in cruel Winter's crest.

Vile houses, jalopies on blocks with rusted hood
are visible now through new, cold windows of wood.
I wish the earth to again be green
for behind leaved trees these sights won't be seen.

I'd trace the source of a spring I know
and lay down and drink like I did years ago
in the untainted woods of County Howe,
my favored uncle alongside, he's dead now.

I think I'll trace that spring today
for winter-dead brush shan't hinder my way.

Clayton Bellamy

Great Marriages

Were there any great marriages ever?
The young girl wondered, watched and listened of young and old.
She was waiting for romance.
Then decided not to marry; for she saw carelessness and struggle,
No evidence of true love.

She thought she was in love again and again.
But again and again was afraid of loneliness in a marriage
And broke off; before lasting decisions were made,
Fearing it would not last.

Then one day met still another love,
This one seemed different, it was different.
This time take time to love,
Take a chance, take time to reflect.
To share thoughts, together brought forth
Tenderness and romance of their souls.

Many years have gone by; Days of joy and pain together faced.
Days of patience and trust.
Their souls are still together.
Their thoughts still sharing, caring.
Example to many of commitment, love and honor.

Barbara Sveitis

Remember The Vet

Vietnam veterans who died for their country
their names engraved on a black granite wall.
They who sacrificed their lives for peace for all.

My father a world war II vet who loved his country saw his
company fall,
In an ambush at Guadalcanal his fellow soldiers sacrificed their
lives for peace for all.

Friends and family shed their tears when given news, their worst
fear of a loved one who died for his country, sacrificing
his life for peace for all.
What I want to say to all, citizens of the USA, please give
thanks from your heart and pray for all veterans who fade
away.
Remember them especially on Memorial Day.

So do not take our country for granted
When so many veterans their names in granite
But give thanks to all Veterans, like the ones remembered on that
wall.
They who sacrificed their lives for peace for all.

Frank J. Alonzo

What's Been

It can be so beautiful out
Then engulf you in its alluring flames
It can be so cloudy out
The attack you with its romantic moon

Everything's so unpredictable—— I just want to know
I want to know
How diseased - How harmful
How venomous this thing's going to be

How curing - How wondrous
How divine this thing's going to feel

I want to take a few moments
Press pause on all life's thoughts
Peel off everyone's head
And see exactly what's been planned

What's been cured
What's been found

What's been hurt
What's been deceived
What's been left to die
Without remorse

Jason Grothaus

Nestling

I held my breath, you took your first step,
Then I watched as our hands slipped apart.
There was hardly a clue that those white baby shoes
Walked away with a piece of my heart.

Years wore the disguise of a moment arrived,
When beauty and poise took their place,
Lending an air of self-confidence
To a young and innocent face.

Go softly now, be kinder still,
Parental reins must fall.
Preen your wings to soar with kings;
The world awaits your call.

As you push away, the nest will sway
With pleasant memories.
The emptiness you leave behind
Is the love that sets you free.

James O. Kelly

Of What Day

Today is yesterday's tomorrow, but if this be,
then that day lost is not so, it must be more,
not one but three.

To put off yesterday, what was not done that today.
Equals what of tomorrow? Of what day?

Work hard enough to need more to do. This rule If
followed will guide you thru. In not tomorrow,
but yesterday's today, to start anew.

These creeds to follow, not to shirk, wash away
the lust for wealth in work. Give thanks to
this god that gave us work. Love is so akin, amen.

Peace, love, and life multiply the same, as three
days lost, not one gained. Do all three to
equal one, Amen. Again, Amen.

Howard L. Wickersham

Oak Leaves

One day a single leaf falls down,
Then there are two upon the ground.
Rake, rake, burn, burn,
Will the season never turn?

Some leaves still cling to branches high,
Stark against the winter sky.
The air is cold, the ground is white.
The trees and I have a cozy night.

Then the robin returns to nest,
Spring is here, and as you guessed,
Old leaves drop from the sky,
Pushed by buds forming on high.

One day a single leaf falls down,
Then there are two upon the ground.
Rake, rake, burn, burn,
Will the season never turn?

Now lush leaves shade me from the summer sun,
The leaf battle is temporarily won.
But Fall will bring a deluge so great.
The colorful refuse will fill many a crate!

Clarice Reinhardt

A Tribute To Dad On His 75th Birthday

It seems throughout our growing years...
There are always lessons to learn...
Like "Mind your manners, sit up straight,"
And while driving, "Watch how you turn!"

Dad taught us many virtues
Like always finish what you start,
Then there's love, respect and honesty
All coming straight from the heart.

How many times I wanted to quit...
My nursing and Dad said "No way!"
If he hadn't been so persistent,
I'd not be where I am today!

We didn't always cooperate
With his discipline and strict rules,
But now that we're all parents,
We know these are valuable tools.

Our lives are filled with memories
Some happy, some that are sad,
But if anyone asked us, we would say...
"He's my Dad, and for that we are glad!!!"

Eileen Shameklis

"The Door To Freedom"

It's hard to explain what runs through my mind
There are so many feelings of an indifferent kind.
I am no longer a subject of a harbored past,
I've come to terms with those demons at last.
It's not about lying or playing the fool,
I've used living and learning as my only tool.
Nothing can be said to alter my view;
I've searched only for love that I've known to be true.
The strength of pain that has come from within
Is my only sign, it's time to begin
To take life on at its greatest age,
And not hand it over to jealousy and rage
So many changes occur each day
But it's a matter of acceptance, no matter what
Role you play.
When you can walk away knowing you're free
Any dream imaginable you will soon begin to see.

Amy L. Luberto

Is There A Place For Me?

I wanted something, I didn't know what.
There are so many idea's in my head.
Some flee as fast as they had entered.
I feel I could reach out and seize one, but which one?
And how could I, a person in a sense imprisoned, make anything
a reality?
I know a lot, but yet I know nothing.
There are brick walls all around.
Will I ever break thru?
Is it I, who wants more than was meant to be?
Or is it I, because of circumstances and choices have cheated my
own self?

Janet Rogan

Father Of The Bride

And right behind the woman in the hat
There came a rather older looking chap.
His head held high, his heart so very low
Both proud and sad to see his daughter go.
Clad in black pants with shiny, wide sideseams
He knew that he no longer filled her dreams.
With dread he thought of all the future days
Which he well knew would soon take her away
To far off places to a strange new land.
She now walks with no need of Daddy's hand.

Brooke Busby

Sunrise

Off in the foggy distance of the dark night,
There comes a twinkling of incoming light,
Just out of our sight,
As the darkness begins to lose its mysterious fight,
That's connecting it to bitterness and fright,
Disappearing with the dewy haze as the rising day
Breaks into new light,
The eye of our earths sight,
Awakening slow and kinda tight,
But soon begins to soar upwards like a rocket taking flight,
It's God's sun shining so high up in our skies,
Lighting our way down here with its beams of light,
Soaring higher and higher upwards like a kite,
Until it's glowing with all God's might,
Then like everything dies just like the night,
Waiting to start a new tomorrow's day when once again
It will arise with brand new light.

David Martin Johnson

A Savior's Glance

The blood cries out across the land, grave have become our sins
There has to be forgiveness before the restoration begins

The heartbreak of the nation in parents and children's lives
Brings such soul sadness and scars that we cannot survive

Oh, blessed Jesus, hear our cry of despair and grief
As we bow our hearts in humble sorrow and ask relief

How great is the love that changes and makes whole
Restoring peace and joy to the needy soul
How tender the mercy, the patience that gives every chance
And sets us free through a fleeting Savior's glance

For the lives that could have been, the wasted years
The stumbling, searching, the unbelief, the bitter tears

For the spiritually blind, the diseased and the lost
Whose lives are worth retrieving at any cost

We repent for the evils that deceive and rob and kill
And ask healing of our land according to the Father's will

How great is the love that changes and makes whole
Restoring peace and joy to the needy soul
How tender the mercy, the patience that gives every chance
And sets us free through a fleeting Savior's glance.

Betty J. Doyle

No Cross - No Crown

Jesus carried his Cross to Calvary's Hill,
There He paid the bill
Must Jesus bear the Cross alone all the
World go free?
No there's a Cross for everyone and there's a
Cross for you and me.
He said that troubles would come and days will be
Dark and dim,
But, I don't have to worry, just call on him...
Jesus said to deny yourself, and take up your Cross
And follow me.
We have to carry our Cross until we are
Called home to Eternity.
You see a Cross will help you, get to your
Eternal resting place
Home with the master, there you can see, the Saviour
Face to Face.
The Bible says to stay faithful until death and
You shall receive a mansion, robe, and crown
And sing with the Angels as they walk around heaven's Town.

Jacquelyn P. Shootes

Paradise

Some people say that in a foreign land,
There is a place that is pleasant, peaceful, and serene
Where a person can be independent; and it is inside that is seen,
Where people stand united; and where criticism ends,
Where people can be themselves and you're always among friends,
Where feelings are considered and sacrifices made,
Where possibilities are endless; and beliefs never fade,
Where actions aren't analyzed; whatever you do is excellent,
Where immediately people agree; and words are always meant,
Where the government isn't shambles; and there is no disease,
Where it is likely you will benefit from things that happen with ease,
If you would like to get there, surprisingly, it isn't far,
It isn't some dream world, or past a distant star,
By using your imagination, and not a motorcart,
You can get to Paradise, because it is in your heart.

Amy D. Dybas

Untitled

When I look through the window of my mind
There is much to see
But as I move through reality
It is another world for me
I don't know when my dreams began to end
Was it my first child?
My working five day's
My second child
My working weekends
Or my final child
I think it was just the struggle of being all alone
feeling like an old lady who's worked too long
I can't turn back time to a place when my life was mine
I can't dream because reality keeps me working too hard
and I can't stop working because I have too many bills to pay
As I walk through the window of my mind I am taken back to the
dreams of my destiny
Which could be the dreams of reality or the reality of my dreaming.

Debra Benacka

Standing Alone

High on a mountain; looking out to the sea,
there stands an old and lonely tree.

It must be sad, for it stands alone,
and yet this place it must call home;

For its roots are deep, burrowing into the ground;
It's probably weeping, but you'll not hear a sound.

Where are the young it used to enfold;
in it's outstretched branches to ward off the cold?

They've gone to more important places, I see;
Who cares for an old and worn out tree.

Jacqueline Hughes Russell

Freedom Stand!

Black and white walk hand in hand!
There's no ban to Freedom Stand!

Don't be feared of your pears!
There's no ban to Freedom Stand!

Make a kind nation of God's creations!
There's no ban to Freedom Stand!

Being friends forever always together!
There's no ban to Freedom Stand!

We are whites they are colors but we are all
sisters and brothers!
There's no ban to Freedom Stand!

We are all the leaders, there are no cheaters in Freedom Stand!

Take my hand, be in good old Freedom Stand!

Aubri Larsen

The Kiss

When Mama and Papa were both in their teens,
They always took caution to kiss where not seen.
And if Papa would catch his son in a trance,
He'd soon know the reason and would fix his pants.
That's why in those days they enjoyed a kiss,
Because it was very seldom and had many risks.
Today it's different, they kiss a galore,
Cause Mama and Papa don't care anymore.
They have kissing contests to see who lasts longest,
Whereas in dad's day he kissed who was strongest.

Carmine Di Bella

"The White Angel Of Death"

As rain drops fall across her gentle face
they appear to be tear drops. So beautiful,
but yet so far away the angel without a face.

She's very smooth, comforting, understanding,
and loving. Her main goal is to conquer your
mind, body and soul. Your desire for the human
flesh vanishes. You only crave for her love and
affection. It's only an illusion.

The hope, strength, confidence, and power you feel
is only an illusion. Wake up you dying soul, you
aren't the winner, she is.

The white angel of death does not have the power
she claims to have. God Almighty has all the power
and controls everything and everyone.

Believe me she loves no one but herself.
It's an illusion, she's not your mother nor your father.
It's an illusion, she's not your spouse nor your lover.
She's an illusion, please, please, wake up before
she destroys you.

Debra Morgan

Tears

Tears is a gift we have.
They are nothing but water.
But what would we do with out them?
We use Tears when we are sad,
We use Tears when we are glad,
Tears run fast, and They run slow
They stain our face
But oh what a joy to know
That my LORD has given me tears
The best part about tears is
That my LORD has collected
and bottled every one of my Tears
because HE loves me so.
Psalms 56:8 Thou Tellest my wanderings: Put Thou my
Tears into Thy bottle: are they not in thy book?

Helen A. Hughes

Our Todays

Capture and hold the Todays you've had.
They are precious as weights of gold,
When thoughts wonder backwards, and you think of them,
They don't seem real, when told.
Because, so long ago, the Todays have been;
We've forgotten the important things;
Like people, family, incidents, the good times—-
That's what Todays all bring.
We strive for years for material things,
Then each day becomes a past.
But if our Todays are memorable ones,
Why not make them last.
Just lock it inside, as a part of you,
And keep every day you knew,
So when you remember, and tell it now,
Everything you say, seems true.

Edna D. Davis

Where Coyotes Play

Where the coyotes run, playful and glee.
Through the sagebrush we see,
where the coyotes dance,
with a yip, and a yap, and a little snap.
Where the coyotes play,
we see tumblin' tumble weeds gone astray.
Where thistles grow tall and the wild flowers bloom.
A coyote will roll over and howl at the moon.

Deanna S. Calderon

They Did Not Know You

They did not know you, they did not care,
they come to take your life and strip you bare.

They beat you, they bruised you, they mocked
and crucified you. Yet you loved them.

"Forgive them Father", you cried. As they
stripped you of all pried. "They know not
what they do," As your crimson blood ran
down your side.

"It is finished," as you hung your head
and died. But it was not finished, it had
only just begun.

What greater love can there be, that Jesus
lived, died and rose again for me.

Betty Gunter

An American Tale

A nation so spoiled, too many demand
They dance on our spirit, but we pay the band
A desperate struggle just to keep pace
The soul unfulfilled by a senseless rat race

Our pockets are picked by elected elite
As political pork leaves little to eat
Our crimes grow more gruesome, but the cage is too crowded
The gavel goes limp, its integrity doubted

We've deserted our cities to escape their demise
But the smog still drifts over suburban skies
The critic condemns and the cynic sneers
Compassion cries out but no one hears

Amazing advancements appear to relieve
But often disguise, distort, and deceive
The media madness, a major distraction
They mess with our minds, then poll our reaction

In the face of adversity, we cannot retreat
Our moral decay will ensure our defeat
Humanity hidden, lost in the hollow
So many roads, which one will it follow?

James McGhin

Just A Thought

In the night they come creeping these silent words of mine
They fill my heart and ease my soul from the struggles of my time

If only they would come out come out, come out words
Are they mere fantasies seeping into my dreams
or, are they hidden thoughts, waiting to be heard

These thoughts fill my mind in the darkness of the night
Thoughts of turmoil in the world and ways to make it right

We as a great people had better stand up and shout
and tell the World, tell the world
Let's stamp the evil out

When I awaken its all just a thought
If only there was a way to bring it out of the
darkness, and into the light
We could all think a better day

Belinda Austin

A Day At The Beach

These men are rarely mentioned (as their fortunes are unknown).
They left this land in sore lament, to sail away alone.
They walked out to the sea in darkness, Down across the shore.
And boarded Sundry, sorry vessels, none would sail before.

Above the howling of the wind, they hear their children crying.
Their women and their kin lament, the Wild Geese are Flying.
And out among the graves, survivors, beat their breasts and moan
Those who live are murdered, them that rule are overthrown.

The Washing of the waves, is pounding bruise upon betrayal.
On saddened eyes, that only rise to seek out ship and sail.
But Solace is a stranger here, and comfort is unknown.
Since men stood crowded on the pier, to sail away alone.

John Lee Stockard

I Will Always Remember

Always give your elders love and respect
They risked their lives for us so they could provide and protect
Some were slaves who paved the way
So that we could have a better life each and every day
Some worked the fields from sun up to sun down
Never going to their families with as much as a frown
Most were never allowed to go to school
And were always happy to add their meager earning to the family pool
The children were glad to do any type of chore
Dreams of a better life were in their minds galore
When the children wanted to migrate north with hopes of getting ahead
Grandma gave them her blessings with hopes to join their stead
The trip north was hard because they rode in boxcars with coal
They were grateful to God they might someday reach their goal
No job was too hard or too low for them to do
Daddy told me "daughter, I did it all for you
So remember to never tell your elders they are in your way
Their sacrifices and hardships paved the way for a better future
For you today

Freda M. Mays

Word of Fear

In Memory of my brothers, Leonard & Joshua Burley

AIDS is a word that people fear
They run from ones we should be near
The help we can give and the love we show
Will help us through the days that follow
Some good, some bad and some not so bright
Especially when we see that fright
In the eyes of our loved ones
Who say I'm not scared
But please oh please always be near (there)
They know more then we, for they can feel
The closeness of God for it is so real.

Havah Sandra Elain Burley Hume

The Flying Dove

Birds don't sing because they have an answer.
They sing because they have a song.
This world may be weak because of darkness,
but because of dreams, we are strong.
If I could touch the stars, would I be reaching too far?
If I could see a dream, would I be looking too hard?
If I could get away, where would I go?
Is there a place where I belong?
Someone tell me, I need to know.
Its been a question for so long-
Then I think of the singing bird, the flying dove.
With a ring of faith, a lift of love.
Take me to her nest, of soaring heights.
There is no fears, no frowns, no frights.
And here I sing my song of love.
For the feather of life...
The Flying Dove.

Freedom M. Staples

"Us"

I've looked at cards, and bought a few
They speak of things for me and you,
Of all the fun, and love we share
But none can say how I really care,
I've grown so close in love with you
And thought of all the things we do,
Just can't explain the reasons why
This love is strong between you and I,
Your warm embrace and loving kiss
Are just two things I've grown to miss,
I love your smile, that special look
That just one touch is all it took,
I like you close, can feel your heart
You stay with me while we're apart,
I hate the times we're not together
I know someday this will all get better.

Jacqueline S. Meek

Opportunity

There are many opportunities lurking behind closed doors, but
they won't come out. Every lock is locked, every bolt bolted.
All doors that are somewhat open are slamming shut. Opportunity
knocks but once, and so many seem to be knocking, I can't decide.
And if I do, it's too late. Too late to try something new, too
late to just peek inside. My world is an endless corridor lined
with doors, but none are open. Those that are open are
unappealing. The unappealing ones don't tempt me. I am tempted
to run. But where? Down my narrowing hallway? To what - more
closed doors? Will it ever end? Why won't it end? Where is
opportunity hiding? In one of the doors I have already passed?
But I can't go back. The past has passed and won't come back.
Who's to blame? Is it me for running, or the unappealing doors,
or my creator for not explaining the rules? When did it all go
wrong? Will it get better? Will opportunity return? Will it
rear its head? Will it beg me to follow? What if it's wrong?
Who will help me? Will you help me?

Alicia Miller

The Little Things That Please

I know our gifts are many of the little
things that please.
I love a cozy fire place when winter is here.
And blowing winds at my window,
A fire place that sends such joy.
The comfort one feels.
A mist of falling rain
A mist of blowing cold wind
Whether its on my face or on my window.
A new snow storm that comes to those that
are still young at heart.
The Cuddling in our beds at night with
blankets pull up on us.
To keep us warm at night.
I get down on my knees to thank
him for everything that he gives me.

Catherine Whittington

Childhood

Comes now, unbidden,
Those forgotten memories,
Fluttering softly like gossamer butterfly wings.
Remembrances of the places long left behind;
Quiet reminders of past years,
of simpler things
Tucked away within the valleys of the mind;
These fragile memories that time has kissed
And gently set aside.

Carol Poel

Obligations

We dream of things we wish were true,
Things unknown, to me and you.
Our fathers dreamed, their fathers, too.
To conquer space, and oceans blue.

We've traveled to the stars and lived beneath the sea.
Not you and I, but those before, who yearned to find the key
To life and love, and time and space, and all eternity.
They sacrificed to make our world a better place to be.

They lived, they loved, they laughed and cried.
But never ran, or tried to hide.
They stood their ground and side by side,
Fought until they won or died.

The legacy they handed down could last million years.
We need to pass it to our sons and vanquish all our fears.
If the world reverts to what it was, they and all their peers
Lose the dream that's made up of blood, sweat and tears.

Charles R. Clark Jr.

Only You

The way I feel right now tears me apart,
thinking about the day you broke my heart.
Leaving me alone again when you said good-bye;
we can't even be friends now, you can't even
give me a "hi".
Now that you are gone for good, I wish in my
dreams your kiss was still real, your hand
clutching my hand was still here, with your warm
gentle words still lingering in my ear.
Wanting for my dreams and wishes to come true,
because I found my world is complete only with you.

Dena Marie Costa

Looking Back

Looking back and thinking.
Thinking of things I should have said.
Should have done.
And now, I regret, it is too late.

Looking back on things like you and me.
Fate was not too good to one of us.
Mostly because you left, and now are free.
And I'm all alone.
Looking back on mistaken love.
Love that was not mine.
Love that I longed for; but could never find.

Looking back on the good times.
Now that I think there weren't as many as I had hoped;
or thought.

Looking back on memories, both good and bad.
All the times I cried, how I could have died.
And all the times I've laughed; it made me feel so good.
But for only a time.

I don't cry over spilled milk; I'm just looking back.

Anastacia C. Garcia

Just For The Moment

Just for a moment, I stood very still
To catch my breath, from climbing the hill
To see all the splendor, in the valley below
I wanted the world to stop, not go.
To see all the beauty, we miss each day
For we are rushing, our lives away.
Lets bow our heads and renew our minds
For the beauty of God, is not hard to find
Bow your head and say a simple prayer
Just Thank God for our every care.

Dorothy Crotts Callahan

Just For A Moment

Sometimes I wonder, as I watch you lying in the warm sun on the lawn this beautiful day, if you think as I thought when I was your age. Do you look at each strand of grass, study the details in the blade, the lines, the shape? Or the sky, do you ask yourself, why is it blue, and not purple or red? And what about the trees, why do they grow so tall and so wide? Do you think about these things as I did? I am watching you closely now, as you ponder and think some thoughts, wrinkle your brow, then roll them off as you run as fast as you can then plunge to the ground in innocent fun. If I could look into that beautiful mind of yours, what would I see? Do you ask the same questions I asked? Do you seek the answers, or simply go on and discover them as you grow and learn about life? Do you make believe when you are alone, pretend to be a prince or a knight or a ninja? Have you ever wished you had more than you do? How do you feel, my sweetheart, about how you look? Are you wishing you were taller or bigger or smarter and always to be older of course! I know I did, for so long until all I wanted was to be younger! I know these are thoughts of an adult...not a child. And in all reality, maybe it is better this way... total innocence, so wonderful only a child has this right. Thank God for children, and to be able to think thoughts of a child once again.....for just a moment.

Joan Huey

Post Semester Pause

Not many moments ago
This corridor bustled boisterously with busy sounds
Locker doors slamming, loud radios jamming
Sounds of incoherent talking and fast-paced walking
Sounds of off-key singing and warning bells ringing

But now I stand alone
And those noises are only echoes faintly reverberating
I pause and ruminate, reflect and contemplate
About term papers done and the semester now gone
About people I met and instructors I won't forget

Perhaps it may have been different
I might have adhered to my goals and regiments
Done research more thoroughly, read more laboriously
Given more to my studies, curtailed some of the parties
Retained all I learned, fulfilled what my brain yearned

Without desire of retrospective alteration
I'll enjoy the positive aspects of my matriculation

Joe Manuel Martinez

"Winter Weather"

Rain, sleet, ice and snow...
This is how my winters go!
When I was young, I had a blast.
The winters seemed to go by so fast!
We had skating, sledding and an occasional snow ball fight.
When I was a child, it was all right.
Now that I'm older, it isn't so much fun...
Shoveling snow takes so long to get done!
My blood is thinner... I get so cold.
Is this what it's like - growing old?!!
Please, I need sunny weather;
So, I can get myself together!
If I stay here, I know I'll die...
The cold, snowy weather is the reason why!

Arlene B. Reed

Loud And Clear

I like the whistle of a train
Tho some call it a mournful sound.
Long ago I heard it often
As the iron monster covered ground.
In dim recesses of my mind
I recall a friendly wave as it passed by
That juggernaut of passing freight
Or people on the move who do not fly.
It sends a warning call to be alert,
To watch and maybe wait a little while
To avert a possible disaster
So it and you can go another mile.
Sometimes we need to be reminded
Not to rush ahead in daring fate
Just to stop and look about us
To be sure before it is too late.

Arlene Hinds

By Pilgrim's Way

By Pilgrim's way He walked through toil,
Thou pure at heart, no sin to spoil,
While yet a child, the world not see,
The Savior's face from Galilee.
On wisdom's eye He did not boast,
But giving thanks to heaven's Host,
His Spirit burned with passions deep,
The Shepherd's love, His flock to keep.
His words of Love we did not hear,
For the world holds not its Savior near,
Through times of trial when flesh grew weak,
His Father's face did Jesus Seek.
With thorns of sorrow His flesh did tear,
And to the cross our sins He bare,
With open arms true love was shown,
By grace alone our sins atone.
And as I sit and ponder still,
Will my life's journey speak so well,
And thou my time be near at hand,
In Jesus arms I shall live again.

Joel O. Severson

Talk To Me

In my dreams she comes softly at night
Though she may be far away.
To my dream's and fantasy's delight—
With me tonight she will stay.

She is warm and tender—yet grown
Through years of learning from within.
She and I gently pass through doors unknown,
Together, taking us closer in.

She says, "Talk to Me", and I start —
but the words do not follow.
My mind is not within my heart
And the sounds are, oh, so shallow.

I stumble and stammer with fear...
Do I dare release the passion from inside?
A lifetime of doing must be undone
No longer can my feelings hide.

She helps me to release my pain
By understanding my cursed plight.
She whispers, "Talk to me...as you can,
And together we'll grow tonight."

Jack E. Durbin

Someday

Someday when God commands that He has joined to be apart
Though the chasm between us be wide, we shall never be
far away, for we shall never part.
If I go first, be not burdened with sadness, but be of
good cheer,
Though you can not see me, I will always be near.
I will be watching and waiting for that glorious day
When God decrees His angels come and from this life
take you away.
And in that glad reunion in Heaven's fair land
We shall walk the streets of gold, hand in hand.
Never more to part or to roam
For we shall be together forever in this our
Heavenly Home!

Franklin Harry

Life

Many choices lie ahead,
Though you follow ones who've led.

All the time you're wondering if
What you're doing is right.

So that at the end .. You hope to see
The enchanting, guiding light.

Our life is full of pain to endure,
While at the same time we must grow and mature.

Every single thought is a twist and a turn,
The more we lose, the more we learn.

Go for your goals, reach for the sky,
When it's all over, you gave it a try.

Life is a gift from God above,
Treat it special. . .Live and love.

Benjamin Rogers

Last Wish

"I wish to be remembered without ceremony except in the thoughts of my friends and loved ones.

Please leave behind on earth only the love of my spirit, the love of your memories, and scatter on the ground the ashes of my flesh and bones.

We all return to the place from whence we came. I go now to see those gone before.

I will wait for you to join us later. Please be with God until we meet again.

God, please know that I thank you for my life and blessings. I hope I have served you well on earth.

Your humble agent

F. C. Hawkins

"The River Of Life"

The river of time, endlessly flows,
through ages and eons, and never slows.
At times, the waters, are storm-tossed and cruel,

Never bending to a human's rule.
At times, the waters are glistening and white
with promises of happiness and might:
Sometimes the waters are placid and still
So utterly boring, you feel you could kill.
The course of the river can change overnight
First this way then that.
The 'River of Life', so full and diverse
with divine intervention can
quickly reverse.

Irene B. Nelson

Sentimental Heart

Just let me love you for the old and for the new,
through good times, bad times, and times that are blue.

Let me make you sing joys to the Lord,
and praise for that I have come.

Let me make your heart beat comfortably fast when I approach you,
talk to you, call out your name.

Let me be the subject of your never ending conversations.
Let me be your only crave, when love rocks your nation.

Let me revive the love that once lived within your heart.
Let me unravel the secret code which cancels your resistance out.

Let me turn your winters to summer, your falls to spring,
your ordinary life to the life of a king.

Let me introduce you to a love that is real,
a love often revealed in fairy tales.

Just let me love you with all of my heart,
and through all eternity.

Debra J. Amy

"As To A Bird"

The wind murmurs my name
Through this pane of glass
As I sit and watch the raindrops fall
This my song I sing to you
From my heart
I cannot render the words
But which I feel as this
Such a longing to understand
This unknown as to a bird
Yet lived by the clouds in wind and storm
Painted across the sky
Held by the paintbrush - lightening
Sounded fury sharpens the images
Into my wandering mind
Racing speed yet gentle stillness
Is this nature
Inside myself.

Jeanne Ewald

Stairways

Eyes are passages
through which minds travel
meeting one another in passing.

Her eyes scream pain
tortured by red-hot nails
driven by demons hiding in by-ways traversed.

His eyes are tired, watery, red.
Fatigue rolls out from depths
like coastal fog in morning — cold, damp.

Sounds penetrate space
but move no light nor
jostle shadows. Eyes don't hear.

Eye meets eye. Her visual reach
is dropped. His mind
shrinks back down passages to safety.

Eyes are passages. Minds move
through these passages
to avoid, to hide, to find solitude.

Brian T. McCauley

Thank God For My Dad And Mother

Thank God for my Dad and Mother,
Through whom,
He gave me life and love,
And a chance to believe, in a home above.

They gave me a good home,
And six brothers to love,
Though one went on early, to that home above.

There's Ray and Gene and Ernest Earl,
Clay and Donovan and Freddie Darrell,
And of course, there's me, (Dottie),
I head the list, it's true, I am the only Miss.

I'm sure there's been many heartaches,
And many hidden tears,
In a love together for fifty years,
And the greatest thrill to me
Is, we all love one another,
Because of the life and love, of our Dad and Mother.

Dortha T. Black

Mom

The strength for us all, she heals our wounds and keeps the strings tied.
For the sake of saying it, she says what she feels, waking up reality
and keeping our feet from falling asleep.
Thrown into this years ago, a fate sealed by a kiss, a life spent
caring for others and coming second.
Keeping spirits alive and rooms clean from an everlasting filth
that makes the stomach churn.
Feelings unlocked they pour, like wine from a bottle into the
giant pot of our fears and emotions.
Always our savior, always our strength, our pride, our love, our
honor, our honesty, our faith in spirit everlasting.

Jennifer Lucchesi

Mannequin

Time in a bottle
Time against time
Numbers are numerous, what happened to mine?

Touch my face
Kiss my lips
Caress my buxom breast
The crone says to her paralytic guest.

Come inside, close the door, sit with us on the
floor as we watch the spirits coalesce with the dead.

Barbwire hair
Eyes of glass
Please don't touch my feet of brass.

Time in a bottle
Time against time
Numbers are numerous
What happened to mine?

Joanna Michelle Lopez

Our Winter Our Christmas

A hard ride North; it will be great,
Through snow we go forth; hope we're not late.
A very special trip; You've waited so long,
You have let it slip; you really miss home.
Mountains covered in snow; what a beautiful sight,
Excitement will grow; there, the Northern lights.
Pine forest everywhere; majestic and bold,
Fresh clean air; no pollen, no mold.
Happy to see you; loved ones of past,
Days are few; time will go fast.
Then a journey home; and more to see,
Together we'll roam; just you and me.

Dale Cravey

Inspiration

Death is something we all deal with, at one
time or another.
It may have been a mom or dad, for me I lost
a brother
He was a very special friend, whose love always
shone through
If you needed a helping hand, he'd be right
there for you
He earned much love and respect, from every
one that knew him
No wonder it's he I emulate, I've learned
so much from Jim
If I can touch a life or two, I'll not have
lived in vain
Because that's what my brother taught me, and
managed to explain
He was gentle, kind and caring, I was filled
with admiration
That is why may brothers life, to me, is such
an Inspiration.

John Sferrazza

To My Sister

In memory I travel a country road,
To a white painted farmhouse I used to know,
It makes me long to drift away,
Back to the scenes of our childhood,
Back to those happy days;

The years have passed, but I remember still,
The trails we wandered, over the hills,
Where we played across the meadows wild and free
And shared happy hours beneath that old fir tree;

I remember the fragrance of wildflowers,
We gathered along the way,
As we followed the trails back home again
On those carefree summer days;

Our barefoot tracks in the dust are gone,
And though we have lived apart,
I will never forget the days we were young
Or that place so dear to my heart.

Florence Hutchinson

The Oracle

I faced a mirror on a wall of time
To behold the reflection of me.
I saw a dream in the heart of youth
an image without enmity.

Teasing the image I smiled at myself
Then rushed to the cogent dream.
To wines of the world where I lost myself
Or somewhere in between.

I sought the mirror a second time
To behold the image once more.
An abstract painting covered the wall
where the mirror had been before.

Through the smears, circles, and colors
There on the wall of time.
A picture was still being painted
And the artist's hand was mine.

I do not attempt to erase the wall
Great entity of reprimand.
To rely on the figure my prerogative
The brush is still in my hand.

JoAnn Lester

Love, Personally

Most people use flowers and candy per se
To bring their love ones joy and cheer
Instead, I decided to use my own words
To tell what my heart feels near

While sitting here thinking about years well spent,
It instills a joy in my heart.
A darkness comes over as I sit and wonder
'What if I hadn't met you to start?'

But the good Lord knew what He was doing
When He placed you in my life.
He knew that my life was incomplete
So He sent you to be my wife

You've stuck with me through ups and downs
Making my life become whole
With you on my side and God up above
I am blessed; I am one happy soul

Henry L. Sowells

Inner Search

I must sit and meditate;
to cleanse my mind of the
riff and raft that's in my head.

To be at peace and loving thoughts,
that God and Mother Nature taught.

My mind so full of heavy woes
must be light to free the soul.

To be me is to be myself
no matter what the day may bring.
You must see me as I am
and except me as I be.

If you do not like me as I am,
I am sorry for I can not be what I am not;
A fraud to life I have not got.

But truth and love is what I give,
Please except me as I live.

To write the thoughts that come to mind,
would take I'm sure a life time.
I am here but so long
can't you help me live along?

Diane Niemiera

"Daddy"

Daddy, why did you leave me all alone?
To climb the ladder of life - unknown
You were my rock and guiding light
Then too soon - you took flight.
You taught me to laugh and skip
You showed me the woods on nature's trip
You taught me to bait a hook and think quietly by a brook
You taught me how to swim and dive
Because of you - I learned to survive.
With respect to clean and shoot a gun
My young life had just begun -
How I missed our continued walks
Your arm around me in buddy talks all your tender love and care
I needed you so many times to share -
Now I've found your grave today
I know why, and I will meet you in heaven one day.
You would be so proud of your grandson
He is all the things you were, and done
Through all your caring skills to me
He is exactly what you'd want him to be.

Dorothy Brown

The Inner Soul

To the ends of the earth, and back again
to every person in and out
deep inside the souls
past the reflections
past the images
to the real thing
where it all begins
and never ends
where it all starts - to find the real thing
the true thing
but where should you begin the search
when should you stop looking
when, when
stop when you find it
stop when you know who you are
and why you are here
never stop
you'll never really know
so never stop - not until
you DIE.

Jennifer Kauffman

That Special Someone

I can't wait to fall in love!
To find that special man to mean
the world to me.
Someone that would do anything for me,
And that I'd do anything for.
Someone I'd love forever and die for.
Someone who'd bring me roses just because,
Or buy me a teddy bear to show his love.
Someone who'd pick me up for a date
with a flower,
And drop me off with a hug.
Who'd steal a kiss when no one's looking.
Who'd make the sun shine on a stormy day.
Someone who's lap I can sit on,
And dance with in the rain.
I can't wait until it's my turn

Amy Tabb

One Last Cry For You

One last cry for you is all I have
to give, one last time to think of
how without you I wouldn't live.
One last look at you is all I
want to remain in my mind. One
last chance to search for what I
couldn't seem to find. One last kiss
from you is all I want to feel.
One last beat from my heart, until
it has time to heal. One last word
sounds from me as I try to think.
One last tear rolls from my eye, as the
others link. One last try to get me
to know you may be letting me go.
One last day to let my love for you show.
One last frown from me as I tell you I understand.
One last cry for you, lost alone where I stand.

Holli McCulloch

My Gifts

I only hope to give you the love you desire.
To give you warmth when you are cold,
A shoulder to lay your weary head upon-
A soft and tender body to hold.

I only hope to be your best friend.
To give you a smile when you are feeling blue,
A gentle kiss upon your lips-
And my soul for you to make love to.

I only hope to be your wife.
To give you a heart that is pure and true,
A love that would always be by your side-
I just want all of me to be inside of you.

Jennifer Lynn Terman

It All In His Hand

For when we are helpless with no place
to go, and our hearts are heavy and our
spirits are low if we place our poor
broken lives in god's hands. He will
walk with you as footprints in the sand.

So praise god for taking you through
trouble that cuts like a knife and
disappointment that shatter our life
for god's only intention is to strengthen
and bless you. Because there is an
opening at the road through which
each must go alone, and there is a light
we can not see, our Father claims his
own. Beyond the gate our loved one finds
happiness and rest. And there is comfort
in the thought that a loving god knows
best. You are not forgotten, loved one, nor will
you every be. As long as life and memory
last, we will remember thee we don't need to know
where. Easy is going just as long as God is leading her.

Gilda A. Finley

It's A Crazy World

When having a gun is the only way,
To handle your problems in a quick way.
It's a crazy world.

When crack is the only way to make your day,
If you keep on six feet under is where you'll have to stay.
It's a crazy world.

When you want to steal to go with the flow,
Don't be stupid, it's not the way to go.
It's a crazy world.

Now I've just explained to you a few simple games,
That will send your whole life going up in flames.
It's not to get you angry, it's not to get you mad,
But if you are doing these things, it's really kind of sad.
It's a crazy world.

Brandy R. Dickerson

Fate

I looked at you, you looked at me,
We had no clue what fate may see.
Two young kids in the same direction,
Bound together by love and affection.
Times are short but memories are long,
We think of each other in the words of a song.
We thought those times would last forever,
For an eternity, they would never.
Say good-bye for yet another year,
Stop thinking of you, I would never my dear.
We spent some time here and there,
But question fate we did not dare.

Dan Ferrucci

"Thank You"

If through the eye you see my soul, I hide.
To know my thoughts, to see my soul unwhole.
You came, you saw, and gave to me inside.
You took my hand and came into my soul.

To feel the love and hear the voice, I cry.
Curtain is drawn away; the warmth! the light!
Captive, to live first I was need to die,
But now the blood has brought me out of night.

Sorrow and pain, the loneliness, the fear,
The torment I had fought, the war was lost,
And then found I He who is coming near.
The chains are broke! He paid my debt, the cost!

To He who reigns and to the Lamb I write,
Thank You for giving me my life this night.

Colin Smith

God's Will

I did not write or send a card
To let you know that I care
In that moment of your greatest despair
But you were in my thoughts and in my prayers
Everyone needs someone on their journey here
And I know that you know our Lord is always there
So when your tears begin to dry
And happy memories begin to arrive
Of your loved one, it helps to ease the pain
And you can surely say that
He/she did not live in vain
So continue to look up to the hills
They will reveal what is God's will

Francenia V. Simmons

Angel

God sent an angel, to brighten our day
to lift our spirits, as we go our way
Her eyes they sparkle, her smile so bright
Her face so round, what a beautiful sight.

She's an angel this we know
nothing so perfect is here below
God lost an angel, when he let her be born
one less angel his heaven to adorn.

Tho, days be long and hard to take
Angel is there our day to make
Her presence is felt, through out each day
because our hearts she melts away.

She shines like gold, and sparkles like dew
on loan from heaven for me and for you
Her beauty is rare, and hard to find
she's made in heaven, one of a kind.

Her wings are set, her halo's in place
a picture of heaven, we see in her face
Thank you Lord for the loan
of this angel, that's blessed our home.

James E. Lamb

Hope

The troubles we see and read about today
We hope and pray that they go away
We were by the lake when spring came around
With the balmy breezes and that nice wave sound
Now the good Lord meant for us to see
The two baby doves in the small pine tree
To show us the world is still full of love
Reassuring us again by watching that mother dove
Now they are gone and we know they will bring
New life and new hope next year in spring

John C. Miller

Untitled

Give wing to my spirit that I may rise
To live above this earth bound tent,
My spirit longs to be set free,
To be on the heights and commune with Thee.
To be on the heights where You alone
Do rule and reign with grace and strength,
Where all my truth is fully known,
And understood, and welcomed home.
To be on the heights where love abounds
Where spirit peace encircles me,
Where time and words cannot hold space,
And light and truth reveals Your holy face.

Ethel Kugler

Escape From Now

With a needle jutting from the vein, I smile -
To myself, eyes pinned, reality softening slowly,
A muted thump barely reaches my ears, as I fall,
Simultaneously into a wall and a stream of eternal bliss.
Here, beneath the lies, God is dead, my friend.
In this tribe, sensation rules supreme, a dream,
Unearthly breath soothing the flesh, and fire -
Shooting up the spine - burning away the pain.
A non-entity I have become, and I only wish to remain,
At peace with what is, inside this asylum, where
the void is my tomb, like a mother's womb,
safe and serene.

Chris Nigro

Angelic Friendship And Love

You took the time from your busy schedules to bring to us much joy,
To open up our hearts and minds and purify our souls.
Angelic thoughts race through our minds, our hearts feel rid of sin,
Since you brought us the Angels and the Wonders there within.

They help us through our sorrows when we stumble and we fall,
But knowing all about them is a treasure most of all.
They can help us through this life that's filled with so much pain,
They can shower down upon us like a holy rain.

We are lucky in this life to have two friends like you
To know your love and your trust are genuine and true.
When we close our eyes in prayer, you're never far away
Because we always thank the Lord, for sending you our way.

We will always love you, until our dying days
For bringing especially just to us the sweet Angelic ways.
So when you read this poem that's written just for you,
Keep in mind it's from the heart, and every word is true.

Jerry H. Marcum

When There's A Cloud

It seems as though a heavy cloud has settled at my door,
the sun doesn't seem to shine as bright as in days before.

The flowers that I planted with such tender loving care,
now seem to look so faded and just a little drear.
Their little heads seem to have drooped instead of standing tall,
it makes me wonder if they, too, know God has made a call.

I sense a bit of sadness in my little feathered friends
as they make their daily visit for the food I place for them.
They seem to linger longer, they're in no hurry to depart,
it's as though they, too can sense, the hurt within my heart.

I know not when there is a cloud what that cloud holds for me,
but I trust the one who made the cloud to know what's best you see.

Edna P. Davis

Our New School

We have built no stately edifice
to our Nation or our State,
Instead, a house of learning where
we instruct and educate.

It has no ancient history or
mem'ries of days gone by.
But nostalgia will build each passing day
as time will swiftly fly.

These walls will shelter everyone
your daughter or your son.
Then others will build for advancing years
on the foundation here begun.

May everyone work together
as long as this house shall stand.
And send them forth with confidence
to other schools throughout the land.

And as we work to help them grow
a challenge is quietly hurled.
Today they are our children
Tomorrow, Leaders of the World!!!

George C. Manning

Near And Far

Like a small atom particle, I move from place
to place without notice.... without knowing.
Far away from you and I'm over here...
But instead I should be there with you;
hugging you, breathing every breath of air you
breathe, making every cell of your body mine
until your heart, and mine unite in one
single beat!...
If someday you get lost in this lifetime and
doubt who loves you, ask your heart for the
answer, if he says that no one loves you, then
you've forgotten me...
But if he says that there's still someone,
is because I will never forget you.

Jorge L. Ferrer

Ode To My Teacher

It has been a long way from ten
To seventy-three in miles and time, and then
The memories at ten spend themselves well
Into the enriched hours at this end.
The gifts of love, and care, and teaching
   You gave me then at ten,
Have grown in rippled circles
   In the sea of life I've seen.

I love those memories you helped me make,
And there is not much more from this life
   That I would wish to take;
But the most enriching thoughts I have these days,
Is the opportunity to again touch the hand
that formed and made these memories stay.

When all of the minds of your children
Are filled with love and care at their ten,
And all of these tokens counted by St. Pete,
To be laid with heavenly care at your feet,
I hope there is room for some of us to stand
When we visit you in your realm so grand.

James O. Matthews

Adoption

Wee one, born to me, I give to you our family tree
To share with those who raise you.
Think of me as your rootstock, and your family the grafted limb,
Together grows a better tree, the strongest there's ever been.
Two families to love you, how doubly blest you are.
One to give you daily care
And one to love afar.

We plant this tree to celebrate and parallel your life.
May her roots give you stability...
May her boughs enfold you and give you love...
May her blossoms give you beauty...
May her fruit be plentiful...
May her arms, reaching for the sun, represent your goals...
May her rains be gentle and her winds but a sigh...
May she shelter birds and be rewarded with song...
May she stand tall and straight
And represent all that I hope you are...
Yes, your two families can share this tree,
Our hopes for you...
From them, from me.....

June W. McFadden

The Color Tree

A sudden quiet settles round
To take the place of Summer's sound
The passing of Summer green, Nature's demand
To be a part of the Season's plan.

Springs first blade of grass, a blooming flower
New fallen snow, or a refreshing Summer shower
Nature's feats are there for all to see,
But none more beautiful than the color tree.

The blending colors, a sight to see
As early frost brings its touch. To the once green tree
The changes come like a fleeting deer
As through Nature's kaleidoscope the colors appear.

From Nature's easel, colors do abound
In the distance a dove, with its mournful sound
Saying Summer's gone, can't you see
The changing hues of the color tree.

Calvin Lunsford

My Children

My children, you have given me a foundation...
To teach you, guide you, and lead you to a better tomorrow
You have inspired me to give you a self-esteem...
That I can see it being nourished by you daily
The "Aloha Spirit" just glows within you, for I have seen
   it in your thoughts and hearts....
Through your sharing with me your thoughtfulness and concerns
A loving, caring, sharing and giving people that I will be
   proud of forever
Your steps through life are light now, but as you grow
   older, it gets heavier
But I have so much faith and hope in you
I know you will always strive for your highest goals...
   Ask, and it shall be given
   Seek, and you will find
   Knock, and doors will be open to you
Give, and receive a reward beyond your ultimate dreams
Love with all your heart, mind, and soul...
The doors to success will befall upon you
Then you can proudly say, "I made it!"

Dolores Bright

Going Home

If each of us could have his way
To tell the time he would pass away,

There would be no one left to grieve
'Cause none of us would ever leave.

We would always stay with those we love
And give none to share with God above.

So when God comes to take us away,
And when we leave this earth that day,

Go with Love and prayers that soon we, too,
Will share his Love and home with you.

John M. Flynn

Untitled

To touch you
To tenderly brush the hair from your cheek
The warmth of you as we embrace
The softness of your lips touching mine
The soft velvet touch of your breath against my face
To touch you, to have you touch me

To love you
To silently hold you close in my arms
The low, almost soundless moan from your lips as
we search for treasures thought beyond our grasp
Loneliness, heartaches, fears of the past disappear
into that one blissful moment only two can share
To love you, to have you love me

To touch you, to love you
This is my dream
This will forever remain my dream
For dreams are fantasies that never come true

Gerald J. Liska

Wildflowers

Though flung on the wind
To trampled gardens, or isolated meadows,
You sing in simple beauty of being on the
mystic journey; spiraling newness
of life unending.

Capricious wonders,
freely you sway delicate petals,
Dancing to the music of the sun.
Solemnly bow to the moonshine.
Morning springs from darkness.

Fragile tenacious webs of splendor,
You captivate my adventurous spirit;
I long rise to be fruitful, to be gone
Knowing that seeds of hope and life
blossom when I am no more.
yet still I be.

Ann Plunkett

Past Remains

Why are people so fast
To want to change their past.
The damage that was done,
Signifies lessons that were learned.
To wipe them all away,
Would mean learning them another day.
Because the lessons are all the same,
It's only damage that may change.
So why dwell on what's been done,
And tackle THE NEW lessons you have learned.
Because there's only one thing that you can to change:
Your future, and its past remains.

Duane E. Patterson

Risks And Chances In Your Lives

To laugh is to risk appearing the fool.
To weep is to risk appearing sentimental.
To reach out for another is to risk involvement.
To expose feelings is to risk exposing your true self.
To place your ideas,
your dreams before a crowd is to risk their loss.
To love is to risk not being loved in return.
To live is to risk dying.
To hope is to risk despair.
To try is to risk failure.

But risks must be taken,
because the greatest hazard in life is to risk nothing.
Those who risk nothing do nothing,
have nothing and are nothing.
They may avoid suffering and sorrow,
but they cannot learn, feel, change, grow, love or live.
Chained by their attitudes,
they are slaves, they have forfeited their freedom.
Only a person who risks is truly free!

John Parisi

"Daydream"

Intricate odessey
today
in me.

It has no name/has no sex
Endless in identity.

It does not intrude/does not include
oneness in harmony.

It is not audible/is not pliable
fluid of serenity.

It does not a moment waste/does not give way to haste
timeless in dimension.

It does not reflect/does not project
No ego to contend with.

it seduces in daylight/infuses with moonlight
shameless in surrender.

It brings no anticipation/leaves no apprehension
Contentment in surreal.

Dianne Damico

Say I Love You Before It's Too Late

I love you, I love you, say it today,
Tomorrow the chance may not come your way.
Three little words, what a difference they make;
I love you, I love you, before it's too late.

To say I love you, why should it be—
So hard to say, for you or for me?
It's commanded by Jesus for us to do,
"Love one another, as I love you."

Three little words, might change one's fate,
Say I love you today, before it's too late.
Moment by moment life passes by,
Don't wait 'til it's over, and have to ask, why?

Just say I love you, and have no regrets,
Those three little words one never forgets.
Say it now, the opportunity take,
Who knows, the next breath, could be too late.

Alta W. Tarpley

Future Dreams

I am young, naive they say,
too innocent to understand.
Money, they say, is the force that guides,
that turns the mill, and tills the land.

Yes, I am young, naive, perhaps,
but still my heart can't understand
why streams flow back and forests fall
and bombs must drop where kids once ran.

For I can see a different world
where small seeds grow to towering trees,
where children play and birds fly free
a world of love, a world of peace.

Yes I believe in a better world,
free of blood and crumbling bones.
An Eden of green 'neath stars and sky
a world that's ruled by love alone.

Alicia Peterson

Mystic Man

You are my mystic man and with your magic touch have given my soul more than any mere mortal can. You have cast your spell and rescued my heart from its hell, my fantasies, my passions, no one had ever been shown, but like magic and with no words spoken your soul had already known.

My hearts wishes fulfilled by your sweet kisses. In your strong arms I am sheltered from all of life's harms and transported to a higher plain, far away from sorrow and pain.

Oh mystic man, what powers you possess, ask of me any want or desire, any request. You will never be denied, about this I would not lie.

You are my mystic man and I, I am your woman.

Carolyn Gunnoe

A Last Wish

SPRING, you joyous youthful knave,
touch me, smile at me, lend me your strength
to brace myself, and to be brave
against the icy winter's length.

SPRING, don't waste the time, come quick, I pray.
I want to greet you just once more
before my breaking spirit goes its way,
to pass eternity's awaiting door.

SPRING, I waited. Hoped so much to catch,
through my slowly closing, tired lid,
your first triumphant thawing patch
to tell me that you'd come.

And SPRING just did...

Ingeborg Hollwoeger

My Prayer

Lord, will you hear my prayer?
To you, my sins I declare.
You are my God of righteousness;
Many times you lifted me while in distress.

Your words are like apples of gold in pictures of silver;
You are my rock and deliverer.
Keep me locked under your wings
And safe from all worldly, ungodly things.

Help me to be pure in heart;
In your path, I shall not depart.

Dorothea J. Dressel

Awakening of a City

You're standing on a small hill, surrounded by
trees, except to the east.

You can hear water running down a
stream bed, a waterfall not too far away tumbles
across the rocks.

The early morning air, fresh, brisk to the
lungs and yet it's soothing because it's pure with no pollution.
The stars starting to fade out as early dawn
emerges to light the sky.

Soft colors of red & orange light the edges of
the horizon. As the colors become brighter,
soft sounds of birds singing and chattering can be heard.

As the sky brightens on the horizon, the yellow
sun appears and dazzles your mind for a few
moments; all too soon other sounds can be heard
in the background swallowing up the sweet sounds of nature.

Car, trucks, buses, trains, people walking & talking
as the city all around you wakes, to start
another day.

John W. Blazin

Journey's End

His walls were full of journeys he had taken every day,
Trips as far as oceans, to mountains far away,
Places of great mystery, he had never seen before.
The life he shared with very few lurked behind the door.

Pictures told the stories that words could not describe,
The world in all its splendor, so wondrous and alive,
He entered lands of fantasies, that gave him lasting pleasure,
Accepting the fact that in his pursuit, he would never
find his treasure.

Dreams he stored within his mind had faded with the years,
Sitting helpless and alone his eyes filled up with tears,
Only he had felt the lose which no one could amend,
Knowing deep within his heart, he had reached his journey's end.

Judy A. Stewart

"True Love Is For Eternity"

True Love is not easy to find.
True Love is a blessing that is divine.

You can tell True Love because time is the key;
For bonding the Hearts of both you and me.

I know my True Love is near,
When I feel the caring and loving appeal.

I pray each day that True Love is with you.
Without your True Love, I feel so blue.

ETERNITY is the bond to True Love,
As sure as I know there's a God above.

He blesses both you and me with this grace,
And it truly reflects in each embrace.

Darling, tell me your True Love is only for me,
As I tell you, with love, my sweet ecstasy;
of sharing True Love ETERNALLY.

Ednarose M. Smith

Of Love-Long Past

Royalty being what is they say,
true love is hard to find.
Kingdoms will fall come what may,
nasty battles are unkind.

It is you my princess, my only love
I'll worship way past death.
For through my fingers will run your hair
your name on my last breath.

On your mount, you play with Jewels
As if they were a toy.
And pass my field no second look
for your love sick peasant boy.

If fate be cruel and destiny true
We'd never be apart.
But I your humble servant
Will always have you in my heart.

Joseph Edward Brown

When I Am Gone

Cry not when I have gone, because I am only sleeping.
Try to understand, replace JOY for your weeping.

I could not stay, or even linger a moment longer.
For I have a very important meeting with my FATHER,
who is ever stronger.

He will open His arms to receive my tired soul.
And, I will cling to Him and His vastness, to see all beauty unfold!

Miss me if you must ...... think of me as I rest ....
But, believe I am always with you, for that is one of life's tests.

To those who really know me, I am sure you will understand.
There is an empty spot where I once stood.
REACH OUT AND TAKE ANOTHER'S HAND.

Andrea R. Silvey

Yester Years

Today I traveled back over roads of yesteryears,
Trying to see the things I thought so dear.
The world I saw thru a child's eyes,
Came back to me as a great surprise.

How did the house get so small,
I could have sworn the trees were a hundred feet tall.
The old school house I thought so great,
Now is so small and about to break.

My friends were thin and in good shape,
Now they all seem to have a problem with weight.
The railroad station so long, I could have sworn,
Now it stands empty and so forlorn.

The big cornfields that dad use to plow,
Now hold herds of city boys cows.
The little road where we kids use to play,
Now has become a super highway.

How strange it seems to these eyes of mine
That things look so different in such short time.
I stopped and looked and wiped a tear,
Knowing that we can never go back to yester year.

Bernice Courtade

Unconditional Love

Reflecting on the past
Trying to theorize exactly what happened
Suddenly someone remarks
Questions the situation, the arrangement
Rouses my soul
Unable to respond satisfactorily
Emotions emerge
What posses staying
Apparent as daylight
"Unconditional Love"
Absolute, perfect, positive
Ultimate love
Need anymore be said

Jolene M. Fetta

White Birches

Far off to where the voices fade, the river
tumbles through a glade of young and tender
trees.

Their leaves are such a summer green, buttered
by the sun and softly fluttered one by one
by a lambent breeze.

Their slender trunks
are satin smooth as children's' faces to my touch,
and the whispered buzzings of winged insects in
their branches accompanies the song
of the river.

Would that I could wander
this delicate wood 'til Vega's rise.

But the voices call to me, and reluctantly
I answer.

Fritzi L. Cahill

News Media

News Media As - is
Turn Select News channel of choice
What do you hear - what do you see
News Media relating mankind's story
as it said - live on dead
Right or wrong
Yours or mine - Hers or His
As - is
The rich the poor and all the rest
Mankind Searching life's highway
for happiness best
Select News channel of choice
Hear and see mankind's story in song
Right or wrong
Best of the Best - worst of the worst
On life's journey from the
Cradle to the grave.

Jessie Turner

The Day My Friend Came Over

The day I picked some clovers,
Was the day my friend came over,
We went to the mall, we bought a new shawl,
We talked in the hall, as we wrote on the wall,
We had a grand ball as we did that all,
It was just us together, and no one to call,
We played with my ball, but she had a great fall,
She seemed too small but yet too tall,
We had a grand ball as we did that all,
But when she left, I looked at my clover,
And knew it was a remembrance of
the day my best friend came over.

Alexis Castillo

Forever Together

Together as one, yet separately,
two lives begin their beginning.

Lives to be forever entwined,
forever together, forever sharing.

Together as one, yet separately,
two lives begin their beginning.

September, oh September,
the tender breath of life shared,
that lovely September.

Two precious gifts from heaven,
that lovely September, forever to share,
forever to remember.

Together as one, yet separately,
two lives begin their beginning.

Filled with wonder at the presence of the other,
knowing gently they will be forever entwined,
forever together.

Barbara Delk Bagley

Reflections Of Life

Can anyone experience life completely
Unless they have lived it to the fullest?
After all we are only mortals.

No more than death can be experienced
Unless we have passed thru its portals.

The wind blows but no one sees its passing—-
You can taste it on your tongue—smell it in your nostrils.
Feel it on your face with reverent
passion - but no one recalls its passing -

Life, like a dormant field in winters
Dead springs to life in a fertile
Field, when plowed of winter's dread.
Nurtured and tended with loving
Care its shackles laid bare

Reaching out with a thirst that
has no bounds, new life abounds all around.

Our present, future or passed, even if
written in stone——can be erased
By our own doing... our own un-doing...
Or by not doing at all — after all we do it alone.

Charles K. Wood

City Boy At A Country Sunset

The night rises, doesn't descend,
Up from the ground on a thousand tiny wings.
And the crickets sing
Just one tune.

The dampness reaches up from the grass
To tug at pants cuffs and tangle shoelaces,
As the daylight races,
Gone too soon.

The dark seeps up, making pretend
It's just more shade under tree limbs and hedges,
Drowned on the edges
Of the land!

The night rises, doesn't descend,
Carried on creature melodies that linger,
With unseen singers
Close at hand.

David G. Vowell

In Loving Memory Of Drew Michael Coffey

All in a sudden, burdens become heavier
upon my shoulders,

Foggy mornings become lost in deep despair
as they develop into evenings of
overwhelming storms.

Even then, I never cease to clinch the desire
to rise above the thought of failure.

With chin up and shoulders back, I emerge
into the merry-go-round of life on earth.

Never resting, never surrendering to the
things that used to complicate my life,

Onward for now!

Greg Carroll

The Time Is Near

As I Sit Silently on this gloom filled day
Vaguely dreaming of Times long gone by the way
When I sailed my proud lady upon the sea
With not another ship in sight just my pretty lady and me
She cresting each white capped wave so effortlessly
My hands guiding her lovingly across the boundless way.
She tossing her head so daintily.
As I dreamed of those glorious days of old.
The gloom was slowly dispelled by a soft radiant light of gold
And some how mysteriously I found myself as of yore
Upon my gallant Lady's pristine white deck in neat array
Her sails were full, as if a steady breeze were blowing
through her stays.
But with a sea so glassy calm this could never be.
And then I knew ere last. My time had come to pass.
This sweet nymph of the sea had been sent for me
To carry my soul before king Neptune's throne
And if I am to be found worthy
To board at last, that great white ship in the quay,
And be with my supreme captain for eternity.

Jerry K. Harbour

"The Poet"

Words written in kind,
  Voices of the mind.
Gifts of views from a romantic soul,
  Bard's songs that never grow old.
Words, simple and sweet,
  With power that affects the strong to the meek.
Tales of lives near and far,
  Lifting hearts to the stars.
Wishes written in form,
  Telling tales of life's storms.
Feeling opened for the world to see,
  Inside views of emotions in you and me.
A gift from today and yester eve,
  Away to let one's heart be free.
Thoughts written in fun,
  Dark dreams brought to the sun.
Words allowed to soar,
  To touch your heart's very core.
A poet, reaches out, touching blank pages,
  Sending Life's message through the ages.

Jo Lemmons

"My Wife"

Green with flecks of fire, these are your eyes,
Vows decades lasting, these are our ties,
Selfless and loving, this is your heart,
You never change, no, not ever, even from the start.

Kind words of love, your mantle, always so true,
The one who loves me best, in all the world is you,
Virtue and honesty, your badge and your claim,
"Compassion" is the translate, of your sweet, sweet name.

"Taking" has never been, any part of your life,
You give of yourself so freely, kindly, my wife,
Your sacrifices are many, your wants are so few,
To know about true love, is to know you.

You seek not fame or fortune, nor silver or gold,
Happiness to you, is love, life, and growing old,
Having much or little, matters not to you,
You care about the pure things, honesty and truth.

You count yourself as no one, why? I don't understand,
You are all and everything, in the life of this man,
In all the world there could be no one, greater in my life,
For by the Grace of God in Heaven, you are my wife.

George Dunagin Jr.

The Dragon In My Closet

A menacing sight if ever I saw one lurked in the closet in my room,
Waiting for me to open the door to all its evil and gloom.
Once a day this horrible creature spit fire and squeaked and groaned,
It puffed up big, its face lit up, and it set off on its own.
It cleared a path wherever it went as it whisked and sucked and hissed,
Then is would turn around, and with another swipe come back
for what it missed.
At last it had indulged enough and returned to its closet lair,
Its fire at last extinguished, it collapsed without a care.
So now my closet's safe and sound, no dragon lurks about,
Until tomorrow at this time when mom takes the vacuum out!

Jaynie Cheney

I Saw A Tree

I saw a tree in a field today
waiting for Spring to come its way;
Waiting for Spring to change its face
from brown-hued wood to greening grace.
Waiting for earth and sky and sun
its stream of sap to gently run.

There was beauty and strength in
the way that it stood,
rooted so firmly midst sod and wood;
Standing alone in that barren field
waiting its leafing branches to yield;
Waiting through snow and ice and rain
for green-tinged leaves to bud again.

And in that tree I saw God's plan:
If a tree must wait, then so must man,
for green to come and sap to flow;
for thoughts to root and minds to grow.

Oh, God, make me patient as that tree,
As I await Your Spring to flow through me.

Geraldine Bartley

Anticipation

Here I sit all alone
Waiting for this quiet old phone
Longing just to hear your voice
And hoping that I've made the right choice

I think of nothing but you all day
Wondering why I feel this way
You've awakened feelings I thought were gone
But now I'm finding they're here...and strong

So now I'm left wondering what to do
I feel the need to see you soon
Wishing we had a little time together
Yet hoping it would last forever

At last it rings...I hope and wonder
No such luck just a wrong number

Christie Savageau

Beyond The Cloud

Have you ever missed someone you didn't know?
Wanted to go some place you can't go?
Dreamed something that cannot be?
Saw something you cannot see?

If you have you are just like me.
For I have seen things that I can't see.
I have gone to places unknown,
And shown things that can't be shown.

I have reached up past that cloud,
And been quiet while still being loud.
I have reached up past my limits,
And I have explored everything in it.

By having imagination and love,
You can explore the world above.
For always remember love is the key
That will lead you to peace and harmony.

It will help you fly above the sky,
And speak the truth, but yet still lie.
For beyond that cloud lie amazing things,
But amazing more are the things you bring.

Brianne Bourcier

The Little Mouse!

The little white mouse,
was looking for a house.
Her name is Miss Quesy,
and life is not easy.
The climbed up a hill,
and the forest was still.
In the distant there was chatter,
when the name closed, birds had a spatter.
She sat on a rock,
it was a beautiful spot.
Branches where moving,
Miss Quesy's heart was soothing.
While looking around,
a very old tree she found.
In amusement she saw,
a wonderful flaw.
The hummed a song,
the search had been long.
Miss Quesy the mouse,
had found her warm cozy house

Josepha P. Peterson

Mister

He sits on the porch in his favorite chair
Watching the children frolic in the summer night
Trying to catch fireflies and putting them in a glass jar.

He wishes he could be carefree like the youth he sees before him.
He tries to remember that it was like when he was a boy,
But he can't.
Too many horrid memories of war and loss
Ar blocking those of happiness and joy.

He sits back, closes his eyes and goes to sleep
On the porch in his favorite chair
On a summer night
While distant laughter of youth dances in the wind.

Christine Burke

It

Standing in the lamplight, darkness seeps in from every way.
Watching, waiting, for IT told me ITs revenge would come today.
Walking slowly away from the light tripping over the wet, damp, ground.
I turn and look and speed my pace, for IT never plays around.
A suspended drop of salty sweat drips into my eyes.
Moments of euphoric pleasure, leading to many vicious lies.
Still can't slow, goosebumps are spreading, glancing, looking round and round.
Legs are pumping, shadows dancing, flying by over the ground.
Clothes are clinging, world is spinning, churning, churning my mind goes.
Hot, sticky breath down my neck, cold and wet rain soaks my toes.
Regrets is on the tip of my tongue, fear in every breath I take.
Stumbling, falling, striking rocks. "I'm sorry's" I'll not live to make.
Rolling, looking into ITs face as suspense pumps through my blood.
As I watch IT jump onto me, In my mind darkness does flood.
Never again will I apologize, regretfully I say.
Never again will I deceive IT. I sealed my fate long before today.

Brenda Jennings

The Tree of Life...

The tree of life is very old and each of us is a flower,
We all are given certain gifts to mold into special powers,

Some of us work very hard to build our natural treasure,
some of us don't work at all and squander our gifts on pleasure,

Like all flowers, ours grow old and cease to bear their beauty,
One would think that to preserve its luster would be our one true duty,

But I've played away my best years and my petals now are withered,
I dallied here and partied there and all the while I've dithered,

Still I know there's more to life than love and wine and song,
I have a duty to the young to help them make their blossoms strong,

I have to try to show them that my fruit could have had more flavor,
And that theirs may be better yet if my advice they savor,

But isn't this the same ole stuff my daddy told to me?
And you can tell by this rhyme that his advice I didn't heed,

So why should anyone follow my advice?
I had my shot, I rolled my dice,

And good or bad, right or wrong, I have done my part,
I dropped a seed from the tree to give another blossom its start.

Jerry A. Martin

The Other Side

There is the other side that we all think is not there
we all have it back deep in our minds, but we really don't care
It's really there, but we are all afraid to face
Our inner thoughts that we always try to erase
Only the ones who really want to live and survive
Are the whole individuals on judgement day will strive
Those who try to deny fate and the true meaning of life's quest
Will be the one's who suffer the torment and the hate the good detest
The other side is the place even the evil see in a dream
But, it will never come to them until the day they redeem
Redemption seems so easy to those that think they believe
Thinking they pray for a day and God's blessing they'll receive
The other side is good for the one's who know the true cost
But, for the evil pretenders the beast prevails, God they have lost.

Dale S. Smith

Searching

In the deep chasms of time,
we all long for love sublime.
We search and yearn along life's way, thinking,
"Maybe I'll find my 'love' today."

We gaze at each passerby,
searching for a spark of
familiarity in the eye;
hoping in the "windows of the soul" to find
a spark of recognition
from a lifetime gone by;
hoping to feel an energy with a vibration
like unto ours—a kindred spirit;
nay, only to meet eyes which are cold, empty, and dour.

Carol Novatnak Short

How Children Learn To Pray

Let's talk to God together, said the mother to her child.
We can thank him for our blessings and visit for a while.
We can tell him that we're grateful for all that he has done,
And that he loved us so much, that he gave his only son.
We can ask him to guide us in the way that we should go,
We can tell him what we're feeling and the reasons that it's so.
And if there's something we can't do, the two of us together,
We can ask God to help us, then we can do it so much better.
For what you ask of God, you know that he can do,
And though he knows beforehand, he wants to hear from you.
So, don't be bashful, now my son, there's nothing you can't say,
For God wants to know you better, in every single way.
He wants to hear your voice, He wants to see your smile.
He wants to spend this time with you because you are his child.
For we should not take for granted that our children understand,
Just why we talk to God, unless we take them by the hand,
And share this blessing with them, so they might know him too.
And maybe someday talk to God, just as now they talk to you.
Though sometimes children listen when we tell them what to do,
It's more likely they will imitate what they see in you.

Ethel White

Depression

Descending slowly into despair
Weighed down by thoughts too foreboding to lift
Overcome by an anguish that smothers
The desire to enjoy life

Trudging through the labyrinth of a darkened mind
Mired in perceptions of helplessness
Neutral, detached it matters not
Bewildered and daunted yearning for release

Shackled to the blackness of the soul
Struggling with the burdens of each day
Blind to the world around
Surrendering to the pain of living

John E. Venlet

Needles And Pins

We've been all through it again
we confess to the right and to the left
if we only knew what was really best,
we would be delighted to be his guest

In living for ourselves, we can only say
let the rest be delivered, and the best be set free,
for out of deliverance comes feelings of great measure,
a deliverance for you and a deliverance for me

When we come forth with our desires in our hearts,
we enter into a covenant, which is far beyond you and me
This is a decree, just designed for you and for me
as we search for more understanding, the truth is always there

We look everywhere, not knowing the answer is so near
Reach me with your presence, receive glory, or Doom...
know in every crevice, every corner, every inch of the way,
He is reaching out to you, you can say yea or nay

Needles and pins, needles and pins,
they ain't much comfort, those needles and pins, needles and pins
Needless to say, if you don't pray,
your sin will befall you again and again

John W.

A Child

We raise a child it costs a lot
we deny ourselves to see she's got.
We worried when she was sick in bed
we sat alone and held her hand.
We got repaid with a special smile
A precious word. I love you mom.
But she grew up and went away
those precious words I never hear her say
my heart is breaking but I understand
my life goes back to when I held her hand
So a needy child is not in years
But in someone who sheds a tear.
So give a smile, hold a hand
show her you understand.
And God hears and lets you know
he has heard when you shed a tear

Helen Matthews

Who's Really Afraid?

Dreading the future, enduring the pain
We huddle in blankets and hide from the rain.
Tears fill our eyes and pour into the gutter.
"Can you spare me a quarter?" "Can you help a sick brother?"

The masses walk by, avoiding a glance;
Tomorrow, perhaps, it may be their "dance".
Fear fills their eyes as they try to avoid us —
A steady reminder are the poor and the homeless.

How uncertain their lives are—they just can't convey
What tomorrow may bring, so they try to remain
Busy and blind to the fear deep within
As they hide from the truth, "I could be just like him".

You cannot ignore us; we're homeless and part
Of the fear and uncertainty deep in your heart.
For a moment our eyes meet, the pity is mine,
For I am what I am; you avoid and deny.

Who's really afraid for the rest of their lives?
"Not us", say the homeless, "We've learned to survive."

Judy Tsoukalas

If

Society looks down upon those below them
We jump at the chance to make fun of them
Tearing away their dignity piece by piece
We never stop to think about what it's doing to our world.
If the poor were rich
And the rich were poor
What would the world be like
If the homeless had a home
And no one was on the street
What would the world be like
If the black man was the white man's friend
And the white man was the black man's friend
What would the world be like
If you could buy anything you wanted
With love and caring
How many people would own nothing
If everyone would accept their neighbor as a person
And love them like a brother
What would the world be like
What would, the world be like?

Brant Pickard

Have You Heard?

Have you heard? Christ the Lord, is coming to reign.
We know not the day, nor the hour;
But what we do know is; that
He has a great and marvelous power.

And those who are doing wrong
And living a life of sin,
Unless they truly repent, will find,
There is no way, that they can win;

But they will live in torment, forever.
Oh, what a terrible shame!
Yet, there is no one earth, but themselves,
Yes, only they themselves, will be to blame.

But those who are living a life of service,
And who the Lord's Commandments Keep,
Will have joy and happiness forever,
And be counted among His sheep.

May we so live, that we will ever be counted worthy,
As each day goes swiftly by;
For when we are living His Glorious Gospel,
On our Precious Savior, we can always rely.

Jennie W. Madsen

"A Little Prayer"

It seems like only yesterday
We laughed and reminisced
About our happy, fun-filled years.

Today is oh, so different
As I try to hide my tears.

Your face is drawn, you seldom smile.
You seem so worried all the while.
You see strange people in your chair,
Unruly children everywhere.

The things you need and use the most
Just seem to vanish in the night,
All tucked away in some strange place.

Dear God, please, please bring back the light
That used to shine in his dear face.

In spite of all life's fading touch
I know you love us very much.

Polly Prindle

Untitled

I love Old Glory flying high, flinging her colors to all passing by.
We learned to love and respect her early in school, to treat her with dignity was always the rule.
I get a lump in my throat when the flag passes by in parades, or just seeing her against the blue sky.
It just breaks my heart when I see what some do to insult her, or burn her as was done by a few.
Our government isn't perfect, oh no, but it's some people not the flag, that need to just go.
Love it or leave it has been said often before, but she signals "Come in" like a wide open door.
Yes I love my flag and my country too, and there's many things we each can do to help our young people learn what we know, of the blood sweat and tears that made our country grow.
We need God in our lives, we need prayer in our school, and we all need to practice the great golden rule.

Elva M. Gross

Life

Life can be a nice dream, about mice,
we love life, it is very nice,
in life we love and grow everyday
just like mice,
roll a dice and your dream will be nice,
we are warm-hearted, not like ice,
roll a dice and your dream about life
will be nice.
It's your life so make it right,
you could be the light,
that shine's for all to see,
even over seas.
In your dream you can be a mice
but not in life,
you may even have a wife,
when it's time to leave,
you may have to say please,
to go were you want to be.

Aggie Snyder

Thoughts On Mothers' Day

Yearly, on the second Sunday in May
We pause to observe Mothers' Day,
To remember what we owe to mothers,
Fonts of love beyond all others.

In her womb we were created,
At her breast our hunger sated,
'Twas she who taught us right from wrong,
And how to play and sing a song.

She saw we got the most from schools,
Learning games and all the rules,
Prepared us for our roles in life,
To achieve success and cope with strife.

One day a year is not enough,
To appreciate such selfless love.
Only in devoting our lives to others,
Do we properly honor mothers.

Carroll F. Sweet

God And Spring

Spring is such a wonderful season
We should look to God for this very reason
He gives us our loved ones, our neighbor and friends
Unnumbered blessings that never finds end.
He fills each flower with buds so bright
O' can't you see, God is our Light?
He died on the cross to save us from sin
So look to Him and Heaven you'll win
Where we'll walk the streets all paved in gold
And live forever where we'll never grow old
It will be just a Paradise up there above
With God in His Mercy, Great Kindness and Love
He is so wonderful-Our God you see
He loves every child, even you and me
This is my way of saying "How I love God So!"
It won't be long before I see Him, I know
Let's start out this spring and remember each day
We must take time to kneel and pray.
So as God gives us this wonderful spring
Let's always remember He's Our "Lord, Master, Saviour and King."

Betty L. Edson

In The End

All throughout life, people live in fear of the truth.
We spend time trying to discover questions
That cannot be answered.
Loved ones die, wars are fought,
Cities are burnt to the ground,
But in the end love is still here.
Love cannot be destroyed.
Where there is love, there is peace,
And where there is peace, there is love.
Without them, we would no longer exist.
Love helps us stand alone and say,
"Nothing is going to hurt me today."
Peace helps us stay together and love one another.
If we learn to love each other,
All good things will follow,
Leaving a trail of peace behind us -

Chris J. Steib

A Thousand Years Of Peace

When we find the gift we were created to share
We will fly like the eagle...alive and floating on air
Sharing the gift frees all of us to fly
So easily and effortlessly soaring high into the sky

There are the dreams to remember and realize
The magic potion manifests...the spell casting surprise
Spellbound for so long for forever it might seem
Then...the age of aquarius dawns again in our dreams

Dawning is the day to let go and release
Moving to a new millennium...a thousand years of peace
The heart at peace is a cup full of love
A promise full of passion all of heaven heals above

The unique gift unlocks the key to all knowing
The stars sharing the sky...a free fall like floating
So quiet and silent hearing only the heart
A clearing in the calmness with a higher healing art

The generous earth gives and gives and gives
In a garden of appreciation much love and magic lives
Dawning is the dream to remember and release
Higher vibrations happening...a thousand years of peace

Deborah Reinhard

Rejoice In This Day!

This is the day which the Lord hath made;
we will rejoice and be glad in it. Psalm 118:24

This is the day the Lord has made,
And each hour will be blessed
If you just ask the Lord for the strength
To do your very best

Whatever path you follow,
He'll be walking by your side
To be your source of comfort
Your friend and constant guide

The Lord is understanding
His mercy will not fail
His love for you is infinite
His wisdom will prevail

Remember this each morning
And you'll not be afraid
To face with growing confidence
The day the Lord has made

Jacquelyn S. Rosier

Time To Mend

The deceased minutes of this day
Weary and made to bleed
This bone and flesh of slow decay
That heart of sound mind and greed
I've swept away this very spot
Where angels tend to die
Of men who look for hearts sought
When they hear the heavens sigh
And the slow winds of many years
Of days tired and old
When woman wipe away bloodied tears
Than the heart is suddenly sold
Growth continues in that pain filled mind
While sleeping children stare at your dreams
When the world is crooked and unkind
There's an angel on these torn seams
Now's the time to mend your veins
Bloodied and cut
Here's the time to end your pains
And close the door of fear and misery tightly shut.

Jaclyn Hare

Dark is night

So, day is light and dark is night.
Well, my friend, who gave you the right
To say this is true and the way it will be
Then turn to say that my country is free.

Math and Physics are real for you but see
These things are not what is real for me.
Real is guilt for not being male
In a society that says this is how I should feel.

Real is realizing that it's only your opinion
And hope one day the things you say shall be forgiven.
Like you say, "Ignorance is bliss" as you pat me on my head
All the while I think the same each night as I go to bed.

So, day is light and dark is night.
If that's what you think, then I'll say you're right.
But don't dare think that this upside down frown
Means that I have let the bastards grind me down.

Catherine Aloi

Too Far Ahead

When my hopes were high, and my dreams
were just a step away.
You were by my side
But for some reason you walked away.

A taller, building was being built
and you wanted to become the steeple
I can't believe you left my dreams for
a room of strange people.

Are you trying to kill me?
Are you trying to shoot me down?
You knew my expectations and you buried
them into the ground.

You have your many followers
or do you call them your pets
You scratch them behind the ears when they obey you
And when they go along with your ignorant pet tricks.

Your followers believe you can fly
But I have yet seen that happen
I'm asking them the question of why
You've made their lives misshappen.

Coren Eckhoff

Beginning With You

Our elders are worried about the youth of today.
We're "slackers," and "losers," and a price we must pay.
There's nothing to prove, they're wrong about us.
When there's sex, and drugs that bury us in dust.

Our future is lost; it seems taken away.
From those who live their life for one day.
Death is the result of one night of fun.
How did we know that war was almost won?

How can it be? This world filled of crass,
There's rape and divorce, and the ones who harass.
When one cannot walk down their very own street,
Without the threat of finding defeat.

There's suicide and hate, and no place to turn,
That feeling of happiness, will forever be yearned.
There's loneliness, there's pain; empty hearts all around.
The friend in the mirror is all that you've found.

The message of hope, in our minds is a lie,
Unless at least one doesn't let life pass by.
One person makes a difference; there IS more we can do
Let us not blame others, let us begin with YOU!

Angela S. Thomas

A Winter Night's Work

Some short little elves all dressed in green,
were the smallest men I've ever seen.
They all dashed around to get their job done
but it seemed to be a lot of fun.
A fat jolly man all dressed in red,
pulled up to my house in a big gold sled.
He whistled and hollered for his reindeer to stop.
But they wouldn't listen, so their heads got a bop.
"Dasher and Dancer your making me crazy"!
"Commit and Cupid quit being so lazy"!
"Prancer and Donor follow my calls"!
"Vixen and Blitzen stop climbing the walls"!
When the sleigh finally stopped, Santa gave a big cheer,
for the jolly old man knew morning was near.
"My jobs almost done. This house is the last.
I love Christmas Eve, it's always a BLAST"!!

Eileen M. Bosiacki

You Kill Me

Thy lover
Thy device
Thy lover
Thy sacrifice

You kill me

Slow and painful
It's most shameful

You kill me

Thy lover
Thy dependent
Thy lover
Is thy defendant

You kill me

Thy lover
Thy keeper
Thy lover
Thy grim reaper

You kill me

Why? "Because I love you!"

Daniel Jay Letchworth

Time

Time it passes,
Time goes by,
We tend to forget the faint
little cry,
of all the people who lived
and then died;

Some who had plenty,
Some who had none,
Some who only just begun;

Let's not forget their
faint little cries:

For we could be next,
the one who dies,
If time decides to
pass us by.

Judith Lynn

Wonderful Wish

Having a wonderful wish
Time you were here
here in my heart
Time for a wonderful wish
Having you here
here in my heart

I wish for a wonderful time
When wonderful wishes come true
I wonder if wishing in time
Will bring wonderful wishes like you

I wish for a wonder sometime
Wish you were here
here in my heart
In wonder I wish for the time
You will be here
here in my heart

Everett R. Simpson

The Value Of A Smile

To add a little sunshine
To a day that seems so blue
Just add a friendly smile
That's all it takes from you.
A smile can mean a lot
To one who feels despair
So do smile more often
Let them know you care.
For a smile not only cheers others
At least that's what they say.
It can even add a little warmth
To brighten up your day.
So every day wear a smile
See what it can do
There will always be someone
Who needs a smile from you.

Estelle Morales

In The Morning I Awaken

In the morning I awaken
To another day alone
A memory day in the making.
The remembering cuts to the bone.

It's tough putting it behind me
When everywhere there's a reminder.
I know it's not a healthy way to be.
But the world's just not kinder.

If I awaken tomorrow
With the same ache as today.
I will be filled with sorrow.
So much that I can't say.

Bobbi Lee Bergsrud

"Can I Give You This Part Of Me?"

Can I give to you this part of me
to be cared for tenderly?

Can I give you this part of me
to be nourished
and to be cherished?

Will you give this part of me the
love and understanding it so desires?
Will you encourage it to grow
from embers to burning fires?

Will you hold it close to you
in times of trouble and in need?
Will you care for it as if it
were your own?

Will you sooth it with a gentle tone?
Can I give to you this part
of me that expresses my love?

Can I give to you this part
that is my heart?

Joseph John Ferraro

Untitled

I took a walk within your eyes,
to golden dunes of the finest sand.
And there, the night
Spread like ink across the heavens.
As I stood among the warm desert winds
There fell to my feet a star,
Trailing blackness behind it.
It pooled before me,
A cool oasis of liquid night,
And I got lost in its dark beauty.

Jesse Harlin

The Mask

Shore wore a mask of cunning illusion
To beguile, to conceal her true feelings
An insincere pretense of wild passion
Filled with only vixenish dealings

A deceitful heart of pretentiousness
Filled with trickery and deception
She wooed me with her venomous charm
And unscrupulous mislaid affection

My soul has been trespassed, laid bear
Exposed to one who little did care
To the game of love, I SALUTE! Is there
no one
Left with whom true love to share.

Irene La Franco

"My God Is Patient"

Today I got my invitation,
to come home to God's salvation.
I have no time to fill my coffer,
For this is not a standing offer.
My God is waiting patiently!

Heavens choir has been put on notice,
the golden bells are ready for service.
As I gaze at heavens' glory,
I remember that old, old story.
My God is waiting patiently!

The choice is mine and mine alone,
my faith is built upon that stone.
The rock of ages stands so tall,
never will it erode or fall.
My God is waiting patiently!

Lord throw open that heavenly gate,
so there will be no wait.
Washed in the blood of the Lamb,
Here my God I am.
Praise my God for waiting patiently.

Joe N. Brown

Untitled

By still waters I rest,
To drink from the brook of life,
Oh how desolate my heart is,
For famine has reached my soul.

How may I be anointed,
That my body runneth over,
With living water,
From the wellspring of life.

My pleasure has contained me,
In moments of haste,
I am consumed.
As fire destroy's a forest.

I have succumbed,
To the want of desire,
The journey of my rest,
Has left me faint.

I have drawn,
From the cup of my portion,
For the pans of misery,
Quenches not my thirst.

Horace Handy III

Lost Cord

Why did my mom take so much time
To find a name to pin on me?
I cannot see
Why I cannot touch her anymore.
Attached we were; detached we are.
Why don't I know her?
'Cause she doesn't know me,
Or perhaps, knows not herself: she?

The one who dropped me
At birth
At the birthplace
After birth
Leaving me to cry outrageous tears
Spilling into forever sorrow, pain
The search in vain!

Why?
Does she - will she
Ever remember the name
Which took so long to find
To pin on me?

Elizabeth Greenlee Goodson

The Answer

I didn't know where to look
To find what I had lost
I didn't know what was gone
I only knew the cost
I didn't know when I slipped
And couldn't see the sun
I didn't know how to change
This game I never won
I didn't know who to be
And so I tried to hide
I didn't know why it hurt
Each time I crawled inside
I didn't know who to ask
To tell me what was wrong
I only know I needed help
And then you came along

Dorothy Stefanik

Wisdom Or Ignorance

Which would you choose,
To follow the elder
Or let a child lead your way?

The unconquerable soul of the innocent,
A vast open mind
Filled with designated input,
Or left open to freely find.

The elder, Captain of his soul.
He's a conqueror of the weak,
Close-minded from life's experiences
Causing the outlook to seem bleak.

Fate rests with neither,
Wisdom or Ignorance,
It makes no difference.
Lead yourself, make your own decision.
Otherwise, you just run circles inside
Life's offbeat precision.

Charel MacIntosh

When Angels Sing

When I lay myself down
to go to sleep
I close my eyes
And hear a sweet sound

From up above
With a gentle whisper
I hear a voice
With lots of love

The voice I hear
I think is an angel
That is singing to me
So I have no fear

The singing has disappeared
The angel flew away
But she left me with
a thought
To never have any fear

Heidi Rorapaugh

Icarus '94

Ah to dream of flying
To imagine never dying
There would be bliss
Life would be effortless
Free of all the trying

Ah to dream of flying
To imagine never dying
Prolonged forever
To cease never
No more vying

Ah to dream of flying
To imagine never dying
Where would we go?
Never slow
Permanent smiling

Ah to dream of flying
To imagine never dying
A chance a chance a chance
To dance to dance to dance
Ah to dream of flying

Edwin L. Cooper

Look to the Sun

When you stop
  to look back,
    At what
      Used to be,
Darkness rules your life.

If you begin
  to look forward,
    to what it
      is you want,
The sun will shine forever.

So if you want to end the darkness,
And let the sun shine every day.
Don't look back, look straight ahead,
To find a better way.

John Rigg

A Prayer For Living

I would that I were just so big
To overlook the little things
Malicious gossip, some sly dig,
The fol-de-rol a liar sings.

I would that I were just so tall
to face my troubles eye to eye
And watch them fade to naught at all
When I have recognized their lie.

I would my view were just so wide
That when a controversy rages
I might see the other side
And give it its due wages.

I would my reach were just so far
That I might find and grasp what's true
And hold it like a flaming star
For all the world to view.

This is my prayer Most Holy One
Please grant it in thy grace
Then when this life of mine is done
I might find mercy in thy face.

Jordan L. Cuthbertson

Hurt

I hurt myself today
  to see if I still feel
I focus on the pain
  the only thing that's real
The needle tears a hole
  the old familiar sting
Try to kill it all away
  look what I've become
My sweetest friend, everyone I know
  goes away in the end
You could have it all
  my empire of dirt
I will let you down
  I will make you hurt
If I could start again
  a million miles away
I would keep myself
  I would find a way.

Jessica Ann Maki

Going Home

I climbed the highest mountain
To see what I could see,
And there among the frothy clouds,
God was looking down at me.

My gaze locked in adoration
The silence was unbroken
I crossed myself and prayed to him
In words conveyed yet, unspoken.

If we live we have to give
We must learn to love all others
It can not be all just take
We must share love with our brothers.

I walk a path I've walked before
This time I'm not alone
I feel the touch of another's hand
This time I'm going home.

Doris Rabenaldt

Untitled

Low and behold a mist appears
to send off its ever spark.
It casts a spell towards the blue
and leaves it there to share.

Though the spark within it shines
It seeks to find out more.
It leaves behind the spoken one
To fill its ever glare.

It's then the spark leaves the eyes
Though deep inside it's there.
It fills the heart forever more to
remind him of what is there.
And soon it'll find the chosen one
to share in its ever glare.

For now the blue casts the spell
to join within the heart.
Forever more the two share shine
its righteous place at heart.
Where no more sparks distill their lives
and peace from them is formed.

Beth Hopkins

December 1994 -

A Tome to Cousin Helen

I thought I'd drop you a line,
To tell you I'm feeling just fine.
Now when we return once again,
To the U.S political scene.
Mr. Ross Perot - was he the goat?
Please let the voters take note.
In Kentucky the horses ran faster,
Especially the filly Flanders.
Timber Country made Lucas look tall,
Having to give his juvenile all.
Battling George Foreman fought Moorer,
While Halloween was filled with horror.
To repeat, I'm fine, a yearly exam,
While O.J. resides in the slam.
I hope that you're up to the game,
May we please root for old Notre Dame?
Meet you at the Texas Cotton Bowl,
Wouldn't doubt if we'd see Robert Dole.
Here's wishing you Holidays so bright,
With feeling of joy and delight.

Charles W. Nelson

I Long To Touch The Sky

The horizon whispers so far away
To the sun that rises high;
I hear their gentle voices call,
And I long to touch the sky.

Golden ribbons of eternity
Dance before my eye,
And I know with hopeful certainty
That I must touch the sky.

The longing is intensified
As moon and stars pass by;
And these sirens say someday
That I will touch the sky.

And then they fade and turn to black
With a single, lonely sigh;
Yet I can almost see them again,
For I long to touch the sky.

Jill Stinson

What Gave You the Right?

What gave you the right to hit me,
to throw me against the wall?
To knock the wind out of me
and to laugh at me when I fall?
to make lies about my black eyes
and the bruises on my face?
Telling people I feel down some stairs.
instead of telling them you hit me
in the face.
I wanted to hit you back, but
I knew what you would do.
Now I know that leaving is the
best thing to do, when the only
way you can communicate with
me is to make me black and blue -

Ben Clare Byard

Last Embrace

When her soul was called to go
To travel to the far off place,
Tears filled his eyes with sorrow
and ran right down his face.

He knew her time had come
But did not want to part,
So he put his arms around her
And loved her with all his heart.

Now that she is gone
To that far off place unknown to man,
She comes to him to visit
In a dream only known to him.

Every now and then
With the help of the Lord's word
She talks to him with dreams
Deep within his head.

Those words she says to him
Although they're short and brief,
Will be with him forever
Even when he's asleep.

Gary Durbin

Oops

When we were young we'd watch the sky
To try to see a falling star.
Back then the tales were weird and wry;
We didn't know it was a meteor.

It was a person's soul just passed away;
We'd pray for its salvation.
We didn't think, that long-passed day
It was going in the wrong direction!

John A. Flood Jr.

Now I See!

If I can't start how can I begin
To waste my time could be a sin
I'm dying to live and living to die
I force a smile so I wont cry
Can I sing a song if I can't sing
Or hear my phone if it won't ring
Time marches on the sages say
Day turns into night and night into day
I found that happiness is what I seek
So I forced a smile for an entire week
I smiled and grinned until I ached
And people smiled back for goodness sake
I then understood what a smile can do
Because you saw me and I saw you.

John Ohara Kirk

To Jackualine

Tomorrow I will cry
Today I mourn,
Yesterday, a sigh,
A life was shorn.
She gave her all
And was received
Most graciously
By those who grieved.

Jackie was born
And raised a lady
A servant to mankind,
Her family and her nation.

As others new her.
We knew her not;
Yet a queen to all
In camelot.
We grieve no more,
At home she rests;
The eternal flame
Soothes an aching breast.

Justin P. Malady

Angels Of Mercy

Angels of Mercy
treading these halls
Angels of Mercy
ministering to all

Loving and tender
sweet, gentle and kind
The service they render
they don't seem to mind

Angels of Mercy
whose cheerful smile
Fill hearts with gladness
make each stay worthwhile

True to their mission
faithfully they serve
Blending compassion
with warmth of their Love

Angels of Mercy
God bless each one
And by thy Spirit
keep true, through Thy son.

Edward M. Williams

Turquoise

Turquoise
Turquoise is my favorite color.
Turquoise is the color of water.
Turquoise is the color of shells.
Turquoise is the color of bells.
Turquoise is up in the skies.
Turquoise is n some people's eyes.
Turquoise is in some kinds of flowers.
Turquoise is in some fire crackers.
Turquoise is the color of a blouse.
Turquoise is the color of a house.
Turquoise

Dana McVay

The Only

There was a hill;
Upon the hill grew but one flower.
There were no others,
Yet the hill was full.

Doug Wynn

Working Girl

Sitting at her desk,
Typing away,
Thinking of what else
She has to do today.
Type a report,
Make some copies,
She'd never have enough
time to get to her hobbies.
The report is due,
She gets it in,
She quotes "I'll do it again
If I have to or else my name
Isn't Lynn." IT'S NOT ! ! !

Diana Zborovsky

Where When Why

Unexpected love
Unexpected pain
Behind windows and doors
A silent wind whips and whirls
Blind and oblivious to its nature
I look it straight faced
It blows me down
Strength from sanity helps me stand
I am standing now
But afraid to move
Unaware of the next whipping wind
But knowing it will come again
And blow me down
Leaving me this time
With only pain
Help me fly with your winds

Gloria Star Whyte

Love

Love is a rollercoaster.
Unknown is the path at which it follows.
Sluggish as it may be,
The track is still a mystery.
Few or numerous times ridden,
The Secret remains hidden.

Andrea Davis

Goodbye, Friend

We were the best of friends
Until the end
When a lie destroyed it all

You came to me
For sympathy
Thinking I would shield you from a fall

We shared laughter together
When I was under the weather
You taught me to believe

But your heart was in another place
I could see it in your face
As you turned and started to leave

You called too late
Because of fate
Our relationship was done

Then you mounted your horse
For your last ride, of course
Into the setting sun.

Gina Hill

Passing Thought

Someone
Usually
Isolates the
Children
Inside until the
Day when it
Ends.

Imagine the
Silence.

Mother and
Young.

Eating
Sleeping
Caring
And
Promises
End.

Darren McCulloch

"Cheyenne Rain"

A rolling slumber of vacant land
vanishing beyond the horizon,
an endless slope of natural beauty
where once did roam the bison.
A tremble of hooves that wake the dust
as horses run wild and free,
the open country of the cowboy man
such a sight for the eyes to see.
A place of barren to some of those
who know not how it became,
Natives knew and blessed it so
it was born of the Cheyenne Rain.

Deana Kyle

The Passing

Life is like the sea
vast, deep and free
undiscovered is the sea
like life, always seems to be
the crash of the waves
are strong and bold
we embrace life
with an untamed hold
the waters run shades
of green, turquoise and blues
the meaning of life
is juxtaposed among the hues
when we need peace and tranquility
just think of the vast, deep blue sea.

James C. Bigelow

Violence Come And Go

Violence come to every town!
Violence is seen at some places!
Violence come from a lot of faces!
Violence come from all sort of sound!
Violence don't act like a clown!
Violence will take you down!
Violence has a lie in it!
Violence come from the Bottom pit!
Violence come from the Devil himself!
Violence from him will be only left!
Violence will be over one of these days!
Because you can go to Jesus when he come
your way!

Darwin Bell

Don't Mean Nothin'

Grunts entering the village that day,
Vengeance permeating their minds,
Stealthily moving from hut to hut,
Weapons ready to grind.

Young man running a fair distance away,
Sensing the impending wrath,
Seen and killed by a sergeants bullet,
Ripping into his path.

Village became a burning inferno,
As wild men hastened the flames.
Destroying families and a way of life,
Why didn't First Louie complain?

Though Country is a distant remnant,
I'll never forget that place.
A tiny hamlet north of Saigon,
An embarrassment forever to face.

Harley E. Sommers

"Times"

Boring days go throw and pass away,
Venture is needed,
Venture is pleaded.
Sitting in the night alone,
No one in sight of my home.
It's Monday again and a new week,
Another troublesome time for the week.
A cat climbed a tree,
Which had no tears of blossoming.
Rain rain it's raining,
It's time for the tree to regain.
The sun has come up.
Which dried the water from the cup.
A pig began to squeal,
A boy began to yell.
Afraid of his love,
Afraid of his dove.
The tree broke in fear,
And then it was the end of the year.

Jonathan Weems

To A Graduate

Sweet girl graduate
walking down the aisle
To an unknown fate
you must reconcile.
Ply your earnest girlhood hope
of your brief career
Into woman's larger scope
of Universal sphere.

Youthful courage can endure
much that age forsakes,
But faith is investiture
when womanhood awakes.

Zealously sustain the truth
and ardently pursue
Dimensions of your eager youth
that contributed to you.

Gladys Rhein

You Need To Have An Iron Rear!

You need to have an iron rear,
To sit upon a cactus,
Or otherwise at least a year,
Of very painful practice.

Erica Pritts

Kiss Me Dear

Kiss me dear with your
Warm wet lips.....
And tell me that I'm
Yours....
Hold me dear so very
Close in those big
Strong arms of yours..
And we'll live our
Lives together....
Today, tomorrow and
Forever.

Helen P. Marino

Terminally Ill

Given to us in some day and time,
was life
Oh how precious to hear the chime.

The chime, the smell, and the air
of life itself
Oh how precious to feel that air.

Sit here on the chair,
look at life
Oh how precious and yet so bare.

Feel how sweet the air
in our life smells
Oh how precious but can we bear.

Can we bear the sound
of life now gone
No chime, no smell or even air.

No we can't and death
is here.

How precious life itself can fee.
Oh how precious life is here.

Abel Salazar

The Legend Of The Dogwood Tree

The trunk of the sturdy dogwood tree
Was used for the cross of calvary.
Legend tells that the tree so grieved
That Jesus its sorrow relieved.
He said henceforth its shape would be
A gnarled bush instead of a tree;
Its flowers' centers like a crown
That on His brow was pressed down.
Four white petals tipped with red
A symbol of the blood He shed
To save a world lost in sin.
He gave His life our souls to win.
Now, each Springtime the dogwood tree
Assures our hope of Eternity.

Frances H. Carmack

Observations Of Uncertainty

I watched my reality,
watched it slap me in the face.
I watched my integrity,
watched it disappear without a trace.
I watched all the religions,
watched them turn into a poem.
I watched all the guns,
watched them destroy a home.
I watched an angel grin,
watched it when it flied
I watched the earth spin,
watched it commit suicide!

Ben Arocho Jr.

Someone Special

Lying beside you
watching you sleep
Moving closer
to feel your body heat.

Your arms devour me
as my cheek you peck
I close my eyes
as your lips brush my neck.

Your touch is so sensual
while your breath mixes with mine
My heart is beating faster
while our bodies then entwine.

Your eyes are so tender
as you gently move with me
I can feel my passion growing
as we become lost in ecstasy.

Lying beside you
watching you sleep
Loving you
Makes my life complete.

DeReé Gould

Reach It

Like naughty boy, is the
way of life.

Lovin', kicking and killing
your friends, your personality.

Flowers and girls, boys and guns,
boys and girls, flowers and guns,

Couples and peace.

Wish we could all be
those naughty boys,
those saviours of life.

but we all have a personality,
our own reality.

Antti Koski

To My Teacher

Mrs. Nelson is very cool,
We enjoy her daily at school

She lets us listen to the radio,
It keeps us happy as we grow

We learn to spell, read and write,
in space and color not too tight

Indoor recess is much fun,
even though we can't yell and run

To multiply and divide,
is more fun than a roller coaster ride

The lollipops were good,
even though they stuck to the wood

About the rats I do recall,
good food is the very best for all

For your help I do say thanks,
and I promise to do no pranks

I like to study Missouri best,
but please don't give too hard of a test

For all your work and plans you made,
thank you for a GOOD FOURTH
GRADE!

Andrew L. Mock

So Simple

Possessed with our living,
We look but do not see.
All the simple little things,
Put there for you and me.

Unwilling to take the time,
To stop and rest a spell.
We hurry by the rose,
Not noticing its smell.

No time for us to enjoy,
Things that heaven sent.
Change! they say is progress,
With asphalt and cement.

Not taking time to thank the Lord,
For giving us the trees.
Sunshine, birds and flowers,
The life beneath the seas.

Progress is important,
Yet it is so sad.
Man will soon destroy,
All the things he had.

Charles R. Martin

"A Question Of Race"

I am black and he is white
We love each other
With all our might

We harm no one,
We cause no fight
We just try to do what's right

People look at us
They swear and curse
They point their fingers
And make gestures

This is nothing new
We are going through
We felt it from our neighbours too

Despite these acts
It is a fact
That our love is solid,
As solid as a rock.

Helena Patricia Evans

I Saw Him

It was cloudy and dreary today,
We passed his corner,
He stood tall and handsome,
Dressed in that grey Charity
Hospital uniform,
His left hand leaning on the cane,
The artificial legs make him a bit
Unsteady as he works,
He's very busy, in his right hand
Is a cloth the size of a handkerchief,
He's wiping the top of his prized
Possession, the old green rusty Buick
Parked in front of his home,
Tears come quickly to my eyes,
I guess no one even noticed him as they
Hurried by,
But I saw him quite clearly,
He's my Daddy

Carol Vella Mockbee

Treasure Chests Of Women

Hold the moments in our lives
We want to keep
But must be put away
Whenever we wish
We can take them out
Feel them
Remember them
Laugh, cry, or just
Be silent with them.
They contain the memories
We hold dear to our hearts
And the pictures
We have taken
With only
Our minds eye.

Julie Gardon

Clouds

I've often sat and watched the clouds
wend their way on high
and wondered where they came from
and how they learned to fly.

Some are large and some are small
and some are in between,
but each and everyone of them
have a shape I've never seen.

George McWatt

We See Ourselves As Others See Us

Just take another look at us.
We're not a bit mysterious.
Respect the values that we trust.
We are substantial, much alive!
for centuries we have survived
and for ourselves we can provide.

David P. Boyd

The Dying Rose

A dying rose,
What a site to see.
What a pity, for you and me.

It was once,
A beautiful fiery red.
Only three days old,
Now it lays on its death bed.

The pretty red petals,
Are now fragile and brown.
One look at this flower,
Will bring a disgraceful frown.

Its turning point has reached.
It's time to move on
The last petal has fallen.
The dying rose, is gone.

Daphne Lewis

It's Just Me

It's just me it is and that is
what I want to be different that
is all I am and that is what I
want to be no one knows my
feelings or not feelings it's just
the way I am can I change
forget about it and what
I am is different.

Erin Michelle Byers

The Answer

If I could see,
What I should be.
Then I would know,
Where I should go.
What should I do?
I wish I knew.

You say to look,
Inside this book?
Oh! Look, I see
Answers for me.
No charge or fee,
The B-I-B-L-E

Bernice Krause Rice

Simple Roads

I have often wondered
What it would be like
To walk down a road
Which did not twist
Which did not turn
A road which had no hills
One that was flat forever
If there is such a road
Would I travel down it?
So I stop and think some more
Such a road is not worth traveling

Dennis R. Derflinger

The Promised Son

"Glory to God in the highest",
What joy had filled the air,
As praises of the angels
Rang out to shepherds there!

This was the night the Babe was born,
The promised Son of God,
For of the stem of Jesse
There should come forth a rod.

He would have authority
To rule and reign forever;
His name is called the Prince of Peace,
The Everlasting Father.

The love which brought Him down to man
Was love beyond all measure,
For through His death upon the cross
He came to be our Saviour.

Anna Sitko

My Fellow

We all expect respect,
when our life is in a wreck,
when we don't know what to do,
and it all comes down to you.

People passing by stop to take a look,
you feel like fictional character in a
cartoon book.

I do not understand
the ways of this great land,
when the only thing I do demand,
is the respect of my fellow man.

Charles Kesler Jr.

"I Understand"

My Life will call soon
What will she say
Gone to find meaning, a new way
I used to know her, will I still
Laughter, spirit, iron clad will

Demons and goblins
In her sky, did fly
I couldn't see them, blind to my eye
A hidden verse she never told
The next morn her spirit they've torn

Ice has a place
For only me to hold
She loves me, it seems too cold
Tears of it should be
Were screams of it's not me

A demon, worse than the beast
She donned armor, prepared a feast
When it is eaten and her life has begun
Lord, please let us watch
your rising sun

Daniel McGuinness

I Wonder If She Thinks Of Me?

I wonder if she thinks of me
when she feels alone?
When no one cares to hear of
the sadness in her soul.

I wonder if she thinks of me
when the lights go out at night?
and her mind begins to wander
feeding on her fright.

I wonder if she thinks of me
when the tears begin to flow?
When the pain seems never-ending
and she's lost all sight of hope.

I wonder if she thinks of me
when the mirror shows her age?
And quicker now than even before
comes the calendars last page.

I hope she knows I think of her
and it brings me to my knees.
For I cannot forget her,
when I'm living times like these.

Eduardo D. Lezcano

Love

Love is blind and have is unkind,
When you love
But you aren't loved in return
You lose all hope in every other person,
Who says they love you too.

You'll feel hurt
You'll feel betrayed
You feel all they want is to get laid.

Can anyone stop this madness
The insanity
That makes you think less
Less of the world
And all of man kind

No matter how long you plan it
Or roll it over and over in your mind
You can't destroy love

Barbie Kerley

My Best Friend My Son

I knew from the moment
When you were born,
Life may not be easy
Come that early morn!

I knew it would be tough
'Cause I did it alone,
I didn't have much
I could call my own.

We've had our problems
And some were many,
But no one said
There wouldn't be any.

You've been my Best Friend
For the last 20 years,
We've laughed and joked
And shed many tears.

One thing is certain
And definitely true,
No matter what happens
I will always Love You.

Janice Harmony

Grandma, Where Did You Go

Grandma, grandma
where did you go.
Grandma, grandma
I love you how much you will
never know.

Grandma, grandma
Where has your time gone.
Grandma, grandma,
You were taken away from me.

Grandma, grandma,
I love you so
Grandma, grandma
How is your life
now that your gone.

Grandma, grandma
you spent your time well.
Grandma, grandma,
Where was I when
you left this world.

Charlene L. Wilson

Zephyr

Distant petals fold to similar shores
Where gazers glide to greet
This mistress to an understatement.
She steps from pebble to pebble
Which, each to each,
Reflect ovarian platitudes
Which form coverlets
For her eyes which smile spaciously
Over rough surfaces.
The two, both as indiscrete figures,
Walk across the grain
of symbolic overtures
To points that rise to meet the expanse.
Layers of colors bleed
From the circle and erase
Images etched from the sea,
Uniting and dividing the two at once
In a languid waltz of fluid thought
Where people other than I have bathed
In waters stagnant with resolve.

Joanne Cherefko

Wait For Me

You were chosen first to go and wait
Where I will meet you at Heaven's gate
Heaven's gates will open wide
Where we'll walk together side by side.

So wait and pray for me
We'll be together wait and see
We'll be together for ever and ever
And I'll leave you no not never.

We'll never have to say goodbye
We'll never have to question why
Our souls will both be free
Because we're safe with God you and me.

I can't wait to be with you
For life is lonely and oh so blue
I'll never find a love that's true
Because I'll always belong to you.

Our loved ones will be sad for awhile
But after awhile they'll learn how to smile
They will have peace and understand
At last we'll take the Masters hand.

Delphinia Buskaritz

Where Is The Hero?

(for the children)
Who is this hero?
Where is he?
I'm too busy!
I don't know the way!

These are the excuses that are
used every day.
The children are walking two by two.
Their eyes are staring, but not at you.
They're staring at the white, the
crystal and the blue.

What have we done?

Caroline Hayes

Fly Fishing

Down, down the water flows,
where it goes nobody knows.
The rocks moving beneath my feet.
Waiting, waiting.
The line going down, down,
my hand moving up and down,
my fly floating, floating beneath
the water.
Waiting, waiting.
Peace and quiet make them come.
Dimples on the water that's where
I'll cast.
Waiting, waiting.
The moon going down, down,
the sun rising, rising, while I wait
the sun came up.
BAM
I got it!

Drusilla A. Bond

Untitled

How many lifetimes to bring us here
to have the courage to feel the fear.

To know the pain, allow the healing
to ascertain, that life is feeling.

Knowing who we are and why we came,
feeling oneness and being sustained.

Elaine Armstrong

My Friend

She's from the bad side
where it's easy to slide
and join the tide
of those who are dark inside
because here love is out of style
sin is in, sin is the thing
The song that they sing
The sugar and spice is vice
if you pay the price
everything's nice
drugs casts its spell
and thrives in this hell
enticing beguiling
its victim entrapping
crime rules
wide is his ring
wicked and evil
he keeps the herd thin

Anthony Thompson

"Passage"

Come lay me rest below the ground
Where sound and sight muffle
Where hot nor cold can touch abreast
Only the grave diggers shuffle.

Yes cold it is, and dark and tore
And ladents creep approach
Where rodents call it peaceful home
The moist cold dirt, they coach

Where paupers rest, breeders nest
A waterfall of spider webbed musk
Cascading air of evergreen
No day, No dawn, No dusk

Wild brown roses
Caress my head of stone
Endless thoughts of life and death
Remembrances of being alone

Come lay a flower on my grave
And shay a salty cry
For there is no preparation for this
passage of devastation
How endless it is, when you die ...

Debra Jean Walker

Radiator

The taking fades in
Whether waking or cold out
The fee is the moment
And left is cloud
Of shadow and light
The shades know no name
But may come when called

Devout believers
The religion is entropy
Taught by hands on a face

Fists that push
Fingers that heal
Hands do the taking

My thoughts are mine
Only for as long as I guard them
From being lost

David Hingorany

The Search

Whether you search far or near
Whether you search with love or fear

Whether you have the strength to fight
Whether you take the flight

Whether you search with passion
Whether you search with relaxation

There are so many wonders
That this world thunders

You'll always come through
With the right path for you

Chandra Mitzel

True Success

Prosperity feeds on envy
While corrupting a willing mind
It deteriorates the body
And affects all of mankind

Its belief of success
Dress with a smile
But elegant material values
Are everything but worthwhile

True happiness we seek
But never seem to find
A never ending chase
To feel more and more divine

Believe and acknowledge
He who created night and day
With one single word
Can bring happiness your way

Let it be known
With your heart, seek his pleasures
True success can be rewarding
As well as unmeasured

Annette Whitaker

O Brother

I sat there crying, weeping,
While my brother gently sleeping,
Sleeping the sleep of eternity,

Never to breathe another breath,
Suffocated by the grip of death,
Watching us with eyelids closed forever,

How can I go another day,
Knowing he will never say,
Brother, brother, I love you so much,

So I sit here barely breathing,
Growing older life is fleeting,
Hoping soon to lay by brother's side.

Gregory A. Williams

Black

On this page of gleaming
White
A Black man hides his face
of sight
For he fears if he is found
He'll be beaten to the ground
There's no reason for his fear
If the white men disappear
Racism here is the case
of the Black man's bloody face.

David W. Hentzell

"Don't Should On Me"

Don't should on me
Who do you think you are
I'm doing my thing
I'm reaching my par

The "shoulders" must think
They know more than me
They just know their thing
So just let me be

Life's hard enough
Finding my own pace
You're not living my life
So get out of my face

Jo Dugger

My Best Friend

Let's do a lot for Jesus
Who does so much for us.
He gave His life for us
You see.

He gives me joy and peace
Of mind and that means
A lot to me.

He really is my best friend
He makes a way for us each
And everyday

My best friend Jesus.
Jesus is the best friend
I know.

Annie Mae Devane

"No-Where"

There once was a feline
who had neither name nor home
She was so petite and fine
even though she lived all alone.

Her home was among the trees
Her day was full of strife
Her daily wish was to conceive
another day of her lonely life

While looking around for a tasty meal
She came upon a lovely house
And talk about a good deal
She received it after catching a mouse

While only asking for a meal
She received much more without delay
She got a much better deal
After she was allowed a bed and also, to stay

Now she has a home of treasured fame
Though she remained thin and bare
She was given a name from whence she
once came
She will now be known as, "No-Where"

Hector Gonzalez III

Envision

The world today is a disgrace
to see the hunger on a child's face
The terror welling in their eyes
And the sight of emaciated thighs.
They wonder if today food will arrive
And pray today they can drive
Away to another place and time
When the word and its people align
To join an everlasting peace and refine.

Angela M. Ficca

Crystal

I have a little girl
who has lots of curl
eyes so blue
a smile that's always new
she loves rap
mama ain't down with that
she is my world
yes.....
sometimes were in a twirl
but that's life with this
beautiful little girl

Dana Lee

Escape

Dreams are for dreamers
who like to escape
from days that are grey
and nights that are dark.
To dream is to coincide
with all that can be real.

To dream is to open any door
and momentarily close it
behind you.
Live to dream.
Dream to live.
Everyone needs to escape.

Jennifer Crabb

Poet

Once there was a poet
Who never wrote a single verse
Once there was a poet
Who never walked upon the Earth
He couldn't write, he couldn't speak
But he could hear and he could see
Always beyond imagination
Only to share his inspiration.

Once there was a poet
Who never wrote a single verse
Once there was a poet
Whose spirit rose above the Earth
We cannot thrive, we cannot heal
If we can't love, if we can't feel
When silence imitates his call
A poem is a precious pearl
Because he cares about us all
A POET CREATED THIS WORLD..

Jacques Seris

Little Black Angels

Oh, famous painter
Who paints little angels
Why don't you paint
Little black angels
For they too are considered
To be creatures of God.

Oh famous painter
Who paints with such fervor
Why deny them their color
If they too are welcome
In the kingdom of God.

Oh, master painter
Who paints in the Churches of God
Paint me a little black angel
With your magic brush.

Angel Isaac Camacho

The Answer

Why flowers?
Why bright, bold, brilliant flowers?
Why let them grow so tall?

Why music?
Why lovely, lilting music?
Why sing that song at all?

For shadows
For predatory shadows
I must construct a wall.

Grete Dollitz

My Grandpa

Now he's gone and I don't understand
Why did God have to take him
When he was such a good man;

Why did he have to go and leave his whole family behind,
He was the best Grandpa,
he was one of a kind;

Jennifer Ann O'Connor

Why Was He Born in a Stable?

Why was he born in a stable,
Why was he laid on the hay,
Why were there animals with him,
On that first Christmas day?

Why was it shepherds who came,
Leaving their flocks far away,
Why did the shepherds come worship,
On that first Christmas day?

Because he was a lamb,
A perfect, spotless male lamb,
Who one day would be,
A sacrifice for sin,
That all who believe,
May enter in-
To life everlasting,
With God, our dear father,
In heaven
In mansions of love.

Jolene Robinson

Life

Why won't it end?
Why won't it all just flow away?
Like a running river.
When I think of you a pain comes to my heart.
How can I go on?
Before I go, I have just one last plea.
Tell me how much you really loved me.
Were you just using me for her?
All that time, all that fun.
Now you're on the run.
Why are you so scared?
Now it's time for me to go.
Things always go with a flow.
Things were not meant to be.
Springs can come and springs can go,
justaslife——

Allison Lazette

Teenage World

Crime is like a storm,
Will it ever die?
What is becoming of our world?

Crime is like a storm,
Are we going to act?
Should we grow up like this?

Crime is like a storm,
Are we like dinosaurs?
Will humans become extinct?

Crime is like a storm,
What are we becoming?
Where is our future?

Crime is like a storm,
Don't destroy us all.
Help! We are sinking.

Brandy Boswell

Winter Rise

Winter rise your heart
Winter rise your soul
Cold as ice
White as snow
Touching you once, as soon as you go
Frost bit my hand, a season ago.

Reasons for seasons
Are all I know
A season for leafing
Gave you reason to go
Hibe from winter
Bud for spring
Summers to love
As fall to leave.

One day you came
One day you left
Talked to me, made me deaf
Telling me once, as sure the reason
The need to winter rise,
Whatever the season.

Dennis E. Poniatowski

The Man

I dwell upon the man
with courage
I dwell upon the man
with wisdom
But most of all
I dwell upon the man
with purpose
and whom is worthy

Alvah W. Reid Sr.

Mother's Love

Into this world of wonder
With eyes so bright with glee;
I looked into the eyes of love
Smiling down on me.

She held me in her loving arms
So gentle was her touch;
With just one look is all it took
To know I meant so much.

The world was big and wonderful
So much to see and feel;
But this I know as I grow
My mother's love is real.

Daniel Martin

Dapper

A small French poodle,
With grayish black hair,
A dog one might cuddle,
As he struts with an air,

A dog of great fame,
With a gait so light,
Called 'Dapper' by name,
He will run with delight.

At the line up ahead,
The dogs of pedigreed,
Await to be led,
To the prize for best breed.

They all walk in line,
Past the judges in row,
The dogs are all fine,
But who'll steal the show?

The award is now given,
To the finest of poodles,
The grand prize, blue ribbon,
For Dapper,—best poodle.

Emma Screpetis

A Winter Phenomenon

Our untraditional winter of 1995,
With its gusts and heavy rains,
Caused many to sigh, and confused the human brain.

The skier ready to take off in his winter gear,
Will have little to rejoice about this year.

For Old Man Winter has failed to deliver,
Snow on the mountains and ice on our rivers.

Disappointed children who can't use their skis and sleds,
Will have to create games of their own instead.

Earthquakes in Japan and the California floods,
Are further signs that Mother Nature has stood us up!

Carol A. Cookson

God's Gift

The red bird of dawn rises
With wispy, ruffled feathers
And touches the shadowed meadow
Colored with hints of heather.

As the now golden orb rises,
Sweet songs of day alight.
And promises of warm brightness
Before turning again to night.

Let us enjoy glorious day
As from God to us it is sent
And do whatever we may
To see it is worthily spent.

God's gift isn't given lightly,
Nor should be lightly taken,
For he stands by us always
When we should have been forsaken.

Betty Raymond

Why Is Life?

Why is life
With passion I find a reason
To survive this season
This season called life
To struggle against its strife
Why is life?
Finding ways to vent frustrations
To defeat life's many aggressions
Friendship gives me strength
For It all
So my love for life shall never fall
Why is Life?
Consoling confusing
Suffocating understanding
Finding the hope
So that I can cope
Why is Life?
To have life is the ultimate struggle
The struggle within
To enjoy life to its fullest
Because you only get ONE
That is LIFE!!!!

John S. King Jr.

"Father's Belt"

Long black thick
with six holes
brass buckle.

Leather cold
on one side
velvety
on the other.

Stitches of black thread
held two strips
together.

One frayed,
leather fell apart,
lying in twisted heap.

Jean B Cheng

The Forest

There grows a mighty forest
With trees so strong and tall
The winds and storms of ages
It has withstood them all.

Home of the Lord's wild creatures
Its branches for birds of the air
Its rippling streams for fishes
Its caves the wild beast's lair

Tho' mighty be its strength
How beautiful its soul
Filled with light and shadow
And colors of green and gold

With music from rustling of the leaves
And the whistle of the wind
The wild life's clarion call
The storm clouds awful din.

Filled with clean pure air
Invigorating every life
With peace and solitude
Free from man's worldly strife.

Fred F. Heitzig

Greetings

Tho' I am but a little babe,
With words I cannot say.
What I would like to speak to you,
Upon this special day.

Tho' I have nothing to offer you,
With my eyes I'll softly tell;
Of all the love and happiness,
Words could express so well.

Through a warm and happy smile,
I sweetly and humbly convey;
Joy, grace and heartfelt devotion,
To glorify this day.

Mom and Dad are by my side;
We're wishing you good cheer.
Hoping that all blessing will abide;
Throughout the coming years.

Joyce E. Smack

To God My Father

You are magnificent in all your glory
Wonderful in all ways
A spirit of love that guides me
And keeps me everyday

You are infinite in your wisdom
Powerful in your rule
A force mysterious and awesome
More precious than any jewel

You are compassionate in your vastness
Merciful with thy love
Creator of the earth
And the heavens above

You are the Lord God Jehovah
The beginning and the end
More loving than a parent
Much closer than a friend

Curtrena M. Turner

"Inside Emotions"

Here I am in the same place,
Wondering if I could only see your face.
Gosh, if only you knew how I feel,
I wonder could our love be real.

I would be so faithful and so true.
Not like other girls who leave you blue.
My heart filled with love and joy,
Everybody just handling it like a toy.

When I think about how we are friends,
I wish the friendship would bend.
Waiting, thinking everyday,
Maybe, Just maybe he will call today.

Too embarrassed to even say,
I haven't even had a chance, yet I pray.
Pray for no shallowness and hate.
Wishing if I could only have one date.

Loving you is just a suggest,
For you to love me back is my only request.
Sitting here waiting to take some action,
Yet afraid to speak, scared of your reaction.

Elaine Carrasco

My Love

Many a night I would sit alone,
wondering when my love would be home.
Night after night I would lie awake,
hoping that he would always be safe.
Time goes by so slowly it seems,
life is like a late night dream.
My love, at last, has made it home,
now I know he is safe from harm.
Making love til morning light,
he is my love, he is my life.

Jamie Stockdale

Christmas Cheer

A simple gift of Christmas cheer
Won't make one wise or wealthy
And there are even those who say
The stuff is none too healthy

But you and I can both agree
That when the time is here
What better way is there to go
Than full of Christmas cheer!

Carl W. Wallstrom

You're My Favorite

Hugs and Kisses,
words and wishes,
isn't that what sisters are made of?

Always from above,
showering me
with so much love,
isn't that what sisters are full of?

Me, with so many questions,
sisters always, with
just the right answers,
isn't that what sisters think of?

Knowing there is
someone there to show their care
and secrets to forever share,
isn't that what sisters have?

Sisters I'll always look up to,
because everything I do,
I've learned from you,
for you have long ago
answered my questions.

Emily Onslow

Shock-'O-Love

I'm in a state
where ya Meditate.

A Sort-'O-Pressure
In search of a treasure.

A shock 'O love
Not an Ordinary Dove.

One that flies while
My heart cries.

God oh God
Turn it on -
Shine your light,
Amidst His flight.

Debra Latimer

Margaret Mary

She never sat upon a throne
Wore a robe of velvet and red
She never had a crown of gold
To place upon her head

Her children there were many
Eleven by count you see
To each she gave her special gift
To live life in harmony

She will never go down in history
For she never had the time
She was busy being our mother
That suited her just fine

How much we took for granted
Thank you not stopping to say
And never knew how much we had
Till He called her home one day

In our hearts and those of people
That she touched along the way
Will always be a thank you prayer
Sent up to her each day

Arlene Kieras

Cellophanes Of Life

The colored cellophane
Wrapped around the branch
Told of happier times
and glad circumstance.

The silence in these halls today
Remind me of the goals outlayed
When I was young and hopeful
And didn't feel betrayed.

Life can be as bleak as the branch
Gray, devoid in outward stance
Hoping at some point of time
A cellophane of color
Will wrap itself around us
And possibly another.

And when the spring buds appear
On our lonely branch
Let's take our wisdom, knowledge and circumstance
And prepare a happy dance
To a song of life's most precious winds
The cellophanes of color, within.

Carolyn O'Donnell

Hate

You can find me in your soul
You can see me in your face
You can identify me
In the whole damn human race
You can hope to purge me
You can pray to win
But I'm the best
And worst of all
I'm the composite
Of all sin..
I like to see all people suffer
I love to see them cry
I call it one small victory
When I cause someone to die
You don't know who I am by now?
Well, you might find out by fate...
My name is evil, ever-present,
And they all call me HATE.

J. E. Hemingway

Death Is Flowers

Death is flowers
you cry for hours.
They're on the grave,
nothing much to save.

You've lost a loved one,
you're not having much fun
But you must move on,
Although it's a con
and think of what awaits you.

Elizabeth Lacasse

Memories

Memories,
you don't leave behind
not all are nice
or even kind.

Memories,
are all the thoughts
of one person
which can't be bought.

Memories,
of old friends and new
and of the time
they made you blue.

Memories,
let you view the past
and makes one wonder
will they last?

Memories,
of more to come
what you know now
are only some.

Jennifer Bentley

Edna

A rare jewel
You have a beauty all your own

Skin the warmth of the caribbean
Eyes of deep brown like pools of autumn
Your statue straight as the wings of
an eagle
Your voice mellow, yet passive

A turmoil rages inside
To let your true self out

If only this inner self did surface
Oh' what sweet embracement would be

Dorothy R. Wade

Silver Bell

Silver bell a gift from my love.
You were fondled with affection.
Sweet sounds like the song of a dove,
You were an omen of protection.

Silver bell, a delight to the ears,
In the midst of all my agony,
You've power to allay my fears,
From one who once spoke with honey.

Ring on and still my troubled brain.
Help me to forget the thunder,
With melody to hush my pain.
Stop my heart from tearing asunder.

Henrietta Block

Why Don't You Know?

Why do you keep asking?
You haven't got a clue.
If you really cared for me.
You'd understand why I'm blue.

You know who's been hurting me.
You see the evidence well.
But why do you have to tell everybody,
that I just fell?

Do you hear me crying?
Do you see that I am sad?
I cry because I'm hurting.
I cry because I'm mad.

And you should know
And you should see.
Are you blind?
He's hurting me.

Shall I show you the scars?
Because you can't see
because you are a man I'll tell you.
he's going to kill me.

Brandi Foster

Books

Open the cover
You may just lover
Turn the page
Now you have more sage
Hours past
Oh at last
A place to mark
It is becoming dark
Time for a break
For thy own sake
Sleep tight
Returning at daylight
Holding the bind
Oh what a find for building my mind

Gary P. Plisko

Far Away

As you sit here next to me
You seem so far away
What can the matter be
Is it true you can not say?

If you were here tonight
instead of far away
We would cuddle all through the
night and dream of all our days

Since your off so far away
There something I might do
Something that'll cheer you up
and say that I LOVE YOU!

Anne Elizabeth Graham

The Little Kitten

Little kitten how nice can you purr?
Without being sure?
Are you warm in the winter?
Do you even get splinter?
How soft can you be?
How much do you love me?
Can you catch any fish?
Do you eat out of a dish?
Oh little kitten how I love
you so.

Christina Michels

Untitled

Oh Martin the marcher, Oh Martin the man,
You were to be our deliverer
To that great promise land

Your stay was so brief
and your message was not long
But God knew what was best
and He wanted you home

The message you sent was
To get it together
It didn't last long and
faded like bad weather

Our men are killing, raping and
robbing each other
There are drive by shootings
of their sisters and brothers

If you could see us today
I believe you would cry
you would ask yourself
For this did I die

Alice E. Phillips

When We Meet

When you meet me
you will know me by my hands,
my hands which were made
to stroke your skin alone,
my long fingers
lingering through your hair,
my palms passing, feather soft,
over your eyes and ears.
I will hold you in these hands
like a cup holds water;
you can sink into me
and I will surround you,
until you see fit
to pour yourself
back out of my hands,
onto your own two feet,
strong and serene and sure
of yourself and of me.

Corby B. Griffin

No Tears

You'll see no tears in daylight
You'll see no sadness in my face.

Every day has some struggles,
obstacles at every place.

My daughter is severely handicapped
"challenged" they say.

She's also very sweet
and shows affection in many ways.

Big bright sparkling blue eyes
show she understands.

Physical and mental weakness
call for many demands.

You'll see no tears in daylight
I save them for the night.

I love my daughter dearly
and for her I'll continue to fight.

Some show kindness and offer a helpful hand;
many are impatient and just can't understand

Until people can learn to accept;
on my pillow I will have wept.

Donna M. Collier

In My Father's Garden

Each Spring renewed,
Young plants carefully sown,
Within the deep rich soil,
In my father's garden.

We laughed and sang,
Memories made again,
As children we played.

We tended and watered,
Life flourishing awaiting harvest,
Pride and accomplishment gained.

Suddenly one Spring,
My father's footprint lain,
Among my tears washing away the soil,
In my father's garden.

Someday again,
With him we will laugh and sing,
Among utmost beauty and pleasure,
In our Father's Garden.

Jeannette M. Monks

Ode To A Cat

Oh, lofty creature-thoughts unknown,
your every movement grace.
Beneath the starlit skies at night
you seek a distant place.

Your eyes glow with the brilliance
of an oriental gem.
You look with scorn and arrogance
upon the race of men.

Your actions high and mighty be,
you heed no master's voice.
Ah, that I might take your place
If I but had the choice.

Ellen S. Potter

Dear Friend

Your warm affectionate eyes
Your sweet tender touch
Your soft gentle smile
Your kind lending ear
Your warm loving embrace
Your caring thoughtful words
Your strong meaningful support
Your helpful honest ways
I pray each day you know
How very special you are
And hope I will be
When my time comes
A loving mother like you.

Christine Swyers

Untitled

Dancing through your light.
Your laughter is my song.
Twirling through ecstasy with you.
Holding you forever.
This is where I always long to be.
A yawn, a sigh, morning light.
I have lost the dream.
Back to sleep I go, to
dance with you again.

Martin Vincent

Untitled

The huge oak tree in the back of
your yard
reminding you of days spent
climbing
and the castles you had up there.

The beautiful old quilt lying on
your bed
with its patches reminding you
of the dresses
that your grandmother made
for you every spring.

The face you see everyday
reminding you of what never
happened
but always reminding of what
might have been.

Ashley Jones

"Midnight Sun"

Tonight
you're only half
the moon you used to be
No! Not radiant!
radiance is for the sun
Your luminous glowing
perfect sphere
lighting up the night
as if it were day
Tonight
you're a piece of pie
revealing every point
curve
shimmering like a jewel
in a black velvet box.
You'll soon be whole again
brandishing your cosmic orb.

Constance E. Radin

You're My Wall

You are my lover.
You're my best friend.
You're the wall, which helps me
to stand.
What's mine is yours.
And yours is ours.
You're my strengths
You're my weakness.
You're the one who picks.
up the pieces.
You're the wall, that helps me
to stand.
You're my today.
You're my tomorrows.
You're the love of my life.
You're my wall, which helps me
to stand
And if ever asked, yes it has name.
Russell Decker because he is
all my strength.

Wendy Kadner

Silence

A walk in silence through a strawberry field of
relieving sighs...
All alone while the sky endures its innocence...

The wind holds its breath while the sunset releases its anger
through a masterpiece of tranquility...

You lay down, as the silence turns to music
and each blade of grass brushes against you as if it felt your
presence and accepted it...

You shut your eyes and suddenly have no desire to speak again...
Alone, yet the most embraced you shall ever know...
A feeling of completely simplicity....

...I shall never leave...

Nicole S. Fernandez

Sacrifice

When you have a cross to bear
Remember Him of long ago
Who bore His Burden for the world
And triumphed that we all might know
The promise of Eternity
In a happier land for you and me

Greater love can never be
Than laying down a life for all
Fulfillment of the Prophesy
Invites the world to heed His call
His call to follow in His ways
That our lives may be blessed for all our days

Marie Latimer

Exploration Of Love

A journey deep inside my heart-the exploration of my soul,
revealed no comprehension as to why I had lost control.

The depth of this emotion is new to me-I try to make my
heart be still, but my heart decides what shall be-as it
now has its own will.

Love, a mystery, the desire and attraction-that just a
glance or smile-arouse such a strong reaction.

This feeling defies all logic-has no basis or explanation-
as if I'm caught now in the middle of an inconceivable riddle
or equation.

Marilyn Hunter Annesi

Alone Again

Alone Again! That empty feeling inside your
rib cage.

Alone Again! No more to hear the words, "You
belong to me."

Alone Again! The dull ache growing until you
want to crawl inside your self and forget.

Alone Again! Always looking on, just a
spectator, no longer a participant.

Alone Again! Loving, but unable to find
someone to return your love.

Alone Again! Grasping at loveless gymnastics
in the dark, touching but not communicating.

But always in the end. Alone Again

Mildred C. Taitch

The Birdwatcher

Before the lark sings, before the waxwings
rise from resting trees; before night dies and crows
cry; before herons stretch their long slim necks
into rosy skies; before the dawn breaks,
before creepers peep or chickadees cheep,
the birdwatcher wakes, wiping sleepy eyes.

He leaves the world of warmth, toast and coffee
to rush to the woods, to find the brush
where thrush may come, to witness the place
where grouse may drum; to hear the first note
of first dawn, like a director sounding a pitch
and into the hush come music and song.

He witnesses, counts, records, but the real Joy
cannot be written down, the smell and feel of
early air, cool still pools and clean green meadows -
or the pleasure of birds greeting the day. This
is his morning prayer, his praise, his meditation,
a birdwatcher's way of counting his blessings.

Tommye Sauer

Flute Player In The City

Delicate..light
rises a sonorous note above the fetid streets
lingering
playfully joyous
a flute plays
somewhere amid the highrise
washing over the streets
lightly touching those that hear
those who wish to capture a moment of beauty
Restful I listen and wait
I close my eyes against the ruin
the waste
The note lifts slowly
magical and sanguine
a melancholy sound
It stops abruptly
the street rushes in
and I retire to sleep and wait
for the next's night solo
and I dream of the someone out there
alone
reaching for beauty

Leslie Lowry

Echoes

Softly, softly, like the petals of a white
rose falling gently in the crisp breeze of
Autumn.

Delicately the sound falls upon my heart-
Echoes, the soft strains of words and
laughter shared in Happy Days.

Magical days - filled with wonder and delight.
And the surreal assurance that life would
Continue to be filled with joy.

The memories, warm and full, fall
softly upon my heart like the petals
of that white rose. They live on -
They shall always softly echo.

Mary Jo Miller

The Rose

The sweet aroma of a newly blooming
rose fills the air, but tomorrow that rose
may not be there.
The kiss of dew from early morning still
remains undisturbed, but the silent cries of that rose
will never be heard.
The gracefulness that the rose portrays, with
the warm embrace of the suns early rays.
The softness in its petals so small an fragile,
with a lady that lands on it for just a while.
Then along comes a dreadful wind with all of its fury
and fire, and to continue to live was the rose's only desire.
But this furry will tear the rose apart, just like
someone can break your heart.
There's a brilliant rose in each of us, but we
try to hide this for we have found those we must.
For to let it be seen would be to give it death,
for its short life will soon run out of our breath.
So the rose within all of us wilts and dies,
for it alone cries all of our silent cries.

Marilynn Leonesse Bradshaw

Wind Of Time

"It's here, it's here!
Run, hide - hurry!"
"You can't run and hide, it's impossible.
Don't you understand?"
Is it true? Can it be here, truly? Why now, why
this year?
Whoooooosshhh________!
"It's here, It's here!"
Has time gone that fast?
Whoooooosshhh________!
It's true, it really is true. Wait! Wait for me. Don't
leave me here! Take me with you!
It's too late.
What? Who's there?
It's gone, gone to another place another time.
Who are you?
It will return, but not for many of years.
Wha.......
Shhh! Don't speak child, and don't cry. It will
return.

Stacie Delaney

Too Busy For God

Running around with our head in the air
Running here and there with no time to spare...

Too busy talking, too busy at work
Too busy shopping, too busy for church

Too busy worrying, no time to share
Too busy to take time out in prayer!

Our lives are so hectic, running all about
With all this pressure, we're ready to shout!

And then it happens, we stumble and fall
We can't think straight from the weight of it all.

We feel so distressed, defeated, and low
With all of our problems, there's only place to go!

So we cry to God and complain of our woes
We expect Him to fix all that we have composed!

Yes, God always has time for His children to hear
Too bad we don't have time to talk to Him in prayer

Too bad, from Him we take time to dodge
Too bad we are too busy for God!

Millie Torzilli

Someday

Look up to the sky, breathing the nice air
Running the extensive plateau
Don't worry about work
Like long time ago, our ancestors didn't.

Look up to the stars, black world around us
Walking middle of the night
Don't worry about time
Like long time ago, our ancestors didn't

Looking at the people, working morning through night
Forgot about the past
Accompanying people
There is no peace, like we did long time ago

Facing to tomorrow
We are having our life
But hopefully we can go back to the past
The time we had peace
The time we were living as a part of nature
The time earth was blue
Hopefully we can go back someday....

Yumie Ota

Fallen Hero

Here I sit beside the bed of my fallen hero, taken down by a ruthless disease that has left him so helpless.

I look into his eyes and wonder where he is and what he feels inside. I pray as he lies silently through his last few days he is viewing the best memories of his life and is filled with peace.

My heart hurts when I think about the days I will need his advice, guidance and reassurance. But I know all the further I have to look is into my own heart, for it's there he will live forever. I know this because half this heart was created by him.

When his struggle is done and he moves into God's care, we will grieve. It is then he will reach back through the clouds and gently push us back into motion, because that is his way.

Dad, we will all miss your daily warmth, but relax knowing you will soon be well. Good bye my hero, I will always love you.

Robb Mack

A Silent Affair

Your sun rises three hours past mine.
Safe in self indulgence.
You began with me in my sun,
Never to set.

You captured me, vulnerable to a kind heart,
Hurting from abuse.
Selfishness your motive,
Heeding not my request.

Your words carefully chosen,
Dare not speak your soul.
The light we shared contained,
A silent affair.

I feel to my child after your
Midnight voice.
Curled in anguish, my strength
Tried once more.

When sharing your light,
Display your truth.
Souls such as mine,
Can see what is real.

Sara Kurtz

Reality Goes Unrealized

A comfortable couch, a place that I can lounge on and relax on, the same as a big bed that I can lay my head on and sleep forever. A breeze through the air, the kind that almost sweeps you off of your feet. A high mountain, a beautiful breeze that allows you great peace for pondering and thinking, where there are no distractions, disturbances, or contrasts of words or spoken ideas....

A cliff, a tall one. A cliff that I can sit on and think of jumping. I can think so clear and so thoroughly that I can feel the wind in my face and its force on my body as I drop. Then I feel no pain, however I can still hear my body hitting the cement, and can foresee my body lying there for days, no one noticing or missing me. No one cares. A little while later I awake in my bed, there is no one lying next to me - there is rain outside, yet the sun shines through in my family and in my friends.
My friends are there. They are quiet, but they are,
that's all that matters, the mystery of being...

Kristen O'Mara

S. F. Poem

Surrounding that old fat woman
San Francisco thundered by.
The staccato rhythm of
straining engines - squealing tires and honking horns
created an appropriate accompaniment.
America's symphony in concert.

At the corner of Hyde and McAllister
the smooth functioning rush hour
was momentarily disturbed as that old woman
listening to some other drummer
marched slowly on her way.

Enmeshed in the rapidly silent crowd
she created swirls and eddys -
Individuality - a stone
caught in a swift running river...

As if it had never been disturbed
the river again flowed smoothly
unheeding between concrete banks
as it empties into suburban oceans.

E. R. Weinard

Eternity

Water, black as coal
Sand, hot as fire
The sun burning bright in the sky
a place borne of desire.
Sphere of flame setting beneath a dimming sky
throwing shadows of light upon the world
saying a final goodbye.
The moon arises, shedding a pale, white glow,
alone on a beach, time moves so slow.
A shadow of darkness envelops our earth
destroying the life that was made in its birth.
Lying on the sand, waves crashing on the shore,
I can't help but wonder, how much longer we'll be here for.

Kimberly Kwedar

Vietnam Legacy

Walking city streets under amber stars
Searching for amnesia in neon signs

Night dreaming of things hidden in the light

My shadow stepping over remembered faces
Taking me back to distant places

Silencing my heart a thousand times...

Michael Evans

Untitled

A lonely man walks across a moonlit beach
Searching for peace and escape.

Just moments before
The woman he loved and adored
Had left him.

But the crashing waves
Had no answer for him.

As the water crept closer and closer
So did he towards an answer.

Finally he fell into the waves
Engulfed by the dark waters.

Down, down, down, the salt water took him
Into a sleep that he would never awake from
He drifted off.

His soul devoured by love.

Molly Brenneis

Shadows

Shadows dance and voices whisper. Darkness contains many unknown secrets. Mysterious eyes watch us in our world of judgement. Skulls smile as we decompose into the very ashes from which we were created. Dead souls roam the night in search of relief from the shattered dreams into which they are forever damned. Once again, the full moon rises in the darkened night's sky. Another soul screams out at night, just as a first breath has been taken. Life and death balance this cycle of existence, which will never change.

Rachelle Hermanson

"Portraits"

A beautiful portrait of a woman
Seemingly perfect in all of her splendor
It has taken so long to find this painting
Fresh brush strokes, bright, intelligent colors
Barriers have been built to withstand such admiration
Barriers which guard against staling brush strokes, fading colors
Walls built around a heart which through eyes has seen
portraits first fade, then crack, then crumble to dust
A heart being protected from the agony of yet another
loss of yet another portrait
It is so hard to admire the beautiful portraits, to take in
all their wonders, beauties, freshness, while gazing
upon these paintings from such a distance seems
to draw the very life-giving substance needed
to keep them from fading, cracking, crumbling

Thayer Andrew McDougle

Growing Old

Time waits for no one is a familiar phrase,
seems like I was a teenager just only yesterday.
As I look in the mirror, I knew it wasn't true,
time is passing by for me and I know for you.
The greys in my hair, the wrinkles on my face,
how did time pass by so fast, what an awful disgrace!
Won't let myself get old and wrinkled, no not yet,
will fool around with Mother Nature, I hope I won't regret.
Maybe I will dye my hair, even get a face-lift,
I'll make myself look younger, for me what a wonderful gift!
Then sometimes I wonder, whom am I trying to fool,
I'll probably get more satisfaction going back to school.
Growing old is not so bad, it's what you do with your life,
if you do the things you want to do, why put up a fight.
I will keep my grey hair, and wrinkles under my eyes.
so what if you're young or old, someday we all will die.
Who am I fooling, trying to buy some time,
the only thing that ages, gracefully, is a bottle of wine.

Michael Graziano

Whispering Shadow

From the moment I saw you I knew it would be, but since you have seen me things have been different.
The heart I have for you is greater than peace, but you ignore me when I'm near.
I follow you because I don't want to lose you, but in the night, you leave me behind.
I just wish you knew how I felt.

As the warm air beat on the windows of every house at dark, the sun slept in its bed, but its shadow slept alone.
The night grew still on this summer evening.
The only light to be seen was the shadowless sight of the moon.
It was full and shining on the rooftop every lifeless house.
As morning rose, night fell and the sun raced throughout the meadow.
Night chased light as day chased the moon, and life is a whispering shadow.

Kathryn A. Schmelzle

Waiting For Snow

Oh when will it snow, Great Father on high?
Send down that stuffing that falls from the sky
In big wafer flakes so icy and bold
For skiing and sledding and catching a cold.

No matter, no matter, for flu we've been shot
Just dust us with white while the coffee is hot.
I'll sit in my chair with a lap full of cat
With seventy-one on the thermostat.

What's this? A white cover caresses the shoulders
Of hills and mountains and softens the boulders,
The shadows designing in purple and blue
I see a quilt pattern coming through.

The batting's hi-loft and the piecing is random
With soft applique and the color is phantom
It's coming together with thimble and thread
I see it, I see it inside of my head.

Hurray, the snow's deeper, the temp drops lower
But alas, it's my MAN that drives the snow blower
And ME, I just sit with a lap full of fur
Sipping hazelnut coffee accompanied by purr.

Mary J. Johnson

Your Birthday

Your birthday is a gift of love
Sent from our Heavenly Father above
Another year He's kept you from all harm
That's because you're safe in His arms
Safe from all the world's fiery darts
That would only seek to tear you apart

So on this your birthday I know you're reminded of
God's Grace, His Mercy, AND His Love
Extended to His servant who preaches His Word
The Word that comes from a true and living God
So continue to preach the gospel and compel men to come
Continue to lift up Jesus
For He is the ONLY ONE!!!

Lastly, be encouraged by the work you do for our Lord
For He has faithfully promised us in His Word
Everlasting life for you and me
When we discharge our Christian duties for all to see
So work on Pastor 'til God says well done
The battle's fought—Praise God!!! Victory's won!!!

Mary J. Huntley

"My Mother's Love"

With the strength of a tiger and a heart of Gold
Seventeen children combined the fold
Knowledge and love instilled in us all
By a caring mother who would not fall
An alcoholic father who seemed not to care
Mother told us he would always be there
Work, learn, dream and play
She taught us these values everyday
Organized, loving and confident
She ruled the roost, the rules were not bent
Now as adults, we still need her so much
She ask us for nothing, just to keep in touch
Life without her would seem fragmented
Life with her total contentment
If you have a problem, she has the solution
Her love and concern comforting resolution
A wish for myself is a selfish one
To be a child once again under mothers bright sun

Philip E. Buckler

Emerald Green

Your eyes are a emerald Green, you look twice as Sexy when your mean.

I've never seen anyone so beautiful and yet So tough. (I guess in attracted to all that stuff)

Your not to tall and that's just fine cause a Body like yours blows my mind.

You temper is shorter then you height. Say the wrong word and your ready to fight

Yet your gentle, sweet, kind and polite And I'll always love you with all my might

Sebastian Acosta

Grandmother

A grandmother is a women of love and gentle care
She always lets us know she is ready to share

She will comfort and love you when times get bad
And makes you realize all the good times you had.

She lends a ear when mom and dad cant be told
Making things all better with one gentle hold

Setting us on the right path in her own special way
So locked deep within our hearts she will always stay

Never turning away when help was at hand
She always stood tall and tall she will always stand.

Even though she has gone to a place we do not know
Her love and tenderness will always show.

Now I know she was Gods gift to me
So deep within my heart I will truly be free

Free from hurt and the will to never need
I thank you grandma for letting me be me.

Thomas L. Haase

Nature Is Free

The whispering of a gentle breeze,
Rustles gently through majestic trees;
Like the constant flow of rushing streams,
Brings to mind forgotten dreams;
Between abstract clouds, we can feel the sun,
To enlighten our lives, for play and fun;
Yet the strength of a sudden thunder shower,
Depicts nature's awesome power;
It can be unpredictable and different, from sea to sea,
Throughout the world, nature is free.

Patrick Creighton

Bewitching Lady Sea

Enchanting and wicked as she can be
She beckons unto you Bewitching Lady Sea

You aren't quite sure, you want to run
But she will not let you, she must have her fun

Her arms outstretched, calling with a voice so mild
You would almost believe, that she's just a child

You simply must obey, this gentle command
Just leave your clothes behind in the sand

She tempts you to enter her silky cool body
And tumbles you around to a siren's melody

You never want to leave her, this strange love affair
But she's all through with you, 'cause she doesn't care

Sandy Krueger Davis

Ode To A Daughter

I have a daughter that I love so,
She cheers me up when I feel low.
She's been with me thru thick and thin,
Always there for me, wherever I've been.
She is worth more to me, than silver and gold,
My love grows deeper, now that I'm old;
If that is possible, which I doubt,
She is such a joy, I want to shout.
What a precious gift God gave to me
That I want all the world to see.
I know her love is the same for me,
So obvious, all the world can see —
I thank the Lord for this precious Gem
That he wanted me to receive from Him.

May Belle Hall

"When It Comes"

The pounding no longer came as a surprise;
She covered her ears and closed her eyes.
She prayed that it would soon go away;
She knew she had to deal with it day by day.
Concentrate on other things and it would soon be gone.
She'd be content to once again be alone.
It never occurred to her to seek help.
That is why she lay on her bed and wept.
She waited for relief but it never came.
If only she had a way to beat it at its own game.

A. Elaine Morrow

The Horse

The horse sees a man lying on the ground, she gets confused.
She does not know what to think.
The horse does not know if he is alive or not.
She knows now that the man is dead,
for the man does not move.

The horse feels sorry for him.
She knows how bad life can be.
She hears the cries of pain and anger.
For every bite of grass is hope to stay alive,
because without it you would surely die.

The horse touches the ground with her hooves,
to show the world that you are still alive.
The horse can feel the pain of the man,
for the horse knows what pain is.

The horse knows that the guy was a lonely man,
filled with pain, anger, and sorrows.
She knew he had felt sorry,
for the horse knew he had done something he had regretted.
The horse knew this for the horse was the symbol of,

LIFE OR DEATH it is your choice in life to make that decision.

Sarah Kelly Young

Ten - Hi Go

She sported blue faded pants, a pure white top,
She is blushingly pregnant, about ready to pop.
It is Saturday night at the Ten - Hi bar,
Rock and hillbilly, side lot full of cars.

She bounces right in, grabbing back the time,
Eight months ago, when she was fresh, so prime.
She hunts for a table, fakes casual and cool,
All eyes are upon her, some are damn cruel.

The dance floor is loaded, a sea of jiggle and jump,
Motion in all direction, hip, arm, leg and rump.
The drummer bangs his cadence, he growls into his mike,
A nasty little ditty, rubbing in her plight:

Go Johnny go, see her shake,
Big belly and all, one little mistake.

But night rushed by, it played out sweet.
Lost in the crowd, a swirl of dancing feet.
She took the floor too, she knew how to take
Life's packages squarely, happily and neat.

Go Johnny go, see her shake,
Big belly and all, one little mistake.

Thomas K. Bullen

Smile

She was 7 when her uncle taught her about sex.
She just smiled and became a klepto and the household thief
She was 9 when her teacher told her she was too ugly.
She just smiled and learned she was worthless
She was 13 when raped by the father of a child she sat for.
She just smiled and became a teenage seductress
She was 14 when gang raped by "friends"
She just smiled and tried promiscuity
She was 15 when they raped her again. This time she knew
that no meant no.
She just smiled because on one believed her
She was 16 when she believed she was beyond redemption.
She just smiled and became a victim of verbal abuse
She was 25 when she realized that a woman, regardless of race,
Creed or color, should be revered, cherished and embraced by
God's design.
Outside she smiled at her children and said,"Mommy loves you
always"
Inside she cried.

Verlisa Washington

She Sat

She sat in the darkness
She sat with her husband
As they watched, the movie on TV drifted into an aerobics scene
The husband worked up a sweat
The movie drifted into plane crash scene
The husband slumped over
The movie drifted into a blazing inferno scene
The husband sweated more, and got slightly burned
One of the characters in the movie shot another
The husband fell to the floor, bleeding
The husband died
She sat
She waited
She sat
She waited
She sighed
She got up, threw the doll away, and ever so slowly
Walked toward the kitchen

William Cullinan

Lovestruck

First sight, my heart be still its might
 She looks beyond compare
Her strength, her grace, alluring face
 Her skin, so wondrous fair

Courage, fear, when she draws near
 A look to steal my heart
I can't explain, exquisite pain
 If only love would start

Her movements dance and just a glance
 Fires burn within
To touch her cheek, her caress, I Seek
 Oh God I must give in

Her laugh, her voice, no other choice
 Take me for awhile
My love, my soul, my being whole
 Are hers for just a smile

Does she care, could love be there
 To hope, and dream, begin
I'll be her friend until life's end
 And pray time helps love win

Richard A. Files

What We Dance

My mother is a Goddess, I know her in the night.
She moves me and I love her.
She shows me secrets no one else will share.

I run to her for comfort, we dance together
when no one else is there.

She is the darkness which is soothing,
the black between the stars.

Regardless of where I am she is there for me.
She loves me and we dance what I am.

Lynda Ferrell

"Yia Yia"

She remembers.
She remembers her youth on the islands
Working and cleaning all through the day.
Dancing and singing with sisters and brothers
She ways young and happy in a Grecian world.

She remembers games she played and friends,
she played them with.
She remembers the dress she wore to church,
that Eastern morn.
She remembers it all.

Today, she forgot her teeth,
Some things aren't as important.

Matthew J. Archambeault

The Reader Of Palms

She seemed foreign, exotic - when I asked
She said she was from Connecticut.

But her accent-gypsies dancing with scarves,
Somewhere in Europe.

Not that I would know -
the only gypsies I've seen were beggars,

Clutching at my clothes on the streets
of Moscow.

Sara Garmon

She Pressed Her Lips Upon My Cheek

She pressed her lips upon my cheek, the day that I was born,
She sang to me a melody, to make me safe and warm.

She pressed her lips upon my knee, the day that I fell down,
She held my hand to steady me, to make my journey sound.

She pressed her lips upon my brow the day I went to school,
She whispered, be want you want to be; there is no rule.

She pressed her lips upon my eyes, the day He broke my heart,
She shared with me her memories; when her true love did part.

She pressed her lips upon my hand, the day I left on my own,
She wished me love and happiness; words to guide me home.

She pressed her lips upon my heart, the day I said I love you,
She joyfully smiled and said, I love you too.

She pressed her lips upon my soul, the day that I was born,
She gave me all she ever had, my life she did adorn.

Nancy L. Graf

Reality

Late at night to escape from life
She takes a trip up very high
Sits on the twinkling stars so bright
Dances with darkness in the sky
Nothing but peace and quiet surrounds her
In the silence she remembers she's all alone
Nobody to talk to, Nobody's at home
She knows who she really is behind her shadow
And jumps off the star, falls into the sky of reality,
Hits the ground
She rides off into the sunset on a motorcycle
Back to what is called life

Mary Marshall

Where Has The Time Gone?

Crystal Lynn Rose:
 She was born, and then she was one.
 She was two, and walking too.
 She was three, and could sing to me.
 She was four, and had birthday cakes galore.
 She was five, and kindergarten was to arrive.
 She was six, and in school she mixed.
 She was seven, a doll from heaven.
 She was eight, growing so straight.
 She was nine, and doesn't always seem to mind.
 She was ten, and at games like to win.
 She was eleven, and we wish she were still seven.
 She's at her twelfth, and baby sitting for wealth.
 She is now thirteen, and going on sixteen.
  Where has the time gone?

Maxine V. Rose

In Loving Memory Of Tina Annette

God plucked a rose bud just at dawn that had hardly
shed the dew of birth.
Like a gentle breeze she was gone, ere she had scarcely
touched the earth.

We watched her go with tear filled eyes, although for her
we could not grieve.
By faith we could see beyond the skies, loving arms
waiting our darling to receive.

Perhaps in his wisdom God fashioned this little bundle of delight
And loaned her to us for a little day
Then took her home with him, so that her little light
shinning from heaven's window, might help us find the way.

J. LaVerne McCawley

Baby Girls

Hair so fair and light;
She's a doll, an angel!
Heart filled with love; so innocent.
Look at the wonder we've made together!

A gift from heaven;
Born of love and faith.
So small, so precious, so loved;
A mother's joy; a father's pride.

Born in a world unsure of tomorrow;
What will it offer to the little ones of today?
I love you, my little one!
I'll care for you, my baby, my child of love.

Mothers worry; fathers protect.
Take care of the babies;
The small, precious ones.
God's most loving gift to us.

Susan B. Swanger

Miy's (Pronounced My Eyes)

Through earth's riches a reflection of your beauty-
shines about my heart shape of tiger's eye.
Once driplets of attraction now harvest decimals of unknown passion
Stored memorabilia palace inner thoughts as if clouds
that gather the just lightened sky
Seasoned memories of yesterday hail suits of armor led by
knights of love fending the enemy off on the run
Challenged to face the feared dragon's of golden fire
Torn by deception and bound by choice;
Saddened days in times of deceit warmed by flowers of desire.
Orchestra of melodies from whispers of a sensual voice;
Loneliness and emptiness lurks about the rhythmic heart
Traveled letters from many distances afar.
Happiness and joy overflows frequent misses of being apart;
How I longed the monthly minutes to connect where you are.

Lamont Lumpkins

Independence

A death quiet stillness. A full moon
shining upon the open meadow shows the
silvery whiteness of the first frost.
Softly and silently it falls upon the land.
A farmer looks out from his kitchen door,
a lantern in his hand, a quiet smile
upon his face, a sparkle in his eye.
Crops been picked, stored away before this
silvery stillness came.
Spring was early, rain substantial all
the blessings he did pray. His calloused
hands, his furrowed brow, his weather
beaten face, can now rest and enjoy the
warmth of the open hearth.

Robert M. Green

My Aunt Violet

Childhood remembrances can be so peaceful.
Sitting in a rocker on her back porch
Sipping cold milk and listening to stories -

This beautiful aunt, with a name so appropriate;
Just as the first soft days of spring
Nourish the tender young plants,
She shows her tenderness and loving gleam

I am thankful GOD brought us together.
Just as I have pressed violets in pages of books,
Her memory will ever be pressed into my heart.

Sheila Nichols Bess

Passage

The silver-glinted waters ebb softly against the bosom of the waiting shore, creeping stealthily toward footprints erratically traversing the sand. They are mine - impressions embedded deeply in evidence of voyage, half filled, half emptied with fragmented presence of time. Fully engrossed in the search for truth that justifies my frangible being, I fail to heed the enshrouding fog manifesting itself through a warp in the unconsciousness of time, absorbing all sight into its nebulous entity, forcing abandonment of any though of flight - then, brief, fragile, fleeting as life, like life, dissipated into a farther eternity, for like the eclipsing sun after light and darkness meld, found no present place to be what it once was. But I, now, in
perfect understanding of who, and why I was, and am, mortal transformed into immortal by passage of soul, no longer traversing shifting sand, or fearing illusory fog or deceptive waters, am distanced from the past, forever refuged from returning to that place where I once was but no more am.

The water, relentless by virtue of motion, and the shore, static by virtue of boundary, in fleeting union, as lovers, embrace and release, embrace and release, ambivalent, unconcerned that all traces of my sojourn are being swept away into obscurity from any who might come seeking an epitaph.

Lena Coapstick

Even When You Don't Hear

God in the sky above,
Shower me with your love.

I've been praying, praying every night.
Still I have no answer when it's light.
Where are you, can't you hear me speak?
I need a sign of your love, for I am weak.

God in the sky above,
Please, shower me with your love.

My little child I hear you call.
But what you don't know is, I never left you at all.
I'm in your heart.
I'm in your soul.
I'll be with you until the day you grow old.
Only time will ease your pain and the words once spoke in vain.
I will carry you through this time of trial.
I will be there for you through life's many miles.
And when the time comes, you will live with me from that day.
For now, I cradle you in my hands and say...

God in the sky above, showers you with his love.
"Even when you don't hear."

Marla Bergland

Weaving Straw Into Gold

Writing quietly in the corner, she sat -
Silently filling her paper with words, phrases - life -
The life around her.
She wanted the world to see it as she saw it -
The warm colors of love and sorrow
Blending together
To be captured
And shared
And not forgotten -
At least by one.

Writing quietly in the corner, she sat -
Silently weaving words of happiness and pain - life -
The life that, to her,
Was filled with allure and excitement -
Needing to be seen in her way,
In her words -
Constantly weaving
The straw
Of this world
Into gold.

Kjersten Ellingson

"The Almighty Baby"

A baby is just an angel without wings
Simple-helpless-can't do things
Considered a dividend of mutual mankind love
Innocent as a little white peace dove

It's an Infant of God giveth and taketh Life
That serves God's purpose in Human Being strife
Personally it has no fear or shame
Nor it seeks no-power-glory or fame

A baby is just a little Human Nobody
With the Almighty power of a SOMEBODY
That makes its infants way
With an almighty suck and cry every-day

A baby -dzieczko—papoose or a bambino
Once was you and me-without a friend or foe
The almighty BOSS-with God blessed Super-Power
With-out the mighty vocabulary-of a Babel Tower

Now—whether it's in Red China?
Russia or Our God blessed America
Every BABY has the same Almighty cry
With a different language LULLABY——-

Wanda Dziedzic

"Daddy's Little Girl"

When I was just a baby, and you would
Sing to me, I knew you were my daddy
with hopes and dreams for me.

When I took my first step how proud
you must have been. Then when I said
My first word you knew that I'd begun,
to strive and grow with each passing day
to become a person in my own special way.

The year's passed very swiftly as your little
girl grew up and before you even knew it
I'd grown so very much.

I brought you joy and some tears too,
but somehow it all seemed worth it to you.

I write this to let you know how much
I love and need you so.

No matter what my life may bring. My
daddy will always be my king. I'll always
be Daddy's little girl.

Linda Starr (Nelson) Scibelli

Down The Road

I sit by my window and watch the sky
Sirens wail, cars scream by
Is someone hurt, or about to die?
Do they rush to the scene of some disaster
There are flashing lights, the cars move faster.
Then all is still
At the top of the hill.

I turn my head to watch the news
But have no patience for someone's views
The direction our country should take
Or decisions our leaders should make;
The number of lives lost to untamed emotions
Or wiped out by Nature and wars beyond the oceans.
I push the button. All is still.
For now. I've had my fill.

Tomorrow's scenery may be better. Or maybe not.
Down the road.

Mary Lou Lanza

One Time After Another

She cries each and every night
Sitting in her room all alone
The pain just keeps happenings and happening
She hopes that night, maybe it won't happen
But then she hears footsteps
Footsteps that are coming closer and closer to her room.
She tries to find a place to hide
Maybe in the closet or maybe behind the dresser.
Her body is trembling and her teeth are shaking
Then he enters her room calling out her name
Hiding, hoping he will not find her
Tears coming down her eyes
And thinking the words "Please don't find me, Please don't hurt me."
Then he finds her, grabs her, pushes her down to the bed
Crying out the word "Help" but no one seems to hear
Or maybe it's just that they don't care
He's so big and strong
She's so tiny and weak
After he gets his way with her he leaves her all alone
Yet letting her cry another night.

Sherri Borenstein

Don't Call My Mother Please

Little chubby tomboy, scabs on both knees,
Sitting in the principal's office-
Don't call my Mother, please.

I don't fight an awful lot
Only when I have to.
That seems like most every day.
Give or take a few.

Lace and frills are not for me.
That's simply not my thing.
What seems to suit me best of all
Is a baseball or a piece of string.

I didn't mean to hit her, sir.
I only wanted to tease,
Oh, she's in the Nurse's office?
Don't call my Mother, please.

Virginia C. Thompson

I Cry

As I enter the circle of stones,
slate grey from years of rain,
worn smooth from age and weather,
set apart from faith and prayer,
the emptiness seeps inside and my search begins.
Where are the humans now,
their carved beliefs, precious as gold,
rare as amber, ancient and old.
The ravens fly beyond the ridge
and the stars move behind me.
Even the clouds allow me to go first.
There is a drifting scent of decay in the woods.
A sense of profound loss in my memory
is felt but the vision is unseen.
My fingers curl into a tight ball
as my eyes lift themselves to the sky,
and I cry.

Larry Miceli

Only Just Begun

About the time I feel so snug
Sleeping soundly in my bed,
I awaken with a sudden start
With cobwebs in my head.
I give a yawn and stretch my legs
Then struggle to my feet;
I stagger to the bathroom door
When my heart skips a beat.
"Well, I don't go to work today,
Nor do I ever again;
I forgot that I am now retired
With a lot of time to spend."
How good to know I don't have to watch
The clock tick away any more,
Quickly washing my face, jumping into my clothes.
And go rushing out the door!
Yesterday I went to work;
We were busier than bees,
Today and tomorrow belong to me
To do with as I please!

Marie Pitt

That Was Then

I can remember when your hands felt safe and warm around us
Sliding down the fingers that held us together;
Laughing and skipping across your lifeline,
Feeling strength and softness enveloping us in your grasp.
And then your hands seemed to shrink and tighten
palms becoming sweaty with no room to play
Too many arms and legs, pushing and kicking from every direction
Suddenly I slipped between your fingers and dropped.
You had to feel me but pretended not to notice
Why didn't you pick me up?
Now your hands are empty and sore, never
to be filled again
...at least not with my children.

Laura A. Kingsley

Sdom Ya (To Know)

The figure as a dream manifested its wreathing self as the smoke from the Sacred grass, undulating slowly as a spectral kind, coruscating in its resplendence; I did not know.

At its scintillating aura long did I gaze, the thoughts in my mind tumultuous; I did not know.

In its far protecting veil as a shepherds flock stand the children of time, silent and unknowing, awaiting the movement of the Earth Mothers clock; and still I did not know.

Then deep within the shadowy folds did I behold an obscure figure of the future to unfold; still I did not know.

There were the eyes so red, nostrils flared, the great white horn, the hopes and dreams of His children forlorn; still I did not know.

Embraced in the radiance of a smile so pure, for those who will see, to behold, resplendent with six feathers so white is the Pipe - Sacred - to the Lakota of old; and still I did not know.

So long did I gaze till from deep within an ethereal sense there came, upward my Spirit Soul to the endless sky whence came the shrill crescendo of the Eagles cry; now - I - know!

Owen R. Britton

Metamorphosis

It is strange how so often when things run
smoothly,
And life just seems to glide along,
It is so easy to laugh and everyone's smiling,
And it takes so little to break into song.

And suddenly — a bolt from beyond — and darkness
descends like a blanket of bleakness.
The ear is soon tuned to life's strife and
sorrow,
And the eye sees nothing but death and
despair.

Then in the morning
the bright golden sun,
Shines down and sparkles —
the day is begun!
A rebirth — a renewal —
sweet juices flow,
As we face the world
with a smile and a glow.

Sally P. Solomon

Snow

Snow! Snow! Falling all around.
Snow! Snow! Falling on the ground.
You fall on the hills and on the trees,
Or on anyone or anything you please!

Everything is painted all shimmering and white
Making a cottony blanket in the stillness of the night.
Like diamonds the snowflakes shine
Forming myriads of crystals in a wintry design.

I'll go out and play in the snow.
To watch and delight and make snowmen grow.
I'll stick out my tongue and catch a snowflake or two.
I'll have fun in the snow.
Snow, do you have fun, too?

Snow, you are lots of fun
As anyone can see.
You are a gift from God,
Falling gently on me!

Lisa Marie Cecil, O.S.U.

The Stout One

To show despair, I would not dare,
So as not to hurt someone, for whom I care.
I have to smile, and bite my lip,
For fear that a longing look would slip.
I laugh a lot, and sing a song,
No one would ever guess, a loved one was gone.
Until I'm alone and in my room,
I shut the door and give vent to my gloom.
The tears they come, no one can see,
So they flow and flow to let out my misery.
And when the light of dawn appears,
Back on, goes the smile, and gone are the tears.

Marie Dibianco

Just Dues

Antigone broke the law of the king that is,
She knew that there was only one true set of laws,
That was of God's.
No one else could match the powers to be,
The King sentenced her to death,
What a harsh thing to do.
Antigone didn't care or even shed a tear.
As long as she is with her
brother, she truly didn't die.

Matthew Brown

Doctor And 3 Year Old Son

"Today is frigid, son," the doctor said.
"So cover your Sternum.. Cover your head"...
"My Tibia, Fibula and phalanges are cold...
Said the child, with voice so bold...

The doctor looked and smiled at him
And placed one hand on his Scapula then;

But something seemed to be the matter;
The young boy's teeth began to chatter...

"Dad, may I shout it in your ear?"
"MY COCCYX NEEDS THE POTTY CHAIR!"

Lila Trapp-Alston

Untitled

When I first met you I didn't know me
So I could not know you
You loved me and cared for me and called me friend
I kept you away
I lingered in the shadows
For I did not know me and could not know you
I lost you and wept
My soul full of sorrow
I hungered and thirst but could not quench
Not knowing me has made me lose you
Help me find myself
So I can find you.

Karen Clements

"Ode To My Friends"

My life should have been better,
So I've been told.
It should have gone somewhere,
It should have been bold!

My friends say it's a shame
A full time mother and housewife.
They never expected this from me.
They never thought this would be my life.

Well, attention my friends
Listen closely and well,
There's nothing I would change
There's nothing for me to dwell.

You see, my life is full.
It has challenge and meaning
When I try to keep four children
From fighting and screaming.

Sharon Dalrymple

To Love You Man

I'll not accept you sir, on just the way you look
Social rating is also not my game
If education has swelled your head, then certainly without rule
I've known some not too smart have gone to school
If you want to be a player, don't spoil my day
Having love should not be used in such a vulgar way
A woman's service on earth, is complimentary to the man
And satisfying my beloved is my true plan
Love expressions from each other is such a beautiful chore
If true love is your goal, then try my door
If it is love that you are after, I can give it
If it is kindness that you want that's all I am
If it is understanding you seek, I'll comprehend for you
If your plan is truth and honesty, I fulfill that too
If your plight is lack of courage, I'll inspire you day by day
If your path needs an enlightening, I shall clear the way
If it is knowledge you are seeking, then understand my book
A woman can do more than, wash, iron, and cook
If fascination is your search, I am enchantment through and through
With all the Love that I will give to you.

Tecca Betty Davison

We Are Coming....We Are Coming...

I think of the young mother, rocking her baby to sleep on her lap, softly humming a lullaby.
She looks sadly at her baby, its tiny mouth misshapen, not like the other new babies in the village.
She is waiting for us. She is praying for us.
She is hoping someone will come and help her and her beautiful new infant daughter.
We are coming. We are coming.

I think of the young child, isolated, the object of ridicule—an outcast.
Does he sit alone, a homemade woolen scarf wrapped loosely around his face, wondering what he did to cause his sad deformity?
Is there anyone, anyone at all who can help him?
Who can remove the shameful badge he wears with such humiliation?
We are coming....we are coming.

A lonely farmer surveys his meager plot of land and dreams of a wife, and children playing happily at his feet.
He wipes a tear from his eyes and sights because he knows it is a dream which can never come true.
No woman in his village could look with anything but fear at one so horribly disfigured.
Resigned to a life of lonely solitude, he digs the dry ground and dreams...

We are coming...we are coming...we are coming...

Robbie Jackson

"Daddy"

To some people it's just another word
some even act like a nerd!

But my Daddy is the very best
he beats out all the rest.

He's the sunshine in my sky,
one day with the Angels he will fly.

As long as he's here with me I'll give him all my Love.
Then with sadness, I'll send him to my God up above.

But for me, please don't cry,
for I'll be joining him in the sweet by and by.

Then I'll pick him out in the crowd,
he'll be the one with his own Golden Cloud!

Never more to be lame, but his loving
smile will be just the same.

So when you see me and my face just glows,
you'll know God picked for me
a Daddy that's perfect as a Rose!

Marie Mathews

Memories Like Shadows

Some days were happy, while others were not
Some I really loathed, and some I liked a lot
But like them or not, they will always be there
Both bad ones and good, both just and unfair
Like shadows they will always remain behind me
In the darkest of moments the bright ones will find me
(Both happy and sad are there to remind me)
That throughout my life I'll be on a scale
To rise once again after each time I fail

Like shadows the dark ones prevail in the light
Like shadows, they're hidden thru sleep in the night
Thru smiles, thru frowns, thru laughs and despair
Both bad and good ones have always been there
In moments of sorrow, some have made me feel nice
While others reap omens, they've made me think twice
They've ruined illusions, but still have come thru
With knowledge to allow other dreams to come true
Like shadows they are behind me to remain
But because of them I know which to repeat again.

Lee Hope

Family

They come in all shapes and sizes.
Some new, some generations long;
happy, sad, weak and strong.
Families can be shaped or shattered
close or spread out thru city, states and towns.
If you look around someone can always be
found, looking for family in every town.
White, Black or Brown any Race, Creed or Color;
Cashiers, Mail persons, Peace Officers and
Hot dog vendors alike, as basic as can be we
all belong to somebody's family.
We should or could help, save and flourish but
instead we hurt, fight and kill.
After all families are made up of individual people;
who care for their own, so why not each other.

Sandy Battisto

What's It All About?

Some people are black, some people are white
Some people think that skin should be light.
That is not true
That is a lie
We would all get along if everyone would just try.

There are some differences between you and them,
But that doesn't mean that you can't be friends.
What's on the outside shouldn't count
What's on the inside is what it's all about.

Samantha Calderan

Two Souls

The other night, I sensed your presence nearby.
Somehow, I knew that you needed me.

For some strange reason our paths never crossed
that night.

We're two souls wanting each other, two souls
not knowing what to do about us.

Perhaps, as times goes by, we'll learn about these
feelings inside of us-perhaps we'll learn the meaning
of it all.

We're two souls wanting each other, two souls not
knowing what to do about us.

Lydia E. Acevedo

My Special Friend

When I look at this person, I see a true friend.
Someone who is always there for me.
When I need a shoulder to cry on,
Or someone to talk to.
...To give me needed advice...

In times of tragedy,
Or of great joy.
When I am depressed,
And need someone to ease the pain.
...To help me solve my problems...

When all these things come into my mind,
So does the name, face, and sound of voice,
Of a friend.
Who to me is worth more than life itself.
...That friend is you!!!!!!!!!...

Sonya Y. Hogans

A Friend

Have you ever had "A Friend?"
Someone you could always trust to the end.
Someone to talk to, from down deep within.
Someone to count on thru thick or thru thin.
I have always prayed to God, "Send me a friend."

How do I find one? Where would I begin?
Someone tell me! Please I cry!
Help me, won't you even try?
All I want is "A FRIEND!"
"A Friend to the End!" Will I ever? Can I ever?

Find me a friend. Someone to trust.
To count on thru thick and thin!
I want you to know, right to the end!
He'll always, always, be my Friend!
Right Here! Right Now! Right to the END!!!
"My Friend" - Is forever and always
And for always and EVER.

Mable Hicks

I Just Wanted To Say - Thank You -

The times that we share are the only times I ever think I am doing
something right.
Because without you I have learned I am nothing.
Thank you for today and everyday you have brought me through.
Thank you for my husband.
Thank you for the children and the one that is to come.
Blessings upon blessings thou has bestowed upon me,
yet still some times I wonder why?
Your love is so perfect.
Guide me Lord, for I have not yet learned perfection.
I don't want to ask for anything,

I just want to say - thank you -
Thank you Father God

Sheronda L. Johnson

Thoughts

Emotions are like the wind.
- Sometimes blowing, softly
So that you could only feel my touch
- Sometimes hard — until you turned away
- Sometimes gently
As to touch your face
- Sometimes in rage
That you should know my anger
- Sometimes warm
When feeling you understood the inside of me
- Sometimes cold
When you counted me void
- Sometimes calm
That you should know my peace within you
- Sometimes uncontrolled
So that you tamed not my direction
I have touched you with all that I am
- Sometimes unnoticed
That I may rest in you
Yet, who? Has (seen) the wind?

Paula E. Goff

Dreams

Dreams. What are dreams? Dream can be
something that happens when you are a sleep at night.
Dreams can be something you want to happen someday.
Those are the best, because you can think about them
everyday and you can work your way up the ladder of dreams.
Just don't stop dreaming those special dreams,
because if you stop dreaming of them, they can never happen.
Climb that ladder of dreams with your special dream no matter
how silly it maybe to other it's not silly to you.

Misty M. Cotterman

My Best Friend

He's not very tall but sometimes he's taller than me
Sometimes he likes to cry
  But then again so do I
I'm always picking up his messes
  But it was fun making them together
He likes to stay up late
  And always gets up too early
Sometimes he makes me mad
  And I'm always sorry I yelled
We watch TV together
  And he falls asleep by my side
We've grown up together
  I'm in my 30's, he jut turned five
He'll ask me a lot of questions
  Always wanting to know why
Mom and dad fight so much
  Yet, he's always in the middle
I know I will miss him and the things we did every day
I just hope by next year He still calls me dad
To my best friend the best friend I'll ever have.

Richard Galbraith

Love

I met a man one day who said
Sometimes I wish I was really dead.
I asked him what his desires might be?
And he looked in my eyes and one word said he.

His whole life was one great remorse
His wife had left him and given him a divorce.
My main problem is hatred said he.
But he looked in my eyes and one word said he.

Just what is a man's deepest desire?
Is it love, hate, peace or sorrow?
Just what is a man entitled to have?
Just one word said he, give me love.

Lloyd Borkholder

Love's Betrayal

Sooner or later it Hurts Us All
Sooner or later we get caught in Loves Betrayal
One gets caught telling lies & your Heart wants to deny
it's True but yet deep down you know the one you love is only
using you your Head Tells you to run the other way but your
Heart takes Control & no matter how much he hurts you he
knows you'll stay even though you know your being used you
stay & let your heart be abused you make that special sacrifice
for the one you love & then he tramples all over your Heart
tearing your whole life apart & you pray everyday that you can
save what you once had Go Back to the day that you once knew
that he was Deep in Love with you before he started playing his
head Games & started calling you everything but by your
own name. Then came the day of ultimate Betrayal he walked
out on you to find someone new you try not to look Back
But you can't help it it's Been so long that you've put
up with this confusion now your in total pain & you
can't help but wonder why must love end like this?
I guess he just doesn't care anymore I guess I just
wasn't what he was looking for.

Laura Christie

In The Mindset Of Sheep

Dark rain falls staining the ground,
Staining the minds of everyone.
The battle has begun, and will never end.
Racist has won over rightist, and evil is live spelled backwards.
A backwards world for backward minds, in a backwards land.
No one can trust anyone, and everyone trusts no one.
Most are sheep, driven by the shepherd named: It Has Been This Way.
All are headed for the same destiny, a cliff looms in their way.

Shoshana Boar

God's Masterpiece In Ice

I saw a little snow man
  Standing so erect,
Such beauty and tranquility
  Demanded my respect.

The sun came out from 'neath the clouds
  And warmed the winter day,
When drop by drop and inch by inch
  He melted fast away.

Now this handsome little snow man,
  God's masterpiece in ice,
Can be compared to human life
  Which costs us quite a price.

For walking down life's pathways,
  As all of us will do,
There are many little snow men
  That we must bid adieu.

Like ice that melts so quickly
  When sunlight shines upon it,
Life is what you make it -
  Let happiness adorn it.

Margaret Mary Leatherberry

Golf Open, USA

Come to the open, see the pros at play!
Star at the open, on this special day!
Come and meet and greet the merry clan!
Playing golf since time began!

Bunker shot! Get your putter out!
On the Dot! Hit that lucky spot!
Swingers hot! That's what it's about!
Just wheel 'n deal 'n squeal 'n shout give it all you've got!

On to the next hole, bunkers galore!
Who put that hole there? Holes are everywhere!
With your heart and soul, make that baby soar!
Stances with a flair, pros are everywhere!

On the green, putter's turn to shine!
Under par, on that birdie shot!
Presidents grace the desert green
Stars of par 'n stars galore 'n stars of stage and screen!

Bob Hope and Trini, Frankie to the fore!
Singin' 'n swingin' — while fans shout for more!
Giants of the game, too numerous to name
Know we all love you 'neath the skies of blue!

Nan Beeson

From The Window

On a night of screaming wind, and a moon of desperate light,
Stood a dark and hooded figure,
That left me cold with fright.
I stood next to the window, and gazed strongly down below,
And the dark, and hooded figure,
Just stood as if to know.
That my heart was beating faster, - and faster it would go,
And then like a ghost he vanished in the night,
No footprints where he was standing,
Just a memory out of sight.
I ran down to the meadow, that I peered at from above,
I saw no trace of anyone, just a metal glove.
I suspected he was a dark knight, that had probably lost his way,
Or maybe he was my true love,
To return to me someday...

Paula Marie Pimentel

The Sacred Garden

Awake;
Stroll among a splendor of tall trees and flowers in bloom;
See the orchids and chrysanthemums as they strive for the sky.
Inside this vast green you view your life, your hopes, your dreams,
Your death; in this sacred garden your vagabond naivete' is brought to its conclusion.

Walk;
Engross yourself now in a movie of your life as you linger about the shadows of the elms and oaks. Adorn a mask, a face from your ancient gallery; do you admire the person in the mirror for the beauty or for the fragile ego? Wander now beyond the woods to a lucent path of dirt and diamonds. Are these transparent rocks that cut and bruise your feet so precious? Misguided vanity is the thorn in your side as you venture the walk of life.

Sleep;
Retire to a myriad of visions that implore your nocturnal life;
Enter the doors of your subconscious and let fly the scant thoughts that lay in waiting. It is only here that you find solace from a cruel and merciless world of murder and plunder. In the immense reality of the sacred garden, dreams and truth become as one.

Mark F. Morrell

Love's Way

Holding her close, tenderly.
Strong arms wrapped around her, protecting for a lifetime.
Mine is the strong hand, with a gentle touch.
An honest heart, of genuine love.

Her eyes are deep, questioning.
Soft hands holding on, uncertain.
Hers is a trust once betrayed,
Always cautious of loves way.

Michael Blaese

Untitled

A tree.
Strong yet weak.
A tough exterior with a soft, fleshy middle
In a forest of many, but still alone.
Roots searching for something to grasp on to.
Reaching for the sky with bare limbs.
Another futile attempt to find a strong hold,
in much bad weather and little sunshine.
Searching, reaching, and blowing in the wind.
Roots unattached, yet alive and still standing straight and tall.
Not needing perfect weather, just water, a ray of sunshine, and life.
That tree is me.

Pamela Paternoster

Reflections On The Mazda Queen

Today Ms. Mazda is forty six,
Surely the fairest on any "pix."
Each year she leases a brand new car,
To take her here, there, and sometimes far.
At seven it was the piano,
She became quite a virtuoso.
Four or more sports she did fairly well,
But too much and her spine would rebel.
An aunt said she had a bright keen mind.
Many times her kidney was unkind.
Always in style, and preferring blue,
She chooses the most becoming hue.
And Kathryn cooks the fanciest meals,
A lot better than meals on wheels!

Her mother, Ruth E. Powers

All It Takes Is A Message

Brilliant yet subtle our founders you see
struggling for freedom that's how it used to be!

Respect and dignity they gave to thee
a world of hope that's how it used to be!

Times sure have changed, for the worst, not the good!
Americans are steady dying like the evil knew they would!

So, what can we do to reclaim that hope?
instead of crack and all other dopes

Pick up a book, instead of a gun
listen to a neighbor, instead of killing their son

Put down the marijuana and plant seeds of life
for our citizens of all races are full of strife

Take time out to talk to a child
instead of beating them and acting wild

There's so many things Americans can do
all it takes is a message from me to you!

Toni D. Davis

End Zone

Only broken shells remain, where once stood homes
Sturdy and proud, and businesses, bustling with life.
Broken windows, sagging doors, fading graffiti, rusty twisted
Back fence wires, barren ground, where even the rubbish strewn/blown about, is poor and bare.
Here and there a scarred, mange-eaten cur, tied-up, hungry
Kicked and despised, shivering, howling, mournfully howling through the cold and the dark.
This place, habitation, corner of the world—decaying, rotting,
Glaring as a death's-head, hollow, stinking, used-up
Used unto weary death. Twisted, uneven, cracked, pounded-down
Falling off. And no one cares. No one.
Zone of living death, owned by those who will not (condemned)
Inhabited by those who cannot, broken souls wandering within it
Muttering to themselves. Humanity? Can these sad wrecks be human?
They love best what kills the pain awhile, seek self-destruction,
Oblivion. They are the lost, who while themselves slowly away.
Hoping, praying, the next lotto ticket will be the ticket out-of-here
Out of this sad ending. But their hope is in illusions...
Which fade 'way to nothing. Even as they, here, in the End Zone.

J. Kenneth Yarnall

Reborn - Again

So this is how it goes, thrown into the fray;
Subjected to ideals of a new generation.
So this is how it goes, ten years gone by;
I succumb to the grip of alienation.

So this is how it goes, re-arranging my existence;
A rebirth I don't fully understand.
Fighting it proved futile, its powerful resistance;
More difficult than counting grains of sand.

But time passes by and begins to heal the wounds;
Thoughts return to today and beyond.
I'm sure now that I'll make it if I just persevere;
Flesh and blood will create an all new bond.

Reborn again, it's time now to accept it;
This time I know I'll do it right.
The path has cleared, all obstacles have vanished;
The future now is finally looking bright.

Randall M. Perrelli

Tira

She slipped away in the noon of life,
Suddenly...
Leaving me to venture the night without her.
Taking a part of me, but leaving precious memories.
Her voice...the laughter,
Her face...the beauty,
Her love, oh, love.
My grieving heart filled with the pain of losing her,
Never to be the same.

I cry...Because my heart aches.
I cry...Knowing I'll never see your face
again...in this world.
But Joy!
I will see you in that other place,
And I'll always love you.

Tira, my sweet Tira, claim your Victory, you are free!
Life's pain and frustrations,
The suffering and aggravations are gone...
I will see you smile, and, all the while
I know that you are with me - Always.

Vivica Aycox

Untitled

I don't remember growing older with beauty
Sunrise sunset sunrise sunset
Swiftly flow the day.
Swiftly years swiftly years.
One season flowing another
Led with happiness and tears.
What word of wisdom can I give them.
Is this the little Girl I carried
Is this the little Boy that played.
I don't remember growing older, when did they
When did she get to be a beauty
How did he get so tall
Wasn't it yesterday when they were small
Sunrise sunset swiftly flow the days
Sunrise sunset swiftly flow the years
One season following another
Led with happiness and tears
What word of wisdom could I give them

Patricia Louise Tillman

The Transition

The tree house is gone.

Tarzan, the elephants, and the jungle are hiding.
Suntanned faces and barefeet that knew the fastest way to the top
have exchanged this play for stories of their children's first steps.
But the tree still stands and beckons to the young.

They've found him.
He holds them now as he camouflages their smiles.
Their echoing giggles and chatter reveal where they've climbed.
The tree house is gone.
We should build another.

Tamie Stockman Heagy

"Take Time"

Take time to watch the flowers grow.
Take time to watch the children playing in the snow.
Take time for a long walk.
Take time to just stop and talk.
Take time to spend with a friend.
Take time to watch a little child grin.
Take time to look up at the beautiful sky.
Take time to wish a loved one "Goodbye!"
Take time just to kneel and pray.
Take time for yourself at least once a day!

Mona R. Rhodes

Style

Soft spoken
Sweet smile
Dynamic motivation, oh what humor
That's style! That's Dottie!

You get the job done
Just look, you have won
For your work seems like it's so much fun
Gosh! That's style, That's Dottie!

Sophistication on all locations
You see, you are known for various vocations
Gee wiz! That's style, That's Dottie!

Caring, daring, courageous, strong will
You keep an open mind to stay focused
Incredible! That's style, That's Dottie!

Thoughtful, concerned, friendly, understanding
You have it all! That's style, That's Dottie!

Dottie will be Dorothus
Dorothus will be Dottie
My, oh my, no change in style
That's Dottie's style!

Marjorie Curl

Man Of The World

Take me somewhere strange.
Take me somewhere foreign.
Take me to a country that I wasn't born in.
Take me far, far away
To a distant land
Where I don't speak the language,
And I'd still understand.
Take me to Iberia, fly me off to Spain,
Where the rain always falls mainly on the plain.
I could keep up with the boys in Barcelona.
I could run along with the bulls in Pamplona.
Converse in Cataluna, or go and stand amid
The people in the barrios all throughout Madrid.
A fish out of water, gasping for air?
You could call me that, but i wouldn't dare.
Because I'm bilingual, I can speak spanish.
I could mingle, I could manage.
I could answer any question that you ask me.
"Se Habla Espanol?"
Oui, Oui!

Michael Gore

Thanks

This little note is here to say,
Thanks to you, my garden is lovelier today.
My garden is one of rare compose.
That's the nicest kind, as everyone knows.
Love blooms in my garden, it never ends,
Cause so many plants are from my friends.
I work in my garden, and relax and share
The touch of beauty the Master Painter put there.
I love the dew in the early morn,
The small green shoots that overnight are born.
To work in my garden is rewarding indeed,
As I reap the harvest from each tiny seed.
The problems of life are wiped away.
Thanks to a walk in my garden today.
It is ever so nice, your plants to share,
As I treasure each one, your love is there.
So thanks again, you're lovely to know.
I'll think of you often, as I watch them grow.

Mary Ellen Willingham

The Light That Severs

The light that severs my opaque darkness
Takes me into its stinging golden arms
And burns me with its love.

It swallows my soul, my breathe;
So it may fill my hallow shell
With its innocence and ignorance.

It leaves me sweaty, trembling,
And convulsing.

It squeezes my heart until I scream;
And all my hatred, and all my animosity,
And all my sarcasm, and all my desperation
Are thrust out of my mind.

Then the light is there
To soothe, to heal, and to protect me.

The light that severs
Does not bother with matters of the flesh,
Does not try to comprehend the "known".

It simply rips, tears, and shreds through the webs
That entangle and ensnare me within the last of my sanity.

The light that severs awakens me.

Sheri Fuller

Changes

Once there was energy to spare!
Tasks from early morn till late;
Dreams got pushed aside for another time.
The children's needs could not wait.

Time sped by us unawares,
Then adult people called us Mom and Dad.
We thought, "What happened to those dreams?"
They were so important once.

Now it's back to just us two.
What once we felt deprived of,
Pleasure, things and such;
Though opportunity affords them now,
Funny, they don't mean as much.

Not wanting to miss some wondrous adventure,
We dust off, and sort with discretion old dreams.
Then we begin to plan,
How best to use this time of new possibilities.

Patsy Arita

Autumn Prayer

Like the October owl, I look wise but have no answers;
Teach me,Lord.
Like the early days of Fall, I blow hot and cold;
Forgive my weakness, Lord.
Like the persimmon not yet frosted, I bite;
Forgive my sourness, Lord.
Like the Halloween ghost, I have no depth;
Discipline my ways, Lord.

Our Father,
You leave us color to excite our eyes;
Thank you, Lord.
You leave us crunch and crispness to please our ears;
Thank you, Lord.
You leave us the music of the wind playing to fill our souls;
Thank you, Lord.
You leave us the vigor of nature scurrying to prepare our minds;
Thank you, Lord.
You leave us memories to warm our nights in January,
Thank you, Lord, for Autumn. Amen.

Rosa Linda Talbert

Silent Prayer

In the silence of the night as I lay awake in bed
Tears upon my pillow, and a sleepless night ahead
I ask the Lord to Guide him as I've done so many times before
To keep him safe from harm until he's home again once more

He's my son and God I love him, he means the world to me
Although I can't convince him that I'm not the enemy
The culprit is the can of beer or bottle in his hand
Why doesn't he see his problem there? Why can't he understand?

Drinking is a way of life which brings him momentary pleasure
It steals away his self respect, the one thing he should treasure
The pain I had when he was born was just a fleeting thing
Not like the pain I feel at night as I wait for the phone to ring

In constant fear I worry that the phone will ring once more
To bring bad news again as it has so many times before
In life we all have choices that decide our fate
I pray that God will help him before it is too late

Muriel Hutchinson

Sweet, Precious Mother

Mother, sweet, precious Mother, I would like to
tell you what my heart has to say, for I'm not with
you everyday.

You gave me life, you gave me love and taught me
of the God above.

I always knew you would be there, no matter what
happened, you would care.

You gave me strength, my life to live, and told me
I had much to give.

You told me I could be, whatever I would like to
be, and to hold my head high for the world to see.

Now that age has come, in pain and agony you
must be, but your sweet smile is all you let me see.

If I had but one wish granted to me, no more
suffering you would see.

Rest, sweet, precious Mother and let me take care,
for you have done your share.

Sue Bishop Boling

What's Life Worth Living For

For every person they kill today
Ten babies will come to play;
It's just a cruelty in despair,
To kill a life, it's just not fair.

For all those people that lost someone
There's no repair on damaged done;
If you're drinking, don't drink and drive,
'Cause you might end up a life.

Just listen to what I've wrote
What thousands to you might say;
If you're using, seek some help,
Save your life, is all I tell.

This girl got killed by gangs
That man just died of aids;
This car ran over a kid,
This other man's life hangs.

Why does it have to be this way
Where everyone is scared to death;
Of walking out in the streets,
Enjoying a sunny day.

Noemi Vega

January Sunday

A green, muddy road leading out to the edge
testing shocks uh! and breath
clouds of color and rain meet the sea
bravery from behind warm windows wanting up closer
winning tug of war with wind and car door
Let's walk! there's the path hurry
smell of salt and wind stings my cheeks
cover up more my ears my nose
feet sink more than they go forward
loud roar deafening
his warm, strong hand squeezes tighter
there's a shell well part of one
foam carried in and left behind to blow and pop amusing a child

Kim Hicks

God's Creation

What more could God send to this earth,
than a vision of heaven, in his work.
Your the beauty of the flowers,
and the glitter of the morning dew.
The sparkle of rain, in the summer sun.
And the glory of the sunset,
as each day is done.
The trill of the song bird,
as he sings Gods praise,
and the majestic rise of the mountains,
we see afar in the haze.
What wonderful thoughts, must have been in Gods mind,
when he sent you to earth,
so rare and so fine.
For like gold your pure,
and a diamond your rare,
and the joy of loving you,
is beyond compare.

Ramona Unruh

Just Say No

The world was much more simple,
than it is now today.
The guns, the drugs, the violent acts,
have all become a way.
A way of life worth dying for
to kids who've barely grown.
The kind of life they can't live out,
their lives will go unknown.
There's so much to be seen yet,
there's so much to be done.
All to live the life they lead,
the one they find so fun.
A life short lived with fancy cars,
the beepers, and the guns.
We can't just ignore it all,
for these may be our sons.
Our sons and daughters are lost to us,
if we don't look and see.
If we don't stop and look around,
and raise them carefully.

Raquel Pierson

To My Wife Alminta

Thanksgiving time is almost here it holds no joy for me.
The festive time will not be known not like it used to be.
We used to sit and talk all day and plan the holiday
Should we stay at home and have the kids or slip quietly away
But now there's no one here with me to plan this holiday
So I'll just find a quiet spot and spend a lonely day,
Lonely nights, lonely days life must go on they say
One day I'll turn the corner and I'll be on my way.

Kenneth Alexander

Beauty Of The Flower

Their once was a flower,
that blew in the wind.
Its beauty was outstanding,
it was a vision, never seen before or again

People would stop and stare,
birds and bees would stop in flight.
animals wild and free, had to stop and see,
the beauty of the flower, as it blew with in the wind

The whole summer, its beauty did shine,
yet, in autumn, it did wilt and die.
It seemed that the whole world did cry,
for the loss of the beauty, gone and never to be seen again.

Yet, I close my eyes, and in my mind,
I see that beauty, forever on.
So I, won't weep nor will I cry,
even though my flower is gone, my love, lives on and on.

Michael Ray Martin

I'll Try

I did not promise, because I knew I could not
That certain feeling came over me
That was impossible to stop

I tried to overcome it but that was so hard to do
Because I know deep down under I wanted to be with you

Playing those certain songs, of course didn't help
They made me more aware of the feelings I felt
So I stopped, sat down and became deeper involved
Thinking strongly of how much I'm really loved

I tried, once again, thinking some day you'll be mine
The tears began to flow, uncontrollably this time
I'm still trying, hoping and praying too
That maybe, just maybe our dreams will come true.

I won't be selfish but be grateful too
For I have tried, yes, I have cried happy tears over you

Sarah E. Moton

"Blessed"

Of all the people in your life
That everyday come and go
There are really very few
That you stop and get to know.

But you are one of those people
That has a special place in my heart.
I've never felt so understood by anyone
And I hope we never grow apart.

If true friendship is considered priceless,
Then the riches and rewards are true
And I know that I am blessed and lucky
Simply because in my life, there's you.

Leslie Edwards

My Secret Garden

The crystal water of the fountain pours from the white flower statue in the center of my garden. The golden leaves fall from the trees to form a hat on my head. Chipmunks rest on my shoulder and their tails wrap around my neck like a scarf. The scent of roses travels through the air and crashes against the wall that protects my garden. The pine needles feel like sharp pencils, and the smell of pine trees makes me feel free and on my own. Sweet strawberries, sour cherries, and crunchy red apples are tasty treats I grow. The buzzing bees and humming birds dance through the air like they're in a ballroom. The wind has its own solo in the garden choir.

Rachelle Brunette

"The Sun"

A fresh new day with a glorious sight
That huge torch in the sky that shines so bright

Good morning world, behold the glow
Prepare yourselves for a sensational show

Grasp a hold of a ray of energy
Saturate yourself and enjoy the scenery

A scientific wonder for us to speculate
Make room in your mind to relax and meditate

The center of attraction, everyone is known to stare
Look out though, it'll scorch with its fiery glare

Piping hot in the summer; smooth warmth in the spring
Power sparkling from heaven to give us zest and zing

Shimmering, spacious, superlative shine
Glimmering, gracious, sentimental, divine

It's so adoring sitting there in the sky
Soon to fade because the evening is nigh

Hold your breath! This performance is splendid
Look! The most beautiful colors so perfectly mended

It cannot be done without the hand of the Lord
Good night, sleep tight and awake for an encore!

Torry L. Black

Destiny

Pluck the roses from my hand
That I have sought out for you
Throw them beneath your feet
And trample them under

I took them from their beauty
And as revenge, my fingers pricked
But no matter to you
Another gift of praise

I could die for you a thousand deaths
But I would never cross a thought —
But the great power in my love
Keeps me hanging on
I will someday build a bridge to your heart
Then burn it as I cross

Kathy "Seropa" Howard

Who Was The Best Clown?

In sickness and in health, til death do us part,
That is the way, the clowning will start,
From the beginning we keep playing a game,
Who is better, or are we both the same?
But as life went on, you think you can tell,
When one of you is no longer well,
Was he the clown, who held it inside?
Or was it I, who spoke no truth, just lied —-
Who convinced who, and did we both know,
And that it was our love, that made it hurt so,
We do not speak of what we fear,
Although I knew that death was near,
Neither mentioned it or wore a frown,
So I'll never know "Who was the best clown?"

Muriel V. Cummings

Imprinted Memory

There is an opened doorway
that is welcoming me
with blind acceptance

I walk through it
hearing echoes of denial and despair
surrounding me

There are four walls
that are painted black
with delusion and distrust

I let a light creep in through the door
slowly creating a distorted shadow.

Suddenly, the light in here has become so blinding
that it has imprinted itself in my mind.
And my soul is now etched on the wall.

Linda Filosa

The Old Home Place

Today I drove down the dusty gravel road
That leads to the Old Home Place.
I stopped my car in front of the house,
And sat while memories flowed.
The good times, the hard times, the best of times-

I could smell the teacakes that Mom just baked,
Feel her soft touch upon my hand.
I could see Dad in his khaki work clothes,
As he walked toward the barn.

The tall cedar trees, the swing where we played,
Peach trees with fruit and smell the fresh cut hay.
Wildflowers in the field, roses near the house,
The large crepe myrtle trees with blossoms of red.

Weekends and holidays we'd all gather,
Sit on the front porch and watch our children play.
Eating good food that Mom had prepared,
Listening to Dad and the stories he'd tell.

I'm glad I traveled this road today,
And I shall travel it again;
Back to The Old Home Place.

Lois Farris Tull

Untitled

I had a dream
That once upon a starlit beach
I took your hand into my own
And under the gentle stars
We danced.

I had a dream
That we sat together upon the sand
And talked about the ways of magic
As the waves gently lapped at our feet
And we danced.

I had a dream
That your breath was mine
That your eyes saw no other
That I lightly kissed the seas salt from your lips
And we danced

I had a dream
That I held your head upon my chest
And gently stroked your flowing hair
As brown as mother earth
And we danced

T. Dey

It's A Dilemma

Perusing the newspaper, I have found
That opportunities often abound.
To this fact may this ditty attest
And my offering be deemed the best.

To write, to write, just what to write?
The poet's dilemma, to not seem trite.
Should it be profound or simply amusing?
Oh Me! Oh My! It's all so confusing.

Since the length of this poem is restricted,
My mind feels it's much too constricted.
Because I know that the ending is near,
The conclusion is most that I fear.

I've thought so much, my brain is pickled,
But nary a phrase has my fancy tickled.
And with each new line along this score,
Finding the right words becomes a chore.

Let this be a lesson, and do take stock,
A poet's worst enemy is writer's block.
When this tragedy strikes, it makes me sob
Which inclines me to keep my regular job.

Peter C. Mirabito

A Query On Latin

On great authority it's been said
That the language called Latin is stone cold dead.
So now I ask you - "how and why?"
Did a bunch of words just up and die.

And why do doctors keep trying to revive
Something that supposedly isn't alive?
And can you imagine a Latin lover
Saying "E Pluribus Unum" while under the cover?

Now isn't this language thing mysterious?
Since "Latins" speak Spanish, how very curious.
Dead or alive, Latin's still being used
By persons who want to keep us confused.

And then there's this Latin known as pig.
Oh, give me a break, I'm starting to dig.
Let's bury this darn thing once and for all.
What's the point of this rhyme? I don't recall.

Marjorie Chapman

Is Any One Here....?

I see sunshine in a dark rain cloud
That thunders in my heart.
Flicks of energy like lightning bolt through my veins.
Soft and gentle with a wild streak running
Like the wind through my soul, touching me
With feelings of desire.
Everything you need in one package.
Everlasting passion with nowhere to turn
Night is black, moon in orbit, with my every
Breath day turns to night.
In one glimpse dreams, hopes and feelings begins and end.
Talk is cheap.
Splinters of pain fill my body with a new sense of being
New days will come upon me.
Now another change will soon follow.

Michelle L. Hendricks

Alone

There are those in this world
that walk in solitude.
They prefer nature to the multitude;
they are like the flag unfurled
riding high on the pole of life,
alone but never really free
always searching for perfect harmony
between life and reality

Many that travel alone
prefer the pleasant land of dreams
to man's evil realms
of greed and business on the telephone.
Those that walk alone but have no loneliness
are those who's life is filled with happiness.

Thomas Sisk

I Had Not

I had a love,
That was never meant.

I had a love,
That I had to let go.

I had a dream,
That brought false hope.

I had a dream,
That I had to let go.

I never had a promise from this love;
Only hurt and doubt.

I never had a feeling of freshness from this dream,
Only a stale feeling of never being.

My heart has been broken!

Give me the broom to sweep up the pieces,
To mend my heart.

For I know one day I can give it to a creature of God's choice.

I have loved!

I have dreamed!

Vickie D. Colenburg

On Top

On top you can see everything,
That you want to see.
While down below everything has to be seen.
Why? I ask, do they on top, see only,
What they on top, want to see,
While we must see everything.
We have to see the hate, the love,
And the death of everything we loved,
While they on top do not care.

If I yelled, to call them down,
To show them what the have done.
Would they see and if they did.
Would they care?
But why their eyes are blind,
To our pains and sorrows,
I do not know.
I guess it's because they're on top
and we're not.

Nicole Krienen

What Is Christmas?

Did Christ not die to save my soul,
That's the story, that has long been told

Yet the world has gone mad,
on a shopping spree.
Buying gifts for the world to see.

The greatest gift of all mankind,
Is to know the Lord
And keep him in mind.

We should hang our heads in sorrow,
Less we should awake,
To find there is no tomorrow

So let us love one another
As Christ loved us,
We should love each other.

The gifts we give should come from the heart
And not from the cart
of the shopping mart.

So what does Christmas mean to me?
It's my love for Christ,
That has set me free.

Virgie Lee Epperson

Radiant Summer Sunset

When the sun is setting in the west,
That's the time that I like best;
To see the glow across the sky,
And watch the birds as they fly by.

The birds are flying to their nest,
There for the night they will rest.
And the honey bees are in the hive.
Man, I feel so much alive.

Down the lane the cows do stroll,
Over the hill and to their stall.
One is calling to her baby calf,
As if stumbles down the path.

It is the end of another glorious day,
And all the children have quit their play.
They are waiting for the morn,
When another radiant day is born.

Verna Ray Humphrey

LIFE

LOVABLE INFANCY-
the age of new life,
nourished by food, love and sound
devotion of husband and wife.

INNOCENT YOUTH-
the age of restless life,
developing body and character
amid the pressures of peer strife.

FAMILY MATURITY-
the age of amorous life,
romance, marriage, children, careers
requires patience were anger is rife.

EARNED LONGEVITY-
the age of serene life,
experiences, adventures and warm memories
are told to prepare the new born life.

William A. Preiss

Sorrow

A soldier rides silently under a pale moon;
The air is filled with gloom;
Not a word is spoken; not a whisper heard;
What is this gloom?
Who is this man?
No armor dose he wear; no smile upon his face;
What is this gloom?
Who is this man?
The stars do not shine; the bells do not chime;
No sword does he carry; no shield in his hand;
What is this gloom?
Who is this man?
Why is he so sad?
There are bags under his eyes;
He is dressed in rags;
What is this gloom?
Who is this man?
Could a loved one have died?
Tears rolling down his face; he is of a different race;
He is a friend of you and I; he has come to say goodbye;

Theresa Kessenger

Something To Think About

Walking hand in hand.
The beaches crowded with couples in love

The taste of salt from our pores
slowly falling into the corners of our mouths.
Trickling down from our cheeks like innocent teardrops.

A gentle, cool breeze overcomes us
Taking our breath away.

The grasses on the dunes
Wave soothingly as we walk by.

Walking some more,
My attention in drawn to others.

I noticed that...
All those in love,
Were in there own creation
Not realizing that we were, too.

From the both of us,
We never thought complete happiness,
Could come with complete
loneliness.

Kim Milligan

In My Grandmother's House

In my grandmother's house we all lived together from
the beginning of my life til the ending of hers.
She was the matriarch and my father learned early that
this was how it ever would be.
But pine floors gleamed softly, laundry was sweet smelling
and our meals were prepared with meticulous care.
In my grandmother's house there wasn't much laughter
and hugs and kisses were precious few.
But her garden was bountiful, arbors hung heavy and
flowers bloomed freely under her watchful eye.
In my grandmother's house a small child was lonely and
grown-ups cautioned silence when she was napping.
But summer nights were peaceful in the porch swing
beside her with neither one of us saying a word.

Sometimes it takes a lifetime to realize that love comes
in many guises.

Martha S. Tanner

Finally

The cut is thin and long across my wrist.
The blood, it dribbles down my hand.
Veins that are sliced gush blood profusely.
But I'll try not to stop it.

One long line of blood down the middle of
my hand that starts to drip at the end of my finger.
I'll let it drip into one big puddle.

I'm getting lightheaded, the room's beginning to spin.

I should fight to stay awake.
Fight to stay alive.
But I can't, because I don't want to live.
I won't fight it because I want to die.

And I will, Finally.

Leah Shultz

Domestic Hell

Complete rigor, posterior liver
The body young, the skin smooth.
Twenty nine years old and a beautiful wife
another victim of domestic life.
Pathologist, scrubs of blue
Mother of three in a gray hue.
Right occipital - Bullet in
tears flow from the next of kin
Left temporal - Bullet out
children weep, in pain she shouts
Gasps and fading screams
another life of shattered dreams
A 38 caliber hits the floor
blood stained husband through the door.
Medical examiners at the scene
Shutters click, flashes scorch
Bullet embedded in the front porch.
Prints lifted, body bag shifted
Mother of three, beautiful wife
Unrenowned to have a hellish life.

Tom Cannon

The Birth Of A Rainbow

Blue is the color of singing puppies dancing in the wind
the color of oceans beating against the withered shore
raging red
the color of the wild ponies eyes
the color of a ripened peach in the spring
purple is the color where dreams often come
it is the freedom of unruly stars struggling to sparkle
greens are the colors
of a new born fawn wobbling on its unstable legs
the color of a hawk soaring through the air
acting as the king of the sky
orange is the sweet color of her wispy hair
as it sways in the gentle breeze
and orange is the color of the melting sun
as it pours over the earth
yellow, the fresh burst of flowers rising from the earth
the color of cotton clouds drifting overhead
and as I recall these colors
a rainbow breaks into the sunlit sky
and I sink into eternal sleep

Taylor Alexandra Gardner

Mid-Summer

The feeling is unbearable,
the coolness untouchable,
the desire unquenchable,
the day unending.

Color floods the sky
blending together as if
it were splashed on to an artists canvas,
carefully placed.

The wind is calling to ones soul,
but the soul does not respond,
total isolation from
the worries of the day.

No-one cares
for no one hears,
the feeling is unbearable,
the coolness untouchable,
the desire unquenchable,
the day unending,
mid-summer.

Pamela A. Peat

Their Life Together

They join hands while walking through
The dark clouds of life together.
Never to know when the storm will
Erupt in their hurts.

Willing to sacrifice their souls
For the love and joy, of life together.
This disease will take over all
They have in sight and will make them
Blind, as they live their life together.

The trouble they will encounter along
The way can never surpass,
What will last, as they live their
Life together.

Reflections of their world will shine.
Shine in a giant mirage, but still the
Masse's of confusion can not
Part, their life together.

Roy Ryder

Living In The Clouds

The sun sets in lustrous clouds of vibrant red and orange
The day ends in silence as night makes its way to the sky.
The only comfort in all the darkness about her is him.
Her vivid thoughts of his touch, his smell, his whole being.
His statuesque pose sets before her eyes with all its majestic
Wonder,
Bringing forth her most intimate dreams never before shared.
The ease of conversation and the warmth of his sensitivity
Awakens her yet undiscovered feelings and emotions.....
As if drifting into unexplored territory.
His power is strong, yet with a casual softness that allows his
Charms to overwhelm her.
Never in her life did she imagine such an exuberant man to
Exist....

Never in her life did she imagine this wondrous creature to
Slip silently into her every thought... Her every dream.

B. Sherr

Friendship

As silently as sunrise comes
The days flow into years,
Some are filled with happiness
And some drenched in tears,

But always it is good to know
That there are those who care,
Who may today lift up your name
With love in fervent prayer.

Your face can wrinkle, hair turn gray,
Even your joints can rust,
You can be a diamond in the rough,
With flaws and covered in dust.

Friends only remember that you were there,
They never notice your age.
They never judge you or shy away,
Or turn your life page by page.

One nice thing about friends,
You needn't be perfect to the end,
They just simply thank God
That your their friend!

Rosemary L. Grant

Twilight

When youth fades
the days grow longer.
Life turns into different shades,
hues with shadows that linger.

Days become shorter,
family more precious -
I tell myself life can only get better,
but the passage of time makes me anxious.

Though the twilight of life nears,
I can still recall the colors,
episodes of my life laid bare.
So bittersweet! I want more!

To my life, I have not one regret.
For my children I leave a legacy
of joy, tears, guidance, and strength to let
their youth live on for others to see.

Pam Burton

Words Not Just Words

Words, a window to open a heart,
The door to one's soul, and steps beyond.
Words, for the one I love.

Words,
Dare my friend to keep in touch!
And show me, you do care very much!
Never deny, what gifts God sent down!
It's lots of love and laughter, not
tears of a clown!

Even if we both go our own way!
Love, God put in our hearts will
bring what may!
Chance is, we'll meet again someday.

Words.
Poetry is really love blooming from the heart!
Love, sweet love, is truly thee part,
Of our souls, that's heaven on earth!
Poetry, is words, awaiting one's birth!
Words, spoken or unspoken, are gifts from God.
And word became, flesh.

Louise Wirtz

Do You Remember Me

I was here when God created the heavens and
the earth. Do you remember me
I was here when God created man and
woman. Do you remember me
I was here when God give you your litter
baby. Do you remember me
I am the one who heal the blind man and
heal sick. Do you remember me
I am the one who take away all the pain
And suffering of this earth do you remember me
I am the one who give you my love
do you remember me
I am the beginning and the end
do you remember me
I am Jesus Christ the Son of God.

William Pruitt

'Denial'

I wake, heavy in a trance, but I have a need to feel
the ecstasy of love, but 'denial' was my deal
My eyes glazed in tears and I want to experience a hug
My idea of true love, but 'denial' is quite a tug
I want... I need... do I ask so much from life?
To wake up and have no 'denial'; just to be someone's wife?
To give a kiss and warm hugs each hour you see them alive
To tell your sweetheart 'I love you', but 'denial' is multiplied
by five.
I walk before the mirror and I'm the pretty girl every guy describes
Why do they cheat? Why can't I trust? 'Denial' gives me bad vibes.
I ache each day to feel the warmth of someone's arm
around my waist, his hand in mine; God? all I get is 'denials' harm
Life is hard, pain follows me in life; doesn't anyone see me as 'me'?
Is there honesty and trust, so I can set my life's 'denials' free?
Crawl inside me and experience what only I know
Show me I'm real, am I alive? Make my 'denials' low
One day I pray before I die, that I feel ecstasy within me
I'll be smiling each day, flushing 'denial' out, cause I'm never
gonna be.... again in 'denial'....

Sherry L. Hargett

The El

(with apologies to Lawrence Ferlinghetti)
Elevated high above my head;
The El with its roaring, rectangular boxes
Races by.
Gazing up,
Flashing blurred lights catch my eye.

The El,
Oh grand, flying God!
I blush in your wonder.

Wait! Stop!
Let me enter your womb.
Deliver me, oh El
To a new place of enchantment.

Thousands crowd inside you,
Sanctified in your motion.

(Can't you see this Lawrence?)

Kathleen B. Heath

Helpless

I feel helpless looking at
the endless fields of wild flowers
I feel lost in this world
that is so close, so close,
to its own destruction
I look for answers.
deep in your big blue seas.
So much is said with your silence
and nothing with your madness.
Teach me...
Help me...
Guide me...
Can you save me?
Can you bring the light to my blind eyes?
Help me find myself,
give me new strength,
Set my sorrows free
because my soul needs relief.
Still I am helpless, Help less.

Sergio Soto

My Sweet Love

Ashes to ashes and dust to dust
The fact that you're gone, isn't fair or just

I can't see you or feel the touch of your lips
The loss of your presence at my heart rips

Always you and me, together forever
Our bond is still strong and never I'll sever

The price of our love, gave you wings up above
And someday I'll join you . . . my sweet love

There was no time for a lover's goodbye
But our love didn't end on the day you died

Why this tragedy happened, no reason, no rhyme
Our special future, destroyed by her crime

The price of our love, gave you wings up above
And someday I'll join you . . . my sweet love

Linda Edwards

Victory

Helmets touch and the whistle blows
the fierce battle begins
blood, sweat and tears carry the team
Fighting ensues, and you get rocked into the nickel seats
getting up you see your enemy
and plan on your line of attack
waiting for the perfect
moment to nail his @#$% to the ground
Late in the game
with only seconds left
he gets a suicide pass from his defender
with teeth clenched and fists tight
you plow towards him hoping to catch him off balance, you do!
Crushing him so hard he has problems getting up
As he staggers off in pain
the whistle blows
and you walk off with a team win
and personal victory.

Matthew T. Dolan

All Of Time

I was there...
The first dance of the dinosaur on a sea of rock
The first step of man in a forest of wild
The birth of a God on a soft bed of straw
I have touched...
The first drop of water that forged the canyons
The first flame of the volcano that formed the islands
The first grain of sand to blow across the deserts
I have seen...
The first ray of light at the start of the new day
The first drop of blood shed for a belief
The first smile of each new born child
I have heard...
The first wave crashing against the shore
The first note of music in an artist's ear
The first drop of rain on the dry ocean floor
From the beginning of time to the end of all days...
I am History...

Melissa Lyons

Treasures

Have you ever seen a rainbow after a summer shower?

Have you ever smelled new-mown hay or picked
the first spring flower?

Have you ever heard a baby's first cry
or a bird call to its mate?

Have you seen the smile on your neighbor's
face as you help her through the gate?

Have you ever sat in Grandma's kitchen and
smelled her homemade bread?

Or walked barefoot in the sand and watched
a sunset painted red?

Did you ever see water in a creek running
fast and free?

And trees with fruit hanging heavy, that
God put there for you and me?

Have you ever watched the wind blow white clouds on a summer day?
Or felt the warmth from a fireplace or heard a small child pray?

If all these things you haven't touched or never hope to see,
Then I'm afraid you haven't lived
for the best things in life are really free.

Leona Ricketts

Remembering

Images and color splashed on canvas in the mind;
The home, the hearth, the family, the treasured ties that bind
Are scenes that give us pleasure as time slips quickly past.
Recalled in vivid shades of light and darkness at the last.

Our minds are a collection of the paintings that we keep;
Of golden days of laughter, dark thoughts that make us weep.
We choose the art to ponder in the gallery of life;
The portraits of our parents, the sculpture of a wife.

Each frame of life a season filled with beauty, warmth, and truth;
The pictures of a life together, babies, children, youth.
Nostalgia, but no sadness, life takes on a different hue;
Once a table filled with many, now reduced to two.

We start each day with fresh supplies, blank canvas and life's oil;
Creating memories of love, of sadness and of toil.
The art is not reality, but our perceptions stand
As tribute to the character that moves the artist's hand.

Stephen E. Proctor

A Leaf Fell

She is the tall tree on the hill. A morning mist spreads
the gentle wash of dew, and the day begins.

The branches are her sentinels. When the winds are
gentle they curve with the subtlety of calm freedom.

When the winds are fierce and mean, they bolt upright
like righteous pride.

The leaves are her children. They dance with happiness
when fingers of the sun caress their tips.

They weep when heavy from the gift of rain that makes it
perilously hard to keep hanging on.

They giggle and whisper tempestuously with the breeze.
The game of teach me, touch me gently Mother tree.

She loves the game. She billows and sways with wonder
at all they can do, and is grateful for the time given.
Mother tree has traversed the life juices through sentinels.

She has given all she has to give, and the leaves have
had their season.

She bows majestically and quivers with a silent shriek
of sorrow for the leaf that fell...
Oh much too soon! And for those that fall tomorrow.

Millie Crowe

Gratitude

As we share this day of love,
The grass, the trees, the stars above,
We think of life and all the love you give.

Sharing all these beautiful things
The birds that fly with outstretched wings,
The sky that holds its color so blue,
The thoughtful words, I love you.

These wonderful sights, and all they bring,
The happiness and all the things from you.
Walking carefully, holding your hand
Marveling at your glorious land of love.

Ron Page

Empty Ballroom

Emptiness graces this great hall.
The guests have all left the ball.
Dying, dying, in my head.
Alone am I, dancing dead.

Silences' domain; the music to a cease.
Sweet tranquility; yet I no peace.
Madness, madness, in my brain.
Still a constant humming of pain.

No illumination vision, the lights to a dim.
All glasses filled with nothing and mine to the brim.
Drinking, drinking, a bittersweet wine.
Yet I am left choking, quietly on the vine.

The shadows flow gently across the floor.
Their thoughts kept in; yet mine outpour.
Twirling, twirling, down am I,
heard only with, the faintest sigh.

Tempting is the joyous event,
yet myself the feast; I must not relent.
Whisper , whisper, a sweet prayer.
The invitation unopened, a party I don't dare.

Kerri K. Tenney

Teenage Rage

As she lay there remembering
the happy times they had,
How he laughed with her during the good times
and cried during the bad,
She couldn't help but wonder
how she could have done,
this crazy act of insanity
she thought he was the one,
she thought about the first time
he looked at her and smiled,
And at that very moment
her emotions had been riled,
And emotions shouldn't be toyed with
at such a tender age,
Being emotionally hurt
can cause quite a rage,
and emotions can be deadly
at the age of a teenage kid,
And that's why she went and done,
that crazy thing she did.

Stephanie Vickers

Where Are Your Children?

PARENTS!

Do you know where your children are?
The hour is late. The skies are grey and dim.
Are your babies home? Are they safe within?

LISTEN!

Do you hear guns popping? They aren't stopping
Screams of police sirens pierce the quiet.
Terror runs rampant throughout the night.

QUICK!

Find your children. Hurry. Look behind closed doors.
Time is swiftly wasting. The enemy is lurking—waiting.
He is hungry as he opens his jaws and loudly roars.

BE BRAVE!

Wipe away the enemy's smirking grin.
Don't give up! Don't let him hear your heart beat.
He's a liar! Don't you dare accept defeat.

MOTHERS! FATHERS!

Surrender your kids to God and pray.
Ask for direction and let Him have His way.
And He will wrap you in His arms of wisdom and love.

Patricia Augustus

Years Pass

They started life together, when they were very young
The intimacy of their love blossomed into a perfect union
Soul meeting Soul
Years pass

They start to follow different paths
Shrouded in secrecy and deception

And as the years pass their paths broaden
Until there is no more trust or belief

Years Pass
Their lives are separate now
No more perfect union
No more soul meeting soul
Only an empty void that nothing and no one can fill

Years pass
She longs for their perfect union
She longs for Soul meeting Soul
She longs to reunite; before too many more
Years Pass

Sue Arment

My Grandma

It's quiet and late and everybody, everywhere is sleeping. I clean the kitchen, tidy the den and make a list of things to do for tomorrow. I go to bed and close my eyes and try to fall asleep. But once again, as so many times before, I think about my Grandma.

I wonder if she's awake too and what she's thinking of, or if she's sleeping - and what she's dreaming of. I wonder how bad her pain was today, and if she cried at all. And then again, as so many times before I start to cry because I miss my Grandma. I wander back in time to when I was a little girl. I'd watch her cook and clean and shovel snow, how I loved her so. "Tell no one but the lamppost," she would always say. But the lamppost is my Grandma. She loved me and taught me and made me understand - "life is very precious and to yourself be true!" This is taught by many teachers and read in many books - but this I wouldn't have believed if my Grandma hadn't told me so.

One day when Grandma and I were walking home, and I was only twelve, I prayed to Him above, "Please, God, don't take away my Grandma until I'm old and gray." And now she's eighty-seven and me - I'm thirty-seven and I look into the mirror every day. I see my hair begin to turn gray and I say a new prayer to Him. "Thank you, God, for answering my prayer, but please...give more time with my Grandma."

Rae Marie Capone

A Parent's Love

As I grow older, I glance back and see,
The love the two of you have for me.
A loving home and helping hands
Are never ceasing like waves on sand.
My love for you is never ending
Because you are so very forgiving.
Now I know you punish me because you love me so,
Not just because I wrecked the house with mud and snow.
I thank you for teaching me about Jesus Christ,
For without Him we would not have everlasting life.
By teaching me just how to read,
Now I do it with grace and ease.
I am growing older now and will soon be gone,
But I will always remember our loving bond.
When I evaluate your life and the many things you do,
I hope when I grow up, I will be just like you.
My love for you grows everyday,
More than words could ever say.
So I'd like to take tonight to say-
"Thank you for loving me everyday!"

Mandy Cline

Friendship Is Forever And Always

Friendship is forever and forever is our love.
The love we share together is what friends are made of.
Friends are good friends, friends are the best
But when the time comes they put you to the test.
You have to be real, you have to be true
You mustn't be lonely, you mustn't be blue.
Cause when at times they need someone
They want you to be there.
Because they just might need to have some fun
To show them that you care
So friendship, understand, is not be a game
Be kind, give out your hand, and be happy that you came
For without friends we are all alone
And always keep in mind; friends that are to be known,
Are the best ones you can find.

Paola Lau

Untitled

So many paths our lives seem to take
The many choices we're forced to make
So overwhelming at times it seems
To keep up your hopes, to follow your dreams

Sometimes just the day seems so hard to face
To deal with reality, or the human race
Do we fit in? Are we part of the plan?
Is existence just fate, a mere slight of hand?

Anger and hate kills our soul, numbs our brains
A boy takes his life, a girl goes insane
Why must we murder, rape, and abuse
Destroy all our land with toxic misuse?

Sometimes I feel cheated till I open my eyes
So selfish we are, so much we deny
Our neighbors are starving, it's children who pay
It's our dreams for the future we're throwing away.

Sandra A. Imperio

"The Martyr"

If this fallow-ground is to produce its bounty,
the martyr's blood must flow.
The womb from which the martyr sprang
is dressed in the heavens with incense and oils,
and shrouded in immortality, majesty, and Godly esteem.

Because the martyr's blood flows,
God's judgment is stayed,
the season's rage is spent,
and the issues of the martyr's heart
echo with the fetal heartbeat
and become the mores of the world that is to come!

Kenneth Allison

Holding On

Because I have not power nor estate
The masks I wear are plain for all to see
Constructed piece by piece through time carefully
Stitch by stitch behold my soul's true face
The tired unwilling slave of life's frantic pace
And I who lack the will to end the game
Will ride atop the stallion wild, untamed
The cautious rider waiting for the race
To finish me or let me finish it
And cross the line where winning matters not
And douse the torch who's flame was barely lit.

Mary L. Sullivan

Untitled

Madness, I whisper to the pain within my breast,
The moonless night's darkness reflecting my thoughts,
For the secrets I have kept will not let me rest.
Praying to feel the peace that oblivion brings,
Waiting, floating upon the gentleness of the North wind.
I will never hear those bells as they ring.

Imagining, pressing my cheek to the softness of your breast,
Gently whispering the tender words of affection,
Nevermore to be parted form the softness of your flesh.
The meanderings of my mind can not comprehend,
That I, and I alone, am the cause of the shadows.
For you had given me your heart on lend.

Left to stare at these glaring white walls,
The remains of your shattered heart enclosed within
my unrelenting fist.
My scattered thoughts and tattered pride left to echo within the halls,
Of my withered dreams and honorable intentions.
My blackened heart burnt, leaving only the ashes you see,
All that is left of the fire that was me.

Larissa Roberts

Beauty

I thank Thee Father for beautiful things
The moonlight and hummingbirds gossamer wings
For the spectrum of colors and every hue
For they each one come, dear Father, from you

The gold of the sunrise, the purple of dawn
When creatures begin to awake with a yawn
The rooster, he crows, as he heralds the day
The wood-nymph relaxes, still hid in the gray

Of the wood that surrounds him on earth's early morn
Not caring nor knowing a new day's been born
And this is the day in which we'll rejoice
And listen intently, we may hear His voice

As He speaks through unlimited thundering's roar
Or tiptoes in easily, shutting the door
Of our conscious alertness of things that surround
He leads us out gently, on to higher ground

So pause in your working and listen awhile
You may hear him speaking, you may see Him smile
Upon you so gently as you move along
Amid the sad crowd, He will give you a song

Laura Spencer Silek

The Mountain Is Me

The mountain is me.
The mountain is me.
From the top of this valley,
From down on my rocky knees,
Looking up, reaching skyward,
I can finally see.

Come and sit by the fire of my gentleness,
And drink from the waters of the lake of my heart.

Come read from the books of the bark of my trees,
Come lay your head down in the lap of my leaves.

Breathe into the essence of the strength of my pain,
And grow with me in spirit as we run through my rain.

Be a part of my vision as I stand forth and scan
The horizons that rest there in the palm of the land.

Lay down in the dew grass, taste and savor fears
Of the emergence of new life that has been there for years.

We are the mountains, and the mountains are we.
I am the mountain and the mountain is me,
Surging and soaring, riding wingtips of song,
The mountain is me and in me I belong.

Vicki Attaway

Morning

Small glimpses of piercing blue peer out of the grey-white sky.
The mountains stand undaunted, unchanged in their changing.
Smoky-green trees bristle from the biting wisps of fog.
The wind whispers secrets to the bending blades of grass.
Air curls lazily around my feet.
Sunbeams sigh, they fail to cut through the sky's blanket.
The secrets of the wind are silenced now,
The air hesitates, waiting.
I wait also, becoming the stillness. Waiting. Watching.
Swiftly the blanket moves, billowing down,
thrown off by the awakening sky.
Warm fingers of gold stretch forth.
They touch my hands, my face.
My soul sings.

Lorinda O'Leary

The Dance

I'm in the halls looking to and fro, wondering where to go.
The music blasting, very long lasting.
What should I do?
I lost my date last night, and my shirt is too tight!
Plus my cotton skirt is very itchy.
I'm not relaxing, how can I be?
I'm going to go bonkers
If I don't go! My feet are too big, I'm too, too, too old.
For all I know I might look like a toad,
And I'm wearing heels that make me look 10 ft more than I already am.
Oh, I think it's over here, 'Oops, sorry!'
Oh my God it's the cutest guy in the world!
That's alright; our eyes met.
He asked me to dance!
Maybe this dance isn't so bad after all.

Shenna Bryan

Ever To Never

The stars could explain
The myriad of Angels that are called by name
Our inability to comprehend
The formidability of the planets
The universe just might explain our position
The one who would know every star
Can call it by its name
Might explain our position
Can we fathom the Universe?
I prefer to wait there is one who knows
All the answers
Man dared go to the moon
Did we learn anything that was
The answers were there before
We decided to go
We can wait and be patient he does
With he who is always
The wisdom of man
Everyone knows learning the wisdom
Of he who is man's lifelong quest
To date man is yet to discover

Robert Jerome Smith

T. L. C.

With hope, understanding, and compassion,
the name that bears the pain, the Nurse.

There is never enough time to fix, mend, and mind,
the suffering faces of various kinds.

The orders that never stop, soft hands and smiles
that touch just the right spots.

The patients, families, and friends,
cry out for their loved ones until the end,
and who is there to comfort and attend.

With pain, suffering, and sorrow,
we will be there to brighten your tomorrows, the Nurse.

Patricia Bross

The Ocean

The rolling waves, the fair blue sea,
The ocean will always be the place for me.
With the saltwater spraying
And the breeze blowing without any harm,
This magical wonderland is quite a charm!
The many fish love the rolling waves,
Jumping up and down
Then going to their secret caves.
The boaters love the gentle sway,
And sightseeing is every which way.
Yes, the ocean is definitely the place for me,
The rolling waves and the fair blue sea.

Sarah Miesner

The Old Man's Story

Treasured moments of love and glory, or imagination of the mind
The old man tells his story, a little different every time
People no longer listen, they have heard it all before
And some hint he lost a little, while fighting in the war

It's hard to tell what goes through his mind
He shows no emotion, when he goes back in time
His tales have no beginning or no end
Only shadowed memories of loved ones and friends

It's sad when he fails with each endeavor
To recall those moments of love and glory
But they fade with time and are lost forever
He waited too long to tell his story

And now the old man's voice is still
Rest in peace I know he will
All that's left of his loves and glory
Are bits and pieces of his story

Melvin G. Cornwell

What Will You Say When Time Runs Out

If only you had known the King;
The one of which the angels sing.
If only you had shared His love;
The one who died and shed His blood.
If only you had shared in His praise;
The one whom the Father raised.
If only you had heard His call;
He who came to redeem us all.
If only you had prayed to Him;
He'd bring light when times were dim.
If only you would seek His face;
He who brought mercy and brought grace.
If only you had just believed;
A life everlasting you would receive.
If only you had heard His voice,
If only you had made the choice.

Teresa Diane Parks

Life's Highway

Life is only a highway,
The one we travel from day to day.
Each day began's with dreams and hopes,
We see and greet many of folks.

Life keeps all moving in one direction,
Each striving to reach a different designation.
We come and we all go, (though) no one (really)
knows the outcome of the flow.

The path get's narrow and Life's Highways gets rough,
that's the time to get morally and spiritually tough.

"It's no fun!! Passenger(s) "There are none;
Careful," Don't fall asleep! Only you're in
control of the driver's seat.

As you travel Live's Highway; travel with caution!
Watch all signs and read the fine lines,
you're surely to reach a piece of mind.

Lennie Graham

"Everyone's Game"

For here I walk on the dew soaked grass,
The sun has come; gone and past.
My memories are such; as most men recall.
The love of the game from spring to fall,
It's a time to rejoice; a time for peers,
A time to remember throughout the years.

Michael C. Irvine

"The Greatest Gifts Of All"

No matter how big a gift or how small
The ones that matter most of all
They are not wrapped in fancy
paper or bows.
They aren't made of gold or a
diamond that glows
There value could never be measured I'm told
They are made out of love
of a Mother and Father
I guess you know
They are my sons and my daughter

Shirley A. Fuller

A Mother's Love

A mother's love is......
The only love in your life, given unconditionally....

A mother's love is..... the only love in your life,
that believes in you, no matter what the odds.....

A mother's love is......
The only love in your life, you can depend on, in any situation...

A mother's love is.....
The only love in your life,
to support you, in spite of your Win/Loss record.........

And for all his mother, I want to 'thank you' and let you know
that you are loved and appreciated very much.......

Mother, I cannot change the Heartache I have caused, I can only say
how sorry I really am and ask to be forgiven......

Mother, I can only promise once released, this time,
I will give it my Best Shot..........

Since there are not enough words in print, or enough paper on which
to write, nor nearly enough time to express just how much you
really mean to me Mother........
I will close by saying "Thank you," for always being there for me,
and that "I love you very much!"........

Vic Wallace

Continuance

A seed,
the origin of life;
Oblivious of the obstacles it may face.
Guided by its miraculous nurturer, the sun;
Fighting its way upward
Towards its provider;
A lime green sprout reaching
for strength.
The wheel turns,
The sprout now a stem,
The stem blossoming forth
with ravishing petals;
The leaves' poison is the
Earth's blessing.
Yet, slowly the petals shrivel;
One by one slipping to the loam.
The stem winds down to the earth,
Leaving only a seed,
oblivious of the distractions
yet to come.

Pamela Ryan

A Baby Is An Innocent Rose

Its colorful personality blooms when it smiles.
The sparkle in its eye is like the soft touch of the
morning dew resting on the body's silky petals.
And like a rose, the baby's sweet - smelling fragrance
Intrigues all who encounter it.

Melissa L. Dortch

Chiconda

The tear on my cheek falls for her,
The pain in my heart grows deeper each day,
Her words are silent now, her pain is gone,
All her dreams are still,
But her memory shall live on,
Her smile so sweet, her eyes so warm,
Little Chiconda your fear is gone,
Your wings will carry you to a better place,
Now I will wait for the time,
When we will meet again,
My little Indian friend,
Chiconda!

Patricia Huotari

Losing A Friend

Losing a friend is the hardest thing to do
The pain you feel
The hurt inside
Losing the most beautiful thing in life

You feel so sad
And really mad
You cry and think
I wish- I wish I could die.

You remember all the things you used to do.
They were always there for you.
They never let you down.
They were always there for you.

Not noticing what you have until you lose it.
That's the hardest thing to face.
But remember—a friend isn't a friend
Until you treat them like one.

Lillian Vigil

The Key

Hold the key the key will know
The path to heart the path to soul
But if the key breaks by the hand
Start to pack, pack up the band

She comes for us to unlock the gate
The key is lost no time to wait
The door is broken no waste of time
The door, the pieces, the heart was mine

Now the puzzle is missing a piece
Can't fit back till again we meet
The day will come, this life or next
The key we'll find, it's time to rest

Till that time the band is lost
Find the piece forget the cost
Maybe peace comes into view
When I realize, the key is You.

Robert Moura

A Valentine For My Fella

Valentine's day is coming and I must find a card
That tells how much I love you, that really will be hard.

I love you for the way you smile, the way you comb your hair.
I love you when you're gone from me, I love you when you're there.

I love you when you're sometimes tough, I love you when you're mellow.
The truth, my dear, to me, is clear, you're really quite a fellow.

There are no words to tell you, so I guess that these will do.
I love you in a thousand ways, just because you're you.

Katherine Hahn

On This Christmas...... (Christmas Blues)

As I remember who, what, and where I am today, I won't forget the price of "FREEDOM", on this Christmas.

While CHILDREN are thanking their parents for their gifts, I'll be thanking our HOLY CREATOR for the health,safety, and happiness of my own too, on this Christmas.

I'll be making SUBSTITUTIONS because I can't make it home on this Christmas, though a part of home is always within me.

I'll send out "APOLOGIES", and "WISH I WAS THERE'S", and, Cards that SMILE of song and poetry will come and WARM my insides,

ON THIS CHRISTMAS, I won't be blue, as I bear the pain of separation, loneliness and wanting, because I know It's Only Temporary.

Some TEARS might be shed, and when I'm alone, some might be MINE, because, On This Christmas I'll be thinking of someone besides myself, AND MAYBE, just maybe, someone will be thinking of ME..... ON THIS CHRISTMAS

Kirby McPhaul Sr.

A Special Day To Remember Was 1975, 18th Day Of December

This sweet baby girl I adore,
The promise of love for evermore.

To look with such joy, as you slept.
The secrets of tears, I just kept.

Just you and I looking at the years.
Wondering what or who might appear.
Please remember this man of your youth.
His commitment to love you, is the truth.

You have grown through happiness and despair,
Still able to love, and show you care.

We are very pleased and proud.
You are still this person, despite the crowd.
We love you dearly, and wish the best.
The future you choose, is yours to test.

Hold all the memories you just past.
Let the gift of love and life forever last.

Remember always give your "Thanks" to above.
That comfort is there for sadness and love.

The tenderness of your heart you share...
Will remind me daily that you care.

Marsha Hardcastle

Finding Light In The Tunnels Of Our Mind

Wandering aimlessly inside my head,
the question of one's existence
is a constant fear and dread.
What do you want from me?
is all I ever ask.
But lonely, empty silence
is where I continuously bask.
Lucky are those who have found the way?
Or is it just an illusion
to keep the rest of us at bay?
But we must keep going,
crazy at it seems,
for therein lies our only hope
and salvation...Our dreams!
It is with this, life must be savored
we must remember at all cost.
For without that hold on reality,
all is lost, all is lost.

Lynnea Rappe

Solitude

It seems these days I often crave,
The quietness of a summer's day.
The sound of waves upon the shore,
And sea gulls with their wings which soar.

Just give to me the peace and quiet,
And time to take the sunsets' sight,
And cherish each and every day
In all I do and all I say.

There seems no time to play or rest,
Or take a walk without a quest.
The world is fast and so are we,
And life goes by so aimlessly.

So, now I take each day I live,
For all I can and it can give.
And treasure it with great delight,
From dawn until the deep of night.

And when I have that summer's day,
I'll take the quiet along the bay,
And watch the sea gulls while they soar,
Keeping the memory forever more.

Mary Lancaster

Colored Trade Only

A Great New Age has dawned today
The Rest of us demand our say
Mere words won't do, we know what's true
Don't think, just do what we tell you.

Reality can take a break
So we can grab your tree and take
Fruits we now claim, you are to blame
Don't think, just do what we tell you.

Lies of the past, Truths of today
We've decided that you will pay
For long ago, we reap, you sow
Don't think, just do what we tell you.

You're a male with light-colored hide
Why did you show? Disqualified
Now for a job, thrown to the mob
Don't think, just do what we tell you.

We are Correct, and you will see
Us deal with Those eventually
Who spurn our Trust, in Causes Just
Don't think, just do what we tell you.

Todd D. Miller

Six Senses

Recognition- that in our tiny part of the world,
the river village, life flows and close friends have not gone mad.

Awareness - that there are vast untapped intellectual resources
in the human brain of each of us...there for our personal
exploitation.

Wonder - that we can observe, at dawn, crescent Venus ascending,
bright moon planet seen through many lenses.

Fulfillment - that in three score of years, more things have
worked out than not; two generations follow, more or less
happily, in our footsteps.

Joy-in discovery of hidden talents in old friends, and creative
people that touch our lives anew as we search for meaning.

Realization - that to be wrong is not a sin, to fail says nothing
about tomorrow, and that He saves some of the best things for last.

Nathan Tufts

"Giving Love"

I love, but this emotion never shares
the same feeling with me, I'm always
giving. I know that God says it's better to
give than to receive, but only God
knows how much I've given to people,
only to receive animosity. I'm always
looking inside of my self, because if I
don't, I'll become that horrible thing I
encounter each and every day of my life.
People only share when it's convenient for
them. I often ask my self why is the world
so beautiful, yet so ugly.

Shirley A. Burks

Dreams

The children know, from times long past
the secrets we've forgotten in the living,
they are the old ones of the world
understanding with the heart
apart from formulas they'll learn
with age.

For in the aging, sense of spirit
often fades,
as shades of those who came before
vanish...and are no more;
their voice, once heard, now stilled
as noises from the present
fill the soul.

But, in the stillness of the night,
when body rests, and mind is free to wander
the sounds are heard once more,
opening the door
to who we are, and why we've come
as children.

G. Lieberman

And The Flower Blooms

And the flower struggles to bloom
The seed is alone in darkness it is held in warmth
The life springs forth to sun and the sun burns
And the flower struggles to bloom
The wind will blow and the sun will burn
The life is fragile the water will refresh
And the flower struggles to bloom
The rains come too hard the life is driven down
And as it fights to stand the sun will burn
And the flower struggles to bloom
The roots strike hold the leaves spread wide
Strength of youth the sun is life
And the flower struggles to bloom
The ground is good the roots are strong
The stem is tall time is kind
And the flower blooms - in its time

Marlene Munday

Spirituality

It is said in the long distance echo of time,
That we dwell in two spheres and gallop between
On silver white steeds with Pegasus wings.

Or a hovering craft of gossamer light,
Sweeps the soul, through the dead of night.
Into Nirvana where Oneness lies, pale and sweet.

That elusive state, so difficult to find,
That Pharaoh sought Death, to taste of its wine!
One foot in each world and balancing there,
The Great Spirit's love builds a bridge from despair.

Sandra Quinlan Streeter

Violets In November

Autumn partings are so sad.
The shorter day,
The longer night,
The cry of the wild geese
Southward in flight,
The threat of winter in the chilling winds:
All these foreshadow summer's end.

The dreams we shared, the joys we knew,
Are but falling leaves
From memory's tree,
And our farewells
Speak of finality.
But suddenly new hope is born-
A hint of spring's return-

There at my feet,
With petals sweet,
Violets in November!

Pearl Dildine Weaver

To Mother!

God made a lot of wonderful things, it is true;
The sky and ocean, he made a heavenly shade of blue -
The stars, the moon and the streams so beautiful;
He made for all of us to enjoy and to live by the Golden Rule.

But more important than all of these to me;
Was the gift he sent down from Heaven for me to know and see.
And it was you, Mother Dear, he chose to be my "Guiding Light";

So now I would just like to say;
In a very simple old fashioned way -
Many thanks for all your kindness and thoughtfulness
throughout my younger years;
You sheltered me and were able to satisfy my many
fears and tears.

I know I wasn't always perfect nor will I ever be;
But you're the sweetest Mother and YOU'll always be
very dear to me!

Mary Ann Fell

My Mother

A mother's love is always there,
The special bond that we share,
A caring heart and gentle touch,
That warm smile I love so much.

In silent whimpers I've called your name,
You've always heard me you've always came.
When I'm so low the depths of the sea seem high,
You lift me up, you make me fly.

Your love is the wind that guides my wings,
With the sound of your voice my heart sings.

With loving hands you've molded my soul,
You sent me forth and watched me grow.

As time goes by, it's been well spent,
You'll never know how much having you has meant.

Michelle L. Wallace

The Long Walk

Walking miles in my moccasin
The walk gets longer
My achy-breaky feet
The hours chipping away as I continue my journey
As I walk the pasture in my moccasin
I narrow my long journey
Thee long walk in my moccasin was a guide to my freedom
My companion, the moccasin

Vonda Nez

Hotline

Hotline, may I help you?
The start of another call
when alone and frightened Stacy attempts to tell me all
Sixteen years old and pregnant, parents no longer there
no job, no money, no future, life just isn't fair.

Is your Dad the father of your baby? I ask as I must pry
I already know the answer as she begins to cry
well, this world is full of Stacy's, my experience tells me so
as so many times the phone rings, and my tears begin to flow.

What's happening to our children? How can people be so cruel?
to abuse, molest, and batter, as if they were a tool
I silently scream in anger to those parents everywhere
the children are God's gift, please give them love, please care!

And once again the phone rings, as I brush away a tear
trying to regain composure for what I'm about to hear
oh God, I feel like quitting before this night is through
yet once again I know I must answer
Hotline, may I help you?

William G. Morris

"Sunshine"

The sun is warm,
The sun is bright,
The sun is beautiful,
Like the rays of the morning light,
And a breezy moonlight summer night,
Like a field of colorful wild flowers,
And bright colored butterflies in the sky,
And the smile of a child at something done right,
As peaceful as birds chirping in the early morning
And crickets chirping late at night,
As refreshing as a spring shower on a mid April night,
As bright as a rainbow high in the sky,
Sunshine truly makes everything, warm, beautiful and bright.
"Sunshine"

Rebecca L. Wagner

Soul's Storm

The storm that raged all night is over,
The sun shines on a world all fresh and sweet;
And now will grow the soft green grass and clover,
The barley and the rye and winter wheat.

The promises I made when we married
I shall keep until my dying day!
No greater love shall mar our life together,
Or my decision ever, ever sway!

Last night I thought the storm would end my living,
And all that lovely was in this small world of mine,
I reckoned not that God's kind hand of mercy
Would still the violence with a wave divine.

Storms may rage again but never
Will I lose faith or falter in my trust,
Always will I know that on a tomorrow
God's Love will make the sun to shine again!

Lillian Mayer

Life's Highway

As we travel down life's highway
There are many hills we must climb
And there are troubles that we can't leave
behind but if we have the faith and
the courage to go on to travel on No
matter how rough the road or heavy
our load one day we will reach our
Heavenly home our heavenly home

Mary B. Taylor

Miracle Of Mothering

You arrived that special day.
The sun was warm and golden,
the air was cool with the
freshness of late autumn.

I will always remember your infant clothes;
sweet, soft yellow,
showing strength of character
yet so mellow.

When I held you in my arms,
your precious newborn scent
touched my very spirit.
Your eyes mirrored my soul.

Your tiny hand touched my cheek
and I saw you were aware
of the intense love we shared.

Mothering comes not from the joining of scientific logic
but is a strong, unyielding, tempered bond
between mother and her daughters
and mother and her sons.

Renee Stauffer

Thank You

Thank you for not making me do it alone.
The terrible nightmares of the incest,
Were so hard to deal with.
The long nights, seeing his face;
Reliving every horrid detail.
All the problems it has caused;
Wondering when it would ever end.
Madness was consuming me entirely.
Until you reached out and gave me your hand.
Without you, I would have slipped over the edge.
Screaming, as I fell down an endless chasm of utter hopelessness.
You rescued me from my thoughts and dreams;
Helped me deal with the pain, and get on with my life.
Thank you for not making me do it alone.

Leslie D. Cottrell

A Farewell To You

A farewell to you for the end is near
The time has come the chance is here
Nothing can change what I feel now,
Peace and Happiness within I never found.

My strength, my pride, my heart have surrender
And the nightmares of the past have not hinder
It is now time for me to leave everything,
The hurt, the anger, the love, and especially the pain.

I no longer desire or care
I just know this darkness I can no longer bare
Nothing remains but an empty space,
I no longer want problems face to face.

I no longer fear, which make me free
My sight is gone, so tears I won't see
I know this pain is not only mines,
But I can no longer face pain of this kind.

You believe I'm as strong as a bear
But no one knows what lurks behind the smile I wear
My load is heavy and my will is weak,
And it is death that I seek.

Twila Lucas

Contrapositive

Will I never forget yesterday's pain?
the time has flown past me, but the memories remain
like an empty reminder that life is moving on
when I slept it was evening, but now it is dawn
whether it's pain or pleasure, it all feels the same
we all become players in life's wicked game
good times are remembered, and bad ones as well
but which is more painful is difficult to tell
a shadow lurks behind every sunshine we see
and when the sun sinks behind the horizon, the shadow is set free
I regret all I did, and all I did not do
I once sat a top a cliff, I jumped off and I flew
the cursed gift of memories does more harm than it does good
but I cannot release myself from it and I ask myself, would I,
If I could

Sahar Shirazi

God's Grace

Sometimes I wonder, as I stroll, o'er the road,
  the trail or the knoll,
How God could be as kind as he is, to a mass
  of his people, so bold.
So bold to commit the sins that we do, that
  He went to the cross for me and for you.
To die there in pain so we might live on, to
  a life of everlasting glory and song.
And when the time comes, to go where we must,
  to know that He's there, and that He died for us.
Thank you oh Lord, for all you have done, to
  show us all just what we have won, we've won
a life everlasting and long to live with you
  Lord, in prayers, word and song.

Kenneth L. Bender

The Struggle

I have been told to think upon
The twins who dwell within
The new man and the aged one
Who fight beneath the skin
The youth who is now born and set
Upon a virgin land,
To think God's thoughts,
And dig his roots, beneath the shifting sand
To embrace eternity.

But familiar ways are wily,
And have power to beguile,
And thoughts still draw me backward,
To wander, yet awhile
Down every wayward path,
That leads me far from home,
Through every maze and morass,
My wandering foot will roam,
And when I grow morose and cold with negativity,
I curse this dammed old man within,
Who will not set the new man free.

Margaret Jean Marsh

Death Of The Dragon

I have come to slay the dragon!
The two headed beast of hatred and greed

I have come to slay the dragon!
No sword or tools of blood shalt I need

I have come to slay the dragon!
My weapons are understanding and the dove

Yes, I have come to slay the dragon!
and those that know me, call me Love.

Mark F. Lerew

"Reflections"

How painful is the journey back;
The whistle of a train,
The falling of a leaf,
The winding ribbon of a highway takes me back in time
to childhood. No longer do I fear the dark of night.
Knowledge sweeps the cobwebs from an ancient room.
How dear the past; the rosy hues of memory transcend the pain of loss.
Night follows day too swiftly, now. Time is so short.
If I could relive the years, what would I change?
The passions of my youth, your love, the children?
No, even though your time in life was brief, our days were rich with living.
You touched my days with joy, and I carried your love as a cloak against the night that came with rapid ease.
The leaf sails gently on the stream; the years of laughter echo softly in my heart and mind.
The train whistle fades in time.
I am content to dream; to catch the graying of my years for a short while. I am content.

Lillian G. Pliskin

Untitled

Wandering through my soul
The why's of life remain a mystery
The depths of which no solving lies
Why - to love as it is perceived
The pain of love lost
Why only one changed
The why of wondering why
The heart is stilled with sorrow
And reshaped forever more.

I feel the pulse —— it is slow
I feel the pain —— it is piercing and deep within.
I look for the answers
And find only questions.
I look for the future
And see what might have been.
So, I search for peace
And still ask why.

Sherry Ackerman

The Candle

Two souls fatefully intertwined,
the wick of an unenlightened candle
ignited by the spark of a mingling match.
Fire, light.
Heat of passion, illumination of life.
In the eyes of the beholder
all appears the burning fervor of happiness.
Golden warmth, tender compassion.
Yet centralized is evil-
the serpent of searing blue
hidden by the mesmerizing yet ominous glow.
But if the ties of commitment are not strong enough,
the erected wax melts-
sometimes slowly, each drop falling bit by bit.
But often suddenly, without warning
the flame diminishes, the wick goes out-
"out brief candle"-
leaving once fulfilled hearts
now despondently overcome
by darkness.

Nicole Meunier

My Enchanted Valley

Peace and contentment fill my day,
The wicked world is far away.
Here and there the fairies dance
And God's creatures aren't here by chance.
They feel the peace and contentment just like me.
God meant this for our place to be.
Spring rains make every thing lush and green
With white dog woods sprinkled in between.
Wild flowers dotted every where
You feel that all is in His care.
Autumn's beauty is a sight to behold
But soon we know we will have the cold
Of winter and its pure white snow
That covers everything below.
The snowflakes fall in disarray,
and make it a wonderful just for today.
Peace and beauty fill this land,
For it's been touched by the savior's hand,
And with the blessings of God's good grace
This shall be my final resting place.

Mae Garland

The Woman

The women I need I don't ever see
The women I want she don't want me.
But I know deep down inside,
A love like ours we shouldn't hide,
So let's let it all out for the world to see
'Cause a love like ours we could set the world free.
So if you should see this little poem of mine
You'll know someday you will be mine.

Michael W. Canzonere

Moontide

Now day is done, the twilight falls, and grasses cease their sighing;
The woodfolk all have settled down and creeping things are hiding.
Far in the distance can be heard a lone bird call his mate,
And things begin to happen fast so wondrous to relate.
Pale shadows deepen into gray, then blended blue, and red,
Now lavender, and indigo paint trees in royal stead.
The nearby fragrant Meadow Sweet distills its heavenly scent,
And Honeysuckle wet with dew now toward the earth is bent.
Beyond the purple ridge at last, a pale light now appears;
It rises slow and deepens to a golden colored sphere.
The opalescent azure sky a curtain now unfolds,
And tiny wispy fireflies dart forth a hundred fold.
The golden lantern in the blue hangs now above the ridge,
It casts a pale white light to earth, the heavens and earth to bridge.
Thus, on it goes 'til night is o'er and wearied with its travel,
The moon's pale light fades into dawn, night's mysteries to unravel.

Mae Williams

Listen...

Listen...as the Gulf waters gently roll in with
their silent roar
Sea gulls, spoonbill roseates glide through the sky
The sand in your toes, your eyes catch the flowers
white in the dunes so high.
Listen...the gentle, never-ceasing breeze, again
it ruffles your hair
The thick gray clouds in the stratosphere obliterate
the warming sunlight
Cool is the wind on your face.
Listen...to the songs of the sea
Splashing, roaring, a gentle roar
Salty air in your eyes make them glisten and wet...
Then you smile.

Mark R. Landry

Racism Of Today And Yesterday

My family faces racism for their origin, language and color of their skin.
Society needs to ask itself, "Do we really want to go back to the racist times again?"
My mother came to America with search of a new life.
But, what she faced was people cutting her down with an invisible knife.
My father was born here in America
in those times he faced total hysteria,
for the color of his skin
and he hopes he never faces that kind of racism again.
For us, their children, society looked down on us.
To have us out about society acted like it was a real fuss.
Now my family looks at racists differently,
thinking what is wrong with you, not me?

Margaret Ann Bell

"Peace of Mind"

"Oh! my mind, please be silence,
Then,
All the problems (of this world) are resolved."
"Yes, it's true."
Because,
The herd of cows
Or the herd of elephants,
Is not "A - Real - Wealth."

A person who has a "peace of mind"
Has got everything.

Therefore,
"OH! my (dear) mind,
Please be at peace."

If you do so,
Then,
"You are the richest-person,
In this whole wide world."

That's it.

Krishna Kulchandra

If You Learn To Love Yourself

If you learn to love yourself as much as I love you,
then all your dreams will come true.

But, if you allow anger, hate and jealousy to dwell in your soul,
then all your dreams will turn to coal.

See, love is the answer to all our pain,
anything else will drive you insane.

There are words from a father who is crying deep down inside
watching his daughter take a walk on life's negative side.
So, this is one of those times I hope you take some advice,
then maybe your dreams won't turn to coal or dry ice.

Anger, hate and jealousy once dwelled in my soul
and my biggest dream turned to coal.

See, a daughter's love for her father should be gold,
but your feeling toward me is like a bucket of coal.

Please, look inside and release this pain
before you drive yourself insane.

Do it for yourself and not for me.
Until that time you won't be free.

William D. Salley

Do I Know You!

A Cherry smile a warm glance so fresh so new
Then softly spoken 'How are you'
Pleasantly shocked I respond as due
But inward I say 'I don't know you'

Some words exchanged not all coherent
Some news true to some extent
Some stories told some views exchanged
Time speeds and heart beat enhanced

Lingering looks are very assuring
Wavy locks from forehead dangling
A glow in face quite alluring
Some moments in life so enduring

Beware faint heart not a step further
Social charm fun hither thither
A carefree gesture or two
May innocently ask 'Do I know you'.

Misbah Ansari

An Angel's Voice

Forty-six years went by so quickly
Then there was no choice
The news came in a vision,
An Angel with a voice.

"It's time for you to leave this home and family you so love
Your Father has a new Home, prepared for you above.
Being a little girl was your favorite time in life
It was filled with happiness and very little strife"

"You'll be a little girl again"
The Angel's sweet voice said
Then she disappeared
From the foot of your Mom's bed.

What a special message,
Sent in the good Lord's name
A wonderful gift of comfort
To help Mom bear the pain.

It's been almost a year now,
Since He took you away
To live with Him forever
To play and play and play!

Vermelle S. Findlay

Help! I'm In A Box

I feel like I'm in a box with no place to go.
There are four big walls which keep me confined to this little room.

No one can look inside and see,
nor can I see out.
And all there is to see,
See is little tiny me.

I can hear no sound round about me,
but my precious little heartbeat.
I want so much to leave this place,
but I can't, I don't even know how I got here.

My mind is blank...
the box is black....
and the air is getting thin.
If someone's there and can hear my yell...
Please help me! I'm in a box.

Karika R. Austin

Climbing The Ladder Of Success

In climbing the ladder to success
There are many steps you will have to make
Sometimes you may start to stumble and fall
But if you have been nice, someone will be there
to cushion that fall.

But if you've been mean, rude and nasty to all.
No one will be there to cushion that fall, no one at all.
You may travel on rough, rocky and dusty roads and the weather is
very cold, you start to turn.
Then you see a tunnel.
You enter, you find it's dark and have a smell of mole.

Finally you see a light at the end.
Low and behold you see your friends.
You see, you may travel on rough and dusty roads, tunnels that
are dark and cold and smell of mole.

Even ladders to reach your goal.
it doesn't matter how far up the ladder you go.
Whether it's to the top or just to the first floor,
Just remember this where ever you go.
Down not the man who is down today but cheer him
up for his sorrow.
For this old world is a funny old world
and you maybe down tomorrow

Mildred Tolbert

Permanence Is Temporary

Permanence is temporary, nothing stays the same,
there are no guarantees in life, you've got to play the game.
Think about the things you have, don't dwell on what is lost,
experience is what you've gained, no matter what the cost.

Things often seem to go awry, it's known as Murphy's law,
and we don't always know why, or what's the reason for.
Just when things seem to be going fine,
there's a fly in the ointment and cork in the wine.

Nothing lasts forever, you wouldn't want it to,
but when there is an ending, you want it planned by you!
Change can make you feel alone, lonely and confused,
it leaves you feeling insecure with a sense of being used.

Change makes you feel uncomfortable you're taken by surprise,
you're lost and feeling vulnerable, but you must realize,
that change is part of growing, part of living, it's God's plan,
accept the things you cannot change, and change the things you can.

Victoria R. Crosby

Always And Forever

How do I love you, let me count the ways
There are only two times I miss you; during the night and
thru the days
I love your touch, so gentle yet strong
It makes my life worth living, this love can't be wrong
Your arms hold me tight, please never let me go.
Just look in my eyes, and your always going to know
When you hold my hand it touches my heart
I'll love you forever. I have from the start
You're the warm Sun in the morning
My shiny stars at night
You can dry my tears and make every thing all right
Just be my friend and walk by my side
I'll love you forever, this love I can't hide.

Pamela C. Hood

Parable Of The Tree

The kingdom of God is like a tree — it is beauty.
There are periods of rest and growth as the seasons change
It is constant.
It is oxygen for those who breathe — it purifies the air,
It refreshes our souls.
It offers shade from the blazing sun — it is protection.
It is home for the fouls of the air — a resting place.
It is food for man and beast for those who hunger.
It is a playground for children at play — it is joy.
It is fuel for those who are cold — it is comfort.
It is a windbreak, with its roots anchored deep in God's
good earth — it is a shield from fierce winds.
It stands in the face of storms, and when the storm is over,
IT IS PEACE.

Vennie Lou Tate

Just One Day

If I could have God to myself for just one day,
There are so many things I'd ask and say.
We'd sit in one of his
Creations a meadows of gold, with many questions
of now and what the future holds.
To end the hatred, bigotry and sin and only you
God know when it all will end.
To be with God for just one day if everyone had
this wish we would surely.
Make God's day.

Vicki S. Morris

The Nursing Home

To those who know not better,
There is a chill of despair
In this place for babies of the 359th degree.
Where time stands still
And identities are measured by a pill.

Professions seem reduced to commonality
While each one goes about the same business.
Those passing through cannot envision the faded brilliance
As morning angels tell the master what to do.

Am I in paradise?
For everything is at a desirable constant
And nothing ill of life can penetrate the shield.
Everyone I meet is a friend
So easy to ignore, yet not offend.

The smells are not unlike the newborn.
In the distance one hears the sounds of a baby's cry,
A comforting voice or singing from the memory of minds.
Where a child's child sits upon a chair
Waiting for the train to yesteryear.

Thomas Shimko

"My Inner Voice"

There is a voice shouting in my head.
There is a voice singing there instead.
There is a choice to which I will listen.
To one the road is long and hard,
To the other yes the road would glisten.
Not a day goes by that I don't think I'm crazy.
Not a day goes by when answers don't seem hazy.
Sometimes I'm lost and down and out.
Then I'm lost and lazy.
If I were lost in the middle of the light,
You know it would surely save me.

Rick James

Dreams

I see myself in a world of constant movement. I feel nothing.
There is always work to be done. I do not move.
I am portrayed as the epitome of the human race and the jerk of
Society. I am not seen.
I excursion to the most beautiful and exotic locales of the world,
Where the days are peaceful the nights are romantic. I do not travel.
I am surrounded by people - people who enjoy my company and despise
My very presence. No one is there.
I encounter decisions that will affect the path in which my life will
Follow, which soon turn out to be meaningless, nominal, childhood
Conflicts. I do not choose.
I accomplish tasks that seem difficult at first with the greatest of
Ease. I do not think.
People ask for my advice and expertise on different subjects.
I do not answer.
I worry about things of great importance and of little value.
I am calm and apathetic.
I am living a brief life, filled with mountains and valleys, highs and
Lows, confusion and tranquility that can change before my eyes.
I dream.

Tom Bodette

Untitled

Eyes downcast, grey masses cry out
There is no silence throughout the black night
The deafening noise cannot be shut off
Like a faucet running full of pain
I place my cup at the foot of the stream
And fill it again and again
I drink in the guilt until I am full
Then I close my eyes and attempt
To drown the noise out of my mind
But the floods have me pinned to the wall
And I am forced to drink until I choke
I am suffocating and am left alone
To live this half-life of greed
Senseless and self-serving
With but an ounce of pity
That I shut off like a faucet

Maura Noonan

When Will It All Stop!

Dark clouds form in the sky
There is thunder but, no rain
The atmosphere is dark
Look at the corner
There they stand
Cops just roll by
They are shooting up,
They are buying,
They are selling,
A little girl watches on
She looks at them and imagines her future
An angry customer, shots are flying
The little girl goes down
As tears roll down my face
I exclaim out loud,
When will the sky be brighter,
When will it all stop!

Sonya Gomes

"Together Forever"

It was night,
There was no light,
But he held her tight.
So she felt no fright.

She loved him she knew,
And he loved her too,
How many times had he said "I love you,"
And told her all his feelings were true.

They'd always be together,
Now and forever,
They'd never part, never,
Their bonds of love will never sever.

They'd be together forever more,
Hang their names together on their front door,
Their children would play happily on the floor,
They'd face together whatever life had in store.

There was a numbing in her head,
What had the police officer just said,
A drunk driver ran a red,
Her husband, her love, her friend was dead.

Sara Jungwirth

Jen

Jen, there's no one like you.
There's no one who cares like you.
There's no one to love like you.
When I was lonely and blue,
You felt what I felt too.

You cared
And you were there.

Jen, I love you
And don't be scared, I'll never hurt you.

Remember, I love you
And there will never be another like you.

Mario Hayes

Our Troubled World

What's to become of this world we live in;
There's violence, hatred and so much sin.
The good and the innocent get hurt everyday,
The bad just seem to always get their own way.

Women getting raped as they walk to their cars,
Men getting killed just sitting in a bar.
The high cost of living gets worse all the time,
And our children are subject to all this crime.

Babies are abused by their parents each day,
Children getting kidnapped when they're outdoors at play
Child pornography, free sex everywhere;
Pushing drugs on these kids, it just isn't fair.

The sounds of gunfire are heard in the night,
Our countries always find another reason to fight.
The muggings in the streets and the riots go on;
One ends up dead, then another is born.

This world is in trouble as anyone can see,
When families have no choice but to pack up and flee.
If we stand united, the difference will show,
Then the criminals will be the ones that will have to go.

Linda Rancatore

Mothers

Mothers are such special people to us;
They are always there to listen and discuss,
Always there to wipe away the tears,
And always there also to offer us those cheers.

Mothers seem to know just when and what to do
During all those times we are feeling down or blue,
They just seem to know without us even saying so
That things just aren't going quite right and it shows.

Mothers are missed more than all the others,
Because, let's face it, they are our MOTHERS,
No one else quite like them in all the world to see
And that's why when they're gone, we miss them terribly.

Mothers are special and it is written there,
God made them that way to show us He cares.
He knows the pain we feel when we lose them,
And He helps us get through it when we trust Him.

Patsy Attaway

Secrets

Secrets are like the monsters of our childhood.
They are creatures arriving from the closet,
Or crawling out from the blackness of night.
Secrets consume friendships, marriages and,
If they are large, evil and fierce enough,
The lives of those who hold them so sacredly
In the dark corners of their hearts and souls.
At times they appear without a clue or warning,
To destroy and threaten our very existence.
Secrets grow from where we have buried them,
Into fire breathing dragons waiting to strike.
If earlier we would of had strength to face them,
And let the light gaze upon their ugly faces,
No size or harm would of been their potential.

Sheila McCoughlin

Why Do Families Treat You So?

Why do families treat you so?
They can't know it,
But they make you feel low.

When they scream,
When they shout
You want them to stop,
You want to get out.

You know they love you,
Or you'd like to think so,
Why do they make you feel so low?

You want it all to go away,
You want to finally have a good day.
You want them to at least be friends,
Even though you can't always make amends.

They know you love them when feelings are bad,
Try not to be so sad.

Do you feel low?
Why do families treat you so?

Stephanie McIntyre

"Thanksgiving"

Thanks to You for all those who have gone....
    Those who will go....
    Those still here....
    And those yet to come..
Bless us past, present and future....
  Amen

Thelma E. Lichlyter

God's Pawns

Amongst the roar and hiss of steam
They catapult their way into the sun's beams
As they fly over the glistening sea
There is no other place they would rather be
Thru the clouds they challenge their fate
For a glimpse of an enemy they're supposed to hate
Time stands still
As the elements test their will
For they know man can't win
When God stirs the wind
Minute upon minute they scan the skies
But on this day only a sea bird flies
With a knowing satisfaction their friends are safe
They turn again for their home base
And for these few moments at heavens gate
These pilots have no fear of being late

Phillip G. Secord

Friendship

Some friends are like the wind:
They fly high and low
And leave you in the end.

Some friends are like the sea:
They rise and fall
And leave you washed ashore.

Some are like a tree:
They bend and sway depending on the day.

I have seen all of these.
And hope none of them to be, for all will flee.

I value your friendship.
You are always here but never in the way.

Our friendship is like the sun.
You shine when I frown, and glow when I'm down.

Our friendship is like a rock.
You're solid and there to lean on,
Not easily moved or chipped away.

I pray when I'm old and gray,
I will be able to look back and say,
Our friendship was the ROCK in every way!

Nicole Prosperie

Side By Side

There's a man and woman whose life they would like to share.
They get together because they really care.
Time goes by, they fall in love and thank the stars above.
They stand side by side knowing their love will abide
as they take their vows side by side.
They both know each other has nothing to hide
but to love each other side by side.
They may drift through the years, cry some tears
but the love for each other takes away their fears.
Side by Side.
It takes two people who really care to open their hearts
and let love be there and reflect upon others to care.
So Side by Side open your heart to stand by each other and care.
Love is always there.

Patricia Arellano

Mama Kin Blues

Oh Mama
They laid your baby down
Oh Mama
From your tears to your knees to the ground
Caught by a bullet from a gun
It took your only son
Mama's world stopped going around

Oh Mama
She cries why couldn't I have been the one
Oh Mama
If you could change what's already been done
She says she just don't understand
What's happening across the land
May God be with you Son

Oh Mama, she cradles the little one
Oh Mama
Can I go outside and play in the sun
She cries out drive by shootings all over town
Raining bullets don't fall on the ground
Stay inside my only one

Shela Cullins

The Trees Remember

The trees remember...
They looked down on us
In our youth...
And in our love...
Protected us with their gracious boughs,
Comforted us with their fine greenery,
And warmed us with the rich colors,
Of their changing leaves.

Yes, the trees remember...
They tenderly guarded us,
Through all our confusions...
And spoke to us of an enduring strength,
That we too might someday find.

Yes, the trees must remember...
How could they forget...
The sheer joy of our being out,
Together under the starlit sky?
How could they forget...
How we marvelled at their majesty,
And our wonder of the great beyond?

Yes, I'm sure the trees remember.

Karyn Ann Taylor

Lead By Inspiration

Many people in the world have the potential to be great.
They possess the intelligence, the skills, and the creativity.
They possess the drive, the energy, and will over fate.
But few people ever become great because greatness cannot
be attained by oneself.
Greatness must be earned through hard work and perseverance.
To have a dream is not greatness but to make that dream
a reality for others is.
To have knowledge is not wisdom but to be able to teach
someone what knowledge can do is.
One must be able to inspire others to greatness.
One commands respect by respecting others.
One is a true leader when one can get others to be strong.
Only one that creates greatness in others is truly great oneself.

Lisa M. Lobue

A Thought In A Grave Yard

Some tombstones are very high
They reach to the sky.
Some are a little small
No matter they also answer the call.
Who knows what they might have been
Some poets, statesmen, kings music men
There are as many dead
Who could have said
If I had lived as long as he
A king I also might be
The grave is marked with their name
Who knows what might have been their fame.
Why did they die so young
Before their song could be sung.
Who decides who should be Master
Why should I have died faster
But the Lord must have His seasons.
No matter what the reasons
We will all know some day
When He will have the final say.

Richard E. Campo

To Eat Among Wild Things

The trash men come on week-ends.
They smile, nod, spit tobacco juice,
Drive a green truck through green trees,
Pick clear plastic bags from brown cans
Placed within reach of each campsite.

They search with diligence,
Pick treasures from the trash,
Salt-topped crackers, mangled tomatoes,
Tangled pretzels, to offer
Bold striped ground squirrels,
Timid, sharp-eared chipmunks.

They sit on grey log benches,
Share lunch with wild things
In cool, close, comradeship
Among vertical conifers
Whose tops whisper secrets
Told by gossipy ridge winds.

Nancy Mottashed Cole

Memories

At your grave there are pinwheels so bright.
They twist and turn keeping birds a flight.
I love you.

Flowers that fade with the suns golden rays.
Oh why did it have to happen this way?
I love you.

I have memories so sweet but they make me cry.
I have questions to ask the biggest is WHY??
I love you.

I look around the house and feel you so near.
I just can't touch you and I want you here.
I love you.

I still have your jeans and tennis shoes too.
Can't seem to part with them, guess I lose.
I love you.

You were kind and gentle, a wonderful son.
Can't play it over, now it's all done.
I love you.

Vickie L. Zastrow

The Wolves And Us

These two wolves are just like you and I,
They will stay together and there's no questions why,

The heart of the baby wolf is bound to its mother,
It loves her like it loves no other.

The mother wolf walks close by its baby's side and
protects it today and forever,
The baby knows it can depend on her through any endeavor.

The mother wolf has taught her baby the wrong from the right,
Just like you mom, and I think about that each and every night.

This mother wolf is so tender, gentle and kind,
And just like you mom she's very special and has a brilliant mind.

This mother and this baby will stay together through the
thick and the thin.
Just like you have done for me mom, and I want to
Thank you once again!

LaJuanna Stokley

Unison

In the wind I watch them bend, I watch the trees all sway.
They're all in motion, in unison
- as if they know that that's the way.

Some are large, and others small.
Some are short, and others tall.
Old and young, colors green, brown, white, and gray.

They are all there, in unison
- as if they know that that's the way.

They have no mind, they have no voice.
yet there's so very much they say
- in unison.

They often may creak, as they grow so old,
or just because it's a windy day.
Look to the trees and you will see it too
- just listen to what they really say.

Watch the trees as they may bend,
watch them as they sway;
though mindless and voiceless as they may be,
they do things in a wonderful way
- in unison!!

Timothy D. Bonney

The Lost Children

Here I search for the things that's lost.
Things of value and of the past.
I see the broken homes and children killed,
By sheer neglect and human ills.

Who's responsible? Who's to blame?
For such tragedy, for such shame.
The teacher tried to do her best,
Two kids in the back were having sex.

Seeing her astonishing glance,
He drew his gun and made a stance
She jumped from her chair and fled,
To remain, she would be dead.

What a shame, what sorrow.
For our children there's no tomorrow.
We all must take our share of blame,
Children today are not the same.

We the parents seem to have lost,
A lesson of the past.
Make the children realize
They must have discipline in their lives.

Leonard L. Lewis

"A White, Unmarked Van"

I lay awake at night,
Thinking of a frozen soil bed,
And my mistakes.

I remember when I forget.
A five table place for now four people,
Or,
When your dress held recital on the clothesline,
Helplessly dancing.

Sometimes in the shed,
I shine your bike
Next to the shovels that dug.

Robert W. Nelson Jr.

Amy's Cries

Silent tears were falling from two lonely eyes
Thinking of him in that moment in time
Hoping to remember what they had,
Knowing that she is feeling more sad
Holding his jacket close to her heart
Not wanting his memory to ever part
Smelling his cologne, feeling him near,
Wearing his necklace, nothing is clear
Hating him for leaving her, but loving him despite
Knowing that it's not his fault, and turning out the light
Lying there quietly thinking of his face
Wanting him beside her, for that is his place
Crying ever so softly, so no one can hear
Thinking of what she meant to him, then feeling fear
"Why did he leave me," she whispered in the night
Hearing no response, she slowly says good night
Sleeping will not come to her, but one visit not received
Death is what took him, just like a sick and desperate thief
Amy's cries are silent, Paul is who they are for,
His memories are not forgotten, And she will never close this door

Sara Coburn

It's Over

I sat in the storm last night for an hour,
thinking of the days past while looking at a flower.

I knew the rain would start just like it has at times before.
The weather always shows my feelings when you're around no more.

The thunder sounds out an anger that inside of me I feel,
and the rain tapping on the ground is the quietness
of my heart that may never heal.

Then the cool breeze as it touches me over and over,
makes me shiver too.

It signals my coldness towards the world for not letting me share
my love with you.

Soon I find myself looking in puddles of water, seeing memories of
"You and Me."

Then I realize it is only the reflections of what
"Use to Be."

As the last drop falls on the petal of my Rose,
it leaves a scent of something new.

For it wasn't the rain, it was my tear, and now
I know It's over with you.

Tana C. Davenport

Tears That Fall Inside

No cure for me to stop the pain
this body hates me sore
I'm tired and worn and feeling the strain
and I just can't take anymore.
My dreams no longer tempt me
to fancy my desires
Yearnings quenched drowned drenched
gone out are the youthful fires.
Dashed are the hopes I held so close
I dreamt to numb the pain
O hope you're gone - it's hard to go on
crazy thoughts now race through my brain.
All the lure and sweet demure
of hopes for finer days
As sorrow waits in turn for fate
and disease has changed my ways.
I can no longer bear the weight
that others just call life
Too hard for me this misery
it cuts me like a knife.
My body aches my skin is hot
as my heart races to keep in stride
With the tears that keep falling one by one
the tears that fall inside.

Mary Ann Ovaduke

Honest Intentions

I will start my diet and lose this weight.
This bulging waistline, I have begun to hate.
So I will start tomorrow with determined will-
No more eating to get my fill.
Those beautiful people who look so trim
After my dieting I, too, will be slim.
Food is for body to make it strong
To overeat excessively will prove to be wrong.
So I will eat a lot of meals today
And tomorrow will be dieting all the way.
There is no reason to be over weight
I must learn to diet and remember the date.
So dieting I will do, just wait and see,
Soon you will look and see a new me.
There will be no problems to bring me sorrow
I will surely start my diet tomorrow.

Luther Berry

One for the Ode

Two lines do not a poem make
This I spoke to him and when all was said and done
My brother said to me just add another one

To my surprise my thoughts had turned to words
I said to him three lines do not a poem make

We laughed and then I thought if
I had another line
A poem or limerick might emerge
That I consider mine

I pondered what we said for the ideas in my head
were jumbled and confused
If I had another line to rhyme
we could surely be amused.

I would say to you that listens to a rhyme
could drink a beer with us
and have an amusing time.

Van B. Perrine

The Future

There is no sky, no clouds, no air.
This is what happened when no one cared.

There are no birds, no trees, no leaves to fall.
This is what happened when no one heard the call.

There are no animals, no areas to roam.
This is what happened to the place they called home.

There are no mountains, no meadows, no fields.
This is what happened when we ignored the appeals.

There is no grass, no bushes, no flowers.
This is what happened when no one used their powers.

There is no food, no crops to grow.
This is what happened when someone said, "So."

There is no beach, no sand, no waves.
This is what happened when no one wanted to save.

There is no music, no songs, no laughter.
This is what happened to happily ever after.

There is no happy, no joy, no love.
This is what happened to the gifts from above.

Tammie J. Barnhouse

The Old House By The Side Of The Road

Alas, 'tis so sad to see,
This old house a home used to be.

Now the aged tin roof is full of rust,
And inside is covered with dust.

Once the yard had flowers galore,
Where happy children played around the door.

Little boys turned cartwheels,
While a rollicking dog jumped at their heels.

Children swinging on an old rubber tire,
Each time going higher and higher.

The old house now stands an empty shell,
But in the hearts of these children dwell,

Memories of the purest gold,
The love of these days are theirs forever to hold

Mildred G. Myers

Untitled

Sensitive to death in every fiber and atom of
this soul will bend to the acts of love and affections
that betrays the senses of the minds idea of what is real.
What is real, other than to the senses which
one interprets subject to opinions of reality.
Sensitive to passions smaller than the atoms of this
soul like fire eternal shifting moods of emotions
and thoughts, cold acts of affections, fueled by
hot and warm expressions of familiarity.
Sensitive to the ghost that passes though me with
ideas of the world in my mind to confuse and shift
my existence as of someone else.
Can't hold back the tears.
Sensitive to the screams in the heart and
soul to explode a riot of emotions and thoughts of chaos.

Michel Edgard Francois

Oysters And Wine

Whenever I dine on oysters and wine
This thought occurs to me.
When shy oysters love who gives them a shove
At the bottom of the sea?

These legless oysters deep in their cloisters
How do they move about?
Do they really not go, never move to and fro?
That I rather doubt.

I've often wondered where oysters blundered
Not having legs to walk.
Do they always sit still like a stone on a hill
Or is it only talk.

I'll never more dine on oysters and wine
'Til it's explained to me.
While oysters aren't dead they just lie in bed
At the bottom of the sea.

Raymond C. Philips

Love

This word can mean many things,
This word can play many roles,
This word can fill empty spaces, or just create more holes.

This word can make you feel joy,
This word can make you feel pain,
This word can give you sunshine, or bring about the rain,

This word creates friendships,
This word creates foes,
This word creates highs, or gives you ultimate lows!

This word creates happiness,
This word creates sadness,
This word creates obsession,
Or just a hint of gladness!

This word is like a secret,
This word is like a story,
This word is like a battle, or just a part of glory!

This word is like a phantom,
This word is like a dove,
This word is like a eagle, or it's just sent from above.

This word is—love!

Scott Percival

Forgotten Lessons

I sit and gaze and wonder why,
This world must go rushing by.
When not one day should ever go,
Without the love we know.

Within this hurrying of today,
Our love is fading fast away.
The love of man and God's creations
Should help our hearts find inspirations.

But in this onward world of ours,
We've forgotten lessons of past hours.
The lessons of love and friendliness,
For which God means us all to bless.

So my friends, Please slow your pace,
Perhaps you'd find a better place.
Yes, a place within this word,
With love instead of constant swirl.

Terri L. Coger

"Welcome"

Welcome to this world, little one-
Tho you won't understand-The ravages that have been done
All in the name of man!
The rivers are polluted- this land of ours is torn,
The animals are being killed, the forests have been shorn!
But Mom and Dad will see to it that all your dreams come true—
They'll have to work doubly hard to make it if they do.
Welcome to our Universe! And as you grow to youth,
Maybe things will turn around and Man will learn the truth!
As how to make this world of ours a better place to live—
And not to let their greed take more than what they have to give.
God willing you will see it through, and when you take your stand—
You'll be proud to say that you were born
in such a gracious land!

Welcome!

Mary E. Lewis

"So Precious To Me"

Just for a moment, I look back to see.
Those day's of home, so precious to me
Through the window of my past, I am there again.
And things look the same, as they were look then

With the thoughts of my childhood days,
Again in mind, my memory strays.
Then my dreams so fond, will again unfold
With pastures of green, and fields of gold.

I see roses blooming, in our garden there.
The smell of spring is in the air.
So lovely and warm, is this spring day.
Makes all of my cares, just fade away.

A voice familiar, I now can hear.
The voice of Mother so very dear
the love in her face, I remember as then.
Isn't it nice, just to go back again?

Those days of home, now so long ago.
My sisters and brothers, that I love so.
The face of my father, again now I see.
When family, and home, were so precious to me.

Marvin K. Snow

Wisdom

The wind winds 'round these withered trees and whispers in my ears
Those secrets remembered, so long ago, those childhood happy years

Where once a child's spirit kept, a wiser one replaced
Left behind to find my way, without the smallest trace

Not yet cried I, not yet I fear, those days have passed too quickly
To have my innocence for just one day, to make up for all the years

I need a light to guide me through, this darkness that consumes me whole
A shoulder to lean on, a voice to soothe, a hand for me to hold

But I learned to see through this darkness, and even to stand on my own
Learned to support myself at times, and I learned to be alone

So now you speak to me, oh wind, of days that once were here
And remind me of a forgotten life, you make things seem so clear

For pain is part of every life, without it you can't be whole
Learn to except it, you tell me now,
'Tis medicine for the soul.

Kathleen Sutherland-Rice

Edgar Poe Cahill

My Papa is a handsome man,
Though he's the oldest of the clan.
When he is really feeling fit,
He can't be beat for charm and wit.

He welcomes all his friends galore,
They can't believe he's ninety-four.
A courteous man, I'm sure you'll agree.
With a "mind of his own" as you quickly will see.

He loves to read the Bible,
And he's read it through and through.
I think each time he reads it, though,
He finds there something new.

He is quite an inspiration—
He's known God all through these years,
His friend, who walked beside him...
How could I have doubts or fears?

Now some folks groan and they bemoan
Their lack of health and fitness.
What's more important on this earth
Than to be God's own witness.

Polly Anne Alspaugh

Thought

There's no copyright on thought
Thought is the power or process of thinking
Mental activity
Intention
Design
Purpose
Conception
Imagination
All human beings are capable of thought

There's no copyright on thought
The brain is infinite
It can will anything into existence
No thought is owned unless it's put to use
But if your thought remains recluse
Someone else will think the same thought and make it produce

So if you have a thought
Will it into existence
When it comes to thought no one steals
Don't feel like a heel
That someone used a particular thought and made it real
There's no copyright on thought

Kristoffer Jackson

Tomorrow

This life of ours comes to us just one day at a time. There are thousands of ways we can spend our tomorrows, and hundreds of days left to fill. Give laughter a voice. Let yesterday's reasons be still, that we may dream, work, and live. Let this day be more than just the hours passing by, Life is definitely a journey. Commit to something you believe in, and start living. Life is a special gift it cannot be left in a parking lot, forgotten for an afternoon. Take note, and feel the world that is yours. Watch a sunset, share a smile with gratitude, for one more way in which to be alive. How far will we progress today? Time is the number of moments we use to fill a lifetime with.

Rose Luper

Through The Eyes Of A Child

What an angelic smile! But, then she's only a child.
Through her eyes, no pain she's seen. Down life's rugged path she's not been.

She lived, she laughed, she loved, she grew. Then one day the Lord said, "Your little task on earth is through." He gently took her by the hand, and told her of the Promised Land.

No doubt was there in her little mind. No one else was so good and kind. Her mother and daddy had taught her well. That Jesus would come and in heaven she would one day dwell.

No excuses did she make that morn - Oh Jesus! I have barely been born, or come again another day - I still have games to play.
Into his eyes she looked - His outstretched hand she took.

Reka A. Bedsole

Dunoon

A gaming road wanders over a low stone wall
Through meadows of dormant green.
The forest waits in the chill of winter's ire
For the day the first colored sail appears on the Clyde.
The blooming of the crocus has promised it.

The violet hills are shrouded in a vail of mist
That hides the beauty of the highlands,
And yet I know it's there.
A sunny day told me so.

The red cheeked babies waiting in their carriages outside the shops
Embrace the cold contentedly and peer at their small Scottish world
Through eyes encircled by warm woollen bunting.
"Mother is coming soon. It's Wednesday, the half day, you know!"

The church tower peers down on its city, taxi cabs all in a row,
Chimneys promising warm homecomings, the coal truck making
its rounds,
Picture pastries in the window of every other store.
"Hurry, the butcher shop is closing"... Dunoon.

Patricia Drapela French

Changes

And there are times when we feel sad
through the destiny we cannot control
and that is when we must take command
and reach deep down into our soul.

And there are things we must understand
or else we will forever remain blind
to what the true objective really is
and whether there really is true happiness to find.

William Colovos

Untitled

The grains of sand, slowly passing
through the hourglass, one by one,
mocking the passage of time
with their eternity.

The waves of the ocean,
beating upon the shore.
Their hum, laughing at the sand,
only to turn, roll away, and return once again.

The power of the moon,
causing turmoil upon the sea,
showing the water
its helplessness.

And two people,
with a love known only to them,
defying the forces of all.

Kristen Bauer

Whispering Fog

Fog whissss-pered
through the valley
tearing kite tails on thickets and glens.

Fog whissss-pered
through the shadows
trailing chiffon veils so white, so thin.

Fog whissss-pered
over the murky meadows
casting spells of hide and seek.

Fog whissss-pered
over the hill hollows
wrapping the landscape in its transparent sheet.

Lorraine Amman-Blau

Little Ones Flight

Watch them go one by one
Through the white clouds and past the sun
These little unborns who song was never sung
Whose faces the cruel world turned to shun

Look neither to heaven nor hell to blame
In this needless death and unbearable shame
It is the legs of morality that have gone lame
And the conscience of man answers to no name

Crushed by their kind in the worlds bitter stare
Away they go these little ones rare
Far out of reach of a mothers tender care
Upon the shoulders of a God where a cross was once bared

May you find peace in that kingdom high
Where hope and love shall never die
And little ones eyes never do cry
In the city of gold where angels fly

Katy Rogers

My Mom

My mom is always ready and there for me
Through times that are sad and even happy
I think I am blessed greatly by the one above
Cause she's the best mom, she like a great dove
People may argue and say theirs is the best
But I don't care cause mine is still above the rest
Even though she is sometimes a mean old witch
I may get up set at her, but which is which
I love my mom no matter what anyone says
Because her and I are like two bee's doing a duet buzz
We belong together forever and ever.

Rachelle Grattan

Take It If I Could

A child's pain shouldn't exist
Throughout the world, in every family and home
A gentle hand's blessing that can't resist
To comfort and sooth the little ones souls

Should this be
That cries of pain are heard
Should this be
That little hearts hurt

I do not agree with the powers that be
Because a child cannot see
The ultimate reason so unseen

Steven Carey Robinson

"Our Love Remembrance Bound"

Man to woman — Woman to man,
Throughout time our life together
The bond of marriage as one
To grow and construct a solidarity foundation
To not be blind, but aware and alert
To reach out with: a hand comfort and support
Our first priority to each.

To seek from living experience and learn
Of and from Our Heavenly Father
And then we will find
Counting the number of tears
Shed for sorrow, shed for love, shed for pain
True love from the heart.

Pauline L. Becker

What Is Love?

Love is a pang that you feel deep inside,
Tickling your stomach like a roller coaster ride.
Love is a smile, a soft touch, or a tease,
Leaving you breathless, dizzy, and weak in the knees.
It's the laughter of children, a puppy's warm lick.
It's a parent who stays by your bed when you're sick.
Love can come quietly as on wings of a prayer,
Found in a friend who will tell you they care.
Love has no boundaries, no borders shape its design.
It's the gift that when shared won't say, "That is mine."
Love knows no score at the end of its day.
But love is kept best when it's given away.

Nancy Olson

The Sparrow And The Owl

The sparrow's morning is highlighted by flight
Time for the night owl to call it quits when daylight
Justifiably fair
Defiantly rare
They'll encompass each other come twilight.

The sparrow's day furious in its right
To finish hers while the owl in the night
Keenly stares
At what's there
They encompass each other come twilight.

The sparrow's day is filled with the Robin's Song
While the night owl's night is silent and long
The sparrow - songs of care
When dark - owl is still there
Yet they encompassed each other come twilight.

Pat Blanks

Time

Time is my enemy....Time is my friend
Time heals all wounds.....Time wounds all heels
I've got too much time on my hands
Sorry, no time for that
Time is the fire in which we burn
The time at the tone will be 10 PM
Time is....
Time was...
Time will be...
Sometime later.....
A stitch in time saves nine
Time is of the essence
Time waits for no man
There's never enough time
As time goes by...Time rolls on
If I could save time in a bottle
I have no yesterdays.....Time took them all away,
But I have tomorrow....So I live today.

Michael G. Sayers

Fall

Fall is in the air!
Tiny, stringy clouds impinge upon the azure blue sky
and string out across the horizon,
and encroach upon the brown coastal hills.

The bright sun is still warm,
but the night-time chill
reminds us that the hoped-for rains of winter
will soon be upon us.

We feel the tinge and beauty of autumn
as we see the gold and red
that starts to fleck the still greenery
of the trees outside my window.

Soon the clouds pile up out of the west and south,
one upon the other, dark gray and ominous
as the thunder and lightning slash through,
and the soft early raindrops fall upon the dry earth
that has yearned so long for this beneficence.

Perhaps the drought will soon be over,
and these early signs will bring us
the relief we have sought for so long.

Robert P. Klein

"Run Away Little Girl"

Tired little girl - when all your wanderings are thru
Tired little girl - I will set up a tent for you
Tired little girl - please don't set and sigh
Just wishing for your mommy to take your hand and cry
Tired little girl - ragged and forborne
When lost in a desert - wishing you weren't born
Tired little girl - stars are your friends
They will always guide you to the destinations end
Happy will be his little girl
When their wanderings are thru
Happy will be his girl
He'll build a campfire for you
He'll keep her snug and war and protect her from the world
storm
Just keep the campfire burning
Someday you'll be returning
Somewhere across the miles
Mom and Dad are there
Happy will be the runaway girl
He will be the love and care.

Mildred V. Talkington

Winter Solstice Of Love

And I just screamed in the wilderness. Blind men lead the way-
to a sunless day, and I just screamed!
Blistering sun, as I screamed in the cold. Blockade the sound
of pain and shivers.

The intensity of life's pleasures has the mind enthralled.
Touch my eyes with clay! Will I see? Will I be clean of
maladies which I abhor.

Give me your eyes that I may see. The mist of pain arising
from my mouth, as I scream in the cold.
Springtime has passed, forever, gone-bye.
I water my couch with tear-drops to moisten my sepulcher.

What will winter, the cold winter, bring? A voice snatched
from my throat, never to express joy in a tune.
In my heart it will never be spring. The four seasons of my
soul: cold; ice; defrosting; and death, dripping from the
stalactites of my soul- screaming in the cold!
Forever frostbitten by love.

Matthew Kowasic

Untitled

You, with your sold-out affliction, spilling your guts
to anyone and everyone who'll listen
you have some obvious bull shit desire to convince
everyone that you're so screwed up inside
reality check, dear
you are not superior just because you have no life
aside from your pills and depression
you're no worse than the rest of us
you simply choose to put yourself in the spotlight
on your demented stage
it's all an act, honey
I can see right to you, right in you, right past you
right through you and your horrific talespin
thanks, but no thanks
I've already read that book, seen that movie, heard that album
I'll bet I've hung myself on your rack
It's all a gamble, anyway
I'll meet your lithium and raise you crack
smack you back into reality.

Stephanie Jo Thorvalson

Untitled

Why must I wait so very long...
To be with the one that I belong?
There are of course so many reasons...
I'll gladly wait the many seasons.
My love for you is so very true...
Sometimes I just don't know what to do.
I spend the weekends holding you tight...
I spend the weekdays alone at night.
I want to marry you one day from tomorrow,
Who cares about money, I guess we'll borrow.
I love you more than words can say...
Our love grows more and more each day.
I gave my heart only to you...
I hope you know just what to do.
I love you sweetheart, I guarantee it...
I hope one day you'll finally see it.
And now I go to sleep alone...
And wait 'till this day when I'll be home.

Randall Lee Rene

Love's Freedom

It is so long ago I gave my Love to you,
to bud, then grow as boughs on trees will do
captured, cultivated...yet somehow free
protected from storms, weeds, thorns even so
sometimes pruned, yet still it strives to be
stretching, seeking to catch each drop of rain
to soak the warmth of sun's rays also
thus strength is gathered to counter time's drain
serene, secure the final fruit ripens still
so, too, our Love enriches, expands fulfilled.
You pleasure me today e'en more than long ago.

Nancy L. Osberg

Spirit

To be or not to be
That is not a question for me.
Trapped to wander with no freeway for escape
My fate has been sealed,
My destiny revealed.
Alone and yet not, I wander this earth
Searching and searching for what it is worth.
Stuck between heaven and hell,
Only time will tell,
If I the damned,
Will be or not.

Steven Rogers

Lament

Love will never be! Impossibility has tightened its grip on me.
To Death belongs the one I love and lost..., to Death belongs!

The flowing morning sun appears; its light sparkling beneath my tears,
banned from reaching beyond the ground where, always at its post,
always in command, Death reigns guarding the one!

Afternoons fall without the glare of years gone,
and Time keeps dripping into this broken jar.

Nights descent in a pilgrimage of pain, one after the other,
wrapped in their mournful gowns, theirs cavernous mouths
murmuring condolences..., yet not one God could heal the pain
which dooms me!

Before my eyes the carelessly-spilled stars downpour their bluish cry.
Awake I hear the sound of a sad song approaching with the soft
September air...,
song of despair coming through the front door half-closed,
invading, searching along the dim-lit corridors, lost, lost, lost!

I am, by impossibility, overpowered; fearing the sounds of life
closing-in on me.
How silent must there be, beneath where my love is sound asleep...
while I cannot release him from Death's grip!

But if neither all light pouring torrential from the sky, nor
life blooming
abundant throughout the land can, how could I, who passes
sweeping dead leaves
off the ground, unbound the one?
To Death belongs the one I love and lost...to Death belongs!

Maritza C. Fonseca

Fade Into Black

All I've ever wanted was to just be me,
To do what I please and to feel like I'm free,
And not have to answer for everything I do,
Because I'm living for me and not for you.

So take a step back and get out of my space,
You're just another critic in a friendly face,
Why can't you just let yourself be my friend,
Standing behind me until the relationship ends.

Things aren't disclosed to get a good laugh,
I do it to retain some sanity on my behalf,
What I'm sharing with you is important to me,
But for you my world is impossible to see.

So my friend the curtain calls,
Watch me from the shadows as the darkness falls,
Try to remember that these are my mistakes to make,
Every time my decisions may make your heart break.

Now all I ask of you is to turn your back,
As my life and your memories of it fade into black...

Lynda M. Wright

What Is The Shell?

What has the body in which we abide,
To do with the person who's living inside?
We are souls, every one, though we have different skin;
Be it white, be it black, be it heavy or thin.
There is hatred, suspicion, and other disgraces,
Heaped upon those presumed of inferior races.
Yet who dares to judge by the way one appears?
He is clouded by ignorance, held captive by fears.
And he is the lowest, and most off the wall,
Who cannot acknowledge that God made us all.
Man looks on the outside, and thinks he's so smart,
Yet the Lord looks within, and He judges the heart.
And if we take caution, we all would do well.
The soul is the person, so what is the shell?

Scott Johnson

Feelings

All this I feel deep in my heart,
to express it all I just can't start,

Feelings too great for simple words alone,
Love much too strong to be known,

And when you stand near me, by my side,
these expressions of love, I just can't hide.

In those hands so soft a touch,
in your kiss I feel so much.

A passion burning in your eyes,
a look of love that never dies.

I feel for you in every way,
I love you more than words can say.

So pull the curtain and close the door,
I'll love you now and forever more.

Suzette Spruck

"On Seeing Schindler's List For The First Time"

The light ... light,
to give meaning to life;
to show the difference in everyman's heart.

The light ... light,
to reveal the evil and the good in mortals;
the reasons for living and the promise in dying.

My heart cries out for the inhumanity;
My whole being weeps for my impotency.

Why the cruelty? Why the killing?
Why the annihilation of the minority?
What reasons are there for all these absurdity?
Why the HOLOCAUST in our memory?

The cries...cries...Oh! all the cries,
the screams, anguish, pains and deaths;
the fighting spirits of the innocents
and the acquiescence of the aged.

To watch the brutality of the uniform on the trodden path of yore;
I could not understand the reasons as I am forlorn.

Must there be HOLOCAUST? Must there be brutality?
Should it not only be PEACE for all eternity?

Marina S. Reyes

A Glimpse Of My Son On A Moonlit Night

I sneak into your room once more;
To glimpse the softness of your sleep;
The moonlight kisses you warm as I;
The breath I take is deep.

The breath I take is deep my son;
This peace so preciously rare;
As I watch you lie there with your friends;
Mr. Bunny, Old Blue, and the Bear.

Mr. Bunny, Old Blue, and the Bear my son;
With them your dreams you share;
With them you slumber unaware of me;
As I brush from your eyes your hair.

I brush from your eyes your hair my son;
And marvel the wonder of your sigh;
As contentedly you call out from your sleep;
Another dream is nigh.

Another dream is nigh my son;
Shared now but with the Bear;
But longfully fervently I beseech the day;
When unhindered you take me there.

Matt A. Colbert

"Mr. Thomas" - The Old Tom Cat

"Mr. Thomas" was gentle, kind and demur
To his lady friend with white fur;
She could feed at his table, eat his food
And it put old Thomas in a kindly mood.

He could spot an enemy by the scent -
When strangers appeared he would resent,
To door he would run - making quick departure
Could not be found for many an hour.

One day he left and didn't look back! -
For Nita had come and stolen his shack;
There is still in my heart a fond memory -
Of old "Mr. Thomas" - Ann's cat so friendly.

Velda H. Booth

Let Your Spirit Soar

In your eyes a fire burns
to know the Universe and what it concerns.
But blocks you raise to suppress the heat
for fear within does strongly beat.

To open your mind and let in the Light
would calm your nerves enough to take flight.
For when you soar you get above it all
and knowledge comes forth like a waterfall.

Joy and peace will follow each flight
and bring balance within to resolve any plight.
And as you rise higher into wisdom's sky
you will no longer question the reasons why.

You simply take note of what has occurred
knowing the wisdom is your cause to endure.
To reach a deeper awareness of your inner worth
and to become one with all, Heaven and Earth.

D. A. Hammond

Angel

Red haired Angel sent from above
To light up my life
To share with me love
My heart was so hard, encased in stone
You tore it down, to build us a home.
The foundation is built
On truth and love
My Red haired Angel, sent from above,
The walls are made, of mutual caring
This home of ours, we'll always be sharing
Our lives, our future, Katy my love
My Red haired Angel, sent from above.

Roy D. Forshee

Untitled

We all have a little time,
To live, to love, to give, to share
Our time is precious, so beware-
Don't waste it on hatred and fear
Love your loved ones while they are near.
For a day may come,
They'll be unable to hear.
Say what you feel about love and caring
This present time is the one for sharing.
You'll never regret the things you feel,
Only those you didn't reveal.
Do it today while the sun still shines,
For we all have only a little time.

Mary Ann Carhart

"Questions Of The Heart"

Yours is a strange kind of relationship
To me it represents the sign of the scales
Sometimes it weighs up, sometimes down
and then balanced again.

What it is about you, I'm not sure I'll ever know
But, I find myself always travelling back toward your path.

Is it a challenge of getting what you
can't have that leads me to this point
or a desire from deep within that only
you control?

Will this continue forever?
only the stars will know.
But for now, you alone hold the
Key to the small special lock on
my heart.

Lori Salerno

Old Friends

How wonderful to sit and talk
to remember (with laughter and pain)
the wonderful/sometimes difficult times
of our shared childhood...

It is pleasant/reassuring to know that
one can always come home.

to return back to the safety/trust of friendship
that remains constant
throughout time/regardless of distance or
periods of absence

To the safety of someone who truly loves you
and loves you merely for what/who you are

Old friends—the good kind
the ones who really "knew you when"
are the best...
the kind that last forever...

Virginia Davis Floyd

For Our Children

To teach our children how to pray we first need to teach them
what to say. When we bring our needs to God above, we know
he's listening with all his love. No matter what problems we
have today, we can take them to God when we pray.
Everyday we face many fears and our faces flow with many tears.
Our tears may flow but still we know that through our prayers we
can grow. We must let them know that God takes care to listen
to what they have to share. We teach our children how to recite
the same old prayer every night. Prayer to God should not be
the same to teach them that would be a shame. Before our
children go to bed at night, before we turn out the light, we
should kiss them, hold them tight. Have them close their eyes
until they get God in their sight. Now we have opened the door,
now they see him as never before. God suddenly is real, now
they understand why we kneel. Now they can tell Him about
their day, the good with the bad they can say.
They can tell him their feelings were hurt today.
They can tell Him how much fun they had at play.
With head bowed low they can begin to say:
Now I lay me down to sleep, my secrets I will no longer keep.
Now I know how to pray, now I know what to say.
Now I'll tell God about my day!

Pamela Joiner Boudreaux

What Is Fair...

To web the human existence into sparkles of stars
To share a life in all its adventures and wonders
To gaze at the universe and awe at the dullest star
To envision the abstract and create the concrete
To crystallize the immortality of our dreams
To open the morning at yesterday's darkness

To play right the cards, loose anyway
To cry an endless sigh of nothingness
To pray for touch, receive confession
To ask the wind an unspoken answer
To journey into the human instinct
To toil from dawn and expire at dusk

To breath the impossible to life
To splint a sliver from decay
To fill of all, an empty glass

To inhale and be
To love and be loved
To exist but for a sprint!
What is fair?

Maria Elena Gomez

With Love In Mind

It is my hope, one of my dreams
to share my heart, my love it seems.
To share my heart, my mind, my soul,
blend mine with yours, and make them whole.

I dream, I hope, I pray one day;
that we shall meet, then I will say,
"My heart is pure, my love is true,
with love in mind, I think of you!"

A kiss, a touch, a gentle caress,
my love for you I'll always stress.
It is strong, so masculine,
yet gentleness that is within!

With love in mind, it is your call,
with love in mind, I'll give my all.
If I should trip, or even stumble;
your heart's a treasure, I shall not fumble!

It is my hope, one of my dreams,
to share my heart, my love it seems.
You are unique, one of a kind,
for you I write, with love in mind!

Phillip R. Krziske

Sleepwalking

Forget it, I say to myself.
Your children are born.
You have no need of it, of him.
Who is he, anyway,
the father of your children?

Beneath the comforter I try
to convince myself
I have no needs.
I am not human.

I remember
how still the mare was
after Daddy sold the stallion.
I sleep standing up.

Susan Spencil

If I Could Be So Bold

If I could be so bold,
What wondrous feats I could achieve.
When life serves me its slop on a silver platter,
I could admire the beauty of the silver platter.
When I've got two strikes against me,
With two outs and bases loaded,
I could swing at the curve ball
with every ounce of strength and confidence I possess.
When my courage falters and my steps become heavy,
I could jump out of my weighted shoes
and sprint the remaining distance.
When my eyesight becomes blurred by doubt and resistance,
I could use my inner eyes to sense my path,
and keep me traveling in my chosen direction.
When the darkness closes about me,
I could shine my inner light to guide me through the mine field.
And when my faith seems to crumble at my feet,
I could rebuild it with a thought
from the foundation that can never be destroyed.
I could be truly and totally happy ... If I could be so bold.

Frank Daniel Banfi

Untitled

A patient sufferer at rest
When a Mother breathes her last farewell,
The stroke means more than time can tell.
The world seems quite another place.
Without the smile of your dear Mother's face
And while she lies in peaceful sleep
Her memory we will always keep.
Her smiling face and pleasant ways
Are a pleasure to recall
She had kindly words for everyone
And died beloved by all.

Gertrude Murt

June

Endlessly thinking of the enchanting moments together.
When eyes seem to sparkle and the heart's impulse heightens.
The spring-like attraction lasts for eternity.
There is nothing more breath - taking

Than the memorable sight of a radiant smile.
This is the beginning of a new life.
The mind produces an enduring image of beauty.
This vision is forever secured in the soul.

Nothing can destroy; nor alter what the mind has created.
Such thoughts of allurement forever rage on day to day.
Everything is a magnificent part of this truly unbelievable;
Yet majestic sight.

Has there ever been anything as remarkably wonderful as this?
Never before, and never again can things be like this.
These things describe what man seeks to experience in life.
Seasonably, people know now what this man knows;
Only these things can be found in June.

Jason Dean Fleeman

The First Crocus

Within my heart I feel a thrill
When first I see a daffodil,
But how my heart with joy does bound
When that first crocus peeps from ground.

"If Winter comes can Spring be far behind?"
So wrote the poet long ago.
All this is true, I know it's so
But I must see that tender bloom
To know there's end to chill and gloom.

Esther Wallace

Going Home

For years I fought my inner fears,
the silent chorus that bid me stay
far from what I love.
I am home now, anxious thoughts
laid to rest while I revel in what
I love the best. Blue sky, as if
painted by an artists brush, mountains
big and bold, into which I
place my trust. I gaze upon a flaming
sunset, and later a bejeweled
night sky and I feel full, complete,
all fears are stilled.
Yes, you can go home again.

Marita Tabor

The Simple Things

A single red rose
The sparkle in a Grandmother's eye
The joyful laughter of a child
A tear when someone cry's

A soft summer shower
A gold band for a wedding ring
Man and a woman just holding hands
A simple song to sing

I love the simple things in life
Look they're all around
Sometimes the simple things in life
Are the best things to be found

A mother's love for her child
A best friend you know who cares
A father and his son at the fishing hole
A simple honest prayer

I love the simple things in life
They're there for you and me
Sometimes God's simple things in life
Are the most beautiful to see

Therese Nichelle Dugan

The Sun And The Sea

Dusk summons their communion.
The Sun dips into the sea.
He brightens her form
As she colors his gaze.
Above her he is, and warmth is his.
Cool is hers.
They ignite and quench at blackness.
In the ripples and the rays,
They brush and breathtake.

Tara Cunningham

Colored Dreams

The sun goes up
The sun goes down
The flowers grow
The flowers die
And then I fly
To see them grow
In shades of red and snow colored white

And all this happens in my dream
And suddenly I see a stream
Of very lightly colored blue.

Maggie Ruth Reitz

The Black Widow Spider

Her language is silence,
The symbol of death.
Her children together,
in one single nest.
The blood she will search for,
The most vital need.
She feels no guilt for,
Her murderous deed.
She walks through the evening,
A victim in sight.
She hunts him slowly,
A perilous fight
Her beauty deceiving,
A poisonous sting.
Her heart beats within
A dead man's ring.
But she loves her children,
She loves the dim light,
The black window spider,
Brings fear through the night.

Sherry Babitz

Gabriel's Horn

There's rumbling in the heavens.
The time of life has come
For Gabriel to take his horn down
And blow those loud, clear, sounds.

The sounds that will be heard
Have never been heard before.
The notes he will be playing
will open heavens door.

Gabriel has blown his horn
The battle has just begun
A heavenly host of angels
Has the devil on the run

His armies are now retreating
Armor and swords laid down
The devil has been defeated
He is nowhere to be found.

Now the war is over
And the dust has settled down
The gates of heaven are open
The Garden of Eden is found.

Samuel L. Levy

The Song

As old as the world
The wait has been long
Straining through ages
To hear from the song.
Set to a rhythm
Life's grim tune played out.
The young are too old
To cry without doubt.

Saw someone slipping
When given a chance.
Cutting in line
For life's short dance...
Behind him the patient,
Knowing their fate,
Regarding his kindness
A break from the hate.

Sara Christian

My Picture Frame

Down in the valley,
The wind is still,
The river runs silently, over the hill.
The sky is clear,
Oh what a sight,
I think I'll stay here,
The rest of the night.
And as I lay here,
I think of you,
And all of the things,
That we used to do.
You smiled so warmly,
You laughed so merry,
You looked so divine,
You were sweet as a cherry.
Now you are gone,
I'm at loss for words,
You remind me of, a pretty singing bird.
I hope you know, you'll always remain,
In my heart forever, in my picture frame.

Tina Marie Shanks

Sun, Sea, And Sky

As I sit upon the dune,
the world fades out of tune.
Drifting into nothingness,
I sit in peaceful bliss.
Nary a care have I,
on what may go by...
Nothing but the sun, sea, and sky.

Tara L. Ribar

No Sparrows Fly Here

Lost souls hiding in the shadows of
their hearts,
So many crowded streets,
No sparrows fly here.

Desert land of memories that played on
ivory keys,
In tune to fading embers that glowed
upon the hearth.

A sparrow's song in early morning
sweetness, gone,
Now only a cracked mirror to reflect
back the image of the truth.

Dark circles etched beneath stricken
eyes that have witnessed the
abomination of stark emptiness.

Black crows picking at the last shreds
of sanity, swallowed by grey skies.
No sparrows fly here.

Laura Chagnon

Sands Of Time

So small and yet so mighty
They seem to be to me;
Nothing slows their eternal journey,
Not even the quirks of fate.
Ever mindful of their purpose—
No one is free of them.
So carefully pick your deeds and works
And those the words you say
For we all must stand
Before the sands of time
To enter those pearly gates.

Patricia Bye

Untitled

People touch-
then move away.
Nothing stays the same.
Different places, times, and faces-
We all must play the game.

and if I stop- to think about-
the people I have known;
a sadness creeps upon my heart
and turns it to a stone.

It's true-
we build our walls up,
never letting others inside,
We may, not be too happy,
but it's easier to hide.

I wish things could be different.

And you-
You've touched my life;
More than you'll ever know.
But I, too, must play the game-
and now it's time to go.

Lynn Baniak

Man In Black

Over by the garden gate
there a man does stand and wait
He is dressed all in black
with a knap sack on his back
He looks so tired, hungry and sad
Wait a minute, I think it's my dad
Many years have come and gone
since we were all at home
Mom was laid to rest
a few years after my dad had left
Oh, such memories flood my mind
of a happy, gentle time
With this man dressed in black
who use to ride me on his back

Shirley Carter

The Ultimate Reality

There are no rocks
There are no rills
There are no flowers
Or distant hills
There are no songs of sad lament
There are no words of discontent
There are no things of "you" or"I"
There are no birds up in the sky
These things you leave here when you die.

There is only spirit.
Immortal soul.
Death brings the ultimate reality.

Peter J. Prato

Untitled

A child's voice is seldom heard,
they so often get passed by.
As fragile as a little bird,
so easily to cry.

Please remember to lend an ear
to hear their little truth,
for soon the passing of the years
will diminish the thing called "youth".

R. Rodriguez

Pa's New Gun

When we got home from school that day
there weren't nobody home.
And me 'n you could act like boys
when we was all alone.
And when we got to my house
we was runnin' outta fun.
And you got so excited when
I showed you pa's new gun.
But papa never taught me
all the things I had to know.
Now you 'n me ain't never gonna
have the chance to grow.
And when I hollered "FREEZE,
SUCKER!"
like they do on T.V.
I thought that when I "squeezed one off"
you'd still play with me.

I just couldn't take it
that I would hurt you.
I just couldn't take it.
I was your best friend.

Michael J. Jablonowski

NEWS ITEM, NOVEMBER 1, 1943

New York has turned on all her lights,
They brighten half the sky,
You cannot tell the days from nights
When New York's feeling high.

She's rubbed the dimout from her eyes
And changed her dingy dresses;
She's gathered stardust from the skies
To decorate her tresses.

Go, take your Paris in the spring,
New York's knee-deep in clover,
And even birds stay up to sing
"Oh, can the war be over?".

Yes, hope rides high in New York town
'Mid toil and tears and pain,
For New York wears a sequinned gown,
Her lights are on again!

Selma D. Kelter

"Best Friend"

Everybody has one,
they come in every size
short, tall, fat and thin
they all are very wise.

You find them in the bedroom,
the bathroom and the kitchen
and when the bugs decide to bite,
they know how to stop the "itchin'"

They have a way of knowing
when you're tired or don't feel good.
Their reasoning for everything is -
"You don't eat the way you should!"

They are always there to guide you,
to lend a helping hand,
nothing seems too much for them,
they always understand.

I'm sure you all have guessed by now
there can't be any other,
your very best friend, your closest pal,
to me she's just called "Mother".

Norma J. Reedy

In Dreamland

All night long
they dreamed of dancing galaxies
and sweet sounding nebulas

spinning out those threads of light
which form the web of life —

he whole of which we cut to pieces
every time we look at any part —

the whole of which our heart
puts back together

every time we stop looking
long enough to feel.

Lanier Graham

Heaven

They say there is no Heaven
They say there's no such place
But I know there is a Heaven
Because I see Heaven in your face.

They say there are no Angels
Celestial Beings from the skies
But I know there must be Angels
Because you're an Angel in my eyes.

With beauty unsurpassed
An Angel...Oh so fair
With sensuous passionate eyes
And Beautiful silken hair.

An Angel here on Earth
For all the world to see
An Angel here on earth
At least you're one to me.

They say there is no Heaven
But this cannot be true
Because I know I'm in Heaven
Whenever I'm with you.

Louis A. Recupero

Understanding My Mother's Pain

Why do men hit the women they love?
They say they're sorry and that it'll
never happen again.
Do they mean it?
Or is it just a game?
A game isn't always fun.
Sometimes you win.
Sometimes you lose.
Which one did you do?
Win or lose?
You think you won by hurting this
woman.
The one you said you loved.
Also by making her the victim of pain,
love, and heartache.
But you lost.
This strength did not come from her body.
Her strength came from fear.
By her fear you LOST the game.

Rayn Fenty

The Birds

O that we could be like the birds
They sing such sweet melody's
Without a care and worry free
A life of real freedom without fear
Not afraid of man or beast,
They are not threatened,
By manmade wars.
Or too much rain, quakes or snow
And other men who choose to harm.
To me, they seem to get along
But maybe that's not so,
I am guessing and hope it's true
For I am not a bird you see

Natalie Ramirez

I Love The Stars

I love the stars.
They twinkle everywhere.
I like the stars with me,
With a star I could go far.
Stars are happy!
Just with me,
The stars twinkle in the sky.
They twinkle everywhere.
I'm flying by a shooting star,
I like going by them every night.
I love the stars.

Rachel Eve Holmes

Your Friend

When you think of me,
think of your best friend
cause if you want me too or not,
I'll be here till the end.
I'll be here till the very end
And you know it's true
I'll be here to help you thru it,
When your sad or blue.
You will never understand,
how true I'd be to you,
But until you realize
I'll be here for you
Think of me, just for now
as your very best friend
Because I'm sure you know,
I'm at the very end.

Wendy Napier

No. 9

Living unmindful
thinking I was content
with my days
and nights
summers spent forgetting
time
not knowing
it was pulling me
to you
forcing me to meet
my soul
then rushing on
to leave me
in ecstasy
in hell
incomplete
in some way
wanting more
wanting none of it
wanting

Susan Humphrey

Muse

Hide and seek,
This damned, blessed seed
Hides deep away, so that
nothing will know...
Not even me.

I poke about to root it out
Nothing
(But grocery lists, laundry lists
And lists of firsts and lasts)

But, then, amidst
The longest list of things to do,
Ears hear, Eyes see
Sounds...Singing free!
It's me!

Wyndy Ellis

Heartache

Why do little children die?
This I'd like to know
They bring such joy into the world
Why do they have to go?

I know that God has called them ,
To join his angels fair.
To bring such joy and laughter
To his castle in the air.

But they bring so much happiness
To those who love them so,
Can't they stay a while longer?
Do they really have to go?

Oh Lord we miss their gentle touch,
We miss their childish cry.
Why do they have to leave us,
Dear God I ask you why?

Palma Bogo

Heavenly Messages

I'm sending a message to heaven
This is what it will say,
"Hello Lord, I've come to tell you,
About my young friend far away."

His language is obnoxious,
He swears most all day long.
It makes me cry to hear him,
And he knows that it is wrong.

Make him see his errors,
And the hurt he spreads today,
I know he can do much good,
Please give him a chance, I pray.

Forgive him one more time Lord,
Bless him with Your love.
Open his eyes to see the joy,
And wonders, from above.

Thank You Lord for listening
To my earnest plea,
To save my special young friend,
From shame and misery.

Maxine Graetz

Have Faith

She said to me, have faith in God.
This phrase helped me as a child.
I prayed when we didn't have food
nor shoes to wear to school. Some how
those prayers were answered

As I grew older and bore the taunts of
others because we were poor, She
said, have faith in mankind. I
found not all felt we were lesser
persons because of poverty. I kept
my faith in mankind.

As years went by she said to me,
have faith in yourself. Apply your
God given gifts and you will
succeed. The gifts of faith in God,
Mankind and yourself are all
you will ever need.

Violet E. Lumetta

Love Me No More

As I sit and think on
this warm spring day,
I wish one more time I
could hear you say,
You love me!
I know that there is something
I did, I wish you would tell me,
so that fault I can rid.
I have this feelings we're
friends no more,
this feeling I have
I, now, know is sure.
I loved you then,
I love you now,
the one lonely question
I ask is, "how?".
How could you love me
so much before,
then all of the sudden,
LOVE ME NO MORE!

Michelle L. Dean

Postcard From A Stranger

You have never seen me
Tho I've... watched you from afar
Afraid to come much closer
I'm different than you are

Side by side yet separate
You live upon your sphere
Imaginary lines you've drawn
You lock your doors in fear

You dream the dreams of
Freedom, peace, democracy
And yet I see no harmony
Just cruel hypocrisy

I'd like to come to see you
Although I don't know when
You won't see me for who I am
Just the color of my skin

I feel that I must tell you
I know that you'll agree
If you can not love each other
How can you love me

C. D. Champagne

No Control

Laying under my bed, I hear
those voices in my head.
rub your stomach, pat your hair
close your eyes and touch
your nose.
No more voices, now just faces
in the blackness of my closed eyes.
Leave me alone.

Libbie Adams

I Was A Sinner On The Run

I was a sinner on the run,
Thought I was having too much fun
To open my heart to let him in;
Thought it was fun living in sin.
Now I've seen the light,
I'm living my life right,
Loving life all the more,
Hear him knocking on your heart's door?
If you are looking for love,
Look toward the Lord above.
If you need Peace in your life today,
Then Jesus is the way.
Are you troubled, is your life blue?
Our Heavenly Father will comfort you.
So come, come pray with me,
The Lord will help you, you will see.
When you welcome him into your heart,
A whole new world will start.

Kimberly Ann Fabri

Traffic

The waves of heat from the city street
Throb up in the hot night's air.
Cars flow slow,
Like a lagging pulse
Or syrup o'er waffle's square.
The traffic vise makes tempers rise;
They honk, resenting the lines.
They feel self pity at life in the city
Stifled by close confines.
STOP, the red light orders a halt.
Then a flash of green and they GO.
The crawl gives way
To the race of the day,
As each one rushes for home.

Peggy G. Clarke

Adsum

My dearest child I reach to you
through days of passing time
and give to you my wisdom learned
upon these simple rhymes.

If I should ever pass away
before to watch you grow,
or miss the days to love you more
you must now always know
that even though we've never met,
I'll always love you so
my leather looking-glass is yours
with memories to bestow.
So hear me now upon the page
do not despair my loss,
we'll meet again you soon shall see
our destined paths shall cross.
I take to chance to speak to you
beyond the fated past
and reach upon the days anon
for time to prove no cast.

Scott A. Osborn

Trees

We struggle to live from year to year
thru the heat and thru the cold.
That we may be tall and graceful,
as our beauty you behold.
The dew drops touch our brow
The sun light lifts our heads;
Our leaves reach upward to the sun,
By God's nature we are fed.
The winds and rain produce our growth.
Our roots are firmly set.
We love the surge of growth we get
When our roots are wet.
We strive for years to reach our gaol.
With graceful pride we grow;
For your purpose we are planted here
And for our beauty to show.

Molly J. Sexton

Wishfulness

Counting the hours
'Till I can realize
The cost of my lifestyle
Emotional wise

I long for a woman
As has been so far
I like the interplay
But I don't like to spar

With infinite stubbornness
All wrapped up inside
I'd rather deal with
Careful thoughts spent with pride

Lacking a partner
Just like most
I'd rather do nothing
And sit like a post

Wrapped up in nothing with nothing to suit
I pray for her body and loving to boot

The cost of reality as least as it seems
Can only be measured in inhuman dreams

Mark F. Coulon

Time To Grow

The time to leave has come at last
Time for me to start my past
Time for me to let you know
That it is time to let go

For many years you have taught me well
I know letting go hurts like hell
But you have taught me right from wrong
And what I need to get along

The time to cut the strings is here
And in my heart I hold you dear
But I must find my own way
And make a past so I can say

Everything important to me
Was given the day you set me free.

Richard Albrecht

The Peaceable Earth

The Angels have come,
To admire our earth,
The Angels were happy,
And filled with mirth.

They admired the mountains,
and river and trees.

While in the background,
The animals romped in the breeze,
The Patriots and the Indians,
Were talking with ease,
About the beautiful land,
And the people needs.

The Angels content,
With the people and animals all
full of delight,
Decided to return to heaven that night,
And as they ascended, to the sky above,
The clouds seemed to be smiling,
While the breezes echoed love.

Maria Stryker

You And I

God made me, I.
To be as I
Until I die.
I must be me,
I cannot see
What else to be.
If I were you,
Perhaps I too
Would do, as you;
So you must be
That which you be,
And leave me, ME!

Robort Andre Dumas Sr.

I Don't Know Do You?

Sometimes it's good to be alone
To be by yourself unknown.
Not able to hear the cries
Or the horrible lies
To be alone in a far off place
To get out of the human race
Which is better alive or dead
These are questions we all dread
Why is the world so cruel.
It's almost like it's some stupid rule.
Are people really that blind
That they don't have time to be kind
If this is what the world is coming to
I really don't know what to do - do you?

Sarah Wrobel

Reflections...

Much too brief is our time to share,
To laugh,
to love,
to cry.
And yet the world
would not be the same
If one of us had never been.
To share this with loving friends
Is the most precious gift of all;
Memories.
To touch just one other heart
Is to feel it's all complete.

Karen Clark

"God's Flower Garden"

If God has a Heavenly garden
To care for - I wish could be
His partner and work the
Heavenly flowers.

I'd plant and tend them with
loving care - Those He gave
for the earth are so wonderful,
How beautiful Heavens flowers
must be.

Only God could create such
Beauty. The "Regal Lily"
and the "Rose", - and my care
for them is not a duty, but, a
task of Love I have chose.

The lovely "Lily of the Valley"
He chose His name sake to be,
and the fragrant "Rose of Sharon"
my God, my Jesus, my keeper is He.

Toni Irene Hanes

The Morning Walks

We roam the woods, my friends and I.
To check the fields and scan the sky.
A goat, a sheep, two dogs and I
Make up the entourage.

Only I have the gift of speech
Yet messages are felt by each
Sometimes I speak just to the air
To note the joy of being there.

Nancy J. Brousseau

Holy Spirit

I am a gift from our Lord God,
to cherish and believe.

I walk with you along your way,
and carry all your load.

As you go through life's long road,
step by step I say.

Remember to give thanks and praise,
to God this very day.

Phyllis B. Clausen

"Homerun"

It is a nice day
to go out to the park.
The crowd is cheering.
But for players it is
different when they
get on the field.
Especially for strong hitters.

They have the sand in
their face.
The grass at their feet.
As they step in the box
they think to themselves.
After they are done
they take a few swings.

The pitcher winds up releases.
But it is a strike.
Another is released.
Strike two is called.
A third pitch comes down the pipe.
He swings and it's going! going! gone!

Ray Sanchez

"Homesick"

To face the world unknown,
To leave what I call home.
Entering this world of darkness,
Leaves but one to rest.
I shudder in the cold,
My heart an empty hole,
The sun forever down
My smile now a frown.
Joyful may I seem,
Torn my soul will be.
Here I am a Beast,
At home I rest in Peace.

Melody Tolentino

A Poet

A poet is the one who knows the verse
To life's sweet song.
A poet knows the words in rhyme,
To what e'er life brings along.

Be it sorrow, be it sweet,
Words in passage are his way
To tell the world the hearts of many,
The words they cannot say.

Life to him is but a story,
One that he must tell.
The verses, the lines, the allegories,
He knows them all so well.

A poet does not ever die,
his rhythm will beat on.
For a poet is the one who knows
The verse to life's sweet song.

Susie Cox

A Slice Of Heaven

To lie beside you, snuggle close,
To listen to your voice;
To touch your skin so silky smooth,
To taste your lips so moist.

To brush my fingers through your hair,
To hold you in my arms;
To whisper gently in your ear,
To tell you of your charms.

To smell your sweetness, feel your glow,
To give my soft caress;
To live the moment, share the joy,
To give my tenderness.

To give you everything I am,
To give what I am made of;
To release unbridled passion -
The ecstasy of love.

To do these things gives life meaning,
And makes it all worthwhile;
For I then see a slice of heaven:
Your warm and loving smile.

P. F. Bowers

Mirror, Mirror On The Wall

As I look into this projectile of me,
This so called mirror — you see.
It's not the same as me.
There is someone trapped inside of me,
Trying to break free
Who? — you tell me.
Mirror, mirror on the wall,
who is the fairest them all?

Tanya R. Autin

The Cemetery

This place is portrayed as peaceful;
to look and mourn and talk,
But as I gaze upon the headstones,
it frightens me to walk.
Images of gone, lost lovers
still longing to be free;
horrid pictures flash through my mind,
that only I can see.
The ground is bare and unforgiving,
the air is cold and sour.
Lying there upon a grave,
is one forgotten flower.
I see the inscription of one know,
I want them back again.
They shouldn't be lying there all alone,
it shouldn't have been the end.
Leaves crumble beneath my feet,
they blend with the blackening sky.
I am standing here all alone,
no one should have to die.

Lauren Rickert

I Tender'd My Heart

I tender'd my heart
To my one love true,
And betroth'd my soul
To no one but you.

Be gentle, my Love,
And sew the lone seed
In deep fertile earth
Of thy breasted need.

Sun and moon and stars
Companion therein,
And sing ancient song
Wing'd on sweet wind.

Water with breathdew
That seedling love, Sweet;
Garden gently its life,
Give to it thy heat.

I tender'd my heart
And swam love's river
To emerge on shore
Of you, my lifegiver.

William R. Douglas

A Summer's Day

A boy, dog and fields
To run and hunt
A sky to see God
And wind from his hand
To cool a summer's day.

A young man, a dog and fields
To walk and think
Of summer days that change
When ways will part,
But friendship remain.

An old man, fields and memories
Of a dog and youth
Gifts from God
And wind from his hand
That blew away a summer's day.

Larry W. Knocke

Untitled

Just a quick note,
To say we're all well.
Ready for Christmas
and broke as all hell.
Bills pouring in
and things breaking down.
Hill's so damn slippery
And can't get to town.
I hate the weather,
I hate Christmas shopping;
Be glad when it's over;
Then I'll be dropping.

Kay Hofmeister

All My Children

I tiptoe, lest I should wake them,
To sit silently in their room.
Just to watch their baby faces
In the pale light from the moon.

It surrounds their heads in silver,
And makes highlights in their hair,
And they look so much like angels
That I kneel to say a prayer.

"Dear God, for all my children,
I ask thee one request:
Please teach their mother patience;
They deserve the very best."

God, they're so young and tender,
Like the first blade of grass in spring,
That it frightens me to remember
They look to me for everything.

"Now tonight, Lord, You see all my children,
Asleep, and how peaceful they seem.
So bless them, and also their mother,
And give all my children sweet dreams.

Rusty Tuck

Tearful Child

I need to fly away tonight
to something of a better kind.
I need to let the soul renew
the ways of leaving out the dew
of terror of a tearful child
to see the way of love revive.

Rest now upon the banks of life
but never ever be contrived
to feel the way the soul is wretched
is of the Father's gracefulness.
It never can reflect His soul
to see the love of hope be blown.

So help the restless of the child;
believe in souls of joining file
to be recovery of the pack
of lost and tortured children's lack.
Come now into the chosen throng
of Love to be of great control
of all that's making children torn
between the Light and love forlorn.

Norma Hobaugh

Desire

This Ghost desires to take its flight
To that fair land of pure delight
Where all is one eternal day
Where joy and love won't pass away

My Lord is there where I will go
The one to whom my praises go
He loved me much - He died for me
He came and set my spirit free

What great love for me he had
That he would choose to make me glad
And give me such a blessed home
Where I will never care to roam

It won't be long before I'll go
To be with him who loved me so
To share his love is pure delight
In that fair land where comes no night

So don't you grieve - this way I take
I do it all for his dear sake
For He who's done so much for me
Gives me this place eternally

Shirley V. Blackman

The Walk

Walk with me
to the place where she lies
under six feet of cold ground.

A lifeless body
placed here to rest
now and forever.

With eyes closed
against a world of hate
and heart stopped
against a hurried world.

A life ended
before it began
stopped short
by accident.

Please help me
and give me your strength
please walk with me
to my sister's grave.

Traci L. Lange

To

To do, to be
To think, to see
To run, to walk
To shout, to talk
To dream, to scheme
To write, to gleam
To sleep, to wake
To tremble, to quake
To jump, to play
To grow up, today
To laugh, to cry
To wonder why
To breathe, to eat
To play ball in the street
To stop and listen
To pet a kitten
To listen to idle chatter
To make every moment matter

Michael Jordan

On Living Today

Yesterday's pain is yesterday's
Today's pain is today's

Why do I want to have yesterday's today?
Can't I let yesterday go?

Tomorrow's pain is tomorrow's
It isn't yet
And I can't know the future

Why do I want to have tomorrow's
pain today?
Isn't today enough?

But then I'd have to give up worrying.
Do I have to give up everything?

Thomas C. Lembcke

"From Rocky Roads To Silken Sand"

We traveled rocky pathways
Together you and I
Until I took a one-way road
And left you asking why.

How could you understand my pain
The turmoil deep inside
When I had lost my will to live
And left my soul to die.

I knew that I must search and find
The fork which bore my name
And then to travel down that road
My own truth to proclaim.

Now when I find a crossroad
I reach for God's right hand
And trust that all my footsteps will
Sink into silken sand.

Ruth Schaefer

Life And Death

Today is today.
Tomorrow is tomorrow.
Death is a new beginning,
And life is never ending.

Life begins as a child
And death renews it.
Like a caterpillar becoming a
Butterfly and then changing
Its life and becoming something new.

A flower that has died
Then comes back in the spring.
This is a sign of a new beginning.

Your life is going to be
With you always.
Death will start it over
Again and renew it.

Mary Patricia Pendzimas

Just Like Me

People are not perfect
They often make mistakes
To judge them or condemn them
Is not our choice to make
But to accept them as they are
Without conditions for them to meet
Is not to make them perfect
But only human - JUST LIKE ME

Marilyn S. Corbin

Do Ya Wanna Play With Me?

I'm too old and
too tired
to play these
endless games.

There are no rules
except those
I impose
on myself.

There are no rules
except those
imposed by
everyone else.

When there is
nothing but rules,
there are
no rules.

Sage Norbury

Freedom

I wrestled to be free,
took off
to roam the wild,
pad the trails of
wilderness.
Aimless rapture,
following the sun,
warm and inviting.
Rolling in the meadow,
Stretching to the rhythm
of silence.
Purring to the freedom.
Sleeping to the peace.

Meg Downey Johnson

Geese, Marshes, And The Coming Of The Deer

Beyond the Palisades curving
towards Newark, the train slowed
down. Peering from the window I
saw a lonely forlorn goose, flapping
its wings frantically over marshes
littered with garbage, abandoned
factories, seeking safety.

Past the marshes, the train
moved south. Deer stared at us
as we rushed by. No one looked up.
We were prisoners of our newspapers.

Released from the train we
walked towards home, embracing
our separateness from nature and
each other.

Tom L. Torosian

Untitled

As I was driving along
Trying to write a song
Thinking of you
For you are so sweet
I had to stop and write
Every fifty feet.

Ronald W. Farris

Untitled

Before the first frost
turns the leaves all to brown,
before the cold wind
blows them all to the ground,

a gift of such beauty
unequaled in splendor
appears in the hillsides
for God's creatures to savor.

A palette of purple,
green, crimson and gold
unite with sienna
to make the hills glow.

'Tis a spirited canvas
we keep in our hearts
through the upcoming months
of wintry nights dark.

Each season begins
with its own unique call,
but none can compare to
the majesty of fall.

Sandra Dunn

Duality

Inside this single body
Two strong hearts compete.
Barbarian and poet,
Neither one complete.

From day to day they battle,
And struggle for control.
To be unchallenged captain
Of this vessel called my soul.

One day I bark with anger,
When the warrior's on the rise.
The next have only gentle words
And the poets anguished sighs.

Will there ever be a victor?
And a single nature be?
Or will the conflict ever roar,
In pained duality?

My lot I fear is not to know
Which one will rule the end.
But only seek to make a choice
And then that choice defend.

Michael E. Wills

Patience

Caterpillars' endless crawl,
up and down the old stone wall.

Wants to see the other side,
but wall's too coarse
wall's too wide.

If patience pays
and doesn't die,
caterpillars' change will fly.

And seek the flowers'
nectar sweet.
Wall is nothing,
wall's discreet.

Robert A. Sabatini

Untitled

All birds perch
Upon a feathered tree
But it is to the Church
That the pigeons flee
For there is not Love
On a feathered tree
Only a torn dove
Watching over thee
Though a set on the steeple
Is the bird of fate
Guiding the people
As if it were late

Robert E. Hole

Man

A man is but a grain of sand
upon this sea of life
Always shifting with the tide
of happiness or strife;
Tossing on the high waves
he moves from place to place
A tiny spot upon the land
a name without a face.
Swimming hard or drifting slowly
millions follow in his wake
And find contentment in
still-waters of the choice he makes.
Drifting, shifting grains of sand
A hope, a dream, a man.

Leona Welch

Wisdom In The Night

Wisdom is not kind
waiting and searching
a treasure hard to find

It's silent as the wind
a breeze so slight
trees daring to bend

A child's early cry
helping and healing
so meek; so shy.

Melissa Toomey

Wilted

Wilted is the flower
Waiting impatiently for the bee
To buzz up along
And pollinate me
Unafraid to caress
My threatening thorns
Willing to be my water, soul and sun
Fertilizing my soul
Bringing life to me once more
Oh, Blessed bee
Where once filthy
I've been cleansed with your honey
My nourished roots
Sprout their praises
Up from the soot
My petals have been dusted
Your wings have brushed
Across them all
Lifted for another season
To peacefully await the fall.

Robert L. Chambers

Haiku For Perry

In red autumn wind
Walking, you clutched my finger
Upward swirl of years.

Thomas B. Trethaway

Silent Flame

There are nights when I lie awake
wanting you with a burning desire
as I watch you in your gentle slumber
like a silent flame in a quiet fire

Sparks dancing in my eyes
wrestle the passion of my soul
I struggle to break free
this beast I cannot control

A thought of you consumes my mind
to ache, to arch, to smile,
to touch your lips, to feel your skin
the promise of a kiss, my beguile

But my longing passes
becoming the morning light
shadow and image
of a dream I had last night

You were standing on a hill
like a picture in a frame
I could see the wind blowing your hair
and I wondered, does she ever feel the
same

Kimberley Russo

Misery

Looking out barred windows
Watching people walk by,
Wishing I could be outside
Waiting to break down and cry.
Smoking cigarettes one after one,
looking into my past,
wanting to run,
I'm only sixteen,
and look where I am,
Trying to be seen
by all my friends
rotting in jail
is like being in Hell;
Nothing to look forward to
getting no mail,
Counting the days
to get out of this hell-hole
wondering if tomorrow will ever come.
I watch the clock as I sit here and rot,
Wishing I could be set free.

Meghan Noonan

"The Pilot"

At the campfire's edge he was
Watching sparks, like ice,
Fly into the dark, snowing air,

Where once, in clouds holding his sound,
He had been.

And with a hand through the snow,
He wrote beneath the sky
How his soul was burning,

Cold and high above,
Hot as the fire's deepest flame.

Larry Coe Prater

As Time Goes By

We come and we go,
We appear, we disappear,
We walk through our life on our way by.

We seem to pass each other by,
Like ships sailing,
You on your way, and me on mine.

You stop and say hi, on your way by.
And me, I watch as time goes by.

No time to cry,
No time to sigh,
Just time for hi,
On our way by.

We grow older each day, on our merry way.
Years come and they go, and we never slow.

Some day it all ends, as time goes by.
Time only for hi, you never really know why,
We never took the time to say more than hi.
Oh my!
Time for each other, time we never had.

Marcia Burns

Untitled

When we meet someone
we change
we bend a little
we give a little
we take a lot

And when that person leaves us
we feel we have lost everything
when if we'd only stop
and think
(which we so rarely do)

We'd realize that we had gained
so much from that person
and even though they are gone now
We can still smile over the memories.

Karen Dunn

Pain

We don't know why
We don't even understand
But always seem to cry
But seem to wear a shield
To help keep the face dry
Always seemed to be happy
Tried hard to hide the pain
The pain that comes at night
And the pain that comes in heavy rain
The pain in pictures that
Aren't really there
But seems so real that you knew
You were there
No I don't understand
The killing, the horror, the shame
That even today is destroying my brain
To Viet-nam we went
From Viet-nam we came
And try as we may to accept all
The shame and the pain

Keith Hall
United States Army 67-68

Couldn't Last

We were wed, back in fifty-four
We had our love, and nothing more
The looks friends cast,
Said this love couldn't last
We traveled the world, east and west
Still our love, passed the test
We've had times, good and bad
Sometimes fun and sometimes sad
Many who shared, the military life
Ended up, without a wife
And the look they oft times cast
Said our love couldn't last
Through the years, we've met the test
And our love, is still the best
And it's why, in June of ninety-four
Barefoot in the sand, we said our vows
once more
They said our love, was bound to end
We knew our love was true, even then
They said it couldn't last
Even now it's still a blast

Russell D. Gifford

Let us conserve our lives
we have only one to live.
Chase our dreams
when reality lets us down.
Look for Love
hoping not to get hurt.
Not stopping when you've been let down
but let time take its course.

Kimberly A. Montgomery

Friends

There comes a time
We have to part
It's a change of season
But not of heart

And as we go our
separate ways
Remember your friends
You'll meet again someday

The miles may be far
And the distance wide
But the memories we've
shared will make up
The gap inside

So remember my friend
As we part it's not
In the distance
It's in the heart.

Reida Butler

Love Of A Dove

We love
We see a dove
Of life and death
Put it to the test
You know the best
At loving
For the life of times
I think your so fine
At loving me

Lawrence Dail

"Our Baby"

Our baby went to heaven,
We never saw his face.
He never had a chance,
to become part of
the human race.
His soul has gone
to heaven,...
His shell has been
erased.
In our hearts we
know, it's God's
"amazing grace."
For we have three
beautiful children,
No one could ever
take their place.
And, we have a baby
in heaven,
someday we will see
his face.

Penny Greener

Untitled

Half of our life is spent waiting
We wait to be served
We wait for a light to change
Never really getting what we deserve
We might as well be locked in a cage
We wait for someone to call
We wait for the birth of our children
We thought we knew it all
Yet we know not more than a pilgrim
We wait for the rain to stop
We wait for the sun
We wait around with a soda pop
My God we must look dumb
We wait in infinite lines
We wait for our favorite song to play
What happened to the good times
What a price we have to pay
We sit and stare and wonder in gloom
I guess having a good life is rare
Some simply never see flowers bloom.

Stephanie Lynn Frenchik

Sweet Love

Oh love, sweet love
were desperate is used of

Each morning, day and night
we continue to fight

For that needed attention
no one seems to mention

Some hearts are surely crying
and love is slowly dying

Oh love, sweet love
we're desperate in need of

Give us another chance
that we may enhance

The life of mankind
before the end of time

Oh love, Oh love
we do...
Thank You ...

Tuwana Arscott

Untitled

Operation Desert Storm.
We're out here all alone.
There's no clouds in the sky.
Just the Sand and I.

We're a long long ways from home.
There's no one I can call, my own.
But the Lord up above.
And he's Mercy of Love

The Desert is Big and Wide.
There's no place, hear to hide,
But the Tanks we in.
And the trench beside.

We were call to Duty
To protect our country
To fight the enemies away
As we boarded the ships to sail, the other side.
Some look back and cried

Now that you own your way, home; and you not alone.
With tears in your eyes.
Your family by your side.

Sanajee Gaddis

Scarlett

Warm, soft
Wet nose
Muddy paws
Big, strong
Brown eyes
Gentle jaws
Playful, loyal
Long tail
Loves treats
Friendly, happy
Floppy ears
Big feet
Yellow, lab
Loves hugs
Doin' fine
Good dog
Scarlett is
All mine

Ryan Joseph Rahe

Best Friends

We've been best friends forever,
We've cried and laughed,
We've shared good ideas,
You've taught me things I would
have never learned.

You'd think we'd be friends forever,
Until that one day everything
came to an end,
You went your own direction
and I went mine.

I called you every day but your
mom said you were busy,
I wanted to save our friendship,
But I guess you didn't want it to last.

Now I'm sitting here wondering
"why",
Then I thought for a while more,
And began to cry.

Taira Jurgena

A Wish

I wish I were a poet —-
What a gift that would be!
To write in rhythmic words
The thoughts that come to me;
But though my mind cries for the beauty
Of flawless singing words,
I only pen the earthly ones —-
Not those my heart has heard.

Each hour, each day,
I hear the sounds
As I move on my way
Doing the common tasks
Each moment demands of me;
So, singing words lie silent
Except inside of me,
Where they hum a song each hour,
And help me to be me.

Mary Humphries Cavender

Christmas Is Here

Christmas is here,
What do we fear?
Of course nothing.
What will we bring to
Grandma's house on
Christmas Eve?
You know it is better to give
than to receive.

Christmas is finally here,
I have some gifts that
I would like to share.
I'll put them under our tree,
For all our guests to see.

Tomorrow I'll go sleighriding
down the snow covered hill.
It'll be nice and warm inside
me
And I won't even have a chill.

Mario A. De Franco

Empty Eyes

Look into my eyes.
What do you see?
The same emptiness that looks at me.
It doesn't matter how long you stare.
Look all you want.
You'll see nothing there.
Empty thoughts.
Famine schemes.
Enter the land of baron dreams.
The view is the same turned around.
Nothing beholds these eyes of brown.
Hollow air.
Shadows of doubt.
Even from the inside out.

Wendy Georgi

"Hope Concealed"

Winter flower
veiled crystal white

Endeared promise
envision the sun's harvest
and dance
with the wind.

Michael Caires

What Would I Do?

If I was a bird,
What kind would I be?
A flying bald eagle
Big, proud, and free.

If I was the sun,
What would I do?
I would shine on the people,
The animals, and you.

If I was a star,
What would I see?
I would see the whole world
Looking at me.

But I am a person.
What do I hear?
I hear kids with guns
Hurting others near.

If I was in charge,
What would I do?
I would stop the kids and guns;
They wouldn't hurt you.

Leah Bennett

Silence

Time after time I ponder,
what oh what shall I do.
Feelings of sorrow keep rising
and silence seems far.

I hope for a day of peace,
but trouble soon knocks.
Why can silence be here
for I long for it so much.

Tomorrow's are full of dreams
and life keeps racing by.
Maybe tonight silence will show
oh I wish it so.

Comforting are those moments
when I alone seem to exist.
Silence, Oh dear silence,
you have finally arrived.

Terri Ridgway

"The Little Things In Life"

Too often we don't realize
What we have until it's gone
Too often we wait too late to say
"I'm sorry, I was wrong"
Sometimes it seems we hurt the ones
We hold dearest in our hearts
And allow stupid things
To tear our lives apart
Far too many times we let
Unimportant things get in our minds
And by then it's usually too late
To see what made us blind
So be sure that you let the people know
How much they mean to you
Take the time to say the words
Before your time is through
Be sure you appreciate
Everything you've got
And be thankful for the little things
In life that mean a lot

Lyndsay Knepper

Fairyland

Last night I went to fairyland
When all the world was still;
I flew on sparkling rain drops
Away beyond the hill.

I sailed through golden moonbeams
And over the rainbow, too;
'Til I came to a misty somewhere
Where all your dreams come true.

And there were all the little friends
My mother told me of;
The air was full of music, too
Like a melody of love.

And when I sadly said "Farewell,"
With moonglow all around;
Like a gentle rain from heaven
On stardust, I drifted down.

But some night when the moon is full
And the stars are sparkling bright;
I hope I may go back again
To the friends I met last night.

Ruby Burke

From The Heart

Where ever you are?
When ever you there.
I want you to know!
I love you so.
I know you are burning!
But, I am hurting.
I just want to know?
Why this is so!
I can't explain,
About all the pain.
But, that is why!
We all cry.
I wish I could see,
What to believe.
This whole world!
Is as small as a squirrel.
Love and hate are so close together,
It reminds me of others!

Rolanda Atkinson

Do You Know What It Is Like

Do you know what it is like,
When in the deep, dark night,
You are staring at the ceiling.

Do you know what it is like,
When in the deep, dark night,
You can't stop the crying.

Do you know what it is like,
When in the deep, dark night,
You hate all the pain and suffering.

Do you know what it is like,
When in the deep, dark night,
You can't stop the heavy drinking.

Do you know what it is like,
When in the deep, dark night,
All you care about is dying.

Steve Hinish

I Wonder

I Wonder if she thinks of me
When it's quiet and she's alone.
I wonder if she remember my number
When she looks at the phone.

I wonder if she hurts inside
When they play our song.
I wonder if she yearns for me
When a couple strolls along.

I wonder if the memories
Keep her awake at night.
I wonder if she wishes
That we never had a fight.

I wonder and question
Until my wonder runs out.
But most of all I wonder
If she's wondering
What I'm wondering about.

Kurt Jarvis

How Do You Think I Feel?

How do you think I feel
When my Mother brings a
doll down from the attic and
says, "Here's my ni**** baby."

Or...

When an African American
family moves in across
the street, and the first
thing my grandfather says
is, "We have to move."

Well??????

Nicole Moro

"Faith Of Love"

Ones gifted with a heart and soul
When one finds a lover the heart unfolds
The souls will fly together
And become as one
Just like the love
That I have won
To both these things
That will not break
Just one more thing
And that is faith

Spencer Vincent Sapp

Cherish The Joy!

Let me go back to the times
When problems were so small.
When all we did was laugh and play
Til night would softly fall.

In to bed so safe and warm
Cause Mom and Dad were near
If dreams were ever troubled
They'd take away my fears.

Awakening to yet another day
Too young to be aware
That time is fleeting very fast
For I'm without a care!

If only we could just grow old
But staying young at heart,
Our life stories could be told
With no regrets til we depart..

Linda M. Collins

I Want To Die In The Spring

I want to die in the Spring, Lord,
When the lark is on the wing,
And the violets smile by the blue brook,
And the dews to the moss rose cling.
I want to die in the morning
With the first wild flush of dawn,
While the sunbeams kiss the green grass
'Til the sparkling dew is gone.
Oh, to lie down and to rest, Lord,
While life surges round rich and free;
To sleep, and to know that above me
A thrush sings his love song for me.
I do not want weeping or night, Lord,
Or to know that funeral bells ring;
But life and laughter and light, Lord,
Please, let me die in the Spring.

Luetta Cole

Seaweed Woman

She walks along the beach at twilight
when the sun turns the water
to butterscotch and fire.
Pausing, she picks up seaweed
strewn along the beach,
the ocean's lingerie.
Tucking it into her belt,
fashioning a seaweed skirt
braiding some into her hair.
Seeds clinging to the seaweed
shimmer like black beads.
Skipping and singing
she kicks the water, laughing.
Demented, most think.
She doesn't care.
She walks along the beach at twilight.

Susan V. Raftery

Definition Of Best Friend

We always have the best times
when we are together;
and that's the way it will always be
today until forever.

I hope you know girlfriend
I'm always here for you;
whenever you need someone to listen to
you know just what to do.

You always know that I'm thinking
or what I'm gonna say;
I think that's cuz we are different
but still the same in every way.

We'll always be best friends
no matter what may be;
We'll always be together
through all eternity.

So long as we are together
there is nothing we can't do,
because now I know the definition of best
friends;
girl, that's me and you.

Nikki Lenkowski

Butterfly, Don't Fly By

Dedicated to Nicholas

What makes a little boy sigh,
When you flutter by,
Without touching his hand,
Without pausing to land,
Butterfly, don't fly by.

What makes a little boy smile,
When you stay a while,
What makes a little boy dance,
Touching you by chance,
Butterfly, don't fly by.

Let the little boy see,
How you fly so gracefully,
Show him your colors,
More beautiful than others,
Butterfly, don't fly by.

Patricia Benson

Hopeful Dream

I had a dream the other night
Where black and white
Came into one
Calming the heat
Of the blood red sun

As shadows chased the day away
Blinking stars came out to play
And shone very bright
In that lonely dark night

A quiet moon rose
As the day came to a close
And in the midst of a dreadful plight
Gave away a comforting light

Sharran Holm

Ode To A Toad

Oh little toad,
Where is your abode?
We see so little of you.
We wonder what you do.
You just sit down there on the ground,
And never make a sound.
If we pick you up, you never make a fuss.
You just wet on us.
So, little toad,
Just hop on down the road.

Mary Esther Jackson

The Forest Of Secrets

Where nobody knows.
Where it never gets dark
and everything grows.
The Forest of Secrets
to others unknown
where storms never hit
and I'm never alone.
The Forest of Secrets
that beautiful land.
Where creatures all listen
and all understand.
The Forest of Secrets
where all that you hear
is the wind in the trees
and the prancing of deer.

Shannon Ochse

The Soldier Is Home

I passed the place
where mothers weep
And fathers spit out
angry words

What made you choose
between the two...
The one more strong
or the one you knew
could not have killed
the other?

And was it for some purpose
to have let him linger so?

But he was broken long ago...
fighting to keep from fighting.

Just bits and pieces of a see
through life that only a
blind man could see.

Miriam Lovito

Untitled

There, a picture frame inside a box
Where poetry abounds
Pondering what isn't there
Beauty will be found
Brightness dreams
Lightning clouds
Pandora's mysteries
Only when the painter seeks
Can visions then unbound

Rob Bolek

An Evening Walk

Come let's spend some time with nature
Where the lacy dogwoods grow,
Where the lofty pine trees whisper
Lullabies so soft and low.

Where violets waltz with buttercups
As night makes her debut grand,
And the silvery moon in splendor
Climbs the hill to view the land.

Moonlight on the placid water
Mirrors the quiet countryside,
As soft shadows slowly gather
Helping tiny creatures hide.

Then when twilight pulls her curtains -
Pins them with a twinkling star,
And the Whippoorwill is calling
To the barred owl from afar.

All the Earth knows peace at sunset,
There's a feeling of delight -
When the hush of tranquil silence
Bids a drowsy world good-night.

Maxine Campbell

Love Without A Looser

The trees blossom as the wind blows.
Walk against the wind as it snows.
The heart flutters beyond the mist.
As I sweetly blow a kiss
to the life beyond the trees
of winter, trees of spring,
like a bird without a wing.

Melissa Kyncy

Tranquility

I took the window seat
where the sun streamed in.
Holding my steaming mug of coffee
I watched morning come to life.

Snow had fallen during the night
and the lawn had not a blemish.
The bright sun made the white
seem almost blue.

Then, a lone Cardinal flew in
his bright red a contrast.
He located the food and
cautiously summoned his mate.

A rabbit ventured out timidly
making the first tracks in the snow.
The beauty, the wonder
of a quiet country morning!

Kathleen Rowe

Falling Shadows

The shadows are falling upon the land
Which once shone with the brilliance
of bright sunlight
They grow deeper and longer with each
passing moment
They usher out the day, and herald
the night.

The shadows are falling upon this life
Which once glowed with the fires to
fight off the night
They grow deeper and longer with each
passing moment
They usher out the flame, and herald
the flight.
And now the shadows have fallen.

Maureen Cummings

The Days Of Rain

In the dead of night
While dawn awaits
The horrid rain cloud
(I sadly state)
Came to its place
Amongst the sky
When morning came
The village cried
"Oh no, what should we do"
The rain poured down
For sixty days
On the very day
The rain stopped
Everybody went outside
And then it started to snow
And snow
And snow

Madeline Woods

Love

Love crept up inside of me
without the slightest notion

Cupid's arrow pierced my heart
with the sweet of the sweetest potion.

A whole life's transformation
occurred in the absence of emotion.

I live, I sleep, I eat, I drink
consumed by my devotion.

Regina Fields

Realization

Thundering storm crashing through
Whipping of the wind
Swirling gales fiercely strew
Won't to resist end.

Telling tales of willful woes
Crashing bolts of light
Thrashing life within the throes
Elucidate insight.

Warning clouds elicit fear
Dust should understand
Time of reckoning draws near
Repentance is at hand.

Recognizing souls obliging
Tempest to appease
Empathizing, realizing
Tumultuousness must cease.

'Tis so ordered grant thus
Forgiveness a decree
Yield to agape love a must
Captives to set free.

Lorraine Powell

Reflections

I look in the mirror,
who do I see?
Someone looks through these eyes,
the reflections not me!
The eyes are the color
mine's always been.
Yet, the hair has turned gray,
and there's loose, wrinkled skin.
Then I look closer.
Oh wait . . . I can see. . .
The person inside of this body is me!

The mirror has grown old,
its edges turned gray.
Now, I realize
I've become the same way.

Although time's changed the house,
it still holds a child.
So, remember it's yours
just for a while.

Toni Hafferty

The Guaranteed Love

There's a woman in my life,
Who I always overlook.
She is always there to help me,
With the problems that I took.

She'll never turn away,
And she'll never put me down.
She always makes me smile,
When I begin to frown.

I know I don't always show,
My love for her the way I should.
But no one can come between us,
Not even if they could.

I can't believe that,
This relationship I never saw.
She's always there for me,
To catch me when I fall.

She isn't a fighter,
She's only a lover.
She's the greatest lady of all,
Her name is ... my Mother.

Kevin Lee Kline

Man Of God

There was a man
Who I once knew.
His head was clear
His heart was true.

He was a man of God,
you see
He hardly ever noticed me.
He always had a gentle smile,
And a kind word for those
in trial
I really do miss him
you see
But he belonged to God
not to me.

Lynn Cauley

"Fate Of A Moth"

I saw a little insect
Who spun himself a home
It had no front or back
"For now," he was alone

In this house their was no
Door to let the daylight in
He could not see the sunrise
Or know when darkness did begin

Now he lived all by himself to
Face each day alone, he could
Not move from place to place
His fate was still unknown

Would he lose to man's desire
And never be a moth,
They instead would take his home
And turn it in to cloth

I could not leave this little
One, with me he had to stay
With much joy, I saw him hatch,
Then slowly fly away

Marion Guttmann

For The Caregiver

Caregiver,
Why can't you let her die?
There she lies—just skin and
bones.
Helpless. Speechless.
Covered with suppurating
bedsores.
You may say you are sustaining life.
Life? No!
Existence only—mere existence.
Not life!
Why must you rush her off to the
hospital,
Time after time,
The ambulance plunging through the
starless night,
Siren screaming, lights ablaze——
Just to hear once again,
"Well, she is stabilized for now"?
Why can't you let her die?

Naidene Stroud Trexler

My Love

My love went dreaming;
Why I cannot say.
It used to be his love was mine,
But it isn't mine today.

My love went gazing;
The daydreams still persist.
This world he cannot cope with
Right now does not exist.

My love went sleeping;
The best for him is over now.
Tomorrow is another day
To be endured somehow.

I lie trembling;
For I have ceased to be
As he crawls into his bottle
To spend eternity.

Shirley Dahn

Deception

He, the wed, removed his ring
With a devilish grin.
All the while his ignorant wife
Allowed him in again.

He, the sly and sinful man,
Hid well his guilt and shame.
Unsuspecting as she was
It was to him she came.

Too pure was she to see his lie
While from the house he crept.
After word spread 'round the town
'Twas on her bed she wept.

She asked when he got home that night,
"Have you betrayed your wife?"
Her eyes met his across the bar—
In vain her heart did writhe.

He packed his bags and left that night.
'Twas her he said he'd miss.
It was only after he was gone
She felt his goodbye kiss.

Karen L. Keith

It

It lives in my heart
with a room of its own,
It takes no part
just sits on its throne.
It moved in fast,
to take me as prey,
It's going to last
every single day.
It's partly yours
and partly mine,
It's just one floor
where we are combined.
"It" has a meaning
that is so true,
The meaning is love
that I feel for you.

Kristal Thompson

Feminism

Foolishly I try to cope
With all the highs and lows,
Mostly though I sit and mope,
This bloating to depose.

Moods go up and moods go down,
Headaches throb and stay.
Cramping belly comes around,
When will it go away!

This late date I'm over the hill,
For ancient puberty.
The culprits are hormonal pills,
It's a worst case history.

Replacing those hot flashes
With tender aching breast,
Water retention and rashes,
Puts "Midol" to be the test.

Doctor, doctor, I'd like to relate,
I really am a mess.
How ridiculous at sixty-eight,
To suffer from PMS !

Louise Harris

The Rose

I wish that I could be a rose
With an abundance of beauty to impose.
I'd bring a smile to every face
And never skip or miss a pace.

Only those with a sincere touch
Could do so without getting stuck.
My color would always be red
To remind me of the blood he shed.

I would represent truth and love
And serve only my father above.
He is the one who gave me breath
And in him only can I rest.

When my usefulness is through
And the red has turned to blue,
I'll just wither up and die
And bloom anew up in the sky.

Lana Burgess

Old Country Roads

I long to find an old country road
With an old house still a'standing,
A picket fence leaning,
A meadow larks keening,
Spreading oaks tall and commanding.

I long to find an old dirt road
One that has no paving,
I'll watch the dust drift,
As my wagon wheels lift,
And swirls high in the air go a'waving.

I long to walk down a shady lane
Dappled in speckles of light,
Trees bending to meet me,
Overhead as they greet me,
And birds sing softly in flight.

I long to find an old grassy pond
With willows and maples nearby,
Grown over with weeds,
Cattails and reeds,
'Tis a dream I dream with a sigh.

E. L. Norris

Fall Poem

Fall is setting in
with colors galore.
It's time to relax and
enjoy the weather more.

Go walking in the park,
and feel the cool air.
The breezes softly blowing,
sweet smell's lingering there.

Enjoy the scents of Autumn,
like smoke, that fills the air.
The autumn leaves are falling,
as winter draws near.

C. Sue McDonald

Flame Of Luv

The candle burns
with every kiss,
every hello,
and moments of bliss.

It flickers and shines
down on us,
every moment we share-
love or lust.

It never wavers or dies
for our love is strong.
When the lights are down
it guides us along.

The flame is our symbol
of love, faith, and devotion.
It dances and twinkles
with every love born emotion.

Sara Slaughter

Heart Of Purest Gold

When you travel through this life,
With hurt and pain to bear,
It's nice to know a friend like you,
My troubles I can share.
He gave to you a loving heart,
To reach and help their pain.
A tender heart for sympathy,
With words of hope to gain.
He gave to you the strongest heart,
To help them carry on.
The gift to help in special ways,
When everything goes wrong.
But, most of all he gave to you,
The Heart of Purest Gold.
A treasure few are blessed to have,
For he has you in his fold.
A special place awaits you,
For you've earned it here below.
God will say well done my child.
With your Heart of Purest Gold.

Mary Nichols

Life, As We Know It

Differences are what make us unique;
With the exception of race and creed.
We are all born with the same innocence;
We are all free of prior prejudice.

As we grow and change in life,
We become what society excepts.
We are born equal and grow separate;
And we reunite in death.

Staci Mellon

Time-Out

I take up pen to write this rhyme
With memories of a younger time

There was a day when words came easy
Poems were written so light and breezy

But now, Alas, I have grown old
My creativity has cooled to cold

Young dreams and thoughts now eludes
Replaced with ramblings and platitudes

Subject matter is lacking some
Waiting for the thoughts to come

The love and fun of words at play
Pump through these veins to this day

These words aren't written to annoy
They're just for fun and to enjoy

For all the deep thoughts you receive
This little ditty is your reprieve!

Sharon L. Terry

The Breaking Up

This has been a nice little country church
With memory untold.
I'm sure it could share with us,
Things more precious than gold.

It has weather many a storm.
It has been around a hundred years.
It rejoice when we rejoice.
And seen us shed many tears.

It's all pretty up now
Standing so proud and tall
Every job in it is important,
No matter how small.

It doesn't matter who do the job,
Just so it is well done.
And the most important thing of all,
That many soul has been won.

It is on the drinks of breaking up.
And hurting all the memory we share.
It don't mean much to some people,
But it does to us who care.

Nellie G. Weaver

Pensive at the Gallery

For all of you are artists:
With perception and with paint!
Well, I too am an artist:
Using words, but never "ain't!"
Each fruit looks so good to eat:
Yet, remains there in its seat!

Every tint and shade seems right:
Is a treat for eye delight!
Lovely blossoms look so swell:
Almost gives a perfumed smell!
As for that old red schoolhouse:
Can be sure it has a mouse!

Too much of a banquet here:
That my appetite can't clear!
Yet, I muse in front of frame:
No two paintings tell the same!
But can only pause a while:
Savor each! Perhaps a smile!

For who am I to judge such art?
Won't pretend it from the heart!

William Soboslay

"As The Lilies Bloom"

As the lilies bloom
With such grace,
They smell like perfume;
And put a smile on my face.
As the lilies bloom
With pedals soft and fair,
I see a groom
And his bride with lilies in her hair.
As the lilies bloom
In the moonlit night,
From my room;
I see a wonderful sight.
As the lilies bloom
As I fall a sleep,
I harken up above
And ask him to safely keep.

Tiffanny Johnson

Ode To Ruffian

Ruffian, Ruffian, Queen of hearts,
With you did many a foal depart.

Filly, Filly, silvery black,
You were mistress of the track.

Tears, tears, a bountiful stream,
Flow down cheeks, sorrows' seam.

Ruffian, Ruffian, fate's design,
You beat that colt to the finish line.

Robert D. O'Farrell

Untitled

Melt me,
With your eager heart
for I am cold,
As a block of ice.
You are the fire
which I need for survival
to help calm my fear,
and let go of my past.
Come to me with great
anxiety and passion.
You are strong,
An I am so weak,
with the help of your
burning fire,
I can be cremated!

Nicole DeLeo

Is It You?

Here I am O great September
Within your heart a kindled ember
While walking through the fields of dew
I stop to ponder, "Is it you?"
I came so far, from early spring
But cannot remember anything
Except for beauty kept so fair
With ne'r a blemish anywhere
And for many months I have been true
So I stop to ask, if it is you.
I keep your warmth inside my heart
Like paintings of exquisite art
Not hung inside elaborate halls
But in my heart of iron walls
And I never dreamt of what could be
But there you stand enchanting me
With love so bright and love so new
I'll love again if it be you.

Michael Keck

Quiet Wisdom

A gentle, knowing smile,
without a spoken word.
A face filled with serenity,
quiet wisdom need not be heard.

A strength that comes from caring,
A heart at peace with love.
Contented is the freest soul,
gentle eyes, patience, and love.

All these things you are quiet wisdom,
with all your strength, stand tall
and teach me always of your quiet ways
your unspoken word, says it all.

Susan L. Federici

This Day

Enjoy life
Without despair
Beauty of youth
Silvering hair

God's gifts
To man and beast
Instincts and love
Never the least

Enjoy the sunrise
Day unfold
Plans for future
Memories to hold

Kind thoughts
Deeds as well
Face toward heaven
Shadow hell

Along with faith
In God and man
Enjoy life
How short the span

Paul R. Reithmayer

One Chance

I cannot take going thru life,
without her by my side.
I cannot take the quietness,
of my children voices dear.

I cannot take the loneliness,
that is felt so very deep.
Oh how I miss my family so.

If only I had one chance,
to see if it could work.
We'd laugh and play and share,
the way things ought to be.

Than it wouldn't be so hard,
to cope with life so cruel.
To see if a family we could be,
"Once forever again"

Mark Borovicka

Weekends At Your Place

Roxy music, candles burning
Zinfandel, two cats purring

You and I end up laughing
Tangled in sheets
On the floor
Totally satisfied

Leo D. Tinkham Jr.

Fears Of Mankind

We fear happiness
Without knowing happiness
We can never be sad

We fear love
Without love
Our hearts can never be broken

We fear success
Without success
There is no failure

We fear people
Without people
There is no loneliness

We fear difference
Without difference
There is no racism

We fear life
For without life
There is no Death

Preston Powell III

The Light

I stand in the spotlight of darkness,
Wondering how to get out.
I hope for the light to reach me
But it is so far away
So far, but I can see,
The tiny speck of light
Coming further towards me.
Finally after what seems like years
It seems to be within reach.
I stand, just looking at it
Imagining the happiness it could bring.
I start to reach out and touch it,
But I can not move.
I am bound with invisible chains
That hold me in the darkness
I scream and fight to break free,
But my chains refuse to budge.
And I am left to only look at the light
That I know will never touch me.

Pia Davies

The Poet

I fell in love with a poet

He was the fusion of
words and flesh
ideas and reality
philosophy and actuality

His poetry
(the words on paper
the rise and fall
of a human voice)
seduced sweat between my legs

He swayed with words,
love sonnets, and tight Levi jeans
he was a word, an idea, a philosophy
one could make love to

He knew how to make love to poetry
he knew how to make love
to a woman

I fell in love with poet

Mary J. Collins

I Love You

I love you so much
Words can never say
I wish I could express
How love grows stronger each day
You're my whole life
Never to change
I'll always love you forever
Forever and Always
What started as Friendship
Seems to have faded away
Something much more deeper
Has come and decided to stay
My lover my Friend
I'll forever be true
Cause your my whole life
I'll always Love You

Vicki Bjork

Poetry

What is this, this Poetry?
Words with life, to be sure;
And beyond life, they endure.

Just say what you feel,
without fear;
If your rhyme is pleasing,
You'll find others near.

Ah, but there's more,
Much more than we know;
And who knows,
Where next we may go?

Or those good people,
That now in words exist;
Are with you always.

The pen is a knife,
And the ink my blood;
My soul it bleeds forth,
Into the flood.

And the paper, it waits...

Mark A. Glenn

Mamma

Our mom helped us to grow up,
Working her fingers to the bone,
And I wore hand-me-down clothes
That my sisters had out grown.
Kids laughed behind my back,
But I really didn't care
It was always hard back then
And we all had to learn to share.
It might have been easier,
If my parents had one or two,
But when you have twelve,
There's always work to do.
Dad worked from dawn to dusk,
Just to make ends meet,
Even though we were poor,
We always had plenty to eat.
So when I think I'm "High and Mighty"
My memories flow to back then,
Of all the Hardship my parents went through
And where my life all began.

Marie Sherrill

Teen Years

The twentieth century is the
worst time to be a teen,
everybody judges them on the
way they look and that's mean.

Every teen's hormones go crazy,
and they become extremely lazy.

They become very mature,
girls before boys but that's
nature.

The girls become self-
conscious of their weight, the
guys wonder if they'll mate.

Being a teen in this day and age,
is like reading a book and
turning a page.

This is the worst time to be a
teen but it's also an easy
time to be one,
it's the peak of your life so
try to have some fun.

Laura Lapointe

A Father's Love

To never know a father's love
would be to never feel
or know a happiness like no other.
He gave his strength without question
never judged or compared.
Strong yet gentle were his hands,
softly spoken for all occasion.
His convictions did him justice
and taught us well,
to stand and speak no matter what.
These attributions were his alone,
for in no other
have they been found...............

LuAnn Herron

A Year To Live

First I would pray, then I
would cry, oh God please
don't pass me by

I knew it was coming but
not this fast, I can not
delay my time has passed
I was born to do this
little task

To live and live well for as
long as it last, don't forget
there is no class

First I would pray, then I
would say, lay me down
in my bed of rose's, I know
longer need one who a poses

For my time has past and
alas, It is time for me to
do my little task

Shirley Clark

Empty Hands?

If I could see the beginning to the end,
Would I see ways that I would mend?
Or would I accept the battles won,
And not regret the work undone?

In my beginning day of life,
Would I see joy, or only strife?
Would my days of fun-filled youth,
Be offset by age-old search for truth?

And what about the middle years,
This mixture of fun and tears?
Would this time be better spent,
In ways our Master meant?

Would words be said, or deeds be done,
That benefited everyone?
So when comes the end of life's demands,
That I not be caught with empty hands.

Raymond P. Lee Jr.

Life's Legend

Life is a legend
written in sand,
That all for the moment
can understand.
Until the inevitable tide
rolls in from the sea
And the beach is smooth
where your tale should be.

Pearl Thomas Clay

Untitled

We are of the same breath
You and I—
Two souls meshed into one
A faithful unity, unsurpassed
Enhanced only by the whimsical
Spirit of tomorrow

Sweet dreams of twilight's caress
Succumb to the rude awakenings
Of the precocious dawn
But tightly we grasp the tranquil
Slumber
And to the muse of hope, we cry
"Hold On."

Seduced no more by yesterday's folly
We no longer fear the obscure
Shadows of today
We are comforted with the blessing
Of our oneness
And it is for these reasons
We are called 'Friend'

Shalayne Petitt Cupo

Sleepwalker

A thousand nights
you've blown into my dreams
like a hot wind
slipping under the window sill,
stripping away my fears,
and overthrowing
my petty fantasies
to sit alone
on the throne
of my imagination.

Michael Psinakis

The Season Of Summer

I have always liked summer best
you can eat fresh tomatoes
from dad's garden
and cucumbers
and squash
the smell of fresh flowers
that are growing in mom's
flower beds
the smell of saltwater
in the air
the sound of the waves
crashing on the seashore
the feeling of sand between
your toes
walking around barefoot
trying to avoid finding
or seeing any snakes
and at night falling fast
asleep to dream about what
tomorrow will bring.

Teresa Perry

Love

I do not know why
you do not love me.

For I love you with
all my heart.

Is it shyness, or do
you not know your feelings?

I know mine, I will
love you forever and I
will be forever waiting for
your love.

You will never be alone
for I will be near you
in my heart.
Because I love you.

Rebecca Rainville

No Longer Matters

Falsely,
you give me that look again
and I know defeat
once more.

You have cried to me
of despair
like some wild
primal scream.

Yet when I
cry out
it is unfair, uncanny
how poorly you respond.

We travel the same territory,
we'll end up in the same grave,
and yet
at that very moment,
with that look,
you are as strange and distant
as the unthinkable.

Murri Banis

Deadly Party

You went to a party,
you had a drink.
You knew it was wrong,
didn't you think?
you partied all night,
you smoked a joint.
Were you acting cool?
What was your point?
These things are
dangerous,
Don't you care?
or do you
actually think
you have a life to spare?

Molly McClain

Importance Of Life

Life's unfair
You live it your best
But who really cares
Until were one less

A friend for years
Gone in one day
Importance of life
Who's to say

A smile and a grin
She always had
She knew the good
She knew the bad

With a heart of gold
She always gave
Her importance to life
Who's to say

We miss you right now
The sorrow, the pain
We'll all live through it
But your memory will remain

Robin Loewen

My Prayer

I say this prayer with thankful heart
You made me who I am
I came to you a broken part
Of who I should have been

A sorrowed soul with trouble sought
Lack of wholeness in my heart
I knew not then my need for you
My ways I need apart

The way for we was long and hard
For strong I was not one
You saw my need for strength and path
You sent a Christian on

She did her job and did it well
I thank you for my friend
For without her I may still be
a lost broken Christian heart

Kathy Lee Davanzo

Love

You measure distance
You measure time
You measure liquids
Which are all just fine

One thing you can't measure
Stands above the rest
Wider and deeper
Is love at its best

Sees through our mistakes
Knows your heart's right
Stands by us always
Each day and each night

Real love is endless
Yes, faithful and true
The power that it has
Is bigger than you

Lester A. Carr

Memories

I was there for you, I knew you needed a friend, who would be there till the end. I was there to share the pain, through the sunshine and through the rain. Though things stepped out in my way you were there, you made everything okay!

We have been through so much together the fun times we've laughed through the sad times you've held me close to you. I would like to bring it back, but you seem so far away. So far from me I guess these are just memories attached to my mind and they will fade away with time. My heart will heal. I'll let it go because you see, it's just a memory.

Tina DeVaney

Baby Face

Your eyes meet mine with their hazy hue,
You seem to know how much I love you.
That toothless grin, brightens my day,
You show your love in such special ways.
Each gurgle, each coo,
Says I love you too.
You grab hold of my finger,
How I wish I could linger.
These moments are fleeting,
There's just no repeating.
I sit here quietly and embrace,
The look of your little baby face.

Kathleen Lane

If Love Was An Ocean

If love was an ocean
You would be my only boat.
Sailing along like a little float.
You think no one is there,
as you sit and cry,
but I'll be there forever
till the day that I die.
When I'm gone and have passed away
I'll still remember you everyday.

Latia Lee

Medford Woods

Old man
You sit there eyes staring
What do you see?
What do you think?
Are you remembering
as the sun slowing sinks
the days of your youth?
She tapped him on the shoulder
it was time to go.
He turned and said
Hi lady who are you?
I am the girl of your youth
You were so handsome and strong
You took my hand
and we have walked
hand in hand over fifty years
His eyes brightened came alive
for one delicious moment
as he muttered Medford Woods.
Ah, you are the lad of my youth!

Winifred J. Munroe

"Stranger In My Dreams"

It took no effort to love you,
You were sitting there,
The sun and sea doing dances on
Your face making you more
Beautiful with every leap and swirl,
A shady palm leaning over offering
A gentle kiss to a strong,
Pondering profile and then flying away.
My fingers knew you.
I knew how you would smell...
Because I'd touched you so
Many times in my dreams.

Renee Beecham

"Lips That Scream Magic"

As you take a look, a really long look
You wish for just a taste.
Maybe a touch or to feel
What do you suppose they think?
How do they react to their magic?

I'm sitting here alone, Alone with my thoughts.
I think about them constantly.
MAGIC, Pure magic.

I feel blood rushing through them
They whisper names, words,
And as I watch extra close
They call me, want me.

But if only I could reach them,
Come to them
Maybe, just maybe they'll want
To feel me, touch me.
TASTE. LET ME TASTE.

Naomi P. Petersen

In Search Of...

"I wandered lonely as a cloud"
Across the darkened plains
Listening to the sounds of the night
Whistling winds, cluttering trains.

If only I were on that train
Alert as an owl in the night
My paranoid; yet lonely soul
Could awaken and take off in flight.

Escaping to a wealthier land
Where harvests freely grow
A place where trees and flowers bloom
Is where I'd like to go

Weeping willows cover me
In actions and in thoughts
Darkened shadows frighten me
My stomach tied in knots.

I can not see my present surroundings.
They are vivid in my mind.
Beautiful colors I once could see
Have disappeared. I am blind.

Tracy Ladurantaye

Life

In life there's a job to be done.
An adventure to be completed.
At the end of your time you will know if you have passed.

For there are many different ways of completing your adventure, you just won't realize it until the time is right.

I don't know my adventure yet, but I know when the time is right it will come to me.

In other words life is precious, don't waste it.

Shallan Fraser

My Family (Way Down Deep Inside)

My family means a lot to me
An anchor to keep me strong
Giving me the strength I need
When everything goes wrong

Showing me how to give and take
And when to slow it down
Knowing the needs of others
Not fussing about my own

Sharing our times of happiness
Or an important family day
Being true to one another
Working to make our way

So know that every one of them
Has a special place with me
I respect and love them dearly
They are my family

Ethel Gregory

Day Dreaming...

There I was at the beach, eating a big old fat juicy peach.
What a great thrill, to see everything was standing still.
It was roughly twelve thirty, and nothing was dirty.
As I spread out the towel, it quickly faded away my scowl.
My feet were sore and tired from all the play, so I buried them in the sand.
They felt as if I had danced all day, with an awesome band.
I could feel the scorching sun, toasting me like I were a hot dog bun.
As I laid there, in a quiet stare,
I could hear off in the distance the sounds of a choo-choo train,
and birds in the sky calling for rain.
The water had no motion then suddenly there was a lot of commotion.
There was a gang of people trying to teach someone tall,
how to play a certain game with a beach ball.
Someone came over and shook me, the surprise took me.
When I came to, it was my foreman telling me to look,
lunch break was over and snatched my book.

Debora L. Hopkins

At Peace In The Sea

They found his body face down in the sea.
What a terrible shock his death is for me.
The newspaper described him as homeless and alone,
but I hear the sadness as his beach-buddies moan.
My job was to help him become substance free.
Oh dear God, was death the only way it could be?
The police say his death was not caused by harm.
The missing food stamps and money give his daughter alarm.
Then I learned that he seizured and shivered in a daze.
Three times the E R released him to Kapaa Town's tangled maze.
I am angry, my friend, you drank, stole and lied.
In anguish, I wonder, is there more I could have tried?

Evelyn Bradberg

Choose Life

Your having a baby, a new little life
What a wonderful glorious thing
And oh what joy and happiness
that new little someone will bring
As the years go by, the choice you made
will make your heart real glad
For you could have chose to end this life
And that would be so sad
For then you'd never watch him grow
You'd never watch him play
And the emptiness you'd feel inside
Would grow worst each passing day
For in your life would be a ghost
of a baby never born
A sad little figure in your mind
As you woke up each morn
Thank God you chose the way you did
For the choice you made that day
Will fill your life with wonder and love
Because you chose that way.

Charlotte A. Martin

Untitled

I think of you and me constantly.
What I would do if I was with you
but there was never you and me
and never will be
You have your heart set someone else
So I just stand back and watch you from a distance
because I can't get too close.
My heart could not take it
Knowing..........
That I could not have you!

John E. Castillo

Butterflies

Look! Oh! Look at those pretty things.
What are they you may say.
Are they birds or planes with beautiful wings?
No! They're butterflies you see today.

Where have they been all winter long?
The mystery we must learn.
They were all tied up in their cocoons
Until the seasons saw fit to turn.

Just think what you would do,
And how happy you would be,
When the long winter was over
And the spring time you would see.

Oh! If I could fly like the butterfly,
I'd go from rose to rose.
I'd be so proud of my colorful wings,
Only goodness knows!

I don't know your favorite
But all have beauty in spite.
These creatures look so fine,
Especially while in flight.

Arthur A. Roller

My Beauty Ran

Laugh, love, laugh, is all we could do,
What caused me to change, to try and hurt you;
With life so short, and time so dear,
Why wouldn't I want you, to be so near;
Fast, fast, fast, the problems would occur,
What made me think, that you'd want to endure;
With actions so bad, and me always the fool,
I know why now, you reacted so cruel;
Pushed to the limit until you screamed,
What does one think while being so mean;
When a friend goes bad, and you learn how to hate,
Always remember us, and please learn to wait;
While hope was eternal, and babe it was great,
But too bad, I couldn't have patience to wait;
With the past behind us, and the future unclear,
You moved yourself eastward so I wouldn't be near;
So to my dear loving friend, who had to go,
I felt a special need, to let you know;
All of my time with you, was the best on earth,
You're not around anymore, and that's the ultimate hurt.

Frank Werhofnik

Untitled

The night is quiet, the night is mysterious
What mysteries does it bring?
All the shadows... All the sounds
What do they do?
They scare some, Others wonder,
But me,
I'm not scared... I don't wonder...
I am a child of the night
The sounds and the shadows call to me
They want me to join in
The games...
The games of the night
Are they fun?
You chase after shadows
The sounds chase after you
You try to remain quiet
But you will be found
You may not be able to find "them"
But who is "them"
"Them" they are the other children of the night

Hilary Lloyd

The Garden Of Life

What type of garden have you grown?
What seeds in your lifetime have you sown?
Are there weeds of sorrow and regret?
Kind deeds still unrooted yet?

Does love bloom where you have passed?
Happiness or sadness in the seeds you've cast?
Have you sown laughter instead of tears?
Helped erase another's fears?

Did you plant wisdom and knowledge of life
Among the rocks of turmoil and strife?
Is your garden full of joy and contentment
instead of anger and resentment?

Do your seeds lie shallow to be blown away?
Or planted deep where they will stay?
Have you been an example for others to follow?
So they can be an example for tomorrow.

These are questions we all should ask
As we go about our daily tasks.
For every person's life is known
By the type of seeds they have sown.

Betty Allen

Plastic Hands

Plastic hands holding time on the quartz clock on the wall
What time is it? Look at the clock.
Plastic ridged sides
Fall off the wall when you close the door
Falling time
Where does time go after it stops,
Or does it stop?
Ever or never
Maybe time doesn't exist in other galaxies
Or does time just runs on machinery that sits on the wall?
Clock hands moving forward forever
Will they ever move backward?
Ridged sides, ridged time
Time falling through millennia of evolution.
Falling, falling, falling
Never ending time.

David Nakamura Hulton

"Our Boy"

Our boy was so loving, he was so much fun,
when I came home he would come at a run.
His fur was soft and shiny black,
we miss him so much, we want him back.

It's hard to explain how strong was our love,
he was so very special, a gift from above.
Our boy was so friendly our neighbors would say,
"Give him to us if you give him away!"

God will watch over him, he brought us such joy;
How could God not love our little boy?
If God loves the innocent, the meek and the mild,
there is simply no way God won't love our child.

A heaven for animals? My God has one.
Our boy will be waiting when our time is done.
There are many who say, "He was only a cat!"
But what do they know, he was much more than that.

We miss you so much, Maverick our boy,
It is hard to imagine where we'll find such joy.
Goodbye, Mr. Maverick, come back if you can,
We both love you, our little man.

Daniel T. Darmody

April Tears

The days turned into months, sometimes I think of you at my side
When I know you are only in my heart

Sweet Hawaiian melodies illicit smiles
Most hear the tenderness in the movement of the voices
For me they are a memory that turns a quiet moment
Into saccharine sadness of...April tears

Places you have been hold the essence of your being
Your space was so vast, no hills or valleys are excluded
The love you shared brings comfort
But when will the memories bring joy
...Instead of April tears

Day transforms to evening too slowly when I miss you
And a simple ring on the phone or passing car
Makes me forget for a second that it cannot be you
And I run to hide...Those April tears

Reality is you are gone to your mansion in the mist
Where we shall meet someday
I long for your comfort and warmth
And know you share, even on sunny days
...My April tears.

Donna-Maria Fasone McLaughlin

One Existence

When you walk, when you smile,
When I look into your eyes,
I crave the intensity of your life,
Don't touch me, you need not to,
Don't talk I hear your words,
I feel your breathe before you breathe
I feel your pain before your hurt
Smile and I will smile with you
Cry and I will die quietly inside
Lay next to me and let me feel the warmth
Of your body, hold me close
And let me feel the strength of your soul
Let me feel your body inside of mine.
Let us be one existence on the same search
If only for a moment
Then I will slowly walk away
Walk away, but I will always remember.

Annette Pangle

Grandpa

One of my most fondest memories took place
when I was a lad.
I would go to the country to visit grandpa,
with mom and dad.
While grandma was in the backyard canning pickles,
grandpa was on the front porch giving me and
my sisters nickels.
I remember him in the field behind his
horse and plow.
Meanwhile I was in the pasture chasing the cow.
It is painful to remember the day he died.
I sat alone in my room and cried.
He was so good at quoting the scriptures and moses.
Oh Lord I thought.
What is tuberculosis?

Don Thomas

Snow

So beautiful on the ground.
When snow falls so peacefully to the ground.
So cold it stays all winter.
Sparkling white just like shining diamonds.

Emmylou Stiffler

"Our Mirror Within"

There seems to be a mystery somehow,
When my reflection looks back at me.

Knowing there's a part of that reflection,
That doesn't know what or where it wants to be.

To wake up each morning feeling unfulfilled,
Unsure and searching for — what!

Looking and searching for the answer within,
If I could do that, then I would fear not.

All our secret ghosts that dwell in us all,
Seem to surface from time to time.

Allowing us to look deep within ourselves,
To ask, is there any mountain I can't climb.

We're only human and will sometimes doubt,
But that's what life and needing to feel special is about.

Joann Patrick

Dark Silence

There is a dark silence between midnight and dawn,
when night rests at last in gentle repose.

Warm breaths of tranquility flow over my being,
like feathery blankets fend off the cold.

In stillness of solitude the mind is alert,
aware of submission to disquieting themes.

Guilt, pain, rejection, hurt light up the black,
those celluloid sequences with no continuity.

Silence breaks fast with deafening thumps of heart,
as siren screams of adrenaline rush to set free.

A trembling mass of humanity lies still in dark silence,
and night rests at last in gentle repose.

Ann Lenore Oppegard

A Friend

A friend is someone who's there,
when no one else cares.
Someone to make you laugh,
when you want to cry.
Someone to make you happy
when you feel sad and blue.
Always there to lend a helping hand
make's you proud to have such a special friend.
Someone to talk to you about your problems
that always understand,
because their your friend.

Jon Hasenbuhler

Jim

Dedicated to Jim Hood

There once was a young man I knew,
when people met him their friendship grew,
So when these people all drew near,
He was one never to show any fear;
As I watched his love for her grow,
It was the one thing he would always show,
Saying she was a gift from heaven above,
Sent to him on the wings of love;
I've known him to work hard,
while he enjoyed living in her yard,
But for all those people he left here,
will always share in the sorrow with a silent tear;
But what happened that day,
To take him away,
when people will think of him,
And so will I always missing Jim...

Earl Lambert

Springtime

I love the springtime of the year
When the crocus peeps above the sod,
The trees are budding, the grass is greening
That's why I know there is a God.

The birds are singing their own little song
Butterflies are flitting from flower to flower,
Spring has come to the earth again
To me this is its finest hour.

Brooks are bubbling up over their banks
Little animals are running free,
The mountains show their lofty heights
And the valleys are fertile as they can be.

When God shall plant us in the earth
As He sad "So shall it be"
We will arise to a new life in Him
And have springtime throughout eternity.

Ada I. Dunn

No One Home

Late night fright let's scare mom and dad tonight
When they come in... We'll jump out with a big loud boo.

Late night fright no one should be home tonight
"Just to be safe I'll hold my gun...hon(ey)"

Cold steel, shiny and bright pointing the way
Into a supposedly empty house.
"The kids are at a friends...
No one should be at home," the wife says.

Noise in the closet
Too muffled to tell it's only giggles.
The cocking sound of the gun
The reluctant feel of a cold stiff hammer.

The click... click sound
Says "This is it... this is it."
Poignant silence then a startling "Boo"
Then an even more startling "Boom."

357 hollow point into the tender neck
The last words for a destroyed man
From a daughter soon dead
"I love you dad"... she said.

Bill Cathey

Rooms

Eyes upon eyes, and I asked, "You're with whom?"
When you appeared in yesterday's room.
To ease my bitter soul, you came
Fading staunch resolves; removing pain.
A glowing within became desire
As you stirred cold ashes to rekindle my fire.

To save me today's burden or gloom
All should you do is come 'cross my room.
Ask of my being, it will speak only your name.
Ceaseless I wonder, "Feel you the same?"
May pleasure between quicken to dance
As passion to recognize repeats in romance.

When dispossessed of all worldly needs
And sweetest memories wind-cast as if seeds
To root in bleak hearts, not many, a chosen few,
Will remember this love when God comes for me and you.
Clasp of my hand, step gently in tune,
As we move, my love, toward tomorrow's room.

Aileen Crawford

Love Song

I love thee with a steadfast heart that iambic beats
When you draw near; I love thee as a soul long dead
And given life and wings by love found new;
My wild heart now flames afire with passion not foretold
By any inward mind of years gone by;
I love thee as the mountain peak on which I stand
And survey a world below — where once I dwelt alone;
I love thee as the husbandman of my heart's secret garden,
Now fragrant with lilies and roses and sweet herbs
You have planted.

Beloved, I cannot tell thee all — I cannot number stars;
But should you wonder more, your answer find
In every look and touch of eye and hand,
And in the silent song my heart sings free —
I do but love thee.

Esther B. Swensen

"Teachers Are The Best Bargain"

When you go to a doctor you never question the price,
When you go to a merchant you buy what is nice.
You buy a new car and the investment is great,
But you make each payment, sure you're not late.
When you go to a lawyer, you pay the fee,
For legal advice is expensive, you see.
You go to a banker, a loan to make,
The interest you pay you know will be great.
When you take your car to the mechanic's shop
You pay what he asks 'cause the price doesn't drop.
It's the same for the butchers and the same for the bakers,
You even pay what is asked to the undertaker.
Who do you think taught these people to be
Intelligent people helping you and me?
It was the teachers they've had along the way,
And if you would ask they'd be quick to say.
So, why do you skimp when it comes to education,
Teachers are the best bargain in this wonderful nation.

Joseph A. Davis

John, I'll Always Wonder!

I wonder what you thought of,
When you laid your head down that night.
What was the final Breaking point?
When you knew the end was near
Was it, thinking of a family never known before?
I always knew you were one of us
although, this I didn't share.
Still I can't help but wonder, if
You knew that I cared!
Or maybe the sad fact no one
tells you they love you until it's too late.
Maybe it was the feeling that our hope
Just can't be saved
I'll never know your last thought as
You slept away.
For you can't tell me; from the grave.

Deborah Lynn Dunlap

"1995"

1995, a royal year to be,
Where love and compassion are very clear to see,
There is so much harmony all around,
There is oneness and friendship to be found,
Where families unite and come closer together,
Where they understand and trust,
Even cherish one another,
May success an prosperity fill us all,
God bless, and much happiness as the new year falls.

Julie Valentine

Listen To The Wind

As the years pass by and we go our own way,
When you listen to the wind
You'll hear it say:
"You still own her heart
You're in her thoughts often.
She wonders if you, too, still remember when...
When smiles made your cheeks hurt,
Stars danced in your eyes,
When lyrics to songs
Could make you both cry."
Along with the wind she's sent you a kiss.
It's just a small piece of
the love you both miss.
So the next time the wind blows,
listen with your heart .
And know as she knows,
Your souls will not part.

Cindy Lamontagne

Untitled

What will you be
when you're away from me.
Who will you become.
What will be your sum.
Where will you turn.
From what teacher will you learn.
When you're away from me.
Who will guide your mind.
What treasures will you find.
What magic will you weave.
What notions to conceive.
When you're away from me.

I think about my three little beings at home. Growing rapidly. Breathing each day - a newness, a freshness, a change. They bring it into their lungs and exhale what does nothing for them. Which is very little. Each task adds to them in some way. With all this change in their tiny selves, I can't help but wonder what they will be like when they grow up. Where will the now take them in the years to come. Who will they be when they're away from me.

Beverly Ryan

The Box

A child's play during long of day
where clovers grow and butterflies flitter.
Girls and boys romp. Without the traffic
noise, glass and litter. Their toys are
simple yet sophisticated. For of this world
they are emancipated and they flourish
freckle and dimple.

They play in a box all their own.
Without prejudice, hatred or wrath;
their world is theirs without clocks
without cares and their toys are the
stairs to the heavens.

Oh to be a child. In my own little box,
free from violence, scorn and pox.
To reshape the world, unlock stoic minds
and leave lack of love to the leaven.

John E. DeGennaro

The Greatest Hug Of All

Sometimes I feel so alone, I'd love a great BIG HUG.
Where do you find it?, OH! Where is LOVE?
I feel small as a sparrow, a bird of low degree;
My life seems of little value, But I know JESUS cares for me.
Some say they love me and always will, so often it seems they have forgotten, but GOD loves me still.
True happiness is not to one person confined, all is found in a contented mind.
"Laugh and all laugh with you, cry, and you cry alone",
This life is a path of sorrow and you walk down that path alone.
Hopefully the future will lead to another time and place where sadness and loneliness is unknown,
I can't reach this blest abode without thorns and thistles in the road.
"WHAT A FRIEND I HAVE IN JESUS, ALL MY SINS AND GRIEFS TO BEAR":
I'm so thankful for that FRIEND, as those on earth seldom care.
I need hugs and understanding; My soul has love and compassion to spare.
When it comes the hour to rest, I pray my last days will be the best.
JESUS will wrap his loving arms around me and whisper in my ear,
"No more despair, for you the child of GOD are now in MY eternal care".

Janice H. Adams

Rose Garden....

Through the mystical mist of confusion and fear,
Where lost are those loved ones in my heart I hold dear.
Where wander the souls of my relatives dead,
To the garden of eden where my spirit has led.
Over mountains of gold and bountiful meadows,
Where mocking birds sing in beautiful crescendos.
Through flourishing forests and fields of white snow,
My true heart has led me where all of us go.
The flowers of spring and the warmness of summer,
Have brought forth a legacy of autumn and winter.
Through the beauty of nature and the welcome of life,
I have strode across deserts and the worst of all strife.
I have come through the darkness and survived easily,
I have lived through depression and war peacefully.
And now I have reached the victory of good,
And have witnessed the rise of my old brotherhood.
So I have reached my destiny and this story now closes,
I can rest peacefully in my garden of roses.

James E. Moore

Our Prodigal Son

Home is where I want to be,
Where no one here can hurt me.

From the outside he brings pain,
Sometimes it's hard to just be sane.

Nobody can tell you just how it is,
When he throws away love that could be his.

It isn't right how he tears apart,
Maybe it's just his own broken heart.

There must be hope deep down inside,
Maybe someday that hope won't hide.

I wish he'd choose his way to go,
So our lives aren't swaying to and fro.

I just want to be free of pain,
It's not too much to want to be sane.

So home is where I shall stay,
Even when others choose to runaway.

Courtney Franke

Let's Be Neighbors In Heaven

Let's be neighbors, neighbors in heaven,
Where the streets are pav'd with gold,
Where we'll never hear the comment,
"My friend, you're growing so old."
Let's be neighbors, neighbors in heaven.
We will leave our burdens here
All we'll bring along is good friends
And lov'd ones near and dear.

Let's be neighbors, neighbors in heaven
We'll live in mansion bright,
Where we'll pay no monthly mortgage,
Or taxes way out of sight.
Let's be neighbors, neighbors in heaven
Soon we'll reach our home above,
Where we'll ever be so grateful
That God is truly love.

George V. Davis

"Destiny"

He said, "I'm going home" to his mother, who was sitting near.
"Where there are no doors or windows, just plenty of fresh air".
He said, "Here is my soul, my greatest love to thee".
This was my brother's humble prayer and God answered his plea.

His needs had all been fulfilled, God answered every prayer.
Here are the gifts He gave my brother, for you and I to share.

A long life would be denied him, Strength would be given instead.
For this gift would be needed, in all his life ahead.

Happiness was my brother's wish, but this he would not find.
Instead God gave him Courage, in his search for peace of mind.

Good health was not in the asking, this God would not fulfill.
But with thought and understanding, the last great gift was Will.

Now his journey started, and these gifts would be his key.
For the road that lay ahead, to life's Destiny.

His strength would make him stronger, for he would suffer heartbreak and pain.
But for this he would be remembered, IN HEAVEN'S HALL OF FAME.

With courage he would not cry out, nor would he beg or plead.
For those of us to help him - in his greatest hour of need.

With will he kept on going - for the road's end he now did see -
His journey now is over, my brother has reached his Destiny.

Dorothy C. Pearson

Untitled

We've come to our crossroads in life
Where you must go left, and I go right
We've shared a part of our journey together
Holding hands through all kinds of weather
But now we have to go in different directions
And can no longer hold on to each other for protection
Even though it hurts to say goodbye
We need to let go, so the other can fly
We've both helped each other in some way
By the obstacles we've gotten through each day
The tears are falling as I come to this part
Because I'm losing a piece of my heart
I wish you love and happiness along your road
Goodbye my love, we no longer have hold.

Carolyn A. Priest

Tomorrow

Uncertain is tomorrow.
Whether joy, grief or sorrow
No one can say.
But ponder not along life's way.

To one who says, "Tomorrow I'll do this!"
Surely he will miss
What is in life for him.
For he came through the past in a skim.

One should learn that tomorrow never comes.
He will, when he adds up his sums
of bills and finds the "tomorrow"
is the cause of sorrow.

Return homeward with a smile
Walk again that happy mile.
For me, I would be alone
Returning, tomorrow, coming home.

Tomorrow lies just beyond the curtain
Just beyond tonight.
But who is so certain
That tomorrow will bring the light?

John W. Perry

I'll Try Again Tomorrow

So many days were filled with sun
Which danced inside my veins.
My very soul was warmed with hope
And dreams that never came.
The years of promise I'd held fast
If only they'd been mine.
I waited for the wonderful
But all that moved was time.
My eyes have dimmed, there bloodshot now
The tears spilled out in sorrow.
The love I had, had not been mine
The time I spent was borrowed.
My heart cries out, the rain pours down
Somehow that soothes the pain.
Tomorrow will be better
And I know I'll try again.

Deona Wootton Grover

Tears Of Light

Sometimes rainbows are made of tears.
which have filled the horizons of our lives.
Like prisms, in the heart they reflect
all the colors of bygone days.
In nature's way, the clouds precede a fragile glory,
a renewed hope, a promise to be kept.
Mindful of this, consider well-
that even tho' you lift your face to the sun
and move so eagerly towards joy and serenity,
you should not close your eyes to all storms of living,
you should not shut your ears to all sounds of discord.
To truly know the value of each day's beginning
and its end,
to fully taste the precious essence of all moments
in between,
your soul must also be touched by
the winds of change and conflict,
the rains of grief.
In fleeing from all that's darkness
you will miss so much that's light.

Barbara H. Lyon

Rain

Listening to the raindrops fall to the ground
while thoughts of you make my heart start to pound
drip by drip I near falling rain
Or is it my tears from all the pain?
As I think of unforgettable times with you
I often wonder if you think of them too
Tears run down from the sides of my eyes
Wishing I didn't have to tell our love goodbye
All of a sudden the rain slows down
As I think of you with a frown
Hoping that one day again you would be mine
And wishing the world weren't so unkind
Just as you the rain fades away
As I live to see another sunny day.

Athena Maika

My Princess

My princess is like the murmur of a soft wind
Whispering a tranquil song that soothes and thrills
My heart and enriches my soul.
Like the fast roll of the drums, my heart's aflutter
When I feel her tender touch. Like the keenest camera
shutter, my eyes capture and hold each segment of her
loveliness. Her eyes are open window to her soul,
Whereby I perceive and understand the very depths of
her being. Like the fleeting pace of the cheetah, I
race to be beside her, there to cherish and behold
her beauty, grace and charm.
This wonderful princess of mine!

Erwin Cox

Two Slightly Used Hearts

Two slightly used hearts
Who claim their life is torn apart

They are really good friends
They don't see what's around the bend

They were meant for each other all along
They don't see their love is getting strong

They can't imagine being together
They've been just friends forever

They didn't know they were destined for each other
Not until they became lovers

They see it's changed their whole life
One day soon he's gonna ask her to be his wife

Now they'll be together until the end
And they said they were just gonna be friends

Heather Moulder

Last Soldier

Memorial Day, all hail to the red, white, and blue
Who did the unknown soldier belong to
Someone's husband, or someone's son
Surely someone's beloved one
Here he lies at his final rest
Proof to the world he met his last test
The honor guard keep the watch, and do their drill
For the one who is a symbol for every man who's blood did spill
Man will always find a reason for war, and with each new battle,
the cries of the dead become a deafening roar
When the last war is done there will be no one
Only the monument will stand barren and alone,
and then we will all be soldiers unknown.

Doris A. Rieth

Borrowed Soul

A borrowed soul
Who for a moment I believe is mine,
Bursts forth purple,
Alive,
Dripping Life.
Silence; eerie in a moment of
Crushing oxygen...
He tries to stare with webbed
And misted eyes.
Can they still see God
Waving goodbye?
A cry hits the walls of a fresh new world
Singing
The only song of joy it knows.
My heart reaches to Heaven and
Sings
The pure melody of love;
Thanking the angels
Who now return to
Heaven.

Heather Rogers

Who Is This Lord

I have a Lord whose hand is always on my life
Who is this Lord? It's Jesus Christ.
He is my friend, He is my love, a soul so pure as a baby dove.
When I'm low and feeling down, I know my Lord is around.
Even when I feel alone, I know that I'm not far from home.
I know my Lord will never leave, despite my failures I will succeed.
Because of the blood that he has shed, my life has changed, there is no death.
He is my life, His love is so true — so perfect, so beautiful and gentle too, yet you still don't listen to what I say,
There is a Lord He's here today.
So even though you refuse to accept,
The grace and love of his Holiness.
I will pray that you will find, His love, His joy, His peace of mind.
But until that time, please know this, He loves you,
He'll protect you, He's never amiss.
So even while you run away He'll wait patiently for that glorious day.
That day in time when you will shout
I have a Lord whose hand is always on my life — who is this Lord?
He's the One and Only Savior, Jesus Christ.

Genevieve T. Lambiase

Grandma And The Parakeet

Once there was a Grandma.
Who lived in this old house.
She didn't have anyone to stay with her
Except a cat, a dog, and a mouse.
The cat named Mopsy,
The dog named Flopsy,
The mouse named Popsy,
Could not get along in this old house.
They fought and fought until Grandma thought
I cannot live with these three.
So she went to the pet shop and what'd she bring back?
A beautiful, bright parakeet.
Grandma through out the cat, through out the dog,
And through out the mouse.
Now they do not live in this old house.
The parakeet whom lives in a golden cage,
Sings in harmony all day.
He does not fight: He does not fuss
Now Mamaw lives happily with her parakeet, Russ.

Jo Graham

Today A Baby

A tiny little bundle lying in his bassinet;
Who never asks a thing of you unless he's
hungry, cold, or wet.

A slippery little creature to hold on to in his tub;
Now sweet and clean and dripping wet,
remember — pat — don't rub.

You oil him up and oil him down, but still
he has a squeak!
So give it up and kiss him once and kiss
him twice upon his cheek.

With fingers, oh, so delicate,
you hardly can believe
They safely made the journey once again
to open end of sleeve.

Now warm and dressed and at his best —
you see, he really smiled.
He is today a baby — will tomorrow be a
child!

Jean E. Lombardo

The Mistress Of Time

She is not a crone
Who plucks at the threads of Life
To ravel them, make them unlovely,
But rather she is a gentle woman
Who draws each strand
Smoothly from the Cloth of Years,
Holding up each gleaming filament
That Love might color it.
She polishes and softens our every hour
'Til it be fitting raiment
Woven for a spirit traveling the long journey
From Eternity to Eternity.
Truly a gentle Woman of Great Skill.

Elizabeth A. Collins

To Travis

To the little fellow who we love so much
Who writes the nicest letters so we can keep in touch.
To the little fellow with the bright, warm smile.
How I wish that we meet if only for a while.

On an airplane you flew many miles away
Just to be with grandma on her 80th birthday.
To the little fellow who was standing there
Whose face I thought I knew, but I could only stare.

To the little fellow who was first to speak
Then coming towards me, gently kissed me on my cheek.
To the little fellow who would swim each day
And underneath the water like fishes he would play.

To the little fellow who just turned seven
We send ALL our good wishes as high as the heaven.
To the little fellow who I miss each day.
In seven years, my dear, you have come a long, long way.

And now it is time to wish you well
And may your birthday be the best you've ever known
And maybe some day you will tell
About this day to me.

Janet L. Ryman

Those Incredible Tears

They are not prejudice, they don't care from
whom they fall.
They show up, without any warning at all.
They really don't care if the occasions is
happy or sad.
They are comfortable weather things are
going good are bad.
They don't discriminate because of race,
color or creed.
They just show up when ever they
feel the need.
Even the strongest person sometimes can't
keep them away,
They come to visit someone each and
everyday.
They never speak a word, yet they seem to
say so much.
They just fade away at the slightest
little touch.
How can something so small, mean so much?

Barbara N. Singleton

Two Halves Equal One

Who me? Yes You!
(Whomever? Or from wherever?)
(Who are we? You and me?)
If I should ask you, or you should ask me, is that you?
Our reply would be the same, yes it is me!
Then if we are both me, and we are both you,
Therefore we are both one instead of two!
If this is so, I would like to know,
Where did (other half? Or which half? Of) everyone go?
Whoever or from wherever we may be?
Half of all of us are you,
Other half of all of us, are me!!

Harvey H. Gimble

Remembrance Day

To my poor sweet darling wife,
whose Spirit is fiery faerie flight,
ensconced unknowingly in body's blight
still ever avows her freedom's might,
and works thereforto, unstintingly bright,
enjoying all blessed to be brought in her sight,
encouraged in Her to undo all loose spite
and embrace this God's world,
lovingly, light,
thus pleasing the one Lord,
her heart's own delight,
to which end I joyously
love my sweet wife.

Alan Dennis McDonald

Unrevealed Appearance

The day of truth will soon darken our souls,
When the day comes, for nobody knows.

My anticipation grows for the cry of the lonely one.
The heat from my reflection is not through, but it is done.

There's only one thing I ask, only one request.
Not to be deceived, but to be put to the test.

The irresistible urge to be shown the way,
Is not here or there, but for where you lay.

The tremors beyond the dark, must finish but not start.
So look outside of my soul and into my heart.

Brian Everingim

As People - We've All Got

We've all got a family we love somewhere,
Who've shown us what it means to care,

Parents everywhere sing the same song,
Stand up! Be counted! And be strong!

What's in a color
I'd really like to know?
Nothing different between you and me,
Then why can't the whole wide world see?
We all eat and drink to stay alive!
Have hopes and dreams and feeling inside!
Bodies that function to keep us all going!
Scholars and others to keep us all knowing!
We work hard to live every-day
Struggling through life in our own unique way!
Then some-day with pride
I hope we all can say -
There is
Nothing! Nothing!
Nothing to any one color!

Brenda T. Blassingame

Why Me, Lord?

How many women have you heard say,
"Why Me, Lord".
There are thousands who say that every day.

The first reaction to hearing breast cancer
Is shock, numbness and then the tears.
And a fleeting thought of how many years.
"Why Me, Lord"?

After the surgery, then comes the treatment.
Chemo, radiation or even both.
Whatever prescribed, we come to loath.
"Why Me, Lord"?

The treatments are over, what a relief!
We can have our life back again.
To go forward, be brave, be thankful and win,
And not be afraid to say "Why Not Me, Lord".

Twenty four years have come and gone
Since that day I distinctly remember;
The doctors saying that day in July
Breast cancer, treatments until September.
And me saying "Why Me, Lord"?

Agnes Victoria Taff

The Edge

Why?
Why when walking on the edge of life and death,
Why does everything good and kind you do
Seem to push you towards death?

Why?
Why when walking on the edge of life and death
Why does everything mean and cruel you do for people
Seem to push you towards life?

Why?
Why when about to fall completely into death,
Why is it then that someone is calling out to help you?
And why is it then that you suddenly realized it's too late.
And quietly slip into the blackness of death?

Brandi Bowdoin

The Magic Of The Unicorn

Somewhere in your dreams, there's a magical land; where the wildflowers grow under a lavender moon.
Somewhere in a magical forest, by a crystal clear waterfall, stands a Unicorn with a mane as white as freshly fallen snow; it has a golden horn that shines as bright as an early morning sunrise.
A place of peace, a place of love, a place of magic... The magic of the Unicorn; the magic only shows in your dreams if you believe. Believe in the magic, and dream those restful, peaceful, loving dreams; and perhaps one day your dreams will come true for you!
And the magic of the Unicorn will shine on through you.

Jennifer Broyles

HIV Lamentation

A cure one day, I hope, I pray
Will come for the one,
the one with AIDS
Silent stalker and time unite
Unite to pose a most difficult fight
A kind of its own, out to destroy
A people so proud, and remove their joy
HIV, how can one be, immune from the sorrow,
the sorrow of thee?

Let us mourn and let us cry
For it's the least we can do to say goodbye
Goodnight dear friend, good sleep to you
When you awaken, your body will be anew
Gone will be the days of disease and fear
I again await to hold you near
But for now all I can do is shed my tears

John Richard Farrington

Wait

When destiny arrives, will the expectation be worth the wait.
Will harvesting forbidden thoughts enhance the process.
Can I taunt the darkness to be my mate,
to walk the edge until it is shone.
Manipulated and suppressed through life's segments.
Conceivably one can be secretly blanketed with angelic perceptions.
And wait.
Summons destiny, I am the judge, jury and the verdict.
Liberate the troubled soul inside of me, to cast into the blackened night with no direction.
Banish the confusion which I dread, dismiss the logic that does not apply.
Find guilty the past, there is no teaching of this destiny.
How must I interpret the soul for it is an illusion not to question, only to be relinquished.
I cannot substantiate our brief encounters.
I must not judge, only anticipate the arrival.
And wait.

Janis P. Thogmartin

The Staircase

I pick myself up, up off the ground
where my life has thrown me, tumbling down
the long narrow stairs
that lead to the beginning of all that is there;
And try as I may, I cannot stand,
for there is a hand pushing me down,
down to the ground; falling, I cry out,
but my cries go unheard and I just wait here
until the time comes for me to begin
the narrow steep climb up to the end;
to the end of this hell, and into heaven.

Jennifer Kunz

Untitled

The sweet smell of the Flowers
Will lure you with there Powers
And you will wonder of the Beauty they hold
While the light shines down in showers

The sound of dragonflies
Flying and Buzzing around the trees
They will put you in a trance
And make you feel like flying in a breeze

Then you see a dear so sweet
Oh, what an amazing treat
And when you look at it you Feel innocents
As it glides away with a quiet beat

You hear and see the forest
It brings innocents and peace
And day by Day the old things go
But the new things take there place

Andrew Page

What Of Man?

Is good bad or is bad good?
Will man ever act the way he knows he should?
Will he look past his desire and his greed,
And lend a helping hand to all the people in need?
Will he control his fury, be it strong or mild,
And never ever again, strike a woman or child?
Will he stay humble in his power and success,
Without stepping all over others while trying to progress?
Will he stop dumping in the oceans and polluting the sky?
And realize that life is something you just cannot buy?
Will he stop treating the youth as an enemy or foe,
And accept them as they are and help them to grow?
Will he open his mind and search for more,
Instead of using every conflict as reason for war?
Will he swallow his pride and open his heart,
And give people a chance right from the start?
Will he work for the future and learn from the past,
So that our next few years on earth won't be our last.
So I ask, "Is Good Bad or Bad Good?
Can man ever act the way he knows he should?

Eric Simonyan

World Understanding

The world doesn't look too good right now.
Will this world's future be good for you and me,
And for all those people fighting to be free?

War doesn't solve anything.
It starts with two people and keeps growing.
Soon the whole world is hating, fighting and creating misery.
BAD SITUATION!

War, being mean spirited, starvation, poverty, inequality,
Differences not accepted,
What can cure this?

Manners have always been important and should be a way of life.
People should try to talk together and work for understanding.
We should do more caring things with our day,
And work to put misunderstandings out of the way.

I don't want wars anymore, anywhere!
They don't solve anything and make a mess for people,
Whether they have more or less.

I'd like to predict, that there will be
A world without conflict,
—YIPPEE!

Jannah Piasetsky

Day By Day

Day by day, we say we may participate in something great
Will we wait? It's not too late!

Day by day, we say we may complete the course that will be the source
To open the doors, we could not before

Day by day, we say we may go overseas on a special tour
Go away, leave this place, but never stop the winning race
We only need a change of pace

Day by day, we say we may earn enough to not need more
And even give to the poor

Day by day, we say we may succeed in life without the strife
And even live a better life
Faith and work go hand in hand
And with God's help we know we can

Procrastination will not pave the way
It's up to you to start today
Day by day, is the only way

Ernest Owens Sykes

Don't Quit

When things go wrong, as they sometimes
Will, when the road you're trudging seems
All up hill, when the funds are low and
The debts are high, and you want to smile,
But you have to sigh, when care is pressing
You down a bit, resist if you must, but don't
You quit. Life is weird with its twists and
Turns, as everyone of us sometimes
Learns. And many a failure turns about
When he might have won had he stuck it
Out. Don't give up though the pace seems
Slow, you may succeed with another blow
Success is failure turned inside out, the
Silver tint of the clouds of doubt.
You never can tell how close you are it
May be near when it seems so far
So stick to the fight when you're hardest
Hit.
It's when things are worst that you must
Not quit.

Gordon D. Richie

August

That summer, the woodchucks came.
Wilted hopes beneath the (invulnerable) fence.
The scraggly garden full of
ravaged fruits:
Those tomatoes, reborn in a tear soaked spring.

Looking closely, so not to die
(One needs to *see* the wound to heal)

Each ripening fruit held the perfectly formed marks of
teeth
The dizzy beauty
the wave at the ocean knocking the breath
The rush of humility
Being fed, without knowing
Mother bear swiping her cub, then offering the breast.

Tiny and green glinted the unexpected pumpkin
in the back of the field
Like a sigh, escaping the humble gardener
Wondering,
hurting,
knowing there is life.

Beth Warner

Pass Through The Storm With Me

Feel each drop of rain, listen to the
wind, feel it blow your hair about. Notice
how it mixed with rain makes you close
your eyes. Feel how the cold goes
through you. See the puddles become
larger and larger. Listen, how you curse the
storm in your mind, each drop of rain
seems to rush you along.

The muddy soil orders you to
move with caution. Finally you reach your
destination, wet, cold and a bit perturbed.
Listen to the rain now mixed with snow
beat like hundreds of tiny little drums
on the windows. See how the wind knocks
things about. It will continue all night
and then finally die. So now, think
how you passed through the storm
with me. Feel each drop of rain,
listen to the wind...

Angelo Secreto

Passage

People pass through time,
Wishing for that special love.
Rare is it all works out,
And together two become one.

I searched for that magical kiss,
And through chance and circumstance
Our two lives crossed paths,
Offering me unending happiness.

For now and ever I offer to be by your side,
Your shoulder to lean on,
A friend to share your joy,
I do this with no regret,
Knowing I will always love you.

Gregory W. Thomas

Hopeless Dreams

Lying on the grass, feeling so sad
wishing he was still the responsibility
of Mom and Dad

Dreaming of a home of even a shed
He'd be happy with a stove, a sink, and a
bed

Smile after smile and tear after tear
he realizes he's been homeless for
nearly a year

He loses hope of a house or a bed
A raindrop or tear just dropped from his
head

He smiles on the outside, but on the
inside it's a lie
He yells "leave me alone!" as he breaks
down and cries

Julie A. Rudolph

Nature's Way

I sit by the sparkling blue lake at dusk
where the fluffy moss tickles my bare feet.
And the sun setting over the horizon is so breathtaking,
for the complexion of the sky can stir the mind.
Such an attractive view aids me to discover,
the beauty of nature that can be found all around us.

Jennifer A. Kolin

Navigator

Fighting the high sea I finally made it
With a ship containing many flaws.
My navigator provided me with what I needed.
I give to him much applause.
I put up my sail and started to pray,
While waiting for the wind to carry me away.
During the years I struggled, many were by my side,
They were braving the seas as I was
But without navigation, they all died.
But I have a different story, a story that is true.
My navigator was there for me, and will be there for you.
Many embark on their journey all alone
While others never even seem to leave home.
A few watch me from the shore
Wondering if I can endure much more.
I wonder why they haven't tried
But without a navigator, they have already died.
As I end my great journey,
I hope many others have luck in the sea.
For I had a special God, which guided me.

Chad Thomas Brazzeal

Maybe Tomorrow

In the springtime there's an awakening
with all its hopes and dreams
and many things to do.
You hear the call to join the march
to change the course of life.
Come now! come now, they call, well
Maybe tomorrow.
Basking in the summer's sun you have it all,
there isn't time to heed the call of hunger,
Three Mile Island, abortion, apartheid.
Of course you care, but
Maybe tomorrow.
Restful autumn, you've earned the right
to sit back and enjoy it now.
You hear the cry, our country needs a change,
get involved in politics, not yet
Maybe tomorrow.
Bleak, cold winter approaches
like a ghostly apparition echoing cries
from the past, too late, too late.

June Carol Roberts

"A New Picture"

I am painting a new picture
with beautiful bright colors.
Yellows like the sun,
to warm even the coldest of hearts
Greens like wide open meadows,
to free any soul.
I will use only my brightest colors.
My blues will be, but only in my sky's.
My rainbows, they'll show off only my happiest shades.
I will use my colors in every direction,
without missing even one corner.
I will keep my eyes open,
as I look for even the slightest mistakes.
I will keep my shapes to no minimum
as I study each line carefully.
This picture will have many colors,
shining far as eyes can see.
For the last one was dark, with limited shapes.
The last one was the old me.

Christina Petrone

Storm Of Sorrow

As the rain fell I thought of you
With each raindrop I repeated your name

As the fog drifted by I thought I saw your shadow
But it was only the shadow of a tree

As the lightening struck I repeated your name
But soon
the rain ended
the lightening phased
and the sound of your name
washed away with the rain

Diane O'Mara

The Runner

The runner postures at the start
with eager limbs and pounding heart
Too long restrained, he aches to flee
uncertain of his destiny

Then, like a shot, he charges free
with confidant agility,
dismissing each of them that warn
of penalties that must be borne
if in his hurry he selects
that branch strewn path he'd best neglect

He sees not stumblers at his side,
nor does he hear their mournful cries
his duty missed, but dream retained
a gilded prize, his only aim

Compelled by dwindling, precious time
too many mountains still to climb
In frenzied haste too late attends
to that which waits at journey's end

Thus twilight finds him lost, alone
and sadly, never reaching Home

Gloria Kersey-Matusiak

A Tribute To Poetry

A book of poetry is so full of life
With everyday happenings of love and strife.
It makes you think, reflect and grow
A treat to read when you're feeling low.

A poem paints pictures so vivid and strong,
Whether it's written short or very long.
I highly recommend a poem or two,
As a quick remedy when you're feeling blue.

Judy Johnson

Blessed Thanksgiving Psalm 103

'Tis a Blessed Thanksgiving we celebrate this year,
With Friends and Family filling us with cheer.
To God Most High we give thanks,
For Family and Friends we esteem so dear.

Tis a Blessed Thanksgiving we celebrate today,
Filled with bounty that our tables display.
To God Most High we give thanks,
For food which sustains us in our way.

Tis a Blessed Thanksgiving we celebrate our call,
Serving God and His Church by "giving" our all.
To God Most High we give thanks,
For the chance to serve in the ranks of His hall.

Dennis Kutzner

Caring For My Soul

As I wander through dark forests, lost and all alone, I'm filled with grief and great sorrow; pent up misery.
I drag my feet and shield my eyes, to pass such destruction.
Caring for my soul.

I leave the forest for the dessert, bleak and hot as hell, I wander aimless; too realistic.
The sand shifts often, as do humans, leaving an empty hole.
Caring for my soul.

I come upon a grassy meadow, filled with bright colors and wonders, the grounds are strange and exotic;
unreal to my senses.
I leap for joy over fields of flowers, reminded of life's sweet pleasures.
Caring for my soul.

The ocean appears upon the horizon, swift and clever, I walk to meet it with open heart;
prepared for my journey.
The road to this water is uncertain, rough or gentle, I cannot do not more then plunge.
Caring for my soul.

Debra L. Merrill

Just A Memory

Tears and anger are entwined
with her fear and pain.
As memories plague her of
things she once attained.

No longer has she the fragile beauty
of youth, nor the soft white hands
as pretty as a dove.
The springs has forgotten her, but not
those she does love.

Though no longer able to touch the roses
or feel the warmth of the sun upon her face.
She bears her burdens with strength and grace.

The flowers are gone shriveled with
winters bitter chill, they await the spring.
But not her, she's waiting to hear the angels sing.

Donna Mullen

Oppressed Spirit

My Spirit is oppressed, with pain and sorrow,
with hurt and sadness, help me oh Lord
to release my spirit, set my spirit free,
Oh Lord to love, to show goodness to
release joy and happiness.
Oh Lord, oh oppressed spirit, through my
children let my spirit fly, give it wings to
soar, to spread cheer and laughter throughout
the land.
Help me, oh Lord to free my spirit, to release
my energy to an unjust world, to show
compassion, to show kindness, to show the world
a whole spirit that can love and be free in an
unjust world.

Ester Spralls

When I Die

When I die will anyone cry
will people be sad that I'm gone
Will anyone say that I brightened their day
even when there was no sun
Will I be missed by the man I kissed
because I loved him so
Or will I be forgotten, alone and rotten
in a casket as dark as hell.

Donna M. Crossley

Seize The Day

One day I sat beside a brook,
With just my pole, line and hook.
I thought about how it would be
If the world was empty except for me.
I'd have no mother to hug when I'm sad,
No father to talk to when I got mad.
There would be no deer amongst the trees,
There would be no plants or ants or bees.
There would be no food when I wanted to eat,
There would be no creek when I wanted to drink.
Then another thought popped into my head;
About what the world would be like
If everything suddenly was dead.
I could not go on thinking that way.
I couldn't waste an entire day
Thinking about life that way;
Carpe Diem,
Seize the day!

Jason Earl Harrison

Everyday's A Holiday

Everyday's a holiday when times are spent with you

We laugh and touch each other hearts
with love that feels brand new

The food, the wine, the songs of joy
puts Christmas in our midst

Instead of presents being shared
our arms hold moments tender cares
and crosses wishes off our list

Everyday's a holiday
when love is standing still

As glittered stars of ecstasy
give way to what we feel

The body heat, the trembling lips
that passion brought our way

Will now engrave our calendars of time
to come what may

Everyday's a holiday
and dreams may now come true

As withered souls of yesterday
wish they had holidays like you

Antoinette Kopperfield

Little Play House Of Long Ago

Little stones in a square,
With my friends I did share.

So very long ago in the woods,
We acted like little Robin Hoods.

Hours and hours we all did stay,
Inside those walls we all would play.

Stopping at times to listen to the lark,
Until, Mom said "It's getting dark.

Down from the hills, running we came,
You'd have thought the trees in flames.

But the very next day, all in a row,
Back to the little Play House we would go.

Doris R. Freeman

Untitled

If I were a blind man
With no hope left but to die,
I'd give up my final days here
For just one look into your eyes.

If I were a beggar
Who owned nothing in this whole land,
I'd give the shirt right off my back
For just five minutes to hold your hand.

If I were an actor
Who's headed straight for the stars,
I'd give up all the fortune and fame
For just one hour in your arms.

If I were a rich man
With enough money to last my whole life,
I'd surely give away every last dime
Just to spend with you one night.

If I were a mortal
Without having to think it through,
I'd surrender my eternal life
Just to spend one life with you.

Dan Perkins

Sometimes

Sometimes my life is an open field
With nothing but grass and sky.
Beautiful and relaxing
But lonely and in need of excitement.

Sometimes my life is a closet
With dark walls pressing in close.
Warm and comforting
But demanding and full of anxiety.

Sometimes my life is a quick-leaving train
With wheels turning and smoke everywhere.
Promising and friendly
But scary and overpowering.

Sometimes my life is a friend's kiss
With two lips touching lightly.
Soft and sweet
But needy and wanting more than you wish.

Sometimes my life is a rocking chair
With old wood and rhythmic creaks.
Peaceful and resting
But fragile and in need of care.

Jenny Lowe

Three PM

Three pm in a suicide house
with Roosevelt stucco and Truman angst
the driveway boxed with hopscotch chalk —
if these old walls could talk.
Waiting for the plumber, waiting all summer
waiting for the birth of Daddy's little jewel
waiting for the boys to get home from school
waiting with the crossword and the hit parade
waiting for Ward Cleaver, waiting to get laid.
Deaf silent living room, eternal afternoon
all boredom all the time
glaring sun wedged in the power lines.
Flannery O'Connor, Sylvia Plath
In Cold Blood, The Grapes of Wrath —
study the razors and run the bath.
Paperboy's footsteps crunch on the path.
Maybe tomorrow I'll be the news
but who knew the world would end here?

Alan K. Lipton

A Fall Train Ride

The train trip I took, was an open book
with pages to be filled.
I wanted to ride as I used to do, and I was very thrilled.

I found myself at the top of the trees,
with leaves of russet and brown.

And roller coasted down the place
where we were on the ground.

Lo, and behold the babbling brook, fed by a waterfall
The water sparkling better than gems,
I found myself enthralled.

This place was pure magic - a secret God planned,
carved through a mountain majestic and grand.

The trees were such show-offs with color so bold
almost too much for my eyes to behold.

As we left the dear mountain, some farmland was there,
neat little rows that were tended with care.

This let us down gently from what we saw,
and one thing is certain - I still am in awe.

Joan A. Duffy

The Path Of Rhythm

It is music that makes Angels move
  With rhythms merging into the night.
Altered perceptions enter with reality
  As you move through ancient doorways,
Following the singing of the magical skins.

A staff of bells awakens on the wings of sound.
  It has come together with the Wisdom
Of a thousand lifetimes and the wand of the raven.

  Within is the middle world of the surreal.
Here the clapping man enters.
  He dances between the worlds.
Making love to an illusion, he becomes

  Invisible with the ease of a soaring eagle.

Driven by the dreams that are yet to come,
  He is created by the sounds of the sacred drum.

Joe Warwick

Shadows

Driving quickly through the early eve
  With shadows passing over me
From brilliant sun to soon-near night,
  In patterns, ever changing, of shadow and light.

With sensations ricocheting in my heart
  Of things with which I've had to part
And feeling in my deepest mind
  A part of me I'd only hoped to find.

For is not life just such as these?
  An endless succession of what will please
Followed in the quickest orderly way
  By the hurts and wounds that come to stay-
And so it is with each new day-
  Morning and Night
    Darkness then Sight
      Shadow and light.

DeAnn Atteberry Luckinhill

A Midsummer's Nightmare

I was alone and in my bed
With strange and dark thoughts in my head.
I closed my eyes to see me stand
Apart from me in some strange land.

Down, down to the land the sky did melt.
I tried to run, it was then I felt
An icy fear that gripped my heart
For I see another me yet stands apart.

Among the trees both stark and bare,
I claw my throat there is no air.
He called to me, I tried to run
And darkness fell there was no sun.
I tried to move but I'd fallen down.
I was floating then, there was no ground.

Two stars were in those melted skies.
They tipped then dripped into my eyes.
Then I was blind with searing pain.
I knew those drops had reached my brain.

When again he called to me I should have fled.
But I couldn't, really couldn't, for I knew that I was dead.

Alan Vickers

Tears

I woke to the beauty of the morning sun
With the pain returning, as it always has done

Fearing not the day, but the emptiness within
Knowing the torment, of lacking tears once again

Seeing despair, beholding an emotional display
Is my awakening struggle, of not being that way

With tears in ones eyes, the trembling in a face
Are my longing sensations, I have yet to embrace

For when the hurt is true, the misfortune so great
Admitting it is there, is a risk I can't take

So why can't I cry and release the fear
Just to know the splendor, of shedding a tear

I must overcome, I must continue the fight
But I give into defeat, for yet another night

And as darkness sets in and stars blanket the sky
I seclude myself, to again shoulder the lie

To ignore the grief, not permitting it to part
Is protecting the memories, is protecting the heart

Even when I know, that no one can hide
From the torture of tears, left un-cried

Cris H. LaDuke

Nature's Awakening

I've walked in deep green pastures.
With twigs snapping under my feet,
With my dogs trailing close behind me.
With a heart that was light and free.
I've dreamed some beautiful dreams in these pastures,
I've solved some difficult problems.
I've found peace and contentment here.
I've looked with clear eyes and clean conscience
To the past and the future ahead.
I've wandered in the slumbering twilight
With the sky a flash of blue and gold.
I've listened to the chatter of the crickets.
I've listened to the love call of the birds.
I've lived in these colorful pastures.
I've found peace of heart and rest of mind.
I've learned that nature is the leader
And example of all mankind.

Johanna Wolfe Dubensky

Making A Living

We all work so hard to make a living today,
With the rising costs, it does not pay.
Here's your paycheck, go pay your bills,
Your rent, utilities, charge cards and meals.
The children get sick, the car breaks down
And we haven't saved a cent,
We fix the car, pay the doctor and look what we spent.
Now taxes are due, and the insurance man is at your door,
Writing check after check until we have no more.
Many of us have goals we would love to make,
Try saving for a house, how long will it take?
How about that vacation you looked forward to for so long,
You now have the time, but your finances are gone.
Tell me, who can save in this day and age,
We just need lower costs and a better wage.
I guess if we were rich, there wouldn't be any dreams to dream,
You would have it all, it would seem.
Life isn't easy, no matter what passes your way,
This is our way of living in the world today.

Gail Thompson

We Need To Know Each Other

The world, the people that it holds
With their love and their hate
Their war and their peace
Filled with happiness and sorrow
Pain and hunger

Each with their own ideas
Their own hopes and their own dreams

Some hungry, some fed
Some rich, some poor
Their religion and color change
As you look throughout the world

Some worry about discovering minerals
Some for discovering homes
Others out to discover the riches they've been told
Then think of discovering all the little things
But instead should discover each other

The Africans, the Asians, Americans and Jews
All the people of the world
Linked by land and sea
Separated by differences

Heather Sourwine

A Writer's Soul

There's a river that flows from a writer's soul,
With waters wide and deep,
Its currents are as swift as the writing it bears,
And its jagged edges are steep,
It can stir your mind, or melt your heart,
Till you feel compelled to weep,
With the rises and swells, the thoughts burst forth,
From the heart and not the head,
It's known only too well, if it's not penned quickly,
Then it will never be read,
What a great sense of loss I feel for the thoughts,
That have flown from a writer's soul,
The words long forgotten now yellow and old,
The beautiful stories that will never be told,
Now lost in the river as it flows.

Jerilyn Jahnke

With You

Sitting out here alone,
with you a few feet from my arms
I feel content and at peace,
knowing your safe from harm.
I look down the hallway, I see
you asleep, off in your own dreamland.
It comes to me out of the blue,
you are the reason I feel like a man.

I look around, a feeling of love,
in everything I see
But now I must get back to you,
because that's where I want
to be...with you

James C. Nelson

Angel Child

Angel child
With your secrets
Please don't hide

Thoughts are mild
In Silence wept
Angel sing
And spread your wings

I saw - you silently crept
Curious eyes wanting not to hide
Bright, sparkling and wide

What lay inside
Wanting to be released?
So timorous
It needed only the sweetness and warmth of love

Angel Child be brave
Show the World - how
Show them to Love

Dulce Petagara

"The Ocean"

What strength and fury pound against the sandy shore,
Withdraw again in foaming sheets to only pound once more.

A constant re-affirming for evermore and now.
I'll be back! I'll be back! Repeats its faithful vow.

The ocean waves so thunderous, an awesome giant roars.
And yet, such peaceful quiet-fills my soul and pores.

I breathe in such serenity, a peace pervades my mind.
The feeling of forever is a calmness hard to find.

A soothing friend in troubled times is always there to hear
Your sorrows and your woes, a silent friend is dear.

The white-capped waves will greet you and beckon you to walk
along its sandy beach, or sit and quietly talk.

The glinting sun darts in and out and sparkles in the waves.
They play a game of hide and seek, such joy they do display.

Its tidal pools are harbors for creatures from the brine,
Its shores are sheltered havens for needy souls like mine.

Cindy Humes

"A Look In The Sky With One Eye"

A blueberry shaded sky
with vanilla malt shake clouds passing by.
Which is surrounded by all sorts of greenish fill
The eye strains to see what it will
Up and beyond sight and sound
The twinkling stars are all around
Amongst the vastness and some where in between.
Lays the beginning to all things

Darrel Lee Keeney

Tis The Man For Me!

Tis The man for me,
without a doubt I can see.
You were only meant for me,
for with your magic I will be.

Tis the man for me,
not as tall as a tree.
You were only meant for me,
only just as tall as to my knee.

Tis the man for me,
rich for all to see.
You were only meant for me,
your pot of gold and rainbow's end of glee.

Tis the man for me,
I'm not Irish as you can see.
You were only meant for me,
A leprechaun that's not suppose to be.

May Schuren

Hope

Hope is not just wishing or dreaming, but believing.
Without believing, there is no receiving.
We all can wish and dream and want to receive,
But to truly hope, we must believe.

Sometimes we feel there is no hope, for life can be cruel
We cannot seem to cope.
Within and without there seems no light;
But where is the winning without a fight?

So press on with hope, we must believe.
Life's dreams can come true, hope does not deceive.

Dorothy Heier

My Brown Eyed Child

I turned back the covers and to my surprise the most
wonderful child with dark brown eyes.

When he looked up at me, my heart leaped for joy as I
Poured out my love on this brown eyed boy.

My child how I love you, now listen to me, the very
best person you'll always be.

Strong and gentle kind and fair, my brown
eyed child with curly hair.

I watch him grow from day to day run and jump
in childish play.

From babe to Lad and then to man, heaven's child
in a human land.

He never caused my heart to ache
Or eyes to weep or hands to shake.

A mother's dream that a child should be.
Both love of God and family
Dear son when I leave this world behind
I'll walk real slow and leave a sign.

I'll sit by the road and watch a while,
For God to send home his brown eyed child.

Carol A. Gatewood

To Sandy

My little daughter, lying there,
With tangles in her soft brown hair,
The imps that skip beneath her lids are fast asleep.
Was ever an angel half so fair,
As my little girl with the soft brown hair.

Betty S. Moss

Life's Greatest Gift

I pondered life's greatest virtue
Wondering, through a forest of thought.
Seeking with fervent attention
One answer, unwavering and final.
From forest leaflets gently parted,
Came a glow of silvery sunshine
Shimmering upon a painting
Of glorious grace and breathless beauty.
Each brush stroke the meaning,
Of loving hearts so full.
Each radiant color,
Tenderness and forgiving.
Each shining reflection,
Abiding courage and devotion.
This painting in beauty so exquisite,
Masterpiece of all life.
Ordained by the holy artist.
Lovely and Precious, Motherhood.

Jules Juillard

Time

Many a night I sit alone,
Wondering where the time has gone.
Time is so short, the future unknown,
To think how I have grown.
I ponder good times and bad,
Those both happy and sad,
Places I've been, places I'll be going.
Often times thoughts bring happiness,
But time brings sadness in so many ways.
Loved ones die, good friends slip away.
Yes, time, it goes so very fast
Live life to its fullest before
it's all past.

Deborah B. Walling

The American Dream

Dedicated to Father

You started on the bottom rung
Working nights while the kids were young
Saving up for dolls and bikes
Feeding your family during strikes

But you shared the American Dream...

You worked with your hands, hard and strong
Planning ahead when the hours were long
Climbing that ladder each day
Taking courses far away

But you shared the American Dream...

Finally you reached your goal
Work is challenging and you have control
Your kids are grown
And we're on our own

And we all share the American Dream!

Debora Mahler

"Ponderings Of A Lover"

Temptation is a walk down the chalkline of desire
With morality beating down like a rainstorm
Washing away your yearnings with puddles of guilt
Confused by the sunlight of pleasure
Content with the warmth of satisfaction
Quench yourself in the pool of fantasy
Cast not a stone of realism
But gaze deep into the mirrored image
For one can not help but see themselves.

Jennifer Rambo

Black

There was a time in my life where I experienced an ever-changing world, but those days are an obscure blur. No more vibrant colors, no more rugged trees, no more smiling faces - BLACK is all I see.

My mind still intact, my sense of humor not erased, deep down inside I am still the same. For the world I once viewed now views me. They see a dependent girl needing others and pity I see.

The warmth of the sun, the whistling of the wind guides me now. Day and night no longer profound. If I could turn back the hands of time the zoo I would see, the more friends I would have made, a nurse I would be.

I discern the gifts GOD has given me like my listening skills and my colorful array of memories. Looking back I never thought diabetes would have this effect, all I know is that I am living more than I have ever lived yet.

I guess I am fortunate in a way, I do not witness the violence, or how sex, money, and jealousy makes one behave. In my mind I can create a more utopian world, without ever losing touch with reality. For my world is BLACK; therefore, BLACK is me.

Jennifer S. Sholler

Hands

Here on my hand...are five fingers, you say; and if this were last year, I'd agree right away. But I just can't look at them that way no more; 'cause I count different now than I used to before. In English we say..'one-two-three-four and five'.—Now you can all say that; it's easy as pie. In Russian they say 'odeen, dvah, tree, chiteery, pyaht'; and if you practice a little you could say that. But it's different now and you'll be convinced when I tell you what happened in Severodvinsk. I was leaving from lunch and standing nearby were five students of English; a little bit shy. Their teacher, God bless her, approached me to say, "Could you stop a few minutes? Is it okay?" I stopped and I told her the conference could wait, and then I met Ann, Olga, Julia, Tanya, and Kate. Their teacher then helped them to know what to do. And shyly one asked me, "Are we different than you?"
"What do I possibly say to this girl?" To show her that God created this world. I took her hand—and I held it with care — her fingers, I showed her, there's five of them there. And then upon my hand, so as to explain, it was simple to show her that I had the same. They giggled and knew that we were no different and out came the questions,—they gave me a present. We talked about everything for a short while. I remember them all, every beautiful smile. So now when I count on my fingers, you see, it's now not the same and never will be.
For numbers don't work any more from that date.
Now I count Ann, Olga, Julia, Tanya and Kate.

Gary C. Violette

Huaha

Huaha!
Yes, that's my name.
Can you pronounce it?
Yes? No?
I bet you just might get it.
Yes, it's an Asian name.
No, not Chinese, Japanese or Vietnamese,
But Hmong.
Yes, Hmong.
Do you want to know the meaning of my name?
Huaha means, "Cloud of Valley."

Huaha Vang

Untitled

Are there ghosts?
Yes, there are ghosts.
You are a ghost.
You come to me in my dreams.
I know you are here.
I can feel your presence when I walk in the room.
Why are you here?
You left me.
Why are you back?
You love me.
I love you too!
Will you wait for me?
I will wait for you.
We will be together soon.
Always and forever.

Jeny Justice

White Velvet

Gentle flakes of silent white ceased their falling for a moment yesterday. I hardly noticed.
Pictured scenery of dressing earth brought to thought by vivid visionals of your voice.

Momentarily drifting caused feelings of warmth from the white velvet blanket now covering frozen earth. Clearly I was being beckoned to its calming beauty by your sonnet.

Transformed into a winter wonderland the scene glittered of its brightest jewels, reflecting from the rays of sun on the earths new masses.

All that you painted drew me deeper into my soul that melted into your spirit...but I don't know why?

What once challenged my anger, my hate - now chipped away towards my love. Again came forth of you a newer day; Tap, Tap, Tapping away at my heart, what wonder it is to be alive!

Cold winter wind brushed past your window. It was not my eyes of frozen brown earth that looked upon the celestial scene - but heavens's deepest velvet blue. Not my voice that created this chorus song for the plea of white velvet.... I don't know why?
I stopped you. It's only snow.

Bonnie Paige

Yesterday's Dreams

Shattered illusions, scattered delusions,
Yesterday's dreams,
Life out of focus, just hocus-pocus,
Or fanciful schemes.
Lost for the instant, yet in a distant
Time memory,
Linger and haunt us, maybe to taunt us,
How it might be.

It seems a shame to say we'll never know
About the dreams we had so long ago,
But still each one is safely stored away,
To savor yet again another day.
The rainbows that we chase we needn't find,
To hold the "pot of gold" within our mind,
For fantasies are made of magic stuff,
And sharing them may simply be enough.

For stardusts that glimmer, or moonbeams that shimmer,
We're never too old.
So dream on with passion, the visions we fashion
Are precious as gold!

James Huble

Time On The Road

The lofty peak is steep and hard to climb, to climb
Yet soon I'll reach the top. Just give me time.

The moon and sun shall serve as guides along my rocky road
All alone, all alone I'll wander on, on, on.
The stars will shine upon the path to light my windy way
All alone, all alone I'll wander on.

The birds hop in the trees to hear my song, my song
The lizards stride my shadows as they speed along.

My eyes behold the beauty while I scan the fields below
All alone, all alone I'll wander on, on, on
My praise salutes the Leadership from the Hand above
All alone, all alone I'll wander on

The lofty peak is steep and hard to climb, to climb
Yet soon I'll reach the top, just give me time!

Edith F. Bondi, Ph.D.

Streetwise

They know their way around,
Yet their feet never leave the ground.

They can hear things that are almost said,
And predict their ending way ahead.

Their thinking is peripherally profound.
Piercing shadows where sunlight abounds.

They know what's behind every door,
But they let you be the one to explore.

They don't have to be abreast with society's changing times.
They see the truth and witness the action behind society's minds.

How do you recognize a "streetwise" from the rest?
Certainly not by a label of i.d. or from their code of dress.

Streetwise, streetwise,
Gaze knowingly into your virgin eyes.

April Lynn Lippet

Baby And Me

You say you care, but you're never there.
You always have an excuse, but I won't take this kind of abuse.
I feel alone and long for love,
This...I don't get much of.
My family loves me, yes they do.
But I need some-ONE to love me, someone like you.
I need strong arms to hold me tight and tell me
that everything's all right.
I need someone to hold my hand and let me know they understand.
These feelings I'm feeling should happy not sad.
I'm going to be a MOTHER, but there is no DAD.
Sometimes I'm happy, sometimes I'm sad,
but most of all it just makes me mad.
This bundle of joy I'm bringing to the world,
will it be a boy or a girl?
It makes no difference for you see, I am the MOTHER and
PROUD to be.
I only wish I could share this baby with a father who cares.
Since the father wants not to be, it looks like BABY AND ME!

Donna Reed

Now Is The Time

Past, Present, Future, three aspects of Time
Yet to treat them as different, Oh what a crime
For when I did this or when I did that
Now was the Time when that was at
Or to think what is to be and to wonder how
Well it just will not happen till it happens Now

Joseph C. Rezuke

When I Want To Talk To You

When I want to talk to you.
You always have something else to do.
Sometimes it's hard to say, what you
want to say
When you feel this way.
To someone who means so much.
To you boy words are just not enough.
Please listen to what I have to say, I
don't want things to end this way.
I want our love to be full of joy and lust.
Don't let a bridge build between us.
Is there somewhere you rather be,
Then to be here with me?
When I want to talk to you?
If that happens to be the case
This is something we have to face.
Like spending more time talking
Not me talking, and you steady walking
So when that time comes to be.
That's when you come to talk to me.

Alice Smith Adams

To My Mother

I have always thought so highly of you
You are my creator and friend it's true
The way I view life is all thanks to you

Everyday I look through your eyes
And everyday I watch your goodness rise
Yet I see your sorrows at an equal size

I share your heart and know what it feels
Your painful secrets securely sealed
The time has come to break that seal
Thank you Mother, now we both can heal.

Everyday we glow with the beauty we share
It lives inside and out, so very rare
My mother and I, an identical pair

You have raised me to believe in all honesty
Taught me to speak with sincerity
Thank you mother for making me be
The wonderful person you're made me to be
The replica of you - A wonderful me

Heidi Lynn Bender

Retirement

The alarm clock is no longer at work,
You awake only to hear the coffee perk.

By dressing your own casual way,
And never rushing through the day.

No warming up a motor on a winter day,
Or trying to beat a flood on the way.

Schedules now are yours to make,
To meet your needs for your own sake.

Happy days are very near,
To do the things you hold so dear.

With Jesus in my heart and soul,
I obtain strength and a bright new goal.

Assembling pictures and history of my past,
Gives me my greatest pleasures at last.

But still trying to help others along my way,
Gives me the greatest joy since my retirement day.

Helon Hazel Dickens

The Way You Make Me Feel

You make me happy,
you bring me joy

The feelings I have for you
can't be ignored.

You make me frown,
you bring me down

But I'm so happy that your
still around.
Although we've had our
hard times, we've had

our good ones to.

And even though you've hurt me, I'm still in
love with you.

No matter what you do,
No matter what you say,
these feelings I have for
you will never go away.
I love you so much with all of my heart
and I hope we never have to be apart.

Ashanta Boyd

Vandalism, Violence, Verbal Abuse

Vandalism, violence, and verbal abuse,
you can get hurt, so what's the use.
Guns and knives and all of those things;
are three bad things that the world brings.
Killing and dying in the streets;
Vandalizing what you see.
Cussing everyone you meet.
All three things that are not so neat.
It needs to stop from here and there;
in homes and schools everywhere.
So, take pride in yourself and make the right choice.
Treat everyone kindly, don't raise your voice.
Life is so short, I'm sorry to say!
If we don't change the world now, then our children will pay.
I pray that you listen to these words that I speak.
This is not the land of dinosaurs;
where the strong kill the weak.
It's an abomination of God when these things go on.
If we don't change things now, the world will be gone.

Angel Collins

The Sea

As you stroll across the sandy beach,
You can hear the sea gull's screeching speech.
When you see the footprints in the sand,
You'll think of people hand-in-hand.

When the waves pound on the sandy shore,
You're lost in time evermore.
The smell of salt that's in the air,
No other place can quite compare.

The sunny glow that warms the place,
Reflects a smile on a child's small face.
The shells that live beneath the waves,
Prepare for their tiny, watery graves.

The sea is a very special place,
Filled with beauty and with grace.
It is a place we have to share,
With all the life whose home is there.

Crystal Spence

What Do It Matter?

No matter which car you're riding in, the fact remains the same
You can only make a living by working, not peddling crack or cocaine.

The U.S. of A is folding from within and our children are the pawns,
You turn on the media or read the papers, it's incest,
rape or Heidi Fleish's Johns.

And ... Revelations is alive 'n well and this too shall pass
in our land,
But ... we must get back to basics and the church,
through Gods' unchanging hand.

Election time is now over and your vote determines us being heard,
We got the vote but Pataki still won, now isn't that absurd?

And ... I sometimes wonder, is it worth our while to really
cast our vote?
'Cause the powers that be have planned all of the tomorrows
as they sit back'n gloat.

And so ... the answers folks lies in your hands and that
ain't no fiction, it's fact,
And does our vote really make the difference?
Well, the powers that be still ain't black.

Barbara Verice Stinnette

Your Day

God gave you this day-to do just as you would,
You can throw it away-or do some good.
You can make someone happy, or make someone sad.
What have you done-with the day that you had,
God gave it to you-to just as you would,
You could do what is wicked, or do what is good.
You can hand out a smile, or just give them a frown,
You can lift someone up, or push someone down.
You can lighten some load, or some progress impede,
You can look for a rose, or just gather a weed.
What did you do-with your beautiful day,
God gave it to you, did you throw it away.

Mildred M. Dugdale

Friendship

In my life was an empty space
you filled it with love and understanding
you understood from the very beginning
I had to be myself

For good or bad you excepted me
never once did I doubt your respect for me
you allowed me to make my mistakes
always present to show me the right way

When I doubted myself you
became my strength
you helped me conquer my biggest foes

Friendship to me use to be merely a word
you gave it a meaning
I easily learned

You've loved me at my worst
you've seen me through my hardest times
I know you'll never forsake me

I know through your love, tolerance,
acceptance and compassion, what it
means to really care!!!

Beverly Farmer

Untitled

I saw you on the shoreline where I was standing
You flew down and landed on the crest of a wave
I spread my wings then soared to you
We rode the wave together
We danced on the sand, teasing the tide
As it beckoned back and forth
I knew it was you so splendid in flight
When you reached for the sky fleeing the shore
I stood watching, waiting your call
You circled a cloud, then returned back to me
The two of us propelled away into night.

Harriet Drucker Hughes

Grandfather's Love

Dear boy come sit and listen to me,
You have wronged others, though yourself more.
You're young and foolish, this I can see;
I do this out of love, so don't be sore.

You've gotten yourself into quite a jam,
Wanting the freedoms that adults do.
Holding your liabilities in like a clam;
The time has come for you to accept them, too.

For sometime now, I have turned a deaf ear
To what others have said of your bad nature.
Do not just listen to me, you need also to hear,
You are only destroying your future.

You needed this small taste of my wrath;
You need to change, and I'm showing you how.
I won't let you go down the wrong path;
I've loved you too long, I won't give up on you now.

So take these solemn words of wisdom,
And like a baby eagle, take flight.
The world, though turbulent, is your kingdom;
Don't be one of its peasants, be one of its knights.

John Beecher

Morning Departure

As I watch the sky I see
You in moonlight close to me
Wishing on a star so bright
Hoping never to end this night

Looking over the horizon I see
The sun is peering out at me
Saying "It's the time for you to go home
Upon this land no more you shall roam"

True to his name day began
My lover gently holds my hand
Taking one look at morning light
Knowing 'tis truly the end of night

Into the car and homeward we go
When we meet again no one knows
Still my heart longs for his touch
As if to prove true love is such

Carrie Ann McLain

My Daughter

My daughter you are brightness and sunshine.
You are the light of day as dawn arises with the sun;
You are all the love and warmth and contentment
any mother could ever hope to have with her child.

But when it's time for you to try your wings,
I will let you fly to face the world with awe and wonderment.
I will try anyway.
And if you should be scared, you can always be safe,
Back in my arms again.

Jean Stires

Sister Brown's Sunday Service

Sister Brown came to church last Sunday and, Lord, what a sight.
You know she won't step in that door until everything's looking
right.
Saw her standing outside long before service could begin,
But she didn't come through that door until everybody else
was in.
Girl, did you see that suit, hat, shoes, and bag to match?
When she walked down that aisle there wasn't an eye she
didn't catch.

When the preacher started preaching, sister had to shout,
Thought somebody had missed her entrance - no doubt.
When we bowed our heads to pray, she got our eye again,
Cause soon as the reverend stopped, she gave a loud - Amen!

And when the service was over, she sighed and smiled once more.
You could tell she was pleased with her performance when she
sashayed out the door
She marched on down the steps and switched on down the street,
Not even the pastor did she stop to greet.

Lord, that woman's something with her frisky, put on self.
Every time I think about her I laugh myself to death.
But we're always glad to see her so we let her go her way,
Cause we know that she'll be back, when it's Sister Brown's Sunday.

Alpha E. Melton Fair

Untitled

You say you fell in love the first time
you laid eyes on him,
But do you have any idea who he is or
what he has done.
This isn't the first time you fell in love
on first sight.
Remember what's his name,
The one you said was the one
and then you found out who he
really was.
So please listen to the ones that care
about you and that you can trust
because these people will be there
when you need them the most.

Helen Louise Marsh

How It Changed Me

Where were you when I needed you,
you left me too.
I remember you as you were,
not who you've become.
I've felt your pain though we're apart.
for no one else can touch my heart.
So every time I try to forget you,
my memory of you comes back.

Where have you gone, why have you gone,
and left me all alone.
I need you here, not where you are,
but how you used to be.
For what I've wanted of you for so long
is something that they can't see.
And I think it was love, because it wasn't wrong,
and because of how it changed me.

Brandy Goyings

Parting

You were my pet, you were my friend,
You loved me till the very end.
Your eyes were filled and mine were too,
You knew that I was losing you.
Your little heart was filled with sorrow,
For you knew with me there'd be no tomorrow.

Barbara Konstanzer

Their Love Looks So Innocent

You can give the ones
You love all your care and heart.

Then they take advantage
Of your heart till it begins
to shattered and shattered.

Then Your love for
Them will lose the
Trust you had care for them

But if you know the Lord,
He keeps telling you to hold on, hold on.
It is nothing but the devil to take away
That sweet love that you have for them.

But the love they have for you becomes
Like A, A, A, poisoning bug
That looks so innocent, but bites so, so dangerous...
And all you want to do is to give up. And you also want
to do is to cry and cry and cry. Let me tell you the best
thing is to pray and pray and pray. And God's unchanging
hands will take care of that innocent bug. Believe me,
God will give back their love they had for you.

Gwen Myers

Grama Gloria

Grama, Grama, you were the one
You made life so much fun
Why did you have to go so soon
I wish I could still talk with you
Memories of just you and me
Made me cry so sadly
The thought of that memory just burns my mind
It's happy and wonderful but sad in my mind
Christmas dinner occasionally
made me eat so happily
I ate whatever was on my plate
and asked for seconds because it was so great
Memories soar through my mind
that is true in my time.

Cheryl Lynn Pecoraro (Age 10)

Untitled

I say no, you say yes
You make me get undressed
Can you see the fear in my eyes?
This is something I have to disguise
"Come on baby, you know you want it"
All I want is for you to stop it.
Why do I feel so helpless?
You laugh at me when you get dressed
I go away crying inside
In that instant a part of me died
Did you think what you did was right?
Only now did I wish that I could fight
I saw you walking around the next day
You walked right past me with nothing to say
I wish that I could have stood up to him.
But at that time my chances were slim
Why do some men love to do that to us?
Now whom can we turn to, who can we trust?
Most men think that this is amusing
But little did they know they were sexually abusing.

Anita Potter

Seasons Of Change

Seeing the tree, beneath a baptism of snow
You may call her barren but is she so?
And for all your watching's on a March night
When the twigs seem dark and the bark feels cold
Can you call her fruitless, and so go?

She smiles, calm in the station of seasons
With the urgency of the sun's warmth in spring.

As for me, you turn away
Impatient with the promises dreamed
But inside I feel the pulse and flow
Of the urgency of green.

I have a season, like the tree
And all your faithless doubts
Will not destroy the rising Spring in me.

Constance Grillo

... Then Comes Tomorrow

When death comes to someone else —
You offer your sympathy,
You feel the sorrow,
... then comes tomorrow.

When grief and death hit home,
You feel so empty and alone,
You search for some answers —
And none come to mind;
You look for a rainbow —
Which seems hard to find.

Why does unhappiness come to those I love?
Lord, up above —
Fill them with no more extra sorrow,
So they look forward to tomorrow.

You ask through these troubled times,
For much faith and hope —
Enough so you can be patient and cope,
Patient enough to accept the sorrow
And brave enough to face what comes TOMORROW!!

Daniel Serratelli Jr.

"Don't Lose Your Faith"

I close my eyes and see you dancing about the room,
You say the music gives you chills,
A woman so full of life, health and happiness,
It seems you should be with us still.

The darkness found its way into our days,
With tender eyes you said you were not ready to go,
It was God's will to take you as He has plans for you,
I guess that was all we needed to know.

In your last breath a tear slowly rolled down your cheek,
Witnessing what we can only hope to behold.
Loved ones nearing to take you to God's heavenly gates of pearl,
To walk with Jesus down the glorious streets paved with gold.

As I linger in your green meadow at sunset,
I hear the melancholy sounds of whippoorwills and locusts,
Sounds of God orchestrating natures evening symphony,
As I struggle with reality but cannot seem to keep my focus.

I know we must wait for God to claim our lives,
For this reason we must present to Him our plight,
No matter how rough life may get we must not lose our faith,
For what a great joy it will be to see you waiting in the light.

Barbara Shepperly

"Of Salt And Sap" (Tears For A Tree)

When small and just three
You stood two hundred years in your majesty;

The wind through your boughs
Souls roaming the earth in whispers and howls;

To fly with those spirits
At life's fleeting end,
Was all a boy wanted
Protector and friend;

To have our fates crossed,
Your roots up and gone;

The mythical weigh station
Lost in the dawn;

While roaming the earth
Old essence of tree;

Blow through the boy's being
And make it like thee.

Dean L. Gordon

A Promise Of Love

When I stopped looking for a man who was nice, generous and loving, you suddenly appeared.

I stand before you with God and our friends as witnesses to pledge my love and support to you.
Our union brings us together as one... to walk along the same path, but not always in the same direction.
We have agreed to respect each others thoughts and opinions...as long as we communicate our disappointments, joys and sorrows with each other our union will grow stronger.

Our blossomed love grew out of admiration and affection.
We visited each others home, wrote letters, sent cards which expressed our feelings, and spent countless hours talking.
Do not forget the moments we spent gazing into each others eyes.

As we stand here confessing our love, warm thoughts of our new beginning embraces my body.
My promise to you today and forever is to respect, love and stand by your side as your friend, wife, companion and lover.

Brenda Sheard

Garbage In, Garbage Out

I don't understand how you do this to me.
You twist my words to cause me pain.
You frustrate my efforts time and again.
My simple desires become complex anxiety.

You seem alive but how can that be?
Electric blood in circuitry veins?
Digital thoughts in silicon brains?
How else could you possibly do this to me?

Mischievous imp, sadistic machine
why do you do what I say and not what I mean?

Craig Coensgen

On The Flip Side

Flip death over, like a nickel, and at the very least...
You'll find life, on the flip side, after death has ceased.
Birth alone is not the light, nor is death by itself the dark,
They are the closest of any friends, two sides of the same part.
Life, in our awareness, shifts from good times to bad,
Then, death, as the flip side, must shift from sad to glad.
So look toward things that are greater than
yourself, be respectful of where you're goin',
Because, to thoroughly grasp all of life's wonders,
you'll have to flip the whole coin.

Beverly Joyce McKenney

Fatherhood

Fatherhood becomes you,
you wear it with such pride.
To see you hold your little girl
warms me deep inside.

I watch you stare at her in awe,
you marvel at her smile.
She is a precious gift from God,
but only for a while.

So, cherish these few precious years,
while she depends on you,
and she'll remember, when she's grown
how much she loves you, too.

Nothing you will do in life,
will ever mean as much,
as the innocent look in your baby's eyes
and the softness of her touch.

I know exactly how you feel,
it's incredible, but true
because I still feel just that way,
each time, I look at you.

Carolyn Whitaker

A Special Woman

As I celebrate your birth today.
You were full of life and happiness.
To be taken from us suddenly.
I remember how beautiful you were.

On your wedding day last month.
I was honored when you spoke for a party.
As you exchanged vows with your husband.
I thanked God for you, wife.

For finding true happiness.
Little did I know, God would call you home.
In only twenty short days.
I know that I'll see you again.

Until that day, life without you.
Will never be the same.
You are gone with in our hearts.
Of those who care your memory lingers.

For a year thoughts of you were a comforts.
We know you are at peace.
Our love we hold for one so dear.
And in our souls your still here.

Evelyn T. Tallman

Recover

Even though we hardly talk I wanted you to know,
you were in my thoughts
We broke up so long ago but it seems like yesterday,
you said you loved me so.

You no longer see a smile upon my face,
just a jealous frown with disgrace.
I wanted what we had to last so long,
but what we had was not very strong.

You said the words and maybe felt them too,
but they weren't as strong as when I said I love you.
You took my heart and broke it into two,
not realizing how much I really loved you.

You didn't mean to do what you did,
and now you've got a kid
You really hurt me and that's no lie,
and I'll recover just before I die.

Frances Sloat

True Nature

The sky's so clear, the air so crisp on this October morn;
You'll want to laugh and cry aloud the day that you were born.

The birds woke up a singing as they wing in early light;
They, too, were happy when they caught a bug before it took flight.

Fall is pretty time of year when leaves start changing color,
And don't forget the flowers bloom and sway to one another.

The acorn, and all nut trees, begin to drop their crop,
And bees, and wasps, and butterflies sip nectar by the drop.

The hunter and the fisherman get all their gear in shape,
For they will soon go to the woods, or fish in some nearby lake.

Much game will now elude them: the fish will never strike,
So, they stop by a store going home for to sate their appetite.

The moon and stars that shined so bright are about to take cover,
The love that bloomed anew last night was made to last forever.

Fall is a pretty time of year to wake to all of this grandeur;
To feel that you've been given time to enjoy God's great wonder.

Dorothy H. Addison

My Mother - The Hostage

A bully now possesses
Your house and your domain;
And you look out of the windows
In bewilderment and pain.
He has bound your legs and ankles
And twisted up your tongue,
And stolen special skills you've had
Since you were very young.
He emptied all the sunny rooms
Where little children played;
Where cakes and pumpkin pies were baked
And traveling plans were made;
Where songs were sung and poems recited
And afghans were crocheted;
Where books were read and green plants grew
And loving words were said.
With vicious blast he left them bare
With only precious memories there.

Elizabeth M. Parrott

Romancing The Rose

You my love, "romance the rose"
You're in love with its velvety petals.
Its beautiful fragrance that fills the air
"Oh the captivating rose".
You love its body so fresh and firm,
The stem, the hip, the fullness of its bloom.
The petals so soft and color so deep.
For whoever picks it, it's theirs to keep.
Her beauty so overwhelming she says.."Pick me", you do
Even she too will prick you and make you bleed too
If you pick this flower that you love so much,
You must feed it, to help it grow.
You mustn't neglect, and let it go dry,
For if you do it will surely die.
Go back and remember, what caught your eye.
Was it the smell or the color? Or what you saw inside?
Most people go through their lives just picking "bouquets".
But if you don't stop to smell the roses,
Then what good are they?

Edie Eggleston

Remembering...

To the memory of Dr. Martin Luther King, Jr.

Today I think of what you gave us;
Your love, your joy, your heart and soul—
Your faith and hope and truth and justice;
Nonviolence was your burning goal...

Today I think of what you gave us;
Your happiness and peace of mind—
You reached to us and filled our beings
With brotherhood for all mankind...

Today I think of what you gave us;
You helped us see the promised land—
You shared with us your dream and courage,
And gave us will to understand!

Hope C. Oberhelman

If a Picture Is Worth a 1,000 Words

If a picture is worth a 1,000 words,
your smile would write a book.

The reader would learn as the pages are turned
that beauty draws a second look.

As birds fly south for the winter
a new season is on the horizon.

Similar to day and night
as the sun sets and the moon rising,
nature is filled with harmony
and is always carried with a tune.
Like the wolf revealing his presence
while howling at the moon.

Love is said to be a destiny,
such as a path through the forest,
valleys, and plains.

Similar to the seed that sprouts after spring
and the soothing summer rains.

Seasons are like emotions,
there will always come a spring and summer
where flowers bloom and birds sing, we all become lovers.

James E. Mesenbrink

To Touch You

I would touch you and soothe away
your tiredness, your aches and pains.
I would hold you within my loving embrace.

I would touch you and be a part of your life.
I would listen to you and hear what you say,
and not agree but love you anyway.

I would touch you and become a part of your heart.
I would be the softest, strongest,
most tender part.

I would touch you and join your soul.
I would be the peace, the gentle quiet,
the part that made you whole.

I would touch you if I could, and through
my touch you would know the depth of love.
Two lives combined, two hearts to beat as one
Together now, and always until time is done.

Christine Dickson

You're Alive

If you wake up in the morning and nothing makes much sense —
You're Alive!
If you can face the fact that reality is sometimes pretty crazy —
You'll Survive!
For the world is full of cruelty — suffering and pain;
And you wonder why a loving God permits these atrocities
On earth to remain.
I don't know the answers,
But feel we need not understand.
Our role is to keep our faith
And trust God to lead us — clinging to His hand!
Only He knows the answers - the purpose that is serves,
Is beyond our ken
We need only pray for strength and courage
As each day we begin.
It's imperative to do God's will,
And for your best to strive;
So, if you wake up in the morning, and nothing makes much sense —
Thank God that you're alive!!!

Betty D. Mason

Sadness

When you're sad,
you're lonely.
Things and people that
make you cry.
you run away, and try to hide
from everyone and the world.
No matter where you turn, your problems
and sadness are there waiting.
You search for thousands of answers,
but can not find one.
And when you do find one,
that problem is already solved.
You try to look through all of the sadness
to find some happiness,
Yet, you can never find it.
Even when your problems are solved,
and you are happy...
That sadness is still there.

Jennifer Groszewski

Understanding

To you who've loved and lost the world's a lonesome place,
You've suffered pain and loss but felt the comforter's grace.
If we had joy less woe each day would seem inane
For what would sunshine mean without contrasting rain?
We learn from suffering, love, compassion gains from grief
And that which seems so cruel may conquer unbelief.
We have a supreme gift sent down from God above,
To know it means to share with those who need His love.
We know our earthly life just cannot end in loss,
"Cause death has died for us with Jesus on the cross.
So 'til we join with Him and in His presence stand,
I offer you my heart,—I know,—and understand!

Alfred A. Mann

Friendship

From different worlds we had come,
to this place so strange.
Full of unfamiliar faces and unexplored places,
all waiting to be discovered.
With the memories of a past life
we struggle for acceptance.
The pains and fears we will both encounter,
are unable to be conquered alone.
So I ask you now to be my friend-
for two have more strength
than one.

Lori Jean Evans

Life

Life is a fortunate journey to some even a pleasure.
To some it's a luxury.
But to some it's a mere distraction
and misunderstanding of a sort.
But what does life really mean to people?
Life is a journey everyone takes some longer than others
no one really knows what life is really expected to bring.
To some, life bring joy and peace but to others
who aren't as fortune,
it brings them poverty and no where to live.
Life has to be discovered by
yourself because people can't look
at you and tell what you dream or who you love or hate.
Just like life you can't look outside
and determine what life is like.
Only you are you and only you can really discover life.

Sabrina Bolen

For My Grandparents

Grandma and Grandpa, this message is for you,
To tell you thank you for all the wonderful things you do.
You are always there for a kiss or a hug,
You know just what to do to make me feel snug.
You spoiled me so much in every way,
But you taught me to be good by the things you say.
You never scolded me too hard or ever too light,
You kindly taught me between the wrong and the right.
Grandma, you were always there to give me a treat,
And Grandpa, you never once forgot to tickle my feet.
I'm too big now to sit on your lap,
And I'm too old now to take an afternoon nap.
But I'm never too old for cookies or pies,
And I'm never too old for you to comfort my cries.
I'm just the right age to help both of you out,
When you need me for something, just give me a shout.
God blessed you both with the gift of kindness,
And he gave you a love that has no boundaries or blindness.
Thank you again for everything the both of you do,
When I'm a grandparent, I hope I'm loved as much as you.

Kim Caudle

San Antonio

From the uneven blocks of Michigan Avenue
to the smooth hayseed hills of Kansas
you careened off track in an Illinois university:
a trainwreck of passion.

Off court, Westy stole glances.
Off point, Bonnie caught the look.

Off in the distance, the train whistle signals.
Smoke leaves a trail of what might have been.
With the utmost faith of lead cars,
you came to the edge of the Pacific
to this valley of plums of peaches.

Now, some 20 years wiser,
towns left for good,
stations gone from the map,
you head off into the black night
to the home city of St. Anthony,
patron saint of finding what is lost.

M. Kathleen Archambeau

Message Of The Mission Bells

They came awake as the dawn did break,
To the sound of the mission bells ringing;
They began their day in a special way,
With the praises unto God all were singing.

One Padre's goal was to save their soul,
And he did this by sharing the Word;
He taught them prayer for God's merciful care,
As soft tones of the bells were heard.

With their soul renewed they toiled for their food,
But with unity their chores were made light.
Another padre would stay to teach the way,
That strength of body was for God's delight.

The bells would toll for body and soul,
To come forth and be replenished for all;
As the day would begin it did also end,
With sweet ringing, God's voice would call.

Laurel Howard

Speechless

Follow the herd and walk with your eyes closed
To the things of this world you know you just can't suppose
That everyone does it and no one could show
What a huge piece of shit — Man this world really blows

And I wanna go where the people see
Clearly through all the shit and sleaze
Where the things I want are all up to me.

Take this young boy that I knew as a kid
Healthy as hell; so young he never did
Foresee that his life would be filled by so much
Feelings of shame, and lies, and be kicked in the dirt

And when that day comes and I am lowered to Earth
Will I feel that one thing; that one thing I deserve
The great peace of mind knowing that they who had sneered
Are Speechless beside me - are speechless beside me

And who's laughing now?

Peter Chen

"Forsaken Love"

Why is it trying to show how I feel?
To utter a love which I know is real.
She professes her love and in turn has your heart.
I had my chance but abandoned my part.
I wish it was me, that I could be her.
That we could go back to what we once were...
The day that you came and told me we're through,
Was the day that I realized, the day that I knew.
All you wanted from me was my love and my heart.
Yet I set sail to your dream with a shot of my dart.
Your heart had crumbled, but I felt so strong.
I knew that I broke you; I knew I was wrong.
And now I must see what I don't want to see:
You're being with her, not being with me.
You're by her at night and with her by day.
There's a void in my arms where you used to lay.
It seems that there's nothing of what we once had.
Just memories and pictures when times weren't so bad.
To tell you I love you is too little too late.
The passage of time consumed is too great.

Natasha Spaleta

A Deserted Farmhouse

I may not pass this way again,
to view a farm house weathered by
the seasons storm.
Where once shouts of laughter merrily
rang out in the early morn.
Winding vines cling to the rusted screened
in porch,
expressing feelings of the forsaken,
a time of skill to build it had taken.
Empty it stands, folk's do not pass this
way anymore,
or stop to knock at the creaking door.
The weeds in the yard are dense,
growing high by the once white picket
fence.
As time passes the old farmhouse will
know longer be,
known only to those in memory.

Viola Straw

I Give Him Thanks

When I arise I lift my hands
To worship him right where I stand.
I give him thanks with all my heart
For his loving spirit that will never depart.

Jesus how I love you dear
You gave me faith and took my fear.
I give him thanks as I rejoice
I praise him with both dance and voice.

My name is written in the book of life
I give him thanks who paid the price.
I'll see him one day face to face
And thank him for unfailing grace.

Oh just to walk those streets of gold
His awesome glory to behold.
I'll worship him and praise his name
For his precious love that will never change.

Lillie P. North

Locust

Much transpiration since last chance
To write literal translations
Summary of circumstance
"Fates worse than death" (Vonnegut would say)
Nightmare's delight; newsreel games
Play, earth movement presto
Storm-bullet, fire, windswept diseases
Leap solar-blazed skies.
Lost flower of hope disappears
Face hungry, nameless, the Locust are here.

Then leapity-hop, when more than ever it counts
Some, wonderful moments come from fountain-bursts
Straight to the heart. This is an art: surrender
To horned-short creatures swarming nothing spared
Holes where pockets once fed life
Friends passing too young, alone with politicians
Assassins recycling misinformation.
Glass at hand the hour has appeared; gracefully
Stately, we're simply being
Now that the Locust are here.

Susan M. Marchese

Shattered Dreams

An old man sits all alone
Tobacco and whiskey his only friends
His life is filled with shattered dreams
His roads all dead ends
He sits on a bench
Just watching the world go by
He's to old to understand
He's to hardened to cry
His shoes don't match
His pants are too short
It doesn't matter to him
His hearing is gone
His vision is dim
He's tired from the race he has run
The people stare as they go by
Saying "Will you look at that dirty old guy"
He doesn't hear what they say
He just sees them on their way
To their own shattered dreams.

Kevin J. Feheley

Love Of Mine

Large, tall man, who makes me feel fragile, a smile that comes
from his toes, to the most blue, blue eyes that I ever did see,
He's a man from my past.

How did he chance to touch my life? I wonder at it all.
Silent but there. I am aware of him, his strength, his hidden power;
He is there. I've traveled on lost and looking for the right way.
I reached for that hand.

The hand who's touch made me feel so safe.
The hand who's touch leaves me in awe.
A hidden strength wrapped in gentleness, that touch.
Please hold my hand forever.

So, he held my hand and I felt much more than safe.
A man beyond what I see with the courage to come from the past,
Roots not forgotten and visions for the future.
Imagine that those still waters run ever so deep.
A natural man, a man of the earth,
A man of the world, who knows more about love than I've ever known.

When he touched me I become his in a way that
I have never been anyone's.
I felt the heat of the sun, The fire of an unquenchable furnace,
The zooming rush of a thousand stars. My lover, I am his, I am his.

He is so many faces into his person.
He touches my life and makes me whole.
He makes me who I am. I'm molded by the strength of his life.
He made me his wife....

Louise A. Molodich

Grandma

An increasing feeling of dread washes over me,
trampling on my inmost thoughts, frighteningly.,..
I find myself too afraid to dream
yet the nights trespass, forcing me to sleep.

She is left, the only one of four souls
and now, she is being targeted by that
selfish fiend called death. He cares not
who he takes, who he swallows whole.

The last link to a certain past of life
lies with a crack open, allowing destruction.
Hanging by fates unknown we wait
in a deafening silent purgatory.

Michelle Serrano

He Gave It All To You

As I think of you this Valentine's Day, I reflect on our time together,
We braved the odds of chance, endured the stormy weather.

As I contemplate your essence, I stand in awe of creation true,
I fall on my knees and give thanks to Him, who has led me
through the maze of life,
To share my heart with you.

When God created the Heavens,
Stars, galaxies, and skies of blue,
He had some beauty left over, so He gave it all to you.

When God created the earth, with birds, mountains and the
morning dew,
He had some beauty left over, so He gave it all to you.

Finally, when God created flowers,
Roses red, and violets, so blue,
He had some beauty left over, so He gave it all to you.

There exists in all creation, a theme of loveliness, a theme of grace,
With all my heart I say this, my Love,
I see it all when I behold your face!

So, on this Valentine's Day, never forget I mean this true,
When God finished the task of creation,
He had, oh, so much beauty left over!
And yes! He gave it all to you!

Mark E. Lawhon

The Old Clipper

A crusty old salt
told me some tales
of old captains and sailors
and ships that he'd sailed

He spoke of a clipper
that sailed the vast seas
how she cut through the water
with grace and with ease

He told me of sailors
that served on her decks
and of ghosts that still roam
on sunken old wrecks

He told me of travel
and places he'd seen
distant and wondrous
like those of my dreams

His love of sailing the adventurous seas
meant more to this man than the air that he breathes

He scans the horizon with watchful old eyes
for captains and sailors and old ships now gone by

Roger H. Waldo

Since The Day You Came Into My Life

Dedicated to Andy

Since the day you came into my life I have felt so secure by your touch. I love you and you love me, together forever happily.

I look into your beautiful blue eyes as I see my sorrows wash away. Knowing you will stay all of my pain fades away.

When I kiss you I know that it really is worth it when I miss you. But seeing you brings a smile to my face knowing that no one could ever take your place.

Holding you so close to me knowing that I will always love you, and you'll always love me. Knowing that we are together is a feeling that could last forever.

Tyna Fallon

Immortal Quest

Lonely adventurer along time's race,
Tomorrow—yesterdays' dust, memory of generations past.
Whence comes my light of life?
Where flees my spark of living source throbbing in pulsing gift?

Oh, God! Fill my being with thoughts profound.
Give my soul voice to write of love's beauty,
Inspire words of faith printed indelibly in time.
Reflect Thy will.

Remember me! Remember me!
Gone so swift as passing cloud.
Exalt my life to illumine the sacredness of life,
Strike some spark within my depths to light the path of sorrow.

All earthly arts record this cry:
"To live eternal, forget not I."
Faith knows that goals of worth live on in some eternal place;
Yet, in weakness, passing flesh, in frantic grief, cries out:
"I live! I love! Forget, not I, Oh, Time!

Lorene Sees

Dear Father God

I find that my faith is so vulnerable and challenged tonight; and I feel that,
I am, maybe... a bit angry with you...

This loss I feel hurts so terribly bad...and I wish that sleep would come and I could lavish in dreams of a time before this threat of separation appeared...

Dear Father God...the thought of facing this loss stuns me! Tears well up deep inside of me and my heart feels like it is splintering.

I feel fragile Lord. And Alone.

I have heard it said that I will grow stronger (in some way) as with precious metal that is formed through its assault from fire.

I have also heard that someday I will come (again) to realize how short and precious life really is - and the memories that I have will always be ingrained deep in my heart...never to be lost...

Dear Father God...I am weak tonight. Grant me the strength to carry on as I say "Goodbye my love".."I WILL see you again someday...

Roberta Raybuck

Loneliness

Loneliness is a long corridor
traveling the distance to an unknown place
without the light of comfort to help you along.

Loneliness is an endless tunnel
you pass through the emptiness like the wind without direction
hoping to find the end to the beginning.

Loneliness is a body of water off course
the turbulent waves unsure where they are to fall
unsure if they will ever find their way.

Loneliness is the inability to love and be loved completely
to allow love to blossom is to begin the eventual end
one must be able to give all not some to find love.

Loneliness is the minds ability to protect the heart
being alone is the ability to be comfortable with oneself
therefore you are prepared to again be alone within the comfortable
place of loneliness.

Vickie Allen

Resurrection

Tulip bulbs sleep in December's cold ground,
Trees are resting; not a leaf to be found.
Both are dead to the untrained eye.
But really just sleeping under a leaden sky.
Waiting for a wake up call to come.
But who will this call ever come from?
No telephone ringing; no whistles are blowing!
No radio alarms; no bright lights are showing!
But when it's Spring God gives them a call
To wake up again until it is Fall.
Tulip bulbs force shoots through the tightly packed sod
To become radiant colors painted by God.
Leaf buds bore through tough bark and escape
To grow into leaves of identical shape.
This resurrection which occurs year after year
Reminds us that we should never have fear
That only death and a grave will be our end!
For God promises we too will live again.

Ralph Le Moon

Tom

Alone, lying, waiting
Twiddling my thumbs, wondering
What is he thinking.
Dreaming, only of him
his golden hair undulating through his fingertips
Sighing, as glimpses of his ice eyes scamper into my wandering thoughts
My fluttering heart skips a beat when I imagine his lips
Only equivalent to rose petals, softer then silk
Wishing, longing that I could run my fingers through his golden locks.
Give stares lovingly into his magnetic eyes
And touch my humble lips to his
Oh so gently

Kristina M. Haas

God's Magnificent Binding

Somewhere in the vast and infinite void of space and time
Two souls will pass, stop, meet and bind.
In all our wisdom and knowledge at hand
The reason for this binding, we may never understand.
The magnificent's of this binding is a wonder to behold
For it is Gods greatest work of art, beginning to unfold.
Energy to matter, god allows to exist
So that the binding of these two souls, will know physical bliss.
When the wonder of this physical love has come to an end,
The transformation of matter back to energy,
Will secure Gods beauty of their love
And bind their souls again and again."

Thomas Stewart

Death

Nobody ever worries about death,
Until it happens to someone close to them.
No one ever tries to think of what it would,
Be like without them,
And then after they're dead,
You just want to end your life, too.
Then after a while after they're gone,
You decide to live on,
Until your time comes to an end, too,
And then everyone will know how it feels.

Natalie Tunnell

Loretta Prayed

I was a young man, and full of life.
Two young children, and a beautiful wife.
I never knew I'd take her this far.
Following our dreams in a new Ford car.
Loretta prayed.

Soon she had gold records, fortune and fame.
No one knew of our trials and pain.
She was constantly in the public eye.
I was down to earth, a common guy.
Loretta prayed.

It was in Missouri on white sheets
I lay in that bed for many long weeks
I'd always been a strong willed man
Trusting in God for a helping hand.
Loretta prayed.

Then one day God heard our prayers
We packed up and headed out of there
No one knows how good it feels
To be going home to Hurricane Mills
Loretta prayed.

Lucy Rudd

Selfless Soldiers

They marched into the war zone,
Unknowingly, unwillingly, and on their own.
They lose their sense of living before they die,
And all they can really do is ask why?
Why me? Why him? Why anyone at all?
Why do we suffer? Why do we fall?
But within they find the courage to live,
Within they find the wisdom they can give.
The power of knowledge and the power of voice,
Knowing that life is as simple as a choice.
A choice to protect, a choice to live on.
A choice they might of had... and now we morn.
Their advice was priceless, their words were true,
Their lives were beautiful, they were lived for you.
You with the choices, you with the mind,
If you use it well you will find,
That life is magnificent and should be cherished forever,
And we should stand and solute together,
The soldiers that marched on until their death,
And the people that lived with AIDS until their last breath.

Stephan Noggle

Time Will Tell

Time will tell when we will love again. I promise you this until the end.

Our love went bad oh yes it went wrong, but you have to be and stay real strong.

I told you I still loved you, I told you I still cared, I tried to tell you I was Scared.

You won't be my friend, I cried so hard to know, but yes I will always love you, this I will try to show.

I never meant to hurt you or make you cry, I swear to you always I will never lie.

I hope that you will love me forever in a day, and when the time comes for us to be together our hearts will surely say.

I LOVE YOU FOREVER !!!

Wendy Jo Felsher

My Tree House (Hansel And Gretel Revisited)

I live in a treehouse,
up amongst the rooftops

You will know it when you see it,
all the windows will be open.
With the sweet, sultry sounds of Sade
drifting down on the breeze.

Come inside, if you dare,
but let me warn you of my hunger,
lest it frighten you

Like the witch in Hansel and Gretel
pushing her sweets,
I too offer many delights to entice you,
all the while, getting you closer to my oven

But, really, I don't think you'll mind,
the walls are velvet soft, and lined with kisses

So, watch carefully, the next time you walk by,
the walkway will be littered with crumbs
spelling out your name.

Marti Baillie

Ode To Vietnam Veterans

Battles hard won, but war was lost
Uphill struggle, belly side down.
Shudders my heart, the human cost
There's no welcome in hometown.

O body falter's mind in vietnam stand —
Jeers, no cheers! Muted is the inner cry.
Changed and shamed by history's hand
anguished and pained, but could not die!

Must I languish in rage unheard —-
O Body's here, but nightmares there?
Friends are dead; and nary a word.
Distrust? Trust? Must I fit nowhere?

Heroes honored, soldiers rest in flanders field
Vietnam restless join with wounded fears.
Fought I too and did not yield!
Are jeers and tears to haunt our years?

O war torn mind, O soldiers wounded heart
O withered spirit, refreshed! Arise —-
O nation weep, may heroes never depart
Without our honor, else it's we who die.

Paul M. D'Amico

Games

Oh what a game we played,
tossing that fragile ball of rose tinted glass.
What a sparkle it had when it twisted and turned in the light above our abusive hands.
How safe it was from our selfish minds.
How bright and beautiful that ball in the warm, southern, sunlight of fall. It was inevitable.
Especially considering our haste and disregard
for our game to end.
With a shattering intensity of that deceptively
beautiful rose tinted ball that once was.
Like the beautiful red and gold leaves that fall from the trees to warn you of winter,
that ball fell straight through our clumsy, foolish grasps, to fall.
Like a crystal dewdrop poised on the tip of a blade of grass,
it smashed into shards of explosive consuming pain.
Leaving the memories to settle around our startled feet,
like glittering fairy dust catching little puffs of wind.
It quietly fell gently sprinkling our hearts with memories of
a once was.

Lydia Bond

Our Mother

God has granted the five of
us a miracle, that is the Gift of Life!
But that's not all,
He gave us you
as Our Mother.

What more can a child ask for,
Not wealth,
Not power,
Not diamonds or jewels,
But a Wonderful Mother like you.

You're Beautiful,
You're smart,
You're Graceful and Caring,
But most of all,
You have the courage and strength of a thousand men.

We Admire you,
We Adore you,
We will always be there for you,
But most of all we will
ALWAYS LOVE YOU!

Renee Gardner

The Night Light

The moon rising casting its glow over the darkness seeming to follow us as its light broadens across the sky; the shadows made by the ultimate night light overcasting the darkness beneath.

The glitter atop the water revealing the coming and going of the tide creating glimmers of what lies below the surface.

The craters of the moon aglow from its light releasing the restlessness within each of us searching for answers to the unknown.

The lovers gazing upon its face feeling the yearnings of romance and passion from deep within.

The rising of the sun overpowering, forcing day as it slowly replaces dreamland with reality.

The moon fading, phasing, quietly hanging in the sky waiting its turn to rise, waiting to give us the peace of night creating dreamland for us again.

Phyllis Mallard

Dusk

A glowing orb above our swiftly spinning world,
Veiled by clouds, soon to be
Unveiled by wind,
Slowly sinking below my land
To light another.
An elder's voice proclaiming it the most beautiful sight,
Enjoy it while you can.
For soon you will come to
The eternal dusk,
And shall see this beauty no more,
Even in Heaven you can not see
More loveliness, because the
Sun is God's gift to Earth,
And its grace may be seen by
Mortals alone.
So cherish this beauty
Whenever you can.

Lisa Williams

Surrounding Walls

Far away sounds, behind prison walls,
very small rooms, and very long halls,
I look but cannot see
the sun is shining, on flowers and trees.
But as I look in each new face,
only to hear the words, man! I hate this place.
There's no use pretending, that I am happy,
when I know damn well it's a lie,
And there's no use in asking the same questions,
when I already know the answers, and the reasons why.
When I had it good, I wanted more
now my greed puts me behind a cold steel door.
But no, I am not alone,
for I know He's with me, behind these walls of stone.
And as I go to sleep at night,
I lay my worries aside.
Only to wake up, and to realize!
Hey!
I still have plenty of time.

Lee Cantu

Losing A Friend

Watching a friend suffer so,
waiting for an end we do not know.
The constant pain and pale face,
how to go with style and grace.

Giving a hug when they feel low,
fighting back the tears that begin to flow.
You try to show courage on your face,
not really knowing how you'd run the race.

Eyes once full of promise and life,
now look through you like a knife.
Seeing past us to a place of light,
brighter than the darkest night.

They see and feel what we fear,
arms outstretched, they pull you near.
"Do not be afraid of where I go,
it's a place of beauty you to will know."

Larry E. Wright

A Child's Dream...

The silent whimper of my baby
wakes me.
The small tears draw me near.

Why does she cry now?
What is her fear?

Have I done something to mislead her?
Can I dry my child's tears?

Lord, how do I help her?
How do I cure her fear?

She breaks the silence of my endless dreams.
She brings me close with silent screams

"Mommy" she calls; and then I appear
to comfort my child, to make her aware.
It's only a dream there's no point in being scared.

Now close your eyes; I'm always here,
and hush my child...
Let the tears clear.

Vicki Koopmeiners

For The Longest Time

For the longest time, there has been you,
walking gently through this heart of glass.
Tip toeing silently one step after another
Holding my hand with patience and grace
For the longest time, there has been you
A vivid reason for continued living
A never changing body and soul
you've pledged to one, with one in mind
For the longest time, there has been you
Severed ties never could be possible
Everlasting truth, binding where it may
always soothing to the ear
For the longest time, there has been you
Guiding a misguided hand
With celestial hopes and mountaintop dreams
A vision of peace appears
For the longest time, there has been you
Protecting, strengthening, creating a path
through this mirrored soul.
Reflecting love, reflecting joy, reflecting you, for the longest time.

Rose A. Sharper

Missing Link

Not a day goes by that I don't think of your smile, your kiss, your warm embrace;
As I close my eyes the only picture I see is the picture of your face;
Pictures of you stored in my mind;
Memories kept so deep within me;
A love such as yours I will never find;
For its difference made it be;
Every night I dream of your dreaming about the past;
As I dream about that passion, my heart begins to beat fast;
But when I awake, reality strikes for I know it was just a dream;
A dream of when once I was in your arms and everything was as bright as it seems;
Although time has gone by it seems it was just yesterday my eyes set on you;
For that was the beginning right there and then my heart already knew;
The chills up my spine and rapid beating of my heart did not allow me to think;
For when I do think of you I think of my missing link.

Virginia Cabello-Durocher

A Child's Love

A child's love is special
warm, loving, and kind.
A child's love is sacred,
and will always be by your side.
A child's love is important,
and always true to heart.
A child's love is strong
never to be torn apart.
A child's love is like a ray of sunshine
on a cloudy day.
A child's love is like a flower
blooming in late May.
A child's love is never to be misunderstood
A child's love will love you,
like no one else could.
A child's love means oh so much to me
for without my child's love,
What would life be like for me?
An empty soul, floating out to sea......

Michelle Robins

Remembering

For the roar of the cannons, the rattle of the gun
Was an early morning battle, the day had just begun
Through the darkness, through the terror
Through the looks of fear and fright
Was the neverending presence
The will to live, to fight
As all came quickly silent and some had turned to flight
Came that beam from heaven, early morning light
As my eyes searched for comrades
Who lay motionless in sight
Was the stark reality, God had claimed their lives
And taken them to heaven away from fear, from strife,
To a sweet and better life
As I walk on through life's venture
And I think about that day
I wait for God to claim me and lead me on my way.

Philip A. Rogers

A Christmas Song

A long time ago, in a manger far away, the Lord Christ was born, was born on Christmas Day.
The wisemen came to see, the King of Bethlehem, the shepherds in the field bowed down and praised the Lamb.
The angels sang their song, "The Little King is here, come see the manger scene, where the Christ child sleeps."
Mary was aglow, a radiance beyond compare, her smile did warm the earthly atmosphere.
Joseph was so proud, he beamed from ear to ear, he wanted to tell the world, that Jesus, his son, was here.
The star of Bethlehem glowed brilliantly in the sky, to guide the men who came to see the Christ child.
Come worship the King, our one and only star, the light of this world, our only saving grace.
Come worship with us now the King of all the earth, come worship with us now the little Jesus' birth.
Christmas is the day we celebrate His birth, we shall sing His praise throughout our days on earth.
Christmas is the day we sing a Christmas song, a song we sing, "Happy Birthday to the King."

Virginia L. Huston

I Looked At God Today

I might have looked at God today here on a busy street,
Was he the one who shuffled by with sore and aching feet?
Or could he be the lonely one I saw beside a door,
The strangeness in whose pain filled eyes I never saw before?
I looked at God today out where the trees are tall,
There, they, so huge and mighty and I so very small.
And as I stood and gazed aloft enthralled by forest hue,
I wondered if by his good grace I could be mighty too.
I looked at God today out where the flower grows,
And marveled that this wondrous power could open up a rose.
I knew that I had looked at God because I bowed my head,
And saw his gentle, rolling earth on which his grass was spread.
I looked at God today and drew a thankful breath,
Because I knew these miracles would linger after death.
I looked at God today my spirit light and free,
And there within my very soul I know he looked at me!

Lewis Lear Quander

"Alicia"

My precious Alicia - I've waited so long,
To share this love that's grown so strong.

With a special little person from my own family tree,
Another GRANDDAUGHTER — how great can life be?

You sure filled the bill, my dear sweet pea,
And made life better for your parents and me!

Linda B. Doerrer

Untitled

How like this day
Was one in my recall,
When Spring's joy burst
The dam of winter,
Compelling my attention,
Like a willful, favored child.
No matter where I turned,
The wonders strung in glittering array
On the loop of April's breeze...
Impossible to concentrate on
Lesser miracles today.
Nature shakes her winter cloistered hair
In sunlight, and is freed from frost-bound sleep.

Lorraine Mae O'Donnell

Analogy

Water rushing to the shore,
watching you walk through my door.
Water kissing the pebbled beach,
the way our eyes cast a glance.
Thundering waves the water makes,
the way I feel when you say my name.
The water chasing the sea gulls away,
the way you make my worries and hurt go away.
The final wave touching the shore,
my heart aching as you close the door.

Shannon Rae Brotherton

"Winter's Edge"

The winter's edge is cold and damp
Way to cold to consider to camp,
It's below zero and dropping more
Your face is cold, chapped, and sore.

The winter's edge is icy and snowy
The wind drift's the snow, and is very blowy,
The snow is deep about hip high
Barely able to move you let out a sigh.

The winter's edge is giving way
Better hide away till the light of day,
The snow is getting deeper and deeper
The winter's edge is certainly not a keeper.

Katina Rice

My Secret

There's a secret I know but so does he
We cannot tell, or can we?
I remember when we made it I was only seven
And now I wonder if I'll ever go to heaven

He told me I was special over and over again
I didn't miss my Dad as much when I was with my friend
He said it wasn't really wrong to do the things we did
I'm not sure why I believed that; but I was just a kid

He listened to me when I had something to say
What he wanted from me seemed a small price to pay
Deep down inside I knew that it was wrong
But I never thought it would go on for so long

Many times I practiced telling Mom and then came the day
I was so scared she would not believe what I had to say
Now I wish I had told Mom a long time ago
Though I thought she wouldn't love me, but she does... I know

Each time I look back on those seven hard years
My eyes can't help but fill up with tears
I will try to forget because that's the best thing to do
But does anyone really forget? Would you?

Theresa A. Corsaut

What We did Not Tell You (Our Kids)

What we told you is all not true
We did not tell you
How our fathers killed people and took their land
Which is ours now
How they spread the Word with disease
In the name of God lives of many tribes were destroyed
We sold the ones who were healthy
Now in the name of peace we are selling them arms
We told you that success was only money and physical strength
We did not tell you that you can lose both
What remains is only love if you have learned it well
And bears are stronger and goats will always run faster
No other animal has learned to sell its own kind
We also told you to be quiet, deaf and blind
Thus enjoy the misery of chance
We did not tell you that monkeys hear, see and talk.
We deceived you as you will deceive others

Yuruk Iyriboz

Untitled

Father we ask of today what is wrong with our kids.
We have taken away the love they should get.
If we must part from another let's not take one from a child.
For though love can grow cold.
We must not let that be shown.
For the judge of our kids is just that of our father.
For no other judge to have to take part of.
Let's not let that be or have any part of.
For two out of love can be a great fate.
If we bring to a child a world that of hate.
For then we might all pay in the future someday.
"For what we all had a part of taken away.
For as of the proof we can just look to our youth.
And their unjustly blame.
For it's of themselves that they blame.
For our mission on earth is to love one another.
May we pray this to end. So our kids can then win."

Sandra Berk

My Childhood Life

I was brought up the hard way, when a dollar was a lot.
We didn't have very much, but was proud of what we got.

We all worked in the fields to earn our daily bread.
Mom and Dad read us the Bible, and we believed in what it said.

Daddy worked very hard and hurried home every night,
Mommy met him at the door, with love that shined so bright.

We the kids would gather around him all talking at one
time, but let it come pay day, Dad give us all a dime.

We spent it very carefully one penny at a time.
We shopped around and looked about till we spent the entire dime.

Then we would be ready to hurry home again to feed the
hogs, milk and cows, and gather the eggs from the hens.

We grew nearly everything we ate, we bought very little from
the store.

We washed and ironed our dirty clothes, and mended them
when they was tore.

Ruby Moore

Mom And Dad

We lost Dad on November 8, 1989
We lost Mom on the 25th of June, 1991
This is when you joined the Lord
When your work on Earth was done
I love you, Mom; I love you, Dad
I'll pray to you every day
And if you have any feedback for me
I'll try to listen to what you say
I know you are both in Heaven, and for this I am glad
It makes me a little less tearful
It makes my heart just a little less sad
I love you, Mom; I love you Dad
This will always be
I will cherish the memories for all of eternity
Please watch over us and protect us; this I ask of you
Be happy in Paradise, Mom and Dad this I pray for too
Now I will end this little poem
I have written just for you
I love you, Mom; I love you, Dad
And Mark and Beau do too

Sandra E. Butterfield

A Winter-Walk

It seemed a simple thing, a winter-walk.
We didn't know we were making memories.
Just two friends sharing mittens on a winter night.
We were still laughing when we fell in the snow.

It seemed a simple thing, a kindred-kiss
That took us both by surprise. Breast to breast
We lingered too long in each other's eyes
And our lips became captives to each other's breath.

It seemed a simple thing, a soulful-sigh
But it took my breath away.
I never really tasted lips before
Or heard the gift of someone else's sigh.

It seemed a simple thing, a forever-more.
Two shy hearts meeting, really for the first time.
Love unmasked friendship's delicate disguise
Exciting us with its promise.

It seemed a simple thing, a magic-moment.
Our spirit-souls resting in each other's arms
Knowing this magic came from beyond ourselves
On a simple winter-walk.

T. J. Quinn

"Brian"

You were here such a little time - but you've touched our hearts so
We miss you already - we wish you didn't have to go

I'm sure you'll miss the memory
of your mother's loving arms
She'll never, ever forget you
your smiles and your charm

She wanted to know you better
to watch and see you grow
To see the joy upon your face
at each new step you'd know

The walk of pain she's feeling
will be one you'll never trod
For joy is yours forever
in the loving arms of God

Heaven is just such a wonderful place
Where the flowers are blooming, and the grass is so green
the mountains and valleys, the rivers so clean
May we find the greatest comfort in the care you'll receive
Where your heart is now mended
Forever to be.

Nancy Pendergast

"The Sea"

With blue majestic waters and swallowing white waves,
We picture memories of new and old in those forgotten days.

We see white birds with snowy wings and think of
Times deep in the spring. When sweet pitched birds
And soft green trees, gave us happiness among other things.

We think of friends, who with their love, brought our Life without a tug. And what we see is not the thing that we all used to dream in spring, but blue clear waters which make our way, to more blue water another day.

So we all picture from the sea, those unforgotten memories.
Which someday may again appear, and make our life once more
So dear. And when those days again they come, we might
Not be so wise or dumb, but love and life shall lead
The way - not like the sea who leads astray.

But then again - the day shall come; when we might not go just as one - but many men with their life gone, will make the sea their willful song. With sleep and dream In seaweed beds. And think one day that the were dead. For life last long only when you see, that someday you'll be back and free. To live life soft with hope and song- and forget the sea that we knew so long...

Richard E. Apuzzo

Why Did We Wait So Long?

Are we procrastinators, all?
We say we want to be together;
Does it take too much effort?
We each have separate families now.
Time has taken us each in different directions.
Are we drifting too far.
Now that time has taken our
Helmsman and our Navigator?
We always enjoy being together,
We have many memories to share;
And we can talk far into the night.
But I, too, wanted to talk with you;
To share memories and build new ones.
To laugh with you, to hug and be hugged,
To say "I love you".
Instead, I must lie here
Forever silent, my spirit reaching out;
Asking, "Where were you?"
Why did we wait so long?

Martha Taylor

"Nocturnal Nanny"

We worship your sincerity
We sought you on your terms
One small step for the seekers
So many lessons learned

A smiling face for children
A mystery to man
A brother to our Earthly plane
Translucent nighttime friend

You dazzled the Egyptians
You dazzle Dallas nights
A beacon in the darkness
Sweet timeless astral sight

The moon will rise, the moon is rising
Above a hazy sky
Twisting our tides, and catching our eyes
Until the day we die

Les J. Ruston

Perseverance

Life is but a role of the dice,
We take a chance not once, but twice.
Often we live in a state of turmoil,
Planning projects which create some toils.
Something our jobs do not work out as planned,
And we often feel trapped in this magnificent land.
We all work hard each and every day
To make our troubles go away.
It is important that each of us tries to do his best,
So that everything we do can be done with zest!
Life with its complexities is not a simple task,
Often we experience difficulties
within our social class.
We must work hard to continue our stride,
For perseverance does not come
without true pride.
In all our endeavors throughout the day,
It is necessary to initiate a say.
If we try to work hard and do our best,
We will be able to hold our heads above the rest.

Wendy Freeman

Miss Malaprop Visits The Zoo!

Our eldest daughter had just turned two
We took her to our city's zoo
The animals to see.
She viewed them calmly... no surprise
Betrayed she, to our watchful eyes
And quite perplexed were we.
She solemnly explored the grounds
Filled with the strangest sights and sounds
And never made a fuss.
But subsequently, day after day
We heard her name them in her play
Just one stood out, quite fabulous
The hippo-pot-a-non-y-mous!

Margaret Condon Cinque

Sunset

We stood upon a mountain high. Saw the desert planes below.
We watched the sunset turn the sand into a golden hue.
We saw the clouds drift overhead on many colored wings.
We watched them being sculpted by the softly blowing winds.
We stood upon a mountain high. Saw the desert planes below.
We watched the sun set deeper 'neath horizons distant sill.
We saw the shadows lengthen o're that still and quiet land.
We watched in awestruck wonder God's artistic hand

Kearby L. Clement

Superior - Maitland, W. Va. Reunion, 1990

Saturday, June 16, was the MOST BEAUTIFUL DAY
   We'd known in many a year.
Our first get-together in fifty years and more
   of old HOME-TOWN FRIENDS of yesteryear.
From all over they came, and it was JOYFUL HUGS
   and KISSES thru out the day.
You could see the question in everyone eyes,
   WHAT DO THEY LOOK LIKE TODAY????

We THANK THE LORD for this bouquet of ROSES
   while we live,
For according to HIS WILL it is HIS to give.
Many a night HE has put us to sleep,
Counting our ROSES instead of sheep.

May we ever labor to reach our goals
To be with HIM who has the power to save our souls.
May we forever give HIM the praise
For the JOY and BEAUTY HE adds to our days.
May GOD BLESS each one of you with HIS LOVE,
For all good things come from HIM up above.

Ted Draus

The Homecoming

The air thickened with refreshed memories, ghosts hover,
WELCOME HOME
Well worn sidewalks received my steps like a familiar lover,
WELCOME HOME
The stately building's bricks shivered at my touch,
WELCOME HOME
And freshly painted portals I loved so much,
WELCOME HOME
Led me back to simpler times and calm comfort for the mind,
WELCOME HOME
And with each greeted classmate now find,
My welcome home.

Robert W. Carman

God

God, we all ask questions and ask why,
We're not supposed to question you, but we all do try,
Everyone at times takes life for granted,
And those are the ones that will be left stranded,
It can be so hard to live in this world at times,
So many killings and so many crimes,
God it can be so painful to lose someone so near and dear,
That's when we should pray so you can take away the fear,
We all have a choice to live wrong or right,
The one's that do live right will be
The ones to see you with such great sight,
God you can ease the pain when it's too much,
But we have to have faith and believe in you
So you can give your special touch.

Sharon Lynn Anderson (Cridlin)

Religion

Religion... has given God a bad name
We've done separated
What always is One and the same
And in the end,
We only have ourselves to blame.

Money... is the root of all evil
First you want it, you get it, but you know it's never enough
Its power here knows no equal
And in the end,
Could sell your soul if you make the wrong deal.

The law... is the politician's tool
They make war on your rights as they dream of that ultimate scheme
The people completely ruled
And in the end,
You'll shut your mouth, unless you're a fool.

Our children... have been robbed of their youth
And their futures the burden of Earth abused too much too long
Time will tell the truth
And in the end,
We all end up inside a pine booth.

DC Englund

The Joy Of My Life

I reached for him
when he wanted to crawl
I held his hand
when he wanted to walk
I cheered him on
when he wanted to run
I gave him a hug
when he needed comfort
I gave him a kiss
when he needed love
I have given him life, security and love
And he has given me even more
as he is the joy of my life and says "I love you mom."

Karen W. Pond

"None So Lovely As He"

Thine works Thou placed before me;
What a picture-perfect painting!
Thy flowers and gardens I see...
Thy way to keep B-e-a-u-t-y remaining
Majestic mountains shout of Thine Glory;
Flowing streams whisper of Thine Peace...
Thy holy Word tells all of thine story;
'Christ, my son, grants thee sweet release!'
Thou art my gift, "L-o-v-e's expression"
If I will only but knock
And Thy love knows no exceptions..
Regardless, thou art The Rock!
Thou shalt put no god before Me;
Thou art to praise none but I.
Accept My Son—My blessing—to be
The Way, the Truth and the Life.

Sherree Olson

A Mind Of Your Own!

Have a mind of your own.
What a wonderful thing!
And a vital component
In a human being.
What better protection of body and soul
Than your own common sense and self control.
There's a danger, ya know, letting others rule
They may only see you as a handy tool.
To be used, forgotten, Then left to rust.
Once you've served their purpose,
and betrayed your trust!
Jealously guard your life and health
and always be thinking for yourself!

Teri J. Carney

I Worry

There was so much time lost.
What absence would escape a patent in waiting.
I had thought ignorantly of an uncommitted crime.
Although I might have imagined; it's not a sound find.

If a refraction could be made of the chair
reposed in eclipse,
Or if images were not perceived
Could I then contend?

Actually, I
vaguely remember that we held a view of premeditated
love and abandon.
But no one saw you at your true point of beauty
The impossibles ignored the request!

There will be no absolute.
I could forever adhere myself, but cannot see it,
Put it but on the table...please.

Ron Ardito

Cherished Children

Where have all my cherished children gone,
When once the garden was full of frolicking free
Infants playing in the dew dropped dawn,
Standing so small beneath the timid tree.
Now it's noon and the children are here to nourish
The growing flesh and blood of my seed;
To thrive and grow and flourish,
Now reaching to the tree's leaves, indeed!
Adolescents as dusk descends, on their own
Yet in need of me to understand life's way.
Now nurtured to the top of the tree's crown,
All have ceased to need me, they stray.
Where have all my cherished children gone?
Night has fallen and my curtain is drawn.

Michele Sorrell

Adding Up

Never mind how long you survive,
What are you doing while you're alive,
Do you wonder about the friends you've got
And whether they are false or true
Would you feel happy or not
Is asked, what kind of friend are you.
What about your job, important or not
Whatever it is you do
Do you give it the best you've got
Or do you just scrape through?
And what about your married life
Are wedding vows kept sacred or not
Did you make her a partner or just a wife
Are you still her lover or is that forgot
Yes, there's a legacy you leave behind
The kids you sire, those images of you
Are what you make them, just your kind
The sort of man you are today,
Is how you'll be remembered, if at all
When you've gone away.

Robert Svensson

The Single Life

Single,
What does it mean?
Feelings of loneliness and uncertainly,
Constantly wondering will I always be alone.

Single,
No one to come home too and talk over the daily challenges,
No one to hold tight at night,
No one to fight, argue, or shout at - maybe,
I'm better off with this statue of life.

Single,
Happy, content, independent,
Relying on no one, but myself,
Knowing God will meet all my needs.
Watching others and wondering do they feel the way I do?

Single,
Yes?? No?? Whatever???

Teresa C. Coonts

The Beauty Of The Rose

Oh, what is a rose so pretty to see,
What does it mean to you and me?
You don't eat its petals, it doesn't have seed,
Just what is there about it we really need?

It gladdens the heart of the lonely and sick,
A broken relation it helps you to fix.
A rose says "I'm sorry" and helps hurt feelings to mend,
and helps restore good relations between old friends.

For the young girl a rosebud is a pleasure to receive,
She'll keep it in her diary, pressed between its leaves.
A rose will say "I love you" for the lad that is shy,
She might give him a kiss when he says goodbye.

A dozen roses will save you just in time they say,
In case you have forgotten your wife's birthday.
A rose will be special you'll keep it for years,
That you take from a casket of a loved one so dear.

Someone has asked if it had another name,
Would this beautiful flower still smell the same?
I'm already convinced and I'll tell it to you,
It would smell just as sweet all covered with dew.

Neil Sewell

Inspiration

You made the best two years of my life,
What else can I say,
Except for thank you
For all the great memories that happened everyday.
From the embarrassing moments,
To the saddest moments -
They will never fade away.
Not today, or any day.
But even though things are not the same,
I've moved onto a bigger change
Without seeing you everyday, after every hour.
But you were an inspiration to me,
From your teaching to your athletic ability.
Those are the things that made me work a little harder,
And accomplish what you see.
Thank you one more time,
And with those memories
You'll never be left behind.

Sally Harker

To My First Born...

How can I begin to put into words
What my heart will always feel;
Of sentiments of pride and joy,
And love so very real?

Not time nor distance nor worldly choice,
Can dim the joy at the sound of your voice.
Though miles may separate us and time keeps marching on,
There's tender feeling deep within, that's been there since day one.

I wasn't that excited when I learned you were on your way;
But the memory of that pain and stress so quickly flew away.
The moment that I heard your cry,
And saw your tiny adorable face,
I knew no one could ever come,
That would ever take your place!

The mystery of maternal love
In palace, hut or condos;
Because ordained by God above
In faith will work its wonders.
Human love is O so sweet, at best it's mighty fine.
But it falls short of the kind of love God has for all mankind.

Thelma Skadal

War: My Life In Vietnam

War is an awfully Terrible thing
When a bullet hits you feel it sting
Boys from around the world will die
And Parents back home soon start to cry.

Some will come home and some will not
Some will go over and die on the spot
Right now they're fighting over in Vietnam
When the battle is ended All will be calm.

They go there some against their will
They go there to fight and now they lay still
And don't ask me why, we all have to die
For Peace we all yell but none of us try.

And when it's all ended and someone asks why
You look at some mother, and see she has cried
So when you say war to you they will tell
Don't start A War Cause All WAR is hell.

Michael Penley

"Whatever Happened To..."

Whatever happened to the good old days,
when children would arise early, so as
not to sleep their whole summer away?
...when they had an imagination,
and could always find something to do,
besides sitting around always expecting
to be entertained by you?
This is a pathetic generation which has been raised.
And it's not the type of thing
which deserves any praise!
...when they had self-respect, as well
as respect for their elders and you?
...when a child would do what he was told to do?
They're selfish, they're lazy, and think
that money grows on trees!
They know not even how to say
"Thank You" or "Please".
A pathetic generation, for which I will take no fault.
This is something to which parents
must put an immediate halt!

Lisa-Marie Kinsman

Untitled

The hushed ringing in my ears
when everything is deliciously silent
disconcerted life - generous to pause
briefly reciting to me with surprising
clarity dwelling in this single, simple
moment residency within the confines
of my soul gaining peaceful admittance
peering out with renewed vigor
incalculable dynamism moving through
my eyes not separate, divergent entities
instead, a pure, harmonious synchronization
meticulously tracing my steps back
possessing more than I can ever fathom
capturing and gathering precious time...
Then inner recognition dimly fades,
my mind becomes mingled in earthly
distractions, and mental sight is
instantaneously consumed I grudgingly
revert back to a day devoid of deep,
reflective emotion.

Robert Pomerhn

Transfer

When the old bard had run out of steam,
When his think tank is drained completely dry;
He may as well be laid on a shelf,
Where, all alone, he can groan and sigh.

Still someone should take up the cause,
For the need of giving encouragement is great;
Out there many are ready to give up in defeat,
So they face a terrible and eternal fate.

Surely there are many who can write,
If only an encouraging note or a line;
They could show appreciation for a friend,
In so doing an unused talent they may find.

So pick up the mantle where it fell,
And begin writing praise in prose and song;
Send the message out both far and near,
'Twill surely help folks to keep on keeping on.

Then when all the pages have been written,
And finally the pen can be laid aside;
Yet the encouraging words will live on,
There in faithful lives where they abide.

Will H. Havens

Talk To Me

Talk to me...
  When I am alone;
Share some faith
  When I can't find my own.

Be silent with me...
  When I don't feel like saying a word;
Listen to me
  When I want so much to be heard.

Try to understand my thoughts;
  Feel my feelings...pick up a few clues.
If only for a second.
  What's there to lose?

In your heart, be by my side.
  In spirit...just be there.
If I feel and know that
  Then everything else I don't care.

Laurel J. Mink

Can You Love Me

Can I call you when it hurts?
When I can't stand the pain?
When once, like a fool, I do it once again?

Will you soothe me with your touch, the one that means so much?
Will you be there when I cry?
When I need a place to hide,
Will you be there by my side?

When the night becomes too long,
Will you make it go away?
Can I count on you to stay?

And when the times become too cold,
Will you find the time to hold, my heart in your hand?
How much can I stand?

Will you be my ear? Always?
Standing near, to listen when I scream?
When the world feels so mean?
Can you love me?

Sherry E. Nakoa

My Beloved

Darlene
When I don't know the way, you are the hand that leads me
when my thoughts are lost.
When I need a star, I can look into our sky and find the brightest
one and know it is you shining back at me.
When I need a song, your voice comes out of nowhere and soothes me
like the enchanting sound of an oboe in the night.
When I thirst, you are the droplets of water that quench it.
When I am hot and it is unbearable, you are the wind,
the mariah that cools me.
When I am cold, you surround me like all the fires of the earth.
And in this warmth I can feel your soul pushing against mine with
a wanting to get closer and warm me even more.
And even when I am alone, you are with me. I think of all these
things and I can almost see you. Your shape, your form, your smile,
your eyes, and I know you love me...
...and I will Love you with all my heart forever.

Kenneth L. Reed

The Night

The night brings loneliness and emptiness into my bed.
When I roll over, there's space.
When I stretch my limbs,
  I only feel the wall and the darkness.
When I call out for love, I can only fantasize.
When I cry, only the night can comfort me.

Lisa D. Smith

"My Daddy"

Here I stand beside my daddy- I'm only three,
When I grow up I wonder what I'll be.
I look up at my daddy so big and tall,
I bet from where he stands things really look small.
There he stands so unafraid as if *his life* has just begun.
I stand proudly next to him because I am his son.
He greets a friend and they shake hands,
Gosh his world is really grand.
He talks and laughs then he smiles,
He introduces me then I'm the big man for awhile.
I remember my manners and watch what I say,
Or daddy will be mad the rest of the day.
My daddy loves my mother and me,
But not because that's the way it should be.
My daddy is proud of me he does not grieve,
I am a young growing branch from his family tree.
In the years to follow my leaves will grow,
And my daddy's pride will glow.
Someday I will marry and have a son,
Mark that as the day that *my life* has just begun.

Marty Martyn

Carrion Heart

Damn passion's dagger that did slash at my heart!
When it attacked me I battled and fought,
But I looked into her eyes, she asked for a kiss,
Then passion lunged! Pierced! From my heart flowed bliss.

I surrendered to passion that night, it was done,
That kiss sealed a pact and she and I became one,
And her pleasurable touch did enhance
My intoxicated bout encountered by chance.

Now it was bliss that flowed, a pleasing touch,
Unaware of my wound I bled to soon ... to much.
Passion soon lost to time and frustration,
But left in its dagger and a cold sensation.

This dagger also cut my soul, sent it squealing,
And now my condition has torn us apart,
This hemorrhage drained me of so much feeling,
Now there's little hope for my carrion heart.

Michael John Ortiz

The Five Senses Of The Desert

Have you seen the Desert's grandeur in the early spring,
When life begins to waken after winter's rain?
Have you seen the Dessert blooming all across the land?
Then you've seen a miracle from God's own hand.

Have you heard the Desert sounds when all the world is still,
When silence seems to dominate every rock and rill?
Have you heard the sounds that only Desert life can make?
Then you've heard another miracle that none can imitate.

Have you felt the Desert breeze softly blowing in your hair,
When walking on the Desert sands among the flowers there?
Have you felt the Desert's vastness stretching out so far, so near?
Then you've felt the miracle of God's presence in the air.

Have you sensed the lovely fragrance of the desert land,
When evening breezes blow across the warming sand?
Have you stopped to smell the tiny flowers growing at your feet?
Then you've breathed the fragrance of a miracle complete.

Have you tasted of the sweetness of God's presence in the Desert land,
When you've seen and heard the wonders of His mighty hand?
Have you felt and smelled the fragrance of the Desert here today.
Then you have to know that miracles will never go away.

Ralph Arthur Allen

"The Sunset"

What is this that happens,
When the day is slowly ending?
You see these different colors,
Across the sky and bending.

You see it sinking lower,
Yes, down below the trees,
And more and more it spreads these colors,
To every bright blue sea.

Now just wait a little longer,
And the sky will get so bright.
How do you suppose nature,
Can make such a pretty sight?

You watch to see more happen,
And the colors fade away.
The sun is almost missing,
Just wait until the next new day!

The scene is always different,
You'll never see the same.
But, stop and think a minute,
What if all this never came?

Melissa Lynn Tedder

The Frosty Festival

It always comes this time of year,
when the frosty festival begins.

All the squirrels gather nuts and chatter,
while the wind starts changing.

The bears get ready for the long winter's nap,
and the birds start flying to a warmer climate.
Unfortunately, some creatures will miss one of
nature's greatest shows.

A frosty world of delight surrounds them,
and the forest is a picture of icicle jewels.
The ground is like a carpet of shimmering silk.

Rita Cavalli

Walk In My Shoes

When the waves of grief come
When the salad reminds me
When every song reminds me
When the scent of his cologne passes by

When the sky's dusky colors remind me
When the beach reminds me
When the restaurant menu reminds me
When a favorite waitress reminds me

When the freeway reminds me
When the dog reminds me
When his tools remind me
When a cloud reminds me

When the sound of a passing truck
When the front door shuts
When the chair scrapes on the kitchen floor
When the very air reminds me

Before you say, "it takes time"
Before you think this pain will dwindle
Before you think that I could ever love another
Before you say "you'll be together again"

Karen K. Asp

You Can Make It

You give me strength
When there is none
You comfort me through all
It only takes a trusting heart
To lean on you, not fall
You give me courage
When there is doubt
You take me by the hand
Your loving arms enfold me
and teach me how to stand
You're there with me through good and bad
You always know the way
And all you want from me Lord
Is to be faithful everyday
I'll walk with you forever
And you will take the lead
And having you so close to me
I surely will succeed.

Kathy De Rosa

Destiny

Destiny, for all of us, is just right down the road.
When we aid another, it helps lighten our load,
The hand of fate can smile on us, each and every one.
It's cool or warm, light or dark, when our day is done.

Saving a kitten from life's forest branch,
Diving from the safety of that thing called chance,
Wrapping in warmth from a blanket of new fallen snow,
Are only a few ways to help a friendship grow.

People meet in daily routine, passing without a word.
Their actions seem as if only the walls have heard.
Down the road, they labor hard for turning the other way.
Possessions fall into place, yet contentment doesn't stay.

Walls come alive and listen to the language there;
Forest dark and wild flowers blossom into stare.
Each turn in the path that life constructs and start to begin
Contests and races each one of us can win.

Which path brings to us the kitten and the snow?
The oak tree doesn't bend at all; it's not that far to go.
Catch the fallen star, and the kitten doesn't fuss.
The hand of fate brings our destiny forth straight to us.

Mary Ann C. Costantini

Granddaughters Galore

Christie, granddaughter; number 1, as they say.
When we watch her, she tries to get her own way.
But Grandma and Grandpa finally learned to say no.
And that is because we love her so.

Jena Lynn is granddaughter number two.
Her eyes are big and so very blue.
She has a mind of her own and will never give in.
Thank God she is not a twin!

Maria Alana granddaughter number three,
Always wants to visit Grandpa and me.
Sweet and pretty; smart as a whip.
Surprised me with the following quip.

When watching Noah and the Ark on TV,
"What a multitude of animals," she said to me.
"What is a multitude?" I asked this child of three.
"So many you can't even count!!" I had to agree.

Ashley Elaine is granddaughter number four.
Could a grandmother ask for anything more?
Even though she wasn't a boy,
At the nursery window I cried with joy.

Theresa Luppowitz

Outsider

Sitting with a midnight query.
When, when will Micki be near me?
She says she'll call; when she gets a break.
So here I wait down by the lake.
Tick, tick, tick. Time is running and D-day is near.
Fear or fun? Which will be here?
I shutter at the thought I might be leavin.
For Joe, who's permanently back from Cleveland.
Snuggling close while he was away.
I hoped his car blew up or just lost its way.
Now he's back and Rog is in second.
Waiting around until she beckons.
Sooner or later the woman of my dreams.
Yes, the one who makes my heart jump to extremes,
will find sometime.
To be all mine.

Roger E. Craig Jr.

Aces

ACES
When you become an ace you are
Superior, and inferior and
Invincible to the eyes of the unimperal
ACES
Now that you are an ace you are a
superb intellectual being
that aces of spade that is the master
of any trade, uniform of silk and
the two colors that match I go along
with you, your training is
behind you and many the ACES of
spade be with you through
all of your journeys the ACE is always
inside of you, that ACE master
that was developed and not born in you ACES
You are an ace, well trained through
and through with you are symbols
Marked on you to represent the ACES
Four level ACES that has made you ACES

Tony L. Lumie

"When Is It Love?"

It's Love -
- When you're never disappointed
- When you have no regrets
- When you have no suspicions
- When you have no jealously
- When you can be open and honest
- When every day is better than the last
- When you realize just how lucky you are
- When the feelings go beyond mere words
- When a smile comes instantly and stays a while
- When everything in your universe has meaning
- When you're comfortable with the person in the mirror
- When you instinctively know the next step
- When words; unspoken; are understood
- When just a smile is a sufficient "O.K."
- When time away is time for missing
- When the hurt you fell is not always your own
- When the meaning of one's self is shared by two
- When the joy is more than you ever imagined
- When the dreams are common, happy ones

J. McCarthy

"Where Angels See And Weep"

In the world beneath the heavens
Where Angels see and weep
The dying child of hunger
gently falls to sleep
To weak to shed a tear, to small to change the world
Their soul escapes the hunger
through the mercy of the Lord

In the world beneath the heavens
Where Angels see and weep
Love is discontinued
by the hatred that we keep
And peace is just a word, that seems
So hard to find
Where Angels see and weep
and pray for all mankind.

Stephen May

Destiny's Companion

Life has many turns and twists.
Where any one choice changes destiny.
Your life seems to have no purpose or meaning.
Knowing that a friend, love, husband or wife
Can not completely fill the void of one's own soul.
Always encountering destiny's little tricks in life
As you travel the road to destiny's final goal.
But down the road the air starts to clear the mists of doubt.
For in the distance there comes a soft glow.
With a warm smile and a giving heart,
That part deep down you have come to know.
Hoping against hope it will stay and not depart.
Finally knowing that you are now complete,
Ready to meet all that is on the road of destiny.
You and destiny's companion.

Terry L. Thomason

Dreams

Dreams take you to a far off land,
Where children play on silver swings.
There are buttercups the size of your hand
And horses that fly on golden wings.
On the trees, diamonds are dew,
Fruits are colored glass.
The unicorn is waiting for you,
In the emerald grass.

Sheila Dillon

One Sad Tale

Ol' Abdul lived in the Bull-bully corral
Where each cow thought she was his own special gal.
But Abdul was tired of keeping them all happy
And having to be every calf's pappy.
Except for Genevieve, that luscious young heifer,
With a flick of her tail could spice his hasenpfeffer.
Then, enter El Toro, a sturdy young blade,
When seeing all those cows, thought, "I've got it made"
He spotted Genevieve, started pawing the ground, and snorted.
Headed straight for her, and around her cavorted.
And fickle young Jenny, fluttered her tail and went to his side
Showing she was willing and ready to become his bride.
Then they took off, nonchalantly, as if for a stroll,
But they were looking for privacy behind some secluded knoll.
Alas, poor Ol' Abdul was retired with no ceremony,
And here he is now, part of my lunch - Oscar Mayer Baloney.

Rita Hodgden

Untitled

I wish I could see myself the way the HE sees me.
Where I see lumps and bulges, HE says he sees only perfect shapes.
I don't feel "perfect," although HE says that I am.
HE calls me beautiful.
"What is beauty?" I ask
"You," he replies,
Then he begins to touch, to kiss, to caress, and all my worries and fears seem to disappear.
I don't feel beautiful, or pretty.
"I love you, I love you," my lover says.
Maybe that's it.
Love. The most beautiful thing of all. I definitely have that. I love HIM.
Maybe because he sees me as I wish I were?
I guess I'll never know.

Lisa Gammon

My Me

Where is it, myself, my real, my me?
Where is it hiding among my "should be"
My "could have been", my "they expect"?
How do I go beneath the thick and heavy veneer
Made impenetrable by all the time and practices
Creating a fortress of defense and make believe
To hide the soft, the vulnerable, the foolish
Even from myself, especially from myself?
What courage must I collect to reveal to myself
My meager possessions? why so fearful?
It is only my eyes to see the truth.
Maybe, just maybe there is lies deep within
The private chamber a small value,
One acceptable virtue. Do you suppose?
Even one small precious talent to be polished
And nurtured into shinning treasure to be admired
by me.

Peggy M. Kirkland

Search For A Better World

Somewhere there has got to be a land
Where people are gentle and kind
That land of beauty and peace I find
Only somewhere deep within my mind.

The lamb will surely lie down with the lion
And together red and yellow, black and white will dine
There will be no hurt, no pain, none insane
The rich man, the poor man is treated the same.

A place where even the blind man sees
The flowers and rivers, the mountains, the trees
All the pain hidden inside is forgotten, put behind
Surely there must be a place like this that I can find.

Yet, though I've searched I cannot find
This place but deep within my mind.

Trudy Tyrone

The Night Returns

The night returns and I,
which gave the day the best I had,
return and quietly seek the havened rest.

Two, it seems ordained,
by some great force unknown, or known,
are numbered right for closing on all odds.

The night returns and one
who gave all he had to give,
returns no more,
and the night is a long, long night.

Tom Clark

Manitou

If there are holy places on earth
Where the humdrum is subtly transformed
into the majestic,
Where our weary selves are freshened
and uplifted,
Where our instinctive communion with nature
reasserts its transcendence,
Where our hearts pulse stronger
with higher resolves,
Where a new hope brings solace
for our fears,
Where our souls are filled with compassion—
If such enchanted spots exist
Surely Great Pond Mountain
is one of them,
Hallowed by its history; wondrous
in its promise.

Stuart Gross

Today

Today two friends walk down an aisle,
Where they'll stand and talk a while,
Today they exchange vows for all to see,
On the most important day of their history.

Today they'll give their lives to each other,
Before all they'll pledge to stay together,
Two separate individuals becoming one,
To smile, to laugh, to have fun.

Today will not be remembered as an ending,
For today is the symbol of a new beginning,
Even if two old lives are being left behind,
One new life with happiness is yet to find.

Today two books close and one book opens,
Instantly a new story begins,
This book bares fresh and unlimited pages,
To be filled throughout the ages.

Today two souls stand together,
And one kiss will bond them forever,
With hope and faith they begin living,
Their love made one by God's own blessing.

Sandra L. Shappy

Lessons In Life

I've been contemplating quietly the lessons found in life
Which aren't gotten from a classroom or a book
Such as how to be compassionate and how to love a pet.
I suppose these things deserve a second look.

How do you teach a child about unconditional love
When his parents are divorced or on the brink?
And generosity comes second to materialistic things.
Some adjustments should be made in how we think.

To acknowledge and to realize our own intrinsic worth
And the fascinating powers of the mind,
Working up to our potential and maintaining self-esteem,
Making sure these things are never left behind.

How do you learn to grieve unless you've lost a friend in death?
And faced with options, what choice should you make?
Methodically we analyze each facet of our lives,
And hopefully we'll learn from our mistakes.

Wendy J. Richmond

The Painting Of Life

Life is a special and unique thing,
Which can be described as a painting.
It's a picture you paint as you go along
In which you try to do what's right, not wrong.

Your canvas is your own decision;
Then you must set out on your mission.
You must start painting in a certain direction,
So pick your paint brush and make your paint selection.

At first your picture will be unclear.
You might get frustrated and shed a tear.
Your picture will soon be colorful and take shape,
And after a while, you might have a beautiful picture of a landscape.

Just as everyone has a different name,
Everyone's picture is not the same.
We all paint with a different color and brush,
And whatever we paint we must not rush.

The day your painting is done will be when you die.
You'll then be remembered for the picture you painted in everyone's
eyes.
Never let your painting consistency decrease or cease
Because if you work hard enough your picture will become a
masterpiece.

Marcus Butts

Priceless Treasure

What priceless treasure Christ is.
Which cannot be bought with millions of earthly dollars.
Yet the poorest of sinner of earthly estate may purchase this
great gift. As but a bended knee, a humble heart,
a cry to God for mercy and forgiveness.

Lester Dean

My Friendship Bouquet

Friends are the flowers one picks along life's way
Which serve as the nucleus of one's friendship bouquet.
Some are picked for their beauty; others, for their stamina or grace,
Whereas some because they compliment others, residing in the vase.

One, or more, is extra special, for some reason maybe unknown,
Yet definitely is outstanding among all others that are grown.
One often has to replace a friend as one travels along life's way,
'Cause friendships just like flowers, sometimes wilt away.

But you're that special flower, in my friendship bouquet,
That never could be replaced if it should fade away.
There would definitely be a void, a loss beyond repair,
If in my friendship garden, you were no longer there.

Friends may come, and friends may go, but our friendship is
meant to last,
It's a friendship of the future, the present, and the past.
So, friend, I hope you're delighted, being special in my friendship
bouquet,
'Cause that's just the way it is as I travel life's highway.

Loraine P. Wright

Little Boys

All little boys will someday grow into men.
While mothers lay to rest their little toy men.

Watching for hours on end as they lay silently in their cribs,
My little boys, weren't even old enough to wear their bibs.

With tears in my eyes and joy in my heart,
I've watched them grow right from the very start.

So, God, give me strength to help them grow
To be tender and loving, happy and wise,
Only that will bring back the tears of joy to my eyes.

Kay Determan

The Hurricane Of Salem

The dark clouds of vengeance were floating in the sky
While clear waters of justice wondered who would die
Shrieks of pain and agony tore the truth apart
For with their false claims, there came many broken hearts

A silhouette of darkness pranced across the moon
The pearly gates stood open, they would be there soon
But the shame of the wicked will all stand on trial
Innocent lives were taken, righteousness defiled

A hurricane of fear swept through the little town
For people within miles could hear its mighty sound
Soon the raging waters were calmed and all seemed to subside
Now it is only history, except to those who died

LeeAnn Gray

These I Love And Do!

Clear water sparkling to the rhythm of the day
While golden sunrise flows upon sweetly labored grain fields.

Emerald shade of forest green painted on the grand horizon
And innocent mountains casting shadows yonder.

Feel the crisp winter wind tingle in your ears
Full of life young and supple leaves of spring time.

While sweet songs of birds I hear
I smell the earthly Nature after showers.

Go for a brisk walk out in the wild woods
On winding trails leading almost to nowhere.

Or listen to rivers flow ever so endlessly
Teasing the warm summer sun along the way.

Silently witness the flawless sunset west
The aura welcoming the night.

Making dreams come true
Experiencing today to tell the world tomorrow.

Oh! the small wonders of love for life in the country
These I love and do in Idaho!

Mansueta D. Pollworth

"Antoinette"

Standing alone but she is there,
While other ask "if", she will dare.

Getting things done before you know,
With spirited heart and smiles aglow.

A lot from life she's never had,
but she'll share her good to shoo your bad.

Bouquets of flowers when spirits are low,
A hot cup of coffee to warm you so.

Taking the time to talk a bit,
Warm, caring hope that's spiced with wit.

She'll hold the hand that's time to go,
'cause someone cares and they will know.

With loving heart and open mind,
God made "Toni", one of a kind!

William H. Collins

A Peaceful Interlude

Darkness lies quite tranquil in my garden
While the moon hangs silver veils upon my wall.
Candles burn serenely in their holders,
Sending dancing flickering shadows down the hall.
Music ebbs and flows in satin ripples
While fire sheds its pure and simple light.
Warm memories wrap themselves around me
And shield me from the loneliness of night.

Karen S. Townsend

"God Bless The Little Children"

God bless the little children,
While they are sleeping or awake.
When they take a crayon in their hand,
be proud of what they make.
God bless the little children,
and all that your children do.
Just remember that those children
are a great big part of you.
God bless the little children,
and treat them all with love.
Treat them as if they were a
beautiful, soft white dove.
God bless the little children,
if they're far or if they're near.
But those little words, "I LOVE YOU",
are what you always like to hear.
God bless the little children,
because when they go away.
Deep down in your hearts and souls,
you wished that they could stay.

Susan I. Rasmussen

Untitled

Misty glens, flowered fields,
Whimsical clowns and ferris wheels ...

Secret longings — fragile, heartfelt —
Of friends and loves long lost ...

Like elusive butterflies fluttering through
My mind, brushing the edges of my heart,
Refusing the captivity of pen and paper.

Kathy Moran

Lord Kṛṣṇa

I hear HIS rhythm,
whispering gently,
The song is sung,
my eyes close slowly....

My heart is bright...glowing,
I feel HIS immense power,
My Lord.... ever knowing,
I will trust in HIM forever.

I feel HIS raga,
I held my hands together,
Chanting the Maha Mantra,
Srī Kṛṣṇa, to you, my Lord, I surrender.

Sumathi Vijayen

The Magic Of Spring

As I lie down under the bright blue sky
Whispering winds and the sweet smell of spring
Birds are singing as they slowly fly by
The grass so soft as I think about things

The sun is shining and bronzing my skin
Not a worry, as the world comforts me
Until the clouds roll in and try to win
Most turning black as far as I can see

It's time to move on as I slowly stand
Pitter patter of droplets falling loud
Running and running as fast as I can
As I beat the clouds I feel real proud

Tomorrow - sunshine and the birds will sing
Predictable? NO. The magic of spring!

Sue Pasko

Freedom

Think of the mothers, wives, daughters and sons
who all lost their loved ones to the cannons and guns.

Think of the veterans of times long ago
they gave all they had in the rain and the snow.

Some take it for granted like a bike or a swing
Those men gave their lives for every living thing

Still there are some who want to see the flag burn
take away all their privileges and it's freedom they'll yearn

It's easy to forget things done and things said
but remember your brethren who fought and bled

It's you and your children that they had in mind
they fought for your country and for all of mankind

Old Glory still waves to all who pass by
reminding us all that some had to die

Our freedom is priceless and abundantly found
take a walk down the street, take a breath, look around.

Stephen Drew Xavier

Who Cares

Who cares if I don't share
Who cares if I'm not aware and ready to spare.
Who cares if my Dog ate my home work
because it was lying on his bowl.
Who cares if I cry because I'm about to die.
Who cares if the school blows up because of a stupid cup.
Who cares if my English teacher dies because
he had a discharge in his garage.
Who cares if I go to hell because
I killed a teacher with a bell.
Who cares if my mom dies by human
eating flies and my Dad is Glad.
Who cares if a train not seen in the rain
Crashes in to a Guy who thought he could fly.
Who cares if my brother is eaten by satan.
Who cares if I try to fly and Die.

Richard Dixon Jr.

For Father, For Father's Day

What are fathers here for? What are fathers dear for?
Who do fathers care for what are fathers there for?
Daddy what would I do - if it were not you?
You took my hand when I was small
And led me so I would not fall!
You watched and guided ever step
And did you best to give me pep!

You spoke to me to mold my mind.
To make my character strong and kind!
To care for me in times when I
was sick in bed, or had a cry.
You always knew just what to say
You've earned you right to an special day!

Thyrza Langer

"I Am Near"

When you think of me I am near.
When you talk to me, I do hear.
Like the wind that blows in all the seasons,
I loved you all, for many reasons.
I am alive now, more than ever,
I have a new body now, even better.
When you think of me and all of my friends,
My love for all of you never ends.
The love I had for you was true and dear,
When you think of me, I am near...

Zelma D. Cagle

Who's Gonna Kneel At My Casket?

If I leave and take my time with all I have left behind.
Who's gonna kneel at my casket?
If I don't rise with the sun and my time has come
Who's gonna kneel at my casket?
When the sun don't shine and all is gray,
When we're troubled and feel as if they're here to stay
Who's gonna kneel at my casket?
When you can't tell the winter from the summer
Or a rainbow from the rain
Who's gonna kneel at my casket?
When my room is empty and dust stricken
And all is left for the pickin
Who's gonna kneel at my casket?
When the paint is chipped and the pages
Are yellow, and all there is left to say is
"He was a nice Fellow". Who's gonna kneel at my casket?
When the fire is out and the ashes have blown,
And the water has drained all that I own
Who's gonna kneel at my casket?
You are, the one I've loved. You are, the one who's loved.

Patrick Duhigg

Forgiving

I was once called a girl with far away eyes
Whose emotions kind of come and go with the tides.
One day I wish someone would stop and hear.
Things that disturb me and bring me to tears

But people don't want to hear things that might.
Dampen their spirit or ruin their night
So you go on with the ritual of everyday living
Hoping one day soon for the time of forgiving

For there is no greater hell than the one we make
To serve our time for our human mistake
But when the time comes for our release
Will we be aware of a subtle ease

To tear down the walls that have been built so high
To laugh and sing and just feel good inside
For the living can't live unless we learn to forgive.

Susan Richards

Untitled

Heavenly father, you who knows all,
Why are children so precious and small?
Death is a part of life, once said a man,
Why an innocent child we don't understand?
You searched the world over for people true,
This time you chose and blessed us two.
Young we may be, though perfect we're not,
Our desires for answers are much needed and sought.
To experience this tragedy at our early age,
Only fills us with confusion hatred and rage.
Lord, console our hearts, and make our minds content,
Explain to us why you took back the angel you sent.
Had you already planned her stay so brief?
Did you know it would bring so much grief?
Taking away the lil cry, and laughter we'd hear,
And replace it with silence, doubt, and fear.
As we wipe our tears, will you wipe away our pain?
See your way into our hearts, give us strength to try again.
You know it's a great honor to watch your child grow,
The lessons, and experiences you get to teach and know.

Manuel Escobar

Where Are You When I Need You?

Where are you? It's dark and cold and you're not around.
Why aren't you around? Don't you love me anymore?
Nobody loves me anymore. I'm scared!
Where are you? There's big, scary people here
and you're not around to protect me.
Why? I'm scared!
Where are you? Have you forgotten about me?
You're always gone, you're never home. Why? I'm scared!
I need you! I need you to hold me tightly
and to me tell me everything is going to
be alright but it's not. You know it, I know it.
I need your shoulder to cry on but you're not here.
Why? I'm scared!
I have a gun. I need you to take it away from me
but you're not here. The gun is at my head and my
fingers are ready to pull. I'm not scared anymore.
Oh, it looks so good at my head.
You're not here to say goodbye. Why?
I'm pulling the trigger now. "Bang"

Summer Horton

Why?

How could she?
Why did she?
He was only 14 months and he was only three
Her friends, her family, the world, and God all
want to know
What made her turn on the children like so
How could she lie?
How could she deny?
The fact of ending her children's lives
She knew what she had done was cruel and mean
Men and children was what she was torn between
Finally with all the stress
She confessed
To taking the breath out of the two she birthed
That once lived on this beautiful earth.

Lindsay Jones

"Lost Innocence"

Oh, sweet innocence, why did you leave me,
Why did you leave me at the age of four,
Didn't you know it was wrong to deceive me,
Leaving me standing in an open door?

Not understanding what I was facing,
Not understanding what life had in store,
Oh, sweet innocence, help me remember,
Please help me remember before age four!

Help me envision my life has as it could be,
Carrying this pain has become such a chore,
Stop the pretending that grows deep within me,
Help me find peace that will last evermore.

Life's not been fair to take so much from me,
Every fiber affected to its very core,
I long to be free from those memories I see,
And return to sweet innocence before age four.

Oh, sweet innocence, can you really help me,
Can you help me believe that life can be more,
Help the bad memories eternally leave me,
Bad memories caused since the age of four!

Mary Lou Gable

Satan

Satan is evil...he's full of sin.
Why do we all listen to him?
He comes around and says, "Sin...let's do,"
"Because that the best things to do."

"Don't go to Church"...that's so dumb.
"Don't pray to God...that's no fun."
"Don't love people...just be mean to them."
"Think of me, and not of Him."

Now God said, "Don't lie or steal,"
But oh, you know, that's no deal,
The more you lie the more fun it gets,
The more you steal the more you get.

Now Gods says, "Honor thy Mother and thy Father."
But why do that because all they do is holler?
God says. "Do unto others as you would want them to do unto you."
But just make sure you do to them before they get a chance at you.

Why love they neighbor...don't you see they hate you the same as me?
Don't kill...what do you mean, that's the most fun game of all to me.

Now listen, people, and listen well.
You listen so Satan and you will go to hell.

Paula Schofield

Gift Of Love

What is it that makes my poor heart sing?
Why does winter suddenly, turn to spring?
Why does it seem, I'm flying without wings?
It's the gift of your love
The gift of your sweet love!
Why is it I take delight in hearing your name?
You're the missing link in my golden chain
When I'm with you the world is not the same
It's the gift of your love
The gift of your sweet love!

Time is fleeting, Gee, it goes so fast
Especially those moments I just want to last
For when I'm with you
It's like a spell has been cast
It's the gift of your love
The gift of your sweet love!

Sandra H. Murphy

A Cruel Sunday

I am walking, Just walking, I do not know
Why, in the pouring rain
Like the missing cloud
Like the thirsty fleeting river
All troubled waves of the world now in my blood
For a poem or to touch your fluty finger
Like the restless wind of this winter, heedless, I am
Walking on a cruel Sunday from East to West.

I will go
From North to South from reality to singed dream
From the bed of mist to the street of solidity
I will be firm from the fluid of my pain
Again from rock
I will be lava, like the paint of your mind
I will walk
Like the billowy water of the broken dam
If you could, pierce him with agony.

I will never say anything about this evening.

Robin Jahangir

Self

I glide along this life; what will I become?
Will I follow in the bloody footprints of my forefathers?
Will I tie on the choking apron strings of my mother's mother?
I will live through my own eyes
My dreams will pave my path
I beg the help of my childhood chums
I beseech them with my casual laugh
Help me, please, oh most wise and innocent
My blood still runs free and wild
My feet dance lightly over the flowers
Will this carefree glee forever roam my heart?
Or will the lead of age invade my soles?
Will my feet now blacken the flowers
which grow so happily along their path?
I hope to remain one with light
I wish to become my music; this music shall envelop me
I grant it permission
The permission to kidnap my child: myself
My only saviour
My guiltless, godless and forever shameless self

Mary L. Colgan

Dusk

Each one describes it new...
Windows and ponds reflecting amber
Golden streaks weave emerald trees and grass
A quiet haze surrounds cooling roof tops
Settling birds are heard near and distant.

The dew is on the earth's carpet
Crickets and frogs have come to have their say
A few twinkling stars on deepening blue are seen
Screen doors no longer bang or children's voices heard
Soft breezes give a final wave to the setting sun
A sadness comes as another day fades away
Dusk has come to me — how has it come to you.

Mary Ann Schokmiller

The Contentment Of Love

I wake in the morning with you at my side
With a feeling of contentment and love I can't hide
The pain of the past has now passed away
And friendship and love is filling my day

No one on earth can fill your place
The feel of your body or sight of your face
My heart fills with joy that the future will be
A lifetime together for you and for me

I pray that each day, that for you I will be
A friend and companion as you are to me
The pain and the heartbreak this world can embrace
Is eased by your comforting arms and dear face

So hold my hand, Darling "Till death do us part"
And be with me always in mind and in heart

Lois Leech

Juanita

Swarthy face, work-reddened hands clutching a purse—
worn, brown, hand-me-down.
Entering the post office, waiting her turn,
exchanging dollars for a money order
to be flown south of the border.
In Mazatenango that once was her home
three brown-eyed children, almost grown,
remember a voice, a mother's soft croon.
Above the garage, alone in her room,
she cries in the night.

Peggy Corbut

Boys And Girls

Don't ever regret falling in love
With a girl, if you think she's right
Cause blue skies will rain from above
And you and your heart will fight
If there is any doubt in your mind
About her, just go to her and explain
And I'm sure you'll always find
If she's right, you had no cause to complain

Girls, if in love, will always be true
As long as you remain that way
They'll stick by when troubles bother you
Even when skies are no longer grey
So fellows, love them with all your heart
No matter how shy you may be
Then there'll be no fear of drifting apart
Like other souls which you see!

William Anderson

What Is A Grandson

Someone who will give you love
With all the warmth of heaven above
Someone who will make you smile
Talk and listen for a while
He'll fill your heart with all his joy
just when he's playing with a toy
when he gets hurt he'll cry a bit
and be in your arms to comfort it
He'll laugh so hardy when having fun
Or just sit silent when having none
He's all the things in the world to you
He'll bring you happiness your whole life through
The posses he makes the first steps he takes
The hug that's there when you awake
And as he grows you will grow to
Because his love is always there for you
So in your heart he is the one
You'll always love and call grandson

Vincent Cea

I Remember Berk Street

I remember when I played and laughed a lot.
With dolls and dishes that I got.
When boys made scooters out of skates in weather hot.
And mom made her dinners in a big big pot.
Where three story houses were tied in a knot.
This was the corner of Berk Street.

I remember my house where six street met berk.
And where Mrs. Irene and Mr. Jimmy lerked.
With their second hand goods so shiny and perked.
And some moms did but all dads worked.
This was our block Berk Street.

Where everyone on 4th to 8th street could dance.
In every bodies house with red light we pranced.
You would pay your waist line in advance.
To bop, two step and slow drag by chance.
This was my neighborhood Berk Street.

I often sit and reminisce about the past.
The houses no longer stand they didn't last. The kids are gone
they all grew fast. But to remember our childhood it all was a blast.
This was my neighborhood, GOOD OLD BERK STREET!

Patricia Harris

Untitled

Today is a miserable day,.....
with drisly thoughts and hopes.

But hopes today are not enchanted;
Because of teary clouds

that sprinkle tears and damp the earth
with a taste of imagination.

The clouds above are misty and gray,
while here below natures bright carpet of grass

has taken pity on tear falling clouds
and has caught their tears on their pillowing blades.

We too can be caught today but not by clouds
But trapped by our thoughts....
that bring restful inspiration.

Sharon Freedline Hovanik

For The Love Of Winter

Falling snow blown into drifts
With each fallen flake my spirit lifts

Winter is the season I like best
I guess I'm different from the rest

Of the people that I know
I love the ice I love the snow

I know four seasons are necessity
But cold and snow just seem the best to me

There is no sight more fair to see
Than icicles glistening on a tree

When the sun is shining bright
And the light hits the tree just right

"Better rain than snow" most people say
But when I hear this I say "No way"

Let me have snow, wind and the rest
Because this is what makes winter best

Maria Timmons

Lonely Butterfly

Butterflies are said, to be free to fly,
With fluttering wings of flight, seen only
during the day light.

Once a caterpillar, but now a monarch, flying
fancy and yes, free.

Something clean and beautiful for spring and me.
Colors of a rainbow, in a scattered design.
The lonely butterfly, in flight, without much time.
Sounds a little sad, but try not to be, once captive
in a cocoon, and then being free, to fly and be seen in
flight seems like a blessed privilege to me.

LaVonne Wilson

The Pear

Spring tree down by the lake
with fruits that only I might take.
The juice so sweet, the skin so soft,
I take the fruit to my hayful loft.
There I dream of robes with flair and looks
and locks of golden hair. I wake
and much too my despair, all
I have is a lonely pear.

Melissa Harper

The White Unicorn

There was a white unicorn
With golden hoof and horn.
She was born to be free
Like the bird and the bee.
Many men sought to hold
The horn and hooves of gold,
For they were thought to hold
Many powers untold.
But those men could have never believed,
The purpose for which the unicorn was conceived;
She was created out of sadness,
But born to spread gladness.
Only those who believe with all their heart
Could ever hope to see that work of art.

Lynn M. Root

"I Miss You"

Mistakes were made out of spitefulness
With hopes of being forgiven
But the pain may now be too much to bare
And away from me you were driven.

A numbness has seemed to come over my body
Sometimes I can't even cry
But my heart is shattered, my thoughts are drained
With emptiness inside.

I wish there were something I could do
To make you come back to me
I want to talk, to listen, to hold you
Or should I let you be?

The days pass by ever so slow
Wondering what you will do
Hoping and praying that we'll be together
Dreading losing you.

I just want you to know that you're in my thoughts
During the time that we're apart
I hope you decide to come back to me soon
For there's and empty place in my heart.

Nicole Davidson

The Bewitching Hour

'Tis the bewitching hour, just now sounded, filled
with horrors and fears unbounded.
With spirits and demons, goblins and hobgoblins too.
Surrounded by the sisters of Hecate forsaking their brew,
Dancing and frolicking with shrouds askew.
In the distance a werewolf gives a mournful howl,
while in the shadows vampire prowls.
The witch gives a disdainful scowl, at the end of this
dance macrabe each gives a courtly bow.
Time after time she invokes the frothy brine, flooding
their bodies with ecstasy sublime.
She chants, "Spine of cat, blood of bat, tongue of rat",
while wreaths of smoke encircle her hat.
In deep meditation or trance she consults her cat.
As though in one voice all hell rejoices as one, for
whatever may come; the unholy deed is done.
With a flurry and scurry each rushes to their grave or crypt,
for with the dawn the veil of darkness begins to lift.

Richard C. Ditsch

Grandmother's Pantry

Grandmother's pantry smelled simply divine,
with pickles, apples, garlic and wine,
spices herbs, peaches and pears,
How my mouth waters, to taste of her wares.

Raisin filled cookies, she kept in a jar,
to serve a young caller, who came from afar.
An old fashion chat, and spicy hot tea,
kept Grandmother's callers, returning with glee.

Especially at christmas, she'd bake up a storm,
I loved to eat cookies while they were still warm.
Always a smile, she wore on her face,
when hungry young callers came to her place.

I'll never forget her, as long as I live,
Grandmother's slogan, "More Blessed To Give"

Sylvia Blakely

My Daughter

She lies sleeping in her bed,
With such abandon and trust,
Arms and legs flung in four
Directions all at once.

Arms and legs, long, tan and graceful,
Like a beautiful young colt,
Weary from a day of play in the meadow.

Her hair, like spun gold,
Spills across the pillow,
Catching moonbeams as they
Steal through the window.

She is resting now,
Preparing to take her place in the world.
Before I can even turn around,
She will take my place in another doorway, like this one,
And wonder what happened to her baby girl.

Lois L. Tarzia

Waves

As I watched the waves roll
with the cool midnight breeze,
I thought of the silken softness
that I once knew.
I remembered how she walked
and how her hair cascaded
over her shoulders like
a waterfall in Spring.
How it gently caressed her brow
as dew just before sunlight.
As she walked, her hair shifted
from side to side
like the tail of a mischievous kitten.
Not a sailor would dare sail those waters;
for he would find his love at sea
and live all his life enthralled with
its beauty.

Michael R. Thompson

Untitled

My love for you submerged and hidden
To speak of it taboo, forbidden. All space and
light mesh between you and I, in glance and feel
in word or sigh. In love no word or deed can steal
the depth and breath our eyes conceal. For you I ache,
for you I shiver, but not too close or truth deliver.

For all of time, for you and I, our love will burn
but never die. Let it heed us not consume.
To share it feed us, to give into it doom.

Sea Cruz

Calling You Home

The mountains are calling you home.
With their tall trees and whispering branches.
With their babbling streams and crystal springs.
With their peace and tranquility.

The lake is calling you home.
With its glass-like surface and its marine life.
With its lapping waves and its hidden mysteries.
With its calm serenity.

The woods are calling you home.
With their quiet harmony.
So full of brush and wildlife.
So full of mother earth and nature.

Your mother is calling you home.
Maybe so full of mothering.
Maybe to be there like never before.
Maybe she is a part of your cure.

I am calling you home.
With attempted understanding and patience.
With loving heart and open arms.
So full of love, desire, to be a part of you.

Sheila Crosby

...Late

Why do you look at me
with those hungering eyes,
that angry mouth,
and your raging voice?
Why do you yell at me
with those hurting words,
your body pacing,
and your fist pounding the counter-top?
Please don't come closer!
No, not again,
leave the children alone,
leave me alone, too.
No, please!
Stop! Don't!
This has to stop,
before it's too...

Leydanit Rivera-Rosado

My Special Angel

My body is weary my strength almost gone
Without a new heart I won't live very long.
How do I tell my children goodbye
Dear Lord, dry my tears and don't let me cry.

The phone rings at ten
The transplant nurse calls to say
A heart has been given
You'll have surgery today.

With family and friends
Gathered at my side
We join hands and pray
The will of God will abide.

The heart of an angel
Now beats in my chest
Her presence is with me
At work and at rest.

And someday I'll meet her
This angel of mine
And thank her in person
When God tells me "It's Time."

Mary L. Engleman

P 51 Pilot

He wanted wings, as young men do
Worked so hard, won them too
Soared thru sky's on wings of speed
A metal mustang was his steed.

Help crush the Nazis was his aim
He asked no part of glory's fame
It was his job he did it well
He and others thru months of Hell.

A member of a gallant band,
The Hunters, based in Britton's land
Meyers Maulers they were named
With this title they flew to fame.

They fought with fury might and main
Krauts they thwarted midst fog and rain
Some came home to fight again
While others screamed to earth in flame
He is lost, there is no trace
Of what became of this near Ace
He makes one more for that long list
Of those who not only are missing, but missed.

Sarah Brannon

Untitled

To know your existence, of life these days.
Would be to know the exit, in a twisting maze.

To turn a corner, and find a long hall.
Is to pick yourself up, after a hard fall.

To believe in your strengths, within yourself.
Is to find your treasures, your sacred wealth.

So find your dreams, within your soul.
Do not stop in the maze, make the exit your goal.

Tammy Raymond

Revolve

Sing me a song of a lover heartbroken,
Write me a poem which speaks when not spoken,

Read me a story ending with a second chance,
Play me a ballad that makes my heart dance,

Act out a drama with the Comedy Face,
Dance a ballet with style and grace,

Paint me a picture of the oppressed and old,
Sculpt me the likeness of one very bold,

Imagine a Carousel whirling around,
Tumble my precious arts and fall to the ground.

REVOLVE 1995

Sing me a song with a synthesized sound,
Write me a program with a low res background,

Read me a sector off of a disc,
Play a video game at your own risk,

With multimedia experience a fine game,
Use virtual reality if fun is your aim,

With computers, camcords, and simulations galore,
Technology is the new art to explore.

Reneé Rojas

A Mother's Day Wish

I hope this day
Years from now you can relay,
As a day of kindness and love
For there is no one else above.

A mother does many things
Including clipping our bird's wings.
So today we made to appreciate
Although we shouldn't make you wait.

Mother's help you through thick and thin
And I can only say thank you over and over again.
I love you for all the things you are
Even when the miles may be far.

Sara Geremski

Because The Son Arose

Now The Sun Truly Rises And Shines

Before the Son arose, men lived in uneasy darkness.
Yes, the sun shone each day, and the plants grew,
But without the Son of God, men lived in unholy quietness.
There could not be the fire of life, the brilliance of the flowers of every hue.

Although the Son of Man was slain,
Even though wicked men killed the precious Lamb,
He did not in the grave remain.
He is alive, the great I AM!

Now we know that all men live by faith, in something or someone, human or divine.
In what or whom does our faith lie, where is our trust?
If it is in the blessed Saviour, there will be joy in life's line.
With belief in His work for sin and because of His resurrection, we are made just.
Praise be to the Lord for Jesus Christ!
Because the Son arose, now the sun truly rises and shines!

Richard Short

When Fallen Angels Fly

There is a breeze that's warm-
yet chilling
each star shines as the sun.

Mother Earth-she's moist and dampened-
blankets of leaves gently padded upon;

Each tiny dew drop glistens- shimmers
of diamonds and sapphires
underneath this haloed moon.

Lonesome trees sway on this breathless
eve- of what many only pray for;
yet held in disbelief.

It can happen in a moment- your heart
lighter than air:
Your eyes heavy with tears.

"Don't weep my child," an inner voice
does reply.

"This is your Resurrection!" when
fallen Angels fly...

Nancy J. Renneberg

Untitled

Love is a word so hard to explain
Yet I feel it each time you call my name

Your touch is so soft it makes me quiver
And your kiss - Well, that makes me shiver

The way you hold me makes me feel so secure
You'd never guess our relationship could be so pure

Your big brown eyes and your long dark hair
Your tall, muscular body - I can't help but to stare

You make me laugh because you're so funny
I think it's cute when you call me your snuggle bunny

You make me feel so comfortable when we're together
I know that's the reason I'll love you forever

You're my inspiration, my life and my love
And we both know who to thank, the Great Lord above

I don't know how else to say it except you're the man of my dreams
I will wait for four years or ten or as long as we need

Whenever I think of you a smile appears on my face
I hope you know there's no one who could ever take your place

I never thought I'd find a love so true
Please don't ever leave me, and I PROMISE I'll never leave you.

Tina Friel

The Greatest Love

So much love to give
Yet no one to receive
What could I possibly say
To make you believe
There's something happening between us

My friends say it's just a phase
But the kiss that night set my heart ablaze
With feelings hidden deep inside
Set off by even your slightest gaze
I'm falling in love with you

I've always believed in taking it slow
But for me, I've got to let you know
That I care so very deeply
And want our friendship to grow
Into the Greatest Love of All

Shane M. Russell

God's Promise In Spring

The chilling blasts, from winter's wrath, makes desolate the earth.
Yet silently we see anew, the sign of our rebirth.

The bright new rays of sun filled days, the drops of liquid gold.
Sing silently the age old song, awake, arise, unfold.

Come forth from out the weathered leaves, the master calls to thee.
Let spring again proclaim thy birth, from grass to tallest tree.

The bursting buds will open wide, to see God's bright new day.
And soon a carpet plush and green, for children's romp and play.

The Lily White will fill the fields, in robes of purest white.
The perfume from the lovely rose, will be for man's delight.

The busy bee we soon will see, as summer breezes blow.
High in the tall and lofty tree, the call of throaty crow.

The birds will sing their summer song, as all the earth renews.
A glimpse we have of paradise, a short and brief review.

May these bright children of the sun, a message speak to man.
We see them die, in victory rise, we too shall live again.

Pearl Todd Miller

"Be Thankful"

Do you sometimes feel that life has dealt
you a lousy hand
And that you carry the heaviest load of any
mortal man,

Well, I'm here to tell you now! that you
are truly "Blessed!"
Just in case you haven't realized, or even
second guessed.

So fall down upon your knees! And thank
Jesus you're alive!
For if it had not been for "His Blood," you
would have "surely died!"

Krystal Robinson-Clark

You Are

I am a flightless bird and you are the wind that makes me soar
...You are my Strength
I am a lonely child, and you are a stray puppy to play with me
...You are my Friend
I am drowning, and you are driftwood floating by
...You are my Hero
It is dark, and you are the sunshine through a window
...You are my Courage
I am sad, and you are a distant memory
...You are my Happiness
I am meek, and you take my hand to guide me
...You are my Mentor
I am ridiculed, and you remind me who I am
...You are my Pride
I am hurt, and you hold me in your arms
...You are my Comfort
Without you, I am less than whole
You are all of this, and more
I Love You

Kathleen Bove

Parkinson Disease

Ole Parkinson, so strong and bold
You attack both young and old
You're so lean and mean, I'm told
You depress people - you make them cry
You invade the brain but don't you try
to be all powerful because this - I do not buy
Even though people stop and stare
I know you're not all that rare
You are stubborn, almost more than we can bare
You make us weak, we fall - we stumble
You slow us down and make us mumble
We have sleepless nights and then we fumble
You take our smile and our pride
You strut along in stride
You have your fun, laugh and chide
You may be old and cold and strong
But in people - you do not belong
We'll conquer you before very long
I pray that you'll be gone forever
Then a life you will not degrade and sever.

Marguerite H. Tripp

Feelings

They were here, part of our lives.
We loved them, they loved us.
He depended on her.
She left us, we cried, he hurt - too much.
He's gone.
They are together, no pain, in peace.
We are left with loneliness and memories.

Suzanne M. Crow

The Tree

You planted a tree when it was just a twig,
You didn't think it would grow,
But you watered it and nurtured it,
But you really didn't know.

But in the spring, you saw a sprout,
Coming out of that little twig,
And soon, after a couple of years,
That tree got, oh so big!

You climbed the tree to the very top,
You could see almost everything,
You built a clubhouse on its limb,
You even put up a swing.

You enjoyed the sweet fragrance,
Of the flowers that you saw,
You even used the fruit from it,
When you picked them in the fall.

The tree is such a magnificent thing,
With its colorful leaves in the fall,
It shades you from the suns hot rays,
You just stand there and look in awe!

Sally Ware

The Nursing Home Resident

You are old and hard of hearing.
You don't understand and sometimes unbearing.
You've lived your life with much caring.
You are no longer strong but weak and seek out sharing.
No one hears, they pass by with no time not even caring.
Your wrinkled hand out stretches with a motion of daring.
To be left unnoticed by all the uncaring.
It doesn't take much to brighten your life, just a smile, a touch and a hint of caring.
Only a few bring happiness in your hours of end nearing.

Randy J. Murray

Changing Tides

Cry out, oh faceless sea of desperation,
you, embracing life,
For liberties, cozened by another generation.
Oh cry out.

Lash hard against the moorings of compliance,
Thou, pursuant ones,
In waves of self-empowering defiance
Do lash hard.

Crash through the strangling paludals of bigotry,
You, transforming time,
With rudder set toward absolute democracy,
Crash on through.

Glide on to rest in tranquil pools of virtue,
Oh triumphant core,
Until the younger, churning streams bestir you,
Glide to rest.

Shelley R. Buhrow

You

You enter the world as a baby, so sweet and so pure
You grow within your environment, the future is unsure
You enjoy the good times in life, the future seems so clear
You hate the bad times in life, the end seems so near
You read this poem and wonder, am I so very strong

You go through the years and ponder, what have I done wrong
Your goal in life is to prosper, so many of you do, yet
Failure is so common, like colds or even the flu
You live from what you've learned, so much evil so much good
You die when your time done, while new life has just begun

Murray T. Johnson Sr.

Thank You Lord

Thank you Lord, for being so good to me.....
for all of the beauty that you have allowed me to see.....
Thank you Lord, for all of the trials and the tribulations.....
Thank you Lord, for meeting all of my expectations.....
Thank you Lord, for giving me food for my soul.....
For teaching me all of the things that you want me to know.....
Thank you Lord, for all of the small things that we all seem to take for granted.....
For the seed in me that you have implanted....
Thank you Lord, for the heavens and earth both.....
For my continued inspiration and for my spiritual growth.....
Thank you Lord, for every day that I wake.....
For all of the technological advances that you allow man to make.....
Thank you Lord, for all of the good as well as all of the bad.....
For all that I have and not the things that I wish I had.....
Thank you Lord, for coming through in times of need.....
Sometimes seemingly slow and other times with incredible speed.....
Thank you Lord, just for being my personal friend....
For showing where I can go in light of where I have been.............

Rolando L. Russell

Together Side By Side

Although you're very quiet, and words from you are few.
You have so many special ways of saying I love you.
Remember the stairs we climbed, when I became your bride?
The first of many step's we've taken side by side.
Some stairs have not been happy, but we took them in our stride.
as we continue climbing, together, side by side.
The happy stairs out weighed the sad, the thin ones and the wide
however we kept climbing them together side by side.
Now thirty years of climbing, and we have more to go;
and they are not so tiring now, because our love will show;
no matter where the stairs may lead our love we'll not hide,
as we continue climbing them together side by side.

Yvonne Wagoner

I'm Home

What more could I want, I have it all here
You know I've looked for many a year
I live on a mountain, with wood you can stack
You can walk to town (a little tough coming back)
Honey suckle at the windows Roses at the side
Trees so tall and green, where birds and squirrels can hide
A wood burning fireplace, a rocking chair too
All I can do is smile, who could ever be blue
Pure water to drink, tastes good too
Healing waters to bathe in, will make a new you
I'll say it now "Ill never roam"
I'll say it again, "This is Home Sweet Home."

Rene Lyman

Living In The Country

Alas, poor city dwellers
You know not what you miss
The breeze that caresses me
Goes unnoticed by you
It does not fill your wings with God's air
But with the chemicals of man and his machines
My air is filled with eagles
Fishing in the Osage River
Gliding motionlessly on the wind
Against a sky that is endless, vast
Not a patch between buildings,
Filled with sun by day
By night, the moon and a million stars.
Ah country, so sweet, so green
Such peace I have never known
There is nothing as uncivilized
As civilization
I miss it not

Maggie Poindexter

In Remembrance Of Poe

I know too well the shadowed path you trod.
You met mind-created images continually, and
welcomed them into your disordered soul.
Some remained constant, while others became
rituals of torment and surfaced only now and then.
You kept them alive to live out their demands
...and then drowned them with bacchanalian fervor
by denying their existence.

When love came trembling toward you, you reached out,
grasped it with eager hands, clung to it with passion,
but lost it to a higher power.
You could not let it leave your starry world
and so you tried to join it in the groping
of wide, strange woods that eventually
took you to the gates of Hell, where you foundered
in dark alleys of torment...until Heaven,
in all its eminence, reached down in despair
and tapped your bloodied pate.

Marian Ford Park

Once Upon A Moment In Time

Does your heart, like mine, in the twilight hours show you pictures of moments long passed? Do they fill your dreams with whispers of songs that once told us that holding love tight would make it last?

These times of our lives, these scenes, painted on living cloth woven from the fragile fiber of our thoughts have become backdrops in memories that, with the passage of time, erased the pain of love's loss. We welcome these parts we played back now and then without fear from where we keep the love of others so near.

So I say to you dwell not, my long ago love, my forever dear friend, on what might have been if we'd held tight each other's dreams but, listen closely to your heart as it reminds you always of life's passionate schemes.

Understand as I that if not for our moments in time there never would have remained this warm emptiness to remind us of now once a love burned brightly, and long enough to guide us each on our way again.

R. Charles Palmer

"The Passenger"

When she leaves this world, she's dead and gone,
you remember her don't you? My chosen one.

I gave her to you to hold, not to abuse and use her,
But that's o.k. For she's only a passenger.

I sent her to you for you to love,
Her wounds you cut open, spilling her precious blood.

Her tiny drops of tears were of blood she shed, I heard,
But that's o.k. she's only a passenger.

I gently knelt down picked her up, and held her in my arms,
I promised her, No more hurts or harms.

She laid her head upon my shoulders, softly she whispered,
Lord, I'm so tired, rest I told her.,
for you are now my passenger...

Tina M. Davenport

Mommy Dearest

Mommy dearest I love you, I'm going to give you a kiss or two.
You tuck me in, you feed me, you and I love each other too.
You work to give me food, water, love and shelter.
Your great to have around.
I'm happy because—your my Mom!!!!

Savannah Broadbent

A Child

To look in your eyes and see them shine
You resemble so much of your father,
But your demeanor is such like mine.
So fragile and dependent upon thine care,
So helpless and sweet and skin so fair.
Oh, I gaze and ponder what the future will bring,
In times of despair and heartache, death and suffering.
I can only be your guide and inspire you with will,
And protect and love you unconditionally until...
You will grow and move on to new endeavors,
God Bless You and love you forever and ever.

Mickie L. Walker

Goodbye, My Friend

You my friend are my life.
You share with me the times of joy,
And comfort me when things aren't quite right.
You know me and I know you;
We are a part of each other.

You are sunshine when it rains
And love and it pours tears.
You understand pain and appreciate happiness.
Together we share in the beauty of life
And in you I find my strength.

We now must take our separate paths
For reality has come and life is ahead.
I cry because of the happiness I've found in you,
And smile for the joy that this love will bring me tomorrow.

Maryanne Howley

For Bo

My Wonderful Son

When you were young and so were we,
You spent many hours upon my knee.
We'd laugh and hug and dream some too,
Sing songs, play games; as little boys do
When their world is still so small
That kisses heal wounds after a fall;
When the sandman still comes and the tooth fairy too,
And friends like Deke, and Dusty, and Pooh.

Now, these precious moments are part of the past;
But they will stay in my heart, so they will last,
To comfort me throughout the days
When you're not here to share the ways
Your life has grown,
And time has flown,
And all the happiness you have known,
Since you were young and on my knee,
And your whole world revolved around me.

Mary Sparks

Sonnet

Insistent so, these voices in my brain;
You surely must have heard them calling me.
In ever reaching circles, struggling free,
They speak through eyes that softly cry again.
Soft spoken words fall heavy on deaf ears,
Though filtered through misinformation's maze
And whispered by the hear's instinctive ways,
Unrecognizable, disguised as tears.
Though it may be my face you will forget
When dust has settled lightly on my grave
And comes the comfort of the peace I crave
My words alone live on with no regret.
While only words survive through all the years,
If not my words remember then my tears.

Sibyl Ashe-Philo

"My Friend Bootsie"

When I first got you,
you was but a pup.
No pedigree
For you was just a mutt
For many years now you have been
at my feet and by my side.
But today my little friend
we must say good-bye.
The years have taken there toll
In a dog's life, you're lived to be very old

My friend the years I've spent
with you have been fun
I've pictures and memories
of cute things you done
For a long time now I've taken you just
about every place I've went
But today my little friend
It must be different
Today I lay you to rest and be
Golden memories of my little friend Bootsie

Sandy McDonald

My Man

I thought I was dreaming when I met you
You were a good man
Your smile gave me that clue

The touch of your hand and the kiss from your lips
Made me feel like I was tasting wine
In very small sips

The smell of your cologne set my heart on fire
I wanted you and wanted you
with burning passionate desire

The feel of your body
Every muscle every curve
Gives me all the pleasure
And passion I deserve

Your sweat and strokes
Make my body want to shout
The vibrations and gyrations
I know you'll soon come out

But just think we can do it all over again
And make it exciting and passionate as we want
Whenever we can

Tonja Danielle Thompson

My Man

As you travel through this life,
You will receive many, many scars,
But, it takes the wounded heart
to separate the men from the boys.

Remember the key to life is endurance,
Being able to stand each new test,
Rising above the complexities of life,
Is what makes a man his best.

Keep smiling, look up, and continue to love,
Give to the world the best of you,
Without grumbling or constant complaints.
And He'll unfold a man that's true.

View each day as your first one,
With a desire to give the best you can,
The hurdles won't seem so very high,
And you'll prove yourself a man.

Shirley Black

You Were Always There

When I was young and still quite weak.
You were always there, someone I could seek.

The times I needed you the most.
You were always there, by my side real close.

Even when I was getting older.
You were always there, when I needed a shoulder.

There never seemed to be a time you didn't care.
When I needed to talk, you were always there.

Through the good times and always through the bad.
I think of the times you cheered me up, whenever I was sad.

When I am sixty you will always be there.
Someone to talk to, someone who will care.

Your like my friend in many a way.
Through out my life will I remember, until my dying day.

I wanted to tell you how much I have cared.
For the love that gave and have always shared.

You are someone special, I know this to be true.
You will always be there, I will always need you.

Marcia M. Lindsey

Maestro

Hail to thee, pretender
You who orchestrate our lives
Step up to the podium.
You are the flowers that have no scent
But whose petals never fall.
You are the vines that cannot climb
And the grass that does not parch in the sun.
You are the familiar sacs
That suffocate the innocent at play
Yet you are the conduit of life-giving fluids
That course in the sick one's veins.
Still you are the maker of explosives
That shatter our all too real flesh and bones
And in your final triumph
You become a shroud for the dead.

Marguerite A. Morris

A Love One

A love one is the number one,
you would write a book about.
The one you love to be with
and you hate to be without.

A love one is knowing that look...
A hand within your own...
The voice you always want to hear
and a smile is what you see.
A love one understand's your moods,
and laughs at things you say,
Or sees you when you're at your worst
but always love you anyway.
A love one is the one you want to kiss
and make up with again, again, again,
When there's a little difference of opinion,
and being open minded now and then.
A love on is someone that you're always thinking of
and in a very special reason,
Why you know that you're in love
And love ones are always in love.

Ronald Taves

A Shooting Star

In your darkest hours of pain or despair,
you'll feel his loving guidance
and in your heart know he is there.
And when you know it's him
to help you light the way,
you will see the past again
which teaches more than anyone can say.
For it's the teachings of our fathers
that paint the future bright,
so we may be the people we might.
It's in their hearts to do what's right,
so that we may see a guiding light.
It's this light that shines so bright
for all to see eternity.
And in our flight we are but a star
for us to see humanity.
But it is His desire that we fly
far beyond the peaceful sky
And when we reach our final site,
it is His love that Fathers and shines the light!

Patricia Perrin

I Want To Always Remember

I want to always remember carrying you in my womb,
Your first step, your first word, those very early years.
I want to always remember how good it made me feel,
When you would run to me to wipe all of your tears.

I want to always remember when you became a young teen,
Watching you face life's changes with each and every day.
I want to always remember the laughter we both shared.
In my heart the good times and the bad will always stay.

I want to always remember you growing into manhood,
Standing strong and tall and making me so glad.
I want to always remember the love you gave to me,
Your family, your friends, your sister, and your dad.

I want to always remember you, my dear son,
My blessing from God that I will always treasure.
I want to always remember you my beloved child,
For having you in my life was indeed a great pleasure.

Sherry P. Hill

Autumn Tree

Autumn tree...
Your leaves are changing...from green...
To varying shades of yellow, orange, red, or brown...
Then they all fall slowly to the gradually, cooling, ground.

Autumn tree...
Standing quite barren of your leaves...
Seemingly so very stark in your solitude...
And from a distance your appear as if dead!

Autumn tree...
Yet, I do see hope...optimism of spring to come...
For there are many buds on each of your bare limbs...
And with these tiny buds the annual cycle begins anew.

Autumn tree...
In silence you stand and patiently wait...for spring...
But not...not in barren desolation...but in expectation...
In expectation and anticipation of renewed and continuing life.

Richard K. Lloyd

A Celebration Of Life

Mother now you must go; you have fulfilled
your life of faith, love, and hope. Your
light shines through the meaning of life and
guides us too. You thought the best for every -
one and enriched our souls and left your mark.
So now the earthly journey ends, and you start
a new beginning. We are sad but we are glad, for your
Savior awaits, and you will surely enrich His
heavenly kingdom.

Lein J. Knudsvig

Our Love

Each day begins with just we two,
your love for me, my love for you.

No better way is there to live,
Than to have so much love to give.

Today we know our love is real,
Together forever is how we feel.

Should our tomorrow's come to an end,
Our love would continue way beyond then.

Regina Arel

The Man I Most Adore

Your the Sun in the morning.
Your the quietness of the dawn.
Your the buck in the forest.
And I'm your fawn.

Your the tides in the ocean.
Your the warmth of the sun.
To sum things up your what
Makes my life fun!

For without you
The Sun would not rise, and,
The dawn would not come.
The buck would vanish, and,
The Fawn would run.
The Sun would grow cold, and,
Shine no more. For you would have left me
The man I most adore.

Tammie L. Colosimo

In Your Memory

It seems like only yesterday when you were taken away from us.
Your thoughts, your dreams, your memories were blown away in the dust.

I still don't understand why God chose to take you.
I often question him, but I guess it was something he had to do.

I look at your picture, I hear your laugh, I see your smile.
Then I sit back, take some time, and cry for a while.

My memories of you continue on as strong as the day we met.
I guess I just haven't been able to come to grips with this yet.

I know you can hear me and I know you can tell how I feel.
Please try and help me to make these feelings heal.

I miss you as much as the day you were taken away.
I think about you, what you're doing, where you are, how you feel, day after day after day.

I love you, miss you, and will never forget you!

Laura A. Colby

Tears Of Joy

We watch you so closely, day by day,
You're dying before us, we know you can't stay.

How do you linger, with the suffering and pain,
Special words we have spoken, were not said in vain.

We hold you so tight, we whisper in your ear,
Tender and loving words, to rid you of fear.

Your body trembles, it weakens by the hour,
To us you still stand, as tall as a tower.

We've fought this battle, few triumphs more dear,
We've come this far, do you still know we're here?

We know that time's close, we see it in your face,
Can we go on, who will fill your place?

We feel so lost, sometimes we wanna go too,
But God has made a place, that is only for you.

We know you didn't want it, to end up this way,
But from your side, we could never stray.

Now go with the angels, to heaven above,
You've filled our hearts so, with your precious love.

It's time to let go, to bid you goodbye,
Only tears of joy, we promised you we'd cry.

Lin Silva

Friday's Miracle

Nathan, you were born today and I am as proud as I can be.
You're indeed a pure delight, as one can plainly see.
You squirm a little and kick a bit and play a little coy,
but we admire your every move, you're such a smiling boy.

I look into that impish face and surely I must pause
and reflect upon the same image that your father was.
You'll bring us joy and happiness in the coming years,
and we will seek to comfort you each time we see your tears.

You're the first grandchild for Grandma Ann and me,
the first child for Tina and Mike who waited patiently.
We've looked forward to your arrival, each and every day,
you're our perfect little one in every single way.

Be strong in character, quick to learn, you'll need to because
you must go a long way to be the boy your father was.
He too was cute like you, and it is so alarming
that someone so self-assured could ever be so charming.

One day you'll become a man and then you'll go away,
but we will always remember that you were born today.
That day, you'll find a lucky girl and she'll become your wife,
until then, enjoy your childhood, my grandson, and have a happy life.

Walter Thompson

The Best Friends Poem

You are my friend, forever we speak
You're often quiet, but suddenly meek.
You are the sun, but can be the rain.
Your feelings and mine, are quite the same.
We feel the ignorance, we feel the pain
Our lives are separate, but quite the same
We often cry, in each other's arms
Seeking happiness, and each others warmth.
You and me, Here and then
Always remember
Those special things
Because we are
The best of friends.

Kimberly O'Donnell Brooks

Reading

In a world of wonder,
Yours to explore.
Thoughts come from a thunder,
Like nothing before.

As you enter the porthole,
Of a dimension unknown,
A rush enters your soul,
For your imagination has just grown.

You experience a strange feeling,
A new one all the time.
You continue on your journey,
No stopping now, just free your mind.

When you come back from the adventure you took,
you suddenly realize it was just a book!

Ryan Ventura

Red And Gold

And the Lord spoke unto man, "You've worked hard my son;
You've brought beauty with your flowers, but now, their season's done.
Have no sadness in your heart because the flowers are gone,
I'll show you beauty in the land that goes far beyond."

"The leaves of green, that bring you shade all during summer's heat,
Shall turn to shades of red and gold, ere dropping at your feet."
The Lord was gone with wave of hand and it seemed overnight,
that leaves were changed from shades of green to colors strong and bright.

With gold and orange, scarlet, brown, and lighter shades of green,
Nature gives us beauty such as man has never seen.
To see these trees so bright adorned, touches deep the soul,
For it shows us the hand of God in colors red and gold.

Leslie L. Goddard

Stephen

It's cold in here, the noise is loud.
Zambonee smells funny, the ice is now wet.

The sound of the buzzer tells us it is time to start.
I will cheer him on proudly he can feel me in his heart.

Here they come now all heads are held high.
The puck is round, black and ready to fly.

He looks up in the stands as if this game is his.
His stick hits the puck a good shot it is.

But here comes a big guy and rushes right in.
Hits my boy hard the fall now begins.

His head goes back stick flies up in the air.
His skates are no help as if they're not there.

The sound of his helmet on the ice I can not take.
Very still he stays not a move he now makes.

I hear sirens sounding. I see flashing lights in my eyes. Dropping to my knees and shaking God are you watching down from the sky?

I'm here for you baby, I'm right by your side.
The tears are now flowing for them I can't hide.

My lips touch his cheek and forehead I'm holding on tight.
He opens his eyes and says "don't cry mama 'cuz I'm alright".

Lisa Annette Engle

Spellbind Star

Among the flowers
a boom of imagination
lain on the grass
touching the light rays
I saw a star passing by.

It was Cynthia going to heaven!
So beautiful Cynthia
Passed through the clouds and smiled
From now on she lives in the heart
of a spellbind star.

...a blue star that flies.

Maria Dalva Junqueira Guimaraes

Epitaph

A few broken sticks,
A glove where a hand should be
A boot where a foot should be
All these tainted memories
A shower of pearls,
A string of words,
All these tainted memories.
This is how it remains with me,
An epitaph. For history.

Rebecca E. Lunn

"Earth Human"

What is this thing called a human?
A man, a woman, put here to share?
To taste the fruit of life.
To bear the burden of despair.
To build a cross, too heavy to carry.
To kill a world filled with their rage.
Against the fates that put them there.
How can this be? What is the end?
But death at hand, to our regret.
For all return from whence they came.
To earth? To earth? To earth?
What must we learn that we have not.
Not man alone, but woman too.
For who are the givers of life?
The builders and destroyers?

May Levandusky

"The Prairie Calls"

Once more-I'd like to be
A prairie child, young, and strong
Freckled face, not a trace
Of anything that might be wrong.

Once more-would God grant to me
A prairie spring, shimmering new
Earthly smells, pale bluebells
All the mornings bright with dew

Once more-I'd like to see
A prairie storm go rolling by
Summer haze, barefoot days
And look a gopher in the eye

Once more—let me be free
To jump on leaves red, and bright
See harvest moon, hear autumn loon
Departing geese in the night

But now- there is an entry
The winter of my life has come
My weary soul, has one goal
Lay me down, where I'm from- THE
PRAIRIE.

Wynne Robinson

A Soul

Mist from beyond reveals
A pulsing soul
That breathes a life,
An eternal existence
Silenced in Heaven
A soul that mystifies
The waves of time
At the speed of love.

Paula Daynes

January '95

January, spring
A Robin sings.
What is that?
Spring, a Robin sings?

January, mild
Records gone wild.
Rain, all the day long
Many days long.
Rivers running high.
Cars on roads.
Too slippery to drive.
Puddles for children
Needing boots to the knee.

January mild,
Elements gone wild.

Joyce M. Kinsey

complexity

pink roses,
and a pig in the middle.
belly up on the beach,
in summer.
hungry people,
with a dark brown bean.
and only a poet,
knows what they mean.

Michele Svejda

The Blueness Of Being

Stillness sweeps over
And blue light moves
Through my dusty veins.

Can you hear my peace?
Feel it travel over countless oceans
Faster than time itself.

Alone in the tree house
You let the blue light
Fill your dusty soul.

Moira Juliebo

Untitled

Listen as I talk
And hear the words I say.
Be patient with me
When I haven't the patience
To accept what may be.
Smile in my sadness
So that smile will show you care.
Be there for me
Though I may sometimes walk away.
Love me, and I'll be yours.

Nancy Jane Burnham

Die With Beauty
Tattooed In My Heart

I follow you unnoticeably
And every step you take I worship
You are like the smoke in my lungs
For you have polluted my heart
And now I suffer from this cancer
That can not be cured

Laying on my death bed
I no longer can follow you around
And as time passes quickly
Ever so slowly I fade away

So I dream
That you can comfort me
Before my soul
Rises to the heavens above
But all I can do is dream
Hence,
I must die.
Die with beauty
Tattooed in my heart

Daryl Michael Lindover

If I Could

If I could make a wish
And know it would come true,
The only thing I would wish for
At this moment would be you.

If I could be a queen
With beauty, gold, and charm,
I would risk it all
Just to hold you in my arms.

If I could build a world
With a single grain of sand,
I would give it all to you
Just to have you take my hand.

If I could say a prayer
And know the Lord would hear,
I would pray with all my heart
That you will be forever near.

Starr Sanson

Our Love

As I am driving down this long
And winding road,

I am thinking of our love;
Therefore I think of you.

I see the trees swiftly passing;
Our love is like a tree:
It grows slowly and is always strong,
But when the wind blows it wavers.

I see flowers in gardens;
Our love is like a flower:
It is beautiful, and may die someday,
But it will always be remembered.

The grass softly blows in the wind;
Swaying back and forth

Like our love.

Then all this becomes a blur as I
Swerve to miss an oncoming car

And land in a ditch with broken
Pieces all around me

Like our love.

Rosalea Klooster

A Message Of Love

Warm sunlight pierces my senses
As day breaks anew,
I grow older each day
But I still think of you.

Were it that I could fly
That I might watch and protect,
From a world filled with pain
Lest your heart should detect.

Alas, but I am a man
Whose heart has been heavy,
I hope you are safe
From the problems of many.

Never take life for granted
Nor what it may bring,
For although there is pain
Life blooms eternal within.

James A. Bleaney

"On The Wind"

Her voice is soft, when e'r she speaks
As on the wind a sound
Echoing from the tall peaks
As it races along the ground.

Her hair tossed by the breeze
Her song, telling you of love
The tall grass brushes her knees
She runs, her eyes lifted above.

On the wind, this, maiden fair
Moves swiftly with grace
Her long flaxen hair
Blows across her lovely face.

Her loveliness, her charm,
Relates a love supreme
You reach out your friendly arm
To find it's but a dream.

On the wind, the maiden fled
Her image, a mirage long past
As you rise up from your bed
The memory simply could not last.

Leslie R. Tidd

I Dream...

I dream of peace
as the missiles fly by,
I dream of love
as I listen to you cry,
I dream of equality
as hate rages on,
I dream of night
when faced by the dawn,
I dream of happiness
as I watch them frown,
I dream of hope
as depression rains down,
I dream of life
as Death sends for me,
I dream of light
as its darkness I see,
I dream of truth
as I hear their lies,
My dreams are shattered
when I look into your eyes.

Holly J. Hancox

Fond Memories

When the evening shadows lengthen
At the closing of the day
There comes a flood of memories
Which will not pass away

In my dreams I see my mother
With her gentle grace and charm
As she guides my stumbling steps
Around our little farm

My daddy waves a greeting
As he works around the barn
We are followed by our collie
Our protector from all harm

The air soon fills with laughter
And we see down the lane
My sisters and my brothers
Who are home from school again

My old eyes are growing misty
With those dreams of long ago
Because they were the best times
That I would ever know.

Gerry Eagan

A Matter Of Taste

I've been thinking a lot
Believe it or not and
I have to say I don't get it:

Once in a restaurant I really did
Justice to the chef
But my date hurriedly left when
He saw my dessert coming
There's no time to waste he
Panicked and then I saw him running

Well one thing I know for sure:
I'm not going to meet him anymore
And there never ever
Can be any "we" that's
A matter of taste
You see

Tanja Hellsten

Creation

Nod your head
Blink your eyes
Sighing willow dry your tears
Waving arms
Rustle your grief
Crying Willow shake your fears
Raise your head
Open your eyes
Tearful Willow you're not alone
Facing forward
Feet on ground
Weeping Willow rise above
Look above
Frail child of dust
Silver Willow tears are gone
No more sorrow
No more sadness
Whispering Willow your Creator is Love

Amy Marlene Russell

Wave Break

Why do the breaking waves
break into me if I am
the breaking wave am I
the movement when I fly
the gull's flight and
wing the waves? If I dipped
the waters or tipped the
snow topped hill
would I then
shed the cloud and
find the blades
of sunset, cut?

Ruth Stern

The Seasons

In the Spring I love to see
Bursting buds upon a tree
Tiny snowdrops peeping through.
In the grass - the crocus too
Wonderful how the seasons go
Spring then Summer and the sun
The buds have burst the flowers come
With different colours - oh so fair
The lovely perfume fills the air
Then comes autumn dull and cold
To turn the leaves from green to gold.
All the colours that you see
Different shades on every tree
But Winter time is very near
Then the trees will all be bare
Until there comes the frost and snow
Covering almost every bough.
Spiders webs with diamonds glow.
On the bushes row by row, if you would only stop and stare you'd see this beauty every where.

A. Hendry

Ode To A Lost Love

I tried forgetting you,
But your eyes were there,
Ranging in sixteen shades
But many more moods
So blue when you're happy,
Grey, misted with tears.
I thought of your lips
In repose, sculpted like a statue.
Pouting to provoke.
Pouting to entice.
I thought of your hands
With their ballerina grace
The animation on that lovely face
Rose petal skin's a phrase too
trite to borrow.
Forget you - Babe I'll try again
Tomorrow.

Leslie Palmer

Second Of Thought

The flow of time
Drifts past-by every moment
Sometimes realizing
And other times not.
Everything happens eventually
Be it slow or fast,
Either way it all goes by
with a blink of an eye

S. Whitney

True Love

Can you hear my heart beat
Can you see it glow
I can feel it burning
Because I love you so.

Look into my eyes
See them shining bright
I want to have you near me
All through the day and night.

Your kiss is sweet as honey
I know you love me true
We can be together
Forever happy too.

Our love for one another
Is something we can share
We'll never die from a broken heart
This promise will be there.

John F. Clouston

Love That Never Ends

No one told me love
Could hurt so much.
When a man could fill your heart
With that one special touch,

And then break loose
From the string of love,
Leaving you clinging
To strands above.

He said that he'd love you
Forever and more.
And now you feel
Like he slammed that door.

He said he was sorry
It turned out like this.
But your love he said,
He would always miss.

What he said was kind,
And you thanked him again.
For the love he gave you
That would never end.

Bree-Ann Bussiere

True Beauty

Her warmth, as sunlight,
creates a radiant glow
Like an eagle in soaring flight
or a Siberian Husky in the snow
She is not exquisite
though her beauty is quite rare
I can see it in her wit
and even when she brushes her hair
Her strength lies in her heart
not in her style or look
She sets herself apart
A little humanity was all it took
This classic beauty is often lost
Irreplaceable at any cost.

J. Semanuik

Life

"Life is like a two tier candle,
Each flicker of flame unique
It burns as we are destined
Only to find a flame, far greater
than the first."
With heart felt thoughts.

Ellen Bruni

Requiem For A Bull Moose

Muscles hunched,
Dark sides heaving,
He bounds for the opening
And disappears
Into the thicket.

An old cycle
As the mighty moose
Harassed by the pack,
Circles,
Doubles back.

And again
Takes to the water.

The sun sets
As he moves downwind -
Doubles back again
And then to sleep,
The sleep of the damned.

Packs of wolves
or a pack of hunters.

William H. Randa

Eternity

Life
death
divided by a
thin line
differentiated by a
breath of air

Spirit, flesh
body, soul
united we live
separated we die

One goes up
one goes down
still in the universe
still under God's care

Judith Huang

Feeling The Loss

It's an emptiness
Deep down inside
It's a love
That will never subside

It's a loss
Too great to tell
It's a loneliness
Deep and black as Hell

It's the hurting
That won't go away
It's the memories
Of that dark and awful day

It's a mother
Who I still hold near
It's the death
Of someone so dear

Charlene Mamo

Unconnected Healing

Suffering and corruption inside my head
Demons and Monsters
Who won't go to Bed.

Hiding
behind
A Big Brass Door
They banish a key
that never fits.

Later ... much later ...
after getting past their Filth
Death screams its rage
While it fornicates and endures.

The Body gets tired
Of failure and defeat
And lifts the keys
Which set it Free.

Now it's Funny you See
When face to face
As the Body grew Stronger
They ceased to be ...

Bobbie Devonport

Grief

I miss her.
Don't say 'She was a good age'
'She had a full life.'
I miss her.
Don't say 'Get on with your life now.'
'You did enough.'
I miss her.
The things I did for her
She did for me
Fifty years ago.
Binding the cuts,
Soothing the bruises,
Calming the fears.
Role reversal.
I miss her.

Pat Constantine

Raindrops

Drip drop,
Drip drop.
Raindrops falling,
In a pattern,
Like they're calling.
Calling me,
Trying to tell me.
What, I don't know,
Maybe, I'll never know.

Jenny Gasparini

My Love For You

The sun rises, the sun sets
each and every day
Just as my love for you is
as real as the mouth of May
Some things in life will always be the
same
One thing is my love for you,
another is your name
But if the day should come,
that we both depart.
Just remember that I love you from
the bottom of my heart

Maureen L. Rilling

A Letter To A Friend

Dear Brandon,

It is nice up here.

I still miss California
especially those nice hot summer days.
The nice beaches with tidepools
A nice ocean smell
A big backyard
Neighborhood kids to play with.

I just know
there is something about California
that makes me want to go back.

Natasha G. Chao

Cats Up At Midnight

Mystique of the night
Eyes glistening bright
Hunters of silence
With no trace of violence
Ferocious claws
Beneath delicate paws.
Mewl in light of the moon
Will it ever be daylight soon?

Alisha Ross

Contemplation

We all go through life
Full of ups and downs
Some fight all the way
While others rather drown
In a sea full of sorrow
Hurt and even hate
How will we get out of it
Before it is too late?

The splendor of life
Often taken for granted
Like a Christmas gift
Forgotten - after its handed!
What is really ours?
What is behind each "I"?

What's our legacy?
What would you remember me by?
Will it be money, fortune or maybe fame?
Or simply kindness, compassion,
Much wisdom blended with humor
And - no more blame!?!

Sabine Mandl

Before It Is Too Late

Get up to date!
Get up to date!
Say everything that couldn't be said
for so long.
Stupefied.
Crushed.
Silent.
Now we must shout it,
write about it, sing about it,
exceed all limits
if necessary.

Because perhaps
there is not much time left
to say it, my love.

Pompeyo Saavedra

Broken Heart

When your loved one
has left you,
the feeling is like shattered glass.
You can never mend it,
and the scars are always there.
Your heart is the shattered glass,
the memories are there forever.
You cannot see the scars
on your heart,
But you can always remember
the hurt and the pain,
long after your loved one
has left you.

Sonia Cowburn

I Love You!

Having done all I could,
Having told you my love,
Having showed you my love,
And having written to you my love.
Now, I can rest at last.

I am satisfied,
I am at peace,
I have come to the point where
Rest is possible at last.

Whether you respond to my love
or whether you choose to be indifferent,
I am happy nevertheless
I have given you my love
as a gift, expecting no return.
You can stay, I will be delighted,
You can go, I am happy also.

All I gave you was free,
There is more happiness in loving,
than being loved
I love you!

Nicole Picot

Dad Goes To Heaven

They're putting make-up on Dad
He looks like a clown
'cause God doesn't like comedies
with ghostly white stars.

My hands are tired and dirty
I've been shining Dad's shoes
Now uncle takes them from my arms
He'll put them on Daddy.

His arms are limp beside his tummy
He won't spank me anymore
His lips are tightly sealed
Good-bye my bedtime stories.

We gather round the bed to pray:
"Dear God, you won't be lonely
'cause Daddy will make you giggle
with all his funny stories."

Annabel Lim

Snow

White bird featherless
Flew form Paradise,
Pitched on the castle wall;
Along come Lord landless
Took it up handless,
And rode away horseless to the Queen's
white hall.

Jerusha Osborne

Why Does Man Destroy

Equal rights for all mankind
Hear the shouts around the globe,
Define the meaning of your outbursts?
Senseless words, relinquish hate.

Cannot be interpreted
From the great book of knowledge,
To satisfy all races. Equalize.

Patronize all human species,
Take away the gift of speech.
Have them tolerate each other,
Keep the inevitable out of reach.

Take a hand of different color
Hold it close, up to your heart
Draw the strength and love within it
Self destruct fools paradise

Instill integrity and show respect
For all mankind put war to rest
Peace and love are insufficient
Intensive thought, refined position.....
Why does man destroy

Carole Simard

"Innocent Young Boys"

Peace in the mind;
Hearts of others;
In the fields;
Where once;
The wars were won and lost.

Boys sent to the fields;
Boys grew to men;
With guns in their hands;
With fear written all over their face.

Innocent young boys;
Blood in the fields;
Innocent young boys;
Bloodstain grass.

4th of July;
Innocent young boys;
Boys sent to battle;
To be slaughter;
All to be slaughter.

Never know when;
If they would returned home—once more.

Chris Lansley

For Mom And Dad At Christmas

Hi mom and dad it's me again
Hi mom and dad your child
Hi mom and dad it's me again
Your son who you make smile

I think of you at Christmas
I think of you all year
I think of you at Christmas
My heart is close and near

I won't be home for Christmas
I won't be by your side
I won't be home for Christmas
I think I'm starting to cry

So have a good one mother
And have a good one dad
'Tis the season to be jolly
Let's all be happy not sad

Barry Dyck

"Awake"

She awoke with a start to find
him at her side
Reading a dusty bible
Transitive phantasm
When she awoke she was beside herself
Transitive reality
She has never awaken
Transcendent dream
She never awoke
Trance

Running in a dream from dream-monsters
dream-lovers
dream-dreamers
She awoke with a start to find
herself at her side
He was beside herself

He lay on the floor
Shivering deep breaths into the carpet

For a start she awoke

Matthew Robinson

Future And Past

I like him so much, I can't let
him know but I want to be with
him even though.

In my heart I can't live without
him, in real life I have no choice.
I'm only one person with a
weak little voice.

My fantasies will probably never
be real, even if I should take
a chance and tell him how
I feel.

I want him to like me, I'm to
Shy to ask, I'll wait for the
future and live on the past

Rikki Haley

Mother/Friend

I just wanted to tell you,
how much I really care,
I appreciate all the things you do,
and the good times that we share.

It's easier to put into words,
how I really feel,
But, most of the times it hurts,
not being able to appeal.

I just wanted to tell you,
how much I really care,
So if you ever need someone,
I will always be there.

Rhonda Bentley

Somebody In The Distance

Somebody I knew yesterday,
I followed with awe!
that distance was somebody.
A life, a person, a distance

A separate table, the conversation.
A different somebody,
even the face spoke of somebody
in the distance.

Tom H. Widdowson

Untitled

The tree
hunched, alone
in a blanket of snow
Like a crippled old man
its branches cold and bare
Only three leaves remain
withered from the biting Winter air

The man alone on the busy street
weakened legs carry him
towards a light
With a wrinkled hand
he reaches into the garbage can

Huddled in the corner of a
dark doorway
wet snow whips his frozen cheeks

The last remaining leaf
blows away with the wind
its branch breaks

Falling into the warm coffin of snow
to sleep under the black December sky

Tanis Dolman

Destiny

My countryland,
I could be a bird
in your woods,
or a fish in your waters....

Once, I sipped
the dew of your tears
and the sap of your trees;

Then, I was feeling
the breath of your wings
on the flowers through
the fields...

Again and again I stuck my ear
on your chest and I listened
the whisper of the mountains
and the roaming of the ocean
like a poet.

Mary Manolake

The Retort

I shouldn't have said a sentence
I didn't want to make
I should have had the senses
To dodge that shamed mistake
My ever-open mouth flapped
The consequence I face
A clever, cunning comeback
To put me in my place

Glenn McFarlane

Dreaming

One night when I was standing there
I felt the wind blow through my hair.
I could feel him close in the air,
I felt his hand on my back
As I was standing there.
To my surprise late that night
As I awoke, he disappeared
I'll never forget that night
As I was standing there
And the wind blow through my hair.

Deanna Brennan

"The Mirror"

Looking in the mirror,
I see a face, not mine.

This one looks so happy.
Not torn apart like mine.

Her eyes will always sparkle,
But mine just rage with fear.

Her smile looks content,
Here mine will just show tears.

This mirror just shows reflections,
But can not see the world.

For looks can be deceiving,
Of what a person feels.

Starla Kingston

Morning

As I look into the sky
I see the sun no longer shines,
But it's the evening,
It's deceiving.

You see the sun it always shines,
It's just the world has turned away
For the moment.
It will turn around.

There is no day without the night.
There is no dark without the light.
You're only sleeping.
Daylight is creeping.

There is love on the horizon,
And I wouldn't be surprised
If the day is long
And the sun shines strong.

Get some rest now,
It's been a long hard day.

Richard James Hassefras

My Feelings

The pain the hurt the emptiness
I'm feeling deep inside.
I wish I were a little girl
so I could go and hide.
But no, I'm all grown up now
and I must carry on.
When I think of you mom
I don't want to think you're gone.
We had almost thirty years together
I wish there could be more.
I'd take another five or ten
or even sixty four.
Remember when you used to say
whatever will be will be.
Or sing the song Kay Sara
the futures not ours to see.
No more hugs, no more kisses
this I have to face.
Memories and dreams are all what's left
sitting in their place.

Theresa Caza

Red Sawdust

I have this recurring nightmare:
In a forest I am clearing,
I am a condemned tree myself!

A chainsaw, roaring, screaming,
sinks its ravenous teeth in me!
My wooden flesh is bleeding,
multiplying my agony
with every cross-cut year-ring!

My whole body, my bones are crushed
and ground up into red sawdust,
a resinous flood, streaming!

There is no one to wake me up,
to tell me: I am dreaming!

Joseph Csinger

Wild Lilies and the Worm Besieged

Wild lilies and the worm besieged,
In autumn pale, the spring must be.
The mother fine, her glances sends,
The poppies fairly conquered,
Slowly transcend.

The sound resists the power in the hour.
The waves slow, descend again,
The nest in pine dry brown,
The colour restrains.

Your eyes fair beneath the stare;
solitude ours alone with despair.
The pleasure pale,
The autumn in with snail.

Peter Haivarlis

Us

I have tomorrow
In my dreams today,
I am the future
I'll find the way.
You are the yesterday
Gone like our sun
You are the memories
fading one by one
today when I saw you
I remembered the past
we shared something wonderful
it just didn't last,
I can't stay any longer,
I have to move on,
To look for the future
yesterday is gone.

Sheri

Memories Of Love

Spring Time is in the air
In my heart you are there.

It was not so long ago
That we felt all aglow.

Love was all that we had
Now I am a mom and your a dad.

Our worlds are far apart
And new families we will start.

My love for you will never die
So for me don't you cry.

God will keep us in his care
While in our lives we can not share.

Trudy A. Ward

"Tie That Binds"

Though in the flesh we are apart
In spirit you bind us together.
Like a tantalizing hydrogen bond,
A puzzle in organic chemistry-
Tie that binds:
Mocker of physical sense
Invisible convex lens,
You focus my mind
To the vanishing point.
And there you stand lit
As if by flames in fields of oil.

The longer the periods of silence
The blacker the veils of night
The starker your beauty is revealed.
Self-luminous thing, uncoverable light:
My love, you yourself are the tie that binds.
How then can you hope to be concealed
Behind barriers fashioned by human minds?

Lade Wosornu

The Cover Up

The snow falls softly to the ground
In stealthy, ghostlike, downy flakes
The earth has carpet, wall to wall
Before the dawn of morning breaks.

It covers all the ugliness
The blackened earth from mass decay
The fallen withered, deadened leaves
Deceitfully, are hid away.

How like the earth our lives can be
Involved with sin and wickedness
We too can fall, turn black and die
From lack of love, from pain and stress.

We also need a cover up
Deceit is practiced, lies are told
We find they seldom satisfy
Like snow, they leave us bare and cold.

Kathy Huber

The World Beyond

Enclosed by mountains
Is a beautiful stream,
Of light blue water
Surrounded by green.
Enjoying the sweet scent
Of aroma in the air,
Kneeling down
For my daily prayer.
Peace and beauty
Is my world in the sky,
War and racism
Is the world I left behind.
When your time comes
You will see the light,
He'll be waiting to take you
Beyond the golden gate.

Shirley Hutt

Psychic Phenomenon

Nurtured my ego
On internal fantasies.
Superego
Grew bigger
Than both of us.
Id swallowed me.
No fertilization.
"i" shriveled and died.

Diane Ferracuti

The Donor Card

The reason that your reading this,
 is because of my demise.
And now you'd like to take from me,
 My heart, my lungs and eyes.

Well that's O.K. I'm done with them,
 So take all that you need.
Give them to someone who may live
 And go there with God's speed.

Please note though, the broken heart.
 The result of the abuse,
Of a million tears and shattered dreams
 I hope there's still some use.

But that is not of your concern,
 For yours is with the living.
So being of sound mind and body...
 My organs I am giving.

I'm otta here!!! Adios!!!

Mike Iannetta

My Partner - My Friend

I often said that happiness
Is being married to your best friend.
Someone you don't take for granted.
But on whom you can always depend.

Someone who'll share your good times
And will always be there too,
When you travel on the rough roads,
Life may have in store for you.

Someone that you can talk with,
And share secrets that are so deep.
Someone that you can laugh with,
And who'll comfort you when you weep.

With all of life's great treasures
You're wealthy when you can share,
The gift of a special partner,
A friend who really does care.

May the vows you've said in marriage
Be blessed by God above
As you travel life's road together,
As partners and friends in love.

Joanne O'Connell

Inspiration

Valley of the pines
Is where I go
Indulging in inspiration
Walking through the snow

Looking at the great horizon
Be it East or West
Watching the great pines
Swaying as they rest

Enjoying the sound
Of a creek flowing by
Never giving thought
To time passing by

Listening to the birds
Observing them nest
Going to the fountain
That never knows rest

This is my religion
In this nature wonder
Absorbing all around me
Turning it to splendor

Jaromir Nerad

Loneliness

Like a knife that cuts and scars
It can tear your life apart
It will tangle up your brain
Till you think you'll go insane

You can feel it coming around
And it slowly wears you down
Like a load upon your shoulders
It will make your days seem darker

Day and night, night and day
It never seems to go away
Till you cannot see the sun
Even when the clouds are gone

It's the rain in the autumn sky
it's a bird that cannot fly
A wheel that just won't turn
A fire that will not burn

And when you think it's left you
And the day starts looking brighter
Like a cloud out of the blue
It comes back even stronger

Claudette Lambert

Love

What is this thing we call love?
It is a word we often use
and, I fear, too often abuse.
Love is everywhere,
and in everything.
It is in my children's eyes,
and in the songs they sing.
People say true love is a rarity.
Due only to our own stupidity.
We build walls of fear and distrust,
then cry alone, no one can reach us.
I pray that my walls will never
be too high, or too heavy to lift,
Because love, you see, is God's
greatest gift.

N. Taylor

Morning Sun

The golden sun is on the breeze
It reaches out and wakes the trees
Gathers up the drops of dew
Paints the morning sky light blue
Causes every bird to sing
Breathes joy on everything
Blue waters turn gold
Closed flowers unfold
The creatures arise
As the sun walks by
It climbs up to the highest hill
And for a moment it stands still
Then reaches up into the sky
And soon the morning passes by

Tina Neufeld

First Love

I let your love into my heart,
Like a helpless burning fire,
You played my prince, the delicate part,
That I could not help admire,
And then one day,
It slipped away,
And your heart had turned to stone,
I realized, I had fantasized,
And I was once again alone.

Catherine M. Plunkett-Kleinlagel

Dancing Of The Minds

When everything clicks
It's so fine,
Dancing of the minds.
They meld together...
Held by silky thread
Passion fed.
Lost in fantasy of mindful pleasure
No limits, as we dance together.
Bright images flash in flight
Soaring into the night.
Emerging, into daylight.
Images of reality,
A tiny speck in the sea
Gradually takes hold.
And although we've just begun,
Daylight won.
Dancing of the Minds will meet again,
Only we
will know when.

Vivian Crawford

Friends

I wonder if you know
Just how much you mean to me.
I can't believe it took this long
For us, true friends, to be.

I'm sure we were destined
Each other to find.
We are, without doubt,
Two of a kind.

It really is uncanny,
The similarities that we share,
And finding the friend I have in you
Is very, very rare.

I know I can count on you
Whatever I may do,
And I hope you know
That I'll be there for you too.

I feel very close to you
And I sense you feel the same,
And I am very thankful
That into my life you came.

Marilyn Corey

Remembering

I am here all alone.
Just like always right?
Wrong because now hear
with me I have a friend, death.

When they die so do you
part by part you do too
it's not about accepting
it's not about moving on
it's about trying to forget the bad
and to only remember the good
it's about accepting that a part of you
had died too.

It's over it's done with
don't try and pretend
cry, scream, hurt,
you probably won't feel much better
but at least you'll realize
that others hurt too.

Tonya Woolford

Cleansing

I sat and thought of silly things,
Like ponytails and plastic rings.
Lost in thought so far away,
Just like tree tops winds do sway.

After while I will come back;
For real life calls to keep on track.
To deal with problems as they are;
And not to drift away so far.

Sometimes though it seems so scary;
Facing all these fears I carry
If only I had wings I'd fly,
And leave my problems in the sky.

I'd then come down to meet the change;
For then my life I could arrange.
And so my mind would then be clear
Free of thoughts that caused me fear.

June Parslow

Soul Mates

Fresh sent of evergreen
Living a life like a dream
Canoeing up a calm black lake
With my one and only soul mate
A wooden paddle at my side
Beautiful sunset, it's our guide
Sitting at the bow faced my way
What an amazingly peaceful day
Silky hair spilling in face
Playing a soft melody with so much grace
Looking up at me with a warm smile
Drifting along for at least a mile
Mysterious eyes gazed into mine
Two soul mates lost in time

Melody-Joy Evon

Living, Life, Love

Living dreams,
Living life;
Loving life, having hope.

Hearts, hate, have.

Happy hearts,
Healing hate;
Have a heart, and listen

Smile, Special, Someone.

Sharing smiles,
Feeling special;
With someone, all mine.

Beauty, Tenderness, Faith

Inner beauty,
Kind tenderness;
Faith above, my strength.

Toward, Future, Peace

Moving toward
Into the future
Peace everlasting, me to you.

Annette Cornish

Plight Of The Eagle From Within

Though it seems so
long ago
I was like a
wounded bird
without much hope

Every now and then
when I sit in a
corner of my patio
listening to my radio
on those lonely quiet nights
the echoing sound of eagles songs
while in flight
prompts me to think that
I too can fly
beyond my limitations and soar
above those higher than
can reach places
and experience the
true meaning
of freedom.

Dorothy Leatherbarrow

Will You Take Me There?

Here I'm sitting on a hill,
looking at a river.
If I were standing by a wind mill,
I would not give a shiver.

Now a rainbow's formed an arch,
In the damp and drizzly sky.
I can't even hear the ants much,
or the birds fly.

As the meandering river flows,
as clear and smooth as air.
I'm unable to see where it goes,
will you take me there?

The tree lined shore,
Is tall and green.
The mossy floor,
Is cool and clean.

As the sky starts to get the dark,
and the sun goes down.
As the shadows fall and make their mark,
I don't want to go back to town.

Erin White

Music, Peaches And Straw

Movement in water ripple through space
looking see pry a hearty laugh
Straw colour full of harmony
gentle breeze cooling temper flair

Touching purple warmth with joy
loving song from deep profound
Light in dark heard inside far
sharing time for moment's care

Hungry sight filled with peaches
air to fill smooth sweet smell whisper
Lips and tongue with fuzzy burn
feel of moist hot music tasting

Gliding wings of wind and softness
lofty free to go and see
Floating sway on upward finding
hanging high for knowing dream

D'Arcy Rheault

My Guardian Angel

Circling round above my head
making sure I'm not mislead
Watching down on every action
help me avoid the needless distractions
Keeping me safe away from harm
holding me close arm in arm
Keeping me on the track I like
help me on my wondrous hike
When I feel I can't go on
you keep me safe so we can bond
My guardian angel my guardian friend
keep me close until the end
And when I reach my one true gold
stay with me as I grow old.

Susan Dalley

Unwritten Symphony

Grey days are written in a
minor key
To match your mood,
A mood that speaks to you
of symphony unborn.
You would write it now,
But time is stealing it,
Phrase by phrase,
As duty claims your eyes and mind,
By nights and crowded days.
I hear, on days cloud - hung,
rain - robbed of light
A soundless song ring in your
soul in ceaseless sad delight.
For they are wrong
Who name such hours
Spheres of dreary duty;
Yes, they lie.
For joy is sadness - sadness beauty,
All hope a sigh.

Dorothy Walke

While My Star Is Shining Above Malibu

My loves are passing
My life is passing too
While my star is shinning
Above Malibu.

I can't forget those eyes
And that pretty face too
I will never meet again
That girl from Malibu.

My loves are passing
Like red roses scent
I know I will be alone
In the end.

The music is playing
On the coast of the sea
Tomorrow I will come back
In Nashville, Tennessee.

Borislav Stanojevic

The Pavement Artist

Care not for the painted frame.
Nor the canvas that lies below
of colours daubed and splashed
with such array
that one would think the
artist on his death bed
did just give way
what majesty, what brush work he
would say unto himself
but that is not as I did see it
on that cold and dismay day
it lay there on the pavement
a cloth cap by its side.
And the man who had painted it
sat there with his eyes on a
distant sight.

Leslie William Beadles

Illogical To Say, Passed Golden Age

Illogical to say passed Golden Age,
O' no! it is ahead.

Gone is the goose that was Golden,
The past was glorious and great,
Enthroned Monarchs were ancestors,
Don't look back, crown is ahead.

Hungry and naked was no one,
Milk and honey flowed in rivers,
Peace and love was all over
Don't lose heart, plenty is ahead.

Religion fosters about drop of Heaven,
Angels bless'th and wiped cheeks dry,
Bogeys are Heavens and Hells,
Look forward, Heaven is ahead.

Digging up will bring no good,
Outskip to value twinkling star of your
fate,
Be roused from sleep for ceaseless
struggle,
Don't brood on past, flash is ahead.

Grandpa asks to face the challenge,
Befall unexpired to perform miracles.

Varuna Godara

Solace

My ship has set sail
O'er these uncharted waters.
I'll visit every port, every town,
Every cove; almost everywhere.
But soon I'll be sailing
My endless sea again;
Leaving those places behind, looking
For new ones.
But seas become stormy
And mine no less than others;
The thunder booms, the waves crush
And my ship is a toy for the surf
Yet, in these troubled times,
It is you, who is my only haven,
My only shore free of rocks;
With a great fiery beacon, beckoning me.
When I reach the shore
You words, your arms drown out the
storm
And you give me comfort,
'Til when storm ends, and I sail again.

Duncan McIntyre

The Mists Of Port Alice

I love the mystical, magical mists
of Alice
that conceal, reveal
and change the contours
of softly veiled mountains,
conjuring landscapes by Onley -
green
green-grey
grey-green
grey.

Mirror lake rimmed
with curling gossamer
reflects fir-treed hills and sky.
Tendrils of vapour drift up the slope,
valleys exude ghostly, feathery spumes
of phantom smoke
ever moving, ever changing
Alice's lovely, chimerical mists.

Ruth M. McVeigh

Hot Mustard

He sang a simple beat
Of what we wanted to eat
And out of the ghastly heat
Were dishes placed at our feet.

He's got to be crazy or nuts
To eat such horrid stuff
A bowl of chocolate soup
That's sprinkled with syrup nuts.

He's ordered two large glasses
The largest that I've seen
Both are sort of lumpy -
It's milk and pickled green.

He doesn't seem to mind
the speckled, smoked blue cheese
And now he's attempting to eat
The chicken-rippled ice cream.

I don't know why I sit here
When it makes my eyeballs turn
He surely must be different
To be loved by someone like me.

Celine R. Calfa

Youth Portrait

There is this look of query,
of years, that lie ahead-
The growing pain and weary,
yet building confidence to set.

Life seems an endless fountain,
time has no impact, no concern-
in faith you climb your mountain
with many lessons still to learn.

The peaks you reach, are no avail,
no place for tranquil rest-
it's motion on the trail
that makes your toughest test.

There is beauty on the way,
with Love its tender flower,
it's in your heart to stay,
hold in the precious hour!

Hans H. Vogt

Mother

Mother, I came here to salute you,
On this lovely Mother's Day,
And I want to thank you,
For the many years you led the way.

I wonder what makes you so special,
Mother, I sure wish I knew,
Among all the beautiful roses,
You're the sweetest the world ever grew.

Thank you for five wonderful sisters,
I shall love as long as I live,
And for three brothers,
The joy only brothers can give.

I'm proud to be part of this family,
I do think it's very nice,
When the Lord picked us a Mother,
He made a wonderful choice.

Irvine Charest

Hardwood Heart

Hardwood is my heart
only for you to burnt.
Soft wind my spirit
only for you to free it.
Liberate my soul from
this ironlike roots.
make me weightless ocean breeze
so I can touch yours sweet skin.
Let me be the perfume
the cedar tree, fragile fragrance
.... coming from the Sea.
Overly I regret not to be
the naked rain, falling
slowly all over your face.
Take as your blanket
all the earth snow will melt on me.
if you reject me, soon
I will suffer frozen ice in
each one of my veins,
I will live in the deepest of my caves.

Rafael Sanchez

The Nature Of Love

To watch a butterfly —
Pausing,
sampling,
batting soft wings —

Is to want it,
to hold it,
to make it our own.

So
we catch it unawares,
cup it in our hands,
little wings tickling our palms.

Cautiously ... we open ...
to peek at our prize ...

A grey-winged insect
limps off our fingertips.

Our hands are stained
with coloured dust.

Vanessa Nicolai

Lost

Precious child whom I'll never know,
Please be safe wherever you go,
Touched my life for a short time,
Now you'll never be mine.

A gift from GOD as precious as gold,
Now you're with HIM, so I'm told.
Be happy, be safe, my little one,
For I loved you one on one.

You changed my life, my very soul,
Let me hold you and then let go.
How I'll miss you, my darling one,
You were here and now you're gone.

Fly unto GOD's breast,
Where I hope you'll rest,
FOREVER. My child, my Christien.

Tina Derzaph

Our Togetherness

The smell of fresh rain
Refreshing. Relaxing.
Never can breathe enough of it.

The coming of it, inevitable.
Yet it's falling, free.

The first whiff of sweetness
The first drop of wetness
Together, yet each
Themselves.

Penelope McGuire

The Barrens

The northern forests disappear,
replaced by only white.
Of snow and ice that's sculptured by
fierce squalls that come at night.
This God forsaken winter land,
is stripped of any life,
by the blinding snow and icy winds
that slice through like a knife.
The vast and vengeful darkening sky
is filled with threatening storms.
That loose their furies to the north,
in angry, icy swarms.
The untamed winds fly through the
plains,
screaming cries of war.
Warning those who venture there,
they might return no more

Lydia Helsdon

Untitled

Happiness
reveals herself
to those
who wish to find he.
Sadness
to those
who seek her out.
I have been
forever
wishing, seeking
and
have found the two
lying
in each other's arms.

Noga Gottesmann

Hardworking Man

Getting up early on mornings
Riding bicycle to Lears
To work for his daily bread
With blood, sweat and tears

Returning home on evenings
To the land he'd go
To weed, fork and hoe
Until dust close.

His mind is contented
He is a hardworking man
Toiling to make a living
In the best way that God plan.

Yvonnette Hinkson

An Edible Jogger

Yummie yuppie jogger
Rolls her 11 stone strawberry track suit
Up and down and up and down and up
down
The sidewalk daily.
Vanilla headband fails to discipline
Chocolate hair.

Day dreams of weight loss
Imagining:
Each pound, pound, pounding step
Crush, crush, crushing calories:
Elusive ants.

End of today's course in sight
Legs of her chassis on fire
She lurches through the franchised door
Wheezes with accomplishment
Her victory speech:
"Gimme a triple neopolitan cone!"

Randy Harrison

Midnight Lovers

Dancing on a moonlight night
round the fire, the spiral glows
midnight, the witching hour
the moon goddesses soft glow.

Velvet thighs soft and warm
touching the lips of a sacred cave
loving until the small hours.
A velvet caress of midnight rites

Gary Trevor Barton

Love

Love is your heart
running through a race
love is as beautiful
as the colour of your face
love is growing larger
as the world goes round and round
me and you together
never to be found
love is the darkness
deep beneath the woods
love is to be secret
never understood
love may feel different
between you and me
but love is always gentle
gentle kind and free

Marci Martin

Isosceles

I don't want to be torn between
Safety and excitement
Anarchy and structure
Peace and turmoil.

I need a place
Where I can be free to love you
And where you can be free to love me
Or not.

I want you to want to stay
I want to want to leave.

I'm scared of you,
Of you ability to feel comfortable
In a world where I can't feel safe.

You can inspire me to greatness
and you have.

I can't go back to what I was
But I cannot go on like this.

The tightrope we walk is giving away
No matter how tightly we cling to each
other.

I can't shake this feeling.

Suzanne Solomon

Nature's Compassion

Sunbeam comfort me
Shadow my pain
Imagine me
Under the rain

Wind blow away
Everything I feel
Eternity
Make it come real

Thunder cry out with me
Light can I die
Only myself
Why

Lightning strike me
Suddenly there
Escape the fantasy
Where

Snowflake fall gently
Reality rise
Within each of us
We hold a surprise

Gabrielle N. Smith

In Memory

Here we stand side by side,
And yet we stand alone.
Sometimes feeling sorrow and grief,
Sometimes feeling none.
The fall has come, the colours fade,
The leaves have blown away,
But everywhere lay seeds of hope
Both planted and astray.
Cultivate the seed you've found
Planted in your heart
And when it's grown and blossomed,
Let it, your memories spark.

Tobi Giles

The Flu Shot

I had a cold all winter
Sick almost every day
I also had the flu shot
But had colds anyway

Since I had the shot
I had colds all the time
And had to stay in the house
Watching T.V. and wine

I could never understand
Being injected with someone's flu
How that's going to help me
Stop catching the flu from you

If I can get through this winter
And then when I get the call
To go down to the clinic
For my flu shot in the fall

I'll have to tell the doctor
The flu shot is not for me
So I'll go through next winter
Without him injecting me

Roy Plichie

Song

Sing me a song for Hosannah
Sing me a song about fate
Sing me a dream or a nightmare
Sing me a song when it's late

Sing me a miracle
Sing me a voice
Sing me a holy song
Sing me a choice

Sing me a destiny
Sing me a hand
Sing me a lost soul
Sing me a land

Sing me a song for Hosannah
Sing me a song about fate
Sing me a dream or a nightmare
Sing to me love when it's late

Erinn Banting

Forlorn Memories

The lonely cross
Sits up on the hillside
With remains of the late soldier.
A shaggy, weathered hat
Shows he was brave.
A large rifle
Stands for his strength.
An old used grenade
Expresses all his power.
Poppies grow tall and proud
To remind us
Of the terrifying wars.
People dying
Families hiding
Suffering for all.
We are thankful
For their unselfish deeds.

Karen Kucharski

Nurse

She's seen those eyes, those dying eyes
so many times before
yet each time as she just stands by
she bows her head once more

She's held the hand, the lifeless hand
as others may not dare
a dying child lays peacefully
she gently strokes his hair

Her nights are long, but wearily
she goes about her way
to mend, to heal, to care for those
who call on her to stay

She's seen those eyes, those dying eyes
again just yesterday
her strength and calmness lose to grief
head bowed, she turns away

Her days do not allow her time
for grieving over fate
so secretly she wipes the tears
another patient waits

Jann Marcoux

The Unborn

Give me life mommy,
So that I can see;
The beautiful world
Our Lord made for you and me.

Give me life mommy,
So that I can hear;
The sweet song birds singing
A melody so dear.

Give me life mommy,
I want so to feel;
Loving arms around me
Something so real.

Give me life mommy,
I want so to speak;
To tell you I love you
It would make me so meek.

Give me life mommy,
I want so to touch;
Your sweet face in the morning
I love you so much!

Alma Deutsch

I Watched a Little Child at Play

I watched a little child at play
somehow that brightened up my day
The little one grew as children can
A little boy became a man

He met his princess made her his wife
Looked forward to a happy life
Soon a baby came on the scene
Adding to their lovely dream

The baby grew up big and strong
And so it wasn't very long
Before I watched a child at play
As I did but yesterday

Jill Geach

The Cheating One

Visions, delusions
Someone's intrusions.
Prying, lying
Someone sighing.

The song was sung
The deal was done
Wishes do come true
Don't be so blue.

Repulsion, depression
Someone's deception.
Love, hate
Is it too late?

Teresa White

Self Absorption

Underlying doubts and fears to adapt,
Soon become real and begin to overlap.
A hidden world beyond my eyes,
Of animate beings who only try,
To be at one with a world so cruel
And lifeless.

So there fool,
A pain or joke or even a pun:
Is it true planets revolve the Sun?
When the answer can be so clear to see,
That my world revolves around only me.

David Sawicki

Broken Angels

A tiny broken tear
Streams down a broken face
Just a broken angel
In a broken place
Broken angels everywhere
In the door ways
On the stairs
Broken angels
What a shame
Maybe God has gone insane
Broken angels cannot dance
Living life
Stuck in the past
Broken angels with love to give
But love is lost
With no life to live.

Richard Radsma

Sunset

Poised, quivering
Tenuous grip at the edge of the world
Awaiting the black cap of night
Daybreak
Execution of eternal dawn

Mary Sellar

Truth

I've often heard in metaphorical guise
That truth is light, pure and chaste
Unspoiled beam say the wise
The darkened corners to illuminate.

But in the rainbow's refracted splendor
Each hue alone stands firm and strong
Will truth itself then thus surrender
And prove our simple notions wrong?

Bob MacDougall

Another Beautiful Brother Bites The Dust

A man of the people
That's what they said
A culture of violence
That's what I read

Sonora's native son
A natural leader
Tears of rage
I continue to shed

Gunned down by my grief
Unaddressed, unreleased
My volunteer messenger
Beaten bloody in the street

A nation stunned
A widow weeps
Deja Vu
Enters my sleep

Dreams of the others
Returning to remind
We are safe, we are peaceful
You will tell all in time

Poppi S. Peace

Angel Of Mercy

I am but one and all
the angel of the night
To all the lonely souls I give
the gift of heaven sight.

I find a heart so full of pain
and heal the wound within
So venture far, and seek for love
you fight so hard to win.

In sleep I hover over thee
a blanket from the fears
In thought a wiseman I become
risen from the tears.

I bring with me the peace and hope
that one day time will tell
I guard the precious gift of life
that from the heavens fell.

Andreja Kovacevic

Lost

The ice is cold and dark
The man he walks alone
Then he stops and points the way
To a tunnel leading below
He turns and walks into the ice
And I am forced to follow
I try to stop-
My legs will not
And we continue on
We come upon a cavern cold
He turns and says to me
"Now you're sealed inside the ice."
"You never can return"
I turn to look, the tunnel's gone
And I an lost in darkness

Nolan Edwards

The World You Live In

Everybody does their time,
the people walk in crooked lines.
Everybody has got their choice
But often we don't use our voice
Let us find what has been so lost
So many people get torn and tossed
We're all in this together
And together we shall be.
You could be my friend
So don't turn your back on me
Cause we'll be here till the end.
We all have that dream
to live in perfect harmony
Don't take away my peace of mind
Don't leave me here to rot and die.
my careless friend.
It's give and take, the more the fake.
The more the pain, the more you lose
Live you life, don't take no sides
Cause the world you live in is full of lies.

Jessica LeBlanc

The Whale Is Beached

Inexplicable;
The sea, the sand, the sun, the sky
and the great gasping beast
with imploring eyes,
And the unanswered questions.

Carolyn Wolfe

We Will Sing

A broken sparrow fell to earth
The sky was gray, the wind was chill.
The frozen ground, no friendly berth
No happy trills, the air did fill!

The passing of this soul was lost
Amidst the hushed and hallowed halls.
If left behind the pain and cost
That pride had buried under walls.

But knowledge that he'd loved and cared
That thirst for new, exiting skies
The soaring trill of music shared
Reflect now in his children's eyes!

They've learned his caring, loving ways
While sharing thrills and flying wide.
The music that now fills their days
Both flows and ebbs like passing tides.

Their grief will soften, as will pain
For he lives on, in sparkling hues.
A testament, not just a name
"Yes Poppa, we will sing for you!"

Sharen Ann Maguire

Untitled

A love like theirs
Only the two could share
Nothing coming in between
for each other they care
A distance kept them apart
Their time together kept close to heart
Many obstacles over came
Still their feelings stayed the same
Nothing worthy to trade
Only wanting to keep the love they made.

Jamie Morton

Stripper's Paradise

The world was sweet;
The world was good.

We strove to acquire all we could;
The more we had, the more we wanted.

Dear GOD, we loved ourselves;
Our load of acquisitions.

And then—it started!
First this, then that;
And on, and on, and on.

Destitute, desolate, depressed—
Stripped of health, wealth, friends;
Stripped of all we had,—
Of all we were!

Hour by hour, transformed to come
Face to face with GOD,
The LOVE of loves that chooses
Not to let us go!

Joyce Cartwright

Untitled

Alone I sit thinking
Thinking about the past
Past was bad why
Why was it so hard
Hard is my heart
Heart is my soul
Soul cry's out loud
Loud is my pain
Pain of memories
Memories I can't find
Find me please
Please let me fly
Fly far away
Away from my memories
Memories I can't find.

Michelle Osborne

Those Eyes

Those Eyes remind me of someone
Those Eyes cry out in pain
You hunger for the bottle;
I can see those eyes again.

Those Eyes are always angry
Those Eyes are full of fright
My father has Those Eyes
Those Eyes are why I fight

I hate to see Those Eyes in you
When once they were so clear
So full of hope and happiness
Now clouded up with fear

You feel you can forget some of;
And someday all your strife
But please don't let me see Those Eyes
That I've seen destroy a life.

Once when I was very small
Those Eyes were all I knew
And now it scares me half to death
To see Those Eyes in you

Kim Hutchinson

Time For The Soul

I took a walk within the woods,
to search within my soul.
For parts of me which I have lost,
that made my spirit whole.

A breath of air caressed my cheek,
and whispered in my ear.
It's been so long since you have come,
We're awful glad your here.

The weeping willow gently reached,
with tendons long and green.
Stay with us for awhile,
We are just what you need.

A nearby brook was bubbling,
with ecstasy and glee.
Oh, won't you take your shoes off,
and come and play with me?

I revelled in the peacefulness,
and beauty everywhere.
My mind subdued, my soul refreshed,
when I departed there.

Nancy Hughes

Angel Song

Sweetly go the children
To the front and then to heaven
Quietly cry the mothers
At the grave with many others
Empty is the house
On a Friday all are praying
Little children come with me
Your mothers all are waiting

Fathers smile and wave goodbye
Tears blocked behind their eyes
Not knowing if they'll ever hold
Their child close to their sides
Empty is the house
On a Friday all are praying
Little children come with me
Your fathers all are waiting

Morag J. McDonald

Hungry For Love

I wish I had a companion who loved me
very much,
but all I could find was a bone and a
bug that I could chew on and such.

If only someone would walk me or put
some food in my dish,
I'd love them so much, anyone would
ever wish.

They always yell and put me down.
I'm a big old dog with one heck of
a frown.

All I want is love, which isn't much
to ask,
A companion to love me forever, and be
able to last.

Lynn Dobson

Remembering

I remember early one morning,
Waking to yells and screams.
Mother and father were fighting,
That's all they do it seems.
I sat at the kitchen stairs,
Listening to them scream and shout.
Then I ran up to Grandma's house,
To tell her what the yelling was about.
Grandma asked me what was wrong,
"Daddy hit Mommy", I started to cry.
Grandma gave me a serious look,
She knew I didn't lie.
All she could do was hug me,
She didn't know what else to do.
I wish all of this was a nightmare,
I wish none of this was true.

Jaimee A. Roach

Untitled

We are all creatures of this earth
We've been together since our birth
Why can't we get along
Join our hands and sing a song
Have we done what we can do
Can we turn it around, and fix this zoo
Pollution and famine, war and greed
Who's gaining from these wasteless needs
It's not you, and it's not me
It's not anyone, that will ever be
The sooner we look, the sooner we see
How better off, we all can be

Robert G. Maude

Loneliness

So much pain deep in your eyes,
What have you seen that now you hide?
Your eyes show wounds faded by time,
But time itself can leave you blind.
You've felt the pain and burning tears,
And now you're wise beyond your years.
Hurt and pain is all you've known,
And through it all you stand alone.

April Jensen

Where Did My Spirit Go

What has happened that I cannot see
When I try and look for thee
I used to find you every night
And now I find your nowhere in sight

What did I do or what did I say
That made you turn the other way
Please give me another chance
So that in your realms I may glance

For when I'm with you seem to say
What I can do for a better day
That if I smile when I start my morn.
It will take away the thoughts of scorn

And if I'm happy with everything I do
It will rub off on others too
You also show me the pure delight
Of loving everything in sight

Please show me where I got off the track
So that I may find the right way back
Give me your guidance and your love
Let me back into your realm above

Michael Cullip

I'm Glad It's Not Summertime

I'm glad it's not summertime
when lovers sit on downtown
park benches
I walk by them now
finger oak bark indentations
where you and I kissed
long and deep
feel the pit of my stomach
contract like an elastic band
snap dull pain through my body
but I don't cry anymore
it's winter
as cold as my heart
emotional hibernation my solace
until Spring
when I'll smell earth heat rebirth
— reminds me of your aftershave

and I will have to deal with
feeling
again

Brenda Biron

The Rose

You gave me a rose
when we were one.
Now you are gone
life isn't fun.
The bright colors are fading
the blooming petals are dead.
One by one they fall off
soon there's only a stem.
I'll save the last petal
when the rose finally dies
To remember the day
you said your final
good-bye.

Colleen Faulkner

Qualification

The color of my eyes
Which is I think grey-blue
Has nothing at all to do
With seeing things in any wise.

What to us both is white
And yet your eyes are brown
Can surely be noted down
To prove the sameness of our sight.

It is in the way we feel
And strictly through the heart
We are sometimes apart:
I might be soft, you hard as steel.

Antonio M. Allego

Frustration

I want to bang my head,
To shout and scream,
What can I do,
What can I say!
Listen to me,
Take time out,
To look and see —
What is happening to your life,
Where are you going? - Nowhere!

Marjorie Masuda

Peace Dome

Canada is the mankind land
Whose ethnic groups is mosaic aggregate
Alteration by the kingdom bound
To independence and autocrat
The immensity of its territory
Its big lakes and immense forest
Are leaving the mark of glory
But also the enclavement of uninvolved
From the East of our Maritimes
To the West of our Columbia
This take us by limousine
Seven beautiful days and nights
Blended by Indians, English and French
We want to give the example
That the yeast of indulgent
As only the foundation of the cognizance
The desire of the human race
No matter the faith or color
Survive the atomic threat
With everybody peace and love

Cau Francis

Leaf Games

Leaves and wind,
Wind and leaves,
Gold and Scarlett,
Interweaves.
Whirling, swirling,
Madly spinning,
Race in circles,
No one winning.

Wind and leaves,
Leaves and wind,
One chase ends
As one begins.
Rattle, prattle,
Sidewalk surfers.
Wind promoted
Fence post skirters.

Claudette M. Dunn

Robert

You lie there so peaceful
with no pain in your eyes
Your hurt all forgotten
and the truth of your lies
My memories of loving you
when no one else would
My thoughts of hating you
yet you lie stiff as you could
The feelings of anger
that I wish I could tell
How your ignorance and selfishness
should send you to hell
And I sit and I wonder
if it matters or not
How I wanted to know you
but your love you forgot
And as I leave your bedside
I think why bother
Because God only knows
you were never my father

Andrea Riopel

Buddha Bookends

Serene cat Buddhas,
with paws folded under,
perched on my porch railing
like black and yellow bookends.

With impassive faces
they patiently sit
on the look out for enemy cat invaders.
longing to spring
"ninja like"
on the slinking invasion.

Crouched unblinking, they wait,
with cat like calm
to launch their attack,
but other yards are being invaded today.

Linda Vigh

Hurting Inside

I'm hurting inside,
With tears in my eyes,
That I cry silently,
And quietly.
I try not to show,
I'm hurt as I go,
Each and everyday,
The hurt seems to stay.
When we were together,
The hurt wasn't there,
But now that we're apart,
It has appeared.
Both my heart and my soul,
Have grown deeply cold,
I'm hurting inside,
But I'm trying to hide,
The feelings I still know,
That hopefully won't show.
Some days I watch the peaceful tide,
And sadly sit, still hurting inside.

Christie McKiel

In For The Kill

I tried to stab her yesterday
With the kitchen carving knife
But she moved towards the oven door
And that move saved her life

I tried to shoot her yesterday
The bullet went too wide
I'd fired right on target, but
She'd stooped to a child that cried

I tried to hang her yesterday
It wasn't any use
Just as I drew in the rope
The wretched noose broke loose

I tried to axe her yesterday
It wasn't worth a candle
I'd brought the chopper down and then
The blade flew off the handle

I'm in a prison cell today
And rue fate's cruellest joke:
Just now she fell under a bus
Which killed her - at a stroke.

Stewart Quentin Holmes

The Angel Sleeps

If I gave you the wise old moon,
Would you take it for a ride?
If I gave you the biggest cloud,
Would you try to jump inside?
If I gave you a gentle rain,
Would you stop to wonder why?
If I gave you the wildest wind,
Would you sail up to the sky?
If I gave you the brightest ray of sun
From God's land up above,
I'd give you all I could in life
To show you all my love.
If I could give you all you need
For all life's favorite things,
I'd give you God's gold halo
And the Angel's softened wings.

Belinda L. Beil

Mask

You think you know me.
You ever say you do.
Are you positive?
For myself knows not who
Lives behind this mask.

You always say to me,
"I read you like a book."
A creature of habit I am —
But a well-read novel, never!

It is safe behind this mask
But comfortable? Oh, no!
You can enjoy my niceness.
But if I remove my mask,
My weakness may weaken you.

You might roar with laughter.
You might quickly run away.
Or I too might run.
But laugh? Never. Never —
I'm crying much too hard.

Patricia Moore

Imperfect Challenge Human

A rope around my neck
You know that it's bad noose
My life is but a speck
Imperfection on the loose

My time is so sublime
Affiliate the stance
To turn the wrong to a rhyme
I think I ate the chance

My mind is a mansion
Stuck up on my hill
It's time for expansion
Renovate with the quill

Turn the clock around
Time just sets me back
Imperfection is my ground
Interferes with my knack

A neck around my rope
You know that it's bad news
A neck what the heck
You know that it will loose

Ryan S. Morin

You Are Supreme

Born with tolerance
You live with endurance
Life's challenges you face
You support the human race.

In anticipation
You live up to man's whims
Nine moons you go through
Heavy with tomorrow's buds.

Mother of virtue
Nurturing the young:
To you,
Toddlers cling
And learn to spring;
You water their skills
They tread life's hills.

In your very frame
Is Patience, Industry, Hope...
You are a mystery.
You are the supreme
The world whispers.

Rosemary Kyarimpa

Why?

You come to me, in my room
You start to talk,
Each word takes away apart of me
My life, my desires, my dreams, my love.

The pain you feel you give to me,
it isn't my fault, is it?
I wish it would stop.
At times you strike out at all of me,
My mind, my body, my soul, my love.

When it is over your pain is gone,
did you ever wonder about mine?
You expect me to stop my crying,
my running, my hurting, my hating.
And once again you drag me back.
Using your powers, your desires,
your touches, your love.

When I think about what you do to me
only one word returns.
Why?

Michele Appleby

The Chores They Must Be Done

Just before the sun comes up
You wash your face and have a cup.
Then yawn until the cows come home
The chores, they must be done.
Hard work with few complaints
Of dirty hands and dirty boots,
Fixing fences and machines
And never enough time or so it seems.
To sleep 'til noon would be a change
Or have weekends off and holidays.
But the chores, they must be done.
You tidy up and put away
Brooms and pails and bales of hay
Just to do the same next day.
The chores, they must be done.
Being midwife and den mother,
Can't be one and not the other.
The whole barn yard will always be,
Part of house and home and family.

Janet Patterson

"Escape"

Treading through the sands of time
you'll find her in her darkest hour
She pushes past the wall of chance
And feels she's losing power
And she swims the angry waters
Walks the anxious plains
Flies up to the passion clouds
To taste the sacred rains
She's in a dream within a dream
But her journey lasts forever
From her dream she'll awake
But after that, she'll never.

Emily Johnston

Mystery History

To show one's love,
You'll make them glad.
A little mystery,
When thoughts are sad.

Late one night,
You'll stew a plan.
Leave a gift,
Where it'll be found.

With only a clue.
To who know's "who"?
Their darkness lights,
When a mystery is in flight.

In lonely thoughts,
Tears are bound.
Teach them good thoughts,
Are still around.

In time, the mystery is history.
But the memory of thoughtfulness,
Will always stay around.
Just maybe, even,
They'll pass it, down.

Bernard Cudmore

Until Death Do Us Part

Your body is so warm against mine,
Your hands are full of care
I feel we will get lost in time
But I don't know how or where.

I pull you close as we kiss,
To show you how I feel.
Your hands grip tight to my waist,
Our passion feels so real.

We share this timed like lovers would,
Embraced for ever more.
We care so deep for one another,
Inside this love we store.

We are lovers until the end,
In which the earth will die.
Our hands held tight, our love so strong,
When in our graves we lye.

Shannon MacVicar

Love

Love is caring
Sharing
Trusting
Not rusting
Love is feeling
Not peeling
That's what love is

Tiffany Johnston

A Touch Of Inspiration

A part of me is lost and sadness I do feel,
Bad thoughts linger making wounds hard to heal.
Day after day I try to forget,
But painful reminders will not let.

There are times, I find, I can barely cope.
These times I fear cause I lose all hope.
I'm so confused, what's happened to me?
Is this the best it'll ever be?

I find myself wandering, alone in despair,
Searching for that something that time can't repair.
When I sit and think the tears want to flow,
For I have no one to turn to and nowhere to go.

You're not alone my troubled friend, in a life so unfair,
The hardships we encounter are not easy to bear.
But burdens could be lifted from the heart and mind,
Receive the Holy Spirit and yourself you shall find.

As a child of God you will have acquired
The blessings that are needed for a mind to be inspired.
Believe, just believe, and you shall see
A heart, once shackled, will soon be free.

Andrew Nickolas Lazor

Through A Portal

It's when the smallest thought overtakes all others in magnitude
Options fall beyond the edges of conscious recognition
You do well to hold your claustrophobia at bay
As the freedom of multitude retreats
And you are left with the oppression of that one pervasive thought
This is when you have reached the portal in this chapter of your life
You either control you rising panic and pass through
To see calm an clarity on the other side as all the other thoughts return
And you have the opportunity to file and categorize
Or you succumb to your panic as your soul swells
And you are wedged in the portal never to get free
This is when you fade to craziness
And are doomed to live stuck in a portal with one swelling panicked thought.

Gina Howard

The Fifth Horse

Summon the Four and they do bring,
A Fifth, a dark and deadly steed,
Whose track is found, in Demon's world,
With rider bound, by deadly need.

For those, whose strident voices' call,
The Horsemen, to this worldly plane,
Should understand, that vengeance kills,
The souls' of those, who use their name.

For those who call, this Four to right,
What they do see, as deadly deed,
Must know, that by their blasphemy,
They seat themselves, on blackened steed.

Dismount this steed, then bid him go!
Give justice, to a wiser hand!
Remember, when their day is done,
Their lot, will be the Devil's band!

Leave them, to their final fate,
For torments theirs, 'till time does end.
Return and be the one we know.
A gentle, wise and caring friend.

Ken Dove

I'll Be There

What is there must go, to haunt every place I tread,
A rippling brook, the gay chatter of the birds.
Will tell you, I am there.
The trees in all their majestic splendor,
The sky, the green grass, the flowers that are in bloom,
Will tell you, I am there.

I walk alone, for there is none to share my inner thoughts,
This vast beauty, the mass creation of God's great love,
Will tell you, I am there.
Tho' the grave shall engulf me, that will not be the end,
Each brook, each bird, each flower and all God's beauty,
Will tell you I'll be there.

The beauty that from within us should show,
The outside being tinsel, changing from year to year,
Will tell you, I'll be there.
Please seek and find what's inside this hidden form,
Salvage and teach it to grow, a beauty unforseen,
Will tell you I'll be there.

Myra McFee

rainmaker

i am a fly trapped in a jar
a treasure, within a crystal palace famous for its mesh skylight and
wilted decor
a prisoner of child's play waiting to be sentenced
a spot of dirt within the polished palace gates

outside the thirsty moat, the people stomp their burning feet
oh bounteous rainmaker, the people collapse on the desiccated earth
you hear their cracking bones and pour life-droplets upon them
their fleshy bodies rise, elate with praise
those fools

i am a fly
oh giver of life, your murderous generosity swats at me
your life-giving waters swarm my wingéd body
you paralyze me with your work
oh creator of this living spa, your mighty currents overwhelm my inert
body
you make me like the dust from the people's feet

the prison-tide swiftly surges
oh loving waters, your angry voice penetrates me
oh deepest oceans of mortality, you stink of bloody dereliction

i succumb to this driven death

Tracy Riley

In Your Smile

In your smile I see a beginning.
A world of laughter, awaiting to start a new day.
Eyes that twinkle, you just can't ignore.

You have a powerful light deep inside you.
Bubbling over to effect all who know you.
So eager am I to be with you, day in and out.

In your smile I see the future,
All your dreams I hope to come true,
All your fantasy's and desires to come alive.

One look, one hope, for all to share.
The type of brilliance, not many can possess.
I see all this in you.

I hope to always remember you as such.
My precious little baby girl.

In your smile I shall always see.
The beautiful love you have given to me.

Lorie Frei

A Feeling Of Christmas

The gentle snowflakes dance down from high
above the sky

Covering Mother earth with a white dreamy blanket,

even the bird feeder has a hood of softness to snuggle
it and quietly lie.

The cards hang greeting us each day as we enter our
haven of peace and make us
smile.

Inside a warm cozy glow as the fire crackles and colours
our cheeks, oh my

a gentle drift of sweet smells comes from the kitchen
as Mom bakes up her wonders
and it tickles my nose as it
passes by.

All these are natures own way of telling us all that a
Special time is oh so near

and it's not the gifts that you buy,

but

what shines from deep down inside that gives us ALL
such a wonderful HIGH!

Ingrid Maria Sestito

Think Of

Think of all the many miles of roads
across the world,
And think of trees.
All the trees in all the forests.
Think of the millions of stars that shine
each night,
And think of how much sky surrounds
these stars.
Now think of the thousands of poems
that have been written to be read,
And all of the songs that have been
sung.
Think also of how many blades of grass
there must be on the earth,
And of how many children's feet have
run across this grass.
And now think of all of these things
combined,
And you'll be thinking of how much I
love you.

Glen Mitchell

View From My Window-Winter

Birch trees-steel etched
Against dark Cedars
Pines bowing to their friend the sun
Snow piled high upon fence and branches
Air so clear, you see each twig in high fidelity.
Small puffs of smoke from a neighbour's chimney
Gusting away on a piercing Westerly wind,
Small puffs of birds, visiting our feeder
For fat and grain to guard against the cold
Of a chill February morning.
The creek gurgling under its mantle of snow
The lake, hard bound, bearing waves, not of water
But of new drifted snow.
A harmony of God, man, and nature
Is the view from my window,
This February morning.

Bill Valentine

Remember When...

Remember when the old dog was just a pup?
All big footed and over grown.
Remember when the pup ran in the fields?
All ears for nature but not for people's words.
Remember when the pup grew up?
All black and white and very handsome too.
Remember when the boy took him hunting?
All nose was he for many years.
Remember when the dog got old?
All black and gray was he.
Remember when the old dog chose to sleep all day long?
All far to tired to rise.
Remember when the old dog fell asleep?
All alone that summer day.
Remember when we remembered the past fourteen years?
All alone that summer day,
We remember them.

Jewel Purves

The World's Rainbow Of Colors

It shined in the air like many gleaming ribbons,
All different colors just floating there
As if a miracle, green, yellow, blue and red.
All in harmony with each other,
Just as the colors of the world should be.

We should take a lesson from the rainbow,
We're just like this miracle of beauty,
All different colors side by side.
But there is one difference between us,
The rainbow's colors are all in harmony.

Holly Lavoie

The Rose Of Friendship

I think of when our friendship was glowing like a rose
All the petals bright and red, sparkling indigos
You looked at it and surely thought that always it would stay
So bright and red and dewy moist, forsaken it would lay
Strong as steel it stood so tall and took whatever thrown
And beautiful it stayed so long, never I would we know
That soon this rose would dry all out and cripple to end dead
I miss that strong and steely rose so bright and glowing red
So when you have a friendship dear remember don't forsake
That this strong rose of friendship dear, only God can make

Rachel Perigny

Untitled

Here I sit,
alone and scared,
not knowing whether you really cared,

It seemed like you liked me,
but now I'm not sure,
my feelings for you are nothing but pure,

I want you to hold me,
all through the night,
and then maybe everything will soon
be alright.

Maybe you're scared,
of what might be,
what can I do to make you love me?

My love for you,
is tearing me apart,
I can't go on without you in my heart.

Kim Pratt

Alone

Here I sit with you, yet I am alone
Alone with my thoughts, my fears, my desires, my dreams

You may think you know all of me
But you never will - because you are not me
I am alone
Alone with my hopes, my obsessions, my feelings, my sadness
You may think you know all of me
But you will never know the real me

No one can make it in this world alone
Is that what everyone thinks?
Yet here I am alone - and I am not dead
I may be with you, but you do not have all of me
Don't you see you can never have all of me?

For fear is what keeps me back
Fear of falling, fear of being hurt, fear of being alone
But most of all - fear of you understanding me
If you do know all of me
Does that not make me vulnerable to hurt, to pain?
Don't you see, I can't allow myself to be hurt

So here I sit - all alone.

Kimberley O'Driscoll

I Love You In Silence

Having all against me: Loneliness, routine and time
Although not being punctual, I now realize that I still
will love you silent.

Like only silence can do, Like only whisper can feel,
Like only life taught me, I now scream and I now
I still will love you silent.

This special way to love you is very important in my life
Because now I can understand that, never is too late love,
And I feel like a magic inside me, because I still
will love you silent.

In silent inside me I don't want forget nothing about you
your smile, your eyes, your way, because today I knew you,
and knew a new way to love you, more free, more personal,
was pretty, was new, was our way, and now I would like said:
The last night was just for us, because was our silent love.

I don't know if you will be remember me, but now every 07th
of the month will be very special to me.

Monica Melendez

Think About It!!

I am saying this as a friend, not as a bottle.
Am your friend, the bottle is not.
If you need to talk, talk to me.
I will listen, the bottle will not.
I will help you out, the bottle will not.
If you need a hug, hug me (I am more huggable)
Don't hug the bottle
the bottle does not hug back (like me).
If you need a hand, hold mine not the bottles.
This bottle is not your friend,
I am and you know it.
I have been here a long time.
I am not going anywhere,
but once you drink that bottle, it's gone.
Then you have to find a new one
You know that's the difference,
the bottle comes and goes, but I always stay.
So hold me, reach for me.
Don't reach for that
STINKEN BOTTLE!

Jean Marjorie Bellerby

Garfield's Christmas

T'was the week before Christmas,
and all through the house,
not a creature was stirring,
not even a mouse,
but a big fat cat shutting the door.
When all of a sudden there was a loud roar!
There was a ping-there was a pouf,
when all of a sudden,
Santa Claus came through the roof!
He said hello there,
he said hello there,
he said ho-ho overwhere!
Garfield sprang to his bed.
leaving a note that said,
"I want to be fed,"

Bobby Layton

Dandelions

I used to pick the dandelions
and bring them to mommy to see her smile.
I used to play in the fields
and felt sorry for the grasshopper
I accidentally stepped on.
I would play in the sandbox,
and the only tears that would fall,
would wash the sand from my eyes.
But now that has all changed,
I'm too old to pick dandelions—
and making mommy smile is harder to do.

I never play anymore, but I still mourn
the grasshoppers' death.
No more sandboxes for this baby,
although the tears still fall frequently.
I miss the life of dandelions.
Now I'm in a much bigger garden
and dandelions just won't do.

Raechelle Passmore

Ode To Mother Earth

Of romance and marriage we've had enough,
And choosing a subject is very tough.

Once again, I picked Mother Earth,
She's always good for a little mirth.

So I called her to task and asked her, "Why
We had such hot weather in the month of July?

"While to a small town, so quiet and serene,
You sent an earthquake, and that was mean.

"To Aylmer, a town so prim and proper,
Along came a hurricane, and it was a whopper".

So, Mother Nature looked me in the eye,
And said, "The Earth is my domain, not the sky.

"This is my answer, and if it doesn't please,
When December comes along, I'll send a deep freeze".

So if you kind folk think I'm somewhat unruly,
I'll just sign off as yours very truly.

Jessica Gavin

"I"

Why am I "I"?
What purpose do I serve,
I've accomplished so little,
Why so much do I deserve.

Stepan Baziuk

Visions Of Love

Oh, but to look upon your face
and delight in beauty's grace,
Into eyes of topaz clear to gaze
hints of laughter it merrily shades,
To shelter in your fragrant hair
and walk through it with fingers bare,
And upon your heaving breast to lay
touched by the hues of a dawning day,
On the hollow of your belly to rest
and linger till midnight's quest,
The softness of rose-red lips to kiss
and drink the honey dew — that love is.

Gavin Aserappa

Nightfall

I walk among the falling autumn leaves,
And dream in silent fields as one who grieves;
And standing in the desert of my years,
I feel my winter's spectral shroud that nears.

Where are the tender songs of days gone by,
The distant hills where bending grasses lie,
The drowsy drone of summer bumble bees,
And breezes sighing through nocturnal trees?

Where are the leaves of childhood's greening ways,
The fresh oasis of my springtime days,
The fleecy clouds that glide beneath the sky,
And golden suns where boyhood's fancies fly?

The falling dark the world with silence stills,
The frosty night engulfs the sunset hills,
The curtain of my greying sky is drawn —
I cannot see again the roses of my dawn.

Alvin Harms

Please

Please hold me tightly in your arms,
And fill me full of all your charms.
Please kiss me softly on the cheek,
And whisper words of love I seek.
Please care for me as I care for you,
And feel the love that's honest and true.
Please keep me safe from all the pain,
And smile away all the rain.
Please just love me forever and more,
And together we'll open the future's door.

Karen Wadden

Salute To A Soldier

As the sky turns dark,
and he begins to tire
he hears a twig snap, and the command to fire!!
He runs like the wind, to a nearby hole.
With shrapnel flying and a bright red glow.
He can feel his heart pounding,
right threw his chest, as he sits and wonders
where are the rest.
He hears mortar fire above his head,
he knows in his heart the others are dead.
Will this be his grave, this hole in the ground,
he's so far from home, with no friends around.
What can we say about these men of war.
We cannot leave them, in that land afar.
All we can do, is bury them at home
and lest we forget, those who died alone.

Stephen Swan

Ticket To Ecstasy

I just got you the other day
and I know I'll have you for a few more.
You're mine now.
I own you - unless you're no good
in which case I'd throw you out with the
rest of the trash of your kind.

You are beautiful, though,
in an almost illegal, sinful way.

Your colour - subtle pink - is the fairest
colour on someone like you I've seen in a long time.

Saying your numbers sends a shiver through my spine!
38-24-33.
You've got other numbers, but those are in more
discreet places.

My mouth salivates at the thought of what you can do to me,
what you can give to me.

I think I'll keep you close and fold you up
and place you in my wallet until the draw Saturday night.

Wish me luck, my dear lottery ticket!!!

Rachel Young

I Live

I've witnessed the fires of hell
And I live
I've scorched the souls of my feet on its embers
And I live
I've singed my lungs breathing its stench
And I live
I've wept an ocean of tears for its lost souls
And I live
I've faced its many demons and evil spirits
And I live
I've encountered its egotistical master
And yet, I live

I live
To feel the gentle warmth of the sun when it rises
I live
To feel the strong caress of the wind when it blows
I live
To feel the soothing coolness of the rain in a downpour
I live
To feel the vibrant chill in the air on a winter's morning

Linda J. Vanin

A Soldier Of Fortune

I have travelled this earth facing hardship and peril
And I've fought 'gainst my own land's, and other lands, foes.
For great causes, and lost ones, I've marched into battle
Seeking fortune and glory where conflicts arose.

Though the cold chill of fear has so often swept through me,
Neither man, neither mountain could stand in my way;
When the odds were against me, I stood my ground boldly:
To the goddess of courage and daring I pray.

Although battles and years leave their scars on my body,
Still my spirit's unbroken, my will drives me on;
And I'm spurred to the chase when my mistress flees from me -
For the battle is yours when the rout has begun.

Diane Elizabeth Maltby

"My Friend"

Time passes and you are always there
And please stay there-
You are necessary in my life.
We share silly moments of laughing and teasing
Then, cover the more difficult times.

To me, you are a beautiful light
That draws people to you
With a strength on which one can lean.

We have shared -
We have cared -
And to me you are

"A very special friend"

Betty Liz Wilkinson

Not For Granted

For every man there is a woman
And so we think it's the order of things
The objective drive that's known as love-
That labour of pure affection that underlines the theme,
Thus seems to play a diminutive role
We dabble into it as a matter of course,
With no deep thoughts for the future of the union
'A family of our own' - our justification for the contract
'A helper in the kitchen - an amusement partner in bed'
But with a little faith, we could after all, strive to make it work!

Godfrey Chux Otiri

The Moon

It illuminates the jet black sky
And soothes the wolves passionate cry.
It guides the night animals to their prey.
As the immense trees in the zephyr meekly sway.
it shimmers bright and provides exotic light.
As the breathtaking twilight begins to come.
And the humming birds begin to hum
Then out blasts the scorching sun
The night has diminished and day has come.

Ramneek Bath

Untitled

The little boy sat under a tree
and there he dreamt of what he would be.
The moon shone bright, the stars twinkled that night
Upon every star he made a wish
that he could catch just one fish to fill his empty dish
As he lost hope — he walked away and began to mope
The next morning he awoke
there lay at least a hundred fish in his boat
He rubbed his eyes—to make sure these were not merely lies
much to his surprise they were still there
He simply stood and stared.
He was puzzled by the Miracle but hungry too
so for a moment he felt his decision lay in smelt
But instead he turned over his bed
Setting them free he thought, He would rather be, A writer of poesy
In both he felt his craft, although his decision would be laughed
He knew he could write better trash
Knowing nothing gave him the chance to out wit the sages
Holding the torch to all tall tales his fish grew more scales,
This narrative ending at the beginning.

Sharon L. Scully

Please Help Me To Study

When books are piled high
and words have no meaning
and my tears fall upon the pages,
Dear Lord, send me a little light,
To shine in the mind you created.

Help me to understand the words you give me,
So vast and unlimited the knowledge.
Give me the patience,
Dear Lord, to continue,
For I need the will and the courage.

Thank You, Dear Lord,
For the intelligence you gave me
And for the will to learn and pray.
For on the road in life,
I'll need what I study today.

Thank You for all the books written.
Someone had the patience to write.
Thank You, Dear Lord, for the light,
Now I can study all day and part of the night.

Clara C. Ouellette

Is It Time?

Is it Time yet?
Are you afraid?
No, just waiting.

Is it Time yet?
No, still some Time to go.
How much Time?
Just Time.

Is it Time yet?
How do you feel?
Tired. Time is running out.

Is it Time yet?
Hush, I'll tell you when the Time comes.

The Time has come. Time to go.

Sabine Exner

At The Bottom Of The Sea

As winter storms howl, swirling ghostly clouds of snow
around my house,
I transpose myself to the day and time when I walked
at the bottom of the sea.

Imagine Low Tide, moist brown mud stretching to the distant horizon
where tree covered hills on an island are resting
in the wide open crescent of a sun filled bay.
There is no sound all around except that of my feet as I retract
them step by step from the bottom of the sea.

I reach a rock, solid and black, anchored in sand, God knows how deep.
Here I feel safe from the strong, sucking mud.
I stroke the rock, rugged and rough, barnacle crusted, netted in
tendrils of woven seaweed, - like a friend, like a saviour -.

A clear pool of water is left in the dent of the granite
from the might of High Tide which has been driven beyond the horizon,
- and still will be back, dictated by heavenly powers -.
Bending over the small sky blue pool my picture winks back at me
smiling reassuringly.
As the vision vanishes I wonder how many feet under water
the rock and my image are buried at the bottom of the wintery sea?!

Heidi Grein

For The Reasons...We Cry

Innocent faces unknown to most,
As a mother we are connected at heart;
We are all God's children,
And this has shattered our world apart.

As mother's we are leaders,
We are taught to provide a sense of security;
Why did it happen, what went so wrong,
And where was Alex, and Micheal's assurity.

To imagine the terror in their darkest moment,
To know we couldn't help, we couldn't be there;
Now all we can do, is feel the loss;
And keep them both, in a prayer.

Blessed are they, who have gone before us,
Unprepared for their time ahead;
Remember, "For God so loved the world"
This is what the Master said.

We weep for the loss, our hearts feel pain,
Their short time on earth we can't understand why;
Innocent faces unknown to most,
These, are for, the reasons.....we cry.

Wendy Hatfield

Silent Graves

I had been torn and tattered by the thought of war,
As I watched my darling walk out that door.
"I'll be back" is what he had said,
But no one knew he'd come back dead.
Cold and unsheltered from the December night air,
I felt that his spirit would always be near.
I rose quietly from beside his forgotten grave,
Thinking of his memories I'd always save.
A silent chill ran through the air where I lay,
And crumbling down, I knew this was forever where I was meant
to stay.
It was there I took one gasping breath,
And there forever my heart would rest.

Loraine Carey

Never Give Up

Where there is hope, there is a way,
As long as you know just what to say.
No matter where you are or what you do,
There'll always be a way that's easy for you.
Don't give up if you ever try,
For birds with no wings never fly.
These "birds" who have never learned how to "fly",
Since they always give up and never try,
Have there goals of success but which have been overpowered,
By the thoughts of a useless and courageless coward.
Forgetting about his worry and distress,
A coward overcomes his fear to success.
Successful is the bird who jumps from his nest,
To struggle and achieve what's his very best.
Life does seem to have its secrets indeed,
And there is a rule that helps one succeed;
Knowing the steps to life's little stairs,
Takes a lot of knowing and quite a few dares.
Take enough time while climbing these steps,
And you'll make it beyond life's secretive depths.

Sandra Patterson

I'm Sad

I'm so sad today.
As you can see, I'm crying.
Sometimes, I just can't stop thinking about my mom.
There's just no use in trying.

She's gone and I'll never see her again.
That's just how I feel.
Sadness is an unhappy feeling,
you can't see it but it's real.

When I'm sad, I just want to be alone,
it's always that way,
but the worse thing of all,
it never goes away.

Nathalie Thibodeau

Blue Like The Sky

The forest is stretching to the horizon.
Behind it shines a cloudless, blue summer sky.
Sometimes a rain cloud passes,
Sometimes a thundercloud.
The rain drops are tears from your eyes,
The lightening the pain in your soul
And the thunder seemingly endless cries of rage.
The rain drops moisten the soil of the forest with magnificent water
Which awakens everything to a new life.
The lightening blows over quickly after it striked,
And some time every thunder dies away.
Then the sky shines even brighter,
The sun is at its zenith
And the view free to the horizon.

Tanja Planko

Oh Happy Days-

Do you recall - when we were small? The sun shone every day
Being specially hot in that favorite spot where we would often play.
Greener grass and bluer skies daily greeted sleepy eyes
Fewer crows and far more larks, cleaner streets and safer parks
Seaside excursions - fussy ferries, happy, healthy, brown as berries
Rabbit stew and home-baked bread, convenience food? Not yet that dread! Two-and-six for joint on Sunday, 'nuff left over cold for Monday
Sunday church - no choice - no flouting worth it for the annual outing
Even winter seemed more jolly, whiter snow and redder holly
Fireside baths - no central heating, bringing laughs - that would take some beating.
Today when winds and hailstone showers snap off branches - wreck the flowers
I sit content with soft-lipped smile then close my eyes and for a while
Enjoy these halcyon days of yore and yearn p'raps for their joys once more
Yet know that they're beyond recall if they were really there at all
In future years in many ways p'raps these will be our halcyon days.

Brynley Richard

My Friend, My Wife

Sometimes I'm not sure how you could care
But life's so much better since you have been there
You've given me strength when my own has failed
My life's colors fading but yours never paled.

There's always a smile on your beautiful face
There's always warmth in my cuddling place
There's always the shine of love in your eyes
There's always the trust, no telling of lies.

Your friendship is special like no other can be
If you asked for the world, you'd receive it from me
With all of my heart my love is only for you
For like no other I've felt, I believe our love to be true.

D. Emberley

The Beauty Of Nature

Oh! how I love to hear the sweet voices of the singing
birds on the trees.
Oh! how I love to touch the lovely blooming flowers
in the garden, guarded by butterflies.
Oh! how I love to look up the sky that appears
the colors of blue and white.
Oh! how I love to reflect as I saw the rising sun
that the whole world would have light.
Oh! how I love to dream as I imagined the moonlight
that shines in the silence of the night.
Oh! how I love to view the colorful green green grasses
grown in the meadows and in fields.
Oh! how I love to glance the clear flowing waters in the river.
Oh! how I love to breath the freshness of the air
that blows everywhere.
Oh! how I love to reach the highest peak of the mountain.
Oh! how I love to be mingle to the different kinds of people
in every side of the world.
Oh! how great and wonderful is the Creator who made
the beautiful nature.

Marinette J. Tomacder

Loneliness

Loneliness has turned my blood,
black from red,
Loneliness has torn my soul,
I'd much rather be dead.

To be all alone, in a world of friendship,
makes my wrists bleed,
black blood starts to drip.

With nobody to talk to,
with nobody at home,
I sit in a corner, feeling alone.

Death seems so simple,
easy and quick I'd much rather be dead,
than lonely and sick

Is death really the answer,
to something so bleak?
my blood is now pouring,
I'm starting to feel weak

I feel like I'm floating,
high up in the sky,
my last word to everyone, forever? Good-bye.

Caryanne Davidson

Seven Bloody Sundays

The acid rain is falling in candy sugar skulls.
Blood runs red the rivers and the burning city falls.
The angels of forgiveness all stagger to their graves.
Christ comes back tomorrow but it's too late to be saved ...

Children turned to ashes in black atomic fire.
The dove is slain by ignorance and God becomes a liar.
Hold your breath and pray for death; the end is on its way;
Lucifer succeeds Santa Claus- and tomorrow's Christmas Day...

The earth becomes a skeleton of what it used to be.
All the stars of hope are doused and love becomes obscene.
Cower as the missiles fall and death lays waste to Kings.
Tongues of fire sing out in praise as Satan spreads his wings...

David Hayman

Always And Forever

A kiss from his lushed lips
burned mine. I love you were
the words he whispered.
His eyes blue they shine
like the bright beautiful moon.
His heart blossomed that
night as we held each other in a warm embrace
The music so soft, he smiled
it was something that lasted
a lifetime. A surge of blood
rushed through me love lasts
a lifetime bad times forgotten
good times remembered and our
dreams come true.
I wanted no other only him
body mind and soul. And
again his kisses burned,
Always and forever I love you.

Jodie Cooper

Have You Ever...

Have you ever waited for the phone to ring
but know he'll never call,
Or waited to see him to say "I love you,"
but instead break down and bawl.

Have you ever waited for him to walk through the door
And embrace his love to you,
Or to tell him what a difference he's made in your life,
but now you both have a life so new.

Have you ever waited for him to drive down the street
looking for that friendly wave and smile,
Or still dreaming of that future together,
Wishing he was only gone awhile.

Have you ever waited for that warm embrace
that seemed to make everything alright,
Or still hoped and prayed you could be as one,
to where your lives seemed forever bright.

Have you ever needed someone so badly but realize he won't ever be there,
the only thing left are his dear memories and a room that's empty and bare.

"Have you ever... needed someone so bad"

Brenda Holman

Begging For Forgiveness

I'll always be dependent, 'cause I love being so
But only when the support, I'm depending on is you
Sometimes I can't support you when you really need it
'Cause I always get your mood...you're my man did you forget
Forgive me please for that mistake
For you control me and never give me a break.
I'm a small particle in an orbit of your own
Rotating in your heavens from night till dawn
Try to understand me and you will have no regret
'Cause the great love between us couldn't melt the ice yet
I'm all yours till the end of time
I'm devoted to you...is that a crime?
For saying I'm myself means nil
But it's different when I say I'm yours and by my will
I mean that you gift me a great value which
without you in my life...I'll never reach
So try to forgive the faults I do
And I swear I'll make it up for you

Dalia Sherif

Date Of Death

As she stepped in the car, she knew the trouble ahead,
By the smell of his breath he was drinking again.
He kept drinking and drinking until the last drop was gone,
Her hope and her prayer was to live her life, long.

He then took a cigarette out of his coat,
Lit it up and started to smoke.
His lady was coughing as smoke filled the car,
He knew that she wished he weren't going far.

As the night dragged on, the boy got weary,
His date was beginning to sense something scary.
They were cruising the highway over the maximum speed,
That girl knew she was in desperate need.

She screamed and she cried as a truck came near,
They collided and crashed in the misty, night air.
Her beautiful smile will be seen no more,
For now she lies dead on the car floor.

Drinking and driving was his horrid mistake,
Because they both know it was now too late.
Those teenagers learned a lesson on that tragic day,
They found out that dying was their price to pay.

Crystal H. Legge

The Wind

The wind blows softly through my hair,
caressing me with its soft touch of nothingness.
I cannot see you, but I know that you are there
in all your mightiness.
You are most annoying at times, but whatever
will we do without you, who brings us rain, our
fountain of life itself. Why is it that you get
so little respect, you the one who can cause
disruptions, consternation, cause wherever you go
in your moment of anger, or is it perhaps
victory.
Victory over us a people, a humble lot
of beings in your flight of fury?
Twisting and twirling causing destruction and
pain wherever you go, until, your moment of glory
peters out and comes to a peaceful end once more, to
be just a prayer answered, a friend, a soft
caress through my hair

Margaret L. Dantu

Untitled

Could you see life as a painting
Coloured by the supreme artist's brush
Can you see and feel the peace and beauty
Behind the turmoil and rush
Do you find joy in the small things
A leaf turning orange and gold
A pure white snowflake falling
On a day turned suddenly cold
Do you find happiness in a child's laughter
Treasure it against sadness that comes after
Can you accept the pain and the joy
That is part of your everyday play
Then take and treasure the painting
Though it is never really your own
For such a short duration
It is yours, just on loan.

Sylvia Elfman Classic

Bird On A Leash

A bird on a leash at her master's command
Controlled by the leash unable to fly
Unable to leave the gilded cage
She was placed in by her master
Trapped, unable to leave

She is not alone. Flocks of these birds
Come to a place where a trap, in the guise of opportunity,
Lurks to catch the flocks, but only the most beautiful
Lovely and gracious birds are kept
And sold for a high price

Their masters then take them home
To a world of glittering glamour
In the confines of the gilded cage
Where the master has absolute control

Forced to wear and look the way the master wants
To sell his products, to make him money
With little in return
In comparison to her master

Just like a prostitute
And her pimp.

Thor Olson

Reflection Of The Wine

It sits in perfect solitude.
Crystal clarity cupping its secrets.
It whispers, of warmth; of ancient passions
Powers of the past. Rising. Falling.
Changing destinies. Splendors eclipsed; and
Embers smoldering in the dust,
And waiting.

See us! See us for we live...
We are one. We are fire.
Now burning, now shining. Now
Dancing in the wine. You, and me. All!
Soaring to infinity. Splendor anew; yet
Embers smoldering in the dust,
And waiting.

Joyce Bickerdike

Door

The door is closed.
Curiosity gets the best of us.
But yet this feeling is unsure.
You want to grab the handle,
Yet your hand will not turn the knob.
You sense that there is evil behind the door,
It is an evil that you can not resist,
It is a pleasurable evil,
One that which you say no to you will regret.
Is this truly something you want?
Yes!
You open the door excitement fills your body.
Joy and love exists once again.
You walk out and close the door.
You feel sadness and fear.
A scare that will not leave your body,
Not until you once again open the door

Antonia Evink

Mockingbird

Emperor of the air
Dawn glitters with the jeweled notes of your realm
Treasure trove, repertoire of brilliant sound
Your silvery serenade, golden trill,
Falling, flat, monotone,
In clipped stanza,
Shrill discord...
Capricious spirit changes tune once more
And liquid music rains down through the trees
Resonating melody pierces morning's haze
Charmed by your chiming lure,
Spell of your bell-like call resounds,
Shimmering on silent air it reverberates...
Remains a whisper... an echo... haunting long after...

Marlene E. Harris

Nothing

Things are changing.
Distance is growing.
Life is good.
Friendships are ending.
Things you want are gone.
There's only one person left.
The thing you thought you found was a mask.
You found yourself in the same place you have always
been in.
You are alone!!!!!
No one to count on.
You open up, just to be shot down.
You find your friends.
What friends?
Times get tough they run.
You give help.
They run.
You end up alone.
Just the way you started.

James C. Storie

Untitled

Does she rip the skin off the animal
Does she eat the flesh off the living creator
Does she hear the rain drops
Do her fingers smooth out the ruffles in her dress.

Does her heart fill your glass with wine
Does she electrify you
Does it feel like she is trying to crucify you
Do you feel like you want to die by her side.

Do you want to climb inside
Does she cry at the birth of day
Does she resurrect your dreams
Is she one by day
And two by night
Is her hair blowin' in the wind.

Patrick John Mills

Advice On Indecision

I think that thought a lot,
but now the thought is gone.
Shall I think the thought forgot?
Was all that thought for naught?

Aye, think that thought a lot,
but only till 'tis gone;
for once the thought ye thought be gone,
'tis time thy thoughts move on!

Thomas Middelveen

Nightfall

Sunset in December in a Nova Scotian town,
Draping the horizon with a lovely fairy gown,
Slanting rays of sunlight glance to upward heights,
Prelude to the darkness of a cold, midwinter night.
Above, the sky is shrouded with clouds of withheld snow,
Across the magic skyline the shadows come and go,
Pale blue near the summit of the ever distant hills,
Edged with wisps of crimson and mellow golden fills.
Trailing smoke of industry floats down through the glen,
Fruit of manual labor, sweat of toiling men,
Bold against the skyline of the busy little town
Of Nova Scotian people as the evening hour comes 'round.
Cares of daylight ended, time for home and rest,
Freedom of the Country, by the Creator blest,
Time for meditation, see God's handiwork,
Colors gently fading, purple shadows lurk
Behind each tree or cottage nestled in the vale,
To merge into the blackness of the ever darkening dale,
The last faint pink remembrance withdraws itself from sight,
The day has passed beyond us, and now, at last, it's night.

Clyde N. Slauenwhite

Production Of Peace

Buddha, Christ and Mohammed are gone
Earth used to be their common home
They sprinkled their wisdom everywhere
To keep the earthly troubles far away

Ism and wisdoms are their proper elixirs
Compounded by art-work of their higher brains

Elixirs as these used to be.
Fresh then still fresh
Needs stirring time and again
By a spiritually tuned spoon

Mind and soul are elixirs' content
Thereby produces peace in consent

Shree C. N. Vaidya

I Love

Kurt I really miss you
Even though I never knew you
I love you
I love your music
I love the way your hair is
I love the way you sing and walk
I love the way you smile
but you did that every mile
Now your not here, I know you had fear
you had lots of problems
but you shouldn't of killed yourself
you could of got help from your fans that melt
maybe it was too late, I don't know
but I wished I could help you, or make you
come back, I know I can't do that
I will never be able to sit by your hat
and I know that's a fact
I just wrote this to tell you how I feel
even though your not standing on your heels
I'll always love you.

Sonia Conca

Leaving Behind A River Of Hope

He ran away with my life leaving behind, a river of hope
He took the innocence of the child in me.
Leaving behind, a river of hope
He left hate at the footsteps of my heart
How can I think of being apart from the man that made me
believe that life was everything.

Florencia Spangano

Be Still

At the height of my loneliness
Fear engulfs me,
I cannot face the challenges
That surround me.

It's a question of self-assurance
And the power it instills
And the stirrings of self-knowledge
Which come to the surface
Or lie still.

It's not easy facing the horrors
Of being all alone -
Of coming up against the steel and barbed wire
And finding there are no pliers
Near to hand.

Be still and be strong,
And fight to the end
Be empowered by love;
And conquer the sin
Of self-indulgence.

Michelle C. M. Johnson

Meant To Be

Our love was born the moment we met.
Finding each other was a blessing, and
Such it was meant.
Finally! No more sorrows, only plenty
Of tomorrows.
How magically our hearts mended, and how
Instantly one they became.
How gently we blended, and how preciously
We'll forever share the same.
Tenderly so we kissed, and embraced.
Fortunately so, we were now blissed and not ashamed.
Together we are strong.
Together we belong!

Love is the strength of life.
Love is stronger than death.

Viviane Kolp

Speak Now For They Are Falling.....

Two lovers die entwined — between enemy lines:
For every life a purpose,
For every life a meaning —
The Angels bent slowly over them——
Tears coming from their eyes;
Compassion filling their souls:
The whole world was hushed,
To see what evil man could do to man:
Will man never learn that nothing is solved by a bullet?
And from the Heavens above came down these words;
"Those with eyes let them see..."
And the world saw:
"Those with ears let them hear..."
And the world heard:
"Those with souls, let them be moved..."
And the world wept:
"Let them not keep silence..."
And the people of the world said;
"LET THERE BE PEACE!"

Sandy MacPherson Henry

If Life Is So Precious

If Life is so precious, then why do I frown?
For whomever I turn to, just lets me down.

No one gives me memories, to cherish, to keep.
Instead I find myself crying to sleep.

If life is so precious, then why do I try?
To flutter broken wings, when there's no way to fly?

Why do I bother living on earth,
When my heart was hollow to begin with at birth?

If life is so precious, when why do I taste,
The salty wet tears that's gone all to waste?

Why do my eyes burns? Why they sting,
When I witness a light, and the reflection it brings?

Why do I hurt? Why do I bleed?
Why am I plant, missing its seed?

Why do I have a body, but don't have a soul?
Why am I a balloon, pierced with a hole?

If life is so precious, then why does life exist?
Why am I faced with temptations, I can't help to resist?

If life is so precious, then why can't they see,
That below all this skin, there's a lonely scared me?

Nanor Sagherian

Autumn Of Life

The bird is free in time and space,
for you and me it's not to be.
We're members of the human race
bound in our own confines we see
just Winter, Summer or the Spring
While birds fly out and in again
Enjoying the exalting songs they sing.

One spot on earth our own domain,
Do we need to plot an scheme?
If rooted to that spot we are so partisan
this Earth is one, is this a dream?
Room enough and some for other man,
let your Autumn softly come,
you'll find that life has just begun...

Ivan Trindell

Decay

Don't let their sins erode you,
For you are old but strong in your ways,
Let they mother overpower their sins,
So you may live without decay.

But now with poison bombs in hand,
You are the real victim,
But for they see the damage done,
The tear you cry are thickening.

You blood which ran clean and pure,
Long ago when you were young,
Is now polluted with their wastes,
The end is soon to come.

But hope still rises from this grim tale,
For it is the children who are close,
They hope to leave a better place,
Than what was left for us.

Darren Scott MacEachern

Master Of Dust

I once had a dream of life, a forgotten time a
forgotten realm. I am here to speak of a dream, so hold
my hand as I guide you through the library of a God.
Dust is left by crying minds. Rays of light shatter
the loneliness of dying hearts. Sheets of paper fall all
around you and the sky is on fire. The God sits with a
lonely scribe who writes all his master says. The God's
voice is unheard by us and we see only his face, fading
as he speaks. Sheet after sheet is added to the book of one
man's life, another that falls to pieces is that of a
woman, a woman who was never born and was rubbed from the slate
of existence; and yet she has left her print, there for was not
truly erased and the chalk had only smudged. A page falls at
your feet and sinks through the floor. What you now stand
on is not really there, you are only a page like the others
falling through an empty time. Generation after generation
until the God himself is but a book in his own library.
Another God looks down upon this tomb and
smiles as the scribe at his side writes all his master says.

Ryan MacFarlane

We Can't Forget

We can't forget the people who
fought, so brave, so strong, so true.
We can't forget the people who died,
just for me and you.
We can't forget how bad it was and
how scary it was too.
But one of the most important things
is, they fought for our rights and freedoms,
So we could live the way we do.

Martine Reid

An Inspiration

Softly speaks the meandering stream,
Gently chides the whispering leaves,
A deer in flight, and so a dream,
Has left my thoughts, another to please.

The kingfisher ever watchful, upon his perch,
His is this water, none dare transgress.
The lotus with the lily does brazenly flirt,
For the emerald brook, its shadows to redress.

The dappled, dancing light of day,
Through the pine and elm, yet another pattern of Life.
Squirrels amongst the acorns and oaks,
The wind and willow in eternal strife.

Wanton, undulating daffodil stalks,
Conqueror of meadow, valley and vale.
Soft words in persuasion from Nature's children,
behold the minstrel, his lyre has begun the tale!

I yearn with all my heart and being,
That this path, I would someday find.
Where my eyes would see without a dream,
And my life would be, in peace enshrined.

Jeshri Inca Uduman

God So Loves

God so loved the little children, he decided to give,
His only begotten son so that they might live.
Christmas is a special day on which we celebrate,
Our Lords birth with gifts of love and joyous songs of faith.

Peace on earth He came to give so that we could love each other.
And we could come to realize that each man is our brother.
When Jesus gave his life for man, he did not wave or quiver.
For he knew he was God's gift to man with a plan he must deliver.

Marlene Mulvina (Cardinal)

Amber Lit Flame

Oh, amber passion lit flame -
Glory is the night breeze -
Upon is thy starlit heavens -
Shining for all to see -
Mind my own I give to you
True feelings bound we suffer -
Fill me with sweet silence -
And I love thee with what I know -
You've chosen to be abide by my side -
A couple we make, an everlasting strength -
You and I, we call our own -
A bond none highest which can be reached -
Attained when you are in my soul -
An eternal choice we have made -
I cherish it all -
For life becomes of what we make and gives us pleasure -
Treasures of gem above all -
Once, twice, both we try -
I give you all that I have and so I say -
I love thee.

Danny J. Wong

Manger To The Cross

He was born in a manger, a shack made of wood,
He came to this world to do what no one else could.
Satan said it couldn't be done,
And the world didn't know that he was the one.

Even from the start, even as a small boy,
He was his mother's delight, truly a joy,
As a youth he followed his father's will,
And only they knew of his death on a hill.

As an adult, He ministered to the sick and the poor
He gave love and mercy where they'd never been before.
And yet His people plotted, concocted a plan,
To hurt the Son of God, to kill the son of man.

And they didn't know, they couldn't see,
That His death on the cross, on Calvary
Nailed up on wood yes even for me.
This was really the greatest victory!

From humble beginnings, to mockery and pain,
He endured it all to wash away our stain
Yes from the manger to the cross, he did bear it all,
yet all we have to do is answer His call.

Wendy Nelson

A Soldier

He buries himself in the dirt
He holds on to mother earth
He is so grateful for just his shirt
Now a man of a humbled birth
So young, so motionless, his spirit already dead.
For the truth was never told...the truth was never said.
He lied watching his brothers, his comrades lay upon the sand.
For they die, in his eyes, on no man's land
A war to end all ward so he thought
Until once again he heard another shot.
He was wounded and instantly killed
in a cold and lonely field
His life and many others taken away
The days before all silence had came.

Sandra M. Cacilhas

Untitled

Little P. H. Junior was fishing in a green river.
He was blind to the song of birds, deaf to the dance of colors,
indifferent to the embrace of the steep sunny blue skies.
Through the headphones of his radio
the boy was listening to beloved dead music,
he was flying over the invented streets of his invented town,
and his invented pride surveyed everything
in the invented jealous eyes of his invented friends.

When the plain grey fish swallowed the bait
the boy felt a sharp pain in his upper lip,
but he paid no attention and continued to fly.
He unhooked the fish, he lit the third cigarette of his life
and came back home.
The boy filled the bath-tub with water
and released still living fish.
All at once with an endless surprise he saw
the fish was dressed in his own school-jacket and, dear me,
on the upper pocket he read his own initials - P.H. Junior.

The boy stood all alone in the stillness of the break
between the end and the beginning of two taped musical hits.

Constantin Sokolov

Midnight

Black as the abyss, she slips into men's hearts,
Her silken touch, a deadly poison, anesthetizing.
Silently moving through dark shadows,
All is feline grace and majesty.
Her luminous eyes, inviting,
Penetrating, suggesting?
Her voice,
The hypnotic voice of a mother soothing her child,
The voice of a vixen.
Lily white lace and roses, all innocence lost.
Filling men's lungs, as smoke inhaled,
The burning sensation as one experiences
The pain of ecstasy or the ecstasy of pain?
To those who survive one last sunrise,
Her perfume leaving bitter-sweet memories...
They remember.
A thrilling dream? Or a nightmare?
The only Evidence?

... A smile on the lips of all those who have plunged a knife through their hearts at her embrace.

Venetia Stelliou

Ancients Rites

Proud and free, they strode their land,
hunting, fishing, in a band.
Though their Gods were many, their fears were few,
trusting in the great white father, ever anew.
They buried their dead in the tribal way,
their ancient rites, passed down to stay.
Then the white man came to steal their land,
and finally won with a powerful hand.
We dig up their dead and hold up our find,
then expect the Indians not to mind.
Would we stand for this if it were turned around,
and they dug up our parents from the ground.
If we were true Canadians as we claim to be,
should we not share this land, so big and free.

Beryl Elizabeth Walls Ranstead

Spirit Of Mankind

I am invisible I am attainable
I am the spirit of mankind

You know me well, within you I dwell
Often I appear, but you deny that I am here
I am the spirit of mankind

I touch many through your soul, getting noticed is my goal
Recognize that I exist; show your spirit, raise a fist!
I am the spirit of mankind

I am power, do not fear, there is no ugly head to rear
It is strength I seek from you, I gain it most from the good you do
I am the spirit of mankind

Don't you see you have it inside — don't let it whither, weaken, and die, there is so much that needs to be done
Wake your spirit with the daily sun.

The strength is there, let it erupt
Voice your opinions - go ahead, speak up!
You can make a difference in whatever you believe
Start today, don't delay, reward is what you'll receive

I am invisible I am attainable
I am the spirit of mankind

Tammy Kalenchuk

Bone Dance

When the spell passes
I can compose myself
And continue on to achieve
Meaningless praises for bravery.

"You're holding up well today, Good Man!"
"Don't let this thing get you down."

Down...down.
With nothing left to look forward to
But bones and stares.
Personal or public, all the same
Except for their eyes.

So for a while I will not be
Me. Once again I shall live
With a light heart.
I will shed this wet cape
With any icy shudder,
Put on a happy face,
And dance.

Kevin Meyer

I Forgot

My memory is so short I don't recall a thing I hear.
I can't remember simple stuff, much less what isn't clear.
My brain has sieve-like qualities that render it inept:
I lose my marbles through the holes till not a thought is kept.
And now my head's so empty, I distinctly feel the lack
Of filling to fill up the space, but I can't get it back.
The things that come in one ear, just go floating into space
And wander 'round until they disappear without a trace.
I don't recall the dates I set (don't ask me where they go),
Like lunch with Mr. What's-his-face and Mrs. So-and-so.
My memory bank is bankrupt and my recollection's shot;
My family longs to see the day I don't say "I forgot".
There's just one consolation here in all this mindless mess—
If I should get Alzheimer's, I am sure no one will guess.

Barbie Cooper

An Angry World

What lies tomorrow we do not know, on the narrow and straight road I desire to go. Destiny eludes our grasp and you wish that life was drawn out like a map. Nuclear tension no longer needs a prescription. Mother nature chants a death song but few are listening.

Financial solutions; says the expert, can solve our troubled evolution but many will be hiding behind religion. Money!, the two face evil that holds the eternal key, will unluck the vault of the soul and set us free. Human behaviour is breeding in the atmosphere of a jungle, the great Tarzan communicated with animals and he was gentle.

Unemployment the stain of human pride has created a welfare of uselessness that we try to hide. Death stalks our neighborhood, searching for the blood of the innocent, their numbers has steadily increased. Tragedy! maybe; is it not a manifestation of what we have release? Civil war, holy war, genocide and starvation, many do not care if it's not television. Peace and harmony among all men, that's all well and good but how long can he be my friend.

Piercing through the dark and pessimistic clouds is a golden ray of light. It beckons my attention and telepathically reassures me that everything will be alright.

Christopher Dwarika

August '94

I don't swim in your toilet, so don't piss in my pool;
I don't pray at the same altar, but don't take me as a fool;
I don't show you my tears, and you continue to be cruel;
I don't mistreat an equal, but you try to ride me like a mule;
I have my own history, but still you see me as a tool,
to benefit your power.
With that you assume I will cower.
I am shy but not enough to lower,
Myself,
to be repressed.
I only love He,
Who,
continually
showers me in a freedom ointment.

S. Ayazi-Hashjin

"Queen Of Flowers"

Your majesty queen of flowers
I feel magically taken by your powers,
and when I smell your fragrance I overdose
simply because you are the Beauty Queen of every rose.
When we come face to face,
I'm overwhelmed by your beauty,
that my heart no longer feels empty.
Your beauty of existence is forever, "Amen."
You joined the essence of love to every woman and man.
You are top of the line, one of a kind,
You shall live on and on,
like a song your life is forever long.
You have touched the hearts of everyone,
even through the eyes of the moon and the sun.
You brought joy to those whose hearts were broken,
therefore, you are to those a gift of love and forever their token.
You are the queen of flowers, the queen of every rose,
you are the final answer to all, and everything you say, goes.

I have only one final request,
for I shall be forever blessed,
so that when time for me has come to die,
all I ask of you Queen of Flowers is
for one last smell-goodbye.

T. J. Way

Is This Love

Oh where is my fantasy?
I long for it - but it's not to be found.
You fooled me into thinking it was here,
I just had to look -
But all I see is truth.

I thought I saw glimpses of it - so long ago.
And wonder if that's what keeps me here.
Have you covered it over with your serenity?
Your peace - your solitude?
And that's why it eludes me so?

In my quest - I invaded your fortress
With my abundance of want.
Like an eagle I have swooped down
To meet you there,
But we were equally matched - the fox that you are.

What can one teach the other
That would gain Profit?
But that you give me a resting place,
While I relate tales of what is
From my domain amongst the clouds.

Doreen Laird

Young Days

Back in the days of my youth,
I often struggled to be uncouth.
It was fashionable to be rough and tough,
Till one day, I had enough.

A pretty girl came strolling by,
She just happened to catch my eye.
She looked at me, who is that bum,
Then she broke into a run.

Was I that bad, that she was scared,
Was I the boy my mother reared?
Certainly not I said out loud,
I will have to fit in with the crowd.

I went home, washed behind the ears,
I began to look like my peers.
I looked handsome, beneath the dirt,
Now I was able to walk and flirt.

I went for a walk all by my self,
I had put my rowdiness on the shelf.
That pretty girl came by with a great big smile,
My man that was really well worth while.

John Korbich

Faces Of Color

I walk down the street
I see four boys
I walk in front of them
They start calling me names
I ran home with tears in my eyes
Thinking why did they call me those names
Was it because of my color or my religion
I want peace and harmony
They don't.

Manj Jaswal

You

You, whenever I look at you I see a beautiful piece of nature.
You are something very valuable to me, that's why I love you.
Every night that I sleep I dream only about you.
I think about you day and night.
You are always on my mind.
I would do anything to have you with me.
Everyday I just wish that I could have you in my arms forever.
If I can't have you my life will end.

Kathy Smith

Untitled

At 18, voting age,
I stare toward my future
With a less than auspicious view.
At dinner, we recite the Lords prayer; redundant.
In this society, what do we (Youth) have to be thankful for?
A society where vacations are sold
in a needle, in a vein
And where our LEADERS lay their burdens
and their mistakes
on us.

A place of placebo liberty spiralling
downwards, Helter Skelter
and all of us are mad/MAD.
Children March and are gunned down;
angered over what their fathers have done.

Desire hangs in a fruit, on a tree, in a garden
and green paper walls surround us all,
somewhere our vanity must fall.
We gave death to that which gives us life.
Help has forgotten us.

Lee David Milton

You Were Worth Waiting For

Sometimes as I sit and ponder what life has given me
I think of you, and how lucky I am to have
finally found the one that makes my life complete.
Before you, I had much turmoil and uncertainty.
Now I don't feel afraid of each passing
moment and what it will bring.
I enjoy being with you and miss you so
very much when we are apart.
You can bring sunshine to my rainy days
and warmth to my cold heart.
You make me happy, even when I'm sad
And though we sometimes quarrel, we always make up quickly
We don't carry on till the hurt is unforgettable.
You are what I dreamed of when I thought
of the perfect relationship. And now it is reality.
And I know that you were the one I was waiting for.
We have the rest of our life to built our hopes and dreams on.
And when we look back, we'll both be glad to know that.
All the trials and pain that we endured in our pasts,
Was what made us the two people we were both looking for.

Amanda Gademans

Leave

I never thought it would be paradise,
I walked the rugged pathway from the start.
No ugliness was hidden from my eyes,
Nor was life's pain a stranger to my heart.
And yet, the earth sprung firm beneath my feet,
And summer winds were gentle to my hair.
I breathed upon the dusk and found it sweet,
I gazed upon the dawn and found it fair.
I know grey moors where shadow mist lie curled,
And sun bright streams and night skies rich with stars.
For all its faults, I so have loved this world,
I found it beautiful, despite its scars.
Though angels sing of glories greater still,
I leave in sadness, much against my will.

Stephanie Haist

My Wish

Five years ago I had a great wish
I wanted something special, not just a fish

I wanted an animal I could cuddle and hold
One that would lie with me when I was sick with a cold

I wanted a soft one, one black and white
One I could cuddle and hold real tight

I needed a friend
Who my secrets would hold
One who'd be wonderful
And who'd not do what he's told

Well I got my wish, last Christmas I did
He's a little rascal just like a kid

He lies on my stomach or drapes on my head
He'll lie on the T.V. or cuddle up on my bed

He steals all my pencils, watches me write like a hawk
I wonder what he'd say; it's a good thing he can't talk

I love him so much, to me he just suits
He's a cute little kitten, whose name.....is Boots!!!

Mandy Birch

A Widow's Guilt

As I placed a wreath upon your grave
I was glad to be free at last
Your repeated torments I forgave -
Burying them with the deadly past.

Yes, I am guilty of loving you less
For wishing you could have loved me more
You replaced my love with hateful stress -
As you wiped my dignity on the floor.

To others you were a paragon of perfection
To our son a hero.. the most perfect dad
But you kept me with hopeless rejection -
Is it wrong to feel relieved and glad.?

Years ago we vowed "till death do us part"
But you killed me slowly before you died
Draining my love and breaking my heart -
Yet I hung on to my hope and pride!

Hyacinth Santiago

Wishes

I wish I may
I wish I might
Make this wish
I wish tonight.
I wish that the Jews shall be free
And the Nazis will leave forever and leave us be.
I wish to have a piece of bread
But more than that, I wish not to be dead.
I wish that my family shall survive
And all of the jews dead in this tragedy shall revive.
G_d, O holy one, are you there?
Are you watching this nightmare?
Why, oh why, was this to be?
Are we ever going to be free?
I wish all my wishes shall come true
But, if they don't, I'll miss you.

Stacey Knecht

Untitled

I am tall and peaceful like a forest.
I wonder why the rainforest must be cut down.
I hear the chirp of a bluejay in a branch.
I see a stream flowing and twisting by my feet.
I want to be pure and serene forever.
I am tall and peaceful like a forest.

I pretend to be a evergreen sometimes.
I feel a bird rest on my branches.
I touch another tree as I sway in the wind.
I cry when I hear the sound of a chain saw.
I worry that acid rain will soon come.
I am tall and peaceful like a forest.

I understand that most of the world is in a fight.
I say I'll live the best I can.
I dream the world will be in peace soon.
I try to be the best person I can.
I hope the violence will stop.
I am tall and peaceful like a forest.

Megan Asselin

Without My Street

Take me, shake me, don't break me,
If I had a dime for every time-
Beat me, eat me, mistreat me,
Then my life'd be yours not mine-

I am an unemployed prostitute, existential whore.

Right me, wrong me, don't wake me,
Hail a cab and try to follow-
Stop me, start me, forsake me,
This shell is frail and the center's hollow-

I am an undiscovered island, severed from the shore.

The argot of thieves, it's my native tongue-
My muted desire, my internal fire-
My corner of life, my unrelenting strife-
Until you find me your map is incomplete-
Without my street...

Book me, cook me, you mistook me,
For someone with an inclination to know-
Free me, be me, look and see me,
Without your home I have no place to go-

I am the smoke of a fire consuming your conscience.

Michael Truscello

Untitled

To the homeless and seemingly unwanted
If only you knew
Just where to look
For everything written in God's free book
The Bible
He'll give you all you need
Here is the seed
Plant carefully and water well
You'll find the cells
Terminate fully into swell
Gifts home, love plants that do well
A lovely place to dwell
Search for God and Jesus
And find them in all of us

Arlie Flook

Untitled

I love thee when the moon doth shine,
I'll love thee cross the hands of time,
And when the rains of autumn fade,
I'll love thee more and more.

I love thee in the rage of May,
I'll love thee when the music fades,
But even when day slips away,
I'll love thee with adore.

I love thee without rule or rhyme,
I'll love thee, less my frame of mind,
Only you could hold my thought in tow,
Safe guard neath cupid's door.

I love thee with a willing heart,
I'll love thee come the season's part,
While sunbeams shine and snow doth fly,
I'll keep thy heart in store.

Colin J. Korney

Love's First Passion

There's a little part
In the center of my heart
That can't let go of the love we once had
I wonder why
We find we must lie
And take for granted a love that's gone bad.

When at first we start
We find it hard to part
Cause our love is a powerful burning passion
But after years together
Through stormy weather
Splitting apart seems to be the fashion.

Yet, if it is true love
That comes from above
Then nothing can ever tear us apart
For each moment we give
In the life we live
Will bring us joy inside our hearts.

Sandra McMurphy

The Sandman

Alone with my thoughts each night grows
Increasingly long,
As my mind whirls and wails against
The approaching light of morrow's dream.

Heavy is my grief, yet in sight there exists
Not one dreamscape of mild relief.
Take me, and embrace me with an attack of
Narcolepsy until my anxiety,
With a vengeance pulls me back.

Sandman where are you this night?

Terrence G. Bray

Untitled

As I walk up to the very first tee
I'd like to hit the ball like on T.V.
I bring my club back and follow through
Ping! I hit the ball and then it flew
It was going as straight as an arrow can be
Then it bounced and rolled as far as I can see
It rolled onto the green and into the hole
I thought this is better than scoring a goal
I'm better than the guys I see on T.V.
Fred Couples, Jack Nicklaus, and then there's
me.

Jon Buysen

Graveyard

Every grave in this cemetery
Is like a sealed envelop
And in every grave there
Is a half read letter.
Tell me if the world is
A dead letter box?

The eternal question comes to mind
Where from I am and where to go.

The life beyond the imaginary horizon
allures me.
My friends read me fully
Before I am posted.
Read my contents and not the address of my
destination.

My friend I don't want, my dead body to be
decorated with dead flowers or bathed with
your salty tears. If you can my friend, dig
my life of a fighter, before you dig my grave.

Rezaur Rahman

Bang!

I hear a noise, what is it?
Is someone in my house that shouldn't be?

I'm so scared, I have reached for my gun,
Oh no!
The person is coming up the stairs.

I don't know what to do,
Do I scream?
Will it make him attack me to shut me up?
Or will it make him leave because he got scared.

He's at my door
My gun is now pointed towards there,
The door has opened,
BANG!
He's dead.

I walked to the door
And who was it I saw?
My boyfriend,
With a dozen red roses in one hand,
And an engagement ring in the other.

All he wanted to do was surprise me...

Linda Delves

Thanking "You"

A moment to give, whether praised or not ...
It comes from down deep and cannot be stopped.
An inner instinct to be who YOU be ...
To give from your depths, to those whom you see.
No cameras are flashing!
No awards being given!
But this is your life and your way of livin'.

Those who are touched know right to their soul...
YOU are a part of what helped them feel whole.
Your touch made a difference,
A tiny "GOD-SPARK"
YOU set them in motion ... towards
Their wholeness mark!

Carell Harder

The Shadow

I see the shadow.
It follows me
wherever I run to,
but I turn to see
who it belongs to
and nothing but tall buildings
and long streets are around me.
I walk again only to see the shadow again.
I stop and turn around
only to stare down the never-ending road.
That's when I see it.
The shadow reaches out his hand
as if he wanted me to follow.
He speaks to me and tells me a story.
When he's done ne turns and runs away.
I am left alone saying,
"That was my Grandfather,
come sit with me
and I will tell you a story."

Kirsten Brouerius

And So Our Journey Begins

Today a bond has been set.
It is not written in stone,
But in something more solid,
Our hearts.
And so our journey begins.
Along many long and winding roads.
The hills we encounter, we will help each other over.
And the valleys we discover, we will help each other through.
Our strength as one, will point us in the right direction.
When we come to a fork in our path, our love will lead the way.
With our hands held tightly,
The mountains will not seem so high and cold,
And the valleys will not be so dark and lonely.
When our eyes are cast upon one another,
We can see the sun rise
And we will watch it soar across the sky.
Its warmth will carry us and keep us safe,
Until our journey together
Is complete.

Julie Wall

A Love Is Shared

In royal times a love is shared
It magnifies your presence there
In honor that will never end
You gave it first of all

Among the great and noble men
You suffered not your children when
You walked into the violet wind
You kept your love around us

And when the breeze of silver lace
Did keep you in an able grace
We shared the joys that touched your face
And love was all around us

A thought to mind you may have missed
The stars wore diamonds when we kissed
And offered up the strongest wisp
Of love that was around us

As rare as roses white as snow
As precious fate could ever show
This love is yours
My dear ... you know

Diane Babcock

"The Joy Of The Lord"

The joy of the Lord flows thru me.
It surges thru like an overflowing brook.
O sing out, o my soul,
Sing the joy of the Lord.

His love fills my whole being.
It fills me to the uttermost,
So much so I can hardly contain it.
O love sweet love, flow on.

I am covered over with the robe of righteousness.
Christ clothes me with holy garb.
He drapes my head with the turban of wisdom.
And shields my heart with the vest of faithfulness.

Sing out, o ye His servants.
Lift up His name on high.
Come and sing along with me.
O sing the joy of the Lord.

Paulyne Cascanette

I Miss You

I was waiting for the train to come, I didn't know, you were the one. It was crowded, too many people, at the same time, in the same space. Only you weren't out of place. I got in using hands and knees, seeing my seat, I felt at ease. I started to walk towards it, as fast as I could. A woman stood in my way, in thought I called her names. My Lord this wasn't my day. Two footsteps from my seat, the compartment door slid open. My heart missed a beat. There we stood gazing each other, from head to toe. What seemed eternity, lasted only two seconds. You sat down on my seat, as if you knew. I sat down, the seat opposite to yours. My eyes could hardly keep away, from you. Brown hair, brown bright eyes, a combination of brown beige clothes. You know how to dress and it shows. It isn't fair, I want you by my side, right now, right here. We played the waiting game, exchanging glances in the reflection on the window. Sometimes direct, the moments you didn't expect. I wonder if you finished the book you were reading, when I was around, you didn't have hard time putting it down. How could I, let you slip away. In my memory, forever you're going to stay. Maybe in future times, we'll meet again, we'll remember how it was back then. As a set free dove, I'm afraid, for now, I've lost my love.

André C. Simmons

"Views From My Patio Door"

Little birds flitting around in the trees,
Larger birds soaring in on the breeze.
Blue birds, cardinals, finches and more.
I see them all from my patio door.
Down the hill to the pond.
Up the hill to the barn.
I'm looking now, at the neighbor's farm.
The hill at the west,
Straight and flat as the floor.
I see it all from my patio door.
Soon the trees will have leaves,
And the flowers will be blooming.
The birds will be nesting high in the eaves.
The fields will be green,
Who could ask for more?
And I will see it all from my patio door.

Olive Bontaine

Untitled

Peeking out the window
Late at night,
I rub my hand
On its cold surface,
Erasing the work of Jack Frost.

Peering at the starlet sky,
My eyes wander
To the dancing fairies
Of the arctic sky,
Wondering how long their party will last.

The howling winds
Never cease to blow,
But, the fairies never stop their merry making.
Protected, like me,
From the fierce world below.

Jennifer Law

A World In Despair

I walked through the door,
Leading nowhere.
Walking,
Letting my eyes wander across the blank walls.
Feet stepping where feet have not gone before me.
I struggle through the emptiness,
Relying on only myself.
To succeed in living,
In a world leading nowhere.
The further I walk
The emptiness is filled with dark faces.
The devil lies within their eyes.
The faces are coming closer
Surrounding me in the darkness.
And they are engulfed in red.
Despair is strong and steady.
I want to wander through another door,
To a world leading somewhere.

Tara Vanwynsberghe

The Fall Of Fall

Cool nights in the early Fall
Leaves in scarlet array
Bedeck the scene
To soon come tumbling down on browning lawns
To mix with the
Other litter of our time.

It is a time of death
The dying summer rears its warming head
Then finally succumbs
To its inevitable
Fate.

Soon will come the blast
Of winter's white
Freezing, the soul
In rigidity.

Like mighty statues
We will be
Immobile.

Caught in an instant
Trance of hope.

John F. Freudeman

Trusting

When you reach the end of your rope
Let go!
Why should you keep hanging on
clutching frustration
and anger and woe
and pride
Or the hurt of some wrong?
Climbing back up with a new-found strength
Will just set you back where you've been
Trapped!
By the height and the length and the breath
Coddled and held ... by routine.
When you reach the end of your rope
Let go!
And, oh! the thrill of the fall!
Caught and held in the strongest of arms
GOD waits.
To give you His all.

Betty Scott

Serenity

Let death grab a hold of you soul,
let it enter your veins,
Inching closer to your heart,
and clasp its endless hand,
Taking your heart in its rein.

Feel the pain,
Bask in the pleasure
of dying, yet still living
but slowly falling away,
from the reality of life.

Death strengthens its hold,
Squeezing the last juice out of your heart,
and embracing your soul.
Taking you with it,
to enter its world.

You have found peace,
Surrendered to the beauty,
let death open its arms,
and welcome you,
to life.

Renee Matiushyk

Untitled

Don't be afraid of the darkness for there is nothing to fear,
Let it take you to the valley, the valley of your soul,
Sit and let the moon caress you as if it were your lover,
Listen to the things the shadows wish to tell,
Reach out your hand and touch the soil, hold and share its riches,
Let the breeze guide you to the tree of time,
Let its leaves surround you with the magic of dreams,
Now drink deeply from the stream beside you for it will give you strength,
Don't be afraid of the darkness for there is much to be learnt.

Doreal G. Perras

Food for Thought

I have loved you from afar
Like a hungry wish upon a star
The fountain of my heart - I feel
My love for you inside - I seal
To save my precious thoughts - I'll hide
My dreams of you - will stay inside
This perfect love - yet incomplete
Stays pure and rich - yet poor and sweet.

Janis Gopeesingh

To The Love Who Inspires Me

There's so much I would like to tell you
Like how much you bring sunshine into my life
You are there when I need someone to talk to;
And you are there, to give me some advice.

When everything seems to go all wrong
You seem to make everything alright
Just like when you hear a sad song;
The ending, somehow turns out right.

After everything we've been through I'd like to say
My pleasure in life, is just having to know you,
That you are the inspiration of my life
And no matter what I say or do,
My love for you, which grows stronger;
Will be cherished, each and every day.

So as I close my eyes at night
It's you that I see, in my dreams
A very comforting thought as you know;
Cause in the morn, the sun shines in, very bright.

Linda M. Laframboise

Stars

Distant stars dotted the blackened sky
Like jewels twinkling in the darkness.
I looked towards the brightest star
I wondered, what secrets it did hide.
What has it seen in its many years,
Of traveling the endless stretch of sky?
Has it seen worlds like ours,
Full of life, full of promise?
Has it seen strange new sights,
That we could only dream of?
I only wish that I
Could catch that star and hold it close
And learn the secrets of its travels.
What it had to tell
I would never know.
But I can look up to the sky,
And wonder whether I am that star
Full of knowledge, roaming through the endless stretch of time,
Ready to share the stories of my travels.

Carrie Hutson

Kind Lips

Lips, so soft, tender and kind —
Lips, like these are hard to find,
Lips, that kissed my cheek, when I was a boy—
Still, fills my heart full of joy.
Lips, that are wrinkling now, with age —
That read the Bible, page after page.
Lips, that long for a roving son —
Beneath moon'lit skies and summers hot sun.
Lips, that are wrinkled, yet! wears a smile,
That never seems to get out of style.
Lips, that has tasted life's storms away.
Beneath bright eyes and hair turned gray.
Wrinkled lips, soft, like no others —
Are the tender lips, of my dear Mother.

William J. Lambert

Love Is...

Love is beautiful, love is kind,
Love is special, love is blind,
Love is something you share with a friend.
Love is something that has no end,
Love is something that last's and last's,
Love will live in the future, present and past.
You can love anyone big or small.
Yes you can love anyone, anyone at all.

Angela Ianni

The Sand, The Sea And Me

I lay face up toward the sky
  Listening to the rolling thunder pass by

I watch as blue turns into grey
  And clouds creep in to enshroud the day

But I care not
  For I drift into a sea of thought

I ponder the universe and all mankind
  Seeking answers I cannot find

But it is not to be
  For me to solve life's mysteries

And as I return from neverland
  I become aware of the sea and the sand

With the storm still threatening all around
  I pick myself up from the ground

Huge droplets begin to fill my space
  As hurriedly I leave that place

Lois-Margaret Sullivan

Tempestuous

Rage seethes chained, is contained,
locked within for a time,
before it comes spewing out
like a volcano erupting.

Vicious forces expelling sheer unholy hell,
unknown reasons for these massive attacks
of our pouring destruction,
surge after surge it levels
upon the undeserving innocent.

Suffering made unbearable,
resulting in such havoc
words only begin to tell.

Lives ruined by forces unheld
within a mind, incapable of changing,
destruction to constructive,
non-violent displays of behavior.

Vera Balla

Untitled

I look out the window with an expressionless stare,
Looking to find the love that's just not there.
I reach out my hand for someone to hold,
My heart sinks into my chest, my hand grows cold.
My love I give but I get none in return,
Your love and respect I want to earn.
Why does nobody care, do they not feel,
This pain and sorrow that needs their love to properly heal?
Can't they see I'm hurting. don't they know.
These feelings of despair are beginning to grow.
Why don't they come to me and lend a hand,
I can't do it alone, for I'm very weak and cannot stand.
I close myself off to the world around me
I take no part, I just sit back and see
Events taking place, no one knows that I'm not there,
This pain was too much that I could not share.
As everyone silently listens to the church bell sound,
My casket is loaded carefully into the ground.
I know now love is something you can't buy or sell,
Regretting that mistake I bid everyone one final farewell.

Debbie McDonough

Love

Love has no boundaries
Love has no lies
Love can make you laugh
Love can make you cry.
Unconditional love is the hardest to find
You'll feel it in your heart and know it in your mind
Don't be a fool and turn it away.
Or you'll be alone, like me someday
Hold him close, oh hold him near.
He's there when you need him to dry up every tear
Remember he's a special gift from above.
And together you'll fly on the wings of a dove.

Margaret Sherwood

Restless Soul

Lying still, thinking of what's not,
Love is lingering in front of my heart,
When I try to grab it, it pulls away,
Then afterwards it sways and sways.
When you have learned to love someone,
That is where it has all begun.
Love is shattered.
Shattered is the love,
The love that sealed my pain with a dove.
But now that pain is out of my heart,
Happiness was built, but you ripped it apart.
Time and time again, day after day,
I think of my love for you in each and every way.
Love so strong and love so deep,
I buried it with my soul, now asleep.

Vanessa Hingst

"Silent Memories"

Oh Lord, will you help me,
Make it through each day
For I have been so lonely
Since my "Mom" passed away.
She was always giving a helping Hand
To her family and her friends
And I know they will miss her
But in time to, this will mend.
I miss your sweet smile "Mom"
And the twinkle of your eyes,
The touch of your soft hands
And your voice saying good-night.
I still feel your presence around me
If I could turn, and meet your face to face
You'll say, "You know I love you, dear,
As I wipe the tears from my face.
I know you're watching over me, "Mom"
Just the way you used to do,
Love you and miss you "Mom"
This poem is From Me To You.

Gerald Knox

"Set Free"

My heart ached
My heart braked
It seemed so easy for you to let go
But for me it wasn't just touch and go

You left such an impression
I was left with nothing but a deception
You led me to believe your love was true
I guess it wasn't meant for me and you

I now know my heart is free
For you no longer have a hold on me
Our love has become a memory
My heart once again belongs to me

Line Duguay

"Musical Trials" "The Band"

Clarinet playing, oh, my what a sound!
My poor head is aching, and spinning around,
My lips are all numb, my fingers are sore,
That darned music teacher keeps asking for more.

She stands on her podium with baton in hand,
Determined and steadfast she ogles the band,
These loafers are out to drive me insane,
Such erratic playing causes me pain.

One hits a wrong note with a thundering jar,
That red headed imp should be hung on a star,
If I had my way they would all get the whip,
Especially that one who is giving me lip.

"Will you please get together and don't miss a note,
The way you are playing is getting my goat,
I came here to teach, and perfection demand,
Now play like I taught you, do you understand?"

Pride and ability each had in store,
Years of hard practice came to the fore,
With excellent playing, a musical team,
Teacher and band are right on the beam.

George Harris MacKay

Just Believe

I walked along as garden path- The sun, was shining bright.
My soul was still - and searching
Then to my hearts delight,
The flowers seemed like people
of every age and creed - some of
them I Had known who loved and filled my need.
The tall trees with their dancing
leaves were reaching to the sky,
Praising God and giving thanks
for blessings now and ones gone by
a little brook began to sing as it bubbled o're each stone-
Behold! God's beauty teaches us - a meaning all its own.
He's always listening when we pray,
He guides us all along the way,
Even when dark clouds appear
You can feel His Presence near
And when the storms have come and gone,
He gives us strength to carry on
So, be ye still and pray, doubt not,
This universe his wonders wrought.

Jean Murray

Decisions

It is night and I am at the edge of water
My thoughts are as dark as the water I stand beside
There are too many roads to travel
Too many decisions to make in this life
How can I go on this way never knowing which way to turn
Making decisions that always are wrong
Hurting most the ones I love so dearly
My life is filled with nothingness.
Now I see out of the corner of my eye
A ray of sunlight coming over the horizon
It is coming toward me shining on my face
Making me radiate with a feeling a peace
Love, yes it's love, filling my everything
All is well with my soul and I feel you
You are walking inside me and leaving your footsteps behind
Each step you take is like a bond to me
I am breathless, and my mind has never felt this way
I can think clearly now, I can see clearly now
It is all I ever dreamed being one is all about

It is love, It is you, It is WE

Elaine A. Schaeffer

My Mother

No more of her delicious cooking,
No more listening to her accordion playing,
No more watching her working in the garden,
No more going on picnics with her,
No more going boating and fishing trips,
No more going for long walks.
No more of her mail,
No more of her phone calls,
No more of her visits,
No more of her smile,
No more of her talk,
No more of her.
Gone beyond a wonderful life,
More so than life on earth.
In which she has rejoiced,
With God's angels in heaven.
Some day I hope to meet her there,
But while I am on this earth,
I hope to follow her footsteps,
So kind, so understanding, and so loving!

Anita Guindon

Lonely

Being lonely, that's what I'm afraid of
No one cares about you
No one loves you
No one wants to be your friend
No one wants to share their happiness with you
No one wants to know your sadness
No one wants to hear your problems
No one can cheer you up
I feel so lonely
I feel like an alien in this world
Am I that boring in their eyes?
But they don't give me a chance
to show who really I am
Oh, I wish I was never born
But, no! it means you're a loser
And I don't wanna be one
I'm gonna show them that I deserve
To get what they get
And I'll never give up

Rannie Zainuri

And The Forest Died

Who killed the forest? Was it the beaver?
No, said the fish,
"The trees he felled were just enough to build his dam,
The dam he built gave life to the stream,
Gave life to the swamp and shelter to our friends."

Who killed the forest? Was it the wind?
"No", said the deer.
"The trees he felled were old and tired,
And longing for peace.
He gave the forest light to share the sun,
To see the stars and worship the moon,
To light our path."

Who killed the forest? Was it the lightning?
"No", said the eagle.
"The trees he burned cleansed the forest's wounds
And sprung the dormant seed to heal that land".

Then who did kill the forest? Was it man?
"Not I," said man. But no one answered.
Not the fish, not the deer, not the eagle.
Only the wind was left to mourn the devastated land.

William M. Robertson

Escaping Into A Lonely World

Alone in a distant memory, trying to escape the fear.
Not knowing who I am, or why I've shed a tear.
Desperate to find the truth, I search within myself,
Wondering who I am.
Alone, I stand, far beyond the sea, looking down at everyone,
Including a vision of me.
Where does one go when they die?
Is it to a better place, away from reality?
Or just to an empty space, above the sky?
Or do they escape into a lonely world?
Far beyond the moon, trapped in a darkened grave, deep beneath the earth.
Alone, stranded.
I see another vision of me, wondering to myself,
How could this ever be?
Did I ever tell you I Love You, before I left you there?
Will you ever forgive me, for leaving you in despair?
If ever you are hurting and need a helping hand, just think of me, and I'll be there.
Placed deep within your heart, you'll know it through and through, that I've never, in my life, loved anyone, as much as I Loved You.

Kristy Marostica

The Girl With Black Hair...

She goes up the stairway, not walking,
not looking, just understanding. She only understands
what she has lost, and unable to find. Floating too
high, touching rough things. Deserves more but nothing
is left but sadness. What has it done? Left all melted,
see how her hair is laughing, laughing from darkness.
She closes her eyes and sees the hole, try to hide
from it. I ask to take away her tears, but fall so
hard, and a distance I have wondered, will I be back?
Trying too hard to help, just leave her to be ... and
watch. Colour in all faults in grey, don't know anything
else. Warm milk and fire put it there, a place or heaven,
for some. To hate all this and to go all alone, to fail,
always nothing but our own. We know not anyone,
and some hair is black.

Tiffany Unsworth

"Forever"

It is not the years I remember most,
Not the sweat and the tears, of our home up the coast,
Nor the days of our birthing a daughter, then son,
Or the way that our spirits with joy had begun.

Tis not the moonlit rides at low tide,
While the phosphorous glow, churning waters did ride,
Nor the sweet smell of rain on a blustery day,
As we'd walk hand in hand, along the hill in the bay.

It isn't the hours that we spent far apart,
Nor is it the morning hours spent talking heart to heart.
Not the times at the farms, nor the long summer days,
Or the children and laughter in their magical ways.

But the time I remember, that always makes me smile,
Was the afternoon we spent after hiking a mile,
The green lush of mother that gently spoke to our hearts,
Was the place that our first real home made its start.

Annette L. Caine

Anniversary Memoriam

It was seven years ago today that we both said, I do,
now all I have of our Anniversary is the memory of you.
I got to share ten years of your life,
almost four of them we spent as man and wife.
You shared in the joy of the birth of your daughter,
and then sadly taken away after the birth of your son.
My heart aches so much and I cry silent tears,
Because you're not here to be part of my life.
Your little girl, she just started school; as she boarded
the bus, the sun shone as if you were here.
Your little boy, he's so much like you,
he has your blonde hair and your eyes of so blue.
All of that can't fill the emptiness as I think of you today,
and of all the joy and happiness we could have shared in every way.
So to that, Happy Anniversary to you and to me,
in a sad, but silent heart-felt way.

Sandra J. McNutt

"Darkness"

O God! Humanity astrayed; please tame
O God! You often send messengers; please name
O God! Nations have become cheats; please send shame
O God! Nations have turned intrigues; bid them to
stop this game.
O God! You confronted one devil; now there are
billions to blame
O God! Your children are molested, raped, and murdered,
method is the same, when you came
O God! Man has raped the moon, the mountains, your holy
monuments
No chance to save your Jerusalem.
O God! Atoms are stored; take care of the flame.
O God! It is the age of Aids, Epidemics and civil wars
save your seed, your own grain.
O God! It is the age of guns, gangs and goons
you must call spade a spade.
O God! Materialism is at large; Honesty has turned in-fame.
O God! Morality has vanished; Prostitution is at gain.
O God! Disheartened we are; repeat your promise again and again.

Hardyal Singh Sara (Vancouver, B.C.)

A Double Entendre!

Soap Time! Always soapy, slippery suds
Of fantasy, mere dreams or illusions...
But, are they? Unfolding life in
Every powered sud, unearthing youth truths
In issues of health, sex, AIDS, emotions
Male/female relationships enduring the stress
The stressors of daily existence and intergenerational crisis
Interfiled, interwoven delicately, meandering
Their soapy path among youth, adults and the golden age of maturity
Morals, ethics, the message permeates the core
The essence of soap dailies
Analysis, critiques of abortion, literacy, the dysfunctional
Families in love, hatred, revenge, the poverty of wealth
Racism, tolerance, false images or themes of survival
A more realistic ethnic composition
Mirroring the true cultural diversity
Shifting comfortably between the Caucasian, African American
African Canadian, or the Pacific Rim...
Culminating into soap suds
Evaporating into REALITY

Rosalind Bryce

A Seed Of Love's Majestic Glory

Out of the impeding darkness
Of life's arena - lonely way
Came a beautiful friend into
My narrow way of living life's pilgrimage.

Surely this relationship I speculated
This new friend I thought
Could help solve my problems and I hers.
But I was wrong.
But sadly speaking one day she just went away
She didn't say goodbye or Hi!
Leaving me hurt-feeling sad-I'd lost a friend.

Lord, forgive me for failing you in this friendship
I tried to show her you
In me
The living Christ.
The way and the Truth - I feel I failed.
We are but instruments
Of thy love.
Weak in ourselves but strong in thee.

Kristin Susan Bethell

A Caring Heart

No one knows the meaning
Of the care that I once felt
No one knows the truth behind it
Or your heart which I once held.

I know now what this word means
With the sparkle of an eye
With the gentle words which you once spoke
Before you wished to die.

I'll remember your touch, your warm caring heart
For the memories I hold in me
Are only yours, my gentle love
As they float through the deep blue sea.

Jolene Schwager

The World Is Hurting

Heavy hearts sink deep into the depths
of the world's soul which is torn.
And abused by hatred, war and pollution
The world is like a man crying for help
But no one is there to help him.

To see a place so beautiful buried by the fog
The fog of darkness and destruction
The voice of the people crying for help
But their voices are memories in our minds
God who created this world is now crying

The world is fading in the distance
And will only be memories to all
A world that is hurting
And is left to feel all the pain
The world is crying out 'stop'

But its voice disappears into the distance
and the hope for happiness and peace
Is only a memory in the minds
and hearts of all the people.

Rochelle Anderson

Beauty

I see Beauty in the misty moon
On a quiet summer's night.
I see her eyes in the drops of dew
That the sun turns to diamonds bright.
I hear her voice in the tinkling laugh
Of children at their play,
And I feel her touch in the quiet time
At the closing of the day.

She moves through every sunbeam's glint
That touches field and flowers,
And she's in each drop of gentle rain
That bathes the earth with showers.
I feel her presence softly near
When I'm with the friends I love-
Then I know that Beauty came to earth
From celestial bands above.

Vera Trogen

awake in a dream

walking
on a well worn hollow trail

across a plain
of long
yellow
grass
waving slowly in a warm wind from the hills
to the left

pausing
to study the distant night

and

feeling the presence
of an old friend
who has crossed

the distance
from the hills
and crossed
my trail

the message is unspoken
follow me.

Colleen Campbell

Let Me Be Your Muse

Your muse came to thee
On soft sandaled feet,
And said, "Let me be the fleeting thoughts
Which your mind may grasp and hold,
And intertwine and fold, through beauteous words,
Into wise images of life:
Resplendent mirrors of the human soul.

Of the worlds of peace and strife:

Of corn fields ripened
By the warmth of sun-drenched days;
Of war fields scarred
By wounds of bleeding days.

Of the worlds of love and hope:

Of childish dreams,
Nebulous mirages, serene and fair,
Inspired and nursed by tender care.
Of youthful dreams, unbridled visions winging high
On ardent clouds of glories unachieved

Yea, let me be thy mind, for I will etch the words
That mirror life and bare the human soul."

Connie Laurent

Two Lovers

I've always thought my mask would be
A face of never coming dawn again,
So I set my hopes to sail
For the Island of the dead.

Though I was to be awakened in Hades
with the coin under the tongue,
God Eros met me naked instead
On the top of Olympus.
He unveiled to me a stone blind sky —
Two snakes intertwined
From the seeds of vacant time.

The one snake with two black holes
Was the demon's serpent causing me to expire,
In the other snake's eyes there was a play of fire,
As I found in me my everlasting twin brother.

Marko Novak

Awakening

Once more white blankets will be lifted
Once more the flowers will bloom
Again sweet voices will be sifted
Thru new born leaves to a heavenly tune.

The birds are busy with their trilling
Above the rooftops in the blue
Your heart will know a secret thrilling
Spring is here in a glorious hue.

The bees are busy with their buzzing
The grass is greening fast
The sun, its warm rays sweetly flooding
The earth whose wakened up at last.

Grace D. King

Untitled

I'd like to pay tribute to a friend of mine
One who went before his time
He was a friend to more than me
He was everyone's friend you see
It's been so hard for us to believe
That God needs you more than those you leave
You were a friend to young and old
We all have memories we will hold
God felt on earth, your job was done
Roles fulfilled of father, brother and son
We wish God had more for you to do
So you could stay, take part in what's new
You were unique and special in so many ways
We should think ourselves lucky for sharing your days
Whenever a good turn needed to be done
Everybody asked for you, you were always the one
To my friend a sad farewell
I'll miss you more than I can tell

Jo Tennant

Prayer For The Dying

Say a prayer for the dying,
for hurt and for crying.
There were flowers and now there are none,
lost is the everlasting warmth of the sun.
Find in your heart, a new place,
make room from all the lost space.
Forgiveness is found within,
live and forget all sin.
Prayer for the dying.

Brittany Gelineau

I've Held A Miracle

I've held a miracle in my arms today
One with tiny fingers and toes
And the cutest little nose.
I can't explain to one who doesn't know,
The feelings in my heart
And the emotions running through my mind,
But there is a new kind of love building inside me,
A love I have never felt before,
One stronger than I've ever known.

I have wishes
And I have dreams for him
But I know he will grow up to become, himself,
As I watch him grow day by day
And I know he will make me proud,
For, he will be then, as he is now,
My son,
The miracle I held in my arms
That beautiful September day.

Kennith W. D. Ciz

Untitled

Clouds forged across the firmament
only to encounter the wind and shrink back again;
lurking on the horizon, the sun gave one, final attempt,
but fell to its demise, far beyond...
the colours of fading light shivered on the verge of night;
then, painfully, all was called to unionize as the moon arose;
a new gaiety shone.

Suddenly, a streak of lightening shot through the sky,
the warning laughter of thunder followed...
rain mocked the pale face who shuddered on his perch;
the stars winked, and bowed their heads;
storming blackness now reigned, obscuring all creation
and then, as it had gone, it came - Light!
In dwelling of darkness a glowing virtue shimmered;
stars twinkled once more, refracting on the fresh, moist mantel.

Creation paused, its breath abated, waiting:

Abruptly then, it happened - the sun broke loose:
Hellishly burning; a glaring, pulsing disc...
dawn screamed its victory around the globe: A new day began!

Melinda Snider-Eising

Life

Skeptics say, "You're born, you live, and then you die!"
Optimists says, "Oh look, at the sun, the moon, and the sky!"
The rest of us, go on our merry way,
Living life as we will, day by day!
Life is a wonderful gift from above,
To be filled with wisdom, courage and love!
These lives and this world, were given to us,
With pleasure and joy, they're put in our trust!
We, with our arrogant, foolish ideas,
Are the ones who decide, who he is or she is!
That's not the way, he meant it to be,
We were meant to be happy, together and free!
Let those without sin, cast the first stone,
Then form your opinions standing alone!
For, in a world of imperfect, human beings,
There's no place for judgement, bigotry or meanness!
There's only room for one mankind,
A perfect one, you'll never find!
So, lets just enjoy this life and this earth,
To its fullest and utmost, for all it's worth!

Holly Williston

Untitled

Mysterious forces are holding me to my chair
or are my thoughts reflecting on a Christmas past?
With dazzling lights and real good cheer a good time had by all?
And now I stare where once a tree so bright, is now all empty space.
Then I get dressed and brave outside.
The magic winter day with snow so white and crystals in the air.
The footsteps sound so crisp and clear.
I walk and walk till I get tired and then return to my sweet fire.
Now I don't reminisce but look forward to spring with bliss.
The force is gone the cob webs too,
so with a smile I wonder about next year Christmas.
But with a bounce in my step I raise my head and say a silent prayer,
let Christmas be as if always is and save a little cheer
through all the year.

Margaret Mikulski

Tropical Childhood

i
out on the porch
in the hammock,
just like yesterday
flowers tired, grass wilting.

a whisper of wind
and before the next breath
a torrent of wet pounding the ridged tin roof
waterwindlightningthunderwater
and then it is gone.

flowers strong, grass straight.
just like yesterday.
in the hammock
out on the porch

i

Elisa Olfert

"Pain Is What I Feel"

Crisp air stabs my chest through and through.
Pain is what I feel!

Radiation rips through my flesh!
Beauty is fading.

I dare not go outside at all.
Fear is what I fear!

Cancer devours my body,
marrow and bone, bone and marrow, marrow and bone.

Hope is a beacon
whose light is fading.

People circle 'round like vultures.
Volcanic rage erupts in me!

Sleep fades in and out of each day
robbing me of time with loved ones!

Loneliness, helplessness,
These are my "companions!"

And pain is what I feel!

Laura McGlynn Weed

The Search For Peace

The search for peace
People care for it - the least.
Severe blows - the storm stops,
Man continues - heaps of dust,
Monstrous inventions - unlocked mysteries,
Man's mementos for earths' service.
A deliberate discovery of death.
So peace lay somewhere far
Far beyond the reach of man.
Far from the destiny of earth.
Far - until it becomes the bomb's story
Covers the front pages of Universal News.
And the devil's reign set loose
The lost shield of nature
Now resides inside the gutter
When so many lives suffer
Far away the star of peace glitters
When love resides deep inside man's heart
He invents more weapons to slain those richest hearts

Lavanya Vijayaraghavan

Alone

Long ago, dancing in a storm
People lived, no one to mourn
Ages ago, tears dried a face
Sorrow's child, everyone's disgrace
She escaped, and lived again
Shunned from people's beliefs, center of all their blame
Ran away, didn't need no one
They asked for forgiveness, but the damage had been done
Then she laughed, their antics so amusing
Listened to her own music, the power of it so soothing
They tried to care, to take away scars of the past
Helped for awhile, but it didn't last
This poor child, left alone for so long
This sad child, what did she do so wrong

Kim Benoit-Muncey

Mind Canyon

The tumultuous minds thirst for knowledge
Quenched by turbulent streams of words
Flowing thunderously from the unharnessed pages
Into the steep crevices of the darkened mind
Pressure cut deep gorges along its course
Swirling in a dramatic basin of fear
Eroding the darkness with each passionate word
Pouring into a precipitous narrow canyon
Draining from its headwaters to its mouth

Eileen Wazny

Mortal Solitude

Crying out from the crevices of despair.
Reaching to surpass the boundary.
Suspended between the balanced and the
unknown - where hope and fear collide.
The bridge has vanished. Turning back
there is none. Here is forever.
Guide by false illusions. Pouring out
all emotion. Drained by the loss of
control. Sensing the near end of a
futile existence.
Still no response from the outside.
Deafened by the echoing of silent screams.
The inequitable product to most of that
kind. Piteous. Every attempt is made in
vain. The cage wires unbending. Led
throughout the shadows they lay, lurking
in every contour. Enveloped by a thick
haze. They are not alone.

Marissa Butcher

Untitled

Shallow hills of hope
Run through with rivers of dreams
Long dry by unsuccessful attempts
To travel across a doubting mind
Mountains crumble as strength of fear
Steps on a weak heart that narrowly escapes
Being condemned to sadness for all time
A cloud of smiles
And a rainbow of light are all that shine
On a desperate world in need of rain
To nourish its drought-driven ego
To green its grass and put the blooms on its barren flowers
And give fruit to a future that has no existence
In a world without faith and love
Let the water come soon as this life ends as it began
In darkness and loneliness as black as a moonless night
Over an empty land

Desti Fairchild

Running Wild

Running wild on ancient ground
Running but not free
For man continues to hunt the lion
To claim his victory

Sitting in a cold iron cage
The monkey is now blind
The scientist tore out her innocent eyes
To experiment with his find

Lying in a shallow grave of blood
He died slowly, confused, in pain
For poachers hacked off his ivory tusks
For riches and for gain

They torture them with wooden clubs
Deaf to their sad cries
For man kills to clothe the rich with furs in which seals die

They harpooned her in the evening in agony, she died at dawn
The lipstick they are selling
Was made from her calf that was never born

Running wild on ancient ground running but not free
God bless the animals of our Land that my children may never see

Tanya Britt Ouzman

The Man Who Walked Alone

You could hear the movements of all the animals
rushing for their lives, running, running
far into the woods when there was a gun shot.
You could hear nothing but a deer.

Tumbling, tumbling down,
then suddenly it just all stopped.
There was no movement, none at all,
except for the footsteps
of the man who walked alone.
Slowly he walked up
to the half-living creature that lay
helplessly on the ground
in a pile of bloody leaves.
Suddenly there was one more gun shot.
You could only hear the yelp
of the creature that no longer lived,
he couldn't try to go free,
but now he will be somewhere
where he won't be hurt again,
by the man who walked alone!

Michelle Desormeau

Westray Mine

The miners in the ground saw a blinding ray of light.
Searching through the ruble, they thought this was an endless fight.
Rescuers above them hoped for any signs of life.
While standing right beside them were the newly widowed wives.
God must have had a reason, a reason no one knew.
By taking them with him, their suffering is through.
Twenty-six of Westray's miners were in the shafts below.
Not knowing that their future was just about to go
People all over the world, as far as Africa and Japan.
Called our local leaders to lend a helping hand
Dealing with the losses and dealing with the pain.
Deep inside their loved ones their memories remain.

Kevin Alexander MacEachern

Mysteries!

I look out in the deep blank sky to
see but, no stars not a trace of the
moon. You wonder where they are write now.
Are they hiding from you? The world?
I wonder where they are at night. I know
there somewhere in the sky so bright but,
without them where is the light and beauty?
You wonder where they are write now and,
who there hiding from. You ask who well I
wish I knew but, that's a mystery just for
you.

Rebeka Boyd

Cowboys Don't Cry

the time for growing up
seems to pass around us so quickly —
four seasons gone
with a touch of the wind.

tears change winds
time after time
and it seems we'll never learn
about being older.

i was older once.
and when sleep arrived each night
it seemed much worse
to have missed the little things
in growing up.

when I was younger
tears never came
through all the little pains.
now I'm young again
and it's hard to remember a place
where little boys keep playing in the rain

and cowboys don't cry.

Steve Clarke

Who Is That Man?

Who is that man dressed in red and white,
Stacking presents under trees which glow in the night?

Who is that man that's sitting there,
Eating cookies and getting crumbs everywhere?

Who is that man which lives at the pole
A belly like jelly as round as a bowl?

The one like no other who strolls in the dark
And comes one night to engage in a lark.

Yes this is Santa I say with a lick
Of the candy he gave me, thank-you Saint Nick!

Melissa Hubble

Age And Experience

Sitting down an old man is like a rock, rough hewn, which a God shaped-shaped here and scoped there with sharp eagerness. Standing and supporting himself with a crook, the weakness creeps out at the knee, and the old man is like a dragon-fly at the painful moment of birth. We are born, and grow. Quietly, imperceptibly, the process unfolds of a baby growing to a baby, a boy to a man. And then suddenly we realize that what we were we no longer are. Then the drama starts it's a fight fitful and feverous of shifting ourselves into this guise and that touching, tasting, testing staining the purity of youth. But relief comes with experience, experience, the pegs of pain piercing to the formless mass of the turmoil inside man. Now the soul is born but gone too is the patterned repetition of traditions. And so sitting down he looks rock-strong but standing is the broken pitcher.

To ...

And so you have gone, gone your usual paradoxical ways meaning to return, but never returning, and you have gone, gone with only one smiling look behind leaving me here to scribble this verse.

Monga Mwanza

She's A Good Living Woman

She's a good living woman, going to heaven when she dies
she deceives her old mother until the day she died
her father was a trusting fool, but she also made him cry
but she's a good living woman, going to heaven when she dies

First there was a good man as trusting as can be
and five wonderful children but she wanted to be free
so she treated them all badly of this she can't deny
but she's a good living woman and going to heaven when she dies

Three sisters and two brothers, they say she used them all
with cheating and lying you know she had a ball
they all say she's evil and mean as she can be
but she's a good living woman, and heaven's where she'll be

They all say she's evil and the devil's in her eye
but she'll just work on them and have them change there mind
and when she's thought with them, they'll never know she lied
cause she's a good living woman, going to heaven when she dies

She's a good living woman, she knows she's done no wrong
she knows she's going to heaven and there she'll sing her song
about all the good she done, you'll never hear her cry
she's a good living woman, and going to heaven when she dies.

Sandra J. Harrison

Regrets

Remembering all the good times
she shared with family and friends

She said those times were so much fun
she hoped they'd never end

One day she pulled out alcohol
and her family and friends didn't know

And the nice controlled person she used to be
just simply did not show

Ever since that very first drink
her life had not been the same

And everyone else's feelings
were just left out in the rain

She ended up crying and hoping and waiting
to make one horrible night end

The night she drank, the night she drove,
and the night she lost her best friend.

Andrea Hoornweg

Unconscious Love

I watch him sleep as I write,
So peacefully he lays on my side of the bed,
His head resting upon my pillow,
Totally oblivious to my observing eye.
I can touch him without him waking.
I can kiss him without him flinching.
But, if I whisper "I love you" in his ear,
He replies the same, without movement.

Laurie Cuthbert

"I Wish That Everybody"

I wish that everyone could visit this island,
So that they could experience our beautiful, clear ocean
And shiny white sand,
And feel the warmth of our people as they sit by the pool and
Listen to a band.

They could watch the sunset brighten the sky,
And watch the beautiful birds as they flew by,
And the coolness of the sea breeze on one's face,
Is enough to fill the night with grace.

To wake up to the waves crashing on the rocks,
And strolling along the moon lit docks,
With the stars twinkling high above,
In the sky that is filled with love.

What a wonderful thing God has planted,
A beautiful island which most of us take for granted,
We never have Winter and so it's always sunny,
And will always have tourism to supply our people with jobs and money.

So I hope that you understand, just how much tourism means to
Cayman,
And I hope that you will help along,
So that Caymanians will always sing a happy song.

Terry-Ann Arch

Are You My Friend?

Someone to talk to, someone who listens,
Someone who cares when I'm sad,
Hugs me when I cry
And rejoices with me when I'm happy.
Someone who is honest and encouraging,
Someone to teach me and whom I can teach,
Someone who shares and allow me to share,
Someone strong, in mind, patient in love, dependable in soul
Can you love me the way I am today?
Are you my friend?
For all the things I ask of you,
You in return shall receive from me.

Jan Desrosier-Traverse

From 28,000 Ft.

Above, enfolded in brilliant blue,
Space, which is boundless, infinite
Bright with shining light.
It lifts the spirit.

Below, soft pillows of cloud
Forming and fashioning in fleecy jackets
Pictures to delight.
It lifts the spirit.

Till suddenly, what the greedy eye has waited for
Dark, jagged, cruel but glorious,
The highest peaks crowned with glittering, virgin snow
Appear the mighty Alps.
It lifts the spirit.

Gillian M. Davidson

Ancestral Legends

Helped by England 1901; Aunt/sister after Aunt/sister
stands on a hill side.
Their bodies glowing, while they pray to the stars
and the heavens for the future legends of their
generation to be born, the way life was meant to be.

Years passed and from their generation after generation
legends were brought to life in a home that was later
knows as "THE DRURY HOUSE".
Six generations lived in that house, ran by the eldest
of knowledge legends.

Legend after legend comes the past now more redeemed
and demented with feelings.

Now the house once filled with life, mystic tales
and magical moments is gone.

Locking up the legends of an era and keeping the key
as a treasure, for the house now starts
a new era of generations.

Two by the heavens and generations by the dozens,
starts a new era of legends and fairy tales.

Christine Linnard

For Strength, For Courage

This is a poem to my former
teacher, and constant influence,
whom I have turned to a million times
whose helpful advise never
fails to bring a smile to my face
or simply a sigh of relief
your never-ending patience and strength
have provided me with the inspiration
to continue
and never lose sight of what I want most
you have taught me more than English
you have taught me determination
and a fighting spirit that brings not only success
but also the ability to keep my vulnerability hidden within
so I write this for strength, for courage
and for gratitude to you,
you've done more than you'll ever know.

Daniella DiPonio

Tara

Ever since I can remember I had her,
that cute little dog named Tara, always listening
to the world around her.
But even life can't last forever 'cause
everyone gets old, older, and even older until
life is no longer a part of them.
That's what happened to Tara, my dog.
The Part terrier, Part Poodle black and white dog
who lived a long happy life, a long happy life
of being a dog.
But somewhere along the way she got too old,
too old to climb the stairs, too old to bark at the birds.
So realizing how much she was suffering
we had to help her, even if it meant giving
her a needle to put her to sleep for many
years to come.
That's what my family did so now
she is not here, but no matter what she
will never be completely gone 'cause I
will always have the memories.

Jennifer Elliott

Spare Baggage

We each carry deep within us, spare baggage from our youth,
That determines our every action and obscures the real truth.
It directs the way we pass our days and even how we breathe,
And how we come and how we go, and whether we stay or leave.

It decides the way we spend our time and how we lead our lives,
How we deal with friend or foe, our husbands and our wives.
It blurs our every waking thought and alters our points of view
Of the way that other people are, and of all the things they do.

It takes much time to remember youth, a great deal of diligent thought
To search for the bags that hold the good, and discard those that do not.
It's a task that each of us must do, to examine the past and see,
If we can't improve our lot in life, and be the person we want to be.

M. Orpen

Gum Trees

So fragrant the blossoms that perfume the gum trees
That grow near the homestead on Galgabba hill
Where honey is gathered and stored by the bees
Beneath the green branches so shady and still.

From lovely young red tips that comes in the spring time
We breath eucalyptus our lungs for to fill
So dear to the natives who slept beneath the time
The stars and the gum trees on Galgabba hill

Oh spare those old gum trees that all through the ages
That sheltered the flowers are the guarding them still
The sweetest of music told of by the sages
Was played on the gum leaves on Galgabba hill.

M. C. McFadyen

Sunset

What a sight!
The colors are quite bright.
Blue orange, red and pink.
It makes you think.
How do they become so unresistibly beautiful.
The colors are, oh, so beautiful
It makes me feel so free.
Free like a bird, free like a bee.
Why can't everything be so wonderful
Life would be great. If every thing was so wonderful.
I wish they could stay.
But they started to fade away.
As the sun goes down.
I put on a frown
I am so disappointed
That it went unappointed.
But I think, do not think in sorrow
It will be back tomorrow.

Manuela Gantenbein

Silent Combat

In my heart of hearts, I wanted you to know
there's a different me inside the me I show.
I often have, briefly, let me out
only to run for cover.
Afraid, somehow, I would be wounded
if you were to discover

In my heart of hearts, I tried to show, in simple ways
the deep unending love that you should know.
Years of hiding, running from, life gone astray
From the way I'd planned.
Insecure love, thoughts not spoken,
too late for you to understand.

Sheila Green

Once In A Lifetime Love

A tear slowly rolls down her cheek
The first one she's cried since last week.
The radio's playing a sweet old song
Bringing back memories, oh so strong.
Of her once in a lifetime love.

She remembers the day they met
A day she will never forget.
He captured her heart and her soul
His love was precious just like gold.
Her once in a lifetime love.

Memories are all she has now
She seems happy with that somehow
It's been several years there apart
But he's still there, deep in her heart.
Her once in a lifetime love.

He was the first and only one
She gave him her life and her love
There will never be another one
He was her once in a lifetime love.

Denise Schiewek

"Remembering"

As I travel down this winding road towards
the place where I was born, fond memories keep
coming back, of the house I once lived in by the
railroad track, and the little stream that ran
out back.

The outward appearance of this place I once called
home, was in need of painting and the shutters
were torn, and the cold wind whistled through the
cracks in the wall, and the trees that surrounded
it were ready to fall.

But the outward appearance doesn't matter at all, it's
what goes on inside these walls that can effect us all.
Remembering the smell of fresh baked bread on the
hearth every day, and the sound of laughter and
chatter as children we played.

These are the fondest memories of all, the house that I
lived in when I was small, and the warmth and
the love that was shared by all, are precious
memories I will always recall.

Irene Shaw

Salute To A Canadian Peace Keeper

He wore the insignia of a Canadian Combat Engineer
The proud young soldier who showed the world no fear
A professional—one of Canada's highly trained few
Disarming booby traps and clearing mine fields, too
He accepted the dangers and he knew them well
One wrong move—you get blown to hell
Orders were received through the chain of command
Deployment as a Peace Keeper in a foreign land
Between the Bosnians and Serbs—he stood in peace
Protecting the innocent—waiting for hostilities to cease
To the helpless victims of the war and strife
He gave the ultimate—he gave his life
He joined the ranks of the fallen—those sent to stand
As pillars of hope and freedom in a war-torn land
Remember the Blue Beret—remember it with pride
It was worn by a proud Canadian—the day that he died.

Robert W. Nicholson

Missing Home

A homeless man walking down the street
The snow was tingling for his feet, like a bird up in the sky.
Time is quickly passing by, the only thing I have to say.
That I miss you everyday, my life is not the very same
Like a person without shame, thought it is better living here
Instead of feeling full of fear, I have overcome my fears today
I have said what I had to say, I'm saying this right now.
I wonder why and wonder how this happened in the fall
Some nights I can not sleep at all
It makes me want to be small
Like a baby deeply sleeping
I would like so start my life over again
But be with the same family
We would be a whole lot better
That is why I am writing this letter
When I write I feel like the moon
I know that we will be together soon
I won't be sitting in this room
I will be out there somewhere having fun
With my dad and mom

James Taylor

Why?

The moon it was full and the sky azure blue.
The sun it was shining and so were you.
The flowers were singing and the rain, well
It danced
Until the reckless day of circumstance.

You knew in your heart you were full of gold
But some where in life a story was told
It filled all the trees with tears and woe
Now there is nothing but ice and cold

Oh what will you do to melt all the snow
The answers within you as you may as well know
I will still love you because I believe it is true
And once again baby the sky will be blue.

I wish I could make all your pain disappear
But only the stars in the night will appear
For the star's they are bright as the sun
Is by day
And the night shall return in its glory to stay

Lois Dunlavy

"Unanswered Wishes"

You are in my wishes and in my dreams
the thought of feeling forever your warm embrace
Hoping your true love will exist only for me
Your kisses taste so sweet and tender

Life is undefined to all
the answers to my wishes and
the meanings of my dreams
Remain all mysteries 'till tomorrow in my heart

Yet, my mind has answered for me the
question of your love
I will adore you and your memory for
an eternity of tomorrows
But still, for each tear that escapes me
there will always be one more unanswered wish

Shannon Allen

Wave Of Emotion

I'm too cold to make heads or tails of this situation
The water keeps surrounding my dreams not allowing me to break free.

Sometimes I feel the light shining over
giving me the spirit of hope
giving me the strength I need to over achieve
giving me the self-esteem the water takes from me

Every day that passes has me asking another question
I live day and night trying to get a grip of this new life
People no-longer understand where I'm speaking from...
just cos my questions are.... unheard of. Are...

Lost out in sea, that's where I'm from when I dream
lost cos my questions are unheard of... are un-believed.
Lost cos when the waves push me under, I can't break free
lost cos the waves hold me under when I want to be me
I just want to be me...

Chris McGregor

The Sky

The farmer was working the fields
then his wife ran out
Husband, something just flew by
What could it have been?
Possibly a plane flying low

Where did it go, the farmer replies
It curved towards the nearby town
Then she clapped her hands in delight
at the nearby cloud rising
from the ground.

I'm afraid we shall have to say good-bye,
he stammers out
Why? Are we going on a journey, his wife asks
Yes, he softly replies, a long journey

Very well then, she says
Goodbye, my sweet husband
And he responds,
good-b.

Casey Ingram

Christmas Tears

Tears slid down her cheeks.
There she sat cold and damp.
Christmas was upon her once more.
It was time once again for the memories to haunt her.

Tears slid down her cheeks.
The winter wind whipped through her warn clothes.
The sound of carolers in the distance, played in her head.
When she was young and full of life, she had sung as well.

Tears slid down her cheeks.
The night brought icy snow,
The sound of people hurrying home to their families.
She remembered when she had somewhere to go, too.

Tears slid down her seeks,
As she closed her eyes,
All went still.
The Christmas memories would haunt her no longer.

Michelle Ruddock

The Healing Process

On my tylenol trip, in my Holy Cross gown
There was many a laugh, an occasional frown
Especially when; my pants would fall down
In this day of technology, how could it be
That this item of clothing is not history?

It is not how I look, but how do I feel
I think that I better make it a practice to kneel
Give thanks to our Creator, the doctors, the nurses
For they have to deal with Ralph's stingy purses
For here is a Holy Spirit that money can't buy
It touches the people on up to the sky.

Give thanks to St. John in the corner of the room
We go there to pray when problems do loom
Help me to pee, have a bowel movement soon
In a week or so, all systems are go
May I go home Doc? don't answer no.

My hearts been replumbed, my life is extended
My journey prolonged; may my ways be amended
A helping hand given with grace and compassion
Truly love one-another, let's start a new fashion.

Ernie Porkka

Fragments Of A Goddess

On the ground withered petals lie.
These same petals were a part of a perfect beauty.
Goddess be not forgotten from so long ago.
She enters our dreams to soothe our cries of help.
The conqueror replaced the nurturer so long ago.
Let no longer concrete and metal monuments
Be a measurement of progress.
A progress that threatens all life!
Goddess be remembered....
Bring back the internal rhythms.
And once again celebrate the moon,
Solstices and the equinox.
Goddess once upon a time embraced...
The hunter and gatherers of the Cro-Magnon Peoples
Had the harmony that we have lost so long ago.
Goddess be quick!
Put the pieces of our hearts back together.
Embrace the goddess within.
Let our energies transcend into the earth's
And once again we'll be united.

Susan George

My Little Angels

My little angels flitter around
they help you out - they save your life
They guide you through the light and in the
right directions
Angels are like little glows at night
they glow like little night lights
They are there to protect you when you are hurt
My little angels — they are there
when you need help the most
They can be like little stars
shining in the dim light
My little angels — they float in
our hearts and in the air, and some
times around the world!

Heather L. Bedford

What Are Dreams?

Dreams are something having great beauty or charm.
They may or may not do you any harm.
Dreams are of the unknown land.
They can be of the lowland or upland.
Dreams are like a huge wonderland, or they can even be of the sands.
Dreams are a fragment of the imagination.
And they go on for generations.
Dreams are of great hope, and are not like the Pope.
Dreams can be very romantic.
They don't have to be dramatic.
Dreams are of a wishful thinker.
They are not like a blinker.
Dreams are something you desperately desire.
They are usually of someone that you greatly admire.
So, while in the land of enchantment,
Let your body have a little enhancement.
And while your in the land of heart's desire,
You may even meet Mr. Meyer.
So, until we meet in dreamland someday.
You never know, it might just be in May.

Teresa A. Lucas

I'm Going To Get Out

I could hear the yelling from my room upstairs,
They were fighting again I could see the anger flair,
I wish it would stop, I wish it would stop
It's the second time this week,
Last time he had left a bruise on her cheek.

Doors slam, it's not ended I know,
By tomorrow the evidence will show,
I wish it would stop, I wish it would stop
When people see the bruises they talk,
Sometimes it gets so bad she can't walk.

It only happens when he's drinking,
The alcohol stops his proper thinking,
I wish it would stop, I wish it would stop
Beer and coolers quench his thirst,
But hard liquor is the worst.

He told her to never leave,
Convinced her that no one would believe,
I wish it would stop, I wish it would stop
She is stuck for life, to cry and pout,
But someday soon I'm going to get out.

Rosie Drew

Mothers

Soon,
They will be here.
With lots of love,
To give to everyone.

Soon,
The new generation will come.
Then our children's children,
Will be the new mothers.

Soon,
There will be people,
we don't even know.
But no one can replace the people who we love.

Such as you....

Mom.

Misa Zima

Ghazal (A Version Of Poetry)

When tired with hard work they will return to their houses
They will get move lived to see the locked doors.

Hungry birds find everything in the abdomen of the earth,
But unsatisfied man is searching the skies.

The siren of the mills are roaring in the ears,
you stop the dancing music more and more.

The birds who have long flights in their fate
Only fly after the confidence in the wings.

They did not know when they will leave their houses
Their own will demolish and look their houses

Nothing is well in these white skinned beauties
To worship them is worshipping white stones.

Bikkar Singh Khosa

Survival

I don't know what to do anymore.
Things are different from days of yore.
Everything's changed.
My life's rearranged.
A new script has been issued out,
And I still don't know what the old one's about.
I just hope that I will make it through.
I just don't know what to do.
So I will just move on day to day.
And hope I do everything the right way.
And if I don't, well, I can't take it.
And I know, on trying, I'll make it.
And when I'm gone, yes, when I die.
I will know—
that I survived.

Regina Brennen

Healing Heart

I thought my heart would never mend,
this wounded memory that lived within.
A love so strong a feeling so deep, a
fleet of soldiers could not keep.
I vowed this I would mend so tight.
A motion I had drawn, is it worth the fight?
To one man I pledged it all.
Blind my eyes over its dwelling ways, to
So no evil threw the haze.
On this darkened night I weep.
I wonder now to him I will seek,
A heart so broken the tears I have
drained, this empty feeling soaring through
my vein.
Kept inside I spaced for you
this moment I now outgrew,
I fell to sleep now to dream not of you
But happier days as each passed through!

So sleep how before the dawn
because I know tomorrow Life must go On!

Lori Lee Minardi

Alone

I looked into your eyes.
Like a raven in flight, they seemed to shift...
far away from my gaze.
Withheld from me; so I felt.
How I longed to see the sparkle in your eyes,
when they sought me again.
Oh, how mine glistened with tears.
So hazy was my sight; I lost all focus.
When I have thought that you turned away,
it has been my face turned, all along.

Chelsea Bowles

Whose To Say

My mind is confined within a prison where voices are heard,
through the cracks in the wall, but human figures are none existent
within this world of pain, the darkest stories
are told with the conscience of fear, all sight
is blinded, except the bars that appear,
fighting for freedom, as insanity sets in.
While looking for memories, that no longer
exist, trying to escape, but never grasping
the key, the more I reach for it, the further it drifts from me.

Who's to say, I'll see another day,
who's to say, I must carry on, whose to say, that this
life of hell isn't real that I tell. Please tell me, whose to say.

The beast appears, through the toxic air I
breath, and the final cut is made to my soul
of agony, my blood is draining from my crippled
body, as I lie here within a hopeless state. I
can see clearly now, I'm going home, mother!
Say no prayer for me, as I let go of your string.
I haven't the strength to speak, nor the words
to say goodbye, so please forgive me.

Tim Felfoldi

"My Love For Thee"

Even if thy stars from the sky shine no more
thy love for thee shall never die
even if thy rivers, streams, and lakes all run dry
thy love for thee will always grow
when thy moon's darkness fades over thee
thy eyes will glow for thee to see
when thy tree has no more a leaf
thy arms will shade thee
and when thy sun forbids to heat
then thy heart will warmth thee
and when they wind creates a storm
thy house of love will protect thee
when thy strength for thee grows weak
thy love for thee, in my own way, will shelter thee forever...

Randy G. Shura

Should I Be Satisfied

I was a sinner once, once lost in the sin!
Till Jesus came along, took me in,
Should I be satisfied?
I saw my Christ to be, hang on the tree!
Yet He in His great love saved even me!
Should I be satisfied?
He gives me grace to live, day by day!
For his great work to give without delay!
Should I be satisfied?
He gives a prayer to ask, whate'ere I need,
He gives on earth a task, to sew his seed,
Should I be satisfied?
Should I be satisfied to live this way?
For one who gave his all! What can I say!
Yes I'll be satisfied! To live for him!
To crown Him Lord of Lords.
Who knew no sin.

Frieda Plantz

Untitled

- Friendship is a bond,
  not of love but of life.
- Life is a map,
  one of which with many pathways.
  - To find a new friend is to find a new pathway.
- This is the direction you will travel,
  until you find a new friend and a new pathway.
- But do not travel in sorrow,
  for there is always the journey home.

Shane Freeman

The Wolf

To the moon the wolf will howl,
To its enemy the wolf will growl.
Its enemy trembles with fear,
For it senses that the wolf is near.

Two shiny eyes peer from the dark,
As it listens to the huskies bark.
As the Eskimos travel through the dark,
Their feet in the snow make a mark.

Then there is a gun shot 'bang, bang',
As the wolf runs slobber drips from its fangs.
Now the wolf is safe and sound,
For a good hiding place he has found.

Now he must rest,
In his newly found nest.
For breakfast in the morning he shall eat a hare,
Which he will find in a hunter's snare.

After breakfast he shall run,
He shall have a lot of fun.
After that the wolf will go back to his den
Where he, shall hide from men.

Brandon Willis

For God And Country

My country, my God, or myself; To whom do I owe allegiance?
To my country I have given my body and life,
Moved about here and there from day to day,
Confined by orders, bound by law, always marching in step;
This uniform restrains more than the heart beneath it.
To my God I have given my devotion and soul,
Followed faithfully all precepts and sacraments,
Confined by dogma, bound by commandments, always singing along;
This religion restrains more than the person within it.
To myself I have left nothing and nobody,
Traveled alone from my God to my country,
Confined by nothing, bound by nothing, always empty and alone;
This empty shell restrains less than the person within it.
My country and my God; Allegiance to all but myself.

Al J. Lemberg

A Very Special Place

There is a special place where I can go
To relax, ponder and dream
It is so beautiful no matter what the time of year
Each season has its own promise and majesty
Where nature seems so pure.

There is water, birds and animals to view
At night the stars seem very bright and near
And morning sunrises too lovely and clear
After a while you lose all track of time and space
The outside world is forgotten and your dreams continue.

How lucky I am to be able to visit this beautiful place.

Carolyn Ainsworth

The Power Of Evil

It creeps through the misty shadows,
feeding on your fears.
Feeling your trembling body,
helpless in the dark of night.
Rising, rising, then slipping away,
into the never ending sea of the unexplained.
Endlessly leading you to the land of the dead,
while you relentlessly try to overcome the power of evil.
You feel death stricken, yearning to defeat
the terrifying eager hand that awaits your destiny.

Lynn Trimble

The Stranger

One day I glanced into a mirror,
To see what I could see,
A stranger's face was staring back,
I no longer looked like me.

Silver strands were in my hair,
My brow was etched with lines,
My skin no longer glowed with youth,
My eyes had lost their shine.

I gazed into my weary eyes,
Life had taken all their light,
I wondered why my youthful dreams,
Were no longer burning bright.

Where was the girl I used to be,
Was she hiding in my soul?
Or had she slowly died each day,
As I was growing old?

My heart no longer beats with hope,
I have no vows to keep,
My soul is simply waiting for,
Its fateful, final sleep.

Penelope Owen-Sears

Childhood Memories

I wish I was a child again
To skip and jump and play
I would cherish every moment
The ones I threw away
The things I took for granted and never could be bought.

To know my mother's waiting
When I get home from school
To smell the dinner cooking, a bucket full of coal
Not a worry in the world, well maybe one or two
But not one lasted very long, with mum to see me through.

Gathering wood to help the coal
With a broken down pram or maybe a sack
We'd collect all we could, then hurry back
To sit in the evening, and watch the fire glow
Is the happiest feeling, I'll ever know.

Jean Henry

Flight Of The Bumblebee

Buzz, buzz, everywhere
To where he lands? Could be anywhere

Far, far off he goes, with his polin
Rows on rows

His wings beat so fast
That you will hardly see him go past!

He returns home with his polin
Out to show

He was welcomed home
With a glow!

For he loves his fellow mates
They even sometimes go out on dates!

But beware, of the midnight stalker
The bat! He is not a good walker!

Mr. Bat will eat the bees, but if he does....
He'll be sure to sneeze

AAAchooo, away go the bees
As happy as can be's.

Lonny Smith

Sunrise

Sunrise sneaks backup over the horizon,
(today the sailors would be displeased).
Crimson phosphorescence,
Slowly gathering intensity,
Like the gentle unfolding
Of a prize rose,
Picking up momentum,
Begins to chase the night's black blanket
To the other end of the earth,
Sweeps it into some colossal closet,
To be held for safekeeping,
Until the day's solar intensity once more tires,
And sinks - slowly into the west,
In yet another blaze of glory.

Gayle Croswell

Trying To Balance The Books

Too many roads made only for leaving on.
Too many jails built just for arriving.
Too many fires, but not enough
warmth in our fingers. Too much rain
on uncovered faces. Too much rain
on unburied faces. Too many battlefields
for all of the plowshares, plowing up
jaw-bones with languages smashed
in their teeth. Too many songs, with too few
singers. Too many interpreters of dreams,
without enough dreams to go round.
Too many politicians beating nothing
but words into plowshares, splintering their smiles.
Too many, or is it too few, saying:
everything's going to be all right.

Roger Nash

Life

Life is something rented - only for a while
Touching hearts and other lives -
Bringing in a child.
Getting educated and giving it sometimes
Loving someone in a special way
Then wedding bells to chime.
Oh pitter patter of little feet,
I must watch you grow
Bounded in the things, I said you ought to know.
Helping out my fellow man
Showing compassion to the poor,
Being sincere and considerate -
Opening a door.
Getting sick - knocking at death's door
Knowing in my heart I lived what life was for.
Jesus knows that His light was never dim
And the life I lived was a life lived for Him!

Vanessa C. Rolle

Children Of The Sea

Sea shells lying in the sand
upon a lazy shore —
Whispering together, beside the
ocean's roar.

Telling salty tales, of life beneath the sea,
where whales swim, and starfish float
and mermaids frolic free.

And when you hold one to your ear
and think you hear a moan —
It's just the ocean's gentle sighs,
calling it back home.

Vilia Milic

The Likeness Of A Leaf

O, leaf of the morning,
unguarded and frail;
Beneath the tree of life,
you rest and remain;
But how do you withstand the harsh, unyielding ways,
associated with nature's brutality?

My delicate contour often deceives,
implying fragility's residency;
But below the exterior of my impressionable silhouette,
lies a strength that is concealed by the slightest imprint;
A paper-thin body, shaped like a spade,
protected by a layer of emerald green;
I sway in the wind,
and shiver in the cold,
but never back down from what the climate beholds;
My sheath is my shield,
my stem is my sword,
and together they fight to conquer all;
But regardless of this, appearance suggest,
that a leaf is a mere vision of weakness.

Melissa Cechetto

Sandman

I can hear the siren's cold
urgent call
not really a sound
but an injection
of pure desire
of a lie that is beyond denying
and I'm forced to wade into waves of sand

Once blindly admired from
a distance now blurred by proximity
now a fatally realized goal
tangible ground between teeth
a taste a texture unavoidable
like the wind in this place

Are these tears of remorse
that I rub or is it
the sand that collects
in every fold of my skin
as the wind curses louder
summoning his next victim

A throat full of my panic cannot quench his thirst

John Cecere

Remembrance Day

Remembrance day is a time of sorrow;
We try to go on and think of tomorrow.
Seasons come and seasons go;
But the pain remains as many of us know.
Many men had left home and would never return.
Freedom for their country they were trying to earn.
Some men were lost and some left to die;
Leaving many a woman and child to cry.
Wives and mothers place poppies at the monument with care;
While sounds of "The Last Post" echo in the air.
We think back when the war had begun,
Of all the soldiers dressed in uniform and with gun.
Now Flander's Field is a remembering spot;
Rows of crosses mark the place where many were shot.
November eleventh is a time of tears, hurt and pain;
Memories of previous years are all that remain.
Poppies became the symbol of the tragedy of war,
The renewal of life and so much more.
So wear your poppy and show it off proud;
Shout "lest we forget" and shout it loud.

Melanie Parker

Moment Of Truth

After pacing to and fro, I finally sit still;
Waiting for information which could determine my life's fate

My mind searches frantically for anything to appease my endless wait;
But still, my anxiety refuses to abate

I glance furtively at the telephone, willing it to come to life;
To put an end to this mystery; to pierce this tension like a knife.

I am alone in this room, my sole witnesses being the four bare walls closing in on me, almost trapping my lithe body, my panic culminating, until I calm myself to my best ability.

I hear my wristwatch ticking, each innocent stroke seeming to me like frightened claws digging deeper into my flesh, thirsting for the unknown. Will it prove itself to be doom, or will everything be wonderful again, with. . . . .

My eyes dart to the ringing instrument, fear almost paralyzing me, but I manage to submit

No longer having to wait, I lift the ear piece, and with trembling voice, greet my caller.
Once I know the reality of my situation, will I want to celebrate, to sob, to flinch, to holler? As I replace the receiver and look up through my tears, I see myself in the future, and smile.
As a silence pervades the room once more, I now see the world as less evil and vile
Everything will be fine after all;
my soul is free, and I can stand tall.

Jane Hillenbrand

Memories

The first time I saw you standing there I knew there was something special about you. The way your hair fell when you moved it when your hand, your beautiful blue eyes which looked at me with intense, and the perfect form your body has, made me realize how special you really are just by first glance. When you said those words as you walked over to me made me want to faint. That's the first memory I have of you.

The second memory is when you and I spent last summer near the ocean. That was the most romantic we ever got, the way you and I sat watching the sunrise and holding each other in arms. The way we danced to the music of romance while we watched the waves come in, made me feel free as the wind. The way we played in the water like a couple of children made me understand how much fun you really are.

As I stand by your grave I can't help wonder the reason, as to why you left me. I do know one thing and that is the meaning of love. You helped me understand love through the year and half we've spent together. I will always treasure you.

Kassie Knauft

Don't Wake Me Yet!

Sitting at peace in the day's waning light,
Watching twists of dusk's violet rays beam,
my lids growing weary, here comes the night.
With my mind's eye on the verge of a dream.

Bursts of utopia flash and then fade.
Painting a picture no Rembrandt could draw.
Mending strings of my heart, broken and frayed,
a vision of beauty, untamed and raw.

I look at you deep, so close, yet so far.
Lips of an angel and skin wrapped in silk,
eyes shining bright like a fiery star,
an illusion of love, never to wilt.

When the orb of the night finally sets,
my final desires is - Don't wake me yet!!

Gordon Lodge

Fall Time

Fall time near the lake.
Water from the lake which thought it would stay.
You could hear faint rapids at a distance away.
White water splashing around and about,
those enormous boulder's shone without doubt.
Your ears became familiar with another sound,
of crackling crisp leaves, which had fallen to the ground.
A rabbit was running keeping his pace,
afraid of hot coals popping from the fire place.
The beavers are busy with delight,
gnawing on poplars but remain out of sight.
The whistle of a loon across in the bay,
sounded like it was only ten feet away.
Assuming his fishing was done for the day,
I could feel the temperature dropping into the night,
as I made my way back to the campsite.
Without any of these rounds it just wouldn't be right.

Micheal Bananish

Struggle

Pages turn, sometimes by hands unknown.
We are surprised, and afraid, and cut to the home.

Cry to understand, though futile at best.
Appreciate finally - you've been put to the test.

Again and again, you have to concede
that patience and strength will make you succeed.

The pages will turn, the test will persist.
The lessons will beckons, and should not be missed.

The pages will turn as the story unfolds.
The story of life by its lessons are told.

Ingrid Slavec

In The Darkness

In the darkness
We cannot see each other,
But we can hear our voices,
And together, we get along fine.
During the day,
You can see my face,
And I can see the hatred in your eyes,
If only we could all live in the darkness.

Michelle Harding

Poppies Still Grow

We remember those who died,
we feel sorrow for those who cried.
At their homes sat the worried wives,
while their husbands spared their lives.
Families and their loved ones so dear,
Sat at home surrounded in fear.
The poor children at the break of dawn,
found out from their mother that their father were gone.
The troubled young man in the plane,
Knew that his family and parents were in pain.
At last the war came to yield,
and there lay the men in the Flander's Fields.
Cross upon cross, row upon row,
yet many years later, poppies still grow.

Annalea Ragan

The Day The Birds Stopped Singing

We were outside having fun just the three of us that day,
we never imagined that something could stand in our way.

Everything seemed so perfect so alive and bright,
the birds in the tree tops were chirping in delight.

But then everything was broken and the sun started to die,
and the songs of the birds turned into a long lonely cry.

The wind started to blow and the trees started to sway,
we decided just then that it was no longer time to play.

We started to walk home slowly but surely,
but when we turned around we started to run in a hurry.

Behind us was a tornado that seemed to draw near,
we grabbed each others hands and started to cry in fear.

We hid behind a tree and hoped it would just pass us by,
but instead it lifted us up and we feared we would die.

It lifted us up and beat us down,
and when it was finished it left us to die on the ground.

I lifted my head and I slowly arose,
one other followed and the other kept her pose.

We tried to revive her but we knew there was no way,
then we sorrowfully walked home just the two of us that day.

Lana Sammut

Mom's Another Name For Love

There is only one who truly understands,
what I go through day by day,
And if she doesn't understand,
she tries to anyway.

She listens with an open mind,
and warmth within her heart,
And helps put me together again,
when I fall apart.

When I'm feeling sad or hurt,
she's there to comfort me,
She helps show me sometimes in life,
that's just how things must be.
She helps me to forget,
the bad feelings I'm thinking of,
That is why I think,
mom's another name for love...

Gerald (Wolf Windwalker) Cook

He Is Still With Us

No, he is not gone.
Whatever is good or kind or gentle or bright in his sons—
that is Herman.
Whoever was helped by his generosity, that is Herman.
The trees, the flowers, the very grass embellishing their home—
that is Herman.
He lives, too, in the hearts and minds and memories of
everyone who knew him.
Grieve not.... He is with us still,
With us in ways that will be a blessing
to those in whom his goodness has found root.
This dear and gentle man lives on in everyone whose life he has
touched.
You have but to look and say, "Yes, that's Herman." But...
Not for Sarah, Sarah his beloved, it is not enough.
Her heart aches to hear his voice, to see his smile, to feel his
touch.
Now — only in memories.
Grateful she will ever be for the years of his loving care.
Content she must be in having filled his life with beauty
and with joy.
Let us not say goodbye. Just say, "Now, it is time for him to rest."

Sadie Stren

"If I Could"

If I could stop the world at some point in time
when life was but a melody and the hills not so steep to climb.
If I could stop the world and make time stand still
maybe sad things that have happened could become void and nil.
If I could slow it down to a mere snails pace
and take the time to savor the beautiful events that took place.
Then maybe all the tears I've cried could somehow change to smiles.
Maybe loved ones far away would no longer be separated by miles.
Maybe all the words left unspoken could be voiced and said.
Maybe it would have made a difference for those now long since dead.
But then, my life would be but remnants
if I'd had that power of control,
empty and meaningless lacking of heart and soul.

Jeannette Wehrhahn

Solitude

Solitude is the murmur of the trees,
When they are moved by a faint breeze.
Solitude is hearing the insects' drone,
And lying in a grassy field all alone.
Solitude is the eagle in the azure sky,
Gliding so regally and majestically by.
Solitude is hearing the screeching of the gulls,
In the morning while they sit on the great ships' hulls
Solitude is peace; solitude is quiet
Solitude: There is so little in this land of riot.

Anita Klyn

The Lamp

In a world full of darkness, there is a lamp, oh what a bright light.
When this light shines it illuminates the night.

In moments of deep sadness this light illuminates leaving sadness
behind,
and creates great peace in the depths of my mind.

The lamp is relentless and in when in need, will be there
for all that it cares for. The lamp is forever selfless
and never shows favor.

The lamp will not tire but will always love. The lamp has
a heart as meek as a dove, compassion that flows as a
river, eyes as bright as the stars, and beauty that
makes all men quiver.

Now you ask who is this lamp, oh I wish I knew, my love
this lamp I speak of is you.

Gilbert Ansah

My First Love

I told everyone I didn't care,
when you dumped me and left me standing there
I'm so confused, I need someone to touch
why does love have to hurt so much?

Sometimes I don't mind being alone
I listen to music or talk on the phone,
but then I wonder why our love died,
and I feel the pain deep deep down inside.

I want to call you, but I can't,
you'd just hang up and laugh at me.
I'm so mixed up, I start to shout,
then I curl up, and cry my heart out.

I hope one day you'll be out of my mind,
and a guy full of love, is what I'll find.
But for now I'm stuck with one sad thought,
That my love for you, will never rot.

Tina Erica Britton

Snow Angels

What is the sense of making angels in the snow,
When your fortune you can not know.
Although the making of the angel's wings,
A certain kind of freedom brings.
One can't rely on winter's snow
to bolster spirits when you're low.
When you roam through winter's fields,
You'll find that faith in God contentment yields.
Thus take note of each flake's design,
And in its shape God's love you'll find.

Michelle Nowak

Peace

Peace!
Where is peace?
Where is peace in the haunting
Mask of suffering of
the emaciated Somali child
Where is peace in the muzzle
of the smoking gun?, and in the
dark depth of the warlords heart?
Where is peace in those liquid pools of
sadness staring you from behind refugee camps.
Where is peace? Somalia? Rwanda?

Where is peace in the cholera racked body?
Where is peace in the hordes of the half submerged canoes to 'safety"?

There is peace in love
"Love your neighbour as you love yourself"
The peace we want is everywhere,
hidden from selfish human eyes.
Peace is in our hearts, let it flow,
Let the bird carry your message of peace to
your neighbour, to the world!

Judith Attyang

Winds Of Time

The breath of love sighs soft on breezes fine
While murmuring sweet whispers of thy name
I long to gentle back the winds of time
Till only our first meeting doth remain.
The first time I beheld thy countenance
Light zephyrs stirred to motion in my soul
Although our sudden meeting was by chance
The sight of thy sweet presence made me whole.
My love, four winds have stolen thee away
The storms of loss still gather in my heart
I thought your love would fill my ever day
Till cruelest fate did sunder us apart.
Blow lightly past these clouds, oh winds of time
Return the love to me, which once was mine.

Lyanne Verschuere

Jargon Of A Drunk

In the name of his unique genius words of wonder,
Who he thinks his dazzle
Will cause a tongue, to cleave to the roof,
Of one's mouth.
When his great mind, now, the unsealed book.
His baffling descriptions, his mortal funk.
Will surge the wind and harrow up the soul,
That always, makes his audiences, "planet struck".
Like a duck, seized in a storm of thunder.
Only to have the message "pass away"
Like the changeables precarious summer clouds.

Joyce H. Haase

The Warriors

The Warrior, strong, obedient and wise approaches the throne of God with a clean heart. The Warrior seeks the Lord's guidance and will to fight the enemy. He is totally covered with the Savior's blood and anointed with the Holy oil. Equipped with the full armour of God he enters the battle field.

He cries out for the lost and hurt people.
He knocks down the walls, tramples the serpent.
He never turns back until the enemy is destroyed. The taste of victory fills the room. The Warrior is weak but yet strong.

The Warrior, like Moses, lifts his arms to the Lord.
The sea is parted, the path is straight before him. The enemies fall at his feet. The battle has been won!
The Warrior looks to heaven, the tears turn to joy.
The rain falls from heaven.

Miriam grabs her weapon. Her spirit is strong!
Her heart is rejoicing. Her grace, her beauty, her strength as she dances for her King. She embraces her weapon with wisdom and she tramples on the enemy. Her strength is in the praisies as she worships her King. Her eyes are upon the Almighty one, her sweet Savior, her sweet Jesus! Her victory cry is like the eagle's. The enemy knows that the victory is the LORD's!

Vera C. Tourangeau

"The Gift"

They say that a dog is man's best friend,
With an unconditional love till the end;
So I dedicate this poem to my little Joe,
My four-legged friend to whom so much I owe.

I'm an only child with no children of my own,
But with this little canine I am never alone;
It is true he's been there unlike any other,
He was my lifeline when I lost my mother.

He gave me a reason to face each new day,
Whether cuddling beside me or bringing toys to play;
And when there were tears he would lick them away,
As if to say Mom don't cry it'll be okay.

He makes me smile and laugh every day,
He creates such a warmth in so many ways;
I cannot put a price on what he is worth,
But he is truly the centre of my universe.

Of all the blessings I received in my time,
One stands apart as being sublime;
His name is "Joey" and he makes me feel tall,
For he has been my greatest gift of all.

Patty Tales

A Wounded Soul

In the stillness of the night
With its silent beauty,
He stood alone on that vast beach
In pain, wounded and lonely.

Why ME?

A cry to a greater presence
And in the mysterious peace of that quiet,
His acceptance
His suffering is eased
As he becomes One
With is God and the Universe.

Merlyn Davidson

Did I?

I was walking down the dark streets,
with the November breeze lightly crawling by,
I thought the wind slapped me on my face,
as we saw each other passing by.

He was looking at me,
or did I imagine he did?
I knew he felt it too,
or do I imagine he does?

I wanted to scream and beat the wind,
wanted to touch his perfect hair.
Suddenly my desire took over my brain,
and I reached out to him, reached out to his hands...
but he wasn't there,
the wind slapped me once again on my face,
or did I imagine it did?

Ece Dizdar

The Racial Bird

If I were a bird what kind of bird would I be
Would I be able to soar high above the clouds like a hawk
Or would my flight be limited to a jump like a barnyard hen
Would my feathers be as glamorous and as beautiful as the peacocks
Or would they be dull and rough like the crows
Would my size be large like the ostrich
Or would I be as tiny as the humming bird
Would I prey on the weak and the defenseless like a vulture
Or would I be a target for shots like the duck
Would my presence be one of peace like the dove
Or would it be one of war like the fighting cock
Would I be praised by a nation like the eagle
Or would I be a blemish on society like the pigeon
Through your eyes what do you see
Is variety the beginning for change

Jonathan Hillman

Exotic Butterflies

Longer than two decades they lay—
Wriggling sedulously to see the light of day.
Breeding in rituals,
Aiming for sparkles,
Crossing all traditions,
To mould into new world creations,
with deliberate care, of arts kindred kind-
unblemished skin, dark long limbs to climb.
They lay awaiting for the great deliverance,
Eventually it came from the chancellors of beauty—
Impressing all deeply.
Out from the city of the sun,
They arrived triumphant in chariot
with sceptures hung,
The women of substance — Indians' pride.

K. N. Prasenna

Shadowmaster

Shadowmaster soldier of death, soldier of evil
You sell your crack vials and powders of design,
You spend your money on cheap women and sex,
you spread the disease, the white powder, your
powder, your powder of hell,
Your baked powder finds its way into mens' pipes,
Smoked a sedative of poison, frying brains,
Men rob, steal, kill imprison themselves, in reality
and in their minds.
Shadowmaster can we turn back the hands of time,
when you suckled on your mother's breast, and didn't
lead a life of crime?
What went wrong, where does it go right?
It is not mine, it is society's fight.

Dion Thomas

Innocent Victims

A little child on the streets of Belfast
Writes with his blood, 'We want peace'.
The poor child! it's time to run and play
Instead he is begging for peace from his forefathers.
He is a victim for no reason of his own,
He doesn't even know what is his sin
It's as if he has born with an accursed life.

We, the human being of this world
Had ever thought, 'What are we leaving behind
for our future generation?'.
Innumerable weapons, arms and ammunitions, the bombs!
A gift from the older generation to the newer
To turn the world into Killing Fields
Showing the paths to destroy the civilization on the Earth.
We failed to begot more Einstein
But succeeded to create more of the War Lords.
Human knowledge and science were more in use
For killing of humans', rather serving the humanity.

Time has come to save those innocent victims
Who being children are unable to voice their opinions
But silently shoulders the crimes of their forefathers.

Manash Mazumder

Forgive But Don't Forget

I live not to claim enemies!
Yet to forgive those who despise my thoughts!
And when I die!
I ask that only tears be shed upon my grave!
And that the anger of injustice be forgotten!
For death is but a door to a new home!
And I shall never leave your hearts,
But only the land you walk on!

Steve Larkman

Impossibleness

You are the sun that makes me shine
You are the wind that blows beneath my
heart and soul
When we've together feelings of emotion
and impossibleness arrive
A blood shot of hazardous becomes of use
Speech of words, are so incompetent,
But yet - to show them
Is the reality of love
With you, I feel as if, I have a reason
to live
But if at death —— I would not.

Rick Hallitt

A Monster's Dinner

If you want to ask a monster to dine,
You can't take him to a restaurant or give him some wine,
If you want to make the dinner a success,
You have to be prepared for any kind of mess!
'Cause the despicable food that monsters eat,
Is not very pleasant and it's sure not sweet,
If you want the monster to like the meal,
You have to think about what would appeal.
Now, for the appetizer I suggest,
Cream of eyeball soup, is surely the best.
Moving on to the main course,
You could offer rabbit ribs, or charred horse.
For dessert peacock pie a la mode is delicious,
Don't give him too much or he'll get suspicious.
For a wonderful beverage, here is a suggestion:
Budgie burgundy (Don't have too much or you'll get indigestion.)
And that is how you make a monster's dinner,
Once you try it, you'll think it's a winner!

Kirsty Jane Large

Abandoned

I helplessly looked into the eyes of a
young child,
Her compelling gaze into mine made
me shiver,
I reached out, mine with warm hands
to touch hers,
Oh so rough, so hard, so trembling.
Her clothes, torn, dirty, an odor made
a bitter lump in my throat.
Coarse hair strung down her contoured
cheek bones.
Do you have a present for me, whispered
a hoarse voice.
I stood speechless, wondering how such
a helpless being could survive.
I took her in my arms, wishing for
a transformation, a miracle.
Her lean shivering body suddenly reached a calm,
I wish I could take her home, for
love, for peace, for comfort.

Zenora Ramotar

Your Choice

I thought I saw you standing over by our tree
Your arms folded across your chest,
Your eyes staring at me.
I wanted to run to you and have you
in my arms once more
but I was held back by the memory
of my heart, you once tore
the feeling inside grows worse each
day whenever I think of you
I kept thinking of our love,
which I thought was true
I don't think you know just how
bad you hurt me inside
every time I see your smile,
a little part of me cries
Those gentle words I long to hear
would never come with your voice
but now when I see your
wicked ways I understand your choice

Heather Thompson-Pharand

Whispers In The Night

Deep into the night,
In a far off place,
Whispers from over the hills,
Fall upon my face.
Whispers from everyone around me,
Keep me wide awake.
These whispers are telling me,
"Stay awake, face the pain!"
I shall not wait!
I try to run! I try to dream!
To keep them away:
I feel so weak.
But to my fear,
They are still here:
To remind me, to remind me.
Suddenly the whispers are gone, back over the hills.
I shall not see them again,
For I'm in a dream.
A dream that lasts forever,
And forever shall I stay there.

Annette Desilets

Survival

As each new leaf appears - As each new bud opens - A change
takes place
A change that is so gradual, only the most observant will notice.
Yet the change is there - ever present.

Until one day - as if overnight -
the air fresh and clean - the water runs free again
the ground is painted with colors only nature can create.

The world is alive - awaken from a deep slumber.
Yet this transformation did not happen without struggle.
For months, the seeds of nature lay dormant, fighting the bitter cold.

As growth begins -
Each new leaf will cling to its branch,
hoping to stave off the ripping fingers of the north wind.

Each new bud will claw its way to the surface,
looking for that single ray of birth light.

And what are the rewards of their battles?
Something few people have ever experienced -

The Peace of Nature - The Satisfaction of Existence

As the cold of yesterday turns into the warmth of tomorrow
We shall each grow
by the strength of our survival and peace of our existence.

Michael Hoskins

The Mountain

The mountain stands defiant,
a challenge steeped to climb -
if rightly paced with proper haste
one can prevail, in time.

The mountain taunts ascension,
a pinnacle of height -
its peak, a dare; each step, a stair...
its summit soon in sight.

The mountain, now a footstool,
the conquest slow but sure -
once scaled, its crest no more the test
of will set to endure.

Randy Almond

Baby Boom

Our fathers killed in lands foreign, fought and toiled
A reluctant adventure due to some rulers' follies
Some were maimed and dead but, some home returned
On the home front the soldiers' warm fluid replaced the warm blood

Flowing at high speed it winded its course into labyrinth
of the womb
The warm over waited, and over ripe womb welcomed the fluid
That wetted and wetted the seeds in the deserted womb
Suddenly offsprings sprang forth: boom boom boom

In their thousands they boomed
With hope and expectations, they blossomed
They saw the world flowing with milk and honey
Boom boom out of the blue the were stumbling, falling, and crying

The boys now have hairs more silvery than their grandpas
The girl's seasonal blood froze faster than their grandmas
They wandered, confused among the cross roads of life
In murky waters some drowned, but some continued to swim

Helter skelter they roved, confused and unmotivated
Poor offsprings of the baby boom

Tanko S. Ahmed

"Love's Not A Game"

It hurts too much that I'm afraid
A strange place this is God made
Broken dreams accompanied by many broken hearts
It tears my heart and soul to parts
A heart is not some sort of a game
Someone gets hurt, another is to blame
When your in love don't play it wrong
Find a love and friendship that will remain
forever strong
Remember, love is not a thing of give and take
It's a strong bond only two people can truly
make.

Nieves Pedreira

A Year Passed

A year has passed since our marriage has begun
A year of love, to grow together and one to become

A carnation forgotten in your lapel
Begins this story, I am about to tell

Me, in my pink, you, in your black
I open my thoughts as they take me back

Knees that were shaking and a voice that croaked
I said my "I do's," my palms were soaked

As I looked into your eyes of blue
I knew our life would be brand new

Together we have found a new home
At Tyee Lake, we have grown

Through trials of love, we have endured
None of which we've seen, can't be cured

Together we are the fate of life
As we carry on as man and wife

I love you my darling, and hope I've shown
A part of me, that only you have known

Lydia E. Clark

My Brother...

I remember when we were kids,
All the things we said and did.
All the times we laughed and played,
I only wished he could have stayed.

He liked to party and have a good time,
And he always made the good times shine.
His pranks, his jokes, his funny smile,
If only he had stayed a while.

I took him for granted all those years,
Now all that is left are memories and tears.
Faded pictures to remind me of long ago days,
Echoes of laughter at his silly ways.

I know he's in a better place,
I'll never forget his handsome face.
Yes, he's gone on to a peaceful land,
Did he know his time was at hand?

I feel we'll meet again one day,
Than I'll tell him what I've wanted to say.
I love my family and a few others,
But no one ever replaced you, my Brother.

Tammy Hitchcock

Salute To A Soldier

As the sky turns dark,
and he begins to tire
he hears a twig snap, and the command to fire!!
He runs like the wind, to a nearby hole.
With shrapnel flying and a bright red glow.
He can feel his heart pounding,
right through his chest, as he sits and wonders
where are the rest.
He hears mortar fire above his head,
he knows in his heart the others are dead.
Will this be his grave, this hole in the ground,
he's so far from home, with no friends around.
What can we say about these men of war.
We cannot leave them, in that land afar.
All we can do, is bury them at home
and lest we forget, those who died alone.

Stephen Swan

Untitled

Years ago, when you kids were small
And I tiredly looked at the mess
I vowed if ever, you were grown
There would be no more of this!

But you're all grown up
And I look around at the many things
that are dear,
And I often think how nice it would be
If you were only here.

A doll, a book - table and chairs
The grand children have out to play
And I'm thankful to God
That he let me live to look at my
mess today.

Mildred H. Kennedy "Grandma Woodsie"

Coyote

He came toward me
and I waited,
beguiled,
wanting a closer look
at this handsome
creature of the wild,
who seemed to have
no fear of me.
Then as he drew near
I grew afraid — and yet
I looked into his eyes
and saw a beauty there
that I cannot forget.

Pauline Trabucco

Snow Birds

We had our first frost in September,
and oh how well I remember
the winter cold and how that north wind can blow
soon I will be wading knee deep in snow.
So it is time for you Snow Birds to go south
and have your fun
Some day it will be my turn to play in the sun.
It must be cheaper than up north where I stay
where winters last from September to May
But for now, I just dream about the warm
beaches where I would like to be
while I look out a frosted window and
the snow covered ground I see.

Wayne Kinghorn

Oh, Child, My Child

Oh, child, my child, you have gone away...
and I will never again be whole
while I am bound upon this earth,
yearning to feel your soul...
a soul I know that, beyond my tears,
rejoices throughout time
to feel the touch of God's Own Hand...
If I could only touch you
with this hand of mine...
Look, how it trembles in lonely pain!
But I must stay awhile
for there are others to love
and things to do
before the glad day I come to you
and, though you'll have beauty
I've never known,
I will still know you...
for you are my own.

Carolyn Strickland

The Seasons Of Life

Life is like the four seasons
And is gone in a fleeting moment.
It starts in the spring and
Matures in the summer.
It mellows in the fall.
When winter is past and the
last snow has melted, life
fades away to start anew,
A new generation.
A newborn infant cries
And the cycle goes on, on and
on until infinity.

Paul Turpin

Fall

Fall comes the apples
Are gray rotting, falling, everyday
They are green, brown, and gold
Too bad they were not sold
Nuts are falling here and there
They are scattered everywhere
Nuts are with the berries, too,
They have fallen just for you!
Crumbled leaves are in your hand
They have crumbled just like sand!

Stefanie Watkins

A Rose In Bloom

The sky is bright blue, with soft fluffy clouds
As I look back on the last year,
I realize the turn around I have made
As I look around at God's beauty,
I know now, he is with me every step of the way
We run in a complete cycle
We start as a seed
As we came each week
We grew into a healthier person
Stronger each day
As we are able, the unhealthy emotions and feelings are shed
Then, we rebloom all over again
We are like a rose
We start out so vulnerable and fragile
As it grows it becomes very strong and vibrant
At the end of a period of time the rose pedals fall to the ground
The new bud fresh and fragile starts again
As we go through the process of life
We shed the old ways
We are blessed with the new and joyful ways of God

Ali

Burdens

Be not afraid to grow old slowly,
Be afraid of not growing old at all!

Be not afraid to grow old and frail
Adulthood is but a stop in time
The body is but a case, a shell
A pod, a steel compartment to house the mind.

If we catch for an instant a thought
That small image or two just to dwell,
To reflect, on life's few impositions
That seem to drive us straight to hell,
But our rigid mind states this is not reality.

While not growing old and failing —-
Life's mission is still complete,
For who is to say, how long
This fragile mind is to remain...,
And this sweet life is not a defeat.

Joseph C. Sheffey Jr.

Lament In The Dark

I know not why you had no trust in me
Because I am not guilty this, I swear.
If all I did was be in love with you
I still do not agree, it is not fair,
I was a helpless lamb but still I died
Although I thought you could not be so cruel,
But you were poisoned by one who to you lied
And so you lost me, your most precious jewel.
My anger blazes like a hot flame now,
And all my love has changed into such hate
Because you did not keep your wedding vow
I must endure this sad untimely fate.
And so in death the truth I've come to see
My husband whom I loved did not love me.

Neuzi Camara-Smith

Gone Forever Is Today

WHEN the sun is slowly setting, and the
birds have gone to rest.
Ask thy self this question, have I
really done my best?
Have I left one thing undone, have I
shirked in any way,
To accomplish my objective, for gone
forever is today.

Greet each morning with a smile, resolved
to do each task,
That God or Man has put before you, no
quarter or question ask.
Then in the blush of evening, when the
moon sends forth its ray.
You can say "well done", for gone
forever is today.

S. Kenneth Tweedt

Snow Man

Snowman, snowman, what do you see?
Do you see a little girl with a doll pram?
Or do you see a little boy with an army man?
Or a dog with a bone? A baker baking bread?
Or a cook cooking? Or how about someone sweeping their porch?
Come now snow man what do you see? Well, says the snowman
I see you but, do you see me?

Hart Scott

Untitled

Leaping,
Bounding,
Jumping high,
My heart
soars up
to the sky.
Exuberance,
Exhilaration,
Happiness inside.
My heart
is so happy
it opens up wide.
It calls everything
to it.
It sings songs
all the time.
It's so happy
at loving
and being loved!

Elsa Mary Koivukangas

In My Head

Sometimes I wish that I were dead
But I know it's all just in my head.
For when I'm happy, I don't think of pain
All in all I have too much to gain.
But when I'm sad and feeling blue
My life is hopeless with nothing to lose.
I think of ways to end my life
So I don't feel anymore strife
I don't know why I feel this way
For I know I'm loved everyday.
I want to know what has happened to me
This isn't the way I wanted it to be.
But when I'm sad and feeling down
I just want to be in the ground.
When I'm sad I feel like this
But when I'm happy, I'm so full of bliss.
I want to know before I'm dead
what's gone wrong inside my head?

M. A. Bautista

"My Dream Girl"

I've met many girls throughout my time
but only one sticks out in the back of my mind

Her image is as clear as the day I met her
and even as time goes on I'll never forget her

Thinking of her takes me to a far off place
where the only thing I see is the beauty of her face

She had lips as full as the moon in the midnight sky
with golden brown hair that glistened in the rays of the warm sunrise

Magnificent brown eyes that burned like wildfire
and to be her one true love was my hearts only desire

And enchanting smile that cast a spell upon my heart
that will always remain even though we're apart

I imagine tasting her sweet kiss over and over again in my mind
and I wish that I could have that moment frozen in time

But she is like a bright star that shines in the night
she will always be out of my reach, but never out of my sight

To spend one night alone in her arms, would be like a dream come true
but to dream is just to wish, just as I do for you

Michael R. Trautz

Germansen Lake

The incessant wind, on Germansen Lake,
Does blow and blow all day!
The only respite from the biting cold,
Is when evening comes our way!
Then, its beauty abounds, as I sit and gaze,
At the millions of wavelets there.
If all the world could see this,
There'd surely be never a care.
Then the wind abates and my campfire's smoke,
Reaches up, to a clear blue sky.
The way that Nature changes like this,
I've no reason to wonder why.
Then dusk; and the Lake is so glassy and smooth.
It tends to reflect my many moods
And my soul, it helps to soothe....

Charles D. Ridgley

The Soul

What is the meaning of a "soul"?
Does man have a soul, own a soul,
Or is he a soul? Is the soul just a
bystander to man's flesh, or is
the soul embroidered into the
flesh of man?

Chris Wenlock

Untitled

Sometimes it seems like
Everything is going on at once
And life pulls you
And rips at you
Until you feel that nothing—
Nothing can save you.
And that's when a real friend comes.
The person who's there
To ease the hurt
To make happiness where none was
And to be there for you—
Just for you.
I hope I can be that friend
That person who cares a little extra
The one who will go the extra mile
Just for you...
Remember, that always
I love and care for you.

Willie F. Jackson Jr.

Untitled

All of the beautiful leaves did die
except for the one way up high
It doesn't want to meet its doom
it's going to wait till others bloom
It watches everything all its day
seeing people and their ways
True sometimes it gets lonely
and its happiness seems a phoney
But it sees the world in a different view
from everybody, me and you
It looks upon the wonders his creator made
and knows one day he too will fade

Heather DeVries

Tears In The New Year

Tears are my only friends this year's end
Fear, my only companion on the long journey ahead.

Dreams to be conquered, resolutions to be made;
Another year to learn how to cope, how to bare.

These feelings of emptiness and feelings of doubt
All surrounded by voices too far to hear yet so loud.

So I wait for compassion and an end to the pain,
in hope the next year brings something to live for,
something to gain.

Nadine Chehab

I Dare Not Wonder

I dare not wonder
For I have foreseen the future
For all its glory and sadness
I stand up tall
So I can feel the sun upon my face
I dare not be afraid for I am man
Yes I can endure pain for glory

I stand to be counted
As we plant the seeds of life
They will grow with love

I dare not wonder why I often cry
To see others die in pain
This is insane

I dare not wonder if this is the end
Because of our sin where do I begin

I dare not wonder
Some things are meant to be
Even when we can't see this is to be

I dare not wonder
I still cry

Kevin Wesley Goodson

My Love

I waited to see you
for such a long time
To see your perfect face
and know that you are mine.

You brighten up my day
and I'll explain why
Your pretty little smile
is a natural high.

You're my ray of sunshine
even when there's rain
And when you are hurting
I'll take away your pain.

The day that you were born
seems so long ago
You are my little girl
and I love you so.

Rebecca Stevens-Artress

Untitled

Something I can feel
but don't yet see...
Mystery with the looking glass,
Sometime in the past,
I believe I've seen you before.
Dark quiet stare
familiar stranger standing there.

Cherylle Burton

depressing words

i have no cheerful words
for what i am thinking

you are there and i am here
in a state of thought without even blinking

i miss you with every breath i take
i would like to just hold you tight

my heart beats, but still it aches
we both know it would be so right

i do not see you for months at a time
i wonder if you are being true

the thought of you with someone else
for i would not know what to do

i would stab myself with something dull
the exact same feeling you put me through

that would be the end of us and of me
then i woulɑ have no more depressing words to speak

Stefanie Jennings

My Mother's Eyes

She looks so tired, she looks so weak
From my mother's eyes tears always leak

Her eyes filled with sadness
Joy and happiness no more...
As her silent tears fall to the floor

In just one look her eyes can tell
A story beyond all tales...
It will make you cry, it never fails...

One mother's bond impossible to break
As I look in her teary eyes...
I wonder how much more can she take

She tells me don't worry...
He's going to be alright...
But her pain and sorrow...
It's never far from sight...

She misses him so much...
As she yearns...for just one last touch...

Stephanie Merrill

Princess In Pain

An untamed collection of masterpieces
furious steps ahead, I see
shall I weep in fear, or play to the masquerade of the castle

Minimizing my dreams in order to contain myself
I run to the Lord's throne and listen to mercy
crying and laughing at the vindictive velvet

Someone save me from this agony
this horrifying atmosphere of gestures
let me hover over the reality of it all
and I will dance a circle on top of stars and nightmares

Indulged in the capture
I potioned my cries into rain
and shimmered my spirit amongst the kingdom

Alas! The souls mingled in contempt of nature
and the ring of fire arose suddenly
leaving no remorse for the witnesses...

Sarah C. Hencsie

Mistakes (Guilt Upon Oneself)

While walking to a restaurant for lunch I was careless and almost got hit by a car
After the incident I was so angry at myself I felt like I had just robbed a bar
My brother saw me and said "Hey-Fred relax we all make mistakes
When I was younger I bought some snakes with my father's money
Instead of the garden rakes.
Your father was madder then a turkey at Thanksgiving and
I felt like I had just hit him with a steel iron ladder."
However mother saw how hard I was being on myself and she told me
"We all learn from our mistakes, because if we didn't none of us would grow
and for today's society that would be one big blow."

Fred Sayin

To My Beloved,

Whom my soul loved since that moment when you put your left hand beneath my head and your right hand embraced me. When I found myself beneath your shadow, cast there by the street lamp; the subdued reflections of my milky white skin against your dark. And you — so sweet to my taste.

There is no more pureness or eternity in love or passion than that of the first time.

My Roebuck, my Impala, you leaped across hills, ran through valleys, sturdy and steadfast — you went.

You ravish my heart in unmeasurable degrees; such sweet pleasures indulged in with thought, but on a moments notice, yet stolen nonetheless.

When I should count myself fortunate to have encountered such as this, instead, I count all of it and find it is not enough. I have settled for my lot in life with respect to love and I will make that enough.

Just as you know my secrets, I know the way to your heart. But knowledge must not be used foolishly and therefore I say goodbye. Not forever — just for now.

Your first Love.

Stephany Howell Davis

Untitled

I see him through a crowded room,
He comes to me at night.
He stays there in the darkness with me,
And awakens me at light.
I see him fading with all the faces,
I watch him disappear.
Every time I think I'm close enough,
My heart gives in to fear.
Every corner that I turn,
And each place that I hide -
He stands there looking the other way,
But kneeling at my side.
I see him at all our places,
Just the way we always were
But there's just one important difference,

Now I see him there with her.

Megan Esser

Untitled

In my eyes childhood is a place with no work but play,
most children adore this place but can't always stay.
We each have a door that no one could ever see
that gets opened by a very secret, and special key;
That lets us see with our hearts and not our eyes, and we
grow more mature by-and-by. Further down the way
down the road lies secrets, and treasures unknown.
Finally we reach the point where we get the course of play,
and deal with the troubles that come with every day.
But don't ever waste your life for it only comes once.

Julie McGowan

Rubies And Diamonds

Driving along the highway at night
Headlights and tail lights shining in view
Not red lights and white lights
But rubies and diamonds
Sometimes many, sometimes few

Traveling down the highway of life
When the darkness sometimes will come
Remember the rubies and diamonds
For they will always come to mind

Try to see that something extra
Of the grief or sorrow you feel
If you can with jewels of the highway
Then why not with life so real

As daylight surely follows the night
And sadness will be followed with joy
Remembering the diamonds and rubies
Makes the journey of life eager to seize

Mary Allmeyer

She's Beautiful

She is beautiful.
Her hair is brown,
as brown as the sands of time.
She has the greenest eyes on the planet.
Her face is the face of a perfect work of art;
neither scar nor scratch would ruin her beauty.
No harsh or improper words could escape her lips.
Her form is the form of a woman;
She has the smile of the next Mona Lisa.
She works hard to support herself.
She has no fears,
but that of aloneness.
She can be as calm as the wind,
as fierce as a storm, or as strong as a tiger.
She has the intelligence of a genius,
and the determination of a child.
Her name reflects the warmth she brings,
as we began our season of love.
Her words and actions can't truly be defined
or be understood by others, except by the one whom she loves.

Joe Bisig

The Nest Is Warm

She stood tiptoe upon the mighty sphere,
Her ties all loosened, like a flag unfurled,
Her voice small sound, with all mankind to hear,
So newly burst from out her childhood world.
New sights to see, diploma in her hand,
No censorious eye to halt her sight of friend,
Vocation's choice lay at her own command,
And like a cloud she'll float to the earth's end.
The words she heard, as she set ship to sail,
Were packed away in trunks she left behind,
She shed the past all shrouded in its veil,
She would sail far, her compass was her mind.
She'll meet with evil in its cruelest form,
God help her to recall the nest is warm.

Elizabeth Dickinson Carson

Our "Dog" Purrs

He runs to the front door when we arrive.
His tail doesn't wag... just twitches a bit.
He loves to play ball with his toy mouse.
He follows us around the house
with the tip of his tongue sticking out.

After dinner, he doesn't sit at our feet...
he has to be right beside us in the recliner.
Instead of howling at the moon he just meows,
"Hey, how about a treat!"

He thinks he's human, we bet..
or at least equal.
He gets away with more than most, we guess.
Just like a puppy, we're wrapped around
his furry little paws.
Our "dog" has the sharpest claws in town.
"OUCH!"

K. Bruce Jordan

Emerald Parts

Quiet a sound, beneath my feet.
I asked the Lord, to take a seat.
He sat he smiled, he touched me with light.
And sent me an angel, far from midnight,
I cried, he laughed, tender he cared,
Parts of rainbows, with me he shared,
He grabbed the sky, and gave it to me,
Without a question, I took its key,
Saying no shadows, will follow you,
He got up from his seat, and off he flew,
I said Lord, you forgot your sky,
He shed a tear, but could not cry.
Understanding, I did not know,
Why he came and why did he go,
My angel appeared, with a rose so red.
This is for love, my Lord had said,
Next to my feet, the rose was laid,
And forever then, the Lord has stayed.

Kenneth E. Romagnano

He Spoke The Truest Words

Come my Child, let me show you
I can give you anything if you believe
I have so much to offer
Only ask, and your wish is my command
Let me give you the treasures of life
Let me help you when you're in need
Let me wash your worries away
Let me stop your tears of pain
Let me whisper words of truth
So you won't doubt or feel confused
Open your heart and let me in
that's when happiness is sure to begin
Open your eyes and look beyond
true love you sought and you have found
Wherever you go, I shall follow
look no further than within your heart
I'll be with you today and tomorrow
take my hand and I will erase your scars.

Esther DelBosque

Forbidden Fantasy

Seeing you has stirred up emotions from our time shared together
I can't seem to get you out of my mind, even though we are both committed to another

Just thinking about you ignite the flames of passion deep within me
Misled dreams of us, is all I see

My soul stripped with disguised yearning
Remembering our passionate love making

I can hardly resist the temptation that consumes my entire body
Whenever you are close to me

Guilt washed my weak heart as the love I feel remains hidden
Clinging to a fantasy that is truly forbidden

Angela Arjun-Bodden

Night's Passion

Frigid Night embrace me, I inhale her icy breath.
I exhale and see her pale skin, only for a moment,
A moment soon repeated.

Above, her diamond studded clock of darkness
conceals her secret folds,
Fire's light will eventually reveal Night's bountiful features
to my impatient eyes.

Crafty spark entices uncertain tinder to emit its fervent energy,
Beads of sweat form on my forehead as I stoke these flames,
Her breath further fuels this glowing ecstasy,

Higher and Hotter the fire blazes, illuminating Night,
I glance down enveloping the silhouette of her fertile valley.

I close my eyes with Night's newly found warmth exciting my senses,
Her heated breath whispers in my ear,
My heart pounds under her pressure,
Lungs collapsing I gasp for breath but the sensation is too intense,

Flames Consume All
Blood Boiling
My Flesh Ignites

Pain, Pleasure, the same.....
...Silence, except for my heavy breathing,
As a strong breeze cools my sweat engrossed face.
The embers provide some heat as Night restores her black cloak.

Sean Walsh

Cruel Grave

Digging the grave of hurt
I found the ashes of your love
Breaking the barriers of my past
Wetting my flesh with unwanted fear.

I remember those eternal days
When our love was rejoicing
Of tenderness and flourishing smiles
By the green nature in the gardens.

But yet I don't come to understand
Why will time one day let die
The fantasy of our life in prose
If my soul still lives in your heart.

And the night seduces me with the stars
When I feel senseless my tears run
In the darkness I stay vacuous of life
Digging day by day my cruel grave of love.

Karina Tholenaar-Panait

Headstone

I didn't know that
I had died
Because you see
I sometimes lied

So on my headstone
Written clear
Hear he lies
That's if he died

Now all my friends
Who know the plight
Let's all believe
Rest easy tonight

Norman F. Pizza

Our Sons

I grieve for the mother who grieves for her son.
I know her not but our souls are one.
I grieve for her loss, the one I can not comprehend.
Many times I fear that together we will stand.

Who cares what the killer, the method be damned.
We are their mothers and we walk hand in hand.
Her pain I must feel, her endless courage I carry.
We have all lost the boy that she now must bury.

Although she goes on she is but a shell,
For look in her eyes, there you'll see she's in hell.
I grieve for the mother who grieves for her son.
Late at night I pray that I'll not be one.

Amanda A. Ciccone

Love For Sure

How could something so good go so wrong
I once had it all but now it's all gone

Everything we had, it seemed so right
We used to laugh and talk every night

He always brought a smile to my face
But those were in the good ole' days.

My life has changed since he left
He's guilty for the crime of theft

He stole my heart and then broke it in two
That's one thing he promised not to do

I always have and always will love him
But right now my world is looking very dim.

I wish we could go back to the way we were
Then I would know it was love for sure.

Avona Ford

"The Snowflake"

At 3:05 I saw a snowflake fall
my heart pitter pattered as I yelled with joy.
It's snowing, it's snow, I yell aloud
as the rest of staff came running over
at 3:10 we looked again
way up high in the sky.
But not another flake did fall
so we watched the birds giving
their call.
Hello, hello, Sandy where is our food"
they skipped and chirped,
Sandy, Sandy we're waiting for you.

Annamarie Laird

Memories Of The Past

On a rock above the flowing creek,
I sat under the old oak tree,
The cows were nearby grazing softly,
so peaceful and so free.

The butterfly's were all around,
The birds were joyfully singing,
The sun was setting in the west,
In the distance a supper bell was ringing.

The field was being plowed
by horses so big and so strong,
The smell of fresh dirt was in the air,
Those days are so long gone.

The cows had to be milked,
The eggs had to be gathered,
The chickens and horses had to be fed
As if nothing else mattered.

One by one, the years went by,
but I still remember that old oak tree,
So many names were carved on it,
for all who went by to see.

Cynthia Harrington

"Diligence"

Look unto thine own reflection, on into the past...
If thou likes not what thou sees, then simply break the glass.
Walk among the broken ages and gently feel the pain...
Then grasp your chosen fragment and slowly start again.

Forget about misfortune for the promised seven years...
Its naught but gypsy garble clinging to the fears.
The future's not contained in broken fragments of the past...
Tis the lore of broken bits of which the dies are cast.

File the bits and pieces until they firmly fit...
Then gently place them in a frame of hope to knit.
Let not the errors of ages go for naught..
Correct the broken bits as thou are taught.

When all the bits and pieces seem to fall in place...
Gently shake them loose and rearrange the future's face.
Drive forever forward and heed not one's rejections...
View the brighter image in one's own new reflection.

Alan Anderson

Deck Of Cards

I'm a deck of card in search of my pairs.
I'm a deck of cards not in search of my heirs.
These fat ugly hands are dealing me out.
"What's that smell!" is what I'd like to shout.

I only have diamonds, spades, and clubs.
I used to be slammed around bars, and pubs.
I remember when I sat in my box so nice.
The order I was in was so precise.

Ace's then two's then three's then fours.
When I was there I have barely any chores.
Fives, then sixes, then sevens, then eights.
And that's where we sat describing our fates.

Nines, then tens, then jacks, and then queens.
And that's where we stayed until we were teens.
But don't you forget those wonderful kings.
The thing that we talked about, those glorious things.

And then one day a woman came here and took us.
First she paid for me and then she caught the bus.
Where she dropped me I was found.
A deck of un-shuffled cards on the ground.

Michael De Rose

One Place

The one place without fear
is high above, but not too lonely,
colored clear with birds
and trees, that finally
let you stop and see.

Words are simple, like
dripping water springs
in some paradise dream...
rimmed with angels
painted perfect pink
as mother's Christmas things...

And lips kiss, and never dry
the sun and sky...
the race is run and won
as fingers touch without regret,
never to forget,
how big or small
it all seems to be.

Gregory R. Stephan

Fly So High

Fly in the clouds so high,
Is it impossible for me to fly, not in an airplane or any machine,
but to enjoy the clouds and the air around me!
To be like a bird to feel the wind in my wings
To touch the clouds with feather softness, cold
The joy of the freeness that no worries surround.
To soar like birds to twirl in the sky, to be part of this picture, to fly so high.

Renee Yarmy

Life

Life is like a dream,
it's there, but it's not,
some of the things you want so bad,
are there, but not to touch.

Things seem so good,
but then you wake up.
You are given a Life,
And then it's taken away.

It's not fair!

I could feel him inside,
moving, growing, breathing,
and all at once, nothing!

The doctor said he was gone,
I didn't want to believe,
but when I lay in bed at night,
and yearn to feel that movement,
I realize he was right,
it was all just a dream.

Lisa J. Ragsdale

Rough

A rock remains suspended
Where my heart used to be.
At one time it was different
As lovely as rough turquoise.

Then it was taken apart.
Pieces were taken from it,
Chunks of its rough beauty.
Only ugly scars remain
Where untouched luster used to be.

Veronica Lopez

Man On The Move

Man on the move to attain more progress
Man on the move to reach some goal
Man on the move to show his power
But what is happening to man' soul?

Man on the move for independence
He wanted freedom from the start
Man on the move to prove his courage
While fear and trembling fill his heart.

Man searching for all things elusive
Things like glory, wealth or fame
Seldom prepared for what may follow
Results of failure, loss or shame.

Man on the move to find a leader
Who will rule without a rod.
Man on the move to find contentment
Demonstrates his need for God.

Man on the move to self destruction
With his selfish aims in view.
Man on the move to a grim tomorrow
Because "God", man has forgotten you."

Marguerite C. Welser

Black America

Malcom X said "By all means necessary"
Martin Luther King believed in non-violence
Jan E. Matzelinger made the shoe last a long time
Daisy Gatson Bates led the Little Rock Nine
Louis Latimer helped us see the light
Rosa Parks put up a fight.

Morgan, McCoy and all the rest I'm very sure they did their best.
They were smart, they knew the time, they saw the light, they were not blind.
Many prices they had to pay so that we could live better right here, today.

In memory of all the Afro-Americans that fought the struggle, picked up the key to knowledge, so that we can unlock the door to SUCCESS!

Tamika Stembridge

"Myself"

TO
MYSELF ...
I belong,
ALONE ...
but not lonely.
NEVER ...
again will I
TRADE ...
myself away.
RESPECT ...
hard won,
FOR ...
what I am.
FALSE ...
images gone,
LOVE ...
is mine.

Jackie Robertson Weathers

Again

In the wee wee hours of the early morn
Nine long months give way and a child is born
You had been here before, a long time ago
And gave birth to a son
Whose smile stole the show.

You catch your breath as you lay and wait
What's that you hear? There it is
That tiny cry "So Dear"

Her angelic face
So precious and sweet
As you think of her loved ones
Just awaiting to meet

As she lay on your chest
There's none to compare
To the love that you feel
And of how much you care

You see the power of love
Is till death do us part
It's what God had intended
To keep in our hearts

Debora Stish

Mysteries

Do I know it all
No, no, there is so much to learn
To understand
It will take more than one lifetime
Though I have lived
Four score and more
The mysteries of the Universe
Discovered and yet to be
Baffle me each day
As the moon and stars
Into my living room
Come and go
Ah my, ah my
I do not want to go yet
For I want to see
What wonders man
Has yet in store
To baffle me
At the coming of each sunrise

Lillian Hoffman

Distance

There was a distance between item,
Not the kind of distance between a woman and a man,
But a distance none the less.
They were apart together
and distant when close by—
They didn't see the difference.
A fire burned between them,
A fire of ice,
Of ignorance, patience, and uncertainty.
But nothing could bring them together,
Not even a star and a wish.
(She knows because she tried. It's her specialty.)
And no matter how he tried,
No matter what he did,
he could not get through the resistance

And close the distance.

Adriana Pineda

53rd Anniversary Pearl Harbor - A Day That Has Lived In Infamy

We the people; oh, those words rang true
Of a land of liberty and skies of blue.
But, not so long ago on a Sunday morn
Filled with anger, hate and scorn: The people
Of Japan, a once quiet and isolated nation
Became the enemy of a neutral land keeping the
Peace at the faraway Hawaii American land station.

With merciless fury, the planes they did fly
Raining terror and destruction from the serene
Quiet Sunday morning sunlit sky.
Without a warning, the enemy flew as ship after
Ship slipped beneath the watery blue.
But, brave men and women saw freedom in despair
And fought back on the beaches, the sea and the air.
Today after war and fury still lingers serene quiet
Men with high tech at their fingers pause to give
Thanks and pray for those who have died for freedoms
Great cause, her laws and her pride.

Charles Ernest Hutton

This One

Blinded by the handsome facade,
Of one whose heart be dead.
Dead to the realm of the emotion
Poured forth, out upon his window sill.
The true, blatantly bared
Before a hollowed shadow.
The thorned truth pierced this heart,
Twisting its wretched poison into this soul.
Break the spirit of one so tender,
One whose purity of love be whole,
And when the heart of this one is shattered,
The skies shall crumble and the sun shall die.
Never had one so sweet and pure
Lived among such reckless ones,
Ones that knew not what a treasure dwelt amongst them,
Until the day that she was destroyed.
The day she died, the sky did cry,
The tears consumed all the earth,
And shall for all eternity.

Joella Taylor

Your Wedding Day

Two very special people
On their wedding day
The moment they've been waiting for
Has finally come their way.

They love each other very much
It's always been like this
Their fondness for each other
Thank God it did exist.

As a sister how I love you
And want the best for you
As a brother-in-law there couldn't be finer
In all the things you do.

As this day is over
You're now husband and wife
May you both have a perfect marriage
To continue the best of your life.

Two very special people
On their wedding day
The moment they've been waiting for
Has finally come their way.

Beverley Revell

"I Ought"

Did you think to tell him you loved him,
or did you wait too long?

Did you think to put your arms around him,
or did you think of it after he was gone?

Did you ever just think of him,
or send a little card?

Did you ever think to visit him,
or was it just too far?

Did you ever think to phone him,
or did you think the price too high?

Did you ever think to write him,
or put it off with a sigh?

Did you ever think to tell him how much
you really cared,

or did you do the usual, neglect him
until he was no longer there?

So, if you have a loved one and you
have not told him your thoughts,

I hope you do not wait too long, for then
you will say "I Ought".

Betty Hines Phillips

What Will It Take

We look at the continuing pollution asking what is the solution
People from countries everywhere persist in polluting the air
Once fresh water was all around soon only bottled will be found
Many throw trash from a moving car to be scattered near and far
Some pitch garbage in the lake how much can those poor fish take
Cutting trees down willy-nilly don't they think this is silly
Constantly removing more bush till leaving barren land once lush
Then complain crops will not grow lack of moisture don't you know
But what is to keep it there now that it is left open and bare
We already have UV warnings and watch out for global warming
Fish start to vanish and die and they've just begun to ask why
Our rain forests continue dying - still we are not really trying
There are many phrases out there to try and make polluters care
Work to reduce - reuse - recycle ride many places on a bicycle
Walk when going a short way try using natural products every day
Join groups cleaning up the mess see if we can throw out much less
What more publicity will it take before we can shock people awake
If it isn't taken seriously soon we may have to move to the moon
It is not polluted just yet....but it wouldn't take long I'd bet
What will our children inherit if we don't take better care of it

Lorna Eastcott

Little Darling

Little Darling
Please don't cry you see.
Mommy was sick
and couldn't get better.
Little Darling,
Let me wipe those tears,
you see, Mommy's up,
with all the teddy bears,
and puppy dogs,
yes even the killers,
So you see,
Mommy's much better now,
and happier,
I know she sends her love,
Just close your eyes,
and you'll see her, waving
Goodbye.

Neil Street

Love

Let great Orpheus, with his sublime arts,
Praise Venus, her hold on human hearts.
Let Cupid, with his swift arrows, strike
The rich, the poor, fools and wise alike.
The sensual love, her trappings, I leave
To those that in Aphrodite believe.
Though I still enjoy a warm and tender kiss,
A stream of tears brings some kind of bliss,
I learned to truly love my brother,
I found this love deeper than any other.
When I lend a hand, visit the sick,
For the helpless poor the tab I pick,
When I comfort the forlorn, the weak,
I realize I found the love I seek.
And when my wounds Nature's powers heal,
The true essence of love they reveal.
In my heart a psalm of praise begins
for God; His forgiveness of our sins,
As it stems from azure skies above,
It surely is the epitome of love.

Michael John Constantinides

The Mission Light

Light is sown for the
righteous, and gladness
for the upright in heart,
and let thy word be a light to
my path.

O send out thy light
and thy truth, and let
it lead me and bring me
to thy holy hill in love
and deed.

O house of Jacob, come
ye and let us walk in the
light of love, we are called
to labor in the light with joy.

Let the mission light
shine through you.

Lois J. Bell

-Progress-

Up go the houses
Row upon row.
I shall never see
The green fields grow,
Or the sun to set
In its orange rosy glow

Up go the houses
All so neat
I shall never see
The dusty back street
Winding its way
The hok hy-way to meek.

Up go the houses
In draft board design
Hiding the view
That once was mine

Pauline Scott

Untitled

That gentle name
Setting my soul
To rest
And bringing my heart
Complete peace
A peace that will never
Be matched
Until that day, that one
Beautiful day
When I will wash his feet
With my imperfect tears

Kathleen Thompson

Nothing

Sitting here alone and afraid
She try's to hold on to hope
for the life she has made.
"It's so hard to smile"
she says, with a tear.
It's so hard to be happy,
while living with that fear.
But if she digs down deep,
somewhere in her soul.
She'll find the strength to fill up
that empty hole.
It might take time,
long hours of pain.
But she has nothing to loose and
nothing to gain.

April Dicus

Quietness, solitude
Silently the snow falls
Covering the bleakness of brown
Hiding the harshness of reality
Swiftly the magnificent moose moves
The deer bounds across the meadows
Undaunted by my presence
They dance the magic of the wild
Stretching gracefully against the glistening whiteness
Frolicking carefree with the crystals
Carefree, beautiful fluid animals
Melting again into the forest
Breathtaking, the fragrance of the wild
Crushing against my chest.
Quietness, solitude
Silently the snow falls.

Ruth Meyer

The Heart Of A Friend

Every once in a while
someone comes into our life,
never to leave us the same.

Someone who walks in
when the rest of the world walks out,
giving us the courage to fight on.

And even when the days are their brightest,
that person shares in our glories
with a promise to be there
during tomorrow's rains.

It is a rare chance to meet someone
whose heart has so much warmth.
I know, because I've found the heart
of such a friend in you...

Sybille C. Pennardt

I, I, I

We are here in the same room,
Sitting all apart;
I wonder to myself;
Where do we start?

Give me one good reason,
To make me think you care;
If so, I wouldn't be here; I'd be there.

Show me some feelings, show me some joy;
Treat me like a lady; not like a toy.

My feelings are deep for you,
They go a long way;
I'm wishing and hoping;
And guess what: I pray.

I pray that you love me,
And let me give you the same,
That way in each others arms we will remain.

So let down your guard,
Show that you can try;
Be true to yourself,
Then you can be true to I.

Sharon A. Thomas

Jungle Nights

The panther, in her sleek brilliance,
slithers across the ground like a poisonous viper.
She searches the nigh with her steel, icy, eyes.
Her sinuous body, and calculating mind,
work as one to find her prey.
She is hauntingly beautiful.
Suddenly, she turns-
swiftness motivates her body.
As she runs,
the wind combs
through her plush,
soft, thick, fur.
Stalking with pride in a murderous silence,
she slows abruptly.
Her prey - caught like the split second crack of a whip!
The weight of death fills the air.
Satisfying warmth encompasses her tired body,
and sleep is the only thing that captures her.

Erica James

How Dare She

She asked me to write for her
something romantic
medieval

She sees me as some sort of
poetic
vending machine

Plug in a kiss
playback a stanza
(H6? no, 14)

I

Two for a sonnet
what does she want for a f*&@?

She will sell her self for platitudes
And I
I am no less the whore

Paul Trottier

Unfinished

Living under siege the memories have fallen on the floor, only to be swept up or swept under a rug. As I dance in the dark, the siege begins. Captivity begins to take its toll being born a captive, and growing up a captive, make becoming expansive much more of a labor.

A troll lives under the bridge — the bridge that lies just beyond the river of dreams, the field of hope. The field of hope is Liberty, it is wilderness. I feel like I am walking on a log, a log that is floating in the water. When I walk the log rolls. And neither goes forward nor backward. Balance is precarious on this log. If I should try to jump from this log, the mud would try to swallow me up, or the old rugged troll that lives under bridge will try to put his guilt on me. As death tries to put its grip on me, 'peace of mind' seems to be latin to me.

So many things I want to learn, but so many roadblocks. Torn like shreds of paper between people. I don't know who to go to. The circle is slowly but constantly closing in. The quicksand has no mercy, I am tired and trapped. A whimper is all that I can muster, the whimper of a wounded animal. My roar as all but left me. A racoon will chew and chew to release him self — but what do I do?

Frankie Harrell

Lifting The Veil

From the dim memory of childhood comes a scene that speaks of more
than all the learning I have known.
On a bright spring morn I woke from my young sleep, and the sound of
a bird song filled my soul so full
I did not feel as though of earth.
Down through the harsh and bitter things I have known, the song
of a bird at dawn has been my promise of the good life.
And when I seem to be lost in the maze that the soulless ones
have made of life,
I think of how much greater the power of that which has brought
a song of happiness to a world of strife.
And thinking so, I can raise my hand to the warm grasp of a fellow
man and believe in him as being kin to the power that brought
me into being.
For in his eyes, as mine, there is a light that sometimes looks a
little far away.
And it seems to me also sees the thing which is quite not seen, and
yet is close as he to me.
That one warm clasp with friendly shake and the kindly light of the
eye raises by one the veils
that cloud the thing we both would see.

Trudy Haggerty McCabe

If

If there is a prayer in heaven
that would rid our lives of war
I would give my life to learn it
no matter how heavy be the score.
I'm sure peace would be contagious
and spread quickly throughout our earth.
It would teach Life, Love and Honesty
and the real meaning of their birth.
If there is a prayer in heaven that
would feed my starving friends, nourish
me with its words and I'll try to
make Amens.
I'll teach it to the young ones
and pray they understand and
maybe when they grow up,
They will take better care of
man.

Albert Dee Sappenfield

"Silent Prayer"

Talked to my neighbor
The other day
And here's what he had to say
My son is over there
A fighting in "Ku-wait"
Then he bowed his head
And I bowed mine
When our heads were bowed together
I saw tears drop from his eyes
Then he said, I guess sometimes
It's wrong to be right
And sometimes it's right to be wrong
And as we prayed, thoughts ran inside my head
I remembered my daughter as she said
Don't worry dad, I'll be back
We'll all be back tomorrow
So I did a little doing
It's not much, but it's worth pursuing
It's just a little prayer
A silent prayer

Jose R. Vitela

Dad

My father, he's a kind and loving man,
the type everyone likes to know.
And if you are down and need a friend,
his love for you he'll show.

All of our lives he's been there,
for the other kids and me.
I often sit back and remember the times,
I sat upon his knee.

His kids in the past made choices
that others might have thought were bad.
But he was there to show us he cared,
he never stopped being our Dad.

No greater man you could ask for,
or even hope to find.
And we are so proud to have him as so,
he's really one of a kind.

Now dad...it's our time to be there,
and return the love that you gave.
Don't worry yourself, things will get done,
SIT BACK....RELAX... and BEHAVE!

Sandra Childers

The Wind

Quiet and dark, a reminiscent
Then, slowly, in rising tide she comes
Like a sharp knife cuts through
The darkness, and the quiet
And she is gone.
What benighted grace she leaves in her wake
And how many stars, through the shadows dark
Must brilliant shine and wane in timeless space
Before her spook steal away to visit another world?
And she is gone.
Her whispers, cold, chilling, sinister
Yet for some reason she must continue in them,
Live in them, in the darkness, in the quiet.
How could thou art,
And you are gone!

Edward M. Ombati

Of All The Things I See In You

Of all the things I see in you,
there comes to mind one pristine thing:
reborn with ev'ry breath anew,
I do believe they call it Spring!

Ben Dooling

Heartbreaker

Before I let you go,
There's something you have to know
I really, really loved you
But you turned stone cold
I know the difference
Between true love and lies.
I'm not ashamed to call you a
Heartbreaker,
Your heart is made of stone
No mercy to any love you own.

Tell me
Why are you so heartless and cruel?
Throwing my love away
And putting me in the blues?
Hey what's the matter!
You made me, oh so blind
To think that you could love me
And double cross my heart
Only a fool, you're just too cruel
Heartbreaker

Miriam Esther Adrien

A Baby

There's nothing quite like a baby,
They gurgle and smile at you so.
There's nothing quite like a baby.
Little sweethearts from head to toe.

We know a baby they won't stay.
All too soon they'll grow up.
As adults they'll make their way,
And drink life's trailsome cup.

But whichever path they wend,
Through much great endeavor.
Parents hope that in the end,
That they'll have joy forever.

Gladys Streich

Fear

They see it in your eyes,
they taste it in your blood
they peal it from your skin like a hidden lie meant to keep secret,
we shall never deceive the ones that are capable of such horror,
though it flows through your veins in daylight,
but it pumps in the night like a shadow of fright
how will we understand such nonsense though we feel it every day,
so if we called it nonsense we would come out of the dark and
face our fears
we can't let our imagination run away with our minds, for if we do
we will be unleashing the horror of something that's been there
since the day we were created,
though we've tried to hid it, it must be unleased if not it will be
torn from our bodies as if we were being peeled like a fruit
waiting to be eaten up by fears and mysteries of the shadows of
darkness.

Cassandra Christides

Show Me The Dark

A change, a risk.
To find something.
To peer past the edge of darkness
And see what's there that excites me.
I have to choose,
Go out of my mind, or into the night.

The tingling, the teasing.
Turning my head to
Catch the ghosts that
Dance on the periphery of sight.

Lead me, lure me
Into the realm of dark conjecture
And show me its secrets.
I want to know because
I am a creature of the visible spectrum.

Corrupting them, destroying them.
To expose the secrets would be to
Pollute the perfect darkness with light,
Yet again escaping my vision and grasp.

Kevin Lamp

Reality

The anger I feel consumes my soul;
tormenting my heart;
threatening my beliefs.

Slam after slam;
punch after punch.

How is it we wake to do it all over again;
Life with so many heart aches
has left me empty, left me with
the feeling of defeat.

No matter what is done or not done
brings no relief;
the tears no longer fall, no longer
bring comfort;
fear used to haunt me, now it no longer
tempts me.

The body and soul grow cold without;
Life's lessons are always surrounding me
near me, within me;
life has no mercy for the likes of me.

Pamela A. MacLaren

To Keep

Kindred soul asleep
upon an azure sea
drifting toward the deep.

Darkened shadows creep
about a dream
dear and hard to keep.

Awake gentle self
accept not this fate.
Hope yet not is late.

Make the leap.
Ready am I not to weep
for a dream
dear and hard to keep.

Marcus H. McGuire

Summer's End

Summer's day will fade away
warm breezes blow no more
The sun hides more and more each day
waiting for winter's roar

The sun sleeps in, no early dawn
the wind in painfully harsh
painted autumn leaves have fallen
the birds have left the marsh

Early signs of winter's edge
are visible everywhere
The flowers on the window ledge
have stems so thin and bare

And winter comes as if on cue
The changes made, so grand
from variegated summer's hue
to a snowy wonderland

We enjoy the season for awhile
and keep the cold at bay
But when the snow begins to pile
we long for a summer's day

Frances G. Weyts

The Little Mouse!

The little white mouse,
was looking for a house.
Her name is Miss Quesy,
and life is not easy.
She climbed up a hill,
and the forest was still.
In the distant there was chatter,
when she came closer, birds had a spatter.
She sat on a rock,
it was a beautiful spot.
Branches where moving,
Miss Quensy's heart was soothing.
While looking around,
a very old tree she found.
In amusement she saw,
a wonderful flaw.
She hummed a song,
the search had been long.
Miss Quesy the mouse,
had found her warm cosy house

Josepha P. Peterson

Within You

It lives in a place
Way down deep inside
And it answers to your touch
When everything is right
When you're feeling as such
When everything is coming together
And it feels a certain way
It comes out threw you
In everything you say

It's in a matter of importance
That it looks to uncover
What is now beneath you
And now what is under
When you've taken its risks
And seen its eternal gifts
And given in
To its wicked bites of mischief
And to its stupendous tricks

Timothy M. Taylor

Endurance

Where did it all go wrong
What tragedy will happen next
I've been fighting this for so long
My life is way out of text

I hope that I am prepared
For what the future holds,
Because it has me so very scared
Of my reaction when it all unfolds

I'm sure I'll deal with it somehow
With what strength I have left
Because I know that the strength I have
God gave to me as a gift...
Faith, Hope, and Charity

Christina N. Haskell

Why

Why should I Dream,
When my dreams will be woken.
Why should I love,
When my heart will be broken.
Why should I feel,
When my feelings will be hurt.
Why should I care,
When they treat me like dirt.
Why do they all talk about me,
When all they think is "I'm shy."
Why does no one like me,
When they do not know this guy.
Why is my life black,
When the lights are on.
Why do I want to die,
When this is my only con.
Why do I love this girl, when our love is love-lorn.
Why should I cry, when my heart is so torn.
Why should I live any more, when my life is all a mess.
Why is the question I ask, when can I stop all this stress?

Brent Bellini

Endure

ENDURE my sister.
When the road seems rough and miles seem long -
hold on - the end is near.
When the heart feels as if it will break with the next heartbeat -
ENDURE.
God will not let you fall. He will not let you carry more than you can bear - for He knows your strength.

ENDURE my sister.
When the next breath you take feels as thought it will be the last breath you take - ENDURE.
God knows your sorrows and He is waiting to breathe hope into your life.
So, for God's sake ENDURE my sister - FOR YOUR OWN SAKE ENDURE!

Vonda Smith

Fame

I had always aspired to be
Someone who could write poetry
A little poem bright and gay
To help others pass the time of day

Somehow I missed this lofty peak
I'm a typist at so much per week
If this is published I can say
I had my "fame" if only for a day.

Trudee Whitaker

A Lazy Spring

Spring, oh spring
Where forth art thou
Do I find you with
My hoe and plow?

If you don't mind
I'd rather find
You with my glass
Of lemonade
And book
And lazy days in shade

Dorothy Meyers

The Spirit

Greater than the prayer is the spirit,
Wherever the holy light of life is lit.
With grace and ease, he is the marvel of age.
Satan's defeat put him at a fit of rage.

Entrusted by the spirit's divine fire.
Caught in a trap, their feet in the mire.
Words conceived in love hold to be true.
In his spirit we long to renew.

Pictures painted by the spoken word,
Conceived and colored and divinely heard.
Man giving allegiance to spiritual conception.
Holy spirit giving away to man's reception.

Man's own life, makes will of God prevail.
In God's victories the angels all hail.
The realm of life encircles our being,
To manifest itself in what were seeing.

Open your eyes to the beauty unknown.
Look on heaven's pleasures now being shown.
Are they not of silent disregard.
Showed on their faces, they are hard.

Thomas D. Alberty

Dreams

Dream can interpret things,
which can be good or bad.
Dreams can predict the future,
whether happy or sad.
Dreams can spur on emotions,
that can control the mind.
Dreams can inspire people,
like Albert Einstein.
Dreams can create ideas,
like the invention of light.
Dreams can become nightmares,
which can give you a fright.
Dreams can be romantic,
erotic, sexy, or nice.
Dreams can be about sex,
done in Chinese food with rice.
In closing dreams can be different,
and about a variety of things.
They can be about emotions,
or wild romantic flings.

Michael M. Buckley

Untitled

Silent and still he walks
through the night
protector of good
and avenger of right.
Ready for action
and for any fight
to protect and do right
He takes a bite
and with all of his might
he tears off the ribbon
which holds down the night.
Faithful and true
he is the protector
who watches over you.

John Iacono

God's Love

Spring is coming ever nearer
The birds are beginning to sing.
The flowers are growing
And my heart is knowing
The wonderful feeling of spring.

God's beautiful world is in bloom now.
His love for us shows everywhere.
The brooks that are flowing
The trees that are growing
Are proof of His love and His care.

The blue skies above us
The sunshine so fair.
All show that He loves us
And He'll always care.

Spring is a special gift from God
To fill our hearts with love.
And tells that He's near us
And He'll always hear us
When we turn to Him above.

Marian L. Dunham

Deaf To His Voice

To shut out all the world, its tribulations,
The noisy clamor of its conflicts,
I stuffed great wads of cotton into my mental ears.

And then I cried, "Talk louder, God, I cannot hear you!"
"Where have you gone, God?" You were much closer yesterday.
"Speak to me!" I'm lonely for you, God.
"Please, please, I want to hear your voice."
"Shout, God! Speak up! Oh, what have you to say?"

Utter weariness made an end to so much begging,
And in my God ward longing I began to realize,—
I had to take from in my ears the cotton of despair,—
Unreasonable and morbid fear, — and clean away the clogging wax
Of self-imposed self-pity. For then and only then
Could I again receive your voice, —the precious, sweet continuation
Of reassurance, ringing loud and clear.

"Why are you afraid of life?" This soft voice asked,
"What does the conflict matter?
"I——am here."

Eleanor Meyering

Today

Today is yours and mine...
Waste it not in petty greed;

Yet stamp a design of love
There or a kindly deed....

Marie Canady

Biographies of Poets

ABRAMS, ROBERT M.
[b.] February 8, 1933, Holyoke, MA; [p.] Samuel, Ida; [m.] Frances, June 29, 1961; [ch.] Joshua, Samuel, Annah, Maury; [ed.] Amherst College, BA, Boston University Medical School MD; [occ.] Pediatrician; [memb.] American Academy of Pediatrics; [hon.] Western Mass Football Hall of Fame; [oth. writ.] Several Medical Articles; [pers.] I believe in the goodness of all humans, and the need of society to promote the welfare of all individuals. The poem recalls my grandparents, who enjoyed being industrious in all their endeavours, which included working on their farm and picking berries.

ABUBAKER, ROOHI
[pen.] Roohi Abubaker; [b.] January 12, 1965, Karachi, Pakistan; [p.] Dr. Mohammed Uzair and Rehana Uzair; [m.] Dr. Yaseen Abubaker, October 9, 1992; [ch.] A son aged 21 months named Mustafa; [ed.] PECHS High School, Karachi St. Joseph's College, Karachi Sind Medical College, Karachi; [occ.] A housewife till I get a license for medical practice.; [hon.] Best Girl of the School Award. Won prizes in debates. Appeared in a T.V. quiz show, when 13 years old.; [oth. writ.] Few other poems, some articles. All unpublished.; [pers.] In contrary to the fact that my mother tongue is urdu, I was always interested in English poetry. I read Byron, Keats Shelley Mainly. I can only write when I am greatly moved by a feeling or an incident.; [a.] Milford, CT

ACKERMAN, DONALD S.
[b.] December 2, 1964, Coco Solo, Panama; [ed.] Bachelor of Science Degree Environmental Health Old Dominion University; [occ.] Environmental Health Officer Indian Health Service.; [memb.] National Environmental Health Association, American Public Health Association; [memb.] USPHS Professional Associations: Member, Commissioned Officer's Association of the U.S. Public Health Service, Life Member, Reserve Officer's Association of the U.S., Professional Affiliations: Member, Association of Military Surgeons of the U.S., Member, National Environmental Health Association, Member, Oklahoma Society for Environmental Health Professionals, Member, American Public Health Association; [hon.] Surgeon Generals Exemplary Service Medal, Unit Citation, Unit Commendation, Crisis Response Service Award, Special Assignment Service Ribbon; [pers.] I would like to see all victims of abuse make a difference in their lives by become the victors of their strife. I can assure you that this is a challenge not to be taken lightly, but one that has great rewards at the end of the journey (edit any this else but please leave this as it is.); [a.] Miami, OK

ADDISON, DOROTHY HOLDER
[pen.] Dorothy H. Addison; [b.] January 23, 1926, Alton, FL; [p.] Jesse F. and Ida Thomas Holder; [m.] Morris S. Addison, December 24, 1942; [ch.] Darrell Keith Addison; [ed.] Pasco High, Dade City, FL Landmark Baptist College, Haines City, FL; [occ.] Housewife; [memb.] Landmark Baptist Church Loughman Civic Center Ass'n; [oth. writ.] Poems Division at Babylon - Book a concise Bible Genealogy - Book Shoots from Noah's Roots - Book, The Books are copyrighted but not published.; [pers.] After beginning College at 50 years of age, teaching and writing the curriculum for Bookkeeping and Office Procedures in the Virgin Islands Bluewater Bible College, I am more curious about a lot of things.; [a.] Loughman, FL

ADRIAN, MANOLACHE
[pen.] Mary Manolake; [b.] June 21, 1952, Romania; [p.] Marin Manolache, Alexandra Manolache; [m.] Lydia Lucaciu, November 15, 1993; [ch.] Marius-Christian, Xenia, Mary-Belle; [ed.] Master in Science; [occ.] Autocad specialist; [hon.] National prize for poetry: Mittv Dragomir Braila - Romania - 1989; [oth. writ.] The tears in the mirror (poems) who killed Marylin (novel) many poems published in several newspapers in Romania; [pers.] Nihil sine deo I have been greatly influenced by the symbolists and I like especially Emily Dickinson.; [a.] New Westminster, Canada

ADRIEN, MIRIAM ESTHER
[pen.] Brownie Merary; [b.] August 11, 1977, St. Lucia; [p.] Peter and Michella Adrien; [ed.] Entrepit Senior Secondary, Basseterre Senior High, College of Further Education; [occ.] Student; [memb.] Literary and Debating Society, S.D.A. Pathfind Club Society; [hon.] Best speller in the local spelling competition; [oth. writ.] Publication for the Junior Voice of the Voice Newspaper; [pers.] In my writings, I attempt to portray the lifestyle of an ordinary person. Poets such as Maya Angelou and Derek Walcoft have been very influential. [a.] Basseterre, St. Kitts

AFFHOLTER, PAUL R.
[pen.] R.; [b.] January 28, 1958, Trenton, MI; [p.] Robert and Virginia; [m.] Renae, August 20, 1977; [ch.] Paul and Joshua; [ed.] High School and Some College; [occ.] Detroit Edison; [oth. writ.] Nothing Published; [pers.] I wrote this poems because my brother died because of alcohol related problems at the young age of 35.; [a.] Wyandotte, MI

AGUILERA, ABEL
[ed.] Graduated from Bowie High School and attended the University of Texas at El Paso, majored in Social Work.; [occ.] Free-lance writer, poet and author of various poems and manuscripts on Chicano cultural and socio-economic issues.; [memb.] President of Project MACHO (Mexican American Committee in Honor of Opportunities and Services), Ex Board of Directors Member and Founding Partner of Centro de Salud Familiar La Fe in South El Paso.; [hon.] Best Community Organizer Award of 1969, won the Best Chicano Poetry Writer Award in 1970 by MECHA.; [pers.] "Always return to your own roots and never forget where you come from."; [a.] South El Paso

AGUILERA, MELISSA A.
[pen.] Lis; [b.] May 8, 1977, Chicago, IL; [p.] Monica and Mario Aguilera; [ed.] I attend George Washington H.S. and will be graduating on June 15, 1995; [hon.] I was a Willye White Winner and received a United States National Leadership Merit Award; [oth. writ.] Several poems which have not been published or looked at by any publisher.; [pers.] Writing brings out my feelings and sometimes a note to other people and really just relaxes my thoughts.; [a.] Chicago, IL

AGUIRRE, JULIAN
[b.] November 15, 1957, La Jolla, CA; [p.] Joaquin and Donna Aguirre; [m.] Gabriella Aguirre, December 17, 1988; [ch.] Julian Manuel Aguirre; [ed.] Carlsbad High School, Point Loma College; [occ.] Self Employed, Independent Sales Broker; [memb.] Boy Scouts of America, Zoological Society of San Diego; [hon.] Eagle Scout; [pers.] I would never want to belong to any club than would have someone like me for a member. Groucho Marx; [a.] Carlsbad, CA

AHMED, TANKO
[pen.] Teekay; [b.] December 14, 1948, Accra; [p.] Hamma; [m.] Rakia alias Aisha; [ch.] Majid Rahman Sule and Abebi; [ed.] B.A. English, M. S.Ed. Education; [occ.] College Professor; [memb.] Tesol Yankasa Assoc. of New York; [hon.] Who's Who Among Students in American Universities and Colleges; [oth. writ.] Brighie, Youass; [pers.] The student that the teacher rejected shall go forth and shine in the world. [a.] New York-Bronx, NY

AKESSON, LASANDRA
[pen.] "Vette" or "Vettita"; [b.] September 15, 1957, Cleveland, OH; [p.] Marvin and Treavie Wimbush; [m.] Johan "Frederick" Akesson, December 31, 1994; [ch.] Akia LaSaundra Morales and Alexander Simone Morales II; [ed.] John Hay/John Adams High, L.A.B.C., L.A.C.C., Metro C.C., L.A.D.W.P. sponsored training and programs.; [occ.] Assistant district clerk with los angeles Dept of Water and power; [memb.] Founder and director, of dream quest enterprises, Inc./NAACP'S San Gabriel Valley Education Committee member/family and education Affirmation Action - Council member and founder; [hon.] Merit thru the City of Los Angeles' Productivity Commission/NAACP'S executive committee/ National - Teen Pageant Winner, "Miss Right On" of 1973/I.I.E. Facilitator; [oth. writ.] Several poems published in other books (such as quill books 94-95); [pers.] Remember: "Without dreams, there would be no fulfillment." My soul of ancient is one of romance, love and spirituality. I express these aspects thru music, art work and poetry. I have found my inner self, and she is now happy and complete.; [a.] Walnut, CA

ALBERTS, JOHAN C.
[pen.] Johnny; [b.] January 14, 1956, Dutch; [p.] Mama and Papa; [m.] Mary Jo Alberts, December 15, 1985; [ch.] Christiaan Dawn Alberts, Allen Oden A., Alex Johan A.; [ed.] 39 years of life; [occ.] Nuts-to life's standards - "totally bonkers"; [memb.] Family; [hon.] I strive to honor God an award to the children; [oth. writ.] Hermit on a hill, child care, winters fury the phanthom, etc. many never published or heard; [pers.] Children an earth need priority. Freedoms come second speech, religion, capitalism, etc; [a.] Cornersville, TN

ALE, DEBRA ANN
[pen.] D.; [b.] September 3, 1965, West Palm Beach, FL; [p.] Wayne and Rosemarie Ale; [m.] Kevin McGee; [ch.] Chelsea Kayla; [ed.] John I. Leonard High School, Palm Beach Community College; [occ.] Housewife, Mother; [pers.] My realm of existence consists of simplicity, persistence, and in this place... shines God's guidance, mercy and grace.

ALEX, MIKE
[b.] June 15, 1966, Bisbee, Arizona; [p.] George and Joan; [m.] Karen, April 12, 1986; [ch.] Zachary; [ed.] Paradise Valley High; [occ.] Truck Driver; [a.] Phoenix, AZ

ALEXANDER, LENNOX
[pen.] Malcolm Xavier; [b.] May 31, 1950, Trinidad and Tobago; [p.] Anna Alexander, Samuel Bournes (Both deceased); [m.] Divorced, July 30, 1975; [ch.] Yusuf, Roxanne and Kelly Alexander; [ed.] Graduate in Political Science, Constitutional Law, and Law.; [occ.] Employee of TNT Express Worldwide; [memb.] Graduate (Diploma) and member of The Newspaper Institute of America, in Journalism and Creative Journalism, Member Rosicrucian Order; [oth. writ.] Several articles published in local newspapers in Trinidad and Tobago. The express, the Guardian, and the T&T mirror.; [pers.] Both man and woman should always endeavour to stand big-

ger than all circumstances that present themselves in their lives.; [a.] Queens, NY

ALFORD, CARRIE
[b.] January 12, 1953, Chandler, OK; [p.] Bob Bailey, Carolyn Shaver Bailey; [m.] Cliff Alford; [ch.] Denise Alford Theroux, Kyle Alford; [ed.] Carney High; [pers.] I have been blessed with a close and loving family, the greatest gift of all; [a.] Wellston, OK

ALLEGO, ANTONIO M.
[p.] Adriano B. Allego, Valentina C. Masucol; [m.] Felicidad A. Collarin; [ch.] Six boys, three girls; [ed.] Journalism; [occ.] Newspaper editor; [memb.] National Press Club of the Philippines; [hon.] Recognized as fiction writer of distinction by The Writers' Union of the Philippines, has had an editorial inserted in the Congressional Record of the House of Representatives, Congress of the United States; [oth. writ.] This Time Yesterday (short stories) Telling Triple (essays, short stories, poems), Time To Go (song); [pers.] One's native language is that language in which he can best express himself; [a.] Marikina Metro Manila, Philippines

ALLEN, BETTY J.
[b.] June 3, 1924, Dunkirk, OH; [m.] Bill Allen, March 28, 1943; [ch.] William and Teresa; [ed.] Dunkirk High School Graduate; [occ.] Retired Hardin Northern School Secretary; [memb.] Trinity U M Church, American Cancer Society, Dunkirk Improvement Corp., Served 4 year term on Hardin Northern School Board-3 years as president.; [hon.] National Honor Society; [oth. writ.] I have been writing poetry for quite a few years for my own enjoyment; [pers.] My goal to help someone each day.; [a.] Dunkirk, Ohio

ALLEN, HILLARY R.
[pen.] Frankly Allen; [b.] September 8, 1975, Des Moines, IA; [p.] Randall and Wendy Allen; [ed.] K-5 Lincoln Elem., Dav., ld, 6th Eisenhower, Dav, Sudlow Jr High, Dav, Central H.S., Dav, Stephens College Col. Mo, freshman year, Iowa State University, Ames, Iowa.; [occ.] Student at Iowa State University; [memb.] Dover Beach Poets Guild, Alpha Betta Pi, ISU Environmental Council.; [oth. writ.] Published in literary journal based out of Utah which is put out by dover beach poet's guild.; [pers.] Through my writing, I struggle to create and unwind my own mental etiquette to help understand myself and the world around me.; [a.] Ames, IA

ALLEN III, ROLLA E.
[b.] December 15, 1944, Champaign, IL; [p.] Freda A. Allen; [m.] Judith L. McSchooler Allen, September 10, 1966; [ch.] Paula J. Judy (Allen), Valerie L. LaRosa (Allen), Jonathan L. Allen, Nathanael J. Allen; [ed.] Ben Davis High 2 1/2 years Indiana Baptist College; [occ.] Conductor Conrail; [memb.] American Legion Marine Corps League Vietnam Veterans of America, Boy Scouts of America, Third Marine Division Association; [hon.] USMC: Presidential Unit Commendation Ribbon, Navy Unit Commendation Ribbon, Good Conduct Medal, National Defense Medal, etc., Boy Scouts: Wood Badge, Order of the Arrow, Fire Crafter, Minisino etc.; [oth. writ.] Marine Coups League, Distinguished Service Medal, Distinguished Citizen Medal, Rainbow Medal, I have written several poems (none published); [pers.] I hope to be a good influence on young people through my writing and story telling. My greatest influence is the Bible. There are too many poets and writers to list all of those I admire.; [a.] Indianapolis, IN

ALLEN, KAY
[pen.] Kay Franzel; [b.] Chicago, IL; [p.] Madeline, Taylor and Flute; [m.] Alphonso Allen Sr., August 15, 1967; [ch.] Alphonso Allen Jr.; [ed.] Currently working on a Masters Degree in Education at Loyola University; [occ.] Substitute teacher at different schools throughout Chicago, Illinois; [memb.] Member of everybody's Methodist Church located on 5958 S. Wabash Chicago, Illinois.; [hon.] 2nd place in Northeastern talent show 1980 - vocals award for participation in the 1987 Chicago park district's talent show honorable mentions on original short stories for young people at loyola.; [oth. writ.] Various short stories (unpublished at this time) original songs - gospel and other categories (also unpublished); [pers.] Kindness is the oil that takes the friction out of life.; [a.] Chicago, IL

ALLEN, LESLIE D.
[b.] May 31, 1958, Detroit, MI; [p.] Doris Murphy, Dan T. Jones; [ch.] Damon, A Paul, Lauren, Twins Anna and Lee; [ed.] Northwestern High, Detroit Inst. of Commerce, Highland Park Comm. College.; [occ.] Research Triangle Inst., Field Interviewer; [oth. writ.] Several poems, editorials, short stories; [pers.] My sincere gratitude to the people who know where I've been yet said I could go anywhere. Especially Path J. and Keith P.; [a.] Detroit, MI

ALLEN, MARQUITA
[b.] May 10, 1984, Cabarrus; [p.] Raynard and Darlene Andrews; [ed.] Fifth Grade Student; [hon.] Terrific Kid Award, Citizenship Award; [a.] Concord, NC

ALLEN, RALPH ARTHUR
[b.] June 22, 1906, Madison, KS; [p.] Arthur Lewis Allen and Wilbertie Allen; [m.] Annetta Louise Allen, July 31, 1936; [ch.] David Ralph Allen, Margaret Louise Estrada; [ed.] Graduate of Delano Joint Union High School, 1926, Courses in Dental Laboratory Tech. in Oakland, CA; [occ.] Retired; [memb.] Central United Methodist Church Stockton, CA, 1935 to 1971, Twain Harte Evangelical Free Church Twain Harte, CA, 1971 to 1995, F and AM Lodge #68 and Scottish Rite Stockton, CA; [oth. writ.] Besides a collection of 64 poems I have a journal containing 116 devotion type 10/15 minute sermonettes, having been Chaplain of a church group for the past 4 years. Other writings consist of a Family History and a few of my poems have been published in some church bulletins, a senior citizen's news column in our local news paper, and a Trailer magazine.; [pers.] What writing I have done began in my last 2 years of High School 1925 and 1926. Hard work and lack of time to write excluded writing for several years, except for publishing bulletins for a church, a camera club, a trailer club and a YMCA Mes's Club. After retirement in 1971, I began to write down my thoughts, poetically expressed, always with a message. My book of poems, I call, "Poems of Love, Faith and Friendship", and at almost 89, "God isn't through with me yet."; [a.] Columbia, CA

ALLEN, TRACEY
[b.] July 18, 1978, Passaic, NJ; [p.] Roy and Judy Allen; [occ.] High School Student; [oth. writ.] Several poems, short stories, and some song lyrics that are not published. Most haven't been read by anyone.; [pers.] When I write, I am inspired by life. Whether or not the things that I write about seem significant to others really doesn't matter to me. However if others can relate to it, I feel good. Life is beautiful, especially when it is understood.; [a.] Flanders, NJ

ALLEN, VICKIE
[b.] February 28, 1955, Brooklyn, NY; [p.] Rose and Richard Donnelly; [m.] Jimmy Allen, December 10, 1988; [ch.] Stephanie and Nicholas; [ed.] Island Trees High School Graduate, Angelo State University Adult Cont. Education.; [occ.] Youth Cane Secretary; [hon.] CASA Volunteer (Cort Appointed Special Advocate); [pers.] Children are our most precious gift and I volunteer my time to insure those that I am involved with have a safe and protective life thru CASA.; [a.] San Angelo, TX

ALLEN, YULIE
[pen.] Io; [b.] June 25, Cairo, Egypt; [p.] Emmanuel, Caliope Pandelson; [m.] Garrick Allen, July 26, 1980; [ch.] Jason, Jacqueline; [ed.] Academy of Performing Arts (WA), Edith Cowan University (Perth Western Australia) Toorak Teacher's College, (Victoria, Australia); [occ.] Director - Music Mosaics - (Private Studio); [memb.] International Assoc. Jazz Educators (IAJE), Australian National Council of Orff Schulwerk (ANCOS), West Aust. Orff Schulwerk Assoc., (WAOSA), Aust. Soc. of Music Education (ASME), Aust. Music Teacher's Assoc (AMTA); [hon.] Honours - piano - (AMTA) scholarship - piano - (WA Academy of Perf. Arts) Honourable mention - Musical - (ASME) Bachelor of Education (WA) A. Diploma Performing Arts (WA) A Diploma Performance - Piano - (WA) Drama Teaching Cert. (WA). Orff Schulwerk Summer Sch. Certificate (Salzburg), Kodaly S.S. Cert. (London), Jazz Ballet Cert. (Vic, Aust), Yamaha J. Mus. (WA); [oth. writ.] Poems, songs and childrens' musicals performed but unpublished yet.; [pers.] "Music mirrors the garden of life through sound, gesture and word, its power is intense as it hones its sword to sharpen wit, prune or destroy......."; [a.] Denver, CO

ALLISON, KENNETH
[b.] September 23, 1934, Detroit, MI; [ed.] Studied Science at the Detroit Institute of Technology and at Wayne State University.; [occ.] Retired; [oth. writ.] I write music, lyrics, poetry, and short stories. One of my songs has been published.; [pers.] I consider myself a traditionalist.; [a.] Detroit, MI

ALLISON, RHONDA
[b.] January 15, 1968, Corinth, NY; [p.] Harold Bordeaux and Bernice Colson Bordeaux; [m.] Jerome Allison, July 5, 1986; [ch.] Amanda Allison, Casandra Allison and Joshua Allison; [ed.] Graduate of Hadley-Luzerne Central School, LK Luzerne New York; [occ.] Teachers Aide, Hadley-Luzerne School; [memb.] Stony Creek Historical Association; [oth. writ.] Several poems for family and friends.; [pers.] I believe there is something special about each individual.; [a.] Stony Creek, NY

AL MAJID, MARIAM
[b.] March 8, 1973, Kabul, Afghanistan; [p.] Khadija, Tabibi, Abdul, Hakim, Al Majid; [ed.] Associate Degree, currently transferred to American Univ; [occ.] Administrative Asst. for int'l import and export firm; [oth. writ.] Working on my book about my experiences of escaping Afghanistan at a very young age with family; [pers.] I have been inspired by the word love itself to write poetry. In this day and age, poetry and love are not taken very seriously; for me poetry is the essence of divine love. Love is not complete without poetry. I strive to speak for the broken hearted through my poetry; [a.] Falls Church, VA

ALMOND, RANDY
[b.] July 28, 1954, Texas; [ed.] BA 1982 UTA (University of Texas a Arlington) Eastern Hills High School; [occ.] Sales representative (former middle school teacher); [memb.] Handley masonic lodge #1140 AF and AM; [hon.] Phi Alpha Theta, Onicron Chapter - National Historical Honor Society; [pers.] Life truly begins at 40!; [a.] Fort Worth, TX

ALSTON, LILA TRAPP
[b.] January 6, 1930, Winnsboro, SC; [p.] Howard Trapp, Roxanna Trapp; [ed.] Bethel High School - Blythewood S.C., Newbury Jr. College Boston State College, EMT Training Cambridge High and Latin, Boston MA. Career Training InstituBostonte the Institute of Childmen's Literature Redding Ridge, CT.; [occ.] MA Cert. Nursing Asst. Private duty-now retired; [memb.] West Haven, CT, Arts Council Nissionary Society - since 1967 Boston MA, an Associate of the Church of God of Prophecy and Asst. Supt. of Sun. School Dept. and Asst. in the Music Dept.; [hon.] Newbury Jr College: Dean's List wrote the school (Bethel High) song at age 15- organized a glee Club that the school adopted and is yet using. Wrote a 3-act play at age 15 that was presented on stage at school. Wrote plays that were presented in local Boston Churches.; [oth. writ.] Poem in local newspaper in Boston, MA for the first men into space, entitled "Men Into Space," poem in local Boston, MA. Newspaper dedicated to men who survived a mine disaster in the 50's entitled "In Touche with God" many poems and articles in a Jamaica plain MA news letter - Boston public school, one play.; [pers.] I never get lonely. Beauty is earth deep and heaven high and nature gives enough light for me to see it all, and hear the trumpets of the earth - for it is my poem and I sing it's songs; [a.] New Haven, CT

ALVEY, WILBUR LEO
[pen.] Wilbur Leo "Bill" Alvey; [b.] December 1, 1912, Kansas City, KS; [p.] Leo and Katie Alvey; [m.] Doris Vivian (Carlile) Alvey, April 21, 1939; [ch.] Delene Lesle and Kevin Dale Alvey; [ed.] Turner High School 1930 Kansas State University, 1935 to 1938, only graduate in history of Kansas State University to complete the Junior and Senior year in one year. Over 60 credit hours.; [occ.] Retired rancher and farmer.; [memb.] National Agricultural hall of fame. Farmers Union, Kansas Horticultural Society, National Democratic Committee Senatorial Kansas State, Life time membership alumni association. Lifetime Kansas teaching certificate in vocational agriculture; [hon.] Phi Kappa Phi, Gamma Sigma Delta, Citation, National Agricultural Hall of Fame, Delegate for Carter to the national Democratic Convention, 1976 New York, City, Designed and had produced the first future farmers of America Uniform in the United States, Year 1939 last uniform in agriculture hall of fame bonner spring, Kan. 1938 Had F.F.A. members sponsor the first future Farmers of America, Corn Shucking Contest. in the United States. Also first F.F.A. Hotbed in U.S.A. while teaching at Auburn Rural High School, Auburn, Kansas. 1939 sold plants; [oth. writ.] Wrote and published first novel by a Kansas State graduate. Title Westport. True Stories and true characters of old Kansas City, MO and the gold fields of Colorado and Montana. Year from 1839 to 1880. Now published by Copley publishing group, Acton, MA. Used as a textbook in the English Departments of Acton Eastern Universities. Published MA 01720 first year 1984.; [pers.] Wrote my first poem at age 8, first novel at age eleven and first song at age 13. It was titled yes, yes, baby I guess I love you. While walking home from school in the 4th grade in Kansas City, I was struck by a car. Over the years I have had two back operations. I always have my organic garden each year. Last year I grew a 42 pound rattlesnake melon. Probably the largest watermelon ever grow in Colorado. I do not drink or smoke.; [a.] Arapahoe, CO

AMARO, SYLVIA
[pen.] Rachel Marin; [b.] August 21, 1956, Racine, WI; [p.] Richard and Josephine Malacara; [m.] Divorced; [ch.] Ricardo - 19, Jennifer - 13, Antonio Jr. - 10; [ed.] Graduated - Washington Park High School, Racine WI, Gateway Tech. College, Racine WI; [occ.] Accounts payable specialist - United Migrant Opportunity Services - 9 yrs.; [hon.] Won an award for Art; [oth. writ.] I also play around with short stories but have never published any.; [pers.] I am a Christian woman and my dream is to either continue to write poems or possibly write songs to my Lord Jesus Christ.; [a.] Milwaukee, WI

AMY, DEBRA J.
[pen.] Zakia Naej; [b.] July 12, 1962, Detroit, MI; [p.] Hattie Clara Amy Brown and Millard Bailey Amy; [ed.] Wayne County Community College, Grad-Detroit Business Institute, Comp-Institute of Children's Lit.; [occ.] Law Enforcement Officer Detroit Police Department Detroit, MI; [memb.] The spiritual Israel Church and It's Army; [hon.] 2 U.S. Navy Battle E Proficiency Awards (ship board) Honor Graduate Detroit Business Inst. Wayne County Comm. College Dean's List Cert of completion from the Institute of Children's literature.; [oth. writ.] Song "Love Essentially," soon to be recorded. Poetry on numerous topics, short stories and other song lyrics.; [pers.] I enjoy the art of writing. It is a special gift that one gives to himself as well as to others. A song is a gift that plays on in the heart. A poem is a gift that reads on in memories. Knowledge is a gift that no one can steal.; [a.] Detroit, MI

ANAS, DAVID
[b.] July 10, 1958, Detroit, MI; [p.] Daniel Anas, Maxine Wethern; [ed.] Franklin H.S., Eastern Michigan University; [occ.] Quality Control, Technicolor Video Services; [memb.] Theta Chi, Co-Founder of APCO; [hon.] ACT Scholarship; [oth. writ.] Song writer for cyclone fenze and former writer for the Boulder Rockers; [a.] Northville, MI

ANDERSON, DANNY R.
[b.] February 5, 1947, Webster, SD; [p.] Ray and Helen Anderson; [ed.] Sacred Heart High School Sacred Heart, MN; [occ.] Engineering Dept. VAMC St. Cloud, MN; [memb.] VFW; [oth. writ.] Several poems unpublished; [pers.] I strive to reflect feelings of the heart and mankind in my writing. I have been greatly influenced by early poets and my high school english teacher; [a.] Sacred Heart, MN

ANDERSON, KELSIE STEWART
[pen.] Kelsie Stewart Anderson; [b.] March 20, 1903, NC; [p.] Mr. and Mrs. Rankins; [m.] Widow, 1922; [ch.] 3 all adults; [ed.] Asso. Degree; [occ.] Retired; [memb.] Wrote and directed a play, Soger at College, Member War, War Mother, Member Church.; [hon.] Written Coop Award outstanding Achievement Award, college; [oth. writ.] Pub. Book 1988; [pers.] Education is the key answer to harmonious living.; [a.] New Haven, CT

ANDERSON, ROCHELLE
[pen.] Rochelle Anderson; [b.] January 18, 1978, Jamaica, West Indies; [p.] Maurice and Jennifer Anderson; [ed.] Vaz preparatory School, Immaculate Conception Preparatory School, St. Andrew High School for girls; [occ.] Student; [oth. writ.] Poem published in local newspaper; [pers.] I strive to be the best at all time. I believe that all men are created equal and should be allowed to expressed themselves in their own way.; [a.] Jamaica, West Indies

ANDERSON, RONALD E.
[pen.] "Rocky Jocky"; [b.] November 17, 1934, Scotland; [p.] Both passed away; [m.] Yes from Thailand, June 13, 1990; [ch.] 3 Daughters in law; [ed.] Scottish GCE: study the works of famous Scottish poet Robert Burns; [occ.] Airport Duty Officer, Hobby Airport Houston TX 77061; [oth. writ.] Some parts of the world have a charm and natural beauty that neither age or custom may stale! One may visit them again and again, and still feel the same magic enchantment of their first visit! Such a place is Scotland! This is where the wild red deer roam where, the little streams become the mighty salmon rivers, and where the grouse soar o'er the heather like elusive shadows: Such a place is scotland!; [pers.] Served 25 years with British airways travelled world wide favorite countries penang Malaysia and Costa Rica

ANDRADE, DANIEL
[b.] September 2, 1919, Taunton, MA; [p.] Manuel and Mary Silva Andrade; [m.] Odessa Seelbach Andrade, June 16, 1952; [ch.] Daniel Andrade, Donald K. Burkett (Step son); [ed.] Walker School Taunton, MA, Taunton High - Taunton, MA; [occ.] Poet, Song writer published - (BMI), Retired; [memb.] Lifetime Membership Rejected Inner Harbor, Membership the Oxford Club (Rejected); [hon.] Nominee Life Time Member International Society of Poets, "Who's Who" in U.S.A world wide; [oth. writ.] Song writer, Contracts - Country Music; [pers.] Put God first in all you do. Wealth won't save your soul. The force of darkness a theist secular humanist are the enemy of all mankind and civilization; [a.] Houston, TX

ANDRADE, DANIEL
[b.] September 2, 1919, Taunton, MA; [p.] Mary Silva Andrade, Manuel Andrade (Deceased); [m.] Odessa Seelbach Andrade, June 16, 1952; [ch.] Daniel Andrade (Son), Donald K. Burkett (Step son); [ed.] Walker School Taunton, MA, Taunton High - Taunton, MA, Chosen-no-n-10ff-medal-fatima research organization; [occ.] Poet, Song riter published - (BMI), Retired; [memb.] Lifetime membership rejected - Inner Harbor, membership the Oxford Club (Rejected); [hon.] Nominee life time member, International Society of Poets, "Who's Who" in U.S.A. Awards too numerous to mention world wide; [oth. writ.] Song writer contracts - Country Music; [pers.] Put God first in all you do. Wealth won't save your soul the force of darkness a theist secular humanist are the enemy of all mankind and civilization.; [a.] Houston, TX

ANDREWS, TIM
[pen.] April 22, 1974, Portage, WI; [b.] Terry and Debra Andrews; [ed.] Home based educators accredited Assc. Cambridge Community College; [hon.] Valedictorian, Class of '91; [oth. writ.] Awaiting Publishing of a private collection; [pers.] I put my pen to the paper to speak golden words in a broken voice and to some day feel them cool gently off my tongue as wisdom; [a.] Bethel, MN

ANGELES, ERIC MICHAEL
[b.] May 25, 1965, New York City, NY; [p.] Dr. Armando Angeles MD., Mary Angeles; [m.] Krista Angeles, July 17, 1987; [ch.] Kyle Angeles; [ed.]

Connersville High School, Indiana University East; [occ.] Student of Elementary Education; [a.] Connersville, IN

ARCH, TERRY-ANN
[b.] October 22, 1982, Cayman Islands; [p.] Beryl and Heber Arch; [ed.] In 8th Grade Cayman Preparatory School; [occ.] Student (talented in poetry and art); [hon.] 1st place in the Tourism Awareness Week Poetry Competition.; [oth. writ.] Several poems; [pers.] My great grandmother, L.E. McTaggart was a poet and song writer. She wrote our national song "Beloved Isle Cayman" she also received several awards. I would like to continue in her footsteps.; [a.] Grand Cayman, Cayman Islands

ARCOS, EVA BORRERO
[b.] May 30, 1961, Philippines; [p.] Loreto Arcos and Felipa Borrero Arcos; [ed.] University of the Philippines, Diliman, Quezon City; [a.] Alamo, TX

AREL, REGINA L.
[b.] June 18, 1949, Vermont; [p.] Raymond E. and Ruth M. Dion; [m.] Divorced; [ch.] Kristina Ann, Stacy Lee; [ed.] Winooski High School VT.; [occ.] Housekeeping; [oth. writ.] None to speak of; [pers.] My boyfriend Paul Davis whom I love very much was my inspiration for writing "Our Love" it was in fact our love that brought these words to me; [a.] Winooski, VT

ARJUNE, RONALD
[pen.] Romuscyjn 305; [b.] March 3, 1936, Guyana, South Africa; [p.] Mrs. Eileen Arjoon, Mr. Balrams Arjoon; [m.] Divorced, August 2, 1985; [ed.] High School; [occ.] Voyer; [pers.] Feelings are precious and should shape your development. If yours are non-existent, purge your will to create the interface with sources that do; [a.] Bronx, NY

ARMSTRONG, JACK THOMAS
[pen.] Jack T. Armstrong; [b.] August 31, 1967, Detroit; [p.] Marion E. and Dolores L. Armstrong; [ed.] Attended Wayne County Community College; [memb.] The International Society of Poets; [hon.] I have received the Editor's Choice Awards for Outstanding Achievement in Poetry presented by that National Library of Poetry in 1993 and 1994. Signed by (editor) Cynthia Stevens and (editor) Caroline Sullivan.; [oth. writ.] I'm published in Dance on the Horizon Winter 1993 - poems able. At days end summer 1994-poem midnight blue. Darkside of the moon winter 1994-poem thanks giving. And also on cassette, the sound of poetry. Musical introduction by the english chamber orchestra. Readings by nationally renowned speaker Ira West Reich, are my poems able - 1993, midnight blue - 1994, and thanks giving - 1994.; [pers.] Bright is the Universe, loud is the sky upon my face the open world wide- a happy note from a poet as I humbly reside in-; [a.] Belleville, MI

ARJUN-BODDEN, ANGELA
[pen.] Angie; [b.] March 12, 1972, Kgn. Jamaica; [p.] Cynderella Scott and Keith Arjun; [m.] Osbourne Bodden, September 26, 1992; [ch.] Gavin L.A. Bodden (2 yrs. old); [ed.] Cayman Islands High School; [occ.] Accounts Administrator, Johnson & Higgins (Cayman Ltd.); [memb.] Associate member of the Int'l Society of Poets, Key Club-Asst. Secretary 1986-87, Secretary 87-88, CIHS Business Club Vice-president, Asst. Editor, member of the National Library of Poetry & Duke of Edinburgh Award Scheme, CASA; [hon.] Golden Poet Awards 1988-91, Outstanding Citizen of the Cayman Islands (1987), Most Likely to Succeed in Business (1989), representative of the Cayman Islands at the Miami Carnival in 1991; [oth. writ.] Poems published in local newspapers, magazines, Great Poems of the Western World Vol II, American Poetry Anthology Vol X book III, Gold and Silver Poets of the 90's and The Best Poems of the 90's; [pers.] Most of my writings are based on the emotions in human relationships. [a.] Georgetown, Cayman Islands, B.W.I.

ARNOLD, KEITH F.
[pen.] Keith F. Arnold; [b.] June 28, 1932, Rochester, MI; [p.] Ora and Martha Arnold; [m.] Harriet M. Arnold, September 30, 1955; [ch.] Mark Gordon Arnold, Sonya Lynne Castanos; [ed.] A.A. Degree - Spring Arbu College 1957, B.S. Ed. Northern Arizona University 1961 M. Ed. Wayne State University 1972, (Rochester High School - June 1951 Rochester, Michigan Choplain (1981- Present); [occ.] Ariz. Dept of Youth Treatment and Rehabilitation; [memb.] Life - Koppa Delta Pi A national Honor Society and Ed. Life National Education Association; [hon.] Many in Certificate, letter and other visual cert former-mainly from students and staff close to my work.; [oth. writ.] Poems of Devotional, Historical, Memory of Childhood, The West, Horses, Civil War and Mr. Lincoln.; [pers.] As one interested in the moral and spiritual aspects of life, teacher, Pastor Choplain - it is fundamental for life to be sensitive, caring and nurtured in the "Faith of Our Fathers" today.; [a.] Mesa, AR

AROCHO JR., BEN
[pen.] Violet Crush; [b.] March 22, 1978, Long Island; [ed.] Currently a Junior in High School; [oth. writ.] Currently working on my first collection of poems, entitled "Indigo Flowers."; [pers.] Poetry is nothing more than words that can evoke feelings and emotions. Poetry is almost human.; [a.] Nesconset, NY

ASERAPPA SR., GAVIN
[b.] June 23, 1939, Kandy, Sri Lanka; [p.] Gordon Aserappa, Violette Aserappa; [m.] Lynette Aserappa (nee Peterson), December 31, 1963; [ch.] Antonie Gavyn, Analiese Chemene, Tashiya Ann; [ed.] St. Peter's College, Bambalapitiya Sri Lanka; [occ.] Art Director, (unemployed); [memb.] Springvale Writer's Circle, (Vic Australia.), Samanala Art Group (Vic Australia); [hon.] Art Exhibitions Guild Hall London Highly Commended citations 3 years consecutively.; [oth. writ.] Advertising copy, Short Stories Catholic Messenger, Articles in Holiday Nepal Magazine and Hotel Soaltee Oberoi Newsletter Kathmandu. A compilation of 5 short stories and a novel are in progress.; [pers.] "One must try to encompass the universe- gather as much knowledge as possible and immerse oneself in it to the best of one's ability, because man is the most vital part of the earth, sky, wind, fire and water. Without him, his dreams and his passions what purpose would it be- the Universe."; [a.] Melbourne, Australia

ASP, KAREN KRISTINE
[b.] April 19, 1963, Lakewood, WA; [p.] Edwin and Thelma Asp; [ed.] B.A. Degree Seattle Pacific University in Language Arts and Elementary Education, Master of Arts Pacific Lutheran University in Education.; [occ.] Elementary Teacher, Dower Elementary; [memb.] The Zoo Society, Pt. Defiance, Zoo Tacoma, WA.; [oth. writ.] "No Flowers" published in Lawrence of Nottingham a poetry anthology to D.H. Lawrence; [pers.] This poem is dedicated to my true love who has received the crown of life with his creator.; [a.] Lakewood, WA

ATKINSON, ROLANDA J.
[b.] November 30, 1972, Madison, WI; [p.] Wayne Lee Roy Anderson, Donna Jean Anderson; [m.] Aaron Francis Atkinson, September 5, 1992; [ch.] Melinda Sue Atkinson; [ed.] Graduated from Adams Friendship High School 1990; [occ.] I'm taking ceramic classes; [memb.] I go to the Trinity United Church of Christ; [pers.] I dedicate this poem, to all the people who never gave up on me! And to the people that put confidence in me, to live life to it's fullest! And my husband who always believed in me!; [a.] Portage, WI

AUGUSTUS, PATRICIA
[pen.] Patsy Ann; [b.] March 17, 1937, Edgar, CO; [p.] Faye E. Shipley, Rev. J. Paul Sisson, Sr.; [m.] Philip E. Augustus, December 27, 1958; [ch.] Eric paul Augustus, Alan Wayne Augustus, Anne-Marie E. Duncan; [ed.] B.S. in Education, August, 1959, Eastern IL. Univ. Charleston, IL.; [occ.] Disabled/retired Elem. School Teacher; [memb.] I was a member of the Radio/T.V. club in College as well as the Journalism Club while at Eastern Il. University.; [hon.] When I was in H.S. I had 2 poems published in a National Poetry Anthology. When I was in College, I had an essay entitled, "Success or failure" published in the school newspaper. Since I have retired from teaching, I have had several essays; [oth. writ.] Published Danville, IL. Local newspaper (Commercial News) I earned a diploma from the Institute of Children's Literature (7/9/87) from redding, Ridge, Connecticut for a course taken in writing for children and teenagers.; [pers.] I base many of my story ideas on incidents from my childhood days. I have collected many recipies and written cookbooks for children, esp. "Latch-key kids cookbook" (with nutritious snacks); [a.] Potomac, IL

AUSTIN, BELINDA
[b.] March 1, 1953, Mexia, TX; [p.] C. W. and Odessa Mims; [m.] Larry Austin, August 18, 1973; [ch.] Latasha Austin; [ed.] Licensed practical nurse Bachelor of Arts degree in Health Education certified Health Education Specialist; [memb.] Little Rock Amezion Church, American Red Cross Bone Marrow, Advisory Committee - CPR Week Committee; [oth. writ.] Several poems that have not been submitted.; [pers.] My poems are a reflection of a spiritual transformation and a voice among many other voices.; [a.] Charlotte, NC

AUSTIN, DAWN D.
[b.] April 29, 1970, Fairbanks, AK; [p.] Jerry Austin, Sharon Austin; [m.] Timothy K. Gross, August 6, 1993; [ed.] Associate degree in nursing (June 1995); [occ.] Student, hoping to specialize in psychiatric nursing; [memb.] National Honor society, Phi Theta Kappa; [hon.] Dean's List; [oth. writ.] Yet to be discovered!; [pers.] Some of my best laughs come from seeing myself in others. My writings put into words what feelings are so often felt by myself and by others I am sure.; [a.] Gladstone, OR

AUSTIN, KARIKA RENEE
[pen.] Cricket; [b.] March 25, 1972, Fox Hills, CA; [p.] Ernestine J. Austin, (Father deceased); [ed.] Lynwood High, Biola University B.A. in Public Interpersonal Communications; [occ.] Law student and actress. Screenwriter in spare time; [memb.] American Heart Association, World Wild Life Fun (WWF), Teens Against Drugs, Biola University Alumni Association; [hon.] Academics, MVP Athletics, expert field and Marksman Badge (ROTC); [oth. writ.] Several poems published in university's newspaper, collections of poems for future

poetry novel.; [pers.] My duty as a human being is to implement the knowledge and talents God has given me and to excell in aspects of life. I have been influenced by friends and family members and various other poets.; [a.] Lynwood, CA

AYAZI-HASHJIN, SHARAREH
[pen.] Sherry Ayazi; [b.] January 6, 1972, Tehran, Iran; [ed.] Central Saint Martins College of Art and Design, Saint Augustines Priory (secondary education); [occ.] Freelance writer, photographer; [hon.] Bachelor of Arts honors in Fashion, Media Communication and Promotion; [oth. writ.] Articles for music and fashion magazines based in the U.K.: Blues and soul, touch, yush, living large, jazz express; [pers.] "The young generation don't want to hear anything about the odds that are against us. What do we care about odds?" Malcolm X; [a.] London, UNITED KINGDOM

BABCOCK, DIANE
[pen.] Dedan; [b.] September 14, 1955, Comox, British Columbia, Canada; [ch.] Tyler Austin Babcock; [ed.] Grade Eleven; [occ.] Office Manager Nu-Dawn Resources Inc; [hon.] Best Waitress Award 1987; [oth. writ.] "Charges" - first published book of inspirational poetry (June 1994) by Carlton Press New York, "Remember Love in a Far Off Place" (Fall 1994) by National Library of Poetry, "The Answered Prayer" in "After The Storm" (Winter 1994) by National Library of Poetry, "Embracing This" (Spring 1995) in "Best Poems of 1995" by National Library of Poetry.; [pers.] Writing for other people is always a challenge for me. This poem was requested by a friend who's father was in palative care and he wanted it from his mother to express how much he was loved by her and their three children. He had suffered a stroke 20 years earlier and his wife took care of him and became a nurse to him for those 20 years. My friend was on his way to see his father when he received this poem and the news that he had passed away at the same time. His mother has put this poem in his father's old room so that he may read it. This poem was the hardest I've ever written and it took something out of me that I didn't know was there. (Very ironic for "The Garden Of Life"); [a.] Nanaimo British Columbia, Canada

BAGLEY, BARBARA DELK
[b.] September 10, 1934, Fresno, CA; [p.] Fletcher Delk - Lois Downen; [m.] Tom Bagley, November 24, 1956; [ch.] Steve Bagley - Beverly Majors - Saralyn Bagley; [ed.] Excelsior Union High Long Beach Junior College; [occ.] Self Employed, Metrin Skin Care; [memb.] Women in Business Alamo Heights Chamber of Commerce Trinity Baptist Church Woodlake Golf and Country Club Petroleum Club of San Antonio; [pers.] I try to live my life by the three E's, enthusiasm, excitement, and expectancy. To be caring of others and to cherish my family.; [a.] San Antonio, TX

BAILEY, CATHERINE VAUGHAN
[b.] September 14, 1957, Saint Charles, IL; [p.] William and Joan Vaughan; [m.] Jesse S. Bailey Jr., February 21, 1981; [ch.] Kelly Gates Bailey; [ed.] Western Connecticut State University; [occ.] Educational Assistant; [memb.] Newtown Educational Assistants Association, International Federation of Professional and Technical Engineers, AFL-CIO, CLC, Parents-Teachers Association (PTA); [pers.] My love of words, and the thought-provoking power they possess, goes back to early childhood. There is a persevering beauty to be found within each day. Writing is my way to explore and release such depths of feeling.; [a.] Sandy Hook, CT

BAILEY, ROLAND J.
[pen.] Bill Bailey; [b.] May 15, 1933, Washington, DC; [p.] Elizabeth D. Bailey (Mother); [m.] Veronica Pamela Littlewood Bailey, August 20, 1955; [ch.] Michael Jay Bailey (son); [ed.] Armstrong High School, Sophomore Community College, Southern Illinois University.; [occ.] Nuclear Physical Security Consultant, Retired, USAF, Chief Master Sergeant; [memb.] Toastmasters International, Air Force Security Police Association, National FBI Academy Graduates; [hon.] Awarded the Bronze Star, Air Force Meritorious Service Medal, Air Force Commendation Medal with 3 Oak Leaf Clusters (OLC). Outstanding Security Police Superintendent of the year 1974.; [oth. writ.] Numerous speeches for my toastmaster CTM and ATM Certifications, (competent and able); [pers.] I want my poetry to help others witness a renaissance of the dynamic and evolving American ideal and spirit. I have been greatly influenced by all whom I have met.; [a.] Burson, CA

BAKER, DEAVONNA ALESIA DEANE
[b.] April 12, 1982, Orange, NJ; [p.] Fonda D. Deane, James F. Baker; [ed.] Our Lady Help of Christian School - Class of "1996"; [occ.] 7th Grade Student (OLHC); [memb.] Philemon Missionary Baptist Church Youth Inspirational Choir Member and Member.; [hon.] First and Second Academic Achievement Awards of OLHC, 7th Grade Classroom Math Tutor.; [pers.] Personal thanks to Mr. Gibbs (Teacher) at OLHC who encouraged me on my "Poetry Writing". Many special thanks to my family members who also supported me with my Gifted Talent, especially my grandnoter Mrs. Caloryn Deane who highly influenced me by seeking forth the entry to The National Library of Poetry Contest. "I will continue to fulfill this Genuine Talent that I have been God fully Blessed with.; [a.] Newark, NJ

BAKER, ELLEN
[pen.] Ellen Baker; [b.] August 28, 1953, Port Jervis, NY; [p.] Charles F, Betty J. Hogencamp; [m.] Kevin J. Baker, July 15, 1978; [ch.] Erin Nicole, Megan Kelly; [ed.] Northview H.S., Covina, CA, California Polytechnic State Univ., San Luis Obispo, CA; [occ.] Resource Teacher Alice G. Mulcahy Middle School Tulare, CA; [memb.] California Teachers Assoc., St. Aloysius Catholic Church Tulare 4-H Club; [hon.] Dean's List, President List, Mentor Teacher, Consultant for California State Department of Education; [oth. writ.] Literature Study guide for Learning Links, Inc., Educational materials for the California State Department of Education in the area of History, Social Science; [pers.] I enjoy writing humorous poetry related to events and people that I know.; [a.] Tulare, CA

BALLARD, HOPE E.
[b.] November 25, 1964, Chillicothe, OH; [pers.] My personal message to all, John 3:16. For God so loved the world, that he gave His only begotten Son, that whosoever believeth in Him should not perish, but have everlasting life. Believe and trust in this.; [a.] Chillicothe, OH

BALLARD, JEAN
[b.] September 23, 1933, Portland, IN; [p.] Kenneth and Onda Stump; [m.] Frank H. Ballard Jr., September 20, 1952; [ch.] Connie, Troy, Terri; [ed.] Madison High; [occ.] Retired; [memb.] Jay County Arts Council, Jay County Friends of the Library; [hon.] DAR Citizenship Award, American Legion Award; [oth. writ.] Short poems, Children's books; [pers.] I hope my poetry will help awaken the conscience of the people, that they will speak up for the things they know are right; [a.] Portland, IN

BALLINGER, JASMINE
[b.] August 12, 1981, Kimbal, NE; [p.] Lois Ballinger; [m.] Single; [ed.] Student in Otis Jr. High (8th grade); [occ.] Student in Otis Jr. High (8th grade); [memb.] Otis High School Band; [oth. writ.] The Rose, The Path, The Lonely Shoe; [a.] Otis, CO

BANIS, MURRI
[b.] July 27, 1965, Long Beach, CA; [p.] Esther and Casey Banis; [ed.] UC Santa Barbara; [occ.] Rehabilitation Coordinator; [pers.] I believe poetry should be an expression of the soul.; [a.] Oakland, CA

BANKER JR., JOHN C.
[b.] December 13, 1931, Westchester, PA; [p.] Deceased; [m.] Mary Sue Banker, June 25, 1963; [ch.] Melanie Lynn, Sandra Jean, and Jennifer Ruth; [ed.] Extensive Military Training (Electronics, digital principals, computers, and satellite systems) retired AF, 1969; [occ.] Retired Technical Writer (Aug 1994); [memb.] VFW Post 4305, Winter Garden, FL, Past member of the society of technical writers. I am an ordained deacon (Baptist). Current teach Old Testament Theology.; [hon.] Many from Military (AF Commendation) and others; [oth. writ.] Several publication in Military Instructor's Journal one unpublished book being edited by several sources (Two wrong's Don't Make a Writer) Another in Draft stage "Journey Into Hell" (about my participation in Atomic Testing); [pers.] As a military/civilian defense technical writer, and later as a writer of computer-based documents, my goal was easy-to-read, easy-to-understand user manuals. My goal was to "keep it simple," explain things in the user language.; [a.] Orlando, FL

BANKS, ALMARINE RUSSELL
[b.] Tuskegee, AL; [p.] Ada Lovey and James Russell; [m.] Cato J. Banks; [ch.] Faye Annette, Jerry, Benjamin, Jessica, Jamin, Jovan, Jeremy, Franchesca, Jerrett, Janine (grandchilren); [ed.] Tuskegee University, University of Buffalo, State Teacher's College; [occ.] Teacher - third grade (Elementary Ed.); [memb.] New York State Teachers' Retirement System, Worldwide Organization of Jehovahs' Witnesses; [oth. writ.] Poems about family, friends, creation and the universe. Also a poem about Voluntary Integration In The Buffalo Schools; [pers.] Whatever is good or virtuous, continue doing this. (Bible) based on Philippians 4:8; [a.] Tuskegee, AL

BANKS, JANE
[pen.] Jane Christian Barnes; [b.] February 12, 1933, Tahlequah, OK; [p.] Marion Haynes Green and E. J. Green; [m.] (ex husband) C. B. Banks, March 27, 1953 - February 28, 1972; [ch.] Marian Sue and Paul Randolph; [ed.] H.S. Plainview High School B.A. English Texas Tech College '53; [occ.] Retired Disabled; [memb.] AARP TACAE, Baptist Church 1995 (College Sigma Tau Delta, FTA (H.S) Y-Teens, Spanish Club, National Honor Society, Plainview High School Band, H.S. newspaper staff, H.S. annual staff; [hon.] LISD Teacher of the Year, Adult Education, 1977, PHS Journalist of the Year - 1950; [oth. writ.] Many unpublished inspirational poems and such; [pers.] Romantic poetry, the writings of John Milton have influenced me to write poetry that is always uplifting and inspirational. I especially love to write patriotic poetry.; [a.] Lubbock, TX

BARDO, CHARLIE
[pen.] Chas or Chuck Bardo; [b.] December 26, 1972, San Jose, CA; [p.] Bonnie Bardo, John Bardo; [m.] Single; [ed.] Live Oak High, De Anza College; [occ.] Manufacturer/wholesale for Pro Sport Ind.; [memb.]

Gumataotao Kajukenbo Emperados Black Belt Society, K.S.D.I; [pers.] Be true to yourself at all costs. Dare to be different!; [a.] Morgan Hill, CA

BARKER, DONALD H.

[pen.] Martin Oliver; [b.] September 21, 1935, Niagara Falls, NY; [ed.] BA, Colgate University; [occ.] Project Engineer; [hon.] Allen Prize for Literature, Colgate University 1957. Honorable Mention 36th Annual Creative Writing Contest. "Atlantic Monthly" Magazine 1957.; [oth. writ.] (As Martin Oliver), McKricken's Christmas 1991 ISBN/856341208, The giggle mirths of Waggledown derry 1991 ISBN 856341860.; [pers.] I am focusing my writing avocation towards the creation of fanciful children's stories. The children are the readers, the writers and the future of all tomorrows.; [a.] Williston, VT

BARNETT SR., RAYMOND B.

[pen.] R. B. or Ray; [b.] July 2, 1952, Mount Holly, NJ; [p.] Donald and Inez Barnett; [m.] Patricia May Barnett; [ch.] Ray Jr., Paul, Dina and Shane; [ed.] Pemberton Twp. High School graduate.

BARNHART, MONIQUE

[pen.] Monique Barnhart; [b.] September 25, 1979, Salinas, CA; [p.] Rick and Pam Barnhart; [ed.] Attending High School; [oth. writ.] Poems and songs; [pers.] I hope by this poem you can truly see how much my granny meant to me. I am inspired to write by my family and friends.; [a.] Castroville, CA

BARTHOLOMEW, DAISY D.

[pen.] Dee Dee, Bartholomew; [b.] July 7, 1925, Hewett West, VA; [p.] Herbert and Spicie Bias; [m.] Charles A. Bartholomew "deceased" 1992, August 18, 1946; [ch.] David A. Bartholomew, Charles E. Bartholomew; [occ.] Retired from 20 yrs. of Antique and Collectible Shop Owner; [hon.] Only from family and friends "Raves" for birthdays Christmas - Graduations - Weddings - Whatever The Occasion! Sickness and death! Lots of letters in form of poetry!; [oth. writ.] Loads of poems put away over the years some good, some sad, some bad just to read over again some lonely day!; [pers.] I try to write as I believe about whatever the subject of thought. But I'm sure my imagination would have to work overtime if for fiction I sought!; [a.] Cleveland, OH

BARTLEY, GERALDINE

[b.] December 22, 1921, Baxter Springs, KS; [p.] W. E. Hiatt, Virginia Hiatt; [m.] Elbridge W. Bartley Jr., August 5, 1943; [ch.] Linda Jeanne, E. W. III, Edwin, John, Robert; [ed.] Baxter Springs, KS High, Phoenix Jr. College, Pittsburgh State Teacher's College; [occ.] Retired (Minister's wife for past 51 years); [memb.] United Methodist Women, King's Highway Chapter DAR; [oth. writ.] Several poems published in church papers and local newspapers; [pers.] I always seek to present the wonder of God and His creation in my poetry.; [a.] Sikeston, MO

BASARA, SHIRLEY

[b.] March 4, 1932, MA; [m.] Walter Basara, 1950; [ch.] Two; [ed.] Deerfield High Kay Hardey School of Cosmetology; [pers.] I am fortunate to be living in the Green Mt State of Vermont the beauty of its woods and rivers inspires me to write and express my gratitude for the privilege.

BASSHAM, P. DENISE

[b.] May 6, 1970, Abilene, Texas; [p.] Larry and Berta Tarrant; [m.] Don Bassham, November 7, 1992; [ed.] Eastland High, Texas Tech University; [occ.] English teacher, Thornton Jr. High, Houston, TX; [memb.] National Council of Teachers of English, Association of Texas Professional Educators, Texas Tech Ex-Students Association; [hon.] Dean's List Texas Tech Univ., Cypress-Fairbanks ISD Spotlight teacher award 1994-95, Vol. X for exemplary teaching; [oth. writ.] Personal narrative writing published in Cypress-Fairbanks Writing Project Anthology 1993; [pers.] My inspiration for writing comes from the bond I share with my family, from Mama Betty and her "Big Red House" to my undying love for my husband, Don. We are all there for each other and for this closeness I am able to express myself through my writing. [a.] Katy, TX

BATHRICK, CONNIE

[pen.] Connie Bathrick; [b.] May 25, 1970, La Jolla; [p.] John and Gloria Wright; [m.] Sean; [ch.] Austin, dog Murphee; [ed.] High School Diploma; [occ.] Housewife; [memb.] Thespian Society, National Forensics League; [hon.] First, Second and Third Place awards for my OPP (Original Prose/Poetry) that I wrote in High School.; [oth. writ.] Longer poems - poems that are typed and 3 pages long, others that I have written over the past 15 years. Personal poetry.; [pers.] I enjoy writing poetry that people can relate to - writings that make people think or feel what I'm trying to say.; [a.] Carlsbad, CA

BATTERTON, DENISE

[pen.] Niecy; [b.] October 21, 1980, Stockton, CA; [p.] Robbie and Robert Morales, Carl and Robin Batterton; [ed.] Edison High School, Marshall Junior School, El Dorado Elementary; [occ.] Student at Edison High School; [memb.] Blockbuster Edison High Marching Band, Band Club, Pacific Little League; [hon.] Citizen of the Year, Author Awards (1st, 2nd) all city, Music Festival (twice), Perfect Attendance 1st Chair for Music Class (the highest you can get); [oth. writ.] Young authors fare, poems 4 mothers and others like you, life's poetry; [pers.] I enjoy writing poetry, its my way of expressing myself. I have been tremendously inspired by the late Emily Dickinson and most of all my late cousin Cindy Batterton; [a.] Stockton, CA

BAUER, KAREN

[b.] September 17, 1971, Trenton, NJ; [p.] Charles and Sharon Bauer; [ch.] Charlie and Jimmy

BEAGLE, BETTY

[b.] September 27, 1947, East Liverpool, OH; [p.] Richard Moffett, Darlene Moffett; [m.] Divorced; [ch.] Mishelle, Kevin, Chad; [ed.] AD in Nursing and AD in Office Admn.; [occ.] Registered Nurse; [memb.] AACN - American Association of Critical Care Nurses; [hon.] "Woman of the Day" 1986, Employee of the Month, 11-86, Nurses Nurse Award in 1990; [oth. writ.] Just for Students - Survival Techniques, Who are We, Nurse Externship, What Is It? Co-authored with C. Campisi; [pers.] I like to write about personal experiences, making serious situations humorous when possible and writing tributes to close friends and family.; [a.] East Liverpool, OH

BEARD, WILLIE EDNA

[pen.] Willabee; [b.] February 20, 1938, Kinston, NC; [p.] William Roberts and Janie Daugherty Roberts; [m.] Divorced; [ch.] Michael, Kelvin, Angela, Brenda and Linda (twins); [ed.] Boylan Haven Boarding School-Jacksonville, FL, Blayton Bus. College Atlanta, GA '58, Antioch U. Phila, PA. Certified in Medical and Psychiatric Assistance.; [occ.] Office Manager, Admin. Assistant to Dir. Jewish Employment and Voc. Service, CCS, OTI; [memb.] 1st Presbyterian Church in Germantown, PA Church of Scientology, American Guild of Hypotherapists; [hon.] Golden Poet Award - 1990 World of Poetry Convention "Love Is A Phoenix"; [oth. writ.] "A Dream Shared", 1991 article for Temple U. Interchange.; [pers.] As children of God, He gives us gifts from a million dollars to a dime He gives his millions to feed the poor and shares His wisdom in the foolishness of Rhyme - Matt. 18:3; [a.] Philadelphia, PA

BEAUDET, ANN CAVIN

[pen.] Ann Blashill; [b.] June 13, 1929, Chicago, IL; [p.] Robert Fisher Cavin and Helen Gordon; [m.] Divorced from Blashill, 1951 and 1968; [ch.] Robert, Alisan and Elizabeth; [ed.] B.A. University of Wn., Seattle, M.A. - San Jose State University, Counselor Education, audit at U of Madrid in Estudios Hispanicas; [occ.] Associate Editor of "Peace Time"; [memb.] N.O.W. WILPF, OWL, Unitarian Church, San Jose Peace Center, Democratic Party; [hon.] Secretary of Student Body U of Wn. '51, Treasurer of Associated Women Students, U of Wn. '47, Vice President, League of Women Voters, pelham, N.Y. Vice President of PTA, Stipe Elementary School, San Jose, Totem Club and Mortar Board - U of W, God "Y", Yakima High School '47.; [oth. writ.] Letters to editors of "Columns" (UW alummag), WORLD (UU national magazine), "Psychology Today", Mercury News, Columnist for UU newsletters, columnist of "The Spanish Scene" for "The Guidepost", Madrid Spain, Columnist for Town Park Towers News (residence newsletter); [pers.] My daughter purchased a commemorative brick for me which lies outside the fountain on the campus of San Jose State University and reads "Ann Beaudet - Peace and Justice". I have written 300 pages of a yet-to-be-published journal called NEXT MORNING THE NEIGHBORS WERE DEAD peopled by illustratrious people I have met around the world in my travels as the wife of a foreign correspondent.; [a.] San Jose, CA

BECERRA JR., MARTIN

[b.] Fresnillo, Zacatecas, NM; [p.] Martin Becerra Sr., Aurora Becerra; [ch.] Laura, Elizabeth; [ed.] Bishop Noll High, Calument College, Indiana University NW.; [occ.] Academic Advisor; [hon.] Kappa Delta Pi, Who's Who in American Universities And Colleges; [pers.] I am always fascinated by words and their power.; [a.] Griffith, IN

BECHARD JR., GARY P.

[b.] August 30, 1968, Newburg, NY; [p.] Virginia and Gary Bechard Sr.; [m.] Ruthanne Bechard, November 17, 1990; [ch.] Matthew Vincent Bechard and Georgerobert Patrick Bechard; [ed.] Beacon High School, Fishkill Ave, Beacon, NY, BOCES Tech - Carpentry; [occ.] Brunetti Contracting; [pers.] I have been greatly influenced by A. E. Housman and Edgar Allen Poe

BECKER, RUTH Z.

[b.] New York City, NY; [p.] Deceased; [m.] Deceased; [ch.] Henry Becker, Jill Becker; [ed.] R. N., B.S. New York University, M.A. New York University; [occ.] Retired

BEIGHEY, GEORGE

[b.] December 17, 1966, Denver, CO; [m.] Kelly, December 17, 1987; [ch.] Robert; [ed.] Self taught; [occ.] Father, husband; [oth. writ.] The Tragedy of God's

Champion (unpublished); [pers.] The trooper was inspired by my son, Robert; [a.] Denver, CO

BEIL, BELINDA LEA
[pen.] Belinda L. Ross (previous writings); [b.] May 2, 1959, Victoria, British Columbia, Canada; [p.] Rose (Duck) and John Lee Ross; [m.] Andrew Patrick James Beil; [ch.] Victoria Kymberly Sakura, Callyn Christa Lea Ross MacDougall; [ed.] University College, New Westminster, BC and Abbotsford, BC (English Major); [memb.] Dallas Community Assoc. in Kamloops (Society Founder), Independent Order of Foresters (Fraternity).; [oth. writ.] Begun writing at age 8, has a diary of unpublished poems titled Secret Places (after the inspirational poem of the same name by Charlotte Bronte), writing a cookbook Great Impressions, regular contributor to local newsletter Dallas Dateline.; [pers.] My high school grad quote (1976): ...and yet we are nearest in twilight here, the work tossed upon the fire year after year like pages of a diary.; [a.] Kamloops British Columbia, Canada

BELL, WILLIE I.
[pen.] Wink; [b.] December 11, 1961, Detroit, MI; [ch.] Marlon, DiJon, and Jovan (all boys); [ed.] Graduate: Specs Howard School of Broadcast Arts.; [occ.] President of Video Production Company.; [memb.] Member of Detroit Newspaper Guild, Member of Word of Faith International Christian Center.; [hon.] Winner of Local Union Press Association Award.; [oth. writ.] Include Poems: "Young Gifted And Black", "It's Nice To Be Loved", "Stir Lean On Me" and more.; [pers.] Currently Working on a book. I am very excited about this book and am looking for a publisher. I'm in the video/film industry, so my books have a great chance of crossing over.; [a.] Detroit, MI

BELLINGER, JOSH
[b.] November 28, 1981, Phoenix, AZ; [p.] John and Conni Bellinger; [ed.] 7th Grade at Sundance Elementary School; [occ.] Student; [memb.] Peoria Presbyterian Church, Peoria Boy and Girls Club; [pers.] I like writing poems, I have quite a extensive collection. Sitting in the darkness is when I usually think of my poems I write poems about what I'm feeling.; [a.] Peoria, AZ

BELLINI, BRENT
[b.] December 1, 1976, Hollywood, California; [p.] Larry and Sue Bellini; [ed.] Newman Central Catholic High School, Sterling, IL. (senior); [occ.] Student; [memb.] Peer minister; [hon.] American Legion Art Award; [oth. writ.] One poem published in local newspaper in 7th grade (Daily Gazette); [pers.] Poetry helps release feelings especially about one's love and one's loss. [a.] Rock Falls, IL

BELLIZZI, JOSEPH
[pen.] Mr. Anonymous; [b.] January 11, 1975, Jersey City, NJ; [p.] Angelo and Anna Bellizzi; [ed.] Hockensack Christian School, Seton Hall University - 2nd year; [occ.] Student; [hon.] Who's Who Among American High School Students 92-93.; [oth. writ.] Poems and short stories all unpublished.; [pers.] Life has a speed limit - infinity. We just have to keep up with it.; [a.] Ridgefield, NJ

BELLOLI, GIAN CARLO
[pen.] Gian Carlo Belloli; [b.] July 25, 1970, Santa Cruz, CA; [p.] Bill and Barbara Belloli; [ed.] New College Of California, presently undergraduate; [occ.] Student; [a.] San Francisco, CA

BENACKA, DEBRA
[b.] April 15, 1958, Chicago, IL; [p.] Orphane; [m.] Single Mom (proud); [ch.] Douglas, Angelo, Arnie and Lisa; [ed.] G.E.D.; [occ.] Clerical; [oth. writ.] Poetry and Editorials in local papers.; [pers.] I grew up in the streets of Chicago. I find a great release in writing and hope to publish a book someday.; [a.] Chicago, IL

BENDER, HEIDI LYNN
[b.] July 11, 1976, Sierra Vista, AZ; [p.] Lynda K. Marshall; [ed.] Barry Goldwater High School; [occ.] Waitress; [memb.] ACDA; [hon.] First place in State Competition for Freshman Class at Barry Goldwater High School. "Beginning of The End"; [oth. writ.] "Pain" Diamonds and Rust ("National Library of Poetry"); [pers.] I write about my personal experiences to let others know they are not alone and that they too can seethe brighter side of life, just as I have; [a.] Phoenix, AZ

BENDER, KENNETH L.
[b.] April 27, 1931, Polo, IL; [p.] William J. and Ethel M. Bender; [m.] Florella C. Bender, December 6, 1969; [ch.] Rick L. Bell, David F. Bender, JoAnne M. Bender and Randy J. Bender; [ed.] Polo Community High School, and Sauk Valley Jr. College.; [occ.] Retired Military, 1sgt, Retired in 1971 after 20 yrs. in U.S. Army; [memb.] Life Member VFW, Life Member American Legion, Life Member 4th Inf. Div. - Life Member - 2nd Inf. Div. - Life Member - 9th Inf. Regt.; [hon.] Bronze Star Medal, Army Commendation Medal, Combat Infantry Badge, (2nd Award) Good Conduct Medal (6 Awards) Korean Service Medal, UN Service Medal, American Defense Service Medal, Army Occupational Medal (Germany) Vietnam Service Medal, Vietnam Campaign medal with 3 campaigns other writings numerous poems unpublished.; [pers.] I remember my Art teacher in high school, Mr. Parrott, and always have tried to live up to his teachings and the standards he maintained.; [a.] Monroe, WI

BENEFIELD, PAM
[b.] May 20, 1947, Hartford, CT; [pers.] This poem was written for my little dog, Chula. She was born on my birthday on May 20, 1977 and she died on November 8, 1994. She truly was a gift and still, even now, she is always with me.

BENNING, ELINOR PAULINE
[pen.] Polly Prindle; [b.] March 12, 1904, Charlotte, VT; [p.] Edwin and Carrie Clark Prindle; [m.] Ernest Katzenberger, November 17, 1956, and Samuel G. Benning, December 2, 1975; [ch.] Sarah B. Carpenter (step-daughter); [ed.] A.B. Degree Oberlin College 1925. I worked 17 years as an Occupational therapist at Sunny Acres Hospital in Cleveland, OH 1943-1960; [occ.] Retired but still retired but busy with toy making and other crafts; [memb.] Formerly Vt. Writers League Charlotte, VT, Congregational Church. My Church has honored me several times for my contributions of various kinds; [oth. writ.] Polly Pringle's "Jolly Jingles" 62 pages, "Polly Pets" 30 pages, children's verses to go with "Polly's Pet's", 15 small stuffed animals designed and hand-made by the author, "What Christmas Means" 20 pages, a collection of Christmas card verses written over the years; [pers.] My advice to friends is develop hobbies or special interests when young that you can enjoy when you retire.; [a.] South Burlington, VT

BENSON, KATHY
[pen.] Kat; [b.] February 10, 1965, Waterloo, IA; [p.] Carl and Jean Seavey; [m.] Deceased; [ch.] Tim Benson, Jason Benson and Christi Benson; [ed.] Finished 10th Grade, received GED.; [occ.] Cook, University of Northern Iowa; [memb.] Waverly Hospital Auxiliary and Health Club; [oth. writ.] Many other unpublished poems we wrote over the years.; [pers.] My writings come from personal experiences and many feelings and thoughts put together.

BENTLEY, RHONDA
[pen.] Rhonda or Roni; [b.] November 9, 1967, Bowmanville, Canada; [p.] Yennette Huber, Gerald Huber; [m.] John Bentlay; [ch.] Jorden Daniel Jackson and Janelle Lynette Rene'; [ed.] Clarke High, Port Perry High; [occ.] Mother - Computer Student at C.I.S.; [memb.] Newcastle Baptist Church; [oth. writ.] Several poems looking to be published, others published in local newspapers; [pers.] The people I meet from day today inspire my writings. When I was younger I dwelt with my feelings by putting them on paper. It paid off, now others can enjoy the feelings I enjoyed.; [a.] Bowmanville Ontario, Canada

BERGIN, WILLIAM A.
[pen.] William A. Bergin; [b.] February 12, 1929, New York, NY; [p.] William and Virginia; [m.] Francisa, June 6, 1955; [ch.] Donny, Jimmy, Jesica-Kim, Pete John; [ed.] University of California Berkely; [occ.] Retired, works part time as driver; [hon.] Alpha-Zeta; [oth. writ.] Miscellaneous poetry; [pers.] I trust in the Lord; [a.] Santa Rosa, CA

BERGSRUD, BOBBI LEE
[b.] February 1, 1963, Great Falls, MT; [p.] Bud Lee, Margie Lee; [m.] Scott; [ch.] Noelle Lee (daughter); [ed.] Graduate of Great Falls High and Central Mt. Barber School; [pers.] My poems are reflections of my feelings at certain stages of my life. Modern poetry is my forte.

BERKLEY, ANNETTE
[b.] August 23, 1960, Washington, MO; [p.] Chester and Dolores Grotewiel; [m.] Terry L. Berkley, October 24, 1992; [ch.] Andy, Erin, Jennifer; [ed.] Hermann High, Charles E. Still School of Radiology; [occ.] Mammographer, X-Ray Technologist; [memb.] ARRT/ASRT; [oth. writ.] This is the first; [pers.] I believe in family. You will always find happiness and acceptance there. My husband is my inspiration; [a.] Albuquerque, NM

BERNITSKY, DAVID
[pen.] Dave; [b.] May 5, 1960, Harrisburg, Pennsylvania; [p.] Bernard and Ruth; [ed.] Didn't graduate from high school; [oth. writ.] Wrote for the Paxton Street Scoop, example: The Fire, From Soul to Soil, Don't Hold onto a Thing that Burns, Thorns and Tweezers; [pers.] I sometimes use Biblical metaphors in my writings. I use personal experience accompanied with this philosophical statement, "You are as big as you think you ARE!" [a.] Harrisburg, PA

BERTRAND, BARBARA A.
[b.] June 18, 1947, Waukegan, IL; [p.] Margaret and Casimer Sowa; [m.] John, August 20, 1966; [ch.] John Jr., Jeff, Joel, Jacob; [ed.] H.S. diploma and 2 yrs. college; [occ.] Student Assistance Aide Poway Unified District; [hon.] Certified Medical Assistant Past Nat'l Leadership for U.S.A. Worldwide Marriage Encounter; [pers.] I like to write about life and nature and how together they bring about hope and healing.; [a.] San Diego, CA

BESS, SHEILA R. NICHOLS
[pen.] S. Bess or Sheila Nichols Bess; [b.] March 17, 1947, Benkelman, NE; [p.] Omar and Eula Nichols; [m.] Divorced, 1965; [ch.] Eric Bess; [ed.] Nicholas Country High School - Summersville, WV; [occ.] Interior Design Specialist - Kahului, HI; [memb.] "Lahaina Arts Society" "Poets At Work" "Hui No'Eau Visual Arts"; [oth. writ.] "Poets At Work"; [pers.] I love touching a person's deepest inner soul with my poems and art.; [a.] Makawao Maui, HI

BETHELL, KRISTIN SUSAN
[b.] November 20, 1958, Nassau, Bahamas; [p.] Mr. and Mrs. C. W. F. Bethell; [ed.] LeRosey, Rolle, Switzerland, Foxcroft High School, Franklin College - Switzerland, University of Miami - Florida Padi College - San Diego; [occ.] Secretary - receptionist at my brother's rock plant; [memb.] BASRA - Bahamas Airsea Rescue Life Member, Bahamas National Trust; [oth. writ.] Precious Treasures, Better than Silver and Gold; [pers.] With the pen history is shapened - Destinies of people and countries can be changed and are with a pen - for good of humanity; [a.] Nassau, Bahamas

BEVINGTON, LINDA A.
[b.] September 2, 1939, Freesoil, MI; [p.] Harry P. and Mildred L. Rasmussen; [m.] Raymond L. Bevington, December 18, 1959; [ch.] Elizabeth Catherine; [ed.] Amphitheater H.S. (Tuczon, AZ) Univ. of Arizona, BA, M. Ed.; [occ.] Classroom teacher (2nd grade); [hon.] Who's Who in American Teachers (1994); [oth. writ.] Three as yet unpublished children's stories; [pers.] I feel that my interests in music and in writing have always been supported by my family.; [a.] Tucson, AZ

BICKERDIKE, JOYCE
[b.] January 17, 1948, Montreal, Quebec, Canada; [ch.] Ravi and Bharath; [ed.] Shawinigan High, Montreal General Hospital School of Nursing, Argyle Institute of Human Relations; [occ.] Psychotherapist; [pers.] My inspiration and my passion is the nature of man's relationship to nature.; [a.] Montreal, Quebec, Canada

BICKNESE SR., KARL S.
[b.] March 6, 1938, Mt. Vernon, NY; [p.] John, Alma; [m.] Martha, July 29, 1972; [ch.] Karl Jr., Ken, Eric; [ed.] High School Graduate, Edison High, Mt Vernon; [occ.] School Bus Driver, (Semi Retired Soft Drink Plant Manager); [memb.] Amer Legion Post 159; [oth. writ.] On going poems for a book of poems; [pers.] Writing poems is a great mind activator which fills empty spaces when you are relaxing; [a.] Venice, FL

BIGELOW, JAMES CHRISTOPHER
[b.] March 10, 1964, Springfield, MA; [p.] Lester Bigelow, Lois Bigelow; [ed.] Classical High, 1982, Westfield State College. 1990 B.A. In Art.; [memb.] Cum Laude, Dean's List.; [pers.] My poem that is published in this anthology, "The Garden Of Life", is dedicated to Josie Dimauro for her courage and strength during the passing of her mother on November 13, 1994 and to my father Lester Bigelow who passed away November 13, 1984.; [a.] Springfield, MA

BIGGS, R. TIPTON
[b.] August 18, 1939, Arbela, MO; [p.] Robert E. and Martha A. Biggs; [m.] C. Maureen Biggs, November 25, 1961; [ch.] Christopher, Adrienne, Erik; [ed.] B.S. in Ed. Northeast MO State, MA Univ of NE - Lincoln; [occ.] Professor of English Iowa Western Comm. College Council Bluffs, IA; [memb.] N.E.A., I.H.E.A., Theatre Arts Guild, Willa Cather Pioneer Memorial; [hon.] Best Director, Come Back Little Sheba, 1980, Best Supporting Actor 1990 Omaha Comm. Playhouse; [oth. writ.] Two unpublished musicals. Several poems in various college publications; [pers.] The best poetry should taste good in the mouth and have some bite to it.; [a.] Omaha, NE

BILLINGTON, WILLIAM F.
[pen.] Bill Billington; [b.] May 8, 1950, Amsterdam, NY; [p.] William and Beverly Billington; [ch.] Michelle, Rachel, Tommy, Timmy, Cassi, Billi Jo; [ed.] Wilbur H. Lynch High; [occ.] Machine Set Up Ct. Spring and Stamping Corp.; [memb.] A.S.C.A.P.; [hon.] Won 8 honors from Billboard Songwriters, 1 honor from Newington Childrens Hosp. for a song "Picture A Rose" and 1 honor from President George Bush for song "For the Heroes"; [oth. writ.] Amsterdam, NY. USA (Bill's Theme) published in The Amsterdam Evening Recorder; [pers.] I try to write about truth, life, and the way it really is, when I write I like to make one really think about the words. Special thanks to Gary L. Billington for inspiring me to write my father's son; [a.] Southington, CT

BINGHAM, KEVIN
[b.] August 15, 1971, Forrest City, AR; [p.] Lewis and Florine Bingham; [ed.] Lee Senior High, Marianna, AR, Oral Roberts University, Tulsa, OK.; [occ.] Case Manager, East Arkansas Regional Mental Health Ctr.; [memb.] National Junior Honor Society, Beta Club, Society of Distinguished American H.S. students, who's who among American H.S. Students, Student Council (President).; [hon.] President Academic Fitness Award, Outstanding Academic Achievement Award, Top 10% H.S., Governor's School Nominee (Gov. Bill Clinton); [oth. writ.] A series of poems expressing Black Positiveness, entitled "Positively Black".; [pers.] When I write, I aim to put the pen in the hands of my heart, for it is the source from where inspiration will start.; [a.] Forrest City, AR

BIRON, BRENDA
[b.] August 28, 1961, Ontario, Canada; [p.] Ken and Shirley Biron; [ed.] Webster University in Vienna, Austria. I received my Bachelor of Arts Degree in International Economy.; [occ.] Director of Building Management; [memb.] Writers' Federation of New Brunswick, Romance Writers of America; [hon.] Howard Grimmar Prize, Honours: Dean's List, University of New Brunswick, Fredericton; [oth. writ.] Poems published in the cormorant, Saint John's Literary Magazine; [pers.] The clearest path toward truth is honesty; [a.] Saint John, New Brunswick, Canada

BISCHOFF, LANA
[b.] April 28, 1947, Loftsgard, IA; [p.] Lila Olson; [m.] Brian Bischoff, August 24, 1968; [ch.] Jonathan Conrad and Christopher Brian; [ed.] University of Tampa; [occ.] 6th Grade Language Arts, Reading Teacher; [oth. writ.] Various short writings for newspapers and magazines throughout the country.; [pers.] I love to write and hope to instill the love for writing in my students. I enjoy writing about those things many would call "not beautiful"; [a.] Matthews, NC

BISHOP JR., MELVIN R.
[b.] September 24, 1922, Charlottesville, VA; [p.] Melvin R. and Pearl B.; [m.] Widow, October 19, 1981; [ch.] By first marriage, Melvin III, Sally G. and Kate P.; [ed.] Lane High - Audited Psychology at Richmond Prof. Institute and Gallaudet College; [occ.] Retired Electrical Building Inspector; [memb.] AARP; [hon.] Author of Two Rules in the National Electrical Code.; [pers.] Dedicated to my wife, Charlotte Ellen, who died in June, 1993; [a.] Leesburg, FL

BLACK, SHIRLEY E.
[b.] July 28, 1936, Saint Louis, MO; [p.] George Dood and Manzella Dood; [m.] Joseph G. Black (Deceased), April 23, 1955; [ch.] Wandamaria, Karen, Suzanne, Joseph, Shelly; [ed.] Cupples Elementary, Summer High School, Lael University; [occ.] Owner - Director (Child and Adult Care) the Learning Tree Intergenerational Center; [memb.] National Association of the Education of Young Children National Black Child Development Institute Coalition for families with children African American Women for Wellness; [hon.] Outstanding Contributions in the Community - 1984; [oth. writ.] Poems published in Church newspapers, Poetry Book "The Mirror Of Her Soul" (unpublished) Copyright January 5, 1995 Plays written for Church Performances; [pers.] It is my desire to have my work reflect God's ability and willingness to substain his children in all circumstances, when they put their total trust in him.; [a.] Saint Louis, MO

BLACKMAN, SHIRLEY CAMPBELL
[b.] November 23, 1934, Cameron, NC; [p.] Claude C. and Dora V. Campbell; [m.] John D. Blackman, September 30, 1951; [ch.] Nora, Doris, Joyce, Linda, Rachel; [oth. writ.] Songs, poems; [pers.] I consider my writings a gift from God for which I am most grateful

BLAIR, ELIZABETH ANNE
[pen.] Siobhan McRae, Shannon McClatchey; [b.] June 6, 1981; [p.] Kenneth W. Blair, Vicki Ray Blair; [ed.] Christ The King School, Benedicts Catholic School; [occ.] Student; [hon.] Highest First Time Composer "1994 Junior Composer Contest" National Federation of Music Club, Indiana State Junior Competition.; [a.] Evansville, IN

BLAKELY, SYLVIA F.
[pen.] Sylvia Blakely; [b.] December 20, 1936, Detroit, MI; [p.] Grace and Edgar Newton Crandell; [m.] Harold Rush (deceased) - 1955, Walter Blakely - 1986; [ch.] Dennis, Daniel, David, Tottie Ann, and 'Dawn' my 'special' child.; [ed.] 8th Grade Jefferson Int. Detroit MI, one course of creative writing in 1985 adukt ed. Pontiac MI; [occ.] Home maker/Part time Care Giver; [memb.] I attend, sporadically poetry readings, colleges and coffee houses. My second love is music. 'Rock' 'country' and some classical I had one song copy write.; [hon.] "5 Alive" a poem about my grandchildren "Gold Metal" winner. "The Rape" short story "Bronze Metal" winner. "Mouse In The Teapot" "Silver Metal" winner also short story. "The gift" (A poem) about my daughter with C.P. cerebral palsy, published in Lapeen County Press 1964; [oth. writ.] An (article) about a missing U-2 Pilot published in a 'Rag' magazine in 1964. Also published in Lapeen County Press "if there was a war and nobody came." Approve, 1968 (poem); [pers.] If an opportunity came to relive my life, I would complete my education. Attend College to obtain a journalism degree, and put off parenthood till I could offer my children a rich and rewarding heritage. God be with us all.; [a.] Pontiac, MI

BLANKENSHIP, BONNIE L.
[b.] October 7, 1949, New Brunswick, NJ; [p.] Alvin O. Schroeder, Bernice Schroeder; [m.] Divorced; [ch.] Tanya Ann Blankenship; [ed.] Hightstown High School, Hightstown, NJ., Philadelphia College of Art, Philadel-

phia PA.; [occ.] Managing Editor, the Jewish Quarterly Review; [memb.] The Plastic Club for Artists, Philadelphia Water Color Club; [pers.] In both my art work and my writing, I seek to explore and to define parts of the total. This has shown me many times that the grace of a minute portion exceeds the grandeur of the whole.; [a.] Philadelphia, PA

BLANKS, STEPHEN PATRICK
[pen.] Pat Blanks; [b.] January 6, 1949, Dallas, TX; [p.] Mary M. and John D.; [m.] Marjorie Anne; [ch.] Shawn Michael, Sidonie Patrice; [oth. writ.] Numerous songs, lyrics, observations of life and heart; [pers.] Life is a gift of breath. Breath is fresh and long, aware of its entity from the first through the last and beyond.; [a.] Fairfax, CA

BLASINGIM, CHRISTY
[b.] November 5, 1978, Houston; [p.] Vickie and John Blasingim; [ed.] 10th grade; [hon.] Honor student

BLAZIN, JOHN W.
[b.] May 9, 1947, Alameda, CA; [p.] John B. Blazin, Gerry Blazin; [m.] Margo Blazin, November 4, 1967; [ch.] James J. Blazin; [ed.] Castro Valley High, Chabot Jr. College; [occ.] Utility Worker II, Alameda County Water Dost. Fremont, CA; [memb.] First Baptist Church of Manteca.; [oth. writ.] Several writings none published yet.; [pers.] My writings are help makes to others, made to cheer up and create positive paths to follow. Awesome insights become great adventures.; [a.] Manteca, CA

BLIZZARD, ANDREA
[b.] February 3, 1926, Sciotoville, OH; [p.] John Rice, Catherine Middleton; [m.] Franklin Blizzard (deceased), January 4, 1946; [ch.] Franklin Jr., Rosanna, Marlene, Retha; [ed.] High School Adult-Ed, Adrian, Mich.; [occ.] Retired; [memb.] Church of Christ Adrian Michigan; [oth. writ.] Numerous poems, country song poems, and the beginning of my autobiography. I have 2 poems in the process of being published in The National Library of Poetry.; [pers.] I have great admiration for several writers of the past, such as, Alfred Lord Tennyson, Robert Louis Stevenson, Robert Browning, Henry Thoreau, and Stephen C. Foster. But my greatest inspiration comes from God and His Holy Word.; [a.] Manitou Beach, MI

BLOUNT, ANGELA LYNN
[b.] September 20, 1964, Georgia; [p.] Carlton and Patricia Allen; [m.] Nicholas Blount, September 24, 1983; [ch.] Dennis Allen Blount, Katie Elizabeth Blount; [ed.] Southwest High School, Macon College, Wesleyan College; [occ.] Mother; [oth. writ.] Other poetry; [pers.] "Writing comes from the soul. Everyone has a soul - Anyone can be a poet."; [a.] Macon, GA

BLUM, KEVIN MICHAEL
[pen.] Kevin Michael Blum; [b.] October 2, 1976, San Francisco, CA; [p.] Arthur Blum, Helga Blum; [ed.] Redwood High School, University of Southern California, Filmic Writing Major. Studied 2 summers in Paris at a French school called "L'Etoile".; [occ.] Student, Screenwriter; [memb.] Actor, Writer, Director in the Ensemble Theatre Company.; [hon.] Bank of America Award for most outstanding student in the Fine Arts Department at my High School.; [oth. writ.] Poem published in "Echoes From the Silence." Articles and film reviews published in local publication "Fast Forward." Author of unpublished book of poetry entitled "Notes on Crossing the Threshold", and author of several unproduced screenplays.; [pers.] There are people who are spectators in this world, and there are people who are participants. I get more satisfaction when I participate. While I live I want to love and be loved, and when I die I just want to be remembered by my words, and for the images and characters I created.; [a.] San Rafael, CA

BOAR, SHOSHANA E.
[b.] November 9, 1976, NH; [p.] Michael and Nicole Boar; [ed.] Presently attending High School; [occ.] Student; [memb.] Dean's List; [oth. writ.] Fiction, fantasy stories, as yet unpublished; [pers.] I have many dreams. Two of which are getting my book published and working with Icelandic horses. I am seeking magazines willing to publish my poems.; [a.] White River Junction, VT

BOGART, MICHAEL D.
[b.] August 23, 1962; [p.] Judith Stamsen, Larry Bogart; [ed.] Georgia State University, Berkeley; [occ.] Gardner, Student; [hon.] Honorable Discharge, US Army; [pers.] I love life; [a.] San Francisco, CA

BOGOLUB, MARIANNE
[pen.] Herma Hoermann; [b.] August 25, 1920, Vienna, Austria; [p.] Gustav Togel, Anna Togel (Toegel); [m.] Sam Bogolub, April 2, 1973; [ch.] Pierre Alexander (Hoermann); [ed.] 8 year Gymnasium in Vienna, Academy for Art (Schottenring Vienna) Nursing School, (Work as Surg. Nurse Saint Vincent LA.) and of curse in Vienna, write Poetry since I was 16 year old.; [occ.] Retired; [hon.] In Israel exipitions in painting and writing, also exipitions in printing in California, and also writing (Fam, Poets Soc. 1994) Hollywood, CA. 1942-45 in Austrien Newsp. (Poetry) and Pollands Newsp. same years. Polnish; [oth. writ.] 1953 Austrien Lyrik, Europ. Kerlag. Wien (Book) also Jubilaumsausgabe 1953 Austr, Lyrik, (Pen name Herma Hoermann) I also write story's for teen. And Illustr, about flower. (Written all in Germany).; [pers.] Somebody gait my hand, to write God give me a talent. I am order by him to use this talent. It make me incredible happy and for a time I forget, all my sorrow, "I enjoy life".; [a.] Los Angeles, CA

BOLDEN, BECKY J.
[Pen.] B.J.; [b.] September 8, 1944, Buffalo, NY; [p.] Thomas and Bessie Robinson; [m.] Divorced; [ch.] Tony, Scott, Phil; [ed.] Bennett High, California College Health Sciences; [occ.] Respiratory Care Practitioner x 28yr; [memb.] St. John United Methodist Church/Pontiac, MI/ AART, MSRT; [hon.] To be the proud mother of 3 very special boys and witness their metamorphosis into 3 wonderful men...my award...their friendship and love; [oth. writ.] Several poems, a few short stories; [pers.] I have been inspired to create many of my works after the experience of life's frequent traumas! Like music, I blend my words to soothe the soul;
[a.] Waterford, MI

BOLEWARE, SANDRA
[b.] February 4, 1960, Clovis, NM; [p.] Harvey Gill and Norman and Sue Unruh; [m.] Robert Hulsey, February 4, 1994; [ch.] Brittany Krystal; [ed.] Rose State College, University of Oklahoma; [occ.] Computer Graphics Artists, Photographer; [hon.] Co-awarded several "Addy" Advertising Awards, Photography Recognition Award; [oth. writ.] Published January '95, Daily Oklahoman Newspaper, various articles in local publications.; [pers.] Reach for the stars, do not accept no as an answer, be happy, because you can have it all, but first decide what is really important.; [a.] Oklahoma City, OK

BOND, DRUSILLA A.
[b.] December 7, 1978, San Diego, CA; [p.] Byron and Nancy Bond; [ed.] Freshman at Reynolds High School; [pers.] The poems, that I write, reflect the mood around me. Whether, the poems are happy are sad. It is my hope, that who ever reads my poems, get that same sense of feeling from them.; [a.] Troutdale, OR

BONDI, EDITH F. (nee Friedlaender)
[pen.] Edith F. Bondi; [b.] September 26, 1919, Berlin, Germany; [m.] Arnold A. Bondi; [ch.] Ardith, Eugene; [ed.] Friedrich Froebel Institute, B.S., M.A. Columbia University, Ph.D. Texas A&M.; [occ.] Professor of English Language and Classroom Teacher at Kossuth University Teacher Training School, Debrecen, Hungary. Director, Museum of Children's Books and Museum Zum Chorlesen Der Bucher Fur Kinder, Houston, Texas and Hungary.; [memb.] International, Texas, German, and Hungarian Reading Assocaitions, Assoc. for Childhood Education, Soc. of Children's Book Writers and Illustrators, American Translators Asso., Goethe Institute, German-Texan Heritage Soc., Camp Morasha, Gimmel Foundation of Israel; [hon.] Harp Soc. Awards for: Raising Reading and Language Development Achievement Levels with Nature Study in Elementary Public Shools and U.S. Dept. of Agriculture Disctricts, Teaching, Writing, Translation, Lectures, Children's Books, Songs, Poetry, and Elementary School Courses of Study.; [pers.] Kids Are Special People!; [a.] Houston, TX

BONDIMA, TOMBWE
[b.] November 20, 1967, Kribi (Cameroon); [p.] Algha, Jean Mawellet; [m.] Armelle Bondima, April 1989; [ch.] Bondima Aigha, Akeva Bondima and Mawellet Bondima; [ed.] College; [occ.] Student; [memb.] Rosicrucian order, AMORC; [oth. writ.] Several poems no published; [pers.] Life has been made to be shared in an equity; [a.] New York, NY

BONGIOVANNI, JEANETTE MADERA
[b.] September 16, 1959, New York, NY; [p.] America and Fernando Madera; [ch.] Marissa Ann, Darla Marie, Frank Joseph; [ed.] Martin Van Buren High School, current student at Nassau Community College; [occ.] Medical Secretary, Heritage Health Products Distributor; [pers.] Nothing is greater than love. God is love, and it is my hope to poetically express the love of Christ within me to others.; [a.] Floral Park, NY

BONO, CHRISTOPHER
[b.] December 31, 1976, Chicago; [p.] Louis and Frances; [ed.] High School Lake Park, Roselle, IL; [occ.] Senior; [hon.] American Legionary Award - 8th Grade, Plus all awards available for that Grade (Presidential Award, Perfect Attendance Award etc.,), Team Captain of JV Volleyball - Freshman, Highest Honor Roll - Freshman and Sophomore, Student Achiever of the Year - Sophomore, Academic All-Conf - Sophomore and Junior, Scholastic Achievement Award IHSA, National Honor Society, Congress-Budestag Youth Certificate of Merit, Coach for two years Little League, Presently a foreign exchange student in Germany; [oth. writ.] An Open Letter:, The Price We Pay, "Dad", Veterans Day '95 - A Report; [pers.] Attached - My poem was published in a Mag. 173rd Airborne, I wrote a letter to explain why I wrote it. If you can fit the 1st par and last - It would be appropriate; [a.] Roselle, IL

BOPP, CLEO
[b.] September 1, 1927, Texas; [p.] Sol and Eula Mae

Murray; [m.] Fred Bopp, May 6, 1945; [ch.] Peggy Sue Lindquist, Helen Elaine Leslie; [ed.] High School; [occ.] Housewife; [hon.] Written for my second grandson Joe Leslie; [oth. writ.] Stories fot my grandsons and poems for them; [pers.] I enjoy writing children's stories.

BORENSTEIN, SHERRI
[b.] July 8, 1978, Bronx, NY; [p.] Enid Borenstein; [ed.] Attending Lehman High School. In Sophomore Year.; [hon.] 1st place in Honors Sophomore English class for my poem. Essay contest winner twice.; [oth. writ.] A Tear, Love Hurts, A Place To Go, A Listener, Love Is Stronger Than Pride, Breaking Up Is Not Easy, Spring Days, Tell Me, A Pain That Never Goes Away; [pers.] If pain is hurting you write about it, if you can't talk about it.; [a.] Bronx, NY

BOSIACKI, EILEEN
[b.] January 30, 1964, Bethesda, MD; [p.] Vernon and Majorie Dempsey; [m.] Richard Eric Bosiacki, December 16, 1983; [ch.] Jackie Dee, Angela Marie, Richard Eric Jr., Logan Raynor; [ed.] Richard Montgomery High School; [occ.] Homemaker; [pers.] Thank you Mom. I love you.; [a.] Jacksonville, FL

BOSWELL, BRANDY M.
[b.] February 14, 1979, Enterprise, AL; [p.] Margit Boswell; [occ.] Student; [hon.] Honor Roll; [pers.] Like to write about the world around me; [a.] Houston, TX

BOWER, MICHAEL W.
[b.] February 19, 1952, Denver, CO; [p.] Don Bower, Louise Bower; [m.] Patricia Bower, March 22, 1975; [ch.] Brooke and Casey; [ed.] University of Colorado, Masters in Architecture; [occ.] Architect; [oth. writ.] 5 Self Published books of Poetry: Scraps and Pieces, Conscious Balance, Smell the Wind, Entangled Chapters, Planetary Air; [pers.] I write to help reconcile my emotions with my experience, but I never let writing become more important than either.; [a.] Sedona, AZ

BOWERS-BRADSHAW, GLORIA P.
[pen.] Penny Bennington; [b.] August 31, 1938, NJ; [p.] W. James and Dorothy Daniels; [m.] Alexander McKinley, December 8, 1990; [ch.] Raymond, Adrianne; [ed.] East Orange U.S. Vocational High School, One year College - Private Piano Student 10 yrs.; [occ.] Freelance Writer; [memb.] Messiah Baptist Church; [hon.] Piano Awards - Certified publication from the National Library of Poetry recognized as "Flower of the month in my (membership) Church February 1995; [pers.] I make a positive statement or declaration when and wherever I feel I am able to achieve a positive reaction. Let us melt down the negative and give structure to the positive in our own little space.; [a.] Avenel, NJ

BOYLE, BRENDAN J.
[pen.] Boyle; [b.] May 28, 1975, Holyoke, MA; [p.] Kevin and Elizabeth Boyle; [ed.] Holyoke Catholic H.S., Holyoke Community College, Quinnipiac College; [occ.] Student; [memb.] Play College Baseball, Play Bass for Hardcore, Funk Band, Frosty Neutral Zone.; [hon.] In Who's Who among American High School Students; [oth. writ.] This is first publication, but writing a book in order to be published.; [pers.] Thanks to everyone, don't let anyone restrict your train of thought, speak your mind. And most important "Be True To Yourself, and you will never fall".; [a.] East Hampton, MA

BRADEN, ESTHER MAYE ROSE
[b.] August 21, 1930, Lawrence, KS; [p.] Harrison and Mary Rose; [m.] Charles J. Braden, October 18, 1978; [ch.] I have four son's and two daughter - Husband has five children; [ed.] High School and Nursing, LPN,; [occ.] Retired; [memb.] Luthern Church, American Nurses Association; [oth. writ.] Lots of poems and non-published, one song copywrited; [pers.] No matter what you got in life, be the best that you can be.; [a.] Topeka, KS

BRADFIELD, KEITH DAVID
[b.] November 3, 1957, Batavia, NY; [p.] David and Jeanette Bradfield; [ch.] Jessica, Justin, Jason; [ed.] High School; [memb.] Marine Corps Officers Club; [hon.] Two Presidential Accommodations, honor graduate of Paris Is. Drill instructor school, and numerous others awards from the Marine Corps.; [pers.] "Righteousness Shall Prevail" inspired by Psalms 94 - if you treat the people and occurrences that enter your life in a truthful and righteous manner you know in your heart you have done no one any harm.; [a.] Havelock, NC

BRADSHAW, JANICE
[b.] December 20, 1951, Donalsonville, GA; [p.] Durell Buckhalter, Jewell Buckhalter; [m.] Al Bradshaw, May 13, 1973; [ch.] Teresa Bradshaw; [pers.] A child is a miracle of love. Look at the world through the eyes of a child, and a smile will appear.; [a.] Lawrenceville, GA

BRAGG, GLIDYS
[pen.] Gigi Bragg; [b.] September 14, Elyria, OH; [p.] Robert and Irene Heath, Charles and Imogene Bell; [ch.] David, Tammie, Julie, Arnold and Christine; [ed.] (Oberlin H.S. grad.) Police Aux School, Kipton Wakeman and Lorain Co Sheriff. Lorain Co. Comm. College - 3 1/2 yrs; [occ.] Independent Freelance Writer.; [memb.] American Legion.; [hon.] Camden Memorial Day Poetry Winner - 1994, Pannel for reconstruction of the Chronicle Telegram 1993, Honor Select Student Famous Writers School 1991; [oth. writ.] Local Column - Oberlin News, Local Correspondent Lorain Journal Letter to the Editor, Chronicle Telegram - 10, Lorain Journal 8 and Cleveland Plane dealer - 2; [pers.] No American novel, no Pulitzer Prize, just to tough people. Lonely for a moment, with words that make a difference to their lives.; [a.] Amherst, OH

BRANNAN, LEA
[pen.] Bebe Brannan; [b.] Manhattan; [ch.] Richard and Peter; [ed.] High School Huntington, N.Y., University of Miami, FL; [occ.] Retired, Art Dealer; [pers.] Raised on the North shore of Long Island. I have been writing prose and poetry since college but have never attempted publication. Hopefully this is just the beginning. I have lived in London for Twelve years and traveled extensively for many years. For this reason, I have a wealth of knowledge and experience from which I can draw and will enjoy putting them on paper.; [a.] Delmar, CA

BRANNON, GENEVIEVE ANNE
[pen.] Genny; [b.] March 19, 1948, Gadsden, AL; [p.] H. K. Downey, Mrs. Clyde Hodges; [m.] Wayne Brannon, June 15, 1973; [ch.] Derryl Brannon; [occ.] Domestic Engineer - Poet - Artist; [memb.] Active Member of Pascagoula Church of God; [oth. writ.] Several poems aired on local Gospel Radio Station, Interviewed on local ABC-TV poem published in "20th Century's Greatest Poems"; [pers.] I believe that my poems are my gift from God - meant to be shared.; [a.] Pascagoula, MS

BREWER, LANA
[pen.] Lana (Foltz) Brewer; [b.] December 21, 1941, Lansing, MI; [p.] Paul and Cleda Foltz; [m.] Divorced; [ed.] Randy, Debbie, Rachelle, Sherie, Stacy Reynolds; [occ.] Lansing Eastern High, Lansing Community College; [memb.] First Presbyterian Church; [hon.] High School Class Officers.; [oth. writ.] I have written several poem's as I crossed the road is my first poem I have let be known.; [pers.] I am a philosopher by nature my grandfather wrote a lot of poetry. One was published in a local newspaper. I have aunts and cousins that write. My love for life has, influenced my writing.; [a.] Lansing, MI

BREWER, NELL SHELTON
[b.] February 28, 1923, Memphis, TN; [p.] Roy P. and Lucille N. Shelton; [m.] Deceased; [ch.] Kay Lynn Beeman and Brenda Nell Kintigh; [ed.] 12 Grade; [occ.] Retired; [memb.] Gibson United Methodist Church Vicksburg, MS: Hospice Foundation, Salvation Army Auxiliary, American Assoc., Retired Persons, National Assoc., Retired Federal Employees.; [hon.] Several for outstanding work at previous work place - Waterways Experiment Station (US Army Engineers), Vicksburg, MS; [oth. writ.] Devotional books for local church; [pers.] Love people, nature and God's beautiful handiwork.; [a.] Vicksburg, MS

BREYMEYER, JUDY ANN
[pen.] Judy Washburn Breymeyer; [b.] April 11, 1945, Decatur, IL; [p.] Helen Eileen Brown, Jewell Washburn (Deceased), Floyd Clark (Step Dad); [ch.] One son; [ed.] Partial College; [occ.] Artist and Administrative Traffic Clerk; [hon.] Various Art Awards; [oth. writ.] Several Unpublished Poems; [pers.] Positive expression helps us understand the miracle of life!; [a.] Edmond, OK

BRIGHT, DOLORES G.
[pen.] Dolly; [b.] March 10, 1936, Kuikuihaele, HI; [p.] Silverio and Fely Gangano; [m.] Roger T. Bright Sr., July 4, 1959; [ch.] Debra Gail Kalani Staples, Kimberly Ann Kekapulani Nahale, Roger Theodore Bright Jr., TamiRene Leiahola Gutina; [ed.] August Ahrens Elementary School, Student Squadron, Waipahu High School, Aircraft Control, and Warning School - Biloxi MI. Keesler AFB, Hawaiian Studies - DOE, Institute of Children Literature; [occ.] Self-employed - Silk Flowers Business in my home.; [memb.] Na Wai Wai 'O Leeward, Pu'uloa Hawaiian Civic Club; [hon.] WAF of the year 1955, Nassau Country, Long Island NY., Silver Medal Award for poems submitted in "The World of Poetry"; [oth. writ.] I have written poems of my youth, religious poems, songs, short stories fiction about Hawaiian Tales and others of reading for ages 5 through 12. My poem - "Always won the Silver Medal Award.; [pers.] Edgar Allan Poe "The Raven" and "Annabelle Lee", John Milton - "Paradise Lost", Maya Angelou, Read her poem during Pres. Clinton's inauguration are a few at the poets that have inspired me. I would like to dedicate my poem: "All Of My Children" to the student's I had at Manana Elem. School, Pearl City, Hawaii.; [a.] Waianae, HI

BRINKLY, MELISSA ANN
[b.] June 2, 1974, Forest Grove, OR; [p.] Terry Harris and Dale Korpi; [m.] John Darin Brinkly, September 25, 1993; [ed.] Forest Grove High School, Business Computer Training Institute; [occ.] General Clerk, First Consumers National Bank; [pers.] I believe that with faith and persistence anything in life is possible, which I try to express in my writing. I am greatly inspired by my hus-

band, who encourages me to strive for perfection.; [a.] Tualatin, OR

BRITTON, OWEN R.
[pen.] R. Machque; [b.] September 25, 1926, Lansing, MI; [p.] Cecil Britton, Anne Britton; [m.] Patricia E. Britton, June 19, 1949; [ch.] Diana Lynn, Walter Riley, Mark, Loran, Ralph Craig, Nora Michell; [ed.] Lakeview and Climax High School Some corses at Kellogg Community College, Battle Creek, Mich.; [occ.] Retired Papermaker.; [memb.] B.S.A., Camp Fire.; [hon.] Silver Beaver, B.S.A. Luther Halsey Gulic Award, Camp Fire.; [oth. writ.] Book of poems (unpublished) three short stories also unpublished.; [pers.] It is my wish to reflect and bring to the public eye the 'Goodness' of the Culture of the indigenous people, the Native Americans of this great land. My life has been greatly influenced by 'The Beautiful People' and their culture.; [a.] Battle Creek, MI

BRITTON, TERRI
[b.] April 9, 1954, Bowling Green, KY; [p.] Anna Montgomery, Robert Tinsley; [m.] Dennis Britton, June 7, 1991; [ch.] Cheridan Ann, Tiffany Lynnette; [ed.] Warren East High, Bowling Green, KY.; [occ.] Corporate Administration Assistant - First National Bank - Kokomo, IN.; [memb.] Member of Beulah Land Church; [pers.] I feel my writing is a God given talent. My goal is to give Him all the glory and praise - and to serve Him with all my mind, heart and soul; [a.] Kokomo, IN

BROADBENT, SAVANNAH SHEENA-MARIE
[b.] January 30, 1986, Newport, NY; [p.] Frank and Heidi Broadbent; [a.] Newport, NY

BROOKS, KIMBERLY O'DONNELL
[b.] June 12, 1974, Delaware County, PA; [p.] Barbara A. Kiger and Daniel J. O'Donnell; [m.] Brian Edward Brooks, April 29, 1993; [ch.] Brian Jr. and Leah-Marie; [ed.] G.E.D. - Cora Neuman; [occ.] Full-time mom; [pers.] I encourage anyone who has a hard time sharing their feelings Pick up a pen and write it down. You would be surprised at the accomplishment it would make.; [a.] Philadelphia, PA

BROOMFIELD, CEDRIC
[b.] December 14, 1971, Los Angeles, CA; [p.] Clarence L. Broomfield Jr., and Etharine Broomfield; [ed.] Westchester High, El Camino College, and University of California, Los Angeles; [occ.] Aspiring Writer; [memb.] N.A.A.C.P.; [hon.] 1992 Mildred C. McCord Memorial Scholarship Recipient.; [pers.] I hope that my poetry will always convey truth and positively affect the lives of readers.; [a.] Inglewood, CA

BROSS, PATRICIA A.
[b.] September 10, 1953, Fayetteville, NC; [p.] Mr. David Paone, Mr. and Mrs. Ralph Hintz; [m.] Nelson Bross, July 6, 1974; [ch.] Alecia Arlene; [ed.] Lakeland Comm. College A.D.N., University of Phoenix B.S.N.; [occ.] Registered Nurse, Critical Care; [memb.] Nursing Scholarship: Why I wanted to be a nurse. Awarded by AMVETS Post 109 Mentor-on-the-Lake, Ohio.; [pers.] To help and nurture others is the greatest gift we can give to ourselves. This poem is dedicated to my family, friends, patients, and peers. A special appreciation and dedication to the AMVETS Post 109 for their generosity.; [a.] Mentor, OH

BROTHERTON, SHANNON
[b.] March 30, 1969; [p.] Ray Doolin, Candace Rhodes; [ch.] Sasha Rae Brotherton, Christian Michael Brotherton; [oth. writ.] Many poems dedicated to my children.; [pers.] My poetry is very heartfelt. I want the reading of my poetry to touch hearts, as it did mine.; [a.] Fenton, MO

BROUSSARD, SAUNDRA LYNN
[pen.] Lynn Tuckson; [b.] March 16, 1952, San Antonio; [p.] Clem Tuckson and Ella Anderson; [m.] Michael Broussard, June 21, 1975; [ch.] Hope Michelle; [ed.] John Martyn High and River Dale Night; [occ.] Referral Coordinator for a NMO Health Plan; [memb.] Current Student of the writers, Digest School; [pers.] All though poetry is my first love, I am also an aspiring mystery writer. I wish I could have known Agatha Christie. She's my favorite author. I have dedicated all of my work to my late brother, Michael.; [a.] Kenner, LA

BROUSSEAU, NANCY J.
[b.] Worcester, MA; [p.] Frank J. and Gertrude (Joyce) Deigman; [m.] Albert P. Brousseau; [ch.] Kevin P., Robert O., Albert P. and Kerry F. Brousseau; [ed.] Univ. of Massachusetts BA, The College of St. Rose, M.A. and Suny - The College of St. Rose, advanced accreditation in reading.; [occ.] Raise Dorset sheep teacher; [memb.] Delta Kappa Gamma, Alpha Nu Chapter, Philmont Hearth Board of Directors, Columbia - Green Reading Council, Sheep and Wool Growers Assoc. Zonmy Chairperson, Philmont Fire Aux; [oth. writ.] The Book of Common and Uncommon Fairies, the Dump Bike, Brendan's Bed, The Fish Tank Mystery; [a.] Philmont, NY

BROWN, ABI DEVILBISS
[p.] Reuben and Alma DeVilbiss; [pers.] The poem was written after hearing this very beautiful music during a personal spiritual experience.

BROWN, ALICE FAYE
[pen.] Ali; [b.] March 21, 1960, Atlantic City, New Jersey; [p.] Clifford "Robbie" and Virginia F. Roberts; [ch.] Robert J.L. Campbell, Rebecca S. Campbell; [ed.] Hueneme High School; [occ.] Full-time student; [pers.] To my mentor and the person who inspires me. Thank you and I love you, Dennis. [a.] Arcadia, CA

BROWN, BARBARA
[b.] February 10, 1943, Taylor, TX; [p.] Joe Zajicek and Sybil Mitchell; [m.] Billy Joe Brown, August 10, 1962; [ch.] Kenneth Dearing Brown; [ed.] Currently attending Sam Houston State University, Huntsville, TX. Graduate Fall '95 in Studio Art - BFA Degree; [occ.] Student, Housewife; [hon.] Dean's List, President's List, Recognization of Outstanding academic record at a Honors Convocation held at Sam Houston State University, Huntsville, TX on April 30, 1995.; [oth. writ.] I have entered the contest last year and my poem was accepted for publication, however, when the book was published The Space Between, I was told my poem "A Poem to Inhale" was in advertenly left out.; [pers.] I feel one should nurture their creative energies and therefore bring joy to themselves as well as others.; [a.] Spring, TX

BROWN, EMELDA J.
[b.] April 3, 1931, North Orleans, LA; [p.] Emanuel Smith, Anaise Valcour; [m.] Manuel Brown, July 31, 1952; [ch.] Emandaline Kelley, Dwan Brown Manuel III, Timothy Brown, Inez Chubb; [ed.] Vallejo High School, Vallejo Jr. College, Vallejo, Cal. Spokane Falls Comm. College, Kinsman Business College, Spokane, WA; [occ.] Homemaker; [memb.] Links Inc. Spokane Chapter, Women of Washington Water Power; [hon.] Honorable Mentions, A certificate from a poetry contest in Washington State, Dean's List from Spokane Comm. College; [oth. writ.] Several articles and poems in Calvary Bap. Church News. Several poems Published in "Linking Together In Love"; [pers.] There is much beauty all around us, we just have to open our eye to see it. My work is a reflection of my experiences of my past, present and future. Its about nature and the elements that exist in the world, thoughts that I remember of family, friends and also my heritage.; [a.] Spokane, WA

BROWN, JOSEPH E.
[b.] May 31, 1965, Westover AFB, MA; [p.] Mr. William Brown, Mrs. Ann B. Kelley, Mr. Terry Kelley; [m.] Patricia Ann, October 7, 1995; [ed.] Hampton High School; [oth. writ.] Extensive Collection in my own library.; [pers.] My inspiration is love, with my wifes' help I will be able to continue my hobby.; [a.] Hampton, VA

BROWN, JUANITA T.
[b.] March 3, 1943, Milton, DE; [p.] George Thompson, Thelma Thompson; [m.] Thurman R. Brown Sr. (Deceased), March 24, 1963; [ch.] Thurman Jr. and Pamela Gordon; [ed.] Central Commercial High School, American Institute of Banking; [memb.] Shaw Temple A.M.E. Zion Church, N.A.C.P., Women's Auxiliary, Prayer Band. International Black Writers Conference, National Authors Registry; [hon.] Amherst Society-Poetic Achievement; [oth. writ.] Poem published in local newspaper, N.Y. Amsterdam News, "Amy's Birthday."; [pers.] During my bereavement period for my late husband, the ford restored my talent to write about the human conditions existing today. A poem to me represents a frozen picture of words of any event that can stimulate and enhance our knowledge of others and ourselves.; [a.] North Babylon, NY

BROWN, LINDA N.
[b.] July 8, 1945, Snowflake, AZ; [p.] Charles Perkins, Ina Perkins; [m.] Ernest A. Brown, July 12, 1963; [ch.] Theresa Lynn, Melissa Doreen; [ed.] Cortez High, Glendale Community College; [occ.] Publications, advertising, Arizona Medical Association; [oth. writ.] Several Poems; [a.] Glendale, AZ

BROWN, MATT
[pen.] Matt Brown; [b.] December 19, 1979, Dover, DE; [p.] Gordon Brown; [m.] Searching; [ed.] Middletown High School; [memb.] Football team R.O.T.C., Drill and Color Guard teams; [hon.] Biggest Pearl Jam Fan; [pers.] "People write letters, hoping you can fix, everything for them." Eddie Vedder lead singer for Pearl Jam; [a.] Odessa, DE

BROWN, REBECCA L.
[b.] October 7, 1976, Oakland, CA; [p.] Thomas and Vicki Brown; [ed.] Currently attended at California State University at Northridge; [oth. writ.] Personal poetry collection; [pers.] Without expression through poetry, my life would be full of insights that could not be comprehended in any other form. When you view everything in a twisted manner, paper is the only haven for your thoughts to inhabit.; [a.] Palmdale, CA

BROWN, WALTER C.
[ed.] Stanford University, Arizona State University, San Francisco State Poetry Writers Workshop; [hon.] Graduating Class Poet, Stanford University, honored with Emmy by Southwestern Area, NATAS.; [oth. writ.] Published in several anthologies of poetry by National Li-

brary, World of Poetry, Threepenny Press, and others.; [pers.] As the world sinks to its lowest common denominator for literacy, only true poetry can top the vein to our souls.; [a.] Bakersfield, CA

BRULEY, LAURIER
[pen.] Laurier Bruley; [b.] July 4, 1968, Heidelberg, West Germany; [p.] Andre Bruley, Melanie Bruley; [m.] Jo Bruley, January 14, 1988; [ch.] Daniel, Micheal, Candace; [pers.] Most of our problems emanate from within ourselves. No one has the power to change life but you do have the power to change how life affects you.; [a.] Desert Hot Springs, CA

BRUNETTE, RACHELLE E.
[b.] August 10, 1981, Lansing; [p.] Mark and Janette Brunette; [ed.] I'm currently in 7th grade at Grand Ledge Hayse Middle School; [occ.] Student; [memb.] Mount Hope Church Youth Alive; [hon.] Academic Awards; [a.] Grand Ledge, MI

BRUNSON, SHARON L.
[b.] December 29, 1955, Fort Pierce, FL; [p.] Charles and Catherine Killings; [m.] Terrence N. Brunson Sr., June 12, 1993; [ch.] Kelvin, Terrence, Tamyka Brunson; [ed.] Two years in College; [occ.] U.S. Army; [oth. writ.] Non-published, My Mother, My Friend, Forgotten Father, Look Inside, Slice of Sunshine, Believe, The Perfect World, and What is a Parent and many more.; [a.] Fort Pierce, FL

BRUSSOW, CLEO
[b.] June 22, 1918, Key West, FL; [p.] Dr. Wm. Kemp, Hazel Kemp; [m.] James Brussow, January 6, 1950; [ch.] Bonnie Lew Prevatt, Kim Fredrick Brussow; [ed.] Key West High School, Florida State University; [occ.] Retired School Teacher; [memb.] Deltona Christian and Missionary Alliance Church; [pers.] I believe God put animals and trees on the earth for us to tend and care for. What other heritage can we leave for our children? My strong faith in God is my inspiration for all I do.; [a.] DeBary, FL

BRYAN, SHEENA LEE
[b.] June 2, 1982, Chattanooga, TN; [p.] Bates and Rosemarie Bryan; [ch.] Captain Ian Bryan, Rebecca Bryan; [ed.] 6th Grade; [occ.] 6th grader - Signal Mountain Middle School; [memb.] Cross Country Team, Mountain Biking Club, Green Cove Camp

BRYANT, LEANDRA HILL
[b.] November 14, 1969, Carbondale, IL; [p.] David Hill, Martha Hill; [m.] Russell M. Bryant, December 15, 1987; [ch.] Lucas Matthew Bryant, Holly Leanna Bryant; [memb.] Pleasant Hill, Christian Church; [pers.] This poem was inspired by Helen Merritt, Eldon Bryant, and Bethany Hull; [a.] Murphysboro, IL

BRYCE, ROSALIND Y.
[ed.] Bachelor of Arts (B.A) (Hons.), Masters in Library Science (M.L.S.), University of Toronto, Canada, Faculty of Information Studies (F.I.S.) Toronto, Canada; [occ.] Librarian; [memb.] Ontario Library Association, Toronto, Canada; [pers.] "Poetry Cements That Moment In Time"

BUCKARD, JOHN
[b.] July 20, 1974, Miami, FL; [p.] John and Lois Buckard; [ed.] Coral Shores High School, Currently attending Valencia Community College; [occ.] Student; [oth. writ.] I've had several poems published in my high school newspaper.; [pers.] I portray my feelings and appreciation the beauty of life, love, and nature through my poems. I've been influenced by Edgar Allan Poe, Walt Whitman, and Robert Frost.; [a.] Key Largo, FL

BUCKLER, PHILIP E.
[pen.] Phil B; [b.] March 1, 1954, La Plata, MD; [p.] Andrew and Edna Buckler; [ch.] Andrea and Analyssia Buckler; [oth. writ.] I constantly play with pen and paper; [pers.] This poem dedicated to my mother who at 79 years young is my best friend. She is always very loving and worked very hard to raise 17 children.; [a.] Oklahoma City, OK

BUCKLEY, JAMES
[b.] June 16, 1953, Brooklyn; [p.] Harry and Alberta Buckley; [ed.] High School Marist College - for one year; [occ.] Contractor; [oth. writ.] I have started writing a book,... but as of yet I still don't know if I am a good enough writer; [pers.] We are all seekers, each one searching for somethings. Seek out truth, and wisdom, which will protect you like a sheltered cloth. Then go forth in your travels and have patients.

BUCKLEY, MICHAEL M.
[b.] August 4, 1980, Philadelphia, PA; [p.] Nancy and Dennis Buckley; [ed.] St. Christopher's Grade School, Archbishop Ryan High School; [occ.] First Honors Student at Archbishop Ryan High School; [hon.] Student of the Month, First Honors-Archbishop Ryan High School, Second Honors-Archbishop Ryan, Parvoli Dei Award-Boy Scouts of America; [a.] Philadelphia, PA

BUDD, CAROLYN J.
[b.] April 29, 1929, Chicago, IL; [ch.] Cliff, Leah, Rhonda, 1 granddaughter - Cory; [occ.] Retired; [pers.] I like to see only the good in people and feel that God never gives you more than you can handle.; [a.] Woodridge, IL

BUECHLER, BETH ANN
[b.] January 1, 1981, Jasper; [p.] Marilyn and Wilfred Buechler; [ed.] Attending Forest Park Jr.-Sr. High School; [hon.] I have a 4.0 average and was invited to read my poetry at the Ohio River Arts Festival.; [oth. writ.] "One Way Or Another" and "Flower's Dew"; [pers.] I believe you shouldn't lock up talent because you may lose the key!; [a.] Huntingburg, IN

BURKE, CHRISTINE
[pen.] Christine Burke; [b.] June 11, 1979, NJ; [p.] Pat and Frank Burke; [ed.] Currently a sophomore, at Paramus Catholic H. S.; [oth. writ.] Many other poems not published

BURKE, RUBY J.
[b.] August 30, 1914, Kanabec, MN; [p.] Joseph Gruver, Gladys Gruver; [m.] Goodwin E. Burke, June 20, 1934; [ch.] Bruce E., Wallace E., Joseph A., Gerald G.; [memb.] Northwest Baptist Church, Denver, CO, American Quilter's Society, Lifetime member of Annual Conifer, Co., Arts and Crafts Fair.; [hon.] Salutatorian, 1927 (2 tied) Kanabec County, MN, 8th grade graduating class. Valedictorian of 1932 Oglivie, MN. High School graduating class.; [pers.] I always loved poetry. As a child I memorized massive amounts of the "masters": Longfellow, Lowell, and others, much of it I still can quote (sometimes with a little prompting); [a.] Arvada, CO

BURKS, SHIRLEY A.
[b.] April 9, 1956, Stuttgart, AR; [p.] Alvin Burks, Alleam Burks; [ch.] Cornelius Burks, Takeysha P. Jones; [ed.] Roosevelt High School, Gary, IN; [occ.] Nurse Aide

BURNS, DAVID
[pen.] Diane Docktor; [b.] Calgary, Alberta, Canada; [p.] Cecelia Molaison; [m.] Bobbie Docktor; [ed.] B.A. Political Science - Calgary 1978, B.Ed. Social Sciences - Calgary 1980, M.A. Curriculum Design - Simon Fraser 1993; [occ.] Steel Buyer; [memb.] 1. Calgary Political Science Alumni Forum, 2. Perpetual Animooooolism Society, 3. American Educational Research Association; [hon.] 1. Valedictorian - 1974, 2. Honorary Membership St. Francis Hockey Heroes - 1988, 3. Distinguished Teacher Award - Calgary 1994.; [oth. writ.] Thesis: Rotating Teaching Models.

BURNS, MARCIA
[b.] August 17, 1949, Tennessee; [p.] Lawrence and Hazel Frady; [m.] Michael Burns, June 8, 1968; [ch.] Stephanie Michelle, Stephen Michael (grandson-Christopher Michael); [ed.] Milton Union High School; [occ.] Homemaker; [pers.] I write for personal enjoyment.; [a.] Piqua, OH

BURTON, GRACE
[b.] March 18, 1950, CA; [p.] John Weiss, Joyce Orr; [m.] John A. Makarewich, September 28, 1985; [ch.] John, Maureen, Eileen; [ed.] Jr. CSUN - Psych. Certified Hypotherapist.; [occ.] Writer; [memb.] AAA, C or Club.; [hon.] Ph. D. Hypotherapy L.N.U. HI. USA.; [oth. writ.] (Unpublished): The Silent Tribe, In The Valley Of The Alpha Wolf; [pers.] The truth is often brutle.; [a.] Simi Valley, CA

BURTON, SCOTT A.
[pen.] Gregory Charlston; [b.] October 20, 1958, Richmond Hill, NY; [p.] Mr. William N. Burton, Mrs. Lucille E. Burton; [ed.] 12th Grade Education Hempstead High School Long Island, New York; [occ.] Food Service The "Grocery Store"; [pers.] The world as we know it, Society as we feel it, People as we see them. My life, myself, my family and friends, they are my content.; [a.] Richmond, VA

BURTON, VICKI
[b.] March 14, 1925, Gulford, CT; [p.] Angelo Benzi, Rosa Benzi; [m.] Elwood Burton, March 20, 1948; [ch.] Lisa Lee and Scott Douglas; [ed.] Guilford High; [occ.] Retired; [pers.] This is my first poem. One day I was thinking of Emily and of how fast she is growing up. My thoughts of her inspired me to write this to let her know how very much her grandfather and I love her. We gave it to her on her third birthday.; [a.] Madison, CT

BUSARI, OLALEKAN IDRIS
[pen.] Lakeside; [b.] April, 19, 1970, Nigeria; [p.] Mr. and Mrs. L. F. Busari; [ed.] Loyola College, Ibadan, Nigeria. University of Ibadan, Ibadan Nigeria.; [occ.] Computer professional (Programmer); [pers.] I want to know the meaning and purpose of man's existence and have inner peace if possible, though I doubt if we can really know why we are here.; [a.] Dayton, OH

BUSBY, BROOKE K.
[b.] October 20, 1977, Salisburg, NC; [m.] Rudy and Karen Busby; [ed.] Graduate Charoltte Country Day School, 1995 Attending Duke University '95-'99; [occ.] Student; [hon.] National Honor Society, Headmasters

List, Pearl S. Buck Award Cum Laude Society, Volleyball Coach's Award.; [a.] Salisbury, NC

BUSTER I, ADAM A.
[b.] July 28, 1965, Queens, NY; [p.] Joseph Sr. and Barbara; [m.] Darlene A., September 17, 1993; [ch.] Shaniqwa (4), Adam (3), Kyle (1); [ed.] BS in Special Education; [occ.] Special Education Teacher for state of CT.; [oth. writ.] A dozen poems that have never been published but are on display in my poetry library.; [pers.] I strive to capture lifes realities in my poetry. My goal is to have my writings provoke thought while supplying clear cut meaning to the reader.; [a.] Ansonia, CT

BUTCHER, HUBERT M.
[pen.] H. Maxwell Butcher; [b.] May 22, 1924, Nairobi, Kenya; [p.] Rev. Hubert and Elizabeth Butcher; [m.] Eva, December 9, 1955; [ch.] Five; [ed.] M.A. (CANTAB) B.D. (Trinity Coll., Toronto) D. Min (San Francisco Theological Seminary); [occ.] Retired Minister; [oth. writ.] Novels: "I Adam" "Rescue At Harper's Landing" (for children) others unpublished. "Story As Away To God - A Guide For Story Tellers"; [a.] Sorrento British Columbia, Canada

BUTLER, JUDITH
[b.] September 24, 1939, Kansas City, KS; [p.] Theodore Chambers, Willa Chambers; [m.] William Butler, October 25, 1958; [ch.] Matthew Scott Butler, Susan Kathleen Butler; [ed.] Argentine High School Kansas City, KS, taken few classes - Penn Valley College, Kansas City, MO; [occ.] Infant Care Giver Creative World School - Independence, MO; [memb.] Six Mile Baptist Church North Shore Animal League, American Heart Association; [pers.] I have spent most of my adult life in a wooded rural area and have developed a deep love for nature. I hope to express this love in future writings. My favorite poet is Emily Dickinson.; [a.] Independence, MO

BUTLER, REIDA
[b.] October 4, 1963, Chadbourn, NC; [p.] Edward and Shirley Butler; [ed.] West Columbus High, Cerro Gordo NC, Southern Pines Comm. College N.C., Saint Petersburg Vo. Tech/SPJC, FL.; [occ.] Nurse, Student of Martial Arts; [oth. writ.] Published in School Newspapers; [pers.] I believe that love and dreams have no boundaries - Romance is in the heart and soul.; [a.] Saint Petersburg, FL

BUXTON, WILLIAM H.
[b.] September 15, 1947, Laurel, MS; [p.] Matt and Emma Buxton; [m.] Gloria, July 14, 1979; [ch.] Byron, Darryl, Isaac; [ed.] Port Clinton H.S., Terra Technical College; [occ.] Graphic Communication; [pers.] I believe God created mankind to strive for excellence. While attaining his goals he must continue to reach out with a willing heart to help othesr.; [a.] Lorain, OH

BYERS, ERIN MICHELLE
[b.] December 14, 1985, Charlotte, NC; [p.] Constance M. Byers, Carl L. Byers Jr.; [ed.] Third Grade Student; [memb.] Studies Gymnastics; [hon.] AB Honor Roll; [oth. writ.] Enjoys writing poems; [a.] Raleigh, NC

CACILHAS, SANDRA M.
[pen.] Sandy; [b.] March 6, 1978, Windsor, Ontario, Canada; [p.] Daniel and Margaret Cacilhas; [ed.] Attending Harrow District High School and I will be graduating in "96".; [hon.] Received the National Authors Registry Honorable Mention Award from Iliad Press.; [oth. writ.] Two other poems have been chosen to be published in hard covered books through other publishers.; [pers.] I enjoy writing because it is a good way for me to release some of the feelings I have towards certain circumstances. I have been greatly influenced by my mother, and her life spent working hard.; [a.] Harrow Ontario, Canada

CADDLE, PETER C.
[pen.] Sir Collinsworth; [b.] November 1, 1959, Barbados; [p.] John Caddle and Clorilda Waterman; [ch.] Christopher D. Caddle, Aishah Yaasmiyn Caddle; [ed.] H. S. Graduate; [occ.] Security Guard, Barnard College N.Y. N.Y.; [memb.] Fifteen years a member of the U. S. Marine Corps; [pers.] "Don't advertise it, if it's not on sale", "Don't tease thee animals if you're not going to feed them."; [a.] Brooklyn, NY

CAGLE, ZELMA D.
[b.] September 30, 1963, Richmond Hts; [p.] Walter and Myrtle Cagle; [ed.] High School graduate, Technical School, some college; [occ.] Waitress; [hon.] Editors choice award from National Library of Poetry; [oth. writ.] Angels; [pers.] My poem is a reflection of my spirituality and beliefs. God is my rock and fortress.; [a.] Medina, OH

CAINE, ANNETTE LEE-ANNE WILLIAMSEN
[b.] February 6, 1963, Port Alberni, BC; [p.] Barri and Margaret Williamsen; [m.] Melvin Edward Caine, January 2, 1982; [ch.] Naomi Yael Louise age 11, Benjamin Ezra Woods Age 9; [ed.] Qualicim Beach High School support worker, Residential resource for mentally ill adults, trained child care worker, Residential Resource for Mentally Ill Adults, Trained Children worker.; [occ.] Support worker, Child care worker with outistic child.; [memb.] British Columbia Federation of foster parents association. Past President and member of Provincial Ethics Committee.; [oth. writ.] Poems and a children's book presently trying to have published.; [pers.] I am committed to the pursuit of pureness in writing from the heart. We all have something to offer as a gift to our Earth mother, mine just happens to be in writing from the heart.

CAIRES, MICHAEL JOHN
[b.] June 28, 1951, Hawaii; [p.] Daniel and Mary Caires; [m.] Jennifer Ann Carvalho, March 9, 1991; [ed.] University of Hawaii (Bachelor Fine arts/ Graphic design).; [occ.] Police Officer (Domestic Violence Unit) Also freelance artist/craftsman; [pers.] The celebration of living encircles good and evil, harmony and discord. Infused in the blend are the virtues of hope and love... Always hope and love.; [a.] Makawao, HI

CALCAGNO, PATRICIA DUGGAN
[b.] March 7, 1931, Reading, PA; [p.] James and Mabel Duggan; [m.] Anthony J. Calcagno, November 27, 1948; [ch.] Carol, Anthony Jr., Philip, Angela; [occ.] Grandmother and Great-grandmother; [pers.] I would personally like to thank my daughters Angela and Carol, my daughter-in-law Cindy, and cousin Doris, and my neighbor Jen for all their love and encouragement. The source of my poetry comes from my family and friends — you are my life, my "Heart".

CALDER, LISA K.
[pen.] Lisa Rutledge Calder; [b.] December 27, 1961, Beaumont, TX; [p.] Albert and Barbara Rutledge; [m.] James H. Calder, December 31, 1992; [ed.] Vidor High School; [occ.] R&R Enterprises Family Embroidery Business; [hon.] National Honor Society - Ecology Awards; [oth. writ.] Several poems printed in local newspapers. I have written slogans for different companies. I like to write poetry for special occasions, anniversaries, birthdays etc.; [pers.] I feel that in my line of work, each item I embroider is personal and reflects on that individual and it is the same in poetry. Each poem I write is very personal. This one was for my one year anniversary to my husband.; [a.] Vidor, TX

CALHOUN, JAMES BRIAN
[b.] April 12, 1969, Van Zandt Co., TX; [ed.] Kaufman High, Richland College A.A., University of North Texas B.A.; [occ.] Musician, Songwriter; [memb.] Dallas Songwriters Association; [hon.] Sigma Tau Delta; [oth. writ.] Include many songs performed either solo or by local acts and several poetic works in progress; [pers.] I have found alot of comfort in the words of others. As a result, I attempt to record my experiences so that someone else who sees the same things many not feel quite so alone. There is a great kinship in shared experience.; [a.] Kaufman, TX

CALICUITT, WILMA L.
[pen.] Lea; [b.] February 14, 1951, Lubbock; [p.] Willie and Marion Pendgraft; [m.] Leroy Calicuitt Jr., June 17, 1987; [ch.] 1 daughter LaVonda McNeal and 1 grandson Shafig Richardson McNeal; [ed.] Dunbar Senior High School, vocational school: Beautician; [occ.] Therapist Technical-3 at Lubbock State School for 21 years; [memb.] Church of the Living God, Motto C.W.F.F., Temple #92.; [hon.] Employee of the Month - February 1983; [oth. writ.] Panther's Jammin', How Will You Love Me and One Wish; [pers.] I enjoy writing poetry, and dramatizing religious poetry. It's my way to escape my troubles. I love working with mentally handicapped people, and spending time with my family.; [a.] Lubbock, TX

CALLAHAN, DOROTHY CROTTS
[b.] Januay 15, 1927, Lexington, NC; [p.] Mr. Edward Lee and Annie Crotts; [m.] Hobert Charles Callahan (deceased), September 22, 1948; [ch.] Donnie Ray Callahan (deceased), Randy Charles Callahan, Roger Dean Callahan; [pers.] Hobbies - Gardening and Traveling

CALLINICOS, JULIE
[b.] June 1, 1964, High Point, NC; [p.] Mr. and Mrs. Thomas Beard; [m.] Brent Callinicos, December 20, 1987; [ed.] BA in Radio, T.V., Motion Pictures-Writing Tract - The University of North Carolina at Chapel Hill, 1986; [occ.] Freelance writer, Competitive Gymnastics Coach; [memb.] United States Gymnastics Federation (USGF), People for Ethical Treatment of Animals (PETA); [hon.] Dean's List, National "Dance Masters" winner, several poems in local publications; [oth. writ.] Coverage of U.S. Olympic Festival - Greensboro News and Record; [pers.] My writing is an expression of my spirituality - an external result of my eternal world. Greatest influence: Wordsworth. Ode: Intimations of Immortality; [a.] Bellevue, WA

CAMPBELL, MAXINE ELIZABETH
[b.] February 26, Wilhurst, KY; [p.] William Holt and Janie Shackelford; [m.] Hobert Campbell, June 5, 1954; [ch.] Venita Kaye, Marc Eugene; [ed.] Ph.D in Education. Taught Elementary School in Northmont City Schools for 34 years. Instructor of Educational Seminars across U.S.; [occ.] Image/Fashion, consultant and public speaker; [memb.] NDEA, OEA, Memorial Methodist Church, Dayton Christian Women's Club, Phi Delta Kappa, International Reading Assoc., WHO Foundation (Women helping others); [hon.] Teacher of the year 1991,

Prom Queen, May Queen, Started young authors conference for students in Northmont. MS in curriculum and supervision numerous awards in image consulting; [oth. writ.] Poems for special events and individuals.; [pers.] All my writing comes from the heart. I am inspired by the beauty of nature and by individuals who have touched my life.; [a.] Dayton, OH

CAMPBELL, O'KEATHER T.
[pen.] "O.T." (Campbell); [b.] June 20, 1956, Forsyth, CO; [p.] The late Ida Mae and Herbert Thompson; [m.] Divorced; [ch.] Herbert Samuel and Sertilya Lea Vern; [occ.] Information Processing Assistant W-S, Forsyth Co., Dept. of Social Services; [memb.] Mt. Nebo TVPH Church of God, Inc., Missionary Dept.; [oth. writ.] Dance to the Tom Tom Tom; [pers.] I strive to cultivate sown seeds of our history in order to obtain a more beautiful bloom each season that we may have a better tomorrow in our Garden of Life!; [a.] Winston-Salem, NC

CAMPERLENGO, GAIL
[pen.] Amanda Gale; [b.] January 31, New York City, NY; [p.] Angelina S. and Vincent J. Camperlengo; [ed.] Pace University (NYC), New York University (NYC); [occ.] Freelance writer; [memb.] American Political Science Association, Irish American Historical Society, Professional Association of Dive Instruction (PADI); [hon.] Pace University's Dean List (4 years); [oth. writ.] Florida Keys Magazine: "A Day To Remember", Irish Echo: "Hungen Shrikes", New York Post: "In Long Kesh"; [pers.] Motto: "Keep smiling it confuses people."; [a.] Ossining, NY

CAMPO, RICHARD E.
[b.] July 6, 1929, Roswell, OH; [p.] Angelo and Mary; [m.] Mary Ann, May 26, 1973; [ch.] 4 step children, Janet, Michael, Theresa, Tracey; [ed.] High School Chadsey; [occ.] Retired; [memb.] American Legion D.A.V.; [oth. writ.] Poems just for my own amusement. This is the first one I ever send in.; [pers.] I have always enjoyed the great english poets and classical composers of Europe in the last four centuries.; [a.] Detroit, MI

CANALE, SHARON
[b.] January 17, 1980, Teaneck, NJ; [p.] Anthony Canale Jr. and Marilyn Canale; [ed.] Notre Dame Interparochial School in Palisade Park, N.J. (elementary) and Academy of the Holy Angels in Demarest, N.J. (high school); [occ.] High School Student; [hon.] 8th Grade General Excellence Award, Presidential Academic Fitness Award, and Principal's List at the Academy of the Holy Angels; [oth. writ.] Poems printed in a high school literary publication; [pers.] My poetry reflects the world as I see it, in times of both joy and sorrow. I thank my parents and friends for their constant encouragement.; [a.] Ridgefield, NJ

CANALES, CARL A.
[b.] January 27, 1972, San Antonio, TX; [p.] Mr. And Mrs. Artemio and Angelita Canales; [m.] Single; [ed.] Central Catholic Marianist High School; [occ.] Working towards a Physics degree at S.W.T.; [oth. writ.] Currently writing a medieval play I wish to publicate, and furthermore direct as a motion picture.; [pers.] Without God, I have no talent.; [a.] San Antonio, TX

CANFIELD, MEGAN
[b.] September 6, 1981, Arizona; [p.] Gerilynn Zeigler; [ed.] 7 Grade - Chaperral, Jr. High Alamogordo NM; [occ.] Student; [pers.] I would like to continue to write about the experiences I have through my life for other people and myself.; [a.] Alamogordo, NM

CANO, SYLVIA
[b.] July 5, 1970, El Paso; [p.] Maura Babb (mother); [ed.] Ysleta High School; [occ.] Secretary - Clinton Industries, Inc.; [hon.] Golden Poet Award; [oth. writ.] Sonnet on life; [pers.] Thanks to all who inspired my writings. Special thanks go to Clinton Industries, Inc. and to my mom.; [a.] El Paso, TX

CARDINAL, MARLENE MULVINA (nee Gallant)
[pen.] Marlene Mulvina; [b.] February 28, 1936, Toronto; [p.] Mabel and Albert Gallant; [m.] Leo Cardinal, May 28, 1954 (1st marriage), August 6, 1995 (2nd marriage); [ch.] Steven Mulvina, Kevin Mulvina, Ken Mulvina, Karen Brace Stan Mulvina, Mark Mulvina, Cherie Mulvina; [ed.] Grade 9, Scarborough Collegiate Institute Ontario; [occ.] Housewife, poet; [oth. writ.] I have written over 50 poems and this poem is my first to publish publicly. It was put in a pamphlet at Cana Place, the old age home where my mother lives in Toronto; [pers.] I have given poems to friends and family in their time of need. The Lord is my inspiration. I pray my work will help others in need.; [a.] Brockville Ontario, Canada

CARIKHOFF, STEVEN
[b.] December 16, 1975, Philadelphia; [p.] David and Joan Carikhoff; [ed.] Holy Ghost Preparatory School in Bensalem, PA., currently attending Saint Joseph's University in Philadelphia, PA.; [occ.] Student; [memb.] American Forensics Assoc., National Forensics Assoc., Villiger Speech and Debate Team at Saint Joseph's.; [hon.] Recipient of the Villiger Scholarship for excellence in communication skills; [oth. writ.] None published - first publication; [pers.] Seldom are my poems about people who did not enter my life. People, to me, are like leaves in autumn, they fall out of your life, but they rest at the bottom of your soul, of who you are, and give you food for thought, growth, and love.; [a.] Bensalem, PA

CARINGER, SHARON
[pen.] Sharon Rose; [b.] June 15, 1961, Sacramento, CA; [m.] Jesse Caringer; [ch.] Kandis, Ami, Kara; [ed.] Graduate of Fair Play High, Graduate of Institute for Children's Literature, San Bernadino Valley College; [occ.] Instructional Aide 3rd Grade, Newmark Elementary; [hon.] Golden Poets Award 1991, Silver Poets Award 1992; [oth. writ.] Poetry, children short stories, science fiction; [pers.] I have been writing short stories and poetry since age 12. I believe that as long as children have their imagination, there will always be new and exciting stories and poems to write; [a.] San Bernardino, CA

CARLILE, THOMAS
[pen.] Tom Carlile; [b.] May 6, 1914, Michigan; [p.] Deceased; [m.] Deceased, August 25, 1937; [ch.] Tom, Craig, Catherine; [ed.] Univ. of Michigan AB and MD; [occ.] Retired; [memb.] American Med. Assn. Pacific Science Center, Past Pres.; [hon.] Distinguished Service Award, American Cancer Society past National President; [oth. writ.] One other poem; [pers.] I write for my own satisfaction and the amusement of my friends. Being published is an additional pleasure.

CARLSON, R. GREG
[b.] January 13, 1960, Boston, MA; [p.] Robert and Dorothy Carlson; [ed.] BA, University of Florida, MLS, San Jose St. University; [occ.] Librarian; [memb.] American Library Association, American Society for Information Science, United States Chess Federation, National Federation of the Blind.; [a.] Clearwater, FL

CARLTON, CANDY
[b.] December 21, 1965, Thorton, CO; [p.] Jack and Pearl Griscko; [m.] William Carlton; [ch.] Michael, Andrea, Tearza, Jessica, and one on the way; [occ.] Foster Parent; [oth. writ.] I have several other poems my family and friends have encouraged me to try to publish. I had never tried before now.; [pers.] I have always wrote in view of life. The beginning, the ending, and all the thoughts and feelings in between; [a.] Lakewood, CO

CARMAN, ROBERT W.
[pen.] Robert Warren; [b.] January 15, 1941, Toronto, OH; [p.] Warren and Audrey Science Carman; [m.] Arlene Carman, August 18, 1962; [ch.] Rene, Christopher, Todd, Amy, Eric; [ed.] Toronto High School, Wabash College; [occ.] Senior Sales Exec., Mitel Telecommunications; [memb.] Southwest Communications Association; [oth. writ.] Local newspapers, college poetry and prose contest, college publications; [a.] Spring, TX

CARNESE, MARY
[pen.] Mari Cee; [b.] August 12, 1917, Stratton, CO; [p.] George Pautler and Louisa Rau-Pautler; [m.] Theodore Carnese, May 31, 1947; [ch.] Rosemarie, Teresa, Gregory; [ed.] Stratton High, Portland Community College; [occ.] Retired Watercolo painting and writing; [hon.] Scholarship to University of Colorado 1937; [oth. writ.] Unpublished poetry and prose; [pers.] It is better to light a candle than curse the darkness.; [a.] Portland, OR

CARPENTER, LYNNETTE
[b.] September 4, 1968, Buffalo, NY; [p.] Frank and Mary Greico; [m.] Graig Scott Carpenter, August 19, 1989; [ch.] Aimee Elizabeth Carpenter; [occ.] Mother; [memb.] N.O.R.M.L.; [pers.] I believe the secret to life is moderation; [a.] Tonawanda, NY

CARRASCO, ELAINE
[b.] July 16, 1978, Odessa, TX; [p.] Aron and Nina Carrasco; [ed.] Currently enrolled in the 11th grade at Odessa High School in Odessa, Texas.; [occ.] Part time Clerical Assistant and part-time sales Associate; [memb.] Member of Office Administration Co-op at Odessa High School. Member and currently standing treasurer for Business Professionals of America at Odessa High School; [hon.] State Qualifier for Business Professionals of America in the Computerized Accounting event. Currently enrolled in a Accounting I honors class.; [oth. writ.] A few but not published or edited.; [pers.] Don't put off what should be done today. For tomorrow may never come." The best rose-bush, after all, is not that which has the fewest thorns, but that which bears the finest roses." Henry Van Dyke; [a.] Odessa, TX

CARROLL, PEGGY M.
[b.] February 6, 1977, Fairbanks; [p.] Harry Carroll Sr. and Jessie Carroll (Grandparents); [ed.] High School Graduate of Tsuk Taih School May 1995; [occ.] EPA/ Americorps; [pers.] May this poem touch and dwell in your hearts forever. In loving memory of my dear father Harry Carroll Sr.; [a.] Chalkyitsik, AK

CARROLL, WILLIAM GREGORY
[b.] October 28, 1965, California; [p.] Pauline Carroll and Andrew Carroll; [ch.] Kalie Lauren James; [ed.] Wilson High, Mt Sal Jr. College, 5 year Union Plumbing School, P.I.P.E; [occ.] Plumber; [memb.] National Wildlife Federation; [oth. writ.] Many (unpublished); [pers.] Peace, love and happiness. If you don't have them, go get them! Now.; [a.] Prescott, AZ

CASSIDY, JOSEPH
[b.] March 20, 1930, Ireland; [m.] Marie Cassidy, October 8, 1958; [ch.] Hugh, Joseph, Michael, Patrick, John; [ed.] Bailiebedo Tech., St. Patrick's College.; [occ.] Retired; [a.] Clearwater, FL

CASTILLO, JOHN
[pen.] Apocalypse; [b.] May 30, 1978, Houston, TX; [p.] Armando B. Castillo and Ernestine O. Castillo; [ed.] Attending Franklin High School 11th Grade; [occ.] Student; [pers.] For me, my poetry are parts of dreams. The wishes, the desires for true love, and the difference between dreams and reality, but one thing you have to remember reality is what you make it!; [a.] Reisterstown, MD

CASTRO, CHRISTINE
[b.] November 4, 1969, Staten Island, NY; [ed.] High school New Dorp Staten Island, New School Culinary Arts Grad.; [occ.] Baker; [pers.] This poem was written in memory of my grandfather. The patriarch of my family, died of cancer peacefully holding my hand. Writing helped me deal with this loss. Now realizing how beautiful life and death are.; [a.] Staten Island, NY

CATCHINGS, MYRIAN ROCHELLE
[b.] March 24, 1975, Meridian, MS; [p.] Myralynn B. Catchings and Haney Catchings Jr.; [ch.] Ariest Dewayne Catchings; [ed.] Meridian High School, Alcorn St. University; [memb.] Biology Club, Honors Club, ASU Cheerleading Squad, Alpha Jewel; [hon.] Honor Roll; [a.] Newton, MS

CAVENDER, MARTHA HUMPHRIES
[pen.] Mary Humphries Cavender; [b.] August 17, 1899, Mexia, TX; [p.] Willie Johnson Humphries (mother), William Barney Humphries Sr.; [m.] John Fletcher Cavender (deceased), July 6, 1919; [ch.] Mary Fletcher Cavender; [ed.] B.A., M.A. with high honors Southern Methodist University, Dallas, TX., Reading in Bodlean Library, Oxford, England, Reading and examination at British Museum, London, England. Travel: USA incl. Hawaii, Mexico, England, France, Italy, Spain, Portugal, Germany, Austria, Bulgaria, East Germany, (under Russian occupation) Holland, and Belgium.; [occ.] Retired; [memb.] Order of Eastern Star (Worthy Matron), Alpha Theta Phi (Phi Beta Kappa provisional chapter) College Spanish Honorary; [oth. writ.] Numerous short stories, sketches, poems and one novel (unpublished).; [pers.] Whatever the odds, keep your chin up and keep on going, try to treat others the way you'd like to be treated.; [a.] Houston, TX

CAZA, THERESA
[b.] August 20, 1964, Saint Petersburg, FL; [p.] Charles G. Troy II, Theresa Troy; [m.] Garry Caza, August 21, 1988; [ch.] Terri-Lyn; [pers.] In memory of my mom eventhough you're not here today within my heart you'll always stay; [a.] Tilbury, Ontario, Canada

CEA, VINCENT
[pen.] Vincent James, James Vincent; [b.] October 14, 1947, New York, NY; [p.] Vincent Cea/Rose Cea; [m.] Carol Ann Cea, June 3, 1988; [ch.] Diane Chiofalo, grandchildren Vincent James, Joseph Paul, Nicholas Anthony, Samantha Lynn; [ed.] Theodore Roosevelt High School; [oth. writ.] Several poems that I am and will try to have them published; [pers.] I think children give life to this earth without them, this world surely has no worth. I have four grandchildren, that are precious to me and through their eyes, this world I'd see; [a.] Selden, NY

CEITHAML, LENORE A.
[b.] July 28, 1949, Chicago, IL; [ch.] Brett L. Callan; [ed.] B.A. University of Michigan, M.A. San Diego State University, J.D. Western State University, School of Law; [occ.] Attorney at Law; [pers.] Inspiration for my poetry is deeply rooted in my strong feelings for my family.; [a.] San Diego, CA

CELLO, FRANCES
[b.] May 14, 1933, Chicago; [p.] Rachel and George Maksud; [m.] John Cello, June 20, 1959; [ch.] Sandra and Cynthia Cello; [ed.] 12 Years, Waller High School - High La Salle School - Grammar; [occ.] Accounts Receivable

CEPHAS, JAMES A.
[m.] Elizabeth; [ch.] Three; [ed.] A.A.S./Respiratory therapy, B.F.A./Exp. Painting Techniques; [occ.] Registered Resp. Therapist; [memb.] NBRC, AARC, Phi-Theta-Kappa, American Heart Assoc.; [hon.] Multiple awards for portraiture, landscape painting, Phi-Theta-Kappa; [oth. writ.] A number of other poems both introspective and worldly.; [pers.] To do the best I can with each day I'm given. I have been inspired by such artists as Henry Tanner and Charles White, and poets such as Sonia Sanchez and Maya Angelou.; [a.] Philadelphia, PA

CHAMBERS, ROBERT LAWNELL
[pen.] R. Free C.; [b.] September 21, 1970, St. Joe, MO; [p.] Lois J. Jackson and Robert D. Chambers Jr.; [ed.] Rogers and Memorial High Schools (Tulsa, OK) and Central High (St. Joe, MO); [occ.] Entertainment Security Officer; [memb.] Lucky Devil Club; [hon.] Best Actor 1988, (St. Joseph Central Theater League); [oth. writ.] Shiver, creating galaxies, put forth the faith; [pers.] "Water the flowers, for you may one day need them for your grave."; [a.] Kansas City, MO

CHAMPION, LAWRENCE
[b.] February 28, 1914, Run, TX; [p.] Deceased; [m.] Deceased, September 1, 1938; [ch.] 2 sons; [ed.] B.S. Degree and Master Degree; [occ.] Retired; [memb.] None anymore - I am a methodist and teacher 4 graders; [hon.] I have many awards from "World of Poetry". Sacramento, California; [oth. writ.] Many poems in my files and home.; [pers.] I started writing poetry in High School, and I still write some as my hobby - no publishing.

CHANDLER, DOROTHY M.
[pen.] Dody; [b.] July 10, 1925, Ithaca, NY; [p.] William and Dorothy Rust; [m.] Floyd L. Chandler (deceased), November 23, 1946; [ch.] Four boys Dayril (deceased), Douglas, Steven and Scott; [ed.] Attended Dryden High School Dryden, NY; [occ.] Housewife; [memb.] A member of 24 years of the Broom County Doll Club; [a.] Endicott, NY

CHAO, NATASHA G.
[b.] May 13, 1987, Mount View, CA; [p.] Irene Kopel and Alfred Chao; [ed.] In second grade at St. Michaels University School, Victoria, B.C. Canada; [occ.] Second Grade student; [hon.] House point winner for third term 1993-1994 school year.; [oth. writ.] I just like to write.; [pers.] My parents made me move from California and I'm still not happy about it!; [a.] Victoria British Columbia, Canada

CHAPMAN, BRIAN K.
[pen.] K-Luv; [b.] November 11, 1966, Tampa, FL; [p.] Earline Chapman Turner and Levy C. Turner; [ch.] Quintavous Lendsey Chapman; [ed.] 1985 King High Grad., one year at Brewton Parker College studying sociology.; [occ.] Independent songwriter, Artist Development manager at Luv Bizarre Entertainment.; [oth. writ.] A catalog of over 300 songs and poems written over the past 3 1/2 years.; [pers.] My poems are merely reflections of the abundance of love that reign over my life. I accept them as blessings from God, and wish to share my gift with the world.; [a.] Atlanta, GA

CHAPMAN, GREG
[b.] November 9, 1964, Houston; [p.] Susie Sheffler; [ed.] BBA, Univ. of Houston; [occ.] Accountant, CPA; [memb.] Honors Program (college), Delta Sigma Di (college), Westbury Baptist Church; [hon.] National Dean's List, Golden Key for Academic Excellence, Beta Gamma Sigma Business Honors, Dale Carnegie, outstanding performance for HR team leader.; [oth. writ.] Unpublished novels, "Beyond Deadzone", "In Search of Doomsday," "Who shall be God."; [pers.] I am a Christian. My Christian beliefs intensified a previously held world view that sees human experience as a struggle between good and evil for dominance over the mass of gray matter in between. My preference is to explore dimensions of this struggle in a SF gene setting.; [a.] Meadows, TX

CHAPMAN, JAMES
[b.] November 9, 1964, Houston; [p.] Susie Scheffler; [ed.] College graduate, Univ. of Houston; [pers.] I perceive existence as a constant struggle to break free. This struggle is commonly manifested in attempts to Control Surroundings and the fire around as a means to secure personal conceptions of liberation. It is the varied forms of resulting competition that intrigues me. The SF genre heavily influences my form or expressions.; [a.] Stafford, TX

CHAPMAN, MICHAEL
[b.] June 24, 1949, Pensacola; [ch.] Elizabeth A. Chapman; [ed.] School, Vietnam, marriage, divorce; [occ.] Offshore worker; [hon.] My name isn't found on the wall on the panels devoted to the years '68-69.; [oth. writ.] A closet full; [pers.] Endeavor to persevere; [a.] Lafayette, LA

CHARD, FREDERICK H.
[b.] June 4, 1915, Dakota, MN; [p.] Herbert J. and Bertha L. Chard; [m.] Beth-Anne B. (Boult) Chard, September 6, 1941; [ch.] Anne C. Hargrove, Ph.D. (deceased), Virginia C. Williams, B.A., Frederick H. Chard, B.A., David W. Chard, B.A., M.A., Martha C. Avery, R.N.; [ed.] B.A. Med. Sc. and M.D., University of Wisconsin, 3 yrs. Residency, Dermatology, Univ. of Michigan Medical School; [occ.] Retired to gardening, gourmet cooking and writing.; [memb.] Am. Medical Association Sedgwick County Medical Society, Kansas Medical Society; [hon.] Diplomate American Board of Dermatology, Adjunct Professor of Dermatology, Wichita State Un. (Physician's Assistant Program), Founder and Chairman, Dept. of Dermatology Wichita Clinic (retired); [oth. writ.] Detailed autobiography in progress; [pers.] "Let me live in the house by the side of the road and be a friend to all of God's creation."; [a.] Wichita, KS

CHAREST, EVA
[b.] May 8, 1891, Chatham, MI; [p.] Ludger and Rose Gagnon; [m.] Frank Charest, January 28, 1913; [ch.] Marcel, Francois, Edna, Irvine, Rosaire, Laurette, Emilda, Juliette, Blanch; [ed.] Three winters of school-

ing at the Beaumont School and 104 years of life.; [occ.] Retirement at St. Joseph's Auxiliary Hospital; [memb.] The Women's Catholic League of St. Ambrose Catholic Church.; [hon.] In honor of Alberta 75th Anniversary in 1980, I received a silver medallion for residing in Alberta for 86 years. Also in celebrating my 100th Birthday I received praise from the Prime Minister of Canada. Governor General of Canada, and many other citizens.; [oth. writ.] Several other poems that just have not been published yet.; [pers.] You want to live your life by working hard and in turn you will be blessed with a happy, healthy life.; [a.] Edmonton Alberta, Canada

CHAREST, IRVINE

[b.] July 23, 1920, Edmonton; [p.] Frank and Eva Charest; [m.] Donnie Charest (2nd wife), December 5, 1992; [ch.] Gilbert, Roland, and Ronald (Charest), Robbie and Joye (Roberts); [ed.] Grade 8 Maple Hill School and the love of a big family.; [occ.] Retired dairy farmer; [memb.] St. Vital Seniors Club, U.F.A. (United Farmers of Alberta), and CO-OP; [hon.] In grade 7, I received a sterling silver pin for sportsmanship.; [oth. writ.] "New Sarepta and Its People" was published in the "New Sarepta: Looking Back" history book. Another poem called "The Plea of an Unborn Child" was published in the "La Nouvelle" of Beaumont, Alberta. A poem called "Time" was printed in the Good Shepherd's monthly newsletter and many other poems written.; [pers.] I cannot complain too much about my life because of so many special events that have happened over the years and I owe it all to my parents.; [a.] New Sarepta Alberta, Canada

CHERNIK, PETER

[b.] January, 23, 1950, New York, NY; [ed.] BA Manhattanville College; [oth. writ.] Eternity Road, Manhattan Wilderness East Coast Line, Railroad Heart (Published poetry book) Trick Bag (Published novel) 7 off - off Broadway play; [pers.] Keep walking mythic road with open heat - feet on ground - touch the sky

CHERUBIN, KETTLY MARIE

[pen.] "Fifie"; [b.] September 20, 1060, Port-au-Prince, Haiti; [p.] Aliette Gaston (mother); [ch.] Regine Bianca Lavaud (11 years old); [ed.] B.S. in Business Administration from La Salle University in Philadelphia in Philadelphia, PA Currently enrolled in Master in Education Program at Florida Atlantic University.; [occ.] Assistant to Department of Decision and Info. Systems at FAU/ Teach for the Florida School Board. Fluent in French, Spanish, Creole and English. Working on a poetry book - would become an offer from a publisher. Hopesto one day meet President Carter if she wins contest.; [hon.] Honor Roll Student - Certificate of Achievement as City of Philadelphia Summer Youth Employment and Educational Program Monitor and Coordinator - 1980; [oth. writ.] Author is planning on writing a book on th story of her grandmother who raised 10 children alone after premature death of husband. She lived to suffer death and rape of two more children, watched her daughter Aliette, suffer throughout 10-year marriage at the hand of an abusive Haitian suffer death herself at the age of 76 years old, the same her day her daughter got killed and her granddaughter laid wounded. It is a story of beauty, love, faith, intrigue and survival; [pers.] My poems aim at reviving the soul I write from personal experiences I often challenge people to look at positive and to overcome all obstacles; [a.] Tamarac, FL

CHISOM, CHEQUETA D.

[b.] November 23, 1950, Rochester, PA; [p.] Robert Allen and Ruby Allen; [m.] Charles G. Chisom, August 17, 1985; [ch.] Matthew Daniel, Cena marie, Charles Brandon; [ed.] East Liverpool High School, Carnegie Mellon University - B.S. The College of William and Mary-MBA; [occ.] Academic Medicine Administrator; [memb.] Medical Group Management Association, MGMA Academic Practice Assembly, Society of Research Administration, National Council of University Research Administrators, Carnegie Mellon Admissions Council, (AIM) Administrator of Internal Medicine; [hon.] Business and Professional Women's Club Young Careerist - Ohio, Finalist, featured profile - Carnegie Mellon Humanities and Social Sciences Recruitment Handbook Quill and Scroll International Award, several High School newspaper Editorials High School Journalism award for excellence; [oth. writ.] One poems - High School Publication, several editorials and articles High School Newspapers; [pers.] My writings reflect the journey of life with all its joy and sorrow. I have great respect for writers and speakers on self-actualization.; [a.] Williamburg, VA

CHO, KYOO-BON

[b.] November 28, 1941, Chunbook, South Korea; [p.] Choonwhan Cho and Wongpong Kang; [m.] Soon-Ja Cho, December 7, 1962; [ch.] Victor K. Cho; [ed.] Dan Kook University, Seoul, Korea, Eastern Michigan University, Michigan.; [occ.] Probation Officer; [oth. writ.] Korean translation of unknown but known published in Seoul, Korea.; [pers.] Man has been built of and from truth in the original architecture to become the truth incarnate. He is not to be treated and live otherwise.; [a.] Jamaica, MI

CHRISTAL

[pen.] Christal; [b.] December 8, 1978, Calgary; [ed.] At present, in grade II; [memb.] Music, Kidney Foundation; [hon.] English grade 9 (writing award) Art, Math, Social; [oth. writ.] Two by the light - two by night. Odessey of Life. Horses, who has seen the "Winds", Parents, "Canada 125" plus more - several have been published.; [pers.] Most of my writings are based on experiences, environment, collector's plates and pictures.; [a.] Canmore, Alberta

CHRISTIANSON, LINDA D.

[b.] October 5, 1958, Portland, OR; [p.] Hazel and David A. Dunn; [m.] Reginald D. Christianson; [ch.] Karl Thomas and Joseph Vernon Christianson

CHRISTIE, LAURA

[pen.] Laura Christie; [b.] December 29, 1971, East Orange, NJ; [p.] Ella and James O'Sullivan; [m.] Donald Christie (X-Husband), May 22, 1990; [ch.] Don Christie, James Christie; [ed.] Whitman-Hanson Regional High School; [oth. writ.] A collection of personal poems based on my life and love that was lost; [pers.] I have been greatly inspired by my mother and future husband who have both taught me a great deal about love and loving unconditionally. All my love to my two sons I could never love anyone more also a special thanks to my sister Patti for always being there for me; [a.] Hanson, MA

CHRISTOPHER, BILLY E.

[b.] July 31, 1934, Devonia TN; [p.] William John and Eva Christopher; [m.] Marilyn Sue, October 31, 1958; [ch.] Billy Jr. Penelope, John; [ed.] Central High School U.S. Navy, Industrial Electronics; [occ.] Retired Cheavy Industry, Manager; [memb.] Petros Baptist Church Friends of Appalachia AARP; [oth. writ.] Numerous poems, songs and short stories published in local newspapers and specialty magazines; [pers.] In the final analysis it is desired that all my writings promote a caring awareness of God's good earth (I keep my own property as a wildlife refuge) and remain an ambassador for Christ; [a.] Petros, TN

CHURCHMAN, VIRGIL IRA

[b.] October 18, 1905, Greenwood Co, KS; [p.] Mr. And Mrs. Wm James Churchman; [m.] Velma Ruth (Chesterman) Churschman (widow), June 9, 1946; [ch.] Kathleen Kay Lewis: Kenneth Duane Chuchman, Marilyn Mae, McKellar; [ed.] Graduate of Eureka High School 1923, At least 85 College Hr Credits at KSTC Emporia Courses taken in summer months and correspondence. Taught in Greenwood County Schools 15 yrs before being inducted into Service of the US Army of WWII Sept. 1942-Sept. 1945, Infantry Weather Btn, Co. Supt of Schools 4 yrs, taught 6 yrs more.; [occ.] Died 12-4-1954 Heart attack He was Poet for his Army group, wrote several while in European Theater of War. - Operations.; [memb.] Masonic Lodge, Fellows Lodge, Kansas State Teachers Association. Member of Christian-Congregational Church Sang in a Men's Quartet at Climax, awhile, Fancy Penmanship/Scrolls to sign Diplomas. Wrote and gave several speeches. He made some wood carvings. Art:draw/paint/chalk. He was an 'Avid Hunter and Fisherman' with his brothers and/or nephews as companions.; [hon.] (Not known or recalled by Virgil sent in his "Biography of Widow Velma.) Booker T. Washington to Kate Smith for a contest or? Widow can't recall outcome. Kate Smith died-June 17-1986. Upper Grade School Teacher- Principal, Coach 2 dtrs were Honor grads of EHS and KSTC/ESU-Emporia.; [oth. writ.] "Saga of the Sage Hen": Poem and Prose. "Musings of a draftee in Uncle Sam's Army": "The Colonel's Dilema': Poem and Prose. Poem and Prose? "Zippers" and Censor Trouble "The Yakiman Incident - First Casualty" New words to: "To Flander Dead" "Home on the Range". Virgil (Magazine) 10-15-1949 sent to The Instructor, Editorial Department, Dansville, New York by Virgil (have letter He submitted the poem "Rainbows". And he sent to Kate Smith, yrs ago, Biography:; [pers.] Virgil liked NATURE and expressed this in his Life-Style. To his wife, he about equaled Norman Rockwell, but without the fame and notariety. He was a quiet person outwardly, who could better express himself (inner-self) excellent 'letter-writer' through his many talents. Courtship mostly by MAIL.; [a.] Eureka, KS

CICCONE, AMANDA

[b.] January 10, 1966, Trenton, NJ; [p.] James and M. Judith Bell; [m.] Franco Ciccone, July 2, 1988; [ch.] James, Vincent, Patrick; [ed.] Mercer County Community College - A.A. degree, currently pursuing B.A. in English at LaSalle University; [occ.] President, AJ Estate Services; [memb.] Crohn's and Colitis Foundation, Sergeant-Auxiliary Police, Office of Emergency Management, Little League Manager; [hon.] Who's Who Among American Junior Colleges 1987, Dean's List LaSalle University; [pers.] This poem is lovingly dedicated to the memory of Andrew Milne for Bobbi Milne and for all mothers who have known her loss. [a.] Ewing, NJ.

CINQUE, MARGARET CONDON

[b.] November 9, 1928, Houston, TX; [p.] Raymond E. Eloise Condon; [m.] Jack J. Cinque, April 22, 1954; [ch.] Susan Kay, John Wm, Charles Alan and Russell Brian Cinque; [ed.] BA/BS in Costume Design and Fashion Illustration from T.S.C.W. in Denton, TX graduated in 1950.; [occ.] Housewife; [memb.] Delta Phi Delta, Art

Fraternity, life member T.W.U. Alumnae Association (formerly T.S.C.W.), American Contract Bridge League; [hon.] I was the 1946 Valedictorian of my high school graduating class in Humble, Texas, i.e. from Charles Bender High School.; [oth. writ.] I was Editor of the London Bridge, the monthly magazine/bulletin of the American Women's Club of London 1979-81, the last two of the four years we lived in London, England; [pers.] What can be more satisfying than composing words in verse form? It gives pleasure to the author, and amazes friends and family when a poem is dedicated to them on a special occasion. Blessings, too, on my mother, from her I inherited the love of language and any gift from rhyme or poetry.; [a.] Missouri City, TX

CIRAOLO, SHELLEY B. LOVE
[b.] February 6, 1951, Bronx, NY; [p.] Harry and Irene Love; [m.] Jack Thomas Ciraolo, August 29, 1987; [ch.] Jake Samuel and Zachary Francis Edward; [ed.] Springfield Gardens High School, John Jay College of Criminal Justice, New York Institute of Technology (MSLIR), Rutgers, The State University of Education (Doctorial Degree); [occ.] Pres./CEO SBL Consulting, Practicing Advocate/Labor Negotiator; [memb.] American Arbitration Ass'n, Industrial Relations Research Association, Who's Who Worldwide, National Ass'n Female Executive's; [hon.] Graduated NYIT with Distinction (Master's Labor and Industrial Relations; [oth. writ.] Should Mediators Be Certified? 1-1984 Amer. A. B. Assoc., Collective Bargaining Grierance Procedures - A Hist. and Practical overview" N.Y. Law Enforce. Journal 1986 2 Police Liability GARDNER (Ireland 1982); [pers.] Would greatly appreciate this poem being dedicated to Mrs. Kari Schwartz-Roosa (Kindergarten Teacher who inspired poem, mom and dad who are always there for me and my two (2) sons who give me the impetus to endure and appreciate them for what they are, my personal rainbows! "Philosophical Statement" "The difficult we do immediately" "The impossible may take a little longer." (As per my dad, my friend); [a.] Hopewell Junction, NY

CITTADINI III, LEO
[b.] October 28, 1977, Philadelphia; [p.] Leo Cittadini Jr. and Linda Cittadini; [ed.] Graduate of St. John Neumann H.S., will be attending a 4 year University in the fall.; [occ.] Part time at a neighborhood pharmacy.; [hon.] American Legion Award, St. John Neumann H.S. Millay Alumni Scholarship - 4 years straight.; [oth. writ.] The mysterious and surreal aspects of life fascinate me and find their way into much of my poetry.; [pers.] Philadelphia, PA

CIZ, KENNITH W. D.
[b.] March 3, 1966, Victoria British Columbia, Canada; [p.] Metodian Ciz, Barba Ciz; [m.] Jessica Ciz, August 24, 1991; [ch.] Izzac Tyler; [occ.] Power Engineer, Wildlife Artist.; [oth. writ.] I have a self published book called "Views from the Minds Eye". It is a collection of poems from ten years of writing; [pers.] I have started to apply my poetry to my paintings to give them a greater impact. I try to write about reality, what I see and what I feel.; [a.] Grand Centre Alberta, Canada

CLADIS, GEORGE
[pen.] George Cladis; [b.] April 22, 1923, New York City, NY; [ch.] Aevonaubical Engineer (1944), College of Aevonaubics NYC, Bachelor of Arts (1957), City College of NY, Master of Arts (1960), New York University; [sib.] Artist/Painter; [hon.] Numerous exhibits and art reviews; [pers.] To quote Picasso if an artist copies the masters, it is necessary. If an artist copies himself it is a tragedy; [a.] Summit, NJ

CLANCY, MICHELLE P.
[pen.] Mishell; [b.] Sept 23, 1971, Bronx, NY; [p.] Gloria M. Clancy, Michael E. Clancy; [ed.] 1 yr. Herbert H. Lehman (self-taught); [occ.] Promotional Assistant for Estee Lauder, Lancome, cosmetics etc.; [memb.] Feed the Children; [oth. writ.] This is the 1st poem published, but it will not be the last. I have a collection of wonderful writings in 4 journal books.; [pers.] Dreams are real. I want the world to see if you put your mind to what you want in life - You can have it. You just have to believe in yourself. Hold God in your heart and let him guide the way.; [a.] Bronx, NY

CLARK, BENJAMIN
[pen.] Benjamin Clark Mantherudder; [p.] Eddie Clark Jr. and Beatric Clark; [ed.] Associate in Science Lake Michigan College, Bachelor of Art in Fine Art and Sociology Fisk University, Bachelor of Fine Arts in Flat Pattern Design, Art Institute of Chicago, Masters of Art Degree in painting and sculpture, Art Institute of Chicago; [occ.] Artist; [hon.] Hines Brook Art Award and Departmental Honors, Fisk University, Flat Pattern Design Departmental Honors Art Institute Chicago, Louis Ritman Award in the Art Institute of Chicago Museum's 70th Annual Exhibition, Carson Pirie Scott Award, Peoria, Illinois Art Guild's 16th Annual Exhibition; [pers.] I am involved in the iridescent spiritual edge of ambient light.; [a.] Chicago, IL

CLARK, BETTY-JO
[b.] August 10, 1949, Dayton, OH; [p.] Martha Marie Medley Short; [ed.] Associate of Arts Degree 1993 at Seminole Community College, Licensed Practical Nurse 1987; [occ.] Student Register Nurse; [memb.] Phi Theta Kappa International Honor Society; [hon.] Won 2 years 1990, 1991, Dr. Wright Poetry Contest "Open Door" Short-Short Story's, Poems, published in the "Catalyst" for 4 years, Presidential Honor Roll and Dean's Honor Roll; [oth. writ.] Several poems published: "Ode To Sugarfoot," "Autumn," "Winter Cabin," "Anger," "Perfect Love," "Love Last," "Democracy," "Old Cabin," "Honesty," "Peace," "Owl of the Night," Short Stories: "Watch Out For Falling Rocks," and "Dream a Nightmare's Dream" and "Poetry's World"; [pers.] Words open up new worlds and helps draw together. Everyday we influence people around us and it's our decision if it's good or bad and our writings touch other people's lives and they relate to us by what we want; [a.] Altamonte Spring, FL

CLARK JR., CHARLES
[b.] July 13, 1943, Sheridan, WY; [p.] C. Robert Clark and Hazel M. Clark; [m.] Neomi Clark, October 24, 1987; [ch.] Dade Walker Clark, Aaron Robert Clark, Greg Aldrin Clark, Connie Hurst; [ed.] BSEE University of Wyoming 1972; [occ.] Electrical Engineer at Naval Warpare Assessment Division Corona, CA; [memb.] Norce Lions Club, BPO&E, American Legion, VFW; [a.] Norco, CA

CLARK, PATSY
[pen.] Patsy Clark; [b.] June 8, 1911, Pittsfield, UT; [p.] Edward and Ella Longley; [m.] Roger Clark (deceased), 1965 (second marriage); [ch.] 6 Children, 29 grand, 24 great and 7 great greats; [ed.] 4 years high school, several college courses; [occ.] Retired; [memb.] Bahai L.S.A. Assembly; [hon.] Good Mother's Award; [oth. writ.] A great many poems and lyrics, news published and except one, "A Part of God" published in "We Sing Our Songs" book. I try to tell a complete story in my poems.; [pers.] A voice wake me up in the middle of the night saying "I want you to write a poem about abortion". I thought I was dreaming but the voice said. "From my precious little human being's point of view "That's what we tried to do.; [a.] Rochester, VT

CLARK, THOMAS LEROY
[pen.] Tom Clark; [b.] June 1, 1936, Prescott, MI; [p.] Ed and Dorothy Clark; [m.] Cecilia Clark, August 15, 1964; [ch.] Brent, Cathy, and Sherri; [oth. writ.] Tom has titled his collection of poems: Rumblings of a Country Boy; [pers.] In December 1993 Tom suffered a severe stroke which left him without the ability to read, speak or write. His family has faith in his recovery. He was a pioneer boy and his over 100 poems reflect his sensitivity to nature, the seasons, and all aspects of life.; [a.] Hale, MI

CLARKE, JIM
[pen.] C. Witsanee; [b.] February 6, 1941, Ashville, NC; [m.] Catherine; [ch.] Four daughters; [occ.] Executive; [oth. writ.] Numerous- to my children referencing the joyful sharing of life and it's occasional trials and tribulations.; [pers.] About: "Remember the goodtimes", A letter left by my uncle and given to my Aunt (88 years) the day after his funeral. These four simple words left to this elegant lady have buffered her loss for many years.; [a.] Kingwood, TX

CLAUSEN, PHYLLIS B.
[b.] November 8, 1920, Alta Loma, TX; [p.] Charles H. and Nettie Johansson M.; [m.] Charles H. Clausen, April 19, 1947; [ch.] Kay C. Gaffney, Margo N. Whale, grandchild Alison; [ed.] High School; [oth. writ.] Other poems; [pers.] I believe if we lived by Matthew 7:12 and Luke 6:31 we would have peace, love and understanding between all people and all nations.; [a.] Boise, ID

CLAY, ALRIC CARTER
[pen.] Alrick C. Clay; [b.] August 22, 1964, Alexandria, VA; [p.] Sgt. Angelo T. and Patricia F. Cucuzzo; [ed.] Hardaway High School Columbus, GA Columbus Technical Last. Columbus Ga Columbus College Columbus, Ga, North Harris County College Kingwood, TX; [occ.] Student of Respiratory Therapy; [memb.] Member of Eastgate Church Dayton, TX, Member of Texas Bijinkan Dojo Houston, TX, under the direction of Dr. Edward F. Jones and James Wood; [hon.] Currently hold a 4th Kyn Rank in Togakure Ryu Ninjutsu.; [oth. writ.] "The Crystal Water's" is the first piece I've ever submitted for publication or contest.; [pers.] Every encounter in our life holds the possibility for personal enlightenment and prepares us for future events. I enjoy the works of Robert Frost, EE Cummings and Algernon Blackwood. The songs "Wooden Ships" by Crosby, Shills, Nash and Young and Steely Dan's "Home at Last" inspired me to write "The Crustal Waters"; [a.] Atascocita, TX

CLAY, BARBARA
[b.] April 4, 1942, Cynthiana, KY; [p.] Addie Laytart and Ransom Whalen; [m.] Gary A. Fields, August 30, 1992; [ch.] Carrie Todd Prebble, Piper Ellen Prebble; [ed.] M.A. - American Studies University of Denver. Cum Laude; [occ.] Marketing Manager Pacemaker Manufacturer; [memb.] Meeting Planners International, International Exhibitors Assoc.; [hon.] Kentucky Colonel, Chair, Exhibitor Committee, AHA, ACC, NASPE, Xth World Congress; [oth. writ.] Non-fiction article of

women and backing - 1985, Master's thesis "Slavery in Kentucky. '83, International Society of Meeting Planners (to be published fall '95) "Pre and Post convention itineraries, newsletters articles on travel.; [pers.] I prefer to write about life's ironies, mostly focused from a woman's point of view.; [a.] Denver, CO

CLAYTON, MARJORIE EVELYN DOWNING LOPEZ
[pen.] "Ebbie"; [b.] April 16, 1921, Florida; [p.] Edward C. and Nellie Mae Downing; [m.] Luciano Lopez (deceased), February 15, 1942, Harry Arden Clayton, married many years; [ch.] Sonia Lopez Benitez (deceased 1973), Sandra Lopez Eubanks; [ed.] High School, a course in law, a course in "Credit" (worked for Credit Bureau of Tampa over 12 years), a course in "Investigation" work.; [occ.] Not any now - just retired; [memb.] Was president for long time of Women's World Fellowship; [hon.] I would not feel well to brag: let's just say "God" has been good to me! My great friends, children, and grandchildren are worth more than life! "Maide" in Queens Court of the Plant City, Fla. Strawberry Fair 1940-1941; [oth. writ.] I love to write poems, I have written poems since I was a young child. I send them to friends all the time instead of a plain "letter", somewhere I also have a book I started long ago; [pers.] Life is too short to be dishonest, "cranky", cheating. Try to love and help all. We should live life to the best of our ability, helping those who need help, praising God, and thanking "Him" for our blessing daily!; [a.] Tampa, FL

CLEGG, MARY MILLER
[b.] November 9, 1913, Oklahoma; [p.] Mr. and Mrs. Harry W. Miller; [m.] Mark R. Clegg, December 31, 1936; [ch.] Mark Robert and James Donald Clegg; [ed.] High School and two year Secretarial and Accounting course in commercial School.; [occ.] Secretary, Treasurer of Family Corporation; [memb.] Former member of International Porcelain Artists and Teachers, Inc., Member of Church of Christ; [oth. writ.] Collection of verse entitled "I Journey by Verse," never submitted for publication. Primarily contains verses about everyday things that happen in most everyone's life. I have written verses since I was a small child. Write my own verses for cards.; [pers.] Have especially enjoyed china painting of vases, tea sets, etc., and if used for a gift, writing, in china paint, an appropriate verse on the bottom of the item. This makes it a lasting gift that can become an heirloom.; [a.] Kansas City, MO

CLEMENTS, KAREN
[b.] December 5, 1967, New York; [p.] Nancy and Theophilus Clements; [ed.] Grover Cleveland High School, Hunter College; [occ.] Television Research Analyst; [oth. writ.] Several poems and essays as yet unpublished; [pers.] I can best express myself through writing, it allows me to clear my thoughts. [a.] Flushing, NY

CLERMONT, HANS PATRICK
[pen.] Hans P. Clermont; [b.] December 6, 1973, Chicago; [p.] Marie T. Clermont; [occ.] Youth-worker

CLEVELAND, THERESA D.
[pen.] Teri Denine; [p.] Haskel and Bettry Cleveland; [pers.] Always follow your dreams for they have no boundaries and are limitless; [a.] Brooklyn, NY

COBB, ISAIAH
[b.] June 21, 1959, Louisville GA; [p.] Frankie Mae and Robert A. Cobb Sr.; [ed.] High School Diploma (Louisville GA) and I.C.S. Diploma (Master Art); [occ.] Stocker (Bilo grocery) Augusta GA; [oth. writ.] Favorite (quotes) and more inspired poems. A poem about "Father" published in the Augusta Chronicle Newspaper.; [pers.] The poem you received, "(Wake Up America)" was inspired to me one morning as I was awaken from my sleep. All the poems I have written were inspired to me, while being awaken from a deep sleep, also I have the dates and times.; [a.] Augusta, GA

CODRINGTON, REV. MARY ELINOR
[b.] January 8, 1935, Springfield, MA; [m.] Divorce; [ch.] David Johnson, Nadirah Shabazz, Leonard Codrington, Richard Codrington, Deborah Codrington, Jerry Codrington; [ed.] Technical High School (1953), B.S. - Springfield MA (5-12-85), Master of Divinity (5-14-88), Howard University School of Divinity Washington D.C.; [occ.] Pastor St. Paul A.M.E. Church - Waynesboro, PA, Bethel A.M.E. Church Greencastle, PA; [memb.] New England Conference Dept. of Evangelist, Vice President 1986-1990, Howard University School of Divinity Student Government Association - Vice President 1987-1988; [hon.] Springfield MA. Dumbar Community Center Volunteer Award, Bethel A.M.E. Church Member service award, Dance award The Gerald Dule, outstanding student award, Howard University School of Divinity, Hines Scholarship - The African Methodist Episcopal Church Scholarship.; [pers.] "I can do all things through Christ who strengthens me". Philippians 4:13; [a.] Waynesboro, PA

COFIELD, SUE
[b.] January 30, 1951, Commerce, GA; [p.] Deceased; [m.] Larry Cofield, September 30, 1972; [ch.] Lori Johanna and Alisha Diane; [ed.] Graduate of Banks County High School - Homer, GA; [occ.] Administrative Assistant - Lanier National Bank, Oakwood, GA; [memb.] Active participant in the March of Dimes - Walk America. Was the top fundraiser for Hall County in 1992 and 1994; [oth. writ.] I have written all my life but never shared my poems until recently. It was by accident my friends found my poems. They had a variety of them bound in a book for me, and encouraged me to submit a poem to you.; [pers.] I strive in all things to be the best I can, but strive the hardest to be just a Mother and a friend. I love poetry for it is the feelings of the heart, put into beautiful words.; [a.] Homer, GA

COHEN, MICHELE D.
[b.] January 29, 1959, Bronx, NY; [ed.] Cherry Hill High School West-CH NJ, C.M. Price School of Advertising and Journalism - Philadelphia PA; [occ.] Advertising, Sales; [memb.] Nature Conservancy, Smithsonian Institute; [hon.] Listed in: Who's Who of American Women (I forgot what year 81? 84?); [oth. writ.] Song lyrics, poems, short stories, scripts.; [pers.] To leave this world, this room, this minute... better for having been there. To encourage compassion, share hope and stand tall.; [a.] Woodbury, NJ

COLBERT, MATT A.
[b.] August 28, 1962, Sacramento, CA; [p.] Ron Colbet, Nancy Kneale; [m.] Louise Tomkinson - Colbert, July 25, 1995; [ch.] Leo Jakob Colbert, Dylan Jade Colbert; [ed.] West Albany High School Simpson College; [occ.] Middle school Teacher, Byron, CA.; [memb.] National Geographic Society California Teachers Association; [hon.] 1993-94 Teacher of the Year: Byron School District Team captain, MVP: Simpson College basketball team, Mentor Teacher: Byron School district; [oth. writ.] None published, have always written for friends, family, and students; [pers.] When writing, I try to express the profound beauty that I believe exists in everyday life. Life's greater joys are those that are simple.; [a.] Antioch, CA

COLBERT, SHANNEN
[b.] February 24, 1983, Georgia Baptist, CT; [p.] Shirley and Willia Colbert; [ed.] Flat Shoaks Em, 6th Grade; [occ.] Student; [memb.] Choirs, sister of the circle, Piano classes, Cheerleading; [hon.] Honor roll and principal list, perfect attendance citizenship, student of the North; [oth. writ.] Stories and poem; [pers.] I strive to best in my writing; [a.] Deactur, GA

COLBERT, SHIRLEY N.
[pen.] Shirley Colbert; [b.] June 30, 1934, Hutchinson, KS; [p.] Zona and John Yehle - both deceased; [m.] 34 yrs, widowed, since 1990; [ch.] 7 children, 6 living, 5 sons - Dennis, Robert, Scott, Kelly and Mike, 1 Daughter - Teresa and 14 grandchildren; [ed.] 10th Grade - obtained GED at age 34; [occ.] Composite lay up at Raytheon (Beech) Aircraft - Wichita, KS; [oth. writ.] This is the 3rd poem being published. I have written many more but have not tried to publish them as of this date.; [pers.] I have deep and intense feelings for home, family, love, America and God and live one day at a time.; [a.] Wichita, KS

COLE, BENITA L.
[b.] March 9, 1919, Painesdale; [p.] Clara and John David Hall; [m.] Fred C. Cole, May 22, 1935; [ch.] David, Douglas, Lynn, Gail, Rosemary and Patricia; [ed.] High school; [occ.] Homemaker (a friend to whoever has a need); [memb.] Lake Orion Women's Club, Church, Red Cross Volunteer, Lake Orion Senior Citizen Housing Board Library, Lake Orion Historical Society; [hon.] Woman of the Year Lake Orion Federation of Women's Club, former March of Dimes, P.T.A. - Band Officer; [oth. writ.] Wrote an article for Detroit Free Press, many letters to local paper, many letters to politicians; [pers.] Memories are the sweet past of whatever we have done or experienced. Our trials are sent that we may help others who suffer that same malady.; [a.] Lake Orion, MI

COLE, SYLVIA H.
[b.] July 17, 1927, Hornell, NY; [p.] Ethel Sturgeon Cole and William S. Cole; [ed.] High School, graduate did take courses in adult evening school, Typing, Art, Child Psychology, Home Nursing; [occ.] Retired from Goodwill Industries Buffalo 1989, NY; [memb.] I belong to the village chorus, here. And in my home town, belonged to my church choir - song for 22 years, and for the Orchard Park Chorale 20 years (Local Musical Org.); [hon.] Have gotten several 1st and 2nd place awards from the National Poetry Assn. I guess a couple of honorable mentions, too.; [oth. writ.] I don't have my poetry published formally. But have completed in International and National Contests since I was a junior in High School. Wrote poetry for Orcnard Park Press for nearly 30 years; [pers.] I love this life and though I've not done anything truly spectacular life itself, has always been beautiful and exciting. I'll never get over marvel of perfection in the Creation of even the smallest things!; [a.] Leesburg, FL

COLE, WILMA M.
[b.] May 22, 1953, Missouri; [p.] Mack and Mary Pennington; [m.] Terry R. Cole; [ch.] Dorothy Mae, Lewis Elmer, Rick Eugene; [occ.] Story teller; [oth. writ.] I have written many poems and prayers to family and friends.; [pers.] Poem inspired by Andrew Euel Arnold Dedicated to Andrew Euel Arnold Jr.; [a.] Modesto, CA

COLENBURG, VICKIE
[pen.] Vickie Colenburg; [b.] May 5, 1965, Natchez, MS; [p.] Rufus and Winnie Mae Colenburg; [ed.] Jackson State University, Jackson, MS, B.S. Speech pathology, Education, M.S. Vocational Rehabilitation Counseling; [occ.] Vocational Evaluator, Workwell, Houston, TX; [memb.] Delta Sigma Theta Sorority, Inc. Jacob's Production (musical), National Association of Rehabilitation Professionals, Houston Wellness Council, Order of Eastern Stars; [hon.] Who's who among American High School Students; [pers.] My writing is inspired by my life events, the words are expressions from the heart. I would like to thank my family and friends for their encouragement and support.; [a.] Houston, TX

COLLINS, ANGEL MARIE
[b.] September 5, 1979, Brazil, IN; [p.] Randy Collins and Diana Braunstein; [ed.] Current student at West Vigo High School, plans to attend St. Mary of the Woods College; [hon.] Honor Roll student; [oth. writ.] Several, not yet recognized; [a.] West Terre Haute, IN

COLLINS, BARBARA
[pen.] Barbara Collins; [b.] September 16, 1958, Marietta, SC; [p.] Alvin L. Huff and Vernelle B. Huff; [m.] Michael Collins, December 24, 1992; [ed.] Parker High School-1976, Greenville Tec College-1984, Associate degree in Health Science with a major in nursing; [occ.] R.N. at Self Memorial Hospital; [memb.] American Heart Asso. National Finch and Softbill Society - The Humane Society; [hon.] School spirit, school beautification, Senator freshman year (high school), several poems published. Won 3 writing contest. "Diamante" style of poetry published in senior year of annual.; [oth. writ.] I also write inspiration poetry; [pers.] I've always dreamed of being a writer. At times when I had trouble expressing myself, I found my pen never fails. I was greatly influenced by my 4th grade teacher, Miss Redmon. Ironically, an essay I wrote about the woman I admired won that year!; [a.] Greenwood, SC

COLLINS, CECILIA
[pen.] Cecilia Collins; [b.] August 29, 1951, Sweetwater, TX; [p.] Betty and Jerry Moykerry; [m.] Arnold E, May 31, 1969; [ch.] Tammy Forest Collins, Timm Eugene Collins; [ed.] Mental Healthy Assoc. Del Mar College; [occ.] Trainer of Teacher at Corpus State school; [memb.] Egule's Lodge; [hon.] Many awards from poetry and job related work for volunteering to help. Being of service to the public.; [oth. writ.] Many poems not published; [pers.] Life is fully rich experiences, if we do our best that's all one man can do. Be satisfied with your self and life.; [a.] Corpus Christi, TX

COLLINS, MARY
[b.] January 14, 1970, Fullerton, CA; [p.] Jack Collins and Carolyn Russell-Collins; [ed.] BA University of Connecticut 1992 major: English concentration, Creative Writing. MAT Quinnipiac College 1995 concentration: English Education; [occ.] English Teacher/Correspondent/graduate student; [hon.] 1992 Best Play, University of Connecticut; [oth. writ.] Newspaper features and articles, poetry, plays, and short stories; [a.] Milford, CT

COLOMA, GARRY GLENN O.
[pen.] J.P Bryan; [b.] March 29, 1977, Manila, Philippines; [p.] Mary Jean and Geronimo J. Coloma; [ed.] High School Graduate; [occ.] College student; [oth. writ.] A collection of unpublished poems and short stories; [pers.] To write subconsciously is a gift to write meditatively is a talent but to write, itself is Innate; [a.] Cathedral City, CA

CONE JR., ALAN W.
[pen.] "A" Cone; [b.] July 23, 1956, Greensboro, NC; [p.] Alan and Emily; [m.] Suzanne, September 30, 1994; [ch.] Salem; [ed.] Woodberry Forest High School, Duke University (BA Economics (Cum laude)), UNC-Chapel Hill MBA; [occ.] Horse Trainer, AHSA Judge, game inventor and manufacturer; [hon.] Invented game called "Play It Smart" - Chicago Tribune's Game of the Year-1993", Fun and Games Magazine's "Game of the Year-1994", invented game called "Nickel and Dime Pool" soon to be every household.; [pers.] I do all my writing and inventing while driving my tractor.; [a.] Huntersville, NC

CONKLIN, PAUL L.
[pen.] Uncle Paul; [b.] June 4, 1912, Sheridan, MI; [p.] Chloa and Melvin Conklin (deceased); [m.] Mary (deceased), December 21, 1941; [ch.] Betty Lee, Nancy Mae; [ed.] New Troy High (Mich.), A.B. Western Michigan Univ., Masters Degree Northwestern Univ.; [occ.] Retired, Entertainer and still sell churches furniture, equipment, robes, etc.; [memb.] Gideons International, National Education Association - life member. Mt. Hope United Methodist Church-Lansing where I was Associate Minister 6 years 1953-59. The youth called me Uncle Paul, and now waitresses and every body call me Uncle.; [hon.] 1930 High School graduation New Troy, Mich. with top honors since I was there just my Senior year. The next highest was the Valedictorian. July 22, 1989 Geri, an 8th grade Graduate in 1934 at Hollywood rural school where I taught grades 5-8 made this plaque and presented to me at the Hollywood reunion.; [oth. writ.] See some poems and news items included in the mailing, School Days was my first poem; [pers.] Most of my poems as you can see are related to my personal experiences. You Little Dickens is about a young girl who rented an apartment from me and helped me with local traveling before I had my eye cater act operation. The whole poem is about things that really happened when we were together. Mt. Hope poems were my Christmas messages when I was Associate Minister there 1953-9 I am still their Uncle Paul; [a.] Eaton Rapids, MI

CONNERY, KATIE
[b.] March 4, 1981, Front Royal, VA; [p.] Rusty Connery and Scott Connery; [ed.] Elementary School, 1 year of High School; [occ.] School; [memb.] FHA in school 1st year; [hon.] 1st place art contest, 3rd place reflections contest for a poem I wrote.; [oth. writ.] "I would if I could" I write a lot of poetry and stories but I hardly ever give them names.; [pers.] My mother influenced me by singing little rhyming songs when I was younger.; [a.] Luray, VA

COOKSEY, GEORGE T.
[b.] February 8, 1954, Washington, DC; [p.] Rose L. Cooksey, Joseph E. (deceased); [m.] Lisa Cooksey, June 25, 1982; [ch.] Nyssa R. Cooksey, Kirstin E. Cooksey; [ed.] Associate in Science Degree; [occ.] Disabled Veteran - 100%; [memb.] American Legion; [hon.] Cum Laude graduate, received Meritorians Service Medal following 18 years active duty - US Army - grade of rank sergeant First class; [pers.] An unshakeable faith in God in the slightest or greatest adversity; [a.] Washington, DC

COOKSON, CAROL A.
[b.] November 18, 1936, Lawrence, MA; [p.] Lloyd and Cecile Cookson; [ed.] 1. St. Mary's High School Lawr. MA, 2. Emmanuel College (Boston, MA) 1963 BA in Teacher Educ. from, 3. Salem State College (Salem, MA) MA in Educ. (Readin Spec.); [occ.] Chapter I Reading Teacher - Tabox School (Lawrence, MA); [memb.] International Reading Assoc. and Merrimack Valley Reading Council; [hon.] Masters and 36 Credits one of the top 10 in high school; [pers.] Perseverance is the key to success! "If at first you don't succeed, try, try, again!"; [a.] Seabrook, NH

COONTS, TERESA
[b.] November 4, 1957, Harrison, AR; [p.] Ralph and Bessie Coonts; [ed.] Mt. Judea High, Univ. of Central Arkansas, Univ. of Ark. at Little Rock.; [occ.] Education Consultant for Deaf/Blind, Ark. Dept. of Edu., Little Rock, AR.; [memb.] TASH, Agape Church; [hon.] Kappa Delta Phi; [oth. writ.] Some poems published in local newspapers.; [pers.] I strive to work from the inside-out in my mental, physical, emotional and spiritual life. I have been greatly influenced by my family and friends.; [a.] Little Rock, AR

COOPER, BARBIE
[b.] December 5, 1967, Coronach, Saskatchewan, Canada; [p.] Ray and Iris Wriksen; [m.] Christopher G. Cooper, August 5, 1989; [ed.] Medicine Hat High School, Medicine Hat, alberta, Canadian Bible College, Regina, Saskatchewan; [occ.] Self-employed baker; [memb.] Evangelical Teachers Training Association; [hon.] Alexander Rutherford Scholarship, Dean's List; [oth. writ.] Several Unpublished poems; [pers.] I write for myself when a topic stirs or amuses me. I want to please the Lord with all I do.; [a.] Thunder Bay Ontario, Canada

COOPER, JOHN GERALD
[pen.] John Kupar; [b.] March 17, 1942, Nanticoke, PA; [p.] John and Julia Cooper; [m.] Susan Cooper, June 27, 1992; [ch.] Jennifer, Carrie, Kim, and Karen; [ed.] Bloomsburg University; [occ.] Teacher; [oth. writ.] "The Loneliest Christmas Tree" copyrighted; [pers.] Life's path is more than curves or bumps. It has hills and valleys. It is the painters, musicians, authors, philosophers..., that tells us the tale of the depths and heights of their journey.; [a.] Binghamton, NY

CORBIN, MARILYN S.
[pen.] Collette Corbin; [b.] October 31, 1953, Des Moines, IA; [p.] Kenneth Hull (deceased) and Mary C. Hull; [m.] Jack L. Corbin, June 25, 1989; [ch.] Frank David and Charles Elbert; [ed.] Harding Jr High - DSM IA, North HS - DSM IA, Grandview Jr Coll - DSM IA, DMACC - Ankeny IA and the School of Hard Knocks; [occ.] Personal tech, State of IA-IA Dept of Personnel; [hon.] 1971 Quill and Scroll Socy.; [oth. writ.] Lyrics to over 75 songs: Scars on My Heart, You're the Woman I'd Marry All Over Again, Tattoos are Just Like Love Sometimes, You'll Always Have My Heart, Thank You for the Pain, The Snake of Many Colors, Be Still My Heart Again, You're Gonna Stomp My Heart; [pers.] Qualification to be a Country-Western songwriter - one broken heart.; [a.] Des Moines, IA

CORCHIA, DEBRA
[pen.] Big Red; [b.] May 9, 1953, New York City; [p.] Jessica and Frank DiPinto; [m.] Robert Corchia, July 19, 1980; [ch.] Jessica; [ed.] Candlewood Bayside High, C.W. Post, N.Y.; [occ.] Owner of the Mica Place, Bronx, NY; [memb.] American Cancer Society, ASCAP; [hon.] National Museum of Women in the Arts, Cannes Music

Festival song of the year 1977; [oth. writ.] Songs published with several publishing companies (words and music) CBS, EMI, BakPhil; [pers.] Carpe Diem; [a.] Bayside, NY

CORELLIS, DANIELLE M.
[b.] December 15, 1981, Albany, NY; [p.] Denise and Anthony Corellis; [ed.] I attend Goff Middle School in E. Greenbush NY; [occ.] Student; [memb.] E. Greenbush Girls Soft Ball League, Goff Middle School Ski Club, E. Greenbush POP Warner Cheerleading; [hon.] 1st place three years in a row Capital District Pop Warner Cheerleading Competition, Presidents award for Educational Excellence; [oth. writ.] I keep a daily journal of my poems and write about my feelings, family and friends; [pers.] I would like to thank my mom and dad for appreciating the poems I write for them and being supportive of me.; [a.] East Greenbush, NY

CORKERY, LINDA C.
[b.] Bronx, NY; [p.] Otto and Agnes Schween; [m.] Terrence M. Corkery; [ch.] Holly and Robert; [ed.] Evander Childs H.S., Bronx, N.Y. and Monroe Business School, Bronx, NY; [occ.] Court Reporter, Dutchess County Grand Jury; [pers.] I have been writing all my life. I enjoy doing personal poems for friends and family. I like to write about different topics and given an idea, enjoy the challenge. I thank my family for their encouragement.; [a.] Staatsburg, NY

CORSON, ALAN
[b.] August 2, 1952, Philadelphia; [p.] Geoffrey and Heidi Corson; [ed.] Harrisburg Area Community College, Penn State University; [occ.] Elementary School Teacher; [memb.] Solor Cookers International; [oth. writ.] Syndication of a cryptogram column in newspapers.; [pers.] I have enjoyed teaching the process of writing and watching students learn to express themselves.; [a.] Dauphin, PA

COTTERMAN, MISTY
[b.] September 1, 1981, Piqua, OH; [p.] Pam and Terry Cotterman; [ed.] Ft. Loramie Elementary J. H.; [a.] Ft. Loramie, OH

COUILLARD, HARMONY H.
[b.] August 22, 1973, Vermont; [ed.] Oxford Hills High School - S. Paris M.E., Elms College - Chicopee, M.A.; [occ.] Student; [memb.] National Organization for Women; [hon.] Field Hockey and Lacrosse Captain - Student Government Asc. President; [oth. writ.] Poetry short story, playwright; [a.] Chicopee, MA

COWEN, BARBARA
[b.] August 10, 1941, Sulphur Springs, TX; [p.] J. P. Glaze and Willie Holcomb Glaze; [m.] Bill Cowen, June 24, 1961; [ch.] Karen Elaine, Cynthia Ann and Valerie Denise; [ed.] Abilene High School, Abilene, TX, North Harris County College, Houston, TX, Extensive Music Studies - concentration in piano pedagogy and theory.; [occ.] Private piano teacher; [memb.] Women's Aglow, Music Teachers Nat'l Assn (MTNA), Texas Music Teachers Assn (TMTA), Cypress Creek Music Teachers Assn (CCMTA); [hon.] Dean's List, NHCC; [oth. writ.] Several unpublished poems and worship songs recently composed; [pers.] My hearts desire is to bring praise and glory to God and to reflect on the goodness of His creation. Also to inspire others to do their best through word and song.; [a.] Spring, TX

COX, KAREN L.
[b.] January 23, 1959, Oakland, CA; [p.] Girver and Gertrude Hudson; [m.] Mobil L. Cox, July 16, 1994; [ch.] Stevie Early Jr., Aaron Early, Kimberly Early; [ed.] Castlemont High School, Laney College, Merritt College.; [occ.] Chemical Dependency Councelor, Children's Hospital; [memb.] N.A.A.C.P. - Oakland, CA, Star Bethal Missionary Baptist Church; [hon.] National Federation of Govt. Employees Women of the year 1988. Dean List; [oth. writ.] Several poems published in various magazines; [pers.] God's grace will not take you, where his love can't keep you...; [a.] Oakland, CA

COX, ROBERT TIMOTHY
[pen.] Tim Cox; [b.] March 11, 1964, Grand Junction, CO; [p.] James and Anna Cox; [ed.] 1970-1982 completed 13 years at DeBeque, High School DeBequelo, correspondence courses at Berean Bible College, Springfield Missouri; [occ.] Certified Nursing Aide at Family Health West; [memb.] Fruita Lion's Club; [hon.] Chaplin for royal rangers at fruita assembly of God; [oth. writ.] Poems in newspaper fruita, times; [pers.] I was a battered child at 2 years old. After that happened, a third family came in and took me in as one of their own. It took love that put the pieces back together again.; [a.] Fruita, CO

COX, SANDRA S.
[pen.] Susie Cox; [b.] July 9, 1961, Port Arthur, TX; [p.] Wilton and Charlotte Golmon; [m.] Bert R. Cox, April 12, 1980; [ch.] Sarah (14), Travis (11), Wilton (8), Colton (6 months); [ed.] High School with a license in Cosmetology (hairdressing); [occ.] Homemaker, Church Librarian; [memb.] Fellowship Baptist Church; [hon.] Currently I am the semi-finals in two other National Contests; [oth. writ.] Several poems written personally for family, friends and teachers; [pers.] Sharing everyday life circumstances with others seems to be the theme of most of my writing. Brining encouragement and understanding to rough times and sharing the joys of life give me the greatest satisfaction.; [a.] Groves, TX

CRAGO, MARY A.
[b.] September 14, 1964, Erie, Pennsylvania; [p.] Dolores Applebee; [m.] James Crago, June 9, 1989; [pet.] dog: "Harley" 6 yr. old Boxer; [occ.] Disabled diabetic housewife; [hon.] The only one I've ever accomplished "is having a mother who is also my friend." [pers.] My biggest hope for today's society is....just because a person may be a "diabetic biker" and live the biker's lifestyle: it does not mean they are an "instant drug addict." Outside appearances and one's lifestyle give no reason for judgement of a person's feelings and inner beauty; [a.] Phoenix, AZ

CRAIN, LAWRENCE J.
[pen.] Larry; [b.] September 14, 1927, Rifle, CO; [p.] Mary Jane Crain; [m.] Opal S. Crain, May 22, 1993; [ed.] 8th Grade Colorado City Texas, High School GED.; [occ.] Retire US Army 23 yrs.; [memb.] Life member of Magonic Temple 914 Huntsville AL; [hon.] 2 Army Commendation Vietnam Aug 68 Aug 69 retired 23 years army Dec. 1945 thur Aug. 1970

CRANDALL, KATIE ZONELLE
[b.] January 16, 1984, Enid, OK; [p.] Charles and Zonelle Rainbolt and the late Darrell Crandall; [ed.] Poems written in 1994 while Katie was in the 4th grade at Sangre Ridge Elementary School in Still water, OK.; [occ.] Currently a 5th grader in Cordell Elementary School; [pers.] Katie loves to write poems, stories, etc. and also illustrates many at her works. Her 4th grade teacher Gina Morris, encouraged and helped Katie so very much.; [a.] Cordell, OK

CRAVEY, DALE
[pen.] Winston Cravey; [b.] December 20, 1960, Brownfield, TX; [p.] Jack Cravey and Ann Hunnicutt; [m.] Cory Olive Cravey, May 20, 1982; [ed.] Breckenridge High, U.S. Air force Personal Study; [occ.] Shop Foreman Mr. Cool Radiator Austin TX; [memb.] Green Peace, National Rifle Assoc.; [hon.] Honor student, High School Honorable Discharge Air Force; [oth. writ.] Several Poems Book called Sluggo; [pers.] I am inspired by my love of nature and the love I share with my family and my beautiful wife Cory; [a.] Austin, TX

CRAWFORD, AILEEN
[b.] January 2, 1946, Beaumont, TX; [m.] Sammy F. Crawford, December 23, 1967; [ch.] Sammy F. Crawford II; [ed.] High School Graduate; [occ.] Homemaker; [oth. writ.] One poem, "Loyce's walk," is appearing in current issue of poet magazine (vol. 6 no. 1). Another, "Falling Gold" to be published in the fall edition of poet magazine. Both winners in the Iva Mary Williams inspirational poetry contest.; [pers.] I enjoy writing poetry that invites the reader to discover layers of deeper meanings presented simply.; [a.] McAllen, TX

CRAWFORD, VIVIAN MAE
[b.] October 2, 1958; [ch.] Courtney Jean Nodine Crawford; [ed.] OLiver Secondary High School Southern Alberta Institute of Technology (SAIT); [occ.] School District #13 (Kettle Valley) Trustee, Secretary; [memb.] Union Board of Health Parent's Advisory Committee Greenwood Curling Club Board of Directors; [hon.] All from World of Poetry Golden Poet Awards - Old age - 1986, Life's message -1987, To Dream - 1989, honorable mention - old age 1986, light of love - 1988, Life's message - 1987, to dream - 1989; [oth. writ.] Numerous poetry published in local newspapers. Reporter for Boundary Community News for 2 yrs. covering news within my area. World of Poetry World Poetry Anthology; [pers.] Emily Dickinson has been my main inspiration for poetry writing because of the depth of her writing. My poetry reflects the depth of personal tribulations and trials that I believe many people experience; [a.] Greenwood, BC

CREEDON, TOM
[b.] April 22, 1987, Hamilton, OH; [p.] John Creedon and Gayle Creedon; [ed.] Hamilton High School (Junior); [occ.] Student; [memb.] National Honor Society, National Organization of Pride, Princeton Pike Church of God; [hon.] 1. 1994 Church of God Southern Ohio Teen Talent winner. Short story division, 2. 1994 Hamilton High Poetry contest winner, 3. Hamilton High Gold Honor Roll, 4. 1993 Miami University Young Author.; [pers.] My feeling and experiences are the basis of my writings.; [a.] Hamilton, OH

CREWS, ARTHUR NEAL
[pen.] Arthur Neal Crews; [b.] December 13, 1957, Jackson, TN; [p.] James and Margaret Crews; [m.] Margaret Denise Mizell, November 18, 1977; [ed.] South Side High School, Jackson State Community College; [occ.] Purchasing/Inventory Control; [memb.] United Way, Woodland Baptist Church; [hon.] U.S. Navy Good Conduct and Meritorious Unit Award; [oth. writ.] Several Religious poems, and two published in Company newsletter.; [pers.] I choose to believe the best in others and write when divinely inspired to do so.; [a.] Jackson, TN

CREWS, PAULA
[pen.] Paula C.; [b.] December 27, 1942, El Paso, TX; [ch.] Patsy Estorga, Anita Casillas, Sylvia Casillas, Veronica Holmes; [ed.] High School Graduate, Usleta High School, 1961, El Paso, Texas; [occ.] Office Manager, Bookkeeper; [oth. writ.] Several poems published in local newsletters.; [pers.] Everything happens for a reason. Even the dark, troublesome times can bring positive results, it we see beyond the storm.; [a.] El Paso, TX

CROMPTON, BRIAN
[b.] July 17, 1981, Somers Point, NJ; [p.] David and Lydia Crompton, Bob and Mary Foltz; [ed.] 8th Grade; [occ.] Student; [memb.] Golf club, National Junior Honor Society, Sports collectibles club, and I am a red belt in Soo Bahk Do Moo Duk Kwan (Karate), consortium for gifted and talented.; [hon.] Principal's list, Superintendent's list, United States National Mathematics Award, National English Award, Science Olympiad Award, and perfect attendance Award (three years in a row); [oth. writ.] Some poems for my own personal enjoyment.; [pers.] I write poetry to express my emotions.; [a.] Mayslanding, NJ

CROSBY, SHEILA
[pen.] Sheila; [b.] June 11, 1967, Hattlesburg, MS; [ed.] Baker High, Mobile, AL; [occ.] Factor, Student; [pers.] Live, love, laugh!!; [a.] O'Fallon, MO

CROSBY, VICTORIA R.
[b.] Cheshire, England; [ch.] 4 sons, all involved in music, one a rock musician; [ed.] Masters degree in Education; [occ.] Private piano teacher part time, former Nursery School teacher, summer camp director; [memb.] Shelley Society of N.Y. Regional Editor Poet to Poet, Lost of Weekly Reading in Glen Cove, volunteer for many local charities, including the Red Cross, St John's Episcopal Church; [hon.] Nassau County Museum of Art, featured in many poetry readings and on T.V. for Poet to Poet. Read poem that I wrote at inauguration of Mayor of City of Glen Cove.; [oth. writ.] Published in local newspaper, poems and publicity articles for many charity organizations. Including Poet to Poet's Literary Review; [pers.] I write in hopes of making my audience laugh, or cry or think. If I can accomplish all of these at a reading then I'm very happy.; [a.] Glen Cove, NY

CROSSLEY, FLOSSIE LAMBERT
[pen.] Margetta Crossley; [b.] June 21, 1928, Monroeville, AL; [p.] John and Lexanna Clausell; [m.] Willie Henry Lambert Sr. and Aaron Crossley (divorced from both), Lambert August 22, 1948, Crossley June 14, 1976; [ch.] Edward, Brenda, Ronald Williett, Jacqulyn, Florastine and Christopher Lambert; [ed.] 12 years high school, B.S. College, work on master's at Alabama State University, worked on finishing the masters at Wayne State University Detroit Michigan; [occ.] Pension and disability complete income 480.00 per month; [memb.] Second Caanan Baptist, Church at Hayes and Wade Detroit, Michigan 48213. Healing Surport Network, Living Faith Mission. Work with Project Bait (Black awareness in television) Channel 50 Detroit; [hon.] No awards or honors. Made Dean's List at the Jr. College in my home town (Monroeville Alabama Patrick Henry for 2 qt. at age 43. I had 7 children and 2 grandchildren Tracy and Chris. I went to College with 3rd son and at one time 4 of my children and my self was in College the same, third child and I finished the same day, ASN Alabama. My oldest son sent me to College bought me a car; [oth. writ.] I have finished my first book and I am half way through the second and 2 children's book and 2 plays. I sent one of the plays for and Artist in resident grant including God's Way, and 2 other poems.; [pers.] My life has been an exciting one, and sometimes lots of fun. My Motto is to "aim at the stars, if you want to walk over the mountain." Nothing beats failing but trying.; [a.] Detroit, MI

CROSWELL, GAYLE SUSAN
[b.] November 25, 1951, Toronto, Ontario; [p.] Jean Wells and Tim Wells; [m.] Frank Robert Croswell, July 8, 1972; [ch.] Melissa Gaylene Croswell; [ed.] Riverdale, Collegiate, Waterloo University, special Education Specialist.; [occ.] English, History, Geography, Art, Drama and special Education Teacher Gr 7 and 8, Swansea Senior School; [hon.] Waterloo University Dean's List, Workshop Leader in both Canada and the U.S. on subjects of: Reading, Language, special Education "Inclusion", Assessment and Homework.; [oth. writ.] (Unpublished) 3 poetry books: 1. The prescription: An Academic Social and emotional bandaid for the ailment of the middle school student. 2. Understanding: When they wear their insides on the outside. 3. Modern day nursery rhymes: Children in Crisis and single poem publications in several educational journals.; [pers.] My focus is poetry is two fold: To enhance our understanding of children "in need" and that of "self-therapy". Using poetry in a therapeutic vein is also an incredible teaching strategy. I use extensively with my students. We all write passionately about importantly, things we adore and perhaps more importantly, things we dislike or fear.; [a.] Etobicoke, Ontario

CRUNCHIE, SHANE ZANE
[b.] 1969, Planet Earth; [oth. writ.] "Put your brain on paper" 1986. "The preliminary phases of self destruction (and other positive moments in time)" 1991.; [pers.] Life is an experiment.; [a.] Beaverton, OR

CRUPI, PAMELA ANN
[b.] May 13, 1954, Troy, NY; [p.] Lebra Mango Crupi and Edward F. Crupi; [ch.] Paula, Peter, Carlo; [ed.] Russell Sage Junior College of Albany, Columbia High School - East Greenbush NY, School of Nursing - Albany County; [occ.] Nurse and homemaker; [memb.] Latham Ridge Pac, Shaker Jr High Pac, Diabetes Association, St. Pius X Church, Heart Fund; [hon.] Valedictorian Nursing class, Phi Theta Kappa-National Honor Society, graduated Dean's List, art awards; [oth. writ.] Poems written to daughter Paula in yearbook, also to mother and father on their birthday.; [pers.] Family love and support is one's greatest gift.; [a.] Colonie, NY

CRUZ, CARLOS
[pen.] Sea Cruz; [b.] December 20, 1968, Brooklyn, NY; [p.] Mr. Florencia Cruz and Manuela Cruz; [ed.] Bishop Loughlin High, John Jay College of Criminal Justice; [memb.] St. Matthews Roman Catholic Church; [hon.] Dean's List, National Dean's List.; [pers.] Life is a mear notion, its chaos just a line. From seas comes my devotion and skies comes your divine. My mom and dad are my sun and moon, creating a world of nature for me to live in tune. Gracias.; [a.] Brooklyn, NY

CRUZ, MARIZ ELIANE ALVES
[pen.] Eliane Cruz; [b.] June 15, 1961, Brazil; [p.] Eloi Alves Cruz and Odette Alves Cruz; [ed.] University of Anchieta St. Paulo.; [occ.] Reporter; [hon.] First and second place award's in poetry contest in Brazil, from the Academia de Letras, The poem for first place was "Amorte" and for second place "A Primavera"; [oth. writ.] In the University of Anonieta I got an award fro second place on an award for second place on a romantic music contest the name of the music was: "Recordacoes"; [pers.] Life is the biggest miracle the biggest miracle is life, 2nd it is registered in Jesus's grave. He's not here because of his resurrection any way he's lives! And that's why life is the biggest miracle....; [a.] Somerville, MA

CSINGER, JOSEPH
[occ.] Writer, Poet; [oth. writ.] Poems published in local papers.; [pers.] Tries to promote public awareness through poetry.; [a.] Nanaimo British Columbia, Canada

CUELLAR, ELVA CAVAZOS
[pen.] Melanie; [b.] December 2, 1956, Weslaco, TX; [p.] Jose Cavazos Jr. and Amelia H. Cavazos; [m.] Ruben Cuellar, February 25, 1991 (2nd); [ch.] Omar, Aimee, and Adam Sandoval, stepchildren: Christopher and Stephanie; [ed.] South Houston High School, San Jacinto College Central and South Campus (graduated in 1975), 72 College credits in Business Administration; [occ.] Management Information System Specialist; [memb.] Parent-teacher Assoc.; [hon.] 2nd Place District Information Communications, 4th Place Area-Information Communications; [oth. writ.] Collection of poems in English and Spanish that reflect triumphs and tragedies in my lifetime.; [pers.] Life and love have greatly influenced my writing. I believe everyone has something they are good at. You must search within yourself to find it.; [a.] Pearland, TX

CULP, DEBRA
[b.] December 20, 1962, Mineral Wells, TX; [p.] Delbert Walker; [m.] Ronald L. Culp, December 31, 1994; [ch.] Elvis Lee Bunnell and Bridgette Ann Bunnell; [ed.] Graduate of Mineral Wells H.S. and Weatherford Jr. College; [occ.] Secretary for Lockheed Fort Worth Company, Ft Worth, TX; [pers.] I hope that "My Heavenly Baby" will bring peace and hope to the hearts of those who read it.; [a.] Fort Worth, TX

CULVER, ANN
[b.] March 7, 1926, Beloit, KS; [p.] Joseph and Anna M. Otter; [m.] Giles Culver, March 9, 1985; [ch.] Joseph A., Mary L., Michael A., Anna M.; [ed.] Nursing School; [occ.] Semi-retired nurse; [oth. writ.] Have written several poems, have not submitted any for publication at this time; [pers.] My children have been and are my inspiration. All my poems are written about and for them, my recent poems are inspired by my eight grandchildren. All poetry related to life experiences.; [a.] Brookfield, IL

CUMMINGS, MAUREEN
[b.] December 19, 1951, New York; [p.] James P. Morris and Mary A. Morris; [m.] Nathan D. Cummings; [ch.] Peace, Leah, Natalia, Jonathan David, Timothy James; [ed.] Bethpage High School; [occ.] Claims department, American Pioneer Life Insurance Co.; [memb.] American Red Cross; [oth. writ.] Many poems; [pers.] Poetry allows us to see through the window of nature of the very heights and depths of the soul. It is the passageway from earth to heaven where we find the connection between body and spirit. It is mystical, it is magical. It unlocks the door to our innermost being and shows us to secrets of the universe.

CUMMINGS, RACHAEL LUJEAN
[pen.] Jeanne Conner Cummings; [b.] December 19, 1927, Dallas, TX; [p.] Rev Merlin E. Conner and Blanche J. Wilkinson Conner; [m.] Donalo W.

Cummings Sr. (deceased), December 26, 1953; [ch.] Don Jr., Rodney Brian (deceased), Bradley Alan; [ed.] North Dallas High School, Central Bible College, University of Akron; [occ.] Retired From AT&T; [memb.] Telephone Pioneers of America, First assembly of God Sanctuary Choir, missions committee, and Educational Dept.; [oth. writ.] Poetry some published in Vancouver BC, Island Christian Herald, Articles and Poetry Published in First family our church monthly news letter.; [pers.] Music and poetry express the heartbeat of my being. Since it flows out from me, it, hopefully, touches others.; [a.] Akron, OH

CURL, MARJORIE ANDERSON

[b.] July 2, Nacogdoches, TX; [p.] Ruth Anderson; [m.] Lavon Curl, June 26; [ch.] Tyrone Curl and Daphne "Peaches" Curl Berry; [ed.] Med (Master Educ), BS Elem Educ, Generic Special Educ, Kindergarten, Early Childhood ED - Handicapped child, Emotionally disturbed, Mentally retarded, Sec'y diploma; [occ.] Teacher; [memb.] Phi Delta Kappa, Business and Professional Women, American Assoc of University Women, Delta Sigma Theta Sorority, Top Ladies of Distinction Inc, National Notary Association; [hon.] Dean's List, Church Honoree, Secretary Appreciation Award, initiated Scholarship Endowment in memory of a 6 grade student, County Fair Home, canning ribbons; [oth. writ.] Church welcomes/responses, children stories and poems.; [pers.] I write what I feel hear and see. To me, it's an expressive language that can be identified by all regardless of age.; [a.] Nacogdoches, TX

CURNUTTE, HELEN P.

[b.] December 23, 1936, Ashland, KY; [p.] Herbert Spradling, Nola Farris; [m.] Robert L. Curnutte Sr., September 24, 1955; [ch.] Cynthia Neff and Robert L. Curnutte Jr.; [ed.] Wayne Co. High School, Courses at U, TN.; [occ.] Homemaker, Consultant-Health care for elderly.; [memb.] Church of Christ; [hon.] National Honor Society, 2 yrs., Employee of year, Collinsville, IL, Nursing home.; [oth. writ.] Presently Working on Manuscript of Poetry Collection and a cook book.; [pers.] I have an unshakeable love of life, hopefully "Painting" a portrait of my mind and soul through my poems to the reader.; [a.] Huntington, WV

CURRAN, JULIE MAE

[pen.] Julie Mae; [b.] November 14, 1931, Minneapolis, MN; [m.] James; [ch.] 3 daughter, 10 grandchildren; [pers.] Lived in Australia for twenty-five years, after returning to U.S.A. last year, began looking over poetry never submitted. I continue creating "pictures from the soul." (Which I have been doing since childhood.)

CURTIS, JERRY

[pen.] Jerry Curtis; [b.] July 11, 1935, Detroit, MI; [p.] Lottie Stracka and Edward (deceased); [m.] Berta Curtis, October 4, 1987; [ed.] Chadsey High (Detroit, MI), Society of Ats and Crafts (Fine Arts Schools in Detroit); [occ.] Artist; [oth. writ.] Book of Poems (unpublished); [pers.] I write from the heart and try to convey love and understanding of human behaviour. Life's simple and complex situations give me food for thought.; [a.] Warren, MI

CZERVINSKI, KATHERINE L. M.

[pen.] Katherine Louette Martin; [b.] November 3, 1946, Ohowekea, Ontario, Canada; [p.] Scott Martin and Norman L. Curley; [m.] George T. Czervinski, May 24, 1975; [ch.] Becky, Ricky, Andy, Angel and David; [ed.] 10th Grade; [occ.] Domestic Engineer, Homemaker; [oth. writ.] Several poems and fillers I have written in spiral note books in longhand, (4 spirals) that have not been published.; [pers.] I have written all my poems about my family, friends and traveling. Only the names had been changed.; [a.] North Tonawanda, NY

D'AMBROSIO, JOSETTA

[b.] August 15, 1977, Pittsburgh, PA; [p.] Salvatore and Diana D'Ambrosio; [ed.] 1995 Graduate of Baldwin High School; [hon.] First place in "Literature" category Reflections Program in 1987-1988; [oth. writ.] This is my first published writing but I have over 30 other poems that someday I hope will be published in books such as this one; [pers.] My writing reflects mostly my life and climaxes which I reflect in my writing instead of violence.; [a.] Pittsburgh, PA

D'AMICO, PAUL M.

[pen.] Paul M. D'Amico; [b.] July 20, 1934, Livingston Manor, NY; [p.] John and Lucy D'Amico; [m.] Barbara L., June 30, 1962; [ch.] 5; [ed.] Georgetown Univ., C. 1956, Columbia Univ: Teachers Coll. C. 1957, Chicago Coll. of Osteopathy, C. 1961; [occ.] Lecturer: Telecomm. Consult., Retired Osteopathic Physician and Addictionist.; [memb.] 25 years N.Y.S. Osteopathic Society, American Soc. of Addiction Medicine, Charter Member of Amer. Acad. of Addictionology.; [hon.] Times Herald Record Community Service Award (1985), Sullivan Co. Cares Coalition Award for Outstanding Svs. Against Substance Abuse; [oth. writ.] Massive Myths with Simple Solutions — Revolutionary Breakthrough in Drug Dependencies (1987), Addictions, Cults and Disease - The Final Solution (1980), Videotape Series (4) - Psychobiology of Drug Dependencies with Spiritual and Social Dimensions and Discharge Instructions.; [pers.] The spirit of God flows through the mind of man, to inspire him. The mind of man flows through the body of man and the human society to heal all things.; [a.] Livingston Manor, NY

D'ARIENZO, SARA

[b.] October 16, 1965, Saint Louis, MO; [p.] Alfred Calvelli, Judy Calvelli; [m.] Carl P. D'Arienzo III, April 30, 1988; [ch.] Emma Noel D'Arienzo; [ed.] Chatsworth High School, San Diego State University; [occ.] Preschool Teacher and Manager, Kinder Care Learning Center, Canyon Country, CA; [oth. writ.] A personal collection which I have not yet sought publication for.; [pers.] I enjoy the challenge of turning thoughts and words into meaningful verse. I am most intrigued by sonnets and iambic pentameter.; [a.] Castaic, CA

DAIGNEAULT, L. PAUL

[b.] July 9, 1932, Ansonville, Ontario, Canada; [p.] Philomene and Armand Daigneault; [m.] Colette Daigneault, October 1, 1955; [ch.] Michael and John; [ed.] Graduate of Kirkland Lake (Ontario), Collegiate and Vocational School, Newspaper Institute of America and DeVry Technical Institute; [occ.] Public Servant in Ottawa Ontario Canada; [oth. writ.] Various poems and now working at the craft of fiction writing; [a.] Nepean Ottawa Ontario, Canada

DALRYMPLE, SHARON L.

[pen.] Sharon Momrow; [b.] June 19, 1954, Miami, FL; [p.] Victor J. Momrow, Phyllis L. Momrow; [m.] Robert B. Dalrymple, July 20, 1979; [ch.] Sharon Nicole, Robert Bruce, Melody Dawn, April Momrow; [ed.] Upper Darby High School, St. Joseph's Evening College; [occ.] Surviving Mother; [pers.] Just starting out, I'm a late bloomer.; [a.] Upper Darby, PA

DAMICO, DIANNE

[b.] July 27, 1948, Heidelberg, Germany; [p.] Lillian Claire and William P. Damico; [m.] Gerald Francis Wagner, November 10, 1985; [ed.] Taipei American School, Taiwan. Art Institute of Pittsburgh, University of Tennessee.; [occ.] Waitress, Stan's, Goodland, Florida.; [a.] Naples, FL

DANTONI, ELVA B.

[b.] August 23, 1922, Port Orange, FL; [p.] Arthur and Stella Bennett; [m.] Joseph L. Dantoni, November 8, 1942; [ch.] Marie, Joseph A. and Linda E. Lise; [ed.] Mainland High School, Southern Baptist School of Nursing, New Orleans LA, Daytona Beach Community College, University South FLorida Diabetes Educators Program.; [occ.] Registered Nurse, Registered Diabetes Educator; [memb.] American Assoc. of Diabetes Educators; [hon.] High Honors from Daytona Beach Community College. Also on the Dean's List.; [oth. writ.] 32 poems, 2 short stories, my autobiography; [pers.] I reflect on life experiences and natures natural beauty. Influenced by Emily Dickenson.; [a.] Holly Hill, FL

DARMODY, DANIEL T.

[b.] January 24, 1952, Los Angeles, CA; [p.] John A. Darmody and Pearline I. Darmody; [m.] Jean Headley Darmody, October 9, 1993; [ed.] Thessaloniki Int'l High School, San Francisco State Univ., (B.A. in Industrial/ Organizational Psychology); [occ.] Game Division Manager, Tesie Meat Company, Oakland, CA; [hon.] Dean's List, (S.F. State Un.), Graduated Magna Cum Laude (S.F. State Un.), Golden Key Nat'l Honor Society (S.F. State Un.); [oth. writ.] "The Shadow" Literary Magazine, Junior and Senior years in High School - Creator, Editor, Contributing Writer. Many other poems over the years.; [pers.] "Our Boy" was inspired by our beloved kitten, Maverick, who was killed on our wedding day. As I have done many times in the past, I use poetry as a catharsis. I try to express what is in my heart and soul.; [a.] Pacifica, CA

DARTU, MARGARET LOUISE

[pen.] Copperbland Hair, Hazel green eyes; [b.] April 17, 1947, Johannesburg; [p.] Thys and Jessie Van Zijl; [m.] Reginald Dartu, February 6, 1966; [ch.] Charmain, Danny, and Michell, 3 grandchildren Dean 5 1/2 yrs, Ashley-John 2 1/2 yrs, Cherise 1 1/2 yr; [oth. writ.] Religious prose, and songs (personal use because of lack of the music) lyrics only.; [pers.] You are never to question the work of a poet, only try to understand it

DAVENPORT, TANA C.

[b.] April 15, 1964, Denver, CO; [p.] Karen K. Damron, Cliff Murphy; [m.] Douglas L. Davenport, June 9, 1990; [ch.] Robert Davenport, Brandon Davenport; [occ.] Vice President of Affordable Legal Aid, Inc.; [pers.] I want to thank my Mom, Karen K. Damron, for her belief in me and without her all of my dreams would only be dreams. Because of my loving husband, adoring children, and beautiful family and friends there are no more storms, only sunshine and roses.; [a.] Sacramento, CA

DAVENPORT, TINA MARIE

[pen.] My husband calls me his "French Fry Angel"; [b.] March 9, 1965, Carrollton, IL; [p.] Claudette Sharks, William E. Broyles; [m.] William M. O. Davenport, November 24, 1993; [ch.] Kevin Ray Carriger Jr.; [ed.] I am a graduated retired Certified Nursing Assistance; [occ.] House wife and mother; [memb.] West fair Baptist Church we help donations fight for Jerry's Kids, also do charity work in side my church and out side of my home.; [oth. writ.] I have many more poems I have written, my goal is to create my poems in a book have them published to the public.; [pers.] I've been writing poems since childhood, a special gift from God, my poems reflect my own feelings of life's trials, the poems I've written or have read of other poets to me are magical and spiritual to the soul.; [a.] Jacksonville, IL

DAVID, MARY ANN

[pen.] M. A. Tata; [b.] May 20, 1936, Newark, NJ; [p.] Constance Space, Edmond Space; [m.] Bernard E. David, September 22, 1957; [ch.] Leslie, Laurie, Gary; [ed.] Kearny H.S., Scottsdale Community College, American University; [occ.] Travel Consultant; [memb.] Goodwill Auxiliary; [hon.] American Legion Medal for Best Essay 1949, "Woman of the Month" 3/1976; [oth. writ.] Poems only; [pers.] I am a romantic and all my poetry reflects this. I haven't written a current poem in forty years.; [a.] Phoenix, AZ

DAVID, VICTOR

[b.] July 29, 1936, Simpson, PA; [p.] Alex David, Ann David; [m.] Luisa Saraimalkah David, November 28, 1962; [ch.] Mercedes David-Sheets; [ed.] Fell Twp. H.S., PA, Penn St. Univ., Temple Univ. Med. School; [occ.] Physician; [memb.] American Medical Association, American Institute of Ultrasound, Planetary Society (Medicine), Astronomical Society, Chabad of the East Bay; [hon.] Dean's List, Diplomat American College OB-Gyn; [oth. writ.] Lifetime of unpublished poems, American Journal Perinatology - article; [pers.] A respect for humankind and everything alive, from a broken flower stem to a superhuman experience; [a.] Berkeley, CA

DAVIDSON, GILLIAN M.

[b.] November 26, 1929, London, United Kingdom; [m.] Married; [ch.] One son; [occ.] Retired School Teacher and Bank Clerk.; [memb.] National Trust, National Association of Decorative and Fine Arts Society, Sainsbury Centre for Visual Arts (U.E.A) Local Church.; [oth. writ.] A few poems published in the U.K.; [pers.] Retirement has offered more time for creative writing and I have also set some poems to music.; [a.] Norwich Norfolk, United Kingdom

DAVIDSON, MERLYN H.

[pen.] "Joe David"; [b.] February 28, 1932, Yorkton, Saskatchewan, Canada; [p.] George and Anna (Laine) Kostenok; [m.] James N. (deceased), 1954; [ch.] Arlene Janet; [occ.] Semi retired from the "business world."; [memb.] Charter member of the Langley Hospice Foundation; [oth. writ.] I started to write poetry and short stories in my 60th year. (Someday I hope to compile a small book of treasured reading for my granddaughters); [pers.] Beauty, courage, poignancy, joy and serenity is what I strive for in my poetic "attempts."; [a.] Lancley British Columbia, Canada

DAVIS, GEORGE V.

[pen.] George V. Davis; [b.] December 12, 1912, Philadelphia, PA; [p.] Roscoe and Gettine V. Davis; [m.] Bernice, September 10, 1989; [ch.] Ros, Elizabeth and Timothy; [ed.] BS in Engineering, LL. B (Law); [occ.] Retired Attorney; [memb.] 1. Connecticut Bar Assn., 2. President of ACAP (Adventist Composers, Arrangers and Poets), 3. The Writer's Arena.; [pers.] Several years ago I started writing gospel poetry and music for the purpose of inspiring others to accept Jesus as their personal Saviour. I am the Editor of ACAP's quarterly newsletter entitled ACAPella.; [a.] Saint George, UT

DAVIS III, JOSEPHUS

[b.] April 20, 1952, Tarrantco Fort Worth, TX; [p.] Josephus Davis Jr. and Lewis Davis, Ollie Marie; [ch.] Josephus Davis IV, Joyce Marie Davis, Tesha Lavon Davis; [ed.] Kirkpatrick Jr. Senior High School, Fort Worth Technical Trade School, Computer Programer and Operator, Aviation Techtraing "U.S. Navy", Cowtown Tractor Traiter Drivers Education"; [occ.] Maintenance Tech "I", Texas Dept of Transportation Dept "Highway"; [memb.] North Tri-etnic Community Center, Donor to the state Trooper Organization; [hon.] Maintenance, Material and Management Certificate Navy Honorable Discharge Navy; [pers.] It is a pleasure for me to write positive writing. There are to many reasons to thank God for the gift of life and humbleness of the thought of love.; [a.] Fort Worth, TX

DAVIS, ROBERTA ANDERSON

[b.] December 17, 1931, Kansas City, KS; [p.] Frank and Dorothy Anderson; [m.] F. Keith Davis, May 25, 1957; [ch.] Mark F. Davis; [ed.] Loretto Academy, Avila College; [occ.] Writer; [memb.] Multiple Sclerosis Society, Homestead Country Club, Smithsonian Institution; [oth. writ.] Several poems and articles published in magazines, newspapers, literary journals, and an anthology of writings on coping with MS; [pers.] I strive for poetry that speaks clearly, concisely and simply to all persons who read it.; [a.] Shawnee Mission, KS

DAVIS, ROLAND B.

[b.] August 24, 1934, Cleveland, OH; [p.] Elizabeth Zelenak, Roland (Hallam) Davis; [m.] Marie Jane Szalay, September 15, 1956; [ch.] Bernadette Marie Furlong, Deborah Anne Blatnik; [ed.] East Technical High, Cleveland, OH, Cuyahoga Community College, Parma, OH, University of Notre Dame, Notre Dame, IN; [occ.] Engineer; [hon.] Eagle Scout, BSA, Scarabaean Honor Society, East Tech., National Honor Society; [pers.] I am a romantic that finds pleasure with people and machines, and I write what comes from within. The solitude of a moment can turn into an eternity of life, enjoy the moment.; [a.] Stow, OH

DAVIS, SANNY

[pen.] Sandy Krueger; [b.] July 13, 1950, Grosse Pointe, MI; [p.] Donald and Earla Krueger; [ch.] Joni 25, Christy 21, and Devon 10, two granddaughters Courtney 3, and Tiffaney 2; [ed.] Fraser High School; [occ.] Waitress (Head) and Hostess at a very unique steak house; [oth. writ.] I have many other poems, mainly written when I was in my teens and twenties. Also, I have some short stories; [pers.] I view poetry as a window into one's mind and soul. Who knows what truly lies therein. Writing is a release letting the inner you project forth, sometimes negative or positive energies.; [a.] Plymouth, MI

DAVIS SR., DANIEL ARMAND

[pen.] D. Armand Longmoon; [b.] April 25, 1957, Sacramento, CA; [p.] Thomas Jefferson and Florence Davis; [m.] Chryl Ann Davis, October 10, 1979; [ch.] Thomas, Daniel Jr. and Johnathon Tyrell; [ed.] I attended school in Templeton, Calif. In listed U.S. Army. Served in 172nd Special Forces Unit, (Alaska); [occ.] Food Service Ind. Mt. Charleston Inn, Mt. Charleston Nevada; [memb.] The Human Race; [hon.] Golden poet 1992, First Place, San Luis Obisp Mid. State Fair for Wood Carving Subject: Tebeton Tower, Prize Winning Singer.; [oth. writ.] Tears for the mother. Peace keepers. Facts. Living in the here and now. Too many castles. Moving Forward. A Bad Mistake. Guardian Child (Golden Poet) Nonsense offense. Spring Child.; [pers.] In my life I have come to see, that the earth, in her endless self giving, is indeed the greatest example of love in it's truest sense. In that knowledge, I have found new joy in each moment.; [a.] Las Vegas, NV

DAVIS, TONI D.

[b.] January 21, 1971, Chicago, IL; [p.] Lea B. Davis and Willie B. Davis Jr.; [ed.] William H. Taft H.S., Fisk University B.A. Degree Political Science, Law; [occ.] Case worker, RTM Family Services, Chicago, IL; [memb.] Citizens for a better West side; [oth. writ.] Several poems published in local newspapers; [pers.] "When excellence is a virtue, there is no limit to what one can or cannot do."; [a.] Forest Park, IL

DAVIS, VICTORIA ELIZABETH

[b.] June 28, 1957, Evansville, IN; [p.] William Oglesby, Rae L. Oglesby; [m.] Rudi Musquez, May 7, 1993; [ch.] S. Eric Davis; [ed.] Junior, Univ. of New Mexico, Freshman, Sophomore at Univ. of Southern Indiana, Graduated Wm. Henry Harrison High School 1975; [occ.] Student, English/ History double major; [hon.] Sigma Tau Delta English Honor Society, Golden Key National Honor Society; [oth. writ.] Poems and essays published in local newspapers, to be published by Sparrograss Publishing in October, 1995 (poem).; [pers.] I believe reading and writing are what makes a civilization: Being a full-time, non-traditional college student, and author must make me civilized indeed.; [a.] Albuquerque, NM

DAVIS, VICTORINE BRADFORD

[pen.] Victorine; [b.] June 20, 1922, Corsicana, TX; [p.] Ruth and Clarence Bradford; [m.] Hugh Donovan Davis (deceased), July 15, 1940; [ch.] Vickie Ruth Kienast - Hugh Bradford Davis; [ed.] High School, Jr. College - made deans list; [occ.] Semi-Retired - Custom Home Builder - Writer; [memb.] Dalls Home Builders Association, ACBL Memphis Tenn., Northway Christian Church; [hon.] Richland College, Dalls, Deans List - Woman Builder of the Year in 1970 Dalls, Texas; [oth. writ.] Stories in local newspaper, wrote for the Hondo Air Force Paper, Hondo Texas during World War II; [pers.] I am a Gemini and do have a dual mind. I have in my time been a model at Neiman Marcus, writer, Custom Home Builder, mother, wife and love any new challenge. I acted in many plays through out high school, the army life and little theatre.

DAYNES, PAULA

[pen.] Jenna Nicole; [b.] February 25, 1976, London, England; [p.] Eileen Daynes (mother); [ed.] Graduate of Handsworth Secondary School, Vancouver, B.C., Canada; [pers.] My writing reflects who I am and what I believe in. I hope when people read my work they come to their own conclusion from their own interpretation. I think it's important to gain something from poetry and to understand it really - is more than just words.; [a.] North Vancouver British Columbia, Canada

DE ANGELIS, CELESTE C.

[b.] June 18, 1956, Italy; [p.] Michael and Nilda Gennarelli; [m.] Peter N. De Angelis, November 4, 1985; [ch.] Gabriella and Louis Step children George and Peter De Angelis; [occ.] Owner and operator of De Angelis Italian Market, in North Wildwood, NJ; [pers.] To live, love and laugh and to give my all to my children and my husband, for they are my greatest works of poetry.; [a.] North Wildwood, NJ

DE BAGGIS, SARA

[b.] July 15, 1978, Attelboro, MA; [p.] Michelle De

Baggis; [m.] Single; [oth. writ.] I have written six notebooks full of poetry. All are about: Life, Love, Death and Memories.; [pers.] My inspiration of most of my writing I've got from my grandfather. A poet needs pain to write and I've had my share. My grandfather recently passed away and I write my feelings about it.; [a.] Medway, MA

DE CHIRICO, DR. CORIN
[pen.] Corin De Chirico; [b.] July 5, 1961, New York; [p.] William and Elain De Chirico; [m.] Dr. Jeremy A. Dzen, September 1, 1991; [occ.] Physician, Internal Medicine, Nashua, N.H.; [memb.] American Medical Association, American Osteopathic Association; [hon.] Dean's list 1983-1984, National Osteopathic Womens Physician Associations Award for Academic Excellence 1990, Intern of the Year Award 1991.; [oth. writ.] Medical: "Common Pyoderms" 1990; [pers.] Carpe Diem!; [a.] Nashua, NH

DE FRANCO, MARIO A.
[b.] November 17, 1986, Paterson; [p.] Mario and Toni De Franco; [ed.] 2nd grade

DE MORGAN, GRISELL
[pen.] Gigi; [b.] July 6, 1961, Cuba; [p.] Amelio Gomez, Maria Gomez; [m.] Perry B. Morgan, October 31, 1981; [ch.] James Perry, Alex Anthony, Perry Bernard Jr., Perri Cristina.; [ed.] Venice High School, West L.A. College; [occ.] Technical Service Especialist, Airtouch Cellular; [memb.] Toast Masters, United Way.; [oth. writ.] Non-Published Book: "From My Heart - To Yours". Collaborated in song writing for R and B Band.; [pers.] From my emotions - "Feelings" are created, and transferred words, but only words that come from my heart. My highest honor to God, and to a dear friends Alejandro Bogle for inspiring me to write again.; [a.] Santa Ana, CA

DE ROSA, KATHY
[b.] February 15, 1948, Brooklyn, NY; [p.] Anthony and Ann Polisano; [m.] Albert De Rosa, September 23, 1967; [ch.] Stacy - 26, Lori - 23, Michael - 19; [occ.] Housewife; [hon.] Inspirational Poetry, Award of Merit Certificate, 2nd Prize Winner Title: The Love of my Life; [pers.] My brother, Anthony Polisano, who in 1981 was diagnosed with cancer and was miraculously healed by prayer was my inspiration to write; [a.] Brooklyn, NY

DEAL, DONALD
[b.] February 22, 1938, Keith, WV; [p.] Emma and Orville Deal; [m.] Widowed, July 4, 1975; [ch.] Marilyn Glazier; [ed.] 8th Grade; [occ.] Mechanic; [pers.] I have been inspired from personal experience to write this simple poem. I have great faith in God and strongly believe that He is the answer to the problems we face on earth.; [a.] West Haven, CT

DEAN, LESTER
[b.] November 23, 1953, Florence, AL; [p.] Bruce L. Dean, Ruth Dean; [sib.] Randy Dean; [ed.] G.E.D., University of North Alabama, Northwest, Shoals Community College; [memb.] Rock of Faith Church, Petersville, AL; [hon.] I have won awards in photography at State Fairs and one of the local museums; [pers.] It is my desire through poetry as one means to be a blessing and inspiration. Also, to reach the unconverted with the Gospel message. And glorify my Lord and Savior Jesus Christ.; [a.] Florence, AL

DEARDEUFF JR., PAUL E.
[pen.] Paul Reeves, Joe Paul Jr.; [b.] June 30, 1943, Ruyle, IL; [p.] Paul and Evelean Deardeuff; [ch.] Marletta Lynn, Charlene Elaine, Tina Marie; [ed.] High School (GED), AA Business Management; [occ.] Ribbon Maker; [memb.] None, not a joiner; [hon.] Bronze Star Air Force Commendation Medal Air force Longevity Service Award Air Force Good Conduct Medal with Loops, National Defence Service Medal Vietnam Service Medal with Two Bronze Stars Republic of Vietnam Campaign Medal Small Arms Expert Marksmanship Ribbon; [oth. writ.] A couple of scifi short stories, and one detective murder story, none published.; [pers.] Age 51, married twice, divorced twice, still looking, hope to find the right woman in the near future.; [a.] Alameda, NM

DECKER, PHILIP H.
[b.] March 15, 1961, Washington, DC; [p.] Allan Decker, Marcia Decker; [m.] Irma Sanchez Decker; [ch.] Rubi, Adriana, and Alejandra; [ed.] University of Maryland Baltimore County, Stanford University, San Diego State University; [occ.] Social Studies Teacher, Middle School; [hon.] UMBC Chancellors, Scholastic Merit, Stanford Public Service, Harcourt Scholar; [oth. writ.] Photo essays and articles published in several magazines and journals.; [pers.] Special thanks to the masculine soul journaling group, at the writing center in San Diego. Adelante!; [a.] San Diego, CA

DEFEYO, JANET
[b.] September 10, 1931, Bronxville, NY; [p.] William DeFeyo and Mary DeFeyo; [ed.] Radford College, Women's Division Virginia Polytechnic Institute, Teachers College, Columbia University; [occ.] Retired Elementary Teacher North Carolina, New York; [hon.] Pi Gamma Mu; [a.] Searsdale, NY

DEGENHARDT, CARA ELIZABETH
[b.] April 24, 1976, Cranford, NJ; [p.] Paul Degenhardt, Bette Degenhardt; [ed.] Cranford High School graduate, previously at Davis and Elkins College, WV, now transferring to Rowan College, NJ; [occ.] Student; [memb.] Member of Division I Field Hockey Team.; [oth. writ.] Several poems that one day I wish to publish, maybe even my own poetry book; [pers.] I started writing poetry a year ago due to my parents divorce. As I started writing about my family many other writings have come out of it. I love my family and I cherish everything that happens to my family and myself.; [a.] Cranford, NJ

DEGENNARO, JOHN E.
[pen.] Effriam Dowser; [b.] January 20, 1958, New Haven; [p.] John B. and Adrian DeGennaro; [m.] Gail Ruth Zercie DeGennaro, November 1, 1980; [ed.] Eli Whitney R.V.T.S.; [occ.] Self-employed; [memb.] N.H.R.H.T.A.; [oth. writ.] "I Love Trains", Trails in the Sand; [pers.] Live for simpler times, love for simpler lives.; [a.] North Branford, CT

DELISLE, ROBIN
[b.] May 26, 1959, Toledo, OH; [p.] Nancy L. Terry; [ed.] Currently working toward a Bachelor of Science and Technical Management Degree at the DeVry Institute of Technology.; [occ.] Electronics Technician; [hon.] Several lyric writing awards from the American Song Festival and Music City Song Festival Lyric Competitions.; [pers.] I feel that poetry is the voice of the spirit, and should therefore be revered.; [a.] Phoenix, AZ

DENIS, ARLY
[b.] October 18, 1971, Haiti; [p.] Annette Denis, Jea C. Denis; [m.] January 28, 1971; [ch.] Patricia, Reginald, J. C. Denis Junior, Irving; [ed.] Brooklyn College, Midwood High School, St. Thomas Aquinas Grammer School; [occ.] Student Brooklyn College; [memb.] Association for the Study of Classical African Civilizations, National Blaer Science Student Organization; [oth. writ.] Reflections: Paradise on the Rocks, The Hidden Meaning, Blissful Imaginings, Woman; [pers.] I am a man of the earth with the potential to do as the earth does, and life - life is a mask of God through which eternity is to be experienced.; [a.] Brooklyn, NY

DERZAPH, TINA L. M.
[b.] February 4, 1967, Reigna, Saskatchewan, Canada; [p.] Ralph and Paulette Sturgean; [m.] Tim M. F. L. Derzaph, August 23, 1986; [ch.] Catherine A., Grayson T., Vincent R., Spencer S.; [ed.] B.A., B.ed., B.Sc.; [occ.] University Lecturer and Researcher; [memb.] South Zone Board; [hon.] General Proficiency; [pers.] Life is all attitude and action.; [a.] Regina Saskatchewan, Canada

DESREVISSEAU, MARCIA A.
[pen.] Marcia Desrevisseau; [b.] April 7, 1945, Plymouth, MA; [p.] George W. and Helen V. Wood; [m.] Edward U. Desrevisseau II, October 30, 1964; [ch.] Edward U. III and George W., grandson Edward U. IV; [ed.] Plymouth HIgh School - 1963, Stenotype Institute of Boston - 1964; [occ.] Administrative Assist.; [hon.] Battelle Award - 1983, Golden Poet Award - 1987 for "Let me Sing Out to America", Typewriting Award - 1964, Perfect Attendance Award - 1964, Certificates of Achievement - 1964, 1982, and 1988, Silver Poet Award; [oth. writ.] Children's book of verses entitled "Those Little Faces"...not yet published. Also "A Profile in Courage" poem written to the memory of President John Fitzgerald Kennedy (written shortly after the assassination.); [pers.] My God eradicate the anguish, grief, misery, pain and undue suffering of the falsely accused with warranted justice to their accusers for their own merit.; [a.] Plymouth, MA

DESROSIER, JANIENE M.
[b.] January 22, 1956, Invermere, British Columbia, Canada; [p.] Don and Anita Traverse; [ch.] Christie Dawn Desrosier, L. Ryan Desrosier; [ed.] 2 yrs College (EKCC), 1 yr University Notre Dane University (which no longer exists); [occ.] Manager of an Esso Bulk Plant; [hon.] Graduated from DISS High School with honors, Graduated EKCC/ Tourism and Hospitality Management with an award for Academic Achievement; [oth. writ.] Other poems none published; [pers.] I am currently taking a 2 yrs computer programming course by correspondence.; [a.] Invermere British Columbia, Canada

DEUTSCH, ALMA M.
[b.] February 12, 1943, Saskachewan, Canada; [p.] Frank and Alma Hordos; [m.] Stanley Deutsch, October 11, 1962; [ch.] Sidney, Shawn, Tina, Todd; [occ.] Farming; [memb.] Involved in my church. I am on the Finance Committee this year.; [oth. writ.] Had an article published in "The Leader Post", "How I Survive the Deep Freeze in '94".; [pers.] I love children, nature, bird watching. Have written a few poems, but never submitted any. Have two lovely grandchildren.; [a.] Raymore Saskachewan, Canada

DEVONE, ANNIE MAE
[pen.] Annie Mae Felder; [b.] June 14, 1935, Clarendon, CO; [p.] Marie Jones; [m.] Leslie James DeVone, Feb-

ruary 14, 1974; [ch.] Patricia Melvin, Robert Lemon, Taquita Barnett, Gloria Bowden, Kenneth Lemon; [ed.] 11th Grade - Manning High School, Manning, South Carolina; [occ.] Owner and Operator of DeVone Daycare; [memb.] New Hope Baptist Church

DEWITT, PAM
[b.] January 21, 1957, Neosho, MO; [ch.] Joseph Dewitt - January 24, 1977; [occ.] I have owned my own business in Pet Grooming for 12 yrs.; [oth. writ.] I have written a book of poetry called Odds and Ends, which I have not had published.; [pers.] I have been writing poetry since I was 13 yrs. old. I strive to catch the inner feelings of my readers, to bring a laugh or a memory of some one dear or to learn about themselves and to realize they are not alone. That's worth all the gold in the world to me, if I can accomplish this feeling.; [a.] North Richland Hills, TX

DEY, TERRY
[pen.] T. Dey; [b.] December 31, 1965, Beneath the Stars; [occ.] Healer; [pers.] Let us not forget from whence we came of spells and magic still the same; [a.] Ramsey, NJ

DIAL, JOHN O.
[pen.] Johnny Latigo; [b.] September 17, 1938, Dinuba, CA; [p.] Lucille Newhall; [m.] Marion C. Dial, July 19, 1972; [ch.] Anne Susan Lennis; [ed.] High School, Hark Knocks University; [occ.] Retired; [oth. writ.] Several other poems submitted for publication but none accepted, yet - I remain hopeful; [pers.] To write poetry is to bare one's soul for all to see. If I must walk naked on the path of my words let them at least be elegant.; [a.] Fremont, CA

DIANE, ELY
[b.] September 17, 1979, Jackson, MI; [p.] Donald B. Ely, Dale A. Ely; [ed.] Fitch Senior High School; [occ.] Student; [memb.] U.S. Soo Bahk (Tang Soo), Do Moo Duk Kwan Assn., New Life Youthful Restoration Choir. Ledyard Ct; [hon.] Degree in Martial Arts, Black Belt, National Forms Champion.; [oth. writ.] Several unpublished poems and songs; [pers.] If you want something done don't look to others, do it yourself, one person can make a difference and that person could be you.; [a.] Groton, CT

DICKENS, HELON HAMILTON
[b.] October 24, 1930, Cross, TX; [p.] Hugh Hamilton, Minnie Hamilton; [m.] Carl Charles Dickens (deceased), August 31, 1953; [ed.] Graduate of High School Freeport, TX 1950; [occ.] Retired Sales Secretary/ C.S. Rep. Accig., 32 yrs. Allstate Ins.; [hon.] Honor student in High School, 101 honor points. "You Make the Difference", Award-Accig., Allstate Ins. Co. and "Good Hands", Award and Many Suggestion Awards-Allstate Insurance Co.; [oth. writ.] Other poetry, "How I Miss You", set to music by lew tobin-five star music masters. Contract 3/10/53, never published, 1990-95 written birthday greetings, memories of lost one in poetry with pictures of family and friends.; [pers.] I love to create, crochet, I love music, and most of all, I enjoy studying God's word and praising Him for the talents he has given me.; [a.] Houston, TX

DILATUSH, TODD CARLETON
[b.] February 6, 1973, Port Pleasent, NJ; [p.] Thomas and Linda Dilatush; [ed.] Bachelor of Science, Mechanical Engineering Lehigh University; [occ.] Student; [memb.] Phi Delta Theta Fraternity; [hon.] Eagle Scout Rank, Boy Scouts of America 1990; [oth. writ.] Several poems, short stories; [pers.] I tend to reflect the things that were and could have been in ones life. I have been greatly influenced by my childhood and by a beautiful person who was once close to my heart.; [a.] Smoke Rise, NJ

DINAN SR., RICHARD P.
[pen.] Dick Dinan; [b.] April 18, 1941, Philadelphia; [p.] John and Helen Dinan; [m.] Ann Marie (Gerger) Dinan, February 23, 1963; [ch.] Deborah Ann, Richard Jr., Jude Mary Bernadette, Beth Ann, Daniel; [ed.] Bishop Neumann H.S., St. Alphonsus, A Vare, St. Rose Lima; [occ.] Driver, Salesman, Stroehmann Bakery Co.; [hon.] Presidents Club; [oth. writ.] Kirsten Re; [pers.] The thoughts that God passes on to you write them down - (Richard Dinan) Dick Dinan; [a.] Philadelphia, PA

DITSCH, BRO. RICHARD C.
[b.] April 2, 1938, Lou., KY; [p.] Sarah and Richard E. Ditsch; [ed.] Asoc. B.A. Pastoral Min. from Simmons Bible College, at present finishing an M.A.R. at St. James Seminary and Christian College, Dale Carnegie graduate, 1961, Life member of U.S.C.F.; [occ.] Student; [memb.] American Assoc. of Christian Counselors, American Assoc. of Family Counselors, seeking certification in Psychology.; [hon.] Charter member of American Assoc. Of Christian Counselors. Appeared on Channel 41 as pianist Louis. Ky.; [oth. writ.] 72 Galaxy, Fugitives Three, The Name of Love.; [pers.] I have been influenced by the works of Poe, Longfellow, Shakespeare, Dante, Nietzsche. I try to write depicting life in its pain, sorrow, joy and triumphs though words are sometimes a poor medium of communication.; [a.] Tampa, FL

DIXSON, DONNA
[b.] December 17, 1963, Munich, Germany; [occ.] Medical Paralegal for a major toxic tort litigation firm, former Designer, Model; [memb.] Dallas Opera Guild, State Bar of Texas - L.A. Division, DALA, National Trust for Historic Preservation, Earth Island Institute Whale Protection Program; [oth. writ.] Poetic writings have been published in a book of anthologies, currently compiling a collection of recent works.; [pers.] I strive to capture the essence of simplicity and embrace the beauty of romance in my writing.; [a.] Dallas, TX

DOBSON, HELEN WILLIAMS
[b.] November 26, 1949, Philadelphia, PA; [p.] Edward B. and Helen S. Williams; [m.] Cred U. Dobson, July 10, 1942; [ch.] William Edward and Michele Lee Williams; [occ.] Wagner Middle School, Science Laboratory Assistant; [pers.] The disease referred to in this poem is Alzheimer's. I commiserate with the millions of families who are experiencing the tragedy of this disease. I believe God gave me the words to express what was in my heart and presented this opportunity to share them.; [a.] Philadelphia, PA

DOBSON, LYNN
[pen.] C. E. Dobson; [b.] August 9, 1979, Moncton, New Brunswick, Canada; [p.] Kathy and Carl Dobson; [ed.] Grade 10 at Moncton High School, (recently going there, only 15 years old); [memb.] Canadian Kennel Club, Canadian Cystic Fibrosis Foundation; [hon.] An award in Pee-Wee Baseball and in Ruth Barnes Modeling Agency, Awards in school, writing and for turning money into the lost and found.; [oth. writ.] Poems such as: Lovers Cove, A Perfect Place, Happiness, Melanie, Friends For Life, A Friend For Me, A Helping Hand, Depending On You, Old And Grey.; [pers.] Writing is very relaxing, and it makes you talk about what you feel inside. All my poems were inspired by family and friends. My mother always said, you could die any day, so live each day to the fullest.; [a.] Moncton New Brunswick, Canada

DOLAND, RHONDA DOUCET
[pen.] Susan Spencil; [b.] February 13, 1960, Jennings, LA; [ed.] Theatre Maj, Psychology Min McNeese State University Lake Charles, LA; [occ.] Wordsmith, Calligrapher, Poet at Large; [memb.] Nat'l Historic Society, Jeff Davis Arts Council, Louisiana Public Broadcasting, Nat'l Public Radio; [hon.] Profiled by Writer's Digest poetry editor Michael Bugeja. Studied under Pulitzer Prize Winner Robert Olen Butler; [oth. writ.] "The Legend of the Cypress Knee Santas"; [pers.] I specialize in commemorative poetry, ballads, and rhyme and rhythm. My motto for 1995 is, "Don't wait to die before you become part of the earth."; [a.] Lake Arthur, LA

DOLL III, RICHARD E.
[b.] February 5, 1979, Alamogordo, NM; [p.] Richard E. Doll II, Leticia M. Doll; [ed.] Alamogordo High School, Vandon High School; [occ.] Student; [pers.] My writings are dedicated to all the friends who help each other through life's little roller coaster. Special thanks to Peter Zemaitaitis and Stacey Burrows.; [a.] Vacaville, CA

DOLLITZ, GRETE
[pen.] Grete Dollitz; [b.] Katden Kirchen, Germany; [p.] Ernst and Charlotte Franke; [m.] Hans J. Dollitz; [ch.] Erika Judy; [ed.] Hunter College NYC, Eastern District High NYC, PS 71 and 121, NYC, also: Parochial (Lutheran) Schools in Germany/Add'l education: Courses U. of NC and U. of CA; [occ.] Producer/Announcer WCUE-FM Radio, Richmond, VA; [memb.] Guitar Foundation of America, Guitar Society in Richmond, Baroque Trio (as guitarist), Consort Firmus (as guitarist); [hon.] Listed in Who's Who in Entertainment also: Personalities of the South; [oth. writ.] 1. Articles in "Soundboard" Magazine, 2. "Virginia Wildlife", 3. "News Leader" on 1. music, 2. Wildflowers, 3. Travel; [pers.] I live an intense inner (personal) life, surrounded by music, my garden, and writing, the beauty of which I try to share with others through my radio programs, as well as greeting cards to friends for which I write the poems especially designed for the person to whom sent.; [a.] Richmond, VA

DONALDSON, CATHERINE L.
[pen.] C. L. Donaldson; [b.] September 29, 1956, Jacksonville, FL; [ed.] Luke M. Powers High School (Flint Michigan), Aquinas College (Grand Rapids, Michigan), Southeast Center for Photographic Studies (at Daytona Beach Community College); [occ.] Research Secretary, St. Vincent's Medical Center, Jacksonville Florida; [pers.] I write poetry as a means to explore and clarify experiences in my life. I derive great satisfaction from the process of transforming a thought into a poem and I challenge myself to recreate the emotion of the experience in each poem I write.; [a.] Jacksonville, FL

DONNELLY, CAROLYN
[b.] September 9, 1984, New Brunswick, NJ; [p.] Catherine and Mike Donnelly; [ed.] 5th grader at Holy Family Academy in Bound Brook; [occ.] Student, Alter Server, Baseball, Basketball, Soccer; [hon.] 1st Place Science Fair, Gymnastics, and Soccer, Honor Roll for 3 years straight.; [oth. writ.] I like to write short stories and I have my own book of poems I wrote.; [pers.] The first shall be last and the last shall be first.; [a.] Manville, NJ

DONOVAN, CHRISTIAN
[b.] November 8, 1972, Philadelphia, PA; [p.] George J. and Catherine M.; [ed.] Wilson Area High School, Univ. of Miami, East Stroudsburg University; [occ.] Student, Writer, Philosopher; [oth. writ.] Only journals which I have yet to attempt publishing; [pers.] I write what I see. Sometimes its happy - sometimes dark or cynical. I try to reflect the state of my environment, whether its my house, country or my mind.; [a.] Riegelsville, PA

DOPWELL, JOSE
[b.] May 27, 1960, Saint Vincent, West Indies; [ed.] Jamaica High School Queens, New York; [occ.] Carpet Installer - blue collar guy; [memb.] Human Race - hope that counts for something; [pers.] I've never written as a type of 'competition'. I've always written as a release for myself or for the benefit of friends. I am both embarrassed and glad that anyone would even consider publishing something I've written; [a.] Cliffside Park, NJ

DORRIS, ROYCE H.
[pen.] Royce H. Dorris; [b.] December 26, 1919, Dermott, AR; [p.] C. L. Dorris and Myrtle V. Dorris; [m.] Blanche E. Dorris, May 15, 1948; [ed.] College; [occ.] Retired; [memb.] Elks, VFW, Independent Methodist Church; [hon.] Gold Tiger Award, Ouachita University, Arkadelphia, AR

DORSETT, BRUCE
[pen.] B. M. Williams; [b.] August 8, 1935, Trenton, TN; [p.] Neal and Edna Dorsett; [ch.] 2; [ed.] B.A. Degree, Chemistry, Physics and Engineering; [occ.] Engineer; [memb.] Optomist Club; [oth. writ.] Personal writings to special friends and relatives; [pers.] Profit from what happened yesterday, keep your hands on today and eyes on tomorrow.; [a.] Baton Rouge, LA

DORST, SHARRON G.
[b.] November 8, 1946, Ottawa, IL; [p.] Dale and Phyllis Mann; [m.] Dennis G. Dorst, July 10, 1965; [ch.] April Morris, Dawn Nickel and Scott Dorst, grandchildren Brandie, Dennis, Kyle Morris and Christopher Nickel; [ed.] Ottawa High School; [occ.] Accounting Clerk; [oth. writ.] Have more poems written but unpublished; [pers.] I hope people enjoy my poem and hopefully I will have some more published in the future; [a.] Slidell, LA

DOUGLAS, RHONDA
[b.] May 17, 1978; [p.] Cleveland and Sonia Douglas; [ed.] High School Junior (Hazelwood West); [occ.] Student; [memb.] Hazelwood Baptist Church Youth Group; [hon.] Manager of Wrestling (certificate), Manager of Track Team (certificate); [pers.] I strive to reflect the experience of daily life in my writing.; [a.] Florissant, MO

DOUGLAS, WILLIAM RICHARD
[b.] October 30, 1950, Portland, OR; [p.] Leonard Douglas, Donna Martin; [m.] Patti Lou Van Den Elsen; [ch.] Hiliary Echo; [ed.] B.A. English, Secondary Teaching Certificate - Portland State University; [occ.] Group Insurance Legal Compliance Supervisor; [pers.] Guinevere, you bless me. You give me beauty, honesty, truth and love. You bless me. I love you. Lancelot; [a.] Portland, OR

DOUGLASS, DON
[b.] January 24, 1927, Saint Anthony, ID; [p.] Lewis and Thera Douglass; [m.] Marie A. Douglass, May 4, 1962; [ch.] Wade J. and Dawn Marie; [ed.] St. Anthony High School, St. Anthony, ID.; [occ.] Mailroom Supervisor; [memb.] National League of Postmasters; [pers.] I write about the positive approach to life, inner feelings and the beauty around us if we only take time to stop and look for it.

DOWLING, FRANCES-ANNE
[pen.] Frances-Anne Dowling; [b.] 1926, New York; [p.] Carlyn and Robert Collins; [m.] John, January 1948; [ch.] 5 children, 6 grandchildren; [occ.] Wife-Mother, Grandmother, Author and Poet; [pers.] The most important part of my life faith in God and family — my parents were the greatest influence in my life; [a.] CA

DOYLE, BETTY J.
[b.] March 27, 1923, Agness, OR; [p.] Leonidas and Mabel Blondell; [m.] James Everett Doyle, March 15, 1942; [ch.] Kerry James, Ronald Everett and Peggy Jean; [ed.] High School; [occ.] Housewife; [memb.] Presbyterian Church; [oth. writ.] Unpublished poems.; [pers.] I hope my words portray a call to reverence, in the God our nation was founded upon, and an appreciation of simple beauty.; [a.] Coquille, OR

DOZIER, LAURIE
[b.] June 21, 1966, Cleveland, OH; [p.] Shirley Dozier and R.C. Clay; [ed.] East High School; [occ.] Senior Underwriting Asst.; [oth. writ.] Various Editorial pieces for the high school newspaper.; [pers.] I base my writing on my own life experiences, creating an equal balance of elation, melancholy and wonder. I've been greatly influenced by Rudyard Kippling, Robert Frost, Edgar Allen Poe and the songwriter "Sting;" [a.] Cleve, OH

DRANGEID, PAUL
[b.] November 28, 1935, Brooklyn, NY; [p.] Deceased; [m.] Miriam Drangeid, June 6, 1958; [ch.] Dana, Jay, Chris, Lindsay; [ed.] B.A. - St. Olaf College - Biology, M.S. - South Dakota State University - Biology; [occ.] Science Teacher, St. Louis Park (MN) Jr. High; [memb.] Minnesota Ed. Assoc. - Bd. Directors, Shepherd of the Hills Luth. Church, Apollo Club - Men's Chorus; [pers.] For along time I have been impressed by the in-sights, into life, I have gained from the people around me - usually after 2nd or 3rd thoughts. I would hope my life and writing would provide this to some others.; [a.] Minnetonka, MN

DRAUS, TED
[b.] June 25, 1919, Old Forge, PA; [p.] John and Agnes Draus-Polish; [m.] Hassie E., March 12, 1940; [ch.] 3; [ed.] High School; [occ.] Retired; [pers.] Altho the poem I entered was dated January 20, 1995, the words came to me about 2 a.m. the next morning after reunion and I got out of bed to write them down before I forgot them. I also have a video of our first reunion. It was a beautiful day! Maybe that should be the name of the poem?

DREW, SHARON LYNN
[pen.] Carol Ann Pike; [b.] March 21, 1955, Detroit, MI; [p.] Dorothy Sandow, Father Unk (birth parents), Thelma Ruth Mathews, Hugh D. Drew (adoptive parents); [m.] Divorced, November 24, 1988; [ch.] Leilah Sempko 4/13/90 (daughter), Brack Scott 1/10/93 (son); [ed.] 12 yrs High School, 1 1/2 yr Comm College Barbizon Graduate Finishing a Modeling School, Criminal Justice Inst. Graduating into Detroit Police Dept. Uncover Operations for street patrol; [occ.] Retired Detroit Police Off., Full time Mom, Part Time Cashier; [memb.] Detroit Northwest and Metro., Seventh-Day Advertise Church, Presenter Speaker-Singer and Organizer, American Lung Association; [hon.] Numerous Certificates and Awards of Achievement as a Detroit Police Officer for 10 years., Between 1975-1985: A minority Hired in as Detroit First Women P.O.s, on Patrol Suffered a severe closed head injury in 1980 and, continuing to work another 5 yrs; [oth. writ.] A Song, Opportunity, Time, A Christians Prayer, Facing Facts, Poker, Forgiveness, Why Goodbye, Having a Friend, Change, How You Make me Feel, Communication Honesty and Under Standing - I'd like to see put to music; [pers.] After growing up in a time period where many of our leaders were assassinated right in front of us on Nat'l TV, riots of 67 in det., an abusive home life situation, a vicious rape and attack by 3 work men, and later having to legally tight the City for Benefits; [a.] Farmington Hills, MI

DUBENSKY, MRS. JOHANNA A. WOLFE
[pen.] J. A. Wolfe Dubensky; [b.] Alamogordo, NM; [p.] H. Joseph Wolfe, Clara C.; [m.] George Dubensky; [ch.] George Jr., Jim and four grandchildren; [ed.] Three Years College continuing Education for Permanent Deacons and Spouse since 1976 to present; [occ.] Retired Fed. Gov., Housewife, Volunteer, Pastoral Care; [memb.] St. Margaret Mary Church Eucharistic Minister, Permanent Diaconate and Spouses; [hon.] (Recognition of service) Command Hf. Kelly AFB, TX, Hz. MPC Randolph, AFB, TX, Hf. Defence Mapping Agency, IAGS, Ft Sam Houston, TX, Outstanding, Ministry 104, Pastoral Counseling, (Seminary, 1985); [oth. writ.] Certificate-dedicated ministry, (Training Program, 1988 Hosp) Certificate, Outstanding Service and Courtesy 1991, Hosp. Certificate-Meritorious and Devotion '94 (Artist) Display Local Library Hosp. Oil Paintings; [pers.] To bring a little sunlight, hope, and cheer into the hearts of all God's Children, (Happy to have my poetry published in two year books 1st in 1946 - Poetry Broadcast "The Exposition Press N.Y."); [a.] San Antonio, TX

DUBNOV, WILLIAM L.
[b.] May 1, 1951, Washington, DC; [p.] I. N. Dubin, Alberta Dubin; [ed.] Ph.D. Bryn Mawr College M.S. Univ. of Pennsylvania; [occ.] Psychologist; [oth. writ.] "Universal Education", "Universal Psychology", "10 Moral Dilemma"; [pers.] My poems have been used extensively as lyrics for popular songs, and are available for such, my poetry is universal, post-modern; [a.] Dallas, TX

DUFF, FLOYD ELTON
[pen.] Fed or F. E.; [b.] February 7, 1924, Holland, VT; [p.] Edmund and Bessie Duff; [m.] Dorothy Alice Darling Duff, June 2, 1944; [ch.] Parris, Paul, Beth Ann, 3 grandsons - 2 granddaughter, 3 great granddaughters; [ed.] Elementary - 8 years, High School - 4 years, 4-H Leader - 3 years; [occ.] Retired - 1989; [memb.] French Club, Polish Club, Senior Citizens 50+, singles, many Historical Socialites, International Poetry Society; [hon.] 4-H Club Member and Leader, American League of Foreign Wars, President of the Senior Citizens of Canterbury in 1992; [oth. writ.] I like good loyal friend so all my life making and keeping good friend has been my life time ambition. This is why I enjoy the poetry, Conv., in Wash., D.C. so much.; [pers.] I do poetry recitals at schools, churches, grange, dinners, family gatherings, historical gatherings etc. I love to recite and I also write poems for special occasions.; [a.] Canterbury, CT

DUFFY, JOAN A.
[b.] December 5, 1934, Holyoke, MA; [p.] Howard and Nellie Doyle - deceased; [m.] William F. Duffy Sr., July 28, 1962; [ch.] Rosemary, William and Catherine; [ed.]

St. Jerome Grammar and High School - Holyoke, MA, Province Hospital School of Nursing - Holyoke, MA; [occ.] R.N. - Not currently employed.; [memb.] Massachusetts Citizens for Life - D.A.V. - Womans Aux.; [oth. writ.] I have more poetry.; [pers.] I like very much to see someone enjoy reading what I have written. I enjoy reading as well as writing poetry. What I write comes from my own experiences as something to write about and capture on paper.; [a.] Chicopee, MA

DUGAN, THERESA NICHELLE
[pen.] T. Nichelle Dugan; [b.] July 13, 1969, Fairfield, Travis AFB CA; [p.] Terrence and Diane Dugan; [ed.] Double degree in Psychology and Film, Media Production from San Diego State University, and Sacramento State Univ. Graduate in Script Supervising from Hollywood Tech. Institute; [occ.] Music Director at CRN in Los Angeles, Script Supervisor, Singer; [memb.] "Women United for fun Organization Sacramento Professional Netwak, NASS; [hon.] Best Director for a Children's TV Show - "The What If Show", Best Actress Scholarship.; [oth. writ.] 3 Articles published in local newspapers, two children's books for a day camp.; [pers.] My poems really don't belong to me at all, they belong to all my life experiences, and the wonderful relations who have influenced my words, especially Gods!; [a.] Sacramento, CA

DUKE, THELMA JEAN
[b.] July 11, 1929, Mesa, AZ; [p.] Will and Esther Duke; [ed.] Mesa High School; [occ.] Small Business Owner; [memb.] ASU Alum.; [oth. writ.] Articles and Song-Poem Published in Local Newspaper; [pers.] Inspired by my sister Margaret (whom I lost in 1994) always there for me - she 'underwrote' the spirit of this poem.; [a.] Phoenix, AZ

DUNCAN, DAVID
[b.] December 20, 1964, Las Vegas, NV; [p.] David L. and Mary E. Duncan; [m.] Elly Bulboaca - fiance; [ed.] New Mexico Tech; [occ.] Co-founder of Decisive Technology; [pers.] I love to put into words the emotions and rhythms I feel inside.; [a.] Palo Alto, CA

DUNLAP, EUGENE W.
[b.] September 14, 1920, Memphis, TN; [p.] Sadie (Mia) Dunlap; [m.] Shirley L. C. Dunlap, August 6, 1960; [ed.] Ed. D, B.S.

DUNLAP, SHIRLEY L. C.
[b.] August 3, 1937, Saint Louis Co., MO; [p.] George and LaVerne Meyer; [m.] Eugene Dunlap, August 6, 1960; [ed.] Univ. of Missouri - Saint Louis, B.S. degree in Education; [occ.] Stain Glass Artist; [memb.] National Wildlife, Missouri Botanical Garden, Missouri Conservation; [hon.] Kappa Delta Pi, National Dean's List; [a.] Hillsboro, MO

DUNLAVY, LOIS
[b.] July 24, 1965, San Diego, CA; [p.] Samuel and Margaret; [ed.] Sydney Academy, St. Francis Xavier University; [occ.] Finance Clerk; [memb.] Community Mental Health Network, Sydney; [pers.] Taking time to look at the world through the eye of a wondrous child helps to strengthen my perception of the beauty that surrounds my life.; [a.] Sydney Cape Breton Nova Scotia, Canada

DUNN, DOROTHY ROBERTSON
[pen.] Dorothy Robertson; [m.] Ulysses S. Dunn, Jr.; [ch.] Deneen Chante Dunn, Danielle Anita Dunn, Felicia Hinton; [occ.] Wachoria Bank of N.C.; [oth. writ.] Commentary in "The News and Observer" and Commentary in "The Carolinian"; [pers.] Character assassination becomes a two-edge sword when one is crucified due to another's criticisms accepted as truths without knowledge.; [a.] Wendell, NC

DUNN, KAREN M.
[b.] January 7, 1956, Detroit, MI; [p.] Coy Green and Mildred Green; [m.] Eldon L. Dunn, December 11, 1992; [ed.] Caro High, David Lipscomb University, Delta Community College, Harding University; [occ.] Corporate Sales Manager; [memb.] National Association of Women Business Owners, San Diego Chamber of Commerce, San Diego Ad Club.; [oth. writ.] Comedy articles for women's newspaper - Citizen.; [pers.] I'm in a constant search for personal growth through the awareness of people's gifts and life's lessons that surround me, while maintaining my sense of humor.; [a.] San Diego, CA

DURBIN, JACK
[b.] January 8, 1953, Monroe, MI; [p.] John J. and Naomi A. Durbin; [m.] Patsy Patterson, March 23, 1990; [ed.] B.S.C.E. and M.S.C.E. from University of Michigan, Ann Arbor; [occ.] Owner, ESET Corp, Civil Engineering Company; [a.] Allen Park, MI

DUTKIEWICZ, THOMAS
[pen.] Thomas Dutkiewicz; [b.] April 27, 1960, Hartford, CT; [p.] Gail Fuller; [m.] Aimee Lyn Dutkiewicz, March 9, 1985; [ch.] Benjamin Robert, Avonlea Autumn, Mandolin Joy, Garth Daniel; [ed.] Bristol Eastern High, Tunxis Community College; [occ.] Hazardous Waste Specialist; [pers.] The words in "Daddy's Tears" are not from a poet - or a writer, but a father's heart that cries out in pain for the death of a daughter, and the love that he had for her. She was only 4 1/2 months old. Wish you were here.; [a.] Bristol, CT

DWARIKA, CHRISTOPHER
[b.] January 2, 1965, Trinidad; [ed.] Couva Gov't Secondary School (Trinidad) Deury Institute (Toronto); [occ.] PC and Customer Support Specialist; [oth. writ.] Wrote and directed four plays for a drama group.; [pers.] You are today where your thoughts have brought you, you will be tomorrow where they take you. I am influenced by social and political issues.; [a.] Carborough Ontario, Canada

DYCK, BARRY
[pen.] Bear; [b.] June 5, 1963, Saint Catharines, Ontario, Canada; [p.] John, Orpha Dyck; [ed.] Grade 12 Diploma; [occ.] Vacuum Cleaner Demonstrator, Filter Queen, General Labor Jobs; [oth. writ.] Grade 12 English Teacher once tome me, you have an effective personal stye of writing. He gave me 90% on my short stories.; [pers.] I write with my heart, if I were to go into a store and pick out a card,(card writing - simple heart to heart poems), I'd like that card to not just affect me, but to affect many other people and they would buy it.; [a.] Saint Catherines Ontario, Canada

EARP JR., TIM
[pen.] Peter Chan; [b.] November 30, 1971, Niagara Falls, NY; [p.] Timothy Earp, Donna Earp; [ed.] Lasalle Sr. High, Niagara County Community College.; [occ.] Student; [pers.] I would like to live my life like a poem or a painting. So everything flows together, not to tell a story, but to show a way of being!; [a.] Niagara Falls, NY

EAST, BEVERLY SUE
[b.] January 14, 1938, Clarksburg, WV; [p.] Madalyn Lynch and Robert Lynch; [m.] Carl E. East, January 17, 1960; [ch.] Lori, Amy, Jenny, Carole, Beth, Carl Jr., Susan; [ed.] Denby High School, Detroit, MI; [occ.] Homemaker; [memb.] Livingston County Wildlife and Conservation Club; [oth. writ.] Poetry locally recognized, article in Detroit News, Articles in County Press; [pers.] Writing has always been an important part of my life. I thank God for the ability to convert my thoughts to the printed word, and my family and friends for their neverending inspiration.; [a.] Howell, MI

EBNER, ROSE BARHM
[pen.] Rose Barhm Ebner; [b.] Columbus, OH; [p.] John and Margaret Schindler; [m.] William E. Ebner; [ch.] Tim, Sue, Thomas; [ed.] Ohio State University Mesa College, San Diego, CA, University of California San Diego; [occ.] Student, UCSD Writer; [oth. writ.] "San Diego Companion" (Resource Book of San Diego County) 1987; [pers.] The poem within, "Beyond the Tomb" is one of a collection of poems (entitled "Over the Hill and Beyond") that reflects one's birth, growth, and aging. That confronts life's end and beyond.; [a.] San Diego, CA

ECKERL, JANE
[pen.] Jane Forbes; [b.] February 10, 1931, Philadelphia, PA; [p.] Edith and Alfred Forbes; [m.] August Eckerl, August 24, 1949; [ch.] Dianne Carol; [ed.] Eastern High - Balto. Essex Comm. Balto. Comm. Coll. PA. and Fla.; [occ.] Retired; [hon.] Honorable mention, World of Poetry for "Promise"; [oth. writ.] "Promise" poems published local newspapers, clubs, and organizations.; [pers.] Writing poetry is my favorite hobby. Was influenced by great teachers at Glenmount Elem., Hamilton Jr. High, and Eastern High, Balto. MD.; [a.] Oviedo, FL

ECKHOFF, COREN
[pen.] Corey; [b.] September 22, 1978, Louisville, KY; [p.] Brenda Eckhoff and Calvin Eckhoff; [ed.] Klondike Elementary, Crosby Middle School, Eastern High School; [memb.] Mope to join PETA; [hon.] 1. English Award - 8th grade 2. Math Award - 8th grade 3. Second Place Medal for Starpower National Dance Competition 4. First place ribbons for numerous other dance competitions; [oth. writ.] School newspaper articles published; [pers.] We wear the mask that grins and lies if hides our cheeks and shades our eyes. Except of "we wear the mask", By Paul Laurence Dunbar, "This poem is very true to life."; [a.] Louisville, KY

EDEL, WILLIAM W.
[b.] March 16, 1894, Baltimore, MD; [p.] John W. and Annie Wilcox Edel; [m.] Louise Bollingsley, July 25, 1917; [ch.] Louise Edel McWhorter, Mary Edel Denman, Wilma Edel McGrath; [ed.] Baltimore City College 1912, Dickinson College, BA(1915), MA (1918), Boston University School of Theology, (1921), Philadelphia Divinity School (1920-21), Church School of the Pacific, Berkeley Ca (1933-35), Pacific School of Religion, Berkeley Ca (1933-35); [occ.] Retired - US Navy Chaplain Corps (1917-1946), (Lt 1920, Lt CMDR 1925, CMDR 1925, Capt 1941) - President of Dickinson College (1947-1959), One of the founders and former President of the Foundation for Independent Colleges of Pennsylvania. President of the Pennsylvania Association of Colleges and Universities, (1957-8), Public member of the US State Department Committee for Promotion, Retention or Retirement of Members of the Foreign Service, 1959), Served as Committee Chairman with the

Brookings Institute.; [memb.] Masonic Order (Knights Templar) Phi Beta Kappa, Tau Kappa Alpha, Omicon Delta Kappa, Pi Gamma Mu, Alpha Chi Rho; [hon.] Dickinson College, DD (1935), Hobart College, DD (1944), Keuka College, LHD (1944), Gettysburg College, LLD (1949), University of Pennsylvania, LLD (1949), Boston University, LHD (1950), Lebanon Valley College, JUD (1956); [oth. writ.] Frequent contributor of articles relating to the history of the US Navy and the Chaplains Corps of the Navy in various periodicals. A book of memories, not an autobiography, titled, MY HUNDRED YEARS, (318 pages, published 1994); [a.] El Cajon, CA

EDSON, BETTY L.
[b.] August 22, 1937, Andalusia, AL; [p.] Conolie R. Johnson, Velma Johnson; [m.] Wilton Roger Edson, February 10, 1984; [ch.] Vicky Amanda, Timothy Roger, David Merril; [ed.] Escamdia Farms High, Tate High; [occ.] Retired - Fiber and Chemical Operator, Monsanto, Pensacola, Fl.; [memb.] Red Oak Baptist Church; [hon.] 17 years Perfect Attendance, Monsanto Co. Basketball Player of the Year, Escambia Farms High; [oth. writ.] Other poems.; [pers.] I strive to touch the lives of others through my writings.; [a.] Pensacola, FL

EDWARDS, DOROTHY L.
[b.] January 8, 1951, Wilson, NC; [p.] Milton and Lucy Evans; [m.] James P. Edwards Jr., June 8, 1971; [ch.] Jawanza, James P. III, and Rodney; [ed.] 1 yr. College; [occ.] Data Entry Spec, Dept of Revenue (State); [memb.] St. Delight MB Church; [pers.] My poems are inspired by God through the life I've lived and the people that made an impression on my life.; [a.] Stantonsburg, NC

EDWARDS, DOROTHY HEMPHILL
[ed.] BLS St. Louis University 1982 MS Ed Southern Il. University 1986; [occ.] Vocational Rehabilitation Counselor; [memb.] St. Louis Counseling Association; [hon.] National Dean's list - Cum Laude - Golden and Silver Poet Awards, World of Poetry; [oth. writ.] My Morning Prayer, Introspection, My Goal, The Challenge, My Own Death; [pers.] My faith in God and Awe of His marvelous creation allows me to experience people, things and events deeply and vividly. I attempt to share this in my writings.; [a.] Saint Louis, MO

EDWARDS, JOAN B.
[pen.] Joann Edwards; [b.] September 16, 1942, Detroit; [p.] Albert and Mildred Edwards; [m.] Divorced; [ch.] Step-son Jim, 2 Grandchildren Steve, Charlene; [ed.] 2 yrs Servite High School, Macomb Community College, University Nevada Las Vegas; [occ.] Casino Cashier; [memb.] DAR Monte's Girls (Golf Team), AGA Golf Tour Partners Community Action, HCAT - Volunteer Group Binions Horseshoe; [hon.] Dean's List, MCC Manager of Month and Employee of Month.; [oth. writ.] Numerous Articles for work newspapers; [pers.] In my writings I strive to bring a little sunshine into the lives of others, and hope through their sorrows and trials.; [a.] Las Vegas, NV

EDWARDS, LILLIAN LOUISE
[pen.] Lillian Louise Edwards; [b.] March 6, 1947, Monroe, LA; [p.] Mr. and Mrs. Barren Jene Newton; [m.] Mr. Lonell James Ward (Boyfriend), July 15, 1988; [ch.] Francine Edwards, Dethra Edwards, Willie Anderson, Geeia Edwards, Raising my grandchild since 2 weeks, Karmeisha Edwards; [ed.] High School Oakland Technical High School; [occ.] Nurse Asst. Home Health Aid Certified; [hon.] Improved two mail machines at the main post office, where I worked; [oth. writ.] Some poems just for myself or for a friend; [pers.] Expressing my feelings.; [a.] Oakland, CA

EGLER, PENNY M.
[pen.] Penny Egler; [b.] March 16, 1967, Michigan; [p.] Martin and Janet Egler; [m.] Joel Vargas, Fiance; [ch.] Mya Victoria Vargas; [ed.] Attending College; [occ.] Floral Designer; [a.] Southgate, MI

EIDENBERG, IRVING B.
[b.] March 13, 1918, Chicago, IL; [p.] Reuben and Etta Eidenberg; [ed.] 2 years City College - Chicago and YMCA Central College - Chicago.; [occ.] Antiquarian Bookseller/formerly merchant seaman, U.S. Merchant Marine, WW II (Veteran of Murmansk run) former printer, railroad fireman, die-casting shops in metal industries.; [memb.] ACLU/Humanist Society, Atheists of San Francisco, American Merchant Marine Veterans, Golden Gate Chapter, San Francisco.; [hon.] Decorated by U.S. and Russian Governments for carrying military cargoes during WW II.; [oth. writ.] Mostly non-paid contributions to Labor periodicals.; [pers.] Personal belief that Man, alone, can and must shape his own destiny.; [a.] San Francisco, CA

EILERMAN, DARIN LEE
[pen.] Darin L. Eilerman; [b.] December 1, 1962, Santa Cruz, CA; [p.] Grege Bev Eilerman, Chris Johnson; [m.] Margaret Critchlow Eilerman, October 16, 1988; [ch.] Courie Lynn, Sarah Anna, Elizabeth Marie, Adam Gregory; [ed.] Woodside High in Redwood, CA. Spokane Community Collage, Fire Science Cert. AAS degree and AA degree working on BA in jour. at EWU.; [occ.] Student of life.; [memb.] Woodside Fire Dept. Muster Team with record times. Spokane Volunteer fire fighter for three years. Firestorm 91 WWP Volunteer. Sixth generation fire fighter; [hon.] First place in show for restored 1930's boat, first found on cliff. Publication in the National Library of Poetry is the highest honor a writer could receive to start with.; [oth. writ.] Five chapters of a wild and wooly autobiography. Thirty plus songs or poems, several works in progress. All unpublished, so far.; [pers.] There is only a thin line between the king and the joker. That line is to learn from one's mistakes instead of being doomed to repeat them.; [a.] Spokane, WA

ELDER, DEBORAH
[pen.] D. S. Elder; [b.] June 27, 1967, Missouri; [p.] Bill and Nancy McGurthy, Helen Albers; [m.] Jeff, April 28, 1990; [ed.] Currently studying to be a Registered Nature at Glendale Community College. Graduate of Shadow Mountain High School; [memb.] Member of Phi Theta Kappa Honor Society; [oth. writ.] Two poems published in literary magazine in High School.; [pers.] I write for the most important people in my life: My family (my people) and friends. The Lord helps me find the words and they are my inspiration.; [a.] Phoenix, AZ

ELLIOTT, JENNIFER
[b.] April 5, 1981, Brockville; [p.] Grace and Barry Elliott; [ed.] Grade 8; [occ.] Student; [memb.] Brockville Figure, Skating Club, Studio C. Majorettes; [hon.] 2 Baton Twirling Trophies, Advertising Award, Creative Writing Award, Shepard's Writing Award, Figure skating medal; [a.] Brockville Ontario, Canada

ELLIOTT, JULIE
[pen.] Julie Elliott; [b.] December 9, 1971, Excelsior Springs, MO; [p.] Ken and Linda Elliott; [m.] To be - Terry Green, September 16, 1995; [ch.] Kendra Krislynn, Andrew Kenneth; [ed.] Graduate of Dekalb High school in Dekalb MO; [occ.] Screen printer Atchison Leather Products - Atchison KS; [hon.] A poem of mine was approved for publication also by sparrow grass poetry; [oth. writ.] I like to write about things that have happened in my life. It always helps to express your true feelings by putting them into words of poetry; [a.] Atchison, KS

ELLIS, EVALYN JEAN
[pen.] E. Jean Ellis; [b.] May 14, 1933, Waynesfield, OH; [p.] Carl and Eva Shaner; [m.] David L. Ellis, February 14, 1982; [ch.] Dianna, Kerry, Kelly, Darren; [ed.] Graduate of Shaw Nee High. Publishing courses at Institute of Children's Literature; [occ.] Housewife and Writer.; [memb.] Women's Aglow - Sunday school teacher at New Covenant Christian Ct. Women only; [hon.] Honor award for service to education and to Youth of Wapakoneta City Schools.; [oth. writ.] Several poems published in local newspaper. (Pen name then E. J. Hasting) Poems written for special Church, and other organizations.; [pers.] I began writing poetry as a young girl. It helped me to express my true feelings. I feel my writings are a gift from God and I like to share this gift with those who like to read, or hear poetry; [a.] Wapakoneta, OH

EMILY, PATRICIA ANN MARIE
[pen.] Lauren Irish; [b.] March 26, 1951, Kansas City, MO; [p.] Virgil Eugene and Nora Mae Phillips; [m.] Russell LeRoy Emily, July 4, 1991; [ed.] St. Pius/Bishop Miege High Blue Springs College of Allied Health Blue Springs Jr. College - Longview College; [occ.] Insurance; [hon.] RMA Registered - Cartoon Book Copyrighted in Washington Winner of Amateur Photo Contests; [oth. writ.] Carton books; [pers.] Poetry is life experiences, and if flows through all our senses.; [a.] Bates City, MO

EMMONS, ELLEN
[b.] December 3, 1980, St. Louis; [p.] Bert and Kris Emmons; [ed.] Currently an 8th grader at Hixson Jr. High in Webster Groves, MO.; [occ.] Student; [memb.] Basketball, soccer, and softball teams; [hon.] Honorable mention for an essay writing contest in 4th grade.; [oth. writ.] I write other poems and reflections and keep a journal.; [pers.] The world illustrates me, love and hate together, peace and war combined.; [a.] St. Louis, MO

ENGLE, DOROTHY ESTELLE
[pen.] Dorothy Estelle Engle; [b.] October 1, 1905, Maplewood, MA; [p.] Lucy L. and Joseph Thackwray; [m.] Frank Engle, 1934; [ed.] High School - US Military US Air Force; [occ.] Retired; [memb.] Westerners-Inter Nat. AZ Historical Society Desert Botanical Society Phoenix Zoo, The Heard Museum; [hon.] Army Commendation Ribbon, changed to US Air force in 1948 - Retired 31 Oct 1963 Lt Colonel.; [oth. writ.] Poems to my husband when I was away on duty; [pers.] Always interested in poetry father read to the family after Sunday dinner mother-father, grandmother and six children in family and me.; [a.] Phoenix, AZ

EVANS, CARRIE D.
[b.] November 13, 1946, Fayetteville, NC; [p.] Mr. Lawence and Omega Evans; [ch.] Fesse Jones, Erick W. Evans, Franklin M. Evans, Issac D. Evans; [ed.] Gratz High, Community College of Philadelphia; [occ.] Homemaker, waiting to go the Nursing Aide Trainee; [pers.] Set and let your energy of your soul explore. Envision infinite peace.; [a.] Philadelphia, PA

EVANS, IMOGENE SACHSE
[pen.] I. Sachse; [b.] March 31, 1922, Dallas, TX; [p.] Beatrice Watson, Herbert C. Watson; [m.] Jack W. Evans, January 8, 1942; [ch.] 3 Boys: Jack Jr., Roy Gene and Craig; [ed.] Woodrow Wilson High School; [occ.] Wife and Home Maker; [memb.] Dallas Museum of Art Waterview Church of Christ Lakewood Country Club Bent Tree Country Club, East Dallas Exchangette Club Arboretum And Botonical garden; [hon.] 8 times winner of Lakewood Golf Ass. Country Club Sold Several Paintings at auction; [pers.] I write poetry to and about my family, relatives and friends. I write only for my entertainment; [a.] Dallas, TX

EVANS, KATONDRIA
[pen.] Nikki; [b.] January 12, 1976, Chicago; [p.] Sharon Evans and Mark Evans; [ed.] Our Lady of Sorrows Elementary School, Lincoln Park High School, Lewis University; [memb.] Voices of Praise Youth Choir; [pers.] As an African-American woman I strive to reflect the love, power and legacy of my black people in my writing, I have been influenced by may A Angelou, Gwendolwyn Brooks, and Langton Hughs; [a.] Chicago, IL

EVANS, MICHAEL L.
[b.] March 18, 1943, San Diego, CA; [p.] Herb and Millie; [m.] Darlene, April 4, 1969; [ch.] Ron, Tim, and Raleigh, Grandchildren: Amanda and Summer; [ed.] Mt. Miguel High 1961 San Diego City College 1976; [occ.] Retired; [memb.] San Diego Chess Club-Board of Directors Southern Calif. Chess Club-Board of Directors; [hon.] 1. AA Business Admin - High Honors 1976 2. Who's Who Among American Jr. College Students 1975-76 3. Alpha Gamma Sigma: Lifetime; [pers.] "Vietnam Legacy" is dedicated to my wife and sons, because they have lived it with me - and for all the disappointments and broken promises.; [a.] El Cajon, CA

EVERSON, DIANNE K.
[pen.] Anna Katherine Fenton; [b.] March 8, 1942, Monteral, Canada; [p.] Ann Moore and C. Clay Welch; [m.] Robert J. Everson, July 15, 1975; [ch.] Jamie Shultz (daughter) and Jon McRoy (son); [ed.] Plainfield High School, Plainfield, IN; [occ.] Homemaker and aspiring writer; [hon.] The birth of my 4 grandchildren, Jonathan Mosier-1986, Kaitlin Shultz-1989, Megan Shultz-1992 and Samantha Shultz-1993. Arrived from Canada, age 11, in 1953 and became an American citizen on 3/6/58.; [oth. writ.] Drop of Heaven, Princess, Wild Irish Rose, Sad Eyes, My Handsome Stranger, Guess Who Called Today, Mother and Sacrifice, A Jar of Bugs, Searching Eyes, Angel in Disguise, My Penny Tree, A Gifted Gentle Soul and The Gift of Love; [pers.] At age 52, I started writing poetry out of frustration. Bad health and rheumatoid arthritis forced me to my bedroom for rest. My poems are positive and center on love, feelings, and thanks for my family, friends and the world in general.; [a.] Indianapolis, IN

EVON, MELODY-JOY
[pen.] Melody-Joy; [b.] December 27, 1974, Windsor, Ontario, Canada; [p.] Dennis Evon and Candi Evon; [ed.] F. J. Brennan High; [oth. writ.] A part of my dream came true by having this poem published in this book, the other half is to get my poetry book published.; [pers.] "I am inspired by nature and truth, and all things real and beautiful."; [a.] Windsor Ontario, Canada

FAGAN SR., WILLIAM W.
[b.] September 7, 1923, Boston, MA; [p.] Harry and Elizabeth Fagan; [m.] Antoinette L. Fagan (Lucier), May 17, 1947; [ch.] William W. Fagan Jr., Nancy Eshleman, Richard J. Fagan and Stephen A. Fagan; [ed.] Newton High School (Mass.) and a graduate of Tufts University (Mass.) Special studies at The University of Georgia and the Univ. of Arkansas; [occ.] Deceased; [memb.] Delta Tau Delta Fraternity, Divine Mercy Catholic Church - Merrit Isl. Fla., American Public Works Assoc., (a past president) Keep America Beautiful, former Director, former Grand Knight of the Knights of Columbus.; [hon.] A citation for Meritorious Service from the President's Committee on Employment of the Handicapped, Commissioned, Kentucky Colonel.; [oth. writ.] A few poems for college newspapers; [a.] Merritt Island, FL

FAIRBANK, BENJAMIN R.
[pen.] Randy; [b.] February 20, 1912, Sheridan, WY; [p.] Lynn Wesley - Anna; [m.] Idella Gertrude, June 9, 1934; [ch.] William Randolph, James Leroy, Larry Randall; [ed.] 8 yrs. grade, 4 yrs. high school; [occ.] Retired - doing wood craft; [pers.] Direct descendant from Jonathan Fairbank and family who came from England in 1636 - who built the first Framehouse and laid out the town of Dedham Mass. Old House still stands. Invented Fairbank scales etc. etc.

FALE, PATRICIA O.
[b.] Emporia, KS; [p.] Berneice and William Quinn; [m.] William A. Fale, July 21, 1965; [ch.] Lorie Ann Fale, William A. Fale Jr.; [ed.] BS University of Maryland; [occ.] Controller

FARISATO, ESTHER
[pen.] Esther Farisato; [b.] January 12, 1923, Italy; [p.] Pasquale and Grace; [m.] Vic Farisato, April 12, 1947; [ch.] Nori Desmas, Victor Farisato; [ed.] Avviamento Proffesionale, Canada College, Santa Clara University; [occ.] Retired; [memb.] Amer. Heart Ass. Young Ladies Institute of Notre Dame, AARP, Catholic Daughters of America; [hon.] Achievement awards from school.; [oth. writ.] Poems, short stories, memoirs, children plays; [pers.] Visualizing vivid memories, bring out the emotions that are later transferred into words.; [a.] Redwood City, CA

FARLEY, MICHAEL R.
[pen.] Mickey Farr; [b.] November 2, 1949, Charleston, SC; [p.] Roy A. Farley, Reby Sineath; [m.] Lan T. Farley, August 19, 1972; [ch.] Micah J. Farley (07-22-88), Michelle L. Farley (05-07-81); [ed.] AS Electrical Eng., Trident Technical College - Charleston, SC; [occ.] Semi-retired; [memb.] Carlisle Military School Alumni; [hon.] One of the most decorated twins during the Vietnam War.; [oth. writ.] Currently writing, "The Adventure of Mickey Farr."; [pers.] As a result of combat duty, my twin brother, Mary and I, suffer Past Traumatic Stress Disorder (PTSD). The extreme sensitivity and feelings I put into my work helps to alleviate some of the psychological burdens of this life long malady.; [a.] Lawrenceville, GA

FARMER, BEVERLY
[b.] February 22, 1956, Harrisburg, PA; [p.] Edna Farmer; [ch.] Nica Farmer; [ed.] Chester High 1974, Hbg Area Comm. College 1983; [occ.] Asst. Manager for restaurant chain; [pers.] I would like to dedicate this poem, my first publication to my greatest inspiration my friend Ms. Patricia Quann; [a.] Harrisburg, PA

FARMER, JESSICA D. CLIFFORD
[b.] January 9, 1964, San Antonio, TX; [p.] Don and Carol Johnson; [m.] Craig Farmer, May 14, 1988; [ch.] Chandler Craig - 5 years, Jenna Sioux - 4 years; [ed.] Labette County HS Altamont Ks., OSLL-OKC, University of Oklahoma; [occ.] Emergency Medical Technician; [memb.] American Heart Association-CPR Instructor, Oklahoma Farm Bureau Young Farmers and Ranchers; [oth. writ.] Other poetry published in "East of the Sunrise"; [pers.] I believe each of us has something significant to share, if we can only find the words.; [a.] Buffalo, OK

FARRELL, MELVIN V.
[pen.] Bud Farrell; [b.] November 5, 1935, Millville, CA; [p.] Mr. and Mrs. Virgil Farrell; [m.] Marcille Farrell, October 29, 1967; [ch.] Sandee, Kenny and Terri; [ed.] Shasta Union High, Western College of Auctioneering - Billings, Montana; [occ.] Rancher, AI Technician, Auctioneer; [memb.] Shasta County Farm Bureau, National Rifle Association, Board of Directors of Millville Cementry District, Lifetime Member of The American Hereford Association; [hon.] Appreciation Award Millville Parade Committee, Shasta County Farm Bureau Director of the Month, Life Time Member of the Oregon Trail Riders, Honorary Service Award Millville PTA; [oth. writ.] I wrote poetry for the Oregon Trail Riders News Letter; [pers.] I strive to do the best I can at all types of Poetry it is fascinating. I like to write Cowboy Poetry, and Poetry of Children; [a.] Millville, CA

FARRINGTON, JOHN RICHARD
[pen.] Richard Rulbacava; [b.] June 26, 1962, San Bernardino, CA; [p.] John Farrington, Elena Maria Lopez; [m.] With long-term companion since 1984; [ed.] Eisenhower High, Bachelor of Arts in Business Administration University of Washington; [memb.] Pilot Light Society of Seattle for Readers of the Urantia Book; [hon.] Beta Alpha Psi, Accounting Society; [pers.] We are all brothers and sisters in one large family created by loving deities. This ideal has given me an incredible amount of happiness and inspiration. Long live love in our lives!; [a.] Seattle, WA

FARROW, RON W.
[b.] August 18, 1938, Iberia, MO; [m.] Linda L. Farrow, July 2, 1976; [ed.] High school graduate; [occ.] Security Guard, Ret. Correctional Officer; [memb.] Leavenworth Christian, Fellowship Church; [oth. writ.] Several not yet published; [pers.] Accept Jesus Christ as your Saviour, practice the golden rule, keep God's Ten Commandments, I believe this is the chosen generation to see the end of time.; [a.] Iberia, MO

FELDMAN, ELIZA JANE
[b.] May 7, 1981, Kansas City, MO; [ed.] Freshman at Bishop Miege High School, Kansas City, MO; [memb.] PETA, Nature Conservancy, World Wildlife Fund, Greenpeace, The Wilderness Society, and Amnesty International.; [pers.] I have two philosophical statements that I hold strong to. Things are not what they seem, they are what they are. The biggest risk in life is not risking.; [a.] Kansas City, MO

FELFOLDI, TIM G.
[pen.] Gypsy T.; [b.] September 17, 1973, Toronto; [p.] Mom, Dad; [m.] My son's mother Theresa; [ch.] Jeorgie and 2 others that lay asleep forever; [ed.] Still working on it, thanks to Bob, Sue, my teachers here, and Jen for seeing me through the fight of my disability "dislexea"; [occ.] Writing for my best friend Jennifer B. and working as a carpenter; [oth. writ.] I've got over 200 that I have done like, Angels Do Weep, and In A Distant Land, as well as Alone. One poem published in newsletter.;

[pers.] I'd love to dedicate this poem to mom Miss Felfoldi, my best friend Jennifer Bester and her mom as well as my kids, Jearyie R. H. Felfoldi and the 2 that past away. I love you all very much; [a.] Kingston, Canada

FELSHER, WENDY JO
[b.] July 22, 1978, Westmoreland, PA; [p.] Steve and Kathy Felsher; [ed.] Frazier High School; [occ.] Cashier at Super K-Mart in Uniontown; [hon.] Dancing awards from Dance Competitions, 1st and 2nd place ribbons and plaques.; [pers.] I write poems that tell of my personal incidents, and I like to share it with others.; [a.] Star Junction, PA

FELTNER, LORI J.
[b.] May 3, 1960, Dayton, OH; [p.] Mary and Charles Bridges; [m.] Michael Feltner, June 30, 1979; [ch.] Rachel Anita, born 6-1-92, adopted at birth; [ed.] Fairmont West High School, 1978 graduate; [occ.] Word Processor; [oth. writ.] 3 poems previously published in other anthologies; [pers.] My greatest desire is to become a country songwriter. I have no musical ability and have not found someone to put music to my lyrics, but I have nearly 20 songs written.; [a.] Franklin, OH

FEMINELLA, LUCILLE A.
[b.] September 2, 1928, Brooklyn, NY; [p.] Deceased; [m.] Joseph C. Feminella, September 25, 1948; [ch.] 2 boys Thomas and John, 2 grandchildren Tom and Joey; [sib.] High School; [occ.] Housewife; [memb.] CMV, DAV; [oth. writ.] Just poetry; [pers.] I dedicate my poem to a very dear friend, Ghori DeGregoria. We have remained good friends for over 50 years.; [a.] New Hyde Park, NY

FERGUSON, BETH ANNA MOONRAY
[pen.] Beth Anna 'MoonRay' Ferguson; [b.] January 18, 1952, Queen, NY; [p.] Louis and Essie Ferguson; [m.] Deceased, July 2, 1994; [ch.] Preparing to adopt; [ed.] Newtown HS - Elmhurst NY, Brooklyn College - Bklyn. NY - Dance and Theatre major, studied dance at: Alvin Ailey's, Nilton Buyo in Kyoto Japan, and Kathak CE. Indian with Gora Singh; [occ.] Intercultural Choreographer of the Jazeast Dance Co. and Lecturer on African and Native American History and Culture; [memb.] Executive Board Member of the NorthEastern Native American Assoc., New Life Christian Fellowship Church, Asian American Alliance, American Indian Community House.; [hon.] Won scholarship to study dance in Japan from Traditional Theatre Training - Dir. Jonah Salz 1986, Citations from City of New York in 1994 for Intercultural Performance of Footpaths - Sub of Jazeast Dance - for HRA, Grant in 1993 from Queen's Council on the Arts, Who's Who-Women 1991 and '92, Who's Who in America - 1993; [oth. writ.] 'Good Morning Mother' - Nat'l Library of Poetry, "Suiting Yourself" - an article written for and published by NY Newsday Daily Paper, writing a new book "Having a Bad Hair Day Life" and various poems, prose, monologues and children's stories.; [pers.] There is a disease that we are all exposed to after birth. It's called ignorance which has a side effect called fear, of which there are only 2 cures: 1) Love of God and 2) The willingness to learn what we do not know or understand.; [a.] New York, NY

FERGUSON, RUBY WHITE
[pen.] Fergie; [b.] September 7, 1949, Houston; [p.] Lewis White, Annie White; [m.] Divorced; [ch.] Crista Ferguson, Jeff Ferguson Jr., Alecia Ferguson; [ed.] 1972 Houston Bapt. Univ. - BSRN, 1975 Interbaptist Theological Seminary - Masters Religious Education, 1968 Honors grad - Jeff Davis Sr HS; [occ.] Administrative Manager - Intra Care Medical Center Hospital; [memb.] Texas Research Society on Alcoholism, Sigma Theta Tau Honor Society in Nursing (Inactive); [hon.] Multiple awards - professional and social semifinalist - 1995 North American Open Poetry Contest; [oth. writ.] Multiple unpublished nursing and religious papers presented as conference speaker across the state of Texas; [pers.] My life is touched daily by genuine goodness of others, my poem is a tribute to one of those persons who will remain a special friend.; [a.] Houston, TX

FERNANDEZ, NICOLE SARINA
[pen.] Nikki; [b.] December 24, 1995, Kingston, NY; [p.] Joseph E. and Jo Ann Fernandez; [ed.] High school senior (graduate June 1995); [occ.] Student, pianist, (musical theater) composer; [memb.] School Drama Club, Jazz Band; [hon.] In music, superior with distinction, state competition on piano, trombone. Thespian festival for acting. Band Director's Award 9th grade; [oth. writ.] More poetry and musical compositions in classical music which I have done and would like to get published.; [pers.] I want to be in musical theater on Broadway, a comedian on Saturday Night Live, and I want to write music for one of Disney's future movies. I'd like to think that my poetry takes you into my world if only for a few moments.; [a.] Palm Bay, FL

FERRER, JORGE L.
[pen.] JLF; [b.] June 21, 1976, Venezuela; [p.] Maria D. Carvajal; [ed.] Miami Springs Senior High Miami Florida; [occ.] U.S. Marine; [hon.] The National Library of Poetry; [oth. writ.] Unknown poems which people have never seen; [pers.] Human being.; [a.] Miami Springs, FL

FERRETTI, JACQUELINE
[b.] July 1, 1959, Philadelphia; [p.] Raymond and Evelyn Winters; [m.] Mark A. Ferretti, September 4, 1993; [ch.] Jade Corrine Kaslov, Jonathan Aaron Kaslov; [ed.] Bishop Neumann Business School; [occ.] Secretary - United States Postal Service; [memb.] St. Bernard's Parish; [pers.] I once read, that a good writer only writes about things that he/she is familiar with or has experienced. These things derive from one's own heart. That is where my writings come from always. Influences: Robert Frost, Carl Sandburg; [a.] Philadelphia, PA

FERRO, BARBARA
[b.] February 3, 1948, Yonkers, NY; [p.] Joseph and Nancy Waldron; [m.] Antonio Ferro, July 9, 1966; [ch.] Antonio Jr. and Maria; [ed.] High School; [occ.] Hairdresser; [oth. writ.] I have written many poems over the years through my life experience and travels.; [pers.] We live in a society which perpetuates stereotypes, which stands in the way of understanding, and then we have the nerve as a society to wonder were we have gone wrong.; [a.] Yonkers, NY

FERTIG, MARLIN K.
[b.] August 20, 1919, New Berlin; [p.] George and Margaret; [m.] Leona, April 6, 1940; [ch.] Bonnie and Cynthia; [ed.] High school, training within industry - 38 yrs. Mill Supervisor in a furniture plant; [occ.] Retired; [memb.] United Church of Christ, American Legion, Vet of foreign wars; [pers.] I have been influenced by the demise of our wildlife in general.

FILES, RICHARD
[b.] June 27, 1948, Bronx, NY; [p.] Margaret, David Files; [m.] Kandra, October 20, 1973; [ch.] Briana Lynn, Kali Davlen; [ed.] Bronx HS of Science, SUNY Maritime Course; [occ.] Principal Engineer Knolls Atomic Power Laboratory; [memb.] Marine Engineers, Benevolent Association - 3rd Assistant, Engineer USNR - Lieutenant (Ret.); [hon.] Dean's List, American Bureau of Shipping Award for Excellence in Marine Nuclear Science; [oth. writ.] Life is God's gift, what we do with it is our gift in return... and in the end, the love we take is equal to the love we make; [pers.] Ballston Spa, NY

FILIOU, EVANTHIA
[b.] July 12, 1976, Upper Darby, PA; [p.] Ann and Paul Filios; [ed.] Graduated from Springfield High School, currently attending Monmouth College; [occ.] Student, waitress - part time; [memb.] West Long Branch, Mentoring Program; [hon.] Never received awards for writing in grammar, middle, and high school, received the Presidential Academic Fitness Award; [oth. writ.] I have written a numerous amount of poems as well as fictional short stories. Although I have been encouraged to submit my writing, I never did. Until now.; [pers.] Writing comes naturally only if we write about what is closest to our hearts. The true essence of writing is lost when we attempt to write about frivolous information.; [a.] Springfield, PA

FINDLAY, VERMELLE
[b.] August 27, 1926, Texas; [m.] Marion B. Findlay, May 19, 1946; [memb.] Austin Women's Club, Save the Children's Federation, Methodist Church, Patient Advisor for the Texas Cancer Center in Austin, Texas; [hon.] Past Pres. of Save the Children Federation-Austin Chptr., Past Pres. Life Underwriters Auxiliary, Volunteer American Cancer "Reach to Recovery" (I am a 7 yr. survivor of cancer), one of Austin's Best Dressed Women.; [a.] Austin, TX

FINNEMAN, STACY
[b.] May 20, 1974, Glendive, MT; [p.] Tony and Sharon Finneman; [ed.] Bachelors in Communications and Bachelors in English; [occ.] Work in a restaurant, DJ in a bar; [oth. writ.] Write for the school paper the University of Mary Summit. Works also published in a book Echoes in the Silence.; [pers.] You don't have to do anything in your life. You choose your destiny, your destiny doesn't choose you.; [a.] Bismarck, ND

FISCHER, WHITNEY
[b.] December 13, 1968, Pensacola, FL; [p.] Thom and Sandra Chandler; [m.] Richie Fischer, June 13, 1992; [ed.] Maranatha Christian Academy, Gainesville High, Lanier Tech. Institute; [occ.] Cosmetologist and singer; [hon.] President's List (Lanier Tech.); [pers.] I am not one of great philosophical words. All I know is that poetry and writing give me great satisfaction and self worth. They are the meaning of life.; [a.] Buford, GA

FITZPATRICK, PATRICK G.
[pen.] Paddy Fitzpatrick; [b.] Ireland; [ed.] Christian Brothers School, Cahirclueen, Co. Kerry, Ireland; [occ.] Gypsy; [memb.] Esoteric Clansmen of Hidden Truths; [hon.] I neither decide nor need any.; [oth. writ.] I am frequently published in NYC publications. I read my work at NYC coffee shops and literary places of worship.; [pers.] I love the work of Rainer Maria R. Lue 'Who Loved the Questions.' I write for the unveiling of the mysteries which may someday reveal me to a truth.; [a.] Queens, NY

FITZSIMMONS, HAROLD J.
[pen.] Hal Fitz; [b.] November 12, 1928, Kansas City, MO; [p.] Harold and Sophie Fitzsimmons; [m.] Arlene L. Fitzsimmons, January 20, 1951; [ch.] Michael, Patricia, Dennis, Kathryn, Timothy, Joan, Terri, James; [ed.] Lillis High School, Metropolitan Jr. College; [occ.] Reporter - McGraw-Hill Inc.; [memb.] Christ the King Church (Catholic), American Legion, Prudential Insurance Co. Builders Association; [hon.] McGraw-Hill reporting Excellence Awards; [oth. writ.] Newspaper "Letters to Editor", Sounding board - K.C. Star, poems published K.C. Star; [pers.] Became a poet as a result of an accident which laid me up for six months - while recuperating it seemed to come naturally as a way to pass the time! Got hooked!; [a.] Kansas City, MO

FLEEMAN, JASON D.
[pen.] Dean Moor; [b.] March 24, 1970, Atlanta, GA; [p.] Randall and Janice Fleeman; [ed.] Bachelor of Science Degree in Psychology; [occ.] Tennis Professional; [memb.] American Psychological Association, American Psychological Society, United States Professional Tennis Registry; [hon.] Golden Key Honor Society, Psi Chi Honor Society, graduated top 5% of class.; [oth. writ.] Several unpublished poems of my own personal thoughts on intimacy and relationships; [pers.] Life is much easier if you live the questions rather than seeking the answers.; [a.] Kennesaw, GA

FLETCHER, KEITH R.
[b.] August 19, 1962, Arlington Heights, IL; [p.] Marolyn Overton, Robert Fletcher; [ch.] Shannon and Shaun; [ed.] University of Rochester, Computer Science and Psychology; [occ.] Associate Director, Network Services for Phillips Van Heusen; [oth. writ.] Reflections - Pub. beginnings 1980; [a.] Andover, NJ

FLOOK, ARLIE M.
[pen.] Arline Small; [b.] August 16, 1924, Stratford, Ontario, Canada; [p.] Mrs. Selina Ellen March, Mr. Wm. Albert Small (both age 58 deceased); [m.] Mr. Harold Flook (Peter), September 5, 1942; [ch.] Mrs. Adrienne Clark, Alfred Leslie Flook (reported dead); [ed.] Sketchy 1st yr University (Queen's) Kingston, Ont; [occ.] Retiree, considered crazy by psychiatrists at any rate various political figures among them - Dr. Schuller and Son-Presidents and Prime Ministers; [memb.] Church of the Redeemer - Vancouver, BC, 1499 Laurier Ave Granville and 24th, looking forward to seeing Jesus' return; [hon.] None as yet however like Christ I am without degrees or even appreciation however, that my change!; [oth. writ.] Poetry on my personal correspondence; [pers.] I adore nature and poetry. I haven't slept thru the night for many a night. I lay awake praying till I must get up and walk; [a.] Vancouver, Canada

FLORES, SARAH JANE
[pen.] Sarah Jane Flores; [b.] February 3, 1945, Spokane, WA; [p.] William James and S. Maxine Shank; [m.] Joe Ralph Flores, June 21, 1980; [ch.] Geneva Inez, Tina Marie, Brenda Louise, and John Paul Chavez (grandson); [pers.] My true feelings can be found through my poetry. Words of poetry can be a cleansing of the soul; [a.] Santa Fe, NM

FLUSS, CHARMAINE
[b.] July 22, 1953, Oakland, CA; [p.] Alphonso and Jeannine Santos; [ch.] Tyson Alphonso Fluss, Shawn Lee Fluss; [ed.] Washington High, Fremont Oak Grove High, San Jose West Valley Jr. College, Saratoga; [occ.] Child Care Aide and YMCA Cook, mother; [memb.] East Valley YMCA; [hon.] Dean's List, West Valley Jr. College, Volunteer Award, East Valley YMCA San Jose; [oth. writ.] Several poems in my personal poem book. A poem titled "Children of the Y," for the East Valley YMCA (inspirational); [pers.] The Golden Rule should rule our lives. I try to live my life accordingly. It's a shame that "Fool's Gold" is the rule that seems to have taken over. Live and let live and your life will truly be golden!; [a.] San Jose, CA

FLYNN, DEVIN MICHELE
[b.] August 19, 1980, Monroe, MI; [p.] Denis and Valerie Flynn; [ed.] I am currently in the 9th grade, but plan on attending college; [occ.] Attend school, studying to be a writer; [oth. writ.] Other poems I have written and submitted to contests; [pers.] I may be only in the 9th grade but I am just as dedicated as anybody else. I hope to have a very promising career in writing.; [a.] Fremont, MI

FONSECA, MARITZA
[b.] July 20, 1958, Sta. Ana, El Salvador; [p.] Pablo Carranza, Evangelina Umana; [m.] Mauricio Fonseca, September 10, 1983; [ch.] Adriana and Camilo Fonseca; [ed.] Los Angeles Valley College; [occ.] English Student; [memb.] Parent Teacher Association; [hon.] Reseda Elm Volunteer Service Award, Leadership Award; [oth. writ.] Several unpublished poems; [pers.] I attempt to reflect the need for spiritual meaning often forgotten in a materialistic world. I have been influenced by the modern symbolist poets.; [a.] Reseda, CA

FORBES, PAULETTE
[b.] November 14, 1958, Jamaica, West Indies; [p.] Marjorie Campbell and Adolph Forbes; [ed.] Shortwood Teachers' College - Jamaica, Holmwood Technical High - Jamaica, St. John's School of Business - W. Spfld, MA; [occ.] Administrative Assistant, Visiting Nurse Association, Spfld. MA; [oth. writ.] Article and poem published in the White Wing Messenger; [pers.] It is amazing, yes, mind-boggling to see how God uses the things of nature to give inspiration — a true reflection of His nature.; [a.] Springfield, MA

FORD, AVONA
[b.] July 9, 1979; [p.] Randy and Theresa Ford; [ed.] Currently a student at Lexington High School (LHS) in Lexington, MO 64067; [memb.] FHA for 2 years, Girls Glee Club, Art Club; [hon.] Poem is being published by Sparrowgrass Poetry.; [pers.] I always look for the best in people, because it's not the outer beauty that counts. It's what's in the heart that makes a person unique; [a.] Lexington, MO

FORSHEE, ROY D.
[pen.] Bee; [b.] May 21, 1955, Saint Louis, MO; [p.] Robert and Helen Forshee; [m.] Kathleen Joy Forshee, September 28, 1994; [ch.] Robin, Mitchell, Rebecca, Chuck Christopher; [ed.] North County High School, US Army, Platte Jr. College; [occ.] Self employed; [memb.] State Pen., Philadelphia Assembly Church; [oth. writ.] Several unpublished poems and songs, spare time hobby.; [pers.] I am a hardened criminal in prison, or so I thought, until the inspiration for this particular poem entered my life, A Red Haired Angel. Sent from God, my wife.; [a.] Jefferson City, MO

FORTIN, BEATRICE O.
[pen.] Bea Fortin; [b.] June 12, 1929, Neshkoro, WI; [p.] Anna Yasick, Frank Yasick; [m.] Working single mom; [ch.] Spencer Fortin, Neal Fortin; [ed.] Princeton High, Oakland Community College, New York University, Columbia University; [occ.] Currently retired, Administrative Analyst, Training Representative; [memb.] Founder's Society of The Detroit Institute of Arts, Detroit Historical Society; [hon.] Dean's List, various commendations for achievement and excellence in performance; [oth. writ.] 30 years writing experience, training manuals, procedures, promotional scripts, analytical studies of various kinds, proposals for change of various kinds, poems, song lyrics, newsletters, editorials in local papers, now am starting to write short stories; [pers.] I believe we are here to learn and grow spiritually. That it is our duty as human beings to help our fellowman and that we should do what we can to make other lives easier because life is difficult enough as it is and that there is no place for greed and selfishness. In my writings I try to take a realistic approach and show life as it is and people as they are with their foibles.; [a.] Royal Oak, MI

FOX, PAULINE MOORE
[b.] April 30, 1910, Platner, CO; [p.] Walter and Dorothy Heise Moore; [m.] Paul Jackson Fox, December 25, 1938; [ed.] High School Graduate, South Denver High 6/16/27; [memb.] First Unitarian Church, San Diego, CA; [oth. writ.] Writing verse since age 12; [pers.] The three verses I have sent are my own; [a.] San Diego, CA

FRANCIS, LINDA
[b.] April 11, 1949, South Gate, CA; [p.] Allen W. and Ruby F. Avery; [m.] Gary Francis Jr., May 20, 1968; [ch.] Tammi and Gary Jr.; [ed.] Manguma Okla. High School, American Red Cross Chair-Side Dental Assistant, Course and Diploma, ARC First Aid Instructor; [occ.] Homemaker, poet; [hon.] Family Ombudsman for Husband's Detachment at Subic Bay Naval Base, Philippines.; [oth. writ.] Poems and remembrances to the family; [pers.] I enjoy researching my family tree and collecting old photographs of and information about my family, for future generations.; [a.] Montgomery, AL

FRANCIS, WALTER CHRISTIAN
[b.] August 15, 1953, Cincinnati, OH; [p.] Elmer W. and Hilda S. Francis; [m.] Rosario Hofilena Francis, April 3, 1981; [ed.] Ferguson High School, Newport News Virginia, Thomas Nelson Community College Hampton Virginia; [occ.] Machinist - Canon Virginia Inc.; [hon.] Magna Cum Laude, Phi Theta Kappa, US Patent 5072720; [a.] Hampton, VA

FRANTZ, JEANNETTE
[b.] Trenton, NJ; [p.] John L. Stout, Edith Stout; [m.] William E. Frantz; [ch.] Yetta Jean Teo and Mary Ann Dansky, Grandchildren Lauren and Sarah Teo; [ed.] Trenton High, Trenton State Teachers College graduate and 1 year at Rider College; [occ.] Retired Teacher: 5th grade, Bear Tavern School, Titusville, NJ; [memb.] Former Regent, National Society Daughters of the American Revolution; [oth. writ.] Wrote 23 plays performed by 5th graders at Bear Tavern School.; [a.] Stamford, NY

FREDA, EDNA M.
[b.] October 8, 1930, Hoboken, NJ; [p.] Wm. and Agnes McLaughlin (deceased); [m.] Mr. Patsy L. Freda, September 20, 1953; [ch.] 2 (also 2 grandchildren), 2 (unofficially adopted); [ed.] High School Graduate; [occ.] Retired secretary; [oth. writ.] Many unpublished poems; [pers.] Go to sleep knowing that you did your best today

FREEMAN, CEDEIRDRE
[b.] August 3, 1973, New York City, NY; [p.] Anita and Leander Rowell; [ed.] Presently attending George Mason University in Fairfax, Virginia; [occ.] Human Resources Dept. - office worker; [memb.] President of Black Student Alliance at GMU, Big Buddy Program, Several Volunteer Positions; [hon.] I consider this an honor. Having my poem published is the ultimate reward for my heart!; [oth. writ.] This is my first published.; [pers.] I take all I hear and observe and put the information together all at once in one giant blast of feeling. I am greatly influenced by black experience poets (Angelou, Giovanni, Hughes, etc.); [a.] Fairfax, VA

FREEMAN, DORIS R.
[b.] February 15, 1947, Mannington, WV; [p.] George and Maude Stevens; [m.] Darrell Freeman, May 20, 1989 (2nd marriage); [ch.] David Brian, Kimberly Sue; [ed.] Mannington High; [occ.] Philips Lighting - Line operator; [memb.] Church of Christ; [hon.] Home Economic Award, Sports trophies; [oth. writ.] Some short stories and poem - unpublished.; [pers.] I try to see, smell and touch the nature God has created for us every day.; [a.] Fairmont, WV

FREEMAN, SHANE
[pen.] L. B. Lemort; [b.] September 17, 1977, Sargent, NE; [p.] Janet Loughran and Mark Freeman; [ed.] I am currently enrolled at Broken Bow High School; [occ.] Student, Lifeguard; [memb.] American Heart Association, Rotary International, Hugh O'Brian Youth Foundation; [hon.] Rotary Exchange Student, Honor Roll; [oth. writ.] Numerous articles in the local newspaper.; [pers.] I would like to dedicate my work to Jaime Spence, my sweet sour Dough. You helped me through those times of impossibility. Belgium, 1994-1995. Thanks!; [a.] Broken Bow, NE

FREEMAN, WENDY
[b.] April 12, 1943, Philadelphia, PA; [p.] Natalie and Phil Weinreich; [m.] Richard Freeman, February 28, 1975; [ch.] Geoffrey, Laura and Sharon; [ed.] Cheltenham High in Wyncote PA, BS in Education - Boston University, graduate schools - Florida Atlantic University and Barry University; [occ.] Learning Disability, Teacher and Adult Ed. Teacher in Child Care Classes; [memb.] NAEYC, Wilderness Organization - Wash. DC; [hon.] Certificate of Appreciation in Special Education 1993; [oth. writ.] Preschool Cookbook; [pers.] I enjoy writing to inspire children and adults who work with young children; [a.] West Palm Beach, FL

FRENCH, KRISTINA JOANN
[pen.] Tina; [b.] June 16, 1981, Pordenone, Italy; [p.] Joann Castro French, Bobby J. French; [ed.] CL Taitano Elem. School, Bishop Baumgartner School, Agueda Johnston Middle School; [occ.] Student; [hon.] Principal's List, Citizenship Award, A Honor Roll, B Honor Roll, Junior Police Cadat, Sports: Most Improved Player, Most Valuable Player in basketball, playing basketball throughout my middle school years.; [oth. writ.] Writing poems on spare time.; [pers.] Life is like a bowl of cherries, but for some they're ripe at a young age.; [a.] Sinajana, GU

FRENCHIK, STEPHANIE LYNN
[pen.] Christina Rae; [b.] December 19, 1972, West Germany; [p.] Norman and Mary Ann Frenchik; [ed.] Merrillville High School; [occ.] Certified Nurses Aid; [oth. writ.] This is the first time I have sent one of my poems anywhere. So this is my very first poem to be published.; [pers.] In all of my writings I try to portray my personality, my outlook, emotions, etc. When someone reads my work I want them to feel what I was feeling when I wrote it. I strive to make people think about what I write.; [a.] Merrillville, IN

FRISCIA, MICHAEL JOSEPH
[pen.] Myke J. Friscia; [b.] February 2, 1969, Bronx, NY; [ed.] Graduate Oak Park HS 1987, AA degree Moorpark College 1990, BA degree in Film Production May 1995; [occ.] Screenwriter and producer; [oth. writ.] A short film based on this poem is currently in production. A full length screenplay which is currently under consideration for production.; [pers.] Everything I write comes from the heart. Anything you do that is important to you, your heart should be in it! If it's not, then you shouldn't be doing it.; [a.] Northridge, CA

FRITZ, DOROTHY
[pen.] Jean Boyce Capra; [b.] February 15, 1931, MO; [p.] A. E. and Ida Boyce; [m.] John Fritz, May 22, 1949, divorced July 26, 1956; [ch.] Judy, Patti, Carol; [ed.] Kansas City Bus. College, Pen Valley College - KC MO, University of Arizona; [occ.] Secretary, Kansas School for the Blind; [memb.] Church of Jesus, Christ of Latter Day Saints - KCKS; [oth. writ.] Poems published in Pierce City Leader Journal, World of Poetry, and American Poetry Association. Have written over 200 poems.; [pers.] I dedicate this poem in Chava and Cho Pan, my adorable puppies, my 16 grandchildren, and all blind children worldwide.; [a.] Kansas City, KS

FRYETT, MEGHAN
[b.] Greenbay, WI; [p.] Roger Fryett, Dorothy Fryett; [oth. writ.] Several poems yet to be discovered; [pers.] I try to describe reality in a more creative form. Life isn't sugar-coated, but sometimes I wish it was.; [a.] Topeka, KS

FULKERSON, MAYUMI
[b.] November 7, 1968, Japan; [p.] Masako and Charles Fulkerson; [ch.] Casey Jessamine; [ed.] Radford High, Honolulu; [occ.] Sheraton, Moana Surfrider Hotel, Front Desk, Hono. HI; [memb.] Allstate Motor Club Association; [hon.] Candidate of Ms. Teen USA Pageant 1984, Golf Tournament awards, ads in local newspaper and magazines.; [pers.] Search deep in your heart and write about your darkest, most secret experiences. Only then, you will find a poet in yourself.; [a.] Honolulu, HI

GABLE, MARY LOU
[b.] October 18, 1950, Laurens, SC; [ch.] Kylie Gable, (daughter); [ed.] Laurens High School, Laurens, S.C. Assoc. of Arts Degree Anderson College, Anderson, S.C.; [occ.] Fraud Investigator, Dept. of Social Services; [memb.] Member of United Council on Welfare Fraud, Served on Board of Directors for three years of South Carolina Council on Welfare Fraud, Member Oakgrove Baptist Church, various organizations; [hon.] President of South Carolina Council on Welfare Fraud for 1995; [oth. writ.] Many poems all relating to "Abuse", several poems released to various organizations dealing with sexual abuse.; [pers.] I have written poetry since a teenager, but never shared any of it until the last two years. I am a survivor of "Incest" and hope to help many other "survivors" through my poetry and life story.; [a.] Spartanburg, SC

GADEMANS, AMANDA D.
[b.] March 11, 1978, Trail, British Columbia, Canada; [p.] Dick and Brandi Gademans; [ed.] Student at J.L. Crowe Secondary School, Trail, B.C., Canada; [memb.] J.L. Crowe Senior Choir; [oth. writ.] This is a first publication of my poetry although I have written many others.; [pers.] I love to write poetry and now I feel that I should be submitting more of my work.; [a.] Trail, British Columbia, Canada

GAINES, REGINA
[pen.] Lady Chaka; [b.] February 26, 1951, Hartford, CT; [p.] William Gaines, Annie Gaines; [ed.] Weaver High, University of Hartford; [occ.] Operations Director: The Joe Picture this show; [memb.] National Urban League Newington Children's Hospital and University; [hon.] Outstanding Young Women of America Award, New Voices in American Literature and Sterling Who's Who executive edition; [oth. writ.] Several poems published in local newspapers, magazines and childrens publications columns on periodic basis). The Joe's Kids page, The City Beat, Media Works, The Northland Agents and The Hartford Courant; [pers.] "Naturaltivity: The profound use of one's abilities and talents by nurturing and developing in harmony with nature one's spiritual being to its fullest potential."; [a.] Hartford, CT

GALE, RICHARD
[pen.] Rebel; [b.] September 27, 1968, North Adams; [p.] William Gale and Joan Gale; [ed.] Hoosac Valley H.S., Berkshire C.C. North Adams S.C.; [occ.] Partner-Gale Floor Covering; [memb.] Central Berkshire Chamber of Commerce, National Rifle Association; [hon.] 1st Ho Bup Sa in Han-Pul Specialized Self Defense; [oth. writ.] In the process of compiling information and photographs in order to depict the legend of Mt. Greylock in Adams, MA; [pers.] To make one person smile every day of my life; [a.] Adams, MA

GALLOWAY, WENDY
[b.] November 10, 1965, Ogden, UT; [p.] Darold and Bonnie Galloway; [ed.] Bonneville High School, In-sync mind and body school; [occ.] Ins. Billing Clerk, Clinical Hypno Therapist; [memb.] National Guild of Hypnotists; [oth. writ.] Self published a small booklet for self-awareness and inner beauty. "The ABC's to a better me." Written many poems and songs.; [pers.] "Free to be Me!" "Regaining one's life and living it to the fullest is more than surviving it is conquering!"; [a.] Ogden, UT

GAMBLE, CINDY L.
[b.] April 26, 1962, Kingsville, TX; [p.] Leeman Arnold, Nicki Arnold; [ch.] Ryan Michael 14 years, Joel David 13 years, Kyle Thomas 10 years, Brad Andrew 8 years; [ed.] Carlson High School International Correspondence School; [occ.] Self employed Computer Processing, San Antonio, TX; [memb.] American Heart Association TX., St. Troopers Ass.; [oth. writ.] not published; [pers.] My children are the pride of my life. If I can teach them to embrace the joy in life and find satisfaction in the simple miracles, rather than allowing themselves to be drown by bitterness, I will have truly succeeded; [a.] San Antonio, TX

GARCIA, CARLOS
[b.] April 23, 1967, Pontiac, MI; [p.] Jim and Sudie Super; [ed.] Walled Lake Central High School, Montcalm Community College/Business Marketing; [memb.] Secretary of Latin American Spanish Speaking Organization.; [oth. writ.] Poem "River" published in Institutional paper; [pers.] Life is too short to sit and wait for your dreams, we must reach for them and count every second as the last. I write from personal experiences; [a.] Muskegon, MI

GARCIA, ELIZABETH
[b.] May 7, 1966, Paterson, NJ; [p.] Thomas and Gloria Vergara; [m.] Omar Garcia, May 30, 1983; [ch.] Omar Jr., Marlene, Mariah, Thomas; [ed.] G.E.D.; [occ.] Home maker; [memb.] Proud member of the Apostolic Penticostal Church; [pers.] Never limit your goals. We can do all things through Christ, who has no limits.; [a.] St. Louis, MO

GARCIA, JESSIE
[b.] November 25, 1952, Waukegan, IL; [m.] Ray Garcia I, August 5, 1989; [ch.] Shannon, Tanya, Ray II, Eric; [ed.] Waukegan Township High School, College of Lake County; [occ.] Business System Analyst, Abbot Laboratories, North Chicago; [hon.] Phi Theta Kappa; [pers.] Phil 3:14 - I press toward the mark for the prize of the high calling of God in Christ Jesus.; [a.] Zion, IL

GARCIA, JOSEPH PAUL
[b.] July 15, 1975, Apple Valley, CA; [p.] Mr. Joseph L. and Mrs. Josie M. Garcia; [ed.] Barstow High, United States Air Force Technical School and Community College of the Air Force; [occ.] Aerospace Ground Equipment Technician; [memb.] U.S.A.F. Honor Guard Roman Catholic Church; [oth. writ.] Mostly un-published love poems to girl friends and personal writings on the spur of the moment.; [pers.] I am motivated by my Lord Jesus Christ to write about life and my feelings towards it, I believe if you don't stand for something, you will fall for anything.; [a.] Luke AFB, AZ

GARDNER, RENEE'
[b.] February 23, 1967, Troy; [p.] Michael and Donna Bergeron; [m.] Bruce Gardner, October 3, 1993; [ch.] Tracy Gardner (16), Justin Gardner (12) (Step Children); [ed.] Mechanicville High School (1985), Hudson Valley Community College (1 year) - (HVCC); [occ.] Receptionist, Cashier, Gregory Chyrsler Jeep Inc., full time student HVCC; [pers.] My writings reflect my inner feelings towards the people and experiences in my life.; [a.] Troy, NY

GARDNER, TAYLOR
[b.] November 23, 1983, Santa Monica, CA; [p.] Pattie Pierce, Tilt Gardner; [ed.] Canyon Charter School 5th grade currently; [occ.] A Student at School; [hon.] Honor Roll for Grades 1995 Scholarly Speller; [a.] Malibu, CA

GARNER, MARY GRACE W.
[pen.] GG; [b.] December 11, 1933, Cabins, WV; [p.] Oscar Obed Wolford, Effie Ann Moyers Wolford; [m.] Russell Land Garner, July 2, 1951; [ch.] Russell Alan Garner, Named to Who's Who 1985 for Colleges and Universities, Steven Everett Garner, Vice President Electric Motor Corp., Mark Eugene Garner, Graduate, United States Air Force Academy, Captain in United States Air Force; [ed.] High School And LPH Schooling have been writing bibliography of my life, however, it is not completed.; [occ.] Retired/LPN; [memb.] Oakland Christian Church The Greatest Gifts in my life have been Jesus, the Son of God, My late husband, and my three sons. I have three daughters-in-law that make my life much happier, and five wonderful grandchildren. (Three granddaughters and two grand sons). My life has been full and rewarding. Many trials and tribulations, however, God has always seen me through each test of faith.; [hon.] Many beneficial suggestions while working for Federal Government, with subsequent monetary awards.; [a.] Suffolk, VA

GARRETSON, KRISTY R.
[b.] July 21, 1968, Oklahoma City; [p.] Bill and Imogene Garretson; [ed.] Moore High School Graduate in 1986. Rose State College graduated in 1989; [occ.] Radiologic Technologist at Midwest City Regional Hospital; [memb.] American Society of Radiologic Technologists, Oklahoma Society of Radiologic Technologists. (ASRT and OSRT); [oth. writ.] Have had two different poems published already; [pers.] I write my poems with great emotions. I want to feel what I write. Poetry is my way to relax.; [a.] Moore, OK

GASPARINI, JENNY
[b.] April 20, 1977, Vancouver, Canada; [p.] Elio Gasparini, Rosetta Gasparini; [ed.] Centennial Senior Secondary High. Planning on attending the University of Victoria in the coming fall.; [occ.] Student; [oth. writ.] personal collection; [pers.] Only through poetry can I express my true self and feelings. Because of this, I have obtained a better understanding of who I am and why I think and act the way I do.; [a.] Coquitlam, British Columbia, Canada

GASSIC, SYLVIA
[pen.] Sylvia Eleman Gassic; [b.] January 28, 1926, England; [p.] Max Tilly Eleman; [m.] Sydney Classic, March 1, 1947; [ch.] 5 Daughters; [occ.] House wife; [memb.] London Hadassah Wizo Congregation or Shalom; [oth. writ.] Lots of poems; [pers.] I write of how I feel about all life, I love mature animals everything that grows. Some of my poems are very sad because I cry inside at what is happening in the world to all living things human and animal.; [a.] London Ontario, Canada

GAVILAN, JAMES
[b.] March 24, 1975, Manhattan, NY; [p.] Caesar and Isabel Gavilan; [ed.] Fordham College at Lincoln Center; [occ.] Investors Services Representative, Blanchard Mutual Funds; [pers.] Disenchanted with the chasms that divide the reality within us and the reality that surrounds us. My motivation in writing is to expose these breaks.; [a.] New York City, NY

GAVIN, JESSIE
[pen.] Jessica Gavin; [b.] November 8, 1897, Montreal, Province of Quebec, Canada; [m.] Charles Gavin, June 15, 1935 (deceased); [ed.] Graduated from St. Patrick's Academy, Montreal in June 1915 [occ.] Retired; [memb.] St. Patrick's Square Association; [hon.] Honors in Literature; [pers.] Sense of humor and kindness to others most essential to live to ninety seven; [a.] Montreal Province of Quebec, Canada

GAYTAN, TIRSO M.
[b.] January 28, 1932, Austin, TX; [p.] Jose and Benita Gaytan; [m.] Esther, March 12, 1950 (first wife deceased), Lupe, March 28, 1983 (present wife); [ch.] Joe, Hector, Mary, Silva (from first marriage); [ed.] None self educated; [occ.] Disabled; [memb.] Our Lady of Guadalupe Catholic Church, Broadcast Music Inc. - BMI represents composers and song writers; [oth. writ.] Songs recorded in Spanish. By various groups song such as "Hay Cosas En La Vida", "Triste En Navidad" and "Como El Perro Y El Gato" among others; [pers.] Respect the right of others. Be in peace with yourself. Live your life to the fullest as our Almighty God intended you to live it in this ever-changing world. Be happy.; [a.] Austin, TX

GEACH, REV. JILL
[b.] July 19, 1927, Croydon, England; [p.] Louise and Alfred Wilkes; [m.] Alwyn, March 29; [ch.] adopted son; [ed.] Ph.D. Physiotherapy Theology; [occ.] Semi Retired; [memb.] Canadian Writers, Swimming Club, Church; [hon.] Chaplaincy at Nursing home Plaque for "Caring Service"; [oth. writ.] Verses - children's annual thesis on homosexuality; [pers.] Important that we love and care for each other; [a.] London, Ontario, Canada

GELBERGER, JUDITH KOPACSI
[b.] February 22, 1946, Hungary; [p.] Sandor Kopacsi, Ibolya Kopacsi; [m.] Peter Paul Gelberger, May 24, 1972; [ch.] Leslie Joseph, Eva Margareth; [ed.] George Brown College Adlerian Institute - Canada; [occ.] Writer, educator, assistant of a film producer; [memb.] Brampton Writer's Guild, The International P.E.N. Club - American Branch.; [oth. writ.] Several poems published in local papers, an autobiography in Heroes Don't Cry" - published in Hungary (1992) an educational hand-book titled "Dealing with behavior problems in a Democratic Society", also in Hungary (1994); [pers.] "Love cures all."

GEORGE, JAMES P. E. WOLF
[pen.] Wolf; [b.] November 11, 1955, NY; [p.] David Lee Clark Sr., Heraldina Clark; [m.] Crystal Daniels, pending; [ch.] Steven Haney, Darius George, Christina Haney, Stakisha Duvall; [ed.] Monroe High School; [occ.] Self Employment; [pers.] Poetry brings out love, hope, and stability we all need. The good Lord and street life experiences influenced me to write.

GEPHART, HELEN
[pen.] Helen Gephart; [b.] February 20, 1928, Comstock, NY; [p.] Helene Warner Glessing and Joseph Glessing; [m.] William Gephart, October 19, 1946; [ch.] Anita Hayes, Jeffrey, Frederick Gephart; [ed.] High School in Attica, NY; [occ.] Home maker and Retired office clerk; [memb.] Honor Lady of the Masonic Order of the Amaranth" Historical Soc.; [oth. writ.] Many poems over my life time in every avenue! In Ocala, Florida I entered, I won a prose story writing of the Ocala Star Banner, (of third place); [pers.] The love of my family and my dear husband have influenced my writing and also in my art painting. My love of history and so many friends fill my days to over flowing!!; [a.] West Valley, NY

GEREMSKI, SARA
[b.] September 23, 1975, Chicago, IL; [p.] Terry and Cece Geremski; [ed.] The Lee Strasberg Theatre Institute; [occ.] Student; [hon.] Who's Who Among American High School Students 1989-93, Student Ambassador to Russia - 1991; [pers.] Only as high as I reach can I grow, only as far as I seek can I go, only as deep as I look can I see, only as much as I dream can I be.; [a.] Los Angeles, CA

GIBBS, JEAN
[b.] January 21, 1924, MO; [p.] Carl and George Ann O'Brion; [m.] Philip Heath Gibbs, June 14, 1947; [ch.] Deborah, Hilarie, Christy, Victoria; [ed.] Deering High School (Portland ME), Westbrook Jr. College (Portland, ME - Assoc. B.A.), University of Texas (Degree not completed); [occ.] Retired corporate Sec/Treasurer; [memb.] Society of Experimental Artists; [oth. writ.] 15 years as the voluntary director of the Cape Cod Cranberry Grower's Association Promotion Committee resulted in lots of writing, none of which was as creative as I might have wished!; [pers.] 40 years post-college-raising, 4 daughters, assisting husband in the business of raising cranberries, and care-taking geriatic family members rather dulled my muse. Now, plunged into painting, poetry has again risen!; [a.] Sarasota, FL

GIFFORD, RUSSELL D.
[b.] June 22, 1932, Minot, ND; [p.] Olen D. Gifford, Ione E. Gifford; [m.] Joan D. Gifford, June 6. 1954; [ch.] Jamie Alyson, David Russell; [ed.] Minot College High, Univ. Maryland Assoc. Electronic Engineer, Quality Engineer and Mechanical Engineer., USAF Technical and Instructor training; [occ.] Quality Assurance Specialist (Electronics) Department of Defense, Defense Contract Management Command, Minneapolis, MN; [memb.] American Society Quality Control, American Society Electronic and Mechanical Engineers, Air Force Sergent Association, American Legion.; [hon.] Citation for Public Service City of Orlando, Fl., performed during Hurricane Donna, Outstanding Performance awards from the Defense Logistics Agency, Outstanding Unit Citations USAF, Germany and Republic of South Korea, Airman of the Defense Logistics Agency for services rendered during Desert Shield and Desert Storm.; [oth. writ.] Poetry published in the "Unknowns" Poetry Publication.; [pers.] It is said that I am a Romantic, and my poems on Family, Love, Friendship, Life and Country convey this to all who have viewed my work. A true Renaissance Man and Western Culture Historian.; [a.] Eagan, MN

GIFFORD, SUSAN HUMPHREY
[pen.] Susan Humphrey; [b.] May 31, 1949, Chula Vista, CA; [p.] Marvin Humphrey and Mary Humphrey; [m.] Charles Randall Gifford, June 1, 1974; [ed.] Grossmont Union High, San Diego State University; [occ.] Design Associate Nettle Creek Interiors; [memb.] The Island Institute, Southport Historical Society, Maine KPBS San Diego, California; [hon.] Catholic Daughters of America, Poetry Competition - 2 awards; [oth. writ.] Advertising copy and trade publication articles; [pers.] I love the drama of poetry and the emotion it can call forth.; [a.] Rancho Santa Fe, CA

GILBERT, ELIZABETH
[b.] November 9, 1982, South Korea; [p.] Betsy Kennedy and Bob Gilbert; [ed.] Mahituck High School. I am in the Seventh grade, and on the honor roll.; [hon.] Numerous student of the month awards and honor roll; [oth. writ.] Personal writings never published

GILCREASE, LARRY
[b.] February 1, 1950, Houston, TX; [p.] Marvin And Roseva Gilcrease; [ed.] B.S., M.Ed. (University of Houston) M.A. (Dallas Seminary); [occ.] School Teacher; [hon.] Honor Graduate, 1989 (Dallas Seminary); [pers.] Work and education are intrinsically good and, when diligence is applied, result in fulfillment. Since true achievement requires maximum effort, "over achievement" and "under achievement" are mutually impossible.; [a.] Houston, TX

GILL, ELIZABETH S.
[b.] January 13, 1936, New London, CT; [p.] William and Elizabeth S. Skoneski; [m.] John F. Gill, November 22, 1958; [ch.] John Frank, Mary Elizabeth, Andrew Joseph; [ed.] Griswold H.S., Jewett City, CT Bryant College, Smithfield, RI-BSS Rowan College, Glassboro, NJ-MAT; [occ.] Retired; [memb.] Treasure Coast Genealogical Society, Rhode Island Genealogical Society; [hon.] Delta Kappa Gamma, Bryant Key Society, Summa Cum Laude Graduate; [oth. writ.] Master's Thesis on need for family life education in school, poem being published by Sparrow-grass poetry forum, WV; [pers.] My poetry is based on the humorous and special qualities of family experiences.; [a.] Port St. Lucie, FL

GIVENS, SIOBHAN NICOLE
[b.] December 24, 1984, Frankfurt, West Germany; [p.] Ricky and Demetri Givens; [ed.] 4th Grader at Crooked Oak Elementary; [memb.] Troop #197 Girl Scouts; [hon.] Principals Honor Roll, Accelerated and Enrichment Student Program, President of Children's Church Choir; [oth. writ.] Several poems; [pers.] My goal is to keep on writing poems, and to influence other writers my age to express their thoughts and feelings.; [a.] Oklahoma, OK

GLASER, DAVID
[b.] September 29, 1919, Brooklyn, NY; [p.] Samuel, Jennie; [m.] Mildred, February 19, 1944; [ch.] Susan, Sherry; [ed.] Thomas Jefferson High School Graduate 1936, Art Student League (Scholar), N.Y. School of Industrial Art, New York School Contemporary Art, Brooklyn Museum Art School, Behring Institute 1954, Teacher Center Island Jewish School. Freeport New York 1959.; [occ.] Artist, Sculptor - Fine Art, writing new age graphic experimentation owner, studio concepts; [memb.] Allied Artists of America, Freeport Art Museum and Conservation, AVC, ACW, Amnesty Int'l Wildness Soc, World Jewish Cong. Greenpeace, American Music of Nat'l history.; [hon.] First poem published 1934 National human review, Nassau City poetry award 1981, Art Students League Scholar 1936, Grand Prize redesign Levitt Home 1967, Numerous graphic awards, Monadnock Mills, Vet Soc. of American Artists, Desi-Grand prize, 3-man show Heckscher Music Huntington 1964, Shows National Arts Club New York 1959, Art Directions 1959, ACA Galleries 1960, Hofstra U., Adelphi U., Nassau Community Call, Pres. Allied Artists of America 1985 exh. Wantagh Levittown, Civilian Conservation Corps 1936 Artist (Adirondacks); [oth. writ.] "My Mother Died Dancing Book 1970, cartoonist, editor, publisher AVS "giggurandom" 1993-4 orientations (sotaus) writings North Pacific 1945, numerous essay on human condition. Inventor: Mosaic reproduction 1948-50 artist, writer 1945 "Bearing Breeze" Aleutians; [pers.] To question to wonder, to accept all possibilities and to explore whenever possible and to accept so called "failure" as a "given" side road to discovery. "To tune in" to the inner universal self and express what is received back in the song of words or the visual. To go "against the grain". Insecurity expressed positively moves me more deeply toward the full potential.; [a.] Wantagh, NY

GLENN, DALE W.
[b.] August 28, 1939, Hoopeston, IL; [p.] Mr. and Mrs. Herbert Glenn; [m.] Joyce, June 14, 1959; [ed.] BS in Ed - Eastern Illinois University Med - University of Illinois; [occ.] Retired, Special Ed. Coordinator - Joliet Twp. H.S. (32 years); [oth. writ.] "The Wolf" is the first poem I have ever submitted.; [pers.] I may be the Grandma Moses of poetry. I believe poetry should reflect our feelings about what we see around us every day the simple things we often take for granted.; [a.] Shorewood, IL

GLENN, SARAH L.
[pen.] Faith Christian; [b.] January 29, 1942, Chesnee, SC; [p.] Jeremiah Glenn and Josel M. Glenn; [ed.] Lincoln High Manpower Development Secretarial Training Center; [occ.] Secretary and Seamstress; [hon.] Valedictorian American Legion School Award Honor Society; [a.] Arcadia, SC

GNEITING, LARRY
[pen.] Larry Dean; [b.] May 12, 1944, CA; [p.] Helen and Ludwig; [m.] Nancy, February 2, 1980; [ch.] Ashley Anne, Devin Michael; [occ.] Personal Growth Consultant, Business Training; [hon.] Who's Who in American Business; [oth. writ.] Articles on personal growth, team building, conflict resolution currently writing a book on "The Care Paradigm" A new model of human behavior; [pers.] We often explain life in a narrative, but the experience of life is only found in poetry.; [a.] Whittler, CA

GNEITING, PHIL
[b.] April 16, 1967, Farmington, PA; [m.] Jennifer, March 4, 1990; [ch.] Kelsey Alfred (4), Kerry Rosanna (2); [memb.] Member of an intentional community, following the sermon of the mount. A life of service, love and joy in others. Our door is open!; [pers.] Trying to regain the joy and spontaneity of a child. What do we have against children anyway?; [a.] Elka Pank, NY

GOBER, GLORIA
[b.] April 2, 1945, Tulsa, OK; [p.] Charles M. and Julia Gober; [ed.] B.A. Oklahoma Baptist University Master of Education East Central University Ada, Oklahoma; [occ.] Teacher; [memb.] Ada Writers Club; [hon.] This poem is my first work published; [oth. writ.] Write and print own books. Book titles are "Poems from the Heart", "The Hedge Lady", "No More Rope" "Lord, Teach Me To Die" "The Road To Submission" "Kick The Cat" and "Hear God Laugh, See God Cry."; [pers.] I write poems, articles and books of encouragement and inspiration; [a.] Ada, OK

GODSEY, WILLIAM W.
[pen.] Hall N. Wood; [b.] September 22, 1902, Hazard, KY; [m.] Geneva C. Godsey, June 15, 1929; [ch.] Mary C.; [ed.] University of Missouri at Columbia; [occ.] Retired; [memb.] Masonic Lodge and Ararat Shrine; [hon.] Golden Poet 1991 Top Automobile Salesman five years in a row; [oth. writ.] Many poems and short stories published in newspapers and magazines since 1938.; [pers.] Writing is a personal way of expressing my views.; [a.] Kansas City, MO

GOLDMAN, SUSAN R.
[b.] December 21, 1971, Queens, NY; [p.] Denise and Mark Goldman; [m.] Single; [ed.] Syosset High School, State University New York At Geneseo; [occ.] Lab Technician, Institute of Paper Science and Technology; [hon.] Norma Gold Award of Human Relations 1988-89; [oth. writ.] Several poems and stories kept in personal journal.; [pers.] My inspiration comes from my mother first. I rejoice in displaying varied emotional states on paper that come from within my soul. Maybe, through my writing I can reach someone in need.; [a.] Gainesville, GA

GOMES, SONYA L.
[pen.] Latoya; [b.] October 11, 1977, Guyana; [p.] George Gomes and Vaulda Gomes; [ed.] Junior in High School; [occ.] Student; [memb.] Metropolitain Baptist Church Youth Choir; [hon.] Community Award; [oth. writ.] Poems (not published); [pers.] Without God, nothing is possible, thank you mom and dad and all my siblings. Special thanks to God for my talent, thanks to my all friends, you know who you are.; [a.] Menands, NY

GOMEZ, JOSEPH A.
[pen.] J.A.G.; [b.] April 12, 1961, Irvington, NJ; [p.] Jose Gomez, Sarah Gomez; [ed.] C. I. High New York, Suffolk Community College N.Y., Miami Dade South, College FL; [occ.] Songwriter, Manager, Producer (Miami FL); [oth. writ.] I am foremost a songwriter, in all styles, Rock, R and B, Funk, Rap, Slow, Love songs, Dance and Pop. Influences: sting, police, G.M., etc.

(Poem H.I.V. influences: The Boss Tom Hanks, Perdro Sommora); [pers.] First I dedicate, this honor to my late brother "Scotty", I love you my talent to my "Heavenly Creator" "Music has no, color" whether in poem, or song, it touches everyone! My reward is to have my words, touch someones, heart, for the better.; [a.] Princeton, FL

GOMEZ, MARIA ELENA

[pen.] Maria Elena; [b.] Cuba; [p.] Valeria and Maximo; [m.] Ted Gonzales; [ch.] Litha, Reymie; [ed.] U.C. Berkeley, Liberal Arts: Language Major; [occ.] Teacher; [memb.] Various organizations that endorse the Arts, Environmental awareness and the rights of every human being; [hon.] Mentor Teacher; [oth. writ.] Poems not published and other writings shared with my students and friends; [pers.] Were "light" reflecting ourselves while receiving energy. As such, I live my life metaphysically and physically...interacting and reacting to all that is awe about me.; [a.] Fremont, CA

GOODMAN, DEBRA L.

[b.] February 26, 1954, Parsons, WV; [p.] Charles and Georgia Shaver; [m.] Mathew J. Goodman; [ch.] Stephen Eric Goodman, Jay Jayson Goodman; [ed.] UAW Parkside College - Business Administration, Technical School - Registered Nurse; [occ.] Homemaker, wife and mother; [memb.] Cub Scouts of America, Den Mother, American Cancer Society, American Leukemia Association; [pers.] Only by our own personal thoughts and actions are we judged so proceed with caution; [a.] Oklahoma City, OK

GOODSON, KEVIN WESLEY

[b.] April 27, 1956, New York; [p.] Arthur and Jane Goodson; [ch.] Kristopher Thomas Goodson; [ed.] Hempstead High School, Morris Brown College, Atlanta Area Tech, North Central Georgia Police Academy, First Aid Instructor Red Cross, Hotel Training in Management, Hotel Intelligence & Security; [occ.] Current (Night Manager); [memb.] Red Cross, Mayors Committee on elections; [hon.] Employee of the Month Residence Inn, 91, Silver Employee of the Year Residence Inn by Marriott, Employee of the Year Regional 94, Residence by Marriott corp., Corporate Minority Business Distinction Award, 1989; [oth. writ.] In Treasured Poems of America Fall of 1993; [pers.] Live life to the extreme, make everyday a special day, love your family, respect others, learn by trial & error. I strive on hope & glory to be the best. Walk by faith & not by sight, I too know why the caged bird sings. [a.] Atlanta, GA

GOOGASIAN, MARY BETH

[b.] January 6, 1965, Detriot, MI; [p.] Richard and Sharon Amluxen; [m.] Steven, July 11, 1987; [ch.] Sara Elizabeth, Henry Steven, and expected sibling!; [ed.] University of Michigan, Ann Arbor, MI; [occ.] Homemaker, Freelance Writer; [memb.] University of Michigan Alumni Association - Lifetime Member, Detriot Zoological Society; [hon.] Nominated outstanding Senior of the year - University of Michigan 1987, Order of Omega Honor Society, Commencement Speaker - 1983; [oth. writ.] Executive speeches, children's stories, poems; [pers.] It was through the encouragement of my parents, and that of my husband Steve, for whom I wrote this poem, that I continue to be inspired to write. Thanks for motivating me!; [a.] Bloomfield Hills, MI

GOPEESINGH, JANIS

[b.] August 22, 1948, Trinidad; [p.] Milton and Phyllis Zaiffdeen; [m.] Horace R. Gopeesingh, January 15, 1972; [ch.] Kerris Laurent, Keisha Tamara; [ed.] Southern Polytechnic High, San Fernando Technical Institute; [occ.] Clerk, Typist; [memb.] Writers Guild of Alberta.; [hon.] Bronze Medal in typing 1968; [pers.] I am new at writing. I have experienced great suffering - and through my writing I am able to secure a measure of inner peace; [a.] Calgary Alberta, Canada

GORDON, DEAN L.

[b.] December 4, 1950, Utica, NY; [p.] Kenneth Gordon, Beverly Gordon; [m.] Mary Hayes Gordon, August 4, 1984; [ch.] David, Philip, Hannah, Max; [ed.] Hartwick College New England School of Law; [occ.] Attorney; [hon.] Seito Shito Ryu Karate Master; [pers.] We all posses unlimited intelligence and ability.; [a.] New Hartford, NY

GORE, JAMES

[pen.] James Lynn; [b.] February 6, 1965; [occ.] Disabled; [pers.] I am living with AIDS, however I have kept my sense of humor and love of life. My only wish is that this terrible disease would not keep spreading. Especially to the innocent children.

GORE, MICHAEL

[b.] February 9, 1976, New London, CT; [p.] Harry Gore Jr. and Pamela Gore; [ed.] Fitch Senior High School, Currently attending the University of Connecticut (A very point campus) as second-semester freshman; [memb.] Editor of the Avery Point Spectrum.; [hon.] Pfizer National Merit Scholar, Vconn Presidential Scholar; [oth. writ.] Poetry in both high school and collage literary magazines; [pers.] I try to write about personal experiences and feelings, usually masked with humor. My poetry is hopefully, enjoyable and accessible to all.; [a.] Groton, CT

GRAF, MARY C.

[b.] Philadelphia, PA; [p.] Patrick and Mary; [m.] Dana T. Graf, July 22, 1988; [ch.] Patrick Dana; [ed.] Bachelor of Science, La Salle College, Philadelphia, PA; [occ.] Professional Pet Sitter - Mary's Little Lambs; [hon.] Alpha Sigma Lambda, Dean's List; [pers.] Let's all join hands to help the world's children.; [a.] Philadelphia, PA

GRAHAM, JARRED ADAM

[b.] October 15, 1976, Garland, TX; [p.] Jan and Linda Graham; [ed.] Currently a Senior at Naaman Forest High School, Garland, TX

GRAHAM, KELLY PAUL

[b.] December 13, 1961, Houston, TX; [p.] Kenneth Graham, and Billie Jean Graham; [ed.] M.B. Lamar High Houston (graduate 1981), Sam Houston State University Hunstville, TX (BS-1985); [occ.] Volunteer Teacher; [memb.] Houston Genealogical Society, Houston Zoological Garden Docent Council. Society for Creativity Anachronism (1987-1988).; [oth. writ.] Clown, (1978), A Young Lad's Prayer Before Battle (1988). A Calm, Cool Breeze (1988); [pers.] As a Christian, I try to see life from God's perspective, and being sightly handicapped, it's been easy to view the world from the outside; [a.] Houston, TX

GRAHAM, LANIER

[b.] March 6, 1940, Shawnee, OK; [p.] Martha and Floyd Graham; [m.] Gloria K. Smith; [ch.] Jennifer; [ed.] B.A. Cultural Affairs American University Washington D.C. 1963, M.A. Art History Columbia University NY City 1966; [occ.] Historian of Art and Architecture, Author, Architectural Planner; [memb.] Society of Architectural Historians. National Society of Literature and the Arts.; [hon.] Who's Who in America. Who's Who in the world.; [oth. writ.] Published 50 collections. The most widely read collections include "Rainbow Haiku" in The Rainbow Book (Shambhala, 1975 and 1976, Vintage/Random House 1979), Heavy Light: A collection of Haiku on the theme of Modern Physics and Ancient Wisdom (Word-Image Press, 1978), Electro-Magnetism: Philosophical Poems on the theme of Complementarity (Word-Image Press, 1982), Fragments of Feeling: Selected Short Poems (Soluna Press, 1994). Numerous books and exhibition catalogues on art and architecture published in six languages.; [a.] Northbank, CA

GRATTAN, RACHELLE

[b.] September 13, 1982, Monroeville, PA; [p.] Lea Ann and Timothy Grattan; [ed.] Milton Hershey School 6th Grade; [occ.] Student in School; [memb.] Girl Scouts of Amer. Jazz band, School Band Play Piano and Trumpet Choir, MHS Today - Schoolwide newscast; [hon.] Distinguished Honor Roll and Honor Roll in school and effort and conduct in school; [a.] New Kensington, PA

GRAVES, AMIE

[b.] February 13, 1981; [p.] Rich and Sue Graves; [occ.] Student at Tom McCall Middle School; [a.] Forest Grove, OR

GREEN, MURIEL

[pen.] Muriel Ratteray Green; [b.] January 4, 1928, Bronx, NY; [p.] Charles, and Joanna Ratteray; [m.] Samuel Green, August 8, 1948; [ch.] Samuel Jr., Valerie, Victor, Glen, Edythe; [ed.] High School Morris H.S. Bronx, NY., Helen Fuld School Practical Nursing; [occ.] Retired Nurse; [oth. writ.] Tapestries, non published autobiography of my life. Typed manuscripts 22 chapters, also on floppy disc. Also "What Jackson Knows". A beautiful story of a cat and his spiritual wisdom of life; [pers.] I would be so grateful to see something of my writings in print. My children would be pleased to know that I am not "daft" from all my scribblings.; [a.] South Ozone Park, NY

GREEN, ROBERT MICHAEL

[pen.] Robert Michael; [b.] June 30, 1940, Methuen; [m.] Grace Marie Green, June 29, 1980; [oth. writ.] Awareness, wars dilemma, a gift, a steady friend, remembered moment; [pers.] To touch by word true feelings within ones soul; [a.] Lawrence, MA

GREENWALD, HERBERT

[b.] January 5, 1921, Yonkers, NY; [p.] Frank and Esther Greenwald, (Deceased); [m.] Bernice Fay (First marriage), Frances (second wife); [ch.] Judith, Miriam, Marion; [ed.] Graduated N.Y. University; [occ.] Accountant; [oth. writ.] Many poems and a novel, not yet published

GREGG, STEVEN PAN I.

[pen.] Christian Blackheart; [b.] March 18, 1962, Virginia Beach, VA; [p.] Philip and Margaret Gregg; [ch.] Ashley Marie Gregg, Jessica Lynn Gregg; [ed.] Currently pursuing matriculation into Hariot-Watt University Edinburg, MBA program for International Rus. and Linguistics; [occ.] Field Teachnician, Special commodities, Nuclear, Industrial waste; [memb.] J. B. Hunt lighthouse team, Transport for Christ. Deliverance Ministries Fellowship. Arbor Day Foundation, World Wildlife Foundation. D.A.R.E.; [hon.] Truly the continued love, acceptance and generous support of my family and friends. They are a constant source of inspiration; [pers.] Jesus sees us as he would like us to the. But love us now just as we are. Be a B.E.A.R.; [a.] Portsmouth, VA

GREGORY, ETHEL IRENE
[b.] November 15, Alberta, Canada; [p.] Harold and Clara Harris; [m.] Marshall A. Gregory, November 1, 1952; [ch.] Roy, Leslie; [occ.] Homemaker; [memb.] Bookkeeper and Steno, Have been Librarian Mile 285, Alaska Highway, B.C. Playschool Teacher, Sunday School Teacher; [hon.] "Our Mother" published in "A Far Off Place" "My Family" To be published in "Best Poems Of 1995" and "The Garden Of Life"; [oth. writ.] Many short poems for family and friends, for births, school, birthdays, weddings, graduations, special events. Some poems published in one city and four small town papers.; [pers.] Asked that my children be honorable. Believe in hard work and trustworthiness. Enjoy doing for others. Greatest influence on my life from the stamina of my parents who came from Oklahoma and Nebraska to Northern Alberta, to the great peace river district.

GRESE, EVELYN D.
[b.] September 4, 1966, Brooklyn, NY; [p.] Keneth and Dolores Russell; [m.] John T. Grese Jr., August 27, 1994; [ch.] Currently expecting first child in August, 1995; [ed.] Liberty Central High School 1984, National Academy of Paralegal studies 1993; [occ.] Paralegal, Housewife; [hon.] During high school I entered a "Voice of Democracy" contest - entitled "What the Constitution Means to Me" and won a monetary award and my paper was published in the local newspaper.; [oth. writ.] I have written several other poems for family and friends which have not seen published. I have also written a few short stories also not published as of yet.; [pers.] Poetry to me is a gift of personal enjoyment. I love to write about the people in my life and make them feel good. Poetry is very good therapy and my expression of love, life and family.; [a.] Parma, OH

GRIFFIN, BETTY G.
[b.] December 10, 1924, Detroit, MI; [p.] Frank and Donna Harrington Gothman; [m.] Russell Cross, June 9, 1945 (deceased), Warren "Jim" Griffin, December 29, 1992 (Remarried); [ch.] Rusty (deceased), Janice (daughter), Dawn (granddaughter), 3 Great Grandchildren; [ed.] Graduated Dearborn High School, Dearborn, MI; [memb.] Methodist Church, Past Matron, order of the eastern star, co-editor news letter class of 1943 dearborn high, sec. of 193 graduation class. Hold 3rd class pilots license "worked" with retarded children little city of the mid-south Memphis, TN; [pers.] Always wanted 6 children gained 4 with second marriage!; [a.] Vaiden, MS

GRIFFIN, CORBY B.
[b.] April 17, 1963, Boothbay Harbor, ME; [p.] Carl R. Griffin Jr. and Gwendolyn B. Griffin; [ed.] Boothbay Region High School BA English, Classics - Tufts University MA Creation Spirituality - Holy Names College; [occ.] MA candidate at JFK University in Transpersonal Psychology; [memb.] Association of Bodywork and Massage Professionals (ABMP); [oth. writ.] I have had several poems and short fiction published in small journals and newspapers, and have developed a presentation of my own and other poets work entitled "The Poetry of Yearning"; [pers.] For me, the sound of language is paramount, my poems are meant to be heard even more thru read, and I strive to evoke an emotional or even Kinesthetic response. My major poetic influences have been W.B. Yeats, William Blake, Robert Graves, Pablo Neruda and David Whyte.; [a.] Orinda, CA

GRIFFITH, RUSSELL DON
[b.] April 1, 1954, East Saint Louis, IL; [p.] Russell L. Griffith, Fairy Mae Griffith; [m.] Kathryn Meyer Griffith, September 2, 1978; [ch.] James L. Olvitt, Danial W. Barks; [ed.] Dupo Community High Belleville Area College Southern Illinois University; [occ.] Carpenter; [memb.] Past Post Commander Post #10 Belleville, IL., AMVETS; [oth. writ.] None, but my wife Kathryn is a published horror writer with Zebra and Leisure books. I helped her with research on her last seven novels, and with different story lines and ideas.; [pers.] I am a former U.S. Marine and Viet Nam Vet. The wall had a great impact on me. It brought together in one place all of those that didn't come home. We must never forget the lessons we learned during that war. We make mistakes because we are human, but we must learn from those mistakes, so we don't ever make the same mistakes twice.; [a.] Cabokia, IL

GROSS, STUART
[b.] September 23, 1909; [m.] Mary Louise La Venture (deceased), 1935; [ch.] David S. and Laurence F. Gross; [occ.] President, Great Pond Mountain Conservation Trust; [memb.] Environmental Societies Sigma Delta Pi; [hon.] Maine Press Association Writing: Local Column (2nd place, 1994 Knight of Civil Service, Spain Honorary President, Sigma Delta Pi, USA Knight of Civil Service, Spain Honorary President, Sigma Delta Pi, National Spanish Honor Society E.M.C. Seminary, Standford University; [oth. writ.] Scattered poems and stories.; [pers.] A lake is she landscape's most beautiful and expressive feature. It is earth's eye, looking into which the beholder measures the depth of his own nature. Those climb the mountains and get their good tidings. Nature's peace will flow into you as sunshine flows into trees. The winds will blow their own freshness into you, and the storms their energy, while cares will drop away from you like the leaves of Autumn.

GROSZEWSKI, JENNIFER
[b.] July 16, 1976, Wilkes-Barre, PA; [p.] Jean Groszewski, Jack Groszewski; [ed.] Hatton Elementary School, Hyre Middle School, Ellet High School; [memb.] Women's International Bowling Congress; [oth. writ.] A lot of personal and unpublished poems.; [pers.] I have been great influenced by my mother, the events in my life, as well as by various poets.; [a.] Akron, OH

GRUBBS, ALLEN P.
[b.] April 7, 1920, Shreveport, LA; [p.] Sydney O. and Mary Pogue Grubbs; [m.] Pearl D. Grubbs, July 12, 1982; [ch.] (Step) Andrienne Ford, Paula Landers, Carole Vinson, Paul Ford and Woody Ford; [ed.] Fair Park HS, Shreveport, La Centenary College, Shreveport, LA; [occ.] Retired Accountant, Exxon Pipeline; [memb.] Mason - Fair Park Lodge #436 F and AM, Eastern Star - Spring Chapter 1105 OES; [oth. writ.] I have written several poems. One has been published in local newspaper; [pers.] I have written several other poems and each poem was inspired by a special event in my life. The poem in this book was inspired by my sitting in the park and watching the children play. Much to my delight, the image I had in my mind as I wrote this poem was personified 3 years ago when my first great-grandchild was born. She is the little girl in the poem.; [a.] Spring, TX

GUALDARAMA SR., HENRY
[pen.] "John"; [b.] January 28, 1949, Honolulu, HI; [p.] Anthony and Dolores Gualdarama; [ch.] Henry J. Gualdarama Jr., Justin D. Gualdarama; [ed.] Thomas Jefferson High, San Antonio, TX; [occ.] Correctional Officer, California, Dept. of Corrections; [pers.] If there is anything, "good" that comes out my writing, then it would be worthwhile! If I make you stop and think, just to better yourselves...; [a.] Salinas, CA

GUBLER, BETTY RAYMOND
[b.] June 2, 1942, Lee, ME; [p.] Pearl Raymond and Peter Raymond Jr.; [m.] Greg Gubler, May 31, 1967; [ch.] Lance Greg, Amy Ruth; [ed.] Graduate of GSTC (now University of Southern Maine) 1964 Graduate work at Brigham Young University Provo, UT; [occ.] Instructor, Author; [hon.] Poems published in newspapers Presenter at Women's Week BYU-H; [oth. writ.] Novel Valentines In The Snow published by Horizon Press November 1993; [pers.] Religious and romantic of nature, I am very interested in the transcendental authors as well as Native American philosophy.; [a.] Laie, HI

GUESS, CHERYL MITCHELL
[b.] February 14, 1950, Nashville, TN; [p.] Reavis and Thelma Mitchell; [m.] Capt. Harry Guess Jr., September 5, 1970; [ch.] Harry III, Cherise, Aaron, Nikki; [ed.] Cathedral High School for Girls, Vanderbilt University (73-BS), Norfolk State University (81-MA) Education of the Gifted; [occ.] Teacher (Grade 7 and 8) English, Writing, Social Studies, St. Vincent School - San Diego Christ the King Catholic Church; [memb.] Alpha Kappa Alpha Sorority, Inc. - Epsilon Xi Omega Chapter, American Association of University Women, U.S. Navy Officer Supply Corps Wives; [pers.] Just when I think that I'm beginning to truly know myself, something happens and I change. Isn't that fantastic!?; [a.] Bonita, CA

GUIDE, ELIZABETH
[pen.] S.C. Welis; [b.] April 29, 1982, Plainfield, NJ; [p.] Colleen and Tony Guide; [ed.] Currently in the 7th Grade at Von E. Mauger Middle School; [occ.] Student; [memb.] Member of the Drama Club at School; [hon.] Went to the Young Authors Conference in 5th Grade; [oth. writ.] Currently writing a series of children's fairy tales; [pers.] My favorite author is C.S. Lewis, when I read his books I was in another world, it really sparked my imagination, and I think all children should experience this.; [a.] Middlesex, NJ

GUIMARAES, MARIA DALVA JUNQUEIRA
[pen.] Madellon; [b.] June 16, 1937, Monte Alegre, ME; [p.] Jose Junqueira De Souza, Maria S. G. De Souza; [ed.] Retired Teacher; [a.] Brasilia DF, Brazil

GUTIERREZ, ARLENE
[pen.] Feathers; [b.] May 14, 1938, Byron, MI; [p.] Edward and Mary Kelly; [m.] Thomas Gutierrez, November 19, 1966, (deceased); [ch.] Thomas Dominic, Vincent Claudio and Leo John; [ed.] Byron High School Northeastern School of Commerce; [occ.] Exec. Secretary, C.P.A. Firm, BS and L; [memb.] Women's Investment Club, School Organizations, Church Organizations; [oth. writ.] Unpublished poetry; [pers.] I am inspired by life itself. Each morning I wake up, I realize that I have been given another gift.; [a.] San Jose, CA

GUTTMANN, MARION
[b.] October 5, 1927, Pensacola, FL; [p.] Louis and Abella Guttmann; [m.] Evelyn Johnson Guttmann, January 18, 1956; [ch.] Michael, Stephen, Rodney Guttmann, Angela Michelle Guttmann (granddaughter), in memory of son's Mark and Gregory Guttmann; [occ.] Real Estate; [oth. writ.] Short Stories; [pers.] "The only thing you take when you leave this world is what you gave away", "Love is action"; [a.] Pensacola, FL

GUYER, MARY E.
[b.] February 3, 1941, Boulder, CO; [p.] Rita Cook and Anthony Collacci; [m.] Donald L. Guyer, January 30, 1990; [ch.] Michael Whitmore, Kelly J. Stanton; [ed.] Park Junior College Denver, CO ABA/CS; [occ.] Data Entry Clerk II; [oth. writ.] One moment in time "Never Alone" winds of the world "Fantasy Planned"; [pers.] Money unwisely spent can sometimes be reobtained time unwisely spent can never be regained.; [a.] Louisville, CO

HAASE, JOYCE H.
[pen.] Heidi Lehman; [m.] Deceased; [ch.] Thomas Charles, Alice Anne; [ed.] Master Art Course, ICS Learning Center, Montreal QC Canada; [occ.] Student, Art; [hon.] Service Awards (Nursing Profession); [pers.] Sometimes my personal desire is to conjuror up a poem to titillate the soul within us warriors.; [a.] Calgary Alberta, Canada

HAASE, THOMAS L.
[b.] October 11, 1960, Omaha, NE; [p.] Raymond and Sharon Bohac; [m.] Doreen L. Haase, May 18, 1993; [ch.] Chrysee Skobis, Jonathan Skobis, Jacob Haase, Crystle Haase; [ed.] South High School - GED; [occ.] Department Manager at Wal-mart.; [memb.] Bone Merrow Donor; [oth. writ.] Having other poems written, I will strive to have more published.; [pers.] As a beginner myself with no education, I would like to influence other people as my mom and dad did for me. If you don't try - to you will never know - go for it.; [a.] Bullhead City, AZ

HADDOX, MAXINE
[b.] 1934, OH; [p.] Sylvia and Glenn Krites; [m.] Donald L. Haddox; [ch.] Jesse and Shan, (Grandchildren) Shawna, Ryan, and Marina; [occ.] Painter - oils Aka Name (Jesshan); [oth. writ.] Several poems (unpublished) one article published by a magazine.; [pers.] Poetry is the "Silent" song within the heart.; [a.] Fairborn, OH

HAIVARLIS, PETER
[b.] November 8, 1947, Greece; [oth. writ.] Hetero - Poetic Epigrams Promethean Farmers; [a.] Toronto, Canada

HAKER, OREN
[b.] February 10, 1974, Manhattan, NY; [p.] Alexander Haker, Laura Haker; [ed.] Amity Regional Senior High, Rice University; [occ.] Student, Rice University, Houston, TX; [a.] Houston, TX

HALE, BILLY MOORE
[pen.] William Leroy Moore; [b.] February 10, 1939, Kingsport, TN; [p.] Mollie Mae Moore; [ed.] Central High School Murfreesboro Tennessee; [memb.] Board of Directors, National Missing Children's Locate Center, Field Investigator, (Committee for Adoption Reform State of Tennessee), (Give Talks on Child Abuse); [oth. writ.] Poems in several newspapers, articles several newspapers across the country. Am writing book on my life, (Broken Trust, A State's Betrayal of it's Children); [pers.] I was kidnapped at age 5 by Georgia Tann (has been made into a movie), Director of the Tennessee Children's Home Society. I was physically, emotionally and sexually abused while in her care, I was later sold. These event's have greatly affected my life and my feelings; [a.] Murfreesboro, TN

HALFORD, JOHN
[b.] January 23, 1950, Augusta, GA; [p.] Mr. and Mrs. J. B. Halford; [m.] Margaret Reed, February 14, 1990; [ch.] (1) Tamra Diane Reynolds, (2) Simon Reed, (3) Leslie Reed; [ed.] High School Graduate El Dorado High, El Dorado Arkansas; [occ.] Mechanic; [oth. writ.] Poems, songs, thoughts; [a.] Amarillo, TX

HALL, BECKY
[b.] April 10, 1953, Ogden UT; [p.] Edward and Helen Bird; [m.] Ronald Hall, May 30, 1975; [ch.] Jeremy, Jocelin, Melissa, Nick and Wendy; [occ.] Housewife; [oth. writ.] I've kept a journal for many years - I often write poetry and short stories, about my children, my garden, my life.; [pers.] Moore, OK

HALL, SAUNDRA LEIGH HUNT
[b.] July 22, 1951, Hyattsville, MD; [p.] Lura B. and Richard W. Hunt; [ch.] Randolph R. II and Ryan Robert, Faith Leigh (Grand-daughter); [ed.] Northwestern High School; [occ.] Data Entry - Quotron Systems, Owner, Operator - Key Strokes Plus; [oth. writ.] I'm trying to gather, enough of my work together, to someday publish a small book of poems.; [pers.] My poems are simple, based on love, conflict and humor. My greatest sources of inspiration and subject matter are Randy, Ryan, Faith and Real Life.; [a.] Bowie, MD

HALLETT, SHERI
[b.] December 20, 1973, Neilburg, Saskatchewan, Canada; [p.] Joan Hallett; [ch.] Cole Chris Kastendieck; [ed.] Neilburg Composite School; [occ.] Cook at Wayside Inn in Lloydmenster, AB; [pers.] I have been writing poems since I was a child but I've never had one published before. So it gives me great pleasure to have this one published.; [a.] Neilburg Saskatchewan, Canada

HALT, ALICE
[b.] June 21, 1925, Chester, IL; [p.] Wallace A., Sr. and Elda H.R. (Gerloch) Halt; [ed.] Assoc. Sc. Belleville Area College 1956 BS. Southwestern University 1958; [occ.] Medical Technologist (part time) (Retired) (laboratory Supervisor); [memb.] Belle-East '21 Business and professional Women's Organization, Phi Tau Omega Sorority Women's of Christian Service of the Methodist Church American Society Medical Technology; [hon.] Woman of the year 1988 in local Business and Professional women's Org. member of Phi Beta Kappa - Scholastic Society - Belleville Area College; [oth. writ.] Procedure Manuals for technical operating analytical instruments.; [pers.] Having had a dramatic conversion to christianity and 49 years of work in the medical field, I have concentrated on helping others to find peace and faith. This is reflected in my writing and poetry.; [a.] Belleville, IL

HAMILTON, ALLENE S.
[b.] December 8, 1925, Concord, NH; [p.] George and Vera Simpson; [m.] Raymond A. Hamilton, August 25, 1946; [ch.] Wade T. Hamilton, Jere M. Hamilton; [ed.] Simonds Free High, The Univ., of New Hampshire, Bridgewater State College, BA in English and MA credits in Lib. Sci.; [occ.] Retired, formerly an English Teacher, child. Librarian and Middle School Librarian; [memb.] Teacher's Assoc., Am. Lib Assoc., Sch. Lib. Assoc., Deaconess First Baptist Church, Hist. Soc., Holiday Lakes Assoc., Lake Todd Assoc., Am. Heart Assoc., Cancer Soc., Audubon Soc., Am. Bapt. Women; [hon.] National Education Association for promoting excellence in Education, DAR award; [oth. writ.] Article for School Library Journal, Bicentennial LOOKING BACK book, THE CHURCHWORD, articles and poems in local papers.; [pers.] I'm very aware of the beauty and mystery of nature and its importance in our lives. I like Frost and Sandburg and Concord Poets. Literature of all ages.; [a.] Bradford, NH

HAMMAN, JULIE L.
[b.] July 20, 1967, Harrisburg, PA; [p.] Lloyd Carl Hamman, Sadie A. Hamman; [ed.] Dauphin County Technical School, Harrisburg Area Community College; [occ.] Computer Programmer/Analyst; [pers.] My gift I share, in hopes that the reader will find themselves experiencing the emotions in my writings. The greatest compliment is the reader's personal interpretation of my work.; [a.] Harrisburg, PA

HAMMERLE, PEARL WEBB
[b.] December 7, 1918, Weesatche, TX; [p.] Elizabeth Hohn Webb and John Leroy Webb; [m.] Colonel (USAF RET) Clarence B. Hammerle; [ch.] George Bernard (1944), Holly Ann (1945); [ed.] U. of Maryland O'seas Campus at Rhein-main Air Base, Germany ('56-'58), Un. of Alabama Montgomery Campus ('65-'66), NO. CA. Comm. College, ('82-'83); [occ.] AF wife, student of languages, graduate genealogist, PINCH HITTER PILOT; [memb.] Ikebana International, Aopa, United Methodist Church, and National Genealogical Society Dewitt C. (TX) Historical Society; [oth. writ.] Poetry: "Seed Pearls", and "A Ring From Tiffany's: History of the Louis A. Hohn Family in Texas" (My Family's history); [pers.] I love poetry! Wife of an Air Force Pilot, I've lived on three continents, in five states, moved 28 times! I've parasailed, ballooned, learned to fly small aircraft. Studied four languages (Spanish, Japanese, German, French). Worked as a Board member in Europe and USA in GSA, BSA and Red Cross, W/US STATE DEPT. on German-American Women's Clubs.; [a.] San Antonio, TX

HAMPTON, ELLEN
[pen.] Ellen Hampton; [b.] August 11, 1957, S.E., MO; [p.] Myrtle and Joe Bollinger; [m.] Carl E. Hampton, April 14, 1992; [ch.] Joel Christopher (R) Hampton; [ed.] Meadow Heights High School and Southeast Missouri State University; [occ.] Wife, Homemaker, Outreach Ministries Director; [oth. writ.] I have written many poems and placed them in a notebook. I hope to publish a book of my poetry.; [pers.] Reading and writing poetry gives me much joy. It helps me to reflect and release. Some of what I am, and the experiences I have had in life. My talent is a gift from my creator.; [a.] Pascagoula, MS

HAMPTON, MARY HELEN
[b.] August 15, 1934, Herrington, KS; [ch.] James Raymond, Robert Carl, Kathleen Noel; [ed.] University of Houston B.S. Cum Laude; [occ.] Business, English Teacher, Houston ISD; [pers.] George Eliot said: "It is never too late to be what you might have been". This keeps me going, writing and teaching.; [a.] Houston, TX

HANCOCK, BRENDA
[pen.] Heather Marshall; [b.] May 1, 1949, Fitzgerald, GA; [p.] J. B. and Lillian Gaines; [m.] Divorced; [ch.] Brandi, Kevin; [ed.] Fitzgerald High, South Georgia College; [occ.] Principal Case Worker, Ben Hill Co., DFCS, Fitzgerald, GA; [memb.] Fitzgerald High Band Boosters; [hon.] South Georgia Coll. - Dean's List; [oth. writ.] Newspaper articles in a nearby area newspaper; [pers.] I hope to have a positive influence on someone.; [a.] Fitzgerald, GA

HANDY III, HORACE
[b.] May 19, 1951, Oakland, CA; [p.] Deceased; [m.] Divorced, May 19, 1990; [ch.] Bryan, Trayvon Barry Christen, Glenda, Hildreath; [ed.] McKinley Jr High, Pasadena High (1 yrs. U.C.L.A.), (Concorde Career Inst. A.A.S. Video Technology); [occ.] Body and Fender Person; [oth. writ.] I have written over three hundred poems.; [pers.] I think mankind has a responsibility to explore their creative talents that they are unaware of in discovering their untapped potential, gifts, and uniqueness.; [a.] Altadena, CA

HANEY, RODERICK
[b.] December 11, 1965, South California; [p.] Sue and Bob Haney; [ed.] B.A. Art History, CSU Stanislaus; [occ.] Student; [pers.] I want to write small but beautiful things that may become monumental to those who feel.; [a.] Santa Cruz, CA

HANLY, ALFRED SHELDON
[pen.] Bo Hanly; [b.] November 4, 1928, Sacramento, CA; [p.] Hilary Norton and Marie Idolian Hanly; [m.] Alyce C. Hanly, November 1, 1977; [ed.] Christian Bros H.S. (Class of '47), Saint Mary's College, Moraga, CA., majored in English (Class of '52); [occ.] USMC Major (retired) after 30 yrs., active duty (1955-1985), wife LPN (retired); [memb.] Marine Memorial Club, S.F., CA, Bennett Valley Seniors Golf Club, Northern CA Tennis Association; [hon.] 1994 Men's Doubles - 65's, player of the year with partner in NCTA play (approx. 25 tennis tourneys), CA Life Teaching Certificate secondary level - taught 8 1/2 years; [oth. writ.] Other romantic poems (unpublished), Animal Short Stories - "Tootsie and Herman", "Freddie Dog and Friends" - (unpublished), Adventures of my Backyard Turtles; [pers.] Romantic poets my favorites; [a.] Santa Rosa, CA

HARALDSEN, KENNETH J.
[pen.] Ken; [b.] December 4, 1922, Buffalo, SD; [p.] Knut and Jennie Haraldsen; [m.] Opal G. Haraldsen, February 24, 1946; [ch.] 4 Daughters Renee, Joy, Marlita Nancy; [ed.] Buffalo, High School Central Bible College, BA, Th.B S.W Baptist Theological Seminary; [occ.] Retired from 27 years in the post office, also 40 years on active and reserve duty.; [memb.] Englewood Lions, Amazing Grace Church, Englewood Schools - Health and Safety Colorado Division of Wildlife, Plains Conservation Center; [hon.] Military, Post Office Plains Conservation Center; [oth. writ.] Articles in the Denver Post Many articles in the Nation's Center News at Buffalo, S. Dakota. Poems in Newspapers, magazines and books.; [pers.] Luck comes to those who seek it. By working with children and wildlife can be very satisfying.; [a.] Englewood, CO

HARDCASTLE, MARSHA TWEEDIE
[pen.] Mar Mar; [b.] April 19, 1953, Kansas; [p.] Jack and Beverly Tweedie; [m.] Howard Hardcastle, October 27, 1977; [ch.] Heather, Michelle and Jack; [sib.] Shawnee Mission West High School; [pers.] Let us live each day with devotion and care so that eternity together, we can share loving memory of my father. 10-5-94 to my mother, husband and children.... I love you!; [a.] Lenexa, KS

HARDING, MICHELLE
[b.] February 28, 1974, Kingston, ON; [p.] Edward Harding, Joan Harding; [ed.] Gananoque Secondary School Trent University; [oth. writ.] Several articles published in local paper; [a.] Gananoque Ontario, Canada

HARGETT, SHERRY L.
[b.] October 30, 1950, Dayton, KY; [p.] Donald and Mildred Julian; [m.] Divorced; [ch.] Julie L. Contessa, Jeffrey L. Julian, Jaclyn S. Troxell. My Grandchildren's: Crystal, Alexis, Vincent and another on the way.; [ed.] Campbell and Boone City, KY., graduated from Cosmetology school; [occ.] Caregiver; [oth. writ.] I have written many poems over the years and I'm in the process over the last year and a half of writing a book.; [pers.] I am striving to reflect "myself" to everyone, especially my children who have been the best support all my life.; [a.] New Port Richey, FL

HARLOW, EVELYN H.
[b.] September 14, 1950, Beaumont, TX; [ch.] Amanda-Jean, James Irwin Trussell III; [ed.] South Houston High School, Houston Community College, University of Houston - currently working on degrees in psychology and anthropology.; [oth. writ.] This is the first submission of any of my poetry for public consumption.; [pers.] My hope is that my poetry will trouble and cause each of us to look deep inside, realizing that, by being so troubled, we are all connected by our psychology, our societies, and our cultures. I am greatly influenced by the writings of Carl Jung, Joseph Campbell, Clarissa Pinkola Estes and Rod McKuen.; [a.] Houston, TX

HARMONY, JANICE M.
[b.] April 21, 1953, Allentown, PA; [p.] Martha and Al Harmony; [ch.] Brandon Matthew; [ed.] Louis E. Dieruff High; [occ.] Candle Maker (Ft.), Emmaus Fire Dept., and Emmaus Police Dept., (Aux.); [oth. writ.] Local Newspaper for our K-9 Police Dog. To NASCAR Drivers printed in their fan club newsletter; [pers.] This poem was written to and for my son Brandon. At 20 yrs., old, he has survived the single parent raising the child. I love you Bud! Also, my poems mostly reflect life around me and everyday situations.; [a.] Emmaus, PA

HARMS, SHARYN
[b.] January 14, 1948, Easton, PA; [p.] Raymond and Shirley Harms; [ed.] Phillipsburg High School Northland College; [occ.] Fifth Grade Teacher at Alpha Public School, Alpha, N.J.; [memb.] Wesley United Methodist Church Parent Teacher's Organization New Jersey Education Association New Jersey Education Association National Education Association; [hon.] Dean's List, Teacher of the Year; [oth. writ.] One poem to be published in a local Christian newsletter, numerous articles for a church bulletin.; [pers.] I strive to glorify God through my Christian writings.; [a.] Phillipsburg, NJ

HARP, MANDY
[pen.] Mandy Harp; [b.] March 9, 1980, Phoenix, AZ; [p.] Kelvie Harp and Robert Harp; [ed.] 8th grade; [occ.] Student; [memb.] Junior Leadership League; [oth. writ.] Poetry and short stories; [a.] Mesa, AZ

HARRELL, FRANCIS D.
[pen.] Frankie Harrell; [b.] November 5, 1974, Jacksonville, FL; [memb.] Am far - Positively Aware NAPWA; [pers.] Paul Monette is the root. My root and my flower. Thanks Paul; [a.] Mayport, FL

HARRIS, MARIE T.
[pen.] Wanderer; [b.] July 13, 1905, Sherman, TX; [p.] V. H. and Martha A. Taylor; [m.] George F. Harris, January 2, 1926; [ed.] High School - Secretarial course in Fort Smith, Ark. Commercial College.; [occ.] Retired after several different employments and 21 years in US Dept. Agri., Washington, D.C.; [memb.] Eastern Star, American Legion Auxiliary Lake Whitney (TX) Humane Society Central Christian Church; [hon.] None - any writing was for personal pleasure no contests entered previously; [oth. writ.] Some poetry published 17 local newspaper.; [pers.] It's a wonderful world!

HARRIS, MARLENE E.
[b.] Montreal, Quebec, Canada; [occ.] President of a non-profit nature organization; [memb.] 1. Zoological Society of Montreal, 2. Canadian Nature Federation, 3. World Wildlife Fund, 4. Nature Conservancy; [oth. writ.] Nature articles printed in related publications, ecotour reviews, poetry editorials; [pers.] Nature's beauty has been the key to unlocking my creativity.; [a.] Montreal Quebec, Canada

HARRIS, YVONNE
[b.] February 8, 1951, Macon, GA; [p.] Mr. and Mrs. Idus Carden Jr. (deceased); [m.] William E. Harris, June 11, 1977; [ed.] High School Graduate, College - 1 yr., Abraham Baldwin Agriculture College; [occ.] Flight Attendant - US Air Airlines - 23 yrs.

HARRISON, BENJAMIN SCOTT
[b.] April 10, 1977, Pensacola, FL; [p.] Jeremiah and Glenda Harrison; [ed.] J.M. Tate High, Pensacola Junior College, University of West Florida; [occ.] Student; [hon.] Servistar "Tools for Tomorrow" for Florida, Departmental Award in Science; [pers.] I have to thank all those that believed loved, and helped me.; [a.] Cantonment, FL

HARRISON, JASON EARL
[b.] March 19, 1979, Fresno, CA; [p.] Teresa MacDonald (Mother); [ed.] Currently a high school sophomore - hopeful of Junior Status by the time of publication! Attending School in Redding, CA.; [occ.] Hoping to obtain part-time employment - soon! In any field directly involved in the care of animals.; [hon.] Received the Presidential Academic Fitness Award for the 1990 - 1991 school year.; [pers.] Due to a life-long neurological condition, I have difficulty with some tasks involving eye, hand coordination (like writing!) In my free time I can usually be found at the nearest body of water - fishing pole in hand!; [a.] Fresno, CA

HARRISON, SANDRA
[b.] Canada; [occ.] Transit Driver; [memb.] Canadian Country Music Association, Songwriters Club of America; [hon.] Certificate of Merit for Lyric Writing.; [oth. writ.] Poems published by the Toronto Sun (years ago) in there poet's corner. I have poems many lyrics and Finished songs and demons out on the Circuit.; [pers.] I try to reflect everyday people and there love's and lives. My big dream in life is to have one of my songs become a hit. This special poem has already been put on Demo.; [a.] Moncton New Brunswick, Canada

HARRY, FRANKLIN
[pen.] Franklin Harry; [b.] May 2, 1936, Hattiesburg, MS; [p.] Robert and Clara Thomas Harry; [m.] Carolyn Moore Harry, February 22, 1986; [ch.] James Charles Moore, Jr.; [ed.] Canton High School (12 years); [occ.] Owner and Operator of welding and machine shop; [memb.] Canton Masonic Lodge #28, Order of Eastern Star #58, Member of First United Methodist Church, Canton, MS.; [hon.] Past Master of Canton Masonic Lodge, Past Worthy Patron of Canton Chapter, Order of Eastern Star, Chapter and Council Mason - York Rite, Past Vice President - Madison County Shriners; [oth. writ.] Poems (listed in First United Methodist Bulletin,

unpublished novels (2); [pers.] I write not for personal gain, but for the enjoyment of others.; [a.] Canton, MS

HART, BRANDON FORREST
[b.] March 18, 1983, Dallas, TX; [p.] Erick and Sheryl Hart; [ed.] Blue Ridge Mid-School, 6th grade; [occ.] Student; [memb.] M.R.A. - National Muzzle Loading Rifleman's Assoc.; [hon.] Read the most books in 4th grade. 89 books; [pers.] I encourage my readers to keep on reading, and further educate themselves as much as they can.; [a.] Pinetop, AZ

HART, DAVID J.
[b.] January 12, 1973, Milford, CT; [p.] Melody Hart, William Hart S.; [ed.] Bullard Havens R.V.I.S. Souther Connecticut State U.; [occ.] Student - English - Education Major; [pers.] I try to show some of the darker sides of adolescence through my writing. It is also important to me to show the light at the end of the tunnel.; [a.] Milford, CT

HATFIELD, WENDY LEAH
[b.] April 12, 1965, Truro, Nova Scotia, Canada; [p.] Mr. and Mrs. Ronald Mingo; [ch.] Raven (age 8 - daughter), Tracy William (age 9 - son); [occ.] Mother of two children ages 8 and 9; [hon.] Winner many times over thru poetry elite. Excelled in English. Local newspaper publishing. Editors Choice Award for "The National Library of Poetry" in 1994.; [oth. writ.] Studying journalism and short story writing, also learning to write books for children and teenagers.; [pers.] Writing is the gift of expression. My writing comes from the heart and is usually based upon everyday life experiences. Earlier influenced by the writings of Robert Frost.

HATZ, MELANIE J. IRWIN
[b.] September 8, 1952, Joliet, Illinois; [p.] William B. Irwin, Janet Lackey; [m.] Donald Alvin Hatz, June 15, 1974; [ch.] David Alan, Deborah Lynn, Diane Marie; [ed.] Minooka Community High School, Joliet Junior college; [occ.] Cake Decorator, Caterer, Poetry, Homemaker, Care Giver all ages, Graphologies; [memb.] American Cancer Society, American Legion, Parapsychology, Graphology, American Heart Assoc., Animal Care League, Doll Collectors Guild, Gone with the Wind Trivia Club, St. Jude's Women's Club; [hon.] Citizen of the Year 1969, Editor's Choice Award 1995, High Salesman (magazine) 1968-71, Wilton Cake Decorating Award 1985; [oth. writ.] "Thank You for My Life" 1979, "We Are But a Bouquet" 1992, "Yesterday's Love" 1995, "Why" 1993; [pers.] I am but a yellow rose, and my friendship is waiting to be picked. [a.] New Lenox, IL

HAUSENFLUCK, J. D.
[pen.] J. D. Hausenfluck; [b.] November 28, 1934, Pharr, TX; [p.] Jake and Viola Hausenfluck; [m.] Yvonne, May 20, 1956; [ch.] Terry Lee, Beverly Ann, and Glyna Kay; [ed.] H.S. 1 1/2 College Military Electronics Electrical Apprenticeship School.; [occ.] Electrical Contractor; [memb.] First Christian Church - Boy Scouts - Gideons; [hon.] District Award of Merit and Silver Beaver in Boy Scouts of America; [oth. writ.] Three unpublished poems; [pers.] To show that through God's grace and love we can help others.; [a.] Harlingen, TX

HAVENS, WILL H.
[b.] November 21, 1910, Douglas County, MO; [p.] B. Ray and Mary E. (Tooley) Havens; [m.] Clara E. Keeler, December 2, 1933; [ch.] Ivan Havens, Ruth Evans, Ann Dowell, Bill R. Havens; [ed.] Self educated beyond high school by home study courses and correspondence; [occ.] Retired Minister; [memb.] Ava General Baptist Church, American Bible Society, AARP; [hon.] Editor's Choice Awards for poems published in "The Desert Sun" and "Edge of Twilight". Award for 50 years pastoring plus eight years award for additional ministry.; [oth. writ.] "Fodder" a book of meditations, "Shallow Waters" a book of poems, "Green Pastures" a book of essays, "The End Time", "Trails Through Trying Times", a book of essays, "Pleasant Moments" a book of poetry. Many articles published in local and area publications.; [pers.] It is my prayer and hope that I may be able to keep writing prose and poetry that will be an encouragement for folks to put their trust in the Lord.; [a.] Ava, MO

HAWKINS, ESTHER
[b.] September 13, 1942, Chicago, IL; [p.] Teo and Pauline Witte; [m.] William (Bill) Hawkins, April 27, 1985; [ch.] Peter Kopel (Age 33 from former marriage), Jeffrey Steve Hawkins (Stepsons from this marriage); [ed.] Thru High School - Thomas Jefferson Dallas, TX. Was Navy wife (1st marriage) for almost 10 years.; [occ.] Sales Manager for Wood and Plastic Pallet Division of W.A. Taylor Co, Inc. Dallas, TX.; [hon.] Recipient of Sales Contests and Performance Awards over 26 years with my company. Recipient of over 55 trophies for 1st, 2nd or 3rd place winner of my age group in running races since age 40.; [oth. writ.] Only write poems and short essays for my own pleasure upon occasion - not on any regular basis. Some poems are user as gifts to family or friends at special events.; [pers.] When not working or fulfilling family obligations, my favorite hobby is running. Often, the ideas for poems come to me as I run. Both running and writing provide excellent stress reduction from the fast Paced Business and Family life most of us maintain.; [a.] Dallas, TX

HAWKINSON, LINDA RICHARDS
[b.] Alice, TX; [p.] Bill and Vonny Richards; [m.] Ron Hawkinson; [ch.] Kelli Harman; [pers.] I was encouraged by my father to pursue anything I thought I could do. Ron encouraged me to pursue my writing. I am indebted to my family and friends for their support.; [a.] Anchorage, AK

HAYES, CAROLINE D.
[b.] October 5, 1937, Vermont; [p.] Richard Lamphere and Della; [m.] Royal S. Hayes, January 8, 1958; [ch.] Tim, Nancy, John and Jennifer; [ed.] Burlington High School - grad. of 1956; [occ.] Day Care Provider; [memb.] V.F.W. Ladies Auxiliary; [oth. writ.] Unpublished short stories for children and adults.; [pers.] Everyone needs love and encouragement, so as to strive to be all they can be.; [a.] Colchester, VT

HAYNES, DAVID W. D.
[b.] March 26, 1969, Chelsea, MA; [p.] Henry D. Haynes, Jean A. Haynes; [ed.] Lynnfield High School, Bentley College; [occ.] Insurance Broker, Colony Insurance Group, Windham NH; [memb.] Derry Village Rotary, Greater Derry Chamber of Commerce; [oth. writ.] Several articles in local newspapers; [pers.] I want to touch the lives of others through my poems and stories; [a.] Lynnfield, MA

HAYNES, LESLIE GRAINGER
[b.] May 7, 1951, Taos, NM; [p.] Mango and Dick Grainger; [m.] Kenneth Haynes, December 27, 1985; [ch.] Lenore Haynes, Thomas Haynes, Perry Haynes; [ed.] Kent School for girls (Denver) University of Colo. B.S. Sorbonne, Paris France Institute Allende, Mexico; [occ.] President Int'l Transition Services; [memb.] American Translation Asso., Colorado Translation Assoc., Colorado Women's Chamber World Trade Assoc., Denver Chamber of Comm.; [oth. writ.] Noble Grees; [pers.] Family has always been the most important. Whether it was the family I lost at a young age - or the family I gained with my blessed marriage.; [a.] Aurora, CO

HEAGY, TAMIE STOCKMAN
[b.] September 24, 1960, Sweet Springs, MO; [p.] Albert and Nora Stockman; [m.] Steve Heagy, September 1, 1990; [ch.] Zachariah Stephen Heagy; [ed.] Sweet Springs High School, Central Missouri State University; [occ.] Word Processing operator; [memb.] Peace Lutheran Church; [pers.] As a Christian, I know there is much more to our lives than we can physically see. Everyone needs help and encouragement at times, and what we do does matter. God always let's us start over and try again with Him. (I personally thank you, Lord.); [a.] Raytown, MO

HEBERT, TRUDY
[b.] September 18, 1960, Montegut, LA; [p.] Acklin and Beulah Blanchard; [m.] Jody Hebert, March 27, 1982; [ch.] Kip Michael, Tad Stefan, and Joy Andrew; [ed.] South Terrebonne High; [occ.] Homemaker; [memb.] Krewe of Bon Terre, Montegut Children's Carnival Club; [oth. writ.] Poems published in the Houma Courier, struggling song writer; [pers.] Thanks to my friend, Dennie for encouraging me to continue writing and to my husband, Jody for his honest criticism.; [a.] Montegut, LA

HEDGE, HEATHER
[pen.] Heather Hedge; [b.] September 11, 1978, AR; [p.] Darlene Freeman and Noble Hedge; [ed.] Currently enrolled in Pontotoc High School; [pers.] I try to reflect my emotions and the emotions and the situation to the reader.; [a.] Pontotoc, MS

HEES, CARL
[b.] September 30, 1932, Eldon, MO; [p.] Irl and Lena Hees; [m.] Ruth L. Hees, June 16, 1957; [ch.] Mike H. Hees; [ed.] 1 - 12; [occ.] Retired 1 Mar 95 Owned an operated for 32 years

HEGDE, RAMESH S.
[b.] May 2, 1960, Sirsi, India; [p.] Satyanarayan G., Mahalaxmi S.; [m.] Sumana R., February 10, 1989; [ch.] Shruti R.; [ed.] Ph.D.; [occ.] Post Doctoral Researcher at University of Oklahoma Health Sciences Center; [memb.] American Society of Agronomy, National Geographic Society; [hon.] Phi Kappa Phi, Gamma Sigma Delta, The Rotary Foundation of Rotary, International Scholar, Government of India National Merit Scholar, Two-time gold medalist in B.Sc (Ag) and M.Sc. (Ag), Government of Karnataka, India, "State award", Jawaharlal Nehru Memorial Award.; [oth. writ.] Several poems and articles in Canada language, my mother tongue, article in The Daily Illini, several "letters to the Editor", in local newspapers and magazines.; [pers.] My poems reflect real life experiences of a cross-cultural nature. I believe that a better international understanding is necessary for a harmonious and peaceful coexistence of humankind of all ethnic, racial and religious background around the globe.; [a.] Norman, OK

HEILMAN, DAVE
[b.] April 13, 1946, Philadelphia, PA; [p.] David and Pat Heilman; [ed.] Central High School University of Pennsylvania; [occ.] Counselor; [hon.] Phi Beta Kappa,

Psi Chi (Psychology Honor Society), Dean's List; [pers.] I would like to create beauty, simple and pure, to show, when I am gone, that I was here.; [a.] Southampton, PA

HEITZIG, FRED F.
[pen.] Fred F. Heitzig; [b.] August 30, 1909, Saint Louis, MO; [p.] Fred C. and Louisa Loellke Heitzig; [m.] Louise B. Wagener, September 6, 1952; [ch.] Margret C. - Janet L., Charles F.; [ed.] High School, Business College; [occ.] Semi-retired Agriculturists; [memb.] Agricultural organizations knights of columbus St. Mary's Church; [hon.] Photographs including the cover and article in historic Illinois Vol. 11 No. 6 Apr 1989 "Log Buildings Thru A Camera Lens"; [oth. writ.] Various Articles on current events; [a.] Fieldon, IL

HELLMUTH, LUCY MARTIN
[pen.] Lucy Martin; [b.] February 12, 1913, Irath Co, TX; [p.] Josephine Latisha Yargrough and Flavios Augustus Bribs; [m.] 1st Ed. N. Martin, 2nd Gus Hellmuth, 1st June 18, 1936, 2nd September 16, 1994; [ch.] Step children 4 (2nd); [ed.] High School (plus 2 years with SWB Telephone 6 Responsible Position in Tax Divn of legal); [occ.] Retired - SWB Tel Co.; [memb.] Past member Texas Poetry Society - member 1st Presbyterian Church - Telephone Pioneers of Amer - member Ret. Police and Fireman's Assn - Past member of Quill and Seroll - (Journalists) B&PW Club; [hon.] Membership in Quill and Seroll in High School - During WW II one of my poems caused me to become a member of the Texas Poetry Society, one of my poems printed in the Dismoaning News, was used in a memorial service for a young man killed in WW II, His father wrote me for permission to use it. Another poem was published in the church papers - it had been in the paper also.; [oth. writ.] I have written at least 4 volumes is poetry - non-published, one book is a story - worthy of publications but too personal about our family entitled "Obituary" - The story of a favorite sister who died; [pers.] The poem submitted "If You Might Return" was written about a family member who died I hope you don't have to change it too much; [a.] Dallas, TX

HELLSTEN, TANJA
[pen.] Tanja Hellsten; [b.] May 18, 1975, Varkaus, Finland; [p.] Elvi Lemmetty, Viljo Hellsten; [ed.] (Comprehensive school), Varkaus Business College and Senior High School; [occ.] Student; [memb.] Varkaus Rheumatism Association; [oth. writ.] My poems have been published in national magazines (but then I of course, used finish, my own language); [pers.] Because English is not my native language, most of my poems have a joke and rhymes, so there is not anything what I would call "A Deeper Meaning". To me its' great when people read my poems, smile and think "I like this girl!"; [a.] Varkaus, Finland

HELSDON, LYDIA
[b.] September 11, 1980, Guelph, Ontario; [p.] Miriam and David Helsdon; [ed.] Grade 8 Straffordville Eden Public School; [occ.] Student (gr.9) at East Elgin Secondary School; [hon.] Winner in the 1993 young playwrights competition (sponsored by the grand theatre of London, Ontario) numerous awards and scholarships in Music festivals (piano, cello, flute); [pers.] Everything I have and am belongs to Jesus.; [a.] Straffordville Ontario, Canada

HELTON, CAROLYN
[pen.] Caroline Helton; [b.] July 29, 1948, Oklahoma City, Oklahoma; [p.] Allen & Martha Heidenbrecht; [m.] Mel Helton, July 12, 1968; [ch.] Todd Dale, Jennifer Brooke; [ed.] Bethany High School, Central State University; [occ.] Vice President - Todd Brooke Group, Inc., dba American Integrity Builders, also Real Estate Investor/Decorator; [pers.] My writing often reflects intense emotions and feelings. I am a true romantic, holding onto my dreams, intensely believing that ultimately they will be realized. [a.] PO Box 32455, Oklahoma City, OK 73123

HENCSIE, SARAH C.
[b.] October 9, 1974, Grosse Pointe, Michigan; [p.] Christine and James Hencsie; [ed.] Henry Ford II High School, Baker College; [occ.] Musician/Poet; [memb.] American Red Cross Volunteers, Detroit Zoological Society, Sigma Pi Sweethearts; [hon.] Academic Scholarship-Baker College; [oth. writ.] Some poems published in chapbooks for college workshops, 2 poems published in Writer's World magazine.; [pers.] My poetry combines the avant-garde and the normal, fused to make one. I am influenced by Edgar Allan Poe, Robert Frost, and William Burroughs; [a.] Sterl. Hgts., MI

HENRY, DOROTHY J.
[pen.] Dottie Henry; [b.] May 8, 1926, Aden, KY; [p.] Milt and Sarah Littleton; [m.] Robert Henry, August 11, 1944; [ch.] Joe, Sara - Judy, Lynn and Cherie.; [oth. writ.] Poems for every member of my family of 5 children and 12 brothers and sisters; [pers.] I wrote this poem for my darling niece I love you Bonnie, you know where home is.; [a.] Jeffrey, WV

HERGERT, PEGGY
[pen.] Peg O'Shea; [b.] December 12, 1940, Hardin County, IL; [p.] Henry M. and Virgie M. Tanner; [m.] Harold Vincent Fredrick Hergert, December 12, 1960; [ch.] Tammie Kay, John Lee, Thomas Leroy; [ed.] Cave - In - Rock High School, Tyler Junior College, Lincoln College, North Harris County College; [occ.] Administrative Assistant For Real Estate Developer And owner of County wide Mgmt. Co.; [memb.] Education Chairperson of Tomball American Business Women's Assn., Member, National Notary Assn., Member, CCUCA, Member Greenspoint Pacesetters, Member, Houston Rose Society; [oth. writ.] Nothing published; [pers.] I am the product of a mother and father who took the time to influence their children with love and wisdom thru action and words... and I thank them.; [a.] The Woodlands, TX

HERMANSON, EDWARD H.
[b.] August 15, 1915, Grand Marais, MI; [p.] Carl and Ida Hermanson; [m.] Nelmi M. Hermanson, May 9, 1934; [ch.] Sidney F. Hermanson; [ed.] High School Graduate; [occ.] Semi-retired caretaker for an author; [oth. writ.] Song writing and song poems descriptive writings depicting old buildings, muddy streets, people and cars. Some published in the Grand Marais Pilot or Grad Marais Gazette. Former member great Lakes Fisherman's Association with Mariners Document. Member of 1st Lutheran Church of Grand Marais, Mich.; [pers.] Interested in writing awaiting for the outcome of the contest; [a.] Grand Marais, MI

HERNANDEZ, FRANK C.
[b.] November 26, 1963, Denver, CO; [p.] Frank and Lorene Hernandez; [ed.] G.E.D. Commercial Arts, Welding. Some Basic and Child Psychology; [occ.] Artist (specializing in cartoons) Poetry (I write a variety); [memb.] 700 Club; [hon.] Having my poem published in "The National Library of Poetry's" "Anthology" is an Honor and also a great award within it's self.; [oth. writ.] I've had a few poems published in some quarterlies like "Street Beat Quarterly".; [pers.] Though I've been writing poetry for years (20), I've only began to seek publishing them in the last year, thanks to my sister Rita and her great encouragement[a.] Denver, CO

HERSH, GERALD LADD
[pen.] G. Ladd; [b.] May 23, 1929, Alma, KS; [p.] Gerald Hersh, Freda Hersh; [m.] Ella Marie Hersh, March 22, 1963; [ch.] Jon Marie Best, John Best III; [ed.] Central High, Highland Jr. College, American Institute of Engineering and Technology, Vocational Instructor—Offset Printing, Paralegal; [occ.] Co-Administrator, Inez Alsop Foundation; [memb.] DeMolay, KS Jaycees, NRA; [oth. writ.] Technical manual of Offset Printing, Gymnastics Handbook — The Highbar, Associate editor of The New Era, editor, Postrock Jaycees Newsletter, president, Consort, Inc. and Editor of Consort, short stories; [pers.] Man will reach the stars one day, if he can first conquer his conceit.; [a.] Manhattan, KS

HESTER, JANA
[b.] April 24, 1979, Saint Petersburg, FL; [p.] Boyce R. and Nancy L. Stewart; [ed.] Currently 10th grade, P.C.C.A. at Gibbs High School (Technical Theatre Major); [occ.] Student; [memb.] AuduBon Society, F.C.A. (Fellowship of Christian Athletes), Apprentice at St. Petersburg Little Theatre.; [hon.] Honor Roll at school. Most improved player (for soccer).; [pers.] Cats Rule and Dogs Drool. (From the movie Homeward Bound); [a.] Saint Petersburg, FL

HEWITT, HEATHER
[pen.] Don't have one; [b.] July 26, 1977, Merced, CA; [p.] Sunny and Dennis Hewitt; [ed.] Attending Baylor University, Waco Texas; [occ.] Student; [memb.] Member, Southeastern Cherokee Confederation, Member, High School Student Council (1994-5), Member, Advanced Symphonic Choir (1991-1995) (local, regional, state, national performances), Varsity/Junior Varsity Cheerleader (1992-4), Member, Spirit Club (1991-5), Member, Letter Club (1992-5), Member, Baptists Youth Group and Choir, Member, Daughters of American Revolution (DAR), Member, Fellowship of Christian Athletes (1991-Date), Coach (1992) and Player (1993-5) — High School 'Powder Puff' Football League; [hon.] High School Honor Roll, Who's Who In American High Schools (Multiple Awards 1993, 1994), Texas Music Educators Association (Feature Performance" (Washington, D.C. 1995), University of Houston Choral Invitational "Feature Performance" (1994), Three Time All-American Nominee — National Cheerleader Association (1992-3, 1993-4, 1994-5), "Top Team" Award Recipient, National Cheerleader Association (1992-3, 1994-5), "Bid to Nationals" Team, National Cheerleader Association (1993-4, 1994-5); [oth. writ.] Contributing Author, Alpha 1994 (High School Literary Magazine); [a.] League City, TX

HICKMAN, WILLIE M.
[b.] February 21, 1927, Caldwell County, Lenoir, NC; [m.] Ray Hickman, June 11, 1949; [ch.] 5 children - Dr. Dennice Herman (daughter), Rebecca Houck (daughter). Barry Hickman (son), Rachelle Duffey (daughter), Adonna Hickman (daughter).; [occ.] Retired Day Care Director; [oth. writ.] One publication in "Collection of Poems", two poems put to music, and several published in church bulletins.; [pers.] As a Christian, I feel that my inspiration for writing poetry comes from God. It is my desire that my poems will be used to glorify God and His goodness to us.; [a.] Hudson, NC

HICKS, KIMBERLY

[pen.] Kim Hicks; [b.] February 16, 1965, Diamond Bar, CA; [p.] Gene and Judy Talley; [m.] Jeff Hicks, June 9, 1990; [ed.] AA Degree in Fashion Design from F.I.D.M., Los Angeles, CA; [occ.] Artist; [hon.] Scholarship from The Niguel Art Association in 1983; [pers.] Fix your thoughts on what is true and good and right. Think about things that are pure and lovely, and dwell on the fine, good things in others. Think about all you can praise God for, and be glad about it. Phil 4:8; [a.] Covina, CA

HICKS, MABLE C. WILSON

[b.] November 2, 1961, Houston, TX; [p.] Charlie Leon Wilson, Verna Mae Freeman; [m.] Llyod C. Hicks, May 1, 1991; [ch.] Paul 13, John 12, Vernon 11; [ed.] G.E.D; [occ.] Wife and Mother; [oth. writ.] I've written other poems, but nothing has been published.; [pers.] My poems come from my heart. I only hope others who read them, will receive knowledge and understanding to help them along life's patches.; [a.] Lucerne Valley, CA

HILARY, ALISA R.

[b.] July 14, 1926, Warwick County, Newport News, VA; [p.] Henry M. and Frankie Showalter Shenk; [m.] Divorced; [ch.] L.A. Hertzler, Kathy Kornhaus, Marie Hertzler, Ashton Hertzler, Ray Hertzler; [ed.] Equivalent of B.A. degree from James Madison College, Harrisonburg, Va.; [occ.] Owner of Alisa's Altering and Sewing Service; [memb.] Port Republic Family and Community Education Club Blue Ridge Poetry and Music Assoc. Christian League Against Poverty; [oth. writ.] Voices On The Wind, Out Of The Depths Cried I and Songs Of The Heart all written and published by Alisa R. Hilary Poems and Music published by United Methodist, women's conference 1990.; [pers.] I endeavor to depict the meaning of life as it applies to the intrinsic value of human beings.; [a.] Grottoes, VA

HILEMAN, LONNIE L.

[b.] September 1, 1967, Oberlin, Kansas; [p.] Judy Rose, Terry Hileman; [m.] Dawn R. Siebold; [ch.] Britney Hileman; [ed.] Clay County Community High School; [occ.] Carpenter; [memb.] "Assembly of God" Christian Church; [hon.] Golden Poet Award 1988 (World of Poetry-Sacramento, CA), was offered publication in their anthology, poem title: "Difference;" [oth. writ.] I have my own collection of poetry that I have been writing and adding to since 1983; [pers.] "Life is full of choices we all have to make, you know the right ones come from your heart, and the others are fake." [a.] Riley, KS

HILL, BECKY

[b.] May 23, 1980, Russelville; [p.] Roy and Trena Wooten; [ed.] Nemo Vista High School; [occ.] Student; [memb.] Girl Scouts, Ameri Corps Explorers, Choir; [hon.] National Achievement Academy Science Award, Grand Champion in Country Fair Livestock Show; [oth. writ.] "Reality", "Thoughts of a Teenage Girl", and "Nevermore"; [pers.] My inspiration for this and my other poems, are my feelings and emotions.; [a.] Center Ridge, AR

HILL, GINA

[b.] February 19, 1965, Latrobe, PA; [p.] Mr. and Mrs. Lawrence Apone; [m.] Leroy J. Hill Jr., September 25, 1985; [ed.] Greensburg Central Catholic High School; [occ.] Brokerage Trading Sun America Securities; [a.] Phoenix, AZ

HILL, MARTIN

[pen.] M. Earl Hill; [b.] June 13, 1949, Medford, MA; [p.] Martin and Mary Hill; [ch.] Christopher Zacary Hill; [ed.] Burlington High (Mass.), College of Marin (Cal.); [occ.] Restaurant Waiter; [memb.] Mensa International; [hon.] Awarded Scholarship to National Broadcasting School; [oth. writ.] Several poems and songs. Unpublished as of this writing. Currently writing my first 3 act play.; [pers.] A love of theatre acting and music. Aspiring to act on the screen and continue writing.

HILL, NICHOLE LEE

[b.] December 28, 1974, Philadelphia, PA; [p.] Frank and Randi Sobolesky; [m.] Lawrence K. Hill III, June 3, 1992; [ch.] Jessica Danielle Hill and Lauren Amber Hill; [ed.] Queen Annes H.S. Centreville, MD and Philadelphia Com. College; [occ.] Housewife and mother; [memb.] Nativity B.V.M. Church; [oth. writ.] Until now my poems were written for my own eyes only; [pers.] I write to expenses what I see going on in our daily lives. In the hope we will all live and learn, live to love.; [a.] Philadelphia, PA

HILL, ROBERT THOMAS

[pen.] Eugene McConnell; [b.] June 23, 1946, Oklahoma City; [ch.] Jason (24) Thomas Hill; [ed.] MS Management, BA Sociology McAlester High School; [occ.] Retired AE Officer (Lt.Col), Military Consultant, Freelance writer, student; [memb.] Retired officers association, 21-club (sociological quasi-professional group), Founder and 1st president of One San Scholarship Foundation in Korea.; [hon.] Dae San, Korea Citizenship Award, Guest Speaker German-American night Pruem, Germany (ERG), Dean's Honor Undergraduate school, Several military decorations including 2 Air Medals and Middle East Expeditionary medal; [oth. writ.] Several editorial in local newspaper, Daily Oklahoma, McAlester News Capitol, Article and AF Times Magazine; [pers.] Beware of those who only answer for no other cloak can cover humanity like that of the egotist's cancer; [a.] Edmond, OK

HILL, SALLY RUTH

[b.] December 19, 1930, Wilson County, Wilson, NC; [p.] Luke Columbus and Victoria Tedder; [m.] M. B. Hill (retired) July 2, 1949; [ch.] Billy Gerald Hill (Pilot, Southwest Airlines), Barbara Ruth Flora (Nurse); [ed.] Chales L. Coon High School, Wilson Technical Community College; [occ.] LRC Secretary Wilson Technical Community College; [memb.] Women's Ministries - Wilson First Pentecostal Holiness Church, Red Cross Volunteer, Falcon Camp Meeting, School Volunteer; [hon.] 1986 Educational Office Person District II, North Carolina Association of Educational Office Personnel, 1984-86 President of Wilson County Chapter North Carolina Office Personnel; [oth. writ.] "Educational Administrators" published in National Education Office Personnel also two articles published in National Education Office Personnel, several writings published in "Gold Minds" publication at Wilson Technical Community College; [pers.] I began writing to help fill the void when my mother died in 1981.; [a.] Wilson, NC

HILL, SHERRY PATRICE

[b.] February 7, 1955, Oak Ridge, TN; [p.] Louella Hill Houston and Eddie Robinson; [ch.] Adrian Jumaane Hill; [ed.] Oak Ridge High Draughon's Business College; [occ.] Secretary Martin Marietta, Oak Ridge, TN; [pers.] I am thankful to God to be able to express myself through writing.; [a.] Oak Ridge, TN

HILLENBRAND, JANE

[b.] March 28, 1969, Montreal; [p.] John Hillenbrand, Lise Hillenbrand; [ed.] Sacred Heart High School, Notre-Dame Secretarial College, Concordia University; [occ.] Secretary; [memb.] John Saul Author Club; [hon.] Won award for speed reading course in 1985.; [oth. writ.] Article for "The Gazette"; [pers.] Dedicated to U.E.; [a.] Montreal Province of Quebec, Canada

HILLIS, CHRISTINA M.

[b.] July 21, 1975, Mexico City, Mexico; [p.] Norman, Janet Hillis; [ed.] Junior at Appalachina State Univ., Boone, NC. Double major Music Performance (Cello) and Accounting; [occ.] Student; [memb.] Kappa Delta Sorority, St. Mary's of the Hills Episcopal Church, Ambassador for A.S.U. Leadership; [hon.] Selected to perform with the LONDON SYMPHONY Orchestra, Aspen Concert Orchestra, Johannsburg Music Festival, Dean's List, ALPHA CHI National Honor Society, Finalist in Elks National Essay Competition.; [oth. writ.] Poem published for school writings. Essay on "What it means to be an American." Dorothy Frasier Music Scholarship, ASU Academic Scholarship Sinfonia Music Scholarship; [pers.] My writngs reflect my inner most feelings and how I relate to the world around me. I am influenced by the poets of the 19th century.; [a.] Boone, NC

HILLMAN, KARA

[b.] July 1, 1982, Waterville; [p.] Jane and Bruce Hillman; [ed.] I am a seventh grader at the Williams Junior High School in Oakland, Me.; [occ.] Junior High Student; [memb.] Student Council; [hon.] Junior High Honor Student; [oth. writ.] Poems published in school News Paper - Cougar Chronicle and Crazy about writing.; [pers.] My philosophy is connected with my poem because on March 8, 1994 my dad had a major stroke and nearly died. Since I am a true believer in God I knew if he fid die he would go on living in a better place. So I dedicated tis poem to my dad.; [a.] Oakland, ME

HIME, JANE

[b.] March 20, 1937, Booneville, MO; [p.] James and Ida Mae Wisherd; [m.] Jesse Hime, May 2, 1956; [ch.] Susan, Beth, Mary, Tim, Mitsy, Katy; [ed.] Graduate Union City, TN High School, 1 yr. UTM, Liberal Arts; [occ.] School Bus Driver; [memb.] St. Elizabeth Ann Seton Church; [oth. writ.] Team Member for Faith Sharing for Small Church Communities St. Anthony Messenger Press, 1993; [pers.] I view nature from the window of my school bus. Frequently it excites me and nudges me to share its beauty. I have a deep faith in God and find my fellow humans truly marvelous. I have been privileged over 23 years to share a little in the lives of countless children who have boarded my bus. I believe that if I can learn to treat each person with dignity it will be "catching" and the world will become a happier place.; [a.] Troy, MI

HINES JR., THOMAS

[pen.] Butch Hines; [b.] July 25, 1964, Baltimore, MD; [p.] Thomas and Faye Hines; [m.] Kim Hines, November 9, 1984; [ch.] Kyle Hines, Kody Hines; [ed.] High School (Glen Burnie High); [memb.] St. Paul's Lutheran Church; [pers.] Wy writings are mainly reflective with an optimistic tone. For without optimism tomorrow is not nearly so bright.

HINKSON, YVONNETTE

[pen.] Yvonnette Hinkson; [b.] November 4, Saint Joseph, Barbados; [p.] Albert (deceased) and Sylvia Hall; [ed.] St. Elizabeth Primary, modern high School; [pers.] I am spiritually inclined and my poems take a biblical direction in that good win over evil. My interest in writing came from reading and I love my native land Barbados and its people.

HIXON, DWAYNE EDWIN
[b.] June 14, 1965, Columbus, OH; [p.] Linda Derenberger and John Hixon; [ed.] Associates Degree in Human Services, Double Baccalaureate Degree in Psychology and Sociology.; [hon.] Cum Laude Graduate, Wilmington College Dean's List; [oth. writ.] Songs, copyrighted as compilation under the title "Song Lyrics from the Heart", many poems, yet to be published.; [pers.] I write my poems and song lyrics as I feel them. Sharing my emotions, my thoughts, my soul is my humble gift to my fellows.; [a.] Columbus, OH

HOBAUGH, NORMA
[b.] Williamsport, IN; [p.] James and Florida Jones; [m.] Deceased; [ch.] Holly Hobaugh, Nichole Elrod; [occ.] Hypnotherapist; [memb.] National Guild of Hypnotists - Search, Inc., The International Society of Poets; [oth. writ.] Book - The "Others" of Light, multiple poems; [pers.] Believe in the power of human ability. Have faith in this human race and know you yourself can make a difference of change.; [a.] Williamsport, IN

HOCKETT, C. C.
[pen.] CC Hockett; [b.] June 8, 1968, Elmendorf AFB, AK; [p.] Charles and Louise Evans; [m.] Sgt. Michael G. Hockett II, January 7, 1993; [ch.] David Ryan Hockett; [ed.] East High School, Anchorage, Alaska; [occ.] Wife of a Sgt. in the U.S. Marine Corps and full time mother; [oth. writ.] This is my first published poem; [pers.] I write from the heart, from personal experience, and what matters most to me in my life. It is there that I find it easiest to write. I wrote this poem for my husband as he was ready to deploy overseas to defend his country once again.; [a.] Camp Pendleton Oceanside, CA

HOFFMAN, AMY
[pen.] Spence Hoffman; [b.] April 7, 1980, Marlton, NJ; [p.] Anthony and Barbara Hoffman; [ed.] Triton Regional High School; [occ.] Student; [memb.] Triton's Literary Magazine; [hon.] "Award of Excellence" for my creativity in related arts areas. Dean's List - grade 1-8; [oth. writ.] Private collection; [pers.] Live life to its fullest, have no regrets, and take nothing for granted. Peace, love and empathy always...; [a.] Blackwood, NJ

HOFFMAN, LILLIAN
[b.] July 6, 1904; [ch.] 1 son; [ed.] Public School; [occ.] Retired; [pers.] Never say never. I wrote my first poem at age 85 by accident, have a book of poems, came to the U.S.A. at age 11 and couldn't read or write in any language; [a.] New York, NY

HOFMEISTER, CHRISTINE
[pen.] Hofmeister Christine; [b.] March 5, 1949, Belgium; [p.] Walter Balij; [m.] Jeffrey Hofmeister, June 29, 1976; [ch.] Anna Marie Hofmeister; [ed.] High School Graduated from whitehall - yearling one year college - Franklin University; [occ.] Bank Teller; [pers.] After being laid off from a job that I had for 27 years - 4 months 12 days I started to write to keep from losing my mind, my poems reflect my feelings and experiencing.; [a.] Howard, OH

HOFSETH, M. MARGARET
[b.] March 12, 1948, Anvik, AK; [ed.] Mount Rainier High School, 1968.; [occ.] Housewife; [pers.] I believe in TRUTH and, writing it explains this, and with understanding what I know and feel from the spiritual influence within that guides me to putting it in words to imprint the heart and mind to meditate on.; [a.] Lynnwood, WA

HOGAN, KATHRYN A.
[pen.] Kathy Hogan; [b.] September 9, 1952, Fayetteville, NC; [p.] Tom (deceased) and Barbara Joan Hogan; [ed.] Ca., School Leadership Academy - Senior Associate, M.A. - Azusa Pacific Univ., B.A. - Cal-Poly, Pomona, Ca.; [occ.] Program Specialist (Elem. level) and Elem. School Teacher Fontana Unified School District; [memb.] Assoc. of Ca., School Administrators, San Bernardino County School Attendance Review Board, National Whale Adoption Project, San Diego Zoological Society, Harvest Christian Fellowship.; [hon.] Who's Who in America 1994 - Silver Anniv., Ed., Continuing Honorary Service Award - Fontana Unified School District - 1991 and 1984, Honorary Service Award - Fontana Unified School District - 1983.; [oth. writ.] Several poems and articles in local newspapers, Christian publications, and educational publications.; [pers.] Our expressions of love, faith, and happiness should be shared unconditionally each and every day. Poetry reflects all of our innermost thoughts and feelings for not only ourselves, but for others.; [a.] San Bernardino, CA

HOGAN, NANCY
[pen.] Nancy L'enz Hogan, Countess Battina; [b.] Cleveland, OH; [p.] Ellis Christian Lenz, Dorothy Smith Lenz; [m.] John D. Hogan; [ch.] David J. Hogan, Timothy C. Hogan, Max J. Hogan; [occ.] Writing, always happily writing; [memb.] The Humane Society of the United States, PETA, International Wildlife Coalition; [oth. writ.] Radio and TV Commercials, Print Advert. for Major Accounts, Humorous Articles for Famous Monsters of Film land, Material for Stand-Up Comics, Youth-Oriented Thrillers, Specif., The Hosty Bell Novels, unpublished. Poetry, including the "Epic" titled "Fall River Summer 1892" - (Re Lizzie Borden) unpublished; [pers.] Herewith, a definition of my personal condition: Penitis: A malady characterized by the compulsive ongoing act of writing (since age 9). Penitis is the one ailment which can be it's own cure.; [a.] Kent, WA

HOLE, ROBERT E.
[b.] February 12, 1969, Germany; [p.] Robert B. Hole, Kathleen M. Gurry; [m.] Carmen E. Hole, September 25, 1993; [ch.] Robert N. Hole, Jeneh E. Johnson; [ed.] St. Martin's College; [hon.] Phi Theta Kappa, National Dean's List; [a.] Redmond, WA

HOLLWOEGER, INGEBORG
[pen.] Inge Borg; [b.] May 3, 1942, Graz, Austria; [p.] Irmgard and Leopold (d) Hollwoeger; [m.] Single; [ed.] Austria (basic education), Language Studies in London, Paris, Moscow; [occ.] Executive Secretary, San Diego, CA.; [oth. writ.] "KHAMSIN" the Devil Wind of the Nile" 175,000 word historical Novel about Ancient Egypt (unpublished as yet) "Mountain Meadows." (In Progress); [pers.] 1995 is the exciting beginning of my true writing career, will devote 100% of my time to it to produce interesting, enjoyable and well-crafted novels.; [a.] La Jolla, CA

HOLM, SHARRAN
[pen.] Sharpoe; [b.] April 7, 1981, Urbana, IL; [p.] Randall and Elizabeth Holm; [ed.] Home schooled; [occ.] Working student, El Rojo Grande Ranch; [memb.] Youth Opportunities United (Church Youth Group); [hon.] 3rd degree brown belt in Classical Okinawan Karate; [oth. writ.] Poem published in Hot Springs AR paper, article published in Sedona Red Rock News.; [pers.] I do my best to be myself when I write, and when people say, my poems have helped them, I'm thrilled! I love to help anyone, in anyway I can!; [a.] Sedona, AZ

HOLMAN, BRENDA G.
[b.] August 20, 1967, Taber, Alberta, Canada; [p.] Jessie Holman, Lenard Holman; [ch.] Tonia Jo; [ed.] W.R. Myers High School; [oth. writ.] Have received certificates from previous poetry contests.; [pers.] My poems are based on my feelings that come from my heart, and I am pleased when the reader can relate to what I write. This poem is dedicated in memory of a very special person who passed away August 18, 1994 in a house fire. His name, Jason William Bradwell; [a.] Taber Alberta, Canada

HOLMAN, YVETTE R.
[b.] April 6, 1973, Aransas Pass, TX; [p.] Emily R. Rangel and George T. Heflin; [m.] Thomas E. Holman Jr., December 23, 1993; [ed.] Allen High School, U.S. Army Basic Training and AIT; [occ.] U.S. Army - Military Police; [hon.] Good Conduct Award - U.S. Army, certificate of appreciation - U.S. Army; [oth. writ.] I have other poetry, I would like to get published to show my talents but have not decided on which ones.; [pers.] Writing poetry gives me the strength to express my feelings of life. I thank the Lord for this blessing of my talent of poetry and being able to share my thoughts with others.; [a.] Plano, TX

HOLMES, JULIE
[pen.] Juls; [b.] August 26, 1952, Willits, CA; [p.] Milton and Lois Kerchenko; [m.] Tommy Holmes, December 30, 1989; [ed.] Fort Bragg High, College of the Redwoods; [occ.] Secretary - California Department of Forestry (CDF); [hon.] A piece of artwork of mine was chosen to hang indefinitely in the Smithsonian Art Institute in...; [pers.] To let every life experience, good or bad, be a learning experience. Never judge.; [a.] Washington, DC

HOLMES, RACHEL EVE
[pen.] Rachel Holmes; [b.] December 31, 1986, Atlanta, GA; [p.] Bryan Holmes, Dana Holmes; [ed.] 2nd grade - Currently; [memb.] Piano club, Brownies, Dance Clayton Student, Singer, Soccer Association. Jonesboro United Methodist Church; [hon.] Honor Roll Student, earlier poem recognized state wide, was submitted school teacher in 1st grade and received special honors.; [a.] Jonesboro, GA

HOLMES, STEWART QUENTIN
[pen.] Stewart Quentin Holmes; [b.] December 25, 1929, London; [p.] Deceased; [ed.] Hendon College, London, Kings Lynn Tech Inst. Norfolk (Higher school Cert.: English, math, shorthand, typewriting, French, German) Hongkong University - Mandarin Chinese; [occ.] Actor and Journalist; [memb.] British Mensa British Actors equity Assoc. Inst. of Journalists Foreign Press Assoc. London; [hon.] Golden Poet 1990 (World of Poetry, Sacramento, Calif.); [oth. writ.] 2 Books of numerous verse: Odes and ends, once upon a rhyme; [pers.] Influenced by the style of the late Ogden Nash, all my poems are either numerous or ridiculous - couldn't be serious if I tried!; [a.] London, UK

HOLODNAK, IRENE
[b.] Glasgow, Scotland; [p.] Catherine and Peter McCulloch; [m.] Joseph E. Holodnak (deceased); [ch.]

David Peter, Stephen Michael, Irene Catherine, William Bruce; [ed.] Queens Park Secondary School and West of Scotland Commercial College.; [oth. writ.] Several other poems; [pers.] I hope to reach others by speaking from the heart with my poems as a child growing up in a beautiful old country, rich in history, ballads and songs I learned to appreciate all types of poetry; [a.] Trumbull, CT

HOLT, BEN EDWARD
[pen.] "The Children's Poet"; [b.] March 29, 1920, Nashville, TN; [p.] Theresa Holt and Ruffin Holt; [m.] Ermine Holt, March 9, 1968; [ch.] Ben Edward Holt Jr., Baritone Opera Singer (Deceased); [ed.] Howard Univ. (B.A), New York Univ. (M.A), Univ. of Mass., Amherst (Ed.D.), Union Institute, Cincinatti (Ph.D.); [occ.] Retired, Former English Teacher, and Director of Academic Services, Division of High Schools, New York City Public Schools; [memb.] College Alumni and English Associations, Alpha Phi Alpha, Pearl Harbor Survivors Assoc., CSA Assoc., NYC., D.A.V., N.A.A.C.P., MLK, Jr. Sr. Center, Hackensack, NJ, others; [hon.] Distinguish teacher, Wall Street Journal Award, Photography Award, Humanities Award, School Administrator Award Purple Heart Medal (Pearl Harbor, December 7, 1941), 7 other Military Battle Stars and Medals; [oth. writ.] "The First Black Doctor in America and Other Short Stories" An African Patriot Fights for His Freedom and Other Historical African - American Short Stories"; [pers.] I believe that multi-ethnic literature, properly written and taught, will motivate school children, irrespective of race, color or creed, to gain greater self-awareness and greater self-awareness and greater sensibility to the concerns of all mankind.; [a.] Wyckoff, NJ

HOLTZCLAW, GERTRUDE
[pen.] Jean Randall; [b.] January 7, 1913; [p.] B. N. and Kitty Shepherd (Foster Parents); [m.] Carrol Holtzclaw, June 17, 1934; [ch.] 3 boys; [ed.] High school and 3 yrs at Baylor University; [occ.] Retired Nurse; [oth. writ.] Religious hymns, easy listening, western music.; [pers.] Enjoy writing poetry and lyrics traveling and camping.; [a.] Odessa, TX

HOOK, BRADFORD
[b.] May 25, 1964, Elwood, IN; [ed.] B.S. - Music Education, Indiana Wesleyan University, M.M. - Saxophone Performance - Univ., of Cincinnati College - Conservatory of Music; [occ.] Inventory Control - factory; [hon.] Dean's List, graduated Cum Laude - Indiana Wesleyan Univ.; [a.] Elwood, IN

HOOKER, JASON R.
[b.] December 4, 1982, Eugene, OR; [p.] Robert and Carol Hooker; [ed.] Dwyer Middle School, Huntington Beach, CA; [hon.] Distinguished Honor Roll; [pers.] Even though my inspiration for this poem was my father, I want to thank my language Arts teacher, Mrs. Gehlke for the assignment.; [a.] Huntington Beach, CA

HOOPER, MARCLON MARY
[pen.] Marky Hooper; [b.] June 6, 1944, Cincinnati, OH; [p.] Trudy and James Corum; [m.] Jerry Sr., December 22, 1965; [ch.] Jerry Lee, Jr., Jeffrey Lee, Jennifer Leigh; [ed.] Woodward H.S., Cincinnati OH., Ohio Wesleyan Univ., Delaware, OH; [occ.] Owner of 2 woman owned companies: Hooper Enterprises, Inc., and Coastal Mfg., and Holding Co., Inc., A parent company for Coastal Bolt and Specialty Co., and Coastal Iron Works.; [oth. writ.] A personal collection of poems from my heart - all of which were created for a particular individual because of a very special occasion.; [pers.] Each poem is base on personal, real - life experiences in which humor has a role. My goal is to put a smile on each recipients face.; [a.] Corpus Christi, TX

HOPE, LEE B.
[b.] January 29, 1971, Stoughton, MA; [p.] Glenn Lee Hope, Margaret D. Hope; [m.] Laurie Mae; [ch.] Brain Anthony; [ed.] Don Bosco Tech.; [occ.] Janitor; [hon.] 1978 Competency Plus Award, 1987 Outstanding English-Level Award, 1987 Essay Contest Gold Medal, 1989 Golden Poet Award, 1991 Poetry Contest Silver Medal; [oth. writ.] Several unpublished songs and poems of assorted topics; [pers.] I write simply because I like to. As far as being able to share it with others is fantastic. We all have dreams about so many different things. If I can reach out and touch someone with my poetry, there's the reason for writing it. My inspirations include - William Blake, Aleister Crowley, Wilfred Owen, Robert Frost and James Montgomery among others.; [a.] Boston, MA

HORNE, EVAN
[b.] January 28, 1980, New Hartford, CT; [p.] Ronald and Karen Horne; [ed.] North West Regional District #7; [oth. writ.] Several short stories about comical events; [pers.] Do what you can and leave the rest to fate.; [a.] New Hartford, CT

HOTZ, KIMBERLY A.
[b.] March 27, 1982, New Jersey; [p.] Robert and Dorothy Hotz; [ed.] 7th grade student at Wandell School; [memb.] Avid Softball and Soccer Player; [hon.] Top 7% - Word Masters Competition. Rogate Student, Honor Roll student, previous student council member, has appeared in school plays, chorus.; [pers.] I hope that by composing this poem, I have made people more aware of the problems in our world. I also hope that people will try harder to help those in need.; [a.] Saddle River, NJ

HOUSTON, FRANCES SERENA
[b.] September 24, 1954, Fontana, CA; [p.] Mr. and Mrs. and E. H. Houston; [m.] Divorced; [ch.] Jeffeson S. Pierce, Jayson R. Pierce, Jennifer A. Pierce; [ed.] AA Degree in Liberal Art Certificate of a Psychiatric Technician; [occ.] Psychiatric Technician; [memb.] Psychiatric Technician, Professional Practice Group and California Association for Psychiatric Technicians; [pers.] Life itself is one of the greatest adventures we can know. People of today's world tend to see the negative side. The old saying "Stop and Smell the Roses", has always spoke to me. I see the world we know today as a classroom. What I have learned is The Garden of Eden is as close to us as are our hearts and our hands and what we do with those we live with until we change ourselves. Blessed be!

HOWARD, EDWARD W.
[b.] June 21, 1950, Upson County; [p.] Rev. and Mrs. Albert Howard Sr.; [m.] Betty Ann Howard, June 2, 1983; [ch.] Edward Martel Howard, Bettina Valencia Howard; [ed.] I attended Drake High School Later on I received my G.E.D. from Flint River Technical Institute in Thomaston, Ga.; [occ.] Textile Worker; [memb.] I am a member of Lincoln Park A.M.E Methodist Church.; [oth. writ.] A poem I wrote was published in the local newspapers and also an article that I wrote was published in the Atlanta Constitution; [pers.] I wrote the poem thousands and thousands miles away for the local military personnel that was deployed to Saudi Arabia hoping to lift their spirits.; [a.] Thomaston, GA

HOWARD, KATHERINE
[b.] December 9, 1974, New Orleans; [p.] Diane Howard; [ed.] High School - Mount Carmel Academy, College - Loyola University; [occ.] Student; [hon.] Dean's List, Phi Eta Sigma, National Honor Society, Alpha Kappa Delta, Sociology Honor Society; [oth. writ.] "It's This Theory" - Published in American Collegiate Poets.; [pers.] Poetry is one of the greatest forms of personal expression.; [a.] Kenner, LA

HOWARD, KATHY
[pen.] Kathy "Seropa" Howard; [b.] May 26, 1978, Washington, DC; [p.] Gerald and Charlene Howard; [ed.] Maranatha Christian School; [occ.] Part time Day Care Teacher; [oth. writ.] Won Presidents Award for Illiad Press. And was published twice in Anthology of Poetry by Young Americans.; [pers.] "Every artists is a cannibal, every poet is a thief, all kill their inspiration and sing about the grief."; [a.] Boise, ID

HOWARD, LAUREL
[b.] November 13, 1936, Waycross, GA; [p.] Clarence Howard, Mytrice Howard; [ed.] Wacona High School, Draughns Business College; [occ.] Co-owner - manager of retail Donut Shop; [memb.] American Center for Law and Justice, Cornerstone Christian Fellowship Church; [hon.] Was awarded scholarship to business college; [oth. writ.] Poem printed in hometown newspaper, others written for friends and family; [pers.] My only desire in writing poetry is to tell and show others of the beauty and the blessings God has wrought in our lives.; [a.] San Bernardino, CA

HOWARD, ROBERT AVEEL
[b.] March 31, 1951, Savannah, GA; [p.] Patch Ford Ancel and Mary Howard; [ed.] Completed 11th grade Lake Charles High School also formally from and Raised in Lake Charles LA.; [memb.] First Baptist Church Lake Charles Louisiana; [oth. writ.] Songs and poems; [pers.] Thru out all it's darkness their will always be greater things in life... people places and stuff and light and love; [a.] Floresville, TX

HOWELL, MARY PAULINE
[pen.] Pauline Myers Howell; [b.] April 1, 1914, Omaha, NE; [p.] Stephen and Dena Myers; [m.] Ernest Howell, November 10, 1934; [ch.] Two: Anita 1939, and Richard Howell 1938; [ed.] Graduated - High School Kennebec, So. Dak.; [occ.] Retired, and tired writing and gardening, I'm 80 years old.; [memb.] The Catholic church. I won many ribbons at fairs in North Dakota and Phoenix Argon's and painted many scenic pictures. I have some of my poems in National Poetry Books); [hon.] 1988 - "Great American Poetry Anthology", 1990 - "Treasured Poems of America", 1992 - "The National Library of Poetry", 1993 - The National Library[oth. writ.] Nine Volumes of my Poetry: - "The Middle Spoke". I wrote and printed (9 volumes in 9 years) printed from 1985 to 1994.; [pers.] "Keep chugging along"; [a.] Rathdrum, ID

HRUBY, EMILY ROSE
[b.] September 10, 1982, Concord, MA; [p.] Leslie Cliff Hruby and B. Frank Michael Hruby; [ed.] Blanchard memorial School, Boxborough, MA, Fay School, South borough, MA.; [occ.] Student, School newspaper reporter; [memb.] Girls Scouts, Clarinet section of the Blanchard Band, School Chorus, Gymnastic Academy of Boston, Cricket Club of Cricket Magazine.; [hon.] First prize for the best 5th grade diary of a three day class trip to Cape Cod, 1994; [oth. writ.] I have many

unpublished poems and short stories.; [pers.] "I view life as a puzzle. Put one piece together at a time and they'll all fall into place."; [a.] Boxborough, MA

HUOTARI, TIMOTHY J.
[b.] March 17, 1962, Highland Park [p.] Basil and Barbara Huotari; [occ.] Materials Management Clerk at William Beaumont Hospital; [memb.] I sing, write songs, and play guitar in the band Conviction, currently playing clubs around the Detroit area; [oth. writ.] I have written many other poems and songs. This is the first publication or contest I have submitted a poem to, although I have sent six songs to various producers and two songs to a contest in the past; [pers.] I thank God for the gift of writing and I thank my parents for their gifts of love and life and all they have taught me. I hope to touch others through my writing as my gift to all who will accept it. [a.] Troy, MI

HUBBARD, FAYE YVONNE
[pen.] Faye Hubbard; [b.] July 28, 1936, Akron OH; [p.] Charles Parnell Sr., Freddie Parnell; [m.] John David Hubbard Sr. (deceased), November 26, 1952; [ch.] Verdetta Trone (deceased), Mildred Ramsey, Charlene Hubbard, Terrance Hubbard, John D. Hubbard Jr., Vince Hubbard; [ed.] North High, Akrow School of Practical Nursing, Napne Pharmacology/LPN - Ohio Board Nursing Intravenous Therapy; [occ.] Licensed Practical Nurse, Barberton Citizens Hospital; [memb.] Mt. Zion Baptist Church, NAACP, Nurse Recruitment and Retention and Task Force of Barberton Citizens Hosp.,; [hon.] Performance Merit Award - Barberton Citizens Hospital; [oth. writ.] Twelve poems of inspiration, none published, several poems printed in Church newsletter; [pers.] I like to write poems of inspiration to uplift other people and myself. My poems are something my grandchildren can reflect upon in later years. I have been inspired by poems written by Helen Steiner Rice.; [a.] Akron, OH

HUBER, KATHY
[b.] December 22, 1938, Bella Coola, British Columbia, Canada; [p.] John and Ruth McHardy; [m.] Earl Huber, February 14, 1981; [ch.] Bryce and Vicky Finlayson, Howard and Tina Kettner, Burton and Cherie Astleford; [occ.] Wife, mother and grandmother; [memb.] S.D.A. Church; [hon.] To have the first two poems I have ever entered into a contest, get to a semi-finalist level and to have them both published in this book gives me joy untold; [oth. writ.] I have written poems for my loved ones. I have shared in their joys and sorrow in the form of a poem.; [pers.] God has given me the ability to put down on paper the burdens on my heart. Poetry can be a cleansing to one's soul. I thank him for this gift.; [a.] Mile House British Columbia, Canada

HUBLE, JAMES
[b.] May 5, 1933; [m.] Sondra; [ch.] Theodore and Peter; [ed.] Bachelor of Arts and Bachelor of Science: University of Minnesota; [memb.] National Wildlife Federation, The Nature Conservancy, Minnesota DNR Safety Enforcement; [oth. writ.] Several Poems and Songs, seldom published but often performed.; [pers.] Play the notes of life, some harmony, some discord. Strike the chords soundly.; [a.] Maple Grove, MN

HUFF, JEANETTE STAMPER
[b.] May 2, 1934, Mayking, KY; [p.] Bill and Manda Stamper; [m.] William Huff, April 6, 1957; [ch.] (2) Kenneth and Tommy, (3 G-Children) Mary Ann, Kenny and Ryan.; [ed.] Graduated from Whitesburg High School Whitesburg KY. 1953; [occ.] None - Disabled have a cancer; [hon.] It's a great honor to me that you have picked 3 of my poem's as Semi-finalist, thank you, you made my day.; [oth. writ.] (Many) I write to survive. It's my Theraphy. My doctor thinks its my attitude is why I am still living. But God is not ready for me yet. Got more thing's to write.; [pers.] My grandchildren love me, and I love them so much I want to live for them. They inspired me to write. My first writing were all about them.; [a.] Maple Heights, OH

HUGHES, GREG
[b.] April 1, 1977, Stanford, CA; [p.] Jim, Becki Hughes; [ed.] Sunset High School graduate 1995; [memb.] Boy Scouts, Eagle Mazamos (Rock Climbing Group), avid dead head, Church Youth Group; [hon.] Eagle Scout, Captain - varsity soccer team, Honor Roll, Olympic Development Soccer Program; [oth. writ.] Student produced literary magazine containing poems, short stories, drawing. Co-founder; [pers.] I look to real life experience as inspiration for poems, not trying to grab little fantasies down our of the clouds that could be more cliche than meaningful.; [a.] Portland, OR

HUGHES, HELEN A.
[pen.] Annie; [b.] April 12, 1943, Steep Falls, ME; [p.] Franklin Hattie Swinington; [m.] Gerarld Hughes, October 7, 1983; [ch.] April L. Steele; [ed.] Graduated Pennell High School, Gray, ME.; [occ.] Housewife; [hon.] Some poems have been aired on radio as a sunday school teacher also children church leader; [oth. writ.] Several; [pers.] Strive to reveal my belief in the Lord. Jesus influenced by my father.; [a.] Carmel, ME

HUGHES, MARK
[pen.] Mark Hughes; [b.] April 26, 1958, Louisville, KY; [p.] Carolyn and Solve Paulley; [m.] Marty, April 21, 1990; [occ.] Freelance Photographer And writer; [oth. writ.] Suicide notes (not published) Ramblings of a Madman's Pen in the Night (not published) and several short stories (Horror and Sci-fi); [pers.] My sister Debbie once told me. "A friend is someone who knows everything about you - but likes you anyway". I've always wanted to thank her for that quote.; [a.] Louisville, KY

HULBERT, ERIN-KELLY
[pen.] Wild Foot; [b.] March 27, 1977, Albany, NY; [p.] Richard and Colleen Hulbert; [ed.] Greenville High, Greenville New York; [occ.] Student; [memb.] Soccer, Track Teams, Soccer Coach; [hon.] 2nd All-Star Team; [pers.] I have been influenced by the passion of Dickinson, the brilliance of wordsworth and the unwritten grace and power of artist Georgia O'Keeffe.; [a.] Greenville, NY

HULL, ERIC VINCENT
[b.] March 8, 1966, New London, CT; [p.] Ruth Trainor, John Hull; [m.] Helia M. Garrido (Fiancee); [ed.] B.S., Providence College MS (Marine Biology), Nova South Eastern Univ, MS (Coastal Zone Mgmt) Nova Southeastern Univ; [occ.] Marine Biologist; [memb.] American Elasmobranch society, American Society of Zoologists, Florida Association of Marine educators; [hon.] Graduated Summa Cum Laude.; [oth. writ.] Articles published in local newspapers, thesis Abstract published in American Society of Zoology.; [pers.] My writing reflect the conflict we all face in understanding our internal feelings while coping with our external experiences. I believe happiness comes to these who stay thru to their feelings; [a.] Fort Lauderdale, FL

HULTON, DAVID NAKAMURA
[b.] March 19, 1983, San Diego, CA; [p.] Vel Nakamura Hulton, David Cleveland Hulton; [ed.] Maria Montessori Elementary; [occ.] Student; [memb.] Junior Golf Association and the United States Tennis Association.; [hon.] Space Camp "Right Stuff" award, Del Mar Fair 1st place in ceramics, 2nd in painting, and the Janet M. Leman Scholarship; [pers.] Every living thing should be treated with as much respect as you would treat yourself.; [a.] Rancho Santa Fe, CA

HUME, HAVAH S. E.
[b.] March 20, 1951, Rochester; [p.] Havah Smith, George Moon; [ed.] 10th yr., GED, some college, East High School, Saint Johns Fisher; [occ.] Own Business; [oth. writ.] Other poems - none published.; [pers.] I've taken care of my family when needed. In the last 4 yrs., I've lost two brothers who I miss and love with all my heart, soul, and took care of them, tell they left to be with God. Both died in my arms at our home. And I couldn't ask for anything else in life, just time to care for who needs it. This poem and others are in memory of my two brothers Leonard and Joshua Burley and all mankind that have die with AIDS and for those who are living with it.; [a.] Rochester, NY

HUMES, CINDY
[b.] June 2, 1937, Sacramento; [ch.] One son 35, one son 30, and One Daughter 33; [ed.] RN - American Nurses Assoc.; [occ.] Home care; [oth. writ.] Never published more poetry - this is my first entry.; [pers.] I try to stay focussed and centered as much as I can and get off balance frequently - working as a nurse balance frequently - working as a nurse helps me achieve this goal - I learn so much caring for others; [a.] Sebastopol, CA

HUNDLEY, MARC L.
[b.] August 25, 1975, Belleville, IL; [p.] Nelson and Ruth Hundley; [ed.] O'Fallon Township High School (OTHS), Southern Illinois Univ., at Edwardsville (SIUE); [occ.] Student - Civil Engineering/Environmental Engineering.; [memb.] Boy Scouts of America; [hon.] Eagle Scout Rank; [oth. writ.] Several personal poems unpublished.; [pers.] My writing takes a personal note to it. I have been greatly influenced by my "One True Love" Jodi.; [a.] O'Fallon, IL

HURDLE, LINDA
[b.] February 25, 1952, Los Angeles, CA; [p.] Nelma and Sam Hurdle; [m.] Never married; [ch.] LaReesha, Shawna and Crystal Page; [ed.] Some college ECE Major Pruitt Business College; [occ.] Pre-School Teacher unemployed'; [hon.] Editors choice award; [oth. writ.] My many writings are in my other biographical data forms that I mailed to your library, in the past.; [pers.] Some of my poems are poems but many can be turned into songs, is that true?; [a.] Sacramento, CA

HUTCHINSON JR., JAMES A.
[b.] March 12, 1962, Battle Creek, MI; [p.] James A. Hutchinson Sr., and Jean-Marie Lett Hutchinson; [m.] Sherise Hutchinson, September 8, 1993; [ch.] Taronday Hutchinson; [ed.] B.S. Criminal Justice Mount Senario College Ladysmith, Wisconsin 1985, Kellogg Community College Battle Creek, Michigan 1980-82. (Graduate of Detroit Mumford HS-1980); [occ.] YSW - Supervisor, Children's Center of Wayne County, Detroit, Michigan.; [memb.] Corinthian Apostolic Church Detroit, Michigan; [hon.] Ten Year's of Service to the Children's Center of Wayne County. Dean's List for Academic Achievement Kellogg Community College, Battle

Creek, Mi.; [oth. writ.] Several poems and short stories never before published.; [pers.] All writings are dedicated to those who before me both anonymous and acclaimed, through perseverance, will and faith endured many inhumanities. For it was in their spirit that a better tomorrow was born, and though a great many injustices remain you and I nevertheless, are blessed with the opportunity of today.; [a.] Detroit, MI

HUTCHINSON, KIMBERLY DAWN YVONNE
[b.] June 13, 1978, Lindsay; [p.] Donna and Donald Hutchinson; [ed.] Ops Elementary, I.E. Weldon Secondary - 11th grade; [occ.] Part time Dairy Queen - student; [hon.] Art honors.; [oth. writ.] Several poems, short stories and essays that haven't been sent for publishing - 'Those Eyes' being my first.; [pers.] Strive for today, tomorrow is mere fantasy.; [a.] Lindsay Ontario, Canada

HUTTON, CHARLES ERNEST
[b.] July 10, 1948, Cleveland, Ohio; [p.] Chester Arthur and Eileen Marie Hutton; [m.] Charlotte Donzetta Hutton, August 3, 1980; [ch.] Holly Donzetta and Walter Hamilton; [ed.] Santa Fe Community College and University of Florida B.S. School of Journalism & Broadcasting; [occ.] Hotel and guest Security Manager, Communications Coordinator; [memb.] Alpha Epsilon Rho, Broadcasting Fraternity-University of Florida; [hon.] Campaign for the World's Fair 1984, Walt Disney World Writers Contest 1st place; [oth. writ.] To My Mother, To Love You, My Dear Dad, For the Children; [pers.] I write to help future generations create, be motivated, and keep alive the pride and great heritage of a great country and its proud people; [a.] Kissimmee, FL.

ILDZA, RUTH MOHR
[b.] November 24, 1920, Detroit MI; [p.] Augusta Maria Steinkopf, Basil Franz Mohr; [m.] Clayton A. Ildza, December 19, 1953; [ch.] Faith, Carol and John, grandchildren Willis, Christina, Danielle, Zachary plus one on the way; [ed.] 30 hrs. toward Doctorate, M.A. in Speech and English, B.A. Elementary Children's Literature; [occ.] Retired, was Elementary Literature teacher for 4 years and High School Speech and English teacher for five.; [memb.] I'm a member of St. Luke Presby. Church of which I'm an elder and called the Poet Laureate. And of Church Women United and our Church Women's Assoc. Also member of Alpha Beta Pi Sorority. Was member of National Honor Society in High School; [hon.] Won 1st place 3 times in adult essay and oratory during Bicentennial and ended up 2nd place winner for the State of Missouri in oratory. Won gold, silver and bronze keys in oratory while in high school. Went on through Wayne State on scholarships won and 2 jobs as both parents were dead when I did. 2 short stories exemplifying all the best in content and delivery in a good story.; [oth. writ.] Had 2 poems in anthologies children's story bought by Jack and Jill winner 1st place, 2nd, 3rd and honorable mention in Story Art Magazines Contests. For stories, sold 3 articles to Detroit News Sun. Magazine, many poems in newsletters. Children's story "Happy Frog" sold to "Jack and Jill". My article "story telling" commissioned for secondary school principal's yearbook one year. Have done much storytelling for children and adults (also workshops postmistress, women's club, girl scouts, churchs. Also given sermons, speechs, stories for church services, church Wm. United World Day of Prayer, etc. and delivered my own poetry as part of services. I also write songs and hymns some of which have been performed by our church. I enjoy writing poems for birth, anniversaries, weddings, deaths for people I care about or who might be forgotten.; [pers.] As a teen I wrote this I try to live by: "I can do anything good that I set out to do, not in my way, but in God's way, not in my time but in God's time!"; [a.] Gladstone, MO

INACIO, DENISE
[b.] November 16, 1979, Modesto; [p.] Frank, Lena Inacio; [ed.] Sophomore at Modesto High School; [oth. writ.] This is my first time publishing or entering one of my poems into a contest.; [pers.] I write through my experiences, and I express my deepest most sacred emotions. I have many inspirations, but mostly they are life and love. Even though most of my poems were written at low times in my life, my friends, boyfriend and God stood beside me.; [a.] Modesto, CA

INCORVAIA, SALVATORE P.
[b.] July 2, 1971, Poughkeepsie, NY; [p.] Nunzio and Tillie Incorvaia; [m.] Julie Incorvaia, May 13, 1995; [ed.] B.A. - Marist College, M.P.A. - Marywood College; [occ.] Public Relations Coordinator/Casework Supervisor - Big Brothers/Big Sisters; [memb.] Big Brothers/Big Sisters of Dutchess County N.Y., Big Brothers/Big Sisters of Lackawanna County P.A., Board of Directors Italian Center of Dutchess County.; [pers.] My writing is a reflection of my inner feelings which at times can't be verbalized. I have been influenced by many poets, including Jim Morrison and William Blake.; [a.] Poughkeepsie, NY

INGRALDI, ROSE
[b.] April 3, 1980, Clifton; [p.] Bart and Darlene Ingraldi; [ed.] Attending Washington Township High School - Vice-President of Freshman Class; [memb.] Member of the WTHS Color guard and "The Way off Broadway Players" drama team, member of the Right to Life Association. Member of an Assemblies of God Youth Group.; [hon.] Principal's List, Honor Roll, various art awards; [pers.] "No matter what your age, you can achieve whatever you put your mind to."; [a.] Sewell, NJ

IVEY, COWANNA
[pen.] Cowanna Raines Ivey; [b.] December 17, 1944, Oklahoma City, OK; [p.] Clarence and Davelene Raines; [m.] Donald Ivey, November 23, 1990; [ed.] G.E.D.; [occ.] Cashier; [memb.] Eastern Star; [pers.] Influenced by the love given to me throughout life. My desire is for the world to appreciate how precious, how powerful love and kindness is, for it lasts beyond a life time. The greatest gift one can give to another. [a.] Shawnee, OK.

IVY, KENDALL
[b.] August 28, 1972, Chicago, IL; [p.] Jimmy Ivy, Brenda Ivy; [ed.] Von Steuben M.S.C., Devry Institute of Technology; [occ.] Security Officer, Mount Sinai Hospital; [hon.] Artwork was used and published by the public relations of Mount Sinai Hospital, Chicago, IL; [pers.] There's a gifted passion bound in every soul which makes everything worthwhile, even more precious.; [a.] Chicago, IL

JACKSON, NKEMDI
[pen.] Nkemdi, Boo and Kem; [b.] October 30, 1979, Chicago, IL; [p.] Wanda and Parker Jackson; [ed.] Evangelical Christian School, Chicago Vocational H.S.; [occ.] Student of Chicago Vocational H.S.; [memb.] Merit Music Program; [hon.] Valedictorian, State Senator Emil Jones Jr. Excellence in Education Award, Girls Basketball M.V.P.; [pers.] I express my true feelings in my writings and feel that someone out there is going through the same problems. This might help them!; [a.] Chicago, IL

JACKSON, ROBBIE
[b.] Bryan, TX; [m.] Roger Jackson, 1966; [ch.] Jason 26, Matt 23; [occ.] Mission Director, Life Enhancement Assoc. for People (LEAP); [oth. writ.] Book, yet to be published "A Healing Wind" about medical mission work in Belize - fiction; [pers.] My work with the LEAP team of Craniofacial surgeons who correct cleft lip and cleft palate on children of the Dominican Republic inspired me to write "We are Coming" as I thought about our patients

JACKSON, VIRGINIA VICKIE
[pen.] Virginia Vickie Jackson; [b.] South Carolina; [ed.] Associate Degree from American Academy of Dramatic Arts, NYC; [occ.] Actress/Writer; [memb.] Unions: Screen Actors Guild, Union: American Federation of TV and Radio (AFTRA); [oth. writ.] Unpublished stage/screen plays, and novels; [pers.] I was born in a small town in South Carolina and raised in the South Bronx in NYC. I worked as a secretary for many years before pursuing a career in the creative arts. My goals are to entertain the world by bringing a little joy into someone's life with my writings and acting, to make a difference.

JACO, DAVID
[pen.] David Jaco; [b.] January 24, 1955, Toledo; [p.] Charles and Betty Jaco; [m.] Wynna, September 15, 1992; [ch.] Adam, Aaron, Kaleigh, Brittany; [ed.] Clay High Oregon, Ohio; [occ.] Retired prize fighter; [hon.] Fought six former Heavyweight World Champions; [oth. writ.] Been profiled in New York Times and Prime Time Live, Television by Judd Rose; [pers.] It's never too late to pursue your dreams; [a.] Sarasota, FL

JACOBS, STEPHEN J.
[pen.] Steven or Stephen; [b.] October 7, 1947, San Francisco; [p.] Martin and Madeline Jacobs; [ed.] W.H. Taft High School, Pierce College, College of the Desert, Monterey Peninsula College, CSU Northridge; [occ.] Musician/Composer/Arranger/Writer/Lyricist. CEO, Chui Productions and Recording Company; [memb.] Amer. Fed. Musicians, Loc 47 voting member: NARAS (National Academy recording Arts and Sciences), Song Writers Guild of America, ASCAP (American Society Composers, Authors and Publishers); [hon.] Dean's List, College of the Desert.; [oth. writ.] 1. Macrotruth and Micropoetry 1984, 2. "This World": a solo album of music and environmental messages on CD and Cassette 1992.; [pers.] I wish my compositions to encourage and help humans rebalance themselves to earth's ecological and environmental systems.; [a.] Los Angeles, CA

JAHNKE, JERILYN A.
[pen.] Jerilyn A. Jahnke; [b.] October 18, 1949, WI; [p.] Charles and Phyllis Wright; [m.] Chad Jahnke, July 24, 1982; [ch.] Denis, Terra and Tim; [ed.] Appleton West High Fox Valley Technical College; [occ.] Machinery Operator Kimberly-Clark Corp.; [oth. writ.] Published in local newspaper in 1985, for a Christmas story.; [pers.] I like to experience life and write it down. Late at night I have most of my ideas. I write these things down on anything, scraps of paper etc. While doing this one night, a writer's soul came to me.; [a.] Neenah, WI

JARRETT, CALVIN
[b.] May 9, 1926, Fieldale, VA; [p.] Samuel Luther Jarrett, Nannie Prillaman Jarrett (both dead); [m.] Martha Gosnell Jarrett-R.N. (deceased), June 14, 1952; [ch.] Christopher (38), Michael (37), Patricia (28); [ed.] Graduate of Graham High School, earned BA degree from Elon College in 1952 with majors History and So-

cial Science. He received his Master of Education degree from UNC. He earned his doctorate in 1979 from the International University - after his retirement - doing his language requirements and course work at UNC-G, UNC-CH, and Duke University. He earned a BS degree from the University of the State of New York in 1983.; [occ.] Retired Educator, former Journalist, Freelance Writer, Cartoonist, Poet; [memb.] Western Writers of America, National Retired Teachers Association , National and International Wildlife Federation, Kentucky Historical Society, the Naval Historical Foundation of Washington DC, is a life member of the National Masque and Gavel - a speech organization.; [hon.] Won markmanship badges in both rifle and .45 sidearm pistol both in the Navy and Marine Corps during World War II, one of his poems "My Dilemma" had received an award of merit as one of the winners in the "Great American Poetry Contest".; [oth. writ.] 150 publications in newspapers, magazines, scholarly journals....; [pers.] I wish to live up to the state motto of North Carolina which is: Esse Quam Videri ("To Be Rather Than To Seem"). I love my country, I love my family and I love God. I wish to entertain people and I wish to spread the Gospel, the Gospel through my writings and my poetry. At the same time I wish to keep my humility. To not be pompous, to be nebulous: However, on the other hand, there were five fingers.

JASWAL, MANJ
[b.] July 15, 1977, Kitimat, British Columbia, Canada; [p.] Manjit Jaswal, Gurmit Jaswal; [ed.] Mount Elizabeth Sec. School; [occ.] Grade 11 Student; [oth. writ.] Other poems published in school yearbook 1. Dreams Of Love, 2. Weapon Of The Mind; [pers.] In my writings I am trying to stop hate and unify mankind; [a.] Kitimat British Columbia, Canada

JEFFERSON, SHIRLEY E.
[pen.] E. J.; [b.] September 3, 1951, Nova Scotia, Canada; [p.] Eunice Johnson and Aubrey Crawford; [m.] Joseph E. Jefferson Jr., March 22, 1980; [ch.] Carmella, Dawn, Joseph Edward III; [ed.] B.A., B.E.D., and M.B.A.; [occ.] Tax Auditor in Houston Texas; [memb.] Wheeler Avenue Baptist Church, Nova Scotia Teachers Association, Bally's Health Club; [pers.] My goal is to stimulate the senses to appreciate the beauty of life and living through verse because these are truly a blessing and not promised to anyone.; [a.] Houston, TX

JENCKS, ROBERT ARNOLD
[b.] Ashton, RI; [p.] Ida and Alden Jencks; [ch.] Belinda A. Jencks, Steven M. Jencks, Robert A. Jencks Jr.; [ed.] High school, two yrs. college, USAF Correspondence; [occ.] Retired U.S. Navy; [memb.] Disabled American Veterans, American Legion, Elks of America; [hon.] Grand Marshal Memorial Day Parade Cape Cod.; [pers.] To my loving daughter Belinda A. Jencks. May God watch over her forever. May we grow in the wisdom and knowledge of God.; [a.] Venice, FL

JENNINGS, BRENDA
[pen.] Andra Williams; [b.] August 18, 1978, Soda Springs, ID; [p.] Richard Jennings, Sharon Jennings; [ed.] Senior at Channing High School; [occ.] Student; [hon.] Louis Armstrong Jazz Award, Outstanding Band Award, Honor Society member.; [oth. writ.] Many unpublished poems and short stories that I plan on putting in one book someday.; [pers.] No matter who you are, anyone can become a literary artist. Letting your feelings concentrate inside and flow out your pen will prove this fact right. Never forget this.; [a.] Seattle, WA

JOHNSON, CLINT
[b.] December 9, 1981, Overland Park, KS; [p.] Martha and Jesse Lumpkin, Brenda and Charles Johnson; [ed.] 7th grader at Hall-McCarter Blue Springs, MO; [memb.] Forensics Team; [hon.] 1993 Missouri State winner of Modern Woodmen of America Oratorical Contest, Presidential Academic Fitness Award 1994, Duke Talent Program; [pers.] Poetry helps me express myself in different ways; [a.] Lee's Summit, MO

JOHNSON, DAVID MARTIN
[b.] August 8, 1957, Des Moines, IA; [p.] Rev. Martin E. Johnson, Hazel Marie Johnson; [ch.] Joshua Martin Johnson; [ed.] Des Moines Independent School District; [memb.] Central Assembly Of God Church; [oth. writ.] A collection of my poems. I call just a simple series of poems by David Martin Johnson; [pers.] As a human race we should always strive for what's true and honest and hold each other accountable for our own.; [a.] Des Moines, IA

JOHNSON, HOLLE E.
[b.] August 28, 1953, Jackson, OH; [p.] Hollie (deceased) and Virginia Hardman; [m.] Robert L. Johnson Jr., September, 1974 (Divorce Pending); [ch.] Stephen Todd, Jefferson Alan, and April Leighanne; [ed.] 1971 Graduate of Jackson High School, 2 years Art Instruction Feb. 1979; [occ.] Teacher's Aide/Monitor; [memb.] Central Elementary School Parent Volunteer Since 1989. Ohio Region 8 Odyssey of The Mind - Coach for 2 years.; [oth. writ.] A children's book entitled It's A Secret, Copyright 1993 as yet unpublished. I wrote and illustrated it.; [pers.] Do the things that please you and make you happy. Never say can't - can't never did do anything.; [a.] Chillicothe, OH

JOHNSON, JEFFREY JAMES
[b.] March 2, 1976, DeSmet, SD; [p.] Ronald and Sharon Johnson; [ed.] Mitchell Senior High, Jamestown College, University of Nebraska; [occ.] Student - Freshman at University of Nebraska (Lincoln); [memb.] Sierra Club, Ducks Unlimited, First Lutheran Church; [oth. writ.] A poem published in Prairie Winds and many poems not yet published.; [pers.] Many of my poems are influenced by my family. I greatly thank the Beastie Boys for inspiration.; [a.] Mitchell, SD

JOHNSON, JOY J.
[b.] November 2, 1921, Laurel Hill, NC; [p.] William and Edith Johnson; [m.] Omega F. Johnson, December 22, 1945; [ch.] Deborah Johnson Killens, Grands Joy and Jeanee; [ed.] Laurinburg Institute - Laurinburg N.C. (High School), Shaw University - Raleigh, NC; [occ.] Minister/Pastor; [memb.] NAACP, Alpha Phi Alpha Fraternity and 33 degrees Mason; [hon.] L.L.D. Shaw University, Raleigh; [oth. writ.] From poverty to power; [pers.] If you trust God, believe in your family, others and yourself and work diligently, you can accomplish anything in life.; [a.] Fairmont, NC

JOHNSON, JUDY
[b.] March 10, 1940, MA; [m.] Richard Johnson, October 1, 1960; [ch.] Dean Johson, Cindy McCarthy; [ed.] Oak Grove School, Colby Sawyer College; [occ.] Library Assistant at Belgrade Central School; [memb.] MEMA (Maine Educational Media Association); [oth. writ.] An article in the Maine entry - a publication for Maine Libraries and Media Centers; [pers.] Working with and guiding children brings many rewards.; [a.] Belgrade Lakes, ME

JOHNSON, KARIMA C.
[b.] October 18, 1974, Baltimore, MD; [p.] Jeanette Jones; [ed.] Baltimore City College High, St. Mary's College of MD; [occ.] Student of St. Mary's College; [hon.] Co-Founder and President of Baltimore City College Chess Team and Founder of "Lords" Chess Team of St. Mary's College. Founder of the New Beatniks Jazz Band.; [oth. writ.] Book 1 Optimistic, Book 2 My First Semester in College, Book 3 Unused Talent, Book 4 Cool Static, Book 5 Tigers on the Ceiling, Smashed to the Floor, Book 6 Enclosed: Dark Gray Collection; [pers.] Life is but a dream but what a dream it is; [a.] Baltimore, MD

JOHNSON, KERRI
[b.] April 20, 1979, Urbandale, IA; [p.] Kurt Johnson, Janice Johnson; [ed.] Urbandale High School; [occ.] Student, YMCA Camp Leader; [hon.] Urbandale High School Honor Roll; [pers.] You must believe in yourself, if you wish to achieve, the more you put in, the more you'll receive.; [a.] Urbandale, IA

JOHNSON, LISA DIANNE JENNINGS
[pen.] "Elise"; [b.] December 7, 1969, Charlotte, NC; [p.] Doris H. Jennings; [m.] Douglas Eugene Johnson, October 9, 1994; [ch.] Brandon Douglas Johnson; [ed.] Starmount High School, Art Instruction Schools - Fine Art Guilford Technical Community College - Commercial Art Department; [occ.] Freelance artist, and a plus-size Fashion model (for Capri & Assoc.); [hon.] Blue Ribbon Art Award - 1989, Frances Larkin McCommon Scholarship - 1988, Gold Key Award - 1988, "Best in the Show" at Sawtooth Gallery ("Celebration of Youth") - 1987, Certificates of Merit from Scholastic Art Awards - one in 1984 four in 1988, Art Honor Society; [oth. writ.] Several poems published in school newspapers. Others for my own enjoyment and a book I'm writing - Private Thoughts. "The Gift", "Shattered Glass", "A Special Gift of Love", "Too Soon", and "Letting Go".; [pers.] I've always admired Edna St. Vincent Millay and Emily Dickinson. In my poetry I try to think with my heart, instead of my head. I like to paint a picture of my feelings through my words, and relate to someone else's feelings.; [a.] Clemmons, NC

JOHNSON, MARGARET ELAINE
[pen.] Maggie Johnson; [b.] January 1, 1955, NYC; [p.] Hazel Holems Phillips, Charles H. Johnson; [ch.] Randy Christopher; [ed.] Juilia Richman High N.Y.C., Tompkins-Cortland Community College A.A.S.-Human Services; [occ.] Youth Division N.Y.S., Corrections Aide; [memb.] Homer Baptist Church; [hon.] The Michele E. McFadden Memorial Scholarship 1990-91, Dean's List: 1988, 1989, 1990, Tompkins-Cortland Community College Nurses Assistant Program's Continuing Education Award 1984-1985; [oth. writ.] Poetry and stories written for children and my own personal enjoyment.; [pers.] Having a poem published is a wonderful way to thank so many teachers who've inspired me to write. They have given me a love for words that I wish to share with others.; [a.] Dryden, NY

JOHNSON, MERRY LYNN
[pen.] Merry Pasco; [b.] November 29, 1938, Berwyn, NB; [p.] Kenneth and Alice Lemon; [ch.] John, Tamera, Rodney, Everett, Paul, Merry; [ed.] Vashon island H.S., Northwest College; [occ.] I work with severely emotionally disturbed children; [memb.] I lived in Mexico for 30 years and helped build churches, two schools, a home for handicapped children.; [oth. writ.] Many poems and articles. I began writing at age 5, and won a boat cruise

at age 15 for a winning essay.; [pers.] I wrote "cadence" for my mentor, Patricia Kelley Cook, who has helped me on my way. She 'reaches out,' which I hope to do in my writing.; [a.] Irving, TX

JOHNSON, MICHELLE CHRISTINA M.
[b.] April 4, 1968, St. Michael, Barbados; [p.] Marjorie Johnson; [ed.] The Smale Preparatory School, Queen's College, University of the West Indies (Cave Hill Campus); [occ.] Bank Clerk, Barclay's Bank PLC - Bridgetown.; [memb.] Queen's College Association, The St. Cyprian's Parochial Church Council, U.W.I. Guild of Graduates.; [oth. writ.] Poem entitled 'Isle-Land' which won prize in a local competition in late 1994. A little book is also kept where inspirations are noted.; [pers.] I write about my feelings, using the poem/story as a remedy for the given emotion - whether it be anger or sorrow, celebration or happiness.; [a.] Barbados, West Indies

JOHNSON SR., MURRAY T.
[pen.] Tee Grundy; [b.] December 24, 1941, Chicago, IL; [p.] Edward Junirs, Inez Junirs; [m.] Willie E. Johnson, October 21, 1961; [ch.] Murray T. Johnson Jr., Timothy B. Johnson, Robert A. Johnson, Jack K. Johnson, and Chad Johnson; [ed.] St. Elizabeth High, U.S. Navy, Unique Beauty School, Seminars on direct sales, stocks and bonds, health, real estate and multi level marketing; [occ.] Advertising; [memb.] President of the Hardy Reynolds Family Club; [hon.] Illinois License in Insurance and Cosmetology, certificate of supervision from Shaklee Corporation, Safety awards from driving and scholarship from cosmetology studies; [oth. writ.] Control Driving, Under Inclement Conditions; [pers.] The mysteries of life, are buried, unless told to all, who want to know. It would be a pleasure to prove some of these mysteries and how dear life can be, and the different physical things a human can do, at the age of 53.; [a.] Chicago, IL

JOHNSON, VINCENT E.
[b.] January 11, 1924, Sommerville, MA; [p.] William and Mary; [m.] Nora L. Johnson, November 11, 1947; [ch.] Kathleen Ann, Nora Marie, Maureen Rose, Lynn Mary; [ed.] High School grad; [occ.] Retired; [hon.] 1st Prize Flower Show Grange Hall, Eastern States Exposition. Four years in a row.; [oth. writ.] The Lemmings, Maintaining Friends, Trees, The Man and the Boy; [pers.] Daughter Kathleen in Who's Who's in Nursing in Library of Congress; [a.] West Springfield, MA

JONES, CAMILLE
[pen.] Camille Charmagne; [b.] November 21, 1964, Manchester, Jamaica, West Indies; [p.] Daphne Graham and Ronald Jones; [ed.] Cleveland Heights High, National University; [occ.] Chief Warrant Officer in the United States Marine Corps; [memb.] Drill Instructors Association, ADFPA - American Drug Free Powerlifting Association; [pers.] My focus when writing my poems is to reflect feelings of the heart and real life situation, so that people can relate and understand my words.; [a.] San Diego, CA

JONES, CAROL SUE
[pen.] Baby Girl Jones; [b.] January 24, 1954, Pensacola, FL; [p.] Duane Jones, Margie Shelby; [m.] Divorced; [ch.] Jessica Diane, Genny Rebbecca, Ruben John, grandchildren Mikie Hughes, Justin Maddalena, Brandon Luke; [ed.] 6th grade - Brentwood Elem., PJ College (GED) didn't complete; [occ.] Caretaker for Elderly's; [oth. writ.] I write poems all the time, haven't never thought that my poem would ever get in a book. This makes me very proud of myself. I always wished to have my poems published. I wished I could sell them.; [pers.] I love children and I love taking care of elderly people. I feel that they have been through a lot, and I feel that we should show kindness with loving hearts. I would like to sell some poems and help the needy.; [a.] Pensacola, FL

JONES, DONNIE
[b.] April 30, 1977, Flora, IL; [p.] Nancy Lane, Donald Jones (Deceased); [educ.] Jr. this year at Wayne City High School; [occ.] Student; [oth. writ.] Some poems around father's death, none other published; [pers.] Poetry is just a feeling I get - it comes I put it on paper. It's like the wind - it comes it goes. It's an expression of feelings - poetry and life walk hand in hand. Poetry is around you everywhere my emotions inspire my writing.; [a.] Wayne City, IL

JONES, JANICE
[b.] November 3, 1941, Texas City, TX; [p.] Ruby and Dennis Lowrey; [m.] Richard A. Jones, February 14, 1959; [ch.] Crystal Jan and Dana Lynn; [ed.] Forest Ave High; [occ.] Medical Claims Examiner; [oth. writ.] This is the only poem I've ever submitted for publication. Other poems have been in a more humorous vein; [pers.] This poem was a tribute to my mother shortly after her death. She was the guiding light in the lives of all of my family.; [a.] Mesquite, TX

JONES, JILL
[b.] July 22, 1980, Fort Worth, TX; [p.] Joe and Jeana Jones; [ed.] Joshua High School; [memb.] National Junior Honor Society; [hon.] High School Freshman: 3 honors classes - English I, Physical Science, World History, Varsity Volleyball as a freshman, freshman basketball team, Honor Roll; [pers.] This was a great personal achievement and I feel honored that my poem was selected. This poem reflects my personal achievement.; [a.] Joshua, TX

JONES, KIMBERLY D. CARTER
[pen.] "Kaecei" Jones; [b.] May 27, 1971, Vicksburg, MS; [p.] Joan Carter Davis; [m.] Roderick K. Jones, May 30, 1992; [ed.] Warren Central High School, Hinds Community College; [occ.] Homemaker; [hon.] National Honor Society, Dean's List, President's List, Phi Theta Kappa, National Art Honor Society, Who's Who Among America's High School Students; [pers.] It was very loving of God to create humans with the ability to express themselves poetically; [a.] New Orleans, LA

JONES, MICHELLE
[b.] July 19, 1978, Eureka, CA; [p.] Ron and Anne Jones; [ed.] Lassen High School; [occ.] Student; [memb.] Spanish Club, California Scholarship Federation (CSF), Golden Grizzlies, Hospital Auxiliary, Varsity Volleyball; [hon.] High Honor Roll, Vice-President Spanish Club, Secretary Golden Grizzlies, Secretary Hospital Auxiliary; [pers.] Every time I'm told I can't do something, I strive to do that and more. You can only do what you put your mind to, you just have to believe in yourself.; [a.] Janesville, CA

JONES, PAUL A.
[b.] July 6, 1965, Pine Bluff, AR; [p.] David Henderson, Bertha Henderson; [m.] Pamela Jones, April 10, 1993; [ch.] Justin Allen, Jordan Antonio; [ed.] Watson Chapel High School; [occ.] Industrial Worker; [memb.] Masonic Lodge; [oth. writ.] Several poems not yet published; [pers.] I try to install my thoughts into the mind of my readers, reality; [a.] Pine Bluff, AR

JONES, PAULETTE M. MCGEE
[b.] March 28, 1957, Prince George, VA; [p.] Alice and LeRoy McGee; [m.] Lesley Jones; [ch.] Jun Quincy, Keijae (deceased), SeDale and SeAira; [ed.] Burlington Twp. High, Burlington County College; [occ.] Correction Sergeant, New Jersey Dept. of Corrections; [oth. writ.] Multitude of other writings; [a.] Willingboro, NJ

JONES, PEARL E.
[pen.] Pearl E. Jones; [b.] June 30, 1924, Galion; [p.] Mr. and Mrs. Walter Ness; [m.] Divorce; [ch.] Kit Earl Jones; [ed.] Twelve years high school; [occ.] Retired from ITT Inc. Inspector and Security Guard, 40 yrs.; [memb.] Women Society of Bloomingrove Methodist Church; [hon.] Published poems in my Hometown newspaper.; [oth. writ.] Did produce my own small book of poetry in 1972 called "The Light"; [pers.] Help with religious education program as, Assistance to the Teacher. Teach school sometimes.; [a.] Galion, OH

JONES, PENNY
[b.] December 31, 1960, Levelland, TX; [p.] Calvin and Marvene Jones; [ed.] Littlefield High - Littlefield TX, South Plains Jr. College - Levelland, TX, Eastern Michigan Univ. - Ypsilanti MI, Texas Tech Univ. - Lubbock TX; [occ.] English and U.S. History teacher, Fabens High School, Fabens, TX; [memb.] Association of Texas Professional Educators (ATPE); [pers.] Poetry is the reflection of a person's thoughts and feelings. Each person will have a different interpretation of a poem because the thoughts and feelings of each person are different.; [a.] Fabens, TX

JONES, REGINA
[pen.] Regina Jones; [b.] January 29, 1969, Sebring, FL; [p.] Willie C. Jones Sr. and Minnie L. Jones; [ed.] Lake Placid High School; [occ.] Sebring Montessori Pre-School; [pers.] I love writing and mostly my writings are dealing with the reality of life. If I can encourage others to read some of my writings I know it will have a positive effect. I like to give a special thanks to God for Blessing me. And also thanks Mom and Dad, Dorothy and Jack Perdue and Ms. Evan Portee for encouragement; [a.] Lake Placid, FL

JONES, ROSEMARY
[pen.] Rosemary Jones-Wylde; [b.] April 4, 1921, Spokane, WA; [p.] Homer and Leona Wylde (deceased); [m.] Ewell Jones (deceased); [ch.] Kathleen McClenahan, C. Jean Strong and 4 grandchildren; [ed.] North Central High School, Kinman Business College - Spokane; [occ.] Retired - Volunteer at church library, attend college/ classes.; [memb.] The Nature Conservancy, Nat'l Audubon Society, several book clubs and a local Senior Writers Network.; [oth. writ.] My family geneological history, consisting of dozens of pages plus years of research. Several articles and poems local newspaper printed with my by-line. And, items for local Audubon Newsletter.; [pers.] I recently discovered joy of creating modern poetry and I enter my mature years retaining the interest of my childhood, the daring of my youth with a life-long inquisitive mind.; [a.] Spokane, WA

JONES, SANDRA K.
[b.] August 19, 1955, Hamilton OH; [p.] Oscar and Marjorie House; [m.] Lee Roy Jones, September 7, 1978; [ch.] Lee Roy Jr. and Elizabeth Jones; [ed.] Hamilton City Schools and Carousel Beauty College in Hamilton;

[occ.] Certified Nurse Aide; [memb.] Wesleyan Fellowship Chapel; [oth. writ.] I have written close to 100 poems since 1970. Religious poems, love poems, and humorous poems.; [pers.] Poetry is a God given talent and I praise him for this gift.; [a.] Hamilton, OH

JONES, TYRONE GRANDERSON
[b.] January 19, 1955, Tampa, FL; [p.] Charles I. Jones and Gwendolyn Shy; [ch.] Celina; [ed.] BA in Theatre from Florida A&M University in Tallahassee, MFA in Acting from UC San Diego in La Jolla; [occ.] Actor, starred in films, CB4, going under!; [memb.] Screen Actors Guild, American Federation of Television and Radio Artist, Actors Equity Association; [hon.] Recipient of 1987 NAACP Image Award for Best Supporting Actor in play "Rounds".; [oth. writ.] Poem play titled "Ain't Got Time To Be Just One Colored Boy", screenplay titled "Johnny Comes Running"; [pers.] I embody and reflect multicultural colors of Americans politically and artistically, exploring surreal dimensions of existence.; [a.] Beverly Hills, CA

JONES, WILEY F.
[pen.] Coyote; [b.] August 23, 1946, Wichita, KS; [p.] Mary and Leo Schmitz; [ch.] Shad Jones and Zachary; [ed.] High School, Training Schools for Large Marine Engines, other schools too many to list; [occ.] Powertrain Mechanic for Road Mach Corp.; [memb.] None are current at this time, except the N.R.A.; [hon.] Various ones at different times, but nothing at this time in space.; [oth. writ.] The poem that I submitted is only a small part of the complete work. I have other works that have never been public.; [pers.] Be responsible for your actions and for your behaviour. Accept the penalties. Our earth is a closed system, every action by each one of us, is very important.; [a.] Gilbert, AZ

JORDAN, K. BRUCE
[b.] December 15, 1949, Caldwell, ID; [p.] Farrel Jordan, Lucille Yowell; [ch.] Aaron; [ed.] 2 years college; [occ.] American Dry Ice; [memb.] Gold Hill Gold Corp., Transcendental Meditation Society; [hon.] Danforth Award, 1968; [oth. writ.] "Sage & Pine"; [pers.] A high degree of mind-body coordination offers everyone continuous enjoyment...of the wonder of Being. [a.] Boise, ID

JORDAN, CAROL
[pen.] Carol Thomas Jordan; [b.] May 8, 1961, Cleveland, OH; [p.] Barney and Grace Thomas; [m.] Brian L. Jordan, August 10, 1985; [ch.] Alan Schuyler, Amelia Grace and Edwin Clark; [ed.] B.A. - Criminal Justice; [occ.] Licensed Daycare Provider; [pers.] My family is my inspiration for writing.; [a.] Longmont, CO

JORDAN, MICHAEL C.
[b.] July 16, 1965, Highland Park, MI; [p.] McKinley and Marjorie Jordan; [m.] Beth Jordan, July 15, 1989; [ch.] Emily Renee; [ed.] Hazel Park High, Oakland University - BA Journalism; [occ.] Stay-at-home Dad, Freelance Writer, Storm chaser.; [oth. writ.] Over 150 articles published in local newspapers, have 100 poems and 150 songs on file. 2 poems published; [pers.] I would like people to be able to relate to things I write...most of my writings are inspired by real life experiences.; [a.] Hazel Park, MI

JOSHUA, SATTY
[pen.] Josh; [b.] Nigeria; [p.] Joshua Amopho, Mary Joshua-Amopho; [m.] Rita Benjamin-Joshua; [ch.] Abigail Kega, Atarah M'Uwani Kebin Gideon, Eella Naomi; [ed.] Morrisville College, NY City College of New York, PACE University, NY; [occ.] Engineer AD/SAT-Skylight Inc., NY; [oth. writ.] Several poems published in World of Poetry Press. Several sayings that are not published yet.; [pers.] 'Tis not enough that you do good work, do it with the best of intentions, and with your soul wrapped around it.; [a.] Montclair, NJ

JOVINELLI, ANTHONY G.
[b.] November 22, 1958, Philadelphia, PA; [p.] George and Eleanor Jovinelli; [m.] Rita K., September 26, 1981; [ch.] Kimberly Patricia, Anthony Nicholas; [ed.] Monsignor Bonner H.S., West Chester State College; [occ.] Asst. Service Manager and Wilkie Chevrolet - Buick-Subaru - Philadelphia, PA; [memb.] Teaching Staff - Holy Cross Church CCD, Westbrook Park Y.A. Coaching Staff; [hon.] Editor's Choice Award - 1994 Competition, 2nd place in local poetry contest.; [oth. writ.] "Peace of a Dream" published in "Edge of Twilight"; [pers.] I try to draw from nature for my poetry. Hoping that people will realize what we could lose from destroying our resources.; [a.] Clifton Heights, PA

JOY, SHEBY
[b.] August 11, 1968, India; [p.] P.K. Joy, Sara Joy; [m.] Sandhya Mary Cherian, December 28, 1992; [ed.] B.S. Engineering, M.S. Marketing; [occ.] Business - Construction, Software, Medical Devices; [pers.] My poems are an outcome of the undying love and constant support of my dear wife Sandhya. Thank you darling. My writings have been greatly influenced by my father's published works, and the values inculcated in me by my mother.; [a.] Madras, India

JOYNER, ANN
[b.] March 26, 1950, Atlanta, GA; [m.] Charles, June 15, 1975,; [ch.] Allison, Molly; [occ.] Teacher

JUILLARD, JULES
[b.] November 26, 1896, Chicago; [p.] David and Ellene Juillard; [m.] Deceased; [ed.] Night classes and reading; [occ.] Retired; [pers.] I was inspired to express the feelings in my heart, by the memory of my mother, toiling in the large vegetable garden, ensuring food for the table. All mothers close to me have shown great love, pain and sacrifice. Motherhood: no greater glory.; [a.] Scottsdale, AZ

KADNER, WENDY
[pen.] Sendy Sue, Winnie "Beky Cakes"; [b.] February 24, 1961, Mitchell County; [p.] Edward and Marcia Mullen; [m.] Russell R. Deeker (partner in life), been together since August 9, 1983; [ch.] Justin 14, Erin 12, Joshua 9, Trevor 4; [ed.] Graduated from Osage High School 1979. Trained Nurses Aide - 15 yrs. experience raising boys; [occ.] A poet and artist and on flipside do the Mom Job; [hon.] I've received Editors Choice Award for "Best Friends" '93 and "So Many Tears" '94 Anthologies with National Library of Poetry; [oth. writ.] Through Famous Poets Society "Four Seasons", "Best Friends" '93, "So Many Tears" '94; [pers.] Just my special `thank you' Sherlock. I thank God I have you. My world would come crashing in without you. You made me whole again. Love ya!; [a.] Floyd, IN

KAITNEY, JEAN ANN
[pen.] Jean Ann (current), Jean Terry-Tobics (previously); [b.] June 15, 1932, Clinton, MA; [p.] John M. and Mary K. Terry; [m.] Bruce E. Kaitner, June 2, 1993; [ch.] 3 daughters, 1 son and 3 stepsons; [ed.] High School, Business Communication - Certification; [occ.] Homemaker; [memb.] Grace Lutheran Church, Redford, MI; [oth. writ.] Between the years 1969 and 1984, several poems were published in anthologies and poetry magazines. Two were aired on WEFG-FM radio and one article was published in an out of State Newspaper. I wrote a social column for the Detroit Suburban Newspapers and wrote a book entitled, love, life and laughter-1973. In 1994-1995, my poems were published in three anthologies and two appointment calendars.; [pers.] I hope that my heartfelt self-expression will, in some small way touch and inspire others.; [a.] Plymouth, MI

KAMENSKY, OLGA
[b.] March 14, 1986, Moscow, Russia; [p.] Alla Kamensky, Victor Kamensky; [occ.] Student, 3rd grade, Salanter Akiba Riverdale Academy; [oth. writ.] About 40 poems. Two published in schools newspaper.; [pers.] My poems used to show much feeling but were a dunce. Now I write about live things and unending beauty. Language is my tool.; [a.] New York, NY

KANTOR, LEONARD R.
[b.] August 21, 1931, Bayonne, NJ; [p.] Sidney-Dorothy Kantor; [m.] Elvira, July 23, 1963; [ch.] Dorothy, Leonard, Debra, Sharon, Brian; [ed.] Bayonne High School; [occ.] Security Co-ordinator; [memb.] Environmental Groups; [pers.] The beauty of what our eyes see, puts love and kindness in our heart and expresses it in words of love. I had put my writing aside to raise my family, but now feel the need to write again. Almost in thanksgiving for what I had growing up as a child and young adult. And in protest against what the world has become. I believe my poetry consists of the words that the soul longs to say aloud, hoping someone will hear. It is almost as if now that my life is less busy, my spirit can get to work.

KAPLAN, SCOTT D.
[b.] May 16, 1969, Long Island, NY; [p.] Irwin Kaplan, Ellen Kaplan; [ed.] John F. Kennedy High Nassau Community College (9/91 - 5/93) Hofstra University (9/93 - Present) 5/96 is expected date of graduation; [memb.] American Heart Association (Nassau Region), Phi Theta Kappa (Omicron Sigma), Psi Chi (The National Honor Society Psychology), International Sports Sciences Association (Certified Fitness Trainer); [hon.] Golden Key National Honor Society (In recognition of outstanding scholastic achievement and excellence), dean's list (1991-present) Academic Honors Scholarship (Hofstra University); [pers.] This is my first publication, and I feel extremely honored to have my work recognized. My poem reflects a topic that I am deeply passionate about. It is imperative that our laws evolve to combat the evil lurking in today's society; [a.] Merrick, NY

KASLIK, GRETCHEN
[pen.] Gretchen Kaslik; [b.] August 30, 1972; [p.] Carolyn and Richard Kaslik; [oth. writ.] A compilation of poems not yet published.; [pers.] Writing has become my religion of self-healing. This piece published is in memory of my beautiful cousin Bruce. The pain that I am capable of releasing through words has made me realize how much I have had to love. To not feel pain would be a true pity, for this would mean one would have never felt love.; [a.] Scottsdale, AZ

KASSIN, RUTH
[b.] February 22, 1930, Brooklyn, NY; [p.] Max and Sara Schneiderman; [m.] Ronald, June 25, 1950; [ch.] Ken Rhonda, grandchild Matthew; [ed.] College: Brooklyn College; [occ.] Retired; [pers.] Love of family; [a.] Fountain Hills, AZ

KASSON, MARY M.
[b.] November 19, 1920, Savannah, GA; [p.] Cris and Penny Martin; [m.] Deceased; [ch.] (2) George Phillip, Leathia Carolyn; [ed.] Savannah High St Therese Hospital School of Nursing.; [occ.] Retired nurse; [memb.] National Assoc Retired Federal Employees.; [oth. writ.] Some unpublished poems and writings; [pers.] Everyone we meet should have MMFI across their chest - "make me feel important" - if we could imagine that, then all people would be better for it.; [a.] Fresno, CA

KAY, DENISE
[b.] March 31, 1947, Brooklyn; [p.] Dennis and Margaret Murphy; [m.] ex - John Andrew Kay, December 30, 1965; [ch.] Christi - Daria, Shannon Patricia and Erin Michael; [occ.] Licensed N.Y.S. Esthetician; [pers.] Treat others as you wish to be treated all else is commentary.

KEARNEY, ELEANOR JOAN
[b.] November 18, 1935, New Rochelle, New York; [p.] Reidar and Lillian Syvertsen; [m.] Ex: Bernard Kearney, Jr., May 8, 1955; [ch.] Laura, Linda, Karen, Kristine, Bernard James III; [ed.] William H. Taft High School, Bronx, NY; [occ.] Retired Homemaker; [memb.] A.A.R.P., Trinity Lutheran Church, St. Anthony's R.C. Church Rocky Point, NY; [hon.] Honor Society, Arista Society High School, New York Classical Club Award for Excellence in Three Years of Latin; [oth. writ.] Two poems titled "Home" and "Autumn Benediction" published by Ideals; [pers.] I strive to leave this world a little bit better place to live in through the accomplishments of my children and grandchildren and my writing of beautiful poetry. [a.] Shoreham, NY.

KECK, MICHAEL AARON
[pen.] Sherif Rashid; [b.] November 4, 1972, Berwick; [p.] Mr. and Mrs. Ray Fred Keck; [ed.] 1992 Graduate of Central Columbia High School, specializing in Music, Art and English; [occ.] Calligrapher; [oth. writ.] Several poems published in the 1994 fall edition of Poetic Voices of America; [pers.] I thank God for my many talents and mom and dad for their continuing support. I strive to get at people's emotions through my poetry.; [a.] Berwick, PA

KEENEY, DARREL LEE
[pen.] Darrel Lee; [b.] September 13, 1948, Saint Louis; [p.] Hoyt and Beulah Keeney; [m.] Linda Kay Keeney, July 20, 1979; [ch.] Keith, Kevin, April, Kyle and Amanda; [ed.] Saint Louis Public Schools, Saint Louis Mo. and Penacola Junior College, Pensacola Florida; [occ.] Warehouseman; [memb.] Local 688 Teamsters; [oth. writ.] Beauty Queen, The Wizard, Music, People, Song, A Summers Day Not So Far Away, The Jokers Gone Wild, The King Has Died, and A Day In The Park; [pers.] To gaze upon the usual. To sense the unique.; [a.] Spanish Lake, MO

KELL, MRS. ALICE B.
[b.] February 5, 1913, Amarillo, TX; [p.] W. A. and Mary Jane Evans; [m.] James Lester Kell, May 1, 1957; [ch.] Bill Ward, Karen Ward, Bernadine Ward, JoAnn Tinsley, Gloria Santag (stepchildren); [ed.] Amarillo High School 1931 - Long Beach City, College 69-76; [occ.] Housewife, retirement with son and daughter in law

KELLOGG, AUREBA G.
[b.] Dallas, TX; [m.] Robert B. Kellogg, (Musician); [ch.] John F. Kellogg IV, (San Ramon, CA) Jeanne M. Keyes, (Renton, WA); [ed.] Administration of justice, creative and report writing, drama and art classes; [occ.] Security/customer service/office supply buyer; [oth. writ.] Other poems, short stories (both fiction and non-fiction), documentaries, song lyrics

KELLY, JAMIE
[b.] April 19, 1977, Detroit, MI; [p.] Pamela and Terry Kelly; [ed.] Graduate of Lakeview High School, student at Wayne State University, Detroit, MI; [memb.] Michigan Young Republicans Association, Volunteer for Macomb County Special Olympics Foundation.; [hon.] 1994 Macomb Daily Ad-Craft, 1994 First place Human Interest Writing at Macomb, English Teachers Association, Third Place Opinion Writer at Michigan State University, MIPA, Summer Journalism workshop, 1994 Journalism scholarship at Michigan State Univ., 1994 1st Place META Columnist.; [oth. writ.] Currently working on a autobiography, "Regarding Girl". And completing a book of my poetry, titled "Poetica".; [pers.] When the rhythm of the soul meets the lyric of the mind, thus creates poetry.; [a.] Saint Clair Shores, MI

KELLY, JOHN
[pen.] John Kelly; [b.] August 16, 1928, Dublin, Ireland; [p.] Peter and Mary Kelly, deceased; [m.] June Kelly, August 29, 1957; [ch.] Erin, Liisa and John F. Kelly; [ed.] B.S. degree from Clark University and has done graduate work at Boston University Law school, Temple University, Holy Cross College Institute of Industrial Relations as well as completing courses at the I.B.M. Educational Center in Philadelphia.; [occ.] Self employed entrepreneur - own business; [memb.] Training manager and educator in the M.B.A. program of a prominent University; [oth. writ.] Wall St. Journal Phila. Inquirer Phila daily news boston globe Norristown, Pr. Times Herald Pottstown, Pr. Mercury Wincester, Mass. Tel. and Gassette many others.; [pers.] poetry offers us all the opportunity to share our unique perceptions with all mankind.; [a.] King of Prussia, PA

KELLY, KENITH
[pen.] Ken Kelly; [b.] July 4, 1941, Los Angeles, CA; [p.] Robert Kelly, Martha Kelly; [ch.] Tammy, Kenny, Julie; [ed.] Hall's High School, Knoxville, Tenn.; [occ.] Master Grill Operator; [hon.] Commander - Director A.W.A.N.A. Clubs of American; [a.] Knoxville, TN

KELLY, MS. OLIVETTE
[b.] March 28, 1955, Chicago, IL; [m.] Single parent; [ch.] Two sons ages 13 and 19; [occ.] Work for the Illinois Dept. of Employment Security for 15 years.; [memb.] Cultural book club "Sister Circle"; [oth. writ.] The Letter, Dream/Life Thoughts of Life, They Got Him, Stress, I Want To Tell My Sons, Over The Edge....; [pers.] In every life there is a story to tell, a poem to write or a song to sing. My writings depict my life and those around me, as I see it and as we live it.; [a.] Chicago, IL

KENO, JOAN E. SHROYER
[pen.] Joan E. Shoryer Keno; [b.] February 14, 1958, Dover, OH; [m.] Jeffrey Bruce Keno, November 4, 1988; [ed.] B.S., 1980 Kent State University, Journalism; [occ.] Administrative Assistant; [hon.] Honorable Mention, 1994 Virginia Highlands Festival; [oth. writ.] Poems published in various national publications; [pers.] For me being a poet means facing the beauty and ugliness within and expressing those inner treasures in an original, thoughtful manner.; [a.] Knoxville, TN

KENYON, COY
[b.] January 31, 1956, Fort Worth, TX; [p.] Virgina Jenkins of Caney, OK. P.E. Kenyon of Denison, TX; [m.] Not married; [ch.] Tony Kenyon, Brandy Kenyon, Candice Kenyon; [ed.] Caney High School in Caney Oklahoma; [occ.] Pest Elimination; [oth. writ.] Several poems, short stories; [pers.] The answer to life is within all of us, love will ask the right questions.; [a.] Fort Worth, TX

KERLEY, BARBIE
[b.] February 20, 1980, Marietta, GA; [p.] James Kerley, Gail Kerley; [ed.] 9th grade, Osborne High School; [pers.] In memory of my mother, Gail Kerley; [a.] Marietta, GA

KERNS, JOHN ANTHONY
[b.] March 17, 1962, French Lick, Indiana; [p.] Amon L. Kerns, Rebecca J. Kerns; [m.] Melissa J. Kerns, March 3, 1986; [ch.] Karma Dawn Kerns, Tyler John Kerns; [ed.] Springs Valley High School, Larry Bird Blvd., French Lick, Indiana; [occ.] Poet; [oth. writ.] Stream of Dreams (copy right '92), A Collective Book of Poetry by John Anthony Kerns; [pers.] Poetry is an art form does not require a degree to produce or understand, only vision. Poetry in its purest form is feeling, it is sampled like a fine wine using the eyes and brain in place of the nose and palate. The value of poetry is not gauged by the number of persons it reaches, rather by the degree of feeling it provokes in each individuals perception. All that I ever hope for when I write a poem is to share those concepts, thoughts, feelings, or emotions that cannot be put into logical order, if only to set them free.; [a.] Indianapolis, IN

KERSCHNER, DARRIN L.
[b.] January 5, 1966, Oklahoma City; [p.] Don and Myrna Kerschner; [m.] Joann Proffitt, May 25, 1990; [ch.] Lauren Marie Kerschner; [ed.] Edmond Memorial High School, University of Central Oklahoma; [occ.] U.S. Coast Guard; [hon.] Numerous Coast Guard and military awards and commendations; [pers.] Before two can truly love, both must first be true to themselves, then honesty and love shall never fail; [a.] Webster, TX

KHOSA, BIKKAR SINGH
[pen.] Bikkar Singh Khosa; [b.] August 18, 1962, Rupana, India; [p.] S. Basank Singh (father), Surjeel Kam (mother); [m.] Gurmail Kam, June 2, 1967; [ch.] Rajdeep (son), Deepinder and Ramandeep (daughter); [ed.] B.A. (Honours) Panjab University Chandigarh, Diploma in Agriculture Science (Panjab Agri-University) Ludhiana; [occ.] Worker in a Company; [hon.] Winner of first prize in short story contest by U.P. Sahit Sabha Kanpur (U.P.) India.; [oth. writ.] My short stories published in the most popular magazines of my mother language Panjabi - named 'Arsee' and Nagmani - one short story published in Indo-Canadian Times - Poems published in anthology of poems and in magazines.; [pers.] I write poems, short stories in Panjabi Song in Hindi and Panjabi. I have studied the foreign literature in English as well as translated in my mother language.; [a.] Surrey British Columbia, Canada

KIDDER, GEORGE
[pen.] Barstool Bard; [b.] September 3, 1930, Ashton, ID; [p.] Jesse Reuben - Gwendolyn Kidder; [m.] Juanita Crislip, Early 1970's; [ch.] 3 of my own - 8 of hers, 2 more hers's by another wedlock; [ed.] They finally kicked me outta high school with a diploma; [occ.] Retired humberjack semi-retired bartender; [memb.] American legion U.F.W. Cowboy poets of Idaho; [hon.] Ulp? Gulp?; [oth. writ.] A few cowboy poems some honky-tonk verse a number of funeral dirges buncha jingles and

junk political puns some rather raneld honky-tonk verse; [pers.] Never had the chance to do much cowboyin' and I am not a pretender, but, I shore put in a passhe of time as a wild west bartender, so I don't reckon you could really call me a cowboy poet, pard, altho I might qualify as a barstool band; [a.] Ashton, ID

KIEFER, NICHOLAS P.
[pen.] Keefah; [b.] September 19, 1960, Pasadena, CA; [p.] Edgar F. Kiefer and Jean G. Morgan; [m.] Darleen Ann, June 6, 1994; [ch.] Jordan Dela Cruz, Tylor Perry; [ed.] B.S. in Computer Science, Univ. of San Francisco, 12/85; [occ.] Systems Analyst/Programmer; [memb.] Grace Bible Church, Hucky Bucky Club; [hon.] Huck Swee Chuh Award; [oth. writ.] Letters to Editors, Poems, Comedy Books; [pers.] Jesus Christ is Lord; [a.] Honolulu, HI

KIERAS, ARLENE P.
[pen.] A. Dillon; [b.] July 16, 1933, Elizabeth, NJ; [p.] Margaret, Michael Tuohy; [m.] John A. Kieras, July 9, 1955; [ch.] Joellen, Barbara, Timothy; [ed.] Blessed Sacrament Grammer, Sacred Heart High Eliz. N.J. Att: Middlesex county college creative writing courses at Sayreville high school; [occ.] Housewife; [memb.] High school paper, march of dimes, cheerleader. Junior women's hospital auxiliary, PTA.; [oth. writ.] Stories for my grandchildren poems for my friends for special occasions, short stories for my own pleasure children stories, hoping to have them published some day; [pers.] I have been writing poetry since I was young, but have never submitted anything until now. I have written many poems, some for birthdays and anniversary and on occasions to console the family at the loss of a loved one.; [a.] Parlin, NJ

KILLINGER, TRACY
[b.] April 27, 1966, Bloomington, IN; [oth. writ.] Currently working on book of poetry, essays and prose. I'm a song writer who has recorded two Albums writing the lyrics and music for both.; [pers.] I hope to capture moments, memories and times in life. I feel that I am a writer as well as a composer, I feel very fortunate to have these ways of expressing my self. Sometimes I haven't a clue where it comes from.; [a.] Spencer, IN

KINARD, JOHN R.
[pen.] Jroll; [b.] December 28, 1940, Henderson, TX; [p.] John and Hetty Kinard - both deceased; [m.] Elsie Lynell, September 10, 1980; [ch.] Scott Kinard son, Kelley Kinard daughter; [ed.] BA, LLB, MBA and JD, University of Texas, Post. Graduate Work. PAN American College to Oxford; [occ.] Woodworker and Boat Builder; [memb.] Delta, Theta, SAE, VT Law School Alum. Assoc., Sierra Club, Cousteau Society; [hon.] (E.A. Thorpe Award, Texas Law). Past President of Rio Grode Society of Financial Analysts, Texas Daily Press League. Acadmy Award Junior Olympics 50 Meter Free Style Champion 1953, 2nd Place. French Broad River. Canoe Race.; [oth. writ.] 2 poems in Hatronal Anthology of High School Poetry. Newspaper Report and Writer for Odessa American and Asheville Citizen; [pers.] Poetry is a reflection on ones life both good and bad. It must be felt and lived. My poems are not for the very young or very old. But beat with the heartbeat of your yesterdays and your tomorrow yet to come.; [a.] Saluda, NC

KING JR., JOHN S.
[pen.] John S. King Jr.; [b.] February 18, 1971, Pontiac, MI; [p.] Linda Evans and John King Sr.; [ed.] Holly High School, Holly, MI, Woodridge Business Institute Major (Medical Secretary); [occ.] Student (UBI); [memb.] Volunteer, Peninsula Regional Medical Center, American Heart Association, Salisbury Blood Bank, and Member of V.F.W.; [hon.] Military: Army Commendation Medal, Southwest Asia Service Medal; [oth. writ.] Unpublished poetry and songs; [pers.] Three most important things in life: 1. Friendship - to have someone to back you up, 2. Love - have someone to share life with, 3. Music - get rid of aggression; [a.] Willards, MD

KING, MARGARET W.
[pen.] Margaret W. King; [b.] November 9, 1938, Boonville, NY; [p.] Alton Reed, Gertrude Reed; [m.] Divorced; [ed.] Central High School, Syracuse, NY, Bachelor's Degree in Sociology, Master's Degree in Counseling, University of New Mexico; [occ.] Social Security Disability Adjudicator, State of New Mexico; [memb.] AARP, AFSCME Union; [hon.] Published poetry and essays in Blue River Anthology, World of Poetry, College Newspaper, Journals, The Now Newsletter and The Syracuse Herald Journal and Tin Pan Alley Music Publications; [oth. writ.] Women in the Twilight Zone, Juvenile Delinquency, Ode to a Therapist, All Alone, Speck of Dust and many more poems.; [pers.] I am a relativist and believe in the resiliency of the human spirit. I was most influenced by Emily Dickinson, Edna St. Vincent Millay, Kahlil Gibran and Bertrand Russell.; [a.] Albuquerque, NM

KINGHORN, WAYNE E.
[b.] December 6, 1931, Machiasport, Maine; [p.] Earl and Gladys Kinghorn; [m.] Lettie C. Kinghorn, June 7, 1951; [ch.] Garry Kinghorn, Carolyn Shaughnessy; [ed.] Washington Academy, East Machias, ME, Cleveland Institute of Radio Electronics; [occ.] Semi-retired insurance agent, substitute teacher; [memb.] Anah Temple Shrine Church Lay Speaker, AARP; [hon.] Insurance marketing awards; [oth. writ.] Industry publications and local newspaper; [pers.] Through poetry we can share life's experiences with others. [a.] Machiasport, ME

KINGSLEY, ANITA
[pen.] Anita Harper Kingsley; [p.] Roland and Chrysolia Harper; [m.] Harold Kingsley; [ch.] Son: Gerald Harper Thomas (Kathleen Gallagher), Grandchildren: Lisa Marie Thomas, Kelly Gallagher Degman (Richard), Margaret Anne Degman (Great), Michael Gallagher; [oth. writ.] Through the years Dear God (Memoir) new inspirations; [pers.] In my writing I try to preserve the past, yet work within the present and contemplate the future.; [a.] Los Angeles, CA

KINGSTON, STARLA
[b.] August 4, 1976, Prince George, British Columbia, Canada; [p.] Leona and Bob Kingston; [ed.] New Westminster Senior, Secondary - grade 12; [pers.] I'd like to say hi to my friends and family - especially my niece Courtney and goddaughter Cera. Love you all.; [a.] New Westminster British Columbia, Canada

KINSEY, JOHN B.
[b.] November 20, 1967, Fort Worth, TX; [p.] Roy and Barbara Kinsey; [m.] Enver Kinsey, October 21, 1994; [ed.] Bachelor of Science in Criminal Justice, Southwest Texas State University; [occ.] Children's Protective Services, State of Texas; [hon.] Dean's List, Alpha Phi Sigma; [pers.] I would hope that each of us never forgets the uniqueness in themselves and others. It is this uniqueness that makes each of us special and with it we can never become just a number or just part of the crowd.; [a.] Round Rock, TX

KIRK, RUTH POWELL
[pen.] Ruth Kirk; [b.] March 11, 1935, Kalamazoo, MI; [p.] Ross and Celesta Powell; [m.] Jessa J. Kirk, September 24, 1935; [ch.] Jesse Joseph II, Timothy Scott Anna Marie, David Evan; [ed.] I did not finish school. I finish the 8th grade at lake wood school in Kalamazoo. I have read a lot. I have gone to many training classes.; [occ.] Home maker; [memb.] Love outreach ministries church.; [oth. writ.] Many poems about childhood memories and family and friends. Also poems about nature. Also christian poems. Poems about poor children and hurting people.; [pers.] I love to write of past experiences. I love to put it into poetry. I write everyday about something - prayers mostly writing helps me to love life.; [a.] Longview, TX

KIRSCH, STEVEN
[b.] August 19, 1976, Montreal, Canada; [p.] A.J. Kirsch, Roselyn Kirsch; [ed.] Shaw High School Columbus College; [occ.] Student; [memb.] Biology Club Medical Exploring CYSA Referee (Soccer); [hon.] Honor roll dean's list poetry awards; [oth. writ.] Several poems published in various publications.; [pers.] "Things may come to those who wait, but only the things left by those who hustle" I always strive to do my best, knowing that if I try hard enough I can achieve anything in life.; [a.] Columbus, GA

KIRSTEIN, JAMES
[b.] May 19, 1930, Fairview, NC; [p.] M. L. and Aleatha Kirstein; [m.] Mary Phyllis, March 1, 1957; [ch.] Laura Lee (January 7, 1959), Charles M. (November 4, 1960), Heather Lyn (July 11, 1965); [ed.] Baylor Univ (BA) 1952, S'wstern Bapt. Theol Sem. (BD) 1956; [occ.] Ordained Minister, Retired Navy Chaplain; [hon.] Captain, USN, Legion of Merit, Meritor. IOUS SVC Medal (2), Navy Comm. (2), Combat Action Ribbon, etc.; [oth. writ.] Many Sermons, Short Stories, Essays and Poems - unpublished.; [pers.] I write for fun and for personal satisfaction.; [a.] Deland, FL

KISKAMP, JOHN C.
[b.] September 30, 1939, Lakewood, OH; [p.] John H. and Beatrice G.; [m.] Patricia L., July 23, 1982; [ch.] 3 sons, 2 stepsons, 3 stepdaughters and 3 grandchildren; [ed.] Avon (OH) High and Navel Electronics; [occ.] Tech Service Eng.; [hon.] Being published in "The Garden of Life"; [oth. writ.] Special occasion poems; [pers.] Enjoy what ever you do. If you don't enjoy it, it probably isn't worth doing.; [a.] North Ridgeville, ON

KITTRELL, IDA SUE
[b.] December 31, 1938, Perryville, MO; [p.] E. B. and Winnie H. Bond; [m.] Thurman Kittrell, March 16, 1963; [ed.] Beaumont High School, 1956. Jones County Jr. College, Ellisville, MS - 1959; [occ.] Retired Public Health Employee; [memb.] Calvary Baptist Church, New Augusta, MS; [hon.] Honor Student, JCJC, Ellisville, MS; [pers.] Blessed are the merciful: for they shall obtain mercy St. Matthews 5:17; [a.] Beaumont, MS

KJELLBERG, NADINE M.
[b.] March 23, 1971, Reading, PA; [p.] Ingvar, Rose-Marie Kjellberg; [ed.] Temple University, School of Communications and Theater; [occ.] Student Photography Lab Instructor; [memb.] American Society of Magazine Editors Golden Key National Honor Society National Press Photographer Association Helennir Student Society; [hon.] American Society of Magazine Editors Intenship Award. Chilton/ABC Writing Award, Spring

1994 PGA Journalism Scholarship, Fall 1994 Kay Krieshbaun Award for Photography Temple University Publishing Contest: First place honor writing, spring 1994; [oth. writ.] 5 poems Treasured poems of America, April fall 1995 editions articles: Themas and expressions, brandweek, artique, Philadelphia People; [pers.] I look for the gems in life to sustain me in my quest for purity and truth. I go forward in this, carried by my inner heart.; [a.] Philadelphia, PA

KLEINLAGEL, CATHERINE PLYNKETT
[b.] October 9, 1957, Brockville; [p.] James Plunkett and Gladys; [m.] Ronald Kleinlagel, July 6, 1985; [ch.] Justin Arthur; [ed.] Thousand Island Secondary, Commercial Artist Course; [occ.] Artist, Chiropractic, Health Assistant; [hon.] Painter for Ducks Unlimited; [oth. writ.] This is my first; [pers.] Poetry is a song of the heart and the spirit of the soul; [a.] Brockville Ontario, Canada

KLINE, KEVIN L.
[b.] September 16, 1979, Harrisburg; [p.] Karen Gorecki, Craig E. Kline Sr.; [ed.] Dauphin County Technical School, Central Dauphin East High School; [occ.] Student; [memb.] Garden Chapel Youth Group, Karate; [hon.] 2nd Degree Green Belt in Isshin Ryu Karate, Scholastic Honor Roll Student; [oth. writ.] Several short stories, several poems; [pers.] It is good to look toward the future... as long as you live in the present; [a.] Oberlin-Steel Town, PA

KNEPPER, LYNDSAY
[b.] October 2, 1980, Houston; [p.] Beth and David Knepper; [ed.] 8th grader now, Wells Middle School, Houston, Texas; [occ.] Student; [memb.] Participate in all School Athletics - Volleyball, basketball, track. Also play softball. Cheerleader and Member of National Charity League - Charity and Philathrophy Work; [hon.] 1. Chosen as member of competitive cheerleading squad, 2. Made all star team in softball, 3. Member of champions superstar drill team that won nationals at Disneyworld.; [oth. writ.] Various for school and personal use; [pers.] "It is the little things in life that can make a difference."; [a.] Houston, TX

KNEZEK, DANE
[b.] July 13, 1982, Olney, TX; [p.] Don Knezek, Jana Knezek; [ed.] 7th Grade so far; [occ.] Student at Oak Crest Middle School; [memb.] Traveling Historians club, student council, Golden readers club; [hon.] Vice-president of the golden readers club; [pers.] You've got to play like there's nobody watching, and sing like you don't need the money.; [a.] San Antonio, TX

KNOCKE, LARRY W.
[b.] August 4, 1937, Sweetwater, TX; [p.] Rudolph and Erna Knocke; [m.] Billye Y. Knocke, July 22, 1967; [ch.] Jon C. Knocke; [ed.] A.C. Jones High, Del Mar College; [occ.] Retired - Social Work; [oth. writ.] Unpublished poems and children's stories; [pers.] Creativity is one of the beauties of life, no matter what the field of endeavor. That beauty for me is the written word. It becomes even more special if someone else takes pleasure or is moved by my creativity.; [a.] Corpus Christi, TX

KNOX, GERALD CLIFFORD
[pen.] Gerald Knox; [b.] March 10, 1952, Huntingdon; [p.] Hartley Knox, Marjorie Lewis Knox; [m.] Jocelyne Krafft Knox, October 25, 1975; [ch.] Melanie, Caroline, Sabrina; [ed.] CVRHS, Chateauguay Valley Regional High School, Ormstown Quebec, Canada; [occ.] Landscaper; [memb.] TLC ... for plants, Plant and Garden, Canadian Small Business Institute; [hon.] Ministere De L'Education Health and Safety on Construction Sites, NAP 242 Thelawn, NNB 241 Botany, NNB 243 Propagation; [pers.] Always keep a pen and paper handy, for no one is smart enough to remember everything he or she knows; [a.] Saint Anicet Quebec, Canada

KOBILJAK, URSULA
[b.] Germany; [m.] Josef M. Kobiljak; [ed.] Gymansium (with Abitur) in Germany, R.N. Degree, University of Heidelberg School of Nursing. Master's Degree in French, Literature, Ph.D. in Modern Languages, Wayne State University (Detroit); [occ.] Lecturer in French, Oakland University, Rochester, Michigan; [memb.] American Literary Translators Association, Univ. of Texas at Dallas, Holderlin Gesellschaft, D-72070 Tubingen, Germany, Association Des Amis de Gustave Roud, CH - 1084 Carrouge, Switzerland; [oth. writ.] A book in "American Univ. Studies" of Peter Lang Publ., Echoes of Germanic Poetry in the Work of Gustave Roud.; [pers.] To compose poetry, I think, a spiritual basis is essential to give substantial depth to our lives, loves and words.; [a.] Warren, MI

KOCH, ERIC
[b.] January 3, 1975, Arlington, MN; [p.] Don Koch and Marti Renville; [ed.] Minnesota Valley Lutheran High School, New Ulm, MN, Willmar Community College, Willmar, MN; [occ.] Student; [memb.] St. Pual's Lutheran Church, Arlington, MN; [oth. writ.] Two other poems written in high school.; [pers.] Never underestimate the power that hope can play in one's life. Use that hope to fly with the birds and to achieve all that which is impossible.; [a.] Arlington, MN

KOEHLER, WILLIAM F.
[b.] February 11, 1922, Milwaukee, WI; [p.] Frank J. Koehler and Erma Butz; [m.] Betty Jane (Pfister) Koehler, October 19, 1945; [ch.] Stephen, Stephanie, Lora and Lisa, 7 grandchildren, 2 great-grandchildren; [ed.] Rufus King High School (1941) Milwaukee, WI; [occ.] Retired from Wisconsin Bell Telephone Company (32 years service); [hon.] "Good Conduct" medal, U.S. Naval Service (WW II) 1941-1947; [oth. writ.] This is my first writing.; [pers.] "Love and compassion"; [a.] Grafton, WI

KOLP, VIVIANE
[b.] October 5, 1957, Arlon, Belgium; [p.] Mrs. Yvette Schever, Father deceased; [ed.] Elementary School in Europe! Montreal High School, followed by several Technical Institutes; [occ.] Therapist, author; [oth. writ.] Die or live drug or supplement. Recently finished writing, projected for publishing, before years end!; [pers.] I believe that it's okay to focus on tomorrow and to look ahead, but for some it never seems to be enough. Please stop the race, slow down the pace and start living. Savor every precious moment life has to offer and hold on to your dreams!; [a.] Vancouver British Columbia, Canada

KONDOLEON, IRENE
[b.] August 15, 1967, Warren, OH; [p.] Louis Kondoleon and Koula Rallis Kondoleon; [ed.] The Ohio State University; [pers.] We have to come to the realization that we are dependent on each other, that our great quest for power and honey, cannot be the sole purpose of our lives. We are all interconnected, and until we understand and accept this fact, we will never truly find peace for ourselves or for our planet; [a.] Warren, OH

KONSTANZER, BARBARA
[b.] June 16, 1935, Manhattan, NY; [p.] Warren Green - Helen Green; [m.] Deceased, May 12, 1953; [ch.] Jeanette Marie; [ed.] William Cullen Bryant New York University; [occ.] Nurse in geriatrics Personal care to 93 year old women; [oth. writ.] Re: A tiny babe to me was born RE: You were my pet, you were my friend. You currently have both of these. I've written other's but have never sent them anywhere.; [pers.] When I write poetry it warms my heart. I usually write poem's about people or friend's that I care a great deal about. This also includes the pet's I've had. I find beauty in everything.; [a.] Long Island City, NY

KONSTANZER, BARBARA
[b.] June 16, 1935, Manhattan, NY; [p.] Warren Green and Helen Green; [m.] Deceased, May 12, 1953; [ch.] Jeanette Marie; [ed.] William Cullen Bryant, New York University; [occ.] Nurse in Geriatrics, personal care to 93 year old woman; [oth. writ.] Re: You Were My Pet, You Were My... you also have this one. I've written others but have never sent them in. Also Re: A Tiny Babe to Me was Born...; [pers.] I'm very sentimental, I write about people and friends that I care very much about also the little pet's I've had. I find beauty in everything.; [a.] Long Island City, NY

KORNEY, COLIN J.
[pen.] Joel Collins; [b.] November 19, 1971, Thompson, Manitoba, Canada; [p.] Jane and Lawrence Korney; [ed.] Olds College, Olds, AB, Sturgis Composite High, Sturgis, SK; [occ.] Carpenter and Part-time Writer; [memb.] Olds College Alumni; [oth. writ.] Editorials in the Progress, a local newspaper, as well as several short stories and unpublished novels.; [pers.] 'I Love' was written as a letter to a beautiful lady, Jackie Stephanyshyn, the inspiration for so many of my poems. I try to relate what I see in life to emotions all people experience.; [a.] Endeavor Saskatchewan, Canada

KOSKI, JAMES
[b.] October 2, 1954, Warren, OH; [p.] George Koski, Dorothy Koski; [m.] Cynthia Wray Koski, December 17, 1989; [ch.] Nathan, Ethan, Jason, and Amelia; [ed.] Ohio Soldiers and Sailors Orphans Home in Xenia, Ohio, also Four Year of Electrical Apprenticeship in Anchorage, Alaska; [occ.] Electrical Contractor; [memb.] 2nd Vice President of the Association of Ex-Pupils of the Ohio Veterans Children's Home (formerly the OS and SO home in Xenia, Ohio.); [hon.] High School Honors including R.O.T.C. Battalion Commander, Military Excellence Award, A.X.P. Essay Award, and Honor Roll; [oth. writ.] News Paper Articles, "The Pride of Ohio Must Remain Open", and "What Price the Children".; [pers.] Orphanages are not as Charles Dickens depicts them, instead they are a place for understanding, guidance and love.; [a.] Beaver Creek, OH

KOSTERA, MELISSA A.
[b.] January 9, 1971, Detroit, MI; [p.] Thomas and Judith Kostera; [ed.] Michigan State University - B.A. English; [occ.] Graphic Production Coordinator; [oth. writ.] Article published in Grand Blanc News, and several articles published for employee and community publications of Bon Secours Hospital, Grosse Pointe, MI; [pers.] I am constantly struck by the world around me and the one within me. My writing is an outlet and escape that I only hope to lead others to as well.; [a.] Detroit, MI

KOTILA, INGA I.
[b.] January 28, 1960, Chicago, IL; [p.] Vilho and Irene

Lehtomaki; [m.] Jeffery V. Kotila, September 19, 1980; [ch.] Iloni, Davin, Teija, and Tomas Kotila.; [ed.] Genesee High School, Genesee, MI - Ranked 4th of 43, 1978, Attended College at Spring Arbor and Suomi College, Michigan; [occ.] Deceased. Buried on family property in Big Rapids, MI; [memb.] National Honor Society 1976; [oth. writ.] Over sixty other poems; [pers.] Inga married young and had four children. She was a good mother, even though she was often sad and melancholy. When she turned 30 she thought her life had passed her by. She committed suicide in 1992. She was survived by a husband and four children. We miss her very much.; [a.] Iron Mountain, MI

KOUVARIS, CATHERINE
[b.] March 9, 1928, Lynnfield, MA; [p.] George Plagianos, Chrisanthy Plagianos; [m.] Charles Kouvaris, January 4, 1953; [ch.] Louis, George, Gregory; [ed.] Women's Garment Trades; [occ.] Housewife; [memb.] St. Demetrius Philoptohos Society, Choir of St. Demetrius, Jamaica, Queens Federation of Choirs, Cultural Committee of St. Demetrius Mr. and Mrs. Club, Parish Council Member, Director and Co-ordinator of Cultural Committee; [hon.] Gold Medal Award in Music; [pers.] He who attempts to write poetry has the desire to unveil all or part of their soul, for it is the soul that moves the pen.

KOVILIC, DANILO
[b.] August 16, 1982, Chicago; [p.] Maryann, Nikola; [ed.] 7th grade, Mary, Seat of Wisdom; [occ.] Student; [memb.] Mary, Seat of Wisdom Band, Track Park Ridge District Baseball, Brown Belt (Karate), Student Council (2 yrs.); [hon.] Band Awards, Karate Championship Trophies; [pers.] The key to life is honor, perseverance, and love, for only the strong survive.; [a.] Park Ridge, IL

KOWASIC, MATTHEW GEORGE
[pen.] Matthew George Kowasic; [b.] December 6, 1969, Charleroi, PA; [p.] George and Elsie Kowasic; [ed.] St. Tikhons Orthodox Theological Seminary, California University of PA; [occ.] Program Assistant for Meukilly Retarded and Physically Handicapped Indiv.; [memb.] Council for exceptional children; [hon.] Many awards for volunteering at Hospitals, Prisons and Hospice Work; [oth. writ.] Currently about 50 poems that were written to help me deal with depression. Prayers written in the Eastern Orthodox Traditional Style.; [pers.] My poems were catharsis for my personal well-being. I hope that those who read them may find a ray of hope in times of despair, and thank God above all for my talent.; [a.] Fayette City, PA

KOZUSZKO, KRISTI ANNE
[b.] December 18, 1958, Burbank, CA; [p.] Clare Vana Kozuszko, John Kozuszko; [ed.] Bachelor of Science Marketing, California State University, Northridge; [occ.] Writer; [pers.] My poem is a gift of inspiration - for me and for you.; [a.] Los Angeles, CA

KRANZLEY, SCOTT HAMILTO
[pen.] Travis Spark; [b.] January 27, 1961, Philadelphia, PA; [p.] Louis S. Kranzley, Doris H. Kranzley; [ch.] Biancha Charne Kranzley; [ed.] Henderson High School, The Pennsylvania State University, West Chester State University; [occ.] Juvenile Correctional Counselor, The Devereux Foundation, West Chester, PA; [hon.] Dean's list, Pennsylvania women's club short story contest winner - 1978.; [oth. writ.] Poem published in supplement to boy's life magazine, short story published in the Pennsylvania women's club magazine; [pers.] This poem is dedicated to the memory of my uncle, Arthur S. Kranzley, who showed me great love and caring in my youth. I strive to guide and inspire the hearts and minds of today's wayward youth.; [a.] Coatesville, PA

KRAUSS, STEPHANIE
[pen.] Stephanie L. Krauss; [b.] June 7, 1983, Boston; [p.] Cheri Zunick, Scott Zunick; [ed.] Baker School, currently enrolled in 6th grade; [occ.] Student; [memb.] Activities - town travel soccer team and town basketball team. Enjoys tennis and swimming and of course writing poetry.; [hon.] D.A.R.E. essay award winner 1st prize in the town wide event. Honor roll student; [pers.] I have always loved to read and write poetry and I was greatly influenced by a child's garden of verses by Robert Louis Stevenson.; [a.] Chestnut Hill, MA

KREBS, ALETHA
[pen.] Aletha Krebs; [b.] November 25, 1946, Austin, Texas; [p.] Ollie and Margarette Wagoner; [m.] James Krebs, October 23, 1965; [ch.] Muzette Krebs, Melody Krebs; [ed.] High school, with Addt'l courses in childrens writing, and other subjects; [occ.] Homemaker; [memb.] New Century club (Pres.) Elgin writers club, A.L.J.C. Dist. ladies auxiliary, Dist. coordinator A.L.J.C. for articles for T.A.W.; [hon.] Reader's choice in poetic eloquence; [oth. writ.] Several poems and articles published in today's apostolic woman and apostolic witness, poems and articles in poetic eloquence.; [pers.] Nature, family and God are important to me and I try to reflect them positively in my writing.; [a.] Elgin, TX

KRIEGER, JOAN
[b.] December 11, 1926, New York, NY; [p.] Arthur and Leona Stone; [m.] Murray Krieger, June 15, 1947; [ch.] Catherine Leona and Eliot Franklin; [ed.] Montclair State University and Ohio State University; [occ.] Graphic artist and author; [memb.] AAUW, Laguna Beach Museum of Art, UCI Town and Gown, UCI Faculty Associates; [hon.] UCI Friends of the Library 1994 Book Award, Achievement award UCI Faculty Associates, Purchase Award from Columbus Museum of Art; [oth. writ.] Touching Places, Foreign and Familiar (book by Fithian Press, 1993), "The Mandolin Hangs on the Wall," (short story), Chariton Review 1992, Epigraph to Poetic Presence and Illusion, 1979, "Varieties of Aesthetic Experience" (translation). In The Problems of Aesthetics.; [pers.] I am excited by the challenge of combining the art of the word and the art of the visual image. I am currently working on graphics to accompany the poems on which I am presently working.; [a.] Laguna Beach, CA

KRZISKE, PHILLIP R.
[b.] June 5, 1964, St. Joseph, MI; [p.] Margaret Bowen and Michael Krziske; [ed.] Parkway west senior High, Ballwin, MO./ National Business Institute, Decatur, GA.; [occ.] Automotive Technician; [oth. writ.] Several poems, some published in school magazines mostly unpublished personal works.; [pers.] The poem included in this book "with love in mind" was written especially for Kelly A. Richards. I would like to thank her for giving me back motivation and meaning to my life.; [a.] Stone Mountain, GA

KUBIK JR., PAUL
[b.] August 24, 1984, Fort Benning, CA; [p.] Paul and Judy Kubik; [ed.] Currently in 5th grade at Harmony Hill School - Cohoes, NY, will be attending St. Ambrose School - Lathan, N.Y., in September '95; [occ.] Student; [hon.] Participant in 1993 Cohoes City School Dist. Math Contest. Have been the recipient of various school awards including, Math, Spelling, Social Studies and attendance.; [pers.] I have played soccer for over 6 years and now I also play hockey. For 3 years now I have been an alterboy. My family is most important to me.; [a.] Cohoes, NY

KUBIK, JULIE A.
[b.] March 10, 1977, Bridgeport, CT; [p.] Joseph and Linda Kubik; [ed.] St. Joseph High School; [occ.] Student; [hon.] Yale Book Award, National Honor Society, Principal's Honor Roll; [oth. writ.] Several poems published in school's Amaranth Literary Magazine, and 21st Century Newspaper; [pers.] It is the privilege of every artist to find the miraculous in the common, it is the duty of every artist to share this gift with others.; [a.] Shelton, CT

KUCHARSKI, KAREN
[b.] November 22, 1980, Windsor, Ontario; [p.] Beverly and Richard; [ed.] Currently in grade 9; [occ.] High School Student; [hon.] Academic award grade 3, language arts award grade 8. I was in the top 25% in gaus math contest for grade 8, students sent from the university of waterloo.; [pers.] I write deep thoughts and feelings straight from my heart, in fluenced by things and feelings in my life.; [a.] Windsor Ontario, Canada

KUEBLER, JOANN G.
[b.] January 22, 1954, Oceanside, NY; [p.] A. John Crue, Grace M. Crue; [m.] James G. Kuebler, September 8, 1979; [ch.] Kathryn Jo and Kevin John, 2 step-children: Kimberly Ann and James Michael; [ed.] Life is an education, some college, graduated an airline-secretarial school, and worked (8) years for a railroad.; [occ.] 100% dedicated mother and Homemaker (a.k.a. - chief cook and bottle washer); [oth. writ.] Never publicly shared (yet); [pers.] A special thanks to my sister, Sue, for having me help her memorize poetry when I was in 3rd Grade! (She was in 10th grade at that time). I've loved poetry ever since. "Poetry is so psycho-therapeutic!"; [a.] Clifton, NJ

KUGLER, ETHEL FLORENCE
[b.] August 13, 1943, Brooklyn, NY; [p.] Robert and Anna Sloan; [m.] Gustan A. Kugler, January 4, 1987; [ch.] Lori, Kim Lori, Michael, Stephen; [ed.] Eastern district H.S. Brooklyn, N.Y.; [occ.] Customer service Rep., Ins. Co.; [memb.] Attends, abundant life christian center, edison, N.J.; [pers.] My poetry is written for the glory of God and for every wounded spirit.; [a.] Bridgewater, NJ

KURTZ, SARA A. SEWEL
[pen.] Sara Kurtz; [b.] March 5, 1962, Spartanburg, SC; [p.] Ann W. Ward, James R. Ward; [m.] Warren "Bud" Kurtz, Jr., June 7, 1992; [ch.] Anna Marie, Matthew Lewis, Brian Monroe; [ed.] B.A. Western Illinois University; [occ.] Writer; [memb.] North Carolina writers network; [oth. writ.] Self published "Menagerie of the palm", 1994, Wilmington, NC.; [pers.] I am influenced by my personal relationships.; [a.] Hampstead, NC

KUTA, DARLENE M.
[pen.] Darcy; [b.] April 9, 1980, Chicago; [p.] Mr. Arnold Kuta; [m.] Mrs. Patricia Kuta, March 27, 1971; [ed.] Graduated from Mark Twain in 1994, going to Kennedy High School.; [hon.] Received Gold Medal for Gymnastics in 1992 from South Side Competition; [pers.] Enjoys helping out at Park District during summer vaca-

tion, loves softball, volleyball, basketball, loves school, will be going to NASA in Alabama for space camp summer of 1996 for her education.; [a.] Chicago, IL

KUTZNER, DENNIS L.
[b.] December 30, 1951, Garrett, IN; [p.] Richard and Joann Kutzner; [m.] Carol S., July 26, 1970; [ch.] Kristine Carol (Kutzner) Reeze Karla Dianne Kutzner; [ed.] 1970 DeKalb High School Grad. 2 yrs 1970-72 College Indiana Univ. (Ft. Wayne) License to preach School, Depaw Univ. 1970; [occ.] Denominational executive (Calony Mintrics, Inc. Int'l; [memb.] Calvary Ministries, Inc., International, Bd of Directors, Global advance; [hon.] National School choir Award, 1970, outstanding young men of America, 1970, 1976; [oth. writ.] Published military articles in Fort Wayne Journal Gazette, regular articles in organizational (CMI) Newsletter, "Together", poem, 1968 with Indiana Agriculture Dept.; [pers.] Attempt to provide practical helps to clergy and churches. When writing military items attempt to left out human interest stories; [a.] Fort Wayne, IN

KYARIMPA, ROSEMARY
[b.] Rukunairo District, South Western Uganda; [p.] Erasmus Tindaburize and Theresa Tibabugira; [ed.] Diploma in Secondary Education, Bachelor of Arts (Social Sciences) (on course); [occ.] Student (Mekerere Univ.); [memb.] Action for Development (ACFODE) Member; [hon.] First class Diploma in Secondary Education (English Language and Literature), Best Actress of the Year 1991-92 - Nkozi Theater Group (National Teachers' College Nkozi); [oth. writ.] Play: The Final Push, The Voice Within, The Beloved Son, Poems: What Beauty?, No More Sanity?, Love Mulled, these are unpublished works; [pers.] Within you is that which many a people label undesirable and that is that which makes you sublime; [a.] Kampala, Uganda

LABA, BENJAMIN
[b.] Perth Amboy, NJ; [ed.] Westside High School, Rutgar's School of Business Administration, Museum of Modern Art Film History with Iris Barry, New York University School of Film.; [occ.] Fur Salesperson-Customers; [oth. writ.] Associate of the Late Ephriam Katz, Author of "The Film Encyclopedia." Owns more than 2000 Books of Film Including 21 Biographies of Greta Garbo Published in "Films in revign," Author of "Funny Bunny", Biography of John Bunny, (1863-1915), First Internationally known American Film Comedian.; [a.] New York, NY

LADUKE, CRIS H.
[b.] October 26, 1953, Middlebury, VT; [p.] Kenneth and Marion LaDuke; [m.] Debbie K. LaDuke, April 17, 1987; [ed.] M.S. - St. Michael's College, B.A. - Johnson State College; [occ.] State of Vermont Employer Resource Consultant; [memb.] Vermont Air National Guards; [oth. writ.] Special poems for family and friends.; [pers.] "When my words convey emotional pleasure, then the true value of my writings is realized." My writings are influenced by and a result of a devoted, encouraging and understanding family.; [a.] Shoreham, VT

LADURANTAYE, TRACY
[b.] September 13, 1976, Ottawa, Ontario, Canada; [p.] Marcella and Clarke Ladurantaye; [ed.] St. Paul's High School, currently attending grade 12 advanced courses; [occ.] Student (full time); [memb.] Peer Mediation Program; [oth. writ.] Several poems and short stories published in school board newspaper; [pers.] 'Expressing your inner feelings on paper is an extremely effective way to relieve any personal stress or temptations.' Remain the same Andrea, Stephanie, Jim and Heather; [a.] Nepean Ontario, Canada

LAFURNO, PAULA MARIE
[b.] August 16, 1974, Bronx, NY; [p.] Gloria Picciano and Joseph LaFurno; [m.] Single; [ed.] I learn every day; [occ.] Writer of Children Lit, Singer, Poet, I also write novels and short stories; [oth. writ.] Two books of poetry "Inside me" and "Children of the Light" both unpublished.; [pers.] I hope to teach the world to neuture and create a better place for our precious children and fill people's hearts with love and heeling through the poignant emotions of poetry; [a.] Yankers, NY

LAINE, ALICIA TARICO
[b.] September 1, 1963, Phoenix, AZ; [p.] L. Frank Tarico, Alice Kuns Tarico; [m.] Paul A. Laine, P.T., May 21, 1988; [ed.] Coronado High, Scottsdale AZ Wheaton College, Wheaton IL American Graduate School of Internatl. Mgmt., Glendale AZ; [occ.] Health Care Marketing; [memb.] Thunderbird Alumni Assoc., A.F.A.A. Aerobics Instructor; [hon.] Phi Theta Kappa Honors Fraternity, Dean's List; [oth. writ.] Compendium of personal unpublished poetry; [pers.] Sparked by the creative flair of an elementary English teacher, I began writing at 9 and am influenced by nature and environmentalism; [a.] Palm Beach Gardens, FL

LALLEGORE, JAMES J.
[b.] May 15, 1924, New York City, NY; [p.] Sinon and Ellen Culligan; [m.] Yvonne B., January 11, 1987; [ch.] 2 Sons, Steven and Jeffrey, 4 Grandchildren; [ed.] Bronx H.S. of Science Utah State University University of Utah, Utah Technical College; [occ.] Instructor on-site training Programs; [memb.] Knights of Columbus, National Education Assn.; [hon.] Governors Craftmanship Award Utah 1978, Master Teacher Utah Technical College; [oth. writ.] I novel "Do you think you will ever go back"; [pers.] I have always been intrigued by the music of languages as seen and heard in their words of their poets. I am particularly fond of poems written with veracular; [a.] San Diego, CA

LAM, FIONA FAY
[pen.] Fiona Lam; [b.] December 10, 1979, Dallas; [p.] Rosalyn; [ed.] 9th grade student at Shepton High school in Plano, TX.; [occ.] Student; [memb.] National Honor Society (Junior) National Member - American College of Musicians 1989 to 86; [hon.] 1992 Renner Middle School Student of the Month 1990-91 Presidential Academic Fitness Awards, 1st Prize Dennisa Performing Art, Piano and String Competition; [pers.] In this poem, meaningless!, I wanted to serve God and try to glorify Him. Hopefully, I'll write more poems to glorify God with. In meaningless! I tried to reflect Solomon's views in Ecclesiastes.; [a.] Dallas, TX

LAMBERT, WILLIAM J.
[b.] December 24, 1919, Camden East; [p.] The late John S. and Winnifred Halland Lambert; [m.] Evelyn, September 21, 1977; [ch.] 3; [ed.] Very little - grade 8; [occ.] Propane Operator, Gardener; [memb.] War Amps of Canada; [hon.] Entered in "Poetry Elite" 1985 Anthology of Canadian Poetry "Nature's Bouquet" by W. J. Lambert Editor's Choice Award 1993 National Library of Poetry, Public Recognition 1939/45 Canadian Forces.; [oth. writ.] I wrote for a local newspaper for 2 years "The Poets Corner" I have 3 books on the market, Vol. 1-2-3 "Treasured Thoughts"; [pers.] Mr. Lambert, a lover of birds, flowers and all nature, now retired, looks back on his childhood years and all nature around him. Putting the love of "Nature" and life thoughts into poems.; [a.] Lyndhurst Ontario, Canada

LAMBIASE, GENEVIEVE T.
[pen.] Genevieve T. Lambiase; [b.] May 18, 1967, Staten Island, NY; [p.] Donald J. Tempone and Mary Anne McCormick Tempone; [m.] Nicholas Lambiase Jr., June 18, 1988; [pers.] I thank God for His grace and mercy and I believe all good things come from God. I give all the glory and honor to my personal Lord and Savior, Jesus Christ.; [a.] Plainsboro, NJ

LAMONT, LUMPKINS
[b.] May 3, 1974, Chicago, IL; [p.] Donna Johnson and Jimmie Johnson George Lumpkins; [ed.] Hyde Park Career Academy; [occ.] United States Marine Corps; [oth. writ.] Several poems and short stories not yet published.; [pers.] For these dreams we have not discovered. I have been influenced by Maya Angelou and my family tree.; [a.] Camp Pendleton, CA

LAMPKIN, JIMMY
[pen.] Foxxy Brown; [b.] February 22, 1978, New Orlean; [p.] Barbara J. Day; [m.] To young; [ed.] Currently attending Eldorado High School (11th Grade) Holticulture, Music Arts, Naval SROTC Training and Education.; [occ.] Music Producer; [memb.] Omega Gentz and Omega PSI PHI Fraternity, NJRSTC. Associates of Mease Management. Association of Naval Aviations. Riffle Drill Team with Arms.; [hon.] Honor and valor Award, Cadet of the Month, Cadet of the Quoter, CNET award, association of Naval Aviation Leaderpship Award, Graduate from Mini-boot Camp Graduate of Leadership Academy.; [oth. writ.] Set me free, as I sit and wonder, assessment of a Brutal crime, contreversy, what can I do, be happy, love no limit, lay a ways.; [pers.] I don't know why but every day I wonna cry to the rules that I went by. If I mean anything to you would it make everything alright. Life is a juice of many taste. Desert sands is dedicated to Antonio Kie 1977-1994 RIP; [a.] Las Vegas, NV

LANDSBERGER, ROBERT C.
[b.] February 11, 1930, St. Cloud, MN; [p.] Nicholas and Clara Landsberger; [ed.] BA Catholic Univ. of America Wash., D.C 1952 M.A Catholic Univ. of America Wash., DC 1953; [occ.] Parish Priest at St. Michael's Parish; [memb.] Motley, MN; [oth. writ.] Master's Thesis at Catholic U Wash., DC in Philosophy; [pers.] I love nature and gardening. I write poems as remembrances for High School Graduates.; [a.] Motley, MN

LANE, STEVEN
[b.] October 23, 1975, Darby, PA; [p.] Charles and Carolann Lane; [ed.] Haverford High School, Delaware County Community College; [occ.] Contractor; [pers.] To the person who made this writing possible. I love you Kerry, always; [a.] Havertown, PA

LANZA, MARY LO
[b.] April 11, 1918, Charleston, MO; [p.] William and Haddie Wright; [m.] Frank Lanza (deceased) for 29 yrs., September 8, 1951; [ch.] Phyllis and Terri, Grandchildren Jennifer, Bryan and Nicole; [ed.] Alma Mater University of MO, Columbia; [occ.] Twenty years, State of Missouri DOLIR, Administrative Secretary (retired 1991); [memb.] St. Joseph Cathedral United Daughters of the Confederacy AARP Capital Region Medical Center Auxiliary and Volunteers; [pers.] Retirement has pro-

vided the time and inspiration to record my thoughts and memories in my poetry.; [a.] Jefferson City, MO

LARKIN, ANNE
[b.] December 26, 1946, Troy, NY; [p.] Ann and (the late) Charles Palladino; [m.] David P. Larkin, April 22, 1972; [ch.] Christopher Larkin (age 17); [ed.] Candidate for BA in English, May 1996, possible combined B.A., MA., minor: Journalism, AAS-Bus Admin.; [occ.] Writer; [memb.] Golden Key Honor Society; [hon.] Honor Student at NY., State University of Albany, Dean's List, AAS. Degree in Business Administration with honors; [oth. writ.] Four poems published in North Country Anthology and several unpublished poems, short stories and prose.; [pers.] If your imagination carries you beyond your hope for today, then, and only then are your dreams attainable.; [a.] Colonie, NY

LASKOS, ROBERT J.
[pen.] Robert J. Laskos; [b.] June 14, 1942, Michigan; [p.] Jerry and Betty Laskos; [m.] Judy A. Laskos, June 28, 1980; [ch.] 3 boys, 3 girls 10-28 yrs. and 5 grandchildren.; [ed.] Turner (Elem), Tappen (Jr. High) Redford High School, Engr. courses and Henry Ford Engr.; [occ.] Sales Engr. for the Allar Co.; [memb.] Saint Mary's of the Hills Parish in Roch. MI., K of C 3rd and 4th deg., Parish Lector, CSA, Parish Founders Fund, Stewards for Tomorrow Prog.; [hon.] High Corp. Sales, Cubmaster Pack 1707 Troy, Northridge Award.; [oth. writ.] My first attempt!; [pers.] The good Lord has blessed me in so many ways that it seems natural to share these life feelings.; [a.] Troy, MI

LASLEY, JEFFERY
[b.] March 6, 1951, Louisville, KY; [p.] Edwin and Margaret Lasley; [m.] Michelle Lasley, November 19, 1974; [ed.] Louisville Male High School, Iowa State University; [occ.] Computer Consultant; [memb.] Dive Master; [a.] Rocky Hill, CT

LATIMER, DEBRA SUE
[pen.] Worth Wright; [b.] September 10, 1954, Tulsa, OK; [p.] Charles R. Latimer Sr. and Barbara L. Root; [ed.] Will Rogers High School, Tulsa Junior College, University of Tulsa; [occ.] International, Export Marketing Coordinator; [hon.] President's Honor Roll, Dean's List; [oth. writ.] Essay's, short stories, tributes and misc. poems.; [pers.] I always give thanks to God for the freedom in expression reflected within my writings or anything I create containing beauty.; [a.] Tulsa, OK

LAUMEYER, ROBERT L.
[b.] August, 31, 1932, Wolf Point, MT; [p.] Joe and Rose Laumeyer; [m.] Kathleen McGlynn Laumeyer, August 31, 1953; [ch.] Mary Runkel, Barbara Miher, Jean O'Leary, Robert A. Laumeyer; [ed.] Nasha Montana High School Northern Mt. College, Harre Mt. University of Montana, Missoula Mt. Arizona St. U., Tempe AZ.; [occ.] Retired Teacher and school adm.; [oth. writ.] Poems published in new voices of American poetry 1980 and 1987; [pers.] The only constant, that we know is that we live in constant change. The only limits to our being, is how far our thoughts will range.; [a.] Sun City, AZ

LAURENT, CONNIE
[b.] March 24, 1928, Mexico City; [m.] Gerard Laurent, September 30, 1946; [ch.] Michel, Pierre, Chantal, Marie - France, Genevieve; [ed.] British and American Schools, Mexico City, Seton Hill College, PA; [occ.] Teaching: Poetry Appreciation Course, Senior Centre; [memb.] Alpha Delta Kappa: International Honorary Sorority, Women Educators," American Society of Mexico, American Benevolent Society, Senior Centre.; [hon.] Sigma Kappa Phi: National Honorary Language Fraternity, Emeritus Professor Award, University of the Americas, Mexico; [oth. writ.] Poem in monthly publication from Alpha Delta Kapp International, Feature article on Poetry Evening in the American Benevolent Society Winter Quarterly, poem in Spring Quarterly.; [pers.] I am interested in human nature, in its strengths and weaknesses, its yearnings and hopes. Thus, my poems are often a comment on human circumstance and on the complexity of human relationships, particularly on some of the life-forces which might affect or control them.; [a.] Mexico City, Mexico

LAWHON, MARK E.
[pen.] Mike Winters; [b.] May 25, 1954, Saint Joseph, MO; [p.] Ival V. Lawhon Sr. and Bertha Lawhon; [m.] Bobby Kay Lawhon, June 16, 1995; [ch.] Jeremy M. Lawhon; [ed.] B.S. Education, Social Science; [occ.] Tutor, counseling positions with educational talent search and upward bound; [memb.] Comedy Writers Assoc., PTA; [oth. writ.] Weekly editorials with the St. Joseph Telegraph (newspaper), photos published: Kansas "Masque" album 1975, Missouri's debut album 1977. Full color layout of The Who Concert News Magazine. Photo editor of college newspaper and yearbook photographer; [pers.] Whatever I do creatively, I strive for ultimate emotion, to achieve peak happiness, sadness, laughter, or reflection; [a.] Independence, MO

LAYTON, ROBERT ZACHARIE
[pen.] Bobby; [b.] February 12, 1985, Burnaby, BC; [p.] Ginger and Bob Layton; [ed.] Currently in grade 4

LAZOR, ANDREW NICKOLAS
[b.] December 17, 1950, Windsor, Ontario, Canada; [p.] Margaret, father deceased March, 1965); [m.] June 5, 1975; [ed.] 1 year Business Administration (St. Clair College, Windsor, Ontario, Canada), acquired Real Estate license (not active); [occ.] Truck driver; [oth. writ.] Yes, not yet released; [a.] Windsor Ontario, Canada

LEE, DIANA
[b.] June 7, 1972, Toronto, Ontario; [ed.] Business Administrations - Marketing 3rd year; [occ.] Math Tutor, Vice President of the Core 3 Incorporated, Secretary; [memb.] Ontario Society for the Prevention of Cruelty to Animals; [hon.] Art award, office procedures, Designed and marketed my own product - a student dayplanner, Grade 6 piano and Theory Grade 1 Rudiments at Royal Conservatory of Music; [pers.] Being successful. "Happiness will always be in the air".; [a.] Mississauga Ontario, Canada

LEE, LATIA STARANDA
[pen.] Star; [b.] May 9, 1982, Florida; [p.] Linda Lee Jones and J.B.; [ed.] Sealey Elementary School, currently enrolled as a 7th grader Griffin Middle School; [occ.] Middle School student; [memb.] Neals Temple Church, Drama Club, Smoke Free Class 2000, Jr. Girl Scout Troop 34; [hon.] Principals Science Fair Award, Tropicana 4 H Public Speaking, YMCA Football Letter, Camp Wild Cat Physical Fitness, Vacation Bible School Recognition; [pers.] I have always been encouraged by my family. There is a writer in me trying to get out. Writers write.; [a.] Tallahassee, FL

LEE, SAMMY S.
[b.] April 27, 1930, Caroleen, NC; [p.] John L. Lee, Mable S. Lee; [m.] Mary Lois Lee, August 7, 1954; [ch.] Belina A., Jame R., Lorie A.; [ed.] HS grd., 2 year bus college; [occ.] Retired-lyric writer-inventor; [memb.] Hill Crest Baptist Church; [hon.] HS grd., 1954, Massey Bus College 1973; [oth. writ.] Lyrics - Be Merry, Child of Bethlehem, Santa Claus Is A Southern Boy, Christmas On The Bayou, Rainy Bow, Please Old Santa Man, Santa Couldn't Take It Anymore, Back When Santa Was Young, Santa's Star, Memo From Santa, Stevie The Star, Just Let Christmas Be, published 1992; [pers.] Cleaning people are the most important people in the world; [a.] Raeford, NC

LEEDOM, RUB
[b.] October 4, 1917, Pike, WV; [p.] Monna Lucas, Harve de Lancy; [m.] Paul W. Leedom (deceased), December 31, 1938; [ch.] Nancy Carol, Judy Lynne, Margaret Suzanne, Michael Paul; [ed.] Pennsboro High, Pennsboro WV, 1938 (high school); [occ.] Retired homemaker; [oth. writ.] Several poems but never published.; [pers.] My poems are my memories and love for the one's whom have touched my life and through my poetry I show my love to them.; [a.] Phoenix, AZ

LELAND, PHYLLIS J.
[b.] June 9, 1955, Plymouth, IN; [ed.] B.A., Indiana University, Bloomington IN 1977, M. Div., Andover Newton Theological School Newton Mass 1981; [occ.] Communications, Marketing Director; [memb.] Bay Area Career Women; [hon.] National Merit Scholar, Dean's List; [oth. writ.] Several articles published in newspapers. Assignment writer for 2 publishers. Edit and write for National Newsletter.; [pers.] The natural expression of life is to create.; [a.] Santa Rosa, CA

LEMBCKE, THOMAS C.
[b.] January 3, 1934, Appleton, WI; [p.] Clarence and Miriam Lembcke; [m.] Gayle, August 29, 1987; [ch.] Karen Sue Hoffman, James Alan Lembcke; [ed.] Lawrence College, Appleton, WI. B. Mus. Garrett Theological Seminary, Evanston IL. M. Div. University of Wisconsin - Milwaukee MSSW.; [occ.] Retired as Clinical Social Worker; [memb.] National Association of Social Workers, Academy at Clinical Social Workers, Board Certified Diplomate in Clinical Social Work; [hon.] Previously listed in Who's Who in the Midwest and Who's Who is the World the thanks Bodge, highest award in Girl Scouting; [oth. writ.] Articles in church publications, sailboat class magazine, music reviews for local paper and letters published in local papers in Michigan and Tennessee; [pers.] I have devoted my life to helping others enrich their lives, develop and justice in their own lives, in their relationships and society through working as a clergyman, marriage and family counselor, psychotherapist, lecturer, workshop leader, consultant and author; [a.] Clinton, TN

LENERT, KYRA LYNN
[b.] October 21, 1983, Vallejo, CA; [p.] Kevin D. and Pimpa Lenert; [m.] Not married; [ed.] 6th Grade, Dan-o-root II Elementary School Suisun CA 94585; [occ.] Child, Dishes, clean room, Mow Lawn; [hon.] Certificate from Suisun city D.A.R.E. program for poem. Honor roll Student Dan-o-root Elementary; [oth. writ.] "Dare To Take A Stand"; [pers.] Just like to put my thoughts in to poems.; [a.] Suisun, CA

LENGEL, BRAD
[b.] August 18, 1973, Kenmore, NY; [p.] Steve and Judy Lengel; [ed.] Mannheim American High, Andress High, University of Texas at El Paso.; [occ.] Sports Freelance Writer, El Paso Herald-Post.; [memb.] UTEP Spirit and Traditional Committee; [hon.] Dean's List, All-area honorable mention soccer player in Germany; [oth. writ.] Several sports articles and editorials published in the herald- post and in the University newspaper, the prospector.; [pers.] Favorite saying: Winners forget they are in a race. They just love to run.; [a.] El Paso, TX

LERCHE, MARILYN
[b.] October 1, 1929, New York, NY; [p.] Estelle and Irving Greenfield; [m.] Will Turner, November 30, 1985; [ch.] 3 sons, 5 grandchildren; [ed.] 2 yrs. College; [occ.] Management Sales and Actress; [oth. writ.] Many poems monologues for acting purposes, and outlines for T.V. program sitcoms; [pers.] I have always enjoyed all the arts especially acting and poetry and feel that all of life is enriched by the creative abilities of artists in any field.; [a.] Riverdale, NY

LEREW, MARK F.
[b.] October 12, 1948, York, PA; [p.] Paul and Paula Lerew; [ch.] Dawn M. Lerew; [ed.] Central York High, University of Alaska, Penn State University; [occ.] Chief; [memb.] Local 669 VA Road Sprinkler fitters - American Legion CCE; [hon.] Best Bar-B-Que for Muscular Dystrophy Fund Raisers; [oth. writ.] "Tracks of Man" Not yet published; [pers.] The only thing you shall ever get out of life is what you share or give away. Favorite Book, Cosmos - Carl Sagan; [a.] York, PA

LERNER, ARTHUR M.
[b.] October 1, 1956, Brooklyn, NY; [p.] Benjamin and Dorothy Sacks; [m.] Laurel, August 9, 1986; [ch.] Jason, Matthew, Keith and MacKenzie; [ed.] BS Suhy C Stomy Brook MS Sung C Stomy Brook MD Ave, NJ Rutgers Med School; [occ.] Physician; [memb.] AACS, PMS, PCMS, AMA; [hon.] Member - Who's Who in Medical Science 1991, Certificate of Merit, Mayor office - for outstanding charity work 1992; [oth. writ.] In search of the dream of other selected works 1992-1994; [pers.] For Ben - who allowed me to dream and was always there to pick up the pieces with all the love and understanding a father could give; [a.] Philadelphia, PA

LERTZMAN, KEN
[b.] December 11, 1956, Salt Lake City, UT; [p.] Joy and Morley Lertzman; [m.] Dana Lepofsky, September, 1987; [ch.] Savia Lertzman-Lepofsky; [ed.] BSC University of Manitoba MSE University of British Columbia Ph D University of British Columbia; [occ.] Assistant Professor forest Ecology, Management and Conservation; [memb.] Ecological Society of America Society for Conservation Biology Association of Professional Biologist of B.C. International Association for Vegetation Science Natural Areas Association; [oth. writ.] Various articles in technical journals of ecology and conservation, contributor of various books such as "The plants of Coastal British Colombia".; [pers.] I have a passion for experiencing me interplay between science and art. The poet with the greatest influence on my thinking is Marge Piercy.; [a.] North Vancouver British Columbia, Canada

LESTER, JOANN
[pen.] Joann Lester; [b.] November 15, 1943; [p.] Brooks McCoy, Birchie McCoy; [m.] Julius Lester Jr., April 29, 1961; [ch.] Randal, Sherry, Vanessa, Michael, Gregory, Christopher; [ed.] Hurley High-Hurley Va, Southwest VA Comm. College; [occ.] Homemaker; [oth. writ.] Poems published in local newspapers; [pers.] I seek to emphasize the ability of mankind to find good within himself. God is my inspiration.

LETCHWORTH, DANIEL JAY
[pen.] Daniel Jay Letchworth; [b.] October 11, 1963, Tampa; [p.] Norma Rumore; [m.] Roger Crouch (Lover); [ch.] Ryan and Erica; [ed.] Graduate of King High; [occ.] Barber; [oth. writ.] Societier Victim, Torn, This Child, Lonely, Ice Berge; [pers.] I've learned reality really does bite. So just smile and say I never did mind the little things.; [a.] Lakeland, FL

LEVY, SAMUEL L.
[b.] May 6, 1932, Twilight Hollow, PA; [p.] Samuel and Dorthia Levy; [m.] Ruth Balas, June 12, 1919; [ch.] Lorraine Ruth, Timothy James, (deceased), Jeffrey Alan (deceased); [ed.] High School Charleroi High School. 12 years; [occ.] Retired; [memb.] U.S.S. Coral sea C143 Association, Applachain Wagon Train Assoc., Wagoners, Rural Letters Carrier Assoc; [oth. writ.] This is my first stab at writing poetry.; [pers.] I hope to put my poems to music in the future as Jesus Christ is my Lord and savior I hope my poetry will glorify his name.

LEWIS, DOROTHY SMITH
[pen.] Dorothy Lewis; [b.] Memphis, TN; [p.] Charlie Smith, Dorothy M. Smith; [m.] Raymond W. Lewis, February 14; [ch.] Edward O. Smith and Vernon D. Smith; [ed.] Auburn High, Rock Valley College, Northern Illinois University; [occ.] Alzheimer's Specialist and Pediatrist, Cancer Specialist; [memb.] Jerusalem Missionary Baptist Church; [hon.] Rockford Head Start Policy Counsel 1975-1977, Rockford Day Nursery Fund Raiser of 1985; [oth. writ.] Several poems has been wrote and recited at some different churches, in Rockford, Illinois; [pers.] I'm people orient, I'm inspired by God, and my own trial and tribulation. I enjoy poetry of Eugene O'Neil, so well that I named my oldest son Edward O'Neil; [a.] Rockford, IL

LEWIS, HILARY
[b.] October 12, 1979, Belgium; [p.] Rebecca Jones and Sterling Lewis; [ed.] Currently a Sophomore at Soquel High School in Soquel, California; [occ.] High School Student and Volleyball Player; [pers.] I strive to write my poetry about my adolescent confusion that other teen ages can relate to. Nothing I write is fiction and that's because it comes from my heart.; [a.] Santa Cruz, CA

LEWIS, LEONARD L.
[pen.] Leanard L. Lewis; [b.] March 12, 1923, Kgn. Jamica, WI; [p.] Prince and Alice Lewis; [m.] Dorothy E., March 1, 1949; [ch.] Eleanor, Leslie, Milton, Winston; [ed.] One year six months college - no diploma. Dutchess Community and Mavist college.; [occ.] Retired Businessman; [memb.] Christ Church, Y.M.C.A. Youth Committee and Board Member. AMORE member.; [oth. writ.] Writer of short stories. Several published articles in local newspaper. (Poughkeepsie Journal.); [pers.] Having a great concern for humanity.; [a.] Poughkeepsie, NY

LEWIS, LISA RENEE
[b.] January 10, 1978, Saginaw, MI; [p.] Peggy and Theodore Desrosier; [ed.] Bridgeport Community High School; [oth. writ.] Several other poems written for an English class in High School.; [pers.] I'd like to thank my boyfriend Gary for inspiring me to write poems that have meaning to them.; [a.] Birch Bun, MI

LEYDEN, PATRICIA M.
[b.] Brooklyn, NY; [m.] John P. Leyden; [ch.] (4 daughters) Katharine, Casey, Margaret, Victoria; [ed.] Graduate of the Mary Lowis Academy, Jamaica, N.Y. and Queens College, Flushing, N.Y.; [occ.] United States Customs Officer; [oth. writ.] A customs affair, a full length suspense - thriller novel. St. James Place, also a suspense - thriller in final stage of completion.; [a.] Whitehouse Station, NJ

LIDDLE, WENDY RENEE
[pen.] Wen or Blondie; [b.] October 5, 1969, Towson, MD; [p.] Donald D. Liddle and Louise Liddle; [ed.] Parkville High and Aberdeen High in Maryland; [occ.] Marketing Home Improvements; [pers.] I love to write poetry because it makes people think and gives them an inner strength.; [a.] Clearwater, FL

LIEBERMAN, GOLDIE
[pen.] Goldie Lieberman; [b.] April 10, 1939, Philadelphia, PA; [p.] Rachel, Louis; [m.] Alan, August 20; [ch.] Richard, Lauren, Martha; [ed.] B.S. - Temple Univ., Masters of Ed., Reading Certif. - Univ. of PA, Curriculum Certif. - Univ. of PA; [occ.] Curriculum Coordinator - Horn School; [memb.] International Reading Association, Phila. Writing Project; [hon.] PA Finalist Tchr. of Year 1986, Rose Lindenbaum Tchg. Award, National Humanities Foundation Fellow, City Council (Phila.) honored for Excellence in Tchg., and contributions to the profession; [oth. writ.] Articles published by Research for Better Schools, poetry published in U. of PA., "The Voice" publication.; [pers.] We're here to serve, to learn and to establish a unity of spirit.; [a.] Philadelphia, PA

LINDIG, GLORIA
[b.] December 29, 1943, WV; [m.] Loren B. Lindig, October 20, 1962; [ch.] Loren B. Lindig Jr., John Paul Lindig; [ed.] High school; [occ.] Housewife; [memb.] Village Baptist Church, AARP; [pers.] My writings come from deep within. I enjoy poems and music. The Lord influences my thoughts and words.; [a.] Coshocton, OH

LINDSEY, MARY ANN K.
[b.] September 30, 1926, Kealakekua; [p.] William and Mary Kelli; [m.] Donald Robert Lindsey, December 2, 1944; [ch.] 3, William M. S. Lindsey (49), Vivian Lindsey Kuhia (42), Linda Ann Lindsey Wong (37); [ed.] Konawaena High School (1944); [occ.] Retired, Hawaiian Bitumuls and Paving Co. Dispatcher Lihue, HI, Hawaiian Telephone Co. Traffic Telephone Opr. Royal Hawaiian Air Service Station Mgr. Kahului, HI Duarte Sales and Service Sales Mgr. Lihue, HI; [oth. writ.] Songs composed for my children great grand children; [pers.] Wendy was a personal friend of mine, she worked part time for Hawaiian Bitumuls, and covered my office when I was sick or went on vacation. Through our busy working life we found the time to make time to go out to birthday luncheons together. We found the time to enjoy little things like boat rides, horse drawn wagon rides through an estate.

LINKS, MARIA M.
[pen.] Maria M. Links; [b.] October 24, 1935, Vienna, Austria; [p.] Dr. Ruddle and Margit Links; [ed.] England and U.S. 1 yr. Floriculture - Cornell Univ., 2 yr. early child Educ. Cornell Univ., 2 yr. Northampton Commercial College, Community, Greenfield College - A.A.; [occ.] At home with mother; [memb.] Roman Catholic Church U.S. Citizen; [hon.] Various scholarships after Ithacia High School to N.Y. State Colleges; [oth. writ.] Aphorisms and short poems with my own musical struc-

ture; [pers.] Played amateur Cello in family string- Quartet for 20 yrs. In poetry I try to lift the heart beyond the promises of this life to eternal happiness.; [a.] Northampton, MA

LIPPET, APRIL LYN
[pen.] Dagney Taggart; [b.] April 17, 1958, NY; [p.] Bob and Naomi; [ed.] Philadelphia College of Art; [occ.] Typesetter/Mac operator; [oth. writ.] "Resume of a Budget Conscious Philadelphia" - Welcomat, "Roller skating-more than a hobby" - view "Secret Notations of a Creative person", "April's Run Away Riddles - a Scrapbook of Typesetting and desktop Jokes"; [pers.] Think God thoughts and good things will happen because good things start with good thoughts; [a.] Collingswood, NJ

LIPTON, ALAN K.
[b.] March 9, 1958, Plainfield, NJ; [p.] Dr. Maurice Lipton and Miriam Lipton; [ed.] North Plainfield High School, Michigan State University, El Camino College, Los Angeles Harbor College, Diabla Valley College, University of California Berkeley; [occ.] Editor and Business Manager; [memb.] U.C. Alumni, Society for the Eradication of Television, Berkeley Creativity Salon, Invisible Theater Radio Workshop, Global Village Idiots; [hon.] National Honor Society, Phi Beta Kappa; [oth. writ.] Information sickness (A self-published magazine of original fiction, music reviews, and socia-political artwork). Music reviews and articles for bam, calendar, magazine, the daily California bay Area live. fiction and poetry for loose (Diablo Valley College); [pers.] Writing is a great gift for the expression of joy, rage, and the entire spectrum of Emotion in evert direction therefrom. The Power is in the Details, and in the use of Words as a give to Combine most other Artistic Media.; [a.] Berkeley, CA

LISKA, GERALD J.
[b.] January 22, 1939, Saint Paul, MN; [p.] Jerry J. and Marie J. Liska; [m.] Jean E. Liska; [ch.] Mike, Steve, Kirk; [occ.] Retired; [memb.] Disabled American Veterans (DAV), Military Order of the Purple Heart (MOPH); [a.] Kansas City, MO

LITTLE, JANET K.
[b.] June 11, 1912, White Sulphur Springs, WV; [p.] John Appleton Kessinger, Donna Virginia Gillesfice Kessinger; [m.] Rev. Haskin V. Little, June 15, 1940; [ch.] Christopher Mark Little, Michael Vincent Little and Jennifer Ann Little (Pinter); [ed.] Covington Virginia High School, Washington Univ. School of Music; [occ.] Traveling the world with my husband and writing and teaching on big ships - like QE2; [memb.] Saint Andrews Epispopal Church Heights Blvd., Houston TX., Member of Houston Apartment Assoc., Texas Apartment Assoc. and National Apartment Assoc.; [hon.] Ladies Golf Champion 4 years, Lampasas Texas, won Archery Tournament contest and Medal (Robinhood Medal the Greenbrier - White Sulphur Springs, W.VA. Am a semi-finalist in the National Library of Poetry - My Best Honor.; [oth. writ.] My book includes poetry, short stories, etc. Have not submitted it for publication. My poem Maui Whales to be published in "The Garden of Life" in the fall.; [pers.] Time us too shall cover if we do not leave a record of what we did, what we thought, what we believed. I do not have grey hair, I am perfectly healthy and happy. I am reader. I buy small houses and rent to families with children, after I restore them

LIUZZI, FRANK R.
[b.] March 12, 1974, Long Island, NY; [p.] Frank Liuzzi and Barbara Liuzzi; [ed.] William Floyd High School; [occ.] United States Marine Corps; [oth. writ.] Personal writings; [pers.] Writings should come from one's heart and soul, where they will be cherished forever.; [a.] Camp Lejeune, NC

LIZARRAGA, CARLOS
[b.] April 16, 1951, Mexicali, Mexico; [p.] Francisco Lizarraga and Maria Franco; [ed.] Imperial Valley College; [occ.] Delivery Driver Px-Drugstore North Hollywood CA; [pers.] A tearful sky, a hopeless love, a wounded spirit, and a vanished feeling of happiness, these are circumstances, that can bring about a melody of sadness to the mind.; [a.] Tujunga, CA

LOBUE, EDIT RUIZ
[b.] October 10, 1921, Melville, LA; [p.] Mary and Morris Ruiz (Deceased); [m.] Louis LoBue, Sr. (Deceased), June 8, 1948; [ch.] Louis and Keith; [ed.] Plaquemine High, Spencer Business College, LSU, and North Western University (Natchitoches); [occ.] Retired Nurse, Non-paid Editor, Forecast (Four page newsletter); [memb.] Presently, American Nurse, Louisiana and Baton Rouge District Nurses's Associations Past, American Heart and Several Non-Profit Organizations; [hon.] Northwestern U., Dean's List, EBR Publicity Scrapbook award, American Heart Assoc. La., Outstanding Contributions to Nursing, BRDN, Private Sector Initiative Commendation from the President of U.S., Ronald Regan, White House, 1986, Outstanding contributions to education for children in Louisiana, by the Superintendent of Education, 1986, Leadership in Nursing Administration from 1962-1981, Founding of Nursing Service Infection Control Committee, 1977 and Establishing an Infection Control Department for The Baton Rouge General Medical Center, 1981, Honored as a Pioneer in Hearts for Contributions to the Development of the Heart Program at the Baton Rouge General Medical Center, 1995. Listed in Who's Who in American Nursing, 1984, by the Society of Nursing Professionals.; [oth. writ.] No formal publications but messages written to Dept. managers and employees written in rhyme, and Poetry in the Oct. and Dec. issues of Forecast.; [pers.] I send messages and express my feelings in my poetry. I enjoy reading about music, flowers, birds, Nature, and love the have been beautifully done published poets.; [a.] Baton Rouge, LA

LOCKHART, VINCENT
[b.] September 11, 1914, Greenville, TX; [p.] William E. and Fannie Lee Lockhart; [m.] Helen Helton Lockhart, June 5, 1938; [ch.] William Welford Lockhart; [ed.] B.J.U. of Mo 1936; [occ.] Retired; [memb.] American Legion, Military Order of the World Wars, Rotary Club; [hon.] From US Army: Legion of Merit, Bronze Star Medal, CIA: Intel Medal of Merit, Cert. of Distinction; [oth. writ.] Author, Book of Military History, "T-Patch To Victory", Spy novel - "Dragons Yet to Slay"; [a.] Canadian, TX

LOMEN, ALLYN FREDRIC
[b.] January 14, 1957, Bemidji, MN; [p.] Arnold and Loraine Lomen; [m.] Joellen Kubista Lomen, May 4, 1985; [ch.] Alexander Michael and Aaron Patrick; [ed.] Bemidji High School, Bemidji State University; [occ.] Systems Analyst/Consultant, Orion Consulting Inc., St. Paul, MN; [memb.] Mount Olivet Lutheran Church, Minneapolis, MN; [hon.] Who's who among American High School Students, National Honor Society (1975) Graduated Cum Laude from Bemidji State University (1979).; [pers.] It is my goal, that my poetry and children's literature reflect the sameness of the human spirit. Despite our differences, we share the same fears, the same wants, the same dreams.; [a.] Burnsville, MN

LONG, FRANCES
[pen.] Liz Hampton; [b.] August 1, 1913, Atlanta, GA; [p.] Rev. and Mrs. H. W. Hampton; [m.] Elmer E. Long, September 27, 1938; [ch.] David (53), Linda (48), Denny (46), grandchildren: Monte, Gwen, Melani, Curtis, Stephanie, Mike, Rodney, and Natalie, great-grandchildren: Hunter, Heather and Amber.; [ed.] High school—grad. 1931 Wesleco High School, Wesleco TX, Massey Business College 1968; [occ.] Housewife, great-grandmother, gardener, and poet-writer; [memb.] Church, National Society of Poets; [hon.] Various Vocal Awards including 3rd place in Rio Grande Valley—Quartet, 1st Place Alto—Rio Grande Valley Area - 1931, Weekly Radio Performance on KCRC Enid OK. - 1931-1940, Church pianist, Sunday School Teacher; [oth. writ.] Various short stories, journals of travels through Jerusalem, and London, currently writing Autobiography.; [pers.] I am a very strong believe in God. He has been my friend all of my life, the best friend I have ever had. Anything that I have ever accomplished or might ever accomplish I give Him all the praise and the Glory. My family is very dear to me and has been a great source of love and support all of my life.

LONG, LISA A.
[b.] January 28, 1965, Springfield, MO; [p.] Clara, Charles; [m.] Jari Wilson, September 16, 1987; [ed.] Missouri Western State College; [occ.] Graphic artist, Local print shop, Topeka, KS; [memb.] NOW, ACLU, NGLTF; [oth. writ.] Poems published in several local and regional magazines and newspapers; [pers.] This poem was inspired by mom's recovery which she discovered through my example of my own recovery. She gave me life - I showed her how to live it.; [a.] Topeka, KS

LONG, MIKHAIL ANN MARSH
[b.] August 16, 1934, Kansas City, MO; [p.] F. Stayton and Margaret Jean Marsh; [m.] Deceased; [ed.] MA English Cal Poly - San Luis Obispo CA, BA English (cum laude) Calif. State-Bakersfield CA; [occ.] Formerly English Professor Cal Poly, and Questa College, San Luis Obispo, CA. Professor-Instructor-Travel and Trade Center Long Beach CA (International Trade); [memb.] Modern Language Association, Sigma Tau Delta - English Honor Society, Huntington Library-Reader; [hon.] President's Honor List - CSLUB 1990, Dean's Starr Award - CSUB 1989, Dean's List - CSUB all quarters 1989, Books donated to Questa College Library include chapters by Mikhail Ann Long.; [oth. writ.] Four poems "Under the Toadstool", "Untitled", "Haiku", "Interiors", Orpheus XVI 1989 — "Wavering, Witless, and Without Council: The Widow in the Eighteenth Century", "Seventeenth Century Women Poets."; [pers.] Whole existence based on love... Verse learned in Sunday School, never forgotten..... "Love, without ceasing, give, without measure, who can exhaust God's limitless treasure."

LONG, SARA SMALLWOOD
[pen.] Sara Smallwood Long; [b.] December 9, 1915, Montevale, NJ; [p.] Roderick F. Smallwood; [m.] Susan M. Smallwood (Sara Smallwood Long and Henry Along, 12/12/52); [ch.] No children; [ed.] Strawbenmuller Textile High School June 1935 (Diploma) (Sara Smallwood Long); [occ.] Retired; [memb.] NARFE (National Association of Retired Federal Employees); [pers.] I am a twin (sister) whose name is Laura M. Wilson and who lives in Honolulu HI; [a.] Honolulu, HI

LONGO, PHILI
[pen.] Philly; [b.] March 7, 1981, Rahway, NJ; [p.] Philip and Julie; [ed.] Attended Strawberry Patch Intro. Ed., Immaculate Conception, Franklin NJ, Bee Meadow, Memorial Jr., School - Whippany NJ; [occ.] Student, entering Whippany Park H.S.; [hon.] Most Favorable Football Player of Hanover Twp. "1992-93-94", 2nd honors; [oth. writ.] Also writes short stories and draws his own illustrations; [a.] Whippany, NJ

LOPEZ, CHRISTINE DANIEL
[b.] March 5, 1983, New York; [p.] Joann Carruci, Michael Lopez; [ed.] Junior High School, student on honor roll. 92 - average I.S. 119; [occ.] Student, gymnast; [hon.] Gymnastics, reading, writing, S.S., Science, good athlete etc.; [oth. writ.] Many others not published; [pers.] I plan to be a model or an actress. I really enjoy gymnastics. I also hope to be in the year 2000 olympics.; [a.] Glendale, NY

LOPEZ, DAVID MICHAEL
[b.] November 19, 1966, Merced, CA; [p.] Manuel J. Lopez, Mary L. Lopez; [m.] Single; [ch.] Joe, Juan, Abe, Tom, Martha, Lilia, and Ana.; [ed.] Modesto high School, Modesto Junior College; [pers.] The search is a lonely one, someday I'll fined her.; [a.] Modesto, CA

LORAH, KIMBERLY
[pen.] Kimberly Lorah; [b.] November 29, 1982, Allentown, PA; [p.] Shirley Lorah and Leroy Lorah; [ed.] 6th Grade, West Penn Elementary School; [pers.] I have been influenced by the people around me. (Family, friends, etc.) I play the organ for 4 years now, and love to read, write stories, and poems; [a.] New Ringgold, PA

LORENZ, LARRY K.
[Pen.] Killer (as in Lady); [b.] February 10, 1960, St. Louis, MO; [p.] Richard and Shirley Lorenz; [m.] Roxane Lorenz, June 16, 1984; [ch.] Danielle, Jake; [ed.] Riverview Gardens High School; [occ.] Machinist/ Trainer at Alco Controls, St. Louis; [memb.] Lodge #1345 I.A.of M.; [pers.] Do something in your life before your life does you in, so when you look back on your life and see where you've been..., you're satisfied! These are my words to live by.; [a.] St. Louis, MO

LOVELESS, MARTHA J.
[b.] November 28, 1950, Louisville, KY; [p.] Joseph and Rita Bischoff; [m.] Michael "Sandy" Loveless, June 19, 1987; [ch.] Beverlee, Jennifer, Donna, Donnie and 6 grandchildren; [ed.] Assumption High - American College; [occ.] Financial Planner, Financial Planning Instructor; [hon.] Outstanding Creativity Frito Lay, Outstanding Service Award, Resource Financial Group - Salesperson of the Year Frito Lay; [pers.] "Life is not a dress rehearsal!"; [a.] Louisville, KY

LOVOY, MICHELLE
[b.] March 24, 1973, West Covina, CA; [p.] Thomas and Patricia Lovoy; [ed.] Chaffey High School Victor Valley College; [occ.] Clerk; [hon.] A plague, and a short poems book my poem was publish in, the in sixty grade; [pers.] I believe that writing helps relieve the street of everyday life, and allows you to really analize your thoughts and feelings, and gives you a chance to know yourself better; [a.] Phelan, CA

LOWE, LAURA
[b.] January 27, 1968, Anaheim, CA; [p.] Ken Hamilton, Milly Fernald; [m.] Matt Lowe, May 28, 1994; [ed.] Clark High School, Cal State Fullerton; [oth. writ.] I've never been published but I've written over 300 poems; [a.] Riverside, CA

LUBERTO, AMY
[pen.] Amy Luberto; [b.] September 30, 1973, Pompton Plains, NJ; [p.] Janet Luberto, Lou Luberto; [ed.] Basic; [occ.] Veterinary Technician; [oth. writ.] 1 poem in American Anorexia, Bulemia Association of America; [pers.] This poem was written to free my feelings of a painful past. It is also a sign of a new dawn, it's time to awaken and enjoy life rather than take advantage of it.; [a.] Pompton Plains, NJ

LUCAS, TWILA JENA
[pen.] Jimmie Lee; [b.] September 18, 1976, Columbus, OH; [p.] William H. Lucas, Roberta Lucas; [ed.] Attending Ohio State University; [occ.] Student; [memb.] AASAC Community Church; [hon.] Who's Who Among Americans High School Students; [oth. writ.] Many other writings, but Farewell to You is the first one published; [pers.] The reason that a reason is a reason is behind a reason.; [a.] Columbus, OH

LUNGER, FLORENCE
[b.] May 31, 1920, Ohio; [p.] Mr. and Mrs. David Kilgore; [m.] Cary L. Lunger, June 19, 1938, April 19, 1980; [ch.] Patricia Canfield, David Eungard, Daniel Eungard; [ed.] Elysia High School Taledo University, Wakeman Elementary Schools, Ohio State University.; [occ.] Retired Nurse, and Vocational Teacher; [memb.] American Legion Auxiliary Senior Center of Sarasota, Arthritis Foundation Art Association; [hon.] Poems written for Fairs, and I am an artist, and have won several best of the show ribbons for my paintings.; [oth. writ.] Poems (The Bikers). (The Christmas Tree).; [pers.] I like to project human and real life happenings into my poems.; [a.] Sarasota, FL

LUNNIE, TONY LAWAYNE
[pen.] Tony Lawayne Saul Lunnie; [b.] March 23, 1969, Little Rock, AR; [ed.] ACES (Rook Master level) in the Education Part, Master ACES (15) schools and still studying 18 yrs+ (private schooling); [occ.] Photography (freelance); [memb.] ACES (Rook Master Education level) known as The ACE Educational Practice AEP; [hon.] Just being on my way to becoming an ACE 23 ongoing through the time method of study and research of ACES, and at the end, I will become councilmaster ACE; [oth. writ.] This is my first 1 and this is it besides researching ACES; [pers.] ACE Training and ACES is my life and I devote all my spare time devoting my life to ACES and to become a better person and ACES is the root of my life before I go or to anything else.; [a.] Little Rock, AR

LUPTON, ROBERT A.
[b.] July 31, 1974, Bayshore, NY; [p.] Shari Lee Warner (mom); [oth. writ.] Many other unpublished pieces; [pers.] This poem is thoughtfully dedicated to Christy M. Stewart. The light of day in my life of darkness. The only true love I've ever known.; [a.] San Angelo, TX

LYKENS, NICOLE
[b.] August 18, 1981, Trenton, NJ; [occ.] Student of Logan Middle School; [memb.] Girl scouts of America Gloucester County Soccer League; [hon.] 1987 Winner of the Tri County Authors Competition. Honor Roll student; [oth. writ.] "The Giant Fly" a short story. Other works published in voices.; [pers.] Write it from the heart. And you can't go wrong.; [a.] Swedesboro, NJ

LYONS, JAMES F.
[pen.] James F. Lyons; [b.] August 31, 1962, Long Island, NY; [m.] Angela R. Lyons, November 29, 1994; [ch.] 1 daughter; [ed.] H.S. grad, 1 year of Suffolk County Community College.; [occ.] Retired because of accident that resulted in losing my leg. I am a handicap person and trying to learn new things to do.; [oth. writ.] I've written many poems of many different natures but this here is the first I've ever tried to do something with.; [pers.] I used to be a Steel Labor Foreman up until 4/19/93 when an accident at work left me without my left leg above the knee. I've been going through many different changes mentally and physically, and I have to tell you that the entering and becoming a semifinalist in your contest is only the second time I've ever won out, something and the first since my accident. So I just want to thank you! Your letter was very uplefting to me at this time. Because of resent financially reason's, I would like a book if my writting is in it. Thank you again. You've really made me happy. And I would like to dedicate this poem to my wife and daughter and future children.

LYRENMANN, JAMES
[b.] October 27, 1966, St. Cloud, MN; [p.] John and Dolores Lyrenmann; [m.] Allison Lyrenmann, August 7, 1993; [ch.] Robert John; [ed.] Greenway High School, Glendale Community College; [pers.] I look for inspiration in everything I see I dedicate my writings to my family, my wife and to my son.; [a.] Phoenix, AZ

MACDOUGALL, BOB
[b.] September 1, 1947, Donkin, Nova Scotia, Canada; [p.] Duncan and Ebbie MacDougall; [m.] Beverly MacDougall, September 23, 1988; [ed.] Donkin-Morien High, Radio College of Canada (Toronto); [occ.] Building Contractor, Wildlife Artist; [hon.] Paintings selected for publication by Regional Hospital Fund Raising Board.; [pers.] Good poetry has the power to reveal that which lies beyond intellect and language.; [a.] Donkin Nova Scotia, Canada

MACEACHERN, KEVIN ALEX
[b.] August 29, 1974, Nova Scotia, Antigonish; [p.] Colin and Heather (mother deceased); [ed.] Dr. John Hugh Gillis Regional High School; [occ.] Packer at a processing plant; [memb.] Member of Nova Scotia 1993 Canada games softball team (won Silver); [oth. writ.] Several poems dealing with a variety of subjects from my girlfriend Paula to trees on to destruction, including my father; [pers.] Need not look farther than the people and places around you to be inspired for poetic expression, but it doesn't hurt to have an imagination; [a.] Antigonish Co. Nova Scotia, Canada

MACIOCE, VIRGINIA F.
[b.] September 10, 1947, Pittsburgh, PA; [p.] John and Irma Macioce; [ed.] Registered Nurse B.A. Business Management, M.A. Public Administration; [occ.] Hospital Administrator Oakland, CA; [memb.] American Organization of Nurse Executives Organization of Nurse Executives - California, American College Health Care Executives, Sigma Theta Tau; [hon.] Tribute to Women in Industry, San Jose, Ca., Nurse Fellow, Wharton School of Business, University of PA; [oth. writ.] Professional articles; [pers.] My deepest thoughts transcribe to words on paper, but the magic of my spirit and soul stays hidden to all but one person.; [a.] Campbell, CA

MACKAY, G. HARRIS
[b.] October 15, 1924, Cape Breton; [m.] Wilhelmina,

August 12, 1948; [ch.] 6; [ed.] VIII; [occ.] Retired; [oth. writ.] Short Stories, many poems, some taken from the Bible the sea, mining etc.; [pers.] I try to paint a true picture of current and past happenings.; [a.] Glace Bay Nova Scotia, Canada

MACVICAR, SHANNON
[b.] July 28, 1976, Guelph, Ontario, Canada; [p.] Suzanne Burt Macvicar and Garry Macvilar; [ed.] Our Lady of Mount Carmel Secondary School, applied to Sheridan College for Fall of '95; [occ.] Student; [memb.] Am member of Mississauga Shotokan Karate Club; [hon.] English Honors Award Presented 1994.; [pers.] A good friend once told me... "Fairy tales do come true if you believe in yourself enough." And I've believed ever since.; [a.] Brampton

MADEY, BETTY SCRIVNER
[pen.] Betty; [b.] June 1, 1933, Lepanto, AR; [p.] Henry Scrivner, Ruby Scrivner; [m.] Richard Madey, January 2, 1990; [ch.] Mark O'Banion, Michael O'Banion, Melba O'Banion; [ed.] Mississippi County High Sch, Arkansas State University, Akron University - OH; [occ.] Retired Elem. Teacher; [pers.] Most of my poetry are stories written in rhyme dealing with happiness, sadness and humor.; [a.] Newport News, VA

MAINA, BENNETT
[b.] February 6, 1971, Kenya; [ed.] Imani International HS, Kenya, Lafayette College, Easton Pa - Mech., Engr., and English double major; [occ.] Student; [memb.] Theta Chi; [pers.] I feel a super-natural bond between me and my universe, my poetry struggles to describe it... Influence range from Ted Hughes to Langston Hughes.; [a.] New Rochelle, NY

MALADY, JUSTIN P.
[b.] July 12, 1909, Watertown, NY; [p.] P. H. Malady, L. C. Malady; [m.] Mary Gould Malady, April 26, 1943; [ch.] Judith Anne Malady; [ed.] High School; [occ.] Retired; [hon.] Awards: Merit, Golden published: 20 books - 1000 poems; [oth. writ.] One collection "Sea Scapes" amateur and hobbyist; [pers.] "Let my poetry speak"

MANDEVILLE, L. ROSE
[b.] August 29, 1928, Indio, CA; [p.] N. Frank and Lillian Mandeville; [ed.] High School Student; [occ.] Part-time, M.D. receptionist; [memb.] Kingman Chamber Swingers Select Choir; [hon.] College Choir Scholarship; [pers.] Jump in - think about it later...; [a.] Kingman, AZ

MANDL, SABIN
[b.] November 24, 1943, Germany; [ch.] Christine, Nicole; [ed.] College (Alternative Medicine in Germany) Real Estate Broker - Canada; [occ.] Assistant Editor German Language Newspaper; [oth. writ.] Weekly Column plus 2 to 3 articles each week, mostly human interest stories in "Kanada Kurier", German Language Newspaper; [pers.] We humans are pupils of life. Whatever we do not learn the first time we'll have to experience again until we get it right! We never stop learning!; [a.] Mississauga Ontario, Canada

MANERI, SHIRLEY M.
[pen.] Shirley Coffey; [b.] August 12, 1963, Berea, KY; [p.] Berry J. Coffey, Luther Coffey; [m.] Michael V. Maneri, December 27, 1990; [ch.] Keven Michael, Kara Jordan; [ed.] Berea Community High School; [occ.] Homemaker Free Lance Writer; [oth. writ.] Several poems and articles; [pers.] Writing is the reflection of the beauty we have within.; [a.] East Islip, NY

MANGES, BOBBIE JO
[b.] December 2, 1979, Waco, TX; [p.] Loyce Manges, Gary Manges; [ed.] I am a freshmen at Axtell High School; [memb.] Member of Axtell Baptist Church, of Axtell Texas; [pers.] Life is a great thing so don't let it pass by you.

MANILLA, ELAINE K.
[b.] June 24, 1923, Covington, KY; [p.] William and Blanche Kathman; [m.] Charles E. Manilla, October 22, 1949; [ch.] Charles A., Steven M., Christine Palmer, Philip J. and Marie E. Manilla; [ed.] La Salette Academy Covington, KY, some college courses; [occ.] Retired; [memb.] Huntington Museum of Art; [hon.] Award of merit certificate for poem "Echoes of Love"; [oth. writ.] "Only today is ours" "My sister my friend" "Celebration of Spring" Manna from Heaven" "Circle of Love"; [pers.] Because of my deep faith most of my poems have a religious orientation.; [a.] Huntington, WV

MANN, CHARLES
[pen.] Chaz; [b.] February 17, 1924, Niagara Falls, NY; [p.] Chas M. and Ida Perry; [ed.] Niagara Falls H.S. Antioch College (4 yrs); [occ.] Gallery Mgr.; [memb.] Am. Mus. of Natl. Hist., Natl. Geographic Society, American Legion, AARP, NCPSS and M., World Wildlife Fund, Democratic Party; [hon.] National Library of Poetry, World of Poetry, N.Y.S. Regents Honor Grad.; [oth. writ.] "Pedigree poems and other genealogy", "Letters from a Pedigreed Past", "Pedigree Cook Book", essays, articles, short stories, dramatic adaptations; [pers.] "I attribute my age to chance". "I no longer let small minds unduly influence me."; [a.] Sag Harbor Long Island, NY

MANN, KATHRYN A.
[pen.] Kalexandra; [b.] February 19, 1950, Hudson, NY; [p.] Henry and Jane Wagner; [m.] Burton Bud Mann, January 20, 1981; [ch.] Ronald, Amy, Jason and Jamie, daughter-in-law Heather, grandchildren Danielle and Jonathan; [ed.] Hudson High School Albany, Medical School of Nursing; [occ.] Home maker; [oth. writ.] Local papers and magazines; [pers.] Problems shared are problems halved, but the joy of writing shared is joy tripled.; [a.] Hudson, NY

MANN, SUSAN
[b.] February 26, 1949, Johnson City, NY; [p.] Charles Lundy, Marjorie Lundy; [m.] John Mann, March 18, 1972; [ed.] Catholic Central High School, attended College of St. Rose, US Army Lab Technician; [occ.] Shipping and receiving clerk in a metal plating shop; [hon.] Honor society CCHS Letter in Sports; [oth. writ.] None Published; [pers.] Life is all about change; [a.] Aurora, CO

MANNAN, HASHAN M.
[pen.] Bunaw; [b.] March 1, 1950, Bangladesh; [p.] Abdul Bari, Sufia Bari; [m.] Shahanara Mannan, May 30, 1982; [ch.] Mahjabin Sabiha Konckon, Suraiyajabin Sania Nikkon; [ed.] GED (P.S.-9, Bklyn, NY); [occ.] Self Employed; [memb.] Executive member of the Noakhali Welfare Association; [hon.] A freedom fighter fought in the Liberation fight of Bangladesh with Pakistan in the year 1971. An active member of mayor's volunteer cop, NYC; [oth. writ.] Several poems published in Bengali newspapers and magazine. One small book named - "303" (three not three) already been published in Bengali in 1988; [pers.] I valued humanity and try to reflect it in my poem. I have been greatly influenced by great Bengali poet "Robi and Nazrul"; [a.] Brooklyn, NY

MANTOOTH, KENNETH WADE
[pen.] Dot Matrix; [b.] October 19, 1960, Oklahoma City, OK; [p.] Joe Jerry Mantooth (deceased), Bertha Mantooth; [m.] Cheryl Ann Mantooth, November 16, 1981; [ch.] Delana Jo Mantooth Walker; [ed.] Chickasha High School, Western Oklahoma State College, Liberty University (Lynchburg, VA), AS - Business; [occ.] Bookkeeper - Hollis Church of Christ Child Care Worker, Westview Boys Home; [memb.] Advisory Board Member: Christian Camp: Lu-jo Kismif, Church of Christ; [hon.] 1989 Outstanding Young Men of America; [oth. writ.] Several poems not published.; [pers.] My desire is to be a servant to God, to my wife, to my daughter, and to others. I am fortunate to be in contact with. When I fail, my hope in Christ lifts me up!; [a.] Hollis, OK

MARCY, JONI L.
[b.] March 18, 1963, Lexington Park, MD; [p.] Beverly and Harry Boggs; [m.] Brian Marcy, June 16, 1984; [ch.] Christopher Scott, Alexis Danielle, Taylor Dianne; [occ.] Secretary to the Controller, Mine Safety Appliances, Pittsburgh, PA; [memb.] Trinity Evangelical Lutheran Church, The Make-A-Wish Foundation of Western Pennsylvania; [pers.] My writing reflects personal experiences-mostly concerning our two growing children and our deceased daughter, Taylor.; [a.] New Kensington, PA

MARSHALL, CASEY
[b.] April 21, 1979, Hayward, CA; [p.] Kenneth and Irene Marshall; [ed.] Currently a sophomore at Irvington High School in Fremont, CA. We are a California distinguished school; [memb.] (Do magazines count?) Rolling Stone.; [hon.] Fifth grade academic achievement award. That's about it.; [oth. writ.] Various short stories and essays that have won praise from peer and superiors.; [pers.] A true sign of intelligence is if one can look at themself understand who they are, and even to laugh a little at themself.; [a.] Fremont, CA

MARSHALL, MICHELE M. M.
[b.] March 29, 1974, Worcester, MA; [p.] Mary Dolan and James Gallo; [m.] Dwayne J. Marshall, May 21, 1994; [ch.] Corey William Michael Marshall; [ed.] Shephard Hill Reg. High, Quinsigmond Community College, Worcester State College.; [occ.] Homemaker; [memb.] Special Olympics Coach; [oth. writ.] Many unpublished poems and short stories; [pers.] "Life is a room filled with many locked doors, leaving you to find the right keys to unlock your dreams." Michelle Marshall I would like to thank my husband for seeing me through those rough times and my son for letting me see life a whole new way.; [a.] Pomfret Center, CT

MARTIN, BILL
[b.] July 27, 1948, Houston, TX; [ed.] University of Texas at Austin: BBA 1976, MBA 1979 Texas A&M University: Ph (but no) D!; [occ.] Consultant, CPA; [memb.] Unity Church of Christianity, Houston Storytellers Guild, The Comedy Gym of Texas; [pers.] I strive to see humor everywhere, the goodness in everyone, and, to never meet a stranger.; [a.] Houston, TX

MARTIN, DANIEL
[b.] February 26, 1957, Hayti, MO; [p.] John and Naomi Martin; [m.] Chris, December 20, 1975; [ch.] Two Boys

and Two Girls; [ed.] High School; [occ.] Pro Horse Trainer and Horse Show Health Food Business; [memb.] President of American Mule Association Sr. Dir world wide mission outreach; [pers.] Foot prints in the sands of time what we say and do is what we will live behind say something good; [a.] Boise, ID

MARTIN, KATHY
[pen.] Kat; [b.] July 26, 1973, Hildebran, NC; [p.] Jerry and Judy Martin; [m.] Patrick Rayfield (fiance), September 16, 1995; [ed.] East Burke High, Appalachian State University, Academy of Artistic Hair Design; [occ.] Housekeeper and laundry personnel - quality Inn, Boone, NC; [memb.] Alpha Phi Omega; [hon.] Distinguished presidents awards (president of Key Club in High School) Presidential Academic Fitness, Who's Who; [pers.] To Patrick - You are the one I waited my whole life for - I Love You! My flower will remain forever.; [a.] Boone, NC

MARTIN, MICHAEL R.
[b.] June 26, 1950, Detroit, MI; [p.] Millard and Donya; [m.] Cynthia, March 29, 1969; [ch.] Michael R. Martin II; [ed.] Allen Park High, MCC College; [occ.] Auto Mechanic; [pers.] Poems I believe, come from the heart and soul. Yet, they are only words, till they touch anothers heart or soul. Only, then are they a poem.; [a.] Warren, MI

MARTIN, NORMA ANNE HOLMES
[b.] May 19, 1948, Long Branch, NJ; [p.] Geo. W. Holmes, Lillian D. W. Holmes; [m.] Jimmie L. Martin (deceased), July 2, 1966; [ch.] Karen Anne Martin, Cynthia Annette Martin Bridges; [ed.] Long Branch Senior High, Monmouth Adult Education Commission, Brookdale Community College, Port Authority of NY and NJ electrical apprenticeship program-women in maintenance; [occ.] Electronic Technician Test Technician but presently Warehouse Shipping Receiving; [memb.] VOCAL (Virginia Organization of Composes and Lyricists); [hon.] Patent/ Copyright on a game I created including handbook "Cocoanutz - A Game" patent, Copyright on "Surface Mount Telecam Audio Video Adapter Model #NA001HM, including instruction sheet.; [oth. writ.] Other poems, songs with lyrics, 2 finished manuscripts, 2 incomplete manuscripts, all the above unpublished and unsubmitted; [pers.] An Edgar Allan Poe Fan. In the past, I've experienced inspirational thoughts, rushing through the fabric of my being, transforming into words unknown to me, just moments before. I continue to experience such moments, and would like to share the words, but leave the interpretation to the reader.; [a.] Richmond, VA

MARTIN, SARA
[b.] December 2, 1980, Omaha, NE; [p.] Gary and Connie Martin; [ed.] Walt Disney Elementary, Walnut Grove Elementary, Pleasant Ridge Elementary and Pioneer Trail Junior High; [occ.] Secretary for Swanson Gentleman Hart, Inc.,; [hon.] Honor Roll, Academic Achievements; [oth. writ.] Poem published in the book "A Moment in Time"; [pers.] My poems are written from my most inner feelings. Poetry comes to me naturally and I believe that you can not force it. To have a great poem, write the feelings that come from your soul.; [a.] Overland Park, KS

MARTIN, SCOTT
[b.] December 25, 1967, Dover, DE; [p.] Gregory Martin, Betty Martin; [m.] Nancy Martin, March 25, 1994; [ed.] Delaware Technical and Community College, Wilmington College; [occ.] Full-time member of Delaware Army National Guard; [hon.] Valedictorian, Summa Cum Laude, Delta Epsilon Rho, Dean's List, Distinguished Graduate of Military Training; [oth. writ.] Several poems and short stories, articles published in military newspaper.; [pers.] All of my work is influenced by the state of the world and the happenings of mankind; [a.] Honolulu, HI

MARTINEZ, JEAN B.
[b.] March 19, 1946, Seine Bight, Belize, CA; [p.] Augustine and Olga Martinez; [ed.] Austin High School University of New Orleans; [occ.] English Teacher St. Mary's Academy, New Orleans; [memb.] Sister of the Holy Family (Religious Community) Alpha Theta Epsilon Honor Society University of New Orleans; [hon.] Honors Certificate 1978, Belize Teachers' College - Belize, CA Academic Excellence 1988 - UNO; [oth. writ.] Two poems published in College Literary Magazines; [pers.] I strive to reflect an appreciation of simple things of life in my writing. I have been greatly influenced by contemporary poets.; [a.] New Orleans, LA

MARTINEZ, LUPE
[pen.] Lupe Martinez; [b.] August 15, 1939, Tumacacori, AZ; [p.] Benino and Lenor Martinez; [m.] Divorced; [ch.] Della M. Ruiz; [ed.] 8th Grade; [occ.] Self-employed in family run mini market.; [memb.] St. Ann's Parish; [hon.] Although I have never received any type of awards, I consider, very much, to have had my daughter a great honor. She has given me a grandson which I also put very highly on my honor list.; [pers.] Being that my father was an immigrant of Mexico, and a citizen of the United States (where he met my mother), myself as well as my four brothers and two sisters were born citizens of the United States. I want to express my gratitude to others in same situations that enjoy and appreciate the many freedoms of our great country.; [a.] Tumacacori, AZ

MARTINEZ, MARA RUTH MEDINA
[pen.] Mara Ruth; [b.] January 1, 1982, Acapulco, Mexico; [p.] Ruth Medina; [ed.] Lamberton, Loesche, Baloli, and soon to be George Washington High School; [occ.] Student; [hon.] I got distinguish and meditorious awards several times, I got an award in 5th grade in Central High School for helping and starting a group to help handicapped children.; [oth. writ.] Several published poems.; [pers.] Life is truly hard to accomplish, but we all must try our best, and strive harder. Give life a chance - before you give up on yourself!; [a.] Philadelphia, PA

MARTINS, KAREN ANTUNES
[b.] April 12, 1977, West Islip, NY; [p.] Mario Martins, Guida Martins; [ed.] St. Anne Brentwood Ross High School; [occ.] Student; [memb.] Future Business Leaders of America, POW WOW, National Honor Society; [hon.] Math and Biology award, varsity letter in soccer and football, FBLA business procedures 1st place; [oth. writ.] Poems and short stories, articles for school newspaper; [pers.] I believe you have to stand for something or you'll fall for anything.; [a.] Brentwood, NY

MARTYN, LO NEDA IRENE
[pen.] Marty Martyn; [b.] March 8, 1940, Detroit, MI; [ed.] High School class of 1958, Berkley High School - Berkley Mich.; [occ.] Retired after 24 yrs with the United Postal Service; [memb.] Church - Our Lady of La Salette Berkley Mi, Michigan Organization of Human Rights; [hon.] Best female athlete of my graduating class. Was a felician nun Sr. Mary Jeffrey from 1966 through 1968 in Livonia Mich., many softball and bowling awards; [pers.] If only you could have known my Daddy, he was my best friend. What is sad is...so many, too many children are growing up without a Daddy. No guidance, no memories I feel truly blessed.; [a.] Berkley, MI

MASCIA, KATHLEEN
[pen.] Kaity Kay; [b.] April 17, 1951, Minneapolis, MN; [p.] George and Dorothy Weins; [m.] Raymond Mascia, January 16, 1988; [ed.] Senior, San Jose State University, English Major and Accounting Major. Working toward a BS in Business with and concentration in Accounting.; [occ.] Bookkeeper, Jr. Accountant; [oth. writ.] Sixty five poems for my titled poetry volume "Loving You". My poetry collection offers insight, introspection and perspective on perhaps the strongest human emotion (love). I have survived not only the pain of separation and loss of my one and only true love but also the cataclysmic joy of being in love once again with Michael who's the love of my life twenty years ago.; [pers.] My poetry focuses upon love, it's joys, dangers, complexities and promises. Through my poetry, I hope you will feel the pain of separation loss and defeat. My poetry will also provide an important view on a deeper both personal and universal, simplistic and impossible. I feel that "Loving You" will provide empathy and solace to those of you who mourn lost love and it will speak to the abandon of those passionately enamored. My poetry could boundaries of age, reason and categorization. I hope that loving you will find an appreciative audience.; [a.] Los Altos, CA

MASON, ELOUISE COLLINS
[pen.] Mary Louise McCoy; [b.] December 17, 1945, Pembroke, VA; [p.] Morriston and Hazel Collins; [m.] Jerry David Mason, June 19, 1978; [ch.] Dennis W. Love and Laura A. Hilton; [ed.] Giles High School New River Community College; [occ.] Disabled; [memb.] Ephesus Free Will Baptist Church, Choir and Ladies Aux; [oth. writ.] Book, A Heart Full of Sunshine and Rainbows, quite a few personal poems for others. And a poem, What is Beauty in a Moment in Time.; [pers.] Live the best you can, love with all your heart, give the most you can for God, and everything will be alright.; [a.] Blounts Creek, NC

MASON, NATALIE R.
[b.] September 10, 1982, Findlay, OH; [p.] Marigail Mason; [ed.] 7th grade student; [occ.] Student; [memb.] St. Michaels Church; [hon.] Honor Roll student; [pers.] I love to read, write short stories and poems.; [a.] Cherokee Village, AR

MASTERVICH, JENNIFER
[b.] March 13, 1976, Maryland; [p.] Mark and Carol Mastervich; [ed.] Central Dauphin H.S., Harrisburg Area Community College; [occ.] Student; [pers.] Everything is possible to those who strive and believe! The worst of your life comes when you look for it, the happiness in life comes on searching and believing in it.; [a.] Harrisburg, PA

MASUDA, MARJORIE
[b.] July 7, 1945, England; [p.] John and Florence Almond; [m.] Glen Masuda, December 17, 1984; [ed.] Educated in England; [occ.] Housewife and volunteer; [memb.] Chedoke - McMaster Hospital Volunteer Assoc.; [oth. writ.] Several Poems and a few short stories; [pers.] I live for today and try to help people whenever I can.; [a.] Hamilton Ontario, Canada

MATA, RICHARD
[pen.] Santowns; [b.] November 28, 1969, Kinshasa, Zaire; [p.] Mata Kilolo Victorine and Mbamu Francois; [ed.] Official School of Limete (Zaire), - Elementary School (Kinshasa/ Zaire), Industrial Technic Institute of Gombe-Sainte Marie (Kinshasa/ Zaire), Winding Electric motor College (Zollikofoen-Bern/ Switzerland); [occ.] Cartoon Art Drawing; [memb.] Jordan Brant Membership, Mont Carmel Church of God; [oth. writ.] Songwriting and Moviewriting Secondary school of Lumumba (Kinshasa)

MATE, BECKY
[b.] December 28, 1953, Denver; [p.] Keith Gettings and Barbara Glazier; [m.] Randy Mate, April 25, 1982; [ed.] Lincoln High, Colorado State Univ (1 year), Colorado Univ. (1 year), Celebrity Center; [occ.] Writer and business owner; [memb.] Glendale Chamber of Commerce, Scientologists for a better Community, International Association of Scientologists, National Parks Assn, Citizens for an alternative tax system.; [hon.] Honorable mention award for a short story submitted to Ron Hubbard's writers of... The Future Contest; [oth. writ.] Published greeting card ideas, short sci-fi stories published, poems published, advertising and press release copy printed; [pers.] Poetry is a great medium for expressing the insight I've learned about the human condition. Much thanks to the National Library of Poetry for their support of the arts!; [a.] Glendale, CA

MATIUSHYK, RENEE
[b.] August 18, 1977, Alberta; [p.] Bob and Frances Matiushyk; [ed.] Ardrossan Jr/Sr High School, NAIT.; [occ.] Student; [hon.] Many academic achievement awards and leadership awards throughout high school.; [oth. writ.] Poems published in stepping stone, an anthology of students literature in Canada; [pers.] I believe that being able to write is a release of the emotions you feel inside. It lets you and you readers escape for a few moments and look inside themselves to see what they feel.; [a.] Sherwood Park Alberta, Canada

MATTHAI, CATHY BACH
[b.] September 16, 1957; [p.] Byron and Marty Bach; [ch.] Richard T. Matthai, Jr.; [occ.] Vice President, Underwriting for IAT; [oth. writ.] Many unpublished; [a.] Nashville, TN

MATTHEWS, DEANA LOUISE
[pen.] Rose; [b.] July 9, 1985, San Francisco, General Hospital; [p.] Louise Avery, Jimmy Matthews; [ed.] Dr. Charles R. Drew; [occ.] Student; [memb.] Chess Club Church. Thank you club; [hon.] Conflic Manager; [oth. writ.] Personal poetry collections; [pers.] My brain told me to sit think and write. Also God told me, and myself.; [a.] San Francisco, CA

MATTHEWS, HELEN M.
[pen.] Bubbles; [b.] January 5, 1935, Kentucky; [p.] Taylor Dora Johnson; [m.] John Smith, October 27, 1951; [ch.] Joyce, Debbie, Lynne, Lisa Smith.; [ed.] 4th Louisville Ky; [occ.] Home care; [memb.] Pentacostal Church; [oth. writ.] None published write for myself.; [pers.] The poem is how I feel we grow old alone no one to care. I, a soft hearted person; [a.] Madisonville, KY

MATTHEWS, JAMES O.
[b.] April 20, 1921, Goliad, TX; [p.] O.C. and Mary G. DuBois Matthews; [m.] Maria Teresa, February 19, 1986; [ch.] James O. Jr., Melanie Kay and Hilary Fagan, Jose Gerardo and Maria Emilia; [ed.] Graduate St. Mary's Univ.-San Antonio (BBA) Northwestern Univ. Chicago (MBA) Minor: Christian Theology; [occ.] Retired Mortgage Banker; [memb.] Confraternity of Christian Doctrine Kiwanis (retired), Mortgage Bankers of America, Bluebird Volunteers (Hospital); [hon.] Four Distinguished Flying Crosses Eleven Air Medals - Three Unit Citations, 1 from Winston Churchill, P.M. 2 from President F.D. Roosevelt Personal Acknowledgement from Pope John XXIII in 1960, for theology teaching in CCD; [oth. writ.] None published nor offered to be published. (This poem was inspired by the reunion of my fifth grade teacher, a Nun who is now retired in Our Lady of the Lake Univ. in San Antonio, after 63 years. She was 25 and I was ten at the time she taught me.) Sister Anicetus Koronosky, born September 1906.; [pers.] Knowledge is the basis of all production and education is the entry door to knowledge.; [a.] San Antonio, TX

MATTOCK JR., RICHARD C.
[pen.] Richard C. Mattock Jr.; [b.] January 12, 1937, East Detroit, MI; [m.] Monica Zinger; [ed.] Pikes Peak Community College Colo, Spgs. Co.; [occ.] Retired USAF Law Office Manager.; [hon.] Poems published in 1978 concours for American Collegiate poets, 1984, 1989-1990 in the World of Poetry Contest, 1989 sparrow grass Poetry Forums Treasured Poems of America and 1995 poetic voices of America hardcover anthology. Poem titles: "The Gift Of Sight", "I Surrender all", "Lord, Draw Me Closer To You Each Day", "God's Time Of Refreshment" and "The Art Of Thanksgiving"; [oth. writ.] Numerous poems published in local newspapers, church bulletins and newsletters, and local Christian writer's newsletters.; [pers.] "I try to provide encouragement, hope and wisdom through my poems. My writings are an extension of my ongoing worship and conversion experience. I consider myself extremely privileged to share my God-given gift with others and want readers to be able to see the rainbows through the storms of life."; [a.] Colorado Springs, CO

MAYER, LILLIAN
[b.] July 4, 1908, Waldeck, MN; [p.] Clarence and Sarah Chute; [m.] Harley Mayer, June 15, 1929; [ch.] David, Willard, and Carol Jean.; [ed.] Two years T. College (High School) graduate of nursing school, Colo. Nursed many years.; [occ.] Retired; [hon.] Two Letters in Basket Ball in Aitkin High School Valedictorian of nursing class.; [oth. writ.] Poetry is a very private matter with me - few friends or family know of my many poems. All I have ever sent to papers have been printed.; [a.] Spokane, WA

MAYES, WANDA L.
[pen.] Wanda L. Mayes; [b.] October 25, 1958, Detroit, MI; [p.] Charles and Dorothy Mayes; [m.] Divorced; [ch.] Rhonda and Janelle Mayes; [ed.] Bachelor of Science Wayne State University in Detroit, MI; [occ.] Labor Relations Specialist; [memb.] Delta Sigma Pi, Cass Tech Alumni, New Grace Missionary Baptist Church; [oth. writ.] Several poems; [pers.] I am determined everyday to see the poetry that God has created in my life.; [a.] Detroit, MI

MAYNARD, RUTH ELLEN
[b.] July 5, 1947, New York; [p.] Frank and Helen Goodenough; [m.] Sidney Perry Maynard Sr., March 10, 1979; [ch.] Staci Rene, Jennifer Sue; [ed.] Camp Verde High, Cosmetology College; [occ.] Second Assistant Mgr. Anne Klien, Sedona, AZ; [memb.] Arizona Women Bowling Assoc.; [hon.] 1st place for High game Bowling Award Scholarship for Cosmetology School.; [oth. writ.] A poem that was a Eulogy for my nephew Doug.; [pers.] I express my feelings in the writing of poems. It's a great release of emotions - great therapy!; [a.] Camp Verde, AZ

MAYS, FREDA M.
[pen.] Freda M. Brockington Mays; [b.] March 24, 1936, Kansas City, MO; [p.] Ferdinand and Ruth Brockington; [m.] Divorced; [ch.] Donald, Terry, Brenda, Helen, Freda, Schenita, Marilyn and Monica; [ed.] High School, 2 years College currently enrolled in Real Estate classes to obtain agent's license; [occ.] Retired Government Emp. current a volunteer tutor for the Adult Literacy Program, San Diego; [memb.] I am a member of the Queen Sheba Order of the Eastern Star; [hon.] Won suggestion awards for former job at Trans World Airlines, and won awards Water Utilities Department; [oth. writ.] I have written a collection of poems that I would like to have published in the near future.; [pers.] My writings are based on personal and true experiences of my life and others in and around my family. My writings help me to heal and understand some of the good and adverse situations that have arisen.; [a.] El Cajon, CA

MCARTOR, JOY DAWN
[b.] May 7, 1947, Mexico, MO; [p.] D. W. and Vineta Stuart; [m.] Charles Marvin McArtor, October 22, 1977; [ed.] Nursing diploma from St. Luke's School of Nursing, Denver CO, Graduated 1968; [occ.] Registered Nurse, Director, Quality Management, St. Joseph's Hospital Hot Springs, AR; [memb.] Arkansas Assn. for Healthcare Quality, National Association for Healthcare Quality Trinity Church Hot Springs, AR, The Witness Productions; [pers.] Writing poetry is an act of worship for me, and my work is reflective of my relationship with God through Jesus Christ.; [a.] Hot Springs, AR

MCBOGG, DUNCAN
[pen.] Duncan McBogg; [b.] September 20, 1975, Denver, CO; [p.] Pamela McKenzie, Bruce McBogg; [ed.] Graduated Wheat Ridge High School, 1994; [occ.] Student; [a.] Wheat Ridge, CO

MCCAFFREY, MICHAEL ANTHONY
[b.] December 19, 1955, Mobile, AL; [p.] Ray and Antonia McCaffrey Jr.; [ed.] B.A. English, Writing Spring Hill College Mobile, AL; [occ.] Active duty U.S. Navy; [memb.] Knights of Columbus, American Legion; [hon.] Published short story: Salute magazine, a submission under consideration for Southern Living Magazine; [pers.] I try to reflect what people feel in their heart, but can't always express in words.; [a.] Smyrna, GA

MCCARTHY, NANETTE METSKAS
[pen.] Nanette McCarthy-Olson; [b.] August 18, 1949; [p.] George and Della Metskas; [m.] Gary Olson, August 15, 1992; [ch.] Sean, Collin and Lauren McCarthy; [ed.] Riverside - Brookfield High School: graduated with Honors in English, B.A. Honors in Liberal Arts and Science at Univ. of Illinois, M.D. Northwestern University Chicago Residency: Michael Reese Hospital Chicago Medical College of Wisconsin; [occ.] Psychiatrist; [pers.] I have urged my patients to express their feelings by writing. I have always done so "privately". This is the first time I have submitted one of my poems.; [a.] Wisconsin Rapids, WI

MCCARTY, DR. L. DWIGHT
[pen.] DeMac; [b.] May 23, 1958, Los Angeles, CA; [p.] Johnye Lea McCarty and Lisbon Carroll McCarty; [m.] Jennifier Ann Sepion (fiancee), 1996 (pending);

[ch.] John Dwight, Keith Jerome McCarthy (Brother); [ed.] Loyola High, University of California, Irvine, Los Angeles College of Chiropractic, Certified Personal Fitness Trainer.; [occ.] Chiropractic Physician, Chiromed Wellness Group, Garden Grove, CA; [memb.] Kappa Alpha PSI Fraternity, California Chiropractic Association, American Chiropractic Association; [hon.] King Kok Scholarship, President's Council of Physical Fitness Award Recipient, Delta Tau Alpha Academic Honor Society for Chiropractic; [oth. writ.] Microtouch Therapy Self Healing Manual, Health and Fitness Articles in Local Newspapers.; [pers.] My early life experiences serve as the muse which allows me to express myself poetically.; [a.] Los Angeles, CA

MCCAULEY, BRIAN T.
[b.] December 10, 1941, Elkader, IA; [p.] Lester and Elisabeth McCauley; [m.] Dale M. McCauley, June 10, 1990; [ch.] Kathleen, Brendan, Morgan; [ed.] BA - Southern Illinois University JD - University of Wyoming; [occ.] Attorney served in Colorado State Senate, 1987-91; [memb.] Bar Associations, Chambers of Commerce, Romanian American Freedom Alliance, local civic boards and advisory boards.; [oth. writ.] Poetry preciously distributed only among family and friends. Published "Mani" in the search, So. Ill. Univ. Press, 1970; [a.] Thornton, CO

MCCLAIN, MOLLY CATHERINE
[b.] October 5, 1977, Kettering Hosp., Kettering, OH; [p.] Larry and Linda McClain; [ed.] I am presently a senior at Beavercreek H.S., next fall, I plan to go to Wright State Univ., to study Elementary Education.; [occ.] I baby sit for a ten year old baby and I am a car hop at the Root Beer Stande.; [hon.] Throughout my years in school I have received many types of awards and accomplishments.; [pers.] In the poems that I write I try to base them on my age level. Many was written containing real life problems I see everyday around me.; [a.] Kettering, OH

MCCLURE, ANNIE L.
[b.] April 28, 1925, Navarro County, TX; [p.] J.H. Rivers and Idah Rivers Williams (deceased); [m.] E. Dean McClure (deceased), June 4, 1943; [ch.] Renee' Anne McClure; [ed.] Ennis High Mountain View College; [occ.] Retired; [hon.] Dean's list. Outstanding Academic Achievement Award; [oth. writ.] Book of poetry "Memories in Flight". Essay, "Family History of World War II."; [pers.] Dedication to each endeavor. Words hold a special magic to stir the imagination and cleanse the soul.; [a.] Duncanville, TX

MCCOMBER, SHARON MARIE
[pen.] Sharon Marie McComber; [b.] December 4, 1958, Saint Louis, MO; [p.] Walter and Ethel McComber; [ed.] Grade 12th Hazelwood Central H.S., MO Baptist College and Baptist Bible College 5 yrs of college in Elementary Education. I transferred and lost credits and that is why I did not graduate.; [occ.] Childcare and Nanny work. I love kids!; [memb.] 1st Baptist Church of Harresteri n St. Charles, MO; [hon.] Being a winner in this contest! 12th grade and 1st 2 yrs of College on Honor Roll.; [oth. writ.] Several other poems. My poetry revolves around God and His great love and how we should love each other and love the life God, gave us. The Lord is precious and gracious.; [pers.] I love the Lord very much. I was adopted at the age of 8 months and on my deathbed from malnutrition. My adoptive parents loved me and gave my (along with God) a second chance at life. I am fine now with only minor health problems but I am determined to do something with the life God gave me.; [a.] Saint Peters, MO

MCCOMBS, NANCY MARIE
[pen.] NanRie; [b.] March 9, 1942, Terre Haute, IN; [m.] Theodore Arnold McCombs (Deceased), October 31, 1960; [ch.] Darrell 30, David 28, Penny 26; [ed.] Degree in Business Mgmt., Degree in Accounting, Three years Architectural drawing, two years creative writing. Languages spoken: German and Persian; [occ.] Graphic Artist for Federal Emergency Management Agency status equals GS-11 Grade C-1; [oth. writ.] For the local paper and a couple of magazine articles. Short stories - The victim, Directions, A Perfect World, Deliverence, Thanksgiving and Solutions. Poetry published in the Amherst Society - A Child's Plea, Life of a Flower, Keeper of the pain and Love Lost. I am also taking courses to write children's stories.; [pers.] I have spent the majority of my existence loving the arts in all its various forms and truly enjoy being a small part of this very rewarding field. I spent a large portion of my married life traveling to Europe and some of the Asian countries teaching English as a Foreign language.; [a.] Douglasville, GA

MCCORMICK, DAN
[pen.] Dan McCormick; [b.] October 9, 1950, Everett, WA; [p.] Milton and Mina McCormick; [m.] Vicki McCormick, May 1, 1971; [ch.] April Christina, Jeremy Daniel; [ed.] Snohomish High Everett Community College; [occ.] Carpenter; [oth. writ.] Many poems that range from the romantic to the humorous, which so far, I have not offered for publication.; [pers.] Inspiration is important. This I receive from Vicki, my wife of 24 yrs. Someday I hope to write a song for her.; [a.] Sedro Woolley, WA

MCCORMICK, WILLIAM SAMUEL
[pen.] William Samuel McCormick; [b.] May 10, 1932, Great Falls, SC; [p.] Will and Mamie McCormick; [m.] Barbara N., October 18, 1955; [ch.] Billi, Joei, Bobbi, Nicki, Ronni, Timmi, Becki, Ricki; [pers.] Southerner, High School Athlete, Marine Corp - Korea, Army - German Occupation, Husband, Father 2 yrs. Vietnam, Divorced, Traveler, Historian, Student and Philosopher.; [a.] Chester, SC

MCCOY, TRACIE
[pen.] Emily Savannah Blake; [b.] April 28; [pers.] Grandpa's Jar Song is dedicated with all my love to Michael A. Harrison...only those who touch my soul become a part of it.; [a.] Kansas City, MO

MCCRACKEN, JUDITH K.
[pen.] Judy Rubidge Koller; [b.] May 4, 1928, Wilmington, DE; [p.] Joseph Peter Koller, Mary Victoria Rubidge Koller; [ch.] James Garth Peiffer Jr., Carroll Anne Peiffer Dayton; [ed.] Wilmington Friends School Beacom College University of DE (BS); [occ.] Retired elementary teacher from Tower Hill School. Wilm - DE; [memb.] Union Methodist Church (Bear, DE) Mt. Cuba Astronomical Observatory, Inc. Life Member of D.F.H.A. Symphony Orchestra; [a.] Hockessin, DE

MCCRAW, GREGORY D.
[pen.] Gregory D. Dawson; [b.] May 24, 1972, California; [p.] Vivian and Ralph McCraw; [ed.] Springstead High School; [occ.] Marina Worker; [pers.] "What man cannot see with the naked eye I strive for and write"; [a.] Spring Hill, FL

MCCULLOCH, DARREN
[pen.] Dmitri Brighton, Deidrich Goth; [b.] March 19, 1979, Poughkeepsie, NY; [p.] Michael McCulloch, Stephanie McCulloch; [ed.] Currently enrolled as Sophomore in Westwood High School (Austin, TX); [memb.] SACA (Student against Cruelty to Animals); [hon.] Honored with the Language Arts Award at age 12 by Hyde Park Elementary School in New York.; [oth. writ.] Poetry published in School publications; [pers.] Somewhere between heaven and hell, love and hate, fantasy and reality lies total ecstasy... find it.; [a.] Austin, TX

MCCULLOCH, HOLLI TYLENE
[pen.] Holli Tylene McCulloch; [b.] May 19, 1981, Eugene, OR; [p.] Rusty and Nancy McCulloch; [ed.] I am in 8th grade, I go to High School next year. I desire to continue my education and attend college; [occ.] School, babysitter and enjoying each day and learning more of life and myself; [memb.] I am going to be trying out for J. V. Rally Soon. Hopefully I will make the squad.; [hon.] Student Honor Roll. My friends constantly ask me to write poems for them. To me that is an honor.; [oth. writ.] I write many poems, and short stories. I got a poem published in our school newspaper. Which I also am a part of publishing and write articles for.; [pers.] When I write, I write about my experiences and the way I'm feeling. I love to write!; [a.] Eugene, OR

MCDANIEL, MARY
[pen.] M. McDaniel, Mary McDaniel; [b.] July 2, 1938, Hoxie, KS; [p.] Fred Conard, Helen Conard; [m.] Lee McDaniel, May 23, 1958; [ch.] Shannon Lynn, Heather Lynn and Elisabeth Lynn; [ed.] Sheridan County High School Hoxie, KS, Bethany College, Lindsborg, KS; [occ.] Unemployed; [memb.] First Presbyterian Church Alton, IL, Deacon of Said Church, Choir member and active in committees of that church member of St. Louis Marfan Chapter; [oth. writ.] One published poem in a religious newsletter. Have written a total of 16 poems but they are unpublished except for the one; [pers.] All of my writings are born out of love of family, remembrances and of my faith. I hope I convey to readers the beauty that is around them.; [a.] Alton, IL

MCDONALD, ALAN
[b.] July 12, 1954, Sydney; [p.] Shirley, Harry, and Moly, Leo; [m.] Anna Karayannis, February 3, 1991; [ed.] Arts Bachelor, James Cook University.; [occ.] Seeking Literary engagement; [memb.] Self realization fellowship; [hon.] N.B.; [oth. writ.] Poems, unpublished; [pers.] Language links mind and soul, and is a sacred enactment of the presence in dwelling every being. Poetry is distilled remembrance of God.; [a.] Encinites, CA

MCDONALD, CAROL SUE
[pen.] Sue McDonald; [b.] May 7, 1943, Ottawa Co, OK; [p.] Loyed Jones, Imogene Jones; [m.] Widow (Duane McDonald); [ch.] Karen Mullens, Sheila Storey, Ann Berry Lee, Charlotte Miller; [ed.] South High, Wichita, KS. Bryan Institute, Wichita, KS; [occ.] Sheetmetal Assy, LearJet Corp. Wichita, KS; [memb.] First United Methodist Church Administrative Board, Wichita, KS C.A.S.A. volunteer (roots and wings); [pers.] I love writing poems of life in general, about people and places.; [a.] Wichita, KS

MCDONALD, SANDY
[b.] March 7, 1944, Jefferson County, IN; [p.] Mr. and Mrs. Aubrey Field; [m.] William McDonald, November 12, 1966; [ch.] Rohn Alan Buffington, Joseph Scott McDonald; [ed.] 12th; [occ.] Psram Sylvania; [oth. writ.] Songs and poems

MCFADDEN, AMBER
[pen.] Paul Harrison; [b.] August 26, 1971, Oklahoma City, OK; [occ.] Secretary for Lee Roy Jordan Redwood Lumber Co., Dallas, TX; [oth. writ.] Although poems are my favorite and easiest thing to write... I hope to write a great fiction novel someday.; [pers.] I think I am one of those people who are in love with love. As long as there is green grass, rolling hills and slow dancing in front of sunsets, I will always write.; [a.] Dallas, TX

MCFADYEN, MARGARET CAMERON
[b.] November 9, 1932, Taree NSW, Australia; [p.] Kenneth McFadyen, Ella McFadyen; [m.] James Ian McFadyen, 1954-1st and 1990-2nd; [ch.] Mecena, Roger, Phillip, Dianne, Gregory; [ed.] Primary School Level only Diplomas Australian College of Journalism The Writing School; [occ.] Company Director and Free Lance Journalist; [oth. writ.] Many poems, short stories; [pers.] I live in both Australia and Canada. For six months each I have a wide interest in Women's Affairs and Genealogy.

MCFEE, MYRA
[pen.] Myra Powell; [b.] January 5, 1928, Dorchester, New Brunswick, Canada; [p.] William and Helen Sollows; [m.] Lawrence McFee, October 14, 1977; [ch.] Karen, Frank, Bill; [occ.] Retired; [oth. writ.] Had a writing - What Happiness Is - published in small magazine.; [pers.] To Tommy - who first gave me the inspiration to seek and find below the surface

MCGEE, MICHAEL J.
[b.] May 10, 1935, San Francisco; [p.] Daniel I. and Regina McGee; [m.] Barbara Joan McGee, June 15, 1957; [ch.] Brian, Michael, Deborah, Lori and Tracy; [ed.] B.S. English Literature, U.S.F. 1957 Graduate School-Accounting; [occ.] Senior Accountant County of Santa Clara; [memb.] First Cavalry Division Association Korean War Veterans Association; [oth. writ.] Poem "The Old Ball Player" published in "Diamond" Magazine.; [pers.] Peace, beauty and justice—everywhere; [a.] San Jose, CA

MCGEEHAN, PATRICK D.
[b.] September 25, 1945, Steubenville, OH; [p.] James and Mary McGeehan; [ed.] Bachelor of Arts in Philosophy, Franciscan University of Steubenville, Associate of Applied Science in Nursing from W. Va. Northern College.; [occ.] Staff Nurse, operating room, Presbyterian University Hospital Pittsburgh Pa.; [memb.] National Sheriffs Association - Oblate of St. Benedict - St. Anselm's Abbey, Washington, D.C., Vietnam Veterans Association, Venerable Order of the Knights of Michael the Archangel; [hon.] Dean's List - Police Academy, Nursing Class Vice President, Area President's Award and National Quality District Award working as a District Executive for the Boy Scouts of America. Highest score ever registered at the National Executives, Institute Final Exam. 1992, "Who's Who in Poetry"; [oth. writ.] Published in "Whispers in the Wind" and "Best poets of 1994". Numerous poems published in local newspaper. Several poems about Vietnam published in National Guard Newsletters. Other poems printed in Hospital Operating Room Newsletter.; [pers.] I try to reflect some part of my personal experience in my poems. I thank Fr. Dennis P. Lyden for opening my heart to the true meaning of poetry and friendship. One of his poems is in this volume. The poem within is dedicated to my mother, who knows the beauty of nature.; [a.] East Liverpool, OH

MCGLYNN, SUZANNE
[b.] November 29, 1953, Scranton, PA; [m.] Kevin P. McGlynn, December 4, 1976; [ch.] Shaun 15 yrs., and Shamus 5 yrs; [ed.] B.S. Special Education Penn State University; [oth. writ.] Currently working on writing and illustrating a children's story and on a book of meditations.; [pers.] This is my first published poem.; [a.] Flower Mound, TX

MCGOWAN, JULIE
[b.] February 22, 1984, Montreal; [p.] Johanne and John McGowan; [ed.] Huntingdon Academy Elementary School; [occ.] Student; [oth. writ.] A poem published in a newspaper article on Christmas; [pers.] I had been influenced to write poetry by my grade four teacher (who loves poetry), Ms. Pamela Mulderrig. I would like to reach deeper in the heart than any poet before me.

MCGREGOR, CHRIS
[b.] February 24, Toronto; [p.] Brian and Sharon; [ed.] Bowmanville High School, currently in Durham College; [pers.] I don't strive. I don't write to reflect. I don't believe writers should have influences. Writing poems should come from within a lost moment and I'm differently lost.; [a.] Bowmanville Ontario, Canada;

MCKENZIE, MARY BURTON
[pen.] M. B. McKenzie; [b.] Baltimore, MD; [p.] Crawford Reaney and Mary B. Haskell; [m.] Kermit E. McKenzie; [ch.] Joan Margaret, Mary Burton, Charles Reid, Mia, Leigh, Max, Wm. and Marcus; [ed.] St. Catherine's School, Richmond, VA, B.A. Westhampton College of the U. of Richmond. M. Ed and Ed S. Georgia State U. Mts, Candler School of Theology of Emory U., Atlanta, GA; [pers.] Several of us have entered this contest, however my husband, Kermit is just about the only one also doesn't unite poems. He is a professor and historian. Any chance of getting us all in one volume, neat and space saving.; [a.] Atlanta, GA

MCKIEL, CHRISTIE
[b.] September 30, 1978, Saint John, New Brunswick, Canada; [p.] Douglas McKiel, Jane McKiel; [ed.] In grade 11 and going in grade 12; [occ.] Student, Simonds High School, Saint John, New Brunswick; [hon.] Academic High Honors; [oth. writ.] Many other poems - none published; [pers.] Poetry expresses your moods and feelings, my inspiration came from a heartbreak in the past and now I write poems as a hobby and to change my moods.; [a.] Saint John New Brunswick, Canada

MCKNIGHT, MEGAN MARIE
[b.] September 12, 1983, Houston, TX; [p.] Glynn and Linda McKnight; [ed.] Currently in 5th grade at Pittman Center Elementary School in the Smoky Mtns., of East Tn.; [occ.] Student; [memb.] 4-H Club; [hon.] Honor Roll, CSA (Children with Special Abilities), 4-H Essay Contest; [pers.] I enjoy writing, reading, soccer, computers, cooking, and crafts.; [a.] Cosby, TN

MCKNIGHT, MELBA JANE
[b.] May 28, Henry Co.; [p.] Robert H. and Cora McLane; [m.] William A. McKnight, July 29, 1967; [ch.] One child - Rickgann; [ed.] Ball State University, Associate of Arts and Sciences Degree in Business Administration; [occ.] Sales Person-part-time Penny's; [pers.] I am of Scotish descent. My writing was inspired by family and teacher and deep feelings.; [a.] New Castle, IN

MCLAIN, CARRIE ANN
[pen.] Carrie Ann; [b.] September 11, 1976, Colorado Springs; [p.] Sue and Charles McLain; [ed.] Elmhurst High School, International Correspondence School; [occ.] Technician at Computer Business Services Inc.; [hon.] National Honor Society, Outstanding Female Voice, Graduating Honors for being 6th in my graduating class; [oth. writ.] Another poem published in "A Moment In Time" several articles published for "The Advance" a newspaper of Elmhurst Publications.; [pers.] It is my Jesus that gives me the air to breathe and the words to write... without him I am nothing.; [a.] Westfield, IN

MCLAUGHLIN, DONNA-MARIA FASONE
[b.] February 1950, Honolulu, HI; [p.] Donald Fasone Sr. and Maria Luz Salve Fasone; [m.] John C. McLaughlin, April 1973; [ed.] Kailua High School, Los Gatos Jt. Unified High School, San Jose State College, University of Hawaii, B. of Education; [occ.] President, One Fas Lube; [memb.] Automotive Oil Change Assn., Natl. Assn. for Female Executives, Natl. Fed of Independent Business, Registered Rep. of the NYSE '78-92; [oth. writ.] AOCA, Oil Change Times; [pers.] Poetry is my way of sharing images and emotions about the essence of experiences from my spirit to the reader. Mahalo for this opportunity!; [a.] Aiea, HI

MCLAUGHLIN, SHELL
[b.] April 17, 1966, Harrisburg, PA; [p.] Shirley and Bill McLaughlin; [occ.] Child Care Worker of a Children's home.; [oth. writ.] This is my first publication and without the support of family and friends I wouldn't have become a reality; [pers.] Special thanks to my mom who always knew I could to Beth who is now and forever my inspirational angel, sent to us from above.; [a.] Elizabethtown, PA

MCLOUGHLIN, CHARLES BOYD
[b.] August 1, 1969, Bronx, NY; [p.] Phylomena and Patrick McLoughlin; [ed.] A.A. Liberal Arts and Humanities Dutchess Community College, B.A. English Literature State University of New York at Albany; [pers.] Thank you parents for your Heritage and your character, thank you Professor Dumbleton, for opening my eyes to the world around us.; [a.] Clinton Corners, NY

MCMURPHY, SANDRA
[b.] June 8, 1958, Ontario, Canada; [m.] Jim, June 6, 1980; [ch.] Chris, Andria, Jamie, Kyle, and Brady; [ed.] Christ the King High School; [occ.] Homemaker; [oth. writ.] Several unpublished poems; [pers.] Poetry is a reflection of the soul. I express my true self through my poetry; [a.] Whitehorse Yukon Territory, Canada

MCMURTRY, AMBER
[pen.] Amber McMurtry; [b.] November 23, 1981, Oklahoma City; [p.] Elmer and Sue McMurtry; [ed.] 7th Grade; [occ.] Student; [memb.] Volunteen Candy Striper; [hon.] Honor Roll; [oth. writ.] Unpublished poems.; [pers.] I work hard in school, with a goal of becoming a teacher. I love to work with kids and animals. I love writing poetry because it makes me feel good.; [a.] Durant, OK

MCNAIRY, HAROLD GABRIEL
[pen.] Hal; [b.] March 30, 1929, Alberdeem, MS; [p.] Frank Billips, Miss Valaria Maria McNairy; [ch.] Three; [ed.] Grade-High School College Graduates. Perfect grades; [occ.] Song writer, Lawyer Hotel-Restaurant Institutes.; [memb.] Three; [hon.] Korea War purple heart hero and others.; [oth. writ.] Songwriter; [pers.] Stop and think what you have, before it is too late.; [a.] St. Louis, MO

MCNEIL, JOHNATHAN
[b.] December 27, 1924, Boston, MA; [p.] Hugh J. McNeil, Lillian P. Gill McNeil; [m.] Carol Ann (Liversidge) McNeil, February 14; [ch.] Christine, Debbie, Frankie, Derek, Grandchildren P.J., Michelle, Jacqueline Christopher, Jillian and Derek Jr.; [ed.] So. Boston High Grad - Fed. Police Acad. Grad. Several Mass criminal Justice sponsored seminars incl. "Terror Hostage Negotiation" D.E.A. seminars on Drugs-Qualified instructor of FBI, NCIC network; [occ.] Retired Fed. Law Enforcement Officer; [memb.] Rep. Pres. Task Force-Rep. Nat'l Senatorial Comm. Area Representative on Rep. Platform Planning Comm. Legion of Merit; [hon.] Numerous Cash awards and commendations in connection with my Federal Service - Designated as and Immigration Officer and Special Deputy US Marshal Region 1 (NE) SORT Team Commander (Special Operations Response Team); [oth. writ.] Author of Social Activities column and philosophical essays for two local newspapers. File cabinet full of "The Unpublished Words and Impressions of Johnathan"; [pers.] Basically, to interpret the words and impressions that come thru me, from a higher source, into the language of human understanding, through detailed "Word Pictures".

MCNUTT, SANDRA JANE
[b.] February 17, 1963, Vancouver, British Columbia, Canada; [p.] Douglas Adams, Maimie Nelmes; [m.] Stephen Henry (died May 8, 1991), November 21, 1987; [ch.] Janice Lynn, Charles Stephen, and Melissa Jean; [ed.] Cobequid Educational Center, Truro, Nova Scotia, Canada; [occ.] Book-keeper, Acct.; [memb.] St. John's Ambulance; [oth. writ.] Many other poems were published in the Truro Daily Newspaper.; [pers.] Other than my three children, my poems and short stories have been my inspiration to go on with life. They are my greatest gifts of all.; [a.] Belmont Nova Scotia, Canada

MCPHERSON, SANDY L.
[b.] June 9, 1962, Oklahoma City, OK; [p.] Marcelle McPherson; [ed.] GED Sociology Major at Oklahoma City University; [occ.] Administrative Assistant; [memb.] PETA People for the Ethical Treatment of Animals; [pers.] My philosophy of life is to keep an open mind and truth will find you.; [a.] Oklahoma City, OK

MCQUEEN, GIGI
[b.] September 21, 1971, Hayward, CA; [p.] Samuel and Delores McQueen; [ed.] B.A. in Mass Communication for California State University Hayward.; [occ.] Data-entry clerk for the I.R.S.; [memb.] Toastmasters International; [oth. writ.] Poems have been published California State University Hayward Escape magazine.; [pers.] To reflect certain segments in society, that are often ignored, overlooked and forgotten. And be one of the many voices wanting to be heard.; [a.] Oakland, CA

MCVEIGH, RUTH M.
[b.] Halifax, NS; [p.] Philip and Marjorie Major; [ch.] David and Bruce Jones, Nancy Solman, Barb Vivian, Thomand Ilana McVeigh plus nine wonderful grandchildren!; [occ.] Semi-retired freelance writer-editor; [oth. writ.] Non-fiction: 'Fogswamp' published by Hancock House, 'Close Harmony' published by Theytus Books. Articles, columns, feature stories and poetry in Canadian publications.; [pers.] The incomparable beauty of Northern Vancouver Island has reawakened the urge to write poetry.; [a.] Port Alice, BC

MCWATT, GEORGE D.
[b.] December 5, 1920, Detroit, MI; [p.] Deceased; [m.] Ruth E. McWatt, August 2, 1946; [ch.] Douglas, Janet Ann and Robert; [ed.] B.S.- Education M.A. Industrial Education Specialist - Administration; [occ.] Retired School Administrator; [memb.] Glen Lake Reformed Church - Lions - Phi Delta Kappa. Michigan Assoc. of retired school personnel. A.A.R.P.; [hon.] High Scholarship at Wayne State University for my B.S. and M.A. degrees; [oth. writ.] Numerous newspaper articles.; [pers.] I strive everyday to do and live the kind of life that God would want me to live.; [a.] Empire, MI

MEADE, BOBBIE VIOLA
[pen.] Bobbie Viola (Meadows) Meade; [b.] Pittsburg, OK; [p.] Andrew Bert Meadows, Willie May Self; [ed.] Studying art in nature years my teachers have ask - did you have art as a child. My cousin Edwina and I always are grateful to Miss Gail who taught us penmanship when we were young. So teachers you do make a difference; [occ.] Retired; [pers.] My greatest vacation. A trip to Israel in 1982 I wish everyone could have such a magnification time in their life.; [a.] Oklahoma, OK

MEEKER, JOYCE
[b.] June 25, 1949, Idaho; [p.] Doris Beebe; [m.] Darrel Hunt, December 5, 1989; [ch.] Trish Dorman; [ed.] Graduated from High School at Foreman Arkansas; [occ.] Raise dogs and write poetry.; [pers.] I like to show people how much easier it is to feel from your heart instead of showing evil and hate. So I write it on paper. Life is so precious.; [a.] Valliant, OK

MEISSNER, DORIS
[b.] October 28, 1944, Many, LA; [p.] Lawrence and Katie Eason; [ch.] Alvin Allen Jr., Tye Allen, grandchildren Dustin and Sarah; [pers.] The love of poetry inspired me to write this poem about my first born.; [a.] Kilgore, TX

MELENDEZ, MONICA
[pen.] Monica Melendez; [b.] August 7, 1961, Callao, Peru; [p.] Franklin Melendez, Laura Melendez; [ch.] Laura Cullell, Andres Cullell; [ed.] Sherisan College, MC Master University, University of Toronto; [occ.] Student Police Management; [hon.] Several poems unpublished; [pers.] I am a women fall in love and the life, and I'd like to send a message for everyone who really need a hope word.; [a.] Miss Ontario, Canada

MELLON, STACI ANN
[b.] March 19, 1976, Fort Lauderdale, FL; [p.] Susan and Chuck Mellon, John Heideman; [ed.] Newport High, South Seattle Culinary; [occ.] Pantry Chef; [hon.] Principles List; [pers.] No matter how chaotic life can seem, there is always time to make a difference. I owe all I have to my family. I love you all!; [a.] Bellevue, WA

MELLOR, RHODA S.
[b.] August 17, 1923, Pawtucket, RI; [m.] Frank R. Mellor (deceased), December 23, 1945; [ch.] Robert Phillip (deceased), Frank Lester, David William, 9 grandchildren, 3 great grandchildren (so far); [ed.] High School graduate, East High School, Pawtucket, RI (The school has undergone at least one change of name since my graduation in 1941); [occ.] Retired bookkeeper and office clerk; [memb.] Ladies auxiliary, Community volunteer fire Co., A.A.R.P.; [hon.] Rhode Island honor Society; [pers.] My husband died in Jan. 1965. Toward the end he could no longer drive so I became his chauffeur, and he became the proverbial back seat drive. "You're going too fast (or too slow) you missed the turn. You're sawing the wheel" he would say, and I stayed silent, though resentful. Shortly after his death I wrote the poem, which immediately put an end to my pent-up frustration. I submitted it to be Philadelphia Bulletin - no longer in existence - and it was printed in its sunday magazine of April 13, 1965; [a.] Deptford, NJ

MERO, JAMES H.
[pen.] James H. Mero; [b.] August 14, 1918, Escanaba, MI; [p.] Joseph and Myrtle (Patterson) Mero; [m.] Leona (Harris) Mero, January 29, 1943; [ch.] Debra Sue; [ed.] Escanaba High School, Cloverland Commercial College, Houghton N.Y.A. School; [occ.] Retired U.S. Civil Service and U.S. Army.; [memb.] Reserve Officers Assn., The Retired Officers Assn., Warrant Officers Assn., four genealogical societies, AF&AM, VA Air and Museum in Britain, First Presbyterian Church, Hampton.; [hon.] Honorary member Masonic Fraternity, Honorary Faculty Member Q. M. School, U.S. Army, Outstanding Meritorious Civilian Svc., Commendation, 30 Yr., Svc., Award, Military Awards: Four medals WW II, Armed Forces Reserve Medal and Meritorious Service Unit Insignia.; [oth. writ.] Books published: Two Research Guides, Family History Book, Editor of two books, and Chief Editor and Compiler of a Church Centennial history; [pers.] Hobbies: Oil protrait paiting and pencil and pastel sketching, genealogy, writing poetry, researching, writing and compiling history and genealogy books.; [a.] Hampton, VA

MERRILL, EILEEN M.
[b.] June 29, 1957, Rollinsford, NH; [p.] Thomas and Juanita Boyle; [m.] Stuart O. Merrill, August 26, 1978; [ch.] Stacie L. Merrill, Lauren M. Merrill, Thomas S. Merrill; [ed.] Somersworth High - Planning to attend College spring 1995; [pers.] All who enter your life are there for a purpose. Relationships are very unique and special. Treat them as such, for you never know which ones are your angels; [a.] Kittery, ME

MERRILL, STEPHANIE
[b.] April 14, 1980, Riverside, California; [p.] Linda Merrill; [ed.] Currently a freshman at Palisade High School; [occ.] Student; [memb.] I am involved in any sport that I can fit into the hours after school and on weekends: volleyball, basketball, soccer, cheerleading; [oth. writ.] Several poems written after the tragic death of my best buddy...my brother "Bryan;" [pers.] "It's not what happens to you in your life that counts most" but rather how you respond to the events. With God as my strength and light and my mother's endless love, the pain in my heart and soul has emerged into words as poems. [a.] Palisade, CO

MESENBRINK, JAMES
[pen.] James Mesenbrink; [b.] August 13, 1964, Hampton, VA; [p.] Dave and Joan Mesenbrink; [ed.] Sunset High School, Computers etc. pltd. Common. College; [occ.] Machinist, Mechanical Engineer; [memb.] Popular Rotorcraft Asscd.l Cystic Fibrosis Foundation; [oth. writ.] Poetry, philosophy and song writing. None have been submitted as of yet.; [pers.] In strong pursuit for balance between man and mother nature. To merge tranquility with reality and to opening minds. I try to reflect a message of balance in my writing.; [a.] Aloha, OR

MICELI, LAWRENCE J.
[pen.] Larry Miceli; [b.] September 28, 1951, Clearfield, PA; [p.] Naomi and Phillip Mitchell; [m.] Divorced; [ch.] Casey son and daughters Naomi, Rebecca and Stephanie; [ed.] BA 1973, University of Pittsburgh, Pittsburgh, PA.; [occ.] Sr. Buyer Lockheed Aircraft Service, Ontario,

California; [memb.] San Secondo D'Asti, Catholic Church, Guasti, CA., Sons of Ilaly (Lodge Due Palme); [oth. writ.] Poems publishes in local magazine; [pers.] It is my belief that through continuous striving, man's spiritual nature will conquer the difficult times we always find ourselves engulfed, and we shall get back to the garden even yet.; [a.] Ontario, CA

MICKLE, KAREN EARLS
[b.] November 17, 1966, Bremerhaven, Germany; [p.] Richard and Rose Earls; [m.] David Jay Mickle, April 27, 1990; [ch.] David and Jayson Mickle (step-children); [ed.] Part-time student of Music at Christopher Newport University, VA; [occ.] Credit Union Teller; [memb.] Pennisula Community Theatre, VA., Previously - Virginia Symphony Chorus, Poquoson Jaycees; [oth. writ.] Many poems, one poetry cycle Eliza, several love songs inspired by my husband, the beginnings of a few fantasy novels, nothing published.; [pers.] Sometimes it is better to think. Sometimes it is necessary to do.; [a.] Hampton, VA

MIDDELVEEN, SHARON L.
[pen.] Sharon L. Scully; [b.] October 27, 1962, Ottawa; [p.] Dr. Edgar and Claire Scully; [m.] Thomas F. Middelveen, August 4, 1990; [ch.] Alexander and Robert Middelveen; [ed.] Attended French schools up to end of grade 13, Baccalaureate in Arts, Honors English from the University of Ottawa.; [occ.] Homemaker; [oth. writ.] One of my poems was published in A Moment in Time by the National Library of Poetry. I have written other poems and am presently working on a book; [pers.] I have a mental illness, manic depression, which both hinders and helps me to write. I try to keep all readers in mind by using different levels in my works. I use philosophy and my knowledge of English Literature in my poetry.; [a.] Gloucester Ontario, Canada

MIDDELVEEN, THOMAS F.
[b.] July 11, 1964, Zweibrucken, Germany; [p.] Frederick and Leona Middelveen; [m.] Sharon (Scully) Middelveen, August 4, 1990; [ch.] Alexander Douglas, Robert Thomas; [ed.] James M. Hill Memorial High, Royal Roads Military College; [occ.] Aero Space Engineer, Canadian Armed Forces; [pers.] No matter how difficult life's challenges might get, one may always take comfort in the knowledge that eventually, all things must pass.; [a.] Gloucester, Ontario

MIKOLAJCZYK, STACY
[pen.] Sam; [b.] March 20, 1980, Bridgeport, CT; [p.] Charlene and William Fardy; [ed.] A 9th grader at Central Magnet High School in Bridgeport; [occ.] Student; [memb.] Tennis Team 3 United States Achievement Academy; [hon.] A first honor student, Valedictorian of my 8th grade class, Science, History, English, French, James Curial Awards; [pers.] I like reading, writing, horses and dolphins. My writings are expressions of me and my surroundings; [a.] Bridgeport, CT

MILHOFER, BILL
[b.] July 22, 1933, Aberdeen; [p.] Henry and Ottilia (decease); [m.] Bonnie Day, June 8, 1952; [ch.] William Perry; [ed.] Bachelor Degree, Business Administration, University of Washington Seattle; [occ.] Retired; [memb.] Life Member Disabled American Veterans; [pers.] A Washington State resident with leisure subjects bird watching, aspiring talent in outdoor photography to bring about self devoted nature sensitivity.; [a.] Aberdeen, WA

MILIC, VILIA
[occ.] Teacher - English (middle school); [oth. writ.] Secular and religious lyrics and music, children's poetry/stories humorous personal essays, educational observations published in "The Apple" (A Hamilton Teachers') Newspaper; [pers.] Poetry and music give wings to the images of the mind which uplift the heart and delight the soul with wonder.; [a.] Hamilton Ontario, Canada

MILLER, CLINTON THOMAS
[pen.] Clinton Thomas Miller; [b.] March 28, 1934, England; [p.] Arnold and Margaret Miller; [ch.] Stephen and Rachelen; [ed.] Hodgesons Sec. Med. College advanced technology Cardiff Sliema College of Commerce Malta; [occ.] Retired; [memb.] Member British Inst. of Mgmt.; [hon.] Degree business administration U.L.C.I. Degree engineering public speaking diploma.; [oth. writ.] Short stories various speech writing.; [pers.] The majority of my poems tend to encourage the reader to give thought to, and reflect upon, many of lifes unanswered questions.; [a.] Fruitland Park, FL

MILLER, JUDITH J.
[b.] September 3, 1951, St. John, KS; [p.] Alice and Russell Fox, Wayne Webster; [m.] Anthony Miller Sr., July 30, 1990; [ch.] 1 son - Jason "Jay" Alan Hensley and 4 step children; [occ.] Radio retiree' currently writing and marketing Energy Management Systems; [oth. writ.] A collection of poetry - song lyrics and a recently completed book.; [pers.] My writing has been enhanced by the emotional charges experienced since the passing of my only child - 25 year old "Jay". The published poem is written for him.; [a.] Wilmington, NC

MILLER, MARY JO
[m.] Garry D. Miller; [ch.] Dannielle; [ed.] Clayton School of Natural Healing - Birmingham, Alabama, earned a Doctor's Degree in Naturopathy; [occ.] Story Teller; [pers.] I believe that we are all put on earth for a specific purpose. Mine is to spread "light" through my words, be they written or spoken. I also write to ease the pain of my wonderful 16 years old son, Adam, passing from this life. May I live and write in the light of his example.; [a.] Edmond, OK

MILLER, RUTH T.
[pen.] Ruth T. Miller; [b.] September 23, 1917, Zion, IL; [p.] Arthur and Vera Taylor; [m.] Wesley G. Miller, September 8, 1939; [ch.] Donald Wesley, Margaret Elaine; [ed.] Morgan Park High, Chicago North Central College, Naperville Aurora Business College, IL; [occ.] Retired (Former Personnel Worker and Development Officer); [memb.] Mount Pleasant Presbyterian Church, Mount Pleasant Renaissance Ensemble; [hon.] Tau Epsilon Honor Society; [oth. writ.] Poems published in "Pleasant News", also some in West Central Tribune, Minnesota; [pers.] I love to write from the heart, sometimes serious, often with a touch of "Whimsy".; [a.] Monroe, OH

MILLINER, ALISHA S.
[b.] February 22, 1981, Abington, PA; [p.] Albert Milliner Jr., Yvonne Milliner; [ed.] Paul V. Fly Elementary School, Stewart Middle School (attended at time of poem's making) and will be entering: Norristown High School in the fall; [memb.] Mt. Zion A.M.E Church; [hon.] D.A.R.E Essay Award SMS Academic honor roll, SMS sports team, National Week Poster Contest Award (Awarded in First Grade); [oth. writ.] Several awards presented by township on literature and art; [pers.] Whenever I write I write what is within myself, not what is acceptable in the minds of others.; [a.] Norristown, PA

MILLS, PATRICK JOHN
[pen.] Patrick; [b.] November 4, 1972, St. Jerome; [p.] June Mills, Joan Mills; [ed.] 4th year University Student, Concordia University; [occ.] Student and Painter; [pers.] In love of my family, and with special memory of my deceased father, John Henry Mills. Love always and forever.; [a.] Montreal, Quebec

MINCEY, DEBRALEE
[pen.] Debra; [b.] August 4, 1981; [p.] Mark Walton (stepfather) and Rose Walter, Ronald P. Mincey; [ed.] Lyon County, Middle School Kuttawa, Ky.; [pers.] Dedicated to my boyfriend, whom I love dearly "William O'Bryan" and my family who surrounds me with love.

MINK, LAUREL J.
[b.] September 15, 1957, Elgin, IL; [ed.] Elgin High School; [occ.] Quality Control Inspector; [memb.] Camp Tu-Endie-Wei Alumni Club; [pers.] I write from my heart. I have alot of deep feelings I try to get down on paper. To make other people feel what I feel.; [a.] Elgin, IL

MINUTI, RICHARD
[pen.] Richard Minot; [b.] August 26, 1951, Philadelphia, PA; [p.] Hector Minuti, Julia Perna; [ed.] Immaculate Conception College, Univ. of Penna.; [occ.] Freelance editor; [memb.] American Heart Association, Mercy Hospice, Morris Animal Refuge; [hon.] Commendations from customers for my work at Bell Atlantic; [pers.] I enjoy reading all types of poetry, and have a special inkling for American poetry.; [a.] Philadelphia, PA

MIRABITO, PETER C.
[b.] October 28, 1936, Amsterdam, NY; [p.] Abbondanzia and Bartolo Mirabito; [m.] Irene E. Mirabito, November 24, 1963; [ch.] Barbara Jeanne, Peter Carmen, Daniel John, Laura Anne; [ed.] St. Mary's Institute; [occ.] Licensed Optician; [memb.] Arizona Association of Dispensing Opticians, Fellow, American board of Opticians; [oth. writ.] Poem published "Young America Sings", National High School Poetry Association; [pers.] Life has been good to me as I enjoy each day without being "bored"; [a.] Scottsdale, AZ

MIRON, BLYTHE
[b.] November 2, 1982, Houston, TX; [p.] Richard Miron, Monica Miron; [ed.] Laurelglen School, Bakersfield, CA; [occ.] Student, 6th grade Perth College, West Australia; [pers.] Enjoy everyday, and share my inner feelings with others. I'm twelve years old and writing poetry makes me happy.; [a.] Bakersfield, CA

MITCHELL, MARY ANN CARRICO
[pen.] Marie Miller; [b.] August 1, 1937, Louisville, KY; [p.] Bernard and Catherine Carrico; [m.] William R. Mitchell, August 25, 1962; [ch.] Mike, Anne and Kate; [ed.] R.N. Grad. B.S.N. Univ. Colo. Boulder August, 1962; [occ.] Retired; [memb.] AAUW Lamer. Assoc. Univ. women.; [pers.] I frequently write from sense of deja vu or personal experiences.; [a.] Littleton, CO

MITCHELL, MAUREEN
[b.] July 9, 1961; [p.] Thomas and Elizabeth Padden; [m.] Richard Mitchell, September 15, 1993; [ch.] Garrett Donnelly Mitchell; [occ.] Mother and wife; [pers.] I love to hear the sounds of children's laughter

MODICA, PEARL V.
[b.] May 28, 1915, Saint Louis, MO; [p.] Bartolomew and Francesca Gambino; [m.] John Modica, June 18,

1939; [ch.] Elizabeth, Frances, Samuel, Barthomew, Marilyn, Joanne, John; [ed.] Grade School; [occ.] Homemaker; [memb.] Christian Hospital N.E. Auxiliary, Grace Assembly of God Church, Camp Chapel of Rocky Mount, MO; [oth. writ.] Poems; [pers.] I strive to honor our Creator, who when honored, provides and upholds all mankind in every endeavor of life.; [a.] Florissant, MO

MOLODICH, LOUISE ANGELINA
[pen.] Angelina Hayes; [b.] May 26, 1953, Monsup, CT; [p.] Henriette Deojay and Ray L. Deojay; [m.] George Molodich, September 3, 1994; [ch.] Jack Tingley, James Hawkins III, Michael Hawkins, Luke Hawkins and Joy Hawkins; [ed.] Killingly Vocational Agricultural High School; [occ.] Wife, mother, grandmother and mill worker; [memb.] All Hallows - St. Joseph's Catholic Community, EKONK Grange, Amalgamated Clothing and Textile Workers Union Local 1196T; [oth. writ.] Local newspaper; [pers.] I believe there is The Goodness of God found in every person. Most of my poems are about the people of this world who have chanced to touch my life.; [a.] Moosup, CT

MONEYMAKER, BREANNE
[pen.] Breanne Leigh; [b.] October 12, 1979, San Leandro, CA; [p.] Loretta Moneymaker, Paul Moneymaker, Steve Grady; [ed.] Castro Valley High, no college yet!; [occ.] Student; [memb.] World wildlife fund; [oth. writ.] Grand Prize poem in the Daily Review; [pers.] Never forget to listen to the song of life.; [a.] San Leandro, CA

MONTOYA, MARIO DOMINGUEZ
[b.] December 8, 1937, Mexico; [p.] Fabiana Dominguez; [m.] Maria Balbina Montoya, December 8, 1974; [ch.] Jaime, Yolanda, Mario Jr., Adrian, Maricela, Moses, Abraham, Faviola, Andrew; [ed.] Technical Schools for General Sheet Metal Mechanics; [occ.] Ornamental Worker; [hon.] Latin American Immigrant Texas Univ., Univ. of North Carolina (Duke), Golden Poet Award of Merit, Canto Al Pueblo Minn. Chicano Arts; [oth. writ.] Tomorrow is coming, seven stars in the Heavens (unpublished with many others); [pers.] My dreams is to published a book of my 150 poems; [a.] San Antonio, TX

MOORE, ALAN THOMAS
[pen.] Alan Thomas Moore; [b.] October 7, 1952, Valley City, ND; [p.] Howard and Carolyn Moore; [ed.] B.A. Degree from Lake Erie College, Painesville, Ohio; [memb.] Greenpeace - Amnesty International; [oth. writ.] poems, 1 play; [pers.] Believe that on the finite planet, so populated with violence, injustice - one should compete to solve problems never forgetting that no amount of money can replace the environment once it is ruined.; [a.] Greensboro, NC

MOORE, DAVID A.
[b.] June 14, 1930, Earle, AR; [p.] Fred and Eunice Moore; [m.] Georgene Moore, October 31, 1993; [ch.] David, Greg, Stacy, Eric; [ed.] BME - Ouachita Baptist Univ., MSME - Baylo Univ., DME - Univ. of Oklahoma.; [occ.] Retired - Part-time Music Director; [memb.] PHi Beta MU, Phi Mu Alpha, Pi Kappa Lambda, Phi Delta Kappa; [pers.] When I was younger, I chuckled at the Conn Corporation's slogan, "The child who blows a horn will never blow a safe," but the older I've gotten, the stronger my belief has grown that the more a child is exposed to a good education in music and the arts, the less likely he or she will be to end up in trouble.; [a.] Heber Springs, AR

MOORE, ELIZABETH L.
[pen.] Betty Moore; [b.] December 8, 1934, Arkansas; [p.] Albert and Flora Sheppard; [ch.] Sue, Lloyd E. Jr., Kathleen, James, Torrence, Gwenetta, Michael; [ed.] Degrees in Broadcasting and Newspaper Journalism; [occ.] Freelancing; [memb.] ABBWA; [hon.] Silver, gold and merit honors for poetry; [oth. writ.] Published small paper 1991-93, have written one full length 3 act play "Snow White Leaves Harlem", a collection of Poetry and Shot Stories; [pers.] As a writer, I try to use my words to uplift, enlighten, encourage, bring peace to an aching heart, and teach love of this space we are in and respect all life, human and animal.; [a.] Oklahoma City, OK

MOORE, GERALDINE E.
[b.] August 27, 1923, Powell, TN; [p.] James E. Elkins and Jessie Greene; [m.] Ralph A. Moore, January 9, 1943; [ch.] Karen Philpot, Steven R. Moore; [ed.] Halls High School, Knoxville Business College; [occ.] Retired; [memb.] Alice Bell Baptist Church Church Organizations AARP; [hon.] Salutatorian High School Graduating Class. Good Citizenship Award from DAR. Runner up in senior class essay contest; [oth. writ.] Poems and essays, editorials for school paper; [pers.] A sincere prayer that my life, words and deeds may bring peace or joy to others.; [a.] Knoxville, TN

MOORE, JEWEL B.
[b.] February 29, 1932, TX; [p.] Verge and Jurdean Brown; [m.] Melvin A. Moore, August 1, 1982; [ch.] Shirley, Charles, Nancy, Grandchildren Sunshine, Nicole, Lashawn, Lamont, Noleta, Anthony; [ed.] High School; [occ.] Retired; [hon.] Good mom - grandma, sweet grandma love children of all kind; [pers.] Inspiration from God, my friend. Writing poems is a joy to me. I love people.; [a.] Poway, CA

MOORE, JOHN D.
[b.] May 9, 1953, Durham, NC; [p.] Ervin D. Moore, Angela G. Moore; [m.] Sherry Y. Moore, June 16, 1973; [ch.] John D. Moore Jr., William Duke Moore; [ed.] Northern High School, Methodist College, University of North Carolina; [occ.] Pharmacist; [memb.] Brevard Co. Pharmacy Association Triangle Dive Club (formerly); [hon.] UNC Dean's List Walgreens Pharmacy of the year; [pers.] The beauty and dynamics of the sea should be witnessed and cherished by everyone. While it can bring out the poet in all of us, it is not limitless and must be respected and preserved.; [a.] Rockledge, FL

MOQUIN, SUSAN M.
[b.] January 23, 1958, Pawtucket, RI; [p.] Irene and Malcolm Goffe; [m.] Divorced; [ch.] Kelly Moquin 17 yrs. old, and Holly Moquin 20 yrs. old; [ed.] 10th grade then quit and accomplished my (GED) 1 yr. of college at CCRI of Rhode Island (Legal Secretary); [occ.] 1 yr. Security officer (D.B. Kelly Security Assoc.) and Gymnastics and dance teacher 22 yrs.; [memb.] Children Museum of Rhode Island and Volunteer in Providence School System for an after school Gymnastics Program 1 a week, St. Anthony's Parish North Prov. RI; [oth. writ.] None yet, but I will keep on writing poems from now on; [pers.] Please indicate my poem to Roy Harwood Ronald Goffe Sr. and my grandchildren and father Malcolms Goffe. To all the people in the world just believe in yourselves the Lord makes everything possible.; [a.] Central Falls, RI

MOREE, EDWINA ANN
[pen.] Annabella Rogers; [b.] December 6, 1972, Greenville, SC; [p.] Samuel and Linda Moree; [ed.] Ged Graduate from Surry Community College, plan to continue ed. to become an Elementary School Teacher; [occ.] Dishwasher, East Bend Dinette, East Bend, NC; [oth. writ.] Published a short story in school literary magazine. Several short stories written at home nonpublished and lots of poems not published; [pers.] I thank God for everyday He gives me and the beautiful country side I now call home with a mate and family that are good to me. Thanks for your support Billy.; [a.] East Bend, NC

MORGAN, ANNE BAILEY
[pen.] Anne Bailey Morgan; [b.] January 23, 1926, Whipple Baracks, AZ; [p.] Dr. and Mrs. Frank Bailey; [m.] Winston Thomas Morgan Jr., July 6, 1995; [ch.] Morgan Stephen Alan, Morgan Bachman and Mark Winston Morgan; [ed.] Little Rock High School University of Arkansas; [occ.] Housewife; [memb.] Trinity Episcopal Cathedral E. CW Outreach Chairman Order of St. Luke, Cathedral Prayer Vigil Chairman ECW Devotional Secretary, Community Bible Study - Little Rock Partners in Prayer, Inc. Active Volunteer weekly at the Arkansas Cancer Research Center Chi Omega Fraternity University of Arkansas Psi Chapter; [oth. writ.] Articles published in Sharing Magazine and Partners in Prayer Breakthrough Mag. Trinity Message publication Christ Church weekly Community Bible Study Sharing Quarterly; [pers.] I pray that all my inspirational and religious articles and poetry will glorify God and bless my readers as they walk Life's paths. To me, "to live is Christ" and He has blessed my family in all ways. We celebrate our 50th Wedding Anniversary this year July 6, 1995.

MORGAN, DEBRA DENISE
[pen.] Morgan Davis; [b.] September 7, 1959, Houston, TX; [p.] Freddie and Cherrie Morgan; [m.] Rogers Davis Jr., March 11, 1985; [ch.] Brittany Davis and Roger Davis III; [ed.] B.A. in Business (1981) on MBA Texas Southern University (1993); [occ.] U.S. Postal Carrier; [memb.] Alpha Kappa Alpha Sorority, National Association of Notary Public, Parent, Teacher Association Futher Business Leaders of America.; [hon.] Marquis Who's Who of American Women 1984, Outstanding Young Women of America - 1982, Dean's List Distinction, School of Business Honor Roll, Miss Texas Southern University Pageant, Miss Texas Pageant, Miss AMS.; [oth. writ.] Several poems none published but, used to read in different church and other organization functions.; [pers.] Through my poetry I hope to reach, someone and make a great affect in their lives. I want to give something make to this world. In my writing you can feel the love, hope and the spirit of an superior force.; [a.] Houston, TX

MORING, EMILEA
[pen.] Summer Lane; [b.] October 26, 1941, Pauls Valley, OK; [p.] Emery and Edith Long; [m.] Eather Moring, March 3, 1956; [ch.] Michael, Tammy, Donna; [occ.] World Bible School Teacher; [memb.] Church of Christ, Friends of the Library, Territory Tellers Story Telling Association; [pers.] I am a story teller and humorist. I stress respect for all authority, for God, country, parents, teachers, veterans, self, and all others. I dress appropriately for the story, and have a great deal of fun. I write heart-felt poems, about what I believe in, and about my family, especially my husband, my best friend.; [a.] Purcell, OK

MORRELL, MARK F.
[b.] April 12, 1972, Newport News, VA; [p.] Frederick Morrell, Judith Morrell; [ed.] Denbigh High; [occ.] Na-

val Rescue Swimmer; [memb.] American Red Cross; [hon.] American Geographic Olympiad Winning Team Member; [oth. writ.] Various other unpublished poetry.; [pers.] Our poetry is life, our love is God. My dreams and experiences greatly influence my writing. Perhaps others can experience my feelings as best as I can portray them in words.; [a.] Newport News, VA

MORRIS, CINDY
[b.] July 1, 1982, Fredricksburg, VA; [p.] Cheryl and James Morris; [ed.] I go to Battlefield Middle School in 6th grade; [hon.] I won Reflections '92 first in my school, second in the county; [pers.] I am always inspired by family members encouraging me to write. I can't thank them enough especially my mom, dad and all my teachers.; [a.] Fredricksburg, VA

MORRIS, MARGUERITE A.
[b.] June 4, 1926, Troy, NY; [m.] John J. Morris; [ch.] Kathleen, Jeanne, John and William; [ed.] St. Vincent's Hospital School of Nursing Queens College; [occ.] Writer, Artist; [memb.] AAUW (American Association of University Women); [hon.] Alpha Sigma Lambda; [a.] Jamaica, NY

MORRISON, MARY J.
[pen.] Mary J.; [b.] March 27, 1955, Watsonville, CA; [p.] Margie and Harold Morris; [m.] Divorced; [ch.] S. Matthew, D. Joshua; [ed.] Watsonville High School; [occ.] Office Manager; [memb.] Boy scouts of America; [oth. writ.] I am in the process of obtaining a publisher for a series of children's books that are not just fun, but will help children with every day problems, ie friendships, new schools, moving, death, racism.; [pers.] Dream the impossible, believe in the impossible, then make it happen! Imagination leads to creation!; [a.] Phoenix, AZ

MORROW, ROGER
[b.] March 31, 1970, Wenatchee, WA; [pers.] My close relationship with nature, and the enduring love of my parents Frank and Margie, have greatly influenced every step taken in my life.; [a.] Wenatchee, WA

MORSE, KATHYANN
[pen.] Thee Elected Lady; [b.] April 23, 1960, Detroit, MI; [p.] Catherine and Norman Thompson; [m.] Richard L., March 26, 1977; [ch.] Robert Anthony, Paul Jerome, Catherine Madonna; [ed.] Self taught public library and Holy Bible; [occ.] Housewife and mother and public servant; [hon.] Acknowledged by Catholic Church as "Thee Saratoga Voice and Thee Elected Lady. Pope John Paul II acknowledged my writings and greetings after many visions I have had"; [oth. writ.] Many poems and spiritual insights broom the spiritual mind and awaken thee dead tribes of this generation. I have already begun to menu a book to feed the people these words given to all of the tribes on earth; [pers.] I rise I stand to "Let the People Know", the son of men shall weave back the brotherhood old man. My writings are a reflection of truth found only in one's heart the true spiritual minds eyes.; [a.] Novi, MI

MOTON, SARAH E.
[pen.] Launey; [b.] New York; [p.] James and Olive Jeffrey; [m.] Ernest Moton Jr., August 15, 1980; [ch.] Larnette, Thomas, Stacey, Rena, Larry, Marie, Teresa; [ed.] High School; [occ.] Retired; [oth. writ.] Yes, just for personal pleasure.; [pers.] Dedicated with love to my husband Ernie and our children, Larnette, Thomas, Stacey, Rena, Larry, Marie and Teresa. Our grandchildren, Simone, E. J., Samantha, Damien, Eugene, Stacey, Larry, Chanell, Dior, Tamika, John, Johrita, Asia, Michael, James 2nd our Great Grandchildren Kellen and Kristian, our God son Curtis my daughter-in-law Nadell, all my nieces and nephews and at last to my very special sisters, Rainey, Gertrude and Sina.; [a.] New York City, NY

MSOMI, SIBUSISO
[pen.] Sibu; [b.] March 20, 1974, Kwa-Mashu; [p.] Joshua and Mumsie; [ed.] Currently doing Biochemical Engineering and Biology double major; [occ.] Student; [hon.] '94 CRC College Chemistry Award; [oth. writ.] Several poems in Zulu; [pers.] "Imbila yaswela umsila ngokulayezela" (Zulu language); [a.] Saint Paul, MN

MULLEN, DONNA
[b.] August 10, 1966, Wilmington, NC; [p.] Jesse and Evelyn Malpass; [m.] Patrick Mullen, November 8, 1985; [ch.] Jacquelyn Mullen, Megan Mullen; [ed.] Hoggard High; [occ.] Homemaker; [oth. writ.] Several writings that are as yet unpublished; [pers.] All my writing comes from the heart.; [a.] Wilmington, NC

MULLINAX, JENNY LYNNE
[pen.] Jen; [b.] August 11, 1958, San Bernardino, CA; [p.] Charles Moore, Marcella Moore; [m.] William E. Mullinax, October 25, 1992; [ch.] Jimmy Lee Jones, Cindy Lynne Ricky Lee, Shawna Dee; [ed.] Pacific High, Sand Bernardino California; [occ.] Housewife; [memb.] First Church of the Nazarene; [hon.] Honor roll student for 3 yrs. Pacific High School CA.; [oth. writ.] Two of my poems have won a special ribbon from two High School, for special recognition, also my poems have been submitted to the states poetry contest; [pers.] Thanks to my wonderful husband and children who have greatly inspired my talent for writing almost 3 yrs. ago; [a.] Fontana, CA

MUNOZ, SIERRA V.
[pen.] Moonbeam; [b.] January 22, 1953, Philadelphia, PA; [p.] Stanley and Bette Hawryluk; [m.] Carlos Munoz, November 29, 1982; [ch.] Brandy and David; [ed.] Highland High School Gloucester County Community College, Berlin Vocational and Technical School; [occ.] Self-employed, Port St. Lucie Movers/Artist; [a.] Fort Pierce, FL

MURRAY JR., MORRIS
[b.] June 6, 1951, Jasper, AL; [p.] Morris Murray Sr., Charlsie Murray; [m.] Brenda Sheryl, July 23, 1971; [ed.] Walker High School, Samford University, Walker College, New Orleans Seminary, Southwestern Seminary, Newport University, University of Alabama - Birmingham, AL; [occ.] Psychology Instructor, Bevill State Community College, Sumiton, AL; [memb.] American Psychological Association, Alabama Education Assoc., National Education Assoc.; [hon.] Advisor, Billy Graham Crusade: Congressional Prayer of U.S. House of Representatives on September 8, 1978; [oth. writ.] "Education Reform: Accenting the wrong syllable?" in Alabama School Journal (February 3, 1995); [a.] Jasper, AL

MYERS, MARY A.
[b.] May 16, 1950, Phoenix, AR; [pers.] Words with love and feelings, are a great pleasure to my mind. I want to share the message: "To let it shine into our souls, of Jesus and the Lords great love for us all!"

MYERS, MELANIE
[b.] January 3, 1980, Philadelphia, PA; [p.] Eugene and Denise Myers; [ed.] Currently student at St. Maria Goretti High School Class of '97; [hon.] Dancing School trophies, Campbell Soup Company wrote a recipe on how to be a "Rock Star" in Second grade won contest; [oth. writ.] Many other poems and short stories unpublished; [pers.] I am very interested in Art, Theatre, Drama and went to dancing school for 8 years. I'm influenced about life and the world today I write about teen life. Stephen King, Edgar Allen Poe and Gene Kelly inspire me.; [a.] Philadelphia, PA

NAKHLE, THERESE JARBOUH
[pen.] T. J. Way; [b.] April 14, 1966, Lebanon; [p.] Assaad and Georgette Jarbouh; [m.] Georges Nakhle, November 4 1984 (divorced); [ch.] One: Crystal Rose, 9 yrs old; [ed.] Grade II; [occ.] Singer, songwriter and poet; [hon.] Other than the greatest award of having my poem published in the "Garden of Life" I haven't received any other rewards.; [oth. writ.] As a singer, poet and songwriter I go by the name T.J. Way and so I would prefer to be called by that name thank you. Hopefully someday I'll be famous: Please note that I'm a Nana Mouskourt look alike.; [pers.] I've recorded four songs and is still working on recording an album - I spend my time writing poetry songs and singing. I dedicate my work to Elvis Presleywho inspired me; [a.] Orleans Ontario, Canada

NAKOA, SHERRY
[b.] March 28, 1958, Hawaii; [p.] Patrick NaKoa, Sr., Gladys NaKoa; [ch.] Gideon Leialiiokeola; [ed.] Radford High School, Kapolani C.C., Travel Institute of the Pacific; [occ.] Human Resources, Brooklyn, N.Y.; [memb.] Keiki O Hawaii Hawaiian Civic Club, Archorage, AK.; [hon.] State of Hawaii Visitors Bureau "Mahalo" Award; [pers.] They come like raindrops, like puddles, like rivers and seas...these are the words that let me be me -; [a.] Brooklyn, NY

NASH, ROGER
[b.] November 3, 1942, Maidenhead, United Kingdom; [p.] Lawrence and Margaret Nash; [m.] Bronnen Nash, May 28, 1966; [ch.] Piers David, Caedmon Huw; [ed.] B.A. (University of Wales) M.A. (McMaster University) Ph.D. (Exeter University); [occ.] Professor of Philosophy, Laurentian University; [memb.] League of Canadian Poets, Canadian Philosophical Association, Canadian Society for Time Study of Higher Education; [hon.] 1st Place, Prisms International Poetry Contest (1986), 1st place, The Fiddlemead's poetry contest (1994), Honorary Fellow of Thorneloe University; [oth. writ.] Books: Settlement in a School of Whales, Psalms From The Suburbs, Night Flying, Ethics, Science, Technology and the Environment (2 vols), The Poetry of Prayer; [a.] Sudbury Ontario, Canada

NAVARRA, CHRISTINA
[pen.] Christina Navarra; [b.] September 4, 1980, Charleston, SC; [p.] Thomas Navarra and Rebecca Robles; [m.] Single; [ed.] Middle School; [occ.] Student; [memb.] YWCA, Howland Middle School Choir.; [pers.] I'm only 14 yrs. old, but I've experienced a lot in my life so far. I've learned something from every success and failure, that's the only thing you can do in such an unpredictable world.; [a.] Warren, OH

NAVEA, CRISTIE
[b.] April 15, 1982, Paterson; [p.] Nilsa Navea and Juan Navea; [ed.] 7th Grade; [a.] Clifton, NJ

NAWLS, DWIGHT
[b.] November 4, 1968, Chicago; [p.] Lillian Nawls; [ed.] Jean B.P. DuSable High Barber - Scotia College - Concord N.C. 1 yr. St. Ambrose University 1 1/2 yr.; [occ.] Bank Teller; [pers.] Our thoughts on romance and love sometimes confuse us and our true feelings are hindred and hid. But a greater love exist when our spiritual side is revealed and our love comes from it.; [a.] Chicago, IL

NEELEY, ALMA
[b.] April 27, 1911, North Bend, OH; [p.] Charles H. Bennett and Myrtle W. (Cummins) Bennett; [m.] James I. Neeley (deceased), April 26, 1946; [ed.] High School - Gods Bible School and Bright High School, Bright IN, Trip to Israel Greece, Corinth and other cities, in 1970; [occ.] Retired pastry cook - Miami University Oxford, OH; [oth. writ.] Poems and songs for friends and acquaintances.; [pers.] I feel I should share the poems since they are an inspiration to me. I enjoy requests for my poems, and often I find pictures to accompany the poems.; [a.] Hamilton, OH

NEFF, NICHOLAS PAUL
[pen.] Nick Neff; [b.] March 1, 1983, Dayton, OH; [p.] Frederick and Tammy Neff; [ed.] Currently attending C.F. Holliday School in West Carrollton - 6th grade; [occ.] Student; [memb.] AWANA, D.A.R.E - Drug abuse resistance education; [hon.] Presidential Academic Fitness Award; [oth. writ.] Speech - for those who overcame - Award Civic Oration - Modern Woodman; [pers.] I think you should always ask questions for example "Why is the sky so high"....; [a.] Dayton, OH

NELSON, CHARLES W.
[pen.] W. J. Hatch; [b.] August 17, 1926, Co Bluffs, IA; [p.] Charles Sr., and Mary Pearl Nelson; [m.] Never married; [ed.] Modale, IA. High School, U.S. Navy NROTC. The state Univ. of Iowa - Iowa Vocat. Rehab.; [occ.] Dorm Desk Clerk at Iowa Veterans Home.; [memb.] Univ. of Iowa alum. Repub. party of Iowa, RNE friends of Iowa RNE Friends of Iowa Public TV., St. Mary's Catholic Church; [hon.] Pres. Of Senior Class '43 - Good Conduct Medal, USN.; [oth. writ.] Compendium on TV - 48 copies - compendium on U.S. Presidents and first ladies - 120 copies poems given to friends and relatives - 11.; [pers.] The devotion of spare time toward a valuable or useful endeavor may prove useful, to one's self or to others. Be not afraid to volunteer service or info.; [a.] Marshalltown, IA

NELSON, KIMBERLY D.
[pen.] K. D. Nelson; [b.] Keene, NH; [p.] Richard and Dorothy Johnston; [m.] Randall Nelson, May 11, 1985; [ch.] Erik Johnston, Jett Chandler, Chandelle Monet; [ed.] Classical High, Our Lady of the Elms College; [pers.] Words touch just the surface of our true feelings - an attempt to express the passions of our soul.

NEUFELD, TINA
[b.] September 10, 1981, Calgary, Alberta, Canada; [p.] Stephen and Beth Neufeld; [ed.] Grade 8 completed, presently in grade nine. Home school.; [occ.] Student; [hon.] "A" Honor Roll in each school year. Editor's Choice Award from National Library of Poetry.; [oth. writ.] "Spring" published in "Echoes of Yesterday".; [pers.] I like to paint word pictures of what I see during my walks in the woods.; [a.] Valleyview Alberta, Canada

NEUMANN, KATHLEEN MAUREEN
[b.] November 29, 1944, Bemidji, MN; [p.] James Edward and Mary Elizabeth; [ed.] Anoka, Minnesota Jr. and Sr. High Schools - Mesa Community College - Mesa, Arizona; [occ.] Final test and assembly worker at Motorola Inc. Mesa, Arizona; [hon.] High School - upper 3rd of class - U.S Army - Distinguished graduate clerk, typist - honor proud to complete basic and training - letters of appreciation from co-workers and other students. Appreciations from teachers.; [oth. writ.] Newspaper Editorials, College Poetry - personal journal writing and poems of recovery - write for employer co. newspaper.; [pers.] Themes of childhood abuse and recovery issues are major components of my writing. My sister Barbara honored me by thanking me for starting the practice of hugging - kissing family members. That will always mean more to me than anything except God. Me - spirituality - most important!; [a.] Chandler, AZ

NEVELS, LOIS ANN
[b.] October 24, 1943, Bellville, IL; [p.] James L. Thomas, Elizabeth Ann Thomas; [m.] Divorced; [ch.] Tracie Elizabeth, Grandchildren - Kristina Ann and Joe; [ed.] Stevenson High School; [occ.] Traffic Administrative Assistant; [a.] Stockbridge, GA

NEYER, KEVIN
[b.] June 23, 1973, Winnipeg, Manitoba, Canada; [p.] Wayne and Cheryl Neyer; [ed.] Sheldon Williams Collegiate, Langara College; [oth. writ.] The Andrea and Lara Poems; [pers.] The best is yet to come. Beauty, eh?; [a.] Vancouver British Columbia, Canada

NEZ, VONDA YVETTE
[pen.] Fuzzy; [b.] May 20, 1983, Phoenix, AZ; [p.] David and Rhoda Nez; [ed.] David Crockett Elementary School, Phoenix, AZ; [occ.] Student; [hon.] Honor Roll, Music, Perfect Attendance, Citizenship, and Achievement Awards. Poetry Awards; [oth. writ.] Poetry contest for school, published in School Newspaper; [pers.] Like to write about things I see and imagine to be that, to make my poems real and interested.; [a.] Phoenix, AZ

NICHOLS, JAMES E.
[pen.] Ed or Jim; [b.] July 31, 1967, Kellyville, OK; [p.] Carol and Theresa Nichols; [m.] Krista G. Nichols, February 19, 1994; [ch.] Cody and Roman; [ed.] Kellyville High; [occ.] Pipe Fitter; [hon.] Trucking Degree Grad. 1993, Welders Degree Grad. 1990

NICHOLSON, JAMES N.
[pen.] James N. Nicholson; [b.] November 5, 1965, Greenville, SC; [p.] Mr. and Mrs. Aaron N. Nicholson; [m.] Gina B. Nicholson, August 8, 1988; [ed.] Mauldin High School, Mauldin S.C. Class of 1984. Management courses in Technical College. "Working man's P.H.D. in school of hard knocks."; [occ.] Research and Development Technician; [oth. writ.] "Recycle my Love" Poem - published in "East of Sunrise." Collaborated with Amateur Guitar Player, I supplied lyrics, he supplied music, title, "Money, Moollah and Bucks" Recorded in a Rock and Roll Format.; [pers.] I believe if only people would explore meaning in things they read in creative writing, and better listen to lyrics in songs they hear, they would find many answers to questions/concerns they have. Even ones they haven't thought of yet.; [a.] Greenville, SC

NICHOLSON, ROBERT W.
[pen.] R. W. Nicholson; [b.] October 17, 1956, Penticton, British Columbia, Canada; [p.] Arlie and Lee Nicholson; [ch.] Cory, Cathy, Scott, Stacie; [ed.] Kumsheen Secondary, Okanagan College; [occ.] Explosives Technician, Private Investigator; [oth. writ.] Publications in local newspapers.; [a.] Midway British Columbia, Canada

NIENSTEDT, LORI-ANN RAFAELLA
[b.] June 8, 1966, Jamaica, NY; [p.] John P. and Lydia J. Nienstedt; [ed.] B. A. - East Stroudsburg University in Sociology/Anthropology, A.A. - County College of Morris in Humanities/Social Science; [occ.] Manager for AT&T; [memb.] Warren County Association of Realtors, N.J. Association of Realtors, Three Angels Seventh-Day Adventist Church Board, Director of Personal Ministries, Certified Counselor for Domestic Abuse/Rape Crisis center; [hon.] Cum Laude - East Stroudsburg University, Individual Performance Award - AT&T, Quality Performance Award - AT&T; [oth. writ.] Poems: "Would You Know Me?" "Autumnal Glory". Several works of fiction include "Run For The Sun", "Through the Tunnel of Time"; [pers.] Believed to have been related to pre-Raphaelite English poet Christina Rossetti (1830-94), Nienstedt a devout Seventh-Day Adventist, shares many of the same tones and subjects in her poems. True joy is found in such: Jesus First, Others Second, Yourself Last.; [a.] Blairstown, NJ

NOLLEY, JACK T.
[b.] February 16, 1946, Shelter Island, NY; [p.] Clarice and John Nolley; [m.] Shirley (Deceased), October 16, 1976; [ch.] Jennifer C. Nolley; [ed.] High School; [occ.] Electronic Technician; [oth. writ.] Poems - Shirley, Who Am I, The Sun, Jenny, The Midnight Desert etc., Books - The Nolley Family Adventures, Montana Jack, The Emergency Rm Follies (All Books unpublished yet) - Plus - Short stories; [pers.] To write is to take a journey into a place in our mind where imagination and fantasy exist. A place where anything can and will happen. To write is to share with others our special place and thoughts.; [a.] Santee, CA

NOONAN, MAURA
[b.] March 17, 1966, Boston, MA; [m.] Steven Noonan, April 24, 1992; [ed.] Plymouth - Carver Regional High, attended U-mass Amherst, attended Fayetteville Tech. College; [pers.] I enjoy the writing process, but usually hide my writing from others. My husband has encouraged me to make my writing public.; [a.] Wahiawa, Hawaii

NORTHROP, BOBBIE J.
[b.] March 5, 1924, Hot Springs, AR; [p.] Standfield and Izetta Parker; [m.] Byron L. Northrop, February 15, 1944; [ch.] James B. Northrop and Robert P. Northrop; [ed.] Hot Springs Public Schools, Adult Education Classes - OK City OK. Floral Design, Sculpture, Oil Painting, Pastels, Calligraphy; [occ.] Retired - Artist, Calligrapher; [memb.] Memorial Christian Church, Ione Branch Y.W.C.A; [hon.] Art work displayed at various state and local art exhibits; [oth. writ.] Nine poems published in Hot Springs Ark. paper - promised August 1995 publication in "Treasured Poems of America" (Sparrowgrass Poetry Forum); [pers.] "We all desire to be heard. To have your creations (poems) published in books seems like a very permanent echo"; [a.] Oklahoma City, OK

NOWAK, MICHELLE
[pen.] Michelle Nowak; [b.] January 11, 1968, Czechoslovakia; [p.] Michael and Zdenka Karnovie; [m.] Jerry Nowak, November 17, 1988; [ed.] Bachelor of Arts of Simon Fraser University in British Columbia Canada. I also have a teaching degree. I teach English and Social Studies; [occ.] Teacher in Summerland, B.C.; [oth. writ.] I have published a teacher's guide to a novel titled The Old Brown Suitcase. The novel was written by Lillian Boraks Nemetz, and my teacher's guide was published

by Ben Simon Publications in Victoria, B.C.; [pers.] Literature is the vehicle which elevates and nourishes the human spirit. Writers and poets alter their reality and express their philosophies through this creative process. In this way they entertain, uplift and inspire others. If my poem achieves only one of these things, I am content.; [a.] Penticton British Columbia, Canada

NUTTALL, KATIE LYNN
[b.] May 30, 1981, Kettering, OH; [p.] Jim and Ruth Nuttall; [ed.] Saint Albert The Great School; [occ.] Student and Baby Sitter; [memb.] Safety Patrol, Recycling Committee, Altar Server, C.Y.O. Sports (track, volleyball, basketball and softball); [hon.] Youth Ministry Award, Honor Roll Student, Ohio Mathematics League, 2nd Place Fair Housing Award; [oth. writ.] (1995) Editorial in Dayton Daily Newspaper, Young Author Writing program (1989); [pers.] In my writings, I try to express my feelings about the world around me.; [a.] Kettering, OH

NUTTER, DEEANN
[b.] February 11, 1969, Little Falls, MN; [p.] Douglas Nutter, Phyllis Nutter; [ch.] Zachary Byron Nutter; [ed.] Sauk Rapids Senior High, Saint Cloud State University, Saint Cloud Technical College; [occ.] Volunteer, self employed; [memb.] Saint Cloud Christian Fellowship Church, Avon Parents and Teachers Association; [oth. writ.] Pearls in a Clam Shell - A collection of poetry by DeeAnn Nutter; [pers.] My favorite writing professor was Steven Klepetar. God's world and it's people are my best sources of poetic inspiration.; [a.] Avon, MN

NYSEWANDER, JUDY
[b.] January 11, 1962, Panama, Canal Zone; [p.] George Dabney and Nury McGaughy; [m.] Jeff Nysewander, August 18, 1984; [ch.] Alexander and Michael; [ed.] Graduated W.A. Berry High School in B'Ham Alabama, attended University of Montevallo.; [occ.] Housewife and Mother; [memb.] Board of Directors for Cystic Fibrosis Foundation, Pittsburgh, PA.; [hon.] Track and Field and Cross Country Awards. Miss Senior Class W.A. Berry High School - Friendliest in Who's Who Berry High School - Chi Omega, University of Mont Dance Company.; [pers.] My poetry reflects true life experiences. I enjoy writing poems for family and friends.; [a.] Birmingham, AL

NYZIO, AMY
[pen.] Scout Parker; [b.] February 27, 1961, Holyoke, Ma; [p.] Raymond and Loraine Chalifoux; [m.] Peter Nyzio, February 27, 1981; [ch.] Adam, Seth, Benjamin; [ed.] Holyoke High, Holyoke Comm. College; [occ.] Merchandiser for Ingram, Merchandising Services, Inc., Asst. Cub Scout Leader Pack 303 South Hadley, MA. President of family business: Nyzio Heating and Air Conditioning, 5th grade CCD teacher for St. Teresa's Parish, South Hadley, MA, also, a freelance radio and T.V. personality, do commercials.,; [hon.] Bravo Arts magazine award for Best Actress of the 1993-94 season in community theatre.; [oth. writ.] Collection of poetry; [pers.] I am grateful for the thread of artistry that runs through my veins. I have my mother, a renowned local artist who passed away in 1992, to thank for her influence and appreciation for all that is beautiful.; [a.] South Hadley, MA

O'CONNELL, JOANNE
[ch.] Three, grandchildren of two; [occ.] In my professional occupation I am employed in several of the major hospitals for the last 25 years in the city of Calgary.; [oth. writ.] In my spare time beside writing poetry, I enjoy doing crafts and spending time with my grandchildren, family and friends. I am also overwhelmed with having my poem published in the forthcoming anthology "The Garden of Life".; [pers.] The poem you have selected is very special to me and I would like to tell you a little about its originality.; [a.] Calgary, Aberta, Canada

O'CONNOR, JAMES C.
[b.] June 28, 1937, New Haven; [p.] Ann O'Connor; [m.] Counsel O'Connor, October 18, 1958; [ch.] Mr. James J. O'Connor, Mrs. Ann Marie Weaver; [ed.] High School graduate; [occ.] Patient equipment mechanic for a major hospital; [oth. writ.] Several short poems 2 short stories both unpublished; [pers.] This was my first attempt at writing, poetry. And I realize there are plenty more yet to surface; [a.] New Haven, CT

O'DONNELL, CAROLYN
[pen.] Carolyn O'Donnell; [b.] April 25, 1953, Albany, NY; [p.] Mr and Mrs Edmund Kowsky; [ed.] Bachelors of Science in Visvalarts, Empire State College; [occ.] Consumer Representative, Niagara Mohawk; [memb.] Rensselaer Co. Council for the Arts Schenectady Photographic Society American Association of Museums Mid Atlantic Associations of Museums; [hon.] February 1995: Two pieces showing in the Rensselaer Artists Movement Society first show. December 1994: One woman photography show at the Albany County Airport Gallery, with an artist's reception on December 8, 1994. October 1994: Eastman Kodak Special Merit Award for photograph "Tranquility". August 1994: Photograph "Tranquility" chosen by the Troy Record Newspapers as a Kodak International Newspaper Snapshot Award. May - June 1994: Honorable Mention Award in the 16th Annual Photography Regional. My "Window Dressing" piece was shown at the Albany Center Galleries. January 1194: Honorable Mention Award in the Evangelist photography contest. April 1993: Second Place winner, the Evangelist photography contest. 1993: Two photographs were chosen for publication in the book "Close Up on the Capital Region". April 1993: Second place winner Art Award Niagara Mohawk's Black History Month contest.; [oth. writ.] An essay on John F. Kennedy in the Kennedy Library, Boston, Massachusetts; [pers.] When I feel a great deal, my waiting reflects the most intense of those feelings. I feel, at times, a need to express my innermost thoughts.; [a.] Rensselaer, NY

O'MARA KRISTEN M.
[b.] July 29, 1977, Philadelphia; [p.] Thomas and Lisa O'mara; [ed.] Nazareth Academy 12th grade; [occ.] Senior in High School; [memb.] SADD, CYO, Prom Committees, Italian Club, Softball Associations; [hon.] American Fitness 1991 several bronze, silver medals in softball; [oth. writ.] Poems published in school magazines, the rest for fun.; [pers.] Through my writing, I reflect upon experience, fear, haze, and imagination. I hope to inspire others, as I have been inspired. My writings help me escape reality, and express things that seem to come better on paper.; [a.] Philadelphia, PA

O'ROURKE, AMY E.
[pen.] Amy Bishop; [b.] October 17, Neptune, NJ; [p.] Robert and Kathleen; [ed.] Communication's major at Brookdale Community College.; [memb.] Assisted in H.S. Magazine Editing (Allentown HS).; [oth. writ.] Under the name Amy O'Rourke featured collection in 1994 college. Several readings in local areas.; [pers.] Breaking through limiting boundaries make the wish gentler man. The untame, uncalculating, make for dashing stories and rhymes.; [a.] Cream Ridge, NJ

OCHMANN, HAMBY ONAONA
[pen.] Hawaiian; [b.] March 31, 1961, Hawaii; [p.] Shem and Hamby Kahawaii; [m.] Bill H. Ochmann, January 19, 1985; [ch.] 5 Beautiful Children: Anthony, Pikake, Kalani, Makana and Billy Jr.; [ed.] Completed High School at the Kona Com. school for adults, studied business law at the UHH West Hawai'i, studied accounting at the knoa community school for adults, attended seminars from S.C.O.R.E. and Small Bus. Admin.; [occ.] Family Business: "Cleaning Services Hi Corp."; [memb.] Member of "The Church of Jesus Christ of Latter day saints" and an assistant to a Hula Teacher of "Halau 'O Kalei'Ulaokala" Hula School; [hon.] In 1985, I entered a valentines poem contest on our local radio and became the first place winner!; [oth. writ.] Writer of more than a dozen songs and poems which has never been publicized except for this poem "hurt!"; [pers.] Aloha! As you go on in your garden of life, learn to release hurt feelings in poetry, see yourself, leave it there in your book of treasures, and go on with your life as best you can, and when appropriate, share it with the world. "You are not alone."; [a.] Waikoloa, Hawaii

OCHOA, BEATRICE
[pen.] Bea Martinez; [b.] March 21, 1960, Texas; [p.] Elena and Zenon Martinez; [m.] Rene Ochoa, September 5, 1985; [ch.] Olivia Marie and Tomas; [ed.] Edinburgh High, Texas Southmost College, UT- Pan Am University,; [occ.] Registered Nurse; [memb.] State Troopers Assoc. Easter Seals, Emergency Nurse's Assoc.; [oth. writ.] One poem in local school paper; [pers.] I write what I feel, and if people can relate to my words, it gives me a great deal of satisfaction.; [a.] La Blanca, TX

OCHSE, SHANNON LEE
[b.] December 14, 1982, Stanford, U; [p.] W. Daniel and Janice A. Ochse; [ed.] I am now in the 6th grade at Borel Middle School. San Mateo, Calif.; [memb.] Girl Scouts; [hon.] I was given awards for being the most 'Physically fit" and for 'Academic Excellence'; [oth. writ.] Many short stories and poems.; [pers.] I adore animals, running, skiing gymnastics, and baseball. I also love spending time with my family.; [a.] San Mateo, CA

ODOM, IRENE SWANNER
[b.] March 17, 1954, Monroeville, AL; [p.] William and Willie Dell Swanner; [m.] John W. Odom; [ch.] Stephen and Amanda Odom; [ed.] Valencia Community College Wilcox County High School; [occ.] Banking (part-time); [memb.] First Baptist Oviedo; [oth. writ.] Article for Orlando Sentinel; [pers.] To share with others as I relate to the world around me.

OGBEVIRE, OGHENEVOVWERO
[b.] April 21, 1970, Nigeria; [p.] Ebue and Rachael Ogbevire; [ed.] Senior: Rutgers University; [occ.] Substitute Teacher at Elizabeth High School, Elizabeth NJ; [hon.] Rutgers Newark Sankofa Award (Academics); [oth. writ.] I had several poems published in school magazine.; [pers.] I strive to give life to the dead in my poetry, and make the living think. I have been deeply influenced by the Harlem Renaissance writers and the poetry of Maya Angelou; [a.] Roselle, NJ

OLDS, KEITH B.
[b.] April 22, 1967, Florida; [p.] Edwin E. and Kay Dean Olds; [m.] Julie A. Olds, August 13, 1993; [ch.] Keenan Keary Olds; [ed.] Westerville South High School, Uni-

versity of Akron; [occ.] Printing Production Team Leader - Murfin Division; [hon.] First Published Poem; [oth. writ.] Numerous poems of varying length and content (Not submitted for publication); [pers.] My writings focus on deep personal feelings and the abounding social and moral decay of the world in which we live. I draw influence from experience and a concern for our future if we continue our present course.; [a.] Athens, GA

OLFUS, EBONESE

[b.] May 27, 1975, Baltimore, MD; [p.] Joy Cromwell, Maurine Olfus; [ed.] Lackey High School, Allegancy Community, College, Broadcasting Institute of Maryland; [occ.] Student; [hon.] 3rd place voice of democracy; [oth. writ.] Personal poems and children's stories (All writings unpublished); [pers.] Don't walk threw life with your head in the ground but up to the sky. You will get the pebbles out of your eyes much easier); [a.] Waldorf, MD

OLSON, THOR

[pen.] YP (Japanese for my first Name); [b.] May 26, 1978, Fairview, Alberta, Canada; [p.] Jim Olson, La Tresa Olson; [ed.] Currently in Grade 10 at Bassano School, Bassano Alberta, Canada.; [occ.] A student at Bassano School; [oth. writ.] A collection of unpublished poetry.; [pers.] Life has the good, the bad, and the ugly, I write about all of them. My favorite writing styles, are, free style, metaphor, and sensory poetry. I would like to give a special thank to Mrs. Pam Allen My English Teacher.; [a.] Bassano Alberta, Canada

OLTMANNS, SONIA

[b.] April 23, 1941, Egnar, CO; [p.] James and Oneta Linnens; [m.] Paul Oltmanns, November 23, 1960; [ch.] Sharon Murray - Sandra Parker - Ron Oltmanns; [ed.] Elementary Lebanon, Colo High School Cortez, Colo N.M.J.C. Hobbs, N.M.; [occ.] Vice President of Hobbs Diesel; [memb.] Taylor St. Church of Christ; [oth. writ.] Numerous essays and poems; [pers.] To evoke a chord of response in those who read my writings

OLUWOLE, MICHAEL K.

[pen.] Kay Oluwole; [b.] November 14, 1955, Nigeria; [p.] James Oluwole, Abigail Oluwole; [m.] Ellen Ely Oluwole, 1993; [ed.] D.V.M. (University of Nigeria) Master of Professional Studies in Communication, M.P.S. (Cornell University, Ithaca, NY); [occ.] Freelance writer; [memb.] American Red Cross, Founder "Youth for Humanity"; [oth. writ.] Over 60 articles covering economics, philosophy, agriculture, health and development issues. Over 20 poems published in newspapers.; [pers.] Don't ever give up - every human being in; [a.] Malvern, PA

ONEIL, THEODORE

[b.] June 25, 1929, Springfield, MA; [p.] Henry and Annie Oneil; [m.] Douglas Oneil, September 20, 1953; [ch.] One son; [ed.] Elementary School; [occ.] Retired; [hon.] 4 years I'm in the air force two years in the navy research. 4 months in the army training, while in the air force. Received 6 medals. Received three certificate air force 4 years, US Navy reserve, 2 years US Army training 4 months; [a.] Boston, MA

OPLINGER, DAVID

[pen.] D.A.O.; [b.] April 29, 1977, Winslow, AZ; [p.] Daniel and Rose Oplinger; [ed.] Winslow High School; [occ.] Teenager; [memb.] Boy Scouts of America; [hon.] Eagle Scout; [oth. writ.] Various unpublished poems.; [pers.] I have been influenced by great philosopher such as yoda from star wars, "Do, or do not, There is no try", and beautiful, heart breaking women who are my inspiration.; [a.] Winslow, AZ

ORPEN, MICHAEL

[pen.] Michael McCarthy; [b.] June 17, 1948, Trenton, Ontario, Canada; [p.] Ron and Eileen; [m.] Pat, June 13, 1970; [ch.] Michael and Sean; [ed.] Arts and Science Matr. St. Joseph's College; [occ.] Commercial Airline Pilot; [memb.] C.A.L.P.A., and B.C.B.U. Assoc. and Can Umpires Assoc.; [oth. writ.] Various other writings for aviation/baseball trade magazines, local papers etc.; [pers.] I tend to draw more or personal experiences as inspiration. Influenced by the poetry and lyrics of E.B. Browning, R.W. Service, R. McKuen, H. Prather and various other 60's and 70's pop musicians; [a.] White Rock British Columbia, Canada

ORTIZ, MICHAEL JOHN

[b.] June 27, 1970, The Bronx; [p.] Patricia Ann Blando (mother); [ed.] Associate in Arts June 1994 Borough of Manhattan Community College, Hunter College English major and Education minor; [occ.] Struggling student and aspiring teacher; [hon.] Dean's list 1992-1994, Certificate of Achievement 1993 Poetry Contest runner up.; [oth. writ.] "Winter Solstice" printed in poems At BMCC: The 1993 Poetry Contest; [pers.] An inspiration and lovely sin, never forgotten is Diana Lynn. . . Mother, what can I say? Thank you, and I love you. Poetic perfection is impossible, but the relentless strive for it is not. Every word is a step towards immortality!; [a.] Bronx, NY

OSBERG, NANCY L.

[b.] April 24, 1931, Mount Prospect, IL; [p.] Oscar and Ingrid Oquist; [m.] E. Art Osberg, Jr., September 17, 1949; [ch.] Lee Ann Ward, Bill Osberg, Scott Osberg; [ed.] A. A. Palomar College, San Marcos, CA, BA in Communication - University of California at San Diego; [occ.] Writer; [memb.] North Coast Presbyterian church; [hon.] Dean's List; [oth. writ.] Article published in college newspaper; [pers.] Only when I became aware of God's unchanging, eternal love for me could I freely love others. The knowledge of God's love for me also allows me to accept unreservedly other people's love. It is the energizing force in my life.; [a.] Carlsbad, CA

OSBORN, SCOTT A.

[b.] December 11, 1969, Stillwater, OK; [p.] Stanley R. Osborn - Carolyn L. Osborn; [ed.] Broken Arrow Senior High School, Upper Merion High School, Montgomery county Community college, Tulsa County Vo-Tech (Photography); [occ.] Industrial Roofer, Lower Providence Ambulance Squad; [oth. writ.] "A Midthoughts Whim" - A collection of poems, short stories, and other assorted literary strands; [pers.] Souls undaunted are souls undone.; [a.] Trooper, PA

OTOSHI, YOSHIYUKI

[b.] July 23, 1920, Hiroshima, Japan; [p.] Asazo Otoshi, Tamano Otoshi; [m.] Betty Kiyoko Otoshi; [ch.] Grant Yukio and Beverly Yukino; [ed.] McKinley High School (Honolulu) American Institute of Banking (Standard Certificate); [occ.] Retired since 1985, after working 43 years with the First Hawaiian Bank as an accountant; [memb.] Honolulu Japanese Chamber of Commerce, Hawaii Economic Study Club Honpa Hongwanji Mission of Hawaii Japanese Cultural of Hawaii; [hon.] Presented with a certificate by the International Society of Poets as a distinguished Member. An Editor's Choice Award was presented to me for "Of Tassels in the Wind," published in anthology Journey Of The Mind.; [oth. writ.] My poem, "Of Tassels in the Wind" was selected for printing in the anthology, Journey Of The Mind, "Bits of Beauty" was selected for printing in the anthology, A Moment In Time, and "A Place on Earth I love to be" in anthology, East Of The Sunrise. Currently, my poem, "The Four Winds of Time and Ozymandias" will be published in the Anthology, The Garden Of Life.; [pers.] I became a naturalized citizen of the United States of America on February 26, 1953. It was a proud and happy moment of my life. To my 1938 Senior Core Studies teacher, Mrs. Mary Robey Harris, I am deeply grateful for first opening my eyes and mind into literature and poetry. With thoughts and deeds, however puny they may be, I am striving to make our world a bit more beautiful.; [a.] Honolulu, Hawaii

OUELLETTE, CLARA C.

[pen.] "Cynthia Diamond"; [b.] November 29, 1941, New Denmark, Victoria Co. NB; [p.] Aurele and Christine Albert; [m.] August 7, 1965; [ch.] Annette, Francis and Danielle; [ed.] Nursing Assistant; [occ.] "Special Home Care Aid"; [memb.] "Writer's Federation of New Brunswick" and "Song Writer's of America"; [oth. writ.] Poem published in the anthology of poetry "Paths Less Treveled" 1990. Poem in "Poetic Voices of America 1990. My first book is to be published in near future. The title is "My Gift of Thoughts" (poetry, fiction short story and reflections.) (Reg. #417896); [pers.] I believe, the spirit of a writer and poet is a heavenly message brought on like a wondering soul, spread across life's restless sea and before me lies revealed upon the written page, the magical thoughts.; [a.] Grand Falls, NB, Canada

OUZMAN, TANYA BRITT

[b.] May 20, 1972, South Africa; [p.] Tom and Sheilach Midgley; [ed.] Kaffrarian High School, King Williams Town; [occ.] General Assistant TMC Real Estate, Cape Town; [memb.] Dolphin Action Protection Group - Volunteer; [oth. writ.] I have written a lot of poetry - but have not sent any in for publication; [pers.] To my parents, sisters, my cousin Robin and my fiancee Marc - I love you. "Don't be afraid of the dark, because it is the only time you can see the stars"; [a.] Claremont Cape Town, South Africa

OWEN, RONDA LEE

[pen.] Ronda Lee Owen; [b.] October 16, 1967, Alliance, OH; [p.] Mildred Scott; [ed.] Graduated Co-Valedictorian Sebring McKinley High School; [pers.] I wrote my poem in memory of my best friend, my cousin. May he be happy in the place he has gone. I miss him.; [a.] East Liverpool, OH

OWENS, STEVEN C.

[b.] September 12, 1967, New York; [m.] Laura A. La Mantia - Owens, October 1, 1994; [ed.] Associates degree in Journalism from Brookdale Community College.; [occ.] Agency service associate at Prudential Insurance; [oth. writ.] Sports writer for the Monmouth college newspaper. Poetry published in another Library Anthology "On a Threshold of a Dream."; [pers.] "The written word is a powerful tool. It has the ability to heal, to teach, to bring cultured together as well as tear them apart. But best of all, to communicate between one another".; [a.] Keyport, NJ

PACE, JAMIE LEANN

[b.] October 12, 1980, Rock Hill, SC; [p.] Lance and Ellen Pace; [ed.] York Comprehensive High School;

[memb.] York Comprehensive High School Cougar Band (1994-95 S.C. State Marching Band Champions).; [hon.] I have made the honor roll every year of my schooling so far. I received a U.S. Achievement Academy 1992 National Award.; [oth. writ.] Another poem published also.; [pers.] I strive to take hold of the most challenging and rewarding opportunities. I take pride in my writing and I believe that when a person finds something they have a talent for, they should grab on to it.; [a.] Rock Hill, SC

PACK, KEVIN R.
[pen.] Boats; [b.] May 7, 1953, Pittsburgh, PA; [p.] Donald and Claire Pack; [m.] Colleen Ann (Miller) Pack, April 30, 1983; [ch.] Morgan Elaine, 10 yrs., James Richard, 8 yrs.; [ed.] Drop-out, 11th grade South Hill H.S. 1971. Obtained G.E.D. University of Maine, 1979.; [occ.] United States Navy 14 June 1972 - 31 January 1996; [memb.] Knights of Columbus; [hon.] Military Awards too numerous to mention in space allotted. All awards received from Vietnam, Granada and desert shield/storm; [oth. writ.] I've started a book (fiction) called R.E.M. It's about 1/10 complete. Most of my writings have been what I consider lyrics but I guess lyrics are just poems without music. I have about 20-30 lyrics/poems that I would consider equal to or better that prozac.; [pers.] Everything a person creates, comes from within, form his heart, his soul based on how he or she feels. Writers block has nothing to do with weather or not a person can write, it's how they are feeling. If you don't believe that just as an artist, a musician, an athlete, ask yourself.; [a.] Hampton, VA

PAGE, DAVID [pen.]
Andrew Page; [b.] March 30, 1983, New Haven, CT; [p.] Samuel and Kimberly Page Jr.; [ed.] Torrington Middle School; [occ.] Student; [hon.] Honor Roll, TAG (Talented and Gifted Program); [pers.] Always plan ahead and cherish time; [a.] Torrington, CT

PAGE, RONALD D.
[b.] March 15, 1948, Fort Worth, TX; [p.] Bob and Joyce Brandt; [ch.] Nikki and Tony Page; [ed.] Marina High School; [occ.] Self-employed; [hon.] Honorary Mention; [oth. writ.] Several poems published by Cader publishers. Iliad publishers and sparrow grass publishers - also a children's book in process called my little pocketbook.; [pers.] I write from the heart and work on personal issues as I write. A lot of my published work has my personal life involved with recovery.; [a.] Redlands, CA

PAIGE SR., CHARLES H.
[b.] June 22, 1944, Boston, MA; [p.] Mr. and Mrs. Milton Paige Sr.; [m.] Judith M. Paige, September 10, 1965; [ch.] Charles II, and Jeffrey; [ed.] Newburry Jr. College, 2 yrs. Management/College Courses, Graduate: Bethel Bible Institute; [occ.] Ministry; [memb.] Member of the Body of Christ; [hon.] Bronze Star Air Medal; [oth. writ.] Various unpublished poems and contemporary Christian songs.; [pers.] You have no life until you give your life to the one who gave you life.; [a.] Ferguson, MO

PAINE, JOHN PAUL
[b.] January 22, 1928, Cincinnati, OH; [p.] Mr. and Mrs. James W. Paine; [ed.] University of Havana, Cuba (Pre-Castro), Lemania College in Lausanne, Switzerland. Spanish Institute of Culture in Madrid, Spain, School of Protocol in Washington, DC.; [occ.] Sub-Contractor; [memb.] Charter Member of US Library of Congress Civilization, Honorary Order of Kentucky Colonels; [hon.] Recipients of Spain's Lighest decoration known as: Isabella La Catolica. 1994 International Citizens of the Principality of Hutt River Province in Australia. Reed Kentucky's Highest Award. - A Kentucky Colonel. Founder of Queen Isabella Day Each April 22 in the USA; [oth. writ.] Wrote and authored a monograph titled: Isabella of Castile - An Historical Tribute, Comments ones the years on current events have been published in the NY times, newsweek, time, The Washington Post, US World news, Intern'l Herald Tribune, The European among others.; [pers.] I'm just right of rush Limbaugh, the doctor of democracy.; [a.] Philadelphia, PA

PALITE, WILLIE RUSSELL
[pen.] Pookey; [b.] February 23, 1960, Philadelphia, PA; [p.] John and Carrie Palite; [m.] Paulette Webb (fiancee); [ch.] Kife, Shannon, Willie Jr., William R. T. Palite; [ed.] E.M. Stanton, Barrett Jr. High, South Phila. High School; [occ.] Banquet Chief and Line Cook at Holiday Inn Hotel; [pers.] What I say comes from the heart, and I was pleased to share my joy with someone who cares.; [a.] Philadelphia, PA

PALMER, ROBERT
[pen.] R. Charles Palmer; [b.] February 12, 1944, Rochester, NY; [p.] Charles and Marie Palmer; [m.] not married; [ch.] 1 daughter; [ed.] Churchville-Chili High School, Monroe Community College, Rochester Institute of Technology; [occ.] Associate Broker Prudential Roaks Realtors; [memb.] N.Y.S. Realtors Association; [oth. writ.] Irish Heart, and notes on the notes of your life; [pers.] Poems are created from observations and experiences of life.; [a.] Rochester, NY

PARENTE, DOROTHY ANN
[pen.] D. Ann Roberts; [b.] May 20, 1930, New Haven, CT; [p.] Joseph and Florence Formato; [m.] Robert Joseph Parente, July 10, 1954; [ch.] Lisa Ann Parente, Suzanne Parente; [ed.] St. John's High, Southern Connecticut State University; [occ.] Former Elementary School Teacher (Retired); [memb.] Leukaemia Society, Southern Connecticut State University Alumni Assoc.; [hon.] P.T.A. Scholarship, Dean's List.; [oth. writ.] Poetry and letters in local newspapers. The American Women's Group in Paris. Editorials.; [pers.] I believe we are firmly rooted in our heritage of the past. Yet we must consciously break with the past to live for the present. To enjoy the love, beauty, and truth in our universe is to fulfill our destiny.; [a.] Clinton, CT

PARISI, JOHN MICHAEL
[pen.] Jonny Pabio; [b.] March 24, 1965, New York City, NY; [p.] Anthony Parisi, Angelina Parisi; [ed.] Alfred G. Berner High School, State University at Coble Skill; [occ.] Certified Chef; [hon.] Honorable mention from Coble Skill College, 94-95; [oth. writ.] I am a hopeless romantic, most of my work is original and unknown!!; [pers.] I dedicate this poem to my entire family, without their love this poem would have not been made possible. "In memory of my lost love" Laura Lee Rini; [a.] Massapequa Park, NY

PARKER, ALICIA
[b.] December 11, 1960, KS; [p.] Gilbert and Marylou Parker; [ch.] Kerren, Destiny and Jessica Parker; [ed.] 11th Grade Business Management Credits; [occ.] Mother; [hon.] My awards are given each day from our creator; [oth. writ.] I have a large amount of poems no one has ever heard their poems about real life love God.; [pers.] I am so thrilled to know my poem will be read by many and understood by few, hopefully those whom understand can relate and know they aren't alone.; [a.] Wichita, KS

PARKER, DENISE
[pen.] Denise Parker; [b.] August 27, 1971, Chester, PA; [p.] Theodore and Cemille Parker; [ed.] Chester High School, Neumann College; [occ.] Registered Nurse; [memb.] Chester AIDS Coalition; [oth. writ.] Two articles on weight loss published in the August 1986 and May 1989 issues of prevention magazine.; [pers.] On a personal note I find writing poetry to be both a cleansing and a healing process which integrates the innermost thoughts and emotions of the author.; [a.] Chester, PA

PARKER, HERMAN
[pen.] Herman Parker; [b.] April 14, 1956, Marshall, TX; [p.] Charlie and Evie Parker; [ch.] Andrea; [ed.] Marshall High School Wiley College MTI Vocational Institute; [occ.] Prison; [pers.] As God uses prisoners in the bible to inspire the hearts of the world. I thank Him for the blessings He has given me.; [a.] Marshall, TX

PARKER, LAURA ELIZABETH
[b.] May 15, 1979, Louisville, KY; [p.] George and Liz Parker; [ed.] Louisville Male Traditional, Saint Francis High School; [occ.] Student, grade 10; [memb.] Walden Theatre, People-to-People International Bon Air Thunder Soccer, Holy Spirit Catholic Church; [hon.] JCPS 15th District Art Award - 1st place Regional Scholastic Student Art Exhibit - 1st place Freshman Class Art Award, Male H.S. Mural Contest - Winner, Principal's List, Academic Excellence Award, Outstanding Freshman JV, MVP Soccer Award, Scholastic Writing Award-1994, Academic Science Team '94-95, Varsity Soccer - District, Regional and State Championships '94, People-to-People Ambassador to Australia/New Zealand.; [oth. writ.] Many stories and poems; [a.] Louisville, KY

PASKO, SUE
[b.] October 3, 1964, Detroit, MI; [p.] Tom and Barbara Elwart; [m.] Stan Pasko, May 23, 1987; [ed.] Centerline High, St. Claire Community College, Macomb County Community College, Oakland University; [occ.] Critical Care RN-Bonsecours Hospital - Grosse Pte, MI; [memb.] Nurses Service Organization; [pers.] I continually strive for improvement in my personal goals and through education. I also believe in commitment to my fellow mankind.; [a.] Saint Clair, MI

PASSI, SONYA
[b.] September 25, 1979, San Diego; [p.] Eduardo and Guadalupe Passi; [ed.] Current enrolled in Sophomore year at Eastlake High School; [hon.] In Junior HIgh, June of 1993, in "The Castle Park Times" poem on graduation, First place in '91 Halloween Poetry contest - "Halloween Night"; [oth. writ.] A collection of poems such as "I'll see you," "Loving You," "Soul Mate," "One Moment," "Eternal Memories," The Gift of Love," and many more.; [pers.] An inspiring line written by my friend, Laurie Hingada: Falling in love is like a rose, each petal falls at its own time.; [a.] Chula Vista, CA

PASSINAULT, SYLVIA J.
[pen.] Kathleen Cornell; [b.] March 22, 1918, Withee, WI; [p.] John and Anna Wing, deceased; [m.] Louis Passinault, June 28, 1952; [ch.] Jeannine Ann, Jonathon Pierre, Timothy L. Gregory Paul, Stepchildren: Tom, Patti, and James; [ed.] Elementary, High School, Secretarial by correspondence and night school, at Parsons Bus. Sch., Cadet Nurse Corp Nazareth Coll. - Borgess Hosp. Kalamazoo and Kaluhozzo State Hospital.; [occ.] Retired; [memb.] Alumnae: Borgess Hospital, etc. Sacred Heart Parish, Munising American Family Assoc. Boystown; [hon.] Mother Agnes Murphy - scholarship

award - as best in Clinical and Academics - Senior Nurse - 1948; [oth. writ.] Wrote parody for my High School Class song (The original was "When It's Dark on Observatory Hill") Some poetry published locally along with several other "poets". "Are You Running Grammar?" "It's Probably Wesley" "This Child and I".; [pers.] I have "words" even as a youngster who insisted on going to school (First Grade - no Kindergarten) at 5 yrs of age. Usually an incident stimulates me something I want to capture so others can see the 'scene' or humor or sensitivity of the person or event, or animals.; [a.] Munising, MI

PATE, CAROL DANIELS
[b.] June 27, 1957, Cuthbert, GA; [p.] Bobby and Becky Daniels; [m.] Randy Pate, December 2, 1978; [ch.] Jason Daniel, Anna Rebecca; [ed.] Tift Co, High School, Abraham Baldwin College; [occ.] Full-time mom, part-time U.S. Postal Service; [memb.] First Baptist Church of Chula, and Baptist Young Women; [pers.] "Rainbows Vs. Reality", In Memory of: Pete Daniels June 13, 1958 - October 27, 1976, Through all the beautiful memories... We will never be apart.; [a.] Chula, GA

PATENTE, MICHELLE SUZETTE
[pen.] Magrant Jensin; [b.] February 21, 1949, Philadelphia; [p.] Robert Marcel and Rose Patente; [ed.] George Washington High (Major: English) They dash school of dance (Certificate of Teaching) Major: TAP, The community college of Philadelphia co-associates degree in library science).; [occ.] Story-writer and poet (free-lance).; [memb.] Twenty-five year member of Nichiren Shushu of America, A Buddist organization for value creation and human revolution; [hon.] Royalties are for drug and alcohol rehabilitation in America, especially street alcoholism, prison system reconstruction, child prostitution and teenage runaways; [oth. writ.] Main words are: Umbrians poetica - Book of Poetry, The Guards of Matilde - Book of Selected poems My Father was a Frenchman, Book of Short Stories, Jesefca and other stories, Book of Selected stories; [pers.] My Cellist and I use the back suites for our performances, at which time I read to an audience and she accompanies me on her musical cello! At that time, John Sebastian's presence can be deeply felt and the audience forms a beautiful soul of it's own.; [a.] Philadelphia, PA

PATTERSON, SANDRA
[b.] April 13, 1973, Winchester, Ontario; [p.] Lloyd and Shirley Patterson; [ed.] Early Childhood Education Graduate (ECE); [occ.] Day Care Teacher; [oth. writ.] I have written a variety of poems hoping to one day publish a book of my own.; [pers.] When your heart aches for something so desperately, secure it's surrounding hope so closely as if to never let it go. That something may one day become yours to keep forever.

PAULIN, STEPHANIE M.
[b.] March 2, 1979, Lewiston, ME; [p.] Reginald and Claudette Poulin; [ed.] Presently Sophomore Mohonasen High School Rotterdam N.Y.; [occ.] Student; [memb.] SADD, Key Club, Mohonasen HS Marching Band, Youth 2000, St Madeleine Sophie RCC; [oth. writ.] None published; [pers.] If you strive to accomplish something go all the way. Don't stop in the middle and quit because it's too hard. If you want any dream bad enough it will happen one day without you even knowing.; [a.] Schenectady, NY

PAVLOUSKY, ANNE B.
[b.] Castalian Springs, TN; [p.] Swaney and Mabel Bentley; [m.] Colonel John D. Pavlousky, April 4, 1970; [ch.] Kathryn, Amanda, John David and Julianne; [ed.] B.S. Degree from Middle Tennessee State University, Master's Degree from the University of Virginia; [occ.] College English Instructor; [oth. writ.] Published OWC monthly newletters, published articles in local newspaper; [pers.] My poems are inspired by the beauty of God's nature and childhood recollections. Perhaps the writers of the romantic era have greatly influenced me.; [a.] San Antonio, TX

PAZIK, GLORIA J.
[b.] February 16, 1946, Little Falls, MN; [p.] Robert and Elsie Clear; [m.] Terry M. Pazik, June 1, 1974; [ch.] Troy, Scott, Heather, Jeremy, and Jay; [ed.] Brookly Center High; [occ.] Painting Contractor; [memb.] Gethsemane Lutheran Church Upsala Lioness Club; [oth. writ.] Several articles printed in the local paper (upsala siren); [pers.] As I get older, I find myself more aware of the beauty around me. I'm constantly writing down my thoughts and my past, for my children and grandchildren to look back on. I feel everyone's life is important to their loved ones.; [a.] Upsala, MN

PEACOCK, HERBERT L.
[pen.] Herbert Peacock; [b.] October 28, 1910, England; [p.] Reid and Caroline Peacock; [m.] Gisele Peacock; [ed.] University of Cambridge, England.; [occ.] Artist and Writer; [memb.] "La Societe Canadienne De L'Aquarelle" (S.C.A), Founder - Member, In England, Elected Member of United Artists (London).; [hon.] Honours degree in history of cambridge University England; [oth. writ.] Short stories a some poetry contributed to "Chamber's Journal" (Edinburgh). Five volumes of history of England, Europe beyond published by Heinemann Educational Publications, Ltd.; [pers.] My early career was in the educational field. I am especially conserved with the twentieth century and its important for the future of man and his philosophy; [a.] Pointe-Claire Quebec, Canada

PEARSON, DOROTHY C.
[b.] December 8, 1928, Gering, NE; [p.] Alex and Amelia Ross; [m.] Donald R. Pearson, January 21, 1951; [ch.] Greg Pearson, Donna Russell, grandchildren - Brian - Jeff - Mark Russell; [ed.] Graduate scottsbluft, Nebraska High School.; [occ.] Housewife; [pers.] In Gering Nebraska - parents Alex and Amelia Ross brothers - Harvey, Jenny, Ernie Ross of Scottsbluff, NE. - Sister Alvina (Ross) Babcock Napa Calif - written poems since fourth grade - as a hobby - and to express press feeling - this poem was written in honor of my brother Ernie - who passed away April 23', 1972 - age 35 - The first two lines - are the actual words - in said to his mother - the poem relates to his life.; [a.] Portland, OR

PEDREIRA, NIEVES
[b.] May 4, 1975, New York; [p.] Nieves and Jose Pedreira; [ed.] In College; [occ.] Student; [hon.] Academic Grant, Dean's List, Alpha Sigma Criminal Justice Honor Society; [pers.] I feel that for me writing is a form of creativity and a form of expression. I feel that I can express any emotion through my poetry and writings. [a.] New York, NY

PENALUNA, GINGER
[pers.] I want to reach enlightenment and help others to reach the same goal. That is all.

PENICK, DIANNA MARIE
[b.] December 12, 1978, Sheffield, AL; [p.] Wanda Terry and Dennis F. Penick; [ed.] I currently attend Charity Chapel Academy as a ninth grade student; [occ.] Student, babysitter; [pers.] I began writing at an early age, my parents were divorcing and writing for me then was an escape from a reality I was unwilling to face at the time.; [a.] Leighton, AL

PENZO, RAQUEL
[b.] May 23, 1975, Brooklyn, NY; [p.] Mercedes Acosta; [ed.] Brooklyn Technical HS, (Civil Engineering major) Alfred University (2nd year, Environmental Studies Major); [occ.] Student at Alfred University; [memb.] Member of IASU (Iberu American student Union) at Alfred U. DJ at College Radio Station (WALF); [hon.] Women in Science Award June 1989, Presidential Academic Fitness Award June 1989; [pers.] I've never considered myself to be an artist, I'm just a person who really knows how to express her feelings with pen and paper.; [a.] Alfred, NY

PERCIVAL, SCOTT
[b.] August 21, 1979, Biloxi, MS; [p.] Michael and Carol Percival; [ed.] High School Sophomore; [occ.] Student, Life Guard; [memb.] Multnomah Athletic Club; [hon.] 6 High School varsity letters. Oregon 13-14 year old State Champion Swimming (1994) 1,500m free style. 2 time Presidential Academic/fitness award winner; [pers.] You have to go all out all the way!; [a.] Portland, OR

PEREIRA, JENNIFER
[b.] March 13, 1976, CA; [p.] Alvaro Pereira, Laura Cabreana, Ernie Cabreara; [pers.] My Lord, Jesus, has inspired me to write, encourage me to trust, and strengthened me with love. I write about him so others may have a chance to experience God's love.; [a.] Dublin, CA

PEREZ, BILL
[pen.] Gib Perez; [occ.] Psychotherapy Clinic Administrator; [oth. writ.] "The Connecting Point" and books. "The Adventures of Willy Wheels and The Skateboard Kings" Poems "Dirt Poor Splendor", "Twist of Fate", "Thinketh"; [pers.] We must always work with what we have and from where we are

PERLIS, RANDY
[b.] September 2, 1955, El Paso, TX; [p.] Anthony F. and Renate Perlis; [m.] Kim Fox, September 2, 1995; [ed.] Killeen High School, University of Texas at Arlington; [occ.] Chemist; [memb.] Aurora Masters Swim Club; [a.] Aurora, CO

PERRAS, DOREAL
[pen.] Doreal Perras; [b.] August 19, 1965, Hamilton, Ontario; [p.] D.A.M. Holmes, Ivan Kolloff (wrestling name) or Ofeal Perras; [ch.] Andre, Heather, Aubre, Dorothy, Grace.; [ed.] Life?; [occ.] Mom, (Do Oil Paintings Part-time); [oth. writ.] Many but I've never let anyone see them.; [pers.] Look up at the sky, watch the clouds as they move, always changing shape, unpredictable, a bit like life.; [a.] Kingston Ontario, Canada

PERRINE, VAN B.
[b.] March 23, 1954, Fort Wayne, IN; [p.] Van and Audrey Perrine; [m.] Betty Perrine, June 25, 1989; [pers.] If you can not fall down with dignity, then fall down with out it. Dedicated to my father. And the Memory of my mother.; [a.] Tampa, FL

PERRY, CONNIE E.
[b.] December 10, 1971, Birmingham, AL; [p.] Kathryn and Jerry Schoenradt; [m.] Bart Perry III, November 5, 1991; [ch.] Steven Nathaniel, Timothy Ryan, De Anna Elise; [ed.] Trevor Brown High, Lamson Jr. College; [occ.] Housewife; [oth. writ.] Published one other poem; [pers.] I have been writing since the eighth grade. I was inspired by my english teacher Mrs. Ireland, and my best friend Kathleen Perry; [a.] Phoenix, AZ

PERRY, PATRICIA A.
[pen.] Patsy Ann; [b.] December 24, 1949, Dallas; [p.] Oleta and Raymond Smith; [m.] Divorced; [ch.] Michael and Chris Perry; [ed.] High School Diploma, Computer Course Diploma; [occ.] Working at Eckerd's Distribution Center

PETAGARA, DULCE
[pen.] Dulce Ledo; [b.] August 2, 1965, San Francisco, CA; [p.] Maria Elena (Ledo) Maltez; [m.] Ernie Petagara, July 6, 1986; [ed.] B.A. Environmental Studies U.C. Santa Cruz, Immaculate Conception Academy High School; [occ.] Hazardous Materials and Safety Coordinator; [oth. writ.] Numerous unpublished poems; [pers.] Nurture the inner child. Always strive to do your best. Take a risk, you might succeed!

PETERS, LILLIAN E.
[b.] January 27, 1956, Warwick, VA; [p.] Kenneth and Bessie Bergman; [m.] Divorced; [ch.] Laura, Benjamin and Ross Peters; [ed.] Mira Costa H.S. Manhattan Beach CA Regional Occupational Program - Truck Driving; [occ.] School Bus Driver and Commercial Truck Driver; [memb.] Carleton Oaks PTA The church of Jesus Christ of Latter-Day Saints.; [oth. writ.] Just my own personal writings. I wrote a lot in high school.; [pers.] To be the best mother and friend that I can be. To be a service to others, and to make positive changes in the lives of those around me.; [a.] El Cajon, CA

PETERSEN, NAOMI P.
[b.] May 11, 1971, Addis Abeba, Ethiopia; [p.] Reome A. Petersen and Tsige Tefera-Petersen; [pers.] I dedicate this poem to Michelle I. White my partner in crime through the madness and to the man who not only inspired this poem, but was the source of our madness Mr. William Bradley Pitt. May your lips live forever.; [a.] Philadelphia, PA

PETERSON, VERTRELL R.
[pen.] Trell; [b.] December 2, 1950, Buffalo, NY; [p.] Arthur and Jannie Davis; [m.] Charles E. (Pete) Peterson, October 27, 1973; [ed.] Elementary High School, Buffalo, N.Y., B.S. Sociology, Wilberforce University, Wilberforce, Ohio Saint Joseph's College, Windham; [memb.] National Association of Female Executives, World of Poetry.; [hon.] Silver Poet '90, Golden Poet '91, Appreciation US Navy '90; [pers.] I wanted to save the world, but once I started working in my field, I realized that the world doesn't want to be saved.; [a.] Charlotte, NC

PETITO, ROZAN
[b.] February 28, 1956, Trenton, NJ; [p.] Salvatore Petito, Dolly Petito; [m.] Ronald E. La Bendig, March 5, 1994; [ch.] Selah Grace, William Stephen, Marisha Katherine; [ed.] Steinert High School, Sarasota School of Massage Therapy; [occ.] Lic. Massage Therapist Pump Haus Health and Fitness, Owner; [memb.] NMTA; [hon.] 1974 American Theatre Assoc. Critics Awards Best Original Playwright/Bucks County Playhouse, 1984, Golden Poet; [oth. writ.] Poetry Today Magazine, local papers; [pers.] To express my heart's desire for every knee to bend and every tongue confess that Christ is Lord.; [a.] Sarasota, FL

PETRIE, CURTIS P.
[b.] June 25, 1970, Edmonton, Alberta, Canada; [p.] Ardis R. Petrie - mother; [ed.] University of Alberta, Concordia University - BFA; [occ.] Design Art Major at Concordia University, (graduating year); [oth. writ.] "Sweet Vexations" - a self produced collection of poems.; [pers.] From the other side of nowhere, springs forth the dream of everywhere.; [a.] Calgary, Alberta, Canada

PFEFFER, ADAM
[b.] December 25, 1957, Queens, NY; [ed.] UCLA, Art Center College of Design (Pasadena, CA); [occ.] Writer; [memb.] Zeta Beta Tau (ZBT) fraternity; [hon.] Statewide awards for UCLA newspaper First Place, Best editorial page Second Place, opinion columns Division and local Dument Investigative Reporting Award. Intern for syndicated columnist Jack Anderson in Wash., D.C.; [oth. writ.] Newspaper Reporter and Magazine editor for about 10 years, investigative article for Jack Anderson appeared in the Congressional Record in 1979.; [pers.] Art is nothing more than signed postcards from the soul.; [a.] Monsey, NY

PHELAN, LYNNE RODGERS
[pen.] Lynne Rodgers; [b.] March 30, 1953, Miami, FL; [p.] Ronald M. Rodgers, Martha Jo Pearson Noble (deceased); [m.] Separated soon to be divorced; [ch.] Kenneth R. Platt, Jonathan M. Phelan, Amanda M. Phelan; [ed.] Palmetto Sr. High, University of Florida; [occ.] Artist, Aerobics Instructor; [memb.] Exer-Safety Association reach of Haywood County - various charities; [hon.] Dean's List, Art Awards; [oth. writ.] Wrote primarily for myself and friends. This is my first submitted writing.; [pers.] My life has not been an easy one so my writing has been my personal journey towards healing. It is my hope and prayer that by sharing my heart, in writing, I could touch other hearts, and in some small way bring comfort.; [a.] Canton, NC

PHILLIPS, DANIEL ROBERT
[b.] March 13, 1976, San Diego; [p.] Bob and Phyllis Phillips; [ed.] Working on College degree at Liberty Univ.; [oth. writ.] I have a lot of poetry I would like to publish and let people read.; [pers.] I believe the Lord Jesus Christ to be my savior. I believe God's word, not man's word, to be the answer of man's problems.; [a.] El Cajon, CA

PHILLIPS, JOSHUA CLAY
[b.] March 16, 1985, New York, NY; [p.] Mark and Patricia Phillips; [ed.] The Mirman School; [occ.] Student; [memb.] U.S. Chess Federation; [oth. writ.] Poem published in "A Moment in Time", poems published in the 1994 and 1995 editions of the Anthology of Poetry by Young Americans".; [a.] Encino, CA

PIASETSKY, JANNAH
[b.] February 28, 1985, New York City, NY; [p.] Eugene and Sheryl Piasetsky; [ed.] Fourth grade student at Jeffrey Elementary School, Madison CT. Gifted and Talented Program.; [memb.] Kodaly Children's Chorus, 1000 Voice Choir (official entertainment for 1995 special olympics), french horn player of Jeffrey School band.; [hon.] 1992 Award winner of Youth Art Exhibit, Carriage House Art Gallery ("Pollution Hurts"). 1995 contributor to K-12 art show, Madison CT.; [oth. writ.] Many stories submitted locally.; [pers.] Life goes on in a circle that never ends. You are born, you live, and, when you die, you go into the ground and turn into grass. The animals eat the grass and we eat the animals. What you write and what you compose lives on in the minds and memories of people.; [a.] Madison, CT

PIERCE, DEBRA L.
[b.] June 30, 1963, New Berln, NY; [p.] Peg and John Gardner; [ch.] John (Jack) Pierce; [ed.] Sauquoit Valley Central, N.Y. Utica School of Commerce, Utica N.Y.; [occ.] Transportation Secretary, Centrex Labs. New Hartford, N.Y.; [pers.] Most of my poems are for someone special, family members and those I love or have loved. All of my poems reflect what's in my heart. My inspiration was my mother, who showed me the greatest love of all.; [a.] Sauquoit, NY

PIERCE, REV. ZEITA M.
[b.] January 22, 1946, Duluth, MN; [p.] Lillian C. and Carl L. Wikstrom; [m.] Rev. Theodore M. Pierce, December 9, 1994; [ed.] Cathedral High School - St Benedict's - St. Joseph's Hospital School of Nrsg - Browning Commercial College - Universal Temple of Truth Foundation - Temple of the Ascended Masters - California College of Hypnosis; [occ.] Minister/Wife/ Clinical Hypnotherapist Counselor - Teacher; [memb.] Universal Temple of Truth Foundation - Temple of the Ascended Masters - American Council of Hypnotist Examiners - Yarnell Senior Center; [a.] Yarnell, AZ

PIMENTEL, PAUL MARIE
[pen.] Paula M. Pimentel; [b.] December 27, 1976, West Sacramento, CA; [oth. writ.] 1,200 poems written in 4 books not yet published, (The Book of Love), (Dream Passage), (The Book of Days), and my current one, (The Dark Decades) and I was published in the National Library of poetry at 13 with the poem, (Gothic); [pers.] Poetry seemed to fade with modern technology taking over, and I keep writing in hope that I can awaken someone to the deep world of a poet.; [a.] West Sacramento, CA

PINKHAM, DANIELLE MARIE
[b.] December 19, 1995, Ellsworth; [p.] Lewis and Carole Anne Pinkham; [ed.] Summer Memorial High School; [occ.] Student; [hon.] Honor Roll, Science Fair Winner, Varsity Cheerleader, Varsity Tennis; [pers.] Cheerleaders are athletes too!; [a.] Gouldsboro, ME

PIPKIN, JAMES
[b.] June 28, 1982, Hildale, UT; [p.] Valerie and Don Pipkin; [ed.] Enoch Elementary School, Colorado City Unified School District #14; [occ.] Student; [hon.] I won a blue ribbon in the Molave County Writing Contest; [oth. writ.] The Father, The Unicorn, No One, What's Wrong With This World (Blue Ribbon) I'll always be there for you psalm for a child, etc.; [pers.] To some, I seem small. To others, I am a giant.

PITT, JAMES M.
[b.] July 26, 1945, St Louis, MO; [p.] Maynard Pitt, Adele Pitt; [m.] Helen Pitt, October 25, 1975; [ch.] Laura Jean, Kathy Lynn, Michael Duane; [ed.] Mater Del High, Southern Illinois University; [occ.] Internal Auditor, U.S. Army, Rancher; [memb.] Oxford Club, National Rifle Association for the People Association; [hon.] Dean's List; [oth. writ.] Several poems offered for publication in local paper or national news letter.; [pers.] Started writing verse late in life completing my first poem the past year. Perhaps inexorably drawn by my perceived breath down in today's value system.; [a.] Laquey, MO

PITTMAN, TERRI

[b.] December 13, 1952, Youngstown, OH; [p.] Ted and Mary Shilling; [m.] Allen Pittman, May 1, 1982; [ch.] Tamara Boles (daughter), Erik Boles (son-in-law); [ed.] Austintown Fitch High Cortez High; [occ.] Waitress, Bitzee Mama's Restaurant, Glendale, AZ; [memb.] Hosanna Christian Fellowship; [oth. writ.] Currently writing a book about my present occupation.; [pers.] I thank my Lord and Savior Jesus Christ for the family and friends he has blessed me with, and I hope to continue to share his love through my writings.; [a.] Glendale, AZ

PIZZA, NORMAN FRANCIS

[b.] April 15, 1921, New Orleans; [p.] Lillian M. Lutz and Norman V. Pizza; [m.] Frances Marie Pizza, February 19, 1949; [ch.] 2 sons; [ed.] Graduate of Fortier High School, graduate of Soulé University as an Accountant, was a soldier scout in 2nd World War; [occ.] retired Computer Programmer Group Leader; [memb.] Realtor for Martha M. Samuel, one of the founders of Terry Town Volunteer Fire Dept, member of "Christ the King Church," member of the "Lions" Club and the Veterans; [hon.] Won meritorious certificate for gov't. work, won medals of honor for expertise at being a soldier scout, was chairman of the publicity committee for Terry Town Trumpet; [oth. writ.] Wrote poems "off & on" then would toss them away. Never saved them! [pers.] Put the entire Bible in my computer and could get any part of it out at the press of a button!

PLACKMEYER, MONA

[pen.] Mona Hand Plackmeyer; [b.] May 3, 1931, Columbia, MO; [p.] Beulah Hand, Howard Hand; [m.] Jerald Plackmeyer (deceased), June 8, 1952; [ch.] Karen, Kathy, Kevin, Kerry; [ed.] Nevada High School, Nevada, MO, Lindenwood College, St. Charles, MO; [occ.] Second grade teacher Lincoln Elementary, St. Charles, MO; [memb.] First United Methodist Church Republican Party, NEA, MO NEA, St. Charles NEA; [hon.] Who's Who among students in American Universities and Colleges 1984-85, Kiwanis Scholastic Award, 1987; [oth. writ.] Many poems in local newspapers, Golden Poet Award for 1989 for poem, Andy; [pers.] I strive to express life along with the influence of nature. I have been influenced by the liberal arts college which I attended.; [a.] Saint Charles, MO

PLANK, TINA

[b.] April 30, 1961, Council Bluffs, IA; [p.] Artie Bedard and Jim Feekin; [m.] Tony Plank, December 3, 1983; [ch.] Andrea Nicole, Nathan Douglas, Tee Daniel; [ed.] GED from Iowa Western Comm. College, Associate Degree in Marketing from Ivy Tech. in Logansport In.; [occ.] Homemaker; [memb.] Arbor Day Society, PTO; [hon.] Dean's List; [oth. writ.] Several children's books submitted, but no answer yet.; [pers.] As a victim of child abuse, both sexual and physical, I would like to use my experiences to change the current laws in this country. I believe through the power of God and the written word my goals are attainable.; [a.] Walton, IN

PLICHIE, ROY

[pen.] Sonny; [b.] July 29, 1931, Glace Bay; [p.] Joesph and Florence Plichie; [m.] Carmel Margaret, December 25, 1952; [ch.] Carol, Tyrone, Rocky; [ed.] St. Annes High College of Cape Breton; [occ.] Safety Co-ordinator, Supervisor; [memb.] Canadian Diabetic Association, Canadian Safety Association, Canadian Liberal Association; [oth. writ.] Poems published in local newspapers.; [pers.] Some of my poems will make you sad, some will make you think, but most will make you feel happy, and that is what I strive to do in life, to make people laugh and be happy.; [a.] Cape Breton, Nova Scotia, Canada

PLISKO, GARY P.

[pen.] Philip; [b.] November 8, 1955, Wheeling, WV; [p.] Alexander Plisko Sr., Caroline Pazzelli Plisko; [m.] Single; [ed.] Northeast High School 1973, St. Petersburg, FL., Flight School-Aeronautics 1980; [occ.] Lithographer; [memb.] Commanders Club (DAV) National Rifle Association; [oth. writ.] Amateur more poetry to come; [pers.] The good Lord lightens the path that guides my feet. I wish to dwell in his house forever; [a.] Saint Petersburg, FL

PLUNKETT, ANN

[pen.] Ann Plunkett; [b.] October 22, 1932, San Francisco, CA; [p.] Mr. and Mrs. Joseph Plunkett; [ed.] B.A. English, Mt. St. Mary's College Los Angeles, CA, Teaching Credential/State of California, Library Credential Certificate/California, Certified Graphoanalyst/California; [occ.] Sister of St. Joseph of Carondelet; [memb.] Former member of Graphoanalysis Assoc. in Oakland, CA; [oth. writ.] Gentle Muses, I "Autumn" go to school; [pers.] I strive to show beauty, wonders and hope in my poetry. I want to give the gift of hope and love to all who read my poems.

PLUNKETT, BERNICE

[pen.] Bernice Plunkett; [b.] May 17, 1944, KY; [p.] Audrey and Orville Jubainville; [m.] Deceased - Donnie E. Plunkett; [ch.] Michael - Walter - Brian - Kristie - Brett - Nathan; [ed.] 12th grade graduate; [occ.] Home maker - Mom; [memb.] None concerning Poetry of Southgate, MI. Church membership - Helps Ministry Word of Life Fellowship Lincoln Park, MI., Pastor's Garris May and Ruby Wood; [hon.] Only honored by my church. They are often used in our Church bulletins and news letters.; [pers.] I am a widow - since 1983 I used to write stories and poems for or in my English-Literature class in high school. Then stopped writing for many years. Got gave me back the talent of writing in 1988.

POEL, CAROL

[b.] June 28, 1937, Chicago, IL; [p.] Eugene and Phyllis Springen; [m.] John Poel, June 20, 1980; [ch.] Linda Murray, Brenda Clouser, Grandchildren: Bryan, Ariel, Matthew; [ed.] Campbell County High, Chapman College; [occ.] Retired (former Teacher's Aide, special education); [oth. writ.] I am currently working on a children's book which I am hoping to publish in the near future; [pers.] My writings usually reflect my feelings. Or experiences I have had.; [a.] Ramona, CA

POMAINVILLE, SONJA

[b.] November 4, 1949, Schenectady, NY; [p.] Walfrid and Dorothy Pirkanen; [m.] Maurice Pomainville, September 27, 1983; [ch.] Sarah Foster; [ed.] UVM, Burlington, Vt. Graduated 1973 with a Degree in Nursing. I previously majored in Music Education from September, 1967 - September, 1970; [occ.] RN (Director of Helen Porter Nursing Home Middleburg, VT. Nursing); [memb.] VSNA, ANA, NADONA, I am co-chair of the Director of Nursing Group in VT. (For long term care); [hon.] Technical Nursing Award 1973, AJN-Award for VT. For article written on Professional Impairment (National Award); [oth. writ.] I have enjoyed writing poetry as a personal quest my entire life. I also am a singer spreading my wings through blues.; [pers.] I believe that writing is a form of spiritual growth and an extension of my soul. Life is a precious gift and one to be treasured.; [a.] Salisbury, VT

POND, KAREN W.

[b.] April 9, 1950, Assumption, IL; [p.] Bernadine R. Wallace; [m.] Charles J. Pond, October 15, 1978; [ch.] Michael Jeffrey; [ed.] Central H.S., Western Michigan University; [occ.] Williamsburg, VA Merchandising-Busch Gardens/Volunteer Caseworker-Ft Eustis, VA; [hon.] First American President - Business and Professional Women Club - Cambridge England 1992-93; [a.] Newsport News, VA

PONIATOWSKI, DENNIS E.

[pen.] Denny Mann; [b.] August 17, 1955, Wayne, MI; [p.] Edward and Irene Poniatowski; [m.] August 13, 1983, Divorced; [ch.] Arden Paige Poniatowski (7), Emily Morgan Poniatowski (5); [ed.] Cody High School Grad. 1973; [occ.] Fine Jewelry Stone Setter, Hand Engraver; [memb.] Q.L.A. (Quality of Life Assoc.); [hon.] Eagle Scout; [pers.] "One does what one has to do, when it's time to do it, and that's how it's done!" "Life needs no excuses, you just live it!"; [a.] Hadley, MI

PORKKA, ERNIE

[b.] March 26, 1928, Lethbridge, Alberta; [p.] Tillie and Walter Porkka; [m.] Lura Mae Porkka, July 17, 1964; [ch.] Lori, Cheryl, Karen; [ed.] Grade 12. Life's experience; [occ.] Retired Farmer; [memb.] Life member of B.P.O.ELKS. McKillop United Church Council Picture Butte Golf Club.; [oth. writ.] Several poems and essays published in local papers.; [pers.] After 50 years of tilling the soil, reaping the benefits of my labor, in partnership with God and nature, it is time to cultivate another field. I strive to nurture, have compassion for others, be concerned for Mother Earth, complete my own journey from the head to the heart.; [a.] Lethbridge Alberta, Canada

POTTER, ANITA

[pen.] Andi; [b.] February 26, 1972, Hannibal, MO; [p.] Charles and Elsie Potter; [ed.] Van-Far Sr. High Albuquerque Technical - Vocational Institute; [occ.] Warehouse Order Parker; [memb.] The Society for Creative Anarchronism; [hon.] Two (2) Honorable mentions in another poetry contest; [oth. writ.] I have written other poems as well as short stories and Movie Scripts. I would also like to publish my children's stories some day.; [pers.] Be the best you can be. If you feel very strongly about something, go for it. Because if you don't, you'll be forever kicking yourself about what could have been.; [a.] Albuquerque, NM

POWELL, A. L.

[b.] October 27, 1925, Australia; [p.] Mr. and Mrs. A. G. Powell; [m.] Barbara Bencini, November 6, 1992; [ch.] Four; [ed.] Kings School Paramatta N.S.W. Australia; [occ.] Consultant; [memb.] Minneapolis Club; [oth. writ.] Poems, essays; [pers.] Greatly influenced by T.S. Elliot, I am fascinated by linking philosophy to poetry; [a.] Minneapolis, MN

POWELL, BARBARA VERICE

[pen.] Barbara Verice Powell; [b.] December 11, 1931, Bronx, NY; [p.] Arthur P. Stinnette, Mary Louise Cordial; [m.] Seldon Powell, September 18, 1954; [ch.] Dr. Cheryl Jean Powell, John Tyler Powell III, Barbara V. Powell Jr.; [ed.] Nassau Community College Flushing, High School, Stoney Brook at Farmingdale; [occ.] Graphic Clerk at Hempstead High School; [memb.] Life paid membership in NAACP, Paid Golden Heritage Member., N.O.W. Organization of Women, Cerebral Palsy of West Hempstead and Professional, National Organization of Business Women, National Cancer Society, Heart Assoc.; [hon.] Govt. Cucomo's Award for African-American's of Distinction 1993, Office of Economic Opportunity, Keeper of the Dream Award 1994, 1990 Martin Luther King A.K.A. Fraternity Community Award from and Professional Nassau Bus. Women. Citations from Mayor Gardener; [oth. writ.] Published in the NAACP Journal from 89-95. Personal Poetry for Parties, end of the year awards, Birthdays. Church Journals etc.; [pers.] I only pass this way but once and whatever I can do for anyone I do it and move on. I only ask that they do the same and pass it on.; [a.] Hempstead, NY

POWELL, LORRAINE
[b.] June 14, 1954, Bakersfield, CA; [pers.] The art provides a way to express ones feelings and thoughts. I endeavor to do this through writing, as others do through music, acting and artistic painting and sculpture.; [a.] San Leandro, CA

POWELL, TERESA A.
[pen.] Juanita; [b.] October 11, 1968, Jackson, TN; [p.] Shirley Hendrix; [ch.] Markita, Lequita, Timothy; [ed.] Tennesse Technical Institute; [occ.] Licensed Practical Nurse; [oth. writ.] Personal poems; [pers.] I write only about things that I feel of experience. Being able to express my most personal, deepest thoughts on paper alleviates much of the sorrow, pain I deal with on this journey called life.; [a.] Jackson, TN

POWERS, RUTH E.
[b.] November 21, 1923; [m.] February 16, 1946; [ch.] Kathryn P. Moore; [ed.] Grand Rapids H.S. Bemidji State Teachers College; [occ.] Retired; [memb.] Arthritis Foundation Science Museum of Minnesota Associate Member of Minnesota State Band; [hon.] Army-Navy "E" Production Award from Northwest Airlines, Nov. '44, Certificate and Pin from Jerry Lewis for Volunteer Work for Muscular Dysthrophy - late 50's; [oth. writ.] I wrote this poem for my daughter's 46th birthday. At 47 1/2 she received her second kidney transplant. Five weeks later she died from many severe complications.; [pers.] Saint Paul, MN

POYNER, JAMES R.
[pen.] James R. Poyner; [b.] February 14, 1950, Brockville, Ontario; [p.] Walter J. Lerma Jean; [ed.] BA, Millikin Univ., Decatur, IL; [occ.] File Clerk, Elek-tek, Inc., Skokie, IL; [hon.] Editor's Choice for "Beauty Flows" in "Reflections of Light"; [oth. writ.] "Soft Feet" in "A Moment in Time", several unpublished novels and "Prairie Woodland", an unpublished, unfinished cycle of verse.; [a.] Chicago, IL

POZO, ADRIANA ROSARIO
[b.] February 5, 1981, Houston, TX; [p.] Gonzalo and Flora Pozo; [ed.] I will be attending Judson High School in Fall of 95. I went to Jr. High at Kitty Hawk Jr. High; [occ.] Student; [memb.] National Jr. Honor Society Savatage Fan Club; [pers.] I'd like to thank my friends April, Brenda, and Lupe, and my brother Gonzo for being there for me; [a.] Selma, TX

PRATO, PETER J.
[pen.] Peter J. Prato; [b.] May 8, 1927, Aguilar, CO; [p.] Peter and Perina Prato; [m.] Janice V. Prato, deceased; [ch.] Elizabeth A. Prato, Stephen D. Prato; [ed.] BA University of Denver 1952, M.S. California Coast University 1993, Ph.D. (Candidate) California Coast University 1994; [occ.] Chairman of Board of following corporations: Gibraltar Capital Corp., Gibraltar Realty and Acceptance Corporation, Leisure Television Corp., Leisure Productions, Inc., Managing Partner - Gunnison County Land Company; [memb.] Veterans U.S. Navy-Pacific Theater 1945-46, Member Colorado Speakers Association, Member of Colorado Trade Contingent to Japan in 1987; [hon.] Selected to Denver Post Hall of Fame, Psi Chi National Honorary Society in Psychology, Black Belt Shotokan Karat May 23, 1988; [oth. writ.] Autobiographical novel "The Cover of Life" 1993, The Miracle of Synchronicity (book in progress); [pers.] A tenet in philosophy of Pierre Teilhard de Chardin was that mankind is continuously evolving on a pathway to an ever higher state of spiritual awareness. This poem (and over 100 other poems written by this author) reflect one man's journey along that spiritual pathway.; [a.] Denver, CO

PRESS, PAULA
[b.] June 28, 1948, Brooklyn, NY; [p.] Harriet Press; [ed.] Hunter College B.F.A. New School for Social Research - M.A. St. John's University P.D.; [occ.] Reading Specialist; [memb.] Phi Delta Kappa, National Academy TV Arts and Sciences; [oth. writ.] Film reviews for council on the Arts film projects.; [pers.] I delicate my writing to sincerity and romance through one's life.; [a.] Flushing, NY

PRESTON, ROBERT A.
[b.] August 10, 1945, New York; [p.] Donald and Ella Preston; [m.] Kathryn E. Preston, March 14, 1967; [ch.] Robert, Tessanie, Shane; [ed.] Painted Post High School Painted Pool, NY., Corning Community College Corning, New York; [a.] Parker, AZ

PREVAUX, LORAIN CAROLE
[b.] November 17, 1965, Dearborn, MI; [ed.] B.S. Biology, University of South Florida, Tampa, Fl. (Aug. 1996). A.S. Medical, Hillsborough Community College, Tampa, Fl. (1993). A.A.S. Allied Health Science, Maxwell A.F.B., Al. (1990). A.A. Emergency Medicine, Hillsborough Community College, Tampa, Fl. (1989).; [occ.] Paramedic and Aeromedical Evacuation Technician in the USAF Reserves.; [memb.] Affiliate Faculty for the American Heart Association, Veterans of Foreign Wars Post 4256, Most Holy Redeemer Catholic Church.; [hon.] Kuwait Liberation Medal, Outstanding Senior NCO, Selected to make welcoming speech to General Schwarzkopf, the event was telebroadcasted live by CNN internationally.; [oth. writ.] "Specialty Training Standard" Authored functional guideline of medical information, standards and regulations for mobile aeromedical staging facilities and aeromedical evacuation technicians. "English Literature Leadership: "Beowulf and Schwarzkopf" - Authored educational material that enables students to identify and develop personal leadership qualities by participating in non-profit drug prevention program. "General Schwarzkopf" - Authored a prize winning essay published in the National League of Pen Women publication.; [pers.] I gain insight about my self-identity when I am able to transform my feelings into words. This insight guides me through this transitional period of my life, while providing a healthy balance between fantasy and reality.; [a.] Tampa, FL

PREYER JR., LEROY
[pen.] Lee; [b.] September 1, 1953, Memphis, TN; [p.] Leroy Preyer Sr., Helen M. Preyer; [m.] Scherry C. Preyer, August 18, 1976; [ch.] James T. Lawson, Tamillia L. Haynes, Leroy Preyer III, Ceakima N. Preyer, Kenneth B. Preyer; [ed.] Millington Central High, George Wallace College; [occ.] Retired Military, Inspector Teledyre Brown Engineering; [memb.] Prosperity Missionary Baptist Church, Choir, W.O.R.K.S.; [hon.] Dean's List, President's List, Army Commodation Medital #2 OLC, 10 AAM, Army Retirement Pin.; [oth. writ.] Many unpublished poem, and songs from 1968 to 1994.; [pers.] An ear to hear of our past, an eye to look toward the future, and a heart to seek our dreams.; [a.] Hardford, AL

PRICE, BEATRICE P.
[b.] January 18, 1918, Reading, PA; [p.] Deceased-Robert and Margaret Wentzel; [m.] Warren H. Price, June 5, 1937; [ch.] Sandra Moyer, Donna Miller; [ed.] High School Graduate of Fleetwood High; [occ.] Retired from Ludems; [oth. writ.] Contributions to "Musings" 15 published so far - in the reading Eagle - Reading, PA (poems); [pers.] Anything accredited to me is the result of positive influence instilled by my father - against all odds of a traumatic childhood. I hope my work relates to many people - conveying comfort - for none of us endure alone!; [a.] Fleetwood, PA

PRICE, JUDY
[b.] November 23, 1944, Tyrone, PA; [p.] Alfred and Mary McMullen; [m.] Calvin Price, September 4, 1971; [ch.] Daughter - Tracy, Son - Michael; [ed.] Tyrone Area School Graduated Class '62'; [occ.] Income Tax preparer; [oth. writ.] Others poem published in church bulletins - devotionals printed in church Lenton Booklet poem published in newspaper.; [pers.] I strive to honor God in writings as my ability comes from Him.; [a.] Warriors Mark, PA

PRICE, RACHEL
[b.] September 15, 1975, New Haven, CT; [p.] Michael Price, Sabra Price; [ed.] Brookline High School, Stanford University; [occ.] Student; [a.] Brookline, MA

PRIDE, VICTORIA MARIE
[b.] October 26, 1982, Staten Island, NY; [p.] Deborah M. Pride and Robin D. Pride'; [ed.] I attended elementary School in South River then moved to E. Brunswick and have attended Hammarsjold M. S. the past two years; [occ.] Student; [memb.] Mentor Club, Corpus Christi Church, South River Drama Club and E. Brunswick Drama Club; [hon.] Picked for student of the month, Energy save award (from PSE&G), Artwork Chosen for Art Exhibit '95, I've enjoyed playing piano for the past six years.; [oth. writ.] This poem came to be made, when my father died on July 19, 1994. I started to think about my feelings, and exactly what they were. I simply just put them on paper, and it came alive!; [pers.] I try to write my innermost feelings through my writings.; [a.] East Brunswick, NJ

PRINGLE, FRONCINE R.
[pen.] "Sunshine" and "Honey Bear"; [b.] May 10, 1963, Philadelphia, PA; [p.] Paulina V. Young and John B. Young Sr.; [ch.] Daniel David III, Da-Yona Danielle, Ka-Vona Victoria Pringle.; [ed.] Martin Luther King High - Berean Institute, Studied Cosmetology Ralph Amodei Barber School, Studied Barber Stylist.; [occ.] Delivery Barcode Sorter Machine Clerk - U.S. Post Office, and inventor....of tiny bops....; [memb.] 1. American Entrepreneurs Association, 2. American Cancer Society, 3. Home and School Association, 4. C.F.C. Key Work "Combined Federal Campaign; [hon.] Several Awards and Trophy's for Honor Roll, Perfect Attendance, Maintaining 95% of average while raising 3 kids as single working parent, and several trophies for Female and Male Hair Styling.; [oth. writ.] Tiny Bops Wee Bop Out Alone:

To be published fall of 95 and several other Children's Books, Children's Poetry, and Children's Songs.; [pers.] I held my mothers hand as she closed her eyes and took her last breath. It was then, I opened my eyes started to live. Don't let life challenge you. Challenge life! For it is you who control your own destiny! Strive for the best because you are!; [a.] Philadelphia, PA

PRITTS, ERICA ELAINE
[b.] January 28, 1984, Mount Pleasant; [p.] Eric and Dana Pritts; [ed.] Dunbar Borough Elem. 5th Grade; [occ.] Student; [memb.] Kid's Club Fox 53; [pers.] "I've done it," overcome the loss of my dad and heading toward a life of success; [a.] Dunbar, PA

PROCTOR, STEPHEN
[b.] June 25, 1951, Port Huron, MI; [p.] Kenneth and Esther Proctor; [m.] Rhonda Hinton Proctor, February 12, 1971; [ch.] Michelle, Eric, Crystal; [ed.] B.S. Elizabethtown College, M.S. University of North Texas; [occ.] Executive, Presbyterian Homes, Inc.; [a.] Dillsburg, PA

PROVIDENCE, DESREE K.
[pen.] Desree Karen; [b.] September 25, 1964, St. Vincent, West Indies; [p.] Clarence Providence, Vivienne Providence-Hollimon; [ch.] Stephanie Vivienne, River Karen; [ed.] 1. St. Vincent Girls' High School 2. St. Vincent Grammar School 3. First Leningrad (St. Petersburg), Institute of Medicine.; [occ.] Having taken a one-year leave from my studies (in St. Petersburg, Russia) I am now a full time mother to my seven-month-old twin daughters.; [oth. writ.] Numerous poems, plays and essays. However, this is my first attempt at publication.; [pers.] Education is the sum total of one's experience, intelligence is the ability to learn from those experiences. Nothing has taught me more than the experiences of motherhood.; [a.] Brooklyn, NY

PROWANT, ROSANNA FISHER
[pen.] Rosanna Fisher; [b.] February 10, 1949, Southern Ohio; [p.] Andrea Blizzard and Franklin Blizzard; [m.] Carl Prowants, April 28, 1993; [ch.] Sherry Anchea and grandchildren: Christa Marie, Daniel Christopher and C. Michael; [ed.] Graduate from Adrian High School in Adrian Michigan and I attended Adrian College; [occ.] In home care and writer; [memb.] Church of Christ Child Abuse Prevention Fund, National Wildlife Association, Veterans of America, American Heart Association and American Cancer Society.; [hon.] I received an Ohio State Scholarship award in the 8th grade. I also received a nomination for "Outstanding College Student of America Award". While I was attending Adrian College.; [oth. writ.] Many other poems and songs, short stories, and beginning of at least 15 novels.; [pers.] I believe that Reverance for God and great respect for family rituals of togetherness is the very essence of an inter sense of well being. In turn enhancing th well being of mankind.; [a.] Manitou Beach, MI

PRUSIN, ANDREA
[b.] July 20, 1947, Brooklyn, NY; [p.] Deceased; [ed.] B.A. English Temple University - Philadelphia PA, R.N. - Frankford Hospital School of Nursing - Philadelphia, PA; [occ.] R.N.; [memb.] Nursing and Medical Professional Organizations; [hon.] 1. Operating Room Award - Frankford Hospital, 2. Teaching Assistant Ship - Temple University; [oth. writ.] Only personal and for school; [pers.] With gratitude 1. C.J.B., Ph.D, 2. D.R.P., Ph.D, 3. J.D.T., Ph.D and "Dr. J" (J.P.H., PhD)., with love Taz, Indigo and Marigold and to all Basenjis everywhere. 4. With appreciation the remarkable gifts and talents of my favorite oxymononic vampires: Kenneth Branagh, Mandy Patawkin, Derek Jacobi, Anthony Andrews, and Her Majesty, Queen Elizabeth I (1533-1603).; [a.] Philadelphia, PA

PURVES, JEWEL LEE
[b.] March 31, 1971, Vanderhoof, BC; [p.] Brien and Darlene Reierson; [m.] John Purves, August 31, 1991; [ch.] Kala Cherie, Bryan George, Jonathan Cole, William Alexander; [ed.] Victoria Correspondence Educational Branch, Nechko Valley College.; [occ.] School Bus Driver; [oth. writ.] Several poem and short stories published in the Western Pruducer as well as a recent publishing in an anthology of verse, entitled Island Sunsets.; [pers.] Born and raised in the remote wilderness of British Columbia, I am inspired by nature.; [a.] Canyon Creek, Alberta, Canada

PYSE, EVERETT E.
[pen.] Sometimes (rarely) I use "Geno"; [b.] September 16, 1973, Sterling, IL; [ed.] Rock Falls High; [occ.] Grocery Clerk; [memb.] Maranatha Baptist Church; [oth. writ.] Two poems in a self-published daily devotional book compiled by a local pastor who is the director of missions of several churches. Plus a few personal notebooks full!; [pers.] The topics and emotions of my poetry vary greatly. While some are likeable and others are a bit too intense - my utmost goal is to love God with all my heart, mind, soul, and strength, and to love my neighbors as myself. Otherwise, my poetry (and life) comes to rough.; [a.] Sterling, IL

QUAID, LEUTY
[b.] February 13, 1917, Allison, OK; [p.] Mr. and Mrs. Robert A. Chestnut; [m.] Laron William Quaid, June 1, 1939; [ch.] Sharon Quaid Harrison, John Laron Quaid; [ed.] B.S. Degree (1937) in Home Economics from Oklahoma College for Women at Chickasha, OK; [occ.] Homemaker; [memb.] Wynnewood Garden Club, Wynnewood Music Club, Wynne Wood Methodist Church.; [hon.] 23 years as a teacher mother of a daughter who has sung 33 different operas. Pres. WW Garden Club, Pres WW Music Club.; [pers.] "To keep within myself a green point growing so that when my leaves are thin and few, I'll have some fruit worth showing"; [a.] Wynnewood, OK

QUINN, LATANYA A.
[b.] October 13, 1960, Philadelphi, PA; [p.] Evelyn Hodges, Walter Williams; [m.] William A. Pugh; [ch.] Lament Jr. Kira, Jeremy, Evelyn; [ed.] Simon Gratz High School Philadelphia, PA.; [occ.] Certified Nursing Assistant.; [hon.] Letter of appreciation given to me by the United States Marine Corps.; [oth. writ.] A poem of mine was published in a Pontiac, MI. Newspaper.; [pers.] I write base on life's experience and from the heart and soul.; [a.] Philadelphia, PA

QUINN, TOM J.
[pen.] T. J. Quinn; [b.] September 22, 1935, Queens, NY; [p.] Martin and Alma; [m.] Barbara Specce, June 18, 1960; [ch.] Karen, Susan, Any; [ed.] University of Dayton, BA Sociology, ordained deacon 1979; [occ.] Typographer; [memb.] Saint Stephen's Society, Marriage Encounter, Charismatic Prayer Group; [oth. writ.] Several poems and short story; [pers.] In my poetry I would like to evoke in the reader the same emotions that I am feeling. Whatever it be joy or sorrow. And I would like to do it in as few words as possible. Above all, it must be clear and simple.; [a.] Massapequa, NY

QUINTO, LLOYD PATRICK B.
[b.] November 3, 1975, San Diego, CA; [p.] Alexander Quinto, Janeta Quinto; [ed.] Mount Carmel High School, San Diego State University; [occ.] Student, Telecommunications and Film Major, San Diego State University; [hon.] Best One-Act Play for Jiffy Mart Dreams, Dean's List; [oth. writ.] Jiffy Mart Dreams (One-Act Play); [pers.] Those who understand the power of words are those who remain quiet.; [a.] San Diego, CA

RABENALDT, DORIS D.
[pen.] Nano Lee; [b.] January 11, 1925, Rosebud, TX; [p.] James and Margaret Knowles; [ch.] Two adopted daughters Kim Marie and Sarena Sharmane.; [ed.] Rosebud High, Steven F. Austin Business School; [occ.] Retired as Steak House Owner (27 yrs.); [memb.] D.O.R.; [oth. writ.] Many poems (unpublished); [pers.] Strive to be worthy of the honor of being a mother and grandmother.

RACKLEY, LAURA L.
[pen.] Laura Lee; [b.] January 26, 1976, Tampa, FL; [p.] Jon and Rita Rackley; [ed.] High School graduate; [occ.] Pre-Bonsai propagator at Jon's Nursery, Inc.; [memb.] First Baptist Church of Mt. Dora, Fl; [oth. writ.] I have written several other poems inspired by special people in my life, nature, everyday life, and romance, and the love of Jesus Christ.; [pers.] I basically use my poetry to reflect the way I feel about something or someone. I have also written poems to cheer people up.; [a.] Eustis, FL

RADIN, CONSTANCE E.
[b.] November 26, 1962, MO; [m.] Anthony E. Radin, April 25, 1987; [ch.] None; [ed.] Associates Degree from Arkansas State University Office Administration Jonesboro, AR; [occ.] Nuclear Fuel Manufacturing Facility (ABB/CE); [memb.] International Society of Poets; [hon.] Friends are not only an inspiration, they are an "Honor" and "Reward".; [oth. writ.] Many poems on every subject, dreams I have had that are extraordinary, short-stories, and a fund raising article for the "Children's Miracle Network."; [pers.] "God helps those who help themselves" in other words, you have to do more than just pray.; [a.] Festus, MO

RAFUSE, JOSEPH P.
[b.] August 25, 1971, Worcester, MA; [p.] David and Nancy Rafuse; [m.] Heather L. Rafuse, January 28, 1995; [ed.] Tahanto Regional High University of Massachussetts, Amherst; [occ.] Health care provider for mentally retarded; [a.] Granby, MA

RAHE, RYAN
[pen.] Ryan Rahe; [b.] August 20, 1981, TN; [p.] Jane M. Rahe; [ed.] 6th grade, Maryville Middle School, Maryville, TN.; [occ.] Student; [memb.] Official Mascot for "Song and Dance". A Showchoir Knoxville Performing Arts Institute, Area 15, Tennessee Special Olympics; [hon.] Silver Medal - Skating - Special Olympics Bronze Medal Skating - Special Olympics, 1st Place - Swimming - Special Olympics, 2nd Place Swimming Special Olympics; [pers.] "Always do your best, try your hardest and be a friend to everyone"; [a.] Maryville, TN

RAHMAN, REZAUR
[b.] February 5, 1957, Dhaka, Bangladesh; [p.] Sheikh Sayeed Bakhsh, Rezia Begum; [m.] Surman Rahman, December 9, 1982; [ch.] Shoumo, Priyoti; [ed.] L.L.B (Hons.), L.L.M. Saint Gregory's High School, Notre Dame College, Dhaka University.; [occ.] Immigration

Counsellor Immigration and Refugee Board, Montreal; [memb.] Canadian Bar Association, American Bar Association, Dhaka Bar Assoc.; [hon.] Who's Who in the world, Marquis Publications, U.S.A. Justice Abu Sayeed Chowdhury Human Rights Award. Jai Jai Din Award. Rotary International, Dhaka Metropolitan Award. 61 Club Gold Medal.; [oth. writ.] Poems published in newspapers. "Senoritader Uddeshya" a book of love poems (1976); [pers.] None of our life is meaningless if we can comprehend that in the first race of life, each one of us defeated our millions of competitors. Out of million sperms you won. Do you think that we have any time to loose. Each one of us is the messenger of the God. You are unique.; [a.] Montreal, Canada

RAINEY, MISTY

[pen.] Nike; [b.] May 26, 1977, Wichita, KS; [p.] Joyce F. Rainey, Kent A. Rainey; [ch.] Trey Ablen Rainey; [ed.] Ozark High School; [memb.] FBLA (Future Business Leaders of America); [hon.] All district center fielder (softball) best defensive player (softball); [oth. writ.] I have no other published writings, but I have a collection of my own writings.; [pers.] Most of my writings are about personal experiences in my life and the life's of my family and friends. I was influenced by the early romantic poets.; [a.] Ozark, MO

RAINVILLE, REBECCA MARIE

[pen.] Rebecca Rainville; [b.] November 16, 1981, Burlington, VT; [p.] Richard and Patti Rainville; [ed.] Eight grade; [occ.] Student; [memb.] 4-H, figure, Skating band french.; [hon.] A-B student honor roll; [oth. writ.] None published.; [pers.] Take risks live life to its full extent.; [a.] Highgate, VT

RALLIS, SUZANNE

[b.] May 11, 1976, Mooresville, NC; [p.] Lauren Rallis, Bruce Rallis; [ed.] South Iredell High School, I semester at Applachian State University, Currently student at Central Piedmont Community College; [occ.] Full-time Student; [memb.] PFLAG, People For The American Way, Student Government Association of CPCC, Contributor to AMFAR and Unicef; [oth. writ.] Poem published in high school newspaper, possible publication in 1995 American Poetry annual; [pers.] I try to give my generation a message that says, "No, you are not the only one who feels this way. Yes, we are living in an uncaring world," feel free to write me at 117 Adventure Lane; [a.] Mooresville, NC

RAMIREZ, NATALIE

[b.] Arizona; [p.] Mariano and Petronila; [m.] Manuel Ramirez, November 3, 1951; [ch.] Mark, Bill, Barbara Ramirez; [ed.] 8th Grade; [occ.] Housewife; [hon.] Got Honorable Mention in July 10, 1991 for poem friendship from World of Poetry Lost my copy.

RAPPETTE, ROSELLE E.

[b.] Milwaukee, WI; [ed.] Licensed Social Worker, Certified Alcohol and Drug Counselor; [occ.] Counseling, Supervisor - Comm. Health Link; [a.] Worcester, MA

RASMUSSEN, SUSAN I.

[b.] April 26, 1966, Neenah, WI; [p.] Violet Rhyner and Darrell Rasmussen; [m.] Unmarried; [ch.] Deanna May Rasmussen and Sierra Kristina Will; [ed.] Winneconne High School and Later Oshkosh North High School. Fox Valley Technical College.; [occ.] Ceramic Tile Installer; [oth. writ.] Many poems published in local papers.; [pers.] All of my poetry is written from my heart. This poem was written for Ronelle "Ronnie" Sue Eichstedt. Born July 16, 1982 - Died August 23, 1992. Given to Ronie's parents, Gary and Charlotte Eichstedt and Ronie's sister, Regina "Regie" God Bless them all. And all who have lost a child.; [a.] Fond de Lac, WI

RATLIFF, D. B.

[pen.] Donnie; [b.] September 21, 1938, Lookout, KY; [p.] Olva and Alma Ratliff; [m.] Mary Ratliff, November 13, 1973; [ch.] Wanda, Ken, Buddy, and Sherry; [ed.] Hellier High School Lookout Grade School; [occ.] Evaporator operator at Golden Gem Growers - Umatilla, FL.; [oth. writ.] Several other poems set to music on Demo Tapes etc.; [pers.] I strive to reflect the goodness of mankind in my writings, and listen to the spirit of God to lead me.; [a.] Umatilla, FL

RAY JR., FRED C.

[b.] February 20, 1968; [occ.] Police Dispatcher Zion Police Department; [pers.] Belmoe, we love you and your memory will live forever. The loss of our friend left a hole in our hearts that could only be filled by the remembrances of the great times we had shared. God bless you David.; [a.] Zion, IL

RAYMOND, TAMMY

[b.] August 27, 1967, Lincoln, NE; [p.] Alice and Leonard Huey; [pers.] Special thanks to my parents, and all the people who have entered my life, for your support. Especially Melinda Westcott, Donna Rivera and Nancy Raymond. I love you all from the bottom of my heart. May God Bless You.; [a.] Phoenix, AZ

REAVES, ANGELA

[pen.] Angela Curl Reaves; [b.] September 5, 1970, Newman, GA; [p.] Ralph Mitch Curl-Vera Boren Curl; [m.] David Glen Reaves, December 7, 1991; [ch.] Elizabeth Curl, Sarah Louise, Merylann Ellen and Bradley Galloway; [ed.] Potts Camp High School, Northwest Junior College.; [occ.] Youth Minister Bells, TN; [memb.] First United Methodist Dyersburg, Tenn.; [hon.] Several creative writing awards; [oth. writ.] "A child's collection of verses"; [pers.] I strive to share what the Lord has done in my life through the words that I write in hopes that others will find sanctity within themselves.; [a.] Dyersburg, TN

REAVLEY, DAWN VERDELL

[pen.] Dawn Verdell; [b.] November 17, 1932, Dekalb, IL; [p.] Lyman and Mildred Prescott; [ch.] Gregory Reavley; [ed.] Rock Falls High School, Rock Falls, IL. Katherine Shaw Bethea School of Nursing, Dixon, IL; [occ.] Retired Registered Nurse and Currently doing book keeping for family business.; [memb.] World wildlife fun consteau society samaritans purse; [oth. writ.] Poems under the book title "Spiritual Reflections"; [pers.] Trust in Jesus, the good shepherd.; [a.] Sterling, IL

REED, NATALIE

[b.] November 11, 1979, Newark, NY; [p.] David and Laurie Rinehart; [ed.] Freshman, attending Clear Lake High School in Houston, TX; [occ.] Student also a big sister to one younger sister and two younger brothers, (Alexandra, Luke and John); [pers.] Life - Take it day by day and everything will be A-okay!; [a.] Houston, TX

REID, JULIE E. HEMINGWAY

[pen.] J. E. Hemingway; [b.] September 27, 1960, Phoenix, AZ; [p.] Robin Jones, Mary Jane Jones (Deceased); [m.] Jerry Wrayman Reid; [ch.] Lindell Reid, Casey Reid, Tatum Reid; [ed.] Apollo High, Nat'l Ed. Center, AZ School of Real Estate; [occ.] Writer, Artist, Pianist and Piano Tuner, Word Processor for Business Planning Analyst, Wife and Mother; [pers.] My mother (deceased) had much to do with the pursuit of my talents. My sister, Angela Jones has further inspired me since our Mother's death. I am compelled to express my political and social viewpoints even thought some may be considered distasteful. Also, I have always needed to write about all issues that affect my life and the people I love.

REID SR., MARKWOOD C.

[pen.] MCR; [b.] February 24, 1923, Gapland, MD; [p.] Daniel and Grace Reid; [m.] Joan Kling Reid, January 14, 1950; [ch.] Markwood Jr., Michelle, Brooke, Matthew; [ed.] High School - Big Spring High School 1942, Newville, PA, 17241; [occ.] Retired Postmaster, Newville, Pa, 17241, with 39 yrs. service, retired 1983.; [memb.] Secretary John Graham Medical Board since 1970 (Built Bldg and Rent Clinic to two Doctors), Treasure, Neighbors in Christ since 1987 (Help needy and troubled families), President - Sarah and Warren Welch Foundation since 1980 (Award Scholarships for Students to go to College), Vice President Big spring area Community Chest since 1970, Deacon in church of the Brethren since 1980.; [hon.] T/Sergeant in U.S. Air Force in South Pacific Theater for 3 1/2 yrs, discharged April 1946, 25 yrs. Sunday School Teacher.; [pers.] I was influenced by my Christian Parents, who put their values in home, church, and country-in that order - Edgar a guest is my favorite, Poet - my one hero is the Rev. Billy Graham.; [a.] Newville, PA

REID SR., ALVAH W.

[b.] September 29, 1940, Montgomery, AL; [p.] Mr. and Mrs. James A. Reid; [m.] Divorced; [ch.] Two children; [ed.] 4 yrs College World Traveled; [occ.] Retired, U.S. Army, National Guard, and Air Guard, Arms Reserve; [memb.] Church and Civic and Community Assoc.; [hon.] Military and Civilian "Only to be Worthy"; [oth. writ.] Over 200 poems written not published on yet or released; [pers.] I have seen all I have heard. Yet I know nothing, for the ears and eyes are limited; [a.] Montgomery, AL

REID, TAKISHA S.

[b.] March 28, 1974, Brooklyn, NY; [p.] Renita Reid and Benjamin Monk; [ed.] High School of Performing Arts (major) Drama Currently LaGuardia College (major) Veterinary Medicine; [occ.] Veterinary Technician; [oth. writ.] "The Man With The Knife", "Fear Of Own", "Pains Of The Heart", "Indian Giver", "After Awhile", "For I Am Is What I'll Be", "My Moral Value".; [pers.] "Never give up on love unless love gives up on you."; [a.] Brooklyn, NY

REYES II, BENITO CRISANTO

[pen.] Cris; [b.] January 23, 1974, Houston, TX; [p.] Ben Reyes and Maria Reyes; [m.] Cassie M. Reyes, February 14, 1994; [ch.] Ariel Alyssandra Reyes; [ed.] Aldine High School, USN Officer Program (Boost); [occ.] Seaman; [oth. writ.] Poems in reflections of light and songs on the wind; [pers.] My favorite saying in life is "It is better to lie about the truth, than to tell the truth about a lie!" Tom Smothers. Also, I thank my devoted family for my inspiration and dedication.; [a.] Houston, TX

REYES, MARINA

[pen.] Violet; [b.] December 12, 1939, Manila, Philippines; [p.] Artemio Reyes, Francisca Silvestre; [m.] Jovito Cruzado; [ch.] Florencia, Ma. Theresa,

Luzviminda, Zenaida; [ed.] B.S. Edu., C.N.A., C.H.H.A., Bonifacio Elem. Sch., Arellano High, Far Eastern Univ., N.C.P. Voc. Sch.; [occ.] Nursing assistant home health aide, Wal-Mart employee; [memb.] Fremont literary workshop; [oth. writ.] A collection of poems reflecting personal views, beliefs and emotions for self enjoyment.; [pers.] As the wind in the sky and the waves of the sea seek love and truth in the universe so do I with all my life. For I do love life as I love my children.; [a.] Union City, CA

REYNOLDS, LESLIE R.
[b.] October 13, 1977, Longview, TX; [p.] Steve Reynolds and Donnarie Long; [m.] Single; [ed.] I am a junior at Community Christian School, I will graduate, in May 1996; [occ.] Student; [memb.] I play basketball, Volleyball, and Tennis.; [hon.] National Youth Leadership Conference, National Honor Roll Student.; [oth. writ.] Several but they are still unpublished.; [pers.] Life is a banquet. Don't go hungry.; [a.] Orange, TX

RHEAULT, D'ARCY ROLLAND RAPHAEL
[b.] January 8, 1963, Timmins, ON; [p.] Gilles and Claudette Rheault; [m.] Alicia Palmer, February 15, 1992; [ed.] Bachelor of Arts with Honours in Philosophy (Brock University, Saint Catharines, ON); [occ.] Graduate Student Trent University, Peterborough, ON; [pers.] Words are the cradle of meaning. Meaning is the definition of life.; [a.] Peterborough, ON

RICASA, BERT R.
[b.] Philippines; [p.] Marcelino Ricasa and Estela Rios Ricasa; [m.] Luretta A. Ricasa (Ex-wife), 1965; [ch.] Michael, Erik and Toni-marie; [ed.] Bachelors Degree - Criminal Justice; [occ.] Retired Police Officer; [memb.] Fraternal Order of Police; [hon.] Dean's list and several commendations awards as a Police Officer; [a.] Catonsville, MD

RICCI, ANTOINETTE T.
[pen.] Tiffany Adams; [b.] August 8, 1958, Philadelphia, PA; [p.] Armand J. and Helen G. Ricci; [m.] Single; [ch.] Francis Armand Ricci, Brandon Lawrence Ricci; [ed.] Saint Adalbert's Grammar '72, John Hallahan Girl's Catholic High '76, LaSalle University '80; [occ.] Motherhood, Tutor, Gardener; [memb.] Phi Gamma NV Sorority Alumnus of LaSalle, Alumni of Hallahan High Home and School Association Saint Adalbert's Spa and Work Life Center; [oth. writ.] Recipes - Correspondence by mail to fellow sorority across the West, 2 short stories never published - private works, News Article in the star in the 80's; [pers.] I never say Never! I Never do Never, I always, try different things in life. Why? Cause, you only live once. So, don't be afraid of "tomorrow" "Wish Upon A Star" and then, live that wish.; [a.] Philadelphia, PA

RICHARDS, JAMES ROOSEVELT
[b.] December 2, 1954, Philadelphia, PA; [p.] Roosevelt and Julia Richards; [m.] Divorced; [ch.] Jamahr Karon; [ed.] Simon Gratz High; [occ.] Student: PBI - Pennsylvania Business Institute.; [hon.] Lifer's Art Contest - Second place 1994, Winner Black History Art Contest 1994 and 1995, Pennsylvania, third place 1976, Black Response to Bicentennial (Poetry); [oth. writ.] Several poems in Christian News Letter and Poetry readings on tape WOL Radio 1976, Washington, DC.; [pers.] God be thanked for the gift and the talent, and eternal life in Christ, by whom I am made free.; [a.] Philadelphia, PA

RICHEY, MARY LOU
[pen.] Mary Lou Oliver; [b.] December 23, 1940, Shallowater, TX; [p.] Mr. and Mrs. S. W. Oliver; [ch.] Lee and Will Richey; [ed.] Smyer High School, Smyer, TX. South Plain College, Levelland, TX. I am a Pilot and love flying. I took cosmetology also.; [occ.] Registrar/Rice Aviation/A and J Enterprises/Houston, TX; [oth. writ.] I have written several other poems, but I have never tried to have them publish.; [pers.] I write poems from the heart. Hope they will help other people. I strive every day to help students so they will have a better life.; [a.] Humble, TX

RICHMOND, WENDY J.
[b.] December 29, 1953, Lakewood, OH; [p.] Will and Jean Richmond; [ed.] BA from Baldwin Wallace College, MA from Cleveland State University; [occ.] Physical Educator Discovery Elementary School, Glendale, AZ.; [memb.] Arizona Education Assoc., National Wildlife Federation, P.E.T.A., Glendale Education Assoc.; [hon.] Honorable Mention Award in community college writing contest, 50 + awards for middle-distance running.; [oth. writ.] On Being Average, What Is Running, Dare to be Different, Double Cross, Culture in Crisis, Green Dragon, Madness by Number, Rebel Without A Clause.; [pers.] Life is a process of change with each day having a special blueprint in the architecture of existence.; [a.] Phoenix, AZ

RICKERT, LAUREN ELIZABETH
[b.] December 7, 1978, Rockford, IL; [p.] Cherie and Edward Rickert; [ed.] Sophomore at McHenry West Campus High School; [hon.] Choir Award - Most outstanding vocalist 1994. Honor roll students; [oth. writ.] Various poems; [pers.] My poetry reflects my most inner thoughts and feelings. I base most of my work on personal experience, as in the cemetery.; [a.] McHenry, IL

RIFORD, RUTH TALLMADGE
[b.] April 20, 1911, Schenectady, NY; [p.] Benjamin, Flora Tallmadge; [m.] Charles P. Riford, April 21, 1956; [ed.] Simmons College; [occ.] Retired; [memb.] Northminster presbyterian Church; [oth. writ.] I write our church's weekly newsletter (32 years so far), sometimes include short, timely verses; [pers.] Climbed many mountains in NY and new hampshire, lassen in Calif. and the highest point in my climbing career was the day I stood on top of rainier.; [a.] Endwell, NY

RIGGS, SONYA WOICINSKI
[b.] October 9, 1935, Newhall, CA; [p.] Jack L. Woicinski and Mittie M. Gillett; [m.] E. G. Riggs, December 21, 1956; [ch.] Georgia, Madeline, Danae; [ed.] B.S. University of Texas, Austin, M.E.D. in Reading Southwest TX. State Univ.; [occ.] Reading specialist bastrop Intermediate School, TX.; [memb.] Association of TX. Professional Educators, American Shih Tzu Club, French Bulldog Club of America, Austin Kennel Club, Mission City Ring Stewards; [hon.] Who's Who in the South and Southwest 1995-1996.; [oth. writ.] The Shih Tzu Reporter (10 times), 1993 French Bulldog Annual (3 poems, 1 line drawing, 2 articles), Golden Retriever World, Winter 1994-95.; [pers.] Everyone should have a profession and a passion. My passion for the past thirteen years has been the little Shih Tzu and French Bulldog (8 have completed AKC championships).; [a.] Elgin, TX

RIKER, BILLYE M.
[pen.] Boo; [b.] March 8, 1923, Miami, OK; [p.] Mack and Mattie Walker; [m.] Franklin Paul Ricker, June 6, 1943; [ch.] Diane, Stephen, David, and Robin; [ed.] Class in High School, Oklahoma City, Okla. Denton College for Women Denton, TX.; [occ.] Retired

RILEY, TRACY
[b.] March 2, 1976, London, Ontario, Canada; [p.] Ron Riley, Wendy Lagerwerf; [ed.] North Middlesex District High School, Parkhill, Ont.; [occ.] University bound, high school student, lifeguard, swimming instructor.; [oth. writ.] Many unpublished poems; [pers.] I am roused not by language but by the presence within. Dance on my friend, dance on.; [a.] Parkhill Ontario, Canada

RIOS, MARISELA
[pen.] Marisela Rios; [b.] July 30, 1965, El Paso, TX; [p.] Juan Manuel Rios and Emma S. Rios; [m.] None; [ch.] Malena Ipiotis; [ed.] Coronado High, University of TX at El Paso, Quinniplac College School at Law, CT.; [occ.] Mother, Student; [pers.] I try to remember poetry goes to the heart at man, woman, or child. Boundaries are imposed but should not be accepted - just because.; [a.] Milford, CT

RIOUX, CHRISTINE
[b.] January 25, 1972, Cloris, NM; [p.] Richard and Carmen Rioux; [ed.] Bay Path College, Southwest Missouri State Univ.; [occ.] Account Executive for an Asset Management Firm; [oth. writ.] Several poems and short stories of which none here been published yet. Ultimate goal is to publish a novel.; [pers.] I write poetry to touch the lives of those who are touched mine.; [a.] Nashua, NH

RITO, ANNA ROSE
[pen.] Anna Rose and Rose Saint Louis; [b.] September 18, 1924, South San Francisco, CA; [p.] Frank and Anna Saint Louis; [m.] Jerry Rito, November 24, 1991; [ch.] Roxanne McLean; [ed.] 1 year College - San Mateo, CA., South San Francisco, CA., High School; [occ.] Retired; [memb.] Friends of Multiple Sclerosis Sun City Support Group; [oth. writ.] Working on Family History - Autobiography's etc.; [pers.] Was a project office manager for a heavy construction Co. for 18 yrs., when diagnosed with M.S. a year after the death of my husband of 43 yrs.. Many of my reflections on life have been brightened; [a.] Sun City, AZ

RIVINIUS, JOANN
[pen.] JoAnn Carucci; [b.] August 19, 1965, New York; [p.] Angela and Anthony; [m.] Richard, April 12, 1991; [ch.] Christine, Jade, Raven, Richie; [ed.] Ged Some College New York Business School; [occ.] Housewife; [oth. writ.] A child's pain, lost to the music published in great poems of our time. In the arms of abuse, our worlds favorite poems, thousands of others not published.; [pers.] Born to be wild, Inspired soley by Jim Morrison; [a.] Glendale, NY

ROBBINS, SUSAN E.
[b.] March 17, 1962, RI; [p.] Bill and Kathy LaSalle; [m.] David; [ch.] Bobby 8, Megan 3; [occ.] Marketing Manager Craft King, Inc.; [oth. writ.] Presently working on a book of inspirational poetry for children. (Not yet published); [pers.] I enjoy writing simple poetry that will inspire children and adults. People need to believe they are important in this world, and that they are loved for who they are inside there is a higher purpose.; [a.] Lakeland, FL

ROBERSON, HOLLY N.
[pen.] Nicoli; [b.] May 22, 1973, CA; [p.] Frank and

Debbi Roberson; [ed.] Laura High School, General College Courses (Fullerton College); [occ.] Receptionist; [pers.] My writing reflects realism with a twist of extremes. I hope to spark thought in the reader to look beyond the words and provoke ideas they don't contemplate, as well as identifying with every aspect of life others can relate to.; [a.] Anaheim, CA

ROBERTS, ANNA HINEMAN
[b.] October 10, 1915, Wilmington, DE; [p.] Florence and George Litz; [ch.] (Five) Edwin, Suzanne, Clifford, (Donald-Martin) (Twins); [ed.] Claymount-Wilmington Del. Schools.; [occ.] Retired; [memb.] Dela. Diamond State Branch NLAPW, Chester County Art, YMCA-Del., and PA. Senior Center - Kennett Sq. PA. International Comm. of YMCA. of Brandy Wine, Dela YMCA; [hon.] Awards from various art shows - 1980-1995 1st place for story in "Chesapeake '95" literary magazine; [oth. writ.] Own book "Fly With Anna" 1972-1993 Trips-Memoirs front page story on Christmas morning Dec 25, '94 edition of "Daily Local" Chester Co. Newspaper.; [pers.] "To live each day as it comes - praise God for health, family, friends and do Good for every body!"; [a.] Kennett Square, PA

ROBERTS, PATRICK
[b.] February 6, 1973, Fayetteville; [p.] Teresa Roberts; [ed.] GED, certified nursing assistant.; [occ.] Recreation worker; [hon.] In job core I received a certificate for center leader and a certificate for search and reserve of a person who fell over a water fall and died.; [oth. writ.] Friends till the end, my heaven on earth a picture, rainbows and roses the old tree by the lake ghost on a hill, my love for you missing you I'm an out law; [pers.] Love your parents, always believe in your self, you can do anything you put your mind to. And most of all spread peace and love through the world; [a.] Fayetteville, NC

ROBINSON, CAROL A.
[b.] August 11, 1957, Philadelphia, PA; [p.] Terry and Bob Stone; [m.] Steven Wayne Robinson, November 26, 1983; [ch.] Andrea, Nicholas and Kira Anne; [ed.] Saint Huberts High School Community College of Phila.; [occ.] Homemaker; [pers.] Poetry, in general, makes the world a more beautiful place. Writing poetry is a necessity to me and a gift from God. It has helped me many times to transcend life's difficulties.; [a.] Philadelphia, PA

ROBINSON, MIA F.
[b.] September 4, 1938, UN; [m.] Albert F. Robinson, November 20, 1973; [ed.] BS Nursing Jem Loma Linda University on 1978 - RN Liance of CA; [occ.] Retired; [memb.] Churches Foster Parent Plan; [hon.] The National Library of Poetry; [oth. writ.] 1) My name is "love" 2) A hero in the future I want to publish my own poems in the market for every one can enjoy my poems; [pers.] Poems is the soul of mankind. I write my poems to express my feelings, my life experiences I've influenced by Asian and European poets I'm a a grand daughter of the popular Asian poet - the Inspirations come to my mind then I write a poem; [a.] Oceanside, CA

ROBINSON, STEVEN CAREY
[b.] July 30, 1964, Kailua, HI; [p.] Wallace Robinson, Diane Robinson; [m.] Hana Soupova-Robinson, September 9, 1989; [ch.] Wendy Bianca; [ed.] Okanogan High, U.S. Air Force Security Police Academy, Washington State Juvenile Security workers academy; [occ.] Residential counselor (staff) St. Joseph's group home; [pers.] If I can give enjoyment to a reader of my work, I have accomplished everything I set out to do.; [a.] Burlington, VT

RODGERS, FLOYD DODD
[pen.] "Cy" Rodgers; [p.] Jennie Berk Dodd (Adopted Parents); [m.] Doris Wilkins Rodgers, November 2, 1946; [ch.] Pat and Mike Rodgers, Kathleen and Jim Rodgers; [ed.] Smithville High School, Smithville Texas 1931, Southwestern University, Georgetown Texas 1941; [occ.] Retired; [memb.] First Baptist Church, AARP, UFW, American Legion, Texas Retired Teacher; [hon.] Student President, Southwestern Univ. 1940-41, Golden Gloves Hall of Fame-Middle Weight; [pers.] Help me to help someone somewhere anytime; [a.] Brenham, TX

RODRIGUEZ, HILDA
[b.] January 31, 1946, Alice, TX; [p.] Jose and Esmeralda Cadena; [m.] Lamar Rodriguez, September 17, 1983; [ch.] Maria Audelia Rodriguez; [ed.] Benavides High School Texas A and I University - BS/MS; [occ.] Secondary English Teacher; [hon.] Dean's list graduated Summa Cum Laude; [oth. writ.] Several unpublished poems; [pers.] My poems reflect some fleeting moments of my life and are dedicated to those who made these fragments of life possible.

RODRIGUEZ, LETICIA
[b.] January 9, 1975, San Antonio, TX; [p.] Saul and Consuelo Rodriguez; [ed.] Currently attending: Our lady of the lake University, San Antonio TX; [occ.] Student; [oth. writ.] One other poem published in 1995 Cera Award for poetry scholarship competition; [a.] San Antonio, TX

ROGERS, BENJAMIN J.
[b.] August 13, 1981, Lafayette, LA; [p.] David and Lana Rogers; [ed.] 8th grade student Mount Carmel Elementary Abbeville, LA; [hon.] Winner Young Author's Contest - 1993-1994, 3rd in State (LA - 1993) Student Council President; [oth. writ.] Several Poems; [a.] Abbeville, LA

ROLLE, VANESSA
[pen.] Vanessa Cordelia/Songbird; [b.] February 18, 1975, New Providence, Bahamas; [p.] Vaneria G. Rolle; [ed.] St. Augustine's College (Bahamas) R.M. Bailey High School (Bahamas); [occ.] Secretary - Compass House - (Bahamas); [memb.] Bahamas Conference of seventh day adventists.; [hon.] Head girl - R.M. Bailey '92, Winner-star of youth speech competition - '92, kay doland award literature '92, winner - breath of life speech competition - '4; [oth. writ.] "One People" - recorded and sung by myself at commonwealth recording studio, "I owe him", why do you claim that you love me, Freedom, "A better world for you", "words"; [pers.] May the beauty of God's unconditional love and free gift of life - free gift of hope, always be seen in my writing. In these trying times I have only been stirred by God's superlative love for me.; [a.] Nassau, New Providence, Bahamas

ROMAN, SANDRA
[b.] July 9, 1948, Wilmington, DE; [p.] Horace and MaryAnn Pedrick; [m.] Roger Longest; [ch.] Jay, Scott and Tracy, Grandchild: Nathaniel; [pers.] The luxury of life is ones true self.

ROMANSKY JR., LOUIS FRANK
[pen.] Lou; [b.] August 1, 1961, East Strousburg, PA; [p.] Louis Sr., and Lois; [ed.] Stroudsburg High School ICS - Associates Degree; [occ.] Chauffeur Bergen Limousine; [memb.] Amfar, EPVA (American Foundation AIDS Research) (Eastern Paralyzed Veterans Association); [hon.] Some High School, College, and Navy honors and awards, (Nothing that stands out); [oth. writ.] None - this was my first attempt!!; [pers.] I would like to thank three wonderful people my mother, Libby, and Paul. Their love, inspiration, and courage has me published.; [a.] Lodi, NJ

ROOT, LYNN M.
[b.] August 5, 1967, Janesville, WI; [p.] Michael and Rosalie Roatch; [m.] Kendrick L. Root, January 12, 1991; [ch.] Elena Marie and Alexander Lewis; [ed.] Graduated from Sturgeon Bay High School on June 6, 1986; [occ.] Secretary and Receptionist; [oth. writ.] Quill books is publishing a book called "Echoes From The Silence" which also contains "The White Unicorn"; [pers.] The mythological Unicorn has always been a source of strength, peace, and freedom to me. My the elusiveness of the Unicorn challenge all of us to be a better people, nation, and world.; [a.] Addison, IL

RORAPAUGH, HEIDI ANN
[b.] May 24, 1982, Painesville, OH; [p.] Jeffery and Cheryl Rorapaugh; [ed.] 7th Grade Ledgemont Middle School; [hon.] Honorable Mention Certificate for Rainbow Kids Cards 95; [pers.] I became interested in poetry when I was ten years old. I like to write about how I feel and would draw pictures to go with my poems. In my spare time I like to write poetry. If I am sad I write about how I feel if I am happy I write happy thoughts.; [a.] Thompson, OH

ROSAS, MARIE
[pen.] Rie Dreamer; [b.] February 4, 1933, Chicago, IL; [p.] Tony and Josephine Barassi; [m.] Edward, January 13, 1953; [ch.] Tony, Michael, Marialaina, and Lisa - 8 Grandchildren and 1 Greatchild; [occ.] Writer of children stories; [oth. writ.] Many children stories; [pers.] I see life as a gift out of control, until a person gets older. At that time, if they have learned anything. Then, and only then, have they realized their gift.; [a.] Las Vegas, NV

ROSE, KIMBERLY
[b.] October 10, 1978, Rockford, IL; [p.] Robert and Ginny Rose; [ed.] Rancho Bernardo High School; [occ.] Life guard, Westwood Club, San Diego, Cal.; [memb.] Diving Team; [pers.] My writings reflect on my dreams, and the hopes people have in their hearts.; [a.] San Diego, CA

ROSIER, JACQUELYN S.
[b.] August 3, 1955, Seymour, IN; [p.] William and Virginia Trujillo; [m.] William W. Rosier Jr., October 6, 1973; [ch.] Jennifer Gayle, Angela Marie, Cynthia Renee'; [ed.] West Hardin High, Monterey Peninsula Community College; [occ.] Pre-School Aide, Saint Paul's Lutheran School; [hon.] National Honor Society; [oth. writ.] Several poems; [pers.] I feel my gift is a gift from God. Therefore, most of my poetry talks about God's greatness and majesty.; [a.] Fort Leavenworth, KS

ROSS, ALISHA TYLA
[pen.] Alisha Tyla Ross; [b.] January 28, 1982, Vancouver, B.C., Canada; [p.] Kelly and Kim Ross; [ed.] Fairview Elementary School - Grade 7; [occ.] Afterschool Child - Care for four children; [hon.] Grades 1-7 academic awards.; [pers.] I love to write children stories and read them to my grade one buddy reading class.; [a.] Maple Ridge, B.C., Canada

ROSS, BONNIE J.
[pen.] Bonnie (Robinson) Ross; [b.] October 18, 1938,

Beulah, KS; [p.] Beulah and Finis Robison; [m.] Larry Ross, March 11, 1978; [ch.] Debbie, Toni, Laine, Lisa, Jenny; [ed.] Tucson HS. Ariz. (A.B.C. Nursing School NY. NY.) (United Cerebal Palsy Medication Adm. NY. NY.) U.S. Health Care NY. NY; [occ.] Certified Nursing Assistant; [memb.] In the process of becoming member D.A.V.; [oth. writ.] Several unpublished poems and I am also currently working on a children's story; [pers.] May my awareness to the needs of others, and my love for writing always inspired them; [a.] Saylorsburg, PA

ROSS, HELEN G.
[b.] January 15, 1948, Baton Rouge, LA; [p.] James and Ruby E. Green; [m.] Matthew Ross III, May 8, 1971; [ch.] Terrance Dwayne, Wyletha Renee; [ed.] McKinley Senior High Southern University; [occ.] Health Care Worker; [memb.] Oasis Christian Center, Usher Board; [oth. writ.] Several poems that are used for various church functions.; [pers.] "I believe my abilities for writing has always been present. It is a gift from God, inspired by the Holy Spirit, suppressed for years, to impress upon others that through God, all things are possible."; [a.] Baton Rouge, LA

ROSS, JESSIE SHOVER
[pen.] Eissej the creator; [b.] November 4, 1982, Berlin, VT; [p.] Pamela Shover and John Ross; [ed.] Elementary Doty Memorial Jr High U-32; [occ.] Student and writer; [oth. writ.] Numerous unpublished works; [pers.] "Doubt all before believing anything."; [a.] Worcester, VT

ROSS, MARY ALICE STANDRING
[pen.] Mary Standring Ross; [b.] October 13, 1914, Tacoma, WA.; [p.] Walter and Aimie Standing; [m.] John A. Ross, July 25, 1942; [ch.] David Albert, Glen Allan; [ed.] Stadium High School Tacoma, WA. Graduate plus many teachers along the way taught me valuable lessons; [occ.] Retired; [memb.] Atlanta Unity Church Unity Choir, Writer's Group Dream Weaver's Drama Group.; [oth. writ.] Inspirational writings children's stories, humorous happenings, experiences of owning a pet store working on my autobiography; [pers.] The present world is hungry for love, humor and inspiration, I wish to base my writing on these healing qualities to help awaken the world to peace; [a.] Atlanta, GA

ROUSE, VERA A.
[pen.] AnnaMae; [b.] December 17, 1935, Pendleton, IN; [p.] Omer G. and Nellie D. Wright; [m.] Lester P. Rouse, October 2, 1955; [ch.] Marilyn K. Hickrod and Russell E. Rouse; [occ.] Retired; [memb.] Order of Eastern Star, Ladies' Oriental Shrine of NA Daughters of the Nile Smyrna Shrine Guild, Life Member of the Tech Alumni Association Greenwood Christian Church; [hon.] Honorary Member of Int'l Order of Job's Daughters.; [oth. writ.] Many other poems written for a special occasion or person that I did not think to save a copy for myself. How unfortunate! Several have been used for informal print in various programs and the like, or making my own greeting cards.; [pers.] The poem "Time To Retire" was written two years ago for someone who returned it to me when I retired last year. How thoughtful of her. I am now collecting my poems. I shall continue to write for the enjoyment of others.; [a.] Indianapolis, IN

ROWDEN, STEPHAN M.
[pers.] I am not a poet. I don't care much for poetry. I wrote this single poem because once, in an unguarded moment, my body was possessed by the spirit of Shel Silverstien.; [a.] Houston, TX

ROWE, BONNIE JOYCE HARLOW
[b.] March 21, 1947, Dayton, OH; [p.] Donald E. and Jeanne K; [m.] Not married; [ch.] Jessica Anne Brock; [ed.] High School Graduate Northridge High School Dayton, OH; [occ.] Cook; [memb.] Bethany Chapel (Church); [hon.] 2 yrs Grand Champion pie, dawson county fair Lamesa, TX; [oth. writ.] Write and perform short Bible stories for my church. Many other poems, which I feel are inspired by God and my surroundings.; [pers.] I feel that God has inspired many of the things I write about. Writing started in 1986, I never thought of doing it before than. Truly enjoy it.; [a.] Lamesa, TX

ROY, KIMBERLY A.
[pen.] Kim Roy; [b.] March 28, 1965, Savannah, Georgia; [p.] Anne and Mike Benedict; [m.] James E. Roy Jr., August 16, 1991; [ch.] Joseph E. Roy; [ed.] Butter H.S., Shelton St. Comm College Tuscaloosa Alabama, Meredith Manor School of Horsemanship waverly, WV.; [occ.] Housewife, horse trainer errand co., saddle/track repair former kennel attendant; [memb.] KACA - Ky Animal Control Ass., NACA - National Animal Control Ass., Coral Ridge Crafters - secretary; [hon.] Volunteers award for pet therapy with darlin' my 3 legged dog, St. helen's art contest - 1st place; [oth. writ.] Currently writing a book on a character based on my life involving rodeo and travel not published.; [pers.] "Animals and children are mirrors. They reflect everything you are and you aren't."; [a.] Fairdale, KY

RUBIO, LOU D.
[b.] September 28, 1967; [p.] Luis and Olga Rubio; [ed.] Archbishop Molloy H.S. Manhattan College; [occ.] Direct Broadcasting Satellites at Home Box Office, Guitar Instructor; [oth. writ.] Poems appearing on internal company publications; [pers.] Writing is the conscious manifestation of the subconscious mind by which we can reflect upon our emotions with regard to what we value or disvalue most in life.

RUBY, STACI C.
[b.] April 26, 1969, Ottumwa, IA; [p.] Janet Brean and Jim Brown; [m.] Stacy M. Ruby, August 22, 1987; [ch.] Ryan William 7 yrs. old, and Lucas James 4 yrs. old; [ed.] Hedrick High School; [occ.] Homemaker; [oth. writ.] "A Christians Prayer" published in Poetic voices of America, Fall, 1994; [pers.] I would like to dedicate this accomplishment to my brother Aaron Lee Brown who passed from our lives March 20, 1994. God bless you Aaron.; [a.] Loveland, CO

RUDDER, DESMOND Y.
[b.] October 27, 1963, Chicago; [p.] William and Earlina-Both are teachers; [ed.] B.A. Degree from Chicago State University - Studied Marketing; [oth. writ.] A poem published in "The Agenda" Magazine; [pers.] I have been greatly influenced by writers like Toni Morrison, Nikki Giovanni, Maya Angelou, Margaret Walker, Dr. Martin Luther King and Malcolm X. My writing, to quote Margaret Walker, is "For my People."; [a.] Chicago, IL

RUDOLPH, JULIE A.
[b.] May 3, 1974, Waukesha, WI; [p.] Robert Rudolph Sr., Lila Rudolph; [m.] Not married; [ch.] Tyler H. Rudolph; [ed.] Spencer High, Mid-state Tech Marshfield WI - Goal Program; [occ.] Machine operator northwest hardwoods dorchester WI; [oth. writ.] I have written several poems and short stories for my own personal satisfaction and enjoyment; [pers.] Writing is my way of getting away from reality but sometimes reality finds me in my writing, reminding me not to take advantage of what I have today as for tomorrow it may not be there; [a.] Medford, WI

RUMJAHN, DIANA
[b.] September 16, 1969, San Francisco, USA; [p.] Edward and June Rumjahn; [ed.] San Francisco State University, Lowell High School of San Francisco; [occ.] Admissions Assistant, San Francisco State University, CA; [memb.] Golden Key National Honor Society, Life Fellow of the International Biographical Association, Sterling Who's Who, National Association for Female Executives; [hon.] Honorary appointed member to the Research Board of Advisors at American Biographical Institute, San Francisco State University Dean's list, lifetime member of Golden key National Honor Society. Published in the world Who's Who of Women 12th Edition, 2000 Notable American Women 5th edition. Sterling Who's Who Executive Directory 1994/1995.; [oth. writ.] Article published in Golden Key National Honor Society Newsletter.; [a.] San Francisco, CA

RUPPE, BILLIE
[b.] August 22, 1975, Rutherfordton, NC; [p.] Lee and Martha Ruppe; [ed.] West Carteret High School; [pers.] Through my writings I express my concern about ecology and the survival of this generation and generations to come.; [a.] Rutherfordton, NC

RUSSELL, DANA JUSTINE
[b.] May 22, 1976, Bronx, NY; [p.] Justin and Sheila Russell; [ed.] University of Rochester; [occ.] Student; [memb.] N.A.A.C.P. Black Students Union, Habitat for Humanity; [hon.] Miss New York State A Phi A Black and Gold 94-95, Dean's List; [oth. writ.] Several poems although this is my first publication.; [pers.] When I look at you, I see myself. If my eyes are unable to see you as my sister.. then it is I who need you..." Lillian Benlow; [a.] Bronx, NY

RUSSELL, JACQUELINE HUGHES
[pen.] Jacque Hughes; [b.] November 17, 1938, Cameron, OK; [p.] Joseph R. Hughes and M. Lenora Taylor; [m.] Marvin G. Russell (deceased); [ch.] Charles Wayne Burch; [ed.] Thomas Jefferson High, Pt. Arthur TX, Jacksonville High, Jacksonville, Ore. Port Arthur College, Pt. Arthur TX; [memb.] First Baptist Church, Pt. Arthur. Dance Works Jazz Co. Groves, TX; [pers.] I am most influenced by my friends, both past and present. And, of course by my family. My mother, my father, my son, my brother Bobby and sister Denise. I love you all.; [a.] Port Arthur, TX

RUSSELL, JOHN FRANCIS
[b.] April 30, 1929, Mount Carmel, IN; [p.] Bertha Leora Major and David Freeman Russell; [m.] Edith Hyde Russell, June 27, 1953; [ch.] Anne Marie Russell; [ed.] Brookville High School, 1947, De Pauw University, B.A., 1951, Indiana University, PG, 1951-52, The Johns Hopkins University, M.A., 1954, Drexel University, M.S.L.S. 1976.; [occ.] Retired Librarian, manager, Park Place Branch, Houston Public Library; [memb.] Texas Library Assoc., American Library Assoc., Pasadena Little Theatre, Festival Angels (Houston Shakespeare Festival and Children's Theatre Festival); [hon.] Phi Eta Sigma, Phi Beta Kappa, Beta Phi Mu., Tusitala (entire writing honorary) American, Shakespeare Festival National Citation of Merit, Mid. Atlantic District, American Theatre Assoc. Award, the Houston Post Critics Choice Award; [oth. writ.] Poetry, Literary and film criticism, journal articles; [pers.] I want to reflect and refract

the world around me and to reveal my relationship with other people and with God.; [a.] Houston, TX

RYDER, ROY
[pen.] Roy Ryder; [pers.] I would like to thank the National Library of Poetry. Also my family and friends for all the support special thanks to my loving Mom. Aloha Roy Ryder PO Box 882; [a.] Hanalei, HI

SAADA, KATHY ANNE
[b.] November 13, 1960, Chatta, TN; [p.] Ann L. and Winston G. Hullander; [m.] Muhanad Saada (ex), May 29, 1991 - December, 1993; [ch.] Anna Marie, Amanda Dawn, Joseph Nasser, Yousef Muhanad; [ed.] A.A. Mass Communications 1987 Gulf Coast Community College; [occ.] Home School Teacher, Full-time Homemaker and Mother; [memb.] Parent to parent of FL Bay County Islamic Society North Bay Clan of Creek Indians; [hon.] Who's who among students in American Jr. Colleges 1987, Phi Theta Kappa 1987, Dean's List 85-87; [oth. writ.] Several articles for local newspaper, articles and poems for student publication Gull's Cry 85-87, parent to parent pamphlet, March of Dimes Newsletter 1986-87,; [pers.] My greatest aim in life lay in my aspiration to share with as many persons as I can that the same GOD who gives our hearts the faith to dare to hope and dream, is the one GOD who will help us make those dreams come true!

SAAVEDRA, PABLO POMPEYO
[pen.] Pompeyo Saavedra; [b.] August 14, 1924, Pitrufquen, Chile; [p.] Nicanor, Maria Elena; [ch.] Ximena, Pablo, Fidel, Esperanza, Daniel, Frank, Geraldine, Yuri, Valentina.; [ed.] Chilean Air Force Academy. University of Chile; [occ.] Journalist, Writer, TV and Radio Host.; [memb.] Chilean Writers Society. Valparaiso Writers Society. University of Chile Club. National Geographic Society. Pilot International Association. Hispanic Press Association of Canada. Native Canadian Centre of Toronto.; [hon.] Best Broadcaster of the year 1992, Toronto, Canada. Best Radio host 1993, Chilean Program Araucania, Toronto.; [oth. writ.] Las Palabras de Siempre (Words of forever), poetry, Santiago de Chile, 1965. The Spring we share, Bilingual edition, poetry, Toronto, 1995. Several poems published in papers and magazines of Chile, Argentina, Germany, United Kingdom and Canada.; [pers.] Without poetry life would be impossible, but poetry is nothing if not authentic.; [a.] Toronto Ontario, Canada

SABATINI, ROBERT A.
[pen.] Robert Sabatini; [b.] February 21, 1957, LA; [p.] Vincent and Willa Sabatini; [ed.] Milby Sr. High School, Houston, Texas San Jacinto Jr. College Pasadena, Texas; [occ.] Engineering; [memb.] Ducks unlimited conservation program; [hon.] Most awards have been granted in my profession, Quality Leader Awards.; [oth. writ.] Continually building manuscripts for possible publications.; [pers.] I would like readers to learn about life in my poetry. I constantly search for peoples' soul, to find out what they are really all about, be it good or not so good!; [a.] Houston, TX

SAHAGIAN, MR. VICTOR
[b.] August 23, 1961, Lebanon; [p.] Nubar, Olga; [ed.] General Equivalency Diploma (GED); [occ.] Grounds dept. and shop stewart of site; [pers.] I hope my writings will let all mankind see, that life is a door of opportunity, and peace is the key.

SAKS, RENNE MORGAN
[b.] April 23, 1983, Lenox Hill, New York City, NY; [p.] Susan E. Morgan-Saks, Steve Saks; [ed.] Elementary School - 6th grade; [occ.] Student; [memb.] Green Peace, People for the Ethical Treatment of Animals; [pers.] I have been creating poems since I was out 3 years old at first I would get an idea for a poem and have my mother write it down. Then as I got older I begun to write them my self.; [a.] New York, NY

SAMIT, SUSAN BACKUS
[b.] December 8, 1954, Battlecreek, MI; [p.] E. Edward Backus, A. Pauline Backus Dill; [m.] John Joseph Samit, April 29, 1986; [ch.] Kristina Monet; [ed.] San Lorenzo High Chabot College, A.A. Degree Golden Gate University: B.A. Degree of M.B.A.; [memb.] Alpha Gamma Sigma Rho East Bay Zoological Society; [hon.] Dean's list, Summa Cum Laude; [pers.] I was a lost child of ten, until my teacher, Mrs. Katherine Brown, recognized and cultivated my writing. She once said she hoped to see me published someday. Here's to you Mrs. Brown!; [a.] San Leandro, CA

SAMMUT, LANA
[b.] January 20, 1981, Cold Lake, Canada; [p.] Charmaine Sammut, John Sammut; [ed.] I am in grade 9 french immersion and have attended St. Dominic's and Assumption.; [occ.] Student of Assumption Jr/Sr High School.; [memb.] I am a member of the Japan Karate Federation (JKF) and I am a student of Royal Conservatory of Music.; [hon.] I have received an academic award in gr. 8 for obtaining the highest average throughout the school year.; [oth. writ.] I keep my own personal poetry journal. I write several poems for school projects.; [pers.] Most of my poems are based on the beauty of nature and I very much enjoy reading Robert Frost and Lucy L. Montgomery; [a.] Cold Lake Alberta, Canada

SAMPSON, DAWN L.
[pen.] Dawn; [b.] June 24, 1943, MO; [p.] Donna and Doug Howard; [m.] Widow, September 13, 1963; [ch.] Dane and Chris; [ed.] 3 yrs. College; [occ.] Work with elderly - CNA and Medical Assistant, Cert; [oth. writ.] Many, many poems, Short stories; [a.] Fremont, MI

SAMPSON, HAROLD L.
[b.] November 25, 1928, Chicago; [m.] Terry Lee, June 24, 1952; [ch.] Roberta Swidersky, Debra Boogaard, Arthur Sampson; [ed.] Two years College; [occ.] Eng. Tech., water Dept.; [pers.] Peace of mind, beauty of thought, and calmness of spirit, are emanations of the body clothed in tranquility and serenity.; [a.] Chicago, IL

SAMUELS, VINCENT
[pen.] Bill Simon; [b.] May 26, 1943, Jamaica, West Indies; [p.] Simeon and Margaret Samuels; [m.] Caren E. Samuels, March 5, 1966; [ch.] Cecille, Karen, Michelle, Vincent Jr. and Max; [ed.] Third Jamaica Local Exam Cert. Aldermaston College, Reading, England, Bronx Community College, Berard Baruch College NY; [occ.] Mechanic; [memb.] Bronx Gospel Chapel, NY. Thru way Home Owners and residents Association, the Academy of American Poets, International Society of Poets; [hon.] Phi Theta Kappa, made Dean's List 5 times at Bronx Community College; [oth. writ.] Several poems published in local and foreign newspapers as well as in literary magazine exposure published by English Dept., Bernard Baruch College, NY; [pers.] I continue to be the humble voice of the disenchanted, the disposed and those who feel there is no hope. I always listen to people I meet in my life daily because there is something I can learn from the stories they tell.; [a.] Bronx, NY

SANCHEZ, RAFAEL
[b.] June 10, 1952, Madrid, Spain; [p.] Serafin Sanchez and Catalina Benitez; [m.] Alicia De Miguel, May 13, 1972; [ch.] Francisco Rafael and Eva Noemi; [ed.] I took my education in Spain, I also have a Electronics Technician Diploma here in Canada.; [occ.] Production Arc, Welder Ford at Saint Thomas Assembly Plant, Talbot Ville. Ontario, Canada; [oth. writ.] I also write poems in Spanish (unpublished); [pers.] I came to Canada with my wife in 1972, actually I'm Spanish/Canadian Citizen. I believe in Liberty and Global Peace.; [a.] London Ontario, Canada

SANDEL, CAMERON M.
[b.] November 4, 1983, Fort Myers, FL; [p.] Marc J. and Melinda Sandel; [ed.] Old Town Elem., Bridgeton Elem., J.T. Barber Elem., Height's Elem.; [occ.] Student; [hon.] Published story in 1992 Young authors Publication - Celebrations III, A-B Honor Roll, D.A.R.E. Graduate.; [oth. writ.] Several poems and short stories.; [pers.] You've only get one life to live, so live it to the fullest!; [a.] Fort Myers, FL

SANDERS, LEO E.
[b.] January 4, 1917, St. Louis, MO; [p.] John T. Sanders - Julia (Quinlan) Sanders; [m.] Betty (Crowe) Sanders, January 17, 1946; [ch.] Maureen Sanders, Peggy (Sanders) Springer, Michael Sanders; [ed.] B.S. Degree - Military Science, University of Maryland, Masters Degree - Education Supervision and Administration Southern Illinois - Edwardsville; [occ.] Retired - Lieutenant Colonel, U.S. Army; [memb.] Retired Officers Ass'n, Army Counter Intelligence Veterans Ass'n, AARP.; [hon.] Several Military Medals Highest of which is Dept. of Defense Joint service commendation medal for meritorious service as commanding officer, 901st Intelligence Corps detachment defense atomic support, Agency.; [oth. writ.] Short story, several poems all unpublished. Energy conservation program for St. Clair County, Ill. Which won award from national Ass'n of counties.; [a.] Belleville, IL

SANTIAGO, HYACINTH
[b.] January 2, 1953, India; [m.] Deceased; [ch.] Marcus Santiago; [ed.] Loretto Convent College, India; [occ.] Secretary; [oth. writ.] Several poems published in "Gulf News Weekly Magazine", "Emirates Woman," "International Indian", "Knaleej Times", "BBME News"; [pers.] "To project triumph over disaster with an emphasis on the positive aspect in every situation ... that every cloud has a silver lining."

SANTOS, EDWARD
[pen.] Eddie; [b.] December 20, 1960, Brooklyn, NY; [p.] Fernando Santos, Raquel Santos; [ch.] Jeanette Christine Santos; [ed.] Educational Assistant for the Board of Education NYC; [hon.] Honorable discharge USAR; [oth. writ.] Poems entitled - Them or You? Published in the National Library of Poetry's Spring 1995 anthology Seasons to come; [pers.] Because of the positive and negative aspects of lifes experiences, I find it to be emotionally and spiritually uplifting to be able to express thoughts combined with emotional content, through poetry. Thanks to Ricardo and Michael Santos 2 of 4 brothers

SARGENT, JANICE A.
[b.] December 9, 1941, Petersburg, MI; [p.] Harry A.

Dowell, Clarrissia Slack; [m.] Lawrence A. Sargent; [ch.] Troy, Felix Jr., Corey, Aron 2nd Steven Tkachuk; [ed.] Summerfield Adult High School, Petersburg MI, North Arkansas Community College, Harrison AR, University of the Ozarks, Clarksville, AR, University of Arkansas, Little Rock, AR; [occ.] Special Education Teacher, Deer Elementary, Deer, AR; [memb.] Association for Supervision and Curriculum Development Council for Exceptional Children. United Methodist Women; [hon.] Gamma Beta Phi, Dean's List, Honor's List, Educational scholarship to University of Arkansas, Little Rock, AR; [oth. writ.] Several poems published poetry anthology; [pers.] I hope to be an asset to all I work with and for. Influenced by Helen Stiener Rice and many of the early romantic poets.; [a.] Jasper, AR

SARNOSKI, ANTOINETTE
[b.] October 19, 1929, Chester, PA

SARRO, TERESA A.
[b.] April 11, 1971, Elizabeth, NJ; [p.] Joseph and Elizabeth Sarro; [ed.] Brick Township High School, Ocean Country College, Rutgers University, Georgian Court College; [occ.] Program Counsellor Preferred Behavioral Health of N.J.; [memb.] PETA - People for the Ethical Treat of Animals, Green peace Ocean Country College Alumni Assoc.; [hon.] Ocean Country Vocational Technical School, Professional Award; [oth. writ.] Articles published in "The Preferred Connection" a total quality management newsletter; [pers.] You can't experience all of the beauty in the world with a closed mind and a cold heart.; [a.] Toms River, NJ

SARRO, TERESA A.
[pen.] Terry Sarro; [b.] April 11, 1971, Elizabeth, NJ; [p.] Betty Sarro, Joseph Sarro; [ed.] Brick Twp. High School, Ocean County College, AA, Rutgers University, Georgian Court College; [occ.] Mental Health Program Counselor; [memb.] World Wildlife Federation PETA, Ocean County College Alumni Assoc. Cousteau Society.; [hon.] OCUTS - most professional award - OCC student tutor award; [oth. writ.] I am currently working on writing a series of children's books and poetry series; [pers.] The beauty of life cannot be seen through closed eyes or experienced through a closed mind.; [a.] Toms River, NJ

SATLIN, LEAH
[b.] October 27, 1983, Boston MA; [p.] Andrew Satlin, Lisa Cooper Satlin; [ed.] Edith C. Baker School, Brookline, MA; [occ.] Student; [memb.] Brookline recreation Department "Dolphins" - Swim Team; [hon.] Honor roll; [a.] Chestnut Hill, MA

SATTERFIELD, TAMMY PELLOM
[b.] April 27, 1963, Knoxville; [p.] James and Lilly Pellom; [m.] E.R. Satterfield - deceased, March 9, 1990; [ch.] James A. Satterfield; [ed.] Graduate of Farragot High School, a Master Caterer and Master Barber; [occ.] Self-employed; [memb.] Northshore Bapt. Church National Rifle Association, National Park Trust; [hon.] Sell and Spell Award 1993; [oth. writ.] Several poems written; [pers.] I guess I write my best work when I see someone hurting I try to reflect a hope in that poem for a word of encouragement; [a.] Lenoir City, TN

SAUER, TOMMYE
[b.] June 5, 1920, Oklahoma; [p.] Thomas and Ermine Miller; [m.] Herbert Sauer, November 23, 1944; [ch.] Constance, Robert, Jeanne Ann, Mary, Dorothy; [ed.] B.A. Oklahoma College for Women, currently called Okla. Univ. of Arts and Science; [occ.] Retired math teacher.; [hon.] Poetic honors have I none, other honors long absulete, forgotten in dusty corners of closets and minds; [oth. writ.] One poem published in Christian Science Monitor, lots of poems in local newspapers. Hundreds (maybe thousands) of poems on floppy discs. My poems are gifts for births, deaths, Christmas, birthdays, hospitalizations, special anniversaries. Computer and printer make small individualized book unique and possible. "The Birdwatcher" was written to cheer a bird watcher friend with a broken hip.; [a.] Cornwall-on-Hudson, NY

SAULTERS, VIRGINIA
[b.] February 6, 1940, Jackson, MS; [p.] Ben and Margie Phillips Pullen; [m.] Billy D. Saulters (Deceased), October 19, 1965; [ch.] Four son's and two daughters also 10 grandchildren.; [ed.] Bachelor's of Science degree in nursing May 1995 from University of Southern Mississippi Hattiesburg, MS.; [occ.] Full time student (after graduation RN at Med. Southwest Regional Center - McComb MS); [memb.] National Student Nurse Assn., National League for Nursing, AARP, United Pentecostal Church International; [hon.] Dean's List, Lily Pate Whitehead Award, Mississippi Institution of Higher Learning Award.; [oth. writ.] Article published in "Pulse Point" Official magazine of Ms. chapter national student nurse Assn., "The Torch" Mississippi United Pentecostal Church Magazine.; [pers.] My inner most thoughts have always been reflected in my poetry and short stories. Seeing the beauty in everyday circumstances fuels my pen, but my children are my inspiration.; [a.] Collins, MS

SAVAGE, NELLIE B.
[pen.] Billie; [b.] July 14, 1921, Haynesville, ME; [p.] David G. Bailey, Elvira K. Bailey; [m.] Carlton H. Savage, November 11, 1941; [ch.] Sharon Sellers, David Savage, Eloise Savage; [ed.] Brewer High; [occ.] Home maker; [oth. writ.] Odds and ends, mostly for personal use. I wrote one for a retiring personnel Mgr., using first letters of his name. It was later used in his eulogy.; [pers.] I am interested in our families' genealogy, indian artifacts and pictures.; [a.] Arrington, ME

SCALES, DONALD
[b.] April 2, 1963, Ann Arbor, MI; [p.] Rodney and Kathryn Scales; [ed.] High School Graduate U.S. Navy Veteran Monessen High School, U.S. Navy Hospital Corps School; [occ.] Steelworker; [memb.] Pittsburgh Jazz Society B.P.O.E. #773 (Elks) United Steelworkers of America Local #7887; [oth. writ.] Numerous selections of unpublished poems, prose, and societal observations.; [pers.] One must always seek for life's truth, only in truth are we able to make the world a better place for self and for all.; [a.] Monessen, PA

SCESNY, MARK
[b.] March 22, 1966; [m.] Donna, July 8, 1995; [pers.] The poem was taken from a few paragraphs written on a card to my fiance' on her birthday during our engagement. It moved her so (which was the intended affect) that she entered it in your contest as a surprise for me.; [a.] Concord, CA

SCHIEWEK, DENISE
[b.] September 24, 1954, Sudbury, Ontario, Canada; [p.] Victor and Madeline Levesque; [m.] Peter Schiewek, May 5, 1973; [ch.] Clayton, Curtis, Cory; [occ.] Bookkeeper; [oth. writ.] A few poems written for friends and family, some of which have been published in local newspapers and a few that have been recorded as songs.; [pers.] The poems I've written are very meaningful, and from my heart "Once in a lifetime Love" is about my mother, Madeleine, whom I love and admire... Forever.; [a.] Val Caron Ontario, Canada

SCHIPPER, JENNY
[b.] November 2, 1950, Upjever, W. Germany; [p.] Dr. Rose Schipper Wightman, Dr. Lewis Schipper; [ed.] B.A. Univ of Wis Madison in History, MA Diguesne Univ Counseling, Swedish Institute Diploma Double Training in N.Y.L. 15 years; [occ.] Massage Therapist Artist in various Mediums and Performance Artist; [oth. writ.] Poems with photos (collaboration/published in Slipstream Magazine short story, film review published in local East Village paper; [pers.] I try to shake up the groove of settled perspective so that a new, more encompassing space of feeling and thinking and seeing is almost unwittingly slipped into.; [a.] New York, NY

SCHLEIS, KRISTEN D. SUTTON
[pen.] Daisy Toes; [b.] April 1, 1972, Worcester, MA; [p.] Pamela A. and A. David Sutton; [m.] Dale W. Schleis, September 11, 1994; [ed.] Doherty Memorial High-Worc. MA, 3 Sem. Psychology Lowell-Lowell, MA Assoc. of Science in equine Ind. Stockbridge School of Agriculture V. Mass Amherst; [occ.] A job I consider a "Day Job:...; [memb.] Abuchon Soc.; [oth. writ.] Many poems as yet unseen; [pers.] My thanks to shakespeare, Poe and Frost (and life as well) for my inspiration; [a.] Hadley, MA

SCHMELZLE, KATY
[b.] May 7, 1978, Kansas City, KS; [p.] Robert Schmelzle and Deborah Schmelzle; [ed.] Summer Academy of Arts and Science (high school); [occ.] Pharmacy Technician at Osco; [memb.] National Honor Society, French National Honor Society; [hon.] Highest Honor Roll, varsity letter,; [pers.] I only write poetry for myself. I do it because it's the easiest way to express my thoughts. I was 11 years old when I wrote "Whispering Shadow".; [a.] Kansas City, KS

SCHMID, DR. DIANE ROSE OKULSKI
[pen.] Diane Rose; [b.] Possaic, NJ; [p.] Laester Okulski; [m.] Marcel Schmid, May 13, 1974; [ch.] Maya Schmid; [ed.] Ph.D. in Eng. Lit. the Union - Cleveland OH '74, M.A. Hunter, NPC '70, BA Montclair, NJ '65; [occ.] Teacher; [memb.] Amer. ACAD poets- New York City, American Alliance for mentally Ill (secretary) National Org. of Women Community Leaders and Noteworthy American; [hon.] Who's who of American women, USA, Int. Acad Poetry - Cambridge - England (Founder-Fellow, N.J. State Scholarship, NE State Scholarship; [oth. writ.] Rest In Peace (Books), Sticks And Stones (Poetry), Daymares (poetry), 100 Ways To Improve Your Relationship - Book

SCHMITT, BILL
[b.] January 16, 1950, Baton Rouge; [p.] William and Evelyn Schmitt; [m.] Becky, April 28, 1973; [ch.] Bill, Betsy, Ben; [ed.] Chemical Engineer LSU - 1972; [memb.] Rotary, United Way, Taft Employee's Credit Union President; [pers.] It is very challenging to put your feelings into words; [a.] Luling, LA

SCHOFIELD, AMANDA
[pen.] Manda; [b.] January 8, 1983, Townsend, MA; [p.] Tom and Tammy; [ed.] 6th grade - Hawthorne Brook Middle School; [memb.] Participates in TYSA soccer, T.A.P. Basketball, Pop warner Cheerleader, Dance Stu-

dent.; [hon.] High Honors student in School.; [oth. writ.] Likes to write for "Fun"; [a.] Townsend, MA

SCHUMANN, PAULA M.
[pen.] Paula M. Libonati Schumann; [b.] October 23, 1938, PA; [p.] Mr. and Mrs. P. Libonati; [m.] Mr. Walt Schumann, June 17, 1967; [ch.] Christian and Larissa; [ed.] Medical Technologist; [occ.] Homemaker; [memb.] Philadelphia Country Medical Society; [oth. writ.] I have written (soon to be released in '95) a book of verse, non-fiction and it tells a story. This book gave me the emotional and moral, courage and strength to go on, having been very seriously ill.; [pers.] Would like to continue an education in writing. Education being the key to intelligence, opening the door to your intellect.; [a.] King of Prussia, PA

SCHWEIGER, CURTIS JR.
[b.] March 14, 1961, Waverly, New York; [p.] Curtis and Mary Schweiger; [ch.] Melody (16) and Dwight (12) Schweiger; [ed.] Waverly Jr. Sr. High School, currently working towards a degree in English Lit.; [occ.] Landscaper, Disc Jockey; [memb.] Songwriters Club of America; [hon.] Won awards for 2 songs, "Nothing Lasts Forever," and "Marilyn;" [oth. writ.] Currently working on 2 books: a compilation of poetry and a creative non-fiction book to be published soon; [pers.] I hope I can touch someone with my work or inspire them. I hope someday to be able to make a living with my writing; [a.] Waverly, NY

SCIBELLI, LINDA STARR
[b.] February 3, 1954, Springfield, MA; [p.] Sherman L and Dorothy N. Nelson; [m.] Divorced; [ed.] Agawan High Graduated 1972, presently attending College for Physical Therapy.; [occ.] Work with Developmentally delayed adults in their home.; [oth. writ.] None published yet "vows of love"; [pers.] This poem is dedicated to my Dad Sherman Nelson, he's truly a wonderful man this poem is also dedicated to my mother Dorothy who in her infinite wisdom chose him.

SCOTT, BETTY
[b.] November 7, 1931, Ontario, Canada; [m.] Walter, 1955; [occ.] Retired; [memb.] Writing Club, Aquatic Club, Library, Music Society, Anglican Church.; [hon.] Honoured to be wife of 40 years. Mother, of 3 boys, 2 girl, grandmother, 2 boys, 3 girls, and nurse - my greatest accomplishments; [oth. writ.] A faith journey - Prose in the form of letters to the Creator - much poetry - 2 others published.; [a.] Madeira Park, BC, Canada

SCOTT, CECILE HART
[b.] May 3, 1982, Charleston, South Carolina; [p.] Dr. Geoffrey Scott and Mrs. Anne Hart Scott; [ed.] Sea Island Academy, James Island Christian School; [hon.] The Presidential Academic Fitness Award, 3rd place in 1995 State Science Fair; [oth. writ.] Anthropology of Young Adults; [pers.] "The secret to staying young is to live honestly, eat slowly, and lie about your age." - Lucille Ball.

SEARS, PENELOPE OWEN
[pen.] Spencer Owen Sears, Penny Sears; [b.] Johnson City, NY; [p.] Frank Owen, Lynne Oliver; [m.] John T. Sears, March 17, 1988; [ch.] Kimberley, Robin and Sarah; [ed.] E.C.E - Georgian College Montessori Teachers Diploma; [occ.] Children's Writer, Nursery School Teacher; [oth. writ.] After thoughts of Life - Collection of poetry. On the edge of a dream - juvenile novel, Big Trouble for Little Bear - Children Story, Rock of Ages, adult novella.; [pers.] I strive to put real, inspiring emotions in all my writing. If I can have just one person "feel" these emotions through my writings than it will have been worthwhile to share it.; [a.] Midland Ontario, Canada

SEAY, CHRISTINA
[b.] November 26, 1976, Morristown, TN; [p.] Pearl Bolling; [ed.] High School -Senior; [occ.] Student; [pers.] My writings come from my heart and from my past experiences. I try to write so other people can understand my point of view on life.; [a.] Cornettsville, KY

SEBREN, SIDNEY DONALD
[b.] June 7, 1957, Jackson, MS; [p.] Ray Sebren and Mary Sebren; [m.] Tammy Sebren, June 5, 1993; [ed.] 12th grade; [occ.] Correctional Officer; [oth. writ.] "The Witcher" that is yet to be published.; [pers.] To put love and faith in Jesus Christ and God. You cannot go to Heaven hating other people no matter what race, creed, or color; [a.] Harrisville, MS

SECORD, PHILLIP GEORGE
[b.] February 1, 1943, Flint MI; [p.] Ernest and Pauline Secord; [m.] Rita Lee, February 14, 1971; [ch.] Kip, Michele, and Richard; [ed.] Millington High, Flint Jr. College; [occ.] Toolmaker, Machinest; [memb.] V.F.W., Lewiston Fun ones; [pers.] Smile and world smiles back. Trouble has to be experienced to be fully understood.; [a.] Birch Run, MI

SEERMON, PAUL
[b.] June 26, 1951, Chicago, IL; [pers.] I wrote the poem to give people something to ponder.; [a.] Flossmoor, IL

SEES, LORENE
[b.] May 30, 1924, Lancaster, MO; [p.] John and Olga Sommer; [m.] Burthol Earl Sees, May 23, 1947; [ch.] Sara Elizabeth Lester; [ed.] Northeast Missouri University Kirksville, Missouri Glendale Community College Glendale, Arizona; [occ.] Taught Elementary School before marriage, Retired; [memb.] Daughters of the American Revolution, First Christian Church, Alpha Sigma Alpha Phi Theta Kappa (Jr. College); [pers.] Poetry is the ultimate medium of expression of the hopes, joys, and sorrows of life as well as promoting a fascination of English to record most effectively ones personal thoughts.; [a.] Phoenix, AZ

SELLAR, MARY
[b.] May 8, 1934, Morden, Surrey, England; [m.] March 29, 1963; [ed.] Ursuline Convent; [occ.] Secretary; [memb.] Thetford and District Writers' Circle; [hon.] 1992 1st prize in Thetford Poetry Comp. For most humorous poem several poems published. Also read on radio.; [oth. writ.] Novel and thriller as yet unfinished; [pers.] Start to write in 1990; [a.] Thetford, Norfolk

SEMANUIK, JOSEPH W.
[b.] November 24, 1966, Edmonton, Canada; [p.] Leonard and Phyllis Semanuik; [m.] Stephanie Semanuik, July 9, 1994; [ch.] Zachary Connor; [ed.] Archbishop MacDonald High School University of Alberta; [occ.] Junior High Teacher, Queen Elizabeth School, Wetaskiwin, Alberta; [oth. writ.] Recently published poem in Echoes From The Silence; [pers.] I strive to let my writing reflect what I see in the world. Poetry is my commentary on issues that have relevance in life. I can only hope it presents some universal ideas.; [a.] Edmonton, Alberta, Canada

SENZAPAURA, KERRI
[b.] April 9, 1966, Redbank, NJ; [p.] Grace Boyer, Bruce C. Boyer; [m.] Angelo Francisco Senzapaura, June 9, 1990; [ch.] Michael Angelo, Christopher, Matthew; [ed.] University of Lowell, Lowell, MA; [occ.] Project Administrator; [pers.] Everyone has the ability to make the most of their lives - It is up to them to tap the faith, strength and desire that is inherent in us all.; [a.] Maynard, MA

SERRANO, DESIREE
[b.] August 12, 1983, Loma Linda; [p.] Daniel Serrano, Cruz Serrano; [ed.] William McKinley Elementary School; [occ.] Student; [memb.] Colton Youth Basketball, Carl Rimbaugh Girls Softball; [hon.] McKinley School - Colton, Honor Student, Perfect attendance; [a.] Colton, CA

SESSIONS, SAMMYE
[pen.] Sam; [b.] August 17, 1943, Winters, TX; [p.] Harry Sanford, Neta Sanford; [ch.] Shannon, Stacey Branden Yarbrough; [ed.] Senior Social Work Major, SWTSU; [occ.] Student; [memb.] OSSW, NTSO; [hon.] PHi Alpha Honor Society; [pers.] I write to express my feelings.; [a.] San Marcos, TX

SEVERINO, ELIZABETH
[pen.] Forrie Gerard-di Carlo; [b.] December 29, 1945, Bryn Mawr, PA; [p.] John Girard-di Carlo, Elizabeth Patton Girard-di Carlo; [m.] Divorced, October 20, 1974; [ch.] Daughter, Nicole; [ed.] A.B. Vassar College, Dean's List M.S., Syracuse University over 150 post graduate courses; [occ.] Computer Company Executive, also, Internationally recognized Consultant, Speaker, Author, Entrepreneur, and Personal fulfillment Advisor; [memb.] National Association of Female Executives, Philadelphia Area Computer Society, Association of Personal Computer Professionals (pres., 1988-91), Institute of Noetic Sciences Robbins Foundation; [hon.] Many Honors and Awards for both corporate and Civic Contributions, Accomplishments are recorded in dozens of Biographical research works Nationally and Internationally; [oth. writ.] Author, Do-it-yourself vibrant neath, 1995, Author, International guide to computer systems architecture, 1974 over 125 articles published on variety of topics; [pers.] God is the source of my creativity and inspiration, helping me to improve the planet, one person at a time.; [a.] Cherry Hill, NJ

SEWELL, NEIL
[b.] November 8, 1923, AL; [p.] Owen and Mamie Sewell; [m.] Doris Sewell, November 10, 1949; [ch.] John 43, Larry 35, Tina 32; [ed.] Lexington High School, Provervial School of Hard Knocks, with the degree of under dog; [occ.] Retired; [memb.] American Legion; [oth. writ.] Poems and numerous stories of life from the good old days printed in the local weekly paper; [pers.] Oh, that I could be all things to everyone, but that is left to God's only Son. To be blessed that I may be a blessing to others, and in times of need help my brothers.; [a.] Lexington, AL

SEXTON, CHARLES J.
[b.] December 3, 1919, Rockford, IL; [m.] Judi Sexton, December 27, 1942; [ch.] Michael, Gerald and Suzanne; [ed.] Bachelor of Arts, San Diego State University, San Diego, California; [occ.] Retired; [oth. writ.] Poetry to amuse.; [pers.] "Never grow old where you were once great!"; [a.] San Diego, CA

SEXTON, MOLLY J.
[b.] May 4, 1920, Drift, KY; [p.] Cleve and Sarah

Baisden; [m.] Charles Sexton, February 29, 1940; [ch.] Ronald E. Sexton; [ed.] High School, Business College, Training for Therapeutic and Dietary work for special diets.; [occ.] Retired; [oth. writ.] "My Son", "A Talk With Myself", "The Awaken Of A City", (Bs. As. Argentina) and others; [pers.] I am touched by moods for writing and awakened from sleep in deep thoughts and words. Always for encouragement or to up lift. The faith in others. Nothing has been sold. Many have been enjoyed. I release in rhyme. Things I cannot in words (orally).; [a.] Valrico, FL

SEYMOUR, MAYA
[pen.] Marilyn Stonne; [b.] February 22, 1981, New Orleans, LA; [p.] Louis Seymour and Ruby Seymour; [ed.] Archbishop Blenk High School; [occ.] Student; [memb.] The Reach Team; [hon.] Poetry Award of 1995 and the A. L. Davis Speaker's Tournament Award of 1993; [oth. writ.] Conflict Prevention published in the program A Lift For Life; [pers.] I love to encourage people of all ages, in my writing, because life is all about being happy.; [a.] New Orleans, LA

SHAFFER, KARYN J.
[b.] March 7, 1943, Bradford, PA; [m.] Clifford J. Shaffer Jr., September 7, 1984; [ed.] B.S., M.E., (Gannon University, Erie, PA); [occ.] Teacher (Glenwood Elementary, Erie); [memb.] E.E.A, P.S.E.A., N.E.A, Director of Erie School Employees Fed. Credit Union; [pers.] Life's personal experiences are my greatest inspiration. I have been fortunate to have good luck - good health - and good times as part of my richly rewarded life!; [a.] Erie, PA

SHAH, LISA DEONNE
[pen.] Lizza; [b.] December 26, 1960, Detroit, MI; [p.] Jam and Alice Shah; [m.] Divorced; [ch.] Keyina Sharif Shah and Emmily Faith Steward; [ed.] Murray Wright High School Wayne County Community, and African Heritage Cultural Center b.; [occ.] Self-employed "I DO", Wedding Rental and Salon/Mailer: Detroit News Agency Newspaper; [memb.] Teamster Union Local 2040; [oth. writ.] No other writings first time experience.; [pers.] I was inspired to write "Found Love", by a special friend Reggie Wright from Toledo Ohio, who help me to trust in love again. Thanks Reggie love always Lisa.; [a.] Detroit, MI

SHANNON, MILTON
[pen.] M. L. Shannon; [b.] January 2, 1939, Mississippi; [m.] Margaret Shannon, June 18, 1970; [ch.] Michelle Shannon, Milton Shannon Jr.; [ed.] Corliss High School; [occ.] Playing my guitar and writing songs; [pers.] I love music and I like writing songs and poems and playing my guitar.; [a.] Chicago, IL

SHAPIRO, DEANNA
[b.] September 19, 1939, Bronx, NY; [p.] Ruth and Abraham Klein; [m.] Charles Shapiro, June 11, 1961; [ch.] Holly Anne, Emily Joy; [ed.] B.A. Hunter College M.S., City College (education), M.S., City College (school psychology) M.S. Th., New Seminary; [occ.] Writer, Artist, Mediator; [memb.] Hudson River Writer's Center Croton Council on the Arts, Academy of Family Mediators, Association of Interfaith Ministers; [hon.] Dean's List, Cum Laude; [pers.] I am inspired by the honesty of women confessional poets, particularly Louise Gliick and Sharon Olds.; [a.] Croton-on-Hudson, NY

SHAPIRO, JILL LYS
[b.] June 10, Brooklyn; [p.] Irving Shapiro, Miriam Myers Shapiro; [m.] Single (unclaimed treasure); [ed.] James Madison High School, Brooklyn College, New York University, York College; [occ.] 'Musing'; [memb.] James Madison High School, Alumni Association, International Center of New York, All the major Department Stores in New York City via my Credit Cards.; [hon.] Citation from the United States Navy American Women's Voluntary Services Music Scholarship with Madame Estelle Liebling (Opera); [oth. writ.] Unpublished; [pers.] 'Make the best of time and time will return the compliment'; [a.] New York, NY

SHAW SR., BASIL D.
[b.] June 13, 1935, Hagerstown, IN; [p.] George and Ellen Shaw; [m.] Ruby, August 29, 1973; [ch.] Basil III, Daniel (deceased), Jennifer, Kelly, Rachel, Roger, Rebecca; [ed.] Whitewater High School (Indiana) Nazarene Bible College (Colorado); [occ.] Pastor, Calcutta Church of the Nazarene, Calcutta, Ohio; [memb.] Calcutta Church of the Nazarene; [pers.] This poems come to me while driving home to officiate at his funeral, a reflection of the privilege of friendship of an elderly christian gentleman.; [a.] Calcutta, OH

SHEFFIELD, DENICE
[b.] October 28, 1970, Houston, TX; [p.] Mary J. Wheeler Hayes; [m.] Frederick Joseph Sheffield, May 8, 1993; [ch.] Tiffany Cy-Reen Sheffield June 30, 1989; [ed.] Caddo-Kiowa practical Nursing Program 1991-1992; [occ.] License Practical Nurse; [memb.] Member of the Church of Jesus Christ of Latter Day Saints; [a.] Mt. View, OK

SHELKOWITZ, MICHAL
[b.] April 27, 1983, Israel; [p.] Hava and Bennett; [oth. writ.] Poem "Rainbow" published in Anthology of Poetry book of young poets; [pers.] When I write a poem, I write it from my feelings. If I'm sad or angry it makes me feel better.; [a.] Bellmore, NY

SHELL, JEWELL
[b.] February 21, 1944, Portland, OR; [ch.] Alexis Allum, Adam Schwartz and Jessica Gagnier; [occ.] Educational Assistant, Buckman Elementary Arts Magnet Portland, OR.; [oth. writ.] Poems for children, other friends and special occasions.; [pers.] Our imaginations, constructively exercised, provide a wellspring of imagery awaiting expression through written and illustrated form. To assist in opening the door to this profoundly exciting resource is a joy unmeasured.; [a.] Portland, OR

SHERBERT, JUDY P.
[b.] September 1, 1950, Spartanburg; [p.] David T. and Myrtle S. Pearson; [m.] William G. Sherbert, January 31, 1970; [ch.] William Bryan Sherbert, Chadwick Lance Sherbert; [occ.] Banker (Nationsbank); [memb.] Canaan Baptist Church (Audit Committee, Choir and Sunday School Teacher); [pers.] Poem written for a very dear friend "Edward Daniel Caston"; [a.] Spartanburg, SC

SHERIF, DALIA MOHAMED
[b.] October 4, 1975, Cairo; [p.] Mohamed Sherif, Bothina El-Deeb; [ed.] EL-Nasr School till 11th grade, then I.G.C.S.E. at Manor House School, and now a student at the American University in Cairo; [memb.] Cairo Friendship Association at AUC.; [oth. writ.] Several Love poems titled My Penultimate Words - Bursting With Your Love - Starting Life Afresh - Living Inside You - Praying To Hate You.; [pers.] I believe that a woman who captures a man's heart eternally is not the one who challenges his strength and power, but the one who tickles his masculinity by showing her weakness and need for him... just to him.; [a.] Cairo, Egypt

SHERWOOD, MARGARET
[pen.] Margaret, Maggie; [b.] August 2, 1950, Saint John, New Brunswick, Canada; [p.] Gerald and Josephine Sherwood; [m.] Divorced; [ch.] Four; [ed.] Grade 10; [occ.] Disability; [hon.] I have had many poems published in local newspaper. I have many dancing awards (Tap, Jazz, Hawaiian); [oth. writ.] Goodbye to drugs. A Santa Claus parade thru the eyes of a child etc. I write many poems; [pers.] I love to write. It is an expression of the heart found in no other way. When I sit to write I don't stop to think what my next line well be. It just flows out naturally; [a.] Alvinston Ontario, Canada

SHIELDS, GINGER
[b.] June 21, 1951, Detroit, MI; [p.] Ruth Rowland, (Deceased); [ch.] Keisha Rena Luckett, Derrick Shields; [ed.] Central Dauphin High School; [occ.] Computer Operator; [memb.] Member of the Goodwin Memorial Baptist Church.; [oth. writ.] I have written several other poems. This is the first time one has been published. I usually write poems for birthdays, or special occasions.; [pers.] I feel that if given time this rare talent could go far. I was told my mother had the same gift. Each poem I write or attempt to write I always pray and ask God for the words. Because through him all things are possible.; [a.] Harrisburg, PA

SHIELDS, SHANESE L.
[pen.] Nese Shields; [b.] September 13, 1980, Kansas City, MO; [p.] Claresta Penn and Kenneth Shields; [ed.] Still in high school. I'm a freshman who attends Grandview High School. Class of 98.; [hon.] Won 2nd place in an ACSI singing competition. Poems published in young writers conference 1995. Also a short story.; [oth. writ.] Write several poems and short stories.; [pers.] I love poetry and I love to read. Maya Angelou and Langston Hughes really inspire me. I'm also very active in sports. My sister Sharese is a journalist who also writes poetry. She's been a real inspiration to me also.; [a.] Grandview, MO

SHIMKO, THOMAS
[b.] December 21, 1946, Cleveland, OH; [p.] Ignatius Shimko, Celia Shimko; [m.] Linda Shimko, May 12, 1973; [ch.] Brian Shimko, Amanda Shimko; [ed.] AAB Cuyahoga Community College, BBA Cleveland State University; [occ.] Credit Manager Southdown, Inc.; [memb.] National Association of Credit Management; [hon.] Credit Executive of the Year, CCE (Certified Credit Executive) Designation; [oth. writ.] Several articles for Business Credit Magazine.; [pers.] Writing is a form of immortality where the writer can affect readers in many different ways which will never be known.; [a.] Beavercreek, OH

SHINKMAN, CLAIRE AMELIA
[b.] April 10, 1080, Philippines; [p.] Bernard and Gillian; [ed.] Currently attending James Madison High School, Fairfax County; [occ.] Student/lover of literature; [memb.] Founder of Dead Poet's Society; [hon.] Fencing Awards, Speech Awards, honor student; [oth. writ.] None published-yet!; [pers.] To all young writers out there: If they say you can't do it, that's one more reason to - on the fast-paced highway of life, strive to be a speed bump!; [a.] Vienna, VA

SHIRAZI, SAHAR
[pen.] Sahar Shirazi; [b.] January 18, 1980, Berkeley, CA; [p.] Ali Shirazi and Sedigheh Taherivard; [ed.] Healdsburg, High School - Sophomore; [occ.] Student; [memb.] California Scholarship Federation, Gifted and Talented Education; [hon.] Board of trustees, Honor roll, Golden State High Honors.; [oth. writ.] Poems in school paper and magazine, essays.; [pers.] I listen to those around me with an open mind and I learn. I am influenced by them, but I shall never let myself become them. I do not want to be lost in the crowd or left behind.; [a.] Windsor, CA

SHOEMATE, MARK W.
[b.] March 15, 1969, Wilmington, DE; [p.] William and Carolyn Shoemate; [ed.] McKean High, Delcastle Votech-Electrical; [occ.] Maintenance, Westuaco, Newark DE; [memb.] Abate of Delaware; [pers.] I usually write about my life, how I feel, my surroundings and the unhappy side of life. Most of my writings I'd like to put music to them.; [a.] Wilmington, DE

SHORT, RICHARD M.
[b.] January 13, 1951, San Francisco, CA; [p.] Richard M. and Elizabeth B. Short; [m.] Reba M. Short, August 16, 1981; [ch.] Ryan, Ruth, and Rachel; [ed.] Southwest Texas State University, Dallas Theological Seminary, University of Texas at San Antonio, Wharton County Junior College; [occ.] Bookkeeper; [hon.] Who's Who in American Colleges and Universities, The National Dean's List; [pers.] Acknowledging the true and living God, the God and Father of Jesus Christ, the Savior of sinners, I seek to reflect Him in word and deed. Poetry has been a favorite way of mine to convey the truth about God and His creation.; [a.] San Antonio, TX

SHRODE, NIKI DAVID
[b.] November 8, 1940, Albuquerque, N.M.; [p.] Walter C. and Katheryn J.; [m.] Elizabeth Dolly "Betty" August 1, 1959; [ch.] Carmine Belle McCausland, Rene' Michelle Werner; [ed.] 5 yrs. College Business and Engineering 1 yr. Art; [occ.] Consulting Systems Engineer at Bank of America - PC Networks; [memb.] Conservative Charismatic Church Walnut Creek, CA; [hon.] Who's Who in Computing in America; [oth. writ.] "Echoes on the Wind" Silver Sands Press 1978; [pers.] "I ride the winds of change... the breath of God."; [a.] Walnut Creek, CA

SIERRA, CHRISTINA
[b.] February 5, 1977, N.Y.C.; [p.] Rosa and George Seyffert; [ed.] Elementary - P.S. 250, Junior High School - 318, (Eugenio Maria De Hostos) I.S. 318, High School - Grover Cleveland, High School Senior 1995 graduate - June; [memb.] The Calvary Spanish Pentecostal Church, NUTS for Christ, Missionettes Club for girls.; [pers.] I can do all things through Christ who strengthens me. Philippians 4:13; [a.] Brooklyn, NY

SIKORA, KEITH
[b.] March 8, 1958, Walnut Creek, CA; [p.] Jenette Green, Stangreen; [m.] Beth Sikora, May 11, 1989; [ch.]Taz, Ozzy, Shadow, and Murphy,; [ed.] Bret Harte Union High, Columbia J.C., School of Animal Science; [occ.] Veterinary Assit.; [oth. writ.] 10 Books of poetry, over 1,000 poems (never published); [pers.] My poetry is a reflection of the way I see the world through my eyes, mind and Heart; [a.] Sand Leandro, CA

SILEK, LAURA SPENCER
[pen.] Laura Spencer Silek; [b.] June 4, 1910, Reynoldsville, PA; [p.] Braden and Rebecca Spencer; [m.] Samuel Silek, July 7, 1932 decease (1984); [ch.] Daughter - Edna, Ruth; [ed.] Grade - High School, Cleveland Bible College (Quaker), Belleville Jr. College (Nursing Course), Olins Nursing School - Licensed, L.P.N.; [occ.] Retired - Ordained Minister with Beulah Fellowship, N.H.; [memb.] Church - And PARA Christians. I still minister Occasionally. I'll be 85 in June So printing is rather shaky.; [hon.] Great Grandmother of 9 and grandmother of 6 with 2 more on the way. I'm thankful. Phi Theta Kappa - Belleville Jr. College - Deans list; [oth. writ.] Published book of 87 poems and have written more since copy right 1981 by Laura Spencer Silek. I read alot cant' really take credit - Just hear them inside me and write them down; [pers.] Born again at age 26, felt call to the ministry. Licensed to preach during W.W. II by the 1st Nazarene Church, Cleveland OH - Moved to VA. after war - where I received my personal pentecost.; [a.] Orange, VA

SILLS, MARY A.
[b.] January 8, 1975, Saint Louis, MO; [p.] Kathryn and Paul Smith; [ed.] Holy Family Grade School, Iron County C-4 High School; [oth. writ.] I have written numerous short stories and poems, but have not published any of them yet.; [pers.] Being able to share my thoughts with such a great audience is truly a wonderful gift. I hope I will have the opportunity to do it again.; [a.] Saint Louis, MO

SILNES, RUTH
[pen.] Ruth Silnes; [b.] March 18, 1915, San Francisco, CA; [p.] Leon and Clarice Goldstein; [m.] Widow; [ch.] Roland Stone and Sandra Goldstein, Grandchildren: Jessica Sears and Gary Goldstein; [ed.] Famous writers Schools and various writers Seminars, Livington's Advertising Art School and numerous fine art Schools and seminars; [occ.] Entrepreneur; [memb.] Manuscripters, Bel Marin Keys Writer's Workshop, Women's National Book Association, Marin Small Book Publishers; [oth. writ.] Book - "Keeping Ahead of Winter" a true life nautical adventure - Public relations for art organizations and international Toastmistress, Newsletter for Bel Marin Keys, Women's Club; [pers.] I am an artist/writer, my long life has taken me through a sea of peaks and valleys worthy of the telling an I delight in painting with words as well as with bushes - My poem "Loneliness" is my first submission for honors; [a.] Bel Marin Keys, CA

SILVEY, ANDREA R.
[b.] July 29, 1939, Jersey City, NJ; [p.] James Silvey and Caroline Silvey; [occ.] Executive Director After-school Math, Science, English, 2nd Computer Literacy program; [oth. writ.] Articles - Oakland Tribune, Oakland Chamber of Commerce (Focus), Computer world; [pers.] To my mother who always told me I was a gift from God. To all of my children around the world - you too, are my gift from God; [a.] Oakland, CA

SIMMONS, FRANCENIA V.
[pen.] Franvisi Files; [b.] April 17, 1933, Bronx, NY; [p.] Viola and Thomas Stewart; [ed.] BA College of New Rochelle NY, HS of Commerce NYC; [occ.] Retired - Nutrition Specialist; [memb.] United Missionary Baptist Church, Golden Ayers Bowling Leagues, Civil Service Retiree Assoc., CWA City Employer Retiree Assoc.; [hon.] Several Service Community Awards, Bowling Achievement Awards, Several Appreciation Certificates for Community Service from City of New York Volunteers Program.; [oth. writ.] Several poems published in community newsletters, other writings for family, friends and co-workers since 1950; [pers.] My biggest aim in life is not to see through people, but to see people through, with my writings and poetry; [a.] Brooklyn, NY

SIMMONS, JANET
[b.] August 30, 1972, Belleville, KS; [p.] Harold and Mary Ann Simmons; [m.] Divorced; [ch.] Destiny Dawn - Nicholas Allen; [ed.] Beatty High, Beatty Nevada; [occ.] Security Officer at Military Range.; [pers.] "I started writing, writing in the eight grade and a teacher once told me to consider having my work published, because I have a talent for it."; [a.] Beatty, NV

SIMMONS, LINDA JEAN
[b.] February 24, 1947, Gadsden, AL; [p.] Troy W. and Jeanette Glenn; [m.] Engaged to Donald E. Utley; [ch.] One son, Troy J. (Chip) Simmons; [ed.] Etowah High School, Gadsden State Jr. College; [occ.] Secretary, Yellow Freight System, Birmingham, AL; [hon.] Beta Club, Dean's List , Phi Theta Kappa.; [oth. writ.] Raindrops", unpublished.; [pers.] I wrote "Twins" from real life experience, I have an identical twin sister, Joan Alexander.; [a.] Birmingham, AL

SIMMONS, SUSIE
[pen.] Sue Lynn; [b.] December 23, 1949, Oklahoma City, OK; [p.] Ray and Betty Simmons; [ch.] Tim - 15, the light of my life; [ed.] John Marshall High School, OCU St. Anthony Hospital School of Nursing, Oklahoma City, OK.; [occ.] Registered Nurse; [memb.] Forest Hills Christian Church, Oklahoma City OK, Consumer and child advocacy. Publicity Committee Chairman Silverstrings of Putnam City School System, Oklahoma City OK.; [oth. writ.] I have written a number of other poems/prose and am hopeful of getting them published one day.; [pers.] This poem was part of my eulogy to my mother who passed away 13 days after my father in July of 1993. I held her hand and watched her die of a broken heart at the young age of 65. I am moved by the world and all the feelings generated from existing in it.; [a.] Oklahoma City, OK

SIMNITT, CHANING
[b.] June 4, 1972, Topeka, KS; [p.] Darrell and Diana Simnitt; [ed.] Jefferson West High School, Washburn University; [occ.] General Contractor; [oth. writ.] Various other poems and songs, none of which have been published.; [a.] Topeka, KS

SIMONE, EILEEN
[pen.] Babe; [b.] January 12, 1946, New York, NY; [p.] John P. Simone, Eileen Simone; [m.] Raymond E. Austin (companion); [ch.] Susan, John and Brian Holland and Jamie Rohler; [ed.] Norland High, No. Miami, FL. and Manatee Community College, Bradenton, FL.; [oth. writ.] Mommy Dearest, Shades of Green, Fifty and Free, Eternal Love and more.; [pers.] I am inspired by mankinds need for spiritual awakening, as well as the personal events of family and friends.; [a.] Palmetto, FL

SIMONSON, ERIC
[pen.] The Kid; [b.] August 13, 1969, Franklin Lks, NJ; [pers.] Inspirations: Peter Tosh, Bob Dylan, Paul Simon, Love, and most important - My Family I do believe man shall prove himself to be worthy. Oh how I do hope.; [a.] Franklin Lakes, NJ

SIMPSON, JOY
[b.] November 1, 1938, Port Arthur, TX; [p.] Milly and Jesse Simpson; [ch.] Taryn Simpson, Tanya Touchstone; [ed.] G.E.D and Lamar University; [occ.] Medical Re-

tirement; [memb.] P.E.T.A. Humane Society P.A.W.S.; [oth. writ.] I am now in the process of writing a book.; [pers.] My goal is to share my life, in hopes and this will cause someone. Somewhere -, to have "second thoughts" on their own lifes journey.; [a.] Antioch, TN

SIMS, BARBARA
[b.] October 22, 1936, CA; [p.] Christina Hanna and Lowell Sims; [m.] Ken Jones (Deceased), 1969; [ch.] Sean Jones, Boone Jones, Mark Bolin, Lance Bolin, Thayne Bolin, Robin Westbrook; [ed.] 12 yrs. through H.S., 3 yrs. Jr. College; [occ.] Self employed Housekeeper and Landscaping; [memb.] Mariposa First Baptist Church; [oth. writ.] Children's stories and many poems - unpublished to date; [pers.] Being orphaned at 10 I felt compelled to write and many stories and poems begin as a dream. I wake up at 3:00 a.m. and begin to write the thoughts that came to me.; [a.] Mariposa, CA

SINGH, HARDYAL SARA
[b.] November 16, 1926, Vill, Bombeli Hoshiar Pur, Punjab, India; [p.] Harbakhsh Singh (deceased), Mankaur; [m.] Mohinder Kaur, February 1, 1962; [ch.] Inder Pall Singh (LLM), Harman Singh Dhana, Amarpall Singh 'Kaka'.; [ed.] Only graduate (Arts) and Diploma in Sports and Physical Education from University of Punjab - India.; [occ.] Reading and writing. Domestic look after prayers in Sikh-Temples, not as professional but as intuitional.; [oth. writ.] My several articles and letters were published in newspapers and weekly's in India as well as Canada (Vancouver) B.C. I am writer at will, not as profession; [pers.] Truthfulness is divine virtue, its practice a divine blessing. The more we practice it, the purer the world shall be.; [a.] Vancouver British Columbia, Canada

SINGLETON, BARBARA
[b.] April 4, 1962, Fort Worth, TX; [p.] Eugene and Liz Andrew; [ch.] Quinton Phillips; [ed.] O.D. Wyatt High, Tarrant County Jr. College; [occ.] Hairdresser; [pers.] I allow God, life and my heart to influence my writing; [a.] Fort Worth, TX

SIRACUSA, DINA L.
[b.] March 31, 1970, Seaford, NY; [p.] Frank Siracusa and Frances Siracusa; [m.] John Keith Carlucci (Fiance), Pending; [ed.] Top ten graduate of Seaford High School Bachelor of Science in a dual major of Elementary Education and English from Hofstra University, Currently obtaining a Master of Science in Foundations of Educational Administration from Hofstra University with aspirations of ultimately earning a Doctorate degree in Education and English.; [occ.] I currently teach fourth grade at Woodward Parkway Elementary School in Farmingdale, New York.; [memb.] I am a proud member of Kappa Delta Pi - The International Education Honor Society, Theta Chapter of Hofstra University and the Education Society. I am the chief editor and developer of a monthly school publication, titled the Woodward Parkway Planet Newspaper.; [hon.] Top ten Distinguished Student Academic Scholarship, Dean's List of Distinguished Students, International Honor Society, National Honor Society Performance awards for piano, clarinet, and voice.; [oth. writ.] Composed an original play for the Drama Department in College.; [pers.] I aspire to uplift the human spirit through the eloquence of the written word, spoken word, convey and inspire great emotion.; [a.] Seaford, NY

SISK, THOMAS H.
[b.] April 9, 1975, Shelby, NC; [p.] Sherry S. Craven; [ed.] Shelby High School, University of Arizona; [occ.] U.S. Navy Midshipman; [oth. writ.] Unpublished Children's Stories, Poems; [pers.] I live for the moment and that's how I write how I feel at the moment.; [a.] Ladson, SC

SITKO, ANNA
[b.] September 8, 1920, Akron, OH; [p.] Thomas and Anna Sitko; [ed.] Graduate of North High School; [occ.] Retired from Firestone Tire and Rubber Co. with 39 years of service; [pers.] I enjoy writing poems about people and sacred poems in which I can express meaningful thoughts.; [a.] Akron, OH

SJOSTEN, KEITH
[b.] 1953, Naha, Okinawa; [occ.] Professional Musician; [oth. writ.] In a monograph titled 'Spiritual Perspectives from the Underground', published at Boston College, I presented archaeological evidence of parthenogenetical (virgin) births. Though the paper earned High Honors, it set him on a path uncontainable by the collegiate mainstream. "That paper proved to be too much to bear, even for the Jesuits." In 1993 his book "Signal Fire' was published, describing spiritual grace as "not genetic or evolutionary, but seeded, and tangible." It also made the case for dis-embodied intelligent evil.; [pers.] I was very fortunate making a living at something for which I had such passion. The success was remaining a commodity in such a fickle business." "That there is a functional suction. That we bump our heads on Heaven, so close does it hover, yet we are unaware of the graze on our brow because of hypnosis by the orthodox. The only thing that matters, and that is apparent in this world and beyond, is the wonder of it all. The indefinable, unchartable, incalculable WONDER.

SLAUENWHITE, CLYDE N.
[b.] March 5, 1926, Liverpool, Nova Scotia, Canada; [p.] Harold and Nellie Slauenwhite; [m.] Irene Slauenwhite, April 9, 1947; [ch.] David Clyde, Sylvia Diane, Gary Albert, Cynthia Irene; [ed.] Liverpool High, Maritime Bible Institute; [occ.] Retired Clergyman; [oth. writ.] Several poems and articles in local newspapers and magazines. Won several writing contests.; [pers.] "I receive great satisfaction in capturing a bit of the wonder and beauty of God's glory in His universe, in my writing (and painting).; [a.] Truro, Nova Scotia, Canada

SLAUGHTER, SARA
[pen.] Sara Slaughter; [b.] November 11, 1981, Nampa, ID; [p.] Karla Peterson/Danny Slaughter; [ed.] I'm in 7th grade at Meridian Middle School in Idaho.; [hon.] I'm in the honor roll, at school; [oth. writ.] 39 other poems that I write about my feelings and my friends. (The quite contrite) Snow White, (all of which are not published):; [pers.] I would have nothing if I didn't have my friends and mom. My mom is my inspirer. A special thanks to Kathrine Peterson for listening to all of my poems.; [a.] Meridian, ID

SLOAN, DIANNE
[b.] April 1, 1960, Memphis, TN; [p.] Ben H. Graham and Jane D. Graham; [m.] William T. Sloan Jr., November 14, 1986; [ch.] Sarah Michelle Sloan, Preston Pierce Sloan, Savannah Lynne Sloan; [ed.] High School St. Agnes Academy College Christian Brothers and Memphis State.; [occ.] Mother and house wife.; [pers.] I usually write to friends and relatives about how I feel. This particular poem I wrote around christmas of 94. My 94 year old great grandmother died January 95 and my 72 year old grandmother died February 95. This poem was read at both funerals; [a.] Memphis, TN

SLOCUM SR., GERALD DON
[b.] October 31, 1955, Dallas, TX; [p.] Floyd Lee and Julia K. Slocum; [ch.] Gerald Don Jr., Barbara Jean, Heather Beam; [ed.] Skyline High, Eastfield College; [occ.] U.S. Navy; [pers.] We live in a beautiful world. Take the time and enjoy her wonders. It's a great influence. God's work!; [a.] Dallas, TX

SMACK, JOYCE ELAINE
[b.] May 24, 1933, Glen Ridge, NJ; [p.] Deceased; [m.] Divorced; [ch.] Deceased; [ed.] B.S. Degree, Rudgers University, Nowark, NJ. June, 1975. M.B.A. Degree Fairleigh Dickinson University, Madison, NJ. - June, 1978; [occ.] Senior Auditor - for a Federal Government Agency; [memb.] National Society of Public Accountants and Toastmasters of America; [hon.] Dean's List, and one Editor's choice Award (1994); [oth. writ.] Poems: "A Dedication To Rickey - 1954", and "The Little Angels". Both of The Aforementioned were published by the National Library of Poetry.; [pers.] It is my great pleasure to be able to share some of my deepest thoughts and emotions with so many others.; [a.] Helmetta, NJ

SMAY, JOLEEN M.
[b.] June 21, 1982, Jhonstown, PA; [p.] Lori Plummer, Gary Smay; [ed.] Lebanon Middle School; [occ.] Seventh grade student at Lebanon Middle School; [hon.] A&B average, top writer for school paper; [oth. writ.] Several poem and articles in school newspaper; [pers.] I would like to thank my Grandma Myrtle Plummer for encouraging me to write; [a.] Lebanon, PA

SMITH, AISHAH
[pen.] Miko; [b.] September 1, 1971, U.S.; [p.] Lillie Smith; [ed.] Graduate of NYU College; [occ.] Phone Operator; [memb.] NAACP; [hon.] One Literary Award for an essay on the homeless in America, Award for excellence in journalism; [pers.] My poetry is art not an art form - but a form of art, that you can close your eyes and feel, touch and taste - and that is Art!; [a.] Brooklyn, NY

SMITH, CATHERYN ANN
[pen.] Cathy; [b.] May 25, 1955, Pratt, KS; [p.] Bernard and Velma Hamilton; [m.] Bill Smith, October 17, 1976; [ch.] Troy Eugene; [ed.] High School took a poetry class; [occ.] Homemaker; [oth. writ.] My own personal book of poetry.; [pers.] I enjoy writing poetry as a pastime hobby. I believe my talent is inherited, as my mother writes beautiful poetry, as did her mother.

SMITH, CINDY A.
[pen.] Cindy Newsum Smith; [b.] November 24, 1958, Peoria, IL; [p.] Joan P. and Milton P. Newsum; [m.] G. Edward Smith Jr., November 25, 1989; [ch.] Erikka Beth Smith; [oth. writ.] My favorites are: We Learn Far Too Young, Every Minute We Spend Spend Dreaming, We Lose A Moment Of Life, Seen But Not Shared.; [pers.] I have been amateur writing my life experiences since a very young age, sharing little of my work with anyone. I felt this particular poem had to be shared and thank this publisher for feeling the same.; [a.] Wernersville, PA

SMITH, DALE S.
[b.] February 4, 1954, EL Paso; [p.] Earl B. Smith, Yolanda Smith; [m.] Joanne Smith, September 30, 1991; [ch.] Derek S. Smith, 13 year old; [ed.] 3 Semester, El Paso Community College, Austin High El Paso.; [occ.] Lost right arm below elbow July 26, 1994, Workman's Comp.; [oth. writ.] I have more poems, bit I have never shared them with the public.; [pers.] I write my poems

strictly from my heart and soul. Read them then join in my these feelings. I want all to share.

SMITH, DAVID M.
[pen.] "Daves"; [b.] April 1, 1966, Phoenix, AZ; [p.] Mike and Margaret Smith; [m.] Not married; [ed.] Graduated High School; [occ.] Janitor/Cook; [memb.] International Churchill Society; [hon.] Chess Club Plack Medal in NJROTC; [oth. writ.] Just one other poem; [a.] Colinsville, IL

SMITH, DENNIS P.
[b.] June 15, 1957, Jackson, MI; [p.] Donald and Patricia Smith; [ed.] Northwest High, Jackson, MI Lansing Community College, Lansing, MI; [occ.] Gas Company Service a Worker Consumers Power Co. Lansing, MI; [memb.] National Wildlife Federation, National Parks and Conservation Assoc.; [hon.] This current recognition for my poem "A Spring Vision" is the first and only - but gives hope that may spring me into a deeper pool of personal writing achievement.; [oth. writ.] Several poems and songs, working on a non-fiction book. Up to this point it has only been a personal hobby. Some people at a writers workshops have encouraged me to get published. This current news has been a tremendous encouragement from the National Library of Poetry. Thank You!; [pers.] It is my desire to live well, laugh often, gain the respect of intelligent adults and the love of children. To always appreciate the earth's beauty and express it. And to be known for bringing out the best in others, and giving my best in writing.; [a.] Lansing, MI

SMITH, DONNA CARTER
[b.] November 1, 1949, Williamsport, PA; [p.] Bob and Arlene Miller; [m.] E. Richard Smith, November 24, 1984; [ch.] Michael Wayne Carter and Steven Allen Carter; [ed.] High School Graduate; [occ.] Ceramic Tile Contractor; [pers.] With God in your life and loving yourself and others, you can accomplish anything you set out to do.; [a.] Arlington, TX

SMITH, EDNAROSE M.
[pen.] "Ednarose"; [b.] September 16, 1934, Queens, NY; [p.] Mildred Schaefer, Charles Schaefer (both deceased); [m.] Bernard Smith (deceased), August 21, 1954; [ch.] Karen Jeanette Smith-Schuster and Maureen Bauer; [ed.] Grover Cleveland High School, St. Joseph's College, N.Y.; [occ.] Freelance writer of poetry and short stories, also clerical worker (insurance); [memb.] Glendale Methodist Church, American Association of Retired persons, Parents without partners.; [hon.] Leadership and human resources development certificate, issued by St. Joseph's College, Brooklyn, NY (1987).; [oth. writ.] "Our Guardian Angels", being published this year in the "Poetry Explosion News Letter, (The Pen)" and "There Is A Miracle", being published this year in the book being published by "The Famous Poets Society", entitled "Famous Poems Of Today".; [pers.] "Love is eternal", is my own poetic way of expressing myself through my writing. I sincerely thank Mr. Andre Anthony Spruile for all his devotion and encouragement to me, with my poetry writing.; [a.] Queens, NY

SMITH, F. PAMELA DEE
[b.] July 5, 1966, Greenville, MS; [p.] Frankie Dee; [m.] Leon Smith, March 24, 1989; [ch.] Matthew, Samantha; [ed.] Greenville High School, El Centro College; [occ.] Computer Operator, College Student; [memb.] Inspiring Body of Christ Church; [pers.] Whatever you can conceive, whatever you can believe, God can achieve.; [a.] Balch Springs, TX

SMITH II, RUSSELL E.
[b.] December 26, 1967, Marion, IN; [p.] Russell Smith and Dale Smith; [m.] Angel Smith, March 4, 1989; [ch.] Kalib Thomas, Brittany Sue; [ed.] Independence H.S.; [oth. writ.] (My Angel) not published "yet"; [pers.] "Poem was written to wife expressing love felt for her."; [a.] Phoenix, AZ

SMITH, JANICE
[b.] November 23, 1951, Allentown, PA; [p.] Robert W. Smith Jr., Lovie M. Smith; [ed.] Northwestern Lehigh High School, Lehigh County Community College; [occ.] Coil insulator, Everson Electric Co., Bethlehem, PA; [pers.] I have been blessed in my life by having met and/or known very special persons which have greatly influenced my creativity I am convinced that individuality is definitely a sacred gift.; [a.] Catasauqua, PA

SMITH, JODELL
[pen.] Jo Smith Jodi Hill; [b.] April 3, 1970, Medina, OH; [p.] Linda Anderson mother, Steve Hill father, Andy Anderson stepfather; [ed.] Currently enrolled in Cuyahoga Community College work towards an associates degree in Science; [occ.] Laboratory Technician; [memb.] Rain Forest Rescue, International Society of Poets; [hon.] Poets editors choice award; [oth. writ.] Other works can be found in Poetry anthologies entitled East of the Sunrise and Journey of the Mind published by The National Library of Poetry; [pers.] I believe poetry has slightly different meaning for different people. As long as a reader has learned something from my writings, my purpose has been achieved.; [a.] Medina, OH

SMITH, RAYMOND
[b.] June 28, 1934; [p.] Rev. R. R. Smith (deceased), Lona Shreve Smith; [ed.] Cairo High - Cairo, W. Va., National School of Aeronautics, Kansas City; [occ.] Retired from Paw American World Airways; [oth. writ.] Poems published in local newspapers; [a.] Parkersburg, WV

SMITH, VICKI
[pen.] V.S. Smith; [b.] April 4, 1982, New York; [p.] Edward and Mary Smith; [pers.] I am me and no one else; [a.] Burnt Hills, NY

SMOTHERS, CORLETTA ALLEN
[b.] March 12, 1952, New Orleans, LA; [p.] Ethel and Lawrence Allen, Sr.; [m.] Earl A. Smothers, Sr, February 26, 1972; [ch.] Carla and Earl, Jr.; [ed.] 1976 B.S. in Accounting - Southern University in New Orleans, LA. 1970, High School Diploma - McDonogh #35 Sr. High in New Orleans, LA.; [occ.] Manual #35 Distri. Clerk U.S. Postal Service; [memb.] McDonogh #35 Alumni Assoc., APWU, NAPFE, Assoc. Mail Handlers; [hon.] 1970 - Southern Univ. in New Orleans 4 yr Scholarship 1976 Cum Laude Graduate; [pers.] I write in order to vent frustrations to express my opinions which often go unheard, and to attempt to explain and come to attempt to explain and come to some self-understanding of my life experiences of which I sometimes find both complicated and overwhelming.; [a.] New Orleans, LA

SNOW, G. R.
[b.] 1964, Iowa; [p.] Herbert and Eloise Snow; [ed.] Knoxville H.S. (Honors Diploma) B.A. Music/religion, Illinois Wesleyan University; [occ.] Director of Music Ministry, Trinity Episcopal Church, Chicago; [memb.] Phi Mu Alpha Sinfonia Music Fraternity (Alpha Lambda '83), American Guild of Organists, Grant Park Symphony Chorus 1995, Chatham Choral Ensemble (rehearsal asst. conductor, soloist); [oth. writ.] The Magi (Christmas Oratorio premiered 1992), Pulses of Iowan Life (poem cycle), several choral anthems, two novels and several poem cycles and short stories, all in various stages of editing and submitting.; [pers.] I consider myself a singer rather than a poet. Occasionally I sing words that are new and thus were a poem without meaning to. The poems thus created are only outgrowths of the song of life, which I take pleasure in singing.; [a.] Chicago, IL

SNYDER, AGGIE
[pen.] Aggie; [b.] October 12, 1981, Graind Rapids; [p.] Allan and Karen Snyder; [ed.] 7 grade

SNYDER, DAINA MARA
[pen.] Daina Marie; [b.] March 12, 1952, Philadelphia; [p.] Mr. Pio D'Carlo and Ilona Lemkins; [m.] Carl David Synder, November 28, 1977; [ch.] Stephen, Joseph Snyder; [ed.] Philadelphia School System; [occ.] Homemaker; [memb.] Needle work guild of America, Delaware county Field and Stream Assoc., Free Letts Society of Philadelphia.; [oth. writ.] Soon to be published, in the near future.; [pers.] Always let your dreams be your guide.; [a.] Paoli, PA

SOETAERT, JAN MICHELLE
[pen.] Jan M. Soetaert; [b.] February 3, 1984, Emporia, KS; [p.] Mr. and Mrs. Tom and Sharon Soetaert; [ed.] Sacred Heart School Elementary School; [occ.] I am a member of Starfire Dance Co.; [memb.] Starfire Dance Co. I play the flute; [hon.] Many many award's for my dance.; [oth. writ.] "When I grow up" I was 8 when I wrote this, it got; [pers.] "Keep your head up and keep trying, stay out of drugs, they can ruin your life"; [a.] Emporia, KS

SOLOMON, SALLY P.
[b.] Bronx, New York; [p.] Blanche and Moe Peterseil; [m.] Robert R. Solomon, June 27, 1960; [ch.] Richard M. Solomon, Susan M. Wolff, Richard M. Wolff (grandchildren-Carina and Cameron Wolff); [ed.] James Monroe High School, B.A. California State University; [occ.] Retired Elementary School Teacher; [oth. writ.] Several songs, yet unpublished.; [pers.] In writing poetry, I try to express a personal mood, feeling or experience. I especially enjoy creating personalized special occasion poems for friends and family as well as song lyrics and parodies.; [a.] Beverly Hills, CA

SONGY, SALLY JO
[b.] November 24, 1951, Superior, WI; [p.] Ralph and Beverly Watt; [m.] John Songy, December 26, 1981; [ch.] Kailee Brienne Songy, Chelsey Nicole Songy; [ed.] Palm Springs High School, La Verne College (Received BA), National University University (Masters in Administration); [occ.] Second Grade Teacher, Katherine Fincy Elementary School; [memb.] Alpha Delta Kappa, Los Compadres; [hon.] Teacher of the Year at Katherine Finchy Elementary School 1985, Certificated Employee of the Month for Palm Spring Unified 1990, Teacher of the Year at Katherine Finchy Elementary School in 1992, District Teacher of the Year for Palm Springs Unified (1992); [pers.] If you live the life of the Lord and believe in yourself, then you can make all things happen.; [a.] Palm Springs, CA

SORRELL, MICHELE
[b.] December 20, 1967, Utica, NY; [m.] Nile A. Sorrell, November 2, 1985; [ch.] Jessica, Rebecca, Amanda; [occ.] Homemaker; [pers.] My children are my greatest

influence in my writing and I hope my writing greatly influences them.; [a.] San Antonio, TX

SOWELLS, HENRY L.
[b.] April 24, 1952, De Ridder, LA; [p.] Paul Sowells, Jeanette Sowells; [m.] Patricia A. Sowells, May 26, 1973; [ch.] Derrick Devaughn, Sonya Trishan, Trinisha Ann; [ed.] Leesville High Southern University; [occ.] Lead Chemical Technician; [memb.] Liberty Baptist Church Deacon Board - Church Choir and Liberty Harmonizers; [hon.] Numerous Church Honors My Poem published in the "Garden of Life"; [oth. writ.] "Giving Thanks", "Why Sing?", "This I Had To Say" and others.; [pers.] I strive to accomplish all things through Christ who strengthens me. I have greatly influenced by my parents, wife and children.; [a.] Houston, TX

SOWERS, SHAWN
[b.] August 21, 1967, Spokane, WA; [p.] Wallace Sowers, Diane Sowers; [ch.] Brendan West; [ed.] High School, R.E.A.L. School College, Spokane Community College; [occ.] Electrician; [pers.] Dedicated to my high school creative writing teacher, John Hanlen, who showed me the wonder and magic within the unstructured written word, and whose example helps me to keep the faith that one man truly can make a difference.; [a.] Spokane, WA

SPANGARO, FLORENCIA
[pen.] Flops; [b.] July 16, 1979, Argentina; [p.] Betty and Norberto; [ed.] Chapel High School Brazil and Lincoln High school; [occ.] Student; [hon.] My life has been the greatest award one can receive.; [oth. writ.] Poems published in High school Newspaper.; [pers.] My words are not letters, like my sentences are not words but feelings. Feelings that were mine and I share with you, for family and friends all my love.; [a.] Buenos Aires, Argentina

SPARKS, MARY L.
[b.] January 10, 1939, Weldon, TX; [p.] Max Koch, Nell Koch; [m.] Jimmy Sparks, March 26, 1959; [ch.] Kelly, Bo, Chad; [ed.] East Bernard High School, East Bernard, Texas; [occ.] Small business owner, Rosenberg, Texas; [pers.] Friends and family are the most important things in my life.; [a.] Rosenberg, TX

SPEARS, BRAD
[b.] May 17, 1976, San Antonio, TX; [p.] Rod and Marty Spears; [ed.] Currently enrolled as a cadet at the United States Air Force Academy in Colorado Springs, Colorado. Graduated from Jonesboro High in Jonesboro, Georgia.; [occ.] Student; [memb.] Mystery Science Theatre 3000 Fan Club. United States Tennis Association.; [hon.] "Nothing Important, or at least nothing anyone would care about wasting their time reading."; [oth. writ.] Only a seldom few that the special people in my life have had a chance to read.; [pers.] Writing is simply your minds expression of life through lyric.; [a.] USAF Academy, CO

SPEARS, CAROLYN HARTWELL
[b.] Mary 26, 1951, Jennings, LA; [p.] Bernard and Eugenie; [m.] Gerald M. Spears, November 18, 1972; [ch.] Laurie Jean, Jason Craig; [ed.] Master of Education; [occ.] Kindergarten teacher of Lake Athur Elem. of Lake Arthur, LA.; [memb.] Our Lady of the Lake Catholic Church, LA., Federation of Teachers/AFT MUS Alumni Ass.; [oth. writ.] Personal Collection; [pers.] I enjoy reading. I encourage all writers to publish whenever they can.; [a.] Lake Arthur, LA

SPEARS, DARREN C.
[b.] November 17, 1970, Marion, SC; [p.] Eunice L. Spears; [ed.] Latta High School; [occ.] United States Marine Corps; [memb.] New Hope Baptist Church; [hon.] Non-Commissioned Officer of the Month, Good Conduct Medal Meritorious Masts; [oth. writ.] Collection of unpublished writings that I wish to have reviewed and published someday.; [pers.] My writing is a way for me to express my inner most feelings. I can say so much more through writing than speaking.; [a.] Latta, SC

SPENCE, NIGEL PATRICK
[b.] February 15, 1957, Darwin, N.J.; [p.] Charles Patrick, Patricia June; [ed.] The Bourne School, Singapore; Eppling Boys' High, Sydney; University of New England (Aust.); [occ.] Free-lance Editor, casual lecturer/tutor (English literature) University of New England (Aust.); [memb.] The English Association, ASAL, CALLS, Aust-NZ American Studies Assoc. (ANZASA); [hon.] B.A. (Hons. 1), Sir Frank Kitto Poetry Prize (1989,1990), Robert Smith Prize, W.G. 1987, Hoddinott Prize 1988 (both academic), Gil McPherson Award 1987 (community service); [oth. writ.] Editor: The Zone (poetry); [pers.] We need to write creatively, all of us; it is catharsis, expression, and self-education. Untrip your tongue. [a.] Armidale, NSW, Australia

SPICER, ELLEN
[pen.] Ellen Spicer; [b.] December 17, 1955, Nashville, TN; [p.] Julie Pursell and Andrew Hollabaugh; [m.] Divorced, March 22, 1980; [ch.] Maggie Spicer; [ed.] St. Bernard Academy, University New Mexico; [occ.] Landscape Artist; [memb.] Smithsonian, Hillsboro Cedar Knob Hounds, Woodford Hounds; [hon.] Graduate from Univ. New Mexico with honors, Pres. Kappa Alpha Theta sorority, college basketball Univ. Tenn. (Pat Head Summit) '1993 Tour de CSI Champion (Biathlon); [pers.] My religion is writing as inspired by my love for God. The relations of all life forms is eternal in the mind, if we allow ourselves to breathe on equal planes. Real time has no limitations.; [a.] Bentwood, TN

ST. LOUIS, ARTHUR
[b.] August 25, 1907, Vernon; [p.] Ernest-Edith St. Louis; [m.] Mildred (Usher) St. Louis, August 24, 1927; [ch.] Fifteen children; [occ.] Retired, was tool and die specialists; [memb.] St. Bernards Church; [hon.] Senior of the year.; [oth. writ.] Own Bio my years in 4-H club work. My years in little league. Ninety or more poems long and short ones; [pers.] Do good for people to-day there will be no regrets to-morrow; [a.] Vernon, CT

STAFFORD, DORIS
[b.] June 11, 1924, Dallas, TX; [p.] Deceased; [m.] Divorced; [ch.] Allan, James, Richard and Raymond Stafford, 9 grandchildren; [ed.] Woodrow Wilson High School 1940, Will graduate from Richland College, Dallas, Texas 1996; [occ.] Retired Banker, but working for my son Allan, who is an attorney; [memb.] Park Cities Baptist Church; [oth. writ.] I have an article published in the December - January 1995 Herb Companion; [pers.] I do not think it is too late to try anything; [a.] Garland, TX

STAGE, BILLY
[b.] October 15, 1976, Oakland, CA; [p.] Robert and Sharon Stage; [ed.] Biloxi High School; [memb.] Students Against Drunk Driving, The Sun Herald Coast Youth Teen Board; [hon.] Who's Who among American High School Students (3 years), 2nd place young Biloxi writer's contest, Honor roll, varsity shot put (letterman); [oth. writ.] Several poems published in Indian Etchings, school collection of literature, several columns in the sun Herald Newspapers; [pers.] The 18th Century and the Romantic age was the best that literature had to offer.; [a.] Biloxi, MS

STALNAKER, BARBARA A.
[b.] October 24, 1937, Belzoni, OK; [p.] A.C. and Laura Morrison; [m.] Robert D. Sr., August 31, 1957; [ch.] Robert Jr. 32 Douglas D. 30, Andrew M. (deceased); [ed.] Masters Guidance, Masters Educ., Bachelors H.S. Rattan, OK 1955; [occ.] Ret. Tchr. (Guthrie, OK), now interning for Lic., Professional Counselor (OK); [memb.] NEA (educ.) (Ret.), OEA, OK Counselors Assn., Logan County Colition (Youth and family problems); [hon.] Certified Teenline (Nat. Hotline) Counselor Certified Literacy Volunteer, Honor Roll (College); [pers.] Early intervention that begets trust and based on understanding can go a long way towards helping neglected youth solve their life problems.; [a.] Edmonton, OK

STANFIELD, JOHNNY A.
[b.] August 11, 1955, Claxton, GA; [p.] Joseph and Effie Stanfield; [m.] Patricia K. Stanfield, June 27, 1976; [ch.] Joy Lynn - 16 yrs old, Brent Lee - 2 1/2 yrs old; [ed.] A.A. in General Education - 1977, BS in Nursing - 1980, Masters Degree in Nursing - 1992; [occ.] Research Clinical Nurse Specialist; [memb.] Sigma Theta Tau - International Society of Nursing, Southern Nursing Research Society, Associates of Clinical Pharmacology American Society of Pain Management Nurses; [hon.] Who's Who in American Nursing, 1990-1991, 1993-1994; [oth. writ.] Several articles in professional nursing, pharmacy journals; [pers.] My poems provide an avenue for me to share my deepest feeling towards someone very special in my life and events that I cannot control.; [a.] League City, TX

STANGER, TRACY
[b.] December 12, 1975, NJ; [p.] Charles and Janet Stanger; [ed.] Friendswood High, University of Texas at Austin; [occ.] Full-time student; [oth. writ.] None, this is the first; [pers.] As a fledgling writer, I'm always open to new ways to express my thoughts, I try to avoid the typical "teen angst" that's found in most teenage writing. Some of my favorite poetry has been by Blake and Wordsworth, and I tend to write like what I like.; [a.] Friendswood, TX

STANOJEVIC, BORISLAV
[b.] Yugoslavia; [p.] Nikola Stanojevic, Jelena Stanojevic; [ed.] Faculty of Law, Faculty of Political Sciences, Music School, University of Belgrade, Europe; [occ.] Musician, Ex-Lawyer, Ex-Judge; [memb.] The Society of Composers (Europe), The Songwriters Club of America (USA); [hon.] Silver Oyster Award, Europe, 1986, Editor's Choice Award, 1994-95, All The National Library of Poetry (3 times). Hollywood Jubilee Song Diploma, USA 1993; [oth. writ.] "To Somebody" (collection of poetry) Yugoslavia, 1981, "Memories" (collection of poetry), Yugoslavia, 1984, "Ana", Yugoslavia, 1984, "Anne", Croatia, 1985, 186 poems published in different magazines and newspapers in Yugoslavia, "Don't Forget" (River of Dreams) 1994, "Old Musicians" ("Poetic Voices of America), "Winter Day" (Dusting off Dreams) 1994, "Can You" (Poetic Voices of America) 1995, anthology, "Please Don't Look So Pretty" (Treasured Poems of America) 1994, anthology, "Can You" (The Toronto Sun) Feb 24, 1995, "The Heart Writes with Tears" (The Toronto Sun) March 14, 1995, "Forget if You Can" (Treasured Poems of America),

1995, anthology, Several poems published in Stoney Creek, Canada (School Newspapers), "A Letter to my Mother" (Echoes of the Silence, USA, Texas) 1995, anthology.; [pers.] I changed professions, countries, and continents. I was a lawyer, a judge, and musician my three songs were published on 3 different albums in Hollywood, and 17 songs were published on albums in Europe (Gramophone Records) I have 10 poems in 10 anthologies in USA in 1994 and 1995. All my songs and poems are about love.; [a.] Hamilton Ontario, Canada

STAPLETON, KARMEL

[b.] September 5, 1986, North Carolina; [p.] Kenneth and Sylvia Stapleton; [ed.] Third grade student at Pearsontown Elementary School in Durham, N.C. Participant in the Academically Gifted Program for Third graders: Explorations Program.; [memb.] Member of the Durham Striders Track Team. Events: 100 and 400 meter races.; [hon.] Reflections Contest at Pearsontown School: First Grade/First Place Winner, Second Grade/ First Place Winner, Third Grade/Second Place Winner.; [oth. writ.] Short stories written for contest: "A WORLD WITHOUT GUNS" First Place winner, "A TRIP TO MARS" Second Place Winner; [a.] Durham, NC

STARR, MIRIAM KATHLEEN

[b.] October 3, 1913, Penna; [m.] 1943; [ch.] Four adult children; [ed.] College graduate -1943 Degree in Theology; [occ.] Retired; [oth. writ.] other poems, short stories, plays (now attempt made to have published. For family only.)

STEBOR, AUSTIN F.

[b.] March 11, 1921, Plainfield, NJ; [p.] Mr. Al. Stebor Sr., Mrs. Catherine McLaughlin; [ed.] Graduated High School, (North Plainfield High); [occ.] Retired R.R. Worker. Worker 40 years for C.R.R. of NJ and Conrail.; [memb.] A.A.R.P, United Seniors Association, Inc., Central R.R. Vets Ass'n. (founded in 1903), All-American Life League, Inc.; [oth. writ.] Two poems, "Freedom", and "St. Patrick's Day Parade" were published in Central R.R. of NJ Vets newsletter in Jan. 1995. I received no money, just a "Thank you" note!; [pers.] I strive to alert my readers to the realities of life on earth. I have been influences by the great poets of America.; [a.] Merritt Island, FL

STEEPLE, TINA L.

[b.] January 22, 1964, Bristol, PA; [p.] John and Elaine Steeple; [ed.] Woodrow Wilson H.S. Class of '81, St. Francis School of Radiologic Technology Class of '87; [occ.] Radiologic Technologist Philadelphia, PA Frankford Hosp.; [oth. writ.] Many other poems in a box under my bed. Never published, never read by anyone else, just you and me.; [pers.] Threats, love and talent the only three times in life that need to be heard to be of any value. Keep writings peace, love and happiness to all.; [a.] Levittown, PA

STELLIOU, VENETIA MARIA

[pen.] Kat, Midnight; [b.] February 23, 1979, Montreal; [p.] Stephen Stelliou, Kathy Stelliou; [ed.] Centennial Regional High School, McGill Conservatory of Music; [occ.] Piano Teacher, Student; [memb.] Maids of Athena Order of Ahepa; [hon.] Silver medal at school science fair, Music (singing, and piano: Competition and exams); [oth. writ.] Miscellaneous poems that have not been published; [pers.] Don't be your own slave, be your own master.; [a.] Montreal Quebec, Canada

STELLMACH, CYNTHIA M.

[b.] December 3, 1960, Saint Claud Hospital; [p.] Alphonse and Mary Wolak; [m.] David Wayne Stellmach, May 30, 1987; [ch.] David Clarence, Ashley Lynn, Scott Thomas, Martin Wayne; [ed.] Diploma from Foley High School; [occ.] Home maker, Mother, Horse trainer/Dietary Aid/Pt.; [memb.] Member of St. Louis Catholic Church; [hon.] Published - "Find Me a Rainbow" American poetry anthology; [oth. writ.] Song in the process of copy righting "Calling Your Name", Horse training memories - in the process of writing for publication; [pers.] Live life fully each day. Use all your talents. Make time for meditation for this is a journey - Don't be afraid to try new things.; [a.] Milaca, MN

STENNIS, MARY JEAN SALMON

[b.] October 30, 1949, Vicksburg, MS; [p.] Mary McGee Robinson, Eugene Salmon; [m.] Kerry P. Stennis Sr., February 8, 1968; [ch.] Kerry P. Stennis Jr., Johnny M. Stennis (Dade), Thelia S. Stennis, Randall, Shelton; [ed.] E.M.T. A, RA, C.N.A., Facilitator, Alzheiners Activity Ade, DCFS Home maker and Home visitations.; [occ.] Writer; [memb.] Missionary of Progressive MB Church Rev. John D. Digby pastor and secretary of the Missions. OWL'S Vice President, Founder of the We Can Make a Difference Club, the Friendship Club and Inner Visions for Building Self-Esteem; [hon.] Works of writing's were on display at City Hall in Kankakee IL, in 1991, Golden Poet Award, Trophy of recognition from Harold Washington Elementary School, Poem's published in The Words Best Poets, and in New York Poets Anthology 88 edition. Children stories and book for Building self esteem, self-publisher for her Non - For - Profit organization "Inner Visions Collective Works of Mary Jean Salmon Stennis poems published to the The Nurses and Elks; [pers.] We can't help people that don't want to help themselves. Know the difference and always leave everything up to God. To the Elk, Nurses Missionary's and Christians everywhere.; [a.] Chicago, IL

STEPHENS, KENNETH R.

[b.] November 2, 1962, Collins, OH; [p.] Barbara Graham and Ervin Stephens; [m.] Missie R. Stephens, April 13, 1994; [ch.] Sarah A. and Lyzzah J. Stephens; [ed.] Cols. South High, Tampa College, Bible Studies (Ind.); [occ.] Gen. Railway Serv.; [memb.] Northgate Baptist Chr. Youth Program; [hon.] Editor's Choice (The way....); [oth. writ.] One published, others awaiting; [pers.] The truth is in God's word. Gifts and promises will not fail. Gain these things and live as Jesus commands.; [a.] Tampa, FL

STEPHENS, R. ISABELLA

[pen.] R. Isabella Stephens; [b.] March 16, 1915, Kintnersville, PA; [p.] Clayton and Myrta Miller; [m.] Arthur R. Stephens, January 1, 1939; [ch.] Carlotta Mannheim and Bruce D. Stephens; [ed.] High School and Home Course in Dressmaking and Designing. I had a Dressmaker's Shop in Allentown for 30 years. Still doing it for family and friends.; [occ.] Artist and Housewife; [memb.] Parkland Art League, I enter my "paintings" in their shows every years.; [pers.] I strive to do my best in every thing that I do, weather it be poetry, sewing, or painting.; [a.] Allentown, PA

STEPP, JUDITH L.

[pen.] Judy Stepp; [b.] April 12, 1940, Rocky Grove, PA; [p.] Harrison and Marien Haney; [m.] Aulton Ray Stepp, February 24, 1960; [ch.] Richard, Delana, Harrison, Arthur; [ed.] Oil City High, Oil City School of Beauty Culture; [occ.] Plumbing Supply Store (owner); [oth. writ.] Several Writings not published at this time.; [a.] Kingston, OK

STERN, RUTH

[b.] May 20, 1926, South Africa; [p.] Freda and Abraham Saretzky; [m.] Gideon Stern, (2nd marriage), 1978 (widowed 1973); [ch.] Gideon Ben Amar, Gilead Ben Amar; [ed.] Boksburg High School (S.A.) Witwatersrand Technical College (S.A.) The Hebrew University, Jerusalem.; [occ.] Voluntary work: 1.) At the Israel Museum, 2.) With disabled soldiers, 3.) With children.; [memb.] 1.) Society for preservation of nature in Israel. 2.) Israel Union for Environmental Defence, 3.) Hebrew Un. Alumni Assoc., 4.) Association of Un. Women.; [hon.] B.A. English Literature. (Summa Cum Laude), M.A. English Literature (Cum Laude); [oth. writ.] Poems printed in local poets' news letters. Poems published in the anthology "Seven Gates" poetry from Jerusalem. Articles in "The English Teachers Journal"; [pers.] After serving as a volunteer in the Israel Med. Corps, in 1948 I became a teacher of teen-agers, sharing their joys and sorrows. To be a teacher is to be a learner. To reach out a helping hand is to be the receiver. In communicating with others and through reading I seek guidance, with humility and tolerance.; [a.] Jerusalem, Israel

STERN, YOLANDA ORTEGA

[b.] November 8, 1947; [m.] Thomas Kim Stern; [ch.] Thomas Montgomery and Marjorie; [ed.] M.A., Ph.D.; [occ.] CEO; [memb.] S.F. Chamber of Commerce World Trade Club Hero Foundation; [pers.] The pursuit of Beauty, Truth and Art in small measures allowed by poetic expression helps me to accept that the human mind is so complex and beyond unraveling.; [a.] Berkeley, CA

STERNBERG, AMY

[b.] August 16, 1971, London, England; [p.] George and Sharon Sternberg; [ed.] Russellville High School, Central Missouri, State University (B.S. in Education); [occ.] 7th grade Language Arts teacher; [memb.] MSTA (Mo. St. Teachers Assoc.), NCTE (NH. Counc. for Teachers of English), MMSA (Mo. Middle School Assoc); [hon.] Missouri State Farmer Degree; [pers.] Hard work, devotion, and love are what most individuals mold their lives around. I try to help us realize how lucky we are to have these gifts.; [a.] Rolla, MO

STEVEN, THOMAS A.

[pen.] Tom Steven; [b.] October 14, 1917, Dryden, OR; [p.] Thomas S. and Nena H. Steven; [m.] Grace D. Steven, September 21, 1945; [ch.] Barbara Jean, James Allen; [ed.] Los Gatos High CA, '35, San Jose State College, AB, '39, Univ. Calif., Los Angeles, Ph.D. '50; [occ.] Retired geologist - USGS Scientist Emeritus - USGS; [memb.] Senior Fellow, Geol. Soc. America, Senior Member, Soc. Econ. Geologists Colorado Scientific Society; [hon.] Dept. Interior Meritorious Service Award, Past Pres., Colo. Sci. Soc.; [oth. writ.] Technical and scientific bibliography - approx. 180 items, Echoes from my mind, 1992 (book of poetry), several poems in press by Mile High Poetry Society; [pers.] I write for personal gratification in a voice that must be honest; [a.] Lakewood, CO

STEVENS, DAVID R.

[b.] July 1, 1971, Southfield, MI; [p.] David and Margaret Stevens; [ed.] Brother Rice H.S. Completed undergraduate degree program in Philosophy at the University of Michigan, Ann Arbor, and is currently working on second major in English.; [memb.] USPA member for 3 years (United States Parachute Assoc.), currently "jumping" for an A-license.; [oth. writ.] Over sixty poems take comfort in a "Personal Portfolio" along with five short stories, dozens I aphorisms, roughly 300 pages of critiques and philosophical writings.; [pers.] The most basic ideas build the foundation for understanding and hold the fortitude of prosperity, novel ideas precipitate therefrom.; [a.] Ann Arbor, MI

STEVENSON, ELIZABETH FAULKNER
[b.] July 28, 1963, Charleston, SC; [p.] Fred W. Stevenson, June F. La Via; [m.] David R. Fairleigh (fiance), June 3, 1995; [ed.] B.A., English Agnes Scott College; [occ.] Public Relations Corporate Communications; [memb.] Public Relations Society of America (PRSA); [hon.] Phoenix Award, Certificate of Excellence, PRSA; [oth. writ.] Poetry collection bi-lined business - related articles; [pers.] Writing poetry is my passion. It is an obsession. My inspiration comes from my own life experiences; [a.] Atlanta, GA

STEWART, JUDY LYNN
[Pen.] ABBA's Child; [b.] December 20, 1959, Morgan City, LA; [p.] Shirley Dupy; [m.] David Bryan Stewart, August 5, 1989; [ch.] Jolie, Larry and Jonathan; [ed.] High School Equivalency; [occ.] Homemaker, and student at the victoria College, Victoria, TX; [memb.] Paralyzed Veterans of America, Focus on the Family, and Concerned Woman of America; [oth. writ.] Poem published in local newspapers.; [pers.] My writing is inspired by God and by the beauty of his creations. To God be the glory.; [a.] Smiley, TX

STIEDE, MARGARET I.
[b.] September 18, 1916, Croswell, MI; [p.] William (Alf.) Hardy and Julia Ann (Crickon) Hardy; [m.] Albert A. Stiede, November 29, 1936; [ch.] Virlee Hope (Stiede) Evans, Delton Bruce Stiede; [ed.] Country School Eighth Grade; [occ.] Homemaker; [oth. writ.] Poem, "Listening to the Rain", published in Kingman, AZ, a Veteran's newspaper; [pers.] I enjoy writing, it keeps my mind active, and fills up my spare time. My writings are an inspiration of God.; [a.] Tempe, AZ

STINER, LOIS
[m.] Nicholas; [ch.] Craig Stiner, Pamela Kasch, Doreen Byrnes; [ed.] Morristown, New Jersey High School Some College Morris County Junior College; [occ.] Retired; [memb.] Attend United Methodist Church - 2nd Circle Group. Volunteer work for WORC (Work Oriented Rehabilitation Center); [hon.] Roller Skating Costume Contest - design and creativity; [oth. writ.] Tooth Fairy Booklet (for my original tooth fairy pillow); [pers.] My goal is aimed at helping others face reality than pleasurable reading.; [a.] Daytona Beach, FL

STINSON, KELLY L.
[b.] June 19, 1960, Waco, TX; [p.] William and Margaret Gibson; [m.] David G. Stinson, July 1, 1990; [ed.] Richfield High School, McLennan Community College, Baylor University - BME 1983; [occ.] Music Consultant, Music Instructor; [memb.] Texas Music Educator's Association American Diabetes Association Word Pounders, Ink. (Writing Club); [hon.] National Honor Society, Phi Beta Kappa, Gamma Beta Phi, National Dean's List; [oth. writ.] Guest column in Waco Tribune Herald; [pers.] I have been greatly blessed by God, and I strive to use my gifts to please Him. It is a great privilege to be able to serve Him and others, and I pray my words will touch those who are in need of encouragement.; [a.] Elm Mott, TX

STINSON, LOLA RHEA
[b.] November 10, 1926, Spickard, MO; [p.] Toud and Juanita Rhea; [m.] Ray Stinson, June 16, 1946; [ch.] Rajean, Ranita and Loray; [pers.] My husband is a musician and artist. He traveled with Henry Busse, Ted Weems Bands. I am also an artist. I dedicate my poem to him and my sister Jean.; [a.] Kansas City, MO

STOCKDALE, JAMIE LYNN
[b.] February 21, 1965, Flint, MI; [p.] Charles and Betty Powell; [m.] Richard Stockdale, November 19, 1986; [ch.] Danielle Lynn Stockdale; [ed.] Oceanside High, ROP, Mira Costa College, ICS Law Studies; [occ.] Crafter, Homemaker and Student; [oth. writ.] Several articles for school papers, poem published in "A Moment in Time". Several others not published; [a.] Oceanside, CA

STOCKMAN, MARION M.
[pen.] Ann McHugh; [b.] September 26, 1932, Baltimore, MD; [p.] Lawrence J. McHugh, Virginia McHugh; [m.] George Warner Stockman, June 20, 1953; [ch.] Sons: Todd Warner, Tracy Mchugh; [ed.] Eastern High School, Strayers Business School.; [occ.] Retired Office Supervisor, Maryland State Police, Pikesville, MD.; [memb.] Women of the MOOSE, Pikesville/ Randallstown Lioness, Club Maryland member.; [hon.] Past president Lioness Club Merit award, Supervisory Management awards, Lioness poem published in Lions International District Newsletter.; [oth. writ.] Music City Song Festival contests, Honorable Mention Awards in 1980 and 1981, Lyric Category. Numerous social and or personal poems.; [pers.] I feel everyone can be reached with pleasurable thoughts, I am inspired by story telling lyrics as in ballads and poems.; [a.] Sykesville, MD

STOEHR, HORST W.
[b.] 1926, Berlin, Germany; [oth. writ.] Non-published poems in the English and German language.; [pers.] Living and working in the United States for more than 30 years. In retirement since 1988. With the reflection of my feelings, impressions and observations in my poems I strive and hope to create and promote respect for and appreciation of all life, all of nature and it's creatures and our universe in my fellow human beings.; [a.] Marco Island, FL

STOLTZFUS, CORALIE AMY
[pen.] Coralie; [b.] July 3, 1979, Lancaster, PA; [p.] Elmer B. and Carol A. Stoltzfus; [ed.] Attending Lampeter - Strasburg High School - 9th grade; [occ.] Amusement Park Employee; [memb.] Reformed Presbyterian Church; [hon.] Honor roll, Track and Field, National Fitness award; [oth. writ.] A lot of short stories, poems, biographies; [pers.] All good things came through God!; [a.] Strasburg, PA

STORM, JOHN A.
[pen.] Storm; [b.] November 21, 1948, Poughkeepsie, NY; [p.] Homer A. and Elizabeth B.; [m.] Cynthia J. Carnan Storm, July 18, 1992; [ch.] Kierston L. Storm, step-children: Erin M. Miller, Thomas C. Miller; [ed.] Attended Franklin and Marshall College, Lancaster PA, majoring in Pre-Medical, and Hartwick College, Oneonta NY, majoring in Philosophy; [occ.] Public Health Information for County Government; [memb.] National Assoc. of County Information officers (NACIO), Hudson Valley Quality Council (HVQC), other professional communicators organizations.; [oth. writ.] Children's short stories: "Admiral of the Fish Pond", "The Too Big Puppy", numerous unpublished poems.; [pers.] This work is dedicated to the memory of my most beloved friend my father, who is buried with this poem as my gift to him forever; [a.] Rhinebeck, NY

STRAIGHT, GRACE M.
[pen.] G.M.S.; [b.] September 19, 1918, Renton, WA; [p.] Alice and Herb Fislar; [m.] James A. Straight, March 9, 1936; [ch.] Naydene Killgore Darlene Johnson; [ed.] Albany-Union High School; [occ.] Retired Nurse and Apartment Manager; [memb.] Assembly of God; [oth. writ.] Jesus picked a little rosebud and other poetry; [pers.] I try to live by the holy Bible to love and to serve to humanity

STRAW, VIOLA
[pen.] Vi Straw; [b.] March 2, 1926, Agar, SD; [p.] William and Eva Mohr, Lewis Compton (step-father); [m.] Loite Straw, June 5, 1945; [ch.] Annette, Floyd, Donna, Donald, Donavan, Danny, Diane, Duane, Bonnie, Ronald, Derwin and Dennis; [ed.] Limestone Mountain School - Moon, S.D., Black Hills of South Dakota; [occ.] Retired.; [memb.] Little White Church; [hon.] Golden and Silver poet awards on several other poems, two merit certificate awards; [oth. writ.] I have written other poems.; [pers.] I like to share in my writings - "The Beauty of Yesterdays Dreams Captured in a Moment of Reflection"; [a.] Hill City, SD

STREETER, SANDRA M.
[pen.] Sandra Quinlan Streeter; [b.] September 16, 1942, Vermont; [p.] Lawrence Quinlan, Edna Lakso; [m.] David W. Streeter, June 24, 1962; [ch.] Son, Keith and daughter, Kristina (my best works); [ed.] Pioneer Valley Regional H.S. Greenfield Community College; [occ.] Artist work in oils and watercolor; [memb.] Traprock Peace Center, Citizen's Awareness Network, Bernardston Zoning Board, United Church of Bernardston; [oth. writ.] Poems in local papers. Drawings and testimony - Alien discussions: Proceedings of the Abduction Study Conference. North Cambridge Press Cambridge, MA. 1994; [pers.] The nuclear insanity of mankind is forcing the reawakening of soul and the science of spirituality. Enlightenment is necessary to end the nightmare.; [a.] Bernardston, MA

STRICKLAN, LOUIS EDDIE
[b.] December 31, 1955, Tennessee; [p.] Louise and Dossie Stricklan; [m.] Divorced; [ch.] Sissy, Joe, Karen, Shawna, Katlin, Nicolas, Dossie; [ed.] High School; [occ.] Disabled; [memb.] International Society of Poetry; [hon.] Gold Poets Award Silver, Who's Who in Poetry two merit awards; [pers.] I'm 39, I have been writing 30 years. I love poetry; [a.] Rockwood, TN

STROBL, JEFFERY MICHAEL
[pen.] J. Michaels; [b.] September 29, 1970, Fort Sill, OK; [p.] Michael and Gail Strobl; [ed.] BS, Communication Studies, South Dakota State University; [hon.] Kermit Sheimo Scholarship, Short Story, Spring 1990; [oth. writ.] Poem This, with Jason Myklegard, poetry/ short writings, December 1992 Published in Oakwood, SDSU college publication, 1993 edition The Agony of Solitude, poetry, February 1995; [a.] Inver Grove Heights, MN

STRYKER, DAVID W.
[b.] March 13, 1946, Oklahoma City, OK; [p.] Harry and Alene Stryker; [ed.] BA Geology; [occ.] Retired Hobbiest; [oth. writ.] "The Essence of Belonging", "Jordan, North Arabia and the Nabatean Cities of Petra and Madain Saleh", and a large collection of poetry (all un-

published).; [pers.] Home made pizza is better.; [a.] Sun City, AZ

STRYKER, MARIA
[pen.] Maria Stryker; [b.] August 14, 1939, New Brunswick, NJ; [p.] John and Mary Saladind; [ch.] Nelson, Debbie, Kenneth; [occ.] Housewife; [oth. writ.] Writing of poetry for fun and relaxation "The Souls", published in a local poetry contest; [pers.] My poetry comes to me amongst the many thoughts that go through my mind depending on my moods that is the theme of my poems; [a.] East Brunswick, NJ

STULTZ, JESSICA SUE
[b.] December 13, 1975, Brazil, IN; [p.] Janice Shelton, Jack Stultz; [ed.] Elem. - East Side Elem. Brazil Jr., High - North Clay Jr. High Brazil High School 9th - 1/2 of tenth - Northview High School, graduated Midterm at Thomas Edison High School '94; [occ.] United States Air force; [oth. writ.] Poem published in "Illusions" School newspaper. Several articles in school paper, editor of school paper.; [pers.] My poetry, reflects a part of me and those close to me. If my words don't have meaning I don't have a poem.; [a.] Lake Station, IN

STUMPH, JOSEPH
[b.] January 13, 1934; [p.] Joseph Stumph, Sr.; [m.] Hazel Lolita Stevens Stumph, September 17, 1959; [ch.] Rebecca, Jodie, Vickie, David and Marty; [ed.] Two years college at Brigham Young University, Weber State Univ. and study or Law with LaSalle Ext. Univ., Chicago. Continuing student in Economics, Law History, Politics, Astronomy and Science.; [occ.] Retired. Worked 27 years for Kennecott Minerals, a large open pit copper mine near Salt Lake City, UT; [memb.] Church of Jesus Christ of Latter-day Saints (Mormon). Founder and member: Committee of 50 States. An organization dedicated to the preservation of the Constitution of the United States in the tradition of the Founding Fathers.; [hon.] Received commendation as the top student of 45 students in U.S. Air Force school of cryptography. Was also top student of about 100 in Air Force Radio School. Received the Liberty Award in 1966 from the Congress of Freedom; [oth. writ.] Books: The Constitution Hanging By a Thread. Saving Our Constitution From The New World Order. Lawful Secession: Key to Peace. All three published by Northwest Publishing Company in Salt Lake City, Utah; [pers.] The Holy Bible is the word of God, as far as it is translated correctly. Jesus Christ is the literal Son of God and his return is imminent, and in the flesh. That the human family are literally children of God, and as children, have the potential to be like him and become equal in knowledge and power as joint heirs with Jesus Christ of all which belongs to our literal Father... the entire universe. That this inheritance is predicated on the individual learning and then obeying God's laws.; [a.] Salt Lake City, UT

STZEMORE, FAYE E.
[pen.] Fe H.; [b.] December 28, 1936, Detroit, MI; [p.] Eileen Hort (Deceased); [m.] Divorced; [ch.] Joyce, Lyle, Lester, Cathy; [ed.] Troy High School, Troy Michigan, Owens College, Toledo, Ohio; [occ.] Retired Telephone Operator; [pers.] Follow your dreams! Don't let others be your pilot! Do what you feel is right!; [a.] Holland, OH

SUBA, RICHARD
[pen.] Richard Suba; [b.] January 30, 1960, Hammond, IN; [p.] Hazel Mae Suba (Wiser); [m.] Divorced, 1980; [ch.] Richard Daniel Suba, four years old; [ed.] Hill Crest High, Country Club Hills, IL and currently taking Business Law at Morine Valley College Palos, IL.; [occ.] Free Lances; [memb.] Lodge 851 A.F. and A.M.; [pers.] Just want to say that I been writing poems for about Twenty years now, and I write to express what I feel most about at that time in my life, love is want I reflect on.; [a.] Burbank, IL

SULLIVAN, MARIAN
[pen.] M. Sullivan; [b.] January 31, 1947, Brooklyn, NY; [p.] Max and Rosalind H. Garber; [ch.] Jennifer Sullivan; [ed.] Sheepshead Bay High, Brooklyn College, NYU, School of Social Work, Graduate School Russell Sage College, Albany, NY; [occ.] Student; [memb.] Tai Chi Association; [hon.] Graduated Cum Laude Brooklyn College, MSW, NYU.; [oth. writ.] Poems published in High School newspapers and wrote articles for college newspaper.; [pers.] I write when I am inspired. Writing is about real things in my life about my feelings, and about nature's beauties and the environment.; [a.] Nassau, NY

SULLIVAN, MICHAEL O.
[b.] October 5, 1952, La Porte, IN; [p.] Howard Sullivan and Marion; [m.] Ann M. Sullivan, December 31, 1990; [ch.] Ryan Michael, Connor Michael, Alexander Thomas; [ed.] Singapore American School, University of Oklahoma B.B.A. Indiana University MBA; [pers.] The best thing I ever did is what I'll do tomorrow; [a.] South Bend, IN

SUMMERS, BARBARA JOAN
[b.] July 3, 1945, Allentown, PA; [p.] Paul and Ann Gehman, Jr.; [m.] Paul Roland Summers, December 16, 1966; [ch.] Ann Blake, Rachel Crank, Paul R. Summers, Jr., (2 grandchildren); [ed.] Nazareth High School, PA, Sellersville School of Nursing, Bob Jones University; [memb.] Cherry St. Baptist Church, The Missouri Right to Life, The Christian Coalition, The Cancer Society - Reach to Recovery; [hon.] National Honor Society, Awana 10 yrs. Service Award; [pers.] I strive to reflect on God's goodness and grace in my life of suffering and to blossom in my valleys so other's can smell the sweet fragrance of God's love in my life.; [a.] Springfield, MO

SUMMERS, WILLIAM LANE
[b.] March 13, 1948, Haward, California; [p.] Clara Leona Newhall, William Luman Summers; [ch.] Salli-Anne; [ed.] Castro Valley High, Chabot J.C., School of Hard Knocks; [occ.] Retired.

SUNCIN, BENJAMIN V.
[pen.] Benjamin V. Suncin; [b.] August 5, 1956, San Francisco; [p.] Manuel V. Suncin and Kathryn De Pineda; [ed.] B.A. Business Management, St. Mary's College of California; [occ.] Telecommunications; [memb.] Founding Member and Vice-President of the "Hispanic Association of AT and T Employees" San Francisco Chapter.; [hon.] Dean's List - Skyline Junior College; [pers.] I have been greatly influenced, and have discovered a kinship, with a few of the great Hispanic writers such as Federico Garcia Lorca, Jorge Luis Borges and Pablo Nevuda. I attempt to delight the senses with the combination of creative imagery, romanticism and raw, unbridled emotion; [a.] San Francisco, CA

SUTO, DEBRA
[b.] June 9, New Haven, CT; [p.] Raymond Carr, Patricia Carr; [m.] Michael Suto, May 10 1975; [ch.] David Michael, Brian Thomas, Scott Raymond; [ed.] Milford High, University Central Florida, Florida State University; [occ.] Child and Adolescent Therapist; [memb.] National Association of Social Workers; [hon.] Phi Theta Kappa, Phi Kappa Phi, Dean's List; [oth. writ.] Poems published in local newspaper.; [pers.] This poem is the first one I ever wrote at age sixteen. This was a high school english assignment.; [a.] Deltona, FL

SUTTERBY, SIM FENTON
[pen.] S. Fenton Sutterby, Fenton Sutterby, Sim F. Sutterby; [b.] June 1, 1948, Orlando, FL; [p.] Sammie Y. T. Frances; [m.] Divorced; [ch.] 4 sons, Sim F. Sutterby Jr., Aaron Caleb Sutterby (deceased), Silas M. Sutterby, Lake M. Sutterby; [ed.] A.S. Computer Science; [occ.] Mortgage Banker and Marketing Consultant; [hon.] Editor of Fine Arts Publication at Seminole College; [oth. writ.] Article published in local newspaper based on first hand experience at wounded knee, South Dak. poem published in sparrow grass poetry forum; [pers.] 7th Generation Floridian personal goal is to learn and achieve the essence of humility before moving on; [a.] Orlando, FL

SVENSSON, ROBERT
[b.] August 27, 1907, Chicago, IL; [p.] Rudolph and Jennie Svensson; [m.] Adele Julia Jacobson, February 2, 1932; [ch.] Carole Linda (Hirsch); [ed.] Venice (CA) High School; [occ.] Retired but active; [memb.] American Heart Assn, ACLU, American Red Cross Sierra Club. etc; [hon.] President CEO Hearing Center of Metropolitan Los Angeles; [oth. writ.] Novel "Marina" (Manor Books) "The Complete Coin Collectors Guide" (Avon Books) Syndicated column "Coins" king features plus scores of magazine stories and articles; [pers.] I dedicate my mind, my pen and my votes to the men, women and institutions whose goal is the protection and preservation of all human life, liberty and rights and the saving of the wild life and the lands of the earth.; [a.] Los Angeles, CA

SVEUM, GLENN CLIFFORD
[pen.] Clifford; [b.] July 27, 1972; [p.] Curtis and Donna Sveum of Missouri; [m.] Angelic Sveum, March 4, 1995; [ch.] no children (yet); [ed.] Burney High School, Shasta College, U.S. Army Infantry and Airborne School. Fire Science/behavior, U.S. Forest Service.; [occ.] Wildland Firefighter; [memb.] Sierra Club, International Association of Firefighters.; [oth. writ.] Great Bear, Hooves of Society, Enter the Moonlight.; [pers.] The absolute power of fire and weather have always inspired me not only in my poetry, but in the way I live my life. "Where has the respect for Mother Nature gone?"; [a.] Albuquerque, NM

SWEENEY, CHRISTOPHER
[b.] April 24, 1986, Farmingdale, NY; [p.] Thomas and Frances Sweeney; [ed.] Presently in the 3rd grade.; [occ.] Student; [memb.] Cub scout in Pack 601-Farmingdale, NY.. Farmingdale PAL-Basketball and soccer. Farmingdale Baseball Mustang League.; [hon.] Golden Egg Award- Northside Elementary School Bird Study. Trophies in various sports (soccer, baseball, basketball.) Good Guy Recreation Award 1993; [oth. writ.] 3 books: Protect the World. Illustory 1994, N.Y. Rangers - 1994, Cub Scouts - 1995 (On loan to Northside School Library); [pers.] I write for enjoyment and to express my thoughts. My favorite authors are: David A. Adler, Dr. Seuss, and Bernard Waber.; [a.] Farmingdale, NY

SWEIS, MIRDAD
[b.] December 3, 1976, Albuquerque, NM; [p.] Rafig and Rehab Sweis; [ed.] Carl Sandburg H.S., graduated in 3 yrs. not 4. Morain Valley Community College.; [occ.]

Student; [hon.] Took 1st place twice in State for playing guitar. 15 different 1st place awards in Art.; [oth. writ.] None that have been published except one on the retirement of Michael Jordan called Omega.; [pers.] All my writings are the truth and come from the heart. I give all thanks of all my writings to God, and savior Jesus Christ.; [a.] Orland Park, IL

SWENSEN, ESTHER B.
[b.] Westfield, MA; [p.] Alexander (deceased) and Helen Brunk; [m.] Divorced; [ch.] Jeffrey E. Swensen (A Mechanical Engineer in Management.); [ed.] Westfield High School - attended American International College, Springfield, MA.; [memb.] The Academy of American Poets, The Smithsonian Institute - (Washington D.C), American Assoc. of Retired persons; [hon.] Salutatorian of High School class, Dean's list in College.; [oth. writ.] A number of poems will e published in Fall '95 edition of "Treasured poems of America."; [pers.] I love to create beauty with words. Much of my poetry is romantic, but I have now begun to write of my deep love for the New England of my childhood.; [a.] Gaithersburg, MD

SWINT, KATHERINE MOON
[p.] Kathe Swint; [b.] December 7, 1917, Muscogee County, GA; [p.] Jacob Clinton and Virginia Woolfolk Moon; [m.] Jesse T. "Jake" Swint, September 7, 1946; [ch.] Merry Katherine De Simone; [ed.] BS in LS, Peabody Library School, Nashville 1943, BS in Education, Oglethorpe University, Atlanta, 1940.; [occ.] Librarian, Retired, Homamaker; [memb.] Oakhurst Baptist Church, Decatur GA, Parkwood Garden Club, President, 1991; [hon.] Master 4-H Club 1035; [a.] Decatur, GA

SYMONS, ROLAND
[pen.] Roland Symons; [b.] April 20, 1909, Canada; [p.] Herbert J. and Polly Agnes Symons; [m.] Present Dorothy A. Symons, November 11, 1988; [ch.] Rolanne, Marilyn, Laurence; [ed.] Franklin High Highland Park CA, Frank Wiggins, Belmont Night School W and P. Supervisors Classes; [occ.] Retired from Los Angeles Water and Power; [memb.] W and P. Choraliers, Ellis Club, Mitchel Boy's Choir Leisure world chorus, Episcopal Church Lay Reader; [hon.] Certificate for 25 yrs. as and lay reader. Order of the Arrow B.S.A; [oth. writ.] What shall I sing for Christmas? "Put To Music." Noelle's Last Word was Roland. What shall we give our children oh Lord the keeper of my soul.; [pers.] I never thought of myself as a poet. My deepest feelings come out as poetry, not for publication, but as thoughts put in poems; [a.] Seal Beach, CA

SZOPINSKI, LAWRENCE J.
[pen.] John Michael Lawrence; [b.] January 14, 1939, Milwaukee, WI; [p.] Clemence and Margerat Szopinski, Suzanne Marie Pelzek; [m.] Divorced; [ch.] Steve, Brian and Amie, Grandsons: Bradley and Zackery; [ed.] Wisc. conservatory of music voice and opera, work shop/U-W-Milw history of music.; [occ.] Delivery Administration; [memb.] Florentine Opera Great Lakes City Opera The Shorewood Players; [oth. writ.] Song published in local newspaper "What Price is Freedom"; [pers.] To believe in your inner spirit and reflect upon life in a way that would make God pleased with my being; [a.] Milwaukee, WI

TABBORA, NADIA
[b.] July 21, 1983, Beirut, Lebanon; [p.] Jeanesette and Anis Tabbara; [ed.] Winchester School System.; [occ.] 6th grade student.; [hon.] Honor student.; [a.] Winchester, MA

TAITCH, MILDRED C.
[b.] March 8, 1936, Big Piney, MO; [p.] Roach and Eva Young; [m.] Michael D. Taitch, August 25, 1981; [ch.] Michael Pigeon, Raymond Pigeon, Patricia Tonkins; [ed.] High School Grad.; [occ.] Bus. Owner Chimney Sweep Co. Firewood Co. Lawn Maint. Co. and Gen. Contractors; [pers.] More time should be spent writing poetry instead of Graffiti on neighbors walls.; [a.] Spokane, WA

TALKINGTON, MILDRED V. KESSEL
[b.] Belfield, ND; [p.] Karol and Agnes Polanchek; [m.] Phil Kessel (deceased) May 30, 1928 and Hrt Talkington, May 30, 1981; [ch.] 16 children, 68 grandchildren, and many grand grandchildren; [ed.] 8th grade and "G.E.D." self educated. Compelled 4 yrs of High School in 3 months Certificate - 1970; [occ.] Housewife; [memb.] American Legion Aux. 58 years, C.D. of America, Charity works of All kinds. Many oil paintings making frames., Quilts-knitting, some Carpenter Works; [hon.] Blue Ribbon - Oil Printing, 2 or 3 stories in the Paper, Deckinson Preer and Bismarck Tribune; [oth. writ.] My Life since I remember. 200 poems - stories about my children and grand children and grand grandchildren.; [a.] Belfield, ND

TALLMAN, EVELYN T.
[b.] November 15, 1922, South Westerloo, NY; [p.] Mrs. Hazel F. Mabie; [m.] January 23, 1940; [ch.] Mr. Ralph R. Tallman; [ed.] Attended Greenville Central High School, Also National Bakers School.; [occ.] Retired Cook and Baker; [memb.] Social Service with Albany, County, Social Security and Benefits; [oth. writ.] Worlds of Poetry

TASSIN, KAMI JO
[b.] January 10, 1980, Houma, LA; [p.] Wendy and Kenneth Tassin; [ed.] (High School) Vandebilt Catholic High School; [occ.] Student; [memb.] Alter Server at Holy Rosary Church, Anne Rices Vampire Lestat Fan Club, Band at School; [pers.] If I would have chosen to explain the "Shadow" in my poem, I could have, but I didn't, because I believe a poem is a little mystery and if I would have told you what the "Shadow" is, the poem wouldn't be.; [a.] Houma, LA

TATARIAN, JOAN E.
[pen.] Joan Reed Tatarian; [b.] March 12, 1935, Province, RI; [p.] Guy H. Reed, Theresa M. Reed; [m.] Nishan M. Tatarian, May 1, 1967; [ed.] Central High School, Course at Prov. College, Course at Roger Williams College; [occ.] Esoteric Astrology teacher; [memb.] American Federation of astrologers - Tempe, AZ; [hon.] Hundreds of "Thank You" cards from my students; [pers.] Philosophy of faith was the first poem I wrote, I was 12 yrs. old in 1947, it was printed in a newspaper called "The Visitor" in Prov., RI. I still retain and adhere to the philosophy of my first poem; [a.] Granby, MA

TATE, VENNIE LOU
[b.] October 12, 1903, Hamilton, MS; [p.] Alford Dabbs, Virgie Lee Smith; [m.] Homer Tate, 1925; [ch.] Two boys - Jerry, Jon Kate; [ed.] High School and 3 year in college; [occ.] Ran as Director seven years as Kindergarten Director, Retired; [memb.] Indianola, MS., United Methodist Church, United Methodist Church Starkville MS., Aldersgate UMC - Starkville, MS.; [hon.] Served as a volunteer in ever town I liked; [oth. writ.] Sacred poems other miscellaneous, Family memoirs, Special people - special services, special occasions; [pers.] Great love for music and served in musical needs in my churches, Served as volunteer's in heart; [a.] Starkville, MS

TATRO, BRENDA L.
[pen.] Louise White; [b.] December 15, 1948, Denver, CO; [p.] Jack and Violet White; [m.] Steve Tatro, September 24, 1985; [ed.] BS Degree from University of Northern Colorado, (Elementary Ed.) and post graduate work in Bilingual Education; [occ.] C.E.O. for non-profit agency dealing with pregnant and parenting teenagers.; [memb.] Rotary Club of San Antonio Executive Directors of United Way Agencies Association; [hon.] Who's Who of American Women 1987/1988, Outstanding Achievement in Public Relations Award NEA 1979-80, March of Dimes certificates of appreciation 1994, National Award for work with homeless children and youth; [oth. writ.] Articles published in local newspaper and non-profit newsletters. Primary books El Carro and La Tortuga; [pers.] I believe that writing impacts on our lives daily and my writing reflects messages from the heart and a cause focus for raising the human spirit to action.; [a.] San Antonio, TX

TAYLOR, BENJAMIN J.
[pen.] Benjamin Taylor Bent; [b.] November 23, 1941, New York, NY; [p.] Clara B. Lette; [m.] Anne F. Taylor, July 11, 1975; [ch.] Marcell Susan, Jordan Benjamin, Rennie B. Taylor, Harvest Chandler Taylor; [ed.] Michigan State University BS 63 Sage Colleges. State University of New York Dartmouth College Poetry Seminar 1971.; [occ.] Director of Community Care New York State Division for Youth; [memb.] American Correctional Association, American Indian Movement, NAACP.; [hon.] Scholarship in Creative Writing Michigan State University 1991, Correctional Leadership Fellowship 1992; [oth. writ.] Zetigiest, 1964. Field Days, 1967, Songs From New Hampshire Traveling, 1971.; [pers.] It is in the search, the journey that the learning takes place. Answers are illusions which lull one into complacency.; [a.] Sarasota Springs, NY

TAYLOR, ERNESTINE D.
[pen.] Kristina Taylor; [m.] Divorced, Mother of four sons; [ch.] Christopher, Michael, Timothy and John; [ed.] Lamar U., Beaumont, Texas: Blair Medical College, Hawthorne, CA. University of Southern Miss, Long Beach, MS; [occ.] Artist: Oils and Pastels Painter, and Portrait Head Sculptor in Clay; [memb.] Gulf Coast Art Assoc., National Federation of Democratic Women, Mensa, Association of Portrait Artists; [hon.] Artist of the week, artist of the year, numerous awards in painting; [oth. writ.] Song, Both words and Music: And Lots of poetry, a few short stories, and AM working on a novel at this time.; [pers.] I try to keep an open mind, always eager to learn. My music (I also play guitar and accordian) expresses my heart and soul, My art shows my appreciation for the beauty and wonders I see and my poetry is my way of laughing at myself and the frailties of life so I don't take things too seriously; [a.]

TAYLOR, JAMES
[pen.] James D. Taylor; [b.] April 25, 1982, Bramalea, Ontario, Canada; [p.] Dean and Anna Taylor; [m.] Single; [ed.] Grade seven student at Greenbriar Senior Public School in Bramalea, Ontario (Almost 13 years old); [occ.] Student at Greenbriar Sr. Public School; [memb.] Left Defense position in Chingua Cousy) Minor Hoskey Club. Intra-city select Hockey team. The Bramalea Boxing Club.; [hon.] Iron Man, Hardest shot award and 3 most valuable player awards and Esso most improved player "A" student working above grade level

in language arts/"Solid strone all around team player, best defense man on his team." The coach; [oth. writ.] This is the first one. Was eleven years old at the time of writing this poem.; [pers.] Writing is a tool I use to vent my frustrations. When I write a good poem I get a warm feeling inside. Just like the crunch of a good clean body check. I can look back and tell myself that I have done a good job.; [a.] Bramalea Ontario, Canada

TAYLOR, JAMES
[b.] September 17, 1955, King Country Hospital; [p.] Clara Welton Taylor; [m.] Elmor Jackson Taylor; [ch.] Rober Taylor, Howard Taylor, Clara Taylor, Charles Taylor, Elle McQueen, Maria Scott, Elnor Taylor, Martha Taylor; [ed.] New Utrecht H.A., C.C.N.Y.; [occ.] Nightmare/Security for therapeutic facility (Denver House); [hon.] St. Cecil Lodge #68 Master Mason, Chief Instructor - Martial Arts Yin Young Martial Arts Studio Brooklyn, NY.; [pers.] I write poetry as a reflection of my spirit, also to give peace and joy to the world, and as a gift to my family and friends.; [a.] Brooklyn, NY

TAYLOR, KARYN
[b.] January 28, 1956, Philadelphia, PA; [p.] Catherine and Lauren Taylor; [ed.] Swarthmore High School, University of Pennsylvania; [oth. writ.] Some unpublished poems and songs; [pers.] I'm grateful to all the teachers along the way who taught me to respect and love the power and beauty hidden in words.; [a.] Swarthmore, PA

TAYMAN, C.R.
[b.] July 1, 1923, Hyndman, Pennsylvania; [p.] Clarence and Edna Tayman; [ed.] Duquesne University, Columbia University; [occ.] Vice President, retired Royers, Inc., smart specialty stores for men, women, children; [memb.] Variety International, Kiwanis, Rotary; [oth. writ.] Satirical tourism political humor columns for Mexico City News; [pers.] At age 49 lost 2/3 of brain cells in auto accident; not expected to live and in no way EVER function on my own after extensive lobotomy. DID however because of positive outlook and faith. [a.] Boca Raton, FL and Acapulco, Mexico

TEGLAND, NAOMI J.
[ed.] B.A. Speech Communication with special emphasis in English Education, SDSU (San Diego State Univ.); [occ.] Customer Service Representative; [memb.] National Teacher's of English., Women In Military Service For America Memorial Foundation., Association for research and Enlightenment, Inc.; [hon.] Sons of the American Revolution Award for leadership. Sailor of the month, NAS Barbers Point, HI, Feb. '89. Top rookie Debater, Aztec Debate Tournament, Oct. '90.; [oth. writ.] "Verify verses" chapbook of poems written in 1992 and 1993.; [pers.] As a U.S. Navy Veteran and a woman, the persian gulf war influenced my views of the world and the U.S. government, as reflected in "Cruel Crude."; [a.] San Diego, CA

TENG, SHIOU YUNG
[b.] December 9, 1981, Taiwan; [p.] Shia Chung Teng and Wang Li Chin; [m.] Single; [ed.] Ashford Elementary (K-4th Grade), Barbara Pierce Bush Elementary, (4th-5th grade), Jane Long Middle School (6th grade) (now) Paul Revere Middle School (7th grade); [hon.] Too many. Can't be named.; [pers.] I am a poet and I don't know it.; [a.] Houston, TX

TENNEY, KERRI K.
[pen.] Kerri K. Tenney or Kerri Kae; [b.] May 6, 1965, Flint, Michigan; [p.] David and Barbara Walker; [m.] John J. Tenney, May 14, 1983; [ch.] Ben B. and David D. Tenney; [ed.] Vassar High School; [occ.] Feature writer for Vassar Pioneer Times (Vassar, MI), Teacher Aide at Vassar High Alternative Education; [memb.] Community active including sons' sporting events; [hon.] Bullar/Sanford Library Writing Contest in Vassar, MI; [oth. writ] Articles in The Pioneer Times, currently working on poetry and children's poetry books; [pers.] The delicacy of the human mind compares to the intricate veins of a rose's petals. To suppose yourself an artist, capable of shifting the order of an individual's mind, is blasphemous. Rather, we are the warmth of the sun and reality of the rain. A writer's purpose should be to prompt growth within. I'm not moved to alter the perfection of the mind, but only to enhance its ability through a different hue. [a.] Vassar, MI

TERMAN, JENNIFER
[b.] August 14, 1966; [p.] Ron and Marilyn Milke; [m.] Chris Terman, November 19, 1988; [ch.] Emily Nicole, Thomas Christopher; [ed.] B.S. in Sociology Midwestern State University Wichita Falls, TX; [occ.] Homemaker; [memb.] Arts Council Co-op; [oth. writ.] Poems published in school paper.; [pers.] I have been fortunate to have been raised in a loving family. I wish every child in the world could be surrounded by love. My husband is my true inspiration.; [a.] Liberal, KS

TERRY, TRACY
[b.] February 24, 1979, Jacksonville, FL; [p.] Lorene and Arthur Terry; [ed.] Currently a sophomore in High School. Studying computers. I want to be able to explore the stars.; [occ.] Sales Associate; [hon.] Won hope of American Award. Won first place for short stories in local contest.; [oth. writ.] 'Lost' and 'For You' are two other poems. An award winning short story called 'Sanity.'; [pers.] Thanks to all who believed in me. Even when I doubted myself. Let your soul speak its words and be free.; [a.] Ogden, UT

THACKER, NETHALYNN
[b.] August 21, 1945, Sanger, CA; [p.] Derrel and Ruth Houdashelt; [m.] Gerald Thacker, November 21, 1964; [ch.] Cynthia Anne, Laura Ellen, Deborah Lynn; [ed.] Samuel Ayer High, San Jose State University; [occ.] Editorial Consultant; [memb.] Future Families Board of Directors; [hon.] Phi Kappa Phi, Kappa Tau Alpha; [oth. writ.] A variety of articles published in national and local journals.; [pers.] My writing reflects my experiences as a woman. I feel honored when others are touched by my words.; [a.] Soquel, CA

THERIAC, CHERYL
[b.] October 16, 1946, Hazleton, IN; [p.] Fremond H. and Daisy M. Frederick; [m.] Willard Andrew Theriac, December 5, 1970; [ch.] Andrea F. Theriac, Daisy F. Theriac; [ed.] 10 1/2 yrs. High School Attended at Princeton, IN.; [occ.] Housewife; [memb.] Membership of United Pente Costal Tabernacle — The Secret Sisters; [oth. writ.] Hours Spent With You, Something Hidden, Rainbows and Dreams, Foolish Heart; [pers.] I try to write about what I feel about my life and do show what is truly important in life; [a.] Vincennes, IN

THEUERKAUF, SHARON
[b.] October 14, 1951, Menominee, MI; [p.] Ben and Alice Mikolas; [oth. writ.] Couples, Guardian Angels published and 30 or more I've written so far.; [a.] Wallace, MI

THIBAULT, MICHELLE
[b.] June 13, 1984, Toms River, NJ; [p.] Dawn Malgieri, Robert Thibault; [ed.] Seaside Park Elementary and H and M Potter Elementary Schools; [hon.] Student of the Month and High Honor Roll; [oth. writ.] Poems in school newspaper; [a.] Bayville, NJ

THOGMARTIN, JANIS P.
[b.] March 11, 1955, Columbus, OH; [p.] Kenneth and JoAnne Damron; [m.] Bruce C. Thogmartin, February 15, 1975; [ch.] Michael Curtis Thogmartin; [ed.] Brookhaven High School; [occ.] Homemaker; [pers.] Creativity is a sanctuary between sanity and madness.; [a.] Charlotte, NC

THOLENAAR-PANAIT, KARINA
[b.] October 10, 1968, Santo Domingo, Dominican Republic; [p.] Francis and Tachy Tholenaar; [m.] Vily Panait, October 30, 1992; [ed.] Santa Teresita High (In Dom. Rep.) Brookdale College, Lincroft, NJ, Travel Agents International, Ocean, NJ; [occ.] Hostess, Water Lot Cafe Restaurant (at the Oyster Point Hotel in Red Bank); [oth. writ.] Hundreds of Poems, which I am starting to translate them to english. (Cruel Grave was originally in Spanish). None published so far. This is the first time I submit my work.; [pers.] I started writing when I was 13. My writing is a reflection of my feelings and the way I think about the world. I live for love, peace, understanding, justice, passion and I feel sorrow, hurt, loneliness, madness, and that's what my writing is about.; [a.] Eatontown, NJ

THOMAS, ESTHER MERLENE
[b.] October 16, San Diego, CA; [p.] Merton Alfred and Nellie Lida (Von Pilz) Thomas; [m.] Single; [ed.] AA with honors, Grossmont College, 1966, BA with honors, San Diego State University, 1969, MA University of Redlands, CA 1977; [occ.] Educator; [memb.] Rep. Presdl. Citizen's Adv. Comm, 1989, Rep. Platform Planning Com, Ca., 1992, at-large del. representing dist. #45, Lakeside, Ca., 1992, Charter Mem. Marine Corps, mem. Lakeside Centennial Com., 1985-1986, Lakeside, Hist. Soc., 1985; [hon.] Recipient Outstanding Svc. award PTA 1972-1974, recognized for various contbns. Commdg. Post Gen., San Diego Bd. Edn., 1989; [oth. writ.] Author: Individualized Curriculum in the Affective Domain, contbg. author: Campbell County, The Treasured Years, 1990, contbg. author: Legends of Lakeside, songs, poems, articles for newspapers; [a.] Lakeside, CA

THOMAS, GREGORY W.
[b.] November 26, 1965, Phoenix, AZ; [p.] William L. Thomas, Ann M. Thomas; [m.] Mary M. Thomas, December 31, 1994; [ed.] B.S. Broadcasting Arizona State University, Grad 1988; [occ.] Production Supervisor, Tav Productions, Video Production House; [oth. writ.] All unpublished and most unread.; [pers.] Writing is both extremely personal and cathartic for me. I do it for no other reason.; [a.] Chandler, AZ

THOMAS, JAYNE ELIZABETH
[b.] June 20, 1964, Northampton, MA; [p.] Richard and Judith Dunn; [m.] David Thomas, April 16, 1993; [ed.] Associate in Science of Dental Hygiene; [a.] South Deerfield, MA

THOMAS, PATRICIA A.
[b.] October 4, 1958, Nashville, NC; [p.] John L. Thomas, Frances Thomas; [ed.] Northern Nash Senior High, East Carolina University, B.A. Psychology, East Caro-

lina University, M.A. I/O Psychology.; [hon.] Psi Chi Psychology Honor Society, Spanish Honor Society, Governor's Award nominee, Honor Roll.; [oth. writ.] "Attitudes toward Job characteristics as a function of Locus of control."; [pers.] "Let your heart and soul guide your pen."; [a.] Philadelphia, PA

THOMPSON, ALEX D.
[b.] June 16, 1970, Los Angeles; [p.] David Thompson, Elyse Thompson; [ed.] Ramona High School, San Francisco City College; [occ.] House Painter and Restorer Part-time Actor; [oth. writ.] America, Balance, One Dark Shadow Among A Sea Of Lights, Other poems to be published in multi cultural Journal by students of mixed heritage from Santa Cruz University.; [pers.] I write to solidify my existence on this planet, to give life a handle so I can grasp it. I write of what brings me pleasure and what causes pain, I am influenced by life, the sounds of John Coltrane and words and music of the last poets.; [a.] San Diego, CA

THOMPSON, GAIL LAUNA
[b.] May 26, 1956, McComb, MS; [p.] Sterling Gillis, Joyce Gillespie; [m.] Anthony M. Thompson, May 25, 1991; [ch.] July Thompson, Kevin Gordon; [ed.] Parklane School, Miramar College, and Academy of Casino Dealing; [occ.] Homemaker; [oth. writ.] I have just completed a book of poems. Titled: "Enjoying Life's Moments" that will be submitted for publication.; [pers.] I thank my family and friends, for giving me the encouragement, and moral support of following through with my writings. I hope to pursue further with my accomplishments.; [a.] Jackson, MS

THOMPSON, ROSEMARIE E.
[pen.] Rosemarie Peters Thompson; [b.] August 20, 1924, Ellensburg, WA; [p.] Richard and Mary Anna Schultz; [m.] Hobert A. Thompson, July 7, 1984 (2nd marriage); [ch.] Bob Peters, Douglas Peters, Donna Fowlks; [ed.] Ellensburg Senior High School, Ellensburg, Washington, Retired from Pacific Northwest Bell The Co Seattle, WA - 1979; [occ.] Homemaker; [memb.] First United Methodist Church - Astoria, OR; [oth. writ.] Freddie the Fly Away Kite and other Children Stories - Book, Magic Moments - Poetry book, Created by His Hands - Poetry book; [pers.] I've always felt the need to create, whether it is in a new poem, or an oil painting or at my sewing machine designing a new sweat shirt or doll I get great joy and satisfaction.; [a.] Astoria, OR

THOMPSON, VIRGINIA
[b.] September 15, 1937, Austin, TX; [p.] Frances and Gus Westerman; [m.] Robert Thompson, March 20, 1959; [ch.] 1 son, Curt Thompson and daughter-in-law Karen; [ed.] Killen High, Temple Jr College, White Design School; [occ.] Free Lance Floral Design (commercial); [memb.] Omega Nu Tau Sorority, Artists Assoc. of Amer. Floral Design, RS Club, American Business Women's Assoc.; [hon.] State Champion in Floral Design (Commercial), Oil paintings selected for show in a Texas gallery. Temple, TX; [oth. writ.] Many poems about life and nature... Book of poems printed and sold in gift shops; [pers.] My poems are written from the heart about love, nature and memories; [a.] Kettering, OH

THOMPSON, WHITNEY TAYLOR
[pen.] Whitney Taylor Thompson; [b.] July 21, 1971, Springfield, MA; [p.] Lynn and David Thompson; [ed.] Dean Junior College, Franklin MA., Assoc. Child Devt.; [occ.] Preschool teacher Mass Mutual Children's House; [pers.] My writings have been greatly inspired by the many experiences, events, and people who have touched my life, even my "angel" who "lives" all around me.; [a.] Springfield, MD

THORNTON, ELIZABETH D.
[b.] February 6, 1949, East Liverpool, OH; [p.] Dale and Frances Thornton; [ed.] East Liverpool High School, Kent State University; [occ.] Retired Teacher; [hon.] Thompson Award; [pers.] I enjoy sharing my life's experiences with others; [a.] East Liverpool, OH

TIBBETTS, KATEY J.
[pen.] Gena McClure; [b.] April 19, 1957, Redding, CA; [p.] Jean and Jim Sullivan; [m.] Rick L. Tibbetts, July 17, 1993; [ch.] 5 children from previous marriage to Matthew Lack; [ed.] Graduated from Trend College (Private College), Majored in Business Management; [occ.] Housewife; [memb.] Church, Christ's Gospel Fellowship; [hon.] Graduated top of Class in High School - Award for Perfect Attendance and 4.0 G.P.A. in college; [oth. writ.] I have been writing poetry since I was in the 6th grade (26 years) I have not have my work published until recently!; [pers.] To notice the positive and happy quality of life. I crave poetry and that in life where there is hope and inspiration. I think we all should live by the Golden Rule with kindness to treat others as you want to be treated!; [a.] Spokane, WA

TICKNOR, NEDRA KIDDER
[pen.] Nedra Ticknor; [b.] July 4, 1958, San Antonio, TX; [p.] Walter Kidder, Clara Kidder; [m.] Jim Ticknor, June 17, 1977; [ch.] 1 son - Bryon Scott Christopher; [ed.] High School - Irving Crown; [occ.] Quality Control inspector, Hoffer Plastics; [oth. writ.] None other than being published in this book, currently working on publishing my first book of poetry.; [pers.] I try to reflect on my own personal experiences as a way to reach out to other people, as way of bringing laughter or a gentle hand to one of God's children.; [a.] Carpentersville, IL

TIEMANN, GEORGANNE G.
[pen.] Jan Greene; [b.] December 20, 1928, Jefferson City, MO; [p.] George Greene, Marvel Green; [m.] Robert C. Tiemann - August 20, 1993 (Exp), September 11, 1953; [ed.] Granite City High School Gradwohl School of Laboratory Technique St. Louis, MO Lindenwood College St. Charles, MO; [occ.] Retired, previously Medical Technologist - Serologist Barnes Hospital, St. Louis; [memb.] Good Shepherd Lutheran Building Comm., American Lung Association, United States Golf Association, National Museum of American Indian.; [hon.] Illinois lives by Walton, Who's Who of American Women Leading Ladies (Metro East Journal) Special Achievement Award from Gradwohl Alumni Association; [oth. writ.] Chapter in Automation for The Laboratory, Article in the American Journal of Clinical Pathology, Poems in four poetry anthologies: Traces Of A Valiant Soul, Magic Of The Muse, Lyrical Voices, A Search Of The Soul; [pers.] Writing verse since a high school junior. "If you keep a strong faith in God, a sense of humor, and remember that knowledge is stored within the brain, but wisdom comes from the heart, you can succeed at whatever you endeavor."; [a.] Troy, IL

TIMBERLAKE, DAVID L.
[b.] April 26, 1935, Akron, OH; [p.] Floyd and Gwen Timberlake; [m.] Anna E. Timberlake, April 5, 1957; [ch.] 5 children, 10 grandchildren; [pers.] This poem is dedicated to the wonderful grace of our Lord Jesus!; [a.] Wilmington, NC

TIMPANARO, TARA A.
[pen.] Tara Timpanaro; [b.] August 23, 1986, Manalapan, NJ; [p.] Joseph and Odessa Timpanaro; [ed.] Currently in 3rd Grade in Taylor Mills School Manalapan, N.J.; [occ.] Grammar School; [oth. writ.] Anthology of poetry by Young Americans; [pers.] Thanks to all my teachers, Mrs. Feingold, Miss Hicks, Mrs. Hecht-Minde and Mrs. Sawyer; [a.] Manalapan, NJ

TODD, JANET E.
[b.] September 1, 1969, Oak Lawn, IL; [p.] Ron Horton, Pat Horton; [ch.] Victoria Kathleen; [sib.] Currently a part time student in college; [ed.] Sales Clerk; [pers.] I tend to write about love and the pursuit of love. I feel that love plays a very important part in all our lives. Everyone should dream of a little romance.; [a.] Export, PA

TOLENTINO, MELODY GRACE E.
[pen.] Melody Tolentino or Dy; [b.] December 27, 1979, Metairie, LA; [p.] Froilan Tolentino, Miguelina Tolentino; [ed.] Zachary Senior High School; [occ.] Student of the Freshmen Class; [memb.] National Beta Club, Spanish Club, St. John's and Zachary High's Choir; [hon.] (8th Grade) Leadership, effort, Honor Roll, Arts, and Presidential Academic Fitness Award (PAFA), (6th grade) PAFA, (9th grade) Principal's Honor Roll, LA music educators association (Superior Rating); [oth. writ.] Some of my poems published in school's anthology and school newspaper ("Hoofprints"); [pers.] Home is always where the heart is and I love the place where I grew up (in Fremont, CA). I am well aware of the problem and heartaches of many young people. I wish to reach their souls with my poems, good or bad.; [a.] Zachary, LA

TOMACDER, MARINETTE J.
[pen.] Angelus; [b.] December 11, 1973, Pangasinan, Philippines; [p.] Phoebec Tomacder, Emilio Tomacder Sr.; [ed.] Binalonan National High, Harris Memorial College; [occ.] Contract Worker; [memb.] I have no such any memberships but I am one of the active youth in our Church and one of the officials in our Youth organization in our community.; [oth. writ.] Some poems published in song Mag.; [pers.] I really want to view of what God had created. I love nature and this is my way of expressing my feelings and through this to be able also to share to others the goodness of our creator.; [a.] Shatin NT, Hongkong

TOMCZYK, ANDREA M.
[pen.] AMT; [b.] January 7, 1965, Decatur, MI; [p.] Ronald and Joan Blahuta; [m.] Dr. Christopher A. Tomczyk, May 1, 1992; [ch.] Sarah Jane, Emily Ann, and Theodore Alan; [ed.] Decatur High, Southwestern, and Kalamazoo Valley Community Colleges.; [oth. writ.] I've only begun.; [pers.] I write to ease my mind, to comfort my soul.; [a.] Hastings, MI

TONN, JULIA A.
[pen.] Julie Tonn; [b.] March 29, 1920, McMurray, Washington; [p.] Charles and Mary Tonn; [ed.] Through College (majored in English and Education). Elementary School teacher (6 years), secretarial work, proofreader for a large pharmaceutical company (23 years).; [occ.] Retired - volunteering on a regular schedule (and loving it) with a child care center.; [oth. writ.] None of my previous "Creations" were ever published, though often shared with and appreciated by others. This poem literally wrote itself: Combine the Monarch's sweet visit with a lucky camera work and simultaneous need for a

perfect message for a faraway, very dear friend, and Viola! "Butterflies... and Friends." The final touch: The poetry contest notice in a local paper leaped out at me that very same day!; [pers.] In these "bonus years" I am joyfully learning - and practicing - the simple philosophy that "love can make a difference." Shared love — written, spoken, expressed by a look or touch or a "random act of kindness," by a special photography, given or received — will make a difference.; [a.] Rutherford, NJ

TORRISI, RANDA LOUISE
[pen.] Randa Torrisi; [b.] May 10, 1946, Portland, OR; [p.] Herbert L. Boutin and Janice Meredith Starr; [m.] Salvatore Torrisi, December 13, 1982; [ch.] Tom, Jess, Steve, Kurt and Fred; [ed.] Cleveland H.S., B.A. Psychology West Virginia State, December, 1990.; [occ.] Homemaker, Photographers and Ing Pipes; [memb.] National Psi Chi; [hon.] Summa Cum Laude, Recipient of 1994 Ingpiping scholarship (Oberlin School of Fine Arts) at Ohio Scottish fames, Best of show photograph 1994 Lake Co. Fair.; [pers.] If something is worth my time, it's also worth my best effort.; [a.] Kirtland, OH

TORZILLI, MILLIE
[pen.] Millie Torzilli; [b.] July 18, 1945, Proctor, VT; [p.] William and Minie vonHofe; [m.] Daniel M. Torzilli III, August 18, 1990; [ch.] Brenda Jean, Edward Alan; [ed.] Yorktown High, Yorktown Heights, New York; [occ.] Wife and Homemaker; [memb.] Church of the Nazarene, Fishkill, N.Y.; [hon.] Certified Model of Estelle and Alfonso Modelling School, Poughkeepsie, N.Y.; [oth. writ.] Many poems not yet published, awaiting their destiny.; [pers.] If I can reach the heart of just one person and show them through my poems that there is hope and love is knowing the Lord, and that there is always an answer to all of life's questions in God's word, then I have accomplished my goal.; [a.] Poughkeepsie, NY

TOWNSEND, KAREN S.
[pen.] Karen Townsend; [b.] January 11, 1938, Seattle, WA; [p.] Frank and Marjorie Shillestad; [m.] Noel E. Townsend (deceased) September 7, 1962; [ch.] Meg, Christopher, Jennie; [ed.] B.A. Degree from the University of Washington; [occ.] Retired Teacher Widow, Community Volunteer; [oth. writ.] Many poems, extensive prose, journals kept on trips, letters to friends. Nothing ever published before.; [pers.] I view the world as my cathedral and I try to express my spirituality in the things I write about.; [a.] Federal Way, WA

TRABUCCO, PAULINE
[b.] April 30, 1917; [p.] Emile and Leslie Trabucco; [ed.] Mariposa High School, Mills College (B.A.), Post-graduate work; [occ.] Retired; [memb.] Mariposa County Arts Council, Mariposa Performing Arts Association, Eastern Star; [hon.] Awards for Paintings, Photography, Mosaics, Flower Arrangements; [oth. writ.] I have written poems for friends and for my own amusement, but have never had any published; [pers.] My poem, "Coyote," was inspired by my meeting with that beautiful creature at the edge of the forest in Yosemite National Park, where I taught for twenty-six years. [a.] Mariposa, CA

TRATHEN, THEODORE M.
[b.] February 8, 1955, Ypsilanti, MI; [p.] Clifford and Marilyn; [m.] Linda Lynette Trathen, July 18, 1992; [ch.] Lynea Lynette Hyde; [ed.] North Farmington High, Oakland Community College; [occ.] Professional Magician. GM auto worker, Orion Assembly, Pontiac, MI; [memb.] U.A.W. 5960, Ward Presbyterian Church, Fellowship of Christian Magicians.; [pers.] My inspiration comes from my family, who teach me about life and love, and from Jesus Christ, my spiritual mentor and emotional pillow.; [a.] Grand Blanc, MI

TREIBER, BECKY
[pen.] Beck; [b.] October 30, 1962, Battle Creek, IA; [p.] Robert Treiber, Judy Schimmer; [ed.] Ida Grove High, Morningside College; [occ.] Management; [memb.] President, Ida Grove Chamber of Commerce, Phi Beta Lambda; [hon.] Dean's List; [a.] Ida Grove, IA

TRESSLER, VALERIE
[b.] August 21, 1977, Elmira, NY; [p.] Larry and Carol Tressler; [m.] Single; [ed.] Senior - Horseheads High School Horseheads, NY; [occ.] Student; [pers.] Every person has a purpose in life. I believe mine is to entertain. I have played the guitar for two years and enjoy writing my own music and lyrics. Lyrics are poetry, whether they rhyme or not. The poetry I write usually portrays an intense emotion. I think the best poet is one who can create something so powerful it can alter a listener's mood.; [a.] Horseheads, NY

TRETHAWAY, THOMAS B.
[b.] January 18, 1957, New York, NY; [p.] John B. and Joy S. Thethaway; [m.] Julia Wu Trethaway, June 16, 1984; [ch.] Perry Lin, Paul Wu; [ed.] The Hotchkiss School, Darthmouth College; [occ.] History/English Teacher, the Hotchkiss School; [memb.] Professional Association of Diving Instructors (Padi), V.S. Master's swimming; [hon.] Undergraduate degree with High Distinction in History, NEH/CEEB Fellowship; [oth. writ.] News Articles in Manchester (VT.) Journal; [a.] Lakeville, CT

TREVINO, SYLVIA L.
[b.] November 2, 1969, Seguin, TX; [p.] Ascension M. Gonzoles, Sara G. Gonzoles; [ch.] Guadalupe L. Bueno; [ed.] G.E.D. Beeville County College; [occ.] Full time student; [pers.] I dedicate this poem to two dear friends of mine Joshue Richins and Robert Owings whom touched my life significantly. I thank you for always being there. I could have never written this poem without your inspiration.; [a.] Mathis, TX

TRIMBLE, LYNN MICHELLE
[b.] September 23, 1979, Lloydminster, SK; [p.] Brian Trimble and Judy Trimble; [ed.] Lloydminster Comprehensive High School - Lloydminster, Alberta Presently enrolled in Grade 10.; [occ.] Student; [hon.] prizes for writing stories, 4-H crafts Dental Association Poetry Award Cdn. Legion Essay award; [pers.] I believe that everyone should strive to do their best and never give up regardless of the obstacles they may face.; [a.] Lloydminster, SK

TRINDADE, BRANDI LEE
[pen.] Brandi Lee Trindade; [b.] October 6, 1981, Merced, CA; [p.] Robert and Patti Trindade; [ed.] I am an 8th grade student at Hilmar Middle School in Hilmar, California.; [hon.] I have won three different poetry awards and three awards for project in Science. I am also a Honor roll student, and I have been a cheerleader of the past six years.; [pers.] I wrote this poem for my God Mother/Aunt Darlene/Wagner for her funeral. My Aunt died of cancer on January 28, 1994.; [a.] Hilmar, CA

TROGEN, VERA
[b.] January 23, 1915, Morrin, Alberta; [p.] Donald (Dan) and Janet (Jessie Grieve) McAllister; [m.] Ray Albert Trogen, October 13, 1940; [ch.] George Gary Trogen 1947-1992; [ed.] Magee High School (Honours) then the school of hard knocks.; [occ.] Retired grain farmer; [memb.] Past matron, Order of the Eastern Star, Highland Chapter Alberta, Blooming Prairie Pioneers, Morrin, Alta; [oth. writ.] The only other poems I have written are an ode to my baby son and a narrative epic concerning a trip to Greece and Egypt; [pers.] Life is a great adventure and I try to enjoy it to the fullest.; [a.] Morrin, Alberta

TROTTER, DONALD R.
[b.] May 24, 1955, Chicago; [p.] Frances and Raymond; [m.] Darcey, January 21, 1989; [ch.] Patricia, Kristen, Andrew, Sydney; [ed.] Marist High School, Cleveland Institute of Electronics.; [occ.] Senior Field Service Engineer, Siemens; [oth. writ.] Numerous Poems and Short stories.; [a.] Rockford, IL

TROY, BURKE
[pen.] Burke Troy; [b.] January 26, 1973, Mississippi; [p.] Jim and Nancy Troy; [ed.] Alton High, Vinncers U.; [occ.] Food Service; [oth. writ.] Working on my own book Memories Of Our Deepest Soul; [pers.] Be true to yourself and the rest will follow.; [a.] Alton, IL

TRUDEAU, VIRGINIA
[b.] October 24, 1966, New Haven, CT; [ch.] Elizabeth; [ed.] Harvard H. Ellis R.V.T.S. Quinneburg Valley College; [memb.] Service Industry; [hon.] Dean's List; [oth. writ.] First Published Piece; [pers.] Thank you God; [a.] Canterbury, CT

TRUSCELLO, MICHAEL
[b.] October 2, 1972, Kitchener, ON; [p.] Anthony Truscello, Valerie Truscello; [ed.] St. Jerome's High, St. Mary's High, University of Waterloo; [occ.] Student, University of Waterloo (MA Programme); [hon.] Dean's List, St. Jerome's College English Award; [oth. writ.] Poem "Tears" appears in "Scaling the Face of Reason" compiled by the Canadian Chamber of Contemporary Poetry; [pers.] Lose what you will: Youth, innocence, beauty. Keep what you can: family, friends, love.; [a.] Kitchener, ON

TURMAN, DEBBIE L.
[pen.] Debbie Leeman; [b.] April 9, 1956, Bonham, TX; [p.] John and Peggy Leeman; [m.] James Turman (Art), June 21, 1986; [ch.] Amanda Marie, Jennifer Nell; [ed.] Skyline High School, Eastfield Jr. College; [occ.] Housewife, Mother; [hon.] Trophy in Billiards medal in Flute "Miss Personality" Trophy; [pers.] My inspiration is the Lord, my husband and the way I feel in my heart.; [a.] Allen, TX

TURNER, WALTER D.
[pen.] Deacon; [b.] September 23, 1948, Gate City, VA; [p.] George and Kedith Turner (both deceased); [m.] Diann W. Turner, May 23, 1979; [ch.] Dyanna W. Turner, Darlene A. Turner; [ed.] Gate City, High School, Morristown Junior College, U.S. Army Sergeants Major Academy; [occ.] Sergeants Major in the U.S. Army; [hon.] Award Numerous Military Decorations for Meritorious Service and Achievement; [pers.] I want to portray my feelings towards the subject in my writings; [a.] Fort Meade, MD

TURNEY, ANNE
[pen.] Anne M. Turney; [b.] January 10, 1980, Butler, PA; [p.] Andrea and Don Turney; [ed.] Still in High School; [occ.] Still in High School; [hon.] Selected as on of the top 12 poetry writers in Tallmadge High School.; [oth. writ.] Sometimes (published last year in Edge of Twilight.); [a.] Tallmadge, OH

TURNIPSEED, PAUL D.
[b.] August 23, 1961, Clarkville, TN; [p.] Johnnie H. Turnipseed, Hattie Turnipseed; [m.] Millie Oates Turnipseed, July 11, 1987; [ch.] Johnnie Terrell Turnipseed, Rakim Kareem Turnipseed; [ed.] Port Gibson High, United States Air Force Hinds Community College; [occ.] Student; [memb.] Church of God in Christ, Computer Science Club; [hon.] (United States Air Force) Longevity Award Outstanding Achievement; [oth. writ.] A poem published in the 1995 summer edition, "A Moment In Time.; [pers.] "You're not an adult, until you've accepted Christ as your personal savior." "Success is not accomplishing the "Goals" that "You" have set for yourself but accomplishing the will of God."; [a.] Port Gibson, MS

TWEEDT, S. K.
[b.] October 11, 1917, Iowa; [p.] Barney and Clara Tweedt; [m.] Dorothy J. Tweedt, June 11, 1943; [ch.] Two girls Norma and Donna; [ed.] 10th Grade plus one Term of English in Tucson, AR; [occ.] Retired; [oth. writ.] Several poems and articles for Yank Magazine when in The Air Force in 1974 I was injured - 4 skull fractures and Brain Damage, I just believe in God and do what I think he wants; [pers.] I just like to write about Normal People and Honestly, I wrote this poem and others when in the air force at Tuscon, AR, I did some writing for Yank Magazine; [a.] Tomball, TX

TYRRELL, TOM
[b.] September 15, 1980, Flint, MI; [p.] Sandra White and Edward Tyrrell; [ed.] I am currently in the 9th grade at Morrice High School; [hon.] I've never really received any major awards, just the kind you get at school for sports and grades.; [oth. writ.] I've always enjoyed writing but never had the courage to show my work to other people, this is one of the rare times that I did.; [pers.] My father always told me, "Don't let anyone steal your dream, Tom." So I guess that's my personal note to you.; [a.] Owosso, MI

ULRICH, BETTY GARTON
[b.] October 28, 1919, Indianapolis, IN; [p.] Harry and Nora (Davis) Gorton; [m.] Louis Ulrich, January 5, 1946; [ch.] Barbara, James, Ruth, John and David, 10 grandchildren; [ed.] So. Side High School, Ft. Wayne Ind. U. of Wisconsin - Madison (B.S. degree); [occ.] Freelance writer and contributing editor to "writer's journal"; [memb.] Wisconsin Regional Winters Assoc., Ure Wisconsin Council for Winters, and Indian head Winters Group, First Lutheran Church of Stone Lake; [hon.] Honorable Mention in Winter's Digest poetry competition; [oth. writ.] Many short stories (including redbook and veritales anthologies) articles (guideports, the Lutherary Lighthouse, etc). and poems, in both secular and religious magazines. Write a bi-weekly column for a Northern Wisconsin Weekly newspaper. Have had 3 books published: by Concordia, Augsburg and Judson Presses.; [pers.] I try to deal in my writing with the impact of the spiritual in our lives and the many ways we handle the (often unrecognized) longing to be reconciled with God.; [a.] Stone Lake, WI

UNRUH, NORMAN
[b.] May 1, 1935, Ringwood, OK; [p.] Harley and Lillie Unruh; [m.] Suzie, July 1, 1988; [ch.] Terra; [ed.] Goltry High, Goltry Okla.; [occ.] Musician; [pers.] God's given talents are the Matrix to share them in the perfection; [a.] Kansas, OK

UNRUH, RAMONA
[pen.] Suzie and Ramon Hulnu; [b.] December 22, 1939, Spiro, OK; [p.] Monroe and Ruth Strickland; [m.] Norman L. Unruh, July 1, 1988; [ch.] Jearold Duawe, Sandra Sue; [ed.] Midwest City High, Nursing, O.V. Extension Course on Pesticides and green house study.; [occ.] Gospel Music Ministry; [hon.] Many Ribbons and Cash prizes on eggery art.; [oth. writ.] 39 gospel and Country songs, copyrighted; [pers.] God gives me all my talents, and dialects my pen. I can do nothing alone.; [a.] Kansas, OK

UPTON, CRYSTAL MARIE
[pen.] Crico; [b.] November 4, 1978, Pontiac, MI; [p.] Fred Upton and Christine Bookie; [ed.] 10th grade at Pontiac Northern High; [occ.] Cashier; [hon.] Honor Roll, Perfect Attendance, Music, and writing awards.; [oth. writ.] Personal poem poetry.; [pers.] My writings comes from my personal experiences and feelings.; [a.] Pontiac, MI

VALDES, LOU J.
[pen.] Lou J. Valdes; [b.] October 12, 1965, El Paso, TX; [p.] Louie Valdes, Susan Valdes; [m.] Juanita Valdes, December 31, 1993; [ch.] Amanda Ryan, Louie Samuel.; [ed.] Saipointe Catholic High, Pima College; [occ.] Retail District Manager, Drug Emporium; [pers.] Hard work and a positive attitude is all you need. give 100% and get 100%!! Respect everyone!! Be happy.!!; [a.] Fremont, CA

VAN DREASON, JEFF
[pen.] Billy Shears, Jeff Barker; [b.] July 11, 1978, Oneida, NY; [p.] Linda Van Dreason, David Van Dreason; [ed.] Currently a sophomore in VVS, High School; [occ.] Student; [memb.] JAM; [oth. writ.] Nothing else published at this time; [pers.] The only way in which we are all the same is that we are all different; [a.] Sherrill, NY

VAN DUSEN, BEVERLY K.
[b.] November 30, 1958, Illinois; [ch.] Dax Moore, Chris Pent; [occ.] Video Store Owner; [pers.] You must look at yourself as if looking at another person and honestly admit your own faults. And work on them until you become a person you truly like or love. If you love and respect yourself. Others will too.; [a.] Arlington, TX

VANACORE, DANIEL
[b.] June 30, 1959, New Haven, CT; [p.] Mr. and Mrs. Raymond Vanacore; [m.] Beverly Vanacore, April 8, 1989; [ch.] Matthew Daniel Vanacore; [ed.] University of New Haven, CT 1980 - A.S. Criminal Justice 1984- B.S. Business Adm.; [occ.] Logistics Manager; [memb.] APICS Membership, ALTA Member; [hon.] Dean's List- College, Dean's List 1978; [oth. writ.] College English and Creative Writing courses; [pers.] Writing to me, is a way to capture a special moment in time; [a.] Lawrenceville, GA

VANN, ALICE
[pen.] Patricia Perrin; [b.] August 4, 1952, Paterson, NJ; [m.] Kenneth Vann; [ch.] Kerry Ann Vann 2, David Christopher Vann 3; [ed.] High School Pequannock, NJ College - Southern Conn. State, New Haven, Conn. University; [occ.] Graphic Designer Owner-Golden Graphics - 17 yrs.; [hon.] American Advertising's Silver Medal, Who's Who in Mississippi, Numerous Addy Awards; [oth. writ.] None published, (Except my commercial copy for brochures and broadcast); [pers.] As much as I have loved commercial copywriting in my career it never fulfilled me as does my personal writing and poetry. I hope it can bring joyful meaning to others.; [a.] Columbus, MS

VANZANT, ROSEMARIE
[b.] November 14, 1960, New Mexico; [p.] John M. and Francis Marie; [m.] Robert L. Vanzant, March 9, 1984; [ch.] Jon Mark, Rebecca Lee, Robert Joseph, Shyla Nicole; [occ.] Homemaker; [oth. writ.] Several poems that have never been published.; [pers.] My word's are from my heart and on deep sometime secret thoughts. I hope that what I write helps others to see with their hearts and not be afraid to feel.; [a.] Taft, CA

VAUGHN, GREGORY REID
[pen.] Gregory Vaughn; [b.] July 13, 1953, Farmville, VA; [p.] Dr. Jones W. Vaughn, Joanne Vaughn; [ed.] 2 yrs. College; [occ.] Pathology Assistant Saint Joseph Health Center, Kansas City, MO; [memb.] Kansas City Society for his to technology.; [hon.] Photography-published in the best of photography annual 1983 by photographs forum magazine; [pers.] I attempt to let my eye for art in photography infiltrate and submerge itself in my poetry.; [a.] Kansas City, MO

VEGA, NOEMI
[pen.] Noemi Vega; [b.] May 19, 1967, Chicago; [p.] Juan Vega and Irma Vega; [m.] Johnny A. Rodriguez; [ch.] Johnny Jr, Xiomara, Wilmans, Joel, Gabriel, Ana I. and Elizabeth Rodriguez; [ed.] Kelvyn Park H.S.; [occ.] Secretary, IL Masonic Hospital; [memb.] American Heart Association, Red Cross; [pers.] This poem is dedicated to the goodness of mankind, also to my great inspiration my husband. Johnny and my daughter Elizabeth and for my loving parents whom have always been my great inspiration.

VELAS SR., ROSEANN
[b.] October 22, 1950, Bethlehem, PA; [p.] Mr. and Mrs. Joseph Velas; [ed.] St. Francis Academy, Bethlehem, PA Kutztown State University - BS Villanova University MSLS; [occ.] Principal - St. Theresa Elementary School; [memb.] NCEA, Member of the School Sisters of St. Francis, Bethlehem, PA Member of American Poetry Society; [hon.] 1st prize in Poetry Unlimited's "Ages and Stages" contest, Listed in Who's who in America-1995, Honorary award by American Family Institute; [oth. writ.] Poems published by "Yes, Press, poetry international, Poetry unlimited, JMW Publishing, and poetry press; [pers.] God is alive in my poetry and his spirit is expressed creatively through my written words. My relationship with him is expressed lovingly and enthusiastically.; [a.] Hellertown, PA

VENNETTILLI, FANNIE BURNELL
[b.] November 5, 1952, Devers, TX; [p.] Lee E. and Annie F. Burnell; [m.] Aldo E. Vennettilli, July 15, 1983; [ch.] Anneke Burnell Allante Burnell (Granddaughter); [ed.] Inkster High, Dorsey Business School; [occ.] Executive Secretary, Michigan Council for arts and cultural affairs; [pers.] My writings reflect the joys and tragedies in my life. "It's still Bare Bronches Straight..." is dedicated to the memory of my father, Lee Edwards Burnell.; [a.] Westland, MI

VERDON, WILLIAM J.
[pen.] Bill Verdon; [b.] October 19, 1922, Philadelphia, PA; [p.] Stephen Verdon and Pauline Kish; [m.] Catherine Hogan, July 7, 1945; [ch.] One daughter Linda Giorgione; [ed.] Stetson Jr. High School, Phila.; [occ.] Retired Steel worker/Boxer and trainer; [memb.] Disabled American Vets. American Legion Nat'l Library of poetry; [hon.] Lightweight and Welterweight Champ Vs. Army "43-45" Boxing; [oth. writ.] 1. "My Son, My Son" - Summer Edition reflections of life, 2. "Care" - Fall edition - Garden of Life.; [pers.] I have written 65 poems in the past 30 years and continue to write poetry about people's feelings. Left School to help out at home 6 brothers. Two sisters.; [a.] Philadelphia, PA

VERSCHUERE, LYANNE
[b.] January 31, 1953, Victoria, British Columbia, Canada; [p.] Julian Verschuere, Evlyn Henderson; [ch.] Christopher, Matthew, Angela, Jesse, Sarah, Douglas.; [ed.] Georges P. Vaniet, Carihi, Career and Continuing Education, Campbell River.; [pers.] I have always held a great love for the written word. Poetry provides me with a freedom of expression that is unequaled in other literary forms.; [a.] Campbell River British Columbia, Canada

VICKERS, A. B.
[b.] June 20, 1920, Xenia, OH; [p.] Josephine Vickers; [ch.] Michael Vickers; [ed.] 2-Univ. Miss State., graduate Airforce Aviation Cadet.; [occ.] Ret.; [memb.] American Legion; [hon.] Military Bronze Star, Air Medal, 2 Oak Lear Clusters Asiatic Pacific Service Medal with 3 Battle Stars; [oth. writ.] Approx. 50 poems; [a.] Bunnell, FL

VICKERS, STEPHANIE
[b.] July 9, 1980, Herrin, IL; [p.] John Vickers, Shirley Vickers; [ed.] I'm in the 9th grade at Sheffield High School; [memb.] Sheffield High Flag Team, Gospel Band: The Vickers Family; [pers.] I know I'll never be a famous poet, but just having my poem published at the age of 14 is enough satisfaction to last me a lifetime; [a.] Sheffield, AL

VICTOR, CARMEL
[ch.] Stanella Victor; [sib.] Sociology major at Brooklyn College; [oth. writ.] Several poems published in local newspapers.; [pers.] My poems are designed to help others look within themselves and make improvements or changes toward their personal happiness as well as others with a realistic approach.; [a.] Brooklyn, NY

VIGIL, LILLIAN
[b.] September 22, 1978, Trinidad, CO; [p.] Lillian Vigil; [ed.] Currently High School Junior at Aguilar High School; [occ.] Student now, plant to become Cosmetology; [memb.] FHA - Future Homemakers of America; [hon.] Cheerleading Squad; [oth. writ.] Reporter for school newspaper; [pers.] I write poetry because it is prettier than stories.; [a.] Aguilar, CO

VINCENT, MARTIN
[b.] May 2, 1969, Saint Louis, MO; [p.] Jane F. Hithcock, Martin E. Vincent (divorced); [occ.] Slacker/Dishwasher; [a.] San Antonio, TX

VINES, WENDY
[b.] February 12, 1978, Caldwell, CO; [p.] Wayne and Donna Vines; [ed.] Currently a Junior at West Caldwell High School in Lenoir, NC; [occ.] Student; [memb.] Omega Beta, Junior Advisory, Image Players, French Club, Save, Key Club; [hon.] Certificate of Appreciation from the Department of Human Resources in the state of North Carolina. American Musical Foundation Band Honors. Presidential Academic Fitness Award, Certificate of Academic Excellence, Who's Who among American High School Students, for being a member for several consecutive years.; [oth. writ.] Life is full of hard work. One of the hardest tasks, however, is opening your eyes to see what you are working for.; [pers.] Lenoir, NC

VIOLETTE, GARY C.
[b.] October 29, 1952, Providence, RI; [p.] Madalene, Donald Violette; [m.] Carol Violette, August 18, 1972; [ch.] Lilia, Erin, Sarah; [ed.] Shelton High School (CT) Hartford State Technical College (A.A.S.) Clarkson College of Technology (B.S.); [occ.] Civil/Structural Engineer; [memb.] Clifton Park Assembly of God, American Society of Civil Engineers; [oth. writ.] None published; [pers.] Some of the most precious memories are the totally unexpected touches of our hearts.; [a.] Clifton Park, NY

VITALE, ANNEMARIE
[b.] January 25, 1976, Warren, Michigan; [ed.] Freshman at Central Michigan University; [occ.] Student; [memb.] Student Government, Forensics, Symphony Band; [hon.] Excellence in Music award for four years in band in high school; [pers.] My poetry does not come from my mind, but from my heart and my imagination. [a.] Warren, MI

VITITOE, JASON
[pen.] Jean Sufo; [b.] March 7, 1978, Chillicothe, OH; [p.] Richard and Marlene Vititor; [ed.] Union-Scioto High School; [occ.] Student at Union-Scioto High School; [memb.] National Honor Society, Chillicothe Civic Ochestra, Pleasant Valley United Methodist Church; [hon.] N.H.S. National Merit Awards - Math, English, Science; [oth. writ.] Several other poems mostly non-published ones.; [pers.] I plan to write and praise the Lord, he inspired my writings and my life.; [a.] Chillicothe, OH

VOGT, HANS H.
[b.] October 27, 1925, Germany; [p.] Hans and Anna; [m.] Irma, September 15, 1951; [ch.] Ludwig; [ed.] High School in Germany Ryerson College in Toronto Seneca College in Toronto Radio College in Toronto; [occ.] Writer for German Papers, Ethnic Publications in Canada; [memb.] Bonchoeffer Lutheran Church German Professional Association Kettleby Home Owners Stiftung Naturschutz, Hamburg; [hon.] Ryerson College, Seneca College; [oth. writ.] Poetry in the German Language, Essays on History and Science Fairy Tales, short stories; [pers.] Influenced by shakespeare, goethe Thomas Mann to give meaning to life by example, to show that this world can be made better by our continuous effort and that good prevails over evil.; [a.] Kettleby, Ontario

VOWELL, DAVID G.
[b.] May 1, 1947, Harlan, KY; [p.] Jesse and Helen Vowell; [m.] Marcy Harris Vowell; [ed.] Alumnus of Stetson, University School of Music; [occ.] Sales and Children's Chess coach.; [memb.] The U.S. Chess Federation, The Willis Bodine Chorale, Alachua County (FL) School Volunteers; [oth. writ.] Lifestyle articles for local newspaper.; [a.] Gainesville, FL

VOYLES, PAMELA
[b.] February 5, 1965, Corpus Christi, TX; [p.] Ms. B. Regmund and Mr. and Mrs. L. Wallace; [m.] Robert Voyles, December 27, 1987; [ch.] Katherine Voyles; [ed.] Del Mar College Corpus Christi State University; [occ.] School teacher; [pers.] I love the challenges, frustrations, and rewards when writing poetry.; [a.] Corpus Christi, TX

WADE, SARAH JANE WOOLF
[b.] March 24, 1936, Boston, GA; [ed.] Tufts University, American University, BA 1957 Boston University, Ed. D. 1980; [occ.] Reading/writing specialist, Brookline, MA., public schools; [memb.] M.R.A., N.E.R.A., I.R.A., N.C.T.E., S.C.B.W.A., B.E.A., M.I.A., N.E.A., Pi Lambda Theta; [oth. writ.] Poems and articles published in Reflections, Inter-Island News, and Journal of the N.J. Teaching Assoc. Self-published a volume, Tidepools.; [a.] New Harbor, ME

WADE, SHERI D.
[pen.] Sheri Wade; [b.] March 8, 1965, Modesto, CA; [p.] Ruth Vance, Gary Wade; [m.] P. Voelker, January 20, 1994; [ed.] Thomas Downey High, Modesto Jr. College.; [occ.] Dental Tech; [memb.] A.A.; [hon.] Won several awards in sports and dancing. A student, High School winner in modelling contest; [oth. writ.] I've written 100's of poems since the age of 4. I love it. I have never been published.; [pers.] I write what I feel every poem is a reflection of me and my experiences. I am greatly inspired by music, music is an emotion.; [a.] Madera, CA

WAGNER, REBECCA L.
[b.] January 10, 1964, Piqua, OH; [p.] Marvin and Delitha Epley; [m.] Chuck Wagner, July 10, 1982; [ch.] Amber Nichole, Chuck Jr., Gregory Allen and Matthew Alan; [ed.] Piqua City School Piqua, OH from 1969-78. Covington School Covington, OH from 1978-82.; [occ.] Homemaker; [memb.] Active in Habit for Humanity.; [oth. writ.] Poem's for my own personal means, as well for family and friends. Other writing interest short stories, plays and songs.; [pers.] To me writing is a wonderful expression of ones thought's and feeling's and the way one see's life, and all things around them.; [a.] Piqua, OH

WAGNER, SANDRA
[b.] May 11, 1946, Albany, NY; [ch.] Brenda and Richard; [pers.] After the loss of my husband, I turned to poetry. By putting into words my emotions, and pain, brought great comfort to me. My husband left me a special gift, the ability to write.; [a.] Cusseta, GA

WAITERS, ERIC EDWARD
[pen.] Eric E. Waiters; [b.] December 6, 1965, New York; [p.] Mr. Ralph E. Waiters and Mrs. Susie M. Waiters; [m.] Mrs. Suleima E. Waiters, July 1995; [ch.] Daughter Ms. Chiquita L. Waiters; [ed.] (H.S.) New York School of printings, U.S. Army 1983-1984 Honorable Discharge, Center for the Media Arts (Audio Engineering); [occ.] Nurses Assistant, Isabella Geriatric Center; [hon.] 2 Appreciation awards for volunteer work at the upper room Aids, ministry in Harlem New York. 1. Army Achievement Medal 2. Good Conduct medals; [oth. writ.] A personal unpublished collection of poetry titled "Paint By Number." All written by Mr. Eric E. Waiters; [pers.] I know how to have sex, it's what comes afterwards. The getting to know you, and I can't get to know you. Until I get to know myself, or I will become you and you will become my life and written "Lost In You"; [a.] New York, NY

WALDEN, J. PAUL
[pen.] J. Paul Walden; [b.] September 26, 1951, Morgantown, WV; [p.] Ben Walden, Freda Walden; [ch.] Kevin James, Joseph Paul; [ed.] Morgantown High, Salem College; [occ.] Assistant Director Finance and Administration West Virginia University, Physical Plant; [memb.] Association of Physical Plant Administrators; [hon.] Magna Cum Laude, Who's Who Among Students in American Universities and Colleges; [oth. writ.] Currently writing a book entitled "It's Hard to Climb Pebble Mountain"; [pers.] No matter what challenge life has in store for us, we must face it with the belief that tomorrow will be a better day.; [a.] Westover, WV

WALKE, DOROTHY
[pen.] D. Daley Walke; [b.] September 20, 1925, Aurora, Ontario, Canada; [p.] Oliver and Lavinia Daley; [m.] James Leslie Walke (dead), July 29, 1956; [ch.] James Oliver Walke; [ed.] Sr. Matriculation, Toronto Normal School, University of Toronto; [occ.] Retired teacher and Case Worker Toronto Soc. Services; [memb.] Alanon (spouse AA) 1961-1974 Aurora Historical Society, 1979-1984; [hon.] General Proficiency Award 5 yrs 1938-1942 Earl Haig C.I.; [oth. writ.] "I remember, I remember" - article about my father. Presently expanding to memoirs a number of poems; [pers.] I enjoy people, good conversation, reading biographies, mysteries, music, my son's writing and paintings. I reflect and try to grow and learn daily.; [a.] Stratford, Ontario, Canada

WALKER, BIRDIE J.
[b.] August 28, 1922, Magnolia, AK; [p.] M. Elina Young, Walter M. Young; [m.] George R. Walker (deceased 1982), October 17, 1942; [ch.] Elizabeth, Carol, George, Patricia, Barbara and Evelyn; [ed.] High School (for me) Harvy C. Couch School, AK; [occ.] Trying to be a loving mom, grandmother and friend; [memb.] Church's Women's Club, TLA (To Live Again), Prayer Group (Light of Intercession); [oth. writ.] None printed. Although through inspiration I have more than one hundred four line poems.; [pers.] The words of my poems vary. Some uplift, encourage some, teach. Others tell what God has done for us and the Beauty of nature; [a.] Deptford, NJ

WALKER, DEBRA JEAN
[pen.] Jean Summerfield; [b.] December 13, 1955, Kingston, NY; [p.] Salvatore and Jean Provenzano; [ch.] 1 son, Christopher Patrick Walker; [ed.] John Jay Senior High School, Dutchess College, Poughkeepsie, New York; [occ.] Property Assets Administrator; [memb.] High School Pep Club, Jr. Varsity Basketball Team, Dollars for Scholars Committee, Leukemia Foundation, Volunteer.; [oth. writ.] I've written poetry, and short stories for close friends; [pers.] For all the Glorious moments of my childhood, I am inspired to write.; [a.] Hopewell Junction, NY

WALKER, GARY
[pen.] G. O. Survivor; [b.] April 2, 1946, Springfield, MA; [p.] Dorothy and Russell; [m.] Mary, July 19, 1968; [ch.] Dorothy Carrie, and Gary A.; [ed.] High School Graduate Technical High Springfield, MA; [occ.] Lock Smith; [hon.] A winter night 50.00 US bond in Junior High School; [oth. writ] Child abuse a road to ruin life as a taxi driver panhandling in style my two grandfathers were brothers I'm sanity alcoholism and several poems; [pers.] I have been writing poetry and stories since I can remember I would like to do it regularly.; [pers.] Bradenton, FL

WALKER, MICKIE LEANN
[b.] October 24, 1963, Colorado Springs, CO; [p.] Barbara and Richard Patton; [m.] Joseph V. Walker, November 27, 1987; [ch.] Meghann Renee, Jacob Ryan; [ed.] Falcon High School 1982, BA - English 1986, Western State College, Gunnison, CO; [occ.] Housewife; [memb.] Co-leader Daisy Girl Scouts, Captain - Recreational Volleyball Team, member - Women's Tennis; [hon.] Full ride scholarship four years at WSC for track "Falcon Girl" honor roll - 4 years. State High Track - 1st place in the 200 dash.; [oth. writ.] Wrote for the "On The Campus" newspaper (sport's stories) at WSC; [pers.] My dream is to publish more poetry and to have a few children's books published. I love to write and enjoy the challenge of utilizing the English language.; [a.] Hayden, CO

WALLACE, CAMILLE
[pen.] Slim; [b.] March 10, 1982, Kingston, Jamaica; [p.] Wayne Wallace, Una Wallace; [memb.] Highlights for Children, Reader's Digest; [hon.] Student of the year, June 17, 1993. Honor Roll. I'm in the Oxford Academy in my school I.S.136.; [pers.] I wrote this poem based on my imagination and some of my dreams.; [a.] New York City, NY

WALLACE, VICTOR
[b.] July 21, 1952, Columbus, OH; [p.] Gloria Jean Michael, Neil L. Michael (Step-father); [m.] Kimberly Kaye Taylor-Wallace, June, 1986; [ch.] Victor Dale, Sonny Michael and Lucky Amanda; [ed.] AA in Soc Sci, Ohio Univ., 1991 AA in Hum Ser, Wilmington Coll, 1994 BA in Psychology, Wilmington Coll, 1995; [occ.] Student/Inmate; [memb.] Red cross, CPR and first aid instructor; [hon.] Dean's lists'; [pers.] Most important! A mother's love...was written for Gloria Jean Michael for mother's day 1990, now dedicated to her loving memory this 19th day of April 1995, marking the blessed day of her passing, by he loving son, Victor "Big Vic" Wallace, an ex-professional boxer with a ring record of 16-8 and a prison Record of 0-3. I love you Mom and I will miss you...; [a.] Columbus, OH

WALLERSTEIN, SUSAN
[b.] April 15, 1972, FL; [p.] Betty and David Wallerstein; [ed.] High, Winston Preparatory College, Sunny New Paltz and Landmark College; [occ.] Student; [hon.] Honor Roll, Dean's List. High School: Drama Award; [oth. writ.] Several poems and short stories. I also wrote my High school senior play, "Time Out".; [pers.] To fully enjoy life, one must first rediscover and childhood and set it free. I continue to be greatly inspired by Sir James M. Barrie and C.S. Lewis, and my writing reflects the inner child in us all.; [a.] New York City, NY

WALLING, JEFFREY G.
[pen.] J. G. Walling; [b.] December 7, 1968, Durant, OK; [p.] Kathy Cheairs, Ronald Walling; [ed.] Evans High School; [occ.] Bellman, Opryland Hotel Nashville, TN; [memb.] Poets Guild; [oth. writ.] "Paper Leaf" published by the Poets Guild "Best New Poems 1994; [pers.] My material focuses on individuals whose lives are forever changed by the most subtle of incidents.; [a.] Hendersonville, TN

WALMSLEY, DEBBIE
[b.] December 10, 1953, Pascagoula, MS; [p.] Tommie and Dorothy Manning; [m.] Steven Walmsley, February 7, 1976; [ch.] Jana Michelle, Stephanie Lyn; [ed.] Pascagoula High; [occ.] Assistant teacher, Arlington Elementary School, Pascagoula, MS; [a.] Pascagoula, MS

WALSH, JEWELL ARDELLE
[b.] August 8, 1937, Bemidji, MN; [p.] Jack and Edna Benson; [m.] Jacob Walsh, August 5, 1955; [ch.] Kristi Marie, Michael Shane, Mark Wayne, Kelly Ann, Shannon Colleen, Ted Andrew, Jacob Maurice, Patrick Henderson; [ed.] Forest Grove High School; [occ.] Homemaker; [memb.] Oregon Right to Life, St. Anthony's Parish (Catholic); [pers.] I want to share the love of God in my poems; [a.] Forest Grove, OR

WALSH SR., JOHN WILLIAM
[pen.] 1995- "Papa Jake"; [b.] August 18, 1924, Roxbury, MA; [p.] John F. and Mary Walsh; [m.] Gladys E. Reardon (deceased), April 7, 1951; [ch.] 2-Girl Donna L. 2/25/64, Boy - John W. Jr. 8/26/65; [ed.] 12 years - Mission Grammar School and High school-Roxbury, MA. (Boston), 18 MO - Boston Univ. Ex. College. 1947-9/1948 - Real Estate Course. No degree but certificate; [occ.] Retired, printer, Linetype Photon operator, Computerized Financial printings; [memb.] St Josephs Church (Catholic) Medford MA., VFW Post 529- Somerville MA., Amvets., AF-Vet, - 20th A.F. Hqs- Gupm Marianas B-29's, In a boy - out as a man Buck Sgt. Intelligence Division and atom Bomb from Tinian Island; [oth. writ.] None published, Readers digest et. Wrote articles for VA-Hospital- Boston. WW II-Stories (True Trivia) Poems and such ask the doctors (Dr. Shocket. Colan); [pers.] I always did things 1-2 and 3- by the numbers in my 70 years. I love music and poetry - as an amateur poet, I write to make people smile or laugh - I'm a jokester. I am a grand father of 2.; [a.] Boston Medford, MA

WALTON, SHARON D.
[pen.] Casi Walton; [b.] December 8, 1961, Saint Louis, MO; [m.] Robert Walton, December 26, 1984; [ch.] Bethlene Nichole, Samantha Walton; [pers.] I love to write poems of, emotions, and spiritual nature. I also am currently writing a book and a novel.; [a.] South Elgin, IL

WANDA, CHRZANOWSKA
[pen.] Iris; [b.] August 3, 1947, Poland; [p.] Michael and Christine Chrzanowska; [ed.] Wroclaw and Warsaw Universities, Poland; [occ.] Teacher and interpreter; [hon.] I'm a debuting author.; [oth. writ.] Short rhymed puzzles published in Polish papers, author of many advertising slogans for Polish cos.; [pers.] Polish romantic and French symbolic poetry are my "guiding lights." My expression is marked by nostalgic hope and faith, hear the music in!; [a.] New York, NY

WANG, PHILEIN
[b.] September 6, 1969, Ann Arbor, MI; [p.] Dr. Ging-Long Wang, Anthena Wang; [ed.] UCLA; [occ.] Modern dancer, choreographer, writer; [memb.] Company member of Winifred R. Harris, between lines, a Modern Dance Company; [hon.] American Dance Festival, Young Artists Scholarship award; [pers.] The process of creating all respective art forms, the act of losing oneself in it, is one of the few forms of freedom I've found in life.; [a.] Sherman Oaks, CA

WARD, BARBARA ANN
[b.] July 4, 1933, MA; [hon.] Silver Poet Award 1990 for This Game of Economics; [oth. writ.] This Game of Economics - published 1985, We Poets published 1985; [pers.] Like Emily Dickenson, most of my work is stuffed into a desk drawer. Like most poets, I write because I have to write!; [a.] North Myrtle Beach, SC

WARD, MRS. TRUDY ARLENE
[b.] October 17, 1952, Newliskeard; [p.] Feda and Roger Belanger; [m.] Art Ward, July 29, 1972; [ch.] Two, Sherry and Joey Ward; [ed.] Grade nine; [occ.] Housewife; [oth. writ.] Many other poems; [pers.] My poems come to me naturally. And I enjoy writing poem's for others my poem's are written from my feelings and love in my heart.; [a.] North Cobalt, Ontario, Canada

WARFE, JENNIFER
[pen.] Jennifer Warfe; [b.] July 22, 1979, San Jose, CA; [p.] Mark and Cynthia Warfe; [ed.] 10th Grade at Del Campo High School; [occ.] Student; [hon.] Honor student, Student Council, AAA award for Basketball. Certificate award for writing a story for the Sacremento Bee.; [oth. writ.] None published; [pers.] I feel that writing poetry helps me express my feelings.; [a.] Carmichael, CA

WARNER, BECKIE
[b.] September 16, 1979, Sault State Marie; [p.] Richard and Carol Warner; [ed.] High School Freshman (now); [occ.] Student; [memb.] Young Author's club, local Y.M.C.A.; [hon.] 2nd - 1st place ribbons in young Author's Club (5th-6th grade), 1st place in area D.A.R.E. poster contests.; [oth. writ.] 2 books for club - "Rainy Day", Taffy and The Polluted Ocean (also illustrated both books), several journals of poems.; [a.] Cassopolis, MI

WARWICK, JOSEPH T.
[b.] March 6, 1956, Fargo, ND; [p.] Dr. Robert and Lu Jean; [ed.] Shanley High, Moorhead State University; [occ.] Poet, Mask maker fungus Painter; [pers.] Disabled since 1975, spends time mask making, painting fungus and writing poetry also creating art out of hidden nature.; [a.] Prescott, AZ

WASHINGTON, ELIZABETH JEAN
[b.] December 25, 1971, Washington, DC; [p.] Nancy O'Glory and Henry B. Washington; [ed.] High School Graduate (Eastern Senior High), Culinary Arts Program, (M.M. Washington); [occ.] Retail Salesperson Gourmet Store; [hon.] Employee of the month (Lawson Gourmet) (most improved student) (honor Roll); [oth. writ.] Written others poetry (not published yet); [pers.] Sunshine was inspired by all the nice, quiet, and peaceful summer days.; [a.] Washington, DC

WATKINS, CARRIE F.
[b.] February 26, 1973, Houston, TX

WATSON, ANNA ELIZABETH
[pen.] E; [b.] October 29, 1979, Charleston, SC; [p.] Harriet and McIver Watson; [ed.] Elizabeth is currently in 9th grade in High School Germantown, TN; [hon.] Black Belt in Karate, President of Church Youth Group, "Honors English" in 9th grade; [oth. writ.]; [pers.] Often times dreams are a representation of life. They express your hopes, goals, and tears, but I believe anything is possible with the love and support of your loved ones. Thanks to all my loved ones!; [a.] Germantown, TN

WATSON, CHARLES R.
[b.] July 11, 1936, Petersburg, MI; [p.] Milo R. and Mary (Cook) Watson; [m.] Janice M. (Haman) Watson, August 9, 1958; [ch.] Gregory David Watson; [ed.] Summerfield High School, Eastern Michigan, Univ., Ypsilanti, Mich. University of Toledo, Toledo, Ohio; [occ.] Fiscal and Budget Officer-Univ. of Toledo-Retired; [memb.] National Fraternity - Theta Chi Sigma, New England Genealogical Society Saint Peters Lutheran Church, My asthenia Gravis Association - Detroit, MI. Chapter; [hon.] National Honor Society, Honor Band, Academic Scholarship; [oth. writ.] Several poems published in local news papers. Children's short stories; [a.] Toledo, OH

WATSON, JENNIFER
[b.] December 19, 1981, Shreveport; [p.] Archie and Rhonda Watson; [ed.] Ridgewood Middle School, Forest Hill Elementary, Youth Writing Project at Louisiana State University - 1993.; [memb.] Fellowship of Christian Athletes, Pep Squad; [hon.] Ridgewood Middle School Principal's Honor Roll, Caddo Parish Career Poetry Contest Winner, State runner up-3rd Grade, Parish and State finalist 5th grade; [oth. writ.] Staff writer for school newspaper-5th grade; [a.] Schreveport, LA

WATTS, JENNY
[pen.] J.; [b.] October 13, 1968, Dallas, TX; [p.] Georgia A. Golden Pitts, James R. Pitts Jr.; [m.] Michael W. Watts, April 21, 1990; [ch.] 1 son, Brandon M. Watts; [ed.] Putnam City West H.S., Rose State College, Oklahoma City Community College; [occ.] Emergency Medical Technician; [pers.] My writing is so dear to me, it is a window to the many different aspects and feelings of my life.; [a.] Oklahoma City, OK

WEATHERS, JACKIE
[b.] October 23, 1939, North Carolina; [p.] Jack and Thelma Robertson; [ch.] Kim Grenwood, Kristi Belote, Beverly Weathers; [ed.] Degree-Art & Design: Fashion Institute of Tech. (NY), degree-Accounting: Dallas Baptist University (TX); [occ.] Advertising Administrator/ Teccor Electronics, Inc.; [memb.] DFW Writers Workshop (Officer), MENSA, Who's Who Worldwide, Toastmasters (Teccor Talkers); [hon.] Who's Who Worldwide, member of MENSA, my paintings have sold all over the U.S., and my commercial art has sold, or been published, worldwide; [oth. writ.] 17 original quotes published in Teleconnect (Int'l. mag.), poem "Ft. Worth Star Telegram" (TX), poem "Metro Singles Lifestyles" (MO), article "Raleigh News & Observer" (NC) plus many others; [pers.] I believe that the more a person is given in talent, brains, money, beauty, etc. -- the more we owe back, the more we should give back to others. [a.] Euless, TX

WEAVER III, ALPHONSO L.
[b.] April 7, 1965, Chicago, IL; [p.] Alphonso Weaver Jr., Carol Godboldo; [m.] Sherrill D. Cooper Weaver, August 26, 1992; [ch.] Shamika, Jonte, Lydell, Brittani; [ed.] Redford High School, Jordan College (Major: Accounting); [occ.] Professional Truck Driver; [memb.] N.A.A.C.P Member, United States Army Vetran; [hon.] Honorable Discharge: U.S. Army Service Ribbon, Overseas Service Ribbon, National Defense Service Medal. Driver badge Sharpshooter marksmanship badge rifle (m-16 rifle); [pers.] I choose this topic so that anyone who reads my poem would get a clear understanding that we are all basically the same inside, and that we should not judge other's by the color of their skin or ethnic.; [a.] Detroit, MI

WEAVER, JOHN R.
[b.] July 24, 1946, Memphis, TN; [ch.] Nicolette LaVee Weaver; [ed.] East Los Angeles College, Univ. of Maryland; [occ.] Retired Police Ofe, Song writer aspirant; [hon.] Above Military awards, Law Enforcement and Educational Dean's List awards. I deem "Eagle Scout" my highest award.; [oth. writ.] "Kinder Than Paradise", "Midnight Cries"; [pers.] My joy is bringing the beauty of the Lord to the hearts of men.; [a.] Denver, CO

WEAVER, NANCY
[b.] June 17, 1948, La Junta, CO; [p.] William and Edith Griffin; [m.] Leland Weaver, May 21, 1967; [ch.] Lori Ann and Dana Jo, Grand "Kids" Jason, Alisha, and Zachary; [ed.] West High-Wichita, KS. Diploma — Paramount High-Paramount, Calif.; [occ.] Housewife and "Bride" of 28 wonderful years!; [memb.] Westside Freewill Baptist Church; [oth. writ.] "Through The Weaver's Needle" (Book printed and sold to friends) 200 sold, "Afterthoughts" - looking for Publisher, of Christian Books.; [pers.] I try to reflect my faith in God and how precious it is to me. I know my poems are given of him and I give him all glory. I have always loved writing and have been influenced by all Christian poets (and songwriters) Examples - Bill Gaither and Helen Steiner Rice.; [a.] Wichita, KS

WEAVER, NELLIE
[b.] April 24, 1923, Vance City; [p.] Julie and Hunter Roberson; [m.] Joe Weaver Jr., April 4, 1941; [ch.] Shirley, Joe III, Layton; [occ.] Housewife; [memb.] Oak Ridge Baptist Church, Sunday School Teacher - 9 years, Bible School Teacher - 5 years; [hon.] Certificate of Completion, The Ambassador College Bible Correspondence Course Award of Merit Certificate for poem "The Little Cloud that Cried"; [pers.] Day Care in home for 5 years wrote and directed Christmas Play at church. Wrote and directed Easter play at church. Visits nursing homes every third Sunday.; [a.] Kittrell, NC

WEBB, KENNETH E.
[b.] December 15, 1924, Montrose, CO; [m.] Patricia M. McHenry, 1952; [ch.] Sharon Arrington, Kim Webb, Sandra Webb; [ed.] Completed High School Education in Ocala, FL, 1946.; [occ.] Worked with Farrens Tree Surgeons 1946-1989.; [memb.] Life member of V.F.W. American Legion, and D.A.V., Active in V.F.W. Post 49 25 years. Trustee 9 years. Active in American Legion Post 76 20 years.; [oth. writ.] Started trying to write poetry in 1967 when Lurleen Wallace became Governor of Alabama. Wrote 25 verses about the inauguration. Resided in Mobile, Ala. 1957-1983.; [a.] Hernando, FL

WEBB, KENNETH E.
[b.] December 15, 1924, Stewartstown, PA; [p.] Walter Webb, Irene Webb; [m.] Patricia Webb, February 1, 1952; [ch.] Sharon, Kim, Sandra; [ed.] Ocala High, Business Management U. of S. Ala., Driving Instructor, First Aid Instructor, Licened Tree Surgeon.; [occ.] Retired Now. Employed by Farrens Tree Surgeons for 42 years.; [memb.] Life member V.F.W. Post 49 active 25 years, life member American Legion Post 76 active 20 years, life member D.A.V. Chapter 70, Member Pi-Kappa-Phi.; [oth. writ.] I have wrote aprox. 200 poems since 1967. Did not enter any of them in competition before.; [pers.] Grew up on our homestead S.W. of Montrose, Colo. Moved to Fla. in 1937. Was in the Army Air Corps 1943-1946 Flight Engineer on B-25. Was inspired to write poetry from my mother, she wrote poetry all of her life. One was put to music.; [a.] Hernando, FL

WEBB, VICKIE R.
[pen.] Stormi Dae; [b.] February 4, 1961, Pawhuska, OK; [p.] John and Myra Shea; [m.] John E. Webb, September 5, 1980; [ch.] Jennifer Renee, Matthew Edward; [ed.] Graduate of Titusville High, Titusville, FL, Florida Community College at Jacksonville; [occ.] Homemaker,

Free lance Graphic Artist; [hon.] Jacksonville Club Gallery of Superb Printing Judges award; [oth. writ.] Numerous unpublished poems and children stories; [pers.] With a big heart and a strong will - dreams become reality.; [a.] Yulee, FL

WEBBER, LISA A.
[b.] October 8, 1965, Oakland, CA; [p.] Barbara Webber, Harold Webber; [ed.] Marina High School; [occ.] Secretary; [memb.] Wayward Hayward Jaycees; [pers.] The only way to let some emotions out is through my writing. It relieves loneliness or shows the happiness in my life.; [a.] San Leandro, CA

WEESE, SANDRA
[b.] August 10, 1948, Skowhegan, ME; [p.] Janet and Hurley Fletcher; [m.] Gary Weese, August 20, 1966; [ch.] Stephanie, Gary II, John, Jessica, Liza, James; [occ.] Certified Nursing Assistant; [pers.] I wrote this poem to bring comfort to my own mind, and perhaps to others who have lost loved members of there families; [a.] Norridgewock, ME

WEIDNER, KENNETH W.
[b.] February 28, 1941, Alexandria, VA; [p.] Elsa and William Weidner; [ch.] Matthew D. Weidner; [ed.] AB, William and Mary 1963; [occ.] Landscape Supervisor, Work Oriented Rehabilitation Center (WORC); [hon.] Geo Wash. University High School Discussion Confercе Scholarship '59 Sang opera with Jan Pearce and Roberta Peeters '65; [oth. writ.] "Courageous Crusader for Peace" Phila Inquirer, Nov. 26, 1963. "Successful Vegetable Gardening" July 1973; [pers.] Success in life is in being the best you can be; [a.] Ormond Beach, FL

WEINBERG, JEREMY JASON
[b.] July 16, 1980, Fredrick, MD; [p.] Patricia Hill Walberg and Brian R. Weinberg; [ch.] Ryan and Mark Weinberg (half-brothers), Steven Walberg (step-brother); [ed.] Hyde Park, and Red Hook NY Central School currently (1994-1995) in Middle School; [occ.] Student; [memb.] Third Evangelical Lutheran Church, Rhinebeck, NY; [oth. writ.] Poems published in local newspapers; [a.] Red Hook, NY

WEISS, DOUGLAS
[b.] June 7, 1959, Webster City, IA; [p.] Jim and Donna Weiss; [ed.] BA in English from Buena Vista College in Storm Lake, IA with a minor in Business Administration; [occ.] Working on my MFA in Creative Writing at Mankato St Univ. in Mankato, MN; [hon.] Hope to win this contest; [oth. writ.] None other published; [pers.] I think Anais Nin said it best: "The artist is not there to be at one with the world, he is there to transform it."; [a.] Mankato, MN

WEISSMULLER, NANCY R.
[b.] October 2, 1939, Providence, RI; [p.] Louis D. and Laura M., Richardson; [m.] Walter T. Weissmuller, November 24, 1962; [ch.] Heather Anne and Thomas Walter; [ed.] Cranston High School University of Rhode Island, BS and MA; [occ.] 2nd grade teacher No. Stonington Elementary School; [memb.] Audubon Society, Mystic Marinelife Aquarium, Mystic Seaport, Wood - Pawcatuck Watershed, Denison Pequotsepos Nature Center, No. Stonington Grange; [hon.] Phi Kappa Phi, Omicron Nu; [oth. writ.] Poems published in children's magazines (Jack and Jill, Children's Playmate) Article in Bird Watcher's Digest; [pers.] The children are our hope for the future. We must teach them to hold our world carefully in their hands.; [a.] North Stonington, CT

WELCH, AMY L.
[b.] November 8, 1966, Norwood, MA; [p.] Francis and Patricia Welch; [ed.] Cedarville College; [occ.] Registered Nurse; [memb.] American Nurses Association, American Association of Critical Care Nurses; [pers.] Much of my poetry reflects on the power of our natural surroundings and its impact on the human spirit.; [a.] San Francisco, CA

WELLS, MARJORIE
[pen.] Marge Wells; [b.] November 7, 1925, Potosi, MO; [p.] Orvil and Daphna Sheppard; [m.] Even Peace Wells, January 1, 1947; [ch.] Brenda Kay Wells, Marshall Lynn Wells; [ed.] 10th Grade; [occ.] Retired; [memb.] Potosi Full Gospel Church; [oth. writ.] Children's short stories religious stories write for local paper weekly have sold very little; [pers.] I wrote this poem he is there back in the seventies. It was truly inspired by God. Was going through a great trial.; [a.] Potosi, MO

WELLS, ROBERT B.
[b.] March 19, 1957, NY; [p.] Florence Wells; [m.] Vicki Wells, September 11, 1993; [ed.] Farmingdale Senior High UNLV; [occ.] Bartender Harrahs Hotel and Casino Las Vegas, NV; [memb.] United Way; [hon.] Chairman's Award, winner Community Service 1991; [oth. writ.] Poems to my wife; [pers.] Writing opens all doors to the world. Its through writing in which we learn about one another. Writing tells of life all life. Writing is universal.; [a.] Las Vegas, NV

WELLS, TERRY L.
[pen.] T. L. Wells; [b.] July 7, 1955, OR; [p.] Donald and Patricia Wells; [ed.] Sweet Home High School, Portland Community College; [occ.] Health Care Technician, aspiring poet and writer; [memb.] State Board of Nursing, Oregon State Poetry Assn. (Portland Chapter), Willamette Writers Assn.: Alzheimer's Society, Willamette-Columbia Parkinsonian Society.; [hon.] Navy Unit Citation; [pers.] "I believe it's what a person becomes in later life, that guides their path.; [a.] Portland, OR

WENGER, HARRY
[b.] October 30, 1920, Pennsylvania; [p.] Laban and Ruth Wenger; [m.] Dorothy, July 31, 1941; [ch.] Ronald, Patricia, Donna, Robert, Pamela, Daryl; [ed.] High School, Shippensburg University, B.S. in Ed, certified in French Eng.. and Latin; [occ.] Retired; [memb.] Church of the Brethren, Chambersburg, PA; [oth. writ.] Published a book of poems (small one); [pers.] I am a devote Christian and have an established philosophy of life with which to rear an intelligent, virtuous family; [a.] Fayetteville, PA

WENLOCK, CHRISTOFFER HENDRIK
[b.] June 23, 1975, Frederiksberg, Denmark; [p.] Nancy and Michael Wenlock [ed.] West High; [occ.] Student, tutor of dyslexic students; [memb.] National Civilian Community Corp (NCCC); [hon.] Principal's Honor Roll, Center of International Studies ambassador of the year '93-'94; [oth. writ.] Nothing previously published; [pers.] I pursue to have my poems reflect new boundaries of spirituality, allowing ourselves to cognize and confront the powers within us, as a being and mind. Thereupon, I leave grace, patience, unlearned knowledge, self exploration, reality, and spiritual freedom for all those who believe in themselves. [a.] Denver, CO

WENNERSTROM, RITA
[b.] December 19, 1931, Saint Louis, MO; [p.] Margaret (deceased) and Marion Svendrowski; [m.] Divorced; [ed.] St. Gabriel St. Louis, MO, Rosati-Kain (High School, St. Louis, MO) Harris Jr. College St. Louis, MO, Tekniskvuxengymnasiet, Goteborg, Sweden; [occ.] Eligibility Worker; [oth. writ.] 40 poems and a few autobiographical essays; [pers.] I began writing poetry while teaching English as a first language in Goteborg, Sweden, where I lived for 30 yrs, and only returned six yrs. ago to the States.; [a.] South Pasadena, CA

WEST, MELISSA
[b.] October 13, 1977, Park Rapids, MN; [p.] Russ and Linda West; [ed.] H.S. Student/Junior; [occ.] Full time student employed by the Dairy Queen; [memb.] E. Club, journalism, class treasurer; [hon.] Varsity Girls Basketball and Varsity Boys Basketball Head Cheerleader; [oth. writ.] Unpublished poetry; [pers.] I base most of my poems on personal experiences. I tend to learn toward the romantic experiences.; [a.] Ennis, MT

WESTIN, CARY S.
[b.] May 10, 1963, Minneapolis, MN; [p.] Jack Westin, Marilyn Westin; [m.] Laurie Westin, June 1, 1985; [ch.] Jennifer Michelle, Jessica Ann; [ed.] Blake High School, Virginia Military Institute, Bachelor of Arts-English; [occ.] U.S. Army Officer; [hon.] Bronze Star, Meritorious Service Medal, Army Commendation Medal, Army Achievement Medal, Desert Storm Campaign Ribbon, Humanitarian Service Medal, Liberation Medal, Deans list; [oth. writ.] Several poems published in college literary magazines.; [pers.] I have been greatly influenced and inspired by my college writing professor and friend, the late T.Y. Greet.; [a.] Huntsville, AL

WESTOVER, DAVID A.
[b.] July 6, 1942, Wilmington, DE; [p.] David and Evelyn Westover; [ed.] B.A. (History), B.A. (Russian), Certificate (Russian Area Studies): Pennsylvania State University: 1968.; [occ.] Seasonal ocean front hotel auditor.; [memb.] National Cathedral Ass'n, Penn State Alumni Ass'n, National Geographic Society, The Planetary Society; [oth. writ.] Over the years, I have published poems and articles in The Pittsburgh Press, Lebanon Cedars, Pivot Poetry Annual, Morning Breeze, and Beachweek Magazine.; [pers.] I am currently seeking a commercial publisher for my novel Crab Nebula, a gothic novel of the Cold War.; [a.] Lewes, DE

WHIPPLE, MARTY
[pen.] Marty, Martha Whipple; [b.] January 11, 1962, Oregon; [p.] Evelyn Roe, Fredrick Cantrell; [m.] Russell Whipple, January 20, 1986; [ch.] Daniel and Tiffany; [ed.] Samuel Clemens High School, St. Philips College TX; [occ.] Consultant for special education; [memb.] Herman Sons Epilepsy and Local Chapters; [hon.] 1st Place Soloist Medal, U.I.L Trinity University 1978; [oth. writ.] Numerous Poems, philosophical comments, lyrics and other writings; [pers.] All my poetry is inspired either by personal experience, people or events in my life. My social consciousness runs deep and is reflected in my writings. "Sweet kindred spirit" was inspired by my Kindred Spirit Michelle Baur.; [a.] Converse, TX

WHITAKER, ANNETTE
[b.] December 21, 1959, Houston; [p.] Lamar and Jackson, Shirley; [m.] Donald Ray Whitaker, February 14, 1980; [ch.] Raenetra Monique and Devin Jamere; [ed.] Forest Brook Sr. High., Houston Community College, Major Finance, Our Lady of the Lake University, major - Business Administration (OLLW); [hon.] Cum Laude; [oth. writ.] Poems unpublished in "Dusting off Dreams

VII, in 1994 and "Echoes from the Silence, 1995; [pers.] My endeavor as a poet is to express the facets of reality from the eyes of a believer and a survivor.; [a.] Houston, TX

WHITAKER, PRISCILLA
[b.] 1930; [ed.] The 1990's Liberal Arts Degree; [oth. writ.] Writing/Publishing into the 30's that's 2,000 and...; [pers.] I know that every experience that has been felt before has been expressed adequately, even brilliantly, before, but it has not been expressed by me, and until I can express it, experience has really only happened to me, not in me.; [a.] Fremont, CA

WHITE, ETHEL FAYE
[b.] May 28, 1942; [p.] Mr. and Mrs. W. G. Townsend; [m.] Alan V. White, January 18, 1964; [ch.] Mark Alan White (5-30-69), Kimberly Faye White (1-25-73); [ed.] Buna High School, Lamar University, Tomball College; [occ.] Homemaker; [oth. writ.] The One Who Needs It Most. This Planet Earth, A Chance to Teach, Prayers of Faith, A Teacher Named Dolly; [pers.] I attend ladies Bible Class at the Magnolia Church of Christ. This poem was written as a result of our study on prayer this year.; [a.] Hockley, TX

WHITE, LERIN MCKENNI
[b.] March 7, 1981, Tulsa, OK; [p.] Dale and Terri White; [ed.] Preschool - Memorial Church of Christ Elementary, Carl Sandburg Middle School - Lewis and Clark; [occ.] 8th grade student; [memb.] Student Council Vice President, yearbook staff, dance committee, Pep Club cheerleading, Pom Squad, Cornerstone chorus, drama group, Garnett Youth Group; [hon.] Student of the Year, 6th place National Dance Comp., painting featured at Gilcrease Museum of Art, 3 awards for Creative Poetry (school), voted "Best-All-Around" by 8th grade class; [oth. writ.] 2 children's "Samples" (Tulsa Schools publication), multiple published poems in Tulsa Tribune, small volume of poetry for the family, several unpublished writings.; [pers.] "Don't be worried about wordly matters, but hold fast to what really counts - family, love and God." My grandpa Orvind white is also in this anthology! Runs in the family.; [a.] Tulsa, OK

WHITE, MARLENE MICHEL
[b.] January 22, 1951, Haiti; [ch.] I have four sons, Reynold, James, Omar and Ali; [ed.] 2 years at City College, New York for Electrical Engineering; [occ.] Electronic Technician U.S. postal service, morgan, GMF, NYC.; [pers.] From childhood, many times in an answer to my letters, it would be an encouragement to write poetry. But, I was really inspired by a poem "Love" dedicated to me by my sons, James and Omar. (I write poetry in French and English); [a.] Corona, Queens NY

WHITE, MARVIN H.
[pen.] Marvin H. White; [b.] June 9, 1910, Killeen, TX; [p.] David and Carew White; [m.] Marcella Reedy White, April 27, 1943; [ch.] David, Richard and Randolph; [ed.] H.S. Peacock, TX., B.A. Howard Payne College, ThM Southwestern Baptist Theo. Seminary, F.S.U.; [occ.] Retired Minister and Math Teacher; [memb.] Myrtle Grove United Meth. Church, Pensacola, FL., Escambia Math Teachers Assoc., REEA., FREA., AARP; [oth. writ.] Various poems published in weekly newspapers. Privately published book of poems "simple Words"; [pers.] I strive to express the greatness and goodness of God and the great blessings that come to men by worshipping him, through my poems.; [a.] Pensacola, FL

WHITE, PATRICIA MARSH
[pen.] Patricia White; [b.] July 26, 1940, Springfield, MA; [p.] John U. and Carolyn R. Marsh; [ch.] Robert J. White, Carrie Lee Powers; [ed.] New London High School and 24 schools previously; [occ.] Antique shop/ owner and Holiday Inn; [oth. writ.] 100's of poems and short stories; [pers.] I write because I feel or care about the people or things in the miles of pink on bits of paper.; [a.] Rose Bud, AR

WHITING, ANN C.
[b.] June 5, 1940; [p.] Lillian Morel Porter and Ewartg Porter; [ch.] Ian B. Whiting, Nathan E. Whiting, Sonja K. Whiting; [ed.] Lawrence High, Beverly Hospital School of Nursing, McGill University; [occ.] Field Supervisor, Hme Health Registry, Clinical Nursing instructor, patient educator; [memb.] Suncoast of Tampa Bay, Tri-county Ig Association, Unity Church of Port Richey Volunteer Assoc.; [oth. writ.] Numerous poems and short prose - published poem by NSCC yearly bulletin; [pers.] My poetry come after a spiritual experience in 1983 and reflects deep emotion and often pain. Often the poems come about in whole pieces - not necessarily from me but form a spirit within me; [a.] Clearwater, FL

WHITLES, LEONA
[pen.] Leanne Wright; [p.] William and Ethel Whitlock; [m.] Divorced; [ch.] Brenda, Rick, Brian, Dwayne and Sharry.; [ed.] Received my grade 9th Diploma than continue my education have completed part of grade 12. After my children were grown.; [occ.] Clerk in an Antique Store.; [memb.] Security officer. I.P.I. Certificate as well as certificates for some courses I completed.; [oth. writ.] Several poems published in the local news papers. Re. the antique store where I am employed at present.; [pers.] Most of the poems and stories I have written are written from the heart. The way I have been reflected by certain thing or the way I see others. I try to make my readers realize there is good in every one we all have a goal, to accp.; [a.] Camrose, Canada

WHITLOW, LILLIAN
[m.] Deceased, July 1, 1951; [ch.] Leo P. Whitlow, Leon J. Whitlow and Leona Whitlow Brown; [ed.] B.A. Degree in music, M.A. Degree in Elementary Education); [occ.] Retired School Teacher, Writer; [memb.] Saint Catholic Church, Alpha Kappa Alpha Sorority, Inc., President of Portland Federation of Women's Organizations, Willamette Writers and Northwest African American Writer's Workshop.; [hon.] "Outstanding Citizen of Dedication from Multnomah Women's Club, top 10 in poetry by U.S. Bank for Black History Month; [oth. writ.] Several poems, plays skits, short story and novel "Brick City" to he released from press Oct. 5, 1995.; [pers.] I strive to learn from yesterday, live for today, dream for tomorrow.; [a.] Portland, OR

WHITMORE, YVONNE R.
[pen.] Y. Regina Whitmore; [b.] January 11, 1955, Chicago, IL; [p.] John and Helen Whitmore; [ed.] Chicago State University, Cook County School of Nursing; [occ.] R.N. at C.I.N.N.; [memb.] American Assoc. of Neuro-Science Nursing; [oth. writ.] Several poems and short stories; [pers.] For me to stop imagining, and writing is to condemn my arias to absolute silence. With help from my mentors: Cynthia A. White and Dr. Vladimir Tkalcevic, I shall sing always.; [a.] Chicago, IL

WHITNER, ROGER DALE
[b.] November 29, 1952, Waynesville, NC; [p.] D.A. Whitner and Ruby Parton Whitner; [ed.] Tuscola Tuscola School 2 quarters, Haywood Community College, Business Administration; [occ.] Dayco Corp. 23 yrs.; [oth. writ.] Several poems only 1 other published in the Haywood County Heritage book vol. 1 a memorial to my mother titled "Guardian Angel"; [pers.] I feel there is "art", in living life. I think art is all around us. It is ever moving through the generations it is in all of God's creations, animals, plants, our earth, universe and you and I.; [a.] Waynesville, NC

WHITTINGTON, CATHERINE
[m.] Donnie Whittington; [ch.] 4 children; [ed.] High School, Trade School; [memb.] America Heart Associate, North Chore Animal League, American Cancer Associate Church contribute

WHITWORTH, CLARENCE O.
[b.] June 3, 1940, St. Louis; [p.] Charles Allen, Martha Ann; [m.] Rosalie Marie, September 15, 1962; [ch.] Richard Charles - Matthew Todd - Lisa Charmaine; [ed.] Pattonsville High School, Jr. College; [occ.] Const. Drywall Taper; [pers.] To uplift my fellow man

WIERZBICKI, MICHAEL E.
[pen.] "Mick #7"; [b.] June 2, 1954, Maspeth Queens, NY; [p.] Stanley J., Madeline R. (Maiden Lynch); [m.] Marija F. (Maiden-Stungurys), June 17, 1983; [ch.] Michael (19), Marlena (17), Bryan (11), Bradd (10), Brett (10); [ed.] High School Diploma Christ the King H.S., Middle Village, NY; [occ.] Traffic Device Maintainer N.Y.C. D.O.T.; [memb.] Founder and Director of Transfiguration Youth Sports Program. Currently applying for Knights of Columbus; [hon.] Various youth services awards; [oth. writ.] Songs written for my past band "Crystal Rose". File consists of 100 poems and songs; [pers.] My writings reflect personal experiences in my life. I believe in touching a person's life through my poems and have them relate to their own lives; [a.] Maspeth, NY

WIGAL, DONALD
[pen.] Silas Wegg; [b.] January 16, 1933, Indianapolis, IN; [p.] Wayne and Louise Wigal; [ed.] U.P. Dayton, U. of Notre Dane, Columbia Pacific U. Institute for Spiritual Theology; [occ.] Information specialist; [memb.] ASCAP, Editorial Freelance Assn.., Spondylitis Assn..; [hon.] Distinguish Alumnus Award, U. of Dayton; [oth. writ.] Experiences in Faith (Herder and Herder), general knowledge (Coleco), Smidget (Xerox) New York time Encyclopedia of film (volume 13), Published a poetry anthology titled Love in New York.; [pers.] We are spiritual beings experiencing a brief human mode. Animals remind us of our post while angels introduce us to our future.; [a.] New York City, NY

WIGGINS, DOLORES ANNE
[b.] March 12, 1945, Bemidji, MN; [p.] Ben and Dorothy Weis; [m.] Charles, July 3, 1982; [ch.] Barbara June and Gary Leland; [ed.] Mount St. Benedict Academy High School and Approximately 2 years of College at Bemidji State University; [occ.] Accountant for Beltrami County Highway Department; [memb.] Poet's Guild, Ridgewood Baptist Church; [oth. writ.] I am in the process of having a book of poetry published; [pers.] Most of my poems are spiritual in content; [a.] Bemidji, MN

WILEY, LEAH K.
[b.] April 11, 1959, Atlanta, GA; [p.] Ronald and Jean Johnson; [ch.] Tony and Kevin; [ed.] Graduate; [occ.] Poet; [hon.] Dance and poetry and friends; [oth. writ.] "You'll never even notice"..."I'm gonna go on believ-

ing"; [pers.] May your days be energy and dance, and your night's poetry and chance!; [a.] Newnan, GA

WILKES, EDWARD BLAKE
[pen.] Ed Wilkes; [b.] October 19, 1959, Niagra Falls, NY; [p.] James Wilkes, Joann Heartbridge; [m.] Divorced, June 14, 1980; [ch.] Kelly Marie, Shelly Lynn, Edward Blake Jr. Eric Patrick, Billie Jean Marie; [ed.] Attended Mohawk Valley Community College, currently studying at Emmaus Bible College PA, Stately High School and Dewitt Clinton Elementary Rome NY; [occ.] Painter; [memb.] Inventors club suny college marcy campus, Moose Lodge Home, NY.; [oth. writ.] Wind of a friend, understanding several others yet to seek publication; [pers.] Without the encouragement of my caring grandmother Florence, I may have never submitted anything for publication, my writings center on real life experiences of myself and others. I stated writing poetry at 13.; [a.] Rome, New York

WILLEY, MARY K.
[b.] Bristow, OR; [p.] Walter C. Williams and Della; [m.] Elmer W. Willey, May 24, 1947; [ch.] One daughter, deceased 1984, and two sons Steven and James; [ed.] High School and a tech. School class in Floral design at Platt College in Tulsa, OR; [occ.] Retired Clerk, Wife - mother - Grandmother and great grandmother; [memb.] W.C.G. (are) women of the Church of God, DAR, Angelette as a wife of an 11th Airborne WWII Veteran servings as "Historian."; [hon.] Perfect attendance award from Platt College. Honor adult III teacher in South Sand Springs Church of God.; [oth. writ.] "My memories" published in a "moment in time by" by the National Library of Poetry. Also some in our High School newspaper at Briston, OR. 1940.; [pers.] I have been raised by my special Christian parents and taught to deal with joy, sorrow and pain and grief. God being in control. I can open up my heart in a poem on paper where I can't talk.; [a.] Tulsa, OR

WILLIAMS, BEVERLY AN
[b.] Brooklyn, NY; [p.] Cornelia Williams and Lester Williams; [m.] Gabriel Esquilin, February 8, 1984; [ch.] David Gabriel Esquilin, Ezekiel Taylor Esquilin; [ed.] John Jay High School, Kingsborough Community College.; [occ.] Peace officer, Fashion Industries High School Board of Education.; [memb.] Bethel Baptist Church; [pers.] Live life to the fullness and love, others with your best.; [a.] Brooklyn, NY

WILLIAMS, BRONTE
[b.] October 4, 1955, Philadelphia, PA; [p.] Elmire and Theodore Price; [ch.] Mark Resinol Montanez, Grand Nore, Desira, Marquis Marquan; [ed.] Germantown, Wilfred Academy; [occ.] I.R.S Reviewer; [memb.] Women Federal Committee; [oth. writ.] Galaxy Heaven, Nam. Misty Passion, 9-15-94, Patience Indeed, I Could Love You, In Touch Warmth, Southern Values, Love U Sweet Juices, Statement of Thought, Destiny.; [pers.] Loving oneself bring out the best of what life can give we are all bless with a talent but we have to learn and seek what it is.; [a.] Philadelphia, PA

WILLIAMS, CAMILLE
[b.] April 25, 1979, Bahamas; [p.] Calvin and Maryann Williams; [ed.] Secondary School Student; [occ.] Student; [a.] Freeport, Bahamas

WILLIAMS, CLARENCE
[b.] June 6, 1954, Philadelphia, PA; [p.] Eugene and Drucilla Williams; [ed.] Simon Gratz High, CEI Tech. School, Philadelphia PA.; [occ.] Computer Operator; [memb.] The National Treasury Employees Union, T.E.P.A.C. Association; [hon.] My first poem published with the national library of poetry; [oth. writ.] Several poems unpublished; [pers.] For some people to write is to communicate to communicate is to write; [a.] Philadelphia, PA

WILLIAMS, DEBORAH R.
[pen.] McCovey; [b.] April 22, 1949, La Jolla, CA; [p.] Alfred and Marguerite Balsley; [m.] John A. Williams (deceased) May 24, 1969; [ch.] Marjorie Ann Williams (21); [ed.] Mount Miguel H.S., Steven Career College; [occ.] Retail Vendor and Night Auditor; [oth. writ.] Unpublished; [pers.] Always look for the love and goodness in each person you meet and know special thanks to V. Fitzpatrick for encouragement and faith and my family for letting me dream.; [a.] Lemon Grove, CA

WILLIAMS, DENA
[b.] October 8, 1980, Philadelphia; [p.] Debra Williams, Keith Copper; [ed.] George Washington High School; [memb.] Lady like Production; [hon.] Creative written; [oth. writ.] "Confused" and "If it's over"

WILLIAMS, EDWARD M.
[b.] February 11, 1931, Rose Hill, NC; [p.] Samuel P. and Laura A. Williams; [ed.] Acquired Education from Private Studies; [occ.] Missionary; [memb.] Seventh Day Adventist Church of Raleigh, National Writers Association, Articles in Church News letters; [oth. writ.] Three Angels, In As Much, The Beautiful Rose of Sharon, The Homeward Bound; [pers.] I draw most of my inspirational thoughts from the holy scriptures especially the sermon on the mount, the golden rule, and the book of nature; [a.] Relaigh, NC

WILLIAMS, LEONARD M.
[pen.] Leonard Williams; [b.] June 16, 1925, Dale Co., AL; [p.] Archie Williams, Alma Vinson Williams; [m.] Bettie Hagler Williams, December 23, 1948; [ch.] Kent Lewis Williams, Tim Bradley Williams; [occ.] Quality Control Coordinator, Rebwood Furniture Company, Headland, AL; [memb.] Napier Baptist Church; [oth. writ.] Many unpublished poems and songs.; [pers.] My writing generally reflects life as we live it.; [a.] Dothan, AL

WILLIAMS, LINDA J.
[b.] November 1, 1946, Drumright, OK; [p.] Cleo and Ruby Bateman; [m.] Charlie Williams, August 30, 1969; [ch.] C.R. Williams (Wife Jan), Lory Estep (Husband Mark); [ed.] Oilton High School - 1963 (OK.), B.A. Liberal Arts, OK. City University December, 1994; [occ.] Executive Secretary to Plant Manager at General Motors Assembly Plant in OK. City.; [memb.] Professional Secretaries International; [hon.] Certified Professional Secretary; [oth. writ.] Personal letters and poems to each of my grandchildren about the day they were born and their first year of life.; [pers.] My grandchildren are my greatest inspiration and influence: Trevin Estep - 7, Brandy Estep - 5, Timmy Williams - 1, and two more due in 1995; [a.] McLoud, OK

WILLIAMS, MEGAN
[pen.] Megs, Airborne; [b.] April 12, 1981, Columbia, AL; [p.] Patsy McMillem and James Williams; [ed.] Eastern York High School; [occ.] Student; [memb.] Girl Scout, Eastern Talks Newspaper, National Geographic Society; [hon.] Several badges and pins for scouts, two for best drawings in th class; [pers.] Practice what you want to be you might just make it. Influenced by: Edgar Allen Poe.; [a.] Wrightsville, PA

WILLIAMS, STEPHANIE LYNN
[b.] March 26, 1969, Wilkesboro, NC; [p.] Jack and Neta Williams; [ch.] Karye Jeanette Williams, Dustin Clinton Call; [ed.] Wilkes Fast High 10th grade; [occ.] Tyson Foods, (fresh plant) (poultry); [oth. writ.] Several poems wrote, waiting for someone to publish.; [pers.] Poems were wrote from experience and feelings from my own life and from the love of both of my deceased parents of whom I'll always respect and love.; [a.] Wilkesboro, NC

WILLIAMSON, SHIRLEY ANN
[b.] February 15, 1963, Sparks, NV; [p.] Mildred Svehla and Lee Berry; [m.] Johnny Lee Williamson, September 24, 1988; [ch.] Steven Williamson, Tiffany Williamson, Sonya LeeAnn Williamson; [ed.] High School and got my G.E.D. Modesto (MJC) I took a writing course. Wrote on the subject of "Why I did not believe that there should be a death penalty; [occ.] Photography; [memb.] P.T.A; [hon.] I have one in a contest before, when I wrote true friends. I also one first place on a California Swimming Team; [oth. writ.] I had several of my poems published in different magazines. True friends, time, colors, family; [pers.] If there is one statement that I try to get across in my poetry it would be, in every thing that you do let it come from the heart; [a.] Turlock, CA

WILLIS, LISA HART
[pen.] Lisa Hart Willis; [b.] October 1, 1958, Dallas; [p.] James Hart, Willis Jr., Terry Armstrong Willis; [ed.] B.A. Rice University '81 Hockaday Preparatory School '76 Sorbonne, Pan's, France '75 University Of North Texas '76 Southern Methodist University '74; [occ.] Public Relations consultant/President Willis public relations; [memb.] The International Society D/FW, Dallas Council on world affairs, Press Club of Dallas, Junior League of Dallas, Dallas Garden Society, The International Podium Society, The United Nations Association; [hon.] Who's who of Emerging leaders in America 1992, who's who among young professionals 1991, outstanding young woman of America 1991, Who's Who of American women 1991, Cardinal Mindszenty Freedom Award 1990, Who's Who of Women Executives 1989, Outstanding Young Woman of America 1987 President's Honor Roll 1976 -1981 J. Rorick Cravens 1978, Benjamin A. Shepherd Award in music 1977, Whittles Music Cup 1976, Orville Thorpe French Cup 1976; [oth. writ.] Articles in the Dallas Morning news and other dailies, weekly's and monthly's, locally and regionally.; [pers.] "God is a concept by which we measure ourselves, therefore let us strive to emulate perfection."; [a.] Dallas, TX

WILLIS, STEVE
[b.] May 7, 1959, Danville, VA; [p.] Paul Willis, Rebecca D. Willis; [ed.] Averett College, University of North Carolina at Greensboro; [occ.] Theatre Director, Instructor; [memb.] North Carolina Writer's Network, Dramatist's Guild; [hon.] Alpha Chi, Magna Cum Laude graduate, Paul Green Playwright's Prize (Honorable Mention); [oth. writ.] Poems published in various literary journals, plays produced locally.; [pers.] Writing teaches me about myself. My writing is often very personal, but I am never shy about sharing it with others.; [a.] High Point, NC

WILSON, ANITA LEOLA JAMES
[pen.] Anita James Wilson; [b.] December 27, 1947,

Orlando, FL; [p.] Motez Nixon-James Alonzo Blaine James, Jr.; [ch.] Theodore Alonzo Wilson; [ed.] St. Francis deSales High School Powhatan, Virginia Rollins College, Winter Park, FL; [occ.] Secretary, Walt Disney CO.; [memb.] Actor's Equity Association (25 yrs) Soka Gakkai U.S.A./International (8 yrs) (Value Creation/ World Peace Organization); [hon.] 10 years Service Award Outstanding Achievement in acting ('88), Most Dedicated Female Performer, Best Entertainment Awards (1983): The Walt Disney Co. Best Director Freddie Award ('80) Rollins College, AUDELCO Certificate of Excellence, Best Supporting Actress ('77-78: NYC); [oth. writ.] Unpublished: 1) Collaboration with William Shakespeare, (1) Musical Drama, (15) Songs (music and lyrics), (1) collective work (prose and poetry), and (1) non-commissioned screen treatment; [pers.] I hope my life and work encourages and inspires peace and harmony. To contribute greatly to the protection and healthy healing of our global community and the environment is my daily prayer.; [a.] Orlando, FL

WILSON, ERNESTINE L.
[b.] March 31, 1935, Clinton, MA; [p.] Raymond and Lillian Fay; [m.] Joseph Wilson, June 22, 1962; [ch.] Rhonda, Roger, Douglas, Joseph, Christopher, Daniel; [ed.] Grammar High School, Nursing, Business; [occ.] Data Entry for Mass Mutual Life Ins Co.; [memb.] Mother against drunk drivers; [oth. writ.] Prepare speeches for mother against drunk driving and than present; [pers.] I like the world to feel the love I have specially my children and spouse, peace and sadness yet acceptance; [a.] Palmer, MA

WILSON, JENNIFER LYNN
[b.] May 3, 1977, St. Petersburg, FL; [ed.] Flat Rock High School; [occ.] Student, Alderson-Broaddus College, Philippi, WV; [memb.] Concert choir, drama club, students against drunk driving; [hon.] National Merit Finalist, National English Merit Award, selected to attend Michigan Department of Education Summer Institute for creative writing; [oth. writ.] Numerous poems and short stories, none yet published; [pers.] I believe poems should be ways of finding words for those things for which words cannot be found.; [a.] Flat Rock, MI

WILSON, LAVONNE
[b.] February 20, 1949, Detroit, MI; [p.] Albert and Lena Broadnax; [m.] Earnest Wilson Sr, October 26, 1968 (divorced); [ch.] Earnest Wilson Jr.; [ed.] Western High Detroit, MI, Carter H. Harrison Chicago, IL, 1 1/2 yr Kennedy King College Chicago, Early Childhood Development; [occ.] Supervisor Staff Residential Aides, Second Stage Housing for Women and Children; [memb.] Currently - WCC West Cluster Collaborative Community Enterprise; [hon.] 1988 Chairperson Westside Youth Boosters 29th Annual Awards Dinner; [oth. writ.] Collection of short poems. "My Garden", "2", "The Last Rose" and a short essay "Big Dog" submitted and qualified for enrollment with Institute of Children Literature; [pers.] I welcome the opportunity for change the good feeling you get from a job well done. The recognition from peers, who may not know where you're been but happy to see the way you're going; [a.] Chicago, IL

WILSON, LETA MAXINE
[pen.] Leta Maxine Wilson; [b.] August 4, 1927, Portland, OR; [m.] Deceased; [ch.] Three Daughters, One son; [ed.] Boise High School - Boise Secretarial Center - I worked for lawyers years ago -; [occ.] Senior citizen who stays home and has constant contact with friends; [hon.] One other poem published 11 years ago in a pamphlet - like brochure which was published locally by a writers' group - limited distribution; [oth. writ.] I have written several poems and some children's stories for the pleasure of family and friends.; [pers.] I believe poetry should sing - be a voice of the soul - my inspiration comes from deep emotional feelings of love for my children and friends, and an intense appreciation and feeling of connection with the pulse of the earth, its smell, wildflowers, and most of all, our beautiful skies in all its moods, stormy and calm.; [a.] Boise, ID

WILSON, RUSSELL R.
[pen.] Russ Wilson; [b.] February 18, 1935, Washington, DC; [p.] Charles Wilson, Flora Wilson (deceased); [m.] Reva Wilson, April 29, 1955; [ch.] Russell E. Wilson, Laura K. Hertlein; [ed.] (High School) School of the Ozarks, Point Lookout MO. (College) University of MO. Columbia MO. BA; [occ.] Retired; [memb.] Retired member (20 yrs.) of Kiwanis Club of Indep.; [hon.] Alpha Kappa Psi; [oth. writ.] None Published; [pers.] As we think, we will grow toward those thoughts, hopefully realizing that the secrets of life are in us all.; [a.] Independence, MO

WINDSOR, CHANDA
[pen.] Angel Erickson; [b.] February 25, 1978, Lawton, OK; [p.] Jimmy and Debbie Windsor; [ed.] Currently a student at Blanchard High School; [occ.] High School Student; [memb.] In school, I'm in Spanish Club, honor Society and Gifted and talented, Science Fiction Book Club; [hon.] International Foreign Language Award, English, Literature awards X B, National Government Award, Congressional Youth Leadership Council; [oth. writ.] Published in Local Newspaper; [pers.] Many of my poems are about people who constantly conform to make others happy and repress the things they'd really enjoy. I've been influenced by the irony and melancholia of Edgar Allan Poe and also Nietzsche.; [a.] Blanchard, OK

WINNIFRED, ROBINSON
[pen.] Robinson Wynne; [b.] January 3, 1921, Birtle, Manitoba, Canada; [p.] Wilhelmina McIntosh, William J. Butcher; [m.] Walter Hollamby Robinson, May 30, 1946; [ch.] Wayne Walter, Tanyse Elaine; [ed.] Registered Nurse from Manitoba, and British Columbia, Canada; [occ.] Retired; [memb.] Baptist Church, Happy Chorister Choral group; [oth. writ.] True anecdote published by Readers Digest January 1995; [pers.] Have been a writer in my head since childhood have finally put pen to paper in my 73rd year.; [a.] Kamloops, British Columbia, Canada

WINTER, SARAH
[b.] June 18, 1982, Oakland, MD; [p.] Paul and Diana Winter; [ed.] Currently in the seventh grade.; [occ.] Student; [memb.] Honor Chorus; [hon.] Spelling Bee (2), Art Awards, Science Fair Award (1st), Dance Awards, 2 other poems published.; [oth. writ.] Moonlight, The Ocean, Out My Window, Dogs, My Soul, Pain of Night; [pers.] My poem was dedicated to "Nanny", my great-grandmother, who passed away on Dec. 7, last year.; [a.] Swanton, MD

WINTERS, RODNEY C.
[b.] June 6, 1969, Brookville, PA; [p.] James C. and Nellie Kay Winters; [ed.] Brookville Area High School, Clarion University of Pennsylvania BSBA in Economics; [occ.] Account Representative Metropolitan Life Insurance Co.; [memb.] National Association of Life Underwriters, First United Methodist Church, life member Theta Xi National Fraternity; [oth. writ.] Several social articles published in local newspapers; [pers.] Success is a series of trials and failures. The only way to be successful is to learn from those trials and failures and never forget that persistence above all wins in the end.; [a.] Brookville, PA

WOJCIK, EDWARD J.
[pen.] E. J.; [b.] May 30, 1960, Detroit; [occ.] Electrician - Amateur Golfer; [a.] Maine

WOLFE, AMY M.
[b.] September 19, 1975, Bethlehem, PA; [p.] Richard and Jean Wolfe; [ed.] Southern Lehigh High School; [occ.] Organist, studying organ student; [oth. writ.] Have written poems on other subjects including my native American heritage. Other poems on the subject of the organ published in Catasauqua High School Literary magazine; [pers.] I believe human beings should care for one another, no matter what the differences. We shouldn't hate or hurt one another because of racial differences or differences in personality.; [a.] Coopersburg, PA

WOOD, STEPHEN T.
[b.] August 25, 1970, Batavia, NY; [p.] Ken and Cindy Wood; [ed.] Attica High School in Attica, NY., Alfred State College in Alfred, NY; [occ.] Equipment Mechanic at Toshiba. In Horseheads, NY; [pers.] We must remember that life is precious, all of life, and that the best thing in life, are free! Example. Ex. (love, friends, trust, etc.); [a.] Elmira, NY

WOODS, DEBORAH
[pen.] Deborah; [b.] June 13, 1952, MI; [p.] Virginia Porter (deceased); [ch.] Franzetta and Misty; [occ.] Social Service; [oth. writ.] Personal writings to my daughters, and loved ones.; [pers.] When I write I don't have to keep my secrets and emotions inside my soul. I release them with words.; [a.] Detroit, MI

WOODWARD, ANDREA
[b.] October 6, 1955, Sandusky, OH; [p.] Nellie Martin; [ch.] Brian W. D. Woodward; [ed.] GED - 1975, classes at Firelands College. Different types of courses.; [occ.] I work at Circon ACMI - as a maintenance person and on weekend - I bartend; [memb.] I belong to the Eagles in Norwalk; [hon.] I received an award for 3rd place in another poetry contest. I had 6 poems published; [oth. writ.] I have a pretty large portfolio of poems that I have written thru out the years.; [pers.] I enjoy writing because it takes me to places that no one else can go. I feel things that are hard to feel in the everyday world. One day I would like to write a novel, or published a paper.; [a.] Norwalk, OH

WORD, J. H.
[pen.] Jack Word; [b.] March 10, 1929, Oklahoma City, OK; [p.] John H. and Patty F. Word; [m.] Patty R. Word, June 2, 1983; [ch.] 2 boys and 2 girls; [ed.] Graduated Lone Grove High School Lone Grove, Okla. 1949 after service in U.S. Marine Corps. (High School drop-out WWII); [occ.] Texas Municipal Court, Judge; [memb.] TX. Municipal Court Association Bowie School Board of Trustees - First Baptist Church, Bowie, TX., Dallas Shrine Temple - Dallas Scottish Rite 32, Rotary International.; [hon.] Honorable Discharge United States Marine Corps 1948 and 1951, Honorary Life Member Texas PTA, Chamber of Commerce "Man Of the Year" 1985. Rotary International "Paul Harris Fellow."; [oth. writ.]

Articles published in local media only - "The Shoe", "The Perfect Shot", "Tribute To The Ostrich", "Reflections" and other human interest type inserts.; [pers.] I believe sincerely that my 66 years in this life are the most exciting, progressive and entertaining years since the beginning of time and I have been blessed with the miracle abilities to read, hear and observe since my earlier years.; [a.] Bowie, TX

WORRALL, MARIAN L.
[b.] December 14, 1906, Pennington, NJ; [p.] Henry L. and May W. Laning; [m.] Edward N. Worrall, June 24, 1933; [ch.] Carolyn, William; [ed.] Hopewell High School, Bachelor of Arts degree from The College of William and Mary; [occ.] Former English teacher in New Jersey and Pennsylvania; [memb.] First Methodist Church of Escondido, North San Diego County Genealogical Society, Hunterson County Historical Society (NJ) Phi Mu Sorority; [hon.] Kappa Delta Pi, Winner of Pi Gamma Mu essay contest; [a.] Escondido, CA

WRIGHT, FANNIE V.
[b.] April 15, 1927, VA; [p.] Hugh and Bernice Wyche; [ed.] High School graduated from Southampton High School, June 1944; [occ.] Retired formerly worked for Suffolk County; [memb.] N.A.A.C.P., A.A.R.P., Southampton Terrace Neighborhood Assoc., American Red Cross, American Heart Assoc.; [oth. writ.] Only write poems or essays for the fun of it. Never submitted anything before.; [pers.] This poem was written in response to the inner turmoil I feel as a result of all the violence, hatred and ugliness which I see daily. Hopefully people will band together and work to make things better.; [a.] Southampton, NY

WRIGHT, JAIME
[b.] March 23, 1980, Fairfax, VA; [p.] Sheila and Richard Hartmann; [ed.] North Stafford High School; [occ.] Student; [memb.] National Music Guild (2 years); [hon.] National Junior Honor Society; [pers.] It is an honor to be considered for this award.; [a.] Stafford, VA

WRIGHT, JOE LAWSON
[b.] July 23, 1938, Morgan Co, AL; [p.] Joe Everett and Lottie Bean Wright; [m.] Margaret McCutcheon Wright, April 22, 1961; [ch.] Melinda J. Wright and Sabrina A. Milner; [ed.] B.S. Athens College; [occ.] Special Agent (Criminal Investigator) U.S. Fish and Wildlife service; [memb.] A.I. Archeology Society TN. Anthropological Society National Audubon Society Mensa; [oth. writ.] Numerous technical writings on anthropology, archaeology and ornithology with the most recent published work being a detailed study of Paleo Man in the Southeastern U.S. and Published in Tennessee Anthropologist Journal by the University of TN. Press (Vol. XIV, no. 2, fall 1989 - Co - Authored with David C. Hulse).; [pers.] "My poems are spontaneous responses to situations at a given moment"; [a.] Alpharetta, GA

WRIGHT, LARRY E.
[b.] February 3, 1950, Kingsport, TN; [p.] Shields E. Wright and Marie Jones; [ch.] Carisa Ann (Wright) Navarro; [ed.] Sullivan West High, Kingsport, TN., Steed Business College, Johnson City, TN.; [occ.] Pediatric Health Aide; [memb.] Bass Anglers Sportsman Society; [pers.] This poem was written for and is dedicated to Jackie Gurley, a good friend, who passed away in Oct. 1994; [a.] Huntington, MA

WYANT, DON R.
[pen.] Damien Ray; [b.] March 29, 1974, Pontiac, IL; [p.] Don and Judy Wyant; [m.] Tara Wyant; [ed.] Graduated school; [occ.] Got a job; [hon.] Schools awards; [oth. writ.] Books and songs; [pers.] Thank you for choosing my poem, I greatly appreciate it!!!; [a.] Waterford, MI

WYMIARKIEWICZ, RENATE S.
[b.] November 30, 1949, Rosenberg, Austria; [p.] Paul and Hildegarde Sumaruck; [m.] Slawomir Wymiarkiewicz, August 10, 1985; [ch.] Makgoszata and Sonia (daughters); [ed.] Richfield High School Waco, TX and one year Univ. of Texas at Arlington; [occ.] Sales Clerk; [pers.] God almighty is number one in my life. His love is ever more a reality through a personal relationship with his son, Jesus Christ. To God be all the Glory!; [a.] San Francisco, CA

XAVIER, ALEXANDRE
[pen.] 'This' and 'That' and yet neither 'This' nor 'That'; [b.] October 25, 1953, Karaikal, South India; [p.] S. Xavier, Marie Antoinette X.; [m.] Josephine Santhosh Mary Luisa A., May 28, 1988; [ch.] Jesuis Gabbriel A.; [ed.] B. Sc. (Maths) - 1st Class - Madras Univ., M.A. (French) 1st Class - Madras University, Ph. D. (Linguistics) Bharathiar University, South India.; [occ.] Reader in French, Avinashilingam Deemed Univ., Coimbatore, South India.; [memb.] 1. Board of Studies in French, Avinashilingam Deemed Univ., 2. Board of Studies in French, Madras Univ. 3. Academic Council, Avinashilingam Deemed University, 4. Executive Committee of the Assoc. of Indian Teachers of the Assoc. of Indian Teachers of French, Madras.; [hon.] 1. Certificate of Merit (1972) in Maths Talent Competition. 2. Consolation Award (1975) in all India Maths Essay Competition - Senior level. 3. Jawaharlal Nehru Memorial Fund Award (1976) by Madras Univ.; [oth. writ.] 1. Some poems were selected in a competition and published (1986) in the Delhi-London Poetry Quarterly, London, U.K. 2. Research articles in Linguistics. 3. Articles on the art of living.; [pers.] Poetry is like the beautiful mystical gaps that one finds in a mist that enshrouds the lofty mountain of truth, and remember, you are that truth so, poetry is the discovery of your 'self'.; [a.] Coimbatore, South India

YAMADA, RYAN
[p.] Roy Yamada, Sandra Yamada; [pers.] Live life to the fullest for you never know when it will all end.; [a.] Honolulu, HI

YEAGER, SHAY
[b.] May 10, 1977, Woodward, OK; [p.] Bill and Sharon Yeager; [ed.] Mooreland Elementary, Cedar Heights Elementary, Woodward Middle School, Woodward High School, Northwestern Oklahoma State; [occ.] Student; [memb.] First Baptist Church, Sub Debs Sorority; [hon.] Writingwood awards, Hugh O'Brian Youth Foundation Ambassador, Girls State Delegate, BPW Girl of the Month; [oth. writ.] A poem was published in a Missouri publication; [a.] Woodward, OK

YOUNG, BETTY
[b.] December 13, 1958, Killarney, WV; [p.] James and Patricia Oliver; [ch.] Christopher Lee and Daniel Lloyd; [ed.] Westland High; [occ.] Training Specialist, FCBMR/DD; [a.] Columbus, OH

YOUNG, RACHEL
[b.] December 24, 1975, Huntsville, Ontario, Canada; [p.] Barb and Harvey Young; [ed.] J.L. Forster S.S., Langara College; [hon.] J.L. Forster S.S. 1994 Valedictorian, Canada Day Youth Award, 1992; [oth. writ.] Several articles published in student publications in Canada.; [pers.] Seize the flowers, smell the day, and make the future what you want.; [a.] Burnaby British Columbia, Canada

YOUNG, SARAH KELLY
[b.] April 2, 1980, California; [p.] Penny Lee Young; [ed.] 9th Grade, High School; [occ.] Student; [hon.] Semifinalist Poetry North American Open; [pers.] Poems are inspired by my mother and my love of Nature; [a.] Pleasant Hill, CA

YOUNG SR., JAMES E.
[pen.] Jimmy; [b.] August 6, 1926, Charlotte, NC; [p.] Frank Young and Florine Kelly Young; [m.] Doris Jean Porter-Young, June 7, 1946; [ch.] Sandra Tyce-Cordone, Sheryl Laurimore, James, Michael, Mark, Scott, Christopher, Cedric Young, Karen, Robin, Avis, Stacey, Crystal Young; [ed.] Robert L. Stevenson H.S., NYC., NY Theological Seminary, NYC, Empire Trade School, NYC.; [occ.] Chauffeur; [pers.] In my writings, I desire to encourage youth in the importance of a good education.; [a.] Bronx, NY

ZAPATA, CATALINA
[b.] February 20, 1968, Leuven, Belgium; [p.] Luis Eduardo Zapata, Soledad Ruiz; [m.] Conrad Vial, April 8, 1995; [ed.] Filology (French and Spanish) Universidad Nacional De Columbia (South America); [occ.] Tutor (Language); [hon.] Canada College Dean's List, 1994, Eric Hedges Memorial Scholarship 1993, John Iliff Scholarship 1993, Certificate of Recognition - Tutorial Center, Canada College 1993; [oth. writ.] Poems (Collected poems published by Centro Colombo-Americano Bogota-Columbia May, 1989); [pers.] Writing in english has been a constant effort aimed at reconciling my native spanish sounds and meanings with new linguistic encounters in North America.; [a.] Menlo Park, CA

ZAVALA, SHANE M.
[b.] March 15, 1975, Sandusky, OH; [p.] Terry and Lori Zavala; [ed.] Sandusky High - Sandusky OH; [occ.] Food Runner - T.G.I. Fridays and Cook; [hon.] Best vignettes Award Best Journal in Terms of Content; [oth. writ.] Unknown heartache - Diversity of the soul - spoiled seeds of youth.; [pers.] To those who read this: Yesterdays experience always shed's light on tomorrow's horizon.; [a.] Sandusky, OH

ZBORAY, GEORGIANNA W.
[b.] January 25, 1961, Staten Island, NY; [p.] Wanda Helen Barbach Zboray and John Stephen Zboray Sr.; [ch.] Misty and Corky; [ed.] Katharine Gibbs Business School; [occ.] Legal Secretary for Wall Street law firm; [memb.] Int'l Society of Poets (Advisory Panel, Admin. Committee), National Wildlife Federation, World Wildlife Fund; [hon.] 2 Editor's Choice Awards (Nat'l Lib. of Poetry): Golden Poet Award, 3 Awards of Merit and Who's Who Status (World of Poetry Society); [oth. writ.] Partners, The Struggle Within, A Dream, No More Heroes, Never Again, Make Love To Me; [pers.] My own life's experiences are what inspire me to write - it's how I release my anger, my depression, my sorrow and even my joy; [a.] Staten Island, NY

ZEHREN, ELIZABETH
[pen.] Zard; [b.] January 5, 1979, Berkeley, CA; [p.] E. R. Z. and K. A. Z; [ed.] Stanley Intermediate, Roosevelt Jr. High, Kingsburg Joint Union High School; [occ.] Student; [hon.] Physical Best Fitness Goals in pull-ups, National Physical Fitness Award, 1990.; [oth. writ.] Poem published in Stanley, Intermediate's Echoes and Reflections, 1992; [pers.] I will always have effort to express myself, the way meant to be by writing.; [a.] Berkeley, CA

ZESSIN, BECKY
[b.] July 24, 1976, Omaha, NE; [p.] Gary and Nancy Zessin; [ed.] Washington Elem. School, Gretna Elem. School, Ralston Middle School, Gretna High School, and Iowa School for the Deaf.; [occ.] Cook and service and teacher's aide; [memb.] Jr. NAD, Dorm Council, Student Council, Class Committee, and Astra Club. I am in Yearbook.; [hon.] Honor Roll, Honor Roll Pin, Second place in Academic Biatholon, and a varsity letter.; [oth. writ.] Two other poems were sent to a contest, one will be published in a book and one was accepted into semi-finals.; [pers.] I have a talent to be creative with words. I have been influenced by reading other poems.; [a.] Council Bluffs, IA

ZIEGLER, SHIRLEY
[ch.] Randy, Sandra Pelletier, Laurie Carey; [ed.] Los Angeles City College; [pers.] For the last 25 years, I've moved at least once a year, working at more than 50 jobs and living in over 20 places along the way. There's nothing more exciting than learning by direct hands on experience!; [a.] Walden, NY

ZIELINSKI, CATHY JEANENE
[b.] March 4, 1959, Abilene, TX; [m.] Russell J. Zielinski, April 28; [ch.] Jarod J. Bell - 20 yrs. old, Melissa M. Bell - 15 yrs. old; [oth. writ.] Published also in Volume Titled "Reflections Of Light" Library of Congress ISBN 1-56167-264-5; [pers.] If you don't know how to say it. "Write it!"; [a.] Peru, NY

ZIMA, MICHAELA
[b.] March 25, 1982, Richmond, CA; [p.] Vera Zima, Ivan Zima; [ed.] Grade 7 at Sacred Heart School; [occ.] Student; [memb.] Western Indoor Tennis Club.; [hon.] Penmanship, Sunshine Hills Jr. Open Tennis Tournament, Bill Gooding Memorial Tournament, Recreational Tennis Tournament, Steveston Jr. Classic, BC Junior Indoor Tennis Tournament.; [pers.] Through my poems, I am able to reveal my inner thoughts and feelings to those who read it.; [a.] Delta British Columbia, Canada

ZIMMERMAN, MALIA M.
[b.] September 6, 1968, Hawaii; [p.] Suzanne and Dennis McLaughlin; [m.] Tom Zimmerman, August 15, 1992; [ch.] Michael David Kekoa Zimmerman; [ed.] Maryknoll Schools, Hon, Hawaii BA, Chaminade University of Honolulu Minors in Business and Drama major - Broad Cast Communications; [occ.] Director of Development (Furdraising, marketing) for Maryknoll Schools; [oth. writ.] Poems published in local papers and in "The Space Between".; [pers.] The reality of life is excitement to be alive, curiosity to see all, and drive to be all. Don't let anyone take that away from you.; [a.] Honolulu, HI

ZOLLER, OLLIE SAUNDERS
[b.] February 16, 1931, Cheyenne, OK; [p.] Andrew F. and Cora F. Saunders; [m.] William Eugene Zoller, June 2, 1952; [ch.] Stanley Blake, Sherry Gay, Dawn Michelle, Debra Lynn; [ed.] Pryor High Graduate (1949); [memb.] Church of Christ; [hon.] Honor Roll (East Prairie High) Queen of the Lake (Wister Dam Dedication, 1951), Silver Poet Award, (World of Poetry, 1989); [oth. writ.] Published: Plight of Eli, Wages of Greed, Sunday Snowflakes, Safari, Sign Resign; [pers.] I believe Jesus Christ is the son of God. My favorite Scripture: Proverbs 25:11 - A word fitly spoken is like apples of gold in pictures of silver.; [a.] Amarillo, TX

ZUISS, KATHLEEN MARY
[b.] December 25, 1941, Southbridge, MA; [p.] Gladys, J. Blinn, Edward R. Zuiss; [ed.] Cathedral High School, American International College; [occ.] Disabled, but previously Medical Library Manager Mercy Hospital; [memb.] Saint Cecilla's Catholic Church, Saint Cecilla's Women's Bible Study; [hon.] Dean's List; [oth. writ.] One other poem published in Saint Cecilla's Newsletter. Many poems written for family and personal enjoyment as an expression of my creative spirit and imagination.; [pers.] I enjoy being able to express myself in poetry, and prose. My exposure to literature in my years at Cathedral and A.I.C. have been a great influence on my poetry writing. My family teachers and professors encouraged and affirmed me. I look for the extraordinary and spiritual in the everyday.; [a.] Wilbraham, MA

ZUKOWSKI, MICHAEL
[pen.] Mike Z.; [b.] November 7, 1929, Chicago, IL; [p.] Adolph and Helen Zukowski; [m.] Geraldine Mary Zukowski, August 24, 1956; [ch.] Deborah Demes and Michelle Tatera; [ed.] United States Air Forces (GED); [occ.] Building Maintenance and security; [memb.] The society of the "Average American"; [hon.] The "first" to receive employee of the month in his company and to receive it twice again in 6 years. Anticipating the honor of having a poem recognized by the National Library of Poetry.; [oth. writ.] A poem I had written called "PSI" unpublished but hold so dear to my heart about man's love for his automobile.; [pers.] Wanting the rest of the world informed of my love for the greatest country in the universe.; [a.] Villa Park, IL

Index of Poets

Index

A

B

D

E

I

J

O

P

Q

R

S

X

Y

Z